2022

the Next EXIT ®

The Most Accurate Interstate Highway Service Guide Ever Printed™

the Next EXIT® will save time, money and frustration.

This tool will help you find services along the USA Interstate Highways like nothing you have ever used.

D1227827

Restaurants • Gas Stations • Hotels • RV Camping • And Much More

www.theNextExit.com

the Next Exit®

USER GUIDE

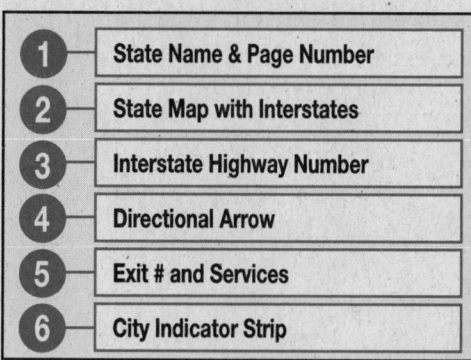

1	State Name & Page Number
2	State Map with Interstates
3	Interstate Highway Number
4	Directional Arrow
5	Exit # and Services
6	City Indicator Strip

Exit

Most states number exits by the nearest mile marker(mm). A few states use consecutive numbers, in which case mile markers are given in ( ). Mile markers are the little green vertical signs beside the interstate at one mile intervals which indicate distance from the southern or western border of a state. Odd numbered interstates run north/south, even numbered run east/west.

Services

Services are listed alphabetically by category 🛢 = gas 🍴 = food 🏠 = lodging Rs = rest stop 🅾 = other services including camping. "Ⓗ" indicates an exit from which a hospital may be accessed, but it may not be close to the exit. Services located away from the exit may be referred to by "access to," or "to" and a distance may be given. A directional notation is also given, such as N, S, E or W

Directional Arrows

Follow exits DOWN the page if traveling from North to South or East to West, UP the page if traveling South to North or West to East.

INTERSTATE 80 Cont'd

Exit #	Services
352b a	US 93, Great Basin Hwy, E Wells, N 🛢 Chevron/dsl/LP, Conoco/dsl, Petro/Dunkin'/dsl/café/casino 🍴 Bella's Diner, Burger King/Subway 🏠 Motel 6, Rest Inn Motel, Sharon Motel, Super 8 🅾 Crossroads RV Park, repair, Tire Factory, S 🛢 ⓕFLYING J/dsl/scales/LP/casino/RV Dump/24hr, LNG, ♥Loves/McDonalds/dsl/scales/24hr 🏠 Hampton Inn 🅾 Great Basin NP
351	W Wells, N 🛢 Wells/dsl/LP 🅾 Family$, Mtn Shadows RV Park, Roy's Foods, USPO, Well's Hardware, S 🅾 Angel Lake RV Park, to Angel Lake RA
348	to Beverly Hills, N 🅾 RV camping
343	to Welcome, Starr Valley, N 🍴 food 🅾 Ⓒ, Welcome RV Park
333	Deeth, Starr Valley
328	to River Ranch
321	NV 229, Halleck, Ruby Valley
318mm	N Fork Humboldt River
317	to Elburz
314	to Ryndon, Devils Gate, N 🛢 Sinclair/cafe/dsl, S 🅾 RV camping
312mm	check sta both lanes
310	to Osino, 4 mi S 🅾 Valley View RV Park

City Indicator Strip: **WELLS**

©2022 by the Next EXIT, Inc. All rights reserved. Reproduction of any kind and/or commercial use of included data is not permitted. Ordering information is available online at *www.theNextExit.com*

the Next EXIT, inc. makes no warranty regarding the accuracy of the information contained in this publication. This information is subject to change without notice.

Copyright 2022 - The Next EXIT ®

Abbreviations & Symbols used in the Next EXIT ®

AFB	Air Force Base	NM	National Monument	st	street, state
B&B	Bed&Breakfast	NHS	Nat Hist Site	sta	station
Bfd	Battlefield	NWR	Nat Wildlife Reserve	TPK	Turnpike
CNG	Compressed Natural Gas	NF	National Forest	USPO	Post Office
Ctr	Center	Ⓗ	Hospital	vet	veterinarian
Coll	College	✈	Airport	whse	warehouse
Cyn	canyon	🎪	Picnic Area/Tables	@	truckstop (full service)
dsl	diesel	NP	National Park	red print	RV accessible
$	Dollar	NRA	Nat Rec Area	♿	Handicapped accessible
EVC	Electric Vehicle Charger	pk	park	☏	Telephone
LNG	Liquid Natural Gas	pkwy	parkway	⛽	Gas
Mem	Memorial	rest.	restaurant	🍴	Food
Mkt	Market	nb	northbound	🛏	Lodging
Mtn	Mountain	sb	southbound	⊡	Other
mm	mile marker	eb	eastbound	℞s	Rest Stop / Rest Area
N	north side of exit	wb	westbound		
S	south side of exit	SP	state park		
E	east side of exit	SF	state forest		
W	west side of exit	Sprs	springs		

More digital options are available at www.theNextExit.com

Copyright 2022 - The Next EXIT ®

YARN OF THE OLD BLACK BAG

Mark Watson – Winter 2022

How do you feel when the time comes to retire an old friend? Some people say goodbye and walk away easy, without even a sentimental glance. Others throw a going-away party celebrating years of service. The "halfway measure" folks ease the old one out and break the new one in little by little. Me? It depends on our relationship. If I have been satisfied, I might call a trusted companion back for contract work. Still, everything ought to be treated with dignity and respect even in decline, right? At least that is what I thought about my black carry-on.

This bag was "free" when I ordered $50 worth of merchandise from an office supply catalog. It arrived folded flat encased in clear plastic underneath paper clips, pads, pens, and staples haphazardly tossed on top. I tore its packaging away, inflated it to full size and was struck by how it seemed to grin sheepishly at me through zippered teeth even as I secretly groused about its cheap, imitation leather exterior. Attaching its wide shoulder strap to the eyelets on each end did however give it the mild look of business and importance, and before long I had peeled back its top flap, inspected the lined in-

sides, and discovered several secret compartments. Thus acquainted, we decided we could get along under an implied agreement: *it* would carry my belongings, and I would carry *it*.

I thought briefly of giving it a name, like people do with a boat, car, or an old truck. I soon shook off that idea though, because really – who names a suitcase?

Over the next 25 years we went everywhere together, driving or flying. To my pleasant surprise, it was the perfect fit for the passenger side foot of my car, which made my necessaries easy to reach. Imagine my delight when I discovered that its dimensions were exact for the little measuring box right next to the flight desk. Overhead compartments? No problem. Under airplane seats? Like a glove. We grew on each other as I learned what its limits were for any given trip. Over time, its seams yielded ever so slightly to accommodate my wayfaring needs and its faux leather construction allowed it to be crammed into almost any shaped compartment required. We traveled to the Orient, New York, New Mexico, and every other U.S. state many times. Overnight, weeks

Continued Next Page

YARN OF THE OLD BLACK BAG

YARN OF THE OLD BLACK BAG

or weekends – the duration made no difference to this patient, squatty hauler of my toiletries and underwear. It rode with me to inspect every exit of every interstate highway in America repeatedly, and never once did I hear a complaint.

But everything in this realm is subject to corruption and decay and the free bag from the office supply catalog was no exception. It began to bulge in its midsection, evidence of the many times I force-fed it with "just one more bite". Threads began to show, cracks and holes appeared in the periphery as it neared middle age. The lining in its gut pulled loose, giving me additional compartments in which to stash stuff. Oftentimes between trips, I didn't bother to fully disgorge it since the next expedition was already being planned. It became a mini-storage bin, housing all the do-dads I never used except when traveling. And yet, like a faithful canine there it sat, its eyelets never looking anywhere but towards me.

I wish I could say my own eyes never wandered, but one day I saw an advertisement for a new genuine leather bag. Manufactured by a company known for its popular leather boots, this satchel was the right size in all the right places. It was not warped out of shape, had no sags, no wrinkles, and no blemishes on its beautiful brown skin. I tried to look away, but it was too late. Then I began seeing it everywhere, first in internet ads and then on TV. Before long I wondered what it would be like to tote that sleek new model through an airport concourse. I felt ashamed, but what could I do? I declared fealty to my ancient companion, loudly and to anyone who would listen, but the images of the younger version would not go away. Then I made the first of several errors by looking it up online, just to see what the seller wanted for it.

Too expensive! Who in their right mind would pay this kind of money for at item they already owned, that did the same job, and was free? Not me! And that was that. Over the next three years, the ads were relentless. I would tell myself things like how smart I was to not be taken in by the sellers' slick campaigns. I would think of all the good times The Old Black Bag and I had enjoyed. Wasn't there something to be said

for loyalty? After all, ordering online is risky. What if I contracted a bad case of shopper's remorse upon receipt after I'd already purchased? I promised myself that unless I could see it in a physical retail location where I could pick it up, smell the leather and examine its construction – I was out.

It wasn't long before I stumbled across a list of outlets, located in destination cities across the USA, places like Aspen, Charleston, and Scottsdale. I felt safe knowing these were not on my frequent visit list. Then I noticed some crossroad cities: Atlanta, Dallas, and Nashville. Well, maybe at some future date on some eventual trip if the circumstances ever arose that placed me near any of these spots, then perhaps I would stop by – just to look. I wouldn't go out of my way for it, though. That was when fate intervened.

My daughter, who lived a rock's throw from the Pacific Ocean, announced that she'd be relocating to a community only a Frisbee toss to Lake Superior. In view of her needing to transport a two-year-old son, husband, two dogs and all her goods to her new home, she asked how I would feel about lending a hand in driving a 24' moving truck complete with car trailer that far. Who wouldn't jump on an adventure like that? I assented and once again began packing the Old Black Bag, secretly hoping it would spontaneously combust – or at least the zipper would tear loose, or one of its major seams, conveniently affording the need for an upgrade. Then, in a separate room away from prying eyelets, I started my research. Firing up my navigation tools, I plotted several separate routes for making the journey. This highway has tolls – *no thanks*. That road is more mountainous – not a good idea with the sizeable rig I'd be hauling. But the best route jumped out at me when I discovered it ran right by a shopping mall in the flatlands of the near-upper mid-west, wherein one of the boot/bag outlets was located. It was the perfect stopping place. Was it divine intervention? Maybe. Inside of ten seconds I had finalized my decision – that was the way my rig and I were headed.

So it was, that on the third day of the moving excursion my excitement ran high. As I hurtled eastward

Copyright 2022 - The Next EXIT ®

across Nebraska on Interstate 80 my single-mindedness was to examine that new leather grip before the store closed that day or die in the attempt. By now, I had realized my motivation for agreeing to this exercise in the first place was related mostly to my flirtations with that new leather bag and helping the daughter of my heart was only an excuse. There was momentary guilt, but that did not stop me from pulling my rig and its trailing appendage into the roomy outskirts of the mall parking lot near Omaha. With the long walk from the parking lot, my heart had plenty of time to reach full speed – pumping with anticipation. The twenty-something year-olds running the store seemed to know a lot less about bags than boots, so I ended up browsing about on my own until I found the luggage display. There, resting prominently amidst the lesser units, the prize was perched all tan and shapely. I could hardly contain my emotions.

But what was this? Marked down to half price? Why? I demanded an explanation from the shop boy who was sauntering over. "Close out", he explained, "the company is moving to another design." I couldn't believe my ears. I'd come too far though, to let reason prevail at this moment of full drama. So, I told him to retrieve it from the back for me. Over his shoulder he asked if I was a veteran. I allowed that I was, which would score me an additional ten percent off, but it didn't much help temper what came next. Suddenly, and without warning I became confused, mildly disappointed and a little upset; Thomas Paine's words whispering in my ear "That which we obtain too easily we esteem too lightly". Plus, my heart was far too set at this point to simply leave empty-handed. I shook off these feelings of hesitancy as best I could, gritted my teeth as I reached for my wallet, paid for the bag, shouldered it, and we both made our way back to the truck.

That first trek across the expansive parking lot was when I noticed how heavy real leather is. The Old Black Bag had weighed less than two and a half pounds empty, but New Brown now approached ten before I added so much as a juggler's scarf. To avoid becoming too dejected, I told myself this one would

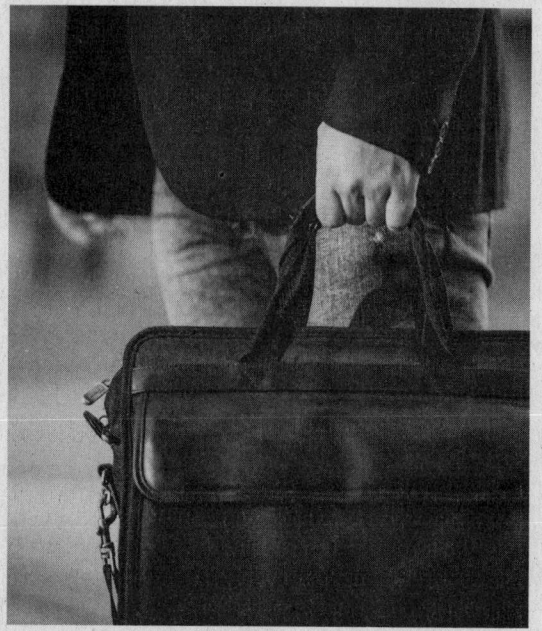

never wear out and was likely the last bag I would ever need, unless of course, I ended up straining my back transporting it. That night in the hotel I reverently and with mixed feelings unloaded faithful Old Black, transferring its contents to their new home. It wasn't easy because every item had molded its own comfortable spot in the former, but now uprooted, had to readjust to new surroundings in the latter.

My original plan had been to discard the Old Black Bag, but this proved to be too much, too soon, and felt a little like switching dates while at the prom, so I stuffed it into the headroom of its replacement, enclosing it with the new industrial-strength zipper. I ended up lugging two bags the remainder of the journey, first to my daughter's new abode, then through three airports en route home. Once there, I unloaded both employees and gently and respectfully placed the retiree on a shelf in my closet. To allow full rest I reduced the strain on its sides by deflating it back to flat and arranging the strap so that its zippered smile was still visible just as I remember on the day we met back in the days of our youth. Then I made sure the eyelets were in a position where I could easily see them, you know, just in case my longtime friend, The Old Black Bag should ever be needed again – for contract work. ◆

YARN OF THE OLD BLACK BAG

ALABAMA

INTERSTATE 10

Exit #	Services
66.5mm	Alabama/Florida state line
66mm	Welcome Ctr, full ♿ facilities, litter barrels, petwalk, 🅒, 🏚, vending
53	rd 64, Wilcox Rd, **N** 🅖 Marathon/Oasis/Chester's/Stuckey's/Subway/dsl/scales/24hr/@ Ⓞ Riverside RV Park, Styx River Resort, **S** 🅖 Chevron/dsl Ⓞ Azalea Acres RV Park, fireworks, Hilltop RV Park (1.5 mi), Wilderness RV Park
49	Rd 68, Baldwin Beach Express, to Gulf Shores, Orange Beach, Gulf SP, **S** 🅖 Buc-ee's/dsl
44	AL 59, Loxley, **N** 🅖 Loves/Arby's/dsl/scales/24hr 🏠 Bay Inn, **S** 🅖 Chevron/dsl, Exxon/dsl, RaceWay/dsl 🍴 Burger King, Hardee's, McDonald's, Waffle House 🏠 Loxley Motel (3mi), WindChase Inn Ⓞ to Gulf SP
38	AL 181, Malbis, **N** 🍴 CA Dreaming, Chick-fil-A, Cracker Barrel, Half Shell Oyster House, IHOP, Logan's Roadhouse, Marble Slab, McDonald's, Moe's SW Grill, Newk's Eatery, Olive Garden, Panera Bread, Pizza Hut, Poor Mexican, Ruby Tuesday, Sonic, Starbucks, Stix Asian, Taco Bell, Waffle House, Wendy's 🏠 Best Western, Comfort Inn, Holiday Inn Express, La Quinta Ⓞ $Tree, Advance Parts, Barnes&Noble, Belk, Best Buy, Dillard's, GNC, Goodyear/auto, Michael's, Old Navy, Petsmart, Publix, Ross, Tuesday Morning, Verizon, Walgreens, World Mkt, **S** 🅖 Chevron/dsl, Shell/LA Subs, Texaco/dsl 🍴 Burger King, Don Carlos, Firehouse Subs, Mellow Mushroom, Zaxby's 🏠 Malbis Motel (1mi), Woodspring Suites Ⓞ AT&T, Honda, Hyundai, Lowe's, Nissan, Sam's Club/gas, Toyota, URGENT CARE, VW
35	US 90, US 98, **N** 🅖 Marathon, Shell 🍴 Beef O'Brady's, China Fun 🏠 Courtyard, Fairfield Inn Ⓞ Bass Pro Shops, JC Penney, Kohl's, Piggly Wiggly, Rite Aid, to Blakeley SP, USPO, **S** 🅖 Exxon/dsl, Shell/dsl 🍴 Arby's, Bangkok Thai, Boudreaux's Cajun Grill, Burger King, Dickey's BBQ, Domino's, Dragon City Buffet, Dunkin', El Rancho Mexican, Firehouse Subs, Five Guys, Foosackly's Chicken Fingers, Hooters, IHOP, Jubilee Diner, Longhorn Steaks, Los Tacos, Maddio's, McDonald's, Mediterranean Sandwich, O'Charley's, Papa John's, Pizza Hut, S China Rest., Smoothie King, Starbucks, Subway, Taco Bell, Waffle House, Waffle House (2), Zaxby's 🏠 Comfort Suites, Eastern Shore Motel, Hampton Inn, Hilton Garden, Homewood Suites, Microtel Ⓞ $Tree, AT&T, Dick's, Fresh Mkt, GNC, Hobby Lobby, Home Depot, 🄷, Office Depot, Petco, TJ Maxx
30	US 90/98, Battleship Pkwy, **N** 🍴 Blue Gill Rest., Ed's Seafood Shed, Oyster House, **S** Ⓞ same as 27
27	US 90/98, Battleship Pkwy, Gov't St, **S** 🍴 Cafe Del Rio, Felix's Fish Camp, R&R Seafood, Ralph&Kacoo's Seafood Ⓞ to USS Alabama
26b	Water St, Mobile, downtown, **N** 🏠 Candlewood Suites, Hampton Inn, Holiday Inn, Quality Inn, Renaissance, to Visitors Ctr
26a	Canal St (from eb) same as 26b
25b	Virginia St, Mobile, **N** 🅖 Shell/dsl
25a	Texas St (from wb, no return)
24	Broad St, to Duval St, Mobile, **N** 🅖 Chevron/dsl
23	Michigan Ave, **N** 🅖 Shell/dsl
22b a	AL 163, Dauphin Island Pkwy, **N** Ⓞ $General, Family$, **S** 🅖 Exxon/Subway, Mobil/dsl 🍴 Checkers, Hart's Chicken, Kim's Palace, Waffle House Ⓞ $General
20	I-65 N, to Montgomery
17	AL 193, Tillmans Corner, to Dauphin Island, **N** 🅖 BP 🍴 Firehouse Subs, Five Guys, Golden Corral, IHOP, Moe's SW, Panda Express, Ruby Tuesday, Zaxby's Ⓞ AT&T, auto repair, 🄷, Lowe's, Office Depot, URGENT CARE, Verizon, Walmart/Subway
15b a	US 90, Tillmans Corner, to Mobile, **N** 🅖 Chevron, Murphy Express/dsl, RaceWay/dsl 🍴 Arby's, Aztecas Mexican, Burger King, Domino's, Godfather's, Hooters, KFC, Krystal, Little Caesar's, McDonald's, Papa John's, Popeye's, Russell's BBQ, Shrimp Basket, Subway, Taco Bell, Waffle House 🏠 Baymont Inn, Best Value Inn, Comfort Suites, Days Inn, EconoLodge, Extended Suites, Hampton Inn, Holiday Inn, Holiday Inn Express, Home 2 Suites, InTown Suites, La Quinta, Motel 6, Quality Inn, Red Roof Inn, Rodeway Inn, Super 8 Ⓞ $General, $Tree, AutoZone, BigLots, Family$, Firestone/auto, Mike's Transmissions, O'Reilly Parts, PepBoys, vet, Walgreens, Winn-Dixie, **S** 🅖 Exxon, RaceWay/dsl, Shell/dsl 🍴 Hardee's, Waffle House Ⓞ Advance Parts, auto repair, B&R Campers, Boutique RV Ctr, Peterbilt, tires, transmissions, USPO, vet
13	to Theodore, **N** 🅖 Clark/dsl, McDonald's, Wendy's/dsl/scales/24hr, Shell/Subway 🍴 Burger King, Church's, Waffle House, Walmart Mkt/dsl Ⓞ Advance Parts, auto repair, Family$, Greyhound Prk, Rouse's Mkt, transmissions, Walgreens, **S** 🅖 Chevron/dsl Ⓞ Bellingraf Gardens, I-10 Kamping, Paynes RV Park (4mi)
10	rd 39, Bayou La Batre, Dawes, **N** 🍴 Waffle House Ⓞ Kenworth
4	AL 188 E, to Grand Bay, **N** 🅖 Exxon, Shell/Subway, TA/Dunkin'/Popeye's/Country Pride/dsl/scales/24hr/@ 🍴 Arby's, McDonald's, Sam's Super Burger, Waffle House Ⓞ $General, Bumper Parts, **S** 🅖 Chevron 🍴 Hardee's Ⓞ Trav-L-Kamp
1mm	Welcome Ctr eb, full ♿ facilities, info, litter barrels, petwalk, 🅒, 🏚, RV dump
0mm	Alabama/Mississippi state line

M O B I L E (left margin)

T H E O D O R E (right margin)

AL

ANNISTON

▲E	INTERSTATE 20
Exit #	Services
215mm	Alabama/Georgia state line, Central/Eastern time zone
213mm	Welcome Ctr wb, 24hr security, full 🛏 facilities, info, litter barrels, petwalk, 🄲, 🄰, RV dump, vending
210	AL 49, Abernathy, N fireworks, S fireworks
209mm	Tallapoosa River, weigh sta wb
205	AL 46, to Heflin, N 🅿 Circle K/dsl, ❤Loves/dsl/scales/24hr 🍽 205 Cafe 🅾 Cane Creek RV Park (2mi), Exit 205 Tire Ctr, Smith Farms, S 🅿 Chevron/dsl/24hr 🅾 Truck Repair
199	AL 9, Heflin, N 🅿 Shell/Subway/dsl 🍽 Hardee's, McDonald's, Vallarta Grill 🛏 Best Value Inn 🅾 Chevrolet, Ford, USPO, S 🅿 Chevron/dsl/24hr, SuperMart/dsl
198mm	Talladega Nat Forest eastern boundary
191	US 431, to US 78
188	to US 78, to Anniston, N 🅿 Samco/dsl, Shell/dsl, Texaco/Subway/dsl 🍽 Cracker Barrel, Fuji Japanese, IHOP, KFC, LoneStar Steaks, Los Mexicanos, Mellow Mushroom, Waffle House, Wendy's, Zaxby's 🛏 Comfort Suites, Country Inn&Suites, Courtyard, Fairfield Inn, Hampton Inn, Hilton Garden, Holiday Inn Express, Home 2 Suites, Quality Inn, Sleep Inn 🅾 Camping World RV Ctr, GS RV Park, Harley-Davidson, Honda, Lowe's, Nissan, O'Reilly Parts, Toyota, S 🅿 Chevron/dsl 🍽 Arby's, Chick-fil-A, Ezell's Fish Camp, Firehouse Subs, Golden Corral, Longhorn Steaks, Mexico Lindo Grill, Moe's SW, Olive Garden, Panda Express, Panera Bread 🅾 AAA, AT&T, Best Buy, Dick's, GNC, Hobby Lobby, Home Depot, Kohl's, Old Navy, Petsmart, Publix, Ross, Sams Club/dsl, Target, TJ Maxx, Verizon
185	AL 21, to Ft McClellan, to Anniston, N 🅿 Chevron/dsl, GrubMart/dsl, Shell/dsl, Texaco 🍽 Applebee's, Arby's, Bojangles, Burger King, Capt D's, China Luck, CiCi's Pizza, Hardee's, HoneyBaked Ham, Jack's Rest., Logan's Roadhouse, Los Mexicanos, McAlister's Deli, McDonald's, Papa John's, Pizza Hut, Red Lobster, Red Pepper Grill, Sonic, Starbucks, Super Buffet, Taco Bell, Waffle House, Western Sizzlin 🛏 Best Value Inn, Red Carpet Inn 🅾 $General, Advance Parts, Aldi Foods, BooksAMillion, CVS Drug, Dillard's, Firestone/auto, Ford, JC Penney, Martin's Foods, Rite Aid, S 🅿 76, Circle K/dsl/scales, Murphy USA/dsl, RaceTrac, RaceWay 🍽 Chick-fil-A, Jefferson's Rest., Outback Steaks, Waffle House, Wendy's 🛏 Comfort Inn, EconoLodge, Key West Inn, Motel 6, Super 8 🅾 $Tree, Cobb Automotive, 🄷, Walmart
179	AL 202, to US 78, to Munford, Coldwater, N 🅿 Chevron/Subway/dsl 🍽 China King, Jack's Rest. 🅾 $General, Anniston Army Depot, Rite Aid, Winn Dixie, S 🅿 Marathon/dsl
173	AL 5, Eastaboga, S 🅿 Mapco/Stuckey's, Sunoco/cafe 🅾 to Speedway/Hall of Fame
168	AL 77, to Talladega, N 🅿 Exxon/QV/Domino's, Marathon/KFC/Taco Bell, 🚛/dsl/scales/24hr 🍽 Jack's Rest., Waffle House, S 🅿 AOC/Burger King, Chevron/Subway/dsl, TA/Popeye's/dsl/scales/24hr 🍽 McDonald's, MT Grill, Rana's Mexican 🛏 Comfort Inn, Days Inn, Lincoln Inn 🅾 Hall of Fame, to Speedway
165	Embry, Lincoln, N 🅿 Hi-Tech/dsl, 🚛/Subway/dsl/scales/24hr 🅾 Paradise Island RV Park, S 🅿 165 TP/Huddle House/dsl, I-20TrkStp/rest./dsl/scales/24hr 🍽 Doghouse Grill 🛏 McCaig Motel
164mm	Coosa River
162	US 78, Riverside, N 🅾 Safe Harbor RV Park, S 🅿 Chevron/dsl 🛏 Best Value Inn/rest
158	US 231, Pell City, N 🅿 Marathon/dsl, Murphy USA/dsl 🍽 Arby's, Azteca Mexican, Buffalo Wild Wings, Chick-fil-A, City Mkt Grill, Cracker Barrel, Golden Rule BBQ, Hwy 55 Cafe, Jade E Chinese,

PELL CITY / LEEDS / BIRMINGHAM

Exit #	Services
158	Continued
	Krystal, Wendy's, Zaxby's 🛏 Comfort Suites, Hampton Inn, Holiday Inn Express 🅾 $Tree, AT&T, City Tire, Home Depot, 🄷, URGENT CARE, Walgreens, Walmart/Subway, S 🅿 Shell/dsl, Texaco/dsl, Valero 🍽 Akita Japanese, Burger King, Dunkin'/Baskin Robbins, Hardee's, Jack's Rest., KFC, Little Caesar's, McDonald's, Pell City Steaks, Pizza Hut, Subway, Taco Bell, Waffle House 🛏 Quality Inn 🅾 $General, AutoZone, Chrysler/Dodge/Jeep, CVS Drug, Ford, O'Reilly Parts, Verizon
156	US 78 E, to Pell City, S 🅿 Chevron/dsl, Shell/dsl
153	US 78, Chula Vista
152	Cook Springs
147	Brompton, N 🅿 Sunoco, Valero TC/dsl/scales/24hr, S 🅿 ❤Loves/McDonald's/Subway/dsl/scales/24hr, Valero/dsl/deli
144	US 411, Leeds, N 🅿 76/dsl, RaceWay/dsl, Shell/Subway 🍽 Arby's, Bojangles, Burger King, Cracker Barrel, Krystal, Logan's Roadhouse, Milo's Burgers, Pizza Hut, Ruby Tuesday, Waffle House, Wendy's, Zaxby's 🛏 Best Western+, Comfort Inn, Super 8 🅾 $Tree, Publix, Verizon, S 🅿 Chevron, RaceWay/dsl 🍽 Capt D's, Chick-fil-A, El Cazador Mexican, Guadalajara Jalisco Mexican, Hardee's, KFC, Little Caesar's, McDonald's, Sakura Steaks, Taco Bell, Waffle House 🛏 Days Inn 🅾 $General, Advance Parts, AT&T, AutoZone, Lowe's, O'Reilly Parts, Walgreens, Walmart/Subway
140	US 78, Leeds, N 🅾 Distinctive Outlets/famous brands, S 🅿 Buc-ee's/dsl, Chevron, Marathon 🍽 Subway 🛏 America's Best Value Inn, Hampton Inn 🅾 Bass Pro Shop
139mm	Cahaba River
136	I-459 S, to Montgomery, Tuscaloosa
135	US 78, Old Leeds Rd, N 🅿 Shell/dsl 🅾 B'ham Race Course
133	US 78, to Kilgore Memorial Dr, (wb return at 132), N 🅿 Chevron, Exxon/Circle K/dsl 🍽 Golden Rule BBQ, Hamburger Heaven, Jack's, Krystal, Waffle House 🛏 Red Roof Inn, same as 132, Siesta Motel, S 🅿 Shell 🍽 McDonald's 🛏 Hampton Inn, Holiday Inn Express, Quality Inn 🅾 Tire Engineers
132b a	US 78, Crestwood Blvd, N same as 133 🅿 Chevron, Exxon/Circle K/dsl 🍽 Golden Rule BBQ, Hamburger Heaven, Jack's, Krystal, Subway, Waffle House 🛏 Red Roof Inn, Siesta Motel 🅾 $General, Aamco, O'Reilly Parts, S 🅿 Chevron, Exxon, Marathon/dsl, Murphy Express/dsl, Shell, Texaco/dsl 🍽 Arby's, Bojangles, Burger King, Capt D's, Chick-fil-A, Domino's, El Cazador Mexican, Honeybaked Ham, IHOP, KFC, King Buffet, Los Arcos Mexican, McDonald's, Milo's Burgers, New China Buffet, Olive Garden, Pancho's Mexican, Shrimp Basket, Starbucks, Taco Bell, Zaxby's 🛏 Comfort Inn, Delux Inn, Garden Suites 🅾 $Tree, Advance Parts, Aldi Foods, Burlington Coats, Firestone/auto, Home Depot, 🄷, Office Depot, Pep Boys, Ross, TJ Maxx, Tuesday Morning, URGENT CARE, Verizon, Walgreens, Walmart
130b	US 11, 1st Ave, N 🅿 Chevron, Petro, Sunoco 🅾 AutoZone, Family$, Piggly Wiggly, S 🅿 Chevron/dsl 🍽 McDonald's, Pacific Seafood 🛏 Relax Inn, Sky Inn
130a	I-59 N, to Gadsden
	I-59 S and I-20 W run together from B'ham to Meridian, MS
129	Airport Blvd, N 🛏 Ramada 🅾, 🎦, S 🅿 Mobil, Shell/dsl, Shell dsl 🍽 Hardee's, Kabob House 🛏 Best Inn, Holiday Inn
128	AL 79, Tallapoosa St, N 🅿 Circle K/Subway/dsl/scales, Shell Wings/dsl
126b	31st St, N 🅿 Shell/dsl, Texaco/dsl 🍽 McDonald's 🅾 Family$
126a	US 31, US 280, 26th St, Carraway Blvd, N 🍽 Church's, KFC, Rally's
125b	22nd St, N 🍽 Subway 🛏 Sheraton, Westin
125a	17th St to downtown

INTERSTATE 20 Cont'd

Exit #	Services
124b a	I-65, S to Montgomery, N to Nashville
123	US 78, Arkadelphia Rd, N 🅖 Chevron, Jet-Pep, 🛢/Wendy's/dsl/scales/24hr (0.5mi), Shell/dsl 🍴 Popeye's 🏠 Days Inn, S 🅞 🏥, to Legion Field
121	Bush Blvd (from wb, no return), Ensley, N 🅖 Exxon, Marathon
120	AL 269, 20th St, Ensley Ave, N 🅖 Jet-Pep 🍴 KFC 🅞 Honda, S 🅖 Chevron 🅞 🏥, Toyota
119b	Ave I (from wb)
119a	Lloyd Noland Pwky, N 🅖 Chevron/dsl, Sunoco/dsl 🍴 Burger King, Fairfield Seafood, McDonald's, Subway, S 🅖 Mobil, Texaco 🅞 🏥
118	AL 56, Valley Rd, Fairfield, S 🅖 Shell 🍴 Papa John's 🏠 Best Inn 🅞 Advance Parts, Home Depot, URGENT CARE
115	Allison-Bonnett Memorial Dr, N 🅖 Marathon/dsl, RaceWay/dsl, Shell/dsl 🍴 Church's, Jack's, Los Reyes, Subway, Zaxby's 🅞 Advance Parts, O'Reilly Parts, USPO
113	18th Ave, to Hueytown, S 🅖 Chevron/dsl/24hr, Marathon 🍴 McDonald's
112	18th St, 19th St, Bessemer, N 🅖 RaceWay/dsl, Shell 🍴 Jack's Rest. 🅞 tire/repair, S 🅖 Chevron, Sunoco/dsl 🍴 KFC, Muffaletta's Italian, Rally's, Subway, Sykes BBQ 🅞 Advance Parts, FMS Drug, Lowe's, NAPA, O'Reilly Parts, Walgreens
110	AL Adventure Pkwy, N 🅞 Splash Adventure Funpark, S 🅞 🏥
108	US 11, AL 5 N, Academy Dr, N 🅖 Circle K 🍴 Applebee's, Carnation Buffet, Catfish Cabin, Cracker Barrel, Waffle House 🏠 Best Western, Comfort Inn, Country Inn&Suites, Fairfield Inn, Holiday Inn Express, Quality Inn, Wood Spring Suites 🅞 Chevrolet, Chrysler/Dodge/Jeep, Nissan, S 🅖 Chevron/Church's/dsl, Murphy USA/dsl, Shell 🍴 Burger King, Domino's, Jade Garden, Little Caesar's, McDonald's, Milo's Burgers, Ruby Tuesday, Sonic, Wendy's, Zaxby's 🏠 Economy Inn, Hamilton Inn, Knights Inn, Motel 6 🅞 $Tree, BigLots, Ford, 🏥, PepBoys, to civic ctr, Verizon, Walmart/Subway
106	I-459 N, to Montgomery
104	Rock Mt Lake, S 🅖 ⛽FLYING J/Subway/dsl/LP/24hr
100	to Abernant, N 🅖 ❤Loves/McDonald's/Subway/dsl/scales/24hr 🍴 Burger King, S 🅖 Citgo, Marathon, Petro/Valero/Iron Skillet/Popeyes/dsl/scales/24hr/@ 🅞 $General, Tannehill Ironworks Camping, Tannehill SP (3mi)
97	US 11 S, AL 5 S, to W Blocton, S 🅖 Chevron/KFC/dsl, Citgo/dsl, Exxon/Subway/dsl 🍴 Jack's Rest., La Tortilla Grill 🅞 Cahaba River NWR
89	Mercedes Dr, N 🏠 Greystone Inn, S 🅞 Mercedes Auto Plant
86	Vance, to Brookwood, N 🅖 Marathon/Huddle House/Subway/dsl, Shell/dsl/rest./24hr
85mm	🆁🆂 both lanes, full ♿ facilities, litter barrels, petwalk, 🅲, 🐾, RV dump, vending
79	US 11, University Blvd, Coaling, S 🅖 Chevron/dsl, Texaco/dsl
77	Cottondale, N 🅖 Chevron/McDonald's, 🛢/Wendy's/dsl/scales/24hr, TA/BP/Taco Bell/dsl/scales/24hr/@ 🍴 Arby's, Pizza Hut, Ruby Tuesday 🏠 Hampton Inn, Microtel 🅞 Blue Beacon, Harley Davidson, SpeedCo, USPO, S 🅞 Chevrolet
76	US 11, E Tuscaloosa, Cottondale, N 🅖 Chevron, Marathon, Shell/dsl 🍴 Burger King, Cracker Barrel, Waffle House 🏠 Centerstone Inn, Howard Johnson, Western Motel, Wingate Inn, Woodspring Suites 🅞 Sunset 2 RV Park, transmissions, S 🅖 🛢/Subway/dsl/scales/24hr, Texaco/dsl 🏠 Rodeway Inn
73	US 82, McFarland Blvd, Tuscaloosa, N 🅖 Chevron/dsl, Circle K, RaceWay, Shell 🍴 Applebee's, Arby's, Buffalo Wild Wings, Burger King, Capt D's, Chick-fil-A, Chipotle, Five Guys,

73	Continued
	Full Moon BBQ, Jason's Deli, Krystal, Longhorn Steaks, Moe's SW Grill, O'Charley's, Olive Garden, Panera Bread, Popeye's, Red Lobster, Shrimp Basket, Starbucks, TCBY, Waffle House 🏠 Best Value Inn, Best Western, Comfort Suites, Guest Lodge, Holiday Inn Express, Masters Inn 🅞 $General, Aamco, Advance Parts, AT&T, Barnes&Noble, Belk, Best Buy, CVS Drug, Firestone/auto, Goodyear/auto, Home Depot, 🏥, JC Penney, Michael's, OK Tire, Old Navy, PepBoys, Rite Aid, Ross, SteinMart, Target, Verizon, vet, S 🅖 Jet-Pep/dsl, Marathon 🍴 Buffet City, Checkers, Cheddar's, Chili's, Hardee's, KFC, Logan's Roadhouse, McDonald's, Papa John's, Pizza Hut, Sonic, Subway, Taco Bell, Taco Casa, Trey Yuen Cinese 🏠 Ambassador Inn, Candlewood Suites, Country Inn&Suites, Days Inn, EconoLodge, La Quinta, Motel 6, Quality Inn, Ramada Inn, Super 8 🅞 $General, $Tree, Chrysler/Dodge/Jeep, NAPA, Office Depot, Rite Aid, Sam's Club/gas, TJ Maxx, U-Haul, Walmart/Subway
71b	I-359, Al 69 N, to Tuscaloosa, N 🅞 🏥, to Stillman Coll, U of AL
71a	AL 69 S, to Moundville, S 🅖 Chevron, Citgo/dsl, Mapco/Quiznos/dsl, Shell/dsl 🍴 Arby's, Baumhower's Rest., Chick-fil-A, Costa BBQ, Hooters, IHOP, LoneStar Steaks, OutBack Steaks, Pizza Hut, Ryan's, Waffle House, Wendy's, Zaxby's 🏠 Baymont Inn, Courtyard, Fairfield Inn, Hilton Garden 🅞 Advance Parts, Goodyear/auto, Kia/Mazda/VW, Lowe's, O'Reilly Parts, PepBoys, to Mound SM, URGENT CARE
68	Northport-Tuscaloosa Western Bypass
64mm	Black Warrior River
62	Fosters, N 🅖 Chevron/Subway/dsl 🅞 $General, Foodland, USPO, vet
52	US 11, US 43, Knoxville, N 🅖 Circle K/dsl
45	AL 37, Union, S 🅖 Chevron/Subway/dsl, Texaco/dsl 🍴 South Fork Rest 🏠 Econolodge, Travel Inn 🅞 Greene Co Greyhound Park
40	AL 14, Eutaw, N 🅞 to Tom Bevill Lock/Dam, S 🅖 🏥, ❤Loves/dsl/scales/24hr, Marathon
39mm	🆁🆂 wb, full ♿ facilities, litter barrels, petwalk, 🅲, 🐾, RV dump, vending
38mm	🆁🆂 eb, full ♿ facilities, litter barrels, petwalk, 🅲, 🐾, RV dump, vending
32	Boligee, N 🅖 Marathon/rest./dsl/24hr, S 🅖 Chevron/Subway/dsl
27mm	Tenn-Tom Waterway, Tombigbee River
23	rd 20, Epes, to Gainesville
17	AL 28, Livingston, S 🅖 Chevron/Subway/dsl, Exxon/L&B/dsl/24hr, Shell/dsl, Spirit 🍴 Burger King, Diamond Jim's/Mrs Donna's, McDonald's, Pizza Hut 🏠 Comfort Inn, Western Inn 🅞 repair/24hr

BESSEMER

TUSCALOOSA

AL

INTERSTATE 20 Cont'd

Exit #	Services
8	AL 17, York, **S** 🅟 Marathon/New Orleans Grill/dsl/scales/@ 🛏 Best Inn
1	to US 80 E, Cuba, **S** 🅟 Citgo/rest./dsl
.5mm	Welcome Ctr eb, full ♿ facilities, litter barrels, petwalk, 🄲, 🚮, RV dump, vending
	I-20 E and I-59 N run together from Meridian, MS to B'ham.
0mm	Alabama/Mississippi state line

INTERSTATE 22

Exit #	Services
96	I-65, N to Nashville, S to Birmingham, **I-22 begins/ends.**
93	rd 77
91	rd 105, to Brookside
89	rd 65, to Adamsville, Graysville
87	rd 112, to Graysville
85	US 78, Birmingham
81	rd 45, W Jefferson
78	rd 81, Dora, Sumiton, **N** 🍴 TJ's/dsl
72	rd 61, Cordova
70	rd 22, Cordova, Parish
65	Bevill Ind Pkwy, Jasper, **N** 🛏 Hampton Inn (3mi) 🄾 🄷, to Walker Co Lake, **S** 🅟 ❤Love's/McDonald's/Subway/dsl/scales/24hr 🍴 Burger King, Cracker Barrel, Waffle House, Zaxby's 🛏 Sleep Inn 🄾 Buick/Cadillac/Chevrolet/GMC
63	AIL 269, Jasper, Parish, **N** 🅟 Chevron/deli/dsl
61	AL 69, Jasper, Tuscaloosa, **N** 🅟 RJ's 🍴 Deano's Hickory Pit
57	AL 118 E, Jasper, **N** 🅟 Chevron, Shell/dsl 🍴 The Barn Rest.
53	to AL 118
52	AL 118, Carbon Hill
46	rd 11, Carbon Hill, Nauvoo, **S** 🅟 Chevron/dsl, Shell
39	AL 13, Natural Bridge, Eldridge
34	AL 233, Glen Allen, Natural Bridge
30	AL 129, Brilliant, Winfield, **S** 🅟 Chevron/deli/dsl, Shell/deli/dsl 🍴 Huddle House 🛏 Hampton Inn
26	AL 44, Brilliant, Guin, **S** 🛏 Holiday Inn 🄾 🄷
22	rd 45
16	US 43, US 278, Hamilton, Guin, **S** 🅟 Shell/deli/dsl
14	Hamilton, **N** 🅟 ❤Love's/dsl/scales/24hr, Texaco/dsl 🍴 Huddle House 🛏 Days Inn (1mi), EconoLodge (1mi), Keywest Inn 🄾 Speedco
11	AL 17, Hamilton, Sulligent, **N** 🅟 Citgo/dsl 🄾 🄷
7	Hamilton, Weston, **N** 🄾 🄷
3	rd 33
0mm	Alabama/Mississippi State Line

INTERSTATE 59

Exit #	Services
241.5mm	Alabama/Georgia state line, Central/Eastern time zone
241mm	Welcome Ctr sb, full ♿ facilities, litter barrels, petwalk, 🄲, 🚮, RV dump, vending
239	to US 11, Sulphur Springs Rd, **E** 🄾 camping
231	AL 40, AL 117, Hammondville, Valley Head, **E** 🄾 camping (5mi), DeSoto SP, **W** 🅟 Fuel City
224	49th St, to Ft Payne, **W** 🅟 Mapco
222	US 11, to Ft Payne, **1 mi E** 🍴 Arby's, Hardee's, Jack's Rest., KFC, Krystal, Pizza Hut, SteviB's Pizza, Subway, Toke Thai Grill, Wingstop 🛏 Quality Inn 🄾 Chevrolet, Foodland/dsl, **W** 🅟 Citgo/dsl 🍴 Waffle King

FT PAYNE / GADSDEN / TRUSSVILLE

Exit #	Services
218	AL35, Ft Payne, **E** 🅟 🍴 Capt D's, Don Chico Mexican, DQ, Jack's, Jefferson's Burgers, Little Caesar's, McDonald's, New China, Papa John's, Sonic, Taco Bell, Western Sizzlin, Zaxby's 🄾 $General, Advance Parts, Alabama Museum, AutoZone, BigLots, Chrysler/Dodge/Jeep, O'Reilly Parts, URGENT CARE, **W** 🍴 Circle K/dsl, MapCo, Mapco/dsl, Murphy USA/dsl 🍴 Applebee's, Burger King, Chick-fil-A, Chow King, Cracker Barrel, Hardee's, Huddle House, Los Arcos, Ruby Tuesday, Santa Fe Steaks, Waffle House 🛏 Days Inn, EconoLodge, Hampton Inn, Holiday Inn Express 🄾 $Tree, AT&T, Ford/Lincoln, GNC, 🄷, Lowe's, Verizon, Walgreens, Walmart, Will's Creek RV Park
205	AL 68, Collinsville, **E** 🅟 Delta 🍴 Jack's Rest. 🛏 Travelers Inn 🄾 to Little River Canyon, Weiss Lake, **W** 🅟 BP/dsl, MapCo 🍴 Burger King
188	AL 211, to US 11, Gadsden, **E** 🅟 Jet-Pep 🄾 Noccalula Falls Camping, **W** 🅟 Marathon/dsl/e85
183	US 431, US 278, Gadsden, **E** 🅟 Jet-Pep/dsl, Shell, Texaco/dsl 🍴 Waffle House 🛏 Days Inn, HomeLodge, Motel 6, Rodeway Inn 🄾 st police, **W** 🅟 Chevron, Exxon, Jet-Pep 🍴 KFC, McDonald's, Pizza Hut, Subway, Taco Bell
182	I-759, to Gadsden
181	AL 77, Rainbow City, to Gadsden, **E** 🅟 Petro/Popeye's/dsl/scales/24hr/@ 🍴 Jack's 🛏 EconoLodge, **W** 🅟 Circle K/dsl, Murphy Express/dsl 🍴 Arby's, Bubba Rito's SW Grill, Cracker Barrel, Domino's, El Patron, Hardee's, Hector's Kitchen, Lucky Wok, McDonald's, Old Mexico Grille, Ruby Tuesday, Subway, Waffle House, Wendy's 🛏 Best Western+, Comfort Suites, Fairfield Inn, Hampton Inn, Holiday Inn Express 🄾 $General, $Tree, O'Reilly Parts, Walmart/Papa John's
174	to Steele, **E** 🅟 ❤Love's/Subway/Chester's/dsl/scales/24hr, **W** 🅟 Marathon/dsl, Sunoco/Molina's/dsl
168mm	🆁🆂 sb, full ♿ facilities, litter barrels, petwalk, 🄲, 🚮, RV dump, vending
166	US 231, Whitney, to Ashville, **E** 🅟 BP, Chevron/dsl, **W** 🅟 Texaco/dsl 🍴 Huddle House, Jack's Rest., Subway
165mm	🆁🆂 nb, full ♿ facilities, litter barrels, petwalk, 🄲, 🚮, RV dump, vending
156	AL 23, to US 11, Springville, to St Clair Springs, **W** 🅟 Murphy USA/dsl, Shell /dsl 🍴 Azteca's Mexican, Burger King, China Stix, KFC, Pizza Hut, Taco Bell, Waffle House, Zaxby's 🄾 $Tree, AT&T, Walmart/Subway
154	AL 174, Springville, to Odenville, **E** 🅟 Exxon/dsl, **W** 🅟 BP/Subway, Chevron, Citgo, MapCo, Shell/dsl 🍴 Choppin Block Rest., Gulf Seafood, Jack's Rest., McDonald's
148	to US 11, Argo, **E** 🅟 Shell 🍴 Jack's, Subway
143	Mt Olive Church Rd, Deerfoot Pkwy, **E** 🅟 Chevron/dsl/CNG, Shell/dsl (1mi) 🍴 Munoz Mexican 🄾 Publix (1mi)
141	to Trussville, Pinson, **E** 🅟 Bama/dsl, Shell/dsl, Texaco/dsl 🍴 Applebee's, Cracker Barrel, Guthrie's, McDonald's, Papa John's, Pizza Hut, Taco Bell, Waffle House, Wendy's 🛏 Comfort Inn, Holiday Inn Express, Quality Inn 🄾 Harley-Davidson, **W** 🅟 Chevron, Marathon, Shell/dsl, Texaco 🍴 Arby's, Buffalo Wild Wings, Burger King, Chick-fil-A, Cici's, Costa's Mediterranean, DQ, East Buffet, Frontera Grill, Full Moon BBQ, Jack's, Konomi Japanese, Krystal, Milo's Burgers, Moe's SW Grill, Momma Goldberg's Deli, Palace Asian, Paul's Hotdogs, Ruby Tuesday, Whataburger, Zaxby's 🄾 $Tree, Ace Hardware, Advance Parts, BigLots, CVS Drug, GNC, Kohl's, Marshall's, Office Depot, Petsmart, Sam's Club/gas, Verizon, vet, Walgreens, Walmart/Subway
137	I-459 S, to Montgomery, Tuscaloosa

⬆️N INTERSTATE 59 Cont'd

Exit #	Services
134	to AL 75, Roebuck Pkwy, **W** 🛢️ BP/Circle K, Chevron, Murphy USA/dsl, Shell/dsl 🍴 Arby's, Burger King, Chick-fil-A, Crab Barrack, Hardee's, McDonald's, Milo's Burgers, Pizza Hut, Subway, Taco Bell 🅾️ $Tree, Aldi Foods, AT&T, CVS Drug, GNC, Honda, �H, NTB, O'Reilly Parts, URGENT CARE, Vo Tires, Walgreens, Walmart/Burger King
133	4th St, to US 11 (from nb), same as 134, **W** 🍴 Papa John's 🅾️ $General, USPO
132	US 11 N, 1st Ave, **E** same as 131, **W** 🛢️ Chevron, Shell/dsl 🍴 Krispy Kreme 🅾️ city park
131	Oporto-Madrid Blvd (from nb), **E** 🛢️ BP/Subway, Chevron 🍴 Church's, Little Caesar's 🅾️ CVS Drug, Family$, O'Reilly Parts, same as 132, U-Haul
130	I-20, E to Atlanta, W to Tuscaloosa
	I-59 S and I-20 W run together from B'ham to Mississippi. See Alabama Interstate 20, exits 129-1.

⬆️N INTERSTATE 65

Exit #	Services
366mm	Alabama/Tennessee state line
365	AL 53, to Ardmore, **E** 🏨 Budget Inn
364mm	**Welcome Ctr sb, full ♿ facilities, info, litter barrels, petwalk, 🚻, 🗑️, RV dump, vending**
361	Elkmont, **W** 🛢️ BP/dsl 🍴 Momma D's Rest. 🅾️ antiques, repair
354	US 31 S, to Athens, **W** 🛢️ Chevron/dsl 🍴 Capt D's, Domino's, Jack's Rest., Little Caesar's, McDonald's, Pizza Hut, Rooster's Cafe, Subway 🏨 Mark Motel 🅾️ $General, Advance Parts, city park, CVS Drug, HomeTown Mkt, �H, Northgate RV Park, Walgreens
351	US 72, to Athens, Huntsville, **E** 🛢️ Exxon, RaceWay/dsl, Shell/Subway, Valero/dsl 🍴 Buffalo Wild Wings, Burger King, Cracker Barrel, Dunkin', Jack's, Las Trejas Mexican, Lawler's BBQ, McDonald's/RV Parking, Taco Bell, Waffle House, Wendy's 🏨 Econolodge, Hampton Inn, Quality Inn, Travel Inn 🅾️ $General, Publix, Russell Stover, Verizon, vet, **W** 🛢️ Chevron/dsl, Citgo/dsl, Marathon, Murphy USA 🍴 Applebee's, Arby's, Bojangle's, Burger King, Catfish Cabin, Chick-fil-A, DQ, Firehouse Subs, Hardee's, IHOP, KFC, Krystal, Logan's Roadhouse, Papa John's, Papa Murphy's, Pizza Hut, Popeye's, Ruby Tuesday, Shoney's, Sonic, Starbucks, Steak-Out, Subway, Zaxby's 🏨 Best Western, Days Inn, Fairfield Inn, Holiday Inn Express, Sleep Inn, Super 8 🅾️ $General, $Tree, Advance Parts, Aldi Foods, AT&T, Big Lots, Chevrolet, Chrysler/Dodge/Jeep, Ford, Goodyear/auto, �H, Lowe's, O'Reilly Parts, Pepboys, SaveALot Foods, Staples, to Joe Wheeler SP, Tuesday Morning, Walmart
347	Brownsferry Rd, Huntsville, **W** 🛢️ Chevron 🅾️ Swan Creek RV Park
340b	I-565, to Alabama Space & Rocket Ctr, to Huntsville
340a	AL 20, to Decatur, **W** 🛢️ Chevron/dsl 🏨 Courtyard (7mi), Hampton Inn (7mi), Holiday Inn Express (7mi)
337mm	Tennessee River
334	AL 67, Priceville, to Decatur, **E** 🛢️ Marathon/dsl, RaceWay/dsl 🍴 JW's Steaks 🏨 Days Inn, Super 8 🅾️ $General, Family$, Foodland, **W** 🛢️ Chevron/dsl, Mapco/dsl, Pilot/Subway/Wendy's/dsl/scales/24hr 🍴 Burger King, DQ, Hardee's, Krystal, McDonald's, Pizza Hut, Taco Bell, Taste of China, Waffle House 🏨 Comfort Inn 🅾️ �H, Johnston RV Ctr, Publix
328	AL 36, Hartselle, **E** 🍴 Cracker Barrel, **W** 🛢️ Chevron/dsl, Cowboys/dsl, Jet-Pep/dsl, Ztrac 🍴 Huddle House 🏨 Red Roof Inn 🅾️ $General, vet

325	Thompson Rd, to Hartselle
322	AL 55, to US 31, to Falkville, Eva, **E** 🛢️ Marathon/Chester's/dsl, **W** 🛢️ Chevron, Loves/McDonald's/Subway/dsl/scales/24hr 🍴 Log Cabin Rest. 🅾️ $General
318	US 31, to Lacon
310	AL 157, Cullman, West Point, **E** 🛢️ 76/dsl, Chevron/Popeye's, Conoco/Subway/dsl, Shell/dsl, Texaco/Wendy's/dsl 🍴 Arby's, Bueno Vista Mexican, Burger King, Cracker Barrel, Denny's, KFC, Lawler's BBQ, Little Caesar's, Logan's Roadhouse, McDonald's, Panda Express, Ruby Tuesday, Taco Bell, Waffle House, Zaxby's 🏨 Best Western, Comfort Suites, Hampton Inn, Holiday Inn Express, La Quinta, Quality Inn, Sleep Inn 🅾️ Buick/GMC, Ford/Lincoln, �H, Verizon, Walmart, **W** 🛢️ Exxon/dsl, Marathon/dsl 🏨 Best Value Inn
308	US 278, Cullman, **E** 🏨 Days Inn 🅾️ Smith Farms, **W** 🛢️ Chevron 🅾️ $General, Chrysler/Dodge/Jeep, flea mkt
305	to Al 69
304	AL 69 N, Good Hope, to Cullman, **E** 🛢️ Exxon/dsl, Jet-Pep/dsl, Pilot/Wendy's/Dunkin'/dsl/scales/24hr, Shell/dsl/scales 🍴 Hardee's, Waffle House 🏨 EconoLodge 🅾️ Good Hope Camping, �H, Johnston RV Ctr, **W** 🛢️ Jet-Pep, to Smith Lake Camping 🅾️ $General
301mm	℞ both lanes, full ♿ facilities, litter barrels, petwalk, 🚻, 🗑️, RV dump, vending
299	AL 69 S, to Jasper, **E** 🛢️ Jet-pep/dsl 🅾️ Millican RV Ctr, repair, tires, **W** 🛢️ Chevron/dsl, Petro/Burger King/Popeye's/Papa John'sdsl/scales/24hr, Shell/McDonald's/dsl 🍴 Jack's Rest., Subway 🅾️ $General
291	AL 91, to Arkadelphia, **E** 🛢️ Jet-Pep/dsl 🅾️ Country View RV Park (1mi), **W** 🛢️ Shell/dsl/24hr/@ 🍴 291 Roadhouse Rest.
291mm	Warrior River
289	to Blount Springs, **W** 🛢️ Citgo 🅾️ to Rickwood Caverns SP
287	US 31 N, to Blount Springs, **E** 🛢️ Jet-Pep/dsl
284	US 31 S, AL 160 E, Hayden, **E** 🛢️ Shamrock/dsl, Sunoco/dsl, Valero Travel Center/dsl 🍴 Jack's 🅾️ URGENT CARE, **W** 🅾️ tires
282	AL 140, Warrior, **E** 🛢️ Chevron/Subway/dsl, Exxon/McDonald's, Shell/Dunkin'/Little Caesar's/dsl 🍴 Hardee's, Pizza Hut, Taco Bell, **W** 🛢️ Marathon 🍴 Huddle House
281	US 31, to Warrior
280	to US 31, to Warrior, **E** 🛢️ Chevron/dsl 🅾️ vet
279mm	Warrior River
275	to US 31, Morris
272	Mt Olive Rd, **E** 🛢️ Shell/dsl 🅾️ LDS Temple, **W** 🛢️ Chevron/dsl, Citgo/dsl 🍴 Jack's Rest. 🅾️ $General
271	Fieldstown Rd, **E** 🛢️ BP/Circle K, Chevron/dsl, Exxon, Murphy USA/dsl, RaceWay/dsl 🍴 Arby's, Buffalo Wild Wings, Capt D's,

A T H E N S

D E C A T U R

C U L L M A N

⬆N INTERSTATE 65 Cont'd

FULTONDALE

271 Continued
Chick-fil-A, DQ, Habanero's Mexican, Jack's, Jim'n Nick's BBQ, Joel's, KFC, Kumo's Asian, Little Caesar's, McDonald's, Milo's Burgers, Moe's SW, Panera Bread, Pasquales Pizza, Pizza Hut, Sonic, Starbucks, Subway, Taco Bell, Waffle House, Wendy's, Zaxby's 🛏 Microtel 🅾 $General, $Tree, Advance Parts, AT&T, AutoZone, CVS, Hobby Lobby, Kia, NAPA, PepBoys, Publix, TJ Maxx, URGENT CARE, Verizon, Walgreens, Walmart/McDonald's, **W** 🅖 Shell/dsl 🍽 Cracker Barrel 🛏 Best Western

267 Walkers Chapel Rd, to Fultondale, **E** 🅖 BP/dsl, Jet-Pep, Murphy Express/dsl, Shell/Subway/dsl 🍽 Applebee's, Arby's, Bojangles, Burger King, Casa Fiesta, Chick-fil-A, Chili's, Domino's, Firehouse Subs, Five Guys, Fullmoon BBQ, Hardee's, Jack's Rest., Logan's Roadhouse, McDonald's, O'Charley's, Outback Steaks, Shoney's, Stix Asian, Waffle House, Whataburger, Wintzell's Oyster House, Zaxby's 🛏 Comfort Inn, Comfort Suites, Fairfield Inn, Hampton Inn, Holiday Inn Express, Home 2 Suites, La Quinta 🅾 $General, AAA, Aldi Foods, AT&T, Best Buy, Books-A-Million, CVS Drug, GNC, JC Penney, Lowe's, O'Reilly Parts, Rite Aid, Ross, Target, URGENT CARE, USPO, Verizon, Volvo/Mack Trucks, Winn-Dixie, **W** 🅖 Chevron/dsl

265b US 31, Fultondale, **E** 🅖 Chevron/dsl 🛏 Days Inn, Econolodge

265a I-22 W, to Memphis

264 41st Ave, **W** 🅖 *FLYING J*/Denny's/dsl/LP/scales/24hr, LNG

263 33rd Ave, **E** 🅖 Chevron/dsl, **W** 🅖 Exxon

262b a 16th St, Finley Ave, **E** 🅖 Chevron, Marathon/dsl, Sunoco/dsl 🅾 Kenworth, **W** 🅖 Chevron, Fuel City/dsl 🍽 Capt D's, McDonald's, Popeye's

261b a I-20/59, E to Gadsden, W to Tuscaloosa

260b a 6th Ave N, **E** 🅖 Citgo, Shell, Texaco 🍽 Mrs Winner's 🛏 Tourway Inn 🅾 Chevrolet, Chrysler/Dodge/Jeep, Hyundai, Nissan, Subaru, **W** 🅖 Chevron/dsl 🅾 Tire Pros, to Legion Field

259b a University Blvd, 4th Ave, 5th Ave, **E** 🅖 Chevron/dsl 🍽 Capt D's, McDonald's, Ted's Cafeteria 🅾 🏥, **W** 🅖 Chevron/dsl 🅾 Goodyear

258 Green Springs Ave, **E** 🅖 Chevron, Shell, Sunoco/dsl 🍽 Exotic Wings

256b a Oxmoor Rd, **E** 🅖 Exxon, Marathon, Mobil/dsl, Shell 🍽 Acapulco Grill, Alfredo's Pizza, Burger King, Domino's, Firehouse Subs, Hunan Rest., KFC, McDonald's, Papa Murphy's, Paw Paw Patch, Popeye's, Purple Onion, San Miguel Mexican, Taco Bell, The Baskits, Zaxby's 🛏 Howard Johnson 🅾 $Tree, Aldi Foods, AutoZone, BigLots, Firestone/auto, Food World, Fred's, Midas, Office Depot, Omega Tire Pros, PepBoys, Publix, Tire Engineers, Tuesday Morning, URGENT CARE, Walgreens, Walmart Mkt, **W** 🅖 Chevron, Texaco/dsl 🍽 Hamburger Heaven, Hardee's, Jim'n Nick's BBQ, Waffle House 🛏 Best Inn, Best Value Inn, Comfort Inn, EconoLodge, Motel 6, Quality Inn, Super 8 🅾 Batteries+, Valley Tire, vet

BIRMINGHAM

255 Lakeshore Dr, **E** 🅖 BP/Circle K 🅾 🏥, to Samford U, URGENT CARE, **W** 🅖 Chevron, Shell 🍽 Arby's, Chick-fil-A, Chili's, Costas BBQ, Hooters, IHOP, La Catrina Mexican, Landry's Seafood, McAlister's Deli, McDonald's, Milo's Burger, Moe's SW Grill, Mr Wang's, O'Charley's, Okinawa Grill, Outback Steaks, Starbucks, Subway, Taco Bell, Taco Casa, Wendy's 🛏 Best Western, Candlewood Suites, Country Inn & Suites, Drury Inn, Extended Stay, Hampton Inn, Hilton Garden, Holiday Inn, La Quinta, Residence Inn, TownePlace Suites 🅾 $Tree, AT&T, Goodyear/auto, Hobby Lobby, Lowe's, Sam's Club/gas, Verizon, Walmart/Subway

HOOVER

254 Alford Ave, Shades Crest Rd, **E** 🅖 Chevron 🅾 vet, **W** 🅖 BP/dsl, Shell/dsl

252 US 31, Montgomery Hwy, **E** 🅖 Chevron, Shell, Sunoco, Texaco/dsl 🍽 Arby's, Backyard Burger, Bruster's, Capt D's, ChuckECheese's, Hardee's, Ichiban Japanese, Milo's Burger, Waffle House 🛏 Baymont Inn, Days Inn 🅾 Aamco, GMC, 🏥, NAPA, PepBoys, Verizon, vet, Volvo, VW, **W** 🅖 Exxon/dsl, Shell/dsl, Sunoco/dsl 🍽 Burger King, Chick-fil-A, FishMkt Rest., Full Moon BBQ, Golden Rule BBQ, Habanero's Mexican, Krispy Kreme, Krystal, Mandarin House, McDonald's, Outback Steaks, Papa John's, Papa Murphy's, Purple Onion, Salvatore's Pizza, Starbucks, Subway, Waffle House 🛏 EconoLodge 🅾 $Tree, Acura, Advance Parts, AutoZone, Cadillac, Chevrolet, Chrysler/Dodge/Jeep, Firestone, Goodyear/auto, Honda, Hyundai, Mr Transmission, Nissan, Publix, Rite Aid, Staples, TJ Maxx, vet

250 I-459, to US 280

247 rd 17, Valleydale Rd, **E** 🅖 BP/Circle K 🍽 Hardee's, Jeffersons Wings 🅾 Goodyear/auto, Lowe's, **W** 🅖 Marathon, RaceWay/dsl, Shell/dsl 🍽 Arby's, Backyard Burger, IHOP, Milo's Burgers, Papa John's, RagTime Café, Subway, Waffle House, Zapatas Mexican 🛏 Homewood Suites, InTown Suites, La Quinta 🅾 Publix, Rite Aid, vet, Walgreens

246 AL 119, Cahaba Valley Rd, **E** 🅾 to Oak Mtn SP, **W** 🅖 Chevron, Circle K/dsl/scales, Murphy USA/dsl, RaceWay/dsl, Shell/dsl 🍽 Applebee's, Arby's, Burger King, Capt D's, Chick-fil-A, Cracker Barrel, DQ, Dunkin', Golden Corral, Hooters, Johnny Ray's BBQ, KFC, Krystal, Margarita Grill, McAlister's Deli, McDonald's, Pizza Hut, Purple Onion, Ruby Tuesday, Sonic, Taco Bell, Two Pesos Mexican, TX Roadhouse, Waffle House, Wendy's, Whataburger 🛏 Best Western, Comfort Suites, Fairfield Inn, Hampton Inn, Holiday Inn Express, Quality Inn, Ramada, Sleep Inn, Travelodge, Woodspring Suites 🅾 $Tree, Advance Parts, AutoZone, Firestone/auto, Harley-Davidson, Kia, Mazda, NAPA, O'Reilly Parts, Verizon, Walmart

PELHAM

242 rd 52, Pelham, **E** 🅖 Chevron/dsl, Exxon/dsl, Shell/dsl 🍽 Johnny Ray's BBQ, Subway 🅾 CVS Drug, Publix, **W** 🛏 Shelby Motel (2mi) 🅾 Good Sam Camping (1mi), 🏥

238 US 31, Alabaster, Saginaw, **E** 🅖 Murphy USA/dsl 🍽 Arby's, Buffalo Wild Wings, Chick-fil-A, DQ, Firehouse Subs, Full Moon BBQ, Habanero's Mexican, HoneyBaked Ham, Jim'n Nick's BBQ, Longhorn Steaks, McDonald's, Mizu Japanese, Moe's SW Grill, Momma Goldberg Deli, O'Charley's, Olive Garden, Panda House, Panera Bread, Ruby Tuesday, Starbucks, Steak'n Shake, Taco Bell 🛏 Candlewood Suites 🅾 $Tree, AT&T, Belk, Best Buy, Books-A-Million, Dick's, GNC, JC Penney, Lowe's, NTB, Old Navy, Petsmart, Ross, Target, TJ Maxx, URGENT CARE, Walmart/Subway, **W** 🅖 Chevron/dsl, Shell/dsl 🍽 Waffle House, Whataburger 🛏 Shelby Motel 🅾 🏥

234 Shelby County Airport, **E** 🅖 BP/Subway/dsl, **W** 🅖 Chevron/dsl, Shell/dsl 🅾 Buick/GMC, Camping World RV Ctr

231 US 31, Saginaw, **E** 🅖 GasBoy, Murphy USA/dsl, Shell/dsl 🍽 Bojangles, Capt D's, Cracker Barrel, Ezell's Catfish Cabin, McDonald's, Milo's Burgers, Pizza Hut, Subway, Taco Bell, Waffle House, Zaxby's, Zopapan Mexican 🛏 Hampton Inn, Quality Inn 🅾 $Tree, AT&T, Burton RV Ctr, Publix, Rolling Hills RV Park, URGENT CARE, Verizon, Walmart/Subway

228 AL 25, to Calera, **E** 🅖 Marathon/dsl, Shell/dsl 🛏 Calera Inn, **W** 🅖 Chevron/dsl 🍽 Little Caesar's, Subway 🅾 $General, Family$, to Brierfield Iron Works SP (15mi)

227mm Buxahatchie Creek

INTERSTATE 65 Cont'd

Exit #	Services
219	Union Grove, Thorsby, **E** 🅿️ Chevron/dsl, Exxon/Subway/dsl 🅾️ Peach Queen Camping, **W** 🅿️ Shell/dsl 🍴 Jack's Rest., Smokey Hollow Rest.
213mm	♿ both lanes, full ♿ facilities, litter barrels, petwalk, 🚻, 🛢️, RV dump, vending
212	AL 145, Clanton, **E** 🅿️ Chevron/dsl 🅾️ Nissan, Toyota, **W** 🅿️ Headco/dsl, Texaco/Subway 🅾️ Buick/Chevrolet/GMC, Chrysler/Dodge/Jeep, 🅷, One Big Peach
208	Clanton, **E** 🅿️ ❤️Loves/Arby's/dsl/scales/24hr 🅾️ Higgins Ferry RV Park (8mi), **W** 🅿️ Exxon/dsl 🍴 Shoney's 🛏️ Clanton Inn 🅾️ Dandy RV Park/Ctr, Heaton Pecans, KOA
205	US 31, AL 22, to Clanton, **E** 🅿️ Jet-Pep/dsl/e85, Shell/dsl, Texaco/dsl 🍴 McDonald's, Waffle House, Whataburger 🛏️ Best Western, Days Inn, Holiday Inn Express, Scottish Inn 🅾️ Peach Park, to Confed Mem Park (9mi), **0-2 mi W** 🅿️ Chevron/dsl, Murphy USA/dsl, Shell/dsl 🍴 Boomerang's Grill, Burger King, Capt D's, Jack's Rest., KFC, New China Buffet, Papa John's, Pizza Hut, San Marcos Mexican, Subway, Taco Bell, Wendy's, Zaxby's 🛏️ Key West Inn 🅾️ $General, $Tree, auto repair, Durbin Farms Mkt, Verizon, Walmart
200	to Verbena, **E** 🅿️ Texaco/dsl, **W** 🅿️ Sunoco
195	Worlds Largest Confederate Flag
186	US 31, Pine Level, **E** 🅾️ Confederate Mem Park (13mi), **W** 🅿️ Chevron/dsl, Exxon/dsl, Texaco/Subway/dsl 🍴 Shann's Kitchen 🅾️ 🅷
181	AL 14, to Prattville, **E** 🅿️ Chevron/dsl/24hr, Entec/dsl 🍴 Jack's, **W** 🅿️ BP, Circle K, QV, Shell/DQ/dsl 🍴 Cracker Barrel, Los Toros, McDonald's, Ruby Tuesday, Subway, Waffle House, Wendy's 🛏️ EconoLodge, Hometowne Suites, La Quinta, Quality Inn, Super 8 🅾️ 🅷
179	US 82 W, Millbrook, **E** 🅿️ Chevron/dsl/24hr 🛏️ Country Inn&Suites, Key West Inn, Sleep Inn, SpringHill Suites 🅾️ K&K RV Ctr/Park, **0-2 mi W** 🅿️ Liberty/dsl, Murphy Express/dsl, RaceWay/dsl, Shell/dsl 🍴 Applebee's, Arby's, Beef'O'Brady's, Bruster's, Burger King, Capt. D's, Chappy's Deli, Chick-fil-A, Chipotle, CiCi's Pizza, City Buffet, El Patron, Five Guys, Hardee's, IHOP, Jim'n Nick's BBQ, KFC, Krystal, Las Casitas Mexican, Logan's Roadhouse, Longhorn Steaks, McAlister's Deli, McDonald's, Mellow Mushroom, Mexico Tipico, Moe's SW Grill, O'Charley's, Olive Garden, Outback Steaks, Panda Express, Popeye's, Sonic, Starbucks, Steak'n Shake, Subway, Waffle House, Zaxby's 🛏️ Courtyard, Days Inn, Hampton Inn, Holiday Inn Express, Howard Johnson, Rodeway Inn 🅾️ $General, $Tree, AT&T, AutoZone, Bass Pro Shops, Belk, Best Buy, BigLots, Books-A-Million, Chevrolet, CVS Drug, Firestone/auto, Ford, GNC, Hobby Lobby, Home Depot, JC Penney, Kohl's, Lowe's, Michael's, O'Reilly Parts, Office Depot, PepBoys, Petsmart, Publix, Ross, Target, TJ Maxx, URGENT CARE, Verizon, vet, Walmart
176	AL 143 N (from nb, no return), Millbrook, Coosada
173	AL 152, North Blvd, to US 231
172mm	Alabama River
172	Clay St, Herron St, **E** 🛏️ Embassy Suites, Hampton Inn, Renaissance Hotel, **W** 🅿️ Chevron/dsl
171	I-85 N, Day St
170	Fairview Ave, **E** 🅿️ Citgo/Subway, Sunoco/dsl 🍴 Church's, McDonald's, Wing Master 🅾️ $General, $Tree, Advance Parts, AutoZone, CVS Drug, Family$, O'Reilly Parts, Piggly Wiggly, Walgreens, **W** 🅾️ Family$
169	Edgemont Ave (from sb), **E** 🅿️ Liberty
168	US 80 E, US 82, South Blvd, **E** 🅿️ Circle K/dsl, Marathon/dsl, TA/Marathon/Country Pride/dsl/24hr/@ 🍴 Arby's, Burger King, Capt D's, KFC, McDonald's, Pizza Hut, Popeye's, Taco Bell, Waffle House 🅾️ 🅷, The Woods RV Park, **W** 🅿️ Chevron/dsl, RaceWay/dsl 🍴 DQ, Hardee's, Wendy's 🛏️ Super 8
167	US 80 W, to Selma
164	US 31, Hyundai Blvd, Hope Hull, **E** 🅿️ Liberty, Saveway/dsl/scales/24hr, Shell/dsl 🍴 El Amigo Mexican 🅾️ auto repair, Montgomery Camping, **W** 🅿️ Chevron, Liberty/Subway, Marathon 🍴 Burger King, Hardee's, McDonald's, Waffle House 🛏️ Comfort Suites, Fairfield Inn, Hampton Inn, Holiday Inn, Motel 6, Quality Inn 🅾️ auto repair
158	to US 31, Tyson, **E** 🅿️ ❤️Loves/Subway/Godfather's/Chester's/dsl/scales/24hr, Shell/DQ/Stuckey's 🅾️ Montgomery South RV Park, **W** 🅿️ FLYING J/Denny's/dsl/scales/24hr
151	AL 97, to Letohatchee, **E** 🅿️ Marathon/dsl, **W** 🅿️ Link
142	AL 185, to Ft Deposit, **E** 🅿️ Petro+/dsl 🍴 Priester's Pecans, Subway 🅾️ auto parts, **W** 🅿️ Chevron
133mm	♿ both lanes, full ♿ facilities, litter barrels, petwalk, 🚻, 🛢️, RV dump, vending
130	AL10 E, AL 185, to Greenville, **E** 🅿️ Chevron/dsl, PaceCar/dsl, Shell 🍴 Arby's, Capt D's, China Town, Hardee's, KFC, McDonald's, Old Mexico, Papa John's, Pizza Hut, Waffle House, Wendy's 🛏️ Days Inn, Quality Inn 🅾️ $General, Advance Parts, CVS Drug, Fred's Store, O'Reilly Parts, Super Foods, to Sherling Lake Park, Walgreens, **W** 🅿️ Exxon/Subway/dsl, Mobil, Murphy USA/dsl, Texaco/dsl 🍴 Bates Turkey Cafe, Burger King, Cracker Barrel, Krystal, Ruby Tuesday, Shoney's, Sonic, Taco Bell, Wintzell's Oyster House 🛏️ Baymont Inn, Best Western, Comfort Inn, Hampton Inn, Holiday Inn Express 🅾️ $Tree, AT&T, Chevrolet, URGENT CARE, Verizon, Walmart/Subway
128	AL 10, to Greenville, **E** 🅿️ Shell/Smokehouse 🅾️ 🅷, **W** 🅿️ Marathon
114	AL 106, to Georgiana, **E** 🅾️ Hank Williams Museum, **W** 🅿️ Chevron, Marathon 🅾️ auto repair
107	rd 7, to Garland
101	to Owassa, **E** 🅿️ Marathon/dsl, **W** 🅿️ Gulf/dsl 🅾️ dsl repair, Owassa RV Park
96	AL 83, to Evergreen, **E** 🅿️ Chevron, Shell 🍴 Burger King, Hardee's, KFC/Taco Bell, McDonald's, Shoney's, Shrimp Basket, Subway, Waffle House, Wendy's, Zaxby's 🛏️ Sleep Inn 🅾️ 🅷, Piggly Wiggly, vet, **W** 🅿️ Spirit/Subway/dsl 🛏️ EconoLodge, Evergreen Inn, Quality Inn
93	US 84, to Evergreen, **E** 🅿️ Liberty/dsl, **W** 🅿️ ❤️Loves/Arby's/dsl/scales/24hr, Shell/dsl
89mm	♿ sb, full ♿ facilities, litter barrels, petwalk, 🚻, 🛢️, RV dump, vending

🅡 = gas   🍽 = food   🛏 = lodging   🅞 = other   🅡ₛ = rest stop   Copyright 2022 - The Next EXIT ®

AL

⤊ INTERSTATE 65 Cont'd

Exit #	Services
85mm	🅡ₛ nb, full ♿ facilities, litter barrels, petwalk, 🚻, 🏤, RV dump, vending
83	AL 6, to Lenox, E 🅡 Marathon/dsl 🅞 RV Park (4mi)
77	AL 41, to Range, to Range, W 🅡 Shell/dsl
69	AL 113, to Flomaton, E 🅡 Chevron/dsl/24hr, Jet-Pep/Subway/dsl, Shell/dsl/scales/24hr 🅞 dsl repair, Magnolia Branch Camping
57	AL 21, to Atmore, E 🅡 Chevron/dsl/24hr, Shell/dsl 🍽 Fairfield Inn, Hardee's, McDonald's, Popeye's, Sonic, Taco Bell, Waffle House 🛏 Hampton Inn, Holiday Inn Express 🅞 Wind Creek Indian Gaming, W 🅡 Shell/dsl 🅞 to Kelley SP
54	Escambia Cty Rd 1, E 🅡 Chevron/Subway/dsl 🅞 to Creek Indian Res, W 🅡 Shell/diner/dsl 🅞 $General
45	to Perdido, W 🅡 Chevron/dsl
37	AL 287, Gulf Shores Pkwy, to Bay Minette, E 🅡 Marathon/dsl
34	to AL 59, to Bay Minette, Stockton
31	AL 225, to Stockton, E 🅞 to Blakeley SP, W 🅡 Shell/Subway/dsl 🅞 Landing RV Park (2mi)
29mm	Tensaw River
28mm	Middle River
25mm	Mobile River
22	Creola, E 🅞 River Delta RV Park (1mi)
19	US 43, to Satsuma, E 🅡 Chevron/dsl/24hr, 🍴/Arby's/dsl/scales/24hr 🍽 McDonald's, Waffle House 🛏 La Quinta, W 🅡 BP/dsl, Chevron/dsl 🅞 I-65 RV Park (1.5mi)
15	AL 41, E 🅡 Chevron, Chevron/DQ/dsl 🍽 China Chef, Church's, Godfather's Pizza, Pizza Hut 🅞 AT&T, AutoZone, CVS, Family$, O'Reilly Parts, Rite Aid, Rouse's Mkt, Walgreens, W 🅡 Shell/Circle K, Shell/Subway/dsl 🅞 $General
13	AL 158, AL 213, to Saraland, E 🅡 Murphy USA/dsl, Shell/dsl 🍽 Goldberg's Deli, Krystal, Marble Slab, Rotolo's Pizza, Ruby Tuesday, Waffle House, Whataburger, Wintzell's Oyster House 🛏 Comfort Suites, Country Inn Suites, Microtel, Motel 6, Quality Inn, Red Lion Inn, Red Roof Inn 🅞 $Tree, AT&T, URGENT CARE, Walmart/McDonald's, W 🅡 Exxon/Subway 🍽 Cracker Barrel 🛏 Baymont Inn, Fairfield Inn, Hampton Inn, Holiday Inn Express, TownePlace Suites 🅞 Publix, to Chickasabogue Campground
10	W Lee St, E 🅡 Shell/Circle K 🛏 M Star Hotel
9	I-165 S, to I-10 E, to Mobile
8b a	US 45, to Prichard, E 🅡 Chevron/Circle K/dsl, Texaco/dsl 🅞 $General, Family$, tires/repair, W 🅡 1st Stop, Energize/dsl, 🅛ₒᵥₑₛ/Subway/dsl/scales/24hr, Texaco/dsl, Valero/dsl 🍽 Burger King, Domino's, Hardee's, McDonald's 🅞 $General, Advance Parts, CVS Drug, Family$, O'Reilly Parts
5b	US 98, Moffett Rd, E 🅡 Exxon/dsl, Texaco/dsl 🍽 BJ's BBQ, Burger King, Church's, McDonald's, Sub King 🅞 AutoZone, Family$, PepBoys, W 🍽 Hardee's 🛏 Super 8 🅞 auto repair
5a	Spring Hill Ave, E 🅡 Burger King 🍽 Dreamland BBQ, McDonald's 🅞 Mr Transmission, PepBoys, W 🅡 Chevron/dsl, Shell/dsl 🍽 Hibachi Express, Starbucks, Subway, Waffle House, Zaxby's 🛏 Extended Stay America, Wingate Inn 🅞 🚑
4	Dauphin St, E 🅡 BP/Circle K/dsl, Shell/dsl 🍽 Checkers, Chick-fil-A, Cracker Barrel, Krystal, McDonald's, Taco Bell, Taco Bell, Waffle House, Wendy's 🛏 Comfort Suites, Extended Suites, Red Roof Inn, Rodeway Inn

Exit #	Services
4	Continued 🅞 $General, Buick/GMC, FoodChamps, Lowe's, Mercedes, same as 3 & 5a, Walmart/McDonald's, W 🅞 🚑
3	Airport Blvd, E 🅡 Shell 🍽 Burger King, Cane's, Logan's Roadhouse, Macaroni Grill, McDonald's, Morrison's Cafeteria, Santa Fe Grill, Starbucks, Waffle House, Wendy's 🛏 Marriott 🅞 $Tree, Acura, Belk, Best Buy, BigLots, Cadillac, Dillard's, Firestone/auto, Ford, Goodyear/auto, Harley-Davidson, Honda, Infiniti, Land Rover, Marshall's, Michaels, Nissan, Old Navy, Sam's Club/gas, Staples, Target, Verizon, W 🅡 BudgetZone/dsl, Shell/dsl 🍽 Arby's, Bamboo Japanese, Baumhowers, Boiling Pot, Burger King, Carrabba's, Cheddar's, China Doll, Chipotle, ChuckECheese, Denny's, Dunkin', Firehouse Subs, Goldberg's Deli, Honeybaked Ham, Hooters, IHOP, Jason's Deli, Lenny's Subs, Los Rancheros Mexican, Marble Slab, Melting Pot, Moe's SW Grill, Newk's Cafe, O'Charley's, Olive Garden, Osaka Japanese, Outback Steaks, Panda Express, Panera Bread, Popeye's, Red Lobster, Ruby Tuesday, Starbucks, Subway, Taco Bell, Waffle House 🛏 Ashberry Suites, Baymont Inn, Best Value Inn, Comfort Inn, Courtyard, Drury Inn, EconoLodge, Fairfield Inn, Family Inn, Hampton Inn, Hilton Garden, Holiday Inn, Homewood Suites, InTowne Suites, La Quinta, Motel 6, Quality Inn, Residence Inn, Woodspring Suites 🅞 $General, $Tree, AT&T, BooksAMillion, Fresh Mkt Foods, Home Depot, 🚑, Jo-Ann Fabrics, Office Depot, PepBoys, Petsmart, Ross, SteinMart, TJ Maxx, to USAL, U-Haul, vet, Walgreens
1b a	US 90, Government Blvd, E 🅡 Raceway/dsl, Shell/dsl 🍽 Dickey's BBQ, Firehouse Subs, Five Guys, McAlister's Deli, Newk's Eatery, Panda Buffet, Starbucks, Steak'n Shake 🛏 Home 2 Suites, Tru Hilton 🅞 $Tree, AT&T, Audi/Porsche/VW, Best Buy, BMW, Chevrolet, Costco/gas, Dick's, Dodge, Family$, Field&Stream, Hobby Lobby, Kia, Lexus, Lincoln/Volvo, Mazda, Old Navy, Petco, Ross, Subaru, Toyota, Verizon, W 🅡 Shell/dsl 🍽 Waffle House
0mm	I-10, E to Pensacola, W to New Orleans. **I-65 begins/ends on I-10, exit 20.**

⤊ INTERSTATE 85

Exit #	Services
80mm	Alabama/Georgia state line, Chattahoochee River
79	US 29, to Lanett, E 🅡 Murphy USA, Shell/Circle K 🍽 Arby's, Burger King, Capt D's, Chuck's BBQ, DQ, Dunkin', KFC, Krystal, Little Caesar's, McDonald's, Pizza Hut, San Marcos Mexican, Subway, Taco Bell, Waffle House, Wendy's, Wing Stop 🅞 $General, $Tree, Advance Parts, 🚑, repair, Verizon, Walmart, W 🅡 Exxon/QV, JetPep, RaceWay/dsl 🍽 Domino's, Jin Japanese Steaks, Sonic 🛏 EconoLodge 🅞 AutoZone, CVS Drug, Kroger, O'Reilly Parts, to West Point Lake, vet
78.5mm	Welcome Ctr sb, full ♿ facilities, litter barrels, petwalk, 🚻, 🏤, vending
77	AL 208, to Huguley, E 🅡 Jet Pep/Church's/dsl, Shell/Circle K/dsl 🍽 Waffle House 🛏 Quality Inn 🅞 Chevrolet, Chrysler/Dodge/Ford/Lincoln, Ford, W 🛏 Hampton Inn 🅞 fireworks
76mm	Eastern/Central time zone
70	AL 388, to Cusseta, E 🅡 BigCat/dsl, Sunoco/Louie's/dsl/scales/24hr/@, W 🅞 fireworks
66	Andrews Rd, to US 29
64	US 29, to Opelika, E 🅡 Sunoco/dsl, W 🅡 Tiger/dsl

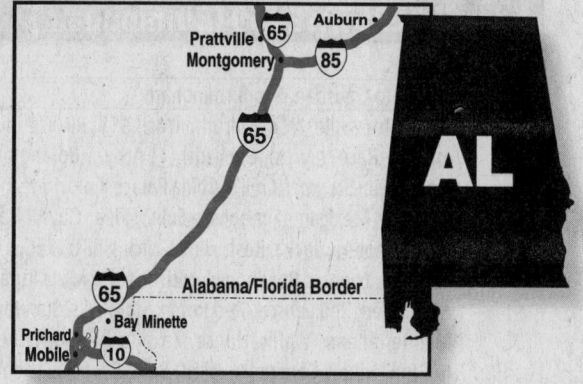

AL

INTERSTATE 85 Cont'd

Exit #	Services
62	US 280/431, to Opelika, **E** 🅿 Chevron/dsl, Eagle/dsl, Marathon/dsl, Shell/Circle K/Church's/dsl 🍴 Burger King, Durango Mexican, McDonald's, Subway, Taco Bell, Wasabi Japanese, Wok'n Roll Rest. 🏨 Days Inn, EconoLodge, Motel 6, Quality Inn, Red Carpet Inn, Red Roof Inn ⭕ $General, **W** 🅿 GrubMart, JetPep 🍴 Capt. D's, Cracker Barrel, Sizzlin Steaks, Waffle House 🏨 Comfort Inn, Magnuson Hotel ⭕ Buick/Chevrolet/GMC, Chrysler/Dodge/Jeep, Ford, H&W Tire, Harley-Davidson, USA Stores/famous brands
60	AL 51, AL 169, to Opelika, **E** 🅿 RaceWay/dsl 🍴 Hardee's ⭕ $General, **W** 🅿 Citgo ⭕ auto repair, Ⓗ
58	US 280 W, to Opelika, **E** 🅿 Eagle/Guthrie's/dsl 🍴 Freddy's, Wild Wing Cafe 🏨 Hampton Inn, Holiday Inn Express, Home 2 Suites, La Quinta ⭕ golf, **W** 🅿 Chevron/Subway/dsl 🍴 Arby's, Brick Oven Pizza, Buffalo Wild Wings, BurgerFi, Chick-fil-A, Chipotle, El Patron Mexican, Huddle House, Jersey Mike's, Jim Bob's, Logan's Roadhouse, Longhorn Steaks, Marble Slab, McDonald's, Moe's SW Grill, New Tokyo, Newk's Eatery, O'Charley's, Olive Garden, Pyro's Pizza, Sonic, Starbucks, Steak'n Shake, Taziki's, Waffle House, Which Wich?, Zaxby's 🏨 Fairfield Inn, Microtel, Motel 6 ⭕ AT&T, Best Buy, Books-A-Million, Dick's, Hobby Lobby, Home Depot, Ⓗ, Kohl's, Kroger/dsl, Lowe's, Office Depot, Old Navy, PetCo, Ross, Target, TJ Maxx, URGENT CARE, World Mkt
57	Bent Creek Rd, **W** 🅿 Exxon, Mapco 🍴 Baumhower's Victory Grille, Moe's Original BBQ, Shakey's Pizza, Venditori's Italian, Waffle House, Wendy's 🏨 Hilton Garden, Sleep Inn ⭕ Sam's Club/gas
51	US 29, to Auburn, **E** 🅿 Chevron/dsl, Grub Mart 🏨 Courtyard, Hampton Inn, Tru ⭕ $General, Cadillac/Chevrolet, Leisure Time RV Park/Camping, Nissan, to Chewacla SP, Toyota, vet, **W** 🅿 Chevron/Subway/dsl, Murphy USA 🍴 Arby's, Burger King, Dunkin', El Dorado Mexican, Firehouse Subs, Jack's, Jim'n Nick's BBQ, KJ's Fish Camp, Krystal, Little Caesar's, McDonald's, Ozzio's Italian, Philly Connection, Pizza Hut, Ruby Tuesday, Shrimp Basket, Sonic, Taco Bell, Waffle House, Wendy's, Zaxby's 🏨 Clarion, EconoLodge, Holiday Inn Express, Microtel, Pannie George's Kitchen, Quality Inn, Sleep Inn ⭕ Advance Parts, Ford/Lincoln, Kia, tires/repair, to Auburn U, URGENT CARE, Walmart, Winn-Dixie
50	Cox Rd
44mm	🆁🆂 both lanes, full 🚹 facilities, litter barrels, petwalk, ⬦, 🚮, RV dump, vending, 24hr security
42	US 80, AL 186 E, Wire Rd, **E** ⭕ dsl repair/tires, to Tuskegee NF, **W** 🅿 Torch 85/rest./dsl/24hr
38	AL 81, to Tuskegee, **E** to Tuskegee NHS, Tuskegee University
32	AL 49 N, to Tuskegee, **E** 🅿 Sunoco/dsl
26	AL 229 N, to Tallassee, **E** 🅿 Chevron/Guthrie's/dsl
22	US 80, to Shorter, **E** 🅿 Loves/McDonald's/Subway/dsl/scales/24hr, Petro/rest./dsl/scales/24hr 🏨 Days Inn ⭕ Wind Drift RV Park
16	Waugh, to Cecil, **E** 🅿 Entec/Circle K/Subway/dsl ⭕ auto repair
15	AL 108 W, Pike Rd
11	US 80, AL 110, to Mitylene, to Mt Meigs, **E** 🅿 BP/dsl, Liberty/dsl, Murphy USA/dsl, Shell/Subway/dsl 🍴 Anthony's Rest., Bruster's, Burger King, Cracker Barrel, Jose's Grill, Krystal, McDonald's, Milo's, Taco Bell, Top China, Waffle House 🏨 Candlewood Suites, Comfort Inn, Country Inn&Suites, Fairfield Inn, Holiday Inn Express, Sleep Inn ⭕ Hobby Lobby, Home Depot, O'Reilly Parts, Walmart/Subway, **W** 🅿 Chevron/dsl 🏨 Microtel
9	AL 271, to AL 110, to Auburn U/Montgomery, **E** 🍴 Arby's, BoneFish Grill, Buffalo Wild Wings, Chick-fil-A, Chili's, Chipotle Mexican, Del Taco, Firebirds Grill, Five Guys, Full Moon BBQ, Genghis Grill, Ixtapa Mexican, La Jolla Rest., Moe's SW Grill, Outback Steaks, Panera Bread, Pieology, Red Robin, Ruby Tuesday, Sonic, Starbucks, Taziki's Cafe, Twin Peaks, TX Roadhouse, Wendy's, Zoe's Kitchen 🏨 Hampton Inn, Staybridge Suites, TownePlace Suites ⭕ AT&T, Books-A-Million, Costco/gas, Dick's, Dillard's, Firestone/auto, Jo-Ann Fabrics, Kohl's, Michael's, Old Navy, Petsmart, Ross, Target, URGENT CARE, Verizon, vet, Whole Foods Mkt, World Mkt, **W** ⭕Ⓗ
6	US 80, US 231, AL 21, East Blvd, **0-2 mi E** 🅿 Chevron, Exxon/dsl, RaceWay/dsl, Shell 🍴 Arby's, Baumhowers Rest., Burger King, Carrabba's, Chick-fil-A, Gangnam Grill, Golden Corral, Hardee's, Jason's Deli, KFC, Longhorn Steaks, Los Cabos, Los Vaqueros Mexican, McDonald's, Ming's Garden, Olive Garden, Piccadilly Cafe, Popeye's, Rock Bottom Cafe, Schlotzsky's, Starbucks, Subway, Sushiyama, Taco Bell, Waffle House, Wendy's, Zaxby's 🏨 Arlington Lodge, Best Inn, Comfort Inn, Country Inn&Suites, Courtyard, Extended Stay America, Home-Towne Suites, La Quinta, Quality Inn, Quality Roof Inn, Residence Inn, Sleep Inn, SpringHill Suites, Wingate Inn, Woodspring Suites ⭕ $General, $Tree, Acura, Best Buy, Books-A-Million, Family$, Ford/Lincoln, Fresh Mkt Foods, Home Depot, Honda, Hyundai, Lowe's, Office Depot, Pepboys, PetCo, Subaru, TJ Maxx, Tuesday Morning, UHaul, USPO, Walmart/McDonald's, Winn-Dixie, **W** 🅿 Chevron, Liberty, Mapco/dsl, Shell 🍴 Arby's, Capt D's, Hardee's, Hibachi Buffet, IHOP, Jan's Rest., Krispy Kreme, Krystal, McDonald's, Outback Steaks, Red Lobster, Saigon Bistro, Taco Bell, Waffle House 🏨 Alabama Hotel, Baymont Inn, Comfort Suites, Drury Inn, Express Inn, Motel 6, Ramada Inn ⭕ $General, Audi/VW, BMW, Buick/Cadillac/GMC, Chevrolet, Chrysler/Dodge/Jeep, Firestone/auto, Infiniti, JC Penney, Kia, Lexus, Mercedes, Nissan, Sam's Club/gas, Toyota, Volvo
4	Perry Hill Rd, **E** 🍴 Chappy's Deli ⭕ Fresh Mkt, **W** 🅿 Chevron, Texaco/dsl 🍴 Hardee's, Subway 🏨 Hilton Garden, Homewood Suites ⭕ $General, Express Oil Change
3	Ann St, **E** 🅿 Chevron 🍴 Arby's, Bojangle's, Capt D's, Domino's, KFC, Krystal, McDonald's, Taco Bell, Waffle House, Wendy's, Zaxby's 🏨 Red Roof Inn ⭕ Pepboys, **W** 🅿 Entec, Murphy USA/dsl, PaceCar, Ztec 🍴 Burger King, Chick-fil-A, CiCi's Pizza, Hardee's, Popeye's 🏨 Stay Lodge ⭕ $Tree, AT&T, O'Reilly Parts, Office Depot, Ross, Verizon, Walmart/Subway
2	Forest Ave, **E** ⭕ CVS Drug, **W** ⭕ Ⓗ
1	Court St, Union St, downtown, **E** 🅿 Marathon/dsl, **W** ⭕ to Ala St U
0mm	**I-85 begins/ends on I-65, exit 171 in Montgomery.**

OPELIKA

AUBURN

MONTGOMERY

AL

⬆N INTERSTATE 459 (Birmingham)

Exit #	Services
33b a	I-59, N to Gadsden, S to Birmingham
32	US 11, Trussville, N ⛽ Marathon/dsl, S ⛽ BP/Wendy's, Chevron/dsl, RaceWay/dsl, Shell/dsl 🍴 Arby's, Bojangles, Burger King, Cajun Steamer, Chili's, China Palace, Coldstone, Dunkin', El Cazador Mexican, Firehouse Subs, Five Guys, Habanero's Rest., Hooters, Jack's Rest., Jim'n Nick's BBQ, KFC, La Bamba Mexican, Logan's Roadhouse, McDonald's, Mizu Japanese, Olive Garden, Red Lobster, Red Robin, Starbucks, Subway, Taziki's Mediterranean, Waffle House, Zaxby's 🏨 Courtyard, Hampton Inn, Hilton Garden Ⓞ AT&T, Belk, Best Buy, Books-A-Million, Buick/GMC, GNC, Home Depot, JC Penney, Lowe's, Mazda, Michael's, Pepboys, Staples, Target, TJ Maxx, Verizon
31	Derby Parkway, N Ⓞ B'ham Race Course
29	I-20, E to Atlanta, W to Birmingham
27	Grants Mill Rd, N 🏨 Hampton Inn Ⓞ Fiat, S ⛽ Chevron/dsl Ⓞ Audi/Porsche, BMW, Chrysler/Dodge/Jeep, Land Rover, Lexus, Mini
23	Liberty Parkway, S 🍴 Billy's Grill, DQ, Taziki's Greek 🏨 Hilton Garden
19	US 280, Mt Brook, Childersburg, N ⛽ Chevron/dsl 🍴 CA Pizza Kitchen, Cheesecake Factory, Chuy's Mexican, Flemings Rest., Johnny Rockets, Lime Tex Mex, Macaroni Grill, Panera Bread, PF Chang's, Seasons Grille, Village Tavern, Which Wich?, Zoe's Kitchen Ⓞ AT&T, Barnes&Noble, Belk, Old Navy, Verizon, 0-3 mi S ⛽ BP/Circle K, Chevron, Marathon, Shell, Shell 🍴 Arby's, Asian Rim, Black Pearl Asian, Buffalo Wild Wings, Burger King, Carrabba's, Chick-fil-A, Chili's, Chipotle Mexican, Cracker Barrel, Edgar's Rest., Full Moon BBQ, Jason's Deli, Jimmy John's, Kobe Japanese, Logan's Roadhouse, Longhorn Steaks, McDonald's, Milo's Burgers, Mooyah Burgers, Newk's Eatery, Pablo's, Papa John's, Pappadeaux, Pizza Hut, Schlotzsky's, Starbucks, Steak'n Shake, Subway, Superior Grill, Suriname 280, Taco Bell, Taziki's Greek, Wendy's, Zaxby's 🏨 Courtyard, Days Inn, Drury Inn, Extended Stay America, Hampton Inn, Hilton, Homewood Suites, Hyatt Place, La Quinta, Marriott, Quality Inn, Residence Inn, SpringHill Suites Ⓞ AT&T, Autozone, Best Buy, CVS Drug, Firestone/auto, Fresh Mkt Foods, Goodyear/auto, Home Depot, Kohl's, NTB, Staples, Target, vet, Walgreens, Winn-Dixie, World Mkt

17	Acton Rd, N ⛽ Shell/dsl 🍴 Krystal, McDonald's, S 🏨 Comfort Inn
15b a	I-65, N to Birmingham, S to Montgomery
13	US 31, Hoover, Pelham, N ⛽ Exxon/dsl, Shell/dsl, Sunoco/dsl 🍴 Burger King, Chick-fil-A, Fish Mkt Rest., Full Moon BBQ, Golden Rule BBQ, Habanero's, Krispy Kreme, Krystal, McDonald's, Outback Steaks, Papa John's, Purple Onion, Salvatori's Pizza, Starbucks, Subway 🏨 Econolodge Ⓞ $Tree, Acura, AutoZone, Cadillac, Chevrolet, Firestone/auto, Goodyear/auto, Honda, Hyundai, Mr Transmission, Nissan, Publix, Rite Aid, Staples, TJ Maxx, vet, S ⛽ Exxon, Jet-Pep, Shell/dsl 🍴 Arby's, Bonefish Grill, CA Pizza Kitchen, Chick-fil-A, Chipotle Mexican, Firebird's Grill, Firehouse Subs, J Alexander's Rest., Jason's Deli, Jim'n Nicks BBQ, La Paz, McDonald's, Moe's BBQ, Moe's SW Grill, Newk's Eatery, Olive Garden, Panera Bread, Pizza Hut, Ruby Tuesday, Steak'n Shake, Stix Asian, Sumo Japanese, Taco Bell, Twin Peaks Rest., Wendy's 🏨 Courtyard, Days Inn, Embassy Suites, Hampton Inn, Hyatt Place, Hyatt Regency/Wynfrey Hotel Ⓞ Barnes&Noble, Belk, Best Buy, Costco/gas, Dick's, GNC, Hancock Fabrics, Home Depot, Infiniti, JC Penney, Jo-Ann Fabrics, Macy's, Mercedes, Michael's, NTB, Office Depot, PepBoys, Petsmart, Ross, Sam's Club/gas, Tuesday Morning, Verizon, Walgreens, World Mkt
10	AL 150, Waverly, N 🍴 Beef o Brady's, Chick-fil-A, Freddy's, Frontera Mexican Grill, Jimmy John's, McDonald's, Starbucks Ⓞ $Tree, Kohl's, Marshall's, PetCo, Sprouts Mkt, Target, URGENT CARE, S ⛽ Circle K/dsl, Shell 🏨 Hampton Inn, Hyatt Place Ⓞ Ford/Lincoln, Publix/deli, Toyota, Walgreens
6	AL 52, to Bessemer, N ⛽ Shell/dsl, S ⛽ Chevron/dsl, Circle K, Texaco/DQ 🍴 Arby's, China Wok, Domino's, McDonald's, Papa John's, Pizza Hut, Railroad Cafe, Subway, Waffle House, Wendy's 🏨 Sleep Inn Ⓞ $General, CVS Drug, RV Camping, Winn-Dixie
1	AL 18, Bessemer, N ⛽ Exxon/dsl, Shell/Dunkin'/dsl 🍴 Burger King, Chick-fil-A, Firehouse Subs, Full Moon BBQ, Habanero's Mexican, Logan's Roadhouse, McAlister's Deli, Taco Bell Ⓞ AAA, AT&T, GNC, Michaels, Petsmart, Publix, Ross, Target, URGENT CARE, S ⛽ Sunoco/dsl 🍴 Bojangles, China King, McDonald's, Meineke, San Antonio Grill, Subway, Zaxby's Ⓞ Advance Parts, CVS Drug, Piggly Wiggly, to Tannehill SP, Verizon
0mm	I-459 begins/ends on I-20/59, exit 106.

BIRMINGHAM

HOOVER

BESSEMER

NOTES

ARIZONA

⬆E   INTERSTATE 8

Exit #	Services
178b a	I-10, E to Tucson, W to Phoenix, **I-8 begins/ends on I-10, exit 199.**
174	Trekell Rd, to Casa Grande, **2-4 mi N** 🅾 🏨, food, gas, lodging
172	Thornton Rd, to Casa Grande, **5-8 mi N** 🚩 gas 🍴 food 🏨 Francisco Grande Resort, Holiday Inn
171mm	Santa Cruz River
169	Bianco Rd
167	Montgomery Rd
163mm	Santa Rosa Wash
161	Stanfield Rd
151	AZ 84 E, Maricopa Rd, to Stanfield, **S** 🅾 Saguaro RV Park
151mm	**picnic area wb,** 🪑, **litter barrels**
149mm	**picnic area eb,** 🪑, **litter barrels**
144	Vekol Rd
140	Freeman Rd
119	Butterfield Trail, to AZ 85, I-10, Gila Bend, **3 mi N** 🚩 Shell/dsl/scales, Shell/Subway/dsl/scales/RV Park/24hr 🍴 Little Italy, Subway 🏨 America's Choice Inn, Best Western, Knights Inn, Palms Inn, Space Age/rest. 🅾 $General
117mm	Sand Tank Wash
115	AZ 85, to Gila Bend, **1-2 mi N** 🚩 Chevron/dsl, Circle K, ❤Loves/Taco Bell/dsl/scales/24hr, Tesla EVC 🍴 Burger King, Carl's Jr, McDonald's, Sofia's Mexican 🏨 Best Western, Palms Inn 🅾 Family$, NAPA
111	Citrus Valley Rd
106	Paloma Rd
102	Painted Rock Rd, **N** 🅾 Painted Rock Petroglyph Site (11mi)
87	Aqua Caliente Rd, Sentinel Rd, Sentinel, Hyder, **N** 🚩 Conde's Gen Store/dsl 🅾 RV Camping
85mm	Ⓡ wb, full 🦽 facilities, litter barrels, petwalk, Ⓒ, 🪑, vending
84mm	Ⓡ eb, full 🦽 facilities, litter barrels, petwalk, Ⓒ, 🪑, vending
78	Spot Rd
73	Aztec, **S** 🅾 Oasis RV Park/dump (4mi)
67	Dateland, **S** 🚩 Chevron/dsl/24hr 🅾 Dateland RV Park, Oasis RV Park/dump (2mi)
56mm	Ⓡ both lanes, full 🦽 facilities, litter barrels, petwalk, Ⓒ, 🪑, vending
54	Ave 52 E, Mohawk Valley
42	Ave 40 E, to Tacna, **N** 🚩 Chevron/dsl 🍴 Jac's Whistlestop Cafe 🅾 USPO, **S** 🚩 Shell/Subway/dsl 🅾 Copper Mtn RV Park
37	Ave 36 E, to Roll
30	Ave 29 E, Wellton, **N** 🚩 Circle K/dsl 🍴 Geronimo Mexican 🏨 Desert Motel 🅾 Family$, NAPA, Tier Drop RV Park, USPO, **S** 🚩 Chevron/dsl 🍴 Dusty's Pizza & Wings, Jack-in-the-Box 🏨 Microtel
24mm	Ligurta Wash
23mm	Red Top Wash
22mm	**parking area/litter barrels both lanes**
21	Dome Valley, **N** 🍴 Ligurta Sta Rest./RV park 🅾 Yuma Proving Ground (16mi)
17mm	insp sta eb, insp sta eb
15mm	Fortuna Wash
14	Foothills Blvd, **N** 🅾 Sundance RV Park, **S** 🍴 Domino's, Foothills Eatery, Jimmy K's 🅾 auto/RV care/lube ctr, Family$, Foothills RV Park
12	Fortuna Rd, to US 95 N, **N** 🚩 Chevron/dsl, ⟲FLYING J/Giant/dsl/scales/24hr 🍴 DayBreakers Cafe, Jack-in-the-Box, Las Palapas Tacos, McDonald's, Pizza Hut, Starbucks, Taco Bell

Left margin labels (top to bottom): G I L A B E N D, **W E L L T O N**

12	Continued 🏨 Comfort Inn, Courtesy Inn 🅾 Caravan RV Park, Oasis RV Park, Shangri La RV Park, **S** 🚩 Chevron/dsl, Mobil/Burger King/dsl 🍴 A&W/KFC, Applebee's, Carl's Jr, Daboyz Pizza, Denny's, Dunkin', Little Caesar's, Papa John's, Subway 🏨 Best Western+ 🅾 $General, $Tree, AutoZone, Big O Tire, CVS Drug, Fry's Foods/dsl, O'Reilly Parts, USPO, Verizon, Walgreens
9	32nd St, to Yuma, **S** 🍴 Del Taco, Panda Express 🅾 RV Parks, Verizon, Walmart/McDonald's
7	AZ 195, Araby Rd, **N** 🚩 Circle K/dsl 🅾 to AZWU, **S** 🚩 Chevron/Jack-in-the-Box/dsl, Circle K/dsl 🅾 RV Parks, RV World
3	AZ 280 S, Ave 3E, **N** 🍴 Arby's 🏨 Candlewood Suites, Holiday Inn Express, **S** 🚩 ❤Loves/Chester's/Subway/dsl/scales/24hr 🅾 CarQuest, Harley-Davidson, to Marine Corp Air Sta
2	US 95, 16th St, Yuma, **N** 🚩 Circle K 🍴 Ah-So Steaks, Black Bear Diner, Buffalo Wild Wings, Chick-fil-A, Chili's, Chipotle Mexican, ChuckeCheese, Coldstone Creamery, Cracker Barrel, Del Taco, Denny's, Famous Dave's BBQ, Five Guys, Freddy's, Hawaiian BBQ, Hooters, In-N-Out, Jack-in-the-Box, Kneaders, Lin's Chinese, Olive Garden, Panda Express, Penny's Diner, Red Lobster, Starbucks, Subway 🏨 Baymont Inn, Best Western, Days Inn, Fairfield Inn, Hampton Inn, Holiday Inn, Homewood Suites, Hotel Inn & Suites, La Fuente Inn, Motel 6, Shilo Inn, SpringHill Suites, TownePlace Suites, Wingate Inn 🅾 AT&T, Best Buy, Dillard's, Discount Tire, GNC, JC Penney, Kohl's, Marshall's, Old Navy, PetsMart, Ross, Sam's Club/gas, Target, Verizon, **S** 🚩 Arco/dsl, Chevron/dsl, Speedway/dsl 🍴 Applebee's, Burger King, Carl's Jr, Chretin's Mexican, Dunkin', Golden Corral, IHOP, Jack-in-the-Box, McDonald's, Subway, TX Roadhouse, Village Inn Pizza, Wendy's 🏨 Budgetel, Quality Inn, Radisson, Super 8 🅾 🏨, BigLots, Family$, Home Depot, Staples
1.5mm	**weigh sta both lanes**
1	Redondo Ctr Dr, Giss Pkwy, Yuma, **S on 4th Ave E** 🚩 Chevron, Circle K/dsl 🍴 Jack-in-the-Box, Yuma Landing Rest. 🏨 Coronado Motel, Hilton Garden, **N** 🅾 to Yuma Terr Prison SP
0mm	Arizona/California state line, Colorado River, Mountain/Pacific time zone

Right margin label: Y U M A

▯ = gas ▯ = food ▭ = lodging ▯ = other ▯ = rest stop   Copyright 2022 - The Next EXIT ®

AZ

	INTERSTATE 10
Exit #	Services
391mm	Arizona/New Mexico state line
390	Cavot Rd
389mm	▯ both lanes, full ♿ facilities, litter barrels, petwalk, ▯, ▯, vending
383mm	weigh sta eb, weigh/insp sta wb
382	Portal Rd, San Simon
381mm	San Simon River
378	Lp 10, San Simon, **N** ▯ 4K Trkstp/Chevron/Noble Romans/Quiznos/dsl/scales/24hrs/@ ▯ auto/dsl/RV repair
366	Lp 10, Bowie Rd, **N** ▯ Shell/Jerky/dsl, **S** ▯ Alaskan RV park
362	Lp 10, Bowie Rd, **N** camping, gas, lodging, **S** to Ft Bowie NHS
355	US 191 N, to Safford
352	US 191 N, to Safford, same as 355
344	Lp 10, to Willcox, **S** ▯ Lifestyle RV Park
340	AZ 186, to Rex Allen Dr, **N** ▯ TA/Shell/Popeye's/Subway/dsl/scales/24hr/@ ▭ Holiday Inn Express, Super 8 ▯ Apple Annie's Country Store, Magic Circle RV Park, RV/Truckwash, truck/auto repair, visitor info, **S** ▯ Chevron/dsl/24hr, Circle K, Texaco/dsl ▯ Burger King, Carl's Jr, McDonald's, Pizza Hut ▭ Days Inn, Quality Inn, Rodeway Inn ▯ ▯ $General, Ace Hardware, auto/tire/RV repair, AutoZone, Beall's, Family$, Grande Vista RV Park, KT's Mkt, Medicine Shoppe, Safeway, to Chiricahua NM, Verizon
336	AZ 186, Willcox, **S** ▯ Chevron/dsl/LP ▭ Royal Western Lodge ▯ Ft Willcox RV Park, Life Style RV Park
331	US 191 S, to Sunsites, Douglas, **S** ▯ to Cochise Stronghold
322	Johnson Rd, **S** ▯ Shell/DQ/dsl/gifts
320mm	▯ both lanes, full ♿ facilities, litter barrels, petwalk, ▯, ▯, vending
318	Triangle T Rd, to Dragoon, **S** ▯ Amerind Museum (1mi), camping, lodging
312	Sibyl Rd
309mm	Adams Peak Wash
306	AZ 80, Pomerene Rd, Benson, **1-2 mi S** ▯ Circle K, Shell ▯ 86 Cafe ▯ CarQuest, El Rio RV Park, Pato Blanco Lakes RV Park, repair, San Pedro RV (2mi)
305mm	San Pedro River
304	Ocotillo St, Benson, **N** ▯ Denny's, Dickey's BBQ, Jack-in-the-Box ▭ Days Inn, Super 8 ▯ Benson RV Park, KOA, **S** ▯ Chevron ▯ Beijing Chinese, Farmhouse Rest, Galleano's Italian-American, Little Caesar's, Magaly's Mexican, Subway, Wendy's ▭ Quality Inn, QuarterHorse Inn/RV Park ▯ ▯ $General, Ace Hardware, Butterfield RV Resort, Dillon RV Ctr, Pardner's RV Park, Safeway, Walmart
303	US 80 (eb only), to Tombstone, Bisbee, **S** ▯ Farmhouse Rest, Little Caesar's, Pablo's Steaks, Reb's Rest, Subway ▭ Quarter Horse Motel/RV Park ▯ auto/dsl/repair, Medicine Shoppe, O'Reilly Parts, Pardners RV Park, to Douglas NHL, to Tombstone Courthouse SHP (26mi), Verizon, Walmart
302	AZ 90 S, to Ft Huachuca, Benson, **S** ▯ Loves/Chester's/Subway/dsl/scales/24hr, Shell/dsl ▯ KFC/Taco Bell, McDonald's ▭ Comfort Inn, Motel 6 ▯ AZ Legends RV Resort, Cochise Terrace RV Park, Ft Huachuca NHS (25mi)
299	Skyline Rd
297	Mescal Rd, J-6 Ranch Rd, **N** ▯ Chevron/dsl
292	Empirita Rd
291	Marsh Station Rd
288mm	Cienega Creek

Exit #	Services
281	AZ 83 S, to Patagonia
279	Colossal Cave Rd, Wentworth Rd, **N** ▯ Chevron/dsl ▯ AZ Pizza Co, DQ, Montgomery's Grill ▯ to Colossal Caves (7mi), USPO
275	Houghton Rd, **N** ▯ Panda Express ▯ Adventure Bound RV Resort, Discount Tire, to Saguaro NP (10mi), Walmart, **S** ▯ to fairgrounds (1mi)
273	Rita Rd, **N** ▯ ▯/Subway/dsl ▯ Burger King ▭ Hampton Inn, **S** ▯ fairgrounds
270	Kolb Rd, **S** ▯ Bay RV Resort, Voyager RV Resort
269	Wilmot Rd, **N** ▯ Chevron/A&W/dsl ▭ Travel Inn, **S** ▯ Shell/pizza/subs/dsl
268	Craycroft Rd, **N** ▯ Circle K, Mr T/dsl/LP, ▯/Subway/Taco Bell/dsl/lp/scales/24hr/@, TTT/rest/dsl/scales/24hr ▯ Crazy Horse RV Park, Freightliner, truck/RV wash, **S** ▯ dsl repair
267	Valencia Rd, **N** ▯ Speedway/Jack-in-the-Box ▯ Pima Air & Space Museum, **S** ▯ Valero/dsl ▯ ▯
265	Alvernon Way, **N** ▯ Davis-Monthan AFB
264b a	Palo Verde Rd, **N** ▯ Circle K/dsl ▯ Denny's, Shell/Wendy's/dsl, Waffle House ▭ Comfort Inn, Crossland Suites, Days Inn, Holiday Inn, Red Roof Inn ▯ Camping World RV Resort, Freedom RV Ctr, **S** ▯ Arby's, McDonald's ▭ Quality Inn, Studio 6 ▯ La Mesa RV Ctr, Lazy Days RV Ctr/Resort, Pedata RV Ctr
263b	Kino Pkwy N, **N** ▯ Shell/dsl ▯ Culver's, Dave&Buster's, In-N-Out, Jimmy John's, Starbucks ▯ AT&T, Costco/gas, Discount Tire, Verizon, Walmart/Subway
263a	Kino Pkwy S, **N** ▯ ▯, **S** ▯ Arco/dsl, Shamrock ▯ Burger King, KFC, Little Caesar's, Mandarin Buffet, Papa John's, Taco Bell ▯ $Tree, AutoZone, Family$, Food City, Fry's Foods, O'Reilly Parts, to Tucson Intn'l Airport, Walgreens
262	Benson Hwy, Park Ave, **S** ▯ Arco/dsl, Chevron/McDonald's/dsl, Circle K/dsl ▯ Carl's Jr. ▭ Best Value Inn, Motel 6, Rodeway Inn, Western Inn ▯ Mack/Volvo Trucks, USPO
261	6th/4th Ave, **N** ▯ GasCo ▯ Little Caesar's, Los Portales ▭ EconoLodge ▯ Discount Tire, Family$, Food City, USPO, **S** ▯ Circle K/dsl ▯ Church's, El Indio, Jack-in-the-Box, Panda Express, Silver Saddle Steaks, Whataburger ▭ Lazy 8 Motel ▯ Big O Tire, El Super Foods, Family$, Midas, O'Reilly Parts
260	I-19 S, to Nogales
259	22nd St, Starr Pass Blvd, **N** ▯ Circle K/dsl, **S** ▯ Kettle, Waffle House ▭ Clarion, Regal Inn, Silverbell Inn, Super 8, Travel Inn
258	Congress St, Broadway St, **N** ▯ Circle K ▭ Hotel Tuscan, **S** ▯ Carl's Jr ▭ Days Inn, Howard Johnson, Motel 6, River Park Inn, Travelodge
257a	St Mary's Rd, **S** ▯ Shell/dsl ▯ Burger King, Church's, Denny's, Eegee's Cafe, Furr's Cafeteria, Jack-in-the-Box, Little Caesar's, Whataburger ▭ Country Inn&Suites, Ramada Ltd. ▯ ▯ Family$, Food City, Pima Comm Coll
257	Speedway Blvd, **N** ▭ Best Western, EconoLodge ▯ ▯ U of AZ, Victory Motorcycles, **S** ▯ Arco/dsl ▯ museum, Old Town Tucson
256	Grant Rd, **N** ▯ Circle K ▯ auto/dsl repair, Burger King, Jack-in-the-Box, Sonic ▯ Walgreens, **S** ▯ Circle K, QT/dsl, Shell/dsl ▯ Arby's, Del Taco, Eegee's Cafe, IHOP, Waffle House ▭ Comfort Inn, Grant Inn, Holiday Inn Express, Super 8 ▯ Ace Hardware, Safeway, Walgreens
255	AZ 77 N, to Miracle Mile
254	Prince Rd, **N** ▯ Circle K, Valero/dsl ▯ $General, O'Reilly Parts, Walgreens, **S** ▯ golf, Kenworth, Prince of Tucson RV Park
252	El Camino del Cerro, Ruthrauff Rd, **N** ▯ Arco ▯ Ruthrauff RV Ctr, **S** ▯ Shell/Jack-in-the-Box/dsl

WILLCOX

BENSON

TUCSON

INTERSTATE 10 Cont'd

Exit #	Services
251	Sunset Rd
250	Orange Grove Rd, **N** 🅿 Arco/dsl, Circle K/dsl 🍴 Burger King, Culver's, Domino's, Firehouse Subs, Golden Corral, Little Caesar's, Subway, Tulioberto's, Wendy's 🅾 Big O Tire, Costco/gas, diesel repair, Home Depot, Petsmart, South Forty RV Park, Sprouts Mkt, Staples, URGENT CARE, vet
248	Ina Rd, **N** 🅿 Chevron/dsl, Circle K/dsl, Shell/dsl 🍴 Bisbee Breakfast Club, Carl's Jr, ChickeNuevo, Chuy's Mesquite, DQ, Eegee's Cafe, Five Guys, Hooters, Jack-in-the-Box, Jade Garden, Losbetos Cafe, Lupita's Cafe, McDonald's, Miss Saigon, Molinitas Mexican, Papa John's, Peter Piper's Pizza, Pollo Loco, Starbucks, Subway, Taco Bell, Waffle House 🏨 InTown Suites, Motel 6 🅾 $Tree, 99c Store, auto repair, AutoZone, BigLots, CarQuest, CVS Drug, Discount Tire, Firestone/auto, Fry's Foods/dsl, Goodyear/auto, Hancock Fabrics, Lowe's, Michael's, Midas, O'Reilly Parts, PepBoys, Target, U-Haul, Walgreens, **S** 🅿 Circle K 🍴 Denny's, Starbucks 🏨 Best Western, Red Roof Inn, Travelodge 🅾 Ace Hardware, Freedom RV Ctr, Harley-Davidson
246	Cortaro Rd, **N** 🅿 Circle K/Arby's/dsl, QT/dsl 🍴 IHOP, Wendy's, **S** 🅿 Shell/dsl 🍴 Boston's Rest, Burger King, Chili's, Chipotle, Chopstix, Cracker Barrel, Dunkin, Eegee's Rest., In-N-Out, Jersey Mike's, Jimmy John's, KFC, Little Caesar's, McDonald's, Nana's Mexican, Native New Yorker, New Town Asian, Panda Express, Starbucks, Subway, Taco Bell, TX Roadhouse 🏨 Comfort Inn, Days Inn, Holiday Inn Express, La Quinta, Super 8, Village Inn 🅾 $Tree, access to RV camping, Ace Hardware, AT&T, Batteries+, GNC, Kohl's, O'Reilly Parts, Petco, Ross, TJ Maxx, USPO, Verizon, Walmart/McDonald's
244	Twin Peaks Rd, **N** 🏨 Hampton Inn 🅾 Tucson Outlets/famous brands
242	Avra Valley Rd, **S** 🅾 🏕, RV camping, Saguaro NP (13mi)
240	Tangerine Rd, to Rillito, **N** 🅾 A-A RV Park, **S** 🅾 USPO
236	Marana, **S** 🅿 Chevron/dsl/LP, Circle K/dsl 🍴 McDonald's, R&R Pizza 🅾 auto repair, Family$, Sun RV Park
232	Pinal Air Park Rd, **S** 🅾 Pinal Air Park (3mi)
228mm	to frontage rd, wb pulloff
226	Red Rock, **S** 🅾 USPO
219	Picacho Peak Rd, **N** 🅿 Shell/DQ, Shell/Subway/dsl, **S** 🅾 Ostrich Ranch, Pichaco Peak RV Park, to Picacho Peak SP
212	Picacho (from wb), **S** 🅾 KOA
211b	AZ 87 N, AZ 84 W, to Coolidge, **S** 🅾 KOA
211a	Picacho (from eb), **S** 🅾 KOA, state prison
208	Sunshine Blvd, to Eloy, **N** 🅿 Pilot/Subway/DQ/dsl/scales/24hr 🅾 dsl repair, **S** 🅿 FLYING J/Denny's/dsl/scales/24hr 🅾 Blue Beacon
203	Toltec Rd, to Eloy, **N** 🅿 Chevron/McDonald's/playplace/24hr, Circle K/dsl 🍴 Carl's Jr, El Caballito Mexican 🏨 Best Value Inn, Super 8 🅾 Desert Valley RV Park, dsl/tire repair, **S** 🅿 Sinclair/dsl, TA/A&W/Taco Bell/dsl/RV dump/24hr/@ 🍴 Pizza Hut 🅾 golf, truckwash
200	Sunland Gin Rd, Arizona City, **N** 🅿 Petro/Iron Skillet/dsl/scales/24hr/@, Pride/Subway/dsl/24hr 🍴 Burger King, Eva's Mexican 🏨 Quality Inn, Rodeway Inn 🅾 Blue Beacon, Eagle Truckwash, Las Colinas RV Park, **S** 🅿 Loves/Arby's/Baskin-Robbins/dsl/24hr 🍴 Golden 9 Rest 🏨 Motel 6 🅾 Speedco Lube
199	I-8 W, to Yuma, San Diego
198	AZ 84, to Eloy, Casa Grande, **N** 🅾 Robson Ranch Rest./golf (3mi)

Exit #	Services
194	AZ 287, Florence Blvd, to Casa Grande, **N** 🅿 Tesla EVC 🍴 Buffalo Wild Wings, Cactus Moon Grill, Cane's, Chick-fil-A, Culver's, In-N-Out, Krispy Kreme, Mimi's Cafe, Olive Garden, Rubio's, Subway 🅾 Dillard's, GNC, JC Penney, Kohl's, Marshall's, Michael's, Petsmart, Ross, Staples, Sunscape RV Park (7mi), Target, Verizon, Walgreens, World Mkt, **0-2 mi S** 🅿 76/DQ, Arco/dsl, Chevron/Little Caesars/dsl, Circle K/gas 🍴 Arby's, Burger King, Carl's Jr, Chili's, China Buffet, Chipotle Mexican, Church's, Coldstone, Cracker Barrel, Del Taco, Denny's, Eegee's, Filiberto's Mexican, Golden Corral, IHOP, Jack-in-the-Box, JB's, Jimmy John's, LJ Silver/Taco Bell, Macayo's Mexican, McDonald's, Panda Express, Papa John's, Papa Murphy's, Peter Piper Pizza, Sonic, Starbucks, Subway, T&M Italian, Wendy's 🏨 Comfort Inn, Holiday Inn Express, Legacy Suites, Mainstay Suites, Quality Inn, Super 8 🅾 🏥, $Tree, 99cents Store, AT&T, AutoZone, Big Lots, Big O Tire, CVS Drug, Discount Tire, Encore Camping (2mi), Family$, Fiesta Grande RV Resort, Food City, Fry's Food/drug/dsl, Goodyear/auto, Home Depot, Jo-Ann Fabrics, Lowe's, U-Haul, URGENT CARE, Verizon, vet, Walgreens, Walmart/McDonald's
190	McCartney Rd, **N** 🅾 to Central AZ Coll, **S** 🅿 Circle K/dsl 🍴 Barro's Pizza (3mi)
185	AZ 387, to Casa Grande, Casa Grande Ruins NM, **S** 🍴 Eva's Mexican (6mi) 🏨 Francisco Grande (6mi), Holiday Inn (6mi) 🅾 Fry's Food/gas (6mi), hwy patrol, to Casa Grande Ruins NM, Val Vista RV camping (3mi)
183mm	℞ₛ wb, full 🚻 facilities, litter barrels, petwalk, 🅲, 🏕, vending
181mm	℞ₛ eb, full 🚻 facilities, litter barrels, petwalk, 🅲, 🏕, vending
175	AZ 587 N, Casa Blanca Rd, Chandler, Gilbert, **S** 🅿 Chevron/dsl
173mm	Gila River
167	Riggs Rd, to Sun Lake, **N** 🅿 Shell/dsl 🅾 Akimel Smoke Shop
164	AZ 347 S, Queen Creek Rd, to Maricopa, **N** 🅿 gas 🅾 to Chandler Airport
162b a	Wild Horse Pass Rd, Sundust Rd, **N** 🅿 Loves/Arby's/dsl/scales/24hr 🍴 McDonald's 🏨 Best Western+ 🅾 MotorCoach Resort, **S** 🅿 Chevron/dsl 🏨 Sheraton Resort, Wildhorse Pass Hotel/Casino 🅾 Firebird Sports Park, Gila River Casino, Phoenix Outlets/famous brands
161	AZ 202 E, Pecos Rd
160	Chandler Blvd, to Chandler, **N** 🅿 Chevron/dsl, Circle K, Circle K/dsl 🍴 Can't Stop Smokin' BBQ, Denny's, Filiberto's Mexican, Marie's Rest., McDonald's, Rudy's BBQ, Sandella's Flatbread Cafe, Starbucks, Subway, US Egg Cafe, Wendy's, Whataburger 🏨 Comfort Inn, Fairfield Inn, Hampton Inn, Hawthorn Suites, Homewood Suites, Motel 6, Quality Inn, Radisson, Super 8 🅾 $Tree, Aamco, ADS Auto Repair, CVS, Firestone/auto, Harley-Davidson, to Compadre Stadium, U-Haul, vet, Walmart Mkt, Williams AFB, **S** 🅿 7-11, Chevron/dsl, Circle K/dsl, Shell/dsl

Vertical side text: **CASA GRANDE** / **CHANDLER**

AZ

	INTERSTATE 10 Cont'd

160 Continued
🍴 Bell Italian Pizza, Brazilian Bull Steaks, Carl's Jr, Cracker Barrel, Del Taco, Dunkin', Hong Kong Buffet, Jersey Mike's, Qdoba, Spinato's Pizzaria, Starbucks, Tukee's Grille, Waffle House, Wendy's 🛏 Extended Stay America, Holiday Inn Express, In-Town Suites, La Quinta 🅞 🅗, AT&T, AutoZone, Discount Tire, Kohl's, URGENT CARE

159 Ray Rd, N 🅟 Circle K, Shell 🍴 Buca Italian, Carrabba's, Charleston's Rest., Chipotle Mexican, Fleming's Steaks, Frederico's Mexican, Genghis Grill, Habit Burger, In-N-Out, Jasons Deli, Jimmy John's, Longhorn Steaks, McDonald's, Nabers Rest., Outback Steaks, Paradise Cafe, Pei Wei Asian, Red Lobster, Roy's Hawaiian, Rumbi Grill, Sandbar Mexican, Starbucks, Subway, Tejas, Zoe's Kitchen 🛏 Courtyard 🅞 AJ's Fine Foods, Audi, BMW, Chevrolet, Ford, Home Depot, Lexus, Lowe's Whse, Mercedes, PetsMart, Sam's Club/gas, Verizon, S 🅟 Circle K/dsl 🍴 Barro's Pizza, Boston Mkt, Chick-Fil-A, Five Guys, Honeybaked Ham, IHOP/24hr, Jack-in-the-Box, Kneaders Cafe, Mellow Mushroom, Mimi's Café, Native Grill, Neo Tokyo, On-the-Border, Peter Piper Pizza, Pizza Hut, Rubio's, Subway, Uncle Bear's Grill, Vincent's Pizza, Wendy's 🛏 Extended Stay America, Extended Stay America 🅞 AT&T, auto repair, Barnes&Noble, Best Buy, Fresh&Easy Mkt, Hobby Lobby, JC Penney, Jo-Ann Fabrics, Marshall's, Michael's, PetCo, Ross, Sprouts Mkt, Target, Verizon

158 Warner Rd, N 🅟 Circle K/dsl, QT 🍴 Carl's Jr, Dunkin', Forefathers Cheesesteaks, Port of Subs, Topical Smoothie 🛏 Drury Inn 🅞 Dick's, IKEA, S 🅟 Circle K/dsl, Minute Mart/dsl 🍴 AZ Sandwich Co., Burger King, ChuckeCheese, DQ, Hillside Spot Cafe, Macayo's Mexican, McDonald's, Nello's Pizza, Panda Garden, Ruffino's Italian, Taco Bell, Zipp's Grill 🅞 Ace Hardware, Basha's Foods, Big O Tire, Goodyear/auto, vet

157 Elliot Rd, N 🅟 Chevron/dsl, QT/dsl, Shell/Circle K/dsl 🍴 Applebee's, Arby's, Burger King, Crackers Cafe, Crazy Buffet, Fuddrucker's, Jimmy John's, Kabab Palace, Kobe Japanese, McDonald's, Olive Garden, Oregano's Pizza Bistro, Panda Express, Red Robin Rest., Sonic, Starbucks, Subway, Taco Bell, Wendy's, YC Mongolian Grill 🛏 Days Inn&Suites 🅞 $Tree, Acura, Buick, Cadillac/GMC, Chrysler/Dodge/Jeep, Costco/gas, Discount Tire, Fiat, Honda, Hyundai, Kia, Mazda, Mini, NAPA, Nissan, PetsMart, Ross, Savers, Staples, Toyota, URGENT CARE, Volvo, Walmart, S 🅟 Circle K/Dsl, Shell/Circle K/dsl 🍴 Biscuits, Cactus Jack's, Niros Gyros, Original Burrito, Pacific Gardens Asian, Starbucks, Sub Factory, Subway 🛏 Clarion, Sheraton 🅞 auto repair, O'Reilly Parts, Safeway, vet, Walgreens

155 Baseline Rd, Guadalupe, N 🅟 Circle K/dsl, Shell/Circle K/Popeye's/dsl 🍴 Carl's Jr, ClaimJumper, Ell Pollo Loco, Joe's Crabshack, KFC, McDonald's, Poliberto's Tacos, Rainforest Cafe, Subway, Taco Bell, Waffle House, Wendy's 🛏 Best Western, Candlewood Studios, Holiday Inn Express, InnSuites, Ramada, Residence Inn, SpringHill Suites, TownePlace Suites 🅞 AutoZone, AZ Mills/Famous Brands, CVS Drug, Food City, Home Depot, Marshall's, Parts Authority, Ross, Walgreens, S 🅟 7-11, Arco/dsl, QT 🍴 Aunt Chilada's Mexican, China Town, Denny's, Little Caesar's, Sonic, Subway 🅞 Fry's Electronics, Fry's Foods, URGENT CARE

154 US 60 E, AZ 360, Superstition Frwy, to Mesa, N 🅞 to Camping World (off Mesa Dr)

153b Broadway Rd E, N 🍴 Denny's 🛏 Comfort Suites, Extended Stay America, La Quinta, Quality Inn, Red Roof Inn, Sheraton 🅞 to Diablo Stadium, S 🅟 Chevron/dsl, Shell/Circle K/Del Taco/24hr 🍴 Goodcents Deli, Panda Express, Papa John's,

---

153b Continued
Pizza Hut, Port of Subs, Taco Bell, Whataburger 🛏 Country Inn & Suites, Homewood Suites 🅞 Staples

153a AZ 143 N, N 🍴 Denny's 🛏 Courtyard, Fairfield Inn, Hilton, Holiday Inn, La Quinta, Sleep Inn 🅞 to Diablo Stadium, S same as 153b

152 40th St, N 🅟 Shell/dsl 🅞 U Phoenix, S 🅟 Shell/Circle K 🍴 Burger King, Quiznos

151mm Salt River

151 b a 28th St, 32nd St, University Ave, N 🍴 Waffle House 🛏 Drury Inn, Extended Stay America, Hilton Garden, Holiday Inn Express 🅞 AZSU, U Phoenix, S 🅟 Circle K/dsl, QT/dsl 🍴 McDonald's

150b 24th St E (from wb), N 🛏 Motel 6 🅞 Air Nat Guard, S 🛏 Best Western/rest.

150a I-17 N, to Flagstaff

149 Buckeye Rd, N 🅞 Sky Harbor Airport

148 Washington St, Jefferson St, N 🅟 Chevron/dsl, Shell, Tiemco/dsl 🍴 Carl's Jr, McDonald's 🛏 Motel 6, Sterling Hotel 🅞 to Sky Harbor Airport, S 🅟 Circle K 🅞 🅗

147b a AZ 51 N, AZ 202 E, to Squaw Peak Pkwy

146 16th St (from sb), N 🅟 Shell/Circle K 🍴 Filiberto's Mexican, S 🅟 Circle K, Shamrock/dsl 🍴 Church's, Jack-in-the-Box, Little Caesar's, Salsita's Mexican 🅞 🅗, O'Reilly Parts, Ranch Mkt

145 7th St, N 🍴 Chicos Tacos, McDonald's, Sonic, Starbucks, Subway, Taco Bell, Whataburger 🅞 🅗, Safeway Foods, Walgreens, S 🅟 Circle K, Shell, Sinclair/dsl 🍴 Jimmy John's 🛏 Holiday Inn Express, Hyatt, Sheraton, SpringHill Suites 🅞 to Chase Field

144 7th Ave, N 🅟 Circle K 🍴 Chipotle, Five Guys, Habit Burger, Jersey Mike's, NY Pizza, Peiwei Asian, Potbelly, Starbucks, Zoe's Kitchen, S 🅟 Circle K 🅞 central bus dist

143c US 60, 19th Ave (from wb), downtown

143b a I-17, N to Flagstaff, S to Phoenix

142 27th Ave (from eb, no return), N 🛏 Comfort Inn

141 35th Ave, N 🍴 Jack-in-the-Box, Rita's Mexican, S 🅟 Shell/Circle K

140 43rd Ave, N 🅟 Arco, Circle K/dsl 🍴 Filiberto's Mexican, KFC, Little Caesar's, Pizza Hut, Salsita's Mexican, Subway 🛏 Woodspring Suites 🅞 AutoZone, Family$, Food City, Fry's Mercado/gas, Walgreens

139 51st Ave, N 🅟 Chevron/dsl, Circle K 🍴 Burger King, Domino's, El Pollo Loco, McDonald's, Sonic 🛏 American Inn, Budget Inn, Holiday Inn, Hometowne Suites, InTown Suites, La Quinta, Motel 6, Red Roof+, Travelodge 🅞 Food City, S 🅟 QT/dsl/scales, Shell/dsl 🍴 Carl's Jr, Filiberto's Mexican, IHOP, Jack-in-the-Box, Port of Subs, Taco Bell 🛏 Baymont Inn, Comfort Inn, Travelers Inn

138 AZ 202, S 🅟 Liberty/Chester's/dsl/24hr 🍴 Waffle House 🅞 Blue Beacon/scales

137 67th Ave, N 🅟 Circle K/dsl, Mobil/dsl, QT/dsl 🍴 Church's, Dunkin', S 🅟 🚛 FLYING J/Denny's/dsl/LP/24hr, Circle K/dsl 🍴 Jack-in-the-Box

136 75th Ave, N 🅟 Chevron/dsl, Circle K 🍴 Applebee's, Chili's, CiCi's Pizza, Denny's, Filiberto's, Hawaiian BBQ, Hooters, IHOP, Lin's Buffet, Longhorn Steaks, McDonald's, Olive Garden, Red Lobster, Starbucks, Subway, Taco Bell, TX Roadhouse, Wendy's, Whataburger, Wing Stop 🅞 $Tree, AT&T, Big Lots, Big O Tire, Dillard's, GNC, Home Depot, La Mesa RV Ctr, Lowe's, Ross, Target, URGENT CARE, Walmart, S 🅟 Arco

135 83rd Ave, N 🅟 Circle K, QT/dsl 🍴 Burger King, Jack-in-the-Box, Waffle House 🛏 Best Western, Premier Inn, Victory Inn 🅞 Sam's Club/gas

P H O E N I X

INTERSTATE 10 Cont'd

PHOENIX

Exit #	Services
134	91st Ave, Tolleson, N ⛽ Circle K/dsl
133b	Lp 101 N
133a	99th Ave, N ⛽ Chevron/Dunkin'/dsl 🍴 Blaze Pizza, Cafe Rio, Cafe Zupas, Cane's, Carrabba's, Chick-fil-A, China City, Chipotle Mexican, ClaimJumper, Coldstone, Dickey's BBQ, El Pollo Loco, Firehouse Subs, Habit Burger, HoneyBaked Ham, Island's Burgers, Jack-in the-Box, Jamba Juice, Jersey Mike's, Jimmy John's, Kneaders Cafe, McDonald's, Native Grill, Panda Express, Panera Bread, Peter Piper Pizza, Pieology, Pita Kitchen, Portillo's Hot Dogs, Potbelly, Red Robin, Rubio's, Smashburger, Starbucks, Subway, Taco Bell, Tokyo Joe's, Village Inn, Waba Grill 🛏 Courtyard ⊡ Best Buy, Costco/gas, Discount Tire, GNC, Hobby Lobby, Marshall's, Old Navy, PetCo, Ross, Tuesday Morning, URGENT CARE, Verizon, S 🍴 Pilot/Subway/Wendy's/dsl/scales/24hr ⊡ CarMax, Chevrolet
132	107th Ave, N ⊡ Walgreens, S 🍴 EVC ⊡ Camping World RV Ctr, Chrysler/Jeep, Dodge/Ram, Fiat, Honda, Hyundai, Kia, Mazda, Nissan, Toyota, VW
131	Avondale Blvd, to Cashion, N ⛽ Circle K/dsl, S 🍴 Culver's, Jack-in-the-Box, Panda Express 🛏 Hilton Garden, Homewood Suites ⊡ CVS Drug, to ISM Raceway
129	Dysart Rd, to Avondale, N ⛽ Chevron/dsl, Shell/Circle K/dsl 🍴 Buffalo Wild Wings, Chick-fil-A, ChuckECheese, El Pollo Loco, Fiesta Mexican, Fired Pie, In-N-Out, Jack-in-the-Box/24hr, Jersey Mike's, Manuel's Mexican, Mimi's Cafe, Nakama Japanese, NYPD Pizza, Ono Hawaiian BBQ, Panda Express, Pei Wei Asian, Starbucks, Subway, Taco Bell, Tomo Japanese 🛏 Holiday Inn ⊡ $Tree, AT&T, AutoZone, Discount Tire, Fry's Foods, JC Penney, Jo-Ann Fabrics, Kohl's, Lowe's, PetsMart, Sprouts Mkt, Verizon, vet, Walmart, S ⛽ QT/dsl 🍴 Black Bear Diner, Del Taco, Golden Corral, IHOP, KFC, Krispy Kreme, McDonald's, Peter Piper Pizza, Pizza Hut, Red Dragon, Subway, Waffle House, Whataburger 🛏 Quality Inn, Super 8 ⊡ Brakemasters, Food City, Home Depot, Pepboys, S&S Tire/repair, Sam's Club/gas, Walgreens
128	Litchfield Rd, N ⛽ Circle K/dsl 🍴 Applebee's, Black Angus Steaks, Chili's, Chipotle Mexican, Cracker Barrel, Denny's, Five Guys, Freddy's Steakburger, Gus' NY Pizza, Hayashi Japanese, Haymaker, Jimmy John's, Macaroni Grill, Macayo's Mexican, McDonald's, MOD Pizza, Raul&Theresa's Mexican, Starbucks, Subway, Wendy's, Wildflower Bread Co. 🛏 Hampton Inn, Red Lion Inn, Residence Inn ⊡ 🄷, Barnes&Noble, Best Buy, Michael's, Ross, Target, to Luke AFB, URGENT CARE, Wigwam Resort/rest (3mi), S ⛽ Circle K/dsl 🍴 Angry Crab Shack, Arby's, Burger King, Little Caesar's, Ramiro's Mexican, Rudy's BBQ, Schlotsky's, Taco Bell 🛏 Best Western, TownePlace Suites ⊡ AutoZone, BigLots, Buick/GMC, Ford, O'Reilly Parts
127	Bullard Ave, N 🍴 PF Chang's, Red Robin
126	PebbleCreek Pkwy, to Estrella Park, N 🍴 Ah-So Steaks, Ariba Mexican, Barro's Pizza, Burger King, Del Taco, Jamba Juice, Native Grill, Olive Garden, Oregano's Pizza, Panera Bread, Popeye's, Red Lobster, Rubio's, Starbucks, Taco Bell, TX Roadhouse ⊡ $Tree, Cal Ranch, Firestone/auto, GNC, Old Navy, PetCo, Staples, TJ Maxx, Walgreens, S ⛽ QT/dsl 🍴 Augie's Grill, Baskin Robbins, Filiberto's Mexican, Jack-in-the-Box, Jimmy John's, Marco's Pizza, McDonald's, Panda Express, Pizza Hut, Robeks Juice, Sammy's Burgers, Senor Taco, Starbucks, Subway, Yan's Chinese 🛏 Comfort Suites ⊡ Ace Hardware, Fletcher Tire, Safeway Foods/dsl, URGENT CARE, Verizon, vet, Walgreens, Walmart
125	Sarival Ave, Cotton Lane (from wb)

125mm	Roosevelt Canal
124	AZ 303
123	Citrus Rd, to Cotton Ln, S ⊡ Destiny RV Park, UHaul
122	Perryville Rd
121	Jackrabbit Trail, N ⛽ Chevron/dsl ⊡ $General, S ⛽ Circle K/dsl ⊡ CarQuest
120	Verrado Way, N ⛽ Shell/dsl 🍴 Culver's, Starbucks ⊡ Verizon
117	Watson Rd, S ⛽ Circle K/dsl 🍴 Carl's Jr, Chipotle Mexican, Cracker Barrel, Denny's, Dunkin', El Pollo Loco, Federico's Mexican, Firehouse Subs, Jack-in-the-Box, Jimmy John's, KFC, Little Caesar's, McDonald's, Palermo's Pizza, Panda Express, Papa John's, Peter Piper Pizza, Subway, Taco Bell, Wendy's 🛏 Holiday Inn Express ⊡ $Tree, AT&T, AutoZone, Discount Tire, Fletcher's Tire, Fry's Foods/dsl, Lowe's, PetsMart, URGENT CARE, Verizon, vet, Walgreens, Walmart/McDonald's
114	Miller Rd, to Buckeye, S ⛽ Chevron/Sam's Deli/dsl/e85/LP/24hr, Loves/Chester's/Subway/dsl/scales/24hr, QT/dsl 🍴 Burger King 🛏 Days Inn ⊡ Ford, Leaf Verde RV Park
112	AZ 85, to I-8, Gila Bend
109	Sun Valley Pkwy, Palo Verde Rd
104mm	Hassayampa River
103	339th Ave, S 🍴 TA/Country Pride/Pizza Hut/Shell/Subway/Taco Bell/dsl/scales/LP/24hr/@ ⊡ truckwash
98	Wintersburg Rd
97mm	Coyote Wash
95.5mm	Old Camp Wash
94	411th Ave, Tonopah, S ⛽ Chevron/dsl, Mobil/dsl, Pilot/Subway/dsl/LP/24hr 🍴 Tonopah Rest. ⊡ Saddle Mtn RV Park, USPO
86mm	🆁🆂 both lanes, full ♿ facilities, litter barrels, petwalk, 🕭, 🛢, vending
81	Salome Rd, Harquahala Valley Rd
69	Ave 75E
53	Hovatter Rd
52mm	🆁🆂 both lanes, full ♿ facilities, litter barrels, petwalk, 🕭, 🛢, vending
45	Vicksburg Rd, N ⛽ Pilot/Subway/dsl/scales/LP/24hr, S 🍴 Pride/Pizza Hut/dsl/scales/24hr ⊡ J&K repair/towing, Kofa NWR, RV Park, tires
31	US 60 E, to Wickenburg, 12 mi N ⊡ camping, food
26	Gold Nugget Rd
19	Quartzsite, to US 95, Yuma, N ⛽ 76/dsl, Arco/dsl, Chevron/dsl 🍴 Taco Mio ⊡ Family$, Roadrunner Foods, RV camping
18mm	Tyson Wash
17	US 95, AZ 95, Quartzsite, N ⛽ Mobil/Burger King/LP/dsl, Pilot/DQ/Subway/dsl/scales/24hr, Tesla EVC 🍴 Carl's Jr, McDonald's, Quartzsite Yacht Grill 🛏 Stagecoach Motel/rest. ⊡ $General, Johnson RV Ctr, tires/repair, S ⛽ Loves/Chester's/Subway/dsl/24hr 🛏 Super 8 ⊡ Desert Gardens RV Park, Lifestyles RV Ctr

QUARTZSITE

⛽ = gas 🍴 = food 🏨 = lodging 🅾 = other ℞ₛ = rest stop Copyright 2022 - The Next EXIT ®

AZ

▲E INTERSTATE 10 Cont'd

Exit #	Services
11	Dome Rock Rd
5	Tom Wells Rd, N ⛽ Chevron/Subway/dsl/scales/24hr
4.5mm	℞ₛ both lanes, full ♿ facilities, litter barrels, petwalk, (📞), (🚮), vending
3.5mm	AZ Port of Entry, weigh sta
1	Ehrenberg, to Parker, N ⛽ 76/dsl, Texaco 🅾 Family$, RV Resorts, S ⛽ *FLYING J*/Wendy's/dsl/LP/scales/lube/repair/tires/24hr 🏨 Best Western
0mm	Arizona/California state line, Colorado River, mountain/pacific time zone

▲N INTERSTATE 15

Exit #	Services
29.5mm	Arizona/Utah state line
27	Black Rock Rd
21mm	turnout sb
18	Cedar Pocket, S 🅾 parking area, Virgin River Canyon RA/camping
16mm	truck parking both lanes
15mm	truck parking nb
14mm	truck parking nb
10mm	truck parking nb
9	Desert Springs, N ⛽ *PILOT*/Chester's/Subway/dsl/scales/24hr
8.5mm	Virgin River
8	Littlefield, Beaver Dam, E 🅾 RV park, 1 mi W 🅾 camping, food, gas/dsl, lodging
0mm	Arizona/Nevada state line, mountain/pacific time zone

▲N INTERSTATE 17

Exit #	Services
341	McConnell Dr, I-17 begins/ends, N ⛽ Chevron/dsl, Circle K, Conoco/dsl, Giant/dsl, Mobil/dsl, Phillips 66/Wendy's/dsl, Shell 🍴 Arby's, August Moon Chinese, Baskin-Robbins, Buffalo Wild Wings, Burger King, Buster's Rest., Cafe Rio, Cane's, Carl's Jr, Chick-fil-A, Chili's, China Garden, Chipotle Mexican, Coco's, Coldstone, Del Taco, Denny's, Domino's, DQ, Dunkin', Five Guys, Freddy's Steakburgers, IHOP, Jack-in-the-Box, Jimmy John's, KFC, Little Caesar's, McDonald's, Native Grill, Ni Marco's Pizza, Olive Garden, Panda Express, Papa John's, Papa Murphy's, Peter Piper Pizza, Picazzo's Pizza, Pizza Hut, Quiznos, Red Lobster, Sizzler, Starbucks, Subway, Taco Bell 🏨 Baymont Inn, Best Inn, Budget Inn, Canyon Inn, Comfort Inn, Courtyard, Days Inn, Drury Inn, EconoLodge, EconoLodge, Embassy Suites, GreenTree Inn, Hampton Inn, Hilton Garden, Knights Inn, La Quinta, Motel 6, Quality Inn, Sleep Inn, SpringHill Suites, Super 8 🅾 🏨, $Tree, AT&T, Barnes&Noble, Basha's Foods, Discount Tire, Jo-Ann Crafts, Kohl's, Michael's, O'Reilly Parts, Petsmart, Ross, Safeway, Sprouts Mkt, Staples, Target, Verizon, Walgreens, Walmart
340b a	I-40, E to Gallup, W to Kingman
339	Lake Mary Rd (from nb), Mormon Lake, E ⛽ Circle K/dsl 🏨 AZ Mtn Inn 🅾 access to same as 341
337	AZ 89A S, to Sedona, Ft Tuthill RA, W 🅾 camping
333	Kachina Blvd, Mountainaire Rd, E 🍴 Mountainaire Rest. (1mi) 🏨 Abineau B&B, W ⛽ Shell/Subway/dsl 🅾 county park
331	Kelly Canyon Rd
328	Newman Park Rd
326	Willard Springs Rd
322	Pinewood Rd, to Munds Park, E ⛽ Shell/dsl, Woody's/dsl 🍴 Lone Pine Rest. 🅾 golf, Motel in the Pines, W ⛽ Chevron/dsl 🅾 Munds RV Park

Exit #	Services
322mm	Munds Canyon
320	Schnebly Hill Rd
317	Fox Ranch Rd
316mm	Woods Canyon
315	Rocky Park Rd
313mm	scenic view sb, litter barrels
306	Stoneman Lake Rd
300mm	runaway truck ramp sb
298	AZ 179, to Sedona, Oak Creek Canyon, 7-15 mi W 🍴 Burger King, Cowboy Club Rest., Joey's Bistro 🏨 Belrock Inn, Diamond Resort, Hilton, La Quinta, Radisson/cafe, Wildflower Inn 🅾 Rancho Sedona RV Park
297mm	℞ₛ both lanes, full ♿ facilities, litter barrels, petwalk, (📞), (🚮), vending
293mm	Dry Beaver Creek
293	Cornville Rd, McGuireville Rd, to Rimrock, E ⛽ McGuireville 🍴 Nikki's Grill, W ⛽ 76/dsl, Conoco/Beaver Hollow/dsl 🍴 El Patio Grill
289	Middle Verde Rd, Camp Verde, E ⛽ Chevron/dsl 🍴 Sonic, The Gathering Rest. 🏨 Cliff Castle Hotel/casino/rest. 🅾 Montezuma Castle NM, W 🅾 Distant Drums RV Park
288mm	Verde River
287	AZ 260, to AZ 89A, Cottonwood, Payson, E ⛽ Shell/Subway/dsl/RV dump/LP/24hr 🍴 Burger King, Carl's Jr, Denny's, DQ, Gabriela's Mexican, Los Betos Mexican, McDonald's, Starbucks, Taco Bell 🏨 Comfort Inn, Days Inn, Super 8 🅾 Territorial RV Park (1mi), Trails End RV Park, Zane Grane RV Park (9mi), W ⛽ Chevron/Wendy's/dsl/24hr 🅾 RV camping, to Jerome SP
285	Camp Verde, Gen Crook Tr, 3 mi E 🍴 Rio Verde Mexican 🏨 Territorial Town Inn 🅾 to Ft Verde SP, Trail End RV Park, Zane Gray RV Park (9mi)
281mm	safety pullout area nb
278	AZ 169, Cherry Rd, to Prescott
269mm	Ash Creek
268	Dugas Rd, Orme Rd
265.5mm	Agua Fria River
263b a	AZ 69 N, Cordes Jct Rd (262 from nb), to Prescott, E ⛽ Chevron, ♥*Loves*/dsl/scales/24hr/@, Shell/Noble Roman's/Subway/dsl/LP/24hr 🍴 Cafe Charo, McDonald's 🏨 Cordes Jct Motel/RV Park 🅾 Family$
259	Bloody Basin Rd, to Crown King, Horse Thief Basin RA
256	Badger Springs Rd
252	Sunset Point, ℞ₛ/scenic view both lanes, full ♿ facilities, (🚮), litter barrels, (📞), vending
248	Bumble Bee, W 🅾 Horsethief Basin RA
244	Squaw Valley Rd, Black Canyon City, E 🍴 Chilleen's on 17 BBQ/Steaks, W ⛽ Shell 🍴 Beni's Pizza 🏨 Mountain Breeze Motel 🅾 Bradshaw Mtn RV Resort (2mi), Family$
243.5mm	Agua Fria River
242	Rock Springs, Black Canyon City, E 🅾 KOA (1mi), W ⛽ 76/dsl, Shell 🍴 Beni's Pizza, Rock Springs Cafe 🏨 Bradshaw Mtn RV Resort, Mtn Breeze Motel 🅾 Ron's Mkt
239.5mm	Little Squaw Creek
239mm	Moore's Gulch
236	Table Mesa Rd
232	New River, E 🍴 RoadRunner Rest.
231.5mm	New River
229	Anthem Way, Desert Hills Rd, E ⛽ Circle K 🍴 Hungry Howie's, McDonald's, Pizza Hut, Rosati's Pizza, Starbucks, Subway, Taco Bell, Wendy's 🅾 CVS Drug, Safeway, URGENT CARE, W ⛽ Chevron/dsl, Circle K/dsl 🍴 Del Taco, Denny's, Fresca's

FLAGSTAFF

CAMP VERDE

ANTHEM

Copyright 2022 - The Next EXIT ®

↗N INTERSTATE 17 Cont'd

A N T H E M

229 Continued
Mexican, Subway Hampton Inn $Store, Anthem Outlets/famous brands/food court, Discount Tire, Harley-Davidson, Meineke, O'Reilly Parts, Tobias Auto, U-Haul, Walmart

227 Daisy Mtn Dr, E Circle K/dsl Cafe Provence, Domino's, Jack-in-the-Box, Roberto's Mexican, Starbucks, Streets of NY Deli, Streets of NY Deli, Subway CVS Drug, Fry's Foods, GNC, Verizon, vet

227mm Dead Man Wash

225 Pioneer Rd, W Pioneer AZ Museum, Pioneer RV Park

223 AZ 74, Carefree Hwy, to Wickenburg, E Chevron AZool Grill, Chili's, Denny's, Good Egg Cafe, In-N-Out, McDonald's, Ray's Pizza, Starbucks, Subway, Taco Bell Albertson's/Osco, GNC, Home Depot, Kohl's, Staples, W Cibola Vista Camping (11mi)

222 Dove Valley

221 AZ 303, Senora Desert Dr

220 Dixileta (from nb)

219 Jomax Rd

218 Happy Valley Rd, E Circle K/dsl, Shell Applebee's, Bajio, Buffalo Wild Wings, Burger King, Carl's Jr, Chipotle Mexican, Coldstone, IHOP, Jack-in-the-Box, Jersey Mike's, L&L Hawaiian BBQ, Logan's Roadhouse, Mellow Mushroom Pizza, Olive Garden, Panda Express, Paradise Cafe, PF Chang's, Rays Pizza, Red Robin, Sauce Pizza, Shane's Ribshack, Smash Burger, Starbucks, Streets of NY Pizza, Subway, TGIFriday's, Zupas Courtyard, Hampton Inn, Homewood Suites, Residence Inn $Tree, Barnes&Noble, Best Buy, Big O Tire, Dick's, Lowe's, O'Reilly Parts, Old Navy, PetCo, Ross, Staples, TJ Maxx, Verizon, vet, Walmart, World Mkt W QT/dsl, Shell/Circle K

217 Pinnacle Peak Rd, E Drury Inn, Hilton Garden Phoenix RV Park

215a Rose Garden Ln, same as 215b

215b Deer Valley Rd, E Shell/Circle K Arby's, Armando's Mexican, Culvers, Dunkin', Jack-in-the-Box, McDonald's, Sonic, Subway, Taco Bell, Wendy's Little Dealer RV Ctr, W Arco/dsl, Circle K/dsl Cracker Barrel, Denny's, Times Square Italian, Waffle House Days Inn, Extended Stay America , U-Haul

214c AZ 101 loop

214b Yorkshire Dr, W 7-11 Chick-fil-A, Chili's, Chipotle, In-N-Out, Jack-in-the-Box, Jimmy John's, Macaroni Grill, Pizza Hut, Wendy's Budget Suites , AT&T, Costco/gas, Michael's, Petsmart, Ross, Target

214a Union Hills Dr, E Circle K/dsl, Valero, W Arco/dsl Comfort Inn, Sleep Inn, Studio 6

S C O T T S D A L E

212b a Bell Rd, Scottsdale, to Sun City, E Chevron/dsl, Circle K, QT, Shell/dsl Big Apple Rest., Caramba Mexican, IHOP, Jack-in-the-Box, LJ Silver, Manuel's Mexican, McDonald's, Schlotzsky's, Shenanigan's Grill, Waffle House Fairfield Inn, Motel 6, Super 8 Big O Tire, Chevrolet, Chrysler/Jeep/Dodge, Discount Tire, Fiat, Ford, Honda, Hyundai, Kohl's, Lincoln, Mazda, Nissan, O'Reilly Parts, Sam's Club/gas, Toyota, U-Haul, Volvo, Walmart, W Applebee's, Denny's, Native New Yorker, US Egg Breakfast Red Roof Inn Fry's Foods/dsl

211 Greenway Rd, E Embassy Suites, La Quinta 7-11

210 Thunderbird Rd, E Circle K/dsl, Valero/dsl/LP Asian Cafe, Barro's Pizza, Hong Kong Chinese, Jack-in-the-Box, Macayo's Mexican, Pizza Hut/Taco Bell, Subway, Wendy's CVS Drug, Home Depot, Walgreens, W   Jamba Juice, McDonald's, Port of Subs, Whataburger Travelodge Best

P H O E N I X

Buy, Fry's Electronics, Lowe's

209 Cactus Rd, W 7-11, Chevron/dsl, QT/dsl China Harvest, Tuliaberto's Mexican Holiday Inn

208 Peoria Ave, E Fajita's, First Watch Cafe, Native Grill, Outback Steaks, Pappadeaux, Sweet Tomatoes Candlewood Suites, Comfort Suites, Crowne Plaza, Extended Stay America, Homewood Suites, Hyatt Place, W QT/dsl Black Angus, Buffalo Wild Wings, Burger King, Cane's, Chili's, Chipotle Mexican, Coldstone, Culvers, Fat Burger, Filiberto's Mexican, Hibachi Grill, Hooters, In-N-Out, Jason's Deli, Longhorn Steaks, Mi Pueblo, Mimi's Cafe, Mongolian BBQ, Old Country Buffet, Olive Garden, Peter Piper Pizza, Red Lobster, Sizzler, Souper Salad, Starbucks, Subway, TX Roadhouse, Wendy's Metro Plaza, Premier Inn $Tree, AT&T, Barnes&Noble, Dillard's, Discount Tire, Firestone/auto, Macy's, Michael's, PetCo, Petsmart, Ross, Staples, Tire Pros/repair, URGENT CARE, Verizon

208.5mm Arizona Canal

207 Dunlap Ave, E Circle K, Shell/dsl Blimpie, Domino's, Fajitas, First Watch Cafe, Fuddrucker's, Jack-in-the-Box, Native Grill, Outback Steaks, Steaken Burger, Subway, Sweet Tomatoes, Wong's Comfort Suites, Courtyard, Mainstay Suites, Sheraton, SpringHill Suites, TownPlace Suites Aamco, CVS Drug, URGENT CARE, W Chevron/dsl Bobby-Q's Rest., Denny's, Schlotzsky's, Subway Woodspring Suites Midas, repair, U-Haul

206 Northern Ave, E Circle K/dsl, Shell/dsl Boston Mkt, Burger King, Del Taco, Denny's, Dunkin', El Pollo Loco, Gyros House, IHOP, Los Compadres, McDonald's, Papa John's, Pizza Hut, Starbucks, Subway, Uncle Tony's Pizza Best Western Albertson's/Osco, AutoZone, Sprouts Mkt, URGENT CARE, Walgreens, W Arco, QT DQ Motel 6, Residence Inn, Super 8 $General, auto repair, vet

205 Glendale Ave, E 7-11, QT Pizza Patron, Subway Ace Hardware, Fry's Foods/dsl, repair, transmissions, vet, W Circle K/dsl Jack-in-the-Box, Lenny's Burger 7-11, O'Reilly Parts, to Luke AFB, Walgreens

204 Bethany Home Rd, E Arco, Chevron/dsl, Shell/Church's/dsl Carl's Jr, Dunkin', KFC, Mandarin Buffet, McDonald's, Papa Joe's, Pizza Hut/Taco Bell, Subway, Tulioberto's Mexican, Whataburger , $Tree, BigLots, Costco/gas, JC Penney, Petsmart, Ross, Target, URGENT CARE, Walgreens, Walmart, W Shell, Valero Burger King, Familia Lorito, Great Dragon Knights Inn auto repair, Food City, Jiffy Lube, Savers

203 Camelback Rd, E Church's, Country Boy's Rest., Filiberto's Mexican, Little Caesars $General, Chrysler/Dodge/Jeep, Discount Tire, Family$, Hyundai, Kia, W Circle K/dsl, QT DQ, Jack-in-the-Box, McDonald's Quality Inn AutoZone, to Grand Canyon U, USPO

🛑 = gas 🍴 = food 🛏 = lodging ⊙ = other Ⓡ = rest stop   Copyright 2022 - The Next EXIT ©

AZ

⬆N INTERSTATE 17 Cont'd

Exit #	Services
202	Indian School Rd, E 🛑 Arco/dsl 🍴 Domino's, Federico's Mexican, Pizza Hut, Subway ⊙ Ace Hardware, CVS Drug, Food City, Little RV Ctr, W 🛑 Shell, Sinclair/dsl, Valero/dsl 🍴 Lenny's Burgers 🛏 Motel 6, Travel Inn ⊙ 7-11, Wide World of Maps
201	Thomas Rd, E 🛑 Chevron/McDonald's 🍴 Arby's, Denny's, Dunkin', Jack-in-the-Box, Starbucks 🛏 Days Inn, La Quinta ⊙ Circle K, W 🛑 🍴 Carl's Jr, Subway ⊙ NAPA
200b	McDowell Rd, Van Buren, E ⊙ Purcell's Tire, W 🛏 Knights Inn
200a	I-10, W to LA, E to Phoenix
199b	Jefferson St (from sb), Adams St (from nb), Van Buren St (from nb), E 🛑 Circle K 🍴 Jack-in-the-Box ⊙ to st capitol, W 🛑 Circle K/gas 🍴 La Canasta Mexican ⊙ Penny Pincher Parts, PepBoys
199a	Grant St
198	Buckeye Rd (from nb)
197	US 60, 19th Ave, Durango St, E 🍴 Jack-in-the-Box, to St Capitol, Whataburger ⊙ $General, AutoZone
196	7th St, Central Ave, W 🛑 Shell/dsl
195b	7th St, Central Ave, E 🛑 Circle K/dsl 🍴 Jack-in-the-Box, McDonald's, Taco Bell 🛏 EZ 8 Motel ⊙ 🏥 NAPA Care
195a	16th St (from sb, no EZ return), E 🛑 Shell/Subway/dsl 🍴 Burger King ⊙ to Sky Harbor Airport
194	I-10 W, to AZ 151, to Sky Harbor Airport
	I-17 begins/ends on I-10, exit 150a

⬆N INTERSTATE 19

Exit #	Services
	I-19 uses kilometers (km)
101b a	I-10, E to El Paso, W to Phoenix. I-19 begins/ends on I-10, exit 260.
99	AZ 86, Ajo Way, E 🛑 Circle K, Speedway 🍴 Eegee's Cafe, Hamburger Stand, Peter Piper Pizza, Pizza Hut, Subway, Taco Bell ⊙ 🏥 $Tree, Fry's Foods, Goodyear/auto, U-Haul, URGENT CARE, vet, Walgreens, W 🛑 QT/dsl, Shell/dsl 🍴 Burger King, Church's, Little Caesar's, Los Betos Mexican, McDonald's ⊙ $General, city park, Family$, Food City, Jiffy Lube, museum, to Old Tucson
98	Irvington Rd, E 🛑 Arco/dsl 🍴 TX Roadhouse ⊙ AutoZone, W 🛑 Circle K/dsl, Speedway 🍴 Buffalo Wild Wings, Chick-fil-A, China Olive Buffet, Chipotle, Firehouse Subs, Five Guys, McDonald's, MOD Pizza, Olive Garden, Panda Express, Peter Piper Pizza, Red Lobster, Starbucks, Subway, Taco Bell ⊙ $Tree, AT&T, Best Buy, Discount Tire, Family$, Food City, GNC, Home Depot, JC Penney, Marshall's, Michael's, Old Navy, Petsmart, Ross, Target, Verizon
95b a	Valencia Rd, E 🛑 Circle K, Speedway 🍴 Chickenuevo, Church's, Donut Wheel, Eegee's Cafe, Jack-in-the-Box, Little Caesar's, McDonald's, Peter Piper Pizza, Sonic, Subway, Whataburger, Yokohama Asian ⊙ $Tree, AutoZone, Brake Masters, Family$, Food City, Jiffy Lube, Midas, O'Reilly Parts, to 🛫, USPO, Walgreens, W 🛑 Circle K/dsl, QT/dsl 🍴 Arby's, Blake's, Burger King, Carl's Jr, Casa Valencia, Chili's, China Dragon, Denny's, DQ, Dunkin', El Taco Tote, Golden Corral, Grand Buffet, Hamburger Stand, Little Caesar's, Papa John's, Papa Murphy's, Pizza Hut, Subway, Taco Bell, Wendy's ⊙ 99¢ Store, Big O Tire, BigLots, CVS Drug, Lowe's, repair, transmissions, URGENT CARE, Walgreens, Walmart
92	San Xavier Rd, W ⊙ to San Xavier Mission (2mi)

Exit #	Services
91.5km	Santa Cruz River
87	Papago Rd
80	Pima Mine Rd, E 🍴 Agave Rest., Diamond Casino
75	Helmut Peak Rd, to Sahuarita, E 🛑 Fry's Fuel, Speedway, dsl/e85 🍴 Dunkin'/Baskin Robbins, EVC, McDonald's, Panda Express, Starbucks, Subway, Taco Bell ⊙ Fry's Foods/drug, USPO, vet
69	US 89 N, Duval Mine Rd., Green Valley, E 🍴 50's Diner, Carl's Jr., Culver's, Denny's, Little Caesar's, Panda House, Pizza Hut, Rigoberto's, Subway ⊙ $Tree, 99¢ Store, Ace Hardware, AutoZone, BigLots, Fletcher's Repair, Jo-Ann Fabrics, O'Reilly Parts, Petco, Ross, Verizon, Walgreens, Walmart/Subway, W 🛑 Circle K 🍴 Arby's, Burger King, Domino's, DQ, Jerry Bob's Rest., Manuel's Mexican, Papa John's, Starbucks, Taco Bell 🛏 Vagabond Inn ⊙ Big O Tire, Ford/Hyundai, Green Valley RV Resort, Safeway/dsl, Titan Missile Museum, URGENT CARE, vet
65	Esperanza Blvd, to Green Valley, E 🛑 Shell/repair/dsl, W 🍴 AZ Family Rest., El Rodeo Mexican 🛏 Best Western/rest., Comfort Inn ⊙ Ace Hardware, Walgreens
63	Continental Rd, Green Valley, E 🍴 Quail Creek Rest. (7mi) ⊙ golf, San Ignacio Golf Club/rest., USPO, W 🛑 Chevron/HotStuff Pizza 🍴 KFC, McDonald's, Starbucks ⊙ CVS Drug, repair/tires, Safeway, to Madera Cyn RA, TrueValue, Verizon, Walgreens
56	Canoa Rd, W 🛏 Canoa Resort
54km	Ⓡ both lanes, full ♿ facilities, litter barrels, petwalk, 🍴, 🛒, vending
48	Arivaca Rd, Amado, 2-3 mi E 🛏 Amado Inn ⊙ DeAnza RV Resort (2mi), Mtn View RV Park, W 🍴 Cow Palace Rest., Longhorn Grill ⊙ $General, Amado Mkt/gas
42	Agua Linda Rd, to Amado, E ⊙ Mtn View RV Park
40	Chavez Siding Rd, Tubac, E ⊙ Tubac Golf Resort
34	Tubac, E 🛑 El Mercado 🍴 Elvira's Cafe, Habaneros Mexican, Italian Peasant, Tubac Deli, Tubac Jack's Rest. ⊙ to Tubac Presidio SP, Tubac Golf Resort, Tubac Mkt, USPO
29	Carmen, Tumacacori, E ⊙ to Tumacacori Nat Hist Park, food, gas, lodging
25	Palo Parado Rd
22	Pec Canyon Rd
17	Rio Rico Dr, Calabasas Rd, E 🛏 Esplendor Resort, W 🛑 Chevron/dsl/LP 🍴 Hua Mei Chinese, Nickles Diner, Subway ⊙ IGA Foods, USPO, vet
12	AZ 289, to Ruby Rd, E 🛑 🍴 Pilot/Wendy's/dsl/scales/24hr, W ⊙ to Pena Blanca Lake RA
8	AZ 82 (exits left from sb, no return), Nogales, E 🛑 Circle K ⊙ Mi Casa RV Park
4	AZ 189 S, Mariposa Rd, Nogales, E 🛑 76, FasTrip/dsl 🍴 Chuyitos Hotdogs, City Salads, Dragon Buffet, Exquisito Mexican, Jack-in-the-Box, KFC, Little Caesar's, McDonald's, Panda Express, Pizza Pollis, Subway, Tacos & Taros, Tito's Pizza 🛏 Mariposa Hotel ⊙ $Tree, AutoZone, Buick/GMC, Chevrolet, Ford, GNC, Hobby Lobby, Home Depot, JC Penney, Marshall's, O'Reilly Parts, Petsmart, Ross, Safeway, Walgreens, Walmart/McDonald's (N Grand Ave), W 🛑 Circle K/dsl 🍴 Carl's Jr, IHOP 🛏 Best Western, Candlewood Suites, Holiday Inn Express ⊙ Mexico Insurance
1b	Western Ave, Nogales
1a	International St
0km	**I-19 begins/ends in Nogales**, Arizona/Mexico Border, 1/2 mi N 🛑 Circle K, Jr's Fuel Depot/dsl, Shell 🍴 Church's, Denny's, Jack-in-the-Box, McDonald's, Peter Piper Pizza, Pizza Hut, Subway ⊙ AutoZone, CarQuest, Family$, Food City, museum, NAPA, O'Reilly Parts, PepBoys

PHOENIX

TUCSON

GREEN VALLEY

AMADO

NOGALES

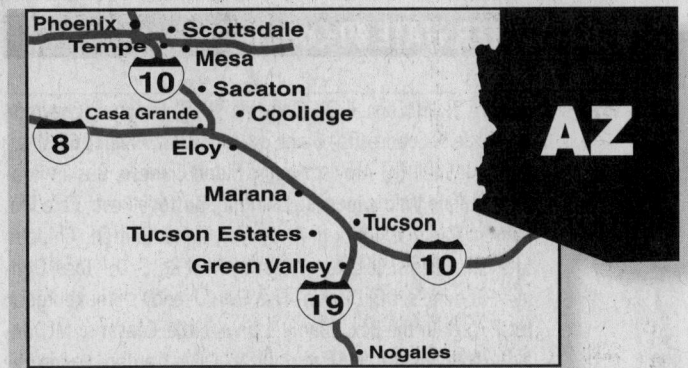

AZ

▲🅴 INTERSTATE 40

359.5mm	Arizona/New Mexico state line
359	Grants Rd, to Lupton, **N** Welcome Ctr/🆁🆂 **both lanes, full** 🦽 **facilities, litter barrels, petwalk,** 🄲, 🄰, 🅕 Speedy's/dsl/rest./24hr 🄾 Tee Pee Trading Post/rest., YellowHorse Indian Gifts
357	AZ 12 N, Lupton, to Window Rock, **N** 🄾 USPO
354	Hawthorne Rd
351	Allentown Rd, **N** 🄾 Chee's Indian Store, Indian City Gifts
348	St Anselm Rd, Houck, **N** 🄾 Ft Courage Food/gifts
347.5mm	Black Creek
346	Pine Springs Rd
345mm	Box Canyon
344mm	Querino Wash
343	Querino Rd
341	Ortega Rd, Cedar Point, **N** 🅖 Armco/gas/gifts
340.5mm	insp/weigh sta both lanes
339	US 191 S, to St Johns, **S** 🅖 Conoco/dsl 🄾 Family$, RV Park, USPO
333	US 191 N, Chambers, **N** 🄾 to Hubbell Trading Post NHS, USPO, **S** 🅖 Mobil/dsl 🏠 Days Inn/rest.
330	McCarrell Rd
325	Navajo, **S** 🅖 Shell/Subway/Navajo Trading Post/dsl/24hr
323mm	Crazy Creek
320	Pinta Rd
316mm	Dead River
311	Painted Desert, **N** 🅖 Painted Desert/dsl 🄾 Painted Desert, Petrified Forest NP
303	Adamana Rd, **N** 🄾 Stewarts/gifts, **S** 🄾 Painted Desert Indian Ctr
302.5mm	Big Lithodendron Wash
301mm	Little Lithodendron Wash
300	Goodwater
299mm	Twin Wash
294	Sun Valley Rd, **N** 🏠 Root 66 RV camping, **S** 🄾 Knife City
292	AZ 77 N, to Keams Canyon, **N** 🅖 Conoco/Burger King/dsl/24hr 🄾 dsl repair
289	Lp 40, Holbrook, **N** 🅖 Chevron/dsl, Hatch's/dsl 🅕 Denny's, Mesa Rest. 🏠 Best Western, Days Inn, EconoLodge, Howard Johnson, Motel 6, Quality Inn, Sahara Inn, Travelodge 🄾 Goodyear
286	Navajo Blvd, Holbrook, **N** 🅖 76/dsl, Circle K, Maverik/dsl 🅕 Aliberto's Mexican, Burger King, Carl's Jr, Hilltop Cafe, McDonald's, Taco Bell, Tom & Suzie's 🏠 66 Motel, Lexington Inn, Super 8 🄾 $General, KOA, OK RV Park, O'Reilly Parts, Econolodge, Taco Bell, **S** 🅖 Chevron/dsl, Fuel Express/dsl, MiniMart/gas, Speedy Dsl 🅕 DQ, Rte 66 Cafe 🏠 Best Value, El Rancho Motel/rest., Knights Inn 🄾 🄷, Dodge/Ford/Lincoln, museum, rockshops, Scotty & Son Repair, SW Transmissions, Little Caesars
285	US 180 E, AZ 77 S, Holbrook, **1 mi S** 🆁🆂, 🄰, **litter barrels,** 🅖 Giant/dsl 🅕 Butterfield Steaks 🏠 Economy Inn, Globetrotter Hotel, Wigwam Motel 🄾 Best Hardware, Family$, Safeway, to Petrified Forest NP
284mm	Leroux Wash
283	Perkins Valley Rd, Golf Course Rd, **S** 🅖 TA/Shell/Popeyes/dsl/scales/24hr/@
280	Hunt Rd, Geronimo Rd, **N** 🄾 Geronimo Trading Post
277	Lp 40, Joseph City, **N** 🅖 **Loves**/Chester's/Subway/scales/dsl/24hr, **S** 🄾 RV camping, to Cholla Lake CP
274	Lp 40, Joseph City, **N** food, gas, lodging, RV camping
269	Jackrabbit Rd, **S** 🄾 Jackrabbit Trading Post
264	Hibbard Rd

257	AZ 87 N, to Second Mesa, **N** 🄾 camping, to Homolovi Ruins SP, **S** 🄾 trading post
256.5mm	Little Colorado River
255	Lp 40, Winslow, **N** 🅖 Winslow Fuel/dsl 🅕 Mi Pueblo Mexican 🏠 Best Western+ 🄾 Take-A-Rest RV Park, **S** 🅖 ⊕FLYING J/Denny's/dsl/LNG/scales/RV Dump/24hr 🅕 Sonic 🄾 Chrysler/Dodge/Jeep, Nissan, 🆁🆂
253	N Park Dr, Winslow, **N** 🅖 Chevron, Maverik/dsl 🅕 Capt Tony's Pizza, Pizza Hut 🄾 $General, Ford, O'Reilly Parts, tires/lube, Walmart/Subway, AutoZone, Carl's Jr, **S** 🅕 Alfonso's Mexican, LJ Silver/Taco Bell, McDonald's, Subway 🏠 Motel 6, Quality Inn, Travelodge 🄾 🄷, Family$, NAPA, Safeway, China Town
252	AZ 87 S, Winslow, **S** 🅖 76/dsl 🅕 Entre Chinese 🏠 EconoLodge, Rodeway Inn
245	AZ 99, Leupp Corner
239	Meteor City Rd, Red Gap Ranch Rd, **S** 🄾 to Meteor Crater
235mm	🆁🆂 **both lanes full** 🦽 **facilities, info, litter barrels, petwalk,** 🄲, 🄰
233	Meteor Crater Rd, **S** 🅖 Mobil/Meteor Crater RV Park/dump 🄾 to Meteor Crater NL
230	Two Guns
229.5mm	Canyon Diablo
225	Buffalo Range Rd
219	Twin Arrows, **N** 🄾 Twin Arrows Resort/Casino
218.5mm	Padre Canyon
211	Winona, **N** 🅖 Shell/dsl/repair
207	Cosnino Rd
204	to Walnut Canyon NM
201	US 89, Flagstaff, to Page, **N** 🅖 76/Express Stop/dsl, Chevron/dsl, Circle K/dsl, Maverik/dsl, Shell, VP/dsl 🅕 Burger King, Del Taco, Denny's, Jack-in-the-Box, LJ Silver/Taco Bell, McDonald's, Pizza Hut, Sizzler, Village Inn, Wendy's 🏠 Best Western, Country Inn Suites, Days Inn, Howard Johnson, Mtn View Inn, Super 8, Travelodge 🄾 🄷, auto repair, Best Buy, Chrysler/Dodge/Jeep/Fiat, CVS Drug, Dillard's, Discount Tire, Evert's RV Center, Family$, Family$, Home Depot, Honda, JC Penney, KOA, Marshall's, Nissan/Subaru, Old Navy, O'Reilly Parts, Pepboys, PetCo, Safeway/dsl, Toyota, Tuesday Morning, VW, World Mkt, **S** 🅖 Mobil/dsl, Shell/dsl 🅕 Oregano's Pizza 🏠 Fairfield Inn, Hampton Inn, Sonesta Suites, Wyndham Resort
198	Butler Ave, Flagstaff, **N** 🅖 Chevron, Conoco/dsl, Shell 🅕 Burger King, Country Host Rest., Cracker Barrel, Culver's, Denny's, McDonald's, Outback Steaks, Sonic, Starbucks, Subway, Taco Bell, Texas Roadhouse 🏠 Comfort Inn, Holiday Inn Express, Howard Johnson, La Quinta, Motel 6, Quality Inn, Ramada, Rodeway Inn, Super 8 🄾 AutoZone, NAPA, Sam's Club/gas, U-Haul, vet, Walgreens, Walmart, **S** 🅖 Mobil, Sinclair/Little America/dsl/motel/@ 🅕 Black Bart's Steaks/RV Park
197.5mm	Rio de Flag

CHAMBERS

HOLBROOK

WINSLOW

FLAGSTAFF

AZ

FLAGSTAFF / WILLIAMS

INTERSTATE 40 Cont'd

Exit #	Services
195b	US 89A N, McConnell Dr, Flagstaff, N ⛽ Chevron, Chevron/dsl, Circle K, Conoco/dsl, Giant/dsl, Mobil/dsl, Phillips 66/Wendy's/dsl, Shell 🍴 Arby's, August Moon Chinese, Baskin-Robbins, Buffalo Wild Wings, Burger King, Buster's Rest., Cafe Rio, Cane's, Carl's Jr, Chick-fil-A, Chili's, China Garden, Chipotle Mexican, Coco's, Coldstone, Country Host Rest., Del Taco, Denny's, Domino's, DQ, Dunkin', Five Guys, Freddy's Steakburgers, IHOP, Jack-in-the-Box, Jimmy John's, Little Caesar's, McDonald's, Native Grill, Ni Marco's Pizza, Olive Garden, Panda Express, Papa John's, Papa Murphy's, Peter Piper Pizza, Picazzo's Pizza, Pizza Hut, Quiznos, Red Lobster, Sizzler, SmashBurger, Starbucks, Subway, Taco Bell 🛏 Baymont Inn, Best Inn, Budget Inn, Canyon Inn, Comfort Inn, Courtyard, Days Inn, Drury Inn, EconoLodge, Embassy Suites, GreenTree Inn, Hampton Inn, Hilton Garden, Howard Johnson, Knights Inn, La Quinta, Motel 6, Quality Inn, Sleep Inn, SpringHill Suites, Super 8 ◎ 🏥 $Tree, AT&T, Barnes&Noble, Basha's Foods, Discount Tire, GNC, Jo-Ann Crafts, Kohl's, Michael's, Natural Grocers, O'Reilly Parts, Petsmart, Ross, Safeway, Sprouts Mkt, Staples, Target, Verizon, Walgreens, Walmart
195a	I-17 S, AZ 89A S, to Phoenix
192	Flagstaff Ranch Rd
191	Lp 40, to Grand Canyon, Flagstaff, 5 mi N ⛽ Chevron, Maverik 🛏 Budget Host, DoubleTree, Super 8 ◎ Home Depot, Kia, Kit Carson RV Park, O'Reilly Parts, vet, Woody Mtn Camping
190	A-1 Mountain Rd
189.5mm	Arizona Divide, elevation 7335
185	Transwestern Rd, Bellemont, N ⛽ Pilot/McDonald's/Subway/dsl/scales/24hr/@ 🛏 Days Inn, S ◎ Harley-Davidson/Roadside Grill, Rte 66 RV Ctr
178	Parks Rd, N ⛽ Texaco/dsl ◎ USPO
171	Pittman Valley Rd, Deer Farm Rd, S 🛏 Mountain Ranch Resort
167	Garland Prairie Rd, Circle Pines Rd, N ◎ KOA
165	AZ 64, to Williams, Grand Canyon, N ⛽ 76 (8mi), Shell/dsl (4mi) ◎ KOA (4mi), to Grand Canyon, S 🛏 Super 8 (1mi)
163	same as 161, Williams, N ⛽ Chevron/dsl, Loves/Arby's/dsl/scales/24hr 🛏 Quality Inn ◎ Canyon Gateway RV Park, S ⛽ Circle K, Mobil/dsl, Mustang/dsl, Shell/dsl 🍴 Jack-in-the-Box, KFC/Taco Bell, McDonald's, Old Town Rest., Pancho's Mexican, Pine Country Rest., Pizza Hut, Red Garter Rest., Rod's Steaks, Rte 66 Diner, Twisters Soda Fountain 🛏 Canyon Motel/RV Park, EconoLodge, El Rancho Motel, Grand Canyon Railway Hotel, Howard Johnson, Knights Inn, Mountainside Motel, Ramada Inn, Rodeway Inn, Rodeway Inn, The Lodge Motel, Travelodge ◎ $General, USPO
161	Lp 40, Golf Course Dr, Williams, N ◎ RV camping, 0-3 mi S ⛽ Circle K, Conoco/dsl/LP, Shell 🍴 Buffalo Pointe Inn, DQ, Jessica's Rest., Maria's Tacos 🛏 AZ Motel, Best Value, Best Western, Budget Host, Canyon Country Inn, Comfort Inn, Days Inn, Grand Canyon Hotel, Highlander Motel, Motel 6, Westerner Motel ◎ 🏥 Family$, Safeway, to Grand Canyon Railway
157	Devil Dog Rd
155.5mm	safety pullout wb, litter barrels
151	Welch Rd
149	Monte Carlo Rd, N ◎ dsl repair
148	County Line Rd
146	AZ 89, to Prescott, Ash Fork, N ⛽ Mobil/dsl, Shell/dsl 🍴 Lulu Belle's BBQ, Ranch House Cafe 🛏 Ash Fork Inn ◎ Family$

SELIGMAN / KINGMAN

Exit #	Services
144	Ash Fork, N 🛏 Ash Fork Inn ◎ Grand Canyon RV Park, museum/info, USPO, S 🍴 Shell/Piccadilly's/dsl, Texaco/dsl/RV Park ◎ auto/RV repair
139	Crookton Rd, to Rte 66
123	Lp 40, to Rte 66, to Grand Canyon Caverns, (same as 121), Seligman, N ⛽ Chevron/A&W, Shell/dsl 🍴 Copper Cart Cafe, Lilo's Rest., Pizza Joint, Snow Cap Burgers 🛏 Canyon Lodge, Deluxe Inn, Stagecoach 66 Motel, Supai Motel ◎ KOA (1mi), repair, USPO, S ⛽ Chevron/Subway/dsl
121	Lp 40, to Rte 66, (same as 123), Seligman, N ⛽ Chevron/A&W, Phillips 66/dsl 🍴 Copper Cart Cafe, Lilo's Rest., Roadkill Cafe 🛏 Canyon Lodge, Route 66 Motel/pizza, Supai Motel ◎ KOA (1mi), repair, to Grand Canyon Caverns, USPO
109	Anvil Rock Rd
108mm	Markham Wash
103	Jolly Rd
96	Cross Mountain Rd
91	Fort Rock Rd
87	Willows Ranch Rd
86mm	Willow Creek
79	Silver Springs Rd
75.5mm	Big Sandy Wash
73.5mm	Peacock Wash
71	US 93 S, to Wickenburg, Phoenix
66	Blake Ranch Rd, N ⛽ Petro/Iron Skillet/dsl/scales/24hr ◎ Blake Ranch RV Park, SpeedCo Lube
60mm	Frees Wash
59	DW Ranch Rd, N ⛽ Loves/Chester's/Subway/dsl/scales/24hr ◎ truckwash, S ◎ Hualapai Mtn Park (9mi)
57mm	Rattlesnake Wash
53	AZ 66, Andy Devine Ave, to Kingman, N ⛽ Flying J/Denny's/dsl/LP/scales/24hr, Chevron/dsl, Maverik/dsl, Terrible's/dsl, Texaco/dsl 🍴 Arby's, Burger King, Denny's, Jack-in-the-Box, McDonald's, Pizza Hut, Taco Bell 🛏 Days Inn, Knights Inn, Motel 6, Red Roof Inn, Super 8, Travelodge ◎ $General, Basha's Foods, Blue Beacon, dsl/tire repair, Freightliner, Harley-Davidson, KOA (1mi), S ⛽ Mobil/dsl, Shell/dsl/repair 🍴 JB's, Oyster's Mexican, Sonic 🛏 Best Western+, Clarion, Days Inn, High Desert Inn, Holiday Inn Express, Ramada Inn, Rodeway Inn, Rte 66 Motel, SpringHill Suites ◎ Chrysler/Dodge/Jeep, Kia, NAPA, Sunrise RV Park, Uptown Drug
51	Stockton Hill Rd, Kingman, N ⛽ Arco/dsl, Chevron, Circle K/dsl 🍴 Carl's Jr, Chili's, Chipotle Mexican, Cracker Barrel, Del Taco, Domino's, Dunkin', Five Guys, Golden Corral, IHOP, In-N-Out, Jimmy John's, KFC, Lin's Little China, McDonald's, Panda Express, Papa John's, Papa Murphy, Plaza Bonita, Sonic, Starbucks, Subway, Taco Bell 🛏 Hampton Inn, La Quinta ◎ 🏥 $General, $Tree, AutoZone, AZ RV Depot/repair, BigLots, BrakeMasters, Buick/Chevrolet, CVS Drug, Discount Tire, Ford/Lincoln, Home Depot, Honda, Hyundai, O'Reilly Parts, PetCo, Petsmart, Ross, Safeway/gas, Smith's Foods/dsl, Staples, Superior Tire, TrueValue, Valvoline, Verizon, vet, Walgreens, Walmart, S ⛽ Circle K 🍴 DQ, Little Caesar's, Pizza Hut 🛏 Home 2 Suites ◎ 99c Store, CarQuest, JC Penney, Safeway/dsl
48	US 93 N, Beale St, Kingman, N ⛽ 76/Little Caesar's/dsl, Chevron/dsl, Diesel, Mobil/dsl, Shell/dsl, TA/Country Pride/Popeye's/dsl/scales/24hr/@, USA/Subway/dsl, Woody's 🍴 Wendy's 🛏 Economy Inn, Tristate Inn ◎ Best Tire Pros, S ⛽ Chevron/Tacos/dsl, Tesla EVC 🍴 Calico's Rest., Carl's Jr, Frederico's 🛏 AZ Inn, Motel 6 ◎ city park, Ft Beale RV Park, Mohave Museum
46.5mm	Holy Moses Wash

▲E INTERSTATE 40 Cont'd

Exit #	Services
44	AZ 66, Oatman Hwy, McConnico, to Rte 66, **S** 🅖 Crazy Fred's/café/dsl 🅞 Canyon West RV Camping (3mi), truckwash
40.5mm	Griffith Wash
37	Griffith Rd
35mm	Black Rock Wash
32mm	Walnut Creek
28	Old Trails Rd
26	Proving Ground Rd, **S** 🅞 AZ Proving Grounds
25	Alamo Rd, to Yucca, **N** 🅞 USPO
23mm	🆁🆂 both lanes, full 🅵 facilities, litter barrels, petwalk, 🄲 ♨ vending

21mm	Flat Top Wash
20	Santa Fe Ranch Rd
18.5mm	Illavar Wash
15mm	Buck Mtn Wash
13.5mm	Franconia Wash, Franconia Wash
13	Franconia Rd
9	AZ 95 S, to Lake Havasu City, Parker, London Br, **S** 🅖 Chevron/dsl, ❤Loves/Carl's Jr/Subway/dsl/scales/24hr, 🅿Pilot/Wendy's/dsl/scales/24hr 🅞 Havasu RV Park, Prospectors RV Resort
4mm	weigh sta both lanes
2	Needle Mtn Rd
1	Topock Rd, to Bullhead City, Oatman, **N** 🅞 camping, food, gas, to Havasu NWR
0mm	Arizona/California state line, Colorado River, Mountain/Pacific time zone

AR

ARKANSAS

▲E INTERSTATE 30

Exit #	Services
	I-30 begins/ends on I-40, exit 153b.
143b a	I-40, E to Memphis, W to Ft Smith
142	15th St, **S** 🅖 Super Stop/dsl
141b	US 70, Broadway St, downtown, **N** 🅖 Exxon, U.S. Fuel 🅕 Burger King 🅞 U-Haul, Verizon Arena, **S** 🅖 Phillips 66, Valero/dsl 🅕 McDonald's, Popeye's, Shark's, Taco Bell, Wendy's 🅛 Econolodge 🅞 Family$
141mm	Arkansas River
141a	AR 10, Cantrell Rd, Markham St (from wb), **W** 🅞 to downtown
140	9th St, 6th St, downtown, **N** 🅖 Shell, SuperStop 🅕 Pizza Hut 🅛 Holiday Inn 🅞 USPO, **S** 🅖 SuperStop 🅛 Comfort Inn
139b	I-630, downtown
139a	AR 365, Roosevelt Rd, **N** 🅖 Exxon 🅕 Sim's BBQ 🅞 AutoZone, O'Reilly Parts, **S** 🅖 Shell 🅞 $Tree, Family$, Kroger
138b	I-530 S, US 167 S, US 65 S, to Pine Bluff
138a	I-440 E, to Memphis, **S** 🅞 ♨
135	W 65th St, **N** 🅖 Exxon/dsl, Shell/dsl, Valero/dsl 🅛 Baymont Inn, **S** 🅛 Rodeway Inn
134	Scott Hamilton Dr, **S** 🅖 Exxon/dsl 🅛 Best Value Inn, Motel 6
133	Geyer Springs Rd, **N** 🅖 Exxon, Hess, Mobil 🅕 Church's, Sims BBQ, Subway, **S** 🅖 Citgo, Phillips 66, Shell 🅕 Arby's, El Chico, KFC, Little Caesar's, McDonald's, Rally's, Sonic, Taco Bell, Waffle House 🅛 Days Inn, Quality Inn, Red Roof Inn, Rest Inn 🅞 CVS Drug, Family$, Goodyear/auto, Kroger/gas, Walgreens
132	US 70b, University Ave, **N** 🅖 RaceWay/dsl, SuperStop, Valero 🅛 Best Value Inn, **S** 🅕 Kum&Go/dsl 🅞 O'Reilly Parts
131	McDaniel Dr, **N** 🅞 U-Haul, **S** 🅛 Economy Inn, Super 7 Inn 🅞 Crain RV Ctr
130	AR 338, Baseline Rd, Mabelvale, 5-8 mi **N** 🅛 Cimarron Inn, EconoLodge, Holiday Inn 🅞 Harley-Davidson, **S** 🅖 Murphy Express/dsl, Shell/dsl 🅕 Asian Buffet, McDonald's, Pizza Hut, Popeye's, Sonic, Taco Bueno, Wendy's 🅞 $Tree, Chevrolet, Crain RV Ctr, GNC, Home Depot, URGENT CARE, Walmart/Subway
129	I-430 N
128	Otter Creek Rd, Mabelvale West, **N** 🅖 ❤Loves/Hardee's/Subway/dsl/scales/24hr 🅕 Chick-fil-A, David's Burger, Hooters, Saltgrass Steaks 🅞 AT&T, Bass Pro Shop, Cavender's, Little Rock Outlets/famous brands, **S** 🅖 Exxon/dsl 🅛 Super 8 🅞 $General, Purcell Tire/auto
126	AR 111, County Line Rd, Alexander, **N** 🅖 Shell/dsl, **S** 🅖 Citgo/Subway 🅞 Cherokee RV Park/dump (4mi)

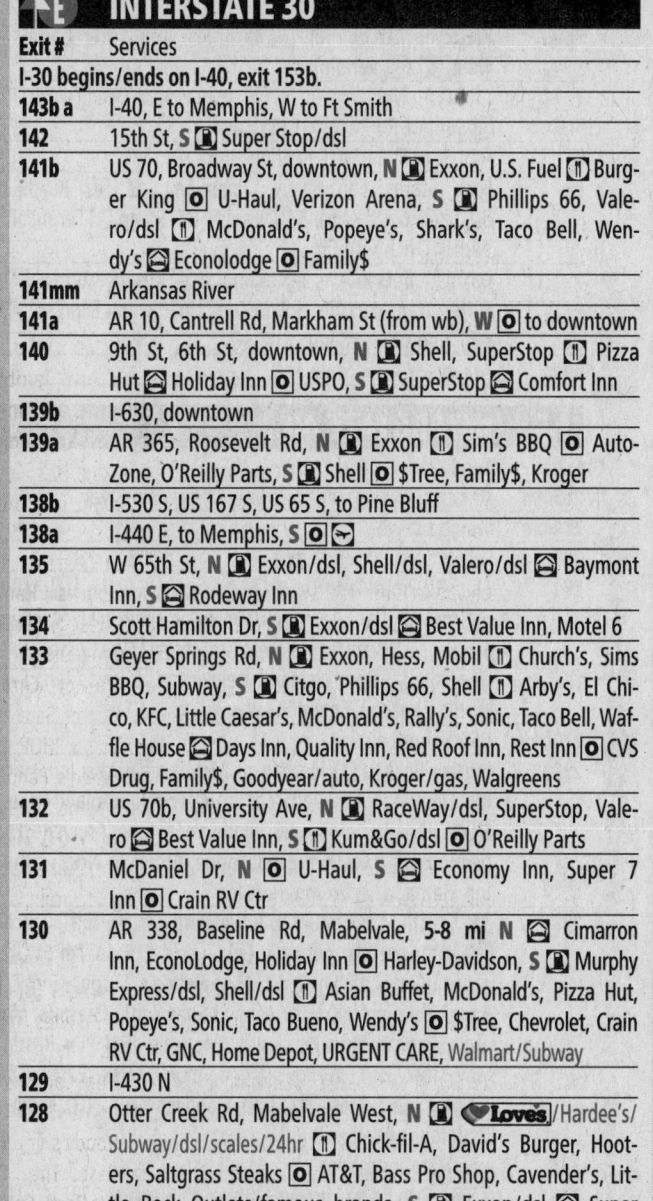

123	AR 183, Reynolds Rd, to Bryant, Bauxite, **N** 🅖 Murphy USA/dsl, Shell 🅕 Arby's, Burger King, Casa Mexicana, Cracker Barrel, David's Burgers, Dickey's BBQ, Domino's, Firehouse Subs, IHOP, KFC, Papa John's, Pizza Hut, Popeye's, Subway, Ta Molly's, Waffle House, Whole Hog Cafe 🅛 Best Value Inn, Comfort Inn, Country Inn Suites, Econolodge, Hampton Inn, Hometown Hotel, La Quinta 🅞 $Tree, AT&T, AutoZone, CVS Drug, Tire Pros, vet, Walgreens, Walmart/Subway, **S** 🅖 Exxon/dsl, Kum&Go/dsl/e85, Mapco/dsl/e85, Valero/dsl 🅕 Bryant Cafe, Chick-fil-A, Dunkin', Little Caesar's, Logan's Roadhouse, McDonald's, Mi Ranchito, Sonic, Taco Bell, Wendy's, Zaxby's 🅛 Super 8 🅞 $General, Family$, Food Giant, Lowe's, O'Reilly Parts, USPO, vet
121	Alcoa Rd, **N** 🅖 EZ Go, 🅿Pilot/Subway/dsl/scales/24hr/@ 🅕 DQ, Freddy's, McDonald's, Pie Five, Red Robin, Slim Chickens, Sonic, Taco Bueno, Tacos 4Life, TX Roadhouse, Zaxby's 🅞 Chrysler/Dodge/Jeep, Discount Tire, Fiat, Firestone/auto, Hobby Lobby, Infinity, Kroger/dsl, Nissan, Petsmart, TJ Maxx, Tuesday Morning, **S** 🅕 Buffalo Wild Wings, Chili's, McAlister's Deli, Moe's SW Grill, Sakura Japanese, Starbucks, Subway 🅛 Holiday Inn Express 🅞 AT&T, Buick/GMC, GNC, Kohl's, PetCo, Target, Verizon

L I T T L E   R O C K

M A B E L V A L E

gas = gas | food = food | lodging = lodging | other = other | Rs = rest stop | Copyright 2022 - The Next EXIT ®

AR

BENTON

	INTERSTATE 30 Cont'd
Exit #	Services
118	Congo Rd, N food Applebee's, Brown's Rest., Domino's, Gino's Grill lodging Fairfield Inn, Relax Inn other Chevrolet, Home Depot, Williams Tire, S gas Exxon, Kum&Go/dsl/e85 food Burger King, Popeye's lodging Days Inn other Ford, I-30 Travel Park, RV City, USPO
117	US 64, AR 5, AR 35, N gas Shell food Papa John's, Waffle House lodging Best Western, EconoLodge, Rodeway Inn, S gas Exxon, Gulf/dsl, Murphy USA/dsl, Valero food Arby's, Backyard Burger, Buffet City, Burger King, Capt D's, Chicken Express, Colton's Steaks, IHOP, KFC, La Hacienda Mexican, Little Caesar's, Mazzio's, McDonald's, Pizza Hut, Rib Crib, Samurai Japanese, Sonic, Subway, Taco Bell, Wendy's lodging Days Inn other $General, $Tree, Advance Parts, AT&T, AutoZone, BigLots, CVS Drug, GNC, H, Kroger/dsl, O'Reilly Parts, Office Depot, URGENT CARE, USPO, Verizon, Walgreens, Walmart/Subway
116	Sevier St, N gas Exxon, Mac's/dsl lodging Troutt Motel, S gas Alon/dsl lodging Capri Inn
114	US 67 S, Benton, S gas Valero/McDonald's/dsl food Sonic other $General
113mm	insp sta both lanes
111	US 70 W, Hot Springs, N other Cloud 9 RV Park, to Hot Springs NP
106	Old Military Rd, N gas Alon/JJ's Rest./dsl/scales/@, S other JB'S RV Park

MALVERN

99	US 270 E, Malvern, S other H
98b a	US 270, Malvern, Hot Springs, N gas Valero/dsl lodging Super 8, S gas Murphy USA/dsl, Phillips 66/dsl, Shell/dsl, Valero, Valero/Baskin-Robbins food Burger King, Chile Peppers, Cotija Mexican, Domino's, El Parian, Great Wall Buffet, Larry's Pizza, McDonald's, Pizza Hut, Popeye's, Sonic, Subway, Taco Bell, Waffle House, Wendy's, Western Sizzlin lodging Best Value Inn, Holiday Inn Express, Quality Inn other $General, $Tree, AT&T, AutoZone, Chevrolet, Chrysler/Dodge/Jeep, city park, Ford, H, O'Reilly Parts, USPO, Verizon, Walmart/Subway
97	AR 84, AR 171, N other Lake Catherine SP, RV camping
93mm	Rs (both lanes exit left), full facilities, litter barrels, petwalk, vending
91	AR 84, Social Hill
83	AR 283, Friendship, S gas Valero/dsl

ARKADELPHIA

78	AR 7, Caddo Valley, N gas Pilot/PJ Fresh Deli/dsl/scales/24hr, Shell/dsl food Chester's, Cracker Barrel, Flying Burger lodging Holiday Inn Express other Arkadelphia RV Park, De Gray SP, dsl repair, to Hot Springs NP, S gas Exxon/Subway/dsl, Valero food Fat Boys Cafe, McDonald's, Taco Bell, Waffle House lodging Best Value Inn, Comfort Inn, EconoLodge, Economy Inn, Hampton Inn, Motel 6, Quality Inn, Super 8
73	AR 8, AR 26, AR 51, Arkadelphia, N gas Phillips 66/dsl, Shell, Stuckey's food Allen's BBQ, Chicken Express, Domino's, Great Wall Buffet, McDonald's, Wendy's, Western Sizzlin other $Tree, to Crater of Diamond SP, Verizon, Walmart/Subway, S gas Exxon/dsl, Shell food Andy's Rest., Big Cheese Pizza, Burger King, Dunkin/Baskin Robbins, Great Wok, Little Caesar's, Ranchito Mexican, Subway other $General, Ace Hardware, AT&T, AutoZone, Brookshire Foods, H, O'Reilly Parts, vet, Walgreens
69	AR 26 E, Gum Springs
63	AR 53, Gurdon, N gas South Fork Trkstp/Citgo/rest./dsl lodging Southfork Inn, S gas Phillips 66/dsl other to White Oak Lake SP
56mm	Rs both lanes, full facilities, litter barrels, petwalk, vending, vending
54	AR 51, Gurdon, Okolona
46	AR 19, Prescott, N gas Phillips 66/cafe/dsl/24hr other Crater of Diamonds SP (31mi), S gas Love's/Hardee's/dsl/scales/24hr food Casa Carlos Mexican

HOPE

44	AR 24, Prescott, N gas TA/Country Pride/Subway/Taco Bell/dsl/scales/24hr/@, S gas Norman's 44 Trkstp/rest/dsl/scales/@ lodging Best Value Inn other to S Ark U, truckwash
36	AR 299, to Emmett
31	AR 29, Hope, N gas SuperStop/dsl lodging Relax Inn, Village Inn/RV park other st police, S gas Exxon/dsl, Valero/dsl food KFC lodging Best Value Inn other H
30	AR 4, Hope, N gas EVC, Murphy USA/dsl, Shell/dsl food Dos Loco Gringos lodging Best Western, Hampton Inn, Holiday Inn Express, Super 8 other Millwood SP, Old Washington Hist SP, Verizon, Walmart/Subway, S gas Exxon/Baskin-Robbins/Wendy's, Valero food Amigo Juan Mexican, Big Jake's BBQ, Burger King, Chicken Express, Little Caesar's, McDonald's, Pizza Hut, Sonic, Subway, Taco Bell, Waffle House lodging Motel 6 other $Tree, AT&T, AutoZone, Buick/Chevrolet/GMC, Bumper Parts, Ford, Fred's, H, O'Reilly Parts, Super 1 Foods/gas, Walgreens
26mm	weigh sta both lanes
18	rd 355, Fulton, N gas Red River Trkstp/dsl
17mm	Red River
12	US 67 (from eb), Fulton
7mm	Welcome Ctr eb, full facilities, info, litter barrels, petwalk, vending
7	AR 108, Mandeville, N gas Flying J/Denny's/dsl/LP/24hr lodging Sunrise RV Park other truckwash
3	I-49, N to Ft Smith, S to Shreveport
2	Four States Fair Pkwy, Texarkana, N gas RoadRunner/dsl, Shell/Circle K/dsl, S gas Camp I-30 Trkstp food Ferguson Fairpark other Nick's RV Ctr
1	US 71, Jefferson Ave, Texarkana, N lodging Best Western+, Comfort Suites, Hampton Inn, Holiday Inn, Holiday Inn Express other KOA, S lodging Country Host Inn
0mm	Arkansas/Texas State line

WEST MEMPHIS

	INTERSTATE 40
Exit #	Services
285mm	Arkansas/Tennessee state line, Mississippi River
284mm	weigh sta wb
281	AR 131, S to Mound City
280	Club Rd, Southland Dr, N gas Blu/dsl/LNG/24hr, Pilot/Wendy's/dsl, S gas Flying J/Denny's/dsl/LP/24hr, Love's/Subway/dsl, Petro/Iron Skillet/dsl/24hr/@ food KFC/Taco Bell, McDonald's lodging Best Western, Deluxe Inn, Express Inn, Super 8 other Blue Beacon, SpeedCo Lube
279b	I-55 S (from eb)
279a	Ingram Blvd, N food Margaritas Mexican lodging Days Inn, Hallmarc Inn, Homegate Inn, Red Roof Inn other Ford, Southland Racetrack, S gas Citgo/dsl, Phillips 66, Shell /dsl food Cross Creek Rest., Waffle House lodging Clarion, EconoLodge, Motel 6, New Hampshire Inn, Ramada, Relax Inn, Rest Inn
278	AR 77, 7th St, Missouri St, N Welcome Ctr/Rs/full facilities, litter barrels, petwalk, gas Shell/dsl, S on 7th St gas Exxon, MapCo, Shell, Shell/dsl food Applebee's, Burger King, Cracker Barrel, Domino's, Krystal, Lenny's Subs, Little Caesar's, McDonald's, Papa John's, Pizza Hut, Popeye's, Red Pier Rest., Subway, Taco Bell, Wendy's lodging Comfort Suites, Extend Suites, Holiday Inn Express other $Tree, Goodyear/auto, H, Kroger/dsl, Walgreens, Walmart
277	I-55 N, to Jonesboro
276	AR 77, Rich Rd, to Missouri St (from eb, same as 278), S gas Exxon, MapCo, Murphy Express/dsl, Phillips 66/dsl, Shell food Applebee's, Burger King, Domino's, Fusion Buffet, Krystal, Lenny's Subs, Little Caesar's, McDonald's, Mi Pueblo Mexican, Papa John's,

INTERSTATE 40 Cont'd

Exit	
276	**Continued** Pizza Hut, Popeye's, Shoney's, Subway, Taco Bell, Wendy's 🛏️ Extend Suites Ⓞ $Tree, AT&T, Family$, Goodyear/auto, Ⓗ, Kroger/dsl, Walgreens, Walmart
275	AR 118, Airport Rd, S 🅿️ Shell/DQ/dsl 🍴 Huddle House Ⓞ city park, URGENT CARE
274mm	weigh sta eb, parking area wb
271	AR 147, to Blue Lake, S 🅿️ Citgo, Exxon/Chester's/dsl, Valero/dsl 🍴 BBQ, produce Ⓞ tires, to Horseshoe Lake
265	US 79, AR 218, to Hughes
260	AR 149, to Earle, N 🅿️ Citgo/Subway, TA/Country Pride/Burger King/Taco Bell/dsl/scales/24hr/@, Valero/dsl 🛏️ Relax Inn Ⓞ Shell Lake Camping, S 🅿️ Citgo Ⓞ dsl repair
256	AR 75, to Parkin Parkin Archeological Park (12mi)
247	AR 38 E, to Widener
245mm	St Francis River
243mm	🆁🆂 wb, full ♿ facilities, litter barrels, petwalk, 🚮, 🛋️, vending
242	AR 284, Crowley's Ridge Rd, N Ⓞ Ⓗ, to Village Creek SP
241b a	AR 1, Forrest City, N 🅿️ Citgo/DQ/dsl, Shell/Popeye's/dsl 🍴 Don Jose Mexican, HoHo Chinese, Wendy's 🛏️ Best Value, Comfort Suites, Days Inn, Econolodge, Hampton Inn, Holiday Inn Express, Luxury Inn, Super 8 Ⓞ st police, S 🅿️ Citgo/dsl, Exxon/dsl, Murphy USA/dsl, Shell/dsl 🍴 Burger King, Domino's, Dragon China, Iguanas Mexican, KFC, McDonald's, Ole Sawmill Cafe, Pizza Hut, Sonic, Subway, Taco Bell, Waffle House 🛏️ Quality Inn, Red Roof Inn Ⓞ $Tree, AT&T, Food Giant, Fred's, O'Reilly Parts, Save-A-Lot Foods, Verizon, Walgreens, Walmart
239	AR 1, to Wynne, Marianna
235mm	🆁🆂 eb, full ♿ facilities, litter barrels, petwalk, 🚮, 🛋️, vending
234mm	L'Anguille River
233	AR 261, Palestine, N 🅿️ 🔵Loves/Chester's/Subway/dsl/scales/24hr 🛏️ Rest Inn, S 🅿️ Exxon/dsl
221	AR 78, Wheatley, N 🅿️ SweetPea/dsl/repair, S 🅿️ MapCo/Subway/dsl, Valero/Pitstop/diner/dsl
216	US 49, AR 17, Brinkley, N 🅿️ Citgo, Mobil/dsl, Road Ranger/dsl 🛏️ Best Inn, Brinkley RV Park, Days Inn, EconoLodge, Super8/RV Park, Sure Stay Ⓞ dsl repair, KFC/Taco Bell, Los Piños Mexican, S 🅿️ Exxon/Baskin-Robbins/dsl, Shell, Victory/dsl 🍴 Gene's BBQ, McDonald's, New China, Pizza Hut, Sonic, Subway, Waffle House Ⓞ $General, AT&T, Family$, Fred's, Kroger, O'Reilly Parts
205mm	Cache River
202	AR 33, to Biscoe
200mm	White River
199mm	🆁🆂 both lanes, full ♿ facilities, litter barrels, no 🚮, 🛋️, vending
193	AR 11, to Hazen, N 🅿️ Exxon/Chester's/dsl Ⓞ Lower White River RV Park, S 🅿️ 🔵Loves/Carl's Jr/dsl/scales/24hr, Mobil/dsl 🍴 El Amigo Mexican 🛏️ Super 8, Travel Inn
183	AR 13, Carlisle, S 🅿️ Citgo, Conoco/dsl, Exxon/Subway/dsl, Valero/dsl 🍴 Nick's BBQ, Pizza 'N More, Sonic 🛏️ Days Inn Ⓞ $General
175	AR 31, Lonoke, N 🅿️ Phillips 66, Valero/dsl 🍴 Burger King, Marachi Mexican, McDonald's, Waffle House 🛏️ Best Western, Days Inn, Economy Inn, Hampton Inn, Holiday Inn Express Ⓞ AT&T, Verizon, Walmart, S 🅿️ Shell/Subway 🍴 KFC/Taco Bell, Pizza Hut, Sonic 🛏️ Perry's Motel Ⓞ $ Tree, $General, Goodyear/auto, O'Reilly Parts, vet
173	AR 89, Lonoke
169	AR 15, Remington Rd
165	Kerr Rd

Exit	
161	AR 391, Galloway, N 🅿️ 🔵Loves/Chester's/subs/dsl/scales/24hr Ⓞ Camping World RV Ctr, S 🅿️ IA-80 TruckOMat/dsl/scales, LNG, Petro/Iron Skillet/dsl/scales/24hr/@, 🔵Pilot/Subway/Pizza Hut/dsl/scales/24hr 🛏️ Days Inn Ⓞ Blue Beacon, dsl repair, Freightliner, Southern Tire Mart, SpeedCo Burger King
159	I-440 W, S 🍴
157	AR 161, to US 70, N 🅿️ Exxon/dsl, S 🅿️ Hess, Mobil/dsl, Shell/dsl, Valero/dsl 🍴 Burger King, McDonald's, Sonic, Taco Bell 🛏️ Days Inn, EconoLodge, Quality Inn, Red Roof Inn, Rest Inn, Super 8 Ⓞ Family$
156	Springhill Dr, N 🅿️ Kum&Go/dsl, Mapco/dsl, Murphy USA/dsl 🍴 Cracker Barrel 🛏️ Candlewood Suites, Fairfield Inn, Hilton Garden, Holiday Inn Express, Residence Inn, Walmart
155	US 67 N, US 167, to Jacksonville (exits left from eb), Little Rock AFB, 0-3 mi N on US 167/McCain Blvd 🅿️ Murphy USA/dsl, Phillips 66/dsl, Shell, Valero/dsl 🍴 Arby's, Bar Louie, BJ's Rest., Buffalo Wild Wings, Burger King, Cactus Jacks, Carino's Italian, Chick-fil-A, Chili's, ChuckECheese's, Chuy's TexMex, CiCi's Pizza, Corky's BBQ, David's Burgers, Dixie Cafe, El Porton Mexican, Firehouse Subs, Five Guys, Fox & Hound, Freddy's, Golden Corral, Hideaway Pizza, Hog Wild Cafe, Hooters, IHOP, Jason's Deli, Jimmy John's, Kanpai Japanese, McDonald's, Newk's Eatery, Old Chicago Pizza, Olive Garden, On-the-Border, Outback Steaks, Panera Bread, Pizza Hut, Popeyes, Rally's, Red Lobster, Saddle Creek Grill, Saltgrass Steaks, Subway, Super King Buffet, Taco Bell, Taziki's Mediterranean, TGIFriday's, TX Roadhouse, US Pizza, Waffle House, Wendy's, Whole Hog Cafe 🛏️ Candlewood Suites, Comfort Inn, Courtyard, Hampton Inn, Hilton Garden, Holiday Inn Express, La Quinta, Motel 6, Super 8, Ⓞ Ⓗ, $Tree, Aamco, AT&T, Barnes&Noble, Best Buy, BigLots, Books-A-Million, Buick/GMC, Chevrolet, Chrysler/Dodge/Jeep, Dick's, Dillard's, Firestone/auto, Ford, Home Depot, Honda, Hyundai, JC Penney, Jo-Ann, Kia, Kroger, Lincoln, Lowe's, Mazda, Michael's, Nissan, Office Depot, PepBoys, PetCo, Petsmart, Ross, Sam's Club/gas, Steinmart, Target, TJ Maxx, Toyota, URGENT CARE, Verizon, vet, VW, Walgreens, Walmart/Subway
154	to Lakewood (from eb)
153b	I-30 W, US 65 S, to Little Rock
153a	AR 107 N, JFK Blvd, N 🅿️ Exxon, Mapco/dsl, Shell 🍴 Schlotzsky's 🛏️ Best Value Inn Ⓞ vet, S 🅿️ Exxon 🍴 Bogie's Grill 🛏️ Best Western+, Motel 6, Quality Inn, Red Roof Inn, Super Stay Inn Ⓞ Ⓗ, USPO Baymont Inn, Murphy Express/dsl, Taco Bueno
152	AR 365, AR 176, Camp Pike Rd, Levy, N 🅿️ Exxon, Shell 🍴 Burger King, KFC, Little Caesar's, McDonald's, Mexico Chiquito, Pizza Hut, Señor Tequila, Sonic, Subway, Taco Bell, US Pizza, Waffle House Ⓞ $General, AutoZone, Family$, Kroger/gas, O'Reilly Parts, S 🅿️ Shell 🍴 Chicken King Ⓞ Family$, Ⓗ, Save a Lot

Map cities (left to right / top to bottom): Conway, West Memphis, 🔵40, N Little Rock, Forrest City, Little Rock, Brinkley, Clarendon, Benton, Malvern, Arkadelphia, 🔵30 Gurdon, Prescott, Hope — **AR**

INTERSTATE 40 Cont'd

Exit #	Services
150	AR 176, Burns Park, Camp Robinson, S ▣ camping, info
148	AR 100, Crystal Hill Rd, N ▣ Shell, S ▣ Citgo/dsl, Exxon/dsl ▣ KOA
147	I-430 S, to Texarkana
142	AR 365, to Morgan, N ▣ Shamrock, Valero/dsl ▢ Razorback Inn ▣ Bumper Parts, Trails End RV Park, S ▣ Kum&Go/dsl, Shell/dsl ⑪ KFC, McDonald's, Razorback Pizza, Smokeshack BBQ, Subway, Waffle House ▢ Best Value Inn, Holiday Inn Express, Quality Inn ▣ $General, Autozone
135	AR 365, AR 89, Mayflower, N ▣ Hess/dsl, S ▣ Exxon/dsl, Valero ⑪ Sonic, Subway ▣ $General, Harp's Mkt
134mm	**truck parking both lanes**
132	Baker-Wills Pkwy, S VP Fuel
129	US 65B, AR 286, Conway, N ▣ Sam's Club/dsl ⑪ On the Border ▣ $Tree, AT&T, BAM!, Buick/GMC, Kia, Michael's, Petco, Ross David's Burgers, Hideaway Pizza, Red Robin, Rita's Custard, Subway, S ▣ Exxon/dsl, MapCo/dsl ⑪ Subway ▣ Chevrolet, Chrysler/Dodge/Jeep, Honda, Ⓗ, st police, to Toad Suck SP, Toyota Burge's Cafe, Meineke, URGENT CARE
127	US 64, Conway, N ▣ Gulf/dsl, Shell, Valero/dsl ⑪ Arby's, Buffalo Wild Wings, Chick-fil-A, Chili's, Chipotle, Freddy's, Golden Corral, Las Palmas Mexican, Logan's Roadhouse, Mulan's Buffet, Popeye's, Sonic, Starbucks, Subway, TGIFriday's, Waffle House ▢ Best Value Inn, Best Western, Comfort Suites, Country Inn&Suites, Days Inn, Hampton Inn, Hilton Garden, Home 2 Suites ▣ $General, AT&T, Belk, Best Buy, Dick's, Firestone/auto, Ford, GNC, Goodyear/auto, Harley-Davidson, Home Depot, Hyundai, Kohl's, Moix RV Ctr, NAPA, Nissan, O'Reilly Parts, Old Navy, Petsmart, repair/transmissions, Staples, Target, TJ Maxx, to Lester Flatt Park, Verizon, vet Blaze Pizza, S ▣ RaceWay, Shell/dsl, Valero/dsl ⑪ Burger King, Church's, Colton's Steaks, Dunkin'/Baskin Robbins, Jimmy John's, LJ Silver, McDonald's, Rally's, Saigon Rest., Taco Bell, Tacos 4 Life, Taziki's Mediterranean, Wendy's, Whole Hog Cafe ▢ Kings Inn ▣ AutoZone, BigLots, Family$, Fred's Drugs, Hobby Lobby, Kroger/gas, tires, Walgreens Captain Hook's, CVS
125	US 65, Conway, N ▣ Conoco/dsl, Exxon/Subway/dsl ⑪ China Town, Cracker Barrel, El Acapulco Mexican, McDonald's, MktPlace Deli ▢ Quality Inn ▣ $Tree, JC Penney, Office Depot, S ▣ Citgo, CNG, Horton's, Mobil/dsl, Murphy USA/dsl ⑪ Burger King, Cast Iron Skillet, CiCi's Pizza, David's Burgers, Dixie Cafe, Firehouse Subs, Fuji Steaks, IHOP, Los Potrillos Mexican, McAlister's Deli, Mexico Chiquito, New China, Outback Steaks, Panera Bread, Ruby Tuesday, Russo's Italian Kitchen, Sonic, Starbucks, Subway, Waffle House, Wendy's ▢ Candlewood Suites, Comfort Inn, Fairfield Inn, Holiday Inn Express, Howard Johnson, La Quinta, Microtel, Motel 6, Super 8 ▣ Advance Parts, AT&T, Ⓗ, Lowe's, tires, Walmart
124	AR 25 N, to Conway, S ▣ Alon/Hess/dsl, Kum&Go/dsl ⑪ DQ, KFC, Popeye's ▣ Ⓗ, vet
120mm	Cadron River
117	to Menifee
112	AR 92, Plumerville, N ▣ Exxon/dsl, S ▣ Country Store/dsl ▣ USPO
108	AR 9, Morrilton, N ▣ Ford/Lincoln, S ▣ Murphy USA, Shell/Pizza Pro/dsl, Valero ⑪ Chop Stix, Colton's Steaks, Hardees, Mama DeLuca's Pizza, McDonald's, Ortega's Mexican, Pizza Hut, Sonic, Subway, Taco Bell, Waffle House, Wendy's ▢ Holiday Inn Express, Super 8 ▣ $General, Ace Hardware, AT&T, Chrysler/

Exit #	Services
108	Continued Dodge/Jeep, Ⓗ, Kroger, NAPA, to Petit Jean SP (21mi), Verizon, vet, Walmart AutoZone, Blue Diamond Cafe
107	AR 95, Morrilton, N ▣ Sunoco/dsl ▢ Best Value Inn ▣ I-40/107 RV Park, S ▣ Loves/Subway/dsl/24hr ⑪ Morrilton Drive Inn, Yesterdays Rest. ▢ Days Inn ▣ Bumper Parts
101	Blackwell, N ▣ Blackwell TrkStp/Citgo/Domino's/diner/dsl/scales/24hr ▣ Utility Trailer Sales
94	AR 105, Atkins, N ▣ Exxon/Subway/dsl, VP/McDonald's/dsl ⑪ El Parian Mexican, Sonic ▣ $General, S ▣ Casey's/dsl ▣ Cash Saver Foods
88	Pottsville, S ▣ $General, truck repair/wash
84	US 64, AR 331, Russellville, N ▣ FLYING J/Denny's/dsl/scales/LP/24hr, Shell/dsl ▣ Ivys Cove RV Retreat, S ▣ Phillips 66, Pilot/Subway/Wendy's/dsl/scales ⑪ Chick-fil-A, CiCi's Pizza, Hardee's, McDonald's, Mulan's Buffet, Sonic, Waffle House ▢ Comfort Inn, Quality Inn ▣ $Tree, AT&T, Belk, Buick/Chevrolet/GMC, Chrysler/Dodge/Jeep, GNC, Hobby Lobby, Ⓗ, Hyundai, JC Penney, K-Mart, Lowe's, Nissan, Petsmart, Ross, Staples, TJ Maxx, Toyota, USPO
83	AK 326, Weir Rd, S ▣ Phillips 66/dsl, Walmart Gas/dsl ⑪ Buffalo Wild Wings, DQ, McAlisters Deli, Popeye's, Starbucks, Steak'n Shake, Subway, Sumo, Taco Bell, Taco John's ▢ Comfort Inn ▣ $General, AutoZone, Firestone/auto, Ford/Lincoln, Mazda, NAPA, O'Reilly Parts, Verizon, Walmart/McDonald's Zaxby's, Chili's
81	AR 7, Russellville, N ▣ SuperStop/dsl ⑪ CJ's Burgers ▢ Motel 6 ▣ $General, Outdoor RV Ctr/Park Courtyard, S ▣ Exxon/dsl, Phillips 66/dsl, Shell ⑪ Arby's, Burger King, Cagle's Mill Rest., Colton's Steaks, Cracker Barrel, Dixie Café, Firehouse Subs, IHOP, La Huerta Mexican, New China, Ruby Tuesday, Subway, Waffle House ▢ Best Value, Best Western, Clarion, Days Inn, Econolodge, Fairfield Inn, Hampton Inn, La Quinta, Super 8 ▣ RV camping, to Lake Dardanelle SP
80mm	Dardanelle Reservoir
78	US 64, Russellville, S ▣ Darrell's Mkt ⑪ Fat Daddy's BBQ ▣ Ⓗ, Mission RV Park, to Lake Dardanelle SP
74	AR 333, London
72mm	▣ wb, full ▣ facilities, litter barrels, petwalk, ▣, ▣, vending
70mm	overlook wb, litter barrels
68mm	▣ eb, full ▣ facilities, litter barrels, petwalk, ▣, ▣, vending
67	AR 315, Knoxville, S ▣ USPO
64	US 64, Clarksville, Lamar, S ▣ Valero/dsl ▣ Dad's Dream RV Park
58	AR 21, AR 103, Clarksville, N ▣ Casey's/dsl, Shell, Valero ⑪ Emerald Dragon Chinese, KFC, La Chiquita Mexican, McDonald's, Pizza Hut, Subway, Taco Bell, Waffle House ▢ Best Western, Executive Inn, Quality Inn, Super 8 ▣ $General, Buick/Chevrolet, Ⓗ, S ▣ Murphy USA/dsl ⑪ Arby's, China Fun, Wendy's ▣ $Tree, AT&T, Chrysler/Dodge/Jeep, Ford, Walmart/Subway
57	AR 109, Clarksville, N ▣ Fuel Stop/dsl ⑪ Sonic, Subway ▣ Family$, Harp's Mkt, S ▣ Shell/Steak'n Shake/dsl ▣ Truckwash, TrueValue
55	US 64, AR 109, Clarksville, N ▣ Hardee's, Kountry Kitchen Grille ▢ Hampton Inn, Holiday Inn Express, Sunset Inn, S ▣ Valero/AutoTruck/dsl ▣ st police
47	AR 164, Coal Hill
41	AR 186, Altus, N ▣ Swiss Family Rest., S ⑪ Wiederkehr Rest. (4mi) ▣ winery (4mi)
37	AR 219, Ozark, S ▣ Loves/Subway/dsl/scales/24hr, Valero/McDonald's/dsl ⑪ KFC/Taco Bell ▢ Best Value Inn ▣ Ⓗ
36mm	▣ both lanes, full ▣ facilities, litter barrels, petwalk, ▣, ▣

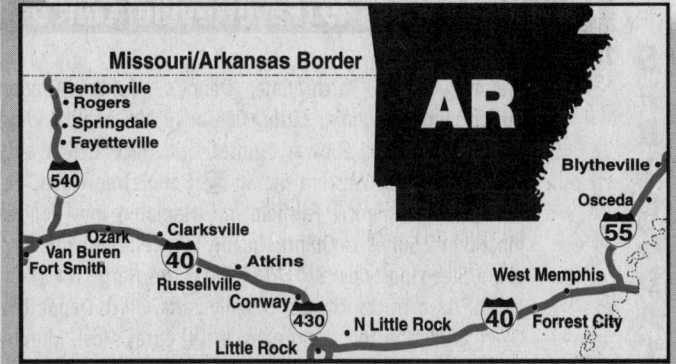

INTERSTATE 40 Cont'd

Exit #	Services
35	AR 23, Ozark, **N** 🅟 Valero/Red Hog BBQ/dsl/scales 🍴 Hillbilly Hideout Rest, **3 mi S** 🛏 Oxford Inn, Ozark Inn 🅾 Aux Arc Park (5mi), 🅷, to Mt Magazine SP (20 mi)
24	AR 215, Mulberry, **S** Vine Prairie Park
20	Dyer, **N** Short Stop/dsl, **S** 🅟 Phillips 66/dsl, Shell/dsl 🛏 Mill Creek Inn
13	US 71 N, to Fayetteville, **N** 🅟 Shell, Sunoco/dsl 🍴 Burger King, Catfish Hole, China Fun, Cracker Barrel, KFC, La Fiesta Mexican, Pizza Parlor, Subway, Taco Bell 🛏 Quality Inn 🅾 $General, Crabtree RV Ctr/Park, KOA (2mi), Lake Ft Smith SP, O'Reilly Parts, to U of AR Bumper Parts, Hog Pizza, **S** 🍴 Murphy USA/dsl, Valero/dsl, Workman's 🍴 Braum's, Geno's Pizza, McDonald's, Pizza Hut, Sonic 🛏 Days Inn 🅾 AT&T, Coleman Drug, Harp's Foods, Shoppers Value Foods, Walgreens, Walmart $Tree
12	I-49 N, to Fayetteville, **N** 🅾 to Lake Ft Smith SP
9mm	**weigh sta both lanes**
7	I-540 S, US 71 S, to Ft Smith, Van Buren, **S** 🅾 🅷
5	AR 59, Van Buren, **N** 🅟 Citgo/dsl, Murphy USA/dsl, VP Fuels 🍴 Arby's, Burger King, Chili's, Domino's, Firehouse Subs, Golden Wok, La Fiesta Mexican, Little Caesar's, McDonald's, Starbucks, Zaxby's 🛏 Best Western, Hampton Inn 🅾 $Tree, Advance Parts, AT&T, CVS Drug, Lowe's, NAPA, USPO, Verizon, Walmart/Subway Aldi, Tropical Cafe, **S** 🅟 Casey's/dsl, Shell/dsl 🍴 Braum's, Geno's Pizza, KFC/Taco Bell, La Fresas Mexican, Sonic, Subway, Waffle House, Wendy's 🛏 Holiday Inn Express, Sleep Inn, Super 8 🅾 $General, Grizzle Tire, Outdoor RV Park, Shoppers Value Foods, truckwash, vet, Walgreens Colton's Steaks, Frank's Italian
3	Lee Creek Rd, **N** 🅟 Sunoco/dsl 🅾 Park Ridge Camping
2.5mm	**Welcome Ctr eb, full** 🅷 **facilities, info, litter barrels, petwalk,** 🅲, 🚗, **vending**
1	to Ft Smith (from wb), Dora
0mm	Arkansas/Oklahoma state line

INTERSTATE 49 (Fayetteville)

Exit #	Services
93	US 71B, Bentonville. **I-49 begins/ends on US 71 N.**
88	AR 72, Bentonville, Pea Ridge, **E** 🅟 Casey's 🍴 River Grille 🛏 Comfort Inn, Courtyard, **W** 🅟 Kum&Go/dsl, Shell/dsl 🍴 Smokin' Joe's Ribs 🅾 Walmart Visitors Ctr
87	8th St
86	US 62, AR 102, Bentonville, Rogers, **E** 🅟 EVC 🛏 TownePlace Suites 🅾 Pea Ridge NMP, Sam's Club/gas, Walmart Mkt, **W** 🅟 McDonald's, Shell/dsl 🍴 Arby's, Dunkin', Sonic, Subway, Taco Bell 🛏 Woodspring Suites
85	US 71B, AR 12, Bentonville, Rogers, **E** 🅟 Conoco/dsl 🍴 Abuelo's, Applebee's, Arby's, Boar's Nest, Cane's, Carino's Italian, Chick-fil-A, Chili's, Colton's Steaks, Freddy's Burgers, IHOP, Logan's Roadhouse, McDonald's, Napoli's Pizza, On-the-Border, Outback Steaks, Quiznos, Red Robin, Rick's Café, Sonic, Starbucks, Tokyo House, Zoe's Kitchen 🛏 Candlewood Suites, Country Inn&Suites, Fairfield Inn, Hampton Inn, Homewood Suites, Hyatt Place, Mainstay Suites, Residence Inn 🅾 AT&T, Barnes&Noble, Belk, Firestone/auto, Jo-Ann, Kohl's, Lowe's, Marshall's, Office Depot, PetCo, Prairie Creek SP, Ross, Staples, Verizon, **W** 🅟 Kum&Go/dsl, Murphy Express/dsl, Shell 🍴 Azul Tequila Mexican, Braum's, Buffalo Wild Wings, Chipotle, Cracker Barrel, Denny's, Firehouse Subs, HoneyBaked Ham, Jimmy John's, Joe's Italian,

Exit #	Services
85	Continued
	Jonny Brusco's Pizza, Krispy Kreme, Lenny's Subs, Lin's Garden, Mama Fu's Asian, McAlister's Deli, Panera Bread, Shogun Japanese, Smashburger, Starbucks, Subway, Taco Bueno, Taziki's Mediterranean Cafe, Village Inn, Waffle House, Whole Hog Cafe, Zaxby's 🛏 Best Western+, Comfort Suites, Days Inn, DoubleTree Hotel, EconoLodge, Element Westin, Hilton Garden, Holiday Inn Express, La Quinta, Microtel, Red Roof Inn, Sheraton, SpringHill Suites, Super 8 🅾 BMW, Buick/GMC, Cadillac, Chevrolet, Christian Bros Auto, Chrysler/Dodge/Jeep, Honda, 🅷, Hyundai, Kia, Mazda, Mercedes, Nissan, Toyota, URGENT CARE
83	AR 94 E, Pinnacle Hills Pkway, **E** 🅟 Phillips 66 🍴 After 5 Grill, Bariola's Pizza, ChuckECheese's, Dickey's BBQ, Firehouse Subs, Five Guys, Jimmy John's, Mojitos Mexican, Olive Garden, Panda Express, Qdoba, Red Lobster, Slim Chickens, Starbucks, Steak'n Shake, Taco Bell 🅾 Home Depot, Horse Shoe Bend Park, 🅷, URGENT CARE, Walgreens, **W** 🍴 Bonefish Grill, Carrabba's, Coldstone, Crabby's Seafood Grill, Grub's Grille, Ruth's Chris Steaks, Subway, The Egg&I, Theo's, Tropical Smoothie 🛏 ALoft, Embassy Suites, Holiday Inn, Staybridge Suites
82	Promenade Blvd, **E** 🍴 Fish City Grill, Longhorn Steaks, Mimi's Cafe, PF Chang's, Twin Peaks 🛏 Courtyard 🅾 AT&T, Bass Pro Shops, Best Buy, Dillard's, Fresh Mkt, GNC, Gordman's, 🅷, JC Penney, Old Navy, Petsmart, Target, TJMaxx, Verizon, **W** 🍴 Chick-fil-A, Chuy's Mexican, Newk's Eatery, Pei Wei, Tacos 4 Life 🅾 Walmart Mkt/dsl
81	Pleasant Grove Rd, **E** 🅟 Murphy USA/dsl 🍴 Backyard Burger, Chick-fil-A, Golden Corral, Gusano's Pizzaria, McDonald's, Moe's SW, Old Chicago, Papa Murphy's, Starbucks, Subway, Taco Bueno, Whataburger 🅾 Burlington, Cavender's, Duluth Trading, Firestone/auto, Walgreens, Walmart, **W** 🅟 Casey's/dsl
78	AR 264, Lowell, Cave Sprgs, Rogers, **E** 🅟 Kum&Go/dsl 🍴 Arby's, auto repair, Dickey's BBQ, Domino's, DQ, McDonald's, Sonic, Subway, Taco Bell 🅾 $General, Camping World RV Ctr, Super 8, **W** 🅟 Kum&Go/dsl, Phillips 66/dsl/scales 🍴 Ozark Mtn Grill
77	AR 612
76	Wagon Wheel Rd, **E** 🅟 Shell/Subway/dsl 🅾 to Hickory Creek Park
73	Elm Springs Rd, **E** 🅟 Kum&Go/dsl, VP/dsl 🍴 Eureka Pizza, Patrick's Burgers, Whataburger 🛏 Woodspring Suites 🅾 Chevrolet, Family$, **W** 🅟 Shell/dsl, Walmart/dsl 🍴 McDonald's, MJ Pizzaria, Panda Express 🅾 🅷, URGENT CARE, Walmart
72mm	**weigh sta nb**
72	US 412, Springdale, Siloam Springs, **E** 🅟 Citgo/dsl, Kum&Go/dsl, Phillips 66 🍴 Angus Jack's Burgers, Applebee's,

Ⓝ INTERSTATE 49 (Fayetteville) Cont'd

72	Continued
	Braum's, Cotton Patch Cafe, Denny's, Golden Dragon Buffet, Jimmy John's, Little Caesar's, McDonald's, Mkt Place Rest., Sonic, Subway, Sunset Grill, Taco Bell, Waffle House, Wendy's, Western Sizzlin 🛏 DoubleTree Hotel, Extended Stay America, Fairfield Inn, Hampton Inn, Holiday Inn, Home 2 Suites, La Quinta, Quality Inn, Residence Inn, Royal Inn, Sleep Inn, Super 8 🅞 AT&T, Big O Tire, Harp's Mkt, Kenworth/Volvo Trucks, Lowe's, O'Reilly Parts, Office Depot, URGENT CARE, Verizon, Walgreens, W 🅟 Casey's/dsl, Murphy Express/dsl, 🄿🄸🄻🄾🅃/Burger King/dsl/scales/24hr 🍴 Arby's, Buffalo Wild Wings, Cracker Barrel, Domino's, Flying Burrito, Freddy's, McDonald's, Pizza Hut, Popeye's, Rib Crib, Slim Chickens, Subway, Taco Bueno, Tacos 4 Life, Tropical Smoothie 🅞 Buick/GMC, Harp's Mkt/dsl, Hobby Lobby, NW RV Ctr, Sam's Club/dsl
71mm	weigh sta sb
70	Don Tyson Pkwy, E 🅟 Casey's/dsl, Walmart/dsl 🅞 Walmart Mkt
69	Johnson Mill Blvd, Johnson, E 🍴 Inn at the Mill Rest. 🛏 Inn at the Mill, TownePlace Suites
67	US 71B, Fayetteville, E 🅞 Ⓗ
66	AR 112, Garland Ave, E 🅟 Phillips 66/dsl, W 🅞 Acura, Chevrolet, Honda, Hyundai, Sam's Club/dsl, Toyota
65	Porter Rd, W 🅞 Subaru
64	AR 16 W, AR 112 E, Wedington Dr, W 🅟 Citgo/McDonald's/dsl, Murphy Express/dsl 🍴 AT&T, Dickey's BBQ, El Matador Mexican, Freddy's, Gusano's Pizza, IHOP, Marco's Pizza, Sonic, Starbucks, Subway, Taco Bell 🛏 Comfort Inn, Hilton Garden, Holiday Inn Express, Homewood Suites 🅞 Harp's Food/gas, Walmart Mkt
62	US 62, AR 180, Farmington, E 🅟 Citgo, Shell/dsl 🍴 Andy's Custard, Arby's, Braum's, Burger King, Cane's, Chick-fil-A, DQ, Ginger Rice&Noodle, KFC, McDonald's, Mexico Viejo, Panda Express, Pieology, Popeye's, Slim Chickens, Sonic, Starbucks, Subway, Taco Bell, Taco Bueno, Thai Wok, Waffle House, Wendy's, Whataburger, Zaxby's 🛏 Best Western, Candlewood Suites, EconoLodge 🅞 Bumper Parts, W 🅟 Murphy USA/dsl 🍴 Firehouse Subs, Jimmy's Egg, King Burrito, Papa Murphy's, Pavilion Buffet, Serrano's 🛏 Baymont Inn, Days Inn, Hampton Inn, Regency 7 Motel, Super 8, Woodspring Suites 🅞 $Tree, Aldi Foods, AT&T, AutoZone, Big O Tire, Lowe's, Verizon, Walgreens, Walmart/McDonald's
61	US 71 (from sb), to Boston Mtn Scenic Lp
60	AR 112, AR 265, Razorback Rd, E 🛏 Staybridge Suites 🅞 Southgate RV Park, to U of AR
58	Greenland, W 🅟 Phillips 66/McDonalds/dsl/scales/24hr 🍴 Sonic
53	AR 170, West Fork, E 🅟 Harp's/dsl 🅞 Harp's Mkt, Winn Creek RV Resort (4mi), W 🅞 to Devils Den SP
45	AR 74, Winslow, W 🅞 to Devils Den SP
41mm	Bobby Hopper Tunnel
34	AR 282, to US 71, Chester, W 🅞 USPO
29	AR 282, to US 71, Mountainburg, 1 mi E 🅞 $General, to Lake Ft Smith SP
24	AR 282, to US 71, Rudy, E 🅟 Loves/Chester's/Subway/dsl/scales/24hr, Phillips 66/dsl 🍴 Red Hog Cafe 🅞 Boston Mtns Scenic Lp, KOA
21	Collum Ln
20	to I-40 (from sb). I-49 N begins/ends on I-40, exit 12.

Ⓝ INTERSTATE 49 (Texarkana)

Exit #	Services
42	I-49 (Texarkana) begins/ends on US 59.
41	Sanderson Ln
37b a	I-30, E to Little Rock, W to Dallas
35	Arkansas Blvd, Four States Pkwy, E 🅞 🐾, fairgrounds, W 🅞 $General
32	US 82, 19th St, 9th St, E 🅟 Shell/dsl, Valero/dsl 🍴 Subway, TA Molly's Mexican 🅞 $General, CashSaver
31	AR 196, Genoa Rd
29b a	US 71, Texarkana, US 59, to Houston, W 🅟 Shell/dsl
26	AR 237
24	Rd 10, Ferguson
18	N Fouke Rd
16	US 71, Fouke
6	Rd 197, Spruell Rd
4	US 71, Doddridge
0mm	Arkansas/Louisiana state line

Ⓝ INTERSTATE 55

Exit #	Services
72mm	Arkansas/Missouri state line
72	State Line Rd, weigh sta sb
71	AR 150, Yarbro
68mm	Welcome Ctr sb, full 🅰 facilities, litter barrels, petwalk, 🄲, 🄰
67	AR 18, Blytheville, E 🅟 Mobil/dsl, Murphy Express/dsl 🍴 Burger King, Hardee's, Las Brisas Mexican, Waffle Inn, Zaxby's 🛏 Best Value Inn, Days Inn/RV park 🅞 Chrysler/Dodge/Jeep, Lowe's, Verizon, Walmart/Subway, W 🅟 Citgo/dsl, Phillips 66/dsl, Shell 🍴 El Puerto Mexican, GreatWall Chinese, Grecian Steaks, Little Caesar's, McDonald's, Olympia Steaks, Perkins, Pizza Hut, Pizza Inn, Sonic, Subway, Taco Bell, Wendy's 🛏 Comfort Inn, Fairview Suites, Hampton Inn, Holiday Inn, Quality Inn, Super 8 🅞 AT&T, AutoZone, Bumper Parts, Family$, Ford/Nissan, Ⓗ
63	US 61, to Blytheville, E 🅟 Loves/IHOP/Chester's/Godfather's/dsl/scales/24hr 🅞 Shearins RV Park (2mi), W 🅟 Citgo/McDonald's/dsl, Dodge's Store/dsl, Exxon/Baskin-Robbins/Chester's/Pizza Hut/dsl 🛏 Deerfield Inn, Relax Inn 🅞 Ⓗ, truckwash
57	AR 148, Burdette, E 🅞 NE AR Coll
53	AR 158, Victoria, Luxora
48	AR 140, to Osceola, E 🅟 Shell/Baskin-Robbins/Chester's/dsl 🍴 McDonald's (3mi), Pizza Inn (3mi), Sonic (3mi), Subway3 (mi) 🛏 Days Inn, Deerfield Inn, EconoLodge 🅞 Ⓗ, Huddle House, Mamma Mia's
45mm	truck parking nb, litter barrels
44	AR 181, Keiser
41	AR 14, Marie, E 🅞 to Hampson SP/museum
36	AR 181, to Wilson, Bassett
35mm	truck parking sb, litter barrels
34	AR 118, Joiner
23b a	US 63, AR 77, to Marked Tree, Jonesboro, ASU, E 🅟 Citgo/chicken/pizza
21	AR 42, Turrell, W 🅟 Valero/pizza/dsl/scales/24hr
17	AR 50, to Jericho
14	rd 4, to Jericho, E 🅟 Citgo/dsl/scales/24hr, W 🅟 Citgo/Stuckey's 🅞 Chevrolet, KOA
10	US 64 W, Marion, E 🅟 Citgo/Baskin-Robbins/Subway/scales, Shell/McDonald's 🍴 KFC/Taco Bell, Sonic, Tops BBQ, Wendy's 🛏 Comfort Inn, Hallmarc Inn 🅞 $General, Family$, Mkt Place Foods, USPO, W 🅟 Exxon/dsl, Shamrock

⬆N INTERSTATE 55 Cont'd

10	Continued
	🍴 Andrey Grill, Burger King, Colton's Steaks, Mi Pueblo, Tropical Cafe, Zaxby's 🛏 Best Value Inn, Fairfield Inn, Hampton Inn, Journey Inn 🅾 AutoZone, to Parkin SP (23mi)
9mm	truck parking nb, weigh sta sb
8	I-40 W, to Little Rock
	I-55 and I-40 run together 3 mi. See I-40, exits 278-279b.
5	(279 a from I-40) Ingram Blvd, **E** Welcome Ctr/🆁🆂/full ♿ facilities, 🛏, litter barrels, petwalk, 🍴 Margaritas Mexican 🛏 Days Inn, Homegate Inn, Knights Inn, Red Roof Inn 🅾 Ford, Southland Racetrack, **W** ⛽ Citgo/dsl, Phillips/dsl, Shell/dsl 🍴 Cross Creek Rest., Waffle House 🛏 Best Value Inn, Clarion Inn, EconoLodge, Hampshire Inn, Motel 6, Ramada, Relax Inn
4	King Dr, Southland Dr, **E** ⛽ *FLYING J*/Denny's/dsl/LP/scales/RV dump, LNG, *Loves*/Subway/dsl/scales/@, Petro/Iron Skillet/rest./dsl/24hr/@, *Pilot*/Subway/Wendy's/dsl/scales/24hr, Tesla EVC, Valero/dsl 🍴 KFC/Taco Bell, McDonald's 🛏 Best Western, Deluxe Inn, Express Inn, Super 8 🅾 Blue Beacon, SpeedCo Lube, **W** 🍴 Pancho's Mexican 🛏 Sunset Inn
3b a	US 70, Broadway Blvd, AR 131, Mound City Rd (exits left from nb), **W** 🛏 Budget Inn
2mm	weigh sta nb
1	Bridgeport Rd
0mm	Arkansas/Tennessee state line, Mississippi River

⬆E INTERSTATE 430 (Little Rock)

Exit #	Services
13b a	I-40. I-430 begins/ends on I-40, exit 147.
12	AR 100, Maumelle, **W** ⛽ Kum&Go/dsl/e85 🅾 NAPA, O'Reilly Parts, vet
10mm	Arkansas River
9	AR 10, Cantrell Rd, **W** 🅾 Maumelle Park, Pinnacle Mtn SP
8	Rodney Parham Rd, **E** ⛽ Conoco/dsl, Kroger/dsl, Phillips 66/dsl, Shell 🍴 Arby's, Baskin-Robbins, Dunkin', Firehouse Subs, McDonald's, Mt Fuji Japanese, Sonic, Starbucks, Subway, Taco Bell, Terri Lynn's BBQ, Tropical Smoothie Cafe, US Pizza 🛏 La Quinta 🅾 $General, AAA, Advance Parts, AutoZone, Drug Emporium, get, Kroger, TJ Maxx, Walgreens, **W** ⛽ Exxon 🍴 Burger King, Chili's, Dixie Cafe, Domino's, Franke's Café, Marco's Pizza, Olive Garden, Ponchito's Mexican, Shorty Small's Ribs, Starbucks, Wendy's 🛏 Best Western 🅾 Audi, Cadillac, Firestone/auto, GNC, vet, Volvo
6b	Kanis Rd, Markham St, to downtown, **E** ⛽ Shell 🍴 Burger King, Kroger, Red Lobster, Subway 🛏 Candlewood Suites, Comfort Inn, Motel 6, SpringHill Suites 🅾 Burlington Coats, Ross, **W** ⛽ Exxon/dsl 🍴 Applebee's, Bobby's Country Cookin', Butcher Shop Steaks, Cactus Jack's, Chi Rest., Church's, Denny's, Famous Dave's BBQ, IHOP, Jason's Deli, KFC, Khalil's Grill, Kobe Japanese, Lenny's Subs, Macaroni Grill, McAlister's Deli, McDonald's, Mexico Cafe, Mimi's Cafe, On-the-Border, Outback Steaks, PF Chang's, Pizza Hut, Popeye's, Purple Cow, Shotgun Dan's Pizza, Slim Chickens, Sonic, Starbucks, Taco Bell, Tokyo House, Twin Peaks, Waffle House, Wendy's, West End Steaks, Whole Foods Mkt 🛏 Courtyard, Crowne Plaza, Embassy Suites, Extended Stay America, Holiday Inn, La Quinta, Ramada Ltd 🅾 $Tree, AT&T, Barnes&Noble, Best Buy, Michael's, Office Depot, PetsMart, Sam's Club/gas, Verizon, Walmart
6a	I-630, E to Little Rock, **E** 🅾 🅷

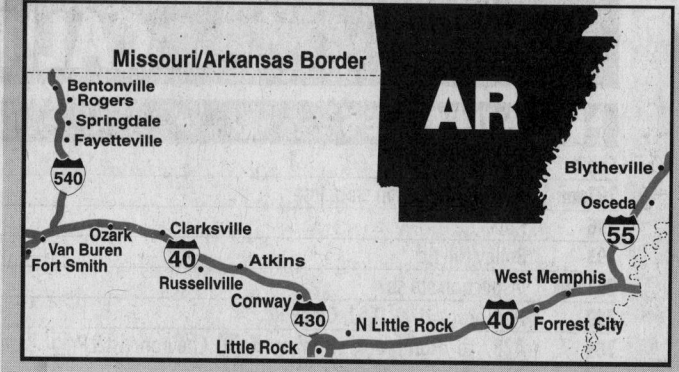

5	Kanis Rd, Shackleford Rd, **E** 🍴 Arby's, BJ's Rest., ChuckE-Cheese, Copeland's Rest., Cracker Barrel, Longhorn Steaks, Panda Garden, Samurai Steaks, TX Roadhouse, Zangna Thai 🛏 Comfort Suites, Home 2 Suites, La Quinta, Towneplace Suites 🅾 AT&T, Gordman's, JC Penney, Jo-Ann, Verizon, Walmart/Subway, **W** 🍴 Shell 🍴 Dunkin', Krispy Kreme, Mooyah Burger, Panera Bread 🛏 Extended Stay America, Hampton Inn, Hilton Garden, Residence Inn, Wingate Inn 🅾 🅷, Lexus
4	AR 300, Col Glenn Rd, **E** 🍴 American Pie Pizza, Subway, Wendy's 🛏 Holiday Inn Express, Woodspring Suites Hotel 🅾 Toyota, **W** 🍴 Valero/Burger King/dsl 🍴 Sonic 🅾 BMW, Chrysler/Dodge/Jeep, Ford, Honda, Hyundai, Infiniti, Jaguar, Land Rover, Mazda, Mercedes, Nissan, Subaru, VW
1	AR 5, Stagecoach Rd, **W** ⛽ Mapco/dsl/e85, Phillips 66, Valero/Domino's 🍴 Down Home Rest., Subway 🅾 $General, CBI Tires, Walgreens
	I-430 begins/ends on I-30, exit 129.

⬆E INTERSTATE 440 (Little Rock)

Exit #	Services
11	I-440 begins/ends on I-40, exit 159.
10	US 70, **W** 🅾 Peterbilt
8	Faulkner Lake Rd
7	US 165, to England, **S** ⛽ Valero/dsl 🅾 Agricultural Museum, Toltec Mounds SP, Willow Beach SP
6mm	Arkansas River
5	Fourche Dam Pike, LR Riverport, **N** ⛽ Exxon/dsl, Shell/Subway 🍴 McDonald's 🛏 Travelodge 🅾 Kenworth, **S** ⛽ Phillips 66/dsl, Valero/dsl
4	Lindsey Rd
3	Bankhead Dr, **N** 🛏 Comfort Inn 🅾 LR Airport, **S** ⛽ Valero 🍴 Boston's Rest., Waffle House 🛏 Days Inn, Holiday Inn, Holiday Inn Express
1	AR 365, Springer Blvd, **S** 🅾 Little Rock Ntl Cemetery
0mm	I-440 begins/ends on I-30, exit 138.

NOTES

🅟 = gas 🍴 = food 🛏 = lodging 🅞 = other 🆁🆂 = rest stop   Copyright 2022 - The Next EXIT ®

CALIFORNIA

⬆N INTERSTATE 5

Exit #	Services
797mm	California/Oregon state line
796	Hilt
793	Bailey Hill Rd
791mm	inspection sta sb
790	Hornbrook Hwy, Ditch Creek Rd
789	A28, to Hornbrook, Henley, **E** 🅟 Chevron/dsl/LP 🅞 Blue Heron RV Park/rest., to Iron Gate RA
786	CA 96, Klamath River Hwy, **W** 🆁🆂 **both lanes, full** ♿ **facilities, info, litter barrels, petwalk,** 🚻, 🅿, to Klamath River RA
782mm	Anderson Summit, elevation 3067
780mm	vista point sb
779mm	Shasta River
776	Yreka, Montague, **E** 🛏 Holiday Inn Express 🅞 Yreka RV Park, **W** 🅟 Mobil/dsl 🍴 Casa Ramos Mexican, J&D Diner, Puerto Vallarta 🛏 Mtn View Inn, Super 8 🅞 Grocery Outlet
775	Miner St, Central Yreka, **W** 🅟 76/dsl, Chevron/dsl 🍴 Grandma's House, Poor George's, RoundTable Pizza, Subway 🛏 Best Western, Budget Inn, EconoLodge, Klamath Motel, Relax Inn, Rodeway Inn, Yreka Motel 🅞 🄷 Ace Hardware, Baxter Parts, CarQuest, Dunn Automotive, museum, NAPA, Rite Aid, USPO
773	CA 3, to Ft Jones, Etna, **E** 🅞 Les Schwab, tires, Trailer Haven RV Park, **W** 🅟 Shell/dsl, Valero/dsl 🍴 BlackBear Diner, Burger King, Carl's Jr, Jefferson's Roadhouse, KFC, McDonald's, Starbucks, Subway, Taco Bell 🛏 Baymont Inn, Comfort Inn, Motel 6 🅞 🄷, $Tree, AAA, AT&T, AutoZone, CHP, Ford, JC Penney, O'Reilly Parts, Raley's Foods, Verizon, Walmart
770	Shamrock Rd, Easy St, **W** 🅟 Beacon/LP, Fuel 24/7/dsl 🅞 RV camping
766	A12, to Gazelle, Grenada, **E** 🅟 Shell/dsl, **W** 🅟 Chevron/dsl/24hr 🅞 RV camping
759	Louie Rd
753	Weed Airport Rd, 🆁🆂 **both lanes, full** ♿ **facilities, litter barrels, petwalk,** 🚻, 🅿
751	Stewart Springs Rd, Edgewood, **E** 🅞 Lake Shasta RA/RV camp (2mi), **W** 🅞 RV camp (7mi)
748	to US 97, to Klamath Falls, Weed, **E** 🅟 Chevron, Shell/dsl, Spirit/dsl 🍴 Ellie's Cafe, Pizza Factory, Subway 🛏 Hi-Lo Motel/rest., Motel 6, Summit Inn, Townhouse Motel 🅞 auto repair, golf, NAPA, Ray's Foods, RV camping
747	Central Weed, **E** 🅞 auto repair, same as 748, **W** Coll of Siskiyou
745	S Weed Blvd, **E** 🅟 Chevron/dsl, ⛽Pilot/Subway/dsl/scales/24hr, Shell/dsl 🍴 Burger King, Dos Amigos Mexican, McDonald's/RV parking, Starbucks, Taco Bell 🛏 Comfort Inn, Quality Inn, Sis-Q Inn 🅞 Friendly RV Park, Grocery Outlet
743	Summit Dr, Truck Village Dr
742mm	Black Butte Summit, elevation 3912
741	Abrams Lake Rd, **W** 🛏 Abrams Lake RV Park
740	Mt Shasta City (from sb), **E** 🅟 Pacific Pride/dsl/LP, Shell/dsl/CFN 🛏 Cold Creek Inn 🅞 KOA, repair, vet
738	Central Mt Shasta, **E** 🅟 76/dsl, Chevron/dsl, Shell/dsl/LP 🍴 BlackBear Diner, Burger King, KFC/Taco Bell, RoundTable Pizza, Subway 🛏 Best Western/Treehouse Rest., Mt Shasta Inn, Travel Inn 🅞 🄷, Best Hardware, NAPA, O'Reilly Parts, Ray's Foods, Rite Aid, USPO, visitors info, **W** 🛏 Lake Siskiyou RV Park, Mt Shasta Resort/rest., Sisson Museum

737	Mt Shasta City (from nb), **E** 🍴 Casa Ramos, LaiLai Chinese, Lily's Rest., Piemont Italian, Wayside Grill 🛏 Alpine Lodge Choice Inn, Evergreen Lodge, Swiss Holiday Lodge 🅞 McCloud RV Park, same as 738
736	CA 89, to McCloud, to Reno, **E** 🛏 Swiss Holiday Lodge
735mm	**weigh sta sb**
734	Mott Rd, to Dunsmuir
732	Dunsmuir Ave, Siskiyou Ave, **E** 🍴 Penny's Diner 🛏 Travelodge, **W** 🅟 Chevron/dsl 🛏 Acorn Inn, Cedar Lodge
730	Central Dunsmuir, **E** 🍴 Burger Barn, Cornerstone Cafe, Dunsmuir Brewery Rest., Pizza Factory 🛏 Dunsmuir Inn, Hotel Dunsmuir/Rest. 🅞 Dunsmuir Mkt, True Value, USPO, **W** 🅟 Chevron/dsl/LP 🍴 Hitching Post, Wild Land Burgers 🛏 Cave Springs Motel 🅞 city park
729	Dunsmuir (from nb), **E** 🍴 Manfredi's/deli/dsl 🛏 auto repair, Dunsmuir Lodge 🅞 to hist dist
728	Crag View Dr, Dunsmuir, Railroad Park Rd, **W** 🅞 Railroad Park Motel/RV Park
727	Crag View Dr (from nb), RV Camping
726	Soda Creek Rd, to Pacific Crest Trail
724	Castella, **W** 🅟 Chevron/dsl 🅞 Castle Crags SP, RV camping, USPO
723mm	vista point nb
723	Sweetbrier Ave
721	Conant Rd
720	Flume Creek Rd
718	Sims Rd, **W** 🅞 RV camping
714	Gibson Rd
712	Pollard Flat, **E** 🅟 Pollard Flat/dsl/LP 🍴 Pollard Flat Diner
710	Slate Creek Rd, La Moine
707	Delta Rd, Dog Creek Rd, to Vollmers
705mm	🆁🆂 **sb, full** ♿ **facilities, litter barrels,** 🚻, 🅿
704	Riverview Dr, **E** 🍴 Klondike Diner 🛏 Lakehead Lodge/RV Camping
702	Antlers Rd, Lakeshore Dr, to Lakehead, **E** 🅟 Chevron/Subway/dsl 🛏 Antlers RV Park, Lakehead Camping, Neu Lodge Motel 🅞 auto repair, USPO, **W** 🅟 Texaco/dsl 🍴 Allyson's Rest., Bass Hole Rest. 🛏 Lakeshore Mkt, Shasta Lake Motel/RV 🅞 Villa RV Park
698	Salt Creek Rd, Gilman Rd, **W** 🛏 Salt Creek Resort/RV Park 🅞 Trail In RV Park
695	Shasta Caverns Rd, to O'Brien
694mm	🆁🆂 **nb, full** ♿ **facilities, litter barrels, petwalk,** 🚻, 🅿
693	Packers Bay Rd (from sb)
692	Turntable Bay Rd
690	Bridge Bay Rd, **W** 🍴 Tail of a Whale Rest. 🛏 Bridge Bay Motel
689	Fawndale Rd, Wonderland Blvd, **E** 🛏 Fawndale Lodge, Fawndale Oaks RV Park, **W** 🛏 Wonderland RV Park
687	Wonderland Blvd, Mountain Gate, **E** 🅟 Chevron/dsl/LP 🍴 La Fogata 🅞 Mountain Gate RV Park, Ranger Sta, **W** 🅟 Shell/dsl/LP
685	CA 151, Shasta Dam Blvd, Project City, Central Valley, **W** 🅟 76/Circle K/dsl, Shell/Burger King/dsl/LP, Valero/dsl 🍴 McDonald's, Pizza Factory, Taco Shop 🛏 Shasta Dam Motel 🅞 NAPA, Rite Aid, Sentry Foods, USPO, vet
684	Pine Grove Ave, **W** 🅟 Valero/dsl/LP
682	Oasis Rd, **E** 🅞 CA RV Ctr, Peterbilt, **W** 🅟 Arco, Shell/Subway/dsl 🅞 CHP, Towtally RV Ctr, U-Haul

Side tabs: CA, YREKA, WEED, MT SHASTA, DUNSMUIR

Copyright 2022 - The Next EXIT ®   🅿️ = gas   🍴 = food   🛏️ = lodging   🅾️ = other   🆁🆂 = rest stop

INTERSTATE 5 Cont'd

Exit #	Services
681b	(from sb, no re-entry) CA 273, Market St, Johnson Rd, to Central Redding, W 🅾️ 🛏️
681a	Twin View Blvd, E 🅿️ Chevron/dsl 🛏️ Motel 6, Ramada Ltd 🅾️ Harley-Davidson, W 🅿️ Pacific Pride/dsl 🍴 El Zarape 🛏️ Best Western+, Comfort Suites, Fairfield Inn
680	CA 299E, 1/2 mi W 🅿️ Arco, Chevron/dsl 🍴 A&W/KFC, Carl's Jr, Giant Burger, Little Caesar's, McDonald's, Papa Murphy's, Popeye's, RoundTable Pizza, Starbucks, Subway 🅾️ AutoZone, O'Reilly Parts, Raley's Foods, Redding RV Camp, Redding RV Park, ShopKO, transmissions, Twin View RV Park, Walgreens

REDDING

677	Cypress Ave, Hilltop Dr, Redding, E 🅿️ Chevron/dsl, Shell/dsl, Valero/dsl, Valero/dsl 🍴 Black Bear Diner, Burger King, Carl's Jr, Cattlemen's Rest., Coldstone, Del Taco, Denny's, Domino's, Gibbs Grille, Grand Buffet, IHOP, Jack-in-the-Box, KFC, Little Caesar's, Logan's Roadhouse, Marie Callender's, McDonald's, Papa Murphy's, Pizza Hut, Popeye's, Starbucks, Subway, Taco Bell, Togo's, Wendy's 🛏️ Baymont Inn, Best Western+, Comfort Inn, Hampton Inn, Holiday Inn, La Quinta, Oxford Suites, Quality Inn, TownePlace Suites 🅾️ 99c Store, AutoZone, Buick/Cadillac/GMC, Chevron/dsl, CVS Drug, Lowe's, Rite Aid, Ross, Safeway/gas, vet, Walgreens, W 🅿️ 76, Chevron/dsl, Mobil/dsl 🍴 Burrito Bandito, CA Cattle Rest., Denny's, Humble Joe's Chophouse, Lumberjack's Rest., RoundTable Pizza, Subway 🛏️ Motel 6, Red Lion Inn, Vagabond Inn 🅾️ America's Tire, Big O Tire, Chevrolet, Dodge, Ford/Lincoln, Honda, Kia, Nissan, Office Depot, Subaru, Toyota, U-Haul, URGENT CARE
675	Bechelli Lane, Churn Creek Rd, E 🅿️ Arco/dsl, Chevron/dsl, Valero 🛏️ Super 8, W 🍴 Chevron/Burger King/dsl 🛏️ Hilton Garden
673	Knighton Rd, E 🅿️ TA/Country Pride/Pizza Hut/Popeye's/dsl/LP/scales/24hr/@, W 🅾️ JGW RV Park (3mi), Sacramento River RV Park (3mi)
670	Riverside Ave, E 🍴 Woodside Grill 🛏️ Gaia Hotel, W 🅾️ Camping World RV Ctr
668	Balls Ferry Rd, Anderson, E 🅿️ Shell/dsl, Valero/dsl 🍴 A&W/KFC, Burger King, Joe's Chophouse, Little Caesar's, McDonald's, Papa Murphy's, Peacock Chinese, Popeye's, Puerto Vallarta Mexican, RoundTable Pizza, Starbucks, Subway, Taco Bell 🛏️ Best Western, Motel 6 🅾️ $Tree, Les Schwab Tire, NAPA, Rite Aid, Safeway/dsl, W 🍴 Players Pizza 🅾️ O'Reilly Parts

REDDING (side tab)

ANDERSON (side tab)

CA

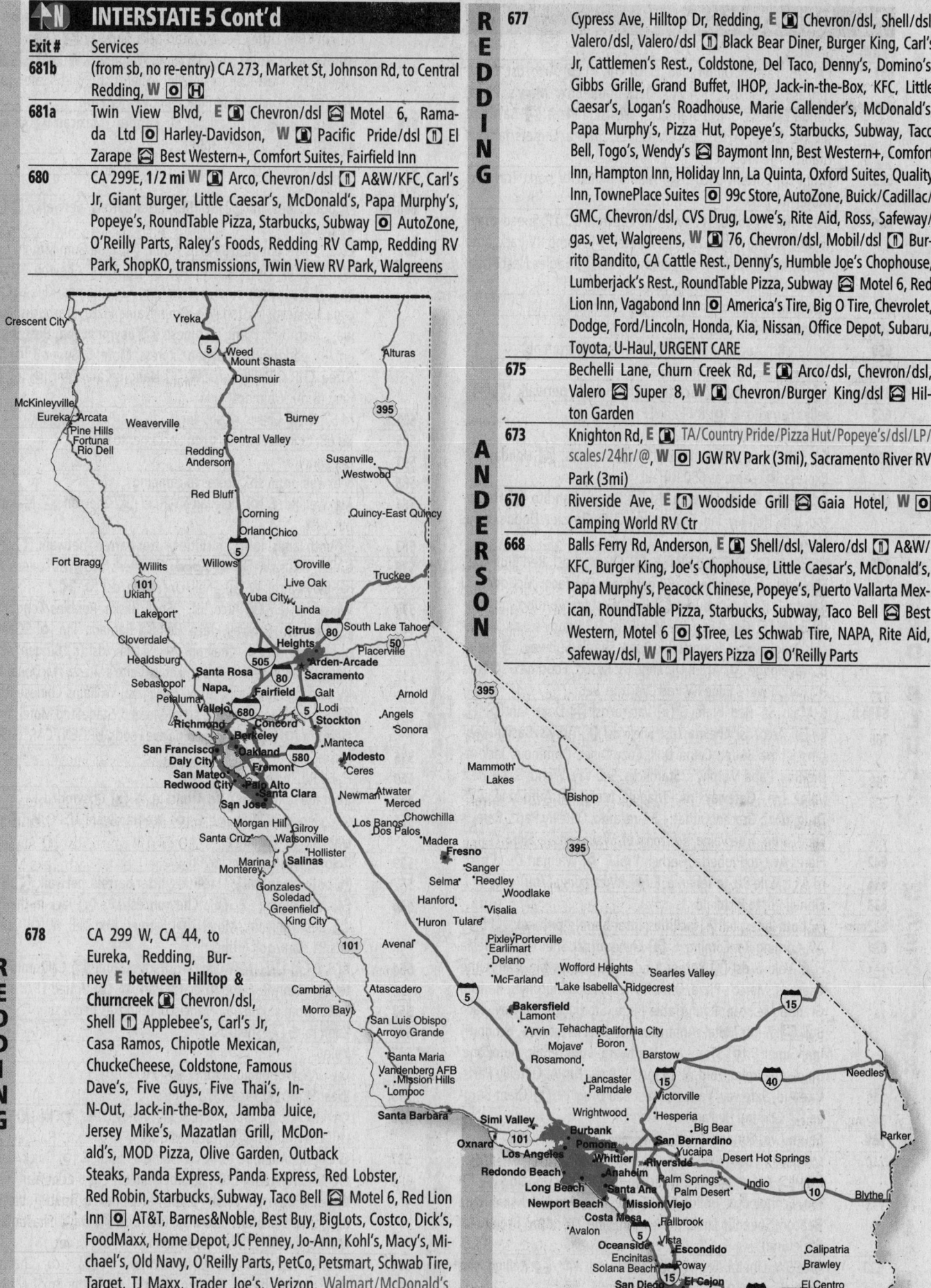

678	CA 299 W, CA 44, to Eureka, Redding, Burney E **between Hilltop & Churncreek** 🅿️ Chevron/dsl, Shell 🍴 Applebee's, Carl's Jr, Casa Ramos, Chipotle Mexican, ChuckECheese, Coldstone, Famous Dave's, Five Guys, Five Thai's, In-N-Out, Jack-in-the-Box, Jamba Juice, Jersey Mike's, Mazatlan Grill, McDonald's, MOD Pizza, Olive Garden, Outback Steaks, Panda Express, Panda Express, Red Lobster, Red Robin, Starbucks, Subway, Taco Bell 🛏️ Motel 6, Red Lion Inn 🅾️ AT&T, Barnes&Noble, Best Buy, BigLots, Costco, Dick's, FoodMaxx, Home Depot, JC Penney, Jo-Ann, Kohl's, Macy's, Michael's, Old Navy, O'Reilly Parts, PetCo, Petsmart, Schwab Tire, Target, TJ Maxx, Trader Joe's, Verizon, Walmart/McDonald's, WinCo Foods, World Mkt

🅖 = gas   🍴 = food   🛏 = lodging   🅞 = other   🆁🆂 = rest stop   Copyright 2022 - The Next EXIT ®

⬆N   INTERSTATE 5 Cont'd

Exit #	Services
667	CA 273, Factory Outlet Blvd, **E** 🅞 vet, **W** 🅖 Arco/dsl, Chevron/dsl, Shell/dsl 🍴 Arby's, Jack-in-the-Box, Mary's Pizza, Panda Express, Sonic, Starbucks, Westside Pizza 🛏 Baymont Inn 🅞 $Tree, AT&T, Grocery Outlet, Shasta Outlets/famous brands, Tire Pros, Verizon, Walmart/Subway
665	(from sb) Cottonwood, **E** 🛏 Alamo Motel/RV park, Travelers Motel/RV Park
664	Gas Point Rd, to Balls Ferry, **E** 🅖 Chevron/dsl/LP, Speedwaay/dsl 🛏 Alamo Motel, Travelers Motel 🅞 Alamo RV Park, auto repair, **W** 🅖 Holiday/dsl, Sunshine/dsl 🍴 Eagles Nest Pizza, Subway 🅞 Ace Hardware, Holiday Foods, vet
662	Bowman Rd, to Cottonwood, **E** 🅖 Chevron/dsl/24hr
660mm	weigh sta both lanes
659	Snively Rd, Auction Yard Rd, (Sunset Hills Dr from nb)
657	Hooker Creek Rd, Auction Yard Rd
656mm	🆁🆂 both lanes, full ♿ facilities, litter barrels, petwalk, 🅲, 🖼
653	Jellys Ferry Rd, **E** 🅞 RV Park/LP
652	Wilcox Golf Rd
651	CA 36W (from sb), Red Bluff, **W** 🅖 Arco/dsl 🛏 Holiday Inn Express 🅞 same as 650, UHaul
650	Adobe Rd, **W** 🅖 Chevron/dsl 🍴 Burrito Bandito 🛏 Hampton Inn, Holiday Inn Express 🅞 CHP, Chrysler/Dodge/Jeep, Home Depot
649	CA 36, to CA 99 S, Red Bluff, **E** 🅖 Chevron/dsl, Red Bluff Gas, Shell/dsl 🍴 Applebee's, Burger King, Del Taco, McDonald's, Rockin' R Rest., Starbucks 🛏 Best Western, Comfort Inn, Motel 6, **W** 🅖 Gas4Less/dsl, Mobil/dsl 🍴 Denny's, Los Mariachis, Luigi's Pizza, RoundTable Pizza, Shari's, Subway 🛏 Super 8, Travelodge 🅞 AT&T, Durango RV Resort, Foodmaxx, O'Nite RV Park, River's Edge RV Park, Verizon, vet
647 a b	S Main St, Red Bluff, **E** 🅖 Valero/dsl 🛏 Days Inn 🅞 🖽, **W** 🅖 Arco/dsl, Chevron/dsl, Shell/dsl 🍴 Arby's, Baskin-Robbins, China Buffet, China Doll, Cozy Diner, Domino's, Jack-in-the-Box, Papa Murphy's, Starbucks, Subway, Wendy's 🛏 Best Value Inn, Gateway Inn, Triangle Motel 🅞 AutoZone, CVS Drug, GNC, Grocery Outlet, I-5 Tire/auto, O'Reilly Parts, Raley's Food/drug, True Value, Verizon, vet, Walgreens, Walmart
642	Flores Ave, to Proberta, Gerber, **1 mi E** 🅞 Walmart Dist Ctr
636	rd A11, Gyle Rd, to Tehama, **E** 🅞 RV camping (7mi)
633	Finnell Rd, to Richfield
632mm	🆁🆂 both lanes, full ♿ facilities, litter barrels, petwalk, 🅲, 🖼
631	A9, Corning Rd, Corning, **E** 🅖 Chevron/dsl, Shell/dsl/LP, Tesla EVC, Valero/dsl 🍴 Burger King, Casa Ramos Mexican, Little Caesar's, Marco's Pizza, Olive Pit Rest., Papa Murphy's, Rancho Grande Mexican, RoundTable Pizza, Starbucks, Subway, Taco Bell 🛏 7 Inn Motel, American Inn, Best Western+, Economy Inn, Super 8 🅞 $Tree, Ace Hardware, auto repair, AutoZone, Buick/Chevrolet, Ford, Heritage RV Park, NAPA, O'Reilly Parts, Rite Aid, Safeway, Verizon, West End Drug, **W** 🍴 Giant Burger 🛏 Corning RV Park
630	South Ave, Corning, **E** 🅖 Loves/Denny's/dsl/LP/RV dump/scales/24hr, Petro/Iron Skillet/dsl/scales/24hr/@, TA/Arby's/Subway/dsl/scales/24hr/@ 🍴 Jack-in-the-Box, McDonald's 🛏 CA Inn, Econolodge, Holiday Inn Express 🅞 Ace Hardware, Blue Beacon, SpeedCo Lube, truck wash/lube, Woodson Br SRA/RV Park (6mi)
628	CA 99W, Liberal Ave, **W** 🅖 Chevron/dsl/24hr 🛏 Rolling Hills Hotel/Casino 🅞 Rolling Hills RV Park
621	CA 7
619	CA 32, Orland, **E** 🅖 Arco, Chevron/dsl 🍴 Berry Patch Rest., Burger King, Little Caesar's, Starbucks, Subway 🛏 Orlanda Inn 🅞 $General, AutoZone, CVS Drug, Walgreens, **W** 🅖 🅿️ Pilot/Wendy's/PJ Fresh/dsl/scales/24hr, Shell/dsl 🍴 I-5 Cafe, Taco Bell 🅞 Old Orchard RV Park, Parkway RV Park
618	CA 16, **E** 🅖 Shell/dsl 🍴 El Potrero Mexican 🛏 Orland Inn 🅞 $Tree, Grocery Outlet
614	CA 27
610	Artois
608mm	🆁🆂 both lanes, full ♿ facilities, litter barrels, petwalk, 🅲, 🖼, RV dump
607	CA 39, Blue Gum Rd, Bayliss, **2 mi E** 🛏 Blue Gum Motel
603	CA 162, to Oroville, Willows, **E** 🅖 Arco, Chevron, Shell/dsl 🍴 Black Bear Diner, Burger King, Casa Ramos, KFC, La Cascada Mexican, McDonald's, RoundTable Pizza, Starbucks, Subway, Taco Bell, Wong's Chinese 🛏 Baymont Inn, Best Western/RV parking, Holiday Inn Express, Motel 6, Super 8 🅞 🖽 $Tree, CHP, O'Reilly Parts, **W** 🍴 Nancy's Café/24hr 🅞 🏥, RV Park (8mi), Walmart
601	rd 57, **E** 🅖 Chevron/dsl/24hr
595	Rd 68, to Princeton, **E** 🅞 to Sacramento NWR
591	Delevan Rd
588	Maxwell (from sb), access to camping
586	Maxwell Rd, **E** 🅞 Delevan NWR, **W** 🅖 Chevron 🛏 Maxwell Inn/rest.
583	🆁🆂 both lanes, full ♿ facilities, litter barrels, petwalk, 🅲, 🖼
578	CA 20, Colusa, **E** 🅖 ♥Loves/Chester's/IHOP/dsl/scales/24hr 🅞 hwy patrol, **W** 🅖 Shell/Orv's Cafe/dsl 🅞 🖽
577	Williams, **E** 🅖 Arco/dsl, Shell/Baskin-Robbins/Togo's/dsl 🍴 Carl's Jr, Subway, Taco Bell 🛏 Ramada Inn 🅞 $General, **W** 🅖 76/dsl, Chevron/dsl, Sinclair/dsl 🍴 Burger King, Denny's, Granzella's Rest., Louis Cairo's Rest., McDonald's/RV parking, Starbucks, Straw Hat Pizza, Williams Chinese Rest. 🛏 Econolodge, Granzella's Inn, Motel 6, StageStop Motel, Travelers Inn 🅞 🖽, NAPA, Shop'n Save Foods, URGENT CARE, USPO
575	Husted Rd, to Williams
569	Hahn Rd, to Grimes
567	frontage rd (from nb), to Arbuckle, **W** 🅖 Chevron/dsl
566	to College City, Arbuckle, **E** 🅞 Ace Hardware, USPO, **W** 🅖 Sinclair/dsl 🅞 $General
559	Yolo/Colusa County Line Rd
557mm	🆁🆂 both lanes, full ♿ facilities, litter barrels, petwalk, 🅲, 🖼
556	E4, Dunnigan, **E** 🅖 Chevron/dsl/LP 🍴 Jack-in-the-Box 🛏 Best Value Inn, Motel 6 🅞 Farmers Mkt Deli, **W** 🅞 Camper's RV Park/golf (1mi)
554	rd 8, **E** 🅖 🅿️ Pilot/Wendy's/dsl/scales/24hr 🛏 California Motel 🅞 Denny's, HappyTime RV Park, **W** 🅖 United TP/dsl
553	I-505 (from sb), to San Francisco, callboxes begin sb
548	Zamora, **E** 🅖 Shell/dsl
542	Yolo
541	CA 16W, Woodland, **3 mi W** 🅞 🏥
540	West St, **W** 🅖 Arco 🍴 Denny's
538	CA 113 N, E St, Woodland, **E** 🛏 Valley Oaks Inn, **W** 🅖 CFN/dsl, Chevron/dsl 🛏 Best Western
537	CA 113 S, Main St, to Davis (same as 536), **E** 🅞 Buick/Cadillac/Chevrolet/GMC, **W** 🅖 Chevron/dsl 🍴 Black Bear Diner, Carl's Jr, Denny's, Dickey's BBQ, McDonald's, RoundTable Pizza, Sonic, Starbucks, Subway, Taco Bell 🛏 Days Inn, Motel 6, Quality Inn 🅞 $Tree, Food4Less
536	rd 102 (same as 537), **E on Main St** 🅖 Arco, Chevron/dsl 🍴 Applebee's, Burger King, Jack-in-the-Box, McDonald's, Subway 🛏 Comfort Suites, Fairfield Inn, Hampton Inn

(side margin labels: RED BLUFF, CORNING, WILLIAMS, WOODLAND)

🧭N INTERSTATE 5 Cont'd

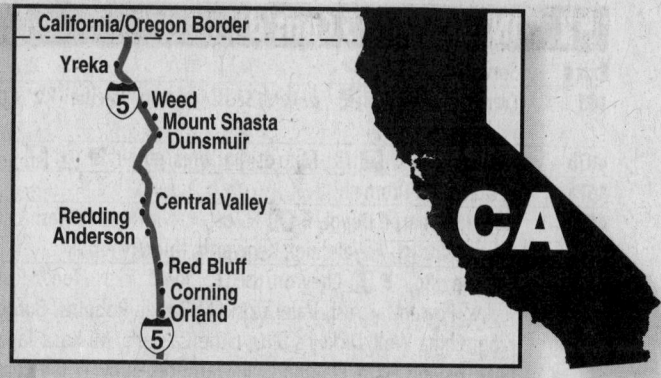

536	**Continued** Holiday Inn Express ⊙ America's Tire, Chevrolet/Buick/GMC, Home Depot, Walmart, **W** 🅿 Circle K/dsl 🍴 In-N-Out, Jimboy's Tacos, MOD Pizza, Panda Express, Red Robin, Starbucks, Subway ⊙ Best Buy, Best Buy, Costco/gas, GNC, Michael's, Target, URGENT CARE, Verizon
531	rd 22, W Sacramento
530mm	Sacramento River
529mm	℞ₛ sb, full 🛏 facilities, litter barrels, petwalk, 🍴, 🏕
528	Airport Rd, **E** 🅿 Arco ⊙ ☎
525b	CA 99, to CA 70, to Marysville, Yuba City
525a	Del Paso Rd, **E** 🅿 Chevron 🍴 A&W/KFC, BurgerIM, Chicken'n Waffles, Denny's, IHOP, In-N-Out, Jack-in-the-box, Jersey Mike's, Jimmy John's, Malabar Rest., Panda Express, Panera Bread, Papa Murphy's, Pizza Guys, Sizzler, Sizzler, Taco Bell 🛏 Hampton Inn, Hilton Garden, Holiday Inn Express, Homewood Suites ⊙ Rite Aid, Safeway Foods/dsl, **W** 🍴 Subway 🛏 Sheraton Four Points ⊙ Walgreens
524	Arena Blvd, **E** 🍴 Huckleberry's, Papa John's, Subway ⊙ Sleep Train Arena, **W** 🍴 Panda Garden, RoundTable Pizza, Starbucks 🛏 Jimboy's Tacos ⊙ Bel-Air Food/Drug/dsl
522	I-80, E to Reno, W to San Francisco
521b	W El Camino Ave (from nb, no return), West El Camino, **W** 🅿 Shell/dsl 🍴 Carl's Jr, Jack-in-the-box, Jamba Juice, Starbucks, Subway, Togo's/Baskin-Robbins 🛏 Courtyard, Hilton Garden, Residence Inn, SpringHill Suites
521a	Garden Hwy, **W** 🛏 Courtyard
520	Richards Blvd, **E** 🅿 Chevron/dsl 🍴 Denny's, McDonald's 🛏 Governor's Inn, Hawthorn Suites, Surestay+, **W** 🅿 Arco, Shell 🍴 Nena's Mexican 🛏 Best Western, Comfort Suites, Days Inn, La Quinta, Motel 6 ⊙ waterfront park
519b	J St, Old Sacramento, **E** 🛏 Holiday Inn, Vagabond Inn, **W** 🛏 Embassy Suites ⊙ Railroad Museum
519a	Q St, downtown, Sacramento, **W** 🛏 Embassy Suites, to st capitol
518	US 50, CA 99, Broadway, **E** services downtown
516	Sutterville Rd, **E** 🅿 76/dsl, Chevron/dsl 🍴 La Bou Cafe, Macau Cafe ⊙ Sprouts Mkt, Wm Land Park, zoo
515	Fruitridge Rd, Seamas Rd
514	43rd Ave, Riverside Blvd (from sb), **E** 🅿 76/7-11
513	Florin Rd, **E** 🅿 Arco, Chevron/dsl 🍴 Carl's Jr, RoundTable Pizza, Starbucks ⊙ $Tree, Bel Air Foods, CVS Drug, O'Reilly Parts, **W** 🍴 Burger King, JimBoy's Tacos, L&L Hawaiian BBQ, Panda Garden, Shari's, Starbucks, Subway, Wingstop ⊙ Marshall's, Nugget Mkt, Petco, Rite Aid
512	CA 160, Pocket Rd, Meadowview Rd, to Freeport, **E** 🅿 Chevron/dsl, Shell/dsl 🍴 Baskin Robbins/Togo's, IHOP, KFC, McDonald's, Starbucks, Wendy's ⊙ AT&T, Home Depot, Schwab Tire, Staples, vet, Walgreens
510	Cosumnes River Blvd, **E** 🍴 Chick-fil-A, Chipotle, El Pollo Loco, Habit Burger, In-N-Out, Jamba Juice, Jersey Mike's, Noodles, Panda Express, Panera Bread, Pieology, Starbucks ⊙ AT&T, Dick's, GNC, Hobby Lobby, Old Navy, Petsmart, Ross, Verizon, Walmart
508	Laguna Blvd, **E** 🅿 76/Circle K/dsl/LP, Chevron/Taco Bell/dsl, Shell 🍴 A&W/KFC, Starbucks, Subway, Wendy's 🛏 Extended Stay America, Hampton Inn ⊙ Jiffy Lube, Laguna Auto Repair, U-Haul
506	Elk Grove Blvd, **E** 🅿 Arco/dsl, Chevron/dsl, Shell/dsl 🍴 Carl's Jr, Flaming Grill Burger, Pete's Grill, Wasabi Grill 🛏 Holiday Inn Express ⊙ vet
504	Hood Franklin Rd

498	Twin Cities Rd, to Walnut Grove
493	Walnut Grove Rd, Thornton, **E** 🅿 CFN/dsl, Chevron/Subway/dsl
490	Peltier Rd
487	Turner Rd
485	CA 12, Lodi, **E** 🅿 ⛽FLYING J/Denny's/Subway/dsl/scales/24hr, Arco/dsl, Chevron/dsl, ❤Loves/Arby's/dsl/scales/24hr, Shell/dsl, Sinclair/Rocky's Rest./dsl/scales/24hr 🍴 Burger King, Carl's Jr, McDonald's, Starbucks, Tortilla Flats 🛏 Best Western, Microtel ⊙ Blue Beacon, Flag City RV Resort, Profleet Trucklube, **W** ⊙ KOA (5mi)
481	Eight Mile Rd, **W** 🅿 Arco/dsl, Chevron/Jack-in-the-Box/dsl 🍴 Baskin-Robbins, Chipotle, El Pollo Loco, GK Mongolian BBQ, Hawaiian BBQ, Jamba Juice, McDonald's, MooMoo's Burgers, Panda Express, Panera Bread, RoundTable Pizza, Sonic, Starbucks, Subway, Sugar Mediterranean, Wendy's ⊙ $Tree, AAA, AT&T, Jo-Ann Fabrics, Kohl's, Lowe's, Mercedes, Petsmart, Ross, Target, Verizon, Walmart/McDonald's, World Mkt
478	Hammer Lane, Stockton, **E** 🅿 76/dsl, Arco 🍴 Adalberto's Mexican, Carl's Jr, KFC, Little Caesar's, McDonald's, Subway ⊙ AutoZone, Food Source, Walgreens, **W** 🅿 Chevron/dsl, QuikStop 🍴 Jack-in-the-Box, Nations Burger, Taco Bell
477	Benjamin Holt Dr, Stockton, **E** 🅿 Arco, Chevron/dsl 🍴 Pizza Guys 🛏 Motel 6 ⊙ QwikStop, **W** 🅿 7-11 🍴 Eddie's Pizza, Lumber Jack's Rest., Lyon's Rest., Mandarin Villa, McDonald's, Starbucks, Subway/TCBY ⊙ Ace Hardware, Marina Foods, vet
476	March Lane, Stockton, **E** 🅿 7-11 🍴 Applebee's, Carl's Jr, Chick-fil-A, Denny's, Domino's, El Torito, Jack-in-the-Box, McDonald's, Olive Garden, Red Lobster, Taco Bell, Toot Sweets Bakery, Wendy's 🛏 Hilton, Motel 6 ⊙ CVS Drug, Marshall's, SMart Foods, **W** 🅿 76/dsl 🍴 Habit Burger, IHOP, In-N-Out, Jamba Juice, Krispy Kreme, RoundTable Pizza, Starbucks, Subway, Wong's Chinese 🛏 Courtyard, Extended Stay America, La Quinta, Residence Inn ⊙ Home Depot
475	Alpine Ave, Country Club Blvd, same as 474 b
474b	Country Club Blvd (from nb), **E** 🅿 Mobil/dsl, **W** 🅿 7-11, Shell/dsl 🍴 Mtn Mike's Pizza, Papa Murphy's, Subway ⊙ BigLots, Safeway/gas
474a	Monte Diablo Ave
473	Pershing Ave (from nb), **W** 🅿 Arco 🛏 Red Roof Inn
472	CA 4 E, to CA 99, Fresno Ave, downtown
471	CA 4 W, Charter Way, **E** 🅿 Arco, Chevron/dsl, Shell 🍴 Burger King, Denny's, Little Caesar's, McDonald's ⊙ $General Mkt, O'Reilly Parts, **W** 🅿 76/dsl/scales/24hr, Valero/Subway 🍴 Carl Jr, Jack-in-the-Box, Taco Bell 🛏 Motel 6 ⊙ Les Schwab Tire, truck repair
470	8th St, Stockton, **W** 🅿 CA Stop/dsl, Shell/dsl 🛏 I-5 Inn
469	Downing Ave, **W** 🍴 China Express, Louie's Chinese, Mtn Mike's Pizza, Papa Murphy's, Subway ⊙ $Tree, AutoZone, Food4Less/gas

🛢️ = gas   🍴 = food   🏨 = lodging   Ⓞ = other   Ⓡˢ = rest stop   Copyright 2022 - The Next EXIT ®

CA

⬆️N   INTERSTATE 5 Cont'd

Exit #	Services
468	French Camp, **E** 🛢️ 76/Togo's/dsl Ⓞ Pan Pacific RV Ctr, **W** Ⓞ Ⓗ
467b	Mathews Rd, **E** 🛢️ J&L Mkt/dsl Ⓞ tires/repair, **W** Ⓞ Ⓗ
467a	El Dorado St (from nb)
465	Roth Rd, Sharpe Depot, **E** 🛢️ FL/dsl, *FLYING J*/PJ Fresh/dsl/scales/24hr Ⓞ Freightliner, Kenworth, truck/rv repair
463	Lathrop Rd, **E** 🛢️ Chevron/dsl/LP, Joe's Trkstp/Togo's/dsl/scales, PowerMart/dsl, Valero/dsl 🍴 Baskin-Robbins, Burger King, China Wok, Dickey's BBQ, Little Caesar's, Mi Kasa Japanese, Milan's Pizza, Platano Grill, Starbucks, Subway 🏨 Comfort Inn, Days Inn, Holiday Inn Express Ⓞ Harley-Davidson, O'Reilly Parts, SaveMart Mkt, Walgreens, **W** Ⓞ Dos Reis CP, RV camping
462	Louise Ave, **E** 🛢️ Arco/dsl, Shell 🍴 A&W/KFC, Carl's Jr, Denny's, Domino's, Golden Bowl, Jack-in-the-Box, McDonald's, Mtn Mike's Pizza, Popeye's, Quiznos, Taco Bell 🏨 Hampton Inn, Quality Inn, **W** Ⓞ Mossdale CP, Target
461	CA 120, to Sonora, Manteca, **E** Ⓞ Oakwood Lake Resort Camping, to Yosemite
460	Mossdale Rd, **E** 🛢️ Chevron/dsl, **W** 🍴 fruit stand/cafe
458b	I-205, to Oakland (from sb, no return)
458a	11th St, to Tracy, Defense Depot, **2 mi W** 🛢️ gas/dsl/food
457	Kasson Rd, to Tracy, **W** 🛢️ Valley Pacific/dsl
452	CA 33 S, Vernalis
449b a	CA 132, to Modesto, **E** Ⓞ The Orchard Campground
446	I-580 (from nb, exits left, no return)
445mm	**Westley Rest Area both lanes, full ♿ facilities, litter barrels, petwalk, Ⓒ, 🚶, RV dump**
441	Ingram Creek, Howard Rd, Westley, **E** 🛢️ 76/dsl, Chevron/dsl, Joe's Trvl Plaza/Denny's/dsl/scales/24hr, Westley Triangle TruckStp/dsl 🍴 Carl's Jr, McDonald's, Subway 🏨 Days Inn, EconoLodge, Holiday Inn Express, Motel 6, **W** 🛢️ Shell/dsl Ⓞ truck repair
434	Sperry Ave, Del Puerto, Patterson, **E** 🛢️ 76/Subway/dsl, Arco/dsl, Chevron, *FLYING J*/Wendy's/PJ Fresh/dsl/scales/24hr, Mobil/dsl, Valero/dsl 🍴 A&W/KFC, Apricot Wood BBQ, Carl's Jr, Denny's, El Rosal Mexican, Golden Lion Chinese, Jack-in-the-Box, Pizza Factory, Starbucks 🏨 Best Western+, Hampton Inn Ⓞ Kit Fox RV Park
430mm	vista point nb
428	Fink Rd, Crow's Landing
423	Stuhr Rd, Newman, **5 mi E** Ⓞ food, lodging, RV camping
422mm	vista point sb
418	CA 140E, Gustine, **E** 🛢️ Chevron/dsl, Sinclair/dsl
409	**weigh sta both lanes**
407	CA 33, Santa Nella, **E** 🛢️ Arco, *Loves*/Del Taco/dsl/scales/24hr, TA/Shell/Country Pride/Popeye's/dsl/scales/24hr/@ 🍴 Andersen's Rest., Carl's Jr, Subway, Wendy's 🏨 Best Western/Andersen's, Quality Inn, **W** 🛢️ 76/dsl, Chevron, Rotten Robbie/dsl/scales, Valero/Circle K/dsl 🍴 Denny's, In-N-Out, McDonald's, Panda Express, Pizza Factory, Starbucks, Taco Bell 🏨 Hotel Mission de Oro, Motel 6 Ⓞ Santa Nella RV Park
403b a	CA 152, Los Banos, **6 mi E** Ⓞ Ⓗ, **1 mi W** 🛢️ Petro/Shell/diner/dsl/24hr 🏨 Motel 6 Ⓞ KOA
391	CA 165N, Mercy Springs Rd, **E** Ⓞ Ⓗ, **W** 🛢️ Shell
388	vista point (from nb)
386mm	Ⓡˢ **both lanes, full ♿ facilities, litter barrels, petwalk, Ⓒ, 🚶**
385	Nees Ave, to Firebaugh, **W** 🛢️ Chevron/CFN/Subway/dsl/scales
379	Shields Ave, to Mendota
372	Russell Ave
368	Panoche Rd, **W** 🛢️ 76/dsl, Chevron/McDonald's, Mobil/Wayback Burger/dsl, Shell/dsl, Valero/dsl 🍴 Subway 🏨 Best Western Ⓞ country store
365	Manning Ave, to San Joaquin
357	Kamm Ave
349	CA 33 N, Derrick Ave
337	CA 33 S, CA 145 N, to Coalinga
334	CA 198, to Lemoore, Huron, **E** 🛢️ Shell/Subway/dsl/24hr Tesla EVC 🏨 Harris Ranch Inn/rest., **W** 🛢️ 76/dsl, Arco/dsl, Chevron/dsl, Valero/Subway/dsl 🍴 Burger King, Carl's Jr, Denny's, McDonald's, Taco Bell 🏨 Best Western, Motel 6, Travelodge Ⓞ Ⓗ, auto repair
325	Jayne Ave, to Coalinga, **W** 🛢️ Shell/Baja Fresh/dsl, Valero 🏨 Sommerville RV Park/LP Ⓞ Ⓗ
320mm	Ⓡˢ **both lanes, full ♿ facilities, litter barrels, petwalk, Ⓒ, 🚶**
319	CA 269, Lassen Ave, to Avenal, **W** 🛢️ Hillcrest TP/76/Subway/dsl/scales/24hr
309	CA 41, Kettleman City, **E** 🛢️ 76/Subway/TCBY, CFN/dsl, Chevron/McDonald's, Mobil/Starbucks/dsl/24hr, Shell/Baja Fresh/dsl, Tesla EVC, Valero/dsl 🍴 Carl's Jr, Denny's, In-N-Out, Jack-in-the-Box, Little Caesar's, Pizza Hut/Taco Bell, Wienerschnitzel 🏨 Best Western, Quality Inn Ⓞ Bravo Farms Mercantile
305	Utica Ave
288	Twisselman Rd
278	CA 46, Lost Hills, **E** 🛢️ Buford Star Mart/dsl/LP Ⓞ to Kern NWR, **W** 🛢️ 76/Quiznos, Arco/DQ/dsl, Chevron/dsl, *Loves*/Arby's/dsl/scales/24hr, Mobil/McDonald's/dsl/LP, *Hilton*, Wendy's/dsl/scales/24hr, Shell/Pizza Hut/Subway/Taco Bell/dsl, Valero/7-11/dsl 🍴 Carl's Jr, Denny's, Jack-in-the-Box 🏨 Days Inn, Motel 6 Ⓞ KOA, Royal Truck Wash/lube
268	Lerdo Hwy, to Shafter
262	7th Standard Rd, Rowlee Rd, to Buttonwillow
259mm	**Buttonwillow Rest Area both lanes, full ♿ facilities, litter barrels, petwalk, Ⓒ, 🚶**
257	CA 58, to Bakersfield, Buttonwillow, **E** 🛢️ 76/Circle K/Quiznos/dsl, Arco/dsl, Chevron/dsl, Shell/dsl, Speedy Fuel/dsl/wash, TA/Mobil/Pizza Hut/Taco Bell/dsl/scales/24hr/@ 🍴 Carl's Jr, McDonald's, Starbucks, Subway, Tita's Mexican, Willow Ranch BBQ 🏨 California Inn, Buttonwillow Inn, Motel 6, Vagabond Inn Ⓞ Castro's Tire/Truckwash, **W** 🛢️ Valero/dsl
253	Stockdale Hwy, **E** 🛢️ Chevron/Subway/dsl, Shell/dsl/24h 🍴 IHOP, Jack-in-the-Box 🏨 Best Western, Vagabond Inn **W** Ⓞ Tule Elk St Reserve
246	CA 43, to Taft, Maricopa, Ⓞ to Buena Vista RA
244	CA 119, to Pumpkin Center, **E** 🛢️ Mobil/dsl, **W** 🛢️ Arco/dsl, scales, Chevron/dsl/LP
239	CA 223, Bear Mtn Blvd, to Arvin, **E** Ⓞ Bear Mtn RV Resort **W** Ⓞ RV camping, to Buena Vista RA
234	Old River Rd
228	Copus Rd, **E** Ⓞ Murray Farms Mkt
225	CA 166, to Mettler, **W** 🛢️ Chevron/Subway/dsl
221	I-5 and CA 99 (from nb, exits left, no return)
219b a	Laval Rd, Wheeler Ridge, **E** 🛢️ Shell/dsl, TA/Shell/Popeye's/Subway/scales/@ 🍴 Baja Fresh, Black Bear Diner, Burger King, Carl's Jr, Habit Burger, Pieology, Pizza Hut, Starbucks, Taco Bell 🏨 Hampton Inn, Microtel Ⓞ Blue Beacon, Tejon Outlets/famous brands, **W** 🛢️ 76/Subway/dsl, Mobil/dsl, Petro/Iron Skillet/Subway/dsl/scales/24hr/@, Tesla EVC 🍴 Arby's, Baskin-Robbins, Chipotle Mexican, Del Taco, Denny's, Firehouse, In-N-Out, McDonald's, Panda Express, Starbucks, Wendy's 🏨 Best Western
218	**truck weigh sta sb**

W E S T L E Y

S A N T A   N E L L A

B U T T O N W I L L O W

INTERSTATE 5 Cont'd

FT TEJON

Exit #	Services
215	Grapevine, **E** 🅿 Valero/dsl 🍴 Denny's, Jack-in-the-Box, **W** 🅿 Shell/dsl 🍴 Don Perico Grill 🛏 Days Inn
210	Ft Tejon Rd, **W** 🅾 to Ft Tejon Hist SP, towing/repair
209mm	brake check area nb
207	Lebec Rd, **W** 🅾 antiques, towing, USPO
206mm	Ⓡs both lanes, full ♿ facilities, petwalk, 🚻, 🗑 litter barrels, vending
205	Frazier Mtn Park Rd, **W** 🅿 ⛟FLYING J/dsl/LP/24hr/@, Arco, Arco/dsl, Chevron/dsl, Mobil/Subway/dsl/24hr 🍴 Jack-in-the-Box, Los Pinos Mexican 🛏 Holiday Inn Express, Motel 6 🅾 auto repair/towing, Carquest, to Mt Pinos RA
204	Tejon Pass, elev 4144, **truck brake insp sb**
202	Gorman Rd, to Hungry Valley, **E** 🅿 76/dsl, Chevron/dsl, LP 🍴 Carl's Jr, El Grullense, Ranch House Rest. 🛏 Motel 6, **W** 🅿 Shell/dsl 🍴 McDonald's 🅾 auto repair

CASTAIC

Exit #	Services
199	CA 138 E, Lancaster Rd, to Palmdale
198b a	Quail Lake Rd, CA 138 E (from nb)
195	Smokey Bear Rd, Pyramid Lake, **E** 🅾 Pyramid Lake RV Park
191	Vista del Lago Rd, **W** 🅾 visitors ctr
186mm	brake inspection area sb, motorist callboxes begin sb
184mm	brake check sb
183	Templin Hwy, **W** 🅾 Ranger Sta, RV camping
176b a	Lake Hughes Rd, Parker Rd, Castaic, **E** 🅿 7-11, Arco/dsl, Castaic Trkstp/dsl/24hr, 🅿LOVE'S/PJ Fresh/dsl/scales/24hr/@, Shell/dsl 🍴 Cajun Chicken, Carl's Jr, Denny's, Domino's, El Pollo Loco, Fosters Freeze, McDonald's, Mike's Diner, Panda Express, Pizza Factory, Red Dot Pizza, Starbucks, Subway, Waba Grill, Wok's Chinese 🛏 Days Inn, Rodeway Inn 🅾 $Tree, Benny's Tire/repair, Castaic Inn, Castaic Lake RV Park, O'Reilly Parts, to Castaic Lake, vet, **W** 🅿 76/repair, Chargepoint EVC, Mobil 🍴 Jack-in-the-Box, Taco Bell 🅾 auto repair, Walgreens

SANTA CLARITA

Exit #	Services
173	Hasley Canyon Rd, **W** 🍴 Pizza Hut, Subway 🅾 Ralph's Foods
172	CA 126 W, to Ventura, **E** 🛏 Courtyard, Embassy Suites
171mm	weigh sta nb
171	Rye Canyon Rd (from sb), **W** 🅿 Arco/dsl, Conserv/dsl 🍴 Del Taco, Jack-in-the-Box, Jimmy Dean's, Starbucks, Tommy's Burgers 🅾 Six Flags
170	CA 126 E, Magic Mtn Pkwy, Saugus, **E** 🍴 Azul Tequila Mexican, Denny's, Rustic Eatery, Sam's Grille, Starbucks 🛏 Best Western/rest., Holiday Inn Express, **W** 🅿 Chevron/dsl, Shell/dsl 🍴 Coffee Bean, McDonald's, Red Lobster, Wendy's 🛏 Hilton Garden 🅾 Six Flags of CA
169	Valencia Blvd, **W** 🍴 Fat Burger, Magic Pizza, Panda Express, Robeks, Starbucks, Subway 🅾 Verizon
168	McBean Pkwy, **E** 🅾 ⊞, **W** 🍴 Cabo Cabana, Chili's, Chucke-Cheese, ClaimJumper, Jamba Juice, Jersey Mikes Subs, Mama Mia Italian, MOD Pizza, Pick Up Stix, Starbucks, Subway, Urbane Cafe 🅾 Michael's, Old Navy, Verizon, Vons Foods, WorldMkt
167	Lyons Ave, Pico Canyon Rd, **E** 🅿 76/Circle K/dsl, Chevron/dsl, Shell/dsl 🍴 Burger King, Wendy's, **W** 🅿 Arco, Shell/dsl 🍴 Cabo Cabana, Carl's Jr, Chuy's, Coco's, Del Taco, Denny's, El Pollo Loco, Fortune Express Chinese, IHOP, In-N-Out, Jack-in-the-Box, Jersey Mike's, McDonald's, Outback Steaks, Spumoni Italian, Taco Bell, Wood Ranch BBQ, Yamato Japanese 🛏 Comfort Suites, Extended Stay America, Fairfield Inn, Hampton Inn, La Quinta, Residence Inn 🅾 AT&T, Camping World RV Ctr, GNC, Jiffy Lube, Marshall's, Old Navy, Petsmart, Ralph's Foods, Ross, Staples, SteinMart, Walmart/McDonald's
166	Calgrove Blvd

SYLMAR

Exit #	Services
162	CA 14 N, to Palmdale
161b	Balboa Blvd (from sb)
160a	I-210, to San Fernando, Pasadena
159	Roxford St, Sylmar, **E** 🅿 Chevron/dsl, Mobil/dsl 🍴 Denny's/24hr, McDonald's 🛏 Good Nite Inn, Motel 6
158	I-405 S (from sb, no return)
157b a	SF Mission Blvd, Brand Blvd, **E** 🅿 76, Arco, Chevron/dsl, Mobil/dsl, Shell 🍴 Carl's Jr, In-N-Out, Little Caesar's, New Asia, Pollo Gordo, Popeye's, Subway, Taco Bell, Winchell's 🅾 ⊞, Honda, Rite Aid, Vallarta Mkt
156b	CA 118
156a	Paxton St, Brand Ave (from nb), **E** 🅿 G&M/dsl 🅾 7-11

ARLETA

Exit #	Services
155b	Van Nuys Blvd (no EZ nb return), **E** 🅿 Arco 🍴 Jack-in-the-Box, KFC/LJ Silver, McDonald's, Pizza Hut, Popeye's 🅾 Discount Parts, USPO, **W** 🍴 Domino's 🅾 auto repair
155a	Terra Bella St (from nb), **E** 🅿 USA
154	Osborne St, to Arleta, **E** 🅿 Arco, Chevron/dsl 🅾 AutoZone, BigLots, Food4Less, Ross, Target, **W** 🅿 76, Mobil/Burger King 🅾 7-11
153b	CA 170 (from sb), to Hollywood
152a	Sheldon St, **E** 🍴 Big Jim's Rest. 🅾 ⊞, auto repair, Big O Parts
152	Lankershim Blvd, Tuxford, **E** 🅿 Superfine/dsl/scales
151	Penrose St

SUN VALLEY

Exit #	Services
150b	Sunland Blvd, Sun Valley, **E** 🅿 76/dsl, Mobil 🍴 Acapulco Rest., Carl's Jr, El Pollo Loco, Old Time Burger, Papa John's, Quiznos, Subway, Town Café, Yoshinoya 🛏 Economy Inn 🅾 $Tree, 7-11, Grocery Outlet, Sunland Produce, **W** 🅿 Chevron/7-11, Shell 🍴 McDonald's, Starbucks
150a	GlenOaks Blvd (from nb), **E** 🅿 Arco/dsl 🛏 Willows Motel
149	Hollywood Way, **W** 🅿 Shell/dsl 🅾 ⏚, U-Haul
148	Buena Vista St, **E** 🛏 Hampton Inn, **W** 🅿 76/dsl 🍴 Jack-in-the-Box 🛏 Quality Inn, Ramada Inn
147	Scott Rd, to Burbank, **E** 🅿 Sevan/dsl, **W** 🍴 HomeTown Buffet, Jamba Juice, Krispy Kreme, Olive Garden, Outback Steaks, Panda Express, Sharky's Mexican, Starbucks, Wendy's 🛏 Courtyard, Extended Stay America 🅾 Best Buy, Lowe's, Marshall's, Michael's, REI, Staples, Target, Verizon
146b	Burbank Blvd, **E** 🅿 76/repair 🍴 Baskin-Robbins, Buffalo Wild Wings, CA Pizza Kitchen, Carl's Jr, Chevy's Mexican, Chipotle, ChuckECheese's, Corner Cafe, El Pollo Loco, Harry's Rest., Hooters, IHOP, In-N-Out, Islands Burger, Jersey Mike's, McDonald's, Pizza Hut, Popeye's, Robek's Juice, Shakey's Pizza, Starbucks, Starbucks, Subway, Taco Bell, Tommy's Burgers, Yoshinoya, Zankou Chicken 🅾 Barnes&Noble, CVS Drug, IKEA, Macy's, Office Depot, Old Navy, Ralph's Foods, Ross, Sprouts Mkt, **W** 🍴 McDonald's, Subway 🅾 Costco/gas, Discount Tire, Walmart

🅖 = gas 🍴 = food 🛏 = lodging 🄾 = other 🆁🆂 = rest stop Copyright 2022 - The Next EXIT ®

LOS ANGELES AREA

⬆N INTERSTATE 5 Cont'd

Exit #	Services
146a	Olive Ave, Verdugo, **E** 🍴 BJ's Rest., Black Angus 🛏 Holiday Inn 🄾 USPO, **W** 🄾 🄷, 7-11, Chevrolet, Metro RV Ctr
145b	Alameda Ave, **E** 🅖 Chevron 🍴 Baskin-Robbins/Togo's, Habit Burger, Starbucks 🄾 CarMax, CVS Drug, Home Depot, IKEA, Ralph's Foods, Trader Joes, Walgreens, **W** 🅖 76/dsl, Arco, Shell 🛏 Burbank Inn 🄾 U-Haul
145a	Western Ave, **W** 🄾 Gene Autrey Museum
144b a	CA 134, Ventura Fwy, Glendale, Pasadena
142	Colorado St
141a	Los Feliz Blvd, **E** 🄾 🄷, **W** 🄾 Griffith Park, zoo
140b	Glendale Blvd, **E** 🅖 76, Valero 🍴 Dunkin', Starbucks, Subway, **W** 🅖 Valero
140a	Fletcher Dr (from sb), **W** 🅖 Arco, Chevron
139b a	CA 2, Glendale Fwy
138	Stadium Way, Figueroa St, **E** 🅖 76, Chevron, USA 🍴 IHOP, McDonald's 🄾 Home Depot, **W** 🄾 to Dodger Stadium
137b a	CA 2, Glendale Fwy, **W** 🅖 76
136b	Broadway St (from sb), **W** 🅖 76
136a	Main St, **E** 🅖 76, Chevron/24hr 🍴 Chinatown Express, Jack-in-the-Box, McDonald's 🄾 🄷
135c	I-10 W (from nb), Mission Rd (from sb), **E** 🍴 Jack-in-the-Box, McDonald's 🄾, 🄷, **W** 🅖 76/dsl
135b	Cesar Chavez Ave, **W** 🄾 🄷
135a	4th St, Soto St, **E** 🅖 Sinclair/dsl 🄾 city park, **W** 🅖 76/dsl
134b	Ca 60 E (from sb), Soto St (from nb)
134a	CA 60 W, Santa Monica Fwy
133	Euclid Ave (from sb), Grand Vista (from nb), **W** 🅖 Mobil
132	Calzona St, Indiana St, **E** 🅖 Arco/dsl
131b	Indiana St (from nb), **E** 🅖 Arco/dsl, Valero/dsl
131a	Olympic Blvd, **E** 🄾 🄷, **W** 🍴 Jack-in-the-Box, King Taco
130c b	I-710 (exits left from nb), to Long Beach, Eastern Ave, **E** 🍴 McDonald's
130a	Triggs St (from sb), **E** 🄾 outlet **W** 🍴 Denny's/24hr 🛏 Destiny Inn
129	Atlantic Blvd N, Eastern Ave (from sb), **E** 🍴 Carl's Jr, Chipotle, Panda Express, Starbucks, Subway 🛏 Doubletree 🄾 Hyundai, outlets/famous brands, **W** 🍴 Denny's, Steven's Steaks
128b	Washington Blvd, Commerce, **E** 🅖 Chevron/dsl/repair/24hr 🍴 McDonald's 🛏 Crowne Plaza Hotel/casino, Doubletree 🄾 Costco/gas, outlets/famous brands, **W** 🅖 Arco 🍴 Del Taco, Subway
128a	Garfield Blvd, **E** 🛏 Crown Plaza/casino 🄾 Home Depot, Office Depot, **W** 🅖 76
126b	Slauson Ave, Montebello, **E** 🅖 Shell/dsl, Valero/dsl 🍴 Mollie's Burger, Ozzie's Diner, Starbucks 🛏 Quality Inn, Travelodge, **W** 🅖 Arco 🍴 Denny's 🛏 Motel 6, Ramada Inn
126a	Paramount Blvd, Downey, **E** 🅖 Shell/Jack-in-the-Box/dsl
125	CA 19 S, Lakewood Blvd, Rosemead Blvd, **E** 🅖 Arco, Mobil 🍴 Arthurs Cafe, Sam's Burgers, Starbucks 🛏 EconoLodge, Guesthouse Inn, **W** 🍴 Chris&Pitt's BBQ, Golden Corral, McDonald's, Subway, Taco Bell, Toppings Pizza 🄾 Ralph's Foods
124	I-605
123	Florence Ave, to Downey, **E** 🅖 Mobil, **W** 🄾 Honda, repair
122	Imperial Hwy, Pioneer Blvd, **E** 🅖 Chevron 🍴 Applebee's, Habit Burgers, IHOP, Jack-in-the-Box, Jimmy John's, McDonald's, Panda Express, Pizza Hut, Subway, Wendy's, Wood Grill Buffet 🄾 O'Reilly Parts, Rite Aid, Target, USPO, **W** 🅖 7-11 🍴 Alberts Mexican, Denny's, Panda King, Pizza Hut, Rally's, Shakey's Pizza, Wienerschnitzel 🛏 Imperial Inn, Keystone Motel, Motel 6 🄾 Toyota, Walmart

NORWALK

121	San Antonio Dr, to Norwalk Blvd, **E** 🍴 IHOP, Jack-in-the-Box McDonald's, Outback Steaks, Starbucks, Wood Grill Buffet 🛏 Doubletree Inn 🄾 Rite Aid, Target, **W** 🅖 Shell 🄾 auto repair
120b	Firestone Blvd (exits left from nb)
120a	Rosecrans Ave, **E** 🅖 76/7-11/dsl 🍴 Casa Adelita, Jim's Burgers, KFC, Little Caesar's, Starbucks, Subway 🄾 🄷, **W** 🅖 Arco/24hr 🛏 Guesthouse Inn 🄾 El Monte RV Ctr
119	Carmenita Rd, Buena Park, **E** 🅖 Arco 🍴 Burger King 🄾 Ford Trucks, Lowe's, **W** 🍴 Galaxy Burgers 🛏 Budget Inn, Dynasty Suites
118	Valley View Blvd, **E** 🅖 Arco/dsl 🍴 In-N-Out, Northwoods Inn, Starbucks, Subway, Wendy's 🛏 Extended Stay America, Holiday Inn Select, Residence Inn, **W** 🄾 Thompson's RV Ctr, to Camping World
117	Artesia Blvd, Knott Ave, **E** 🅖 Chevron 🛏 Extended Stay America 🄾 CarMax, **W** 🄾 Knotts Berry Farm, to Camping World RV Ctr
116	CA 39, Beach Blvd, **E** 🅖 Chevron 🛏 Travelodge 🄾 BMW, Buick/GMC, CarMax, Chevrolet, Honda, Mercedes, Nissan, Tesla, Toyota, **W** 🅖 Chevron 🍴 Arby's, Black Angus, Denny's, Fuddruckers, KFC, Pizza Hut, Subway, Wendy's 🛏 Hilton, Holiday Inn 🄾 🄷, Stater Bros, Target, to Knotts Berry Farm, Verizon
115	Manchester (from nb), same as 116
114b	CA 91 E, Riverside Fwy, **E** 🄾 to 〰
114a	Magnolia Ave, Orangethorpe Ave, **E** 🅖 Mobil/dsl 🍴 Burger King, Burger Town, Taco Bell 🄾 7-11, Harley-Davidson
113c	CA 91 W (from nb)
113b a	Brookhurst St, LaPalma, **E** 🅖 Chevron/dsl 🍴 Subway, **W** 🅖 Arco, Texaco/dsl 🍴 Burger King, Carl's Jr, Starbucks 🄾 Home Depot, Staples
112	Euclid St, **E** 🅖 Arco 🍴 Happy Dragon, IHOP, Marie Callender's, McDonald's, Rubio's, Starbucks, Subway, Taco Bell, Wendy's 🄾 AAA, El Super, GNC, Old Navy, PetCo, Ross, TJ Maxx, Verizon, Walmart, **W** 🅖 76, Mobil 🍴 Charley's Subs, Denny's, KFC/LJ Silver, Subway, Wok Experience 🄾 Aldi Foods, Target, Verizon
111	Lincoln Ave, to Anaheim, **E** 🍴 La Villa Mexican, Ruby's Diner, Starbucks 🄾 vet
110b	Ball Rd (from sb), **E** 🅖 7-11, Chevron/dsl, Shell 🍴 Burger King, Carolina's Italian, El Pollo Loco, KFC, McDonald's, Shakey's Pizza, Starbucks, Subway, Taco Bell 🛏 Best Value Inn, Days Inn, Frontier Inn, Sheraton 🄾 Anaheim RV, Traveler's World RV Park, **W** 🅖 Arco/24hr, Shell/dsl 🛏 Best Western, Budget Inn, Holiday Inn, Majestic Garden Hotel, Staybridge Suites, Super 8, Travelodge 🄾 Disneyland, USPO
110a	Harbor Blvd, **E** 🅖 Chevron, Shell 🍴 Shakey's Pizza, Starbucks, Taco Bell 🛏 Days Inn, Frontier, Ramada 🄾 Anaheim Harbor RV Park, **0-2 mi W** 🍴 Captain Kidd's, Coldstone, Dennys, IHOP, McDonald's, Mimi's Cafe, Mortons Steaks, Panera Bread, Tony Roma's 🛏 Anaheim Resort, Best Western+, Camelot Inn, Candy Cane Inn, Castle Inn Suites, Clarion, Courtyard, Del Sol Inn, Fairfield Inn, Hampton Inn, Hilton Garden, Howard Johnson, Hyatt House, ParkVue Inn, Portofino Inn, Ramada Inn, Red Lion, Sheraton, Travelodge, Tropicana Inn 🄾 multiple hotels & restaurants, same as 109, to Disneyland
109	Katella Ave, Disney Way, **E** 🅖 Arco 🍴 Baskin-Robbins, Carl's Jr, Denny's, McDonald's, Panda Express, Starbucks, Subway, Togo's 🛏 TownePlace Suites 🄾 Angels Stadium, **W** 🅖 Chevron 🍴 Bubba Gump Shrimp, CA Pizza Kitchen, Cheesecake Factory, McCormick&Schmick, PF Chang's, Roy Roy's, Subway 🛏 Best Value Inn, Cambria, Comfort Inn, Desert Palms Suites

ANAHEIM

⬆N INTERSTATE 5 Cont'd

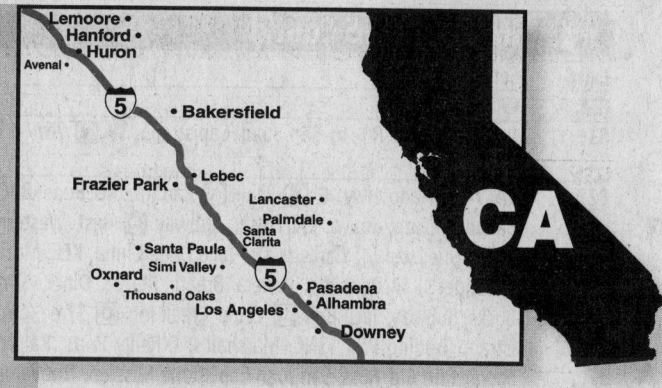

Exit	Description
109	Continued
	Extended Stay America, Hilton, Hotel Indigo, Hyatt House, Kings Inn, Little Boy Blue, Marriott, Peacock Suites, Ramada Inn, Residence Inn, Riviera Motel, SpringHill Suites, Staybridge Suites, Worldmark, Wyndham Garden 🅾 7-11, CVS, to Disneyland
107c	St Coll Blvd, City Drive, **E** 🍴 Del Taco 🛏 Embassy Suites, **W** 🛏 Alo Hotel, Ayres Hotel, Doubletree Hotel
107b a	CA 57 N, Chapman Ave, **E** 🍴 Burger King, Del Taco, Denny's, Jack-in-the-Box, Waba Grill 🛏 Motel 6, **W** 🍴 Chevron 🍴 Krispy Kreme, Lucille's BBQ, Starbucks, Taco Bell, Wendy's 🛏 Ayres Inn, DoubleTree 🅾 H, Best Buy
106	CA 22 W (from nb), Garden Grove Fwy, Bristol St
105b	N Broadway, Main St, **E** 🅿 7-11 🍴 Baskin-Robbins, CA Pizza Kitchen, Carl's Jr, Chipotle, Corner Bakery Cafe, Habit Burgers, Jamba Juice, Olive Garden, Papa Johns, Polly's Café, Rubio's Grill, Starbucks, Subway, Taco Bell, Togo's 🛏 Days Inn, Red Roof Inn 🅾 H, Barnes&Noble, CVS Drug, JC Penney, Macy's, Staples, Verizon, **W** 🛏 Golden West Motel, Travel Inn 🅾 Bowers Museum
105a	17th St, **E** 🅿 76/dsl/24hr 🍴 Hometown Buffet, IHOP, McDonald's 🅾 Chevrolet, CVS Drug, same as 104b, Walgreens, **W** 🅿 Chevron 🍴 YumYum Donuts 🅾 7-11
104b	Santa Ana Blvd, Grand Ave, **E** 🍴 Gavilan, Hometown Buffet, IHOP, KFC/LJ Silver, Marie Callender, McDonald's, Popeye's, Starbucks, Subway, Taco Bell, Taco Sinaloa, Waba Grill 🅾 $Tree, AT&T, CVS Drug, O'Reilly Parts, Target, vet, Walgreens, **W** 🅾 Kia
104a	(103c from nb), 4th St, 1st St, to CA 55 N, **E** 🅿 Chevron, Shell, US Gas 🍴 Del Taco
103b	CA 55 S, to Newport Beach
103a	CA 55 N (from nb), to Riverside
102	Newport Ave (from sb), **E** 🍴 Arby's, Jack-in-the-Box, **W** 🅿 Arco 🍴 Carl's Jr, Domino's, Little Caesar's 🅾 American Tire Depot
101b	Red Hill Ave, **E** 🅿 Mobil/dsl, Shell/repair 🍴 Del Taco, Denny's, Starbucks, Wendy's 🛏 Key Inn 🅾 BigLots, U-Haul, **W** 🅿 Arco/24hr, Chevron/24hr, Valero 🍴 Pizza Shack, Taco Bell 🅾 7-11, Stater Bros
101a	Tustin Ranch Rd, **E** 🍴 McDonald's 🅾 Acura, Buick/GMC, Cadillac, Chrysler/Dodge/Jeep, Costco, Ford/Lincoln, Hyundai, Infiniti, Lexus, Mazda, Nissan, Toyota
100	Jamboree Rd, **E** 🅿 Shell 🍴 Baja Fresh, BJ's Rest., Boston Mkt, Burger King, CA Pizza, Carl's Jr, Chick-fil-A, Corner Bakery, Daphne's Greek, DQ, El Pollo Loco, In-N-Out, Islands Burger, Lazy Dog Cafe, Macaroni Grill, Miguel's Mexican, Panda Express, Panera Bread, Pick-up Stix, Rubio's, Starbucks, Subway, Taco Bell, Taco Rosa 🅾 AAA, AT&T, Barnes&Noble, Best Buy, Costco, Dick's, Home Depot, Old Navy, Petsmart, Ralph's Foods, REI, Rite Aid, Ross, Sprouts Mkt, Target, TJ Maxx, Verizon
99	Culver Dr, **E** 🅿 Shell/24hr 🅾 vet, **W** 🍴 Buffalo Wild Wings, Domino's
97	Jeffrey Rd, **E** 🅿 Arco 🍴 Baskin-Robbins, Juice-it-Up, Starbucks, Subway 🅾 Albertson's, Kohl's, **W** 🅿 76/dsl 🍴 China Garden, Thai Cafe 🅾 99 Ranch Mkt, vet
96	Sand Canyon Ave, Old Towne, **W** 🅿 76/dsl 🍴 Denny's, Jack-in-the-Box, Knowlwood Burgers 🛏 La Quinta 🅾 H
95	CA 133 (**toll**), Laguna Fwy, N to Riverside, S Laguna Beach
94b	Alton Pkwy, **E** 🅿 Shell/Subway/dsl 🍴 Carl's Jr, Starbucks 🛏 Extended Stay America 🅾 Costco/gas, Office Depot, Walmart, **W** 🍴 Brio, CA Pizza, Capital Grill, Cheesecake Factory, Chipotle Mexican, Dave&Buster's, Johnny Rockets,

**Side labels (left margin):** TUSTIN / IRVINE

Side labels (right margin): LAGUNA HILLS / MISSION VIEJO

Exit	Description
94b	Continued
	Panda Express, PF Chang's, Pieology, Ruby's Diner, Starbucks, Wahoo's Fish Tacos, Wood Ranch, Yardhouse Rest. 🛏 Doubletree Inn 🅾 Barnes&Noble, Nordstrom, Old Navy, Target
94a	I-405 N (from nb)
92b	Bake Pkwy, **W** 🅾 CarMax, Toyota, same as 92a
92a	Lake Forest Dr, Laguna Hills, **E** 🅿 Chevron/24hr, Shell/dsl 🍴 Buffalo Wild Wings, Dickey's BBQ, IHOP, Jack-in-the-Box, McDonald's, Panera Bread, Peppino's Italian, RoundTable Pizza, Starbucks, Subway, Taco Bell, The Hat, Waba Grill, Which Wich? 🛏 Best Western, Holiday Inn, Quality Inn 🅾 America's Tire, AT&T, Chevrolet, Chrysler/Dodge/Jeep, Ford/Lincoln, Honda, Hyundai, Mazda, Nissan, Subaru, VW, **W** 🅿 Chevron/24hr, Shell 🍴 Carl's Jr, Coco's, Del Taco, McDonald's, Pizza 900, Subway 🛏 Comfort Inn, Courtyard 🅾 AZ Leather, Best Buy, BMW/Mini
91	El Toro Rd, **E** 🅿 Chevron/dsl, USA 🍴 Arby's, Asia Buffet, Baskin-Robbins, Cafe Rio, Chipotle Mexican, Corner Baker Cafe, Del Taco, Denny's, Dunkin', El Pollo Loco, Fuddrucker's, Habit Burger, Honeybaked Ham, Jack-in-the-Box, Jamba Juice, Jersey Mike's, Lucille's BBQ, Luna Grill, McDonald's, Mr Wok, Panda Express, PeiWei Asian, Sizzler, Subway, Tommy's Burgers 🅾 99c Store, AT&T, CVS Drug, Firestone/auto, Home Depot, Petsmart, Ralph's Foods, Ross, Staples, Verizon, **W** 🅿 76, Chevron/dsl 🍴 BJ's Rest., CA Pizza Kitchen, Cane's, Chick-fil-A, El Torito, FarmerBoys, In-N-Out, King's Fishhouse, Ruby's Diner, Starbucks, Subway 🛏 Laguna Hills Lodge 🅾 H, CVS Drug, Firestone/auto, Just Tires, Marshall's, Trader Joe's, USPO, Walgreens
90	Alicia Pkwy, Mission Viejo, **E** 🍴 Del Taco, Denny's, Five Guys, Subway 🅾 $Tree, America's Tire, AT&T, CVS Drug, O'Reilly Parts, Target, **W** 🅿 Chevron 🍴 Carl's Jr, Little Caesar's, Stefano's, Togo's, Wendy's 🅾 AAA, BigLots, Dick's, URGENT CARE, vet
89	La Paz Rd, Mission Viejo, **E** 🅿 Arco/24hr, Shell 🍴 Pizza Hut, Ralph's, Starbucks, Taco Bell, TK Burgers 🅾 vet, **W** 🅿 76/dsl 🍴 Cecilia's Grill, DQ, Dunkin', Flamingos Mexican, Hot Off the Grill, Jack-in-the-Box, Krispy Kreme, McDonald's, Outback Steaks, Starbucks, Villa Roma, Wienerschnitzel 🛏 Hills Hotel 🅾 7-11, Best Buy, Jo-Ann Fabrics, Midas, PetCo, to Laguna Niguel Pk
88	Oso Pkwy, Pacific Park Dr, **E** 🅿 76/dsl/repair, Chevron/repair 🍴 Carl's Jr, Starbucks, Subway 🛏 Fairfield Inn 🅾 golf
86	Crown Valley Pkwy, **E** 🅿 76, Arco, Chevron 🍴 Buffalo Wild Wings, Cheesecake Factory, Chili's, Islands Grill, Ruby's Diner 🅾 H, Macy's, vet, **W** 🅿 Chevron/dsl 🅾 Costco/gas
85b	Avery Pkwy, **E** 🅿 Shell/dsl 🍴 Broken Yolk, Coco's, Del Taco, Jack-in-the-Box, Jimmy John's, Mongolian BBQ, Papa John's, Starbucks, Subway 🛏 Hampton Inn 🅾 Acura, America's Tire/auto, Audi/Infiniti, Burlington, Jaguar/Land Rover, Lexus, Volvo, World Mkt, **W** 🅿 Arco/dsl, Chevron 🍴 A's Burgers, Carl's Jr, In-N-Out 🛏 Best Value Laguna Inn 🅾 American Tire Depot, Cadillac/GMC, Costco/gas, Hyundai, Mercedes

INTERSTATE 5 Cont'd

Exit #	Services
85a	CA 73 N (toll)
83	Junipero Serra Rd, to San Juan Capistrano, W 🅿 76/7-11, Shell
82	CA 74, Ortego Hwy, E 🅿 Shell 🍴 Bad to the Bone BBQ, Ballpark Pizza, Bravo CA Fresh, Subway 🛏 Best Western, W 🅿 Shell/dsl 🍴 Carl's Jr, Del Taco, Jade China, KFC, Marie Callender's, McDonald's, Panera Bread, Ruby's Diner, Starbucks, Subway, Taco Bell 🛏 Cedar Creek Inn 🅾 $Tree, Capistrano Trading Post, GNC, Marshall's, O'Reilly Parts, Ralph's Foods, Rite Aid, Ross, San Juan Capistrano Mission, TrueValue, Verizon
81	Camino Capistrano, E 🅾 W on Capistrano 🅿 Shell 🍴 Baskin Robbins, Domino's, El Adobe Rest., Eng's Chinese, KFC, Pizza Hut, Ricardo's Mexican, Starbucks 🛏 Residence Inn 🅾 CHP, Chrysler/Dodge/Jeep, Ford, Goodyear/auto, Honda, Nissan, PetCo, Rite Aid, Ross, San Juan Capistrano SP (1mi), Toyota, Trader Joe's, Vons Foods
79	CA 1, Pacific Coast Hwy, Capistrano Bch, Capistrano, W 🅿 Arco/24hr, Chevron/dsl, Costco/gas 🍴 A's Burgers, Carl's Jr, Del Taco, Denny's, El Pollo Loco, Jack-in-the-Box, McDonald's, Subway 🛏 Best Western, DoubleTree 🅾 $Tree, Aamco, AutoZone, Petsmart, Ralph's Foods, Rite Aid, Staples, USPO, vet
78	Camino de Estrella, San Clemente, E 🅿 76/dsl 🍴 China Well, Flame Broiler, Habit Burger, RoundTable Pizza, Rubio's, Starbucks, Subway, Wahoo's Fish Taco 🅾 🄷 AAA, CVS Drug, Ralph's Foods, Stater Bros Foods, Trader Joe's, vet, W 🅿 USA/dsl 🍴 Las Golondrinas 🅾 O'Reilly Parts, Sprouts Mkt, TJ Maxx
77	Ave Vista Hermosa
76	Ave Pico, E 🅿 Mobil/Circle K 🍴 Chipotle, Golden Spoon, Juice it Up, McDonald's, Panda Express, SmashBurger 🅾 Albertson's/Sav-On, GNC, W 🅿 Chevron 🍴 Del Taco, Denny's/24hr, Pick-up-Stix, Pizza Hut, Stuft Pizza, Subway 🛏 Holiday Inn Express 🅾 99c Store, Outlets/famous brands, Staples, tires/repair, Tuesday Morning, USPO, vet
75	Ave Palizada, Ave Presidio, W 🅿 Valero 🍴 Baskin-Robbins, Mr. Pete's Burgers, Sonny's Pizza, Starbucks, Subway, Taka-O Japanese 🛏 Holiday Inn 🅾 7-11, AutoZone, CVS Drug, Rite Aid, TrueValue
74	El Camino Real, E 🅿 Chevron/dsl 🛏 Budget Lodge, San Clemente Inn, Tradewinds Motel 🅾 same as 75, W 🅿 76/dsl 🍴 Biggie's Burger, Subway, Taco Bell, Tommy's Rest. 🅾 7-11, O'Reilly Parts, Ralph's Foods
73	Ave Calafia, Ave Magdalena, E 🅿 76/dsl, Shell 🍴 Jack-in-the-Box, Molly Bloom's Cafe, Pedro's Tacos, Sugar Shack Cafe 🛏 Calafia Beach Motel, C-Vu Inn, Hampton Inn, LaVista Inn, San Clemente Motel, Travelodge 🅾 7-11, repair/tires, W to San Clemente SP
72	Cristianitos Ave, E 🍴 Cafe Del Sol, Carl's Jr. 🛏 Comfort Suites, San Clemente Surf Inn 🅾 San Mateo RV Park/dump, W 🅾 to San Clemente SP
71	Basilone Rd, W 🅾 San Onofre St Beach
67mm	**weigh sta both lanes**
66mm	**viewpoint sb**
62	Las Pulgas Rd
59mm	**Aliso Creek** 🆁🆂 **both lanes, full 🅰 facilities, litter barrels, petwalk, 🄲, 🕭, RV dump, vending**
54c	Oceanside Harbor Dr, W 🅿 Chevron, Mobil 🍴 Del Taco, Denny's/24hr 🛏 Days Inn, Harbor Inn, Holiday Inn 🅾 to Camp Pendleton
54b	Hill St (from sb), to Oceanside, W 🅿 Chevron, Mobil 🍴 Denny's, In-N-Out 🛏 Days Inn, Holiday Inn, Rodeway Inn
54a	CA 76 E, Coast Hwy
53	Mission Ave, Oceanside, E 🅿 7-11/dsl, Arco/24hr, Mobil, dsl 🍴 Alberto's Mexican, Arby's, Armando's Tacos, Armando's Tacos, Burger King, Jack-in-the-Box, KFC, McDonald's, Starbucks 🛏 Ramada, Travelodge 🅾 Bussry's Automotive, CarQuest, El Super Mkt, W 🍴 El Pollo Loco, Panda Express, Subway, Wendy's 🅾 99c Store, AutoZone, Walmart Mkt
52	Oceanside Blvd, E 🅿 Arco 🍴 Alberto's Mexican, IHOP, McDonald's, Pizza Hut, Starbucks, Subway, Taco Bell, Wienerschnitzel 🅾 $Tree, CVS Drug, Frazier Farms Mkt, W 🅿 GM/dsl 🛏 Best Western
51c	Cassidy St (from sb)
51b	CA 78, Vista Way, Escondido, E 🅿 Chevron/dsl, Shell 🍴 Applebee's, Boston Mkt, Buffalo Wild Wings, Burger King, Carl's Jr, Cheesecake Factory, Chili's, Chipotle, ChuckECheese's, Dave&Buster's, Domino's, Islands Rest., Jersey Mike's, Macaroni Grill, McDonald's, Mimi's Café, Olive Garden, Outback Steaks, QuikWok, Red Lobster, Rubio's, Starbucks, Subway, TX Roadhouse 🅾 $Tree, Best Buy, CVS Drug, Dick's, Firestone/auto, JC Penney, Macy's, Marshall's, Michael's, PetCo, Sprouts Mkt, Staples, Stater Bros Foods, Target, Tuesday Morning, Verizon, Vons Foods, Walmart, World Mkt, W 🍴 Hunter Steaks
51a	Las Flores Dr
50	Elm Ave, Carlsbad Village Dr, E 🅿 Shell 🍴 Lotus Thai Bistro, W 🅿 7-11 🍴 Al's Cafe, Carl's Jr, Denny's/24hr, Jack-in-the-Box, KFC/Taco Bell, Mikko Japanese, Subway 🛏 Extended Stay America, Motel 6 🅾 Albertson's, TrueValue
49	Tamarack Ave, E 🅿 76/dsl, Chevron 🍴 Village Kitchen 🛏 Days Inn 🅾 Rite Aid, Vons Foods, W 🅿 Arco 🍴 Stag&Lion Grille
48	Cannon Rd, Car Country Carlsbad, E 🅾 Acura, Buick/GMC/Cadillac, Chevrolet, Chrysler/Dodge/Jeep, Ford, Honda, Kia, Lexus, Lincoln, Mazda, Mercedes, VW, W 🅿 West Mart 🍴 West Steak&Seafood 🛏 Hyatt House, West Inn
47	Carlsbad Blvd, Palomar Airport Rd, E 🅿 7-11, Chevron, Mobil/dsl 🍴 BJ's Rest., Carl's Jr, Corner Bakery Cafe, Islands Burgers, Kings Fish House, Panda Express, PF Chang's, Ruby's Diner, SeaFire Rest., Starbucks, Strauss Brewery Rest., Subway, Taco Bell 🛏 Carlsbad by the Sea, Motel 6 🅾 AT&T, Carlsbad Ranch/Flower Fields, Chrysler/Dodge/Jeep, Costco/gas, Ford, GNC, outlet, W 🅿 Shell/dsl 🍴 In-N-Out, McDonald's, Miguel's Mexican, Pisco Rotisserie 🛏 Hilton Garden 🅾 S Carlsbad St Bch
45	Poinsettia Lane, W 🅿 Shell/dsl 🍴 Benihana, El Pollo Loco, Jack-in-the-Box, Pick-Up Stix, Starbucks, Subway 🛏 Holiday Inn Express, La Quinta, Motel 6, Ramada 🅾 Ace Hardware, Porsche/Volvo, Ralph's Foods, Rite Aid
44	La Costa Ave, E vista point, W 🅿 Chevron/dsl
43	Leucadia Blvd, E 🛏 Quality Inn, W 🅿 Shell/service 🍴 Starbucks
42b	Encinitas Blvd, E 🅿 Chevron/dsl, Mobil, Valero 🍴 Honey Baked Ham, In-N-Out, Oggi's Pizza 🅾 CVS Drug, NAPA, Petco, to Quail Botanical Gardens, vet, W 🅿 Shell 🍴 Denny's, Little Caesar's, Subway, Wendy's 🛏 Best Western/rest., Days Inn
41a	Santa Fe' Dr, to Encinitas, E 🅿 Shell 🍴 Carl's Jr, El Nopali, to 🅾 7-11, W 🍴 Domino's, Schooner Pizza 🅾 🄷, Rite Aid, vet, Vons Foods
40	Birmingham Dr, E 🅿 Chevron, Valero 🍴 El Pueblo 🛏 Holiday Inn Express, W 🅿 Arco
39mm	**viewpoint sb**
39	Manchester Ave, E 🅿 🅾 to MiraCosta College

Side labels: CA / CAPISTRANO / SAN CLEMENTE / OCEANSIDE / CARLSBAD / ENCINITAS

INTERSTATE 5 Cont'd

Exit #	Services
37	Lomas Santa Fe Dr, Solana Bch, **E** 🍴 Baskin-Robbins, Habit Burger, Jersey Mike's, Pizza Nova, Samurai Rest., Starbucks Ⓞ Vons Foods, We-R-Fabrics, **W** 🅶 Mobil 🍴 Carl's Jr, Jamba Juice, Panda Express, Panera Bread, Starbucks Ⓞ AT&T, CVS Drug, Discount Tire, GNC, Marshall's, Sprouts Mkt, Staples
36	Via de La Valle, Del Mar, **E** 🅶 Chevron, Mobil 🍴 Chipotle, Coffee Bean, McDonald's, Milton's Deli, Taste of Thai, Urban Pizza Ⓞ Albertson's/SavOn, Gelson's Mkt, PetCo, Verizon, Whole Foods Mkt, **W** 🅶 Arco/24hr, Shell/dsl 🍴 Denny's, FishMkt Rest., Red Tracton's Rest. 🛏 Hilton Ⓞ racetrack
34	Del Mar Heights Rd, **E** 🅶 Shell/dsl, **W** 🅶 7-11 🍴 Broken Yolk Cafe, Bushfire Kitchen, Jack-in-the-Box, Jersey Mike's, Starbucks Ⓞ AAA, CVS Drug, vet, Vons Foods
33	Carmel Mtn Rd, **E** 🅶 Arco, Shell/repair 🍴 Ruth's Chris, Taco Bell, Tio Leo's Mexican 🛏 DoubleTree Hotel, Hampton Inn, Marriott, Residence Inn
32	CA 56 E, Carmel Valley Rd
31	I-805 (from sb)
30	Sorrento Valley Rd
29	Genesee Ave, **E** Ⓞ 🅷
28b	La Jolla Village Dr, **E** 🛏 Embassy Suites, Hyatt, Marriott Ⓞ 🅷, to LDS Temple, **W** 🅶 Mobil/dsl 🍴 BJ's Rest., CA Pizza Kitchen, Chipotle Mexican, Dominos, Flame Broiler, Islands Burgers, Jamba Juice, Mrs Gooch's, RockBottom Café, Rubio's, Starbucks 🛏 Sheraton Ⓞ AT&T, Best Buy, CVS Drug, Marshall's, PetsMart, Ralph's Foods, Ross, Trader Joe's, Verizon, Whole Foods Mkt
28a	Nobel Dr (from nb), **E** 🛏 Hyatt Ⓞ LDS Temple, **W** same as 28b
27	Gilman Dr, La Jolla Colony Dr
26b	CA 52 E
26a	La Jolla Rd (from nb)
23b	CA 274, Balboa Ave, **E** 🍴 Del Taco, Starbucks Ⓞ 🅷, Costco/gas, **W** 🅶 7-11, 76/repair 🍴 In-N-Out, McDonald's, Rubio's, Sonic, Wienerschnitzel 🛏 Holiday Inn Express, La Quinta, Red Roof Inn, San Diego Motel Ⓞ Discount Tire, Ford, Mission Bay Pk, Nissan, Toyota
23a	Grand Ave, Garnet Ave, same as 23b
22	Clairemont Dr, Mission Bay Dr, **E** 🅶 Shell, USA 🛏 Best Western Ⓞ Chevrolet, VW, **W** to Sea World Dr
21	Sea World Dr, Tecolote Dr, **E** 🅶 Shell 🛏 Seaside Inn Ⓞ Aamco, Circle K, PetCo, **W** 🛏 Hilton Ⓞ Old Town SP, Seaworld
20	I-8, **W** to Nimitz Blvd, **E** to El Centro, CA 209 S (from sb), to Rosecrans St
19	Old Town Ave, **E** 🅶 Arco, Shell 🛏 Courtyard, La Quinta
18b	Washington St, **E** 🛏 Holiday Inn Express
18a	Pacific Hwy Viaduct, Kettner St
17b	India St, Front St, Sassafras St, **E** 🅶 Mobil, **W** Ⓞ 🖃
17a	Hawthorn St, Front St, **E** Ⓞ 🅷, **W** 🅶 Mobil/dsl 🛏 Motel 6, Sheraton
16b	6th Ave, downtown
16a	CA 163 N, 10th St, **E** Ⓞ 🅷, AeroSpace Museum, **W** 🅶 Shell 🍴 Burger King, Del Taco, Jack-in-the-Box, McDonald's 🛏 Days Inn, Downtown Lodge, El Cortez Motel, Holiday Inn, Marriott
15c b	CA 94 E (from nb), Pershing Dr, B St, **W** Ⓞ civic ctr
15a	CA 94 E, J St, Imperial Ave (from sb)
14b	Cesar Chavez Pkwy
14a	CA 75, to Coronado, **W** toll rd to Coronado

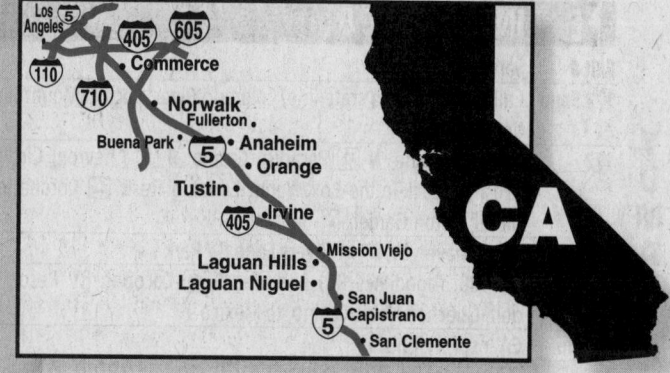

Exit #	Services
13b	National Ave SD, 28th St, **E** 🍴 Jack-in-the-Box, Little Caesar's, Panda Express, Starbucks, Subway Ⓞ AutoZone, **W** 🅶 Shell 🍴 Burger King, Del Taco, El Pollo Loco, McDonald's
13a	CA 15 N, to Riverside
12	Main St, National City
11b	8th St, National City, **E** 🅶 Arco 🍴 Jack-in-the-Box 🛏 Cassia Hotel, Howard Johnson, National City Inn, Ramada Inn, Rodeway Inn
11a	Harbor Dr, Civic Center Dr
10	Bay Marina, 24th St, Mile of Cars Way, **E** 🍴 Chick-fil-A, Chipotle, Denny's, Freddy's, In-N-Out, Jersey Mike's, Starbucks, **W** 🛏 Best Western+
9	CA 54 E
8b	E St, Chula Vista, **E** 🍴 Arco, Black Angus, Denny's, Taco Bell 🛏 Days Inn, Motel 6, **W** 🛏 GoodNite Inn
8a	H St
7b	J St (from sb)
7a	L St, **E** 🅶 76, Shell/dsl 🛏 China Vista Inn Ⓞ NAPA
6	Palomar St, **E** 🅶 Arco 🍴 Carl's Jr., DQ, HomeTown Buffet, IHOP, KFC, Little Caesar's, McDonald's, Panda Express, Starbucks, Subway 🛏 Palomar Inn Ⓞ $Tree, 7-11, Costco/gas, Food4Less, Jack-in-the-Box, Michael's, Office Depot, Petco, Ross, Target, Walmart, Yoshinoya, **W** 🅶 Valero
5b	Main St, to Imperial Beach, **E** 🅶 Arco
5a	CA 75 (from sb), Palm Ave, to Imperial Beach, **E** 🅶 Arco, USA 🍴 Armando's Mexican, Papa John's, Starbucks Ⓞ 7-11, Discount Tire, Soto's Transmissions, **W** 🅶 7-11, 76, Arco, Shell 🍴 Boll Weevil Diner, Burger King, Carl's Jr, Coldstone Creamery, IHOP, McDonald's, Rally's, Subway, Wienerschnitzel 🛏 Prime Inn, Super 8 Ⓞ 99c Store, AutoZone, CVS Drug, GNC, Home Depot, Von's Foods, Walmart
4	Coronado Ave (from sb), **E** 🅶 Chevron/service, Shell/service 🍴 Taco Bell 🛏 EZ 8 Motel Ⓞ 7-11, **W** 🅶 Arco, Hollister/dsl 🍴 Denny's 🛏 Motel 6 Ⓞ to Border Field SP
3	CA 905, Tocayo Ave, **W** 🅶 7-11
2	Dairy Mart Rd, **E** 🅶 Arco/24hr 🍴 Burger King, Carl's Jr, Coco's, KFC, McDonald's 🛏 Best Western Ⓞ Pacifica RV Resort, **W** 🛏 Quality Inn
1b	Via de San Ysidro, **W** 🅶 Chevron, Mobil/dsl 🍴 Denny's 🛏 Knights/RV park, Motel 6, Travelodge
1a	I-805 N (from nb), Camino de la Plaza (from sb), **E** 🍴 Burger King, Jack-in-the-Box, KFC, McDonald's, Subway 🛏 Holiday Motel Ⓞ AutoZone, **W** 🍴 Achiato Mexican, IHOP, Iron Wok, McDonald's, Starbucks, Sunrise Buffet Ⓞ $Tree, Baja Duty-Free, border parking, factory outlet, Marshall's, Old Navy, Ross, TJ Maxx

California state line, US/Mexico Border, customs, I-5 begins/ends.

Side margin labels: LA JOLLA · SAN DIEGO AREA · SAN DIEGO AREA · SAN YSIDRO [gas icon] = gas   [food icon] = food   [lodging icon] = lodging   [other icon] = other   [Rs] = rest stop   Copyright 2022 - The Next EXIT ®

INTERSTATE 8

Exit #	Services
172.5mm	California/Arizona state line, Colorado River, Pacific/Mountain time zone
172	4th Ave, Yuma, N [other] Paradise Casino, S [gas] Chevron, Circle K/dsl [food] Jack-in-the-Box, Yuma Landing Rest. [lodging] Coronado Motel, Hilton Garden [other] to Yuma SP
170	Winterhaven Dr, S [other] Rivers Edge RV Park
166	CA 186, Algodones Rd, Andrade, S [other] Cocopah RV Resort/golf, Quechan Hotel/Casino, to Mexico
165mm	CA Insp/weigh sta
164	Sidewinder Rd, N [other] st patrol, S [gas] Chevron/LP/dsl [other] Pilot Knob RV Park
159	CA 34, Ogilby Rd, to Blythe
156	Grays Well Rd, N Imperial Dunes RA
155mm	[Rs] both lanes (exits left), full facilities, litter barrels, petwalk, [icon]
151	Gordons Well
146	Brock Research Ctr Rd
143	CA 98, to Calexico, Midway Well
131	CA 115, VanDerLinden Rd, to Holtville, 5 mi N [other] food, gas, lodging, RV camping
128	Bonds Corner Rd
125	CA 7 S, Orchard Rd, Holtville, 4 mi N [other] food, gas/dsl
120	Bowker Rd
118b a	CA 111, to Calexico, N [other] Country Life RV Park
116	Dogwood Rd, S [gas] Arco/dsl, Tesla EVC [food] Buffalo Wild Wings, Burger King, Carino's, Chili's, ChuckeCheese, Denny's, Famous Dave's BBQ, Fortune Garden, Jack-in-the-Box, Olive Garden, Sombrero Mexican, Starbucks, Subway [lodging] Fairfield Inn, Hampton Inn, TownePlace Suites [other] $Tree, 99c, AT&T, Best Buy, Dillard's, Discount Tire, JC Penney, Kohl's, Macy's, Marshall's, Michael's, PetCo, Ross, Staples
115	CA 86, 4th St, El Centro, N [gas] 7-11/dsl, Arco/dsl, Chevron/dsl, FillCo/dsl, Shell/dsl [food] Carl's Jr, Exotic Thai, Jack-in-the-Box, Las Palmitas Tacos, Lucky Chinese, McDonald's [lodging] Holiday Inn Express, Motel 6 [other] Family$, O'Reilly Parts, U-Haul, S [gas] 7-11/Subway, Mobil/dsl/scales [food] Habit Burger, IHOP, In-N-Out, Johnny's Burritos, Korean BBQ, Panda Express, Starbucks, Taco Bell [lodging] Best Value Inn, Best Western, Comfort Inn, Mainstay Inn [other] AutoZone, Buick/Chevrolet/GMC/Cadillac, Desert Trails RV Park, Home Depot, Honda, Hyundai
114	Imperial Ave, El Centro, 0-3 mi N [gas] 7-11/dsl, Arco, Chevron/dsl, USA/dsl [food] Applebee's, Broken Yolk Cafe, Burrito Factory, Carl's Jr, Carrow's, Church's, Coldstone, Del Taco, Denny's, Domino's, El Pollo Loco, Farmer Boys, Hamburger Stand, Jack-in-the-Box, Jack-in-the-Box, KFC, La Resaca, Little Caesar's, McDonald's, Papa John's, Pizza Hut, Rally's, Sizzler, Sonic, Starbucks, Subway, Taco Bell, Wendy's [lodging] Crown Motel, Days Inn, Quality Inn, Super 8, Travelodge/RV Park, Value Inn [other] [H], $General Mkt, $Tree, 99c Store, Aldi Foods, Chrysler/Dodge/Jeep, Costco/gas, CVS Drug, Discount Tire, Food4Less, Ford, Goodyear/auto, Jo-Ann, Kia, Lowe's, Nissan, O'Reilly Parts, PepBoys, Petsmart, Rite Aid, Ross, st patrol, Target, Toyota, Verizon, Von's Foods, VW, Walgreens, Walmart
111	Forrester Rd, to Westmorland
108mm	Sunbeam Rest Area both lanes, full [icon] facilities, litter barrels, petwalk, [icon], RV dump
107	Drew Rd, Seeley, N [other] Sunbeam RV Park, to Sunbeam Lake, S [other] Rio Bend RV Park
101	Dunaway Rd, elev 0 ft, Imperial Valley, N [other] st prison

89	Imperial Hwy, CA 98, Ocotillo, N [other] Red Feathers Mkt/Cafe, RV camping, USPO, S [gas] Chevron/dsl [other] Desert Museum
87	CA 98 (from eb), to Calexico
81mm	runaway truck ramp eb
80	Mountain Springs Rd
77	In-ko-pah Park Rd, N [food], towing
75mm	brake insp area eb
73	Jacumba, S [gas] Chevron/dsl, Shell/Subway/dsl/24hr
65	CA 94, Boulevard, to Campo, S [gas] MtnTop/dsl [food] Manzanita Diner [lodging] Back Country Inn [other] to McCain Valley RA (7mi), USPO
63mm	Tecate Divide, elev 4140 ft
62mm	Crestwood Summit, elev 4190 ft
61	Crestwood Rd, Live Oak Springs, S [gas] Golden Acorn Trkstp/casino/dsl [other] info
54	Kitchen Creek Rd, Cameron Station, S food, RV camping
51	rd 1, Buckman Spgs Rd, to Lake Morena, [Rs] both lanes, full [icon] facilities, litter barrels, petwalk, [icon], [icon], RV dump S food, gas/dsl/LP, Lake Morena CP (7mi), lodging, Potrero CP (19mi), RV camping
48	insp sta wb
47	rd 1, Sunrise Hwy, Laguna Summit, elev 4055 ft, N to Laguna Mtn RA
45	Pine Valley, Julian, N [food] Frosty Burger, Major's Diner [lodging] Pine Valley Inn [other] city park, Mtn Mkt, Pine Valley/gas, to Cuyamaca Rancho SP, USPO, vet
44mm	Pine Valley Creek
42mm	elev 4000 ft
40	CA 79, Japatul Rd, Descanso, N [food] Descanso Rest. [other] to Cuyamaca Rancho SP
37mm	vista point eb, elev 3000 ft
36	E Willows, N [other] Alpine Sprs RV Park, casino, Viejas Indian Res
33	W Willows Rd, to Alpine, same as 36, N [other] Alpine Sprs RV Park, casino, Viejas Outlets/famous brands, S [other] ranger sta
31mm	elev 2000 ft
30	Tavern Rd, to Alpine, N [gas] Chevron/dsl, Shell/dsl, S [gas] Phillips 66/Circle K, Tesla EVC [food] American Grill, Carl's Jr, Greek Village Grill, La Carreta, Little Caesar's, Mananas Mexican, Mediterraneo Grill, Panda Machi Chinese [lodging] Ayre's Lodge [other] Ace Hardware, CVS Drug, Rite Aid
27	Dunbar Lane, Harbison Canyon, N [other] Flinn Sprgs CP, RV camping
25mm	elev 1000 ft
24mm	[icon]
23	Lake Jennings Pk Rd, Lakeside, N [gas] Mobil/Jack-in-the-Box, dsl/24hr, to Lake Jennings CP [other] RV camping, S [gas] 7-11 [food] Burger King, Marechiaro's Pizza
22	Los Coches Rd, Lakeside, N [gas] 7-11, Eagle/dsl/LP, East County Gas [food] Albert's Mexican, Giant Pizza, Laposta Mexican [other] RV camping/dump, S [gas] Shell/dsl [food] Denny's, McDonald's, Panda Express, Subway, Taco Bell [other] Walmart
20b	Greenfield Dr, to Crest, N [gas] Chevron/dsl, Sky Fuel dsl [food] Jack-in-the-Box, Janet's Cafe, Marieta's Mexican, McDonald's, Panchos Tacos, Subway [other] 7-11, 99c Store, Albertson's, auto repair, AutoZone, Ford, RV camping, st patrol, URGENT CARE, vet, S [gas] Mobil/dsl/LP
20a	E Main St (from wb, no EZ return), N [lodging] Budget Inn [other] Ford Vacationer RV Park, S [gas] Arco [other] Combs RV Ctr
19	2nd St, CA 54, El Cajon, N [gas] Arco, Chevron/dsl, Phillips 66 dsl [food] Marechiaro's Italian, Pancake House [other] CVS Drug, Genie Auto Ctr, USPO, S [gas] Gas Depot, Golden State/dsl, Shell [food] Arby's, Baskin-Robbins, Carl's Jr, Chipotle, El Charrito, El Compadre Tacos, IHOP, Jack-in-the-Box, Jamba Juice, KFC, Little Caesar's, McDonald's, Popeye's, Starbucks, Subway, Taco Bell

Vertical side labels: YUMA, CA, EL CENTRO, LAKESIDE

INTERSTATE 8 Cont'd

19	Continued
	Wing Stop, Wings n Things 🏠 Best Value Inn 🅾 $Tree, 7-11, CarQuest, Firestone/auto, Grocery Outlet, Jiffy Lube, PepBoys, PetCo, Sprouts Mkt, Walgreens, Walmart Mkt
18	Mollison Ave, El Cajon, **N** 🅶 Chevron 🍴 Denny's, Starbucks 🏠 Best Western, Days Inn, Quality Inn, **S** 🅶 Arco, QuickTrip/dsl 🍴 Los Garcia's 🏠 EconoLodge
17c	Magnolia Ave, CA 67 (from wb), to Santee, **N** 🅶 Arco 🍴 Black Angus Steaks, Del Taco, El Pollo Loco, Jack-in-the-Box, Jersey Mike's, Panda Express, Starbucks 🅾 AT&T, Food4Less, Target, **S** 🅶 EVC, Shell/service/dsl 🍴 Panda Express, Perry's Cafe, Rubio's, Super Buffet 🏠 Courtyard, Motel 6, Super 8 🅾 Nudo's Drug, Ross
17b	CA 67 (from eb), same as 17 a&c
17a	Johnson Ave (from eb), **N** 🅶 EVC 🍴 Applebee's, Black Bear Diner, Boston Mkt, Burger King, Carl's Jr, Dunkin', Five Guys, Fuerte's NY, Hacienda Mexican, In-N-Out, Jamba Juice, KFC, Little Caesar's, LJ Silver, McDonald's, New Century Buffet, O's American Kitchen, Panera Bread, Rubio's, Subway 🅾 $Tree, Best Buy, CVS Drug, Dick's, Home Depot, Honda, JC Penney, Lexus, Macy's, Marshall's, Mercedes, Office Depot, PetsMart, Subaru, Tire Choice/auto, Toyota, Walmart, **S** 🅾 Aamco, Kia, Mazda, vet
16	Main St, **N** 🅶 Arco 🍴 Denny's, Sombrero Mexican 🏠 Relax Inn 🅾 7-11, **S** 🅶 Chevron/dsl, Super Star 🅾 brakes/transmissions, Nissan
15	El Cajon Blvd (from eb), **N** 🏠 Rodeway Inn, **S** 🅶 76/dsl 🍴 Wrangler BBQ 🅾 BMW
14c	Severin Dr, Fuerte Dr (from wb), **N** 🅶 Shell/dsl, Tesla EVC 🍴 Anthony's Fish Grotto, Charcoal House Rest., La Casa Blanca 🏠 Best Western+, **S** 🍴 Brigantine Seafood Rest.
14b a	CA 125, to CA 94
13b	Jackson Dr, Grossmont Blvd, **N** 🅶 Chevron 🍴 BJ's Rest., Casa de Pico, Chili's, ChuckeCheese, ClaimJumper, Fuddrucker's, Olive Garden, Panda Express, Panera Bread, Red Lobster, Starbucks, Vallarta Express 🅾 🅷 $Tree, Best Buy, CVS Drug, Macy's, Office Depot, O'Reilly Parts, Petco, Target, USPO, Verizon, vet, Walmart, World Mkt, **S** 🅶 Phillips 66/Circle K 🍴 Honeybaked Ham, Jack-in-the-Box, Jersey Mike's 🅾 Discount Tire, Ford, Hobby Lobby, Hyundai, Ross, Walmart Mkt
13a	Spring St (from eb), El Cajon Blvd (from wb), **S** 🍴 El Pollo Loco, El Torito, Starbucks, Subway 🏠 Hitching Post 🅾 99c Store, AutoZone
12	Fletcher Pkwy, to La Mesa, **N** 🅶 Shell/dsl 🍴 Carl's Jr, Chick-fil-A, Chipotle Mexican, Habit Burger, McDonald's, Pick Up Stix 🏠 Heritage Inn, Holiday Inn 🅾 7-11, Costco, **S** 🍴 El Torito, Starbucks, Subway 🏠 Motel 6 🅾 99c Store, Chevrolet, San Diego RV Resort
11	70th St, Lake Murray Blvd, **N** 🅶 Shell/dsl 🍴 Subway, **S** 🅶 Shell/7-11/dsl 🍴 Akin's Deli, Denny's, Marie Callender's 🅾 🅷 auto repair, URGENT CARE
10	College Ave, **N** 🅶 Chevron/dsl 🅾 Windmill Farms Mkt, **S** 🅾 🅷 to SDSU
9	Waring Rd, **N** 🏠 Days Inn, Rodeway Inn
8	Fairmount Ave (7 from eb), to Mission Gorge Rd, **N** 🅶 7-11, Arco/dsl, Mobil, Sky/dsl 🍴 Black Angus, Carl's Jr, Chili's, Denny's, El Pollo Loco, Jack-in-the-Box, Jamba Juice, Jersey Mike's, McDonald's, Rolando's Tacos, Rubio's, Sombrero Mexican, Starbucks, Subway, Szechuan Chinese, Taco Fiesta, Wendy's 🅾 🅷 AutoZone, CVS Drug, Discount Tire, Home Depot, Honda, Rite Aid, Toyota, Tuesday Morning, Vons Foods
7b a	I-15 N, CA 15 S, to 40th St
6b	I-805, N to LA, S to Chula Vista

SAN DIEGO AREA / POINT LOMA

6a	Texas St, Qualcomm Way, same as 5, **N** 🍴 Dave&Buster's
5	Mission Ctr Rd, **N** 🅶 Chevron, EVC 🍴 Broken Yolk Cafe, Buffalo Wild Wings, Chipotle Mexican, Corner Cafe, El Pollo Loco, Habit Burger, Hooters, In-N-Out, King's Fish House, Lazy Dog Rest., Mimi's Cafe, On The Border, Outback Steaks, Panda Express, Pei Wei, Pick-Up Stix, Robek Juice, Rubio's, Sammy's Woodfired Pizza, Starbucks, Subway, Taco Bell 🏠 Marriott, SpringHill Suites 🅾 AT&T, Best Buy, Chevrolet, Lincoln, Marshall's, Michael's, Nordstrom Rack, Old Navy, Staples, Target, Trader Joe's, **S** 🍴 Benihana, Denny's, Fuji Japanese, Wendy's 🏠 Hilton, Homewood Suites, La Quinta, Quality Suites, Sheraton 🅾 Buick/GMC/Cadillac, Chrysler/Dodge/Jeep, Mazda
4c b	CA 163, Cabrillo Frwy, **S** 🅾 to downtown, zoo
4a	Hotel Circle Dr (from eb), CA 163 (from wb)
3a	Hotel Circle, Taylor St, **N** 🍴 Hunter Steaks 🏠 Comfort Suites, Crowne Plaza, Handlery Hotel, Motel 6, Town&Country Motel 🅾 golf, **S** 🅶 Tesla EVC 🏠 Best Western, Candlewood Suites, Courtyard, Days Hotel, DoubleTree Inn, Extended Stay America, Hampton Inn, Holiday Inn Express, Homewood Suites, Hotel Iris, Howard Johnson, King's Inn/rest., Quality Inn, Residence Inn, Super 8 🅾 vet
2c	Morena Blvd (from wb)
2b	I-5, N to LA, S to San Diego
2a	Rosecrans St (from wb), CA 209, **S** 🅶 Shell 🍴 Chipotle Mexican, ChuckECheese, Del Taco, Denny's, In-N-Out, Panda Express, Starbucks, Subway 🏠 Goodnite Inn, Sheraton 🅾 Staples
1	W Mission Bay Blvd, Sports Arena Blvd (from wb), **N** 🅾 to SeaWorld, **S** 🍴 Arby's, Buffalo Wild Wings, Chick-fil-A, Chili's, Denny's, Jack-in-the-Box, McDonald's, Phil's BBQ, Red Lobster, Wendy's 🏠 Green World Inn, Holiday Inn Express, Wyndham Garden 🅾 Dick's, Home Depot, Ralph's, Target, U-Haul, Von's
0mm	I-8 begins/ends on Sunset Cliffs Blvd, 1/4 mi **W** 🅶 Phillips 66, Shell/repair 🍴 Jack-in-the-Box, Kaiserhof Cafe, **N** 🅾 Mission Bay Park

INTERSTATE 10

Exit #	Services
245mm	California/Arizona state line, Colorado River, pacific/mountain time zone
244mm	inspection sta wb
243	Riviera Dr, **S** 🅾 The Cove RV Park
241	US 95, Intake Blvd, to Needles, Blythe, **N** 🅶 Mobil/dsl, Shell/Baja Fresh/dsl 🍴 Steaks'n Cakes Rest. 🏠 Magnuson Motel, Relax Inn 🅾 auto/RV repair/24hr, Burton's RV Park, **S** 🏠 Hampton Inn 🅾 McIntyre Park
240	7th St, **N** 🅶 EZ Mart, Valero/dsl 🍴 China Garden, Little Caesar's, Starbucks 🏠 Blue Line Motel, Budget Inn, Knights Inn, Motel 6 🅾 $General, Albertson's, AutoZone, Ford, repair, Rite Aid, **S** 🅾 Buick/Chevrolet, Chrysler/Dodge/Jeep

= gas = food = lodging = other = rest stop Copyright 2022 - The Next EXIT

▲E INTERSTATE 10 Cont'd

BLYTHE / INDIO

Exit #	Services
239	Lovekin Blvd, Blythe, N Mobil/dsl Shell/Quiznos Carl's Jr, Del Taco, Domino's, Jack-in-the-Box, McDonald's, Popeye's, Sizzler, Starbucks Best Western, Clarion, Emerald Inn, Red Roof Inn, Regency Inn H, $Tree, Ace Hardware, Goodyear/auto, O'Reilly Parts, Verizon, S Chevron/dsl, R/dsl/24hr, Valero/Circle K, VP/dsl Ampola Mexican, Burger King, Denny's, Pizza Studio, Subway, Taco Bell Comfort Suites, Motel 6, Quality Inn, Super 8 city park
236	CA 78, Neighbours Blvd, to Ripley, N Valero/dsl, S to Cibola NWR
232	Mesa Dr, N BB TC/scales/24hr/@, Valero/dsl
231	weigh sta wb
222mm	Wileys Well Rd, N both lanes, full facilities, litter barrels, petwalk, , , S to st prison
217	Ford Dry Lake Rd
201	Corn Springs Rd
192	CA 177, Rice Rd, to Lake Tamarisk, N camping, USPO
189	Eagle Mtn Rd
182	Red Cloud Rd
177	Hayfield Rd
173	Chiriaco Summit, N Chevron/Foster's Freeze/dsl/24hr Chiriaco Rest. camping, Patton Museum, truck/tire repair
168	to Twentynine Palms, to Mecca, Joshua Tree NM
162	frontage rd
159mm	Cactus City Rest Area both lanes, full facilities, litter barrels, petwalk,
147mm	0 ft elevation
146	Dillon Rd, to CA 86, to CA 111 S, Coachella, N Chevron, Loves/Carl's Jr/dsl/24hr Del Taco, S Chevron, TA/Shell/Country Pride/Taco Bell/dsl/24hr/@ Santiago's Mexican Spotlight Casino, truckwash
145	CA 86 S (from eb)
144	CA 111 N, CA 86 S, Indio, N Arco/dsl Holiday Inn Express, Quality Inn Fantasy Sprgs Casino/Hotel/Cafe, Indio Sprgs RV Park
143	Jackson St, Indio, N Arco/dsl Carl's Jr, Domino's, Dunkin', IHOP, KFC, McDonald's, Panda Express, Starbucks, Subway, Taco Bell Fairfield Inn $Tree, AT&T, AutoZone, BigLots, CVS Drug, GNC, Home Depot, Marshall's, PetCo, Ramona Tire/auto, Ross, Verizon, Walgreens, WinCo Foods, S 7-11
142	Monroe St, Central Indio, N Circle K/dsl Starbucks Walmart, S Circle K, Mobil/dsl/LP, Phillips 66/dsl Mexicali Cafe, Subway, Taco Jalisco Days Inn $General
139	Jefferson St, Indio Blvd, N hwy patrol, Shadow Hills RV Resort
137	Washington St, Country Club Dr, to Indian Wells, N Arco, Chevron/dsl, EVC Burger King, Coco's, Del Taco, Legends & Icons Grill, Mario's Italian, McDonald's, Papa John's, Popeye's, Starbucks, Taco Bell, Winchell's Comfort Suites, Motel 6 Buick/GMC, Chrysler/Dodge/Jeep, Ford, Holland RV Ctr, Honda, Palm Springs RV Park, Rite Aid, Stater Bros, Toyota, TrueValue, VW, Walgreens, S 76, Mobil/Circle K Carl's Jr, China Wok, Domino's, Goody's Cafe, La Casita Mexican, Pizza Hut, Subway, TJ's Steaks, Victor's Mexican, Wendy's Firestone/auto, Goodyear/auto
134	Cook St, to Indian Wells, S Arco, Mobil/Circle K/dsl Applebee's, Billy Q's, Buccatini, Carl's Jr, Castenada's Mexican, Firehouse Grill, Jack-in-the-Box, Pueblo Viejo Grill, Starbucks, Subway Courtyard, Fairfield Inn, Hampton Inn, Homewood Suites, Residence Inn vet

PALM SPRINGS / BANNING

Exit #	Services
131	Monterey Ave, Thousand Palms, N Arco Jack-in-the-Box, S Castenada's Mexican, Chipotle, Clark's Cafe/Food Mkt, Del Taco, El Pollo Loco, Firehouse Subs, Hibachi City, IHOP, Krispy Kreme, Maracas Cantina, McDonald's, Panda Express, Panera Bread, Red Robin, Starbucks, Subway, Wendy's $Tree, 99c Store, America's Tire, AutoZone, Costco/gas, Home Depot, Jo-Ann, Kohl's, Lowe's, Mountain View Tire/auto, PetsMart, Sam's Club/gas, Verizon, Walmart
130	Ramon Rd, Bob Hope Dr, N FLYING J/dsl/LP/rest./24hr, Chevron/dsl, Shell/dsl, Valero/dsl Carl's Jr, Del Taco, Denny's, Domino's, Goody's Cafe, In-N-Out, McDonald's, San Miguel Mexican, Starbucks, Taco Bell Motel 6 truckwash, S H, Agua Caliente Casino/rest.
126	Date Palm Dr, Rancho Mirage, S Arco/dsl, EVC, Mobil, Valero DQ Walgreens
123	Palm Dr, to Desert Hot Sprgs, N Arco/dsl, Chevron/Jack-in-the-Box/dsl Caliente Springs Camping, S to Gene Autry Trail
120	Indian Ave, to N Palm Sprgs, N Arco/dsl, Phillips 66/Circle K, Shell/dsl Denny's Motel 6 Harley-Davidson, S Chevron, /Wendy's/dsl/scales/24hr Del Taco, Jack-in-the-Box H
117	CA 62, to Yucca Valley, Twentynine Palms, to Joshua Tree NM
114	Whitewater, many windmills
113mm	both lanes, full facilities, litter barrels, ,
112	CA 111 (from eb), to Palm Springs
110	Haugeen-Lehmann
106	Main St, to Cabazon, N Shell/dsl Burger King, S 7-11, Circle K/dsl $General
104	Cabazon, same as 103
103	Fields Rd, N Chevron, Morongo/dsl, Tesla EVC Blaze Pizza, Chipotle, Coldstone, In-N-Out, Jersey Mike's, McDonald's, Panda Express, Ruby's Diner, Starbucks, Taco Bell Hadley Fruit Orchards, Morongo Reservation/casino, Premium Outlets/famous brands
102.5mm	Banning weigh sta both lanes
102	Ramsey St (from wb)
101	Hargrave St, Banning, N Arco/dsl, Mobil/Church's Consuelo's Mexican Country Inn, Stagecoach Motel tires
100	CA 243, 8th St, Banning, N Chevron/dsl IHOP, Jack-in-the-Box, Subway Rite Aid
99	22nd St, to Ramsey St, N Arco/dsl, Shell/dsl Carl's Jr, Del Taco, KFC, Little Caesar's, Los Victor's, McDonald's, Pizza Hut, Russo's Italian, Sizzler, Starbucks, Taco Bell, Wall Chinese Days Inn, Travelodge $General, Banning RV, Family$, Goodyear/auto
98	Sunset Ave, Banning, N Chevron/dsl Domino's, Gramma's Kitchen, Gus Jr #7 Burger Holiday Inn Express $Tree, AutoZone, Boyd's RV Ctr, Buick/Chevrolet/GMC, repair, Rio Ranch Mkt, vet
96	Highland Springs Ave, N Arco, Chevron/dsl, Shell/dsl Applebee's, Burger King, Denny's, FarmHouse Rest, Guy's Italian, Jack-in-the-Box, Little Caesar's, Papa John's, Subway, Thai Orchid, Wendy's Hampton Inn H, Hardware, Food4Less, Stater Bros Foods, Walgreens, S Mobil Carl's Jr, Chili's, Dickey's BBQ, El Pollo Loco, FarmerBoys, Firehouse Subs, Good China, La Casita, McDonald's, Panda Express, Panera Bread, Patsy's Country Kitchen, Sonic, Starbucks, Taco Bell, Waba Grill, Wienerschnitzel, Wingstop $Tree, Albertson's, Aldi, Best Buy, GNC, Hobby Lobby, Home Depot, hwy patrol, Kohl's, Marshall's, PetCo, Ramona Tire/auto, Rite Aid, Ross, Verizon, Walmart/Subway

INTERSTATE 10 Cont'd

Exit #	Services
95	Pennsylvania Ave (from wb), Beaumont, **N** 🍴 Country Jct Rest., Marla's Rest. 🛏 Rodeway Inn 🅾 AutoZone, Meineke, Miller RV Ctr
94	CA 79, Beaumont, **N** 🅖 76/dsl, USA 🍴 Baker's DriveThru, Casa Palacios, Juan Pollo, McDonald's, Popeye's, YumYum Donuts 🛏 Best Value Inn, Motel 6 🅾 Family$, NAPA, O'Reilly Parts, **S** 🅖 Arco/dsl, Chevron/dsl, Shell/Circle K/dsl 🍴 Del Taco, Denny's, Jack-in-the-Box, Subway 🅾 vet
93	CA 60 W, to Riverside
92	San Timoteo Canyon Rd, Oak Valley Pkwy, **N** 🅖 Chevron/dsl 🍴 Sand Trap Grill, Subway 🛏 Holiday Inn Express 🅾 golf, Rite Aid, **S** 🅾 golf
91mm	🆁🆂 wb, full 🦽 facilities, litter barrels, petwalk, 🅲, 🏕
90	Cherry Valley Blvd, **N** 🅾 truck/tire repair
89	Singleton Rd (from wb), to Calimesa
88	Calimesa Blvd, **N** 🅖 Arco/dsl, Chevron/dsl, Shell/dsl 🍴 Best Wok, Burger King, Carl's Jr, Denny's, McDonald's, NY Pizzaria, Starbucks, Subway, Taco Bell 🛏 Calimesa Inn 🅾 $Tree, Stater Bros Foods, Walgreens, **S** 🍴 Big Boy, Jack-in-the-Box
87	County Line Rd, to Yucaipa, **N** 🅖 FasTrip/dsl, Shell/dsl 🍴 Baker's DriveThru, Del Taco 🛏 Best Value 🅾 $General, 99c Store, USPO, vet
86mm	Wildwood Rest Area eb, full 🦽 facilities, litter barrels, petwalk, 🅲, 🏕
85	Live Oak Canyon Rd, Oak Glen, **N** 🅖 Arco/dsl
83	Yucaipa Blvd, **N** 🅖 Arco/dsl, Chevron/dsl, Mobil 🍴 Baker's DriveThru, Corky's Kitchen, In-N-Out, Starbucks, **S** 🍴 Subway
82	Wabash Ave (from wb)
81	Redlands Blvd, Ford St, **S** 🅖 Phillips 66 🍴 Starbucks
80	Cypress Ave, University St, **N** 🅾 to U of Redlands, **S** 🅾 🏥
79b a	CA 38, 6th St, Orange St, Redlands, **N** 🅖 Arco, Chevron 🍴 Domino's 🛏 Budget Inn, Stardust Motel 🅾 Stater Bros Foods, **S** 🅖 Phillips 66, Shell 🍴 Chipotle Mexican, Corner Cafe, Eureka Burger, Jersey Mike's, Las Fuentes Mexican, Phoenicia Greek, Pieology, Rubio's, Starbucks 🅾 Firestone/auto, Office Depot, O'Reilly Parts, Sprouts Mkt, Trader Joe's, Verizon, Von's Foods
77c	(77b from wb) Tennessee St, **N** 🅖 7-11 🍴 Jack-in-the-Box, Shakey's Pizza 🅾 Home Depot, Toyota, **S** 🅖 Shell 🍴 Arby's, Bakers DriveThru, Burger King, Carl's Jr, Coco's, El Burrito, El Pollo Loco, Papa John's, Subway, Taco Bell 🛏 Ayers Hotel, Comfort Suites, Dynasty Suites, Motel 6 🅾 American Tire Depot, Ford, USPO, vet
77b	(77c from wb) CA 210, to Highlands
77a	Alabama St, **N** 🅖 Phillips 66/Circle K/dsl 🍴 Buffet Star, Cafe Rio, Chick-fil-A, Chili's, Chipotle, Coldstone Creamery, Denny's, Famous Dave's BBQ, Farmer Boys, Five Guys, Habit Burger, Hawaiian BBQ, Jamba Juice, Jersey Mike's, Jimmy John's, Macaroni Grill, Magic Wok, MOD Pizza, Noodle 21 Asian, Red Robin, Starbucks, Subway, Tom's Burgers 🛏 Best Value Inn, Motel 7 West, Super 8 🅾 Barnes&Noble, GNC, Hobby Lobby, JC Penney, JoAnn Superstore, Kohl's, Marshall's, Michael's, PetCo, Ross, Target, Tuesday Morning, U-Haul, Verizon, World Mkt, **S** 🅖 Chevron, Shell 🍴 Del Taco, IHOP, McDonald's, Mr Taco, Nick's Burgers, Old Spaghetti Factory, Pizza Hut 🛏 Country Inn&Suites, GoodNite Inn 🅾 $Tree, 7-11, 99c Store, BigLots, Chevrolet, CVS Drug, Discount Tire, Goodyear/auto, Lowe's, Midas, Nissan, PepBoys
76	California St, **N** 🍴 Mill Creek Rest. 🅾 funpark, museum, **S** 🅖 Arco, EVC, Shell/LP/dsl 🍴 Applebee's, Bravo Burger, Jack-in-the-Box, Jose's Mexican, Little Caesar's, Panda Express, Red Chili Szechuan, Subway, Wendy's, Wienerschnitzel 🅾 AT&T, AutoZone, Food4Less, Mission RV Park, Walmart

75	Mountain View Ave, Loma Linda, **N** 🅖 Valero/dsl, **S** 🅖 Shell/Circle K/dsl 🍴 Alberto's Mexican, Domino's, FarmerBoys Burgers, Subway
74	Tippecanoe Ave, Anderson St, **N** 🍴 BJ's Rest., Cane's, Chipotle Mexican, El Pollo Loco, Hawaiian BBQ, In-N-Out, Jack-in-the-Box, Jamba Juice, Jimmy John's, Panera Bread, Pick-Up Stix, Pollo Campero, Starbucks, Subway, Tasty Goody 🛏 Fairfield Inn, Hampton Inn, Homewood Suites, Residence Inn 🅾 Best Buy, Costco/gas, Sam's Club/gas, Staples, Verizon, **S** 🅖 Phillips 66/dsl 🍴 Baker's DriveThru, Del Taco, HomeTown Buffet, KFC, Napoli Italian, Waba Grill 🅾 auto repair, Honda, Hyundai, to Loma Linda U
73b a	Waterman Ave, **N** 🅖 Chevron, G&M/dsl 🍴 Baja Fresh, Black Angus, Buffalo Wild Wings, Chili's, ChuckeCheese, ClaimJumper, Cutting Board Rest., El Torito, Five Guys, Golden Corral, IHOP, King Buffet, Lotus Garden Chinese, Mimi's Café, Olive Garden, Outback Steaks, Panda Express, Red Lobster, Sizzler, Souplantation, Star Crab, Subway, TGIFriday's 🛏 Days Inn, DoubleTree, Hilton Garden, La Quinta, Quality Inn, Super 8, SureStay+ 🅾 7-11, Aldi Foods, Home Depot, Office Depot, PetsMart, **S** 🅖 Arco 🍴 Burger King, Carl's Jr, Gus Jr Burger #8, McDonald's, Popeye's, Starbucks 🛏 Motel 6 🅾 Camping World RV Ctr, El Monte RV Ctr, repair
72	I-215, CA 91
71	Mt Vernon Ave, Sperry Ave, **N** 🅖 7-11, Trkstp/dsl/LP 🍴 Alberto's Mexican 🛏 Colony Inn, Colton Motel, Comfort Inn 🅾 repair
70b	9th St, **N** 🅖 Mobil 🍴 Denny's, Domino's, McDonald's, P&G Burgers, Starbucks, Subway 🛏 Best Western+ 🅾 NAPA, Stater Bros Foods, USPO
70a	Rancho Ave, **N** 🍴 Del Taco, Jack-in-the-Box, KFC/Taco Bell, Wienerschnitzel
69	Pepper Dr, **N** 🅖 Arco/Chelo's/dsl, Chevron 🍴 Baker's DriveThru
68	Riverside Ave, to Rialto, **N** 🅖 Chevron/dsl, EVC, I-10 Trkstp/dsl/scales, USA 🍴 Burger King, Burger King, Coco's, El Pollo Loco, HomeTown Buffet, Jack-in-the-Box, McDonald's, Panda Express, Starbucks, Subway, Taco Joe's 🛏 American Inn, Days Inn, Welcome Inn 🅾 American Tire Depot, dsl repair, Pepboys, Walmart, **S** 🅖 Shell/Circle K/dsl
66	Cedar Ave, to Bloomington, **N** 🅖 Arco, Valero/dsl 🍴 Baker's DriveThru, Burger King, DQ, FarmerBoys Burgers, Subway, Taco Bell, **S** 🅾 7-11
64	Sierra Ave, to Fontana, **N** 🅖 76/dsl, Arco, Mobil, Shell 🍴 Billy J's Rest., Cajun Crab, ChuckeCheese, Del Taco, Denny's, El Gallo Giro, Hawaiian BBQ, IHOP, In-N-Out, Jack-in-the-Box, KFC, Little Caesar's, McDonald's, Pancho Villa's, Papa John's, Popeye's, Sizzler, Starbucks, Subway, Taco Bell, Tom's Burgers, Wendy's, Wienerschnitzel, Yoshinoya 🛏 Best Value Inn, EconoLodge,

BEAUMONT

REDLANDS

SAN BERNARDINO

🔟 INTERSTATE 10 Cont'd

64 Continued
Motel 6, Valley Motel 🅾 🏥, $Tree, American Tire Depot, AutoZone, BigLots, Cardenas Foods, CVS Drug, Food4Less, GNC, PepBoys, Rite Aid, Stater Bros Foods, Verizon, **S** 🅰 Chevron/dsl 🍴 Brandon's Diner, Chipotle, Circle K, Del Taco, Five Guys, National Buffet, Pizza Hut, Shakey's Pizza, Starbucks, Subway, Tasty Goody 🏠 Hilton Garden 🅾 AutoZone, O'Reilly Parts, Ross, Target, TJ Maxx

63 Citrus Ave, **N** 🅰 🍴 Baker's DriveThru, Subway 🅾 Ford, **S** 🅰 7-11/dsl, Arco/dsl

61 Cherry Ave, **N** 🅰 Arco, Chevron, Fontana Trkstp/dsl/24hr, One Stop/dsl 🍴 Carl's Jr, Del Taco, Jack-in-the-Box 🅾 Mack/Volvo, truck sales, **S** 🅰 3 Sisters Trkstp/dsl/@, North American Trkstp/dsl, Phillips 66/Circle K 🍴 Farmer Boy's Rest., La Chiquita 🅾 Peterbilt

59 Etiwanda Ave, Valley Blvd

58b a I-15, N to Barstow, S to San Diego

57 Milliken Ave, **N** 🅰 76/dsl, Arco/24hr, Chevron, Mobil/Cherony's/dsl, Shell 🍴 Applebee's, Baja Fresh, BJ's Rest., Burger King, Carl's Jr, Chevy's Mexican, Chick-fil-A, Chipotle, Dave&Buster's, Del Taco, Denny's, El Pollo Loco, Famous Dave's BBQ, Fat Burger, Fourth and Mill, Fuddrucker's, Hooters, IHOP, In-n-Out, Jack-in-the-Box, Jamba Juice, Jersey Mike's, KFC, Krispy Kreme, McDonald's, Mkt Broiler, New York Grill, Olive Garden, Outback Steaks, Panda Express, Panera Bread, Rain Forest Cafe, Ramona's Mexican, Red Lobster, Rubio's, Sonic, Starbucks, Subway, Taco Bell, Tokyo Wako, Wendy's, Wienerschnitzel 🏠 Ayre's Suites, Country Inn&Suites, Courtyard, Hampton Inn, Hilton Garden, Holiday Inn Express, Homewood Suites, Hyatt Place, TownePlace Suites 🅾 $Tree, America's Tire, Carmax, Costco/gas, Jo-Ann Fabrics, Kohl's, Marshall's, Ontario Mills Mall, Petsmart, Ross, Sam's Club/gas, Staples, Target, Verizon, **S** 🅰 TA/Shell/Pizza Hut/Subway/Taco Bell/dsl/rest./24hr/@ 🏠 Rodeway Inn

56 Haven Ave, Rancho Cucamonga, **N** 🅰 Mobil 🍴 Benihana, Black Angus, El Torito, Five Star Pizza, Hamburger Mary's 🏠 Aloft Hotel, Best Western, Extended Stay America, La Quinta, Ontario Airport Hotel, Ontario Grand Inn, **S** 🍴 Panda Chinese, TGIFriday's 🏠 Embassy Suites, Fairfield Inn

55b a Holt Blvd, to Archibald Ave, **N** 🅰 Arco, Mobil/dsl 🍴 Baker's Drive-thru, Burgertown USA, Joey's Pizza, Starbucks, Subway, Weinerschnitzel

54 Vineyard Ave, **N** 🅰 76/Circle K 🍴 Carl's Jr, Del Taco, El Pollo Loco, Great China, Pizza Hut/Taco Bell, Popeye's, Rocky's Pizza, Subway 🅾 AutoZone, Rite Aid, Stater Bros Foods, **S** 🅰 76/dsl, Mobil, Quick Gas/dsl 🍴 Denny's, In-N-Out, Jack-in-the-Box, Marie Callenders, Porter's Steaks, Rossa's Italian, Spires Rest., Starbucks, Subway, Wendy's, Yoshinoya Japanese 🏠 Azure Suites, Best Western, Comfort Suites, DoubleTree Inn, Folk Inn, Holiday Inn, Motel 6, Ontario Airport Inn, Quality Inn, Ramada Inn, Red Roof Inn, Residence Inn, Sheraton 🅾 Buick/Cadillac/Chevrolet/GMC, to Airport, USPO

53 San Bernardino Ave, 4th St, to Ontario, **N** 🅰 7-11, Arco, Shell 🍴 Carl's Jr, Domino's, Golden Corral, Jack-in-the-Box 🏠 EconoLodge, Motel 6, **S** 🅰 Arco/24hr, Chevron, Ontario Fuel/dsl 🍴 Denny's, Little Caesar's, McDonald's, Subway, YumYum Donuts 🏠 Days Inn, Travelodge 🅾 city park

51 CA 83, Euclid Ave, to Ontario, Upland, **N** 🅾 🏥

50 Mountain Ave, to Mt Baldy, **N** 🅰 Chevron, Mobil/Circle K/dsl, Shell/dsl 🍴 Corky's Kitchen, Dunkin', El Torito, Hawaiian BBQ, HoneyBaked Ham, Panda Express, Subway, Wendy's 🏠 Super 8

50 Continued
🅾 $Tree, AT&T, CVS Drug, GNC, Hobby Lobby, Home Depot, Michaels, Staples, **S** 🅰 76/dsl 🍴 Carl's Jr, Casa Jimenez, Chopstix, Coldstone, Juice it Up, Starbucks, Wingnuts 🅾 vet, Walmart/Subway

49 Central Ave, to Montclair, **N** 🍴 Carl's Jr., Chipotle Mexican, El Pollo Loco, Gen Korean BBQ, John's Incredible Pizza, McDonald's, Panda Garden Buffet, Paradise Buffet, Pizza Hut, Rodrigo's Mexican, Starbucks, Subway, Taco Bell, Waba Grill 🅾 $Tree, 99c Store, America's Tire, AutoZone, Barnes&Noble, Best Buy, Firestone/auto, Giant RV Ctr, Harley-Davidson, JC Penney, Just Tires, Macy's, PepBoys, PetCo, Ross, same as 48, Target, vet, **S** 🅰 Chevron, USA 🍴 Dickey's BBQ, Fulin Chinese, Jack-in-the-Box, Jersey Mike's, Starbucks, Subway, Tommy's Burgers, Wienerschnitzel 🅾 7-11, Acura/Honda/Infiniti/Nissan, AT&T, Costco/gas, Stater Bros

48 Monte Vista, **N** 🍴 Acapulco Mexican, Applebee's, Black Angus, Chilis, Elephant Bar Rest., Olive Garden, Red Lobster 🅾 Macy's, Nordstrom's, same as 49, **S** 🅾 🏥

47 Indian Hill Blvd, to Claremont, **N** 🅰 Shell/dsl 🍴 BC Cafe 🏠 Claremont Lodge, Knights Inn, **S** 🅰 76/dsl, Chevron/ McDonald's 🍴 Carl's Jr, Chipotle, Denny's, In-N-Out, Norm's Rest., Popeye's, RoundTable Pizza, Starbucks, Subway 🏠 Motel 6 🅾 Hyundai, Toyota, Verizon

46 Towne Ave, **N** 🅰 7-11, Chevron/dsl 🍴 Jack-in-the-Box

45b Garey Ave, to Pomona, **N** 🅰 USA/dsl 🅾 🏥, vet, **S** 🅰 Chevron, Shell/dsl 🍴 Del Taco

45 White Ave, Garey Ave, to Pomona

44 (43 from eb) Dudley St, Fairplex Dr, **N** 🅰 Arco/dsl 🍴 Coco Palm, Denny's 🏠 LemonTree Motel, **S** 🅰 Chevron/24hr 🍴 Jack-in-the-Box, McDonald's, Starbucks 🅾 7-11

42b CA 71 S (from eb), to Corona

42a to I-210, CA 57 S

41 Kellogg Dr, **S** 🅾 to Cal Poly Inst

40 Via Verde

38b Holt Ave, to Covina, **N** 🍴 Hamiltons Steaks 🏠 Vanllee Suites

38a Grand Ave, **N** 🅰 76, Arco/dsl 🍴 Denny's, Misky Misky Peruana 🏠 Best Western+ 🅾 7-11

37b Barranca St, Grand Ave, **N** 🅰 🍴 BJ's Rest., Carl's Jr, Chili's, Chipotle Mexican, El Torito, Habit Burgers, Hawaiian BBQ, Hooters, Islands Rest., Marie Callender, Mariposa Mexican, Pacific Fish Grill, Starbucks, Waba Grill 🏠 Fairfield Inn, Hampton Inn, Holiday Inn 🅾 $Tree, Albertsons, CVS Drug, Dick's, Hobby Lobby, IKEA, Marshalls, Petsmart, Ross, Target, Verizon, **S** 🍴 In-N-Out, McDonald's 🏠 5 Star Inn, Days Inn, same as 37a

37a Citrus Ave, to Covina, **N** 🅰 Chevron 🍴 Buffalo Wild Wings, Burger King, Del Taco, IHOP, Jack-in-the-Box, Jersey Mike's, Millie's Rest., Starbucks, Subway, TGIFriday's, Yum Yum Donuts 🅾 Acura, Albertsons, AT&T, Baja Ranch Foods, Buick/GMC, Chevrolet, CVS Drug, Kia, Marshall's, Nissan, Office Depot, VW, Walmart, **S** 🅰 76/7-11 🍴 Classic Burger 🅾 Cadillac, same as 37b

36 CA 39, Azusa Ave, to Covina, **N** 🅰 76/dsl, Arco/24hr 🍴 Denny's, Green Field Brazillian, McDonald's, Norm's Rest., Papa John's, Subway 🅾 $Tree, American Tire Depot, BigLots, Chrysler/Dodge/Jeep, CVS Drug, Food4Less, Stater Bros, **S** 🅰 Mobil, Shell/dsl 🅾 Audi, Ford, Honda, Mercedes, Toyota

35 Vincent Ave, Glendora Ave, **N** 🅰 Chevron 🅾 auto repair, **S** 🅰 🍴 Blaze Pizza, Chipotle, Five Guys, Gen Korean BBQ, Jamba Juice, Lazy Dog Rest., Lucille's BBQ, Mikomi Japanese, Panera Bread, Pizza Hut, Red Robin, Starbucks, Subway, Wienerschnitzel 🅾 Best Buy, Firestone/auto, JC Penney, Macy's, Michael's, USPO, Verizon

INTERSTATE 10 Cont'd

Exit #	Services
34	Pacific Ave, **N** 📷 76, **S** 📷 Shell ⊙ 🏠, Discount Tire, same as 35
33	Puente Ave, **N** 📷 Chevron 🍴 Denny's, Farmer Boy's, Guadalajara Grill, McDonald's, Panda Express, Sizzler, Starbucks 🏠 Courtyard, Motel 6 ⊙ AT&T, Home Depot, Verizon, Walmart, **S** 🍴 Jack-in-the-Box 🏠 Regency Inn ⊙ Harley-Davidson
32b	Francisquito Ave, to La Puente, **N** 📷 Valero, **S** 📷 🍴 Carl's Jr, In-N-Out, Wienerschnitzel 🏠 Grand Park Inn ⊙ hwy patrol
32a	Baldwin Pk Blvd, **N** 📷 Chevron/McDonald's 🍴 IHOP, Jack-in-the-Box, Papa Johns, Pizza Hut/Taco Bell, Starbucks, Subway, Wendy's, Yum Yum Donuts ⊙ CVS Drug, Food4Less, Target, transmissions, **S** ⊙ 🏠
31c	(31b from wb) Frazier St, **N** ⊙ 7-11
31b a	(31a from wb) I-605 N/S, to Long Beach
30	Garvey Ave, **S** 📷 Rte 66
29b	Valley Blvd, Peck Rd, **N** 📷 Chevron 🍴 Baskin-Robbins, Burger King, Carl's Jr., Denny's, Jamba Juice, KFC, Papa Johns, Shakey's Pizza, Subway, Taco Bell, Yoshinoya 🏠 Motel 6 ⊙ Honda, Hyundai, Lexus, Nissan, Toyota, Walgreens, **S** 🍴 McDonald's, Tommy's Burgers, Waba Grill
29a	S Peck Rd (from eb)
28	Santa Anita Ave, to El Monte, **S** 📷 76/dsl ⊙ 7-11, vet
27	Baldwin Avenue, Temple City Blvd, **S** 📷 Arco/24hr 🍴 Denny's, same as 26b a
26b	CA 19, Rosemead Blvd, Pasadena, **N** 🍴 Habit Burger, Chipotle, Coldstone, IHOP, Jamba Juice, Starbucks, Subway ⊙ $Tree, GNC, Office Depot, Target, **S** 🍴 Del Taco, Jack-in-the-Box, Starbucks
26a	Walnut Grove Ave
25b	San Gabriel Blvd, **N** 📷 Shell 🍴 Carl's Jr, Popeye's, Taco Bell 🏠 Budget Inn, **S** 📷 7-11
25a	Del Mar Ave, to San Gabriel, **N** 📷 Mobil ⊙ auto repair, **S** 📷 Shell/dsl, USA 🏠 Travelodge
24	New Ave, to Monterey Park, **N** 🍴 KFC, to Mission San Gabriel
23b	Garfield Ave, to Alhambra, **S** 📷 76, Arco 🏠 Grand Inn ⊙ 🏠, auto repair
23a	Atlantic Blvd, Monterey Park, **N** 📷 🍴 Pizza Hut, Popeye's, Starbucks ⊙ 🏠, **S** 🏠 Courtyard, Monterey Park Inn ⊙ Ralph's Foods
22	Fremont Ave, **N** ⊙ 🏠, **S** 🍴 Papa Johns, Subway ⊙ 7-11
21	I-710, Long Beach Fwy, Eastern Ave (from wb)
20b a	Eastern Ave, City Terrace Dr, **S** 📷 Chevron/service, Mobil 🍴 Burger King, McDonald's
19c	Soto St (from wb), **N** 📷 Chevron/dsl ⊙ 🏠, city park, **S** 📷 76, Mobil
19b	I-5 (from wb), US 101 S, N to Burbank, S to San Diego
19a	State St, **N** ⊙ 🏠
17	I-5 N
16b	I-5 S (from eb)
16a	Santa Fe Ave, San Mateo St, **S** 📷 76/dsl, Mobil ⊙ industrial area, Penske Trucks
15b	Alameda St, **N** 📷 76/dsl 🍴 Jack-in-the-Box, to downtown, **S** industrial area
15a	Central Ave, **N** 📷 Shell/repair, **S** 📷 Shell
14b	San Pedro Blvd, **S** industrial
14a	LA St, **N** ⊙ conv ctr, **S** 🍴 El Pollo Loco, McDonald's ⊙ 99c Store, O'Reilly Parts, Rite Aid, URGENT CARE
13	I-110, Harbor Fwy
12	Hoover St, Vermont Ave, **N** 📷 Chevron 🍴 Burger King, McDonald's, Subway ⊙ AutoZone, CVS Drug, PepBoys,

12	Continued **S** 📷 76, Chevron 🍴 Jack-in-the-Box, Papa Johns, Yoshinoya ⊙ Ralph's Foods
11	Normandie Ave, Western Ave
10	Arlington Ave, **N** 📷 76, Chevron
9	Crenshaw Blvd, **N** 📷 Mobil, **S** 📷 76, Chevron 🍴 El Pollo Loco, McDonald's, Subway, Taco Bell, Yoshinoya ⊙ U-Haul
8	La Brea Ave, **N** 📷 Valero/dsl ⊙ USPO, **S** 📷 Chevron ⊙ AutoZone
7b	Washington Blvd, Fairfax Ave, **S** 📷 Mobil, same as 8
7a	La Cienega Blvd, Venice Ave (from wb), **N** 📷 Chevron/24hr, Mobil 🍴 Carl's Jr., Del Taco ⊙ Aamco, Firestone/auto, **S** 🍴 Subway
6	Robertson Blvd, Culver City, **N** 📷 Chevron/dsl, Valero 🍴 Domino's, Taco Bell ⊙ EZ Lube, **S** 🍴 Del Taco
5	National Blvd, **N** 📷 🍴 Papa John's, Starbucks, Subway, Taco+ ⊙ Rite Aid, Von's Foods, **S** 📷 Arco
4	Overland Ave, **S** 📷 Mobil/dsl
3b a	I-405, N to Sacramento, S to Long Beach
2c b	Bundy Dr, **N** 📷 Chevron, Shell/dsl 🍴 Taco Bell ⊙ Cadillac/GMC, Staples
2a	Centinela Ave, to Santa Monica, **N** 🍴 Taco Bell, **S** 🍴 McDonald's, Trader Joe's 🏠 Travelodge
1c	20th St (from wb), Cloverfield Blvd, 26th St (from wb), **N** 📷 76/dsl, Chevron, Shell/repair ⊙ 🏠
1b	Lincoln Blvd, CA 1 S, **N** 🍴 Denny's, McDonald's, Starbucks ⊙ BrakeMasters, Toyota, Tuesday Morning, USPO, Vons Foods, **S** 📷 Chevron/dsl, Shell 🍴 Dominos, Jack-in-the-Box, Subway 🏠 Doubletree Suites ⊙ 7-11, Firestone/auto, U-Haul
1a	4th, 5th, (from wb)
0	Santa Monica Blvd, to beaches, **I-10 begins/ends on CA 1.**

INTERSTATE 15

Exit #	Services
298	California/Nevada state line, services in NV
291	Yates Well Rd
289	weigh sta sb
286	Nipton Rd, **E** Mojave Nat Preserve, to Searchlight
281	Bailey Rd
276mm	brake check area for trucks, nb
272	Cima Rd, **E** 📷 Shell/cafe/dsl/towing
270mm	Valley Wells Rest Area both lanes, full ♿ facilities, litter barrels, petwalk, 🚻
265	Halloran Summit Rd
259	Halloran Springs Rd
248	to Baker (from sb), same as 246

[gas] = gas [food] = food [lodging] = lodging [other] = other [Rs] = rest stop   Copyright 2022 - The Next EXIT ®

INTERSTATE 15 Cont'd

BAKER

Exit #	Services
246	CA 127, Kel-Baker Rd, Baker, to Death Valley, **W** [gas] Tesla EVC, 76/dsl, Arco, Chevron/Subway/Fatburger/Pizza Hut/dsl, Chevron/Taco Bell, Shell/DQ/dsl, Shell/Jack-in-the-Box/dsl, Valero, Valero/A&W/Pizza Hut/Subway/dsl [food] Arby's, Burger King, Carl's Jr, Del Taco, Denny's, Mad Greek Café [lodging] BunBoy Hotel, Santa Fe Motel [other] Alien Fresh Jerky, Baker Mkt Foods, Country Store, repair, USPO, World's Tallest Thermometer
245	to Baker (from nb), same as 246
239	Zzyzx Rd
233	Rasor Rd, **E** [gas] Shell/Rasor Sta/dsl/towing/24hr
230	Basin Rd
221	Afton Rd, to Dunn, **W** [other] Mini Mkt
217mm	[Rs] both lanes, full [facilities] facilities, litter barrels, petwalk, [C], [picnic]
213	Field Rd
206	Harvard Rd, to Newberry Springs
198	Minneola Rd, **W** [gas] Cali Burger, Shell/dsl
197mm	agricultural insp sta sb
196	Yermo Rd, Yermo
194	Calico Rd, **E** [gas] Eddie World/dsl, Tesla EVC
191	Ghost Town Rd, **E** [gas] Arco/24hr, Mohsen Oil Trkstp/dsl/24hr [food] Jack-in-the-Box, Peggy Sue's 50s Diner, Penny's Diner [lodging] Baymont Inn, **W** [gas] Chevron/dsl, Shell/Subway/dsl/24hr [other] Calico GhostTown (3mi), KOA
189	Ft Irwin Rd
186	CA 58 W, to Bakersfield

BARSTOW

Exit #	Services
184	E Main, Barstow, Montera Rd (from eb), to I-40, **E** [gas] Phillips 66/dsl [food] Grill It, McDonald's, Mega Tom's Burgers, Panda Express, Popeye's, Starbucks, Subway [lodging] Arco, Best Western, Travelodge [other] Walmart, **W** [gas] Chevron, Circle K, EVC, Mobil/dsl, USA/dsl [food] Alberto's, Burger King, Carl's Jr, China Town Buffet, Del Taco, Denny's, Di Napoli's Italian, IHOP, Jack-in-the-Box, Jenny's Grill, Little Caesar's, Rigoberto's, Wienerschnitzel [lodging] Astro Budget Motel, Best Motel, Budget Inn, CA Inn, Days Inn, Desert Inn, EconoLodge, Economy Inn, Motel 6, Quality Inn/rest., Ramada Inn, Rodeway Inn, Super 8 [other] $Tree, 99c Store, AutoZone, O'Reilly Parts, U-Haul/LP
184a	I-40 E (from nb), **I-40 begins/ends**
183	CA 247, Barstow Rd, **E** [food] Circle K, Valero/7-11/dsl [food] Jimenez Mexican, Pizza Hut, Subway [other] $General, Rite Aid, **W** [gas] Food4Less/dsl, Shell [other] [H], Food4Less, Marshall's, Mojave River Valley Museum, st patrol
181	L St, W Main, Barstow, **W** [gas] Arco/dsl, Chevron, USA [food] Foster's Freeze [lodging] Baymont Inn [other] Firestone/auto, Home Depot, NAPA, tires/towing
179	CA 58, to Bakersfield
178	Lenwood, to Barstow, **E** [gas] ⊛FLYING J/Denny's/dsl/24hr, 76/dsl, Arco/dsl, Chevron, Shell/dsl, Valero [food] Arby's, Big Boy, Burger King, Carl's Jr, Chili's, Chipotle Mexican, Del Taco, Denny's, El Pollo Loco, Fatburger, Habit Burger, IHOP, In-N-Out, Jack-in-the-Box, Jersey Mike's, Oggi's, Panda Express, Panera Bread, Starbucks, Subway, Tommy's Burgers [lodging] Ayres Hotel, Comfort Suites, Hampton Inn, Holiday Inn Express [other] Blue Beacon, Old Navy, Tanger Outlet/famous brands/food ct, **W** [food] ⊛Loves /Chester's/Godfather's/dsl/scales/24hr/@, [Pilot]/Subway/dsl/scales/24hr, TA/Shell/Country Fare/Subway/dsl/scales/24hr/@ [food] McDonald's [lodging] Days Inn [other] repair, truckwash, Zippy Lube
175	Outlet Ctr Dr, Sidewinder Rd
169	Hodge Rd
165	Wild Wash Rd

Exit #	Services
161	Dale Evans Pkwy, to Apple Valley
157	Stoddard Wells Rd, to Bell Mtn
154	Stoddard Wells Rd, to Bell Mtn, **E** [other] Shady Oasis Camping/LP, **W** [gas] 76/dsl, Mobil [food] Franky's Diner [lodging] Motel 6, Queens Motel
153.5mm	Mojave River
153b	E St
153a	CA 18 E, D St, to Apple Valley, **E** [gas] Arco [other] [H], repair, **W** [gas] Arco/Subway/dsl

VICTORVILLE

Exit #	Services
151b	Mojave Dr, Victorville, **E** [gas] Mobil/dsl [lodging] Rodeway Inn, **W** [gas] Valero/dsl [lodging] Economy Inn, Sunset Inn
151a	La Paz Dr, Roy Rogers Dr, **E** [gas] Chevron, Shell/dsl [food] Burger King, Carl's Jr, El Pollo Loco, HomeTown Buffet, IHOP, Jack-in-the-Box, McDonald's, Wendy's, Wienerschnitzel [other] $General, $Tree, 99c Store, AutoZone, BigLots, Costco/gas, Fiat, Food-4Less, Goodyear/auto, Harley-Davidson, Pepboys, Rite Aid, Toyota, **W** [gas] Arco [food] Carl's Jr, Dickey's BBQ, Domino's, Farmer Boys, Golden ChopStix, Hawaiian BBQ, In-N-Out, Panda Express, Papa John's, Starbucks, Subway [other] Americas Tire, Buick/GMC, Chrysler/Dodge/Jeep, Home Depot, Honda, Kia, Nissan, Stater Bros, Verizon, Walgreens, WinCo Foods
150	CA 18 W, Palmdale Rd, Victorville, **E** [food] Baker's Drive-Thru, Burger King, Denny's, KFC, Richie's Diner [lodging] Greentree Inn, Red Roof Inn, **W** [gas] 76/dsl, Arco, Circle K [food] Coco's, Del Taco, House of Joy, La Casita Mexican, McDonald's, Pizza Hut, Raul's Mexican, Starbucks, Subway, Taco Bell, Tom's Rest. [lodging] Budget Inn, Days Inn, Holiday Inn [other] [H], $General, Aamco, AutoZone, CVS Drug, Ford, Hyundai, Kamper's Korner RV, Mazda, Target, Town&Country Tire, vet
148	La Mesa Rd, Nisquali Rd, **E** [lodging] Red Roof Inn, **W** [food] Baskin-Robbins, Buffalo's, ChuckeCheese, Fatburger [other] AT&T, Petsmart
147	Bear Valley Rd, to Lucerne Valley, **0-2 mi E** [gas] 76/Circle K, dsl, Arco, Chevron, Mobil [food] Arby's, Baker's Drive-Thru, Burger King, Carl's Jr, Del Taco, Dragon Express, John's Pizza, KFC, Los Alazanes Mexican, Los Toritos, Marie Callender's, McDonald's, Panda Express, Red Robin, Starbucks, Steak'n Shake, Steer'n Stein, Tacos Mexico, Wienerschnitzel [lodging] Best Value Inn, Comfort Suites, Day&Night Inn, EconoLodge, Extended Stay, Extended Studio Hotel, La Quinta, Travelodge [other] Affordable RV Ctr, America's Tire, AutoZone, Firestone/auto, Home Depot, Michael's, O'Reilly Parts, Range RV, Rite Aid, Scandia Funpark, Tire Depot, Vallarta Foods, vet, Walmart/McDonald's, auto, **W** [gas] 76/Circle K, Arco, Chevron/dsl, Valero/dsl [food] Applebee's, Archibald's Drive-Thru, Baja Fresh, Carino's, Chili's, Chipotle Mexican, Cracker Barrel, Del Taco, El Pollo Loco, Tio Pepe Mexican, Farmer Boy's Rest., Freddy's Custard, Guseppe's, Jack-in-the-Box, Little Caesar's, McDonald's, Mimi's Cafe, Olive Garden, Outback Steaks, Pancho Villa's, Red Lobster, RoadHouse Grill, Sonic, Starbucks, Subway, Tokyo Steak, Wendy's [lodging] Hawthorn Suites [other] 99c Store, AAA, Barnes&Noble, Best Buy, CVS Drug, Dick's, Goodyear/auto, Hobby Lobby, JC Penney, Kohl's, Lowe's, Macy's, Rite Aid, Stater Bros., Verizon, Walgreens, Walmart

HESPERIA

Exit #	Services
143	Main St, to Hesperia, Phelan, **E** [gas] Chevron/dsl, Mobil [food] Alberto's, Shell/Popeye's/dsl [food] Arby's, Burger King, Chipotle, Del Taco, Denny's, IHOP, In-N-Out, Jack-in-the-Box, Panda Express, Quiznos, Starbucks [lodging] Courtyard, SpringHill Suites [other] Walmart/Subway, **W** [gas] 76/dsl, Arco/dsl [food] Baker's Drive-thru, FarmerBoys, Five Guys, Golden Corral, Subway, Waba Grill [lodging] Holiday Inn Express, Motel 6 [other] Desert Willow RV Park, GNC, Jo-Ann Fabrics, Marshall's, Ross, SuperTarget, URGENT CARE, Verizon

INTERSTATE 15 Cont'd

Exit #	Services
141	US 395, Joshua St, Adelanto, W Arco/dsl, Pilot/Wendy's/dsl/scales/24hr Outpost Café repair, RV supply ctr, truck/RV wash, Zippy Lube
140	Ranchero Rd
138	Oak Hill Rd, E Chevron/dsl Summit Inn Café, W Oak Hills RV Village/LP
137mm	**brake check sb,** Cajon Summit, elevation 4260
131	CA 138, to Palmdale, Silverwood Lake, E Chevron McDonald's Silverwood SRA, W 76/Circle K/Del Taco/LP, Shell/Subway/dsl/LP Best Western
130mm	**weigh sta both lanes,** elevation 3000
129	Cleghorn Rd
124	Kenwood Ave
123	I-215 S, to San Bernardino, E Arco to Glen Helen Park
122	Glen Helen Parkway
119	Sierra Ave, W Arco/dsl, Chevron/dsl, Shell/Del Taco/dsl, Valero/dsl Jack-in-the-Box, McDonalds to Lytle Creek RA
118	Duncan Canyon Rd
116	Summit Ave, E 7-11, Chevron Chili's, Coldstone, Del Taco, El Ranchero, Five Guys, Hawaiian BBQ, Jack-in-the-Box, Juice It Up, Little Caesar's, Panera Bread, Quiznos, Roundtable Pizza, Starbucks, Subway, Taco Bell, Wendy's $Tree, CVS Drug, GNC, Kohl's, Marshall's, Michael's, Petsmart, Ross, Staples, Stater Bros, Target, Verizon
115b a	CA 210, Highland Ave, E to Lake Arrowhead
113	Base Line Rd, E USA Denny's, Jack-in-the-Box, Logans Roadhouse, Pizza Hut, Rosa Maria's, Starbucks Comfort Inn
112	CA 66, Foothill Blvd, E Chevron Asia Buffet, ClaimJumper, Golden Spoon, In-N-Out, Panda Express, Subway, Taco Bell, Wienerschnitzel $City, Food4Less, Jiffy Lube, Walmart, 1-2 mi W 76/dsl, Chevron/dsl Baker's, Buffalo Wild Wings, Carino's, Cheesecake Factory, Chick-fil-A, Chipotle Mexican, Del Taco, Denny's, El Pollo Loco, El Torito, Flemings Steaks, Islamadora Fish Co, Jack-in-the-Box, Joe's Crab Shack, Johnny Rockets, Kings Fishouse, Lucille's BBQ, Old Spagetti Factory, Paisano's Rest., PF Chang's, Popeyes, Red Robin, Richie's Diner, Shakey's Pizza, Starbucks, TGIFriday's, The Hat Grill, Wendy's Sheraton 4 Points AT&T, AutoZone, Bass Pro Shops, Best Buy, Fresh&Easy Mkt, Home Depot, JC Penney, Macy's, Office Depot, Sears Grand
110	4th St, E Arco/dsl Baker's, Subway, W 76/dsl, Arco, Chevron/Alberto's Mexican/dsl, Shell/dsl Applebee's, Arby's, Baja Fresh, Baskin-Robbins, BJ's Rest., Boston's, Burger King, Carl's Jr, Chevy's Mexican, Chick-fil-A, Chipotle, Chop Sticks, Coco's, Daphne's Greek, Del Taco, Denny's, El Pollo Loco, Famous Dave's BBQ, Fat Burger, Fuddruckers, Hooters, IHOP, In-N-Out, Jack-in-the-Box, Jamba Juice, Juice It Up, KFC, Krispy Kreme, Lazy Dog Cafe, McDonald's, Mkt Broiler, New City Buffet, NY Grill, Olive Garden, Outback Steaks, Panera Bread, Rain Forest Cafe, Red Brick Pizza, Red Lobster, Rubio's, Sonic, Starbucks, Subway, Tokyo Tokyo, Wendy's, Wienerschnitzel, Wing Place Ayre's Suites, Country Inn&Suites, Courtyard, Hampton Inn, Hilton Garden, Holiday Inn Express, Homewood Suites, Hyatt Place, TownePlace Suites $Tree, America's Tire, Costco/gas, JC Penney, Jo-Ann Fabrics, Kohl's, Marshall's, Ontario Mills Mall, Petsmart, Sam's Club/gas, Staples, Target, Tire Pros, Verizon
109b a	I-10, E to San Bernardino, W to LA
108	Jurupa St, E Chevron/dsl Burger King, Del Taco, El Gran Burrito, Starbucks, Subway Affordable RV, BMW, Chrysler/Dodge/Jeep, Family RV Ctr, Fiat, Honda, Hyundai, Lexus, Mazda, Mini, Nissan, Subaru, Toyota, Volvo, VW, W Arco Carl's Jr Ford, Kia, Scandia funpark

CUCAMONGA

ONTARIO

Exit #	Services
106	CA 60, E to Riverside, W to LA
105	Cantu-Galleano Ranch Rd
103	Limonite Ave, E Asado Grill, Carl's Jr, Del Taco, Denny's, Five Guys, Hawaiian BBQ, Jamba Juice, Subway Lowe's, Michael's, PetCo, Ross, W Chevron Applebee's, Blaze Pizza, Buffalo Wild Wings, Carino's, Chipotle, Coldstone, Dickey's BBQ, Domino's, Farmer Boys, Habit Burger, Jersey Mike's, Juice it Up, Little Caesar's, McDonald's, On-the-Border, Pacific Fish Grill, Panda Express, Panera Bread, Pick Up Stix, Starbucks, Subway, Taco Bell, Tutti Frutti Yogurt, Wendy's AT&T, Best Buy, GNC, Home Depot, Kohl's, Nestle Tollhouse, Petsmart, Ralph's Foods/gas, Staples, Target, TJ Maxx, Verizon, Vons Foods/gas, Walgreens
100	6th St, Norco Dr, Old Town Norco, E 76/dsl, Chevron Jack-in-the-Box, McDonald's Rite Aid, W Arco, Valero/dsl Big Boy, Norco's Burgers, Starbucks, Wienerschnitzel Fairfield Inn Brake Masters, Jiffy Lube, USPO, vet
98	2nd St, W Mobil, Shell/dsl, Thrifty Baja Fish Tacos, Burger Basket, Burger King, Carl's Jr, Del Taco, In-N-Out, Pancake House, Pizza Hut, Polly's Cafe, Subway $Tree, 7-11, Ace Hardware, Chrysler/Dodge/Jeep, Ford, Norco Tires, Schwab Tire, Stater Bros
97	Yuma Dr, Hidden Valley Pkwy, E 7-11 Chick-fil-A, Hot Dog Shoppe, Marco's Pizza, Shogun Japanese, Starbucks, Starbucks, Subway, Waba Grill Kohl's, Stater Bros, W 76/dsl, Chevron, Shell/dsl Alberto's Mexican, Burger City Grill, Carl's Jr, Chipotle, Denny's, Domino's, Fantastic Cafe, Five Guys, Hawaiian BBQ, Hickory Joe's BBQ, Jack-in-the-Box, Jamba Juice, Jersey Mike's, Jimmy John's, KFC, McDonald's, Miguel's Jr, Papa John's, Pieology, Popeye's, Rodrigo's Mexican, Rubio's, Taco Bell, Wahoos Fish Taco Hampton Inn, Howard Johnson Express America's Tire, AT&T, AutoZone, BigLots, GNC, Hobby Lobby, O'Reilly Parts, Staples, Target, URGENT CARE, Verizon, Walgreens, Walgreens, Winco
96b a	CA 91, to Riverside, beaches
95	Magnolia Ave, E Chevron/Jack-in-the-Box/dsl Islands Burgers, Shamrock's Grill Residence Inn AAA, Lowe's, Office Depot, W Mobil/Circle K, Shell Baskin-Robbins, Broken Yolk, Coco's, Jersey's Pizza, Little Caesar's, McDonald's, Sizzler, Subway, Waba Grill Holiday Inn Express $Tree, AT&T, CVS Drug, El Super Mkt, O'Reilly Parts, Sonic, Stater Bros Foods
93	Ontario Ave, to El Cerrito, E Shell/dsl Sombrero Mexican, Starbucks Mtn View Tire, vet, W 76/Circle K, Arco, Chevron Chipotle, Chopstix, Del Taco, Denny's, El Pollo Loco, Hawaiian BBQ, In-N-Out, Jack-in-the-Box, Jersey Mike's, Juice It Up, KFC, Magic Wok, McDonald's, Miguel's Jr, Papa John's, Pieology, Porky's Pizza, Rubio's, SpringHill Suites, Subway, Taco Bell, Tommy's Burgers, Wienerschnitzel Albertson's/Sav-On, America's Tire, AutoZone, CVS Drug, Home Depot, Sam's Club/gas, USPO, Walmart

NORCO

EL CERRITO

CA

📵 = gas 🍴 = food 🛏 = lodging ⭕ = other Ⓡs = rest stop Copyright 2022 - The Next EXIT ®

INTERSTATE 15 Cont'd

Exit #	Services
92	El Cerrito Rd
91	Cajalco Rd, **E** 🍴 BJ's Rest., Buffalo Wild Wings, Chick-fil-A, Chili's, Chipotle, Five Guys, Jamba Juice, King's Fish House, Macaroni Grill, Panera Bread, Rock Brews Rest., Starbucks, Wendy's ⭕ AT&T, Barnes&Noble, Best Buy, Kohl's, Marshall's, Michael's, Old Navy, PetCo, Ross, See's Candies, Staples, Target, Verizon, World Mkt, **W** 📵 Mobil/dsl 🍴 Jack-in-the-Box, NY Pizza, Subway ⭕ Stater Bros, vet
90	Weirick Rd, Dos Lagos Dr, **E** 📵 Arco/dsl 🍴 Citrus City Grille, Fatburger, Miguel's, Tap's Rest., TGIFriday's, Wood Ranch BBQ 🛏 Staybridge Suites ⭕ 7 Oaks Gen Store, Trader Joe's
88	Temescal Cyn Rd, Glen Ivy, **E** 📵 Shell, **W** 📵 Arco/dsl 🍴 Carl's Jr, Tom's Farms/BBQ
85	Indian Truck Trail, **W** 🍴 Pizza Hut, Starbucks, Subway ⭕ CVS Drug, Von's Foods/dsl
81	Lake St
78	Nichols Rd, **W** 📵 Arco/dsl ⭕ Outlets/famous brands
77	CA 74, Central Ave, Lake Elsinore, **E** 📵 Arco, Chevron, Mobil/Circle K/dsl 🍴 Archibald's, Burger King, Chili's, Del Taco, Dickey's BBQ, Douglas Burgers, Golden Corral, Hawaiian BBQ, Juice It Up, Panda Express, Submarina, Taco Del Mar, Tom's ChiliBurgers, Wendy's ⭕ $Tree, AT&T, Costco/gas, Lowe's, Petsmart, Staples, Valvoline, **W** 🍴 El Pollo Loco, Farmer Boys, Golden Chop Stix, IHOP, McDonald's, Papa John's, Starbucks, Subway, Wienerschnitzel ⭕ 99c Store, Aldi Foods, Home Depot, Marshall's, PetCo, Target, Verizon, Walgreens
75	Main St, Lake Elsinore, **W** 📵 Main St Gas/dsl ⭕ 7-11, tires/repair
73	Railroad Cyn Rd, to Lake Elsinore, **E** 📵 76/7-11, Shell/Circle K/dsl 🍴 Alberto's Mexican, Denny's, El Pollo Loco, In-N-Out, KFC, Peony Chinese, Starbucks 🛏 Holiday Inn Express ⭕ GNC, Jiffy Lube, O'Reilly Parts, URGENT CARE, Verizon, vet, Von's Foods, Walmart/McDonald's, **W** 📵 Arco, Chevron, Mobil/Circle K/dsl 🍴 Annie's Cafe, Cafe China, Carl's Jr, Del Taco, Don Jose's Mexican, King Kabob, McDonald's, Pizza Hut, Sizzler, Subway, Taco Bell, Vincenzo's 🛏 Best Western+, Quality Inn, Travel Inn ⭕ $Tree, 7-11, AutoZone, BigLots, Buick/GMC, Chevrolet, CVS Drug, Express Tire/auto, Firestone/auto, Ford, Stater Bros, vet, Walgreens
71	Bundy Cyn Rd, **E** 📵 Shell/Circle K, **W** 📵 Arco 🍴 Jack-in-the-Box
69	Baxter Rd
68	Clinton Keith Rd, **E** 📵 Chevron/dsl, USA 🍴 Denny's, Golden Spoon, Los Jilbetos Tacos, Los Reyes Grill, McDonald's, Panda Express, Starbucks, Subway ⭕ 🅗, Ace Hardware, Albertsons/Sav-on, **W** 📵 7-11, Arco/dsl 🍴 Del Taco, Jack-in-the-Box, Stadium Pizza, Starbucks, Tresino's Italian, Yellow Basket Burgers ⭕ Baron's Mkt, Rite Aid, Stater Bros
65	California Oaks Rd, Kalmia St, **E** 📵 76/Circle K/dsl, Chevron, Shell/7-11/dsl 🍴 Burger King, Carl's Jr, Chili's, Chipotle, DQ, Jade Chinese, Jamba Juice, Jersey's Pizza, Jimenez Mexican, KFC, Little Caesar's, McDonald's, Papa John's, Starbucks, Subway, Wings'N Things 🛏 Comfort Inn ⭕ $Tree, Albertson's/Sav-On, AutoZone, Express Tire, O'Reilly Parts, Rite Aid, Target, Tuesday Morning, vet, Walgreens, **W** 📵 Arco/dsl, Chevron 🍴 Applebee's, Chick-fil-A, Farmer Boys, Jack-in-the-Box, Juice it Up, Pick Up Stix, Sizzlin Steer, Taco Bell ⭕ America's Tire, Giant RV Ctr, Kohl's, Lowe's, Office Depot, PetCo
64	Murrieta Hot Springs Rd, to I-215, **E** 📵 7-11, Shell/dsl 🍴 Buffalo Wild Wings, Carl's Jr, El Pollo Loco, Hungry Bull, Richie's Diner, Rubio's, Sizzler, Starbucks, Wendy's ⭕ Ralph's Foods,

64	Continued
	Rite Aid, Ross, Sam's Club/gas, Walgreens, **W** 📵 7-11, Shell, Popeye's/dsl 🍴 Arby's, Chuy's, Coldstone, Denny's, IHOP, Jersey Mike's Subs, McDonald's, Panda Express, Starbucks, Subway, Tom's Burgers, Wienerschnitzel ⭕ 99c Store, AAA, American Tire Depot, AT&T, Best Buy, BigLots, CarMax, Home Depot, Petsmart, Staples, Walmart/McDonald's
63	I-215 N (from nb), to Riverside
62	French Valley Pkwy (from sb, no return), **W** 🍴 Los Cabos ⭕ BMW, O'Reilly Parts, VW
61	CA 79 N, Winchester Rd, **E** 📵 76/dsl, Chevron 🍴 Baja Fresh, Baskin-Robbins/Togo's, BF Greek Rest., BJ's Rest., Burger King, CA Pizza Kitchen, Chick-fil-A, Chipotle Mexican, Coldstone, Corner Cafe, Del Taco, Dickey's BBQ, El Torito, Famous Dave's, Fatburger, Five Guys, Freebirds Burrito, Harry's Grill, Hometown Buffet, Islands Burgers, Jamba Juice, Lazy Dog Cafe, Lucille's BBQ, Macaroni Grill, McDonald's, Mimi's Cafe, Ming's, Olive Garden, Outback Steaks, Panda Express, Panera Bread, PF Chang's, Red Ginger Chinese, Red Lobster, Red Robin, Shakey's Pizza, Shogun Chinese, Souplantation, Starbucks, Subway, Taco Bell, TGIFriday's, Tilted Kilt, Wahoo's, Yellow Basket Hamburgers ⭕ $Tree, 99c Store, America's Tire, AT&T, AutoZone, Barnes&Noble, Costco/gas, CVS Drug, Express Tire, Express Tire, Food4Less, GNC, Hobby Lobby, Hyundai, JC Penney, Jo-Ann Fabrics, Lowe's, Macy's, Nissan, Office Depot, Old Navy, PepBoys, PetCo, Ramona Tire, Roots Mkt, See's Candies, TJ Maxx, Trader Joe's, Verizon, WinCo Foods, World Mkt, **W** 📵 Arco, Chevron/dsl 🍴 Arby's, Banzai Japanese, Chin's Gourmet Chinese, Del Taco, El Pollo Loco, Farmer Boys, In-N-Out, Jack-in-the-Box, Patsy's Country Kitchen, Serrano's Grill, Starbucks, Subway, Super China, Tacos El Gallo, Vail Ranch Steakhouse, Wendy's 🛏 Best Western, Extended Stay America, Fairfield Inn, Holiday Inn Express, La Quinta, Quality Inn ⭕ NAPA, Richardson's RV Ctr, st patrol, tires/repair, vet
59	Rancho California Rd, **E** 📵 Arco, Mobil/Circle K/dsl, Shell/dsl 🍴 Black Angus, Chili's, ClaimJumper, Del Taco, Golden Spoon, Jilberto's Mexican, Little Caesar's, Marie Callender's, Pat&Oscar's Rest., Peony Chinese, Pizza Hut, RoundTable Pizza, Rubio's, Starbucks, Subway, Times Square NY Pizza 🛏 Embassy Suites ⭕ BigLots, CVS Drug, Ford, Mazda, Michael's, Subaru, Target, URGENT CARE, Verizon, vet, Von's Foods, **W** 📵 76/Circle K/dsl, Chevron 🍴 Alberto's Mexican, Denny's, McDonald's, Kabob Grill, Penfold's Cafe, Rosa's Café, Starbucks, Vince's Spaghetti 🛏 Hampton Inn, Motel 6, Rancho California Inn, Rodeway Inn, SpringHill Suites ⭕ to Old Town Temecula, USPO
58	CA 79 S, to Indio, Temecula, **E** 📵 Mobil/Circle K/dsl, Valero/Circle K/dsl 🍴 Carl's Jr, Del Taco, Domino's, Domino's Francesca's Italian, Golden Bowl Asian, In-N-Out, Los Jilbeto's, Starbucks, Utopizza, Wing-n-Things ⭕ 7-11, Ace Hardware, America's Tire, CVS Drug, Valvoline, **W** 📵 Arco, Shell/dsl 🍴 Baskin-Robbins, Eldorado Mexican, Garage Rest., Hungry Howie's, Leinzo Charro Mexican, Wienerschnitzel 🛏 Ramada Inn ⭕ Express Tire, Harley-Davidson
55mm	check sta nb
54	Rainbow Valley Blvd, **2 mi E** 📵 gas 🍴 food, **W** ⭕ CA Insp S
51	Mission Rd, to Fallbrook, **W** ⭕ 🅗
46	CA 76, to Oceanside, Pala, **E** ⭕ RV camp, **W** 📵 Mobil/Circle K 🍴 McGrath's Grill 🛏 Quality Inn ⭕ Pala Meas Mkt
44mm	San Luis Rey River
43	Old Hwy 395
41	Gopher Canyon Rd, Old Castle Rd, **1 mi E** 🛏 Welk Resort ⭕ RV camping
37	Deer Springs Rd, Mountain Meadow Rd, **W** 📵 Arco
34	Centre City Pkwy (from sb)

INTERSTATE 15 Cont'd

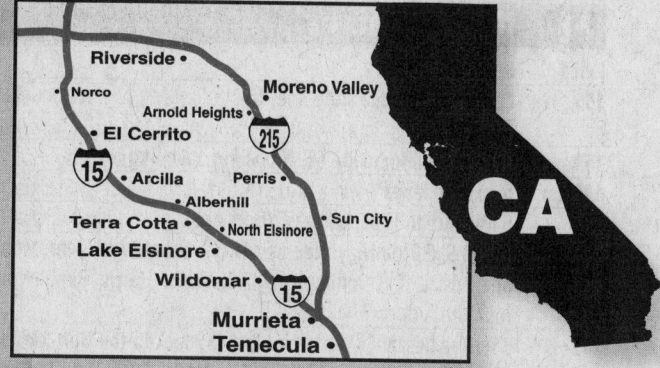

Exit #	Services
33	El Norte Pkwy, **E** ⛽ Arco, Shell/dsl 🍴 Arby's, DQ, IHOP, Papa John's, Starbucks 🏠 Best Western 🅾 CVS Drug, Express Tire/auto repair, RV Resort, vet, Von's Foods, **W** 🍴 76/7-11/dsl, Circle K 🍴 Jack-in-the-Box, Killer Pizza, Rita's Custard, Subway, Wendy's 🅾 vet, Von's Foods
32	CA 78, to Oceanside
31	Valley Pkwy, **E** ⛽ Arco 🍴 Chili's, ChuckeCheese, Cocina del Charro, Firehouse Subs, McDonald's, Olive Garden, Panda Express, Rock'N Jenny's Subs, Thai Kitchen 🅾 🏥, Barnes&Noble, Meineke, Michael's, PetCo, URGENT CARE, **W** ⛽ Express 🍴 Applebee's, Burger King, Carl's Jr, Chipotle Mexican, Coco's, Del Taco, El Pollo Loco, Five Guys, In-N-Out, Jamba Juice, Mike's BBQ, Panera Bread, Pick Up Stix, Port of Subs, Primo's Mexican, Soup Plantation, Starbucks, Subway, Wendy's 🏠 Comfort Inn, Holiday Inn Express 🅾 7-11, Albertson's, AT&T, BigLots, CVS Drug, Dick's, GNC, Home Depot, Lexus, Ross, Staples, Target, TJ Maxx, Verizon, World Mkt
30	9th Ave, Auto Parkway, **E** 🅾 Infiniti, Mercedes, **W** same as 31
29	Felicita Rd
28	Centre City Pkwy (from nb, no return), **E** 🍴 Center City Café 🏠 Escondido Lodge 🅾 vet
27	Via Rancho Pkwy, to Escondido, **E** ⛽ Chevron/dsl, Shell 🍴 BJ's Rest., Cheesecake Factory, Macaroni Grill, On-the-Border, Panera Bread, Red Robin 🅾 JC Penney, Macy's, Nordstrom, San Diego Animal Park, Target, **W** ⛽ Shell/Quiznos/dsl 🍴 McDonald's, Starbucks, Subway 🅾 Verizon
26	W Bernardo Dr, to Highland Valley Rd, Palmerado Rd
24	Rancho Bernardo Rd, to Lake Poway, **E** ⛽ Arco, Mobil/Circle K 🍴 Chef Chin, Cojita's Taco, Pizza Hut, Soup Plantation, Starbucks, Stirfresh, Sub Marina, Subway 🏠 Hilton Garden 🅾 AT&T, Barons Mkt, GNC, Von's Foods, **W** ⛽ 76/Circle K, Chevron/7-11 🍴 Elephant Bar Rest., Starbucks 🏠 Holiday Inn Express, Radisson
23	Bernardo Ctr Dr, **E** ⛽ Chevron 🍴 Burger King, Carl's Jr, Coco's, Denny's, Hibachi Buffet, Jack-in-the-Box, Little Caesar's, McDonald's, Quiznos, Robeks Juice, RoundTable Pizza, Rubio's 🅾 7-11, CVS Drug, Express Tire/auto, Firestone/auto, vet
22	Camino del Norte
21	Carmel Mtn Rd, **E** ⛽ Chevron, Shell/dsl 🍴 Athens Greek, Baskin-Robbins, Boston Mkt, Broken Yolk Cafe, CA Pizza Kitchen, Carl's Jr, Chick-fil-A, China Fun, Chipotle Mexican, ClaimJumper, DQ Orange Julius, El Pollo Loco, Habit Burgers, In-N-Out, Islands Burgers, Jamba Juice, Little Tokyo, Marie Callender's, McDonald's, Olive Garden, O's American Kitchen, Panda Express, Panera Bread, Rubio's, Sombrero Mexican, Subway, Taco Bell, TGIFriday's, Wendy's, Which Wich? 🏠 Residence Inn 🅾 AT&T, Barnes&Noble, Best Buy, Costco/gas, GNC, Home Depot, Marshall's, Michael's, PetCo, Ralph's Foods, Rite Aid, Ross, Sears Outlet, See's Candies, Sprouts Mkt, Staples, TJ Maxx, Trader Joe's, USPO, Valvoline, Verizon, **W** ⛽ Chevron 🍴 Jack-in-the-Box, Starbucks 🅾 7-11, Albertson's, Big O Tire, Office Depot
19	CA 56 W, Ted Williams Pkwy
18	Rancho Penasquitos Blvd, Poway Rd, **E** ⛽ Arco 🍴 Alvero's Mexican, Papa John's 🅾 AAA, **W** ⛽ 76/dsl, Mobil/dsl 🍴 IHOP, McDonald's, Mi Ranchito Mexican, MXN Cafe, NY Pizza, Starbucks, Subway 🏠 La Quinta 🅾 7-11
17	Mercy Rd, Scripps Poway Pkwy, **E** ⛽ USA/dsl 🍴 Chili's, Wendy's, Yanni's Grill 🏠 Residence Inn, SpringHill Suites, **W** ⛽ Chevron 🍴 KFC, Que Pasa Mexican, Starbucks
16	Mira Mesa Blvd, to Lake Miramar, **E** 🍴 Bruski Burgers, ChuckeCheese, Denny's, Filippi's Pizza, Filippi's Pizza, Gyu-Kaku Japanese, Lucio's Mexican, Nok Thai, Pizza Hut, Shozen BBQ 🏠 Comfort Suites, Holiday Inn Express 🅾 Trader Joe's, USPO, **W** ⛽ Arco, Shell 🍴 Applebee's, Arby's, Buca Italian, Coldstone, El Patron, In-N-Out, Islands Burgers, Jack-in-the-Box, Jamba Juice, Jersey Mike's Subs, McDonald's, Mimi's Café, MXN Mexican, On the Border, Panera Bread, Pick Up Stix, Popeye's, Rubio's, Starbucks, Subway, Wings n Things 🅾 Albertson's/Sav-On, AutoZone, Barnes&Noble, Best Buy, BigLots, CVS Drug, Discount Tire, GNC, Home Depot, Old Navy, Ralph's Foods, Rite Aid, Ross, USPO, Verizon
15	Carroll Canyon Rd, to Miramar College, **E** 🍴 Carl's Jr, Subway
14	Pomerado Rd, Miramar Rd, **W** ⛽ Chevron/dsl, Mobil, Shell/dsl, USA/dsl 🍴 Carl's Jr, Chin's Rest., IHOP, Rice King, Subway 🏠 Best Western, Holiday Inn, Quality Inn 🅾 Audi/Porsche, aviation museum, Land Rover, vet
13	Miramar Way, US Naval Air Station
12	CA 163 S (from sb), to San Diego
11	to CA 52
10	Clairemont Mesa Blvd, **W** 🍴 Boll Weevil Rest., Carl's Jr, China Express, Giovanni's, Giovanni's Pizza, Jack-in-the-Box, Jersey Mike's, La Salsa, McDonald's, Panda Express, Primo's Mexican, Robeks, Rubio's, Spice House Cafe, Starbucks, Subway, Sunny Donuts, Taco Bell, Taco Bell, Togo's, Wendy's 🅾 7-11, vet
9	CA 274, Balboa Ave
8	Aero Dr, **W** ⛽ Arco, Chevron/dsl 🍴 Baskin-Robbins/Togo's, Jack-in-the-Box, McDonald's, Papa John's, Pick Up Stix, Rubio's, Sizzler, SmashBurger, Starbucks, Submarina, Subway, Taco Bell 🏠 Holiday Inn 🅾 $Tree, AT&T, Express Tire/auto, Fry's Electronics, Petsmart, Verizon, Von's Foods, Walmart/McDonald's
7b	Friars Rd W, **W** 🍴 Coldstone, Dragon Chinese, IHOP, Islands Burgers, Luna Grill, McDonald's, Oggi's Pizza, Playa Grill, Starbucks, Subway 🅾 Costco/gas, Lowe's, San Diego Stadium
7a	Friars Rd E
6b	I-8, E to El Centro, W to beaches
6a	Adams Ave, downtown
5b	El Cajon Blvd, **E** ⛽ Pearson/dsl/E85/NG 🍴 Subway 🅾 Carquest, Ford, **W** ⛽ Chevron/dsl, United Oil 🍴 Church's 🅾 PepBoys
5a	University Ave, **E** ⛽ Chevron/dsl 🍴 Burger King, Jack-in-the-Box
3	I-805, N to I-5, S to San Ysidro
2b	(2c from nb) CA 94 W, downtown
2a	Market St, **E** 🅾 Costco/gas
1c	National Ave, Ocean View Blvd
1b	(from sb) I-5 S, to Chula Vista
1a	(from sb) I-5 N. **I-15 begins/ends on I-5.**

CA

NEEDLES / BARSTOW — INTERSTATE 40

Exit #	Services
155	California/Arizona state line, Colorado River, pacific/mountain time zone
153	Park Moabi Rd, to Rte 66, N boating, camping
149mm	insp both lanes
148	5 Mile Rd, to Topock, Rte 66 (from eb)
144	US 95 S, E Broadway, Needles, N ☐ Chevron/dsl/24hr, Mobil, Shell/dsl/LP ☐ Domino's ☐ AutoZone, Harris Repair/towing, Rite Aid
142	J St, Needles, N ☐ American/dsl ☐ Jack-in-the-Box, McDonald's ☐ Quality Inn ☐ Big O Tire, NAPA, S ☐ Days Inn, Motel 6 ☐ ☐
141	W Broadway, River Rd, Needles, N ☐ Porky's BBQ, River City Pizza ☐ Best Motel, Desert Mirage Inn, River Valley Motel, S ☐ Chevron/Circle K/dsl, Mobil/dsl, Shell/DQ/Subway/dsl, Tesla EVC ☐ Carl's Jr, Giggling Cactus, Panda Garden, Wagon Wheel Rest. ☐ Best Western, Budget Inn, Red Roof Inn, Rio Del Sol Inn ☐ auto/RV/tire/repair
139	River Rd Cutoff (from eb), N ☐ Desert View RV Park, KOA, Hist Rte 66, rec area
133	US 95 N, to Searchlight, to Rte 66
120	Water Rd
115	Mountain Springs Rd, Mountain Springs Summit, elev 2770, elev 2770, High Springs Summit
107	Goffs Rd, Essex, N ☐ Hi Sahara Oasis/dsl/snacks, Hist Rte 66
106mm	☐ both lanes, full ☐ facilities, litter barrels, petwalk, ☐, ☐
100	Essex Rd, Essex, N Mitchell Caverns, to Providence Mtn SP
78	Kelbaker Rd, to Amboy, E Mojave Nat Preserve, Kelso, S Hist Rte 66
50	Ludlow, N ☐ 76/DQ, S ☐ Chevron/dsl ☐ Ludlow Cafe ☐ Ludlow Motel
33	Hector Rd, to Hist Rte 66
28mm	☐ both lanes, full ☐ facilities, litter barrels, petwalk, ☐, ☐
23	Ft Cady Rd, to Newberry Spgs, N ☐ Mobil/Circle K/dsl, S ☐ Newberry Mtn RV Park
18	Newberry Springs, N ☐ Chevron/dsl/24hr, S ☐ Shell/Subway/dsl/LP
12	Barstow-Daggett Airport, N ☐ ☐ ☐
7	Daggett, N ☐ RV camping (2mi), to Calico Ghost Town
5	Nebo St (from eb), to Hist Rte 66
2	USMC Logistics Base, N ☐ Desert Rat RV Park
1	E Main St, Montara Rd, Barstow, 1 mi N ☐ Chevron, Circle K/dsl, EVC, Mobil/dsl, Phillips 66/dsl, USA/dsl ☐ Alberto's Mexican, Burger King, Carl's Jr, China Town Buffet, Del Taco, Denny's, Di Napoli's Italian, Grill It, IHOP, Jack-in-the-Box, Jenny's Grill, Little Caesar's, McDonald's, Panda Express, Popeye's, Rigoberto's, Starbucks, Subway, Taco Bell, Tom's Burgers, Wienerschnitzel ☐ Astro Budget Motel, Best Motel, Best Western, Budget Inn, CA Inn, Days Inn, Desert Inn, EconoLodge, Economy Inn, Motel 6, Quality Inn/rest., Ramada Inn, Rodeway Inn, Super 8, Travelodge ☐ $Tree, 99c Store, AutoZone, O'Reilly Parts, U-Haul/LP, S ☐ Arco ☐ Walmart/McDonald's
0mm	I-40 begins/ends on I-15 in Barstow.

INTERSTATE 80

Exit #	Services
208	California/Nevada state line
201	Farad
199	Floristan
194	Hirschdale Rd, N Stampede Dam, to Boca Dam, S RV Park
191	(from wb), inspection sta, weigh sta

TRUCKEE / COLFAX — INTERSTATE 80 (continued)

Exit #	Services
190	Overland Trail
188	CA 89 N, CA 267, to N Shore Lake Tahoe, N ☐ Coachland RV Park, USFS, S same as 186
186	Central Truckee (no eb return), S ☐ 76/dsl, Beacon ☐ Burger Me, Casa Baeza Mexican, El Toro Bravo Mexican, Jax Truckee Diner, Marg's Taco Bistro, Wagon Train Café ☐ Hilltop Lodge, Truckee Hotel ☐ CA Welcome Ctr
185	CA 89 S, to N Lake Tahoe, N ☐ DQ, Golden Rotisserie, Panda Express, Port of Subs, RoundTable Pizza, Starbucks, Zano Pizza ☐ ☐, 7-11, Ace Hardware, NAPA, New Moon Natural Foods, Rite Aid, Safeway Foods, URGENT CARE, Verizon, S ☐ Shell/dsl ☐ McDonald's, Pizzaria, Starbucks, Subway ☐ auto repair, CVS Drug, O'Reilly Parts, SaveMart Foods, to Squaw Valley
184	Donner Pass Rd, Truckee, N ☐ Shell/dsl ☐ La Bamba Mexican, Smokey's Kitchen ☐ Sunset Inn ☐ vet, S ☐ Chevron/dsl ☐ Taco Bell ☐ Truckee Donner Lodge ☐ chain services, RV camp/dump, to Donner SP
181mm	vista point both lanes
180	Donner Lake (from wb), S ☐ Donner Lake Village Resort
177mm	Donner Summit, elev 7239, ☐ both lanes, full ☐ facilities, litter barrels, petwalk, ☐, ☐, view area
176	Castle Park, Boreal Ridge Rd, S ☐ Boreal Inn/rest. ☐ Pacific Crest Trailhead, skiing
174	Soda Springs, Norden, S ☐ Sugar Bowl/dsl ☐ Summit Rest ☐ Donner Summit Lodge ☐ chain services
171	Kingvale, S ☐ Shell
168	Rainbow Rd, to Big Bend, S ☐ Rainbow Lodge/rest. ☐ RV camping
166	Big Bend (from eb)
165	Cisco Grove, N ☐ RV camp/dump, skiing, snowmobiling, S ☐ Chevron/dsl/24hr ☐ Subway ☐ chain services
164	Eagle Lakes Rd
161	CA 20 W, to Nevada City, Grass Valley
160	Yuba Gap, S ☐ boating, camping, ☐, ☐, skiing, snowpark
158	Laing Rd, S ☐ Sierra Woods Lodge/café ☐ USPO
157mm	brake check area, wb
158a	Emigrant Gap (from eb), S ☐ Sierra Woods Lodge/café ☐ USPO
156	Nyack Rd, Emigrant Gap, S ☐ Shell/Burger King/dsl ☐ Nyack Café ☐ USPO
156mm	brake check area
155	Blue Canyon
150	Drum Forebay
148b	Baxter, N ☐ chainup services, food, ☐, RV camping
148a	Crystal Springs
146	Alta
145	Dutch Flat, N ☐ Monte Vista Rest., S ☐ 76/dsl ☐ chainup services, Dutch Flat RV Resort, hwy patrol
144	Gold Run (from wb), N chainup, food, gas/dsl, ☐
143mm	☐ both lanes, full ☐ facilities, litter barrels, petwalk, ☐, ☐
143	Magra Rd, Gold Run, N chainup services
140	Magra Rd, Rollins Lake Rd, Secret Town Rd
139	Rollins Lake Road (from wb), RV camping
135	CA 174, to Grass Valley, Colfax, N ☐ 76/dsl, Beacon/dsl ☐ McDonald's, Pizza Factory, Starbucks, Taco Bell, TJ's Roadhouse ☐ Colfax Motel ☐ $General, NAPA, Sierra Mkt Foods, S ☐ Chevron/dsl, Valero/dsl ☐ Shang Garden Chinese, Subway
133	Canyon Way, to Colfax, S ☐ Dine'n Dash Cafe ☐ Chevrolet, Plaza Tire
131	Cross Rd, to Weimar

🅴 INTERSTATE 80 Cont'd

Exit #	Services
130	W Paoli Lane, to Weimar, **S** 🅖 Weimar Store/dsl
129	Heather Glen, elev 2000 ft
128	Applegate, **N** 🅖 Valero/dsl/LP 🅞 chainup services
125	Clipper Gap, Meadow Vista
124	Dry Creek Rd
123	Bell Rd
122	Foresthill Rd, Ravine Rd, Auburn, **N** 🅛 Marriott, **S** 🅕 Awful Annie's Rest., Burger King, Ikeda's Cafe, Sizzler, Starbucks, Subway 🅛 Best Western, Rodeway Inn 🅞 same as 121
121	Lincolnway (from eb), Auburn, **N** 🅖 Mobil, Mobil/dsl, Valero/dsl 🅕 JimBoy's Tacos, Starbucks, Taco Bell, Wienerschnitzel 🅛 Red Lion Inn, Foothills Motel, Motel 6, Super 8, **S** 🅖 Arco, Auburn/dsl, Chevron/dsl, Gas&Shop, Shell/dsl 🅕 Awful Annie's Rest., Black Bear Diner, Burger King, Burrito Shop, Carl's Jr, Hawaiian BBQ, Jack-in-the-Box, Joe Caribe Bistro, KFC, McDonald's, Pete's Grill, Sierra Grill, Sizzler, Starbucks, Subway 🅛 Best Western, Rodeway Inn 🅞 Ikeda's Cafe, Raley's Foods, Verizon
120	Russell Ave (from wb), same as 121, to Lincolnway from eb
119c	Elm Ave, Auburn, **N** 🅖 76/dsl, Shell/dsl 🅕 Burger&Cream, Roundtable Pizza, Starbucks 🅛 Holiday Inn 🅞 CVS Drug, Grocery Outlet, Rite Aid, SaveMart Foods, Staples, Verizon
119b	CA 49, to Grass Valley, Auburn, **N** 🅖 76/dsl, Shell/dsl 🅕 In-N-Out 🅛 Holiday Inn 🅞 RV Connection, Staples
119a	Maple St, Nevada St, Old Town Auburn, **S** 🅖 Valero 🅕 Cafe Delicias, Tio Pepe Mexican 🅞 USPO
118	Ophir Rd (from wb)
116	CA 193, to Lincoln
115	Indian Hill Rd, Newcastle, **N** 🅞 transmissions, USPO, **S** 🅖 Mobil/dsl, Valero/dsl 🅕 Denny's 🅞 CHP
112	Penryn, **N** 🅖 76/dsl, Chevron/dsl 🅕 Subway
110	Horseshoe Bar Rd, to Loomis, **N** 🅕 Burger King, RoundTable Pizza, Starbucks, Taco Bell 🅞 Raley's Food
109	Sierra College Blvd, **N** 🅖 7-11/dsl, Arco/dsl, Chevron/McDonald's/dsl 🅕 Blast Pizza, Carl's Jr, Chipotle, Mooyah Burger, Noodles&Co, Panera Bread, Subway 🅞 Camping World RV Ctr, GNC, Rocklin RV Ctr, Ross, Steinmart, Target, Tesla, Verizon, **S** 🅖 Shell/dsl 🅕 Dickey's BBQ, In-N-Out, Jimboy's Tacos, Mod Pizza, Panda Express, Starbucks, Wing Stop 🅞 AT&T, Bass Pro Shop, Petsmart, TJ Maxx, Walmart
108	Rocklin Rd, **N** 🅖 Valero/dsl 🅕 A&W/KFC, Adalberto's Mexican, Arby's, Baskin-Robbins, Denny's, Golden Dragon, Jack-in-the-Box, Jamba Juice, Koja Kitchen, Milo's, Papa Murphy's, RoundTable Pizza, Starbucks, Subway, Taco Bell 🅛 Comfort Inn, Days Inn, SureStay Inn 🅞 CVS Drug, GNC, Land Rover, Mercedes, Porsche, Safeway Foods, **S** 🅖 Arco 🅕 Little Caesar's 🅛 Rocklin Park Hotel 🅞 vet
106	CA 65, to Lincoln, Marysville, **1 mi N on Stanford Ranch Rd** 🅖 76, Arco, Shell 🅕 Black Bear Diner, Carl's Jr, Cheesecake Factory, Chipotle, IHOP, Jack-in-the-Box, KFC, McDonald's, Olive Garden, On-the-Border, PF Changs, Ruth's Chris Steaks, TGIFriday 🅛 Courtyard, Holiday Inn Express, Homewood Suites, Hyatt Place 🅞 AutoZone, Barnes&Noble, Best Buy, Costco/dsl, JC Penney, Macy's, Marshall's, Michael's, Nordstrom's, Old Navy, Ross, Sprouts Mkt, Staples
105b	Taylor Rd, to Rocklin (from eb), **N** 🅕 Cattlemen's Rest., **S** 🅖 76/Burger King/dsl, Chevron 🅕 Islands Burgers, Subway, Tahoe Joe's 🅛 Courtyard, Fairfield Inn, Hilton Garden, Holiday Inn Express, Larkspur Suites, Residence Inn 🅞 🄷, funpark

Exit #	Services
105a	Atlantic St, Eureka Rd, **S** 🅕 76/7-11/dsl, Shell/Circle K 🅕 Brookfield's Rest., Chicago Fire Rest., In-N-Out, Taco Bell, Wendy's 🅞 🄷, Acura, America'sTire, Buick/GMC, Carmax, Chevrolet, Chrysler/Dodge/Jeep, Fiat, Ford, Home Depot, Honda, Hyundai, Infiniti, Kia, Lexus, Mazda, Nissan, Petsmart, Subaru, Target, Toyota, VW
103b a	Douglas Blvd, **N** 🅖 76/dsl, Arco/dsl, Chevron/7-11, Shell/dsl 🅕 Burger King, Carolina's Mexican, Claim Jumper, McDonald's, Mongolian BBQ, Popeye's, Starbucks, Subway 🅛 Best Western, Extended Stay America, Heritage Inn 🅞 $Tree, Ace Hardware, Autozone, Big O Tire, BigLots, BrakeMasters, Goodyear, Grocery Outlet, Midas, O'Reilly Parts, Rite Aid, Trader Joe's, **S** 🅕 Carl's Jr, Chevy's, Del Taco, Denny's, Jack-in-the-Box, Lorenzo's Mexican, Outback Steaks, Panera Bread, Rubio's, Sizzler, Subway 🅛 Best Western, Hampton Inn 🅞 🄷, Fry's Electronics, Hobby Lobby, Office Depot, Ross, Target
102	Riverside Ave, Auburn Blvd, to Roseville, **N** 🅖 Arco/dsl, Chevron/dsl 🅕 Starbucks 🅞 auto repair, Meineke, **S** 🅖 Chevron/7-11, Shell, Towne Mart 🅕 Back 40 TX BBQ, Baskin-Robbins, CA Burgers, Jack-in-the-Box, Subway 🅞 $General, auto repair, AutoZone, BMW Motorcycles, Camping World RV Ctr, NAPA, Schwab Tire
100	Antelope Rd, to Citrus Heights, **N** 🅖 🅕 Carl's Jr, Extreme Hummus, Giant Pizza, McDonald's, Papa Murphy's, Popeye's, RoundTable Pizza, Subway, Taco Bell, Wendy's 🅞 $Tree, 7-11, O'Reilly Parts, Raley's Foods, vet
100mm	weigh sta both lanes
98	Greenback Lane, Elkhorn Blvd, Orangedale, Citrus Heights, **N** 🅕 Baskin Robbins, Carl's Jr, Little Caesar's, McDonald's, Pizza Hut, Starbucks, Subway, Taco Bell 🅞 $General, CVS Drug, Safeway Foods
96	Madison Ave, **N** 🅖 Chevron/dsl, Mobil/dsl 🅕 Brookfield's Rest., Denny's, Jack-in-the-Box, Mongolian BBQ, Ninja Asian, Starbucks 🅛 Motel 6, Super 8 🅞 funpark, to McClellan AFB, **S** 🅖 Arco, Shell/dsl 🅕 Burger King, Chick-fil-A, Chipotle Mexican, El Pollo Loco, IHOP, In-N-Out, Jack-in-the-Box, McDonald's, Panda Express, Starbucks, Subway, Wienerschnitzel 🅛 Crowne Plaza, La Quinta 🅞 7-11, Acura, AT&T, Chevrolet, Firestone/auto, Ford, Office Depot, PepBoys, Schwab Tire, Target, Verizon, Volvo, Walgreens
95	CA 99 S
94b	Auburn Blvd
94a	Watt Ave, **N** 🅖 76/dsl, Arco 🅕 Carl's Jr, Del Taco, Golden Corral, Jack-in-the-Box, KFC, McDonald's, Panda Express, Starbucks, Subway, Taco Bell 🅛 Best Value Inn 🅞 $Tree, Firestone/auto, McClellan AFB, Walmart, **S** 🅖 76/dsl, Arco, Chevron, Shell 🅕 Denny's, Jimboy's Tacos, Quiznos, Starbucks, Wendy's 🅛 Red Roof Inn 🅞 AutoZone, Grocery Outlet

Vertical side labels: **AUBURN** · **ROCKLIN** · **CITRUS HEIGHTS** · **CA**

🅴 INTERSTATE 80 Cont'd

CA — SACRAMENTO / DAVIS

Exit #	Services
93	Longview Dr
92	Winters St
91	Raley Blvd, Marysville Blvd, to Rio Linda, **N** 🅖 Arco, Chevron/dsl, **S** 🅞 $General, Hooten Tires, USPO, Valley Tire, Viva Mkt
90	Norwood Ave, **N** 🅖 Arco/Jack-in-the-Box, Valero 🅕 Little Caesar's, McDonald's, RoundTable Pizza, Starbucks, Subway 🅞 Rite Aid, Viva Foods, Walgreens, **S** 🅞 $General
89	Northgate Blvd, Sacramento, **N** 🅕 Cilantro's Mexican, L&L Hawaiian BBQ, Subway 🅞 Fry's Electronics, **S** 🅖 Arco, Shell, Valero/Circle K 🅕 524 Mexican, Carl's Jr, Classic Burgers, El Pollo Loco, IHOP, KFC, LampPost Pizza, LJ Silver, McDonald's/playplace, Subway, Taco Bell 🅛 Econolodge, Extended Stay America 🅞 $Tree, Foodsco Foods, O'Reilly Parts, PepBoys, Schwab Tire
88	Truxel Rd, **N** 🅖 Chevron/McDonald's, Shell/dsl 🅕 Applebee's, BJ's Rest, Buffalo Wild Wings, Casa Ramos, Chili's, Chipotle Mexican, Del Taco, Firehouse Subs, Hooters, In-N-Out, Logan's Roadhouse, On the Border, Panda Express, Panera Bread, Rubio's, Sandwich Spot, Starbucks, Subway, Tokyo Steakhouse 🅛 Staybridge Suites 🅞 AT&T, Barnes&Noble, Best Buy, GNC, Home Depot, Michael's, Old Navy, Petsmart, Power Balance Pavilion, Ross, See's Candies, Staples, Target, TJ Maxx, Verizon, Walmart, World Mkt
86	I-5, N to Redding, S to Sacramento, to CA 99 N
85	W El Camino, **N** 🅖 49er Trkstp/Silver Skillet/dsl/scales/24hr/@, Chevron/Subway/dsl/24hr 🅕 Black Bear Diner, Burger King 🅛 Fairfield Inn, Super 8, **S** 🅖 Arco
83	Reed Ave, **N** 🅖 Chevron/dsl 🅕 Jack-in-the-Box, Panda Express, Starbucks, Subway 🅛 Extended Stay America, Hampton Inn, SpringHill Suites, **S** 🅖 Arco/24hr, Shell/McDonald's/dsl 🅕 Burger King, Chipotle, Five Guys, IHOP, In-N-Out, Taco Bell 🅞 America's Tire, Firestone/auto, GNC, Home Depot, IKEA, Petco, Ross, Walmart
82	US 50 E, W Sacramento
81	Enterprise Blvd, W Capitol Ave, W Sacramento, **N** 🅖 Arco/dsl, Chevron 🅛 Granada Inn, **S** 🅖 7-11 🅕 Eppie's Diner, Starbucks, Subway 🅞 KOA
78	Rd 32A, E Chiles Rd, **S** 🅞 Fruit Stand
75	Mace Blvd, **N** 🅖 Arco 🅞 Target, TJ Maxx, to Mace Ranch, Verizon, **S** 🅖 Chevron/dsl, Gas&Shop/dsl, Sinclair/dsl, Valero/dsl 🅕 Cindy's Rest., Domino's, McDonald's, Starbucks, Subway, Taco Bell 🅛 Days Inn, Motel 6 🅞 American River RV Ctr, Chevrolet, Chrysler/Dodge/Jeep, Honda, Kia, La Mesa RV Ctr, Nissan, Nugget Mkt Foods, Toyota
73	Olive Dr (from wb, no EZ return)
72b a	Richards Blvd, Davis, **N** 🅖 Shell 🅕 In-N-Out, Redrum Burger 🅛 University Park Inn 🅞 NAPA, **S** 🅖 Chevron/dsl 🅕 Applebee's, Carl's Jr, IHOP, KFC, Starbucks 🅛 Holiday Inn Express, La Quinta 🅞 Jiffy Lube, O'Reilly Parts
71	to UC Davis
70	CA 113 N, to Woodland, **N** 🅞 🅷
69	Kidwell Rd
67	Pedrick Rd, **N** 🅖 76/LP, Chevron/dsl/24hr 🅞 produce
66b	Milk Farm Rd (from wb)
66a	CA 113 S, Currey Rd, to Dixon, **S** 🅖 Chevron/dsl, Shell/dsl, Valero/Popeye's/dsl 🅕 Cattlemen's Rest., Jack-in-the-Box, La Cocina, Papa Murphy's, Subway, Wendy's 🅛 Country Inn Suites 🅞 Schwab Tires, Walmart
64	Pitt School Rd, to Dixon, **S** 🅖 Chevron/24hr, Valero/24hr 🅕 Arby's, Asian Garden, Baskin Robbins, Burger King, Capital China, Denny's, IHOP, Little Caesar's, Maria's Mexican, Mary's

CA — VACAVILLE

Exit #	Services
64	Continued Pizza, McDonald's, Pizza Guys, Solano Bakery, Starbucks, Subway, Taco Bell 🅛 Best Western+, Motel 6 🅞 Safeway/dsl
63	Dixon Ave, Midway Rd, **N** 🅖 Truck Stp/dsl, **S** 🅖 Arco LP/lube, Chevron/dsl 🅕 Alheli's Drive Thru, Carl's Jr, M Taco 🅛 Super 8 🅞 Dixon Fruit Mkt
60	Midway Rd, Lewis Rd, Elmyra, **N** 🅞 Produce Mkt, RV campin (3mi)
59	Meridian Rd, Weber Rd
57	Leisure Town Rd, **N** 🅞 🅷, Camping World, **S** 🅖 76/M Donald's, Arco, Chevron/dsl, QuikStop 🅕 Black Oak Rest Clay Oven Grill, Hideaway Grill, Jack-in-the-Box, King's Buffe Popeye's, Starbucks, Subway, Taco Bell 🅛 Comfort Suites, Ex tended Stay America, Fairfield Inn, Holiday Inn Express, Mot 6, Quality Inn, Residence Inn 🅞 Buick/GMC, Chevrolet, Chrys ler/Dodge/Jeep, Harley-Davidson, Home Depot, Honda, Kohl Mazda, Nissan, Toyota, VW
56	I-505 N, to Winters
55	Nut Tree Pkwy, Monte Vista Dr, Allison Dr, **N** 🅖 7-11, 76/Ci cle K, Chevron 🅕 Boudin SF Sourdough, Buckhorn BBQ, Bu falo Wild Wings, Burger King, Chipotle, Denny's, El Pollo Loc Fenton's Creamery, Firehouse Subs, Five Guys, Food Court, Hab it Burger, Hawaiian BBQ, Hisui Japanese, IHOP, Jamba Juic Krispy Kreme, McDonald's, Murillo's Mexican, Nations Burge Noodles&Co, Panda Express, Panera Bread, Pelayo's Mexica Pieology Pizza, Round Table Pizza, Rubio's, Starbucks, Subwa Taco Bell, Wendy's, Yen King Chinese 🅛 Best Value Inn, Be Western, Super 8 🅞 America's Tire, Best Buy, Big O Tire, CV Drug, Firestone/auto, Lowe's Whse, Michael's, Nugget Food Old Navy, Petsmart, See's Candies, U-Haul, Verizon, Worl Mkt, **S** 🅖 Arco/24hr, Chevron/24hr 🅕 Applebee's, BJ's Gri Black Oak Rest., Carl's Jr, Chick-fil-A, Chili's, Coldstone Cream ery, Dickey's BBQ, Favela's Mexican Grill, Freebirds Burrit Grocery Outlet, Home Towne Buffet, In-N-Out, Jack-in-the-Bo Jamba Juice, Mel's Diner, Olive Garden, Popeye's, Red Robi Starbucks, Starbucks, String's Italian, Subway, Tahoe Joe Steaks, Togo's 🅛 Comfort Suites, Courtyard, Fairfield In Holiday Inn Express, Motel 6, Residence Inn 🅞 🅷, GMC, GN Jo-Ann Fabrics, Marshall's, PetCo, Ross, Safeway, Sam's Clu dsl, Staples, Target, Vacaville Stores/famous brands, Walmar McDonald's
54b	Mason St, Peabody Rd, **N** 🅖 Chevron/7-11, Conservati Fuel/dsl 🅛 Hampton Inn 🅞 CVS Drug, NAPA, O'Reilly Par Schwab Tire, **S** 🅖 Shell 🅕 Carl's Jr, Domino's, Starbuck Subway 🅞 $Tree, 7-11, Costco/gas
54a	Davis St, **N** 🅖 Chevron/McDonald's 🅕 Outback Steal 🅛 Hampton Inn, **S** 🅕 DQ, Sonic 🅞 repair, WinCo Foods
53	Merchant St, Alamo Dr, **N** 🅖 Chevron, Merchant/dsl, She dsl 🅕 Baldo's Mexican, Baskin-Robbins, Black Bear Dine RoundTable Pizza, Tony's Rest. 🅛 Alamo Inn 🅞 BigLo **S** 🅖 76/dsl 🅕 Jack-in-the-Box, KFC, McDonald's, Pizza H Rita's Custard, Starbucks, Subway 🅞 Walmart Mkt
52	Cherry Glen Rd (from wb)
51b	Pena Adobe Rd, **S** 🅛 Ranch Hotel
51a	Lagoon Valley Rd, Cherry Glen
48	N Texas St, Fairfield, **S** 🅖 Arco/24hr, Chevron/dsl, Shell 🅕 Pollo Loco, Jim Boy's Tacos, McDonald's, Panda Express, Roun Table Pizza, Starbucks, Subway, Texas Roadhouse 🅛 Best Va ue Inn 🅞 CVS, Lowe's, Raley's Foods
47	Waterman Blvd, **N** 🅕 Dynasty Chinese, RoundTable Pizz Starbucks, Subway 🅞 Chevrolet/Subaru, Safeway, to Austi Place, **S** 🅞 museum, to Travis AFB

INTERSTATE 80 Cont'd

Exit #	Services
45	Travis Blvd, Fairfield, **N** ⛽ Arco/24hr, Chevron 🍴 Baskin-Robbins, Burger King, Denny's, Domino's, Huckleberry's Cafe, In-N-Out, McDonald's, Peking Rest., Subway, Taco Bell, Togo's 🛏 Courtyard, Motel 6 ⭕ $Tree, CHP, Meineke, PetCo, Raley's Foods, **S** ⛽ 76/dsl 🍴 Buffalo Wild Wings, Carino's Italian, Chevy's Mexican, Chick-fil-A, Chipotle Mexican, Coldstone, Five Guys, Fuddrucker's, HomeTown Buffet, Jamba Juice, Mimi's Café, Panda Express, Panera Bread, Pieology, Red Lobster, Red Robin, Rubio's, Starbucks, Subway, Wing Stop 🛏 Hilton Garden ⭕ 🅗, AT&T, Barnes&Noble, Best Buy, Firestone/auto, JC Penney, Macy's, Michael's, Ross, Trader Joe's, Verizon
44	W Texas St, same as 45, Fairfield, **N** ⛽ A&A/dsl, KwikServ/dsl 🍴 ChuckeCheese, Gordito's Mexican, Popeye's, Starbucks 🛏 Extended Stay America ⭕ Staples, **S** ⛽ Valero/dsl 🍴 Baldo's Mexican, McDonald's, Paleyo's Mexican ⭕ 99c Store, Acura/Honda, CarMax, Chrysler/Jeep/Dodge, Ford/Lincoln, Home Depot, Hyundai, Infiniti, Mercedes, Nissan, O'Reilly Parts, Target, Toyota, VW, Walgreens
43	CA 12 E, Abernathy Rd, Suisun City, **S** ⭕ Budweiser Plant, Walmart
42mm	weigh sta both lanes, 🅲
41	Suisan Valley Rd, **N** 🛏 Homewood Suites, Staybridge Suites, **S** ⛽ 7-11, 76, Chevron/dsl, Shell/dsl, Valero/dsl 🍴 Arby's, Burger King, Carl's Jr, Cenario's Pizza, Del Taco, Denny's, Green Bamboo, Jack-in-the-Box, Jersey Mike's, McDonald's, Starbucks, Straw Hat Pizza, Subway, Taco Bell, Wendy's 🛏 Best Western, Comfort Inn, Fairfield Inn, La Quinta, Motel 6, Travelodge ⭕ Fairfield RV Ctr, Scandia FunCtr, vet
40	I-680 (from wb)
39b	Green Valley Rd, I-680 (from eb), **N** 🍴 Happy Garden, Hawaiian BBQ, Hinata, Peloyas Mexican, RoundTable Pizza, Starbucks, Subway 🛏 Homewood Suites, Staybridge Suites ⭕ Costco/gas, CVS, Safeway, TJ Maxx, **S** ⛽ Arco ⭕ Kia
39a	Red Top Rd, **N** ⛽ Chevron 🍴 Jack-in-the-Box
36	American Canyon Rd
34mm	Rs wb, full 🅰 facilities, info, litter barrels, petwalk, 🅲, 🅰, vista parking
33b a	CA 37, to San Rafael, Columbus Pkwy, **N** ⛽ Chevron/dsl, Valero/dsl 🍴 Baskin-Robbins, Carl's Jr. 🛏 Best Western, Courtyard ⭕ funpark, **S** same as 32
32	Redwood St, to Vallejo, **N** ⛽ Chevron 🍴 Denny's, Panda Garden 🛏 Best Value Inn, Motel 6 ⭕ 🅗, **S** ⛽ Shell, Valero 🍴 Applebee's, Black Angus, Black Bear Diner, Chevy's Mexican, Chick-fil-A, Chipotle, Coldstone, Habit Burger, IHOP, Jamba Juice, Jimmy John's, Little Caesar's, McDonald's, Mtn. Mike's Pizza, Olive Garden, Panda Express, Papa Murphy's, Red Lobster, Rubio's, Starbucks, Subway, Taco Bell, Wendy's, Wing Stop 🛏 Comfort Inn, Ramada Inn ⭕ $Tree, AT&T, AutoZone, Best Buy, Cadillac/Chevrolet, Chrysler/Dodge/Jeep, Costco/gas, CVS, Home Depot, Honda, Hyundai, Kohl's, Lowe's, Marshall's, Mazda, Michael's, PepBoys, PetCo, Ross, Safeway, Target, Toyota, Verizon, vet
31b	Tennessee St, to Vallejo, **S** ⛽ Flyers, Valero/dsl 🍴 Jack-in-the-Box, Pizza Guys 🛏 Great Western Inn, Howard Johnson ⭕ Grocery Outlet, USPO
31a	Solano Ave, Springs Rd, **N** 🍴 Burger King, Church's, Subway, Szechuan, Taco Bell 🛏 Rodeway Inn, Super 8 ⭕ Mi Pueblo Mkt, Rite Aid, U-Haul, **S** ⛽ Chevron, Grand Gas, QuikStop 🍴 DQ, McDonald's, Pizza Hut, Subway 🛏 Express Inn ⭕ Island Pacific Foods, O'Reilly Parts
30c	Georgia St, Central Vallejo, **N** ⛽ Safeway/gas, **S** ⛽ Chevron/Starbucks/dsl 🍴 McDonald's 🛏 California Motel
30b	Benicia Rd (from wb), **S** ⛽ Chevron/dsl 🍴 McDonald's, Starbucks
30a	I-780, to Martinez
29b	Magazine St, Vallejo, **N** ⛽ Gas&Shop/dsl 🍴 Starbucks, Subway 🛏 7 Motel, Economy Inn, El Rancho ⭕ Tradewinds RV Park, **S** 🍴 McDonald's 🛏 Travel Inn ⭕ 7-11
29a	CA 29, Maritime Academy Dr, Vallejo, **N** ⛽ 5 Star Gas, Chevron/dsl 🛏 Motel 6
28mm	pay toll from eb, toll plaza
27	Pomona Rd, Crockett, **N** 🍴 Dead Fish Seafood, vista point
26	Cummings Skyway, to CA 4 (from wb), to Martinez
24	Willow Ave, to Rodeo, **N** 🍴 Straw Hat Pizza, Subway ⭕ Safeway, USPO, **S** ⛽ 76/dsl 🍴 Burger King, Mazatlan, Mtn Mike's Pizza, Starbucks, Willow Garden Chinese
23	CA 4, to Stockton, Hercules, **N** ⛽ Shell 🍴 Extreme Pizza, Jack-in-the-Box, Starbucks, **S** 🍴 Dragon Terrace, McDonald's, RoundTable Pizza, Subway, Taco Bell ⭕ BigLots, Home Depot, Lucky Foods, Rite Aid
22	Pinole Valley Rd, **S** ⛽ Arco/24hr, Chevron/dsl 🍴 Chipotle, Five Guys, Jack-in-the-Box, Jamba Juice, Krispy Kreme, Mod Pizza, Red Onion Rest., Subway ⭕ 7-11, Trader Joe's, Walgreens
21	Appian Way, **N** ⛽ Pinole Express 🍴 China Delights, McDonald's, Pizza Hut ⭕ CVS, O'Reilly Parts, Safeway, **S** ⛽ Valero/dsl 🍴 Burger King, Carl's Jr, ChuckECheese, Coldstone, Dickey's BBQ, Due Rose Italian, Hawaiian BBQ, HomeTown Buffet, In-N-Out, KFC, Mel'sOriginal Shakes, Mtn Mike's Pizza, Panda Express, Papa Murphy's, RoundTable Pizza, Sizzler, Starbucks, Subway, Taco Bell, Wendy's, Wing Stop 🛏 Days Inn, Motel 6 ⭕ $Tree, AT&T, AutoZone, Best Buy, Goodyear/auto, Grocery Outlet, Lucky Foods
20	Richmond Pkwy, to I-580 W, **N** ⛽ Chevron/dsl 🍴 IHOP, McDonald's, Me&Ed's Pizza, Subway ⭕ 99c Store, Buick/GMC, Chrysler/Dodge/Jeep, Ford, Hyundai, Kia, Nissan, Ross, Toyota, VW, **S** ⛽ Shell/dsl 🍴 Applebee's, Cheese Steak, In-N-Out, Mel's Original Shakes, Outback Steaks, Panda Express, Panera Bread, RoundTable Pizza ⭕ FoodMaxx, Michael's, O'Reilly Parts, Petsmart, Staples, Target, TJ Maxx
19b	Hilltop Dr, to Richmond, **N** ⛽ Chevron 🍴 Chevy's Mexican 🛏 Courtyard, Extended Stay America ⭕ Firestone/auto, Macy's, Walmart, **S** ⛽ Hilltop Fuel/dsl
19a	El Portal Dr, to San Pablo, **S** ⛽ Shell 🍴 McDonalds, Mtn. Mike's Pizza, Starbucks, Subway ⭕ Raley's Foods, vet, Walgreens
18	San Pablo Dam Rd, **N** ⛽ Chevron 🍴 Burger King, Denny's, El Pollo Loco, Empire Buffet, Jack-in-the-Box, Jamba Juice, Nations Burgers, Pizza Guys, Popeye's, RoundTable Pizza, Starbucks, Subway, Taco Bell 🛏 Holiday Inn Express ⭕ 🅗, $Tree, AutoZone, Big Lots, FoodMaxx, Ross, Walgreens

CA

EL CERRITO BERKELEY

⬆E INTERSTATE 80 Cont'd

Exit #	Services
17	Macdonald Ave (from eb), McBryde Ave (from wb), Richmond, N 🔲 Arco/24hr 🍴 Burger King, S 🔲 Chevron/24hr 🍴 Wendy's 🅾 auto repair
16	San Pablo Ave, to Richmond, San Pablo, S 🔲 Chevron 🍴 KFC, LJ Silver, Subway, Wendy's
15	Cutting Blvd, Potrero St, to I-580 Br (from wb), to El Cerrito, N 🔲 Arco 🍴 Panda Express 🅾 Target, S 🔲 Valero/dsl 🍴 Church's, Denny's, IHOP, Jack-in-the-Box, McDonald's, Starbucks, Trevino's Mexican 🅾 $Tree, Home Depot, Honda, Safeway, Staples, Walgreens
14b	Carlson Blvd, El Cerrito, N 🔲 KwikServ 🏨 40 Flags Motel, S 🏨 Best Value Inn
14a	Central Ave, El Cerrito, S 🔲 76, Shell/dsl, Valero 🍴 Burger King, Chipotle, KFC, Nations Burgers
13	to I-580 (from eb), Albany
12	Gilman St, to Berkeley, N 🅾 Golden Gate Fields Racetrack, S 🅾 Target
11	University Ave, to Berkeley, S 🔲 Element/dsl, 76, Econo Gas 🏨 La Quinta 🅾 to UC Berkeley
10	CA 13, to Ashby Ave
9	Powell St, Emeryville, N 🔲 Shell 🍴 Chevy's Mexican 🏨 Hilton Garden, S 🔲 🍴 Black Bear Diner, Burger King, CA Pizza Kitchen, Denny's, Jamba Juice, PF Chang's, Starbucks, Togo's 🏨 Courtyard, Hyatt House, Sheraton 🅾 Barnes&Noble, Marshall's, Old Navy, Petco, Ross, Trader Joe's
8c b	Oakland, to I-880, I-580
8a	W Grand Ave, Maritime St
7mm	toll plaza wb
5mm	SF Bay
4a	Treasure Island (exits left)
2c b	Fremont St, Harrison St, Embarcadero (from wb)
2a	4th st (from eb), S 🔲 Shell
1	9th st, Civic Ctr, downtown SF
1b a	I-80 begins/ends on US 101 in SF.

⬆E INTERSTATE 110 (Los Angeles)

Exit #	Services
21	I-110 begins/ends on I-10.
20c	Adams Blvd, E 🍴 Chevron 🅾 Audi, Chrysler/Dodge/Jeep, LA Convention Ctr., Mercedes, Nissan, Office Depot, VW
20b	37th St, Exposition Blvd, W 🔲 Chevron/McDonald's 🏨 Radisson 🅾 Chevrolet
20a	MLK Blvd, Expo Park, W 🔲 Chevron 🍴 McDonald's, Subway
19b	Vernon Ave, E 🔲 Mobil 🍴 Tacos El Gavilan, W 🔲 76/24hr, Shell 🍴 Burger King, Jack-in-the-Box, Tom's Burger 🅾 Rite Aid, Ross
18b	Slauson Ave, E 🔲 Mobil, W 🔲 76
18a	Gage Blvd, E 🔲 Arco 🍴 Church's, Hercules Burgers
17	Florence Ave, E 🔲 Shell 🍴 Jack-in-the-Box, W 🔲 Chevron, Valero 🍴 Burger King, Little Caesar's, McDonald's, Pizza Hut, Subway
16	Manchester Ave, E 🔲 Arco 🍴 El Pollo Loco, Little Caesar's, McDonald's, Subway, Winchell's 🅾 AutoZone, W 🔲 🍴 Church's, Jack-in-the-Box, Popeye's, Tam's Burgers
15	Century Blvd, E 🔲 Arco, Shell/Subway/dsl 🍴 Burger King, McDonald's, W 🔲 76/dsl
14b	Imperial Hwy, W 🔲 Chevron/dsl 🍴 Jack-in-the-Box, McDonald's
14a	I-105

LA AREA

Exit #	Services
13	El Segundo Blvd, E 🍴 Taco Bell, W 🔲 Shell
12	Rosecrans Ave, E 🔲 Arco/24hr, Valero, W 🔲 Chevron/McDonald's, Sinclair 🍴 Jack-in-the-Box, KFC/LJ Silver, Pizza Hut, Popeye's, Subway, Yoshinoya 🅾 7-11, casino
11	Redondo Beach Blvd, E 🍴 McDonald's, W 🔲 Mobil 🍴 Farmer Boys, Subway 🅾 H, casino, Ross, Staples
10b a	CA 91, 190th St, W 🔲 Arco 🍴 Jack-in-the-Box, Krispy Kreme, McDonald's, Subway, Taco Bell 🅾 Food4Less, Ranch Mkt, Sam's Club
9	I-405, San Diego Fwy
8	Torrance Blvd, Del Amo, E 🍴 Burger King, Chile Verde, Starbucks, Waba Grill, W 🔲 Mobil, Shell/Subway/dsl
7b	Carson St, E 🍴 KFC 🏨 Cali Inn 🅾 vet, W 🔲 Harbor Fuel, Shell 🍴 Carl's Jr., FatBurger, In-N-Out, Jack-in-the-Box, Los Paisas Mexican, McDonalds, Pizza Hut, Starbucks, Subway, Wienerschnitzel 🅾 H, Autozone, Bella Vida Drug, Numero Uno Mkt, O'Reilly Parts, Rite Aid
5	Sepulveda Blvd, E 🍴 McDonald's, Starbucks 🅾 Albertson's, Home Depot, Staples, Target, W 🔲 Arco/24hr, Chevron, Mobil/dsl 🍴 Burger King, Carl's Jr, McDonald's, Popeye's, Starbucks, Subway, Taco Bell 🏨 Motel 6 🅾 $Tree, 99c Store, AT&T, Big Lots, Food4Less, Ross
4	CA 1, Pacific Coast Hwy, E 🔲 Arco 🍴 Jack-in-the-Box, Pizza Hut, Wienerschnitzel 🅾 $Tree, W 🔲 76, Mobil, United/dsl 🍴 Del Taco, Denny's, El Pollo Loco, Subway 🏨 Best Western 🅾 H, PepBoys, Rite Aid, transmissions
3b	Anaheim St, E 🔲 🍴 Dunkin'
3a	C St
1b	Channel St, W 🔲 Arco, Chevron 🍴 Big Nick's Pizza, Larry's Hamburgers 🅾 7-11, Home Depot, Target
1a	CA 47, Gaffey Ave
0mm	I-110 begins/ends.

⬆N INTERSTATE 205 (Tracy)

Exit #	Services
12	I-205 begins wb, ends eb, accesses I-5 nb.
9	MacArthur Dr, Tracy, S 🔲 Chevron/Jack-in-the-Box/Subway/dsl 🅾 Tracy Outlet Ctr/famous brands
8	Tracy Blvd, Tracy, N 🔲 76/Mean Gene's Burger/dsl, Chevron, Shell/dsl 🍴 Denny's 🏨 Holiday Inn Express, Motel 6, S 🔲 Arco 🍴 Arby's, Burger King, In-N-Out, Lyon's Rest., McDonald's, Milano Pizza, Nations Burgers, Pizza Guys, Starbucks, Straw Hat Pizza, Subway, Wendy's 🏨 Best Western, Microtel, Quality Inn 🅾 H, CHP, CVS Drug, Mi Pueblo Mkt, O'Reilly Parts
6	Grant Line Rd, Antioch, N 🔲 Chevron/dsl 🍴 Applebee's, Buffalo Wild Wings, Burger King, Dickey's BBQ, Famous Dave's BBQ, Five Guys, Golden Corral, Hometown Buffet, IHOP, Jamba Juice, Olive Garden, Panda Express, Red Robin, RoundTable Pizza, Rubio's, Sonic, Squeeze Inn Burger, Starbucks, Strings Italian, Subway, Taco Bell, TX Roadhouse, Wienerschnitzel 🏨 Extended Stay America, Fairfield Inn, Hampton Inn 🅾 America's Tire, AT&T, Barnes&Noble, Best Buy, Chevrolet, Chrysler/Dodge/Jeep, Costco/gas, Ford, Home Depot, Honda, Hyundai, JC Penney, Les Schwab Tire, Macy's, Marshall's, Michael's, Nissan, Petsmart, Ross, See's Candies, Staples, Target, Toyota, Verizon, VW, Walmart/McDonald's/auto, WinCo Foods, World Mkt, World Mkt, S 🔲 7-11, 76/Subway/dsl, Arco, Shell/dsl 🍴 A&W, KFC, Black Bear Diner, Carl's Jr, Chili's, Hawaiian BBQ, Mtn Mike's Pizza, Popeye's 🅾 Rite Aid
4	11th St (from eb), to Tracy, Defense Depot
2	Mtn House Pkwy, to I-580 E
0mm	I-205 begins eb/ends wb, accesses I-580 wb.

TRACY

⮏E INTERSTATE 210 (Pasadena)

Exit #	Services
85a	I-210 begins/ends on I-10, exit 77.
84	San Bernardino Ave, **W** 🍴 Habit Burger 🅾 Hobby Lobby, Old Navy, Ross, TJ Maxx
83	W 5th St, Greenspot Rd, **E** 🅿 Chevron/dsl 🍴 Del Taco, Dickey's BBQ, In-N-Out, Subway, Waba Grill 🅾 AT&T, Lowe's, Staples
82	Base Line Rd, **E** 🅿 Arco, Valero 🍴 Carl's Jr, KFC/Taco Bell, McDonald's, Subway, Wendy's 🅾 Albertson's, CVS Drug, Walgreens, **W** 🅿 76/dsl 🍴 Baker's, Popeye's, Starbucks 🅾 AutoZone, CVS Drug, Family$
81	CA 330 N, to Big Bear
79	Highland Ave, **N** 🅿 Chevron/Subway, Shell/dsl 🍴 Baker's, Coco's, IHOP, Taco Bell, Wienerschnitzel/Tastee Freez, **S** 🍴 Del Taco, El Pollo Loco, KFC 🅾 $Tree, 99c Store, O'Reilly Parts, Rite Aid, Target, Walmart Mkt
78	Del Rosa Ave, **N** 🅿 7-11, Shell 🍴 Del Taco, **S** 🅿 Circle K, Exxon, Valero 🍴 Jack-in-the-Box, McDonald's 🅾 CVS Drug, Stater Bros, Walgreens
76	Waterman Ave, **S** 🅿 Mobil/7-11/dsl 🅾 🏨
75	CA 259 (from wb), H St
74	I-215 N to Barstow S to San Bernardino
73	State St, University Pkwy, **N** 🅿 American, USA 🅾 $General
71	Riverside Ave, **N** 🅿 Chevron 🍴 Carl's Jr, Del Taco, Panda Paradise, Starbucks, Subway 🅾 GNC, Ralph's Foods, Rite Aid, Verizon, Walgreens, **S** 🅿 Arco 🍴 Chipotle, In-N-Out, Jack-in-the-Box 🅾 7-11, URGENT CARE
70	Ayala Dr, **S** 🅾 city park
68	Alder Ave, **N** 🅿 Arco/Subway/dsl
67	Sierra Ave, **N** 🍴 Applebee's, Boston's, Carl's Jr, Dickie's BBQ, El Pollo Loco, Jamba Juice, McDonald's, Mimi's Cafe, Panda Express, Papa Murphy's, Pizza Hut, Starbucks, Subway, Tio's Mexican, Waba Grill 🅾 $Tree, 7-11, Costco/gas, Jo-Ann, Lowe's Whse, Petco, Schwab Tire, Verizon, **S** 🍴 Burgerim Burgers, Cane's 🅾 Chevrolet, Honda, Nissan, Sprouts Mkt
66	Citrus Ave, **N** 🍴 El Ranchero, FarmerBoys Rest., Jimmy John's, Juice It Up, Pick Up Stix, Popeye's, Red Brick Pizza, Taco Bell 🅾 America's Tire, AutoZone, Home Depot, Ralph's Foods, Walgreens, **S** 🅿 Arco/dsl
64	Cherry Ave
63	I-15 N to Barstow, S to San Diego
62	Day Creek Blvd, **S** 🅿 Arco/dsl, Shell 🍴 Chinese Food, Jack-in-the-Box, Starbucks, Subway, Wendy's 🅾 Ralph's Foods
60	Milliken Ave, **S** 🅿 Mobil/Circle K/dsl 🍴 Subway, Taco Bell 🅾 $Tre, Albertsons, CVS Drug, Verizon, vet
59	Haven Ave, **N** 🅿 7-11, 76, Mobil 🍴 Corky's Kitchen, Del Taco, Domino's, Jack-in-the-Box, McDonald's, Subway, Tio's Mexican 🅾 Trader Joe's, vet, Vons Foods, Walgreens
58	Archibald Ave, **S** 🍴 Bamboo Garden, Barboni's Pizza, Carl's Jr 🅾 Stater Bros, vet
57	Carnelion St, **S** 🅿 🍴 Baskin-Robbins, Del Taco, El Ranchero Mexican, Juice It Up, Papa John's, Starbucks, Subway 🅾 Rite Aid, Vons Foods, Walgreens
56	Campus Ave, **N** 🅿 Arco/dsl 🍴 In-N-Out, **S** 🍴 Carl's Jr, Chick-fil-A, Chili's, Chipotle, El Pollo Loco, Golden Spoon Yogurt, Habit Burger, Hawaiian BBQ, Jersey Mike's, Magic Wok, Panera Bread, Pick Up Stix, Pieology Pizza, Qdoba Mexican, Starbucks, Subway, Which Wich? 🅾 AT&T, Dick's, GNC, Goodyear/auto, Haggen Mkt, Home Depot, Kohl's, Office Depot, Petsmart, Target, TJ Maxx, Verizon
54	Mtn Ave, Mount Balde

52	Baseline Rd, **S** 🍴 Corky's Kitchen, Jersey Mike's, MOD Pizza, Starbucks, Waba Grill 🅾 CVS Drug, Whole Foods Mkt
50	Towne Ave
48	Fruit St, Via Verde, **S** 🅿 Shell 🍴 Chipotle, El Pollo Loco, In-N-Out, Jersey Mike's, Jimmy John's, McDonald's, Myabi Japanese, Panda Express, Panera Bread, Pizza Hut, Round Table Pizza, Rubio's Grill, Starbucks, Subway 🅾 Kohl's, Marshall's, Staples, Target, U of LaVerne, vet
47	Foothill Blvd, LaVerne, **N** 🅿 Mobil 🍴 Mr D's, **S** 🅿 76/dsl 🍴 IHOP, Jack-in-the-Box, Starbucks, The Grill House, Togo's 🅾 GNC
46	San Dimas Ave, San Dimas, **N** San Dimas Canyon CP
45	CA 57 S
44	Lone Hill Ave, Santa Ana, **N** 🍴 Panda Express, **S** 🅿 Chevron 🍴 Baja Fresh, Chili's, Chipotle, Coco's, Corner Bakery Cafe, In-N-Out, Olive Garden, Subway, Wendy's 🅾 Barnes&Noble, Best Buy, Chevrolet, Chrysler/Dodge/Jeep, Costco/gas, Ford, Home Depot, Hyundai, Kohl's, Old Navy, Petsmart, Sam's Club/gas, Staples, Toyota, Verizon, Walmart/auto
43	Sunflower Ave
42	Grand Ave, to Glendora, **N** 🅿 76, Valero/dsl 🍴 Carl's Jr, Denny's, El Pollo Loco 🅾 🏨
41	Citrus Ave, to Covina
40	CA 39, Azusa Ave, **N** 🅿 Arco/24hr, Chevron/dsl, Mobil/dsl, Shell/Del Taco 🍴 Jack-in-the-Box 🏨 Rodeway Inn, Super 8, **S** 🅿 Chevron 🍴 In-N-Out 🏨 Best Value 🅾 7-11, Family$, Rite Aid
39	Vernon Ave (from wb), same as 38
38	Irwindale, **N** 🅿 Arco, Shell/Subway/dsl 🍴 Carl's Jr, FarmerBoys Rest., McDonald's, Taco Bell 🅾 Costco/gas
36b	Mt Olive Dr, **N** 🅿 Mobil/dsl 🍴 Subway 🅾 CVS, Fresh&Easy Mkt
36a	I-605 S
35b a	Mountain Ave, **N** 🅿 Arco, Chevron 🍴 Del Taco, Denny's, Old Spaghetti Factory, Qdoba, Sonic, Taco Bell, Tommy's Hamburgers, Wienerschnitzel 🏨 Oak Park Motel 🅾 Best Buy, BMW/Mini, Buick/Chevrolet, CarMax, Chrysler/Dodge/Jeep, Fiat, Ford, Goodyear/auto, Honda, Infiniti, Mazda, Staples, Subaru, Target, Walgreens, **S** 🍴 IHOP, Panda Express, Subway 🅾 Home Depot, Ross, Verizon, Walmart/McDonald's
34	Myrtle Ave, **S** 🅿 76, Chevron/dsl 🍴 Jack-in-the-Box
33	Huntington Dr, Monrovia, **N** 🅿 Shell/dsl 🍴 Applebee's, Black Angus, Burger King, Chili's, Chipotle, ChuckeCheese, Domenico's Italian, Domino's, Jack-in-the-Box, Jersey Mike's, Jimmy John's, LeRoy's Rest., McDonald's, Mimi's Cafe, Panda Express, Panera Bread, Papa Murphy's, Popeye's, RoundTable Pizza, Rubio's, Smashburger, Starbucks 🏨 Courtyard 🅾 Baja Ranch Foods, GNC, Kohl's, Marshall's, Pepboy's, Petsmart, Rite Aid,

(vertical side labels) **SAN DIMAS**   **MONROVIA**

CA

⬆️Ⓔ INTERSTATE 210 (Pasadena) Cont'd

33	Continued
	Sprouts Mkt, Trader Joe's, vet, Walgreens, **S** 🏪 🍴 Baja Fresh, BJ's Grill, Capistrano's, Capital Seafood, ClaimJumper, Derby Rest., Golden Dragon, Olive Garden, Outback Steaks, Pieology, Red Lobster, Robeks Juice, Soup Plantation, Starbucks, Subway, Taisho Rest., Togo's, Tokyo Wako, Zen Buffet 🛏 DoubleTree, Embassy Suites, Extended Stay America, Extended Stay America (2), Hampton Inn, Hilton Garden, OakTree Inn, Residence Inn, SpringHill Suites 🅾 Verizon
32	Santa Anita Ave, Arcadia, **N** 🏪 76, Arco 🍴 McDonald's, Pizza Hut, Subway 🅾 Ralph's Foods, Rite Aid, Walgreens, **S** 🏪 Chevron/dsl 🍴 In-N-Out 🅾 carwash, vet
31	Baldwin Ave, to Sierra Madre
30b a	Rosemead Blvd, **N** 🏪 76/dsl, Arco 🍴 Baskin Robbins, ChuckeCheese, Corner Bakery Cafe, Del Taco, Habit Burger, Island Burger, Jamba Juice, Panda Express, Panera Bread, Pick Up Stix, Starbucks, Subway 🅾 AT&T, CVS Drug, Marshall's, Ralph's Foods, Rite Aid, Toyota, Verizon, Whole Foods Mkt, **S** 🏪 🍴 Coco's, Jack-in-the-Box 🛏 Best Value Inn, Best Western 🅾 Big O Tires, Sprouts Mkt, Staples, World Mkt
29b a	San Gabriel Blvd, Madre St, **N** 🏪 🍴 Chipotle Mexican, El Torito, Pizza Rey, Starbucks, Togo's 🅾 Best Buy, Dick's, Old Navy, Petsmart, Ross, **S** 🏪 🍴 Subway 🛏 Best Western, Holiday Inn Express, Hotel La Reve 🅾 Buick/Chevrolet/GMC, Cadillac, Land Rover Staples, Target
28	Altadena Dr, Sierra Madre, **S** 🏪 Chevron, Mobil 🅾 Just Tires
27b	Allen
27a	Hill Ave
26	Lake Ave, **N** 🏪 Mobil/Circle K/dsl 🅾 AutoZone
25b	CA 134, to Ventura
25a	Del Mar Blvd, CA Blvd, CO Blvd (exits left from eb)
24	Mountain St
23	Lincoln Ave, **S** 🛏 Lincoln Motel 🅾 tire service
22b	Arroyo Blvd, **N** 🍴 Jack-in-the-Box, **S** to Rose Bowl
22a	Berkshire Ave, Oak Grove Dr
21	Gould Ave, **S** 🏪 Arco, Chevron 🍴 McDonald's, RoundTable Pizza, Subway, Trader Joe's 🅾 Firestone/auto, Just Tires, La Canada Automotive, Petco, Ralph's Foods
20	CA 2, Angeles Crest Hwy, **S** 🏪 76, Shell
19	CA 2, Glendale Fwy, **S** 🅾 🇭
18	Ocean View Blvd, to Montrose
17b a	Pennsylvania Ave, La Crescenta Ave, La Crescenta, **N** 🏪 76, Shell/7-11, Valero 🍴 Baja Fresh, Burger King, Domino's, Little Caesar's, Starbucks, Subway, Togo's, Wienerschnitzel 🅾 Office Depot, O'Reilly Parts, Ralph's Foods, Rite Aid, Toyota, USPO, Verizon, vet, Vons Foods, Walgreens, **S** 🅾 Gardenia Mkt/deli
16	Lowell Ave
14	La Tuna Cyn Rd
11	Sunland Blvd, Tujunga, **N** 🏪 Chevron, Mobil/dsl, Shell 🍴 Coco's, Jack-in-the-Box, Panda Express, Pizza Hut, Starbucks, Subway, Yum Yum Donuts 🅾 7-11, city park, O'Reilly Parts, Ralph's Foods, Rite Aid, Verizon
9	Wheatland Ave
8	Osborne St, Lakeview Terrace, **N** 🍴 Ranch Side Cafe 🅾 7-11
6a	Paxton St
6b	CA 118
5	Maclay St, to San Fernando, **S** 🏪 76/dsl, Chevron 🍴 El Pollo Loco, KFC, McDonald's, Quizno's, Subway, Taco Bell 🅾 Home Depot, Office Depot

S A N   B E R N A R D I N O

R I V E R S I D E

4	Hubbard St, **N** 🏪 Chevron 🍴 Denny's, Yum Yum Donuts 🅾 99c Store, AutoZone, Fresh&Easy, **S** 🏪 Mobil/dsl, Shell 🍴 El Caporal Mexican, Jack-in-the-Box, Shakey's Pizza, Starbucks, Subway 🅾 USPO, Von's Foods
3	Polk St, **S** 🏪 Arco, Chevron/dsl 🍴 KFC 🅾 🇭, 7-11
2	Roxford St, **N** 🏪 Arco/dsl 🍴 Fresh&Fast Mexican 🅾 🇭, Jiffy Lube, **S** 🛏 Travelodge
1c	Yarnell St
1b a	I-210 begins/ends on I-5, exit 160.

⬆️Ⓝ INTERSTATE 215 (Riverside)

Exit #	Services
55	**I-215 begins/ends on I-15.**
54	Devore, **E** 🏪 Arco/dsl, Shell, **W** 🍴 Tony's Diner
50	Palm Ave, Kendall Dr, **E** 🏪 7-11, Arco 🍴 Albertacos, Burger King, Mi Cocina Mexican, Starbucks, Subway, **W** 🍴 Denny's
48	University Pkwy, **E** 🏪 76/Circle K, Chevron/dsl 🍴 Alberto's, Baskin Robbins/Togo's, Carl's Jr, Del Taco, Domino's, IHOP, KFC, Little Caesar's, McDonald's, Papa John's, Starbucks, Subway, Wienerschnitzel 🅾 AT&T, Jiffy Lube, Ralph's Foods, Staples, **W** 🏪 Arco, Mobil/dsl/LP 🍴 Don Martin Grill, Jack-in-the-Box, Taco Bell 🛏 Days Inn, Motel 6 🅾 Verizon, Walmart/Subway
46c a	CA 210, Redlands, to Pasadena, **E** 🅾 golf, **W** 🅾 golf
46b	Highland Ave
45a	CA 210 E, Highlands
45	Baseline Rd, **E** 🏪 76, Arco
44a	CA 66 W, 5th St, **E** 🍴 In-N-Out 🛏 Best Value Inn, Country Inn, Golden Star Inn, Leisure Inn, Rodeway Inn
43	2nd St, Civic Ctr, **E** 🏪 Chevron/dsl 🍴 Del Taco, Honeybaked Ham, In-N-Out, McDonald's, Starbucks, Subway, Taco Bell 🛏 Best Value Inn 🅾 $Tree, Food4Less, Ford, Marshall's, Ross
42b	Mill St, **E** 🍴 Carl's Jr, Jack-in-the-Box 🅾 AutoZone, **W** 🏪 Shell 🍴 Yum-yum Donuts
42a	Inland Ctr Dr, **E** 🏪 Chevron/dsl 🍴 Carl's Jr, Jack-in-the-Box, Wienerschnitzel 🅾 AutoZone, Macy's, O'Reilly Parts, **W** 🏪 Arco/dsl
41	Orange Show Rd, **E** 🏪 76/dsl, World 🍴 Burger Mania, ChuckECheese, Jose's Mexican, Subway, Sundowners Rest., Viva Villa Grill 🛏 Knights Inn, Orange Show Inn 🅾 7-11, 99c Store, BigLots, Chrysler/Dodge/Jeep, Firestone/auto, Kelly Tire, Target, **W** 🅾 AT&T, Kia, Mitsubishi, Nissan, Subaru, Toyota, VW
40b a	I-10, E to Palm Springs, W to LA
39	Washington St, Mt Vernon Ave, **E** 🏪 5 Point/repair, 76/Circle K, Arco 🍴 Baker's Drive-Thru, China Town, DQ, George's Burgers, Siquio's Mexican, Starbucks, Taco Joe's 🛏 Colton Inn 🅾 BigLots, Goodyear/auto, Jiffy Lube, **W** 🍴 Buffet Star, Carl's Jr, Church's, Del Taco, Denny's, Graziano's Pizza, Jack-in-the-Box, McDonald's, Starbucks, Subway, Taco Patron 🛏 Red Tile Inn 🅾 99c Store, GNC, multiple RV dealers, Ross, Walmart/auto
38	Barton Rd, **E** 🏪 Arco, Shell/Circle K/dsl 🍴 Miguel's Mexican, Quiznos 🅾 AutoZone, Stater Bros., **W** 🍴 Demetri's Burgers 🅾 vet
37	La Cadena Dr, (Iowa Ave from sb), **E** 🏪 Shell/dsl 🍴 Jack-in-the-Box 🛏 Holiday Inn Express
36	Center St, to Highgrove, **E** 🏪 Chevron/Subway/dsl, **W** 🏪 Valero/dsl
35	Columbia Ave, **E** 🏪 Arco/dsl, **W** 🅾 Circle K
34b a	CA 91, CA 60, Main St, Riverside, to beach cities
33	Blaine St, 3rd St, **E** 🏪 76, Shell, Valero 🍴 Baker's Drive-Thru, Jack-in-the-Box, Starbucks 🅾 Stater Bros., Valvoline
32	University Ave, Riverside, **W** 🏪 Mobil/dsl, Shell, Thrifty 🍴 Canton Chinese, Carl's Jr, Coco's, Denny's, Domino's, Fatburger,

▲N INTERSTATE 215 (Riverside) Cont'd

32	Continued Gus Jr, IHOP, Jack-in-the-Box, Jersey Mike's, Little Caesar's, Mandarin Chinese, Papa John's, Pizza Hut, Rubio's, Santana's Mexican, Shakey's Pizza, Starbucks, Subway, Taco Bell, Wiener-schnitzel 🛏 Comfort Inn, Courtyard, Motel 6 🅾 $Tree, AT&T, Food4Less, O'Reilly Parts, Rite Aid, USPO, Walgreens
31	MLK Blvd, El Cerrito
30b	Central Ave, Watkins Dr
30a	Fair Isle Dr, Box Springs, **E** 🅾 Marjon RV Ctr, **W** 🅶 76/Circle K/Subway/dsl 🍴 Jack-in-the-Box 🅾 Ford, Nissan
29	CA 60 E, to Indio, **E** 🅶 Arco, Shell/dsl 🍴 Applebee's, Baffalo Wild Wings, Baker's Drive-Thru, BJ's Rest., Burger Boss, Carl's Jr, Chick-fil-A, Chili's, Chipotle Mexican, El Pollo Loco, Five Guys, Golden Chop Stix, Hawaiian BBQ, Home Town Buffet, Hooters, Jamba Juice, Jason's Deli, Jersey Mike's, John's Pizza, McDonald's, Miguel's Mexican, Mimi's Cafe, Olive Garden, Outback Steaks, Panda Express, Panera Bread, Portillo's Hot Dogs, Round Table Pizza, Rubio's, Starbucks, Subway, Waba Grill, Wendy's, Wienerschnitzel 🛏 Ayres Hotel, Hampton Inn 🅾 $Tree, 99c Store, Best Buy, Costco/gas, JC Penney, Jo-Ann Fabrics, Lowe's, Macy's, Marshall's, Michael's, Old Navy, PetCo, Petsmart, Ross, Staples, Target, TJ Maxx, Verizon, Walmart, WinCo Foods, World Mkt
28	Eucalyptus Ave, Eastridge Ave, **E** 🍴 Bravo Burgers, Hooters 🅾 Sam's Club/gas, Target, Walmart, 🅾 same as 29
27b	(27c from sb) Alessandro Blvd, **E** 🅶 Arco/dsl 🅾 auto repair, Big O Tire, **W** 🅶 Chevron 🍴 Farmer Boys
27a	Cactus Ave to March ARB, **E** 🅶 76/Circle K/dsl, Chevron/dsl 🍴 Carl's Jr, Gus Jr
25	Van Buren Blvd, **E** 🅾 March Field Museum, **W** 🅾 Riverside Nat Cem
23	Harley Knox Blvd
22	Ramona Expswy, **E** 🅶 Arco, Chevron/dsl, Mobil/Circle K, Shell/Subway/dsl 🍴 Farmer Boys, Harry's Cafe, McDonald's, Papa John's, Starbucks, Subway, Valentino's Pizza, **W** 🅶 76/Circle K/dsl/LP, Arco/dsl/scales/24hr 🍴 Jack-in-the-Box
19	Nuevo Rd, **E** 🅶 Arco, Chevron/dsl, Mobil/Circle K 🍴 Baskin-Robbins, Burger King, Carl's Jr, China Palace, Del Taco, El Pollo Loco, IHOP, Jenny's Rest., McDonald's, Pizza Hut, Sizzler, Starbucks, Subway 🅾 AutoZone, Food4Less, GNC, Rite Aid, Stater Bros Foods, Walmart
17	CA 74 W, 4th St, to Perris, Lake Elsinore, **E** 🅶 Shell, **W** 🅶 Chevron 🍴 Del Taco, Denny's, Jack-in-the-Box, Jimenez Mexican, Little Caesar's, Popeye's 🛏 Holiday Inn Express 🅾 AutoZone, Chrysler/Dodge/Jeep/Kia
15	CA 74 E, Hemet, **E** 🍴 Jack-in-the-Box 🛏 Sun Leisure Motel
14	Ethanac Rd, **E** 🍴 KFC/Taco Bell 🅾 Richardson's RV, **W** 🅶 76/dsl, Circle K/dsl 🍴 Carl's Jr, Del Taco, Ono Hawaiian BBQ, Starbucks, Subway 🅾 Home Depot, Just Tires, Verizon, WinCo Foods
12	McCall Blvd, Sun City, **E** 🅶 Valero/dsl 🍴 Wendy's 🛏 Best Value Inn, Motel 6 🅾 🏥, **W** 🅶 Chevron/dsl, United Oil 🍴 Coco's, Domino's, McDonald's, Papa Murphy's, Santana's Mexican, Subway 🅾 $Tree, Rite Aid, Stater Bros, Von's Foods, Walgreens
10	Newport Rd, Quail Valley, **E** 🅶 Shell/Del Taco/dsl 🍴 Cathay Chinese, Jack-in-the-Box, Papa John's, Subway, Taco Bell 🅾 $Tree, AutoZone, GNC, Ralph's Foods, Ross, vet, **W** 🅶 Circle K/dsl 🍴 Applebee's, Baskin-Robbins, BJ's Rest., Chipotle Mexican, In-N-Out, Miguel's Mexican, NY Pizza, Panda Express, Panera Bread, Red Robin, Starbucks, Subway, TX Roadhouse, Yellow Basket Cafe 🅾 AT&T, Best Buy, CVS Drug,

*(left margin, vertical)* P E R R I S

M U R R I E T A

10	Continued Kohl's, Lowe's, Michael's, Old Navy, PetCo, Staples, SuperTarget, TJ Maxx, URGENT CARE, Verizon, vet
7	Scott Rd, **E** 🅶 7-11, Arco/dsl 🍴 Carl's Jr, Del Taco, Jack-in-the-Box, Submarina, Subway, Wood Rock Fire Pizza 🅾 Albertson's/SavOn, Verizon, vet, Walgreens, **W** 🍴 Marco's Pizza
4	Clinton Keith Rd, **W** 🅶 Arco/dsl 🍴 Del Taco, Jersey Mike's, Juice It Up, Starbucks, Subway 🅾 Mtn View Tire, Target, URGENT CARE, Verizon, Walgreens
2	Los Alamos, **E** 🅶 Shell 🍴 Board'z Grill, Cojito's Mexican, In-N-Out, Miguel's Jr Mexican, Peony Chinese, Starbucks, Taco Bell 🅾 USPO, **W** 🅶 Mobil/Circle K/dsl 🍴 ChuckeCheese, Jack-in-the-Box, McDonald's, Pizza Hut, Starbucks, Subway, TJ's Pizza 🅾 CVS Drug, Stater Bros., vet
1	Murrieta Hot Springs, **E** 🅶 7-11, Shell/dsl 🍴 Alberto's Mexican, Buffalo Wild Wings, Carl's Jr, El Pollo Loco, Habit Burger, Hungry Bull, Richie's Diner, Rubio's, Sizzler, Starbucks, Submarina, Wendy's 🅾 $Tree, Dick's, Ralph's Foods, Rite Aid, Ross, Sam's Club/gas, Verizon, vet, Walgreens, **W** 🍴 Richie's Diner, Starbucks
0mm	I-215 begins/ends on I-15.

▲E INTERSTATE 280 (Bay Area)

Exit #	Services
58	**4th St, I-280 begins/ends, N** 🅾 Whole Foods Mkt, **S** 🅶 Shell
57	7th St, to I-80, downtown
56	Mariposa St, downtown
55	Army St, Port of SF
54	US 101 S, Alemany Blvd, Mission St, **E** 🅶 Shell
52	San Jose Ave, Bosworth St (from nb, no return)
51	Geneva Ave
50	CA 1, 19th Ave, **W** 🅶 Chevron 🅾 SFSU, to Bay Bridge
49	Daly City, Daly City, **E** 🅶 76/dsl/LP, Flyers 🅾 Toyota, Walgreens, **W** 🅶 76, Arco 🍴 Carl's Jr, Domino's, IHOP, In-N-Out, Krispy Kreme, McDonald's, Val's Rest. 🛏 Hampton Inn
47a	Serramonte Blvd, Daly City (from sb), 🅾 same as 47b
47b	CA 1, Mission St (from nb), Pacifica, **E** 🍴 Chipotle, Hawaiian BBQ, Popeye's, RoundTable Pizza, Sizzler, Starbucks 🅾 🏥, $Tree, Chevrolet, Chrysler/Jeep/Dodge, Ford, Fresh Choice Foods, Hyundai, Lexus, Michael's, Nissan, Target, Verizon, VW/Subaru, **W** 🅾 JC Penney, Target
46	Hickey Blvd, Colma, **E** 🅶 Chevron/dsl, Shell/dsl, **W** 🅶 Shell/dsl/24hr 🍴 Boston Mkt, Celia's Rest., Habit Burger, Koi Palace, Max's Filipino, Moonstar, Outback Steaks, Panera Bread, Pieology 🅾 7-11, AT&T, CVS, Petsmart, Ross, Sprouts Mkt, Target
45	Avalon Dr (from sb), Westborough, **W** 🅶 Arco/24hr, Valero/dsl 🍴 Five Guys, McDonald's, Subway, Take One Pizza 🅾 AT&T, Pacific Mkt, Safeway, Skyline Coll, Walgreens/24hr

◻ = gas ◻ = food ◻ = lodging ◻ = other ◻ = rest stop   Copyright 2022 - The Next EXIT ®

↑E INTERSTATE 280 (Bay Area) Cont'd

SAN FRANCISCO

Exit #	Services
44	(from nb), W ◻ same as 45
43b	I-380 E, to US 101, to SF Airport
43a	San Bruno Ave, Sneath Ave, E ◻ Au's Kitchen, Baskin-Robbins, Cafe Grillades, Carl's Jr, Extreme Pizza, Jamba Juice, Nueve Mexican, Pasta Pomodoro, Starbucks ◻ CVS, GNC, Mollie Stones Mkt, W ◻ 76, Chevron, Kwik Serv ◻ Shari's ◻ 7-11
42	Crystal Springs (from sb), E ◻ county park
41	CA 35 N, Skyline Blvd (from wb, no EZ return), to Pacifica, **1 mi** W ◻ Chevron
40	Millbrae Ave, Millbrae, E ◻ Chevron
39	Trousdale Dr, to Burlingame, E ◻ ◻
36	Black Mtn Rd, Hayne Rd, W ◻ vista point, golf
36mm	Crystal Springs ◻ wb, full ◻ facilities, litter barrels, petwalk, ◻, picnic table
35	CA 35, CA 92W (from eb), to Half Moon Bay
34	Bunker Hill Dr
33	CA 92, to Half Moon Bay, San Mateo
32mm	vista point both lanes
29	Edgewood Rd, Canada Rd, to San Carlos, E ◻ ◻
27	Farm Hill Blvd, E ◻ Cañada Coll
25	CA 84, Woodside Rd, Redwood City, **1 mi** W ◻ Chevron/dsl ◻ Buck's Rest., Firehouse Bistro ◻ Robert's Mkt, USPO
24	Sand Hill Rd, Menlo Park, **1 mi** E ◻ Shell ◻ Starbucks ◻ CVS, Safeway
22	Alpine Rd, Portola Valley, E ◻ ◻, W ◻ Shell/autocare ◻ Amigos Grill, Lobster Shack ◻ Bianchi's Mkt
20	Page Mill Rd, to Palo Alto, E ◻ ◻, to Stanford U
16	El Monte Rd, Moody Rd
15	Magdalena Ave
13	Foothill Expswy, Grant Rd, E ◻ Chevron/24hr ◻ Red Pepper Grill, Starbucks, Subway ◻ Rite Aid, Trader Joe's, Verizon, W ◻ to Rancho San Antonio CP
12b a	CA 85, N to Mtn View, S to Gilroy
11	Saratoga, Cupertino, Sunnyvale, E ◻ Chevron/dsl ◻ Chipotle, Starbucks ◻ Cupertino Inn ◻ Goodyear/auto, Michael's, Rite Aid, Ross, Safeway, SteinMart, W ◻ 76, Chevron, Valero ◻ BJ's Rest., Outback Steaks, Starbucks, Willy's BBQ ◻ Aloft, Juniper Hotel ◻ Apple Computer HQ, Sprouts Mkt
10	Wolfe Rd, E ◻ Arco/24hr ◻ Mod Pizza, Panchero's, Starbucks ◻ Courtyard, Hilton Garden ◻ Ranch Mkt, W ◻ ◻ Alexander Steaks, Benihana, Vallco Dynasty Chinese ◻ FreshChoice Foods, JC Penney, Vallco Fashion Park
9	Lawrence Expswy, Stevens Creek Blvd (from eb), N ◻ El Pollo Loco, McDonald's, Panda Express, Starbucks ◻ AT&T, Marshall's, Nissan, Safeway, Verizon, S ◻ Rotten Robbie, Shell ◻ IHOP, Subway ◻ Woodcrest Hotel ◻ 7-11
7	Saratoga Ave, N ◻ Arco/24hr, Chevron/24hr ◻ Burger King, Happi House, Harry's Hofbrau, Lion Foods, McDonald's, Starbucks, Subway, Taco Bell, Togo's ◻ TownePlace Suites ◻ 7-11, Chevrolet, Ford, PepBoys, Walmart Mkt, S ◻ 76, Shell, Valero ◻ Applebee's, Lyon's Rest. ◻ Sheraton
5c	Winchester Blvd, Campbell Ave (from eb)
5b	CA 17 S, to Santa Cruz, I-880 N, to San Jose
5a	Leigh Ave, Bascom Ave
4	Meridian St (from eb), N ◻ ◻ Big Lots, FoodMaxx, Harley Davidson, S ◻ Chevron ◻ Subway ◻ 7-11
3b	Bird Ave, Race St, N ◻ Chevron
3a	CA 87, N ◻ Hilton, Marriott, Westin
2	7th St, to CA 82, **N** conv ctr
1	10th St, 11th St, **N** ◻ 7-11, to San Jose St U
0mm	**I-280 begins/ends on US 101.**

SAN JOSE

↑N INTERSTATE 405 (Los Angeles)

LOS ANGELES AREA

Exit #	Services
73	I-5, N to Sacramento, I-5, S to LA.
72	Rinaldi St, Sepulveda, E ◻ Chevron/dsl ◻ Arby's, McDonald's, Presidente Mexican, Starbucks, Subway ◻ ◻, Nissan, Toyota, W ◻ Shell ◻ Best Value Inn
71	CA 118 W, Simi Valley
70	Devonshire St, Granada Hills, E ◻ 76, Arco, Sinclair/dsl ◻ Mandarin Island, Millie's Rest., Papa John's, Safari Room Rest., Starbucks, Subway ◻ Rite Aid, Verizon, Vons Foods
69	Nordhoff St, E ◻ Mobil/dsl ◻ China Wok, Coldstone, Del Taco, KFC, Panda Express, Pollo Campero, Starbucks, Subway ◻ Hillcrest Inn ◻ 7-11, Marshalls, Vallarta Foods, Walgreens, W ◻ 76/dsl, Arco ◻ Jack-in-the-Box, Pizza Hut
68	Roscoe Blvd, to Panorama City, E ◻ 76/dsl, Shell ◻ Burger King, Denny's, Horseless Carriage Rest., Jack-in-the-Box, Kountry Folks Rest., Little Caesar's, McDonald's, Panda Express, Taco Bell, Yoshinoya ◻ Holiday Inn Express ◻ 7-11, AutoZone, Ford, Jaguar/Volvo, Lincoln, U-Haul, W ◻ Chevron/dsl, Shell/dsl ◻ Tommy's Burgers ◻ Motel 6
66	Sherman Blvd, Reseda, E ◻ Chevron, Mobil/LP ◻ McDonald's, Starbucks ◻ Motel 6 ◻ ◻, BigLots, CVS Drug, Jon's Foods, W ◻ 76/dsl/24hr ◻ Taco Bell ◻ USPO
65	Victory Blvd, Van Nuys, E ◻ Carl's Jr, El Pollo Loco, Fatburger, Jack-in-the-Box, Subway, Wendy's ◻ ◻, Costco/gas, CVS Drug, El Monte RV Ctr, Office Depot, PepBoys, Staples, W ◻ Arco/24hr
64	Burbank Blvd, E ◻ Chevron, Shell ◻ Denny's, Zankou Chicken ◻ Best Western, Hampton Inn ◻ Target
63b	US 101, Ventura Fwy
63a	Ventura Blvd (from nb), E ◻ Mobil ◻ Cheesecake Factory, El Pollo Loco, PF Chang's ◻ Whole Foods Mkt, W ◻ ◻ Ameci Pizza, CA Chicken Cafe, Corner Bakery Cafe, IHOP, McDonald's ◻ Courtyard, Valley Inn
63a	Valley Vista Blvd (from sb)
61	Mulholland Dr, Skirvall Dr
59	Sepulveda Blvd, Getty Ctr Dr, W ◻ to Getty Ctr
57	Sunset Blvd, Morega Dr, E ◻ 76/dsl, Chevron/24hr ◻ to UCLA, W ◻ Luxe Hotel
56	Waterford St, Montana Ave (from nb)
55c b	Wilshire Blvd, E ◻ ◻, downtown
55a	CA 2, Santa Monica Blvd, E ◻ Chevron, Mobil, Mobil, Shell ◻ Coffee Bean, Del Taco, Fatburger, Jack-in-the-Box, Jamba Juice, Jin Jiang Chinese, Starbucks ◻ 7-11, LDS Temple, Porsche, Staples, Tesla, W ◻ 76, Chevron/dsl ◻ Subway ◻ Holiday Inn Express ◻ vet
54	Olympic Blvd, Peco Blvd, E ◻ Mobil ◻ Islands Burgers, Starbucks, Subway ◻ USPO, W ◻ Big Tomy's Rest. ◻ Best Buy, Marshall's, Michael's, Petsmart
53	I-10, Santa Monica Fwy
52	Venice Blvd, E ◻ Chevron/service, Shell/dsl ◻ Carl's Jr, Subway ◻ Ramada ◻ 7-11, **services W on Sepulveda** ◻ SP/dsl ◻ FatBurger
51	Culver Blvd, Washington Blvd, E ◻ Dear John's Café, Domino's, Taco Bell ◻ vet, W ◻ 76/repair, CIC Gas
50b	CA 90, Slauson Ave, to Marina del Rey, E ◻ Arco/24hr ◻ Del Taco, El Pollo Loco, HoneyBaked Ham, Shakey's Pizza, Winchell's ◻ $Tree, BigLots, Goodyear/auto, Just Tires, Office Depot, Old Navy
50a	Jefferson Blvd (from sb), E ◻ Coco's, Jack-in-the-Box ◻ PetsMart, Rite Aid, Target, W to LA Airport

▲N INTERSTATE 405 (Los Angeles) Cont'd

Exit #	Services
49	Howard Hughes Pkwy, to Centinela Ave, **E** 🅟 Chevron/dsl, Mobil/dsl 🅕 BJ's Brewhouse, Five Guys, Lucille's BBQ, Qdoba, Sizzler, Subway 🅛 Courtyard, Sheraton 🅞 Best Buy, CVS Drug, Ford, Honda, JC Penney, Macy's, Marshall's, Target, Tesla, **W** 🅟 Chevron 🅕 Buffalo Wild Wings, Chick-fil-A, Chuy's Mexican, Dinah's Rest., Habuki Japanese, Islands Burgers, Starbucks 🅛 Extended Stay America 🅞 Howard Hughes Ctr, Nordstrom
48	La Tijera Blvd, **E** 🅟 Mobil/sl 🅕 Burger King, ChuckeCheese, El Pollo Loco, Jamba Juice, KFC, McDonald's, Starbucks, Subway, Taco Bell, TGIFriday's 🅛 Best Western 🅞 99c Store, CVS Drug, Ralph's Foods, Ross, Vons Foods, **W** 🅟 76, Arco 🅕 Wendy's 🅞 USPO
47	CA 42, Manchester Ave, Inglewood, **E** 🅟 76/Circle K/dsl/24hr 🅕 Carl's Jr, Subway 🅛 Best Western, Economy Inn 🅞 7-11, **W** 🅟 76, Arco, Mobil/7-11, Shell 🅕 Arby's, Burger King, Denny's, El Pollo Loco, Jack-in-the-Box, Subway 🅛 Days Inn 🅞 CarMax, Home Depot
46	Century Blvd, **E** 🅕 El Pollo Loco, Hawaiian BBQ, Little Caesar's, Panda Express, Rally's 🅛 Best Western, Motel 6, Quality Inn, Tivoli Hotel 🅞 7-11, **W** 🅟 76, Arco/24hr, Chevron/dsl, Shell 🅕 Carl's Jr, Denny's, McDonald's, Taco Bell 🅛 Crowne Plaza, Embassy Suites, Hilton, Holiday Inn, La Quinta, Marriott, Residence Inn, Travelodge, Westin Hotel 🅞 to LAX
45	I-105, Imperial Hwy, **E** 🅟 76/dsl, Shell, Valero 🅕 El Pollo Loco, Jack-in-the-Box, McDonald's, Starbucks 🅛 Best Value Inn, Candlewood Suites, Hampton Inn, Holiday Inn Express
44	El Segundo Blvd, to El Segundo, **E** 🅟 76, Chevron/dsl, Thrifty 🅕 Burger King, Cougars Burgers, Jack-in-the-Box, Subway 🅛 El Segundo Inn 🅞 transmissions, **W** 🅕 Denny's 🅛 Ramada Inn
43b a	Rosecrans Ave, to Manhattan Beach, **E** 🅟 76, Shell 🅕 Denny's, El Pollo Loco, Pizza Hut, Starbucks, Subway, Waba Grill 🅞 Best Buy, CVS Drug, Food4Less, Ford/Lincoln, Home Depot, Marshall's, Michael's, Ross, TJ Maxx, Verizon, Walmart Mkt, **W** 🅟 Arco 🅕 Blaze Pizza, Cafe Rio, Carl's Jr, Chipotle Mexican, Coffee Bean, Flemings Rest., Hawaiian BBQ, Houston's, Jamba Juice, Luigi's Rest., McDonald's, Robeks Juice, Sansai Japanese, Starbucks, Subway 🅛 Ayres Hotel, Hyatt, SpringHill Suites, TownePlace Suites 🅞 REI, AT&T, Barnes&Noble, Costco/gas, CVS Drug, Office Depot, Old Navy, Porsche, Subaru, Trader Joe's, VW
42b	Inglewood Ave, **E** 🅟 Arco, Shell 🅕 Del Taco, Denny's, Domino's, In-N-Out, Panda Wok 🅞 CVS Drug, Marshall's, PetCo, Vons Foods, Walmart Mkt, **W** 🅟 Chevron/dsl, Chevron/dsl (2) 🅕 Chile Verde Mexican, Subway 🅞 99c Store, repair
42a	CA 107, Hawthorne Blvd, **E** 🅟 Chevron 🅕 Carl's Jr, Jack-in-the-Box, McDonald's, Panda Express, Papa John's, Spires Rest., Starbucks, Wendy's, Wienerschnitzel 🅛 Baymont Inn, Best Western, Days Inn 🅞 99c Store, CVS Drug, El Super Foods, O'Reilly Parts, PepBoys, vet, **W** 🅟 Arco/24hr, USA/dsl 🅕 Boston Mkt, Del Taco, Sizzler, Starbucks, Subway, Taco Bell, Yoshinoya 🅞 AutoZone, Macy's, Nordstrom, Walgreens
40b	Redondo Beach Blvd (no EZ sb return), Hermosa Beach, **E** 🅟 76, Arco/24hr 🅕 ChuckeCheese, Jack-in-the-Box 🅞 golf, **W** 🅕 Coldstone, RoundTable Pizza, Starbucks 🅞 $Tree, AutoZone, CVS Drug, Walgreens
40a	CA 91 E, Artesia Blvd, to Torrance, **W** 🅟 Chevron 🅞 Carl's Jr, Starbucks, YumYum Donuts

TORRANCE

39	Crenshaw Blvd, to Torrance, **E** 🅟 Arco/24hr, Shell 🅕 Coffee Bean, El Pollo Loco, McDonald's 🅞 USPO, **W** 🅟 Shell/Subway/dsl 🅞 Jiffy Lube
38b	Western Ave, to Torrance, **E** 🅟 76/dsl, Arco, Chevron 🅕 Chipotle, Del Taco, Denny's, In-N-Out, Jersey Mike's, Local Place, Panda Express, Papa John's, Quiznos, Starbucks, Wendy's 🅛 Dynasty Inn 🅞 Albertson's/Sav-On, AT&T, GNC, Toyota, **W** 🅟 Mobil 🅛 Courtyard
38a	Normandie Ave, to Gardena, **E** 🅛 Travelodge, **W** 🅟 Shell/dsl 🅕 Carl's Jr, Hong Kong Cafe, On + On Asian, Pizza Hut/Taco Bell, Quiznos, Starbucks, Subway, Wienerschnitzel 🅛 Extended Stay America 🅞 $Tree, AT&T, AutoZone, Office Depot, Walmart
37b	Vermont Ave (from sb), **E** 🅕 Paradise Rest., **W** 🅛 Holiday Inn
37a	I-110, Harbor Fwy
36	Main St (from nb)
36mm	**weigh sta both lanes**
35	Avalon Blvd, to Carson, **E** 🅟 Chevron, Mobil 🅕 Buffalo Wild Wings, Carson Buffet, Chili's, Chipotle, ChuckeCheese, Denny's, Five Guys, Jack-in-the-Box, Jamba Juice, Jersey Mike's, Jersey Mike's, McDonald's, Olive Garden, Panda Express, Panera Bread, Pieology, Pizza Hut, Shakey's Pizza, Sizzler, Smashburger, Starbucks, Subway, Tokyo Grill, Tony Roma, WingStop 🅛 Motel 6 🅞 America's Tire, AT&T, Firestone/auto, IKEA, JC Penney, Just Tires, Old Navy, PepBoys, Target, Verizon, Walmart Mkt, **W** 🅟 Arco, Mobil 🅕 Carl's Jr, McDonald's 🅞 Kia, O'Reilly Parts, Ralph's Foods, USPO
34	Carson St, to Carson, **E** 🅛 EconoLodge, **W** 🅟 76/dsl, Mobil 🅕 Carl's Jr, Jack-in-the-Box, Subway 🅛 DoubleTree Inn
33b	Wilmington Ave, **E** 🅟 Shell/dsl 🅕 Carson Burgers, **W** 🅟 Chevron/Jack-in-the-Box/dsl, Shell/Subway/dsl 🅕 Del Taco, Spires Rest. 🅞 Chevrolet/Hyundai, Honda, Nissan, Toyota
33a	Alameda St
32d	Santa Fe Ave (from nb), **E** 🅟 SC Fuels, **W** 🅟 76, Chevron/24hr, Oasis/dsl 🅕 Fantastic Burgers, Tom's Burgers
32c b	I-710, Long Beach Fwy
32a	Pacific Ave (from sb)
30b	Long Beach Blvd, **E** 🅟 Arco/dsl 🅕 Subway 🅞 7-11, **W** 🅟 United 🅞 🅗
30a	Atlantic Blvd, **E** 🅟 🅕 Arby's, Carl's Jr, Denny's/24hr, El Torito, Jack-in-the-Box, Polly's Cafe 🅞 CVS Drug, Staples, Target, vet, Walgreens, **W** 🅕 Applebee's, Chipotle, In-N-Out, Starbucks 🅞 🅗, $Tree, Home Depot, PetCo, Ross
29c	Orange Ave (from sb)
29b a	Cherry Ave, to Signal Hill, **E** 🅟 Mobil/dsl 🅕 Fantastic Burgers 🅞 Ford, Lincoln, Mazda, **W** 🅟 76/dsl 🅞 America's Tire, Best Buy, Buick/GMC, Cadillac, Chrysler/Dodge/Jeep, Costco/gas, Home Depot, Honda, Mercedes, Mini, Nissan

(left margin) HAWTHORNE

(right margin) TORRANCE / CARSON

(far right) **CA**

= gas = food = lodging = other = rest stop   Copyright 2022 - The Next EXIT ®

INTERSTATE 405 (Los Angeles) Cont'd

Exit #	Services
27	CA 19, Lakewood Blvd, E Marriott , W Chevron, Shell Spires Rest., Subway Extended Stay America, Holiday Inn, Residence Inn , Goodyear/auto, Verizon
26b	Bellflower Blvd, E Burger King, Carl's Jr, Denny's, Jamba Juice, KFC, Papa John's, Starbucks, Subway, Togo's Ford, Lowe's, Verizon, W Chevron, Mobil/dsl Hof's Hut, IHOP, McDonald's, Pick-Up Stix, Pieology, Wendy's , AT&T, BigLots, CVS Drug, Goodyear/auto, See's Candies, Target, TJ Maxx, Trader Joe's, USPO
26a	Woodruff Ave (from nb)
25	Palo Verde Ave, W Del Taco, Domino's, Starbucks, Subway, Taco Bell
24b	Studebaker Rd (from sb)
24a	I-605 N
23	CA 22 W, 7th St, to Long Beach
22	Seal Beach Blvd, Los Alamitos Blvd, E 76/dsl, Chevron/repair/24hr, Mobil/dsl Baja Fresh, CA Pizza Kitchen Daphne's Greek, Chick-fil-A, Chipotle, Hot Off the Grill, In-N-Out, Islands Burgers, Jamba Juice, Kobe Japanese, Macaroni Grill, Marie Callenders, Peiwei Asian, Pick-Up Stix, Rubio's, Spaghettini Grill, Starbucks, Subway Ayres Hotel AT&T, CVS Drug, GNC, Kohl's, Marshall's, Ralph's Foods, Sprouts Mkt, Staples, Target, Verizon, 1 mi W 76/dsl, Chevron Carl's Jr, Del Taco, Denny's, Domino's Hampton Inn
21	CA 22 E, Garden Grove Fwy, Valley View St, E Dillon RV Ctr
19	Westminster Ave, to Springdale St, E 76/dsl, USA Café Westminster, Carl's Jr, Chipotle, In-N-Out, KFC, McDonald's, Pizza Hut, Popeye's Motel 6, Quality Inn $Tree, 7-11, Albertson's, America's Tire, AutoZone, BigLots, Home Depot, O'Reilly Parts, Rite Aid, Ross, W 76/dsl, Chevron/dsl/24hr Ranchito Mkt, Starbucks, Subway Best Western, Courtyard Inn
18	Bolsa Ave, Golden West St, W Mobil/dsl Del Taco, El Torito, Jack-in-the-Box, Outback Steaks, Rodrigo's Mexican, Starbucks, TGIFriday, Wendy's $Tree, CVS Drug, JC Penney, Jo-Ann Fabrics, Jons Foods, Macy's, Target
16	CA 39, Beach Blvd, to Huntington Bch, E Chevron Jack-in-the-Box, Subway Hotel 39 , Infiniti, PepBoys, Toyota, U-Haul, W Mobil/service Arby's, BJ's Rest., Buca Italian, Burger King, CA Pizza Kitchen, Cheesecake Factory, Chick-fil-A, Chipotle Mexican, Islands Burgers, Jack-in-the-Box, Macaroni Grill, Marie Callender's, McDonald's, Panera Bread, Starbucks, Subway Comfort Suites, SpringHill Suites AT&T, Barnes&Noble, Chrysler/Dodge/Jeep, Costco/gas, Firestone/auto, Kohl's, Old Navy, REI, See's Candies, Staples, Target, Verizon, Whole Foods Mkt
15b a	Magnolia St, Warner Ave, E Del Taco, Mel's Diner, Sizzler, W Chevron, Mobil/Circle K Magnolia Café, Quang Trang Rest., Starbucks, Tommy's Burgers, Winchell's Motel 6 7-11, Aldi Foods, CVS Drug, Tuesday Morning
14	Brookhurst St, Fountain Valley, E Arco/24hr, Chevron, Mobil, Shell Carl's Jr, Del Taco, KFC, Sabrosada Mexican, Taco Bell Ayres Inn, Courtyard, Residence Inn Sam's Club/gas, Thompson's RV Ctr, W Arco, Berri Bros/dsl, Shell/dsl, USA/dsl Applebee's, Black Angus, ClaimJumper, Coldstone, Corner Bakery Cafe, Dickey's BBQ, Dunkin', Islands Burgers, Jamba Juice, Jersey Mike's, Mandarin Chinese, Mimi's Cafe, Pick Up Stix, Rubio's, Starbucks, Subway, Wendy's ,

Exit #	Services
14	Continued Albertson's, Office Depot, Ralph's Foods, Rite Aid, TJ Maxx, Verizon, vet
12	Euclid Ave, E Tesla EVC Cancun Fresh, Coffee Bean, FlameBroiler, Jimmy John's, McDonald's, Panda Express, Souplantation, Starbucks, Subway, Taco Bell , $Tree, Costco/gas, PetsMart, Ross, Tire Whse
11b	Harbor Blvd, to Costa Mesa, E Hooters La Quinta, W Arco, Chevron, Mobil Cane's, Chick-fil-A, Denny's, El Pollo Loco, Five Guys, Flame Broiler, IHOP, In-N-Out, Jack-in-the-Box, McDonald's, Panera Bread, Sonic, Starbucks, Subway, Taco Bell Motel 6, Super 8, Vagabond Inn Acura, AutoZone, CarMax, Chevrolet, Chrysler/Dodge/Jeep, Honda, Nissan, Rite Aid, Sprouts Mkt, Target, Vons Foods
11a	Fairview Rd, E Starbucks Best Buy, Marshall's, Old Navy, Verizon, W 76, Chevron, Shell Del Taco, Jack-in-the-Box, Round Table Pizza CVS Drug, O'Reilly Parts, Stater Bros
10	CA 73, to CA 55 S (from sb), Corona del Mar, Newport Beach
9b	Bristol St, E Chevron/dsl Antonello's Italian, Baskin-Robbins, Boudin SF Cafe, Buffalo Wild Wings, Capital Grill, Chick-fil-A, China Olive, Chipotle Mexican, ClaimJumper, Corner Bakery, In-N-Out, Jack-in-the-Box, Maggiano's Rest., McDonald's, Morton's Steaks, Pizza Hut, Red Robin, Starbucks, Subway, TGIFriday Marriott Suites, Westin Hotel $Tree, AT&T, BigLots, Bloomingdale's, CVS Drug, Firestone/auto, GNC, Macy's, Michael's, PetCo, Rite Aid, Staples, Trader Joe's, Vons Foods, W 76/Circle K/dsl, Chevron/dsl Del Taco, El Pollo Loco, Subway, Wahoo's Fish Taco Crowne Plaza, Hilton 7-11, PepBoys, vet
9a	CA 55, Costa Mesa Fwy, to Newport Bch, Riverside
8	MacArthur Blvd, E Chevron, Mobil/Subway Carl's Jr, Jersey Mike's, McDonald's, Starbucks Embassy Suites, Homewood Suites, W Chevron El Torito, Gulliver's Ribs, IHOP Atrium Hotel, Hilton, to
7	Jamboree Rd, Irvine, E Shell Andrei's Rest., Del Taco, Soup Plantation Courtyard, Hotel Irvine, Hyatt, Residence Inn, W Houston's, Melting Pot, North Italia, Panini Cafe, Ruth's Chris Steaks, Starbucks, Subway, Wahoo's Fish Taco, Which Wich? Marriott Verizon
5	Culver Dr, W Alfie's Gas, Chevron/dsl Carl's Jr, Subway Ace Hardware, Rite Aid, Wholesome Choice Mkt
4	Jeffrey Rd, University Dr, E Chevron, Mobil/Circle K CA Pizza Kitchen, El Pollo Loco, Golden Spoon, I Can Korean BBQ, McDonald's, Mooyah Burgers, Olive's Branch, Pick-Up Stix, Pizza 90, Square One Pizza, Starbucks, Togo's , CVS Drug, Gelson's Mkt, Ralph's Foods, Verizon, Walgreens, W Mobil/dsl Korean House, Subway vet, ZionMart
3	Sand Canyon Ave, E , URGENT CARE, W Arco/dsl Johnny's NY Pizza, Sharkey's Mexican, Starbucks, Subway, Thai Bamboo, Thai Bamboo, Two Left Forks Albertson's, CVS Drug, vet
2	CA 133, to Laguna Beach, E Courtyard, DoubleTree Inn
1c	Irvine Center Dr, E Cheesecake Factory, Chipotle Mexican, Dave&Buster's, Panda Express, PF Chang's, Pieology, Wahoo's Fish Tacos Barnes&Noble, Macy's, Nordstrom, Target, W 7-11 Burger King, Puesto Mexican, Starbucks, Togo's Big O Tire, URGENT CARE, Whole Foods Mkt
1b	Bake Pkwy, W Carmax, Toyota
1a	Lake Forest
0mm	I-405 begins/ends on I-5, exit 132.

Side markers: COSTA MESA, IRVINE

CA

▲N INTERSTATE 505 (Winters)

Exit #	Services
33	I-5. I-505 begins/ends on I-5.
31	CR 12A
28	CR 14, Zamora
24	CR 19
21	CA 16, to Esparto, Woodland, W ⛽ Guy's Food/fuel 🍴 La Plazita
17	CR 27
15	CR 29A
11	CA 128 W, Russell Blvd, W ⛽ Arco/Burger King/dsl, Chevron/24hr 🍴 RoundTable Pizza, Starbucks, Subway, Taco Bell ⊙ $General, Lorenzo's Mkt
10	Putah Creek Rd, no crossover, same as 11
6	Allendale Rd
3	Midway Rd, E ⊙ RV camping
1c	Vaca Valley Pkwy, E ⊙ 🛏, W ⛽ Vaca Valley TC/Chevron/Blimpie/dsl 🍴 Burger King
1b	I-80 E. I-505 begins/ends on I-80.

▲E INTERSTATE 580 (Bay Area)

Exit #	Services
79	I-580 begins/ends, accesses I-5 sb.
76b a	CA 132, Chrisman Rd, to Modesto, E ⛽ 76/dsl ⊙ RV camping (5mi)
72	Corral Hollow Rd
67	Patterson Pass Rd, E 🍴 Subway, W ⛽ Shell/7-11/dsl
65	I-205 (from eb), to Tracy
63	Grant Line Rd, to Byron
59	N Flynn Rd, Altamont Pass, elevation 1009, S Brake Check Area, many wind-turbines
57	N Greenville Rd, Laughlin Rd, Altamont Pass Rd, to Livermore Lab, S ⛽ 76/7-11/dsl 🛏 Best Western, La Quinta ⊙ Harley-Davidson
56mm	**weigh sta both lanes**
55	Vasco Rd, to Brentwood, N ⛽ 7-11, Arco, Chevron/dsl, Gas&Shop/dsl, QuikStop/dsl 🍴 A&W/KFC, Country Waffles, McDonald's, Wienerschnitzel/Tastee Freez ⊙ Toyota, S ⛽ 7-11, Valero/dsl 🍴 Jack-in-the-Box, Taco Bell 🛏 Quality Inn
54	CA 84, 1st St, Springtown Blvd, Livermore, N ⛽ Chevron/dsl 🍴 Zpizza 🛏 DoubleTree, Motel 6, Springtown Inn ⊙ 7-11, S ⛽ 76, Chevron, Shell, Valero/Circle K 🍴 Applebee's, Burger King, Chili's, Chipotle, IHOP, Jamba Juice, McDonald's, Panda Express, Panera Bread, Peking Chinese, Starbucks, Subway, Taco Bell, Togo's ⊙ America's Tire, Big Lots, CVS Drug, GNC, Lowe's Whse, Petco, Ross, Safeway/gas, Target, TJ Maxx, vet
52	N Livermore Ave, S ⛽ 7-11, Chevron 🍴 Baja Fresh, Coldstone, Denica's Kitchen, In-N-Out, Jack-in-the-Box, Popeye's, Quizno's, String's Italian 🛏 Hawthorn Suites ⊙ AT&T, Home Depot, Honda, Kohl's, Schwab Tire, Subaru, USPO, Walmart/Subway
51	Portola Ave, Livermore (no EZ eb return), S ⊙ Ford/Lincoln
50	Airway Blvd, Collier Canyon Rd, Livermore, N ⛽ Chevron/dsl 🍴 Wendy's 🛏 Comfort Inn, Courtyard, Hampton Inn, Hilton Garden, Holiday Inn Express, Residence Inn ⊙ Costco/gas, S 🍴 Carl's Jr, Cattlemen's Rest., Cholula's, Starbucks, Subway 🛏 Extended Stay America ⊙ 7-11
48	El Charro Rd, O'Fallon Rd, N ⛽ Chevron/dsl 🍴 BJ's Rest., Fresh Pixx, Jersey Mike's, Panera Bread, Starbucks ⊙ Dick's, Target, S ⊙ Chrysler/Dodge/Jeep, SF Outlets/famous brands

47	Santa Rita Rd, Tassajara Rd, N 🍴 Baja Fresh, Buffalo Wild Wings, Coco Cabana ⊙ Buick/GMC, GNC, Kia, Lowe's, Safeway, S ⛽ Shell 🍴 McDonald's, Ozora Steaks, Pizza Guys, Subway ⊙ $Tree, Acura, AutoZone, BMW/Mini, Chevrolet/Cadillac, CVS Drug, Goodyear/auto, Lexus, Ranch Mkt, Trader Joe's
46	Hacienda Dr, Pleasanton, N ⛽ Shell 🍴 Applebee's, Black Angus, Chipotle, Five Guys, Fuddruckers, Habit Burger, Lazy Dog Rest., Mimi's Cafe, On-the-Border, Papa John's, Quiznos, Starbucks, Urban Plates 🛏 Hyatt Place ⊙ Barnes&Noble, Best Buy, Old Navy, TJ Maxx, Toyota, Verizon, Whole Foods Mkt, S 🍴 Red Robin, Subway ⊙ 🛏, Kohl's, Walmart/McDonald's
45	Hopyard Rd, Pleasanton, N ⛽ 76, Chevron/dsl, Shell/dsl 🍴 IHOP, Subway 🛏 La Quinta ⊙ America's Tire, El Monte RV Ctr, Fiat, Honda, Hyundai, Mazda, Nissan, Office Depot, O'Reilly Parts, U-Haul, VW, S ⛽ Chevron/dsl, Shell/dsl 🍴 Arby's, Black Bear Diner, Burger King, Chili's, Denny's, Faz Rest., In-N-Out, Nations Burgers, Specialty's Cafe Bakery, Starbucks, Taco Bell 🛏 Best Western, Courtyard, Doubltree, Larkspur Landing, Motel 6, Sheraton ⊙ Home Depot, Mercedes, Verizon
44b	I-680, N to San Ramon, S to San Jose
44a	Foothills Rd, San Ramon Rd, N ⛽ 76/dsl, Chevron/dsl, Shell/dsl, Valero 🍴 Baskin Robbins, Burger King, Casa Orozco, Chipotle Mexican, ChuckeCheese, Country Waffles, Elephant Bar Rest., Frankie Johnnie & Luigi's Too, Freebirds Burrito, Habit Burger, Hana Japan, Hooters, Korean BBQ, McNamara's Steaks, Outback Steaks, Panda Express, Panera Bread, Popeye's, RoundTable Pizza, Starbucks, Subway, Togo's 🛏 Holiday Inn ⊙ $Tree, Big Lots, CVS Drug, Hobby Lobby, Jo-Ann, Marshall's, Michael's, O'Reilly Parts, PetCo, PetsMart, Ranch Mkt Foods, REI, Ross, Safeway/gas, Sprouts, Target, S 🍴 Baja Fresh, CA Pizza Kitchen, Cheesecake Factory, PF Chang's 🛏 Marriott, Residence Inn, Sheraton ⊙ JC Penney, Macy's, Nordstrom
39	Eden Canyon Rd, Palomares Rd, S ⊙ rodeo park
37	Center St, Crow Canyon Rd, N 🍴 Dickey's BBQ, Panda Express, Subway ⊙ GNC, Petco, Rite Aid, Safeway, S ⛽ 76/dsl, Chevron/dsl
36	Redwood Rd, Castro Valley, N ⛽ 76/dsl, Chevron/dsl 🍴 Chipotle Mexican, KFC, Round Table Pizza, Starbucks, Taco Bell ⊙ CVS, Goodyear, Lucky Foods, Rite Aid, Safeway, Walgreens
35	Strobridge Ave, N 🍴 Burger King, McDonald's, Starbucks, Wendy's 🛏 Comfort Suites, Holiday Inn Express ⊙ 🛏
34	I-238 W, to I-880, CA 238, W off I-238 🍴 Jack-in-the Box ⊙ 99c Store
33	164th Ave, Miramar Ave, E ⛽ Chevron/dsl, National 🛏 Fairmont Inn
32	150th Ave, Fairmont, E ⊙ 🛏, W ⛽ 76/dsl, Mash/dsl, Shell 🍴 Arby's, Burger King, Chili's, Denny's, Jamba Juice, Starbucks, Subway, Tito's Cafe ⊙ $Tree, CVS, Goodyear, Kohl's, Lucky Foods, Michael's, Old Navy, Pepboys, Ross, Staples, Target

Side labels: PLEASANTON · CASTRO VALLEY · LIVERMORE · CA

🅿 = gas 🍴 = food 🏠 = lodging 🅾 = other 🆁🆂 = rest stop Copyright 2022 - The Next EXIT ©

CA

🏁E INTERSTATE 580 (Bay Area) Cont'd

Exit #	Services
31	Grand Ave (from sb), Dutton Ave, **W** 🅿 Valero 🅾 Rite Aid
30	106th Ave, Foothill Blvd, MacArthur Blvd, **W** 🅿 Arco
29	98th Ave, Golf Links Rd, **E** 🅿 Shell 🅾 Oakland Zoo, **W** 🅿 76/dsl, Valero
27b	Keller Ave, Mtn Blvd, **E** 🅾 repair
27a	Edwards Ave (from sb, no EZ return), **E** 🅾 US Naval Hospital
26b	Seminary Rd, **E** 🅾 Observatory/Planetarium, **W** 🍴 Seminary
26a	CA 13, Warren Fwy, to Berkeley (from eb)
25b a	High St, to MacArthur Blvd, **E** 🅿 🍴 Razzo's Pizza, Subway 🅾 O'Reilly Parts, USPO, vet, **W** 🅿 Valero 🅾 Walgreens
24	35th Ave (no EZ sb return), **E** 🅿 Chevron 🍴 Taco Bell, **W** 🅿 Energy, QuikStop
23	Coolidge Ave, Fruitvale, **E** 🅿 Shell/dsl 🍴 Little Caesar's, McDonald's, Subway 🅾 CVS, Farmer Joe's
22	Park Blvd, **W** 🅿 Arco 🅾 🅷
21b	Grand Ave, Lake Shore, **E** 🅿 76/24hr, Chevron/dsl 🍴 Chipotle, KFC, Subway 🅾 CVS, Trader Joe's, USPO, Walgreens
21a	Harrison St, Oakland Ave, **E** 🅿 Quikstop, **W** 🅾 Honda
19d c	CA 24 E, I-980 W, to Oakland
19b	West St, San Pablo Ave, **E** 🍴 Panera Bread 🏠 Extended Stay America 🅾 Best Buy, Home Depot, Michael's, Office Depot, Safeway, Target
19a	I-80 W
18c	Market St, to San Pablo Ave, downtown
18b	Powell St, Emeryville, **E** 🅿 🍴 Burger King, CA Pizza Kitchen, Denny's, Elephant Bar/Grill, Jamba Juice, PF Chang's, Starbucks, Togo's 🏠 Courtyard, Sheraton, Woodfin Suites 🅾 Barnes&Noble, Old Navy, Ross, Trader Joe's, **W** 🅿 Shell 🍴 Chevy's Mexican 🏠 Hilton Garden
18a	CA 13, Ashby Ave, Bay St, same as 18b
17	University Ave, Berkeley, **E** 🅿 76, University Gas 🏠 La Quinta 🅾 to UC Berkeley
16	Gilman St, **E** 🅾 Golden Gate Fields Race Track, **W** 🅾 Target
13	Albany St, Buchanan St (from eb)
12	Central Ave (from eb), El Cerrito, **E** 🅿 Shell/dsl, Valero, **W** 🅾 Costco/gas
11	Bayview Ave, Carlson Blvd
10b	Regatta Blvd, **E** 🅿 Golden Gate/dsl
10a	S 23rd St, Marina Bay Pkwy, **E** 🍴 Subway, **W** 🍴 Artisan Kitchen 🅾 CVS
9	Harbour Way, Cutting Blvd, **E** 🅿 Arco, **W** 🍴 Burger King
8	Canal Blvd, Garrard Blvd, **W** 🅿 Chevron/dsl 🏠 Days Inn, Marina Inn Suites
7b	Castro St, to I-80 E, Point Richmond, downtown industrial
7a	Western Drive (from wb), Point Molate
5mm	Richmond-San Rafael Toll Bridge
2a	Francis Drake Blvd, to US 101 S, **E** 🏠 Extended Stay America 🅾 BMW, Home Depot, Honda
1b	Francisco Blvd, San Rafael, **E** 🅿 76, Beacon, Circle K 🍴 Burger King, La Croissant 🏠 Motel 6, Travelodge 🅾 Mazda, tires, U-Haul, **W** 🍴 Subway 🅾 $Tree, Office Depot, to San Quentin, USPO
1a	US 101 N to San Rafael, **I-580 begins/ends on US 101.**

OAKLAND AREA

🏁N INTERSTATE 605 (Los Angeles)

Exit #	Services
27c	**I-605 begins/ends.** Huntington Dr. 🅿 Mobil/dsl 🍴 Subway 🅾 CVS Drug, Fresh&Easy Foods
27	I-210
26	Arrow Hwy, Live Oak, **E** 🅾 Santa Fe Dam, **W** 🅾 Irwindale Speedway
24	Lower Azusa Rd, LA St

Exit #	Services
23	Ramona Blvd, **E** 🅿 Mobil 🍴 Del Taco/24hr
22	I-10, E to San Bernardino, W to LA
21	Valley Blvd, to Industry, **E** 🅿 76, Chevron/Chester's/Subway dsl 🍴 Taco Nazo, Winchell's Donuts 🏠 Valley Inn
19	CA 60, Pamona Fwy
18	Peck Rd, **E** 🅿 Shell, **W** 🅾 Ford Trucks
17	RoseHills Rd
16	Beverly Blvd
15	Whittier Blvd, **E** 🅿 76/dsl 🍴 Carl's Jr, Taco Bell, YumYum Donuts 🏠 GoodNite Inn 🅾 7-11, **W** 🅿 Arco, Shell 🍴 Pizza Hut, Shakey's Pizza, Starbucks, Subway, Tommy's Burgers 🏠 Howard Johnson 🅾 AutoZone, Rite Aid
14	Washington Blvd, to Pico Rivera, **E** 🅾 Firestone/auto
13	Slauson Ave, **E** 🅿 Arco, Mobil 🍴 Denny's 🏠 Motel 🅾 🅷
12	Telegraph Rd, to Santa Fe Springs, **E** 🅿 76, Chevron 🍴 Del Taco, Jack-in-the-Box, Jersey Mike's, KFC, Subway, Yoshinoya, **W** 🅿 Arco/dsl
12mm	I-5
11	Florence Ave, to Downey, **E** 🅿 Arco 🅾 Honda
10	Firestone Blvd, **E** 🅿 🍴 ChuckeCheese, KFC, McDonald's, Sam's Burgers, Starbucks, Subway, Waba Grill 🏠 Best Western 🅾 99c Store, Audi/BMW/Porsche, Costco/gas, CVS Drug, Food4Less, Verizon, Walgreens, **W** 🅿 Chevron/repair 🍴 Starbucks 🅾 Chrysler/Dodge/Jeep, Office Depot, Target
8	I-105, Imperial Hwy, **E** 🅿 Chevron 🍴 Domino's, KFC, LJ Silver, McDonald's, Taco Bell 🅾 CVS Drug, Food4Less, **W** 🅿 Arco
9	Rosecrans Ave, to Norwalk, **E** 🅿 Chevron, Mobil 🍴 Little Caesar's, McDonald's, Pizza Hut, Starbucks, Subway 🅾 🅷, Walgreens, **W** 🏠 Motel 6 🅾 7-11
7	Alondra Blvd, **E** 🅿 7-11, Chevron 🍴 Frantone's Rest., In-N-Out, KFC, RC Burgers 🅾 CVS Drug, Home Depot, Staples, **W** 🅿 Shell 🍴 Del Taco
6	CA 91
5	South St, **E** 🍴 Baja Fresh, BJ's Rest., Blaze Pizza, Buffalo Wild Wings, CA Pizza Kitchen, Carl's Jr, Cheesecake Factory, Chick-fil-A, Coco's, Coldstone, DQ, Five Guys, Four Seasons Buffet, Gen Korean BBQ, Jamba Juice, Lazy Dog Cafe, Lucille's BBQ, Olive Garden, Panda Express, Panera Bread, Panera Bread, Peking Wok, Starbucks 🅾 Aldi Foods, AT&T, Dick's, Firestone/auto, Macy's, Nordstrom's, Target, Verizon, **W** 🅿 Shell/service, Valero 🅾 Acura, Buick/GMC, Chevrolet, Chrysler/Dodge/Jeep, Ford, Honda, Hyundai, Infiniti, Kia, Land Rover, Lexus, Mazda, Nissan, Toyota, VW
4	Del Amo Blvd, to Cerritos, **E** 🍴 Del Taco, Loft Hawaiian, Omega Burgers, Starbucks
3	Carson St, **E** 🅿 🍴 Little Caesar's, McDonald's, Popeye's, Starbucks, Subway, Wienerschnitzel 🏠 Lakewood Inn 🅾 7-11, CVS Drug, Food4Less, O'Reilly Parts, **W** 🅿 Chevron/Subway/dsl, Sam's Club Gas 🍴 Carl's Jr, Chick-fil-A, Del Taco, Denny's, El Pollo Loco, El Torito, In-N-Out, Island's Burgers, Jack-in-the-Box, Lucille's BBQ, Panda Express, Roadhouse Grill, Starbucks, SuperMex, TGIFriday's 🅾 America's Tire, Barnes&Noble, Lowe's, Michael's, Old Navy, Petsmart, Ross, Sam's Club, Verizon, Walmart/auto
1	Katella Ave, Willow St, **E** 🅿 Shell 🍴 Madera's Steaks, McDonald's, Polly's Cafe, Starbucks 🅾 🅷, CVS Drug, **W** Eldorado Regional Park
0mm	**I-605 begins/ends on I-405.**

LA AREA

INTERSTATE 680 (Bay Area)

Exit #	Services
71b a	I-80 E, to Sacramento, W to Oakland, **I-680 begins/ends on I-80.**
70	Green Valley Rd (from eb), Cordelia, W ⓞ Kia, N ⛽ Arco ⓞ Costco/gas, CVS, Safeway
68	Gold Hill Rd, W ⛽ Chevron/dsl
65	Marshview Rd
63	Parish Rd
61	Lake Herman Rd, E ⛽ Texaco/Jack-in-the-Box/dsl, W ⛽ Chevron/Carl's Jr/dsl/24hr, Gas City/dsl ⓞ vista point
60	Bayshore Rd, industrial park
58	I-780, to Benicia, **toll plaza**
56	Marina Vista, to Martinez
55mm	Martinez-Benicia Toll Br
54	Pacheco Blvd, Arthur Rd, Concord, W ⛽ Chevron/dsl, Shell/dsl
53	CA 4 E to Pittsburg, W to Richmond, Pittsburg
52	CA 4 E, Concord, Pacheco, E 🍴 Blaze Pizza, Buffalo Wild Wings, Habit Burger, Hometown Buffet, Jimmy John's, Noodles&Co, Starbucks, Subway, Taco Bell 🏨 Clarion, Crowne Plaza ⓞ Ford/Lincoln, Home Depot, Hyundai, Infiniti/VW, Kia, Petco, Sam's Club, Seafood City Mkt, Toyota, Trader Joe's, USPO, W ⛽ Grand Gas, Shell/24hr, Valero/dsl 🍴 A&W/KFC, Burger King, Denny's, In-N-Out, Lucille's BBQ, McDonald's, Round Table Pizza, Taco Bell, Wendy's ⓞ AutoZone, Firestone/auto, Harley Davidson, Nordstrom's, O'Reilly Parts, Pepboys, Ross, Safeway/dsl, Schwab Tire, Target
51	Willow Pass Rd, Taylor Blvd, E 🍴 Benihana Rest., Claim Jumper, Denny's, Elephant Bar Rest., Fuddruckers, Jamba Juice, Krispy Kreme, Lazy Dog Rest., Lin's Buffet, Panera Bread 🏨 Hilton ⓞ Hobby Lobby, Old Navy, REI, Willows Shopping Ctr, World Mkt, W 🍴 Baja Fresh, Red Robin, Tahoe Joe's Steaks ⓞ JC Penney, Macy's, See's Candies, URGENT CARE
50	CA 242 (from nb), to Concord
49b	Monument Blvd, Gregory Lane (from sb), E ⛽ 76/dsl 🍴 Country Waffles, Hawaiian BBQ, Panda Express, Pieology, Rubio's, Starbucks, Wing Stop ⓞ $Tree, AT&T, Dick's, Kohl's, Marshall's, W ⛽ Chevron/dsl 🍴 Boston Mkt, Chipotle, Corner Bakery Cafe, Five Guys, Jack-in-the-Box, Jack's Rest., Jamba Juice, McDonald's, Mtn Mike's Pizza, Nations Burgers, Original Pancakes, Pizza Hut, Starbucks, Subway, Sweet Tomatoes, Taco Bell 🏨 Courtyard, Hyatt ⓞ Big O Tire, Grocery Outlet, Michael's, Rite Aid, Ross, Safeway Foods, Staples, Tuesday Morning
49a	Contra Costa Blvd (from nb)
48	Treat Blvd, Geary Rd, E ⛽ Chevron 🍴 Back 40 BBQ, Heavenly Cafe, Starbucks, Subway 🏨 Embassy Suites, Extended Stay America ⓞ 7-11, Best Buy, Office Depot, W ⛽ Chevron, Shell 🍴 Black Angus, Chick-fil-A, Freebirds Burrito, Habit Burger, IHOP, Jimmy John's, Starbucks, Wendy's, Yan's China Bistro ⓞ Volvo, Walgreens
47	N Main St, to Walnut Creek, E ⛽ Chevron 🍴 Fuddrucker's, Jack-in-the-Box, Taco Bell 🏨 Marriott, Motel 6 ⓞ Cadillac, Chrysler/Dodge/Jeep, Honda, Jaguar, Land Rover, Mercedes, Nissan, Target, VW, W ⛽ 76/7-11/dsl/24hr 🍴 Domino's 🏨 Holiday Inn Express ⓞ NAPA, Porsche, Subaru
46b	Ygnacio Valley Rd
46a	SR-24 W
45b	Olympic Blvd, Oakland
45a	S Main St, Walnut Creek, E ⓞ H
44	Rudgear (from nb)
43	Livorna Rd
42b a	Stone Valley Rd, Alamo, W ⛽ Chevron/dsl, Shell/dsl 🍴 Alamo Grill, Don Jose's, Panera Bread, Papa Murphy's, Round Table Pizza, Starbucks, Subway, Taco Bell, Xenia's ⓞ CVS, Rite Aid, Safeway, USPO, vet
41	El Pintado Rd, Danville
40	El Cerro Blvd
39	Diablo Rd, Danville, E ⛽ Chevron 🍴 China Gourmet, Taco Bell ⓞ Mt Diablo SP (12mi), W ⛽ Valero
38	Sycamore Valley Rd, E ⛽ Shell 🍴 Black Bear Diner, Esin, Maria Maria, Starbucks, Subway 🏨 Best Western, W ⛽ 76/dsl, Valero/dsl ⓞ CVS, Lucky Foods
36	Crow Canyon Rd, San Ramon, E ⛽ Shell/dsl 🍴 Baskin Robbins, Burger King, Carl's Jr, Cheese Steak Shop, Chili's, Dickey's BBQ, Habit Burger, Jamba Juice, On Fire Pizza, Panda Express, Panera Bread, Primavera Ristorante, Round Table Pizza, Ruggie's Rest., Starbucks, Starbucks (2), Subway, Zachary's Pizza 🏨 Extended Stay America ⓞ H, Big O Tire, Costco, GNC, Marshall's, Office Depot, PetCo, Rite Aid, Sea's Candies, Sprouts, W ⛽ 76, Chevron/dsl, Shell/autocare, Valero 🍴 Chipotle Mexican, Giuseppe's Italian, In-N-Out, McDonald's, Nation's Burger's, Subway, Taco Bell, Togo's 🏨 Hyatt House Hotel ⓞ 7-11, CVS Drug, Home Depot, Safeway, Staples, Verizon, vet
34	Bollinger Canyon Rd, E ⛽ Valero 🍴 Baja Fresh, Buffalo Wild Wings, Izzy's Steaks, Jimmy John's, Pasta Pomodoro 🏨 Marriott, Residence Inn ⓞ AT&T, CVS Drug, Target, Whole Foods Mkt, W ⛽ Chevron/dsl 🍴 Chevy's Mexican, Clementine's Grill 🏨 Courtyard, Extended Stay America
31	Alcosta Blvd, to Dublin, E ⛽ 76/dsl ⓞ 7-11, W ⛽ Chevron, Shell/dsl 🍴 DQ, McDonalds, Papa Murphy's, Peking Delight, Subway, Taco Bell ⓞ Lucky Foods, Walgreens
30	I-580, W to Oakland, E to Tracy
29	Stoneridge, Dublin, E 🏨 DoubleTree, W 🍴 Baja Fresh, Cheesecake Factory, PF Chang's, Taco Bell 🏨 Sheraton ⓞ JC Penney, Macy's, Nordstrom
26	Bernal Ave, Pleasanton, E ⛽ Chevron/Jack-in-the-Box/dsl 🍴 Dickey's BBQ, Habit Burger, Jamba Juice, Jersey Mike's, Lindo's Mexican, Panda Express, Round Table Pizza, Starbucks, Subway ⓞ CVS, Safeway/dsl
25	Sunol Blvd, Pleasanton
21b a	CA 84, Calvaras Rd, Sunol, W to Dumbarton Bridge
20	Andrade Rd, Sheridan Rd (from sb), E ⛽ Sunol Super Stp/dsl
19mm	weigh sta nb
19	Sheridan Rd (from nb)
18	Vargas Rd
16	CA 238, Mission Blvd, to Hayward, E ⛽ Shell 🍴 McDonald's, W ⓞ H
15	Washington Blvd, Irvington Dist, E ⛽ QuikStop
14	Durham Rd, to Auto Mall Pkwy, W ⛽ 76/Subway/24hr, Jack-in-the-Box ⓞ Fry's Electronics, Home Depot, Walmart

Map labels: 580, Hercules, El Sobrante, East Richmond, El Cerrito, Albany, Berkeley, Orinda, 980, Piedmont, Oakland, Alameda, 880, Concord, Pleasant Hill, Waldon, Walnut Creek, Lafayette, Alamo, Danville, 680, San Ramon, CA

Side labels: CONCORD, WALNUT CRK, SAN RAMON, FREMONT

🛢 = gas 🍴 = food 🏠 = lodging Ⓞ = other 🅿️ = rest stop Copyright 2022 - The Next EXIT ®

⬆️Ⓔ INTERSTATE 680 (Bay Area) Cont'd

Exit #	Services
12	CA 262, Mission Blvd, to I-880, Warm Springs Dist, W 🛢 76, Valero 🍴 Burger King, Carl's Jr, Denny's, Jack-in-the-Box, KFC, RoundTable Pizza, Subway, Taco Bell 🏠 Extended Stay America, Motel 6 Ⓞ CVS, Ross, Safeway
10	Scott Creek Rd
9	Jacklin Rd, E Ⓞ Bonfare Mkt, W 🛢 Shell/dsl
8	CA 237, Calaveras Blvd, Milpitas, E 🛢 76, Shell/repair 🍴 King Wah, Round Table Pizza, Shabu House, Starbucks, Subway 🏠 Executive Inn Ⓞ 7-11, Oceans SuperMkt, W 🛢 Shell 🍴 El Torito, Giorgio's Italian, IHOP, Jamba Juice, McDonald's, Mtn Mike's Pizza, Panda Express, Red Lobster, Starbucks, Subway 🏠 Embassy Suites, Extended Stay America Ⓞ CVS, Safeway, Staples
6	Landess Ave, Montague Expswy, E 🛢 76, Arco, Chevron 🍴 Burger King, Jack-in-the-Box, McDonald's, Starbucks, Subway, Taco Bell, Togo's Ⓞ Firestone/auto, Lucky Foods, Rite Aid, Target, vet, Walgreens
5	Capitol Ave, Hostetter Ave, E 🛢 Shell 🍴 Carl's Jr, Popeye's Ⓞ Lucky Foods, W Ⓞ 7-11
4	Berryessa Rd, E 🛢 Arco/24hr, Shell/dsl 🍴 Denny's, Lee's Sandwiches, McDonald's, Round Table Pizza, Starbucks, Taco Bell Ⓞ $Tree, AutoZone, CVS, Safeway
2b	McKee Rd, E 🛢 76, Chevron, Shell/dsl 🍴 Burger King, Chipotle, HomeTown Buffet, Jamba Juice, Panda Express, Popeye's, Starbucks, Togo's, Wienerschnitzel, Wingstop Ⓞ $Tree, GNC, Grocery Outlet, Marshall's, Mi Pueblo Mkt, Ross, Target, Walgreens, W 🛢 World Gas 🍴 Baskin-Robbins, Lee's Sandwiches, McDonald's, RoundTable Pizza, Subway, Wendy's, Yum Yum Donuts Ⓞ 🏥, Kohl's
2a	Alum Rock Ave, E 🛢 Shell/dsl/24hr 🍴 Jack-in-the-Box, Taco Bell, W 🛢 Chevron, Valero 🍴 Carl's Jr Ⓞ AutoZone
1d	Capitol Expswy
1c	King Rd, Jackson Ave (from nb), E 🛢 L&D Gas, Shell 🍴 El Pollo Loco, Jack-in-the-Box, Kings Burger, Starbucks, Subway, Tropicana Buffet Ⓞ AT&T, Target, Verizon, Walgreens
1b	US 101, to LA, SF
1a	(exits left from sb) I-680 begins/ends on I-280.

⬆️Ⓔ INTERSTATE 710 (Los Angeles)

Exit #	Services
23	I-710 begins/ends on Valley Blvd. E 🛢 Arco
22b a	I-10
20c	Chavez Ave
20b	CA 60, Pamona Fwy, E 🍴 King Taco, Monterey Hill Rest., W 🛢 Shell Ⓞ AutoZone
20a	3rd St
19	Whittier Blvd, Olympic Blvd, W 🍴 McDonald's
17b	Washington Blvd, Commerce, W 🛢 Commerce Trkstp/dsl/rest.
17a	Bandini Blvd, Atlantic Blvd, industrial
15	Florence Ave, E 🍴 Alfredo's Mexican, Applebee's, Coldstone, Dunkin', El Pollo Loco, IHOP, Jack-in-the-Box, KFC, Little Caesar's, McDonald's, Panda Express, Starbucks, Subway, Taco Bell 🏠 Quality Inn Ⓞ $Tree, casino, Food4Less, Marshall's, Rite Aid, Ross, W 🛢 Chevron
13	CA 42, Firestone Blvd, E 🛢 Arco 🍴 Burger King, Denny's, Golden Bowl, Hooters, McDonald's, Panda Express, Starbucks, Subway 🏠 Guesthouse Inn Ⓞ El Super Foods, Ford, GNC, Sam's Club, Target

L A A R E A

12b a	Imperial Hwy, E 🛢 GM/dsl 🍴 Carl's Jr., El Pollo Loco, Subway, W 🛢 76, Arco, Chevron/dsl 🍴 Church's, KFC, McDonald's, Panda Express, Starbucks, Subway, Taco Bell, Wiener schnitzel, Winchell's Ⓞ AutoZone, El Super Mkt, Manny' Repair, Walgreens
11b a	I-105
10	Rosecrans Ave
9b a	Alondra Ave, E 🛢 Chevron/dsl 🍴 Jack-in-the-Box Ⓞ Home Depot
8b a	CA 91
7b a	Long Beach Blvd, E 🛢 76/dsl, Chevron, Mobil, Sinclair 🍴 El Cortez Mexican, McDonald's, Sizzler Ⓞ CVS Drug, W 🛢 Arco/24hr 🍴 Jack-in-the-Box, Subway 🏠 Luxury Inn
6	Del Amo Blvd
4	I-405, San Diego Freeway
3b a	Willow St, E 🛢 Arco, Chevron/dsl 🍴 Baskin-Robbins, Domino's, Pizza Hut, Wienerschnitzel Ⓞ Albertson's, Walgreens, W 🛢 76, Arco 🍴 KFC, Popeye's Ⓞ AutoZone
2	CA 1, Pacific Coast Hwy, E 🛢 76/dsl, Arco/mart, Chevron, Mobil 🍴 Hong Kong Express, KFC, McDonald's 🏠 Best Western, La Mirage Inn, Travel Eagle Inn Ⓞ Ranch Mkt, W 🛢 76/service, PCH Trkstp/dsl, Shell/Carl's Jr/dsl 🍴 Alberto's Mexican, Golden Star Rest., Jack-in-the-Box, McDonald's, Taco Bell, Tom's Burgers, Winchell's 🏠 Hiland Motel, SeaBreeze Motel
1d	Anaheim St, W Ⓞ auto repair
1c	Ahjoreline Dr, Piers B, C, D, E, Pico Ave
1b	Pico Ave, Piers F-J, Queen Mary
1a	Harbor Scenic Dr, Piers S, T, Terminal Island, E 🏠 Hilton

I-710 begins/ends in Long Beach.

⬆️Ⓔ INTERSTATE 780 (Vallejo)

Exit #	Services
7	I-780 begins/ends on I-680.
6	E 5th St, Benicia, N 🛢 Fast&Easy, S 🛢 7-11, 76/dsl 🍴 China Garden 🏠 Holiday Inn Express Ⓞ Big O Tire, repair
5	E 2nd St, Central Benicia, N 🛢 Valero/dsl 🏠 Best Western, S 🍴 Kimono Steaks, McDonald's, Nations Burger, Subway
4	Southampton Rd, Benicia, N 🍴 Burger King, Ensenada Mexican, Huckleberry's, Jamba Juice, Panda Express, RoundTable Pizza, Starbucks, Subway Ⓞ $Tree, Ace Hardware, AT&T, Raley's Foods
3b	Military West
3a	Columbus Pkwy, N 🛢 Chevron/dsl 🍴 Burger King, McDonald's, Mtn Mike's Pizza, Napoli Pizza, Papa Murphy's, Starbucks, Subway Ⓞ CVS, Jiffy Lube, S to Benicia RA
1d	Glen Cove Pkwy, N Ⓞ Hwy Patrol, S 🍴 Domino's, J's Garden, Subway Ⓞ GNC, Safeway
1c	Cedar St
1b a	I-780 begins/ends on I-80.

⬆️Ⓝ INTERSTATE 805 (San Diego)

Exit #	Services
28mm	I-5 (from nb), I-805 begins/ends on I-5.
27.5	CA 56 E (from nb)
27	Sorrento Valley Rd, Mira Mesa Blvd
26	Vista Sorrento Pkwy, E 🛢 Mobil/dsl 🍴 Chili's, Flame Broiler, Jamba Juice, McDonald's, Quizno's, Rubio's, Starbucks, Subway 🏠 Country Inn, Courtyard, Extended Stay America, Holiday Inn Express, Hyatt House Ⓞ Staples
25b a	La Jolla Village Dr, Miramar Rd, 1 mi E 🛢 76/dsl Ⓞ Discount Tire, Firestone, W 🍴 Corner Cafe, Cozymel's Cantina, Donovan's Grill, Harry's Grill, PF Chang's, Seasons Fresh Grill 🏠 Embassy Suites, Marriott Ⓞ 🏥, Macy's, Nordstrom's, Sears

Side labels: CA | SAN JOSE | L A AREA | BENICIA

INTERSTATE 805 (San Diego) Cont'd

Exit #	Services
24	Governor Dr
23	CA 52
22	Clairemont Mesa Blvd, E 🅿 7-11/dsl, Chevron/dsl, Mega/Subway/dsl, Shell 🍴 Arby's, Burger King, Carl's Jr, Chipotle Mexican, Coco's, Godfather Rest., Jersey Mike's, McDonald's, Rubio's Grill, Souplantation, Starbucks, Subway, Tommy's Burgers ⊙ Food4Less, Ford/Kia, Nissan, Ranch Mkt, Verizon, Walmart, W 🅿 Gas 🍴 Buga Korean BBQ, Subway 🛏 Best Western, CA Suites, Motel 6
21	CA 274, Balboa Ave, E 🅿 7-11, 76, Arco/dsl, Chevron/dsl 🍴 Applebee's, Islands Burger, Jack-in-the-Box ⊙ CarMax, Chevrolet, Chrysler/Dodge/Jeep, Jaguar, VW
20	CA 163 N, to Escondido
20a	Mesa College Dr, Kearney Villa Rd, W ⊙ 🏩
18	Murray Ridge Rd, to Phyllis Place
17b	I-8, E to El Centro, W to beaches
16	El Cajon Blvd, E 🅿 Arco, Ultra ⊙ Pancho Villa Mkt, W 🅿 🍴 Carl's Jr, Jack-in-the-Box, Rudford's Rest., Subway, Wendy's ⊙ O'Reilly Parts
15	University Ave, E 🅿 Chevron 🍴 Subway, W 🅿 76/dsl, USA/dsl 🍴 Starbucks ⊙ CVS Drug, Fresh&Easy Mkt, Walgreens
14	CA 15 N, 40th St, to I-15
13b	Home Ave, MLK Ave
13a	CA 94
12b	Market St
12a	Imperial Ave, E 🅿 Homeland Gas/dsl, United, W 🍴 Asia Wok, Cojita's Taco, Domino's, KFC/LJ Silver, Sizzler, Subway ⊙ 99c Store, Home Depot
11b	47th St
11a	43rd St, W 🍴 Giant Pizza, Jack-in-the-Box, Subway ⊙ AutoZone, CVS Drug, Northgate Mkt
10	Plaza Blvd, National City, E 🍴 Chow King, McDonald's, Pizza Hut, Popeye's, Starbucks, Subway, Winchell's ⊙ 🏩, AutoZone, Firestone/auto, Vallarta Foods, vet, Walgreens, Well's Drug, W 🅿 USA 🍴 Bistro City Chinese, Carl's Jr, Family House Rest., IHOP, Jubilee Chicken/burgers, Little Caesar's, Papa John's, Subway, Wings n Things 🛏 Holiday Inn Express, Motel 6, Stardust Inn ⊙ AT&T, Big Lots, CVS Drug, Discount Tire, Firestone/auto, Jo-Ann Fabrics, O'Reilly Parts, Walmart
9	Sweetwater Rd, E 🍴 Applebee's, Outback Steaks 🛏 Sweetwater Inn ⊙ 7-11, JC Penney, Macy's, W 🅿 Chevron/7-11/dsl 🍴 Ben's Rest., Carl's Jr, Denny's, Hanaoka Japanese, Mike's NY Pizza, Pizza Hut, Pizza Hut, Starbucks, Subway, Taco Bell ⊙ CVS Drug, Food4Less, Goodyear/auto, Staples
8	CA 54
7c	E St, Bonita Rd **E on Bonita Plaza Rd** 🍴 Applebee's, El Torito, Outback Steaks, Red Robin, Starbucks, Subway ⊙ JC Penney, Macy's, Target, W 🅿 Chevron/dsl, Circle K, Shell/dsl 🍴 Burger King, Denny's, La Tequila Mexican 🛏 Comfort Inn, La Quinta
7b a	H St, E 🅿 Shell 🍴 China China, Coldstone, Daphne's CA Greek, D'Lish Pizza, Honeybaked, Jack-in-the-Box, Robeks Juice, Subway, Taco Bell ⊙ CVS Drug, Marshall's, Vons Foods, W 🍴 Caffe Tazza
6	L St, Telegraph Canyon Rd, E 🅿 Arco/dsl 🍴 Little Caesar's, Mandarin Canyon, McDonald's, Starbucks, Subway ⊙ 🏩, Olympic Training Ctr, Rite Aid, vet, Von's Foods, W 🅿 76/Circle K/dsl, USA 🍴 Canada Steakburger ⊙ 7-11
4	Orange Ave, E 🛏 Olympic Training Ctr
3	Main St, Otay Valley Rd, E 🅿 Shell/dsl 🍴 Panda Express, Souplantation ⊙ Ford/Kia, Honda, Kohl's, Nissan, PetsMart, Staples, Toyota, W 🅿 Circle K/dsl 🛏 Best Western
2	Palm Ave, E 🅿 Arco, Chevron 🍴 Carl's Jr, Hometown Buffet, Starbucks, Subway, Taco Bell ⊙ AT&T, Home Depot, Meineke, Tire Pros, USPO, Von's Foods, Walmart/McDonald's, W 🅿 Chevron 🍴 Golden House Chinese, KFC, Little Caesar's, McDonald's
1b	CA 905, E Brown Field Airport, Otay Mesa Border Crossing
1a	San Ysidro Blvd, E 🅿 Shell/dsl, Valero 🍴 Church's ⊙ 99c Store, CVS Drug, Factory2U, O'Reilly Parts, W 🅿 76, Chevron, Mobil/dsl, Shell 🍴 Denny's, McDonald's 🛏 Motel 6
0	I-805 begins/ends on I-5.

INTERSTATE 880 (Bay Area)

Exit #	Services
46b a	I-80 W (exits left). I-80 E/580 W.
44	7th St, Grand Ave, downtown
42b a	Broadway St, E 🍴 KFC, McDonald's 🛏 Marriott, W 🛏 Jack London Inn ⊙ to Jack London Square
41a	Oak St, Lakeside Dr, downtown
40	5th Ave, Embarcadero, E 🍴 Burger King, W 🍴 Starbucks, Subway 🛏 Best Western, Executive Inn, Homewood Suites, Motel 6
39b a	29th Ave, 23rd Ave, to Fruitvale, E 🅿 Shell 🍴 Boston Mkt, DonutStar, Popeye's, Starbucks ⊙ AT&T, AutoZone, FoodMaxx, W 🅿 7-11
38	High St, to Alameda, E 🅿 Mash/dsl 🛏 Bay Breeze Inn, Coliseum Motel, W 🅿 Shell/dsl 🍴 McDonald's ⊙ Home Depot
37	66th Ave, Zhone Way, E coliseum
36	Hegenberger Rd, E 🅿 Arco/24hr, Shell/dsl 🍴 Burger King, Chubby Freeze, Denny's, Jack-in-the-Box/24hr, McDonald's, Taco Bell 🛏 Comfort Inn, Day's Hotel, La Quinta, Motel 6, Quality Inn ⊙ Freightliner, GMC/Volvo, W 🅿 76/dsl, Chevron/Del Taco/dsl, Shell 🍴 Black Bear Diner, Chipotle, Francesco's Rest., In-N-Out, Jamba Juice, Panda Express, Red Brick Pizza, Starbucks, Subway, Subway, Wing Stop 🛏 Best Western, Courtyard, Econolodge, Hilton, Holiday Inn, Holiday Inn Express, Red Lion ⊙ Harley-Davidson, Infiniti, Lexus, to Oakland Airport, Toyota
35	98th Ave, W ⊙ 🖐
34	Davis St, W 🅿 Shell/Burger King 🍴 Hawaiian BBQ, Togo's ⊙ $Tree, Costco/gas, Home Depot, Office Depot, See's Candy, Verizon, Walmart/McDonald's

🅿 = gas 🍴 = food 🛏 = lodging 🅾 = other 🆁🆂 = rest stop   Copyright 2022 - The Next EXIT ®

INTERSTATE 880 (Bay Area) Cont'd

Exit #	Services
33b a	Marina Blvd, E 🅿 Chevron/dsl, Valero 🍴 Jack-in-the-Box, La Salsa Mexican, Panda Express, Pieology, Starbucks, Taco Bell 🅾 Chevrolet, Ford/Lincoln, Honda, Hyundai, Kia, Marshall's, Nissan, Nordstrom's, Volvo, W 🅿 Flyers/dsl 🍴 A&W/KFC, Denny's
32	Washington Ave (from nb), Lewelling Blvd (from sb), W 🅿 76/dsl, Arco, Chevron 🍴 Jack-in-the-Box, McDonald's, Mtn Mike's Pizza, Papa Murphy's, Subway 🛏 Nimitz Motel 🅾 99c Store, Big O Tire, CVS, Food Maxx, GNC, Jo-Ann, Safeway, same as 30, Walgreens/24hr
31	I-238 (from sb), to I-580, Castro Valley
30	Hesperian Blvd, E 🅿 National 🍴 In-N-Out, Starbucks, Taco Bell 🅾 O'Reilly Parts, Walmart/Subway, Wheel Works, W 🅿 76, Arco, Chevron 🍴 Black Angus, Peking Garden, Round Table Pizza 🛏 Hilton Garden, Nimitz Inn 🅾 99c Store, CVS, Food Maxx, Lucky Foods, same as 32, USPO
29	A St, San Lorenzo, E 🅿 880/dsl/e85 🍴 McDonald's 🛏 Best Western 🅾 Costco, tires/repair, W 🅿 76/7-11/dsl, Valero/dsl 🍴 Burger King, Chef Ming, Five Guys, Hawaiian BBQ, Jamba Juice, Pizza Hut, Rigatoni's Italian, Starbucks, Subway 🛏 Days Inn, La Quinta, Rodeway Inn 🅾 $Tree, Home Depot, Mi Pueblo Foods, Target
28	Winton Ave, W 🅿 Chevron 🍴 Applebee's, Buffalo Wild Wings, Coldstone, Elephant Grill, Famous Dave's BBQ, Hawaiian BBQ, Hometown Buffet, Olive Garden, Panda Express, Panera Bread, Sizzler, Subway 🅾 Dick's, Firestone/auto, Goodyear/auto, JC Penney, Macy's, O'Reilly Parts, Ross, Verizon
27	CA 92, Jackson St, E 🅿 76/dsl, Valero 🍴 Asian Wok, Hawaiian BBQ, Mtn Mike's Pizza, Nations Burgers, Papa John's, Popeye's, Round Table Pizza, Starbucks, Subway, Taco Bell 🅾 7-11, CVS, Grocery Outlet, Lucky Foods, Safeway, Walgreens, W San Mateo Br
26	Tennyson Rd, E 🅿 76, All Star dsl, Shell 🍴 Jack-in-the-Box, KFC 🅾 O'Reilly Parts, Walgreens, W 🅿 🅾 🏥
25	Industrial Pkwy (from sb), E 🅿 Golden Gate/dsl, Industrial/dsl 🍴 Fuzhou Kitchen, Starbucks, Straw Hat Pizza, Subway, W 🛏 Pheonix Lodge
24	Whipple Rd, Dyer St, E 🅿 76/dsl, Chevron/dsl/24hr 🍴 Country Waffles, Denny's, Hawaiian BBQ, McDonald's, Panda Express, Starbucks, Subway, Taco Bell, Wing Stop 🛏 Best Value Inn, Motel 6 🅾 FoodMaxx, Home Depot, PepBoys, Target, W 🅿 Shell 🍴 Andersen Baker a Cafe, Applebee's, Baskin-Robbins, Buckhorn Grill, Buffalo Wild Wings, Chevy's Mexican, Chili's, Chipotle, Coldstone, Fuddrucker's, IHOP, In-N-Out, Jamba Juice, Jollibee, Krispy Kreme, La Salsa Mexican, Mtn Mike's Pizza, Pasta Pormadora, Starbucks, Texas Roadhouse, TGIFriday, Togo's, Tomatina Italian 🛏 Extended Stay America, Hampton Inn, Holiday Inn Express 🅾 AT&T, Best Buy, GNC, Lowe's Whse, Lucky Foods, Michael's, PetCo, Tuesday Morning, Verizon, Walmart
23	Alvarado-Niles Rd, E 🅿 Shell 🛏 Crowne Plaza 🅾 7-11, W 🅿 Shell 🍴 Burger King 🅾 Walmart, (same as 24)
22	Alvarado Blvd, Fremont Blvd, E 🍴 Fortune Kitchen, Subway 🛏 Motel 6 🅾 Lucky Foods
21	CA 84 W, Decoto Rd to Dumbarton Br, E 🅿 7-11 🍴 McDonald's 🅾 Walgreens
19	CA 84 E, Thornton Ave, Newark, E 🅾 U-Haul, W 🅿 Chevron/dsl, Shell 🍴 Carl's Jr, KFC, Mtn Mike's Pizza, My Cafe, Round Table Pizza, Subway, Taco Bell 🅾 7-11, BigLots, Home Depot

FREMONT

17	Mowry Ave, Fremont, E 🅿 76/Circle K, Chevron/dsl, QuikStop, Valero 🍴 Applebee's, Chick-fil-A, Denny's, Olive Garden, Papa Murphy's, Starbucks, Subway 🛏 Best Western, Extended Stay America, Residence Inn 🅾 🏥, Lucky Foods, W 🅿 🍴 Arby's, BJ's Rest., Bombay Garden, Jack-in-the-Box, Little Caesar's, McDonald's, Papa John's, Ray's Chinese, Ray's Crabshack, Red Robin, Subway, Taco Bell 🛏 Chase Suites, Comfort Inn, EZ 8 Motel, Homewood Suites, Towneplace Suites 🅾 Chrysler/Dodge/Jeep, Firestone/auto, Ford, JC Penney, Jiffy Lube, Lion Mkt, Macy's, Mazda, Target, VW
16	Stevenson Blvd, E 🅿 Arco/dsl, Shell 🍴 Jack-in-the-Box, Outback Steaks 🅾 $Tree, W 🅿 Chevron 🍴 Carl's Jr, Chucke-Cheese, Isla Filipino, Nijo Castle Japanese, Starbucks, Subway, World Gourmet Buffet 🛏 Doubletree 🅾 Fiat, Ford, Walmart
15	Auto Mall Pkwy, E 🅿 Arco, Chevron/dsl, W 🅿 Shell/dsl 🍴 Applebee's, Asian Pearl, Bennigan's, Blaze Pizza, Buffalo Wild Wings, Chick-fil-A, Chipotle, ClaimJumper, Coldstone, Dickey's BBQ, Dog Haus, Firehouse Subs, Five Guys, Habit Burger, Hawaiian BBQ, In-N-Out, Jamba Juice, Krispy Kreme, MilkCow Cafe, Mkt Broiler, Panchero's, Panda Express, Panera Bread, PF Chang's, Rubio's, Starbucks, Subway, Wendy's, Which Wich?, Wing Stop 🛏 Holiday Inn Express 🅾 Acura, AT&T, BMW, Buick/GMC/Cadillac, Chevrolet, Costco/gas, Dick's, Honda, Jo-Ann Fabrics, Kia, Kohl's, Lexus, Lowe's Whse, Mercedes, Nissan, Nordstrom's, Old Navy, Target, TJ Maxx, Toyota, Verizon, Volvo
14mm	weigh sta both lanes
13	Fremont Blvd, Irving Dist, W 🅿 Chevron/Subway 🍴 McDonald's 🛏 Extended Stay America, GoodNite Inn, La Quinta, Marriott
13a	Gateway Blvd (from nb), E 🛏 Comfort Inn
12	Mission Blvd, E 🅿 🍴 Burger King, Carl's Jr, Denny's, Jack-in-the-Box, KFC, Subway, Taco Bell 🛏 Comfort Inn 🅾 CVS, Safeway, to I-680, W 🛏 Courtyard, Hampton Inn, Hyatt Place
10	Dixon Landing Rd, E 🍴 McDonald's 🛏 Residence Inn 🅾 7-11
8b	CA 237, Alviso Rd, Calaveras Rd, to McCarthy Rd, Milpitas, E 🅿 76/7-11/dsl, Arco 🍴 Black Bear Diner, Burger King, Chili's, Denny's, King Egg Roll, Lee's Sandwiches, Milpitas Buffet 🛏 Best Western, Chili Palace, Days Inn, Heritage Inn 🅾 7-11, BigLots, Grocery Outlet, O'Reilly Parts, Walgreens, W 🍴 Applebee's, Black Angus, Happi House, In-N-Out, Macaroni Grill, McDonald's, On the Border, Starbucks, Subway, Taco Bell, Togo's 🛏 Crowne Plaza, Extended Stay America, Hampton Inn, Hilton Garden, Larkspur Landing Hotel, Staybridge Suites 🅾 $Tree, AT&T, Best Buy, Chevron, GNC, Michael's, Petsmart, RanchMkt Foods, Ross, Verizon, Walmart/McDonald's/auto
8a	Great Mall Parkway, Tasman Dr, E 🅾 Honda, Toyota
7	Montague Expswy, E 🅿 Shell/dsl, Valero 🍴 Carl's Jr, Jack-in-the-Box 🛏 Quality Inn 🅾 U-Haul, W 🅿 Chevron/dsl 🛏 Beverly Heritage Hotel, Sheraton
5	Brokaw Rd, W 🅾 America's Tire, CHP, Ford Trucks, Fry's Electronics
4d	Gish Rd (nb only), W 🅾 auto/dsl repair/transmissions
4c b	US 101, N to San Francisco, S to LA
4a	1st St, E 🅿 Chevron/dsl, Shell/repair 🍴 Subway, W 🅿 🍴 Cathay Chinese, Denny's/24hr, Genji Japanese 🛏 Caravelle Inn, Comfort Suites, Country Inn Suites, Days Inn, Extended Stay America, EZ 8 Motel, Holiday Inn, Residence Inn, SpringHill Suites, Vagabond Inn, Wyndham Garden 🅾 7-11

SAN JOSE AREA

Copyright 2022 - The Next EXIT ®   🅟 = gas   🅕 = food   🅛 = lodging   🅞 = other   🆁🆂 = rest stop

⬆N INTERSTATE 880 (Bay Area) Cont'd

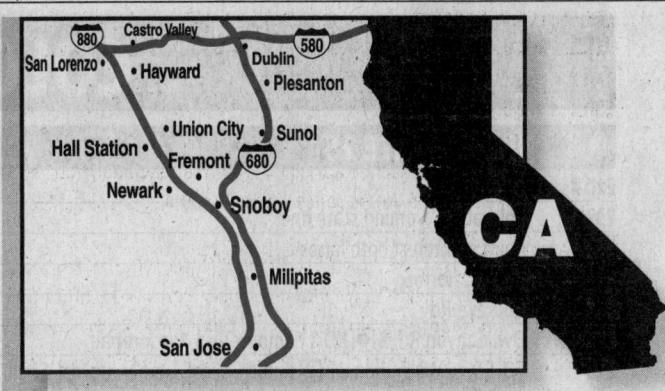

Exit #	Services
3	Coleman St, **E** 🅟 Valero/dsl, **W** 🅟 Chevron/dsl 🅕 Chipotle, In-N-Out, Mod Pizza, Smoking PIG BBQ, Starbucks, Which Wich? 🅞 🖂, Staples
2	CA 82, The Alameda, **W** 🅟 Shell/repair 🅕 Bill's Cafe, Round Table Pizza, Starbucks, Subway, Taco Bell 🅛 Best Western, Santa Clara Inn, St. Francis Hotel, Sterling Motel, Valley Inn 🅞 Safeway, Santa Clara U
1d	Bascom Ave, to Santa Clara, **W** 🅟 Rotten Robbie/dsl, Valero 🅕 Burger King
1c	Stevens Creek Blvd, San Carlos St, **E** 🅟 Valero/dsl, Valley/dsl 🅛 The Row Hotel 🅞 🅗, **W** 🅟 🅕 Arby's, CheeseCake Factory, Jack-in-the-Box, Yard House 🅞 7-11, Audi/VW, Best Buy, Chevrolet, CVS, Ford, Goodyear/auto, Kia, Lexus, Macy's, Nordstrom's, Old Navy, Safeway, Subaru
1b	I-280. I-880 begins/ends on I-280.
1a	Ca 17 to Santa Cruz.

NOTES

⛽ = gas 🍴 = food 🛏 = lodging Ⓞ = other Ⓡⓢ = rest stop   Copyright 2022 –The Next EXIT ©

COLORADO

CO

INTERSTATE 25

Exit #	Services
299	Colorado/Wyoming state line
296	point of interest both lanes
293	to Carr, Norfolk
288	Buckeye Rd
281	Owl Canyon Rd, E Ⓞ KOA Campground, truck repair
278	CO 1 S, to Wellington, W ⛽ Kum&Go/dsl, Loaf'N Jug/dsl, Shell/dsl 🍴 Burger King, Domino's, McDonald's, Subway, Taco Bell, Taco John's 🛏 Days Inn Ⓞ Family$, Ridley's Mkt, USPO, vet
271	Mountain Vista Dr, W Ⓞ Budweiser Brewery
269 b a	CO 14, to US 87, Ft Collins, E ⛽ Maverick/dsl 🍴 McDonald's 🛏 Best Value Inn, W ⛽ Shell/dsl 🍴 Denny's, Hacienda Real, Waffle House 🛏 9 Motel, Comfort Inn, Days Inn, EconoLodge, La Quinta, Motel 6, Red Lion Inn, Rodeway Inn, Super 8 Ⓞ to CO St U, vet
268	Prospect Rd, to Ft Collins, W Welcome Ctr/Ⓡⓢ both lanes, full ♿ facilities, litter barrels, 🛒, petwalk Ⓞ Ⓗ
267mm	weigh sta both lanes
265	Harmony Rd, Timnath, E ⛽ Murphy USA/dsl 🍴 Chick-fil-A, Freddy's, Starbucks, Taco Bell, Wendy's Ⓞ Costco/dsl, Schwab Tires, Walmart/Subway, W ⛽ Sinclair/dsl 🍴 Austin's Grill, BJ's Rest., Carrabba's, Chipotle, Famous Dave's, Firehouse Subs, Five Guys, HuHot, IHOP, Jersey Mike's, Macaroni Grill, McAlister's Deli, Old Chicago, Outback Steaks, Panera Bread, Papa John's, Potbelly, Qdoba, Red Robin, Rustic Oven, SmashBurger, Sprouts Mkt, Starbucks, Subway, Texas Roadhouse, Tom+Chee, Village Inn, Wahoo's, Which Wich? 🛏 Cambria Suites, Comfort Suites, Courtyard, Fairfield Inn, Hampton Inn, Hilton Garden, Holiday Inn Express, Home 2 Suites, Homewood Suites, Residence Inn Ⓞ AT&T, Ⓗ, Kohl's, Lowe's, Office Depot, Safeway/gas, Sam's Club, Staples, Target, Verizon, Walgreens, World Mkt
262	CO 392 E, to Windsor, E ⛽ 7-11/dsl, Shell/Subway/dsl 🍴 Arby's, Pueblo Viejo, Taco John's 🛏 AmericInn Ⓞ vet, W Ⓞ Powder River RV Ctr
259	Crossroads Blvd, E ⛽ 7-11/dsl, Kum&Go/dsl, Shell/dsl 🍴 Boot Grill, Carl's Jr, Nordy's, Palomino Mexican, Perkins, Qdoba Mexican, Subway 🛏 My Place, Candlewood Suites, Embassy Suites, Holiday Inn Express, Microtel, Woodspring Suites, W 🍴 Hooters Ⓞ BMW, Buick/GMC, CarMax, Chevrolet, Harley-Davidson, Hyundai, Mercedes, Mini, Subaru, to ✈
257 b a	US 34, to Loveland, E ⛽ 7-11/dsl, Shell/dsl 🍴 Bent Fork Grill, Biaggi Italian, BoneFish Grill, Culver's, East Coast Pizza, On-the-Border, PF Chang's, Qdoba, Red Robin, Rock Bottom Rest., Starbucks Ⓞ AT&T, Barnes&Noble, Best Buy, Dick's, GNC, Macy's, See's Candies, Verizon, W ⛽ Conoco/dsl 🍴 Buffalo Wild Wings, Carino's Italian, Chick-fil-A, Chili's, Chipotle Mexican, Cracker Barrel, IHOP, Jimmy John's, KFC/Taco Bell, LoneStar Steaks, McDonald's, Mimi's Cafe, Noodles&Co, Old Chicago, Panera Bread, Starbucks, Subway, Wendy's 🛏 Best Western+, Fairfield Inn, Hampton Inn, Residence Inn Ⓞ Ⓗ, Jo-Ann Fabrics, Loveland Outlets/famous brands, Loveland RV Resort, Marshall's, museum, Old Navy, Petsmart, Ross, Sportsman's Whse, Staples, Target, to Rocky Mtn NP
255	CO 402 W, to Loveland
254	to CO 60 W, to Campion, E ⛽ Johnson's Corner/Sinclair/café/dsl/scales/motel/24hr 🛏 Budget Host Ⓞ Lazydays RV Ctr/retreat
252	CO 60 E, to Johnstown, Milliken, W ⛽ Loaf'n Jug/Subway/dsl

Exit #	Services
250	CO 56 W, to Berthoud, W ⛽ ♥Loves/Subway/Taco John's dsl/scales/24hr Ⓞ to Carter Lake
245	to Mead
243	CO 66, to Longmont, Platteville, E ⛽ Conoco/dsl, Kum&Go/dsl, Shell/7-11 🍴 Rancheros Rest., Red Rooster Rest. Ⓞ Camping World/K&C RV Ctr, tires, vet, W Ⓞ to Estes Park, to Rocky Mtn NP
241mm	St Vrain River
240	CO 119, to Longmont, E ⛽ Murphy Express/dsl, Shell/7-11/dsl 🍴 Burger King, Carl's Jr, Del Taco, Good Times Grill, KFC, Pizza Hut, Popeye's, Qdoba, Starbucks, Wendy's 🛏 Best Western, Comfort Suites, Woodspring Suites Ⓞ Century RV Ctr, Home Depot, Kia, Lexus, Toyota, Transwest RV Ctr, Verizon, W ⛽ 7-11/Subway/dsl, Phillips 66/dsl/scales/24hr, Shell/Circle K/dsl 🍴 Arby's, McDonald's, Taco Bell, Waffle House 🛏 1st Inn, Best Value Inn, Quality Inn, Super 8, Travelodge Ⓞ museum, to Barbour Ponds SP, truckwash, Valley Camper RV Ctr
235	CO 52, Dacono, E ⛽ Kum&Go/dsl 🍴 Burger King Ⓞ Ford, Infiniti, W ⛽ Conoco/dsl/LP 🍴 McDonald's, Pepper Jacks Grille, Starbucks, Subway Ⓞ Harley-Davidson, to Eldora Ski Area
232	to Erie, Dacono
229	CO 7, to Lafayette, Brighton, E 🍴 Buffalo Wild Wings, Chick-fil-A, Chili's, Famous Dave's BBQ, Goodtimes Burgers, Gunther Toody's, La Fogata, Starbucks, Subway, Village Inn Ⓞ AT&T, Costco/gas, Dick's, Home Depot, Petsmart, Sears Grand, W ⛽ Murphy Express/dsl 🍴 Sonic, Wendy's Ⓞ King's Sooper/dsl
228	E-470 (tollway), to Limon
226	144th Ave, E ⛽ Murphy Express/dsl 🍴 Arby's, Cuba Cuba, Firehouse Subs, Five Guys, Freddy's, Freddy's, Panda Express, Potbelly, Wendy's 🛏 Candlewood Suites, Hilton Garden Ⓞ Cabela's, Hobby Lobby, Steinmart, W 🍴 HuHot Mongolian, Mimi's Cafe, Mooyah Burgers, Panera Bread, Red Robin, Rusty Bucket, Starbucks, Which Wich? Ⓞ $Tree, AT&T, Ⓗ, JC Penney, Macy's, Marshall's, Old Navy, REI, Ross, Staples, Target, Verizon
225	136th Ave, E ⛽ Kum&Go/dsl Ⓞ Denver Outlets/famous brands, W ⛽ Valero/dsl 🍴 Big Burrito, Carl's Jr, KFC/LJ Silver, Starbucks, Subway Ⓞ Advance Parts, Firestone/auto, Lowe's, URGENT CARE, Walmart/McDonald's
223	CO 128, 120th Ave, to Broomfield, E ⛽ Conoco, Valero/dsl 🍴 Applebee's, Bad Daddy's Burger Bar, Burger King, Café Rio, Chick-fil-A, Chipotle Mexican, Coldstone, Fazoli's, First Watch Cafe, Jim'N Nick's BBQ, Jimmy John's, Krispy Kreme, LoneStar Steaks, Longhorn Steaks, McDonald's, Olive Garden, Outback Steaks, Panda Express, Panera Bread, Smashburger, Sonic, Starbucks, Subway, Taziki's Cafe, Tequila's Mexican, TGIFriday's 🛏 DoubleTree, EconoLodge, Hampton Inn, Holiday Inn Express, Ramada Inn Ⓞ $Tree, Albertson's, AT&T, Barnes&Noble, Big O Tire, Brakes+, CarQuest, Discount Tire, GNC, Meineke, Michael's, O'Reilly Parts, PetCo, Sprouts Mkt, Target, Tires+, Verizon, vet, Walgreens, W ⛽ Conoco/dsl, Shell/Circle K/Popeye's/dsl, Valero/dsl 🍴 CB Potts Rest., Chili's, Cracker Barrel, DQ, Hooters, Laguna's Mexican, Perkins, Qdoba, Starbucks, Subway, Village Inn Rest., Wendy's 🛏 Comfort Suites, Cottonwood Suites, Extended Stay America, Fairfield Inn, La Quinta, Super 8
221	104th Ave, to Northglenn, E ⛽ Conoco, Shell 🍴 Buffalo Wild Wings, Burger King, CiCi's Pizza, Denny's, DQ, Firehouse Subs, Old Chicago, Qdoba, Subway, Texas Roadhouse Ⓞ GNC, Home Depot, Ⓗ, King's Soopers, Tires+, Walgreens, W ⛽ 7-11, Shell/Circle K/dsl 🍴 Applebee's, Atlanta Bread, Blackeyed Pea, Cinzzetti's Italian, GoodTimes Burger, Gunther Toody's,

Side labels: FT COLLINS · LOVELAND · LONGMONT · BROOMFIELD

INTERSTATE 25 Cont'd

THORNTON

221 Continued
McDonald's, Seoul BBQ, Sheplar's, Starbucks, Taco Bell, The Armadillo 🅾️ Best Buy, Fiat, Firestone/auto, Ford, Goodyear/auto, Hyundai, Jo-Ann Fabrics, Lowe's, Marshalls, Office Depot, Petsmart, Ross

220 Thornton Pkwy, E 🍴 Golden Corral, Rico Pollo 🅾️ AT&T, Hobby Lobby, Ⓗ, Sam's Club/gas, Thornton Civic Ctr, Walmart/McDonald's, W 🛢️ Shell, Valero/dsl, Western/dsl 🍴 Subway

219 84th Ave, to Federal Way, E 🛢️ Shell/dsl, Valero/dsl 🍴 Arby's, McDonald's, Quiznos, Sonic, Starbucks, Subway, Taco Bell, Taco Star, Waffle House 🅾️ O'Reilly Parts, W 🛢️ Econogas, Valero/dsl 🍴 Burger King, DQ, El Fogon, McDonald's, Popeye's, Santiago's Mexican, Village Inn Rest. 🏠 Motel 6 🅾️ AutoZone, CarQuest, Discount Tire, Ⓗ, Meineke, Save-A-Lot, vet

217 US 36 W (exits left from nb), to Boulder, W 🛢️ Ammco 🍴 Subway 🅾️ Chevrolet, Toyota

216 b a I-76 E, to I-270 E

215 58th Ave, E 🍴 Burger King, McDonald's, Steak Escape, Subway, Wendy's 🏠 Comfort Inn 🅾️ URGENT CARE, W 🛢️ Conoco/dsl, Shamrock/dsl 🏠 Super 8 🅾️ O'Reilly Parts

214c 48th Ave, E 🅾️🚂, coliseum, W 🍴 Village Inn Rest. 🏠 Clarion, Quality Inn

214 b a I-70, E to Limon, W to Grand Junction

213 Park Ave, W 38th Ave, 23rd St, downtown, E 🛢️ Conoco 🍴 Domino's, McDonald's, Starbucks 🏠 La Quinta, W 🏠 Town&Country Motel

DENVER AREA

212c 20th St, downtown, Denver

212 b a Speer Blvd, E 🅾️ museum downtown, W 🛢️ Conoco/dsl, Shell/dsl 🍴 Starbucks, Subway 🏠 AutoZone, Hampton Inn, Ramada, Residence Inn, Super 8 🅾️ Walgreens

211 23rd Ave, E 🅾️ funpark

210c CO 33 (from nb)

210b US 40 W, Colfax Ave, W 🍴 Denny's, KFC 🏠 Ramada Inn/rest. 🅾️ Mile High Stadium

210a US 40 E, Colfax Ave, E 🅾️ civic center, U-Haul downtown

209c 8th Ave

209b 6th Ave W, US 6, W 🛢️ Shell/dsl

209a 6th Ave E, downtown, Denver

208 CO 26, Alameda Ave (from sb), E 🛢️ Shamrock/dsl 🍴 Burger King, Denny's 🅾️ Home Depot, same as 207b, W 🛢️ Conoco/dsl

207b US 85 S, Santa Fe Dr same as 208

207a Broadway, Lincoln St, E 🍴 Griff's Burgers 🅾️ USPO

206b Washington St, Emerson St, E 🅾️ Whole Foods Mkt, W 🅾️ Ⓗ

206a Downing St (from nb)

205 b a University Blvd, W 🅾️ to U of Denver

204 CO 2, Colorado Blvd, E 🛢️ Conoco/dsl, Loaf'n Jug, Shamrock, Shell/Circle K 🍴 Arby's, Black Eyed Pea, Chili's, Domino's, GoodTimes Grill, Hacienda Colorado, IHOP, Jimmy John's, McDonald's, Noodles&Co, Old Chicago Pizza, Pizza Hut, Qdoba, Smashburger, Starbucks, Subway, Taco Bell, Tokyo Joe's, Village Inn Rest., Wahoo's, Whole Foods Mkt 🏠 Belcaro Motel, Courtyard, Fairfield Inn, Hampton Inn 🅾️ Barnes&Noble, Best Buy,

204 Continued
Chevrolet, Home Depot, Mercedes/BMW, Petco, Ross, Safeway Foods, Staples, vet, VW, Walgreens, W 🛢️ Conoco 🍴 A&W/KFC, Dave&Buster's, McDonald's, Pei Wei, Perkins, Which Wich 🏠 La Quinta 🅾️ Natural Grocers, Office Depot, USPO

203 Evans Ave, E 🏠 Rockies Inn, W 🏠 Cameron Motel 🅾️ Ford

202 Yale Ave, W 🛢️ King's Sooper 🍴 BeauJo's CO Pizza, Chipotle Mexican 🅾️ GNC, Michaels

201 US 285, CO 30, Hampden Ave, to Englewood, Aurora, E 🛢️ Conoco/Circle K/LP, Shamrock, Shell 🍴 Chick-fil-A, Chipotle Mexican, Coldstone, Domino's, Firehouse Subs, Jimmy John's, McDonald's, Noodles&Co, NY Deli, Panera Bread, Qdoba, Smashburger, Starbucks, Subway, Wahoos Fish Taco, Zanitas Mexican 🏠 Embassy Suites 🅾️ Discount Tire, King's Sooper/dsl, Omaha Steaks, Petco, Target, URGENT CARE, Verizon, vet, Walgreens, Whole Food Mkt, W 🛢️ Conoco/7-11 🍴 Burger King, Starbucks 🅾️ Safeway

200 I-225 N, to I-70

199 CO 88, Belleview Ave, to Littleton, E 🍴 Baker St Grill, Chipotle Mexican, Cool River Cafe, Fiocchi's Pizzeria, Fornaio Rest., Garcia's Mexican, Great Northern Rest., Noodles&Co, Pancake House, Panera Bread, Qdoba, Starbucks, Wendy's, Which Wich? 🏠 Hampton Inn, Hilton Garden, Hyatt Place, Marriott, W 🛢️ Conoco, Shamrock 🍴 McDonald's, Pappadeaux Café, Pizza Hut/Taco Bell 🏠 Extended Stay Am, Extended Stay America 🅾️ Lexus

198 Orchard Rd, E 🍴 Del Frisco's Steaks, Shepler's, W 🛢️ Shell/Circle K/dsl 🍴 Subway 🏠 DoubleTree 🅾️ vet

197 Arapahoe Blvd, E 🛢️ Conoco/dsl, Shell/Circle K/dsl 🍴 A&W/KFC, Bros BBQ, Burger King, Chick-fil-A, Del Taco, Dickie's BBQ, Domino's, El Parral, El Tapatio Mexican, Gunther Toody's Rest., Hoong's Palace, McDonald's, Outback Steaks, Pat's Cheesesteak, Pizza Hut, Qdoba, Schlotsky's, Smashburger, Sonic, Starbucks, Subway, Volcano Chinese, Wendy's 🏠 Best Western, Courtyard, Extended Stay America, Hawthorn Suites, Hyatt House, LaQuinta, Motel 6, Sleep Inn 🅾️ Chrysler/Jeep, Discount Tire, Ford, Home Depot, Honda, Hyundai, Kia, Lowe's Whse, Mazda, Nissan, Subaru, Target, Toyota, USPO, Walmart, W 🛢️ Phillips 66/dsl, Shell/dsl, Valero/dsl 🍴 Arby's, Boston Mkt, CB & Potts, Chipotle Mexican, DQ, Elephant Bar Rest., Five Guys,

⬆N   INTERSTATE 25 Cont'd

DENVER AREA

197 Continued
Garbanzo Grill, Goodtimes, Jamba Juice, Jimmy John's, Macaroni Grill, McDonald's, Papa Murphy's, Qdoba, Red Robin, Starbucks, Subway, Taco Bell, Twin Peaks Grill 🏨 Residence Inn, Wingate Inn ⊙ Advance Parts, AT&T, Big O Tire, Brakes+, Firestone/auto, GNC, Goodyear/auto, Office Depot, Safeway, Sprouts Mkt, URGENT CARE, vet

196 Dry Creek Rd, E 🍴 IHOP, Landry's Seafood, Maggiano's Italian, Purple Ginger Asian 🏨 Comfort Suites, Days Inn, Extended Stay America, Holiday Inn Express, La Quinta, Quality Inn, Sheraton, Staybridge Suites, W ⛽ 7-11/dsl 🍴 Bono's BBQ 🏨 Drury Inn

195 County Line Rd, E 🍴 Fleming's 🏨 Courtyard, Homewood Suites, Residence Inn, W ⛽ Conoco 🍴 Buffalo Wild Wings, Burger King, CA Pizza Kitchen, Chick-fil-A, Chipotle Mexican, Earl's Kitchen, Firehouse Subs, Genghis Grill, J Alexander's, Jason's Deli, Panda Express, PF Changs, Red Lobster, Red Robin, Rock Bottom Brewery/Cafe, Smashburger, Starbucks, TGIFriday's, Thai Basil, Tokyo Joe's 🏨 Hyatt Place ⊙ AT&T, Barnes&Noble, Best Buy, Costco/gas, Dick's, Dillard's, Home Depot, JC Penney, Jo-Ann Fabrics, Macy's, Marshall's, Michaels, Nordstrom, Old Navy, PetsMart, REI, Ross, Verizon

194 CO 470 W, CO 470 E (tollway)

193 Lincoln Ave, to Parker, E ⛽ 7-11/dsl, Circle K/dsl, Conoco 🍴 Carl's Jr, Hacienda Colorado, Kneaders, Starbucks, Subway 🏨 Hilton Garden, Quality Inn, W ⛽ Phillips 66/mkt/dsl 🍴 Chili's, Chipotle Mexican, Firehouse Subs, Five Guys, Heidi's, McDonald's, Noodles&Co, Papa John's, Papa Murphy's, Qdoba, Starbucks, Subway 🏨 Hampton Inn, Marriott ⊙ Discount Tire, Ⓗ, Safeway, Sprouts Mkt, Target

192 Ridgegate Pkwy, W 🏨 TownePlace Suites ⊙ Cabela's, Ⓗ

191 no services

190 Surrey Ridge, Surrey Ridge

188 Castle Pines Pkwy, W ⛽ Conoco/dsl, Shell/Circle K/Taco Bell/dsl 🍴 La Dolce Vita, Las Fajitas Mexican, Papa John's, Papa Murphy's, Starbucks, Subway, Wendy's ⊙ Big O Tires, Discount Tire, King's Sooper/dsl, Safeway, URGENT CARE, vet, Walgreens

CASTLE ROCK

187 Happy Canyon Rd, W ⊙ services 2 mi

185 Castle Rock Pkwy, W ⛽ Phillips 66/7-11 🍴 Berry Blends Smoothies, Chick-fil-A, Cuba Cuba, Del Taco, La Loma, Panda Express, Starbucks, Whole Foods Mkt ⊙ Petco, Sam's Club/dsl, TJ Maxx, Verizon

184 Founders Pkwy, Meadows Pkwy, to Castle Rock, E 🍴 Conoco/dsl, Shell/Circle K/dsl 🍴 A&W/KFC, Applebee's, Baskin-Robbins, Canes, Chick-fil-A, Chipotle Mexican, Coldstone, Five Guys, Goodtimes Grill, Jimmy John's, Little Caesar's, Noodles&Co, Outback Steaks, Panera Bread, Parry's Pizza, Qdoba, Red Robin, Sonic, Starbucks, Subway, Taco Bell, Wendy's ⊙ $Tree, Advance Parts, AT&T, Brakes+, Discount Tire, Firestone/auto, GNC, Goodyear/auto, Grease Monkey, Home Depot, Just Brakes, King's Sooper, Kohl's, Michael's, Natural Grocers, O'Reilly Parts, Office Depot, Petsmart, Sprouts Mkt, Target, Verizon, vet, Walgreens, Walmart, W ⛽ Loaf'n Jug/dsl 🍴 Arby's, Blackeyed Pea, Cafe Rio, Chili's, Food Court, Freddy's Steakburger, IHOP, McDonald's, MOD Pizza, Popeye's, Potbelly, Rockyard Grill, Smashburger 🏨 Best Western+, Comfort Suites, Days Inn, Hampton Inn, Holiday Inn Express ⊙ Castle Rock Outlet/famous brands, King's Sooper/dsl, Lowe's, Midas, st patrol

LARKSPUR

182 CO 86, Castle Rock, Franktown, E ⛽ 7-11/dsl, Conoco/dsl 🍴 Augustine Grill, B&B Cafe, Castle Cafe, El Meson Mexican 🏨 Castle Pines Motel ⊙ vet, W ⛽ Shell/Circle K/dsl, Valero/dsl 🍴 Burger King, Domino's, Guadalajara Mexican, Jack-in-the-Box, McDonald's, Old West BBQ, Santiago's Mexican, Village Inn, Waffle House, Wendy's 🏨 Castle Inn, LaQuinta, Super 8 ⊙ NAPA

181 CO 86, Wilcox St, Plum Creek Pkwy, Castle Rock, E ⛽ Phillips 66, Valero/dsl, Western/dsl 🍴 Blimpie, DQ, El Meson Mexican, Jimmy John's, Papa John's, Papa Murphy's, Pizza Hut, Quiznos, Starbucks, Stumpy's Pizzaria, Subway, Taco Bell 🏨 Castle Rock Motel ⊙ AutoZone, Big O Tire, Buick/Chevrolet/GMC, Chrysler/Dodge/Jeep, Ford, Midas, Safeway/dsl, Tuesday Morning, URGENT CARE, USPO, Walgreens

174 Tomah Rd, W ⊙ Yogi Bear's Campground

173 Larkspur (from sb, no return), 3 mi W ⛽ Conoco/Larkspur Cafe/dsl/🍴

172 Upper Lake Gulch Rd, Larkspur, 2 mi W ⛽ Conoco/dsl/🍴 🍴 Larkspur Pizza Cafe, Spur Grill ⊙ USPO

167 Greenland

163 County Line Rd

162.5mm elev 7352, Monument Hill

162mm weigh sta both lanes

161 CO 105, Woodmoor Dr, E ⛽ Kum&Go/dsl, Sinclair/dsl 🍴 3 Margaritas Mexican, Jimmy John's, Papa John's 🏨 Ramada, Sundance Mtn Lodge/rest. ⊙ CO Hts RV Park (2mi), vet, W ⛽ 7-11, Phillips 66/dsl 🍴 Arby's, Domino's, La Casa Fiesta New Mexican, McDonald's, Rosie's Diner, Starbucks, Subway, Taco Bell, Village Inn ⊙ Big O Tire, Natural Grocers, Safeway/dsl, USPO, Walgreens

158 Baptist Rd, E ⛽ Murphy USA/dsl, Shell/Circle K/Popeye's/dsl/24hr 🍴 Borriello Bros. Pizza, Carlos Miguel's, Chili's, Coldstone, Freddy's Steakburgers, McDonald's, Mexican Grill, Papa Murphy's, Qdoba, Subway, TX Roadhouse 🏨 Fairfield Inn ⊙ Advance Parts, AutoZone, Christian Bros. Auto, Discount Tire, GNC, Home Depot, King's Sooper, Kohl's, Natural Grocers, O'Reilly Parts, Petsmart, Staples, URGENT CARE, Verizon, Walgreens, Walmart/Subway, W ⛽ 🍴/Arby's/dsl/scales/24hr, Shamrock/dsl/scales

156b N Entrance to USAF Academy, E ⛽ Loaf'n Jug/Subway/dsl 🍴 Bourbon Bros Kitchen, C B & Potts Rest., Costa Vida, Jimmy John's, Kneaders Cafe, Wendy's ⊙ AT&T, Bass Pro Shops, W ⊙ visitors center

156a Gleneagle Dr, E ⊙ mining museum

155 new exit

153 InterQuest Pkwy, E ⛽ Cheddar's, Kum&Go/dsl 🍴 CO Mtn Brewery/rest., Dickey's BBQ, Freddy's, Jersey Mike's, Starbucks, Taco Bell, Zoup! 🏨 Drury Inn, Great Wolf Lodge, Hampton Inn, Holiday Inn Express, Residence Inn

152 scenic overlook on sb

151 Briargate Pkwy, E ⛽ 7-11 🍴 Biaggi's, CA Pizza Kitchen, Garbanzo Grill, Marco's Pizza, Panera Bread, PF Changs, Qdoba, Salsa Brava Mexican, Starbucks, Ted's MT Grill 🏨 Hilton Garden, Homewood Suites ⊙ AT&T, to Black Forest

150b a CO 83, Academy Blvd, E ⛽ Shamrock/dsl, Shell/Circle K/dsl 🍴 A&W, Amanda's Fonda, Applebee's, Baskin-Robbins, Buffalo Wild Wings, Burger King, Chick-fil-A, Chipotle Mexican, Coldstone, Cracker Barrel, Crave Burgers, Culver's, Del Taco, Denny's, Drifters Hamburgers, Egg&I Café, Elephant Bar Rest., Extreme Pizza, Famous Dave's, Firehouse Subs, Five Guys, HuHot Mongolian, IHOP, Jason's Deli, Jimmy John's, KFC, McDonald's, Mimi's Café, Noodles&Co, Olive Garden, On-the-Border,

INTERSTATE 25 Cont'd

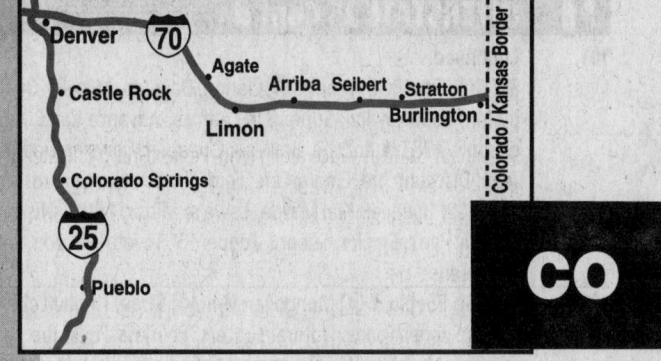

150b a Continued
Panera Bread, Pei Wei, Qdoba, Red Robin, Salt Grass Steaks, Schlotzsky's, Sonic, Starbucks, Steak'n Shake, Subway, Tokyo Joe's Grill, Wendy's 🛏 Academy Hotel, Comfort Suites, Days Inn, Drury Inn, EconoLodge, Howard Johnson, Super 8 🔲 $Tree, Advance Parts, AT&T, Barnes&Noble, Best Buy, Chevrolet, Dick's, Dillard's, Firestone/auto, Ford, Hobby Lobby, Home Depot, Hyundai, JC Penney, Kia, King's Sooper, Macy's, Marshall's, Michael's, Midas, Natural Grocers, O'Reilly Parts, Old Navy, PepBoys, Petsmart, REI, Ross, Sam's Club/gas, to Peterson AFB, URGENT CARE, Verizon, VW, Walmart/Subway, Whole Foods Mkt, **W** S Entrance to USAF Academy

149 Woodmen Rd, **E** 🍴 Carl's Jr, Carraba's 🔲 Nissan, **W** 🔲 Shell/Circle K/dsl 🍴 Hooters, Old Chicago Pizza, Outback Steaks, TGI-Friday's 🛏 Comfort Inn, Embassy Suites, Fairfield Inn, Hampton Inn, Holiday Inn Express, Microtel, Staybridge Suites

148 Corporate Ctr Dr, Nevada Ave, **E** 🍴 BJ's Rest., Bonefish Grill, Chipotle Mexican, Hacienda Colorado, Noodles&Co, Panera Bread, Pita Pit, Smashburger, Tokyo Joe's Grill, Which Wich? 🛏 The Lodges 🔲 BMW, Costco/gas, Harley-Davidson, Kohl's, Lowe's, Petco, SteinMart, Trader Joe's, **W** 🔲 Shell/Circle K 🛏 Crestwood Suites, Extended Stay America, Hyatt House, Marriott 🔲 to Rodeo Hall of Fame

146 Garden of the Gods Rd, **E** 🔲 Conoco/7-11, Shell/Circle K/dsl 🍴 Carl's Jr, Caspian Cafe, Drifter's Burgers, McDonald's 🛏 Best Value Inn, La Quinta 🔲 Aamco, **W** 🔲 Circle K/dsl, Conoco/7-11, Exxon/dsl 🍴 Applebee's, Arby's, Arceo's Mexican, Blackeyed Pea, Chick-fil-A, Freddy's Steakburgers, Jimmy John's, Mollica's Italian, Sonic, Souper Salad, Subway, Taco Bell, Taco Bueno, Village Inn, Wendy's 🛏 Days Inn, Hyatt Place, Quality Inn, Super 8 🔲 $Tree, AutoZone, Discount Tire, to Garden of Gods, vet

145 CO 38 E, Fillmore St, **E** 🔲 Conoco/7-11, Shamrock/dsl, Western/dsl 🍴 Arby's, Burger King, Carl's Jr, DQ, Lucky Dragon, McDonald's, Subway, Taco Bell 🛏 Budget Host 🔲 Advance Parts, 🅷, Walgreens, **W** 🔲 Kum&Go/dsl 🍴 Waffle House 🛏 Best Western+, Motel 6, Super 8

144 Fontanero St

143 Uintah St, **E** 🔲 7-11 🔲 Uintah Fine Arts Ctr

142 Bijou St, Bus Dist, **E** 🛏 The Antlers Hotel 🔲 Firestone/auto, visitor info, **W** 🍴 Denny's 🛏 Clarion, Holiday Inn Express, Quality Inn

141 US 24 W, Cimarron St, to Manitou Springs, **W** 🔲 Shell/7-11/dsl, Sinclair/dsl 🍴 Arby's, Capt D's, La Casita Mexican, McDonald's, Popeye's, Sonic, TX Roadhouse 🔲 Acura, Audi, AutoZone, Brakes+, Buick/GMC, Cadillac, Chevrolet, Chrysler/Dodge/Jeep, Discount Tire, Ford, Grease Monkey, Hobby Lobby, Hyundai, Infiniti, Kia, Land Rover/Jaguar, Lexus, Lincoln, Mazda, Meineke, Mercedes, NAPA, Office Depot, Porsche, Subaru, to Pikes Peak, Toyota, Volvo, VW, Walmart/McDonald's

140b US 85 S, Tejon St, **E** 🔲 Peerless Tires, **W** 🔲 Conoco/dsl 🔲 access to same as 141

140a Nevada Ave, **E** 🔲 Kum & Go/dsl 🛏 Chateau Motel, Howard Johnson 🔲 repair, **W** 🔲 7-11, Shamrock 🍴 Angry Chicken, Arceo's Mexican, Burger King, China Kitchen, Chipotle Mexican, Dunkin', Five Guys, IHOP, KFC, McDonald's, Noodles&Co, On the Border, Panda Express, Panera Bread, Rancho Alegre Mexican, Red Robin, Starbucks, Subway, Taco Bell, Taco Express, Wendy's 🛏 Rodeway Inn, Sunsprings Motel, Travel Star Inn 🔲 $Tree, access to auto dealers at 141, Big O Tire, Family$, Michael's, Midas, Natural Grocers, O'Reilly Parts, Office Depot, Petsmart, Ross, Safeway Foods, Tuesday Morning, Walgreens

139 US 24 E, to Lyman, Peterson AFB

138 CO 29, Circle Dr, **E** 🔲 Phillips 66, Shell/Circle K/dsl 🍴 McDonald's 🛏 Hotel Elegante, SPC, Super 8 🔲 🖂, Kohl's, URGENT CARE, **W** 🔲 Conoco/7-11 🍴 Arby's, Buffalo Wild Wings, Carl's Jr, Carrabba's, Chili's, ChuckeCheese, Culver's, Denny's, Fazoli's, Macaroni Grill, Outback Steaks, Smoothie King, Subway 🛏 Best Western, Comfort Inn, Courtyard, DoubleTree Hotel, Fairfield Inn, Hampton Inn, Home2 Suites, La Quinta, Quality Inn, Residence Inn 🔲 AT&T, GNC, PetCo, Target

135 CO 83, Academy Blvd, **E** 🔲 to 🖂, **W** 🍴 Freddy's, Jersey Mike's, MOD Pizza, Qdoba, Starbucks 🛏 Holiday Inn Express 🔲 Ft Carson, Sam's Club/gas, to Cheyenne Mtn SP, Verizon, Walmart/Subway

132 CO 16, Wide Field Security, **E** 🔲 🛢Loves/Subway/dsl 🛏 Microtel 🔲 Camping World RV Ctr, KOA, Windish RV Ctr

128 to US 85 N, Fountain, Security, **E** 🔲 7-11, Loaf'n Jug/Subway/dsl 🔲 Family$, USPO, **W** 🔲 Tomahawk/Exxon/rest./dsl/24hr/@ 🛏 Fountain Inn, Super 8 🔲 Freightliner

125 Ray Nixon Rd

123 no services

122 to Pikes Peak Meadows, **W** 🔲 Pikes Peak Intn'l Raceway

119 Rancho Colorado Blvd, Midway

116 county line rd

115mm Ⓡ🔲 nb, full ♿ facilities, litter barrels, petwalk, 🏕

114 Young Hollow

112mm Ⓡ🔲 sb, full ♿ facilities, litter barrels, petwalk, 🏕

110 Pinon, **W** 🔲 atm

108 Purcell Blvd, Bragdon, **E** 🔲 racetrack, **W** 🔲 KOA

106 Porter Draw

104 Eden, **W** 🔲 🛢Loves/Chester's/Subway/dsl/scales/24hr 🔲 Peterbilt

102 Eagleridge Blvd, **E** 🔲 Loaf'n Jug/dsl 🍴 Burger King, Subway, TX Roadhouse 🛏 Candlewood Suites, Holiday Inn Express 🔲 Big O Tire, Home Depot, Sam's Club/gas, **W** 🔲 Conoco/dsl 🍴 Buffalo Wild Wings, Cactus Flower Mexican, Chili's, Cracker Barrel, IHOP, Mexican Grill, Starbucks, Village Inn, Wonderful Bistro 🛏 Best Western+, EconoLodge, Hampton Inn, La Quinta, Quality Inn, Ramada, Wingate Inn 🔲 Best Buy, Cavender's Boots, Dick's, frontage rds access 101, Harley-Davidson, Kohl's, PetCo

101 US 50 W, Pueblo, **E** 🍴 Capt D's, Coldstone, Fritangas Mexican, Margaritas Mexican, Ruby Tuesday 🛏 Baymont Inn 🔲 Barnes&Noble, CO Tire, Dillard's, JC Penney, Jo-Ann, Petsmart, Ross, Target, TJ Maxx, U-Haul, Verizon, Walmart/Subway, **W** 🔲 Circle K/dsl, Conoco/7-11, Loaf'n Jug/dsl, Shell/dsl 🍴 Applebee's, Arby's, Arriba Mexican, Blackeyed Pea, Carl's Jr, Chipotle Mexican, Country Kitchen, DJ's Steaks, DQ, Fazoli's, GG's BBQ, Golden Corral, Jack-in-the-Box, Little Caesar's, Manhattan's Pizza, McAlister's Deli, McDonald's, Noodles&Co, Old Chicago, Olive Garden, Papa John's, Papa Murphy's, Pass Key Rest., Popeye's, Red Lobster, Simple Simon Pizza, Starbucks, Subway,

🅶 = gas 🍴 = food 🛏 = lodging 🅾 = other 🆁🆂 = rest stop   Copyright 2022 - The Next EXIT ®

INTERSTATE 25 Cont'd

Exit	Services
101	Continued
	SW Grill, Taco Bell, Wendy's 🛏 Clarion, Days Inn, Motel 6, Quality Inn, Rodeway Inn, Super 8 🅾 Aamco, Advance Parts, Albertson's, AT&T, AutoZone, Brakes+, Chevrolet, Chrysler/Dodge/Jeep, Discount Tire, EmergiCare, Ford/Lincoln, frontage rds access 102, Hyundai, Kia/Mazda, Lowe's, Midas, NAPA, Nissan, O'Reilly Parts, Staples, Subaru, Topper RV, Toyota, Verizon, vet, Walgreens
100b	29th St, Pueblo, **E** 🍴 Mongolian Grill 🅾 $Tree, Hobby Lobby, King's Sooper Foods, Natural Grocers, Peerless Tires, tire svc, Tuesday Morning, **W** 🅶 Conoco 🍴 Sonic 🛏 USA Motel 🅾 Family$, Grease Monkey
100a	US 50 E, to La Junta, **E** 🅶 Loaf'n Jug/dsl, Shell 🍴 Little Caesar's, Los Carnales Mexican, McDonald's, Pizza Hut, Wendy's 🅾 Advance Parts, AutoZone, Belmont Tire/repair, Save-A-Lot Foods, Walgreens
99b a	Santa Fe Ave, 13th St, downtown, **W** 🍴 Black Swan Cafe, Chelsey's Burgers, Momo Japanese, Subway, Taco Bell, Wendy's 🛏 Bramble Tree Inn, Santa Fe Inn 🅾 Buick/Cadillac/GMC, Honda, �H
98b	CO 96, 1st St, Union Ave Hist Dist, Pueblo, **W** 🅶 Loaf'n Jug/dsl 🍴 Carl's Jr 🛏 Courtyard
98a	US 50E bus, to La Junta, **W** 🍴 Sonic
97b	Abriendo Ave
97a	Central Ave, **W** 🅶 $General, Alta/dsl 🍴 McDonald's
96	Indiana Ave, **W** 🅾 H
95	Illinois Ave (from sb), **W** 🅾 to dogtrack
94	CO 45 N, Pueblo Blvd, **W** 🅶 Loaf'n Jug/dsl, Phillis 66/dsl 🍴 Subway, Taco Bell 🛏 Hampton Inn, Microtel 🅾 Forts RV Park, to Lake Pueblo SP
91	Stem Beach
88	Burnt Mill Rd
87	Verde Rd
83	no services
77	Hatchet Ranch Rd, Cedarwood
74	CO 165 W, Colo City, **E** 🅶 Shamrock/deli/dsl/24hr 🍴 Obie's BBQ 🅾 KOA, **W** 🆁🆂 both lanes, full 🦽 facilities, litter barrels, petwalk, 🚻, 🐾, vending, 🅶 Exxon/Subway/dsl 🍴 Max's Place 🛏 Days Inn/rest.
71	Graneros Rd
67	to Apache
64	Lascar Rd
60	Huerfano
59	Butte Rd
56	Redrock Rd
55	Airport Rd
52	CO 69 W, to Alamosa, Walsenburg, **W** 🅶 Conoco/dsl, Loaf'n Jug/dsl (2mi), TA/Phillips 66/A&W/dsl 🍴 Carl's Jr (2mi), George's Rest., KFC/Taco Bell, Subway (2mi) 🛏 Best Western 🅾 Dakota RV Park/camping, Family$ (2mi), San Luis Valley, to Great Sand Dunes NM
50	CO 10 E, to La Junta, **W** 🅾 H
49	Lp 25, to US 160 W, Walsenburg, **E** 🅶 Loves/Subway/Godfather's/dsl/scales/24hr, 1 mi **W** 🅶 Loaf'n Jug/dsl 🍴 Carl's Jr., Subway 🅾 Lathrop SP, to Cuchara Ski Valley
42	Rouse Rd, to Pryor
41	Rugby Rd
34	Aguilar
30	Aguilar Rd, **W** 🅾 Green Earth RV Park
27	Ludlow, **W** 🅾 Ludlow Memorial
23	Hoehne Rd
18	El Moro Rd, **W** 🆁🆂 full 🦽 facilities, litter barrels, petwalk, 🚻
15	US 350 E, Goddard Ave, **E** 🍴 Burger King, Pizza Hut 🛏 Super 8 🅾 Art Cartopia Museum, AutoZone, Big R Ranch Store, Family$, �H, **W** 🍴 Shell/dsl 🛏 Frontier Motel/café
14	Commercial St, downtown, Trinidad same as 13b
13b	Main St, Trinidad, **E** CO Welcome Ctr, 🅶 Exxon/dsl 🍴 KFC/Taco Bell, McDonald's, Sonic 🛏 Days Inn 🅾 CarQuest, �H, Safeway Foods/dsl, Travelodge, **W** 🅶 Conoco/dsl 🅾 Monument Lake, to Trinidad Lake
13a	Santa Fe Trail, Trinidad, **E** 🅾 RV camping
11	Starkville, **E** 🅶 Shell/Wendy's/dsl/24hr 🍴 Tequila's Mexican 🛏 Budget Host/RVPark, Holiday Inn Express, Rodeway Inn 🅾 Summit RV Park, to Santa Fe Trail, weigh/check sta, **W** 🛏 La Quinta, Quality Inn/rest 🅾 Big O Tire, O'Reilly Parts, Walmart
8	Springcreek
6	Gallinas
2	Wootton
1mm	scenic area pulloff nb
0mm	Colorado/New Mexico state line, Raton Pass elev 7834, **weigh sta sb**

INTERSTATE 70

Exit #	Services
450mm	Colorado/Kansas state line
438	US 24, Rose Ave, Burlington, **N** 🛏 Hi-Lo Motel, Sloan's Motel 🅾 $General, Bomgaars, Buick/Cadillac/Chevrolet/GMC, CarQuest, Family$, Ford/Lincoln, �H, NAPA, O'Reilly Parts, Outback RV Park, Safeway Foods, **S** 🅶 Sinclair/Reynaldo's Mexican/dsl/24hr 🅾 truck repair
437.5mm	Welcome Ctr wb, full 🦽 facilities, historical site, info, litter barrels, petwalk, 🚻, 🚻
437	US 385, Burlington, **N** 🅶 Conoco/dsl, Phillips 66/dsl 🍴 Arby's, Burger King, Dish Room, McDonald's, Pizza Hut, Subway 🛏 Burlington Inn, Burlington Stay Inn, Chaparral Motel, Quality Inn, Western Motel 🅾 �H, ShopKO, **S** 🅶 Loves/Carl's Jr/dsl/scales/24hr/@ 🛏 Best Western+, Fairfield Inn, Woodspring Suites
429	Bethune
419	CO 57, Stratton, **N** 🅶 Cenex/dsl, Conoco/dsl 🍴 Dairy Treat 🛏 Claremont Inn/café, Rodeway Inn 🅾 Marshall Ash Village Camping, Trails End Camping
412	Vona, 1/2 mi **N** 🅾 gas, 🚻
405	CO 59, Seibert, **N** 🅾 Shady Grove Camping/RV dump, **S** 🅶 Conoco/dsl 🅾 tire repair
395	Flagler, **N** 🅶 Loaf'N Jug/dsl 🍴 I-70 Diner, Subway 🛏 Little England Motel 🅾 Flagler SWA, G&B RV camping, NAPA, **S** 🅶 Cenex/dsl 🅾 golf
383	Arriba, **N** 🅶 DJ/café/dsl, motel, **S** 🆁🆂 both lanes full 🦽 facilities, litter barrels, petwalk, 🚻, point of interest, RV camping
376	Bovina
371	Genoa, **N** food, gas, 🚻, point of interest, **S** 🅾 H
363	US 24, US 40, US 287, to CO 71, to Hugo, Limon, 13 mi **S** 🅾 H
361	CO 71, Limon, **N** 🅾 Ace Hardware, **S** 🅶 Shell/Wendy's/dsl, Sinclair/dsl 🍴 Golden China, Pizza Hut 🛏 1st Inn Gold, Coyote Motel 🅾 KOA, RV camping, st patrol
360.5mm	**weigh/check sta both lanes**

Sidebars: CO · TRINIDAD · BURLINGTON · LIMON · WALSENBURG

INTERSTATE 70 Cont'd

LIMON

Exit #	Services
359	to US 24, to CO 71, Limon, **N** 🅿️ 🔷FLYING J/IHOP/dsl/scales/LP/24hr 🛏️ La Quinta ⊙ dsl repair, RV camping, **S** 🅿️ Qwest/dsl, Sinclair/dsl, TA/Phillips 66/Subway/Country Pride/dsl/scales/24hr/@ 🍴 Arby's, McDonald's, Microtel, Oscar's Grill, Taco Bell 🛏️ Baymont Inn, Comfort Inn, EconoLodge, Holiday Inn Express, Quality Inn, Super 8 ⊙ Chrysler/Dodge/Jeep
354	no services
352	CO 86 W, to Kiowa
348	to Cedar Point
340	Agate, 1/4 mi **S** gas/dsl, 🅒
336	to Lowland
332mm	📱 wb, full 🛏️ facilities, info, litter barrels, petwalk, 🅒, 🅰️, vending
328	to Deer Trail, **N** 🅿️ Phillips/dsl, **S** 🅿️ Shell/dsl ⊙ USPO
325mm	East Bijou Creek
323.5mm	Middle Bijou Creek
322	to Peoria
316	US 36 E, Byers, **N** 🅿️ Sinclair/dsl 🛏️ Budget Host ⊙ Thriftway Foods/Drug, **S** 🅿️ Tri Valley 🍴 Country Burger Rest. ⊙ USPO
310	Strasburg, **N** 🅿️ Conoco/dsl, Coronas Mexican 🍴 KT's BBQ, Patio Cafe, Subway ⊙ Country Gardens RV Camping (3mi), dsl/auto repair, KOA, NAPA, USPO, vet, Western Hardware
306	Kiowa, Bennett
305	Kiowa (from eb)
304	CO 79 N, Bennett, **N** 🅿️ Conoco/Hotstuff Pizza/dsl, 💚Loves /McDonald's/dsl/scales/24hr 🍴 Carl's Jr, China Kitchen, High Plains Diner, Starbucks, Subway, Taco Bell ⊙ Family$, King Soopers Foods/dsl, O'Reilly Parts, USPO, **S** 🅿️ ⊙ Ace Hardware
299	CO 36, Manila Rd, **S** 🅿️ Shamrock/dsl
295	Lp 70, Watkins, **N** 🅿️ Shell/Tomahawk/rest/dsl/24hr/@ 🍴 Biscuit's Cafe, Lulu's Cafe 🛏️ Country Manor Motel ⊙ USPO
292	CO 36, Airpark Rd
289	E-470 Tollway, 120th Ave, CO Springs
288	US 287, US 40, Lp 70, Colfax Ave (exits left from wb)
286	CO 32, Tower Rd, **N** 🅿️ Murphy Express/dsl 🍴 Chick-fil-A, Chili's, Chipotle Mexican, Del Taco, DQ, Firehouse Subs, McAlister's Deli, Noodles&Co, Panda Express, Starbucks, Wendy's ⊙ $Tree, AT&T, Best Buy, Brakes+, Discount Tire, GNC, Home Depot, Les Schwab Tire, O'Reilly Parts, Office Depot, PetCo, Verizon, Walmart/Subway
285	Airport Blvd, **N** ⊙ Denver Int Airport, **S** 🅿️ 🔷FLYING J/Denny's/dsl/scales/24hr, Conoco/McDonald's/dsl 🛏️ Comfort Inn, Quality Inn ⊙ Harley-Davidson
284	I-225 N (from eb)
283	Chambers Rd, **N** 🅿️ Conoco, Shell/Circle K/Popeye's 🍴 A&W/KFC, Anthony's Pizza, Applebees, Chicago Grill, Jimmy John's, LJ Silver/Taco Bell, Outback Steaks, Pizza Hut, Qdoba, Sonic, Subway, Ted's MT Grill, Urban Sombrero, Wendy's, Zume Asian 🛏️ A Loft, Cambria Suites, Country Inn&Suites, Crowne Plaza, Econolodge, Hampton Inn, Hilton Garden, Homewood Suites, Hyatt Place, Marriott, Residence Inn, TownePlace Suites, Woolley's Suites ⊙ Tires+, U-haul, **S** 🅿️ Shamrock 🍴 Burger King, Jack-in-the-Box 🛏️ Crossland Suites, Woodspring Suites ⊙ RV America, URGENT CARE
282	I-225 S, to Colorado Springs
281	Peoria St, **N** 🅿️ 7-11, Conoco/dsl, Shell/dsl 🍴 Ajua Mexican, Burger King, Del Taco, Domino's, GoodTimes Burgers, McDonald's, Peoria Grill, Quizno's, Starbucks, Subway 🛏️ Holiday Inn Express, La Quinta, Rodeway Inn, Timbers Motel ⊙ Big O Tire, Family$, **S** 🅿️ Phillips 66/dsl, Shamrock/dsl 🍴 Bennett's BBQ,

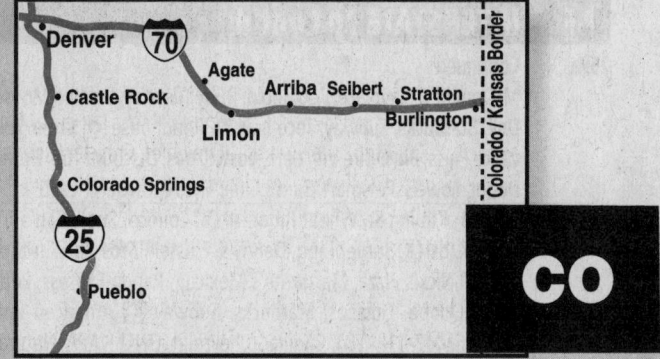

CO

DENVER AREA

281	Continued Denny's, Ho Mei Chinese, Taco Bell, Taco Mex 🛏️ Motel 6, Rodeway Inn, Star Hotel, Stay Inn ⊙ auto/RV repair, Goodyear/auto
280	Havana St, **N** 🛏️ Embassy Suites
279	I-270 W, US 36 W (from wb), to Ft Collins, Boulder
279b	Central Ave, **N** 🛏️ Drury Inn, Residence Inn
278	CO 35, Quebec St, **N** 🅿️ Sapp Bros/Sinclair/Subway/dsl/@, TA/dsl/rest./24hr/@ 🍴 Bar Louie, Coldstone, Del Taco, Islamorada Fish Co, Jim'n Nick's BBQ, La Sandia Cantina, Marco's Pizza, Olive Garden, Qdoba, Red Lobster, Red Robin, Starbucks, Subway, TGIFriday's, TX Roadhouse, Wahoo's, Which Wich? 🛏️ Best Inn, Comfort Inn, Staybridge Suites ⊙ Bass Pro Shops, JC Penney, Macys, Old Navy, Super Target, **S** 🅿️ Walmart Gas 🍴 Arby's, Buffalo Wild Wings, Country Buffet, Famous Dave's BBQ, IHOP, Jimmy John's, La Mariposa, McDonald's, Panda Express, Panera Bread, Papa John's, Smashburger, Sonic, Subway 🛏️ Best Western, Courtyard, DoubleTree Hilton, DoubleTree Hotel, Holiday Inn, Renaissance Inn, Super 8 ⊙ AT&T, GNC, Home Depot, Office Depot, Petsmart, Ross, Sam's Club, Tires+, Walgreens, Walmart/Subway
277	to Dahlia St, Holly St, Monaco St, frontage rd
276b	US 6 E, US 85 N, CO 2, Colorado Blvd, **S** 🅿️ Conoco/Subway/dsl 🍴 Carl's Jr, Domino's, KT'S BBQ, Starbucks
276a	Vasquez Ave, **N** 🅿️ 🅿️/Wendy's/dsl/scales/24hr 🛏️ Western Inn ⊙ Blue Beacon, Ford Trucks, Peterbilt, **S** 🅿️ 7-11 🍴 Burger King
275c	York St (from eb)
275b	CO 265, Brighton Blvd, Coliseum, **N** 🅿️ 7-11
275a	Washington St (from wb), **N** 🅿️ 7-11 🍴 Pizza Hut, **S** 🅿️ Conoco/dsl 🍴 McDonald's
274b a	I-25, N to Cheyenne, S to Colorado Springs
273	Pecos St, **N** 🅿️ Conoco/7-11/dsl ⊙ Family$, SavALot Foods, **S** 🅿️ 7-11 🍴 Quiznos ⊙ Autocare
272	US 287, Federal Blvd, **N** 🅿️ Phillips 66/dsl, Sinclair 🍴 Burger King, Goodtimes Burgers, Little Caesar's, McCoy's Rest., McDonald's, Pizza Hut, Rico Pollo, Subway, Taco Bell, Village Inn, Wendy's, Winchell's 🛏️ Motel 6 ⊙ $Tree, 7-11, Advance Parts, Family$, tires, **S** 🅿️ Conoco/Mkt/dsl 🍴 El Padrino Mexican, Popeye's, Starbucks 🛏️ Travelers Inn
271b	Lowell Blvd, Tennyson St (from wb)
271a	CO 95, **S** ⊙ funpark
270	Sheridan Blvd, **N** 🅿️ Shell/dsl, **S** 🅿️ Murphy Express/dsl 🍴 El Paraiso Mexican, Grammy's Pizza ⊙ Family$, Firestone/auto, fun park, Schwab Tire, Walmart
269b	I-76 E (from eb), to Ft Morgan, Ft Collins
269a	CO 121, Wadsworth Blvd, **N** 🅿️ 7-11, Conoco, Shell/dsl 🍴 Anthony's Pizza, Applebee's, BeauJo's, Bennet's BBQ, Chick-fil-A, Chipotle Mexican, Coldstone, Country Buffet, El Tapatio Mexican, Fazoli's, HuHot, IHOP, Jimmy John's, Kukoro Japanese,

⛽ = gas 🍴 = food 🛏 = lodging ⊙ = other Ⓡⓢ = rest stop Copyright 2022 - The Next EXIT

🔼 INTERSTATE 70 Cont'd

Exit	Services
269a	Continued McDonald's/playplace, Red Robin, Ruby Tuesday, Smiling Moose Deli, Starbucks, Subway, Taco Bell, TX Roadhouse ⊙ $Tree, Advance Parts, Big O Tire, city park, Costco/gas, Discount Tire, Home Depot, Lowe's, Petsmart, Sam's Club, Tires+, URGENT CARE
267	CO 391, Kipling St, Wheat Ridge, N ⛽ Conoco, Shell/Carl's Jr/Circle K/dsl 🍴 Burger King, Denny's, Einstein Bros, Jack-in-the-Box, Lil Nick's Pizza, Margarita's Mexican, Panda Express, Popeye's, Qdoba, Quiznos, Starbucks, Subway 🛏 American Inn, Motel 6 ⊙ 7-11, AT&T, Cadillac/Chevrolet, GNC, NAPA, Natural Grocers, repair, Target, Verizon, vet, S ⛽ Conoco/Mkt/dsl, Shell 🍴 Taco Bell, Three Agaves Mexican, Village Inn, Winchell's 🛏 Affordable Inn, Best Value Inn, Comfort Inn, Holiday Inn Express, Super 8 ⊙ Ketelesen RV Ctr
266	CO 72, W 44th Ave, Ward Rd, Wheat Ridge, N ⛽ Conoco/dsl ⊙ transmissions, S ⛽ TA/Country Pride/dsl/scales/24hr/@, Valero/dsl 🛏 Howard Johnson ⊙ Trailer Source RV Ctr
265	CO 58 W (from wb), to Golden, Central City
264	Youngfield St, W 32nd Ave, N ⛽ Phillips 66/mkt 🍴 Denny's, GoodTimes Burgers 🛏 La Quinta, S 🍴 Abrusci's Italian, Chili's, Chipotle, DQ, McDonald's, Noodles&Co, Pizza Hut, Pizza Hut/Taco Bell, Qdoba, SmashBurger, Starbucks, Subway ⊙ Four Seasons RV Ctr, King's Sooper/24hr, Petsmart, Tuesday Morning, Walgreens, Walmart/Subway
263	Denver West Blvd, N 🛏 Marriott/rest., S 🍴 Coldstone, Freddy's, Jamba Juice, Keg Steaks, Macaroni Grill, Mimi's Cafe, Noodles&Co, Olive Garden, Qdoba, Twin Peaks ⊙ Barnes&Noble, Best Buy, Old Navy, same as 262, Whole Foods Mkt
262	US 40 E, W Colfax, Lakewood, N ⛽ Sinclair/dsl 🍴 El Señor Sol Mexican, Jack-in-the-Box, Lil' Ricci's Cafe, Subway 🛏 Hampton Inn, Holiday Inn Express ⊙ Buick/GMC, Camping World RV Ctr, Chrysler/Jeep, Dodge, Home Depot, Honda, Hyundai, Kohl's, PetCo, Staples, Subaru, transmissions, U-Haul, vet, S ⛽ Shell/Circle K/dsl/LP 🍴 Bonefish Grill, Cafe Rio, Carrabba's, Chick-fil-A, Chipotle Mexican, Five Guys, Garbanzo Grill, Jamba Juice, Jimmy John's, Marshall's, Mimi's Cafe, Mod Mkt Eatery, Native Foods Cafe, On-the-Border, Outback Steaks, Panera Bread, Pei Wei Asian, Pieology, Wendy's, Which Wich?, Yard House 🛏 Courtyard, Days Inn/rest., Mtn View Inn, Residence Inn ⊙ Chevrolet, Lexus, mall, Old Navy, same as 263, Target, Toyota, Verizon, World Mkt
261	US 6 E (from eb), W 6th Ave, to Denver
260	CO 470, to Colo Springs
259	CO 26, Golden, N ⛽ Shamrock/dsl 🛏 Hampton Inn (2mi), Holiday Inn Express (2mi) ⊙ Heritage Sq Funpark, S ⊙ Music Hall, to Red Rocks SP
257mm	runaway truck ramp eb
256	Lookout Mtn, N ⊙ to Buffalo Bill's Grave
254	Genesee, Lookout Mtn, N ⊙ to Buffalo Bill's Grave, S ⛽ Conoco/Genesee Store 🍴 Chart House Rest., Guido's Pizza, Hideaway Cafe ⊙ vet
253	Chief Hosa, S ⊙ RV Camping 🍴
252	(251 from eb), CO 74, Evergreen Pkwy, S ⛽ Phillips 66 🍴 El Señor Sol, Illegal Burger, McDonald's, Qdoba, Starbucks 🛏 Comfort Suites ⊙ Big O Tire, Echo Mtn Ski Area, Home Depot, King Sooper (2mi), Walmart/Subway
24	(247 from eb), Beaver Brook, Floyd Hill, S ⊙ antiques
244	US 6, to CO 119, to Golden, Central City, Eldora Ski Area
243	Hidden Valley, N ⛽ Valero/dsl
242mm	tunnel

Exit	Services
241b a	rd 314, Idaho Springs West, N ⛽ Conoco/dsl, Exxon/dsl, Phillips 66/McDonald's/dsl, Sinclair 🍴 Carl's Jr, Eric's Asian, Marion's Rest., Picci's Pizzaria, Smokin' Yards BBQ, Starbucks, Subway, Wildfire Rest. 🛏 6&40 Motel, Argo Inn, Columbin Inn, H&H Motel, Idaho Springs Hotel, JC Motel ⊙ CarQuest, Safeway Foods/Drug, USPO
240	CO 103, Mt Evans, N ⛽ Kum&Go/dsl, Shell/dsl, Sinclair/dsl 🍴 2 Bros Deli, Azteca Mexican, Beaujo's Pizza, Buffalo Rest., Jiggie's Cafe, Main St Rest., same as 241, Tommy Knocker Grill West Winds Cafe ⊙ vet, S to Mt Evans
239	Idaho Springs, S ⊙ camping
238	Fall River Rd, to St Mary's Glacier
235	Dumont (from wb)
234	Downeyville, Dumont, N ⛽ Sinclair/Subway/dsl 🍴 Starbucks Taco Bell ⊙ ski rentals, S ⊙ weigh sta both lanes
233	Lawson (from eb)
232	US 40 W, to Empire, N ⊙ Rocky Mtn NP to Berthoud Pass, Winterpark/Sol Vista ski areas
228	Georgetown, S ⛽ Circle K/dsl, Exxon/Subway/dsl, Shell/dsl 🍴 Blue Sky Cafe, Mountain Buzz Pizza 🛏 Best Value Inn, Chateau Chamonix ⊙ Family$, visitors ctr
226.5mm	scenic overlook eb
226	Georgetown, Silver Plume Hist Dist, N ⊙ repair
221	Bakerville
220mm	Arapahoe NF eastern boundary
219	parking area (eb only)
218	no services
216	US 6 W, Loveland Valley, Loveland Basin ski areas
214mm	Eisenhower/Johnson Tunnel, elev 11013
213mm	parking area eb
205	US 6 E, CO 9 N, Dillon, Silverthorne, N ⛽ 7-11, Kum&Go/dsl Shell/7-11/dsl, Sinclair/dsl, Tesla EVC 🍴 Cafe Toro, Chipotle Mexican, Dominos, Mint Cafe, Mtn Lyon Café, Murphy's Cafe, Old Chicago, Quiznos, Wendy's, Which Wich? 🛏 1st Interstate Inn, Days Inn, La Quinta, Luxury Suites, Quality Inn, Silver Inn ⊙ AutoZone, Buick/Cadillac/Chevrolet/GMC, CarQuest, Chrysler/Dodge/Jeep, Ford, Lowe's, Murdoch's, Outlets/famous brands, Subaru, Target, TrueValue, S ⛽ Conoco, Shell/dsl 🍴 Arby's, Bamboo Garden, Blue Moon Deli, Burger King, Chimayo Burrito, Dam Brewery/Rest., DQ, Fiesta Mexican, Jimmy John's, McDonald's, Nick'n Willy's Pizza, Noodles&Co, Nozawa Japanese, Pizza Hut, Qdoba, Red Mtn Grill, Ruby Tuesday, SmashBurger, Smiling Moose Cafe, Starbucks, Subway, Sunshine Cafe 🛏 Comfort Suites, Dillon Inn, Hampton Inn, Super 8 ⊙ AT&T, City Mkt Foods/gas, GNC, Natural Grocers, Outlets/famous brands, Petco, Tuesday Morning, Verizon, vet, Walgreens
203.5mm	scenic overlook both lanes
203	CO 9 S, to Breckenridge, Frisco, S ⛽ 7-11, Conoco/Wendy's/dsl, Shell/dsl, Valero/dsl 🍴 Hacienda Real Mexican, KFC, Q4U BBQ, Rio Grande Mexican, Spinelli's Pizza/Subs, Sporting News Grill, Starbucks, Subway, Szechuan Chinese, Taco Bell 🛏 Alpine Inn, Baymont Inn, Holiday Inn, Ramada Ltd, Summit Inn ⊙ Big O Tire, Meadow Creek Tire/auto, NAPA, RV Resort (6mi), Safeway Foods, to Breckenridge Ski Area, Verizon, Walmart, Whole Foods Mkt
201	Main St, Frisco, S ⛽ Loaf N' Jug 🍴 Backcountry Brew Pub, Bagali's Italian, Blue Spruce Inn, Boatyard Pizzaria, Butterhorn Cafe, Frisco Emporium, Greco's Pastaria, Log Cabin Cafe, Lost Cajun Rest., Moosejaw Cafe, Rainbow Ct Rest. 🛏 Frisco Lodge, Hotel Frisco, Snowshoe Motel ⊙ museum/visitor info, RV camping, to Breckenridge Ski Area, USPO
198	Officers Gulch emergency callbox

Side tabs: CO · WHEAT RIDGE · LAKEWOOD · IDAHO SPRINGS · SILVERTHORNE · FRISCO

🔼E INTERSTATE 70 Cont'd

Exit #	Services
196mm	scenic area (wb only)
195	CO 91 S, to Leadville, **1 mi S** 🛢 Conoco/dsl 🍴 Healthy Tomato Deli 🛏 Copper Lodging 🅾 to Copper Mtn Ski Resort
190	**S** 📶 **both lanes, full** ♿ **facilities, litter barrels,** 🚮, 🏞
189mm	elev 10662 ft, **parking area both lanes,** Vail Pass Summit
180	Vail East Entrance, **services 3-4 mi S**
176	Vail, **S** 🅾 🏥, ski info/lodging
173	Vail Ski Area, **N** 🛢 Phillips 66, Shell/dsl 🍴 Casa Mexico, May Palace, McDonald's, Old Forge Pizza, Qdoba, Subway, Westside Cafe 🛏 Holiday Inn 🅾 Ace Hardware, City Mkt Foods/deli, Safeway Food/Drug, USPO, **S** 🛢 Conoco/dsl/LP 🛏 Marriott/Streamside Hotel
171	US 6 W, US 24 E, to Minturn, Leadville, **N** 🅾 Ski Cooper ski area, **2 mi S** 🛢 Shell 🍴 Magusto's Italian, Minturn Steaks 🛏 Minturn Inn 🅾 RV Camping, USPO
169	Eaglevale (from wb), no return
168	William J. Post Blvd, **S** 🍴 Castle Peak Grill 🅾 Home Depot, Verizon, Walmart/McDonald's
167	Avon, **N** 🛢 Exxon/7-11/dsl, Shell 🍴 Northside Kitchen 🅾 vet, **S** 🍴 Boxcar Rest., Burger King, Domino's, Fiesta Jalisco Mexican, Gondola Pizza, Montana's Smokehouse, Pazzo's Pizza, Starbucks, Subway 🛏 Avon Ctr Lodge, Christie Lodge, Comfort Inn, Sheraton, Westin 🅾 City Mkt/drugs, GNC, ski info, to Beaver Creek/Arrowhead Ski, URGENT CARE, USPO, Walgreens
163	Edwards, **S** 📶 **both lanes, full** ♿ **facilities, litter barrel,** 🏞, **RV dump** 🛢 Conoco/dsl, Shell/Wendy's/dsl 🍴 Cafe Milano, Dive Cafe, East Asian, Fiestas Cafe, Gashouse Rest., Gore Range Brewery, Henry's Chinese, Main St Grill, Marble Slab Creamery, Marko's Pizza, Old Forge Pizza, Smiling Moose, Starbucks, Subway, Zino's Italian 🛏 Riverwalk Inn 🅾 AT&T, to Arrowhead Ski Area, USPO, Village Mkt
162mm	scenic area eb
159mm	Eagle River
157	CO 131 N, Wolcott, **N** to Steamboat Ski Area
147	Eagle, **N** 🛢 Kum&Go/dsl 🍴 Burger King, Roberto's Italian, Starbucks 🛏 AmericInn, Comfort Inn, Holiday Inn Express 🅾 AT&T, City Mkt Foods, **S** 📶 **both lanes, full** ♿ **facilities, info,** 🛢 Conoco/dsl, Shell/dsl, Sinclair/Subway/dsl 🍴 Eagle Diner, Gourmet China, Grand Ave Grill, Moe's Original BBQ, Pazzo's Pizzaria, Primavera Mexican, Taco Bell, Wendy's 🛏 Best Western, Eagle Lodge&Suites, Hawthorn Suites 🅾 AutoZone (3mi), Costco/dsl (3mi), USPO, vet
140	Gypsum, **S** 🛢 Conoco, Kum&Go/dsl, Shell/dsl 🍴 Asian Fusion, Buffalo Grill, Gypsum Grill, Ridley's Mkt, Tu Casa Mexican 🅾 🖥, Family$, O'Reilly Parts, River Dance Resort camping, USPO
134mm	Colorado River
133	Dotsero, **N** 🅾 River Dance RV Camping (3mi)
129	Bair Ranch, **S** 📶 **both lanes, full** ♿ **facilities, litter barrels, pet-walk,** 🏞
128.5mm	parking area eb
127mm	tunnel wb
125mm	tunnel
125	to Hanging Lake (no return eb)
123	Shoshone (no return eb)
122.5mm	exit to river (no return eb)
121	to Hanging Lake, Grizzly Creek, **S** 📶 **both lanes, full** ♿ **facilities, litter barrels,** 🏞
119	No Name 📶 **both lanes, full** ♿ **facilities), rafting, RV camping**
118mm	tunnel
116	CO 82 E, to Aspen, Glenwood Springs, **N** 🛢 Kum&Go/dsl, Shell/dsl 🍴 Chomp's Rest., Fiesta Guadalajara, KFC, Qdoba, Subway, Tequilas Rest., Village Inn 🛏 Best Western, Glenwood Springs Inn, Hampton Inn, Holiday Inn Express, Hotel Colorado, Hotel Glenwood Springs, La Quinta, Silver Spruce Motel, Starlight Motel 🅾 Hot Springs Bath, Land Rover, **0-2 mi S** 🛢 Conoco, Phillips 66/dsl, Shamrock/dsl, Shell, Sinclair 🍴 19th St Diner, Chang Thai Cuisine, China Town, Domino's, Jimmy John's, McDonald's, Pizza Hut, Starbucks, Subway, Taco Bell, Taipei Japanese, Wendy's 🛏 Caravan Inn, Cedar Lodge, Frontier Lodge, Hotel Denver 🅾 7-11, Alpine Tire, AutoZone, B.Thornal DDS, Chrysler/Dodge/Jeep, City Mkt Foods, city park, 🏥, Midas, NAPA, Office Depot, Rite Aid, Safeway Foods, to Ski Sunlight, USPO, Walmart
115mm	📶 eb, full ♿ facilities, litter barrels, 🏞
114	W Glenwood Springs, **N** 🛢 7-11, Exxon/Arby's/dsl, Shell/dsl 🍴 Culver's, Jilberito's Mexican, Rte 6 Grill House, Vicco's Charcoal Burger 🛏 Affordable Inn, Hanging Lake Inn, Ponderosa Motel, Red Mtn Inn, Rodeway Inn 🅾 Big O Tire, Carquest, Chevrolet, Discount Tire, Ford, Honda, O'Reilly Parts, Ross, Subaru, Toyota, Verizon, **S** 🛢 Kum&Go/DQ/dsl 🍴 Chili's, Moe's SW Grill, Russo's Pizza, Starbucks, Zheng Asian 🛏 Courtyard, Glenwood Suites, Quality Inn, Residence Inn 🅾 AT&T, Audi/VW, Harley-Davidson, Lowe's, Natural Grocers, PetCo, Target, URGENT CARE, Verizon
111	South Canyon
109	Canyon Creek
108mm	parking area both lanes
105	New Castle, **N** 🛢 Conoco/dsl, Kum&Go/dsl 🍴 Hong Kong Chinese, Hong's Garden, McDonald's, Tapatios 🛏 The Lodge 🅾 City Mkt Foods/deli, Elk Creek Campground (4mi)
97	Silt, **N** 🛢 Kum&Go/dsl, Sinclair/dsl, Tim's/dsl 🍴 Brickhouse Italian, Miner's Rest. 🛏 Red River Inn 🅾 $General, to Harvey Gap SP, **S** 🛢 Golden Gate/dsl 🛏 Holiday Inn Express 🅾 Heron's Nest RV Park, KOA
94	Garfield County Airport Rd
90	CO 13 N, Rifle, **N** 📶 both lanes, full ♿ facilities, litter barrels, **NF Info,** 🏞, **RV dump,** 🛢 Conoco/dsl, Kum&Go/dsl, Shell 🍴 Dickey's BBQ 🛏 Gateway Lodge 🅾 Rifle Gap SP (10mi), USPO **S** 🛢 Kum&Go/dsl, Phillips 66/Subway/dsl 🍴 Burger King, Domino's, Dunkin', Little Caesar's, McDonald's, Rib City Grill, Sonic, Starbucks, Subway, Taco Bell 🛏 Comfort Inn, Hampton Inn, La Quinta, Rodeway Inn 🅾 AutoZone, 🏥, O'Reilly Parts, Verizon, Walmart/Subway
87	to CO 13, West Rifle
81	Rulison
75	Parachute, **N** 📶 both lanes, full ♿ facilities, info, litter barrels, **petwalk,** 🚮, 🏞, 🛢 CNG, Exxon/dsl, Sinclair/dsl 🍴 El Tapatio Mexican, Hong's Garden Chinese, Nalini's Rest., Subway 🛏 Grand Vista, Parachute Inn 🅾 NAPA, USPO, vet **S** 🛢 Phillips 66/Domino's/dsl, Shell/Wendy's/dsl 🍴 Shommy's Rest. 🛏 Candlewood Suites, Grand River Hotel 🅾 Family$, RV Park (4mi)

VAIL AVON EAGLE

GLENWOOD SPGS RIFLE

CO

▲E INTERSTATE 70 Cont'd

Exit #	Services
72	US 6, W Parachute
63mm	Colorado River
62	De Beque, N 🅿 Kum&Go/Subway/dsl
50mm	Colorado River, **parking area eastbound**, tunnel begins eastbound
49mm	Plateau Creek
49	CO 65 S, to CO 330 E, to Grand Mesa Powderhorn Ski Area
47	Island Acres St RA, N Ⓞ CO River SP, RV camping, S 🅿 Exxon/rest./dsl
46	Cameo
44	Lp 70 W, to Palisade, 3 mi S Ⓞ food, gas, lodging
43.5mm	Colorado River
42	US 6, Palisade, S 🅿 Golden Gate/dsl 🛏 Wine Country Inn Ⓞ Fruitstand/store, wineries
37	to US 6, to US 50 S, Clifton, Grand Jct, 0-1 mi S 🅿 Conoco/dsl, Maverik/dsl, Shamrock/dsl, Shell/dsl, Sinclair/dsl ⑪ Burger King, Chin Chin Oriental, China Jade, Denny's, Dos Hombres, Enzo's Pizza, Jimmy John's, KFC, Little Caesar's, McDonald's/playplace, Papa John's, Papa Murphy's, Pizza Hut, Qdoba, Sonic, Starbucks, Starvin Arvin's Steaks, Subway, Taco Bell, Taco John's, Wendy's 🛏 Best Western Ⓞ Ace Hardware, AutoZone, City Mkt Food/dsl, Family$, GNC, Murdoch's Store, O'Reilly Parts, repair, RV Ranch, URGENT CARE, USPO, vet, Walgreens, Walmart/gas (2mi)
31	Horizon Dr, Grand Jct, N 🅿 Shell/dsl ⑪ Pantuso Mexican, Peppers Rest., Tepanyaki Rest., Village Inn, Wendy's 🛏 Best Value Inn, Clarion, Comfort Inn, Courtyard, Econolodge, Grand Vista Hotel, Holiday Inn, La Quinta, Motel 6, Ramada Inn, Residence Inn Ⓞ 🛫, Harley-Davidson, Zarlingo's Repair, S 🅿 Exxon/Subway/dsl, Shell/dsl ⑪ Applebee's, Aztecas, Burger King/playland, Denny's, Enzo's Pizza, Freddy's, Good Pastures Rest., Nick'n Willy's Pizza, Sang Garden, Starbucks, Taco Bell 🛏 Days Inn, Doubletree Hotel, Mesa Inn, Quality Inn, Rodeway Inn, Super 8, Super 8, Travelodge Ⓞ CO NM, golf, Ⓗ, Safeway Food/drug/gas, Shop'n Save, to Mesa St Coll, visitors ctr
28	Redlands Pkwy, 24 Rd, N Ⓞ Kenworth, 0-2 mi S 🛏 Candlewood Suites, city park, same as 26, Woodspring Suites Ⓞ Subaru, VW
26	US 6, US 50, Grand Jct, N 🅿 ♥Loves/Carl's Jr/dsl/scales/Lp/24hr, 🛢🛢/PJ Fresh/dsl/scales/24hr Ⓞ Hyundai, Jct W RV Park, 0-4 mi S 🅿 TA/Conoco/A&W/dsl ⑪ Boston's Grill, Buffalo Wild Wings, Burger King, Cafe Rio, Chick-fil-A, Chili's, Chipotle Mexican, ChuckeCheese, Citrolas Italian, Coldstone, Costa Vida, Del Taco, Famous Dave's BBQ, Genghis Grill, Golden Corral, Grand Buffet, Honeybaked Ham, IHOP, Jimmy John's, McDonald's/playplace, Mi Mexico, Noodles&Co, Olive Garden, Outback Steaks, Papa Murphys, Qdoba, Red Lobster, Red Robin, Schlotzky's, Sonic, Starbucks, Subway, Taco Bell, Tequila's, Wendy's, Which Wich? 🛏 Holiday Inn Express, Red Roof Inn Ⓞ $Tree, AT&T, AutoZone, Barnes&Noble, Best Buy, Big O Tire, Buick/Chevrolet, Cabela's, Chrysler/Dodge/Jeep, City Mkt/dsl, Ford, Freightliner, Hobby Lobby, Home Depot, JC Penney, Kohl's, Lowe's, Michael's, Mobile City RV Park, Natural Grocers, Nissan, Office Depot, Old Navy, PetCo, Petsmart, Ross, Sam's Club/dsl, Scott RV Ctr, Sprouts Mkt, Target, TJ Maxx, Toyota, Verizon, Walmart/McDonald's
19	US 6, CO 340, Fruita, N 🅿 Sinclair/dsl ⑪ Burger King, Munchie's Burgers/Pizza 🛏 Balanced Rock Motel Ⓞ City Mkt Foods/deli/24hr, city park, Ⓗ, NAPA, USPO, Walgreens, S Welcome Ctr, full 🛫 facilities, litter barrels, petwalk, ⟨🅿⟩, 🛫, RV dump

19	Continued
	🅿 Exxon/dsl, LNG, Shell/Wendy's/dsl/24hr ⑪ DQ, Drago Treasure Chinese, El Tapatio Mexican, FeedLot Rest., Jimmy John's, McDonald's/playplace, Pablo's Pizza, Rib City Grill, Starbucks, Starvin Arvin's, Subway, Taco Bell 🛏 Comfort Inn, La Quinta, Super 8 Ⓞ dinosaur museum, Monument RV Park, Peterbilt/Volvo, to CO NM, vet
17mm	Colorado River
15	CO 139 N, to Loma, Rangely, N gas/dsl, to Highline Lake SP
14.5mm	weigh/check sta both lanes
11	Mack, 2-3 mi N Ⓞ food, gas/dsl
2	Rabbit Valley, N Ⓞ to Trail Through Time
0mm	Colorado/Utah state line

▲E INTERSTATE 76

Exit #	Services
185mm	I-76 begins/ends on NE I-80, exit 102.
184mm	Colorado/Nebraska state line
180	US 385, Julesburg, N Welcome Ctr/🆁🆂 both lanes, full 🛫 facilities, info, RV dump, 🅿 Shell ⑪ Subway 🛏 Budget Host Ⓞ Ⓗ RV dump, S 🅿 Conoco/dsl
172	Ovid
165	CO 59, to Haxtun, Sedgewick, N ⑪ Lucy's Cafe
155	Red Lion Rd
149	CO 55, to Fleming, Crook, S 🅿 Sinclair/dsl/café
141	Proctor
134	Iliff
125	US 6, Sterling, 0-3 mi N 🆁🆂 both lanes, full 🛫 facilities, 🛫, litter barrels, petwalk, vending, RV dump, 🅿 Cenex/dsl, HR/dsl ⑪ Arby's, Bamboo Garden, Burger King, Domino's, DQ, Jimmy John's, Little Caesar's, McDonald's, Papa Murphy's, Pizza Hut, Sonic, Subway, Taco Bell, Taco John's, Village Inn, Wendy's 🛏 1st Interstate Inn, Best Western, Holiday Inn Express Ⓞ $Tree, AutoZone, Bomgaars, Buick/Chevrolet, Chrysler/Dodge/Jeep, Family Food Mkt, Ford/Lincoln, Home Depot, Ⓗ, museum, N Sterling SP, NAPA, O'Reilly Parts, st patrol, USPO, Verizon, vet, Walgreens, Walmart, S 🅿 Reata/dsl 🛏 Budget Inn, Quality Inn, Ramada Inn, Super 8 Ⓞ RV Camping
115	CO 63, Atwood, N 🅿 Sinclair/dsl Ⓞ Ⓗ
102	Merino
95	Hillrose
92	to US 6 E, to US 34, CO 71 S
90b a	CO 71 N, to US 34, Brush, N 🅿 Brush Trkstp/Shell/Subway/dsl/24hr, Tesla EVC ⑪ China Dragon, Pizza Hut, Wendy's 🛏 Rodeway Inn, S 🅿 Conoco/dsl ⑪ McDonald's 🛏 Microtel
89	Hospital Rd, S 🅿 ♥Loves/Carl's Jr/dsl/scales/24hr Ⓞ golf, Ⓗ
86	Dodd Bridge Rd
82	Barlow Rd, N ⑪ The Mav Grill 🛏 Best Western+, Comfort Inn, Rodeway Inn Ⓞ Silver Spur Camping, S 🅿 Reata/dsl/scales ⑪ Burger King 🛏 Fairfield Inn Ⓞ $Tree, Walmart/Subway
80	CO 52, Ft Morgan, N Ⓞ City Park, Golf, RV Camping, S 🅿 Conoco/dsl, Conoco/dsl, Maverik/dsl, Sinclair/dsl ⑪ Arby's, DQ, McDonald's, Sonic, Subway, Taco Bell, Taco John's, Wonderful House Chinese 🛏 Hampton Inn, Sands Inn, Super 8 Ⓞ AutoZone, Family$, Ⓗ, Toyota, Verizon, Walgreens
79	CO 144, to Weldona, (no wb return)
75	US 34 E, to Ft Morgan, S 🅿 Shell/pizza/dsl ⑪ Embers Rest. 🛏 Baymont Inn Ⓞ GS RV Park, st patrol
74.5mm	weigh sta both lanes
73	Long Bridge Rd
66b	US 34 W (from wb), to Greeley

Side labels (vertical): PARACHUTE · GRAND JCT · FRUITA · STERLING · FT MORGAN · CO

INTERSTATE 76 Cont'd

Exit #	Services
66a	CO 39, CO 52, to Goodrich, N Shamrock/dsl RV Camping, to Jackson Lake SP, S both lanes, full facilities, litter barrels, petwalk, vending Sinclair/cafe/dsl/e-85
64	Wiggins
60	to CO 144 E, to Orchard
57	rd 91
49	Painter Rd (from wb)
48	to Roggen, N Conoco/dsl, S USPO
39	Keenesburg, S Shell/dsl Deno's Rest. Keene Motel Family$, Tim's Car Clinic
34	Kersey Rd
31	CO 52, Hudson, N Loves/Subway/Carl's Jr/scales/24hr/dsl Best Western+, S Conoco/dsl, Shell/dsl Pepper Pod Rest. Pepper Pod Camping, USPO
25	CO 7, Lochbuie, N Shell/dsl
22	Bromley, N Circle K/dsl KFC/LJ Silver, Wendy's Hampton Inn (4mi) , Lowe's, S Kum&Go/dsl/e85 Barr Lake SP, Freightliner
21	144th Ave, Eagle Blvd, N Arby's, Buffalo Wild Wings, Chick-fil-A, Chili's, McDonald's, Old Chicago, Panda Express, Red Robin, Subway, Taco Bell Candlewood Suites, Comfort Suites, Holiday Inn Express $Tree, AT&T, Dick's, GNC, Hobby Lobby, Home Depot, , JC Penney, Kohl's, Michael's, Office Depot, Petsmart, Ross, Target, Verizon
20	136th Ave, N Barr Lake RV Park same as 21
18	E-470 tollway, to Limon (from wb)
16	CO 2, Sable Blvd, Commerce City, N to Denver Airport
12	US 85 N, to Brighton (exits left from eb), Greeley
11	96th Ave, N dsl repair, S Buick/GMC
10	88th Ave, N Shell/dsl La Quinta, Super 8, S flea mkt
9	US 6 W, US 85 S (no EZ wb return), Commerce City, S Shell/dsl st patrol, transmissions
8	CO 224, 74th Ave (no EZ eb return), 1 mi N NAPA
6b a	I-270 E, to Limon to , to I-25 N
5	I-25, N to Ft Collins, S to Colo Springs
4	Pecos St
3	US 287, Federal Blvd, N Shamrock/dsl, S Advance Parts, vet
1b	CO 95, Sheridan Blvd
1a	CO 121, Wadsworth Blvd, N 7-11/gas; EVC, Exxon, Shell/dsl Anthony's Pizza, Applebee's, BeauJo's, Bennet's BBQ, Chick-fil-A, Chipotle Mexican, Coldstone Creamery, Country Buffet, El Tapatio Mexican, Fazoli's, HuHot, IHOP, Jimmy John's, Kukoro Japanese, McDonald's/playplace, Red Robin, Ruby Tuesday, Smiling Moose, Starbucks, Subway, Taco Bell, TX Roadhouse $Tree, Advance Parts, Big O Tire, Costco/gas, Discount Tire, Home Depot, Lowe's Whse, Petsmart, Sam's Club, Tires+, URGENT CARE

I-76 begins/ends on I-70, exit 269b.

INTERSTATE 225 (Denver)

Exit #	Services
12b a	I-70, W to Denver, E to Limon
10	US 40, US 287, Colfax Ave, E 7-11, Conoco/dsl, Shell/dsl, Sinclair Burger King, Del Taco, Domino's, DQ, El Pelicano Seafood, KFC, McDonald's, Pizza Hut/Taco Bell, Popeye's, Starbucks, Subway, Village Inn, Wendy's Aamco, Advance Parts, Chevrolet, Family$, King's Sooper/gas, NAPA, Walgreens, W Conoco/dsl, Shamrock/dsl Caribou Coffee, Chipotle Mexican,

Exit #	Services
10	Continued Noodles&Co, Panera Bread, Smashburger, Which Wich? SpringHill Suites , U-Haul
9	Co 30, 6th Ave, E Conoco/dsl Denny's Travelodge, Woodspring Suites, W Shell/dsl
8	Alameda Ave, E Valero/dsl Atlanta Bread, BJ's Rest., Chick-fil-A, Chili's, Coldstone, FatBurger, Jamba Juice, Jimmy John's, L&L BBQ, Macaroni Grill, Mimi's Cafe, Panda Express, Sabor Mexican, Starbucks, TGIFriday, Wingstop AT&T, Barnes&Noble, Dillards, Hobby Lobby, JC Penney, Macy's, Michael's, Petsmart, Ross, Super Target, W Conoco/dsl, Shell/Circle K $Tree
7	Mississippi Ave, Alameda Ave, E Arby's, Burger King, Chubby's Mexican, ChuckeCheese, CiCi's, Fazoli's, Guadalajara Mexican, McAlister's Deli, Schlotsky's, Sonic, Starbucks, Subway, Tokyo Joe's, Village Inn Best Western, Holiday Inn Express, La Quinta Best Buy, Burlington Coats, Home Depot, JoAnn Fabrics, Sam's Club/gas, Tires +, Verizon, Walmart, W IHOP, McDonald's, Mirage Rest., Senor Ric's, Waffle House 7-11, AutoZone, Pepboys
5	Iliff Ave, E 7-11 Ajuua Mexican, Applebee's, Boston Mkt, Carrabba's, Hibachi Japanese, Joe's Crabshack, Outback Steaks, Real de Minas Mexican, Rosie's Diner, Ruby Tuesday, Sweet Tomatoes, TX Roadhouse Comfort Inn, Crestwood Suites, Extended Stay America, Extended Stay America (2), Fairfield Inn, Motel 6, W Conoco Dragon Boat, Legends Grill, Subway DoubleTree 7-11
4	CO 83, Parker Rd, E Radisson Cherry Creek SP, W Shell/dsl Big Burrito, DQ, Little Caesar's, Popeye's, Starbucks, Subway, Taco Bell, Wendy's $Tree, 7-11, Firestone/auto, King Sooper/dsl
2b	Yosemite St
2	DTC Blvd, Tamarac St, W Conoco/7-11 Fel Fel Mediterranean, La Fogata Mexican, Sonic, South Garden Chinese, Subway $Tree, Goodyear/auto
1b a	I-25. I-225 begins/ends on I-25, exit 200.

INTERSTATE 270 (Denver)

Exit #	Services
4	I-70
3	N TA/Burger King/Country Pride/Popeye's/Pizza Hut/dsl/24hr/@, S Sapp Bros/Sinclair/Subway/dsl/@
2b a	US 85, CO 2, Vasquez Ave, N Arby's, Carls Jr, Chipotle Mexican, Jack-in-the-Box, KFC/LJ Silver, McDonald's, Taco Bell, Wendy's TDS Tire, Walgreens, Walmart
1b	York St
1a	I-76 E, to Ft Morgan
1c	I-25 S, to Denver

DENVER

DENVER

CO

CONNECTICUT

⬆E INTERSTATE 84

Exit #	Services
98mm	Connecticut/Massachusetts state line
74(97)	CT 171, Holland, S 🍴 Traveler's Book Rest. 🄾 Campers Inn RV Ctr
95mm	weigh sta wb
73(95)	CT 190, Stafford Springs, N 🄾 motor speedway, Roaring Brook camping (seasonal)
72(93)	CT 89, Westford, N 🏨 Ashford Motel, Roaring Brook camping (seasonal)
71(88)	CT 320, Ruby Rd, S 🍴 TA/Shell/Burger King/Country Pride/dsl/scales/24hr/@ 🍴 Dunkin' 🏨 Rodeway Inn
70(86)	CT 32, Willington, N 🄾 🄷, Wilderness Lake Camping, S 🍴 Mobil/dsl, Sunoco/dsl
85mm	🆁 both lanes, campers, full 🅰 facilities, info, litter barrels, petwalk, 🄲, 🄴, vending
69(83)	CT 74, to US 44, Willington, S food, gas, 🄲, RV camping, st police
68(81)	CT 195, Tolland, N 🍴 Gulf/dsl, Mobil 🍴 Dunkin', Papa T's Rest., Subway 🄾 NAPA, S 🍴 Citgo 🍴 Camille's Pizza, Lee's Garden 🄾 Big Y Foods, Verizon, vet
67(77)	CT 31, Rockville, N 🍴 Mobil, Shell/dsl 🍴 Beni's Grill, Burger King, China Taste, Dunkin', McDonald's, Subway 🄾 🄷, S 🄾 Nathan Hale Mon
66(76)	Tunnel Rd, Vernon
65(75)	CT 30, Vernon Ctr, N 🍴 Cumberland/dsl, Mobil/dsl, Shell 🍴 Brick Oven Pizza, Burger King, Dunkin', KFC, Oki Asian, Rein's Deli, Simply Thai, Vernon Diner, Wang's Buffet 🏨 Days Inn, Red Roof Inn 🄾 Firestone/auto, Meineke, Stop&Shop/gas
64(74)	Vernon Ctr, N 🍴 Sunoco 🍴 99 Rest., Angellino's Italian, Anthony's Pizza, D'angelo's, Denny's, Dunkin', Friendly's, McDonald's, Moe's SW, Rita's Custard, Starbucks, Taco Bell, Wendy's, Wood'n Tap 🏨 Holiday Inn Express 🄾 $Tree, AutoZone, CVS Drug, GNC, Goodyear/auto, Staples, TJ Maxx, vet, S 🏨 Motel 6 🄾 Chevrolet, VW
63(72)	CT 30, CT 83, same as 62, Manchester, S Windsor, N 🍴 Azteca Mexican, BurgerIM, Chipotle Mexican, Dunkin', HomeTown Buffet, IHOP, Longhorn Steaks, McDonald's, Outback Steaks, Panera Bread, Red Robin, Smashburger, Starbucks, Subway, TGIFriday's 🏨 Courtyard, Residence Inn 🄾 AT&T, Best Buy, Marshall's, PetCo, Verizon, Walgreens, Walmart, S 🍴 Best, BP/dsl, EVC, Shell/dsl, Sunoco/dsl, Xtra 🍴 Shea's Pizzaria 🏨 Best Value Inn, Extended Stay America, Motel 6 🄾 🄷, Big Y Mkt, Hyundai, Kohl's, Nissan, Subaru, Toyota, U-Haul, USPO
62(71)	Buckland St, same as 63, N 🍴 Mobil/Dunkin'/dsl, Tesla EVC 🍴 Artisanal Burger, Boston Mkt, Burton's Grill, Chili's, Dave&Buster's, Five Guys, Friendly's, Hooters, Jersey Mike's, Maggie McFly's, Market Grille, Moe's SW Grill, Olive Garden, Panera Bread, Sakura Garden, Starbucks, Taco Bell, Ted's MT Grill 🏨 Fairfield Inn, Hampton Inn, Homewood Suites 🄾 $Tree, Barnes&Noble, BigLots, Dick's, Hobby Lobby, Home Depot, JC Penney, Jo-Ann Fabrics, LL Bean, Lowe's, Macy's, Michael's, Old Navy, PetsMart, Target, Town Fair Tire, Trader Joe's, Verizon, S 🍴 Shell/dsl 🍴 Buffalo Wild Wings, Burger Fi, ChuckeCheese, EVC, Golden Dragon, Joey Garlic's, Kobe Asian, McDonald's, Sonic, Subway, TX Roadhouse, Wendy's 🄾 BJ's Whse/gas, Firestone/auto, GNC, Honda, USPO
61(70)	I-291 W, to Windsor
60(69)	US 6, US 44, Burnside Ave (from eb)
59(68)	I-384 E, Manchester
58(67)	Roberts St, Burnside Ave, N 🍴 Margaritas Grill, Nolita Ristorante 🏨 Comfort Inn, S 🍴 Mobil, Sunoco 🍴 Dunkin', Queen Pizza, Taco Bell 🄾 Cabela's, vet
57(66)	CT 15 S, to I-91 S, Charter Oak Br
56(65)	Governor St, E Hartford, S 🄾 🔀
55(64)	CT 2 E, New London, downtown
54(63)	Old State House, N 🄾 Audi, Chevrolet, Chrysler/Dodge/Jeep, Ford, Kia, Lexus, Lincoln, S 🏨 Hampton Inn
53(62)	CT Blvd (from eb), S 🏨 Holiday Inn
52(61)	W Main St (from eb), downtown
51(60)	I-91 N, to Springfield
50(59.8)	to I-91 S (from wb), N 🏨 Red Lion, S 🏨 Hilton, Residence Inn
48(59.5)	Asylum St, downtown, N 🏨 Red Lion, S 🏨 Capitol Hotel, Homewood Suites 🄾 🄷
47(59)	Sigourney St, downtown, N 🄾 Hartford Seminary, Mark Twain House
46(58)	Sisson St, downtown (from wb, exits left), N 🄾 UConn Law School
45(57)	Flatbush Ave (from wb, exits left)
44(56.5)	Prospect Ave, N 🍴 Mobil, Shell/dsl 🍴 Burger King, Goldroc Diner, Hibachi Grill, McDonald's, Prospect Pizza, Wendy's 🄾 ShopRite Foods
43(56)	Park Rd, W Hartford, N 🄾 to St Joseph Coll
42(55)	Trout Brk Dr (exits left from wb), to Elmwood
41(54)	S Main St, Elmwood, N 🄾 American School for the Deaf
40(53)	CT 71, New Britain Ave, S 🍴 Sunoco/dsl, Tesla EVC 🍴 Brick Grille, Burger King, CA Pizza, Chili's, China Pan, Chipotle Mexican, McDonald's, Olive Garden, Panera Bread, PF Chang's, Red Robin, Starbucks, Subway, Wendy's 🏨 Courtyard 🄾 AT&T, Barnes&Noble, Best Buy, Costco/dsl, JC Penney, Macy's, Michael's, Nordstrom, Old Navy, PetCo, Target, TJ Maxx, Trader Joe's, Verizon
39a(52)	CT 9 S, to New Britain, Newington, S 🄾 🄷
39(51.5)	CT 4, (exits left from eb), Farmington, N 🄾 🄷
38(51)	US 6 W (from wb), same as 37, Bristol
37(50)	Fienemann Rd, to US 6 W, N 🍴 Dunkin', Subway 🏨 Hampton Inn, Marriott, S 🍴 Noble/Dunkin'/dsl 🏨 Extended Stay America
36(49)	Slater Rd (exits left from eb), S 🄾 🄷
35(48)	CT 72, to CT 9 (exits left from both lanes), New Britain, S 🄾 🄷
34(47)	CT 372, Crooked St, N 🍴 EVC, Gulf/dsl, Sunoco 🍴 Applebee's, Friendly's, McDonald's, Starbucks, Taco Bell/LJ Silver, Wendy's 🏨 Fairfield Inn 🄾 $Tree, AT&T, Big Y Mkt, Dick's, Ford/Lincoln, Kohl's, Lowe's, Marshall's, Old Navy, Petsmart, VW
33(46)	CT 72 W, to Bristol (exits left from eb)
32(45)	Ct 10, Queen St, Southington, N 🍴 Cumberland Farms, Exxon, Shell/dsl 🍴 Buffalo Wild Wings, Burger King, Chick-fil-A, Chili's, Chipotle, D'angelo, Denny's, Dunkin', Gobi Mongolian, IHOP, JD's Rest., KFC, Luen Hop Chinese, McDonald's, Moe's SW Grill, Noodles&Co, Outback Steaks, Puerto Vallarta, Smashburger, Starbucks, Subway, Taco Bell, Vivaldi Pizza 🏨 Motel 6 🄾 🄷, $Tree, 7-11, Aldi, AutoZone, BJ's/gas, CVS Drug, GNC, Home Depot, Jo-Ann, O'Reilly Parts, PetCo, ShopRite Foods, Staples, TJ Maxx, TownFair Tire, Verizon, S 🍴 Gulf, Mobil, Sunoco 🍴 Aziagos Italian, Dunkin', Eddie's Sombrero, Friendly's, Nardelli's Cafe, Noble Japanese, Panera Bread, Rita's Custard, Subway, Tokyo Japanese, Wendy's, Wood'n Tap Grill 🏨 Days Inn, Holiday Inn Express 🄾 Advance Parts, AT&T, Firestone/auto, Midas, Monro, PriceChopper Foods, URGENT CARE, Walmart

HARTFORD (vertical label)

VERNON CTR (vertical label)

WINDSOR (vertical label)

SOUTHINGTON (vertical label)

CT (side tab)

INTERSTATE 84 Cont'd

Exit #	Services
31(44)	CT 229, West St, **N** 🅖 EVC, Mobil/dsl, Sunoco/dsl 🍴 Chip's, Dunkin', Popeye's, Starbucks 🏨 Courtyard, Homewood Suites 🅞 Lowe's, Michael's, Target, **S** 🅖 Citgo, Gulf/dsl 🍴 Dunkin', Giovanni's Pizza, Subway 🏨 Residence Inn
30(43)	Marion Ave, W Main, Southington, **N** 🅞 ski area, **S** 🅖 Mobil/dsl 🅞 🅗
29(42)	CT 10, from wb, exits left, Milldale (exits left from wb)
41.5mm	🆁🆂 eb, full ♿ facilities, info, litter barrels, petwalk, 🄲, 🚯
28(41)	CT 322, Marion, **S** 🅖 Fleet/dsl, Mobil, TA/Popeye's/Taco Bell/dsl/scales/24hr/@ 🍴 Blimpie, Burger King, DQ, Dunkin', Manor Inn Rest., Subway, Young Young Chinese 🏨 Comfort Suites, EconoLodge 🅞 Home Depot
27(40)	I-691 E, to Meriden
26(38)	CT 70, to Cheshire, **N** 🍴 Blackie's Cafe
25a(37)	Austin Rd, **N** 🅖 Winzz/dsl 🍴 Asian Garden, Subway, Tiramisu Italian 🅞 Costco/gas, Kohl's
25(36)	Harper's Ferry Rd, Reed Dr, Scott Rd, E Main St, **N** 🅖 Mobil/dsl 🍴 Dunkin' 🅞 AT&T, NAPA, **S** 🍴 Burger King, Dunkin', Golden Wok, McDonald's, Nino's Rest., Subway, TX Roadhouse 🏨 Quality Inn 🅞 Aldi Foods, BJ's Whse/gas, Cadillac/Chevrolet, CVS Drug, Super Stop&Shop/gas
23(33.5)	CT 69, Hamilton Ave, **N** 🍴 Buffalo Wild Wings, Chili's, IHOP, McDonald's, Olive Garden, TGIFriday's 🅞 🅗, Barnes&Noble, JC Penney, Macy's, Michael's, Petco, Save-a-Lot Foods, TJ Maxx, **S** 🅖 Shell 🍴 Dunkin'
22(33)	Baldwin St, same as 23, Waterbury, **N** 🅖 Gulf 🏨 Courtyard 🅞 🅗, USPO
21(33)	Meadow St, Banks St, **N** 🍴 7-11, **S** 🅖 Exxon/dsl 🅞 Home Depot, PetsMart
20(32)	CT 8 N (exits left from eb), to Torrington
19(32)	CT 8 S (exits left from wb), to Bridgeport
18(32)	W Main, Highland Ave, **N** 🅖 ProFuel/dsl 🍴 Dunkin', Lena's Deli, Starbucks, Subway, Wayback Burger 🏨 Hampton Inn 🅞 🅗, CVS Drug
17(30)	CT 63, CT 64, to Watertown, Naugatuck, **N** 🍴 Maggie McFly's Rest., **S** 🅖 Mobil/dsl 🍴 Dunkin', Leo's Rest., Maples Rest., Subway
16(25)	CT 188, to Middlebury, **N** 🅖 Mobil 🍴 Patty's Pantry Deli 🏨 Crowne Plaza
15(22)	US 6 E, CT 67, Southbury, **N** 🅖 Citgo/deli, Mobil, Shell/repair 🍴 Dunkin', McDonald's, Panera Bread, Subway 🏨 Heritage Hotel 🅞 AT&T, Stop&Shop, TJ Maxx, Verizon, **S** 🅞 to Kettletown SP
14(20)	CT 172, to S Britain, **N** 🅖 Mobil 🍴 Dunkin', Maggie McFly's, **S** 🅞 st police
20mm	motorist callboxes begin eb, end wb
13(19)	River Rd (from eb), to Southbury
11(16)	CT 34, to New Haven
10(15)	US 6 W, Newtown, **N** 🍴 Fig's Rest., Foundry Kitchen, Subway, Villa Rest., **S** 🅖 Citgo/dsl, Mobil/dsl 🍴 Blue Colony Diner, Pizza Palace, Starbucks
9(11)	CT 25, to Hawleyville, **N** 🅞 USPO
8(8)	Newtown Rd, **N** 🅖 Global, Mobil/dsl 🍴 Applebee's, Dunkin', Outback Steaks 🏨 La Quinta, Quality Inn 🅞 Best Buy, Harley-Davidson, Lowe's, Volvo, **S** 🅖 Shell/dsl, Sunoco 🍴 99 Rest.,

8(8)	Continued Black Angus, Boston Mkt, Burger King, Chili's, Denny's, Dunkin', Ichiro Steaks, Little Caesar's, McDonald's, Popeye's, Puerto Vallarta, Rizzuto's, Starbucks, Subway, Taco Bell, TX Roadhouse, Wayback Burger 🏨 Best Western, Courtyard, Days Inn, Hampton Inn, Holiday Inn/rest., Microtel 🅞 $Tree, Aldi Foods, Marshall's, Staples, Stop&Shop, Subaru, Target, TJ Maxx, Town Fair Tire, Verizon, Walmart/Subway
7(7)	US 7N/202E, to Brookfield (exits left from eb), New Milford, **1 mi N on Federal Rd** 🅖 Irving, Mobil, Sunoco 🍴 Arby's, Burger King, Chick-fil-A, Dunkin', Five Guys, Jersey Mike's, KFC, McDonald's, Moe's SW, Panera Bread, Starbucks, Wendy's 🅞 AT&T, Bj's Whse/gas, Costco/gas, CVS Drug, Firestone/auto, Ford, GNC, Home Depot, Jo-Ann Fabrics, Kohl's, Michael's, Petco, ShopRite Foods, Stew Leonards, Town Fair Tire, Toyota, Verizon, Walgreens
6(6)	CT 37 (from wb), New Fairfield, **N** 🅖 Gulf 🍴 Burger King, Castello's Italian, Dunkin', Elmer's Diner, Grand Century Buffet, McDonald's, Moon Star Chinese, Starbucks 🅞 $Tree, CVS Drug, Rite Aid, **S** 🅖 Shell 🍴 KFC
5(5)	CT 37, CT 39, CT 53, Danbury, **N** 🅖 Exxon/dsl, Shell 🏨 Best Value Inn, **S** 🅖 Mobil 🍴 Dunkin', Taco Bell 🅞 🅗, to Putnam SP
4(4)	US 6 W/202 W, Lake Ave, **N** 🅖 Gulf/dsl, Orbit/dsl, Shell/dsl 🍴 Dunkin', McDonald's 🏨 Ethan Allen Hotel, Maron Hotel, Super 8 🅞 CVS Drug, Stop&Shop Foods, **S** 🍴 Chuck's Steaks 🏨 Residence Inn, to mall
3(3)	US 7 S (exits left from wb), to Norwalk, **S** 🅖 EVC, Mobil/Burger King/dsl, Tesla EVC 🍴 Agave Mexican, Brio Grille, Buffalo Wild Wings, Cheesecake Factory, Chipotle, Coldstone, Olive Garden, Panera Bread, Red Lobster 🅞 AT&T, Barnes&Noble, Dick's, JC Penney, LL Bean, Lord&Taylor, Macy's, Petco, Whole Foods Mkt
2b a(1)	US 6, US 202, Mill Plain Rd, **N** 🅖 Mobil/dsl 🍴 Chipotle, Rosy Tomorrows, Starbucks, Tuscanero's Pizza 🏨 Hilton Garden, Holiday Inn Express 🅞 Rite Aid, Staples, Trader Joe's, **S** Welcome Ctr/weigh sta, full ♿ facilities, info, 🚯 litter barrels, petwalk 🏨 Crowne Plaza, Hotel Zero Degrees, SpringHill Suites 🅞 to Old Ridgebury
1(0)	Saw Mill Rd, **N** 🏨 Hilton Garden, Holiday Inn Express, Maron Hotel
0mm	Connecticut/New York state line

SOUTHBURY (vertical left margin)

DANBURY

🄴

CT

🅶 = gas 🍴 = food 🛏 = lodging Ⓞ = other 🆁🆂 = rest stop   Copyright 2022 - The Next EXIT ®

CT

WINDSOR AREA | **ROCKY HILL** | **WALLINGFORD**

🔼N INTERSTATE 91

Exit #	Services
58mm	Connecticut/Massachusetts state line
49(57)	US 5, to Longmeadow, MA, E 🅶 Pride/dsl 🍴 Dunkin', McDonald's 🛏 Holiday Inn Ⓞ Meineke, repair, W 🅶 Sunoco/dsl 🍴 Baco's Pizza, Cloverleaf Café, DQ, Dunkin', Pizza Palace Ⓞ $General, Chrysler/Dodge
48(56)	CT 220, Elm St (same as 47), E 🅶 Mobil/Dunkin'/dsl 🍴 Burger King, Denny's, Dunkin', Figaro, First Wok, Friendly's, Jason's Seafood, McDonald's, Outback Steaks, Panera Bread, Starbucks, TGIFriday's, Wendy's Ⓞ $Tree, AutoZone, Best Buy, Costco/gas, Dick's, Firestone/auto, Home Depot, Honda, Hyundai, Jo-Ann Fabrics, Kohl's, Nissan, Target, TownFair Tire, Toyota, USPO, VW
47(55)	CT 190, to Hazardville (same as 48), E 🍴 99 Rest., Acapulcos Mexican, Cheng's Garden, Chick-fil-A, Chipotle, D'angelo, Dunkin', Longhorn Steaks, McDonald's, Moe's SW Grill, Olive Garden, Red Robin, Starbucks, Subway, Taco Bell 🛏 Hampton Inn, Motel 6, Red Roof Inn Ⓞ 🏥, Advance Parts, Aldi Foods, AT&T, Barnes&Noble, Big Y Foods, CVS Drug, Ford, Marshall's, Michael's, NAPA, Old Navy, PetCo, Petsmart, Rite Aid, ShopRite, Staples, Stop&Shop/gas, Suburban Tire/auto, URGENT CARE, Verizon, Walgreens
46(53)	US 5, King St, to Enfield, E 🅶 Mobil 🍴 Astro's Rest., W 🛏 Enfield Inn
45(51)	CT 140, Warehouse Point, E 🅶 Shell 🍴 Burger King, Chen's Chinese, Cracker Barrel, Dunkin', Sofia's Rest., Subway, Wayback Burgers 🛏 Comfort Inn Ⓞ to Trolley Museum, W 🅶 Sunoco/dsl 🛏 Rodeway Inn Ⓞ Advance Parts
44(50)	US 5 S, to E Windsor, E 🅶 Sunoco/dsl 🍴 Big Y Mkt, Dunkin', Elizabeth's Rest., KFC, Taco Bell, Wendy's 🛏 Baymont Inn Ⓞ Walmart
49mm	Connecticut River
42(48)	CT 159, Windsor Locks, E Longview RV Ctr, W same as 41
41(47)	Center St (exits with 39), W 🍴 Ad's Pizzaria 🛏 HillPoint Hotel
40(46.5)	CT 20, W Ⓞ🛏, Old New-Gate Prison
39(46)	Kennedy Rd (exits with 41), Community Rd, E Ⓞ vet, W 🅶 Shell/Dunkin'/dsl 🍴 Char Koon, Chili's, Starbucks Ⓞ $Tree, AT&T, GNC, PetCo, Stop&Shop Foods, Target
38(45)	CT 75, to Poquonock, Windsor Area, E 🅶 Mobil/Circle K/dsl 🍴 Asian Bistro, Buffalo Wild Wings, Dunkin', Moe's SW, Pizzarama, Subway Ⓞ PriceChopper Foods, to Ellsworth Homestead, W 🍴 The Bistro 🛏 Courtyard, Hilton Garden, Hyatt House Suites, Marriott
37(44)	CT 305, Bloomfield Ave, Windsor Ctr, E 🅶 Mobil/dsl 🍴 McDonald's, W 🅶 Sunoco 🛏 Residence Inn
36(43)	CT 178, Park Ave, to W Hartford
35b(41)	CT 218, to Bloomfield, to S Windsor, E food, gas/dsl
35a	I-291 E, to Manchester
34(40)	CT 159, Windsor Ave, E 🅶 Sunoco/dsl, W 🅶 Citgo/dsl 🛏 RanchHouse Rest. Ⓞ🏥
33(39)	Jennings Rd, Weston St, E 🅶 Tesla EVC Ⓞ Cadillac, Fiat, Jaguar, VW, W 🅶 Mobil/dsl 🍴 Burger King, Dunkin', McDonald's, Subway 🛏 Super 8, Travel Inn Ⓞ CarMax, Honda, Hyundai, Infiniti, Mazda, Mercedes, Midas, Nissan, Subaru, Toyota
32b(38)	Trumbull St (exits left from nb), W 🛏 Hilton, Red Lion Ⓞ🏥, Goodyear, to downtown
32a	(exit 30 from sb), I-84 W
29b(37)	I-84 E, Hartford
29a(36.5)	US 5 N, CT 15 N (exits left from nb), W Ⓞ🏥, capitol, civic ctr, downtown
28(36)	US 5, CT 15 S (from nb), W 🅶 Citgo 🍴 Burger King, Dunkin', Wendy's
27(35)	Brainerd Rd, Airport Rd, E 🅶 Mobil/Dunkin'/Subway/dsl, Shell/Dunkin'/dsl 🍴 McDonald's, USS Chowder Pot 🛏 Best Western, Days Inn Ⓞ Regional Mkt
26(33.5)	Marsh St, W Ⓞ CT MVD, Silas Deane House, Webb House
25(33)	CT 3, Glastonbury, Wethersfield
24(32)	CT 99, Rocky Hill, Wethersfield, E 🅶 Phillips 66/dsl 🍴 Algarve Grill, Chuck's Steaks, Dakota Steaks, Dunkin', McDonald's, On-the-Border, Rita's Custard, Rockyhill Pizza, Saybrook Seafood, Subway 🛏 Holiday Inn Express, Howard Johnson, Super 8 Ⓞ Aldi Foods, Kohl's, Meineke, Monro, W 🅶 Mobil, Shell/dsl, Valero/dsl 🍴 Buffalo Wild Wings, Burger King, Chip's Rest., Chipotle, D'Angelo, Denny's, Friendly's, Ginza Cuisine, KFC, Panera Bread, Red Lobster, Sake Japanese, Sofia's Pizzaria, Starbucks, Subway, Townline Diner, Wendy's, Wood-n-Tap Grill 🛏 Comfort Inn, Motel 6 Ⓞ $Tree, AT&T, CVS Drug, Goodyear/auto, Marshall's, Stop&Shop, TJMaxx, TownFair Tire, Verizon, Walgreens, Walmart/Subway
23(29)	to CT 3, West St, Rocky Hill, Vet Home, E 🛏 Sheraton Ⓞ to Dinosaur SP, W 🅶 Cumberland Farms/dsl, Exxon/dsl, Mobil 🍴 DeNovellis, Michelangeo's Pizza, Starbucks, Subway 🛏 Residence Inn Ⓞ Westside Mktplace
22(27)	CT 9, to New Britain, Middletown
21(26)	CT 372, to Berlin, Cromwell, E 🅶 Sunoco/dsl/repair 🛏 Quality Inn, Red Lion Inn Ⓞ Krauszer's Foods, Lowe's, W 🅶 Citgo/Subway/dsl, Mobil/dsl 🍴 Baci Grill, Burger King, Chili's, Cromwell Diner, Dunkin', McDonald's, Mizzu Asian, Nardelli's 🛏 Courtyard, Super 8 Ⓞ Firestone/auto, PriceRite Foods, URGENT CARE, Verizon, vet, Walmart
20(23)	Country Club Rd, Middle St
22mm	🆁🆂/weigh sta nb, full ♿ facilities, info, litter barrels, petwalk, 🍴, 🏤, RV dump, vending
19(21)	Baldwin Ave (from sb)
18(20.5)	I-691 W, to Marion, access to same as 16 & 17, ski area
17(20)	CT 15 N (from sb), to I-691, CT 66 E, Meriden
16(19)	CT 15, E Main St, E 🅶 Gulf/dsl, Mobil/dsl, Valero 🍴 American Steaks, Gianni's Rest., Huxley's Cafe, Kings Garden Chinese, Olympos Diner, Subway 🛏 Extended Stay America, Hawthorn Inn, Red Roof Inn, The Meridan Inn, W 🅶 Gulf/repair, Shell/dsl 🍴 Boston Mkt, Boston Mkt, Burger King, Dunkin', KFC, Les' Dairy Bar, Little Caesar's, McDonald's, Nardelli's, Subway, Taco Bell, Wayback Burgers, Wendy's 🛏 Comfort Inn Ⓞ🏥, CVS Drug, Hancock's Drug, Walgreens
15(16)	CT 68, to Durham, E 🛏 Hilton Garden Ⓞ golf, W 🛏 Courtyard, Fairfield Inn, Homewood Suites
15mm	🆁🆂 sb, full ♿ facilities, info, litter barrels, petwalk, 🍴, 🏤
14(12)	CT 150 (no EZ return), Woodhouse Ave, Wallingford
13(10)	US 5 (exits left from nb), Wallingford, **services 2 mi W on US 5** Ⓞ to Wharton Brook SP
12(9)	US 5, Washington Ave, E 🅶 Exxon, Sunoco, Valero 🍴 Boston Mkt, Burger King, D'angelo's, DQ, Dunkin', McDonald's, Popeye's, Starbucks, Subway Ⓞ CVS Drug, Stop&Shop Food, TownFair Tire, USPO, Verizon, Walgreens, W 🅶 BP, Mobil, Shell/dsl 🍴 Arby's, Athena II Diner, Dunkin', Outback Steaks 🛏 Best Western+/Harry's Grill Ⓞ Advance Parts, BigY Foods/drug, vet
11(7)	CT 22 (from nb), North Haven, same as 12
10(6)	CT 40, to Cheshire, Hamden
9(5)	Montowese Ave, W 🅶 Gulf/dsl, Sunoco 🍴 Buffalo Wild Wings, Chick-fil-A, Dunkin', Friendly's, Longhorn Steaks, McDonald's, Olive Garden, Panera Bread, Red Lobster, Ruby Tuesday

N **INTERSTATE 91 Cont'd**

9(5)	Continued
	Subway, Wendy's 🅾 $Tree, AT&T, Barnes&Noble, Best Buy, BigLots, BJ's Whse/gas, CVS, Dick's, GNC, Home Depot, Michael's, Nissan/Jeep, PetCo, Petsmart, Target, TJMaxx, URGENT CARE, Verizon
8(4)	CT 17, CT 80, Middletown Ave, E 🅿 7-11, Global/dsl, Mercury/dsl, Shell 🍴 91 Diner, Burger King, Dunkin', KFC, McDonald's, Popeye's, Seasons, Taco Bell 🛏 Days Inn 🅾 Advance Parts, Aldi Foods, AutoZone, Lowe's, vet, Walgreens, Walmart/Subway
7(3)	Ferry St (from sb), Fair Haven, W 🍴 Exxon/dsl 🅾 NAPA
6(2.5)	Willow St (exits left from nb), Blatchley Ave, E 🅾 repair
5(2)	US 5 (from nb), State St, Fair Haven
4(1.5)	State St (from sb), downtown
3(1)	Trumbull St, downtown, W 🅾 Peabody Museum
2(.5)	Hamilton St, downtown, New Haven
1(.3)	CT 34W (from sb), New Haven, W 🅾 🏥, downtown
	I-91 begins/ends on I-95, exit 48.

N **INTERSTATE 95**

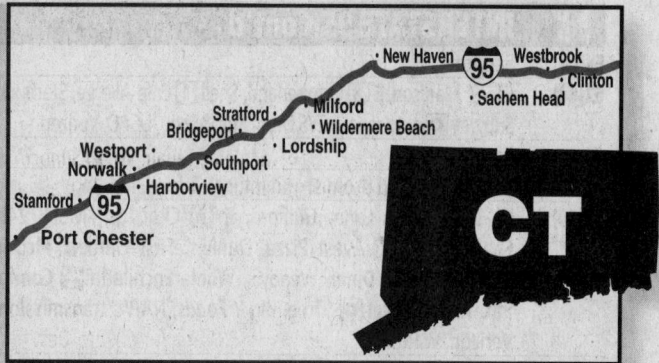

Exit #	Services
94mm	Connecticut/Rhode Island state line
93(111)	CT 216, Clarks Falls, E 🅿 Citgo/dsl/repair 🍴 Subway, to Burlingame SP 🅾 $General, W 🅿 Mobil/dsl, Pilot/Shell/Stuckey's/Sbarro's/dsl/scales/24hr 🍴 Dunkin' 🛏 Budget Inn, Stardust Motel
92(107)	CT 2, CT 49 (no EZ nb return), 🆁🆂 sb, **full facilities**, Pawcatuck, E 🅿 Shell 🍴 Dunkin', McDonald's 🛏 La Quinta 🅾 🏥, Stop&Shop, W 🛏 Cedar Park Suites 🅾 FoxWoods (8mi), KOA
91(103)	CT 234, N Main St, to Stonington, E 🅾 🏥
90(101)	CT 27, Mystic, E 🅿 Shell/Domino's/Dunkin/dsl, Tesla EVC 🍴 Friendly's, Go Fish, McDonald's, Mystic Diner, Peking Tokyo, Starbucks, Steak Loft 🛏 Hilton, Holiday Inn Express, Howard Johnson, Hyatt Place, Rodeway Inn 🅾 aquarium, Mystic Outlet Shops, W 🅿 Mobil/Subway/dsl 🍴 Cristo's Pizza, Dunkin', Frank's Grille 🛏 Days Inn, Hampton Inn, Mystic River Inn, Quality Inn, Residence Inn 🅾 Chevrolet, Chrysler/Dodge/Jeep, Ford, TrueValue, VW
89mm	Mystic River, scenic overlook nb, scenic overlook
89(99)	CT 614, Mystic St, Allyn St, W 🅾 camping (seasonal)
88(98)	CT 117, to Noank, E 🅾 🍴, W 🍴 Octagon Steaks, Starbucks 🛏 Marriott
87(97)	Sharp Hwy (exits left from sb), Groton, E 🍴 Applebee's 🛏 Hampton Inn 🅾 🍴, to Griswold SP
86(96)	rd 184 (exits left from nb), Groton, E 🍴 99 Rest., Applebee's, Olio Rest. 🛏 Hampton Inn, Motel 6, Rodeway Inn 🅾 Walgreens, W 🅿 Gulf/dsl, Mobil/dsl, Shell/dsl, Xpress Fuel 🍴 Chinese Kitchen, Domino's, Dunkin', Five Guys, Flanagan's Diner, Groton Rest., KFC, Moe's SW, Panera Bread, Pick Pockets Deli, Subway, Taco Bell 🛏 Days Inn, Groton Inn, Hilton Garden, Ramada, Super 8 🅾 Advance Parts, GNC, Honda, Kia, Kohl's, Midas, Stop&Shop, to US Sub Base, Verizon
85(95)	US 1 N, Groton, downtown, E 🍴 Norms Diner 🛏 Sleep Inn
84(94)	CT 32 (from sb), New London, downtown
83(92)	CT 32, New London, E 🅾 to Long Island Ferry
82a(90.5)	frontage rd, same as 82, New London, E 🅿 Mobil/dsl 🍴 Denny's, TX Roadhouse 🅾 Advance Parts, AutoZone, Goodyear/auto, NSA Foods, Staples, TownFair Tire, W 🅿 Sunoco 🍴 Chili's, Outback Steaks, Panda Buffet 🛏 Clarion, Red Roof Inn, SpringHill Suites 🅾 Marshall's, Petsmart, ShopRite Foods
82(90)	CT 85, to I-395 N, New London, W 🅿 Mobil/Dunkin' 🍴 Buffalo Wild Wings, Coldstone, Jersey Mike's, Longhorn Steaks, Moe's SW, Olive Garden, Panera Bread, Ruby Tuesday, Smashburger, Starbucks, Subway 🅾 BAM, Best Buy, Dick's, Home Depot, JC Penney, Macy's, Michael's, PetCo, Target, Verizon
90mm	**weigh sta both directions**
81(89.5)	Cross Road, W 🛏 Rodeway Inn 🅾 $Tree, BJ's Whse/gas, Lowe's, Walmart/McDonald's
80(89.3)	Oil Mill Rd (from sb), W 🛏 Rodeway Inn
76(89)	I-395 N (from nb, exits left), to Norwich
75(88)	US 1, to Waterford
74(87)	rd 161, to Flanders, Niantic, E 🅿 Citgo/dsl, Mobil, Niantic/dsl/repair 🍴 Burger King, Country Gourmet, Dunkin', Illiano's Grill, Starbucks 🛏 Days Inn, Motel 6, Niantic Inn, Sleep Inn 🅾 Ford, Monro Automotive, Stop&Shop/gas, Verizon, W 🅿 Shell 🍴 Flanders Seafood, King Garden, McDonald's, Osaka Japanese, Shack Rest., Smokey O'Grady's BBQ, Subway, Yummy Yummy Pizza 🅾 CVS Drug, Tri Town Foods, TrueValue, Walgreens
74mm	🆁🆂 sb, full ♿ facilities, st police
73(86)	Society Rd
72(84)	to Rocky Neck SP, **2 mi** E food, lodging, RV camping, to Rocky Neck SP
71(83)	4 Mile Rd, River Rd, to Rocky Neck SP, **1 mi** E 🅾 KOA (seasonal), beaches
70(80)	US 1, CT 156, Old Lyme, W 🅿 Shell/dsl 🍴 Dock 11 Cafe, Dunkin', Subway 🛏 Old Lyme Inn/dining 🅾 Big Y Foods, Griswold Museum, Rite Aid, USPO, vet
69(77)	US 1, CT 9 N, to Hartford, W 🍴 Otter Cove 🛏 Quality Inn
68(76.5)	US 1 S, Old Saybrook, E 🅿 Mobil, Shell/dsl 🍴 Cloud 9 Deli, Mystic Mkt Kitchen, W 🅾 Buick/GMC, Chevrolet, Chrysler/Dodge/Jeep, Hyundai, Kia, Nissan, VW
67(76)	CT 154, Elm St (no EZ sb return), Old Saybrook, E 🅾 same as 68
66(75)	to US 1, Spencer Plain Rd, E 🅿 Citgo/dsl 🍴 Alforno Trattoria, Cuckoo's Nest Mexican, Dunkin', Five Guys, Sal's Pizza, Samurai Japanese, Wayback Burgers 🛏 EconoLodge, Saybrook Motel, Super 8 🅾 Big Y Mkt, Kohl's, NAPA, transmissions, URGENT CARE, vet
65(73)	rd 153, Westbrook, E 🅿 Mobil/Dunkin', Valero 🍴 Cafe Routier, Cristy's Rest., Denny's 🅾 Honda, 🏥, Old Navy, Toyota, USPO, Walgreens, Westbrook Outlets/famous brands
64(70)	rd 145, Horse Hill Rd, Clinton
63(68)	CT 81, Clinton, E 🅿 Shell, Shell/dsl/LP, Sunoco/dsl 🍴 Chester's BBQ, Chips Rest., McDonald's, Subway 🅾 CVS Drug, USPO, vet, W 🍴 Coldstone, Dunkin' 🅾 AT&T, Clinton Crossing Premium Outlets/famous brands, PetCo
62(67)	E 🅾 beaches, RV camping, to Hammonasset SP
66mm	**service area both lanes**, 🅿 Mobil/dsl (both) 🍴 Dunkin' (nb) McDonald's (sb), Popeye's (sb), Subway (both) 🅾 atm

🅖 = gas 🍴 = food 🏠 = lodging 🅞 = other 🆁🆂 = rest stop   Copyright 2022 - The Next EXIT ®

MADISON

BRANFORD

NEW HAVEN

CT

	INTERSTATE 95 Cont'd
Exit #	Services
61(64)	CT 79, Madison, E 🅖 Cumberland, Shell 🍴 Cafe Allegre, Starbucks, Subway 🅞 auto repair, CVS Drug, Stop&Shop, USPO, Verizon
61mm	East River
60(63.5)	Mungertown Rd (from sb, no return), E food, lodging
59(60)	rd 146, Goose Lane, Guilford, E 🅖 Citgo/dsl, Mobil/24hr, Shell/DQ/dsl 🍴 Avest Pizza, Dunkin', First Garden, McDonald's, Shoreline Diner, Wendy's, Whole Enchilada 🏠 Comfort Inn, Tower Motel 🅞 $Tree, Big Y Foods, NAPA, transmissions, Verizon, Walmart
58(59)	CT 77, Guilford, E on US 1 🅖 Gulf/dsl, Mobil, Wave/dsl, Xpress 🍴 Dunkin' 🅞 CVS Drug, to Henry Whitfield Museum, Walgreens, on US 1, W 🅞 vet
57(58)	US 1, Guilford, E 🅞 Shell/Dunkin'/dsl, W 🅞 Fresh Mkt, Michael's, Petco, Verizon, vet
56(55)	rd 146, to Stony Creek, E 🏠 Rodeway Inn, W 🅖 Mobil, Shell/dsl, TA/Popeye's/Starbucks/Subway/dsl/scales/24hr/@ 🍴 56 Diner, Dunkin', USS Chowderpot 🏠 American Inn, Baymont Inn 🅞 Freightliner, Stop&Shop Foods
55(54)	US 1, E 🅖 Branford/repair, Cumberland, Shell/dsl 🍴 Carson's Rest., Dunkin', Hornet's Nest Deli, Lynn's Rest., Marco Pizzaria 🏠 Holiday Inn Express, Motel 6 🅞 Ford, vet, Walgreens, W 🅖 Gulf, Mobil/Dunkin'/dsl 🍴 Brother's Deli, Cafe Fiore, Gourmet Wok, Parthenon Diner 🏠 Days Inn
54(53)	Cedar St, Branford, E 🅖 Mobil, Stop&Shop Gas 🍴 Dragon East Chinese, Dunkin', La Luna Ristorante 🅞 Kia, Staples, Subaru, W 🅞 Krauszer's Foods, NAPA
52mm	**service area both lanes**, 🅖 Mobil/dsl (both) 🍴 Dunkin' (sb), McDonald's (nb), Subway (nb)
52(50)	rd 100, North High St, E 🅞 to Trolley Museum
51(49.5)	US 1, Easthaven, E 🅖 Sunoco, Valero/dsl, Xpress/dsl 🍴 Boston Mkt, Chili's, Dunkin' 🏠 Quality Inn 🅞 $Tree, Big Lots, Chevrolet, Hobby Lobby, Lexus, TJ Maxx, W 🍴 Golden Dragon, Wendy's 🅞 AutoZone, CarMax, Home Depot, Hyundai
50(49)	Woodward Ave (from nb), E 🅖 Shell 🅞 Ft Nathan Hale, US Naval/Marine Reserve
49(48.5)	Stiles St (from nb)
48(48)	I-91 N, to Hartford
47(47.5)	CT 34, New Haven, W 🅖 Mobil/Dunkin'/dsl 🍴 Brazi's Italian, Greek Olive Diner 🏠 La Quinta 🅞 Ikea, Long Wharf Theater, same as 46
46(47)	Long Wharf Dr, Sargent Dr, E 🍴 Lenny & Joe's Rest., W 🅖 Mobil/Dunkin'/dsl 🍴 Brazi's Italian, Greek Olive Diner 🏠 La Quinta 🅞 Ikea, Long Wharf Theater
44(46)	CT 10 (from nb), Kimberly Ave, E 🏠 Super 8, W 🍴 DQ, Dunkin', McDonald's, Popeye's, Townhouse Pizza 🅞 same as 45
43(45)	CT 122, 1st Ave (no EZ return), West Haven, W 🅖 1st Fuel/dsl, Xtra 🅞 🅗, NAPA, to U of New Haven, vet
42(44)	CT 162, Saw Mill Rd, E 🅖 Mobil/Dunkin' 🏠 EconoLodge, W 🅖 Shell 🍴 Chipotle, Denny's, Dunkin', McDonald's, Starbucks, Subway, TX Roadhouse 🏠 Best Western, Hampton Inn 🅞 Aldi Foods, Firestone/auto, Walmart/Subway
41(42)	Marsh Hill Rd, to Orange, E 🏠 Homewood Suites, W 🍴 Outback Steaks 🏠 Courtyard
41mm	**service area both lanes**, 🅖 Mobil/dsl, Tesla EVC 🍴 Dunkin', McDonald's, Panda Express
40(40)	Old Gate Lane, Woodmont Rd, E 🅖 Citgo/dsl, [Pilot]/Wendy's/dsl/scales/24hr, Shell, Sunoco 🍴 Cracker Barrel, Duchess Rest., Dunkin', Gipper's Rest., Popeye's 🏠 Hilton Garden, Holiday Inn Express, Hyatt Place, Mayflower Motel, Milford Inn 🅞 Midas ▸

MILFORD

39(39)	US 1, to Milford, E 🅖 Cumberland Farms/dsl 🍴 Athenian Diner, Dunkin', Hooters, Mama Teresa's, Mexico Tipico 🏠 Howard Johnson, Super 8 🅞 $Tree, CVS Drug, Firestone/auto, Mazda/Volvo, ShopRite Foods, vet, Walgreens, W on US 1 🅖 Mobil, Tesla EVC 🍴 Boston Mkt, Buffalo Wild Wings, Burger King, Chili's, Chipotle Mexican, DiBella Subs, Domino's, Dunkin', Golden Corral, HoneyBaked Ham, McDonald's, Panera Bread, Rustica Rest., Smashburger, Sonic, Starbucks, Subway, Taco Bell 🅞 Acura, Advance Parts, AT&T, Barnes&Noble, BigLots, Chrysler/Dodge/Jeep, Costco/gas, Dick's, Jo-Ann Fabrics, Macy's, Marshall's, Michael's, Old Navy, PetCo, Rite Aid, Shop&Shop/gas, Staples, Target, TownFair Tire, Walmart/Subway, Whole Foods Mkt
38(38)	CT 15, Merritt Pkwy, Cross Pkwy
37(37.5)	High St (no ez nb return), E 🅖 Citgo, Gulf 🍴 Subway 🅞 7-11, Toyota, vet
36	Plains Rd, E 🅖 Cumberland Farms, EVC, Mobil 🍴 Dunkin', Gusto Italian 🏠 Hampton Inn 🅞 Aldi Foods
35(37)	Bic Dr, School House Rd, E 🅖 EVC 🍴 Wendy's 🏠 Motel 6 🅞 AutoZone, Chevrolet, CVS Drug, Dennis' Parts, Ford/Lincoln, Honda, Land Rover, Nissan, Stop&Shop Foods/gas, Subaru, Walgreens, W 🏠 Red Roof Inn, Residence Inn, SpringHill Suites
34(34)	US 1, Milford, E on US 1 🍴 Dunkin', McDonald's, Ming Feng Chinese, Subway, Taco Bell 🏠 Devon Motel 🅞 $Tree, Hyundai, Walgreens
33(33.5)	US 1 (from nb, no EZ return), CT 110, Ferry Blvd, E 🅖 Shell/dsl, Sunoco/dsl 🍴 Boathouse Cantina Grill, Danny's Drive-In, Riverview Bistro, Subway 🅞 $Tree, BJ's Whse, PetCo, W 🅖 EVC 🍴 99 Rest., McDonald's, Popeye's, Villa Pizza 🅞 Home Depot, Marshall's, ShopRite Foods, Stop&Shop/dsl, USPO, Walmart/Subway
32(33)	W Broad St, Stratford, E 🅖 Sunoco/dsl, W 🅖 Gulf/dsl 🍴 Acropolis Pizza, Dunkin'
31(32)	South Ave, Honeyspot Rd, E 🅖 Gulf 🏠 HoneySpot Motel, Quality Suites 🅞 NAPA, W 🅖 Citgo/dsl 🍴 TownFair Tire
30(31.5)	Lordship Blvd, Surf Ave, E 🅖 Gulf/dsl, Shell/dsl 🍴 Dunkin' 🅞 URGENT CARE, W 🅖 Massey/dsl
29(31)	rd 130, Stratford Ave, Seaview Ave, same as 28, W 🅞 🅗
28(30)	CT 113, E Main St, Pembrook St, E 🅖 EVC 🍴 Chipotle, Starbucks, Uncle Buck's Grill 🅞 Bass Pro Shop
27(29.5)	Lafayette Blvd, downtown, W 🍴 Dunkin' 🅞 🅗, Barnum Museum
27a(29)	CT 25, CT 8, to Waterbury
26(28)	Wordin Ave
25(27)	CT 130 (from sb, no EZ return), State St, Commerce Dr, Fairfield Ave, E 🅞 Audi, Infiniti, Mercedes, Porsche, USPO, W 🍴 McDonald's
24(26.5)	Black Rock Tpk, E 🍴 Blackrock Oyster Bar, Fairfield Pizza, Ric Bravo, Sweet Basil 🏠 Best Western+ 🅞 Audi, BJ's Whse/Subway, Lexus, Porsche, Staples, USPO, Verizon, W 🅖 Gulf 🅞 Firestone/auto, Nissan
23(26)	US 1, Kings Hwy, E 🅖 EVC, Sunoco/dsl 🍴 Chipotle, Five Guys 🅞 CVS Drug, Home Depot, Petco, Whole Foods Mkt
22(24)	Round Hill Rd, N Benson Rd
23.5mm	**service area both lanes**, 🅖 Mobil/dsl 🍴 Dunkin', McDonald's, Qdoba, Subway
21(23)	Mill Plain Rd, E 🅖 Citgo/dsl, Mobil/dsl 🍴 Avellino's Italian, DQ, Geronimo SW Grill, Rawley's Drive-In, Shu Chinese, Starbucks, Subway, Tequila Revolucion 🅞 Hemlock Hardware, Hyundai, Rite Aid
20(22)	Bronson Rd (from sb)
19(21)	US 1, Center St, W 🅖 Exxon, Shell, Shell/7-11/dsl 🍴 Athena Diner, Baskin-Robbins/Dunkin', Border Grill, Panera Bread, Shake Shack, Starbucks, Subway 🏠 Westport Inn 🅞 Balducci's Mkt, Honda, Michael's, Stop&Shop, TownFair Tire

⬆N INTERSTATE 95 Cont'd

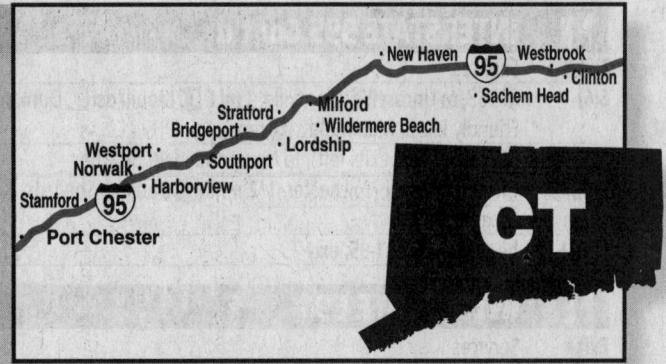

Exit #	Services
18(20)	to Westport, **E** 🅾 beaches, Sherwood Island SP, **1 mi W on US 1** 🅶 Gulf 🍴 Angelina's Trattoria, Five Guys, Fresh Mkt, Little Barn, McDonald's, Sakura Japanese, Sherwood Diner, Starbucks 🅾 Barnes&Noble, Marshall's, Toyota, URGENT CARE, vet, Walgreens
17(18)	CT 33, rd 136, Westport
16(17)	E Norwalk, **E** 🅶 Citgo, Mobil/Dunkin'/dsl, Shell/dsl 🍴 Baskin-Robbins, Mike's Deli, Penny's Diner, Subway 🅾 Rite Aid
15(16)	US 7, to Danbury, Norwalk
14(15)	US 1, CT Ave, S Norwalk, **E** 🍴 Shell 🅾 Walgreens, **W** 🍴 Exxon, Global, Shell 🍴 Burger King, Dunkin', Post Road Diner, Silver Star Diner, Starbucks, Subway, Wendy's 🅾 🅷, $Tree, Best Buy, CVS Drug, GNC, Kohl's, Petsmart, REI, same as 13, ShopRite Foods, Stop&Shop, TJ Maxx, TownFair Tire
13(13)	US 1 (no EZ return), Post Rd, Norwalk, **W** 🍴 EVC, Mobil, Shell, Sunoco 🍴 American Steaks, Bertucci's, Blue Wave Taco, Chipotle Mexican, Darien Diner, Driftwood Diner, KFC, McDonald's 🛏 DoubleTree 🅾 AT&T, Costco, Home Depot, Mini, same as 14, vet, Walmart
12.5mm	**service area nb,** 🍴 Mobil/dsl, Tesla EVC 🍴 McDonald's, Sbarro's, Subway, Taco Bell
12(12)	rd 136, Tokeneke Rd (from nb, no return), **W** 🍴 SoNo Cafe
11(11)	US 1, Darien, **E** 🍴 EVC, EVC, Exxon 🛏 Shake Shack 🅾 Chevrolet, Land Rover/Jaguar, repair, vet, **W** 🍴 Gulf 🍴 Dunkin' BMW, CVS, Whole Foods Mkt
10(10)	Noroton, **W** 🍴 Mobil, Shell 🍴 Jake's Place, Subway 🅾 vet
9.5mm	**service area sb,** 🍴 Mobil/dsl, Tesla EVC 🍴 Chipotle, Dunkin', McDonald's, Subway
9(9)	US 1, rd 106, Glenbrook, **E** 🛏 Red Carpet Inn, **W** 🍴 Gulf 🍴 Dunkin', McDonald's, Subway 🅾 Advance Parts, Meineke
8(8)	Atlantic Ave, Elm St, **E** 🍴 Sunoco 🍴 Dunkin', **W** 🛏 Marriott 🅷
7(7)	CT 137, Atlantic Ave, **W** 🍴 Capital Grille 🛏 Hampton Inn, Marriott 🅾 Barnes&Noble, same as 8
6(6)	Harvard Ave, West Ave, **E** 🍴 Stamford Diner, Starbucks 🛏 La Quinta 🅾 Advance Parts, Petsmart, Subaru, USPO, **W** 🍴 Shell 🛏 Super 8 🅾 🅷
5(5)	US 1, Riverside, Old Greenwich, **W** 🍴 BP, Mobil, Shell 🍴 Boston Mkt, Chipotle, Corner Deli, McDonald's, Starbucks, Taco Bell, Valbella Ristorante 🛏 Hyatt Regency 🅾 Acme Mkt, CVS Drug, GNC, Staples, USPO, Walgreens
4(4)	Indian Field Rd, Cos Cob, **W** 🅾 Bush-Holley House Museum
3(3)	Arch St, Greenwich, **E** 🅾 Bruce Museum, **W** 🍴 Shell 🅾 🅷, Cadillac, Lexus
2mm	**weigh sta nb**
2(1)	Delavan Ave, Byram
0mm	Connecticut/New York state line

⬆N INTERSTATE 395

Exit #	Services
55.5mm	Connecticut/Massachusetts state line
53(54)	E Thompson, to Wilsonville
50(50)	rd 200, N Grosvenor Dale, **W** 🅾 W Thompson Lake Camping (seasonal)
49(49)	to CT 12 (from nb, exits left), Grosvenor Dale
47(47)	US 44, to E Putnam, **E** 🍴 Dunkin', Empire Buffet, McDonald's, Subway, Wendy's 🅾 $Tree, Advance Parts, CVS Drug, Giant Pizza, GNC, Stop&Shop/gas, **W** 🍴 Citgo/dsl/repair, Mobil 🅾 AutoZone, Walmart/Subway
46(46)	to CT 12, Putnam, **W** 🛏 Best Value Inn 🅾 🅷
45(45)	Kennedy Dr, to Putnam, **E** 🅾 Ford, **W** 🅾 🅷
43(43)	Ballouville, **W** 🛏 Comfort Inn
41(41)	CT 101, to Dayville, **E** 🍴 Gulf, Shell/dsl 🍴 Burger King, China Garden, Dayville Mexican, Domino's, Dunkin', Subway, Yamato Japanese, Zip's Diner 🛏 Budget Inn 🅾 $General, $Tree, Aldi Foods, Kohl's, O'Reilly Parts, Town Fair Tire, Walgreens, **W** 🍴 Mobil/Taco Bell/dsl, Shell/dsl 🍴 99 Rest., Dunkin', McDonald's, Railside Tavern 🅾 AT&T, city park, GNC, Lowe's, Michael's, PetCo, Staples, Stop&Shop, Target, TJ Maxx, Verizon
38(39)	to S Killingly, **W** 🍴 Dunkin', Giant Pizza 🅾 st police
37(38)	US 6 W, to Danielson, to Quinebaug Valley Coll
35(36)	to US 6 E (from nb), to Providence
35mm	🆁🆂 both lanes, full ♿ facilities 🍴 Mobil/dsl 🍴 Dunkin', Subway
32(32)	CT 14, to Sterling, Central Village, **E** 🍴 Cumberland, T&S/repair 🍴 Edi's Place, Pizza Pizzaz 🅾 RV camping, USPO, Walgreens, **W** 🍴 Citgo, Valero/dsl 🍴 Dunkin', Frank O's Pizza, Subway 🛏 Knights Inn 🅾 $General, transmissions
29(30)	CT 14A to Plainfield, **W** 🍴 Mobil
28(28)	Lathrop Rd, to Plainfield, **E** 🍴 Shell/Domino's/dsl 🍴 Dunkin', HongKong Star Chinese, Subway, Wendy's 🛏 La Quinta, Quality Inn 🅾 Big Y Foods, Ford, Hyundai/VW, Mazda, **W** 🍴 Ardmore Fuel, Sunoco/dsl 🍴 Bakers Dozen Cafe, McDonald's, Mr Z's Rest. 🅾 Advance Parts, CVS Drug
24(24)	rd 201, Hopeville, **E** 🅾 Hopeville Pond SP, RV camping
22(23)	CT 164, CT 138, to Pachaug, Preston, **E** 🍴 Exxon/Petro Max/Dunkin'/dsl 🅾 $Tree, Campers World, **W** 🛏 AmericInn
21(21)	CT 12, Jewett City, **E** 🍴 Chili's, Panera Bread, Ruby Tuesday, Starbucks 🅾 Aldi Foods, AT&T, Dick's, GNC, Home Depot, Kohl's, Lowe's, PetCo, Target, Verizon, Walmart/Dunkin', **W** 🍴 Mobil/Dunkin'/dsl, Shell/dsl 🍴 McDonald's 🅾 Val-U Foods, vet
19a(20)	CT 169 (from nb), Lisbon, **E** 🅾 Hidden Acres RV camping
18(18)	rd 97, Taftville, **E** 🍴 Shell/dsl, **W** 🍴 7-11/dsl
14(14)	to CT 2 W, CT 32 N, Norwichtown, **E** 🍴 Friendly's 🅾 tires, **W** 🍴 Global/Dunkin'/dsl, Mobil/dsl, Shell/dsl 🍴 Illiano's Grill, Prime 82 Rest., Subway, Yantic River Inn 🛏 Courtyard, Rosemont Suites 🅾 Ace Hardware
13b a(14)	CT 2 E, CT 32 S, Norwich, **E** 🅾 🅷
11(12)	CT 82, Norwich, **E** 🍴 Mobil, Shell/dsl 🍴 99 Rest., Burger King, Chinese Buffet, Dunkin', Five Guys, KFC/Taco Bell, Little Caesar's, McDonald's, Popeye's, Starbucks, Subway, Wendy's 🅾 $Tree, AT&T, Jo-Ann Fabrics, Rite Aid, ShopRite Foods, Staples, TJ Maxx, TownFair Tire, Verizon, **W** 🛏 Holiday Inn 🅾 Big Y Foods, Walmart
9a(10)	CT 2A E, to Ledyard, to Pequot Res
8.5mm	**service plaza sb,** 🍴 Mobil/dsl (sb) 🍴 Dunkin' (sb), Subway (sb) 🅾 st police (nb)

Map labels: New Haven, Westbrook, Clinton, Sachem Head, Stratford, Milford, Wildermere Beach, Bridgeport, Lordship, Southport, Westport, Norwalk, Harborview, Stamford, Port Chester, CT

Side tabs: NORWALK, GREENWICH, PUTNAM, PLAINFIELD, NORWICHTOWN, CT

📛 = gas   🍴 = food   🏠 = lodging   🅾 = other   ℞ = rest stop   Copyright 2022 - The Next EXIT ©

🚩N INTERSTATE 395 Cont'd

Exit #	Services
6(6)	rd 163, to Uncasville, Montville, **1 mi E** 📛 Mobil/dsl 🍴 Dunkin', Friendly Pizza, McDonald's 🅾 repair
5(5)	CT 32 (from sb, exits left), to New London, RI Beaches
2(2)	CT 85, to I-95 N, Colchester, 1/2 mi **E** 📛 Dunkin', Shell/dsl 🏠 Oakdell Motel
	I-95. I-395 begins/ends on I-95, exit 76.

🚩E INTERSTATE 691

Exit #	Services
	I-691 begins/ends on I-91.
12(12)	Preston Ave
11(11)	I-91 N, to Hartford
10(11)	I-91 S, to New Haven, CT 15 S, W Cross Pkwy
9	Berlin Tpk

Exit #	Services
8(10)	US 5, Broad St, **N** 📛 HH Gas, Irving, Shell/dsl 🍴 DQ, Gourme Chinese Kitchen
7(9)	downtown (no ez wb return), Meriden (from wb)
6(8)	Lewis Ave (from wb, no EZ return), to CT 71, **N** 🍴 Ruby Tuesday 🅾 🏥, Best Buy, Dick's, Macy's, Old Navy, Target, TJ Maxx, **S** 📛 7-11 🍴 Subway
5(7)	CT 71, to Chamberlain Hill (from eb, no EZ return), **N** 🅾 🏥, Bes Buy, Target, **S** 📛 7-11/gas 🍴 Subway
3mm	Quinnipiac River
3(1)	CT 10, to Cheshire, Southington, **N** 🍴 Sam's Clams Rest., Tony' Rest.
2(0)	I-84 E, to Hartford
1(0)	I-84 W, to Waterbury
	I-691 begins/ends on I-84.

NOTES

DELAWARE

🔼N INTERSTATE 95

Exit #	Services
23mm	Delaware/Pennsylvania state line, motorist callboxes for 23 miles sb
11(22)	to I-495 S, DE 92, Naamans Rd, **E** 🅾 $General, Burlington Coats, Goodyear/auto, Jo-Ann Fabrics, SaveALot, WaWa, **W** 🍴 Shell/Circle K/dsl, WaWa/dsl 🍴 KFC/Taco Bell 🏠 Crowne Plaza 🅾 CVS Drug, Home Depot, Rite Aid
10(21)	Harvey Rd(no nb return)
9(19)	DE 3, to Marsh Rd, **E** 🍴 Dunkin' 🅾 Rockwood Museum, st police, to Bellevue SP
8b a(17)	US 202, Concord Pike, to Wilmington, **E** 🅾 Home Depot, to Brandywine Park
7b a(16)	DE 52, Delaware Ave
6(15)	DE 4, MLK Blvd, **E** 🍴 Joe's Crabshack, McDonald's 🅾 AAA, Fresh Grocer Foods, Rite Aid, **W** 🍴 Liberty 🅾 Family$
5c(12)	I-495 N, to Wilmington, to DE Mem Bridge
5b a(11)	DE 141, to US 202, to New Castle, Newport, **E** 🏠 Sheraton
4b a(8)	DE 1, DE 7, to Christiana, **E** 🍴 Bahama Breeze, Brio Tuscan Grille, CA Pizza Kitchen, Cheesecake Factory, Don Pablo, Foodcourt, JB Dawson's Rest., Panera Bread, Ted's MT Grill 🅾 Barnes&Noble, Cabela's, Costco, Dick's, JC Penney, Macy's, Michael's, Nordstrom, PetCo, Target, **W** 🍴 Applebee's, Dunkin', Firebird's Grill, Fuddrucker's, Jimmy John's, Marble Slab Creamery, Michael's Rest., Olive Garden, Red Lobster 🏠 Country Inn&Suites, Courtyard, Days Inn, Extended Stay America, Hampton Inn, Hilton, Quality Inn, Red Roof Inn 🅾 🏥 AAA, Best Buy, casino/racetrack, Home Depot, Petsmart, TJ Maxx, Verizon
3b a(6)	DE 273, to Newark, Dover, **E** 🅖 BP, Exxon/dsl 🍴 Bertucci's, Bob Evans, Boston Mkt, Ciao Pizza, Famous Dave's BBQ, Olive Grill Italian, Red Robin, Shell Hammer's Grille, Wendy's 🏠 Ramada Inn, Residence Inn, Sheraton, Staybridge Suites, TownePlace Suites 🅾 Acme Foods, Boscov's, Jo-Ann Fabrics, Old Navy, Staples, Walgreens, **W** 🍴 Getty, Shell/dsl 🍴 Denny's, Dunkin' 🏠 Comfort Inn, Holiday Inn Express, Motel 6 🅾 7-11
5mm	service area both lanes(exits left from both lanes), 🍴 Sunoco/dsl 🍴 Baja Fresh, Burger King, Famiglia, Popeye's, Starbucks 🅾 info
1b a(3)	DE 896, to Newark, to U of DE, Middletown, **W** 🍴 Exxon, Shell/dsl, Sunoco 🍴 Boston Mkt, China Garden, Dunkin', Friendly's, Jersey Mike's, Malin's Deli, Mario's Pizza, McDonald's, TGIFriday's 🏠 Baymont Inn, Candlewood Suites, Embassy Suites, Homewood Suites, Red Roof Inn, Rodeway Inn 🅾 DE Tire Ctr
1mm	toll booth, st police
0mm	Delaware/Maryland state line, motorist callboxes for 23 miles nb

🔼N INTERSTATE 295 (Wilmington)

Exit #	Services
15mm	Delaware/New Jersey state line, Delaware River, Delaware Memorial Bridge
14.5mm	toll plaza
14	DE 9, New Castle Ave, to Wilmington, **E** 🍴 🍴 Giovanni's Cafe 🅾 Advance Parts, CVS Drug, Family$, Firestone/auto, Harley-Davidson/rest., Rite Aid, Super G Foods, **W** 🍴 Shell, Super/dsl 🍴 Dunkin', McDonald's 🏠 Best Night Inn, Budget Inn, SuperLodge

13	US 13, US 40, to New Castle, **E** 🍴 BP, Shell/dsl, Speedway/dsl, Sunoco/dsl, WaWa 🍴 Applebee's, Arby's, Arner's Rest, Burger King, Checkers, DogHouse, Dove Diner, Dunkin', Hooters, IHOP, KFC, Krispy Kreme, Little Caesar's, McDonald's, Popeye's, Season's Pizza, Taco Bell, TGIFriday's, Wendy's 🏠 Quality Inn, Super 8 🅾 $General, $Tree, Acura, AutoZone, Big Lots, BJ's Whse/gas, Chevrolet, Chrysler/Jeep/Dodge, Cottman Transmissions, Fiat, Ford, GNC, Home Depot, Hyundai, Lincoln, Mazda, Nissan, PepBoys, repair, Ross, Save-a-Lot, Staples, Toyota, URGENT CARE, Verizon, Walgreens, Walmart, **W** 🍴 WaWa/dsl 🍴 Dunkin' 🏠 Clarion, Fairfield Inn 🅾 Ford Trucks, Lowe's
12	I-495, US 202, N to Wilmington
I-295 begins/ends on I-95.	

🔼N INTERSTATE 495

Exit #	Services
11mm	I-95 N. I-495 begins/ends on I-95.
5(10)	US 13, Phila Pike, Claymont, **W** 🍴 BP, Exxon/dsl, Sunoco/dsl, WaWa/dsl 🍴 Arby's, Boston Mkt, Burger King, Dunkin', McDonald's 🏠 Milan Motel 🅾 Aamco, Family$, Food Lion, USPO
4(5)	US 13, rd 3, Edgemoor Rd, to Fox Point Park
3(4)	12th St
2(3)	rd 9A, Terminal Ave, Port of Wilmington
1(1)	US 13, **E** 🍴 WaWa/dsl 🍴 Dunkin' 🏠 Clarion 🅾 Ford Trucks, Lowe's
0mm	I-95 S. I-495 begins/ends on I-95.

NEWARK

WILMINGTON

FLORIDA

FL

INTERSTATE 4

DELTONA

Exit #	Services
132	I-95, S to Miami, N to Jacksonville, FL 400. **I-4 begins/ends on I-95, exit 260b.**
129	to US 92 (from eb, exits left)
118	FL 44, to DeLand, N ⛽ BP/dsl Ⓞ Ⓗ
116	Orange Camp Rd, Lake Helen
114	FL 472, to DeLand, Orange City, N Ⓞ Clark Campground (1mi), Orange City Resort, to Blue Sprgs SP, S ⛽ RaceTrac/dsl 🍴 Dunkin', Subway
111b a	Deltona, N ⛽ RaceTrac/dsl, Shell/Circle K, Wawa/dsl 🍴 Applebee's, Baskin-Robbins/Dunkin', Bob Evans, Chick-fil-A, Chili's, Denny's, Five Guys, Fujiyama, Jimmy John's, KFC, Moe's SW, Olive Garden, Papa John's, Perkins, Pizza Hut, Popeye's, Ruby Tuesday, Sonny's BBQ, Starbucks, Steak'n Shake, Subway, Taco Bell, Tijuana Flats, Woody's BBQ, Zaxby's 🛏 Holiday Inn Express Ⓞ Ⓗ, $General, Firestone/auto, Hobby Lobby, Home Depot, Lowe's, Office Depot, Publix/deli, Save-A-Lot Foods, Target, Tire Kingdom, Tires+, URGENT CARE, Verizon, Walgreens, Walmart, S ⛽ Citgo/repair 🍴 Wendy's Ⓞ Family$, Publix, Walgreens
108	Dirksen Dr, DeBary, Deltona, N 🍴 Burger King, IHOP 🛏 Hampton Inn, S ⛽ Citgo/dsl, Valero 🍴 McDonald's, Subway (2mi), Waffle House 🛏 Travelodge Ⓞ Publix (2mi)
104	US 17, US 92, Sanford, N Ⓞ La Mesa RV Ctr, S ⛽ Marathon/Subway/dsl Ⓞ Myers RV Ctr
101c	rd 46, to Mt Dora, Sanford, N ⛽ 7-11 🍴 IHOP, Subway, Tijuana Flats Ⓞ Ace Hardware, Audi, Ford, vet, S ⛽ 7-11, Chevron/dsl, Mobil, Murphy USA/dsl, RaceTrac/dsl, Shell/dsl 🍴 Buffalo Wild Wings, Burger King, Carrabba's, Cheddar's, Chianti's Pizza, Chipotle, Cracker Barrel, Don Pablo, Dunkin', El Paso Mexican, Firehouse Subs, Habaneros, Honeybaked Ham, Hooters, Joe's Crabshack, LJ Silver/Taco Bell, Logan's Roadhouse, Longhorn Steaks, McDonald's, Mellow Mushroom, Olive Garden, Orlando Alehouse, Outback Steaks, Panda Express, Panera Bread, PDQ Grill, Pollo Tropical, Red Lobster, Red Robin, Rte 46 Smokehouse, Smokey Bones BBQ, Steak'n Shake, Subway, Wendy's 🛏 Comfort Inn, SpringHill Suites Ⓞ Ⓗ, $Tree, Aldi Foods, AT&T, Beall's, Best Buy, Big Lots, BJ's Whse/gas, Books-A-Million, Chrysler/Dodge/Jeep, CVS Drug, Dick's, Dillard's, GNC, Goodyear/auto, Harley-Davidson, JC Penney, Jo-Ann Fabrics, Macy's, Marshall's, Michael's, Old Navy, PetCo, Ross, Target, Tire Kingdom, Tuesday Morning, Tuffy Auto, URGENT CARE, Verizon, Walmart, World Mkt
101a b	rd 46a, FL 417 (**toll**), FL 46, Sanford, Heathrow, N 🍴 Applebee's, Coldstone, Crisper's, Duffy's Grill, F&D Cafe, FishBones, Friendly Confines Grill, McDonald's, Moe's SW Grill, Papa Joe's Pizza, Ruth's Chris Steaks, Shula's 347 Grill, Subway, Terra Mia Pizza 🛏 Hampton Inn, Marriott, Residence Inn, Westin Ⓞ Publix, URGENT CARE, Walgreens, S 🍴 Giovanni's, Jersey Mike's, Marco's Pizza, Smokey Joe's BBQ Ⓞ 7-11, Acura, CarMax, CVS Drug, Honda, Infiniti, Kohl's, Mercedes, Publix, Sam's Club/gas, Toyota
98	Lake Mary Blvd, Heathrow, N ⛽ Shell 🍴 Casey's Grill, Luigino's Italian, Panera Bread, RW Blue Grill, Stonewood Grill, Subway 🛏 Courtyard, Hyatt Place Ⓞ CVS Drug, Walgreens, Winn-Dixie, S ⛽ 7-11, BP/24hr, Marathon/Kangaroo/dsl, Mobil/dsl 🍴 Arby's, Baskin-Robbins/Dunkin', Bob Evans, Boston Mkt,

HEATHROW

98	Continued Burger Fi, Burger King, Chick-fil-A, Chili's, China King, Chipotl Mexican, Chop Stix, Domino's, Dunkin', Firehouse Subs, Fred Mkt, Jason's Deli, Jimmy John's, KFC, Longhorn Steaks, Mar ble Slab, McDonald's, Mikado Japanese, Noodles&Co, Paner Bread, Papa Joe's Pizza, Papa John's, Papa Murphy's, Sta bucks, Steak'n Shake, Subway, Taco Bell, Tilted Kilt, Wendy' Which Wich? 🛏 Candlewood Suites, Extended Stay Ameri ca, Hilton Garden, Homewood Suites, La Quinta Ⓞ Advanc Parts, AT&T, Fresh Mkt, GNC, Goodyear/auto, Home Depo Office Depot, Petsmart, Publix, Ross, Staples, Target, Tires+, T Maxx, USPO, Verizon, Walgreens
95mm	Ⓡˢ both lanes, 24hr security, full ♿ facilities, litter barrels, pe walk, 🐾, 🚮, vending
94	FL 434, to Winter Springs, Longwood, N ⛽ 7-11, Chevron Mobil/7-11/dsl 🍴 Burger King, China Gate, FirstWatch Cafe Imperial Dynasty, Jimmy John's, Kobe Japanese, Melting Po Rest., Mykonos Greek, Panera Bread, Papa Joe's Pizza, Sta bucks, Starbucks, Tijuana Flats, Wendy's Ⓞ CVS Drug, Publi vet, S 🍴 Bonefish Grill, Boston Mkt, Carmela's Rest., Pickle NY, Smokehouse Ⓞ Ⓗ
92	FL 436, Altamonte Springs, N ⛽ 7-11, Chevron/dsl, Shel Circle K/dsl 🍴 Boston Mkt, Checkers, Chick-fil-A, Chipotl Mexican, ChuckeCheese, Cracker Barrel, Kobe Japanese, Littl Caesar's, Longhorn Steaks, McDonald's, Olive Garden, Per kins, Pollo Tropical, Popeye's, Red Lobster, Sweet Tomatoe Taco Bell, Twin Peaks, Waffle House, WingHouse 🛏 Days In Hampton Inn, Howard Johnson, Quality Inn, Ramada, Rem ington Inn, Residence Inn, SpringHill Suites Ⓞ Best Buy, CV Drug, Family$, Firestone/auto, O'Reilly Parts, Tire Kingdom U-Haul, URGENT CARE, Walgreens, S ⛽ BP/Circle K, Chevro Mobil/dsl, Speedway/dsl 🍴 Bahama Breeze, Burger King Chili's, Coldstone, Denny's, Duffy's Grill, Dunkin', Five Guys, Ja son's Deli, Moe's SW Grill, Orlando Alehouse, Panda Express Pei Wei, Starbucks, Steak'n Shake, Subway, Wendy's 🛏 Em bassy Suites, Extended Stay America, Hilton Ⓞ Ⓗ, Advanc Parts, Albertson's, AT&T, Barnes&Noble, CVS Drug, Dillard's, Penney, Marshall's, PetCo, Publix, Ross, Whole Foods Mkt
90b a	FL 414, Maitland Blvd, N ⛽ 7-11 🍴 Applebee's, Chick-fil-A Oak Grill, Wendy's 🛏 Extended Stay America, Extended Sta America (2), Homewood Suites, Sheraton, S Ⓞ Maitland Art C
88	FL 423, Lee Rd, N ⛽ 7-11 🍴 Christner's Rest., IHOP, Littl Caesar's, LJ Silver/Taco Bell, McDonald's, Popeye's, Shell Rest., Wild Rice Buffet 🛏 Europe Inn, InTown Suites, Motel Quality Inn Ⓞ Advance Parts, Family$, Firestone/auto, Hom Depot, O'Reilly Parts, VW, S ⛽ Chevron/dsl, Sunoco 🍴 Den ny's Ⓞ Aamco, BMW
87	FL 426, Fairbanks Ave (no eb re-entry), N ⛽ Speedway Dunkin'/dsl
86	Par St (from eb, no re-entry), S ⛽ Shell/Circle K
85	Princeton St, S ⛽ 7-11 🍴 Wendy's 🛏 Comfort Suites Ⓞ Ⓗ
84	FL 50, Colonial Dr, Ivanhoe Blvd, N 🛏 Crowne Plaza
83b	US 17, US 92, FL 50, Amelia St (from eb), N 🛏 Crowne Plaza
83a	FL 526 (from eb), Robinson St
83	South St (from wb), downtown
82c	Anderson St E, Church St Sta Hist Dist, downtown
82b	Gore Ave (from wb), S Ⓞ Ⓗ, downtown
82a	FL 408 (**toll**), to FL 526
81b c	Kaley Ave, S ⛽ Mobil Ⓞ Ⓗ

ALTAMONTE SPGS

INTERSTATE 4 Cont'd

ORLANDO

Exit	Description
81a	Michigan St (from wb), **N** 🅟 Citgo/dsl
80b a	US 17, US 441 S, US 92 W, **S** 🅟 7-11, Chevron, Citgo, Mobil, RaceTrac, Shell 🍴 Checkers, McDonald's, Subway 🛏 Days Inn ⊙ $General, Aldi Foods, AutoZone, Save-A-Lot Foods, Walgreens
79	FL 423, 33rd St, John Young Pkwy, **N** 🛏 Ramada Inn ⊙ Harley-Davidson, Toyota, **S** 🅟 RaceTrac/dsl, Wawa/dsl 🍴 IHOP 🛏 Days Inn
78	Conroy Rd, **N** 🅟 7-11 ⊙ Audi, **S** 🍴 BJ's Rest., Bloomingdale's, Brio Grille, Burger 21, Cheesecake Factory, Duffy's Grill, Elephant Bar Rest., Jimmy John's, Krispy Kreme, La Madeleine, McDonald's, Moe's SW Grill, Olive Garden, Panda Express, PF Chang's, Pollo Tropical, Subway, TGIFriday's, Wendy's, Zaxby's ⊙ $Tree, AT&T, Best Buy, BJ's Whse/gas, Costco/gas, Dick's, Home Depot, Infiniti, Jaguar, Macy's, Marshall's, Mercedes, Old Navy, PetCo, Ross, Super Target
77	FL 527, FL TPK (**toll**)
75b a	FL 435, International Dr (exits left from both lanes), **N** 🅟 Chevron, Mobil 🍴 Burger King, Carrabba's, TGIFriday's 🛏 Clarion, Comfort Suites, DoubleTree, Extended Stay America, Fairfield Inn, Holiday Inn, Holiday Inn Express, Hyatt Place, InTowne Suites, La Quinta ⊙ to Universal Studios, Walgreens, **S** 🅟 7-11, Chevron/dsl, Speedway/dsl 🍴 Black Angus Steaks, Burger King, Del Taco, Denny's, IHOP, Red Lobster, Sonic, Subway, Sweet Tomatoes 🛏 Best Western, Day Inn, Hampton Inn, Hilton Garden, Homewood Suites, International Palms Inn, La Quinta, Motel 6, multiple hotels & resorts, Sheraton, Sunsol Hotel, Super 8 ⊙ Artegon/famous Brands, Bass Pro Shops, Walgreens
74b	**N** ⊙ Universal Studios (from wb)
74a	FL 482, Sand Lake Rd, **N** 🅟 7-11, Chevron 🍴 Chick-fil-A, Dunkin a Donuts, Fresca Italian, McDonald's, O'Charley's, Pei Wei, Wendy's, Zoe's Kitchen 🛏 Drury Inn ⊙ 🅗 $Tree, GNC, Michael's, Publix, Tire Kingdom, Walgreens, Walmart/McDonald's, Whole Food Mkt, **S** 🅟 BP/Circle K/dsl, Shell/Circle K/dsl 🍴 Bahama Breeze, BJ's Rest., Boston Lobster, Brickhouse Grill, Buffalo Wild Wings, Burger King, Capital Grille, Carrabba's, Charley's Steaks, Checkers, Chili's, China Jade, ChuckE-Cheese, Chuy's Mexican, CiCi's Pizza, Coldstone, Dave&Buster's, Del Frisco's, Denny's, Domino's, Don Pablo's, Fish Bones Rest., Friendly's, Golden Corral, Hooters, IHOP, Joe's Crabshack, Kobe Japanese, Longhorn Steaks, Maggiano's, McDonald's, Miller's Alehouse, Ming Court, Olive Garden, Outback Steaks, Panda Express, Perkins, Pizza Hut, Ponderosa, Popeye's, Red Robin, Senor Frogs, Subway, TGIFriday's, Tommy Bahama's, Tony Roma's, Twin Peaks, Uno, Vito's Chophouse, Yardhouse 🛏 Avanti Resort, Best Western, Castle Hotel, Comfort Inn, Courtyard, Crowne Plaza, EconoLodge, Embassy Suites, Extended Stay America, Fairfield Inn, Hampton Inn, Hampton Inn (2), Holiday Inn Express,

ORLANDO

Exit	Description
74a	Continued Homewood Suites, Hyatt Place, Hyatt Regency, La Quinta, La Quinta (2), Ramada Inn, Residence Inn, Rosen Suites, Sonesta Suites, SpringHill Suites, Wyndham Resort ⊙ Harley-Davidson, Ripley's Believe-it-or-not!, Walgreens
72	FL 528 E (**toll, no eb re-entry**), to Cape Canaveral, **N** ⊙ USPO, **S** 🛏 Hilton ⊙ to ✈
71	Central FL Pkwy (from eb no re-entry), **S** 🅟 7-11/dsl, Chevron, Wawa/dsl 🍴 Bonefish Grill, Buffalo Wild Wings, KFC, McDonald's, Mellow Mushroom, Panera Bread, Starbucks, Taco Bell, TGIFridays, Wendy's 🛏 Fairfield Inn, Hampton Inn, Hilton Garden, Renaissance Resort, Residence Inn, SpringHill Suites, to SeaWorld ⊙ CVS, Publix, Walgreens
68	FL 535, Lake Buena Vista, **N** 🅟 7-11, Mobil/dsl, Shell/Circle K/dsl 🍴 AleHouse, Black Angus Steaks, Black Fire Brazilian Steaks, Buffalo Wild Wings, Burger King, Chevy's Mexican, Chili's, China Buffet, CiCi's Pizza, Denny's, Domino's, Dragon Super Buffet, Dunkin', El Patron, Firehouse Subs, Flipper's Pizzaria,

INTERSTATE 4 Cont'd

ORLANDO

68 Continued
Fuddrucker's, Giordano's, Hooters, IHOP, Jamba Juice, Joe's Crabshack, Johnnie's Rest., Kobe Japanese, Macaroni Grill, McDonald's, Noodles&Co, Olive Garden, Papa John's, Perkins, Pizza Hut, Qdoba, Red Lobster, Seadog Brewing, Shoney's, Sofrito Latin Cafe, Steak'n Shake, Subway, Sweet Tomatoes, Taco Bell, TGIFriday's, The Knife Argentinian Steaks, Tom+Chee, Uno, Waffle House 🅛 B Resort, Clarion, Comfort Inn, Courtyard, Delta Orlando, DoubleTree, Embassy Suites, Extended Stay America, Fairfield Inn, Hampton Inn, Hawthorn Suites, Hilton, Hilton Garden, Holiday Inn, Holiday Inn Express, Homewood Suites, Hyatt Place, Quality Inn, Radisson, Residence Inn, Sheraton, StayBridge Suites, Wyndham 🅞 Gooding's Foods/drug, Walgreens, Winn Dixie, S 🅖 7-11, Chevron/dsl, Shell/dsl 🅵 Applebee's, Bahama Breeze, BJ's Rest., Carrabba's, Chick-fil-A, CiCi's Pizza, Dunkin', Golden Corral, Landry's Seafood, LoneStar Steaks, Longhorn Steaks, Panera Bread, Pollo Tropical, Santa Fe Steaks, Starbucks, Subway, Wendy's 🅛 Blue Heron Resort, Buena Vista Suites, Courtyard, Fairfield Inn, Holiday Inn Resort, Marriott Village, Residence Inn, Sheraton, SpringHill Suites 🅞 $Tree, CVS Drug, GNC, Orlando Premium Outlets, Verizon, Walgreens

67 Fl 536, to Epcot, N 🅞 DisneyWorld, **1 mi** S 🅖 7-11 🅵 Fusion Rest. 🅛 Buena Vista Suites, Caribe Royale, Marriott 🅞 CVS Drug, multiple resorts, to 🛈

65 Osceola Pkwy, to FL 417 (toll), N 🅞 Animal Kingdom, Epcot, to DisneyWorld, Wide World of Sports

64 b a US 192, FL 536, to FL 417 (toll), to Kissimmee, N 🅞 Harley-Davidson, Hollywood Studios, to DisneyWorld, **0-3 mi** S 🅖 7-11, Mobil/dsl, RaceTrac/dsl 🅵 Applebee's, Arby's, Bob Evans, Boston Lobster Feast, Burger King, Charley's Steakhouse, Checkers, Chick-fil-A, Chili's, Chinese Buffet, Chipotle, CiCi's Pizza, Cracker Barrel, Denny's, Dunkin', Five Guys, Golden Corral, IHOP, Joe's Crabshack, KFC, Kobe Japanese, Krispy Kreme, Little Italy, Logan's Roadhouse, Longhorn Steaks, Macaroni Grill, McDonald's, Olive Garden, Pacino's Italian, Panda Express, Panera Bread, Papa John's, Pei Wei, Perkins, Pizza Hut, Pizza Hut, Ponderosa, Popeye's, Red Lobster, Rio Mexican Grill, Smokey Bones BBQ, Starbucks, Subway, Taco Bell, TGIFriday's, Uno, Waffle House, Wendy's 🅛 Celebration Suites, Comfort Suites, Days Inn, Embassy Suites, Fairfield Inn, Holiday Inn, Howard Johnson, Motel 6, Parkway Resort, Quality Suites, Radisson, Red Roof Inn, Rodeway Inn, Seralago Hotel, Sun Inn, Super 8, Travelodge 🅞 🅷, $General, AT&T, Camping World RV Ctr, CVS Drug, Jo-Ann Fabrics, Marshall's, Publix, Sam's Club/dsl, Target, USPO, Walgreens

62 FL 417 (toll, from eb), World Dr, Celebration, N 🅞 to DisneyWorld, S 🅞 to 🛈

60 Fl 429 N (toll), Apopka

58 FL 532, to Kissimmee, N 🅖 7-11, BP/Circle K/dsl 🅵 Chili's, China One, Dunkin', McDonald's, Pizzaria, Subway, Wendy's 🅛 Championship Gate Resort 🅞 Publix, Walgreens, S 🅛 Reunion Resort (2mi)

55 US 27, to Haines City, N 🅖 7-11, Chevron/dsl, 🅛Loves/Arby's/dsl/scales/24hr, Sunoco/dsl 🅵 Burger King, Cracker Barrel, Denny's, McDonald's, Waffle House, Wendy's 🅛 Comfort Inn, Hampton Inn, Holiday Inn Express, Quality Inn 🅞 FL Camp Inn (5mi), Ford, S 🅖 7-11, Marathon/dsl, RaceTrac/dsl, Wawa/dsl 🅵 Bob Evans, CiCi's Pizza, Davenport's Ale House, Grand China, Perkins, Popeye's, Sake Steaks, Subway, Taco Bell 🅛 Days Inn, Ramada Inn 🅞 🅷, $Tree, AT&T, Best Buy, Books-A-Million, Deer Creek RV Resort, Dick's, Family$, GNC, JC Penney, KOA, Michael's, Petsmart, Ross, Staples, Target, Theme World RV Park, to Cypress Gardens, tourist info

LAKELAND

48 rd 557, to Winter Haven, Lake Alfred, S 🅖 Marathon/dsl

46mm 🆁🆂 both lanes, 24hr security, full 🅰 facilities, litter barrels, pet-walk, 🅲, 🅰, vending

44 FL 559, to Auburndale, S 🅖 🅛Loves/Arby's/dsl/scales/24hr, Shell/Subway/dsl/scales/24hr

41 FL 570 W toll, Auburndale, Lakeland

38 FL 33, to Lakeland, Polk City

33 rd 582, to FL 33, Lakeland, N 🅖 7-11, Exxon/dsl 🅵 Applebee's, Cracker Barrel, Five Guys, McDonald's, Starbucks, Subway, Wendy's 🅛 Baymont Inn, Crestwood Suites, Days Inn, Hampton Inn, Holiday Inn Express, La Quinta, Quality Inn, Sleep Inn 🅞 BMW, CVS Drug, GNC, Publix, S 🅖 Marathon/dsl 🅵 Waffle House 🅛 Woodspring Suites 🅞 🅷, Harley-Davidson, Lakeland RV Resort, Mercedes, Nissan

32 US 98, Lakeland, N 🅖 7-11, Marathon, Mobil/dsl, Murphy USA/dsl, Wawa/dsl 🅵 Beef o' Brady's, Buffalo Wild Wings, Checkers, Chick-fil-A, Chili's, Chipotle, ChuckeCheese, CiCi's Pizza, Domino's, DQ, Dunkin', Firehouse Subs, Golden Corral, Hooters, Hungry Howie's, IHOP, KFC, Little Caesar's, Longhorn Steaks, McDonald's, Moe's SW Grill, Olive Garden, Outback Steaks, Panda Express, Panera Bread, Papa John's, Pizza Hut, Red Lobster, Smokey Bones BBQ, Sonny's BBQ, Starbucks, Steak'n Shake, Subway, Taco Bell, Wendy's, Zaxby's 🅛 Comfort Inn, La Quinta, TownPlace Suites, Travelodge 🅞 $General, $Tree, Advance Parts, Aldi Foods, AT&T, AutoZone, Beall's, Best Buy, Big Lots, Chrysler/Dodge/Jeep, CVS Drug, Dick's, Dillard's, Discount Tire, Firestone/auto, Goodyear/auto, Hobby Lobby, JC Penney, JoAnn Fabrics, Lowe's, Michael's, Old Navy, O'Reilly Parts, PepBoys, PetCo, Petsmart, Publix, Ross, RV World, Sam's Club/gas, Save a Lot, Staples, Target, Tire Kingdom, Tires+, TJ Maxx, Toyota, Verizon, Walgreens, Walmart (2mi), S 🅖 7-11, Coastal, RaceTrac/dsl, Sunoco/dsl 🅵 Bob Evans, Burger King, Denny's, Dunkin', McDonald's, Popeye's, Waffle House 🅛 Howard Johnson, Motel 6, Ramada 🅞 🅷 $Tree, AutoZone, Beall's, Family$, Home Depot, NAPA, U-Haul

31 FL 539, to Kathleen, Lakeland, N 🅖 Circle K/dsl, Marathon 🅵 Romeo's Pizza, Subway, Wendy's 🅞 Publix/dsl, Walgreens, S hist dist

28 FL 546, to US 92, Memorial Blvd, Lakeland (from eb re-entry), 🅖 Citgo, Shell/Circle K/dsl, Sunoco/dsl 🅵 Hardee's

27 FL 570 E toll, Lakeland

25 County Line Rd, S 🅖 Mobil/dsl, Shell/Circle K/Subway 🅵 McDonald's, Wendy's 🅛 Fairfield Inn 🅞 FL Air Museum

22 FL 553, Park Rd, Plant City, N 🅵 Smokin Aces BBQ 🅞 Chevrolet, S 🅖 Shell/Circle K/Subway 🅵 Arby's, Burger King, Denny's, Popeye's 🅛 Comfort Inn, Holiday Inn Express

21 FL 39, Alexander St, to Zephyrhills, Plant City on FL 39, S 🅖 BP/dsl, Mobil/dsl 🅛 Knights Inn, Red Rose Inn/rest.

MANGO

19 FL 566, to Thonotosassa, N 🅖 Marathon/dsl, S 🅖 RaceTrac/dsl, Wawa/dsl 🅵 Applebee's, BuddyFreddy's Rest., Burger King, Carrabba's, Lin's Chinese, Little Caesar's, McDonald's, Mi Casa, OutBack Steaks, Pizza Hut/Taco Bell, Sonny's BBQ, Starbucks, Subway, Waffle House 🅛 Hampton Inn 🅞 🅷, $General, AT&T, GNC, Publix, Walgreens

17 Branch Forbes Rd, N 🅖 Citgo/dsl, Marathon/dsl 🅞 Dinosaur World, S 🅖 BP, Citgo/dsl, Shell/Circle K/Subway/dsl 🅞 Advance Parts, AutoZone

14 McIntosh Rd, N 🅖 BP/dsl 🅞 Camping World RV Ctr, Windward RV Park (2mi), S 🅖 7-11/dsl, Marathon/dsl, RaceWay/dsl, Speedway/dsl 🅵 Burger King, McDonald's/playplace 🅞 East Tampa RV Park, General RV Ctr, Tampa RV Ctr

12mm weigh sta both lanes

🏁 INTERSTATE 4 Cont'd

Exit #	Services
10	rd 579, Mango, Thonotosassa, N 🅶 ✈FLYING J/Denny's/dsl/LP/scales/24hr, Sunoco, TA/Arby's/Popeye's/dsl/scales/24hr/@ 🍽 Bob Evans, Cracker Barrel 🏨 Country Inn&Suites, Hampton Inn 🅾 Ford/Lincoln, Hillsboro River SP, Lazy Day's RV Ctr/Resort, S 🅶 Shell/Circle K/dsl 🍽 Hardee's, Subway, Wendy's 🏨 Masters Inn
9	I-75, N to Ocala, S to Naples
7	US 92W, to US 301, Hillsborough Ave, N 🅶 Mobil/dsl, Mobil/rest./dsl/scales/24hr, Wawa/dsl 🍽 Waffle House 🅾 Hard Rock Hotel/casino, S 🅶 BP, Speedway/Dunkin'/dsl, Wawa/dsl 🍽 Five Guys, WingHouse 🏨 Comfort Suites, Holiday Inn Express, La Quinta, Red Roof Inn 🅾 FL Expo Fair
6	Orient Rd (from eb)
5	FL 574, MLK Blvd, N 🍽 McDonald's 🅾 truck/rv wash, S 🅶 BP, Mobil, Sunoco/Subway 🍽 Wendy's 🏨 Fairfield Inn 🅾 Kenworth
3	US 41, 50th St, Columbus Dr (exits left from eb), N 🅶 Chevron/dsl, Shell/Subway/dsl 🏨 Days Inn, Quality Inn 🅾 $General, to Busch Gardens, S 🅶 Marathon/dsl, Sunoco/Circle K/dsl 🍽 Burger King, Checkers, Church's, KFC, McDonald's, Salem's Subs, Subway, Taco Bell 🏨 Rodeway Inn 🅾 Advance Parts, Family$, Save-A-Lot, URGENT CARE
1	FL 585, 22nd, 21st St, Port of Tampa, S 🅶 Sunoco 🍽 Burger King, McDonald's 🅾 museum
	I-4 begins/ends on I-275, exit 45b.

🏁 INTERSTATE 10

Exit #	Services
363mm	I-10 begins/ends on I-95, exit 351b.
362	Stockton St, to Riverside, S 🅶 BP, Gate 🅾 🅷
361	US 17 S (from wb)
360	FL 129, McDuff Ave, S 🅶 Sunoco 🍽 Popeye's
359	Luna St, to Lenox Ave (from wb)
358	FL 111, Cassat Ave, N 🅶 Shell/Subway/dsl, Sunoco/Godfather's/dsl 🍽 Burger King, McDonald's, Popeye's 🅾 AutoZone, S 🅶 BP/dsl, EVC, RaceWay/dsl 🍽 Domino's, Dunkin'/Baskin-Robins, Krispy Kreme, Pizza Hut, Royal Buffet, Taco Bell, Wendy's 🅾 $Tree, Advance Parts, Lowe's, Walgreens
357	FL 103, Lane Ave, N 🅶 CNG, Speedway/dsl 🍽 Andy's Sandwiches 🏨 Knights Inn, Stars Rest Inn, S 🅶 BP, Shell/dsl 🍽 Applebee's, Bono's BBQ, Cross Creek Steaks, Hardee's, KFC, Lee's Dragon, McDonald's 🏨 Diamond Inn, Sleep Inn 🅾 CVS Drug, Firestone/auto, Home Depot, Office Depot, PepBoys
356	I-295, N to Savannah, S to St Augustine
355	Marietta, N 🅶 Flash, S 🅶 Speedway/Dunkin'/dsl 🍽 Domino's
354	Hammond Blvd
351	FL 115, Chaffee Rd, to Cecil Fields, N 🅶 Kangaroo/dsl 🅾 $General, Campers RV Ctr, S 🅶 Shell/Subway/dsl, Valero 🍽 Cracker Barrel, King Wok, McDonald's, Mr Chubby's Wings, Perard's Italian, Subway, Wendy's 🏨 Best Western, Fairfield Inn, Hampton Inn, Holiday Inn Express 🅾 Family$, Winn-Dixie
350	FL 23, Cecil Commerce Ctr Pkwy
343	US 301, to Starke, Baldwin, S 🅶 🅶🍽🏨🅾/Subway/dsl/scales/24hr, TA/Shell/Arby's/dsl/scales/24hr/@, Valero 🍽 Burger King, McDonald's, Waffle House 🏨 Red Roof Inn
336	FL 228, to Maxville, Macclenny, N 🅶 Murphy USA/dsl 🍽 Starbucks 🅾 🅷, fireworks, GNC, Walmart/Subway

Exit #	Services
335	FL 121, to Lake Butler, Macclenny, N 🅶 Mobil, Shell/dsl 🍽 China Dragon, Crystal River Seafood, Domino's, Firehouse Subs, Hardee's, KFC, Krystal, McDonald's, Pier 6, Pizza Hut, Subway, Taco Bell, Waffle House, Wendy's, Woody's BBQ, Zaxby's 🏨 Motel 6 🅾 🅷, $General, $Tree, Advance Parts, AutoZone, Save-A-Lot Foods, USPO, Verizon, vet, Walgreens, Winn-Dixie, S 🅶 Exxon/dsl, RaceWay/dsl 🍽 Burger King, China Buffet, San Jose Mexican 🏨 EconoLodge, Travelodge
333	rd 125, Glen Saint Mary, N 🅶 Citgo/dsl/e85
327	rd 229, to Raiford, Sanderson
324	US 90, to Olustee, Sanderson, S 🅶 Mobil/dsl, Osceola NF, to Olustee Bfd
318mm	🆁🆂 both lanes, 24hr security, full ♿ facilities, litter barrels, petwalk, 🚰, 🏧, vending
303	US 441, Lake City, N 🅶 Chevron/dsl 🅾 Lake City Camping (1mi), Lake City RV Resort, S 🅶 Shell/dsl, Sunoco/dsl 🍽 Huddle House 🏨 Days Inn 🅾 🅷
301	US 41, to Lake City, N 🅶 Marathon/Busy Bee/dsl 🅾 to Stephen Foster Ctr, S 🅾 🅷
296b a	I-75, N to Valdosta, S to Tampa
294mm	🆁🆂 both lanes, 24hr security, full ♿ facilities, litter barrels, petwalk, 🚰, 🏧, vending
292	rd 137, to Wellborn
283	US 129, to Live Oak, N 🅶 Busy Bee/Burger King/Dunkin'/dsl/24hr, to Boys Ranch, S 🅶 BP, Chevron/dsl, Exxon/dsl, Murphy USA/dsl, Shell/dsl 🍽 China Buffet, Hungry Howie's, Krystal, McDonald's, Subway, Taco Bell, Waffle House, Wendy's, Zaxby's 🏨 EconoLodge, Holiday Inn Express, Quality Inn 🅾 🅷, $Tree, GNC, Lowe's, Verizon, Walmart
275	US 90, Live Oak, N 🅾 to Suwannee River SP, S 🅾 🅷
271mm	truck insp sta both lanes
269mm	Suwannee River
265mm	🆁🆂 both lanes, 24hr security, full ♿ facilities, litter barrels, petwalk, 🚰, 🏧, vending
264mm	weigh sta both lanes
262	rd 255, Lee, N 🅾 to Suwannee River SP, S 🅶 Jimmy's/Chevron/Red Onion Grill/dsl/scales/24hr/@, Loves/Arby's/dsl/scales/24hr
258	FL 53, N 🅶 Chevron/McDonald's/dsl, Mobil/DQ/Subway/Wendy's/dsl/scales/24hr 🍽 Denny's, Waffle House 🏨 Best Western, Days Inn, Super 8 🅾 🅷, S 🏨 Deerwood Inn 🅾 Jellystone Camping, Madison Camping
251	FL 14, to Madison, N 🅶 Mobil/Arby's/24hr 🅾 🅷
241	US 221, Greenville, N 🅶 Mobil/DQ
234mm	🆁🆂 both lanes, 24hr security, full ♿ facilities, litter barrels, petwalk, 🚰, 🏧
233	rd 257, Aucilla, N 🅶 Shell/dsl

= gas = food = lodging = other = rest stop   Copyright 2022 - The Next EXIT

INTERSTATE 10 Cont'd

Exit #	Services
225	US 19, to Monticello, N Camper's World Camping, S Chevron/McDonald's/dsl, Mobil/Arby's/dsl, Sunoco/dsl Days Inn, Super 8 A Stones Throw RV Park, KOA
217	FL 59, Lloyd, S BP/rest/dsl/scales/24hr, Shell/Subway/dsl EconoLodge
209b a	US 90, Tallahassee, N Staybridge Suites, S Circle K/dsl, Shell/Subway/dsl Eastern Chinese, Waffle House Best Western, Country Inn&Suites auto museum, Publix, Tallahassee RV Park
203	FL 61, US 319, Tallahassee, N BP/dsl, Shell/Circle K, Sunoco/dsl Baskin-Robbins/Dunkin', Bonefish Grill, Burger Bar, Chipotle, Far East Asian, Firehouse Subs, Five Guys, Hungry Howie's, Jimmy John's, McDonald's, Moe's SW Grill, Newk's Eatery, Panda Buffet, Panera Bread, Pepper's Cantina, Popeye's, Shogun Japanese, Smashburger, Sonny's BBQ, Starbucks, Subway, Taco Bell, Trader Joe's, Waffle House, Wendy's, Which Wich? $Tree, AT&T, Books-A-Million, CVS Drug, Discount Tire, Fresh Mkt Foods, GNC, Hobby Lobby, Petco, Publix, SteinMart, SuperLube, TJ Maxx, Walgreens, Walmart (3mi), S Citgo, Marathon/dsl Carrabba's, Chick-fil-A, McDonald's, Osaka Japanese, Outback Steaks, Steak'n Shake, Subway, Ted's MT Grill, TGIFriday's, TX Roadhouse, Village Inn, Zaxby's Courtyard, Extended Stay America, Hampton Inn, Hilton Garden, Holiday Inn Express, Mainstay Suites, Residence Inn , Advance Parts, Goodyear/auto, Home Depot, Infiniti, Office Depot, O'Reilly Parts, Petsmart, U-Haul, URGENT CARE
199	US 27, Tallahassee, N Chevron/dsl, Kangaroo/dsl, McKenzie/dsl Burger King, Domino's, McDonald's, Papa John's, Pizza Hut, Starbucks, Subway, Taco Bell, Waffle House Baymont Inn, Baymont Inn, Best Western, Country Inn&Suites, Fairfield Inn, Holiday Inn, Microtel, Quality Inn $General, Ace Hardware, Advance Parts, AutoZone, Big Oak RV Park (2mi), CVS Drug, Family$, USPO, vet, Walgreens, Walmart, Winn-Dixie, S Chevron/dsl, Shell, Shell/Circle K Arby's, Boston Mkt, Chick-fil-A, China Buffet, ChuckECheese, Cracker Barrel, Crystal River Seafood, Denny's, DQ, Dunkin', El Jalisco, Firehouse Subs, Golden Corral, Guthrie's, Hardee's, Hooters, IHOP, Kacey's Rest, Krispy Kreme, Little Caesar's, Longhorn Steaks, McDonald's, Melting Pot, Papa John's, Red Lobster, Sonic, Sonny's BBQ, Starbucks, Subway, Wendy's, Whataburger, Zaxby's EconoLodge, Howard Johnson, La Quinta, Motel 6, Red Roof Inn, Rodeway Inn, Suburban Hotel, Travelodge, Wingate Advance Parts, AT&T, AutoZone, Barnes&Noble, Belk, city park, CVS Drug, PepBoys, Publix, Ross, Staples, Sun Tire, Tuffy Auto, U-Haul, Verizon, vet, Walgreens
196	FL 263, Tallahassee, S Chevron/dsl, Inland/dsl, Murphy USA/dsl, Shell/dsl, Stop'n Save Gas Applebee's, DQ, Dunkin', Firehouse Subs, KFC, McDonald's, Sonic, Steak'n Shake, Subway, Taco Bell, Waffle House, Wendy's, Zaxby's Sleep Inn $Tree, Advance Parts, , AutoZone, Chrysler/Dodge/Jeep, Harley-Davidson, Home Depot, Hyundai, Lowe's, Mazda, Office Depot, Toyota, Verizon, Walgreens, Walmart
194mm	both lanes, 24hr security, full facilities, litter barrels, petwalk, , , vending
192	US 90, to Tallahassee, Quincy, N FLYING J/Denny's/dsl/LP/scales/24hr, BP Comfort Inn, Howard Johnson Camping World RV Ctr (2mi), S /Subway/dsl/scales/24hr Waffle House Best Western

Exit #	Services
181	FL 267, Quincy, 1 mi N Murphy USA/dsl Domino', Mayflower Chinese , Walmart, S BP/dsl, Citgo/d Hampton Inn, Holiday Inn Express, Parkway Inn, to Lak Talquin SF
174	FL 12, to Greensboro, N Marathon/dsl, Shell/Burger King/d
166	rd 270A, Chattahoochee, N to Lake Seminole, S Shel dsl to Torreya SP, Triple C RV Park (1mi)
161mm	both lanes, 24hr security, full facilities, litter barrels, pe walk, , , vending
160mm	Apalachicola River, central/eastern time zone
158	rd 286, Sneads, N Lake Seminole, to Three Rivers SP
155mm	weigh sta both lanes
152	FL 69, to Grand Ridge, Blountstown, N Exxon/dsl, Marathon/dsl
142	FL 71, to Marianna, Oakdale, N Murphy USA/dsl, /Arby's/dsl/scales/24hr Beef'O'Brady's, Burger King, Firehous Subs, Hong Kong Chinese, Pizza Hut, PoFolks, Ruby Tuesda San Marco's Mexican, Sonny's BBQ, Waffle House Comfo Inn, Days Inn, Econolodge, Fairfield Inn, Marianna Inn, Microte Quality Inn, Super 8 , $Tree, AT&T, Lowe's, to FL Cavern SP (8mi), Verizon, Walmart/Subway, S Chevron/dsl, TA/Piz Hut/Popeye's/Taco Bell/dsl/scales/24hr/@ Dickey's BBQ, D McDonald's Best Value Inn Dove Rest RV Park
136	FL 276, to Marianna, N to FL Caverns SP (8mi)
133mm	both lanes, 24hr security, full facilities, litter barrels, pe walk, ,
130	US 231, Cottondale, N Chevron, Sunoco/dsl Hardee's, Su way, S Loves/Chester's/McDonald's/dsl/scales/24hr/@
120	FL 77, to Panama City, Chipley, N Exxon/Burger King/Stud ey's, Marathon/dsl, Murphy USA/dsl, Shell/dsl Angel's B fet, Arby's, Cancun Mexican, Dunkin', Hardee's, Hungry Hov ie's, JinJin Chinese, KFC, McDonald's, Pizza Hut, Sonic, Subwa Waffle House, Wendy's Comfort Inn, Days Inn/rest., Exec tive Inn, Quality Inn, Super 8 , $General, $Tree, Advan Parts, Brickyard Mkt, NAPA, O'Reilly Parts, Verizon, Walma S Falling Water SP
112	FL 79, Bonifay, N Chevron, Shell/dsl, Tom Thumb/ Burger King, Cancun Mexican, Castaway Cafe, Ha ee's, Hungry Howie, McDonald's, Pizza Hut, Subway, Waf House Bonifay Inn, Holiday Inn Express, Tivoli Inn FL Springs RV Camping, Fred's, S Panama City Beach
104	rd 279, Caryville
96	FL 81, Ponce de Leon, N $General, to Ponce de Leon S Vortex Spring Camping (5mi), S both lanes, full faciliti , , litter barrels, petwalk, 24hr security Shell/dsl, noco, Sunoco/Subway/dsl Ponce de Leon Motel
85	US 331, De Funiak Springs, N Murphy USA/dsl, Sunoc dsl Arby's, Beef O'Brady's, Burger King, Hungry Howi McLain's Steaks, Pizza Hut, Sonic, Subway, Taco Bell, Wa House Econolodge, Regency Inn, Sundown Inn, Su 8 $General, $Tree, AT&T, Buick/Chevrolet, Lowe's, Veriz Walgreens, Walmart, winery, Winn-Dixie, S Sunoco, Su co/dsl, Sunoco/dsl KFC, McDonald's, Whataburger B Western
70	FL 285, to Ft Walton Bch, Eglin AFB, N Loves/ Donald's/Subway/dsl/scales24hr, RaceWay/dsl Sleep I-10 Truck Ctr, S Econolodge Dixie RV Ctr
60mm	both lanes, 24hr security, full facilities, litter barrels, p walk, , , vending
56	FL 85, Crestview, Eglin AFB, N BP/dsl, Mobil/Chester's/ Applebee's, Beef O'Brady's, Burger King, Capt D's, Ch 1, Dunkin', Firehouse Subs, Golden Asian, Hungry Howi

TALLAHASSEE

QUINCY

QUINCY

CHIPLEY

CRESTVIEW

FL

▲E INTERSTATE 10 Cont'd

CRESTVIEW

56 Continued
Hunon Chinese, Krystal, Lenny's Subs, McDonald's, Mia's Italian, Panera Bread, Papa Murphy's, Ryan's, Sonic, Starbucks, Taco Bell 🛏 Country Inn&Suites, EconoLodge ⊙ 🅷, $General, Advance Parts, AT&T, AutoZone, BigLots, GNC, Lowe's, Publix, Staples, URGENT CARE, Verizon, Walgreens, Walmart, **S** 🗔 Exxon/dsl, Tom Thumb/dsl 🍴 Arby's, Cracker Barrel, Hardee's, Hooters, LaRumba Mexican, Waffle House, Wendy's, Whataburger, Zaxby's 🛏 Baymont Inn, Best Value Inn, Comfort Inn, Holiday Inn Express, Quality Inn, Super 8 ⊙ Buick/GMC, Chevrolet, Chrysler/Dodge/Jeep, Ford, Stay Suites

45 rd 189, to US 90, Holt, **N** 🗔 Marathon (1mi) ⊙ Eagle's Landing RV Park, to Blackwater River SP, **S** ⊙ River's Edge RV Park (1mi)

31 FL 87, to Ft Walton Beach, Milton, **N** 🗔 Exxon/dsl 🍴 Waffle House 🛏 Holiday Inn Express ⊙ Blackwater River SP, KOA, **S** 🗔 BP, Shell/dsl 🛏 Blackwater Inn, Milton Inn

31mm Rs both lanes, 24hr security, full 🚻 facilities, litter barrels, petwalk, 🅲, 🔀

28 rd 89, Milton, **N** ⊙ 🅷

27mm Blackwater River

26 rd 191, Bagdad, Milton, **N** 🗔 Shell/Circle K/dsl ⊙ 🅷, $General, **S** 🗔 Chevron/DQ/Stuckey's ⊙ Pelican Palms RV Park

22 N FL 281, Avalon Blvd, **N** 🗔 RaceWay/dsl, Tom Thumb 🍴 McDonald's, **S** 🗔 Shell/Circle K/Subway/dsl 🍴 Waffle House 🛏 Red Roof Inn ⊙ Avalon Landing RV Park (3mi)

18mm Escambia Bay

17 US 90, Pensacola, **N** 🗔 Marathon/dsl, **S** 🗔 Exxon/DQ 🛏 Quality Inn/rest.

PENSACOLA

13 FL 291, to US 90, Pensacola, **N** 🗔 Exxon, Shell/dsl 🍴 Arby's, Capt D's, Denny's, La Hacienda Mexican, McDonald's, Santino's Cafe, Subway, Taco Bell, Waffle House 🛏 Comfort Inn, Days Inn, Holiday Inn, La Quinta ⊙ 🅷, $Tree, CVS Drug, Ross, U-Haul, Walgreens, **S** 🍴 Cheddar's, ChuckECheese, Dickey's BBQ, Egg&I Cafe, Fazoli's, HoneyBaked Ham, Jimmy John's, Moe's SW, O'Charley's, Shrimp Basket Rest, TX Roadhouse, Waffle House, Wendy's, Whataburger 🛏 Baymont Inn, Best Value Inn, Courtyard, Econolodge, Extended Stay America, Fairfield Inn, Hampton Inn, Mainstay Suites, Red Roof Inn, SpringHill Suites, Super 6 Inn, TownePlace Suites ⊙ $General, Big Lots, Books-A-Million, Firestone/auto, GNC, Hobby Lobby, JC Penney, Jo-Ann Fabrics, Mr Transmission, PepBoys, Petsmart, TJ Maxx, Tuesday Morning, U-Haul, Verizon

12 I-110, to Pensacola, Hist Dist, Islands Nat Seashore

10b a US 29, Pensacola, **N** 🗔 Kangaroo/dsl/scales, Murphy USA/dsl 🍴 Church's, Hardee's, Ryan's, Sonic ⊙ $Tree, Advance Parts, AT&T, AutoZone, Carpenter's RV Ctr, GNC, Office Depot, O'Reilly Parts, Tires+, Walmart, **0-2 mi S** 🗔 RaceWay/dsl, Shell/Circle K, Tom Thumb 🍴 3D Burgers, Capt D's, IHOP, McDonald's, Pizza Hut, Smokey's BBQ, Subway, Waffle House, Wendy's, Whataburger 🛏 Best Value Inn, Executive Inn, Key West Inn, Luxury Suites, Magnuson Hotel, Motel 6, Pensacola Inn ⊙ $General, Buick/Cadillac/GMC, Chevrolet, Chrysler/Dodge/Jeep, Ford, funpark, Harley-Davidson, Honda, Hyundai, Kia, Lincoln, Mazda, NAPA Autocare, Nissan, Subaru, Toyota

7b a Fl 297, Pine Forest Rd, **N** 🗔 Chevron 🍴 Beef'O'Brady's, Starbucks, Wendy's 🛏 Best Western, Garden Inn, Quality Inn, Woodspring Suites ⊙ Publix, transmissions, Walmart Mkt, **S** 🗔 Raceway/dsl, Shell, Tom Thumb 🍴 Burger King, Cracker Barrel, Hardee's, McDonald's, Ruby Tuesday, Sonny's BBQ, Subway, Waffle House, Wayne's Diner 🛏 Country Inn&Suites, Days Inn, Econolodge, Hampton Inn, Holiday Inn Express, Red Roof Inn ⊙ Big Lagoon SRA (12mi)

5 US 90 A, **N** 🗔 Shell/Circle K, Shell/dsl 🍴 Beef'O Brady's, Hot Head Burrito, Jersey Mike's, Ollie's Grill, Papa Murphy's, Starbucks, Wendy's ⊙ AT&T, Publix/gas, Verizon, Walgreens, **S** ⊙ Leisure Lakes Camping

4mm Welcome Ctr eb, 24hr security, full 🚻 facilities, info, litter barrels, petwalk, 🅲, 🔀, vending, wi-fi

3mm weigh sta both lanes

1mm inspection sta eb

0mm Florida/Alabama state line, Perdido River

▲N INTERSTATE 75

Exit #	Services
471mm	Florida/Georgia state line
469mm	Welcome Ctr sb, full 🚻 facilities, info, litter barrels, petwalk, 🅲, 🔀, vending
467	FL 143, Jennings, **W** 🗔 Marathon/dsl 🛏 N Florida Inn ⊙ fireworks, Jennings Camping
460	FL 6, Jasper, **E** 🗔 Indian River Fruit/gas, Marathon/Burger King/dsl, Marathon/Huddle House/dsl 🛏 Budget Inn, **W** 🗔 Pilot/Subway/dsl/scales/24hr, Shell/dsl, Sunoco/dsl 🛏 American Inn ⊙ Suwanee River SP
451	US 129, Jasper, Live Oak, **E** 🗔 Love's/Arby's/dsl/scales/24hr, Mobil/DQ/Subway/dsl, **W** 🗔 Marathon/Wendy's/dsl ⊙ Suwanee Music Park (4mi), to FL Boys Ranch
448mm	weigh sta both lanes
446mm	insp sta both lanes
443mm	Historic Suwanee River
439	to FL 136, White Springs, Live Oak, **E** 🗔 Gate/dsl/e-85, Shell/dsl 🍴 McDonald's ⊙ Suwanee RV Camping (4mi), to S Foster Ctr, **W** 🛏 Best Value Inn
435	I-10, E to Jacksonville, W to Tallahassee
427	US 90, to Live Oak, Lake City, **E** 🗔 Chevron/dsl, Exxon, Murphy USA/dsl, Shell/dsl, Tesla EVC 🍴 Arby's, Bojangles, Buffalo Wild Wings, Burger King, Cedar River Seafood, Chick-fil-A, CiCi's, Cracker Barrel, Domino's, DQ, Dunkin', El Potro, Elliano's Coffee, Firehouse Subs, Five Guys, Gondolier Italian, Hardee's, IHOP, Jersey Mike's, Krystal, Longhorn Steaks, McDonald's, Moe's SW Grill, Neapolitan Pizza, Ole Times Buffet, Olive Garden, Panda Express, Panera Bread, Papa John's, Red Lobster, Ruby Tuesday, Sonny's BBQ, Starbucks, Steak'n Shake, Subway, Taco Bell, TX Roadhouse, Waffle House, Wendy's, Zaxby's 🛏 Best Inn, Cypress Inn, Days Inn, Driftwood Inn, Holiday Inn, Quality Inn, Ramada Ltd, Rodeway Inn ⊙ 🅷, $Tree, Advance Parts, Aldi Foods, AT&T, AutoZone, Belk, BigLots, CVS Drug, Discount Tire, Ford/Lincoln, Hobby Lobby, Home Depot, Inn&Out RV Park, JC Penney, Kia, Lowe's, Michael's, Petsmart, Publix, Tire Kingdom, TireMart, TJ Maxx, Toyota, Verizon, Walgreens,

LAKE CITY

⬆N INTERSTATE 75 Cont'd

LAKE CITY

427 Continued
Walmart, W 🅿 Chevron/dsl, Circle K/dsl, Marathon/Subway 🍴 Bob Evans, China One, Denny's, Salsa's Mexican, Waffle House 🛏 Baymont Inn, Best Value Inn, Best Western+, Comfort Suites, EconoLodge, Fairfield Inn, Gateway Inn, Hampton Inn, Home 2 Suites, Travelodge, Tru Hilton ⭕ $General, Cadillac/Chevrolet, Camping World RV Ctr, Chrysler/Dodge/Jeep, Family$, Harvey's Foods, Honda, Nissan, vet

423 FL 47, to Ft White, Lake City, E 🅿 Shell/dsl ⭕ Mack/Volvo Trucks, W 🅿 Inland/dsl, Stop-N-Go/USPO 🍴 Little Caesar's, Subway, Wendy's 🛏 Super 8 ⭕ $General, Casey Jones RV Park, Freightliner

414 US 41, US 441, to Lake City, High Springs, E 🅿 Chevron/dsl, Exxon, Pitstop 🛏 Traveler's Inn ⭕ $General, W 🅿 Marathon/dsl, Shell/Wendy's/dsl 🍴 Country Skillet, Subway ⭕ antiques, to O'Leno SP (5 mi)

413mm ℞ˢ both lanes, 24hr security, full ♿ facilities, litter barrels, pet-walk, ⎗, 🚮, vending

409mm Santa Fe River

404 rd 236, to High Springs, E 🅿 Chevron/fruits/gifts, Citgo/dsl, Marathon, W ⭕ High Springs Camping

399 US 441, to High Sprs, Alachua, E 🅿 BP, Kangaroo 🍴 Domino's, El Toro, McDonald's, Mi Apa Latin Cafe, Moe's SW Grill, NY Pizza, Pizza Hut, Sonny's BBQ, Subway, Taco Bell, Waffle House 🛏 EconoLodge, Quality Inn ⭕ $General, Advance Parts, AT&T, AutoZone, CVS Drug, Family$, Hitchcock's Foods, Lowe's, Traveler's Campground (1mi), Verizon, vet, Walgreens, W 🅿 Exxon/Kangeroo, Kangaroo/Wendy's, Mobil/Dunkin'/dsl, RaceWay/dsl 🍴 Hungry Howie's, Zaxby's 🛏 Best Value Inn, Royal Inn ⭕ Publix

390 FL 222, to Gainesville, E 🅿 Circle K/Subway/dsl, Marathon/McDonald's/dsl, Valero/dsl 🍴 Burger King, Chan's Chinese, Pomodoro Cafe, Sonny's BBQ, Wendy's ⭕ Publix, Walgreens, W 🅿 Shell/DQ/Dunkin'/dsl 🍴 Wahoo Grill 🛏 Best Western ⭕ Harley-Davidson, vet

387 FL 26, to Newberry, Gainesville, E 🅿 Chevron/dsl, Shell/dsl, Sunoco 🍴 BJ's Rest., Bono's BBQ, Boston Mkt, Buffalo Wild Wings, Burger King, Dunkin', FoodCourt, HoneyBaked Ham, Jason's Deli, McAlister's Deli, McDonald's, Ocean Buffet, Panda Express, Panera Bread, Perkins, Red Lobster, Red Robin, Ruby Tuesday, Starbucks, Subway, Wendy's 🛏 La Quinta ⭕ 🇭, AT&T, Belk, Books-A-Million, Dillard's, Hobby Lobby, JC Penney, Office Depot, PetCo, to UF, Verizon, W 🅿 BP, Chevron/dsl, Exxon/dsl, Marathon/dsl 🍴 Applebee's, Hardee's, Krystal, Moe's SW Grill, Napolatanos Rest., Peppers Mexican, Pizza Hut, Taco Bell, Waffle House 🛏 Baymont Inn, Best Value Inn, Days Inn, EconoLodge, TownePlace Suites ⭕ $Tree, Advance Parts, Goodyear/auto, Home Depot, PepBoys, Publix, tires/repair, TJ Maxx, vet, Walgreens

GAINESVILLE

384 FL 24, to Archer, Gainesville, E 🅿 Exxon/dsl, Shell, Valero/dsl 🍴 Arby's, Asian Wok, Blaze Pizza, BoneFish Grill, Burger King, BurgerFi, Carrabba's, Chick-fil-A, Chili's, Chipotle Mexican, Chuy's Mexican, CiCi's Pizza, Coldstone, Domino's, DQ, Firehouse Subs, Five Guys, Gainesville Alehouse, Hungry Howie's, KFC, McAlister's Deli, McDonald's, Moe's SW Grill, Olive Garden, Outback Steaks, Panda Express, Panera Bread, Panera Bread, Papa John's, Pizza Hut, Pollo Tropical, Sonny's BBQ, Starbucks, Steak'n Shake, Subway, Taco Bell, TGIFriday's, Tijuana Flats, TX Roadhouse, Waffle House, Wendy's, Wing House, Zaxby's, Zoe's Kitchen 🛏 Comfort Inn, Courtyard, Extended Stay America, Hampton Inn, Hilton Garden, Homewood Suites, Motel 6, Red Roof Inn, Residence Inn, Sleep Inn, SpringHill Suites,

384 Continued
Super 8, The Lodge ⭕ $Tree, AT&T, AutoZone, Best Buy, CVS Drug, Discount Tire, Firestone/auto, GNC, Jo-Ann, Kohl's, Lowe's, Michael's, Old Navy, Petsmart, Publix, Publix, Ross, Target, Trader Joe's, Tuesday Morning, Verizon, Walgreens, Walmart, W 🅿 Marathon/dsl 🍴 Cracker Barrel 🛏 Country Inn&Suites, Holiday Inn Express ⭕ to Bear Museum

382 FL 121, to Williston, Gainesville, E 🅿 Marathon/dsl, Mobil/dsl 🍴 First Wok, Little Caesar's, McDonald's, Subway ⭕ Publix, USPO, W 🅿 Chevron/dsl, Circle K/dsl, Shell/dsl 🍴 43rd Deli 🛏 Quality Inn, Rodeway Inn, Woodspring Suites ⭕ Fred Bear Museum

381mm ℞ˢ both lanes, 24hr security, full ♿ facilities, litter barrels, pet-walk, ⎗, 🚮, vending

374 rd 234, Micanopy, E 🅿 BP, Chevron/dsl ⭕ antiques, to Paynes Prairie SP, W 🛏 Micanopy Inn ⭕ repair

368 rd 318, Orange Lake, E 🍴 Jim's/BBQ, Petro/BP/Iron Skillet/dsl/scales/24hr/@ 🍴 Wendy's ⭕ Grand Lake RV Park (3mi), W ⭕ Ocala N RV Camping

OCALA

358 FL 326, E 🅿 Marathon/McDonald's/dsl, 🄿🄸🄻🄾🅃/Arby's/dsl/scales/24hr, 🄿🄸🄻🄾🅃/Wendy's/dsl/scales/24hr, Sunoco/FL Citrus Ctr/dsl ⭕ auto/truck repair, Freightliner, W 🅿 ♥Love's Chester's/Subway/dsl/scales/24hr, Shell/Circle K/dsl 🍴 DQ

354 US 27, to Silver Springs, Ocala, E 🅿 Marathon/dsl, RaceTrac/dsl 🍴 Burger King, Rascal's BBQ 🛏 Golden Palms Inn, W 🅿 BP/dsl, Chevron/dsl, Shell/dsl 🍴 Blanca's Cafe, China Taste, Ci Ci's, Darrell's Diner, McDonald's, Pizza Hut, Roma Italian, Subway 🛏 Budget Host, Comfort Suites, Days Inn, Howard Johnson, Motel 6 ⭕ $General, $Tree, AT&T, Family$, GNC, Nelson's Trailers, Oaktree Village Camping, Publix, Walgreens, Winn-Dixie

352 FL 40, to Silver Springs, Ocala, E 🅿 Chevron/dsl, Mobil/Circle K/dsl, RaceTrac/dsl, Sunoco/dsl, Valero/dsl 🍴 Dunkin' McDonald's, Subway, Taco Bell, Waffle House, Wendy's, Zaxby's 🛏 Days Inn/café, Motor Inn/RV ⭕ Family$, to Silver River SP (8mi), W 🅿 Shell/dsl 🍴 Burger King, Denny's, Waffle House 🛏 Red Roof Inn, Super 8 ⭕ Holiday Trav-L Park

350 FL 200, to Hernando, Ocala, 0-2 mi E 🅿 BP/dsl, Citgo/dsl, Texaco/dsl 🍴 Applebee's, Arby's, Black Bear Smokehouse, Bob Evans, Boston Mkt, Burger King, Carrabba's, Checkers, Chick-fil-A, Chili's, Chipotle, ChuckECheese, Cody's Roadhouse, Coldstone, Crisper's, Domino's, El Toreo Mexican, Firehouse Subs, Five Guys, Freddy's, Golden Corral, Hardee's, Hungry Howie's, Jersey Mike's, Jimmy John's, Krystal, Lee's Chicken, Logan Roadhouse, Maddio's Pizza, McDonald's, Moe's SW Grill, Ocean Buffet, Olive Garden, Outback Steaks, Panda Express, Panera Bread, Papa John's, Papa Murphy's, PDQ Grill, Pizza Hut, Red Lobster, Ruby Tuesday, Smoothie King, Sonic, Sonny's BBQ, Starbucks, Stevie B's Pizza, Subway, Taco Bell, Wendy's, Yummy House, Zaxby's 🛏 Country Inn&Suites, Hilton, La Quinta, Quality Inn ⭕ 🇭, $Tree, Acura, Advance Parts, Aldi Foods, Belk, Best Buy, Chevrolet, CVS Drug, Discount Tire, Goodyear/auto, Hobby Lobby, Home Depot, Honda, Hyundai, JC Penney, Jo-Ann Fabrics, Kia, Lowe's, Macy's, Mazda, Michael's, Nissan, Office Depot, O'Reilly Parts, PepBoys, Petsmart, Ross, Staples, Target, Tire Kingdom, TJ Maxx, Toyota, Tuesday Morning, Tuffy Auto, URGENT CARE, Verizon, Walgreens, Walmart, W 🅿 Marathon, RaceTrac/dsl, Tesla EVC, Valero/Kangaroo, WaWa/dsl 🍴 Bonefish Grill, Burger King, Cheddar's, Cracker Barrel, Crazy Cucumber, Dunkin', Edo Japanese, Gator's Dockside, KFC, La Margaritas, McAlister's Deli, McDonald's, Mimi's Cafe, Panera Bread, Starbucks, Steak'n Shake, Tijuana Flats, Waffle House, Yamato Japanese 🛏 Best Western, Courtyard, Fairfield Inn

⬆N INTERSTATE 75 Cont'd

350	Continued
	Hampton Inn, Holiday Inn, Homewood Suites, Residence Inn ⊙ **H**, AT&T, Barnes&Noble, BMW, Buick/GMC, Cadillac, Dick's, Dillard's, Kohl's, Ocala RV Park, Old Navy, PetCo, Porsche, Sam's Club/gas, Tires+, Verizon, vet, VW, Walgreens
346mm	Rs both lanes, 24hr security, full ♿ facilities, litter barrels, petwalk, 🅒, 🚮, vending
341	rd 484, to Belleview, **E** 🍴 Exxon/dsl, Marathon/fruit, RaceTrac/dsl, Shell/dsl 🍴 Baskin-Robbins/Dunkin', Cracker Barrel, KFC/Taco Bell, Sonny's BBQ, Zaxby's 🏠 Microtel, Sleep Inn ⊙ drag racing museum, FL Citrus Ctr, **W** 📁Pilot DQ/Wendy's/dsl/scales/24hr 🍴 McDonald's, Subway, Waffle House 🏠 Hampton Inn ⊙ Ocala Sun RV Resort, outlets
338mm	weigh sta both lanes
329	FL 44, to Inverness, Wildwood, **E** 🍴 Marathon/dsl, 📁Pilot Steak'n Shake/dsl/scales/24hr, Sunoco 🍴 Burger King, McDonald's, Waffle House, Wendy's ⊙ FL Citrus Ctr, KOA, **W** 🍴 Citgo/dsl/repair/24hr, 📁Pilot/dsl/scales/24hr, TA/BP/Pizza Hut/Popeye's/Subway/dsl/scales/24hr/@ 🍴 IHOP, KFC 🏠 Budget Inn, Days Inn, Motel 6 ⊙ truck repair, truckwash
328	FL TPK (from sb), to Orlando
321	rd 470, to Sumterville, Lake Panasoffkee, **E** 🍴 Spirit/deli/dsl/scales/24hr ⊙ Coleman Correctional, **W** 🍴 Chevron/Circle K/dsl, Mobil/Hardee's/Subway/dsl ⊙ Countryside RV Park, KOA
314	FL 48, to Bushnell, **E** 🍴 Citgo, Murphy USA/dsl, Shell/Circle K/Subway 🍴 Hong Kong Chinese, KFC/Taco Bell, Little Caesar's, McDonald's, Wendy's 🏠 Bushnell Inn ⊙ $Tree, AutoZone, BlueBerry Hill RV Camp, Red Oaks Camp (1mi), to Dade Bfd HS, Verizon, vet, Walmart, **W** 🍴 ❤Loves/Arby's/dsl/scales/24hr, Sunoco/dsl 🍴 Beef'O'Brady's, Sonny's BBQ 🏠 Microtel ⊙ Flagship RV Ctr
309	rd 476, to Webster, **E** ⊙ Breezy Oaks RV Park (1mi), Sumter Oaks RV Park (1mi)
307mm	Rs both lanes, 24hr security, coffee, full ♿ facilities, litter barrels, petwalk, 🅒, 🚮, vending
301	US 98, FL 50, to Dade City, **E** 🍴 RaceTrac/dsl 🍴 Beef'O'Brady's, Cracker Barrel, Dunkin', McDonald's, Monticello's Pizzaria, Subway, Taco Bell, Waffle House, Wendy's 🏠 Days Inn, Holiday Inn Express ⊙ $General, Advance Parts, Winn-Dixie, **W** 🍴 Burger King 🏠 Hampton Inn, Microtel, Quality Inn ⊙ **H**
293	rd 41, to Dade City, **E** 🍴 Citgo (2mi) ⊙ to Sertoma Youth Ranch, **W** ⊙ Travelers Rest Resort RV Park (3mi)
285	FL 52, to Dade City, New Port Richey, **E** 🍴 ✈FLYING J/Denny's/dsl/LP/scales/24hr ⊙ **H**, Blue Beacon
279	FL 54, to Land O' Lakes, Zephyrhills, **E** 🍴 Speedway/Dunkin'/dsl 🍴 Applebee's, Burger King, Chili's, China Wok, City Grill, Gonna China, Las Vallartas, Papa's John's, Pizza Hut/Taco Bell, Sonny's BBQ, Subway, Waffle House, Wendy's ⊙ Ace Hardware, Advance Parts, Beall's, Fiat, Ford, Happy Days RV Camping (9mi), Kia, Leisure Days RV Park (7mi), Nissan, Publix, Ralph's RV Camping (7mi), to Hillsborough River SP (18mi), Toyota, Walgreens, Walmart, **W** 🍴 7-11, Marathon, Mobil/Dunkin', Shell/Circle K/dsl 🍴 Beef'O'Brady's, ChuckeCheese, Cody's Roadhouse, Cracker Barrel, DQ, Hardee's, Hungry Howie's, Marco's Pizza, McDonald's, Outback Steaks, Winghouse 🏠 Best Western, EconoLodge, Rodeway Inn, Sleep Inn ⊙ $General, $Tree, Advance Parts, Best Buy, Chevrolet, CVS Drug, Dick's, GNC, Goodyear/auto, Honda, Hyundai, Mazda, Michael's, Old Navy, Petsmart, Quail Run RV Camping, Ross, Tire Kingdom, TJ Maxx, Tuffy Auto, URGENT CARE, Verizon, Winn Dixie

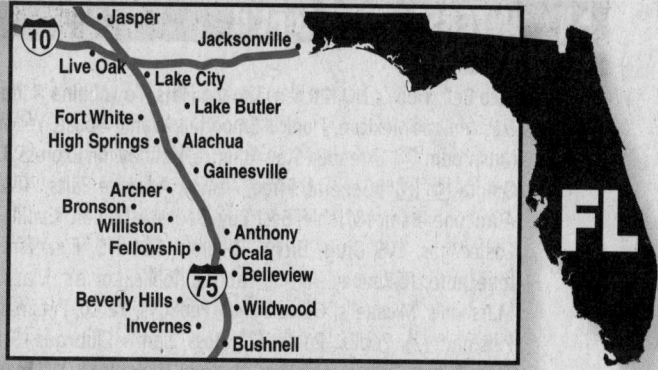

277mm	Rs both lanes, 24hr security, full ♿ facilities, litter barrels, petwalk, 🅒, 🚮, vending
275	FL 56, Land O Lakes, Tarpon Springs, **E** 🍴 BP/Dunkin'/dsl, Gate/dsl, RaceTrac/dsl 🍴 Buffalo Wild Wings, TX Roadhouse 🏠 Hampton Inn, Holiday Inn Express ⊙ Mercedes, Mini, Publix (2mi), vet, **W** 🍴 Shell/dsl 🍴 Abuelo's, Culver's ⊙ Tampa Outlets/famous brands, Walgreens
274	I-275 (from sb), to Tampa, St Petersburg
270	rd 581, Bruce B Downs Blvd, **E** 🍴 7-11, Mobil, Shell/Circle K/Taco Bell/dsl, Speedway/dsl 🍴 Baskin-Robbins/Dunkin', Boston Mkt, Chick-fil-A, Chili's, Chipotle, Coldstone, DQ, Glory Days Grill, Jimmy John's, Kobe Japanese, Kobe Japanese, Liang's Asian Bistro, McDonald's, Moe's SW Grill, Panera Bread, Papa John's, Pizza Hut, Ruby Tuesday, Senor T's, Starbucks, Steak'n Shake, Subway, TGIFriday's, Tijuana Flats, Wendy's 🏠 Holiday Inn Express, La Quinta ⊙ AT&T, Best Buy, CVS Drug, GNC, Home Depot, Kauffman Tire, Michael's, Publix, Tires+, Verizon, vet, Walgreens, Walmart/Subway, **W** 🍴 7-11 🍴 McDonald's, Olive Garden, Red Lobster, Stonewood Grill 🏠 SpringHill Suites ⊙ $Tree, BJ's Whse/Subway/gas, CVS Drug, Jo-Ann Fabrics, Lowe's, Petsmart, Ross, Staples, USPO
266	rd 582A, Fletcher Ave, **W** 🍴 Shell/Circle K/dsl 🍴 Baskin-Robbins/Dunkin', Bob Evans, Lenny's Subs, Starbucks, Wendy's 🏠 Courtyard, Extended Stay America, Fairfield Inn, Hampton Inn, Hilton Garden, Holiday Inn Express, Residence Inn, Sleep Inn, Sleep Inn ⊙ **H**
265	FL 582, Fowler Ave, Temple Terrace, **E** ⊙ flea mkt, Happy Traveler RV Park, **W** 🍴 Marathon, Sunoco, Value/dsl 🍴 IHOP, Marco's Pizza 🏠 Ramada Inn ⊙ to Busch Gardens, to USF
261	I-4, W to Tampa, E to Orlando
260b a	FL 574, to Mango, Tampa, **E** 🍴 Citgo/dsl, Mobil, Shell/Circle K/Subway 🍴 Baskin-Robbins/Dunkin', China Wok, Domino's, Waffle House ⊙ Walgreens, Winn Dixie, **W** 🍴 Citgo, Mobil 🏠 Quality Inn, Residence Inn, Sheraton, Staybridge Suites ⊙ Family$
257	FL 60, Brandon, **E** 🍴 Mobil (2), Mobil/dsl, Shell/Circle K, Tesla EVC, WaWa/dsl 🍴 Bahama Breeze, Boston Mkt, Brandon Ale House, Buffalo Wild Wings, Checkers, Cheddar's, Cheesecake Factory, Chick-fil-A, Chili's, Chipotle, ChuckECheese, Corner Bakery Cafe, Denny's, Dunkin', Firehouse Subs, Five Guys, Ford's Garage, Honeybaked Ham, Hungry Howie's, Jimmy John's, KFC, Kobe Japanese, Krispy Kreme, Little Caesar's, LJ Silver, Longhorn Steaks, Macaroni Grill, McDonald's, McDonald's (2), Mission BBQ, Moe's SW Grill, Olive Garden, Outback Steaks, Panda Express, Panera Bread, Papa John's, Popeye's, Portillo's, Qdoba, Red Lobster, Smokey Bones BBQ, Smoothie King, Starbucks, Steak'n Shake, Subway,

*(left margin vertical text: INVERNESS ... DADE CITY)*
TAMPA ... BRANDON

FL

⬆N INTERSTATE 75 Cont'd

257 Continued
Taco Bell, Tibby's NO Kitchen, Tijuana Flats, Tops China Buffet, Tres Amigos Mexican, Tropical Smoothie, Waffle House, Yellow Mushroom 🏨 Extended Stay America, Holiday Inn Express, La Quinta 🅾 🏥 $General, $Tree, Aamco, Advance Parts, AT&T, AutoZone, Barnes&Noble, Best Buy, Books-A-Million, Cadillac, Costco/gas, CVS Drug, Dick's, Dillard's, Family$, Fiat, Firestone/auto, JC Penney, Jo-Ann Fabrics, Kohl's, Lowe's, Macy's, Marshall's, Michael's, Office Depot, PepBoys, PetCo, Petsmart, Petsmart (2), Publix, Publix (2), Ross, Sam's Club/gas, Staples, Target, Tires+, TJ Maxx, Verizon, Walgreens, Walmart, **W** ⛽ Citgo/dsl, Marathon, Shell 🍴 Bob Evans, Burger King, Hooters, McDonald's, Sonny's BBQ, Subway, Sweet Tomatoes, Wendy's 🏨 Clarion, Comfort Suites, Country Inn&Suites, Courtyard, Embassy Suites, Fairfield Inn, Homewood Suites, La Quinta, Motel 6, Red Roof Inn, SpringHill Suites 🅾 Bass Pro Shops, Buick/GMC, Chevrolet, Chrysler/Dodge/Jeep, Ford, Harley-Davidson, Home Depot, Honda, Hyundai, Kia, Mazda, Nissan, Office Depot, Toyota, VW

256 FL 618 W (toll), to Tampa

254 US 301, Riverview, **E** ⛽ Thornton's/dsl, WaWa/dsl 🍴 Panda Express, Steak'n Shake 🅾 CVS Drug, Firestone/auto, Home Depot, Target, **W** ⛽ 7-11/dsl 🍴 China 1, Crazy Cafe, Dunkin', McDonald's, Pizza Hut, Smokin' Pig BBQ, Starbucks, Subway 🏨 Hilton Garden 🅾 GNC, Publix

250 Gibsonton Dr, Riverview, **E** ⛽ 7-11/dsl, RaceWay/dsl, Victory Lane/dsl, WaWa/dsl 🍴 Beef'O'Brady's, Burger King, DQ, Hungry Howie's, Jola Pizza, Little Caesar's, McDonald's, New China, Pizza Hut, Ruby Tuesday, Subway, Taco Bell, Wendy's 🅾 $Tree, Alafia River RV Resort, Beall's, CVS Drug, Family$, Hidden River RV Resort (4mi), Lowe's, Save-a-Lot, USPO, Walgreens, **W** ⛽ Murphy USA/dsl 🅾 Walmart/McDonald's

246 rd 672, Big Bend Rd, Apollo Bch, **E** ⛽ 7-11, Speedway/dsl, Thornton's/dsl 🍴 Applebee's, Beef'O'Brady's, Buffalo Wild Wings, Burger King, China Taste, DQ, East Coast Pizza, Firehouse Subs, First Watch Cafe, Little Caesar's, McDonald's, Mi Casa, Panera Bread, Papa John's, PDQ Cafe, Pita's, Pizza Hut, Popeye's, Qdoba, Sakura Japanese, Sonic, Starbucks, Subway, Taco Bell, Tijuana Flats, Village Inn, Wendy's 🅾 $General, $Tree, Ace Hardware, Advance Parts, AT&T, AutoZone, Beall's, Dunkin', Firestone/auto, GNC, Goodyear/auto, 🏥, Kauffman Tire, Marshall's, Publix, Sam's Club/gas, Tire Choice, Tuffy Auto, URGENT CARE, Verizon, vet, Walgreens, Walmart Mkt, WaWa/dsl, Winn Dixie, **W** ⛽ Shell/Circle K/Dunkin'/dsl

240b a FL 674, Sun City Ctr, Ruskin, **E** ⛽ Shell 🍴 Beef'O'Brady's, Bob Evans, BubbaQue's BBQ, Burger King, Checkers, China Star, Denny's, Dunkin', Hungry Howie's, Little Caesar's, Pizza Hut, Popeye's, Sonny's BBQ, Subway, Taco Bell, Wendy's 🏨 Comfort Inn 🅾 🏥, AT&T, Beall's, GNC, Home Depot, to Little Manatee River SP, Verizon, **W** ⛽ Circle K/dsl, Marathon/dsl, RaceTrac/dsl 🍴 China Wok, KFC, McDonald's 🏨 Ruskin Inn 🅾 $General, auto repair, BigLots, NAPA, SunLake RV Resort (1mi)

237mm Rs both lanes, 24hr security, full 🏨 facilities, litter barrels, petwalk, 🅲, 🚻, vending

229 rd 683, Moccasin Wallow Rd, to Parrish, **E** 🅾 Little Manatee Sprs SRA (10mi), **W** 🅾 Circle K, Fiesta Grove RV Park (3mi), Frog Creek RV Park (3mi), Terra Ceia RV Village (2mi), Winterset RV Park (3mi)

228 I-275 N, to St Petersburg

B R A D E N T O N

224 US 301, to Bradenton, Ellenton, **E** ⛽ Mobil, Shell/Circle K/dsl 🍴 Applebee's, Checkers, Chili's, Dunkin', Hungry Howie's, King's Wok, McDonald's, Peach's Rest., Ruby Tuesday, Subway, Taco Bell, Wendy's, Winghouse, Woody's River Grill 🏨 Hampton Inn, Sleep Inn 🅾 $General, $Tree, Ace Hardware, Beall's, Ellenton Outlets/famous brands, GNC, TJ Maxx, USPO, Walgreens, **W** ⛽ 🚂/dsl 🍴 Anna Maria's, Waffle House 🏨 Red Roof Inn, Super 8

223 Manatee River

220b a FL 64, to Zolfo Springs, Bradenton, **E** 🅾 Lake Manatee SRA, **W** ⛽ Citgo/dsl, Marathon/dsl, RaceTrac/dsl, Shell/Circle K/dsl 🍴 Burger King, Cracker Barrel, Dunkin', IHOP, KFC/LJ Silver, McDonald's, Sonny's BBQ, Starbucks, Subway, Waffle House, Wendy's 🏨 Best Value Inn, Best Western+, Days Inn, Motel 6, Quality Inn, Sunrise Inn 🅾 🏥, Encore RV Resort (1mi), Gerzeny's RV Ctr, Harley-Davidson, Toyota, Walmart

217b a FL 70, to Arcadia, **E** ⛽ Speedway/dsl 🍴 Burger King, Culver's, Hungry Howie's, Jersey Mike's, Menchie's, PDQ Cafe, TX Roadhouse, Wasabi Foods 🏨 Holiday Inn Express 🅾 GNC, Tire Choice/auto, Walmart/Subway, **W** ⛽ 7-11/dsl, Marathon, Dunkin'/dsl, RaceTrac/dsl, Shell/Circle K 🍴 Applebee's, Bob Evans, Bogey's Rest., Boneyard BBQ, Chick-fil-A, DQ, Freddy's, Gecko's Grill, Jimmy John's, LJ Silver/Taco Bell, McDonald's, Papa John's, Rice Bowl, Starbucks, Subway 🏨 Country Inn&Suites 🅾 $Tree, Beall's, CVS Drug, Lowe's, Pleasant Lake RV Resort, Publix, Tire Kingdom, Tires+, Tuffy Auto, Verizon

---

S A R A S O T A

213 University Parkway, to Sarasota, **E** ⛽ Mobil/Subway/dsl 🍴 Alamo Steaks, Broken Egg Cafe, Chili's, First Watch Cafe, Little Greek, Pizza Hut 🏨 Fairfield Inn, Holiday Inn, Hyatt Place 🅾 🏥, GNC, Publix, URGENT CARE, Walgreens, **W** ⛽ WaWa/dsl 🍴 Apollonian Mediterranean, Blaze Pizza, BoneFish Grill, Brio, Buffalo Wild Wings, BurgerFi, Capital Grille, Carrabba's, Cheesecake Factory, Chicken Kitchen, Chipotle Mexican, Daily Eats, Five Guys, Jason's Deli, Jersey Mike's Subs, Jimmy John's, Kumo Japanese, Moe's SW Grill, Newk's Eatery, Panera Bread, Pei Wei, Ruby Tuesday, Seasons Rest., Selmon's Rest., Starbucks, Stonewood Grill, Subway, Sweet Tomatoes, Tijuana Flats, Tom+Chee, Valentino's, Wendy's, Zoe's Kitchen 🏨 Homewood Suites, Courtyard, Hampton Inn 🅾 $Tree, AT&T, Best Buy, BJ's Whse/gas, CVS Drug, Dillard's, Fresh Mkt Foods, Home Depot, Jo-Ann Fabrics, Kohl's, Macy's, Marshall's, Michael's, Old Navy, PetCo, Ross, Staples, SteinMart, Target, TJ Maxx, to Ringling Museum, Verizon, vet, Whole Foods Mkt

210 FL 780, Fruitville Rd, Sarasota, **E** 🅾 Sun-N-Fun RV Park (1mi), **W** ⛽ Marathon/dsl, Mobil/7-11/dsl, RaceTrac/dsl, Shell/dsl 🍴 Applebee's, Bob Evans, Burger King, Checkers, Chick-fil-A, Chipotle, Culver's, Daruma Japanese, Dunkin', Firehouse Subs, Five Guys, Gecko's Grill, Gonzalez Asian, Jersey Mike's, Jets Pizza, Longhorn Steaks, McDonald's, Perkins, Ping's Chinese, Pollo Tropical, Rodizio Grill, Starbucks, Subway, Super Buffet, Taco Bell 🏨 Homewood Suites (2mi), La Quinta, Mainstay Suites, Sleep Inn 🅾 $Tree, Advance Parts, AT&T, CVS Drug, GNC, Lowe's, Office Depot, Publix, Sam's Club, Target, Tire Kingdom, Winn-Dixie

207 FL 758, Sarasota, **E** ⛽ RaceTrac/dsl, **W** ⛽ BP/Subway/dsl, Marathon/Dunkin'/Subway 🍴 Arby's, Chili's, Domino's, First Watch Cafe, Jimmy John's, Joey D's Eatery, McDonald's, Panera Bread, Pizza Hut, Sarasota Alehouse, Starbucks, Steak'n Shake, Taco Bell 🏨 Hampton Inn 🅾 🏥, Beall's, Home Depot, Publix, to Selby Botanical Gardens (8mi), Verizon, vet, Walgreens, Walmart

INTERSTATE 75 Cont'd

Exit #	Services
205	FL 72, to Arcadia, Sarasota, E ⊡ Myakka River SP (9mi), W 🅿 7-11/dsl, Marathon/Jimmy John's/dsl, Mobil/7-11/dsl, Shell/Circle K 🍴 Applebee's, Burger King, Chick-fil-A, Dunkin', Gecko's Grill, McDonald's, Starbucks, Subway, Waffle House, Wendy's 🛏 Days Inn, Holiday Inn Express, Quality Inn ⊡ Acura, Audi, Beall's, BMW, CVS Drug, Infiniti, Jaguar, Land Rover, Lexus, Mercedes/Smart, O'Reilly Parts, Publix, Tire Kingdom, Turtle Beach Camping (8mi), USPO, vet, Walgreens, Walmart Mkt, Windward Isle RV Park
200	FL 681 S (from sb), to Venice, Osprey, Gulf Bchs
195	Laurel Rd, Nokomis, E 🅿 Shell/USPO/dsl 🍴 Subway, W ⊡ Encore RV Park (2mi), Scherer SP (6mi)
193	Jaracanda Blvd, Venice, W 🅿 RaceTrac/dsl, Shell, Speedway/dsl, WaWa/dsl 🍴 BrewBurgers, China Taste, Cracker Barrel, Culver's, Dunkin', McDonald's, Ping's Chinese, Tomatillo's 🛏 Best Western+, Fairfield Inn, Holiday Inn Express ⊡ CVS Drug, Publix, Verizon
191	rd 777, Venice Rd, to Englewood, W ⊡ Encore RV Park (3mi), KOA (6mi), to Myakka SF (9mi)
182	rd 771, Sumter Blvd, to North Port
179	rd 779, Toledo Blade Blvd, North Port, W 🅿 Mobil/Subway/dsl, Shell//dsl 🍴 Burger King ⊡ Publix
170	rd 769, to Arcadia, Port Charlotte, E 🅿 7-11/dsl, Murphy USA/dsl, RaceTrac/dsl 🍴 Applebee's, Culver's 🛏 Hampton Inn, Holiday Inn Express ⊡ Lettuce Lake Camping (7mi), Riverside Camping (5mi), Walmart, W 🅿 Mobil/Circle K/DQ/dsl, Shell/Circle K/Dunkin', Speedway/dsl 🍴 Burger King, Cracker Barrel, Domino's, DQ, Golden China, Jets Pizza, McDonald's, Papa John's, Pizza Hut, Starbucks, Subway, Taco Bell, Top China, Waffle House, Wendy's 🛏 Country Inn&Suites, La Quinta, Sleep Inn ⊡ 🅷 $General, $Tree, Ace Hardware, Advance Parts, Beall's, CVS Drug, Publix, vet, Walgreens, Winn-Dixie
167	rd 776, Port Charlotte
164	US 17, Punta Gorda, Arcadia, E 🅿 7-11/dsl, RaceWay/dsl, Shell/Circle K/dsl 🍴 King House Chinese, RV camping, Subway, vet ⊡ $General, Winn-Dixie, W 🍴 Fisherman's Village Rest. (2mi) ⊡ 🅷
161	rd 768, Punta Gorda, W 🅿 Marathon/DQ, Murphy USA/dsl, 🚛/Arby's/dsl/scales/24hr, Shell/dsl 🍴 Burger King, McDonald's, Pizza Hut, Subway, Waffle House, Wendy's 🛏 Best Value Inn, Holiday Inn Express, Knights Inn ⊡ Encore RV Park (2mi), Walmart
160mm	weigh sta both lanes
158	rd 762, Tropical Gulf Acres, Tuckers Grade, E ⊡ Babcock-Wells Wildlife Mgt Area
143	FL 78, to Cape Coral, N Ft Myers, E 🅿 Marathon/dsl ⊡ Seminole Camping (1mi), Up River Camping, W 🅿 Loves/Subway/Wendy's/dsl/scales/24hr 🛏 Encore RV Camping
141	FL 80, Palm Bch Blvd, Ft Myers, E 🅿 Marathon, Sunoco/dsl 🍴 Cracker Barrel, Waffle House 🛏 Comfort Inn, Woodspring Suites, W 🅿 Gulf, Mobil, Speedway/Dunkin'/dsl 🍴 Domino's, Hardee's, KFC, Papa John's, Popeye's, Subway, Taco Bell ⊡ $General, BigLots, CVS Drug, Family$, North Trail RV Ctr, Save-A-Lot, USPO, vet
139	Luckett Rd, Ft Myers, E ⊡ Camping World RV Service/supplies, Cypress Woods RV Resort, W 🅿 🚛/Subway/dsl/scales/24hr/@
138	FL 82, to Lehigh Acres, Ft Myers, E 🅿 7-11/dsl 🛏 Hyatt Place, W 🅿 Mobil/dsl, RaceTrac/dsl, Sunoco/dsl ⊡ Peterbilt

136	FL 884, Colonial Blvd, Ft Myers, E 🅿 7-11/dsl 🍴 Bajio, Bella Mozzarella, Buffalo Wild Wings, Domino's, Firehouse Subs, Five Guys, McAlister's Deli, Moe's SW, Pizza Hut, Starbucks, Subway 🛏 Candlewood Suites, Holiday Inn Express ⊡ GNC, Home Depot, PetCo, Ross, Staples, Target, Winn Dixie, W 🅿 7-11/dsl, Marathon/dsl, Murphy USA/dsl, RaceTrac/dsl, Shell/Circle K/dsl 🍴 Applebee's, Bellacino's, Bob Evans, Burger King, Chick-fil-A, Chili's, China King, Chipotle, Culver's, Dickey's BBQ, Dunkin', First Watch Cafe, Golden Corral, LJ Silver/Taco Bell, McDonald's, Panda Express, Pollo Tropical, Steak'n Shake, Subway, Tijuana Flats, Tropical Cafe, TX Roadhouse 🛏 Woodspring Suites ⊡ 🅷 $Tree, AT&T, Beall's, BJ's Whse/gas, Hobby Lobby, Kohl's, Lowe's, Petsmart, Publix, Tire Choice/auto, Verizon, Walmart/McDonald's
131	rd 876, Daniels Pkwy, to Cape Coral, E 🆁🆂 both lanes, full ♿ facilities, 🅲 vending, 🪑 litter barrels, petwalk, 24hr security 🅿 RaceTrac/dsl, Shell/Subway/dsl 🍴 Cracker Barrel, Fat Katz 🛏 Comfort Inn, Dsys Inn, Sheraton ⊡ 🍴 Audi, CVS Drug, Harley Davidson, Porsche, W 🅿 7-11, RaceTrac/dsl, Shell/Circle K/dsl, Speedway/Dunkin'/dsl 🍴 Arby's, Beef'O'Brady's, Burger King, Denny's, DQ, La Grotia, McDonald's, New China, Papa John's, Sports Page Grill, Starbucks, Subway, Taco Bell, Two Meatballs Italian, Waffle House, Wendy's 🛏 Baymont Inn, Best Western, Hampton Inn, La Quinta, Quality Inn, SpringHill Suites, Travelodge ⊡ 🅷 AT&T, CVS Drug, Publix, Tire Choice/auto, Tuffy Auto, Walgreens
128	Alico Rd, San Carlos Park, E 🅿 7-11 🍴 Arby's, Aurelio's Pizza, BJ's Rest., BurgerFi, Carrabba's, Cheddar's, Chick-fil-A, Chili's, Chipotle, Connor's Steaks, Culver's, Famous Dave's BBQ, First Watch Cafe, Jason's Deli, Jimmy John's, Longhorn Steaks, McDonald's, Miller's Alehouse, Moe's SW Grill, Olive Garden, Outback Steaks, Panera Bread, PDQ Cafe, Pei Wei, PF Chang's, Pincher's Crabshack, Pita Pit, Pollo Tropical, Red Robin, Rita's, Starbucks, Subway, Taco Bell, Tijuana Flats, Twin Peaks, Zaxby's 🛏 Courtyard, Drury Inn, Hilton Garden, Holiday Inn, Homewood Suites, Residence Inn ⊡ $Tree, AT&T, Bass Pro Shop/Islamorada Fish Co, Belk, Best Buy, Costco/gas, Dick's, GNC, JC Penney, Jo-Ann Fabrics, Marshall's, PetCo, Ross, Staples, Target, Verizon, W 🅿 7-11/dsl, Marathon/Dunkin'/dsl, RaceTrac/dsl ⊡ Family$
123	rd 850, Corkscrew Rd, Estero, E 🅿 Marathon/7-11/dsl, Shell/Dunkin'/dsl 🍴 Beef'O'Brady's, China Gourmet, Duffy's Grill, Dunkin', Ford's Garage, Marsala's Italian, McDonald's, Naples Flat Bread, Perkins, Subway, Wasabi Steaks ⊡ CVS Drug, GNC, Johnson Tire/auto, Miramar Outlet/famous brands, Publix, W 🅿 7-11, Mobil/dsl, Speedway/Dunkin'/dsl 🍴 Applebee's, Arby's, Culver's, Rib City, Ruby Tuesday 🛏 Embassy Suites, Hampton Inn ⊡ Chevrolet, Koreshan SHS (2mi), Lowe's, Tire Choice/auto, Woodsmoke RV Park (4mi)

⬆N INTERSTATE 75 Cont'd

NAPLES

Exit #	Services
116	Bonita Bch Rd, Bonita Springs, E 🅿 7-11, Mobil/7-11/dsl, RaceTrac/dsl 🍴 China A, Dolce Rita's, Subway 🅾 Advance Parts, Publix, Tire Choice/auto, W 🅿 Chevron/dsl, Shell/McDonald's, Speedway/dsl, Speedway/dsl (2) 🍴 Culver's, Waffle House 🛏 Days Inn 🅾 CVS Drug, Home Depot, Imperial Bonita RV Park, Tire Kingdom, to Lovers Key SP (11mi), Walgreens
111	rd 846, Immokalee Rd, Naples Park, E 🅿 7-11, Mobil/dsl 🍴 Bob Evans, Burger King, Chili's, Fuzzy's Tacos, L'Appetito Pizza, Panera Bread 🛏 Hampton Inn 🅾 GNC, Petsmart, Staples, Target, World Mkt, W 🅿 Shell/Circle K/dsl 🍴 McDonald's, Skillets, Subway 🅾 Ⓗ, Publix, to Delnor-Wiggins SP, Verizon, Walmart
107	rd 896, Pinebridge Rd, Naples, E 🅿 BP/McDonald's/dsl 🍴 China Garden, Giovanni Ristorante, Subway, Tropical Smoothie 🅾 Ⓗ, Publix, vet, Walgreens, W 🅿 RaceTrac/dsl, Shell/Circle K/dsl 🍴 Burger King, Five Guys, Hooters, IHOP, Napoli Pizza, Perkins, Senor Tequilas, Sophia's Rest., Starbucks, Waffle House 🛏 Best Western, Hawthorn Suites, Spinnaker Inn 🅾 Harley-Davidson, Johnson Tire/auto, Nissan, URGENT CARE, vet
105	rd 886, to Golden Gate Pkwy, Golden Gate, E 🍴 Subway 🅾 CVS Drug, W 🅿 to 🛫, zoo
101	rd 951, to FL 84, to Naples, E 🅿 Shell/Subway/dsl 🛏 Fairfield Inn, SpringHill Suites, Woodspring Suites 🅾 Ⓗ, W 🅿 Marathon/Subway/dsl, Mobil/Subway/dsl, Shell/dsl 🍴 Chili's, China Dragon, Cracker Barrel, Dunkin', McDonald's, Taco Bell, Waffle House 🛏 Comfort Inn, Holiday Inn Express, La Quinta, Super 8 🅾 $Tree, AT&T, Club Naples RV Resort, KOA (7mi), vet, Walmart
100mm	toll plaza eb
80	FL 29, to Everglade City, Immokalee, W 🅾 Big Cypress NR, Everglades NP, Smallwoods Store
71mm	Big Cypress Nat Preserve, hiking, no security
63mm	W 🆁🆂 both lanes, 24hr security, full ♿ facilities, litter barrels, petwalk, Ⓒ, 🏕, vending
49	rd 833, Snake Rd, Big Cypress Indian Reservation, E 🅿 Miccosukee Service Plaza/deli/dsl 🅾 museum, swamp safari
41mm	rec area eb, litter barrels, 🏕
38mm	rec area wb, litter barrels, 🏕
35mm	W 🆁🆂/rec area both lanes, 24hr security, full ♿ facilities, litter barrels, petwalk, Ⓒ, 🏕, vending
32mm	rec area both lanes, litter barrels, 🏕
25mm	motorist callboxes begin/end, toll plaza wb
23	US 27, FL 25, Miami, South Bay
22	FL 84 W, NW 196th, Glades Pkwy, W 🅾 Publix, same as 21
21	FL 84 W (from nb), Indian Trace, W 🅿 Exxon/dsl, Shell 🍴 Las Rikuras, McDonald's, Papa John's, Spain's Cuisine 🅾 CVS Drug
19	I-595 E, FL 869 (toll), Sawgrass Expswy
15	Royal Palm Blvd, Weston, Bonaventure, W 🅿 Chevron, Mobil 🍴 BurgerFi, Carolina Ale House, Flanigan's Rest, La Granja, Los Verdes, Lucille's Cafe, Moon Thai, Offerdahl's Grill, Pollo Tropical, Subway, Wendy's 🛏 Comfort Suites, Courtyard, Residence Inn 🅾 Ⓗ, Meineke, Tires+, USPO, VW
13b a	Griffin Rd, E 🅿 Shell/dsl, Usave/dsl 🍴 Burger King, Donato's Rest., DQ, Outback Steaks, Waffle House 🅾 Goodyear/auto, LDS Temple, Porsche, Publix, vet, W 🅿 7-11/dsl, Tom Thumb/dsl 🍴 Anthony's Pizza, Aprezo 2 Venezuelan, Bone Fish Grill, Chick-fil-A, Chili's, Chipotle, Coldstone, Domino's, Dunkin', HoneyBaked Ham, Jimmy John's, McDonald's, Panera Bread, Pei Wei, Pizza Heaven, Starbucks, Weston Diner 🅾 AT&T, Fiat, Home Depot, Honda, Hyundai, Nissan/Volvo, Office Depot, Publix, Toyota, vet, Walgreens

MIAMI

Exit #	Services
11b a	Sheridan St, E 🅿 Chevron 🍴 Cracker Barrel, Wendy's 🛏 Hampton Inn, Holiday Inn Express 🅾 Audi, BMW, Ⓗ (3mi), Piccolo Park, W 🅿 Shell/dsl 🍴 China One, Coldstone, Little Caesar's, McDonald's, Original Pancake House, Piola Pizza, Romeus Cuban, Starbucks, Subway, TGIFriday's 🅾 Firestone/auto, Lowe's, Publix, URGENT CARE, Verizon, vet, Walgreens
9b a	FL 820, Pine Blvd, Hollywood Blvd, E 🅿 Marathon, Shell 🍴 BJ's Rest., Boston Mkt, Brimstone Woodfire Grill, Brio Italian, Cheesecake Factory, Chick-fil-A, Chili's, First Watch Cafe, Fuddrucker's, Habit Burger, Havana 1957, HoneyBaked Ham, Jason's Deli, La Granja, Lime Mexican Grill, McDonald's, Sal's Italian, Sergio's Grill, Starbucks, Subway, The Pub, Tijuana Flats, Twin Peaks, Village Tavern, Wendys 🅾 Ⓗ, Barnes&Noble, BJ's Whse/gas, Chrysler/Dodge/Jeep, Dick's, Mercedes, Old Navy, Petsmart, Publix, Trader Joe's, USPO, Verizon, Walgreens, Walmart, W 🅿 Chevron/dsl, Marathon/dsl, Mobil 🍴 Burger King, BurgerFi, Chipotle Mexican, Corner Bakery Cafe, Dickey's BBQ, Firehouse Subs, KFC/Taco Bell, La Granja, Las Vegas Cuban, Marco's Pizza, Mazda Mediterranean, Panda Express, Sal's Italian, SmashBurger, Starbucks, Sweet Tomatoes, Wasabi, Wendy's, Wingstop 🅾 $Tree, Acura, Advance Parts, AT&T, AutoZone, Costco/gas, CVS Drug, GNC, Lexus, Petco, Publix, Ross, Sedano's Foods, Subaru, Tires+, TJ Maxx, Tuesday Morning, vet, Walgreens, Whole Foods Mkt
7b a	Miramar Pkwy, E 🅿 Chevron 🍴 Baskin-Robbins/Dunkin, Blue Ginger Rest., Jimmy John's, La Carreta, McDonald's, Papa John's, Pollo Tropical, Sal's Italian, Starbucks, Subway, Tijuana Flats, Wendy's 🛏 Courtyard, Hilton Garden, Residence Inn, Wingate Inn 🅾 $Tree, Publix, USPO, vet, Walgreens, W 🅿 Mobil, Shell 🍴 Anthony's Pizza, Benihana, Chick-fil-A, Chili's, Chipotle, Coldstone, Jersey Mike's, McDonald's, Orient Chef, Panera Bread, Primo's Pizza, Starbucks, Subway, TX Roadhouse 🅾 Ⓗ, city park, CVS Drug, GNC, Home Depot, Marshall's, Ross, SuperTarget, Verizon, Winn-Dixie
5	to FL 821 (from sb), FL TPK (toll)
4	FL 860, NW 186th, Miami Gardens Dr, E 🅿 Chevron, Mobil 🍴 Carrabba's, Dunkin', McDonald's, Subway 🅾 AT&T, CVS Drug, GNC, Publix/deli, Sedanos Foods, vet
2	NW 138th, Graham Dairy Rd, W 🅿 Mobil, Shell/dsl 🍴 China Casa, China Wok, IHOP, Latin Cuban Cafe, Little Caesar's, McDonald's, Pollo Tropical, Starbucks, Subway, Wendy's 🅾 $General, Aldi Foods, AT&T, GNC, Publix, Ross, vet, Walgreens
1b a	I-75 begins/ends on FL 826, Palmetto Expswy, multiple services on FL 826.

⬆N INTERSTATE 95

Exit #	Services
382mm	Florida/Georgia state line, St Marys River
381mm	inspection sta both lanes
380	US 17, to Yulee, Kingsland, E 🅾 Osprey RV Park, W 🅿 Shell/dsl
378mm	Welcome Ctr sb, 24hr security, full ♿ facilities, litter barrels, petwalk, Ⓒ, 🏕, vending
376mm	weigh sta both lanes
373	FL 200, FL A1A, to Yulee, Callahan, Fernandina Bch, E 🅿 Flash, Krystal, Marathon/dsl, RaceWay/dsl 🍴 Burger King, DQ, KFC, McDonald's, Wendy's 🛏 Best Western, Comfort Inn, Holiday Inn Express 🅾 to Ft Clinch SP (16mi), W 🅿 BP/Subway/dsl, Flash/dsl
366	Pecan Park Rd, E 🅿 Loves/Chester's/Subway/dsl/scales/24hr, W 🅾 Flea&Farmer's Mkt, Pecan Park RV Camping
363b a	Duval Rd, E 🅿 Mobil/7-11/dsl 🍴 Arby's, BJ's Rest., Blaze Pizza, Boston's, Buffalo Wild Wings, Buffalo's Philly, Carrabba

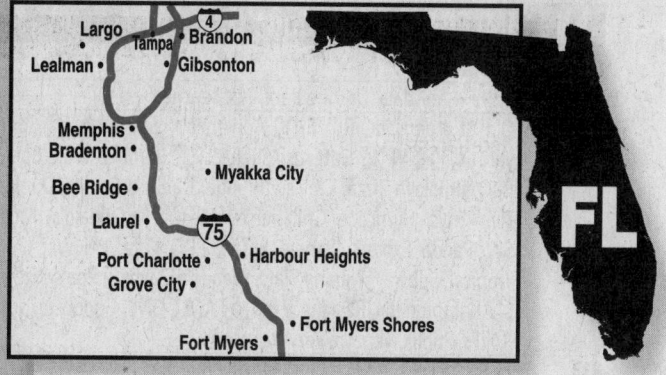

⬆N INTERSTATE 95 Cont'd

J A C K S O N V I L L E

363b a	Continued Chick-fil-A, Chili's, Chipotle, Coldstone, Cracker Barrel, Firehouse Subs, Five Guys, Green Papaya, Hardee's, Jimmy John's, Logan's Roadhouse, McDonald's, Mellow Mushroom Pizza, Moe's SW Grill, Newk's Eatery, Olive Garden, Outback Steaks, Panda Express, Panera Bread, Pollo Tropical, Red Lobster, Starbucks, Sticky Fingers, Subway, Taco Bell, Wasabi, Wendy's 🏨 A Loft 🅾 $Tree, AT&T, AutoZone, Best Buy, Dick's, Discount Tire, GNC, Goodyear/auto, Hobby Lobby, Lowe's, Marshall's, Michael's, Old Navy, Petsmart, Ross, Tire Kingdom, URGENT CARE, Verizon, Walgreens, Walmart/Subway, W 🅿 BP/dsl, Flash/dsl, Sunoco/Subway, Valero/dsl 🍴 Denny's, Longhorn Steaks, Millhouse Steaks, Ruby Tuesday, Waffle House, Zaxby's 🏨 Airport Inn, Best Airport Inn, Comfort Suites, Courtyard, Crowne Plaza, Days Inn, Econolodge, Fairfield Inn, Hampton Inn, Hilton Garden, Holiday Inn Express, Hyatt Place, Jacksonville Plaza Hotel, Microtel, Red Roof Inn, Residence Inn, SpringHill Suites, Travelodge 🅾 🔁 Gore's RV Ctr
362b a	I-295 S, FL 9A, to Blount Island, Jacksonville
360	FL 104, Dunn Ave, Busch Dr, E 🅿 Gate/dsl 🍴 Hardee's, Waffle House 🏨 Woodspring Suites 🅾 NAPA, Sam's Club/gas, USPO, W 🅿 BP/dsl, Chevron/dsl, Marathon/dsl, Shell/dsl, Sunoco, Valero 🍴 Arby's, Burger King, Capt D's, Chan's Chinese, Checker's, China Buffet, CiCi's, Country Cabin Rest., Dunkin', Firehouse Subs, KFC, Krystal, Little Caesar's, McDonald's, New China, Papa Murphy's, Pizza Hut, Popeye's, Sonny's BBQ, Starbucks, Subway, Taco Bell, Wendy's 🏨 Knights Inn, Motel 6, River City Inn 🅾 $Tree, Aamco, Advance Parts, Camping World RV Ctr, CVS Drug, Family$, PepBoys, Publix, Tires+, Walgreens
358b a	FL 105, Broward Rd, Heckscher Dr, E 🅾 zoo, W 🅿 BP/dsl
357mm	Trout River
357	FL 111, Edgewood Ave, W 🅿 BP/dsl, Texaco/dsl
356b a	Fl 115, FL 117, Lem Turner Rd, Norwood Ave, E 🍴 Hardee's, W 🅿 BP/dsl, RaceWay/dsl, Shell, Speedway/Dunkin' 🍴 Burger King, Checker's, Golden EggRoll, Ho-Ho Chinese, Krystal, Popeye's, Subway, Taco Bell 🅾 Advance Parts, King Tires, Save-A-Lot, Walgreens
355	Golfair Blvd, E 🅿 Shell, W 🅿 Chevron/dsl, RaceWay/dsl
354b a	US 1, 20th St, to Jacksonville, to AmTrak, MLK Pkwy
353d	FL 114, to 8th St, E 🍴 McDonald's 🅾 🏥, Walgreens
353c	US 23 N, Kings Rd, downtown
353b	US 90A, Union St, 🅾 Sports Complex, downtown
353a	Church St, Myrtle Ave, Forsythe St, downtown
352d	I-10 W, Stockton St (from sb), Lake City
352c	Monroe St (from nb), downtown
352b a	Myrtle Ave (from nb), downtown
351d	Stockton St, W 🅾 🏥, downtown
351c	Margaret St, downtown
351b	I-10 W, to Tallahassee
351a	Park St, College St, 🏥, to downtown
351mm	St Johns River
350b	FL 13, San Marco Blvd, E 🅾 🏥
350a	Prudential Dr, Main St, Riverside Ave (from nb), to downtown, E 🅿 🏨 Extended Stay America, Hampton Inn, W 🍴 Panera Bread 🏨 Hilton Garden, Homewood Suites
349	US 90 E (from sb), to beaches, W 🅿 Shell/dsl 🏨 Scottish Inn, downtown
348	US 1 S (from sb), Philips Hwy, W 🏨 Scottish Inn, Super 8
347	US 1A, FL 126, Emerson St, E 🅿 Chevron/dsl, Shell 🍴 Hot Wok 🅾 Advance Parts, Family$, O'Reilly Parts, W 🅿 BP/dsl, Gate, Gate/dsl, Speedway/dsl 🍴 Dunkin', McDonald's, Taco Bell 🏨 Emerson Inn 🅾 Chevrolet, Goodyear/auto

J A C K S O N V I L L E

346b a	FL 109, University Blvd, E 🅿 BP, Shell, Speedway/dsl, Sunoco/dsl 🍴 Baldino's Subs, Capt D's, Checkers, DQ, Firehouse Subs, Happy Garden Chinese, Hungry Howie's, Korean BBQ, Krystal, Pizza Hut, Subway, Ying's Chinese, Zaxby's 🅾 🏥, Ace Hardware, CVS Drug, Family$, Fresh Fields Mkt, Meineke, NAPA, Sun Tire, Tires+, Tires+, Winn-Dixie, W 🅿 BP/dsl, RaceTrac/dsl 🍴 Baskin-Robbins/Dunkin', Burger King, Famous Amos, KFC, Krispy Kreme, McDonald's, Papa John's, Sonny's BBQ, Taco Bell, Wendy's, Whataburger 🏨 Days Inn, Econolodge, Super 8 🅾 $Tree, auto repair, AutoZone, Family$, TJ Maxx, U-Haul
345	FL 109, University Blvd (from nb), E 🅿 Gate/dsl/24hr, Mobil, Subway/dsl, Speedway/dsl 🍴 Bono's BBQ, Parisian Sandwich, Vino's Pizza 🅾 🏥
344	FL 202, Butler Blvd, E 🅿 Gate/dsl 🍴 Dave&Buster's 🏨 Best Western, Candlewood Suites, Country Inn Suites, Extended Stay America, Holiday Inn Express, Marriott, Radisson 🅾 🏥, USPO, W 🅿 BP/dsl, Shell, Texaco/dsl 🍴 Applebee's, Baskin-Robbins/Dunkin', Chick-fil-A, Cracker Barrel, Jimmy John's, McDonald's, Sonic, Starbucks, Waffle House, Wendy's, Whataburger/24hr, Zaxby's 🏨 Baymont Inn, Courtyard, Extended Stay America, Extended Stay America (2), Fairfield Inn, Hampton Inn, Hometown Inn, La Quinta, Red Roof Inn, TownePlace Suites
341	FL 152, Baymeadows Rd, E 🅿 BP/dsl, Gate/dsl, Shell/dsl 🍴 Arby's, Chili's, Four Rivers Smokehouse, Hardee's, Jimmy John's, Krystal, Panda Express, Subway 🏨 Comfort Suites, Embassy Suites, Extended Stay America, Ramada Inn 🅾 Advance Parts, Autozone, Publix, Tires+, Walgreens, W 🅿 Mobil/Kangaroo, Shell 🍴 Al's Pizza, Denny's, Dunkin', Firehouse Subs, Gator's Dockside, IHOP, Jersey Mike's, KFC, Larry's Subs, Little Caesar's, McDonald's, Pagoda Chinese, Red Lobster, Taco Bell, Waffle House, Wendy's, Woody's BBQ 🏨 Best Inn, Days Inn, Hawthorn Suites, InTown Suites, Knights Inn, La Quinta, Motel 6, Quality Inn, Residence Inn, Sheraton, Suburban Inn 🅾 $Tree, AT&T, BJ's Whse/gas, CVS Drug, Discount Tire, Harley-Davidson, Lowe's, Office Depot, Pepboys, Verizon
340	FL 115, Southside Blvd (from nb)on FL 115, E 🅿 Marathon/Kangaroo 🍴 Five Guys, Fusion Buffet, Longhorn Steaks, Newk's Eatery 🅾 Aldi, AT&T, Home Depot, Michael's, Petsmart, same as 339, Target
339	US 1, Philips Hwy, E 🅿 BP/Circle K/dsl, Exxon/Kangaroo/dsl, RaceTrac/dsl 🍴 Arby's, Bono's BBQ, Buca Italian, Buffalo Wild Wings, Burger King, Chick-fil-A, Coldstone, Latitude 360 Grille, McDonald's, Mikado, Moe's SW Grill, Olive Garden, Ruby Tuesday, Starbucks, Taco Bell 🅾 $Tree, Belk, Best Buy, Chevrolet, Dillard's, Ford, JC Penney, Mazda, Nissan, Tire Kingdom, Toyota, vet, Volvo, Walmart, W 🅿 BP/dsl 🍴 Benito's Italian, Salsa's Mexican, Steak&Shake, Subway

🅖 = gas 🍴 = food 🛏 = lodging 🅞 = other 🆁🆂 = rest stop Copyright 2022 - The Next EXIT ®

▲N INTERSTATE 95 Cont'd

Exit #	Services
337	I-295 N, to rd 9a, Orange Park, Jax Beaches
335	Old St Augustine Rd, **E** 🍴 Applebee's, Starbucks 🛏 Courtyard 🅞 �H, **W** 🅖 Gate/dsl, Shell/dsl 🍴 Bamboo Wok, Bono's BBQ, Brooklyn Pizza, Chili's, Chipotle, Daruma Steaks, Dunkin', Five Guys, Hurricane Grill, Jersey Mike's, McDonald's, Moe's SW, Panda Express, Panera Bread, PDQ Cafe, Pei Wei, Pollo Tropical, Subway, Tijuana Flats, Wendy's, Zaxby's, Zoe's Kitchen 🛏 Hampton Inn, Residence Inn 🅞 AT&T, GNC, Goodyear/auto, Kohl's, Publix, Verizon, vet, Walgreens
333	FL 9b, to US 1, I-295, N Jacksonville Beaches
331mm	🆁🆂 both lanes, 24hr security, full 🅖 facilities, litter barrels, petwalk, 🛈, 🚻, vending
329	rd 210, Green Cove Springs, Ponte Vedra Beach, **E** 🅖 ⛽🍴🛏 McDonald's/dsl/scales/24hr, Sunoco/fruit, TA/Mobil/Subway/dsl/scales/24hr/@ 🍴 Waffle House, **W** 🅖 Circle K/dsl, Mobil/Subway/dsl/USPO, Shell/dsl 🍴 Burger King, China Wok, Domino's, Dunkin', Firehouse Subs, Jenk's Pizza, Los Portales, Papa John's, Starbucks, Tropical Smoothie, Yummy Asian 🅞 AT&T, CVS Drug, fireworks, Goodyear/auto, vet, Winn-Dixie
323	International Golf Pkwy, **E** 🅖 BP/dsl/USPO, Shell/Subway/dsl 🛏 St Augustine Suites, **W** 🍴 Cino's Pizza, King Wok, Village Grill/Subs 🛏 Renaissance Resort 🅞 vet, World Golf Village
318	FL 16, Green Cove Sprgs, St Augustine, **E** 🅖 Chevron/DQ/dsl, Gate/dsl/fruit, Mobil/Kangaroo/dsl, Shell/dsl 🍴 Burger King, Dunkin', Krystal, McDonald's, NY Diner, Starbucks, Subway 🛏 Comfort Inn, Courtyard, Fairfield Inn, Holiday Inn Express, La Quinta, Quality Inn, St Augustine Motel 🅞 Cadillac, Camping World RV Ctr, Ford/Lincoln, Gore's RV Ctr, St Augustine Outlets/Famous Brands, **W** 🅖 Exxon, RaceTrac/dsl 🍴 Cracker Barrel, Denny's, Giovanni's Italian, IHOP, KFC, Lemongrass Asian, Ruby Tuesday, Sonny's BBQ, Taco Bell, Wendy's 🛏 Best Western, Days Inn, Hampton Inn, Howard Johnson, Scottish Inn, Super 8, Wingate Inn 🅞 Discount Tire, funpark, St Augustine Outlets
311	FL 207, St Augustine, **E** 🅖 BP/Subway/dsl, RaceTrac/dsl 🍴 Burger King, Dunkin' 🅞 H, flea mkt, Indian Forest RV Park (2mi), KOA (7mi), St Johns RV Park, to Anastasia SP, **W** 🛏 Quality Inn
305	FL 206, to Hastings, Crescent Beach, **E** 🅖 ⛽FLYING J/Denny's/Subway/dsl/LP/scales/24hr 🅞 to Ft Matanzas NM, truck repair, **W** 🅞 truck repair
302mm	🆁🆂 both lanes, 24hr security, full 🅖 facilities, litter barrels, petwalk, 🛈, 🚻, vending
298	US 1, to St Augustine, **E** 🅖 BP/dsl, Indian River Fruit, Marathon 🅞 to Faver-Dykes SP, **W** 🅖 Mobil/DQ/dsl, Sunoco/dsl
293	Matanzas Woods Pky
289	to FL A1A (**toll** br), to Palm Coast, **E** 🅖 Exxon, Mobil/7-11, RaceTrac/dsl, Shell 🍴 Anthony's Pizza, China Express, Cracker Barrel, Denny's, Dunkin', Grand China, Hungry Howie's, KFC, McDonald's, Metro Diner, Salsa's Mexican, Starbucks, Wendy's 🛏 Best Western, Fairfield Inn, Microtel, Red Roof Inn 🅞 Beall's, CVS Drug, Publix, Staples, Walgreens, **W** 🅖 Citgo, Exxon, Exxon/Kangaroo/dsl, Kangaroo/dsl, Shell/dsl 🍴 Baskin-Robbins/Dunkin', Bob Evans, Bruster's, Carrabba's, Chick-fil-A, China King, China One, Golden Corral, Houligan's, Joe's NY Pizza, McDonald's, Nathan's Cafe, Outback Steaks, Ruby Tuesday, Sakura Japanese, Sonny's BBQ, Steak'n Shake, Subway, Taco Bell, Wendy's, Zaxby's 🛏 Days Inn 🅞 $General, $Tree, Advance Parts, AutoZone, Beall's, Belk, CVS Drug, Ford, GNC, Home Depot, Kohl's, Lowe's, Publix, Tire Kingdom, Tuffy Auto, USPO, Verizon, Walgreens, Walmart, Winn-Dixie

286mm	weigh sta both lanes
284	FL 100, to Bunnell, Flagler Beach, **E** 🅖 Mobil/dsl, Shell/ds 🍴 Burger King, Domino's, Joe's Pizza, McDonald's, Oriental Garden, Subway, Woody's BBQ 🛏 Hampton Inn, Holiday Inn Express 🅞 Ace Hardware, Winn-Dixie, **W** 🅖 Interstate 100 🍴 McDonald's, Panda Express, Pizza Hut, Subway 🛏 Hilton Garden 🅞 H, $Tree, AT&T, Chevrolet, Chrysler/Dodge/Jeep, Dunkin', Michael's, Olive Garden, Panera Bread, Petsmart, Ross, Target, TJ Maxx, Verizon
278	Old Dixie Hwy, **E** 🅖 7-11 🍴 King Chinese, Mezzaluna Pizza 🅞 Bulow RV Park (3mi), Publix, to Tomoka SP, vet, **W** 🅖 BP/dsl 🅞 Holiday Travel Park, vet
273	US 1, **E** 🅖 Mobil, RaceTrac/dsl 🍴 McDonald's, Waffle House 🛏 La Quinta, Motel 6 🅞 fruit/fireworks, Giant Rec RV Ctr, **W** 🅖 Exxon/Burger King, ⭕Loves/Arby's/dsl/scales/24h 🍴 Daytona Pig Stand BBQ, DQ, Houligan's 🛏 Days Inn, Econolodge, Howard Johnson, Scottish Inn, Super 8 🅞 Encore RV Park, Harley-Davidson
268	FL 40, Ormond Beach, **E** 🅖 Speedway/dsl, Sunoco/dsl, Valero/dsl 🍴 Agave Cantina, Applebee's, Boston Mkt, Chick-fil-A, Chili's, Chipotle, Denny's, Dustin's BBQ, Houligan's, Jersey Mike's, Mama Mia's Pizza, Panera Bread, Papa John's, Pie Five, Red Bowl, Starbucks, Steak'n Shake, Subway, Taco Bell, Takeya Steaks, Wendy's, Wok&Roll 🛏 Sleep Inn 🅞 H, $General, $Tree, Beall's, Discount Tire, GNC, Love Whole Foods, Lowe's, Petco, Publix, Ross, Tire Kingdom, to Tomoka SP, USPO, vet, Walmart, **W** 🅖 7-11, BP/Dunkin', Citgo/dsl, RaceTrac/dsl, Texaco 🍴 Cantina Mezcal, Cracker Barrel, Little Italy, McDonald's 🛏 Baymont Inn, Hampton Inn 🅞 Walgreens
265	LPGA Blvd, Holly Hill, Daytona Beach, **E** 🅖 7-11, Shell/Circle K/Dunkin'/dsl 🍴 Vince Carter Rest., Wendy's 🅞 CVS Drug, Tanger Outlets/famous brands, **W** 🛏 Holiday Inn 🅞 BMW, Chrysler/Dodge/Jeep, Fiat, Ford, Infiniti, Lincoln, Mazda, Mercedes, Mini, Nissan, VW
261b a	US 92, to DeLand, Daytona Bch, **E** 🅖 7-11, Citgo/dsl, RaceWay/dsl, Speedway/Dunkin'/dsl, Sunoco/dsl 🍴 Applebee's, Asian Grill, Bahama Breeze, BJ's Rest., Bob Evans, Buffalo Wild Wings, Burger King, Carrabba's, Checkers, Cheddar's, Chick-fil-A, Chili's, Chipotle Mexican, Cracker Barrel, Daytona Ale House, Firehouse Subs, Five Guys, Honeybaked Ham, Hooters, IHOP, Jersey Mike's Subs, Jimmy John's, Krystal, Krystal, Longhorn Steaks, McDonald's, Olive Garden, Outback Steaks, Panda Express, Panera Bread, Red Lobster, Ruby Tuesday, Smoke Shack BBQ, Starbucks, Subway, Taco Bell, Tijuana Flats, Waffle House, Wendy's, Winghouse 🛏 Best Western, Courtyard, Extended Stay America, Hampton Inn, Hilton Garden, Holiday Inn Express, Homewood Suites, La Quinta, Quality Inn, Residence Inn 🅞 H, $Tree, AT&T, Barnes&Noble, Bass Pro Shops, Beall's, Best Buy, BigLots, Books-A-Million, Dick's, Dillard's, Firestone/auto, Hobby Lobby, Home Depot, JC Penney, Jo-Ann Fabrics, Macy's, Michael's, Old Navy, Pep Boys, Petsmart, Staples, SteinMart, Target, TJMaxx, to Daytona Racetrack, Tuesday Morning, Verizon, World Mkt, **W** 🅖 BP/dsl, RaceTrack/dsl 🍴 McDonald's 🛏 Days Inn, Motel 6 🅞 flea mkt, KOA
260b a	I-4, to Orlando, FL 400 E, to S Daytona, **E** 🅖 RaceTrac/dsl/e85 Shell/Circle K/dsl
256	FL 421, to Port Orange, **E** 🅖 BP, Murphy USA/dsl, Shell/dsl, WaWa/dsl 🍴 Applebee's, Bob Evans, Boston Mkt, Burger King, Chicken Salad Chick, Chick-fil-A, Chili's, Chipotle, Culver's, Daily Grind Burgers, Denny's, Domino's, Dustin's BBQ

ST AUGUSTINE

PALM COAST

ORMOND BEACH

DAYTONA

INTERSTATE 95 Cont'd

256 Continued

Golden Corral, Houligan's, KFC, McDonald's, Mellow Mushroom, Moe's SW, Monterrey Grill, Panera Bread, Papa John's, Pollo Tropical, Red Bowl Asian, Smoothie King, Sonny's BBQ, Starbucks, Stonewood Grill, TGIFriday's, Tijuana Flats Country Inn&Suites, La Quinta BigLots, BJ's/gas, CVS Drug, Daytona Beach RV Park, Home Depot, Lowe's, Save-a-Lot, Super Target, Tuffy Auto, Verizon, vet, Walgreens, Walmart, W 7-11/dsl, Marathon/dsl China Chef, ChuckECheese, Coldstone, Five Guys, Luigi's Pizzaria, Malibu Beach Grill, McDonald's, Olive Garden, Panda Express, Popeye's, Red Robin, Subway, Takara Steaks, TX Roadhouse, Waffle House, Wendy's $Tree, AT&T, Belk, Firestone/auto, GNC, Kohl's, Love Whole Foods, Marshall's, Michael's, PetCo, Publix, Walgreens

249b a FL 44, to De Land, New Smyrna Beach, E New Smyrna RV Camp (3mi), W Chevron/dsl McDonald's Walmart/Subway

244 FL 442, to Edgewater, E Marathon/dsl truck repair

231 rd 5A, Scottsmoor, E BP/Stuckey's/dsl Crystal Lake RV Park

227mm sb, 24hr security, full facilities, litter barrels, petwalk, , , vending

225mm nb, 24hr security, full facilities, litter barrels, petwalk, , , vending

223 FL 46, Mims, E McDonald's, W BP, Chevron/dsl $General, KOA/LP, Seasons RV Park

220 FL 406, Titusville, E BP/dsl, Shell/Hungry Howie's/dsl Beef O'Brady's, First Wok, Kelsey's Pizza, McDonald's, Subway, Valentino's Rest., Wendy's Executive Garden Inn , $General, $Tree, Advance Parts, GNC, O'Reilly Parts, Publix, Tires+, to Canaveral Nat Seashore, Walgreens

215 FL 50, to Orlando, Titusville, E BP/KFC/dsl, Chevron/Subway/dsl, Exxon/Circle K, Murphy USA/dsl, Shell/Dunkin'/dsl Burger King, Denny's, Durango Steaks, McDonald's, Panda Express, Sonny's BBQ, Starbucks, Taco Bell, Waffle House, Wendy's Best Western, Ramada Inn Aldi Foods, AT&T, Ford, GNC, Home Depot, Lowe's, Marshall's, Pepboys, PetCo, Staples, Target, Tire Kingdom, to Kennedy Space Ctr, Walmart, W Cracker Barrel, IHOP Days Inn, Fairfield Inn, Hampton Inn, Holiday Inn, Quality Inn Christmas RV Park (8mi), Great Outdoors RV/golf Resort

212 FL 407, to FL 528 **toll** (no re-entry sb)

208 Port St John

205 FL 528 (**toll 528**), to Cape Canaveral & Cape Port AFS, City Point

202 FL 524, Cocoa, E FLYING J/Wendy's/dsl/scales/24hr, Shell/dsl Museum of History&Science, W BP/dsl Days Inn

201 FL 520, to Cocoa Bch, Cocoa, E BP/dsl, Exxon/Circle K, Pilot/Subway/dsl/scales/24hr IHOP, Waffle House Best Western, Budget Inn , fireworks, Sams Club/gas, W Chevron/dsl, Shell/Burger King, Sunoco/dsl McDonald's Holiday Inn Express Camping World RV Ctr

195 FL 519, Fiske Blvd, E 7-11, Mobil/dsl Baci Pizza, Ruby Tuesday Swiss Inn , Discount Tire, Lowe's, Space Coast RV Park

193 Viera Blvd, E Brooklyn Pizza, Long Doggers Earth Fare Mkt, Walgreens, W Mobil/pizza Dunkin', El Leoncito, Kimbo Chinese, McDonald's, Publix, Slow&Low BBQ, Vincinos Pizza

191 rd 509, to Satellite Beach, Viera, E 7-11, BP, Speedway/dsl, Sunoco/dsl Bob Evans, Carrabba's, Chick-fil-A, Domino's, DQ, Firehouse Subs, Jimmy John's, McDonald's, Papa John's,

191 Continued

Perkins, Pizza Hut/Taco Bell, Sonny's BBQ, Subway, Uno Grill, Wendy's Hampton Inn, Holiday Inn AT&T, CVS Drug, Publix, Tires+, to Patrick AFB, Tuffy Auto, URGENT CARE, Walgreens, zoo, W Murphy USA/dsl, Shell/dsl Asian Wok, Bonefish Grill, Buffalo Wild Wings, Burger King, Chili's, Chipotle, Coldstone, Cracker Barrel, Five Guys, Longhorn Steaks, Melting Pot, Moe's SW Grill, Outback Steaks, Panera Bread, Pizza Gallery, Pollo Tropical, Starbucks, Steak'nShake, Subway, Tijuana Flats, Which Wich? La Quinta , $Tree, AT&T, Belk, Books-A-Million, GNC, Hobby Lobby, Kohl's, Lexus, Michael's, Office Depot, Old Navy, PetCo, Petsmart, Ross, SuperTarget, Tire Kingdom, TJ Maxx, Verizon, Walmart/McDonald's, World Mkt

188 FL 404, Patrick AFB, Satellite Beach

183 FL 518, Melbourne, Indian Harbour Beach, E 7-11, BP/dsl, Marathon/Dunkin', RaceTrac/dsl, WaWa/dsl , art museum, AT&T, W Flea Mkt

180 US 192, to Melbourne, E BP/dsl, Cumberland/dsl, Mobil/dsl, RaceTrac/dsl, Shell/Circle K, Sunoco/dsl ChuckECheese, Denny's, Dunkin', Waffle House Best Value Inn, Budget Inn, Days Inn, Fairfield Inn, Hampton Inn, Holiday Inn Express, La Quinta, Melbourne Suites, Woodspring Suites , Ace Hardware, fireworks, Lowe's, Sam's Club/gas, Subaru, Volvo

176 rd 516, to Palm Bay, E 7-11, BP/Circle K/dsl, Murphy USA/dsl, Pro Energy, RaceTrac/dsl Baskin Robbins/Dunkin', Chick-fil-A, Cracker Barrel, Denny's, Golden Corral, Popeye's, Starbucks, Tijuana Flats Hampton Inn, Quality Inn Aldi Foods, Bass Pro Shops, BJ's Whse/gas, GNC, Harley-Davidson, Office Depot, Verizon, Walgreens, Walmart, W 7-11, Mobil/dsl, Shell Buffalo Wild Wings, Burger King, Firehouse Subs, Five Guys, Long Doggers, Longhorn Steaks, McDonald's, Michelli's Pizzeria, Moe's SW Grill, Panda Express, Panera Bread, Pollo Tropical, Subway, Wendy's $Tree, AT&T, CVS Drug, Discount Tire, Giant RV Ctr, Kohl's, Marshall's, Michael's, PetCo, Publix, Ross, Target, URGENT CARE, vet, Walgreens

173 FL 514, to Palm Bay, E RaceTrac/dsl, Shell, Sunoco/dsl Holiday Inn Express , Firestone/auto, Ford, truck/RV repair, W Mobil/dsl, Speedway, Sunoco/dsl Arby's, Burger King, Chick-fil-A, IHOP, Japanese Buffet, McDonald's/playplace, Panda Express, Sonic, Sonny's BBQ, Subway, Taco Bell, TX Roadhouse, Waffle House, Wendy's Comfort Suites, Motel 6 $General, Advance Parts, CVS Drug, Gatto's Tire/auto, Home Depot, Lowe's, Publix, Tire Kingdom, URGENT CARE, USPO, Verizon, Walgreens, Walmart

168mm both lanes, 24hr security, full facilities, litter barrels, petwalk, , , vending

166 St John's Heritage Pkwy

= gas = food = lodging = other Rs = rest stop   Copyright 2022 - The Next EXIT

↑N INTERSTATE 95 Cont'd

Exit #	Services
156	rd 512, to Sebastian, Fellsmere, E ⛽ BP/DQ/Stuckey's/dsl, Chevron/McDonald's, RaceWay/dsl ◻ ⊞, Encore RV Park, Sebastian Inlet SRA, W ◻ St Sebastian SP
147	FL 60, Osceola Blvd, E ⛽ 7-11, BP/dsl, Citgo/dsl, Mobil/dsl, Sunoco, TA/BP/Popeye's/Subway/dsl/scales/24hr/@, Valero/dsl, WaWa/dsl ⊞ Dunkin', IHOP, McDonald's, Wendy's 🛏 Comfort Suites, Howard Johnson, Motel 6, Vero Beach Resort, Vero Beach Suites ◻ ⊞, Hyundai, USPO, vet, W ⊞ Shell/dsl ⊞ Cracker Barrel, McDonald's, Steak'n Shake 🛏 Country Inn&Suites, Hampton Inn, Holiday Inn Express ◻ Vero Beach Outlets/famous brands
138	FL 614, Indrio Rd, 3 mi E ◻ Oceanographic Institute
133mm	Rs both lanes, 24hr security, full ♿ facilities, litter barrels, petwalk, ◻, 🚮, vending
131b a	FL 68, Orange Ave, E ◻ ⊞, to Ft Pierce SP, W ⊞ ⭐FLYING J/Denny's/Subway/dsl/LP/scales/24hr, Loves/Hardee's/dsl/scales/24hr ◻ Blue Beacon
129	FL 70, to Okeechobee, E ⛽ Citgo, Murphy USA, RaceTrac/dsl, Shell, Sunoco/dsl ⊞ Applebee's, Cowboys BBQ, Golden Corral, Sonic, Waffle House ◻ ⊞ $General, $Tree, Advance Parts, AT&T, Firestone/auto, Home Depot, URGENT CARE, Walgreens, Walmart/Subway, W ⛽ Citgo, Loves/Arby's/dsl/24hr/@, Marathon/scales/dsl, Mobil/Dunkin'/Subway, Pilot/McDonald's/dsl/scales/24hr ⊞ Burger King, Cracker Barrel, Golden Bear Rest., KFC, La Granja, LJ Silver, McDonald's, Red Lobster, Steak'n Shake, Subway, Waffle House, Wendy's 🛏 Best Value Inn, Comfort Suites, Days Inn, Fairfield Inn, Hampton Inn, Holiday Inn Express, La Quinta, Motel 6, Quality Inn, Rodeway Inn, Sleep Inn ◻ to FL TPK, Treasure Coast RV Park
126	rd 712, Midway Rd, E ⛽ Marathon/Subway/dsl
121	St Lucie West Blvd, E ⛽ 7-11, Mobil/Dunkin', Murphy USA/dsl, Shell/Subway/dsl ⊞ Arby's, Bob Evans, Burger King, Carrabba's, Cheddar's, Chili's, Chipotle Mexican, First Watch, Five Guys, Frank&Al's Pizza, Friendly's, Hokkaido, Jersey Mike's, Jimmy John's, KFC, Little Caesar's, McDonald's, Moe's SW Grill, Outback Steaks, Panda Express, Panera Bread, Pollo Tropical, Ruby Tuesday, Starbucks, Subway, Taco Bell, TGIFriday's, Tijuana Flats, Wendy's 🛏 Hampton Inn, Holiday Inn Express, Residence Inn, SpringHill Suites, TownePlace Suites ◻ $Tree, AT&T, Beall's, CVS Drug, GNC, Outdoor Resorts Camping (2mi), PetCo, Publix/deli, Ross, Staples, SteinMart, Tire Kingdom, Tires+, URGENT CARE, USPO, Verizon, Walgreens, Walmart, W ⛽ Chevron/dsl 🛏 Hilton Garden, MainStay Suites, Sheraton Resort, Sleep Inn ◻ PGA Village
120	Crosstown Pkwy
118	Gatlin Blvd, to Port St Lucie, E ⛽ BP/dsl, Chevron/Dunkin'/Subway/dsl, Mobil/Dunkin', RaceTrac, Sunoco/e85 ⊞ McDonald's, Taco Bell, Wendy's ◻ AutoZone, Bass Pro Shops, Home Depot, Sam's Club/gas, Tire Kingdom, Tires+, vet, Walgreens, Walmart, W ⛽ WaWa/dsl ⊞ Culver's, Longhorn Steaks, McDonald's, Olive Garden, Panda Express, Panera Bread, Recovery Grill, Subway, Tropical Smoothie 🛏 Homewood Suites ◻ ⊞, AT&T, GNC, Michael's, Old Navy, Petsmart, Publix, Target, TJ Maxx
114	Becker Rd
112mm	weigh sta sb
110	FL 714, to Martin Hwy, Palm City, E ◻ ⊞
106mm	Rs both lanes, vending, 24hr security, full ♿ facilities, litter barrels, petwalk, ◻, 🚮
102	Rd 713, High Meadow Ave, Palm City

Left margin: O K E E C H O B E E **FL**

101	FL 76, to Stuart, Indiantown, E ⛽ Chevron/dsl, RaceTrac/ds Sunoco/dsl ⊞ Popeye's, Baskin-Robbins/Dunkin', Cracker Bar rel, La Forchetta Pizza, McDonald's, Wendy's 🛏 Courtyar Holiday Inn Express ◻ ⊞, city park, Publix, Walgreens, W ⛽ Marathon/DQ/dsl, Mobil/dsl
96	rd 708, to Hobe Sound, E ◻ Dickinson SP (11mi), RV campin
92mm	weigh sta nb
87b a	FL 706, to Okeechobee, Jupiter, E ⛽ Citgo, Mobil/dsl, Shell/ds Sunoco ⊞ Cheeseburgers&More, Chipotle, Domino's, Duffy Rest., Dunkin', First Watch Cafe, Five Guys, Giuseppe's, Hurr cane Grill, IHOP, Jersey Mike's Subs, KFC, McDonald's, Paner Bread, Park Ave Grill, Pollo Tropical, Rancho Chico, Starbuck Subway, Taco Bell, Tijuana Flats, Tomato Pie, Vinny's Pizz YumYum 🛏 Comfort Inn, Fairfield Inn ◻ ⊞, Advance Part AT&T, BMW, GNC, Home Depot, PepBoys, Petsmart, Publi Tire Kingdom, to Dickinson SP, URGENT CARE, vet, Walgreen Walmart, Winn-Dixie, W ⛽ Sunoco ◻ CVS Drug, to FL TPK
83	Donald Ross Rd, E ⛽ Marathon/Subway, Shell/deli ⊞ M Donald's 🛏 Hampton Inn (3mi), Holiday Inn Express (3mi Homewood Suites ◻ ⊞, AT&T, CVS Drug, Publix, stadium Walgreens
79c	FL 809 S (from sb), Military Tr, W same services as 79b, to FL TP
79a b	FL 786, PGA Blvd, E ⛽ Shell/dsl ⊞ Chili's, Moe's SW, Yar house Rest. 🛏 Hilton Garden, Marriott ◻ ⊞, Best Bu Michael's, PetCo, Publix, Whole Foods Mkt, W ⛽ Shell/d ⊞ Blaze Pizza, Bonefish Grill, Chipotle Mexican, J Alexa ders, Outback Steaks, Panera Bread, Starbucks, Three Fork Rest. 🛏 DoubleTree Hotel, Embassy Suites ◻ CVS Dru Publix
77	Northlake Blvd, to W Palm Bch, E ⛽ Shell/dsl, Speedwa ⊞ Applebee's, Arby's, Burger King, Checkers, Chick-fil-A Giovanni's Rest., Habit Burger, Jersey Mike's, Jimmy John's, L Granja, McDonald's, Miami Subs, Panera Bread, Pollo Tropica Starbucks, Taco Bell ◻ ⊞, $Tree, AT&T, Buick/Chevrolet GMC, Chrysler/Dodge/Jeep, Costco, CVS Drug, Ford, Ford, Hob by Lobby, Home Depot, Hyundai, Jo-Ann, Kia, Lowe's, PepBoy Ross, Staples, Target, vet, VW, Walgreens, W ⛽ Chevro Mobil/dsl, Shell, Sunoco/dsl ⊞ Duffy's Grill, Dunkin', Origin Pancakes, Papa John's, Pizza Hut, Subway, Wendy's 🛏 In of America ◻ Advance Parts, CVS Drug, Publix, Tires+, ve Winn-Dixie
76	FL 708, Blue Heron Blvd, E ⛽ Marathon/dsl, Shell/ds WaWa/dsl ⊞ Wendy's 🛏 Travelodge ◻ Honda, Nissa W ⛽ 7-11/dsl, Chevron/dsl, Cumberland Farms, Marathon Subway/dsl, RaceTrac/dsl ⊞ Burger King, Denny's, McDo ald's 🛏 Super 8
74	FL 702, 45th St, E ⛽ 7-11/dsl ⊞ Burger King, IHOP 🛏 Day Inn ◻ ⊞, Cadillac, URGENT CARE, Walgreens, W ⛽ Rac Trac/dsl ⊞ Cracker Barrel, McDonald's, Pollo Tropical, Subwa Taco Bell, Wendy's 🛏 Courtyard, Extended Stay America, Ho iday Inn Express, Homewood Suites, Red Roof Inn, Residenc Inn, SpringHill Suites ◻ FoodTown, Harley-Davidson, Sam Club/gas, Walmart
71	Lake Blvd, Palm Beach, E ⛽ Marathon/Dunkin'/dsl ⊞ BJ Rest., McDonald's, Pei Wei, Red Robin, Starbucks 🛏 Be Western, Hawthorn Suites ◻ ⊞, Best Buy, Home Depo Old Navy, Petsmart, Ross, Target, TJ Maxx, Whole Foods Mk W ⛽ Texaco/dsl, Valero ⊞ Chick-fil-A, Chipotle Mexican Dunkin', Hooters, Raindancer Steaks, Red Lobster, Sweet Toma toes, Tijuana Flats, Twin Peaks 🛏 La Quinta, Ramada ◻ U GENT CARE, vet, Walgreens

Right margin: **W P A L M B E A C H** / **P A L M B E A C H**

INTERSTATE 95 Cont'd

Exit #	Services
70b a	FL 704, Okeechobee Blvd, E 🍴 Ruth's Chris Steaks 🛏 Hilton, Marriott, W 🅖 BP/dsl, Chevron/dsl, Mobil/dsl, Shell, Speedway, Valero/dsl 🍴 Arby's, Burger King, Checkers, ChuckECheese, Denny's, Firehouse Grill, IHOP, McDonald's, PDQ Cafe, Pizza Hut, Pollo Tropical, Starbucks, Subway, Taco Bell 🅞 $Tree, Advance Parts, Aldi Foods, AT&T, Audi/Porsche, BMW/Mini, Chevrolet, Firestone/auto, GNC, Hyundai, Mercedes, Michael's, Office Depot, Staples, Verizon, VW
69b	W 🅞 to ✈
69a	Belvedere Rd, W 🅖 BP, Shell, WaWa/dsl 🍴 Burger King, IHOP, Wendy's 🛏 Courtyard, DoubleTree, Embassy Suites, Hampton Inn, Hilton Garden, Holiday Inn/rest., Stay Inn, Studio 6
68	US 98, Southern Blvd, E 🍴 Coastal, W Palm Gas 🍴 Subway 🅞 CVS Drug, Publix, W 🛏 Hilton
66	Forest Hill Blvd, W 🅖 Chevron/dsl, Sunoco 🍴 Dunkin' 🅞 Advance Parts
64	10th Ave N, W 🅖 Citgo, Marathon/Circle K/dsl, Mobil/dsl, Murphy USA/dsl 🍴 Chili's, Dunkin', Flanigan's Grill, Taco Bell, Wendy's 🛏 Woodspring Suites 🅞 CVS Drug, Ford, President Foods, Ross, Tires+, Walgreens, Walmart/Subway
63	6th Ave S, W 🅞 🅗
61	FL 812, Lantana Rd, E 🅖 Shell 🍴 Domino's, Dunkin', KFC, Little Caesar's, McDonald's, Riggins Crabhouse, Subway 🛏 Motel 6 🅞 $General, 7-11, Ace Hardware, AutoZone, CVS Drug, Publix, W 🅞 🅗, Costco/gas
60	Hypoluxo Rd, E 🅖 Chevron/dsl, Mobil/dsl, RaceTrac/dsl, Shell/dsl 🍴 Popeye's, Subway, Taco Bell, Wendy's 🛏 Comfort Inn, Holiday Inn Express, Super 8 🅞 Family$, NAPA, Tire Kingdom, Tire Pros, Tires+, Winn-Dixie, W 🅖 Valero/dsl 🍴 Anchor Inn Rest. 🅞 Advance Parts
59	Gateway Blvd, W 🅖 Mobil/7-11/dsl 🍴 Bonefish Grill, Boynton Alehouse, BurgerFi, Carrabba's, Chili's, Egg&I Cafe, Firehouse Subs, Golden Phoenix Chinese, McDonald's, PizzaRox, Starbucks, Subway, Tropical Smoothie 🛏 Hampton Inn, TownePlace Suites 🅞 $Tree, AT&T, CarMax, CVS Drug, Kohl's, Publix, Ross, Tuesday Morning, vet
57	FL 804, Boynton Bch Blvd, E 🅖 Marathon/dsl 🍴 KFC 🛏 Boynton Beach Inn 🅞 🅗, USPO, W 🅖 BP, Chevron/dsl, Mobil, Shell 🍴 Applebee's, Burger King, Checkers, Chick-Fil-A, Dunkin', Golden Corral, KFC, La Brasa, Little Caesar's, Olive Garden, Sonic, Starbucks, Steak'n Shake, Subway, TGIFriday's, Tijuana Flats, TX Roadhouse, Wendy's 🅞 $Tree, 7-11, Barnes&Noble, BJ's Whse/gas, CVS Drug, Dick's, GNC, Office Depot, Old Navy, PetCo, Petsmart, Publix, SteinMart, TJ Maxx, USPO, vet, Walgreens, Walmart
56	Woolbright Rd, E 🅖 Shell 🍴 McDonald's, Panera Bread, Smashburger, Subway, Tijuana Flats, Wendy's 🅞 🅗, 7-11, GNC, Jo-Ann Fabrics, Publix, vet, Walgreens, W 🅖 Marathon/McDonald's, RaceTrac/dsl 🍴 Burger King, Cracker Barrel, Dunkin' 🅞 Advance Parts, Home Depot, Lowe's, Staples, Walgreens
52b a	FL 806, Atlantic Ave, W 🅖 Chevron/dsl, Shell/dsl 🍴 Dunkin', Sandwich Man, Silver Wok, Subway 🅞 🅗, Tires+, transmissions, Verizon, vet, Walgreens
51	rd 782, Linton Blvd, E 🅖 Shell 🍴 Arby's, Chick-fil-A, Chipotle Mexican, DQ, Duffy's Grill, Five Guys, KFC, McDonald's, Outback Steaks, Pollo Tropical, Starbucks, Steak'n Shake, Subway, Taco Bell, Tijuana Flats, Wendy's 🅞 $Tree, AT&T, Chevrolet, Ford, Home Depot, Marshall's, Mercedes, Michael's, Petsmart, Publix, Ross, Target, Tire Kingdom, TJ Maxx, W 🅖 Shell 🍴 Dunkin', Little Caesar's 🅞 🅗, AutoZone, URGENT CARE

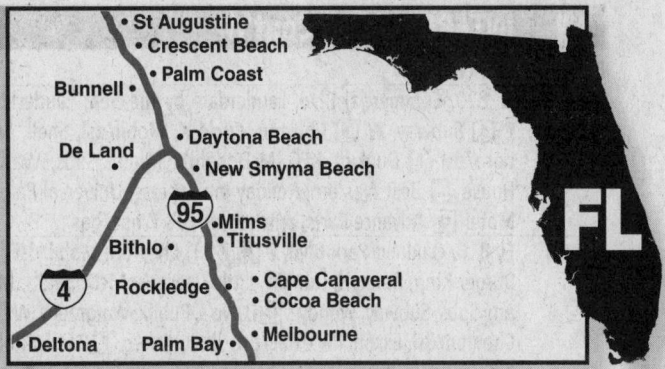

Exit #	Services
50	Congress Ave, W 🅖 Mobil 🛏 Hilton Garden, Residence Inn 🅞 Costco/gas
48b a	FL 794, Yamato Rd, E 🅖 Mobil 🍴 Panera Bread 🅞 CVS Drug, W 🅖 BP/dsl, Mobil 🍴 Blue Fin, Dunkin', Jersey Mike's Subs, Jimmy John's, McDonald's, Miller's Alehouse, Sal's Italian, Starbucks, The Grille, Wendy's 🛏 Embassy Suites, Hampton Inn, Ramada, SpringHill Suites, TownePlace Suites
45	FL 808, Glades Rd, E 🅖 Mobil/dsl 🍴 J Alexander's Rest., Jamba Juice, PF Chang's 🛏 Fairfield Inn 🅞 Barnes&Noble, CVS Drug, Whole Foods Mkt, W 🅖 Marathon 🍴 Brewzzi Cafe, Brio Italian Grill, CA Pizza Kitchen, Capital Grille, Cheesecake Factory, Chili's, Chipotle Mexican, Farmer's Table, Hooters, Houston's Rest., Madison's Grill, Maggiano's Italian, Moe's SW Grill, Morton Steaks, Season's Rest., Starbucks 🛏 Courtyard, Marriott, Renaissance, Wyndham Garden 🅞 Publix
44	Palmetto Park Rd, E 🅖 Valero/dsl 🍴 Denny's, Dunkin', Subway, Taco Bell, Tomasso's Pizza 🅞 Publix, USPO
42b a	FL 810, Hillsboro Blvd, E 🅖 Marathon, Shell/dsl 🍴 Dunkin', Hook Fish&Chicken, McDonald's, Popeye's, Wendy's 🛏 Doubletree, Hampton Inn, La Quinta 🅞 Advance Parts, W 🅖 Chevron/dsl, Mobil/dsl, WaWa/dsl 🍴 Checkers, Dunkin', Subway 🛏 La Quinta 🅞 CVS Drug, Home Depot, Walgreens
41	FL 869 (toll), SW 10th, to I-75, E 🅖 Mobil/7-11 🍴 Cracker Barrel, Pizza Express 🛏 Extended Stay America, Woodspring Suites, W 🛏 Best Western+, Quality Suites
39	FL 834, Sample Rd, E 🅖 Marathon/dsl, Shell/dsl, Speedway/dsl 🍴 Taco Bell 🅞 🅗, $General, AutoZone, Save-A-Lot, U-Haul, W 🅖 Chevron, Citgo/dsl, Mobil, Mobil/dsl, Solo/dsl, Sunoco/dsl, WaWa/dsl 🍴 Burger King, Checkers, IHOP, La Granja, McDonald's, Miami Subs, Subway 🅞 CarMax, Costco/gas, CVS Drug, Family$, Seabra Foods, vet
38b a	Copans Rd, E 🅖 Marathon/7-11 🍴 McDonald's 🅞 Land Rover, Mercedes, PepBoys, Porche/Audi, W 🅖 Chevron, Mobil/dsl 🅞 Home Depot, NAPA
36b a	FL 814, Atlantic Blvd, to Pompano Beach, E 🅖 RaceTrac/dsl 🍴 KFC/Pizza Hut/Taco Bell, Miami Subs, **1 mi** W 🅖 Marathon, Mobil/dsl, Murphy USA/dsl 🍴 Baskin-Robbins/Dunkin', Burger King, Golden Corral, KFC/LJ Silver, McDonald's, Pollo Tropical, Subway, Wendy's 🅞 $Tree, Chevrolet/Mazda, CVS Drug, to FL TPK, USPO, Walmart/Subway
33b a	Cypress Creek Rd, E 🅖 Marathon, Speedway 🍴 Duffy's Diner, Subway 🛏 Extended Stay America, Hampton Inn, Westin Hotel 🅞 7-11, W 🅖 Shell/repair 🍴 Arby's, Blaze Pizza, Burger Freak, Burger King, Carlucci's Italian, Chili's, Five Guys, Hooters, Jersey Mike's, Jimmy John's, Longhorn Steaks, McDonald's, Moonlite Diner, Starbucks, Subway, Sweet Tomatoes, Wendy's 🛏 Courtyard, La Quinta, Marriott, Sheraton Suites 🅞 AT&T, GNC, Jaguar, Office Depot, Tires+, URGENT CARE

POMPANO BEACH

FL

🅿 = gas 🍴 = food 🛏 = lodging 🅾 = other ℞ = rest stop   Copyright 2022 - The Next EXIT

🔼N INTERSTATE 95 Cont'd

Exit #	Services
32	FL 870, Commercial Blvd, Lauderdale by the Sea, Lauderhill, E 🍴 Subway, W 🅿 Chevron, Circle K, Mobil/dsl, Shell, Sunoco/dsl 🍴 Dunkin', KFC, McDonald's, Miami Subs, Waffle House 🛏 Best Western, Holiday Inn Express, Universal Palms Motel 🅾 Advance Parts, auto repair, BJ's Whse/gas
31b a	FL 816, Oakland Park Blvd, E 🅿 7-11, Chevron, Mobil/dsl 🍴 Burger King, Denny's, Dunkin', Little Caesar's, McDonald's, Miami Subs, Subway, Wendy's 🅾 Lowe's, Publix, Walgreens, W 🅿 Chevron/dsl, Exxon, RaceTrac/dsl, Shell, Valero 🍴 Baskin-Robbins/Dunkin', Burger King, Checkers, KFC, Subway 🛏 Days Inn 🅾 $General, Home Depot, Toyota, USPO, Walgreens
29b a	FL 838, Sunrise Blvd, E 🅿 Marathon/dsl, Mobil/dsl, Shell, Sunoco/dsl/e85 🍴 Burger King, Miami Subs, Popeye's 🅾 Advance Parts, auto repair/tires, AutoZone, Family$, to Birch SP, W 🅿 BP, Exxon/dsl, Marathon, Shell, Valero 🍴 China Bowl, Church's, Dunkin', KFC, McDonald's, Snapper's Fish&Chicken, Subway 🅾 🛏 Family$
27	FL 842, Broward Blvd, Ft Lauderdale, E 🅿 Marathon 🍴 Burger King, Dunkin 🛏 Days Inn 🅾 🛏 Walgreens, W 🅿 RaceTrac/dsl, WaWa/dsl 🍴 Charley's, Checkers, Chen's, Chipotle, McDonald's 🅾 Verizon, Walmart/Burger King
26	I-595 (from sb), FL 736 (from nb), Davie Blvd, E 🅾 to ℞
25	FL 84, E 🅿 7-11, Marathon, Marathon/dsl, RaceTrac/dsl, Sunoco/dsl, Texaco 🍴 Dunkin', Li'l Red's BBQ, McDonald's, Ruby Chinese, Subway, Wendy's 🛏 Best Western, Candlewood Suites, Hampton Inn, Holiday Inn Express, Motel 6, Sky Motel 🅾 $Tree, BigLots, Firestone/auto, U-Haul, Walgreens, Winn-Dixie, W 🛏 Ramada Inn, Red Carpet Inn, Rodeway Inn
24	I-595 (from nb), to I-75, E 🅾 to ℞
23	FL 818, Griffin Rd, E 🛏 Ft Lauderdale Hotel, W 🅿 Mobil 🍴 Dunkin', Subway, Wendy's 🛏 Courtyard, Fairfield Inn, Homewood Suites, Residence Inn 🅾 Bass Pro Shops, Publix
22	FL 848, Stirling Rd, Cooper City, E 🅿 Mobil/Dunkin'/dsl 🍴 AleHouse Grill, Burger King, Chipotle Mexican, Dave&Buster's, Firehouse Subs, McDonald's, Moonlite Diner, Red Lobster, Sal's Italian, Subway, Sweet Tomatoes, Taco Bell, TGIFriday's, Wendy's, Yum Berry Yogurt 🛏 Hampton Inn, Hilton Garden, Hyatt House, Hyatt Place, La Quinta, Quality Inn, SpringHill Suites 🅾 Advance Parts, BJ's Whse, GNC, Home Depot, Marshall's, Michael's, Old Navy, Petsmart, Ross, to Lloyd SP, Verizon, W 🍴 Las Vegas Cuban, Subway 🛏 Best Western, Cambria Suites, Comfort Suites, Home 2 Suites 🅾 CVS Drug, PepBoys, Tire Kingdom, vet, Walgreens
21	FL 822, Sheridan St, E 🅿 Chevron/dsl, Cumberland Farms/gas, Marathon/Dunkin'/dsl 🍴 Domino's, W 🅿 Shell 🍴 Denny's, McDonald's 🛏 Days Inn, Holiday Inn
20	FL 820, Hollywood Blvd, E 🅿 Shell 🍴 IHOP, Miami Subs 🛏 Hollywood Gateway Inn 🅾 Goodyear/auto, U-Haul, vet, W 🅿 Chevron/dsl, Marathon 🍴 Boston Mkt, Burgers&Shakes, China Hollywood, Coldstone, McDonald's, Offerdahl's Grill, Starbucks, Subway, Taco Bell, Waffle Works, Wendy's 🅾 🛏 Publix, Target, Walgreens
19	FL 824, Pembroke Rd, E 🅿 Orion/dsl, Shell 🅾 Family$, W 🅿 Mobil/dsl
18	FL 858, Hallandale Bch Blvd, E 🅿 7-11, Exxon, Shell 🍴 Baskin-Robbins/Dunkin', Burger King, Denny's, IHOP, KFC, La Granja, Little Caesar's, McDonald's, Miami Subs, Pollo Tropical, Subway, Taco Bell, Wendy's, Won Ton Garden 🛏 Best Western+ 🅾 Family$, Goodyear/auto, Tire Kingdom, vet, Walgreens, Winn-Dixie, W 🅿 Mobil/dsl, RaceTrac/dsl 🅾 🛏 Advance Parts

Exit #	Services
16	Ives Dairy Rd, E 🅾 🛏, W 🅿 Marathon/7-11 🍴 Subway
14	FL 860, Miami Gardens Dr, N Miami Beach, E 🅾 🛏, Oleta River SRA, W 🅿 Shell/dsl, Valero/dsl
12c	US 441, FL 826, FL TPK, FL 9, E 🅿 7-11, Chevron, Exxon/dsl, Marathon/dsl, Marathon/dsl, Speedway, Valero/dsl 🍴 Baskin-Robbins/Dunkin', Burger King, La Granja, McDonald's, Starbucks, Subway, Taco Bell/Pizza Hut, Wendy's 🛏 Rodeway Inn 🅾 🛏, PepBoys, Toyota
12b	US 441 (from nb), same as 12c
12a	FL 868 (from nb), FL TPK N
11	NW 151st (from nb), W 🅿 Sunoco/dsl 🍴 McDonald's 🅾 Advance Parts, Winn-Dixie
10b	FL 916, NW 135th, Opa-Locka Blvd, W 🅿 Chevron, Mobil/dsl 🍴 Checkers, Pizza Hut, Subway
10a	NW 125th, N Miami, Bal Harbour, W 🅿 Shell 🍴 Burger King, Wendy's 🅾 $General
9	NW 119th (from nb), W 🅿 7-11/dsl, Marathon/McDonald's 🍴 KFC, Pollo Tropical, Popeye's 🅾 Advance Parts, AutoZone, CVS Drug, Family$, Walgreens, Winn-Dixie
8b	FL 932, NW 103rd, E 🅿 Chevron, Shell 🅾 7-11, W 🅿 Sunoco, Sunshine/dsl 🍴 $General, Baskin-Robbins/Dunkin', Brave Foods
8a	NW 95th, E 🅿 Chevron, W 🅿 7-11/dsl, CR/dsl, Mobil/dsl 🍴 McDonald's 🅾 🛏, Advance Parts, Walgreens
7	FL 934, NW 81st, NW 79th, E 🅿 Chevron/dsl, Valero/dsl, W 🅿 Sunoco 🍴 Checkers
6b	NW 69th (from sb)
6a	FL 944, NW 62nd, NW 54th, W 🍴 China Town, McDonald's, Subway 🅾 Family$, Presidente Mkt, Walgreens
4b a	I-195 E, FL 112 W (toll), Miami Beach, E downtown, W 🅾 ℞
3b	NW 8th St (from sb)
3a	FL 836 W (toll) (exits left from nb), W 🅾 🛏, to ℞
2d	I-395 E (exits left from sb), to Miami Beach
2c	NW 8th, NW 14th (from sb), Miami Ave, E 🅾 Port of Miami
2b	NW 2nd (from nb), downtown Miami
2a	US 1 (exits left from sb), Biscayne Blvd, downtown Miami
1b	US 41, SW 7th, SW 8th, Brickell Ave, E 🅿 Chevron, Citgo 🍴 Burger King, Graziano's, McDonald's, Pepper's Mexican Grill, Subway, Wendy's 🛏 Extended Stay America, Hampton Inn 🅾 CVS Drug, GNC, Publix, W 🅿 Shell 🍴 Papa John's
1a	SW 25th (from sb), downtown, to Rickenbacker Causeway, E 🅾 to Baggs SRA
0mm	I-95 begins/ends on US 1. 1 mi S 🅿 Mobil

🔼N INTERSTATE 275 (Tampa)

Exit #	Services
59mm	I-275 begins/ends on I-75, exit 274.
53	Bearss Ave, E 🅿 Citgo/dsl, Wawa/dsl 🍴 Culver's 🅾 Carmax, Walmart, W 🅿 BP, Chevron/dsl, Marathon/Dunkin', RaceTrac/dsl, Shell/dsl 🍴 Burger King, IHOP, McDonald's, Popeye's, Subway 🛏 Vista Inn 🅾 Aldi Foods, BigLots, CVS Drug, GNC, Ross
52	Fletcher Ave, E 🅿 Citgo/dsl, Marathon, Mobil/dsl, RaceTrac/dsl, Speedway, Sunoco, Wawa/dsl 🍴 Arby's, Bruno's Pizza, Church's, DQ, Krystal, McDonald's, Popeye's 🛏 Days Inn 🅾 🛏, Aldi Foods, Family$, to USF, Toyota, Walmart, W 🅿 Citgo, Marathon, Mobil 🛏 Super 8 🅾 Cadillac, Family$, Jaguar, Save-A-Lot
51	FL 582, Fowler Ave, E 🅿 Citgo/dsl, Marathon/dsl, Mobil/dsl, Shell/Circle K 🍴 A&W/LJ Silver, Burger King, Chili's, Chipotle Mexican, Denny's, Firehouse Subs, Five Guys, Jason's Deli, Jimmy John's, KFC, Longhorn Steaks, McDonald's, Panda Express, Pizza Hut, Shell Rest., Sonic, Starbucks, Steak'n Shake, Subway

◤N INTERSTATE 275 (Tampa) Cont'd

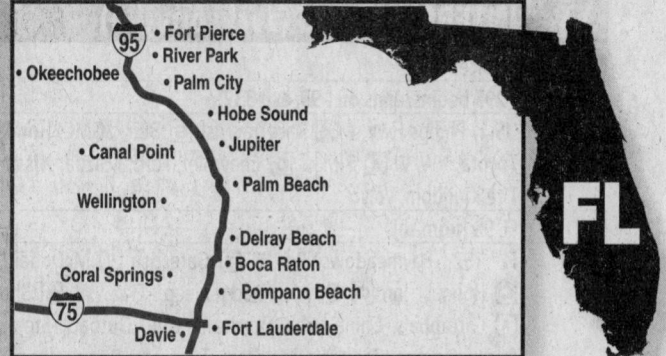

51	Continued
	Taco Bell, TGIFriday's, Waffle House, Wendy's 🅐 Clarion, Embassy Suites, Holiday Inn, Hyatt Place, La Quinta, Wingate Inn 🅞 $General, $Tree, Advance Parts, AT&T, CVS Drug, O'Reilly Parts, Verizon, Walgreens, Winn Dixie, **W** 🅐 Rodeway Inn 🅞 Audi, BMW, Chevrolet, NAPA, Porsche, VW
50	FL 580, Busch Blvd, **E** 🅖 Citgo, Marathon 🅕 Burger King, McDonald's, Olive Garden, Popeye's, Red Lobster, Subway, Taco Bell 🅐 Hampton Inn, Holiday Inn Express, La Quinta, Red Roof Inn 🅞 $General, Advance Parts, AutoZone, Busch Gardens, Family$, Walgreens, **W** 🅕 Burger King 🅞 $Tree, Advance Parts, CVS Drug, Family$, Firestone/auto, Home Depot, Walmart Mkt
49	Bird Ave (from nb), **E** 🅞 Family$, **W** 🅕 Checkers, KFC, Krispy Kreme, McDonald's, Subway, Wendy's 🅞 $General, Save-A-Lot
48	Sligh Ave, **E** 🅖 Marathon, Sunoco 🅞 USPO, **W** 🅞 zoo
47b a	US 92, to US 41 S, Hillsborough Ave, **E** 🅖 Marathon, Mobil/dsl, Shell/Circle K 🅕 Burger King, Checkers, McDonald's, Popeye's, Subway, Taco Bell, Wendy's 🅞 Advance Parts, Ross, vet, Walgreens, Walmart, **W** 🅖 BP, Shell/Circle K 🅕 Papa John's, Starbucks 🅐 Dutch Motel
46b	FL 574, MLK Blvd, **E** 🅖 🅞 Advance Parts, Walgreens, Winn Dixie, **W** 🅖 Chevron/dsl 🅕 McDonald's 🅞 🅗
46a	Floribraska Ave (from sb, no return)
45b	I-4 E, to Orlando, I-75
45a	Jefferson St, downtown E
44	Ashley Dr, Tampa St, downtown W
42	Howard Ave, Armenia Ave, **W** 🅖 Marathon/dsl 🅕 Popeye's
41c	Himes Ave (from sb), **W** 🅞 RJ Stadium
41b a	US 92, Dale Mabry Blvd, **E** 🅖 Marathon, Marathon (2), Mobil/dsl, Shell/Circle K, Wawa/dsl 🅕 Brickhouse Grill, Burger King, Carrabba's, Chick-Fil-A, Crispers, Don Pan Cuban, Donatello Italian, Grill 116, IHOP, J.Alexanders Rest, Jersey Mike's Subs, Little Caesar's, Pei Wei, Pizza Hut, Ruby Tuesday, Shells Rest., Starbucks, Subway, Village Inn 🅐 Best Western, Courtyard, Quality Inn, Tahitian Inn/cafe 🅞 AT&T, Barnes&Noble, CVS Drug, Office Depot, Publix, Tire Kingdom, to MacDill AFB, Trader Joe's, Verizon, **W** 🅖 Marathon/Dunkin' 🅕 Burger King, Chili's, China 1, Chipotle, Denny's, Jimmy John's, Joe's Pizza, McDonald's, Moe's SW Grill, Sonic, Starbucks, Subway, Sweet Tomatoes, Wendy's 🅐 Fairfield Inn, Hilton, Howard Johnson, Residence Inn 🅞 Best Buy, Chrysler/Dodge/Jeep, Family$, Home Depot, Honda, Petsmart, Staples, Target, to RJ Stadium, Walmart, Whole Foods Mkt, Winn Dixie
40b	Lois Ave, **W** 🅖 Marathon/dsl 🅕 Charley's Rest. 🅐 DoubleTree Hotel, Sheraton
40a	FL 587, Westshore Blvd, **E** 🅖 BP, Chevron/dsl, Citgo/Subway 🅕 Burger King, Chipotle Mexican, Gogo's Greek, Jimmy John's, Maggiano's Rest., McDonald's, Panera Bread, PF Chang's, Season's Grill, Starbucks, Taco Bell, Waffle House 🅐 Crowne Plaza, Embassy Suites 🅞 Firestone, JC Penney, Macy's, Old Navy, PetCo, Walgreens, **W** 🅖 Shell/Subway 🅕 Blue Water Grill 🅐 Hampton Inn, Holiday Inn, Marriott, Ramada Inn, SpringHill Suites
39b a	FL 60 W, **W** 🅞 to ✈
32	Fl 687 S, 4th St N, to US 92 (no sb re-entry)
31b a	9th St N, MLK St N (exits left from sb), 🅞 ✈, info
30	FL 686, Roosevelt Blvd, 0-2 mi **W** 🅖 Rally 🅕 Bascom's Chophouse, Burger King, Chil-fil-A, Cracker Barrel, Mamma Mia's, McDonald's, Starbucks, Subway, Taco Bell, Wendy's 🅐 Comfort Inn, Courtyard, Extended Stay America, Fairfield Inn, Hampton Inn, Holiday Inn, La Quinta, Marriott, Quality Inn, Red Roof Inn, Sleep Inn, SpringHill Suites, Super 8 🅞 CVS Drug, Publix

28	FL 694 W, Gandy Blvd, Indian Shores, 0-2 mi **W** 🅖 Citgo, Murphy USA/dsl, Speedway/dsl, WaWa/dsl 🅕 Applebee's, BJ's Brewhouse, Bob Evans, Buffalo Wild Wings, Burger King, Cheddar's, Chick-fil-A, Chili's, Chipotle, Coldstone, Dunkin', Firehouse Subs, Five Guys, IHOP, McDonald's, Moe's SW, Panda Express, Panera Bread, Pizza Hut/Taco Bell, Pollo Tropical, Sonny's BBQ, Starbucks, Subway, Wendy's 🅐 La Quinta 🅞 $Tree, Bentley, BMW, Cadillac, GNC, Home Depot, Honda, Marshall's, Michael's, Office Depot, PetCo, Publix, Rolls Royce, Target, U-Haul, Walgreens, Walmart
26b a	54th Ave N, **E** 🅖 Cracker Barrel 🅐 Comfort Inn, Holiday Inn Express, **W** 🅖 RaceTrac/dsl 🅕 Waffle House 🅐 Knights Inn 🅞 🅗, Harley-Davidson, NAPA
25	38th Ave N, to beaches, **W** 🅖 Citgo/dsl, Wawa/dsl 🅕 Burger King, Hardee's 🅞 Subaru, VW, Walgreens
24	22nd Ave N, **W** 🅖 Citgo/dsl, RaceTrac/dsl, Wawa/dsl 🅕 Dunkin', Little Caesar's 🅞 Advance Parts, Home Depot, Lowe's
23b	FL 595, 5th Ave N, **E** 🅞 🅗
23a	I-375, **E** 🅞 The Pier, Waterfront, downtown
22	I-175 E, Tropicana Field, **E** 🅞 🅗
21	28th St S, downtown
20	31st Ave (from nb), downtown
19	22nd Ave S, Gulfport, **W** 🅖 Chevron, Citgo, Shell/dsl 🅕 Church's, KFC 🅞 Family$
18	26th Ave S (from nb)
17	FL 682 W, 54th Ave S, Pinellas Bayway, **W services on US 19 (34th St)** 🅖 7-11, Sunoco/dsl 🅕 Beef'O'Brady's, Bob Evans, Burger King, China Wok, Domino's, Dunkin', IHOP, McDonald's, Papa John's, Pizza Hut, Portofino Italian, Subway, Taco Bell, Wendy's 🅐 Bayway Inn, Crystal Inn 🅞 $Tree, AT&T, Beall's, CVS Drug, GNC, Publix, St Pete Beach, to Ft DeSoto Pk, vet, Walmart/McDonald's
16	Pinellas Point Dr, Skyway Lane, to Maximo Park, **E** 🅐 Magnuson Resort, **W** 🅞 marina
16mm	toll plaza sb
13mm	N Skyway Fishing Pier, **W** 🆁🆂 both lanes, full ♿ facilities, litter barrels, petwalk, 🗑, ⛽, vending
10mm	Tampa Bay
7mm	S Skyway Fishing Pier, **E** 🆁🆂 both lanes, full ♿ facilities, litter barrels, petwalk, 🗑, ⛽, vending
6mm	toll plaza nb
5	US 19, Palmetto, Bradenton
2	US 41, (last nb exit before **toll**), Palmetto, Bradenton, **E** 🅞 Circle K, Fiesta Grove RV Resort, Frog Creek Campground, Terra Ceia Village Campground, Winterset RV Resort, **W** 🅖 Shell/DQ/Subway/dsl
0mm	I-275 begins/ends on I-75, exit 228.

S T P E T E R S B U R G

🅶 = gas 🍴 = food 🛏 = lodging 🅾 = other Ⓡ = rest stop   Copyright 2022 - The Next EXIT ®

◣◥ INTERSTATE 295 (Jacksonville)

Exit #	Services
61b a	I-295 begins/ends on I-95, exit 337.
60	US 1, Philips Hwy, **E** 🅶 RaceTrac/dsl 🅾 Buick/GMC, Honda, Toyota, VW, **W** 🅶 BP/dsl 🅾 Chevrolet, Ford, Mazda, Nissan, Tire Kingdom, Volvo
58	FL 9b (from sb)
56	FL 152, Baymeadows Rd, **E** 🅶 Gate/dsl 🍴 McDonald's 🛏 Holiday Inn 🅾 Chrysler/Dodge/Jeep, Fiat, **W** 🅶 Shell 🍴 Carrabba's, China Wok, Hurricane Grill, Outback Steaks, Sticky Fingers, Tequila's Mexican, Tony D's Pizza, Wendy's 🛏 Hampton Inn 🅾 Publix, SteinMart, URGENT CARE, Walgreens, Winn Dixie
54	Gate Pkwy, **W** 🍴 Melting Pot, Otaki Japanese Steaks
53	FL 202, Butler Blvd, **1 mi W on Gate Pkwy** 🅶 Shell/dsl 🍴 Arby's, Bahama Breeze, BJ's Rest, Bono's BBQ, Brio Grille, Burger-Fi, Cantina Laredo, Capital Grill, Cheesecake Factory, Chick-fil-A, Chipotle Mexican, Cooper's Hawk, J Alexander's, Maggiano's Italian, McDonald's, Mimi's Cafe, Moxie Kitchen, Ovinte, Panda Express, Panera Bread, Pei Wei, PF Chang's, Pollo Tropical, Seasons Rest, Ted's MT Grill, Wasabi, Wendy's, Zaxby's, Zoe's Kitchen 🛏 Sheraton 🅾 $Tree, AT&T, Barnes&Noble, Best Buy, Costco, CVS Drug, Dick's, Dillard's, Jo-Ann, Nordstrom, Old Navy, Petsmart, REI, Ross, Staples, Target, Verizon
52	U of NF Dr, Town Center Pkwy, same as 53
51	US 90, Beach Blvd, **E** 🍴 Burger King, Dunkin', Jimmy John's, **W** 🅶 Shell 🍴 Arby's, Checkers, McDonald's, Pizza Hut, Sonic, Taco Bell 🛏 InTown Suites 🅾 $Tree, Advance Parts, Sam's Club/gas, USPO, vet, Walgreens, Winn-Dixie
49	St John's Bluff Rd (from nb), **E** 🅶 BP, Shell 🍴 Papa John's 🛏 Holiday Inn Express, InTown Suites 🅾 $Tree, Nissan, O'Reilly Parts
48	FL 10, to Atlantic Blvd
47	Monument Rd, **E** 🅶 Marathon/Kangaroo/dsl 🍴 Domino's, Hong Kong Chinese, Mudville Grille 🅾 vet, **W** 🅶 Gate/dsl 🍴 Ruby Tuesday 🛏 Courtyard, Hampton Inn 🅾 Walmart/McDonald's
46	FL 116 E, Wonderwood Connector, Merrill Rd, **E** 🛏 Candlewood Suites, **W** 🛏 Woodspring Suites
44mm	St John's River
41	FL 105, Heckscher Dr, Zoo Pkwy, **E** 🅶 Gate/dsl, **W** 🅶 Valero/Kangaroo/dsl 🍴 Wendy's 🛏 Holiday Inn Express 🅾 zoo
40	Alta Dr, **E** 🍴 Molly Brown's Grill, Viva Mexican
37	Pulaski Rd, **E** 🅶 Marathon/Kangaroo/dsl
36	US 17, Main St, **E** 🅶 Kangaroo/dsl 🍴 DQ, McDonald's 🅾 Winn-Dixie, **W** 🍴 Subway
35b a	I-95, S to Jacksonville, N to Savannah
33	Duval Rd, **W** 🍽
32	FL 115, Lem Turner Rd, **E** 🅶 7-11/dsl 🍴 Burger King, China Wok, McDonald's (1mi), Subway, Waffle House, Wendy's 🅾 $Tree, Home Depot, Walmart/McDonald's, **W** 🅾 Flamingo Lake RV Resort, Lakeside Cabins/RV Park
30	FL 104, Dunn Ave, **E** 🅶 7-11/dsl, Gate/dsl, Shell (1mi), Valero (1mi) 🍴 McDonald's (1mi), **W** 🅾 Big Tree RV Park
28b a	US 1, US 23, to Callahan, Jacksonville, **E** 🅶 Kangaroo/dsl, **W** 🅶 BP/DQ/dsl, RaceTrak/dsl 🍴 Wendy's 🅾 auto repair, **S** 🅶 Valero/Kangaroo/Subway/dsl
25	Pritchard Rd, **W** 🅶 Kangaroo/Subway/deli/dsl/24hr

22	Commonwealth Ave, **E** 🅶 BP/dsl 🍴 Burger King, Hardee's, Waffle House, Zaxby's 🛏 Quality Inn 🅾 dogtrack, **W** 🍴 Wendy's 🛏 Comfort Suites, Country Inn&Suites
21b a	I-10, W to Tallahassee, E to Jacksonville
19	FL 228, Normandy Blvd, **E** 🅶 BP/dsl, Murphy USA/dsl 🍴 Burger King, Capt D's, El Potro, Firehouse Subs, Golden Corral, Hot Wok, McDonald's, Panda Express, Papa John's, Sonic, Waffle House, Wendy's 🅾 $Tree, AT&T, CVS Drug, Save-A-Lot, Walgreens, Walmart, **W** 🅶 BP, RaceTrac/dsl, Shell/dsl, Speedway/dsl 🍴 Famous Amos, Golden China, Hardee's, KFC, Larry's Subs, McDonald's, Pizza Hut, Popeye's, Sam's Seafood Rest., Whataburger 🅾 Advance Parts, CVS Drug, Family$, Publix, Walgreens, Winn-Dixie
17	FL 208, Wilson Blvd, **E** 🅶 7-11/dsl, BP/Subway/dsl, Speedway/Dunkin'/dsl 🍴 China Wok, Hardee's 🅾 $General, Advance Parts, FL RV Ctr, Walmart Mkt, **W** 🅶 Kangaroo
16	FL 134, 103rd St, Cecil Field, **E** 🅶 BP/dsl, Gate/dsl, Murphy Express/dsl, RaceTrac/dsl, Speedway 🍴 Applebee's, Capt D's, Firehouse Subs, Krispy Kreme, Krystal, Papa John's, Pizza Hut, Popeye's, Sonic, Wendy's, Ying's Chinese 🛏 Hospitality Inn 🅾 $General, $Tree, Advance Parts, AT&T, CVS Drug, GNC, Goodyear/auto, NAPA, Save-A-Lot Foods, Tires+, U-Haul, URGENT CARE, Walmart/McDonald's, **W** 🅶 BP/dsl, Exxon/dsl, Shell 🍴 Burger King, DQ, Dunkin', IHOP, KFC, Little Caesar's, McDonald's, Subway, Taco Bell, Waffle House 🅾 Aamco, AutoZone, Family$, Goodyear/auto, O'Reilly Parts, Publix, Sun Tires, vet, Walgreens
12	FL 21, Blanding Blvd, **E** 🅶 BP, RaceTrac/dsl, Speedway/Dunkin'/dsl, Texaco 🍴 Burger King, Dunkin', Larry's Subs, McDonald's, Pizza Hut, Subway 🅾 $General, Acura, Audi, Best Buy, BMW, Buick/GMC, Cadillac, CarMax, Chrysler/Dodge/Jeep, CVS Drug, Fiat, Ford, Honda, Hyundai, Infiniti, Lexus, Lincoln, Mazda, Mercedes/Smart, Nissan, Office Depot, Subaru, U-Haul, USPO, VW, Walgreens, **W** 🅶 BP, Carrabba's, Marathon/Kangaroo/dsl, Shell 🍴 Applebee's, Arby's, Buffalo Wild Wings, Burger King, Chick-fil-A, Chili's, China Buffet, Chipotle Mexican, ChuckeCheese, Denny's, Dick's Wings, Firehouse Subs, Five Guys, HoneyBaked Ham, Hooters, KFC, Krystal, Kyodai Steaks, Longhorn Steaks, Mission BBQ, Olive Garden, Orange Park Ale House, Outback Steaks, Panda Express, Panera Bread, Papa John's, Red Lobster, Ruby Tuesday, Starbucks, Steak'n Shake, Sweet Tomatoes, Taco Bell, Ted's MT Grill, TGIFriday's, Thai Garden, Wendy's 🛏 Country Inn Suites, La Quinta, Motel 6, Quality Inn, Red Roof Inn, Super 8 🅾 🏥, $Tree, AT&T, Belk, Books-A-Million, Dick's, Dillard's, Discount Tire, Firestone/auto, Goodyear/auto, Home Depot, JC Penney, Jo-Ann Fabrics, Michael's, O'Reilly Parts, PepBoys, Petsmart, Publix, Sam's Club/gas, Tires+, TJMaxx, Toyota, Verizon, Walgreens, Walmart/dsl
10	US 17, FL 15, Roosevelt Blvd, Orange Park, **E** 🛏 Best Western, **W** 🅶 BP/dsl, Chevron/dsl, RaceTrac/dsl, Speedwaydsl 🍴 Aron's Pizza, Cracker Barrel, Dunkin', Four Rivers Smokehouse, Krystal, McDonald's, Subway, Waffle House, Wendy's 🛏 Courtyard, Days Inn, Fairfield Inn, Hampton Inn, Hilton Garden, Holiday Inn, Rodeway Inn 🅾 🏥, $Tree, CVS Drug, General RV Ctr, Harley-Davidson, Sun Tire, vet, Winn-Dixie
7mm	St Johns River, Buckman Br

FL

INTERSTATE 295 (Jacksonville) Cont'd

Exit #	Services
5b a	FL 13, San Jose Blvd, E 🅿 Speedway/dsl, Valero/DQ/dsl 🍴 Arby's, Bob Evans, Bono's BBQ, Carrabba's, Chick-fil-A, Crystal River Seafood, Dickey's BBQ, Domino's, Famous Amos, Firehouse Subs, Five Guys, HoneyBaked Ham, Krystal, McDonald's, Outback Steaks, Popeye's, Red Elephant Pizza, Smoothie King, Starbucks, Steak'n Shake, The Loop Pizza, Village Inn, Which Wich?, Zaxby's 🏨 La Quinta, Ramada Inn 🅾 Aamco, Advance Parts, BigLots, CVS Drug, Firestone/auto, Office Depot, PepBoys, Publix, Save-A-Lot, Sun Tire, Target, Tire Kingdom, Tires+, URGENT CARE, Verizon, Whole Foods Mkt, W 🅿 BP, Citgo, Shell 🍴 Al's Pizza, Bonefish Grill, Bruster's, Chili's, Chipotle Mexican, Dunkin', Golden Corral, Hardee's, Jimmy John's, Krispy Kreme,

5b a	Continued
	Mama Fu's, Mandarin Ale House, McDonald's, Moe's SW Grill, Newk's Eatery, Osaka Grill, Panera Bread, Papa John's, Papa Murphy's, Pizza Hut, Pollo Tropical, Starbucks, Subway, Taco Bell, Tree Steakhouse 🅾 $Tree, Advance Parts, AT&T, AutoZone, Barnes&Noble, Goodyear/auto, Marshall's, Michael's, NAPA, PetCo, Publix, Staples, SteinMart, Tire Kingdom, TJ Maxx, U-Haul, vet, Walgreens, Walmart, Winn-Dixie, World Mkt
3	Old St Augustine Rd, E 🅿 BP/dsl, Shell/dsl 🍴 Burger King, Little Caesar's, Little China, McDonald's, Pizza Hut, Salento Steaks, St Mary's Seafood, Taco Bell, Wendy's 🏨 Holiday Inn Express 🅾 $General, $Tree, CVS Drug, GNC, Hobby Lobby, Publix/deli, Winn-Dixie, W 🅿 Gate/dsl, Marathon/Kangaroo/dsl 🍴 Firehouse Subs, KFC, Rosy's Mexican, Subway, Vino's Pizza 🅾 Lowe's, vet, Walgreens

NOTES

FL

GEORGIA

⬆️🅴 INTERSTATE 16

Exit #	Services
167b a	W Broad, Montgomery St, **I-16 begins/ends in Savannah.** Savannah, 0-1 mi **N** 🛢️ Chevron, Enmarket, Parker's 🛏️ Best Western, Courtyard, DoubleTree, Fairfield Inn, Hampton Inn, Hilton Garden, Holiday Inn, Quality Inn, Residence Inn, SpringHill Suites, **S** 🍴 Burger King, Popeye's, Wendy's ⬜ Family$
166	US 17, Gwinnet St, Savannah Savannah Visitors Ctr
165	GA 204, 37th St (from eb), to Ft Pulaski NM, **N** ⬜ Savannah College
164b a	I-516, US 80, US 17, GA 21
162	Chatham Pkwy, **S** 🛢️ Shell/dsl 🍴 Kan Pai Japanese, Larry's Subs, Nicky's Pizza, Sunrise Rest. ⬜ Acura, Chrysler/Dodge/Jeep, Kia, Lexus, Subaru, Toyota
160	GA 307, Dean Forest Rd, **N** 🛢️ Parker's/dsl, Pilot/Subway/dsl/scales, Shell/dsl 🍴 Ronnie's Rest., Waffle House
157b a	I-95, S to Jacksonville, N to Florence
155	Pooler Pkwy, **N** 🛢️ EnMarket/dsl, Murphy USA/dsl, to Airport 🍴 Jalapeno's Mexican, Papa John's, Subway, Wasabi Fusion ⬜ Lowe's, Savannah Tire, Verizon, **S** 🛢️ BP/dsl, Parker's/dsl
152	GA 17, to Bloomingdale
148	Old River Rd, to US 80
144mm	**weigh sta both lanes**
143	US 280, to US 80, **N** 🛢️ Loves/dsl/scales/24hr/@, **S** 🛢️ BP/Subway/dsl, Marathon/dsl
137	GA 119, to Pembroke, Ft Stewart
132	Ash Branch Church Rd
127	GA 67, to Pembroke, Ft Stewart, **N** 🛢️ BP/dsl, EnMarket/dsl 🍴 Sallie Mae's Kitchen ⬜ antiques
116	US 25/301, to Statesboro, **N** 🛢️ Chevron/PoJo Diner/dsl/scales/24hr ⬜ Magnolia Springs SP (45 mi), to GA Southern U, **S** 🛏️ Patriot Inn
111	Pulaski-Excelsior Rd, **S** 🛢️ Citgo/Grady's Grill/dsl ⬜ Beaver Run RV Park, tires/repair
104	GA 22, GA 121, Metter, **N** 🛢️ BP/dsl/scales/24hr, Enmark, EVC, Parker's/dsl, Shell/dsl 🍴 Bevrick's Grille, Burger King, DQ, El Mariachi, Jomax BBQ, KFC/Taco Bell, McDonald's, Papa Buck's BBQ, Pizza Hut, Shogun, Subway, Waffle House, Zaxby's 🛏️ American Inn, Days Inn, Econo Inn, Garden Inn ⬜ Chevrolet, 🅷, info, O'Reilly Parts, to Smith SP, Walgreens, **S** 🛢️ Chevron/dsl, Marathon/dsl ⬜ Ford
101mm	Canoochee River
98	GA 57, to Stillmore, **S** 🛢️ BP/dsl/24hr, Chevron/dsl ⬜ to Altahama SP
90	US 1, to Swainsboro, **N** 🛢️ Chevron/Subway/dsl, Marathon/dsl
88mm	Ohoopee River
84	GA 297, to Vidalia, **N** ⬜ truck sales
78	US 221, GA 56, to Swainsboro
71	GA 15, GA 78, to Soperton, **N** 🛢️ Chevron/dsl
67	GA 29, to Soperton, **S** 🛢️ Marathon/dsl 🍴 Huddle House
58	GA 199, Old River Rd, East Dublin
56mm	Oconee River
54	GA 19, to Dublin, **S** 🛢️ Chevron/dsl/24hr
51	US 441, US 319, to Dublin, **N** 🛢️ BP/Subway/dsl, EVC, Exxon/dsl, Flash/gas, Pilot/dsl/scales/24hr 🍴 Arby's, Asian Buffet, Burger King, KFC, King's Inn/rest., McDonald's, Ruby Tuesday, Salsa's Mexican, Taco Bell, Wendy's 🛏️ Baymont Inn, Days Inn, Holiday Inn Express, Motel 6, Quality Inn, Relax Inn, Super 8 ⬜

Exit #	Services
51	Continued $General, Chrysler/Dodge/Jeep, 🅷, Steve's RV, **S** 🛢️ Chevron/dsl, Tesla EVC 🍴 Cracker Barrel, Longhorn Steaks, Waffle House, Zaxby's 🛏️ Fairfield Inn, Hampton Inn, La Quinta ⬜ to Little Ocmulgee SP, visitor ctr
49	GA 257, to Dublin, Dexter, **N** 🍴 Friendly Gus/dsl ⬜ Honeysuckle Farm RV Park, 🅷, **S** 🛢️ Loves/Chester's/Subway/dsl/scales/24hr
46mm	🆁🆂 wb, full 🚻 facilities, litter barrels, petwalk, 📶, 🏧, RV dump, vending
44mm	🆁🆂 eb, full 🚻 facilities, litter barrels, petwalk, 📶, 🏧, RV dump, vending
42	GA 338, to Dudley
39	GA 26, to Cochran, Montrose
32	GA 112, Allentown, **S** 🛢️ Chevron/dsl
27	GA 358, to Danville
24	GA 96, to Jeffersonville, **N** 🛢️ Marathon/dsl, **S** 🛢️ Exxon/Huddle House/dsl/24hr 🛏️ Suburban Inn ⬜ museum, to Robins AFB
18	Bullard Rd, to Jeffersonville, Bullard
12	Sgoda Rd, Huber, **N** 🛢️ Marathon/dsl
6	US 23, US 129A, East Blvd, Ocmulgee, **N** 🛢️ Shell/Circle K/DQ, Texaco/dsl 🍴 McDonald's, Waffle House ⬜ GA Forestry Ctr, 📶, **S** 🛢️ Chevron/Huddle House/dsl/scales/24hr, Friendly Gus 🍴 Subway
2	US 80, GA 87, MLK Jr Blvd, **N** 🛏️ Marriott ⬜ conv ctr, 🅷, Ocmulgee NM, **S** 🛢️ Marathon/dsl ⬜ to Hist Dist
1b	GA 22, to US 129, GA 49, 2nd St (from wb), **S** ⬜ 🅷
1a	US 23, Gray Hwy (from eb), **N** 🛢️ Exxon, Flash/dsl, Valero 🍴 Arby's, Bojangles, Burger King, Chen's Wok, DQ, El Sombrero Mexican, Fincher's BBQ, Hardee's, Hong Kong Express, Krispy Kreme, Krystal, McDonald's, Nu-Way Weiners, Papa John's, Subway, Taco Bell, Wendy's ⬜ Attaway Tire, CVS Drug, Family$, 🅷, Kroger, O'Reilly Parts, U-Haul, Walgreens, **S** 🛢️ Jumbo's, Sunoco/dsl 🍴 Burger King, Checker's, Krystal, Pizza Hut, Waffle House, Zaxby's
0mm	I-75, S to Valdosta, N to Atlanta. **I-16 begins/ends on I-75, exit 165 in Macon.**

⬆️🅴 INTERSTATE 20

Exit #	Services
202mm	Georgia/South Carolina state line, Savannah River
201mm	**Welcome Ctr wb, full** 🚻 **facilities, litter barrels, petwalk,** 📶, 🏧, **vending**
200	GA 104, Riverwatch Pkwy, Augusta, **N** 🛢️ Pilot/Wendy's/dsl/scales/24hr 🍴 Waffle House 🛏️ Baymont Inn, Best Western +, Candlewood Suites, Comfort Suites, Extended Stay, Microtel, Sleep Inn, Woodspring Suites ⬜ Freightliner, **S** ⬜ $Tree, Cabela's, Costco/gas
199	GA 28, Washington Rd, Augusta, 0-3 mi **N** 🛢️ BP, RaceWay, Shell/Circle K, Sprint 🍴 Applebee's, Baskin-Robbins/Dunkin', Burger King, CA Dreaming, Capt D's, Checkers, Chick-fil-A, Denny's, Domino's, DQ, Fujiyama Japanese, Krystal, Longhorn Steaks, McDonald's, Mi Rancho Mexican, Piccadilly, Pizza Hut, Rhinehart's Seafood, Starbucks, Steakout, Veracruz Mexican, Waffle House, Wife Saver Rest, Wild Wing Cafe 🛏️ Clarion, Courtyard, Econolodge, Hampton Inn, Hilton Garden, Holiday Inn Express, Homewood Suites, La Quinta, Masters Inn, Scottish Inn, Sheraton, Sunset Inn, Super 8, Travelodge ⬜ $Tree, AutoZone,

GA (side tab)

OCMULGEE MACON (vertical side tab), METTER DUBLIN (vertical side tab), AUGUSTA (vertical side tab)

🚏 INTERSTATE 20 Cont'd

199   Continued
Buick/GMC, Chevrolet, Chrysler/Dodge/Jeep, Hyundai, Infiniti, Lexus, Mercedes, NAPA, Nissan, Toyota, Tuesday Morning, **S** 🍴 BP, Circle K/dsl, Shell/Circle K/dsl 🍴 Arby's, BoneFish Grill, Carrabba's, Crazy Turk's Pizza, Five Guys, HoneyBaked Ham, Hooters, Krispy Kreme, McDonald's, Moe's SW Grill, New Peking, Olive Garden, Outback Steaks, Red Lobster, Roadrunner Cafe, Shangri La, Straw Hat Pizza, Subway, T-Bonz Steaks, Taco Bell, Teresa's Mexican, TGIFriday's, Thai Jong Rest., TX Roadhouse, Vallarta Mexican, Waffle House, Wendy's, Zaxby's 🛏 Best Western, Country Inn&Suites, Knights Inn, Magnolia Inn, Motel 6, Parkway Inn, Staybridge Suites, Westbank Inn ⚫ $Tree, AT&T, CVS Drug, Firestone/auto, Fresh Mkt Foods, Goodyear/auto, Kroger/dsl, Midas, PepBoys, Publix, SteinMart, Tire Kingdom, Verizon, Walgreens, Whole Food Mkt

196b   GA 232 W, **N** 🍴 Enmark, Murphy Express/dsl 🍴 Checkers, Golden Corral, Krystal, Salsa's Grill, Stevi B's Pizza 🛏 Baymont Inn, Travel Inn ⚫ Aldi Foods, Discount Tire, GNC, Home Depot, Lowe's, NTB, O'Reilly Parts, Sam's Club/dsl, Sprouts Mkt, URGENT CARE, Walgreens, Walmart

196a   I-520, Bobby Jones Fwy, **S** 🍴 Atlanta Bread Co, Buffalo Wild Wings, Carolina Alehouse, Chick-fil-A, Chili's, Dunkin', Genghis Grill, Logan's Roadhouse, Macaroni Grill, McDonald's, O'Charley's, Panera Bread, Starbucks, Sticky Fingers, Subway, Waffle House 🛏 DoubleTree Hotel ⚫ Best Buy, Hobby Lobby, ℍ, Michael's, Office Depot, Old Navy, Petsmart, Rite Aid, Staples, Target, Tires+, to ⚫, Verizon, vet

195   Wheeler Rd, **N** 🍴 Sprint 🍴 Farmhaus Burgers 🛏 Hyatt Place ⚫ CarMax, Gander Outdoors, **0-2 mi S** 🍴 BP/dsl, Shell/Circle K 🍴 Guiseppe's Pizza, Sonic 🛏 Days Inn ⚫ Harley-Davidson, ℍ, URGENT CARE, Walgreens

194   GA 383, Belair Rd, to Evans, **N** 🍴 Shell/Circle K/dsl, Sprint 🍴 Bojangles, Burger King, Hungry Howie's, Popeye's, Sun Kwong Chinese, Taco Bell, Waffle House, Wendy's 🛏 GA Inn ⚫ Family$, Food Lion, Fun Park, **S** 🍴 BP/DQ/dsl, Fuel Express, 🚚/Subway/dsl/scales/24hr 🍴 Cookout, Cracker Barrel, McDonald"s, Steak'n Shake, Waffle House 🛏 Augusta Inn, Best Suites, Best Value Inn, Best Western, Comfort Inn, Hampton Inn, Hawthorn Suites, Holiday Inn, Howard Johnson, Quality Inn, Red Roof Inn, Super 8, Wingate Inn ⚫ Goodyear/auto, Kenworth

190   GA 388, to Grovetown, **N** 🍴 Waffle House, **S** 🍴 Murphy Express/dsl 🍴 Applebee's, Arby's, Chick-fil-A, Culver's, Jersey Mike's, Mi Rancho 🛏 Avid Hotel, Home 2 Suites ⚫ Verizon, Walmart

189mm   **weigh sta both lanes**

183   US 221, to Harlem, Appling, **S** 🍴 Exxon/dsl ⚫ to Laurel&Hardy Museum

182mm   🅿 both lanes, full ♿ facilities, litter barrels, petwalk, 🚻, 🐾, RV dump, vending

175   GA 150, **N** 🍴 Chevron/rest/dsl/24hr 🛏 Express Inn ⚫ to Mistletoe SP

172   US 78, GA 17, Thomson, **N** 🍴 Loves/Chester's/Subway/dsl/scales/24hr, Sprint/dsl 🍴 Waffle House ⚫ Chrysler/Dodge/Jeep, **S** 🍴 76/dsl, Circle K/dsl, Citgo/DQ/dsl, Marathon/dsl, RaceWay/dsl 🍴 Arby's, Bojangles, Burger King, Checkers, Chick-fil-A, Domino's, Habaneros Mexican, Krystal, LJ Silver, Lucky Chinese, McDonald's, MingWah Chinese, Popeye's, Taco Bell, Tasty Wings & Seafood, Waffle House, Wendy's, Zaxby's 🛏 Comfort Inn, Days Inn, EconoLodge, Hampton Inn, White Columns Inn ⚫ $General, Advance Parts, AutoZone, Family$, ℍ, O'Reilly Parts, URGENT CARE, Verizon, Walgreens

169   Thomson

165   GA 80, Camak

160   E Cadley Rd, Norwood

154   US 278, GA 12, Barnett

148   GA 22, Crawfordville, **N** 🍴 BP ⚫ to Stephens SP

138   GA 77, GA 15, Siloam, **N** 🍴 FLYING J/Denny's/dsl/LP/scales/24hr, **S** 🍴 Chevron/dsl

130   GA 44, Greensboro, **N** 🍴 BP/dsl, Valero/Subway 🍴 DQ, McDonald's, Pizza Hut, Waffle House, Wendy's, Zaxby's 🛏 Holiday Lodge, Quality Inn ⚫ $General, Buick/Chevrolet, Greensboro Tire/repair, **S** 🍴 Chevron/dsl 🍴 Chick-fil-A ⚫ Home Depot/gas, ℍ

121   to Lake Oconee, Buckhead, **S** 🍴 Sunoco/dsl ⚫ Museum of Art (3mi)

114   US 441, US 129, to Madison, **N** 🍴 Chevron/Subway/dsl, Citgo/dsl, 🚚/Huddle House/dsl/scales/24hr, RaceWay/dsl 🍴 Arby's, Burger King, Chick-fil-A, Cracker Barrel, Hong Kong Buffet, KFC, Krystal, McDonald's, Pachos Mexican, Pizza Hut, Steak'n Shake, Taco Bell, Waffle House, Wendy's, Zaxby's 🛏 Comfort Inn, Hampton Inn, Quality Inn ⚫ $General, $Tree, Advance Parts, AutoZone, ℍ, Ingles Foods/gas, Lowe's, O'Reilly Parts, Rite Aid, Verizon, Walmart, **S** 🍴 Flash/dsl, Shell, TA/BP/Country Pride/Popeye's/dsl/scales/24hr/@ 🍴 Waffle House 🛏 Deerfield Inn, Holiday Inn Express, Super 8, Wingate Inn ⚫ Country Boys RV Park (1mi), truckwash/service

113   GA 83, Madison, **N** 🍴 BP/dsl, Loves/Hardee's/Godfather/dsl/scales/24hr/@ ⚫ Speedco, st patrol, **S** 🍴 Exxon/dsl

108mm   **N** 🅿 wb, full ♿ facilities, litter barrels, petwalk, 🚻, 🐾, RV dump, vending

105   Rutledge, Newborn, **N** 🍴 Valero/pizza/dsl ⚫ Hard Labor Creek SP

THOMSON

MADISON

GA

🛢 = gas   🍴 = food   🏠 = lodging   🔵 = other   🅿️ = rest stop   Copyright 2022 - The Next EXIT

⬆️E INTERSTATE 20 Cont'd

Exit #	Services
103mm	**S** 🅿️ eb, full 🛗 facilities, litter barrels, petwalk, 🚹, 🖼, RV dump, vending
101	US 278, Stanton Spgs Pkwy
98	GA 11, to Monroe, Monticello, **N** 🏠 Blue Willow Inn (4mi), **S** 🛢 BP/dsl
95mm	Alcovy River
93	GA 142, Hazelbrand Rd, **N** 🔵 Home Depot, **S** 🛢 QT/dsl 🍴 Bullrito's Cafe, Chili's, IHOP, Jersey Mike's, McDonald's, Shane's Rib Shack, Subway, Taco Bell, Waffle House, Wendy's 🏠 Hampton Inn, Holiday Inn Express, Quality Inn 🔵 $Tree, Aldi Foods, AT&T, �H, Mavis Tire & Brakes, Verizon, Walmart/Subway
92	Alcovy Rd, **N** 🛢 Chevron/dsl, Shell/dsl 🍴 Waffle House 🏠 Baymont Inn, Days Inn, HomeTowne Lodge, Oyo Inn, Super 8, **S** 🔵 �H
90	US 278, GA 81, Covington, **S** 🛢 Citgo/dsl, QT, RaceWay/dsl 🍴 Applebee's, Arby's, Bojangles, Burrito Loco, Capt D's, Checkers, Chick-fil-A, Church's, Covington Diner, DQ, Dunkin'/Baskin-Robbins, Firehouse Subs, Hardee's, Just Dogs/Burgers, KFC, Krystal, Little Caesar's, LJ Silver, Longhorn Steaks, Mama Maria's, McDonald's, Moe's SW Grill, Pacho's Mexican, Papa John's, Pizza Hut, Stalvey's Rest., Stevi B's Pizza, Subway, Taco Bell, Waffle House, Wendy's, Zaxby's 🏠 La Quinta 🔵 $General, Ace Hardware, Advance Parts, AutoZone, BigLots, Chevrolet, CVS, Family$, Food Depot, GNC, Ingles Foods, K-Mart, Kroger/dsl, O'Reilly Parts, Rite Aid, vet, Walgreens
88	Almon Rd, to Porterdale, **N** 🛢 Chevron/dsl, **S** 🛢 Marathon/Dunkin'/deli, Texaco 🍴 McDonald's 🔵 Chrysler/Dodge/Jeep, Riverside Estates RV Park, transmission repair
84	GA 162, Salem Rd, to Pace, **N** 🛢 BJ's Whse/gas, Marathon/dsl 🔵 Leer Truck Accessories, **S** 🛢 Exxon, QT, RaceWay/dsl, Shell/dsl 🍴 Baskin-Robbins, Burger King, Dunkin', KFC, Los Bravos Mexican, McDonald's, Subway, Taco Bell, Waffle House, Wendy's 🔵 Advance Parts, Family$, Food Depot, Ingles/gas, O'Reilly Parts, Olympic Auto, PepBoys, Southern Tire Auto
82	GA 138, GA 20, Conyers, **N** 🛢 QT 🍴 Applebee's, Bruster's, Chili's, ChuckECheese, Coldstone, Cracker Barrel, Don Tello's, Golden Corral, IHOP, O'Charley's, Outback Steaks, Red Lobster, Sonic, Subway 🏠 Best Western Premier, Country Inn&Suites, Courtyard, Econo Lodge, Hampton Inn, Jameson Inn, La Quinta 🔵 AT&T, Belk, charging sta, Chevrolet/Buick/GMC, Ford, Harley-Davidson/charging sta, Home Depot, Jo-Ann, Kohl's, Michael's, Old Navy, Petsmart, Tires+, TJ Maxx, U-Haul, Walmart, **S** 🛢 Chevron, QT, Shell/dsl 🍴 Burger King, Capt D's, Checkers, Chick-fil-A, Dunkin'/Baskin-Robbins, Firehouse Subs, Frontera Mexican, HoneyBaked Ham, Hooters, Jim'n Nick's BBQ, KFC, Krystal, Kumo Sushi, Little Caesar's, Mandarin Garden, McDonald's, Mellow Mushroom, Milano Cafe, Moe's SW Grill, Panda Express, Panera Bread, Popeye's, Starbucks, Subway, Taco Bell, Waffle House 🏠 Microtel 🔵 $General, $Tree, Aldi Foods, BigLots, Discount Tire, Firestone/auto, GNC, Goodyear/auto, Hobby Lobby, Honda, Kauffman Tire, Kroger/gas, Office Depot, PepBoys, Publix, Ross, Target, USPO, Verizon, Walgreens
80	West Ave, Conyers, **N** 🛢 Shell/dsl, Valero/dsl 🍴 Domino's, DQ, Subway, Waffle House 🏠 Best Value Inn, Motel 6 🔵 Conyers Drug, Family$, Meineke, Piggly Wiggly, **S** 🛢 QT/dsl, Texaco/dsl 🍴 Fish House, Longhorn Steaks, McDonald's 🏠 Comfort Inn 🔵 Nissan, vet
79mm	parking area eb
78	Sigman Rd, **N** 🛢 Shell/dsl, Texaco 🍴 Waffle House
75	US 278, GA 124, Turner Hill Rd, **N** 🛢 BP/dsl, QT/dsl, **S** 🍴 Applebee's, Arizona's, Belinda's Rest, Chick-fil-A, Chili's, Don Tello's Mexican, Double Scoop Ice Cream, Firehouse Subs, Grand China, IHOP, Kampai Sushi & Steak, McDonald's, Olive Garden, Panera Bread, Smokey Bones BBQ, Steak n'Shake, Subway, Taco Bell, TGIFriday, Zaxby's 🏠 Comfort Suites, Fairfield Inn, Hilton Garden, Holiday Inn Express 🔵 $Tree, AT&T, Dillard's, JC Penney, Kia, Macy's, Marshalls, PetCo, Ross, Staples, Tires+, Toyota, Verizon, Walmart
74	Evans Mill Rd, GA 124, Lithonia, **N** 🛢 BP/Circle K, Chevron, Texaco 🍴 Burger King, Capt D's, McDonald's, Pizza Hut, Robert's Rest., Subway 🔵 Advance Parts, CVS Drug, O'Reilly Parts, **S** 🛢 Citgo/dsl 🍴 Da-Bomb Wings/Seafood, DQ, Dudley's Rest., Krystal, Waffle House 🏠 Microtel 🔵 $General
71	Hillandale Dr, Farrington Rd, Panola Rd, **N** 🛢 QT/dsl, Shell/dsl 🍴 Burger King, Checkers, Cook Out, It's The Rib Tips, KFC, McDonald's, Waffle House 🏠 Knights Inn, Quality Inn, Super 8 🔵 Family$, **S** 🛢 BP/dsl, Murphy USA/dsl, Shell/dsl, Stop & Shop 🍴 A-Town Wings, Dunkin', IHOP, Marco's Pizza, New China, Popeye's, Ruby Tuesday, Subway, Taco Bell/LJ Silver, Wendy's 🏠 Red Roof Inn 🔵 Lowe's, Publix, Tires+, Verizon, Walgreens, Walmart
68	Wesley Chapel Rd, Snapfinger Rd, **N** 🍴 Capt D's, Checkers, Chick-fil-A, China Cafeteria, Church's, Dunkin', KFC, Little Caesar's, Subway, Taco Bell, Waffle House, Wings & Burger 🏠 Haven Inn 🔵 $General, DJ's Repair, Home Depot, Kroger, NTB, 🛢 Chevron/dsl, QT, Shell/dsl, Texaco 🍴 Dragon Chinese, JJ's Fish& Chicken, McDonald's, Popeye's 🏠 Oyo 🔵 Family$, USPO
67b a	I-285, S to Macon, N to Greenville
66	Columbia Dr (from eb, no return), **N** 🛢 Chevron
65	GA 155, Candler Rd, to Decatur, **N** 🛢 Chevron, Citgo, Valero/dsl 🍴 Pizza Hut, Popeye's, Red Lobster, Wendy's 🏠 Best Value Inn, Discovery Inn, Motel 6 🔵 CVS Drug, U-Haul, **S** 🛢 BP, Chevron, Shell/dsl, Texaco 🍴 Baskin-Robbins/Dunkin, Burger King, Checkers, Church's, DQ, KFC, McDonald's, Subway, Taco Bell, Waffle King 🏠 Budgetel Inn 🔵 BigLots, Firestone/auto, Macy's
63	Gresham Rd, **N** 🛢 Chevron, Citgo/dsl 🍴 American Deli 🔵 Walmart/Subway, **S** 🛢 Citgo, Marathon, Shell, Texaco/dsl 🍴 Church's
62	Flat Shoals Rd (from eb, no return)
61b	GA 260, Glenwood Ave, **N** 🛢 Chevron, Shell/dsl
61a	Maynard Terrace (from eb, no return)
60b a	US 23, Moreland Ave, **N** 🛢 Texaco, Valero 🏠 Atlanta Motel 🔵 Advance Parts, **S** 🛢 Citgo/dsl, Shell 🍴 Checkers, Krystal, LJ Silver, McDonald's, Wendy's
59b	Memorial Dr, Glenwood Ave (from eb), **S** 🛢 Kroger/gas
59a	Cyclorama, **N** 🛢 Chevron/Blimpie/dsl 🔵 MLK Site, **S** 🛢 BP/Subway 🔵 Confederate Ave Complex, CVS
58b	Hill St (from wb, no return), **N** 🛢 Shell 🍴 Mrs. Winners
58a	Capitol St (from wb, no return), **N** to GA Dome, **S** Capital Inn downtown
57	I-75/85
56b	Windsor St (from eb)
56a	US 19, US 29, McDaniel St (eb only), **N** 🛢 Chevron/dsl
55b	Lee St (from wb), Ft McPherson, **S** 🛢 Exxon, Shell 🍴 Church's, Popeye's, Taco Bell, West Inn Food Court 🔵 $Family, Maxway, Sav-A-Lot
55a	Lowery Blvd, **S** 🛢 Exxon/dsl, Shell 🍴 Church's, Popeye's, Taco Bell, West Inn Food Court 🔵 Family$, Maxway, Sav-A-Lot
54	Langhorn St (from wb), to Cascade Rd
53	MLK Dr, to GA 139, **N** 🛢 Chevron, Shell/dsl, **S** 🛢 Texaco/dsl 🔵 auto repair

Vertical side labels (left column): **COVINGTON**, **CONYERS**

Vertical side labels (right column): LITHONIA, **ATLANTA AREA**

GA

INTERSTATE 20 Cont'd

ATLANTA AREA

Exit #	Services
52b a	GA 280, Holmes Dr, High Tower Rd, S 🅿 Chevron 🍴 Hong Kong Chinese, McDonald's, Wendy's 🄾 $General, AutoZone, CVS Drug
51b a	I-285, S to Montgomery, N to Chattanooga
49	GA 70, Fulton Ind Blvd, N 🅿 Citgo/dsl 🍴 Wendy's 🛏 Budgetel, Extended Stay, Quality Inn 🄾 🖂, FleetPride Truck Parts, S 🅿 BP/dsl, Chevron/dsl, Valero 🍴 Grand Buffet, Waffle House 🛏 Economy Hotel, OYO 🄾 U-Haul
48mm	Chattahoochee River
47	Six Flags Pkwy (from wb), N 🅿 BP 🛏 EconoLodge, S 🛏 Knights Inn, Sleep Inn, Wingate Inn 🄾 Six Flags Funpark
46b a	Riverside Parkway, N 🅿 Citgo/Church's, Marathon, QT/dsl 🍴 Hong Kong Buffet, Waffle House 🛏 Super 8 🄾 Family$, S 🅿 Texaco 🍴 Wendy's 🛏 Knights Inn, Sleep Inn, Wingate Inn 🄾 Six Flags Funpark
44	GA 6, Thornton Rd, to Lithia Springs, N 🅿 BP, QT, RaceTrac/dsl, Shell/dsl, Valero 🍴 Applebee's, Bojangles, Burger King, Chick-fil-A, Cod Tail Rest., Domino's, Firehouse Subs, Fred's BBQ, Hardee's, IHOP, KFC, McDonald's, Olive Tree Rest., Popeye's, Sonic, Subway, Taco Bell, Waffle House, Wendy's, Wings R Us, Zaxby's 🛏 Budget Inn, Holiday Inn Express, InTowne Suites, Knights Inn, Quality Inn 🄾 $General, AT&T, Atlanta West Camping (2mi), Autozone, Carmax, Chevrolet, Ford, Harley Davidson, Home Depot, Honda, Hyundai, Kroger/gas, Nissan, Tires+, Verizon, vet, VW, Walgreens, S 🅿 Shell 🍴 Bei Jin China, Cracker Barrel, Fiesta Mexican 🛏 Baymont Inn, Candlewood Suites, Country Inn&Suites, Courtyard, Hampton Inn, Hilton Garden, Motel 6, SpringHill Suites 🄾 Chrysler/Dodge/Jeep, Kia, to Sweetwater Creek SP, Toyota, Walmart
42mm	weigh sta eb
41	Lee Rd, to Lithia Springs, N 🅿 Marathon/dsl

DOUGLASVILLE

37	GA 92, to Douglasville, N 🅿 RaceTrac/dsl, Shell/dsl 🍴 Blimpie, Checker's, Chick-fil-A, Church's, DQ, Kenny's Rest., Krystal, Longhorn Steaks, Martin's Rest., McDonald's, Pizza Hut, Popeye's, Subway, Taco Bell, Waffle House, Wendy's 🛏 Best Value Inn, Comfort Inn, Days Inn, EconoLodge, Quality Inn, Ramada Ltd, Royal Inn 🄾 AutoZone, CVS Drug, Family$, 🄷, Kroger/dsl, NAPA, O'Reilly Parts, Tires+, Walgreens, S 🅿 Chevron/dsl, QT, Texaco/dsl 🍴 Domino's, Waffle House 🄾 $General, Aamco, Advance Parts, Ingles Foods
36	Chapel Hill Rd, N 🄾 🄷, S 🅿 QT, Shell/dsl 🍴 Arby's, Carrabba's, China Garden, Coldstone, Daruma, Five Guys, Joe's Crabshack, Johnny's Subs, Logan's Roadhouse, McDonald's, O'Charley's, Olive Garden, Outback Steaks, Panda Express, Provino's Italian, Shane's Rib Shack, Starbucks, Subway, TX Roadhouse, Waffle House 🛏 Hampton Inn 🄾 $Tree, Aldi Foods, Belk, BigLots, Dillard's, Discount Tire, Firestone/auto, Hobby Lobby, JC Penney, Kohl's, Macy's, Marshall's, Michael's, Old Navy, Petsmart, Rite Aid, Ross, Target, Verizon
34	GA 5, to Douglasville, N 🅿 RaceTrac/dsl, Texaco/dsl 🍴 Atlantic Grill, Cracker Barrel, Stevie B's Pizza, Waffle House, Williamson Bros BBQ, Zaxby's 🛏 Holiday Inn Express, La Quinta, Sleep Inn 🄾 $Tree, Kauffman Tires, Sam's Club, URGENT CARE, Walmart, S 🅿 Chevron/dsl, Circle K, Shell/dsl 🍴 Applebee's, Bruster's, Buffalo Wild Wings, Burger King, Chick-fil-A, ChuckE-Cheese, DQ, Dunkin, El Tio Mexican, Fiesta Mexican, Folk's Rest., Golden Corral, HoneyBaked Ham, IHOP, KFC, King Buffet, Krystal, La Salsa, LJ Silver, McDonald's, Moe's SW Grill, Monterrey Mexican, Papa John's, Pizza Buffet, Popeyes, Red Lobster,

34	Continued
	S'more BBQ, Seabreeze Seafood, Sonic, Steak'n Shake, Subway, Taco Bell, Taco Mac, Waffle House, Wasabi Japanese, Wendy's 🛏 InTown Suites 🄾 Advance Parts, AT&T, Batteries+, Best Buy, Goodyear/auto, Home Depot, Jo-Ann Crafts, Kroger/dsl, Lowe's, Meineke, NTB, O'Reilly Parts, Office Depot, PepBoys, Publix, Tuesday Morning, U-Haul, vet, Walgreens
30	Post Rd, S 🅿 Shell/dsl

VILLA RICA

26	Liberty Rd, Villa Rica, N 🅿 Shell/dsl, Swifty/dsl 🍴 China Wok, Johnny's Pizza, McDonald's, Mex-Grill, Olive Tree Rest., Subway, Sumo Japanese, Waffle House 🄾 $General, 🄷, Publix, vet, Walgreens, S 🅿 Chevron, 🅿Pilot/Subway/dsl/scales/24hr 🛏 American Inn
24	GA 101, GA 61, Villa Rica, N 🅿 BP/dsl, RaceTrac/dsl, Shell/dsl 🍴 Arby's, Chick-fil-A, Hardee's, KFC/Taco Bell, Krystal, Lin's Garden Chinese, McDonald's, Pizza Hut, Romero's Italian, Sonic, Stix Grill, Subway, Waffle House, Wendy's 🛏 Comfort Inn, Days Inn, EconoLodge, Super 8 🄾 Advance Parts, AT&T, AutoZone, CVS Drug, 🄷, Ingles Foods, Rite Aid, Walgreens, S 🅿 QT, Shell/dsl 🍴 Bojangles, Burger King, Capt D's, Domino's, El Ranchito Mexican, O'Charley's, Papa John's, Waffle House, Zaxby's 🄾 $Tree, Chevrolet, GNC, Home Depot, to W GA Coll, URGENT CARE, Verizon, Walmart/Subway
21mm	Little Tallapoosa River
19	GA 113, Temple, N 🅿 FLYING J/dsl/scales/24hr, 🅿Pilot/Subway/Wendy's/dsl/scales/24hr/@ 🍴 Bojangles, El Tapatio's, Fortune Star Chinese, Hardee's, Marco's Pizza, McDonald's, Waffle House 🄾 Ingles Foods/gas
15mm	weigh sta wb

BREMEN

11	US 27, Bremen, Bowdon, N 🅿 Chevron/dsl, Murphy USA/dsl, Valero/Domino's/dsl 🍴 Arby's, Capt D's, Chopsticks Chinese, Cracker Barrel, Jack's, Juanito's, KFC/Taco Bell, Little Caesar's, Mama Deluca's, McDonald's, Papa John's, Waffle House, Wendy's, Zaxby's 🛏 Hampton Inn, Holiday Inn Express, Microtel, Motel 6, Quality Inn 🄾 $General, Advance Parts, Ford, 🄷, Ingles Foods/gas, URGENT CARE, Verizon, Walmart/McDonald's, S 🅿 BP/dsl, Circle K/dsl 🍴 Subway 🄾 John Tanner SP
9	Waco Rd, N 🅿 ❤Loves/Chesters/Subway/dsl/scales/24hr 🄾 Jellystone RV Park (2mi)
5	GA 100, Tallapoosa, N 🅿 Exxon/dsl, Robinson's/dsl/24hr 🍴 Waffle House 🄾 Big Oak RV park, S 🅿 Newborn TrkStp/rest/dsl/24hr/@, 🅿Pilot/KFC/Taco Bell/dsl/scales/24hr, Robinson & Son 🍴 DQ, GA Diner, Smokin' Pig 🛏 Super 8 🄾 to John Tanner SP, truck repair/wash
1mm	Welcome Ctr eb, full 🚻 facilities, litter barrels, petwalk, 🄲, 🄰, vending
0mm	Georgia/Alabama state line, Eastern/Central time zone

🅿 = gas 🍴 = food 🛏 = lodging Ⓞ = other Rs = rest stop   Copyright 2022 - The Next EXIT ©

INTERSTATE 59 N

Exit #	Services
	I-59 begins/ends on I-24, exit 167. For I-24, turn to TN Interstate 24.
20mm	I-24, W to Nashville, E to Chattanooga
17	Slygo Rd, to New England, W 🅿 Citgo/dsl Ⓞ KOA (2mi)
11	GA 136, Trenton, E 🅿 Chevron/dsl, Mobil 🍴 Asian Garden, Guthrie's, Hardee's, McDonald's, Pizza Hut, Subway 🛏 Days Inn Ⓞ $Tree, Advance Parts, CVS Drug, Ingles, O'Reilly Parts, to Cloudland Canyon SP, W 🅿 BP, Citgo/dsl, Marathon/Circle K/dsl 🍴 Huddle House, Krystal, Larry's Buffet, Little Caesar's, Taco Bell, Wendy's Ⓞ $General, Food City, Food Outlet
4	Rising Fawn, E 🅿 Marathon, W 🅿 BP/dsl, 🅿Pilot/Subway/dsl/scales/24hr Ⓞ camping
0mm	Georgia/Alabama state line, eastern/central time zone

INTERSTATE 75 N

Exit #	Services
355mm	Georgia/Tennessee state line
354mm	Chickamauga Creek
353	GA 146, Rossville, E 🅿 Marathon 🛏 Cloud Springs Lodge, W 🅿 BP/Subway/dsl, Shell/dsl Ⓞ Costco/gas
352mm	Welcome Ctr sb, full 🚻 facilities, info, litter barrels, petwalk, 🄲, 🛢, vending
350	GA 2, Bfd Pkwy, to Ft Oglethorpe, E 🅿 Chevron/dsl/24hr, Mobil/Circle K/dsl 🍴 Farm to Fork 🛏 Hampton Inn, Hometown Inn, SpringHill Suites, W 🅿 RaceTrac/dsl, Shell 🍴 Subway Ⓞ Battleground Camping, Ⓗ, to Chickamauga NP
348	GA 151, Ringgold, E 🅿 BP/Circle K/dsl, Mapco 🍴 Cracker Barrel, Hardee's, KFC, Little Caesar's, McDonald's, Pizza Hut, Sonic, Subway, Taco Bell, Waffle House 🛏 Holiday Inn Express, Super 8, Tru Hilton Ⓞ $General, Advance Parts, AutoZone, Chevrolet, CVS Drug, Hyundai, Ingles, vet, Walgreens, W 🅿 Exxon/dsl 🍴 Arby's, Bojangles, Burger King, Domino's, Guthrie's, Krystal, New China, Wendy's Ⓞ Ace Hardware, Chrysler/Dodge/Jeep, Dunlap RV Ctr, Family$, Food Lion, Northgate RV Ctr, Peterbilt, truck repair
345	US 41, US 76, Ringgold, E 🅿 BP, W 🅿 Circle/Subway/dsl/scales/24hr, Cochran's TP/rest./dsl/scales/24hr/@, Shell 🍴 Waffle House
343mm	weigh sta both lanes
341	GA 201, to Varnell, Tunnel Hill, W 🅿 BP/Mapco Ⓞ carpet outlets
336	US 41, US 76, Dalton, Rocky Face, E 🅿 Mapco, Murphy USA/dsl, RaceTrac/dsl 🍴 Burger King, Checkers, Mr Biscuit, Waffle House Ⓞ Ford/Lincoln, Home Depot, Ⓗ, Kohl's, PetCo, Verizon, Walmart/Subway, W 🅿 BP/dsl, Victory Fuels 🍴 Los Pablos, Wendy's 🛏 Baymont Inn, carpet outlets, Econolodge, Guest Inn, Motel 6, Staylodge
333	GA 52, Dalton, E 🅿 BP/dsl, RaceTrac/dsl, Sexton's/dsl 🍴 Applebee's, Bruster's, Burger King, Chick-fil-A, CiCi's Pizza, Cracker Barrel, Five Guys, Fuji Japanese, IHOP, Jersey Mike's Subs, KFC, Krispy Kreme, Las Palmas Mexican, Longhorn Steaks, McDonald's, Outback Steaks, Panda Express, Panera Bread, Pizza Hut, Schlotzsky's, Shoney's, Sonic, Starbucks, Steak'n Shake, Subway, Taco Bell, Waffle House 🛏 Days Inn, Hampton Inn, Holiday Inn Express, Holiday Inn Express, Red Roof Inn, Super 8 Ⓞ $Tree, AT&T, BigLots, Chevrolet, Chrysler/Dodge/Jeep, Food City, Harley-Davidson, Kroger/dsl, Petsmart, TJ Maxx, Tuesday Morning, Walgreens, W 🍴 Bojangles, Chili's, Red Lobster, Zaxby's 🛏 Comfort Inn, Country Inn Suites, Courtyard, Hilton Garden, Holiday Inn Express, Howard Johnson, La Quinta, Quality Inn, Super 8 Ⓞ NW GA Trade/Conv Ctr

328	GA 3, to US 41, E 🅿 BP/Circle K/dsl, 🅿Pilot/Arby's/dsl/scales/24hr 🍴 Waffle House, Wendy's 🛏 Best Value Inn, W Ⓞ carpet outlets
326	Carbondale Rd, E 🅿 LNG, 🅿Pilot/McDonald's/Subway/dsl/scales, W 🅿 BP
320	GA 136, to Lafayette, Resaca, E 🅿 ⓕFLYING J/Denny's/dsl, LP/24hr Ⓞ Dollar General Mkt, truck repair/parts
319mm	Oostanaula River, Rs sb, full 🚻 facilities, litter barrels, pet walk, 🄲, 🛢, vending
318	US 41, Resaca, E 🅿 🅿Pilot/DQ/Wendy's/Dunkin'/scales/dsl/24hr 🍴 Hardee's 🛏 Rodeway Inn, W 🅿 Marathon, Shell/dsl 🍴 Chuckwagon Rest. 🛏 Best Inn, Budget Inn, Duffy's Motel, Executive Inn
317	GA 225, to Chatsworth, E New Echota HS, Vann House HS, W 🅿 BP/Circle K 🛏 Express Inn
315	GA 156, Redbud Rd, to Calhoun, E 🍴 Subway, Waffle House Ⓞ AOK Camping (2mi), Food Lion, W 🅿 BP/dsl, Liberty 🍴 Arby's, Shoney's 🛏 Quality Inn Ⓞ Ⓗ, URGENT CARE, Walgreens
312	GA 53, to Calhoun, E 🅿 Shell/dsl 🍴 Applebee's, Cracker Barrel, Longhorn Steaks, Wendy's 🛏 Country Inn&Suites, EconoLodge, Fairfield Inn, La Quinta Ⓞ Calhoun Outlets/famous brands, W 🅿 BP/Arby's, Circle K, Exxon/dsl, Murphy USA, RaceTrac/dsl, Shell 🍴 Bojangles, Burger King, Capt D's, Checkers, Chick-fil-A, China Palace, DQ, Dunkin', El Nopal Mexican, Five Guys, Gondolier Pizza, Hardee's, Hibachi Buffet, Huddle House, IHOP, KFC, Krystal, Little Caesar's, McDonald's, Panda Express, Popeye's, Ruby Tuesday, Starbucks, Subway, Taco Bell, Tokyo Steaks, Waffle House, Zaxby's 🛏 Baymont Inn, Motel 6, Red Roof Inn, Scottish Inn, Super 8 Ⓞ $General, Advance Parts, Aldi Foods, AT&T, AutoZone, GNC, Goodyear/auto, Home Depot, Kroger/dsl, NAPA, Office Depot, Verizon, vet, Walmart
310	Union Grove Rd, E 🅿 Buc-ee's/dsl, 🅿Loves/Burger King/dsl/scales/24hr
308mm	Rs nb, full 🚻 facilities, litter barrels, petwalk, 🄲, 🛢, vending
306	GA 140, Adairsville, E 🅿 Click/dsl, Patty's Tkstp/rest./dsl, QT/dsl/scales/24hrs, Valero/dsl 🍴 Cracker Barrel, Wendy's 🛏 Hampton Inn Ⓞ truck repair, W 🅿 BP/dsl, Chevron/dsl, Shell/dsl 🍴 Burger King, Hardee's, McDonald's, Subway, Taco Bell, Waffle House, Zaxby's 🛏 Magnuson Hotel, Oyo Hotel, Quality Inn Ⓞ Advance Parts, AutoZone, Family$, Food Lion, Harvest Moon RV Park
296	Cassville-White Rd, E 🅿 🅿Pilot/McDonald's/Subway/dsl/scales, TA/BP/Burger King/Pizza Hut/Popeye's/Taco Bell/dsl/scales/24hr/@, Texaco/dsl 🛏 Baymont Inn Ⓞ truckwash, W 🅿 Chevron, Citgo/dsl, Marathon/dsl 🛏 Country Hearth Inn Ⓞ KOA
293	US 411, to White, E 🅿 Sunoco/dsl, Texaco/dsl 🛏 Quality Inn, W 🅿 Chevron/dsl, Marathon, Tesla EVC, Valero/Subway 🍴 Waffle House 🛏 Motel 6 Ⓞ Harley-Davidson, mineral museum
290	GA 20, to Rome, E 🅿 Chevron/dsl, Circle K/dsl, Exxon/Subway/dsl 🍴 Arby's, Fire it Up BBQ, McDonald's, Wendy's 🛏 Best Value Inn, Best Western, Country Inn Suites, EconoLodge, Motel 6, Red Roof Inn, Super 8, W 🅿 Murphy USA (1.5mi), Shell/dsl, Texaco/dsl 🍴 Cracker Barrel, Shoney's, Waffle House, Zaxby's 🛏 Days Inn, Hampton Inn, Holiday Inn Express Ⓞ $Tree, Ⓗ, Lowe's, Walgreens, Walmart/McDonald's
288	GA 113, Cartersville, 0-2 mi W 🅿 Exxon/Circle K/dsl, RaceTrac/dsl, Shell/dsl 🍴 Applebee's, Bojangles, Bruster's, Burger King, Chick-Fil-A, Chili's, CiCi's, Firehouse Subs, Five Guys, Freddy's, Gondolier Pizza, IHOP, KFC, Krystal, Larry's Subs, Longhorn Steaks, McDonald's, McDonald's, Ming Moon, Moe's SW Grill, Papa John's, Red Lobster, Shane's Ribshack, Starbucks,

Side labels: TRENTON · DALTON (left margin); RESACA · CALHOUN · ADAIRSVILLE (right margin); GA

⬆N INTERSTATE 75 Cont'd

288 Continued
Steak'n Shake, Subway, Taco Bell, Waffle House, Wendy's, Willy's Mexicana 🛏 Fairfield Inn, Hilton Garden, Home 2 Suites, Knights Inn 🅞 $General, $Tree, AT&T, Belk, Big Lots, Chrysler/Dodge/Jeep, Discount Tire, GNC, Hobby Lobby, Honda, Kohl's, O'Reilly Parts, Petsmart, Publix, Staples, Target, TJ Maxx, to Etowah Indian Mounds (6mi), USPO, Verizon

286mm Etowah River

285 Emerson, E 🅖 Sunoco 🛏 Red Top Mtn Lodge 🅞 to Red Top Mtn SP, **W** 🅞 to Allatoona Dam

283 Allatoona Rd, Emerson, W 🍴 ♥Loves/McDonald's/Subway/dsl/scales/24hr 🍴 Arby's, Chick-fil-A, Starbucks, Taco Bell, Tokyo Steaks, Wendy's 🛏 Hampton Inn, MainStay Suites, Sleep Inn

280mm Allatoona Lake

278 Glade Rd, to Acworth, E 🅖 Exxon/Circle K/dsl, Shell 🛏 Best Value 🅞 McKinney Camping (3mi), to Glade Marina, **W** 🅖 RaceTrac/dsl 🍴 Bojangles, KFC, Krystal, Papa John's, Pizza Hut, Taco Bell, Waffle House 🛏 Red Roof Inn 🅞 AutoZone, Ingles/cafe, O'Reilly Parts

277 GA 92, Acworth, E 🅖 BP/Dunkin'/dsl, RaceTrac/dsl 🍴 Hardee's, Shoney's, Waffle House 🛏 Comfort Inn, Days Inn, Holiday Inn Express 🅞 Cabela's, **W** 🅖 Chevron/dsl, Shell/DQ/dsl 🍴 Arby's, Bamboo Garden, China Chef, Domino's, La Bamba Mexican, McDonald's, Sonic, Subway, Waffle House, Wendy's, Zaxby's 🛏 Best Western, Deerfield Lodge, Econolodge, Fairfield Inn, Quality Inn, Super 8 🅞 $General, Advance Parts, CVS Drug, Family$, Goodyear/auto, Publix, Walgreens

273 Wade Green Rd, E 🅖 BP/dsl, RaceTrac/dsl 🍴 Arby's, Burger King, Coldstone, Dunkin', Firehouse Subs, Happy Panda, Las Palmas Mexican, Marco's Pizza, McDonald's, Papa John's, QT/dsl, Subway, Taco Bell, Waffle House 🛏 Red Roof Inn, Sleep Inn 🅞 $Tree, BigLots, GNC, O'Reilly Parts, Pepboys, Publix, Tires+, **W** 🅖 Shell, Texaco/dsl 🍴 Bojangles, Johnny's Pizza/Subs, Mandarin Cafe, Starbucks, Wendy's, Wing Zone 🅞 Home Depot, Kroger/gas, Mavis Tire, Verizon, Walgreens

271 Chastain Rd, to I-575 N, E 🅖 Chevron/Circle K, Tesla EVC 🍴 Chick-Fil-A, Chipotle, Cookout, Cracker Barrel, Del Taco, Dunkin'/Baskin Robbins, Five Guys, O'Charley's, Panda Express, Panera Bread, Ruth's Chris Steaks, Starbucks, Taco Mac, Taziki's, Tin Lizzy Cantina, Willy's Mexicana, Zaxby's 🛏 Comfort Suites, Embassy Suites, Fairfield Inn, Hampton Inn, Kennesaw Inn, Residence Inn, **W** 🅖 Shell/dsl, Swifty Save Gas/Blimpie, Taco Bell 🍴 Arby's, Burger King, Jimmy John's, Mellow Mushroom, Waffle House, Wendy's 🛏 Baymont Inn, InTown Suites, SpringHill Suites 🅞 museum

269 to US 41, to Marietta, E 🅖 EVC, Shell/dsl 🍴 Anchor Grill, Applebee's, Honey Baked Ham, J Christopher's, Jimmy John's, McDonald's, Olive Garden, Penang Malaysian, Provino's, Red Lobster, Shogun Japanese, Smoothie King, Starbucks, Subway, Twin Peaks 🛏 Comfort Inn, Country Inn Suites, Holiday Inn Express, Red Roof Inn 🅞 Belk, Firestone/auto, Home Depot, JC Penney, Macy's, Marshall's, Midas, Pepboys, TJ Maxx, Verizon, **W** 🅖 BP/dsl, Chevron, Tesla EVC 🍴 Bahama Breeze, Burger King, Carrabbas, Chick-fil-A, Chili's, Chipotle, ChuckeCheese, Chuy's Mexican, Coldstone, Copeland's Grill, Golden Corral, Jason's Deli, Jersey Mike's, Longhorn Steaks, Melting Pot, On-the-Border, Outback Steaks, Panera Bread, Rafferty's, Sivas Tavern, Starbucks, Steak'n Shake, Sweet Tomato, Ted's MT Steaks, TGIFriday, Willy's Mexicana 🛏 Courtyard, Day's Inn, Hampton Inn, Hilton Garden, Homewood Suites, La Quinta, Quality Inn 🅞 Aldi Foods, Best Buy, Buick/GMC, CarMax, Chevrolet,

269 Continued
Costco/gas, Dick's, Ford/Lincoln, Jo-Ann Fabrics, Kia, Michael's, Nissan, NTB, Old Navy, PetsMart, REI, Subaru, Target, to Kennesaw Mtn NP, Toyota, VW

268 I-575 N, GA 5 N, to Canton

267b a GA 5 N, to US 41, Marietta

265 GA120, N Marietta Pkwy, W 🍴 Chevron/dsl, Shell/dsl 🛏 Days Inn 🅞 Advance Parts, Family$, O'Reilly Parts, Office Depot

263 GA 120, to Roswell, E 🅖 Chevron, QT, Shell, **W** 🅖 QT, repair 🍴 Applebee's, China Kitchen, DQ, Haveli Rest., Piccadilly's, Subway, Tasty China 🛏 Econolodge, Ltd Suites, Radisson, Super 8, Wyndham Garden 🅞 U-Haul

261 GA 280, Delk Rd, to Dobbins AFB, E 🅖 Chevron/dsl, RaceTrac/dsl, Shell, Shell/Subway/dsl 🍴 Delray Diner, Hardee's, KFC/Taco Bell, Little Caesar's, Marco's Pizza, McDonald's, Ruby Tuesday, Waffle House 🛏 Courtyard, Drury Inn, Motel 6, Ramada, Rodeway Inn 🅞 Kroger, **W** 🅖 BP, Chevron/dsl 🍴 Bojangles, Cracker Barrel, Dave&Busters 🛏 Baymont Inn, Days Inn, Economy Hotel, Holiday Inn Express, Quality Inn

260 Windy Hill Rd, to Smyrna, E 🅖 BP/dsl 🍴 Boston Mkt, Jersey Mike's Subs, Mellow Mushroom, Pappadeaux Seafood, Pappasito's Cantina, Schlotzsky's, Subway 🛏 Best Western, Country Hearth Inn, Extended Stay America, Extended Stay America (2), Hilton Garden, Hyatt Regency, Marriott 🅞 CVS Drug, USPO, **W** 🅖 Chevron, Conoco, Shell, Texaco/dsl 🍴 Chick-fil-A, McDonald's, Panda Express, Popeye's, Starbucks, Waffle House, Wendy's 🛏 Comfort Inn, Country Inn&Suites, Courtyard, Days Inn, DoubleTree, Masters Inn, Motel 6, Red Roof Inn 🅞 🅗 Target

259b a I-285, W to Birmingham, E to Greenville, Montgomery

258 Cumberland Pkwy, E 🛏 Hyatt House, **W** 🍴 Chick-fil-A, Chipotle Mexican, Copeland's Rest., Firehouse Subs, Hooters, Longhorn Steaks, Moe's SW Grill, Shane's Ribshack, Subway 🛏 Homewood Suites 🅞 Kroger

257mm Chattahoochee River

256 to US 41, Northside Pkwy

255 US 41, W Paces Ferry Rd, E 🅖 Chevron, Shell/dsl 🍴 Blue Ridge Grill, Chick-fil-A, Flying Biscuit Cafe, Houston's Rest., McDonald's, OK Café, Pero's Pizza, Smoothie King, Starbucks, Steak'n Shake, Whole Foods Mkt, Willy's Mexicana 🅞 Ace Hardware, CVS Drug, 🅗 Publix, **W** 🅖 Exxon

254 Moores Mill Rd

252b Howell Mill Rd, E 🅖 Shell/auto 🍴 Chick-fil-A, Chipotle, Domino's, Jersey Mike's, McDonald's, Willy's Mexicana 🅞 Goodyear/auto, Publix, USPO, Walgreens, **W** 🅖 Shell 🍴 Arby's, Chin Chin Chinese, Dunkin', La Parrilla Mexican, Starbucks, Subway, Taco Bell, Waffle House, Wendy's 🅞 Ace Hardware, Firestone/auto, GNC, Kroger, NTB, Office Depot, Petsmart, TJ Maxx, Verizon, Walmart

🅿 = gas 🍴 = food 🛏 = lodging Ⓞ = other 🆁🆂 = rest stop   Copyright 2022 - The Next EXIT

⬆N INTERSTATE 75 Cont'd

Exit #	Services
252a	US 41, Northside Dr, E Ⓞ 🅷, W 🅿 Shell 🍴 Little Azio's 🛏 InTown Suites
251	I-85 N, to Greenville
250	Techwood Dr (from sb), 10th St, 14th St, E 🛏 Hilton Garden
249d	10th St, Spring St (from nb), E 🅿 BP, Chevron/24hr 🍴 Checker's, Domino's, Pizza Hut, The Varsity 🛏 Fairfield Inn, Regency Suites, Renaissance Hotel, Residence Inn, W 🍴 McDonald's 🛏 Comfort Inn, Courtyard Ⓞ 🅷, to GA Tech
249c	Williams St (from sb) downtown, to GA Dome
249b	Pine St, Peachtree St (from nb), downtown, W 🛏 Hilton, Marriott
249a	Courtland St (from sb), downtown, W 🛏 Hilton, Marriott Ⓞ GA St U
248d	Piedmont Ave, Butler St (from sb), downtown, W 🛏 Courtyard, Fairfield Inn, Radisson Ⓞ Ford, 🅷, MLK NHS
248c	GA 10 E, Intn'l Blvd, downtown, W 🛏 Hilton, Holiday Inn, Marriott Marquis, Radisson
248b	Edgewood Ave (from nb), W Ⓞ downtown, 🅷, hotels
248a	MLK Dr (from sb), W st capitol, to Underground Atlanta
247	I-20, E to Augusta, W to Birmingham
246	Georgia Ave, Fulton St, E 🛏 Comfort Inn, Country Inn& Suites, Holiday Inn Ⓞ stadium, W 🅿 BP 🍴 KFC Ⓞ GSU, to Coliseum
245	Ormond St, Abernathy Blvd, E 🛏 Comfort Inn, Country Inn& Suites Ⓞ stadium, W Ⓞ st capitol
244	University Ave, E 🅿 Chevron, Exxon Ⓞ NAPA, W 🍴 Mrs Winner's
243	GA 166, Lakewood Fwy, to East Point
242	I-85 S to 🔁
241	Cleveland Ave, E 🅿 BP, Chevron/Subway/dsl 🍴 Checkers, Church's, McDonald's Ⓞ Advance Parts, W 🅿 Citgo/dsl, ExpressZone, Marathon 🍴 Amecian Deli, Burger King, Krystal, Papa John's 🛏 American Inn Ⓞ $Tree, AutoZone, Big Lots, CVS Drug, Family$, Kroger, Walgreens
239	US 19, US 41, E 🅿 Chevron/dsl 🍴 Waffle House Ⓞ USPO, W 🅿 Texaco 🍴 Chick-fil-A, IHOP, McDonald's, Wendy's 🛏 Best Western, to 🔁
238b a	I-285 around Atlanta
237a	GA 85 S (from sb)
237	GA 331, Forest Parkway, E 🅿 BP, Chevron/dsl, Shell/McDonald's, SunPetro/dsl 🍴 Burger King, Mr Taco, Subway, Waffle House 🛏 Econolodge Ⓞ Farmer's Mkt, W 🅿 BP, Exxon/Subway/dsl 🍴 Quizno's 🛏 Atlanta Inn, Ramada Ltd Ⓞ Lee Tires/repair
235	US 19, US 41, GA 3, Jonesboro, E 🅿 Chevron/dsl, Circle K/Subway/dsl, Texaco/dsl 🛏 Super 8, Travelodge, W 🅿 Chevron/dsl, Citgo, Texaco/dsl 🍴 Applebee's, Burger King, Checkers, ChuckeCheese, Dunkin', Hibachi Grill, Hooters, Little Caesar's, McDonald's, Popeye's, Red Lobster, Waffle House, Zaxby's 🛏 Amercan Inn, Econolodge, Motel 6 Ⓞ $General, $Tree, 🅷, Little Giant Farmers Mkt, O'Reilly Parts, Office Depot
233	GA 54, Morrow, E 🅿 BP/dsl, Citgo, Gulf 🍴 Cookout, Cracker Barrel, IHOP, Krystal, Taco Bell, Waffle House, Wendy's 🛏 Best Western, Comfort Suites, Days Inn, Drury Inn, Red Roof Inn Ⓞ Walmart, W 🅿 Chevron/dsl, Exxon/dsl, QT/dsl 🍴 China Café, Golden Buddha, KFC, Lenny's Subs, Olive Garden, Subway, Three$ Cafe, Waffle House, Wendy's 🛏 Hampton Inn, Quality Inn Ⓞ Acura, Buick/GMC/Mazda, Burlington Coats, Cadillac, Costco/gas, Fiat, Harley-Davidson, Kia, Macy's, Nissan, Sam's Club/gas, Sears/auto, TJ Maxx, Toyota

231	Mt Zion Blvd, E 🅿 QT Ⓞ Chrysler/Dodge/Jeep, Ford/Lincoln, Honda, W 🅿 BP/Circle K/Subway/dsl, Chevron, Texaco/dsl 🍴 Arby's, Atlanta Bread, Bruster's, Burger King, Carrabba's, Chili's, China King, Chipotle, City Cafe Diner, Joe's Crabshack, Longhorn Steaks, McDonald's, Mo-Jo's Wings, Moe's SW Grill, Panda Express, Papa John's, Pizza Hut, Skyboxx Rest., Steak 'n Shake, Taco Bell, TGIFriday, Truett's Rest., Waffle House, Wendy's, Wok Asian, Zaxby's 🛏 Best Value Inn, Country Inn&Suites, Extended Stay America, Sun Suites Ⓞ AT&T, Barnes & Noble, Best Buy, Home Depot, NTB, Petsmart, Publix, Ross, Verizon
228	GA 54, GA 138, Jonesboro, E 🅿 Raceway/dsl 🍴 Applebee's, Broadway Diner, Chick-fil-A, Frontera Mexican, Golden Corral, Honeybaked Ham, IHOP, Krystal, Marco's Pizza, O'Charley's, Piccadilly's, Stevi B's Pizza, Subway, Taco Mac, Tokyo Seafood, Waffle House, Wing Nuts 🛏 Comfort Inn, Day's Inn, Express Inn, Hampton Inn, Holiday Inn, La Quinta, Red Roof Inn Ⓞ 🅷, Kroger/dsl, Lowes Whse, Office Depot, Tires+, URGENT CARE, Verizon, W 🅿 Marathon, Mobil, Raceway/Wendy's/dsl 🍴 Dragon Garden Chinese, McDonald's, Ranchero's Mexican 🛏 Fairfield Inn Ⓞ CarMax, CVS Drug, Kohl's
227	I-675 N, to I-285 E (from nb)
224	Hudson Bridge Rd, E 🅿 Shell/dsl, Texaco/dsl 🍴 Chick-fil-A, China Wok, DQ, Italian Oven, Johnny's NY Pizza, KFC, La Hacienda, Outback Steaks, Pueblo Mio, Serafino Itlian, Starbucks, Sticky Cactus Mexican, Subway, Waffle House, Wendy's 🛏 Quality Inn Ⓞ 🅷, Kauffman Tire, Publix, Rite Aid, Walgreens, W 🅿 Murphy USA/dsl, QT 🍴 Arby's, China Cafe, Firehouse Subs, McDonald's, Mellow Mushroom, Taco Bell, Zaxby's 🛏 Super 8 Ⓞ $Tree, AT&T, AutoZone, Discount Tire, GNC, Verizon, Walmart
222	Jodeco Rd, E 🅿 Citgo, Shell, Texaco 🍴 Hardee's, W 🍴 Fifteenth St Pizza Ⓞ Atlanta So. RV Camping
221	Jonesboro Rd, E 🅿 QT/dsl, Shell/dsl Ⓞ Kauffman Tire, Kroger/gas (2mi), W 🍴 American Deli, Arby's, Burger King, Cheddar's, Chili's, Firehouse Subs, Golden Corral, Hong Kong Cafe, Hooters, La Parrilla, Logan's Roadhouse, Longhorn Steaks, Marble Slab Creamery, McDonald's, Mike's Burger, O'Charley's, Olive Garden, Red Lobster, Rocky's Pizza, Starbucks, Subway, Truett's Grill, Wendy's, Wild Wing Cafe, Yuki Hibachi 🛏 Courtyard, Fairfield Inn, Home 2 Suites Ⓞ AT&T, AutoZone, Belk, Best Buy, Books-A-Million, Dick's, Home Depot, Marshall's, Michael's, Old Navy, PetsMart, Ross, Sam's Club/gas, Staples, Target, Verizon
218	GA 20, GA 81, McDonough, E 🅿 BP/dsl, Murphy USA/dsl, QT, Texaco 🍴 American Deli, Applebee's, Arby's, Burger King, China King, China Star, Cracker Barrel, DQ, IHOP, KFC, Maritza& Frank's Rest., McDonald's, Mesquite Mexican, Moe's SW Grill, Montego Bay Cafe, OB's BBQ, Pizza Hut, Popeye's, Ruby Tuesday, Sakura Hibachi, South Side Diner, Taco Bell, Three $ Cafe, Waffle House, Zaxby's 🛏 Baymont Inn, Best Western, Economy Inn, Howard Johnson, Super 8 Ⓞ $General, $Tree, Aamco, Discount Tire, Goodyear, Lowe's Whse, Office Depot, Rite Aid, URGENT CARE, Walmart, W 🅿 RaceTrac/dsl, Shell 🍴 Chick-fil-A, Dunkin', El Agade Mexican, Firehouse Subs, Folks Rest., Freddy's, Hampton Inn, Hardee's, Ichiban Express, Jimmy John's, Starbucks, Subway, Waffle House 🛏 Comfort Suites, Econolodge, Fair Bridge Inn, Hilton Garden, Holiday Inn Express, Motel 6 Ⓞ Advance Parts, AT&T, Hobby Lobby, Honda, JC Penney, Kia, Kohl's, NTB, TJ Maxx, Toyota, Verizon
216	GA 155, McDonough, Blacksville, E 🅿 Shell/dsl, Sunoco 🍴 Honk Kong Express, Sonic 🛏 Best Value, Day's Inn, Hyundai, Rodeway Inn Ⓞ Chevrolet/Buick/GMC, Ford, GMC, Tire South,

GA

⬆N   INTERSTATE 75 Cont'd

216	Continued
	W 🅟 BP, Chevron, Citgo/dsl/24hr, Exxon/dsl, QT 🍴 Bass BBQ, Da Vinci's Pizza, El Jimador, Graffiti's Oizza, Krystal, Kuma Japanese, Steve's Cafe, Subway, Waffle House 🏨 Country Inn& Suites, Quality Inn, Sleep Inn
212	to US 23, Locust Grove, **E** 🅟 BP/McDonald's/dsl, Chevron/ Burger King, Marathon/Quizno's, Murphy USA/dsl, QT/dsl, Shell/dsl 🍴 American Deli, Capt D's, Denny's, Hamburger Mike's, IHOP, KFC/Taco Bell, Koji Japanese, Little Caesar's, Pizza Hut, San Diego Mexican, Shane's Ribshack, Subway, Sunrise China, Waffle House, Wendy's, Zaxby's 🏨 Executive Inn, La Quinta, Ramada, Red Roof Inn 🅾 $Tree, Advance Parts, AT&T, Ingles/gas, NapaCare, Tanger Outlet/famous brands, Verizon, Walmart, **W** 🅟 Exxon/dsl, Shell/DQ/dsl 🍴 Subway 🏨 Comfort Suites, Scottish Inn, Sundown Lodge, Super 8 🅾 Bumper Parts
205	GA 16, to Griffin, Jackson, **E** 🅟 BP, **W** 🅟 Chevron/Subway/dsl 🍴 Hogfather's BBQ 🅾 Forest Glen RV Park
201	GA 36, to Jackson, Barnesville, **E** 🅟 ⬤Loves/McDonald's/ dsl/grill/scales/24hr, 🅿🅸🅻🅾🆃/DQ/Wendy's/dsl/scales/24hr/@, TA/Subway/Taco Bell/dsl/scales/24hr/@ 🅾 Blue Beacon, **W** 🅟 BP/dsl, ✈FLYING J/Denny's/dsl/LP/24hr 🍴 Waffle House 🅾 Speedco Lube, truckwash
198	Highfalls Rd, **E** 🅟 Exxon (1mi) 🍴 High Falls BBQ 🏨 High Falls Lodge 🅾 High Falls SP, HighFalls RV Park (1mi)
193	Johnstonville Rd, **W** 🅟 Marathon/dsl
190mm	weigh sta both lanes
188	GA 42, **E** 🅟 Shell 🏨 Budget Inn, Hill Top Garden Inn 🅾 RV camping, to Indian Springs SP
187	GA 83, Forsyth, **E** 🏨 Econolodge, KOA, Regency Inn, **W** 🅟 Citgo/dsl, Exxon/Circle K, Marathon, Shell, Valero/dsl 🍴 Burger King, Capt D's, DQ, Hardee's, McDonald's, Subway, Taco Bell, Waffle House, Wendy's 🏨 Day's Inn 🅾 $Tree, Advance Parts, Family$, Freshway Foods, O'Reilly Parts, Verizon, Walmart/dsl
186	Tift College Dr, Juliette Rd, Forsyth, **E** 🅾 Jarrell Plantation HS (18mi), KOA, **W** 🅟 BP/dsl, Chevron/dsl, Marathon 🍴 Waffle House 🏨 Holiday Inn Express, Motel 6, Super 8 🅾 CVS Drug, H, Ingles/Deli
185	GA 18, **E** 🅾 L&D RV Park (2mi), **W** 🅟 Exxon/Circle K, Shell/dsl 🍴 Shoney's 🏨 Comfort Inn 🅾 Ford, st patrol
181	Rumble Rd, to Smarr, **E** 🅟 BP/dsl
179mm	🆁🆂 sb, full 🚻 facilities, litter barrels, petwalk, 🖨, 📶, vending
177	I-475 S around Macon (from sb)
175	Pate Rd, Bolingbroke (from nb, no re-entry)
172	Bass Rd, **E** 🍴 McDonald's, Zaxby's 🅾 Bass Pro Shop, **W** 🅟 Citgo/dsl, Flash/DQ/dsl 🍴 Chick-fil-A, Genghis Grill, Homewood Suites, Magarita's Mexican, Mellow Mushroom, Natalia's Rest., Subway, Taco Bell, Zheng's Wok 🏨 Microtel, Woodspring Suites 🅾 CVS, Publix, to Museum of Arts&Sciences
171	US 23, to GA 87, Riverside Dr, **E** 🅟 BP, Marathon/dsl 🍴 Barbarito's Cantina, Bonefish Grill, Buca Italian, Chili's, Firehouse Subs, GA Bob's BBQ, Jersey Mike's, La Parrilla, TX Roadhouse, Wild Wing Cafe 🏨 SpringHill Suites 🅾 Acura, AT&T, Barnes & Noble, Belk, BMW, Dick's, Dillard's, GNC, Hobby Lobby, Jo-Ann, Mercedes, Petsmart, Subaru, Verizon, Volvo, **W** 🅾 Lexus, Toyota
169	to US 23, Arkwright Dr, **E** 🅟 Shell/Circle K/24hr 🍴 Carrabba's, Logan's Roadhouse, Outback Steaks, Waffle House, Wager's Grill 🏨 Candlewood Suites, Comfort Inn, Country Inn & Suites, Courtyard, Fairfield Inn, Hampton Inn, Holiday Inn, Home 2 Suites, La Quinta, Red Roof Inn, Residence Inn, Sleep Inn 🅾 Buick/Cadillac/GMC, **W** 🅟 Chevron/dsl, Marathon/dsl
169	Continued 🍴 Arby's, Buffalo Wild Wings, Burger King, Cheddar's, Chick-fil-A, Chipotle, Cracker Barrel, Dunkin', Five Guys, Guitarras Mexican, Hooters, IHOP, Joy's Buffet, KFC, Krystal, Little Caesar's, Longhorn Steaks, Mandarin Chinese, McDonald's, Panda Express, Panera Bread, Papa John's, Starbucks, Steak'n Shake, Steve B's Pizza, Subway, Taco Bell, Waffle House, Wendy's 🏨 Baymont Inn, Budgetel, Days Inn, Extended Stay America, Quality Inn, Rodeway Inn, Travelodge, Wingate Inn 🅾 $General, $Tree, Ace Hardware, Chrysler/Jeep/Dodge, GNC, Goodyear/auto, H, Hyundai, Kia, Kroger/dsl, Mazda, O'Reilly Parts, Publix, Tuesday Morning
167	GA 247, Pierce Ave, **E** 🏨 United Inn, **W** 🅟 Exxon, Fastrip/dsl, Shell/Circle K/dsl, Shell/dsl 🍴 Applebee's, Loco's Grill, Marco's Pizza, Metropolis Mediterranean, S&S Cafeteria, Shogun Japanese, SteakOut, Waffle House 🏨 Best Western/rest., Holiday Inn Express, Howard Johnson, Magnuson Hotel, Palmtree Extended Stay 🅾 Firestone/auto, Rite Aid
165	I-16 E, to Savannah
164	US 41, GA 19, Forsyth Ave, Macon, **E** 🍴 Sid's Rest. 🅾 hist dist, H, **W** 🅟 Citgo/dsl 🅾 museum
163	GA 74 W, Mercer U Dr, **E** 🏨 Hilton Garden 🅾 to Mercer U, **W** 🅟 Citgo
162	US 80, GA 22, Eisenhower Pkwy, **W** 🅟 Citgo/dsl, Lo-lo Gas, Sunoco/dsl 🍴 Burger King, Capt D's, Checker's, Krispy Kreme, Krystal, McDonald's, Mrs Winners, Overtyme Grill, Subway, Wendy's 🏨 InTown Suites 🅾 $Tree, O'Reilly Parts, PepBoys, Save-A-Lot Foods, Walgreens
160	US 41, GA 247, Pio Nono Ave, **E** 🅟 Flash/dsl, RaceWay/Dunkin'/ dsl 🍴 Waffle House, **W** 🅟 BP, Enmark/dsl 🍴 Arby's, DQ, KFC, McDonald's, Subway, Waffle House 🅾 $General, Advance Parts, Family$, O'Reilly Parts, Piggly Wiggly, Raffield Tire, Roses
156	I-475 N around Macon (from nb)
155	Hartley Br Rd, **E** 🅟 Shell/KFC/dsl 🍴 Domino's, Subway, Waffle House, Wendy's 🅾 Kroger/dsl, Verizon, **W** 🅟 Citgo/dsl, Flash/ DQ/dsl 🍴 McDonald's, Zaxby's 🏨 Best Value Inn 🅾 Advance Parts, CVS Drug
153	Sardis Church Rd, **E** 🅟 Citgo/dsl
149	GA 49, Byron, **E** 🅟 Chevron/dsl, Shell/dsl 🍴 Burger King, Casa Mexico, Denny's, GA Bob's BBQ, Krystal, Marco's Pizza, McDonald's, Pizza Hut, Subway, Waffle House, Wendy's, Zaxby's 🏨 Best Western, Comfort Suites, Holiday Inn Express, Super 8 🅾 Campers Inn RV Ctr, Mid-State RV Ctr, Peach Stores/famous brands, **W** 🅟 Citgo/dsl/24hr, Flash/dsl, Marathon/dsl, RaceWay/dsl, Texaco/dsl 🍴 DQ, Hardee's, Hudson's BBQ, Waffle House 🏨 Budget Inn, Days Inn, EconoLodge, Quality Inn 🅾 $General, Advance Parts, Bumper Parts, Camping World RV Ctr, Chevrolet, Ford, Interstate RV Ctr/park, O'Reilly Parts, Verizon

FORSYTH

MACON

MACON

 = gas   = food   = lodging   = other   = rest stop   Copyright 2022 - The Next EXIT ®

INTERSTATE 75 Cont'd

Exit #	Services
146	GA 247, to Centerville, **E** Exxon/dsl, Flash/dsl, Shell Subway, Waffle House Comfort Lodge, EconoLodge to Robins AFB, **W** Chevron/dsl, /Arby's/dsl/24hr
144	Russel Pkwy, **E** aviation museum, Robins AFB
142	GA 96, Housers Mill Rd, **E** Shell/dsl Ponderosa RV Park
138	Thompson Rd, **E** Valero/dsl , **W**
136	US 341, Perry, **E** Flash/dsl, Murphy Express/dsl, Shell/Circle K/dsl Burger King, Capt D's, Chick-fil-A, China House, George & Bob's BBQ, Hibachi Buffet, Jalisco Grill, KFC, Krystal, Little Caesar's, Longhorn Steaks, McDonald's, Pizza Hut, Red Lobster, Sonny's BBQ, Steamers Seafood, Subway, Taco Bell, Waffle House, Wendy's, Zaxby's Great Inn, Hampton Inn, Howard Johnson, Jameson Inn, Motel 6, Rodeway Inn, Super 8 $General, $Tree, Ace Hardware, Advance Parts, Boland's RV Park, GNC, , Kroger/dsl, NAPA, Verizon, Walmart, **W** Shell/Circle K/dsl Applebee's, Grill Master BBQ Days Inn, EconoLodge, Hardee's, Holiday Inn Express, Knights Inn, Passport Inn, Quality Inn, Ramada Inn Crossroads Travel Oark
135	US 41, GA 127, Perry, **E** Chevron/dsl, Flash/dsl, Flash/dsl (2), Shell, Texaco/dsl Cracker Barrel, DQ, Subway, Waffle House Best Western, Budget Inn, Comfort Inn, Relax Inn, Travelodge Chrysler/Dodge/Jeep, GA Nat Fair, Kia, **W** Fair Harbor RV Park, st patrol
134	South Perry Pkwy, **W** Microtel Buick/Chevrolet/GMC, Ford
127	GA 26, Henderson, **E** Twin Oaks Camping, **W** Shell/dsl
122	GA 230, Unadilla, **E** Chevron/dsl Chevrolet/Ford
121	US 41, Unadilla, **E** Borum/repair, Flash/DQ/dsl Subway Scottish Inn $General, Family$, Firestone, Piggly Wiggly, Southern Trails RV Resort, USPO, **W** Citgo/rest./dsl/scales/24hr
118mm	sb, full facilities, litter barrels, petwalk, , , RV dump, vending
117	to US 41, Pinehurst, **W** GasnGo/Subway/dsl
112	GA 27, Vienna
109	GA 215, Vienna, **E** /McDonalds/dsl/scales/24hr, **W** Shell/dsl, Sunoco Popeye's Executive Inn $General Mkt, Cotton Museum
108mm	nb, full facilities, litter barrels, petwalk, , , RV dump, vending
104	Farmers Mkt Rd, Cordele
102	GA 257, Cordele, **E** Sunoco/dsl, **W** Smoothie's BBQ
101	US 280, GA 90, Cordele, **E** BP/dsl, /Arby's/dsl/scales/24hr, Shell Denny's, Golden Corral, Waffle House Fairfield Inn, Holiday Inn Express, Motel 6, Ramada Inn Ford, st patrol, **W** Flash/dsl, Gas'n Go, Sunoco, VP/Subway Burger King, Capt D's, Chick-fil-A, Cracker Barrel, DQ, Hachi Japanese Grill, Hardee's, KFC, Krystal, Little Caesar's, Los Compadres, McDonald's, New China, Pizza Hut, Sonic, Subway, Taco Bell, TJ's Rest, Wendy's, Zaxby's Ashburn Inn, Athens 8 Motel, Baymont Inn, Best Western, EconoLodge, Hampton Inn, Quality Inn, Travelodge $General, $Tree, Advance Parts, AT&T, AutoZone, Belk, Harvey's Foods, Home Depot, J Carter HS, Kauffman Tire, O'Reilly Parts, Save-A-Lot, to Veterans Mem SP, Verizon, Walgreens, Walmart
99	GA 300, GA/FL Pkwy, **E** Marathon/DQ/dsl, **W** Waffle House Comfort Inn to Chehaw SP
97	to GA 33, Wenona, **E** Cordele RV Park, dsl repair, **W** KOA, truckwash

Exit #	Services
92	Arabi, **E** Shell/Plantation House, **W** Southern Gates RV Park
85mm	nb, full facilities, litter barrels, petwalk, , , vending
84	GA 159, Ashburn, **W** Chevron/DQ/Blimpie/dsl/24hr Ashburn Inn/RV Park
82	GA 107, GA 112, Ashburn, **W** BP, Shell Carroll's Sausage & Country Store/RV Park, KFC, McDonald's, Pizza Hut, Shoney's, Subway, Waffle House, Zaxby's Best Western, Days Inn, Holiday Inn Express, Super 8 Buick/Chevrolet/GMC, O'Reilly Parts, O'Reilly Parts, Piggly Wiggly, Rite Aid, to Chehaw SP
80	Bussey Rd, Sycamore, **W** Allen's Tires
78	GA 32, Sycamore, **E** to Jefferson Davis Mem Pk (14mi)
76mm	sb, full facilities, litter barrels, petwalk, , , vending
75	Inaha Rd
71	Willis Still Rd, Sunsweet, **W** Citgo/dsl
69	Chula-Brookfield Rd, **E** Sunoco/dsl
66	Brighton Rd
64	US 41, Tifton, **E** BP/dsl Waffle House $General, Harvey's Foods, , **W** Shell
63b	8th St, Tifton, **E** Flash/dsl/e85 El Patron, Firehouse Subs Jo-Ann, Publix, TJ Maxx, **W** Pit Stop BBQ GA Museum of Agriculture
63a	2nd St, Tifton, **E** BP/dsl, Marathon Arby's, Asahi Xpress, Barberito's, Checkers, El Metate, JoJo's Rest., KFC, Krystal, McDonald's, Pizza Hut, Red Lobster, Subway, Surcheros Grill, Taco Bell, Waffle House EconoLodge, Super 8 $General, $Tree, Big Lots, **W** Bob's/dsl El Cazadore Mexican Motel 6, Quality Inn
62	US 82, to US 319, Tifton, **E** Flash/dsl Applebee's, Bojangles, Charles Seafood, Chili's, Cracker Barrel, DQ, Golden Corral, Hardee's, King Buffet, Logan's Roadhouse, Ole Times Buffet, Sonic, Tokyo Japanese, Waffle House, Zaxby's Comfort Inn, Country Inn&Suites, Fairfield Inn, Hampton Inn, Holiday Inn Express, Microtel $Tree, Advance Parts, AutoZone, BigLots, Chrysler/Dodge/Jeep, Family$, Ford/Lincoln, NAPA, O'Reilly Parts, Pecan Outlet, Save-A-Lot, Staples, **W** Burger King, EZ Mart, Flash/dsl, Murphy USA/dsl, Shell/dsl, Tesla EVC Buffalo Wild Wings, Capt D's, Chick-fil-A, Cookout, HogBones BBQ, Little Caesar's, Longhorn Steaks, McDonald's, Oishi Japanese, Olive Garden, Panera Bread, Pizza Hut, Ruby Tuesday, Starbucks, Taco Bell, Waffle House, Wendy's Days Inn, Hilton Garden $General, AT&T, Chevrolet, Hobby Lobby, Honda, Lowe's, Toyota, URGENT CARE, Verizon, Walmart/Subway
61	Omega Rd, **E** Nissan, **W** Shell/Waffle King/pizza/dsl/24hr Howard Johnson Harley-Davidson, Pines RV Park
60	Central Ave, Tifton, **E** Chevron Dragon 1 Chinese, **W** /Steak'n Shake/Subway/dsl/scales/24hr Blue Beacon, KOA
59	Southwell Blvd, to US 41, Tifton, **E** /Hardee's/dsl/scales/24hr
55	to Eldorado, Omega, **E** Shell/Magnolia Plantation/dsl
49	Kinard Br Rd, Lenox, **E** Dixie/dsl Lenox Inn, **W** BP/dsl/24hr, Chevron
47mm	both lanes, full facilities, litter barrels, petwalk, , , vending
45	Barneyville Rd
41	Rountree Br Rd, **E** Citgo, **W** to Reed Bingham SP
39	GA 37, Adel, Moultrie, **E** Citgo/dsl, Dixie Gas, McDonald's, Quick Gas DQ, Hardee's, Subway, Waffle House Super 8, Zaxby's $General, $Tree, Ace Hardware, Advance Parts, Family$, , O'Reilly Parts, Piggly Wiggly, Rite Aid, **W** BP, Citgo/Huddle House/dsl/scales, Shell Burger King, Capt D's,

PERRY / **CORDELE** (left margin) · **ASHBURN** / **TIFTON** (right margin) · **GA**

INTERSTATE 75 Cont'd

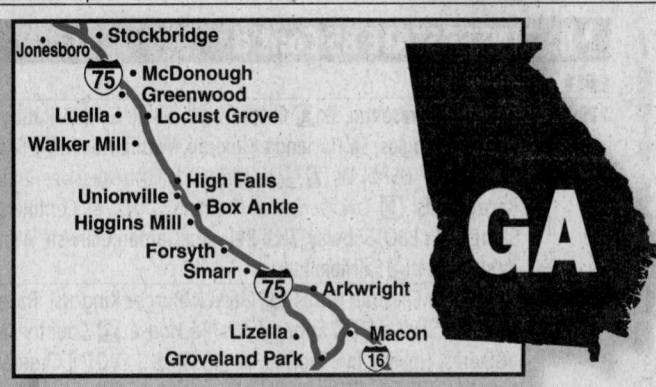

39	**Continued**
	Don Julio's, Taco Bell, Wendy's, Western Sizzlin 🛏 Hampton Inn 🅾 to Reed Bingham SP, Verizon, Walmart
37	Adel, **E** 🅿 Liberty/dsl 🅾 GMC
32	Old Coffee Rd, Cecil, **E** 🅿 Citgo/dsl 🛏 Stagecoach Inn, **W** 🅿 Chevron/dsl 🅾 Cecil Bay RV Park
29	US 41 N, GA 122, Hahira, Sheriff's Boys Ranch, **E** 🍴 Down Home Pizza, Harvey's Mkt, Huddle House 🅾 NAPA, vet, **W** 🅿 Citgo/dsl, Shell/Big Foot/cafe/dsl/24hr 🛏 Hahira Inn
23mm	**weigh sta both lanes**
22	US 41 S, to Valdosta, **E** 🍴 BP, Shell/Subway/dsl 🍴 Waffle House 🛏 Best Western+ 🅾 Buick/Chevrolet/GMC, 🔩, Mazda, **W** 🍴 Citgo/dsl 🍴 Burger King 🛏 Howard Johnson 🅾 Valdosta Oaks RV Park
18	GA 133, Valdosta, **E** 🅿 Flash, Mobil, Tesla EVC 🍴 Applebee's, Arby's, Beijing Cafe, Buffalo Wild Wings, Burger King, Chick-fil-A, Chili's, Chow Town, CiCi's Pizza, Cookout, Cracker Barrel, Crystal River Seafood, Denny's, Dick's Wings, El Toreo, Fazoli's, Firehouse Subs, Five Guys, Honeybaked Ham, Hooters, KFC, Krystal, Little Caesar's, Longhorn Steaks, McDonald's, Mellow Mushroom, Ole Times Country Buffet, Olive Garden, Outback Steaks, Panda Express, Panera Bread, Red Lobster, Sonny's BBQ, Starbucks, Steak'n Shake, Subway, Taco Bell, TX Roadhouse, Waffle House, Wendy's, Zaxby's 🛏 Baymont Inn, Candlewood Suites, Comfort Suites, Country Inn&Suites, Courtyard, Drury Inn, Hilton Garden, Holiday Inn Express, InTown Suites, La Quinta, Motel 6, Oyo Hotel, Quality Inn 🅾 $Tree, AT&T, Belk, Best Buy, Books-A-Million, Discount Tire, Family$, Goodyear/auto, Hobby Lobby, Home Depot, JC Penney, Kohl's, Lowe's, Michael's, Old Navy, Petsmart, Publix, Ross, Target, TJ Maxx, URGENT CARE, Verizon, Walgreens, **W** 🍴 BP/dsl, RaceWay/dsl 🛏 Days Inn, EconoLodge, Sleep Inn, Super 8 🅾 River Park Camping, Toyota
16	US 84, US 221, GA 94, Valdosta, **E** 🍴 BP/dsl, Exxon/dsl, Murphy Express/dsl, Shell/dsl, Sunoco 🍴 Aligatou Japanese, Bojangles, Bubba Jax Crab Shack, Burger King, Cajun Wild Crab, Cheddar's, IHOP, McDonald's, Pizza Hut, Sonic, Waffle House, Wendy's 🛏 Comfort Inn, Days Inn, Fairfield Inn, Hampton Inn, Holiday Inn, Motel 6, Super 8, Super Value Inn 🅾 Sam's Club/gas, Walmart/Subway, **W** 🍴 Citgo/dsl/24hr, Sunstop/Moe's SW/dsl 🍴 Austin's Steaks 🛏 Briarwood Inn, Kinderlou Inn, Oyo Inn
13	Old Clyattville Rd, Valdosta, **W** 🅾 Wild Adventures Park
11	GA 31, Valdosta, **E** 🅿 LNG, PILOT/Dunkin'/dsl/scales/24hr, PILOT/Subway/dsl/24hr/@ 🍴 Waffle House 🛏 Travelers Inn 🅾 truckwash, **W** 🍴 Quick Gas 🅾 $General
5	GA 376, to Lake Park, **E** 🍴 Flash Foods/Stuckey's/dsl, RaceWay/dsl, Shell 🍴 Chick-fil-A, Cowboys Grill, Domino's, Farmhouse Rest., Krystal, Lin's Garden Chinese, Rodeo Mexican, Subway, Taco Bell, Waffle House, Zaxby's 🛏 Lake Park Express, Motel 6 🅾 $Tree, antiques, Day Bros RV Ctr, Eagles Roost Camping, Family$, Horizon RV Ctr, USPO, Winn-Dixie, **W** 🍴 Camping World RV Ctr, Exxon/dsl 🍴 Cracker Barrel, McDonald's, Pizza Hut, Wendy's 🛏 Best Value Inn, Days Inn, Hampton Inn, Holiday Inn Express, Travelodge 🅾 Lake Park Camping
3mm	**Welcome Ctr nb, full** ♿ **facilities, litter barrels, petwalk,** 🚻, 🐾, **vending**
2	Lake Park, Bellville, **E** 🍴 TA/BP/Arby's/dsl/scales/24hr/@ 🅾 SpeedCo, **W** 🍴 FLYING J/Denny's/Subway/dsl/LP/scales/24hr 🛏 Stay Inn Suites 🅾 lube/tires/wash
0mm	Georgia/Florida state line

INTERSTATE 85

Exit #	Services
179mm	Georgia/South Carolina state line, Tugaloo River, Lake Hartwell
177	GA 77 S, to Hartwell, **E** 🍴 BP/gifts/dsl 🍴 Dad's Grill 🅾 to Hart SP, **W** 🅾 Tugaloo SP
176mm	**Welcome Ctr sb, full** ♿ **facilities, info, litter barrels, petwalk,** 🚻, 🐾, **vending**
173	GA 17, to Lavonia, **E** 🍴 Raceway/dsl 🍴 Bojangles, Cracker Barrel, La Cabana Mexican, McDonald's, Subway, Taco Bell, Waffle House 🛏 Days Inn, EconoLodge, Rodeway Inn 🅾 $General, Lavonia Foods, Rite Aid, **W** 🍴 Exxon/dsl 🍴 Burger King, Chic, DQ, Hardee's, J Peters Grill, Pizza Hut, Shoney's, Zaxby's 🛏 Hampton Inn, Holiday Inn Express, Super 8 🅾 Chrysler/Dodge/Jeep, Ford, to Tugaloo SP
171mm	**weigh sta nb**
169mm	**weigh sta sb**
166	GA 106, to Carnesville, Toccoa, **E** 🍴 Exxon/dsl, PILOT/Dunkin'/DQ/Wendy's/dsl/scales/24hr 🍴 Little Caesar's, **W** 🍴 Echo Trkstp/Chevron/Echo Rest./dsl/scales/24hr
164	GA 320, to Carnesville
160	GA 51, to Homer, **E** 🍴 Marathon/Subway/dsl/24hr 🅾 to Russell SP, Ty Cobb Museum, Victoria Bryant SP, **W** 🍴 FLYING J/dsl/24hr, Petro/BP/Iron Skillet/dsl/scales/24hr/@ 🅾 Blue Beacon
154	GA 63, Martin Br Rd
149	US 441, GA 15, to Commerce, Homer, **E** 🍴 EVC, Murphy USA, QT/dsl, TA/Shell/Country Pride/dsl/scales/24hr/@ 🍴 Bojangles, Capt D's, Grand Buffet, Koji Japanese, Krispy Kreme, Little Caesar's, Longhorn Steaks, Outback Steaks, Papa John's, Sonny's BBQ, Taco Bell, Waffle House, Zaxby's 🛏 Days Inn, Hampton Inn, Red Roof Inn, Scottish Inn 🅾 $General, $Tree, AT&T, Chrysler/Dodge/Jeep, Funopolis, GNC, 🔩, O'Reilly Parts, URGENT CARE, Walmart/Subway, **W** 🍴 BP/Krystal/dsl, Petro Express/dsl, RaceTrac/dsl 🍴 Applebee's, Arby's, Burger King, Chick-fil-A, Cracker Barrel, Culver's, DQ, Five Guys, Hawg Wild BBQ, La Hacienda, McDonald's, Pizza Hut, Popeye's, Ruby Tuesday, Ryan's, Sonic, Starbucks, Subway, Wendy's 🛏 Best Western, Comfort Suites, Country Inn&Suites, Fairfield Inn, Holiday Inn Express, Howard Johnson, Motel 6, Quality Inn, Super 8, Travelodge 🅾 Home Depot, Pritchett Tires, Tanger Outlet/famous brands, Verizon
147	GA 98, to Commerce, **E** 🍴 Citgo/dsl, Loves/Dunkin'/dsl/24hr 🅾 🔩, **W** 🅾 Chevron
140	GA 82, Dry Pond Rd, **E** 🍴 Circle K Trkstp/dsl/scales 🅾 Freightliner, **W** 🅾 Truck Repair
137	US 129, GA 11 to Jefferson, **E** 🍴 RaceTrac/dsl 🍴 Arby's, Bojangles, El Jinete Mexican, KFC/Taco Bell, McDonald's, Waffle House, Zaxby's 🛏 Quality Inn 🅾 museum, **W** 🍴 QT/dsl/scales/24hr 🍴 Burger King, Waffle House, Wendy's 🅾 flea mkt

INTERSTATE 85 Cont'd

J E F F E R S O N

Exit #	Services
129	GA 53, to Braselton, **E** 🅿 Chevron/dsl, Shell/Golden Pantry/dsl 🍴 Bojangles, La Hacienda Mexican, Waffle House 🛏 Best Western 🅾 USPO, **W** 🅿 ▭/McDonald's/dsl/scales/24hr, RaceTrac/dsl 🍴 Cracker Barrel, Domino's, DQ, El Centinela, Stonewall's BBQ, Subway, Taco Bell, Tea Garden Chinese, Wendy's, Zaxby's 🛏 Fairfield Inn
126	GA 211, to Chestnut Mtn, **E** 🅿 Circle K/Burger King/dsl, RaceTrac/dsl, Shell/dsl 🍴 Subway, Waffle House 🛏 Country Inn&Suites, Holiday Inn Express, **W** 🅿 BP/dsl, EVC 🍴 Chateau Elan Winery/rest., China Garden, Papa John's 🛏 Baymont Inn, Hampton Inn 🅾 Publix, Verizon, vet
120	to GA 124, Hamilton Mill Rd, **E** 🅿 BP, QT/dsl 🍴 Arby's, Buffalo's Café, Burger King, Caprese Rest., Firehouse Subs, Five Guys, McDonald's, Moe's SW Grill, Riverside Pizza, Starbucks, Wendy's, Zaxby's 🅾 Aldi Foods, auto repair, Home Depot, Kohl's, Publix/Deli, RV World of GA (1mi), vet, **W** 🅿 Chevron, EVC, Murphy USA/dsl, Shell/dsl 🍴 Barberito's, Chick-fil-A, Chili's, Dunkin', El Molcajate, Hardee's, Italy's Pizza, Krystal, Little Caesar's, Taco Bell 🅾 $Tree, Advance Parts, AT&T, CVS Drug, O'Reilly Parts, Tires+, USPO, Verizon, Walmart/Subway
115	GA 20, to Buford Dam, **E** 🅿 QT 🍴 Waffle House 🅾 Pepboys, **W** 🍴 Arby's, Atlanta Bread, Bonefish Grill, Bruster's, Burger 21, Burger King, Cheesecake Factory, Chick-fil-A, Chili's, Chipotle, ChuckeCheese, East Coast Wings, Einstein's Bagels, Firehouse Subs, Genghis Grill, Honeybaked Ham, Kani House, Krispy Kreme, Longhorn Steaks, Macaroni Grill, Maddio's Pizza, McDonald's, Mimi's Cafe, Moe's SW Grill, O'Charley's, Olive Garden, On-the-Border, Panda Express, Panera Bread, PF Chang's, Provino's Italian, Red Lobster, Shogun Japanese, Sonny's BBQ, Starbucks, Steak n' Shake, Subway, Taco Mac, Ted's MT Grill, TGIFriday's, Tilted Kilt, Waffle House, Wendy's, Which Wich? 🛏 Country Inn&Suites, Courtyard, Hampton Inn, SpringHill Suites, Wingate Inn 🅾 $Tree, AT&T, Barnes&Noble, Belk, Best Buy, Buick/GMC, Costco/gas, Dick's, Dillard's, Discount Tire, Fiat, Firestone/auto, Honda, Hyundai, JC Penney, Lowe's, Macy's, Marshall's, Mazda, Michael's, Nissan, Nordstrom Rack, PetCo, Petsmart, REI, Ross, Sam's Club/gas, Staples, SteinMart, Target, TJ Maxx, to Lake Lanier Islands, Toyota, Tuesday Morning, Verizon, Von Maur, VW, Walmart
113	I-985 N (from nb), to Gainesville
111	GA 317, to Suwanee, **E** 🅿 BP/dsl, Valero/dsl 🍴 Applebee's, Arby's, Checker's, Chick-fil-A, Cracker Barrel, Dunkin', Orient Garden, Outback Steaks, Philly Connection, Pizza Hut, Schlotsky's, Subway, Taco Bell, Waffle House, Wendy's 🛏 Comfort Suites, Courtyard, Fairfield Inn, Motel 6, Quality Inn, Sun Suites 🅾 CVS Drug, GNC, O'Reilly Parts, **W** 🅿 Chevron/dsl, Murphy USA/dsl, QT/dsl, Raceway/dsl, Shell 🍴 Dunkin', Greek Island, HoneyBaked Ham, IHOP, Jimmy John's, KFC, McDonald's, Moe's SW Grill, Sonic, Subway, Taco Mac 🛏 Red Roof Inn, Super 8 🅾 $Tree, Advance Parts, AT&T, Lowe's, Office Depot, Walmart
109	Old Peachtree Rd, **E** 🅿 QT 🍴 McAlister's, McDonald's, Mi Casa Mexican 🛏 Hampton Inn, Homewood Suites 🅾 Bass Pro Shops, Publix, **W** 🍴 Arena Tavern, Carrabba's, Chick-fil-A, China Delight, Firehouse Subs, Five Guys, Jim&Nicks BBQ, Starbucks, Subway, Tilted Kilt, Waffle House 🛏 Hilton Garden, Holiday Inn, Residence Inn 🅾 Home Depot
108	Sugarloaf Pkwy (from nb), **E** 🛏 Hampton Inn, Homewood Suites, **W** 🍴 Carrabba's, Chick-fil-A, Tin Lizzy Cantina 🛏 Hilton Garden, Holiday Inn 🅾 Gwinnett Civic Ctr

S U W A N E E

D U L U T H

GA

A T L A N T A   A R E A

Exit #	Services
107	GA 120, to GA 316 E, Athens, **E** 🅿 Shell 🍴 Burger King, Carino's, Dave&Busters, Dunkin', Subway, Zaxby's 🅾 Bass Pro Shops, Books-a-Million, Burlington Coats, Discount Tire, Rite Aid, Ross, Saks 5th Ave, Suburban Tire, **W** 🅿 BP/dsl, Chevron 🍴 Bojangles, China Gate, McDonald's, Subway, Waffle House 🛏 La Quinta, Suburban Lodge
106	Boggs Rd (from sb, no return), Duluth, **W** 🅿 QT/dsl/24hr 🅾 Mercedes
104	Pleasant Hill Rd, **E** 🅿 Chevron/e85, QT/dsl, Shell/dsl, Valero/dsl 🍴 Bahama Breeze, Burger King, Chick-fil-A, Costas Nayaritas, Don Pedro Mexican, East Pearl, Fung Mei Chinese, GA Diner, Golden House, Joe's Crabshack, McDonald's, Popeye's, Schlotsky's, Stevi B's Pizza, Subway, Super Buffet, TGIFriday's, Waffle House, Wendy's 🛏 Best Western, Candlewood Suites, Comfort Suites, Fairfield Inn, Hampton Inn Suites, Holiday Inn Express, Residence Inn, Sonesta 🅾 $General, $Tree, Advance Parts, Best Buy, Family$, Home Depot, Publix, URGENT CARE, Walgreens, **W** 🅿 BP/Dunkin'/dsl, Chevron/dsl, Valero/dsl 🍴 Applebee's, Arby's, Barnacle's, Bruster's, Burger King, Checker's, Chili's, Chipotle Mexican, Hooters, IHOP, Jimmy John's, KFC, Krispy Kreme, McDonald's, Melting Pot, Olive Garden, On the Border, Panda Express, Red Lobster, Starbucks, Steak'n Shake, Subway, Taco Bell, Wendy's 🛏 Courtyard, Extended Stay America, Haven Hotel, Hyatt Place, Quality Inn, Wingate Inn, Wyndham Garden 🅾 AT&T, Audi, Batteries+, Belk, BMW, Buick/GMC, Firestone/auto, Ford, Fry's Electronics, Goodyear/auto, Honda, Hyundai, Infiniti, JC Penney, Jo-Ann Fabrics, Kia, Macy's, Marshall's, Nissan, PetCo, Rite Aid, Staples, Subaru, TJ Maxx, Toyota, Verizon
103	Steve Reynolds Blvd (from nb, no return), **W** 🅿 QT/dsl, Shell 🍴 Dave&Buster's, Waffle House 🛏 InTown Suites 🅾 $Tree, Big Lots, Costco/gas, Kohl's, Petsmart, Sam's Club, same as 104
102	GA 378, Beaver Ruin Rd, **E** 🅿 QT, Shell/dsl, Valero/dsl 🍴 Subway, **W** 🅿 Citgo
101	Lilburn Rd, **E** 🅿 QT, Shell/dsl 🍴 Blimpie, Bruster's, Burger King, Domino's, Hong Kong Buffet, Jimmy John's, KFC, Krystal, McDonald's, Starbucks, Taco Bell, Waffle House 🛏 Guesthouse Inn, InTown Suites, Super 8 🅾 Jones RV Park, **W** 🅿 Chevron, Marathon/dsl, QT 🍴 Arby's, China Panda, El Taco Veloz, Papa John's, Pizza Plaza, Subway, Waffle House, Wendy's 🛏 Knights Inn, Red Roof Inn 🅾 CarMax, Chrysler/Dodge/Jeep, Lowe's
99	GA 140, Jimmy Carter Blvd, **E** 🅿 Shell/dsl 🍴 Checker's, Chick-fil-A, Cracker Barrel, Denny's, Dunkin', McDonald's, Papa John's, Pollo Campero, Subway, Taco Bell 🛏 Congress Suites, Courtyard, Horizon Inn, La Quinta, Motel 6, Rite4Us Inn 🅾 Advance Parts, Aldi Foods, Family$, U-Haul, Walgreens, **W** 🅿 Chevron/dsl, QT/dsl, Valero/dsl 🍴 Hibachi Grill, Hong Kong Buffet, Pappadeaux Steak/seafood, Sonic, Waffle House, Wendy's 🛏 Country Inn&Suites, Days Inn, Microtel, Rodeway Inn 🅾 AutoZone, CarQuest, NTB, O'Reilly Parts, PepBoys
96	Pleasantdale Rd, Northcrest Rd, **E** 🍴 Burger King, Pleasantdale Chinese, **W** 🅿 Exxon/dsl, QT/dsl 🍴 Subway 🛏 Atlanta Lodge
95	I-285
94	Chamblee-Tucker Rd, **E** 🅿 Chevron/Subway/dsl, Shell/dsl 🅾 to Mercer U, **W** 🅿 QT/dsl 🍴 DQ, Waffle House 🛏 Motel 6, Super 8
93	Shallowford Rd, to Doraville, **E** 🅿 Shell 🍴 Hop Shing Chinese, Marco's Pizza, Subway 🅾 Publix, U-Haul, **W** 🅿 Shell/dsl 🛏 Quality Inn
91	US 23, GA 155, Clairmont Rd, **E** 🅿 Chevron/dsl, QT/dsl, URGENT CARE 🍴 IHOP, Mo's Pizza, Popeye's 🅾 repair, **W** 🅿 BP 🍴 McDonald's, Waffle House 🛏 Extended Stay America, Holiday Inn Express, Marriott 🅾 NTB, Sam's Club/dsl

INTERSTATE 85 Cont'd

Exit #	Services
89	GA 42, N Druid Hills, **E** 🅿 Chevron/Subway/dsl, QT, Shell/dsl 🍴 Arby's, Boston Mkt, Burger King, Chick-fil-A, El Torero, Fortune Cookie, Grub Burger, Jersey Mike's, McDonald's, Moe's SW Grill, Newk's Eatery, Panera Bread, Penn Sta Subs, Piccadilly's, Starbucks, Taco Bell, Tin Roof Cantina, Willy's Mexicana, Zoe's Kitchen 🏨 Courtyard 🅾 $Tree, Firestone/auto, GNC, Target, Walgreens, **W** 🅿 Chevron/dsl, Exxon/dsl, Shell 🍴 HoneyBaked Ham, Krystal, McDonald's, Waffle House 🏨 DoubleTree, Hampton Inn, Red Roof Inn 🅾 CVS Drug, Just Brakes
88	Lenox Rd, GA 400 N, Cheshire Br Rd (from sb), **E** 🅿 Valero/dsl 🍴 McDonald's 🏨 La Quinta
87	GA 400 N (from nb)
86	GA 13 S, Peachtree St, **E** 🅿 BP, Chevron 🍴 Papa John's, Wendy's 🏨 Intown Inn 🅾 Sprouts Mkt, vet
85	I-75 N, to Marietta, Chattanooga
84	Techwood Dr, 14th St, **E** 🅿 BP, Shell 🍴 CheeseSteaks, La Bamba Mexican, Thai Cuisine, VVV Ristorante Italiano 🏨 Best Western, Hampton Inn, Marriott, Sheraton, Travelodge 🅾 Woodruff Arts Ctr, **W** 🍴 Blimpie 🏨 Courtyard, Knights Inn 🅾 CVS Drug, Dillard's, Office Depot, to Georgia Tech
77	I-75 S
76	Cleveland Ave, **E** 🅿 Citgo/dsl 🍴 Burger King, Papa John's 🅾 $Tree, AutoZone, BigLots, CVS Drug, Family$, 🏥, Kroger, Walgreens, **W** 🅿 Shell/dsl, Texaco/dsl 🍴 Chick-fil-A, Church's 🅾 CVS, O'Reilly Parts
75	Sylvan Rd, **E** 🅿 Shell/dsl
74	Loop Rd Aviation Commercial Center
73b a	Virginia Ave, **E** 🅿 Citgo/dsl 🍴 Jimmy John's, Jonny's Pizza, Landmark Diner, Malone's Grill, McDonald's, Pizza Hut, Ruby Tuesday, Schlotsky's, Spondivit's Rest., Waffle House, Wendy's, Willy's Mexican 🏨 Courtyard, Drury Inn, Hilton, Motel 6, Renaissance Hotel, Residence Inn, **W** 🅿 Chevron/Subway, Shell 🍴 Arby's, BBQ Kitchen, Blimpie, Giovanna's Italian, Happy Buddha Chinese, KFC, La Fiesta Mexican, Waffle House 🏨 Country Inn&Suites, Crowne Plaza, DoubleTree, EconoLodge, Fairfield Inn, Hampton Inn, Hilton Garden, Holiday Inn, Homewood Suites, Hyatt Place, Palms Hotel, Staybridge Inn, Wellesley Inn
72	Camp Creek Pkwy
71	Riverdale Rd, Atlanta Airport, **E** 🍴 Ruby Tuesday 🏨 Courtyard, Fairfield Inn, Hampton Inn, Holiday Inn, Hyatt Place, La Quinta, Microtel, Sheraton/grill, Sleep Inn, Super 8, **W** 🏨 Days Inn, Embassy Suites, Hilton Garden, Holiday Inn Express, Marriott, Westin Hotel
70	I-85 (from sb)
69	GA 14, GA 279, **E** 🅿 Chevron/dsl, Citgo, Exxon/dsl, Valero 🍴 Blimpie, Bojangles, Burger King, Checker's, China Cafe, Church's, Cozumel, KFC, Krystal, McDonald's, Piccadilly Cafeteria, Subway, Taco Bell, Waffle House, Wendy's 🏨 Comfort Inn, Days Inn, Quality Inn, Super 8, Travelodge, Windsor Atl Hotel 🅾 AutoZone, Family$, U-Haul, URGENT CARE, **W** 🅿 Chevron/dsl, Texaco 🍴 Waffle House 🏨 EconoLodge
68	I-285 Atlanta Perimeter (from nb)
66	Flat Shoals Rd, **W** 🅿 BP, Chevron/dsl/24hr, Shell/Blimpie 🍴 King's Rest., Waffle House 🏨 Motel 6
64	GA 138, to Union City, **E** 🅿 BP/dsl, RaceTrac/dsl 🍴 Waffle House 🏨 EconoLodge, Western Inn 🅾 BMW/Mini, Chevrolet, Chrysler/Dodge/Jeep, CVS Drug, Ford/Lincoln, Honda, Infiniti, Kia/Nissan, Lexus, Toyota, VW, **W** 🅿 Chevron/dsl, QT, Shell/dsl 🍴 Arby's, Burger King, Capt D's, China Garden, China King,
64	Continued Corner Cafe, Dunkin', IHOP, KFC, Krystal, McDonald's, Papa John's, Pizza Hut, Sonic, Southern Grill, Subway, Taco Bell, Wendy's, Zaxby's 🏨 Best Western, Comfort Inn, Country Hearth Inn, Garden Inn, La Quinta, Magnuson Hotel, Microtel 🅾 $Tree, Advance Parts, AT&T, BigLots, Firestone/auto, Kroger/dsl, NTB, O'Reilly Parts, PepBoys, vet, Walgreens, Walmart/Subway
61	GA 74, to Fairburn, **E** 🅿 BP/Huddle House/dsl/scales/24hr, QT/dsl, RaceWay/dsl, Shell, Starbucks 🍴 Bojangle's, Chick-fil-A, Cracker Barrel, Dunkin', Hardee's, Krystal, Marco's Pizza, McDonald's, Taco Bell, Waffle House, Wendy's, Zaxby's 🏨 Best Western+, Country Inn&Suites, Fairfield Inn, Hampton Inn, Holiday Inn Express, Wingate Inn 🅾 Fairburn Tires, vet, **W** 🅿 Chevron/dsl, Sun Petro/dsl 🏨 Efficiency Motel
56	Collinsworth Rd, **W** 🅿 Marathon/dsl, Shell 🍴 Frank's Rest. 🅾 South Oaks Camping
51	GA 154, to Sharpsburg, **E** 🅿 Marathon/dsl, Texaco/Subway/dsl 🍴 Hardee's, **W** 🅿 Chevron/dsl, Shell/Circle K/dsl 🍴 Waffle House
47	GA 34, to Newnan, **E** 🅿 Chevron/dsl, Marathon/Subway/dsl, QT, Shell/dsl 🍴 Applebee's, Arby's, Asian Chef, Capt D's, Chin Chin, Chipotle, Dunkin', Fried Tomato Buffet, Hooters, La Hacienda, Longhorn Steaks, Marco's Pizza, Moe's SW Grill, Panda Express, Red Lobster, Ruby Tuesday, Sprayberry's BBQ, Starbucks, Steak'n Shake, Stevi B's Pizza, TX Roadhouse, Waffle House, Wendy's 🏨 Country Inn&Suites, Hampton Inn, Quality Inn, SpringHill Suites 🅾 Aldi Foods, GNC, Goodyear/auto, Hobby Lobby, Home Depot, 🏥, Jo-Ann, Kauffman Tire, Kohl's, Lowe's, Petsmart, Ross, Walmart/McDonald's, **W** 🅿 RaceTrac/dsl 🍴 Burger King, Checkers, Chick-fil-A, Coldstone, Cracker Barrel, Firehouse Subs, Five Guys, Goldberg's Deli, Golden Corral, HoneyBaked Ham, IHOP, Jimmy John's, KFC, Krystal, La Parrilla Mexican, Newk's Cafe, O'Charley's, Olive Garden, Panera Bread, Red Robin, Rockback Pizza, Shane's BBQ, Shoney's, Starbucks, Taco Bell, Taco Mac, Thai Heaven, Tokyo Japanese, Yogli Mogli, Zaxby's 🏨 Best Western, Comfort Inn, La Quinta, Motel 6, Newnan Inn 🅾 $General, $Tree, AT&T, Barnes&Noble, Belk, Best Buy, BigLots, BJ's Whse/gas, Buick/Cadillac/GMC, Chevrolet, Dick's, Dillards, Ford/Lincoln, Hyundai, JC Penney, Michael's, Office Depot, Old Navy, Publix, Target, Tires+, TJ Maxx, Toyota, Verizon, vet, Walgreens
44	Poplar Rd, **E** 🅾 🏥
41	US 27/29, Newnan, **E** 🅿 Huddle House/Subway/Wendy's/dsl/scales/24hr 🅾 Little White House NHS, Roosevelt SP, **W** 🅿 BP/dsl 🍴 Huddle House, McDonald's, Waffle House 🏨 Best Value Inn, Falcon Inn, Home Lodge, Red Carpet 🅾 $General, repair
35	US 29, to Grantville, **W** 🅿 BP/dsl, Marathon/dsl

P = gas   ⑪ = food   ⊟ = lodging   O = other   Rs = rest stop   Copyright 2022 - The Next EXIT ®

⬆N INTERSTATE 85 Cont'd

Exit #	Services
28	GA 54, GA 100, to Hogansville, **E** P Valero/dsl, **W** P ✦Loves/Arby's/dsl/scales/24hr, Marathon/dsl, Shell/dsl ⑪ McDonald's, Roger's BBQ, Subway, Waffle House, Wendy's, Wendy's ⊟ Garden Inn, Woodstream Inn O Ingles
23mm	Beech Creek
22mm	**weigh sta both lanes**
21	I-185 S, to Columbus
18	GA 109, to Mountville, **E** P Marathon/Domino's ⊟ Rodeway Inn, Wingate Inn O Little White House HS, to FDR SP, **W** P BP/dsl, Exxon/Circle K/dsl, Mobil/dsl, RaceTrac/dsl, Shell/dsl, Valero ⑪ Applebee's, Banzai Japanese, Burger King, Chick-fil-A, Cracker Barrel, Firehouse Subs, IHOP, Juanito's Mexican, Longhorn Steaks, Los Nopales, McDonald's, Mi Casa Mexican, Moe's SW Grill, Starbucks, Subway, Waffle House, Wendy's, Zaxby's ⊟ Baymont Inn, Comfort Inn, Holiday Inn Express, La Quinta, Lafayette Garden Inn, Quality Inn, Super 8 O AT&T, Belk, Chrysler/Dodge/Jeep, Ford/Lincoln, Hobby Lobby, Home Depot, Honda, Hyundai, JC Penney, TJ Maxx, Verizon
14	US 27, to La Grange, **W** P Exxon, Marathon, Shell/Summit/dsl, Waffle House ⊟ Hampton Inn
13	GA 219, to La Grange, **E** P Exxon/dsl/scales/24hr ⑪ Waffle House ⊟ EconoLodge, **W** P Pilot/Subway/Wendy's/dsl/scales/24hr, ⑪ Arbys, McDonald's ⊟ Great Wolf Lodge, Home 2 Suites O H
10mm	Long Cane Creek
6	Kia Blvd, **W** Kia Plant
2	GA 18, to West Point, **E** P Chevron/dsl, Shell/Summit/dsl ⊟ Best Value, **W** P BP/dsl ⑪ Subway (1.5) O camping, to West Point Lake
.5mm	**Welcome Ctr nb, full** ♿ **facilities, litter barrels, petwalk,** ⑪, ⊟, **vending**
0mm	Georgia/Alabama state line, Chattahoochee River

⬆N INTERSTATE 95

Exit #	Services
113mm	Georgia/South Carolina state line, Savannah River
111mm	**Welcome Ctr/weigh sta sb, full** ♿ **facilities, info, litter barrels, petwalk,** ⑪, ⊟, **vending**
109	GA 21, to Savannah, Pt Wentworth, Rincon, **E** P Enmark/dsl, Pilot/McDonald's/Subway/dsl/scales/24hr ⑪ Waffle House ⊟ Best Western, Country Inn&Suites, Hampton Inn, Mulberry Grove Inn O Freightliner, **W** P Flash/dsl, Murphy Express/dsl, Shell/Circle K/Blimpie/dsl ⑪ Bojangles, Dunkin', El Ranchito, Happy Wok, Island Grill, Port Side Seafood, Sweet Tea Grill, Wendy's, Zaxby's ⊟ Comfort Suites, Days Inn, Holiday Inn Express, Palm Extended Stay, Quality Inn, Savannah Inn, Sleep Inn, Super 8 O CVS Drug, Family$, Food Lion, Whispering Pines RV Park (3mi)
107mm	Augustine Creek
106	Jimmy DeLoach Pkwy
104	Savannah Airport, **E** P BP, Shell/Wendy's/dsl ⑪ Sam Sneed's Grill, Waffle House, Waffle House ⊟ Candlewood Suites, Comfort Suites, Country Inn&Suites, DoubleTree, Fairfield Inn, Hampton Inn, Hilton Garden, Holiday Inn Express, Hyatt Place, SpringHill Suites, Staybridge Suites, TownePlace Suites, Wingate Inn O to ✈, **W** P Murphy USA, Parkers/dsl, Shell/Subway ⑪ Applebee's, Arby's, Buffalo Wild Wings, Cheddar's, Chick-fil-A, Chili's, Chipotle, CookOut, DQ, Fatz Cafe, Firehouse Subs, Five Guys, Hilliard's Rest., IHOP, Jalapeños, Jersey Mike's,

104	Continued
	Jimmy John's, Krystal, Little Caesar's, Logan's Roadhouse, Longhorn Steaks, McAlister's Deli, McDonald's, Mellow Mushroom, Moe's SW, Olive Garden, Panda Express, Panera Bread, Ruby Tuesday, Shane's Rib Shack, Sonic, Starbucks, Steak'n Shake, TX Roadhouse, Wild Wing Cafe, Zaxby's ⊟ Embassy Suites, Holiday Inn, Red Roof Inn, Residence Inn O AT&T, Chevrolet, Dick's, GNC, Goodyear, Hobby Lobby, Home Depot, Michael's, Petsmart, Publix, Ross, Sam's Club/gas, Savannah Tire, Tanger Outlets/famous brands, TJ Maxx, URGENT CARE, Verizon, Walmart/McDonald's
102	US 80, to Garden City, **E** P El Cheapos/Baldinos Subs, Enmarket/dsl, Flash/dsl ⑪ Bojangles, Cracker Barrel, Dickey's BBQ, Guerrero Mexican, Hiranos Steaks, Jersey Style Subs, KFC, Krystal, Larry's Subs, Los Bravos Mexican, McDonald's, Peking Chinese, Spanky's, Subway, Taco Bell, Waffle House ⊟ Best Western, Microtel, Motel 6, Quality Inn, Travelodge O Camping World RV Ctr, Family$, Food Lion, museum, to Ft Pulaski NM, **W** P Gate/dsl, Marathon, Shell ⑪ Burger King, Domino's, El Potro Mexican, Hardee's, Italian Pizza, Pizza Hut, Wendy's, Western Sizzlin ⊟ EconoLodge, Holiday Inn, La Quinta, Magnolia Inn, Ramada, Sleep Inn O $General
99b a	I-16, W to Macon, E to Savannah
94	GA 204, to Savannah, Pembroke, **E** P 76/dsl/e85, BP/dsl, Exxon, Murphy USA/dsl (2mi), Shell/dsl ⑪ Applebee's, Cracker Barrel, Denny's, Hardee's, Houlihan's, IHOP, McDonald's, Perkins, Ruby Tuesday, Sonic ⊟ Baymont Inn, Best Inn, Best Western, Clarion, Comfort Suites, Country Inn Suites, Days Inn, EconoLodge, Fairfield Inn, Hampton Inn, Holiday Inn, Holiday Inn Express, Howard Johnson, La Quinta, Quality Inn, Red Roof Inn, San's Boutique Hotel, Scottish Inn, Sleep Inn, SpringHill Suites, Super 8, Travelodge O Factory Stores/Famous Brands, GNC, H, Walmart (2mi), **W** P Chevron/dsl, Sunoco O ⑪ Hooters, Shellhouse Rest, Subway, Waffle House ⊟ Motel 6, Rodeway Inn O Harley-Davidson, Indian Motorcycles, Savannah Oaks RV Park (2mi)
91mm	Ogeechee River
90	GA 144, Old Clyde Rd, to Ft Stewart, Richmond Hill SP, **E** P Exxon/dsl, Parkers ⑪ DQ, Jalapeno's, Pizza Hut, Subway, Zaxby's O AT&T, Kroger/deli/dsl, URGENT CARE, Verizon, **W** P ✦Loves/McDonald's/dsl/scales/24hr, Marathon/dsl O Gore's RV Ctr
87	US 17, to Coastal Hwy, Richmond Hill, **E** P BP/Subway, Chevron/dsl, RaceWay/dsl ⑪ China 1, Denny's, Domino's, Fuji Japanese, Molly McPherson's Grill, Papa Murphy's, Smokin' Pig BBQ, Southern Image Rest., Steamer's Rest., Waffle House ⊟ Days Inn, Motel 6, Royal Inn, Scottish Inn, Travelodge O Food Lion, URGENT CARE, **W** P McDonald's, Shell/dsl, Sunoco/dsl, TA/BP/Pizza Hut/Popeye's/dsl/scales/24hr/@ ⑪ Arby's, KFC/Taco Bell, Waffle House, Wendy's ⊟ Best Western+, EconoLodge, Fairfield Inn, Hampton Inn, Holiday Inn Express, Quality Inn, Super 8 O KOA
85mm	Elbow Swamp
80mm	Jerico River
76	US 84, GA 38, to Midway, Sunbury, **E** hist sites, **W** P Gulf/McDonald's/dsl, Parker's/dsl, Shell/dsl/scales ⑪ Huddle House, Smokin' Pig BBQ O H
67	US 17, Coastal Hwy, to S Newport, **E** P BP/Subway/dsl, Citgo/dsl, El Cheapo, Shell/McDonald's ⑪ Jones BBQ O Harris Neck NWR, **W** P Texaco
58	GA 99, GA 57, Townsend Rd, Eulonia, **E** P BP/dsl, Citgo O $General, USPO, **W** P Exxon/dsl, Shell/Stuckey's/dsl, Snappy ⑪ Huddle House ⊟ Motel 6 O Lake Harmony RV Park, McIntosh Lake RV Park

(side tabs: LAGRANGE, GA, SAVANNAH on left; SAVANNAH on right)

⬆️N INTERSTATE 95 Cont'd

Exit #	Services
55mm	weigh sta both lanes
49	GA 251, to Darien, E 📵 Mobil/dsl 🍴 DQ, McDonald's, Waffle House 🅾 Ford, Inland Harbor RV Park, W 📵 BP/dsl/scales, Parker's 🍴 Burger King, KFC/Taco Bell, Wendy's 🏠 Days Inn, Econolodge, Hampton Inn, Quality Inn, Super 8
47mm	Darien River
46.5mm	Butler River
46mm	Champney River
45mm	Altamaha River
42	GA 99, E to Hofwyl Plantation HS
41mm	📢 sb, full 🚻 facilities, info, litter barrels, petwalk, 📵, 📶, vending
38	US 17, GA 25, N Golden Isles Pkwy, Brunswick, E 📵 RaceTrac/dsl 🍴 McDonald's, Millhouse Steaks 🏠 Comfort Suites, Country Inn&Suites, Embassy Suites (2mi), Fairfield Inn, Holiday Inn, Microtel 🅾 🏥, Nissan, W 🍴 Flash, Marathon/dsl, Parker's, Shell/dsl 🍴 China Town, Denny's, Huddle House, Subway, Toucan's, Waffle House 🏠 Best Western+, Courtyard, EconoLodge, Guest Cottage Motel, Hampton Inn, Quality Inn, Sleep Inn 🅾 $General, Family$, Harley-Davidson, Toyota, Winn Dixie
36b a	US 25, US 341, to Jesup, Brunswick, E 📵 Chevron/Subway/dsl, Exxon/dsl, RaceWay/dsl 🍴 Burger King, Cracker Barrel, IHOP, KFC, Krystal, McDonald's, Pizza Hut, Starbucks, Taco Bell, Waffle House, Wendy's 🏠 Days Inn, Jameson Inn, La Quinta, Motel 6, Red Roof Inn, Tropical Inn 🅾 Jack's Tires, W 🍴 Parker's/dsl, Shell/dsl 🍴 Capt Joe's Seafood, China Buffet, Huddle House, Larry's Subs, Sonny's BBQ, Waffle House 🏠 Clarion, Comfort Inn, Economy Inn, Magnuson Inn, Ramada Inn, Stay Express, Super 8 🅾 $General, Advance Parts, AutoZone, CVS Drug, Family$, Fred's, URGENT CARE, Winn-Dixie
33mm	Turtle River
30mm	S Brunswick River
29	US 17, US 82, GA 520, S GA Pkwy, Brunswick, E 📵 Exxon/dsl, Flash, 🟡Loves/Godfather's/Subway/Chester's/dsl/scales/24hr, Mobil/dsl 🍴 Bubba Jack's Crab Shack, Huddle House, Krystal, McDonald's, Zaxby's 🏠 Comfort Suites 🅾 Blue Beacon, SpeedCo, W 📵 🍴 ⛽FLYING J/Denny's/dsl/LP/scales/24hr, Shell/Dunkin'/dsl, TA/BP/Burger King/Starbucks/Subway/dsl/24hr 🍴 Domino's, Larry's Subs, Waffle House, Zachry's Rest 🏠 EconoLodge, Motel 6, Super 8 🅾 $General, Family$, Golden Isles Camping, TA Truck Service, Winn Dixie
27.5mm	Little Satilla River
26	Dover Bluff Rd, E 📵 Mobil/Stuckey's/dsl
22	Horse Stamp Church Rd
21mm	White Oak Creek
19mm	Canoe Swamp
15mm	Satilla River
14	GA 25, to Woodbine, W 📵 Chevron/Sunshine/rest/dsl/scales/24hr 🏠 Stardust Motel (3mi)
7	Harrietts Bluff Rd, E 📵 Flash/dsl, Shell/Subway, W 📵 BP/dsl 🅾 Walkabout Camping/RV Park
6.5mm	Crooked River
6	Laurel Island Pkwy, E 📵 Gtrac Express/dsl, Shell/Chester's/dsl
3	GA 40, Kingsland, to St Marys, E 📵 Chevron, El Cheapo/dsl, Flash/dsl, Mobil, Murphy USA/dsl, Shell/Subway, Sunoco 🍴 Angelo's Italian, Applebee's, Burger King, Capt D's, Chick-fil-A, DQ, Dunkin', Firehouse Subs, KFC, Little Caesar's, Longhorn Steaks, McDonald's, OPS Kitchen, Papa John's, Ruby Tuesday, Sonny's BBQ, Taco Bell, Waffle House, Wendy's, Zaxby's 🏠 Best Western, Comfort Suites, Country Inn&Suites, Days Inn,

ST MARYS

3	Continued
	Fairfield Inn, Hawthorn Suites, Magnolia Inn, Microtel, Motel 6, Quality Inn, Red Roof Inn, Rodeway Inn, Sleep Inn 🅾 $Tree, Buick/Chevrolet, Chrysler/Dodge/Jeep, CVS Drug, Ford, GNC, 🏥, Lowe's, NAPA, Publix, Tire Kingdom, to Crooked River SP, to Submarine Base, URGENT CARE, Verizon, Walgreens, Walmart, Winn-Dixie, W Welcome Ctr/info 📵 Flash/dsl, Petro/Popeye's/dsl/scales/24hr/@, RaceWay/dsl, Shell/dsl 🍴 Cracker Barrel, Denny's, Domino's, IHOP, Millhouse Steaks, Waffle House 🏠 Baymont Inn, EconoLodge, Hampton Inn, La Quinta, Springfield Suites, Travelers Inn 🅾 Ace Hardware, Advance Parts, Fred's, Kiki RV Park
1	St Marys Rd, to Cumberland Is Nat Seashore, E Welcome Ctr nb, full 🚻 facilities, 📵, vending, 📶, litter barrels, petwalk, 📵 Pilot/Subway/PJ Fresh/dsl/scales/24hr, Shell/dsl W 📵 BP/dsl, Chevron/dsl, Pilot/Dunkin'/Wendy's/dsl/scales/24hr 🍴 Little Pearl's Bistro 🅾 Country Oaks RV Park, KOA
0mm	Georgia/Florida state line, St Marys River

⬆️N INTERSTATE 185 (Columbus)

Exit #	Services
48	I-85. I-185 begins/ends on I-85.
46	Big Springs Rd, E 📵 Shell/dsl, W 🅾 tires
42	US 27, Pine Mountain, E 📵 Marathon/dsl, Summit/dsl 🍴 Waffle House 🅾 Little White House HS, Pine Mtn Camping, to Callaway Gardens
34	GA 18, to West Point, E 🅾 to Callaway Gardens
30	Hopewell Church Rd, Whitesville, W 📵 Shell/dsl 🅾 $General
25	GA 116, to Hamilton, W 🅾 RV camping
19	GA 315, Mulberry Grove, W 📵 Chevron/dsl/24hr
14	Smith Rd
12	Williams Rd, W Welcome Ctr/rest rooms 📵 Chevron, Summit/dsl 🏠 Country Inn&Suites, Microtel
10	US 80, GA 22, to Phenix City, W 🅾 Springer Opera House
8	Airport Thruway, E 🍴 Bojangles, Great Wall 🅾 $Tree, GNC, Home Depot, Walmart/Subway, W 📵 Marathon/dsl, Shell 🍴 Applebee's, Baskin Robbins, Ben's Chophouse, Blue Iguana Grill, Burger King, Cafe Le Rue, Capt D's, Country Road Buffet, Fuddruckers, Hardee's, Houlihan's, IHOP, McDonald's, Mikata Japanese, Outback Steaks, Pickle Barrel Cafe, Stevi B's Pizza, Subway, Taco Bell 🏠 Comfort Suites, DoubleTree, Extended Stay America, Hampton Inn, Sleep Inn 🅾 AAA, BigLots, Office Depot
7	45th St, Manchester Expswy, E 🍴 Applebee's, Burger King, Carino's Italian, Krystal, Ruby Tuesday 🏠 Courtyard, La Quinta, Super 8 🅾 Best Buy, Cadillac/Chevrolet, Dillard's, JC Penney, Macy's, W 📵 BP/dsl, Chevron/dsl, Circle K/dsl, Marathon

C O L U M B U S

INTERSTATE 185 (Columbus) Cont'd

7 Continued
🍴 Arby's, Chick-fil-A, China Express, Dunkin', Goldberg's Deli, Golden Corral, Jimmy John's, KFC, Little Caesar's, Logan's Roadhouse, Lucky China, McDonald's, Pizza Hut, Ryan's, Shogun Japanese, Sonic, Starbucks, SteakOut, Subway, Waffle House 🏠 Fairfield Inn, Holiday Inn, TownePlace Suites 🅾 $General, Advance Parts, Big T Tire/repair, Civil War Naval Museum, 🄷, Midas, Mr Transmission

6 GA 22, Macon Rd, **E** 🅿 Chevron/dsl, Circle K/dsl 🍴 Bruster's, Burger King, DQ, Little Caesar's, Taco Bell, Waffle House 🏠 Best Western, Comfort Inn, Days Inn 🅾 $General, Rite Aid, U-Haul, vet, Walgreens, **W** 🅿 Chevron/dsl, Shell/dsl 🍴 American Deli, Capt D's, ChuckeCheese, Cici's, Country's BBQ, Denny's, Dunkin'/Baskin Robbins, Firehouse Subs, Jimmy John's, Longhorn Steaks, McDonald's, Subway, Zaxby's 🏠 Efficiency Lodge, La Quinta 🅾 AT&T, CVS Drug, Fred's, GNC, Goodyear/auto, Publix, TJ Maxx, Tuesday Morning, Verizon

4 Buena Vista Rd, **E** 🅿 BP, Circle K, Solo 🍴 Burger King, Capt D's, Checkers, Church's, Krystal, McDonald's, Papa John's, Pizza Hut, Subway, Taco Bell, Waffle House, Zaxby's 🅾 $Tree, AutoZone, Family$, Firestone/auto, Goodyear/auto, O'Reilly Parts, Rainbow Foods, repair, USPO, vet, Walgreens, Walmart, Winn-Dixie, **W** 🅿 Marathon

3 St Marys Rd, **E** 🍴 Domino's 🏠 Microtel 🅾 Family$, **W** 🅿 FuelTech/dsl, Shell/dsl 🍴 Hardee's, Shark Seafood/Chicken 🅾 $General, Ace Hardware, Piggly Wiggly

1b a US 27, US 280, Victory Dr, **0-3 mi W** 🅿 Chevron/dsl, Circle K, Liberty, RaceWay/dsl 🍴 Burger King, Capt D's, Checkers, Krystal, McDonald's, Papa John's, Sonic, Subway, Taco Bell, Waffle House, Wendy's 🏠 Candlewood Suites, Columbus Inn, EconoLodge, Holiday Inn Express, Motel 6, Suburban Lodge 🅾 $General, Advance Parts, AutoZone, CVS Drug, Family$, O'Reilly Parts, Piggly Wiggly, Verizon

0mm **I-185 begins/ends on Victory Dr.**

INTERSTATE 285 (Atlanta)

Exit #	Services
62	GA 279, S Fulton Hwy, Old Nat Hwy, **N** 🅿 Chevron/dsl, Texaco 🍴 Waffle House 🏠 Econolodge, **S** 🅿 Chevron, Citgo, Exxon, Shell, Valero 🍴 American Deli, Blimpie, Bojangles, Burger King, Checker's, China Cafeteria, Church's, Cozumel Mexican, KFC, Krystal, McDonald's, Piccadilly Cafeteria, Subway, Taco Bell, Waffle House, Wendy's 🏠 Baymont Inn, Day's Inn, Quality Inn, Super 8, Travelodge, Windsor Atl Hotel 🅾 AutoZone, Family$, Midas, O'Reilly Parts, U-Haul
61	I-85, N to Atlanta, S to Montgomery
60	GA 139, Riverdale Rd, **N** 🏠 Fairfield Inn (2mi), Microtel (2mi), Wingate Inn (2mi), **S** 🅿 QT/dsl, Shell/dsl, Valero/dsl 🍴 Checkers, Church's, McDonald's, Papa John's, Waffle House 🏠 Best Western, Day's Inn, Quality Hotel 🅾 $General, Advance Parts, Family$
59	Clark Howell Hwy, **N** 🅾 air cargo
58	I-75, N to Atlanta, S to Macon (from eb), to US 19, US 41, to Hapeville, **S** 🅿 BP/dsl, Citgo/dsl, Exxon/dsl 🍴 American Deli, Jimmy John's, Subway, Tijuana Joe's, Waffle House, Wendy's 🏠 Home Lodge Motel
55	GA 54, Jonesboro Rd, **N** 🏠 Super 8, **S** 🅿 BP/dsl, Citgo/dsl, Shell/dsl, Texaco/dsl 🍴 DaiLai Vietnamese, McDonald's 🅾 Family$, Home Depot, repair

A T L A N T A   A R E A

53	US 23, Moreland Ave, to Ft Gillem, **N** 🅿 BP/dsl, Citgo/dsl, **S** 🅿 Chevron/dsl, Citgo 🍴 Wendy's 🏠 EconoLodge 🅾 USPO
52	I-675, S to Macon
51	Bouldercrest Rd, **N** 🅿 BP, [____]/Wendy's/dsl/24hr 🍴 Checkers, Domino's; Hardee's, KFC, WK Wings 🅾 Family$, Wayfield Foods, **S** 🅿 Exxon/dsl, Shell/Blimpie/dsl, Texaco/dsl
48	GA 155, Flat Shoals Rd, Candler Rd, **N** 🅿 BP, Chevron, Citgo/dsl, Shell/dsl, Texaco/dsl 🍴 Burger King, Checkers, Church's, DQ, Dunkin'/BR, KFC, McDonald's, Taco Bell, Waffle King, WK Wings 🏠 Gulf American Inn 🅾 BigLots, Macy's, **S** 🅿 Citgo, QT, Texaco/dsl 🍴 Burger King, China One, Sonic, Subway 🅾 Family$
46b a	I-20, E to Augusta, W to Atlanta
44	GA 260, Glenwood Rd, **E** 🅿 Sunoco/dsl 🏠 EconoLodge, **W** 🅿 Exxon/dsl, Texaco/dsl, Valero/dsl
43	US 278, Covington Hwy, **E** 🅿 Chevron/Subway, Texaco/dsl 🍴 Waffle House 🅾 U-Haul, **W** 🅿 Mystik/dsl, QT, RaceTrac/dsl, Texaco/dsl 🍴 HoneyBaked Ham, Wendy's 🏠 Best Inn 🅾 Advance Parts, Family$
42	(from nb) Marta Station
41	GA 10, Memorial Dr, Avondale Estates, **E** 🅿 Citgo, Mystik 🍴 Applebee's, Baskin-Robbins/Dunkin', Burger King, Church's, Domino's, IHOP, Pancake House, Pizza Hut, Subway, Taco Bell, Waffle House, Wendy's 🏠 Best Value Inn, Budgetel, United Suites 🅾 $Tree, Advance Parts, Atl Tires, AutoZone, Family$, Firestone/auto, GNC, Office Depo, Ross, transmissions, U-Haul, USPO, Walgreens
40	Church St, to Clarkston, **E** 🅿 Chevron, Marathon/dsl, Texaco 🅾 auto repair, **W** 🅾 🄷
39b a	US 78, to Athens, Decatu
38	US 29, Lawrenceville Hwy, **E** 🅿 Citgo, QT/dsl, RaceTrac/dsl 🍴 Bojangle's, Waffle House 🏠 Best Value Inn, Knights Inn 🅾 🄷 **W** 🅿 Citgo/dsl 🍴 Bruster's 🏠 Masters Inn, Motel 6 🅾 AutoZone, CVS Drug
37	GA 236, to LaVista, Tucker, **E** 🅿 Chevron/dsl, Exxon 🍴 Checkers, Folks Rest., Hudson Grille, IHOP, O'Charley's, Piccadilly's, Pollo Tropical, Waffle House 🏠 Comfort Suites, Days Inn 🅾 DeKalb Tire/auto, Firestone/auto, Target, **W** 🅿 BP/Domino's, Chevron, Shell/dsl 🍴 Blue Ribbon Grill, Capt D's, Chick-fil-A, Chipotle, Coco Cabana Cuban, Dunkin', Eduardo's Mexican, HoneyBaked Ham, Jason's Deli, Kacey's Rest., Kobe Steaks, Lucky Key Chinese, Maddio's Pizza, Marlow's Tavern, McDonald's, Mellow Mushroom, Moe's SW, Monterrey Mexican, Panda Express, Panera Bread, Pizza Hut, Popeye's, Red Lobster, Starbucks, Subway 🏠 Courtyard, DoubleTree, Holiday Inn, Quality Inn 🅾 $Tree, Aldi Foods, AT&T, Best Buy, Goodyear/auto, JC Penney, Kohl's, Kroger, mall, Michael's, Office Depot, Petsmart, Publix, Sears/auto, TJ Maxx, Verizon
36	Northlake Pkwy (from sb, no return)
34	Chamblee-Tucker Rd, **E** 🅿 Texaco/dsl 🍴 $3 Cafe, China Star, Galaxy Diner, Hunan Inn, Jersey Mike's Subs, KFC/Taco Bell, Moe's SW Grill, Wendy's 🅾 Advance Parts, Goodyear/auto, Kroger, Rite Aid, USPO, **W** 🅿 Citgo, Shell 🍴 McDonald's, Subway 🅾 BigLots, vet
33b a	I-85, N to Greenville, S to Atlanta
32	US 23, Buford Hwy, to Doraville, **E** 🅿 BP/dsl 🍴 Baldino's Subs, Bojangle's, Burger King/playland, Checkers, Chick-fil-A, McDonald's, Waffle House, White Windmill Café, Zaxby's 🅾 Advance Parts, Firestone/auto, Marshalls, PepBoys, **W** 🅿 Citgo, QT/dsl 🍴 McDonald's, Monterrey Mexican, Subway, Waffle House 🏠 Clarion 🅾 $Tree, Aamco, Meineke

GA

INTERSTATE 285 (Atlanta) Cont'd

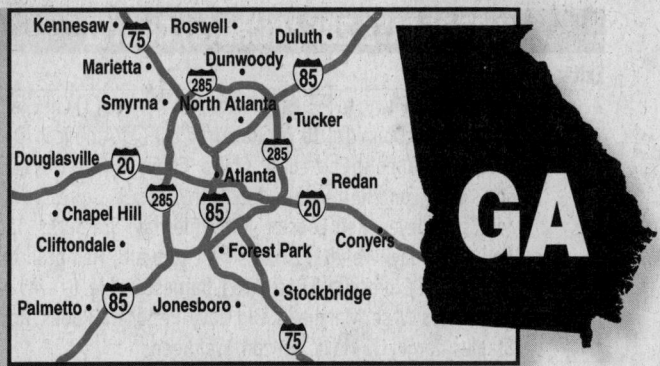

Exit #	Services
31b a	GA 141, Peachtree Ind, to Chamblee, **W** 🅿 QT 🍴 Arby's, Baskin-Robbins/Dunkin', Chick-fil-A, IHOP, McDonald's, Pizza Hut, Subway, Wendy's 🅾 Acura, Advance Parts, AT&T, Audi, Brandsmart, Buick/GMC, Chevrolet, Chrysler/Dodge/Jeep, CVS Drug, Firestone/auto, Ford, Honda, Hyundai, Infiniti, Kia, Lexus, Mazda, Mini, Nissan, Office Depot, Porsche, Toyota, VW, Walgreens
30	Chamblee-Dunwoody Rd, N Shallowford Rd, to N Peachtree Rd, **N** 🅿 BP/dsl, BP/Dunkin', Shell, Texaco/dsl 🍴 Bagel&Co. Deli, Burger King, Marco's Pizza, McDonald's, Starbucks, Subway, Takorea, Waffle House 🅾 Kroger, Tuesday Morning, **S** 🅿 Exxon/dsl, Mobil, Shell, Texaco/dsl, Valero 🍴 La Botana Mexican, Mad Italian Rest., Papa John's, Taco Bell, Wendy's, Wild Ginger Thai 🏨 Residence Inn
29	Ashford-Dunwoody Rd, **N** 🅿 Exxon/Subway 🍴 Brio Tuscan, Broken Egg, CA Pizza Kitchen, Capital Grille, Cheesecake Factory, Chick-fil-A, Chili's, Corner Bakery&Cafe, Fogo de Chao, J. Alexander's, Jason's Deli, Maddio's Pizza, Maggiano's Little Italy, McDonald's, McKendrick Steaks, Memphis BBQ, Newk's Eatery, Olive Garden, PF Chang's, Popeye's, Schlotzsky's, Seasons 32 Grill, Starbucks, Wild Wing Cafe 🏨 Crowne Plaza, Hampton Inn 🅾 Barnes&Noble, Best Buy, Dillard's, Hobby Lobby, Macy's, mall, Marshalls, Nordstrom, Old Navy, USPO, Walmart, **S** 🅾 Hilton Garden
28	Peachtree-Dunwoody Rd (no EZ return wb), **N** 🍴 Arby's, Chuy's Mexican, Domino's, Five Guys, Panera Bread, Subway, Uncle Julio's Mexican, Willy's Mexican 🏨 Comfort Suites, Courtyard, Extended Stay America, Extended Stay America (2), Fairfield Inn, Hampton Inn, Hilton Suites, Holiday Inn Express, La Quinta, Marriott, Microtel, Residence Inn, Sheraton, Westin 🅾 Costco/gas, GNC, Home Depot, mall, Publix, Rite Aid, Ross, Target, TJ Maxx, **S** 🅾 🏥
27	US 19 N, GA 400, **2 mi N** 🅾 LDS Temple
26	Glenridge Dr (from eb), Johnson Ferry Rd
25	US 19 S, Roswell Rd, Sandy Springs, **N** 🅿 BP, Shell/dsl, Shell/dsl 🍴 Andres Mexican, Bobbys Burgers, Boston Mkt, Burger King, Chick-fil-A, Chipotle Mexican, Domino's, Dunkin', Egg Harbor Café, El Azteca Mexican, Firehouse Subs, Five Guys, Hudson Grille, IHOP, Jimmy John's, Longhorn Steaks, Maya Steaks, McDonald's, Mellow Mushroom, Moe's SW Grill, Pizza Hut, Roasters, Starbucks, Steak'n Shake, Subway, Taco Bell, Waffle House, Wendy's, Willy's Mexican, Zaxby's 🏨 Comfort Inn 🅾 $Tree, Aldi Foods, AT&T, CVS Drug, DeKalb Tire, Lowe's, Marshalls, Mr Tire, NAPA AutoCare, Office Depot, PepBoys, PetCo, Publix, Target, Toyota, Trader Joe's, Tuesday Morning, URGENT CARE, Verizon, Walgreens, Whole Foods Mkt, **S** 🅿 Chevron/dsl, Citgo, Shell 🍴 Barberitos, El Taco Veloz, Five Seasons Rest., Marlow's Tavern, Panda Express, Starbucks, Taco Mac 🅾 Publix, Staples, Target, URGENT CARE
24	Riverside Dr
22	New Northside Dr, to Powers Ferry Rd, **N** 🅿 Shell/Subway/dsl 🏨 Extended Stay America, **S** 🅿 BP, Chevron/dsl 🍴 McDonald's, Ray's Rest., Rio Bravo, Subway, Waffle House 🏨 Wyndham 🅾 CVS Drug, Publix, vet
21	(from wb), **N** 🅿 Chevron 🍴 Harry's Pizza, Homestead Village 🏨 Extended Stay America 🅾 BMW/Mini
20	I-75, N to Chattanooga, S to Atlanta (from wb), to US 41 N
19	US 41, Cobb Pkwy, to Dobbins AFB, **N** 🅿 BP/dsl, Marathon, QT 🍴 Applebee's, Bruster's, Burger King, Carrabba's, ChuckeCheese, Del Taco, Dunkin', IHOP, Jade Palace, KFC, McDonald's,

ATLANTA AREA *(vertical, left margin)*

Exit #	Services
19	Continued Olive Garden, Panda Express, Papa John's, Red Lobster, Scalini's Italian, Subway, Taco Bell, Thompson Bros BBQ, Waffle House, Wendy's, Wingate Inn, Zaxby's 🏨 DoubleTree, Extended Stay America, Hampton Inn, Holiday Inn Express, Hyatt, Residence Inn 🅾 $Tree, Aldi Foods, Best Buy, Braves Stadium, Cadillac, Chevrolet, Discount Tire, Honda, Hyundai, Kia, Lexus, Marshall's, Michael's, NTB, Office Depot, PetsMart, Ross, Target, Verizon, Walgreens, **S** 🍴 Buffalo Wild Wings, Cheesecake Factory, Chick-fil-A, Chipotle Mexican, Corner Bakery Cafe, Firehouse Subs, Hooters, Jason's Deli, Longhorn Steaks, Maggiano's Italian, PF Chang's, Pizza Hut, Pollo Tropical, Schlotsky's, Stoney River Steaks, Subway, Tilted Kilt, Zoe's Kitchen 🏨 Courtyard, Hampton Inn, Homewood Suites, Renaissance, Sheraton Suites 🅾 AT&T, Barnes&Noble, Costco/gas, Macy's, Old Navy, USPO
18	Paces Ferry Rd, to Vinings, **N** 🍴 Panera Bread 🏨 Fairfield Inn, La Quinta, **S** 🅿 QT/24hr 🍴 Chick-fil-A, Starbucks, Subway, Willy's Grill 🏨 Extended Stay America 🅾 Goodyear/auto, Home Depot, Publix, Verizon
16	S Atlanta Rd, to Smyrna, **N** 🍴 Five Guys, Waffle House 🏨 Days Inn 🅾 🏥, **S** 🅿 Chevron/Subway/dsl, Shell/dsl 🍴 Jersey Mike's 🅾 Kroger
15	GA 280, S Cobb Dr, **E** 🏨 Araamda 🅾 U-Haul, **W** 🅿 BP/dsl, Mobil, RaceTrac/dsl, Shell 🍴 Arby's, Chick-fil-A, China Cafe, Dunkin', IHOP, Jimmy John's, Krystal, McDonald's, Subway, Taco Bell, Zaxby's 🏨 Baymont Inn, Comfort Inn, Country Inn Suites, Knight's Inn, Sun Suites
14mm	Chattahoochee River
13	Bolton Rd (from nb)
12	US 78, US 278, Bankhead Hwy, **E** 🅿 Petro/Iron Skillet/dsl/scales/24hr/@, Shell/dsl/24hr, Valero/dsl 🍴 Burger King 🅾 Blue Beacon, **W** 🅿 BP, Texaco
10b a	I-20, W to Birmingham, E to Atlanta (exits left from nb), **W** 🅾 to Six Flags
9	GA 139, MLK Dr, to Adamsville, **E** 🅿 Quikmart, Shell 🅾 Family$, O'Reilly Parts, Wayfield Foods, **W** 🅿 Chevron, Shell, Texaco/dsl 🍴 Checker's, Church's, KFC/Taco Bell, McDonald's 🅾 $General, Family$
7	Cascade Rd, **E** 🅿 Exxon/dsl 🍴 Papa John's 🅾 Kroger, **W** 🅿 BP/dsl, Shell/dsl 🍴 Applebee's, China Express, KFC, Little Caesar's, McDonald's, Pizza Hut, Starbucks, Subway, Wendy's 🅾 GNC, Home Depot, Publix, Tires+, Walgreens, Walmart
5b a	GA 166, Lakewood Fwy, **E** 🅿 Chevron, Shell 🍴 Burger King, Capt D's, Checker's, KFC, Little Caesar's, Subway, Wendy's 🅾 CVS Drug, Firestone, Goodyear/auto, Kroger, Macy's, **W** 🅿 BP, RaceWay/dsl, Shell/dsl, Texaco/dsl, Valero 🍴 Church's 🏨 Deluxe Inn 🅾 AutoZone, Family$, O'Reilly Parts

ATLANTA AREA

GA *(state outline graphic with cities: Kennesaw, Roswell, Duluth, Marietta, Dunwoody, Smyrna, North Atlanta, Tucker, Douglasville, Atlanta, Redan, Chapel Hill, Cliftondale, Forest Park, Conyers, Palmetto, Jonesboro, Stockbridge)*

INTERSTATE 285 (Atlanta) Cont'd

Exit #	Services
2	Camp Creek Pkwy, to 🖼, **E** 🅕 Exxon/dsl, Texaco 🅕 Checker's, Church's, McDonald's, **W** 🅕 RaceTrac/dsl 🅕 American Deli, Bruster's, Carino's, Chick-fil-A, Chili's, China 1, Five Guys, Jason's Deli, LongHorn Steaks, Moe's SW, Panda Express, Papa John's, Popeyes, Red Lobster, Ruby Tuesday, Starbucks, Taco Bell, TGIFriday, Wendys, Zaxby's 🅛 Courtyard, Hampton Inn, Holiday Inn Express 🅞 $Tree, AT&T, Barnes&Noble, BJ's Whse/gas, Lowes Whse, Marshall's, Old Navy, PetsMart, Publix, Ross, Staples, Target, TJ Maxx, Verizon, Walgreens
1	Washington Rd, **E** 🅕 Texaco/dsl, **W** 🅕 Chevron/dsl

⬆N INTERSTATE 475 (Macon)

Exit #	Services
16mm	I-475 begins/ends on I-75, exit 177.
15	US 41, Bolingbroke, **1 mi E** 🅕 Exxon/dsl/LP, Marathon/dsl
9	Zebulon Rd, **E** 🅕 Marathon/dsl, Shell/Circle K/24hr 🅕 Applebee's, Buffalo's Café, Chick-fil-A, Johnny's NY Pizz, Krystal, Macon Pizza Co, Margarita's Mexican, McAlister's Deli, McDonald's, Moe's SW, NU Way Wieners, Papa John's, Pizza Hut, Sonic, Subway, Taco Bell, Taki Japanese, Tutti Frutti, Waffle House, Wendy's 🅛 Baymont Inn, Comfort Suites, Fairfield Inn, Sleep Inn 🅞 Goodyear/auto, 🅗, Kohl's, Kroger/dsl, Lowe's, URGENT CARE, USPO, Verizon, Walgreens, Walmart/Subway, **W** 🅕 Marathon/dsl, Sunoco/dsl 🅕 Marco's Pizza, Polly's Cafe, Zaxby's 🅞 Advance Parts, CVS Drug
8mm	🆁🆂 nb, full 🖼 facilities, litter barrels, petwalk, 🄲, 🖼, vending
5	GA 74, Macon, **E** 🅕 RaceWay/dsl 🅕 Waffle House 🅞 Harley-Davidson, to Mercer U, **W** 🅕 Flash/Subway/dsl, Texaco/Church's/dsl 🅕 Capt D's 🅛 A1 Economy 🅞 $General, Tires+, to Lake Tobesofkee, vet
3	US 80, Macon, **0-2 mi E** 🅕 Marathon/dsl, Murphy USA/dsl, RaceWay, Shell/Circle K/Subway 🅕 Aldi Foods, Applebee's, Burger King, Chick-fil-A, China Buffet, Cracker Barrel, DQ, Firehouse Subs, Golden Corral, JL's BBQ, Margarita's Mexican, McAlister's Deli, McDonald's, Papa John's, S&S Cafeteria, Silver Bay Seafood, Smokin' Pig BBQ, Taco Bell, Waffle House, Zaxby's 🅛 Best Inn, Best Western, Bridgeview Inn, Comfort Suites, Days Inn, Discovery Inn, EconoLodge, Hampton Inn, Holiday Inn Express, La Quinta, Motel 6, Quality Inn, Ramada Inn, Red Roof Inn, Super 8, Woodspring Suites 🅞 $Tree, AT&T, Best Buy, BigLots, CVS Drug, Dick's, Discount Tire, Firestone/auto, GNC, Home Depot, Honda, Kroger/gas, Lowe's, Macy's, mall, Marshall's, Michael's, Nissan, Office Depot, Old Navy, Petsmart, Ross, Sam's Club/gas, Staples, Target, Verizon, vet, VW, Walmart/Subway, **W** 🅕 Shell/Circle K, Sunoco/dsl 🅕 Burger King 🅛 Best Value Inn, Windsor Economy Inn
1	Hartley Bridge Rd same as I-75 exit 156
0mm	I-475 begins/ends on I-75, exit 156.

⬆N INTERSTATE 575

Exit #	Services
30mm	I-575 begins/ends on GA 5/515.
27	GA 5, Howell Br, to Ball Ground
24	Airport Dr
20	GA 5, to Canton, **E** 🅕 BP 🅕 Bojangles, Buffalo's Cafe, Casey's Rest., Chick-fil-A, Dos Margaritas Mexican, Jin's Buffet, Stevi B's Pizza, Waffle Wouse, Wendy's 🅛 Econolodge, Homestead Inn, Motel 6 🅞 AT&T, Chevrolet, Chrysler/Dodge/Jeep, GNC, Toyota, Verizon, Walmart, **W** 🅕 RaceTrac/dsl, Shell/Subway,

Exit #	Services
20	Continued Texaco/dsl 🅕 Applebee's, Arby's, Cracker Barrel, Five Guys, Honeybaked Ham, Longhorn Steaks, McDonald's, O'Charley's, Okinawa Steaks, Outback Steaks, Panda Express, Provino's Red Lobster, Seven Tequilas Mexican, Starbucks, Zaxby's 🅛 Best Western, Hampton Inn, Holiday Inn Express 🅞 Belk, Home Depot, 🅗, Michaels, Publix, Ross
19	GA 20 E, Canton, **E** 🅕 Bobby's Burgers, Chick-fil-A, Chipotle, IHOP, Jimmy John's, La Parrilla Mexican, Maddio's Pizza, McDonald's, Olive Garden, Starbucks, Subway, Taco Mac, Waffle House, Which Wich?, Zaxby's 🅞 Best Buy, BooksAMillion, Dick's, Goodyear/auto, Kohl's, Lowe's, NTB, Petsmart, Target, TJ Maxx
17	GA 140, to Roswell (from sb), Canton
16	GA 20, GA 140, **W** 🅕 Citgo, RaceTrac/dsl 🅕 Burger King, KFC, Mandarin House, Papa John's, Subway, Taco Bell, Waffle House 🅞 $General, Advance Parts, Rite Aid
14	Holly Springs, **E** 🅕 Texaco/dsl 🅕 Domino's, Ichiban Buffet, Las Palmas Mexican, Pizza Hut 🅛 Pinecrest Motel 🅞 vet, Walmart, Subway, **W** 🅕 Chevron, Family$, Shell/dsl 🅕 Dunkin', Golden China, McDonald's, Subway, Taste of Italy, Viva Mexico, Wendy's, Zaxby's 🅞 Autozone, Kauffman Tire, Kroger/dsl, Publix, Verizon, Walgreens
11	Sixes Rd, **E** 🅕 Chevron/dsl, Home Depot, QT 🅕 Shane's Rib shack, Zaxby's 🅞 Verizon
9	Ridgewalk Pkwy, **E** 🅕 Applebee's, Chick-fil-A, Five Guys, McDonald's, Panda Express 🅞 outlets/famous brands
8	Towne Lake Pkwy, to Woodstock, **E** 🅕 Shell/dsl 🅕 Subway, Waffle House 🅞 Ford, **W** 🅕 Phillips 66, QT 🅕 Chili's, Longhorn Steaks 🅞 Tuesday Morning, Walgreens
7	GA 92, Woodstock, **E** 🅕 Chevron, QT 🅕 Arby's, Bubba Q Rest., Burger King, Capt D's, Checker's, Chick-fil-A, Chin Chin, Del Taco, DQ, Dunkin', Firehouse Subs, Folk's Kitchen, Honeybaked Ham, Maddio's Pizza, McDonald's, Moe's SW Grill, O'Charley's, Resturante Mexico, Ruby Tuesday, Starbucks, Stevi B's Pizza, Subway, Taco Bell, Waffle House 🅛 Comfort Suites, Hampton Inn, InTown Suite 🅞 Camping World, Firestone/auto, Goodyear/auto, **W** 🅕 Texaco/dsl 🅕 Hacienda Vieja Mexican, IHOP, Jimmy John's, Schlotzky's, Steak'n Shake, Taco Mac 🅛 Microtel 🅞 AT&T, Atlanta Bread, Big Lots, BJ's Whse/gas, Discount Tire, GNC, Home Depot, Honda, Kohl's, Lowe's Whse, Old Navy, Petsmart, Target, Verizon
4	Bells Ferry Rd, **W** 🅕 QT, RaceTrac/dsl, Shell/dsl 🅕 Arby's, Burger King, Dunkin', Pizza Hut, Ralph's Grill, Subway, Waffle House 🅞 Pepboys, Publix, Walgreens
3	Chastain Rd, to I-75 N, **W** 🅕 Chevron 🅕 CA Dreaming, Cookout, Cracker Barrel, Del Taco, Firehouse Subs, Five Guys, Los Reyes, Maddio's Pizza, Marlow's Tavern, O'Charley's, Panda Express, Papa's Cuban, Ruth's Chris Steaks, Starbucks, Taco Mac 🅛 Best Western, Comfort Suites, Embassy Suites, Fairfield Inn, Residence Inn, SpringHill Suites 🅞 to Kennesaw St Coll
1	Barrett Pkwy, to I-75 N, US 41, **E** 🅕 Murphy USA/dsl, QT 🅕 Buffalo Wild Wings, Burger King, Cheeseburger Bobby's, Fuego Tortillo, Pacific Buffet, Starbucks, Texas Roadhouse, Twisted Kitchen, Waffle House, Wendy's, Zaxby's 🅞 $Tree, AT&T, Barnes&Noble, CVS Drug, Mavis Tire, Petco, Publix, Ross, SteinMart, Tuesday Morning, Walmart/Subway, **W** 🅕 Shell/dsl 🅕 Anchor Grill, Applebee's, Honeybaked Ham, Jimmy John's, McDonald's, Olive Garden, Provino's Italian, Red Lobster, Shogun Japanese, Starbucks, Subway, Twin Peaks 🅛 Comfort Inn, Country Inn&Suites, Holiday Inn Express, Red Roof Inn 🅞 Belk, Firestone/auto, Home Depot, Marshall's, Midas, Pepboys, TJ Maxx, Verizon
0mm	I-575 begins/ends on I-75, exit 268.

Side labels: GA · MACON · CANTON · WOODSTOCK

S T O C K B R I D G E

🔼🔽 INTERSTATE 675

Exit #	Services
10mm	I-285 W, to Atlanta Airport, E to Augusta. **I-675 begins/ends on I-285, exit 52.**
7	Anvil Block Rd, Ft Gillem, **E** 🅿 Chevron/dsl 🍴 Waffle House, Walmart/Subway, Wendy's 🅾 $Tree, **W** 🅿 Exxon/dsl
5	Forest Pkwy, **E** 🅿 Texaco/dsl, **W** 🅿 BP/dsl, QT/dsl/scales, Texaco/dsl 🍴 McDonald's, Waffle House
2	US 23, GA 42, **E** 🅿 BP, Texaco, Valero/Subway/dsl 🍴 El Granero Mexican, **W** 🅿 Chevron/dsl, Citgo 🍴 Waffle House 🅾 Family$, Food Depot, GoodTime/auto, Rite Aid, USPO
1	GA 138, to I-75 N, Stockbridge, **E** 🅿 Citgo/dsl, Exxon/dsl, Murphy USA/dsl, QT, Sunoco/dsl 🍴 Burger King, Capt D's, Checker's, Church's Chicken, DQ, Dunkin', Golden Corral, Hibachi Buffet, KFC, Krispy Kreme, Little Caesar's, McDonald's, Olympia Pizza, Papa John's, Popeye's, Taco Bell, Waffle House, Wendy's, Zaxby's 🛏 Best Value, Econolodge, Knights Inn, Magnolia Inn, Quality Inn, Sleep Inn, Stay Inn, Stockbridge Inn 🅾 $General, $Tree, Advance Parts, Aldi Foods, BigLots, CVS Drug, Goodyear/auto, NAPA, Pepboys, Walmart, **W** 🅿 Raceway/dsl 🍴 Applebee's, Broadway Diner, Chick-fil-A, Frontera Mexican, Honeybaked Ham, IHOP, Krystal, O'Charley's, Piccadilly's, Subway, Taco Mac, Tokyo Seafood, Waffle House 🛏 Comfort Inn, Day's Inn, Express Inn, Hampton Inn, Holiday Inn, La Quinta, Red Roof Inn 🅾 Kroger/dsl, Lowes Whse, Office Depot, Tires+, URGENT CARE, Verizon
0mm	**I-675 begins/ends on I-75, exit 227.**

🔼🔽 INTERSTATE 985 (Gainesville)

Exit #	Services
24.5	**I-985 begins/ends on US 23, 25mm.**
24	to US 129 N, GA 369 W, Gainesville, **N** 🅿 QT/dsl 🍴 McDonald's, Papa John's, Taco Bell 🅾 Autozone, 🛏 Kroger/dsl, **S** 🅿 BP/dsl, Chevron/dsl, Subway 🍴 Double B Burger, Rabbittown Cafe
22	GA 11, Gainesville, **N** 🅿 QT/dsl, Shell/dsl 🍴 Burger King, **S** 🅿 Chevron/dsl, Shell/dsl 🍴 Waffle House 🛏 Motel 6 🅾 $General

G A I N E S V I L L E

20	GA 60, GA 53, Gainesville, **N** 🅿 RaceTrac/dsl, **S** 🅿 Kangaroo/Subway/dsl 🍴 Waffle House
17	GA 13, Gainesville
16	GA 53, Oakwood, **N** 🅿 Arby's, Burger King, Capt D's, DQ, Dunkin', El Sombrero Mexican, Firehouse Subs, Hardee's, KFC, McDonald's, Napoli's Pizza, Pizza Hut, Steak'n Shake, Taco Bell, Waffle House, Zaxby's 🛏 Best Western, Jameson Inn 🅾 $Tree, Aldi Foods, Camping World RV Ctr, Chrysler/Dodge/Jeep, Sam's Club/dsl, Walmart/Subway, **S** 🅿 O'Reilly Parts, QT/dsl 🍴 Ace Hardware, Buffalo's Cafe, Chick-Fil-A, Krystal, La Parilla Mexican, Sonic, Sonny's BBQ, Subway, Waffle House, Wendy's 🛏 Quality Inn 🅾 AutoZone, Kauffman Tire, Publix, Slack Parts, Toyota, Walgreens
12	Spout Springs Rd, Flowery Branch, **N** 🅿 Exxon/dsl, **S** 🅿 Chevron/dsl, Marathon/Subway/dsl 🍴 Burger&Shake, Chick-fil-A, Chili's, China Garden, CrossRoads Grill, Domino's, El Sombrero Mexican, Firehouse Subs, Little Caesar's, Napoli's Pizza, Shane's Ribshack, Shogun Japanese 🛏 Hampton Inn 🅾 AT&T, GNC, Home Depot, Kohl's, Petsmart, Publix, Rite Aid, Ross, Target, TJ Maxx, Verizon, Walgreens
8	GA 347, Friendship Rd, Lake Lanier, **N** 🅿 Chevron/dsl, QT/dsl, Shell/dsl 🍴 Blimpie, Burger King, Cracker Barrel, McDonald's, Mykonos Cafe, Shoney's, Subway, Vinny's NY Grill, Waffle House, Wendy's, Zaxby's 🛏 Holiday Inn Express 🅾 $General, Advance parts, Family$, O'Reilly Parts, Publix, URGENT CARE, Verizon, vet, **S** 🅾 Camper City RV Ctr, Harley Davidson
4	US 23 S, GA 20, Buford, **N** 🅿 QT, Shell/dsl 🍴 Arby's, Bojangles, Burger King, Capt D's, Golden Buddah, Golden Corral, Hardee's, IHOP, KFC, McDonald's, Pizza Hut, Subway, Taco Bell, Waffle House, Wendy's, Zaxby's 🛏 Best Value Inn, Holiday Inn Express 🅾 Ace Hardware, Chrysler/Dodge/Jeep, Hobby Lobby, Home Depot, Kia, NAPA Autocare, NTB, O'Reilly Parts, **S** 🅿 Chevron/dsl, Exxon/dsl, Mtn Express/dsl 🍴 Asia Buffet, Sonny's BBQ, Stevi B's Pizza, Viva Mexico 🅾 $Tree, Firestone/auto, Honda, Kauffman Tire, Lowes Whse, Walmart
0mm	**I-985 begins/ends on I-85.**

GA

NOTES

■ = gas   ⑪ = food   ⌂ = lodging   ◙ = other   ℞ = rest stop   Copyright 2022 - The Next EXIT

IDAHO

⬆N INTERSTATE 15

Exit #	Services
196mm	Idaho/Montana state line, Monida Pass, continental divide, elev 6870
190	Humphrey
184	Stoddard Creek Area, E◙ Historical Site, RV camping, W◙ Stoddard Creek Camping
180	Spencer, E⑪ Opal Country Café/gas ◙ High Country Opal Store, W⑪ Spencer Grill/RV Park
172	no service
167	ID 22, Dubois, E℞ both lanes, full ♿ facilities, litter barrels, petwalk, ℂ, ♨, ■ Phillips 66/dsl ◙ city park, USPO, W◙ Nez Pearce Tr, to Craters NM
150	Hamer, E◙ Ron's Tire, USPO, W◙ Camus NWR
143	ID 33, ID 28, to Mud Lake, Rexburg, W◙ Sacajawea Hist Bywy, weigh sta both lanes
142mm	hist site, roadside parking
135	ID 48, Roberts, E■ Exxon/cafe/dsl/LP ◙ city park
128	Osgood Area, E■ Osgood/dsl ◙ camping (6mi)
119	US 20 E, to Rexburg, Idaho Falls, E on Lindsay ■ Sinclair/dsl ⑪ Denny's, Jaker's Steaks, Outback Steaks, Sandpiper Rest. ⌂ Best Western+, Fairbridge Inn, Hampton Inn, Hilton Garden, Le-Ritz Hotel, Motel 6, Quality Inn, Safari Inn, Shilo Inn/rest., Super 8, Tru Hilton ◙ LDS Temple, same as 118, Snake River RV Park/camping, W■ Sinclair/dsl
118	US 20, Broadway St, Idaho Falls, E■ Phillips 66/dsl, Walmart/dsl ⑪ Applebee's, Arctic Circle, Buffalo Wild Wings, Carl's Jr, Cedric's Rest., Chili's, Culver's, Domino's, Famous Dave's BBQ, Jimmy John's, MacKenzie River Grill, Olive Garden, Panda Express, Shari's Rest., Smitty's Pancakes, Starbucks, Wendy's ⌂ Candlewood Suites, Fairfield Inn, Hampton Inn, Hilton Garden, Residence Inn, SpringHill Suites ◙ 🏥, Candy Jct, Ford, Harley-Davidson, LDS Temple, same as 119, tires, URGENT CARE, Verizon, Walmart/Subway, W■ Exxon/dsl, Phillips 66/dsl, Sinclair/McDonald's ⑪ Arby's, Burger King, Fiesta Ole, Five Buck Pizza, Hong Kong Rest., Jack-in-the-Box, Los Adalberto's Mexican, O'Brady's, Papa Murphy's, Pizza Hut, Subway ⌂ Comfort Inn, Motel 6, Motel West ◙ Albertsons, AutoZone, Camping World RV Ctr, O'Reilly Parts, Walgreens
116	US 26, Sunnyside Rd, Ammon, Jackson, E◙🏥, BMW, Chevrolet, Honda, Sunnyside Acres RV Park, Toyota, VW, W■ Exxon/diesel ⑪ DoubleDown Grill ⌂ Sleep Inn
113	US 26, to Idaho Falls, Jackson, E■ Blu LNG/dsl, Chevron/Burger King/dsl, ✈FLYING J/Subway/dsl/24hr/@, Loves/McDonald's/dsl/scales/24hr ⑪ Subway ◙🏥, Jack's Tires, Peterbilt
108	Shelley, Firth Area, 1 mi E◙ RV Park/dump
101mm	℞ both lanes, full ♿ facilities, geological site, litter barrels, petwalk, ℂ, ♨
98	Rose-Firth Area
94.5mm	Snake River
93	US 26, ID 39, Blackfoot, E■ Chevron/Jimmy John's/dsl, Maverik/dsl, Sinclair/Stinker/dsl ⑪ Arby's, Burger King, Domino's, Homestead Rest., Hong Kong Garden, Little Caesar's, McDonald's, Papa Murphy's, Pizza Hut, Roberto's Mexican, Subway, Taco Bell, Taco Time, Wendy's ⌂ Best Western, Super 8 ◙ $Tree, AutoZone, Bealls, Chrysler/Dodge/Ford/Jeep, city park, Kesler's Foods, O'Reilly Parts, Point S Auto, Ridley's Mkt, Schwab Tire, URGENT CARE, Verizon, Walgreens, Walmart/Subway, W■ Sinclair/A&W/dsl ◙ Riverside Boot/saddleshop (4mi)

90.5mm	Blackfoot River
89	US 91, S Blackfoot, W■ Sinclair/Sage Cafe/dsl
80	Ft Hall, W■⑪ Phillips 66/rest./dsl/casino ⌂ Shoshone Bannoc Hotel/casino
72	I-86 W, to Twin Falls
71	Pocatello Creek Rd, Pocatello, E■ Chevron/Burger King/ds Phillips 66/dsl, Shell/dsl ⑪ Applebee's, Jack-in-the Box, Per kins, Sandpiper Rest., Subway ⌂ Best Western, Clarion, L Quinta, Quality Inn, Red Lion Inn, Super 8 ◙ KOA (1mi), 0-mi W■ Exxon, Maverik/dsl ⑪ Arby's, Bamboo Garden, Butt Burr's Lickety Split, Butter Burr's Rest., Café Rio, Carl's Jr, Chang Garden Chinese, Coldstone, El Caporal, Golden Corral, Jamb Juice, KFC, Mandarin House, McDonald's, Papa Murphy's, Ri ley's Mkt, Senor Iguana's Mexican, Sizzler, Sonic, Starbuck Subway, Taco Bell, Taco Time, Thai Kitchen, Wendy's, Winger ◙ $Tree, Advance Parts, AutoZone, BigLots, Buick/GMC, Chev rolet, Fred Meyer/dsl, Harley-Davidson, Hyundai, O'Reilly Part Subaru, Tuesday Morning, Walgreens, WinCo Foods
69	Clark St, Pocatello, E■ Chevron/cafe/dsl, Maverik/dsl, Sinclai Arctic Circle/dsl ⑪ Jakers Grill ⌂ Hampton Inn, Holiday Inn E press, TownePlace Suites ◙🏥, W◙ museum, to ID St U
67	US 30/91, 5th St, Pocatello, E■ Exxon/dsl, 1-2 mi W■ Chevron/dsl, Shell/dsl ⑪ Elmer's Dining, Goody's Deli, Jimm John's, McDonald's, Pizza Hut, Subway, Taco Bell ⌂ Rodewa Inn, Thunderbird Motel ◙🏥, city park, info, museum, Old Fo Hall, RV dump
63	Portneuf Area, W◙ RV camp/dump, to Mink Creek RA
59mm	weigh sta both lanes
58	Inkom (from sb), 1/2 mi W■ Sinclair/café/dsl ◙ Bisharat Mkt, Pebble Creek Ski Area, repair, USPO
57	Inkom (from nb), same as 58
47	US 30, to Lava Hot Springs, McCammon, E■ ✈FLYING J/ds scales/LP/RV dump/24hr, Chevron/A&W/Taco Time/dsl ⑪ Sub way ◙ Lava Hot Springs RA, McCammon RV Park, to KOA
44	Lp 15, Jenson Rd, McCammon, E access to food
40	Arimo, E◙ USPO
36	US 91, Virginia
31	ID 40, to Downey, Preston, E■ Shell/Flags West/café/dsl/mo tel/24hr/@ ◙ Downata Hot Springs RV camping (6mi)
25mm	℞ sb, full ♿ facilities, litter barrels, petwalk, ℂ, ♨
24.5mm	Malad Summit, elevation 5574
22	to Devil Creek Reservoir, E RV camping
17	ID 36, to Weston, to Preston
13	ID 38, Malad City, W■ Chevron/Burger King, Chevron/dsl Phillips 66/café/dsl ⑪ Me&Lou's Rest., Pines Rest., Sperow' BBQ, Subway ⌂ Village Inn Motel ◙🏥, 3R's Tire, Family$ pioneer museum, repair, RV dump
7mm	Welcome Ctr nb, full ♿ facilities, info, litter barrels, petwalk ℂ, ♨, vending
3	to Samaria, Woodruff
0mm	Idaho/Utah state line

⬆E INTERSTATE 84

Exit #	Services
275mm	Idaho/Utah state line
270mm	℞ both lanes, full ♿ facilities, geological site, litter barrels petwalk, ℂ, ♨
263	Juniper Rd
257mm	Sweetzer Summit, elev 5530
254	Sweetzer Rd

🔼🔽 INTERSTATE 84 Cont'd

Exit #	Services
245	Sublett Rd, to Malta, **N** 📕 Sublett/dsl/café
237	Idahome Rd
234mm	Raft River
229mm	🅁🅂/weigh sta both lanes, full ♿ facilities, litter barrels, petwalk, 🚻🏃
228	ID 81, Yale Rd, to Declo
222	I-86, US 30, E to Pocatello
216	ID 77, ID 25, to Declo, **N** 📕 Phillips 66/Food Court/dsl ◻🏨, to Walcott SP, Village of Trees RV Park, **S** 📕 Sinclair/Pit Stop Grill/dsl
215mm	Snake River
211	ID 24, Heyburn, Burley, **N** 📕 Sinclair/A&W/café/dsl 🍽 Wayside Cafe 🏨 Tops Motel ◻🏨, Country RV Village/park, **S** 📕 Loves/Carl's Jr./dsl/scales/24hr ◻ Riverside RV Park, truck repair, truck wash
208	ID 27, Burley, **N** 📕 Phillips 66/dsl 🍽 Conner's Cafe 🏨 Super 8 ◻ Kenworth, **S** 📕 Chevron/Subway/dsl/24hr, Maverik/dsl, Shell/dsl, Sinclair/dsl 🍽 Aguila's Mexican, Arby's, Burger King, Denny's, El Caporal, Guadalajara Mexican, Jack-in-the-Box, KFC, Little Caesar's, McDonald's, Morey's Steaks, Perkins, Taco Bell, Wendy's 🏨 Best Western+, Budget Motel, Fairfield Inn ◻🏨, $Tree, Beall's, Buick/GMC, Cal Ranch Store, CarQuest, Chrysler/Dodge/Jeep, Commercial Tire, NAPA, O'Reilly Parts, to Snake River RA, URGENT CARE, Verizon, Walmart
201	ID 25, Kasota Rd, to Paul, **N** ◻ Kasota RV Park
194	ID 25, to Hazelton
188	Valley Rd, to Eden
182	ID 50, to Kimberly, Twin Falls, **N** 📕 Sinclair/dsl ◻ Gary's RV Ctr/park/dump, **S** 📕 Shell/Blimpie/Taco Time/dsl/scales/24hr @ 🍽 Garden of Eden Cafe 🏨 Amber Inn ◻🏨, auto/truck/rv repair, to Shoshone Falls scenic attraction
173	US 93, Twin Falls, **N** 📕 FLYING J/dsl/LP/24hr/@, Phillips 66/dsl 🍽 Subway 🏨 Comfort Inn, Red Lion Inn ◻ Blue Beacon, Freightliner, KOA (1mi), to Sun Valley, **5 mi S** 📕 Chevron/Subway/dsl, Maverik/dsl, Phillips 66/dsl, Shell/dsl, Sinclair, Walmart Fuel/dsl 🍽 Applebee's, Arby's, Arctic Circle, Baskin-Robbins, Blaze Pizza, Buffalo Wild Wings, Burger King, Cafe Rio, Carino's, Chick-fil-A, Chili's, Coldstone, Costa Vida, Culver's, Denny's, Dickey's BBQ, DQ, Five Guys, Golden Corral, Habit Burger, Idaho Joe's, IHOP, IHOP, Jack-in-the-Box, Jakers Grill, Jamba Juice, Jimmy John's, KFC, La Fiesta, Mandarin Chinese, McDonald's, Noodles&Co, Outback Steaks, Panda Express, Papa John's, Papa Murphy's, Perkins, Pizza Hut, River Rock Grill, Shari's, Sizzler, Sonic, Starbucks, Subway, Taco Bell, Tomato's Italian, Wendy's, Wok In Grill 🏨 Best Western, Fairfield Inn, Hampton Inn, Hilton Garden, Holiday Inn Express, La Quinta, Motel 6, Quality Inn, Red Lion, Super 8 ◻🏨, $Tree, AT&T, AutoZone, Barnes&Noble, Best Buy, Buick/GMC, Chevrolet, Chrysler/Dodge/Jeep, Coll of S ID, Commercial Tire, Costco/gas, Dick's, Ford/Lincoln, Fred Meyer/dsl, Home Depot, Honda, Hyundai, JC Penney, Jo-Ann Fabrics, LDS Temple, Les Schwab Tire, Lowe's, Mazda/VW, Michael's, Nissan, Old Navy, O'Reilly Parts, Petco, Petsmart, Point S Automotive, Ross, ShopKO, Sportsmans Whse, Target, TJ Maxx, Verizon, visitors ctr, Walgreens, Walmart/Subway, WinCo Foods

171mm	🅁🅂/weigh sta eb, full ♿ facilities, litter barrels, petwalk, 🚻🏃, vending
168	ID 79, to Jerome, **N** 📕 Blu/LNG/dsl, Chevron/dsl/24hr, Shell/Wendy's/dsl, Tesoro/dsl 🍽 Burger King, Domino's, DQ, Garibaldi's Mexican, Little Caesar's, McDonald's, Pizza Hut 🏨 Best Western, Crest Motel, Holiday Motel ◻🏨, $Tree, AutoZone, Brockman RV Ctr, Family$, Les Schwab Tire, NAPA, O'Reilly Parts, Verizon, Walmart/Subway, **S** 🍽 Subway ◻ Chevrolet
165	ID 25, Jerome, **N** 📕 Sinclair/dsl 🏨 Holiday Motel (1mi) ◻🏨, RV camping/dump, vet
157	ID 46, Wendell, **1 mi N** 🍽 Subway ◻🏨, CarQuest, Family$, Intermountain RV Park, **S** 📕 Phillips 66/dsl 🍽 Farmhouse Rest.
155	ID 46, to Wendell, **N** ◻ Intermountain RV Camp/ctr
147	to Tuttle, **S** ◻ High Adventure RV Park/cafe, to Malad Gorge SP
146mm	Malad River
141	US 26, to US 30, Gooding, **N** ◻🏨, **S** 📕 Phillips 66/café/dsl, Sinclair/dsl 🏨 Amber Inn, Hagerman Inn (9mi) ◻ Hagerman RV Village (8mi)
137	Lp 84, to US 30, to Pioneer Road, Bliss, **2 mi S** 📕 Sinclair/Stinker/dsl/24hr ◻ camping
133mm	🅁🅂 both lanes, full ♿ facilities, info, litter barrels, petwalk, 🚻🏃
129	King Hill
128mm	Snake River
125	Paradise Valley
122mm	Snake River

BURLEY (left margin)
TWIN FALLS (left margin)
JEROME (center margin)
ID (right margin)

ID

◆E INTERSTATE 84 Cont'd

Exit #	Services
121	Glenns Ferry, 1 mi S 🅿 Sinclair/dsl, Veltex/dsl 🛏 Hansen Motel/cafe, Redford Motel 🅾 Carmela Winery/rest., Family$, fudge factory, NAPA, tires, to 3 Island SP, Trails Break RV camp/dump
120	Glenns Ferry (from eb), same as 121
114	ID 78 (from wb), to Hammett, 1 mi S access to gas/dsl, to Bruneau Dunes SP
112	to ID 78, Hammett, 1 mi S food, gas/dsl, to Bruneau Dunes SP
99	ID 51, ID 67, to Mountain Home, 2 mi S 🛏 camping
95	US 20, Mountain Home, N 🅿 Chevron/KFC/dsl, [Pilot]/Arby's/dsl/scales/24hr 🍽 AJ's Rest., Jack-in-the-Box, Subway, Wingers 🛏 Best Western, Hampton Inn, Mtn Home Inn, S 🅿 USA 🍽 Jade Palace, McDonald's, Smoky Mtn Pizza, Wendy's 🛏 Hilander Motel (1mi), Towne Ctr Motel (1mi) 🅾 🅷, $Tree, AT&T, Chrysler/Dodge/Jeep, Ford/Lincoln, to Mtn Home RV Park, Verizon, visitors ctr, Walmart/Subway
90	to ID 51, ID 67, W Mountain Home, S 🅿 Chevron/Burger King/dsl 🍽 McDonald's (4mi) 🛏 Maple Cove Motel (4mi), to Hilander Motel (4mi), Towne Ctr Motel (4mi) 🅾 KOA
74	Simco Rd
71	Orchard, Mayfield, S 🅿 Sinclair/rest./StageStop Motel/dsl/24hr 🅾 truckwash
66mm	weigh sta both lanes
64	Blacks Creek, Kuna, historical site
62mm	📶 both lanes, full ♿ facilities, litter barrels, OR Trail info, petwalk, 🚰, 🛏, vending
59b a	S Eisenman Rd, Memory Rd
57	ID 21, Gowen Rd, to Idaho City, N 🅿 Sinclair 🍽 Domino's, Jack-in-the-Box, McDonald's, Subway, Taco Del Mar 🛏 Best Western/NW Lodge 🅾 Albertsons/Sav-On, Peterbilt, to Micron, S 🅿 Chevron/dsl 🍽 Burger King, FoodCourt 🅾 Boise Stores/famous brands, ID Ice World
54	US 20/26, Broadway Ave, Boise, N 🅿 ⊕FLYING J/dsl/LP/24hr, Chevron/dsl, Fred Meyer/dsl, Shell/dsl 🍽 A&W/KFC, Arby's, Fiesta Mexican, IHOP, Jack-in-the-Box, Mongolian Noodles, Pizza Pie Cafe, Port Of Subs, Sonic 🛏 Courtyard (3mi) 🅾 Big O Tire, Firestone/auto, Fred Meyer, Goodyear/auto, Home Depot, Jo-Ann Fabrics, O'Reilly Parts, PetCo, Ross, ShopKO, to Boise St U, vet, Walgreens, S 🅿 TA/Country Pride/Taco Bell/Subway/dsl/24hr/@ 🛏 Red Lion Inn 🅾 Bretz RV Ctr, Kenworth, Mtn View RV Park
53	Vista Ave, Boise, N 🅿 Shell/dsl, Texaco/dsl 🍽 Applebee's, Pizza Hut 🛏 Comfort Inn, Comfort Suites, Extended Stay America, Fairfield Inn, Hampton Inn, Holiday Inn/rest., La Quinta, Super 8, Wyndham Garden 🅾 museums, st capitol, st police, zoo, S 🅿 Chevron/dsl 🍽 Denny's, Kopper Kitchen 🛏 Best Western, InnAmerica, Motel 6, Quality Inn, Rodeway Inn 🅾 🔲
52	Orchard St, Boise, N 🅿 Maverik/dsl, Shell/dsl 🍽 Subway 🅾 BMW Motorcycles, Fiat, GMC
50b a	Cole Rd, Overland Rd, N 🅿 Chevron/dsl, Shell, Sinclair 🍽 Cancun Mexican, Cobby's Sandwiches, Eddie's Rest., McDonald's, Outback Steaks, Pizza Hut, Subway, Taco Bell, Taco Time 🅾 Grocery Outlet, LDS Temple, transmissions, S 🅿 Phillips 66/dsl, Shell/dsl 🍽 A&W/KFC, Black Bear Diner, Burger King, Carino's, Carl's Jr, Chapala Mexican, Chuck-a-Rama, Cracker Barrel, Del Taco, Goodwood BBQ, Jimmy John's, Lucky Palace Chinese, McGrath's FishHouse, Nato's Mexican, On the Border, Panda Express, Papa John's, Sonic, Starbucks, Tucano's Brazilian Grill, Twin Peaks 🛏 Hampton Inn, Hilton Garden, Homewood Suites,

Exit #	Services
50b a	**Continued** Howard Johnson's, Oxford Suites 🅾 Commercial Tire, Costco gas, Dillon RV Ctr, Discount Tire, Einstein Oilery, Les Schwab Tire, Lowe's, Meineke, USPO, Verizon, vet, Walmart/McDonald's
49	I-184 (exits left from eb), to W Boise, N 🅾 🅷
46	ID 55, Eagle, N 🅿 Chevron/McDonald's/dsl 🍽 Buffalo Wild Wings, Del Taco, Ling&Louie's, Los Beto's, Mi Casa, Smash Burger, Starbucks, Subway 🛏 Hampton Inn, Holiday Inn Express, La Quinta 🅾 🅷, S 🅿 Chevron/dsl 🍽 Beef'O'Brady's, Chicago Connection, Dickey's BBQ, Dutch Bros Coffee, Happy Teriyaki, Jack-in-the-Box, Jimmy John's, Joy Garden, Panda Garden, Pita Pit, Qdoba, Rudy's Grill, Sakana Japanese, Subway, Taco Bell, TCBY, The Griddle 🛏 Candlewood Suites, Courtyard, TownePlace Suites, Tru 🅾 AAA, Harley-Davidson, Indian Motorcycles, URGENT CARE, vet
44	ID 69, Meridian, N 🅿 Chevron/dsl, Maverik/dsl, Sinclair 🍽 50 Cafe, A&W/KFC, China Wok, DQ, Jimmy John's, McDonald's, Panda Express, Pizza Hut, Shari's, Starbucks, Subway, Taco Bell, Taco Time, Wendy's 🛏 Best Western+, Motel 6 🅾 AT&T, Home Depot, Johnny's Autocare, Les Schwab Tire, Sierra Trading Post, Verizon, WinCo Foods, S 🅿 Shell/dsl 🍽 Starbucks, Carl's Jr, JB's, Papa John's 🛏 Mr Sandman Inn 🅾 Camping World RV Ctr, Ford, Lowe's, O'Reilly Parts, Walgreens, Walmart, waterpark
42	Ten Mile Rd
38	Garrity Blvd, Nampa, N 🅿 Chevron/dsl, Walmart Gas/dsl 🍽 Dutch Bros Coffee, Jack-in-the-Box, Los Betos, Port of Subs, Sonic 🛏 Hampton Inn, Home 2 Suites 🅾 Buick/GMC, Cadillac/Chevrolet, Chrysler/Dodge/Jeep, Ford, Hyundai, Infiniti, Kia, Nissan, Toyota, Walmart/Subway, S 🅿 Phillips 66/dsl, Shell/dsl 🍽 Fiesta Guadalajara, Jimmy John's, McDonald's, Panda Express, Papa Murphy's, Pizza Hut, Popeye's, Starbucks, Subway, Taco Bell, Wendy's 🛏 Holiday Inn Express 🅾 🅷, Freddy's, Garrity RV Park, JC Penney, Verizon, War Hawk Museum, Winco Foods
36	Franklin Blvd, Nampa, N 🅿 Blu/LNG/dsl, Maverik/dsl 🍽 Jack-in-the-Box 🛏 Shilo Inn/rest., S 🅿 Chevron/dsl, Shell/Subway/dsl/RV dump/scales/4hr 🛏 Sleep Inn 🅾 🅷, Bretz RV Ctr, Freightliner, Honda, Mason Cr RV Park
35	ID 55, Nampa, S 🅿 Maverik/dsl, Shell/dsl 🍽 Denny's 🛏 Nampa Inn, Rodeway Inn, Super 8
33b a	ID 55 S, Midland Blvd, Marcine, N 🍽 Blaze Pizza, Chick-fil-A, Cracker Barrel, Dickey's BBQ, Habit Burger, McDonald's, Olive Garden, Panera Bread, Qdoba Mexican, Sonic, Subway, TGIFriday's, Winger's 🛏 Fairfield Inn, Holiday Inn 🅾 AT&T, Best Buy, Costco/gas, Dick's, Discount Tire, Gordmans, Hobby Lobby, 🅷, Kohl's, Michael's, Old Navy, PetCo, Petsmart, Sportsmans Whse, Target, TJ Maxx, Verizon, World Mkt, S 🅿 Shell/dsl 🍽 Applebee's, Arby's, Baskin-Robbins, Blimpie, Buffalo Wild Wings, Carl's Jr, Chipotle, Coldstone, Costa Vida, DQ, Golden Corral, IHOP, Jack-in-the-Box, Jade Garden, Jalapeno's Grill, Jimmy John's, Mongolian BBQ, Outback Steaks, Papa Murphy's, Pizza Hut, Red Robin, Shari's Rest, Smashburger, Smokey Mtn Grill, Starbucks, Subway, Taco Bell, TX Roadhouse, Wendy's, Zupa Kitchen 🅾 $Tree, Home Depot, Jo-Ann Fabrics, Lowe's, Nampa Tire, NAPA, Point S Automotive, Ross, Savers, Shopko, Staples, U-Haul, Verizon, Verizon (2), vet, Walgreens, WinCo Foods
29	US 20/26, Franklin Rd, Caldwell, N 🅿 ⊕FLYING J/Denny's/dsl/LP/scales/24hr 🅾 Ambassador RV camping, RV dump, S 🅿 Sage/Sinclair/cafe/dsl/24hr 🍽 Burger King, Dutch Bros 🛏 Best Western+, La Quinta
28	10th Ave, Caldwell, N 🅿 Maverik/dsl 🅾 city park, U-Haul, S 🅿 Chevron/dsl, Shell/dsl 🍽 Carl's Jr, Fiesta Mexican, Jack-in-the-Box, Mr V's Rest., Pizza Hut, Subway, Wendy's 🅾 🅷, AutoZone, Point S Automotive, Walgreens

Vertical side labels: MOUNTAIN HOME / BOISE (left column); EAGLE / NAMPA / CALDWELL (right column)

INTERSTATE 84 Cont'd

Exit #	Services
27	ID 19, to Wilder, 1 mi **S** 📮 Chevron/dsl 🄾 visitor info
26.5mm	Boise River
26	US 20/26, to Notus, **N** 🄾 Caldwell Campground, **S** 📮 Sinclair/dsl 🄾 RV Resort
25	ID 44, Middleton, **N** 📮 Sinclair/dsl 🍴 44 Burgers/shakes, **S** Insp sta eb
17	Sand Hollow, **N** 🍴 Sinclair/Sand Hollow Café/dsl 🄾 Country Corners RV Park
13	Black Canyon Jct, **S** 📮 Sinclair/rest./motel/dsl/scales/24hr
9	US 30, to New Plymouth
3	US 95, Fruitland, **N** 📮 Chevron/A&W/dsl 🄾 Neat Retreat RV Park (5mi), to Hell's Cyn RA (26mi)
1mm	**Welcome Ctr eb, full ♿ facilities, info, litter barrels, petwalk, 🄲, 🅿**
0mm	Idaho/Oregon state line, Snake River

INTERSTATE 86

Exit #	Services
63b a	I-15, N to Butte, S to SLC. **I-86 begins/ends on I-15, exit 72.**
61	US 91, Yellowstone Ave, Pocatello, **N** 📮 Exxon, Maverik/dsl, Shell/dsl 🍴 Arby's, Arctic Circle, Burger King, Chapala Mexican, Domino's, Five Mile Café, Jack-in-the-Box, Lei's BBQ, Papa Murphy's, Subway, Tres Hermanos, Wendy's 🛏 Motel 6, Travelodge 🄾 $Tree, AutoZone, Bargain Tire, Crossroads RV Ctr, Family$, O'Reilly Parts, Smith's Foods/dsl, vet, **S** 📮 Exxon/dsl, Phillips 66/dsl 🍴 Buffalo Wild Wings, Chili's, Costa Vida, Denny's, Firehouse Subs, Five Guys, Freddy's, Great Wall, IHOP, Jimmy John's, MacKenzie River Grill, McDonald's, Noodles&Co, Panda Express, Panera Bread, Pizza Hut, Pizza Pie Café, Popeye's, Red Lobster, Red Robin, Starbucks, TX Roadhouse 🄾 AT&T, Cal Ranch Store, Chrysler/Dodge/Jeep, Costco/gas, Dick's, Discount Tire, Ford/Lincoln, Hobby Lobby, Home Depot, Honda, JC Penney, Jo-Ann Fabrics, Kia, Lowe's, NAPA, Nissan, PetCo, Petsmart, Ross, Schwab Tire, ShopKo, TJ Maxx, Toyota, Verizon, Walgreens, Walmart
58.5mm	Portneuf River
58	US 30, W Pocatello, **N** 🄾 Batise Springs RV Park/dump (1mi-seasonal)
56	**N** 🄾 Pocatello Reg Airport, **S** 📮 Sinclair/dsl/24hr
52	Arbon Valley, **S** 📮 Phillips 66/Bannock Peak/dsl 🄾 casino
51mm	Bannock Creek
49	Rainbow Rd
44	Seagull Bay
40	ID 39, American Falls, **N** 📮 Sinclair/dsl (1mi), Texaco 🍴 Pizza Hut, Subway, Tres Hermanos Mexican 🛏 American Motel 🄾 🄷, auto repair, Family$ (1mi), Jiffy Lube, NAPA, Schwab Tire, to Am Falls RA, Willow Bay RV Park/dump, **S** 🛏 Hillview Motel
36	ID 37, to Rockland, American Falls, 2 mi **N** 📮 Shell/dsl 🛏 Falls Motel 🄾 🄷, 2 mi **S** 🄾 Indian Springs RV Resort
33	Neeley Area
31mm	🆁🆂 wb, full ♿ facilities, hist site, litter barrel, petwalk, 🄲, 🅿, vending
28	**N** 🄾 Register Rock Hist Site, RV camping/dump, to Massacre Rock SP
21	Coldwater Area
19mm	🆁🆂 eb, full ♿ facilities, hist site, litter barrel, petwalk, 🄲, 🅿, vending
15	Raft River Area
1	I-84 E, to Ogden. **I-86 begins/ends on I-84, exit 222.**

INTERSTATE 90

Exit #	Services
74mm	Idaho/Montana state line, Pacific/Central time zone, Lookout Pass elev 4680
73mm	scenic area/hist site wb
72mm	scenic area/hist site eb
71mm	**runaway truck ramp wb**
70mm	**runaway truck ramp wb**
69	Lp 90, Mullan, **N** 📮 Sinclair/dsl 🄾 Mullan Trail grocery/RV Park, museum, USPO
68	Lp 90 (from eb), Mullan, same as 69
67	Morning District, Morning District
66	Gold Creek (from eb)
65	Compressor District
64	Golconda District
62	ID 4, Wallace, **S** 📮 Conoco 🍴 Pizza Factory, Smokehouse Rest. 🛏 Brooks Hotel, Stardust Motel 🄾 Harvest Foods, museum, Wallace RV Park
61	Lp 90, Wallace, **S** 📮 Conoco/dsl 🍴 Pizza Factory, Smokehouse Rest., Trailside Cafe 🛏 Brooks Hotel/rest., Wallace Inn 🄾 auto repair, info ctr, same as 62
60	Lp 90, Silverton, **S** 🄾 RV camping
57	Lp 90, Osburn, **S** 📮 76/dsl 🄾 Blue Anchor RV Park, Stein's Foods, USPO
54	Big Creek, **N** 🄾 hist site
51	Lp 90, Division St, Kellogg, **N** 📮 Conoco/dsl 🛏 Trail Motel 🄾 🄷, Bender Drug, Buick/Cadillac/Chevrolet/GMC, Chrysler/Dodge/Jeep, Schwab Tire, Stein's Foods, vet, **S** 🍴 Moose Creek Grill 🄾 USPO
50	Hill St (from eb), Kellogg, **N** 🍴 Humdinger Drive-In 🛏 Trail Motel 🄾 Ace Hardware, Benzer Drug, NAPA, Stein's Foods, tires, **S** 📮 Conoco/dsl 🄾 museum, Silver Mtn Ski/summer resort/rec area, Yoke's Foods
49	Bunker Ave, **N** 📮 Conoco/dsl 🍴 McDonald's, Sam's Drive-In, Subway 🛏 Silverhorn Motel/rest. 🄾 🄷, **S** 🍴 Noah's Canteen, Silver Mtn Rest. 🛏 Fairbridge Inn, Morning Star Lodge 🄾 city park, museum, RV dump, Silver Mtn RA
48	Smelterville, **S** 🄾 Dave Smith Tire, O'Reilly Parts, USPO, Walmart
45	Pinehurst, **S** 📮 Chevron/dsl/repair, Conoco/dsl 🄾 By-the-way Camping, Harvest Foods, TrueValue, USPO
43	Kingston, **N** 📮 Conoco/dsl, **S** 📮 Exxon/dsl/rv dump, USPO
40	Cataldo, **N** 🍴 Timbers Roadhouse, USPO, **S** 🄾 RV Park
39.5mm	Coeur d' Alene River
39	Cataldo Mission, **S** 🄾 Nat Hist Landmark, Old Mission SP

POCATELLO

WALLACE

KELLOGG

ID

■ = gas ⑪ = food ⌂ = lodging ⊙ = other ℞ = rest stop   Copyright 2022 - The Next EXIT

� ⁊E INTERSTATE 90 Cont'd

Exit #	Services
34	ID 3, to St Maries, Rose Lake, **S** ■ Conoco/dsl, Rose Lake/dsl ⑪ Rose Lake Cafe ⊙ White Pines Scenic Rte
33	chain removal eb
32mm	chainup area/weigh sta wb
31.5mm	4th of July Cr, Panhandle NF eastern boundary
28	4th of July Pass, elevation 3069, Mullen Tree HS, turnout both lanes, ski area, snowmobile area
24mm	chainup eb, removal wb
22	ID 97, to St Maries, L Coeur d' Alene Scenic ByWay, Wolf Lodge District, Harrison, **1 mi N** ⊙ Wolf Lodge Camping, **S** ⊙ Lake Coeur d'Alene RV Park
20.5mm	Lake Coeur d' Alene
17	Mullan Trail Rd
15	Lp 90, Sherman Ave, Coeur d' Alene, **N** ⊙ forest info, Lake Coeur D' Alene RA/HS, **S** ■ Chevron, Exxon/dsl, Mobil/dsl/LP ⑪ Jimmy's Cafe, Michael D's Eatery, Moontime Cafe, O'Shay's Rest., Roger's Burgers, Zip's Rest. ⌂ Baymont Inn, BudgetSaver Motel, El Rancho Motel, Flaming Motel, Holiday Motel, Japan House Suites, State Motel, Two Lakes Motel ⊙ auto repair, Harvest Foods, tourist info
14	15th St, Coeur d' Alene, **S** ■ TAJ Mart ⊙ Jordon's Grocery
13	4th St, Coeur d' Alene, **N** ■ A&D/dsl ⑪ Atilano's Mexican, Baskin Robbins, Carl's Jr, Davis Donuts, Denny's, DQ, IHOP, Jimmy John's, Little Caesar's, Original Mongolian BBQ, Panda Express, Starbucks, Subway, Taco Time, Wendy's ⌂ Ramada Inn ⊙ AutoZone, BigLots, Costco/gas, NAPA, same as 12, Schwab Tire, Verizon, **S** ■ Exxon/dsl ⑪ Thai Bamboo ⊙ Maserati/Alfa Romeo
12	US 95, to Sandpoint, Moscow, **N** ■ Exxon/dsl, Holiday/dsl, Mobil/dsl, Walmart/dsl ⑪ Applebee's, Arby's, Buffalo Wild Wings, Cafe Rio, Chili's, China Town, Del Taco, Elmer's, Golden Corral, JB's Rest., Jimmy John's, MacKenzie River Pizza, McDonald's, Olive Garden, Panda Express, Panera Bread, Pizza Hut, Red Lobster, Taco Bell, Tomato St., TX Roadhouse ⌂ Best Western+, Comfort Suites, Fairbridge Inn, Motel 6, Quality Inn, Super 8 ⊙ $Tree, Advance Parts, Albertson's, AT&T, Best Buy, Blue Dog RV, Buick/GMC, Cadillac, Combs RV, Discount Tire, Ford/Subaru, Fred Meyer/dsl, Grocery Outlet, Home Depot, JC Penney, Jo-Ann Fabrics, Kia, Kohl's, Michael's, Natural Grocers, O'Reilly Parts, PetCo, Ross, Safeway/dsl, Super 1 Foods, Target, TireRama, TJ Maxx, Toyota, Tuesday Morning, U-Haul, URGENT CARE, Verizon, Walgreens, Walmart/Subway, **S** ■ Conoco/dsl, Mobil ⑪ Asian Twist, Jack-in-the-Box, Jamba Juice, Papa Murphy's, Qdoba Mexican, Shari's, Starbucks ⌂ La Quinta ⊙ H, Albertson's, AT&T, GNC, Rite Aid, same as 13, ShopKO/drugs, Staples
11	Northwest Blvd, **N** ■ Conoco/dsl ⑪ Cracker Barrel, Firehouse Subs, Jack-in-the-Box, MOD Pizza, Subway, Sweet Burrito, Thai Express ⊙ Lowe's, WinCo Foods, **S** ■ Exxon/dsl, SpeeDee ⑪ Anthony's, Azteca Mexican, Bullman's Woodfired Pizza, Coldstone, Ipanema Brazilian, Martino Tuscan, McDonald's, Outback Steaks, Red Robin, SF Sourdough, Starbucks ⌂ Days Inn, Hampton Inn, Holiday Inn Express, SpringHill Suites, Staybridge Suites ⊙ H, Honda, Riverwalk RV Park, Verizon
8.5mm	**Welcome Ctr/weigh sta eb, ℞ both lanes, full ♿ facilities, info, litter barrels, petwalk, ⊙, ⌂**
7	ID 41, to Rathdrum, Spirit Lake, **N** ■ 76/dsl ⑪ Burger King, Del Taco, Domino's, NY Pizza, Papa Murphy's, Pita Pit, Popeye's, Sonic, Starbucks, Subway, Wendy's ⊙ $Tree, AT&T, auto repair, Chevrolet, Chrysler/Dodge/Jeep, Couer d'Alene RV Park, Hyundai, Nissan, VW, Walmart/Subway, **S** ■ Chevron/dsl, Coleman/dsl

Exit #	Services
7	Continued ⑪ A&W/KFC, Capone's Grill, DQ ⌂ Quality Inn ⊙ Robins R Ctr, truck repair, Verizon, vet
6	Seltice Way, **N** ■ 7-11 ⑪ La Cabana Mexican, Paul Bunyan Burgers, Pizza Hut ⊙ NAPA, Super 1 Foods, Walgreens, **S** ■ 76/dsl/LP ⑪ Denny's, Dueling Irons Cafe, Fuki Japanese, Litt Caesar's, McDonald's, Old European Cafe, Rancho Viejo Mex can, Taco Bell, Timbers Rest. ⊙ Ace Hardware, O'Reilly Par TireRama, USPO, vet, Yoke's Foods
5	Lp 90, Spokane St, Treaty Rock HS, **N** ■ 76/dsl, Exxon/dsl Corner Cafe, Golden Dragon, Hunter's Rest., Papa John's, Rob Seafood/burgers, Subway, WhiteHouse Grill ⊙ AutoZone, Blu Dog RV Ctr, Meineke, Perfection Tire/repair, Schwab Tire, **S** Handy Mart/Pacific Pride/dsl ⌂ Red Lion Inn ⊙ visitors ctr
2	Pleasant View Rd, **N** ■ ⊕FLYING J/Conoco/Subway/dsl/LP scales/24hr, Exxon/dsl, ♥Loves/Carl's Jr/dsl/scales/24hr McDonald's, Toro Viejo Mexican ⌂ Sure Stay Inn+ ⊙ RV truckwash, Suntree RV Park, **S** ■ Exxon/dsl ⑪ Zip's Drive-⌂ Riverbend Inn, Sleep Inn ⊙ dogtrack
1	Beck Rd, **N** ⑪ Panda Express ⊙ Cabela's, Walmart/Subway, ⊙ greyhound track
0mm	Idaho/Washington state line

⁊E INTERSTATE 184 (Boise)

Exit #	Services
6mm	**I-184 begins/ends on 13th St**, downtown, ■ Shell ⑪ Bonefis Grill, Chandler's Steaks, Five Guys, PF Chang's ⌂ Hampton Inn Safari Inn, The Grove ⊙ Office Depot, USPO
5	River St (from eb), **W** ■ Chevron ⑪ McDonald's ⊙ Red Lion
4.5mm	Boise River
3	Fairview Ave, to US 20/26 E, **W** ⑪ Joe's Crabshack, Tepanyal Japanese ⌂ Boise Inn, Cottonwood Suites, Riverside Hotel ⊙ Commercial Tire
2	Curtis Rd, to Garden City, **E** ■ Shell ⊙ H
1 b a	Cole Rd, Franklin Rd, **E** ■ Chevron/Subway/dsl ⊙ Acur Chrysler/Dodge/Jeep, Honda, Jaguar, Land Rover, Mercede Volvo, **W** ■ Chevron/dsl, Sinclair/dsl ⑪ Applebee's, Cafe Ol Cafe Rio, Carl's Jr, Cheesecake Factory, Chick-fil-A, Chili's, Ch potle, Dave&Buster's, Fujiyama Japanese, Golden Corral, IHO Jalapeno's, McDonald's, Noodles&Co, Old Chicago Pizza, Oliv Garden, Port of Subs, Red Lobster, Red Robin, Rumbi Islan Grill, Shari's, Sizzler, Smash Burger, Starbucks, Wendy's ⌂ Car dlewood Suites, La Quinta, Residence Inn ⊙ AT&T, AT&T, Audi VW, Best Buy, Cabela's, Dick's, Dillard's, JC Penney, Kohl's, Ma cy's, Michael's, Old Navy, PetCo, Petsmart, REI, Ross, Target, T Maxx, Tuesday Morning, Verizon
0mm	I-184 begins/ends on I-84, exit 49.

NOTES

ILLINOIS

⬆E INTERSTATE 24

Exit #	Services
38mm	Illinois/Kentucky state line, Ohio River
37	US 45, Metropolis, **N Rs both lanes, full ♿ facilities, info, litter barrels, petwalk, 🛣, vending, S P** BP/dsl **¶** Bill's BBQ, China House, El Tequila, Huddle House, McDonald's, Pizza Hut, Sonic **⌂** Best Value Inn, Holiday Inn Express, Motel 6, Quality Inn, Super 8 **O H**, $General, Buick/Chrysler/Dodge/GMC/Jeep, camping, Chevrolet, Ft Massac SP, O'Reilly Parts, Plaza Tire, to Riverboat Casino
27	to New Columbia, Big Bay
16	IL 146, Vienna, **S P** BP/dsl, Citgo/dsl, FastStop **¶** DQ, McDonald's, Smokin Daddy's Grill, Subway, Vienna Diner **⌂** Hotel 7 **O** vet
14	US 45, Vienna, **S O** camping
7	to Goreville, Tunnel Hill, **N O** winery (7mi), **S O** camping, to Ferne Clyffe SP
1	I-57, N to Chicago, S to Memphis. **I-24 begins/ends on I-57, exit 44.**

⬆N INTERSTATE 39

Exit #	Services
122.5	**I-39 and I-90 run together into Wisconsin. See Illinois Interstate 90, exits 15mm-1.**
122b a	US 20 E, Harrison Ave, to Belvidere (last nb exit before **toll rd**), **W P** Fas Fuel/Subway/dsl, Mobil, Tesla EVC **¶** Arby's, Bergner's, Burger King, DQ, Granite City Rest., Lung Fung, Rosati's, Rosati's Pizza, Sonic, Taco Bell, TGIFriday's **O** Barnes&Noble, BMW, Buick/Chevrolet/GMC, Collier RV Ctr, Goodyear/auto, Harley-Davidson, JC Penney, Macy's, Menards, Schnuck's Foods/gas, Tires+, vet, VW, Walgreens
119	US 20 W, Alpine Rd, to Rockford
116.5mm	Kishwaukee River
115	Baxter Rd, **E P** Shell/Subway/dsl/scales/24hr/@
111	IL 72, to Monroe Center, **E P** BP/Sunrise Family Rest./dsl/24hr, Marathon (1mi)
104	IL 64, to Oregon, Sycamore, **W ¶** Grubsteakers Rest/truck parking (2mi)
99	IL 38, to De Kalb, Rochelle, **E P** [🚂]/dsl/scales/24hr, **0-2 mi W P** Murphy USA/dsl, Murphy USA/dsl, Petro/Iron Skillet/dsl/scales/RV Dump/@, Phillips 66/Circle K/dsl, Road Ranger/Subway/dsl/scales/24hr, Shell/dsl **¶** Arby's, Butterfly Rest, China Wok, Culver's, Dunkin', Jimmy John's, Little Caesar's, McDonald's, New China, Pizza Hut, Subway, Taco Bell, Wendy's **⌂** Comfort Inn, Country Hearth Inn, Holiday Inn Express, Super 8 **O H**, $General, $Tree, Blue Beacon, GNC, O'Reilly Parts, Sullivan's Foods, Verizon, Walgreens, Walmart
97b a	I-88 **tollway**, to Moline, Rock Island, Chicago
93	Steward
87	US 30, to Sterling, Rock Falls, **E O** to Shabbona Lake SP, **W O** Yogi Bear Camping (16mi)
84.5mm	**Rs both lanes, full ♿ facilities, litter barrels, petwalk, 🛣, playground, vending**
82	Paw Paw, **3 mi E P** Casey's (3mi), **W** many wind turbines
72	US 34, to Mendota, Earlville, **W P** BP/Cindy's/dsl/scales/24hr, Road Ranger/Subway/dsl/scales/24hr **¶** KFC/Taco Bell, McDonald's **⌂** Quality Inn, Super 8/truck parking **O H**
67.5mm	Little Vermilion River

66	US 52, Troy Grove, **E O** KOA (6mi)
62.5mm	Tomahawk Creek
59 a	I-80, E to Chicago, W to Des Moines
57	US 6, to Peru, La Salle, **1-2 mi W P** Casey's **⌂** Daniel's Motel **O** city park
56mm	Illinois River, Abraham Lincoln Mem Bridge
54	Oglesby, **E P** BP/dsl, Casey's, Phillips 66/dsl, Shell **¶** Burger King, Delaney's Rest., KFC/Taco Bell, McDonald's, Root Beer Stand, Subway **⌂** Best Western, Days Inn **O** Starved Rock SP, **W P** ❤Loves/Hardee's/dsl/scales/24hr
52	IL 251, to La Salle, Peru
51	IL 71, to Hennepin, Oglesby
48	Tonica, **E P** Casey's **O** city park
41	IL 18, to Streator, Henry
35	IL 17, to Wenona, Lacon, **E P** BP/dsl, Casey's (2mi), Shell/Burger King/dsl/RV dump **¶** Subway **⌂** Best Value Inn/truck parking
27	to Minonk, **E P** Casey's (2mi), Road Ranger/Subway/Woody's Rest./dsl/24hr **⌂** Motel 6 **O** NAPA
22	IL 116, to Peoria, Benson
14	US 24, to El Paso, Peoria, **E P** BP/Subway/dsl/24hr, Casey's/dsl, Freedom/dsl **¶** DQ, Hardee's, McDonald's, Woody's Family Rest. **⌂** Days Inn **O** Buick/Chevrolet/GMC, city park, Ford, IGA Foods, USPO, **W ¶** Monical's Pizza **⌂** Super 8 **O** $General, Hickory Hill Camping (4mi), PROMPT CARE
9mm	Mackinaw River
8	IL 251, Lake Bloomington Rd, **E O** Lake Bloomington, **W O** Evergreen Lake, to Comlara Park
5	Hudson, **1 mi E P** Casey's/dsl
2	US 51 bus, Bloomington, Normal
0mm	**I-39 begins/ends on I-55, exit 164.**

= gas ☐ = food ⌂ = lodging ◉ = other Ⓡˢ = rest stop   Copyright 2022 - The Next EXIT ®

INTERSTATE 55

CHICAGO AREA

Exit #	Services
295mm	I-55 begins/ends on US 41, Lakeshore Dr, in Chicago.
293a	to Cermak Rd (from nb)
292	I-90/94, W to Chicago, E to Indiana
290	Damen Ave, Ashland Ave (no EZ nb return), E 🅖 Marathon, Shell ☐ Starbucks ◉ Target
289	to California Ave (no EZ nb return), E 🅖 Marathon, Road Ranger/Subway/dsl, Thornton's/dsl
288	Kedzie Ave, (from sb no ez return), E 🅖 Citgo
287	Pulaski Rd, E 🅖 BP/dsl, Shell ☐ Burger King, Domino's, Dunkin', Subway, Wendy's ◉ Advance Parts, Aldi Foods, AT&T, Dodge, Honda, Marshall's, Michael's, Pete's Mkt, Petsmart, Ross, Target, Walgreens
286	IL 50, Cicero Ave, E 🅖 BP, Mobil/dsl, Shell/dsl ☐ Dunkin', McDonald's, Starbucks, Subway ◉ AutoZone, O'Reilly Parts, to 🅡ˢ
285	Central Ave, E 🅖 BP/dsl, Grand Prix/Dunkin', Minuteman/Dunkin' ☐ Burger King, Donald's HotDogs
283	IL 43, Harlem Ave, E 🅖 Shell ☐ Baskin-Robbins/Dunkin', Burger King, Domino's, Little Caesar's, Portillo HotDogs, Potbelly's, Subway ◉ Aldi Foods, AT&T, AutoZone, Fannie May Candies, Walgreens
282b a	IL 171, 1st Ave, W ◉ Brookfield Zoo
279b	US 12, US 20, US 45, La Grange Rd, 0-2 mi W 🅖 BP, Mobil, Shell, Circle K ☐ Andy's Custard, Applebee's, Arby's, Baskin-Robbins/Dunkin', Boston Mkt, Burger King, Chick-fil-A, Cocula Rest., Dragon Buffet, Dunkin', Hooters, JC Georges Rest., Jimmy John's, Ledo's Pizza, LoneStar Steaks, McDonald's, Nonno's Pizza, Panda Express, Pizza Hut, Popeye's, Starbucks, Subway, Taco Bell, Taco Tico, Time Out Grill, TX Roadhouse, Via Bella, Wendy's, White Castle ⌂ Best Western+, Holiday Inn ◉ $Tree, Aldi Foods, Best Buy, Buick/Cadillac/GMC, Chevrolet, Chrysler/Dodge/Jeep, Discount Tire, Firestone/auto, Ford, GNC, Harley Davidson, Home Depot, Honda, Jo-Ann Fabrics, Kohl's, Mazda, Menards, NAPA, Nissan, NTB, O'Reilly Parts, PepBoys, PetCo, Petsmart, Sam's Club/gas, Subaru, Target, Toyota, Verizon, VW, Walmart
279a	La Grange Rd, to I-294 toll, S to Indiana
277b	I-294 toll (from nb), S to Indiana
277a	I-294 toll, N to Wisconsin
276c	Joliet Rd (from nb)
276b a	County Line Rd, E ☐ Capri Rest., China King, Ciazza's Grill, Cooper's Hawk, Eddie Merlot's, Patti's Sunrise Cafe, Starbucks, Subway, Topaz Rest. ⌂ Extended Stay America, Marriott, Quality Inn ◉ Tuesday Morning, W ⌂ SpringHill Suites
274	IL 83, Kingery Rd, E 🅖 Shell, W 🅖 BP/dsl, Mobil/dsl, Shell ☐ Bakers Square, Buffalo Wild Wings, Chick-fil-A, Chipotle Mexican, Denny's, Dunkin', Jamba Juice, Jimmy John's, MOD Pizza, Panera Bread, Papa John's, Patio BBQ, Portillo's HotDogs, Potbelly's Rest., Starbucks, Wendy's ⌂ Econolodge, Holiday Inn, La Quinta, Red Roof Inn ◉ Ford/KIA, GNC, Marshall's, Marshall's, Michael's, Staples, Target, Verizon
273b a	Cass Ave, W 🅖 Shell ☐ Al Chile Mexican, Chuck's Rest., Rosati's Pizza, Uncle Mao's Chinese
271b a	Lemont Rd, E ⌂ Extended Stay America, W 🅖 Shell
269	I-355 toll, to W Suburbs
268	(from sb only), Joliet, same as 267
267	IL 53, Bolingbrook, E 🅖 55 Trkstp/rest./dsl/scales/24hr/@, BP/dsl ☐ McDonald's ⌂ Ramada Ltd, Super 8 ◉ Chevrolet, W 🅖 Shell/Circle K, Speedway/dsl ☐ Burger King, Cheddar's, Denny's, Dunkin', El Burrito Loco, Family Square Rest., Golden Chopsticks, Golden Corral, McDonald's, Popeye's, Starbucks, Subway, Wendy's, White Castle ⌂ Hampton Inn, Hilton Garden,

BOLINGBROOK

JOLIET

Exit #	Services
267	Continued Holiday Inn, Quality Inn, Residence Inn, SpringHill Suites ◉ $Tree, Aldi Foods, Fiesta Mkt, NAPA, Tony's Mkt, U-Haul, Walgreens, Walmart
266mm	weigh sta both lanes
263	Weber Rd, E 🅖 7-11, BP/dsl, Speedway/Dunkin'/dsl/e85 ☐ Burger King, Burrito's, Culver's, Doc Watson's Smokehouse, KFC, Little China, McDonald's, Michael's Pizza, Popeye's, Subway, Todake Steaks, White Castle ⌂ Days Inn, Holiday Inn Express ◉ Ace Hardware, BB Rest., Discount Tire, GNC, Reba's Automotive, Walgreens, W 🅖 Mobil/Jimmy John's/dsl, Shell ☐ Circle K ☐ Arby's, Cracker Barrel, Wendy's ⌂ Comfort Inn, Country Inn&Suites, Extended Stay America, Woodspring Suites
261	IL 126 (from sb), to Plainfield
257	US 30, to Joliet, Aurora, E 🅖 Shell/Circle K ☐ Anthony's Rest. Applebee's, Baskin-Robbins/Dunkin', Burger King, Chipotle, ChuckeCheese, Denny's, Diamand's Rest., Five Guys, Fresh Thyme Mkt, Hooters, LoneStar Steaks, McDonald's, Outback Steaks, Panera Bread, Red Lobster, Steak'n Shake, Subway, Taco Bell, TGIFriday's, TX Roadhouse, Wendy's ⌂ Best Western+, Comfort Inn, Fairfield Inn, Hampton Inn, Home 2 Suites Motel 6, Super 8 ◉ $Tree, Aldi Foods, AT&T, AutoZone Barnes&Noble, Best Buy, Dick's, Discount Tire, Firestone/auto Home Depot, Honda, JC Penney, Jo-Ann Fabrics, Macy's, Michael's, NTB, Old Navy, Petsmart, Ross, Target, Verizon, W 🅖 Mobil/dsl ☐ Blue's BBQ, Luigi's Pizza ◉ Chevrolet, Ford
253b a	US 52, Jefferson St, Joliet, E 🅖 Citgo/dsl, Mobil/dsl, Shell ☐ Joe's Rest., McDonald's ⌂ Best Western, Econolodge, Elk's Motel, La Quinta, Wingate Inn ◉ Ⓗ, 🅡ˢ, Ford, Freedom Automotive, Freightliner, Harley-Davidson, Rick's RV Ctr, W 🅖 BP/dsl Shell ☐ Burger King, Casa Maya, DQ, Rosati's Pizza, Starbucks Subway ◉ 7-11, Chrysler/Dodge/Jeep, Jewel-Osco, vet
251	IL 59 (from nb), to Shorewood, access to same as 253 W
250b a	I-80, W to Iowa, E to Toledo
248	US 6, Joliet, E 🅖 ☐ ▦/Dunkin'/Subway/dsl/24hr, Speedway dsl ☐ Taco Burrito King, W 🅖 BP/McDonald's, Thornton's/dsl scales
247	Bluff Rd
245mm	Des Plaines River
244	Arsenal Rd, E ◉ Exxon/Mobil Refinery
241	to Wilmington
241mm	Kankakee River
240	Lorenzo Rd, E 🅖 BP/dsl, W 🅖 Mobil/pizza/dsl/scales/24hr, Petro/Shell/Iron Skillet/dsl/scales/24hr/@ ⌂ Knights Inn
238	IL 129 S, to Wilmington (from nb), Braidwood
236	IL 113, Coal City, E ◉ EZ Living RV Ctr, Fossil Rock Camping, W 🅖 Casey's, Shell/DQ/dsl ☐ KFC/Taco Bell, Little Caesar's, Lo 3 Burritos, WhistleStop Cafe
233	Reed Rd, E 🅖 Marathon/dsl ☐ Jones-sez BBQ
227	IL 53, Gardner, E 🅖 Casey's ☐ Gardner Rest., Subway ◉ $General, truck/tire repair, W 🅖 BP/dsl
220	IL 47, Dwight, E 🅖 BP/Burger King/dsl, Loves/Hardee's dsl/scales/24hr, Marathon/Circle K/dsl/24hr ☐ Arby's, Dwight Chinese, Dwight Pizza, McDonald's, Pete's Rest., Subway ⌂ Classic Motel, Super 8
217	IL 17, Dwight, E 🅖 Casey's, Shell/Circle K/dsl/24hr ☐ DQ, Rt 66 Rest. ◉ Ace Hardware, CVS Drug, Family$, NAPA, ShopKO
213mm	Mazon River
209	Odell, E 🅖 ◉ USPO
201	IL 23, Pontiac, 0-3 mi E ☐ DQ, La Mex ◉ 4H RV Camp (seasonal) RV Ctr, Pontiac RV Ctr, W ◉ truck repair
198mm	Vermilion River

⬆N INTERSTATE 55 Cont'd

Exit #	Services
197	IL 116, Pontiac, E 📶 BP/dsl, Shell/dsl, Thornton's/dsl 🍴 Arby's, Baby Bull's Rest., Burger King, Cafe Fontana, Dunkin', KFC, LJ Silver, McDonald's, Monical's Pizza, Pizza Hut, Subway, Taco Bell, Wendy's 🛏 Best Western, Hampton Inn, Quality Inn, Super 8 🅾 $General, $Tree, Advance Parts, Aldi Foods, AT&T, AutoZone, Big R Store, Buick/Chevrolet/Cadillac/GMC, Chrysler/Dodge/Jeep/Lincoln, Firestone/auto, Lincoln, Verizon, Walgreens, Walmart/Subway, W 🍴 Mobil/dsl 🅾H
193mm	🅿️ both lanes, full 🚻 facilities, litter barrels, petwalk, 🅲, 🛢, vending
187	US 24, Chenoa, E 📶 Casey's/dsl, Phillips 66/McDonald's/dsl, Shell/Subway/dsl 🍴 Best Value Inn, Chenoa Family Rest.
179mm	Des Plaines River
178	Lexington, E 📶 BP/McDonalds/dsl, Freedom/dsl 🍴 Subway 🅾 $General, W 🅾 Chevrolet
178mm	Mackinaw River
171	Towanda, E 📶 FastStop/dsl
167	Lp 55 S Veterans Pkwy, to Normal, 0-3 mi E 📶 BP/Circle K, Marathon/Circle K/dsl 🍴 Alexander's Steaks, Applebee's, Bandana's BBQ, Biaggi's Ristorante, Bob Evans, Burger King, Carlos O'Kelly's, Chick-fil-A, Chili's, Chipotle Mexican, ChuckeCheese, Coldstone, Destihl Rest., DQ, Fazoli's, Fiesta Ranchera Mexican, FlatTop Grill, Hardee's, IHOP, Jason's Deli, Jimmy John's, Jimmy John's (2), Krispy Kreme, Logan's Roadhouse, Lonestar Steaks, McDonald's, Monical's Pizza, Noodles&Co, Olive Garden, Outback Steaks, Panda Express, Panera Bread, Papa John's, Pizza Hut, Pizza Ranch, Popeye's, Portillo's, Potbelly, Qdoba Mexican, Red Lobster, Red Robin, Schlotzsky's, Smashburger, Sonic, Starbucks, Steak'n Shake, Subway, Taco Bell, Tony Roma's, Wendy's, Wild Berries Rest. 🛏 Baymont Inn, Candlewood Suites, Chateau, Comfort Suites, Courtyard, Hampton Inn, Holiday Inn Express, Motel 6, Quality Inn, Super 8 🅾H, $Tree, Advance Parts, Aldi Foods, AT&T, AutoZone, Barnes&Noble, Best Buy, CVS Drug, Dick's, Fresh Mkt, GNC, Goodyear/auto, Gordman's, Hobby Lobby, Home Depot, Honda, Hyundai, HyVee, Jewel-Osco, Jo-Ann Fabrics, Kohl's, Kroger/dsl, Lowe's, Meijer/dsl, Meineke, Menards, Michael's, Midas, Office Depot, Old Navy, O'Reilly Parts, PetCo, Sam's Club/gas, Schnuck's Foods, Target, TJ Maxx, to 🛢, Tuesday Morning, Tuffy, Verizon, Von Maur, Walgreens, Walmart/Subway
165 b a	US 51 bus, to Bloomington, E 📶 BP/Circle K, Mobil/Arby's/dsl, Qik-n-EZ, Shell/Burger King/dsl 🍴 Denny's, Dunkin', McDonald's, Moe's SW Grill, Rosati's Pizza, Smoothie King, Starbucks, Steak'n Shake, Subway, Uncle Tom's Pancakes, Wendy's 🛏 Baymont Inn, Motel 6, Radisson, Super 8 🅾H, $General, $Tree, Discount Tire, Schnuck's Foods, to Ill St U, Verizon, Walgreens, W 🅾 dsl repair
164	I-39, US 51, N to Peru
163	I-74 W, to Peoria
160 b a	US 150, IL 9, Market St, Bloomington, E 📶 BP/Circle K, Freedom/dsl, 🛢/Wendy's/dsl/scales/24hr, Shell/repair, TA/Country Pride/dsl/scales/24hr/@ 🍴 Arby's, Cracker Barrel, Culver's, KFC, McDonald's, Popeye's, Subway, Taco Bell 🛏 Days Inn, EconoLodge, Hawthorn Suites, Quality Inn, Quality Suites, Red Roof Inn 🅾H, Advance Parts, Blue Beacon, Family$, Peterbilt, W 🍴 Marathon/Circle K/dsl, Murphy USA/dsl 🍴 Bob Evans, Fiesta Ranchera Mexican, Steak'n Shake/24hr 🛏 Comfort Suites, Country Inn&Suites, Fairfield Inn, Hampton Inn, Holiday Inn Express, Ramada Ltd 🅾 Aldi Foods, Farm&Fleet, Walmart
157b	Lp 55 N, Veterans Pkwy, Bloomington, E 🅾H, to 🛢
157a	I-74 E, to Indianapolis, US 51 to Decatur
154	Shirley

149	W 🅿️ both lanes, full 🚻 facilities, litter barrels, petwalk, 🅲, 🛢, playground, vending
145	US 136, E 🅾 Quality RV Ctr, W 🍴 Dixie/Road Ranger/Subway/dsl/scales/24hr, Mobil/dsl 🍴 McDonald's, Rte 66 Drive Thru 🛏 Super 8
140	Atlanta, E 🅾 RV camping (3mi), W 📶 Casey's/dsl 🍴 Country-Aire Rest. 🛏 Atlanta Inn 🅾 $General, NAPA
133	Lp 55, Lincoln, 2 mi E 🅾H, Camp-A-While Camping
127	I-155 N, to Peoria
126	IL 10, IL 121 S, Lincoln, 0-2 mi E 📶 BP/Arby's/dsl/24hr, Casey's/dsl, Thornton's/🛢/dsl/scales/24hr 🍴 Bonanza Steaks, Burger King, Cracker Barrel, Culver's, Daphne's Rest., DQ, Dunkin', El Mazatlan Mexican, Hardee's, McDonald's, Pizza Hut, Rio Grande Grill, Steak'n Shake, Subway, Taco Bell, Wendy's 🛏 EconoLodge, Hampton Inn, Holiday Inn Express, Super 8 🅾H, $General, $Tree, Aldi Foods, AT&T, AutoZone, Chrysler/Dodge/Jeep, CVS Drug, Ford/Lincoln, Kroger, O'Reilly Parts, Russell Stover, Verizon, Walgreens, Walmart/Subway
123	Lp 55, to Lincoln, E 🅾H
119	Broadwell
115	Elkhart
109	IL 123, Williamsville, E 📶 Casey's 🍴 Subway, W 🍴 Loves/McDonalds/dsl/scales/24hr 🍴 Huddle House 🅾 New Salem SHS
107mm	weigh sta sb
105	Lp 55, to Sherman, W 📶 Casey's 🍴 Cancun Mexican, China King, Fairlane Diner, Fire&Ale Grill, Ricco's Pizza, Sam's Too Pizza, Subway 🅾 Conv Ctr, County Mkt Foods, hist sites, Military Museum, repair, Riverside Park Campground, Verizon, vet, Walgreens
103mm	🅿️ sb, full 🚻 facilities, litter barrels, petwalk, 🅲, 🛢, vending
102mm	Sangamon River
102mm	🅿️ nb, full 🚻 facilities, litter barrels, petwalk, 🅲, 🛢, vending
100b	IL 54, Sangamon Ave, Springfield, W 📶 BP/Circle K, Marathon/Circle K, Murphy USA/dsl, Shell/dsl 🍴 Arby's, Buffalo Wild Wings, Burger King, Culver's, DQ, Hickory River BBQ, Jimmy John's, McDonald's, Panda Express, Parkway Cafe, Penn Sta Subs, Sonic, Steak'n Shake, Taco Bell, Thai Basil, Wendy's, Wings Etc, Xochimilco Mexican, Yummy House 🛏 Northfield Suites, Ramada 🅾 🛢, Aldi Foods, AT&T, GNC, Harley-Davidson, Lowe's, Menards, to Vet Mem, Verizon, Walmart/Subway
100a	IL 54, E to Clinton, E 📶 Road Ranger/Subway/dsl/scales/24hr 🅾 Kenworth/Ryder/Volvo, truckwash
98b	I-72, IL 97, Springfield, W 📶 Casey's, Circle K, Shell/dsl 🍴 Chesapeake Seafood House, Freddy's, Hardee's, Mario's Pizza, McDonald's, Starbucks, Subway 🛏 Best Western, Lincoln's Lodge 🅾H, city park, Ford Trucks, to Capitol Complex, Walgreens
98a	I-72 E, US 36 E, to Decatur
96 b a	IL 29 N, S Grand Ave, Springfield, W 📶 Marathon/dsl 🍴 Godfather's, Popeye's 🛏 Red Roof Inn, Super 8 🅾 $General, Advance Parts, AutoZone, Buick/GMC, County Mkt, Hyundai, JC Penney, museum, O'Reilly Parts

INTERSTATE 55 Cont'd

Exit #	Services
94	Stevenson Dr, Springfield, **E** KOA (7mi), **W** 🅖 Circle K/dsl, Shell/dsl, Subway 🍴 Applebee's, Arby's, Blue Margaritas, Bob Evans, Cancun Mexican, Dew Chili, Gallina Pizza, Hardee's, Hooters, IHOP, La Fiesta Mexican, LJ Silver, McAlister's Deli, McDonald's, Panera Bread, Papa John's, Red Lobster, Smokey Bones BBQ, Steak'n Shake, Taste of Thai 🏠 Candlewood Suites, Comfort Suites, Country Inn Suites, Crowne Plaza, Drury Inn, Hilton Garden, Holiday Inn Express, Microtel, Residence Inn, Wingate Inn 🅞 $General, auto repair, BigLots, CVS Drug, GNC, Walgreens
92b a	I-72 W, US 36 W, 6th St, Springfield, **W** 🅖 Marathon/dsl, Thornton's 🍴 Arby's, Burger King, Chadito's Tacos, Cozy Drive In, Golden Corral, Jimmy John's, KFC, Marco's Pizza, McDonald's, Pizza Hut, Pizza Ranch, Sgt. Pepper's Cafe, Starbucks, Subway, Taco Bell 🏠 Comfort Inn, La Quinta, Route 66 🅞 🏥 Aldi, AT&T, AutoZone, CarX, County Mkt Foods, Mazda, Walgreens, Walmart/McDonald's
90	Toronto Rd, **E** 🅖 Qik-n-EZ/Wendy's/dsl, Shell/Circle K 🍴 Antonio's Pizza, China Express, Cracker Barrel, Head West Subs, Hen House, McDonald's, Subway, Taco Bell 🏠 Baymont Inn, Day's Inn, Motel 6, **W** 🅖 Road Ranger/dsl/24hr
89mm	Lake Springfield
88	E Lake Dr, Chatham, **E** 🅞 KOA, to Lincoln Mem Garden/Nature Ctr, **W** 🅞 JJ RV Park/camping (2mi)
83	Glenarm, **W** 🅞 JJ RV Park/camping (4mi)
82	IL 104, to Pawnee, **E** 🅞 to Sangchris Lake SP, **W** 🅖 Mobil/Auburn Trvl Ctr/Subway/scales/dsl/rest/24hr 🍴 Toni's Cafe 🅞 antiques/crafts
80	Hist 66, Divernon, **W** 🅞 antiques
72	Farmersville, **W** 🅖 Phillips 66/Subway/dsl/24hr, Shell
65mm	🆁🆂 both lanes, full ♿ facilities, litter barrels, petwalk, 🚰, 🏞, playground, vending
63	IL 48, IL 127, to Raymond
60	IL 108, to Carlinville, **E** 🅞 Kamper Kampanion RV Park, **W** 🅖 Shell/dsl/LP/café 🏠 Magnuson Grand Hotel/café 🅞 antiques, to Blackburn Coll
56mm	weigh sta nb
52	IL 16, Hist 66, Litchfield, **E** 🅖 BP, Casey's, Faststop/deli/dsl/scales, Murphy USA/dsl, Phillips 66/Jack-in-the-Box/dsl, Shell 🍴 A&W/LJ Silver, Arby's, Ariston Café, Burger King, China Town, Denny's, DQ, El Rancherito Mexican, Huddle House, Jimmy John's, Jubelt's Rest., KFC, Maverick Steaks, McDonald's, Pizza Hut, Ruby Tuesday, Subway, Taco Bell, Wendy's 🏠 Best Value Inn, Hampton Inn, Holiday Inn Express, Quality Inn, Super 8 🅞 🏥 $General, $Tree, Aldi Foods, AT&T, Buick/Cadillac/Chevrolet/GMC, Ford, Goodyear/auto, IGA Foods, NAPA, O'Reilly Parts, Rte 66 Museum, Verizon, vet, Walgreens, Walmart/Subway, **W** 🅞 st police
44	IL 138, to Benld, Mt Olive, **E** 🍴 Crossroads Diner, Rte 138 Cafe 🅞 Mother Jones Mon
41	to Staunton, **E** 🅞 Country Classic Cars, **W** 🅖 Casey's 🍴 DQ 🏠 Super 8 🅞 🏥 $General, Chrysler/Dodge/Jeep
37	Livingston, New Douglas, **W** 🅖 Shell/dsl 🍴 Gasperoni's Café 🏠 Country Inn/cafe 🅞 AutoCare, IGA Foods, USPO
33	IL 4, to Staunton, Worden
30	IL 140, Hamel, **E** 🅖 ❤Loves❤/McDonald's/Subway/dsl/scales/24hr 🏠 Innkeeper Motel, **W** 🅖 Shell 🍴 Weezy's Grill
28mm	🆁🆂 both lanes, full ♿ facilities, litter barrels, petwalk, 🚰, 🏞, vending
23	IL 143, Edwardsville, **E** 🅖 Phillips 66/dsl
20b	I-270 W, to Kansas City

Exit #	Services
20a	I-70 E, to Indianapolis
I-55 S and I-70 W run together 18 mi.	
18	IL 162, to Troy, **E** 🅖 Casey's/dsl, Phillips 66/Circle K/dsl, Pilot/Arby's/dsl/scales/24hr, TA/BP/Country Pride/dsl/scales/24hr/@ ZX 🍴 Alfonzo's Pizza, Burger King, China King, Domino's, DQ, Dunkin', El Potro Mexican, Jack-in-the-Box, Little Caesar's, McDonald's, Pizza Hut, Subway 🅞 🏥 $General, Ace Hardware, O'Reilly Parts, Schuette's Mkt, Speedco, truckwash, USPO, vet, Walgreens, **W** 🍴 Cracker Barrel, Fire'n Smoke Kitchen, Joe's Pizza, Taco Bell 🏠 Best Western, Holiday Inn Express, Motel 6, Red Roof Inn, Super 8 🅞 Freightliner, Verizon
17	US 40 E, to Troy, to St Jacob
15b a	IL 159, Maryville, Collinsville, 0-2 mi **E** 🅖 Phillips 66/Circle K/dsl, VP/dsl, Zx Gas 🍴 Asia Garden, Carisillo's Mexican, KFC, McDonald's, Sonic, Subway 🅞 $General, Advance Parts, Aldi Foods, AutoZone, CVS Drug, Ford/Lincoln, O'Reilly Parts, vet, Walgreens, **W** 🏠 Loyalty Inn
14mm	weigh sta sb
11	IL 157, Collinsville, **E** 🅖 Casey's 🍴 A&W/LJ Silver, Denny's, Golden Corral, Little Caesar's, McDonald's, Penn Sta Subs, Qdoba Mexican, St Louis Bread Co, Starbucks, Waffle House, Wendy's 🏠 Best Value Inn 🅞 AT&T, Dobbs Tire, Gateway RV Ctr, GNC, Home Depot, Midas, Verizon, Walgreens, Walmart, Subway, **W** 🅖 Motomart/dsl/24hr 🍴 Applebee's, Arby's, Bandana's BBQ, Bob Evans, Burger King, Colton's Steaks, Culver's, DQ, Jimmy John's, Pizza Hut, Porter's Steaks, Ruby Tuesday, Steak'n Shake, White Castle/24hr, Zapata's Mexican 🏠 Comfort Inn, Days Inn, DoubleTree Inn, Drury Inn, Fairfield Inn, Hampton Inn, La Quinta, Super 8 🅞 Buick/GMC, st police
10	I-255, S to Memphis, N to I-270
9	Black Lane (from nb, no return), **E** Fairmount RaceTrack
6	IL 111, Great River Rd, Fairmont City, **E** 🅖 Exxon 🏠 Relax Inn, Royal Budget Inn 🅞 auto repair, **W** 🅞 Horseshoe SP
4b a	IL 203, Granite City, **E** 🅖 BP/dsl 🏠 Western Inn, **W** 🅖 Pilot/Subway/Taco Bell/dsl/scales/24hr/@ 🅞 Gateway Int Raceway
3c	Exchange Ave
3b	I-70 W, to KC
3a	I-64 E, IL 3 N, St Clair Ave
2b	3rd St
2a	M L King Bridge, to downtown E St Louis
1	IL 3, to Sauget (from sb)
I-55 N and I-70 E run together 18 mi.	
0mm	Illinois/Missouri state line, Mississippi River

INTERSTATE 57

Exit #	Services
358mm	I-94 E to Indiana, **I-57 begins/ends on I-94, exit 63 in Chicago.**
357	IL 1, Halsted St, **E** 🅖 BP, Gulf/dsl 🅞 auto repair, **W** 🅖 Shell, Dunkin', Supersave 🍴 McDonald's, Shark's
355	111th St, Monterey Ave, **W** 🅖 BP, Citgo
354	119th St, **W** 🅖 Citgo/Dunkin' 🍴 Chili's, Panda Express, Subway 🅞 $Tree, AT&T, GNC, Jewel-Osco, PetCo, Pizza Hut
353	127th St, Burr Oak Ave, **E** 🅖 Citgo, GoLo, Shell 🍴 Burger King, Dillinger's Drive-In, Dunkin', McDonald's, Wendy's 🏠 Days Inn, M Hotel, Plaza Inn 🅞 Ace Hardware, Advance Parts, Family$, Walgreens, **W** 🅖 BP, Citgo/dsl 🍴 Egg Shack 🅞 🏥 J, Fish&Chicken
352mm	Calumet Sag Channel
350	IL 83, 147th St, Sibley Blvd, **E** 🅖 Marathon/dsl 🍴 Checkers, Domino's, Harold's Chicken, McDonald's, Subway 🅞 $General, Aldi Foods, Family$, O'Reilly Parts, **W** 🅞 USPO
349	I-294 (from nb)

INTERSTATE 57 Cont'd

Exit #	Services
348	US 6, 159th St, **E** 🅿 BP/dsl, Clark, Marathon/dsl 🍴 Baskin-Robbins/Dunkin', Burger King, McDonald's, Popeye's, Subway, Taco Bell, White Castle 🅾 $Tree, AutoZone, U-Haul, **W** 🅿 Shell/dsl
346	167th St, Cicero Ave, to IL 50, **E** 🅿 BP, Shell/dsl, Tesla EVC 🍴 Baskin-Robbins/Dunkin', Harold's Chicken, Kenny's Ribs, McDonald's, Panda Express, Pizza Hut, Shark's Fish&Chicken, Sonic, Starbucks, Wendy's 🏨 Best Western 🅾 GNC, Walmart/Subway, **W** 🅿 Shell 🅾 7-11
345b a	I-80, W to Iowa, E to Indiana, to I-294 **N toll** to Wisconsin
342	Vollmer Rd, **E** 🅿 Shell/Circle K/dsl 🅾 🅷
340b a	US 30, Lincoln Hwy, Matteson, **E** 🅿 BP, Marathon/dsl 🍴 A Fusion Asian, A&W/LJ Silver, Bar Louie, Bocce's Grill, Burger King, Chipotle, ChuckeCheese, Culver's, Dunkin', Dusties Buffet, Five Guys, Fuddrucker's, Giordano's, Harold's Chicken, IHOP, Jimmy John's, KFC, McDonald's, Olive Garden, Panda Express, Panera Bread, Pepe's, Perros Bros Gyros, Pizza Hut, Potbelly, Red Lobster, Rosati's, Shark's, Starbucks, Subway, White Castle 🏨 Comfort Inn, Country Inn&Suites, Hampton Inn, Holiday Inn, Quality Inn 🅾 $Tree, Aldi Foods, Best Buy, Chrysler/Dodge/Jeep, Discount Tire, Firestone/auto, GNC, Home Depot, JC Penney, Marshall's, Menards, NTB, PepBoys, Petsmart, Ross, USPO, Verizon, Walgreens, **W** 🅾 Buick/Cadillac/GMC, Ford/Lincoln, Honda, Hyundai, Kia, Nissan, Toyota, Walgreens
339	Sauk Trail, to Richton Park, **E** 🅿 BP/dsl, Marathon/dsl 🍴 Blue Sharks, Domino's, McDonald's 🅾 Family$, Walgreens, **W** 🅾 Walmart/dsl
337	Stuenkel Rd
335	Monee, **E** 🅿 BP/Dunkin'/Subway/dsl, Petro/Iron Skillet/dsl/e85/scales/24hr/@, 🄿🄸🄻🄾🄲/McDonald's/dsl/scales/24hr 🍴 Burger King, Culver's, KFC/Taco Bell, Lucky Burrito, Pizza Hut, Schoops Rest. 🏨 Country Host Motel, Quality Inn, Red Roof Inn, Super 8 🅾 Advance Parts, Blue Beacon
332mm	**Prairie View Rest Area both lanes, full** ♿ **facilities, info, litter barrels, petwalk,** 🚻, 🛢, **vending**
330mm	**weigh sta both lanes**
327	to Peotone, **E** 🅿 Casey's, Circle K 🍴 McDonald's/RV parking
322	Manteno, **E** 🅿 BP/McDonald's/dsl, Casey's/dsl, Phillips 66/Subway 🍴 DQ, Jimmy John's, KFC/Taco Bell, Monical's Pizza, Pizza Hut, Wendy's 🏨 Country Inn&Suites, Howard Johnson 🅾 Harley-Davidson, vet, **W** 🅿 BP/Dunkin'/dsl
320	E. 6000N Rd
315	IL 50, Bradley, **E** 🅿 Circle K/Burger King, EVC, F&F 🍴 Buffalo Wild Wings, Chipotle, Cracker Barrel, Firehouse Subs, Five Guys, Jimmy John's, KanSai Japanese, McDonald's, Noodles&Co, Olive Garden, Panera Bread, Red Lobster, Starbucks, Taco Bell, TGIFriday's, Tucci's Rest., White Castle 🏨 Comfort Inn, Fairfield Inn, Hampton Inn, Holiday Inn Express, Magnuson 🅾 Aldi, AT&T, Barnes&Noble, Best Buy, Chrysler/Dodge/Jeep, Dick's, Discount Tire, GNC, JC Penney, Kohl's, Marshall's, Michael's, PetCo, Petsmart, Ross, Staples, Target, Verizon, Walmart/Subway, **W** 🅿 BP/dsl, Circle K/dsl, CircleK/dsl, Speedway/dsl 🍴 Applebee's, Arby's, Bakers Square, Checkers, Coyote Canyon, Denny's, IHOP, Mancino's Pizza, McDonald's, Oberweis Ice Cream, Panda Express, Steak'n Shake, Subway, Texas Roadhouse, Wendy's 🏨 Quality Inn, Super 8 🅾 $Tree, AT&T, Bradley RV Ctr, Buick/GMC, Chevrolet, Hobby Lobby, Honda, Hyundai, Jo-Ann Fabrics, Kia, Lowe's, Menards, Nissan, O'Reilly, to Kankakee River SP, URGENT CARE, Verizon, vet
312	IL 17, Kankakee, **W** 🅿 BP/dsl, Circle K, Marathon/dsl 🍴 McDonald's, PoorBoy Rest. 🅾 🅷, $ General, Advance Parts, Family$

310.5mm	Kankakee River
308	US 45, US 52, to Kankakee, **E** 🍴 ♥Love's/Arby's/dsl/scales/24hr 🅾 🍴, KOA (3mi), **W** 🅿 Murphy USA, Speedway/Dunkin'/Subway/dsl 🍴 El Mexicano, KFC/Taco Bell 🏨 Fairview Motel, Hilton Garden 🅾 $Tree, Aldi Foods, Walmart/Subway
302	Chebanse, **W** 🅾 truck repair
297	Clifton, **W** 🅿 Phillips 66/Circle K/DQ/dsl 🅾 $General
293	IL 116, Ashkum, **E** 🅿 BP/Subway/dsl 🅾 st police, tires, **W** 🍴 Beans and Barley
283	US 24, IL 54, Gilman, **E** 🍴 K&H Trkstp/BP/dsl/scales/24hr/@, Mobil/dsl, 🄿🄸🄻🄾🄲/Denny's/dsl/scales/24hr 🍴 Burger King, DQ, McDonald's, Monical's Pizza 🏨 Motel 6, Super 8, **W** 🅿 BP/dsl
280	IL 54, Onarga, **E** 🅿 Casey's, Phillips 66 🅾 USPO, **W** 🅾 Lake Arrowhead RV camping
272	to Roberts, Buckley
268.5mm	℞ₛ **both lanes, full** ♿ **facilities, litter barrels, petwalk,** 🚻, 🛢, **vending**
261	IL 9, Paxton, 0-1 mi **E** 🅿 Casey's, Phillips 66/dsl 🍴 Hardee's, Monical's Pizza, Pizza Palace, Subway 🅾 Buick/Cadillac/Chevrolet/GMC, IGA Foods, NAPA, TrueValue, USPO, **W** 🅿 Phillips/dsl 🍴 Country House Rest. 🏨 Cobblestone Inn, Paxton Inn
250	US 136, Rantoul, 0-1 mi **E** 🅿 BP/Circle K, Casey's/dsl, Circle K/dsl 🍴 Arby's, Burger King, Dunkin', McDonald's, Monical's Pizza, Papa John's, Red Wheel Rest., Subway 🏨 Heritage Inn, Holiday Inn Express, Knights Inn, Super 8 🅾 $General, Chrysler/Dodge/Jeep, Ford, NAPA, vet, Walgreens, Walmart
240	Market St, **E** 🅿 Road Ranger/McDonald's/dsl/scales 🅾 Kenworth/Volvo, truck/tire repair, **W** 🅾 D&W Lake Camping/RV Park
238	Olympian Dr, to Champaign, **W** 🅿 Circle K/dsl 🍴 DQ 🏨 Microtel 🅾 RV/dsl repair
237b a	I-74, W to Peoria, E to Urbana
235b	I-72 W, to Decatur
235a	University Ave, to Champaign, **E** 🅾 🅷, U of Ill
232	Curtis Rd
229	to Savoy, Monticello
221.5mm	℞ₛ **both lanes, full** ♿ **facilities, litter barrels, petwalk,** 🚻, 🛢, **vending**
220	US 45, Pesotum, **E** 🅾 st police
212	US 36, Tuscola, **E** 🅿 FuelMart/dsl, **W** 🅿 BP/dsl, Circle K, Road Ranger/dsl/scales/24hr 🍴 Burger King, Denny's, DQ, Jimmy John's, McDonald's, Monical's Pizza, Pantry Cafe, Pizza Hut, Subway, Taco Bell 🏨 Baymont Inn, Holiday Inn Express, Super 8 🅾 $General, Ford, IGA Foods, O'Reilly Parts, Tuscola Outlets/Famous Brands, Verizon
203	IL 133, Arcola, **E** 🏨 Best Western+, **W** 🅿 Phillips 66/Subway/dsl, Sunrise/dsl 🍴 DQ, El Toro Mexican, Hen House, McDonald's, Monical's Pizza 🏨 Arcola Inn, Quality Inn 🅾 $General, city park, NAPA, vet
192	CtyRd 1000 N, Rd 18

Ⓝ INTERSTATE 57 Cont'd

Exit #	Services
190b a	IL 16, to Mattoon, **E** 🅿 BP/dsl 🅾 🎗, Fox Ridge SP, to E IL U, **W** 🅿 Huck's, Murphy USA/dsl, Phillips 66/Subway/dsl 🍴 A&W/ LJ Silver, Alamo Steaks, Arby's, Buffalo Wild Wings, China Wok, Cracker Barrel, Denny's, Domino's, Don Sol Mexican, DQ, El Vaquero Mexican, Freddy's, Japanese Steaks, Jimmy John's, KFC, Lee's Chicken, McDonald's, McHugh's, Papa Murphy, QQ Buffet, Stadium Grill, Starbucks, Steak'n Shake, Taco Bell, Wendy's 🛏 Baymont Inn, Comfort Suites, Hampton Inn, Holiday Inn Express, Suite Dreams, Super 8 🅾 $General, $Tree, Aldi Foods, AT&T, BigLots, CVS Drug, GNC, Home Depot, JC Penney, JoAnn, O'Reilly Parts, Petsmart, Verizon, Walgreens, Walmart/Subway
184	US 45, IL 121, to Mattoon, **E** 🅿 Phillips 66/Subway/dsl, **W** 🍴 McDonald's 🛏 Motel 6, Quality Inn 🅾 to Lake Shelbyville
177	US 45, Neoga, **E** 🅿 FuelMart/Subway/dsl/e-85 🅾 NAPA, **W** 🅿 Casey's/dsl (1mi) 🅾 $General
166.5mm	🆁🆂 both lanes, full ♿ facilities, litter barrels, petwalk, 🄲, 🄰, vending
163	I-70 E, to Indianapolis
162.5	I-57 S and I-70 W run together 6 mi
162	US 45, Effingham, **E** 🅿 Motomart 🅾 Harley-Davidson, **W** 🅿 ⬜/McDonald's/dsl/scales/24hr 🍴 Subway 🅾 Camp Lakewood (2mi), truck repair
160	IL 33, IL 32, Effingham, **E** 🍴 Domino's, Jimmy John's, McAlister's Deli, Papa John's, Pizza Hut 🛏 Best Western, Fairfield Inn, Quality Inn 🅾 🎗, $General, Aldi Foods, AutoZone, Save-a-Lot, Verizon, vet, **W** 🅿 ⓕFLYING J/Denny's/dsl/LP/scales/24hr, Murphy USA/dsl, Phillips 66/dsl, TA/Popeye's/dsl/@ 🍴 Arby's, Buffalo Wild Wings, Burger King, Chili's, Chipotle, Cracker Barrel, Denny's, El Rancherito Mexican, Fujiyama Steaks, KFC, LJ Silver, McDonald's, Panda Express, Panera Bread, Starbucks, Steak'n Shake, Taco Bell, TGIFriday's, Wendy's 🛏 Country Inn&Suites, Days Inn, Hampton Inn, Holiday Inn, La Quinta, Super 8 🅾 $Tree, AT&T, Blue Beacon, Camp Lakewood RV Park, Ford/ Lincoln, Hodgson Mill Mercantile, Kohl's, Menards, Peterbilt, SpeedCo, Verizon, Walmart/Subway
159	US 40, Effingham, **E** 🅿 Phillips 66/dsl, Speedway/Speedy's Cafe/dsl/24hr 🍴 China Buffet, Culver's, Hardee's, Little Caesar's, Niemerg's Rest, Subway 🛏 Abe Lincoln Motel, Best Value Inn, Comfort Suites, EconoLodge, Lexington Inn 🅾 Honda, O'Reilly Parts, tires/repair, Walgreens, **W** 🅿 Petro/Iron Skillet/ dsl/24hr/@ 🛏 Baymont Inn 🅾 Blue Beacon, Freightliner
	I-57 N and I-70 E run together 6 mi.
157	I-70 W, to St Louis
151	Watson, 5 mi **E** 🅾 Percival Springs RV Park
150mm	Little Wabash River, Little Wabash River
145	Edgewood, **E** 🅿 Phillips 66/dsl 🅾 city park
135	IL 185, Farina, **E** 🅿 Shell/Subway/dsl 🅾 $General, Ford
127	to Kinmundy, Patoka
116	US 50, Salem, **E** 🅿 Circle K/dsl, Huck's/dsl, Motomart, Tesla EVC 🍴 Burger King, China King, Denny's, Domino's, Hardee's, La Cocina Mexican, McDonald's, Pizza Hut, Pizza Man, Subway, Taco Bell, Village Garden, Wendy's 🛏 Holiday Inn Express 🅾 🎗, $General, AutoZone, Chrysler/Dodge/Jeep, CVS Drug, GMC, NAPA, O'Reilly Parts, Save-A-Lot, to Forbes SP, USPO, Verizon, **W** 🅿 Murphy USA/dsl, Phillips 66/dsl 🍴 Applebee's, Arby's, El Rancherito, KFC, Mi Pueblo 🛏 Days Inn, Quality Inn, Super 8 🅾 $Tree, AT&T, Buick/Chevrolet, Carlisle Lake (23mi), Ford, Salem Tires, Walmart
114mm	🆁🆂 both lanes, full ♿ facilities, litter barrels, petwalk, 🄲, 🄰, playground, vending

109	IL 161, to Centralia, **W** 🍴 Biggie's General Store/cafe/dsl
103	Dix, **E** 🅿 Phillips 66/dsl 🛏 Red Carpet Inn
96	I-64 W, to St Louis
95	IL 15, Mt Vernon, **E** 🅿 Circle K/dsl, Hucks 🍴 Agave Mexican, Asian Buffet, Bandana's BBQ, Domino's, El Rancherito Mexican, Fazoli's, Hardee's, KFC, Little Caesar's, LJ Silver, McAlister's Deli, McDonald's, Moe's SW Grill, Panda Express, Panera Bread, Pizza Hut, Starbucks, Steak'n Shake, Subway, Taco Bell, The Grille, Waffle Co, Wendy's 🛏 Best Value Inn, Comfort Suites, Drury Inn, Motel 6, Super 8 🅾 🎗, AT&T, AutoZone, Big Lots, Chevrolet/Cadillac, CVS Drug, Harley-Davidson, Hobby Lobby, JC Penney, Kroger/dsl, Midas, O'Reilly Parts, Plaza Tire, Prompt Care, Ross, Verizon, Walgreens, **W** 🅿 Circle K/dsl, ⓕFLYING J, Hucks/Huddle House/dsl/scales/24hr, ⬜/Denny's/dsl/ scales/24hr, TA/Country Pride/Popeye's/dsl/24hr/@, Tesla EVC 🍴 Applebee's, Arby's, Bob Evans, Buffalo Wild Wings, Burger King, Chili's, Cracker Barrel, Double Overtime Grill, Jimmy John's, McDonald's, Ryan's, Sonic, Subway 🛏 Days Inn, Doubletree, Fairfield Inn, Hampton Inn, Holiday Inn Express, Quality Inn 🅾 $Tree, Archway RV Park, Buick/GMC, Freightliner, Kohl's, Lowe's, NAPA, Staples, Toyota, truckwash, Walmart
94	Veteran's Memorial Dr, **E** 🅿 Phillips 66/dsl 🍴 Culver's 🅾 🎗 **W** 🅾 Menards
92	I-64 E, to Louisville
83	Ina, **E** 🅿 ♥Love's/McDonald's/dsl/scales 🍴 Uncle Joe's BBQ 🅾 tire/trailer repair, **W** 🅾 to Rend Lake Coll
79mm	🆁🆂 sb, full ♿ facilities, info, litter barrels, petwalk, 🄲, 🄰, playground, vending
77	IL 154, to Whittington, **E** 🅿 Phillips 66/dsl 🛏 Surestay Inn 🅾 Whittington Woods RV Park, **W** 🛏 Seasons at Rend Lake Lodge/rest. 🅾 golf, to Rend Lake, Wayne Fitzgerrell SP
74mm	🆁🆂 nb, full ♿ facilities, litter barrels, petwalk, 🄲, 🄰, playground, vending
71	IL 14, Benton, **E** 🍴 Arby's, Hardee's, KFC/Taco Bell, Pizza Hut 🛏 Country Hearth Inn, Gray Plaza Motel, Phillips 66/dsl 🅾 AutoZone, CVS Drug, KOA (1.5mi), O'Reilly Parts, Plaza Tire, **W** 🅿 Casey's/dsl, Circle K/dsl, Murphy USA/dsl 🍴 Applebee's, Burger King, McDonald's, Subway 🅾 $Tree, AT&T, to Rend Lake, Verizon, Walmart
65	IL 149, W Frankfort, **E** 🅿 Circle K/dsl, ROC/dsl 🍴 China Star, Dixie Cream Deli, Don Luna Mexican, Hardee's, La Fiesta Mexican, LJ Silver, Mike's Drive-In, Opie's Rest., Sonic, Subway 🛏 Gray Plaza Motel 🅾 CVS Drug, NAPA, **W** 🅿 Casey's/dsl, Phillips 66/dsl 🍴 Bonnie's Cafe, McDonald's, Taco Bell 🛏 Best Value Inn 🅾 $General, $Tree, Buick/Chevrolet/GMC, Chrysler/ Dodge/Jeep, Kroger
59	to Herrin, Johnston City, **E** 🅿 ROC/dsl/e85, Stuckey's/dsl, ZX/ dsl 🍴 DQ, McDonald's, Subway 🅾 $General, Bandy Drug, camping (2mi), **W** 🅾 🎗, camping (4mi)
54b a	IL 13, Marion, **E** 🅿 Circle K/dsl 🍴 Arby's, Fazoli's, Hardee's, KFC, La Fiesta Mexican, Little Caesar's, LJ Silver, Papa John's, Pizza Hut, Subway, Tequila's Mexican, Wendy's 🛏 Best Value Inn, EconoLodge 🅾 $General, Advance Parts, Aldi Foods, AutoZone, Ford/Hyundai/Lincoln, Kroger/gas, Plaza Tire, USPO, Walgreens, **W** 🅿 Huck's/dsl, Phillips 66/dsl, ⬜/Subway/dsl/scales/24hr 🍴 17th St Grill, Applebee's, Backyard Burger, Bob Evans, Buffalo Wild Wings, Burger King, Culver's, Don Sol Mexican, Freddy's, Hong Kong BBQ, IHOP, Jimmy John's, Krispy Kreme, Logan's Roadhouse, Mackie's Pizza, McAlister's Deli, McDonald's, O'Charley's, Panda Express, Panera Bread, Red Lobster, Sonic, Starbucks, Steak'n Shake, Taco Bell, Wok'n Roll Buffet 🛏 Comfort Inn, Country Inn&Suites, Drury Inn, Fairfield Inn, Hampton Inn

Side labels: MATTOON / EFFINGHAM / SALEM (left); MT VERNON / BENTON / MARION (right); IL

⬆️🅽 INTERSTATE 57 Cont'd

54b a	Continued
	Holiday Inn Express, Super 8 🅾 🏨, $Tree, AT&T, Buick/Chevrolet/GMC, Chrysler/Dodge/Jeep, Dillard's, GNC, Harley-Davidson, Home Depot, Honda, Menards, Mercedes, Nissan, Sam's Club/gas, Subaru, Target, Toyota, Verizon, Walmart/Subway
53	Main St, Marion, **E** 🅿 Casey's/dsl 🍴 DQ 🅾 🏨, Marion Camping/RV Park, NAPA, **W** 🍴 Motomart 🍴 Cracker Barrel, HideOut Steaks, Huddle House 🏨 Baymont Inn, Best Western, Quality Inn
47mm	weigh sta both lanes
45	IL 1481 mi **E** 🍴 Marathon/dsl 🏨 Lake Tree Inn 🅾 camping, vet, **W** 🅾 dsl repair
44	I-24 E to Nashville
40	Goreville Rd, **E** 🅾 camping, Ferne Clyffe SP, scenic overlook
36	Lick Creek Rd, **W** 🅾 vineyards
32mm	Trail of Tears Rest Area both lanes, full ♿ facilities, info, litter barrels, petwalk, 🚻, 🪑, playground, vending
30	IL 146, Anna, Vienna, **W** 🅾 🏨, auto/RV repair
25	US 51 N (from nb, exits left), to Carbondale
24	Dongola Rd, **W** 🍴 BP/dsl 🅾 $General
18	Ullin Rd, **W** 🍴 Fast Stop/dsl 🍴 EEE BBQ 🏨 Best Value Inn 🅾 Chevrolet, st police
8	Mounds Rd, to Mound City, **E** 🍴 Huckleberry's Rest.
1	IL 3, to US 51, Cairo, **E** 🏨 Quality Inn 🅾 $General, camping, Mound City Nat Cem (4mi), **W** 🅾 camping
0mm	Illinois/Missouri state line, Mississippi River

⬆️🅴 INTERSTATE 64

Exit #	Services
131.5mm	Illinois/Indiana state line, Wabash River
131mm	Skeeter Mtn Welcome Ctr wb, full ♿ facilities, litter barrels, petwalk, 🚻, 🪑, vending
130	IL 1, to Grayville, **N** 🍴 Casey's (2mi), Road Ranger/dsl/scales/24hr 🍴 Guadalajara Mexican, Subway 🏨 Super 8, Windsor Oaks Inn/rest. 🅾 Beall Woods SP (10mi)
124mm	Little Wabash River
117	Burnt Prairie, **S** 🍴 CountryMark/dsl 🍴 ChuckWagon Charlie's Café 🅾 antiques
110	US 45, Mill Shoals
100	IL 242, to Wayne City, **N** 🍴 Citgo/dsl
89	to Belle Rive, Bluford
86mm	🆁🆂 wb, full ♿ facilities, litter barrels, petwalk, 🚻, 🪑, vending
82.5mm	🆁🆂 eb, full ♿ facilities, litter barrels, petwalk, 🚻, 🪑, vending
80	IL 37, to Mt Vernon, 2 mi **N** 🍴 Hucks/dsl/24hr, Phillips 66/Circle K/Burger King/dsl 🅾 $General
78	I-57, S to Memphis, N to Chicago
	I-64 and I-57 run together 5 mi. See I-57, exits 95-94.
73	I-57, N to Chicago, S to Memphis
69	Woodlawn
61	US 51, to Centralia, Richview
50	IL 127, to Nashville, **N** 🅾 to Carlyle Lake, **S** 🍴 BP/dsl, Citgo/dsl/e85/rest., Little Nashville/Conoco/rest/dsl/scales/24hr 🍴 McDonald's 🏨 Best Western 🅾 🏨
41	IL 177, Okawville, **S** 🍴 Road Ranger/dsl/24hr 🍴 Burger King, DQ, Subway 🏨 Original Springs Motel, Super 8 🅾 $General, tires/repair, USPO
37mm	Kaskaskia River
34	to Albers, 3 mi **N** 🍴 Casey's
27	IL 161, New Baden, **N** 🍴 Casey's/dsl, Shell/dsl 🍴 A Fine Swine BBQ, China King, Good Ol Days Rest., McDonald's, Subway 🅾 $General, **S** 🍴 💗Loves/Hardee's/dsl/scales/24hr

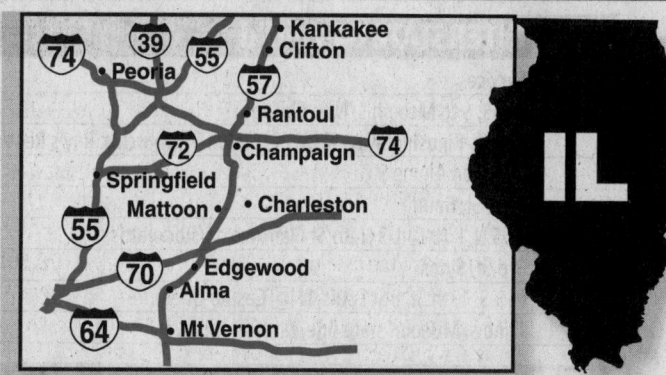

25mm	🆁🆂 both lanes, full ♿ facilities, info, litter barrels, petwalk, 🚻, 🪑, vending
23	IL 4, to Mascoutah, **N** 🍴 Phillips 66/Huddle House/dsl/RV dump 🍴 Domino's 🏨 Best Western+, **S** 🅾 🖨
21	Rieder Rd
19b a	US 50, IL 158, **N** 🍴 Motomart/dsl 🍴 Subway 🏨 Super 8 🅾 🏨, **S** 🅾 to Scott AFB
18mm	weigh sta eb
16	to O'Fallon, Shiloh, **N** 🍴 Bella Milano, Dewey's Pizza, Lion's Choice, Sonic, Sugarfire Smokehouse, The Egg & I 🏨 Hampton Inn, Hilton Garden, TownePlace Suites 🅾 CVS Drug, Harley-Davidson, 🏨, URGENT CARE, **S** 🍴 Motomart/dsl 🍴 54th St. Grille, Applebee's, Arby's, Aroy Thai, Buffalo Wild Wings, China King, Coldstone, Cracker Barrel, Freddy's, Golden Corral, Hop House Rest., Jersey Mike's, Jimmy John's, La Casa Mexicana, Little Caesar's, McAlister's Deli, McDonald's, Noodles&Co, Qdoba, St. Louis Bread Co., Starbucks, Subway, TX Roadhouse, White Castle 🏨 Drury Inn, Holiday Inn Express 🅾 $Tree, AT&T, Carmax, Dierbergs Foods, Dobb's Tire, GNC, Menard's, Michael's, Target, vet
14	O'Fallon, **N** 🍴 Circle K/dsl, Motomart, Shell/dsl 🍴 IHOP, Steak'n Shake, Subway 🏨 Best Western, Extended Stay America, HomeTowne Suites, La Quinta, Sleep Inn 🅾 Cadillac, Chevrolet, Ford, O'Reilly Parts, **S** 🍴 Chevy's Mexican, Culver's, Hardee's, Jack-in-the-Box, KFC, McDonald's, O'Charley's, Panda Express, Papa Murphy's, Sake Grill, Starbucks, Syberg's Rest., Taco Bell 🏨 Baymont Inn, Candlewood Suites, Quality Inn 🅾 Aldi Foods, BMW, Home Depot, Honda, Hyundai, Kia, Mazda, Nissan, Petsmart, Sam's Club/gas, Toyota, VW, Walmart
12	IL 159, to Collinsville, **N** 🍴 Circle K/dsl 🍴 Agostino's, Bob Evans, Ginger Buffet, Lotawata Creek Grill, Olive Garden, Red Lobster, Rio Grande, Shogun Japanese, TGIFriday's 🏨 Comfort Suites, Drury Inn, EconoLodge, Hampton Inn, Holiday Inn, Sheraton, Super 8, Wingate Inn 🅾 Fiat, Gordman's, **S** 🍴 BP/dsl, Motomart/dsl 🍴 Arby's, Boston Mkt, Burger King, Capt D's, Cheddar's, Chick-fil-A, Chili's, Chipotle Mexican, ChuckECheese, Domino's, Dunkin', Fazoli's, Firehouse Subs, Five Guys, Honeybaked Ham, Hooters, Imo's Pizza, Jimmy John's, Krispy Kreme, Little Caesar's, LJ Silver, Longhorn Steaks, McAlister's Deli, McDonald's, Popeye's, Red Robin, Ruby Tuesday, St. Louis Bread, Subway, Taco Bell, Wasabi, Wendy's, White Castle 🅾 $General, $Tree, Aamco, Aldi Foods, AT&T, Barnes&Noble, Best Buy, BigLots, Burlington Coats, CarX, Dick's, Dillard's, Dobb's Tire, Firestone/auto, Fresh Thyme Mkt, Hobby Lobby, JC Penney, JoAnn Fabrics, Kohl's, Lowe's, Macy's, Marshall's, Meineke, Midas, NTB, Old Navy, O'Reilly Parts, PetCo, Ross, Russell Stover, Schnuck's Foods, TJ Maxx, Verizon, vet, Walgreens
9	IL 157, to Caseyville, **N** 🍴 Gulf/Subway, Huck's/dsl 🍴 Hardee's 🏨 Western Inn, **S** 🍴 🍴 Cracker Barrel, Domino's, DQ, McDonald's, Taco Bell 🏨 Best Inn, Fairbridge Inn, Motel 6, Quality Inn

MARION (vertical side label)   O'FALLON (vertical side label)   COLLINSVILLE (vertical side label)   IL

🔼E INTERSTATE 64 Cont'd

Exit #	Services
7	I-255, S to Memphis, N to Chicago
6	IL 111, Kingshighway, N 🛢 BP, Crown 🍴 Church's, Ray's Rest.
5	25th St
4	15th St, Baugh
3	I-55 N, I-70 E, IL 3 N, to St Clair Ave, to stockyards
2b a	3rd St, S gas
1	IL 3 S, 13th St, E St Louis, N 🅾 Casino Queen
0mm	Illinois/Missouri state line, Mississippi River

🔼E INTERSTATE 70

Exit #	Services
156mm	Illinois/Indiana state line
154	US 40 W
151mm	weigh sta wb
149mm	🆁🆂 wb, full ♿ facilities, info, litter barrels, petwalk, 🕻, 🏕, vending
147	IL 1, Marshall, N 🛢 Road Ranger/Church's/dsl/scales/ 24hr 🍴 Crossroads Rest., S 🛢 Casey's (1mi), DQ, Marathon/Arby's/dsl, Phillips 66/dsl 🍴 Burger King, Los Tres Caminos, McDonald's, Pizza Hut, Sam's Steaks, Subway, Wendy's 🛏 Lincoln Suites, Relax Inn, Super 8 🅾 antiques, Ford, Lincoln Trail SP, Walmart
136	to Martinsville, S 🛢 Phillips 66/dsl/24hr
134.5mm	N Fork Embarras River
129	IL 49, Casey, N 🅾 KOA (seasonal), RV service, S 🛢 Casey's, DQ, Marathon/Circle K/dsl, Phillips 66/dsl 🍴 Hacienda Mexican, McDonald's, Pizza Hut, Subway 🛏 Days Inn 🅾 $General, IGA Foods
119	IL 130, Greenup, S 🛢 Casey's/dsl, 💙Loves/Chester's/IHOP/dsl/scales/24hr, Phillips 66/dsl 🍴 Backyard BBQ, DQ, Subway 🛏 Budget Host, Greenup Motel 🅾 $General, hist sites, NAPA
105	Montrose, N 🅾 Spring Creek Camping (1mi), S 🛢 BP/dsl, Phillips/dsl 🛏 Fairview Inn
98	I-57, N to Chicago. I-70 and I-57 run together 6 mi. See I-57, 159-162.
92	I-57, S to Mt Vernon
91mm	Little Wabash River
87mm	🆁🆂 both lanes, full ♿ facilities, info, litter barrels, petwalk, 🕻, 🏕, playground, RV dump, vending
82	IL 128, Altamont, N 🛢 Casey's/dsl, Phillips 66/Subway/dsl/24hr 🍴 Dairy Bar, Joe's Pizza/pasta, McDonald's 🛏 Altamont Motel, Cobblestone Inn 🅾 $General, city park, S 🛏 Relax Inn
76	US 40, St Elmo, N 🛢 Casey's 🛏 Waldorf Motel 🅾 Timberline Camping (2mi)
71mm	weigh sta eb
68	US 40, Brownstown, N 🅾 Okaw Valley Kamping, S 🅾 truck repair
63.5mm	Kaskaskia River
63	US 51, Vandalia, N 🍴 Chuck Wagon Cafe, LJ Silver 🛏 Best Value Inn, S 🛢 Casey's, Phillips 66, Phillips 66/Burger King/24hr 🍴 Arby's, China Gate, DQ, McDonald's, Pizza Hut, Rancho Nuevo Mexican, Sonic, Subway, Wendy's 🛏 Economy Inn, Jay's Inn 🅾 Aldi Foods, city park, County Mkt Foods, hist site
61	US 40, Vandalia, N 🛢 Fast Stop/Denny's/dsl/scales/24hr, S 🛢 Murphy USA/dsl 🍴 China King, Embers Pizza, Huddle House, KFC/Taco Bell, Ponderosa 🛏 Holiday Inn Express, Ramada 🅾 $Tree, AT&T, AutoZone, Verizon, Walmart
52	US 40, Mulberry Grove, N 🛢 Casey's/dsl 🅾 Timber Trail Camp-In (2mi), S 🅾 Cedar Brook Camping (1mi)

(side tab: IL)

(side tab: VANDALIA)

45	IL 127, Greenville, N 🛢 💙Loves/Subway/dsl/scales/24h Shell/dsl 🍴 Chang's Buffet, Domino's, Huddle House, KFC/Taco Bell, Los Amigos, Lu-Bob's Rest., McDonald's 🛏 EconoLodge, Red Carpet Inn, Super 8 🅾 🍴, S 🛏 Comfort Inn 🅾 America Farm Heritage Museum, RV Service, to Carlyle Lake
41	US 40 E, to Greenville
36	US 40 E, Pocahontas, S 🛢 BP/dsl, Phillips 66/dsl 🍴 Funderburk's Grill 🛏 Lighthouse Lodge, Powhatan Motel/rest., Taho Motel 🅾 truck/tire repair
30	US 40, IL 143, to Highland, S 🛢 Shell/dsl/wifi 🍴 Blue Spring Café 🅾 🍴, Tomahawk RV Park (7mi)
26.5mm	Silver Lake 🆁🆂 both lanes, full ♿ facilities, litter barrels, pe walk, 🕻, 🏕, vending
24	IL 143, Marine, 4 mi S 🅾 🍴
21	IL 4, Troy
15b a	I-55, N to Chicago, S to St Louis, I-270 W to Kansas City
	I-70 and I-55 run together 18 mi. See I-55, exits 1-18.
0mm	Illinois/Missouri state line, Mississippi River

🔼E INTERSTATE 72

Exit #	Services
183mm	I-72 begins/ends, E 🛢 Gas Depot, Thornton's/dsl 🍴 Arby's, Burger King, Dunkin', Garcia's Pizza, Jets Pizza, Jimmy John's, KFC, La Bamba Mexican, McDonald's, Monical's Pizza, Original Pancakes, Papa John's, Pizza Hut, Sonic, Subway, Taco Bell, T. Roadhouse 🅾 $General, Advance Parts, AutoZone, Big Lots, CVS Drug, O'Reilly Parts, Schnuck's Foods/e85, ValuCheck Mkt, Walgreens
182b a	I-57, N to Chicago, S to Memphis, to I-74
176	IL 47, to Mahomet
172	IL 10, Lodge, Seymour
169	White Heath Rd
166	IL 105 W, Market St, N 🅾 🍴, Ford, S 🛢 Circle K/dsl 🍴 Re Wheel Rest. 🛏 Best Western, Foster Inn 🅾 city park, railway museum
165mm	Sangamon River
164	Bridge St, 1 mi S 🛢 Circle K/dsl 🍴 DQ, Golden Kitchen, Hardee's, McDonald's, Monical's Pizza, Pizza Hut, Subway 🅾 🍴 $General, Buick/Chevrolet, Chrysler/Dodge/Jeep, USPO, vet
156	IL 48, to Weldon, Cisco, N 🅾 Friends Creek Camping (may-oct 3mi)
153mm	🆁🆂 both lanes, full ♿ facilities, litter barrels, petwalk, 🕻, 🏕, vending
152mm	Friends Creek
150	Argenta
144	IL 48, Oreana, S 🛢 Pilot/McDonald's/Subway/dsl/scales/24hr 🛏 Sleep Inn 🅾 🍴, Chrysler/Dodge/Jeep, Honda, Hyundai, Pressley RV Ctr (3mi)
141b a	US 51, Decatur, N 🛢 Casey's/dsl, Circle K 🍴 Applebee's, Buffalo Wild Wings, Burger Theory, Cheddar's, Cracker Barrel, McDonald's, Panda Express, Penn Sta Subs, Pizza Hut, Red Lobster, Steak'n Shake, Subway, Taco Bell, TX Roadhouse 🛏 Baymont Inn, Country Inn&Suites, EconoLodge, Fairfield Inn, Hampton Inn, Homewood Suites, Quality Inn, Ramada Ltd, Residence Inn 🅾 $Tree, AT&T, Best Buy, Buick/Cadillac/GMC, GNC, Harley-Davidson, Hobby Lobby, Kohl's, Lowe's, Menards, Petsmart, Ross, Staples, TJ Maxx, Verizon, Von Maur, S 🛢 Arby's, Burger King, El Rodeo Mexican, Fuji Japanese, La Fondita, Monical's Pizza, Olive Garden, Panera Bread, Papa Murphy's, Starbucks 🅾 🍴, Jo-Ann Fabrics, Sam's Club, Target, Verizon, Walgreens, Walmart/Subway

(side tab: URBANA)

(side tab: DECATUR)

D E C A T U R

INTERSTATE 72 Cont'd

Exit #	Services
138	IL 121, Decatur, S 🅖 Loves/Hardee's/dsl/scales24hr 🅞 🎗
133b a	US 36 E, US 51, Decatur, S 🅖 Shell/Subway/dsl 🛏 Best Value Inn, Decatur Hotel/rest.
128	Niantic
122	to Mt Auburn, Illiopolis, N 🅖 FastStop/dsl 🅞 $General
114	Buffalo, Mechanicsburg, 2 mi S 🅖 Gas Depot/dsl 🅞 USPO
108	Riverton, Dawson
107mm	Sangamon River
104	Camp Butler, 2 mi N 🅞 golf
103b a	I-55, IL 97.
I-72 and I-55 run together 6 mi. See I-55, exits 92-98.	
97b a	Loop 55 N (from eb), 6th St, I-55 S, N 🅖 Road Ranger 🍴 Golden Corral, McDonald's, Pizza Ranch 🛏 Comfort Inn, La Quinta, Rte 66 🅞 Aldi Foods, Lincoln, Mazda, Walmart

S P R I N G F I E L D

96	MacArthur Blvd, N 🅖 Tesla EVC 🍴 Engrained Brewing Co 🛏 SpringHill Suites 🅞 Scheels
93	IL 4, Springfield, N 🅖 Hucks, Thorntons/dsl 🍴 Applebee's, Arby's, Bakers Square, Burger King, Casa Real, Chick-fil-A, Chili's, Chipotle Mexican, Cooper's Hawk Rest., Dew's Chili, Five Guys, Indigo, Jersey Mike's, Jimmy John's, Kiku Japanese, Longhorn Steaks, Los Rancheros Mexican, McDonald's, Noodles&Co, Olive Garden, Outback Steaks, Panda Express, Panera Bread, Pasta House, Penn Sta Subs, Popeye's, Qdoba, Red Robin, Sonic, Starbucks, Subway, Taco Bell, TGIFriday's, TX Roadhouse, Wendy's 🛏 Courtyard, Fairfield Inn, Quality Inn, Sleep Inn 🅞 Aldi Foods, AT&T, Barnes&Noble, Best Buy, Big Lots, County Mkt Foods, Dick's, Discount Tire, Fannie May, Gordman's, Hobby Lobby, Jo-Ann Fabrics, Kohl's, Lowe's, Macy's, Marshall's, Michael's, Office Depot, Old Navy, PetCo, Petsmart, Ross, Sam's Club/gas, Target, TJ Maxx, Verizon, Walgreens, Walmart, S 🅖 Meijer/dsl/e85 🍴 Bob Evans, Monical's Pizza, Steak'n Shake 🛏 Hampton Inn, Staybridge Suites 🅞 Cadillac, CarMax, Chevrolet, Chrysler/Jeep, Fiat, Ford, Honda, Menards
91	Wabash Ave, to Springfield, N 🅖 Qik-n- EZ/dsl 🍴 Bella Milano, Buffalo Wild Wings, Culver's, Freddy's, IHOP, McDonald's, Mimosa Thai, Papa Frank's Italian 🅞 Audi/VW, Dodge/Ram, Kia, Subaru, Nissan, Toyota, S 🅞 Colmans RV Ctr
82	New Berlin, S 🅖 Road Ranger/Subway/dsl 🅞 $General
76	IL 123, to Ashland, Alexander
68	to IL 104, to Jacksonville, 2 mi N 🅖 Casey's/dsl, Circle K 🅞 🎗
64	US 67, to Jacksonville, 2 mi N 🅖 Circle K/dsl, FastStop/dsl, Loves/IHOP/dsl/scales/24hr, Qik-n-EZ/Subway/dsl 🍴 KFC, Little Caesar's, McDonald's 🛏 Baymont Inn, Comfort Inn, Holiday Inn Express, Sleep Inn 🅞 🎗, $General, CVS Drug, Family$, Hopper RV Ctr, Walgreens
60	to US 67 N, to Jacksonville, 6 mi N on IL 104 🅞 🎗, food, gas, lodging
52	to IL 106, Winchester, N 🅞 golf, 2 mi S food, gas, lodging
46	IL 100, to Bluffs
42mm	Illinois River
35	US 54, IL 107, to Pittsfield, Griggsville, 4 mi N food, gas, lodging, S 🅞 🎗, Jellystone Camping (6mi), st police
31	to Pittsfield, New Salem, 5 mi S 🅞 🎗, Jellystone Camping, food, gas, lodging
20	IL 106, Barry, S 🅖 FastStop/dsl/24hr, Shell/dsl 🍴 Wendy's 🛏 Ice House Inn 🅞 $General
10	IL 96, to Payson, Hull
4a	I-172, N to Quincy
1	IL 106, to Hull

0mm	Illinois/Missouri state line, Mississippi River.
Exits 157 & 156 are in Missouri.	
157	to Hannibal, MO 179, S 🅖 Ayerco, BP, Pickadilly, Shell/dsl 🍴 Mark Twain Dinette, Subway 🛏 Best Way Inn, Best Western, Country Hearth Inn, Hotel Mark Twain 🅞 auto repair, visitor info
156	US 61, New London, Palmyra. **I-72 begins/ends in Hannibal, MO,** N on US 61 🅖 BP, Casey's/dsl, Murphy USA/dsl 🍴 Arby's, Burger King, Country Kitchen, Domino's, Gabriella's Mexican, LJ Silver, McDonald's, Mi Mexico, Pizza Hut, Royal Garden, Rustic Oak Grill, Saints Ave Steaks, Sonic, Subway, Taco Bell 🅞 $General, $Tree, Aldi Foods, BigLots, Ford, JC Penney, Lowe's, Walmart, 0-2 mi S 🅖 Ayerco, Shell/dsl 🍴 Cassano's Subs, China King, DQ, Gran Rio Mexican, Hardee's, Jimmy John's, KFC, Little Caesar's, Logue's Rest, Wendy's 🛏 Comfort Inn, Days Inn, Economy Inn, Hannibal Inn, Motel 6, Super 8 🅞 $General, AT&T, AutoZone, Buick/Chevrolet, Chrysler/Dodge/Jeep, County Mkt Foods, CVS Drug, O'Reilly Parts, Walgreens

INTERSTATE 74

Exit #	Services
221mm	Illinois/Indiana state line, Central/Eastern Time Zone

D A N V I L L E

220	Lynch Rd, Danville, N 🍴 Marathon/dsl/scales (1mi), Shell/dsl 🍴 Border Cafe 🛏 Best Western, Hampton Inn, Holiday Inn Express, Motel 6, Quality Inn, Red Roof Inn, Sleep Inn, Super 8, TownePlace Suites
216	Bowman Ave, Danville, N 🅖 Mobil/dsl, Phillips 66/dsl 🍴 Burger King, Godfather's, KFC, McDonald's 🅞 city park, CVS Drug, Walgreens
215b a	US 150, IL 1, Gilbert St, Danville, N 🅖 BP/Circle K/dsl 🍴 Arby's, El Toro, La Potosina, LJ Silver, McDonald's, Pizza Hut, Steak'n Shake, Subway, Taco Bell 🛏 Best Western, Days Inn 🅞 🎗, Aldi Foods, BigLots, S 🅖 Casey's/dsl, Marathon/Circle K/dsl, Marathon/dsl 🍴 Burger King, Green Jade Chinese, Mike's Grill, Monical's Pizza, Rich's Rest. 🅞 $General, $Tree, AutoZone, Big R, Buick/Chevrolet/GMC, County Mkt, Family$, Forest Glen Preserve Camping (11mi), Toyota
214	G St, Tilton
210	US 150, MLK Dr, 2 mi N 🅖 Marathon 🍴 Little Nugget Steaks 🅞 🎗, to Kickapoo SP
206	Oakwood, N 🅖 Loves/Hardee's/dsl/scales/24hr, S 🅖 Casey's (1mi), Phillips 66/Subway/dsl/scales, 🚚/PJ Fresh/dsl/scales/24hr 🍴 McDonald's 🅞 $General
200	IL 49 N, to Rankin
197	IL 49 S, Ogden, S 🅖 Phillips 66/Godfather's/dsl 🍴 Rich's Rest. 🅞 city park
192	St Joseph, S 🅖 Casey's, Shell/dsl 🍴 DQ, Monical's Pizza, Subway 🅞 antiques
185	IL 130, University Ave

CHAMPAIGN

INTERSTATE 74 Cont'd

Exit #	Services
184	US 45, Cunningham Ave, Urbana, N ⓖ F&F ⓞ Hyundai, Kia, Mazda, Toyota, VW, S ⓖ Marathon/Circle K/Subway/dsl, Shell/dsl ⓕ Arby's, Cracker Barrel, Hickory River BBQ, McDonald's, Steak'n Shake, Toro Loco, Wendy's ⓛ Eastland Suites, Motel 6 ⓞ $General, auto repair, vet
183	Lincoln Ave, Urbana, S ⓖ Circle K/dsl, Marathon/Circle K/dsl ⓕ Urbana Garden Rest. ⓛ Comfort Suites, Holiday Inn Express, Knights Inn, Ramada Inn, Sleep Inn, Wyndham Garden ⓞ Ⓗ, Harley-Davidson, to U of IL
182	Neil St (same as 181), Champaign, N ⓕ Alexander's Steaks, Bob Evans, Buca Italian, Food Court, McDonald's, Old Chicago, Olive Garden, Panera Bread, Taco Bell, TGIFriday's, Za's Italian ⓛ Baymont Inn, La Quinta, Quality Inn, Red Roof Inn, Super 8 ⓞ Barnes&Noble, Bergner's, Cadillac/Chevrolet, Chrysler/Dodge/Jeep, Dick's, Field&Stream, Gordman's, Hobby Lobby, Kohl's, Macy's, Mercedes/Volvo, Office Depot, Sears Hometown, TJ Maxx, Tuesday Morning, Verizon, S ⓖ Mobil/Circle K
181	Prospect Ave (same as 182), Champaign, N ⓖ Murphy USA/dsl ⓕ Applebee's, Best Wok, Blaze Pizza, Buffalo Wild Wings, Burger King, Chili's, Chipotle, Culver's, Denny's, Denny's, Fazoli's, Firehouse Subs, Five Guys, HuHot Mongolian, Longhorn Steaks, O'Charley's, Oishi Asian, Outback Steaks, Panda Express, Penn Sta Subs, Portillo's, Red Lobster, Ruby Tuesday, Starbucks, Steak'n Shake, Subway, Super Niro's Gyros, Super Niro's Gyros, Wendy's ⓛ Candlewood Suites, Country Inn&Suites, Courtyard, Drury Inn, Extended Stay America, Fairfield Inn, Quality Inn, Residence Inn, Residence Inn, Wingate Inn, Woodspring Suites ⓞ $Tree, Advance Parts, Aldi Foods, AT&T, Best Buy, Ford/Lincoln, Ford/Lincoln, Jo-Ann, Jo-Ann, Lowe's, Meijer/dsl, Menards, Michael's, Nissan, Nissan, Petsmart, Sam's Club/gas, Staples, Target, Tires+, Verizon, Walmart/Subway, S ⓖ Marathon/Circle K, Mobil/Jimmy John's, Phillips 66/dsl, Shell/dsl ⓕ Arby's, Dos Reales Mexican, Dunkin', LJ Silver, McDonald's, Popeye's ⓛ Best Value Inn, Days Inn ⓞ $General, CarX, Home Depot, NAPA, Tire Barn, Walgreens
179b a	I-57, N to Chicago, S to Memphis
174	Lake of the Woods Rd, Prairieview Rd, N ⓖ BP, Casey's, Mobil/Circle K/dsl ⓞ $General, auto repair, Lake of the Woods SP, Tin Cup RV Park, S ⓖ Marathon/Subway/dsl ⓕ McDonald's
172	IL 47, Mahomet, N ⓞ R&S RV Sales, S ⓖ Exxon/Domino's/dsl, Mobil/dsl ⓕ Arby's, Azteca, DQ, El Toro Mexican, HenHouse Rest., Los Zerapes, Monical's Pizza, Peking House, Subway, The Wok ⓛ Heritage Inn ⓞ Ace Hardware, CVS Drug, IGA Foods, NAPA, Walgreens
166	Mansfield, S ⓖ Phillips 66/dsl ⓞ Mansfield Gen. Store/Rest.
159	IL 54, Farmer City, S ⓖ Casey's/dsl, Huck's/Godfather's/dsl ⓕ Imo's Cafe, Subway ⓛ Budget Motel, Days Inn ⓞ $General, NAPA, to Clinton Lake RA, USPO
156mm	Ⓡ both lanes, full ⓖ facilities, litter larrels, petwalk, ⓒ, ⓐ, playground, vending
152	US 136, to Heyworth
149	Le Roy, N ⓖ Casey's/dsl, Loves/Arby's/dsl/scales/24hr ⓕ Jack's Cafe, McDonald's, Roma Pizza, Subway ⓛ Holiday Inn Express ⓞ $General, IGA Foods, NAPA, to Moraine View SP, TrueValue, S ⓖ Shell/Woody's Rest./dsl/scales/24hr ⓛ Days Inn ⓞ camping, Clinton Lake
142	Downs, N ⓖ Mobil/Pizza/Subs/dsl/24hr ⓞ USPO
135	US 51, Bloomington, N ⓖ Huck's/dsl, Mobil/Circle K/dsl ⓕ McDonald's, Pizza Hut ⓞ $General, S ⓖ BP/dsl
134b[157]	Veterans Pkwy, to Bloomington, N ⓞ Ⓗ, to ⓐ

BLOOMINGTON

	I-74 and I-55 run together 6 mi. See I-55, exits 157b-160b a.
127[163]	I-55, N to Chicago, S to St Louis, I-74 W to Peoria
125	US 150, to Bloomington, Mitsubishi Motorway
123mm	weigh sta wb
122mm	weigh sta eb
120	Carlock, N ⓖ BP/dsl/repair ⓕ Carlock Rest., S ⓞ Kamp Komfort Camping (Apr-Oct)
114.5mm	Ⓡ both lanes, full ⓖ facilities, litter barrels, petwalk, ⓒ, ⓐ vending
113.5mm	Mackinaw River
112	IL 117, Goodfield, N ⓖ Shell/Subway/dsl ⓕ Busy Corner Res ⓞ Eureka Coll, Jellystone Camping (1mi), Reagan Home, Timberline RA, USPO
102b a	Morton, N ⓖ Mobil/Arby's/dsl/scales/24hr ⓕ Baskin Robin Dunkin', Burger King, Cracker Barrel, Culver's, Steak'n Shak Taco Bell ⓛ Baymont Inn, Best Value Inn, Days Inn, Holiday Ir Express, Park Inn, Quality Inn ⓞ Chrysler/Dodge/Jeep, Farm Fleet, Freightliner, Walmart/Subway, S ⓖ BP/Circle K, Casey' dsl, Marathon/Circle K, Subway ⓕ China Dragon, Domino' Great Harvest Bread Co, Jimmy John's, La Fiesta, Lin's Buffe McDonald's, Monical's Pizza, Pizza Hut, Pizza Ranch ⓞ $Tre Buick/GMC, CVS Drug, Ford, Kroger/dsl, O'Reilly Parts, Verizo
101	I-155 S, to Lincoln
99	I-474 W, ⓞ ⓐ
98	Pinecrest Dr
96	95c (from eb), US 150, IL 8, E Washington St, E Peoria, N ⓖ Fa Stop/dsl ⓕ Subway, Super Gyros ⓛ Super 8 ⓞ O'Reilly Part
95b	(from eb) IL 116, to Metamora
95a	N Main St, Peoria, N ⓖ Shell/dsl ⓕ Burger King ⓛ Ham ton Inn, Paradice Hotel/Casino, S ⓖ BP/Circle K ⓕ A&W/ Silver, Bob Evans, Chick-fil-A, Chipotle Mexican, Firehouse Pi za, Hardee's, IHOP, Jason's Deli, Jersey Mike's, Jimmy John Johnny's Italian Steaks, McDonald's, Moe's SW, Noodles&C Panda Express, Papa Murphy's, Pizza Hut, Popeye's, Potbel Red Robin, Subway, Taco Bell, Tequilas Grill, Wendy's ⓛ Be Value Inn, Best Western+, Fairfield Inn, Holiday Inn ⓞ $Tre Advance Parts, Aldi Foods, AT&T, Costco/gas, CVS Drug, GN Goodyear/auto, Gordman's, Kohl's, Kroger, Ross, Target, Ve zon, Walgreens
94	IL 40, RiverFront Dr, S ⓖ Hucks/Godfather's/dsl ⓕ Arby's, B falo Wild Wings, Chili's, Culver's, Granite City Grill, Logan's Roa house, Lorena's Mexican, Panera Bread, Papa John's, Qdo Mexican, Shogun, Slim Chickens, Steak'n Shake, TX Roadhou Uncle Buck's Grill ⓛ Embassy Suites, Holiday Inn Express ⓞ Ba Pro Shop, Lowe's, PetsMart, Verizon, Walmart/Subway
93.5mm	Illinois River
93b	US 24, IL 29, Peoria, N ⓖ BP, S ⓛ Mark Twain Hotel ⓞ civic c
93a	Jefferson St, Peoria, N ⓖ BP, S ⓕ Two 25 Grill ⓛ Mark Twa Hotel, Marriott, Sheraton ⓞ to civic ctr
92b	Glendale Ave, Peoria, S ⓞ Ⓗ, downtown
92a	IL 40 N, Knoxville Ave, Peoria, S ⓛ Sheraton ⓞ Ⓗ
91	University St, Peoria
90	Gale Ave, Peoria, S ⓖ Marathon ⓞ to Bradley U, $General
89	US 150, War Memorial Dr, Peoria, N on War Memorial ⓖ B Circle K, Marathon/dsl ⓕ Burger King, Dunkin', Golden Cor IHOP, McDonald's, Papa Murphy's, Perkins, Popeye's, Stea Shake, Wendy's ⓛ Baymont Inn, Comfort Suites, Courtya EconoLodge, Extended Stay America, Quality Inn, Red R Inn, Residence Inn, Super 8 ⓞ Aldi Foods, AT&T, AutoZo Barnes&Noble, Best Buy, Chevrolet/Cadillac, Hobby Lob Lowe's, Midas, NAPA, PetsMart, Target, Tires+, U-Haul, Walgreens, Walmart/Subway

IL

🔼🔽 INTERSTATE 74 Cont'd

Exit #	Services
88	to US 150, War Memorial Dr, **N** 🅿 Shell 🍴 Arby's, Avanti's Rest., Baskin Robins/Dunkin', Biaggi's, Chick-fil-A, Chipotle, ChuckE-Cheese, Firehouse Subs, Five Guys, Panda Express, Panera Bread, Portillo's, Red Lobster, Sonic 🛏 Motel 6, SpringHill Suites 🅾 $Tree, JC Penney, Michael's, Ross, Verizon, Walgreens
87b a	I-474 E, IL 6, N to Chillicothe, **S** 🅾 🔄
82	Edwards Rd, Kickapoo, **N** 🅿 Mobil/dsl/service, Shell/Subway/dsl 🍴 Jubilee Café 🅾 to Jubilee Coll SP, **S** 🅾 USPO, Wildlife Prairie SP
75	Brimfield, Oak Hill, **N** 🅿 Casey's/dsl
71	to IL 78, to Canton, Elmwood
62mm	℞ **both lanes, full** 🚻 **facilities, litter barrels, petwalk**, 🕳, 🖼, **vending**
61.5mm	Spoon River
54	US 150, IL 97, Lewistown, **N** 🅾 TravL Park Camping (1mi), **S** 🅿 Mobil/dsl (2mi) 🍴 Alfano's Pizza (2mi)
51	Knoxville, **S** 🅿 BP/dsl, ♥Loves/Subway/Chester's/dsl/scales/24hr, Phillips 66/Charley's Subs/dsl/scales 🍴 Hardee's, McDonald's 🛏 Best Value Inn
48b a	E Galesburg, Galesburg, **N** 🛏 Best Western 🅾 Harley-Davidson, **S** 🅿 BP/Circle K/dsl, HyVee/dsl, Phillps 66/Beck's/dsl 🍴 DQ, Hardee's, Jalisco Mexican, KFC, Marco's Pizza, McDonald's, Pizza Hut, Subway, Taco Bell 🛏 Baymont Inn, Holiday Inn Express 🅾 Family$, HyVee Foods, Lincoln-Douglas Debates, Sav-A-Lot Foods, to Sandburg Birthplace, Walgreens
46b a	US 34, to Monmouth, **N** 🅾 Nichol's dsl Service, **1 mi S** 🍴 Buffalo Wild Wings, Crazy Buffet, Mi Casa Mexican, Pizza Ranch 🅾 🏥, Aldi Foods, AT&T, Kohl's, Menards, Toyota, Verizon, vet, Walmart/Subway
32	IL 17, Woodhull, **N** 🅿 BP/dsl, Shell/dsl 🍴 Subway 🅾 $General, **S** 🅿 🚛/dsl/scales/24hr 🅾 Shady Lakes Camping (8mi)
30mm	℞ **wb, full** 🚻 **facilities, litter barrels, petwalk**, 🕳, 🖼, **playground, RV dump, vending**
28mm	℞ **eb, full** 🚻 **facilities, litter barrels, petwalk**, 🕳, 🖼, **playground, RV dump, vending**
24	IL 81, Andover, **N** 🍴 Casey's (2mi) 🅾 camping
14mm	I-80, E to Chicago, I-80/I-280 W to Des Moines
8mm	weigh sta wb
6mm	weigh sta eb
5b	US 6, Moline, **S** 🅿 Shell/dsl 🍴 Bare Bones BBQ, McDonald's, MT Jack's 🛏 Best Inn, Country Inn&Suites, Hampton Inn, Holiday Inn Express, La Quinta, Motel 6, Quality Inn 🅾 🔄
5a	I-280 W, US 6 W, to Des Moines
4b a	IL 5, John Deere Rd, Moline, **N** 🅿 BP/7-11, Phillips 66, Shell/dsl 🍴 Applebee's, Burger King, Chipotle Mexican, Culver's, Hungy Hobo, Osaka Buffet, Panera Bread, Ryan's, Starbucks, Steak'n Shake, Subway, Wendy's 🛏 Residence Inn 🅾 $Tree, Cadillac, Farm&Fleet, Honda, Hyundai, Lowe's, Menard's, Staples, Subaru, Tires+, Toyota, Volvo, Walmart/Subway, **S** 🅿 BP/7-11 🍴 A&W/LJ Silver, Arby's, Buffalo Wild Wings, China Cafe, Denny's, KFC, Los Agaves, McDonald's, New Mandarin Chinese, Qdoba Mexican, Taco Bell 🛏 Best Western, Comfort Inn, Fairfield Inn, Motel 6 🅾 $General, Best Buy, Buick/GMC, Chevrolet, Chrysler/Dodge/Jeep, Dillards, Firestone/auto, Ford/Lincoln, Goodyear/auto, Gordman's, JC Penney, Mazda, Nissan, PetCo, Von Maur, Walgreens, Younkers
3	23rd Ave, Moline, **N** 🛏 Economy Inn
2	7th Ave, Moline, **S** 🅿 QuikStop 🍴 La Casa Mexican 🅾 riverfront, to civic ctr, USPO
1	3rd Ave (from eb), Moline, **S** 🅿 QuickStop 🛏 Stoney Creek Inn

0mm	Illinois/Iowa state line, Mississippi River
	Exits 4-1 are in Iowa.
4	US 67, Grant St, State St, Bettendorf, **N** 🅿 BP/dsl 🍴 Hardee's, McDonald's, Subway 🛏 Waterfront Conv Ctr 🅾 CarQuest, **S** 🍴 Village Inn Rest. 🛏 City Ctr Motel 🅾 $General
3	Middle Rd, Locust St, Bettendorf, **S** 🅿 BP/dsl 🍴 China Taste, Grinders Rest., Jimmy John's, McDonald's, Pizza Ranch, Red Ginger Asian, Starbucks, Subway 🛏 Hilton Garden 🅾 🏥, AT&T, Burlington Coats, Hobby Lobby, Home Depot, Marshall's, Schuck's Foods, Verizon, Walgreens
2	US 6 W, Spruce Hills Dr, Bettendorf, **N** 🅿 BP/dsl, Phillips 66 🍴 Domino's, Old Chicago Pizza 🛏 Courtyard, EconoLodge, Ramada Inn, Super 8, The Lodge Hotel/rest. 🅾 U-Haul, **S** 🅿 Hyvee Gas 🍴 Applebee's, KFC, Panera Bread, Red Lobster 🛏 AmericInn, Days Inn, Holiday Inn, La Quinta 🅾 Buick/GMC, Gordman's, Kohl's, Lowe's, PetCo, Sam's Club/gas, st patrol
1	53rd St, Hamilton, **N** 🅿 🍴 Bad Boyz Pizza, Biaggi's Italian, Buffalo Wild Wings, Chili's, Coldstone, Granite City Rest., Los Agaves, Maggie Moo's, Moe's SW, Osaka Steaks, Panchero's Mexican, Red Lantern Chinese, Red Robin, TX Roadhouse 🛏 Hampton Inn, Homewood Suites, Staybridge Suites 🅾 🏥, GNC, Harley-Davidson, HyVee Foods, Michael's, Natural Grocers, Old Navy, TJ Maxx, Walgreens, **S** 🅿 Murphy USA/dsl, Shell/dsl 🍴 Arby's, Azteca Mexican, Burger King, Chick-fil-A, China Cafe, Chipotle Mexican, DQ, Dynasty Buffet, Golden Corral, HuHot, Hungry Hobo, IHOP, La Rancherita, Noodles&Co., PepperJax Grill, Sonic, Starbucks, Steak'n Shake, Subway, Taco Bell, Village Inn Rest., Wendy's 🛏 Sleep Inn 🅾 $Tree, Aldi Foods, AT&T, Best Buy, Costco/dsl, Dick's, Discount Tire, Field&Stream, Meineke, PetsMart, Staples, Target, Verizon, Walmart
	I-74 begins/ends on I-80, exit 298. Exits 1-4 are in Iowa.

🔼🔽 INTERSTATE 80

Exit #	Services
163mm	Illinois/Indiana state line
161	US 6, IL 83, Torrence Ave, **N** 🅿 🍴 Burger King, Chili's, Culver's, Dunkin', Hooters, IHOP, Kenny's Ribs, Liang's Garden, New China Buffet, Olive Garden, Outriggers, Ranch Grande, Subway, Wendy's 🛏 Comfort Suites, Extended Stay America, Holiday Inn Express, Red Roof Inn, Sleep Inn, Travelodge 🅾 $General, $Tree, Aldi Foods, Best Buy, CarX, Chrysler/Jeep/Dodge, Fannie May Candies, Firestone/auto, Home Depot, Honda, JustTires, PepBoys, Starway Inn, **S** 🅿 Gas For Less, Marathon, Mobil 🍴 Burger King, Checkers, China Chef, DQ, Dunkin', Johnny K's Cafe, McDonald's, Popeye's, Round the Clock, Subway 🅾 AT&T, Auto Clinic, Chevrolet, O'Reilly Parts, Saab, SunRise Foods, vet, Walgreens, Walmart/Subway
160b	I-94 W, to Chicago, **tollway begins wb, ends eb**

INTERSTATE 80 Cont'd

Exit #	Services
160a	IL 394 S, to Danville
159mm	Oasis, 🛢 EVC, Mobil/7-11/dsl 🍴 McDonald's, Panda Express, Starbucks, Subway
2	IL 1, Halsted St, N 🛢 Quick Fuel 🍴 Maxwell St Grill 🛏 Clarion, Days Inn, Motel 6, Quality Inn, Red Carpet Inn, Super 8, Travelodge, S 🛢 Delta Sonic, Shell, Speedway, Walmart/dsl 🍴 Boston Mkt, Buffalo Wild Wings, Burger King, Chick-fil-A, Chili's, Chipotle, Culver's, Dunkin', Freddy's, KFC, Krispy Kreme, McDonald's, Panda Express, Panera Bread, Popeye's, Portillo's Hot Dogs, Potbelly, Starbucks, Subway, Wendy's, White Castle 🅾 $Tree, Aldi Foods, Best Buy, Chevrolet, Fanny May Candies, Firestone/auto, GNC, Home Depot, Jewel-Osco, Kohl's, Menards, Old Navy, PepBoys, PetCo, Ross, Target, TJ Maxx, Walgreens, Walmart
4	Dixie Hwy (from eb, no return), S 🛢 Mobil 🍴 Belagio, Dunkin' 🅾 golf
155	I-294 N, Tri-State Tollway, **toll plaza**
154	Kedzie Ave (from eb, no return), N 🛢 Speedway, S 🅾 H
151b a	I-57 (exits left from both directions), N to Chicago, S to Memphis
148b a	IL 43, Harlem Ave, N 🛢 Speedway/dsl 🍴 Buffalo Wild Wings, Burger King, Cracker Barrel, Culver's, Dunkin', Hamada of Japan, Joy Yee Asian, Pop's Italian Beef, Side Street Tavern, Tin Fish Grill, Wendy's 🛏 Comfort Suites, Fairfield Inn, Hampton Inn, Holiday Inn, La Quinta, Sleep Inn, Wingate Inn, Woodspring Suites 🅾 AT&T, Tinley Park Convention Center, Verizon, S 🛢 EVC 🍴 Arby's, Panera Bread, Subway, Taco Bell, TGIFriday's 🅾 ampitheater, Best Buy, CarMax, Dick's, GNC, Kohl's, Michael's, Old Navy, PetsMart, Ross, SuperTarget, TJ Maxx
147.5mm	**weigh sta wb**
145b a	US 45, 96th Ave, N 🍴 Arby's, Arrenello's Pizza, Baskin-Robbins/Dunkin', Tokyo Steaks, TX Roadhouse 🛏 Country Inn&Suites, Hilton Garden 🅾 Harley-Davidson, vet, **0-2 mi** S 🛢 BP, Shell/Circle K/dsl/24hr 🍴 Beggar's Pizza, Chipotle, Denny's, Doc's Smokehouse, Domino's, DQ, Legends, Mindy's Ribs, Mobil, Rising Sun Chinese, Starbucks, Stoney Pt Grill, Subway, Wendy's, White Castle 🛏 Super 8 🅾 Firestone/auto, repair, vet
143mm	**weigh sta eb**
140	SW Hwy, I-355 N Tollway, US 6 S, N 🅾 H
137	US 30, New Lenox, N 🍴 Williamson's Rest., S 🛢 Shell/Circle K/dsl, Speedway/dsl 🍴 Al's Hotdogs, Beggar's Pizza, Buffalo Wild Wings, Burger King, Keys's Chophouse, KFC, McDonald's, Paisano's Pizza, Subway, Taco Bell 🅾 Ace Hardware, Goodyear/auto, Jewel-Osco/dsl, Walgreens
134	Briggs St, N 🛢 Speedway, S 🛢 Mobil/dsl, Shell/dsl 🅾 Martin Camping
133	Richards St
132b a	US 52, IL 53, Chicago St, N 🛢 BP, Shell 🍴 Dunkin', Shark Fish Chicken
131.5mm	Des Plaines River
131	US 6, Meadow Ave, N 🅾 to Riverboat Casino
130b a	IL 7, Larkin Ave, N 🛢 Delta Sonic/dsl, Marathon/24hr, Mobil/CircleK/dsl, Shell, Speedway 🍴 Baskin-Robbins/Dunkin', Bob Evans, Boston Mkt, Burger King, Checkers, Culver's, DQ, JJ Fish&Chicken, KFC, Little Caesar's, McDonald's, Subway, Taco Bell, Wendy's, White Castle 🛏 Budget Inn, Clarion, Joliet Inn, Motel 6, Quality Inn, Red Roof Inn 🅾 H, 7-11, AT&T, auto repair, Cadillac/Chevrolet, Discount Tire, Goodyear/auto, Meineke, Pepboys, Sam's Club/gas, to U of St Francis, USPO, S 🛢 Mobil/dsl

Exit #	Services
127	Houbolt Rd, to Joliet, N 🛢 7-11, BP/deli 🍴 Burger King, Burger Theory, China Kitchen, Cracker Barrel, Dunkin', Heros Sport Grill, Jimmy John's, Jimmy K's, McDonald's, Subway 🛏 Comfort Inn, Fairfield Inn, Hampton Inn, Holiday Inn, TownePlace Suites 🅾 Riverboat Casino
126b a	I-55, N to Chicago, S to St Louis
125.5mm	Du Page River
122	Minooka, N 🛢 Circle K/dsl, S 🛢 BP, 🍴/Arby's/scales/dsl/24hr 🍴 2-Fers Pizza, Baskin-Robbins/Dunkin', McDonald's, Rosati's Pizza, Subway, Taco Bell, Wendy's, Wings Etc 🛏 Hampton Inn, TownePlace Suites 🅾 $General, 7-11
119mm	Rs wb, full 🚻 facilities, litter barrels, petwalk, 🅲, 🦽, playground, vending
117mm	Rs eb, full 🚻 facilities, litter barrels, petwalk, 🅲, 🦽, playground, vending
116	Brisbin Rd, CR 3000 E
112	IL 47, Morris, N 🛢 Citgo/dsl, 🍴/Subway/dsl/scales/24hr TA/BP/RPlace/scales/dsl/24hr/@ 🍴 Bellacino's, Chili's, IHO 🛏 Comfort Inn, Days Inn, Holiday Inn Express, Quality Inn 🅾 $General, Menards, S 🛢 BP/dsl, Circle K/dsl, Shell 🍴 Buffalo Wild Wings, Burger King, Culver's, DQ, Dunkin', Hong Kong Chinese, KFC/LJ Silver, Maria's Ristorante, McDonald's, Morris Diner, Pizza Hut, Rosati's Pizza, Sherwood Oaks Rest., Subway, Taco Bell, Wendy's 🛏 Park Motel, Super 8 🅾 H, $Tree, Aldi Foods, AT&T, AutoZone, Big R Store, Buick/Cadillac/Chevrolet, Chrysler/Dodge/Jeep, Fisher Parts, Ford, GMC, GNC, Jewel-Osco, to Stratton SP, transmissions/repair, Verizon, Walgreens, Walmart/Subway
105	to Seneca
97	to Marseilles, S 🛢 Shell/dsl 🅾 Four Star Camping (5mi), Glenwood Camping (4mi), to Illini SP
93	IL 71, Ottawa, N 🛢/🍴/Road Ranger/Subway/dsl/scales/24hr Shell/rest./dsl, S 🍴 Hank's Farm Rest., New Chiam 🅾 H
92.5mm	Fox River
90	IL 23, Ottawa, N 🛢 BP/Subway 🍴 Arby's, Cracker Barrel, Fonta Mexican, Rosati's Pizza, Taco Bell 🛏 Comfort Inn, Hampton Inn 🅾 AT&T, F&F, GNC, Honda, Toyota, Verizon, Walmart/McDonald's, S 🛢 BP/dsl/LP, Thornton's/dsl 🍴 China Inn, Culver's, DQ, Dunkin', Hardee's, KFC/LJ Silver, Sunfield Rest. 🛏 Fairfield Inn, Holiday Inn Express, Quality Inn, Super 8, Surrey Motel 🅾 H, $Tree, Aldi Foods, Ford/Lincoln/Kia, Harley-Davidson, Kroger, O'Reilly Parts, USPO, Verizon
81	IL 178, Utica, N 🛢 Loves/McDonald's/Subway/dsl/scale 24hr 🅾 KOA (2mi), S 🛢 Casey's/dsl, Shell/Jimmy Johns/dsl repair, to Starved Rock SP, visitor info
79b a	I-39, US 51, N to Rockford, S to Bloomington
77.5mm	Little Vermilion River
77	IL 351, La Salle, S 🛢 FLYING J/Denny's/dsl/scales/24hr 🍴 UpTown Grill (3mi) 🛏 Daniels Motel (1mi) 🅾 st police
75	IL 251, Peru, N 🛢 Mobil, Shell/rest./dsl/24hr 🍴 Arby's, Four Star Rest., McDonald's, Olive Garden, Starbucks, Taco Bell 🛏 Holiday Inn Express, Quality Inn, Super 8 🅾 Kohl's, Petsmart, Walmart/Dunkin', S 🛢 BP, Shell, Tesla EVC 🍴 Applebee's, Buffalo Wild Wings, Burger King, Culver's, DQ, IHOP, Jalepeno Mexican, Jersey Mike's, Jimmy John's, Master Buffet, McDonald's, Pizza Hut, Red Lobster, Steak'n Shake, Subway, Wendy's 🛏 Fairfield Inn, Hampton Inn, La Quinta 🅾 H, $Tree, Advance Parts, Aldi Foods, AT&T, AutoZone, BigLots, Buick/GMC, Chevrolet, Chrysler/Dodge/Jeep, CVS Drug, Ford/Hyundai/Lincoln, Goodyear/auto, Hobby Lobby, Home Depot, HyVee Food/dsl, Jo-Ann Fabrics, Marshall's, Menards, Mercedes, Midas, NAPA, Nissan, O'Reilly Parts, Staples, Target, Verizon, Walgreens

(left margin vertical text) CHICAGO AREA IL

MORRIS OTTAWA PERU

INTERSTATE 80 Cont'd

Exit #	Services
73	Plank Rd, **N** ⓖ Sapp Bros/Burger King/Subway/dsl/scales/@, Speedway/Speedway Cafe/dsl ⓕ Big Apple Rest. ⓞ Mack Trucks
70	IL 89, to Ladd, **N** ⓖ Casey's, **S** ⓛ Spring Valley Motel ⓞ Ⓗ golf
61	I-180, to Hennepin
56	IL 26, Princeton, **N** ⓖ Road Ranger/scales/dsl/@ ⓛ Super 8, **S** ⓖ BP/Beck's/dsl, Casey's, Shell/dsl ⓕ Big Apple Rest., Burger King, Coffee Cup Rest., Culver's, McDonald's, Subway, Wendy's ⓛ AmericInn, Days Inn, EconoLodge ⓞ Ⓗ $General, Auto-Zone, Buick/Cadillac/Chevrolet, O'Reilly Parts, Sullivan's Food/gas/e85, vet, Walmart
51mm	ⓡˢ both lanes, full Ⓐ facilities, litter barrels, petwalk, Ⓒ, Ⓐ, playground, RV dump, vending
45	IL 40, **N** ⓞ antiques, to Ronald Reagan Birthplace (21mi), **S** ⓞ Hennepin Canal SP
44mm	Hennepin Canal
33	IL 78, to Kewanee, Annawan, **N** ⓖ Shabbona RV Ctr/Camp (3mi), **S** ⓖ Cenex/dsl, FS/dsl/e85, Shell/Subway/dsl ⓛ Best Western ⓞ to Johnson-Sauk Tr SP
27	to US 6, Atkinson, **N** ⓖ Casey's (1mi), ♥Loves/Chester's/Godfathers's/Subway/dsl/scales24hr
19	IL 82, Geneseo, **N** ⓖ BP/dsl, Casey's/dsl ⓕ Culver's, DQ, Happy Joe's Pizza, Hardee's, McDonald's, New China, Pizza Hut, Subway, Sweet Pea's Grill ⓛ Best Western ⓞ Ⓗ $General, Ford, SaveALot Foods, Verizon, Walgreens, Walmart, **S** ⓕ Los Ranchitos Mexican
10	I-74, I-280, W to Moline, E to Peoria
9	US 6, to Geneseo, **N** ⓕ Lavender Crest Winery/Cafe, **S** ⓞ Niabi Zoo
7	Colona, **N** ⓖ Shell/dsl
5mm	Rock River
4a	IL 5, IL 92, W to Silvis, **S** ⓞ Lundeen's Camping
4b	I-88, IL 92, E to Rock Falls
2mm	weigh sta both lanes
1.5mm	Welcome Ctr eb, full Ⓐ facilities, info, litter barrels, petwalk, Ⓒ, Ⓐ, scenic overlook
1	IL 84, 20th St, Great River Rd, E Moline, **N** ⓖ BP/dsl ⓕ Bros Rest. ⓞ The Great River Rd, **3 mi S** ⓞ camping
0mm	Illinois/Iowa state line, Mississippi River

GENESEO

INTERSTATE 88

Exit #	Services
139.5mm	I-88 begins/ends on I-290.
139	I-294, S to Indiana, N to Milwaukee
138mm	toll plaza
137	IL 83 N, Cermak Rd, **N** ⓕ Cheesecake Factory, Clubhouse Rest., Ditka's Rest., McDonald's ⓛ Marriott ⓞ Barnes&Noble, Lord&Taylor, Macy's, Nieman-Marcus
136	IL 83 S, Midwest Rd (from eb), **N** ⓖ Shell/Circle K ⓕ Chipotle Mexican, Denny's, Devon Steaks, Giordano's Rest., Jamba Juice, Jimmy John's, McDonalds, Noodles&Co, Redstone Grill, Starbucks, Subway, Twin Peaks, Which Wich? ⓛ Courtyard, Holiday Inn, La Quinta, Staybridge ⓞ AT&T, Big Lots, Costco/gas, Home Depot, Nordstrom's, Old Navy, REI, TJ Maxx, Walgreens, World Mkt
134	Highland Ave (no EZ wb return), **N** ⓕ Barbokoa, Benihana, Brick House, Brio Grille, Buca Italian, Burger King, Capital Grille, Chama Guacha Brazilian, Champps Grill, Chick-fil-A, Chipotle, Claimjumper Rest., Fuddruckers, Harry Caray's, Honey-Jam Cafe,

OAKBROOK

134	Continued
	Hooters, Kona Grill, Kyoto, McCormick & Schmick's, Melting Pot, Miller's Rest., Noodles&Co, Olive Garden, Olive Therapy Pizza, Panera Bread, PF Chang's, Portillo's Hotdogs, Potbelly, Red Lobster, Rockbottom Brewery, Ruby Tuesday, Starbucks, Starbucks, Subway, TGIFriday's, Tom&Eddie's Burgers, Uncle Julio's ⓛ Comfort Inn, Embassy Suites, Extended Stay America, Holiday Inn Express, Hyatt Place, Marriott, Red Roof Inn, Westin Hotel ⓞ Ⓗ $Tree, Best Buy, Dick's, Home Depot, JC Penney, Kohl's, Marshall's, Michael's, Petsmart, Ross, Target, Tuesday Morning, Verizon, Vonmaur, **S** ⓕ Parkers Ocean Grill
132	I-355 N (from wb)
131	I-355 S (from eb)
130	IL 53 (from wb), **1 mi N** ⓖ BP, Mobil ⓕ McDonald's ⓞ Walmart
127	Naperville Rd, **N** ⓕ Mullen's Grill ⓛ Hilton, Sheraton, **S** ⓖ Mobil ⓕ Arby's, Buona Beef, Butterfield's Pancakes, Chipotle, Coopers Hawk, Fogo de Chao Brazilian, Granite City, HoneyBaked Ham, Jason's Deli, Maggiano's, McDonald's, Ming Hin, Morton's Steaks, Paisan's Pizza, Panera Bread, Pizza Hut, Subway, Tom & Eddie's Burgers, Uncle Julio's, Wendy's, White Chocolate Grill ⓛ Best Western, Country Inn & Suites, Courtyard, Embassy Suites, Extended Stay America, Fairfield Inn, Hampton Inn, Marriott, Motel 6, Regency Inn ⓞ $Tree, CVS, Staples, Subaru
125	Winfield Rd, **N** ⓖ BP, Mobil ⓛ Hyatt House, Hyatt Place, Residence Inn ⓞ Ⓗ Walgreens, **S** ⓕ Buffalo Wild Wings, CA Pizza Kitchen, Chipotle Mexican, Corner Bakery Cafe, Eddie Merlot, Masala, McDonald's, Potbelly, Red Robin, Rockbottom Brewery, Starbucks, Twin Peaks, Zoup ⓛ Hilton Garden, SpringHill Suites ⓞ SuperTarget
123	IL 59, **N** ⓖ Speedway/dsl ⓞ CarMax, **S** ⓖ BP/Domino's, Delta Sonic, Speedway ⓕ Baskin Robbins/Dunkin', Cracker Barrel, Firehouse Subs, Jimmy John's, McDonald's, Oberweis, Starbucks, Subway, TX Roadhouse, Wendy's ⓛ Extended Stay America, Fairfield Inn, Red Roof Inn, Sleep Inn, Towneplace Suites ⓞ $Tree, 7-11, CVS Drug
119	Farnsworth Ave, **N** ⓖ BP, Shell, Thornton's/dislike ⓕ Chipotle, McDonald's, Noodles&Co, Panera Bread, Papa Bear Rest., Quizno's, Sonic, Starbucks ⓛ Fox Valley Inn, Motel 6 ⓞ Advance Parts, AT&T, Firestone/auto, GNC, Premium Outlets/Famous Brands, Verizon, Walgreens, Walmart/Subway, **S** ⓖ Marathon, Moble, Shell, Speedway ⓕ Baskin-Robbins/Dunkin', Goody's, Little Caesar's, McDonald's, Mike&Denise's Pizza, Subway, Taco Bell ⓞ $General, 7-11, AutoZone, Family$, Walgreens
118mm	toll plaza
117	IL 31, IL 56, to Aurora, Batavia, **N** ⓖ BP/dsl ⓕ A&W ⓞ 7-11, **S** ⓖ Mobil, Speedway/dsl, Thornton's/dsl ⓕ Baskin-Robbins/Dunkin', Burger King, Culver's, Denny's, McDonald's, Nikarry's, Popeye's, Subway, Taco Bell, Wendy's, White Castle ⓛ Baymont Inn ⓞ Ⓗ $General, $Tree, Ace Hardware, Advance Parts, AutoZone, Cermak Foods, Family$, Firestone, GNC, O'Reilly Parts, Ross, U-Haul, Walgreens

NAPERVILLE

IL

INTERSTATE 88 Cont'd

Exit #	Services
115	Orchard Rd, **N** 🍴 Dunkin', McDonald's, Subway ⊙ $Tree, Best Buy, Chrysler/Dodge/Jeep, Ford/Lincoln, Hyundai, JC Penney, Kia, Michaels, Nissan, PetCo, Subaru, Target, Verizon, Woodman's/dsl, **0-2 mi S** 🅟 7-11 🍴 Arby's, Buffalo Wild Wings, Chili's, Chipotle, IHOP, Jimmy John's, Panera Bread, Papa Saverio's, Pizza Hut, Starbucks, Wendy's 🛏 Candlewood Suites, Hampton Inn, Holiday Inn ⊙ AT&T, CVS Drug, Discount Tire, Home Depot, Office Depot
114	IL 56W, to US 30 (from wb, no EZ return), to Sugar Grove
109	IL 47 (from eb), Elburn
94	Peace Rd, to IL 38, **N** ⊙ 🅷
93mm	**Dekalb Oasis/24hr both lanes,** 🅟 Mobil/dsl 🍴 McDonald's, Panda Express, Starbucks, Subway
92	IL 38, IL 23, Annie Glidden Rd, to DeKalb, **2-3 mi N** 🅟 BP, Road Ranger/dsl, Shell 🍴 Baskin-Robbins, Burger King, Chipotle Mexican, Culver's, Dunkin', Fatty's, Happy Wok Chinese, IHOP, Jct Rest., Jersey Mike's, McDonald's, Miki MOto, Molly's Eatery, Panda Express, Papa John's, Pizza Hut, Pizza Pros, Pizza Villa, Potbelly, Starbucks, Subway, Taco Bell, Tom&Jerry's, Topper's Pizza 🛏 Baymont Inn, Hampton Inn, Red Roof Inn, Super 8 ⊙ CVS, Ford, Illini Tire, Schnuck's Food/Drug, to N IL U, Walgreens
86mm	toll plaza
78	I-39, US 51, S to Bloomington, N to Rockford
76	IL 251, Rochelle, **N** 🅟 BP/dsl, Casey's, Shell ⊙ 🅷, Ford, tires/repair, **S** 🅟 ♥Loves♥/Hardee's/dsl/scales/24hr
56mm	toll plaza
54	IL 26, Dixon, **N** 🅟 Murphy USA/dsl, Road Ranger/dsl/24hrs 🍴 Hardee's, Las Palmas, Panda Chinese, Pizza Hut 🛏 Comfort Inn, Super 8 ⊙ 🅷, $Tree, Aldi, GNC, to John Deere HS, to Ronald Reagan Birthplace, to St Parks, URGENT CARE, Verizon, Walmart
44	US 30 (last free exit eb), **N** ⊙ Leisure lake RV Ctr (2mi), food, gas, lodging
41	IL 40, to Sterling, Rock Falls, **1-2 mi N** 🅟 Mobil/dsl, Shell 🍴 American Grill, Arby's, Arthur's Deli, Burger King, Candlelight Rest., Culver's, Gazi's Rest., Hardee's, Jimmy John's, McDonald's, Perna's Pizza, Pizza Hut, Red Apple Rest., Subway 🛏 Country Inn&Suites, Days Inn, Holiday Inn Express, Super 8 ⊙ 🅷, $General, AutoZone, Harley-Davidson, O'Reilly Parts, Sava-Lot, Verizon, Walgreens, Walmart
36	to US 30, Rock Falls, Sterling
26	IL 78, to Prophetstown, Morrison, **N** ⊙ to Morrison-Rockwood SP
18	to Albany, Erie
10	to Port Byron, Hillsdale, **S** 🅟 Phillips 66/dsl, Shell/Subway/scales/dsl/24hr
6	IL 92 E, to Joslin, **N** 🍴 Jammerz Roadhouse (2mi), **S** ⊙ Sunset Lake Camping (1mi)
2	Former IL 2
1b a	I-80, W to Des Moines, E to Chicago
0mm	IL 5, IL 92, W to Silvis. Lundeen's Camping, to Quad City Downs. **I-88 begins/ends on I-80, exit 4b.**

INTERSTATE 90

Exit #	Services
0mm	Illinois/Indiana state line, **Chicago Skyway Toll Rd begins/ends.**
1mm	US 12, US 20, 106th St, Indianapolis Blvd, **N** 🅟 Mobil 🍴 Burger King, Starbucks, Taco Bell ⊙ Aldi Foods, AutoZone, casino, Jewel-Osco, **S** 🅟 Citgo 🍴 Beggars Pizza, McDonald's ⊙ auto repair
2.5mm	🅟 Skyway Oasis 🍴 McDonald's ⊙ toll plaza
3mm	87th St (from wb)
4mm	79th St, services on 79th St and Stoney Island Ave

5.5mm	73rd St (from wb)
6mm	State St (from wb), **S** 🅟 Citgo
7mm	I-94 N (mile markers decrease to IN state line)
	I-90 E and I-94 E run together. See I-94, exits 43b - 59a.
84	I-94 W, Lawrence Ave, **N** 🅟 BP/dsl
83b a	Foster Ave (from wb), **N** 🅟 🍴 Elly's Pancakes, Subway ⊙ Advance Parts, Firestone/auto, Walgreens
82c	Austin Ave, to Foster Ave
82b	Byrn-Mawr (from wb)
82a	Nagle Ave
81b	Sayre Ave (from wb)
81a	IL 43, Harlem Ave, **S** 🅟 Gas Depot, Shell 🍴 Dunkin', Popeye's, Sally's Pancakes, Wendy's ⊙ $Tree, AutoZone
80	Canfield Rd (from wb), **N** ⊙ Walgreens
79b a	IL 171 S, Cumberland Ave (from wb), **N** 🅟 7-11, Mobil 🍴 Al's Burgers, Dunkin'/Baskin Robbins, Hooters, McDonald's, Nancy's Pizza, Outback Steaks 🛏 Marriott, SpringHill Suites, Westin Hotel ⊙ Hampton Inn, Mariano's Mkt, **S** 🍴 Bar Louie's, Starbucks 🛏 Holiday Inn, Hyatt, Renaissance
78	I-294, I-190 W, **N** 🅟 Mobil 🍴 McDonald's 🛏 Hampton Inn, Westin, **S** 🛏 Hyatt ⊙ to O'Hare Airport
76	IL 72, Lee St (from wb), **N** 🍴 Buona, Chili's, Chipotle, Culver's, IHOP, Jimmy John's, Longhorn Steaks, Panda Express, Steak'n Shake, Subway 🛏 Extended Stay America, Radisson, Residence Inn ⊙ Target, **S** 🍴 McDonald's 🛏 Best Western, Holiday Inn Express, Holiday Inn Select, Sheraton Gateway
73	Elmhurst Rd (from wb), **S** 🅟 Shell 🍴 Burger King, McDonald's, Subway, White Castle 🛏 Best Western, Days Inn, InTowne Suites, La Quinta, Motel 6, Super 8, Wyndham Garden
70	Arlington Hts Rd, **S** 🅟 Mobil, Shell 🍴 Subway 🛏 Sheraton ⊙ Chevrolet, **N on Algonquin** 🅟 BP/dsl, Shell/dsl 🍴 Arby's, Buona Beef, Chef Ping, Chipotle Mexican, Coopers Hawk, Denny's, Five Guys, Honey Baked Ham, Jimmy Johns, McDonald's, Noodles&Co, Panda Express, Panera Bread, Pie Five, Potbelly's, Steak'n Shake 🛏 Comfort Inn, Courtyard, DoubleTree, Holiday Inn Express, Red Roof Inn, Wingate Inn ⊙ AT&T, GNC, Lowe' Whse, Meijer/dsl, NTB, Staples, vet, Walmart
68	I-290, IL 53, **N on Algonquin** 🛏 Embassy Suites, Holiday Inn, Holiday Inn Express, Renaissance Inn, **1 mi S on Golf Rd** 🍴 C... Pizza Kitchen, Cheesecake Factory, Chevy's Mexican, Hooters, Joe's Crabshack, Longhorn Steaks, Maggiano's, Olive Garden, Panera Bread, Qdoba, Red Robin, Starbucks, Subway, TGI Friday's, Uno 🛏 Extended Stay America, Hyatt, Residence Inn ⊙ AT&T, Costco/gas, Firestone/auto, JC Penney, Lord&Taylor, Macy's, Marshall's, Michael's, Nordstrom, Old Navy, Petsmart, Trader Joe's
65	Roselle Rd (from wb, no return), **N** ⊙ Medieval Times Funpark, **S** 🅟 Mobil 🍴 Boston Mkt, Chipotle Mexican, Denny's, Fox &Hound, Jimmy John's, KFC, McDonald's, Melting Pot, Outback Steaks, Panda Express, Papa John's, Subway, Taco Bell, Wendy's 🛏 Country Inn&Suites, Extended Stay America, Extended Stay America (2), Holiday Inn Express, Radisson ⊙ 7-11, Buick GMC, Carmax, Chrysler/Dodge/Jeep, Fiat, Firestone/auto, Jewel-Osco, Mazda, Office Depot, O'Reilly Parts, PetCo, TJ Maxx, Walgreens
62	Barrington Rd (from wb), **N** 🍴 Apple Villa Pancake House, Gino's East, Hunan Beijing, Jersey's Grill, Jimmy John's, Lucky Monk 🛏 Hilton Garden ⊙ vet, **S** 🅟 BP, Mobil/dsl 🍴 Buona Beef, Burger King, Chili's, Domino's, IHOP, Macaroni Grill, McDonald's, Moretti's, Starbucks, Steak'n Shake, Subway, Swe... Caroline's 🛏 Hampton Inn, Hawthorne Suites, Hyatt Place, La Quinta, Quality Inn, Red Roof Inn ⊙ U-Haul

DEKALB DIXON E MOLINE (left vertical tab)

CHICAGO AREA SCHAUMBURG (right vertical tab)

IL (left margin tab)

INTERSTATE 90 Cont'd

Exit #	Services
59	IL 59, N 🍴 Buffalo Wild Wings, Chipotle Mexican, Claim Jumper Rest., Cooper's Hawk Rest., Culver's, Dunkin', Firehouse Subs, Jersey Mike's, Jimmy John's, Moe's SW Grill, Noodles& Co, Panda Express, Panera Bread, Potbelly, Red Robin, Rookie's Grill, Ruth's Chris Steaks, Starbucks, Subway, Which Wich? 🛏️ Marriott 🅾️ Cabela's, CVS Drug, Duluth Trading, GNC, Petsmart, Ross, Target, TJ Maxx, Verizon, World Mkt
58	Beverly Rd (from wb)
56	IL 25, N 🛏️ Lexington Inn, S 🅿️ BP/dsl, Shell/dsl, Speedway/dsl 🍴 Arby's, Baker Hill Pancakes, Subway, Wendy's 🅾️ Advance Parts, city park, NAPA AutoCare
54b a	IL 31, N 🅿️ BP, Thornton's 🍴 Alexander's Rest., Baskin-Robbins/Dunkin' 🛏️ Courtyard, Hampton Inn, Holiday Inn, Quality Inn, Super 8, TownePlace Suites
53.5mm	Elgin Toll Plaza, 🄫
52	Randall Rd, N 🅿️ Shell 🍴 Big Sammy's Hot Dogs, Burnt Toast, Cafe Roma, DQ, Jimmy John's, Jimmy's Charhouse, Mr Wok, Panera Bread, Rookies Grill, Starbucks, Village Pizza 🛏️ Comfort Suites, Country Inn&Suites 🅾️ Honda, VW, S 🅿️ 7-11 🛏️ Candlewood Suites 🅾️🄷, Subaru
46	IL 47, to Woodstock, N 🅾️ Ford, General RV Ctr, Huntley Outlets/famous brands
42	US 20, Marengo, N 🅿️ Citgo/Mexican Grill/dsl/scales/24hr, ♥Loves/Arby's/dsl/scales/24hr, Road Ranger/Subway/dsl/scales/24hr, Speedway/Speedy's Cafe/dsl/24hr, TA/BP/Country Pride/Burger King/Popeye's/dsl/scales/24hr/@ 🍴 McDonald's, Wendy's 🛏️ Super 8 🅾️ access to services at exit 46 (6mi), Ford, Huntley Outlets, to museums
38mm	Marengo Toll Plaza (from eb)
25	Genoa Rd, to Belvidere, N 🅿️ Murphy USA/dsl 🍴 Applebee's, Rosati's Pizza, Starbucks, Subway 🅾️ Verizon, Walmart/Dunkin'
24mm	Belvidere Oasis both lanes, 🅿️ Mobil/7-11/dsl/24hr 🍴 Food Court, McDonald's, Panda Express, Sbarro, Starbucks, Subway 🅾️🄫
20	Irene Rd
18mm	Kishwaukee River
17mm	I-39 S, US 20, US 51, to Rockford, S funpark
15	US 20, State St, N 🅿️ Mobil/dsl, Phillips 66/Subway/dsl 🍴 Cracker Barrel 🛏️ Baymont Inn, Clocktower Resort, Days Inn, 0-2 mi S 🅿️ FasFuel/dsl, Mobil/dsl 🍴 Applebee's, Buffalo Wild Wings, Burger King, Chick-fil-A, Chili's, Chipotle Mexican, City Buffet, Coldstone, Culver's, Denny's, Dos Reales, Fiesta Cancun, Five Guys, Gerry's Pizza, Giovanni's Rest., Hoffman House Rest., Hooters, IHOP, Jason's Deli, Jersey Mike's, Jimmy John's, KFC/LJ Silver, Lino's Italian, LoneStar Steaks, Longhorn Steaks, Machine Shed Rest., McDonald's, Noodles&Co, Old Chicago Grill, Olive Garden, Outback Steaks, Panda Express, Panera Bread, Panino's Drive-Thru, Perkins, Pizza Hut/Taco Bell, PotBelly, Red Lobster, Red Robin, Ruby Tuesday, Starbucks, Steak'n Shake, Stone Eagle Tavern, Subway, ThunderBay Grille, TX Roadhouse, Wendy's 🛏️ Candlewood Suites, Comfort Inn, Courtyard, Extended Stay America, Fairfield Inn, Hampton Inn, Hilton Garden, Holiday Inn, Motel 6, Quality Suites, Radisson, Red Roof Inn, Residence Inn, Sleep Inn, Staybridge Suites, Super 8 🅾️🄷, $Tree, Advance Parts, Aldi Foods, AT&T, Best Buy, BigLots, Burlington Coats, Cadillac, Chrysler/Dodge/Jeep, Dick's, Discount Tire, GNC, Gordman's, Hobby Lobby, Home Depot, Hyundai, JoAnn Fabrics, Kohl's, Lowe's, Marshall's, Mazda, Michael's, Nissan, Old Navy, Old Time Pottery, PetCo, Petsmart, Ross, Sam's Club/gas, Schnuck's Foods, Subaru, Target, Tuesday Morning, Valli Foods, Verizon, Walgreens, Walmart/McDonald's

12	E Riverside Blvd, Loves Park, N 🅿️ EVC 🅾️ Costco/gas, 🄷, 0-2 mi S 🅿️ BP, Mobil/dsl, Phillips 66/dsl, Road Ranger/Subway/dsl, Shell/dsl 🍴 2nd Cousin's Grill, Arby's, BeefARoo, Ciaobella, Culver's, DQ, Greenfire Rest., India House, Japanese Express, KFC, McDonald's, RBI Rest., Rosatti's Pizza, Sam's Ristorante, Singapore Grill, Subway, Taco Bell, Wendy's 🛏️ Holiday Inn Express, Home 2 Suites, Quality Inn 🅾️ Audi/Honda/Mercedes, Autowerks, Farm&Fleet, funpark, Lexus, to Rock Cut SP, Toyota, Tuffy Auto, Walgreens
8	Il 173, S to Rock Cut SP
3.5mm	S Beloit Toll Plaza
3	Rockton Rd, S 🅿️ ♥Loves/Hardee's/dsl/scales/24hr
1.5mm	Welcome Ctr/🆁🆂 eb, full 🛏️ facilities, info, litter barrels, petwalk, 🄫, 🄿, playground, RV dump
1	US 51 N, IL 75 W, S Beloit, N 🅿️ Fas Fuel/McDonald's/dsl S 🅿️ Flying J/Denny's/dsl/scales/24hr, Road Ranger/Subway/dsl/E85/scales/24hr 🛏️ Best Western, Tollway Inn 🅾️ Finnegan's RV Ctr
0mm	Illinois/Wisconsin state line

INTERSTATE 94

Exit #	Services
77mm	Illinois/Indiana state line
	I-94 and I-80 run together 3 mi. See I-80, exit 161.
74[160]b	I-80/I-294 W
74a	IL 394 S, to Danville
73b a	US 6,159th St, N 🅿️ ♥Loves/Hardee's/dsl/scales/24hr, Mobil 🍴 Applebee's, Buffalo Wild Wings, Continental Rest., Denny's, Outback Steaks, Panda Express, Sonic, Starbucks, Taco Bell, Tilly's, White Castle 🅾️ BigLots, Cadillac, Goodyear Commercial Tire, Hyundai, JC Penney, Kia, Lincoln, Macy's, Marshall's, Nissan, PetCo, Ross, Sam's Club, Toyota, USPO, vet, S 🅿️ BP, Marathon 🍴 Checkers, Harold's Chicken, Little Caesar's, McDonald's, Papa John's, Popeye's, Shark's, Subway 🛏️ Holland Inn 🅾️ Aldi Foods, Family$, Jewel-Osco, O'Reilly Parts, Stanfa Tire/repair
71b a	Sibley Blvd, N 🅿️ BP/dsl, Citgo, Mobil/dsl 🍴 McDonald's, Nick's Gyros, Popeye's, Shark's, Subway 🛏️ Baymont Inn 🅾️ $Tree, Family$, Pete's Mkt, S 🅿️ Circle K/Checkers/dsl, Marathon/dsl, Shell 🍴 Baskin-Robbins/Dunkin', Burger King, KFC, Taco Bell, Wendy's, White Castle 🛏️ Best Motel 🅾️ $General, Advance Parts, AutoZone, Family$, Food4Less/gas, Menards, Walgreens
70b a	Dolton
69	Beaubien Woods (from eb), Beaubien Woods Forest Preserve
68b a	130th St
66b	115th St, S 🍴 McDonald's
66a	111th Ave, S 🅿️ Citgo/dsl, Shell 🅾️🄷, $Tree, Firestone/auto, Ross, Walmart
65	103rd Ave, Stony Island Ave
63	I-57 S (exits left from wb)

🅖 = gas 🍴 = food 🛏 = lodging 🅞 = other 🆁🆂 = rest stop Copyright 2022 - The Next EXIT ©

INTERSTATE 94 Cont'd

Exit #	Services
62	Wentworth Ave (from eb), N 🅖 Citgo 🍴 Burger King, KFC, S 🍴 McDonald's
61b	87th St, N 🅖 BP, Shell/dsl 🍴 Burger King, McDonald's, S 🍴 Starbucks, Subway 🅞 $Tree, AutoZone, Burlington Coats, Food4Less, Home Depot, Jewel-Osco, Marshall's, O'Reilly Parts, Staples, Verizon
61a	83rd St (from eb), N 🅖 Shell 🍴 Subway 🅞 st police
60c	79th St, N 🅖 Mobil, Shell 🅞 Walgreens, S 🅖 Falcon 🍴 Church's, Subway
60b	76th St, N 🅖 BP, Mobil, Shell 🅞 Walgreens, S 🍴 KFC, Popeye's
60a	75th St (from eb), N 🅖 BP, Shell 🅞 Aldi Foods, S 🍴 KFC, Popeye's
59c	71st St, N 🅖 BP, S 🍴 McDonald's
59a	I-90 E, to Indiana Toll Rd
58b	63rd St (from eb), N 🅖 BP, S 🅖 Mobil
58a	I-94 divides into local and express, 59th St, S 🅖 Mobil
57b	Garfield Blvd, N 🍴 Checker's 🅞 Family$, Walgreens, S 🅖 Citgo, Mobil, Shell/24hr 🍴 Wendy's
57a	51st St
56b	47th St (from eb)
56a	43rd St, S 🅖 BP/Subway/dsl, Citgo/dsl
55b	Pershing Rd
55a	35th St, S 🅞 to New Comiskey Park
54	31st St
53c	I-55, Stevenson Pkwy, N to downtown, Lakeshore Dr
53b	I-55, Stevenson Pkwy, S to St Louis
52c	18th St (from eb), N 🅞 Whole Foods
52b	Roosevelt Rd, Taylor St (from wb), N 🅖 Citgo 🍴 Chipotle 🅞 Best Buy, Home Depot, Walgreens, Whole Foods Mkt
52a	Taylor St, Roosevelt Rd (from eb), N 🅖 Citgo
51h-i	I-290 W, to W Suburbs
51g	E Jackson Blvd, downtown
51f	W Adams St, downtown
51e	Monroe St (from eb), downtown, S 🛏 Crowne Plaza 🅞 Walgreens, Whole Foods
51d	Madison St (from eb), S 🛏 Crowne Plaza 🅞 Walgreens, Whole Foods, downtown
51c	E Washington Blvd, downtown
51b	W Randolph St, downtown
51a	Lake St (from wb)
50b	E Ohio St, S 🅖 Marathon, downtown
50a	Ogden Ave
49b a	Augusta Blvd, Division St, N 🅞 Acura, Lexus, Mercedes, S 🅖 BP, Shell
48b	IL 64, North Ave, N 🅖 BP, S 🅞 Mercedes
48a	Armitage Ave, N 🅞 Best Buy, Kohl's, Lexus, S 🅖 Shell 🅞 Jaguar, Land Rover, Volvo
47c b	Damen Ave, N 🅖 car/vanwash
47a	Western Ave, Fullerton Ave, N 🅖 Mobil 🍴 Burger King, Dunkin', Popeye's, Starbucks, Subway 🅞 Costco/gas, Home Depot, Jo-Ann Fabrics, Pepboys, Petsmart, Staples, Target, S 🅖 Marathon
46b a	Diversey Ave, California Ave, S 🍴 IHOP/24hr, Popeye's 🅞 Walgreens
45c	Belmont Ave
45b	Kimball Ave, N 🅖 Marathon/dsl 🅞 CVS Drug, Home Depot, S 🅖 Shell 🍴 Dunkin', Subway 🅞 Aldi Foods, Best Buy, Walgreens
45a	Addison St
44b	Pulaski Ave, Irving Park Rd, N 🅖 Mobil/Subway, Shell/dsl
44a	IL 19, Keeler Ave, Irving Park Rd, N 🅖 Mobil/Subway, Shell/dsl 🅞 to Wrigley Field

Exit #	Services
43c	Montrose Ave
43b	I-90 W
43a	Wilson Ave
42	W Foster Ave (from wb), S 🅖 Marathon/service, Mobil 🍴 Subwa
41mm	Chicago River, N Branch
41c	IL 50 S, to Cicero, to I-90 W
41b a	US 14, Peterson Ave, N 🅞 Whole Foods Mkt
39b a	Touhy Ave, N 🅖 BP/dsl, Shell/Circle K 🅞 Cassidy Tire, Toyota, S 🅖 BP, Citgo, Mobil, Shell 🍴 Bar Louie's, Baskin-Robbins Dunkin', Brickhouse Rest., Buffalo Wild Wings, Burger King Chili's, Chipotle Mexican, ChuckeCheese, Corner Bakery Cafe Jersey Mike's, Jimmy John's, McDonald's, Noodles&Co, Outback Steaks, Panda Express, Penn Sta Subs, Red Robin, Sand er's Rest., Shallot's Bistro, Starbucks, Subway, Tilted Kilt 🛏 Holiday Inn 🅞 Barnes&Noble, Best Buy, Dick's, Fresh Farms Mk GNC, Jewel-Osco, Michael's, Nissan, PepBoys, Petsmart, Ros Tuesday Morning, vet, Walgreens, Walmart
37b a	IL 58, Dempster St, N 🅖 Shell 🍴 Panda Express, Subway, S 🅖 BP/dsl, Shell 🍴 Pizza Hut 🅞 Midas
35	Old Orchard Rd, N 🅖 BP, Shell 🍴 Bloomingdale's, Buffalo Wil Wings, CA Pizza Kitchen, CheeseCake Factory 🅞 🅷, Lord&Taylor, Macy's, Nissan, Nordstrom's, S 🍴 Ruby Tuesday 🛏 Extended Stay America, Hampton Inn, Residence Inn
34c b	E Lake Ave, N 🅖 BP/dsl 🍴 Corner Bakery Cafe, Five Guys, Panda Express, Starbucks, Subway 🅞 Fresh Mkt Foods, GNC, Walgreens, S 🅖 Shell 🍴 DQ, Jimmy John's, Starbucks 🅞 auto repa
34a	US 41 S, Skokie Rd (from eb)
33b a	Willow Rd, S 🅖 Shell 🍴 Dunkin', Starbucks 🅞 Mariano's Mkt USPO, Walgreens
31	E Tower Rd, S 🅞 BMW, Carmax, Infiniti, Land Rover, Mercedes Toyota, vet, Volvo
30b a	Dundee Rd (from wb, no EZ return), S 🅖 Citgo/dsl 🍴 Barnaby Rest., Chipotle, Morton's Steaks, Noodles&Co, Panera Brea Potbelly, Roti Mediterranean, Ruth's Chris Steaks, Starbucks 🛏 Renaissance 🅞 Mariano's Mkt
29	US 41, to Waukegan, to Tri-state tollway
28	IL 43, Waukegan Rd (from eb), N 🅖 BP, Shell 🍴 Dunkin Baskin Robbins, Mod Pizza, Noodles&Co, Starbucks 🛏 Courtyard, Embassy Suites, Red Roof Inn 🅞 Hobby Lobby, Hom Depot, Jewel-Osco, Just Tires
25	I-294 S, Lake-Cook Rd (from sb), E 🛏 Embassy Suites, Hyatt, 🍴 J Alexander's Rest.
24	Deerfield Rd (from nb), W 🅖 Mobil 🛏 Marriott Suites
21	IL 22, Half Day Rd, E 🍴 Leaf Cafe 🛏 La Quinta, W 🛏 Hom wood Suites
19	IL 60, Town Line Rd, E 🅞 🅷, W 🛏 Hilton Garden, Residen Inn 🅞 Costco/gas
18mm	Lake Forest Oasis both lanes, 🅖 Mobil/7-11/dsl 🍴 KFC/Ta Bell, McDonald's, Panda Express, Starbucks, Subway 🅞 info
16mm	IL 176, Rockland Rd (no nb re-entry), E 🅞 Harley-Davidson, Lamb's Farm
14mm	IL 137, Buckley Rd, E 🅞 Chicago Med School, to VA 🅷
11mm	IL 120 E, Belvidere Rd (no nb re-entry), E 🅞 🅷
10mm	IL 21, Milwaukee Ave (from eb, no eb re-entry), E 🅞 🅷, S Flags
8mm	IL 132, Grand Ave, E 🅖 Speedway/dsl 🍴 Baskin-Robbin Dunkin', Burger King, ChuckeCheese, Cracker Barrel, Cra ings Red Hots, Culver's, Golden Corral, Ichibahn, IHOP, Jimm John's, Joe's Crabshack, KFC/LJ Silver, Mama K's Zpizza, M Donald's, Oberweiss, Old Chicago Red Hots, Olive Garden, Ou back Steaks, Rosati's Pizza, Starbucks, Subway 🛏 Baymont In

CHICAGO AREA

IL

CHICAGO AREA

⬆E INTERSTATE 94 Cont'd

8mm   Continued

Country Inn&Suites, Extended Stay America, Hampton Inn, Key Lime Cove Resort, La Quinta, Super 8 🅞 Six Flags Park, **0-2 mi W** 🅟 Shell/Circle K 🍴 Bakers Square, Boston Mkt, Buffalo Wild Wings, Chili's, Chipotle Mexican, Denny's, Five Guys, Giordano's Pizza, Jersey Mike's Subs, Jimano's Pizza, LoneStar Steaks, McDonald's, Noodles&Co, Panda Express, Panera Bread, Penn Sta Subs, Pizza Hut, Portillo's, Potbelly's, Red Lobster, Red Robin, Ruby Tuesday, Starbucks, Steak'n Shake, Taco Bell, TGIFriday's, Uno Grill, Wendy's, White Castle 🏠 Comfort Inn, Fairfield Inn, Holiday Inn 🅞 $Tree, AT&T, AutoZone, Bass Pro Shops, Best Buy, Buick/GMC, Chrysler/Dodge/Jeep, Goodyear, Gurnee Mills Outlet Mall/famous brands, Home Depot, Honda, Hyundai, Jewel-Osco, Kohl's, Macy's, Mariano's Mkt, Marshall's, Menards, Michael's, Old Navy, Petsmart, Ross, Sam's Club, Sears Grand/auto, Target, TJ Maxx, Tuesday Morning, Verizon, VW, Walgreens, Walmart

5mm	**Waukegan toll plaza**
2	IL 173 (from nb, no return), Rosecrans Ave, **E** 🅞 to IL Beach SP
1b	US 41 S, to Waukegan (from sb)
1a	Russell Rd, **E** 🅞 I-94 RV Ctr, **W** 🅟 Citgo/dsl/scales, ♥Loves /dsl/scales/24hr/@, TA/Country Pride/dsl/scales/24hr/@ 🅞 Peterbilt
0mm	Illinois/Wisconsin state line

⬆N INTERSTATE 255 (St Louis)

Exit #	Services
	I-255 begins/ends on I-270, exit 7.
30	I-270, W to Kansas City, E to Indianapolis
29	IL 162, to Glen Carbon, to Pontoon Beach, Granite City
26	Horseshoe Lake Rd, **E** st police
25b a	I-55/I-70, W to St Louis, E to Chicago, Indianapolis
24	Collinsville Rd, **E** 🅟 🍴 Jack-in-the-Box 🅞 Shop'n Save, **W** 🅞 Fairmount Racetrack
20	I-64, US 50, W to St Louis, E to Louisville. **Services 1 mi E off I-64, exit 9.**
19	State St, E St Louis, **E** 🏠 Western Inn, **W** 🅞 Holten SP
17b a	IL 15, E St Louis, to Belleville, Centreville, **E** 🅟 ⬦FLYING J/Denny's/dsl/scales/24hr, **W** 🅟 Phillips 66 🅞 auto repair
15	Mousette Lane, **E** 🅟 ♥Loves/Chester's/Godfather's/Subway/dsl/scales/24hr/@ 🅞🅗, **W** 🅞 Peterbilt
13	IL 157, to Cahokia, **E** 🅟 Phillips 66, **W** 🅟 BP, MotoMart 🍴 Capt D's, China Express, Classic K Burgers, Domino's, Hardee's, KFC, Little Caesar's, McDonald's, Pizza Hut, Rally's, Subway, Taco Bell, White Castle 🏠 Comfort Inn 🅞 $General, $Tree, Advance Parts, Aldi Foods, AutoZone, Dobb's Tires, Family$, Schnuck's, Shop'n Save Foods, Walgreens, Walmart
10	IL 3 N, to Cahokia, E St Louis, **W** 🅟 Fuelmart/Subway/dsl
9	to Dupo, **W** 🅟 Hucks
6	IL 3 S, to Columbia (exits left from sb), **E** 🅟 Phillips 66, Shell/dsl/24hr 🏠 Hampton Inn (2mi) 🅞 Chevrolet
4mm	Missouri/Illinois state line, Mississippi River
3	Koch Rd
2	MO 231, Telegraph Rd, **N** 🅟 Conoco, Shell/Circle K 🍴 Great Wall, Little Caesar's, McDonald's, Pizza Hut/Taco Bell, Steak'n Shake, Waffle House 🅞 Advance Parts, AT&T, Jefferson Barracks Nat Cem, Petco, SaveALot, Walmart/Subway, **S** 🅟 Phillips 66/dsl, QT, Shell/Circle K/dsl 🍴 China Wok, DQ, Dunkin' 🅞 Verizon

1d c	US 50, US 61, US 67, Lindbergh Blvd, Lemay Ferry Rd, accesses same as I-55 exit 197 E, **N** 🅟 Phillips 66 🍴 Applebee's, Arby's, Buffalo Wild Wings, ChuckeCheese, CiCi's Pizza, Dillard's, Hometown Buffet, HoneyBaked Ham, Hooters, IHOP, Imo's Pizza, Krispy Kreme, McAlister's Deli, Noodles&Co, Penn Sta Subs, Qdoba Mexican, Starbucks, Steak'n Shake, Subway, Taco Bell, Tucker's Place, Wendy's 🏠 Holiday Inn 🅞 AT&T, Best Buy, Chrysler/Dodge/Jeep, Costco/gas, CVS Drug, Dick's, Ford/Lincoln, Home Depot, JC Penney, Macy's, Marshall's, NTB, Verizon, vet, **S** 🍴 Phillips 66 🍴 Jack-in-the-Box, Jimmy John's, McDonald's, Rich & Charlie's Italian, White Castle 🅞 $General, $Tree, BigLots, Firestone, Old Navy, Petsmart, Sam's Club/gas, Walgreens
1b a	I-55 S to Memphis, N to St Louis.
	I-255 begins/ends on I-55, exit 196.

INTERSTATE 270

See Missouri Interstate 270 (St Louis)

⬆E INTERSTATE 294 (Chicago)

Exit #	Services
	I-294 begins/ends on I-94, exit 71.
	I-294 & I-80 run together 5 mi. See I-80, exits 155-160.
39.5mm	toll booth eb
5mm	I-80 W, access to I-57
5.5mm	167th St, **toll booth**, Ⓒ
6mm	US 6, 159th St, **E** 🅟 Citgo, Exxon/dsl, Marathon, Mobil/dsl, Shell/dsl 🅞 $Tree, AutoZone, Family$, **W** 🅟 BP/dsl 🍴 Baskin-Robbins/Dunkin', Burger King, McDonald's, Popeye's, Subway, Taco Bell, White Castle 🏠 Chicago Inn&Suites 🅞 $Tree, AutoZone, U-Haul, Walgreens
11mm	Cal Sag Channel
12mm	IL 50, Cicero Ave, **E** 🅟 BP, Shell/dsl 🍴 Dunkin', Subway, White Castle 🅞 Home Depot, O'Reilly Parts, **W** 🅟 BP, Shell/dsl 🍴 Applebee's, Boston Mkt, Chipotle, Culver's, IHOP, Lone Star Steaks, Panda Express, Pizza Hut, Popeye's, Portillo's Dogs, Potbelly, Starbucks, Subway 🏠 Baymont Inn, Days Inn, DoubleTree, Holiday Inn Express 🅞 AT&T, Best Buy, GNC, Jo-Ann, Kohl's, NTB, PepBoys, Petsmart, Ross, Target, TJ Maxx, Ultra Foods, Walgreens, Walmart/Subway
18mm	US 12/20, 95th St, **E** 🅟 Marathon 🍴 Buffalo Wild Wings, Chick-fil-A, Starbucks, TX Corral 🅞🅗, CarMax, Discount Tire, Mazda, **W** 🅟 7-11, BP, Shell, Speedway/dsl 🍴 Arby's, Baskin-Robbins, Burger King, Denny's, Dunkin', Jimmy John's, Les Bros Rest., McDonald's, Papa John's, Prime Time Rest., Subway, Taco Bell, The Pit Ribhouse, Wendy's 🏠 Motel 6 🅞 $Tree, AutoZone, Jewel-Osco, Walgreens
20mm	toll booth, Ⓒ
22mm	75th St, Willow Springs Rd

🅴 INTERSTATE 294 (Chicago) Cont'd

Exit #	Services
23mm	I-55, Wolf Rd, to Hawthorne Park
25mm	**Hinsdale Oasis both lanes,** 🅖 Mobil/7-11/dsl 🍴 KFC/Taco Bell, McDonald's, McDonald's, Panda Express, Sbarro, Subway
28mm	US 34, Ogden Ave, **E** 🅞 zoo, **W** 🅖 BP, Shell/deli 🍴 Dunkin', McDonald's, Starbucks 🅞 🅷, Ferrari/Maserati, Firestone/auto, LandRover, Whole Foods Mkt
28.5mm	Cermak Rd (from sb, no return)
29mm	I-88 tollway
30mm	toll booth, 🅲
31mm	IL 38, Roosevelt Rd (no EZ nb return), **E** 🅖 Shell/dsl 🅱 Hillside Manor Motel 🅞 vet
32mm	I-290 W, to Rockford (from nb)
34mm	I-290 (from sb), to Rockford
38mm	**O'Hare Oasis both lanes,** 🅖 Mobil/7-11/dsl 🍴 KFC, McDonald's, Panda Express, Sbarro, Starbucks, Subway, Taco Bell, TCBY
39mm	IL 19 W (from sb), Irving Park Rd, **E** 🅖 Citgo, Marathon/dsl, Shell/dsl 🍴 Dunkin', McDonald's, Starbucks, Subway, Wendy's 🅱 Comfort Suites 🅞 7-11, Aldi Foods, Walgreens, **W** 🅖 BP/Subway/desk 🍴 Mirage Rest. 🅱 Candlewood Suites, Hampton Inn, Sheraton
40mm	I-190 W, **E** 🅖 Mobil 🍴 Basil's Kitchen, McDonald's, Starbucks 🅱 Courtyard, Doubletree, Embassy Suites, Hampton Inn, Hilton, Hilton Garden, Holiday Inn, Hyatt, Hyatt Regency, Marriott, Rosemont Suites, Westin
41mm	toll booth, 🅲
42mm	Touhy Ave, **W** 🅖 Mobil/service 🍴 Tiffany's Rest. 🅱 Comfort Inn, Radisson
43mm	Des Plaines River
44mm	Dempster St (from nb, no return), **E** 🍴 Wendy's 🅞 🅷, CVS Drug, **W** 🍴 Dunkin', Subway
46mm	IL 58, Golf Rd, **E** 🅖 Mobil/Dunkin'/dsl, Shell/Subway/dsl 🍴 Omega Rest. 🅱 Wyndham 🅞 CVS Drug, Golf Mill Mall, Meijer, Meineke, Target, **W** 🅞 🅷
49mm	Willow Rd, **W** 🅖 BP/Subway/dsl 🍴 Chipotle, Jimmy John's, McDonald's, Pie Five Pizza, Starbucks, TGIFriday's 🅱 Best Western, Country Inn Suites, Courtyard, Motel 6 🅞 CVS Drug, Mariano's Mkt
53mm	Lake Cook Rd (no nb re-entry), **E** 🅱 Embassy Suites, Hyatt, **W** 🍴 J Alexander's
I-294 begins/ends on I-94.	

🅽 INTERSTATE 355 (Illinois)

Exit #	Services
31mm	I-355 begins/end on I-290.
30	US 20, W Lake St, **E** 🅖 Marathon, Mobil/dsl 🍴 Baskin-Robbins/Dunkin', Burger King, Chipotle, Culver's, Famous Dave's BBQ, Firehouse Subs, IHOP, Jimmy John's, La Hacienda Mexican, Panda Express, Panera Bread, Ristorante de Marco's, Starbucks 🅱 Hampton Inn 🅞 Midas, Sam's Club/gas, Verizon, Walmart/Subway, **W** 🅖 Shell 🍴 Dave&Buster's, Venuti's Rest.
29	Army Trail Rd, **E** 🅖 Mobil/dsl, Shell/dsl 🍴 Serino's Deli, **W** 🅖 BP/dsl, Mobil/dsl 🅱 Hilton Garden
27	IL 64, E North Ave, **E** 🅖 BP/Subway/dsl, Burger King, Comfort Suites, Fairfield Inn, McDonald's, Shell/Circle K, Thornton's/dsl 🍴 Jimmy John's, **W** 🅖 Speedway/dsl 🅱 Ramada 🅞 Art's RV Ctr, Suburban Tire/auto

Exit # (col 2)	
24	Roosevelt, **E** 🅖 Mobil 🍴 Dunkin', Subway 🅱 Crowne Plaza 🅞 Cadillac, Mariano's Mkt, Toyota. **W** 🍴 Jimmy John's 🅞 NAPA, Pete's Mkt
22	IL 56, Butterfield Rd, **E** 🍴 Arby's, Brick House Rest., Burger King, Chama Gaucha Brazilian, Chipotle Mexican, Fuddrucker's, Hooters, Melting Pot, Olive Garden, Panera Bread, Portillo's, Red Lobster, Ruby Tuesday, Starbucks, Subway, Zoup! 🅱 Comfort Inn, Extended Stay America, Holiday Inn Express, Marriott, Red Roof Inn 🅞 $Tree, Best Buy, Kohl's, Michael's, Petsmart, Ross, Verizon, **W** 🍴 Carlucci Italian 🅱 DoubleTree Suites 🅞 7-11, Home Depot
20mm	I-88 E/I-355 run together.
19	US 34, Ogden Ave, **E** 🅖 Shell 🍴 Culver's, Jimmy John's, McDonald's 🅱 InTown Suites 🅞 AT&T, Buick/GMC, Chrysler/Dodge/Jeep, Ford, **W** 🍴 Baskin-Robbins/Dunkin' 🅱 Extended Stay America 🅞 Chevrolet, Speedway/dsl, vet
18	Maple Ave, 1 mi **W** 🅖 BP, Mobil, Shell/Circle K 🍴 KFC/Taco Bell, McDonald's 🅞 Jewel Osco, Walgreens
16	63rd St, Hobson Rd, **E** 🅖 Mobil/dsl, Thornton's/McDonald's/dsl 🍴 Steven's Rest, Subway 🅞 AutoZone, Familia Fresh Mkt, GNC, Target, Walgreens
15	W 75th St, **E** 🅖 Mobil 🍴 Arby's, Bakers Square Rest 🅞 Hobby Lobby, Home Depot, Sam's Club/gas, **W** 🅖 Marathon 🍴 Dunkin', El Burro Loco, McDonald's, Pizza Italiano 🅞 Jewel-Osco
14	87th St, Baughton Rd, **E** 🅖 BP, Shell 🍴 Al's Pizza, Dunkin', McDonald's, Oberweiss, Subway, Wendy's 🅞 Costco/gas, CVS Drug, **W** 🅖 Mobil 🍴 Bar Louie, Buffalo Wild Wings, Famous Dave's BBQ, Five Guys, IHOP, Jimmy John's, Longhorn Steak, Panda Express, Panera Bread, Potbelly, Starbucks, Ted's M Grill 🅱 ALoft 🅞 AT&T, Barnes&Noble, Bass Pro Shops, Discount Tire, IKEA, Macy's, Meijer/gas, Verizon, Walgreens
12	I-55
8	127th St, **E** 🍴 Burger King, Jimmy John's, KFC, McDonald's, Starbucks, Subway, Taco Bell 🅞 Aldi Foods, AT&T, Firestone/auto, Jewel-Osco, Jiffy Lube, Pepper's Autocare, USPO, Verizon, Walgreens
6	IL 171, Archer Ave, 143rd St, **E** 🅞 Kohl's, Target, vet
4	159th Ave, IL 7, Orland Park, Homer Glen, **E** 🅖 Citgo/dsl, **W** 🅞 URGENT CARE
3mm	toll booth both directions
1	US 6, **E** 🅖 Rte 6 Food'n Fuel/Dunkin'/dsl, **W** 🅞 🅷
0mm	I-80 E, W, I-355 begins/ends on I-80 exit 140.

🅴 INTERSTATE 474 (Peoria)

Exit #	Services
15	I-74, E to Bloomington, W to Peoria
9	IL 29, E Peoria, to Pekin, **N** 🅖 Shell/Arby's/dsl, Thornton's 🍴 DQ, Driftwood Pizza, Taco John's 🅞 $General, Riverboat Casino (6mi), **S** 🅖 BP/Subway/dsl, Casey's 🍴 Denny's, Domino's, Lian Wang, McDonald's, Rosati's Pizza 🅞 Chrysler/Dodge/Jeep, Toyota
8mm	Illinois River
6b a	US 24, Adams St, Bartonville, **S** 🅖 BP/dsl, Mobil/dsl 🍴 Hardee's, KFC, McDonald's, Tyroni's Café
5	Airport Rd, **S** 🅖 Mobil/e85/dsl 🅞 🖼
3a	to IL 116, Farmington, **S** 🅞 Wildlife Prairie Park
0b a	I-74, W to Moline, E to Peoria.
I-474 begins/ends on I-74, exit 87.	

IL

P E O R I A

INDIANA

✈ E   INTERSTATE 64

Exit #	Services
124mm	Indiana/Kentucky state line, Ohio River
123	IN 62 E, New Albany, **N** 🅿 Marathon/dsl, Shell/Circle K 🍴 DQ 🅾 Family$, Firestone/auto, 🏨, Save-A-Lot, **S** 🅿 Shell/Circle K, Valero 🍴 Daisy's Cafeteria, Subway, Waffle House 🏨 Best Western, Holiday Inn Express
121	I-265 E, to I-65 (exits left from eb), **N** access to 🏨
119	US 150 W, to Greenville, **N** 🅿 Marathon 🍴 Bean St Cafe, Bearno's Buffet, Beef O'Brady's, Chillburger, China Cafe, Domino's, DQ, El Nopal, McDonald's, Papa John's, Sam's Family Rest., Subway, Taco Bell, Tumbleweed SW Grill 🅾 AutoZone, JayC Foods, Rite Aid, URGENT CARE, Walgreens
118	IN 62, IN 64W, to Georgetown, **N** 🅿 Marathon/dsl/24hr, Shell/Circle K 🍴 Korner Kitchen, McDonald's 🏨 Red Roof Inn 🅾 CashSaver Foods, Mr. Hardware, **S** 🅿 Marathon/dsl
115mm	Welcome Ctr wb, full ♿ facilities, vending, 🄲, 🚮, litter barrels
113	to Lanesville
105	IN 135, to Corydon, **N** 🅿 Marathon/dsl, Shell 🍴 Big Boy 🏨 Comfort Inn, **S** 🅿 5 Star, BP/dsl 🍴 Alberto's Italian, Arby's, Beef O'Brady's, Burger King, Cracker Barrel, Culver's, Domino's, DQ, El Nopal Mexican, Hong Kong Buffet, Jimmy John's, KFC, Lee's Chicken, LJ Silver, McDonald's, O'Charley's, Papa John's, Papa Murphy's, Pizza Hut, Ryan's, Subway, Taco Bell, Waffle House, Wendy's, White Castle 🏨 Baymont Inn, Hampton Inn, Holiday Inn Express, Super 8 🅾 $Tree, Advance Parts, AT&T, AutoZone, Big O Tire, Buick/Chevrolet, Chrysler/Dodge/Jeep, CVS Drug, Family$, Ford, 🏨, Verizon, Walgreens, Walmart/Subway
100mm	Blue River
97mm	parking area both lanes
92	IN 66, Carefree, **N** 🅾 Marengo Caves, **S** 🅿 Marathon/dsl/rest./24hr, 🄿🄸🄻🄾🅃/Subway/dsl/scales/24hr 🍴 Big Dadd's Rest., Country Style Rest. 🏨 Red Carpet Inn 🅾 Carefree Truckwash, Harrison Crawford SF, repair, to Wyandotte Caves
88mm	Hoosier Nat Forest eastern boundary
86	IN 37, to Sulphur, **N** to Patoka Lake, **S** gas, food, scenic route
79	IN 37, to Tell City, St Croix, **S** 🅿 Marathon/Subshop/pizza/dsl 🅾 to Hoosier NF, to OH River Br
76mm	Anderson River
72	IN 145, to Birdseye, **N** 🅾 to Patoka Lake, **S** 🅾 St Meinrad Coll, winery (2mi) gas
63	IN 162, to Ferdinand, **N** 🅿 Sunoco/dsl 🍴 China Garden, McDonald's, Subway, Taco Bell, Wendy's 🏨 Comfort Inn, Red Roof Inn 🅾 CVS Drug, Ferdinand SF, **S** 🅾 Lake Rudolph RV Camping (8mi)
58mm	Ⓡⓢ both lanes, full ♿ facilities, info, vending, 🚮, litter barrels, 🄲
57	US 231, to Dale, Huntingburg, **N** 🅾 🏨, **S** 🅿 Chuckles/dsl 🍴 Denny's, Wendy's 🏨 Baymont Inn, Motel 6 🅾 Lincoln Boyhood Home, Lincoln SP
54	IN 161, to Holland, Tennyson
39	IN 61, Lynnville, **N** 🅿 Marathon 🍴 Monterrey Mexican 🅾 USPO
32mm	**N** 🅾 Wabash & Erie Canal
29 b a	I-69 N, IN 57 N&S, to Evansville
25b a	US 41, to Evansville, **N** 🅿 ⛟FLYING J/Denny's/dsl/scales/24hr, ⓛⓞⓥⓔⓢ/Wendy's/dsl/24hr, 🄿🄸🄻🄾🅃/Subway/Taco Bell/dsl/24hr 🏨 Baymont Inn 🅾 Blue Beacon, truck repair/lube, **S** 🅿 Marathon/dsl 🍴 Arby's, Denny's, McDonald's, Stoll's Amish Rest.

25b a	Continued
	🏨 Holiday Inn Express, Quality Inn, Red Roof Inn, Super 8 🅾 st police, to U S IN
18	IN 65, to Cynthiana, **S** 🅿 Motomart/dsl/24hr
12	IN 165, Poseyville, **S** 🅿 CountryMark/Subway/dsl 🍴 Red Wagon Rest. 🅾 NAPA, New Harmonie Hist Area/SP
7mm	Black River Welcome Ctr eb, full ♿ facilities, 🄲, 🚮, litter barrels, petwalk
5mm	Black River
4	IN 69 S, New Harmony, Griffin, **1 mi N** USPO, **S** Harmony St Park
2mm	Big Bayou River
0mm	Indiana/Illinois state line, Wabash River

✈ N   INTERSTATE 65

Exit #	Services
262	I-90, W to Chicago, E to Ohio, **I-65 begins/ends on US 12, US 20.**
261	15th Ave, to Gary, **E** 🅾 Mack/Volvo Trucks, **W** 🅿 Citgo
259b a	I-94/80, US 6W
258	US 6, Ridge Rd, **E** 🅿 Luke/dsl, Marathon/dsl 🍴 Diner's Choice Rest., **W** 🅿 Citgo, Save Gas
255	61st Ave, Merrillville, **E** 🅿 Family Express/dsl, Speedway/dsl 🍴 Arby's, Cracker Barrel, McDonald's, Pizza Hut/Taco Bell, Wendy's 🏨 Comfort Inn, Days Inn 🅾 Chevrolet, 🏨, I-65 Repair, Menards, **1 mi W** 🅿 Clark 🍴 Burger King, Subway 🅾 AutoZone, Walgreens
253b	US 30 W, Merrillville, **W** 🅿 Blue, Speedway/dsl 🍴 Abuelo's Mexican, Applebee's, Bar Louie, Baskin-Robbins/Dunkin', Gino's Rest., Golden Corral, Hooters, House of Kobe, La Carreta Mexican, McAlister's Deli, McDonald's, Old Chicago Pizza,

*Left margin:* CORYDON   **MERRILLVILLE**

*Right margin tab:* IN

⛽ = gas 🍴 = food 🛏 = lodging 🅾 = other Ⓡˢ = rest stop   Copyright 2022 - The Next EXIT ®

M E R R I L L V I L L E

⬆️N INTERSTATE 65 Cont'd

253b	Continued
	Oriental Buffet, Panda Express, Panera Bread, Pepe's Mexican, Pizza Hut, Portillo's Hot Dogs, Qdoba, Starbucks, Steak'n Shake, Subway, TX Corral Steaks, Wendy's, White Castle 🛏 Baymont Inn, Clarion, Fairfield Inn, Hampton Inn, Knights Inn, Microtel, Red Roof Inn, Residence Inn 🅾 $Tree, Acura, Aldi Foods, Buick/GMC, Cadillac, CarX, Chrysler/Dodge/Jeep, CVS Drug, Discount Tire, Fanny May Candies, Ford/Lincoln, Ⓗ, Hyundai, Infiniti, Meijer/dsl, Midas, NTB, Old Time Pottery, Subaru, U-Haul, USPO, Verizon, Walgreens
253a	US 30 E, E ⛽ BP/Luke/dsl, Speedway/dsl 🍴 Bakers Square, BC Osaka, Bob Evans, Buffalo Wild Wings, Chick-fil-A, Chili's, Chipotle Mexican, ChuckeCheese, Culver's, Dunkin', Firehouse Subs, IHOP, Jimmy John's, KFC/LJ Silver, Longhorn Steaks, McDonald's, Olive Garden, Outback Steaks, Popeye's, Potbelly, Red Lobster, Red Robin, Sheffield's Rest., Starbucks, Starbucks (2), Taco Bell, TGIFriday's, Wendy's 🛏 Best Value Inn, Best Western, Candlewood Suites, Comfort Suites, Country Inn&Suites, Economy Inn, Extended Stay America, Hilton Garden, Home 2 Suites, La Quinta, Motel 6, Quality Inn, Staybridge Suites, Super 8, Woodspring Suites 🅾 AT&T, Audi/VW, AutoZone, Best Buy, BigLots, Carmax, Costco/gas, Dick's, Firestone/auto, Hobby Lobby, Home Depot, Honda, JC Penney, Jo-Ann, Kia, Kohl's, Lowe's, Macy's, Michael's, Nissan, Office Depot, Old Navy, PetCo, Petsmart, Ross, Sam's Club/gas, Target, Tire Barn, TJ Maxx, Toyota, Tuesday Morning, vet, Walmart/McDonald's
249	109th Ave, W ⛽ Speedway/dsl 🍴 Aldi, Buffalo Wild Wings, China Garden, Culver's, Dunkin', Golden Apple Rest., Jimmy John's, La Quesadilla, Marco's Pizza, Rosati's Pizza 🅾 $Tree, GNC, Verizon, Walgreens
247	US 231, Crown Point, W ⛽ Family Express 🅾 Ⓗ
241mm	weigh sta sb
240	IN 2, Lowell, E ⛽ ⊕FLYING J/Denny's/dsl/24hr/@, [Pilot]/Wendy's/dsl/scales/24hr, truck repair 🍴 Arby's, McDonald's, Subway 🛏 Comfort Inn, Super 8 🅾 truck wash, W 🅾 st police
234mm	Kankakee River
231mm	Ⓡˢ both lanes, full 🚻 facilities, 🛒, info, 🌳 litter barrels, vending, petwalk
230	IN 10, Roselawn, E ⛽ ◆Loves/Arby's/dsl/scales/24hr, TA/BP/Country Pride/dsl/scales/24hr/@, W ⛽ Family Express/e85, Marathon/Subway 🍴 China Wok, J&J Pizza, Sycamore Drive-In 🅾 $General, CVS Drug, Lake Holiday Camping, Oak Lake Camping, SaveALot, TrueValue
220	IN 14, Winamac, W ⛽ BP/dsl, CNG, Tesla EVC 🅾 Fair Oaks Farms Store
215	IN 114, Rensselaer, E ⛽ Family Express/dsl/e85/24hr 🍴 Arby's, DQ, KFC, McDonald's, Taco Bell 🛏 Baymont Inn, Comfort Suites, Interstate Motel 🅾 Ⓗ, W ⛽ Marathon/Trail Tree Rest./dsl/24hr 🍴 Burger King 🛏 Economy Inn 🅾 fireworks, tires/repair/towing/24hr
212mm	Iroquois River
205	US 231, Remington, E ⛽ Crazy D/dsl 🅾 Ⓗ, to St Joseph's Coll
201	US 24/231, Remington, E 🅾 Caboose Lake RV Camping, W ⛽ Family Express/dsl, Petro/Shell/Iron Skillet/dsl/scales/24hr/@, [Pilot]/Subway/dsl/scales/24hr 🍴 KFC, McDonald's 🛏 Sunset Inn, Super 8
196mm	Ⓡˢ both lanes, full 🚻 facilities, vending, 🛒, info, 🌳 litter barrels, petwalk
193	US 231, to Chalmers, E ⛽ Marathon/DQ
188	IN 18, to Brookston, Fowler many windmills

IN

L A F A Y E T T E

178	IN 43, W Lafayette, E ⛽ Phillips 66/Subway/dsl, Speedway/Taco Bell 🍴 McDonald's, Wendy's 🅾 museum, st police, to Tippecanoe Bfd, W 🅾 to Purdue U
176mm	Wabash River
175	IN 25, Lafayette, E ⛽ Family Express/dsl/e85, Marathon/dsl W 🅾 Ⓗ
172	IN 26, Lafayette, E ⛽ Tesla EVC 🍴 Cracker Barrel, DQ, Dunkin, El Rodeo, Fox's Pizza, Starbucks, Steak'n Shake, Subway, White Castle 🛏 Baymont Inn, Candlewood Suites, Comfort Inn, Comfort Suites, Days Inn, La Quinta, Motel 6, TownePlace Suites 🅾 Meijer/dsl/e85, visitor's ctr, W ⛽ Luke/dsl, Shell/Circle K/dsl, Speedway/dsl, Tesla EVC, Tesla EVC 🍴 Arby's, Bob Evans, Burger King, Cheddar's, Chick-fil-A, Chili's, Chipotle, ChuckeCheese, Coldstone, Culver's, Denny's, Fazoli's, Firehouse Subs, Golden Corral, Grindstone Charlie's, HuHot, IHOP, Jets Pizza, Jimmy John's, KFC, Logan's Roadhouse, Longhorn Steaks, McAlister's Deli, McDonald's, Moe's SW Grill, Mtn Jack's, Noodles&Co, Olive Garden, Outback Steaks, Panera Bread, Pizza Hut, Qdoba, Red Lobster, Sonic, Spageddie's, Starbucks, Steak'n Shake, Subway, Taco Bell, TGIFriday's 🛏 Courtyard, Doubletree, EconoLodge, Fairfield Inn, Hampton Inn, Holiday Inn Express, Home 2 Suites, Homewood Suites, Quality Inn, Red Roof Inn, Residence Inn, Super 8, Travelodge 🅾 $General, $Tree, Aamco, Chevrolet, CVS Drug, Discount Tire, Fresh Thyme Mkt, Gordman's, Harley Davidson, Hobby Lobby, Home Depot, Ⓗ, Hyundai, Lowe's, Nissan, Office Depot, Sam's Club/gas, Target, TJ Maxx, to Purdue U, Toyota, USPO, Verizon, vet, Walmart/Subway
168	IN 38, IN 25 S, Dayton, E ⛽ BP/Subway, CNG, Shell/Circle K/dsl
158	IN 28, to Frankfort, E ⛽ BP/Subway/dsl 🅾 Mack/Volvo, 2 mi W 🛏 Lincoln Lodge Motel
150mm	Ⓡˢ sb, full 🚻 facilities, info, 🌳 litter barrels, 🛒 vending, petwalk
148mm	Ⓡˢ nb, full 🚻 facilities, info, 🌳 litter barrels, 🛒 vending, petwalk
146	IN 47, Thorntown, W 🅾 camping
141	US 52 W (exits left from sb), Lafayette Ave, E 🅾 Ⓗ
140	IN 32, Lebanon, E ⛽ BP/repair, Marathon/dsl 🍴 Denny's, McDonald's, White Castle 🛏 Quality Inn 🅾 AutoZone, Goodyear auto, Ⓗ, Menards, O'Reilly Parts, Pomp's Tires, W ⛽ McClure/dsl/e85, Shell 🍴 Arby's, Flapjacks Pancakes, KFC, Steak'n Shake, Subway, Taco Bell 🛏 Best Value Inn, EconoLodge, Holiday Inn Express, Motel 6 🅾 truckwash
139	IN 39, Lebanon, E ⛽ Speedway/dsl 🍴 Penn Sta Subs, Starbucks, Wendy's 🅾 $General, W ⛽ ⊕FLYING J/Huddle House/dsl/LP/scales/24hr 🅾 Donaldson's Chocolates
138	to US 52, Lebanon, E ⛽ BP/dsl
133	IN 267, Whitestown, W ⛽ ◆Loves/McDonald's/Subway/dsl/scales/24hr
130	IN 334, Zionsville, E ⛽ Marathon/Fazoli's/dsl, Shell/Circle K/Subway/dsl, Tesla EVC 🍴 Buffalo Wild Wings, Burger King, City BBQ, Cracker Barrel, Dunkin', El Rodeo Mexican, Flamm Burger, Flapjacks Pancakes, Fox's Pizza, McAlister's Deli, McDonald's, Panda Express, Panera Bread, Qdoba, Starbucks, Taco Bell, Verizon, Wendy's, Which Wich? 🛏 Hampton Inn, Holiday Inn Express, Woodspring Suites 🅾 AT&T, CVS Drug, Ⓗ, Lowe's, Meijer/dsl, Petco, Ross, TJ Maxx, Toyota, vet, W ⛽ TA/BP/Popeye's/dsl/scales/24hr/@
129	I-865 E, to I-465 E, US 52 E (from sb)
126mm	Fishback Creek
124	71st St, 1 mi E ⛽ BP 🍴 Hot Box Pizza, Starbucks, Steak'n Shake, Subway 🛏 Best Western+, Candlewood Suites, Courtyard, Hampton Inn, Hilton Garden, Holiday Inn Express, Residence Inn, W 🅾 Eagle Creek Park
123	I-465 S, S 🅾 to 🛏

L E B A N O N

INTERSTATE 65 Cont'd

Exit #	Services
121	Lafayette Rd, same as 119 W, **E** 🅖 Speedway (2), Speedway/dsl 🛏 Quality Inn, **W** 🅖 Shell/Circle K 🍴 Arby's, Church's, Fazoli's, La Bamba Burritos 🛏 Executive Inn 🅞 $Tree, Aldi Foods, AT&T, Batteries+Bulbs, Best Buy, Discount Tire, Family$, GNC, 🅷, Hyundai, Kia, Mazda, Nissan, PepBoys, SaveALot, Tire Barn, Walmart/Subway
119	38th St (no nb return), same as 121, Dodge, **W** 🅖 Phillips 66, Speedway/dsl 🍴 KFC, McDonald's, Papa John's, Pizza Hut, Red Lobster, Taco Bell 🅞 Advance Parts, Aldi Foods, Best Buy, Chevrolet, Hyundai, Meijer/dsl, Tires+
117.5mm	White River
117	MLK St (from sb), **W** 🅖 Marathon/dsl
116	29th St, 30th St (from nb), **W** 🅞 Marian Coll
115	21st St, **E** 🅖 Shell/Circle K 🅞 🅷, **W** 🅞 museums, zoo
114	MLK St, West St downtown
113	US 31, IN 37, Meridian St, to downtown, **E** 🅞 🅷
112a	I-70 E, to Columbus
111	Market St, Michigan St, Ohio St, **E** 🍴 Hardee's 🅞 museum, **W** 🅞 City Market
110b	I-70 W, to St Louis
110a	Prospect St, Morris St, East St
109	Raymond St, **E** 🅞 🅷, **W** 🅖 BP, Speedway/dsl 🍴 Little Caesar's, White Castle 🅞 CVS Drug, Family$, Safeway
107	Keystone Ave, **E** 🅖 Mystick 🛏 Best Value Inn 🅞 🅷, **W** 🅖 Phillips 66/dsl, Speedway/dsl, Valero 🍴 Big Kahuna Pizza, Burger King, Denny's, DQ, McDonald's, Subway, Wendy's 🛏 Comfort Inn 🅞 $General, U of Indianapolis, Walmart Mkt
106	I-465 and I-74
103	Southport Rd, **E** 🅖 BP/McDonald's, Shell/Circle K 🍴 Arby's, Chicago Grill, Chick-fil-A, Hardee's, Hotbox Pizza, Jersey Mike's, Jimmy John's, Leonardo's Mexican, Longhorn Steaks, Monical's Pizza, Mr Wok, Noble Roman's, O'Charley's, Panda Express, Panera Bread, Penn Sta Subs, Pizza Hut, Qdoba, Rally's 🅞 Aldi Foods, AT&T, Firestone/auto, Harley-Davidson, Home Depot, Kohl's, Meijer/dsl/e85, Menards, Staples, Target, **W** 🅖 EVC, Marathon/Circle K, Phillips 66, Speedway/dsl 🍴 Bob Evans, Burger King, Carrabba's, Cheeseburger Paradise, Cracker Barrel, McDonald's, Stacked Pickle, Starbucks, Steak'n Shake, Subway, TX Roadhouse, Waffle House, Wendy's 🛏 Baymont Inn, Comfort Suites, Country Inn&Suites, Courtyard, Fairfield Inn, Hampton Inn, Motel 6, Quality Inn, Super 8 🅞 🅷
101	CountyLine Rd, **E** 🍴 Candlewood Suites, **W** 🅖 Murphy USA/dsl, Shell/Circle K/dsl 🍴 Buffalo Wild Wings, Cheddar's, Culver's, El Meson Mexican, Freddy's, Leon Mexican, Lindo Mexico, McAlister's Deli, Newk's Eatery, Popeye's, Primanti Bros, Sonic, Taco Bell, Tokyo Buffet, Zaxby's 🛏 Hilton Garden, Holiday Inn Express, Home 2 Suites, Residence Inn, Woodspring Suites 🅞 Costco/dsl, 🅷, Kroger/dsl, Verizon, Walmart/Subway
99	Greenwood, **E** 🅖 Road Ranger/🍴/Subway/dsl/scales/24hr, **W** 🅖 Marathon, Shell/Circle K 🍴 Arby's, China Wok, Denny's, Main St Grille, McDonald's, Papa John's, Puerto Vallarta, Starbucks, Subway, Taco Bell, Waffle House, White Castle 🛏 InTown Suites, La Quinta, Red Carpet Inn, Red Roof Inn 🅞 Camping World RV Ctr, 🅷, Sam's Club, vet
97	Worthsville Rd, **W** 🅖 Circle K/dsl
95	Whiteland, **E** 🅖 *FLYING J*/Denny's/scales/dsl/LP/RV dump/24hr 🅞 Blue Beacon, SpeedCo, tires, **W** 🅖 *Loves*/Arby's/dsl/scales/24hr, 🍴/McDonald's/dsl/scales/24hr/@
90	IN 44, Franklin, **W** 🅖 Marathon/Subway/dsl, Shell/Circle K 🍴 Burger King, McDonald's/RV Parking, Waffle House 🛏 Baymont Inn, EconoLodge, Motel 6, Quality Inn 🅞 golf, 🅷
85mm	Sugar Creek
82mm	Big Blue River
80	IN 252, to Flat Rock, Edinburgh, **W** 🅖 Marathon/dsl, Shell/dsl
76b a	US 31, Taylorsville, **E** 🅖 Shell/Circle K/dsl, Speedway/dsl 🍴 A&W/KFC, Burger King, El Toreo Mexican, Waffle House 🛏 Red Roof Inn 🅞 $ General, 🅷, Toyota, **W** 🅖 EVC, GetGo/dsl, Marathon, Thornton's/café/dsl 🍴 Applebee's, Arby's, Cracker Barrel, Hardee's, Max&Erma's, McDonald's, MT Mikes, Ruby Tuesday, Snappy Tomato Pizza, Subway, Taco Bell 🛏 Best Western, Comfort Inn, Hampton Inn, Hilton Garden, Holiday Inn Express 🅞 antiques, Express Outlets/famous brands, Goodyear, Harley-Davidson, repair
73mm	🆁🆂 both lanes, full ♿ facilities, 🅒, vending, info, 🅐, litter barrels, petwalk
68mm	Driftwood River
68	IN 46, Columbus, **E** 🅖 Shell/Circle K, Speedway/dsl 🍴 Buffalo Wild Wings, Burger King, Culver's, IHOP, Jimmy John's, Lincoln Sq Rest., McAlister's Deli, McDonald's, Panda Express, RuYi Asian, Starbucks, Subway, TX Roadhouse, Waffle House, Wendy's 🛏 Fairfield Inn, Holiday Inn, Sleep Inn, Super 8 🅞 AutoZone, Belle Tire, Chevrolet, 🅷, Menards, Sam's Club/gas, Verizon, Walgreens, Walmart/Subway, **W** 🅖 BP 🍴 Arby's, Bob Evans, Chicago's Pizza, El Nopal Mexican, Freddy's, Marco's Pizza, Noble Roman's, Papa John's, Papa's Grill, Taco Bell 🛏 Courtyard, Days Inn, EconoLodge, La Quinta, Residence Inn 🅞 $General, CVS Drug, Jay-C Foods, to Brown Co SP, vet
64	IN 58, Walesboro, **W** 🅖 Circle K/dsl, GetGo/dsl
55	IN 11, to Jonesville, Seymour
54mm	White River
51mm	weigh sta both lanes
50b a	US 50, Seymour, **E** 🅖 Circle K/dsl, Sunshine Cafe/Waffle House, TA/BP/Country Pride/dsl/24hr/@ 🍴 McDonald's 🛏 Allstate Inn, Days Inn, EconoLodge, Economy Inn, Motel 6, Travelodge, **W** 🅖 Circle K/dsl, Murphy USA/dsl, Shell/Circle K/dsl, Speedway/dsl 🍴 Applebee's, Arby's, Bonanza, Buffalo Wild Wings, Buffet China, Burger King, Capt D's, Chili's, Cracker Barrel, Domino's, DQ, El Nopal Mexican, Freddy's, Hardee's, KFC, Little Caesar's, McDonalds, Papa John's, Pizza Hut, Popeye's, Rally's, Steak'n Shake, Subway, Taco Bell, Wendy's, White Castle 🛏 Fairfield Inn, Hampton Inn, Holiday Inn Express, Knights Inn, Quality Inn 🅞 $General, $Tree, Advance Parts, Aldi Foods, AT&T, AutoZone, BigLots, Buick/Cadillac/Chevrolet/GMC, Chrysler/Dodge/Jeep, CVS Drug, Ford, GNC, Home Depot, 🅷, Jay-C Foods, JC Penney, O'Reilly Parts, Verizon, Walgreens, Walmart/Subway
41	IN 250, Uniontown, **E** 🅞 tires, **W** 🅖 Marathon/dsl
36	US 31, Crothersville, **W** 🅖 Marathon/dsl
34a b	IN 256, Austin, **E** 🅖 Shell/Circle K 🅞 Clifty Falls SP, to Hardy Lake, **W** 🅖 Fuelmart/dsl/scales, Sunoco/Huddle House/dsl

(left margin: INDIANAPOLIS AREA • GREENWOOD)
*(center margin: COLUMBUS • SEYMOUR)*
*(right margin: IN)*

⬆N INTERSTATE 65 Cont'd

Exit #	Services
29b a	IN 56, to Salem, Scottsburg, **E** 🅖 MotoMart/dsl, Speedway/dsl, Sunoco 🍴 Burger King, China Wind, Cracker Barrel, Denny's, Domino's, First Wok, KFC, Mariann Inn, Papa John's, Ponderosa, Popeye's, Sonic, Subway, Taco Bell 🏠 Holiday Inn Express 🅞 Ace Hardware, Advance Parts, AutoZone, CVS Drug, 🅷, O'Reilly Parts, **W** 🅖 Circle K, Murphy USA 🍴 Arby's, Chillers, LJ Silver, McDonald's, Pizza Hut, Puerto Vallarta, Roadhouse USA, Waffle House, Wendy's 🏠 Hampton Inn, Quality Inn, Red Roof Inn 🅞 Big O Tire, Buick/Chevrolet, Jellystone Camping (4mi), Verizon, Walmart/Subway
22mm	🆁🆂 both lanes, full ♿ facilities, info, 🚻, 🏞, litter barrels, vending, petwalk
19	IN 160, Henryville, **E** 🅖 Circle K, Marathon/Subway/dsl 🅞 $General, USPO
16	Memphis Rd, Memphis, **E** 🅖 ♥Loves/McDonald's/Subway/dsl/scales/24hr, **W** 🅖 Pilot/Arby's/dsl/scales/24hr/@ 🅞 Customers First RV Ctr
9	IN 311, to New Albany, Sellersburg, **E** 🅖 Circle K, Sunoco 🍴 Arby's, Cracker Barrel, DQ, Waffle House 🏠 Days Inn, Ramada Inn 🅞 Carmerica/repair, Ford, O'Reilly Parts, **W** 🅖 Circle K 🍴 Burger King, El Nopal Mexican, McDonald's, Taco Bell 🏠 Quality Inn
7	IN 60, Hamburg, **E** 🅖 BP/dsl, **W** 🍴 Cricket's Cafe, KFC/Pizza Hut 🏠 Travelodge
6b a	I-265 W, to I-64 W, IN 265 E, New Albany
5	Veterans Parkway, **E** 🅖 Marathon/dsl 🍴 Boombozz Pizza, Bubba's BBQ, Culver's, Krispy Kreme, Popeye's, Wild Eggs 🅞 AT&T, Hobby Lobby, 🅷, Menards, Tire Discounters, **W** 🍴 Buffalo Wild Wings, Cheddar's, Chick-fil-A, Chuy's Mexican, DQ, First Watch, IHOP, Jimmy John's, Kansai, Longhorn Steaks, McAlister's Deli, Mission BBQ, Olive Garden, Outback Steaks, Panda Express, Panera Bread, Papa Murphy's, Pizza Hut, Qdoba, Red Robin, Storming Crab, Subway, Taco Bell 🏠 Candlewood Suites, Home 2 Suites, Suburban Inn 🅞 Bass Pro Shops, Best Buy, Buick/Chevrolet/GMC, Lowe's, Michael's, Old Navy, Old Time Pottery, Petsmart, Ross, Sam's Club/gas, Staples, Target, Verizon, Walgreens, Walmart/Subway
4	US 31 N, IN 131 S, Clarksville, New Albany, **E** 🅖 Thorntons/dsl 🍴 Momma's Pizza, White Castle 🏠 Woodspring Suites 🅞 Raben Tire, **W** 🅖 Speedway/dsl 🍴 Applebee's, Arby's, Bob Evans, Burger King, Capt D's, Chili's, China Buffet, Chucke-Cheese, Denny's, Fazoli's, Golden Corral, Hooters, LJ Silver, Logan's Roadhouse, McDonald's, Mr Gatti's, Outback Steaks, Papa John's, Rally's, Red Lobster, Senor Iguana, Steak'n Shake, TX Roadhouse, Wendy's, Zesto 🏠 Best Western, Candlewood Suites, Hampton Inn, Suburban Lodge 🅞 $Tree, AT&T, AutoZone, BigLots, Books-A-Million, CVS Drug, Dick's, Dillard's, Discount Tire, Ford, Home Depot, Honda, JC Penney, Jo-Ann Fabrics, Kia, Kroger/gas, Nissan, O'Reilly Parts, PepBoys, TJ Maxx, Towery Tire/auto, Toyota, Tuesday Morning, USPO, VW, Walgreens
2	Eastern Blvd, Clarksville, **E** 🏠 Days Inn, Quality Suites, Red Carpet, Value Inn 🅞 🅷, U-Haul, **W** 🅖 Circle K 🏠 Best Inn
1	US 31 S, IN 62, Stansifer Ave, **E** 🅖 Thornton's/dsl 🍴 DQ, Subway 🅞 $General, Advance Parts, CVS Drug, 🅷, Walgreens, **W** 🏠 Radisson 🅞 Stinnett RV Ctr
0	Jeffersonville, **E** 🅖 Thornton's/dsl 🍴 Hardee's 🅞 Chrysler/Jeep/Dodge, CVS Drug, 🅷, Hyundai, to Falls of OH SP, Walgreens, **W** 🍴 Hooters, Kingfish Rest., Kobe 🏠 Fairfield Inn, Hawthorne Suites, Sheraton
0mm	Indiana/Kentucky state line, Ohio River

⬆N INTERSTATE 69

Exit #	Services
358mm	Indiana/Michigan state line
357	Lake George Rd, to IN 120, Fremont, Lake James, **E** 🅖 Petro/Iron Skillet/dsl/LP/scales/24hr/@ 🅞 Freightliner/Western Star Truck Repair, Kenworth, **W** 🅖 Marathon/dsl, Pilot/Wendy's/dsl/scales/24hr, Shell/Subway/dsl 🍴 McDonald's, Red Arrow Rest. 🏠 Holiday Inn Express, Redwood Inn 🅞 Freemont Outlets/Famous Brands, GNC, Jellystone Camping (5mi), to Pokagon SP
356	I-80/90 Toll Rd, E to Toledo, W to Chicago
354	IN 127, to IN 120, IN 727, Fremont, Orland, **E** 🅖 Tesla EVC 🏠 American Inn, Comfort Inn, Quality Inn, Ramada, Travelers Inn 🅞 golf, **W** 🅖 Marathon/dsl 🏠 Holiday Inn Express 🅞 Freemont Outlets/Famous Brands, Jellystone Camping (4mi), to Pokagon SP
350	rd 200 W, to Lake James, Crooked Lake, **E** 🅖 Sunoco/dsl 🅞 fireworks, **W** 🅖 Marathon, Sunoco/Subway 🍴 Caruso's Rest. Tasty Pizza 🅞 Marine Ctr
348	US 20, to Angola, Lagrange, **E** 🅖 Marathon/Subway/dsl Speedway/Taco Bell/dsl 🍴 McDonald's 🏠 Happy Acres Camping (1mi), University Inn (2mi) 🅞 🅷, **W** 🅖 ♥Loves/Hardee's/dsl/scales/24hr 🅞 KOA (2mi)
345mm	Pigeon Creek
344mm	🆁🆂 sb, full ♿ facilities, info, 🚻, 🏞, litter barrels, vending, petwalk
340	IN 4, to Hamilton, Ashley, Hudson, **1 mi W** 🅖 Marathon/Subway/dsl
334	US 6, to Waterloo, Kendallville, **E** 🍴 Subway 🅞 $General, **W** 🅖 BP/dsl, Marathon/dsl/24hr 🍴 Kathy's Kountry Kitchen
329	IN 8, to Garrett, Auburn, **E** 🅖 BP, Lassus, Speedway/dsl, Speedway/dsl (2) 🍴 Applebee's, Arby's, Burger King, Culver's, DQ, Jimmy John's, KFC, Little Caesar's, McDonald's, Papa John's, Peking Buffet, Penguin Point Rest., Pizza Hut, Richard's Rest. Starbucks, Steak'n Shake, Subway, Taco Bell, Wendy's 🏠 Auburn Inn, Baymont Inn, Comfort Suites, Days Inn, Red Roof Inn, Wingate Inn 🅞 $General, $Tree, Advance Parts, Aldi Foods, AT&T, AutoZone, Buick/Chevrolet/RV Ctr, Chrysler/Dodge/Jeep, CVS Drug, Davis RV Ctr, Ford, GNC, 🅷, Kroger/dsl, Monro, Save A Lot, Walmart/Subway, **W** 🅖 Marathon/dsl 🍴 Buffalo Wild Wings, Cebolla's Mexican, Cracker Barrel, Paradise Buffet, Subway 🏠 Hampton Inn, Holiday Inn Express 🅞 Home Depot, Verizon
326	rd 11A, to Garrett, Auburn, **E** 🅞 Auction Park, **W** 🅞 Fireside Camping
324mm	🆁🆂 nb, full ♿ facilities, info, 🏞, litter barrels, vending
317	Union Chapel Rd, **E** 🅞 🅷
316	IN 1 N, Dupont Rd, **E** 🅖 Lassus/Elmo's/dsl, Phillips 66/Burger King 🍴 Arby's, Arcos Mexicano, Culver's, Taco Bell 🏠 Comfort Suites, Hampton Inn, Holiday Inn Express 🅞 🅷, **W** 🅖 Speedway/dsl 🍴 Bagger Dave's Burgers, Bob Evans, Domino's, Jimmy John's, McDonald's, Panera Bread, Pine Valley Grill, Starbucks, Trolley Grill 🏠 Baymont Inn, La Quinta
315	I-469, US 30 E, **W** 🏠 Woodspring Suites
312b a	Coldwater Rd, **E** 🅖 BP/dsl, Marathon, Sunoco 🍴 Agaves Mexican, Arby's, Bill's Smokehouse, Buffalo Wings & Rings, Chili's, Cork'N Cleaver, Firehouse Subs, Hall's Factory Rest., IHOP, Jimmy John's, Koto Japanese, Mister Coney, Papa John's, Rally's, Red Lobster, Subway, Taco Bell, Wendy's, Wu's Fine Chinese 🏠 Hyatt Place, Ramada Plaza 🅞 $Tree, Aldi Foods, Dick's, Hobby Lobby, Hyundai, JoAnn Fabrics, O'Reilly Parts, PetCo, Tuesday Morning, U-Haul, Walmart/Subway, **W** 🅖 Marathon 🍴 Salsa Grille

SCOTTSBURG

CLARKSVILLE

IN

AUBURN

⬆N INTERSTATE 69 Cont'd

Exit #	Services

311b a   US 27 S, IN 3 N, **E** 🅿 Shell/dsl, Sunoco/dsl 🍴 Arby's, BJ's Rest., Cheddar's, Chick-fil-A, ChuckECheese's, DQ, Fazoli's, Golden Corral, Hall's Rest., Longhorn Steaks, McDonald's, Olive Garden, Starbucks, TGIFriday's, Tim Horton's 🛏 Candlewood Suites, Hawthorn Suites, TownePlace Suites, Tru Hilton 🅾 Barnes&Noble, Chevrolet, Chrysler/Dodge/Jeep, Costco/gas, Discount Tire, Fiat, Ford/Lincoln, Honda, Infiniti, JC Penney, Macy's, Nissan, Subaru, Toyota, Verizon, **W** 🅿 BP/dsl, Lassus/Elmo's Pizza/dsl, Marathon/dsl 🍴 Applebee's, Burger King, Chipotle, Cracker Barrel, Culver's, Hardee's, IHOP, Logan's Roadhouse, McDonald's, Panda Express, Sapporo Japanese, Starbucks, Subway, Taco Bell, TX Roadhouse 🛏 Best Value Inn, Best Western+, Comfort Inn, Days Inn, EconoLodge, Extended Stay America, Fairfield Inn, Fairfield Inn, Guesthouse Motel, Hampton Inn, Quality Inn, Travelodge, Wyndham Garden 🅾 Belle Tire, CVS Drug, Home Depot, Lowe's, Meijer/dsl/e85, Sam's Club/gas, VW

309b a   US 33, Goshen Rd, Ft Wayne, **E** 🅿 Phillips 66/dsl, [Pilot]/dsl/scales/24hr, Shell 🍴 Liberty Diner, McDonald's 🛏 Ft Wayne Inn, Knights Inn, Motel 6, Red Roof Inn, Rodeway Inn, Travel Inn 🅾 auto/dsl repair, Blue Beacon, 🇭, NAPA

305b a   IN 14 W, Ft Wayne, **E** 🅿 Lassus, Murphy USA, Shell/Subway/dsl, Speedway/Speedy's Cafe/dsl 🍴 Arby's, Biaggi's, Chick-fil-A, Chipotle Mexican, Coldstone, Domino's, Eddy Merlot Rest., Firehouse Subs, Flat Top Grill, Great Wall Buffet, Little Caesar's, Logan's Roadhouse, McAlister's Deli, Noodles&Co., O'Charley's, Panda Express, Panera Bread, Penn Sta Subs, Smokey Bones BBQ, Starbucks, Steak'n Shake, Subway, Taco Bell, Tuscanos Brazilian, Wendy's 🛏 Klopfenstein Suites 🅾 $General, $Tree, Acura, Advance Parts, Audi/Porsche, Barnes&Noble, Belle Tire, Best Buy, BigLots, BMW, Buick/GMC, Cadillac, Chevrolet, Chrysler/Dodge/Jeep, Dick's, Ford/Lincoln, Gordman's, Harley-Davidson, 🇭, Kia, Kohl's, Lexus, Lowe's, Marshall's, Mazda, McMahon's Tire/auto, Meijer/dsl, Menards, Michael's, NAPA, Old Navy, Petsmart, Target, to St Francis U, Toyota, Tuesday Morning, Verizon, vet, Volvo, Walmart/Subway

302   US 24, to Jefferson Blvd, Ft Wayne, **E** 🍴 Subway (1mi), Taco Bell (1mi) 🛏 Extended Stay America, Fairfield Inn, Hampton Inn, Residence Inn 🅾🇭, IN Wesleyan Ft Wayne, **W** 🅿 Lassus, Marathon/dsl 🍴 Applebee's, Arby's, Bob Evans, Buffalo Wild Wings, Coventry Tavern Rest., McDonald's, Naked Chopstix, Outback Steaks, Pizza Hut, Salsa Grille, Sara's Rest., Starbucks, Wendy's, Zesto Drive-In 🛏 Best Western, Comfort Suites, Hilton Garden, Holiday Inn Express, Homewood Suites, Staybridge Suites 🅾 Kroger/dsl, Meineke, st police, Walgreens

299   Lower Huntington Rd, **E** 🅾 to ↩

296b a   I-469, US 24 E, US 33 S, **E** 🅾 to ↩

286   US 224, to Huntington, Markle, **E** 🅿 Marathon/dsl, Phillips 66/Subway/dsl, Sunoco/dsl 🍴 DQ 🛏 Guesthouse Inn, Heritage Place Inn 🅾🇭, repair/tires, **W** 🅾 Roush Lake, to Huntington Reservoir

280mm   weigh sta sb/parking area nb

278   IN 5, to Warren, Huntington, **E** 🛏 Huggy Bear Motel, **W** 🅿 Marathon/Subway/dsl, Shell/Diner/dsl/scales/24hr 🍴 McDonald's, Ugalde's Rest. 🛏 Arlington Inn, Comfort Inn 🅾 fireworks, 🇭, RV camping, to Salamonie Reservoir

276mm   Salamonie River

273   IN 218, to Warren

264   IN 18, to Marion, Montpelier, **E** 🅿 Loves/McDonalds/dsl/scales/24hr, **W** 🅿 BP/Subway/dsl, Flying J/Wendy's/dsl/scales/24hr 🍴 Arby's 🛏 Best Value Inn 🅾 Harley-Davidson, 🇭, Ram

260mm   Walnut Creek

259   US 35 N, IN 22, to Upland, **E** 🅿 Shell/Subway 🍴 Burger King, Casa Grande Mexican, China 1, Cracker Barrel 🛏 Best Western+, Super 8 🅾 Mar-Brook Camping, Taylor U, **W** 🅿 Marathon/dsl, McClure Trkstp/dsl/24hr, Phillips 66/dsl 🍴 Hardee's, Starbucks, Taco Bell 🛏 Holiday Inn Express 🅾 to IN Wesleyan

255   IN 26, to Fairmount

250mm   🆁🆂 both lanes, full ♿ facilities, info, 🔌, 🚮, litter barrels, vending, pet walk

245   US 35 S, IN 28, to Alexandria, Albany, **E** 🅿 Petro/Shell/Iron Skillet/Subway/dsl/scales/24hr/@ 🅾 RV Camping

241   IN 332, to Muncie, Frankton, **E** 🅿 BP/Subway/dsl 🅾🇭, to Ball St U

234   IN 67, to IN 32, Chesterfield, Daleville, **E** 🅿 [Pilot]/Subway/dsl/scales/24hr, Shell 🍴 Arby's, Pizza Hut, Smokehouse BBQ, Taco Bell, Waffle House, White Castle 🛏 Budget Inn 🅾🇭, **W** 🅿 McClure/dsl/e85, [Pilot]/Denny's/dsl/scales/24hr, Speedway/dsl 🍴 McDonald's, Subway, Wendy's 🛏 Travel Inn 🅾 Timberline Valley Camping (3mi)

226   IN 9, IN 109, to Anderson, **E** 🍴 A&W/KFC, Culver's, Golden Corral, MT Mike's 🛏 Fairfield Inn, Hampton Inn, Holiday Inn Express, Quality Inn, Red Roof Inn 🅾 Belle Tire, Meijer/dsl, Menards, visitors ctr, **W** 🅿 BP, Marathon/dsl, Speedway/dsl 🍴 Applebee's, Arby's, Bob Evans, Buffalo Wild Wings, Burger King, Cracker Barrel, Fazoli's, IHOP, Jimmy John's, McDonald's, Olive Garden, Panda Express, Panera Bread, Papa Murphy's, Payless Mkt/dsl, Penn Sta Subs, Perkins, Pizza Hut, Ponderosa, Popeye's, Qdoba, Red Lobster, Riviera Maya, Ruby Tuesday, Starbucks, Steak'n Shake, Subway, Taco Bell, TX Roadhouse, Waffle House, Wendy's, White Castle 🛏 Baymont Inn, Best Value Inn, Best Western+, Comfort Inn, Days Inn, Motel 6 🅾 $Tree, AT&T, Big Lots, Cadillac/Chevrolet, Chrysler/Dodge/Jeep, GNC, Hobby Lobby, Honda, 🇭, Kohl's, Marshall's, Nissan, O'Reilly Parts, Petsmart, Tire Barn, to Anderson U, to Mounds SP, Verizon, vet, Walmart/Subway

222   IN 9, IN 67, to Anderson, **W** 🅿 Speedway/dsl 🍴 Skyline Chili 🅾🇭

219   IN 38, Pendleton, **E** 🅿 Ricker's/dsl 🍴 Burger King, McDonald's, Subway, **W** 🅾 Pine Lakes Camping

214   IN 13, to Lapel, **E** 🅿 BP/dsl, Loves/McDonald's/dsl/scales24hr 🍴 Waffle House, **W** 🅿 [Pilot]/Subway/dsl/scales/24hr 🅾 camping

210   IN 238, to Noblesville, Fortville, **E** 🅿 BP/dsl 🍴 Arby's, Culver's, DQ, Starbucks, Subway, Taco Bell, Wendy's 🅾🇭, **W** 🅿 EVC, Shell/dsl 🍴 Aspen Grill, BJ's Rest., Chick-fil-A, Chuy's, Coldstone, Famous Dave's, Five Guys, Fresh to Order Cafe, Houlihan's, McAlister's Deli, McDonald's, Olive Garden, Panda Express, Perkins, Potbelly, Qdoba, Red Robin, Stone Creek Rest.,

IN

INDIANAPOLIS AREA

RICHMOND

⬆N INTERSTATE 69 Cont'd

210 Continued
Tuscano's 🛏 Cambria Suites, Embassy Suites, Holiday Inn Express 🅞 $Tree, AT&T, Cabela's, CVS Drug, Dick's, Duluth Trading, Earth Fare Foods, Firestone/auto, JC Penney, Old Navy, Sleepy Bear Camping, Steinmart, Verizon

205 IN 37 N, 116th St, to Noblesville, Fishers, E 🅖 BP 🍽 Bent Cafe Asian, Penn Sta Subs, Sunrise Cafe 🅞 Kroger, W 🍽 Shell/Circle K, Speedway 🍽 Brixx Pizzaria, Five Guys, Handel's Ice Cream, Happy Dragon, Jet's Pizza, Marco's Pizza, McAlister's Deli, McDonald's, Moe's SW Grill, O'Charley's, Original Pancakes, Pure Eatery, Qdoba, Starbucks, Steak'n Shake, Subway, Verde Mexican, Wendy's, Wild Ginger Asian 🛏 Hampton Inn 🅞 AT&T, CVS Drug, Firestone/auto, Target, URGENT CARE

204 E 106th St, W 🛏 Fairfield Inn

203 96th St, E 🅖 Marathon/dsl (2), Murphy USA/dsl, Shell/Circle K, Village Pantry/dsl 🍽 Applebee's, Bubba's Rest., Cracker Barrel, Donato's Pizza, Dunkin', Hot Box Pizza, IHOP, Jersey Mike's, Jimmy John's, McDonald's, Noodles&Co., Panda Express, Panera Bread, Qdoba, Red Habanero, Rita's, Ruby Tuesday, Sahm's Grill, Slimm's Pizza, Smoothie King, Starbucks, Steak'n Shake, Tijuana Flats, Wendy's 🛏 AmericInn, Baymont Inn, Hilton Garden, Holiday Inn Express, Studio 6 🅞 $Tree, AT&T, Fry's, GNC, Kohl's, Meijer/dsl, PepBoys, PetCo, Staples, Tuesday Morning, Verizon, Walmart, W 🅖 Marathon/dsl 🍽 Arby's, Bob Evans, Burger King, Chicotes Mexican, Culver's, DJ's Hotdogs, Izakya Japanese, Journey Rest., Peterson's Steaks/seafood, Riviera Maya, Starbucks, Taco Bell, Tire Discounters, Wolfie's Grill 🛏 Comfort Suites, Residence Inn, SpringHill Suites, Staybridge Suites 🅞 Aldi Foods, Home Depot, Menards, NAPA, Sam's Club/gas, vet

201 82nd St, Castleton, E 🍽 Boston Mkt, Burger King, Jet's Pizza, Red Robin 🛏 Drury Inn, Extended Stay America, Red Roof Inn, Super 8 🅞 CVS Drug, �H, Lowe's, vet, Walgreens, W 🍽 Speedway/Speedy's Cafe/dsl 🍽 Applebee's, Arby's, Burger King, Charleston's Rest., Dave & Buster's, Denny's, Domino's, Fazoli's, Firehouse Subs, Formosa Buffet, Hooters, Jimmy John's, Joe's Grill, KFC, LJ Silver, Longhorn Steaks, Los Cabos Mexican, McAlister's Deli, McDonald's, Olive Garden, Panda Express, Penn Sta Subs, Pizza Hut, Popeye's, Red Lobster, Skyline Chili, Starbucks, Subway, Taco Bell, Thai Orchid, Twin Peaks, Wendy's 🛏 Candlewood Suites, Days Inn, Hampton Inn, Suburban Suites, Surestay+ 🅞 Aamco, Advance Parts, AutoZone, Best Buy, CarX, Dick's, Discount Tire, Firestone/auto, fireworks, Goodyear/auto, JC Penney, Macy's, Midas, O'Reilly Parts, Tire Barn

200mm I-465 around Indianapolis. I-69 begins/ends on I-465, exit 37, at Indianapolis.

⬆E INTERSTATE 70

Exit #	Services
156.5mm	Indiana/Ohio state line, **weigh sta**

156b a US 40 E, Richmond, N 🅖 Petro/BP/Iron Skillet/dsl/24hr/@ 🛏 Fairfield Inn 🅞 Blue Beacon, S 🅖 Murphy USA/dsl, Shell/dsl, Speedway/dsl, Sunoco 🍽 A&W/LJ Silver, Applebee's, Arby's, Big Boy, Buffalo Wild Wings, Buffalo Wings&Rings, Burger King, Chili's, Chipotle Mexican, Cracker Barrel, El Rodeo Mexican, Fazoli's, Galo's Italian, Golden Corral, IHOP, Jade House Chinese, Jimmy John's, KFC, McAlister's Deli, McDonald's, MCL Cafeteria, O'Charley's, Olive Garden, Papa Murphy's, Pizza Hut, Rally's, Red Lobster, Starbucks, Steak'n Shake, Subway, Taco Bell, TX Roadhouse, Yamato Japanese 🛏 Best Western, Days Inn, EconoLodge, Hampton Inn, Holiday Inn, Motel 6, Quality Inn

RICHMOND

156b a Continued
🅞 $General, $Tree, Advance Parts, Aldi Foods, AT&T, Best Buy, Big Lots, Buick/GMC, Chevrolet, Chrysler/Dodge/Jeep, Dick's, Dillard's, Firestone/auto, Ford, Hobby Lobby, JC Penney, Jo-Ann Fabrics, Kohl's, Kroger/dsl, Lowe's, Menards, O'Reilly Parts, Save-A-Lot Foods, Tires+, TJ Maxx, Toyota/Nissan, U-Haul, Verizon, Walgreens, Walmart/Subway

153 IN 227, to Whitewater, Richmond, 2 mi N 🅞 KOA

151b a US 27, to Chester, Richmond, N 🍽 Fricker's Rest. 🅞 Honda, KOA, S 🅖 Shell 🍽 Bob Evans, Burger Time, Carver's Rest., El Bronco Mexican, Hardee's, McDonald's, Subway, Taco Bell, Wendy's 🛏 Comfort Inn, Red Roof Inn 🅞 CVS Drug, Harley-Davidson, �H, Meijer/dsl/E85

149b a US 35, IN 38, to Muncie, N 🍽 Loves/Hardee's/dsl/scales/24hr, S 🍽 Shell/dsl 🅞 Camping World RV Ctr

148mm weigh sta wb

145 Centerville, N 🅖 Marathon/DQ/Godfather's/dsl 🛏 Super 8 🅞 Goodyear/truck repair, S 🅞 Warm Glow Candles/cafe

145mm 🅞 Nolands Fork Creek

144mm 🆁ｓ wb, full ♿ facilities, info, vending, 🚻, 🏞, litter barrels, petwalk

141mm Greens Fork River

137 IN 1, to Hagerstown, Connersville, N 🅞 Amish Cheese, S 🅖 BP/Arby's/dsl/24hr, Shell/Burger King, Speedway/dsl/e85 🍽 McDonald's

131 Wilbur Wright Rd, New Lisbon, S 🍽 Shell/Pizza Hut/Taco Bell/dsl/scales/24hr/@ 🅞 New Lisbon RV park

126mm Flatrock River

123 IN 3, to New Castle, Spiceland, N 🛏 All American Inn (3mi), Holiday Inn Express (3mi) 🅞 �H, S 🍽 FLYING J/Denny's/Subway/dsl/LP/scales/24hr, Mr Fuel/rest./dsl/scales/24hr 🍽 Montgomery's Steaks 🅞 tires/repair

117mm Big Blue River

115 IN 109, to Knightstown, Wilkinson, N 🍽 Loves/McDonald's/Subway/dsl/scales/24hr, Speedway/rest./dsl/scales/24hr 🍽 Burger King 🅞 Jellystone Camping

107mm 🆁ｓ both lanes, full ♿ facilities, vending, 🚻, 🏞, litter barrels, petwalk

104 IN 9, Greenfield, Maxwell, N 🍽 Speedway/dsl, S 🍽 Circle K/dsl, Murphy USA/dsl, Shell/Circle K, Speedway/dsl 🍽 Applebee's, Arby's, Bamboo Garden, Bob Evans, Buffalo Wild Wings, Burger King, Chicago's Pizza, China Inn, Cracker Barrel, Culver's, Firehouse Subs, Hardee's, Jimmy John's, KFC, Little Caesar's, McDonald's, Mi Casa Mexican, MT Mike's Steaks, O'Charley's, Papa John's, Papa Murphy's, Penn Sta Subs, Pizza Hut, Ponderosa, Popeye's, Qdoba, Starbucks, Steak'n Shake, Subway, Taco Bell, Waffle House, Wasabi, Wendy's, White Castle 🛏 Comfort Inn, Country Inn&Suites, Fairfield Inn, Greenfield Inn, Hampton Inn, Holiday Inn Express, Quality Inn, Super 8 🅞 $General, $Tree, Advance Parts, Aldi Foods, AutoZone, Big Lots, CVS Drug, GNC, Home Depot, �H, Kohl's, Kroger/dsl, Petsmart, Verizon, Walgreens, Walmart

96 Mt Comfort Rd, N 🅖 ▦/Pizza Hut/dsl/scales/24hr, Speedway/Subway/dsl 🍽 Burger King, Wendy's, S 🍽 Shell/Circle K 🍽 McDonald's 🅞 KOA (seasonal), Mt Comfort RV Ctr

91 Post Rd, to Ft Harrison, N 🅖 Mobil/Circle K 🍽 Cracker Barrel, Denny's, Outback Steaks, Steak'n Shake, Wendy's 🛏 InTown Suites, La Quinta 🅞 Lowe's, st police, S 🅖 Admiral, BP/dsl, Shell/dsl, Speedway 🍽 Hardee's, Jack-in-the-Box, KFC/Taco Bell, Little Caesar's, Waffle House 🛏 Country Hearth Inn, Days Inn 🅞 CVS Drug, Family$, Home Depot

90 I-465 (from wb)

GREENFIELD

INTERSTATE 70 Cont'd

Exit #	Services
89	Shadeland Ave, I-465 (from eb), **N** 📭 Marathon/dsl 🍴 Bob Evans 🛏 Baymont Inn, Comfort Inn, Holiday Inn Express, Welcome Inn 🅾 Toyota, U-Haul, **S** 📭 Admiral/dsl, Circle K, Exxon/dsl, Marathon, Speedway/dsl 🍴 Arby's, Burger King, Damon's, Domino's, Four Seasons Diner, Jimmy John's, Lincoln Sq Rest., McDonald's, Papa John's, Penn Sta Subs, Rally's, Red Lobster, Starbucks, Subway, Taco Bell, TX Roadhouse, Wendy's 🛏 Always Inn, Best Value Inn, Candlewood Suites, Delta Hotel, Express Inn, Fairfield Inn, Marriott, Quality Inn 🅾 $General, CarX, Chevrolet, Chrysler/Dodge/Jeep, CVS Drug, Honda, Kia, Kroger/gas, Mazda, Nissan
87	Emerson Ave, **N** 📭 BP/McDonald's, Speedway/dsl, **S** 📭 Shell 🅾 ⊞
85 b a	Rural St, Keystone Ave, **N** 📭 Shell 🍴 Church's 🅾 fairgrounds, **S** 📭 Shell/dsl
83b(112)	I-65 N, to Chicago
83a(111)	Michigan St, Market St, **S** 🍴 Hardee's downtown
80(110a)	I-65 S, to Louisville
79b	Illinois St, McCarty St downtown
79a	West St, **N** 📭 Speedway/dsl 🛏 Holiday Inn, Holiday Inn Express, Hyatt, JW Marriott, Staybridge Suites 🅾 Govt Ctr, ⊞, Lucas Oil Stadium, zoo
78	Harding St, to downtown, **S** 📭 Marathon/Subway 🍴 Wendy's
77	Holt Rd, **N** 📭 Phillips 66/dsl 🍴 Rally's, Steak'n Shake, **S** 📭 Speedway/Speedy's Cafe/dsl 🍴 McDonald's
75	Airport Expswy, to Raymond St (no EZ wb return), **N** 📭 Marathon/dsl, Speedway/dsl 🍴 Indy's Rest., Jimmy John's, Library Rest., Subway, Waffle House 🛏 Candlewood Suites, Courtyard, Extended Stay America, Fairfield Inn, Hyatt Place, La Quinta, Ramada, Red Roof Inn, Residence Inn, Super 8, Wyndham 🅾 NAPA, to ✈
73 b a	I-465 N/S, I-74 E/W
69	(only from eb) to I-74 E, to I-465 S
68	Six Points Rd, **N** 🅾 ✈, **S** 📭 Mobil/dsl 🍴 Burger Theory, Subway 🛏 Hampton Inn, Hilton Garden, Holiday Inn, Home 2 Suites
66	IN 267, to Plainfield, Mooresville, **N** 📭 Blu/dsl, BP, Shell/Circle K, Speedway/dsl, Thornton's/dsl 🍴 Arby's, Bob Evans, Burger King, Coachman Rest., Cracker Barrel, Golden Corral, McDonald's, Narita Japanese, Nonna's Italian, Steak'n Shake, Subway, Taco Bell, Waffle House, White Castle 🛏 Baymont Inn, Best Western+, Budget Inn, Comfort Inn, Days Inn, Embassy Suites, Hampton Inn, Holiday Inn Express, Homewood Suites, Indianapolis Airport Suites, La Quinta, Quality Inn, Staybridge Suites, Super 8, Wingate Inn, Woodspring Suites 🅾 Buick/GMC, Chateau Thomas Winery, Harley-Davidson
65mm	Rs both lanes, full 🚻 facilities, info, vending, 🕽, 🛢, litter barrels, petwalk
59	IN 39, to Belleville, **N** 📭 Loves/McDonald's/Subway/dsl/scales/24hr, **S** 📭 TA/Country Pride/dsl/scales/24hr/@, truckwash
51	rd 1100W, **S** 📭 Koger's/Sunoco/dsl/rest./24hr 🅾 repair/towing/24hr
41	US 231, to Greencastle, Cloverdale, **S** 📭 BP/dsl, Casey's (2mi), Marathon/dsl/scales/24hr 🍴 Arby's, Chicago's Pizza, El Cantarito, McDonald's, Subway, Taco Bell 🛏 Days Inn, EconoLodge, Holiday Inn Express, Motel 6, Super 8 🅾 $General, Family$, Jordan's Carcare, NAPA, Taylor's Hardware, to Lieber SRA, Value Mkt Foods
37	IN 243, to Putnamville, **S** 📭 Marathon/dsl 🅾 Misty Morning Campground (4mi), to Lieber SRA

Exit #	Services
23	IN 59, to Brazil, **N** 📭 Pilot/McDonald's/Subway/dsl/scales/24hr, Speedway/dsl 🅾 ⊞, truck repair, **S** 📭 BP/dsl, Petro/Iron Skillet/dsl/scales/24hr/@, Road Ranger/Pilot/Subway/dsl/scales 🍴 Burger King, Family Table Rest. 🛏 Best Western+, Travelodge
15mm	Honey Creek
11	IN 46, Terre Haute, **N** 📭 Pilot/Subway/dsl/scales/24hr, Thornton/dsl 🍴 Arby's, Burger King, Holiday Inn Express, McDonald's, Monical's Pizza, Real Hacienda, Sonic, Taco Bell 🛏 Home 2 Suites 🅾 $Tree, ☕, Aldi Foods, GNC, Meijer/dsl, Verizon, Walmart, **S** 🅾 KOA
7	US 41, US 150, Terre Haute, **N** 📭 Casey's/dsl, Marathon/dsl, Sunoco/dsl, Thornton's/dsl 🍴 Applebee's, Bandana's BBQ, Bob Evans, Coyote's Mexican Hacienda, Cracker Barrel, Dunkin', East Star Buffet, Fazoli's, IHOP, Moe's SW Grill, NewDay Cafe, Pizza Hut, Real Hacienda Mexican, Starbucks, Steak'n Shake, Tokyo Japanese, TX Roadhouse 🛏 Comfort Suites, Days Inn, Drury Inn, Fairfield Inn, La Quinta, PearTree Inn, Super 8 🅾 AT&T, AutoZone, Chrysler/Jeep, O'Reilly Parts, URGENT CARE, **S** 📭 Speedway/dsl, Thornton's/dsl 🍴 Arby's, Baskin-Robbins, Buffalo Wild Wings, Burger King, Cheddar's, Chick-fil-A, Chili's, Denny's, DQ, Five Guys, Fuddrucker's, Golden Corral, Hardee's, Jimmy John's, KFC, LJ Silver, Longhorn Steaks, Los Tres Caminos, McDonald's, Monical's Pizza, Olive Garden, Outback Steaks, Panda Express, Panda Garden, Panera Bread, Papa John's, Penn Sta Subs, Popeye's, Qdoba, Rally's, Red Lobster, Ruby Tuesday, Starbucks, Subway, Taco Bell, TGIFriday's, Wendy's, White Castle 🛏 Hampton Inn, Holiday Inn, Motel 6, SpringHill Suites 🅾 $Tree, Aldi Foods, AT&T, Best Buy, Big O Tire, BigLots, BooksAMillion, Buick/Cadillac/GMC, Burlington Coats, Chevrolet, Dodge, Ford, Fresh Thyme Mkt, Goodyear/auto, Harley-Davidson, Hobby Lobby, ⊞, Hyundai, JC Penney, Jo-Ann Fabrics, Kohl's, Kroger/dsl, Lowe's, NAPA, Nissan, Old Navy, Petsmart, Ross, Sam's Club/gas, Staples, Tire Barn, TJ Maxx, Verizon, Walgreens, Walmart
5.5mm	Wabash River
3	Darwin Rd, W Terre Haute, **N** 🅾 to St Mary of-the-Woods Coll
1.5mm	Welcome Ctr eb, full 🚻 facilities, info, 🛢, litter barrels, 🕽, vending, petwalk
1	US 40 E (from eb, exits left), to Terre Haute, W Terre Haute
.5mm	**weigh sta eb**
0mm	Indiana/Illinois state line

INTERSTATE 74

Exit #	Services
171.5mm	Indiana/Ohio state line
171mm	**weigh sta wb**
169	US 52 W, to Brookville, **S** 🅾 Chevrolet
168.5mm	Whitewater River
164	IN 1, St Leon, **N** 📭 Shell/Subway/dsl, Sunoco/Pizza/dsl, **S** 📭 BP/Blimpie/dsl 🍴 Skyline Chili

INTERSTATE 74 Cont'd

Exit #	Services
156	IN 101, to Sunman, Milan, S 🅖 BP/dsl 🅞 KOA (2mi)
152mm	🆁🆂 both lanes, full 🚻 facilities, 🅲, 🚶, litter barrels, vending, petwalk
149	IN 229, to Oldenburg, Batesville, N 🅕 Marathon, Shell/dsl 🅕 China Buffet, McDonald's, Pizza Hut, Pizza King, Subway, Toros Mexican, Wendy's 🛏 Best Western 🅞 $General, Advance Parts, Kroger/dsl, URGENT CARE, Verizon, S 🅖 BP 🅕 Arby's, DQ, KFC/Taco Bell, La Rosa's Pizza, Skyline Chili 🛏 Quality Inn 🅞 CVS Drug, 🅷, O'Reilly Parts
143	to IN 46, New Point, N 🅖 Petro/Iron Skillet/dsl/scales/24hr/@, S 🅖 BP 🛏 Hwy 46 Inn
134b a	IN 3, to Rushville, Greensburg, S 🅖 BP/dsl, Marathon/DQ/Subway, Speedway/dsl 🅕 A&W, Arby's, Big Boy, Buffalo Wings&Rings, Burger King, Chili's, El Chile Poblano, El Reparo Mexican, Great Wall Buffet, Jimmy John's, KFC/LJ Silver, Lincoln St Grill, Little Caesar's, McDonald's, Papa John's, Pizza Hut, Taco Bell, Waffle House, Wendy's 🛏 Baymont Inn, Holiday Inn Express, Quality Inn 🅞 $General, $Tree, Aldi Foods, AT&T, AutoZone, Buick/Chevrolet, Chrysler/Dodge/Jeep, CVS Drug, Ford, GNC, O'Reilly Parts, TrueValue, Verizon, Walgreens, Walmart/Subway
132	US 421, to Greensburg, S 🅖 Amoco/Sonic/dsl, CNG, Shell, Sunoco/rest./dsl 🅕 Sonic 🛏 Hampton Inn, Holiday Inn Express (2mi)
130mm	Clifty Creek
123	Saint Paul, S 🅖 Loves/McDonald's/Subway/dsl/scales/24hr 🅞 repair
119	IN 244 E, to Milroy
116	IN 44, to Shelbyville, Rushville, N 🅖 Circle K/dsl, S 🅖 BP/dsl, Country Mark/dsl, Marathon, Murphy USA/dsl, Sunoco/dsl 🅕 Agustin's Mexican, Applebee's, Arby's, Bellacino's, Bob Evans, Buffalo Wild Wings, Burger King, China Wok, Cholula Mexican, Denny's, Domino's, DQ, Dunkin', Fazoli's, Jimmy John's, KFC, King Buffet, McDonald's, Papa John's, Penn Sta Subs, Pizza Hut, Rally's, Starbucks, Subway, Taco Bell, Wendy's, White Castle 🛏 Quality Inn 🅞 $General, $Tree, Ace Hardware, Advance Parts, Aldi Foods, AT&T, AutoZone, BigLots, Chevrolet, Ford, GNC, 🅷, Kroger/dsl, Midas, O'Reilly Parts, Verizon, Walgreens, Walmart/Subway
115mm	Little Blue River
113mm	Big Blue River
113	IN 9, to Shelbyville, N 🅖 Speedway/dsl 🅕 Cracker Barrel, TX Corral, Wendy's, S 🅖 Shell, Shell/Circle K/Subway/dsl 🅕 Casey's, McDonald's, Waffle House, Zaxby's 🛏 Comfort Inn, EconoLodge, Hampton Inn, Holiday Inn Express, Super 8 🅞 🅷
109	Fairland Rd, N 🅖 PILOT/McDonald's/dsl/scales/24hr 🅞 Indiana Grand/casino, S 🅞 Brownie's Marine
103	London Rd, to Boggstown
102mm	Big Sugar Creek
101	Pleasant View Rd, N 🅖 Country Mark/dsl/repair
99	Acton Rd
96	Post Rd, N 🅖 Marathon/Subway/dsl/24hr 🅕 McDonald's, S 🅖 Circle K/dsl 🅕 Taco Bell, Wendy's 🅞 Chevrolet
94b a	I-465/I-74 W, I-465 N, US 421 N.
	I-74 and I-465 run together 21 miles. See I-495, exits 2-16, and 52-53.
73b	I-465 N access to same services as 16a on I-465
73a	I-465 S, I-74 E
71mm	Eagle Creek

Exit #	Services
68	Ronald Reagan Pkwy, N 🅞 🅷
66	IN 267, Brownsburg, N 🅖 Circle K, Citgo/dsl 🅕 Applebee's, Asia Wok, Buffalo Wild Wings, Dunkin', Papa's Pizzaria, Starbucks, Steak'n Shake, Subway, Tequila Mexican 🛏 Hampton Inn, Quality Inn 🅞 Big O Tire, Midas, S 🅖 BP/dsl, GetGo, Speedway/dsl 🅕 Arby's, Arnie's Rest., Bob Evans, Burger King, China's Best, Elegance Rest., Firehouse Subs, Five Guys, Hotbox Pizza, IHOP, Jimmy John's, KFC, McAlister's Deli, McDonald's, Mediterranean Pizza, Papa Murphy's, Penn Sta Subs, Qdoba, Starbucks, Taco Bell, The Toros Mexican, Wendy's, White Castle 🛏 Comfort Suites, Super 8 🅞 AT&T, Belle Tire, Firestone/auto, Ford, GNC, Kohl's, Kroger/gas, Lowe's, O'Reilly Parts, USPO, Verizon, Walmart/Subway
61	to Pittsboro, S 🅖 Loves/Godfather's/Subway/dsl/scales/24hr
58	IN 39, to Lebanon, Lizton, S 🅖 Sunoco/dsl/e85 🅞 $General
57mm	🆁🆂 both lanes, full 🚻 facilities, 🅲, 🚶, litter barrels, vending, petwalk
52	IN 75, to Advance, Jamestown, 2 mi S gas, food, camping
39	IN 32, to Crawfordsville, S 🅖 PILOT/Subway/dsl/scales/24hr
34	US 231, to Linden, S 🅖 Circle K/dsl, Marathon/dsl, McClure/dsl, Speedway, Sunoco/dsl/cng 🅕 Cracker Barrel, McDonald's, Subway 🛏 Best Western+, Comfort Inn, Hampton Inn, Holiday Inn Express, Knights Inn, Motel 6, Super 8 🅞 🅷, KOA (1mi), Sugar Creek Campground (4mi)
25	IN 25, to Wingate, Waynetown
15	US 41, to Attica, Veedersburg, S 🅖 BP/Subway, Casey's/dsl, Marathon/dsl 🅕 Suzie Q's 🅞 $General, camping, Family$, to Turkey Run SP
8	Covington, N 🅖 Marathon/dsl, Valero/dsl 🅕 Benjamin's, Overpass Pizza 🅞 fireworks
7mm	Wabash River
4	IN 63, to Newport, N 🅖 One9/Arby's/dsl/scales/24hr 🅕 Beefhouse Rest.
1mm	Welcome Ctr eb, full 🚻 facilities, info, 🅲, 🚶, litter barrels, vending, petwalk
0mm	Indiana/Illinois state line, Eastern/Central Time Zone

INTERSTATE 80/90

Exit #	Services
157mm	Indiana/Ohio state line
153mm	toll plaza, litter barrels
144	I-69, US 27, Angola, Ft Wayne, N 🅖 Petro/Iron Skillet/dsl/scales/24hr/@, PILOT/Wendy's/dsl/scales, Shell/Subway/dsl 🅕 McDonald's, Red Arrow Rest. 🛏 Redwood Inn 🅞 Freightliner/Western Star/truck repair, S services on IN 120 🅖 Marathon/dsl 🛏 Comfort Inn, Holiday Inn Express, Quality Inn, Travelers Inn 🅞 Freemont Outlet Shops/famous brands, GNC, golf/rest, Jellystone Camping (5mi), to Pokagon SP
131.5mm	Fawn River
126mm	Ernie Pyle TP both lanes 🅖 Sunoco/dsl 🅕 Popeye's, Starbucks 🅞 RV dump
121	IN 9, to Lagrange, Howe, 2 mi N 🅖 Golden Buddha, Marathon, Murphy USA/dsl, Speedway/dsl 🅕 Applebee's, Buffalo Wild Wings, Burger King, Culver's, Fiesta Mexican, Hot'n Now, KFC, King Dragon, Little Caesar's, McDonald's, Pizza Hut, Subway, Taco Bell, Wendy's 🛏 American Inn, Best Western+, Hampton Inn, Travel Inn, Travelodge 🅞 $Tree, AT&T, CarQuest, Family$, Ford, GNC, 🅷 (4mi), Kroger, Meijer/dsl, Rite Aid, Walgreens, Walmart/Subway, S 🅖 Marathon/dsl 🛏 Holiday Inn Express, Super 8 🅞 🅷 (8mi)

IN

Exit #	Services

INTERSTATE 80/90 Cont'd

Exit #	Services
120mm	Fawn River
108mm	trucks only ℞ₛ both lanes
107	US 131, IN 13, to Middlebury, Constantine, 0-3 mi N 🅖 Marathon/dsl, Speedway/dsl 🍴 Country Table Rest., McDonald's 🛏 Patchwork Quilt Inn, Plaza Motel 🅞 $General, 1 mi S 🅖 BP/dsl 🍴 Yup's DairyLand 🛏 McKenzie House B&B 🅞 Dollar General, Eby's Pines RV Park, KOA (apr-nov)
101	IN 15, to Goshen, Bristol, 0-2 mi S 🅖 Mobil/7-11, Speedway/dsl 🍴 Subway 🅞 Eby's Pines Camping (3mi), USPO
96	Rd 1, E Elkhart, 2 mi S 🅖 BP/dsl, Marathon, Mobil/7-11 🍴 Arby's, China Star, DQ, McDonald's, Subway, Taco Bell 🅞 Ace Hardware, RV/MH Hall of Fame
92	IN 19, to Elkhart, N 🅖 Marathon, Mobil/7-11/dsl, Phillips 66/Subway/dsl 🍴 Chubby Trout, Cracker Barrel, Perkins, Steak'n Shake 🛏 Best Western, Candlewood Suites, Comfort Suites, Country Inn&Suites, Diplomat Motel, EconoLodge, Fairfield Inn, Fairway Inn, Hampton Inn, Hilton Garden, La Quinta, Microtel, Quality Inn, Sheraton, Sleep Inn, Staybridge Suites, Turnpike Motel 🅞 $General, Aldi Foods, CVS Drug, Elkhart Campground (1mi), Martin's Foods, Montana RV Ctr, Walgreens, 0-2 mi S 🅖 Exxon, Marathon/dsl, Speedway/dsl 🍴 Arby's, Buffalo Wild Wings, Burger King, Callahan's, Culver's, DQ, Dunkin', El Camino Real, Jets Pizza, Jimmy John's, KFC, King Wha Chinese, LJ Silver, Marco's Pizza, McDonald's, MOD Pizza, Noodles&Co, North Garden Buffet, Olive Garden, Panda Express, Papa John's, Penn Sta Subs, Pizza Hut, Qdoba, Red Lobster, Subway, Taco Bell, TX Roadhouse, Wendy's, Wings Etc. 🛏 Baymont Inn, Budget Inn, Daylite Inn, Garden Inn, Red Roof Inn, Super 8 🅞 $Tree, Advance Parts, AT&T, AutoZone, Belle Tire, CarQuest, Family$, Honda, Ⓗ, Indian Motorcycles, Lowe's, Menards, O'Reilly Parts, Petsmart, Ross, Verizon, Walmart/Subway
91mm	Christiana Creek
90mm	Schricker TP both directions 🅖 Sunoco/7-11/dsl 🍴 Starbucks 🅞 RV Dump, Z Mkt
83	to Mishawaka, N 🅖 BP/dsl, Phillips 66/dsl, Phillips 66/Subway/dsl 🍴 Applebee's, Bar Louie, Five Guys, Granite City Grill, Longhorn Steaks, Olive Garden, Starbucks, Subway, Wendy's 🛏 Best Western+, Country Inn&Suites, Fairfield Inn, Hampton Inn, Holiday Inn Express, Quality Inn 🅞 Barnes&Noble, Best Buy, Costco/dsl, CVS Drug, JC Penney, KOA (mar-nov), Macy's, Martin's Foods/gas, Menards, Ross, Target, Verizon, Walgreens, S 🅞 Ⓗ
77	US 33, US 31B, IN 933, South Bend, 2 mi N on frtge rd 🅖 Admiral, Mobil/dsl, Murphy USA/dsl 🍴 Arby's, Burger King, DQ, Dunkin', Fazoli's, Hacienda Mexican, Jimmy John's, Jimmy John's, KFC, Little Caesar's, Marco's Pizza, McDonald's, McDonald's, Papa John's, Pizza Hut, Ponderosa, Sonic, Starbucks, Steak'n Shake, Subway, The Farmhouse 🛏 Comfort Suites, Hampton Inn, Rodeway Inn, Staybridge Suites, Suburban Lodge, Waterford Lodge 🅞 $Tree, Ace Hardware, Aldi Foods, AT&T, AutoZone, Belle Tire, BMW/Mazda, Meijer/dsl/24hr, NAPA, O'Reilly Parts, vet, Walgreens, Walmart/Subway, S 🅖 Marathon, Phillips 66/Subway/dsl 🍴 American Pancake House, Bob Evans, HoPing House Chinese, King Gyros, Perkins, Pizza King, Taco Bell, Wendy's 🛏 Best Value Inn, Hilton Garden, Holiday Inn Express, Microtel, Quality Inn, St Marys Inn 🅞 CarX, Ⓗ, to Notre Dame
76mm	St Joseph River
72	US 31, to Niles, South Bend, N 🅖 🅿️Pilot/Subway/dsl/scales/24hr, Speedway/Subway/dsl 🍴 Chivo's Pizza, El Arriero, Taco Bell 🛏 Super 8, S 🅞 🍴, to Potato Creek SP (20mi)
62mm	Eastern Time Zone/Central Time Zone
56mm	TP both lanes 🅖 Sunoco/dsl 🍴 Burger King, Starbucks
49	IN 39, to La Porte, N 🅖 Hampton Inn, 3 mi S 🅖 Family Express, Phillips 66/dsl 🍴 DQ, El Bracero Mexican 🛏 Best Western+, Blue Heron Inn, Cassidy Inn & RV, Holiday Inn Express, Travelodge
39	US 421, to Michigan City, Westville, S Purdue U North Cent
38mm	trucks only ℞ₛ both lanes, litter barrels
31	IN 49, to Chesterton, Valparaiso, N 🅖 Family Express/dsl, Phillips 66, Speedway/dsl 🍴 AJ's Pizza, Bob Evans, Clock Rest., Culver's, Subway 🛏 Hilton Garden 🅞 CVS Drug, Dean's Tire/auto, Sand Creek RV Park (3mi, Apr-Oct), Strack&Van Til Mkt, to IN Dunes Nat Lakeshore, S 🛏 Hampton Inn (8mi), Super 8 (8mi)
24mm	toll plaza
23	Portage, Port of Indiana, 0-2 mi N 🅖 Luke, Marathon 🍴 Denny's, Mark's Grill 🛏 Baymont Inn, Best Western+, Country Inn&Suites, Days Inn, Hampton Inn, Quality Inn, Rodeway Inn, Super 8, S 🅖 BP, Speedway/dsl 🍴 Burger King, CiCi's Pizza, DQ, Dunkin', Jimmy John's, KFC, Little Caesar's, McDonald's, Rosewood Rest., Subway, Wendy's 🅞 Ace Hardware, Advance Parts, AutoZone, Family$, GNC, O'Reilly Parts, USPO, Walgreens
22mm	TP both lanes 🅖 Sunoco/dsl 🍴 Ladson Grill
21mm	I-90 and I-80 run together eb, separate wb. I-80 runs with I-94 wb. For I-80 exits 1 through 15, see Indiana Interstate 94.
21	I-94 E to Detroit, I-80/94 W, US 6, IN 51, Lake Station, S 🅖 🟥FLYING J/Denny's/dsl/scales/24hr/@, Mr Fuel/dsl/scales/24hr, 🅿️Pilot/Road Ranger/Subway/dsl/scales, TA/BP/Popeye's/dsl/scales/24hr/@ 🅞 Blue Beacon, Blue Beacon
17	I-65 S, US 12, US 20, Dunes Hwy, to Indianapolis
14b	IN 53, to Gary, Broadway, S 🅖 Citgo
14a	Grant St, to Gary, S 🅞 Ⓗ
10	IN 912, Cline Ave, to Gary, N 🅞 🍴, casino
5	US 41, Calumet Ave, to Hammond, S 🅖 GoLo, Nice'n Easy, Speedway/dsl 🍴 Aurelio's Pizza, Dunkin', Gorditas, Johnel's Rest., KFC, McDonald's, Subway, Taco Bell, White Castle 🛏 EconoLodge, Ramada Inn, Super 8 🅞 Aldi Foods, AutoZone, O'Reilly Parts, Walgreens
3	IN 912, Cline Ave, to Hammond, N 🅞 to Gary Reg Airport, S 🅖 Shell
1.5mm	toll plaza
1mm	US 12, US 20, 106th St, Indianapolis Blvd, N 🅖 BP, Citgo/Dunkin', Luke/dsl 🍴 IHOP, Popeye's, Starbucks 🅞 $Tree, AT&T, casino, Ross, Walmart, S 🍴 Burger King, KFC, McDonald's, Pizza Hut, Subway 🅞 Aldi Foods, O'Reilly Parts
0mm	Indiana/Illinois state line

ELKHART

MISHAWAKA

SOUTH BEND

SOUTH BEND

PORTAGE

IN

🅿 = gas   🍴 = food   🏨 = lodging   🅾 = other   🆁🆂 = rest stop   Copyright 2022 - The Next EXIT ®

INTERSTATE 94

Exit #	Services
46mm	Indiana/Michigan state line
43mm	**Welcome Ctr wb, full ♿ facilities, info, 🄲, 🚰, litter barrels, vending, petwalk**
40b a	US 20, US 35, to Michigan City, N 🅾 🄷, S 🅿 Speedway/dsl
34b a	US 421, to Michigan City, N 🅿 BP/dsl, Family Express/e85, Marathon, Speedway/dsl, Speedway/White Castle/dsl 🍴 Arby's, Baskin-Robbins/Dunkin', Buffalo Wild Wings, Burger King, Chili's, Chipotle, Crawford's Eatery, Culver's, Denny's, El Bracero Mexican, Five Guys, Hardee's, IHOP, Jimmy John's, KFC, LJ Silver, McDonald's, Olive Garden, Panda Express, Panera Bread, Pizza Hut, Popeye's, Red Lobster, Sake Asian Fusion, Schoop's Rest., Sonic, Sophia's Pancakes, Starbucks, Subway, Taco Bell, TX Corral, Wendy's 🏨 ABC Motel, Baymont Inn, Comfort Suites, Country Inn&Suites, Dunes Inn, Hampton Inn, Holiday Inn Express, MI City Inn, Microtel, Quality Inn, Red Roof Inn, Super 8, Travel Inn 🅾 $General, $Tree, Advance Parts, Aldi Foods, AT&T, AutoZone, Belle Tire, BigLots, Discount Tire, Family$, Fannie May Candies, Ford/Lincoln, GNC, Hobby Lobby, 🄷, Jo-Ann Fabrics, Kohl's, Lowe's, Meijer/dsl, Menards, Midas, Petsmart, Ross, Save-a-Lot, TJ Maxx, Verizon, Walgreens, Walmart/Subway, S 🅿 Speedway/Subway/dsl/scales/24hr 🅾 Buick/Chevrolet/GMC, Harley-Davidson
29mm	weigh sta both lanes
26b a	IN 49, to Valparaiso , Chesterton, N 🅾 to IN Dunes SP, S 🅿 BP/White Castle, Speedway/dsl 🍴 A&W/KFC, Arby's, Burger King, Domino's, DQ, Dunkin', El Salto Mexican, Gelsosomo's Pizza, Gino's Grill, Happy Wok, Jimmy John's, Lemon Tree Grill, Little Caesar's, McDonald's, Papa John's, Pizza Hut, Subway, Taco Bell, Tao Chen's, Third Coast Cafe, Wendy's 🏨 Best Western, EconoLodge, Hilton Garden (3mi), Lakeside Inn, Quality Inn 🅾 Advance Parts, AutoZone, 🄷, Jewel-Osco, Sand Cr Camping (5mi), Verizon, Walgreens
22b a	US 20, Burns Harbor, N 🅿 Shell/Subway/dsl/scales/LP, TA/BP/Country Pride/Pizza Hut/Popeye's/Taco Bell/dsl/scales/24hr/@ 🏨 Comfort Inn 🅾 fireworks, S 🅿 Luke/dsl, �val/McDonald's/Subway/dsl/scales/24hr 🅾 Camp-Land RV Ctr, Chevrolet, fireworks, Ford, Kia, Nissan, repair, Toyota
19	IN 249, to Port of IN, Portage, N 🅿 Family Express/dsl/e85 🍴 DQ, El Salto, Hooters, Longhorn Steaks, McDonald's, Quaker Steak&Lube, Starbucks, Subway, Taco Bell 🏨 Affordable Suites, Country Inn&Suites 🅾 Bass Pro Shops, S 🅿 Luke, Marathon/dsl 🍴 Denny's, Dunkin', Shenanigans Grill 🏨 Best Western+, Days Inn, Hampton Inn, Holiday Inn Express, Rodeway Inn, Super 8, Travel Inn
16	access to I-80/90 toll road E, I-90 toll road W, IN 51N, Ripley St same as 15b&a

I-94/I-80 run together wb.

15b	US 6W, IN 51, N 🅿 *FLYING J*/Denny's/dsl/scales/24hr/@, Mr Fuel/dsl/scales/24hr, TA/BP/Popeye's/Subway/dsl/scales/24hr/@ 🍴 Wing Wah 🅾 Blue Beacon, Blue Beacon
15a	US 6E, IN 51S, to US 20, S 🅿 GoLo, Road Ranger/�val/Subway/dsl/scales/24hr, Shell/Luke 🍴 Burger King, DQ, Dunkin', LJ Silver, Papa John's, Ruben's Café, Wendy's 🅾 Ace Hardware, Walgreens
13	Central Ave (from eb)
12b	I-65 N, to Gary and toll road
12a	I-65 S (from wb), to Indianapolis
11	I-65 S (from eb)
10b a	IN 53, Broadway, N 🅿 Clark 🍴 Tommy's Philly Steak, S 🅿 GoLo 🍴 Checkers, DQ
9	Grant St, N 🅿 Clark 🅾 $General, $Tree, Advance Parts, County Mkt Foods/gas, Walgreens, S 🅿 Citgo, ❤Loves/Denny's/dsl/scales/LP/24hr/@, Petro/Iron Skillet/Pizza Hut/dsl/scales/24hr Speedway/dsl 🍴 Burger King, Dunkin', McDonald's, Subway 🅾 $Tree, Aldi Foods, AutoZone, Firestone/auto, Midas
6	Burr St, N 🅿 🔪val/Subway/dsl/scales/24hr/@, TA/Country Pride/Pizza Hut/Taco Bell/dsl/scales/24hr/@ 🍴 J&J Fish & Chicken, Philly Steaks, Rico's Pizza 🅾 SpeedCo, S 🅿 GoLo, Mr Fuel/dsl/24hr
5	IN 912, Cline Ave, S 🅿 BP, Speedway/dsl 🍴 Arby's, Culver's, DQ, Dunkin', Jedi's Garden Rest., KFC, McDonald's, Pizza Hut, Popeye's, Subway, Taco Bell, Wendy's, White Castle 🏨 Best Western, Hometowne Lodge, Motel 6 🅾 $Tree, Family$, Fannie May Candies
3	Kennedy Ave, N 🅿 GoLo, Speedway 🍴 Burger King, Domino's, Dunkin'/Baskin Robbins, McDonald's 🅾 repair, Walgreens, S 🅿 Sixers 🍴 Buffalo Wild Wings, Cracker Barrel, Squigi's Pizza, Subway, Wendy's 🏨 Courtyard, Fairfield Inn, Hampton Inn, Holiday Inn Express, Residence Inn 🅾 IN Welcome Ctr, USPO
2	US 41S, IN 152N, Indianapolis Blvd, N 🅿 GoLo, Luke, SavAStop 🍴 Dunkin', House Of Pizza, Papa John's, Pepe's Mexican, Petros Rest., Pizza Hut, Popeye's, Rally's, Schoop's Burgers, Subway, Taco Bell, Wendy's, Wheel Rest. 🅾 CarX, Chevrolet, Family$, Midas, vet, S 🅿 🔪val/dsl/scales/24hr 🍴 JJ Fish, Starbucks, White Castle 🏨 Comfort Inn 🅾 Aldi Foods, Cabela's, Walmart/Subway
1	US 41N, Calumet Ave, N 🅿 Speedway/dsl 🍴 Baskin-Robbins/Dunkin' 🅾 Walgreens, S 🅿 BP, CT Fuel, GoLo, Marathon 🍴 Arby's, Baskin-Robbins/Dunkin', Boston Mkt, Burger King, Canton House Chinese, Chipotle, Edwardo's Pizza, Five Guys, Fortune House, Munster Gyros, Panera Bread, Pizza Hut, Subway, Taco Bell, Wendy's 🅾 $Tree, AT&T, Jewel-Osco, Staples, Target, URGENT CARE, Verizon
0mm	Indiana/Illinois state line

INTERSTATE 465 (Indianapolis)

Exit #	Services
	I-465 loops around Indianapolis. Exit numbers begin/end on I-65, exit 106.
53b a	I-65 N to Indianapolis, S to Louisville
52	Emerson Ave, N 🅿 BP/dsl, Marathon, Shell/Circle K, Speedway/dsl 🍴 Burger King, Domino's, El Mariachi, KFC, LJ Silver, Subway, Taco Bell, Waffle House 🏨 Motel 6 🅾 $General, 🄷, 🅿 Murphy USA/dsl, Speedway/dsl 🍴 Arby's, Bamboo House, China Buffet, DJ's Hotdogs, DQ, Egg Roll, El Puerto Mexican, Fazoli's, Firehouse Subs, Fujiyama, Hardee's, Jets Pizza, Jimmy John's, Little Caesar's, McDonald's, Papa John's, Papa Murphy's, Pizza Hut, Ponderosa, Rally's, Starbucks, Steak'n Shake, Subway, Taco Bell, Wendy's, White Castle 🏨 Holiday Inn Express, La Quinta, Red Roof Inn, Super 8 🅾 $Tree, Advance Parts, AT&T, AutoZone, CarX, GNC, Goodyear/auto, Kroger/dsl, Lowe's Whse, Meineke, O'Reilly Parts, Verizon, vet, Walgreens, Walmart/Subway

I-74 W and I-465 S run together around S Indianapolis 21 miles.

49	I-74 E, US 421 S
48	Shadeland Ave (from nb)
47	US 52 E, Brookville Rd, E 🅿 Marathon, Speedway/dsl 🍴 Bugsy's Grill, Burger King, McDonald's, Subway, Taco Bell 🏨 Baymont Inn 🅾 CVS Drug, Family$, vet
46	US 40, Washington St, E 🅿 Marathon, Phillips 66, Shell/dsl, Speedway/dsl 🍴 Arby's, Blueberry Hill Pancakes, Church's, LJ Silver, Olive Garden, Skyline Chili, Steak'n Shake, Yen Ching Chinese 🅾 $General, Advance Parts, AutoZone, Ford, Meineke,

INTERSTATE 465 (Indianapolis) Cont'd

Exit	Services
46	Continued O'Reilly Parts, **W** 🅿 Thornton's/dsl 🍴 Applebee's, Bob Evans, Fazoli's, McDonald's, Subway 🏠 Comfort Stay 🅾 Buick/GMC, Hyundai, PepBoys
44b	I-70 E, to Columbus
44a	I-70 W, to Indianapolis
42	US 36, IN 67 N, Pendleton Pike, **E** 🍴 Cafe Heidelberg, Chile Verde, Hardee's, Papa's Rest., Popeye's, Skillet Rest., Wendy's 🅾 $General, $Tree, Menards, Save-A-Lot Foods, U-Haul, **W** 🅿 GetGo/dsl, Speedway/dsl, Thornton's/dsl 🍴 Arby's, Domino's, Dunkin', KFC, LJ Silver, Los Rancheros, McDonald's, Rally's, Subway, Taco Bell, Waffle House, White Castle 🅾 Advance Parts, Aldi Foods, CVS Drug, Family$, 🏥, Meineke, Menards, O'Reilly Parts
40	56th St, Shadeland Ave, **E** 🅿 Marathon, to Ft Harrison SP
37b a	I-69, N to Ft Wayne, IN 37, **E** 🅾🏥, **W** 🅾 services on frontage rds
35	Allisonville Rd, **N** 🍴 Bravo Italian, Buca Italian, Buffalo Wild Wings, Dave&Buster's, Hardee's, MCL Cafeteria, Melting Pot, On-the-Border, Outback Steaks 🏠 Courtyard 🅾 Costco/gas, Firestone/auto, JC Penney, Jo-Ann Fabrics, Macy's, REI, Sears/auto, Van Maur, **S** 🅿 Shell, Speedway/dsl 🍴 Chipotle, Chucke-Cheese, Five Guys, Noodles&Co, Panera Bread, Papa John's, Pie Five, Qdoba, White Castle 🏠 Quality Inn 🅾 $Tree, Michael's, Petsmart, Ross, TJ Maxx, Trader Joe's
33	IN 431, Keystone Ave, **N** 🅿 BP/McDonald's, Marathon/dsl 🍴 Bob Evans, Coopers Hawk, Steak'n Shake 🅾 Acura, BMW/Mini, Chevrolet, Fiat, Ford, Harley-Davidson, Honda, Hyundai, Infiniti, Kia, Mercedes, Nissan, Porsche, Subaru, Toyota, **S** 🍴 Benihana, Champp's, Cheesecake Factory, Chipotle, Fleming's Steaks, LePeep Rest., Maggiano's, McAlister's Deli, PF Chang's, Pizza Hut, Ruth Chris Steaks, Seasons 52, Starbucks, Sullivan's Steaks, TGIFriday's 🏠 Hyatt Place, Marriott, Sheraton 🅾 Kohl's, mall, Nordstrom's
31	US 31, Meridian St, **N** 🏠 Comfort Inn, Courtyard, Holiday Inn 🅾🏥, **S** 🅿 Marathon/DQ/dsl, Shell/Circle K/dsl 🍴 Another Broken Egg Cafe, Arby's, Firebirds Grill, Granite City, McAlister's Deli, McDonald's, Paradise Cafe Bakery, Starbucks 🏠 Drury Inn
27	US 421 N, Michigan Rd, **N** 🅿 Marathon, Speedway/dsl 🍴 Applebee's, Burger King, DQ, HoneyBaked Ham, Jimmy John's, KFC/Taco Bell, McDonald's, Olive Garden, Outback Steaks, Red Robin, Subway, Wendy's 🏠 Holiday Inn Express, Red Roof Inn 🅾 AutoZone, Best Buy, Buick/GMC, Chevrolet, Chrysler/Dodge/Jeep, Home Depot, Kohl's, Marshall's, PetCo, Target, Walgreens, **S** 🅿 Citgo/dsl, Marathon, Shell/Circle K 🍴 Arby's, Blaze Pizza, Burger King, Chick-fil-A, Chipotle Mexican, CiCi's, Cracker Barrel, Denny's, El Meson Mexican, Famous Dave's, Five Guys, Hardee's, Jack-in-the-Box, McAlister's Deli, McDonald's, Noodles&Co, Panda Express, Panera Bread, Papa Murphy's, Pizza Hut, Popeye's, Qdoba, Rally's, Ruby Tuesday, Steak'n Shake, Subway, Taco Bell, Tilted Kilt, TX Roadhouse, Wendy's, White Castle, Yen Ching Chinese, Zaxby's 🏠 Best Western, Comfort Inn, Days Inn, Drury Inn, Embassy Suites, Extended Stay America, Extended Stay America (2), Gatehouse Suites, Homewood Suites, InTown Suites, La Quinta, Motel 6, Quality Inn, Rodeway Inn 🅾 $General, $Tree, Aamco, Aldi Foods, BigLots, Costco/gas, Discount Tire, Firestone, GNC, JC Penney, Lowe's Whse, Office Depot, Staples, Walgreens, Walmart
25	I-865 W, I-465 N to Chicago
23	86th St, **E** 🅿 BP, Speedway/dsl 🍴 Abuelo's, Arby's, Chili's, Coldstone, DiBella Subs, Jimmy John's, Longhorn Steaks, Macaroni Grill, Monical's Pizza, Noodles&Co, Panera Bread, Qdoba, Starbucks, Subway, Taco Bell, Ted's MT Grill, Tom+Chee, Traders Mill Grill, Wendy's 🏠 Extended Stay America, Fairfield Inn,

Exit	Services
23	Continued InTown Suites 🅾 AT&T, Big-O Tires, BooksAMillion, Dick's, 🏥, Michael's, Old Navy, Petsmart
21	71st St, **E** 🅿 BP/dsl 🍴 Chef Mike's, Hardee's, McDonald's, Steak'n Shake, Subway 🏠 Candlewood Suites, Clarion Inn, Courtyard, Hampton Inn, Holiday Inn Express, TownePlace Suites, **W** 🍴 Gatsby's, Hotbox Pizza, Jimmy John's, LePeep, Starbucks 🏠 Hilton Garden, Residence Inn, Wingate Inn
20	I-65, N to Chicago, S to Indianapolis
19	56th St (from nb), **E** 🅿 Marathon, Speedway/dsl
17	38th St, **E** 🅿 BP, Marathon/dsl, Shell/Circle K, Speedway 🍴 DQ, El Maguey Mexican, Golden Corral, Jack-in-the-Box, Little Caesar's, Red Lobster, Steak'n Shake, Subway, White Castle 🅾 $General, $Tree, AutoZone, Chevrolet, CVS Drug, Family$, Home Depot, Meijer, O'Reilly Parts, **W** 🍴 Arby's, Burger King, Chili's, Cracker Barrel, IHOP, Jersey Mike's, McDonald's, Taco Bell, TGIFriday's 🏠 Baymont Inn 🅾 Target
	I-74 W and I-465 S run together around S Indianapolis 21 miles
16b	I-74 W, to Peoria
16a	US 136, to Speedway, **E** 🅿 Circle K, Shell/Circle K, Thornton's/dsl 🍴 Applebee's, Arby's, Buffalo Wild Wings, Burger King, Chicago's Pizza, Chipotle, Denny's, El Rodeo, Firehouse Subs, Grindstone Charley's, Hardee's, Jimmy John's, KFC, LJ Silver, McDonald's, Papa Murphy's, Pizza Hut, Starbucks, Subway, Taco Bell, White Castle 🏠 $Inn, Courtyard 🅾 $General, $Tree, Advance Parts, AT&T, Big Lots, CarX, CVS Drug, Firestone/auto, GNC, Goodyear/auto, Kohl's, Kroger/dsl, PetCo, TJ Maxx, Tuesday Morning, Verizon, **W** 🅿 BP/dsl 🏠 Clarion
14b a	10th St, **E** 🍴 Peking Chinese, Penn Sta, Pizza Hut, Wendy's 🅾 🏥, Lowe's Whse, Walmart Mkt, **W** 🅿 Shell/Circle K, Speedway/dsl 🍴 Arby's, Fazoli's, Flapjacks, Marco's Pizza, McDonald's, Rally's, Starbucks, Taco Bell 🅾 CVS Drug, Walgreens
13b a	US 36, Rockville Rd, **E** 🅿 Mobil 🍴 Kazablanka Grill 🏠 Holiday Inn Express, Microtel, Motel 6, Wingate Inn 🅾 Sam's Club, **W** 🅿 Speedway/dsl 🍴 Bob Evans 🏠 Best Western
12b a	US 40 E, Washington St, **E** 🅿 BP/dsl 🍴 Burger King, China Inn, Church's, Fazoli's, McDonald's, Papa John's, Pizza Hut, Taco Bell, Wendy's, White Castle 🅾 $General, $Tree, $Tree, Ace Hardware, Advance Parts, AutoZone, CVS Drug, Family$, Kroger/gas, O'Reilly Parts, Speedway Parts, U-Haul, vet, **W** 🅿 Circle K/dsl, Phillips 66/dsl, Thornton's/dsl 🍴 Arby's, Hardee's, Jimmy John's, LJ Silver, McDonald's, Steak'n Shake, Subway 🏠 Regal 8 Inn 🅾 $General, CarX, Goodyear/auto, K-Mart, Save-A-Lot Foods
11b a	Sam Jones Expwy, **E** 🅿 Marathon/dsl, Speedway/dsl 🍴 Jimmy John's, Library Rest., Subway, Waffle House 🏠 Candlewood Suites, Comfort Suites, Courtyard, Delta Marriott, Extended Stay America, Fairfield Inn, Hyatt Place, Hyatt Place, La Quinta, Quality Inn, Ramada Inn, Red Roof Inn, Residence Inn, Super 8, Wyndham, **W** 🏠 Crowne Plaza, Radisson

🅿 = gas 🍴 = food 🛏 = lodging 🅾 = other 🆁🆂 = rest stop   Copyright 2022 - The Next EXIT ®

INTERSTATE 465 (Indianapolis) Cont'd

Exit #	Services
9b a	I-70, E to Indianapolis, W to Terre Haute
8	IN 67 S, Kentucky Ave, **E** 🅿 Phillips 66/dsl 🅾 🛏, **W** 🅿 BP/McDonald's/dsl, Shell/Subway/dsl, Speedway/dsl 🍴 Burger King, Culver's, Denny's, KFC, Rally's 🛏 Country Inn&Suites 🅾 Walmart Mkt
7	Mann Rd (from wb), **E** 🅾 🛏
4	IN 37 S, Harding St, **N** 🅿 Mr Fuel/dsl/scales, 🅿Pilot🅿/Subway/dsl/scales/24hr 🍴 Indian & American 🛏 Motel 6, Quality Inn 🅾 Blue Beacon, 🛏, **S** 🅿 ⊕FLYING J/Arby's/dsl/LP/scales/24hr/@, Marathon 🍴 Hardee's, McDonald's, Taco Bell, Waffle House, White Castle 🛏 Knight's Inn 🅾 Freightliner, SpeedCo, TruckoMat/scales
2b a	US 31, IN 37, **N** 🅿 BP/dsl, Marathon/Dunkin'/dsl 🍴 Arby's, China Garden, CiCi's, Domino's, El Azabache, Golden Wok, KFC, King Gyros, Little Caesar's, LJ Silver, MCL Cafeteria, Penn Sta Subs, Pizza Hut, Qdoba, Steak'n Shake 🅾 $General, $Tree, Advance Parts, Aldi Foods, AT&T, AutoZone, CarQuest, Family$, Firestone/auto, GNC, Kroger/gas, Marshall's, Meineke, Midas, Save-A-Lot, U-Haul, **S** 🅿 BP/dsl, Speedway/dsl 🍴 8 Lucky Buffet, Bob Evans, El Jalapeño, McDonald's, Red Lobster, Subway, Taco Bell, Wendy's 🛏 Comfort Inn, Holiday Inn Express, Indy Lodge, Super 8, Travel Inn 🅾 CVS Drug, Walgreens
53b a	I-65 N to Indianapolis, S to Louisville

I-465 loops around Indianapolis. Exit numbers begin/end on I-65, exit 106.

INTERSTATE 469 (Ft Wayne)

Exit #	Services
31c b a	I-69, US 27 S, Auburn Road. I-469 begins/ends.
29mm	St Joseph River
29b a	Maplecrest Rd, **W** 🅿 Lassus/DQ/Subway/dsl, Marathon/dsl
25	IN 37, to Ft Wayne, **W** 🅿 Murphy USA/dsl 🍴 Agaves Mexican, Antonio's Pizza, Applebee's, Arby's, Bob Evans, Buffalo Wild Wings, Cracker Barrel, DQ, Starbucks, Steak'n Shake, Subway, Wendy's, Wings Etc, Zianos Italian 🅾 AT&T, Discount Tire, Kohl's, Marshall's, Meijer/dsl, Menards, Michael's, Petsmart, Verizon, Walgreens, Walmart/McDonald's
21	US 24 E
19b a	US 30 E, to Ft Wayne, **E** 🅿 ⊕FLYING J/Huddle House/Subway/dsl/LP/scales/24hr, Sunoco/Taco Bell/dsl 🅾 Freightliner, Mack/Volvo, Peterbilt, truck/tire repair, **W** 🅿 Marathon 🍴 Mancino's Grinders, Richard's Rest., Zesto Drive-In 🛏 Holiday Inn Express 🅾 $General
17	Minnich Rd
15	Tillman Rd
13	Marion Center Rd
11	US 27, US 33 S, to Decatur, Ft Wayne, **E** 🅿 Shell/Subway/dsl
10.5mm	St Marys River
9	Winchester Rd
6	IN 1, to Bluffton, Ft Wayne, **W** 🅾 to ✈
2	Indianapolis Rd, **W** 🅾 to ✈
1	Lafayette Ctr Rd

NOTES

IOWA

⬆N   INTERSTATE 29

Exit #	Services
152mm	Iowa/South Dakota state line, Big Sioux River
151	IA 12 N, Riverside Blvd, **E** 🍽 Casey's, 🅾 $General, Fareway Foods, Pecaut Nature Ctr, Riverside Park, to Stone SP
149	Hamilton Blvd, **E** 🍽 Central Mart 🍽 Horizon Rest. 🛏 Rodeway Inn 🅾 JiffyLube, to Briar Cliff Coll, **W** Iowa Welcome Ctr sb, **full facilities** 🍽 Bev's on the River Rest. 🛏 Hilton Garden 🅾 Riverboat Museum
148	US 77 S, to S Sioux City, Nebraska, **W** 🍽 Casey's, Conoco/dsl, Sam's 🍽 DQ, McDonald's, MiFamilia, Pizza Hut, Taco Bell 🛏 Marina Inn, Regency Inn 🅾 Advance Parts, camping/picnic area, Family $, O'Reilly Parts
147b	US 20 bus, Sioux City, **E** 🍽 Kum&Go/dsl 🍽 Arby's, Burger King, Chili's, Famous Dave's BBQ, Hardee's, IHOP, Perkins 🛏 Holiday Inn, Ramada, Stoney Creek Inn 🅾 🅷 , Chevrolet, USPO, Walgreens
147a	Floyd Blvd, **E** 🍽 Sinclair/dsl 🅾 Home Depot
146.5mm	Floyd River
144b	I-129 W, US 20 W, US 75 S
144a	US 20 E, US 75 N, to Ft Dodge, **1 mi E on Lakeport Rd** 🍽 Casey's 🍽 A&W/LJ Silver, Applebee's, Buffalo Wild Wings, Burger King, Chick-fil-A, Chipotle, ChuckeCheese, Firehouse Subs, Golden Corral, Hardee's, HuHot Chinese, Iron Hill Grill, Japanese Steaks, Jimmy John's, McDonald's, Mr Stirfry, Old Chicago, Olive Garden, Outback Steaks, Panda Express, Panera Bread, Qdoba, Red Lobster, Red Robin, Starbucks, TX Roadhouse 🛏 Candlewood Suites, Comfort Inn, Fairfield Inn, Hampton Inn, Holiday Inn Express, Quality Inn 🅾 Barnes&Noble, Best Buy, Buick/Honda, Fareway Mkt, Gordman's, Hobby Lobby, Hy-Vee Foods/gas, JC Penney, Jiffy Lube, Kohl's, Lowe's, Marshall's, Michael's, Old Navy, Petsmart, Scheel's, Staples, Target, URGENT CARE, Verizon, Younkers
143	US 75 N, Singing Hills Blvd, **E** 🍽 Cenex/dsl, Murphy USA/dsl, 🅿ilot/Burger King/Subway/dsl/scales/24hr 🍽 China Buffet, Culver's, Four Bros Grill, Hunan Palace, KFC, McDonald's, Pizza Hut, Taco Bell, Taco John's 🛏 AmericInn, Days Inn, Victorian Inn 🅾 $Tree, AT&T, Buick/Cadillac/GMC, Ford/Lincoln, Kia, Mazda, Nissan, Sam's Club/gas, Sgt Floyd Mon, Subaru, Toyota, URGENT CARE, VW, Walmart/Subway, **W** 🍽 ❤Loves/Subway/dsl/scales/24hr/ @ 🍽 Wendy's 🛏 Super 8 🅾 Peterbilt, truckwash/repair
141	D38, Sioux Gateway Airport, **E** 🍽 Cenex, Shell/dsl 🍽 Aggies Rest., Pizza Ranch, Subway 🛏 DeSoto Inn 🅾 $General, **W** 🛏 Travelodge 🅾 🚻, museum
139mm	🆁🆂 both lanes, full ♿ facilities, info, litter barrels, 🅲, 🚮, RV dump, wireless internet
135	Port Neal Landing
134	Salix, **W** 🅾 camping

132mm	🆁🆂 parking only nb, weigh sta sb, 🚮 litter barrels
127	IA 141, Sloan, **E** 🍽 Casey's/dsl, Kum&Go/Subway/dsl 🛏 Homestead Inn, WinnaVegas Inn 🅾 RV Park, **W** 🍽 Pony Express (3mi) 🅾 to Winnebago Indian Res/hotel/casino (3mi)
120	to Whiting, **W** 🅾 camping
112	IA 175, Onawa, **E** 🍽 Cenex/dsl, Conoco/Subway/dsl 🍽 DQ, McDonald's, Michael's Rest. 🛏 Super 8 🅾 🅷, NAPA, On-Ur-Wa RV Park, repair, ShopKo, **2 mi W** 🅾 Keel Boat Exhibit, KOA, Lewis&Clark SP
110mm	🆁🆂 both lanes, full ♿ facilities, info, litter barrels, petwalk, 🅲, 🚮, RV dump, wireless internet
105	E60, Blencoe
96mm	Little Sioux River
95	F 20, Little Sioux, **E** 🍽 gas 🅾 Loess Hills SF (9mi), **W** 🅾 Woodland RV Park
92mm	Soldier River
91.5mm	🆁🆂 both lanes, parking only, litter barrels
89	IA 127, Mondamin, **1 mi E** 🍽 Jiffy Mart/dsl
82	F50, Modale, **1 mi W** 🍽 Heartland/dsl
79mm	🆁🆂 both lanes, full ♿ facilities, info, litter barrels, 🅲, 🚮, RV dump, wireless internet
75	US 30, Missouri Valley, **E** Iowa Welcome Ctr (5mi), 🍽 Shell/dsl/24hr 🍽 Arby's, McDonald's, Penny's Diner, Subway 🛏 Oaktree Inn 🅾 🅷 (2mi), to Steamboat Exhibit, **W** 🍽 Cenex/dsl, PetroMart/dsl 🍽 Burger King, Taco John's, The Edge Rest. 🛏 Best Value Inn, DeSoto Inn, Rath Inn 🅾 Buick/Chevrolet
72.5mm	Boyer River
72	IA 362, Loveland, **E** 🍽 Desoto/dsl, **W** 🅾 to Wilson Island SP (6mi)
71	I-680 E, to Des Moines
I-29 S & I-680 W run together 10 mi.	
66	Honey Creek, **W** 🅾 RV Camping
61b	I-680 W, to N Omaha, **W** Mormon Trail Ctr
I-29 N & I-680 E run together 10 mi.	
61a	IA 988, to Crescent, **E** 🍽 Casey's/dsl
56	IA 192 S (sb only, exits left), Council Bluffs, **E** 🅾 🅷, URGENT CARE, Walmart

(Map of Iowa showing major cities and highways appears at top center, with labels for Sioux City, Council Bluffs, Des Moines, Waterloo, Cedar Rapids, Iowa City, Dubuque, Davenport, and interstate routes 29, 35, 80, 380.)

Sidebar labels: SIOUX CITY (left margin), **MO VALLEY** (right margin), **IA**

🅿 = gas   🍴 = food   🛏 = lodging   Ⓞ = other   ℞ = rest stop   Copyright 2022 - The Next EXIT ®

IA

⬆N INTERSTATE 29 Cont'd

Exit #	Services
55	N 25th, Council Bluffs, **E** 🅿 Cenex/dsl, Sinclair Ⓞ URGENT CARE (1mi), Walmart/Subway (1mi)
54b	N 35th St (from nb), Council Bluffs
54a	G Ave (from sb), Council Bluffs
53b	I-480 W, US 6, to Omaha (exits left from nb)
53a	9th Ave, S 37th Ave, Council Bluffs, **E** 🅿 Phillips 66, Shell 🛏 Days Inn, **W** Ⓞ Harrah's Hotel/Casino
52	Nebraska Ave, **E** 🅿 Phillips 66/dsl 🍴 Hooters, Quaker Steak, Ruby Tuesday 🛏 Comfort Suites, Holiday Inn Express, Microtel, SpringHill Suites, Woodspring Suites Ⓞ Bass Pro Shops, **W** 🛏 AmeriStar Hotel/casino, Hampton Inn, Holiday Inn
51	I-80 W, to Omaha
I-29 and I-80 run together 3 miles. See Iowa I-80, exits 1b-3.	
48	I-80 E (from nb), to Des Moines, **E** Ⓞ ℍ
47	US 275, IA 92, Lake Manawa, **E** Ⓞ Iowa School for the Deaf, **W** 🍴 Buffalo Wild Wings, Famous Dave's, Firehouse Subs, Freddy's, Longhorn Steaks, Olive Garden, Panda Express, Panera Bread, Pepperjax Grill, Pizza Ranch, Qdoba, Starbucks Ⓞ $Tree, AT&T, Dick's, Hobby Lobby, Kohl's, Petsmart, Target, TJ Maxx, Verizon
42	IA 370, to Bellevue, **W** Ⓞ K&B Saddlery, to Offutt AFB, truck parts
38mm	℞ both lanes, full ♿ facilities, info, litter barrels, petwalk, ⓒ, 🚽, RV dump, wireless internet
35	US 34 E, to Glenwood, **E** 🍴 McDonalds (4mi) 🛏 Western Inn (4mi) Ⓞ RV Park, **W** 🅿 BP/rest/dsl, ⬥Loves/Subway/dsl/scales/24hr 🛏 Bluff View Motel Ⓞ Harley-Davidson
32	US 34 W, Pacific Jct, to Plattsmouth
24	L31, to Tabor, Bartlett
20	IA 145, Thurman
15	J26, Percival, **1-2 mi E** gas/dsl
11.5mm	weigh sta nb
10	IA 2, to Nebraska City, Sidney, **E** Ⓞ to Waubonsie SP (5mi), **W** 🅿 Cenex/Godfathers/dsl/E85, ⬥Pilot/Subway/dsl/scales/24hr, Sapp Bros/Apple Barrel Rest/dsl/scales/24hr 🍴 Wendy's 🛏 Motel 6, Super 8 Ⓞ antiques, dsl/tire repair, IA Info, Lewis&Clark Ctr (3mi), to Arbor Lodge SP, Victorian Acres RV Park (3mi)
1	IA 333, Hamburg, **1 mi E** 🅿 Casey's/dsl 🍴 Blue Moon Grill 🛏 Hamburg Inn Ⓞ ℍ, NAPA, Stoner Soda Fountain
0mm	Iowa/Missouri state line

⬆N INTERSTATE 35

Exit #	Services
219mm	Iowa/Minnesota state line
214	rd 105, to Northwood, Lake Mills, **E** 🛏 Royal Motel (7mi), **W** Welcome Ctr both lanes, full ♿ facilities, litter barrels, petwalk, 🚽, RV dump, vending, wireless internet, 🅿 BP/Burger King/dsl, Kum&Go/dsl 🛏 Country Inn&Suites, Holiday Inn Express Ⓞ casino,
212mm	℞ nb, weigh sta sb, 🚽, litter barrels
208	rd A38, to Joice, Kensett, windmills
203	IA 9, to Manly, Forest City, **W** Ⓞ to Pilot Knob SP
202mm	Winnebago River
197	rd B20, **8 mi E** Lime Creek Nature Ctr
196mm	℞ both lanes, litter barrels, parking only
194	US 18, to Mason City, Clear Lake, **E** 🅿 KwikStar/dsl/24hr Ⓞ Chevrolet, Freightliner, ℍ (8mi), **W** 🅿 Casey's/dsl, Kum&Go/dsl, ⬥Pilot/Subway/dsl/scales 🍴 Arby's, Bennigan's, Culver's,

Exit #	Services
194	**Continued** DQ, KFC/Taco Bell, McDonald's, Perkins, Wendy's 🛏 AmericInn, Best Western, Best Western, Microtel Ⓞ Ford
193	rd B35, to Mason City, Emery, **E** 🅿 Kum&Go/Taco John's/dsl/e85 🛏 Super 8 Ⓞ truckwash, **W** 🍴 Seven Stars Rest. Ⓞ to Clear Lake SP
190	US 18, rd 27 E, to Mason City
188	rd B43, to Burchinal
182	rd B60, to Rockwell, Swaledale
180	rd B65, to Thornton, **W** 🅿 Cenex (2mi) Ⓞ camping
176	rd C13, to Sheffield, Belmond
170	rd C25, to Alexander
165	IA 3, **E** 🍴 Dudley's Corner/Rest./dsl 🛏 AmericInn (9mi), Hampton Motel (9mi) Ⓞ ℍ (7mi)
159	rd C47, Dows, **W** ℞ both lanes, full ♿ facilities info, litter barrels, petwalk, ⓒ, 🚽, RV dump, vending, wireless internet 🅿 BP/Arby's/Godfather's/dsl/24hr
155mm	Iowa River
151	rd R75, to Woolstock
147	rd D20, to US 20 E
144	rd D25, Williams, **E** 🅿 Boondocks Trkstp/cafe/dsl 🛏 Best Western, Boondocks Motel Ⓞ RV camping, **W** 🅿 ⬥FLYING J/Subway/dsl/scales/24hr
142b a	US 20, to Webster City, Ft Dodge
139	rd D41, to Kamrar
133	IA 175, to Jewell, Ellsworth, **W** 🅿 Kum&Go/Subway/dsl, ⬥Loves/rest./dsl/scales/24hr
128	rd D65, to Stanhope, Randall, **5 mi W** Little Wall Lake Pk
124	rd 115, Story City, **W** 🅿 Casey's, Kum&Go/dsl 🍴 DQ, KFC/Taco Bell, McDonald's, Pizza Ranch, Royal Cafe, Subway 🛏 Comfort Inn, Super 8, Viking Motel/rest Ⓞ antiques, Ford, Goodlife RV Ctr, VF Factory Stores/famous brands, Whispering Oaks Camping
123	rd E18, to Roland, McCallsburg
121mm	prairie area sb
120mm	℞ nb, full ♿ facilities, info, litter barrels, ⓒ, 🚽, RV dump/scenic prairie area sb, vending, wireless internet
119mm	℞ sb, full ♿ facilities, litter barrels, ⓒ, 🚽, RV dump, vending, wireless internet
116	rd E29, to Story, **2 mi W** Story Co Conservation Ctr
113	13th St, Ames, **W** 🅿 Kum&Go/Burger King/dsl/E-85, Phillips 66/Arby's 🍴 Burger King, Jimmy John's, Pizza Ranch 🛏 Holiday Inn Express, Quality Inn Ⓞ ℍ, Harley-Davidson, ISU, to USDA Vet Labs
111b a	US 30, to Nevada, Ames, **E** Twin Acres Campground (11mi), **W** 🅿 Kum&Go/DQ/Subway/dsl 🍴 El Azteca Mexican 🛏 AmericInn, Baymont Inn, Country Inn&Suites, EconoLodge, Fairfield Inn, Hampton Inn, Microtel, Red Roof, Super 8, TownePlace Suites Ⓞ Chrysler/Dodge/Jeep, to IA St U
109mm	S Skunk River
106mm	℞ nb, weigh sta sb, no restrooms
102	IA 210, to Slater, **3 mi W** 🍴 Subway
100mm	℞ both lanes, full ♿ facilities, 🚽, litter barrels, petwalk
96	to Elkhart, **W** Ⓞ to Big Creek SP (11mi), Saylorville Lake
94	NE 36th St, Ankeny, **W** 🅿 Kum&Go/dsl 🍴 Subway
92	1st St, Ankeny, **W** 🅿 Kum&Go, QT 🍴 Applebee's, Arby's, Burger King, Cazador Mexican, Fazoli's, Guadalajara Mexican, KFC, Subway, Tokyo Steaks, Village Inn 🛏 Days Inn, Fairfield Inn, Quality Inn, Ramada, Super 8 Ⓞ Goodyear/auto, O'Reilly Parts, Tires+
90	IA 160, Ankeny, **E** 🅿 Casey's/dsl 🍴 Outback Steaks, Waterfront Seafood 🛏 AmericInn, Comfort Inn, Country Inn&Suites

Side labels: **COUNCIL BLUFFS** · **CLEAR LAKE** · **AMES** · **ANKENY**

INTERSTATE 35 Cont'd

ANKENY

90	Continued
	Courtyard, Holiday Inn Express, Homewood Suites ◻ Buick/GMC, **W** ⛽ Casey's 2, Casey's/dsl, MurphyUSA/dsl 🍴 B-bops Rest., Buffalo Wild Wings, Burger King, Chick-fil-A, Chili's, China Buffet, Chipotle, Culver's, Fuzzy's Tacos, HuHot Chinese, IHOP, Jimmy John's, Los Charro, Maid Rite, Marble Slab, McDonald's, Noodles&Co, Okoboji, Old Chicago, Olive Garden, Panchero's Mexican, Panda Express, Panera Bread, Pepperjax, Perkins, Starbucks, Subway, Taco Bell, Tasty Tacos, Wendy's ◻ AT&T, Best Buy, Big O Tires, Chevrolet, Chrysler/Dodge/Jeep, Duluth Trading, Ford, GNC, Home Depot, Jo-Ann Fabrics, Kohl's, Menards, Michael's, Petsmart, Staples, Target, TJ Maxx, to Saylorville Lake (5mi), Tuesday Morning, Tuffy Auto, Verizon, Walgreens, Walmart/Subway
89	Corporate Woods Dr, **E** 🛏 Hampton Inn, **W** 🛏 Woodspring Suites ◻ F&F/dsl, Sam's Club/dsl
87b a	I-235, I-35 and I-80

I-35 and I-80 run together 14 mi around NW Des Moines. See I-80, exits 124-136.

DES MOINES

72b	I-80 W
72a	I-235 E, to Des Moines
70	Civic Pkwy, Mills, **E** ⛽ Kum&Go/McDonald's 🍴 Fire Creek Grill, Legend's Grill, Starbucks ◻ Hy-Vee Foods/gas, Verizon, vet, Walgreens, **W** ⛽ Casey's/dsl 🍴 Applebee's, Bar Louie, BoneFish Grill, Bravo Italiana, Buffalo Wild Wings, Caribou Coffee, Cheesecake Factory, Chick-fil-A, Draught House 50, Fleming's Rest., Fuddruckers, Iron Wok, Jimmy John's, Joe's Crabshack, Johnny's Italian Steaks, Joseph's Steaks, Monterrey Mexican, Noodles&Co, On-the-Border, Panda Express, Panera Bread, PF Chang's, Red Robin, Tasty Tacos, Wellman's Grill 🛏 Courtyard, Drury Inn, Hilton Garden, Holiday Inn, Residence Inn ◻ 🅷, $Tree, Aldi Foods, Barnes&Noble, Best Buy, Costco/gas, Dick's, Dillards, Firestone/auto, Kohl's, Lowe's, Old Navy, PetCo, Scheel's Sports, Target, TJ Maxx, Trader Joe's, Verizon, Walmart, Younkers
69b a	Grand Ave, W Des Moines
68.5mm	Racoon River
68	IA 5, 7 mi **E** ◻ to ✈, to Walnut Woods SP
65	G14, to Norwalk, Cumming, **W** ◻ John Wayne Birthplace (14mi), Madison Co Museum (14mi)
61mm	North River
56	IA 92, to Indianola, Winterset, **W** ◻ Good Life RV Ctr
56mm	Middle River
53mm	℞s nb, litter barrels, no restrooms
52	G50, St Charles, St Marys, **W** ⛽ Casey's/dsl ◻ John Wayne Birthplace (14mi), museum (14mi)
51mm	℞s sb, litter barrels, no restrooms
47	rd G64, to Truro, **W** ⛽ Kum&Go (4mi)
45.5mm	South River
43	rd 207, New Virginia, **E** ⛽ Kum&Go/Subway/dsl
36	rd 152, to US 69, 3 mi **E** 🛏 Blue Haven Motel, Evergreen Inn, **W** ◻ st patrol

OSCEOLA

34	Clay St, Osceola, **W** ⛽ 🅿🅸🅻🅾🆃/Subway/dsl/scales/24hr ◻ Lakeside Casino Resort/camping
33	US 34, Osceola, **E** ⛽ Casey's/dsl/scales 🍴 McDonald's, Pizza Hut, Subway 🛏 Best Value Inn, Quality Inn, Super 8 ◻ 🅷, Ford, Goodyear, Hy-Vee Foods, O'Reilly Parts, **W** ⛽ BP/Arby's/dsl 🍴 KFC/Taco Bell 🛏 AmericInn ◻ Harley-Davidson, Walmart
32mm	℞s both lanes, full ♿ facilities, litter barrels, petwalk, ⚟, 🐾, RV dump, vending, wireless internet

31mm	parking area sb, weigh sta nb
29	rd H45
22	rd J14, Van Wert
18	rd J20, to Grand River
12	rd 2, Decatur City, Leon, 5 mi **E** ⛽ Shell/dsl 🛏 Little River Motel (5mi) ◻ 🅷
7.5mm	Grand River
7mm	℞s both lanes, full ♿ facilities, info, litter barrels, petwalk, ⚟, 🐾, RV dump, vending, wireless internet
4	US 69, to Davis City, Lamoni, **E** to 9 Eagles SP (10mi), **W** IA Welcome Ctr, ⛽ Casey's (2mi), Kum&Go/dsl/e85 🍴 Maid-Rite Cafe, Pizza Hut (2mi), QC Rest., Subway (2mi) 🛏 Chief Lamoni Motel, Super 8 ◻ auto/truck repair
0mm	Iowa/Missouri state line

INTERSTATE 80

Exit #	Services
307mm	Iowa/Illinois state line, Mississippi River
306	US 67, to Le Claire, **N** ⛽ BP/A&W (2mi), Shell/dsl 🍴 Bierstube Grill, Hungry Hobo, McDonald's, Pizza Hut, Steventon's Rest., Subway 🛏 Comfort Inn, Holiday Inn Express, Super 8 ◻ Buffalo Bill Museum, Slagles Foods, **S** 🍴 BP (2mi)
301	Middle Rd, to Bettendorf
300mm	℞s both lanes, full ♿ facilities, litter barrels, petwalk, ⚟, 🐾, RV dump, vending, WiFi
298	I-74 E, to Peoria, **S** ◻ st patrol, to 🅷

DAVENPORT

295b a	US 61, Brady St, to Davenport, **N** ⛽ BP/dsl ◻ Fiat, to Scott CP, 0-2 mi **S** ⛽ BP, Kwik$tar/dsl, Shell 🍴 Burger King, Cracker Barrel, Happy Joe's Pizza, Hardee's, Hooters, Los Agaves Mexican, McDonald's, Mo Brady's Steaks, Olive Garden, Papa John's, ThunderBay Grille, Village Inn Rest. 🛏 Baymont Inn, Best Western+, Casa Loma Suites, Clarion, Country Inn&Suites, Motel 6, Quad City Inn, Quality Inn, Residence Inn, Super 8, Travelodge, Wickliffe Inn ◻ $General, AutoZone, CarQuest, Firestone/auto, Honda, Hyundai, JC Penney, Lexus, Menards, Nissan, Tires+, Toyota, US Adventures RV Ctr, vet, Von Maur, VW
292	IA 130 W, Northwest Blvd, **N** ⛽ ⚑FLYING J/Denny's/dsl/LP/scales/24hr, ♥Loves/Arby's/dsl/scales/24hr 🛏 Comfort Inn ◻ Farm&Fleet, Interstate RV Park (1mi), Peterbilt, truckwash, **S** ⛽ BP/McDonald's/dsl, Shell 🍴 Machine Shed Rest. 🛏 Days Inn ◻ Freightliner
290	I-280 E, to Rock Island
284	Y40, to Walcott, **N** ⛽ 🅿🅸🅻🅾🆃/Arby's/dsl/24hr/scales, TA/IA 80/BP/DQ/Pizza Hut/Taco Bell/Wendy's/dsl/scales/24hr/@ 🍴 Checkered Flag Grille, Gramma's Rest. 🛏 Comfort Inn ◻ Blue Beacon, IA 80 Trucking Museum, IA 80 Truck-o-Mat, SpeedCo Lube, tires, **S** ⛽ 🅿🅸🅻🅾🆃/Subway/dsl/24hr 🍴 McDonald's 🛏 Days Inn ◻ Cheyenne Camping Ctr, Walcott CP

🅿 = gas   🍴 = food   🛏 = lodging   🅾 = other   ℞s = rest stop   Copyright 2022 - The Next EXIT ®

INTERSTATE 80 Cont'd

Exit #	Services
280	Y30, to Stockton, New Liberty
277	Durant, 2 mi S 🅿 Casey's/dsl, Fifth St Petro/dsl 🍴 Subway
271	US 6 W, IA 38 S, to Wilton
270mm	℞s both lanes, full 🛗 facilities, info, litter barrels, petwalk, 🅲, 🛗, RV dump, vending, WiFi
268mm	parking areas
267	IA 38 N, to Tipton, N 🅿 Kum&Go/Subway/dsl/e85 🅾 Cedar River Camping
266mm	Cedar River
265	to Atalissa, S 🅿 𝗣𝗶𝗹𝗼𝘁/dsl only/scales/24hr
259	to West Liberty, Springdale, S 🅿 BP/dsl 🛏 EconoLodge 🅾 Little Bear Camping
254	X30, West Branch, N 🅿 BP/dsl, Casey's 🅾 Hoover NHS, Jack&Jill Foods, USPO, S 🅿 Kum&Go 🍴 Casa Tequila Mexican, McDonald's 🛏 Days Inn 🅾 Chrysler/Dodge/Jeep
249	Herbert Hoover Hwy, N 🅾 winery (2mi), S 🍴 Wildwood Smokehouse 🅾 golf
246	IA 1, Dodge St, N 🅿 BP/Subway/dsl 🍴 Jimmy John's, Joensy's 🛏 Clarion 🅾 URGENT CARE, S 🅿 Sinclair 🍴 Bob's Pizza 🛏 Travelodge
244	Dubuque St, Iowa City, N Coralville Lake, S 🅾 🅷, museum, to Old Capitol
242	to Coralville, N 🍴 Twelve 01 Kitchen 🛏 Hampton Inn, Radisson, S 🅿 BP, Kum&Go/dsl 🍴 30 Hop Cafe, Applebee's, Arby's, Back Pocket Brewing, Bandana's BBQ, Burger King, Casa Azul, DQ, Dunkin', Edge Water Grill, Hardee's, IA Riverpower Rest., McDonald's, Milio's Sandwiches, Mondo's Cafe, Monica's Rest., Old Chicago Grill, Panera Bread, Papa John's, Peking Buffet, Perkins, Sparti's Gyros, Subway, Taco John's, Wig&Pen Rest. 🛏 Baymont Inn, Best Western, Big Ten Inn, Comfort Inn, Heartland Inn, Homewood Suites, IA Lodge, Marriott, Quality Inn, Super 7, Super 8 🅾 🅷, auto repair, vet, Von Maur, Walgreens
240	IA 965, to US 6, Coralville, N Liberty, N 🅿 BP, Casey's/dsl 🍴 Buffalo Wild Wings, Cheddar's, Culver's, Jimmy John's, La Cava Mexican, McDonald's, Steak'n Shake, TX Roadhouse, Village Inn, Wendy's 🛏 AmericInn, Country Inn&Suites, Suburban Lodge 🅾 Colony Country Camping (3mi), Costco/gas, Gordman's, Harley-Davidson, Kohl's, Michael's, PetCo, TJ Maxx, URGENT CARE, Walgreens, Walmart/Subway, S 🅿 Casey's/dsl 🍴 Caribou Coffee, Chili's, Coldstone, Food Court, Huhot Mongolian, IHOP, Jimmy John's, Longhorn Steaks, Mellow Mushroom, Noodles&Co, Olive Garden, Panchero's Mexican, Papa Murphy's, Pizza Hut, Red Lobster, Starbucks, Taste of China, Which Wich? 🛏 Comfort Suites, Holiday Inn Express, Residence Inn 🅾 Ace Hardware, Advance Parts, Barnes&Noble, Best Buy, Dillard's, Discount Tire, Hobby Lobby, HyVee Foods/dsl, JC Penney, Lowe's, Old Navy, Scheel's Sports, Target, Tires+, U-Haul, Verizon, Younkers
239b	I-380 N, US 218 N, to Cedar Rapids
239a	US 218 S
237	Tiffin, N 🅿 Kum&Go/Subway/dsl 🍴 Jon's Rest (1mi) (seasonal), S 🅾 Sun& Fun RV Ctr
236mm	℞s both lanes, full 🛗 facilities, litter barrels, petwalk, 🅲, 🛗, RV dump, vending, wireless internet
230	W38, to Oxford, N 🅾 Sleepy Hollow Camping, S 🅾 Kalona Village Museum (15mi)
225	US 151 N, W21 S, N 🛏 Heritage Inn, to Amana Colonies, S 🅿 Casey's 🍴 7 Villages Rest., MaidRite Cafe 🛏 Motel 6, Ramada
220	IA 149 S, V77 N, to Williamsburg, N 🅿 BP, Casey's/Landmark Rest./dsl 🍴 Arby's, McDonald's, Subway 🛏 Cozy House Inn,

220	Continued
	Crest Motel, Super 8 🅾 factory outlets/famous brands, GNC, Old Navy, S 🛏 Days Inn 🅾 $General, Williamsburg Tire/auto
216	to Marengo, N 🅿 Kum&Go/Subway/dsl 🅷 (8mi)
211	to Ladora, Millersburg, S 🅾 Lake IA Park (5mi)
208mm	℞s both lanes, full 🛗 facilities, litter barrels, petwalk, 🅲, 🛗, RV dump, vending, wireless internet
205	to Victor
201	IA 21, to Deep River, N 🅿 𝗣𝗶𝗹𝗼𝘁/Subway/dsl/scales/24hr 🛏 Pleasant Stay Inn, S 🅿 KwikStar/Denny's/dsl/scales/24hr/@, truck repair
197	to Brooklyn, N 🅿 TA/Country Pride/Dunkin'/dsl/scales/24hr/@
191	US 63, to Montezuma, S 🅾 to Diamond Lake SP (9mi)
182	IA 146, to Grinnell, 0-2 mi N 🅿 Casey's, Kum&Go/Subway/dsl/24hr 🍴 Casa Margaritas, Grinnell Steakhouse, KFC/Taco Bell, McDonald's, Pizza Ranch 🛏 Best Western, Comfort Inn, Country Inn, Quality Inn, Super 8 🅾 $General, Ace Hardware, Buick/Chevrolet/GMC, Chrysler/Dodge/Jeep, 🅷 (4mi), HyVee Foods, O'Reilly Parts, Verizon, vet, Walmart
180mm	℞s both lanes, full 🛗 facilities, litter barrels, petwalk, 🅲, 🛗, playground, RV dump (eb) wireless internet, vending, weather info
179	IA 124, to Oakland Acres, Lynnville
175mm	N Skunk River
173	IA 224, Kellogg, N 🅿 Phillips 66/Best Burger/dsl/24hr 🅾 Kellogg RV Park, Rock Creek SP (9mi), S 🅾 Pella Museum
168	SE Beltline Dr, to Newton, 1 mi N 🅿 Casey's/dsl, Murphy USA/dsl 🍴 Arby's, Taco John's 🅾 $Tree, KOA (seasonal), Walmart, S 🅿 Loves/Chester's/McDonald's/dsl/scales, Valero/dsl 🛏 AmericInn, Boulders Inn 🅾 Iowa Speedway
164	US 6, IA 14, Newton, N 🅿 Casey's/dsl, Phillips 66/Subway/dsl 🍴 Culver's, KFC/Taco Bell, MT Mikes, Okoboji Grill, Perkins, Pizza Ranch 🛏 Days Inn, EconoLodge, Quality Inn, Super 8 🅾 🅷, museum, S 🛏 Best Value Inn 🅾 Cadillac/Chevrolet, Chrysler/Jeep/Dodge, Ford/Lincoln, to Lake Red Rock
159	F48, to Jasper, Baxter
155	IA 117, Colfax, N 🅿 BP/McDonald's/dsl 🍴 Subway 🛏 Colfax Inn, Microtel 🅾 truck repair, S 🅿 Casey's, Kum&Go/pizza/dsl/e85/24hr
153mm	S Skunk River
151	weigh sta wb
149	Mitchellville
148mm	℞s both lanes, full 🛗 facilities, litter barrels, petwalk, 🅲, 🛗, RV dump, vending, wireless internet
143	Altoona, Bondurant, S 🅿 Casey's/dsl, Kum&Go/dsl 🛏 Hampton Inn, Holiday Inn Express 🅾 RV One Ctr
142b a	US 65, Hubble Ave, Des Moines, S 🅿 BP, ⊘FLYING J/Max's Diner/dsl/scales/24hr/@, Git'n Go 🍴 Bianchi Boys Pizza, Big Steer Rest., Burger King, Culver's, Jethro's BBQ, KFC/Taco Bell, McDonald's, Perkins, Pizza Hut, Subway, Taco John's 🛏 Adventureland Inn, Best Western+, Comfort Inn, Motel 6, My Place, Quality Inn 🅾 Adventureland Funpark, Blue Beacon, camping, casino, Freightliner, Peterbilt
141	US 6 W, US 65 S, Pleasant Hill, Des Moines, S 🍴 Uncle Buck's Grill 🅾 Bass Pro Shops
137b a	I-35 N, I-235 S, to Des Moines

I-80 W and I-35 S run together 14 mi.

| 136 | US 69, E 14th St, Camp Sunnyside, N 🅿 BP/dsl, Casey's 🍴 Bonanza Steaks, MT Mikes 🛏 Budget Inn, Motel 6, Quality Inn, Rodeway Inn 🅾 Allied Tire, antiques, Volvo, 0-1 mi S 🅿 Casey's/dsl, QT/Burger King/dsl/scales/24hr, Star Gas 🍴 Arby's, |

IOWA CITY (vertical left margin)

NEWTON (vertical right margin)

IA (left margin tab)

✈ INTERSTATE 80 Cont'd

136	**Continued** Fazoli's, Hardee's, KFC, McDonald's, Papa Murphy's, Pueblo Viejo Mexican, Subway, Taco Bell, Taco John's, Village Inn, Wendy's 🛏 Baymont Inn, Travelodge ⊙ $General, Advance Parts, Aldi Foods, AutoZone, CarX, Family$, O'Reilly Parts, Tires+, TruckLube, USPO
135	IA 415, 2nd Ave, Polk City, **N** 📱 Kum&Go/dsl 🍴 Smokey D's BBQ ⊙ antiques, Harley-Davidson, Ryder Trucks, **S** 📱 Git'n Go, QT, Shop&Save ⊙ Earl's Tire, NAPA, st patrol
133mm	Des Moines River
131	IA 28 S, NW 58th St, **N** 📱 Casey's, QT 🍴 Bandit Burrito, Chopsticks, DQ, El Mariachi Mexican, Greenbriar Rest., Jimmy John's, Pagliai's Pizza, Panera Bread, Sonic, Subway, VanDee's Icecream/Sandwiches 🛏 AmericInn ⊙ Ace Hardware, Acura, Audi/VW, Goodyear/auto, Hy-Vee Food/dsl, USPO, vet, **S** 📱 BP/dsl/LP/24hr, Casey's, QT 🍴 Applebee's, Arby's, Bamboo Buffet, Bennigan's, Buffalo Wild Wings, Burger King, Carlos O'Kelly's, Chipotle Mexican, Cici's Pizza, Dunkin', Famous Dave's BBQ, Fazoli's, Hardee's, IHOP, Jimmy John's, KFC, McDonald's, Noodles&Co, Old Chicago, Panda Express, Perfect Taco, Perkins, Pita Pit, Popeye's, Starbucks, Subway, Taco John's, Wendy's 🛏 Days Inn, EconoLodge, Holiday Inn, Quality Inn, Ramada/Rest., Super 8 ⊙ $Tree, Advance Parts, AT&T, Big Lots, BigLots, CarX, Chevrolet, Dahl's Food/Fuel, Firestone/auto, Ford, Goodyear/auto, Hobby Lobby, Kia, Kohl's, NAPA, Nissan, Office Depot, Old Navy, PriceChopper, Staples, Target, Toyota, URGENT CARE, Verizon, vet, Younkers
129	NW 86th St, Camp Dodge, **N** 📱 Kum&Go 🍴 Burger King, Legends Grill, McDonald's, Okoboji Grill, Panchero's Mexican, Planet Sub, Starbucks, TX Roadhouse, Village Inn 🛏 Hilton Garden, Stoney Creek Inn, TownePlace Suites ⊙ Dahl's Foods, Verizon, **S** 📱 Casey's, Kum&Go/dsl 🍴 Arby's, B-Bops Burgers, Culver's, Friedrich's Coffee, Overtime Grill, Papa Murphy's, Pizza Ranch, Ruby Tuesday, Subway, Viva La Bamba 🛏 Fairfield Inn, Hampton Inn, Holiday Inn Express, Microtel ⊙ Walgreens
128	NW 100th St
127	IA 141 W, Grimes, **N** 📱 BP/dsl, QT/dsl 🍴 MaidRite Cafe, McCoy's Grill, Subway ⊙ to Saylorville Lake, Toyota, **S** 📱 Kum&Go/dsl/e85 🍴 McDonald's ⊙ Firestone/auto, Home Depot, Target
126	Douglas Ave, Urbandale, **E** 📱 Casey's/dsl 🛏 EconoLodge, Extended Stay America ⊙ Chevrolet, **W** 📱 Kum&Go/dsl, ⬥Pilot/Subway/dsl/scales/24hr/@ 🍴 Mama Lacona's
125	US 6, Hickman Rd, **E** 🍴 IA Machine Shed Rest., Starbucks, Subway 🛏 Clive Hotel, Hotel Renovo, Sleep Inn ⊙ CarMax, Fiat, Honda, Hyundai, to Living History Farms, **W** 📱 Kum&Go/dsl, ⬥Loves/Denny's/dsl/scales/LP/24hr ⊙ Chrysler/Dodge/Jeep, Menards
124	(72c from I-35 nb), University Ave, **E** 📱 Git'n Go/dsl 🍴 Applebee's, Bakers Square, Chili's, Chuck-fil-A, Huhot Mongolian, Jason's Deli, KFC, Little Caesars, McDonald's, Mi Mexico, Mi Mexico, Outback Steaks, Qdoba Mexican, RockBottom Rest./brewery, Starbucks, TCBY, Twin Peaks, Wobbly Boots BBQ 🛏 Courtyard, Days Inn, Sheraton, Sterling Suites, Super 8, Wildwood Lodge ⊙ AT&T, Barnes&Noble, Best Buy, Home Depot, Kohl's, Lowe's, Marshall's, Office Depot, Petsmart, Target, Verizon, Whole Foods Mkt, World Mkt, **W** 📱 Kum&Go/Burger King, QT 🍴 Biaggi's Rest, Caribou Coffee, Cracker Barrel, El Rodeo Mexican, Jersey Mike's, Other Place Grill, Panera Bread, Red Rossa Pizza, Wendy's, Z'Marik's Cafe 🛏 Best Western, Country Inn&Suites, La Quinta ⊙ 🄷, Granite City Food, Walgreens

I-80 E and I-35 N run together 14 mi.

123b a	I-80/I-35 N, I-35 S to Kansas City, I-235 to Des Moines
122	(from eb) 60th St, W Des Moines, **N** ⊙ 🄷, same as 121
121	74th St, W Des Moines, **N** 🍴 Biaggi's Rest., Panera Bread, Red Rossa Pizza 🛏 Hampton Inn, Staybridge Suites ⊙ 🄷, Granite City Foods, HyVee Food/gas, Walgreens, **S** 📱 Kum&Go/Subway 🍴 Arby's, Burger King, Culver's, McDonald's, Perkins, Taco John's 🛏 Candlewood Suites, Fairfield Inn, Marriott, Motel 6, SpringHill Suites, vet
118	Grand Prairie Pky, **N** 📱 Kum&Go/dsl
117	R22, Booneville, Waukee, **N** 📱 Kum&Go/dsl/e85 🍴 Organic Farm Rest. ⊙ Timberline Camping (2mi), **S** 📱 Rube's Steaks, Waveland Rest. (2mi)
115mm	weigh sta eb
113	R16, Van Meter, 1 mi **S** 📱 Casey's ⊙ Veteran's Cemetary
112mm	N Racoon River
111mm	Middle Racoon River
110	US 169, to Adel, DeSoto, **N** ⊙ camping (6mi), **S** 📱 Casey's/dsl, Kum&Go/dsl/e85 🛏 Countryside Inn, Edgetowner Motel ⊙ $General, John Wayne Birthplace (14mi), USPO
106	F90, P58, **N** ⊙ KOA (apr-oct)
104	P57, Earlham, **S** 📱 Casey's (1mi)
100	US 6, to Redfield, Dexter, **N** 📱 Casey's (2mi) 🍴 Drew's Chocolate (2mi)
97	P48, to Dexter, **N** 📱 camping, Casey's (2mi)
93	P28, Stuart, **N** 📱 Casey's/dsl/scales, Kum&Go/dsl/e85 🍴 Burger King, McDonald's, Subway 🛏 AmericInn, Best Value Inn ⊙ $General, Chevrolet, city park, Hometown Foods, **S** 📱 Phillips 66/dsl 🍴 Country Kitchen 🛏 Economy Inn ⊙ NAPA
88	P20, Menlo
86	IA 25, to Greenfield, Guthrie Ctr, **N** ⊙ to Spring Brook SP, **S** ⊙ Hospital (13mi)
85mm	Middle River
83	N77, Casey, 1 mi **N** 📱 Kum&Go ⊙ camping
80.5mm	🅁ₛ both lanes, full ♿ facilities, litter barrels, petwalk, 📱, 🛏, RV dump, vending, wireless internet
76	IA 925, N54, Adair, **N** 📱 Casey's/dsl, Kum&Go/Subway/dsl 🍴 Chuck Wagon Rest. 🛏 Adair Budget Inn, Super 8 ⊙ camping, city park
75	G30, to Adair
70	IA 148 S, Anita, **S** to Lake Anita SP (6mi)
64	N28, to Wiota
61mm	E Nishnabotna River
60	US 6, US 71, to Atlantic, Lorah, **S** 📱 Conoco/dsl/24hr 🛏 Sunset Inn

IA

INTERSTATE 80 Cont'd

Exit #	Services
57	N16, to Atlantic, N 🅞 Nelsen RV Ctr, S 🅞 🅷 (7mi)
54	IA 173, to Elk Horn, 6 mi N Welcome Ctr/wifi, 🛏 Tivoli Inn 🅞 Windmill Museum
51	M56, to Marne
46	M47, Walnut, N 🅟 Cenex/McDonald's/dsl 🍴 Emma Jean's Rest. 🛏 Super 8 🅞 to Prairie Rose SP (8mi), S 🅟 Kum&Go/pizza/dsl 🛏 EconoLodge/RV Park, tires/repair
44mm	weigh sta wb/parking area eb
40	US 59, to Harlan, Avoca, N 🅟 ⓕ FLYING J/Taco John's/MaidRite Cafe/dsl/24hr/scales 🍴 Subway 🛏 Cobblestone Inn, Motel 6 🅞 🅷 (12mi), truckwash, S 🅟 Casey's/dsl, Shell/dsl 🍴 Embers Rest. 🛏 Acova Motel, Capri Motel 🅞 Avoca Foods, Farmall-Land Museum (seasonal), Nishna Museum
39.5mm	W Nishnabotna River
34	M16, Shelby, N 🅟 BP/rest./dsl/e85, Shell/Cornstalk Cafe/dsl 🍴 DQ, Godfather's 🛏 Shelby Country Inn/RV Park, S 🅟 ♥Loves/McDonald's/Chester's/dsl/scales/24hr
32mm	🆁🆂 both lanes, parking only
29	L66, to Minden, S 🅟 Casey's/dsl 🛏 Midtown Motel (2mi) 🅞 winery (4mi)
27	I-680 W, to N Omaha
23	IA 244, L55, Neola, S 🅟 Kum&Go/dsl/e85 🅞 camping, to Arrowhead Park
20mm	Welcome Ctr eb/🆁🆂 wb, full ♿ facilities, litter barrels, petwalk, ♿, 🚮, RV dump, vending, Wireless Internet
17	G30, Underwood, N 🅟 Cenex/Subway/dsl/24hr 🛏 Underwood Motel 🅞 truck/tire repair
8	US 6, Council Bluffs, N 🅟 Casey's/dsl (1mi) 🅞 $General, 🅷 (3mi), S 🅞 st patrol
5	Madison Ave, Council Bluffs, N 🅟 BP/dsl 🍴 Burger King, FoodCourt, Great Wall Chinese, KFC, McDonald's, Papa Murphy's, Starbucks, Subway 🛏 AmericInn 🅞 HyVee Foods/drug, Verizon, Walgreens, S 🅟 Phillips 66 🍴 DQ, Village Inn Rest. 🛏 Western Inn 🅞 Family Fare Mkt
4	I-29 S, to Kansas City
3	IA 192 N, Council Bluffs, N 🅞 to Hist Dodge House, S 🅟 Casey's/dsl, Shell/dsl, TA/Valero/Country Pride/dsl/scales/24hr/@ 🍴 Applebee's, Beijing Rest., Burger King, Cracker Barrel, Dickey's BBQ, DQ, Fazoli's, Golden Corral, Hardee's, Huhot Mongolian, Jimmy John's, La Mesa Mexican, LJ Silver, McDonald's, Perkins, Red Lobster, Subway, Taco Bell 🛏 Days Inn, Fairfield Inn, Motel 6, Red Roof Inn 🅞 Advance Parts, Aldi Foods, Best Buy, Buick/GMC, Cadillac/Chevrolet, Chrysler/Dodge/Jeep, Ford, Freightliner, Gordman's, Home Depot, Hyundai/Subaru, Kia, Menards, Nissan, Outdoor Recreation RV, Sam's Club/gas, truck/dsl repair, U-Haul, Walmart/Subway
1b	S 24th St, Council Bluffs, N 🅟 BP, Casey's, PILOT/Arby's/scales/dsl/24hr, Sapp Bros/Burger King/dsl 🍴 Famous Dave's BBQ, Hooters, Quaker Steak&Lube, Ruby Tuesday, Uncle Buck's 🛏 American Inn, Best Western, Country Inn&Suites, Hilton Garden, Holiday Inn Express, Microtel, SpringHill Suites, Super 8 🅞 Bass Pro Shop, Blue Beacon, Camping World RV Ctr, casino, Horseshoe RV Park, Peterbilt, SpeedCo, S Welcome Ctr, full facilities, 🍴 Culver's, TX Roadhouse 🅞 JC Penney, PetCo
1a	I-29 N, to Sioux City
0mm	Iowa/Nebraska state line, Missouri River

INTERSTATE 235 (Des Moines)

Exit #	Services
15	I-80, E to Davenport
12	US 6, E. Euclid Ave, E 🅟 Casey's 🍴 Burger King, Drago House Chinese, Papa John's, Perkins, Tasty Tacos 🅞 $Tree, HyVee Foods/drug, Walgreens, W 🅟 QT/dsl 🅞 Midas, NAPA
11	Guthrie Ave, W 🅟 Kum&Go/dsl 🅞 CarQuest
10b a	IA 163 W, E University Ave, Easton Dr
9	US 65/69, E 14th, E 15th, N 🍴 Subway 🅞 Walgreens, 🅟 🍴 McDonald's, Tasty Tacos 🅞 🅷, st capitol, URGENT CARE, zoo
8b	E 6th St, Penn Ave (from wb), N 🅞 🅷
8a	3rd St, 5th Ave, N 🛏 Holiday Inn 🅞 🅷, S 🛏 Embassy Suites, Marriott, Quality Inn 🅞 Conv Ctr
7	Keo Way
6	MLK Blvd/31st St, N 🅞 Drake U, S 🅞 🅡🆂, Governor's Mansion
5b	42nd St, Science & Art Ctr, N 🅟 Git'n Go 🍴 Papa John's 🅞 Drake Automotive
5a	56th St (from wb), N 🅞 golf
4	IA 28, 63rd St, to Windsor Heights, S 🅞 Historic Valley Jct, zoo
3	8th St, W Des Moines, N 🅟 Kum&Go 🍴 B-Bop's Café, Burger King, Papa Murphy's, Starbucks 🅞 HyVee Foods, PetCo, Sam's Club/gas, Walmart/Subway, S 🅟 BP, Kum&Go/dsl/e85 🍴 Dunkin', Jimmy John's, Lemon Grass Thai, Tacos Andreas 🛏 Days Inn
2	22nd St, 24th St, W Des Moines, N 🅟 BP, Casey's/dsl, Kum&Go/dsl, QT/dsl 🍴 Arby's, ChuckeCheese, Culver's, Famous Dave's BBQ, Hardee's, Hibachi Buffet, Jethro's BBQ, McDonald's, SmashBurger, Taco Bell, Village Inn 🅞 $Tree, CarX, Firestone/auto, Gordman's, Meineke, Michael's, Midas, Walgreens
1b	Valley West Dr, W Des Moines, N 🅟 BP/dsl 🍴 Chipotle Mexican, Cozy Cafe, Hamilton's Rest., Hurricane Grill, Jimmy John's, La Hacienda, Noodles&Co, Olive Garden, Panda Express, Panera Bread, Red Lobster, Subway 🛏 Valley West Inn 🅞 AT&T, Best Buy, Home Depot, HyVee Foods, JC Penney, Marshall's, Target, Von Maur, Whole Foods Mkt

I-235 begins/ends on I-80, exit 123.

INTERSTATE 280 (Davenport)

Exit #	Services
18b a	I-74, US 6, Moline, S 🅟 Shell/dsl 🍴 Bare Bones BBQ, McDonald's, MT Jack's 🛏 Best Inn, Country Inn&Suites, Hampton Inn, Holiday Inn Express, La Quinta, Motel 6, Quality Inn 🅞 🅡🆂
15	Airport Rd, Milan, 1 mi N 🍴 Hardee's, MaidRite Café, McDonald's, Subway 🅞 auto repair, Buick/Chevrolet, Firestone
11b a	IL 92, to Andalusia, Rock Island, S 🛏 Jumer's Hotel/casino/rest. 🅞 KOA Camping
9.5mm	Iowa/Illinois state line, Mississippi River
8	rd 22, Rockingham Rd, to Buffalo
6	US 61, W River Dr, to Muscatine, W 🅞 camping, 🅟
4	Locust St, rd F65, 160th St, E 🅞 🅷, St Ambrose U, to Palmer Coll, W 🅟 Shell/Subway/dsl
1	US 6 E, IA 927, Kimberly Rd, to Walcott, 3 mi E 🅟 Murphy USA/dsl 🍴 Applebee's, Culver's, Harlan's Rest., Steak'n Shake, Subway, Wendy's 🅞 Discount Tire, GNC, Walmart

I-280 begins/ends on I-80, exit 290.

D E S   M O I N E S

C O U N C I L   B L U F F S

IA

⬆E INTERSTATE 380 (Cedar Rapids)

WATERLOO

Exit #	Services
73mm	I-380 begins/ends on US 218, 73mm in Waterloo. **E** 🅿 BP/dsl, **W** 🅿 Clark 🍴 Pizza Hut
72	San Marnan Dr, **W** 🅿 Casey's, Kwik Star/Dallas/e85 🍴 A&W/LJ Silver, Applebee's, Burger King, Carlos O'Kelly's, Chick-fil-A, DQ, Freddie's, Hardee's, IHOP, Jimmy John's, Little Ceasar's, Lone Star, Longhorn Steaks, McDonald's, Noodles&Co, Olive Garden, Panchero's, Panda Express, Panera Bread, Red Lobster, Starbucks, Subway, Taco Bell, Taco John's, Tokyo Bay, Wendy's 🏠 Baymont Inn, Candlewoods Suites, Comfort Inn, Country Inn&Suites, Days Inn, Fairfield Inn, Hampton Inn, Holiday Inn Express, Motel 6, Super 8 ⊙ Advance Parts, Aldi Foods, AT&T, Barnes & Noble, Best Buy, Chevrolet, Chrysler/Dodge/Jeep, CVS Drug, Dick's, Dillards, Ford, Gordman's, Hobby Lobby, Home Depot, HyVee Foods, Jo-Ann Fabrics, KIA, Menards, PetCo, PetsMart, Staples, Target, Tires+, TJ Maxx, Verizon, Walmart
71	I-380, US 20, IA 27, Cedar Rapids, Cedar Falls, Dubuque, **W** on US 18 🏠 Isle Hotel/Casino
70	River Forest Rd
68	Elk Run Heights, Evansdale Dr, **E** 🅿 ⊕FLYING J/Denny's/dsl/scales/24hr, 🚛/RR/Junie's/Subway/dsl/scales/24hr/@ 🍴 Arby's, McDonald's 🏠 Days Inn ⊙ Freightliner, Paine's RV Ctr, truckwash/repair
66	Gilbertville, Raymond
65	US 20 E, Dubuque
62	rd d-38, Gilbertville
55	rd v-65, Jesup, La Port, **W** ⊙ Hickory Hills Park, McFarlane Park
54mm	weigh sta sb
51mm	weigh sta nb
49	rd d-48, Brandon, **1 mi W** food, gas
43	IA 150, Independence, Vinton, **E** 🅿 Casey's/dsl 🏠 Urbana Inn Suites ⊙ truckwash
41	Urbana, **E** ⊙ Lazy Acres RV Park, **W** 🅿 Casey's/dsl ⊙ $General
35	rd w-36, Center Point, **E** 🅿 BP, Casey's, Sinclair/McDonald's/Subway/dsl/scales/24hr ⊙ $General, Chrysler/Dodge/Jeep/Ford, **W** ⊙ Pleasant Creek SRA (5mi)
28	rd e-34, Robins, Toddville, **E** 🅿 BP/dsl, **W** ⊙ Wickiup Outdoor Learning Ctr (5mi)
25	Boyson Rd, Hiawatha, **E** 🅿 Casey's 🍴 Culver's ⊙ Buick/GMC/Cadillac, Ketelsen RV Ctr, Kia, Nissan, Subaru, **W** 🅿 ⊙ Toyota/Mazda

CEDAR RAPIDS

Exit #	Services
24	IA 100, Blairs Ferry Rd, **E** 🅿 KwikShop/dsl 🍴 Buffalo Wild Wings, Domino's, Hardee's, KFC, Las Glorias Mexican, McDonald's, Scott Family Rest., Wendy's 🏠 Comfort Inn, Country Inn&Suites, Days Inn, Residence Inn ⊙ Advance Parts, Chrysler/Dodge/Jeep, CVS Drug, Honda, O'Reilly Parts, Target, **W** 🅿 Fas Fuel 🍴 Adelitas Mexican, Arby's, Burger King, Dunkin' Donuts, Freddy's, Pizza Hut, Starbucks, Subway, Taco Bell ⊙ Aldi Foods, AutoZone, GNC, Lowe's, Sam's Club/gas, Walmart
22	Glass Rd, 32nd St, **E** 🅿 KwikShop/dsl 🍴 Papa Johns
21	H St, Cedar Rapids, downtown
20b	7th St E, Cedar Rapids, **E** ⊙ 🏥, downtown
20a	US 151 Bus, **E** 🏠 DoubleTree
19b	1st Ave W, **W** ⊙ NAPA
18	Wilson Ave, ⊙ museums
17	33rd ave SW, Hawkeye Downs, **W** 🅿 Casey's, Casey's/dsl (2) 🍴 Burger King, Cancun, McDonald's, Taco Bell, Wendy's 🏠 Clarion, Econolodge, Economy Inn, Fairfield Inn, Hampton Inn, Holiday Inn Express, Hometown Inn, Motel 6, Quality Inn, Red Roof Inn, Residence Inn, Super 8, Super 8
16	US 30 W, US 151 S, US 218 N, Tama
13	Ely, **E** 🅿 🚛/Arby's/dsl/scales/24hr, **W** 🅿 Casey's/A&W/dsl, Casey's/dsl/scales, Kwik Star/dsl/e85 🍴 McDonald's, Subway 🏠 AmericInn, Country Inn&Suites ⊙ ☺
12mm	Rs both lanes, littler barrels, petwalk, (C), 🚻, RV Dump, vending, wireless internet
10	rd f-12, Shueyville, Swisher, **E** 🅿 BP/dsl ⊙ Lake Mcbride SP, **W** ⊙ Amana Colonies
8mm	Iowa River
4	rd f-28, North Liberty, **E** 🅿 Casey's/Blimpie, Kum&Go/dsl/e85 🏠 Sleep Inn ⊙ Colony Country RV Park (5mi)
0b a	I-80 E to Iowa City, W to Des Moines, **I-380 begins/ends on I-80.**

IA

NOTES

KANSAS

INTERSTATE 35

Exit #	Services
235mm	Kansas/Missouri state line
235	Cambridge Circle
234b a	US 169, Rainbow Blvd, E 🅿 QT 🍴 Sonic, Subway, Taqueria Mexico 🛏 Oak Tree Inn 🅾 KU MED CTR, O'Reilly Parts, W 🅿 Sinclair/dsl
233a	SW Blvd, Mission Rd
233b	37th Ave (from sb)
232b	US 69 N, E 🅿 Phillips 66/dsl, QT 🍴 Burger King, China Star, Cici's, McDonald's, Subway, Taco Bell 🅾 Aldi Foods, Lowe's, Price Chopper, Walgreens, Walmart
232a	Lamar Ave, E 🅿 QT 🛏 Wood Spring Suites
231b a	I-635 (exits left from sb)
230	Antioch Rd (from sb)
229	Johnson Dr, E 🅿 QT/dsl 🍴 Chili's, China Garden, Jack-in-the-Box, Jimmy John's, McDonald's, Starbucks, Subway, Taco Bell 🅾 AT&T, Dick's, GNC, Hen House Mkt, Hobby Lobby, Home Depot, IKEA, Marshall's, Old Navy, Petsmart, Verizon, Walgreens, W 🅿 Cenex/dsl
228b	US 56 E, US 69, Shawnee Mission Pkwy, E 🅿 Shell 🍴 Caribou Coffee, Denny's, Krispy Kreme 🛏 Drury Inn, Extended Stay America, Super 8 🅾 BMW/Mini, W 🍴 A&W, Arby's, LJ Silver, McAlister's Deli, Panera Bread, Pizza Hut, Subway 🅾 AutoZone, Discount Tire, Famil$, Firestone/auto, Ford, Goodyear/auto, Jo-Ann Fabrics, O'Reilly Parts, Russell Stover, Walgreens
228a	67th St, E 🛏 Quality Inn 🅾 CarMax, W 🅿 Phillips 66/dsl 🅾 Hyundai, Infiniti, Jaguar, Land Rover, Lexus, Maserati, Mercedes, Porsche Smart, Toyota
227	75th St, E 🍴 McDonald's 🛏 Extended Stay America 🅾 Acura, Audi, Ⓗ, Walmart, W 🅿 QT/dsl 🍴 Domino's, Sonic, Starbucks, Subway, Taco Bell, Wendy's 🛏 Hampton Inn 🅾 Hyundai, URGENT CARE
225b	US 69 S (from sb), Overland Pkwy
225a	87th St, E 🅿 BP 🍴 Green Mill Rest, Wendy's 🛏 Holiday Inn, W 🅿 Phillips 66/dsl 🍴 Dunkin', Taco Bell, Zarda BBQ
224	95th St, E 🍴 Applebee's, BD Mongolian BBQ, Burger King, Cheddar's, Chick-fil-A, Chipotle Mexican, Five Guys, Houlihan's, Jimmy John's, KFC, McDonald's, Noodles&Co, On-the-Border, Outback Steaks, Panda Express, Pie Five, Subway, Taco Bell, Winstead's Cafe, Zoe's Kitchen 🛏 Crossland Suites, Crowne Plaza, La Quinta, Motel 6, Quality Inn, Super 8 🅾 Advance Parts, Barnes&Noble, Best Buy, Dillard's, Firestone/auto, Hobby Lobby, Ⓗ, JC Penney, Kohl's, Macy's, mall, Nordstrom, Office Depot, PetCo, Ross, Sam's Club/gas, Target, Verizon, W 🅿 Phillips 66 🍴 Costco/gas, Mi Ranchito, O'Reilly Parts, U-Haul
222b a	I-435 W & E
220	119th St, E 🅿 Conoco/7-11, Phillips 66, Phillips 66/dsl 🍴 A&W, Buffalo Wild Wings, Burger King, Chick-fil-A, Chipotle Mexican, Chuy's, Coldstone, Cracker Barrel, Firehouse Subs, Five Guys, Five Guys, Freddy's, Granite City Cafe, Hira's Steak, IHOP, Jimmy John's, KC Joe's BBQ, KC Super Buffet, LJ Silver, Master Wok, McDonald's, Mr Gyros Greek, Noodles&Co, Old Chicago, Olive Garden, Panda Express, Panera Bread, Papa Murphy's, Pei Wei, Penn Sta Subs, Pie Five, Planet Sub, Popeye's, Red Lobster, Schlotzsky's, Smashburger, Starbucks, Steak'n Shake, Subway, Taco Bell, Twin Peaks, TX Roadhouse, Wendy's, Zaxby's, Zoe's Kitchen 🛏 Fairfield Inn, Hampton Inn, Hilton Garden,
220	Continued Holiday Inn Express, Residence Inn, Wood Spring Suites 🅾 AT&T, Best Buy, Chrysler/Dodge/Jeep, Dick's, Fiat, GNC, Goodyear/auto, Home Depot, Honda, Marshall's, Michael's, Natural Grocers, NTB, Old Navy, Petsmart, Ross, Target, U-Haul, Verizon, Whole Foods Mkt, W 🍴 Houlihan's, Jason's Deli, Longhorn Steaks, Starbucks 🅾 Bass Pro Shops
218	135th, Santa Fe St, Olathe, E 🅿 Phillips 66/dsl 🍴 Applebee's, Burger King, Chapala Mexican, China Buffet, Church's, McDonald's, Other Place Grill, Papa John's, Perkins, Pizza St, Sheridan's Custard, Subway, Taco Bell 🅾 $General, $Tree, Ace Hardware, Aldi Foods, AutoZone, BigLots, Discount Foods, Ford/Lincoln, GNC, Hobby Lobby, Kohl's, Midas, Office Depot, vet, W 🅿 QT 🍴 Domino's, KFC, McDonald's, Subway, Taco Bell, Waffle House 🛏 Rodeway Inn 🅾 Aamco, Advance Parts, Buick GMC, Chevrolet, Harley-Davidson, Hyundai, Kia, Meineke, Nissan, O'Reilly Parts, Subaru, Toyota, VW
217	Old Hwy 56 (from sb) same as 215
215	US 169 S, KS 7, Olathe, E 🅿 Phillips 66/dsl, QT/dsl 🍴 Chipotle Mexican, IHOP, Jimmy John's, MOD Pizza, Panera Bread, Red Robin 🛏 Candlewood Suites, Quality Inn 🅾 Aldi Foods, Discount Tire, GNC, Home Depot, Jiffy Lube, NTB, Target, W 🅿 Phillips 66/dsl/scales/24hr 🍴 54th St Grill, Chili's, McDonald's, Taco Bell, Wendy's 🛏 Best Western, Days Inn, Econolodge, La Quinta, Motel 6 🅾 Burlington Coats, Ⓗ, Mazda
214	Lone Elm Rd, 159th St
213mm	weigh sta both lanes
210	US 56 W, Gardner, W 🅿 Phillips 66/dsl, QT/dsl 🍴 Arby's, Burger King, KFC, McDonald's, Perkins, Pizza Hut, Sonic, Subway, Taco Bell, Waffle House 🛏 Super 8 🅾 AutoZone, Price Chopper, Walgreens, Walmart
207	US 56 E, Gardner Rd, E 🅾 Olathe RV Ctr, W 🅿 Phillips 66/dsl, Phillips 66/dsl (2)
205	Homestead Lane
202	Edgerton
198	KS 33, to Wellsville, W food, gas
193	Tennessee Rd, Baldwin
188	US 59 N, to Lawrence
187	KS 68, Ottawa, W 🅿 Phillips 66/dsl 🅾 Central RV Ctr, Midwest RV Ctr
185	15th St, Ottawa
183	US 59, Ottawa, E 🅿 Loves/Hardee's/dsl/scales/24hr, 🅿 BP, Ottawa/dsl, Phillips 66/dsl 🍴 Applebee's, Burger King, Freddy's, McDonald's, Nagoya Japanese, Old 56 Rest., Pizza Hut, Sirloin Stockade, Taco Bell, Wendy's 🛏 Best Western, Comfort Inn, Days Inn, EconoLodge, Super 8 🅾 $General, $Tree, Advance Parts, Ford, Ⓗ, Walmart
182b a	US 50, Eisenhower Rd, Ottawa
176	Homewood, W 🅾 RV camping
175mm	Rs both lanes, full ♿ facilities, litter barrels, petwalk, Ⓒ, Ⓑ, RV dump, vending, wireless internet
170	KS 273, Williamsburg, W 🅿 Gas&Food
162	KS 31 S, Waverly
160	KS 31 N, Melvern
155	US 75, Burlington, Melvern Lake, E 🅿 Conoco/Subway/dsl, TA/Shell/Wendy's/dsl/scales/24hr/@ 🛏 Wyatt Earp Inn 🅾 dsl repair
148	KS 131, Lebo, E 🅿 Casey's, Cenex/dsl 🛏 Universal Inn 🅾 $General, W 🅾 to Melvern Lake

Side markers: KANSAS CITY AREA, KS, OLATHE, OTTAWA

Map of Kansas showing interstate and highway routes including I-70, I-135, I-335, I-35, and cities such as Goodland, Colby, Hays, Salina, Topeka, Kansas City, Wichita, Dodge City, Garden City, Liberal, and others.

INTERSTATE 35 Cont'd

Exit #	Services
141	KS 130, Neosho Rapids, E🅾 NWR (8mi)
138	County Rd U
135	County Rd R1, W🅾 Dieker RV Ctr, RV camping/🚽
133	US 50 W, 6th Ave, Emporia, 1-3 mi E🍴 Casey's 🏠 Budget Host
131	KS 57, KS 99, Burlingame Rd, E📮 Phillips 66/Circle K/dsl 🍴 Goodcents Subs, Hardee's 🅾 Dillon's Food, repair, Tire Pros
130	KS 99, Merchant St, E📮 Phillips 66/dsl 🍴 Subway 🅾 CVS Drug, Emporia SU, Lyon Co Museum
128	Industrial Rd, E🍴 Arby's, Bruff's Steaks, Burger King, China Buffet, Gambino's Pizza, Ichiban Japanese, Spangles, Subway 🏠 EconoLodge, Knights Inn, Motel 6 🅾 $General, Aldi Foods, AT&T, 🏥, JC Penney, Walgreens, W🍴 Phillips 66/WhichWich?/dsl 🍴 Applebee's, Braum's, Domino's, IHOP, KFC, McDonald's, MT Mike's Steaks, Pizza Hut, Pizza Ranch, Planet Sub, Starbucks, Taco Bell 🏠 Candlewood Suites, Comfort Inn, Hampton Inn, Holiday Inn Express, La Quinta, Quality Inn 🅾 $Tree, Staples, Verizon, Walmart/Subway
127c	KS Tpk, I-335 N, to Topeka
127b a	US 50, KS 57, Newton, E 🍴FLYING J/Huddle House/dsl/LP/scales/24hr, Casey's/dsl 🍴 Arby's, China Buffet, Papa John's 🏠 Best Inn, Best Western/rest., Days Inn, Rodeway Inn, Super 8 🅾 Buick/Chevrolet, Chrysler/Dodge/Jeep, dsl repair, Ford/Lincoln, Kenworth, NAPA, Nissan, PriceChopper Foods, Tires4Less, Toyota, W🅾 Emporia RV Park
127mm	I-35 and I-335 KS Tpk I-35 S and KS tpk S run together, toll plaza I-35 S and KS Tpk S run together.
125mm	Cottonwood River
111	Cattle Pens
97.5mm	Matfield Green Service Area (both lanes exit left), 📮 Phillips 66/dsl 🍴Hardee's/Dunkin'
92	KS 177, Cassoday, E📮 Fuel'n Service, 🚽
76	US 77, El Dorado N, E📮 Casey's, Phillips 66/dsl 🍴 Pizza Hut, Taco Bell 🏠 Stardust Motel 🅾 $General, Ace Hardware, city park, Dillon's Foods/dsl, El Dorado SP, Walgreens
71	KS 254, KS 196, El Dorado, E📮Casey's/dsl, Phillips 66/dsl, QT/dsl 🍴 Arbys, Braum's, Burger King, Domino's, Freddy's, Gambino's Pizza, Hog Wild BBQ, Jimmy's Egg, KFC, LJ Silver, McDonald's, Pizza Hut, Sonic, Spangles, Subway 🏠 Days Inn, Holiday Inn Express, Motel 6, Red Coach Inn, Sunset Inn, Super 8 🅾 $General, AutoZone, Buick/Cadillac, Bumper Parts, Deer Grove RV Park, 🏥, KS Oil Museum, O'Reilly Parts, Verizon, Walmart
65mm	Towanda Service Area (both lanes exit left), 📮 Phillips 66/dsl 🍴 Hardee's/Dunkin'
62mm	Whitewater River
57	21st St, Andover, W golf, 🚽
53	KS 96, Wichita
50	US 54, Kellogg Ave, E on Kellogg Ave, 🍴 Beijing Bistro, BJ's Rest., Bubba's Rest., Burger King, Carlos Kelly's, Chipotle Mexican, Denny's, Firehouse Subs, Golden Corral, Green Mill Rest., IHOP, LJ Silver, Logan's Roadhouse, Longhorn Steaks, McDonald's, Noodles&Co, Old Chicago Pizza, Panda Express, Red Lobster, Subway, Taco Bell, 🏠 Best Western, Comfort Inn, Days Inn, Extended Stay America, Fairfield Inn, Hampton Inn, Hawthorn Suites, Holiday Inn, La Quinta, Marriott, Motel 6, Super 8, 🅾 $Tree, Acura, AT&T, AT&T, Bosley Tires, Cadillac/Chevrolet, CarMax, CarQuest, Chrysler/Dodge/Jeep, Costco/dsl, Dillard's, Fiat, Firestone/auto, Ford, Honda, Infiniti, JC Penney, Lincoln, Lowe's, Mazda, Michael's, Nissan, Petsmart, Ross, Sears/auto, Subaru, TJ Maxx, Toyota, USPO, Verizon, Von Maur, VW, Walmart/Subway
45	KS 15, Wichita, E🅾 Spirit Aero Systems
44.5mm	Arkansas River
42	47th St, I-135, to I-235, Wichita, W📮 QT/dsl 🍴 Applebee's, Arby's, Braum's, Burger King, Carlos O'Kelly's, Domino's, Godfather's, Goodcents Subs, Heritage Rest., Hog Wild BBQ, IHOP, KFC, Little Caesar's, LJ Silver, McDonald's, New China, Pizza Hut, Spangles Rest., Subway, Taco Bell 🏠 Best Western, Days Inn, Holiday Inn Express, Quality Inn, Springfield Inn, Super 8, Woodspring Suites 🅾 $General, $Tree, Air Capital RV Park, Dillon's Foods/dsl, K-Mart, O'Reilly Parts, Verizon
39	US 81, Haysville, W📮 JumpStart 🍴 Sonic, Subway 🏠 Express Inn, Sleep Inn

EMPORIA

WICHITA

KS

🅝 INTERSTATE 35 Cont'd

Exit #	Services
33	KS 53, Mulvane, **E** 🅞 Mulvane Hist Museum, **W** 🅛 Hampton Inn, Kansas Star Casino/Hotel 🅞 Wyldewood Winery
26mm	**Belle Plaine Service Area (both lanes exit left)**, 🅖 Phillips 66/dsl 🅕 McDonald's
19	US 160, Wellington, **3 mi W** 🅕 KFC, McDonald's, Penny's Diner 🅛 OakTree Inn 🅞 KOA
17mm	toll plaza
I-35 N and KS TPK N run together.	
4	US 166, to US 81, South Haven, **E** 🅖 Phillips 66/dsl 🅛 Motel 6 🅞 repair/tires, **W** 🅞 Oasis RV Park
1.5mm	weigh sta nb
0mm	Kansas/Oklahoma state line

🅔 INTERSTATE 70

Exit #	Services
424mm	Kansas/Missouri State Line
423b	3rd St, James St
423a	5th St (from eb, exits left)
422d c	Central Ave, service rd
422b a	US 69 N, US 169 S
421b	I-670
421a	**S** 🅞 railroad yard
420b a	US 69 S, 18th St Expswy, **N** 🅖 Cenex/dsl, Sinclair/Subway/dsl 🅕 China Town, Jack-in-the-Box, Tapatio Mexican 🅞 GNC, SunFresh Foods
419	38th St, Park Dr access to 10 motels
418b	I-635 N (eb only)
418a	I-635 S
417	57th St
415a	KS 32 E (from eb)
415b	to US 24 W, State Ave, Kansas City, **N on US 24** 🅕 Papa John's, Taco Bell 🅛 Gables Motel 🅞 Lowe's
414mm	**parking area both lanes, vehicle insp sta wb**
414	78th St, **N on US 24** 🅖 Phillips 66, QT/dsl 🅕 Arby's, Burger King, Capt D's, CVS Drug, Domino's, Hardee's, KFC, Krispy Kreme, Lucky Chinese, McDonald's, Papa John's, Papa Murphy's, Sonic, Subway, Taco Bell, Wendy's 🅛 Days Inn 🅞 $Tree, Advance Parts, BigLots, Buick/GMC, Firestone/auto, Ⓗ, Marshall's, O'Reilly Parts, Petsmart, PriceChopper Foods, SavALot, Tires+, Walgreens, XPress/auto/tire, **S** 🅖 BP 🅛 American Motel, Comfort Inn
411b	I-435 N access to Woodlands Racetrack, to KCI Airport
411a	I-435 S
410	110th St, **N** 🅛 Chateau Avalon, Great Wolf Lodge 🅞 Cabela's, KS Speedway
225mm	**I-70 W and KS TPK W run together.**
224	KS 7, to US 73 (last free exit wb before KS TPK), Bonner Springs, Leavenworth, **N** 🅖 Phillips 66/7-11/dsl, QT/dsl 🅕 El Potro Mexican, KFC/Taco Bell, Waffle House 🅛 Holiday Inn Express, Super 8 🅞 museum, **S** 🅖 BP 🅕 Arby's, Burger King, Goodcents Subs, Lin's Chinese, McDonald's, Papa Murphy's, Pizza Hut, Taco John's 🅞 $Tree, Ace Hardware, AutoZone, Cottonwood RV Camp, Nachbar Automotive, PriceChopper Foods, Walgreens, Walmart/Subway
217mm	toll booth
212	Eudora, Tonganoxie
209mm	**Lawrence Service Area (both lanes exit left), full facilities,** 🅖 Phillips 66/dsl 🅕 McDonald's

204	US 24, US 59, to E Lawrence, **S** 🅖 Cenex/dsl, Phillips 66/Subway 🅕 Burger King 🅛 Motel 6, SpringHill Suites (1mi) 🅞 $General, O'Reilly Parts
203mm	Kansas River
202	US 59 S, to W Lawrence, **S on US 40** 🅖 Conoco, Phillips 66/dsl, Zarco/dsl 🅕 Burger King, Domino's, Dunkin', Jimmy John's, Kobe Japanese, McDonald's, Sonic, Subway, Taco Bell, Taco John's, Wendy's 🅛 Best Value Inn, Baymont Inn, Comfort Inn, Days Inn, DoubleTree, EconoLodge, Hampton Inn, Quality Inn 🅞 $General, Advance Parts, Dillon's Foods/gas, Ⓗ, O'Reilly Parts, to Clinton Lake SP, to U of KS, vet, Walgreens
197	KS 10, Lecompton, Lawrence, **N** 🅞 Perry Lake SP, **S** 🅞 Clinton Lake SP
188mm	**Topeka Service Area, full** 🅖 **facilities,** 🅖 Phillips 66/dsl 🅕 Dunkin', Hardee's, Pizza Hut, Taco Bell
183	I-70 W (from wb), to Denver
367mm	toll plaza
366	I-470 W, to Wichita
I-70 E and KS TPK E run together.	
365	21st St, Rice Rd access to Shawnee Lake RA
364b	US 40 E, Carnahan Ave, to Lake Shawnee
364a	California Ave, **0-1 mi S** 🅖 BP/dsl, Phillips 66/dsl 🅕 Arby's, Baskin-Robbins, Burger King, Domino's, DQ, McDonald's, Pizza Hut, Subway, Tacos Mexicano 🅞 $General, $Tree, Ace Hardware, Advance Parts, AutoZone, Dillon's Food/gas, O'Reilly Parts, repair, vet, Walgreens, Walmart/Subway
363	Adams St, **S** 🅖 Phillips 66/dsl
362c	10th Ave (from wb), **N** 🅛 Ramada Inn, **S** 🅞 st capitol
362b a	to 8th Ave, **N** 🅛 Ramada, **S** 🅞 to St Capitol downtown
361b	3rd St, Monroe St
361a	1st Ave, **S** Ryder
359	MacVicar Ave, **S** 🅞 Ⓗ, Kenworth
358b a	Gage Blvd
357b a	Fairlawn Rd, 6th Ave, **S** 🅖 Phillips 66, Valero/dsl 🅛 Best Western, Motel 6 🅞 $General, NAPACare, vet
356b a	Wanamaker Rd, **N** 🅕 Red Robin 🅛 Hyatt Place 🅞 KS Museum of History, **S** 🅖 BP, Murphy Express/dsl, Phillips 66/dsl 🅕 Applebee's, Arby's, AutoZone, Buffalo Wild Wings, Burger King, Chick-fil-A, Chili's, Chipotle Mexican, ChuckECheese, CiCi's Pizza, Coldstone, Cracker Barrel, Denny's, Five Guys, Freddy's Steakburgers, Golden Corral, Hardee's, Hooters, HuHot Chinese, IHOP, Jason's Deli, Jersey Mike's Subs, Jimmy John's, Jose Pepper's, Longhorn Steaks, McAlister's, McDonald's, Noodles&Co, Old Chicago, Olive Garden, On-the-Border, Panda Express, Panera Bread, Papa John's, Perkins, Pie Five Pizza, Pizza Hut, Qdoba, Red Lobster, Sonic, Spangles, Starbucks, Steak'n Shake, Taco Bell, Taco John's, TX Roadhouse, Wendy's 🅛 Baymont Inn, Candlewood Suites, Clubhouse Inn, Comfort Suites, Country Inn&Suites, Courtyard, Days Inn, Econolodge, Fairfield Inn, Hampton Inn, Hilton Garden, Holiday Inn Express, Homewood Suites, Quality Inn, Relax Inn, Residence Inn, Sleep Inn, Super 8, Woodspring Suites 🅞 $Tree, AAA, Aldi Foods, AT&T, Barnes&Noble, Best Buy, Dick's, Dillard's, Goodyear/auto, Hobby Lobby, Home Depot, JC Penney, Jo-Ann, Kohl's, Lowe's, Menards, Michael's, Natural Grocers, Old Navy, PetCo, Sam's Club/gas, Target, TJ Maxx, Tuesday Morning, URGENT CARE, Verizon, Walmart/Subway
355	I-470 E, US 75 S, to VA MED CTR, Topeka, **1 mi S** same as 356 air museum
353	KS 4 W, to Auburn Rd
351	frontage rd (from eb) Mission Creek
350	Valencia Rd

Side markers: **KS** · **KANSAS CITY** · **BONNER SPGS** · **LAWRENCE** · **TOPEKA**

⁅E INTERSTATE 70 Cont'd

Exit #	Services
347	West Union Rd
346	Carlson Rd, to Rossville, Willard
343	Ranch Rd
342	Keene-Eskridge Rd access to Lake Wabaunsee
341	KS 30, Maple Hill, S 🅿 24-7/Subway/café/dsl/RV dump
338	Vera Rd, S 🅿 Valero/Baskin-Robbins/dsl
336mm	🆁🆂 (exits left from both lanes), full ♿ facilities, litter barrels, petwalk, 🅲, 🕭, RV parking, wireless internet
335	Snokomo Rd, Paxico Skyline Mill Creek Scenic Drive
333	KS 138, Paxico, N 🅾 Mill Creek RV Park, winery
332	Spring Creek Rd
330	KS 185, to McFarland
329mm	weigh sta both lanes
328	KS 99, to Alma, S Wabaunsee Co Museum
324	Wabaunsee Rd, N 🅾 Grandma Horners Store&Factory
322	Tallgrass Rd
318	frontage rd
316	Deep Creek Rd
313	KS 177, to Manhattan, 8 mi N 🅿 Phillips 66 🍴 Chili's, IHOP, Longhorn Steaks, McAlister's Deli, McDonald's, Olive Garden, Sonic, Taco Bell, TX Roadhouse, Wendy's 🏨 Best Western, Candlewood Suites, Comfort Inn, Fairfield Inn, Hampton Inn, Hilton Garden, Motel 6, Quality Inn, Super 8 🅾 Aldi Foods, JC Penney, to KSU, Walmart/Subway
311	Moritz Rd
310mm	🆁🆂 both lanes, full ♿ facilities, litter barrels, petwalk, 🅲, 🕭, RV dump
307	McDowell Creek Rd, scenic river rd to Manhattan
304	Humboldt Creek Rd
303	KS 18 E, to Ogden, Manhattan, N 🅾 to KSU
301	Marshall Field, N 🅾 Cavalry Museum, Custer's House, KS Terr Capitol, to Ft Riley
300	US 40, KS 57, Council Grove, S hist church
299	Flinthills Blvd, to Jct City, Ft Riley, N 🅿 Cenex/dsl 🍴 Stacy's Rest. 🏨 EconoLodge, Grandview Plaza Inn, Great Western Inn
298	Chestnut St, to Jct City, Ft Riley, N 🅿 Shell/dsl/24hr 🍴 Arby's, Cracker Barrel, Family Buffet, Freddy's Steakburgers, JC's BBQ, La Fiesta, Pizza Hut, Qdoba, Starbucks, Taco Bell, Tokyo Steaks 🏨 Best Western, Candlewood Suites, Comfort Inn, Courtyard, Quality Inn 🅾 $General, $Tree, CVS Drug, Verizon, Walmart/Subway
296	US 40, Washington St, Junction City, N 🅿 Casey's, Cenex/dsl, Phillips 66, Shell/dsl 🍴 IHOP, McDonald's, Munson's Prime, Peking Chinese, Sonic, Subway 🏨 Budget Host/RV park, Express Inn, Hampton Inn, Jct City Inn, Super 8, Woodspring Suites 🅾 Cadillac/Chevrolet, Haas Tire, Harley-Davidson, vet
295	US 77, KS 18 W, Marysville, to Milford Lake, N 🅿 Sapp Bros/A&W/dsl/24hr 🏨 Motel 6 🅾 Ford/Lincoln/Kia/Chrysler/Dodge/Jeep, 🏥, RV Ctr, S 🅾 Owls Nest Camping, truckwash
290	Milford Lake Rd
286	KS 206, Chapman, S 🅿 Casey's/dsl, Cenex/dsl 🅾 $General, Chapman Creek RV Park, KS Auto Racing Museum
281	KS 43, to Enterprise, N 🅿 Phillips 66/dsl 🅾 4 Seasons RV Ctr/Park
277	Jeep Rd
275	KS 15, to Clay Ctr, Abilene, N 🍴 Brookville Hotel/rest., Holiday Inn Express, S 🅿 24-7/Arby's/dsl, KwikShop, Sips 🍴 Burger King, M&R Grill, McDonald's, Pizza Hut, Sonic, Subway 🏨 Budget Inn, Super 8 🅾 $General, Auburn Drug, AutoZone, Buick/Cadillac/Chevrolet, CountryMart Foods, 🏥, O'Reilly Parts, ShopKO, to Eisenhower Museum

J C T   C I T Y (vertical, left margin)

A B I L E N E (vertical, left margin)

S A L I N A

R U S S E L L

Exit #	Services
272	Fair Rd, to Talmage, S 🅿 💛Loves/Hardee's/dsl/scales/24hr 🅾 Russell Stover Candies
266	KS 221, Solomon
265mm	🆁🆂 both lanes, full ♿ facilities, litter barrels, petwalk, 🅲, 🕭, RV dump, vending
264mm	Solomon River
260	Niles Rd, New Cambria
253mm	Saline River
253	Ohio St, N 🅾 RV park, S 🅿 FLYING J/Huddle House/dsl/LP/scales/24hr, LNG 🅾 Harley-Davidson, 🏥, Kenworth
252	KS 143, 9th St, Salina, N 🅿 24-7/Subway/dsl/24hr, Petro/Shell/Starbucks/Popeye's/dsl/24hr/@ 🍴 IHOP, Iron Skillet, McDonald's 🏨 Days Inn, Holiday Inn Express, La Quinta, Motel 6, Red Carpet, Rodeway Inn, Super 8 🅾 Blue Beacon, dsl repair, Freightliner, KOA, S 🅿 Pilot/dsl/scales/24hr/@ 🏨 Comfort Inn, EconoLodge
250 b a	I-135, US 81, N to Concordia, S to Wichita
249	Halstead Rd, to Trenton
244	Hedville, S 🅿 Phillips 66/dsl 🅾 Rolling Hills Park (2mi)
238	to Brookville, Glendale, Tescott
233	290th Rd, Juniata
225	KS 156, to Ellsworth, S 🅿 D&S/dsl 🅾 Ft Harker Museum, Ft Larned HS
224mm	🆁🆂 both lanes, full ♿ facilities, litter barrels, petwalk, 🅲, 🕭, RV dump
221	KS 14 N, to Lincoln
219	KS 14 S, to Ellsworth, S 🅿 Conoco/dsl
216	to Vesper
209	to Sylvan Grove
206	KS 232, Wilson, N 🅿 Travel Shoppe/rest. 🅾 Wilson Lake (6mi), S 🅾 RV camping
199	Dorrance, N 🅾 to Wilson Lake, S 🅿 Agco/dsl/food
193	Bunker Hill Rd, N 🅿 Conoco/Sunmart/pizza/dsl/24hr, to Wilson Lake WA
189	US 40 bus, Pioneer Rd, Russell
187mm	parking area both lanes, 🕭, litter barrels
184	US 281, Russell, N 🅿 24-7/dsl, Cenex/Fossil Sta./dsl 🍴 A&W, McDonald's, Meridy's Rest., Pizza Hut, Sonic, Subway 🏨 Days Inn, Fossil Creek Hotel, Quality Inn, Russell's Inn 🅾 $General, Bumper Parts, CarQuest, Fossil Creek RV Park, 🏥, JJJ RV Park, Klema Mkt, Shopko, st patrol
180	Balta Rd, to Russell
175	Gorham, 1 mi N 🅿 Co-Op/dsl
172	Walker Ave
168	KS 255, to Victoria, S 🅿 255 Diner/dsl, to Cathedral of the Plains
163	Toulon Ave
161	Commerce Parkway, S 🅾 Volvo/Mack Trucks

⛽ = gas   🍴 = food   🛏 = lodging   🅾 = other   🆁🆂 = rest stop   Copyright 2022 - The Next EXIT

▲E INTERSTATE 70 Cont'd

Exit #	Services
159	US 183, Hays, N ⛽ Cenex/Taco Grande/dsl, EVC, Qwest/dsl 🍴 Applebee's, IHOP, Old Chicago, Pasta Jay's, Sims BBQ, Wendy's 🛏 Best Western+, Comfort Inn, Fairfield Inn, Hampton Inn, Holiday Inn Express, Sleep Inn, TownePlace Suites 🅾 AT&T, Chrysler/Dodge/Jeep, Ford/Lincoln, Harley-Davidson, Home Depot, Tesla EVC, Toyota, Verizon, Walmart/Subway, S ⛽ 24-7/dsl, 🟡Loves, Phillips 66/dsl, Phillips 66/dsl/24hr, Sinclair/dsl 🍴 A&W/LJ Silver, Arby's, Burger King, China Garden, Domino's, Freddy's, Jimmy John's, KFC, Lucky Buffet, McDonald's, Pheasant Run Pancakes, Pizza Hut, Qdoba, Sonic, Starbucks, Subway, Taco Bell, Taco Grande, Thirsty's Grill, Vernie's Hamburger House, Wendy's, Whiskey Creek Grill 🛏 Baymont Inn, Days Inn, EconoLodge, Ft Hays Inn, Quality Inn, Rodeway Inn, Super 8 🅾 $Tree, Ace Hardware, Advance Parts, Chevrolet, Dillon's Foods/gas, Hobby Lobby, 🅷, JC Penney, O'Reilly Parts, Tires 4 Less, Verizon, Walgreens
157	US 183 S byp, to Hays, N 🅾 Peterbilt, S 🅾 museum, st patrol, to Ft Hays St U, tourist info
153	Yocemento Ave
145	KS 247 S, Ellis, S ⛽ Casey's, 🟡Loves/DQ/Subway/dsl/scales/24hr 🍴 Cancun Mexican 🛏 Days Inn 🅾 Railroad Museum, RV camping, to Chrysler Museum, USPO
140	Riga Rd
135	KS 147, Ogallah, N ⛽ Frontier Selfserve/dsl, S 🅾 to Cedar Bluff SP (13mi)
132mm	🆁🆂 both lanes, full ♿ facilities, litter barrels, petwalk, 🍴, RV dump
128	US 283 N, WaKeeney, N 🛏 Super 8
127	US 283 S, WaKeeney, N 🍴 Jake & Chet's Cafe, Pizza Hut, Tropical Mexican 🛏 Best Western+, KS Kountry Inn 🅾 $General, S ⛽ 24-7/McDonald's/dsl/24hr, Conoco/Subway/dsl 🛏 EconoLodge 🅾 antiques, auto repair, KOA
120	Voda Rd
115	KS 198 N, Banner Rd, Collyer
107	KS 212, Castle Rock Rd, Quinter, N ⛽ Sinclair/dsl 🛏 First Inn/rest. 🅾 $General, 🅷 Cobblestone Inn, S ⛽ Conoco/dsl/24hr 🍴 DQ, Pizza Sta
99	KS 211, Park, 1 mi N ⛽ Sinclair/dsl
97mm	🆁🆂 both lanes, full ♿ facilities, litter barrels, petwalk, 🍴, RV dump, vending
95	KS 23 N, to Hoxie
93	KS 23, Grainfield, N ⛽ Sinclair/dsl
85	KS 216, Grinnell
79	Campus Rd
76	US 40, to Oakley, S ⛽ TA/Shell/Buckhorn Rest./Subway/dsl/e-85/scales/24hr/@ 🛏 Rodeway Inn, Sleep Inn 🅾 Blue Beacon, Fick Museum, 🅷
70	US 83, to Oakley, N 🛏 Free Breakfast Inn, S ⛽ Cenex/dsl 🍴 Colonial Steaks 🅾 antiques, Fick Museum, High-Plains RV Park, 🅷
62	rd K, Mingo, S ⛽ gas/dsl/🍴
54	Country Club Dr, Colby, N ⛽ LNG, 🟡LNG/Subway/dsl/scales/24hr 🛏 Hampton Inn 🅾 🅷, truck/dsl repair
53	KS 25, Colby, N ⛽ 24-7/Subway/dsl 🍴 Arby's, Burger King, China Buffet, Jimmy John's, McDonald's, MT Mike's Steaks, Pizza Hut, Sonic, Subway, Taco John's 🛏 Days Inn, Holiday Inn Express, Motel 6, Quality Inn, Sleep Inn, Super 8 🅾 $General, Dillon's Foods/dsl, dsl repair, Ford/Lincoln, Haas Tire, 🅷, O'Reilly Parts, Prairie Museum, Quilt Cabin, RV park/antiques, visitors ctr, Walmart, S ⛽ Petro/Phillips 66/scales/dsl/@ 🍴 City Limits Grill, Qdoba, Starbucks, Village Inn 🛏 American Inn, Comfort Inn 🅾 Chrysler/Dodge/Jeep, truck repair

▲N INTERSTATE 70 Cont'd (right column top)

Exit #	Services
48.5mm	🆁🆂 both lanes, full ♿ facilities, litter barrels, petwalk, 🍴, RV park/dump, vending
45	US 24 E, Levant
36	KS 184, Brewster, N ⛽ Fuel Depot/dsl
35.5mm	Mountain/Central time zone
27	KS 253, Edson
19	US 24, Goodland, N 🍴 Pizza Hut 🅾 $General, High Plains Museum, KOA, NAPA
17	US 24, KS 27, Goodland, N ⛽ Cenex/dsl, Conoco, Phillips 66/dsl 🍴 DQ, McDonald's, Reynaldo's Mexican, Sonic, Subway, Taco John's 🛏 Best Value Inn, Econolodge, Motel 6, Quality Inn, Super 8 🅾 CarQuest/Firestone, Chevrolet/GMC, Ford, 🅷 Walmart, S ⛽ 24-7/dsl/scales 🍴 Steak'n Shake 🛏 Holiday Inn Express 🅾 Mid-America Camping, Tesla EVP
12	rd 14, Caruso
9	rd 11, Ruleton
7.5mm	Welcome Ctr eb/🆁🆂 wb, full ♿ facilities, info, litter barrels, petwalk, 🍴, 🚮, RV dump, vending, wireless internet
1	KS 267, Kanorado, N food, gas
.5mm	weigh sta eb
0mm	Kansas/Colorado State Line

▲N INTERSTATE 135 (Wichita)

Exit #	Services
95b a	I-70, E to KS City, W to Denver, US 81 N. **I-135 begins/ends on I-70, exit 250.**
93	KS 140, State St, Salina, E 🅾 art ctr, museum
92	Crawford St, E ⛽ 24-7/dsl, KwikShop, Shell, Sinclair 🍴 Arby's, Braum's, Cotijas Mexican, Great Wall Chinese, Gutierrez Mexican, Hickory Hut BBQ, Jim's Chicken, KFC, La Casita, La Hacienda, McDonald's, Russell's Rest., Spangles, Subway, Taco Bell, Western Sizzlin 🛏 Ambassador Hotel, AmericInn, Baymont Inn, Days Inn, Econolodge, Value Inn&Suites 🅾 $General, $Tree, Advance Parts, Dillon's Foods, Kansas Land Tires, NAPA, O'Reilly Parts, Walgreens, W ⛽ Phillips 66/dsl 🛏 Quality Inn
90	Magnolia Rd, E ⛽ Casey's, Phillips 66/dsl 🍴 Buffalo Wild Wings, Burger King, Carlos O'Kelly's, Chick-fil-A, Chili's, Coyote Canyon Café, Domino's, Freddy's Burgers, Goodcents Subs, Hog Wild BBQ, Hong Kong Buffet, IHOP, Jalisco Mexican, Longhorn Steaks, Marco's Pizza, McDonald's, Papa Murphy's, Qdoba, Schlotzsky's, Sonic, Spangles, Starbucks, Subway, Taco Bell 🛏 Best Value Inn, Candlewood Suites 🅾 $General, $Tree, Aldi Foods, AT&T, AutoZone, BigLots, Cadillac/Chevrolet, Dick's, Dillard's, Dillon's Foods/dsl, Hobby Lobby, Honda, JC Penney, JoAnn Fabrics, Kohl's, Marshall's, O'Reilly Parts, Old Navy, PetCo, Ross, Subaru, Toyota, Verizon, W ⛽ Cenex/dsl 🅾 Menard's
89	Schilling Rd, E ⛽ KwikShop/dsl 🍴 Applebee's, Daimaru Steaks, Five Guys, Olive Garden, Pizza Hut, Red Lobster, Rib Crib BBQ, Taco John's, Tucson's Steaks, Wendy's 🛏 Country Inn&Suites, Courtyard, Hampton Inn, Hilton Garden, Holiday Inn 🅾 Lowe's, Sam's Club/gas, Target, URGENT CARE, Walmart/Subway, W ⛽ Casey's 🛏 Best Western, Comfort Suites, Super 8
88	Water Well Rd, E 🛏 Sleep Inn 🅾 Chrysler/Dodge/Jeep, Ford, Nissan
86	KS 104, Mentor, Smolan
82	KS 4, Falun Rd, Assaria, E 🅾 RV Camping
78	KS 4 W, Lindsborg, W 🅾 to Sandz Gallery/Museum
72	Lindsborg, 4 mi E 🅾 Maxwell WR, McPherson St Fishing Lake, W 🅾 camping, food, gas, 🅷, lodging, museum
68mm	🆁🆂 (both lanes exit left), full ♿ facilities, litter barrels petwalk, 🍴, 🚮, RV dump
65	Pawnee Rd

INTERSTATE 135 (Wichita) Cont'd

Exit #	Services
62	Mohawk Rd
60	US 56, McPherson, Marion, **E** 🅖 ♥Love's/Hardee's/dsl/LP/scales/24hr, **W** 🅖 24/7/Burger King/dsl, Phillips 66/dsl 🍴 Applebee's, Arby's, Braum's, Freddy's Burgers, Golden Dragon Chinese, KFC/LJ Silver, La Fiesta Mexican, McDonald's, MT Mike's, Perkins, Pizza Hut, Subway, Taco Bell, Taco John's, Woodie's BBQ 🛏 Best Western, Days Inn, EconoLodge, Fairfield Inn, Hampton Inn, Holiday Inn Express, Knights Inn 🅾 AutoZone, Buick/Cadillac/GMC, Chrysler/Dodge/Jeep, Ford, Ⓗ, Walgreens, Walmart
58	US 81, KS 61, to Hutchinson, McPherson
54	18th Ave, Comanche Rd, Elyria
48	KS 260 E, Moundridge, **2 mi W** gas
46	KS 260 W, Moundridge, **2 mi W** 🅾 truck repair food, gas
40	Lincoln Blvd, Hesston, **E** 🍴 Panda Kitchen 🛏 AmericInn 🅾 Cottonwood Grove RV Camping, **W** 🅖 Casey's/dsl/24hr 🍴 El Cerrito Grill, Lincoln Perk Coffee, Pizza Hut, Sonic, Subway 🛏 Best Value Inn 🅾 city park
34	KS 15, N Newton, to Abilene, KS 15, **E** 🅾 RV camping, **W** 🍴 Papa John's (1mi), Subway (1mi), Taco Bell (1mi) 🅾 Kauffman Museum
33	US 50 E, to Peabody (from nb)
31	1st St, Broadway St, **E** 🅖 LoneStar/dsl, Newell TC/dsl/@ 🍴 Applebee's, CJ's Rest., KFC 🛏 Days Inn, Holiday Inn Express, Newton Inn 🅾 Cadillac/Chevrolet, Chrysler/Dodge/Jeep, Ford/Lincoln, **W** 🍴 Braum's, MT Mike's 🛏 Comfort Inn, Red Coach Inn
30	US 50 W, KS 15 (exits left from nb), to Hutchinson, Newton, **W** 🅖 KwikShop/dsl 🍴 Arby's, Panda Kitchen, Papa Murphy's, Pizza Hut, Sonic, Subway 🅾 $Tree, AutoZone, Buick/GMC, Dillon's Foods, Ⓗ, R Tires, Verizon, Walmart
28	SE 36th St, **W** 🅖 Phillips 66/dsl 🍴 Burger King 🅾 Chisholm Trail Outlets/famous brands
25	KS 196, to Whitewater, El Dorado
23mm	🆁🆂 both lanes, full ♿ facilities, litter barrels, petwalk, 🅒, 🛏, RV dump, vending
22	125th St
19	101st St, **W** 🅾 RV camping
17	85th St, Valley Ctr
16	77th St, **E** 🛏 Motel 6 🅾 Wichita Greyhound Park
14	61st St, **E** 🅖 QT/dsl 🍴 Applebee's, Chopstix, Cracker Barrel, Pizza Hut, Spangles Rest., Subway, Taco Bell, Wendy's 🛏 Red Roof Inn 🅾 Chevrolet, **W** 🅖 Phillips 66/dsl 🍴 KFC, McDonald's 🛏 Quality Inn, Super 8 🅾 Goodyear/auto

Exit #	Services
13	53rd St, **E** 🅾 Freightliner, Harley-Davidson, Volvo/Mack Trucks, **W** 🅖 Phillips 66/dsl 🍴 Arby's, Country Kitchen 🛏 Best Western, Days Inn
11b	I-235 W, KS 96, to Hutchinson
11a	KS 254, to El Dorado
10b	29th St, Hydraulic Ave
10a	KS 96 E
9	21st St, **E** 🅖 Valero 🍴 Sonic 🅾 $General, Wichita St U
8	13th St, **E** 🍴 $General, **W** 🍴 Pig In Pig Out BBQ
7b	8th St, 9th St, Central Ave., **E** 🅾 School of Medicine
7a	downtown
6b	1st St, 2nd St downtown
5b	US 54, US 400, Kellogg Ave, **E** 🍴 QT/dsl
5a	Lincoln St, **E** 🍴 DQ, **W** 🅖 QT/dsl
4	Harry St, **1 mi E** 🍴 Arby's, Bionic Burger, Burger King, Denny's, Hardee's, Jimmy's Egg, LA Fried Chicken, Little Caesar's, McDonald's, NuWay Drive-Thru, Poblano Mexican, Shanghai Chinese, Spangles Rest., Subway, Taco Bell, Wendy's 🅾 BigLots, CVS Drug, Firestone/auto, Goodyear/auto, Ⓗ, **W** 🅖 BD-C/dsl
3	Pawnee Ave, **E** 🅖 QT 🅾 Family$, O'Reilly Parts, **W** 🅖 Jumpstart/dsl 🍴 Burger King, Pizza Hut, Spangles 🅾 $General, AutoZone
2	Hydraulic Ave, **E** 🅖 KwikShop, **W** 🍴 McDonald's, Subway
2mm	Arkansas River
1c	I-235 N, **2 mi W** 🛏 Hilton
1b a	US 81 S, 47th St, **E** 🅖 QT/dsl 🛏 Days Inn, Holiday Inn Express, Quality Inn, Super 8, **W** 🍴 Applebee's, Arby's, Braum's, Burger King, Carlos O'Kelly's, Domino's, Godfather's, Goodcents Subs, Heritage Rest., Hog Wild BBQ, IHOP, KFC, Little Caesar's, LJ Silver, McDonald's, New China, Pizza Hut, Spangles Rest., Subway, Taco Bell 🛏 Best Western, Springfield Inn, Woodspring Suites 🅾 $General, $Tree, Air Capital RV Park, Dillon's Foods/dsl, O'Reilly Parts, Verizon

I-135 begins/ends on I-35, exit 42.

KS

NOTES

KENTUCKY

⬆️E INTERSTATE 24

Exit #	Services
93.5mm	Kentucky/Tennessee state line
93mm	Welcome Ctr wb, full ♿ facilities, litter barrels, petwalk, 🅒, 🏕, vending
91.5mm	Big West Fork Red River
89	KY 115, to Oak Grove, **N** 🅞 to Jeff Davis Mon St HS, **S** 🅖 Pilot/McDonald's/dsl/scales/24hr, Shell/Subway/dsl 🅞 truck repair
86	US 41A, to Ft Campbell, Pennyrile Pkwy, Hopkinsville, **N** 🅖 Loves/Hardee's/dsl/scales/24hr/@, Marathon/dsl/scales/24hr/@, **S** 🅖 FLYING J/Denny's/dsl/LP/scales/24hr, Exxon/dsl, Pilot/Subway/Wendy's/dsl/scales/24hr 🍴 McDonald's, Waffle House 🛏 Candlewood Suites, Days Inn, Hampton Inn, Holiday Inn Express, Oak Grove Inn, Quality Inn, Sleep Inn 🅞 🅗, truck wash
81	Pennyrile Pky N, to Hopkinsville
79mm	Little River
73	KY 117, to Gracey, Newstead
65	US 68, KY 80, to Cadiz, **S** 🅖 BP/dsl, Marathon/dsl, Shell/dsl 🍴 Cracker Barrel, Harper House Rest., KFC, McDonald's, Subway, Taco Bell, Triplets BBQ, Wendy's 🛏 Knights Inn, Quality Inn, Red Roof Inn, Super 7 Inn 🅞 Chevrolet, golf, 🅗, to NRA
56	KY 139, to Cadiz, Princeton, **S** 🅖 Marathon/dsl 🅞 KOA (9mi), NRA
47mm	Lake Barkley
45	KY 293, to Princeton, Saratoga, **S** 🅖 Marathon/dsl 🅞 Mineral Mound SP, RV Camping, to KY St Penitentiary
42	I-69 N, to W KY Pkwy, Elizabethtown
40	US 62, US 641, Kuttawa, Eddyville, **N** 🛏 Regency Inn (2mi), Relax Inn 🅞 Mineral Mound SP, **S** 🅖 BP/Wendy's/dsl/24hr, Exxon, Pilot/Huck's/Godfather's/dsl/scales/24hr 🍴 Huddle House, SW Grill 🛏 Days Inn, Hampton Inn 🅞 KY Lake Rec Areas, to Lake Barkley
36mm	weigh sta both lanes
34mm	Cumberland River
31	KY 453, to Grand Rivers, Smithland, **N** 🅖 BP/dsl 🛏 Patti's Inn, **S** 🅖 Marathon/dsl 🍴 Miss Scarlett's 🛏 Green Turtle Resort (3mi), Lighthouse Landing Resort, Motel 6 🅞 Exit 31 RV Park, NRA
29mm	Tennessee River
27	US 62, to KY Dam, Calvert City, **N** 🅖 BP/dsl, Marathon/dsl 🍴 Cracker Barrel, DQ, Mama D's Italian, McDonald's, Waffle House 🛏 Days Inn, KY Dam Motel, Super 8 🅞 Cypress Lakes Camp, Freightliner, KOA, O'Reilly Parts, vet, **S** 🅖 Loves/Arby's/dsl/scales/24hr, Speedway/Subway/dsl/scales/24hr 🍴 Subway 🛏 Econolodge
25 b a	I-69 S, Carroll/Purchase Pkwy, to Calvert City, **N** 🅞 services 1 mi **S** to KY Lake RA
16	US 68, to Paducah, **S** 🅖 BP/Southern Pride/Subway/dsl/scales/24hr 🅞 flea mkt
11	rd 1954, Husband Rd, to Paducah, **N** 🅖 BP/dsl, FiveStar/dsl 🛏 Best Western 🅞 Duck Creek RV Park, **S** 🅞 Harley-Davidson
7	US 45, US 62, to Paducah, **N** 🅖 FiveStar/dsl 🍴 Burger King, Taco Bell 🅞 🅗, **S** Welcome Ctr both lanes, full ♿ facilities, litter barrels, petwalk, 🅒, 🏕, vending, 🅖 BP, Marathon/dsl 🍴 Arby's, Backyard Burger, Chong's Chinese, Domino's, Hardee's, KFC, Los Amigo's Mexican, McDonald's, Papa John's, Popeye's, Sonic, Subway, Waffle House, Wendy's

*(left margin: P A D U C A H)*

*(left margin tab: KY)*

7	Continued
	🛏 Travelers Inn 🅞 AT&T, Banks Mkt/gas, CVS Drug, Family$, O'Reilly Parts, Plaza Tires, Verizon
4	US 60, to Paducah, **N** 🅖 BP, Exxon/dsl 🍴 Applebee's, Bob Evans, Burger King, McDonald's, O'Charley's, Outback Steaks, Rafferty's 🛏 Auburn Place, Candlewood Suites, Comfort Inn&Suites, Courtyard, Days Inn, Drury Inn, Fairfield Inn, Hampton Inn, Holiday Inn Express, Homewood Suites, La Quinta, Residence Inn, Westowne Inn 🅞 Toyota, **S** 🅖 BP, Murphy USA/dsl 🍴 Arby's, Buffalo Wild Wings, Cap'n D's, Chick-fil-A, Chong's Chinese, ChuckeCheese, Cracker Barrel, Culver's, Domino's, Fazoli's, Firehouse Subs, Five Guys, Hardee's, IHOP, Jimmy John's, La Juicy Seafood, Logan's Roadhouse, Longhorn Steaks, Los Amigos, Los Garcia's, McAlister's Deli, Olive Garden, Panera Bread, Pizza Hut, Qdoba, Red Lobster, Sonic, Starbucks, Steak'n Shake, Taco Bell, Taco John's, Tokyo Hibachi, TX Roadhouse, Wendy's, Zaxby's 🛏 Country Inn&Suites, Drury Suites, EconoLodge, PearTree Inn, Quality Suites, Super 8 🅞 $General, $Tree, AAA, Advance Parts, Aldi Foods, AT&T, Best Buy, Books-A-Million, Dick's, Dillard's, Goodyear/auto, Hobby Lobby, Home Depot, JC Penney, Kohl's, Lowe's, Menard's, Michael's, Office Depot, Old Navy, Petsmart, Plaza Tire, Sam's Club/gas, TJ Maxx, Tuesday Morning, Verizon, Walmart
3	KY 305, to Paducah, **N** 🅖 Shell/dsl, Superway/dsl 🛏 Best Value Inn, Comfort Inn/rest., Red Roof Inn, **S** 🅖 Marathon/Charley's Noble Romans/dsl/e85, Pilot/Subway/dsl/scales/24hr 🍴 El Torito, Waffle Hut 🛏 Baymont Inn 🅞 Fern Lake Camping
0mm	Kentucky/Illinois state line, Ohio River

⬆️E INTERSTATE 64

Exit #	Services
192mm	Kentucky/West Virginia state line, Big Sandy River
191	US 23, to Ashland, 1-2 mi **N** 🅖 Exxon, Marathon/Subway/dsl, Speedway/dsl 🍴 Arby's, Little Caesar's, McDonald's, Waffle House, Wendy's 🛏 Ramada Ltd 🅞 🅗, IGA Foods, Rite Aid, USPO
185	KY 180, Cannonsburg, **N** 🅖 Exxon/dsl, Marathon/dsl, Shell, McDonald's/USPO, Superquik 🍴 Arby's, Bob Evans, Burger King, DQ, Gatti's Pizza, Hermanos Nunez Mexican, KFC, Subway, Taco Bell, Waffle House, Wendy's 🛏 Days Inn, Fairfield Inn, Hampton Inn, Holiday Inn Express 🅞 $Tree, 🅗, Walmart/Subway, **S** 🅖 FLYING J/Denny's/dsl/LP/scales/24hr
181	181 US 60, to Princess, **N** 🅖 BP/dsl, **S** 🅖 Marathon/dsl
179	rd 67, Industrial Pkwy, **N** 🅞 KOA/@
174mm	🆁🆂 eb, full ♿ facilities, litter barrels, petwalk, 🅒, 🏕, vending
173mm	🆁🆂 wb, full ♿ facilities, litter barrels, petwalk, 🅒, 🏕, vending
172	rd 1, rd 7, Grayson, **N** 🅖 Marathon/dsl, Superquik/dsl/24hr 🍴 A&W/LJ Silver, Huddle House, KFC, Pizza Hut, Shoney's, Subway 🛏 Days Inn, Econolodge, Quality Inn 🅞 $General, $Tree, Chrysler/Dodge/Jeep, Ford, K-Mart, Save-A-Lot Foods, URGENT CARE, **S** 🅖 BP, Exxon/Hardees, Loves/Wendy's/scales/dsl/24hr, Marathon, Shell/dsl, Speedway/dsl 🍴 Arby's, Biscuit World, China House, DQ, Little Caesar's, McDonald's, Papa John's, Taco Bell, Toro Loco 🛏 Super 8 🅞 $General, Advance Parts, AT&T, AutoZone, Family$, Food Fair, O'Reilly Parts, Rite Aid, USPO, Verizon
161	US 60, to Olive Hill, **N** 🅖 BP 🛏 Spanish Manor Motel 🅞 to Carter Caves SP

(right margin: G R A Y S O N)

INTERSTATE 64 Cont'd	

Exit #	Services
156	rd 2, to KY 59, to Olive Hill, S BP
148mm	weigh sta wb
141mm	both lanes, full facilities, litter barrels, petwalk, vending
137	KY 32, to Morehead, N BP/dsl, Speedway/dsl DQ, Huddle House AT&T, Big Lots, Kroger/dsl, Lowe's, Walmart/Subway, S BP/McDonald's/dsl/24hr, Marathon/dsl China Star, Cracker Barrel, Domino's, Don Señor, Hardee's, Lee's Chicken, Reno's Roadhouse Best Western, Days Inn, Hampton Inn, Motel 6, Red Roof Inn $General, Ace Hardware, auto repair, AutoZone, st police
133	rd 801, to Sharkey, Farmers, N Shell/dsl Chrysler/Dodge/Jeep/Ford, S BP/Subway/dsl Comfort Inn Outpost RV Park (4mi)
123	US 60, to Salt Lick, Owingsville
121	KY 36, to Owingsville, N BP/dsl, Exxon/dsl, Valero/dsl DQ, McDonald's, Subway $General, Family$, S Save-a-Lot Foods
113	US 60, to Mt Sterling, N Shell/dsl, S /McDonald's/Subway/dsl/scales/24hr
110	US 460, KY 11, Mt Sterling, N Shell/Krystal/Subway/dsl, Valero/dsl Cattleman's Roadhouse, Cracker Barrel Comfort Inn, Ramada Ltd, S BP/dsl, Exxon, Marathon, Marathon/dsl, Murphy Express/dsl, Speedway/dsl Applebee's, Arby's, Asian Buffet, Bojangle's, Burger King, Capt D's, City King Buffet, Don Señor, El Camino Real, Hardee's, KFC, Lee's Chicken, Little Caesar's, LJ Silver, Los Rodeos, McDonald's, Pizza Hut, Subway, Taco Bell, Waffle House, Wendy's Budget Inn, Days Inn $Tree, Advance Parts, Advance Parts, AT&T, AutoZone, Chevrolet, Chrysler/Dodge/Jeep, CVS Drug, Family$, Ford, JC Penney, Kroger, Lowe's, O'Reilly Parts, Verizon, Walmart/Subway
101	US 60
98.5mm	eb, full facilities, litter barrels, petwalk, vending
98	KY 402 (from eb), S Natural Bridge Resort SP
96b a	KY 627, to Winchester, Paris, N 96 Truck Plaza/dsl/rest./scales, BP/dsl, S Baymont Inn, Hampton Inn, Red Roof Inn Buick/Chevrolet/GMC

94	KY 1958, Van Meter Rd, Winchester, N Marathon/dsl/24hr, Shell/scales/dsl Comfort Inn, Value Stay Inn, S BP/dsl, Marathon/dsl, Murphy Express/dsl, Shell/dsl, Speedway/dsl Applebee's, Arby's, Big Boy, Bojangle's, Burger King, Capt D's, Dickey's BBQ, Domino's, Don Señor, DQ, El Camino Real, Fazoli's, Golden Corral, Great Wall Chinese, Hardee's, Jade Garden Chinese, Jimmy John's, KFC, Little Caesar's, McDonald's, Papa John's, Pizza Hut, Puerta Grande, Rally's, Sakura Express, Sir Pizza, Sonic, Starbucks, Subway, Taco Bell, Taste Of China, Waffle House, Wendy's Holiday Inn Express $Tree, Advance Parts, AT&T, auto repair, AutoZone, Chrysler/Dodge/Jeep, Kroger/dsl, Lowe's, O'Reilly Parts, Office Depot, Rite Aid, Tire Discounters, to Ft Boonesborough Camping, Verizon, Walgreens, Walmart/Subway
87	KY 859, Blue Grass Sta
81	I-75 S, to Knoxville
I-64 and I-75 run together 7 mi. See I-75, exits 113-115.	
75	I-75 N, to Cincinnati access to KY Horse Park
69	US 62 E, to Georgetown, N antiques (6mi), to Georgetown Coll., S Equus Run Vineyards (2mi)
65	US 421, Midway, S BP/dsl, McDonald's, Shell/dsl Subway
60mm	both lanes, full facilities, litter barrels, petwalk, vending
58	US 60, Frankfort, N BP/dsl, Five Star/dsl, Shell/dsl, Speedway/dsl Arby's, Buffalo Wild Wings, Capt D's, Cattleman's Roadhouse, DQ, KFC, McDonald's, Miguel's Mexican, Starbucks, Subway, Taco Bell, Waffle House, Wendy's, White Castle, Zaxby's Best Western, Bluegrass Inn, Fairfield Inn $General, $Tree, Buick/Chevrolet/GMC, Chrysler/Dodge/Jeep, Dick's, ElkHorn Camping (5mi), Ford/Lincoln, GNC, Honda, Kohl's, Kroger/gas, KYSU, Michael's, Nissan, TireDiscounters, TJMaxx, to KY St Capitol, to Viet Vets Mem, Toyota, Walgreens, S Cracker Barrel, Logan's Roadhouse
55mm	Kentucky River
53b a	US 127, Frankfort, N Marathon, Speedway/dsl, Speedway/dsl Applebee's, Arby's, Baskin-Robbins, Beef O'Brady's, Big Boy, Burger King, Capt D's, Carino's Italian, Chili's, China Buffet, CookOut, DQ, Fazoli's, Ginza Japanese, Hardee's, KFC, Longhorn Steaks, McDonald's, My Guadalajara, O'Charley's, Panera Bread, Penn Sta Subs, Qdoba Mexican, Sonic, Starbucks, Staxx BBQ, Steak'n Shake, Subway, Taco Bell, Tacos n More, Wendy's

Side labels: MOREHEAD, WINCHESTER, FRANKFORT, KY

⬆E INTERSTATE 64 Cont'd

Exit	Services
53b a	**Continued** 🛏 Best Value Inn, Days Inn, Hampton Inn, Holiday Inn Express Ⓞ $General, Advance Parts, Ancient Age Tour, AT&T, AutoZone, Big-O Tire, BigLots, Family$, GNC, Goodyear/auto, 🄷, JC Penney, Kroger/gas, Lowe's, Midas, Office Depot, Petco, Rite Aid, st police, Staples, to KY St Capitol, URGENT CARE, USPO, Verizon, Walgreens, Walmart/Subway, **S** 🍴 BP/dsl
48	KY 151, to US 127 S, **S** 🍴 Marathon/dsl, Valero/dsl
43	KY 395, Waddy, **N** ⛽ ✈FLYING J/Denny's/dsl/LP/scales/24hr, **S** ⛽ 🔵Loves/McDonald's/Subway/dsl/scales/24hr
38.5mm	weigh sta eb
35	KY 53, Shelbyville, **N** 🍴 Marathon/dsl, Shell/Circle K/dsl, Speedway/dsl 🍴 Cracker Barrel, KFC, Little Caesar's, McDonald's (1mi), Subway, Taco Bell, Waffle House Ⓞ $General, Advance Parts, Family$, Ford, Kroger/deli/dsl, Lake Shelby Camping (3mi), vet, **S** 🍴 Huck's/White Castle/dsl, Valero/Subway/dsl 🛏 Holiday Inn Express Ⓞ golf
32b a	KY 55, Shelbyville, **1-2 mi N** ⛽ Murphy USA/dsl, Valero/dsl 🍴 Arby's, Asian Buffet, Bojangle's, El Nopal, Firefresh BBQ, Hardee's, McDonald's, Pizza Hut, Subway, Taco Bell, Waffle House, Wendy's, Zaxby's 🛏 Best Western, Econolodge, Red Roof Inn Ⓞ $Tree, AutoZone, Big O Tire, Buick/Chevrolet/GMC, Chrysler/Dodge/Jeep, CVS Drug, 🄷, Lowe's, Rolling Hills Camping (16mi), Verizon, Walgreens, Walmart, **S** 🍴 Cattleman's Roadhouse 🛏 Ramada Ⓞ Taylorsville Lake SP
28mm	Ⓡˢ eb, full ♿ facilities, info, litter barrels, petwalk, 🄲, 🄰, vending
28	KY 1848, Veechdale Rd, Simpsonville, **N** ⛽ Pilot/Wendy's/dsl/scales/24hr 🍴 DQ, Subway, Zaxby's 🛏 Hampton Inn Ⓞ golf, **S** 🍴 Bob Evans, Culver's, McDonald's Ⓞ Blue Grass Outlets/famous brands
19b a	I-265, Gene Snyder Fwy, **N** to Tom Sawyer SP
17	S Blankenbaker, **N** ⛽ Shell/Circle K/dsl 🍴 Mellow Mushroom Pizza, Zaxby's 🛏 Staybridge Suites Ⓞ Harley-Davidson, **S** ⛽ Marathon, Speedway/Subway/dsl, Thornton's/dsl 🍴 Arby's, BackYard Burger, Burger King, Cracker Barrel, El Caporal Mexican, HomeTown Buffet, KFC, Kingfish Rest., LJ Silver/Taco Bell, Logan's Roadhouse, McDonald's, Penn Sta Subs, Qdoba, Ruby Tuesday, Starbucks, Waffle House, Wendy's 🛏 Comfort Suites, Country Inn&Suites, Extended Stay America, Fairfield Inn, Hampton Inn, Hawthorn Suites, Hilton Garden, Holiday Inn Express, La Quinta, Microtel, Quality Inn, Sleep Inn, Wingate Inn, Woodspring Suites Ⓞ Lexus, Sam's Club/gas
15	Hurstbourne Pkwy, Louisville, **0-2 mi N** ⛽ Shell/Circle K/dsl, Speedway, Thorton's/dsl 🍴 Arby's, Bob Evans, Bonefish Grill, Carrabba's, Chili's, Fazoli's, Firehouse Subs, IHOP, Jimmy John's, Macaroni Grill, McDonald's, Mimi's Cafe, Momma's BBQ, Noodles&Co, Olive Garden, Panda Express, Panera Bread, Papa John's, PF Changs, Pita Pit, Qdoba, Sichuan Garden, Skyline Chili, Smashburger, Starbucks, Subway, Waffle House 🛏 Baymont Inn, Courtyard, Days Inn, Drury Inn, Holiday Inn, Hyatt Place, Red Roof Inn, Residence Inn Ⓞ Barnes&Noble, Kroger/gas, Lowe's, Towery's Auto, Tuesday Morning, Walgreens, **S** 🍴 Kroger/gas 🍴 Applebee's, BoomBozz Pizza, Buca Italian, Buffalo Wild Wing, Burger King, Cattleman's Roadhouse, Chick-fil-A, ChuckeCheese, Coldstone, DQ, El Marlin Seafood, El Torazo Mexican, Famous Daves, Happy China, Home Run Burgers, J Gumbo's Cajun, Jason's Deli, Jumbo Buffet, Kansai Japanese, Longhorn Steaks, McAlister's Deli, McDonald's, Melting Pot, Moe's SW Grill, O'Charley's, Old Chicago, Panera Bread, Penn Sta. Subs, Pizza Hut, Qdoba,

Exit	Services
15	**Continued** Shogun Japanese, Smokey Bones BBQ, Starbucks, Steak Shake, Taco Bell, Tumbleweed SW Grill, Wendy's, White Castle, Yen Ching 🛏 Best Western, Extended Stay America, Marriott, Ramada, Red Carpet Inn Ⓞ $Tree, AutoZone, BMW, Buick/GMC, Cadillac, Carmax, Chevrolet, Discount Tire, GNC, Home Depot, Honda, Infiniti, Michael's, Office Depot, Staples, Subaru, Target, Verizon, Volvo, VW, Walgreens, Walmart
12b	I-264 E, Watterson Expswy, **1 exit N on US 60** 🍴 Thornton's/dsl 🍴 Arby's, Big Boy, Bravo Cucina Italin, Buffalo Wild Wings, CPizza, Cheesecake Factory, Chick-Fil-A, Chuy's Mexican, Jason's Deli, Logan's Roadhouse, McDonald's, Outback Steaks, Panera Bread, Red Robin, Speedway/dsl, Taco Bell, Wendy's Ⓞ Acura, Best Buy, Dick's, Dillard's, Ford/Lincoln, Goodyear/auto, Hyundai, JC Penney, Jo-Ann, Kia, Kohl's, Macy's, mall, Old Navy, Sears/auto, Staples, SteinMart, Toyota, Von Maur, Whole Foods Mkt
12a	I-264 W access to 🄷
10	Cannons Lane
8	Grinstead Dr, Louisville, **S** 🍴 gas 🍴 Le Moo
7	US 42, US 62, Mellwood Ave, Story Ave
6	I-71 N (from eb), to Cincinnati
5a	I-65, S to Nashville, N to Indianapolis
5b	3rd St, Louisville, **N** 🍴 Joe's CrabShack, **S** 🛏 Galt House Hotel, Marriott Ⓞ 🄷
4	9th St, Roy Wilkins Ave, **S** Ⓞ KY Art Ctr, science museum, downtown
3	US 150 E, to 22nd St, **S** 🍴 Marathon/dsl, Shell/Circle K 🍴 DQ, McDonald's Ⓞ Family$
1	I-264 E, to Shively, **S** Ⓞ 🔄, zoo
0mm	Kentucky/Indiana state line, Ohio River

⬆N INTERSTATE 65

Exit #	Services
138mm	Kentucky/Indiana state line, Ohio River
137	I-64 W, I-71 N, I-64 E, **W** Ⓞ to Galt House downtown
136c	Jefferson St, Louisville, **E** Ⓞ 🄷, Walgreens, **W** 🍴 Shell 🍴 McDonald's, Papa John's, Subway, White Castle 🛏 Courtyard, EconoLodge, Fairfield Inn, Hampton Inn, Hyatt, Marriott, SpringHill Suites Ⓞ Tires+
136b	Broadway St, Chestnut St (from nb), **E** Ⓞ 🄷, NAPA, Walgreens, **W** 🍴 Shell, Thornton's 🍴 McDonald's, Subway, White Castle 🛏 Courtyard, Fairfield Inn, Hampton Inn, Hyatt, Marriott, SpringHill Suites Ⓞ same as 136c, Tires+
135	W St Catherine, **E** 🍴 Shell
134b a	KY 61, Jackson St, Woodbine St, **W** 🍴 Shell/Circle K 🛏 Days Inn, Quality Inn Ⓞ Harley-Davidson
133b	US 60A, Eastern Pkwy, Taylor Blvd, **E** 🍴 Denny's, Subway, **W** 🍴 Speedway/dsl 🍴 Cracker Barrel, McDonald's, Papa John's Ⓞ Churchill Downs, museum, U of Louisville
133a	Crittenden Dr (132from sb), **E** 🍴 Denny's, same as 133, **W** 🍴 BP 🍴 Arby's, Burger King, Cracker Barrel, Hall of Fame Cafe 🛏 Country Inn&Suites, Hilton Garden, Holiday Inn, Ramada Inn, Sheraton, Super 8
131b a	I-264, Watterson Expswy, **W** Ⓞ 🔄, Cardinal Stadium, Expo Center
130	KY 61, Preston Hwy, **E on Ky 61** 🍴 Shell/Circle K, Speedway/dsl, Thornton's 🍴 Bob Evans, Domino's, Fazoli's, Little Caesar's, McDonald's, Papa John's, Popeye's, Rally's, Slabhouse BBQ, Subway, Waffle House, Wendy's 🛏 EconoLodge, Red Roof Inn, Super 8 Ⓞ $General, $Tree, Aamco, AutoZone, Big O Tire, BigLots, Chevrolet/Kia, Dodge, Ford, GNC, O'Reilly Parts, Sav-A-Lot Foods, Tires+, U-Haul

INTERSTATE 65 Cont'd

Exit #	Services
128	KY 1631, Fern Valley Rd, E 📱 BP, Mapco/dsl/e85, Marathon/Circle K, Thornton's/dsl 🍴 Big Boy, Dunkin', El Nopal Mexican, Hardee's, Indi's Rest., McDonald's, Outback Steaks, Shoney's, Subway, Taco Bell, Waffle House, Wendy's, White Castle, Zaxby's 🛏 Baymont Inn, Comfort Suites, Days Inn, Holiday Inn, InTown Suites ⊙ Sam's Club/gas, Walgreens, W ⊙ UPS Depot
127	KY 1065, outer loop, E 🍴 Cheddar's, TX Roadhouse, W 🍴 McDonald's/RV Parking
125b a	I-265 E, KY 841, Gene Snyder Fwy
121	KY 1526, Brooks Rd, E 📱 BP, Marathon 🍴 Burger King, Cracker Barrel, McDonald's, Subway, Tumbleweed Grill 🛏 Comfort Inn, Fairfield Inn, Holiday Inn Express ⊙ 🏥, W 📱 BP/dsl, Pilot/Subway/dsl/scales/24hr 🍴 Taco Bell, Waffle House 🛏 Baymont Inn, EconoLodge, Hampton Inn, Quality Inn
117	KY 44, Shepherdsville, E 📱 BP/dsl, Valero 🍴 Denny's 🛏 Best Western/rest., Garden Inn ⊙ KOA (2mi), vet, W 📱 Marathon, Speedway/dsl 🍴 Arby's, Big Boy, Cattlemans Roadhouse, China Buffet, Domino's, DQ, El Nopal, El Tarasco, Fazoli's, KFC, Little Caesar's, LJ Silver, McDonald's, Mr Gatti's, Papa John's, Penn Sta Subs, Sonic, Starbucks, Subway, Taco Bell, Waffle House, Wendy's, White Castle 🛏 Country Inn&Suites, Motel 6, Sleep Inn, Super 8 ⊙ $General, Advance Parts, AT&T, AutoZone, BigLots, Family$, Kroger/dsl, Lowe's, NAPA, O'Reilly Parts, Rite Aid, SaveALot, Towery Tire/auto, Walgreens, Walmart/dsl
116.5mm	Salt River
116	KY 480, to KY 61, E 📱 Loves/Chester's/Subway/dsl/scales/24hr, Valero/dsl ⊙ House of Quilts, W 📱 Marathon/dsl ⊙ Grandma's RV Park/flea mkt
114mm	🅿 sb, full 🚻 facilities, litter barrels, petwalk, 🕭, 🦮, vending
112	KY 245, Clermont, E 📱 Valero/dsl ⊙ Bernheim Forest, Jim Beam Outpost, to My Old Kentucky Home SP (15mi)
105	KY 61, Lebanon Jct, W 📱 Pilot/McDonald's/Subway/dsl/scales/24hr/@, Speedway/dsl
102	KY 313, to KY 434, Radcliff, W to Patton Museum
94	US 62, Elizabethtown, E 📱 BP/dsl, Marathon/dsl 🍴 Denny's, Waffle House, White Castle 🛏 Days Inn, Quality Inn, Super 8 ⊙ $General, W 📱 BP/dsl, Speedway/dsl 🍴 Arby's, Burger King, Chalupa's Mexican, Cracker Barrel, Gatti's Pizza, HoneyBaked Ham, KFC/Taco Bell, McDonald's, Papa John's, Pizza Hut, Ruby Tuesday, Ryan's, Shoney's, Subway, TX Outlaw Steaks, TX Roadhouse, Wendy's 🛏 Baymont Inn, Comfort Suites, Fairfield Inn, Hampton Inn, Holiday Inn Express, La Quinta, Motel 6, Ramada Inn, Wingfield Inn ⊙ $General, Advance Parts, AutoZone, Crossroads Camping, 🏥, Kroger/gas, Skagg's RV Ctr, st police, USPO, visitors ctr, Walgreens
93	to Bardstown, to BG Pky, E ⊙ Maker's Mark Distillery (27mi), to My Old KY Home SP (25mi)
91	US 31 W, KY 61, WK Pkwy, Elizabethtown, E 📱 Marathon/dsl 🍴 LJ Silver, Subway 🛏 Best Value Inn, Royal Inn ⊙ $General, to Lincoln B'Place, W 📱 Doug's/dsl, Marathon ⊙ 🏥
90mm	weigh sta sb only
86	KY 222, Glendale, E 📱 Pilot/McDonalds/dsl/scales/24hr ⊙ Glendale Camping, trk repair, W 📱 Petro/Dunkin'/dsl/scales/24hr/@ 🛏 Glendale Economy Inn ⊙ Blue Beacon
83mm	Nolin River
81	KY 84, Sonora, E 📱 Pilot/Subway/dsl/scales/24hr ⊙ to Lincoln B'Place, W 📱 Five Star/dsl
76	KY 224, Upton, E 📱 Marathon/dsl, W ⊙ to Nolin Lake

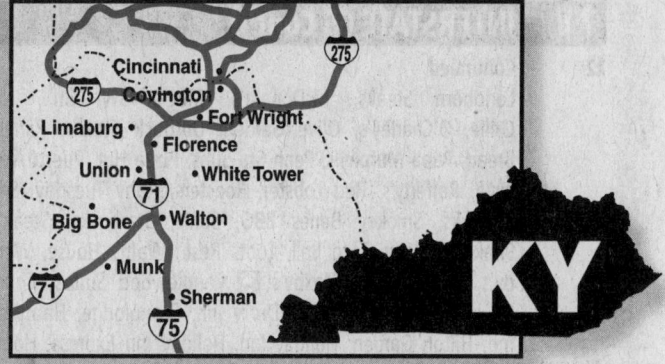

75mm	eastern/central time zone
71	KY 728, Bonnieville
65	US 31 W, Munfordville, E 📱 BP/Subway/dsl, FiveStar/dsl 🍴 DQ, El Mazatlan, King Buffet, McDonald's, Pizza Hut, Sonic 🛏 Super 8 ⊙ $General, Advance Parts, Fred's Store, IGA Foods, Save-A-Lot, W 📱 Marathon/dsl, Shell 🍴 Bucky Bee's BBQ, to Nolin Lake
61mm	🅿 both lanes, full 🚻 facilities, Green River, info, litter barrels, petwalk, 🕭, 🦮, vending
58	KY 218, Horse Cave, E 📱 Loves/McDonald's/dsl/scales/24hr/@ ⊙ 🏥, W 🛏 Hampton Inn, Quality Inn ⊙ KOA, to Mammoth Cave NP
53	KY 70, KY 90, Cave City, E 📱 BP/dsl, Gulf/dsl/repair, Shell, Subway/Sonic/dsl 🍴 A&W/LJ Silver, Cracker Barrel, El Mazatlan, KFC, McDonald's, Pizza Hut, Wendy's 🛏 Baymont Inn, Comfort Inn, Days Inn/rest., Motel 6, Red Roof Inn, Sleep Inn, Super 8 ⊙ $General, Barren River Lake SP (24mi), 🏥, Olde General Store, W 🍴 Watermill Rest. ⊙ Jellystone Camping, Mammoth Cave NP, Onyx Cave
48	KY 255, Park City, E 📱 Shell/Subway/dsl ⊙ $General, Park Mammoth Resort, W ⊙ Diamond Caverns Resort, to Mammoth Cave NP
43	Nun/Cumberland Pky, E ⊙ to Barren River Lake SP
38	KY 101, Smiths Grove, W 📱 Exxon/dsl/scales, Marathon/Subway/dsl, Shell/Schlotsky's/dsl 🍴 Bestway Pizza, McDonald's, Miss Betty's Diner, Wendy's 🛏 Bryce Inn ⊙ $General, auto repair, city park, IGA Foods
36	US 68, KY 80, Oakland (no nb return)
31	to Bristol Rd
28	rd 446, to US 31 W, Bowling Green, W 📱 Huck's/dsl, Shell/dsl 🍴 Hardee's, Jerry's Rest., McDonald's, Wendy's 🛏 Best Value Inn, Country Hearth Inn, Super 8, Value Lodge ⊙ Corvette Museum/cafe, 🏥, to WKYU
26	KY 234, Bowling Green, W 📱 Shell/dsl 🍴 Subway ⊙ 🏥, IGA Foods
22	US 231, Bowling Green, E 📱 Exxon/dsl, Marathon/Godfather's, Shell, Shell/dsl 🍴 Cracker Barrel, Culver's, Domino's, El Maguey, El Mazatlan, Hardee's, Motor City Grill, Ryan's, Sonic, Waffle House, Zaxby's 🛏 Baymont Inn, Best Western, Days Inn, Greenwood Hotel, HomeTowne Suites, Jameson Inn, La Quinta, Microtel, Quality Inn, Ramada Inn, Sleep Inn, Super 8 ⊙ $General, Camping World, Harley-Davidson, URGENT CARE, USPO, W 📱 Marathon/dsl, Speedway/dsl 🍴 Applebee's, Arby's, Beijing Chinese, Bob Evans, Bojangles, Bruster's, Buffalo Wild Wings, Burger King, Capt D's, Chick-fil-A, Chipotle, ChuckeCheese, Chuy's Mexican, Corner Bakery Cafe, Double-Dog's Chowhouse, Fazoli's, Firehouse Subs, Five Guys, Freddy's, Gondolier Italian, Honeybaked Ham, IHOP, Jersey Mike's, Jimmy John's, KFC, Krystal, Kyoto Steaks, Logan's Roadhouse,

🚗 = gas   🍽 = food   🛏 = lodging   🅾 = other   ℞s = rest stop   Copyright 2022 - The Next EXIT ®

INTERSTATE 65 Cont'd

22	Continued
	Longhorn Steaks, McDonald's, Moe's SW Grill, MT Grille, O'Charley's, Olive Garden, Outback Steaks, Panera Bread, Papa Murphy's, Penn Sta Subs, Pizza Hut, Puerto Vallarta, Rafferty's, Red Lobster, Roosters, Ruby Tuesday, Saladworks, Smokey Bones BBQ, Sonic, Starbucks, Steak'n Shake, Subway, Taco Bell, Toots Rest., Waffle House, Wendy's, White Castle, Zaxby's 🛏 Candlewood Suites, Country Inn&Suites, Courtyard, Drury Inn, Econolodge, Hampton Inn, Hilton Garden, Holiday Inn, Holiday Inn Express, Home 2 Suites, Motel 6, Red Roof Inn 🅾 $General, $Tree, Advance Parts, AT&T, AutoZone, Barnes&Noble, Best Buy, BMW/Mercedes, Buick/GMC/Cadillac, Cabela's, Chevrolet, Chrysler/Dodge/Jeep, CVS Drug, Dick's, Dillard's, Ford/Lincoln, Goodyear/auto, Hobby Lobby, Home Depot, Honda, 🏥, Hyundai, JC Penney, Kia, KOA, Kohl's, Kroger/gas, Lowe's, Meijer, Michael's, Nissan, Old Navy, PetCo, Petsmart, Sam's Club/gas, Sears, Staples, Target, TJ Maxx, Toyota, Tuesday Morning, U-Haul, URGENT CARE, Walgreens, Walmart/McDonald's
20	WH Natcher Toll Rd, to Bowling Green, access to W KY U, W 🅾 st police
6	KY 100, Franklin, E 🚗 Shell/dsl/24hr 🅾 truckwash, W 🚗 🛢Subway/dsl/scales/24hr, 🛢Wendy's/dsl/scales/24hr 🍽 El Potrero 🛏 Comfort Inn, Days Inn, Knights Inn 🅾 Bluegrass RV Park, 🏥, SpeedCo, TA Truck Service, truck&tires/repair, truckwash, Volvo Trucks
4mm	weigh sta nb
2	US 31 W, to Franklin, E 🚗 ⓕFLYING J/Denny's/dsl/LP/scales/24hr, Keystop/Marathon/Burger King/dsl/24hr, W 🚗 BP/dsl 🍽 Cracker Barrel, Franklin Steakhouse, McDonald's, Oasis SW Grill, Solazteca, Waffle House 🛏 Baymont Inn, EconoLodge, Hampton Inn, Holiday Inn Express, Quality Inn, Super 8 🅾 antiques, 🏥
1mm	Welcome Ctr nb, full 🅿 facilities, litter barrels, petwalk, 🚗, 🍽, vending
0mm	Kentucky/Tennessee state line

INTERSTATE 71

Exit #	Services
100	Kentucky/Ohio state line, Ohio River
	I-71 and I-75 run together 19 miles. See I-75, exits 175-192.
77[173]	I-75 S, to Lexington, N 🅾 🏥, S 🅾 to Dans Mt SP
75mm	weigh sta sb
72	KY 14, to Verona, E 🚗 BP/dsl, Marathon/dsl 🅾 Oak Creek Camping (5mi)
62	US 127, to Glencoe, E 🚗 62 TrkPlaza/rest./dsl, W 🚗 Valero/dsl/rest. 🛏 127 Motel
57	KY 35, to Sparta, E 🚗 Marathon/dsl 🅾 Eagle Valley Camping (10mi), Sparta RV Park (3mi), W 🚗 BP/dsl 🛏 Ramada 🅾 KY Speedway
55	KY 1039, W 🚗 🛢Loves/McDonald's/Subway/dsl/scales/24hr 🅾 casino, KY Speedway
44	KY 227, to Indian Hills, W 🚗 Marathon/dsl, Marathon/dsl, Murphy USA/dsl, Valero/dsl 🍽 Arby's, Burger King, El Nopal, Hometown Pizza, KFC, McDonald's, Mi Viejo Mexican, New China, Subway, Taco Bell, Waffle House 🛏 Hampton Inn, Holiday Inn Express, Quality Inn, Red Roof Inn, Super 8 🅾 $General, $Tree, AutoZone, Chevrolet, Ford, Gen. Butler SP, 🏥, Kroger/dsl, Save-a-Lot Foods, URGENT CARE, Verizon, Walmart
43.5mm	Kentucky River
43	KY 389, to KY 55, English

INTERSTATE 65

34	US 421, New Castle, Campbellsburg, W 🚗 Marathon/dsl, Valero/Subway/dsl 🅾 st police
28	KY 153, KY 146, to US 42, Pendleton, E 🚗 🛢/Subway/dsl/scales/24hr/@, Valero/dsl, W 🚗 🛢/McDonald's/scales/dsl/24hr 🅾 truck repair
22	KY 53, La Grange, E 🚗 Murphy USA/dsl, Speedway/Rally's/dsl, Valero/dsl 🍽 Applebee's, Beef O'Brady's, Burger King, Jumbo Buffet, Papa John's, Papa Murphy's, Subway, Waffle House, Wendy's 🛏 Best Western-Ashbury, Comfort Inn 🅾 $General, AT&T, Big-O Tire, GNC, 🏥, Kroger/gas, Towery's Tire/auto, Verizon, Walgreens, Walmart/Subway W 🚗 Marathon/dsl 🍽 Arby's, Cracker Barrel, Domino's, DQ, El Nopal, Hometown Pizza, KFC, LJ Silver, McDonald's, Taco Bell 🛏 Quality Suites, Super 8 🅾 $Tree, Advance Parts, Buick/Chevrolet/GMC, Lee Tires, NAPA, Rite Aid, USPO, vet
18	KY 393, Buckner, W 🚗 Marathon/dsl 🍽 Subway 🅾 Ford
17	KY 146, Buckner, W 🚗 Thornton's/dsl/24hr 🅾 USPO
14	KY 329, Crestwood, Pewee Valley, Brownsboro, **2 mi** E 🚗 BP/dsl 🍽 DQ, Hometown Pizza, McDonald's, Sonic, Starbucks, Subway
13mm	℞s both lanes, full 🅿 facilities, litter barrels, petwalk, 🚗, 🍽, vending
9b a	I-265, KY 841, Gene Snyder Fwy, E 🛏 Drury Inn, Hilton Garden 🅾 Cabela's, Costco/gas, 🏥, to Sawyer SP
5	I-264, Watterson Expswy (exits left from sb), E 🅾 to Sawyer SP
2	Zorn Ave, E 🅾 VA 🏥, W 🚗 Shell/dsl, Valero 🍽 El Nopal Mexican, KingFish Rest. 🛏 Ramada Inn 🅾 WaterTower Art Museum
1b	I-65, S to Nashville, N to Indianapolis

INTERSTATE 75

Exit #	Services
193mm	Kentucky/Ohio state line, Ohio River
192	5th St (from nb), Covington, E 🚗 BP/dsl, Shell/Circle K, Speedway/dsl 🍽 Big Boy, Burger King, GoldStar Chili, McDonald's, Popeyes, Riverfront Pizza, Skyline Chili, Subway, Taco Bell, Waffle House, Wendy's, White Castle 🛏 Courtyard, Extended Stay America, Holiday Inn, Radisson 🅾 Lexus, Riverboat Casino, W 🛏 Hampton Inn
191	12th St, Covington, E 🅾 🏥, museum, same as 192
189	KY 1072, Kyles Lane, W 🚗 BP/dsl, Shell/dsl 🍽 Big Boy, Skyline Chili, Substation II Subs 🛏 Rodeway Inn 🅾 same as 188, Walgreens
188	US 25, US 42, Dixe Hwy, E 🚗 Marathon 🍽 Starbucks, Subway 🅾 GNC, Kroger/dsl, Tuesday Morning, W 🛏 Rodeway Inn 🅾 Mercedes, same as 189
186	KY 371, Buttermilk Pike, Covington, E 🚗 BP/dsl, Marathon/DQ dsl 🍽 Graeter's Ice Cream, Oriental Wok, Papa John's 🛏 Montgomery Inn, Super 8, W 🚗 BP, Speedway/dsl, Sunoco dsl 🍽 Arby's, Baskin-Robbins/Dunkin', Bonefish Grill, Burger King, Cancun Mexican, Chipotle Mexican, Domino's, Empire Buffet, Firehouse Subs, GoldStar Chili, Jimmy John's, La Rosa Pizza, Marco's Pizza, McDonald's, Miyako Steaks, Outback Steaks, Skyline Chili, Subway, Sweet Basil Thai 🅾 $Tree, Field & Stream, Home Depot, Petco, Remke Foods, Staples, Verizon, Walgreens
185	I-275 E and W, **W** to 🅿
184	KY 236, Donaldson Rd, to Erlanger, E 🚗 BP, Erlanger Dunkin' 🍽 Double Dragon Oriental, W 🚗 Racers/Subway/dsl, Speedway/dsl 🍽 Peecox Grill, Waffle House 🛏 Country Hearth Inn, EconoLodge, Red Roof Inn, Wingate Inn 🅾 Goodyear/auto

FRANKLIN

LOUISVILLE

COVINGTON

KY

🔼 Ⓝ INTERSTATE 75 Cont'd

Exit #	Services

182 KY 1017, Turfway Rd, E ⛽ BP/dsl, Shell/dsl 🍴 Bamboo Garden, Big Boy, China City, Lee's Chicken, McDonald's, Papa John's, Subway, Taco Bell 🛏 Baymont Inn, Courtyard, Days Inn, Woodspring Suites ⊙ BigLots, CVS Drug, Family$, Office Depot, Remke Foods, USPO, W 🍴 Applebee's, Chick-fil-A, Chili's, Ci-Ci's Pizza, Cracker Barrel, Famous Dave's BBQ, Firebowl Grill, Longhorn Steaks, Noodles&Co., O'Charley's, Potbelly, Rafferty's, Skyline Chili, Steak'n Shake, Subway, Wendy's 🛏 Comfort Inn, Extended Stay America, Hampton Inn, Hilton, Hyatt Place, La Quinta, SpringHill Suites ⊙ Best Buy, Dick's, Home Depot, 🅗, Jo-Ann, Kohl's, Lowe's, Meijer, Michael's, Petsmart, Sam's Club, Target, Turfway Park Racing

181 KY 18, Florence, E ⛽ Speedway/dsl, TA/Valero/Pizza Hut/Popeye's/Subway/dsl/24hr/@ 🍴 Kiwha Korean, Waffle House 🛏 Best Value Inn, Best Western, Heritage Inn ⊙ Chevrolet, W ⛽ BP/dsl, Marathon/dsl, Speedway/dsl 🍴 Buffalo Wild Wings, Cheddar's, Chipotle Mexican, Chuy's Mexican, City BBQ, Currito Burrito, El Rio Grande, Fazoli's, Firehouse Subs, Fuji Steaks, Hooters, IHOP, Jersey Mike's, La Rosa's, Laughing Noodle, Logan's Roadhouse, Miyoshi Japanese, Panda Express, Panera Bread, Red Robin 🛏 Homewood Suites, Stay Lodge ⊙ AT&T, Buick/GMC, Chrysler/Jeep/Dodge, Ford, Honda, Hyundai, Mazda, Nissan, Tire Discounters, Toyota, URGENT CARE, Verizon, VW, Walmart/Subway

180a Mall Rd (from sb), W 🍴 Asian Buffet, BJ's Rest., Buca Italian, ChuckeCheese, GoldStar Chili, HoneyBaked Ham, Jimmy John's, Olive Garden, Pizza Hut, Qdoba, Skyline Chili, Smokey Bones BBQ, Starbucks, Subway, Taco Bell, Which Wich? ⊙ $General, $Tree, AT&T, Barnes&Noble, Harley Davidson, Hobby Lobby, JC Penney, Kroger/dsl, Macy's, Old Navy, same as 180, Staples, TJ Maxx, Tuesday Morning

180 US 42, US 127, Florence, Union, E ⛽ BP/dsl, Speedway/dsl 🍴 Big Boy, Bob Evans, Capt D's, Chipotle Mexican, El Nopal Mexican, Mai Thai, McDonald's, Penn Sta Subs, Rally's, Red Lobster, Subway, Wendy's 🛏 Holiday Inn, Howard Johnson, Knights Inn, Motel 6, Quality Inn, Super 8 ⊙ Cadillac, funpark, Subaru, W 🍴 Marathon/dsl, Murphy USA/dsl, Speedway/dsl 🍴 Arby's, Chick-fil-a, Dave&Buster's, KFC, Little Caesar's, LJ Silver, outback, Ponderosa, Waffle House, White Castle 🛏 Magnuson Hotel, Travelodge ⊙ CarX, Costco/dsl, Midas, O'Reilly Parts, PepBoys, Tire Discounters, Tires+, Walgreens

178 KY 536, Mt Zion Rd, E 🍴 Marathon/Rally's/dsl, Speedway/dsl, Sunoco/Subway/dsl 🍴 Buffalo Bob's, Chopsticks, GoldStar Chili, Hot Head Burritos, Jersey Mike's Subs, La Fuentes Mexican, La Rosa's Pizza, Mad Mike's Burgers, Sonic, Steak'n Shake, Taco Bell ⊙ AutoZone, Goodyear/auto, Kroger

177mm Welcome Ctr sb/Ⓡⓢ nb, full ♿ facilities, litter barrels, 🚻, 🐾, RV dump, vending

175 KY 338, Richwood, E 🍴 Ⓟⓘⓛⓞⓣ/Subway/dsl/24hr, TA/BP/Country Pride/Taco Bell/dsl/24hr/@ 🍴 Arby's, Burger King, White Castle 🛏 Richwood Inn, W 🍴 BP/dsl, Ⓟⓘⓛⓞⓣ/Subway/dsl/scales/24hr, Shell/dsl 🍴 GoldStar Chili, Gourmet Cafe, Hong Kong Cafe, McDonald's, Papa Dino's Pizza, Penn Sta Subs, Skyline Chili, Snappy Tomato Pizza, Waffle House, Wendy's 🛏 EconoLodge, Holiday Inn Express ⊙ to Big Bone Lick SP

173 I-71 S, to Louisville

171 KY 14, KY 16, to Verona, Walton, E 🍴 BP/dsl, Marathon/DQ/dsl 🍴 China Moon, El Toro Mexican, McDonald's, Pizza Hut, Starbucks, Subway, Waffle House ⊙ AT&T, AutoZone, Kohl's, Kroger/dsl, Tire Discounters, URGENT CARE,

171 Continued
Walton Drug, W 🍴 ⚜FLYING J/Denny's/dsl/scales/24hr ⊙ Blue Beacon, Delightful Days RV Ctr, Oak Creek Camping (1mi), to Big Bone Lick SP, vet

168mm ⊙ weigh sta/rest haven sb

166 KY 491, Crittenden, E ⛽ BP/dsl, Sunoco/dsl 🍴 McDonald's ⊙ Chrysler/Dodge/Jeep, Cincinnati S Camping (2mi), W 🍴 Marathon/dsl, Shell/Gold Star Chili 🍴 China Castle, Subway, Wendy's ⊙ $General, Grant Co Drugs

159 KY 22, to Owenton, Dry Ridge, E 🍴 BP, Shell/dsl, Speedway/dsl 🍴 Arby's, Burger King, Happy Dragon Chinese, KFC/Taco Bell, La Rosa's, LJ Silver, McDonald's, Pizza Hut, Skyline Chili, Subway, Waffle House, Wendy's 🛏 Microtel, Red Roof Inn ⊙ $General, Buick/Chevrolet, 🅗, O'Reilly Parts, Verizon, Walmart, W 🍴 Marathon/dsl, Speedway/dsl 🍴 Beavis Cafe/Bakery, Big Boy, Cracker Barrel 🛏 Hampton Inn, Quality Inn ⊙ Camper Village, Dry Ridge TowneCtr, Sav-A-Lot, Tire Discounters, Toyota

156 Barnes Rd, E ⊙ 🅗

154 KY 36, Williamstown, E 🍴 Marathon/dsl, Shell/dsl ⊙ 🅗, to Kincaid Lake SP, W 🍴 Sunoco/dsl 🍴 El Jalisco Mexican 🛏 Best Value Inn, Sunrise Inn

144 KY 330, to Owenton, Corinth, E 🍴 Noble's Trk Plaza/rest./dsl, Sunoco/dsl, W 🍴 BP 🍴 North Star Cafe 🛏 North Star Inn

136 KY 32, to Sadieville, E 🍴 Ⓛⓞⓥⓔⓢ/Hardee's/dsl/scales/24hr

130.5mm weigh sta nb

129 rd 620, Cherry Blossom Wy, E 🍴 Ⓟⓘⓛⓞⓣ/Wendy's/dsl/scales/24hr/@ 🍴 Waffle House 🛏 Days Inn, Motel 6, W 🍴 Ⓟⓘⓛⓞⓣ/McDonald's/dsl/scales/24hr, Shell ⊙ Whispering Hills RV Park (3mi)

127mm Welcome Ctr sb/Ⓡⓢ both lanes, full ♿ facilities, litter barrels, petwalk, 🚻, 🐾, vending

126 US 62, to US 460, Georgetown, E 🍴 Marathon/dsl, Murphy USA/dsl 🍴 Applebee's, Asian Royal Buffet, Big Boy, Buffalo Wild Wings, Gold Star Chili, Jimmy John's, McDonald's, O'Charley's, Papa John's, Penn Sta Subs, Pepe's Mexican, Qdoba, Starbucks, Steak'n Shake, Subway 🛏 Holiday Inn Express ⊙ AT&T, Kohl's, Lowe's, Tire Discounters, URGENT CARE, Verizon, Walmart/Subway, W 🍴 Marathon, Shell/Subway, Speedway/dsl 🍴 Cane's, Chick-fil-A, Cracker Barrel, Culver's, Fazoli's, KFC, Panera Bread, Ruby Tuesday, Waffle House 🛏 Baymont Inn, Best Western, Comfort Suites, Country Inn&Suites, Fairfield Inn, Hampton Inn, Hilton Garden, Microtel, Super 8 ⊙ Buick/Chevrolet, Chrysler/Dodge/Jeep, 🅗, same as 125, to Georgetown Coll

125 US 460 (from nb), Georgetown, E 🍴 BP, Shell 🍴 FatKats Pizza 🛏 Knights Inn, W 🍴 Swifty/dsl, Valero/dsl 🍴 Arby's, DQ, Little Caesar's, LJ Silver, Taco Bell, Wendy's 🛏 Winner's Circle Motel ⊙ $Tree, Advance Parts, BigLots, Camping World, Midas, Outlets/Famous Brands, same as 126

*(left margin, vertical) FLORENCE*
*(right margin, vertical) DRY RIDGE   GEORGETOWN*
KY

INTERSTATE 75 Cont'd

Exit #	Services
120	rd 1973, to Ironworks Pike, KY Horse Park, E 🅞 KY Horse Park Camping, W 🅖 BP/dsl, Shell/dsl 🅞 H
118	I-64 W, to Frankfort, Louisville
115	rd 922, Lexington, E 🅖 Shell/Subway/dsl 🍴 Cracker Barrel, McDonald's, Waffle House 🛏 Best Western Global, Fairfield Inn, La Quinta, Sheraton 🅞 SaddleHorse Museum (4mi), W 🍴 Marathon/dsl 🍴 Cortland's Kitchen, Denny's, Happy Dragon Chinese 🛏 Clarion, Embassy Suites, Marriott/rest. 🅞 museum
113	US 27, US 68, to Paris, Lexington, E 🅖 BP/dsl, Speedway/dsl 🍴 Waffle House 🛏 Ramada Inn, W 🍴 Marathon/dsl, Shell, Shell/dsl 🍴 Arby's, Burger King, Capt D's, Donato's Pizza, DQ, Fazoli's, Golden Corral, Hardee's, Horseshoes Grill, Little Caesar's, McDonald's, Penn Sta Subs, Rally's, Subway, Taco Bell, Wendy's, Zaxby's 🛏 Catalina Motel, Days Inn, Red Roof Inn 🅞 Advance Parts, AutoZone, Bluegrass RV Ctr, Chevrolet, CVS Drug, Northside RV Ctr, O'Reilly Parts, Rupp Arena, to UK, Walmart
111	I-64 E, to Huntington, WV
110	US 60, Lexington, E 🅖 AC&T/dsl, W 🅖 Exxon/dsl, Murphy USA/dsl, Shell/dsl, Speedway/dsl, Sunoco/dsl, Thorntons/dsl 🍴 A&W Cafe, Arby's, Bob Evans, Calistoga Cafe, Cane's Chicken, China 88, Cracker Barrel, FirstWatch Cafe, McDonald's, McDonald's, Smashing Tomato, Starbucks, Subway, Tom+Chee Rest., Waffle House, Waffle House, Wendy's 🛏 Baymont Inn, Comfort Inn, Country Inn&Suites, Guesthouse Inn, Hampton Inn, Holiday Inn Express, Howard Johnson, Microtel, Motel 6, Quality Inn, Red Roof Inn, Super 8 🅞 auto repair, Hobby Lobby, H, KOA (4mi), Lowe's, Rite Aid, Walmart/Subway
108	Man O War Blvd, E 🅖 Shell 🍴 Freddy's 🅞 Cabela's, Costco/gas, Rite Aid, W 🅖 Marathon/dsl, Meijer/dsl, Shell/KFC/Pizza Hut/Wendy's/dsl 🍴 Applebee's, Arby's, Asuka Grill, Backyard Burger, BD Mongolian Grill, Big Boy, Blaze Pizza, BoneFish Grill, Carino's, Carrabba's, Cheddar's, Chick-fil-A, Chipotle Mexican, Coldstone, Culver's, Fazoli's, GoldStar Chili, IChing Asian, Logan's Roadhouse, Malone's, McDonald's, Old Chicago, Outback Steaks, Qdoba, Rafferty's, Red Lobster, Saul Good Rest., Starbucks, Steak'n Shake, Subway, Taco Bell, Ted's MT Grill, TGIFriday's, Waffle House 🛏 Courtyard, Hilton Garden, Homewood Suites, Hyatt Place, Residence Inn, Sleep Inn, TownePlace Suites 🅞 AT&T, Audi, Barnes&Noble, Best Buy, BigLots, Dick's, GNC, Gordmans, Harley-Davidson, H, Kohl's, Marshall's, Michael's, Old Navy, Petsmart, Ross, Staples, Target, Tire Discounters, Verizon, Walgreens
104	KY 418, Lexington, E 🅖 BP/dsl, Shell/McDonald's 🛏 Clarion, Comfort Inn, Days Inn, EconoLodge, La Quinta, W 🅖 BP/dsl, Speedway/dsl 🍴 Wendy's 🅞 H
99	US 25 N, US 421 N, Clays Ferry
98mm	Kentucky River
97	US 25 S, US 421 S, Clay's Ferry, W 🍴 WOW/dsl/scales/24hr
95	rd 627, to Boonesborough, Winchester, E 🅖 💗 Loves/Arby's/dsl/scales/24hr 🅞 camping, Ft Boonesborough SP, Speedco, W 🍴 Shell/Subway/dsl
90	US 25, US 421, Richmond, E 🅖 Shell 🍴 Cracker Barrel 🛏 La Quinta, Red Roof Inn, Relax Inn, Super 7, W 🅖 BP, Gulf/dsl, Marathon, Shell, Valero 🍴 Big Boy, DQ, Hanger's Rest., Hardee's, McDonald's, Pizza Hut, Subway, Taco Bell, Waffle House, Wendy's 🛏 Days Inn, Super 8 🅞 $General, vet
87	rd 876, Richmond, E 🅖 BP/dsl, Marathon/dsl, Shell/dsl, Speedway/dsl 🍴 A&W/LJ Silver, Arby's, Casa Fiesta Mexican, Cook-Out, Domino's, Fazoli's, Fong's Chinese, Hardee's, Hooters,

87	Continued
	King Buffet, Lee's Chicken, Little Caesar's, McAlister's Deli, McDonald's, Papa John's, Qdoba, Rally's, Subway, Taco Bell, Waffle House, Wendy's 🛏 Best Western, Country Hearth Inn, Quality Quarters Inn 🅞 $General, Aamco, Ace Hardware, AT&T, BigLots, Goodyear/auto, H, Rite Aid, to EKU, vet, W 🅖 Marathon/Circle K, Shell/dsl 🍴 Bob Evans, Buffalo Wild Wings, Burger King, Cane's, Chick-fil-A, Culver's, Firehouse Subs, Golden Corral, IHOP, Koto Japanese, Logan's Roadhouse, Olive Garden, Panera Bread, Ryan's, Starbucks, Steak'n Shake, Subway 🛏 Comfort Suites, Hampton Inn, Holiday Inn Express, Quality Inn, TownePlace Suites 🅞 Belk, Dick's, GNC, JC Penney, Meijer/dsl, Michaels, Petsmart, Tire Discounters, TJ Maxx, Verizon
83	to US 25, rd 2872, Duncannon Ln, Richmond, E 🅞 Bluegrass Army Depot
77	rd 595, Berea, E 🅞 H, KY Artisan Ctr/Cafe/Travelers Ctr, to Berea Coll, W 🍴 Shell/dsl, Valero/Subway/dsl 🍴 Smokehouse Grill 🛏 Motel 6, Quality Inn, Red Roof Inn 🅞 $General
76	KY 21, Berea, E 🅖 BP, Circle K, Shell/Burger King, Speedway/dsl 🍴 A&W/LJ Silver, Arby's, Cracker Barrel, Dinner Bell Rest., Gold Star Chili, Hong Kong Buffet, Mario's Pizza, McDonald's, Old Town Amish Rest., Papa John's, Pizza Hut, Subway, Taco Bell, Wendy's, Wings Etc, Yamato Japanese 🛏 Best Value Inn, Holiday Motel, Knights Inn 🅞 $General, $Tree, H, URGENT CARE, Walmart, W 🍴 76 Fuel/dsl, BP/dsl, Marathon/dsl 🍴 Lee's Chicken 🛏 EconoLodge, Fairfield Inn, Holiday Inn Express 🅞 Oh! Kentucky Camping, tires, Walnut Meadow RV Park
62	US 25, to KY 461, Renfro Valley, E 🍴 Derby City/rest./dsl, Shell 🍴 Hardee's, Little Caesar's 🛏 Baymont Inn 🅞 KOA (2mi), Renfro Valley RV Park/rest, W 🅖 BP, Marathon/dsl, Marathon/Wendy's/dsl, Shell 🍴 Arby's, El Dorado Mexican, Godfather's/Subway, KFC, Limestone Grill, McDonald's, Taco Bell 🛏 Days Inn, EconoLodge 🅞 H, Lake Cumberland, Rite Aid, to Big South Fork NRA
59	US 25, to Livingston, Mt Vernon, E 🍴 Shell, TravelCtr/dsl 🍴 El Cazador Mexican, Pizza Hut 🛏 Kastle Inn, W 🅖 BP 🛏 Mtn View Inn
51mm	Rockcastle River
49	KY 909, to US 25, Livingston, E 🅞 Camp Wildcat Bfd, W 🍴 49er/dsl/24hr 🅞 RV Park, truck/tire repair
41	rd 80, to Somerset, London, E 🍴 Speedway/dsl 🍴 Arby's, Azteca Mexican, Burger King, Gondolier Italian, KFC, McDonald's, Subway, White Castle 🛏 Days Inn, EconoLodge, Quality Inn, Red Roof Inn, Super 8 🅞 $General, Advance Parts, AutoZone, CVS Drug, H, Kroger/deli, Parsley's Tire/repair, st police W 🅖 BP/Home Cooker/dsl/24hr, Marathon/McDonald's, Shell, pizza, Sunoco/dsl, Valero/dsl 🍴 Buffalo Wings&Rings, Cheddar's, Cracker Barrel, LJ Silver, Old Town Grill, Shiloh Roadhouse, Smokin' Barrel BBQ, Subway, Taco Bell, Waffle House, Wendy's 🛏 Budget Host, Fairfield Inn, Hampton Inn 🅞 Dog Patch Ctr
38	rd 192, to Rogers Pkwy, London, E 🅖 BP/dsl, Marathon, Murphy USA/dsl, Shell/Mama's Subs/dsl, Speedway/dsl 🍴 Big Boy, Burger King, Capt D's, Dino's Italian, Domino's, DQ, Dunkin'/Baskin Robins, El Dorado Mexican, Fazoli's, Golden Corral, Great Wall Chinese, Hardee's, Huddle House, Krystal, McDonald's, Penn Sta Subs, Pizza Hut, Starbucks, Steak'n Shake, Subway, Sun Buffet, Taco Bell 🛏 Baymont Inn, Comfort Suites, Country Inn&Suites, Holiday Inn Express, Microtel 🅞 $Tree, Advance Parts, 🔧, AT&T, camping

LEXINGTON

BEREA

LONDON

RICHMOND

KY

INTERSTATE 75 Cont'd

38 Continued
E Kentucky RV Ctr, Ford/Lincoln, Kroger/dsl, Lowe's, NAPA, Nissan, Office Depot, Peterbilt, Rogers Pkwy to Manchester/Hazard, to Levi Jackson SP, USPO, Verizon, Walgreens, Walmart/Subway, W 🅾 🄷, to Laurel River Lake RA

34mm truck haven, weigh sta both lanes

30.5mm Laurel River

29 US 25, US 25E, Corbin, E 🅰 Marathon, Murphy USA, 🄿🄸🄻🄾🅃/McDonald's/Subway/dsl/scales/24hr, Spur Oil 🍴 David's Steaks, DQ, Huddle House, Mi Jalisco Mexican, Taco Bell 🛏 Super 8 🅾 Aldi Foods, AutoZone, Blue Beacon, Lowe's, to Cumberland Gap NP, Walmart/Subway, W 🍴 BP/Krystal/dsl, ♥Love's/Hardee's/dsl/scales/24hr/@, Marathon, Shell/dsl 🍴 Cracker Barrel, Sonny's BBQ 🛏 Baymont Inn, Fairfield Inn, Hampton Inn, Knights Inn, Quality Suites 🅾 KOA, tires/repair, to Laurel River Lake RA

25 US 25W, Corbin, E 🅰 Speedway/dsl 🍴 Applebee's, Arby's, Bojangle's, Burger King, Cayenne SW Grill, CB's Grill, Dino's Italian, McDonald's, Taco Bell, Wendy's 🛏 EconoLodge, Holiday Inn Express, Landmark Inn, Red Roof Inn 🅾 auto repair/tires, 🄷, W 🍴 Shell 🍴 El Dorado Mexican, Subway, Waffle House 🛏 Best Western 🅾 to Cumberland Falls SP

15 US 25W, to Williamsburg, Goldbug, W 🍴 Shell, Xpress/dsl 🅾 Cumberland Falls SP

14.5mm Cumberland River

11 KY 92, Williamsburg, E 🍴 BP/dsl, Shell 🍴 Arby's, El Dorado Mexican, Hardee's, KFC, Little Caesar's, McDonald's, Pizza Hut, Subway, Taco Bell 🛏 Budget Inn, Cumberland Inn, Super 8 🅾 $General, Advance Parts, AutoZone, Family$, museum, Sav-A-Lot, Windham Drug, W 🍴 🄿🄸🄻🄾🅃/Wendy's/dsl/scales/24hr, Shell 🍴 Burger King, DQ, Huddle House, Krystal, LJ Silver 🛏 Hampton Inn 🅾 $Tree, to Big South Fork NRA, Walmart

1.5mm Welcome Ctr nb, full 🅰 facilities, litter barrels, petwalk, 🄲, 🛏, vending

0mm Kentucky/Tennessee state line

INTERSTATE 275 (Cincinnati)

Exit #	Services
84	I-71, I-75, N to Cincinnati, S to Lexington, Louisville

83 US 25, US 42, US 127, S 🍴 Shell/Circle K/dsl, Thornton's/dsl 🍴 Abuelo's Mexican, Buffalo Wings&Rings, Carrabba's, Chipotle, Coldstone, Dewey's Pizza, Donato's Pizza, First Watch Cafe, Five Guys, Gold Star Chili, Jimmy John's, KFC, Max&Erma's, McAlister's Deli, McDonald's, Moe's SW Grill, Panera Bread, Starbucks, Subway, Taco Bell, The Pub, Wendy's 🅾 $Tree, CarX, Dillard's, GNC, K-Mart, Verizon, Walgreens

82 rd 1303, Turkeyfoot Rd, S 🍴 TGIFriday's 🅾 🄷

80 KY 17, Independence, N 🍴 Speedway/dsl, United/dsl 🍴 Arby's, Big Boy, Bob Evans, Buffalo Wild Wings, Burger King, El Ranchero Mexican, Golden Corral, Hot Head Burrito, Penn Sta Subs, Snappy Tomato Pizza, Subway, Taco Bell, TX Roadhouse, Wendy's, White Castle 🅾 AT&T, Petco, TireDiscounters, Verizon, Walmart/Subway, S 🍴 Thornton's/dsl 🍴 McDonald's, Waffle House

79 KY 16, Taylor Mill Rd, N 🍴 BP, Marathon, Speedway/dsl 🍴 Domino's, Goldstar Chili, McDonald's, Peking Chinese, Subway, Wendy's 🅾 $General, $Tree, Big Lots, Burlington Coats, CVS Drug, Kroger/gas, URGENT CARE, Walgreens,

79 Continued
S 🍴 BP/dsl 🍴 El Jinete Mexican, Graeter's Rest., KFC/Taco Bell, La Rosa's Pizza, Marco's Pizza, McDonald's, Original Wok, Skyline Chili, Subway 🅾 Remke's Mkt, Verizon, vet

77 KY 9, Maysville, Wilder, N 🛏 Hampton Inn, S 🍴 Speedway/dsl, Thorntons/dsl, UDF/dsl 🍴 DQ, Goldstar Chili, McDonald's, Mellow Mushroom Pizza, Subway, Waffle House 🛏 Country Inn Suites

76 Three Mile Rd

74a Alexandria (exits left from sb), to US 27

74b I-471 N, Newport, Cincinnati, N 🅾 🄷

73mm OH River, OH/KY state line

72 US 52 W, Kellogg Ave, S 🍴 Coney Island Funpark, Marathon (2mi)

71 US 52 E, New Richmond

69 5 Mile Rd, W 🍴 BP/dsl 🍴 Big Boy, Carrabba's, Firehouse Subs, IHOP, La Rosa's Mexican, McDonald's, Moe's SW Grill, Outback, TGIFriday's 🅾 CVS, 🄷, Kroger/gas, TireDiscounters

65 OH 125, Beechmont Ave, Amelia, E 🍴 Shell, Speedway, UDF/dsl 🍴 Hibachi Grill, Los Cazadores, Red Lobster, Ron's Chinese, Tender Towne, Wendy's 🛏 Beechmont Motel 🅾 CarX, Family$, Ford, Lowe's, Tires+, Walgreens, W 🍴 BP, Marathon, Speedway/dsl 🍴 Big Boy, Bob Evans, Burger King, Butterbee's Grille, Chick-fil-A, Chipotle Mexican, McDonald's, Olive Garden, Peking Chinese, Skyline Chili, Smashburger, Starbucks, Waffle House, White Castle 🛏 Best Western, Days Inn, Red Roof Inn 🅾 $Tree, Aldi Foods, AT&T, Audi, AutoZone, BigLots, Goodyear/auto, Home Depot, Honda, Kroger, O'Reilly Parts, Staples, Sumerel Tire/repair, Target, TireDiscounters, TJ Maxx, Toyota, Tuesday Morning, Verizon

63b a OH 32, Batavia, Newtown, E 🍴 UDF 🍴 Applebee's, Big Boy, Bob Evans, Burger King, Chick-fil-A, China Buffet, Chipotle, ChuckE-Cheese, City BBQ, Firehouse Subs, Five Guys, Fuji Steaks, Golden Corral, Hwy 55 Cafe, Jimmy John's, KFC, LaRosa's Pizza, LJ Silver, Logan's Roadhouse, Longhorn Steaks, McDonalds, O'Charley's, Panera Bread, Penn Sta Subs, Pizza Hut, Popeye's, Skyline Chili, Skyline Chili, Sonic, Starbucks, Steak'n Shake, Taco Bell, Wendy's, White Castle 🛏 Comfort Inn, Fairfield Inn, Hampton Inn, Holiday Inn 🅾 $Tree, Advance Parts, Aldi Foods, AT&T, Best Buy, Dick's, Dillard's, Firestone/auto, Hobby Lobby, JC Penney, Jo-Ann Fabrics, Jungle Jim's Mkt, Kohl's, Kroger/dsl, Marshall's, Meijer/dsl, PepBoys, Petsmart, Sam's Club/gas, Sears, URGENT CARE, Walmart/Subway, W 🍴 Marathon, Speedway/dsl, Sunoco 🍴 Gold Star Chili, Gramma's Pizza 🅾 Kroger, Midas

59 OH 452, US 50, Milford Pkwy, Hillsboro, S 🍴 UDF/dsl 🍴 Buffalo Wild Wings, Cracker Barrel, Dos Amigos, Goldstar Chili, Mint Bistro, Quaker Steak&Lube, Red Robin, Roney's Rest., Ruby Tuesday, Subway, TX Roadhouse, Wendy's 🛏 Homewood Suites 🅾 Office Depot, Petsmart, Target, Verizon, Walmart

INTERSTATE 275 (Cincinnati) Cont'd

Exit #	Services
57	OH 28, Blanchester, Milford, **0-1 mi N** 🅕 Arby's, Burger King, Chipotle Mexican, Donato's Pizza, DQ, Dunkin', Goldstar Chili, IHOP, KFC, Panera Bread, Papa John's, Penn Sta Subs, Skyline Chili, Sonic, Steak'n Shake, Subway, Taco Bell, Wendy's, White Castle 🅞 GNC, Home Depot, Kroger/dsl, Lowe's, Meijer/dsl, Petco, URGENT CARE, **S** 🅕 Thornton's/dsl 🅕 Bob Evans, Cazadore's Mexican, Putter's Grill, Roosters Grill 🛏 Holiday Inn Express 🅞 Goodyear/auto, vet
54	Wards Corner Rd, **N** 🅖 BP, **S** 🅖 UDF/dsl 🅕 Big Boy, Dominos, Goldstar Chili, Subway 🛏 Hilton Garden
53mm	Little Miami River
52	Loveland, Indian Hill, **N** 🅖 Marathon/Circle K/dsl, Shell, Speedway/dsl 🅕 Arby's, Burger King, Penn Sta Subs, Pizza Hut, Skyline Chili, Starbucks, Subway, Taco Bell, Wendy's 🅞 CVS Drug, Indian Motorcycles, URGENT CARE, Verizon, vet, Walgreens
50	US 22, OH 3, Montgomery, **N** 🅖 Shell 🅕 Buffalo Wild Wings, Chili's, deSha's Tavern, Dewey's Pizza, Donato's Puzza, DQ, Johnny Chan's, Melting Pot, Panera Bread, Starbucks, Subway, Taco Casa, Which Wich? 🅞 Acura, AT&T, Fresh Thyme Mkt, GNC, Hyundai, Kroger/dsl, TJ Maxx, **S** 🅖 BP/dsl, Shell/Subway/Dunkin' 🅕 El Jinete, Goldstar Chili, McDonald's, Merlot's Rest., Skyline Chili, Wendy's 🅞 Ⓗ
49	I-71 N to Columbus, S to Cincinnati
47	Reed Hartman Hwy, Blue Ash, **S** 🅕 Chipotle, Jersey Mike's, Jimmy John's, Kanpai Japanese, Ruby Tuesday, Smashburger, Starbucks, Tropical Cafe 🛏 DoubleTree, Hyatt Place, Quality Inn, Residence Inn
46	US 42, Mason, **N** 🅖 BP 🅕 Chipotle, KFC, Marie's Scrambler, Max&Erma's, McDonald's, Skyline Chili, Taco Bell, Wendy's, White Castle 🛏 Holiday Inn, Motel 6, Woodspring Suites 🅞 Advance Parts, CVS Drug, Goodyear/auto, Kroger/dsl, Walgreens, **S** 🅖 Marathon/dsl, Shell, Speedway/dsl, UDF/dsl 🅕 Arby's, El Rancho Grande, Waffle House 🛏 Days Inn 🅞 Midas, Mr Transmission, Tire Discounters
44	Mosteller Rd, **N** 🅕 Subway, **S** 🛏 Homewood Suites
43b a	I-75, N to Dayton, S to Cincinnati
42	OH 747, Springdale, Glendale, **N** 🅖 Sunoco, Thorntons 🅞 $General, Staples, **S** 🅖 Shell/dsl 🅕 BJ's Brewhouse, Blue Agave Mexican, Chick-fil-A, Chipotle, Firehouse Subs, La Rosa's Pizza, McDonald's, Noodles&Co, Panera Bread, Steak'n Shake, TGIFriday's 🅞 BigLots, Chevrolet, Chrysler/Dodge/Jeep, Dillard's, Hancock Fabrics, Hobby Lobby, Lowe's, Macy's, Michael's, Office Depot, Petsmart, Sears/auto, TJ Maxx, Verizon
41	OH 4, Springdale Pkwy, **N** 🅖 Shell, Speedway/dsl, Sunoco/dsl 🅕 Burger King, Hooters, Olive Garden, Pappadeaux, Rib City, Skyline Chili, SmoQ Rest., Wendy's 🛏 La Quinta, **S** 🅖 BP, UDF/dsl 🅕 Beef'O'Brady's, DJ's Tavern, DQ, Goldstar Chili, Outback Steaks, Penn Sta Subs, Subway, White Castle 🛏 Extended Stay America, Howard Johnson, Super 8 🅞 CVS Drug, Family$, O'Reilly Parts
39	Winton Rd, Winton Woods, **N** 🅖 BP 🅕 Asian Buffet, Chipotle, Golden Corral, IHOP, McDonald's, Old Spaghetti Factory, Panera Bread, Red Lobster, Steak'n Shake 🛏 Comfort Suites, Hampton Inn 🅞 Bass Pro Shops, CarMax, Home Depot, Kohl's, Meijer/dsl, Tire Discounters, **S** 🅖 Marathon/dsl, Shell/dsl, UDF/dsl 🅕 Big Boy, Cancun Mexican, China Garden, Cracker Barrel, Izzy's Cafe, Jade House Chinese, Jax Tavern, KFC, La Fiesta Mexican, Papa John's, Penn Sta Subs, Popeye's, Skyline Chili, Starbucks, Subway, Taco Bell, Wendy's

39	Continued 🛏 Quality Inn, SpringHill Suites 🅞 $Tree, AAA, Aldi Foods, A⎯ toZone, Kroger/gas, Tires+, vet, Walmart
36	US 127, Hamilton, Mt Healthy, **N** 🅖 Marathon/Circle⎯ dsl, Speedway 🅕 Wendy's 🅞 CVS Drug, **S** 🅖 Shell/dsl, S⎯ noco, UDF 🅕 Big Boy, China Island, La Rosa's Pizza, Lit⎯ Caesars, McDonald's, Rally's, Subway, Taco Bell 🅞 Advan⎯ Parts, Family$, O'Reilly Parts
33	US 27, US 126, Colerain Ave, **N** 🅖 Speedway/dsl 🅕 Burg⎯ King, Skyline Chili, Steak'n Shake, Wendy's 🅞 Dick's, J⎯ Ann, Lowe's, Petsmart, TireDiscounters, Walmart/Subw⎯ **S** 🅖 Shell 🅕 Applebee's, Arby's, Big Boy, Bob Evans, Buffa⎯ Wild Wings, Burger King, Cheddar's, Chipotle, Five Guys, Ho⎯ eybaked Ham, IHOP, KFC, La Piñata Mexican, La Rosa's Pizza,⎯ Silver, Logan's Roadhouse, Longhorn Steaks, McDonald's, O⎯ ive Garden, Outback Steaks, Panera Bread, Pizza Hut, Po⎯ eye's, Potbelly, Qdoba, Red Lobster, Starbucks, Taco Bell, TGIF⎯ day's, White Castle 🅞 Aldi Foods, AT&T, Best Buy, GNC, Hob⎯ Lobby, JC Penney, Kroger, Macy's, Marshalls, Meijer/dsl, M⎯ chael's, Old Navy, Sumerel Tire/auto, Tires+, Tuesday Mor⎯ ing, URGENT CARE, Verizon, Walgreens
31	Ronald Reagan Hwy, Blue Rock Rd
28	I-74, US 52, E to Cincinnati, W to Indianapolis
25	I-74, E to Cincinnati, W to Indianapolis
21	Kilby Rd 🅞 Indian Springs Camping (3mi)
18mm	Ohio/Indiana State Line
16	US 50, Greendale, Lawrenceburg, **W** 🅖 Ameristop/dsl, She⎯ Circle K/Subway, Sinclair/dsl 🅕 Buffalo Wings&Rings, Burg⎯ King, KFC, La Rosa's Pizza, Maverick's Grill, McDonald's, Ta⎯ Bell, Waffle House, White Castle 🛏 Baymont Inn, Holiday I⎯ Express, Quality Inn, Riverside Inn 🅞 casino, Chevrolet, Chry⎯ ler/Dodge/Jeep, Ford, TireDiscounters, Walgreens
14mm	Kentucky/Indiana state line, Ohio River
11	Petersburg
8	Worldwide Blvd
6b a	KY 237, Hebron, **N** 🅖 Shell/DQ/dsl, UDF/dsl 🅕 Agave Me⎯ ican, Arby's, China Wok, Hebron Grille, Jets Pizza, Jimm⎯ John's, Longnecks Grill, Papa John's, Penn Sta Subs, Pizz⎯ Hut, Poseidon's Pizza, Strong's Pizza, Wendy's 🅞 Remke⎯ Mkt, URGENT CARE, **S** 🅖 Speedway/Subway/dsl 🅕 Burg⎯ King, Chipotle, Skyline Chili, Sonic, Waffle House
4a b	KY 212, KY 20, **N** 🅖 Shell/dsl 🛏 Comfort Suites, Country Inn⎯ Suites, Hampton Inn, Marriott, **S** 🛏 DoubleTree (2mi) 🅞 🅞,⎯
2	Mineola Pike, **N** 🅖 Marathon/Rally's/Subway/dsl 🅕 Ra⎯ ly's 🛏 Holiday Inn, Quality Inn, **S** 🅖 Shell/dsl 🅕 Hot Hea⎯ Burrito, Subway 🛏 Courtyard Inn, Residence Inn

NOTES

LOUISIANA

◥E INTERSTATE 10

Exit #	Services
274mm	Louisiana/Mississippi state line, Pearl River
272mm	West Pearl River
270mm	Welcome Ctr wb, full 🛏 facilities, info, litter barrels, petwalk, 🅲, 🅿, RV dump
267b	I-12 W, to Baton Rouge
267a	I-59 N, to Meridian
266	US 190, Slidell, **N** 🅿 RaceTrac/dsl, Shell/dsl, TA/Country Pride/dsl/scales/24hr/@ 🍴 Baskin-Robbins, Cane's, Chick-fil-A, Copeland's Rest., Firehouse Subs, Golden Dragon Chinese, Los Tres Amigos, McDonald's, NO Rest., NOLA Southern Grill, Panda Express, Rotolo's Pizza, Sonic, Subway, Taco Bell 🛏 Best Value Inn, Best Western+, Country Inn Suites, Motel 6, Red Roof Inn 🅾 🛏 CVS Drug, Firestone/auto, GNC, Harley-Davidson, Hobby Lobby, Office Depot, O'Reilly Parts, PepBoys, Petco, Rouse's Mkt, U-Haul, Walgreens, **S** 🅿 Chevron/dsl, Murphy USA/dsl, RaceTrac/dsl 🍴 Applebee's, Big Easy Diner, Cracker Barrel, Fuji Yama Hibachi, Hooters, McAlister's Deli, Outback Steaks, Popeye's, Sonic, Starbucks, TX Roadhouse, Waffle House 🛏 Days Inn, La Quinta, Wingate Inn 🅾 🛏 $General, $Tree, AT&T, CVS, Home Depot, Lowe's, repair/transmissions, vet, Walgreens, Walmart/Subway
265	US 190, Fremaux Ave, **N** 🅿 RaceTrac/dsl 🍴 BJ's Rest., Cheddar's, Chipotle, Five Guys, Longhorn Steaks, Lost Cajun, Panera Bread, Red Robin, Saltgrass Steaks, Starbucks, Which Wich? 🛏 TownePlace Suites 🅾 BAM, Best Buy, Dick's, Dillard's, GNC, Goodyear/auto, Kohl's, Michael's, Petsmart, TJ Maxx, Verizon
263	LA 433, Slidell, **N** 🅿 Exxon/Circle K/dsl, Shell/dsl, Valero 🍴 Oishii Buffet, Waffle House 🛏 Hampton Inn, Super 8 🅾 repair, **S** 🅿 Circle K/Subway/scales/dsl, Exxon/Circle K/dsl 🍴 McDonald's, Taco Bell, Wendy's 🛏 Holiday Inn 🅾 Buick/GMC, Chevrolet/Cadillac, Chrysler/Dodge/Jeep, Ford, Honda, Hyundai, Kia, Nissan, NO East RV Park (1mi), Pinecrest RV Park, Toyota
261	Oak Harbor Blvd, Eden Isles, **N** 🅿 Exxon/Circle K/dsl 🍴 Waffle House 🛏 Sleep Inn, **S** 🅿 Shell/Subway/dsl 🅾 Bayou Country Store
255mm	Lake Pontchartrain
254	US 11, to Northshore, Irish Bayou
251	Bayou Sauvage NWR, **S** 🅾 swamp tours
248	Michoud Blvd
246 b a	I-510 S, LA 47 N, S to Chalmette, N to Little Woods
245	Bullard Ave, **N** 🅿 Chevron/dsl, Shell/dsl 🍴 Bullard Diner, Waffle House 🛏 Comfort Suites, Holiday Inn Express 🅾 Family$, Honda, **S** 🅿 Chevron/dsl, Shell 🍴 Burger King, IHOP, KFC/Taco Bell, McDonald's, NO Rest., Papa John's, Subway, Super Cajun Seafood, Wendy's 🛏 Motel 6, Quality Inn 🅾 Chrysler/Dodge/Jeep, Home Depot, Nissan, NTB, PepBoys, Toyota, Walgreens, Walmart
244	Read Blvd, **N** 🅿 Shell/dsl 🍴 McDonald's 🅾 Walgreens, **S** 🅿 EZ Stop/dsl 🍴 Popeye's, Subway, Waffle House, Wendy's 🛏 Days Inn, Knights Inn, Wyndham Garden 🅾 🛏 CVS, SaveALot Foods

242	Crowder Blvd, **N** 🅿 Chevron, **S** 🅿 Crowder Ctr, Exxon/dsl 🍴 Subway 🛏 Rodeway Inn 🅾 Family$, Walgreens, $General
241	Morrison Rd, **N** 🅿 Big E-Z/dsl, FuelXpress/dsl
240b a	US 90 E, Chef Hwy, Downman Rd, **N** 🅿 Shell/dsl 🛏 Super 8 🅾 Chevrolet, U-Haul, USPO, **S** 🅾 DZ/dsl, DZ/dsl 🅾 Delta Tires
239b a	Louisa St, Almonaster Blvd, **N** 🅿 Big Easy TP/rest./dsl, Chevron/dsl, FuelZone/dsl 🍴 Burger King, Cane's, Church's, McDonald's, Min Moon Chinese, Popeye's, Rally's, Subway, Taco Bell, Waffle House, Wendy's 🛏 Days Inn, EconoLodge, Motel 6 🅾 $General, Family$, Goodyear/auto, Walgreens, Walmart, Winn-Dixie, **S** 🅿 Day&Night/dsl
238b	I-610 W (from wb)
237	Elysian Fields Ave, **N** 🍴 Mardi Gras Trkstp/Subway/dsl 🅾 Lowe's
236c	St. Bernard Ave
236b	LA 39, N Claiborne Ave
236a	Esplanade Ave, downtown
235a	Orleans Ave, to Vieux Carre, French Qtr, **S** 🅿 Chevron/dsl 🛏 Clarion, Marriott, Sheraton
235b	Poydras St, **N** 🅾 🛏, **S** 🅾 to Superdome, downtown
234a	US 90A, Claiborne Ave, to Westbank, **S** 🅾 Superdome
232	US 61, Airline Hwy, Tulane Ave, **N** 🍴 Burger King, **S** 🅿 Exxon, Shell 🍴 McDonald's, Popeye's, Rallys, Subway, Wendy's 🅾 Costco/gas, CVS, Family$, Firestone/auto, Pepboys, to Xavier U, USPO, vet
231b	Florida Blvd, WestEnd
231a	Metairie Rd
230	I-610 E (from eb), to Slidell
229	Bonnabel Blvd

LA

S L I D E L L

🅖 = gas   🍴 = food   🛏 = lodging   🅞 = other   🆁🆂 = rest stop   Copyright 2022 - The Next EXIT ©

INTERSTATE 10 Cont'd

Exit #	Services
228	Causeway Blvd, **N** 🅖 Exxon/dsl, Shell/dsl 🍴 Buffalo Wild Wings, Cheesecake Factory, Cucina Italiana, Outback Steaks, PF Chang's, Red Lobster, Ruth's Chris Steaks, TGIFriday's 🛏 Best Western, Hampton Inn, Ramada 🅞 Dick's, Dillard's, JC Penney, Macy's, Whole Foods Mkt, **S** 🅖 DZ, Exxon/Circle K 🍴 IHOP, Little Tokyo 🛏 Courtyard, Extended Stay America, Holiday Inn, La Quinta, Ramada Inn, Residence Inn, Sheraton
226	Clearview Pkwy, Huey Long Br, **N** 🅖 Chevron/dsl, Exxon/Circle K/dsl 🍴 Cafe Dumonde, Cane's, Chili's, Copeland's Cheesecake Bistro, Corky's BBQ, Don's Seafood Hut, Hooters, Houston's Rest., Izzo's Burrito, Jimmy John's, Popeye's, Romano Italian, Starbucks, Taco Bell, Taco Tico, Zea Rotisserie 🛏 Sleep Inn 🅞 NTB, Target, Walgreens, **S** 🅖 Chevron, Danny&Clyde 🍴 Beijing Chinese, Burger King, Piccadilly, Smoothie King, Subway 🛏 In Town Suites, Super 8 🅞 🅗 AT&T, Buick/GMC, Firestone/auto
225	Veterans Blvd, **N** 🅖 Chevron, DZ/dsl, Shell 🍴 Bonefish, Burger King, Coyote Blues, Denny's, Hooters, McDonald's, Panera Bread, Pei Wei 🛏 La Quinta 🅞 CVS Drug, Honda, Hyundai, Rite Aid, Rouses Mkt, URGENT CARE, **S** 🅖 Shell/dsl 🍴 Burger King, Casa Garcia, ChuckeCheese, Little Caesar's, Louisiana Purchase Kitchen, New Orleans Burgers, O'Henry's, Popeye's, Starbucks, Subway, Tiffin Pancakes, Wendy's 🛏 Evergreen Inn, Wyndham Garden 🅞 $General, Acura, Best Buy, BigLots, BMW, Chevrolet, GNC, Home Depot, Jo-Ann Fabrics, Kia, Lexus, Michael's, Nissan, Office Depot, PepBoys, Petsmart, TJ Maxx, Verizon, vet, VW, Walgreens, Walmart
224	Power Blvd (from wb)
223b a	LA 49, Williams Blvd, **N** 🅖 DZ/dsl, Exxon/dsl, Shell/dsl 🍴 Cafe Dumonde, Cane's Chicken, Fisherman's Cove, IHOP, Popeye's, Rally's, Subway, Taco Bell, Wendy's 🛏 Fairfield Inn 🅞 $Tree, AutoZone, Carmax, Dillards, Family$, Ford, Office Depot, PetCo, Save-a-Lot Foods, Target, TrueValue, Walmart Mkt, **S** 🅖 Exxon/Circle K/dsl, Shell 🍴 American Pie Diner, Brick Oven, Chick-fil-A, Don Jose's Grill, Dot's Diner, KFC/LJ Silver, McDonald's, Pollo Campero, Sonic, Subway, Taco Tico 🛏 Comfort Suites, Contempra Inn, Crowne Plaza, DoubleTree, EconoLodge, Extended Stay America, Holiday Inn, La Quinta, Radisson, Woodspring Suites 🅞 $General, CVS Drug, Family$, Goodyear/auto, NAPA, NTB, Toyota, U-Haul, USPO, Winn-Dixie
221	Loyola Dr, **N** 🅖 Circle K, Exxon/Circle K/dsl, Shell, Shell/dsl 🍴 Church's, Little Caesar's, McDonald's, Popeye's, Rally's, Subway, Taco Bell, VooDoo BBQ 🅞 Advance Parts, Sam's Club/gas, **S** 🅖 Citgo/dsl, DZ 🛏 Red Roof Inn 🅞 $General, 📧, Family$
220	I-310 S, to Houma
214mm	Lake Pontchartrain
210	I-55N (from wb)
209	I-55 N, US 51, to Jackson, LaPlace, Hammond, **N** 🅖 Shell/Huddle House/casino/dsl 🛏 Suburban Lodge, **S** 🅖 Chevron/dsl, Circle K/dsl, 🛢/Subway/dsl/24hr/scales 🍴 Burger King, McDonald's, Waffle House, Wendy's 🛏 Best Western, Days Inn, Hampton Inn, Holiday Inn Express, Quality Inn, TownePlace Suites
207mm	weigh sta both lanes
206	LA 3188 S, La Place, **S** 🅖 Circle K/dsl, Marathon/dsl, Shell/dsl 🛏 Fairfield Inn 🅞 🅗, Chrysler/Dodge/Jeep, Ford, Goodyear/auto
194	LA 641 S, to Gramercy, 4-6 mi **S** 🅖 Marathon, Shell, Taylors/dsl 🍴 Golden Grove Rest., McDonald's, Popeye's 🅞 🅗, plantations
187	US 61, N to Sorrento, S to Gramercy

Exit #	Services
182	LA 22, Sorrento, **N** 🅖 Shell/Popeye's/dsl, Texaco/dsl, Marathon/Subway/dsl/scales/24hr, SJ/dsl 🍴 McDonald's Waffle House 🅞 tourist info
179	LA 44, Gonzales, **1 mi N** 🅖 Exxon/Popingo's Cafe/dsl, Murphy USA/dsl 🍴 Alabasha Cafe, Subway 🅞 $General, Buick/GMC, Chabill's Automotive, Fred's Store, Walgreens
177	LA 30, Gonzales, **N** 🅖 Circle K/dsl, Shell/dsl 🍴 Buffalo Wild Wings, Burger King, Chick-fil-A, El Paso Mexican, Jack-in-the-Box, McDonald's, Outback Steaks, Taco Bell, Waffle House, Zaxby' 🛏 Best Value Inn, Budget Inn, Clarion, Days Inn, Highland Inn Western Inn 🅞 🅗, Home Depot, O'Reilly Parts, **S** 🅖 Marathon dsl, RaceTrac/dsl, Shell/dsl 🍴 Bergeron's, Chili's, Cracker Barrel Don's Seafood Hut, Firehouse Subs, KFC, Logan's Roadhouse, Mooyah Burger, Popeye's, Sonic, Starbucks, Tang Buffet, Tilted Kilt, Wendy's, Which Wich? 🛏 Best Western+, Candlewood Suites, Comfort Suites, Hampton Inn, Holiday Inn Express, Home 2 Suites, La Quinta, Quality Inn, SpringHill Suites, TownePlace Suites 🅞 Cabela's, Tanger/famous brands, Vesta RV Park
173	LA 73, to Geismar, Prairieville, **N** 🅖 Circle K/dsl, Shell/dsl 🅞 vet, **S** 🅖 Exxon/dsl, Marathon/dsl, Mobil/McDonald's/dsl, RaceTrac/dsl, Sunoco/dsl 🍴 Burger King, DQ, Griffin Grill, Ho Wok, Las Palmas Mexican, Pizza Hut, Popeye's, Smoothie King, Sonic, Subway 🛏 Mainstay Suites, Sleep Inn 🅞 O'Reilly Parts, repair, Twin Lakes RV Park (1mi), Walgreens
166	LA 42, LA 427, Highland Rd, Perkins Rd, **N** 🅖 Circle K/Church's dsl, Exxon/Circle K/dsl 🍴 Las Palmas Mexican, Popeye', Ruffino's Italian, Sonic, Starbucks, Waffle House, Zoe's Kitchen 🅞 Alexander's Mkt, funpark, Goodyear/auto, Home Depot, Tire Engineers/auto, **S** 🅖 Shell/dsl, Texaco/dsl 🍴 Subway
163	Siegen Lane, **N** 🅖 Marathon/dsl, RaceTrac/dsl, Shell/Circle K dsl 🍴 Burger King, Cane's, CC's Coffee, Chick-fil-A, China 1, Ci's Pizza, Firehouse Subs, Freddy's, Hooters, IHOP, Jason's Deli McDonald's, Olive Garden, PoBoy Express, Ribs Chophouse, Smoothie King, Subway, Taco Bell, Twin Peaks Rest., Waffle House, Whataburger, Whataburger, Which Wich? 🛏 Best Value Inn, Hampton Inn, Holiday Inn Express, Home 2 Suites, La Quinta, Microtel, Motel 6, Siegen Inn, Super 8 🅞 $Tree, Advance Parts, AT&T, BigLots, Cadillac, CarMax, Firestone auto, GNC, Harley-Davidson, Hobby Lobby, Honda, Kia, Office Depot, PetCo, Ross, Target, Verizon, **S** 🍴 Backyard Burger, Chili's, ChuckeCheese, Honeybaked Ham, Joe's Crabshack, T Roadhouse 🛏 Courtyard, Residence Inn 🅞 Jo-Ann, Kohl', Lowe's/Subway, Old Navy, Petsmart, Sam's Club/gas, TJ Maxx, Walmart/Subway, World Mkt
162	Bluebonnet Rd, **N** 🅖 Exxon/Circle K/dale 🍴 Albasha Rest Cadillac Cafe, Francois Cafe 🛏 Wyndham Garden 🅞 vet **S** 🍴 BJ's Brewhouse, Copeland's Cheesecake Bistro, J Alexander's, King Buffet, Longhorn Steaks, Pluckers Wing Bar, Ralph&Kacoo's, Red Lobster, Red Robin 🛏 Hyatt Place, Renaissance 🅞 🅗, Best Buy, Dick's, Dillard's, JC Penney, Macy's
160	LA 3064, Essen Lane, **S** 🅖 Exxon/Circle K/dsl, RaceTrac/dsl 🍴 Burger King, Copeland's Bistro, Domino's, Gatti's Pizza, India's Rest., Jimmy John's, McDonald's, Omi Japanese, Piccadilly, Popeye's, Subway, Taco Bell, Wendy's 🛏 Drury Inn, Fairfield Inn, SpringHill Suites 🅞 🅗, $General, Albertson's, NTB, O'Reilly Parts, URGENT CARE, Walgreens
159	I-12 E, to Hammond
158	College Dr, Baton Rouge, **N** 🅖 Speed Zone 🍴 Broken Egg Cafe, Cane's, Firehouse Subs, Hooters, Izzo's Grill, Jason's Deli, Mansurs Rest., Marble Slab Creamery, Subway, Sullivan's Rest, Waffle House, Wendy's 🛏 Candlewood Suites, Cloverleaf Suites, Extended Stay America, Homewood Suites, Marriott

Vertical side labels: NEW ORLEANS AREA, GONZALES, BATON ROUGE

B A T O N   R O U G E

🔼E   INTERSTATE 10 Cont'd

158	Continued
	Richmond Inn, Tru Hilton 🅾 �H, Barnes&Noble, Meineke, Midas, **S** 🅟 Exxon/Circle K/dsl, Shell/Circle K 🍴 Chick-fil-A, Chili's, Don Jose's, Gino's Rest., IHOP, McDonald's, Panda Express, Ruth's Chris Steaks, Starbucks, Subway, Taco Bell, Tio Javi's Mexican 🛏 Best Value, Comfort Inn, Comfort Suites, Crowne Plaza, DoubleTree, Embassy Suites, Hampton Inn, Holiday Inn 🅾 $Tree, Albertson's, AutoZone, Hobby Lobby, Office Depot, USPO, Verizon, Walgreens, Walmart/Subway
157b	Acadian Thwy, **N** 🅟 Chevron/dsl 🍴 Mestizo Grill, Rib's Rest. 🛏 La Quinta, Radisson 🅾 �H, **S** 🅟 Shell/Circle K/dsl 🍴 Acme Oyster House, Juban's Rest., Outback Steaks, Provisions, Saltgrass Steaks 🛏 Courtyard 🅾 AT&T, PetCo, Trader Joe's, Tuesday Morning
157a	Perkins Rd (from eb), same as 157b
156b	Dalrymple Dr, **S** 🅾 to LSU
156a	Washington St
155c	Louise St (from wb)
155b	I-110 N, to Baton Rouge bus dist, **N** 🅾 ✈
155a	LA 30, Nicholson Dr, Baton Rouge, **N** 🛏 Belle Hotel, **S** 🅟 Shell/Circle K/dsl 🅾 to LSU
154mm	Mississippi River
153	LA 1, Port Allen, **N** 🅟 Chevron, Shell/Circle K/dsl 🍴 Church's, Pizza Hut 🅾 AutoZone, Family$, Kenworth, NAPA, O'Reilly Parts, repair, Walgreens **S** 🅟 LA 1S TP/Exxon/Casino/dsl/scales/24hr, RaceTrac/dsl, Sunoco 🍴 Domino's, Hardee's, Waffle House 🛏 Red Roof Inn 🅾 $Tree, Verizon, Walmart/Subway
151	LA 415, to US 190, **N** 🅟 Cash's Trk Plaza/dsl/scales/casino, Chevron/dsl, Emerald Plaza Trkstp/Champs Chicken/dsl, Exxon/dsl, Nino's/dsl/casino, Shell/Circle K/dsl 🍴 Burger King, KFC/Taco Bell, McDonald's, Popeye's, Subway, Waffle House 🛏 Best Western, Comfort Suites, Hampton Inn, Holiday Inn Express, La Quinta, Quality Inn, TownePlace Suites, West Inn 🅾 $General, **S** 🅟 🚂 Loves/Arby's/dsl/scales/24hr, Mobil/dsl/24hr 🛏 Audubon Inn, Motel 6, Super 8, Super 8 🅾 truck repair
139	LA 77, Grosse Tete, **N** 🅟 Shell/Subway/dsl 🍴 Big Heads BBQ 🅾 Chevrolet, **S** 🅟 Tiger/Country Store/dsl/rest./@
135	LA 3000, to Ramah
127	LA 975, to Whiskey Bay
126.5mm	Pilot Channel of Whiskey Bay
122mm	Atchafalaya River
121	Butte La Rose, **N** Visitors ctr/🆁🆂 both lanes, full facilities, litter barrels, petwalk, 🍴, tourist info, vending, **S** 🍴 Lazy Cajun Grill (2mi) 🅾 Frenchman's Wilderness Camground (.5mi)
115	LA 347, to Cecilia, Henderson, **N** 🅟 Exxon/dsl/24hr, Shamrock/dsl, Texaco/dsl 🍴 Chicken on the Bayou, Landry's Seafood 🛏 Holiday Inn Express 🅾 casinos, **S** 🅟 Chevron/dsl, Exxon/Subway/dsl, Shell/McDonald's/dsl, Texaco/dsl, Valero/dsl 🍴 Popeye's, Waffle House 🅾 $General
109	LA 328, to Breaux Bridge, **N** 🅟 Shell/dsl, Texaco/Hardee's/dsl/casino 🛏 Microtel, **S** 🅟 Exxon/Domino's/dsl, Murphy USA/dsl, 🚂 Pilot/Arby's/dsl/scales/24hr, Valero/Popeye's/dsl 🍴 Burger King, City Buffet, Crazy Bout Cajun, Hacienda Real, McDonald's, Pizza Hut, Sonic, Taco Bell, Waffle House, Wendy's, Zapote Mexican 🛏 Best Value Inn, Super 8 🅾 $General, $Tree, AT&T, AutoZone, Chevrolet, Chrysler/Dodge/Jeep, city park, Dixie RV Ctr, Family$, Ford/Lincoln, O'Reilly Parts, Pioneer RV Park, Super 1 Foods, USPO, Walgreens, Walmart/Subway
108mm	weigh sta both lanes

L A F A Y E T T E

C R O W L E Y

104	Louisiana Ave, **S** 🅟 RaceTrac/dsl 🍴 Chick-fil-A, McDonald's, Subway, Taco Bell 🅾 AT&T, GNC, JC Penney, Office Depot, PetCo, Ross, Target, Verizon
103b	I-49 N, to Opelousas
103a	US 167 S, to Lafayette, **S** 🅟 Circle K, Murphy USA/dsl, RaceTrac/dsl, Shell/dsl 🍴 Checkers, McDonald's, Popeye's, Sonic, Subway, Taco Bell, Waffle House, Wendy's 🛏 Baymont Inn, Best Western, Fairfield Inn, Holiday Inn, Howard Johnson, La Quinta, Motel 6, Quality Inn, Super 7, Super 8 🅾 �H, $Tree, Home Depot, Super 1 Foods/gas, transmissions
101	LA 182, to Lafayette, **N** 🅟 McDonald's, Shell/Circle K/Subway/dsl, TA/Country Pride/dsl/scales/24hr/@ 🍴 Burger King, Waffle House, Whataburger 🛏 Red Roof Inn, **S** 🅟 Chevron/dsl, Citgo, Exxon 🍴 Church's, Cracker Barrel, KFC 🛏 Days Inn, Drury Inn, Hilton Garden (2mi), King Motel, Peartree Inn 🅾 �H, $General, Advance Parts, Family$, O'Reilly Parts, 🅟 Valero/dsl
100	Ambassador Caffery Pkwy, **N** 🅟 Exxon/dsl 🅾 Gauthier's RV Ctr, Peterbilt, Ryder Trucks, **S** 🅟 Chevron/dsl, RaceTrac/dsl, Shell/Circle K/dsl 🍴 Burger King, McDonald's, Sonic, Taco Bell, Waffle House, Wendy's 🛏 Ambassador Inn, Hampton Inn, Microtel, Sleep Inn 🅾 �H, Southern Tire Mart
97	LA 93, to Scott, **N** 🍴 La Rumba Mexican 🅾 Super 1 Foods/dsl, **S** 🅟 Chevron/McDonald's, Shell/Church's/dsl 🍴 Billy's Cracklings, Fezzo's Seafood, Huddle House, Popeye's, Rochetto's Pizza 🛏 Comfort Inn, Holiday Inn Express, Howard Johnson 🅾 Harley-Davidson, KOA
92	LA 95, to Duson, **N** 🅟 Exxon/dsl/casino/RV dump/scales/24hr, 🚂 Loves/Chester's/Wendy's/dsl/scales/24hr, **S** 🅟 Chevron/dsl, Marathon/Subway/dsl/casino, Roady's/cafe/dsl/casino 🛏 Super 8 🅾 Frog City RV Park
87	LA 35, to Rayne, **N** 🅟 Chevron/dsl, Shell/Subway/casino/dsl 🍴 Burger King, Chef Roy's Rest., McDonald's, Taco Bell 🛏 Days Inn 🅾 $General, **S** 🅟 Circle K/dsl, Citgo/dsl, Frog City/Exxon/Cajun Rest./dsl, Shop Rite, Texaco/dsl 🍴 Candyland Ice Cream, Domino's, DQ, Gabe's Café, Great Wall Chinese, Pizza Hut, Popeye's, Sonic 🛏 Best Western 🅾 Advance Parts, Family$, O'Reilly Parts, Super 1 Foods, Walgreens
82	LA 1111, to E Crowley, **S** 🅟 Chevron/dsl, Murphy USA 🍴 Chili's, Wendy's 🅾 �H, AT&T, GNC, Lowe's, Walgreens, Walmart/Subway
80	LA 13, to Crowley, **N** 🅟 Conoco/Exit 80/dsl/rest./24hr 🍴 DQ, Fezzo's Seafood/steaks, Waffle House 🛏 Crowley Inn, Days Inn, Motel 6 🅾 Buick/Chevrolet, vet, **S** 🅟 Chevron/dsl, Exxon, Raceway/dsl, Tobacco+/gas, Valero/dsl 🍴 Asian Buffet, Burger King, Cajun Way, China Dragon, El Dorado Mexican, Gatti's Pizza, KFC, Little Caesar's, McDonald's, Pizza Hut, PJ's Grill, Popeye's, Sonic, Subway, Taco Bell 🅾 $General, $Tree, AutoZone, Ford, O'Reilly Parts, Super 1, Verizon

LA

🔷E   INTERSTATE 10 Cont'd

Exit #	Services
76	LA 91, to Iota, S 🅿 Petro/Shell/Subway/dsl/scales/24hr
72	Egan, N 🅾 Cajun Haven RV Park
65	LA 97, to Jennings, S 🅿 Shell/dsl/casino 🛏 Howard Johnson
64	LA 26, to Jennings, N 🍴 Los Tres Potrillos 🅾 LA Oil & Gas Park, RV Park, S 🅿 Circle K/dsl, Exxon/dsl, EZ Mart, Murphy USA/dsl, Shop Rite/dsl/casino 🍴 Burger King, Domino's, Gatti's Pizza, General Wok Chinese, KFC, La Rumba Mexican, McDonald's, Pizza Hut, Popeye's, Shoney's, Sonic, Subway, Taco Bell, Waffle House, Wendy's 🛏 Days Inn, Hampton Inn, Motel 6 🅾 🅷, $General, $Tree, AT&T, AutoZone, O'Reilly Parts, Verizon, Walgreens, Walmart/Subway
59	LA 395, to Roanoke, N 🅿 Peto's TrvlCtr/Chevron/dsl/scales/24hr
54	LA 99, Welsh, S 🅿 Citgo, Exxon/dsl/24hr, Valero 🍴 DQ, Subway
48	LA 101, Lacassine, S 🅿 Exxon
44	US 165, to Alexandria, N 🅾 Quiet Oaks RV Park (10mi), S 🍴 Rabideaux's Cajun
43	LA 383, to Iowa, N 🅿 Loves/Hardee's/dsl/scales/24hr, Pilot/Arby's/PJ Fresh/dsl/scales/24hr 🍴 Burger King 🛏 Howard Johnson Express, La Quinta, S 🅿 Citgo/dsl, Shell/McDonald's/dsl, Texaco 🍴 Boudreaux's Cajun, Sonic, Subway 🅾 $General, I-10 Outlet/famous brands
36	LA 397, to Creole, Cameron, N 🅾 Jean Lafitte RV Park (2mi), S 🅿 Cash Magic/grill/dsl/RV Dump, Chevron/dsl 🍴 Los Ponchos 🛏 Red Roof Inn 🅾 casino, Country Oaks RV Park
34	I-210 W, to Lake Charles
33	US 171 N, N 🅿 Chevron/dsl, Conoco/dsl, RaceWay/dsl/E85, Shell/dsl, Time/dsl 🍴 Burger King, Church's, KFC, Subway, Taco Bell 🛏 Best Western, Comfort Suites, Motel 6, Richmond Suites 🅾 $General, AutoZone, Family$, O'Reilly Parts, to Sam Houston Jones SP, S 🛏 EconoLodge, Holiday Inn Express, Super 10
32	Opelousas St, N 🅿 Exxon, S 🛏 EconoLodge, Holiday Inn Express, Super 10
31b	US 90 E, Shattuck St, to LA 14, N 🅿 Chevron/dsl/casino, S 🅿 Valero/dsl
31a	US 90 bus, Enterprise Blvd, S 🅿 Valero/dsl 🍴 Popeye's
30b	downtown
30a	LA 385, N Lakeshore Dr, Ryan St, N 🅿 Citgo 🍴 Steamboat Bill's Rest., Waffle House 🛏 Days Inn, Oasis Inn, S 🍴 Wendy's 🛏 Quality Suites
29	LA 385 (from eb), same as 30a
28mm	Calcasieu Bayou, Lake Charles
27	LA 378, to Westlake, N 🅿 Chevron/dsl, Conoco/dsl, Texaco/dsl, Valero 🍴 Burger King, El Tapatia Mexican, McDonald's, Popeye's, RoundTop Burger, Sonic, Subway 🛏 La Quinta 🅾 $General, Bumper Parts, Family$, Fred's, MarketBasket, O'Reilly Parts, to Sam Houston Jones SP (6mi), S 🛏 Inn at the Isle 🅾 Riverboat Casinos
26	US 90 W, Southern Rd, Columbia, N 🅿 Exxon/dsl
25	I-210 E, to Lake Charles
23	LA 108, to Sulphur, N 🅿 Chevron, Circle K, Exxon/dsl, Murphy USA, Shell 🍴 Bergeron's Cajun Diner, Burger King, Cane's, Chili's, China Wok, Kyoto, McDonald's, Popeye's, Subway, Taco Bell, Wendy's 🛏 Quality Inn 🅾 $General, $Tree, AT&T, Bumper Parts, Lowe's, Verizon, Walgreens, Walmart/Subway, S 🅿 Chevron/Jack-in-the-Box/dsl, Citgo/Cash Magic/dsl, Sulphur Trkstp/Shell/Subway/dsl/casino 🍴 Cracker Barrel, Waffle House 🛏 Best Western+, Comfort Suites, Days Inn, Holiday Inn Express, HomeTowne Studios, Studio 6, Super 8 🅾 Southern Tire Mart

Exit #	Services
21	LA 3077, Arizona St, N 🅿 Conoco/dsl, Shell 🍴 Boiling Po Cajun, China Taste, Papa John's, Starbucks 🅾 🅷, $Gener AT&T, Chevrolet, CVS Drug, Ford, GNC, Kroger/gas, NAPA, W greens, S 🅿 Chevron/dsl, Shell/dsl, Valero/dsl/casino 🅾 H den Ponds RV Park
20	LA 27, to Sulphur, N 🅿 Chevron/dsl, Circle K, Conoco/dsl, G Valero/dsl 🍴 Burger King, Casa Ole Mexican, Checkers, Gat Pizza, Hollier's Cajun, Hong Kong Chinese, Joe's Pizza/pasta, Rumba Mexican, LeBleu's Landing Cajun, Little Caesar's, N Donald's, Pitt Grill Cajun, Popeye's, Ruiz's Steaks, Subway, Ta Bell, Wendy's 🛏 Best Value, Hampton Inn, Motel 6 🅾 🅿 Brookshire Bros/gas, Family$, Firestone/auto, Goodyear/au Jiffy Lube, S 🅿 Chevron/dsl/24hr, Shell/dsl 🍴 Navrosk Burgers, Pizza Hut, Sonic, Waffle House 🛏 Baymont Inn, Ca dlewood Suites, Days Inn, Fairfield Inn, Holiday Inn, Red Rc Inn, Wingate Inn 🅾 Stine, to Creole Nature Trail
8	LA 108, Vinton, N 🅿 Chevron/dsl, Exxon/dsl 🍴 Cajun Co boy's Rest. 🅾 V RV Park
7	LA 3063, Vinton, N 🅿 FuelStop/dsl 🍴 Burger King, Sc ic, Subway 🛏 Cobblestone Inn 🅾 $General, casino, S 🅿 Loves/Arby's/dsl/scales/24hr
4	US 90, LA 109, Toomey, N 🅿 Cash Magic/dsl/grill/casino, Ch ron/dsl/casino, Shell/dsl 🅾 truck repair, S 🅿 Conoco/dsl, E on/dsl, Valero/dsl/rest. 🍴 Subway 🛏 Best Western 🅾 ca nos, RV Park
2.5mm	weigh sta wb lanes
1.5mm	Welcome Ctr eb, full 🛗 facilities, litter barrels, petwalk, Ⓒ,
1	(from wb), Sabine River Turnaround
0mm	Louisiana/Texas state line, Sabine River

🔷E   INTERSTATE 12

Exit #	Services
85c	I-10 E, to Biloxi. **I-12 begins/ends on I-10, exit 267.**
85b	I-59 N, to Hattiesburg
85a	I-10 W, to New Orleans
83	US 11, to Slidell, N 🅿 Circle K/dsl, Exxon/dsl 🍴 Burger Kir McDonald's, Sonic, Waffle House, S 🅿 RaceTrac/dsl, She Subway/dsl 🅾 🅷
80	Airport Dr, North Shore Blvd, N 🅿 Circle K/Krystal/dsl 🍴 Dic ey's BBQ, IHOP, PJ's Coffee, Sonic 🛏 Comfort Inn 🅾 AT& Petsmart, Ross, Target, S 🅿 Chevron, Shell/dsl 🍴 Burg King, Chili's, ChuckECheese's, Domino's, McDonald's, Oli Garden, Starbucks, Subway, Taco Bell, Waffle House, Wendy Zea Grill 🛏 Candlewood Suites, Holiday Inn Express, Hom wood Suites, La Quinta 🅾 $Tree, Burlington, Dillard's, Goo year/auto, Home Depot, Jo-Ann, Marshalls, Sam's Club/ga Walgreens, Walmart
74	LA 434, to Lacombe, N 🅿 Chevron/Subway/dsl 🅾 🅷, Steve RV Ctr, S 🅾 Big Branch Marsh NWR
68	LA 1088, to Mandeville
65	LA 59, to Mandeville, N 🅿 Chevron/dsl, Exxon/Danny Clyde's/cafe/dsl, Shell/dsl 🍴 Fat Spoon Cafe, Popeye Smoothie King, Sonic, Subway, Waffle House 🛏 Comfo Suites, S 🅿 Circle K/Arby's/dsl, Valero/Domino's/dsl 🍴 Rancho Mexican, Liu's Wok, McDonald's, PJ's Coffee 🅾 cam ing, to Fontainebleau SP, vet, Winn-Dixie
63b a	US 190, Covington, Mandeville, N 🅿 Chevron/dsl, Exxon, Rac Trac, Shell/Circle K 🍴 Acme Oyster House, Applebee's, Burg King, Cane's, Chick-fil-A, Copeland's Grill, Dakota Rest., Dol Seafood, Dunkin', Four Seasons Chinese, HoneyBaked Ham, IHC Jimmy John's, Johnny's Pizza, La Carreta, Lee's Hamburge

LA

INTERSTATE 12 Cont'd

63b a	Continued
	McAlister's Deli, Mellow Mushroom Cafe, North Shore Empress Asian, Osaka Japanese, Outback Steaks, Papi's Fajita Factory, Piccadilly, Sonic, Starbucks, Subway, Thai Chili, Waffle House, Wendy's, Zea Rotisserie 🛏 Best Western, Clarioh, Comfort Inn, Country Inn&Suites, Courtyard, Hampton Inn, Hilton Garden, Holiday Inn, Homewood Suites, Residence Inn, Staybridge Suites, Super 8 ⭕ Ace Hardware, AT&T, AutoZone, Chevrolet, Chrysler/Dodge/Jeep, CVS Drug, Firestone/auto, GNC, Home Depot, Honda, Hyundai, Lowe's, Nissan, Office Depot, Petsmart, Rouse's Mkt, Subaru, Toyota, Verizon, Walmart/McDonald's, S ⭕ 🅷, st police, to New Orleans via toll causeway
60	Pinnacle Pkwy, to Covington, same as 59
59	LA 21, to Covington, Madisonville, N 🅿 Chevron/dsl, Kangaroo, Shell/dsl 🍴 Buffalo Wild Wings, Cafe Du Monde, Carreta's Grill, Chili's, Cracker Barrel, Firehouse Subs, Five Guys, Golden Wok, Isabella's Pizza, Italian Pie, Izzo's Burrito, Jimmy John's, McDonald's, Olive Garden, Panda Buffet, Panera Bread, PJ's Coffee, Safa Mediterranean, Sake Steaks, Seafood Grill, Smoothie King, Steak'n Shake, Subway, TX Roadhouse 🛏 La Quinta ⭕ 🅷, $Tree, AT&T, AutoZone, CVS Drug, Hobby Lobby, Kohl's, Petco, URGENT CARE, Walgreens, Winn-Dixie, S 🅿 Valero/Domino's 🍴 Chick-fil-A, ChuckECheese's, Dickey's BBQ, Habaneros Mexican, Longhorn Steaks, Pardo's Grill, Taco Bell, Wendy's, Which Wich?, Zoe's Kitchen 🛏 Holiday Inn Express ⭕ Belk, Best Buy, Fairview Riverside SP, GNC, JC Penney, Marshall's, Michael's, Ross, Sam's Club/dsl, Target, Verizon, World Mkt
57	LA 1077, to Goodbee, Madisonville, S 🅿 QuickWay/PoBoys/dsl 🍴 Best Wok, Pizza Hut, PJ's Coffee, Subway ⭕ to Fairview Riverside SP, vet
47	LA 445, to Robert, **1-3 mi** N 🍴 Jellystone Camping, to Global Wildlife Ctr, S 🅿 Chevron/dsl
42	LA 3158, to Airport, N 🅿 Chevron/dsl/24hr, Texaco/dsl 🍴 McDonald's, Popeye's 🛏 Friendly Inn, S 🅿 Shell/Subway/dsl ⭕ 🅷, Berryland RV Ctr
40	US 51, to Hammond, N 🅿 RaceTrac/dsl, Shell/Circle K 🍴 Burger King, Cane's, Chick-fil-A, China Garden, Church's, Coldstone, Don's Seafood, East of Italy, IHOP, Jimmy John's, McDonald's, Nagoya Rest., Olive Garden, Ryan's, Santa Fe Steaks, Shane's Rib Shack, Smoothie King, Sonic, Subway, Taco Bell, Wendy's, Which Wich? 🛏 Best Western, Courtyard, Holiday Inn, Quality Inn ⭕ AT&T, Best Buy, Books-A-Million, Dillard's, GNC, Harley-Davidson, JC Penney, Rite Aid, Target, TJ Maxx, U-Haul, Verizon, Walgreens, S 🅿 Petro/Mobil/Subway/dsl/scales/24hr/@, 🚛 Arby's/dsl/scales/24hr, Shell/dsl 🍴 Waffle House 🛏 Colonial Inn, Days Inn, La Quinta ⭕ 🅷, $General, Blue Beacon, SpeedCo
38b a	I-55, N to Jackson, S to New Orleans
37mm	**weigh sta both lanes**
35	Pumpkin Ctr, Baptist, N 🅿 Texaco/dsl ⭕ $General, Dixie Camping World RV Service/Supplies, Punkin RV Park (2mi), S 🅿 Chevron/Bayou Boyz/Subway/dsl
32	LA 43, to Albany, N 🅿 Chevron/Subway/dsl, Exxon/dsl, Shell/Big River/dsl 🍴 McDonald's, S ⭕ to Tickfaw SP (11mi), tourist info
29	LA 441, to Holden, N 🅿 Sunoco/dsl ⭕ Berryland Campers
22	LA 63, to Frost, Livingston, N 🅿 Chevron/dsl, Marathon/dsl 🍴 Pizza Hut, Subway, Wayne's BBQ ⭕ Carters Foods, Family$, Thrift Town Drug, USPO, S ⭕ Lakeside RV Park (1mi)
19	to Satsuma, Colyell, N 🅿 Exxon/dsl 🍴 Subway

15	LA 447, to Walker, N 🅿 Murphy Express/dsl, Shell/Subway/dsl, Texaco/dsl 🍴 Burger King, China Wok, Domino's, Foochow Buffet, Jack-in-the-Box, McDonald's, Papa John's, Papa Murphy's, Pizza Hut, Popeye's, Sherwood PoBoy's, Sombrero Mexican, Sonic, Taco Bell, Waffle House, Wendy's 🛏 La Quinta ⭕ $General, $Tree, AT&T, AutoZone, NAPA, O'Reilly Parts, Verizon, Walgreens, Walmart/Subway, Winn-Dixie, S 🅿 Chevron/dsl/24hr ⭕ 🅷
12	LA 1036, Juban Rd, N 🍴 Marble Slab, Moe's SW ⭕ Belk, Kohl's, Michael's, Old Navy, Petsmart, Ross, Rouse's Mkt, TJ Maxx, Verizon, S 🅿 Shell/dsl
10	LA 3002, to Denham Springs, N 🅿 Chevron, Exxon, RaceTrac/dsl, Shell/Circle K/dsl 🍴 Arby's, Baskin-Robbins, Burger King, Cactus Café, Cane's, Chili's, Church's, Domino's, Don's Seafood, Gatti's Pizza, IHOP, McDonald's, Papa John's, Papi's Fajita, Pizza Hut, Popeye's, Ron's Seafood, Ryan's, Sonic, Starbucks, Subway, Taco Bell, Waffle House, Wendy's 🛏 Best Value Inn, Candlewood Suites, Carom Inn, Comfort Suites, Hampton Inn, Motel 6 ⭕ $General, $Tree, Advance Parts, Albertsons, AT&T, AutoZone, CVS Drug, Home Depot, Meineke, NTB, Office Depot, O'Reilly Parts, PetCo, Rite Aid, Tire Pros, Walgreens, Walmart/Subway, S 🅿 🚛 Subway/dsl/scales/24hr, Shell 🍴 Cafe Phoenicia, El Rancho Mexican, Hardee's, Hooters, Islamorada Fish Co, Longhorn Steaks, Piccadilly, Rotolo's Pizza, VooDoo BBQ 🛏 Days Inn, Highland Inn ⭕ Bass Pro Shops, Cavender's, Chrysler/Dodge/Jeep, Ford, KOA, Sam's Club/dsl, Walgreens
8.5mm	Amite River
7	O'Neal Lane, N 🅿 Mobil, RaceTrac/dsl 🛏 La Quinta, Quality Inn ⭕ Hobby Lobby, Toyota, S 🅿 Murphy USA/dsl, RaceTrac/dsl, Shell, Texaco/Subway/dsl 🍴 China King, Hardee's, Las Palmas Mexican, Little Caesar's, LoneStar Steaks, McDonald's, Popeye's, Rice Bowl, Sonic, Taco Bell, Waffle House, Wendy's ⭕ 🅷, $Tree, AutoZone, O'Reilly Parts, Walgreens, Walmart/Subway
6	Millerville Rd, N 🅿 Chevron/dsl 🍴 Chick-fil-A, Chili's, Golden Corral ⭕ Best Buy, Honda, Lowe's, Office Depot, Petsmart, Super Target, S 🅿 Texaco/dsl 🍴 Rotolo's Pizza, Subway ⭕ Ace Hardware
4	Sherwood Forest Blvd, N 🅿 Exxon, Shell/Circle K/dsl 🍴 Burger King, ChuckECheese, Egg Roll King, Jack-in-the-Box, McDonald's, Pizza Hut, Popeye's, Sonic, Subway, Taco Bell, Waffle House 🛏 Crossland Suites, Red Roof Inn, Super 8, Woodspring Suites ⭕ Fred's, Goodyear/auto, Rite Aid, S 🅿 RaceTrac/dsl, Shell/dsl 🍴 Cane's, DQ, Dunkin', Hardee's, Nagoya, Piccadilly, Podnuh's BBQ, Sherwood PoBoys 🛏 Calloway Inn ⭕ AT&T, auto care
2b	US 61 N, N 🅿 Chevron/dsl, Mobil/dsl, Rende's/dsl, Shell/Circle K 🍴 Applebee's, Chinese Inn, Cracker Barrel, Little Caesar's, McDonald's, Taco Bell 🛏 Days Inn, Holiday Inn, Knights Inn,

B A T O N   R O U G E

INTERSTATE 12 Cont'd

Exit	Services
2b	Continued
	Magnuson Hotel, Microtel, Motel 6, Sleep Inn 🅾 $Tree, Albertsons/gas, Burlington Coats, Dodge/Ram, GNC, Marshall's, Michael's, Nissan, PepBoys, SteinMart, Toyota, Walgreens, Walmart Mkt
2a	US 61 S, S 🅿 Circle K, Exxon/Circle K/dsl 🍴 Burger King, China 1, Fernando's Mexican, Isabella's Pizza, Jimmy John's, McDonald's, Subway, Waffle House 🅾 $Tree, Costco/gas, Home Depot, Hyundai, Volvo
1b	LA 1068, to LA 73, Essen Lane, N 🅿 Shell/Circle K/dsl 🍴 Cane's, China Wok, McDonald's, VooDoo BBQ 🅾 Family$, Le Blanc's Mkt, S 🅾 �H
1a	I-10 (from wb). I-12 begins/ends on I-10, exit 159 in Baton Rouge.

INTERSTATE 20

Exit #	Services
189mm	Louisiana/Mississippi state line, Mississippi River
187mm	weigh sta both lanes
186	US 80, Delta, S 🅿 Chevron/Subway/dsl/24hr
184mm	🆁s wb, full 🚻 facilities, litter barrels, petwalk, 🛈, 🚮, RV dump
182	LA 602, Mound
173	LA 602, Richmond
171	US 65, Tallulah, N 🅿 Chevron/Subway/dsl, Shell/dsl 🍴 Chopsticks Buffet, McDonald's, Wendy's 🛏 Days Inn, Super 8 🅾 �H, S 🅿 Exxon/dsl/scales, Loves/Arby's/dsl/scales/24hr, TA/Country Pride/dsl/scales/24hr/@, Texaco 🍴 Red Top Grill
164mm	Tensas River
157	LA 577, Waverly, N 🅿 Waverly Trkstp/rest./dsl/24hr, S 🅿 Chevron/Hunt Bros Pizza/dsl/24hr, Madison/rest./dsl/24hr 🅾 Casino, to Tensas River NWR
155mm	Bayou Macon
153	LA 17, Delhi, N 🅿 Chevron/Subway, Texaco/dsl 🍴 Boomers, Burger King, Pizza Hut, Sonic 🅾 �H, $General, AT&T, Brookshire's Foods, Family$, Fred's, USPO, S 🅿 Central/dsl 🛏 Best Western, Executive Inn
148	LA 609, Dunn
145	LA 183, rd 202, Holly Ridge
141	LA 583, Bee Bayou Rd
138	US 425, Rayville, N 🅿 Bud's, [Murphy]/Wendy's/dsl/scales/24hr 🍴 Fox's Pizza, McDonald's, Sonic 🛏 Days Inn 🅾 �H, $General, $Tree, AutoZone, Brookshire's Foods, Buick/Chevrolet, Family$, repair, Verizon, Walmart, S 🅿 Chevron/Subway/dsl/24hr, Exxon/Circle K/dsl, RaceWay/dsl 🍴 Big John's Rest., Popeye's, Waffle House 🛏 Super 8
135mm	Boeuf River
132	LA 133, Start, N 🅿 Exxon/dsl
128mm	Lafourche Bayou
124	LA 594, Millhaven, N 🅿 Shell/dsl 🅾 st police, to Sage Wildlife Area
120	Garrett Rd, Pecanland Mall Dr, N 🅿 Chevron/dsl 🍴 Applebee's, ChuckECheese, Copeland's Rest., Fiesta Linda, IHOP, Longhorn Steaks, McAlister's, O'Charleys, Olive Garden, Red Lobster, Ronin Habachi, Sonic 🛏 Courtyard, Residence Inn, TownePlace Suites 🅾 $Tree, AT&T, Belk, Best Buy, Dick's, Dillard's, Firestone/auto, Home Depot, JC Penney, Kohl's, Michael's, Old Navy, PetCo, Petsmart, Ross, Stein Mart, Target, TJ Maxx, S 🅿 Shell/dsl 🛏 Best Western, Days Inn, Hampton Inn 🅾 Harley-Davidson, Hope's Campers, Lowe's, Ouachita RV Park, Pecanland RV Park, Sam's Club/gas

R A Y V I L L E

LA

M O N R O E

Exit	Services
118b a	US 165, N 🅿 Valero/dsl 🛏 Clarion, Motel 6, Stratford Hou Inn 🅾 Hyundai, Kia, Nissan, to NE LA U, S 🅿 Chevron, Cono dsl, Exxon, Now Save/dsl, Shell/Circle K 🍴 Burger King, C D's, Church's, KFC, McDonald's, Popeye's, Sonic, Subway, Ta Bell, Wendy's 🛏 Comfort Suites, Motel 6, Quality Inn, Super
117b	LA 594, Texas Ave, N 🅿 Now Save/deli/dsl
117a	Hall St, Monroe, N 🅾 �H, Civic Ctr
116b	US 165 bus, LA 15, Jackson St, N 🅾 �H
116a	5th St, Monroe
115	LA 34, Mill St, N 🅿 Chevron
114	LA 617, Thomas Rd, N 🅿 Murphy USA, RaceWay/dsl 🍴 Bu er King, Cane's, Capt D's, Cheddar's, Chick-fil-A, El Chico Chile Verde, Five Guys, Grandy's, Hibachi Grill, IHOP, KFC, M ister's Deli, McDonald's, Podnuh's BBQ, Popeye's, Subw Taco Bell, Waffle House, Wendy's 🛏 Best Value Inn, Supe Wingate Inn, Woodspring Suites 🅾 �H, AT&T, BigLots, Hol Lobby, Office Depot, Rite Aid, Walgreens, Walmart/McD ald's, S 🅿 Chevron, Exxon/Circle K/Subway/dsl 🍴 Buff Wild Wings, Chili's, Cracker Barrel, El Sombrero, Four Bros Re Genghis Grill, Hooters, Logan's Roadhouse, Outback Stea Peking Chinese, Pizza Hut, Ronin Hibachi, Sonic, TX Roadho Waffle House 🛏 Best Western, Comfort Inn, La Quinta, M 6, Quality Inn, Red Roof Inn
113	Downing Pines Rd, S 🛏 Fairfield Inn, Hampton Inn, Hilton den, Holiday Inn Express, Home 2 Suites 🅾 Chrysler/Dod Jeep, Hyundai
112	Well Rd, N 🅿 Conoco, Now Save/dsl, Pine Stop/dsl, Shell/ cle K/dsl 🍴 Burger King, DQ, McDonald's, Sam's Eatery, Francisco TexMex, Sonic, Subway, Taco Bell, Waffle House, Z by's 🅾 Advance Parts, CVS Drug, Mac's Fresh Mkt, vet, W greens, Walmart Mkt/dsl, S 🅿 [Murphy]/Subway/Wendy's/ scales/24hr 🅾 Pavilion RV Park
108	LA 546, to US 80, Cheniere, N 🅿 Central/dsl, Smart 🅾 $General, S 🅿 Exxon/Subway/dsl
107	Camp Rd, rd 25, Cheniere
103	US 80, Calhoun, N 🅿 Chevron, Exxon/USA/dsl/24hr 🍴 Jc ny's Pizza (1mi) 🛏 Motel 103
101	LA 151, to Calhoun, S 🅿 Chevron/Huddle House/Subway/ Exxon 🍴 Sonic 🅾 101 RV Park
97mm	🆁s wb, full 🚻 facilities, litter barrels, petwalk, 🛈, 🚮, RV du
95mm	🆁s eb, full 🚻 facilities, litter barrels, petwalk, 🛈, 🚮, RV d
93	LA 145, Choudrant, S 🅿 Choudrant 🅾 camping, Jimmie D SP (28mi)
86	LA 33, Ruston, N 🅿 Murphy USA, RaceWay/dsl, Shell/Circl dsl, Texaco/dsl 🍴 Arby's, Cane's Chicken, Cheeburger Ch burger, Chili's, El Jarrito Mexican, Hot Rod BBQ, Huddle Ho Log Cabin Grill, Logan's Roadhouse, Portico Grill, Ronin Hiba Ryan's, Sonic, Taco Bell, Whataburger, Z Buffet 🛏 Comfort Days Inn, Home 2 Suites 🅾 $Tree, AT&T, Buick/GMC, Cadi Chevrolet, Chrysler/Dodge/Jeep, Ford/Lincoln, Fred's, L Lowe's, Toyota, vet, Walmart/Subway, S 🅿 Spirit/dsl 🛏 Western, Fairfield Inn, Holiday Inn Express
85	US 167, Ruston, N 🅿 Chevron/Subway, Exxon, Shell/Circ 🍴 Applebee's, Burger King, Capt D's, Little Caesar's, McL ald's, Peking Chinese, Wendy's 🛏 Courtyard, Hampton Relax Inn 🅾 $General, Office Depot, Super 1 Foods, TrueVa Walgreens, S 🅿 Texaco, Valero/dsl 🍴 Pizza Hut 🛏 Best ue Inn, Sleep Inn 🅾 �H, Advance Parts, Verizon
84	LA 544, Ruston, S 🅿 Chevron/dsl, Exxon 🍴 Domino's, J ny's Pizza, Pizza Inn, Smoothie King, Starbucks, Subway, W House 🛏 Super 8
83	LA 818, Tarbutton Rd

R U S T O N

INTERSTATE 20 Cont'd

Exit #	Services
81	LA 149, Grambling, S 🔲 Chevron/Church's/dsl, Exxon 🔲 to Grambling St U
78	LA 563, Industry, S 🔲 Texaco/dsl
77	LA 507, Simsboro
69	LA 151, Arcadia, N 🔲 Chevron/dsl, Mobil/Burger King/dsl 🔲 La Fogata Mexican 🔲 Ford, S 🔲 Exxon/dsl, Gulf/dsl, Texaco/Church's/dsl 🔲 El Jarrito Mexican, McDonald's, Sonic, Subway 🔲 Days Inn 🔲 Ⓗ, $General, Brookshire Foods, Bumper Parts, Factory Stores/famous brands, Fred's, tires/repair
67	LA 9, Arcadia, N 🔲 to Lake Claiborne SP, S 🔲 Shell/dsl/repair
61	LA 154, Gibsland, N 🔲 to Lake Claibourne SP
55	US 80, Ada, Taylor
52	LA 532, to US 80, Dubberly, N 🔲 Exxon/dsl, Valero/dsl
49	LA 531, Minden, N 🔲 ⭕Loves/Arby's/dsl/scales/24hr, Murphy USA (3mi), Quick Draw TrkStp/Shell/dsl/rest./24hr, QuickDraw/Subway/dsl 🔲 KFC (3mi), Pizza Hut (3mi), Taco Bell (3mi) 🔲 Walmart (3mi), S 🔲 truck/tire repair
47	US 371 S, LA 159 N, Minden, N 🔲 Chevron/dsl, Exxon/dsl, Valero/dsl 🔲 Beanie&Bubba's Grill 🔲 Best Western, Exacta Inn/rest., Holiday Inn Express, Southern Inn 🔲 Ⓗ, Ford, S 🔲 camping, to Lake Bistineau SP
44	US 371 N, Cotton Valley, N 🔲 Exxon/Huddle House/dsl 🔲 Crawfish Hole #2, Nicky's Cantina, Sonic 🔲 Minden Motel (2mi) 🔲 Cinnamon Creek RV/camping, Family$, Lakeside RV Camping
38	Goodwill Rd, S 🔲 Valero/Rainbow Diner/dsl/24hr 🔲 Ammo Plant, truck/trailer repair
33	LA 157, Fillmore, S 🔲 Exxon, ⭕Pilot/Arby's/dsl/scales/24hr 🔲 Pizza Hut, Waffle House 🔲 $General, Family$, Lake Bistineau SP, USPO
26	I-220, Shreveport, 1 mi N 🔲 RaceWay/dsl 🔲 Comfort Suites, Holiday Inn, SpringHill Suites 🔲 Casino
23	Industrial Dr, N 🔲 Chevron/dsl/24hr, Shell/Circle K, Valero/dsl 🔲 McDonald's, Popeye's, Sue's Country Kitchen, Taco Bell, Wendy's 🔲 Ramada Inn 🔲 O'Reilly Parts, RV Repair, st police, S 🔲 Mobil/dsl 🔲 Budgetel 🔲 Peterbilt, Southern RV Ctr
22	Airline Dr, N 🔲 Citgo/dsl, Mobil/McDonald's/dsl, Shell/Circle K, Valero/dsl 🔲 Applebee's, Arby's, Burger King, Chili's, China Flag, DQ, Five Guys, Gatti's Pizza, IHOP, Johnny's Pizza, Logan's Roadhouse, Notini's Italian, Popeye's, Red Lobster, Shogun Steaks, Sonic, Starbucks, Subway, Taco Bell, TX Street Steaks, Waffle House 🔲 Crossland Suites, Rodeway Inn, Super 8 🔲 Ⓗ, Albertsons, BigLots, Books-A-Million, CVS Drug, Dillard's, Firestone/auto, JC Penney, Meineke, Michael's, Office Depot, PepBoys, Tuesday Morning, Verizon, Walgreens, S 🔲 Exxon/dsl, Gulf/dsl 🔲 Beard's Catfish/seafood, Capt John's, Church's, Griff's Burgers, Outback Steaks 🔲 Microtel, Quality Inn, Red Carpet Inn 🔲 AutoZone, Fred's, Super1 Foods, to Barksdale AFB
21	LA 72, to US 71 S, Old Minden Rd, N 🔲 Shell/Circle K/dsl, Valero 🔲 DAQ's Grill, Denny's, Johnny's Pizza, McDonald's, Pancho's Mexican, Podnah's BBQ, Posado's Mexican, Ralph&Kacoo's, Subway, TX Roadhouse, Whataburger 🔲 Best Value Inn, Hampton Inn, Hilton Garden, Homewood Suites, La Quinta, MainStay Suites, TownePlace Suites 🔲 $General, Bayou RV Ctr, O'Reilly Parts, USPO, VW, S 🔲 RaceWay 🔲 Waffle House, Wendy's 🔲 Days Inn, Motel 6, Woodspring Suites
20c	to US 71 S, to Barksdale Blvd
20b	LA 3, Benton Rd, same as 21

20a	Hamilton Rd, Isle of Capri Blvd, N 🔲 Circle K 🔲 Quality Inn, Wingate Inn, S 🔲 Exxon 🔲 Bossier Inn, Travelodge 🔲 casino
19b	Traffic St, Shreveport, N 🔲 Courtyard 🔲 Bass Pro Shop, casino, Chevrolet, S 🔲 casino, downtown
19a	US 71 N, LA 1 N, Spring St, Shreveport, N 🔲 Chateau Suites, Hilton, Shreveport Hotel
18b-d	Fairfield Ave (from wb), S 🔲 Ⓗ, downtown Shreveport
18a	Line Ave, Common St (from eb), S 🔲 Ⓗ, downtown
17b	I-49 S, to Alexandria
17a	Lakeshore Dr, Linwood Ave
16b	US 79/80, Greenwood Rd, N 🔲 Ⓗ, S 🔲 Citgo/dsl 🔲 El Chico 🔲 Travelodge
16a	US 171, Hearne Ave, N 🔲 Shell/dsl 🔲 Subway 🔲 Ⓗ, vet, S 🔲 Raceway/dsl 🔲 KFC, Wendy's 🔲 Cajun Inn
14	Jewella Ave, Shreveport, N 🔲 Clark/dsl, Phillips 66/dsl, Valero 🔲 Burger King, Church's, McDonald's, Popeye's, Sonic, Subway, Whataburger 🔲 AutoZone, County Mkt Foods, Family$, O'Reilly Parts, Rite Aid, Super 1 Foods, Walgreens
13	Monkhouse Dr, Shreveport, N 🔲 Bro's Cafe 🔲 Best Western, Days Inn, Residence Inn, Super 8, Value Inn, S 🔲 Citgo/dsl, Exxon/Subway/dsl, Valero/dsl 🔲 Waffle House 🔲 Baymont Inn, Hampton Inn, Holiday Inn Express, Merryton Inn, Moonrider Inn, Motel 6, Quality Inn, Regency Inn 🔲 to 💬
11	I-220 E, LA 3132 E, to I-49 S
10	Pines Rd, N 🔲 Chevron/dsl 🔲 DQ, Johnny's Pizza, Pizza Hut, Popeye's, Sam's Eatery, Subway 🔲 Meineke, S 🔲 Circle K, Exxon/dsl, Murphy USA/dsl, Shell/Circle K/dsl 🔲 Burger King, CiCi's Pizza, Cracker Barrel, Domino's, Dragon Chinese, Great Wall Chinese, IHOP, KFC, McDonald's, Nicky's Mexican, Papa John's, Sonic, Taco Bell, Waffle House, Wendy's, Whataburger 🔲 Comfort Suites, Courtyard, Fairfield Inn, Hilton Garden, Holiday Inn, Homewood Suites, La Quinta, Sleep Inn, Woodspring Suites 🔲 $Tree, CVS Drug, Family$, GNC, Home Depot, O'Reilly Parts, Rite Aid, USPO, Verizon, Walgreens, Walmart/Subway
8	US 80, LA 526 E, N 🔲 Red Roof Inn 🔲 Freightliner, repair, tires, S 🔲 Chevron/dsl, Citgo/dsl, Petro/Shell/Iron Skillet/dsl/scales/@ 🔲 Wendy's 🔲 Blue Beacon, Blue Beacon, Camper's RV Ctr/park, Tall Pines RV Park (1mi)
5	US 79 N, US 80, to Greenwood, N 🔲 Outpost Travel Ctr/dsl, TA/Valero/Country Pride/Subway/dsl/scales/24hr/@ 🔲 Country Inn, Mid Continent Motel 🔲 RV park, S 🔲 Pizza Hut 🔲 $General, Southern Living RV Park
3	US 79 S, LA 169, Mooringsport, N 🔲 Gator's RV Park (4mi), S 🔲 ⛽FLYING J/Denny's/dsl/LP/scales/24hr, ⭕Loves/Arby's/dsl/scales/24hr 🔲 Sonic 🔲 SpeedCo
2mm	Welcome Ctr eb, full ♿ facilities, litter barrels, petwalk, 🔲, 🆁🆂, RV dump
1mm	weigh sta both lanes
0mm	Louisiana/Texas state line

LA

LA

INTERSTATE 49

SHREVEPORT

Exit #	Services
246.5mm	Louisiana/Arkansas state line
245	LA 168, Ida, Rodessa
241	Rd 16, Mira Myrtis Rd, to Mira, E ⛽ Exxon/pizza/dsl
237	LA 2, Plain Dealing, Hosston
234	US 71, Gilliam, Hosston
231	LA 170, Gilliam, Vivian, W Ⓞ Ⓗ
228	LA 530, Belcher, Oil City
223	LA 169, Mooringsport
221	LA 173, Dixie, Blanchard
215	LA 1, N Market St, E Ⓞ Family$, vet, W ⛽ Exxon/dsl, Walmart/dsl 🍴 China Wok, Johnny's Pizza, McDonald's, Popeye's, Sonic, Subway, Taco Bell, Trejo's Mexican, Wendy's, Zaxby's Ⓞ Verizon, Walmart
211	LA 3194, MLK JR Dr, E ⛽ Chevron/dsl 🍴 Checkers, Domino's, Pizza Hut, Sonic, Subway, Waffle House, Whataburger Ⓞ Brookshire's/gas, Walgreens
210b a	I-220, I-49 begins/ends in Shreveport on I-20, exit 17.
206	I-20, E to Monroe, W to Dallas.
205	King's Hwy, E ⛽ Tesla EVC 🍴 Cane's, McDonald's, Piccadilly, Taco Bell Ⓞ Dillard's, W ⛽ Circle K/dsl 🍴 Burger King, LJ Silver, Subway 🏨 Sleep Inn Ⓞ Ⓗ
203	Hollywood Ave, Pierremont Rd, W ⛽ Chevron/dsl
202	LA 511, E 70th St, E ⛽ RaceWay/dsl, W ⛽ Circle K 🍴 SC Chicken Ⓞ $General, Family$
201	LA 3132, to Dallas, Texarkana
199	LA 526, Bert Kouns Loop, E ⛽ Chevron/Arby's/dsl/24hr, Shell/Circle K 🍴 Burger King, KFC, Taco Bell, Wendy's 🏨 Comfort Inn Ⓞ Home Depot, W ⛽ RaceWay/dsl 🍴 McDonald's, Sonic, Starbucks, Subway, Waffle House Ⓞ Audi/Porsche, Brookshire Foods, Verizon, Walmart Mkt
196	Southern Loop
196mm	Bayou Pierre
191	LA 16, LA 3276, to Stonewall, W Ⓞ Chevrolet/Buick
186	LA 175, to Frierson, Kingston, E Ⓞ Trailerhood RV Park (3mi), W ⛽ Relay Sta./rest./casino/dsl/scales Ⓞ Heart of Haynesville RV Park (7mi)
177	LA 509, to Carmel, E ⛽ Texaco/Eagles Trkstp/casino/dsl/rest., W Ⓞ Hwy 509 RV Park (4mi)
172	US 84, to Grand Bayou, Mansfield, W Ⓞ Civil War Site, New Rockdale RV Park (4mi)
169	Asseff Rd
162	US 371, LA 177, to Evelyn, Pleasant Hill
155	LA 174, to Ajax, Lake End, W Ⓞ Country Livin' RV Pk, Cowboys/dsl
148	LA 485, Powhatan, Allen
142	LA 547, Posey Rd

NATCHITOCHES

Exit #	Services
138	LA 6, to Natchitoches, E ⛽ French Mkt/cafe/dsl, RaceWay/dsl 🍴 Cane's (5mi), IHOP, Popeye's, Wendy's 🏨 Best Western, Comfort Suites, Days Inn, Fairfield Inn, Holiday Inn Express Ⓞ Ⓗ, Walmart (5mi), W ⛽ Chevron/dsl/24hr, Exxon, Texaco/dsl 🍴 Burger King, El Patio, Huddle House, McDonald's, Ribfin's, Subway 🏨 EconoLodge, Hampton Inn, Quality Inn Ⓞ Nakatosh RV Park, to Kisatchie NF
132	LA 478, rd 620
127	LA 120, to Cypress, Flora, E ⛽ Exxon/dsl Ⓞ to Cane River Plantations
119	LA 119, to Derry, Cloutierville, E to Cane River Plantations
113	LA 490, to Chopin, E ⛽ Express Mart TrkStp/dsl
107	to Lena, E Ⓞ USPO
103	LA 8 W, to Flatwoods, E ⛽ Chevron/dsl, W Ⓞ RV camping, to Cotile Lake

ALEXANDRIA

Exit #	Services
99	LA 8, LA 1200, to Boyce, Colfax, 6 mi W Ⓞ Cotile Lake RV Campir
98	LA 1 (from nb), to Boyce
94	rd 23, to Rapides Sta Rd, E ⛽ Rapides/dsl, W ⛽ Loves Arby's/dsl/scales/24hr Ⓞ Alexandria RV Park (2mi), I-49 RV C
90	LA 498, Air Base Rd, W ⛽ Chevron/dsl/CNG/24hr, Exxon/Su way/dsl, Shell/dsl, Texaco/Eddie's BBQ/dsl 🍴 Burger Kir Cracker Barrel, McDonald's 🏨 Comfort Suites, Hampton Ir La Quinta, Rodeway Inn, Super 8 Ⓞ Cabana RV Park
86	US 71, US 165, MacArthur Dr, 0-2 mi W ⛽ Conoco/dsl, Exxor dsl, Mobil/dsl, Shell/Circle K/dsl, Texaco/dsl, Valero, Valero/ 🍴 Applebee's, Burger King, Cane's, Chick-fil-A, Church's, CiC Pizza, Dominos, DQ, Eddie's BBQ, El Paso Mexican, El Repa Mexican, Firehouse Subs, Golden Corral, Little Caesar's, M Donald's, Outlaw's BBQ, Piccadilly, Popeye's, Schlotzsky's, Son Steamboat Bill's, Subway, Taco Bell, TX Roadhouse 🏨 Alexa dria Inn, Baymont Inn, Best Value Inn, Best Western, Candlewo Suites, Comfort Inn, Guesthouse Inn, Holiday Inn Express, Mot 6, Quality Inn, Red Roof Inn Ⓞ $General, $Tree, Advance Par AutoZone, Buick/GMC, Kia, Kroger/gas, NAPA, Office Dep O'Reilly Parts, Petco, Super 1 Foods, Tuesday Morning, Verizon
85b	Monroe St, Medical Ctr Dr (from nb), E Ⓞ Ⓗ
85a	LA 1, 10th St, MLK Dr, downtown
84	US 167 N, LA 28, LA 1, Pineville Expswy (no EZ nb return)
83	Broadway Ave, E ⛽ Fuel+ Ⓞ $General, 1 mi W 🍴 Murp USA/dsl 🍴 Checker's, Little Caesar's, Sonic, Wendy's Ⓞ $Tre AutoZone, Harley-Davidson, Walmart
81	US 71 N, LA 3250, Sugarhouse Rd, MacArthur Dr (from sb), same as 80 and 83
80	US 71 S, US 167, MacArthur Dr, Alexandria, 0-3 mi W ⛽ Che ron/dsl, Exxon/dsl, Shell 🍴 Buffalo Wild Wings, Burger Kir Capt D's, Carino's Italian, Chili's, IHOP, KFC, Logan's Roadhou McDonald's, Outback Steaks, Panda Express, Pizza Hut, Po eye's, Sonic, Taco Bell 🏨 Courtyard, Fairfield Inn, Home 2 Suit TownePlace Suites Ⓞ $General, Albertson's, Best Buy, Dillar Family$, Ford/Lincoln, Hyundai, JC Penney, Marshall's, Maze Michael's, Old Navy, Petsmart, Sam's Club/gas, U-Haul
73	LA 3265, rd 22, to Woodworth, W ⛽ Chevron/dsl/24hr Ⓞ Conf Ctr, RV camping, to Indian Creek RA
66	LA 112, to Lecompte, E ⛽ Chevron/dsl/24hr 🍴 Burger King, ⛽ Exxon/dsl Ⓞ museum (10mi)
61	US 167, to Meeker, Turkey Creek, E Ⓞ to Loyd Hall Plantation (3
56	LA 181, Cheneyville
53	LA 115, to Bunkie, E ⛽ Sammy's/Chevron/dsl/casino/2 🏨 Knights Inn
46	LA 106, to St Landry, W Ⓞ to Chicot SP
40	LA 29, to Ville Platte, E ⛽ Pilot/PJ Fresh/Subway/dsl/scales/2
35mm	E 🅿️s/rec area both lanes, full ♿ facilities, litter barrels, pe walk, 🐕, RV dump, vending
27	LA 10, to Lebeau
25	LA 103, to Washington, Port Barre, W ⛽ Citgo Ⓞ Family$
23	US 167 N, LA 744, to Ville Platte, E ⛽ Chevron/Subway/Stu ey's/dsl/scales/casino, Valero/dsl/casino, W ⛽ Texaco/dsl/ca no Ⓞ visitors ctr

OPELOUSAS

Exit #	Services
19b a	US 190, to Opelousas, E Ⓞ Evangeline Downs Racetrack, ⛽ Chevron/dsl, Exxon/dsl, RaceTrac/dsl, Valero Ⓞ Ⓗ, C Drug, Lowe's, USPO
18	LA 31, to Cresswell Lane, E ⛽ Murphy USA/dsl 🍴 Waf House 🏨 Comfort Inn, Hampton Inn, Holiday Inn Ⓞ $Tre Chrysler/Dodge/Jeep, Ford/Lincoln, URGENT CARE, Veriz Walmart/Subway, W ⛽ Chevron/dsl, Circle K/dsl, Shell/ 🍴 Burger King, Cane's, Cresswell Lane, Domino's, Gatti's Piz

INTERSTATE 49 Cont'd

18	Continued
	Jimmy John's, McDonald's, Pedro's Mexican, Peking Buffet, Pizza Hut, Subway, Taco Bell, Wendy's 🛏 Days Inn, Super 8 ⊙ AT&T, Buick/GMC, Cashsaver, Danny's Tires, Family$, Walgreens
17	Judson Walsh Dr, E 📓 Valero/dsl
15	LA 3233, Harry Guilbeau Rd, W 🛏 Motel 6 ⊙ Ⓗ, Courvelle RV Ctr, Nissan, Toyota
11	LA 93, to Grand Coteau, Sunset, E 📓 Chevron, Exxon/Popeye's/dsl, Texaco/Huddle House/dsl/24hr 🍴 McDonald's ⊙ Primeaux RV Ctr, vet, W 🍴 Subway ⊙ $General, Family$, Janise's Foods
7	LA 182, W ⊙ Primeaux RV Ctr
4	LA 726, Carencro, E 🍴 Dickey's BBQ, Don's, Hardee's, La Pizzaria, Pizza Hut, Popeye's, Rotolo's Pizza, Taco Bell, Tropical Cafe ⊙ $Tree, AT&T, GNC, Super 1 Foods/gas, URGENT CARE, Walmart, W 📓 Chevron/dsl, Texaco/dsl 🍴 Burger King, King Wok, McDonald's 🛏 Economy Inn ⊙ $General, Champagne's Mkt, Family$, Fred's, USPO
2	LA 98, Gloria Switch Rd, E 📓 Chevron/deli/dsl 🍴 Chili's, IHOP, Prejean's Rest., Wendy's ⊙ Lowe's, W 📓 Shell/Circle K/Church's/dsl 🍴 Domino's, El Paso Mexican, Great Wall Buffet, Subway
1c	Pont Des Mouton Rd, E 📓 Circle K/dsl, Shell/dsl, Texaco/dsl 🍴 Buffalo Wild Wings, Burger King 🛏 Plantation Inn, Rodeway Inn ⊙ CVS, Walgreens, W 📓 Exxon/dsl ⊙ Firestone/auto, Ford
0 b a	I-10, W to Lake Charles, E to Baton Rouge, US 167 S 📓 Circle K, Murphy USA/dsl, RaceTrac/dsl, Shell/Circle K/dsl 🍴 Checker's, McDonald's, Popeye's, Sonic, Subway, Taco Bell, Waffle House, Wendy's 🛏 Baymont Inn, Best Western, Express Inn, Fairfield Inn, Garden Plaza Hotel, Holiday Inn, Howard Johnson, La Quinta, Motel 6, Quality Inn, Super 8 ⊙ Ⓗ, $Tree, Home Depot, Super 1 Foods/gas, transmissions

I-49 begins/ends on I-10, exit 103.

INTERSTATE 55

Exit #	Services
66mm	Louisiana/Mississippi state line
65mm	Welcome Ctr sb, full ♿ facilities, litter barrels, petwalk, 📓, 🛏, tourist info
64mm	weigh sta nb
61	LA 38, Kentwood, E 📓 Chevron/dsl/24hr, Texaco 🍴 Jam Chicken, Popeye's, Sonic ⊙ $General, AutoZone, Family$, Fred's, IGA Foods, Super$, W 📓 Kangaroo/dsl, Kangaroo/dsl (2)
58.5mm	weigh sta sb
57	LA 440, Tangipahoa, E ⊙ to Camp Moore Confederate Site
53	LA 10, to Greensburg, Fluker, W ⊙ Ⓗ
50	LA 1048, Roseland, E 📓 Chevron/dsl 🍴 Subway (1mi)
46	LA 16, Amite, E 📓 Exxon/dsl, Murphy USA/dsl, RaceTrac/dsl 🍴 Burger King, Master Chef, McDonald's, Mike's Catfish, Panda Garden, Popeye's, Smoothie King, Sonic, Subway, Taco Bell, Waffle House, Wendy's, Yamato Japanese 🛏 Comfort Inn ⊙ Ⓗ, $Tree, AutoZone, Fred's, O'Reilly Parts, to Bogue Chitto SP, Verizon, Walgreens, Walmart/Subway, Winn-Dixie, W 🛏 Colonial Inn, Holiday Inn Express ⊙ Buick/Chevrolet/GMC
40	LA 40, Independence, E 🛏 Best Stop ⊙ Ⓗ, W ⊙ Indian Cr Camping (2mi)
36	LA 442, Tickfaw, E 📓 Chevron/dsl/24hr ⊙ to Global Wildlife Ctr (15mi), W 📓 Exxon/dsl
32	LA 3234, Wardline Rd, E 📓 Chevron, Kangaroo/dsl, Texaco 🍴 Burger King, McDonald's, Popeye's, Sarita Grill, Sonic, Subway, Taco Bell, Wendy's 🛏 Lexington Inn ⊙ Tony's Tire

31	US 190, Hammond, E 📓 Chevron/dsl/scales/24hr, Exxon/dsl, Murphy USA/dsl, RaceTrac/dsl 🍴 Applebee's, Baskin-Robbins, Buffalo Wild Wings, Burger King, Cane's, Chili's, CiCi's Pizza, Cracker Barrel, Firehouse Subs, Hi-Ho 1 BBQ, McDonald's, Pizza Hut, Sonic, Starbucks, Taco Bell, Voodoo BBQ, Waffle House, Wendy's 🛏 Comfort Inn, Hampton Inn, Super 8, Western Inn, Woodspring Suites ⊙ Ⓗ, $General, $Tree, Advance Parts, AT&T, AutoZone, Chrysler/Dodge/Jeep, CVS Drug, Family$, Hobby Lobby, LeBlanc's Foods Lowe's, Lowe's, Office Depot, Ross, Sav-A-Lot Foods, Tuesday Morning, URGENT CARE, Walgreens, Walmart/Subway, Winn-Dixie
29 b a	I-12, W to Baton Rouge, E to Slidell
28	US 51 N, Hammond, E 📓 Exxon, RaceTrac/dsl, Valero/dsl 🍴 Don's Seafood/Steaks, Great Wall Chinese 🛏 Best Value Inn, Red Roof Inn ⊙ Ⓗ, Buick/GMC, dsl repair, Mitchell RV Ctr, Toyota
26	LA 22, to Springfield, Ponchatoula, E 📓 Chevron/dsl, Exxon/dsl, Murphy Express/dsl, RaceTrac/dsl/e85, Shell/dsl 🍴 Burger King, China King, Hi-Ho BBQ, McDonald's, Papa John's, Pizza Hut, Popeye's, Smoothie King, Sonic, Subway, Taco Bell, Waffle House, Wendy's 🛏 Microtel ⊙ AutoZone, Bohning's Foods, CVS Drug, Family$, Ford, O'Reilly Parts, Rouse's Mkt, Walgreens, Walmart/Subway, W 📓 Kangaroo/Domino's/dsl ⊙ $General, Tickfaw SP (13mi)
23	US 51, Ponchatoula
22	frontage rd (from sb)
15	Manchac, E 🍴 Middendorf Café ⊙ 📓, swamp tours, USPO
7	Ruddock
1	US 51, to I-10, Baton Rouge, La Place, S 📓 Chevron/dsl, Circle K/dsl, 🍴/Subway/dsl/24hr/scales, Shell/Huddle House/casino/dsl 🍴 Burger King, McDonald's, Waffle House, Wendy's 🛏 Best Western, Days Inn, Hampton Inn, Holiday Inn Express, Quality Inn, Suburban Lodge, TownePlace Suites

I-55 begins/ends on I-10, exit 209.

INTERSTATE 59

Exit #	Services
11	Louisiana/Mississippi state line, Pearl River Turnaround, ⊙ to Bogue Chitto NWR
5b	Honey Island Swamp
5a	LA 3081, Pearl River
3	US 11 S, LA 1090, Pearl River, 0-1 mi W 📓 Chevron/dsl, Interstate Fuels/dsl, Shell/Subway/dsl, Texaco 🍴 McDonald's, Sonic, Taco Bell, Waffle House 🛏 Microtel ⊙ AutoZone, Family$, Jubilee Foods/drug, NAPA
1.5mm	Welcome Ctr sb, full ♿ facilities, info, litter barrels, petwalk, 📓, 🛏, RV dump
1c b	I-10, E to Bay St Louis, W to New Orleans
1a	I-12 W, to Hammond. I-59 begins/ends on I-10/I-12.

INTERSTATE 210 (Lake Charles)

Exit #	Services
12	I-210 begins/ends on I-10, exit 34.
11	US 90, Broad St, Fruge St, E📵 Exxon/dsl, Shell/dsl, W🛏 Best Value Inn
10	Legion St, E📵 Shell/dsl 🅾 🔧, Luke's RV Ctr, W🅾 Kia, Nissan
8	LA 14, Gerstner Mem Dr, N📵 Citgo/dsl 🍴 Chili's, IHOP 🅾 Hobby Lobby, S📵 Murphy USA/dsl, Valero 🍴 ChuckE-Cheese, Kyoto, Logan's Roadhouse, Outback, Panda Buffet, Sonic, Taco Bell, Wendy's 🛏 Quality Inn, Woodspring Suites 🅾 $Tree, AT&T, Chrysler/Jeep/Dodge, GMC, Home Depot, Lowe's, Old Navy, Toyota, VW, Walmart
7b	Enterprise Blvd, LA Blvd, N📵 Conoco/dsl, Exxon/dsl 🍴 Sonic, Subway 🛏 Best Western, Super 8 🅾 $General, AutoZone, O'Reilly Parts, S📵 Shell/dsl 🅾 Chevrolet/Cadillac, Ford, Honda, Hyundai
6a	LA 385, Ryan St, N🍴 Burger King, McDonald's, Popeye's, Tony's Pizza 🛏 Comfort Inn 🅾 Aamco, S🍴 Church's, CiCi's, Gatti's Pizza, Jason's Deli 🅾 $General, Firestone/auto, Goodyear/auto, Tuesday Morning
5	Lake St, N🍴 McAlister's Deli, Wendy's 🛏 Best Value Inn 🅾 🏥, AT&T, Best Buy, Dick's, Dillard's, Kohl's, Petco, Verizon
4	LA 1138, Nelson Rd, N🍴 Buffalo Wild Wings, Jo Jo's Chinese, Mongolian Grill, O'Charley's, Olive Garden, Sonic, Subway 🛏 Candlewood Suites, Courtyard, Hampton Inn, La Quinta, Residence Inn, SpringHill Suites, Wingate Inn 🅾 Marshall's, Ross, Sam's Club/gas, Target, S📵 Murphy USA/dsl, Tobacco+ 🍴 Chick-fil-A, Panera Bread, Starbucks, TX Roadhouse 🅾 Walmart/Subway
3	Golden Nugget Blvd, Prien Lake Rd, N🅾 casino/hotel
1b a	I-210 begins/ends on I-10, exit 25.

INTERSTATE 220 (Shreveport)

Exit #	Services
	I-220 begins/ends on I-20, exit 26.
17b	I-20, W to Shreveport, E to Monroe
17a	US 79, US 80, N📵 RaceWay/dsl, Shell/Circle K 🍴 Taco Bell, Waffle House 🛏 Comfort Suites, Holiday Inn, SpringHill Suites 🅾 Racetrack/casino, S📵 Chevron/Huddle House/dsl🍴 Silver Star Smokehouse
15	Shed Rd
13	Swan Lake Rd

Exit #	Services
12	LA 3105, Airline Dr, N🍴 Baskin-Robbins, Chick-fil-A, Dickey's BBQ, Firehouse Subs, Izzo's Burrito, McAlister's Deli, Newk's Eatery, Olive Garden, Papa Murphy's, Santa Fe Steaks, Starbucks, Subway, TaMolly's 🅾 🏥, AT&T, Belk, Best Buy, GNC, Old Navy, Petsmart, Ross, Sam's Club/gas, Target, Verizon, Walgreens, S📵 Exxon/dsl, Murphy USA/dsl, Valero/dsl 🍴 Applebee's, Burger King, Cane's, Capt D's, China Flag, McDonald's, Nicky's Rest., Panda Express, Ruby Tuesday, Ryan's, Smashburger, Sonic, Taco Bell, Trejo's Mexican, Wendy's 🛏 Hampton Inn 🅾 $Tree, Gateway Tire, Hobby Lobby, Home Depot, Kroger/dsl, Lowe's, vet, Walmart
11	LA 3, Bossier City, N📵 RaceWay/dsl 🅾 🏥, Buick/GMC, Ford, Harley-Davidson, Lexus, RV Park, Subaru, Suzuki, Toyota, S📵 Valero/dsl 🅾 Chrysler/Dodge/Jeep, Nissan
7b a	US 71, LA 1, Shreveport, N📵 Chevron/dsl, Exxon/dsl 🍴 Checkers, Domino's, Johnny's Pizza, Papa John's, Pizza Hut, Sonic, Subway, Waffle House, Whataburger/24hr 🅾 Brookshire Foods/gas, Family$, Walgreens, S📵 RaceWay/dsl, Shell 🍴 Burger King, Carl's Jr, Church's, KFC, McDonald's, Podnah' BBQ, Popeye's, Taco Bell, Wendy's 🛏 Royal Inn 🅾 Advance Parts, AutoZone, CVS Drug, Family$, O'Reilly Parts, repair, transmissions, Shoppers Foods, U-Haul
6	I-49 N
5	LA 173, Blanchard Rd, N📵 Citgo/dsl
2	Lakeshore Dr
1a	Jefferson Paige Rd, S🛏 Days Inn, Hampton Inn, Merryton Inn, Ramada Inn, Residence Inn, Super 8, Value Inn
1b c	I-20, E to Shreveport, W to Dallas. I-220 begins/ends on I-20 exit 11.

INTERSTATE 610 (New Orleans)

Exit #	Services
	I-610 begins/ends on I-10.
4	Franklin Ave (from eb)
3	Elysian fields, S📵 B Express, Shell 🍴 Burger King, McDonald's, Waffle House 🅾 🏥, Lowe's
2b	US 90, N Broad St, New Orleans St (from wb)
2c	Paris Ave (from wb, no return), S📵 Jimmy's, Shell/24hr 🍴 Popeye's
2a	St Bernard Ave (from eb), to LSU School of Dentistry, S🅾 auto racetrack
1a	Canal Blvd
1b	I-10, to New Orleans
	I-610 begins/ends on I-10.

NOTES

MAINE

INTERSTATE 95

Exit #	Services
305mm	US/Canada border, Maine state line, US Customs. **I-95 begins/ends.**
305	US 2, to Houlton, E🅾 DFA Duty Free Shop, Houlton Airport
303mm	Meduxnekeag River
302	US 1, Houlton, E📟 Irving/Circle K/dsl/24hr 🍴 Burger King, Domino's, McDonald's, Pizza Hut, Tang's Chinese 🅾 🏥, IGA Foods, Mardens, O'Reilly Parts/VIP Service, Rite Aid, W🆁🆂 **both lanes, full ♿ facilities, litter barrels, petwalk, 🚻, 🛒,** 📟 Citgo/Subway/dsl, Irving/Circle K/dsl/scales/@, Shell/Dunkin'/dsl 🍴 Tim Hortons/Coldstone 🛏 Ivey's Motel, Shiretown Motel 🅾 Arrowstook SP, Family\$, Ford, Hannaford Mkt, Toyota, Walmart
301mm	B Stream
291	US 2, to Smyrna, E🛏 Brookside Motel/rest.
286	Oakfield Rd, to ME 11, Eagle Lake, Ashland, W📟 Irving/Circle K/dsl, Sunoco/dsl 🍴 A Place To Eat 🅾 USPO
277mm	Mattawamkeag River, W Branch
276	ME 159, Island Falls, E🍴 Islands Falls Onestop, Porter's/rest. 🅾 Bishop's Mkt, USPO, W🅾 to Baxter SP (N entrance)
264	to ME 11, Sherman, E🍴 Shell/dsl/LP/rest., W📟 Irving/Circle K/dsl 🛏 Katahdin Valley Motel 🅾 to Baxter SP (N entrance)
259	Benedicta (from nb, no re-entry)
252mm	scenic view Mt Katahdin, nb
247mm	Salmon Stream
244	ME 157, to Medway, E Millinocket, W📟 Irving/Circle K/dsl 🛏 Gateway Inn 🅾 🏥, city park, Katahdin Shadows Camping, to Baxter SP (S entrance), USPO
244mm	Penobscot River
243mm	🆁🆂 **both lanes, full ♿ facilities, litter barrels, petwalk, 🚻, 🛒**
227	to US 2, ME 6, Lincoln, 4 mi E🅾 🏥, RV camping, food, gas, lodging
219mm	Piscataquis River
217	ME 6, Howland, E📟 Irving/95 Diner/dsl 🅾 camping, Citgo/95er Towing/repair, LP
201mm	Birch Stream
199	ME 16 (no nb re-entry), to LaGrange
197	ME 43, to Old Town, E gas/dsl
196mm	Pushaw Stream, Pushaw Stream
193	Stillwater Ave, to Old Town, E📟 Citgo/dsl, Gulf/dsl, Irving/Circle K/dsl 🍴 Burger King, China Garden, Dunkin', Governor's Rest., McDonald's, Wendy's 🛏 Black Bear Inn 🅾 \$Tree, IGA Foods, O'Reilly Parts/VIP Service
191	Kelly Rd, to Orono, 2-3 mi E camping, food, gas, lodging
187	Hogan Rd, Bangor Mall Blvd, to Bangor, E📟 Citgo 🍴 Denny's 🛏 Courtyard, Hampton Inn, Hilton Garden, TownePlace Suites 🅾 Audi/VW, Buick/GMC, Cadillac/Chevrolet, Chrysler/Dodge/Jeep, Firestone/auto, Ford, Honda, Hyundai, Mazda, Mercedes, Nissan, Sam's Club/gas, Subaru, Volvo, W📟 Citgo/dsl, Irving/Circle K/dsl 🍴 Applebee's, Buffalo Wild Wings, Burger King, Chicago Grill, Chick-fil-A, Chili's, Chipotle, Dunkin', Elevation Burger, Five Guys, Green Tea Japanese, Happy China, KFC, Kobe Japanese, Las Palapas, Longhorn Steaks, McDonald's, Miguel's Mexican, Olive Garden, Papa Johns, Pizza Hut, Starbucks, Subway, TX Roadhouse, Wendy's 🛏 Bangor Motel, Comfort Inn, Country Inn, Quality Inn 🅾 \$Tree, AT&T, AutoZone, Best Buy, BJ's/gas, BooksAMillion, Dick's, Hannaford Foods, Hobby Lobby,

187	Continued
	Home Depot, JC Penney, Jo-Ann Fabrics, Kia, Kohl's, LL Bean, Lowe's, Old Navy, O'Reilly Parts/VIP Service, PetCo, Petsmart, Staples, Sullivan Tire/auto, Target, Town Fair Tire, URGENT CARE, Verizon, Walmart
186	Stillwater Ave, same as 187
185	ME 15, to Broadway, Bangor, E📟 Irving/Circle K/dsl 🍴 Tri-City Pizza 🅾 🏥, W📟 Citgo 🍴 Amato's, China Light, Coldstone/Tim Hortons, Governor's Rest., KFC, McDonald's, Moe's BBQ, Pizza Hut, Subway, Taco Bell 🅾 Advance Parts, Hannaford Foods, TJ Maxx, Walgreens
184	ME 222, Union St, to Ohio St, Bangor, E📟 Citgo, Irving 🅾 Walgreens, W📟 Citgo, Shell/dsl 🍴 Burger King, Dunkin', McDonald's, Nicky's Rest., Wendy's 🛏 Sheraton 🅾 \$Tree, auto repair, Hannaford Foods, Marshall's, Midas, to 🏕
183	US 2, ME 2, Hammond St, Bangor, E📟 Citgo, Shell 🍴 Angelo's Pizza, Papa Gambino's Pizza 🅾 Corner Store, Fairmont Hardware, Fairmont Mkt, NAPA, W🅾 🏕
182b	US 2, ME 100 W, W📟 Irving/Circle K/Subway/dsl, Shell/dsl 🍴 Dunkin', Ground Round, Tim Hortons 🛏 Fairfield Inn, Holiday Inn, Howard Johnson, Motel 6, Quality Inn, Ramada Inn, Rodeway Inn, Super 8, Travelodge 🅾 O'Reilly Parts/VIP Service, Pumpkin Patch RV Resort, Tire Whse
182a	I-395, to US 2, US 1A, Bangor, downtown
180	Cold Brook Rd, to Hampden, E📟 Citgo 🍴 Angler's Rest. (1mi), W📟 Citgo/dsl/24hr/@, Dysarts Fleet Fuel/dsl 🛏 Best Western 🅾 dsl repair, Mack, Volvo
178mm	🆁🆂 sb, full ♿ facilities, info, litter barrels, petwalk, 🚻, 🛒, vending, wireless internet

HOULTON

BANGOR

ME

🅿 = gas 🍴 = food 🛏 = lodging 🅾 = other Rs = rest stop   Copyright 2022 - The Next EXIT

🔼N INTERSTATE 95 Cont'd

Exit #	Services
177mm	Soudabscook Stream
176mm	Rs nb, full 🚻 facilities, info, litter barrels, petwalk, 🍴, 🚮, vending, wireless internet
174	ME 69, to Carmel, E 🅿 Citgo/dsl, W 🅾 Shady Acres RV camping
167	ME 69, ME 143, to Etna
161	ME 7, to E Newport, Plymouth, W 🅾 LP, RV camping
159	Ridge Rd (from sb), to Plymouth, Newport
157	to US 2, ME 7, ME 11, Newport, W 🅿 Irving/Circle K/dsl/24hr, Shell/dsl 🍴 Burger King, China Way, Dunkin', McDonald's, Pizza Hut, Sawyers Dairy Bar 🛏 Lovley's Motel 🅾 Advance Parts, Aubuchon Hardware, Auto Value Parts, AutoZone, Chrysler/Dodge/Jeep, Hannaford Mkt, Rite Aid, Verizon, Walmart/Deli
151mm	Sebasticook River
150	Somerset Ave, Pittsfield, E 🅿 Irving/dsl 🍴 Dunkin', Subway 🛏 Pittsfield Motel 🅾 🚫 Advance Parts, Chevrolet, Family$, Rite Aid, Shop'n Save Foods
138	Hinckley Rd, Clinton, E 🅿 Citgo/dsl
134mm	Kennebec River
133	US 201, Fairfield, E 🍴 Purple Cow Pancakes
132	ME 139, Fairfield, E 🅿 EVC, Gene's Mkt/dsl, W 🅿 Irving/Circle K/Subway/dsl/scales/24hr
130	ME 104, Main St, Waterville, E 🅿 Citgo 🍴 Dunkin', Firehouse Subs, Five Guys, Governor's Rest., Little Caesar's, McDonald's, Ruby Tuesday, Starbucks, Subway, Wendy's 🛏 Best Western+, Fireside Inn, Holiday Inn Express 🅾 🚫 Advance Parts, Audi/Mazda/VW, GNC, Hannaford Foods, Home Depot, JC Penney, O'Reilly Parts/VIP Service, Staples, Verizon, Walmart
129mm	Messalonskee Stream
127	ME 11, ME 137, Waterville, Oakland, E 🅿 EVC, Irving/dsl/24hr, Xpress/dsl 🍴 Applebee's, Burger King, DQ, Dunkin', KFC/Taco Bell, McDonald's, Pad Thai, Pizza Hut, Subway, Supreme Buffet 🛏 Budget Host, Hampton Inn 🅾 🚫 AutoZone, Buick/Chevrolet, Chrysler/Dodge/Jeep/Fiat, CVS Drug, Hannaford Foods, Jo-Ann Fabrics, Marden's, Shaw's Foods/Osco Drug, Tire Whse, TJ Maxx, Toyota, Verizon, W 🅿 Shell/dsl 🅾 Aubuchon Hardware, Ford/Lincoln, NAPA
120	Lyons Rd, Sidney
117mm	weigh sta both lanes
113	ME 3, Augusta, Belfast, W 🅾 🚫
112	ME 27, ME 8, ME 11, Augusta, E 🅿 Citgo, Tesla EVC 🍴 Chipotle, Denny's, DQ, Dunkin', Elevation Burger, IHOP, Longhorn Steaks, Olive Garden, Panera Bread, Red Robin, Ruby Tuesday, Sam's Italian, Subway 🛏 Best Western+ 🅾 Barnes&Noble, Dick's, GNC, Home Depot, Kohl's, Michaels, Old Navy, Sam's Club, TJ Maxx, TownFair Tire, Verizon, Walmart, W 🅿 Irving/Circle K/dsl/24hr 🍴 99 Rest., Great Wall Chinese, KFC/Taco Bell, Wendy's 🛏 Comfort Inn, Fairfield Inn 🅾 Advance Parts
109	US 202, ME 11, ME 17, ME 100, Augusta, E 🅿 Citgo/dsl, Irving/Circle K/dsl 🍴 Amato's Rest., Amazing Garden, Applebee's, Arby's, Burger King, Damon's Italian, Domino's, Five Guys, Little Caesar's, McDonald's, Pizza Hut, Starbucks, Subway, Wendy's 🛏 Senator Inn 🅾 $Tree, Best Buy, BigLots, Lowe's, O'Reilly Parts/VIP Service, Petsmart, Shaw's Foods/Osco Drug, Staples, Target, U-Haul, USPO, vet, Walgreens, W 🅿 Kenoco 🍴 Margarita's Mexican, TX Roadhouse 🛏 Days Inn, Hampton Inn, Homewood Suites, Quality Inn, Super 8 🅾 CarQuest, Chrysler/Dodge, Hannaford Foods, Honda, Hyundai, Jeep, Kia, Nissan, PetCo, Subaru, Toyota
103	to I-295 S (from sb), ME 9, ME 126, to Gardiner, **service plaza**, 🅿 Citgo 🍴 Burger King, Popeye's, Starbucks 🅾 ZMkt

102	to I-295 S (from nb), rd 9, rd 106, **service plaza**, E 🅿 Citg 🍴 Burger King, Popeye's, Starbucks 🅾 ZMkt
100mm	**toll plaza**
99mm	Cobbosseecontee Stream
86	to ME 9, Sabattus
84mm	Sabattus Creek
80	ME 196, Lewiston, W on ME 196 🅿 Coast Fuels, Gendron's/ds Shell/dsl, XPress/dsl 🍴 Burger King, Canton Wok, D'Angel Domino's, Dunkin', Governor's Rest., KFC/Taco Bell, McDonald's Papa John's, Sam's Italian, Subway 🛏 Advance Parts, Motel 6 Ramada Inn, Super 8 🅾 🚫 $Tree, NAPA, Staples, USPO
78mm	Androscoggin River
75	US 202, rd 4, rd 100, to Auburn, E 🅿 Irving/Circle K/dsl, Mo bil/Subway/dsl 🍴 Dunkin', Peking Chinese 🛏 Fireside Inn, W 🅾 🚫
71mm	Royal River
66mm	**toll plaza**
63	US 202, rd 115, rd 4, to ME 26, Gray, E 🅿 Citgo, Cumberlan Farms/dsl, Mobil, Sunoco 🍴 China Gray, Dunkin', Goody's Piz za, McDonald's, Subway 🅾 $General, $Tree, Ace Hardware NAPA, Shop'n Save Mkt
59mm	**service plaza both lanes,** 🅿 Citgo/dsl 🍴 Burger King
55mm	Piscataqua River
53	to ME 26, ME100 W, N Portland, E 🅿 Irving/Circle K/Subway dsl 🍴 Dunkin', Maddens Grill 🅾 🚫 Hannaford Foods
52	to I-295, US 1, Freeport
48	ME 25, to Portland, E 🍴 Applebee's, Asian Bistro, Panda Ga den, Subway 🛏 Portland Inn 🅾 $Tree, BigLots, BJ's Whse/ga Chevrolet, CVS Drug, Fiat, Jo-Ann Fabrics, Lowe's, Sullivan Tir vet, W 🅿 Irving/Circle K/dsl, Mobil 🍴 Amato's Rest., Burge King, Chipotle, Dunkin', Egg&I Cafe, KFC/Taco Bell, McDonald' Panera Bread, Pizza Hut, Ruby Tuesday, Wendy's 🛏 Firesid Inn, Motel 6, Ramada, Super 8 🅾 Advance Parts, AT&T, Chry ler/Dodge/Jeep, Ford, Harley-Davidson, Home Depot, Hyunda Kohl's, Lexus/Toyota, Lincoln, Midas, NAPA, O'Reilly Parts/VI Service, Shaw's Foods/Osco Drug, Sullivan Tire, Tire Whse, vet
47	to ME 25, Rand Rd
47mm	Stroudwater River
46	to ME 22, Congress St, same as 45
45	to US 1, Maine Mall Rd, S Portland, E 🅿 Citgo/dsl, Sunocc dsl, Tesla EVC 🍴 Burger King, Chili's, Chipotle Mexican, Crac er Barrel, Dunkin', Five Guys, Food Court, Friendly's, Great Wa Chinese, Heidi's Brooklyn Deli, HomeTown Buffet, IHOP, Imp rial China, Kobe Steakhouse, Longhorn Steaks, Macaroni Gri McDonald's, Olive Garden, On the Border, Panda Express, Pan ra Bread, Popeye's, Qdoba, Sebago Brewing Rest., Starbuck Tuscan Table, UNO Pizzaria, Villa Italian, Wendy's 🛏 Comfo Inn, Courtyard, Days Inn, DoubleTree, EconoLodge, Fairfie Inn, Hampton Inn, Home 2 Suites, Homewood Suites, Tru Hilto 🅾 $Tree, Best Buy, BooksAMillion, Carmax, Dick's, Hannafor Foods, Honda, JC Penney, Macy's, Michael's, Nissan, Old Nav PetCo, Staples, TJ Maxx, TownFair Tire, Verizon, W 🍴 Appl bee's, Starbucks 🛏 Holiday Inn Express, Sheraton 🅾 Target
44	I-295 N (from nb), to S Portland, Scarborough, **1 mi** E on M 114 🍴 Cumberland 🍴 Chia Sen Chinese, KFC/Taco Bell, Le oux Kitchen, Little Caesar's, Red Robin, Subway, TX Roadhou 🛏 Candlewood Suites, Extended Stay America, Homewoo Suites, Residence Inn 🅾 🚫 AT&T, Lowe's, Marshall's, NAP O'Reilly/VIP Parts/service, Sam's Club/gas, Shaw's Foods/Os Drug, Walmart/Dunkin'
42mm	Nonesuch River

INTERSTATE 95 Cont'd

Exit #	Services
42	to US 1, **E** 🅿 🍴 Famous Dave's, Portland Pie 🅾 Cabela's, Scarborough Downs Racetrack (seasonal)
36	I-195 E, to Saco, Old Orchard Beach, **E** 🏨 Hampton Inn 🅾 KOA, Paradise Park Resort RV
35mm	**E** 🏨 Ramada Inn/Saco Hotel Conference Ctr
33mm	Saco River
32	ME 111, to Biddeford, **E** 🅿 Irving/Circle K/Subway/dsl 🍴 Amato's Sandwiches, Dunkin', Wendy's 🏨 Best Value Inn, Holiday Inn Express 🅾 🏥, AAA, AutoZone, O'Reilly/VIP Parts/Service, Walmart, **W** 🅿 Cumberland/dsl 🍴 Applebee's, Casa Fiesta Mexican, Kobe Japanese, Longhorn Steaks, Panera Bread 🅾 GNC, Home Depot, Kohl's, MarketBasket Foods, Michael's, Petsmart, Staples, Target, TJ Maxx, TownFair Tire, Verizon
25mm	Kennebunk River
25	ME 35, Kennebunk Beach, **service plaza both lanes E** car repair, vet, **W** 🅿 Shell 🏨 Hampton Inn, Kennebunk Lodge, 🅿 Citgo/dsl, Tesla EVC (nb&sb) 🍴 Burger King (sb), Popeye's (nb), Starbucks (nb&sb) 🅾 Zmkt
24mm	Mousam River
19.5mm	Merriland River
19	ME 9, ME 109, to Wells, Sanford, **W** 🅾 to Sanford RA
7mm	Maine Tpk begins/ends, **toll booth**
7	ME 91, to US 1, The Yorks, **(last exit before toll rd nb), E** 🅿 Irving/Circle K/dsl, Mobil/dsl, Shell 🍴 Bamboo Garden, Norma's Rest., Ruby's Grill, Wild Willy's Burgers, York 54 Pizza 🏨 Best Western, Microtel 🅾 🏥, Ford, Hannaford Foods, Rite Aid, vet
5.5mm	**weigh sta nb**
5mm	York River
4mm	**weigh sta sb**
3mm	**Welcome Ctr nb, full** 🅿 **facilities, info, litter barrels, petwalk,** 🅿, 🚻, **vending, wireless**
2	(2 & 3 from nb), US 1, to Kittery, **E on US 1** 🍴 7-11/dsl, Irving/Circle K/dsl/scales 🍴 Burger King, DQ, McDonald's, Robert's Maine Grill, Starbucks, Subway, Sunrise Grill, Tasty Thai, Weathervane Seafood Rest. 🏨 Days Inn, Hampton Inn, Kittery Inn, Northeaster Hotel, Ramada Inn 🅾 Outlets/Famous Brands, vet
1	ME 103 (from nb, no re-entry), to Kittery
0mm	Maine/New Hampshire state line, Piscataqua River

INTERSTATE 295

Exit #	Services
52mm	**I-295 begins/ends on I-95 exit 103.**
51	ME 9, ME 126, to Gardiner, Litchfield, **toll plaza, W service plaza,** 🅿 Citgo 🍴 Burger King, Popeye's, Starbucks 🅾 ZMkt
49	US 201, to Gardiner
43	ME 197, to Richmond, **E** 🅿 Irving/dsl 🍴 Dunkin', Subway, **W** 🅾 KOA (5mi)
37	ME 125, Bowdoinham, **W** 🅾 USPO
31 b a	ME 196, to Lisbon, Topsham, **E** 🅿 EVC, Gibbs/dsl, Irving/Circle K/Dunkin'/Subway 🍴 99 Rest., Arby's, Fairground Cafe, Firehouse Subs, Little Caesars, McDonald's, Panera Bread, Romeo's Pizza, Ruby Tuesday, Starbucks, Wendy's 🅾 $Tree, AT&T, Best Buy, Dick's, Hannaford Foods, Home Depot, Jo-Ann Fabrics, Meineke, Nissan, O'Reilly Parts/VIP Service, PetCo, Rite Aid, Target, Tire Whse, Town Fair Tire, Toyota, Verizon, **W** 🅿 Xpress Stop/dsl
30mm	Androscoggin River
28	US 1, Bath, **1 mi E on US 1** 🅿 Cumberland/dsl, Irving/dsl, Shell 🍴 Amato's, Dunkin', McDonald's, Pancho Villa, Subway 🏨 Best Value Inn, Comfort Inn, Fairfield Inn, Relax Inn, Travelers Inn 🅾 🏥, Chevrolet/Mazda, Chrysler/Dodge/Jeep

Exit #	Services
24	to Freeport (from nb), **services 1 mi E on US 1**
22	ME 125, to Pownal, **1 mi E on US 1** 🅿 Irving/Circle K 🍴 Azure Cafe, Jameson Rest., Linda Bean's ME Kitchen, McDonald's, Mediterranean Rest., Sam's Italian, Starbucks, Subway, Tuscan Bistro 🏨 Harraseeket Inn, Hilton Garden 🅾 CVS Drug, LL Bean, outlets/famous brands, USPO, **W** 🅾 to Bradbury Mtn SP
20	Desert Rd, Freeport, **E** 🅿 Irving/Circle K 🍴 Antonia's Pizza, Buck's BBQ, Dunkin', Thai Garden Rest. 🏨 Econolodge, Hampton Inn, Holiday Inn Express, Quality Suites, Super 8 🅾 Shaw's Foods
17	US 1, Yarmouth, **E** ℞ **both lanes, full** 🅿 **facilities, info,** 🍴 Day's Takeout, Muddy Rudder Rest. 🏨 Best Western 🅾 Delorme Mapping, Ford, **W** 🅿 Citgo/Dunkin'/dsl, Cumberland/dsl 🍴 Pat's Pizza 🅾 Ace Hardware, Hannaford Foods, O'Reilly Parts/VIP Service, Tire Whse
15	US 1, to Cumberland, Yarmouth, **W** 🅿 Mobil, Sunoco/dsl 🍴 233 Grill, Chopstick Asian, Romeo's Pizza, Subway 🅾 AT&T, Rite Aid
11	to I-95, ME Tpk (from sb)
10	US 1, to Falmouth, **E** 🅿 Citgo/dsl, Irving/dsl 🍴 Dunkin', Foreside Rest., Leavitt & Sons Deli, McDonald's, Orchid Thai, Ricetta's Pizza, Starbucks, Subway 🏨 Falmouth Inn 🅾 Ace Hardware, Audi/VW, Mazda, Rite Aid, Shaw's Foods, Staples, Sullivan Tire/auto, vet, Walmart
9mm	Presumpscot River
9	US 1 S, ME 26, to Baxter Blvd
8	ME 26 S, Washington Ave, **E** 🅾 U-Haul
7	US 1A, Franklin St, **E** 🍴 Miss Portland Diner 🅾 AT&T, Tire Whse, Trader Joe's, Verizon, Walgreens, Whole Foods Mkt
6 b a	US 1, Forest Ave, **E** 🅿 Citgo 🍴 Chipotle, Leavitt & Son Deli 🅾 🏥, USPO, **W** 🅿 Mobil/dsl 🍴 Burger King, Leonardo's Pizza, Stavros Pizza 🅾 CVS Drug, Hannaford Foods, U of SME, Walgreens
5 b a	ME 22, Congress St, **E** 🍴 Amato's Rest., D'Angelos, Denny's, Dunkin', McDonald's, Subway 🏨 La Quinta 🅾 🏥, Sullivan Tire, **W** 🅿 Gulf, Mobil/dsl 🍴 Anania's Italian 🏨 Clarion
3mm	Fore River, Fore River
4	US 1 S, to Main St, to S Portland, **E** 🅾 services on US 1
3	ME 9, to Westbrook St, no sb return, **W** 🅿 Citgo/dsl, Irving/Circle K/dsl 🍴 Buffalo Wild Wings, El Rodeo Mexican, Guerrero Maya, Olive Garden, Seadog Brew Co., Subway 🅾 Chevrolet, Home Depot
2	to US 1 S, S Portland, E on US 1 🅿 Irving/Circle K/dsl, Mobil 🍴 Dunkin' 🏨 Best Western, Budget Inn, Howard Johnson, Quality Inn
1	to I-95, to US 1, **multiple services E on US 1**
	I-295 begins/ends on I-95, exit 44.

NOTES

ME

🅿 = gas   🍴 = food   🛏 = lodging   🅾 = other   Rs = rest stop   Copyright 2022 - The Next EXIT

MARYLAND

🏴 E INTERSTATE 68

HANCOCK

Exit #	Services
82c	I-70 W, to Breezewood. I-68 begins/ends on I-70, exit 1.
82b	I-70 E, US 40 E, to Hagerstown
82a	US 522, Hancock, **S** 🅿 Mobil/dsl, Sheetz/dsl 🍴 Hardee's, Park'n Dine, Pizza Hut, Subway 🛏 Hancock Motel, Super 8 🅾 $General, Chevrolet, Happy Hills Camping, NAPA, Save-A-Lot Foods
77	US 40, MD 144, Woodmont Rd, **S** 🅾 RV camping
75mm	runaway truck ramp eb
74mm	Sideling Hill Rs/exhibit both lanes, full ♿ facilities, vending, 1269 ft (seasonal)
74	US 40, Mountain Rd (no return from eb)
73mm	Sideling Hill Creek
72mm	no service
72	US 40, High Germany Rd, Swain Rd, **S** 🅿 Citgo/dsl 🍴 Oak Barrel Cafe
68	Orleans Rd, **N** 🅿 Exxon/dsl
67mm	Town Hill, elevation 940 ft, Town Hill
64	MV Smith Rd, **S** 🅾 scenic overlook, elevation 1040 ft, to Green Ridge SF HQ
62	US 40, 15 Mile Creek Rd, **N** 🅾 Billmeyer Wildlife Mgt Area
58.7mm	Polish Mtn, elevation 1246 ft
57mm	Town Creek
56mm	Flintstone Creek
56	MD 144, National Pike, Flintstone, **S** 🅿 Billie's Gas&Grub 🛏 Seven C's Lodge 🅾 USPO
52	MD 144, Pleasant Valley Rd (from eb), National Pike
50	Pleasant Valley Rd, **N** 🅿 Tesla EVC 🍴 Lakeside Grill, Signature's Grill 🛏 Rocky Gap Lodge/golf/rest. 🅾 to Rocky Gap SP
47	US 220 N, MD 144, Dehaven Rd (from wb), Old National Pike, Bedford, **S** 🅿 Loves/Arby's/dsl/scales/24hr 🛏 Sleep Inn
46	US 220 N, Dehaven Rd, Baltimore Pike, Naves Crossroads, **N** 🅿 Sheetz/dsl 🛏 Cumberland Motel 🅾 $General, Advance Parts, **S** 🅿 Loves/Arby's/dsl/scales/24hr 🍴 Puccini's Rest. 🛏 Sleep Inn
45	Hillcrest Dr, **S** 🅿 Sunoco/dsl
44	US 40A, Baltimore Ave, Willow Brook Rd, to Allegany Comm Coll, **N** 🛏 Hampton Inn, **S** 🅾 🚑 to Allegany Comm Coll
43d	Maryland Ave, **N** 🛏 Ramada 🅾 USPO, **S** 🅿 Gulf/7-11/Subway 🍴 Chick-fil-A, Papa John's 🅾 🚑 AT&T, AutoZone, Martin's Foods/gas
43c	downtown, same as 43b
43mm	Youghiogheny River
43b	MD 51, Industrial Blvd, **N** 🍴 McDonald's, Subway 🛏 Ramada 🅾 Family$, SaveALot Foods, **S** 🅿 Sunoco/dsl 🍴 Roy Rogers, Taco Bell, Wendy's 🛏 Fairfield Inn
43a	to WV 28A, Beall St, Industrial Blvd, to Cumberland, Johnson St, **N** 🅿 Sheetz
42	US 220 S, Greene St, Ridgedale
41	Seton Dr (from wb, no directory turn)
41mm	Haystack Mtn, elev 1240 ft
40	US 220 S, to US 40A, Vocke Rd, La Vale, **N** 🅿 BP/dsl, Sheetz/dsl, Tesla EVC 🍴 Arby's, Asian Garden, Bob Evans, Burger King, Cracker Barrel, D'Atri Rest., Denny's, DQ, KFC, LJ Silver, McDonald's, New Orient, Pizza Hut, Rio Grande Mexican, Rita's Custard, Ruby Tuesday, Subway, TX Grill, Wendy's 🛏 Best Western,

FROSTBURG

Exit #	Services
40	Continued
	Comfort Inn, Holiday Inn Express, Super 8 🅾 $General, Advance Parts, AT&T, AutoZone, CVS Drug, Harley-Davidson, Jo-Ann Fabrics, Lowe's, Mr Tire, NAPA, st police, Staples, URGENT CARE, **S** 🍴 Applebee's, Buffalo Wild Wings, Chick-fil-A, Wasabi Japanese 🛏 Motel 6 🅾 $Tree, Aldi Foods, JC Penney, Kohl's, Martin's Foods/gas, Petsmart, Walmart/McDonald's
39	US 40A (from wb), same as 40
34	MD 36, to Westernport, Frostburg, **N** 🅿 Sheetz/dsl, Valero/dsl 🍴 Burger King, Fox's Pizza, Mario's Italian, McDonald's, Pizza Hut, Subway 🛏 Hampton Inn, Quality Inn 🅾 🚑 $General, Rite Aid, Save-A-Lot, Weis Mkt, **S** 🅾 to Dans Mtn SP
33	Midlothian Rd, to Frostburg, **N** 🅾 🚑 **S** 🅾 to Dans Mt SP
31mm	weigh sta eb
30mm	Big Savage Mtn, elevation 2800 ft
29	MD 546, Finzel, **N** 🍴 Hen House Rest. (2mi) 🅾 Mason-Dixon Camping (4mi/seasonal), **S** 🍴 Savage River Lodge/rest. (4mi)
25.8mm	eastern continental divide, elevation 2610 ft
24	Lower New Germany Rd, to US 40A, **S** 🅾 to New Germany SP, to Savage River SF
23mm	Meadow Mtn, elevation 2780 ft
22	US 219 N, to Meyersdale, **N** 🅿 Pilot/Arby's/dsl/scales/24hr, Sunoco/dsl 🍴 Burger King, IHOP, Little Caesar's, Penn Alps Rest., Subway 🅾 $General, Ford, Hilltop Fruit Mkt, NAPA, Rite Aid, Shop'n Save, TrueValue, **S** 🅿 Valero/dsl 🛏 Comfort Inn 🅾 New Germany SP, Savage River SF
20mm	Casselman River
19	MD 495, to US 40A, Grantsville, **N** 🅿 Exxon/Subway/dsl, Sunoco/dsl 🛏 Casselman Motel/rest. 🅾 Medicine Shoppe, USPO
15mm	Mt Negro, elevation 2740 ft
14mm	Keyser's Ridge, elevation 2880 ft
14b a	US 219, US 40 W, Oakland, **N** 🅿 7-11/dsl, Liberty/Ridge/rest/dsl 🍴 McDonald's, repair
6mm	Welcome Ctr eb, full ♿ facilities, info, litter barrels, petwalk 🚻, 🛏, vending
4.5mm	Bear Creek
4	MD 42, Friendsville, **N** 🅿 Exxon/dsl, Liberty/dsl 🛏 Yough Valley Motel 🅾 S&S Mkt, USPO, **S** 🛏 Sunset Inn 🅾 to Deep Creek Lake SP
0mm	Maryland/West Virginia state line

🏴 E INTERSTATE 70

BALTIMORE

Exit #	Services
	I-70 begins/ends in Baltimore at Cooks Lane.
94	Security Blvd N, **S** 🅿 Shell
91b a	I-695
87b a	US 29 (exits left from wb) to MD 99, Columbia, **2 mi S** on US 40 🅿 BP/dsl, Exxon/dsl, Gulf, Shell/dsl, Sunoco 🍴 Arby's, Baskin Robbins/Dunkin', Boston Mkt, Burger King, Checkers, Domino's, Jimmy John's, McDonald's, Papa John's, Pizza Hut, Qdoba, Starbucks, Subway 🅾 7-11, Acura, Advance Parts, Cadillac/Chevrolet, Carmax, CVS Drug, Giant Foods, Goodyear/auto, H Mart Food, Home Depot, Honda, Infiniti, Kia, Mars Foods, Midas, Mr Tire, Nissan, Rite Aid, Safeway Foods, Verizon, Walgreens, Walmart
83	US 40, Marriottsville (no EZ wb return), **2 mi S** 🛏 Turf Valley Hotel/Country Club/rest.
82	US 40 E (from eb), same as 83
80	MD 32, Sykesville, **N** 🅾 golf, **S** 🅿 High's/dsl 🍴 Subway, Tony's Pizzeria

MD

INTERSTATE 70 Cont'd

Exit #	Services
79mm	weigh/insp sta wb, 🌐
76	MD 97, Olney, S 🅿 High's/dsl 🍴 Subway
73	MD 94, Woodbine, N 🅿 High's/dsl 🍴 Baskin Robbins, China Yee, Dunkin', Harvest Chicken, McDonald's, Pizza Hut, Subway 🅾 $Tree, Food Lion, Ramblin Pines RV Park (6mi), Verizon, S 🅿 BP/dsl, Citgo 🍴 Town Grill
68	MD 27, Mt Airy, N 🅿 7-11, Liberty/dsl 🍴 Arby's, Baskin-Robbns/Dunkin', Burger King, Chipotle, Chong Yet Yin Chinese, Domino's, Five Guys, J&P Pizza, Jersey Mike' Subs, KFC/Taco Bell, Ledo's Pizza, McDonald's, Papa John's, Pizza Hut, Rita's Custard, Starbucks, Subway 🅾 Ace Hardware, Advance Parts, AT&T, Food Lion, GNC, Goodyear, Mr Tire, Rite Aid, Safeway, Verizon, Walmart, S 🅿 Exxon/dsl, Shell/dsl 🏨 Budget Inn
66mm	truckers parking area eb
64mm	weigh/insp sta eb
62	MD 75, Libertytown, N 🅿 Falcon Fuels, High's/dsl 🍴 Asian Bistro, Baskin Robbins, Burger King, Domino's, Dunkin', Mc-Donald's, Morgan's Grill 🅾 CVS Drug, Food Lion, New Market Hist Dist
59	MD 144
57mm	Monocacy River
56	MD 144, N 🅿 BP, Sheetz 🍴 Beijing, Burger King, JR's Pizza, McDonald's, Roy Rogers, Taco Bell, Wendy's 🅾 to Hist Dist, S 🅾 Chesaco RV Ctr
55	South St, 1 mi N 🅿 BP, Sheetz/dsl 🅾 same as 56
54	Market St, to I-270, N 🅿 Costco/gas 🏨 Super 8, S 🅿 7-11, Sheetz/dsl, Shell/dsl, SouStates/dsl, Valero/dsl, Wawa/dsl 🍴 Applebee's, Arby's, BJ's Rest., Burger King, Checker's, Chick-fil-A, ChuckeCheese, Cracker Barrel, Golden Corral, KFC/Taco Bell, Longhorn Steaks, McDonald's, Olive Garden, Panera Bread, Papa John's, Peking Gourmet, Popeye's, Red Robin, Ruby Tuesday, Sonic, Subway, Waffle House 🏨 Clarion, Country Inn Suites, Courtyard, Days Inn, EconoLodge, Extended Stay America, Fairfield Inn, Hampton Inn, Hilton Garden, Residence Inn, Sleep Inn 🅾 $Tree, AAA, Aamco, Audi, Barnes&Noble, Best Buy, Buick/GMC, Chrysler/Dodge/Jeep, Dick's, Home Depot, Honda, Hyundai, JC Penney, Kia, Kohl's, Lincoln, Lowe's, Macy's, Michael's, Mr Tire, Nissan, Petsmart, Ross, Sam's Club/dsl, Staples, Target, Tires+, TJMaxx, Toyota, Volvo, Walmart
53b a	I-270 S, US 15 N, US 40 W, to Frederick
52b a	US 15 S, US 340 W, Leesburg
49	US 40A, Braddock Heights, N on US 40 🅿 Carroll/dsl, Citgo/dsl, Exxon/dsl, GetGo, Shell/dsl, Sunoco, WaWa/dsl 🍴 Arby's, Bob Evans, Boston Mkt, Burger King, Casa Rico Mexican, Chipotle, Denny's, Domino's, Dunkin', Famous Dave's BBQ, Flaming Grill, HoneyBaked Ham, KFC, Los Trios, McDonald's, Mtn View Diner, Outback Steaks, Pizza Hut, Popeye's, Red Horse Rest., Red Lobster, Roy Rogers, Starbucks, Subway, Taco Bell, Wendy's 🏨 Comfort Inn, Motel 6 🅾 H, $General, $Tree, 7-11, Aldi Foods, AT&T, AutoZone, Boscov's, CVS Drug, Giant Eagle Foods, Home Depot, Meineke, Mr Tire, NTB, PepBoys, PetCo, Subaru, Verizon, Weis Foods, S 🅾 camping, to Washington Mon SP

48	US 40 E, US 340 (from eb, no return), 1 mi N same as 49
42	MD 17, Myersville, N 🅿 Exxon, Sunoco/dsl 🍴 Burger King, McDonald's, Old Town Diner 🅾 Greenbrier SP (4mi), to Gambrill SP (6mi), S 🅿 Crown/dsl 🍴 Subway
39mm	🆁🆂 both lanes, full ♿ facilities, litter barrels, petwalk, 🌐, 🖼, vending
35	MD 66, to Boonsboro, S 🅿 Sheetz/dsl (1mi) 🅾 camping, to Greenbrier SP
32b a	US 40, Hagerstown, 0-3 mi N 🅿 7-11/dsl, BP, Exxon/dsl, Sheetz/dsl, Sunoco 🍴 Baskin-Robbins/Dunkin', Bob Evans, Burger King, Cancun Cantina, Checkers, Coldstone, Denny's, DQ, El Ranchero Mexican, Family Diner, Five Guys, Jimmy John's, KFC, Ledo's Pizza, Little Caesar's, McDonald's, Papa John's, Pizza Hut, Popeye's, Sonic, Subway, Supreme Buffet, Taco Bell, TX Roadhouse, Wendy's 🏨 Baymont Inn, Comfort Suites, Days Inn, Garden Plaza Hotel, Hampton Inn, Quality Inn, Super 8 🅾 H, $General, $Tree, Advance Parts, Aldi Foods, AT&T, AutoZone, Cadillac/Chevrolet, Chrysler/Dodge/Jeep, CVS Drug, Family$, Martin's Foods, Mercedes, Midas, Mr Tire, Nissan, Tires+, Toyota, URGENT CARE, Walgreens, Weis Foods, S 🅾 Buick/GMC, Honda, Kia, Subaru/Mazda/VW
29b a	MD 65, to Sharpsburg, N 🅿 EVgo EVC, Exxon/Subway/dsl, Sheetz/dsl, Tesla EVC 🍴 FoodCourt, Longhorn Steaks 🅾 H, Prime Outlets/famous brands, S 🅿 EVC, Liberty/7-11/dsl 🍴 Burger King, Cracker Barrel, McDonald's, Waffle House, Wendy's 🏨 Sleep Inn 🅾 Jellystone Camping, st police, to Antietam Bfd, Walmart
28	MD 632, Hagerstown
26	I-81, N to Harrisburg, S to Martinsburg
24	MD 63, Huyett, N 🅿 Pilot/Subway/dsl/24hr, Sheetz/dsl (2mi), S 🏨 Red Roof Inn 🅾 C&O Canal, KOA (2mi)
18	MD 68 E, Clear Spring, N 🅿 BP/dsl, Liberty 🍴 Al's Grill, McDonald's 🏨 Holiday Inn Express, Sleep Inn, S 🅿 Exxon/dsl 🍴 Wendy Hill Café
12	MD 56, Indian Springs, S 🅿 Exxon/dsl 🅾 Ft Frederick SP
9	US 40 E (from eb, exits left), Indian Springs
5	MD 615 (no immediate wb return), N 🅾 Log Cabin Rest. (2mi)
3	MD 144, Hancock (exits left from wb), S 🅿 ACT/Exxon/dsl, Liberty/rest./dsl/24hr 🍴 Hardee's, Park'n Dine 🏨 Hilltop Inn 🅾 Blue Goose Mkt

F R E D E R I C K

H A G E R S T O W N

➤E INTERSTATE 70 Cont'd

Exit #	Services
1b	US 522 (exits left from both lanes), Hancock, **S** 🅖 Mobil/dsl, Sheetz/dsl 🅕 Hardee's, Park'n Dine, Pizza Hut, Subway 🛏 Hancock Motel, Super 8 🄾 $General, Chevrolet, Happy Hills Camp, NAPA, Save-A-Lot Foods
1a	I-68 W, US 40, W to Cumberland
0mm	Maryland/Pennsylvania state line, Mason-Dixon Line

➤N INTERSTATE 81

Exit #	Services
12mm	Maryland/Pennsylvania state line
10b a	Showalter Rd, **E** 🄾 🔄
9	Maugans Ave, **E** 🅖 BP, Sheetz/dsl, Shell/Domino's/dsl 🅕 Fox's Pizza, Hometown Diner, McDonald's, Papa Murphy's, Pizza Hut, Pollo Loco, Subway, Taco Bell, Waffle House 🛏 Hampton Inn 🄾 $General, AutoZone, CVS Drug, Food Lion, Martin's Foods/gas, Meineke, vet, Walgreens, **W** 🅕 Burger King, Dunkin' 🛏 Microtel 🄾 Kenworth, Volvo
7b a	MD 58, Hagerstown, same as 6
6b a	US 40, Hagerstown, **E** 🅖 Shell 🄾 🛏, **W** 🅕 Arby's, Chipotle Mexican, Five Guys, IHOP, Jersey Mike's Subs, KFC, McDonald's, Number One Chinese, Panera Bread, Ryan's, Starbucks, Subway, TGIFriday's, Uno Pizza, Wendy's 🄾 $Tree, AT&T, Best Buy, Dick's, GNC, Home Depot, Marshall's, Petsmart, Walmart
5b a	Halfway Blvd, **E** 🅖 AC&T/dsl 🅕 Bob Evans, Boston Mkt, Boston Mkt, Buffalo Wild Wings, Burger King, Chick-fil-A, ChuckE-Cheese's, CiCi's Pizza, Cinco de Mayo, Coldstone, El Ranchero Mexican, Fireside Rest., Golden Corral, Hard Times Cafe, Jimmy John's, McDonald's, Nikko Japanese, Noodles&Co, Olive Garden, Outback Steaks, Papa John's, Pizza Hut, Popeye's, Red Lobster, Red Robin, Roy Rogers, Ruby Tuesday, Sakura Steaks, Starbucks, Taco Bell, Tilted Kilt, Wendy's 🛏 Country Inn&Suites, Courtyard, Holiday Inn Express, Homewood Suites, Motel 6, Ramada, SpringHill Suites 🄾 $Tree, BigLots, BonTon, CVS Drug, Firestone/auto, Ford, Hobby Lobby, Hyundai, JC Penney, Kohl's, Lowe's, Martin's Foods/gas, Michael's, PetCo, Ross, Sam's Club/gas, Staples, Target, **W** 🅕 Exxon/dsl/scales/24hr, 🅿🄻🄾🅃/McDonald's/Subway/dsl/scales/24hr 🛏 Super 8 🄾 Freightliner
4	I-70, E to Frederick, W to Hancock, to I-68
2	US 11, Williamsport, **E** 🅖 AC&T/dsl, **W** 🅖 Exxon/dsl, Sunoco/dsl 🅕 China 88, McDonald's, Subway, Waffle House 🛏 Red Roof Inn 🄾 auto repair, KOA (4mi)
1	MD 63, MD 68, Williamsport, **E** 🅖 Bowman/dsl 🄾 Jellystone, to Antietam Bfd, **W** 🅖 Citgo 🄾 $General, KOA, NAPA
0mm	Maryland/West Virginia state line, Potomac River

➤N INTERSTATE 83

Exit #	Services
38mm	Maryland/Pennsylvania state line, Mason-Dixon Line
37	to Freeland (from sb)
36	MD 439, Bel Air, **W** 🅖 Filler-Up 🅕 Maryland Line Inn Grill 🄾 Holiday Travel Park (5mi), Merry Meadows Camping (5mi)
35mm	weigh/insp sta sb
33	MD 45, Parkton, **E** 🄾 USPO
31	Middletown Rd, to Parkton, **E** 🄾 golf
27	MD 137, Mt Carmel, Hereford, **E** 🅖 Exxon/dsl 🅕 Michael's Pizza, Monkton Grill, Subway 🄾 7-11, Graul's Foods, Hereford Drug, Mt Carmel Drug, USPO, vet
24	Belfast Rd, to Butler, Sparks

20	Shawan Rd, Hunt Valley, **E** 🅖 Exxon/dsl, Mobil 🅕 Burger King, CA Pizza, Carrabba's, Chick-fil-A, Chipotle Mexican, Coal Fire Cafe, Joe's Crabshack, McDonald's, Noodles&Co, Outback Steaks, Panera Bread, Pei Wei, Sakura Hibachi, Subway 🛏 Courtyard, Embassy Suites, Holiday Inn Express, Hunt Valley Inn, Residence Inn 🄾 Burlington Coats, Dick's, Giant Foods, Goodyear/auto, Marshall's, Verizon, vet, Wegman's Foods
18	Warren Rd (from nb, no return), Cockeysville, **services E on York Rd**
17	Padonia Rd, Deereco Rd, **E** 🅖 7-11, BP/dsl, Gulf/dsl, Marathon/dsl 🅕 Applebee's, Bob Evans, Chili's, Macaroni Grill, Wendy's 🛏 Extended Stay America, Hampton Inn, Holiday Inn 🄾 Audi/VW, Chevrolet, Goodyear/auto, Lowe's Whse, Mars Mkt, Mr Tire, Porsche, Rite Aid, Sam's Club, services E on York Rd, Subaru, Target, USPO
16b a	Timonium Rd, **E** 🅖 Sunoco/dsl 🅕 Baja Fresh, Firehouse Subs, Little Caesar's, McDonald's 🛏 N Baltimore Plaza Hotel, Red Roof Inn 🄾 Infiniti/Nissan, Petsmart, REI, Rite Aid, ShopRite Foods, **services E on York Rd**
14	I-695 N
13	I-695 S, Falls Rd, **E** 🄾 🛏, **W** 🄾 st police
12	Ruxton Rd (from nb, no return)
10b a	Northern Parkway, **E** 🅖 Exxon, Shell, **W** 🄾 🛏
9b a	Cold Spring Lane
8	MD 25 N (from nb), Falls Rd
7b a	28th St, **E** 🄾 🛏, **W** 🄾 Baltimore Zoo
6	US 1, US 40T, North Ave, downtown
5	MD Ave (from sb), downtown
3	Chase St, Gilford St, downtown
2	Pleasant St (from sb), downtown
1	Fayette St, downtown Baltimore, **I-83 begins/ends.**

➤N INTERSTATE 95

Exit #	Services
110mm	Maryland/Delaware state line
109b a	MD 279, to Elkton, Newark, **E** 🅖 CF/dsl, ✈FLYING J/Golden Corral/dsl/scales/24hr/@ 🅕 Cracker Barrel, KFC/Taco Bell, McDonald's, Waffle House 🛏 Days Inn, Elkton Lodge, Hampton Inn, Knights Inn, La Quinta, Motel 6 🄾 🛏, Blue Beacon, **W** 🅖 7-11, TA/Country Pride/dsl/24hr/@, WaWa/dsl 🛏 Holiday Inn Express 🄾 to U of DE
100	MD 272, to North East, Rising Sun, **E** 🅖 ✈FLYING J/Denny's dsl/LP/24hr, Sunoco/dsl 🅕 Burger King, Dunkin', Frank's Pizza, Little Caesar's, McDonald's, Waffle House, Wendy's 🛏 Comfort Inn, Holiday Inn Express 🄾 $General, $Tree, Advance Parts, AT&T, auto repair, Food Lion, Lowe's, PetCo, st police, to Elk Neck SP, Verizon, Walgreens, Walmart/Subway, **W** 🅖 High's/dsl 🅕 Hunan Wok, Pizza Hut 🛏 Best Western 🄾 zoo
96mm	Chesapeake House service area (exits left from both lanes) 🅖 Sunoco/dsl 🅕 Burger King, Peets Coffee, Pizza Hut, Popeye's, Wendy's
93	MD 275, to Rising Sun, US 222, to Perryville, **E** 🅖 Exxon/dsl 🅿🄻🄾🅃/Subway/dsl/scales/24hr 🅕 Denny's 🛏 Days Inn 🄾 🛏
92mm	weigh sta/toll booth
91.5mm	Susquehanna River
89	MD 155, to Havre de Grace (last nb exit before toll), 1-3 mi **E** 🅕 Burger King, Chesapeake Grill, Dunkin', MacGregor Rest., McDonald's, Waffle House 🛏 Super 8, Van Divers B&B 🄾 🛏, **W** 🄾 to Susquehanna SP
85	MD 22, to Aberdeen, **E** 🅖 7-11, Crown/dsl, Royal Farms/dsl, Shell/dsl 🅕 Applebee's, Baskin-Robbins/Dunkin', Bob Evans, Burger King, Chap's Pit Beef, Chick-fil-A, IHOP, KFC, La Tolteca Mexican, Little Caesar's, McDonald's, Olive Tree Italian

H A G E R S T O W N (vertical, left margin)

B A L T I M O R E (vertical, center margin)

A B E R D E E N (vertical, lower center margin)

MD

A B E R D E E N

INTERSTATE 95 Cont'd	
85	Continued
	Panera Bread, Papa John's, Rita's Custard, Subway, Taco Bell, Wendy's 🛏 Comfort Inn, Days Inn, Hampton Inn, Hilton Garden, Holiday Inn Express, La Quinta, Red Roof Inn, Super 8, Travelodge ⊙ $General, $Tree, Firestone/auto, GNC, Home Depot, Rite Aid, ShopRite Foods, Target, Verizon, Walgreens, **W** 🛏 Courtyard, Residence Inn
81mm	**MD House service area (exits left from both lanes)** ⛽ Sunoco/dsl 🍴 Dunkin', Jerry's, Phillips Seafood, Starbucks, Wendy's
80	MD 543, to Riverside, Churchville, **E** ⛽ 7-11, BP/Burger King, Shell/dsl, Sunoco 🍴 Arby's, China Moon, Cracker Barrel, Lee's Asian Bistro, McDonald's, Pizza Hut, Riverside Grille, Riverside Pizzeria, Ruby Tuesday, Subway, Waffle House 🛏 Candlewood Suites, Country Inn&Suites, Extended Stay America, Homewood Suites, SpringHill Suites, Wingate Inn ⊙ Bar Harbor RV Park (4mi), Rite Aid, ShopRite Foods
77b a	MD 24, to Edgewood, Bel Air, **E** ⛽ Exxon/dsl, Royal Farms/dsl, Sunoco/dsl 🍴 Denny's, My 3 Sons Rest., Subway, Waffle House 🛏 Comfort Inn, Hampton Inn, Holiday Inn Express, La Quinta, Motel 6, Ramada, Red Roof Inn, Sleep Inn ⊙ Old Navy, **W** ⛽ Exxon/dsl, WaWa/dsl 🍴 Boston's, Chick-fil-A, Dickey's BBQ, KFC/Taco Bell, McDonald's, Panda Express, Panera Bread, Starbucks ⊙ Ⓗ, $Tree, BJ's Whse, GNC, JC Penney, Lowe's, Petsmart, Target, Walmart/Subway, Wegman's Foods
74	MD 152, Fallston, Joppatowne, **E** ⛽ CF/dsl, Exxon/dsl, WaWa/dsl 🍴 Friendly's, Subway 🛏 Super 8 ⊙ Toyota (1mi), **W** ⛽ Royal Farms/dsl
70mm	⊙ Big Gunpowder Falls
67b a	MD 43, to White Marsh Blvd, US 1, US 40, **E** ⛽ BP/dsl 🍴 Applebee's, Chick-fil-A, Chipotle, Five Guys, Jimmy John's, Ledo Pizza, McDonald's, Noodles&Co, Panda Express, Panera Bread, Pie Five, Qdoba, Starbucks, Subway, Zoe's Kitchen 🛏 Home 2 Suites ⊙ Best Buy, Carmax, Chevrolet, Dick's, Lowe's, Michael's, Petco, Target, TJ Maxx, **W** ⛽ 7-11, Exxon/dsl 🍴 All About Burger, Bertucci's, Buffalo Wild Wings, Burger King, Chili's, China Wok, Coldstone, Don Pablo, Kobe Japanese, McDonald's, Olive Garden, PF Chang's, Red Brick Sta., Red Lobster, Red Robin, Starbucks, Taco Bell, TGIFriday's, Tilted Kilt, TX Roadhouse, Wendy's 🛏 Fairfield Inn, Hampton Inn, Hilton Garden, Residence Inn, Woodspring Suites ⊙ AT&T, Barnes&Noble, Giant Foods, IKEA, JC Penney, Macy's, Mr Tire, Old Navy, Staples, to Gunpowder SP, USPO, Verizon
64b a	I-695 (exits left), E to Essex, W to Towson
62	to I-895 (from sb)
61	US 40, Pulaski Hwy, **E** ⛽ BP, Shell/dsl 🍴 McDonald's
60	Moravia Rd
59	Eastern Ave, **W** ⛽ BP/dsl, Exxon, Royal Farms/dsl, WaWa 🍴 Broadway Diner, McDonald's, Subway, Wendy's ⊙ Ⓗ, Home Depot, Shoppers Foods
58	Dundalk Ave, (from nb), **E** ⛽ Citgo
57	O'Donnell St, Boston St, **E** ⛽ TA/Buckhorn/Country Pride/Subway/dsl/scales/motel/@ 🍴 McDonald's 🛏 Best Western
56	Keith Ave
56mm	McHenry Tunnel, **toll plaza (north side of tunnel)**
55	Key Hwy, to Ft McHenry NM, last nb exit before **toll**
54	MD 2 S, to Hanover St, **W** ⊙ Ⓗ, Harris Teeter, downtown
53	I-395 N, to MLK, **W** ⊙ Oriole Park, downtown
52	Russell St N, **W** ⊙ Ⓗ
51	Washington Blvd

C O L U M B I A

50.5mm	inspection sta nb
50	Caton Ave, **E** ⛽ Marathon/dsl, Shell/dsl, US/dsl 🍴 Caton House, Loafers Grill, McDonald's 🛏 Motel 6 ⊙ 7-11, Aldi Foods, auto repair, Midas, Toyota, **W** ⊙ Ⓗ
49b a	I-695, E to Key Bridge, Glen Burnie, W to Towson, to I-70, to I-83
47b a	I-195, to MD 166, to BWI Airport, to Baltimore
46	I-895, to Harbor Tunnel Thruway
43b a	MD 100, to Glen Burnie, **1 mi E on US 1** ⛽ Exxon/Wendy's/dsl, Xtra 🛏 Best Western
41b a	MD 175, to Columbia, **E** ⛽ BP/dsl, Exxon/dsl, Shell/dsl, TA/Country Pride/Subway/dsl/scales/24hr/@ 🍴 Arby's, Burger King, Frank's Diner, IHOP, McDonald's, Panda Express, Starbucks 🛏 Comfort Suites, Holiday Inn, La Quinta, Red Roof Inn, Sleep Inn, Super 8 ⊙ $Tree, Advance Parts, Mom's Organic Mkt, **W** ⛽ Exxon 🍴 Bob Evans, Fat Burger, Houlihan's, Jersey Mike's, McDonald's, Mimi's Cafe, Olive Garden, On the Border, TGIFriday's 🛏 Extended Stay America, Homewood Suites ⊙ Ⓗ, Best Buy, Costco/gas, CVS Drug, Lowe's, Loyola U, Office Depot, Royal Farms, to Johns Hopkins U, Trader Joe's
38b a	MD 32, to Ft Meade, **2 mi E on US 1** ⛽ BP/dsl, Exxon/Wendy's/dsl, Royal Farms, Shell/dsl 🍴 Burger King, Dunkin', McDonald's, Subway, Taco Bell 🛏 Comfort Inn, Extended Stay America ⊙ Ⓗ, to BWI Airport
37mm	**Welcome Ctr both lanes, full ♿ facilities, info, litter barrels, petwalk, ⊙, ♿, RV Dump, vending**
35b a	MD 216, to Laurel, **E** ⛽ Exxon, Shell/dsl 🍴 McDonald's, Subway ⊙ Weis Food/drug
34mm	Patuxent River
33b a	MD 198, to Laurel, **E** ⛽ Exxon ⊙ Ⓗ, **W** ⛽ Exxon/Blimpie/dsl, Shell 🍴 Outback Steaks 🛏 Holiday Inn
31	MD 200 (**toll**), to I-270
29	MD 212, to Beltsville, **E** ⊙ Cherry Hill RV Resort, **W** ⛽ Exxon/Blimpie/dsl 🍴 Baskin-Robbins, Danny's Subs, KFC, McDonald's, Taco Bell, The Villa Rest., TJ's Rest., Wendy's 🛏 Comfort Inn, Sheraton ⊙ CVS Drug, Giant Foods
27	I-495 S around Washington
25b a	US 1, Baltimore Ave, to Laurel, College Park, **E** ⛽ 7-11, BP/dsl, Exxon/dsl, Shell, Sunoco, Wawa/dsl 🍴 Arby's, Buffalo Wild Wings, Burger King, Chipotle, Domino's, Dunkin', McDonald's, Moose Creek Steaks, Panera Bread, Papa John's, Pizza Hut/Taco Bell, Potbelly's, Starbucks, Subway, Wendy's 🛏 Holiday Inn ⊙ Advance Parts, Aldi Foods, AutoZone, Cherry Hill RV Resort, Costco/gas, CVS Drug, IKEA, PetCo, Rite Aid, URGENT CARE, US Agri Library, Verizon, **W** ⛽ BP/24hr, Exxon, Shell, Xtra 🍴 Azteca, Burger King, College Park Diner, Denny's, Dunkin', Hard Times Cafe, IHOP, Mamma Lucia, McDonald's, Pizza Hut, Sakura Seafood Buffet, Starbucks, Taco Bell 🛏 Clarion, Days Inn,

B A L T I M O R E

MD

⬆N INTERSTATE 95 Cont'd

25b a	Continued EconoLodge, Hampton Inn, Holiday Inn Express, Howard Johnson, Red Roof Inn, Super 8 🅾 CVS Drug, GNC, Home Depot, Honda, Hyundai, Nissan, Shoppers Foods, to U of MD, vet
24	(from sb), to metro
23	MD 201, Kenilworth Ave, E 🛏 Marriott/rest., **1 mi W on Greenbelt** 🍴 Boston Mkt, Checker's, Chipotle Mexican, Domino's, Jersey Mike's, Joe's Crabshack, KFC, McDonald's, Popeye's, Silver Diner, TGIFriday's, Wendy's 🛏 Courtyard, Hilton Garden, Residence Inn, Shell 🅾 AutoZone, Buick/GMC/Cadillac, CVS Drug, Giant Food/drug, Jo-Ann Fabrics, Marshall's, Staples, Target, URGENT CARE
22	Baltimore-Washington Pkwy, E 🅾 to NASA
20b a	MD 450, Annapolis Rd, Lanham, E 🍴 Burger King, McDonald's, Red Lobster 🛏 Best Western, Days Inn/rest., Red Roof Inn 🅾 Ford/KIA, NTB, W 🅿 7-11/dsl, BP, Citgo, Shell 🍴 Bojangles, Chipotle, Dunkin', El Gran Chaparral, Jersey Mike's, KFC, King Pollo, Papa John's, Popeye's, Starbucks, Subway, Wendy's 🛏 Metro Points Hotel 🅾 🅷, Advance Parts, Chrysler/Dodge/Jeep, CVS Drug, Family$, Foodway Foods, JustTires, Lowe's, Meineke, SaveALot, Shoppers Foods, Staples
19b a	US 50, to Annapolis, Washington
17	MD 202, Landover Rd, to Upper Marlboro, E 🍴 Chipotle, Copper Canyon, Jasper's Rest., Kobe Japanese, Outback Steaks, Ruby Tuesday 🛏 Doubletree, Hampton Inn, Holiday Inn Express 🅾 Best Buy, Costco/gas, Old Navy, Petco, Wegman's, W 🅾 FedEx Center
16	Arena Dr, E 🍴 Carolina Kitchen, Chick-fil-A, ChuckeCheese, Famous Dave's, Five Guys, Golden Corral, Kobe Japanese, Longhorn Steaks, Panda Express, TGIFriday's 🛏 Courtyard, Residence Inn, W 🅾 to FedEx Field
15	MD 214, Central Ave, E 🛏 Extended Stay America, Hotel Largo 🅾 to Six Flags, W 🅿 BP, Exxon/dsl, Shell 🍴 Checker's, Dunkin', IHOP, KFC, McDonald's, Panda Express, Taco Bell, Wendy's 🛏 Fairbridge Inn&Suites, La Quinta 🅾 Family$, Goodyear/auto, Home Depot, NTB, U-Haul, URGENT CARE
13	Ritchie-Marlboro Rd, Capitol Hgts, W 🅿 WaWa/dsl 🍴 Chick-fil-A, Chipotle, Dave&Buster's, Five Guys, Ledo Pizza, McDonald's, Popeye's, Sonic, Tropical Cafe 🅾 $Tree, Advance Parts, Big Lots, BJ Whse/gas, Honda, Hyundai, Tires+, TJ Maxx
11	MD 4, Pennsylvania Ave, to Upper Marlboro, W 🅿 Exxon, Shell, Sunoco 🍴 Applebee's, Arby's, Domino's, IHOP, LJ Silver, Starbucks, Subway, Taco Bell, Wendy's 🅾 $Tree, CVS Drug, JC Penney, Marshall's, PetCo, Shoppers Foods, Target
9	MD 337, to Allentown Rd, E 🅿 Exxon, Shell/repair 🍴 Checker's, Dunkin', McDonald's, Popeye's 🛏 Days Inn, Quality Inn, Rodeway Inn, Super 8 🅾 to Andrews AFB, U-Haul, W 🅿 Sunoco
7	MD 5, Branch Ave, to Silver Hill, E 🅿 Citgo, Exxon, Sunoco 🍴 Dunkin', Wendy's, W 🅿 Shell/Subway/dsl 🍴 Red Lobster 🛏 Country Inn Suites, Hampton Inn, Holiday Inn Express 🅾 🅷, BMW, Chrysler/Dodge/Jeep, Ford, Infiniti, KIA, Mazda, Nissan, Toyota
4b a	MD 414, St Barnabas Rd, Marlow Hgts, E 🅿 Citgo/dsl, Zip-in 🍴 Bojangle's, Burger King, Checker's, IHOP, KFC, McDonald's, Outback Steaks, Wendy's 🛏 Red Roof Inn 🅾 $Tree, CVS Drug, GNC, Home Depot, Petsmart, Ross, Safeway Foods, Staples, W 🅿 Exxon/7-11/dsl, Shell/autocare 🍴 China Best, McDonald's, Subway 🅾 Family$
3b a	MD 210, Indian Head Hwy, to Forest Hgts, E 🅿 Gulf, Sunoco 🍴 Popeye's, Subway, Taco Bell 🛏 Comfort Inn, Ramada 🅾 Advance Parts, Aldi Foods, MGM Casino, Sav-A-Lot Foods,

3b a	Continued Shoppers Foods, Tanger Outlets/famous brands, USPO, W 🅿 BP/dsl, Citgo, Shell 🍴 7-11, Burger King, CVS Drug, Family$, Giant Foods, Goodyear/auto, McDonald's, Papa John's, Popeye's, Rite Aid, Subway, S 🅿 Exxon/dsl 🍴 Pizza Hut, Rita's 🅾 Marshall's, Safeway
2b a	I-295, N to Washingon
0mm	Maryland/Virginia state line, Potomac River, Woodrow Wilson Bridge

⬆N INTERSTATE 97

Exit #	Services
17	I-695. I-97 begins/ends on I-695.
16	MD 648, Ferndale, Glen Burnie, E 🅿 BP, Crown 🍴 Dunkin', Hong Kong Cafe, McDonald's, Rita's Custard, Wendy's 🅾 $General, Giant Foods, Roses, W 🅿 Carroll 🅾 UHaul
15b a	MD 176 W, Dorsey Rd, Aviation Blvd, E 🅿 BP, Crown 🍴 Dunkin', McDonald's, Wendy's, W 🅾 st police, to BWI
14b a	MD 100, Ellicott City, Gibson Island
13b a	MD 174, Quarterfield Rd, E 🅿 7-11, Gulf, Liberty/dsl 🍴 Squisito Pizza, Subway, The Grill, W 🅿 Shell/dsl, WaWa/dsl 🍴 Chick-fil-A, Ichiban, Pizza Hut 🅾 AT&T, Kohl's, Lowe's, Rite Aid, Sam's Club/dsl, Shoppers Foods, Walmart/Subway
12	MD 3, New Cut Rd, Glen Burnie, E **on Veterans Hwy** 🅿 BP, Exxon, Gulf, Royal Farms, Sunoco, WaWa/dsl 🍴 Burger King, Domino's, Dunkin', Fortune Cooky, Hardee's, KFC, McDonald's, Popeye's, Steak'n Shake, Subway, Taco Bell, Wendy's 🅾 CVS Drug, Giant Foods, Goodyear/auto, Shoppers, Target, Verizon, vet, Walgreens
10b a	Benfield Blvd, Severna Park, E 🅿 BP/dsl, Exxon/dsl, Transit/dsl/scales 🍴 Baskin-Robbins/Dunkin', Hella's Rest., Ledo's Pizza 🅾 $General, 7-11, access to same as 12
7	MD 3, MD 32, Bowie, Odenton, E 🛏 White Gables Motel, W 🅾 KOA
5	MD 178 (from sb, no EZ return), Crownsville
	I-97 begins/ends on US 50/301.

⬆N INTERSTATE 270 (Rockville)

Exit #	Services
32	I-270 begins/ends on I-70, exit 53.
31b a	MD 85, N 🅿 7-11, Sheetz/24hr, Shell/dsl, SouStates/dsl, Valero/dsl, Wawa/dsl 🍴 Applebee's, Arby's, BJ's Rest., Bob Evans, Burger King, Checker's, Chick-fil-A, ChuckeCheese, Golden Corral, Jersey Mike's, KFC/Taco Bell, Longhorn Steaks, McDonald's, Olive Garden, Panera Bread, Papa John's, Peking Gourmet, Pizza Hut, Popeye's, Red Robin, Roy Rogers, Ruby Tuesday, Smashburger, Sonic, Subway, Tilted Kilt, UNO Grill, Waffle House 🛏 Country Inn Suites, Days Inn, EconoLodge, Holiday Inn, Sleep Inn, Super 8 🅾 $Tree, AAA, Aamco, Audi, Barnes&Noble, Best Buy, Buick/GMC, CarMax, Chrysler/Dodge/Jeep, Costco/gas, Dick's, Harley-Davidson, Home Depot, Hyundai, JC Penney, Kohl's, Lincoln, Lowe's, Macy's, Michael's, Mr Tire, Nissan, Office Depot, Petsmart, Ross, Sam's Club/dsl, Staples, Target, Tires+, TJ Maxx, Verizon, Volvo, Walmart, S 🅿 🍴 Cafe Rio, Chipotle Mexican, Cici's, Cracker Barrel, Firehouse Subs, Five Guys, IHOP, Jimmy John's, Macaroni Grill, McDonald's, Noodles&Co, Panda Express, Starbucks, TGIFriday's, TX Roadhouse 🛏 Comfort Inn, Courtyard, Extended Stay America, Fairfield Inn, Hampton Inn, Hilton Garden, Homewood Suites, MainStay Suites, Residence Inn, TownePlace Suites 🅾 Honda, Toyota
30mm	Monocacy River
28mm	scenic view wb, no rest rooms

⬆N INTERSTATE 270 (Rockville) Cont'd

Exit #	Services
26	MD 80, Urbana, **N** 🅿 7-11, Exxon, Royal Farms/dsl, Shell/dsl 🍴 Black Hog BBQ, Buffalo Wild Wings, Burger King, China Taste, Dunkin', Jimmy John's, Ledo's Pizza, McDonald's, Waffle House 🅾 Advance Parts, CVS Drug
22	MD 109, to Barnesville, Hyattstown, **N** 🅿 Carroll/dsl 🍴 Denise Deli, Dunkin', Laurienzo Cafe 🅾 Food+
21mm	weigh/insp sta both lanes
18	MD 121, to Clarksburg, Boyds, **N** Little Bennett Pk, **S** 🅾 Clarksburg Outlets/famous brands, Blackhill Pk
16	MD 27, Father Hurley Blvd, to Damascus, **N** 🅿 Exxon, Free State/dsl, Sunoco, Washington Express 🍴 Applebee's, Bob Evans, Jersey Mike's Subs, McDonald's, Starbucks 🏨 Extended Stay America 🅾 AT&T, Best Buy, Giant Foods, GNC, Home Depot, Kohl's, Michael's, PepBoys, Petsmart, Target, TJ Maxx, Verizon, Walmart
15b a	MD 118, to MD 355, **N** 🏨 Holiday Inn Express, **S** 🅿 7-11, BP/dsl, Exxon/Circle K, Sunoco/dsl 🍴 Baja Fresh, Burger King, Carrabba's, Chick-fil-A, Chipotle, Domino's, Firehouse Subs, Five Guys, Greene Turtle, IHOP, Longhorn Steaks, McDonald's, Panda Express, Panera Bread, Pizza Hut, Red Robin, Ruby Tuesday, Senor Tequilas, Starbucks, Taco Bell, Wendy's, Zoe's Kitchen 🏨 Extended Stay America, Fairfield Inn 🅾 Giant Foods, Honda, Mercedes/Smart Car, Nissan, Petco, Rite Aid, Safeway Foods
13b a	Middlebrook Rd (from wb)
11	MD 124, Quince Orchard Rd, **N** 🅿 Exxon, Exxon 🍴 Boston Mkt, ChuckeCheese, Ichiban Rest., KFC, McDonald's, Panera Bread, Popeye's, Subway 🏨 Hampton Inn, Hilton, Holiday Inn, Homewood Suites, TownePlace Suites 🅾 Aamco, Acura, AT&T, Costco, CVS Drugs, Ford, Hyundai/Subaru, JC Penney, Lincoln, Lord&Taylor, Macy's, Mazda, Mini, Ross, Sam's Club, Toyota, Verizon, VW/Kia, **S** 🅿 Shell/dsl 🍴 Buffalo Wild Wings, Dunkin', Jerry's Subs, Jimmy John's, McDonald's, Starbucks 🏨 Motel 6 🅾 Advance Parts, Aldi Foods, Chevrolet, Chrysler/Dodge/Jeep, Fiat, Giant Foods, JoAnn Fabrics, Rite Aid, Seneca Creek SP, Staples
10	MD 117, Clopper Rd (from wb), same as 11
9b a	I-370, to Gaithersburg, Sam Eig Hwy, **S on Washington Blvd** 🍴 Copper Canyon Grill, Corner Cafe Bakery, Joe's Crabshack, Pizza Hut, Uncle Julio's 🏨 Courtyard 🅾 Barnes&Noble, Dick's, Kohl's, Target
8	Shady Grove Rd, **N** 🅿 Shell/dsl 🍴 Burger King, Five Guys, Red Lobster, Subway 🏨 Red Roof Inn, Sheraton 🅾 7-11, Best Buy, Home Depot, Office Depot, vet, **S** 🍴 Thatsamore 🏨 Courtyard, Marriott, Radisson, Residence Inn, Sleep Inn, SpringHill Suites 🅾 🅷
6b a	MD 28, W Montgomery Ave, **S** 🅿 Shell 🏨 Best Western
5b a	MD 189, Falls Rd
4b a	Montrose Rd, **S** 🍴 Elevation Burger, Starbucks, Zoe's Kitchen 🅾 Harris Teeter, Walgreens
2	I-270/I-270 spur diverges eb, converges wb
1b a	MD 187, Old Georgetown Rd, **S** 🅿 Exxon 🍴 Chipotle, Not Your Joe's, Subway 🅾 🅷, Balducci's Foods, Giant Foods, Verizon
1	(I-270 spur)Democracy Blvd, **E** 🏨 Marriott, **W** 🅿 Exxon/dsl, Shell/dsl 🅾 Macy's, Nordstrom, Sears
I-270 begins/ends on I-495, exit 35.	

⬆N INTERSTATE 495 (DC)

See Virginia Interstate 495 (DC)

INTERSTATE 695 (Baltimore)

Exit #	Services
48mm	Patapsco River, Francis Scott Key Br
44	Broening Ave (from nb)
43	MD 157, **toll plaza**
42	MD 151 S, Sparrows Point (last exit before **toll** sb), **E** 🅿 Citgo/dsl 🅾 North Point SP
41	MD 20, Cove Rd, **W** 🅿 Royal Farms/dsl, WaWa 🍴 Burger King, McDonald's
40	MD 150, MD 151, North Point Blvd, (nb only)
39	Merritt Blvd, **W** 🅿 🍴 Burger King, Dunkin', McDonald's, Rita's 🅾 $Tree, Aldi Foods, Ford, Giant Foods, Honda, Hyundai, JC Penney, Mazda, Mr Tire, Walmart
38b a	MD 150, Eastern Blvd, to Baltimore, **E** 🅿 Royal Farms, **W** 🍴 Applebee's, Arby's, Checker's, Chick-fil-A, Dunkin', Hibachi Buffet, Hip Hop Fish&Chicken 🅾 $Tree, AT&T, JC Penney, Kia/Nissan, Staples
36	MD 702 S (exits left from sb), Essex
35	US 40, **N** 🅿 Sunoco, WaWa/dsl 🍴 Arby's, Chipotle Mexican, DQ, Dunkin', IHOP, Longhorn Steaks, Panda Express, Panera Bread, Sonic 🅾 Aldi Foods, Best Buy, Harley-Davidson, Home Depot, Mr Tire, NTB, Office Depot, PetCo, same as 34, Sam's Club/gas, U-Haul, Walmart
34	MD 7, Philadelphia Rd, **N** 🍴 McDonald's, Panda Express, Popeye's 🏨 La Quinta 🅾 🅷, $General, $Tree, Giant Foods, Goodyear/auto, Marshall's, **S** 🅿 Exxon/dsl 🅾 same as 35, Walgreens
33b a	I-95, N to Philadelphia, S to Baltimore
32b a	US 1, Bel Air, **N** 🅿 Exxon 🍴 Bob Evans, Burger King, Dunkin', Golden Corral, IHOP, McDonald's, Peking House, Taco Bell 🅾 $Tree, 7-11, BJ's Whse, Giant Foods, Merchants Tire/auto, Mr Tire/auto, Nissan, Toyota, Verizon, vet, Walmart, **S** 🅿 Shell 🍴 Baskin-Robbins/Dunkin', Carrabba's, Papa John's, Rita's Custard, Subway, Szechuan Taste 🅾 7-11, Goodyear/auto, Verizon
31c	MD 43 E (from eb, exits left)
31b a	MD 147, Harford Rd, **N** 🅿 7-11/dsl, BP, CF/dsl, CF/dsl (2), Sunoco 🍴 Dunkin', Wendy's 🅾 Chrysler/Dodge/Jeep, CVS Drug, Honda, VW, Walgreens, Weis Foods
30b a	MD 41, Perring Pkwy, **N** 🅿 Shell 🍴 Bateman's Bistro, Burger King, Checker's, Chick-fil-A, Denny's, Dunkin', Five Guys, Hibachi Buffet, KFC, McDonald's, Popeye's, Rita's Custard, Starbucks, Subway, Taco Bell 🅾 $Tree, Advance Parts, Chevrolet, Ford/Lincoln, Goodyear/auto, Home Depot, Jo-Ann Fabrics, NTB, Office Depot, Ross, Safeway Foods, Shoppers Foods, Tuesday Morning, Verizon

MD

INTERSTATE 695 (Baltimore) Cont'd

Exit #	Services
29b	MD 542, Loch Raven Blvd, **S** 🅿 BP, Gulf, Marathon, Royal Frms 🍴 Dunkin', Hooters, McDonald's, Papa John's, Pizza Hut, Subway 🛏 Comfort Inn, Days Inn, Welcome Inn 🅾 Mr Tire, PepBoys
29a	Cromwell Bridge Rd, **S** 🛏 Best Western
28	Providence Rd, **S** 🍴 Sunoco
27b a	MD 146, Dulaney Valley Rd, **N** 🅾 Hampton NHS, **S** 🍴 Exxon 🍴 BJ's Rest., Bonefish Grill, Cheesecake Factory, PF Chang's, Starbucks, Stoney River Steaks 🛏 Sheraton 🅾 Barnes&Noble, Fresh Mkt, Macy's, Trader Joe's
26b a	MD 45, York Rd, Towson, **N** 🅿 BP, Citgo, Exxon/dsl, Oceanic, Sunoco/dsl 🍴 Dunkin', Ocean Pride Rest., Pizza Hut, Subway 🅾 Best Buy, Firestone/auto, Kia, Mazda, Mr Tire, NTB, Petco, Rite Aid, **S** 🅿 Exxon, Shell 🍴 Burger King, Five Guys, Mc-Donald's, Towson Diner 🅾 CVS Drug, Goodyear/auto, Honda, Hyundai, Lexus, Safeway Foods, Verizon, vet, Walgreens
25	MD 139, Charles St, **S** 🅾 🏥
24	I-83 N, to York
23b	MD 25, Falls Rd, Baltimore, **N** 🅿 Exxon/Circle K/dsl
23a	I-83 S, MD 25 N, Baltimore
22	Greenspring Ave
21	MD 129, to Stevenson Rd, Park Hghts Rd
20	MD 140, Reisterstown Rd, Pikesville, **N** 🅿 Exxon/7-11/dsl 🍴 Chipotle Mexican, Starbucks 🅾 AT&T, Barnes&Noble, Trader Joe's, **S** 🅿 BP/dsl, Shell/dsl, Sunoco/Subway 🍴 Mc-Donald's, Olive Branch Italian 🛏 Doubletree, Ramada Inn 🅾 Target, vet
19	I-795, NW Expswy
18b a	MD 26, Randallstown, Lochearn, **E** 🅿 Shell/dsl, Sunoco/dsl 🍴 Baskin-Robbins/Dunkin', KFC, Popeye's, Subway 🅾 $General, Family$, **W** 🅿 BP, Exxon/dsl, Shell/dsl 🍴 Burger King, Dunkin', McDonald's, Sonic, Subway, Taco Bell 🅾 🏥, 7-11, Firestone/auto, Giant Foods, Shoppers Foods, vet, Walgreens
17	MD 122, Security Blvd, **E** 🅿 BP/repair, Shell 🍴 City View Grill, Dunkin', Little Caesar's, McDonald's, Subway, Taco Bell 🛏 Days Inn, Knights Inn, Motel 6 🅾 Chevrolet, Family$, Nissan, PriceRite Foods, Rite Aid, **W** 🅿 Carroll/dsl, Exxon/dsl 🍴 Burger King, Chipotle, Five Guys, McDonald's, Panera Bread, Popeye's, Rita's Custard 🛏 Hampton Inn, Quality Inn 🅾 Ford, Macy's, Old Navy, Rite Aid, Weis Foods
16b a	I-70, E to Baltimore, W to Frederick
15b a	US 40, Ellicott City, Baltimore, **E** 🅿 🍴 Burger King, Checker's, Chick-fil-A, ChuckECheese's, KFC, McDonald's, Panda Express,
15b a	Continued Shirley's Diner, Subway 🛏 Holiday Inn Express, Quality Inn 🅾 $Tree, BigLots, CVS Drug, Dodge, Firestone/auto, Lowe's, Marshall's, Mr Tire, Rite Aid, Ross, Safeway Foods/gas, Sam's Club/gas, Shoppers Foods, U-Haul, Walgreens, **W** 🅿 BP/dsl, Exxon/dsl, Shell, Shell 🍴 Applebee's, Bob Evans, McDonald's, Popeye's, Starbucks, Starbucks, Subway, Taco Bell, TT Diner 🛏 Ramada 🅾 $Tree, Aamco, Aldi Foods, Chrysler/Jeep, Firestone/auto, Giant Foods, Goodyear/auto, Home Depot, Hyundai, NTB, Office Depot, Office Depot, PepBoys, Petsmart, Staples, Toyota, Verizon, Walgreens, Walmart/McDonald's
14	Edmondson Ave, **E** 🍴 Grilled Cheese&Co 🅾 Royal Farms, **W** 🅿 Carroll 🍴 Papa John's
13	MD 144, Frederick Rd, Catonsville, **W** 🅿 BP, Gas+, Gulf 🍴 Baskin-Robbins/Dunkin', McDonald's, Subway 🅾 7-11
12c b	MD 372 E, Wilkens, **E** 🅾 🏥
11b a	I-95, N to Baltimore, S to Washington
10	US 1, Washington Blvd (from wb only), **E** 🅿 Royal Farms/dsl, WaWa 🍴 3 Bros Pizza, Chick-fil-A, Dunkin', IHOP, Wendy's 🛏 Beltway Motel/rest. 🅾 Home Depot, Office Depot, PetCo, Walmart, **W** 🍴 Burger King
9	Hollins Ferry Rd, Lansdowne, **E** 🅿 Carroll/Circle K/Subway, Sunoco/7-11/dsl 🍴 Victor's Deli 🅾 Royal Farms
8	MD 168, Nursery Rd, **N** 🅿 Exxon, Shell 🍴 Hardee's, KFC, Mc-Donald's, Taco Bell, Wendy's 🛏 Motel 6, **S** 🅿 BP, Carroll 🍴 Dunkin', G&M Rest., Happy Garden Chinese, Rita's Custard, Seasons Pizza
7b a	MD 295, **N** to Baltimore, **S** 🅾 BWI Airport
6b a	Camp Mead Rd (from eb)
5	MD 648, Ferndale, **N** 🅿 Exxon/7-11/dsl, Shell/dsl 🍴 Checker's, Dunkin' 🛏 Best Western, Comfort Inn 🅾 NAPA, 🍴 Hot Wok
4b a	I-97 S, to Annapolis
3b a	MD 2, Brooklyn Park, **S** 🅿 Exxon, Royal Farms/dsl, Shell/dsl 🍴 Bob Evans, BoneFish Grill, Checker's, Chick-fil-A, ChuckE-Cheese's, Coldstone, Denny's, Five Guys, Golden Corral, Hibachi Buffet, HipHop Fish&Chicken, Ledo Pizza, McDonald's, Moe's SW, Noodles&Co, Panera Bread, Pappas Rest., Pie Five, Pizza Hut, Qdoba, Starbucks, Subway, Taco Bell, Wendy's 🛏 Days Inn, Extended Stay America, Hampton Inn, La Quinta 🅾 $Tree, Advance Parts, Aldi Foods, AT&T, AutoZone, Best Buy, BigLots, Buick/GMC, Dick's, Hyundai, Just Tires, Lowe's, Office Depot, PetCo, Salvo Parts, ShopRite Foods, Subaru, Target, Tuesday Morning, Verizon, Walgreens, Walmart
2	MD 10, Glen Burnie, **S** 🍴 McDonald's 🅾 Costco/gas, Home Depot, Petsmart
1	MD 174, Hawkins Point Rd, **S** 🅿 Citgo/deli/dsl

NOTES

MASSACHUSETTS

S T U R B R I D G E

🅴 INTERSTATE 84

Exit #	Services
4(11)	I-84 begins/ends on I-90, Exit 9.
3b a(9)	US 20, Sturbridge, 0-2 mi N 🅿️ Citgo, Cumberland Farms, EVC 🍴 Burger King, CVS Drug, Dunkin', Empire Village, Friendly's, McDonald's, Panera Bread, Sturbridge Coffeehouse, Sturbridge Seafood, Subway, Village Pizza 🛏️ EconoLodge, Hampton Inn, Holiday Inn Express, La Quinta, Old Sturbridge Lodges, Super 8 🅾️ USPO, 0-2 mi S 🍴 S&S, Shell/Dunkin'/Subway 🍴 Applebee's, Cracker Barrel, Uno Pizzaria, Wendy's 🛏️ Comfort Inn 🅾️ Marshall's, Michael's, Petco, Staples, Stop&Shop, Verizon, vet, Walmart/Subway
2(5)	MA 131, to Old Sturbridge Village, Sturbridge, 2 mi S 🛏️ Publick House, RV camping
4mm	picnic area wb, litter barrels
1(3)	Mashapaug Rd, to Southbridge, S 🅿️ Mobil/dsl, 🚚/deli/dsl/scales/24hr/@ 🛏️ Days Inn 🅾️ H
2mm	weigh sta both lanes
.5mm	picnic area eb
0mm	Massachusetts/Connecticut state line

B O S T O N   A R E A

🅴 INTERSTATE 90

Exit #	Services
140mm	I-90 begins/ends near Logan Airport
25	to I-93, to downtown Boston
24	to I-93, to downtown Boston
22(134)	Presidential Ctr, downtown
20(132)	MA 28, Alston, Brighton, Cambridge, N 🛏️ Courtyard, Doubletree Inn 🅾️ H, S 🅿️ Mobil
131mm	toll plaza
18(130)	MA Ave (from eb), N 🍴 IHOP, Starbucks
17(128)	Centre St, Newton, N 🍴 Bertucci's, Starbucks 🛏️ Crowne Plaza 🅾️ Honda, Walgreens
16(125)	MA 16, W Newton, N 🅿️ Shell/repair 🍴 Blue Ribbon BBQ 🅾️ CVS Drug
15(124)	I-95, N 🅿️ Speedway 🛏️ Marriott
123mm	toll plaza
14(122)	MA 30, Weston
117mm	**Natick Travel Plaza eb**, 🅿️ EVC, Gulf/dsl 🍴 Dunkin', McDonald's, Papagino's/d'Angelo's
13(116)	MA 30, Natick, S 🅿️ Cumberland, EVC, Mobil, Shell, Tesla EVC 🍴 Boston Mkt, Burger King, Chick-fil-A, Dunkin', Five Guys, Lotus Flower Chinese, McDonald's, Panera Bread, Stop&Shop

Exit #	Services
13(116)	Continued 🛏️ Courtyard, Monticello Inn, Red Roof+ 🅾️ Best Buy, BJ's Whse, Home Depot, Kia, Kohl's, Lowe's, Marshall's, REI, Target, TJ Maxx, USPO, Walmart
114mm	**Framingham Travel Plaza wb**, S 🅿️ EVC, 🅿️ Gulf/dsl 🍴 Boston Mkt, McDonald's, Starbucks
12(111)	MA 9, Framington, N 🅿️ BP, Speedway 🍴 Dunkin', Godavari Framingham, Wendy's 🛏️ Motel 6, Sheraton, S 🍴 China Gourmet 🅾️ Toyota
11a(106)	I-495, N to NH, S to Cape Cod
105mm	**Westborough Travel Plaza wb**, 🅿️ Gulf/dsl 🍴 Boston Mkt, D'angelo, Dunkin', Papagino's
11(96)	MA 122, to Millbury, N 🅾️ UMA Med Ctr
10a(95)	MA 146
94mm	Blackstone River
10(90)	I-395 S, to Auburn, I-290 N, Worcester, N 🍴 Outback, Papa Gino's 🛏️ Comfort Inn, La Quinta, S 🅿️ Shell, Shell/repair/24hr 🍴 Applebee's, D'angelo, Dunkin', Friendly's, Wendy's 🛏️ Fairfield Inn, Hampton Inn, Holiday Inn Express 🅾️ CVS Drug, Hyundai, Park'n Shop, TJ Maxx
84mm	**Charlton Travel Plaza wb**, 🅿️ Gulf/dsl 🍴 McDonald's, Papa Gino's/d'Angelo's
80mm	**Charlton Travel Plaza eb**, 🅿️ Gulf/dsl 🍴 McDonald's, Papa Gino's 🅾️ st police
79mm	toll plaza
9(78)	I-84, to Hartford, NYC, Sturbridge, access to same services as I-84, exit 3, S 🅾️ access to H
67mm	Quaboag River
8(62)	MA 32, to US 20, Palmer, S on MA 32 🅿️ Pride, Shell/dsl 🍴 Domino's, Dunkin', McDonald's, Subway, Wendy's 🅾️ H, Big Y Foods, Chevrolet, CVS Drug, repair/transmissions, Rite Aid, vet
58mm	Chicopee River
56mm	**Ludlow Travel Plaza wb**, 🅿️ Gulf/dsl 🍴 Papa Gino's, Starbucks

⬆E INTERSTATE 90 Cont'd

Exit #	Services
55mm	**Ludlow Travel Plaza eb**, 🅖 Gulf/dsl 🍴 McDonald's, Starbucks
7(54)	MA 21, to Ludlow, **N** 🅖 Cumberland Farms, Pride/dsl, Sunoco 🍴 Burger King, Dunkin', McDonald's, Starbucks, Subway 🅞 Ace Hardware, Big Y Foods, CVS Drug, **S** 🅖 Shell/dsl 🍴 Dominos, Taco Bell 🛏 Holiday Inn Express
6(51)	I-291, to Springfield, Hartford CT, **N** 🅖 Pride/50's Diner/Subway/dsl 🍴 Dunkin', McDonald's, Po's Chinese 🛏 Motel 6 🅞 🄷, Basketball Hall of Fame, Mercedes, to Bradley Int Airport
5(49)	MA 33, to Chicopee, Westover AFB, **N** 🅖 Tesla EVC 🍴 99 Rest., Applebee's, Arby's, Buffalo Wild Wings, Chick-fil-A, Chipotle Mexican, Denny's, Dunkin', Five Guys, Friendly's, Little Caesar's, McDonald's, Panera Bread, Popeye's, Royal Buffet, Starbucks, Subway, Wendy's 🛏 Hampton Inn, Quality Inn, Residence Inn 🅞 $Tree, Aldi Foods, Big Y Foods, BJ's Whse/gas, Chrysler/Dodge/Jeep, Home Depot, Honda, Marshall's, Monro, Nissan, Petsmart, Staples, Staples, Stop&Shop/gas, TownFair Tire, U-Haul, Verizon, Walmart/Subway, **S** 🅖 Pride/Dunkin'/Subway/dsl 🅞 Buick/GMC
46mm	Connecticut River
4(46)	I-91, US 5, to Holyoke, **W** Springfield, **N on US 5** 🅖 Shell 🍴 Dunkin' 🛏 Welcome Inn, **S on US 5** 🅖 Pride/dsl 🍴 Donut Dip, Five Guys, Hooters, On the Border, Outback Steaks, Subway 🛏 Hampton Inn, Red Roof+, Residence Inn, Springfield Inn, Super 8 🅞 BMW, Honda/Lexus/Toyota
41mm	st police wb
3(40)	US 202, to Westfield, **N** 🅖 Mobil 🍴 Alessio's Pizza, **S** 🅖 Citgo/Subway/dsl, Shell/dsl 🍴 Dunkin', Friendly's, McDonald's, Wendy's 🛏 Hampton Inn, Quality Inn 🅞 🄷, repair, vet
36mm	Westfield River
35.5mm	runaway truck ramp eb
29mm	Blandford/Ludlow TP both lanes, 🅖 Gulf/dsl 🍴 McDonald's 🅞 info
20mm	highest point on MA Tpk, 1724 ft
14.5mm	Appalachian Trail
2(11)	US 20, to Lee, Pittsfield, **N** 🅖 Citgo, Shell/dsl, Sunoco 🍴 Athena's Rest., Dunkin', Friendly's, McDonald's, Rose's Rest., Subway 🛏 Morgan House/rest., Pilgrim Inn, Sunset Motel, Super 8 🅞 Rite Aid, True Value, **S** 🅖 Big Y/dsl 🍴 Orient Taste, Subway, Villa Pizza 🅞 Big Y Foods, Lee Outlets/famous brands
10.5mm	Hoosatonic River
8mm	**Lee Travel Plaza both lanes**, 🅖 EVC, Gulf/dsl 🍴 McDonald's, Papa Gino's 🅞 info
4mm	**toll booth**, 🅒
1(2)	MA 41 (from wb, no return), to MA 102, W Stockbridge, the Berkshires, **N** 🛏 Pleasant Valley Motel 🅞 to Bousquet Ski Area
0mm	Massachusetts/New York state line

⬆N INTERSTATE 91

Exit #	Services
55mm	Massachusetts/Vermont state line
54mm	**parking area both lanes**, 🆁🆂
28(51)	US 5, MA 10, Bernardston, **E** 🛏 Fox Inn, **W** 🅖 Sunoco 🍴 Antonio's II Ristorante, Four-leaf Clover Rest., Hillside Organic Pizza 🅞 Country Corner Store, USPO
27(45)	MA 2 E (exits left from sb), Greenfield, **E on US 5** 🅖 Cumberland Farms, Speedway, Stop&Shop, Sunoco/dsl 🍴 Denny's Pantry, Domino's, Dunkin', McDonald's, Subway 🅞 🄷, $General, AT&T, Aubuchon Hardware, AutoZone, Chrysler/Dodge/Jeep, Honda, O'Reilly Parts, Walgreens
26(43)	MA 2 W, MA 2A E, Greenfield, **E** 🅖 Mobil/dsl, Planet/dsl, Shell/dsl 🍴 Applebee's, Athens Pizza, China Gourmet, D'Angelo, Dunkin' 🅞 🄷, Chevrolet, Ford/Lincoln, Toyota, **W** 🅖 Shell 🍴 99 Rest., Friendly's, KFC/Taco Bell, Kobe Asian, McDonald's, Subway 🛏 Days Inn, Hampton Inn 🅞 $General, $Tree, Big Y Foods, BJ's Whse, Home Depot, Staples, to Mohawk Tr, Verizon
39mm	Deerfield River
37mm	**weigh sta both lanes**
25(36)	MA 116 (from sb), S Deerfield, camping, hist dist, same as 24
24(35)	US 5, MA 10, MA 116, Deerfield (no EZ return), **E** 🅖 Irving/Circle K/Dunkin'/Subway/dsl 🛏 Red Roof+ 🅞 vet, Yankee Candle Co, **W** 🅖 Roady's Trkstp/diner/dsl/24hr 🍴 24hr Diner
34.5mm	**parking area both lanes**
23(34)	US 5 (from sb), **E** 🍴 Tom's Hot Dog 🅞 Orchard Trailers, Rainbow Motel/camping
22(30)	US 5, MA 10 (from nb), **N** Hatfield, **W** 🅞 Diamond RV Ctr
21(28)	US 5, MA 10, Hatfield, **W** 🅖 Sunoco/dsl 🍴 Subway 🛏 Hatfield Inn 🅞 st police
20(26)	US 5, MA 9, MA 10 (from sb), Northampton, **W** 🅖 Pride/dsl, Speedway/dsl 🍴 Burger King, D'angelo's, Domino's, KFC, McDonald's, Moe's SW, Taco Bell 🅞 🄷, AutoZone, Big Y Food/Drug, BigLots, Chevrolet, Chrysler/Dodge/Jeep, CVS Drug, Firestone/auto, Ford, Goodyear/auto, Honda, Hyundai, Stop&Shop/gas, TownFair Tire, Toyota, U-Haul, Verizon, VW, Walgreens, Walmart/Subway
19(25)	MA 9, to Amherst, Northampton, 0-2 mi **E** 🅖 Big Y/dsl, Cumberland Farms, Phillips 66, Pride/Subway/dsl 🍴 Primo Pizza 🛏 Hampton Inn 🅞 Nissan, to Elwell SP, vet
18(22)	US 5, Northampton, **W** 🅖 Shell/Dunkin' 🛏 Fairfield Inn, Quality Inn 🅞 to Smith Coll
18mm	scenic area both lanes
17b a(16)	MA 141, S Hadley, **E** 🅖 Mobil/dsl, Shell/dsl 🍴 Dunkin', Real China, Subway 🛏 Motel 6 🅞 Meineke, Walgreens
16(14)	US 202, Holyoke, **W** Soldier's Home
15(12)	to US 5, Ingleside, **E** 🅖 Shell/Dunkin' 🍴 Applebee's, Chicago Grill, Chipotle, Cracker Barrel, JP's Rest., McDonald's, Red Robin 🛏 Fairfield Inn 🅞 🄷, Barnes&Noble, Best Buy, CVS Drug, Hobby Lobby, JC Penney, Macy's, Old Navy, PetCo, Target, TJ Maxx, **W** 🛏 Homewood Suites
14(11)	to US 5, to I-90 (Mass Tpk), **E** to Boston, **W** to Albany, **E** 🅞 🄷
13b a(9)	US 5 N, W Springfield, **E** 🅖 Pride/dsl 🍴 Donut Dip, Five Guys, Hooters, On-the-Border, Outback Steaks, Shallot Thai, Subway, Tap House Grill 🛏 Express Inn, Red Roof+, Residence Inn, Springfield Inn, Super 8 🅞 BMW, Lexus/Toyota, **W** 🅖 Pride/dsl, Shell/dsl, Tesla EVC 🍴 99 Rest., Burger King, Cal's Grill, Carrabba's, Chili's, D'angelo's, Dunkin', Friendly's, IHOP, KFC, Longhorn Steaks, McDonald's, Nippon Grill, Olive Garden, Panera Bread, Pizza Hut, Tokyo Cuisine, Wendy's 🛏 Bel Air Inn, Best Western, Candlewood Suites, Clarion, Courtyard, EconoLodge, Hampton Inn, Quality Inn, Red Carpet Inn, Travel Inn 🅞 $Tree, Aldi Foods, AT&T, Chrysler/Dodge/Jeep, Costco, CVS Drug, Dick's, Fiat, GNC, Home Depot, Honda, Kohl's, Mazda, Michael's, Nissan, Staples, Stop&Shop, Subaru, TownFair Tire, Verizon
12(8.5)	I-391 N, to Chicopee
11(8)	Birnie Ave (from sb), **E** 🅖 Mobil 🅞 🄷
10(7.5)	Main St (from nb), Springfield, **E** 🅖 Mobil
9(7)	US 20 W, MA 20A E (from nb), **E** 🍴 McDonald's, **W** 🅖 Pride/Subway/dsl
8(6.5)	I-291, US 20 E, to I-90, **E** downtown
7(6)	Columbus Ave (from sb), **E** 🅖 Pride/Subway/dsl 🛏 Sheraton, Tower Square, **W** 🅞 to Basketball Hall of Fame
6(5.5)	Springfield Ctr, **E** 🅖 Pride/Dunkin'/Subway/dsl 🍴 Starbucks, **W** 🍴 Coldstone, Plan B Burger 🅞 Basketball Hall of Fame

(Left margin vertical labels: PITTSFIELD)
(Right margin vertical labels: GREENFIELD, NORTHAMPTON, SPRINGFIELD)

MA

🅝 INTERSTATE 91 Cont'd

Exit #	Services
5(5)	Broad St, same as 4, **E** 🅖 Shell/dsl 🄐 Hampton Inn 🄞 Hyundai, **W** 🅖 Sunoco/dsl 🅕 Chicago Grill, Subway 🄐 Hilton Garden 🄞 Buick/GMC
4(4.5)	MA 83, Broad St, Main St, same as 5, **E** 🅖 Shell/dsl 🅕 Antonio's Grinders 🄞 Hyundai, **W** 🅖 Sunoco/dsl 🅕 Chicago Grill, Subway 🄐 Hilton Garden 🄞 Buick/GMC, Chevrolet
3(4)	US 5 N, to MA 57, Columbus Ave, W Springfield, **E** 🅖 Sunoco 🅕 Antonio's Pizza, **W** 🄞 Chevrolet
2(3.5)	MA 83 S (from nb), to E Longmeadow
1(3)	US 5 S (from sb)
0mm	Massachusetts/Connecticut state line, callboxes begin/end

🅝 INTERSTATE 93

Exit #	Services
47mm	Massachusetts/New Hampshire state line, callboxes begin/end
48(46)	MA 213 E, to Methuen, **E** 🄞 🄗
47(45)	Pelham St, Methuen, **E** 🅖 Sunoco 🅕 Dunkin', Heavenly Donuts, McDonald's, Outback Steaks, **W** 🅖 BP, Irving/Circle K/Subway/dsl 🅕 Fireside Rest. 🄐 Day's Hotel/rest. 🄞 Chrysler/Dodge/Jeep
46(44)	MA 110, MA 113, to Lawrence, **E** 🅖 BP/repair, Mobil, Shell 🅕 Burger King, Dunkin', KFC/Taco Bell, McDonald's, Pizza Hut 🄞 🄗, $Tree, MktBasket Foods, Rite Aid, **W** 🅖 Super 🅕 Anthony's Roast Beef, Dunkin', Irish Cottage, Royal Roast Beef 🄐 Passport Inn
45(43)	Andover St, River Rd, to Lawrence, **E** 🄐 Courtyard, Doubletree, Homewood Suites, **W** 🅖 Mobil/Dunkin' 🅕 Chateu Italian, Chili's 🄐 La Quinta, Residence Inn, Sonesta Suites, SpringHill Suites 🄞 vet
44b a(40)	I-495, to Lowell, Lawrence, **E** 🄞 🄗
43(39)	MA 133, N Tewksbury, **E** 🅖 Mobil/Dunkin', **W** 🅕 99 Rest.
42(38)	Dascomb Rd, East St, Tewksbury, **W** 🅖 Citgo/dsl 🅕 Dunkin', Luna Rossa Italian, Subway 🄞 7-11
41(35)	MA 125, Andover, **E** 🅖 EVC 🅕 Dunkin' 🄐 Hampton Inn 🄞 Target
40(34)	MA 62, Wilmington
39(33)	Concord St, **E** 🅕 Dunkin', Mona's Kitchen 🄞 Shriners Auditorium, URGENT CARE
38(31)	MA 129, Reading, **W** 🅖 Mobil/Dunkin'/Subway/dsl 🅕 Burger King, Pacific Grove Chinese, Red Heat Tavern
37c(30)	Commerce Way, Atlantic Ave, **W** 🅕 Chipotle Mexican, Firehouse Subs, Starbucks 🄐 Red Roof+, Residence Inn 🄞 PetCo, Petsmart, Target, Verizon
37b a(29)	I-95, S to Waltham, N to Peabody
36(28)	Montvale Ave, **E** 🅖 Mobil/Circle K 🅕 Deli Works, Dunkin' 🄐 Courtyard, **W** 🅖 BP, Gulf, Speedway/dsl 🅕 Bickford's Grille, Dunkin', McDonald's, Polcari's Italian, Wendy's 🄐 Best Western+, Comfort Inn 🄞 🄗
35(27)	Winchester Highlands, Melrose, **E** 🄞 🄗 (no EZ return to sb)
34(26)	MA 28 N (from nb, no EZ return), Stoneham, **E** 🅖 Mobil/Circle K/dsl 🅕 Friendly's, **W** 🄞 🄗
33(25)	MA 28, Fellsway West, Winchester, **W** 🄞 🄗
32(23)	MA 60, Salem Ave, Medford Square, **W** 🄐 Hyatt Place 🄞 🄗, to Tufts U
31(22)	MA 16 E, to Revere (no EZ return sb), **W** 🅖 Fred's Gas, Mobil/dsl, Mr. C's/dsl 🅕 Avellino's Italian, Burger King, Dunkin' 🄞 AutoZone, Chrysler/Dodge/Jeep, Infiniti, Nissan
30(21)	MA 28, MA 38, Mystic Ave, Somerville, **W** 🅖 Mr. C's/dsl 🅕 Burger King 🄞 AutoZone, VW
29(20)	MA 28 (from nb), same as 30, Somerville, **E** 🅕 99 Rest., Dunkin', Starbucks 🄐 La Quinta 🄞 Home Depot, Staples, TJ Maxx, Trader Joe's, **W** 🅖 Gulf, Speedway 🅕 Dunkin' 🄞 Stop&Shop
28(19)	Sullivans Square, Charles Town, downtown
27	US 1 N (from nb)
26(18.5)	MA 28 N, Storrow Dr, North Sta, downtown
25	Haymarket Sq, 🄞 Gov't Center
24(18)	Callahan Tunnel, **E** 🄞 🔄
23(17.5)	High St, Congress St, **W** 🄐 Harborside Inn
22(17)	Atlantic Ave, Northern Ave, South Sta, 🄞 Boston World Trade Ctr
21(16.5)	Kneeland St, ChinaTown
20(16)	I-90 W, to Mass Tpk
19(15.5)	Albany St (from sb), **W** 🄞 🄗
18(15)	Mass Ave, to Roxbury, **W** 🄞 🄗
17(14.5)	E Berkeley (from nb)
16(14)	S Hampton St, Andrew Square, **W** 🅕 Applebee's, Chipotle, Olive Garden, Panera Bread, Wahlburgers 🄐 Courtyard, Holiday Inn Express 🄞 Best Buy, Home Depot, Marshall's, Old Navy, Stop&Shop/gas, Target, TJ Maxx
15(13)	Columbia Rd, Everett Square, **E** 🄐 DoubleTree 🄞 JFK Library, to UMA, **W** 🅖 Gulf, Speedway
14(12.5)	Morissey Blvd (from nb no return), **E** 🄞 JFK Library, **W** 🅖 Shell
13(12)	Freeport St, to Dorchester, (from nb), **W** 🅖 7-11, Citgo 🅕 Deadwood Cafe, Dunkin', Ruritan Pizza, Subway 🄐 Comfort Inn, Ramada 🄞 CVS Drug, Honda, Lambert's Mkt, Stop&Shop, Toyota
12(11.5)	MA 3A S (from sb, no EZ return), Quincy, **E** 🅖 Express, tires 🄐 Best Western, **W** 🅖 Gulf/Dunkin', Speedway/dsl 🅕 PapaGino's 🄞 AutoZone, CVS Drug, Staples, Verizon, Walgreens
11b a(11)	to MA 203, Granite Ave, Ashmont
10(10)	Squantum Ave (from sb), Milton, **W** 🄞 🄗
9(9)	Adams St, Bryant Ave, to N Quincy, **E** 🅕 Dunkin', House of Pizza, **W** 🅖 Shell/repair 🄞 USPO
8(8)	Brook Pkwy, to Quincy, Furnace, **E** 🅖 Gulf/dsl, Mobil/dsl
7(7)	MA 3 S, to Cape Cod (exits left from sb), Braintree, **E** 🄐 Marriott
6(6)	MA 37, to Holbrook, Braintree, **E** 🅖 EVC, Mobil/dsl 🅕 99 Rest., Buffalo Wild Wings, CA Pizza Kitchen, Cheesecake Factory, Chicago Grill, Chipotle, D'angelo, Dave&Buster's, Five Guys, Legal Seafood, Potbelly, Qdoba, Red Robin, Starbucks, TGIFriday's, Tokyo Japanese 🄐 Hyatt Place 🄞 AT&T, Lord&Taylor, Macy's, Nordstrom's, Sullivan Tire/auto, Target, URGENT CARE, **W** 🅖 Citgo 🄐 Best Western, Candlewood Suites, Extended Stay America, Hampton Inn 🄞 Barnes&Noble, Ford, VW

METHUEN (vertical left margin)

BOSTON AREA (vertical margins)

MA

⛽ = gas 🍴 = food 🛏 = lodging 🅾 = other 🆁🆂 = rest stop   Copyright 2022 - The Next EXIT ®

⬆N INTERSTATE 93 Cont'd

Exit #	Services
5b a(4)	MA 28 S, to Randolph, Milton, **E** ⛽ Mobil/dsl, Shell/dsl 🍴 Domino's, Dunkin', La Scala, Lombardo's, Randolph Cafe, Wong's Chinese 🛏 Comfort Inn 🅾 AT&T
4(3)	MA 24 S (exits left from sb), to Brockton
3(2)	MA 138 N, to Ponkapoag Trail, Houghtons Pond
2b a(1)	MA 138 S, to Stoughton, Milton, **E** 🅾 golf, **W** ⛽ BlueHill/dsl, Mobil/dsl, Shell/dsl 🍴 Blue Hills Grill, Dunkin' 🛏 Homewood Suites
1(0)	I-95 N, S to Providence. **I-93 begins/ends on I-95, exit 12.**

⬆N INTERSTATE 95

Exit #	Services
89.5mm	Massachusetts/New Hampshire state line, **Welcome Ctr**/🆁🆂 sb, **full** ♿ **facilities, litter barrels,** 🏞
60(89)	MA 286, to Salisbury, beaches, **E** ⛽ Mobil/dsl 🍴 Cosmos Rest., Dunkin', Lena's Seafood Rest. 🅾 Black Bear Camping (seasonal)
59(88)	I-495 S (from sb)
58b a(87)	rd 110, to I-495 S, to Amesbury, Salisbury, **E** ⛽ Sunoco/Dunkin'/Subway/dsl 🍴 China Buffet, Niko's Place, Sylvan St Grille, Winner's Circle Rest. 🅾 $Tree, Ford, U-Haul, vet, **W** ⛽ EVC, Irving Gas/Circle K, Mobil, Sunoco/dsl, Tesla EVC 🍴 Acapulco's Mexican, Burger King, Dunkin', Friendly's, McDonald's, Subway 🛏 Fairfield Inn, Hampton Inn 🅾 AT&T, Chevrolet, Stop&Shop, Verizon
57(85)	MA 113, to W Newbury, **E** ⛽ Mobil/dsl, Shell/dsl/repair, Sunoco 🍴 China Wok, Dunkin', Giuseppe's Italian, Hana Japan, McDonald's, Moe's SW, Panera Bread, Wendy's 🅾 🄷, 7-11, CVS Drug, GNC, Marshall's, Midas, MktBasket Foods, Shaw's Foods, Verizon, Walgreens
56(83)	Scotland Rd, to Newbury, **E** 🅾 st police
55(82)	Central St, to Byfield, **E** 🍴 Rusty Can, **W** ⛽ Prime/dsl/repair
54b a(78)	MA 133, E to Rowley, W to Groveland, **E** 🅾 vet
77mm	weigh sta both lanes
53b a(76)	MA 97, S to Topsfield, N to Georgetown
52(74)	Topsfield Rd, to Topsfield, Boxford
51(72)	Endicott Rd, to Topsfield, Middleton
50(71)	US 1, to MA 62, Topsfield, **E** ⛽ Gulf/dsl, Mobil/dsl 🅾 Honda, **W** ⛽ S&S 🍴 Break Away Rest., Supino's Rest., TX Roadhouse 🛏 DoubleTree, Knights Inn 🅾 CVS Drug, st police, Staples, Stop&Shop, USPO
49(70)	MA 62 (from nb), same as 50, Danvers, Middleton
48(69)	Hobart St (from sb), **W** 🍴 Calitri's Italian 🛏 Best Western+, Comfort a Inn, Motel 6 🅾 Home Depot
47b a(68)	MA 114, to Middleton, Peabody, **E** ⛽ Gulf/Dunkin', Sunoco 🍴 Dunkin', Honey Dew Donuts, McDonald's, Olive Garden, Outback Steaks, Pizza Hut 🅾 Audi, CarMax, Chevrolet, Chrysler/Dodge/Jeep, Infiniti, Lexus, Lowe's, NTB, Petsmart, Subaru, TJ Maxx, Toyota, Trader Joe's, Verizon, vet, VW, Walmart/Subway, on US 1, **W** ⛽ Cumberland Farms, Speedway/dsl 🍴 Chili's, Hardcover Rest., TGIFriday's 🛏 Motel 6, Residence Inn, TownePlace Suites 🅾 Costco/gas, Home Depot, Land Rover, Mazda, Meineke, NAPA
46(67)	to US 1, **W** ⛽ Best, Gulf/dsl, Mobil, Sunoco/dsl 🍴 Dunkin', Dunkin' (2), Honey Dew Donuts 🅾 auto repair
45(66)	MA 128 N, to Peabody
44b a(65)	US 1 N, MA 129, **E** 🅾 🄷, **W** ⛽ 7-11, Gulf, Shell 🍴 Bertucci's, Bros Kouzina Rest., Dunkin', Marco's Italian, Santarpio's Pizza, Sonic, Wendy's 🛏 Hampton Inn, Holiday Inn, Homewood Suites, Plaza Inn, SpringHill Suites

43(61)	Walnut St, Lynnfield, **E** 🍴 99 Rest. 🅾 golf, to Saugus Iron Works NHS (3mi), **W** 🍴 Panera Bread, Starbucks, Yardhouse 🛏 Sheraton 🅾 EVC, Whole Foods
42(62)	Salem St, Montrose, **E** ⛽ Irving/Circle K/Subway, Sunoco 🍴 Dunkin', **W** 🛏 Sheraton
41(60)	Main St, Lynnfield Ctr, **E** ⛽ Shell, **W** 🅾 vet
40(59)	MA 129, Wakefield Ctr, N Reading, **E** 🍴 Bellino's Italian, Honey Dew Donuts 🅾 city park, vet, **W** ⛽ Cumberland Farms 🍴 Dunkin', Mandarin Chinese 🅾 Chevrolet, Mazda, REI
39(58)	North Ave, Reading, **E** 🛏 Lakeside Inn 🅾 city park, Subaru, **W** ⛽ Shell/dsl 🍴 Anthony's Pizza, Bertucci's, Chili's, Chipotle, Fuddrucker's, Longhorn Steaks, Oye's Rest., Starbucks 🅾 Home Depot, Honda, Mkt Basket Foods, Staples, Stop&Shop Foods, URGENT CARE, Verizon
38b a(57)	MA 28, to Reading, **E** ⛽ Gulf/repair, Mobil, Speedway/dsl 🍴 99 Rest., Burger King, D'Angelo's/PapaGino's, Dunkin', Dunkin', Five Guys, Loui Loui 🅾 Advance Parts, AutoZone, Ford, GNC, Marshall's, Michael's, Stop&Shop/gas, Target, Verizon, Walgreens, **W** ⛽ Citgo, Mobil/dsl, Shell 🍴 Anthony's Roast Beef, Burger King, Calareso's Farm Stand, China Moon, Domino's, Dunkin', Harrow's Chicken Pies, McDonald's, Starbucks 🅾 Meineke
37b a(56)	I-93, N to Manchester, S to Boston
36(55)	Washington St, to Winchester, **E** ⛽ 🍴 B Good, Chick-fil-A, Dunkin', Red Robin, Sal's Pizza, Starbucks, Subway 🛏 Hilton 🅾 BJ's Whse/gas, Hogan Tire/auto, Nissan, Staples, Toyota, **W** ⛽ Sunoco 🍴 99 Rest., Bertucci's, China Pearl, Dave&Buster's, Dunkin', Joe's Grill, On the Border, Qdoba 🛏 Courtyard, Fairfield Inn, Holiday Inn Express, Red Roof+ 🅾 $Tree, AT&T, CVS Drug, Kohl's, Lowe's, Mkt Basket Foods, NTB, TJ Maxx, Town Fair Tire, USPO
35(54)	MA 38, to Woburn, **E** 🍴 Scoreboard Grill 🛏 Crowne Plaza 🅾 🄷, **W** ⛽ Mobil/dsl 🍴 Applebee's, Dunkin', Sichuan Garden 🛏 Extended Stay America 🅾 city park, CVS Drug, Stop&Shop Foods
34(53)	Winn St, Woburn
33b a(52)	US 3 S, MA 3A N, to Winchester, **E** 🍴 Bickford's Grille, Café Escadrille, Capital Grille, Coldstone, Dunkin', NYA Joe's Grill, Panera Bread, Potbelly, Seasons 52 Grill, Starbucks, Subway 🛏 Hyatt House 🅾 CVS Drug, Honda, LL Bean, Marshall's, Michael's, **W** ⛽ EVC, Prime, Speedway 🍴 Chopps Grill 🛏 Marriott 🅾 🄷, Audi/Porsche, Kia, Mercedes, repair
32b a(51)	US 3 N, MA 2A S, to Lowell, **E** ⛽ Mobil/dsl, Shell 🍴 Burger King, Burton's Grill, Chateau Italian, Dunkin', Five Guys, McDonald's 🛏 Hilton Garden, Sonesta Suites 🅾 Best Buy, Jo-Ann, Midas, Mkt Basket Foods, Nordstrom, Old Navy, PetCo, Trader Joe's, **W** 🍴 Border Cafe, Buffalo Wild Wings, Cheesecake Factory, Chipotle, Del Frisco's Grill, Legal Seafoods, Macaroni Grill, Wendy's 🛏 Candlewood Suites, Extended Stay America 🅾 AT&T, Barnes&Noble, Kohl's, Lord&Taylor, Macy's, Nordstrom, Staples, URGENT CARE, Verizon
31b a(48)	MA 4, MA 225, Lexington, **E** ⛽ Gulf, Mobil/dsl/repair 🍴 Alexander's Pizza, Qdoba, Starbucks 🅾 Stop&Shop, Walgreens, **W** ⛽ Gulf, Shell 🍴 Chipotle, Dunkin', Great Wall, Margarita's, McDonald's, Minuteman Diner 🛏 Bedford Plaza Hotel, Quality Inn 🅾 Stop&Shop, TJ Maxx, vet
30b a(47)	MA 2A, Lexington, **E** ⛽ Sunoco/Dunkin'/dsl 🅾 🄷, **W** 🛏 ALoft, Element Hotel 🅾 Hanscom AFB, to MinuteMan NP
46.5mm	**travel plaza nb,** ⛽ Gulf/dsl/CNG 🍴 Honey Dew Donuts, McDonald's, Original Boston Pizza

Side margins (vertical text): **A M E S B U R Y** / **P E A B O D Y** (left); **R E A D I N G** / **L E X I N G T O N** (right)

⭡N INTERSTATE 95 Cont'd

Exit #	Services
29b a(46)	MA 2 W, Cambridge
28b a(45)	Trapelo Rd, Belmont, **E** ⛽ Gulf/dsl, Mobil/dsl 🍴 Boston Mkt, Burger King, Dunkin', Panera Bread, Papa Gino's, Starbucks, Subway 🅾 city park, Star Mkt/Osco Drugs, Verizon
27b a(44)	Totten Pond Rd, Waltham, **E** ⛽ Shell 🍴 Copper House, D'Angelo, Dunkin', Osteria Posto, Ruth's Chris 🏠 Best Western+, Courtyard, Extended Stay America, Extended Stay America (2), Hilton Garden, Holiday Inn Express, Home Suites, Hyatt, Westin Hotel, **W** 🍴 Bertucci's Rest., Green Papaya Thai 🏠 Embassy Suites/The Grille, Hampton Inn 🅾 AT&T, Costco, Home Depot
26(43)	US 20, to MA 117, to Waltham, **E** ⛽ Sunoco/dsl, **W** ⛽ Mobil/dsl 🍴 Dunkin' 🅾 NTB, vet
25(42)	I-90, MA Tpk
24(41)	MA 30, Newton, Wayland, **E** ⛽ Speedway 🏠 Marriott/rest.
23(40)	Recreation Rd (from nb), to MA Tpk
22b a(39)	Grove St, **E** 🏠 Hotel Indigo 🅾 golf
38.5mm	travel plaza sb, ⛽ Gulf/dsl 🍴 McDonald's
21b a(38)	MA 16, Newton, Wellesley, **E** 🅾 **H**, **W** ⛽ Sunoco 🍴 Dunkin', North End Pizza, Papa Razzi, Starbucks 🅾 CVS Drug
20b a(36)	MA 9, Brookline, Framingham
19(35)	Highland Ave, Newton, Needham, **E** ⛽ EVC, Speedway 🍴 Anthony's Pizza, Chef Mike's, Chipotle Mexican, Five Guys, Mandarin Cuisine, Mighty Subs, Panera Bread, Petsmart, Starbucks 🏠 Residence Inn, Sheraton/rest. 🅾 AAA, Advance Parts, CVS Drug, Marshall's, Michael's, PetCo, Staples, TJ Maxx, **W** 🍴 Three Squares Rest. 🅾 Chevrolet, Ford
18(34)	Great Plain Ave, W Roxbury
33.5mm	parking area sb
17(33)	MA 135, Needham, Wellesley
32mm	truck turnout sb
16b a(31)	MA 109, High St, Dedham, **W** ⛽ Mobil/dsl
15b a(29)	US 1, MA 128, 0-2 mi **E** ⛽ Gulf 🍴 Dunkin', Harrow's Chicken Pies, Hooters, Joe's Grill, Panera Bread, PapaGino's, PF Chang's, Qdoba, Starbucks, Subway, TGI Friday's, Victory Grille, Yard House Rest. 🏠 Fairfield Inn, Holiday Inn, Residence Inn 🅾 AT&T, AutoZone, Best Buy, BJ's Whse, Costco/gas, CVS Drug, LL Bean, NTB, PepBoys, PetCo, Staples, Star Mkt, Tesla, Verizon, vet, Whole Foods Mkt, 0-2 mi **W** ⛽ Irving/dsl, Shell/dsl 🍴 Burger King, Dunkin', Jade Chinese, McDonald's 🏠 Budget Inn 🅾 AAA, Acura, AT&T, Audi, Buick/GMC, Chevrolet, Chrysler/Dodge/Jeep, Fiat, Honda, Hyundai, Kia, Mercedes, Porsche, Toyota
14(28)	East St, Canton St, **E** 🏠 Hilton
27mm	🅿️s sb, full 🚻 facilities, litter barrels, ℂ, 🚶
13(26.5)	University Ave, **W** ⛽ EVC 🍴 Anthony's Pizza, Chipotle, Del Frisco's, Joe's Grill, Panda Express, Panera Bread, Smashburger, Starbucks, Which Wich? 🅾 GNC, Michael's, Petsmart, Target, Verizon, Wegman's Mkt
12(26)	I-93 N, to Braintree, Boston, motorist callboxes end nb
11b a(23)	Neponset St, to Canton, **E** ⛽ Citgo/repair, Sunoco/dsl 🍴 Dunkin', **2 mi W** on US 1 ⛽ Gulf/dsl, Sunoco 🍴 Jake&Joe's, The Chateau 🏠 Hampton Inn 🅾 **H**, Chevrolet, Ferrari, Ford, Honda, Hyundai, Maserati, Nissan, Toyota, Volvo
22.5mm	Neponset River
10(20)	Coney St (from sb, no EZ return), to US 1, Sharon, Walpole, **1 mi W** on US 1 ⛽ BJ's Gas, Mobil 🍴 99 Rest., Bertucci's, Chili's, Chipotle Mexican, Dunkin', Five Guys, Friendly's, IHOP, McDonald's, Panda Express, Panera Bread, Starbucks, Subway, Taco Bell, TX Roadhouse, Wendy's 🏠 Courtyard, Holiday Inn Express, Residence Inn, Sheraton 🅾 Advance Parts, Barnes&Noble, CarMax, Home Depot, Jo-Ann, Kohl's, Old Navy, O'Reilly Parts, PetCo, Petsmart, Staples, Stop&Shop, TownFair Tire, VW, Walgreens

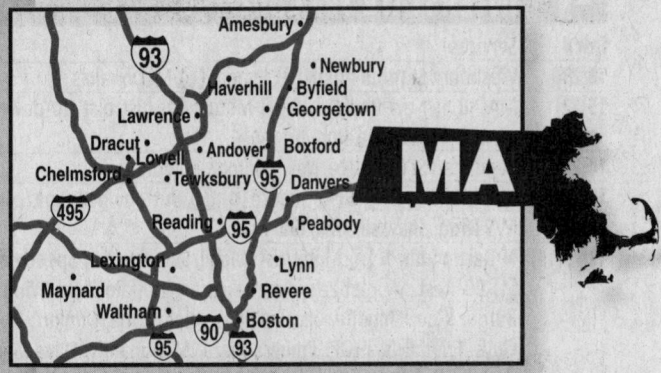

9(19)	US 1, to MA 27, same as 10, Walpole, **W** ⛽ Gulf, Mobil/dsl 🍴 Applebee's, Dunkin', Starbucks 🏠 Best Western+, EconoLodge 🅾 BigY Foods/drug, Lexus, Walmart
8(16)	S Main St, Sharon, **E** 🍴 Dunkin', Starbucks 🅾 Shaw's Foods
7b a(13)	MA 140, to Mansfield, **E** 🍴 99 Rest., Jake'nJoe's Grille 🏠 Comfort Inn, Courtyard, Holiday Inn, Red Roof+, Residence Inn 🅾 Stop&Shop/gas, **W** ⛽ Shell/HoneyDew Donuts/dsl 🍴 Dunkin', PapaGino's 🅾 $Tree
6b a(12)	I-495, S to Cape Cod, N to NH
10mm	Welcome Ctr/🅿️s nb, full 🚻 facilities, info, litter barrels, petwalk, ℂ, 🚶
9mm	truck parking area sb
5(7)	MA 152, Attleboro, **E** 🅾 **H**, **W** ⛽ Gulf/dsl 🍴 Barett's Alehouse, Wendy's 🅾 Shaw's Foods/Osco Drug
4(6)	I-295 S, to Woonsocket
3(4)	MA 123, to Attleboro, **E** ⛽ Shell/dsl 🍴 Dunkin' 🅾 **H**, zoo
2.5mm	parking area/weigh sta both lanes, litter barrels, no restrooms
2b a(1)	US 1A, Newport Ave, Attleboro, **E** ⛽ Mobil/dsl 🍴 McDonald's, Olive Garden 🅾 Hobby Lobby, Home Depot, Market Basket Foods, TJ Maxx, Verizon, **W** ⛽ Grampy's/dsl 🅾 Kia
1(.5)	US 1 (from sb), **E** 🏠 Attleboro Inn 🅾 Rite Aid, Volvo, **W** ⛽ Speedway/dsl
0mm	Massachusetts/Rhode Island state line

⭡N INTERSTATE 195

Exit #	Services
22(41)	I-495 N, MA 25 S, to Cape Cod. **I-195 begins/ends on I-495, exit 1.**
21(39)	MA 28, to Wareham, **N** 🍴 BB's Rest., Casa Cancun, Cosi, Gourmet Garden, Longhorn Steaks, Qdoba Mexican, Red Robin 🅾 Aldi, AutoZone, GNC, JC Penney, LL Bean, Lowe's, Michael's, Old Navy, PetCo, Staples, Target, TJ Maxx, Verizon, Walmart/Subway, **S** ⛽ Gateway Star/dsl, Mobil/Dunkin/Subway/dsl 🍴 99 Rest., Five Guys, Saga Fusion 🏠 TownPlace Suites 🅾 **H**
37mm	parking area eb, boatramp, info
36mm	Sippican River
20(35)	MA 105, to Marion, **S** 🅾 RV camping (seasonal)
19b a(31)	to Mattapoisett, **S** ⛽ Mobil 🍴 Dunkin', Nick's Pizza, Ying Dynasty 🅾 USPO
18(26)	MA 240 S, to Fairhaven, **1 mi S** ⛽ 7-11 🍴 99 Rest., Burger King, Frontera Grill, Jake's Diner, McDonald's, PapaGino's, Pasta House, Riccardi's Italian, Subway, Taco Bell, Wendy's 🏠 Hampton Inn 🅾 $Tree, AutoZone, Brahmin Handbags, Buick/GMC, GNC, Marshall's, Mazda, Staples, Stop&Shop/gas, Sullivan Tire, TownFair Tire, Walgreens, Walmart/Subway
25.5mm	Acushnet River
17(24)	Coggeshall St, (from wb only), same as 16, New Bedford, **N** ⛽ 7-11/gas, Petro/dsl, Sunoco 🍴 HoneyDew Donuts, Little Caesar's, McDonald's, Popeye's, Subway, Taco Bell 🅾 GNC, Market Basket Foods, URGENT CARE

N E W T O N   D E D H A M *(left margin)*

A T T L E B O R O *(right margin)*

MA *(bottom right)*

⛽ = gas   🍴 = food   🏨 = lodging   🅾 = other   🆁🆂 = rest stop   Copyright 2022 - The Next EXIT ®

▲▼N INTERSTATE 195 Cont'd

Exit #	Services
16(23)	Washburn St (from eb), N ⛽ Sunoco 🍴 McDonald's
15(22)	MA 18 S, New Bedford, S ⛽ Mutual 🅾 hist dist, to downtown, Whaling Museum
14(21)	Penniman St (from eb), New Bedford, downtown
13b a(20)	MA 140, N 🅾 🖕, S ⛽ Sunoco 🅾 🏨, Buttonwood Park/zoo, CVS Drug, Shaw's Foods, Walgreens
12b a(19)	N Dartmouth, S ⛽ Mobil/dsl, Mobil/Subway/dsl, Speedway 🍴 99 Rest., Applebee's, Azuma Asian, Buffalo Wild Wings, Burger King, Chipotle, ChuckeCheese, Coldstone, Dunkin', Five Guys, Friendly's, IHOP, Jimmy's Pizza, McDonald's, Olive Garden, Panera Bread, Peking Garden, Starbucks, Subway, Taco Bell, TGIFriday's, Tropical Smoothie, TX Roadhouse, Wendy's 🏨 Residence Inn 🅾 $Tree, AT&T, Barnes&Noble, Best Buy, BJ's Whse/gas, Chevrolet, Dick's, Firestone/auto, Home Depot, JC Penney, Jo-Ann, Kia, Kohl's, Lowe's, Macy's, Michael's, Nissan, Old Navy, PetCo, Stop&Shop/gas, Target, TJ Maxx, TownFair Tire, Toyota, USPO, Walgreens, Walmart
11b a(17)	Reed Rd, to Dartmouth, **2 mi** S ⛽ Shell 🍴 Dunkin'
10(16)	MA 88 S, to US 6, same as 9, Westport, S ⛽ Cumberland 🅾 CVS Drug
9(15.5)	MA 24 N (from nb), Stanford Rd, Westport, S ⛽ Rte 6 Gas, Supreme, Valero 🍴 Dunkin', Galley Grill 🏨 Hampton Inn 🅾 White's Hospitality
8b	MA 24 N, (exits left from eb)
8a(15)	MA 24 S, Fall River, Westport
7(14)	MA 81 S, Plymouth Ave, Fall River, N ⛽ Speedway 🍴 99 Rest., Boston Mkt, Burger King, Dunkin', HoneyDew Donuts, KFC, Subway, Wendy's 🅾 🏨, CVS Drug, Hyundai, S ⛽ Gulf, Shell 🍴 Applebee's, McDonald's 🅾 Stop&Shop, Sullivan Tire, Walgreens
6(13.5)	Pleasant St, Fall River, downtown
5(13)	MA 79, MA 138, to Taunton, S ⛽ 7-11, Speedway/dsl 🍴 Dunkin'
12mm	Assonet Bay
4b a(10)	MA 103, to Swansea, Somerset, N ⛽ Wilbur's 🍴 Rogers Rest. 🅾 repair, vet, S ⛽ Shell 🍴 Jillian's Grill 🏨 Riverview Inn
3(8)	US 6, to MA 118, Swansea, Rehoboth, N ⛽ Mobil/Dunkin', Speedway 🍴 Five Guys, Friendly's, McDonald's, Subway, Thai Taste, Wendy's 🅾 $Tree, AT&T, BigLots, Firestone/auto, Jo-Ann Fabrics, Marshall's, Petsmart, Price Rite Foods, Target, Verizon, Walmart/Subway, S ⛽ Cumberland Farms/dsl 🍴 Umi Japanese 🏨 Holiday Inn Express, Rodeway Inn 🅾 Kia, NAPA, USPO
5.5mm	parking area wb
2(5)	MA 136, to Newport, S ⛽ Mobil/24hr, Shell/24hr 🍴 Dunkin', McDonald's, Subway 🅾 CVS Drug, Toyota
3mm	weigh sta eb
1(1)	MA 114A, to Seekonk, N ⛽ Exxon, Global/Subway/dsl, Shell/dsl 🍴 99 Rest., Dunkin', Newport Creamery 🏨 Motel 6 🅾 vet, S ⛽ Mobil/24hr, Speedway/dsl, Stop&Shop Gas/repair, Sunoco 🍴 Applebee's, Buffalo Wild Wings, Burger King, Chick-fil-A, Chili's, Chipotle, Dunkin', Five Guys, Ichigo Ichie Japanese, IHOP, Joe's Kitchen, Longhorn Steaks, McDonald's, Moe's SW, Outback Steaks, Panera Bread, Papa John's, PapaGino's, Rebeco Mexican, Starbucks, Subway, Taco Bell, TGIFriday's, Wendy's 🏨 Best Western, Clarion, Extended Stay America, Hampton Inn, Knights Inn, Mary's Motel, Quality Inn 🅾 $Tree, Acura, Advance Parts, AT&T, Best Buy, BigLots, BJ's/gas, Bob's Stores, Dick's, Firestone/auto, GNC, Hobby Lobby, Home Depot, Kohl's, Lowe's, Michael's, PepBoys, Petco, Staples, Stop&Shop Foods, Target, TJMaxx, TownFair Tire, Verizon, Walmart

FALL RIVER
SEEKONK

PROVIDENCE

0mm	Massachusetts/Rhode Island state line. **Exits 8-1 are in RI.**
8(5)	US 1A N, Pawtucket, S ⛽ Mobil/dsl 🍴 Dunkin', Subway 🅾 CVS Drug, Walgreens
7(4)	US 6 E, CT 114 S, to Barrington, Seekonk
6(3)	Broadway Ave, N 🅾 Monro
5(2.5)	RI 103 E, Warren Ave
4(2)	US 44 E, RI 103 E, Taunton Ave, Warren Ave
3(1.5)	Gano St, S ⛽ EVC 🅾 Hilton Garden
2(1)	US 44 W, Wickenden St, India Pt, downtown, N ⛽ Shell/dsl, ⛽ EVC 🏨 Hilton Garden
1(.5)	Providence, downtown

I-195 begins/ends on I-95, exit 20 in Providence, RI. Exits 1-8 are in RI.

▲►E INTERSTATE 290

Exit #	Services
26b a(20)	I-495. I-290 begins/ends on I-495, exit 25.
25b a(17)	Solomon Pond Mall Rd, to Berlin, N ⛽ EVC 🍴 Bertucci's, Olive Garden, TGIFriday's 🏨 Quality Inn, Residence Inn 🅾 Best Buy, JC Penney, Macy's, Old Navy, Target, S ⛽ 🍴 Cafe Norma
24(15)	Church St, Northborough
23b a(13)	MA 140, Boylston, N ⛽ Gulf/Dunkin'/dsl, Shell/dsl
22(11)	Main St, Worcester, N 🍴 Dunkin'
21(10)	Plantation St (from eb), N 🍴 Dunkin', same as 20
20(8)	MA 70, Lincoln St, Burncoat St, N ⛽ Gulf/Subway/dsl, Shell/dsl 🍴 Crown Chicken, Denny's, Dunkin', Five Guys, KFC, Kyoto, McDonald's, PapaGino's/D'Angelo, Ruby Tuesday, Subway, Taco Bell, TX Roadhouse, Wendy's 🏨 Quality Inn, Suburban Inn 🅾 $Tree, Aldi Foods, AT&T, AutoZone, Barnes&Noble, CVS Drug, Dick's, Kohl's, Lowe's, Staples, Stop&Shop, Target, URGENT CARE, USPO, Walgreens
19(7)	I-190 N, MA 12
18	MA 9, Framington, Ware, N 🅾 Worcester Airport, S 🅾 🏨
16	Central St, Worcester, N 🍴 99 Rest., Starbucks 🏨 Hilton Garden, Holiday Inn Express 🅾 USPO
14	MA 122, Barre, Worcester, downtown
13	MA 122A, Vernon St, Worcester, downtown
12	MA 146 S, to Millbury
11	Southbridge St, College Square, N ⛽ Shell/dsl 🍴 Culpepper's Cafe, Wendy's 🅾 Family$
10	MA 12 N (from wb), Hope Ave
9	Auburn St, to Auburn, E ⛽ Shell 🍴 Arby's, Auburn Town Pizza, Dunkin', McDonald's, Outback, PapaGino's, Starbucks, Subway, Yong Shing 🏨 Comfort Inn, Holiday Inn Express (1mi), La Quinta 🅾 Acura, AutoZone, Big Lots, Firestone/auto, Macy's, Midas, Monro, Petco, Shaw's Foods, Staples, TownFair Tire, USPO, Verizon
8	MA 12 S (from sb), Webster, W ⛽ Shell 🏨 Holiday Inn Express
7	I-90, E to Boston, W to Springfield. I-290 begins/ends on I-90.

WORCESTER

▲▼N INTERSTATE 395

Exit #	Services
12.5	I-395 begins/ends on I-290, exit 10.
7(12)	to I-90 (MA Tpk), MA 12, same as 6b, E 🏨 Holiday Inn Express, W ⛽ Shell 🍴 Bentley Cafe
6b a(11)	US 20, E ⛽ Cumberland 🍴 Major League Roast Beef, Tiny Tim's 🅾 NAPA, truck tires/repair, VW, W ⛽ Shell 🍴 Applebee's, Chuck's Steakhouse, D'angelo, Dunkin', Friendly's, Wendy's 🏨 Fairfield Inn, Hampton Inn 🅾 BJ's Whse/dsl, Buick/Cadillac/GMC, Chevrolet, CVS, Ford, Home Depot, Hyundai, Nissan, TJ Maxx
5(8)	Depot Rd, N Oxford

OXFORD

INTERSTATE 395 Cont'd

Exit #	Services
4b a(6)	Sutton Ave, to Oxford, **E** 🅿 Shell/Dunkin'/dsl ⊡ $Tree, Home Depot, MktBasket Foods, URGENT CARE, **W** 🅿 Mobil/dsl 🍴 Dunkin', McDonald's, NE Pizza, Subway ⊡ Cumberland Farms, CVS Drug
3(4)	Cudworth Rd, to N Webster, S Oxford
2(3)	MA 16, to Webster, **E**⊡ RV Camping, Subaru, **W** 🅿 BP/repair, Gulf, Sunoco 🍴 Burger King, D'angelo, Dunkin', Empire Wok, Friendly's, HoneyDew Donuts, KFC/Taco Bell, Little Caesar's, McDonald's, Mexicali Grill, Panera Bread, PapaGino's, Wendy's ⊡ 🏥 $Tree, Advance Parts, AutoZone, Big Lots, CVS Drug, Ford, GNC, O'Reilly Parts, PriceChopper Foods, Rite Aid, Verizon, Walgreens
1(1)	MA 193, to Webster, **E** ⊡ 🏥, **W** 🅿 Mobil/dsl 🍴 Golden Greek Rest., Wind Tiki Chinese ⊡ Goodyear/auto
0mm	**Massachusetts/Connecticut state line**

INTERSTATE 495

Exit #	Services
119	**I-495 begins/ends on I-95, exit 59.**
55(119)	MA 110 (from nb, no return), to I-95 S, **E**🅿 EVC, Irving/Circle K, Mobil, Sunoco/dsl 🍴 Acapulco Mexican, Burger King, Dunkin', Friendly's, McDonald's, Subway 🛏 Fairfield Inn, Hampton Inn ⊡ AT&T, Chevrolet, Stop&Shop, Verizon, **W** 🅿 Cumberland Farms/dsl ⊡ CVS, NAPA
54(118)	MA 150, to Amesbury, **W** ⊡ RV camping
53(115)	Broad St, Merrimac, **W** 🍴 Dunkin', Osaka
114mm	**parking area sb, litter barrels (6AM-8PM), 🛏, restrooms**
52(111)	MA 110, to Haverhill, **E** ⊡ 🏥, **W** 🅿 Mobil, Racing Mart 🍴 Biggart Ice Cream, Dunkin'
110mm	**parking area nb, litter barrels, 🛏**
51(109)	MA 125, to Haverhill, **E** 🅿 Gulf, Mobil 🍴 Bros Pizza, China King, Dunkin' ⊡ 🏥, **W** 🅿 Mobil/dsl 🍴 Applebee's, Burger King, Dunkin', Five Guys, Friendly's, Li's Asian, Longhorn Steaks, Lucky Corner Chinese, McDonald's, Mr Mikes Grill, Starbucks, Taco Bell, Wendy's ⊡ Monro Service
50(107)	MA 97, to Haverhill, **W** 🍴 Starbucks ⊡ Ford, Target
49(106)	MA 110, to Haverhill, **E** 🅿 Cumberland Farms, Sunoco 🍴 99 Rest., Athens Pizza, Dunkin', McDonald's, Oriental Garden, PapaGino's 🛏 Best Western, Hampton Inn ⊡ Buick/Chevrolet/GMC, Chrysler/Dodge/Jeep, CVS Drug, Marshall's, MktBasket Foods, Tire Whse, Walgreens
105.8mm	Merrimac River
48(105.5)	MA 125, to Bradford, **E** 🅿 BJ's Whse/Subway/gas
47(105)	MA 213, to Methuen, 1-2 mi **W** 🅿 EVC, Haffner's, Shell 🍴 Burger King, Chick-fil-A, Chipotle, ChuckeCheese, Joe's Grill, Margaritas Mexican, McDonald's, Olive Garden, Starbucks, TGIFriday's, Wendy's ⊡ 🏥, Home Depot, Marshall's, MktBasket Foods, Old Navy, Stop&Shop, Target, The Mann Orchards/Bakery, Walmart/Subway
46(104)	MA 110, **E** 🅿 Giovanni's Deli, Sunoco 🍴 Tekila's Mexican, **W** ⊡ 🏥
45(103)	Marston St, to Lawrence, **W**⊡ Chevrolet, Honda, Kia, Nissan, VW
44(102)	Merrimac St, to Lawrence
43(101)	Mass Ave, **W**⊡ Mobil
42(100)	MA 114, **E** 🅿 Gulf, Mobil, Wave 🍴 Bollywood Grill, Boston Mkt, Burger King, Burtons Grill, Chipotle Mexican, Dunkin', Friendly's, Lee Chin Chinese, Panera Bread 🛏 Holiday Inn Express ⊡ Ace Hardware, AT&T, CVS Drug, Kohl's, MktBasket Foods, PetCo, Staples, TJ Maxx, Walgreens, **W** 🅿 Gas'n Go

Exit #	Services
42(100)	Continued 🍴 Dunkin's, KFC, Little Caesar's, Starbucks, Subway, Taco Bell, Wendy's ⊡ 🏥, Advance Parts, America's Food Basket, Family$, Marshall's, Monro Service, O'Reilly Parts/VIP Service, vet
41(99)	MA 28, to Andover, **E** 🍴 Dunkin' ⊡ Cadillac/Chevrolet
40b a(98)	I-93, N to Methuen, S to Boston
39(94)	MA 133, to Dracut, **E** 🅿 Speedway 🍴 Longhorn Steaks, McDonald's 🛏 Extended Stay America, **W** 🅿 Mobil/Circle K/dsl 🍴 Cracker Barrel, Wendy's 🛏 Fairfield Inn, Holiday Inn/rest., Residence Inn, TownePlace Suites
38(93)	MA 38, to Lowell, **E** 🅿 Cumberland Farms/dsl, EVC, Petroil/dsl 🍴 99 Rest., Applebee's, Burger King, Dunkin', Harrow's Chicken Pie, IHOP, Jade East, Vic's Waffle House 🛏 Motel 6 ⊡ AT&T, Home Depot, Honda, TownFair Tire, Toyota, URGENT CARE, Verizon, Walmart, **W** 🅿 Citgo, Mobil, NTB, Sunoco 🍴 Dunkin', Jillie's Rest., McDonald's, Milan Pizza, Wendy's ⊡ Buick/GMC, Chevrolet, Chrysler/Dodge/Jeep, CVS Drug, Hannaford Foods, Hogan Tire/auto, Marshall's, Mazda, MktBasket Foods
37(91)	Woburn St, to S Lowell, **W** 🅿 Gulf/Dunkin'/Subway
35c(90)	to Lowell SP, Lowell ConX, 0-2 mi **W** on US 3 🍴 Chili's, Outback Steaks 🛏 Courtyard ⊡ Kia/VW, Lincoln, Shop&Save, Target, Walgreens
35b a(89)	US 3, S to Burlington, N to Nashua, NH
34(88)	MA 4, Chelmsford, **E** 🅿 Ampet, EVC, Mobil, Sunoco 🍴 110 Grill, Domino's, Dunkin', Jimmy's Pizza, PapaGino's 🛏 Radisson ⊡ CVS Drug, USPO, Walgreens, **W** 🅿 Shell 🍴 Moonstone's Rest. 🛏 Best Western+
33	MA 4, N Chelmsford (from nb)
87mm	℞s both lanes, (8AM-8PM), full 🚻 facilities, litter barrels, 🚰, 🛏, vending
32(83)	Boston Rd, to MA 225, **E** 🅿 Cumberland Farms, EVC, Gulf, Mobil 🍴 British Beer Co, Burton's Grill, Chili's, Chipotle, Dunkin', Evviva Trattoria, Five Guys, McDonald's, Panera Bread, Starbucks, Subway 🛏 Hampton Inn, Regency Inn, Residence Inn ⊡ CVS Drug, GNC, Jo-Ann Fabrics, Marshall's, MktBasket Foods, Petco, to Nashoba Valley Ski Area, Verizon, vet, Walgreens, Whole Foods Mkt
31(80)	MA 119, to Groton, **E** 🅿 Gulf, Mobil/dsl, Shell/Dunkin' 🍴 Dunkin', Littleton Subs, Subway, Yangtze River Chinese ⊡ Auburchon Hardware, CVS Drug, Donelan's Foods, Toyota, Verizon, vet, **W** 🍴 Anthony's Pizza, Moe's SW, Starbucks 🛏 Courtyard ⊡ AT&T, Market Basket, Town Fair Tire
30(78)	MA 110, to Littleton, **E**🅿 EVC 🍴 Littleton Cafe, **W**🅿 Mobil/Dunkin' 🍴 vet ⊡ 🏥
29b a(77)	MA 2, to Leominster, **E**⊡ to Walden Pond St Reserve

MA

🔼N INTERSTATE 495 Cont'd

Exit #	Services
28(75)	MA 111, to Boxborough, Harvard, **E** 🗲 Gulf/Dunkin' 🍴 Bravo Pizza 🛏 Boxboro Regency, **W** ⊡ vet
27(70)	MA 117, to Bolton, **E** 🗲 Mobil/dsl 🍴 Dunkin', Subway, **W** ⊡ vet
26(68)	MA 62, to Berlin, **E** 🗲 Gulf/Dunkin', Tesla EVC 🍴 110 Grill, Panera Bread, Qdoba, Subway 🛏 Holiday Inn Express ⊡ BJ's Whse/gas, Cabela's, GNC, Lowe's, Market Basket, Michael's, Petsmart, TJ Maxx, URGENT CARE, Verizon, **W** 🗲 Mobil/dsl
66mm	Assabet River
25b(64)	I-290, to Worcester
25a	to MA 85, Marlborough, **1 mi E** 🗲 Cumberland Farms, Mobil/dsl, Stop&Shop Gas 🍴 99 Rest., Applebee's, Burger King, Checkerboards Rest., Dunkin', HoneyDew Donuts, KFC/Taco Bell, McDonald's, PapaGino's ⊡ $Tree, AutoZone, Chevrolet, CVS Drug, GMC Trucks, Hogan Tire/auto, PetCo, Shaw's Foods, Stop&Shop, Verizon, Walgreens, Walmart/Subway, **W** 🛏 Residence Inn
24b a(63)	US 20, to Northboro, Marlborough, **E** 🗲 Mobil/dsl 🍴 D'angelo, Dunkin', Lake Williams Pizza 🛏 Holiday Inn, **W** 🗲 EVC, EVC, Gulf/Dunkin', Shell 🍴 99 Rest., Boston Mkt, Chick-fil-A, China Taste, Chipotle Mexican, Five Guys, Friendly's, Japan 1, Jersey Mike's, Longhorn Steaks, McDonald's, Panera Bread, Qdoba, Starbucks, Subway, Wendy's 🛏 Best Western, Courtyard, Embassy Suites, Extended Stay America, Fairfield Inn, Hampton Inn, Hyatt Place ⊡ $Tree, AT&T, Hannaford Foods, Sullivan Tire/auto, URGENT CARE
23c(60)	Simrano Dr, Marlborough
23b a(59)	MA 9, to Shrewsbury, Framingham, **E** 🗲 Cumberland/Dunkin', Gulf 🍴 Wendy's 🛏 Red Roof Inn ⊡ Cadillac, Volvo, **0-2 mi W** 🗲 Mobil/dsl, Shell 🍴 Bertucci's, Chateau Rest., Chipotle Mexican, Dunkin', Harry's Rest., Mandarin, McDonald's, Starbucks, Subway 🛏 Courtyard, Doubletree Inn, Extended Stay America, Extended Stay America (2), Extended Stay America (3), Hampton Inn, Residence Inn ⊡ 🏥, Buick/GMC, CarMax, Chrysler/Dodge/Jeep, Marshall's, Staples, Stop&Shop, VW
22(58)	I-90, MA TPK, E to Boston, W to Albany
21b a(54)	MA 135, to Hopkinton, Upton, **E** 🗲 Cumberland, Mobil/Dunkin' 🍴 110 Grill, Dynasty Chinese, Hiller's Pizza, Starbucks ⊡ Verizon
20(50)	MA 85, to Milford, **E** 🍴 Dunkin', **W** 🗲 Gulf/dsl/LP, Mobil/dsl 🍴 99 Rest., Pizza 85/deli, TGIFriday's, Wendy's 🛏 Best Western, Courtyard, Fairfield Inn, Holiday Inn Express ⊡ 🏥, Best Buy, Lowe's, PetCo, Staples, Target, Toyota
19(48)	MA 109, to Milford, **W** 🗲 Mobil/Circle K/dsl, Shell 🍴 Applebee's, Burger King, Chipotle, Dunkin', Five Guys, IHOP, KFC, McDonald's, Panera Bread, PapaGino's, Red Heat Tavern, Starbucks, Subway 🛏 Doubletree, La Quinta ⊡ $General, $Tree, AutoZone, Big Y Foods, CVS Drug, Jo-Ann Fabrics, Kohl's, Stop&Shop, TJ Maxx, TownFair Tire
18(46)	MA 126, to Bellingham, **E** 🍴 Chili's, McDonald's, Moe's SW ⊡ Barnes&Noble, Michael's, MktBasket Foods, Old Navy, Staples, Verizon, Walmart/Subway, Whole Foods Mkt, **W** 🗲 Mobil, Speedway/dsl, Sunoco/dsl 🍴 Chicago Grill, Dunkin', Outback Steaks ⊡ Home Depot, Petsmart
17(44)	MA 140, to Franklin, Bellingham, **E** 🗲 BP/7-11, Mobil/dsl, Shell/dsl 🍴 3 Rest., British Beer Co, Burger King, Chipotle, Dunkin', Firehouse Subs, Five Guys, HoneyDew Donuts,

17(44)	Continued
	Longhorn Steaks, Panera Bread, PapaGino's, Pepper T race Thai, Starbucks, Subway, Taco Bell, Wendy's ⊡ AT& AutoZone, Buick/GMC, CVS Drug, GNC, Marshall's, Mid Stop&Shop, URGENT CARE, Verizon, **W** ⊡ Stop&Shop G 🍴 99 Rest., Ichigo Ichie Hibachi 🛏 Residence Inn ⊡ B Whse/Subway/gas
16(42)	King St, to Franklin, **E** 🗲 BP/7-11 🍴 Dunkin', King St Ca Spruce Pond Creamery 🛏 Hampton Inn, **W** 🛏 Hawtho Suites
15(39)	MA 1A, to Plainville, Wrentham, **E** 🍴 Assisi Pizza ⊡ repa **W** 🗲 Mobil/dsl 🍴 Chicago Grill, Cracker Barrel, Dunkin', Ru Tuesday ⊡ Premium Outlets/famous brands
14b a(37)	US 1, to N Attleboro, **E** 🗲 Shell/dsl 🍴 Luciano's Rest. 🛏 A bor Motel ⊡ Bass Pro Shops (4mi), **W** 🗲 Mobil 🍴 Chili Dunkin', Panera Bread 🛏 Holiday Inn Express ⊡ casin Lowe's, NTB, Pete's RV Ctr, Stop&Shop, Target, TJ Maxx, vet
13(32)	I-95, N to Boston, S to Providence, **W** ⊡ 🏥
12(30)	MA 140, to Mansfield, **E** 🗲 Tesla EVC 🍴 Bertucci's Italian, B falo Wild Wings, Chipotle Mexican, Coldstone, Dunkin', Longho Steaks, Papa Gino's, Qdoba Mexican, Sake Japanese, TGIFriday ⊡ AT&T, Best Buy, Firestone/auto, GNC, Home Depot, Kohl's, Bean, Michael's, PetCo, Shaw's Foods, Staples, Verizon
11(29)	MA 140 S (from sb), **1 mi W** 🗲 Cumberland, Mobil 🍴 Be Sandwich, Dunkin', Fiesta Mexican, Mandarin Chinese, McDo ald's ⊡ $Tree, Roche Bros Mkt
10(26)	MA 123, to Norton, **E** 🍴 Dunkin' ⊡ QuickStop, **W** ⊡ 🏥
9(24)	Bay St, to Taunton, **E** 🍴 Chateau Rest., **W** 🍴 Dunkin', Jayl Cafe, Ruby Tuesday, Subway, Wendy's 🛏 Extended Stay Ame ica, Holiday Inn ⊡ $Tree, BJ's Whse, Tadeschi Foods, Watsc Pond SP
8(22)	MA 138, to Raynham, **E** 🗲 Mobil/dsl, Speedway/dsl 🍴 Ho eyDew Donuts, **W** 🗲 AARC/dsl/repair, Gulf/Dunkin', Stop Go/dsl 🍴 Brothers Pizza, Cape Cod Cafe, D'angelo, HoneyDe Donuts, Lucky Corner Chinese, McDonald's, PieZoni's Pizz ⊡ 🏥, Ace Hardware, Mkt Basket Foods, O'Reilly Parts, USPC Walmart
7b a(19)	MA 24, to Fall River, Boston, **1/2 mi E** 🗲 Mobil/dsl 🍴 Burge King
18mm	weigh sta both lanes
17mm	Taunton River
6(15)	US 44, to Middleboro, **E** 🗲 Super/dsl 🍴 Burger King, Dunkir Friendly's, PapaGino's, Subway, **W** 🗲 Irving/Circle K/Dunkin dsl 🛏 Fairfield Inn, Holiday Inn Express
5(14)	MA 18, to Lakeville, **E** 🗲 Shell, Super/dsl 🍴 D'Angelo, Dave Diner, Harry's Grille, Lorenzo's Rest, PapaGino's, Persy's Plac Cafe ⊡ CVS Drug, Kelly's Tire, Trucchi's Mkt, **W** ⊡ Massaso SP, RV camping (seasonal)
4(12)	MA 105, to Middleboro, **E** 🗲 Cumberland/dsl, PetroMa 🍴 Best Pizza, China Sails, DQ, Dunkin', McDonald's ⊡ Aut Zone, Family$, Hannaford Mkt, Rite Aid
11mm	parking area eb
10mm	parking area both lanes
3(8)	MA 28, to Rock Village, S Middleboro, **E** 🗲 GeKo/dsl ⊡ re pair, **W** 🗲 Mobil/Dunkin'/Subway/dsl
2(3)	MA 58, W Wareham, **E** 🗲 Mobil/dsl (2mi) 🍴 Dunkin' (2mi ⊡ RV camping, to Myles Standish SF, **W** 🗲 Shell/dsl
2mm	Weweantic River
I-495 begins/ends on I-195, MA 25 S.	

MICHIGAN

⬆N INTERSTATE 69

Exit #	Services
273mm	Welcome Ctr/🆁🆂 eb, full ♿ facilities, 🛍 litter barrels, petwalk
199	Lp 69 (from eb, no return), to Port Huron, **0-2 mi S** on Lp 69 🅖 Mobil/dsl, Speedway 🅕 Arby's, Burger King, Jimmy John's, KFC, Little Caesar's, Mc-Donald's, Subway, Taco Bell, Tim Horton's, Wendy's 🅞 $General, Advance Parts, AutoZone, Kroger/gas, repair, Sam's Club/gas, to Port Huron, USPO
	I-69 E and I-94 E run together into Port Huron. See I-94, exits 274-275mm.
198	I-94, to Detroit and Canada
196	Wadhams Rd, **N** 🅖 BP/Wendy's, Marathon, Speedy Q/dsl 🅕 Hungry Howie's, McDonald's, Peking Kitchen, Subway, Taco Bell 🅞 KOA (1mi), Vinckier Foods, Wadham's Drugs, **S** 🅖 🅛🅞🅥🅔🅢/Subway/dsl/scales/24hr 🅞 golf
194	Taylor Rd, **N** 🅞 Goodells CP, RV camping
189	Wales Center Rd, to Goodells, **S** 🅞 golf
184	MI 19, to Emmett, **N** 🅖 Sunoco/dsl/scales/24hr 🅞 repair, USPO, **S** 🅖 Marathon/dsl/24hr
180	Riley Center Rd, **N** 🅞 KOA
176	Capac Rd, **N** 🅖 BP/dsl/scales, ♦Loves♦/Chester's/McDonald's/dsl/scales/24hr
174mm	🆁🆂 wb, full ♿ facilities, litter barrels, petwalk, 🅒, 🛍, vending
168	MI 53, Imlay City, **N** 🅖 BP/dsl, Speedway/dsl 🅕 Big Boy, Burger King, DQ, Hungry Howie's, Jet's Pizza, John's Country Kitchen, Little Caesar's, Lucky's Steaks, McDonald's, New China, Taco Bell, Wah Wong Chinese, Wendy's/Tim Horton 🏠 Days Inn, M53 Motel, Super 8 🅞 AutoZone, Chevrolet, Chrysler/Dodge/Jeep, CVS Drug, Ford, GNC, Kroger/dsl, NAPA, O'Reilly Parts, Verizon
163	Lake Pleasant Rd, to Attica
160mm	🆁🆂 eb, full ♿ facilities, litter barrels, petwalk, 🅒, 🛍, vending
159	Wilder Rd
158mm	Flint River
155	MI 24, Lapeer, **1 mi N** 🅖 Speedy Q/dsl, Sunoco/dsl 🅕 Apple Tree Rest., Applebee's, Arby's, Blind Fish Rest., Brian's Rest., Buffalo Wild Wings, Burger King, Checkers, DQ, Jet's Pizza, Jimmy John's, KFC, Leo's Coney Island, Little Caesar's, Mancino's, McDonald's, Nick's Grill, Sonic, Starbucks, Subway, Taco Bell, Tim Horton, Wah Wong Chinese, Wendy's 🏠 Best Western, Holiday Inn Express 🅞 🏥, $Tree, Aldi Foods, AT&T, AutoZone, Belle Tire, Home Depot, Honda, Kohl's, Kroger/gas, Marshall's, Meijer/dsl, Michael's, Office Depot, O'Reilly Parts, Rite Aid, st police, URGENT CARE, Verizon, vet, Walgreens, **S** 🅖 Mobil/dsl 🅞 Chrysler/Dodge/Jeep, Harley Davidson
153	Lake Nepessing Rd, **S** 🅞 camping, golf, to Thumb Correctional
149	Elba Rd, **N** 🅞 Torzewski CP, **S** 🅞 Country Mkt, RV/truck repair
145	MI 15, Davison, **N** 🅕 Marathon, Speedway/dsl, Sunoco/dsl 🅕 Apollo Rest., Applebee's, Arby's, Big Boy, Burger King, Chee Kong Chinese, Flag City Diner, Hungry Howie's, Italia Gardens, Jimmy John's, KFC, Little Caesar's, Lucky's Steaks, McDonald's,

145	Continued Pizza Hut, Senor Lucky, Subway, Taco Bell, Tim Horton, Tropical Smoothie 🏠 Best Western 🅞 AutoValue Parts, Buick/GMC, Davison Automotive, GNC, Monro Tire, Rite Aid, Verizon, Walgreens, YaYa Chicken, **S** 🅖 Mobil/dsl 🅕 Sicilian Pizza 🅞 vet
143	Irish Rd, **N** 🅖 Speedway/dsl 🅞 Menard's, **S** 🅖 Sunoco/McDonald's/24hr 🅞 Meijer/dsl/e85
141	Belsay Rd, Flint, **N** 🅖 Marathon/Wendy's/dsl/24hr, Mobil 🅕 Halo Burger, KFC, McDonald's, Subway, Taco Bell 🅞 $Tree, Walmart/Subway, **S** 🅖 Sunoco/Tubby's/dsl 🅕 Little Caesar's
139	Center Rd, Flint, **N** 🅖 Speedway/dsl 🅕 Applebee's, Domino's, El Cozumel Mexican, Empire Wok, Halo Burger, Leo's Coney Island, Quiznos, Starbucks, Subway, Tim Horton 🅞 Aldi Foods, Big Lots, Discount Tire, GNC, Home Depot, JC Penney, Jo-Ann Fabrics, Staples, **0-2 mi S** 🅕 China 1, Coney Island, DQ, Hungry Howie's, McDonald's, Red Baron Rest., Subway 🏠 Burton Inn 🅞 $Tree, AT&T, Belle Tire, Meijer/dsl, TJ Maxx, Verizon
138	MI 54, Dort Hwy, **N** 🅖 BP/dsl, Speedway/dsl, Sunoco/dsl 🅕 Big John's Rest., Little Caesar's, Rally's, Tom's Coney Island, YaYa's Chicken 🅞 🏥, $General, KanRock Tires, Rite Aid, Save-a-Lot, Walgreens, **0-2 mi S** 🅖 Marathon, Marathon, Sunoco 🅕 American Diner Coney Island, Arby's, Big John Steak, Burger King, Church's, Empress of China, KFC, McDonald's, Taco Bell, The Coney Grill 🏠 Travel Inn 🅞 $General, Advance Parts, AutoZone, Burton Tire/auto, Family$, O'Reilly Parts, Tuffy Auto, U-Haul, Walgreens

LAPEER (vertical left margin)

FLINT (vertical right margin)

MI

⬆️N INTERSTATE 69 Cont'd

Exit #	Services
137	I-475, UAW Fwy, to Detroit, Saginaw
136	Saginaw St, Flint, N 🅖 Sunoco/dsl 🅞 🅗, U MI at Flint
135	Hammerberg Rd, industrial area
133b a	I-75, S to Detroit, N to Saginaw, US 23 S to Ann Arbor
131	MI 121, to Bristol Rd, 1/2 mi N on Miller Rd 🅕 Bar Louie, BD Mongolian BBQ, Buffalo Wild Wing, Casa Real, Chili's, Chipotle, ChuckeCheese, Famous Dave's BBQ, Golden Corral, Golden Moon Chinese, Halo Burger, Hooters, Jimmy John's, Leo's Coney Island, LJ Silver, Logan's Roadhouse, Olive Garden, Osaka Buffet, Outback Steaks, Panda Express, Panera Bread, Red Robin, Subway, Taco Bell, Telly's Coney Island, TX Roadhouse 🅞 $Tree, AT&T, Barnes&Noble, Belle Tire, Best Buy, BigLots, Hobby Lobby, JC Penney, Jo-Ann Fabrics, Kohl's, Macy's, Michael's, Old Navy, PetCo, Petsmart, Target, TJ Maxx, USPO, Valley Tire, Verizon
129	Miller Rd, S 🅕 Arby's, Burger King, McDonald's, Subway, Taco Bell, Wendy's 🅞 Kroger/gas, O'Reilly Parts
128	Morrish Rd, N 🅞 Meijer/dsl/e85, S 🅖 Admiral, Mobil/dsl 🅕 Hungry Howie's
126mm	🆁🆂 eb, full 🅗 facilities, info, litter barrels, petwalk, 🅒, 🅟
123	MI 13, to Saginaw, Lennon, N 🅖 Speedway/dsl 🅞 USPO
118	MI 71, to Corunna, Durand, N 🅞 Durand Automotive, S 🅖 Shell/dsl, Valero 🅕 China House, Hungry Howie's, McDonald's, Subway, Wendy's 🅛 Quality Inn 🅞 Ace Hardware, CarQuest, Chevrolet, Family$, golf, Rite Aid
115mm	Shiawassee River
113	Bancroft, S 🅖 BP/dsl (1.5mi) 🅞 RV camping
105	MI 52, to Owosso, Perry, S 🅖 Citgo/Subway/dsl, Exxon/7-11, Mobil/dsl, Sunoco/dsl/scales/24hr 🅕 Burger King, Cafe Sports, China Garden, Hungry Howie's, McDonald's, Taco Bell 🅛 Heb's Inn 🅞 $General, Carl's Mkt, Family$, Rite Aid, truck repair (1mi), USPO
101mm	🆁🆂 wb, full 🅗 facilities, litter barrels, petwalk, 🅒, 🅟
98.5mm	Vermilion River
98	Woodbury Rd, to Laingsburg, Shaftsburg
94	Lp 69, Marsh Rd, to E Lansing, Okemos, S 🅖 Speedway/dsl 🅕 McDonald's 🅞 Gillette RV Ctr, Meijer/Subway/dsl/e85, Monticello's Mkt
92	Webster Rd, Bath
89	US 127 S, to E Lansing
87	Old US 27, to Clare, Lansing, N 🅖 Marathon, Speedway/Speedy's Café/dsl 🅕 Arby's, Bob Evans, Burger King, China Gourmet, FlapJack Rest., Little Ceasar's, Mancino's, McDonald's, Subway, Tim Horton 🅛 Sleep Inn 🅞 Chevrolet, Meijer/dsl, Price Rite RV Ctr, Verizon, vet, S 🅖 Speedway/dsl 🅛 American Inn
85	DeWitt Rd, to DeWitt
84	Airport Rd
81	I-96 (from sb), W to Grand Rapids, Grand River Ave, Frances Rd, W 🅖 ⚡FLYING J/Denny's/dsl/24hr, 💙Loves/Hardee's/Subway/dsl/scales/24hr
93b a	MI 43, Lp 69, Saginaw Hwy, to Grand Ledge, 0-2 mi N 🅖 EVC, Shell, Speedway/dsl 🅕 Applebee's, Buffalo Wild Wings, Burger King, Carrabba's, Cheddar's, Chick-fil-A, Chipotle, Denny's, Finley's Grill, Frank's Grill, Hibachi Grill, Honeybaked Ham, Houlihan's, Jets Pizza, Logan's Roadhouse, Longhorn Steaks, Marco's Pizza, McDonald's, Outback Steaks, Panera Bread, Qdoba, Red Robin, Subway 🅛 Comfort Inn, Fairfield Inn, Hampton Inn, Hilton Garden, Motel 6, Quality Inn, Ramada Inn, Red Roof Inn, Residence Inn 🅞 🅗, $Tree, Aldi, AT&T,

93b a	Continued
	Barnes&Noble, Best Buy, BigLots, Chrysler/Dodge/Jeep, Hobby Lobby, JC Penney, Kohl's, Kroger/dsl, Meijer/dsl/24hr, Target, TJ Maxx, vet, Walgreens, S 🅖 QD, Shell/Dunkin', Sunoco/McDonald's 🅕 Arby's, Biggby Coffee, Bob Evans, Cancun Mexican, Cracker Barrel, Culver's, Steak'n Shake 🅛 SpringHill Suites 🅞 Belle Tire, Buick/GMC, Discount Tire, Lowe's, Mazda/Volvo, Menards, Michael's, PetsMart, Staples, Walmart/Subway
95	I-496, to Lansing
72	I-96, E to Detroit, W to Grand Rapids
70	Lansing Rd
68mm	🆁🆂 nb, full 🅗 facilities, litter barrels, petwalk, 🅒, 🅟, vending
66	MI 100, to Grand Ledge, Potterville, W 🅖 BP/dsl, Shell/Subway/dsl 🅕 Charlie's Grill, McDonald's, to Fox Co Park
61	Lansing Rd, E 🅖 Murphy USA/dsl 🅕 Applebee's 🅛 Comfort Inn 🅞 $Tree, AT&T, AutoZone, Buick/Chevrolet/GMC, Verizon, Walmart/Subway, W 🅖 QD, Speedway/dsl 🅕 Arby's, Big Boy, Biggby Coffee, Burger King, Jersey Subs, Jet's Pizza, KFC, Little Caesar's, McDonald's, Pizza Hut, Rally's, Taco Bell, Tasty Twist, Top Chinese, Wendy's 🅞 🅗, Ace Hardware, Advance Parts, Family$, Ford, NAPA, O'Reilly Parts, Tire City, vet
60	MI 50, Charlotte, E 🅛 Holiday Inn Express 🅞 Meijer/dsl, URGENT CARE, W 🅖 Admiral 🅛 Best Value Inn 🅞 🅗
57	Lp 69, Cochran Rd, to Charlotte
51	Ainger Rd, 1 mi E 🅖 gas 🅕 food 🅞 RV camping
48	MI 78, to Bellevue, Olivet, 1 mi E 🅖 Cenex/Subway/dsl 🅞 to Olivet Coll
42	N Drive N, Turkeyville Rd, W 🅕 Osprey Grille
41mm	🆁🆂 sb, full 🅗 facilities, litter barrels, petwalk, 🅒, 🅟
38	I-94, E to Detroit, W to Chicago
36	Michigan Ave, to Marshall, E 🅖 Admiral, Citgo/dsl/e85, Shell/Subway/dsl 🅕 Applebee's, Arby's, Biggby Coffee, Little Caesar's, McDonald's, Pizza Hut, Speedy Chick, Starbucks, Taco Bell, Wendy's, Yin Hai Chinese 🅛 Quality Inn 🅞 $General, $Tree, Ace Hardware, AT&T, AutoZone, Chevrolet, Family Fare Mkt/gas, NAPA, O'Reilly Parts, Rite Aid, Save-A-Lot, Tuffy Auto, Verizon, W 🅛 Arbor Inn 🅞 🅗, Chrysler/Dodge/Jeep
32	F Drive S, E 🅖 Shell/dsl 🅞 RV Camping
25	MI 60, to Three Rivers, Jackson, E 🅖 BP/dsl, Sunoco/dsl, TA/Shell/Country Pride/dsl/scales/24hr/@ 🅕 McDonald's, Subway 🅞 $General, Auto Value Parts, RV camping
23	Tekonsha, W access to RV camping
16	Jonesville Rd, W 🅞 Waffle Farm Camping (2mi)
13	US 12, to Quincy, Coldwater, E 🅖 Speedway/dsl 🅕 Applebee's, Biggby Coffee, Bob Evans, Buffalo Wild Wings, Grand Buffet 🅛 Hampton Inn, Holiday Inn Express, Red Roof Inn 🅞 $Tree, Aldi Foods, AT&T, AutoZone, Belle Tire, BigLots, Buick/Chevrolet/GMC, GNC, Haylett RV Ctr, Home Depot, Meijer/dsl, Verizon, Walmart/Subway, W 🅖 Citgo/dsl, Speedway/dsl 🅕 Arby's, Burger King, Coldwater Garden Rest., Cottage Inn Pizza, Culver's, Dickey's BBQ, Jimmy John's, KFC, Little Caesar's, McDonald's, Pizza Hut, Subway, Taco Bell 🅛 Best Western+, Quality Inn 🅞 🅗, auto repair, Ford/Lincoln, O'Reilly Parts, Rite Aid, st police, Walgreens
10	Lp 69, Fenn Rd, to Coldwater, W 🅞 Harbor Cove RV Park (4mi)
8mm	weigh sta nb
6mm	Welcome Ctr nb, full 🅗 facilities, litter barrels, petwalk, 🅒, 🅟, vending
3	Copeland Rd, Kinderhook, W 🅖 BP/dsl
0mm	Michigan/Indiana state line

M A R S H A L L

C O L D W A T E R

L A N S I N G

INTERSTATE 75	
Exit #	**Services**
395mm	US/Canada Border, Michigan state line, **I-75 begins/ends at toll bridge to Canada.**
394	Easterday Ave, **E** 🔲 Citgo/Krist/dsl 🏠 Holiday Inn Express, Ramada Inn (2mi) 🅾 🅷, to Lake Superior St U, **W Welcome Ctr**/🆁🆂, **info** 🔲 Admiral/dsl, Holiday/dsl/currency exchange
392	3 Mile Rd, Sault Ste Marie, **E** 🔲 Admiral/dsl, Holiday/dsl, Marathon/dsl, Shell/dsl, Sunoco/dsl 🍴 Applebee's, Arby's, Asian Buffet, Buffalo Wild Wings, Burger King, Domino's, DQ, Fuji Steaks, Great Wall Chinese, Indo China Garden, Jimmy John's, Little Caesar's, McDonald's, Pizza Hut, Subway, Taco Bell, Wendy's 🏠 Best Value Inn, Best Western, Comfort Inn, Days Inn, Hampton Inn, Plaza Motel, Skyline Motel, Super 8 🅾 🅷, $Tree, Advance Parts, AT&T, AutoZone, BigLots, Buick/Chevrolet/GMC, Family$, Goodyear/auto, Jo-Ann Fabrics, Kohl's, NAPA, O'Reilly Parts, Save-a-Lot, Soo Locks Boat Tours, st police, TJ Maxx, Verizon, Walgreens, Walmart/Subway, **W** 🅾 Meijer/dsl
389mm	🆁🆂 nb, full 🅰 facilities, info, litter barrels, petwalk, 🚻, 🅰
386	MI 28, **W** 🅾 to Brimley SP
379	Gaines Hwy, **E** to Barbeau Area
378	MI 80, Kinross, **E** 🔲 BP/dsl 🅾 🍴, golf, to Kinross Correctional
373	MI 48, Rudyard, **2 mi W** 🔲 gas/dsl 🍴 food 🏠 lodging
359	MI 134, to Drummond Island, **W** 🅾 National Forest Camping
352	MI 123, to Moran, Newberry
348	H63, to Sault Reservation, St Ignace, **0-2 mi E** 🍴 Jose's Cantina 🏠 Bavarian Haus, Baymont Inn, Bayview Motel, Bear Cove Inn, Best Value Inn, Birchwood Motel, Breakers Resort, Cedars Motel, Evergreen Motel, Great Lakes Motel, Holiday Inn Express, NorthernAire Motel, Pines Motel, Quality Inn 🅾 🅷, 🍴, casino, Castle Rock Camping, st police, to Mackinac Trail, **W** 🅾 Castle Rock Gifts
346mm	🆁🆂/scenic turnout sb, full 🅰 facilities, litter barrels, petwalk, 🅰
345	Portage St (from sb), St Ignace
344b	US 2 W, **W** 🔲 BP/dsl, Holiday/dsl, Shell/dsl 🍴 Big Boy, Burger King, Clyde's Drive-In, McDonald's, Subway, Suzy's Pasties 🏠 Quality Inn, Sunset Motel, Super 8 🅾 Ford, golf, KOA, Lakeshore RV Park
344a	Lp 75, St Ignace, **0-2 mi E** 🔲 Shell 🍴 BC Pizza, Bentley's Cafe, Galley Rest., Mackinac Grille, MI Patio Grill 🏠 Aurora Borealis Motel, Boardwalk Inn, Cedar Hill Lodge, Colonial House, Moran Bay Motel, Normandy Motel, Thunderbird Motel, Village Inn/rest., Voyager Motel 🅾 🅷, $General, Ace Hardware, Bay Drug, Family Fare Mkt, Family$, NAPA, public marina, st police, Straits SP, to Island Ferrys, TrueValue, USPO
343mm	**E Welcome Ctr** nb, full 🅰 facilities, litter barrels, 🚻, 🅰, **W** museum, **toll booth to toll bridge**
341mm	**toll** bridge, Lake Huron, Lake Michigan
339	US 23, Jamet St, **E** 🍴 Audie's Rest. 🏠 Days Inn, Knights Inn, LightHouse View Motel, Parkside Motel, Riviera Motel, Super 8, **W** 🔲 Shell 🍴 Bridgeview Diner, Darrow's Rest., Mackinaw Cookie Co 🏠 Holiday Inn Express, Vindel Motel 🅾 Wilderness SP
338	US 23 (from sb), same as 337, **E** 🔲 Marathon/dsl 🍴 BC Pizza, Burger King, DQ, KFC, Mama Mia's Pizza, Pancake Chef, Subway, Wienerlicious 🏠 Baymont Inn, Court Plaza Hotel 🅾 Mackinaw Mkt, Mackinaw Outfitters, USPO, **W** 🏠 Holiday Inn Express
337	MI 108 (from nb, no EZ return), Nicolet St, Mackinaw City, **E Welcome Ctr**/🆁🆂, 🔲 Citgo/dsl/LP, Tesla EVC 🍴 Blue Water Grill, Lighthouse Rest., Mackinaw Pastie&Cookie Co., Starbucks 🏠 Bayside Inn, Beach House Cottages, BeachComber Motel,

337	**Continued** Bell's Melody Motel, Best Value Inn, Best Western, Bridge Vista Beach Motel, Bridgeview Motel, Budget Inn, Capri Motel, Clarion, Clearwater Lakeshore Motel, Comfort Inn, Crown Choice Inn, Days Inn, EconoLodge, Fairview Inn, Great Lakes Inn, Hamilton Inn, Mackinaw Inn, North Winds Motel, Quality Inn, Rainbow Motel, Ramada Ltd, Sundown Motel, Sunrise Beach Motel, Super 8, Thunderbird Inn, Waterfront Inn 🅾 Harley-Davidson, Old Mill Creek SP, Tee Pee Camping, to Island Ferrys, **W** 🅾 KOA, Wilderness SP
336	US 31 S (from sb), to Petoskey
328mm	🆁🆂 sb, full 🅰 facilities, info, litter barrels, petwalk, 🚻, 🅰
326	C66, to Cheboygan, **E** 🔲 Andy's/dsl 🅾 🅷, Sea Shell City/gifts
322	C64, to Cheboygan, **E** 🅾 🅷, 🍴, LP, st police
317mm	🆁🆂/scenic turnout nb, full 🅰 facilities, info, litter barrels, petwalk, 🚻, 🅰
313	MI 27 N, Topinabee, **E** 🏠 Indian River RV Resort/Camping, Topinabee Motel
311mm	Indian River
310	MI 33, MI 68, **E** 🏠 Hometown Inn 🅾 Michigan Oaks Camping (3mi), **W** 🔲 Marathon, Shell/McDonald's 🍴 Burger King, Subway, Wilson's Rivers Edge Rest. 🏠 Coach House Motel, Indian River Motel 🅾 auto repair, Family$, Ken's Mkt/gas, to Burt Lake SP, to Indian River Trading Post/RV Resort
301	C58, Wolverine, **E** 🔲 Marathon/dsl 🍴 Whistle Stop Rest. 🅾 Elkwood Campground (5mi), **W** 🅾 Sturgeon Valley Campground (3mi)
297mm	Sturgeon River
290	Vanderbilt, **E** 🔲 Marathon/dsl/LP/RV dump, Spirit/dsl 🍴 Elk Horn Grill 🅾 USPO, Village Mkt Foods, **W** 🔲 Mobil/dsl 🅾 Black Bear Golf Resort (2mi)
287mm	🆁🆂 sb, full 🅰 facilities, info, litter barrels, 🚻, 🅰
282	MI 32, Gaylord, **E** 🔲 Family Fare/dsl, Holiday, Speedway/dsl 🍴 Arby's, Arlene's Diner, Big Buck Steaks, Burger King, DQ, Jet's Pizza, KFC, La Senorita Mexican, McDonald's, Qdoba Mexican, Subway, Wendy's 🏠 Alpine Lodge, Baymont Inn, Fairfield Inn, Quality Inn 🅾 🅷, Advance Parts, Family FareMkt, Harley-Davidson, Rite Aid, st police, **W** 🔲 Marathon/dsl, Marathon/dsl (2), Mobil/dsl, Murphy USA/dsl, Shell/dsl 🍴 Applebee's, BC Pizza, Big Boy, Biggby Coffee, Bob Evans, Buffalo Wild Wings, China Buffet, Coldstone/Tim Horton, Culver's, El Rancho Mexican, Five Guys, Jimmy John's, Little Caesar's, Mancino's Pizza, Panera Bread, Ponderosa, Ruby Tuesday, Starbucks, Taco Bell 🏠 Best Western, Hampton Inn, Holiday Inn Express 🅾 $Tree, Aldi Foods, AT&T, BigLots, Chrysler/Dodge/Jeep, GNC, Hobby Lobby, Home Depot, Kenworth, Kohl's, Lowe's, Meijer/dsl, Northern MI RV Ctr, O'Reilly Parts, Petsmart, Save-A-Lot Foods, TJ Maxx, Verizon, Walgreens, Walmart/Subway

Side labels: **SAULT STE MARIE** · **MACKINAW CITY** · **GAYLORD**

MI

↑N INTERSTATE 75 Cont'd

Exit #	Services
279mm	45th Parallel, halfway between the equator and North Pole
279	Old US 27, Gaylord, E 🛢 Marathon/Subway/dsl, Mobil/dsl, Shell 🍴 Burger King, Mama Leone's 🛏 Best Value Inn 🅾 Ace Hardware, auto repair, Buick/GMC, Chevrolet, Ford/Lincoln, st police, W 🍴 Bennethum's Rest., Porter Haus 🛏 KOA (3mi)
277mm	Ⓡ🅂 nb, full 🚻 facilities, info, litter barrels, petwalk, 🅲, 🗑
270	Waters, E 🛢 Marathon/dsl 🍴 Hilltop Rest., W 🛢 BP/dsl, Waters Inn 🅾 Freeway RV Ctr, to Otsego Lake SP, USPO
264	Lewiston, Frederic, W 🍴 access to food 🅾 camping
262mm	Ⓡ🅂 sb, full 🚻 facilities, litter barrels, petwalk, 🅲, 🗑
259	MI 93, E 🅾 Hartwick Pines SP
256	(from sb), to MI 72, Grayling, access to same as 254
254	MI 72 (exits left from nb, no return), Grayling, 1 mi W 🛢 Admiral/dsl, Marathon/dsl, Shell, Speedway/dsl 🍴 Burger King, DQ, Keg'O'Nails, Little Caesar's, McDonald's, Pizza Hut, Subway, Taco Bell, Wendy's 🛏 Days Inn, Ramada 🅾 Ⓗ, $General, 7-11, Ace Hardware, AT&T, Auto Value Parts, Family Fare Mkt, Family$, Ford, NAPA, O'Reilly Parts, Save-A-Lot Foods, Verizon, Walgreens
251mm	Ⓡ🅂 nb, full 🚻 facilities, info, litter barrels, petwalk, 🅲, 🗑, vending
251	4 Mile Rd, E 🅾 Jellystone RV Park (5mi), W 🛢 Marathon/Arby's/dsl/scales/RV Dump/24hr 🛏 Super 8
249	US 127 S (from sb), to Clare
244	MI 18, Roscommon, 3 mi E 🛢 Shell/dsl 🍴 McDonald's, W 🛢 Valero/dsl 🅾 Higgins Lake SP, KOA (1mi)
239	MI 18, Roscommon, S Higgins Lake SP, 3 mi E 🛢 Shell/McDonald's/dsl 🅾 camping, W 🅾 camping, Higgins Lake SP
235mm	Ⓡ🅂 sb, full 🚻 facilities, info, litter barrels, petwalk, 🅲, 🗑, vending
227	MI 55 W, rd F97, to Houghton Lake, 5 mi W 🍴 food
222	Old 76, to St Helen, 2-4 mi E 🍴 food 🛏 lodging 🅾 camping
215	MI 55 E, West Branch, E 🛢 Shell/dsl 🅾 Ⓗ
212	MI 55, West Branch, E 🛢 Mobil/dsl, Murphy USA/dsl, Shell/Subway/dsl 🍴 Applebee's, Arby's, Big Boy, Burger King, KFC, Lumberjack Rest., McDonald's, Ponderosa, Rally's, Taco Bell, Tim Hortons, Wendy's 🛏 Quality Inn, Super 8 🅾 Ⓗ, Home Depot, st police, Walmart/Subway, West Branch Outlets/famous brands, W 🛢 Marathon/dsl
210mm	Ⓡ🅂 nb, full 🚻 facilities, info, litter barrels, petwalk, 🅲, 🗑, vending
202	MI 33, to Rose City, Alger, E 🛢 Marathon/Narski's Mkt/jerky, Mobil/jerky outlet/dsl, Shell/Subway/dsl 🅾 Greenwood Camping
201mm	Ⓡ🅂 sb, full 🚻 facilities, litter barrels, petwalk, 🅲, 🗑, vending
195	Sterling Rd, to Sterling, 6 mi E 🛢 gas 🅾 Riverview Camping (seasonal)
190	MI 61, to Standish, E 🅾 Ⓗ, W 🛢 Marathon, Mobil/jerky/dsl
188	US 23, to Standish, 2-3 mi E 🛢 gas 🍴 food 🅾 camping
181	Pinconning Rd, E 🛢 Shell/McDonald's/dsl 🍴 Cheesehouse Diner 🛏 Pinconning Inn (2mi), W 🛢 BP/pizza/dsl/24hr
175mm	Ⓡ🅂 nb, full 🚻 facilities, litter barrels, petwalk, 🅲, 🗑, vending
173	Linwood Rd, to Linwood, E 🛢 Mobil/dsl/jerky 🍴 Arby's (2mi)
171mm	Kawkawlin River
168	Beaver Rd, to Willard, E 🅾 to Bay City SRA, W 🛢 Mobil/jerky
166mm	Kawkawlin River
164	to MI 13, Wilder Rd, to Kawkawlin, E 🍴 Cracker Barrel, Lucky Steaks, Ponderosa, Uno Pizzaria 🛏 AmericInn, Holiday Inn Express 🅾 KanRock Tire, Meijer/dsl, Menards

SAGINAW

162b a	US 10, MI 25, to Midland
160	MI 84, Delta, E 🛢 Mobil, Shell/Subway/dsl, W 🛢 Speedway/dsl 🍴 Berger's Rest., Burger King, KFC/Taco Bell, McDonald's 🛏 Econolodge 🅾 RV World Super Ctr, to Saginaw Valley SU
158mm	Ⓡ🅂 sb, full 🚻 facilities, litter barrels, petwalk, 🅲, 🗑, vending
155	I-675 S, to downtown Saginaw, 4 mi W 🍴 Outback Steaks 🛏 Hampton Inn
154	to Zilwaukee
153mm	Saginaw River
153	MI 13 E Bay City Rd, Saginaw
151	MI 81, to Reese, Caro, E 🛢 BP/McDonald's/dsl 🅾 Volvo Trucks, W 🛢 🏳FLYING J/Wendy's/dsl/LP/24hr
150	I-675 N, to downtown Saginaw, 6 mi W 🍴 Outback Steaks 🛏 Hampton Inn
149b a	MI 46, Holland Ave, to Saginaw, W 🛢 BP, Speedway/dsl 🍴 Arby's, Big John's Steaks, Burger King, McDonald's, Popeye's, Subway, Taco Bell 🛏 Red Roof Inn, Welcome Inn 🅾 Ⓗ, Advance Parts, USPO
144b a	Bridgeport, E 🛢 ❤Loves/Hardee's/dsl/scales/24hr, Speedway/dsl 🅾 Jellystone Camping (9mi), W 🛢 Mobil/dsl/e85, TA/Country Pride/dsl/scales/24hr/@ 🍴 Arby's, Big Boy, Cracker Barrel, Hungry Howie's, McDonald's, Subway, Taco Bell, Wendy's 🛏 Baymont Inn, Knights Inn 🅾 $General, Family$, Kroger/gas, Rite Aid, st police, USPO
143mm	Cass River
138mm	pull off both lanes
136	MI 54, MI 83, Birch Run, E 🛢 Mobil/dsl/24hr 🍴 Halo Burger, KFC, Subway 🛏 Best Value Inn, Best Western, Comfort Inn, Hampton Inn, Holiday Inn Express 🅾 Advance Parts, General RV Ctr, Mejier/dsl/e85, Totten Tires, W 🛢 BP, Citgo/7-11, Marathon 🍴 A&W, Applebee's, Arby's, Bagger Dave's Burgers, Beijing Express, Bob Evans, Buffalo Wild Wings, Culver's, DQ, Dunkin', Jimmy John's, Leo's Coney Island, Little Caesar's, McDonald's, Sonic, Starbucks, Taco Bell, Tony's Rest., Uno Grill, Victor&Merek's Pizza, Wendy's 🛏 Country Inn&Suites 🅾 Birch Run Outlet/famous brands, Buick/Chevrolet, Family$, GNC, Old Navy, USPO
131	MI 57, to Montrose, E 🛢 🍴 Arby's, Big John's Steaks, Burger King, DQ, KFC, McDonald's, Oriental Express, Subway, Taco Bell, Tim Hortons, Twins Pizza, Wendy's 🅾 AutoZone, Chevrolet, Chrysler/Dodge/Jeep, KanRock Tire, Tradewinds RV Ctr, vet, W 🛢 Mobil/Rally's/dsl, Murphy USA/dsl 🍴 Applebee's, Big Boy, Lucky Steaks, Tropical Smoothie Cafe 🅾 $Tree, auto repair, Menards, Verizon, Walmart/Subway
129mm	Ⓡ🅂 both lanes, full 🚻 facilities, litter barrels, petwalk, 🅲, 🗑, vending
126	to Mt Morris, E 🛢 B&B/A&W/dsl/scales/24hr, W 🛢 BP/dsl
125	I-475 S, UAW Fwy, to Flint
122	Pierson Rd, to Flint, E 🛢 BP/dsl, Marathon/dsl 🍴 McDonald's, Papa's Coney's, Subway 🅾 Family$, O'Reilly Parts, Tuffy Auto, W 🛢 Citgo/dsl, ClicMart/dsl 🍴 Arby's, Big John's, Cracker Barrel, Domino's, Halo Burger, Red Lobster, Taco Bell, Tim Hortons, YaYa Chicken 🛏 Baymont Inn 🅾 $General, $Tree, Aldi Foods, AT&T, Belle Tire, Discount Tire, Home Depot
118	MI 21, Corunna Rd, E 🛢 🍴 Badawest Lebanese, Big John's Steaks, Burger King, Church's, Hungry Howie's, Little Caesar's, Taco Bell, Wing Fong Chinese, YaYa Chicken 🅾 Ⓗ, Advance Parts, Family$, Kroger/gas, Rite Aid, W 🛢 BP/dsl, Marathon/Wendy's, Mobil, Speedway/dsl, Valero 🍴 Burger King, KFC, Mega Diner, Rally's, Tim Horton, White Castle 🛏 Economy Motel 🅾 $General, Aldi Foods, AutoZone, Buick, Chevrolet, GMC,

GRAYLING

⬆N INTERSTATE 75 Cont'd

F L I N T

118 Continued
Home Depot, KanRock Tire, Kroger/gas, O'Reilly Parts, Rite Aid, Sam's Club/gas, st police, Verizon, Walgreens, Walmart

117b Miller Rd, to Flint, **E** 🅖 Speedway/dsl 🍴 Applebee's, Arby's, Cottage Inn Pizza, Domino's, Fuddrucker's, McDonald's, Popeye's, Qdoba, Sonic, Subway, Vehicle City Diner, West Side Diner 🏨 Knights Inn, Quality Inn, Rodeway Inn 🅞 Harley Davidson, Tuffy Auto, **W** 🅖 Mobil 🍴 Bar Louie, BD's Mongolian BBQ, Bob Evans, Buffalo Wild Wings, Casa Real, Chili's, Chipotle, ChuckeCheese, Famous Dave's BBQ, Five Guys, Golden Corral, Golden Moon, Halo Burger, HoneyBaked Ham, Hooters, IHOP, Italia Garden, Jimmy John's, Logan's Roadhouse, Olive Garden, Outback Steaks, Panda Express, Panera Bread, Pizza Hut, Red Robin, Starbucks, Subway, Taco Bell, Telly's Coney Island, Tim Horton, TX Roadhouse 🏨 Red Roof Inn, Super 8 🅞 AT&T, Barnes&Noble, Belle Tire, Best Buy, Big Lots, Hobby Lobby, JC Penney, Jo-Ann Fabrics, Macy's, Michael's, Midas, Office Depot, Old Navy, Petsmart, Target, U-Haul, Valley Tire, Verizon, vet

117a I-69, E to Lansing, W to Port Huron

116 MI 121, Bristol Rd, **E** 🅖 Mobil, Speedway/dsl 🍴 Capitol Coney Island, KFC, McDonald's, Subway 🅞 Advance Parts, AutoZone, **W** 🅖 Marathon/dsl 🅞 ☹

115 US 23 (from sb), **W on Hill Rd** 🅖 Citgo, Mobil 🍴 Arby's, Hill Rd Grille, Jimmy John's, McDonald's, Redwood Steaks, Subway, Taco Bell, Tim Hortons 🏨 Best Western+, Courtyard, Hampton Inn, Holiday Inn, Residence Inn 🅞 $Tree, Meijer/dsl

111 I-475 N (from nb), UAW Fwy, to Flint

109 MI 54, Dort Hwy (no EZ return to sb)

108 Holly Rd, to Grand Blanc,. **E** 🅖 Sunoco/dsl 🍴 Bagger Dave's Burgers, Big Apple Bagels, Buffalo Wild Wings, Culver's, Freakin' Burger, Qdoba, Taco Bell 🏨 Fairfield Inn, Holiday Inn Express, Quality Inn 🅞 BMW/Mercedes/Toyota, Nissan, URGENT CARE, **W** 🅖 BP/McDonald's/dsl 🍴 Arby's 🅞 🅗

106 Dixie Hwy (exits left from sb, no nb return), Saginaw Rd, to Grand Blanc

101 Grange Hall Rd, Ortonville, **E** 🅖 Shell/dsl 🅞 Groveland Oaks Camping, Holly RA, KOA, **W** 🅖 Shell/dsl 🅞 to Seven Lakes SP

98 E Holly Rd, **E** 🅖 Mobil/Tubby's/dsl 🅞 Ford, golf

96mm 🆁🆂 nb, full ♿ facilities, info, litter barrels, petwalk, 🚬, 🔁, vending

95mm 🆁🆂 sb, full ♿ facilities, info, litter barrels, petwalk, 🚬, 🔁, vending

93 US 24, Dixie Hwy, Waterford, **E** 🅖 BP/dsl 🍴 McDonald's 🅞 Chrysler/Dodge/Jeep, General RV Ctr, Kroger/gas (2mi), **W** 🍴 Kruse's Deer Lake Inn, Wendy's 🅞 CVS Drug, Office Depot, to Pontiac Lake RA, Walgreens

91 MI 15, Davison, Clarkston, **E** 🅖 Sunoco/dsl, **W** 🅖 BP/dsl 🍴 Andiamo Italian 🅞 URGENT CARE

89 Sashabaw Rd, **E** 🅖 Mobil/dsl 🍴 Arby's, Culver's, Ruby Tuesday, Taco Bell, Tropical Smoothie Cafe 🅞 county park, **W** 🅖 BP, Citgo 🍴 Chicken Shack, Dunkin', E Ocean Chinese, Guido's Pizza, Hong Kong Chinese, Hungry Howie's, Jimmy John's, Leo's Coney Island, Little Caesar's, McDonald's, Sagano Japanese, Starbucks, Subway, Tim Horton, Wendy's 🅞 $Tree, AT&T, CVS Drug, Kroger/dsl, vet

86mm weigh sta sb

84b a Baldwin Ave, **E** 🅖 BP/dsl 🍴 Arby's, Big Boy, Chipotle, Joe's Crabshack, Longhorn Steaks, Panera Bread, Patty Burger, Potbelly, Starbucks, Taco Bell, Wendy's 🅞 $Tree, Best Buy, Costco/gas, Discount Tire, Kohl's, Michael's, Nordstrom Rack, Old Navy, PetCo, Staples, **W** 🅖 Mobil 🍴 Bar Louie, Chili's, Five Guys,

84b a Continued
Jimmy John's, Kerby's Coney Island, McDonald's, On-the-Border, Oriental Forest Buffet, Qdoba Mexican, Rainforest Cafe, Starbucks, Steak'n Shake, Subway 🏨 TownePlace Suites 🅞 AT&T, Bass Pro Shops, Batteries+Bulbs, Great Lakes Crossing Outlet/famous brands, Hampton Inn, Holiday Inn Express, Marshall's, TJ Maxx, USPO, Verizon, Vitamin Shoppe

83b a Joslyn Rd, **E** 🅖 Tesla EVC 🍴 Biggby Coffee, Checkers, Logan's Roadhouse, Olive Garden, Panda Express, Subway 🅞 Belle Tire, Home Depot, Jo-Ann Fabrics, Meijer/dsl, Sam's Club/gas, Target, **W** 🅖 BP

81 MI 24, Pontiac (no EZ return), **E** 🅞 The Palace Arena, to Bald Mtn RA

79 University Dr, **E** 🅖 🍴 BD Mongolian, Blaze Pizza, Dibella's Subs, Domino's, Dunkin', Jersey Mike's, Jimmy John's, Spargo Coney Island, Starbucks, Subway, Taste of Thailand, Ziggy's Cheesesteak 🏨 Extended Stay America 🅞 AT&T, **W** 🅖 Mobil, Speedway/dsl 🍴 Burger King, KFC, Lelli's Steaks, McDonald's, Taco Bell, Wendy's/Tim Horton 🏨 Baymont Inn, Comfort Suites, Courtyard, Crowne Plaza, Extended Stay America, Extended Stay America (2), Hampton Inn, Hawthorn Suites, Hilton, Holiday Inn Express, Hyatt Place, Quality Inn, Rodeway Inn, Sonesta Suites, Staybridge Suites 🅞 🅗

78 Chrysler Dr, **E** 🅞 Chrysler, Chrysler Museum, Oakland Tech Ctr

77b a MI 59, to Pontiac, **2 mi E on Adams** 🍴 112 Pizza, Five Guys, Grand Tavern, Kerby's Coney Island, Panera Bread 🏨 Holiday Inn Express, Woodspring Suites 🅞 GNC, Meijer/dsl, Petsmart, Walmart/Subway

75 Square Lake Rd (exits left from nb), to Pontiac, **W** 🅞 🅗, St Mary's Coll

74 Adams Rd

72 Crooks Rd, to Troy, **W** 🅖 EVC 🍴 Cedar Grille, Jimmy John's, Kerby's Coney Island, Loccino Italian, Papa Romano's Pizza, Red Robin, Starbucks 🏨 Embassy Suites

69 Big Beaver Rd, **E** 🍴 Kona Grill, TGIFriday's 🏨 Drury Inn, Marriott, **W** 🅖 🍴 Benihana, Bonefish Grill, Capital Grille, Carrabba's, Chipotle Mexican, Granite City Rest., J Alexander's, Jersey Mike's, Jimmy John's, Maggiano's Italian, Melting Pot Rest., Morton's Steaks, Noodles&Co, Papa Romano's Pizza, PF Chang's, Potbelly, Ruth's Chris Steaks, Shake Shack, Starbucks 🏨 Hampton Inn, Hilton Garden, Somerset Inn 🅞 AT&T, Macy's, Neiman Marcus, Nordstrom, Verizon

67 Rochester Rd, to Stevenson Hwy, **E** 🅖 BP, Shell/dsl, Sunoco 🍴 Bahama Breeze, Burger King, Detroit Burger Bar, Domino's, El Charro, First Watch, Gran Castor Mexican, Hills City Grille, Hungry Howies, Jimmy John's, McDonald's, Mission BBQ, MOD Pizza, Orchid Cafe, Panera Bread, PeiWei, Picano's Italian, Qdoba, Sakura Japanese, Subway, Taco Bell, Tim Hortons, Troy Deli,

A U B U R N   H I L L S   T R O Y

MI

⬆N INTERSTATE 75 Cont'd

Exit	
67	Continued
	Wendy's ⚪ Discount Tire, Fresh Thyme Mkt, Nordstrom Rack, Petsmart, REI, Tuesday Morning, vet, **W** ⛽🍴🛏 Courtyard, Quality Inn, Red Roof Inn ⚪ Pepboys
65b a	14 Mile Rd, Madison Heights, **E** ⛽ Mobil/dsl, Shell/dsl 🍴 Bob Evans, Burger King, Chili's, Chipotle, ChuckeCheese, Coldstone, Grand Azteca, Jersey Mike's, Jimmy John's, Krispy Kreme; Logan's Roadhouse, McDonald's, Panda Express, Panera Bread, Pizza Hut, Pizza Papalis, Red Robin, Sonic, Starbucks, Steak'n Shake, Taco Bell, Wendy's 🛏 Motel 6, Red Roof Inn ⚪ $Tree, AT&T, Barnes&Noble, Belle Tire, Best Buy, BigLots, CVS Drug, Dick's, Field & Stream, Firestone/auto, Ford, JC Penney, Jo-Ann Fabrics, Kohl's, Macy's, Michael's, Target, TJ Maxx, Verizon, **W** ⛽ Mobil 🍴 Applebee's, McDonald's, NY Coney Island, Outback Steaks, Twin Peaks 🛏 Baymont Inn, Courtyard, Days Inn, Extended Stay America, Fairfield Inn, Hampton Inn, Holiday Inn Express, Residence Inn, Rodeway Inn, TownPlace Suites ⚪ Costco/gas, Value Ctr Foods
63	12 Mile Rd, **E** ⛽ Marathon/dsl 🍴 Culver's, Green Lantern Rest., McDonald's, Penn Sta Subs, Red Lobster, Sero's Rest., Starbucks, Tim Hortons, TX Roadhouse ⚪ Home Depot, Lowe's, Midas, Sam's Club/gas, Uncle Ed's Oil, USPO, vet, **W** ⛽ Marathon, Mobil/dsl, Speedway ⚪ Chevrolet, Costco/gas, Family$
62	11 Mile Rd, **E** ⛽ Exxon/dsl, Mobil 🍴 Biggby Coffee, Boodles Rest., Happy's Pizza, Jets Pizza, Telway Burgers ⚪ 7-11, Advance Parts, CVS Drug, repair/tires, Save-a-Lot, Tirezfactory, Walgreens, **W** ⛽ BP, Marathon/dsl 🍴 Taco Bell, Tim Hortons, Tubby's Subs ⚪ Belle Tire, vet
61	I-696 E, to Port Huron, W to Lansing, to Hazel Park Raceway
60	9 Mile Rd, John R St, **E** 🍴 Checkers, China 1 Buffet, Hardee's, McDonald's, Subway, Tim Hortons ⚪ $General, CVS Drug, Kroger/gas, O'Reilly Parts, USPO, **W** ⛽ Exxon, Marathon, Mobil 🍴 Tubby's Subs, Wendy's ⚪ Hasting's Parts, repair
59	MI 102, 8 Mile Rd
58	7 Mile Rd, **W** ⛽ BP/dsl
57	McNichols Rd, **E** ⛽ Mobil/dsl 🍴 LA Coney Island
56b a	Davison Fwy
55	Holbrook Ave, Caniff St, **E** ⛽ Mobil/dsl, **W** 🍴 Grandy's Coney Island
54	E Grand Blvd, Clay Ave, **W** ⛽ Mobil/dsl
53b	I-94, Ford Fwy, to Port Huron, Chicago
53a	Warren Ave, **E** ⛽ Mobil, **W** ⛽ BP
52	Mack Ave, **E** ⛽ Exxon/dsl 🍴 McDonald's
51c	I-375 to civic center, tunnel to Canada, downtown
51b	MI 3 (exits left from nb), Gratiot Ave, downtown
50	Grand River Ave, downtown
49b	MI 10, Lodge Fwy, downtown
49a	Rosa Parks Blvd, **E** ⚪ Firestone, Tiger Stadium, **W** ⛽ Mobil/dsl
48	I-96 begins/ends
47b	Porter St, **E** MI Welcome Ctr, bridge to Canada, DutyFree/24hr
47a	MI 3, Clark Ave, **E** ⛽ BP/Subway/dsl, **W** ⛽ Marathon
46	Livernois Ave, to Hist Ft Wayne
45	Fort St, Springwells Ave, **W** ⛽ Mobil 🍴 McDonald's
44	Deerborn St (from nb)
43b a	MI 85, Fort St, to Schaefer Hwy, **E** ⛽ Exxon/dsl, **W** ⛽ Marathon Refinery ⚪ to River Rouge Ford Plant
42	Outer Dr, **E** ⛽ Marathon/dsl 🍴 Happy's Pizza, **W** ⛽ Quick Fuel/dsl ⚪ Family$, truck tires
41	MI 39, Southfield Rd, to Lincoln Park, **E** 🍴 A&W, Tim Hortons, White Castle ⚪ Aldi Foods, Family$, O'Reilly Parts, Walgreens,

D E T R O I T   A R E A (left margin)

Exit	
41	Continued
	W ⛽ Citgo/Tim Hortons, Mobil 🍴 Burger King, Checkers, Hungry Howie, McDonald's, Pizza Hut, Starbucks, Taco Bell, Wendy's 🛏 Royal Choice Inn ⚪ $Tree, AT&T, Belle Tire, Kroger/gas, Verizon
40	Dix Hwy, **E** ⛽ AAA/A&W/dsl, Marathon/dsl, Sunoco, Welcome 🍴 Baskin-Robbins/Dunkin', China Bowl, Sonic, Tomato Coney Island ⚪ 7-11, CVS Drug, Dix Parts, Meijer, **W** ⛽ Citgo, Marathon 🍴 Big Boy, Burger King, Checkers, DQ, McDonald's, Papa John's, Pizza Hut, Starbucks, Taco Bell, Wendy's ⚪ $Tree, AT&T, Belle Tire, Family$, Kroger/gas, Tire Trax Auto/repair, Verizon
37	Allen Rd, North Line Rd, to Wyandotte, **E** ⛽ BP/dsl, Shell/Tim Hortons 🛏 Hampton Inn, Holiday Inn ⚪ Ⓗ, Sam's Club/gas, **W** ⛽ Citgo/dsl, Sunoco 🍴 Arby's, Burger King, Mallie's Grill, McDonald's, Wendy's 🛏 Comfort Suites, La Quinta, Motel 6
36	Eureka Rd, **E** ⛽ Speedway, Sunoco 🍴 Bob Evans, Burrito Express, Denny's, Golden Corral, Tim Hortons 🛏 Super 8 ⚪ vet, **W** 🍴 Culver's, Famous Dave's, HoneyBaked Ham, Hooters, Jimmy John's, Leo's Coney Island, Little Daddy's Grill, McDonald's, Olga's Kitchen, Panera Bread, Penn Sta Subs, Pizza Papalis, Primanti Bros, Qdoba, Starbucks, Subway, Tropical Smoothie, TX Roadhouse, Wahlburgers, Wendy's 🛏 Red Roof Inn ⚪ $Tree, AT&T, Belle Tire, Best Buy, Big Lots, Dick's, Discount Tire, Hobby Lobby, Home Depot, JC Penney, Jo-Ann, Kohl's, Macy's, Meijer/dsl, Petsmart, Target, Verizon, Walgreens
35	US 24, Telegraph Rd, (from nb, exits left)
34b	Sibley Rd, Riverview, **W** ⛽ Sunoco/Baskin-Robbins/Dunkin', Subway ⚪ General RV Ctr
34a	to US 24 (from sb), Telegraph Rd
32	West Rd, to Trenton, Woodhaven, **E** ⛽ EVC, EVC, 🚩FLYING J/Detroiter/IHOP/dsl/LP/scales/24hr/@, Speedway/dsl 🍴 Applebee's, Baskin-Robbins/Dunkin', Blue Margarita, Bob Evans, Buffalo Wild Wings, Chipotle, Christoff's Rest., Coldstone, Firehouse Subs, Five Guys, Jersey Subs, MOD Pizza, Olga's Kitchen, Panda Express, Panera Bread, Qdoba, Starbucks, Steak'n Shake, Subway, Taco Bell, Tim Hortons, Wendy's, White Castle ⚪ Aldi Foods, Belle Tire, Chevrolet, Chrysler/Dodge/Jeep, Discount Tire, Firestone/auto, Ford, GNC, Home Depot, Kohl's, Lowe's, Marshall's, Meijer/dsl, Michael's, Office Depot, O'Reilly Parts, Petsmart, Target, URGENT CARE, Verizon, Walmart/Subway, **W** ⛽ BP, BP/Tim Hortons, Circle K/Hardee's/dsl 🍴 Andy's Pizza, DQ, Jimmy John's, Little Caesar's, McDonald's, Sparta Coney Island, Subway 🛏 Best Western/rest., Holiday Inn Express, Westwood Inn ⚪ Ⓗ, $Tree, AT&T, CVS Drug, Kroger/dsl, Walgreens
29	Gilbralter Rd, to Flat Rock, Lake Erie Metropark, **E** ⛽ Citgo/dsl 🍴 McDonald's, Peking Chinese, Sammy's Pizza, Subway, Tim Horton, Wendy's ⚪ Ⓗ, GNC, Kroger/gas, **W** ⛽ Marathon/Burger King/dsl 🛏 Baymont Inn ⚪ Ford
28	rd 85 (from nb), Fort St, **E** ⚪ Ⓗ
27	N Huron River Dr, to Rockwood, **E** ⛽ Marathon/7-11/dsl 🍴 Benito's Pizza, Marco's Pizza, Subway ⚪ $General, Rite Aid, SaveALot, USPO, **W** ⛽ Speedway/dsl 🍴 River Village Rest.
26	S Huron River Dr, to S Rockwood, **E** ⛽ Sunoco/dsl 🍴 Dixie Cafe ⚪ USPO
21	Newport Rd, to Newport, **E** ⛽ BP/Subway/dsl, **W** ⛽ Marathon/Burger King/dsl/24hr
20	I-275 N, to Flint
18	Nadeau Rd, **E** ⛽ ❤Loves/Hardee's/dsl/scales/24hr, **W** ⛽ 🚩Taco Bell/dsl/scales/24hr ⚪ Ⓗ

D E T R O I T   A R E A (right margin)

INTERSTATE 75 Cont'd

Exit #	Services
15	MI 50, Dixie Hwy, to Monroe, **E** 🅟 Citgo 🍴 Burger King, Red Lobster, Subway 🏠 Best Value Inn, Days Inn, Hampton Inn, Holiday Inn Express 🅾 to Sterling SP, **W** 🅟 🍴/Subway/dsl/scales/24hr, TA/BP/Fazoli's/Popeye's/Tim Hortons/dsl/scales/24hr/@ 🍴 Cracker Barrel, Denny's, El Maguey, IHOP, McDonald's, Taco Bell, Wendy's 🏠 Quality Inn 🅾 🏥, to Viet Vet Mem
14	Elm Ave, to Monroe
13	Front St, Monroe
11	La Plaisance Rd, to Bolles Harbor, **W** 🅟 Marathon/Taco Bell/dsl, Speedway/dsl 🍴 McDonald's, Monroe's Hotdogs 🏠 Econolodge, Harbor Town RV Resort
10mm	Welcome Ctr nb, full ♿ services, info, litter barrels, petwalk, 🅲, 🚻, vending
9	S Otter Creek Rd, to La Salle, **W** 🅾 antiques
7mm	weigh sta both lanes
6	Luna Pier, **E** 🅟 Sunoco/Subway/dsl/scales 🍴 Beef Jerky Un-Ltd., Ganders Rest. 🏠 Pier Inn 🅾 USPO
5	to Erie, Temperance
2	Summit St (no nb re-entry)
0mm	Michigan/Ohio state line

INTERSTATE 94

Exit #	Services
275mm	I-69/I-94 begin/end on MI 25, **N** Pinegrove Ave in Port Huron, 🅟 BP, Shell/dsl, Speedway/dsl 🍴 Arby's, McDonald's, Tim Horton, Wendy's 🏠 Comfort Inn, Days Inn 🅾 Family$, Honda, Rite Aid, **toll**bridge to Canada
274.5mm	Black River
274	Water St, Port Huron, **N** 🅟 Tesla EVC 🍴 Cracker Barrel 🏠 Best Western 🅾 Lake Port SP, Port Huron RV Park, **S** 🅟 SpeedyQ/dsl 🍴 Bob Evans 🏠 Fairfield Inn, Hampton Inn, Holiday Inn Express, Quality Inn 🅾 Menard's, O'Reilly Parts
273mm	Welcome Ctr/🆁🆂 wb, full ♿ facilities, 🚻, litter barrels, petwalk
271	I-69 E and I-94 E run together eb, Lp I-69, 0-2 mi **S** on Lp 69 🅟 Mobil/dsl, Speedway 🍴 Arby's, Burger King, Jimmy John's, KFC, Little Caesar's, McDonald's, Subway, Taco Bell, Tim Horton's, Wendy's 🅾 $General, Advance Parts, AutoZone, Kroger/gas, repair, Sam's Club/gas, to Port Huron, USPO
269	Dove St, Range Rd, **N** 🅟 Speedway/dsl 🍴 Theo's Rest. 🏠 Baymont Inn
266	Gratiot Rd, Marysville, 0-2 mi **S** 🅟 BP, Marathon/dsl/scales/24hr, Speedway/dsl 🍴 Arby's, Big Boy, Burger King, China Lite, Dairy Boy, Daliono's, Four Star Grille, Hungry Howie's, Jets Pizza, Jimmy John's, KFC, Little Caesar's, McDonald's, Mr Pita, Pelican Café, Subway, Taco Bell, Tim Horton 🏠 Super 8 🅾 🏥, $General, $Tree, Advance Parts, AutoZone, CVS Drug, Meijer/dsl, O'Reilly Parts, Rite Aid, Verizon, vet, Wally's Mkt
262	Wadhams Rd, **N** 🅟 Loves/Subway/dsl/scales/24hr, **S** 🅟 Mobil/dsl
257	St Clair, Richmond, **N** 🅟 Sunoco/dsl, **S** 🅟 BP/dsl
255mm	🆁🆂 eb, full ♿ facilities, info, litter barrels, petwalk, 🅲, 🚻
251mm	🆁🆂 wb, full ♿ facilities, info, litter barrels, petwalk, 🅲, 🚻
248	26 Mile Rd, to Marine City, **N** 🍴 McDonald's (2mi), **S** 🅟 Mobil/7-11, Shell 🍴 Subway, Taco Bell, Tim Horton 🅾 Mejier/dsl
247mm	Salt River
247	MI 19 (no eb return), New Haven

Exit #	Services
243	MI 29, MI 3, Utica, New Baltimore, **N** 🅟 BP/Dunkin', EVC, Marathon/dsl, Sunoco/dsl 🍴 Applebee's, Arby's, Buffalo Wild Wings, Burger King, Chapo's Tacos, Chipotle, Chophouse, Coldstone, Coney Island, Dave's Pizza, Del Taco, Detroit Wings, Dimitri's Rest., Eagles Grill, Happy's Pizza, Jersey Mike's, Little Caesar's, McDohald's, MOD Pizza, Noodles&Co, Olga's Kitchen, Panda Express, Panera Bread, Potbelly, Qdoba, Ruby Tuesday, Starbucks, Tim Horton, TX Roadhouse, Wendy's, White Castle 🅾 $Tree, AutoZone, Belle Tire, Best Buy, Big Jim's Automotive, Big Lots, Dick's, Discount Tire, GNC, Hobby Lobby, Home Depot, JC Penney, Jo-Ann Fabrics, Kohl's, Lowe's, Meijer/Subway/dsl, Michael's, NAPA, Old Navy, O'Reilly Parts, PetCo, PetsMart, Rite Aid, Staples, Target, TJ Maxx, URGENT CARE, Verizon, Walgreens, **S** 🅟 Marathon/dsl/24hr, Speedway/dsl/24hr 🍴 Big Boy, Buscemi's Pizza, Checkers, Taco Bell 🏠 LodgeKeeper 🅾 Chevrolet
241	21 Mile Rd, same as 240, Selfridge, **N** 🅟 Exxon/dsl/e85, Speedway/dsl 🍴 China King, Hungry Howie's, Jets Pizza, Jimmy John's 🅾 Advance Parts, AT&T, CVS Drug, Verizon, vet
240	to MI 59, **N** 🅟 7-11/gas, BP, Mobil 🍴 Arby's, Bob Evans, Burger King, Coney Island, Culver's, KFC, McDonald's, Taco Bell, Twisted Rooster 🏠 Fairfield Inn, Hampton Inn, Holiday Inn Express 🅾 $Tree, Ford, Harley-Davidson, Kia, Menard's, Subaru, Toyota, Walmart
237	N River Rd, Mt Clemens, **N** 🅟 BP/dsl, Mobil/Subway/dsl 🍴 Clinton River Cruise Co, McDonald's 🅾 🏥, General RV Ctr
236.5mm	Clinton River
236	Metro Parkway, **S** 🍴 Big Apple Bagels, Empire Chinese, Little Caesar's, McDonald's, Subway 🅾 🏥, CVS Drug, Kroger, URGENT CARE, Verizon
235	Shook Rd (from wb)
234b a	Harper Rd, 15 Mile Rd, **N** 🅟 BP/McDonald's, Marathon/dsl, SpeedyQ, Sunoco/dsl 🍴 Domino's, Gina's Cafe, Tim Horton's 🅾 Family$, vet, **S** 🅟 Shell 🍴 China Moon, Subway, Travis Rest., Winners Grill
232	Little Mack Ave (from wb only), same as 231, **N** 🅟 Marathon, Mobil, Shell, Sunoco 🍴 Chipotle, Coldstone, Denny's, Hooters, McDonald's, Pizza Hut, Potbelly, Red Robin 🏠 Hampton Inn, Holiday Inn Express, Red Roof Inn, Relax Inn, Super 8, Victory Inn 🅾 Advance Parts, Aldi Foods, AT&T, Belle Tire, Discount Tire, Firestone/auto, O'Reilly Parts, Sam's Club/gas, Target, Tuesday Morning, **S** 🅟 Kroger/dsl, Speedway/dsl 🍴 Cracker Barrel, Culver's, IHOP 🏠 Baymont Inn 🅾 Home Depot, Jo-Ann Fabrics, Kroger, Meijer/dsl/24hr, PetsMart, URGENT CARE
231	(from eb), MI 3, Gratiot Ave, **N** 🅟 Exxon/dsl, Marathon 🍴 Applebee's, Arby's, Bob Evans, Burger King, Chili's, Chipotle, ChuckeCheese, Del Taco, Denny's, Famous Dave's BBQ, Huddle Grill, Jersey Mike's, Logan's Roadhouse, McDonald's,

M O N R O E (side tab, left)

P O R T   H U R O N (side tab, left)

D E T R O I T   A R E A (side tab, right)

MI

🛣 INTERSTATE 94 Cont'd

231	Continued National Coney Island, Panera Bread, PetCo, Pizza Hut, Potbelly, Qdoba, Ruby Tuesday, Starbucks, Subway, Tim Horton, TX Roadhouse 🏨 Days Inn, Extended Stay America, Hampton Inn, Microtel ⚪ Belle Tire, Best Buy, Dick's, Discount Tire, Firestone/auto, Honda/Acura, Kia, Kohl's, Kroger, Michael's, Nissan, Sam's Club/gas
230	12 Mile Rd, **N** 🚗 Mobil/dsl, Sunoco/dsl ⭐ Jimmy John's, Outback Steaks, Starbucks, Taco Bell ⚪ $Tree, AT&T, CVS Drug, Marshall's, Verizon, Walmart/Subway, **S** 🚗 Marathon
229	I-696 W, Reuther Fwy, to 11 Mile Rd, **S** 🚗 Shell/dsl, Speedway/dsl ⚪ $General, 7-11
228	10 Mile Rd, **N** 🚗 7-11, BP ⭐ Baskin-Robbins, Donna's Rest., Eastwind Chinese, Jet's Pizza, Little Italy Pizza, Sugarbush Rest. ⚪ $General, Save Mor Drugs, URGENT CARE
227	9 Mile Rd, **N** 🚗 BP, Metro, Mobil/dsl, Speedway/dsl ⭐ DQ, McDonald's, Milestone Grill, Popeye's, Subway, Taco Bell, Tim Horton's, Wendy's ⚪ $Tree, Aldi Foods, CVS Drug, Family$, Fresh Choice Mkt, Office Depot, TrueValue, vet, **S** 🚗 Mobil/dsl 🏨 Shore Pointe Motel ⚪ Cadillac, Mercedes
225	MI 102, Vernier Rd, 8 Mile Rd, **S** 🚗 BP/Subway, Mobil, Sunoco/dsl ⭐ Coney Island, KFC, Taco Bell, Wendy's ⚪ Kroger, Walgreens
224b	Allard Ave, Eastwood Ave
224a	Moross Rd, **S** 🚗 Citgo ⚪ 🅷 Family Foods Mkt
223	Cadieux Rd, **S** 🚗 BP/Subway, Marathon/dsl, Mobil, Sunoco ⭐ Checkers, Papa's Pizza, Popeye's, Tubby's Subs, Wendy's, White Castle ⚪ Family$, Rite Aid
222b	Harper Ave (from eb), **S** ⚪ Hastings Auto Parts
222a	Chalmers Ave, Outer Dr, **N** 🚗 76, BP/Subway/dsl ⭐ Coney Island, KFC, Little Caesar's ⚪ Family$
220b	Conner Ave, **N** 🚗 BP, Sunoco
220a	French Rd, **S** 🚗 Mobil
219	MI 3, Gratiot Ave, **N** 🚗 76, Marathon/Subway ⭐ Coney Island, McDonald's ⚪ $General, Farmer John's Foods, USPO, **S** 🚗 Citgo ⭐ Burger King
218	MI 53, Van Dyke Ave, **N** 🚗 BP, Mobil/dsl
217b	Mt Elliott Ave, **S** 🚗 Citgo, Mobil/dsl ⭐ Royal BBQ
217a	E Grand Blvd, Chene St, **S** 🚗 Marathon
216b	Russell St (from eb), to downtown
216a	I-75, Chrysler Fwy, to tunnel to Canada
215c	MI 1, Woodward Ave, John R St
215b	MI 10 N, Lodge Fwy
215a	MI 10 S, tunnel to Canada, downtown
214b	Trumbull Ave, **N** ⚪ to Ford Hospital
214a	(from wb)Grand River Ave
213b	I-96 W to Lansing, E to Canada, bridge to Canada, to Tiger Stadium
213a	W Grand (exits left from eb)
212b	Warren Ave (from eb)
212a	Livernois Ave, **S** 🚗 BP/dsl, Marathon/Subway/dsl
211b	Cecil Ave (from wb), Central Ave
211a	Lonyo Rd, **S** 🚗 Sunoco ⚪ Ford
210	US 12, Michigan Ave, Wyoming Ave, **N** 🚗 Mobil/dsl, **S** 🚗 BP/dsl, Sunoco/dsl ⭐ Checkers
209	Rotunda Dr (from wb)
208	Greenfield Rd, Schaefer Rd, **N** 🚗 Mobil/dsl ⭐ Senate Coney Island, Wendy's/Tim Horton ⚪ 7-11, **S** ⚪ River Rouge Ford Plant
207mm	Rouge River

D E T R O I T   A R E A

206	Oakwood Blvd, Melvindale, **N** 🚗 EVC, Marathon, Shell ⭐ Applebee's, Biggby Coffee, Chili's, Chipotle, Coldstone, Coney Island, Five Guys, Jimmy John's, Little Caesar's, Longhorn Steaks, Olga's Kitchen, On-the-Border, Panda Express, Panera Bread, Potbelly, Qdoba, Starbucks, Subway, Taco Bell ⚪ AAA, Barnes&Noble, Best Buy, GNC, Greenfield Village Museum, Home Depot, Jo-Ann Fabrics, Lowe's, Meijer, Michael's, Old Navy, PetCo, Staples, Target, TJ Maxx, USPO, Verizon, **S** 🚗 BP/dsl ⭐ Burger King, McDonald's, Ming Sun Chinese, Mr Steve's Pizza, Sabina's, Tim Horton's 🏨 Best Western, Comfort Inn ⚪ $General, $Tree, 7-11, CVS Drug, O'Reilly Parts, Rite Aid
205mm	Largest Uniroyal Tire in the World
204b a	MI 39, Southfield Fwy, Pelham Rd, **N** 🚗 Mobil, Valero/dsl ⚪ 7-11, to Greenfield Village, **S** 🚗 Exxon/dsl, Marathon/dsl, Marathon/dsl ⚪ Walgreens
202b a	US 24, Telegraph Rd, **N** 🚗 Citgo, Mobil, Sunoco ⭐ Burger King, Checkers, Dunkin', Jets Pizza, KFC, McDonald's, Papa John's, Pizza Hut, Ram's Horn Rest., Subway, Taco Bell, Wendy's ⚪ Advance Parts, Aldi Foods, Walgreens, 0-2 mi **S** 🚗 BP, Citgo/dsl, Marathon/dsl, Valero/dsl ⭐ Arby's, Big Boy, Burger King, Dunkin', Hungry Howie's, Jersey Mike's, Jimmy John's, KFC, Leon's Rest., Leo's Coney Island, Little Caesar's, Lucky Star Buffet, Marina's Pizza, McDonald's, New Hong Kong, Pancho's Mexican, Pizza Hut, Popeye's, Subway, Taco Bell, Teppanyaki, Tim Horton's/Coldstone, Tubby's, Wendy's 🏨 Comfort Inn ⚪ $Tree, AT&T, AutoZone, Family$, Firestone/auto, Home Depot, 🅷, Rite Aid, st police, U-Haul, Verizon, vet, Walgreens, Walmart/Burger King
200	Ecorse Rd, (no ez eb return), to Taylor, **N** 🚗 Marathon/Subway/dsl/scales ⭐ Tim Horton's, **S** 🚗 Citgo/dsl, Rich
199	Middle Belt Rd, **S** 🚗 BP/dsl ⭐ Checkers, McDonald's, Wendy's 🏨 Days Inn, Knights Inn, Quality Inn
198	Merriman Rd, **N** 🚗 Citgo/dsl, Marathon, Speedway/Speedy Cafe/dsl ⭐ Big Boy, Bob Evans, Capitol Bistro, Fortune Chinese, Leonardo's Italian, McDonald's, Merriman St Grill, Subway, Urban Steak 🏨 Baymont Inn, Best Value Inn, Clarion Comfort Inn, Courtyard, Delta Hotel, Embassy Suites, Extended Stay America, Fairfield Inn, Hampton Inn, Hilton Garden, Holiday Inn, Holiday Inn Express, Howard Johnson, La Quinta, Magnuson Hotel, Marriott, Rodeway Inn, Sheraton, Sheraton Four Points, SpringHill Suites, Travelodge, Wyndham Garden Hotel **S** ⚪ Wayne Co Airport
197	Vining Rd
196	Wayne Rd, Romulus, **N** 🚗 Shell/dsl ⭐ Little Caesar's, McDonald's, Taco Bell ⚪ $General, **S** 🚗 Mobil/dsl ⭐ Burger King, Jimmy John's, Subway
194b a	I-275, N to Flint, S to Toledo
192	Haggerty Rd, **N** 🚗 BP/Tubby's/dsl, Mobil/dsl, **S** ⚪ Lower Huron Metro Park
190	Belleville Rd, to Belleville, **N** 🚗 EVC, Marathon, Mobil/dsl ⭐ Applebee's, Arby's, Asian Garden, Coney Island, Cracker Barrel, Culver's, Dunkin', Happy's Pizza, Hungry Howie's, McDonald's, Qdoba, Starbucks, Taco Bell, Tim Horton, Twisted Rooster, Wendy's 🏨 Hampton Inn, Holiday Inn Express, Red Roof Inn ⚪ $Tree, Aldi Foods, AT&T, AutoZone, Belle Tire, Camping World RV Ctr, CVS Drug, Firestone/auto, Ford, Meijer/dsl, Menards, National RV Ctr, O'Reilly Parts, Verizon, Walgreens, Walmart, **S** 🚗 Shell ⭐ Burger King, China City, China King, Dos Pesos Mexican, Subway 🏨 Baymont Inn, Super 8 ⚪ URGENT CARE, USPO
189mm	🅁🅂 wb, full 🚻 facilities, info, litter barrels, petwalk, ☎, 🏪 vending

Copyright 2022 - The Next EXIT ®   🅿=gas 🍴=food 🏠=lodging ⊙=other ℞=rest stop

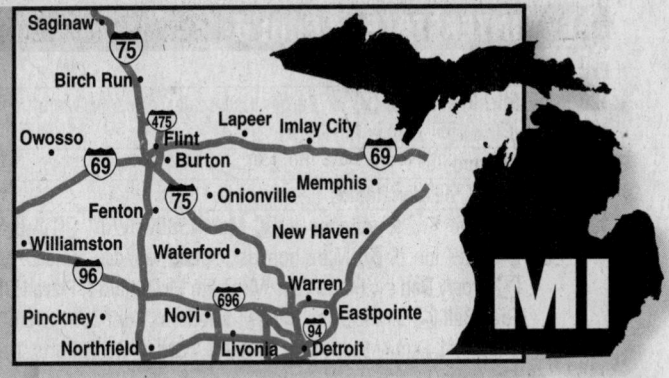

INTERSTATE 94 Cont'd

Exit #	Services
187	Rawsonville Rd, N ⊙ Freightliner, S 🅿 Mobil/dsl, Speedway/dsl 🍴 Burger King, Denny's, KFC, Little Caesar's, McDonald's, Pearl River Chinese, Pizza Hut, Taco Bell, Tim Horton, Wendy's ⊙ $General, $Tree, Detroit Greenfield RV Park
185	US 12, Michigan Ave (from eb, exits left, no return), to frontage rds, N ⊙ 🚻
184mm	S ⊙ Ford Lake
183	US 12, Huron St, Ypsilanti, N 🅿 Citgo/dsl ⊙ H, to E MI U, S 🅿 Shell 🍴 Buffalo Wild Wings, Coney Island, Jet's Pizza, McDonald's, Tim Horton's 🏠 Fairfield Inn, Marriott ⊙ Kroger/dsl, USPO
181b a	US 12 W, Michigan Ave, Ypsilanti, N 🅿 Speedway/dsl 🍴 Dunkin', Hong Kong Chinese, Koney Island, Popeye's, Taco Bell, Tim Horton/Wendy's ⊙ H, Aamco, BigLots, GNC, Walmart/Subway, 0-2 mi S 🅿 Mobil/Circle K, Shell/Subway/dsl, Sunoco/dsl 🍴 Harvest Moon Cafe, McDonald's ⊙ Sam's Club/gas
180b a	US 23, to Toledo, Flint
177	State St, N 🅿 BP, Mobil, Shell/dsl 🍴 Bravo Italiana, Buffalo Wild Wings, Burger King, CA Pizza, Chipotle, Los Amigos, Macaroni Grill, Mediterrano Rest, Olive Garden, Panda Express, PF Chang's, Red Robin, Relish Rest., Wendy's 🏠 Comfort Inn, Courtyard, Extended Stay America, Extended Stay America, Fairfield Inn, Hampton Inn, Hilton Garden, Holiday Inn, Holiday Inn Express, Kensington Court Inn, Red Roof Inn, Sheraton, Sonesta Suites, TownePlace Suites ⊙ Firestone/auto, Honda, JC Penney, Macy's, Porsche, to UMI, URGENT CARE, Von Maur, VW, World Mkt, S 🅿 Citgo/Subway/dsl, Speedway/dsl 🍴 Black Rock Grill, Coney Island, Jimmy John's, McDonald's, Taco Bell, Tim Horton's 🏠 Motel 6, Staybridge Suites ⊙ Belle Tire, Costco/gas, U-Haul
175	Ann Arbor-Saline Rd, N 🅿 Shell/Tim Horton's 🍴 Applebee's, Blaze Pizza, Dibella Subs, Moe's SW Grill, Panera Bread, Potbelly, Tropical Smoothie, Zamaan Cafe 🏠 Candlewood Suites ⊙ REI, to UMI Stadium, vet, Whole Foods Mkt, S 🅿 Tesla EVC 🍴 Bob Evans, Buddy's Pizza, ChuckECheese's, Five Guys, Jets Pizza, McDonald's, Nick's Pancakes, Outback Steaks, Panchero's, Starbucks, Subway, TGIFriday's, TX Roadhouse ⊙ AT&T, Best Buy, BigLots, Dick's, Jo-Ann Fabrics, Kohl's, Meijer/dsl/e85, Petsmart, Target
172	Jackson Ave, to Ann Arbor, S 🅿 Marathon 🍴 Weber's Rest. 🏠 Hampton Inn, Wyndham Garden ⊙ Belle Tire, Chevrolet, Cadillac, Ford, Hyundai, Mini, Nissan, Subaru, Toyota, N on Stadium Ave 🅿 Marathon, Shell/dsl 🍴 Cottage Inn Pizza, DQ, Jersey Mike's, McDonald's, Noodles&Co, Quarter Rest., Subway, Taco Bell, Zingerman's Roadhouse ⊙ H, CVS, Goodyear/auto, Kroger, Midas, O'Reilly Parts, Plum Mkt, Rite Aid, Staples, TJ Maxx, Verizon, Walgreens
171	MI 14 (from eb, exits left), Ann Arbor, to Flint by U.S. 23
169	Zeeb Rd, N 🅿 BP/dsl 🍴 Grand Traverse Pies Co, Kathy's Pancakes, McDonald's, Metzger's Rest. 🏠 Holiday Inn Express, S 🅿 Citgo/dsl 🍴 Arby's, Burger King, Culver's, Domino's, Panera Bread, Standard Grill, Subway, Taco Bell, Wendy's ⊙ AutoZone, CVS Drug, Discount Tire, Lowe's, Meijer/dsl, Menard's, vet
167	Baker Rd, Dexter, N 🅿 🚛/Subway/scales/dsl/24hr, S 🅿 🚛/Arby's/dsl/scales/24hr, TA/BP/Popeye's/dsl/scales/24hr/@ 🍴 McDonald's ⊙ Blue Beacon
162	Jackson Rd, Fletcher Rd, S 🅿 Marathon/Krispy Chicken/dsl/24hr 🍴 Stiver's Rest.
161mm	℞ eb, full 🚻 facilities, litter barrels, petwalk, 🅰, 🏧, vending
159	MI 52, Chelsea, N 🅿 Shell/dsl, Speedway/dsl, Sunoco/dsl 🍴 Big Boy, Biggby Coffee, China Garden, Chinese Tonite, Jimmy John's, KFC/Taco Bell, McDonald's, Subway, Uptown Coney Island, Wendy's 🏠 Baymont Inn, Comfort Inn ⊙ H, $Tree, Ace Hardware, AutoZone, Chrysler/Dodge/Jeep, Country Mkt Foods/drug, CVS Drug, Travel Land RV Ctr, USPO, Verizon, S ⊙ Buick/Chevrolet
157	Jackson Rd, Pierce Rd, N ⊙ Gerald Eddy Geology Ctr
156	Kalmbach Rd, N ⊙ to Waterloo RA
153	Clear Lake Rd, N 🅿 Marathon/dsl
151.5mm	weigh sta both lanes
150	to Grass Lake, S 🅿 Mobil/Dunkin'/Subway/dsl
150mm	℞ wb, full 🚻 facilities, litter barrels, petwalk, 🅰, 🏧, vending
147	Race Rd, N ⊙ Hideaway RV Park, to Waterloo RA, S 🏠 Joy Motel ⊙ Holiday RV Camp
145	Sargent Rd, S 🅿 BP, Marathon/145 Auto Trk Plaza 🍴 McDonald's, Wendy's 🏠 Colonial Inn ⊙ $General
144	Lp 94 (from wb), to Jackson
142	US 127 S, to Hudson, 1 mi S 🅿 Meijer/dsl, Speedway/dsl 🍴 Arby's, Bob Evans, KFC, McDonald's, Taco Bell, Wendy's ⊙ $General, $Tree, Advance Parts, AT&T, Rite Aid, to MI Speedway, Verizon, Walgreens
141	Elm Rd, N 🏠 Travelodge ⊙ Chevrolet, Chrysler/Dodge/Jeep, Ford/Lincoln, Honda, Nissan, S ⊙ H
139	MI 106, Cooper St, to Jackson, N ⊙ st police/prison, S 🅿 Citgo/Subway ⊙ H, Meekhof Tire
138	US 127 N, MI 50, to Lansing, Jackson, N 🍴 Red Lobster, Yen King Chinese 🏠 Baymont Inn, Comfort Inn, Fairfield Inn, Hampton Inn, Super 8 ⊙ vet, S 🅿 Admiral, BP/dsl, Shell/dsl 🍴 Arby's, Bob Evans, Buffalo Wild Wings, Burger King, Dunkin', Fazoli's, IHOP, KFC, LJ Silver, Los Tres Amigos, McDonald's, Outback Steaks, Panda Express, Panera Bread, Papa John's, Potbelly, Qdoba, Rally's, Starbucks, Subway, TX Roadhouse, Wendy's 🏠 Best Value Inn ⊙ $Tree, Advance Parts, Aldi Foods, AT&T, AutoZone, Belle Tire, Best Buy, BigLots, Discount Tire, Home Depot, JoAnn Fabrics, Kohl's, Kroger/gas, Lowe's, Michael's, Midas, O'Reilly Parts, Petsmart, Target, TJ Maxx, Verizon, Walgreens
137	Airport Rd, N 🅿 Marathon/dsl, Shell/Taco Bell 🍴 Burger King, Denny's, McDonald's, Steak'n Shake, Subway, Wendy's 🏠 Holiday Inn ⊙ 7-11, Meijer/dsl, S 🅿 BP/dsl 🍴 Cracker Barrel, Culver's, Olive Garden 🏠 Holiday Inn Express ⊙ Sam's Club/gas, Save-A-Lot Foods
136	Lp 94, MI 60, to Jackson
135mm	℞ eb, full 🚻 facilities, litter barrels, petwalk, 🅰, 🏧, vending
133	Dearing Rd, Spring Arbor, S ⊙ to Spring Arbor U
130	Parma, S ⊙ $General

MI

Exit #	Services
	INTERSTATE 94 Cont'd
128	Michigan Ave, N 🅟 BP/Burger King/scales/dsl/24hr, Marathon/deli/dsl 🅞 Zephyr Hill Farms
127	Concord Rd
124	MI 99, to Eaton Rapids
121	28 Mile Rd, to Albion, N 🅟 Mobil/Subway/dsl 🍴 Arby's 🛏 Days Inn, S 🅟 Marathon/dsl, Speedway/dsl, Sunoco/dsl 🍴 Frosty Dan's, KFC, La Casa Mexican, McDonald's, Pizza Hut, Taco Bell 🛏 Super 9 Inn 🅞 H, $General, AutoZone, Buick/Chevrolet, Family Fare Foods, Family$, Ford, O'Reilly Parts, Tire City/auto
119	MI 199, 26 Mile Rd
115	22.5 Mile Rd, N 🅟 Citgo/115 Rest./dsl/24hr
113mm	🆁🆂 wb, full ♿ facilities, litter barrels, petwalk, 🅲, 🚗, vending
112	Partello Rd, S 🅟 ♥Love's/Hardee's/scales/dsl/24hr 🍴 Schuler's Rest. (2mi)
110	Old US 27, Marshall, N 🅟 Shell/Country Kitchen/Subway/dsl/24hr, S 🅟 Citgo/dsl, Tesla EVC 🍴 Denny's, Schuler's Rest. (2mi) 🛏 Hampton Inn, Holiday Inn Express 🅞 H, sheriff
108	I-69, US 27, N to Lansing, S to Ft Wayne
104	11 Mile Rd, Michigan Ave, N 🅟 Pilot/McDonald's/dsl/scales/24hr, TA/Country Pride/dsl/scales/24hr/@, S 🅟 Citgo/Subway/dsl/e85 🛏 Quality Inn/rest. 🅞 casino
102mm	Kalamazoo River
100	rd 294, Beadle Lake Rd, N 🍴 Moonraker Rest., S 🅟 Citgo/dsl/repair 🅞 Binder Park Zoo
98b	I-194 N, to Battle Creek
98a	MI 66, to Sturgis, same as 97, S 🅟 Citgo/Tim Horton/dsl 🍴 Chili's, Los Aztecas, McDonald's, Ruby Tuesday, Schlotzsky's, Starbucks, Steak'n Shake 🛏 Courtyard, Holiday Inn, TownePlace Suites 🅞 AT&T, Best Buy, Discount Tire, Kohl's, Lowe's, Meijer/dsl, Menards, Michael's, PetCo, Sam's Club/gas, Staples, TJ Maxx, Verizon, Walgreens, Walmart/Subway
97	Capital Ave, to Battle Creek, N 🅟 BP, Marathon 🍴 Arby's, Domino's, Lux Cafe, McDonald's, Old China, Red Lobster 🛏 Knights Inn, Quality Inn, S 🅟 BP/Subway, Shell/dsl 🍴 Applebee's, Bob Evans, Buffalo Wild Wings, Burger King, Cracker Barrel, Culver's, Denny's, Fazoli's, Hibachi Steaks, Jimmy John's, La Cocina, Panera Bread, Pizza Hut, Qdoba, Taco Bell 🛏 Baymont Inn, Best Value Inn, Best Western, Fairfield Inn, Hampton Inn, Red Roof Inn, Rodeway Inn, Travelodge 🅞 $Tree, AAA, Barnes&Noble, Belle Tire, BigLots, Firestone/auto, Harley Davidson, Hobby Lobby, Jo-Ann Fabrics, Target, Uncle Ed's Oil Shoppe, URGENT CARE, vet
96mm	🆁🆂 eb, full ♿ facilities, litter barrels, petwalk, 🅲, 🚗, vending
95	Helmer Rd, 2 mi N 🅟 Citgo/dsl 🍴 Arby's, Big Boy 🅞 Meijer/dsl/e85
92	Lp 94, rd 37, to Battle Creek, Springfield, N 🅟 BP/Arlene's Trkstp/dsl/rest./24hr, Shell 🅞 to Ft Custer RA
88	Climax, N 🅞 Galesburg Speedway
85	35th St, Galesburg, N 🅟 Shell/dsl 🍴 McDonald's, Subway 🅞 Galesburg Speedway, River Oaks CP, to Ft Custer RA, S 🅞 Colebrook CP, Scott's Mill CP
85mm	🆁🆂 wb, full ♿ facilities, litter barrels, petwalk, 🅲, 🚗, vending
81	Lp 94 (from wb), to Kalamazoo
80	Cork St, Sprinkle Rd, to Kalamazoo, N 🅟 Marathon/dsl, Speedway/dsl, Sunoco/dsl 🍴 Arby's, Burger King, Crew Rest., Denny's, Godfather's, Taco Bell 🛏 Baymont Inn, Clarion, Holiday Inn Express, Red Roof Inn, Sheraton 🅞 Monro, vet, S 🅟 BP/dsl, Speedway/dsl 🍴 McDonald's, Michelle's Rest., Nob Hill Grill,

Exit #	Services
80	Continued Subway, Wendy's 🛏 Candlewood Suites, EconoLodge, Fairfield Inn, Motel 6, Quality Inn
78	Portage Rd, Kilgore Rd, N 🅟 Mobil/Circle K 🍴 China Hut, Summer Thyme Cafe 🛏 Comfort Inn, Residence Inn 🅞 H, repair, 🅟 Marathon/dsl, Shell, Speedway 🍴 Angelo's Italian, Biggby Coffee, Bravo Rest., Brewster's Jct., Café Meli, McDonald's, Pizza King, Subway, Taco Bell, Travelers Cafe 🛏 Country Inn&Suites, Days Inn, Hampton Inn 🅞 AutoValue Parts, Fields Fabrics
76	Westnedge Ave, N 🅟 Meijer/dsl, Speedway/dsl 🍴 Grand Traverse Pie Co, Hibachi Buffet, IHOP, Jersey Giant Subs, Lee's Chicken, McDonald's, Old Chicago Grill, Outback Steaks, Papa Murphy's, Pizza Hut, Qdoba, Riviera Mayo, Root Beer Stand, Steak'n Shake, Subway, Taco Bell, Theo&Stacy's Rest. 🛏 Courtyard, Homewood Suites 🅞 $Tree, Advance Parts, Discount Tire, Earth Fare, Firestone/auto, Goodyear/auto, Lowe's, Midas, Walgreens, S 🅟 Shell 🍴 Antique Kitchen Rest., Applebee's, Biggby Coffee, Blaze Pizza, Bob Evans, Brann's Steaks, Burger King, Carrabba's, Chick-fil-A, Chili's, ChuckECheese's, Coldstone, CoreLife Eatery, Culver's, Five Guys, HoneyBaked Ham, Jimmy John's, KFC, Little Caesar's, Logan's Roadhouse, Los Amigos Mexican, McDonald's, Moe's SW Grill, Noodles&Co, Olive Garden, Panera Bread, Penn Sta Subs, Qdoba Mexican, Red Lobster, Red Robin, Schlotzsky's, Starbucks, Subway, Taco Bell, Tim Horton, TX Roadhouse, Wendy's, Zoup! 🛏 Holiday Motel 🅞 $Tree, Aldi Foods, AT&T, AutoZone, Barnes&Noble, Belle Tire, Best Buy, BigLots, Buick/Cadillac/GMC, Dick's, Fannie May Candies, Firestone/auto, Harding's Mkt, Hobby Lobby, Home Depot, JC Penney, JoAnn Fabrics, Kohl's, Macy's, Michael's, Monro, Old Navy, O'Reilly Parts, PepBoys, Petco, Sam's Club/gas, Target, TJMaxx, Tuesday Morning, Tuffy Auto, Verizon, Walgreens, World Mkt
75	Oakland Dr
74b a	US 131, to Kalamazoo, N 🅞 Kalamazoo Coll, to W MI U
72	9th St, Oshtemo, N 🅟 Citgo/dsl, Speedway/dsl 🍴 Arby's, Culver's, McDonald's, Starbucks, Taco Bell, Wendy's 🛏 Hampton Inn, S 🛏 Fairfield Inn, Microtel, Towne Place Suites
66	Mattawan, N 🅟 Citgo/dsl, Speedway/Subway/dsl/scales/24hr 🍴 Chinn Chinn, Mancino's Italian 🅞 $General, Family$ Freightliner, R&S RV Service, vet, S 🅟 Shell/dsl 🍴 Pizza Hut, Subway 🅞 USPO, Wagoner's Foods
60	MI 40, Paw Paw, N 🅟 Citgo, Speedway/dsl 🍴 Arby's, Biggby Coffee, Burger King, Chicken Coop, Copper Grille, McDonald's, Pizza Hut, Red's Root Beer, Subway, Taco Bell, Wendy's 🛏 Comfort Inn, EconoLodge, Travelodge 🅞 H, Advance Parts, AT&T, Buick/Chevrolet/GMC, Chrysler/Dodge/Jeep, Family Fare Mkt, Ford, O'Reilly Parts, St Julian Winery, Walgreens, S 🅞 Walmart/Subway
56	MI 51, to Decatur, N 🅞 st police, S 🅟 Citgo/dsl, Marathon/dsl
52	Lawrence
46	Hartford, N 🅟 Shell/dsl 🍴 McDonald's, Panel Room Rest., Subway
42mm	🆁🆂 wb, full ♿ facilities, litter barrels, petwalk, 🅲, 🚗, vending
41	MI 140, to Niles, Watervliet, N 🅟 Casey's/dsl, Citgo, Marathon/dsl, Shell/dsl 🍴 Burger King, Chicken Coop, Frosty Boy, Mill Creek Charlie's Rest., Subway, Taco Bell 🛏 Fairfield Inn 🅞 H, KOA (Apr-Oct) (7mi)
39	Millburg, Coloma, Deer Forest, 0-1 mi N 🅟 BP/dsl, Shell/dsl, Speedway/dsl, Wesco/dsl 🍴 DQ, El Asadero Mexican, Friendly Grill, McDonald's, Subway 🅞 Family$, Krenek RV Ctr, 🅞 fruit mkt, wine tasting
34	I-196 N, US 31 N, to Holland, Grand Rapids
33	Lp I-94, to Benton Harbor, 2-4 mi N 🅞 🍴

INTERSTATE 94 Cont'd

Exit #	Services
30	Napier Ave, Benton Harbor, **N** 🅖 Pilot/Wendy's/dsl/LP/24hr/@, Shell/dsl 🛏 American Inn 🅞 H, Blue Beacon
29	Pipestone Rd, Benton Harbor, **N** 🅕 Applebee's, Asian Grille, Burger King, El Rodeo Mexican, IHOP, McDonald's, Popeye's, Sophia's Pancake House, Steak'n Shake, Super Buffet, TX Corral 🛏 Best Western, Days Inn, Hilton Garden, Red Roof Inn, Travelodge 🅞 Aldi Foods, Best Buy, Big Lots, Chrysler/Dodge/Jeep, Home Depot, JC Penney, Jo-Ann Fabrics, Lowe's, Meijer/dsl, Staples, USPO, Walmart/Subway, **S** 🅖 BP/dsl 🅕 Bob Evans 🛏 Comfort Suites, Holiday Inn Express
28	US 31 S, MI 139 N, Scottdale Rd, to Niles, **N** 🅖 Citgo/dsl, Marathon/dsl 🅕 Burger King, Chicken Coop, Country Kitchen, Henry's Burgers, Jimmy John's, Joey C Pizza, KFC, Little Caesar's, Pizza Hut, Sonic, Subway, Taco Bell, Wendy's 🛏 Best Value Inn, Loyalty Inn 🅞 H, $General, $Tree, AutoZone, Belle Tire, Chevrolet/Buick/GMC, Family$, Kohl's, M&W Tire, Michael's, Midas, NAPA, O'Reilly Parts, Petsmart, radiators/repair/transmissions, Save-A-Lot, TJ Maxx, U-Haul, vet, Walgreens
27mm	St Joseph River
27	MI 63, Niles Ave, to St Joseph, **N** 🅖 Citgo 🅕 Nye's Apple Barn, **S** 🅖 Tesla EVC 🅕 Five Guys, Moe's SW Grill, Panera Bread 🅞 Goodyear
23	Red Arrow Hwy, Stevensville, **N** 🅖 Admiral, BP/Taco John's, Marathon/dsl, Mobil/Dunkin', Shell/dsl 🅕 Big Boy, Burger King, Coach's Grill, Cracker Barrel, Crimson Cafe, Culver's, DQ, LJ Silver, McDonald's, Papa John's 🛏 Baymont Inn, Candlewood Suites, Comfort Suites, Fairfield Inn, Super 8 🅞 Honda, Walgreens, **S** 🛏 Hampton Inn 🅞 Meijer/dsl
22	John Beers Rd, Stevensville, **N** 🛏 Chalet on the Lake 🅞 to Grand Mere SP, **S** 🅖 Marathon/dsl
16	Bridgman, **N** 🅖 BP/Quiznos/dsl 🅞 camping, to Warren Dunes SP, **S** 🅖 Citgo 🅕 Early Bird Eatery, Lydia's Rest., McDonald's, Pizza Hut, Roma Pizza, Subway 🛏 Bridgman Inn 🅞 auto repair, Chevrolet, Chrysler/Dodge/Jeep, Ford/Mazda, vet
12	Sawyer, **N** 🅖 Marathon/deli/dsl/scales/24hr 🅕 truck wash, **S** 🅖 TA/Burger King/Popeye's/Taco Bell/scales/dsl/24hr/@ 🅕 Greenbush Brewing 🛏 Super 8 🅞 Family$, USPO
6	Lakeside, Union Pier, **N** 🅞 Round Barn Winery, St Julian Winery, **S** 🅞 RV camping
4b a	US 12, to Three Oaks, New Buffalo, **N** 🅕 Pizza Hut, Redamak's Hamburgers, Roma Pizza
2.5mm	weigh sta both lanes
1	MI 239, to Grand Beach, New Buffalo, 0-2 mi **N** 🅖 Shell/Subway/dsl 🅕 Brewster's Italian, Casey's Grille, McDonald's, Nancy's, Rosie's Rest., Stray Dog Grill, Subway 🛏 Baymont Inn, Fairfield Inn, Holiday Inn Express, Quality Inn, Super Inn 🅞 $General, **S** 🛏 Days Inn 🅞 casino
.5mm	Welcome Ctr eb, full ♿ facilities, info, litter barrels, petwalk, 🚻, 🛏, vending
0mm	Michigan/Indiana state line

INTERSTATE 96

Exit #	Services
	I-96 begins/ends on I-75, exit 48 in Detroit.
191	I-75, N to Flint, S to Toledo, US 12, to MLK Blvd, to Michigan Ave
190b	Warren Ave, **N** 🅖 BP/dsl
190a	I-94 E to Port Huron
189	W Grand Blvd, Tireman Rd, **N** 🅖 Citgo/dsl, Mobil
188b	Joy Rd, **N** 🅕 Church's
188a	Livernois, **N** 🅖 Exxon/Subway, Mobil 🅕 Burger King, KFC, McDonald's, Wendy's
187	Grand River Ave (from eb)

Exit #	Services
186b	Davison Ave, I-96 local and I-96 express divide, no exits from express
186a	Wyoming Ave
185	Schaefer Hwy, to Grand River Ave, **N** 🅖 Citgo, Mobil 🅕 Coney Island, McDonald's 🅞 CVS Drug, **S** 🅖 Sunoco/dsl
184	Greenfield Rd
183	MI 39, Southfield Fwy, exit from expswy and local
182	Evergreen Rd
180	Outer Dr, **N** 🅖 BP/dsl/lube
180mm	I-96 local/express unite/divide
179	US 24, Telegraph Rd, **N** 🅖 BP, Marathon/dsl 🅕 Arby's, Baskin-Robbins/Dunkin', China King, Little Caesar's, McDonald's, Tim Horton's, White Castle 🅞 AutoZone, Chevrolet, Family$, Family$, O'Reilly Parts, URGENT CARE, **S** 🅖 Marathon/dsl, Shell/dsl
178	Beech Daly Rd, **N** 🅖 Sunoco
177	Inkster Rd, **N** 🅖 BP/Tim Horton 🛏 Best Value Inn 🅞 $General, 7-11, URGENT CARE
176	Middlebelt Rd, **N** 🅕 Bob Evans, IHOP, Olive Garden 🛏 Comfort Inn 🅞 Aldi Foods, H, 0-1 mi **S** 🅕 Applebee's, Chili's, Culver's, Del Taco, Five Guys, Jimmy John's, Leo's Coney Island, Logan's Roadhouse, McDonald's, MOD Pizza, Noodles&Co, Outback, Panda Express, Panera Bread, Pizza Hut, Popeye's, Potbelly, Qdoba, Red Lobster, Starbucks 🛏 Hampton Inn, Holiday Inn Express, Hometowne Suites 🅞 $Tree, AT&T, AutoZone, BigLots, Costco/gas, Dick's, Firestone/auto, GNC, Goodyear/auto, Home Depot, Jo-Ann Fabrics, Marshall's, Meijer, Menard's, Michael's, Office Depot, Petsmart, Target, URGENT CARE, Verizon, Walgreens, Walmart
175	Merriman Rd, **N** 🅖 Mobil/dsl, Speedway/dsl, **S** 🅖 Exxon/dsl 🅕 Prime Grill
174	Farmington Rd, **N** 🅖 Mobil/dsl, Sunoco 🅕 Looney Baker, **S** 🅖 🅕 KFC 🅞 vet
173b	Levan Rd, **N** 🅞 H, to Madonna U
173a	Newburgh Rd
	I-275 and I-96 run together 9 miles.
170	6 Mile Rd, **N** 🅕 Bar Louie, Big Boy, Buffalo Wild Wings, Jersey Mike's, Jimmy John's, Johnny's Italian, Panera Bread, Qdoba, Red Robin 🛏 Best Western, Courtyard, Holiday Inn, Marriott 🅞 H, Ace Hardware, AT&T, Busch's Foods, GNC, O'Reilly Parts, Rite Aid, Verizon, Walgreens, **S** 🅖 Marathon, Mobil 🅕 Applebee's, Brann's Steaks, Bravo Italian, Buca Italian, Charlie's Grille, Claddagh Rest., Fleming's, Hyde Park Steaks, Leo's Coney Island, McDonald's, Mitchell's Fish Mkt, Noodles&Co, Panchero's, PF Chang, Potbelly, Tahini Grill, Tim Horton, Wendy's 🛏 Fairfield Inn, Residence Inn, TownePlace Suites 🅞 Barnes&Noble, CVS, Kroger, Office Depot, Petsmart, REI

BENTON HARBOR

DETROIT AREA

🅿 = gas 🍴 = food 🛏 = lodging 🅾 = other ℞ = rest stop   Copyright 2022 - The Next EXIT

MI

INTERSTATE 96 Cont'd

Exit #	Services
169b a	7 Mile Rd, **N** 🍴 Dave&Buster's, Los Amigos 🛏 Embassy Suites, **S** 🅿 EVC 🍴 Andiamo's Cafe, Bahama Breeze Rest., BJ's Rest., Burger Fi, Chipotle, Gaucho Brazilian, Granite City Grill, J Alexander's Rest., Jimmy John's, Macaroni Grill, MOD Pizza, Rusty Bucket Rest. 🛏 Hyatt Place 🅾 AT&T, Home Depot, Trader Joe
167	8 Mile Rd, to Northville, **S** 🅿 BP/dsl, Speedway/dsl 🍴 Benihana, Big Boy, Chili's, Five Guys, Kerby's Koney Island, McDonald's, Mission BBQ, On-the-Border, Panera Bread, Qdoba, Starbucks, Taco Bell, Twin Peaks, Zoup! 🛏 Country Inn Suites, Extended Stay America, Hampton Inn, Holiday Inn Express, Sheraton 🅾 Best Buy, Costco/gas, Dick's, Firestone/auto, Kohl's, Meijer/dsl, Target, to Maybury SP, Verizon
165	I-696, I-275, MI 5, Grand River Ave.
	I-275 and I-96 run together 9 miles.
163	I-696 (from eb)
162	Novi Rd, to Walled Lake, Novi, **N** 🅿 🍴 Bar Louie, Black Rock Rest., Buddy's Pizzaria, Buffalo Wild Wings, CA Pizza, Carrabba's, Cheesecake Factory, ChuckECheese's, Coldstone, McDonald's, Novi Chophouse, Red Lobster, Starbucks, Subway, Taco Bell 🛏 Hilton Garden, Renaissance, Residence Inn 🅾 BigLots, Dick's, JC Penney, JoAnn Fabrics, Kohl's, Lord&Taylor, Macy's, Marshalls, Michael's, Midas, Nordstrom, Old Navy, **S** 🅿 Mobil/dsl, Sunoco/dsl 🍴 Athenian Coney Island, Bagger Dave's Burgers, BD Mongolian BBQ, Blaze Pizza, Bonefish Grill, Boston Mkt, Chipotle, Famous Dave's, Genji Japanese, Honeybaked Express, IHOP, Jersey Mike's, Maisano's Italian, Noodles&Co, Olive Garden, Panda Express, Panera Bread, Pei Wei, Pizza Hut, Potbelly, Primanti Bros, Qdoba, Red Robin, Steve&Rocky's, TGIFriday's, Tony Sacco Pizza, Wasabi, Wendy's 🛏 Courtyard, DoubleTree, Homewood Suites, Towne Place Suites 🅾 🏥, Advance Parts, AT&T, Belle Tire, Better Health Mkt, Chevrolet, Discount Tire, Hobby Lobby, Kia, Monro/auto, NAPA, O'Reilly Parts, TJ Maxx, URGENT CARE, Verizon, Walmart
160	Beck Rd, 12 Mile Rd, **S** 🅿 EVC, Shell/Tim Horton 🍴 Applebee's, China King, Guido's Pizza, La Herraduro Mexican, Leo's Coney Island, Olga's Kitchen, Outback Steaks, Starbucks, Subway, Zoup! 🛏 Hyatt Place, Staybridge Suites 🅾 🏥, GNC, Home Depot, Kroger, Staples, to Maybury SP
159	Wixom Rd, Walled Lake, **N** 🅿 Marathon/dsl, Sunoco/dsl 🍴 Culver's, Denise's Grill, Quiznos, Wendy's 🛏 Holiday Inn Express, My Place, SpringHill Suites 🅾 Aldi Foods, General RV Ctr, Meineke, Menard's, to Proud Lake RA, **S** 🅿 Exxon, Mobil/dsl, Valero/dsl 🍴 A&W/KFC, Arby's, Baskin-Robbins/Dunkin', Burger King, Dickey's BBQ, Grand Diner, Jimmy John's, McDonald's, Red Olive Rest., Shakers Grill, Stinger's Grill, Taco Bell, Tropical Cafe 🛏 Comfort Suites 🅾 AutoZone, Lincoln, Meijer/dsl, Sam's Club/gas, Target
155b a	to Milford, New Hudson, **N** 🅾 Camp Dearborn (5mi), Ford, to Lyon Oaks CP, **S** 🅿 Sunoco 🍴 Applebee's, Arby's, Biggby Coffee, Jet's Pizza, Jimmy John's, Kensington Grill, Leo's Coney Island, McDonald's, Starbucks, Subway, Tim Horton's 🅾 AAA, AT&T, Belle Tire, Chevrolet, Discount Tire, Hyundai, Lowe's, URGENT CARE, Verizon, Walmart
153	Kent Lake Rd, **N** 🅾 Kensington Metropark, **S** 🅿 BP/dsl 🛏 Country Meadows Inn (3mi)
151	Kensington Rd, **N** 🅾 Kensington Metropark, **S** 🅾 Island Lake RA
150	Pleasant Valley Rd (no return wb)

HOWELL

Exit #	Services
148b a	US 23, N to Flint, S to Ann Arbor
147	Spencer Rd, **N** 🅿 Mobil/dsl 🍴 Cheryl's Cafe 🅾 st police, 🅾 to Brighton St RA
145	Grand River Ave, to Brighton, **N** 🅿 BP, Shell/dsl 🍴 Arby's, Baskin-Robbins/Dunkin', Cracker Barrel, Outback Steaks, Pizza Hut 🛏 Courtyard 🅾 🏥, $General, Buick/GMC, Ford, Honda, Mazda, URGENT CARE, vet, **S** 🅿 Marathon/Subway 🍴 Big Boy, Burger King, Chili's, Chipotle, Firehouse Subs, Five Guys, Gourmet Garden, IHOP, Jimmy John's, Leo's Coney Island, Li Chef, McDonald's, MOD Pizza, Olga's Kitchen, Panda Express, Panera Bread, Pi's Asian, Potbelly, Red Robin, Starbucks, Taco Bell, Tim Horton, Wendy's 🛏 Homewood Suites, Wingate Inn 🅾 $Tree, AAA, Advance Parts, Aldi Foods, AT&T, Belle Tire, Best Buy, Bob's Tire, CVS Drug, Home Depot, JoAnn Fabrics, Marshalls, Meijer/dsl, Michael's, O'Reilly Parts, Petsmart, Staples, Target, to Brighton Ski Area, USPO, Verizon, Walgreens
141	Lp 96 (from wb, return at 140), to Howell, **0-2 mi N** 🅿 BP, dsl, Shell/Tim Horton/dsl, Speedway, Sunoco/dsl 🍴 Applebee's, Arby's, Asian Fusian Buffet, Aubree's Pizzaria, Biggby Coffee, Bluefin Steaks, Bob Evans, Buffalo Wild Wings, Jimmy John's, KFC, Leo's Coney Island, Little Caesar's, Los Tres Amigos, McDonald's, Panera Bread, Qdoba, Subway, Taco Bell, White Castle 🅾 $Tree, AT&T, Belle Tire, Big Lots, Chevrolet, Discount Tire, GNC, Home Depot, Kohl's, Lowe's, Meijer, O'Reilly Parts, Petsmart, URGENT CARE, Walmart
140	S Latson Rd, same as 141
137	D19, to Pinckney, Howell, **N** 🅿 Marathon, Mobil/dsl, Speedway/dsl, Sunoco/Baskin-Robbins/Dunkin'/dsl 🍴 All Star Coney Island, Block Brewing Co, Joanna's 2 Go, Taco Bell, Wendy's 🛏 Kensington Inn 🅾 🏥, Parts+, Spartan Tire, True Value, USPO, **S** 🍴 Wooly Bully's Rest. 🛏 Magnuson Hotel
135mm	℞ eb, full 🚻 facilities, litter barrels, petwalk, 🐾, 🏕, vending
133	MI 59, Highland Rd, **N** 🅿 Marathon/McDonald's/dsl 🍴 Arby's, Jersey Giant Subs, Leo's Coney Island 🛏 Baymont, Holiday Inn Express 🅾 Tanger Outlets/famous brands
129	Fowlerville Rd, Fowlerville, **N** 🅿 BP/dsl, Marathon/dsl, Sunoco/dsl 🍴 Great Lakes Rest., McDonald's, Pizza Hut/Taco Bell, Wendy's 🛏 Magnuson Hotel 🅾 Chevrolet, O'Reilly Parts, Walmart, **S** 🅿 Mobil/dsl 🍴 Subway 🅾 Chysler/Dodge/Jeep, Ford
126mm	weigh sta both lanes
122	MI 43, MI 52, Webberville, **N** 🅿 Mobil/dsl/24hr 🍴 McDonald's
117	to Dansville, Williamston, **N** 🅿 Marathon/Jersey's Giant Subs/dsl, **S** 🅿 Sunoco/dsl
111mm	℞ wb, full 🚻 facilities, litter barrels, petwalk, 🐾, 🏕, vending
110	Okemos, Mason, **N** 🅿 Marathon/dsl, Sunoco/Dunkin' 🍴 Applebee's, Arby's, Backyard BBQ, Big John's Steaks, Biggby Coffee, Coldstone/Tim Horton, Cracker Barrel, Culver's, Grand Traverse Pie Co., Hibachi Grille, Jimmy John's, Leaf Salad Bar, Little Caesar's, Lucky's Steaks, McDonald's, Ozzy Mediterranean, Panchero's Mexican, Starbucks, Stillwater Grill, Subway, Taco Bell 🛏 Comfort Inn, Fairfield Inn, Hampton Inn, Holiday Inn Express, Staybridge Suites 🅾 7-11, BMW/Porsche, Mercedes, to stadium, Verizon
106b a	I-496, US 127, to Jackson, Lansing, **N** 🅾 St Police
104	Lp 96, Cedar St, to Holt, Lansing, **N** 🅿 Admiral, Speedway/dsl 🍴 Applebee's, Arby's, Asia's Finest, Big John's, Biggby Coffee, Blimpie, Bob Evans, Boston Mkt, Burger King, China King, Domino's, Fazoli's, Happy's Pizza, Hooters, Jet's Pizza, KFC, Los Tres Amigos, Mikado Grill, Panda Gourmet, Pizza Hut, Steak'n Shake, Taco Bell, TX Roadhouse, Wendy's, Zeus Coney Island

LANSING

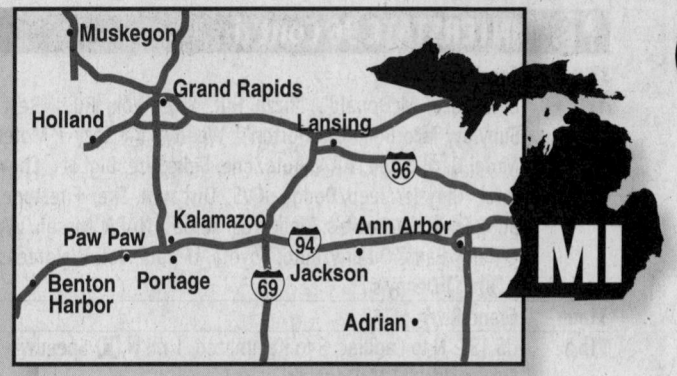

✈E INTERSTATE 96 Cont'd

L A N S I N G

Exit	Description
104	**Continued** 🛏 Best Value Inn 🅾 �H, $Tree, Aldi Foods, AT&T, auto repair, Belle Tire, Cadillac, Chevrolet, Chrysler/Dodge/Jeep, Discount Tire, Family$, GNC, Kia, Lexus, Meijer/dsl, Menards, Target, Toyota, Tuffy Auto, Verizon, vet, **S** 🅶 Speedway/dsl 🍴 Aldaco's Taco Bar, Burger King, Champion's Grill, China East Buffet, Dairy Dan, Hungry Howie's, McDonald's, Starbucks, Subway, Taco Bell 🛏 Causeway Bay Hotel 🅾 Advance Parts, AutoZone, Budget Tire, CVS Drug, Family$, Kroger/gas, Lowe's, NAPA, O'Reilly Parts, Rite Aid, URGENT CARE, Verizon
101	MI 99, MLK Blvd, to Eaton Rapids, **0-3 mi N** 🅶 QD, **S** 🅶 Mobil/Tim Horton, Speedway/Subway/dsl 🍴 Coach's Grill, McDonald's, Wendy's
98b a	Lansing Rd, to Lansing, **N** 🍴 Arby's, Wendy's 🛏 Comfort Inn, Holiday Inn Express 🅾 Harley-Davidson, **S** 🅾 st police
97	I-69, US 27 S, S to Ft Wayne, N to Lansing
95	I-496, to Lansing
93b a	MI 43, Lp 69, Saginaw Hwy, to Grand Ledge, **0-2 mi N** 🅶 Shell, Speedway/dsl 🍴 Applebee's, Buffalo Wild Wings, Burger King, Carrabba's, Cheddar's, Chick-fil-A, Chipotle, Denny's, Finley's Grill, Frank's Grill, Hibachi Grill, Honeybaked Ham, Houlihan's, Logan's Roadhouse, Longhorn Steaks, McDonald's, Outback Steaks, Panera Bread, Qdoba, Red Robin, Subway 🛏 Comfort Inn, Fairfield Inn, Hampton Inn, Motel 6, Quality Inn, Ramada Inn, Red Roof Inn, Residence Inn 🅾 �H, $Tree, Aldi, AT&T, Barnes&Noble, Best Buy, BigLots, Chrysler/Dodge/Jeep, Hobby Lobby, JC Penney, Kohl's, Kroger/dsl, Macy's, Meijer/dsl/24hr, Target, TJ Maxx, vet, Walgreens, **S** 🅶 QD, Shell, Dunkin', Sunoco/McDonald's 🍴 Arby's, Biggby Coffee, Bob Evans, Cancun Mexican, Cracker Barrel, Culver's, Steak'n Shake 🛏 SpringHill Suites 🅾 Belle Tire, Buick/GMC, Discount Tire, Lowe's, Mazda/Volvo, Menards, Michael's, Petsmart, Staples, Walmart/Subway
92mm	Grand River
91	I-69 N (from wb), US 27 N, to Flint
90	Grand River Ave, to 🖨 (from wb), **E** 🅶 Loves/Hardee's/dsl/scales/24hr/@, **N** 🅶 Loves/Hardee's/Subway/dsl/scales/24hr, **S** 🅶 FLYING J/Denny's/dsl/24hr
89	I-69 N, US 27 N (from eb), to Flint
87mm	🆁🆂 eb, full ♿ facilities, litter barrels, petwalk, 🚰, 🐾, vending
86	MI 100, Wright Rd, to Grand Ledge, **S** 🅶 Mobil/McDonald's/dsl, Speedway/Subway/24hr
84	to Eagle, Westphalia
79mm	🆁🆂 wb, full ♿ facilities, info, litter barrels, petwalk, 🚰, 🐾, vending
77	Lp 96, Grand River Ave, Portland, **N** 🅶 Citgo/dsl, Shell/Subway, Speedway/dsl 🍴 Arby's, Biggby Coffee, Burger King, Little Caesar's, McDonald's, New China Buffet, Red Tomato Pizza 🛏 American Heritage Inn 🅾 CarQuest, Family$, Rite Aid, Tom's Foods, Verizon, **S** 🅶 Tom's/dsl 🍴 Wendy's
76	Kent St, Portland
76mm	Grand River
73	to Lyons-Muir, Grand River Ave
69mm	**weigh sta both lanes**
67	MI 66, to Ionia, Battle Creek, **N** 🅶 Pilot/Subway/dsl/scales/24hr 🍴 Corner Landing Grill 🛏 Midway Motel, Super 8 🅾 �H, Alice Springs RV Park (3mi), Lakeside Camping, Meijer/dsl (4mi), Walmart (4mi)
64	to Lake Odessa, Saranac, **N** 🅾 Ionia St RA, **S** 🅾 I-96 Speedway
63mm	🆁🆂 eb, full ♿ facilities, litter barrels, petwalk, 🚰, 🐾, vending
59	Clarksville

C A S C A D E

Exit	Description
52	MI 50, to Lowell, **N** 🅶 Mobil/Subway/dsl, **S** 🅶 Marathon/dsl (2mi)
46mm	Thornapple River
46	rd 6, to rd 37
44	36 St, **S** 🅾 🖨
43b a	MI 11, 28th St, Cascade, **N** 🍴 Bagger Dave's, Biggby Coffee, Brann's Steaks, Culver's, Dan's Diner, Dunkin'/Baskin Robbins, Firehouse Subs, Freddy's, Gipper's Grill, Jet's Pizza, Jimmy John's, Korean BBQ, Leo's Coney Island, New Beginnings Rest., Panera Bread, Pit Stop BBQ, Pizza Hut, Qdoba, Starbucks, Subway, Sundance Grill, Taco Bell 🛏 Baymont Inn, Best Western, Country Inn&Suites, Crowne Plaza, EconoLodge, Holiday Inn Express 🅾 Ace Hardware, AT&T, Audi/Porsche/Subaru, Fresh Mkt, GNC, Meijer/dsl, Mercedes/Volvo/VW, Verizon, Walmart, **0-3 mi S** 🅶 Citgo, Shell, Speedway/dsl 🍴 Applebee's, Arby's, Arby's, Arnie's Rest., Bob Evans, Buddy's Pizza, Burger King, Cantina Mexican, Chick-fil-A, Chipotle Mexican, ChuckeCheese, Dave&Buster's, Denny's, Five Guys, Grand Coney, Grand Traverse Pie Co, Honey Baked Ham, IHOP, Jersey Mike's, Jimmy John's, Krispy Kreme, Longhorn Steaks, McDonald's, Moe's SW Grill, Noodles&Co, Old Chicago, Olive Garden, Osaka Japanese, Outback Steaks, Panera Bread, Pizza Hut, Pizza Ranch, Potbelly, Red Lobster, Smokey Bones, Starbucks, Steak'n Shake, Subway, Taco Bell, Tropical Cafe, TX Roadhouse, Wendy's 🛏 Clarion, Comfort Inn, Courtyard, Delta Marriott, DoubleTree, Drury Inn, Extended Stay America, Fairfield Inn, Hampton Inn, Hawthorn Suites, Homewood Suites, Motel 6, Red Roof Inn, Residence Inn, Sleep Inn, SpringHill Suites, Tru Hilton, Wyndham Garden 🅾 $General, $Tree, Advance Parts, Aldi Foods, Belle Tire, Best Buy, Big Lots, Costco/gas, Dick's, Ford/Mazda, Hobby Lobby, Home Depot, Honda, Hyundai/Kia, Jo-Ann Fabrics, Lowe's, Michael's, Monro Auto, Nissan, Old Navy, Petsmart, Sam's Club/gas, Staples, Target, TJ Maxx, Trader Joe's, Tuesday Morning, U-Haul, World Mkt
40b a	Cascade Rd, **N** 🅶 BP/dsl, Forest Hills Fuel 🍴 Biggby Coffee, Great Harvest, Jets Pizza, Little Bangkok, Little Caesar's, Manna Cafe, Noco Provisions, Subway 🅾 Forest Hills Mkt, vet, Walgreens, **S** 🅶 Shell/dsl, Speedway/dsl 🍴 Bonefish Grill, Jimmy John's, Zoup! 🅾 �H
39	MI 21 (from eb), to Flint
38	E Beltline Ave, to MI 21, MI 37, MI 44, **N** 🅶 🍴 Applebee's, Fuji Yama Japanese, Red Hot Inn Rest., Wendy's 🅾 Meijer/dsl, URGENT CARE, Verizon, **S** 🍴 Gravity Grille 🛏 Country Inn&Suites 🅾 �H
37	I-196 (from wb, exits left), Gerald Ford Fwy, to Grand Rapids
36	Leonard St, **2 mi S** 🍴 Arby's, Jimmy John's, McDonald's
33	Plainfield Ave, MI 44 Connector, **N** 🅶 Citgo/dsl, Speedway/dsl 🍴 Anna's House, Arby's, Biggby Coffee, Charlie's Grille, Cheers Grill, Freddy's, Fred's Italian, Jimmy John's, KFC, Little Caesar's,

= gas   = food   = lodging   = other   = rest stop   Copyright 2022 - The Next EXIT

INTERSTATE 96 Cont'd

33	Continued
	Loco Taco, McDonald's, Pizza Hut, Rice Wok, Russ' Rest., Subway, Taco Bell, Tim Horton's, Wendy's 🛏 Lazy T Motel, Motel 6 ⊙ $Tree, AAA, AutoZone, Belle Tire, BigLots, Chevrolet, Chrysler/Jeep/Dodge, CVS, Discount Tire, Firestone/auto, Ford, Kia, Lowe's, Meijer/dsl, Midas, NAPA, Nissan/VW, O'Reilly Parts, Quality/auto, Toyota, U-Haul, vet, Walgreens, S 🛢🍴 Denny's
31mm	Grand River
31b a	US 131, N to Cadillac, S to Kalamazoo, 1 mi N 🛢 Speedway/Subway/dsl 🍴 McDonald's
30b a	Alpine Ave, Grand Rapids, N 🛢 BP/dsl, Marathon/dsl, Mobil 🍴 Applebee's, Buffalo Wild Wings, Checkers, ChuckeCheese, Culver's, El Burrito Mexican, Empire Buffet, Firehouse Subs, First Wok, Five Guys, Freddy's, Golden Corral, Hibachi Grill, IHOP, Jersey Mike's, Jimmy John's, Little Caesar's, Logan's Roadhouse, McDonald's, MOD Pizza, Olive Garden, Outback Steaks, Panda Express, Panera Bread, Qdoba, Russ' Rest., Sonic, Starbucks, Steak'n Shake, Subway, Taco Bell, TGIFriday's, Three Happiness Chinese 🛏 Hampton Inn, Holiday Inn Express, SpringHill Suites ⊙ $Tree, Aldi Foods, AT&T, AutoZone, Belle Tire, Best Buy, Discount Tire, Ford, GNC, Hobby Lobby, Jo-Ann, Kohl's, Marshall's, Menards, Michael's, NAPA, PepBoys, PetCo, Sam's Club/gas, Target, TJ Maxx, Verizon, Walgreens, Walmart, S 🛢 Admiral/dsl, Speedway/dsl 🍴 Arby's, Burger King, Fazoli's, Jimmy John's, KFC, LJ Silver, McDonald's, Papa John's, Wendy's 🛏 Best Value Inn ⊙ Goodyear/auto, Home Depot, Meijer/dsl, Midas, O'Reilly Parts, U-Haul, URGENT CARE
28	Walker Ave, S 🛢 Meijer/dsl/24hr 🍴 Bob Evans, McDonald's 🛏 Baymont Inn, Quality Inn
26	Fruit Ridge Ave, N 🛢 Citgo/dsl, S 🛢 Marathon/deli/dsl
25mm	🅿 eb, full 🚻 facilities, litter barrels, petwalk, 🆑, 🛢
25	8th Ave, 4Mile Rd (from wb), S 🛢 Marathon/dsl 🛏 Wayside Motel
24	8th Ave, 4Mile Rd (from eb), S 🛢 Marathon/dsl 🛏 Wayside Motel
23	Marne, N ⊙ tires, S 🍴 Depot Café, Rinaldi's Café ⊙ Ernie's Mkt, fairgrounds/raceway, USPO
19	Lamont, Coopersville, S ⊙ LP
16	B-35, Eastmanville, N 🛢 Citgo/Subway/dsl, Shell/Burger King/dsl, Speedway/dsl/24hr 🍴 #1 Chinese, Arby's, Biggby Coffee, Hungry Howie's, Little Caesar's, McDonald's, New Beginnings Rest., Taco Bell 🛏 Rodeway Inn ⊙ Buick/Chevrolet, Chrysler/Dodge/Jeep, Family Fare Foods, Family$, Ford, Fun 'N Sun RV Ctr, Rite Aid, vet, S 🛢 Pacific Pride/dsl ⊙ RV camping
10	B-31 (exits left from eb), Nunica, N 🍴 Turk's Rest., S ⊙ Conestoga RV camping, golf course/rest.
9	MI 104 (from wb, exits left), to Grand Haven, Spring Lake, S 🛢 Marathon/dsl ⊙ to Grand Haven SP, vet
8mm	🅿 wb, full 🚻 facilities, litter barrels, petwalk, 🆑, 🛢, vending
5	Fruitport (from wb, no return)
4	Airline Rd, S 🛢 Speedway/dsl, Wesco/dsl 🍴 Burger Crest Diner, McDonald's, Norm's Ice Cream, Subway, Village Inn ⊙ $General, Grover Drug, Orchard Mkt Foods, to PJ Hoffmaster SP, USPO
1c	Hile Rd (from eb), S 🛢 Tesla EVC 🍴 Arby's, Asian Buffet, Bob Evans, Brann's Grille, Buffalo Wild Wings, Burger King, ChuckeCheese, Five Guys, Golden Corral, Grand Traverse Pie Co, Kazumi Steaks, KFC/Taco Bell, Logan's Roadhouse, McDonald's, Olive Garden, Qdoba, Red Lobster, Red Robin, Starbucks,

1c	Continued
	Subway, TX Roadhouse 🛏 Baymont Inn, Fairfield Inn, Hampton Inn ⊙ $Tree, Aldi Foods, AT&T, Barnes&Noble, Belle Tire, Best Buy, Dick's, Hobby Lobby, JC Penney, Jo-Ann Fabric, Kohl's, Meijer/dsl, Menards, Old Navy, PetCo, Target, TJ Maxx, Verizon, VW/Audi/Nissan/Subaru/Toyota
1b a	US 31, to Ludington, same as 1c, Grand Haven, 2 mi N 🛢 Sherman Blvd 🍴 Applebee's, Arby's, Fazoli's, Los Amigos, McDonald's, Panera Bread, Pizza Ranch, Red Wok, Subway, Taco Bell, Tim Horton, Wendy's 🛏 Airline Motel, Alpine Motel, Bel-aire Motel, Quality Inn/rest. ⊙ 🏥, $Tree, All Seasons Mkt Ctr, Big Lots, GNC, Lowe's, Marathon/dsl, Norton Automotive, Petsmart, Sam's Club/gas, Staples, Walmart

I-96 begins/ends on US 31 at Muskegon.

INTERSTATE 196 (Grand Rapids)

Exit #	Services
81mm	I-196 begins/ends on I-96, 37mm in E Grand Rapids.
79	Fuller Ave, N ⊙ sheriff, S 🛢 Shell/dsl, Speedway 🍴 Biggby Coffee, Bill's Rest., Checkers, Elbow Room, KFC, Subway, Taco Bell, Wendy's ⊙ 🏥, Ace Hardware, Family$, Verizon, Walgreens
78	College Ave, S 🛢 Mobil/Circle K 🍴 McDonald's, Omelet Shop ⊙ 🏥, Ford Museum
77c	Ottawa Ave, S ⊙ Gerald R Ford Museum, downtown
77b a	US 131, S to Kalamazoo, N to Cadillac
76	MI 45 E, Lane Ave, S ⊙ Gerald R Ford Museum, John Ball Park&Zoo
75	MI 45 W, Lake Michigan Dr, S ⊙ to Grand Valley St U
74mm	Grand River
73	Market Ave, N ⊙ to Vanandel Arena
72	Lp 196, Chicago Dr E (from eb)
70	MI 11 (exits left from wb), Grandville, Walker, S 🛢 Citgo/dsl, Shell 🍴 New Beginnings 🛏 Best Western+ ⊙ USPO, vet
69c	Baldwin St (from wb)
69b a	Chicago Dr, N 🛢 Speedway 🍴 Biggby Coffee, Culver's, Dickey's BBQ, Domino's, Fazoli's, Jimmy John's, KFC, McDonald's, Peppino's Pizza, Subway, Taco Bell ⊙ $Tree, Advance Parts, Aldi Foods, AutoZone, Meijer/dsl, O'Reilly Parts, USPO, Walgreens, S 🛢 Admiral, Speedway/dsl 🍴 Adobe Mexican, Arby's, Brann's Steaks, Little Caesar's, Rainbow Grill, Russ' Rest., Wings&More 🛏 Grand Village Inn, Holiday Inn Express ⊙ NAPA
67	44th St, N 🛢 Mobil/dsl 🍴 Burger King, Cracker Barrel, Panera Bread, Steak'n Shake 🛏 Comfort Suites ⊙ Honda, Walmart/Subway, 0-2 mi S 🍴 Anna's House, Applebee's, Big Boy, Carrabba's, China One, Famous Dave's, IHOP, Jimmy John's, Logan's Roadhouse, Noodles&Co, Olive Garden, On the Border, Qdoba, Red Lobster, Red Robin, Sakura Japanese, Starbucks, Subway, TGIFriday's, Tropical Smoothie, TX Roadhouse, Uccello's Ristorante, Wendy's 🛏 Residence Inn ⊙ $Tree, Barnes&Noble, Best Buy, Chrysler/Dodge/Jeep, Costco/gas, Dick's, Discount Tire, Family Fare Foods, Fiat, Gordman's, Hobby Lobby, Home Depot, JC Penney, Kohl's, Lowe's, Macy's, Marshall's, Meijer/zeal, Michael's, Old Navy, Petsmart, Verizon, World Mkt
64	MI 6 E, to Lansing (exits left from wb)
62	32nd Ave, to Hudsonville, N 🛢 BP/dsl, Citgo/dsl 🍴 Arby's, Biggby Coffee, Burger King, Hudsonville Grille, Little Caesar's, McDonald's 🛏 Quality Inn ⊙ Chevrolet, S 🛢 Mobil/Subway/dsl/24hr, Tesla EVC 🍴 Rainbow Grill, Wendy's 🛏 Travelodge ⊙ Harley-Davidson, Harvest Foods, Meijer/dsl

✈️E INTERSTATE 196 (Grand Rapids) Cont'd

Exit #	Services
58mm	🆁🆂 eb, full ♿ facilities, litter barrels, petwalk, 🚻, 🛒, vending
55	Byron Rd, Zeeland, N 🅿 Citgo/7-11 🍴 Blimpie, McDonald's ⭕ 🏥, to Holland SP
52	16th St, Adams St, 2 mi N 🅿 Speedway/dsl 🍴 Burger King, Jimmy John's, Papa Murphy's, Pizza Ranch, Wendy's ⭕ 🏥, Meijer/dsl/e85, S 🅿 Loves/Hardee's/dsl/scales/24hr, Mobil/Subway/dsl
49	MI 40, to Allegan, N 🅿 BP/McDonald's/dsl 🛏 Residence Inn, S 🅿 Pilot/Arby's/dsl/scales/24hr, Tulip City/Marathon/Subway/dsl/scales/24hr ⭕ truck repair, truck wash
44	US 31 N (from eb), to Holland, 3-5 mi N ⭕ 🏥, food, gas
43mm	🆁🆂 wb, full ♿ facilities, info, litter barrels, petwalk, 🚻, 🛒, vending
41	rd A-2, Douglas, Saugatuck, N 🅿 Marathon/dsl, Marathon/dsl, Shell/Subway/dsl 🍴 Burger King, Dairy Dayz, Spectators Grill 🛏 Best Western (1mi) ⭕ $General, NAPA, to Saugatuck SP, S 🍴 Belvedere Inn/Rest.
38mm	Kalamazoo River
36	rd A-2, Ganges, N 🅿 Shell 🍴 Christo's Rest., Pizza Mambo, Saugatuck Brewing Co 🛏 AmericInn, Blue Star Motel
34	MI 89, to Fennville, N ⭕ to West Side CP, S 🅿 Shell ⭕ Cranes Pie Pantry (4mi), Lyons Farm Mkt
30	rd A-2, Glenn, Ganges, N ⭕ to Westside CP (4mi)
28mm	🆁🆂 eb, full ♿ facilities, litter barrels, petwalk, 🚻, 🛒, vending
26	109th Ave, to Pullman, N ⭕ Dutch Farm Mkt
22	N Shore Dr, N ⭕ Cousin's RV Camping/rest., to Kal Haven Trail SP
20	rd A-2, Phoenix Rd, N 🅿 BP/dsl, Marathon/dsl 🍴 Arby's, China Buffet, Taco Bell ⭕ 🏥, $Tree, AutoZone, Meijer/dsl, Walgreens, S 🅿 Murphy USA/dsl, Shell/dsl 🍴 Big Boy, McDonald's, Sherman's Dairybar, Wendy's 🛏 Baymont Inn, Comfort Suites, Hampton Inn, Holiday Inn Express ⭕ $General, Aldi Foods, Menards, Walmart
18	MI 140, MI 43, to Watervliet, 0-2 mi N 🅿 Shell/dsl 🍴 Burger King, Little Caesar's, McDonald's, Pizza Hut 🛏 Great Lakes Inn, LakeBluff Motel ⭕ 🏥, auto repair, AutoValue Parts, Buick/Cadillac/GMC, Chevrolet, Chrysler/Dodge/Jeep, Ford/Lincoln, Village Mkt Foods, 7 mi S ⭕ KOA (Apr-Oct)
13	to Covert, N ⭕ RV camping, to Van Buren SP
7	MI 63, to Benton Harbor, N 🍴 DiMaggio's Pizza
4	to Coloma, Riverside, S 🅿 Shell/dsl ⭕ KOA (Apr-Oct)
2mm	Paw Paw River
1	Red Arrow Hwy, N ⭕ SW Michigan Airport
0mm	I-94, E to Detroit, W to Chicago

I-196 begins/ends on I-94, exit 34 at Benton Harbor.

✈️N INTERSTATE 275 (Livonia)

Exit #	Services
	I-275 and I-96 run together 9 miles. See I-96, exits 165-170.
29	I-96 E, to Detroit, MI 14 W, to Ann Arbor
28	Ann Arbor Rd, Plymouth, E 🅿 BP/Dunkin', Mobil, Shell/dsl 🍴 Little Caesar's, Los Tres Amigos, McDonald's 🛏 Red Roof Inn ⭕ $Tree, Verizon, W 🍴 Burger King, Firehouse Subs, Grand Traverse Pie Co., Lee's Coney Island, Tropical Smoothie 🛏 Comfort Inn ⭕ Cadillac, CVS Drug, Lincoln, vet
25	MI 153, Ford Rd, Garden City, E 🍴 Logan's Roadhouse, Parthenon Coney Island, Starbucks, Subway ⭕ Home Depot, Sam's Club, Walmart, W 🅿 BP, Speedway, Sunoco/dsl 🍴 Applebee's, Arby's, Basement Burger Bar, BD Mongolian BBQ,

LIVONIA

25	Continued
	Black Rock Grill, Bob Evans, Boston Mkt, Bowery Grill, Buffalo Wild Wings, Burger King, Carrabba's, Carvel Ice Cream, Chili's, Chipotle, Chopstick House, ChuckeCheese, Coldstone, Dunkin'/Baskin-Robbins, Five Guys, Jersey Mike's, Jimmy John's, KFC, Little Caesar's, McDonald's, Mexican Fiesta, MOD Pizza, Olga's Kitchen, Outback Steaks, Panera Bread, Potbelly, Qdoba, Starbucks, Subway, Taco Bell, TGIFriday's, Tim Hortons, Wendy's, White Castle 🛏 Baymont Inn, Comfort Suites, Extended Stay America, Fairfield Inn, Hampton Inn, La Quinta, TownePlace Suites ⭕ Advance Parts, Aldi Foods, CVS Drug, Discount Tire, Firestone/auto, GNC, Hobby Lobby, IKEA, JC Penney, Jo-Ann, Kohl's, Lowe's, Marshall's, Meijer/dsl, Michael's, Midas, PetCo, Target, Tuesday Morning, URGENT CARE, Verizon, vet, Walgreens
23	🆁🆂 nb, full ♿ facilities, info, litter barrels, 🚻, 🛒
22	US 12, Michigan Ave, to Wayne, E 🅿 BP/dsl, Mobil/dsl, Shell, Valero/dsl 🍴 Arby's, Jonathan's Rest., McDonald's, Quiznos, Subway, Wendy's 🛏 EconoLodge, Fellows Cr Motel, Holiday Inn Express, Super 8, Willo Acres Motel, W 🅿 Marathon/dsl 🍴 Jimmy John's ⭕ Kia, Nissan, vet
20	Ecorse Rd, to Romulus, E 🅿 Mobil/7-11, Shell/Tubby's/dsl, W 🅿 BP/Burger King/scales/dsl/24hr
17	I-94 E to Detroit, W to Ann Arbor, E ⭕ 🔁
15	Eureka Rd, E 🅿 Shell/Subway/dsl ⭕ 🔁
13	Sibley Rd, New Boston, W 🅿 Mobil/Subway/dsl ⭕ to Lower Huron Metro Park
11	S Huron Rd, W 🅿 Sunoco/Burger King/dsl 🍴 Iron Mike's Rest.
8	Will Carleton Rd, to Flat Rock
5	Carleton, South Rockwood, W 🅿 Speedway/dsl, Sunoco/Subway/dsl ⭕ $General, USPO
4mm	🆁🆂 sb, full ♿ facilities, litter barrels, 🚻, 🛒
2	US 24, to Telegraph Rd, W 🅿 BP/dsl, Marathon/Subway/dsl ⭕ $General
0mm	I-275 begins/ends on I-75, exit 20.

✈️N INTERSTATE 475 (Flint)

Exit #	Services
17mm	I-475 begins/ends on I-75, exit 125.
15	Clio Rd, W 🅿 ⭕ Chevrolet
13	Saginaw St, E 🅿 🍴 Hungry Howie's, KFC, McDonald's, Taco Bell ⭕ Advance Parts, Kroger/gas, O'Reilly Parts, W 🅿 Marathon 🍴 Burger King, Little Caesar's
11	Carpenter Rd
10	Pierson Rd
9	rd 54, Dort Hwy, Stewart Ave E 🅿 BP/dsl 🍴 McDonald's
8mm	Flint River
8b	Davison Rd, Hamilton Ave
8a	Longway Blvd W 🛏 Holiday Inn Express ⭕ 🏥, USPO
7	rd 21, Court St, downtown Flint

FLINT

🅖 = gas 🍴 = food 🏨 = lodging 🅞 = other 🆁🆂 = rest stop   Copyright 2022 - The Next EXIT ®

MI

INTERSTATE 475 (Flint) Cont'd

Exit #	Services
6	I-69, W to Lansing, E to Port Huron
5	Atherton Rd (from sb) **E** 🅖 Marathon/dsl
4	Hemphill Rd, Bristol Rd **E** 🅖 Speedway/dsl 🍴 Rally's, Subway 🅞 Rite Aid, **W** 🅖 Speedway/dsl 🍴 Little Caesar's, Tim Horton/Wendy's 🅞 $General, Kroger/dsl, vet
2	Hill Rd **E** 🅖 Speedway 🍴 Applebee's, Bob Evans 🏨 Wingate Inn 🅞 vet, **W** 🅖 Mobil, Speedway/dsl 🍴 Arby's, Burger King, Burger St Grill, Little Caesar's, McDonald's, Starbucks, Taco Bell, Wendy's 🅞 Rite Aid

I-475 begins/ends on I-75, exit 111.

INTERSTATE 696 (Detroit)

Exit #	Services

I-696 begins/ends on I-94.

28	I-94 E to Port Huron, W to Detroit, 11 Mile Rd, **E** 🅖 7-11, Shell/dsl, Speedway/dsl 🅞 $General
27	MI 3, Gratiot Ave, **N** 🅖 BP, Marathon, Valero 🍴 Checkers, Firehouse Subs, McDonald's, National Coney Island, Tubby's Subs 🅞 Costco/gas, **S** 🅖 Marathon, Mobil/McDonald's/dsl, Shell 🍴 Biggby Coffee, Burger King, JW Ice Cream, KFC, Subway, Taco Bell, Tim Horton's, White Castle 🅞 Belle Tire, Chrysler/Dodge/Jeep, Family$, Firestone/auto, GNC, Kroger/gas, Rite Aid, Sav-A-Lot Foods, TJ Maxx
26	MI 97, Groesbeck Ave, Roseville, **N** 🅖 BP/dsl, **S** 🍴 Tim Horton
24	Hoover Rd, Schoenherr Rd, **N** 🅖 🍴 Burger King, KFC, **S** 🅖 BP/dsl, Mobil/7-11 🍴 Boston Mkt, Del Taco, DQ, Grubhouse, Little Caesar's, Popeye's, Red Lobster, Subway, Taco Bell, Tim Horton, Wendy's 🏨 Holiday Inn Express 🅞 $Tree, Advance Parts, CVS Drug, GNC, Home Depot, Kroger
23	MI 53, Van Dyke Ave, **N** 🅖 BP, Marathon, Mobil/dsl 🍴 Applebee's, Arby's, Baskin-Robbins/Dunkin', McDonald's, Simple Palate Rest., Subway 🅞 $General, Cadillac, Dodge/Ram, Toyota, Walmart, **S** 🍴 Luca's Coney Island 🅞 Chevrolet/Buick/GMC, Discount Tire, Ford, Rite Aid, USPO, vet
22	Mound Rd, **N** 🅖 BP/Burger King, Mobil/dsl
20	Ryan Rd, Dequindre Rd, **N** 🅖 Citgo, Mobil/7-11, Sunoco 🏨 Knights Inn, Red Roof Inn 🅞 auto repair, BigLots, vet, **S** 🍴 Church's, LA Coney Island, McDonald's 🏨 Best Inn, Victory Suites 🅞 transmissions

DETROIT

19	Couzens St, 10 Mile Rd, **S** 🅞 Hazel Park Racetrack
18	I-75 N to Flint, S to Detroit
17	Campbell Ave, Hilton Ave, Bermuda, Mohawk, **S** 🅖 Marathon/ds
16	MI 1, Woodward Ave, Main St, **N** 🅞 zoo, **S** 🅖 Sunoco
14	Coolidge Rd, 10 Mile Rd, **S** 🅖 Speedway 🍴 Hungry Howie's, Jade Palace Chinese, Little Caesar's, Sahara Grill, Subway 🅞 CVS Drug, Family$, URGENT CARE
13	Greenfield Rd, **N** 🅖 Marathon, Mobil 🍴 L George Coney Island, McDonald's, Popeye's, Subway, White Castle 🅞 $Tree, Aldi Foods, Family$, Save a Lot Foods, Sol's Automotive, URGENT CARE, **S** 🅖 Shell, Sunoco 🍴 Baskin-Robbins/Dunkin', Front Page Deli, Pita Cafe, Starbucks 🅞 Rite Aid
12	MI 39, Southfield Rd, 11 Mile Rd, **N** 🍴 Panera Bread 🅞 Discount Tire, **S** 🅖 Shell 🍴 Happy's Pizza 🅞 AT&T
11	Evergreen Rd, **S** 🅖 Mobil, Speedway/dsl 🍴 Benito's Pizza, China Gourmet, Chipotle, Coldstone/Tim Horton's, Fuddrucker's, Jimmy John's, Potbelly, Qdoba, Subway, TGIFriday's 🏨 Hawthorn Suites, Holiday Inn Express
10	US 24, Telegraph Rd, **N** 🅖 Marathon, Mobil, Sunoco 🍴 Chipotle, DiBella Subs, Five Guys, Jimmy John's, Mezzanine Mediterranian, Noodles&Co, Panera Bread, Popeye's, Potbelly, Qdoba, Starbucks, Wendy's 🏨 Extended Stay America, Red Roof Inn, SpringHill Suites 🅞 AT&T, Belle Tire, Best Buy, Buick/GMC, Chevrolet, Chrysler/Dodge/Jeep, Ford, Honda, Hyundai, Kia, Lexus, Lincoln, Lowe's, Meijer/dsl, Michael's, Mini, Nissan, Office Depot, Petsmart, Subaru, Verizon, **S** 🅖 Mobil/7-11, Sunoco 🍴 Kerby's Koney Island, Starbucks, Tim Horton's 🏨 Best Western, Candlewood Suites, Courtyard, Holiday Inn Express, Marriott, Quality Inn 🅞 AutoZone, Family$
8	MI 10, Lodge Fwy
7	American Dr (from eb), **S** 🏨 Extended Stay America, Hilton Garden
5	Orchard Lake Rd, Farmington Hills, **N** 🅖 BP/dsl, Marathon, Mobil/dsl, Sunoco 🍴 Arby's, Burger King, Camelia's Mexican, Hong Hua Chinese, Jet's Pizza, Jimmy John's, Kabuki Japanese, Marie's Scrambler, Roberto's, Ruby Tuesday, Starbucks, Subway, Wendy's 🏨 Comfort Inn, Extended Stay America, Fairfield Inn, Radisson 🅞 CVS, Discount Tire, Holocaust Museum, Petco, to St Mary's Coll, Verizon
1	(from wb), I-96 W, I-275 S, to MI 5, Grand River Ave

NOTES

MINNESOTA

⊕N   INTERSTATE 35

D U L U T H

Exit #	Services
260mm	I-35 begins/ends on MN 61 in Duluth.
259	MN 61, London Rd, to Two Harbors, North Shore, W 🅿 BP/dsl, Holiday/dsl, Holiday/dsl (2), ICO/dsl 🍴 Blackwoods Grill, Dunn Bros Coffee, KFC, McDonald's, Perkins, Subway, Taco John's, Wendy's 🛏 Days Inn, Esdgewater Inn
258	21st Ave E (from nb), to U of MN at Duluth same as 259
256b	Mesaba Ave, Superior St, E 🍴 ICO/DQ 🍴 Bellisio's, Caribou Coffee, Famous Dave's BBQ, Grandma's Grill, Greenmill Rest., Grizzly's, Little Angie's Cantina, Old Chicago, Red Lobster, Smokehouse Rest., Subway, Timberlodge Steaks 🛏 Canal Park Lodge, Comfort Suites, Hampton Inn, Inn at Lake Superior, Suites Hotel, W 🛏 Holiday Inn, Radisson, Sheraton
256a	Michigan St, E 🅾 waterfront, W 🅾 🅷 downtown
255a	US 53 N (exits left from nb), W 🅿 Mobil 🅾 Kia downtown
255b	I-535 spur, to Wisconsin
254	27th Ave W, W 🅿 Holiday/Burger King/dsl, KwikTrip/dsl 🍴 Duluth Grill, Little Caesar's, Subway 🛏 Motel 6 🅾 USPO
253b	40th Ave W, W 🅿 Holiday/dsl/CNG 🍴 Perkins 🛏 Comfort Inn, Super 8
253a	US 2 E, US 53, to Wisconsin
252	Central Ave, W Duluth, W 🅿 Holiday/dsl, Mobil/Charley's/dsl 🍴 China King Buffet, Domino's, Jimmy John's, KFC, McDonald's, Pizza Hut, Subway, Taco John's 🅾 $Tree, Advance Parts, CVS Drug, K-Mart, Menards, O'Reilly Parts, Super 1 Foods, USPO, Walgreens
251b	MN 23 S, Grand Ave
251a	Cody St, E 🛏 Allyndale Motel 🅾 zoo
250	US 2 W (from sb), to Grand Rapids, 1/2 mi W 🅿 Holiday/dsl, Mobil/dsl/LP 🍴 Blackwoods Grill 🛏 AmericInn
249	Boundary Ave, Skyline Pkwy, E 🅿 Holiday/dsl 🍴 McDonald's 🛏 Best Western 🅾 to ski area, to Spirit Mtn RA, W 🆁🆂 both lanes, full 🛁 facilities, info, 🄲, 🚮, litter barrels, vending 🅿 Exxon/Subway/dsl 🍴 Blackwoods Grill 🛏 AmericInn, Best Value Inn 🅾 Mack/Volvo
246	rd 13, Midway Rd, Nopeming, W 🅿 Armor/dsl 🍴 Dry Dock Rest.
245	rd 61, E 🍴 Buffalo House Rest./camping
242	rd 1, Esko, Thomson, E 🅿 Mobil
239.5mm	St Louis River
239	MN 45, to Cloquet, Scanlon, E 🅾 Jay Cooke SP, KOA (May-Oct) (3mi), W 🅿 Holiday, KwikTrip/dsl/e85 🍴 dsl repair, Trapper Pete's Steaks 🛏 Golden Gate Motel 🅾 Coates RV Ctr, 🅷
237	MN 33, Cloquet, 1 mi W 🅿 Lemon Tree/dsl, Mobil, Murphy USA/dsl 🍴 Applebee's, Arby's, DQ, Erbert&Gerberts, Little Caesar's, McDonald's, Papa Murphy's, Perkins, Pizza Hut,

Exit #	Services
237	Continued South Gate Pizza, Subway, Taco John's/Steak Escape, Wendy's 🛏 AmericInn, Super 8 🅾 $Tree, AT&T, AutoZone, Chrysler/Dodge/Jeep, Family$, Ford, 🅷, NAPA, O'Reilly Parts, Super 1 Foods, Verizon, Walgreens, Walmart/Subway
236mm	weigh sta both lanes
235	MN 210, to Cromwell, Carlton, E 🅿 BP/rest./dsl, ICO/dsl/24hr 🍴 Spirits Rest. 🛏 AmericInn, Royal Pines Motel 🅾 to Jay Cooke SP, W 🅾 Black Bear Casino/Hotel/rest.
235mm	Big Otter Creek
233mm	Little Otter Creek
227	rd 4, Mahtowa, E 🅾 camping, W 🅾 TJ's Country Store/gas (2 mi)
226mm	🆁🆂 nb, full 🛁 facilities, 🄲, 🚮, litter barrels, vending, petwalk
220	rd 6, Barnum, E 🅾 Bear Lake Camping, W 🅿 Mobil/café/dsl/24hr 🍴 Lazy Bear Rest. 🛏 Northwoods Motel 🅾 Munger Tr
219mm	Moose Horn River
218mm	Moose Horn River
216	MN 27 (from sb, no EZ return), Moose Lake, 1-2 mi W 🅿 Cenex/dsl, Holiday/dsl 🍴 Art's Café, DQ, Lazy Moose Grille 🛏 Days Inn (4mi), Moose Lake Motel 🅾 1918 Museum, Ace Hardware, AutoValue Parts, 🅷, Mkt Place Foods, O'Reilly Parts, to Munger Trail
214	rd 73, E 🅾 camping, Moose Lake SP (2mi), 2 mi W 🅿 KwikTrip/dsl/e85/scales, McDonald's, Mobil/dsl 🍴 Subway 🛏 Days Inn, Moose Lake Motel 🅾 🅷, Munger Trail, Red Fox Camping
209	rd 46, Sturgeon Lake, E 🅿 Mobil/dsl 🍴 Doc's Café 🅾 Sturgeon Lake, W 🍴 Ernie's Rest. (seasonal) 🛏 Sturgeon Lake Motel 🅾 camping (3mi)

⛽ = gas 🍴 = food 🏨 = lodging ⊙ = other Ⓡ = rest stop   Copyright 2022 - The Next EXIT ®

INTERSTATE 35 Cont'd

Exit #	Services
209mm	Ⓡ sb, full ♿ facilities, ⦶, 🏕, litter barrels, vending, petwalk
206.5mm	Willow River
205	rd 43, Willow River, W ⛽ BP/cafe/dsl ⊙ camping (2mi)
198.5mm	Kettle River
198mm	Ⓡ nb, full ♿ facilities, ⦶, 🏕, litter barrels, vending, petwalk
195	rd 18, rd 23 E, to Askov, E ⛽ Cenex/cafe/dsl 🍴 Banning Jct Cafe 🏨 Best Value Inn ⊙ camping, to Banning SP, W ⊙ camping
191	MN 23, rd 61, Sandstone, E ⛽ Casey's/dsl, Victory/dsl 🍴 Subway 🏨 Sandstone 61 Motel (2mi) ⊙ Chris' Food Center/dsl
184mm	Grindstone River
183	MN 48, Hinckley, E ⛽ Holiday/Hardee's/dsl, KwikTrip/dsl, Marathon/Tobie's Rest./dsl/E-85 🍴 Burger King, DQ, McDonald's, Subway, Taco Bell 🏨 Days Inn, Grand Northern Inn ⊙ casino, to St Croix SP (15mi), W ⛽ Mobil, Mobil/White Castle/dsl 🍴 Cassidy's Rest. 🏨 Best Value Inn ⊙ Family$, Hinckley Fire Museum
180	MN 23 W, rd 61, to Mora
175	rd 14, Beroun, E ⛽ Marathon/dsl
171	rd 11, Pine City, E ⛽ SA/dsl 🍴 McDonald's ⊙ Ace Hardware, Chrysler/Dodge/Jeep, Verizon, W ⊙ camping
170mm	Snake River
169	MN 324, rd 7, Pine City, E ⛽ Holiday/dsl, Marathon/dsl, Murphy USA/dsl 🍴 A&W, DQ, KFC, Pizza Hut, Subway ⊙ $Tree, Campbell Auto/tire, Ford, O'Reilly Parts, USPO, vet, Walmart/Subway, W ⊙ to NW Co Fur Post HS
165	MN 70, to Grantsburg, Rock Creek, E ⛽ Marathon/dsl ⊙ camping, W ⛽ Heidelbergers/dsl 🍴 Rock Creek Cafe
159	MN 361, rd 1, Rush City, E ⛽ Holiday/Burger King/dsl ⊙ $General, Rush City Foods, W ⊙ camping (2mi)
154mm	Ⓡ nb, full ♿ facilities, ⦶, 🏕, litter barrels, vending, petwalk
152	rd 10, Harris, 1 mi E ⛽ Harris 61/dsl 🍴 Kaffe Stuga Caffe
147	MN 95, to Cambridge, North Branch, E ⛽ Casey's, Holiday/dsl 🍴 China Taste, Domino's, DQ, McDonald's, Oak Inn Rest., Perkins, Subway, Taco Bell 🏨 AmericInn, Budget Host ⊙ Family$, Fisk Tire, NAPA, O'Reilly Parts, to Wild River SP (14mi), vet, W ⛽ Holiday/dsl/e85 🍴 Burger King, Denny's, Dickey's BBQ, Don Lulu Mexican, Papa Murphy's ⊙ Chevrolet, County Mkt Foods, Ford, North Branch Outlets/famous brands, USPO, Verizon
143	rd 17, W ⛽ Tesoro/dsl
139	rd 19, Stacy, E ⛽ Gas+ 🍴 Rustic Inn Rest., Stacy Grill, Subway ⊙ city park, W ⛽ KwikTrip/dsl/e85 ⊙ A-1 Tires
135	US 61 S, rd 22, Wyoming, E ⛽ Casey's, Sinclair/dsl 🍴 DQ, Linwood Pizza, Subway, Tasty Asia ⊙ CarQuest, Ⓗ, IGA Foods, WY Drug, W ⛽ Shell/dsl 🍴 McDonald's, Village Inn Rest. ⊙ camping (10mi), golf, vet
132	US 8 (from nb), to Taylors Falls
131	rd 2, Forest Lake, E ⛽ BP, Holiday/dsl, SA/dsl 🍴 Applebee's, Arby's, Burger King, Culver's, Joy Garden, KFC, McDonald's, Papa John's, Perkins, Quack's Cafe, Subway, Taco Bell, White Castle 🏨 AmericInn ⊙ Aldi Foods, AutoZone, O'Reilly Parts, RV/Auto repair, Target, Tires+, Verizon, Walgreens, Walmart/Subway, W ⛽ Holiday/dsl 🍴 Famous Dave's BBQ, Jimmy John's, Papa Murphy's, Starbucks, Taco John's, Wendy's 🏨 Country Inn&Suites ⊙ AT&T, Buick/GMC, Cadillac/Chevrolet, Chrysler/Dodge/Jeep, Cub Foods, GNC, Home Depot, Jiffy Lube, Menards
131mm	Ⓡ sb, full ♿ facilities, ⦶, 🏕, litter barrels, vending, petwalk
129	MN 97, rd 23, E ⛽ Kwik Trip/dsl/e85 ⊙ camping (6mi), W ⛽ Holiday/dsl ⊙ camping (1mi), Coates RV Ctr
128mm	weigh sta both lanes
127	I-35W, S to Minneapolis. See I-35W.

Exit #	Services
123	rd 14, Centerville, E ⛽ Kwik Trip 🍴 Blue Heron Grill, Dunn Bros Coffee, McDonald's, Papa Murphy's ⊙ Festival Foods, vet White Bear RV Ctr, W ⛽ Mobil, Shell/Circle K 🍴 DQ, Fiesta Cancun, WiseGuys Pizza ⊙ auto repair
120	rd J (from nb, no return)
117	rd 96, E ⛽ SA/dsl 🍴 Burger King, Carbone's Pizza 🏨 AmericInn ⊙ Goodyear/auto, NAPA, W ⛽ Holiday 🍴 $5 Pizza Applebee's, Arby's, Caribou Coffee, Culver's, McDonald's, Noodles&Co, Punch Pizza, Subway, Zen Asia ⊙ AutoZone, Cub Foods, Tires+, USPO, Walgreens
115	rd E, E ⛽ BP/repair, SA/dsl 🍴 Jimmy John's, Jimmy's Rest. Perkins, Savoy Pizza 🏨 Country Inn&Suites, Fairfield Inn, Holiday Inn Express ⊙ URGENT CARE, W 🍴 Chipotle Mexican, KFC, Mad Jack's Cafe, Panera Bread, Papa Murphy's, Wendy's ⊙ $Tree, AT&T, Fresh Thyme Mkt, GNC, Target, Walmart
114	I-694 E (exits left from sb)
113	I-694 W
112	Little Canada Rd, E ⛽ BP, W 🍴 Porterhouse Rest.
111a/b	MN 36 E, to Stillwater/MN 36 W, to Minneapolis
110b	Roselawn Ave
110a	Wheelock Pkwy, E ⛽ BP, Gulf 🍴 May's Deli, Roadside Pizza Subway
109	Maryland Ave, E ⛽ SA/dsl, W 🍴 Wendy's ⊙ K-Mart
108	Pennsylvania Ave downtown
107c	University Ave, E ⛽ SA/dsl, W ⊙ Ⓗ, to st capitol downtown
107b a	I-94, W to Minneapolis, E to St Paul.
	I-35 and I-94 run together.
106c	11th St (from nb), Marion St downtown
106b	Kellogg Blvd (from nb), E 🍴 Eagle St Grill 🏨 Holiday Inn ⊙ Ⓗ downtown
106a	Grand Ave, E ⊙ Ⓗ
105	St Clair Ave
104c	Victoria St, Jefferson Ave
104b	Ayd Mill Rd (from nb)
104a	Randolph Ave
103b	MN 5, W 7th St, E 🍴 Burger King, W ⛽ SA/dsl ⊙ Midas, USPO
103a	Shepard Rd (from nb)
102mm	Mississippi River
102	MN 13, Sibley Hwy, W ⛽ BP, Holiday/Subway
101b a	MN 110 W, E ⛽ BP/dsl 🍴 Caribou Coffee, McDonald's, Subway, Teresa's Mexican, Tommy Chicago's Pizza ⊙ Verizon, Walgreens, W ⛽ SA/dsl/e85
99b a	I-494 W/I-494 E
98	Lone Oak Rd, E 🏨 Extended Stay America, Microtel ⊙ Sam's Club/gas, URGENT CARE, USPO, W ⛽ Shell 🍴 Farmer Grandson's Eatery 🏨 Hampton Inn, Sonesta Suites
97b	Yankee Doodle Rd, E 🍴 Applebee's, Arby's, Buffalo Wild Wings, Burger King, Chipotle, Coldstone, Culver's, Domino's, DQ, Genghis Grill, Houlihan's, Jake's Grille, Jersey Mike's, Jimmy John's, KFC, Noodles&Co, Old Chicago Pizza, Panda Express, Panera Bread, Papa John's, Papa Murphy's, Perkins, Pizza Man, Potbelly, Qdoba, Smashburger, Taco Bell ⊙ $Tree, AT&T, Barnes&Noble, Best Buy, BigLots, GNC, Home Depot, Kohl's, Lunds&Byerly's Mkt, Michael's, O'Reilly Parts, Old Navy, Petsmart, TJ Maxx, Verizon, Walgreens, Walmart/Subway, W ⛽ BP/dsl, SA/dsl 🍴 El Loro Mexican, Granite City, Starbucks, Subway 🏨 Best Western, Extended Stay America ⊙ Hobby Lobby, HyVee Foods, Marshall's, NAPA
97a	Pilot Knob Rd, E ⛽ Holiday, Speedway 🍴 Chili's, McDonald's, Wendy's 🏨 SpringHill Suites, TownePlace Suites ⊙ Discount Tire, Excel Repair, Firestone/auto, Jiffy Lube, Kohl's, Tires+, Walmart/Subway, W ⛽ BP/dsl, Speedway/dsl 🍴 Dunkin', Starbucks 🏨 Best Western+, Holiday Inn Express same as 97b

MN (vertical tab)

HINCKLEY (vertical label)

FOREST LAKE (vertical label)

ST PAUL (vertical label)

INTERSTATE 35 Cont'd

Exit #	Services
94	rd 30, Diffley Rd, to Eagan, **E** 🅿 Holiday/dsl 🍴 Andiamo Italian 🅾 CVS Drug, Kowalski's Mkt/Starbucks, URGENT CARE, **W** 🅿 Sinclair/dsl 🅾 Goodyear/auto
93	rd 32, Cliff Rd, **E** 🅿 Holiday/dsl 🍴 Bonfire Grill, Sarpino's Pizza, Subway 🅾 Ace Hardware, **W** 🅿 Holiday/dsl 🍴 Burger King, Caribou Coffee, Casper's Rest., Chipotle Mexican, Dolittle's Grill, DQ, Green Mill Rest., Hong Wong Chinese, Jimmy John's, Leeann Chin's, Noodles&Co, Papa John's, Papa Murphy's, Pizza Hut, Starbucks, Taco Bell, Wendy's, Which Wich? 🛏 Hilton Garden, Quality Inn, Staybridge Suites 🅾 $Tree, Cub Foods, O'Reilly Parts, Target, USPO, Walgreens
92	MN 77, Cedar Ave, **E** 🅾 Zoo, **1 mi W** access to Cliff Rd services
90	rd 11, **E** 🅿 KwikTrip 🍴 Pizza Man, Subway 🅾 Valley Natural Foods, vet, **W** 🅿 Speedway/dsl
88b	rd 42, Crystal Lake Rd, **E** 🍴 Chianti Grill 🅾 Lund's&Byerly's Mkt, Petsmart, **W** 🅿 BP, Holiday/dsl, Shell, Speedway/dsl 🍴 Applebee's, Arby's, Buca Italian, Burger Jones, Burger Jones, Burger King, Cam Ranh Bay, Chick-fil-A, Chili's, Chipotle Mexican, ChuckECheese, HoneyBaked Ham, IHOP, Jimmy John's, KFC, LeeAnn Chin, Little Caesar's, McDonald's, Noodles&Co, Old Country Buffet, Olive Garden, Outback Steaks, Panera Bread, Papa John's, Papa Murphy's, Pizza Hut, Porter Creek Grill, Red Lobster, Roasted Pear, Royal Buffet, Shogun Japanese, Smashburger, Starbucks, Taco Bell, TGIFriday's, Wendy's 🛏 AmericInn, Best Western, Fairfield Inn, Hampton Inn, InTown Suites 🅾 $Tree, Ace Hardware, Advance Parts, AT&T, Barnes&Noble, Best Buy, Costco/gas, Cub Foods, Dick's, Discount Tire, Home Depot, 🅷, JC Penney, Kohl's, Macy's, mall, Michael's, Old Navy, PetCo, Sears/auto, Target, Tires+, Tuesday Morning, Verizon, VW, Walgreens
88a	I-35W (from nb), N to Minneapolis. **See I-35W.**
87	Crystal Lake Rd (from nb), **W** 🅿 Kwik Trip/dsl 🅾 Honda/Nissan, Hyundai, Mazda, Subaru, Toyota
86	rd 46, **E** 🅿 KwikTrip/dsl, Speedway/dsl 🍴 KFC, Starbucks 🅾 Harley-Davidson, **W** 🍴 McDonald's 🅾 auto repair, O'Reilly Parts
85	MN 50, **E** 🅿 F&F/dsl, SA/dsl 🍴 Caribou Coffee, Culver's, Domino's, DQ, Eddie Cheng, Gerbert's Sandwiches, Green Mill Rest., Jimmy John's, Lakeville Chinese, Little Caesar's, Starbucks, Subway, Taco Bell, Wendy's 🛏 Quality Inn 🅾 $Tree, Advance Parts, Cub Foods, CVS Drug, GNC, Goodyear/auto, NTB, O'Reilly Parts, Verizon, Walgreens, **W** 🅿 Holiday/dsl 🍴 Cracker Barrel, Perkins, Pizza Ranch 🛏 Baymont Inn 🅾 Camping World
84	185th St W, Orchard Trail, **E** 🅿 Speedway/dsl 🍴 Applebee's, Buffalo Wild Wings, Caribou Coffee, Quiznos, SawaJapan 🅾 Marshall's, Target
81	rd 70, Lakeville, **E** 🅿 Holiday/dsl 🍴 Baldy's BBQ, McDonald's, Min Garden, Porterhouse Steaks, Subway 🛏 Holiday Inn/rest., Motel 6, **W** 🅿 Speedway/dsl 🍴 Harry's Cafe 🛏 Candlewood Suites 🅾 Aldi, Walmart/Subway, **N** 🛏 Hampton Inn
76	rd 2, Elko, **W** 🍴 Endzone Grill 🅾 Elko Speedway
76mm	Ⓡ🅢 sb, full 🚻 facilities, 🅲, 🛋, litter barrels, vending, petwalk
69	MN 19, to Northfield, New Prague, **7 mi E** 🅿 KwikTrip 🍴 Applebee's, Big Steer Rest., Caribou Coffee, McDonald's, Quarterback Rest., Subway, Taco Bell 🛏 AmericInn, College City Motel, Country Inn&Suites, Super 8 🅾 Carleton Coll, 🅷, St Olaf Coll, **W** 🍴 🅙 *FLYING J*/Subway/dsl/scales/24hr
68mm	Ⓡ🅢 nb, full 🚻 facilities, 🅲, 🛋, litter barrels, vending, petwalk
66	rd 1, to Dundas, **1 mi W** 🍴 Boonie's Grill

59	MN 21, Faribault, **0-2 mi E** 🅿 KwikTrip, Speedway/Family Diner/dsl/scales/24hr 🍴 A&W, Arby's, Burger King, DQ, Hardee's, Joe's Cafe, KFC, Pizza Hut, Taco Bell, Taco John's 🛏 Best Value Inn, Days Inn, Grandstay 🅾 Aldi Foods, Buick/Chevrolet/GMC, Chrysler/Dodge/Jeep, O'Reilly Parts, repair, Satakah St Trail, vet, **W** 🅾 Harley-Davidson, **0-2 mi S** 🅾 Ford/Lincoln
56	MN 60, Faribault, **E** 🅿 KwikTrip 🍴 A&W, Asian Buffet, Burger King, Jimmy John's, KFC, Little Caesar's, McDonald's, Perkins, Subway, Taco John's 🅾 $Tree, Aldi Foods, AutoValue Parts, AutoZone, Buick/Chevrolet/GMC, Chrysler/Dodge/Jeep, Family$, Goodyear/auto, 🅷, Hy-Vee Foods/dsl, Jo-Ann, O'Reilly Parts, Petsmart, TrueValue, Verizon, Walmart/Subway, **W** 🍴 DQ 🛏 Regency Inn 🅾 Sakatah Lake SP same as 59
55	rd 48, (from nb, no return), **1 mi E** 🅿 KwikTrip, Mobil/dsl, SA/dsl 🍴 A&W, Arby's, Broaster Rest., Burger King, DQ, El Tequila Mexican, KFC, Southern China Cafe, Subway, Taco John's
48	rd 12, rd 23, Medford, **E** 🅿 Casey's/dsl, **W** 🍴 McDonald's 🅾 Outlet Mall/famous brands
45	rd 9, Clinton Falls, **W** 🅿 KwikTrip/dsl/scales 🍴 Caribou Coffee, Famous Dave's BBQ, Sportsman's Grille, Subway, TimberLodge Steaks, Wendy's 🛏 Comfort Inn, Motel 6 🅾 Buick/Chevrolet/Cadillac, Cabela's Sporting Goods, Russell-Stover Candies
43	rd 34, 26th St, Owatonna, **E** 🅾 Camping World, **W** 🅾 🅷
42b a	US 14 W, rd 45, to Waseca, Owatonna, **E** 🍴 Hardee's, Kernel Rest. 🛏 Valu Stay Inn 🅾 AutoZone, CashWise Foods, Chrysler/Dodge/Jeep, Ford/Lincoln, O'Reilly Parts, repair, vet, **W** 🅿 KwikTrip/dsl 🍴 Buffalo Wild Wings, Culver's, Don Juan Cantina, East Wind Buffet, McDonald's, Olivia's Rest., Panda Express, Perkins 🛏 Best Budget Inn, Super 8 🅾 $Tree, Aldi, GNC, Kohl's, Lowe's, Verizon, Walmart/Subway
41	Bridge St, Owatonna, **E** 🅿 Holiday/dsl 🍴 Applebee's, Arby's, Asian Kitchen, Burger King, DQ, Jimmy John's, KFC, Papa Murphy's, Red&Green Burrito, Starbucks, Subway, Taco Bell 🛏 Baymont Inn, Country Inn&Suites 🅾 Verizon, **W** 🅿 F&F/dsl 🛏 Microtel 🅾 Target
40	US 14 E, US 218, Owatonna, **1 mi E on rd 45** 🍴 Godfather's, Little Caesar's, Taco John's 🛏 Oakdale Motel 🅾 Hy-Vee Foods/dsl, vet, Walgreens, WholesaleTire
38mm	Turtle Creek
35mm	Ⓡ🅢 both lanes, full 🚻 facilities, 🅲, 🛋, litter barrels, vending, petwalk
34.5mm	Straight River
32	rd 4, Hope, **1/2 mi E** 🅾 Hope Oak Knoll Camping, **1 mi W** 🅿 gas 🍴 food
26	MN 30, to Blooming Prairie, Ellendale, **W** 🅿 Casey's/dsl/scales
22	rd 35, to Hartland, Geneva, **1 mi E** 🍴 food

Vertical labels: FARIBAULT, OWATONNA

🅖 = gas 🍴 = food 🛏 = lodging 🄾 = other 🆁🆂 = rest stop Copyright 2022 - The Next EXIT ®

INTERSTATE 35 Cont'd

Exit #	Services
18	MN 251, to Hollandale, Clarks Grove, W 🅖 BP/dsl/LP
17mm	weigh sta both lanes
13b a	I-90, W to Sioux Falls, E to Austin, W 🄾 🄷
12	US 65 S (from sb), Lp 35, Albert Lea same as 11
11	rd 46, Albert Lea, E 🅖 ⬭Loves⬭/Wendy's/dsl/scales/24hr, Petro/Iron Skillet/McDonald's/Pizza Hut/dsl/scales/24hr/@ 🍴 Comfort Inn, Holiday Inn Express 🄾 dsl repair, KOA (may-oct/6mi), to Myre-Big Island SP, W 🅖 Casey's, KwikTrip 🍴 Burger King, Casa Zamora Mexican, GreenMill Rest., KFC, Perkins, Subway, Taco John's, Taco King, Trumble's Rest., Wok'n Roll 🛏 Best Value Inn, Country Inn&Suites, Countryside Inn, Heritage Hotel, Motel 6 🄾 $Tree, Advance Parts, AutoValue Parts, AutoZone, Buick/GMC, CarQuest, Chrysler/Dodge/Jeep, Ford, Home Depot, Honda, 🄷, Lincoln, NAPA, Nissan/VW, O'Reilly Parts, Volvo Trucks, Walmart/Subway
9mm	Albert Lea Lake
8	US 65, Lp 35, Albert Lea, 2 mi W 🅖 Freeborn City Co-op/dsl 🍴 DQ, Hardee's
5	rd 13, to Glenville, Twin Lakes, 3 mi W 🄾 camping
2	rd 5
1mm	Welcome Ctr nb, full 🅢 facilities, 🄲, 🄿, litter barrels, vending, petwalk
0mm	Minnesota/Iowa state line

INTERSTATE 35 West

Exit #	Services
41mm	I-35W begins/ends on I-35, exit 127.
36	rd 23, E 🅖 Holiday/dsl, W 🅖 Minnoco/dsl 🍴 Caribou Coffee, Don Julio, DQ, McDonald's, Subway, Tasty Asia 🛏 Hampton Inn 🄾 AT&T, Discount Tire, Kohl's, Super Target, Verizon
33	rd 17, Lexington Ave, E 🅖 F&F/dsl, Holiday/dsl 🍴 Burger King, Walmart/Subway 🄾 Aldi Foods, W 🍴 Applebee's, Arby's, Bonfire Rest., Caribou Coffee, Green Mill Rest., Taco Bell, Wendy's, Zantigo's Mexican 🄾 Cub Foods, GNC, Home Depot, Michael's, Walgreens
32	95th Ave NE, to Lexington, Circle Pines, W 🄾 Nat Sports Ctr
31b a	Lake Dr, E 🅖 Shell/Circle K/dsl 🍴 Quizno's, Red Ginger Asian 🛏 Country Inn&Suites
30	US 10 W, MN 118, to MN 65
29	rd I, W 🅖 Cenex/dsl
28c b	rd 10, rd H, W 🅖 BP 🍴 McDonald's, Mermaid Café, Taco Bell 🛏 AmericInn, Days Inn
28a	MN 96, E 🅖 Holiday/dsl, W 🛏 Homewood Suites
27b a	I-694 E and W
26	rd E2, W 🅖 Exxon/Circle K/dsl 🍴 Jimmy John's, Limu Coffee 🄾 USPO
25b	MN 88, to Roseville (no EZ return to sb) same as 25a
25a	rd D (from nb), E 🅖 BP/dsl 🛏 Courtyard, Fairfield Inn, Residence Inn, W 🅖 Marathon/dsl, SA/dsl, Shell 🍴 Barley John's, Caribou Coffee, Jake's Café, McDonald's, New Hong Kong, Perkins/24hr, Sarpino's Italian, Subway
24	rd C, E 🍴 Burger King, India Palace Rest., Joe Senser's Rest. 🛏 Hampton Inn, Home 2 Suites, Key Inn, Motel 6, Radisson 🄾 USPO, Walmart, W 🛏 Holiday Inn Express 🄾 Buick/GMC, Chevrolet, Chrysler/Dodge/Jeep, Norm's Tires
23b	Cleveland Ave, MN 36
23a	MN 280, Industrial Blvd (from sb)

Exit #	Services
22	MN 280, Industrial Blvd (from nb), E 🛏 Ramada Plaza
21b a	Broadway St, Stinson Blvd, E 🅖 Ford/Isuzu Trucks, W 🍴 Baj-Sol, Burger King, Caribou Coffee, Leeann Chin, McDonald's, Taco Bell 🄾 Cub Foods, GNC, Home Depot, Target
19	E Hennepin (from nb)
18	US 52, 4th St SE, University Ave, to U of MN
17c	11th St, Washington Ave, E 🛏 Courtyard, W 🅖 Mobil 🄾 🄷, US Bank Stadium
17b	I-94 W (from sb)
17a	MN 55, Hiawatha
16b a	I-94 (from nb), E to St Paul, W to St Cloud, to MN 65
15	31st St (from nb), Lake St, E 🍴 McDonald's, Taco Bell 🄾 Auto Zone, 🄷
14	35th St, 36th St
13	46th St
13mm	Minnehaha Creek
12b	Diamond Lake Rd
12a	60th St (from sb), W 🅖 Mobil 🄾 Cub Foods
11b	MN 62 E, to 🔄 🄾 to 🔄
11a	Lyndale Ave (from sb)
10b	MN 62 W, 58th St
10a	rd 53, 66th St, E 🅖 SA
9c	76th St (from sb)
9b a	I-494, MN 5, to 🔄 🄾 to 🔄
8	82nd St, E 🄾 BMW, W 🍴 Applebee's, Caribou Coffee, Jimmy John's, Panda Express, Red Lobster, Sonic, Starbucks, Subway, Timberlodge Steaks, Wendy's 🛏 Embassy Suites 🄾 Chevrolet, Chrysler/Dodge/Jeep, GNC, Infiniti, Kia, Kohl's, TJ Maxx, Verizon, Walgreens
7b	90th St
7a	94th St, E 🄾 Goodyear/auto, W 🛏 Holiday Inn
6	rd 1, 98th St, E 🍴 Applebee's, Bakers Square, Domino's, Jimmy John's, Leeann Chin, McDonald's, Starbucks, Subway, Wendy's, White Castle 🄾 Bloomington Drug, Festival Foods, Ford, URGENT CARE, Walgreens, W 🅖 SA/dsl
5	106th St
5mm	Minnesota River
4b	113th St, Black Dog Rd
4a	Cliff Rd, E 🄾 Dodge, Subaru, Walmart
3b a	MN 13, Shakopee, Canterbury Downs, W 🍴 Perkins
2	Burnsville Pkwy, E 🅖 BP 🍴 Carbone's Pizza, W 🅖 Holiday 🍴 Clive's Roadhouse, Denny's, Gourmet Chinese, Perkins 🛏 Best Value Inn, LivInn, Norwood Inn, Prime Rate Motel 🄾 auto repair, vet
1	rd 42 (from sb), Crystal Lake Rd, E 🅖 Shell 🍴 Arby's, Burger King, Chianti Grill, HoneyBaked Ham, McDonald's, Old Country Buffet, Roasted Pear, Taco Bell 🛏 AmericInn, Best Western, Fairfield Inn, Hampton Inn 🄾 Home Depot, 🄷, Lunds&Byerly's Mkt, PetsMart, W 🅖 Holiday/dsl, SA/dsl 🍴 Applebee's, Buca Italian, Burger Jones, Burger King, Cam Ranh Bay, Chick-fil-A, Chili's, Chipotle, ChuckECheese, IHOP, Jimmy John's, KFC, LeAnn Chin, Little Caesar's, Noodles&Co, Olive Garden, Outback Steaks, Panera Bread, Papa John's, Papa Murphy's, Pizza Hut, Porter Creek Grill, Red Lobster, Royal Buffet, Shogun Japanese, Smashburger, Starbucks, TGIFriday's, Wendy's 🛏 InTown Suites 🄾 $Tree, Ace Hardware, Advance Parts, AT&T, Barnes&Noble, Best Buy, Costco/gas, Cub Foods, Dick's, Discount Tire, JC Penney, Kohl's, Macy's, mall, Michael's, Old Navy, PetCo, Sears/auto, Target, Tires+, Tuesday Morning, Verizon, VW, Walgreens
	I-35W begins/ends on I-35, exit 88a.

INTERSTATE 90

Exit #	Services
278mm	Minnesota/Wisconsin state line, Mississippi River
276	US 14, US 61, to MN 16, La Crescent, **N** Welcome Ctr wb, full 🅐 facilities, info, 🅒, 🅐, litter barrels, vending, petwalk, **S** 🅖 Kwik Trip (1mi)
273b a	Dresbach
271	Dakota
270	US 14, US 61, to Winona (from wb), **N** to OL Kipp SP/camping
267	rd 12, Nodine, **N** 🅞 Great River Bluffs SP, **S** 🅖 Kwik Trip/Hearty Platter Rest./dsl/e-85/scales/24hr/@
261mm	weigh sta both lanes
258	MN 76, to Houston, Ridgeway, Witoka, **N** 🅖 gas, **S** 🅞 camping
252	MN 43 N, to Winona, 7 mi **N** 🅕 Taco Bell 🅐 Express Inn, Holiday Inn Express, Plaza Hotel, Quality Inn 🅞 🅗, **S** 🅞 vet
249	MN 43 S, to Rushford, **N** 🅞 Peterbilt Trucks/repair
244mm	🆁🆂 eb, full 🅐 facilities, 🅒, 🅐, litter barrels, vending, petwalk
242	rd 29, Lewiston
233	MN 74, to Chatfield, St Charles, **N** 🅖 Kwik Trip/LP/24hr (2mi) 🅕 A&W (2mi), Subway (2mi) 🅞 Whitewater SP, **S** 🅖 BP/Amish Ovens Rest./dsl/RV dump/LP
229	rd 10, Dover
224	MN 42, rd 7, Eyota, **N** 🅖 KwikTrip/dsl/e85 (3mi) 🅕 Country Cafe (3mi)
222mm	🆁🆂 wb, full 🅐 facilities, 🅒, 🅐, litter barrels, vending, petwalk
218	US 52, to Rochester, **S** 🅖 BP/dsl 🅞 KOA (Mar-Oct) (1mi)
209b a	US 63, MN 30, to Rochester, Stewartville, 8-10 mi **N** 🅐 Clarion, EconoLodge, Hampton Inn, Super 8, **S** 🅖 KwikTrip/dsl 🅕 DQ, Pizza Ranch, Subway 🅐 Best Inn 🅞 Family$, Verizon
205	rd 6
202mm	🆁🆂 eb, full 🅐 facilities, 🅒, 🅐, litter barrels, vending, petwalk
193	MN 16, Dexter, **N** 🅖 BP/Oasis Rest./dsl, **S** 🅐 Windmill Motel
189	rd 13, to Elkton
187	rd 20, **S** 🅞 Jellystone Camping
183	MN 56, to Rose Creek, Brownsdale, **S** 🅖 Freeborn County Co-op/dsl/LP
181	28th St NE
180b a	US 218, 21st St NE, to Austin, Oakland Place, **S** 🅖 Shell 🅐 Rodeway Inn
179	11th Dr NE, to Austin, **N** 🅖 KwikTrip/dsl/24hr
178b	6th St NE, to Austin, **S** 🅞 Spam Museum
178a	4th St NW, **N** 🅕 Culver's, Jimmy John's, Perkins, Torge's Grille 🅐 AmericInn, Days Inn, Holiday Inn 🅞 Buick/Chevrolet/GMC, vet, **S** 🅖 KwikTrip/dsl 🅕 Burger King, Hardee's, Subway 🅞 🅗
177	US 218 N, to Owatonna, Austin, Mapleview, **N** 🅕 Applebee's, Arby's, China Star, El Patron Mexican, KFC, King Buffet, Pizza Hut, Pizza Ranch, Wendy's 🅞 $Tree, Aldi Foods, AT&T, AutoZone, Hy-Vee Foods/gas, JoAnn Fabrics, O'Reilly Parts, Verizon, Walmart/Subway, Younkers, **S** 🅖 Sinclair/McDonald's/dsl 🅐 Super 8
175	MN 105, rd 46, to Oakland Rd, **N** 🅐 Econolodge, **S** 🅖 BP/dsl, Shell/dsl 🅞 Chrysler/Dodge/Jeep, Ford/Lincoln, vet
171mm	🆁🆂 wb, full 🅐 facilities, 🅒, 🅐, litter barrels, petwalk
166	rd 46, Oakland Rd, **N** 🅞 KOA/LP
163	rd 26, Hayward, **S** 🅖 Freeborn County Co-op/dsl 🅕 McDonald's (4mi), Pizza Hut (4mi), Trails Rest. (4mi) 🅐 Holiday Inn Express (4mi) 🅞 KOA, Myre-Big Island SP
161.5mm	🆁🆂 eb, full 🅐 facilities, 🅒, 🅐 litter barrels, petwalk
159b a	I-35, N to Twin Cities, S to Des Moines

Exit #	Services
157	rd 22, Albert Lea, **N** 🅞 dsl repair, **S** 🅖 HyVee/dsl, KwikTrip/dsl 🅕 Applebee's, Arby's, Caribou Coffee, DQ, McDonald's, Pizza Ranch, Plaza Morina Mexican, Qdoba 🅐 AmericInn, Best Western+ 🅞 Ace Hardware, Chevrolet, Harley-Davidson, 🅗, Hy-Vee, Hy-Vee Foods, Verizon
154	MN 13, to US 69, to Manchester, Albert Lea, **N** 🅖 Speedway/dsl
146	MN 109, to Wells, Alden, **S** 🅖 Cenex/dsl/rest., Freeborn Co-Op Gas/dsl/E-85 🅞 truck/dsl repair
138	MN 22, to Wells, Keister, **N** 🅖 Casey's (6mi)
134	MN 253, rd 21, to Bricelyn, MN Lake
128	MN 254, rd 17, Frost, Easton
119	US 169, to Winnebago, Blue Earth, **S** 🅖 Blue Earth/dsl, Shell/dsl 🅕 Country Kitchen, DQ, McDonald's, Pizza Hut, Subway 🅐 AmericInn, Super 8 🅞 $General, 🅗, Jolly Green Giant Bomgaars
119mm	🆁🆂 both lanes, full 🅐 facilities, 🅒, 🅐, litter barrels, petwalk, playground
113	rd 1, Guckeen
107	MN 262, rd 53, to East Chain, Granada, **S** 🅞 camping (May-Oct) (1mi), gas/dsl
102	MN 15, to Madelia, Fairmont, **N** 🅖 Verizon, Walmart/Subway, 0-2 mi **S** 🅖 Cenex/dsl, KwikTrip, Speedway/dsl/24hr 🅕 Arby's, Bean Town a Grill, Burger King, China Buffet, DQ, Green Mill Rest., Hardee's, McDonald's, Perkins, Pizza Ranch, Ranch Family Rest., Subway 🅐 Budget Inn, Hampton Inn, Holiday Inn, Quality Inn, Super 8 🅞 $Tree, Ace Hardware, Advance Parts, auto repair, Chevrolet, Chrysler/Dodge/Jeep, Fareway Foods, Ford, Freightliner, Goodyear/auto, 🅗, Hy-Vee Foods, NAPA, O'Reilly Parts, USPO, Walgreens
99	rd 39, Fairmont
93	MN 263, rd 27, Welcome, 1/2 mi **S** 🅖 camping, Casey's/dsl
87	MN 4, Sherburn, **N** 🅞 Fox Lake Camping (3mi), **S** 🅖 Casey's/dsl, Kum&Go/Subway/dsl/E-85
80	rd 29, Alpha
73	US 71, Jackson, **N** 🅖 Speedway/dsl 🅕 Burger King 🅐 EconoLodge, Super 8 🅞 KOA, to Kilen Woods SP, **S** 🅖 BP/DQ, Casey's/dsl 🅕 Pizza Ranch, Santee Rest., Subway 🅐 AmericInn, Earth Inn, Prairie Winds Motel 🅞 Ace Hardware, Buick/Chevrolet, Chrysler/Dodge/Jeep, city park, Family$, 🅗, Sunshine Foods, to Spirit Lake
72.5mm	W Fork Des Moines River
72mm	🆁🆂 wb, full 🅐 facilities, 🅒, 🅐, litter barrels, vending, petwalk
69mm	🆁🆂 eb, full 🅐 facilities, 🅒, 🅐, litter barrels, vending, petwalk
64	MN 86, Lakefield, **N** 🅖 gas/dsl 🅕 food 🅞 camping, to Kilen SP (12mi)
57	rd 9, to Heron Lake, Spafford
50	MN 264, rd 1, to Brewster, Round Lake
47	rd 3 (from eb, no return)

AUSTIN

ALBERT LEA

FAIRMONT

🛢 = gas 🍽 = food 🛏 = lodging ⊙ = other 🅁🅂 = rest stop   Copyright 2022 - The Next EXIT ®

🛡 INTERSTATE 90 Cont'd

Exit #	Services
46mm	weigh sta eb
45	MN 60, Worthington, N 🛢 BP/Blueline Cafe/dsl/scales, S 🛢 Holiday/dsl/scales/24hr ⊙ dsl repair, truckwash
43	US 59, Worthington, N 🛢 Casey's/dsl 🛏 Comfort Suites, Norwood Inn, S 🛢 Casey's, Cenex/dsl, Shell 🍽 Arby's, Burger King, DQ, Ground Round, Hardee's, Jimmy John's, KFC, McDonald's, New City Buffet, Perkins, Pizza Hut, Pizza Ranch, Subway, Taco John's 🛏 AmericInn, Holiday Inn Express ⊙ $General, Ace Hardware, CarQuest, Chevrolet, Fareway Foods, Ford, Ⓗ, Hy-Vee Foods/dsl, NAPA, O'Reilly Parts, Verizon, Walgreens, Walmart/Subway
42	MN 266, rd 25, to Reading, S 🛏 Days Inn, Super 8
33	rd 13, to Wilmont, Rushmore
26	MN 91, Adrian, S 🛢 Cenex/dsl, Kum&Go/Subway/dsl/E-85/24hr 🍽 Countryside Steaks ⊙ $General, Adrian Camping, city park
25mm	🅁🅂 wb, full 🅳 facilities, 🅲, 🖼, litter barrels, petwalk
24mm	🅁🅂 eb, full 🅳 facilities, 🅲, 🖼, litter barrels, petwalk
18	rd 3, Kanaranzi, Magnolia, N ⊙ camping
12	US 75, Luverne, N 🛢 BP/dsl/E-85, Casey's/dsl, Holiday/Subway/dsl 🍽 McDonald's, Papa's Place Rest., Taco John's, Tasty Drive-In 🛏 Cozy Rest Motel (1mi), GrandStay Hotel, Quality Inn ⊙ $General, Buick/Cadillac/Chevrolet/GMC, Chrysler/Dodge/Jeep, Ford, Ⓗ, Lewis Drugs, Pipestone NM, Sturdevant's Parts, to Blue Mounds SP, S 🍽 Blue Stem Rest. 🛏 Super 8
5	rd 6, Beaver Creek, N 🛢 Local/dsl
3	rd 4 (from eb), Beaver Creek
1	MN 23, rd 17, to Jasper, N ⊙ access to gas/dsl, to Pipestone NM
0mm	Minnesota/South Dakota state line, Welcome Ctr eb, full 🅳 facilities, info, 🅲, 🖼, litter barrels

🛡 INTERSTATE 94

Exit #	Services
259mm	Minnesota/Wisconsin state line, St Croix River
258	MN 95 N, to Stillwater, Hastings, Lakeland, N 🍽 Bungalow Rest.
257mm	Welcome Ctr wb, full 🅳 facilities, 🅲, 🖼, litter barrels, vending, petwalk, weigh sta wb
253	MN 95 S, rd 15, Manning Ave, N ⊙ StoneRidge Golf, S ⊙ ski area, to Afton Alps SP
251	rd 19, Keats Ave, Woodbury Dr, S 🛢 KwikTrip, Speedway/dsl 🍽 Applebee's, Arby's, Burger King, Caribou Coffee, Chili's, Chipotle Mexican, ChuckECheese, Culver's, Dino's Rest., Dunn Bros Coffee, Fiesta Brava, Jersey Mike's, Lakes Grill, LeeAnn Chin, Little Chopstix, McDonald's, Noodles&Co, Papa Murphy's, Quiznos, Ray J's Grill, SmashBurger, Starbucks, Subway, Which Wich? 🛏 Extended Stay America, Holiday Inn Express ⊙ $Tree, AT&T, Discount Tire, Hobby Lobby, Michael's, Sam's Club/gas, Staples, Target, Trader Joe's, Verizon, Walmart/Subway, Woodbury Lakes Outlets/famous brands
250	rd 13; Radio Dr, Inwood Ave, N 🍽 Buffalo Wild Wings, Caribou Coffee, Five Guys, Machine Shed Rest., Milio's Rest., Olive Garden, Red Lobster 🛏 Hilton Garden, Holiday Inn ⊙ Best Buy, S 🛢 Holiday/e85 🍽 Domino's, DUC Vietnamese, Firehouse Subs, Jamba Juice, Little Caesar's, Pei Wei, Piada Italian, Pie Five, Potbelly, Qdoba, Starbucks, Taco Bell, Tamarack Rest., Wendy's, Wild Bill's Grill, Zupas 🛏 Courtyard, Residence Inn ⊙ Aldi Foods, BigLots, Cabela's, Cub Foods, CVS Drug, Dick's, Fannie May, GNC, Gordman's, Heppner's Auto Ctr, Home Depot, JC Penney, Jo-Ann, LandsEnd Inlet, Old Navy, Petsmart, Tires+, Verizon, vet

Exit #	Services
249	I-694 N & I-494 S
247	MN 120, Century Ave, N 🍽 Denny's 🛏 LivInn ⊙ Harley-Davidson, S 🛢 SA/dsl 🍽 GreenMill Rest. 🛏 Country Inn/rest. ⊙ CarQuest, Chevrolet
246c b	McKnight Ave, N ⊙ 3M, S 🛏 Holiday Inn 🍽
246a	Ruth St (from eb, no return), N 🛢 BP 🍽 Culver's, Domino's, Hoho Chinese, Jimmy John's, Leeann Chin ⊙ $Tree, Cub Foods, Firestone/auto, GNC, TJ Maxx
245	White Bear Ave, N 🛢 SA/dsl 🍽 Subway 🛏 Motel 6 ⊙ Walgreens, S 🛢 BP 🍽 Arby's, Davanni's Pizza/subs, Los Ocampo, McDonald's, Papa John's, Popeye's, Sonic, Taco Bell, Wendy's ⊙ Aldi Foods, Family$, NAPA, O'Reilly Parts, Target
244	US 10 E, US 61 S, S ⊙ Mounds/Kellogg
243	US 61, Mounds Blvd, S River Centre
242d	US 52 S, MN 3, 6th St, (exits left from wb), N 🛢 Holiday/dsl 🍽 Subway
242c	7th St, S 🛢 SA
242b a	I-35E N, US 10 W, I-35E S (from eb)
241c	I-35E S (from wb)
241b	10th St, 5th St to downtown
241a	12th St, Marion St, Kellogg Blvd, N 🛏 Best Western+, S ⊙ St Paul's Cathedral
240	Dale Ave
239b a	Lexington Pkwy, Hamline Ave, N 🛢 BP, SA 🍽 DQ, Hardee's, Leeann Chin, Noodles&Co, Popeye's, White Castle ⊙ $Tree, Aldi, AutoZone, Cub Foods, Discount Tire, Herberger's, O'Reilly Parts, Target, TJ Maxx, Verizon, S ⊙ Ⓗ
238	MN 51, Snelling Ave, N 🍽 Culver's, Little Caesar's, McDonald's, Peking Garden, Perkins ⊙ CVS Drug, Family$, GNC, Rainbow Foods, same as 239, Walgreens, Walmart/Subway, S ⊙ Tires+
237	Cretin Ave, Vandalia Ave to downtown
236	MN 280, University Ave to downtown
235b	Huron Blvd
235mm	Mississippi River
235a	Riverside Ave, 25th Ave, N 🛢 Fina 🍽 Starbucks, S 🍽 Perkins, Taco Bell
234c	Cedar Ave downtown
234b a	MN 55, Hiawatha Ave, 5th St, N 🛏 Courtyard ⊙ to downtown
233b	I-35W N, I-35W S (exits left from wb)
233a	11th St (from wb), N downtown
231b	Hennepin Ave, Lyndale Ave to downtown
231a	I-394, US 12 W to downtown
230	US 52, MN 55, 4th St, 7th St, Olson Hwy, N ⊙ US Bank Stadium, S ⊙ Ⓗ, Int Mkt Square
229	W Broadway, Washington Ave, N 🛢 EZ Stop/dsl, Holiday/dsl 🍽 Broadway Pizza, S 🛢 Winner 🍽 Burger King, Little Caesar's, McDonald's, Subway, Taco Bell, Wendy's ⊙ $Tree, AutoZone, Cub Foods, Family$, Walgreens
228	Dowling Ave N
226	53rd Ave N, 49th Ave N
225	I-694 E, MN 252 N, to Minneapolis
I-94 and I-494 run together. See I-494/694, exits 28-34.	
216	I-94 W and I-494
215	rd 109, Weaver Lake Rd, N 🛢 SA/dsl, Shell 🍽 Angeno's, Arby's, Broadway Pizza, Burger King, Caribou Coffee, Chin Yung, ChuckECheese's, Domino's, DQ, El Rodeo Mexican, Famous Dave's BBQ, Frankie's Pizza, Golden Corral, Great Harvest Bread Co., Jimmy John's, McDonald's, Papa John's, Papa Murphy's, Rita's, Starbucks, Subway, Taco Bell, Wendy's ⊙ AT&T, Barnes&Noble, Cub Foods, GNC, Goodyear/auto, JC Penney, Kohl's, Lund&Byerly's Foods, Michael's, Midas, Old Navy, PetCo, same as 28, Tires+, USPO, Verizon, Walgreens, S 🍽 Applebee's

🅴 INTERSTATE 94 Cont'd

Exit #	Services
214mm	🆁🆂 eb, full 🅰 facilities, 🄲, �Ⓐ, litter barrels
213	rd 30, 95th Ave N, Maple Grove, **N** 🅿 SA/dsl 🍴 Chipotle Mexican, Subway 🛏 Cambria Suites 🄾 Aldi Foods, GNC, Home Depot, Ⓗ, Target, **S** 🅿 Holiday/dsl 🍴 Caribou Coffee, Culver's, Jersey Mike's, Jets Pizza, Leeann Chin, McDonald's, Starbucks, Teresa's Mexican, Which Wich?, White Castle 🄾 $Tree, AT&T, BigLots, Discount Tire, Firestone/auto, Goodyear/auto, Hobby Lobby, KOA (2mi) (Apr-Oct), Menards, Sam's Club/gas, Verizon, Walgreens, Walmart/Subway
212	101st Ave (from eb)
207	MN 101, to Elk River, Rogers, **N** 🅿 Holiday/dsl, SA/dsl, TA/Country Pride/dsl/scales/24hr/@ 🍴 Applebee's, Arby's, Burger King, China Kitchen, Chipotle, Culver's, Davanni's Pizza, Denny's, Dickey's BBQ, Domino's, DQ, Hardee's, Jimmy John's, Maynard's, McDonald's, Noodles&Co, Papa Murphy's, Starbucks, Subway, Taco Bell, Wendy's 🛏 Hampton Inn, Holiday Inn Express, Super 8 🄾 $Tree, AT&T, Cabela's, Camping World, Cub Foods, Discount Tire, GNC, Kohl's, NAPA, NTB, O'Reilly Parts, Target, Tires+, Verizon, vet, Walgreens, **S** 🅿 BP/Circle K/dsl, Holiday 🍴 BoBo Asian, Guadalajara Mexican, Minne's Diner 🛏 AmericInn 🄾 Chevrolet, CVS Drug, TrueValue, URGENT CARE, USPO
205.5mm	Crow River
205	MN 241, rd 36, St Michael, **S** 🅿 KwikTrip/dsl, SA/dsl
202	rd 37, Albertville, **N** 🅿 Shell/dsl 🍴 Emma Krumbee's Rest., **S** 🅿 BP/dsl, SA/dsl, same as 201
201	rd 19 (from eb), Albertville, St Michael, **N** 🍴 Andy's Pizza, Burger King, Five Guys, Hana Steaks, Michael B's Grill, Subway 🛏 Country Inn&Suites 🄾 Albertville Outlets/famous brands, Old Navy, **S** 🅿 Casey's, Mobil/Circle K 🍴 Caribou Coffee, China Dragon, Culver's, Little Caesar's, Papa Murphy's, Space Aliens Grill, Subway, Taco Bell 🄾 Ace Hardware, auto repair, Coburn's/dsl, Goodyear/auto, Verizon
194	rd 18, rd 39, Monticello, **N** 🅿 KwikTrip/dsl 🍴 Caribou Coffee, Little Caesar's 🄾 AT&T, GNC, Home Depot, Ⓗ, Marshall's, Petsmart, Target, Verizon
193	MN 25, to Buffalo, Monticello, Big Lake, **N** 🅿 Holiday/dsl 🍴 Burger King, Caribou Coffee, KFC, Papa Murphy's, Perkins, Quiznos, Rancho Grande Mexican, Taco Bell 🛏 AmericInn 🄾 AutoValue Parts, Cub Foods, USPO, Walgreens, **S** 🅿 Holiday/dsl, SA/dsl 🍴 Applebee's, Arby's, Buffalo Wild Wings, China Buffet, Culver's, DQ, Jimmy John's, McDonald's, Pizza Ranch, Subway, Taco John's 🛏 Best Western, Days Inn, Super 8 🄾 $Tree, Aldi Foods, AutoZone, Buick/GMC, Chevrolet, Goodyear/auto, Lake Maria SP, NAPA, O'Reilly Parts, Verizon, Walmart/Subway
187mm	🆁🆂 eb, full 🅰 facilities, 🄲, �Ⓐ, litter barrels, vending, petwalk
183	rd 8, to Silver Creek, Hasty, Maple Lake, **S** 🅿 SA/rest./dsl/scales/24hr/@ 🄾 camping, to Lake Maria SP
178	MN 24, to Annandale, Clearwater, **N** 🅿 Holiday/Petro/dsl/scales/24hr/@ 🍴 Burger King, DQ, Kettle, Subway, Taco Gringo 🛏 Best Value Inn 🄾 Clearwater Hardware, Coburn's Foods/gas, Parts City, repair, USPO, **S** 🄾 A-J Acres RV Camping (Apr-Oct), Recreation Outdoor RV Ctr
178mm	🆁🆂 wb, full 🅰 facilities, 🄲, �Ⓐ, litter barrels, petwalk, vending
173	Opportunity Dr
171	rd 7, rd 75, St Augusta, **N** 🅿 Pilot/dsl/scales/24hr, Shell/Burger King/dsl 🍴 McDonald's, RJ's Grill, Subway 🛏 AmericInn, Holiday Inn Express, Travelodge 🄾 Goodyear/auto, Ⓗ, **S** 🅿 BP 🄾 Freightliner, Pleasureland RV Ctr

*(left margin vertical text:* MONTICELLO)

167b a	MN 15, to St Cloud, Kimball, **4 mi N** 🅿 Holiday, SA/dsl 🍴 Applebee's, Arby's, Bonanza, Boulder Taphouse, Buffalo Wild Wings, Burger King, Caribou Coffee, Chick-fil-A, Chipotle, ChuckE-Cheese's, Coldstone, Famous Dave's BBQ, Five Guys, Granite City Grill, Grizzly's Grill, IHOP, La Casita Mexican, Leeann Chin, McDonald's, Noodles&Co, Old Chicago Pizza, Olive Garden, Panda Express, Perkins, Pizza Ranch, Red Lobster, Red Robin, Sammy's Pizza, Starbucks, Subway, Taco Bell, Taco John's, TX Roadhouse, Wendy's, White Castle 🛏 Country Inn&Suites, Days Inn, Fairfield Inn, Hampton Inn, Holiday Inn, Homewood Suites, Quality Inn, Super 8 🄾 AT&T, Barnes&Noble, Best Buy, CashWise Foods, Dick's, Fresh Thyme Mkt, Hobby Lobby, Home Depot, Ⓗ, JC Penney, Jo-Ann Fabrics, Kohl's, Macy's, Michael's, Office Depot, Old Navy, Petsmart, Sam's Club, Save-A-Lot, Scheel's Sports, Sears/auto, Subaru, Target, Walgreens, Walmart
164	MN 23, to St Cloud, Rockville, **4-6 mi N** 🅿 KwikTrip/dsl, SA/dsl 🍴 Culver's, IHOP, KFC, Subway, Wendy's 🛏 Astaria Inn 🄾 $Tree, Discount Tire, Grande Depot Gourmet Foods, Honda, Hyundai, Kia, Menards, Petsmart, same as 167, Toyota
162.5mm	Sauk River
160	rd 2, to Cold Spring, St Joseph, **N** 🅿 BP 🄾 Coll of St Benedict
158	rd 75 (from eb exits left), to St Cloud, **3 mi N** same as 160
156	rd 159, St Joseph, **S** 🄾 St Johns U
153	rd 9, Avon, **N** 🅿 Casey's/dsl, Tesoro/McDonald's/dsl 🍴 Subway 🛏 Budget Host 🄾 city park, USPO, **S** 🄾 El Rancho Manana Camping (10mi)
152mm	🆁🆂 both lanes, full 🅰 facilities, 🄲, �Ⓐ, litter barrels, vending, petwalk
147	MN 238, rd 10, Albany, **N** 🅿 Holiday/dsl, Shell/Godfather's/dsl 🍴 A&W/Subway, DQ, Hillcrest Rest. 🛏 Baymont Inn 🄾 CVS Drug, golf, Ⓗ, **S** 🅿 Chrysler/Dodge/Jeep, NAPA, vet
140	rd 11, Freeport, **N** 🅿 Cenex/dsl, Sinclair/dsl 🍴 Ackie's Pioneer Rest., Charlie's Café 🄾 auto repair, vet
137	MN 237, rd 65, New Munich
137mm	Sauk River
135	rd 13, Melrose, **N** 🅿 Sinclair/dsl/repair, Victory/Subway/dsl 🍴 Burger King, Cornerstone Buffet 🄾 $General, Ⓗ, **S** 🅿 Casey's/dsl 🍴 DQ, El Portal Mexican 🛏 Super 8 🄾 TrueValue, vet
132.5mm	Sauk River
131	MN 4, to Paynesville, Meire Grove
128mm	Sauk River
127	US 71, MN 28, Sauk Centre, **N** 🅿 Casey's, Holiday/dsl, Trillium CNG 🍴 DQ, Four Seas Buffet, Hardee's, McDonald's, Subway 🛏 AmericInn, Best Value Inn 🄾 Ace Hardware, Coburn's Foods, Ford, Ⓗ, NAPA, O'Reilly Parts, Sinclair Lewis Home, Verizon, Walmart/Subway, **S** 🅿 Shell/café/dsl/scales/24hr/@ 🄾 Buick/Chevrolet/Chrysler/Dodge/Jeep, Kenworth

*(vertical text between columns:* ST CLOUD)

 = gas   = food   = lodging   = other   = rest stop   Copyright 2022 - The Next EXIT ®

MN

INTERSTATE 94 Cont'd

Exit #	Services
124	Sinclair Lewis Ave (from eb), Sauk Centre
119	rd 46, West Union
114	MN 27, rd 3, to Westport, Osakis, **3 mi N** gas A&W, lodging, Subway
105mm	wb, full facilities, , , litter barrels, vending, petwalk
103	MN 29, to Glenwood, Alexandria, **N** F&F/dsl, Holiday/dsl, Simonson/dsl Arby's, Burger King, Caribou Coffee, China Buffet, Culver's, Dolittle's Grill, Great Hunan, Hardee's, Jimmy John's, KFC, McDonald's, Perkins, Qdoba, Subway, Taco Bell, TN Roadhouse, Wendy's AmericInn, Best Western, Days Inn, Hampton Inn, Super 8 $Tree, Aldi Foods, AT&T, AutoZone, Cadillac/Chevrolet/Mazda, Cub Foods, Goodyear/auto, Harley-Davidson, Herberger's, , Jo-Ann Fabrics, Mazda, Menards, Target, Verizon, Walmart/Subway, **S** Holiday/dsl Country Inn&Suites, Holiday Inn Alexandria RV Ctr, Buick/GMC
100	MN 27, **N** /Subway/dsl/scales/24hr/@ Best Inn/Alexandria RV Park (2mi) , **S** camping
100mm	Lake Latoka
99mm	eb, full facilities, , , litter barrels, vending, petwalk
97	MN 114, rd 40, to Lowry, Garfield
90	rd 7, Brandon, **S** camping, ski area
82	MN 79, rd 41, to Erdahl, Evansville, **2 mi N** BP/dsl , **S** camping
77	MN 78, rd 10, to Barrett, Ashby, **N** gas/dsl camping, **S** camping
69mm	wb, full facilities, , , litter barrels, petwalk, vending
67	rd 35, Dalton, **N** camping, **S** camping
61	US 59 S, rd 82, to Elbow Lake, **N** Tesoro/café/dsl/LP/24hr camping (4mi), , **S** camping
57	MN 210 E, rd 25, Fergus Falls, **N**
55	rd 1, to Wendell, Fergus Falls, **N** antiques
54	MN 210 W, Lincoln Ave, Fergus Falls, **N** Cenex/dsl, F&F/dsl, Tesoro/dsl Applebee's, Arby's, Burger King, Family Diner, Hardee's, Hunan Spring Buffet, Kenworth, McDonald's, Papa Murphy's, Perkins, Pizza Hut, Pizza Ranch, Subway, Thrifty White Drug AmericInn, Best Value Inn, Best Western, Comfort Inn, Motel 7, Super 8 $Tree, Aldi Foods, AT&T, Chrysler/Dodge/Jeep, Ford/Lincoln, GMC, Herberger's, Home Depot, , museum, NAPA, O'Reilly Parts, SunMart Foods/dsl, Target, Tires+, Toyota, USPO, **S** Mabel Murphy's Rest. Walmart
50	rd 88, rd 52, to US 59, to Fergus Falls, Elizabeth camping
38	rd 88, Rothsay, **S** Tesoro/cafe/dsl/24hr Powerhouse Grill Comfort Zone Inn tires
32	MN 108, rd 30, to Pelican Rapids, Lawndale, **19 mi N** Maplewood SP
24	MN 34, Barnesville, **N** Renee's Drive-in, **1 mi S** Cenex/dsl, Tesoro/dsl DQ, Subway $General, city park, Wagner Park Camping (May-Oct)
22	MN 9, Barnesville, **1 mi S** Cenex/dsl, Tesoro/dsl DQ, Subway $General
15	rd 10, Downer
8mm	Buffalo River
6	MN 336, rd 11, to US 10, Dilworth, **N** to Buffalo River SP
5mm	Red River weigh sta eb
2b	34th St, Moorhead, **2 mi N** Casey's/dsl, Holiday/dsl/e-85, Tesoro Arby's, Fry'n Pan, Hardee's, McDonald's, Perkins, Pizza Ranch, Subway Travelodge $Tree, CVS Drug, , Menards, Target, Tires+, Walmart/Subway
2a	no service

MOORHEAD

1mm	Welcome Ctr eb, full facilities, info, , , litter barrels, vending
1b	20th St, Moorhead (from eb, no return)
1a	US 75, Moorhead, **N** Cenex/dsl Burger King, Crave Burger Co., Jimmy John's, Little Caesar's, Noodles&Co, Papa Murphy's, Qdoba, Starbucks, Village Inn Courtyard Family Fare Foods, Verizon, **S** Casey's, Holiday/dsl, Microtel Panchero's Mexican, Sarpino's Pizza, Snapdragon Asian, Speak Easy Rest., Subaru, Subway Days Inn, Grand Inn, Super 8 CVS Drug, Hornbacher's Mkt, vet, Walgreens
0mm	Minnesota/North Dakota state line, Red River

INTERSTATE 494/694

Exit #	Services
	I-494/I-694 loops around Minneapolis/St Paul.
71	rd 31, Pilot Knob Rd, **N** Courtyard, Fairfield Inn, **S** Holiday Inn
70	I-35E, N to St Paul, S to Albert Lea
69	MN 149, MN 55, Dodd Rd, **S** Caribou Coffee, Jimmy John's, McDonald's Country Inn&Suites, Omni
67	MN 3, Roberts St, **1 mi N** BP, Holiday Applebee's, Arby's, Baker's Square, Burger King, Chick-fil-A, Chipotle Mexican, Culver's, Jimmy John's, KFC, Noodles&Co, Panda Express, Panera Bread, Papa Murphy's, Taco Bell, White Castle $Tree, Aamco, Aldi Foods, AT&T, Best Buy, Buick/GMC, Chevrolet, Cub Foods, Discount Tire, Ford, Home Depot, Honda, Hyundai, Kia, Lincoln, Lowe's, Mazda, NAPA, Nissan, NTB, O'Reilly Parts, PepBoys, Petco, Target, Toyota, VW, Wagreens, Walmart
66	US 52, **S** SA Applebee's, B-52 Burger, Outback Steaks AmericInn, Holiday Inn Express, Microtel
65	7th Ave, 5th Ave
64b a	MN 56, Concord St, **N** KwikTrip/dsl/scales Burger King, Subway Envision Hotel Goodyear, Peterbilt, Stockmens/dsl, **S** Holiday/dsl Chrysler/Jeep/Dodge, Parts+
63mm	Mississippi River
63c	Maxwell Ave
63b a	US 10, US 61, to St Paul, Hastings, **S** BP, Speedway Burger King, Subway Boyd's Motel NAPA
60	Lake Rd, **E** SA/dsl Carbone's Pizza, Milio's Sandwiches, **W**
59	Valley Creek Rd, **E** BP/repair, Speedway/dsl/LP Applebee's, Chipotle Mexican, Coldstone, DQ, Jersey Mike's, Jimmy John's, Noodles&Co, Panda Express, Papa Murphy's, Perkins, Potbelly, Red's Savoy Pizza, Starbucks, Yang's Chinese Key Inn $Tree, Barnes&Noble, GNC, Kohl's, Lunds&Byerly's Mkt, Marshall's, PetCo, Target, URGENT CARE, USPO, Walgreens, **W** Shell Bonfire Rest., Burger King, Keys Cafe, McDonald's, Sole Mio Italian, Subway Hampton Inn Ace Hardware, Goodyear,
58c	Tamarack Rd, **E** Tavern Grill, Woodbury Cafe La Quinta, Sheraton, **W** Woodspring Suites Costco/gas, URGENT CARE
58b a	I-94, E to Madison, W to St Paul. **I-494 S begins/ends, I-694 N begins/ends.**
57	rd 10, 10th St N, **E** SA/dsl IHOP, Pizza Man, Sgt Peppers Grill, Wild Boar Grill Best Western, **W** Holiday/dsl Burger King, Caribou Coffee, Hardee's, Hunan Buffet, KFC, Papa Murphy's, Starbucks $Tree, Cub Foods, HyVee/dsl
55	MN 5, **E** SA/dsl McDonald's Target, **W** Holiday/dsl, KwikTrip/dsl Subway Menards, st patrol
52b a	MN 36, N St Paul, to Stillwater, **W** F&F/dsl Burger King, Caribou Coffee, DQ

INTERSTATE 494/694 Cont'd

Exit #	Services
51	MN 120, **E** 🍴 BP, SA/dsl 🍴 Dulano's Pizza, Jethro's, Tacos Fresh, **W** 🍴 The Corner/gas 🅾 vet
50	White Bear Ave, **N** 🍴 SA/dsl 🅾 Cub Foods, Sam's Club/gas, **S** 🍴 Acapulco, Arby's, Bakers Square, Buffalo Wild Wings, Caribou Coffee, Chili's, Chipotle, Denny's, Great Moon Buffet, IHOP, Jake's Grill, Jimmy John's, McDonald's, Noodles&Co, Olive Garden, Osaka, Outback Steaks, Perkins/24hr, Pizza Hut, Pizza Ranch, Popeye's, Red Lobster, Taco Bell, TGI Friday, Wendy's 🏠 Emerald Inn 🅾 Aamco, Barnes&Noble, Best Buy, Firestone/auto, Hobby Lobby, JC Penney, Jo-Ann Fabrics, Kohl's, Macy's, mall, Marshall's, Michael's, Sears/auto, Tires+, Verizon, Walgreens
48	US 61, **N** 🍴 KwikTrip/dsl 🅾 Acura, Chrysler/Dodge/Jeep, Ford, Honda, Hyundai, Kia, Lincoln, Subaru, **S** 🍴 Chili's, Jake's Grill, McDonald's, Olive Garden, Subway 🅾 Audi/Porsche, CarMax, Costco/gas, 🏠, Lexus, Mercedes, Nissan, Toyota, Venburg Tire, Volvo
47	I-35E, N to Duluth
46	I-35E, US 10, S to St Paul
45	rd 49, Rice St, **N** 🍴 Gas+, Mobil/dsl 🍴 Subway, Taco Bell, **S** 🍴 Burger King, Caribou Coffee
43b	Victoria St
43a	Lexington Ave, **N** 🍴 Greenmill Rest., Red Robin 🏠 Best Western+, Hilton Garden, **S** 🍴 Exxon/Circle K/dsl 🍴 Arby's, Cane's, Caribou Coffee, Chipotle, Davanni's Pizza, Five Guys, Jimmy John's, Leeann Chin, Noodles&Co, Papa John's, Papa Murphy's, Perkins, Potbelly, Starbucks, Subway, Wendy's 🏠 Quality Inn 🅾 AT&T, Cub Foods, GNC, Target, Trader Joe's
42b	US 10 W (from wb), to Anoka
42a	MN 51, Snelling Ave, 1 mi **S** 🍴 Shell/dsl 🍴 Flaherty's Grill, Lindey's Steaks, McDonald's 🏠 Country Inn&Suites 🅾 vet
41b a	I-35W, S to Minneapolis, N to Duluth
40	Long Lake Rd, 10th St NW
39	Silver Lake Rd, **N** 🍴 BP 🍴 Acapulco Mexican, McDonald's, Subway 🅾 Ford, U-Haul
38b a	MN 65, Central Ave, **N** 🍴 Holiday/dsl 🍴 Subway, **S** 🍴 SA 🍴 A&W/KFC, Applebee's, Asia Rest., Big Marina Deli, Chipotle, Domino's, Embers Rest., Flameburger Rest., Jimmy John's, La Casita Mexican, Leeann Chin, Little Caesar's, McDonald's, Papa John's, Pizza Hut, Sonic, Starbucks, Subway, Taco Bell, Wendy's 🏠 LivInn Hotel 🅾 $General, Advance Parts, Aldi Foods, AT&T, AutoZone, Discount Tire, Menards, Noodles&Co, PetCo, Target, Tires+, vet, Walgreens
37	rd 47, University Ave, **N** 🍴 Holiday, SA/dsl 🍴 Burger King, McDonald's, Panchero's, Papa Murphy's Pizza, Zantigo's Rest. 🅾 Cub Foods, CVS Drug, Duluth Trading, Home Depot, NTB, **S** 🍴 Bona Bros/repair, Shell
36	E River Rd
35mm	**I-494 W begins/ends, I-694 E begins/ends.**
35c	MN 252, **N** 🍴 Holiday, SA
35b a	I-94 E to Minneapolis
34	to MN 100, Shingle Creek Pkwy, **N** 🍴 Denny's 🏠 Best Western, Country Inn&Suites, Doubletree, Extended Stay America, Motel 6, Norwood Inn, Quality Inn, Super 8, **S** 🍴 Ocean Buffet, Panera Bread, Rose Garden 🏠 Embassy Suites 🅾 AT&T, Target, Tires+, Walmart
33	rd 152, Brooklyn Blvd, **N** 🍴 SA/dsl 🍴 Culver's, Slim's Café, Subway 🅾 Buick/GMC, Chevrolet, Honda, Toyota, USPO, VW, **S** 🍴 BP 🅾 AutoZone, Family$, Sun Foods, Walgreens
31	rd 81, Lakeland Ave, **N** 🍴 SA/dsl 🍴 Chipotle Mexican, Wagner's Drive-In, Wendy's 🅾 CarMax, Target, U-Haul, **S** 🏠 Northstar Inn

30	Boone Ave, **N** 🏠 La Quinta, Marriott, **S** 🅾 Home Depot
29b a	US 169, to Hopkins, Osseo
28	rd 61, Hemlock Lane, **N on Elm Creek** 🍴 Arby's, Benihana, Biaggi's Italian, Buca Italian, Chick-fil-A, Chipotle Mexican, Coldstone, Dave&Buster's, Dickey's BBQ, Firehouse Subs, Five Guys, Freddy's, Granite City Rest., Leeann Chin, Malone's Grill, Mongo's Grill, Noodles&Co, Olive Garden, Panda Express, Panera Bread, Patrick's Cafe, PF Chang's, Pittsburgh Blue, Potbelly's, Red Lobster, Redstone Grill, Starbucks, Subway, TGIFriday's, Wild Bill's Café, Zupas 🏠 Courtyard, Hampton Inn, Holiday Inn, Staybridge Suites 🅾 $Tree, Best Buy, Costco/gas, Dick's, Jo-Ann Fabrics, Lowe's, Marshalls, Petsmart, REI, Trader Joe's, Verizon, Whole Foods Mkt, World Mkt, **S** 🍴 BP 🍴 Perkins 🏠 Asteria Suites
27	I-94 W to St Cloud, I-94/694 E to Minneapolis
26	rd 10, Bass Lake Rd, **E** 🍴 Freedom 🍴 Caribou Coffee, Culver's, McDonald's, Subway 🏠 Extended Stay America 🅾 vet, **W** 🍴 BP, Holiday/dsl 🍴 Jimmy John's, Pancake House, Pizza Hut, Rusty Taco, Solos Pizza 🏠 Hilton Garden 🅾 auto repair, CVS Drug
23	rd 9, Rockford Rd, **E** 🍴 Holiday 🍴 Chili's, Domino's, Five Guys, Sunshine Factory Grill 🅾 AT&T, GNC, Kohl's, O'Reilly Parts, PetsMart, Target, TJ Maxx, Walgreens, **W** 🍴 BP, Freedom/dsl 🍴 DQ, LeAnn Chin, Subway, Toppers Pizza 🍴 Caribou Coffee
22	MN 55, **E** 🍴 Holiday/dsl 🍴 Broadway Pizza, Caribou Coffee, Green Mill Rest., Jimmy John's, McDonald's, Red Robin, Solos Pizza, Starbucks, Subway 🏠 Crowne Plaza, Ramada, Red Roof Inn, Residence Inn, **W** 🍴 Holiday/dsl 🍴 Arby's, Burger King, Davanni's Rest., Firehouse Subs, Jake's Rest., Perkins, Wendy's 🏠 Comfort Inn, Days Inn 🅾 Goodyear/auto, Tires+
21	rd 6, **E** 🍴 KwikTrip 🅾 Discount Tire, Home Depot
20	Carlson Pkwy, **E** 🍴 Holiday/dsl 🍴 Pizza Hut, Subway, **W** 🍴 Grizzy's Grill 🏠 Country Inn&Suites
19b a	I-394 E, US 12 W, to Minneapolis, 1/2 mi **W** 🍴 BP, Holiday 🍴 Chipotle, Goodyear/auto, KFC, McDonald's 🅾 BMW, Chevrolet, Lexus, Nissan, 1 mi **E** off of I-394 🍴 Wendy's 🅾 Barnes&Noble, Best Buy, Ford, JC Penney, Jo-Ann Fabrics, Lunds&Byerly's Foods, Mazda, Mercedes, Office Depot, Petco, Subaru, Target, Tires+, Whole Foods
17b a	Minnetonka Blvd, **E** 🍴 Minnoco Gas 🍴 DQ, Royal Subs
16b a	MN 7, 1 mi **W** 🍴 Christo's Rest., Davanni's Rest., Famous Dave's BBQ, Taco Bell 🅾 Goodyear
13	MN 62, rd 62
12	Valleyview Rd, rd 39 (from sb)
11c	MN 5 W same as 11 a b
11b a	US 169 S, US 212 W, **N** 🍴 Don Pablo's, Jets Pizza, Subway 🏠 Comfort Inn, Courtyard, Fairfield Inn, Hyatt Place, Residence Inn 🅾 vet, **S** 🍴 BP, Holiday 🍴 Caribou Coffee, Champp's,

🅿 = gas 🍴 = food 🛏 = lodging Ⓞ = other Ⓡ🅂 = rest stop Copyright 2022 - The Next EXIT

↑E INTERSTATE 494/694 Cont'd

11b a	Continued
	Davanni's Rest., Jake's Grill, Leeann Chin, McDonald's, Old Chicago, Osaka Japanese, Panera Bread, Papa John's, Popeye's, Qdoba, Redstone Rest., Starbucks, Wildfire Steaks 🛏 Discount Tire, Extended Stay America, JC Penney, Office Depot, Sears/auto, SpringHill Suites, Target, TownePlace Suites, Walgreens, Walmart Ⓞ $Tree, Barnes&Noble, Best Buy, Costco/gas, Cub Foods, Petco
10	US 169 N, to rd 18
8	rd 28 (from wb, no return), E Bush Lake Rd same as 7 a b
7b a	MN 100, rd 34, Normandale Blvd, **N** 🅿 Shell/dsl 🍴 Burger King, Chili's, DQ, Jimmy John's, Starbucks, Subway, TGIFridays 🛏 Days Inn, Doubletree, Sheraton, **S** 🅿 Holiday/dsl 🍴 El Loro 🛏 Country Inn&Suites, Crowne Plaza, Hampton Inn, Hilton Garden, La Quinta, Staybridge Inn
6b	rd 17, France Ave, **N** 🅿 Mobil 🍴 Fuddrucker's, Perkins 🛏 Holiday Inn Express, Park Plaza Hotel, Residence Inn Ⓞ 🅷, Marshall's, Michael's, Staples, Trader Joe's, World Mkt, **S** 🍴 Denny's, Joe Senser's Grill, Olive Garden 🛏 AmericInn, Hilton Ⓞ Buick/GMC, Hyundai, Mercedes, Toyota
6a	Penn Ave (no EZ eb return), **S** 🍴 Applebee's, Caribou Coffee, Home 2 Suites, Jimmy John's, McDonald's, Red Robin, Starbucks, Subway, Which Wich? 🛏 Embassy Suites Ⓞ AT&T,

6a	Continued
	Chevrolet, Chrysler/Jeep/Dodge, Fresh Thyme Mkt, Herberger's, Hobby Lobby, Kohl's, Target, TJ Maxx, Walgreens
5b a	I-35W, S to Albert Lea, N to Minneapolis
4b	Lyndale Ave, **N** 🅿 BP, SA 🍴 Boston Mkt, Chipotle Mexica DQ, Eddie Cheng's, Noodles&Co, Papa John's, Potbelly, Sarpno's Pizza, Starbucks, Subway 🛏 Candlewood Suites, Sheratc Ⓞ Best Buy, Honda, Lands End, PetsMart, **S** 🛏 Extended Sta America Ⓞ Acura/Subaru, Lincoln, REI
4a	MN 52, Nicollet Ave, **N** 🅿 SA/dsl 🍴 Taco Bell Ⓞ Menards, **S** 🅿 Holiday/dsl 🍴 Culver's, McDonald's 🛏 La Quinta, Super 8 Ⓞ Home Depot, Sam's Club
3	Portland Ave, 12th Ave (from eb), **N** 🍴 Arby's, Khan's BBQ 🛏 AmericInn, **S** 🅿 BP 🍴 $Tree, Denny's, Jimmy John's, Outba Steaks, Pizza Hut, Subway 🛏 Comfort Inn, Microtel, Quali Inn, Residence Inn Ⓞ Walgreens, Walmart/Subway
2c b	MN 77, **N** 🅿 SA 🛏 Motel 6, **S** 🍴 Outback Steaks 🛏 Comfo Inn, Courtyard, Fairfield Inn, Hampton Inn, Hilton Garden, Marriott, Marriott, Northwood Inn, Radisson, Residence In SpringHill Suites, TownePlace Suites Ⓞ IKEA, Macy's, Mall America, Nordstrom's, Sears
2a	24th Ave same as 2c b
1b	34th Ave, Nat Cemetary, **N** 🅿 Holiday/dsl, **S** 🛏 Crowne Plaz Embassy Suites, Hilton, Hyatt Place, Hyatt Regency
1a	MN 5 E, **N** Ⓞ 🚉
0mm	Minnesota River. **I-494/I-694 loops around Minneapolis/St Pa**

NOTES

MISSISSIPPI

M O S S   P O I N T

🅴 INTERSTATE 10

Exit #	Services
77mm	Mississippi/Alabama state line, **weigh sta wb**
75	Franklin Creek Rd
75mm	Welcome Ctr wb, full ♿ facilities, Ⓒ, 🏪, litter barrels, petwalk, RV dump, weigh sta eb
74mm	Escatawpa River
69	MS 63, to E Moss Point, **N** 🅶 Raceway/dsl, Shell/Circle K/Domino's/dsl/24hr 🍴 Waffle House 🏠 Best Value, La Quinta, Motel 6, **S** 🅶 Chevron/dsl/24hr, Exxon/Subway/dsl, 🅿🆃🅻🅾🆃/Moe's SW/dsl/scales/24hr, Shell 🍴 Burger King, Cracker Barrel, Hardee's, KFC, McDonald's, Pizza Hut, Ruby Tuesday, San Miguel Mexican, Taco Bell, Waffle House, Wendy's 🏠 Best Western, Comfort Inn, Days Inn, EconoLodge, Hampton Inn, Holiday Inn Express, Quality Inn 🅾 🏥, Toyota
68	MS 613, to Moss Point, Pascagoula, **N** 🅶 Chevron/dsl, Texaco/dsl 🍴 Coco Loco Mexican, Tugus' Rest. 🏠 Super 8, **S** 🅶 Marathon/dsl 🅾 🏥, Pelican Landing Conf Ctr
64mm	Pascagoula River
63.5mm	Ⓡs both lanes, full ♿ facilities, Ⓒ, 🏪, litter barrels, petwalk, RV dump, 24hr security
61	to Gautier, **N** 🅾 MS Nat Golf Course, **1-3 mi S** 🅶 Marathon/dsl 🍴 Hardee's, KFC, McDonald's, Pizza Hut, Sonic, Wendy's 🏠 Best Western, Suburban Lodge 🅾 Sandhill Crane WR, Shephard Camping
57	MS 57, to Vancleave, **N** 🅶 Chevron/dsl/24hr 🍴 Shed BBQ 🅾 Journey's End Camping, tires/repair, **S** 🅶 Exxon
50	MS 609 S, Ocean Springs, **N** 🅶 Shell/Circle K/Domino's/dsl 🍴 Waffle House 🏠 Best Western+, Country Inn&Suites, Motel 6, Quality Inn, Ramada Ltd, Red Roof Inn, Super 8 🅾 Martin Lake Camping (1mi), tires/repair, **S** 🅶 Chevron/McDonald's, Circle K/Subway/dsl, Marathon/dsl, RaceTrac/dsl 🍴 Denny's, El Rancho Mexican, Waffle House, Wendy's 🏠 Comfort Suites, Days Inn, Hampton Inn, Holiday Inn Express, Magnuson 🅾 $General, $Tree, Nat Seashore

B I L O X I

46b a	I-110, MS 15 N, to Biloxi, **N** 🅶 Chevron/dsl, Murphy USA/dsl 🍴 Beef O'Brady's, Beijing Chinese, Buffalo Wild Wings, Chick-fil-A, Chili's, Cici's, Dickey's BBQ, Five Guys, IHOP, Logan's Roadhouse, Moe's SW Grill, Newk's Cafe, Olive Garden, Osaka Japanese, Outback Steaks, Panda Palace, Papa John's, Red Lobster, Ruby Tuesday, Salsarita's, Samurai, Sonic, Starbucks, Subway, Twin Peaks, Waffle House, Wendy's, Whataburger, Which Wich? 🏠 Comfort Inn, Courtyard, Home2 Suites, Regency Inn 🅾 AT&T, Best Buy, CVS, Dick's, GNC, Kohl's, Lowe's, Marshall's, Mercedes, Michaels, NTB, Office Depot, Petsmart, Ross, Target, URGENT CARE, Verizon, vet, VW, Walgreens, Walmart, **S** 🅾 BMW, Buick/GMC, 🏥, to beaches
44	Cedar Lake Rd, to Biloxi, **N** 🅶 ❤Loves/Subway/dsl/scales/24hr 🅾 Chevrolet, **S** 🅶 Exxon/Circle K/dsl, Shell/dsl 🍴 Applebee's, El Saltillo, KFC/LJ Silver, McDonald's, Pop's Pizza, Sonic, Subway, Taco Bell, Waffle House 🏠 La Quinta 🅾 $General, Biloxi Nat Cem, Cedar Lake Drug, Harley-Davidson, Home Depot, 🏥, O'Reilly Parts, to Jeff Davis Shrine (Beauvoir), vet
41	MS 67 N, to Woolmarket, **N** 🅶 Chevron/dsl, Texaco/dsl 🅾 golf (6mi), **S** 🅾 Camping World, Freightliner, Mazalea RV Prk, Parkers Landing RV Prk, Southern Tire Mart
39.5mm	Biloxi River

G U L F P O R T

38	Lorraine-Cowan Rd, **N** 🅶 Chevron/dsl, Exxon/Subway, Shell/Circle K/dsl 🍴 Domino's, McDonald's, Sonic 🅾 Toyota, **S** 🅶 RaceTrac/dsl 🅾 Baywood RV Park (3mi), Foxes RV Park (8mi), to beaches
34b a	US 49, to Gulfport, **N** 🅶 Circle K/dsl, Exxon, Shell/Circle K/dsl 🍴 Buffalo Wild Wings, Burger King, Cane's, Chick-fil-A, Chili's, ChuckeCheese, Cracker Barrel, Dickey's BBQ, Domino's, Firehouse Subs, Five Guys, Golden Corral, Hardee's, KFC, Krystal, Little Caesar's, Logan's Roadhouse, Longhorn Steaks, Marble Slab, McDonald's, Newk's Cafe, O'Charley's, O'Neal's PoBoy, Panda Palace, Papa John's, Pepper's Deli, Pizza Hut, Popeye's, Sicily's Italian Buffet, Sonic, Starbucks, Subway, Taco Bell, Taco Sombrero, TGIFriday's, TX Roadhouse, Waffle House, Wendy's, Whataburger 🏠 Hampton Inn, Home 2 Suites, Sleep Inn 🅾 $Tree, Advance Parts, AT&T, Barnes&Noble, Belk, Best Buy, Buick/Cadillac/Chevrolet, CVS Drug, Foley's RV Ctr, Food Giant/gas, Fred's Store, Goodyear/auto, Hobby Lobby, Honda, 🏥, Michael's, NTB, Office Depot, Old Navy, Petsmart, Rite Aid, Ross, Sam's Club/dsl, TJ Maxx, URGENT CARE, USPO, Walgreens, Winn-Dixie, **S** 🅶 Circle K/dsl, Murphy USA, RaceWay/dsl, Shell/dsl, Shell/Subway 🍴 Applebee's, Arby's, Aztecas Mexican, Burger King, Food Court, Hibachi Express, Hooters, IHOP, Jimmy John's, Krispy Kreme, McAlister's Deli, McDonald's,

GULFPORT

▲E INTERSTATE 10 Cont'd

34b a	Continued
	Shrimp Basket, Sonic, Taco Bell, Waffle House, Wendy's 🛏 Best Western, Comfort Suites, Days Inn, EconoLodge, Fairfield Inn, Hilton Garden, Holiday Inn, In Town Suites, Luxury Inn, Motel 6, Quality Inn, Red Roof Inn, Residence Inn, Super 8, Woodspring Suites 🅞 Ford/Lincoln, GNC, Home Depot, Mazda, Nissan, Petco, Premium Outlets/famous brands, repair, Verizon, Walmart/McDonald's
31	Canal Rd, to Gulfport, N 🅟 Exxon/Subway/dsl 🅞 Bayberry RV Park, S 🅟 ⊘FLYING J/Denny's/dsl/LP/scales/24hr, Pure Country/McDonald's/dsl/24hr 🍴 Waffle House, Wendy's 🛏 Comfort Inn, Legacy Inn
28	to Long Beach, N 🅟 ♥Love's/McDonald's/dsl/scales/24hr, S 🅟 Chevron/dsl, Shell/dsl 🍴 Subway 🅞 NAPA, tires/repair
27mm	Wolf River
24	Menge Ave, N 🅟 Chevron/Subway/dsl/scales 🅞 $General, S 🅟 Interstate/dsl 🅞 flea mkt/RV Park, golf, to beaches
20	to De Lisle, to Pass Christian, N 🍴 Kin-Mart
16	Diamondhead, N 🅟 Chevron/Domino's, Shell/dsl 🍴 Burger King, DQ, Pizza Hut, Red Zone Grill, Subway, Waffle House 🛏 Diamondhead Resort 🅞 $Tree, CVS, Family$, Rouse's Mkt, TrueValue, URGENT CARE, USPO, S 🅟 Giterdone/dsl 🍴 Harbor House Rest., La Rumba 🛏 EconoLodge
15mm	Jourdan River
13	MS 43, MS 603, to Kiln, Bay St Louis, N 🅞 McLeod SP, S 🅟 Exxon/Subway/dsl, Interstate/dsl 🅞 🅗, RV Camping (8-13mi)
10mm	weigh sta eb
2	MS 607, to Waveland, S Welcome Ctr both lanes, full ♿ facilities, 🚻, 🏤, litter barrels, RV dump, petwalk, 24hr security Buccaneer SP, camping, to beaches, 🅞 NASA Visitor Ctr
1mm	weigh sta wb
0mm	Mississippi/Louisiana state line, Pearl River

▲E INTERSTATE 20

Exit #	Services
172mm	Mississippi/Alabama state line. I-20 W and I-59 S run together to Meridian.
170mm	weigh sta both lanes
169	US 11, US 80, Kewanee, S 🅟 Kewanee Trkstp/BBQ/dsl 🅞 Simmons-Wright Gen Store
165	to US 11, Toomsuba, N 🅟 Dee's/dsl, Sunoco/Subway, S 🅟 ♥Love's/Arby's/dsl/scales/24hr 🅞 KOA (2mi)
164mm	Welcome Ctr wb, full ♿ facilities, 🚻, vending, 🏤, litter barrels, petwalk, RV dump, wi-fi, 24hr security
160	to Russell, N 🅟 TA/Country Pride/dsl/scales/24hr/@ 🅞 Nanabe RV Camping (1mi), S 🅟 Chevron/dsl/24hr 🅞 KOA (4mi)
157b a	US 45, to Macon, Quitman
156	Jimmie Rodgers Pkwy
154b a	MS 19 S, MS 39 N, Meridian, N 🅟 MapleLeaf/dsl, Shell, Texaco/dsl 🍴 Applebee's, Buffalo Wild Wings, Cracker Barrel, IHOP, Logan's Roadhouse, Penn's Rest, Waffle House, Western Sizzlin 🛏 Days Inn, Drury Inn, Fairfield Inn, Hampton Inn, Hilton Garden, Holiday Inn, Home 2 Suites, Relax Inn, Rodeway Inn, Sleep Inn, Super 8, Super Inn, Western Motel 🅞 Back Country RV Ctr, Chrysler/Dodge/Jeep/Kia, Kia, U-Haul, S 🅟 Chevron/dsl, Texaco/dsl 🍴 Chick-fil-A, Chili's, CiCi's, Dickey's BBQ, Honey Baked Ham, McAlister's Deli, McDonald's, O'Charley's, Olive Garden, Outback Steaks, Popeye's, Red Lobster, Ryan's, Taco Bell 🛏 Baymont Inn, Comfort Inn, Country Inn&Suites, Microtel 🅞 $Tree, AT&T, Belk, Best Buy, Books-A-Million, Dillard's,

MERIDIAN

154b a	Continued
	Harley-Davidson, Jo-Ann Fabrics, PetCo, Ross, Sam's Club/gas, TJ Maxx, Tuesday Morning
153	MS 145 S, 22nd Ave, Meridian, N 🅟 Shell, Xpress Lane 🍴 Arby's, Bumper's Drive-In, Burger King, Capt D's, China Buffet, Hardee's, KFC, McDonald's, Pizza Hut, Subway, Wendy's 🅞 $General, CarQuest, Cash Saver Foods, Ford/Nissan, Fred's, Goodyear/auto, 🅗, S 🅟 Exxon/dsl, Murphy USA/dsl, Texaco/dsl, Valero/dsl 🍴 A&W/LJ Silver, Checkerboard Kitchen, E Norte Mexican, Waffle House 🛏 Astro Motel, Budget 8 Motel, EconoLodge, Extended Suites, Hamilton Inn, Holiday Inn Express, La Quinta, Red Roof Inn, Sleep Inn 🅞 Chevrolet, Lowe's, Office Depot, Verizon, Walmart/McDonald's
152	29th Ave, 31st Ave, Meridian, N 🅟 Chevron/dsl 🛏 Best Value Inn, S 🛏 Royal Inn
151	James Chaney Dr, N 🅞 tires, S 🅟 Pilot/Subway/dsl/scales/24hr 🅞 stockyards
150	US 11 S, MS 19 N, Meridian, N 🅟 Exxon/dsl, Queen City Trkstp dsl/rest./@ 🍴 McDonald's, Waffle House 🅞 Okatibbee Lake RV camping, S 🅟 Chevron/Stuckey's/Subway/dsl, Shell/dsl 🅞 🍴, Peterbilt
130[149]	I-59 S, to Hattiesburg. I-20 E and I-59 N run together.
129	US 80 W, Lost Gap, S 🅟 Mr Fuel/ Dunkin'/Subway/dsl/RV Dump/24hr
121	Chunky
119mm	Chunky River
115	MS 503, Hickory
109	MS 15, Newton, N 🅟 Shell/Jct Deli/dsl/24hr 🍴 Los Parrillero 🛏 Thrifty Inn 🅞 🅗, lube/repair, S 🅟 Chevron/dsl, Newto Jct/dsl, Texaco/dsl 🍴 Cooks BBQ, Hardee's, KFC/Taco Bell, Mc Donald's, Panda Buffet, Pizza Hut, Sonic, Subway, Zack's Steak 🛏 Days Inn 🅞 $General, Advance Parts, AT&T, AutoZone Fred's, Piggly Wiggly, Walmart/Subway
100	US 80, Lake, Lawrence, N 🅟 Marathon/rest/dsl
96	Lake, S 🅟 ♥Love's/Chester's/Subway/dsl/scales/24hr
95mm	Bienville NF, eastern boundary, Bienville Nat Forest Bienvil Nat Forest
90mm	🆁🆂 eb, full ♿ facilities, 🚻, 🏤, litter barrels, petwalk, RV dump 24hr security
88	MS 35, Forest, N 🅟 Murphy USA/dsl, Shell, Texaco/Chester's dsl, Valero/dsl 🍴 KFC, Las Parrillas Mexican, McDonald's, Po eye's, Taco Bell, Waffle House, Wendy's, Zhen's Garden 🛏 Be Value Inn, Days Inn, EconoLodge, Holiday Inn Express 🅞 $Tre AT&T, 🅗, O'Reilly Parts, Walgreens, Walmart/Subway, S 🅟 Chevron/dsl/24hr 🍴 Penn's Rest.
80	MS 481, Morton, S 🅞 RV Camping
77	MS 13, Morton, N 🅟 Exxon/McDonald's/dsl, Texaco/dsl [Green Tree RV Park (4mi), 🅗, to Roosevelt SP, S 🅟 Shell/Su way/dsl
76mm	Bienville NF, western boundary
75mm	🆁🆂 wb, full ♿ facilities, 🚻, 🏤, litter barrels, petwalk, R dump, 24hr security
68	MS 43, Pelahatchie, N 🅟 Chevron/Subway/dsl, Texaco/res dsl/24hr 🅞 Jellystone Camping, S 🅟 Marathon/dsl
59	US 80, E Brandon, 2 mi S 🅟 Shell/dsl
56	US 80, Brandon, N 🅟 Shell/dsl 🍴 El Potrillo Mexican, Kryst Sonny's BBQ, Taco Bell 🛏 Microtel 🅞 AT&T, AutoZone, O'Rei Parts, USPO, Verizon, S 🅟 BP, Chevron, Exxon, Mac's Gas, Te aco/dsl 🍴 DQ, Penn's Rest., Sonic, Waffle House, Wendy's 🛏 Best Value Inn, Red Roof Inn 🅞 Auto+, to Ross Barnett Rese voir, vet

MERIDIAN · **NEWTON** · **FOREST** · **BRANDON**

MS

MS

INTERSTATE 20 Cont'd

Exit #	Services
54	Crossgates Blvd, W Brandon, **N** 🅖 Circle K/dsl, Exxon, Murphy USA 🅕 Abner's Chicken, Applebee's, Burger King, Chick-fil-A, China Buffet, Fernando's Fajita Factory, KFC, Little Caesar's, Mazzio's, McAlister's Deli, McDonald's, Newk's Rest, Papa John's, Pizza Hut, Popeye's, Subway, Waffle House 🅞 $Tree, Big-gLots, Buick/GMC, Chevrolet, CVS Drug, Ford/Lincoln, GNC, 🅗, Kroger/dsl, Nissan, Office Depot, Piggly Wiggly, Scotty's Tire/repair, Toyota, Tuesday Morning, Walgreens, Walmart/Subway, **S** 🅖 Circle K/dsl, Exxon/dsl, Mobil/Domino's/dsl 🅕 Steak Escape, Wendy's 🅛 La Quinta 🅞 Home Depot, Honda, Tire Pros
52	MS 475, **N** 🅖 Exxon/Subway/dsl, RaceWay/dsl, Texaco/dsl 🅕 Waffle House 🅛 Quality Inn, Ramada, Sleep Inn, Super 8 🅞 Peterbilt, to Jackson Airport
48	MS 468, Pearl, **N** 🅖 Exxon/dsl, Shell/dsl, Texaco 🅕 Arby's, Baskin Robbins, Bumpers Drive-In, Cracker Barrel, Domino's, DQ, Dunkin', Jose's Rest., KFC, Kobe Japanese, Logan's Roadhouse, LoneStar Steaks, Los Parrilleros, McAlister's Deli, McDonald's, Mikado, Mikado Japanese, Moss Creek Fishouse, O'Charley's, Popeye's, Ruby Tuesday, Sonic, Subway, Waffle House, Wendy's 🅛 Baymont Inn, Best Western, Comfort Inn, Courtyard, Days Inn, Fairfield Inn, Hampton Inn, Hilton Garden, Holiday Inn Express, Motel 6 🅞 AT&T, CarCare, **S** 🅖 Exxon/dsl, Mobil/dsl 🅛 Candlewood Suites, Country Inn&Suites, La Quinta 🅞 $General, Family$
47b a	US 49 S, Flowood, **N** 🅖 *FLYING J*/Denny's/dsl/LP/RV dump/24hr, ♥Loves/Subway/dsl/scales/24hr 🅕 Western Sizzlin 🅛 Airport Inn, Holiday Inn 🅞 Bass Pro Shop, MS Outlets/famous brands, Sam's Club/dsl, SpeedCo, **2-3 mi S** 🅖 RaceWay/dsl 🅕 Waffle House 🅞 Freightliner, Kenworth, tires
46	I-55 N, to Memphis
45b	US 51, State St, to downtown
45a	Gallatin St, to downtown, **N** 🅖 Marathon/dsl, Petro/Iron Skillet/dsl/scales/24hr/@, Shell 🅞 Blue Beacon, tires/truck repair, vet, **S** 🅖 Pilot/McDonald's/dsl/scales/24hr 🅛 Hilltop Inn 🅞 Nissan
44	I-55 S (exits left from wb), to New Orleans
43b a	Terry Rd, **N** 🅖 Exxon/dsl, Jasco 🅞 Apache RV Ctr
42b a	Ellis Ave, Belvidere, **N** 🅖 BP, Citgo/dsl, Shell 🅕 Capt D's, Church's, McDonald's, Pizza Hut, Popeye's, Sonny's BBQ, Wendy's 🅛 Best Inn, Metro Inn, Scottish Inn, Super 8 🅞 $Tree, Advance Parts, AutoZone, CarQuest, Family$, Firestone/auto, O'Reilly Parts, Sav-a-Lot Foods, transmissions, U-Haul, zoo, **S** 🅖 Citgo/dsl, Exxon/dsl 🅕 DQ
41	I-220 N, US 49 N, to Jackson
40b a	MS 18 W, Robinson Rd, **N** 🅖 Exxon/dsl, Jasco/dsl, Shell/dsl 🅕 Arby's, Krystal, Mazzio's, Piccadilly, Popeye's 🅞 $General, AT&T, Office Depot, USPO, **S** 🅖 Chevron, Citgo/dsl, Murphy USA, RaceWay/dsl, Shell/Church's/dsl 🅕 Chan's Garden, IHOP, McDonald's, Subway, Waffle House, Wendy's 🅛 Quality Inn 🅞 $Tree, GNC, 🅗, Lowe's, Walmart/Subway
36	Springridge Rd, Clinton, **N** 🅖 Chevron/Burger King, Citgo/dsl, Murphy USA/dsl, Shell 🅕 Capt D's, Chick-fil-A, China Buffet, Chopstick Buffet, DQ, El Sombrero, Hungry Howie's, KFC, Kroger/dsl, Little Ceasar's, Mazzio's, McAlister's, McDonald's, Newk's Cafe, Smoothie King, Sonic, Starbucks, Subway, Taco Bell, Waffle House, Wendy's, Zaxby's 🅛 Comfort Inn, Days Inn, Fairfield Inn 🅞 $Tree, Advance Parts, AT&T, BigLots, CVS Drug, Family$, Fred's, Home Depot, Kroger/gas, O'Reilly Parts, Verizon, Walgreens, Walmart (2mi), **S** 🅖 Exxon/Baskin-Robbins/Quiznos/dsl, Valero/dsl 🅕 Applebee's, Bonsai, Froghead Grill,

36	Continued
	Pizza Hut, Popeye's, Salsa's Mexican, Shoney's 🅛 Best Western, Econolodge, Hampton Inn, Holiday Inn Express, Quality Inn, Super 8 🅞 $General, Davis Tire, Springridge RV Park, vet
35	US 80 E, Clinton, **N** 🅖 Chevron, Circle K/dsl, Shell/dsl 🅞 vet
34	Natchez Trace Pkwy
31	Norrell Rd
27	Bolton, **S** 🅖 Chevron/dsl
19	MS 22, Edwards, Flora, **N** 🅞 Askew's Landing Camping (2mi), **S** 🅖 Exxon/dsl, Shell/dsl 🅛 Relax Inn
17mm	Big Black River
15	Flowers, **N** 🅖 ♥Loves/Arby's/Chester's/dsl/scales/24hr
11	Bovina, **N** 🅖 Texaco/Subway/dsl/24hr 🅞 RV camping
10mm	weigh sta wb
8mm	weigh sta eb
6.5mm	parking area eb
5b a	US 61, MS 27 S, **N** 🅖 Exxon/dsl, Shell/dsl 🅕 Sonic, **S** same as 4a
4b a	Clay St, **N** 🅖 Shell 🅛 Hampton Inn, Motel 6, Super 8, Vicksburg Inn 🅞 🅗, RV Park, to Vicksburg NP, **S** 🅖 Shell/dsl, Texaco 🅕 Baskin Robbins, Bumper's Drive-In, China Buffet, Cracker Barrel, Little Caesar's, McAlister's deli, Pizza Inn, Rowdy's Rest., Subway, Waffle House, Wendy's 🅛 Beechwood Inn/rest., Comfort Suites, Courtyard, Econolodge, Holiday Inn Express, La Quinta, Quality Inn, Scottish Inn 🅞 $General, Outlet Mall/famous brands/deli, same as 5
3	Indiana Ave, **N** 🅖 Shell/Subway/dsl 🅕 China King, McDonald's, Papa John's, Waffle House 🅛 Best Western, Deluxe Inn 🅞 Chevrolet, Chrysler/Dodge/Jeep, Corner Mkt Foods, Ford/Lincoln, Honda, Mazda, Nissan, Rite Aid, Toyota, **S** 🅖 Shell/dsl 🅕 Goldie's BBQ, Heavenly Ham, KFC 🅛 Best Inn 🅞 Buick/Cadillac/GMC, Family$
1c	Halls Ferry Rd, **N** 🅖 Exxon/dsl 🅕 Burger King, Sonic 🅛 Travel Inn 🅞 CVS Drug, Durst Drugs, 🅗, **S** 🅖 Shell/dsl 🅕 Asian Kitchen, Capt D's, Chick-fil-A, DQ, El Sombrero Mexican, Garfield's Rest., Goldie's Express, Little Caesar's, Newk's Eatery, Pizza Hut, Popeye's, Shoney's, Subway, Taco Bell, Taco Casa, Wendy's, Whataburger 🅛 Candlewood Suites, Holiday Inn, Howard Johnson, Ramada Inn, Red Roof Inn 🅞 $General, Advance Parts, AT&T, Belk, BigLots, Dillard's, Fred's, Hobby Lobby, Home Depot, Kroger/dsl, TJ Maxx, USPO, Walgreens
1b	US 61 S, **S** 🅖 Murphy Express/dsl, Shell/Domino's/dsl 🅕 McDonald's, Panda Buffet, Waffle House 🅞 $Tree, same as 1c, Verizon, Walmart/Subway
1a	Washington St, Vicksburg, **N** Welcome Ctr both lanes full ♿ facilities, 🅟, 🅖 Shell/dsl 🅛 AmeriStar Hotel/Casino/RV Park **S** 🅕 Waffle House 🅛 Best Value Inn, Days Inn
0mm	Mississippi/Louisiana state line, Mississippi River

BRANDON
PEARL
JACKSON
CLINTON
VICKSBURG

⛽ = gas 🍴 = food 🛏 = lodging 🅾 = other Ⓡⓢ = rest stop Copyright 2022 - The Next EXIT ®

⬆E INTERSTATE 22

Exit #	Services
118mm	Alabama/Mississippi State Line
115mm	**Welcome Ctr/Rest Area wb, 🚻, litter barrels, petwalk, vending, RV dump**
113	rd 23, Tremont, Smithville
108	rd 25 N, Belmont, Iuka
106mm	**weigh sta, both lanes**
104	rd 25 S, Fulton, Amory, **N** ⛽ Shell/cafe/dsl/scales, Texaco/dsl 🍴 Burger King, Ft Smith BBQ, Hardee's, Huddle House, McDonald's, Mi Toro Mexican, Sonic, Subway 🛏 Days Inn, Holiday Inn Express 🅾 $General, AutoZone, Food Giant/dsl, Fred's, O'Reilly Parts, RV camping, Whitten HS, **S** ⛽ Murphy USA/dsl 🍴 Peking Palace 🅾 AT&T, KFC, Los Compadres Mexican, Pizza Hut, URGENT CARE, Walmart, Wendy's
104mm	Tombigbee River/Tenn-Tom Waterway
101	rd 178, rd 363, Peppertown, Mantachie, **N** ⛽ Marathon, **S** ⛽ Dorsey Fuel/dsl (2mi)
97	Fawn Grove Rd
94	rd 371, Mantachie, Mooreville, **N** ⛽ Woodchuck's/pizza/dsl
90	Auburn Rd, **N** ⛽ Chevron/dsl
87	Veterans Blvd, **N** ⛽ Shell/Chix Rest/dsl 🍴 Huddle House 🛏 Wingate Inn 🅾 E. Presley Campground/Park, **S** 🅾 Tombigbee SP
86	US 45 N, Tupelo, to Corinth, **1 exit N** ⛽ Shell/dsl, Texaco, Valero 🍴 Abner's Rest., Applebee's, Baskin Robbins, Buffalo Wild Wings, Burger King, Capt D's, Chick-fil-A, Chili's, ChuckeCheese, Cracker Barrel, Crossroads Rib Shack, D'Casa Grill, Dickey's BBQ, Five Guys, IHOP, Kyoto Japanese, Lenny's Subs, Logan's Roadhouse, Longhorn Steaks, Margaritas Mexican, McDonald's, Mt Fuji Japanese, New China Buffet, Newk's Eatery, O'Charley's, Olive Garden, Pizza Hut, Pizza Pro, Red Lobster, Ryan's, Sake Japanese, Sonic, Subway, Taco Bell, Thai Garden, Waffle House, Wendy's 🛏 Best Inn, Best Western, Econolodge, Fairfield Inn, Hampton Inn 🅾 $Tree, AT&T, AutoZone, Barnes&Noble, Belk, Best Buy, CarMax, Dick's, Ford/Lincoln, Hobby Lobby, Home Depot, Hyundai, JC Penney, Jo-Ann, Kohl's, Kroger/gas, Lowe's, Mazda, Midas, NAPA, Nissan, Old Navy, Petsmart, Ross, Sam's Club/gas, Sears, Staples, TJ Maxx, Toyota, Tuesday Morning, URGENT CARE, Verizon, Walgreens, Walmart
85	Natchez Trace Pkwy
82	Barnes Crossing Rd, Coley Rd
81	rd 178, McCullough Blvd, **N** ⛽ 🐾Loves/McDonald's/dsl/scales/24hr 🛏 Best Value Inn, **S** ⛽ Exxon/dsl, Shell/dsl 🍴 Old Venice Pizza, Sonic 🛏 Super 8 🅾 $General, USPO
76	rd 9 S, Sherman, Pontotoc, **N** ⛽ Wild Bill's/dsl 🅾 Sherman RV Ctr
73	rd 9 N, to Magnolia Way, Blue Springs
64	rd 15, rd 30 E, Pontotoc, Ripley, **N** ⛽ 76/dsl, **S** ⛽ Circle K/dsl 🐾Pilot/Arby's/scales/dsl/24hr
63	New Albany, **N** ⛽ Dee's Oil/dsl 🅾 Buick/Chevrolet/GMC, Ford
62mm	Tallahatchie River
61	rd 30 W, W New Albany, **N** ⛽ Dee's 🍴 China Buffet, Cracker Barrel, McAlister's Deli, McDonald's, Pizza Hut, Subway, Waffle House, Wendy's 🛏 Hampton Inn 🅾 🅷, Rite Aid, Walgreens, **S** ⛽ Exxon, Murphy USA/dsl, Shell 🍴 Burger King, Capt D's, Domino's, El Agave Mexican, Huddle House, KFC, Mi Pueblo Mexican, Taco Bell, Zaxby's 🛏 Comfort Inn, Economy Inn, Hallmarc Inn, Holiday Inn Express 🅾 $Tree, AT&T, Lowe's, to U of MS, Verizon, Walmart
60	Glenfield, to Oxford, **N** ⛽ Pure 🛏 Budget Inn 🅾 Tire Pros, **S** 🅾 to U of MS
55	Myrtle

CORINTH (vertical side text)

48	rd 178, Hickory Flat, **S** ⛽ Exxon/Trkstp/rest/dsl/24hr
41	rd 346, Potts Camp, **S** ⛽ Flicks/dsl 🅾 $General, NAPA
41mm	Tippah River
37	Lake Center, **N** 🅾 Chewalla Lake/RV camping
30	rd 7, rd 4, Holly Springs, Oxford, **N** ⛽ Exxon, Shell/Chester's/BBQ 🍴 Burger King, Domino's, El Nopalito, Huddle House, KFC, Little Caesar's, McDonalds, Panda Buffet, Pizza Hut, Popeye's, Sonic, Subway, Taco Bell, Wendy's 🛏 Magnolia Inn 🅾 $General, AT&T, AutoZone, Liddy's Drug, O'Reilly Parts, Save-a-Lot, Wall Doxey SP/RV camping, **S** ⛽ 🐾Loves/Arby's/dsl/scales/24hr, Shell/dsl 🛏 Days Inn, Quality Inn 🅾 Walmart
26	W Holly Springs
21	Red Banks, **N** ⛽ Dee's Oil/dsl, Valero/dsl
18	Victoria, E Byhalia, **N** ⛽ Marathon/dsl, **S** ⛽ Victoria/dsl
14	rd 309, Byhalia, **N** ⛽ BP/dsl, Shell/dsl 🛏 Best Value Inn 🅾 Autozone
12	I-269, MS 304
10	W Byhalia, **N** ⛽ Exxon/dsl
6	Bethel Rd, Hacks Crossroad, **N** ⛽ ✈FLYING J/Subway//dsl/scales/LP/RV dump/24hr, Exxon/Baskin Robbins/dsl, Shell 🍴 JR's Grill, Rancho Grande, Tops BBQ 🛏 Best Western+, Super 8 🅾 truck repair, **S** 🅾 🅷
4	rd 305, Olive Branch, Independence, **N** ⛽ Shell/Circle K, Valero 🍴 DQ, Old Style BBQ, Pizza Hut 🛏 Holiday Inn Express 🅾 $General, Piggly Wiggly, USPO, **S** ⛽ Exxon/dsl 🅾 CVS Drug
3.5mm	**weigh sta both lanes**
2	rd 302, Olive Branch, **N** ⛽ Murphy Express/dsl 🍴 Abbay's Rest., Baskin-Robbins, Buffalo Wild Wings, Chick-fil-A, Chili's, Colton's Steaks, IHOP, Krystal, Lenny's Subs, McAlisters Deli, Mis Pueblos Mexican, O'Charley's, Starbucks, Wendy's 🛏 Candlewood Suites, Comfort Suites, Hilton Garden 🅾 $Tree, Ford, Home Depot, Lowe's, Verizon, Walmart/Subway, **S** ⛽ Chevron/dsl, Shell/Circle K 🍴 Applebees, Backyard Burger, Burger King, Casa Mexicana, Honeybaked Ham, Hunan Chinese, McDonald's, Panera Bread, Papa John's, Steak Escape, Subway, Taco Bell, Waffle House, Zaxby's 🛏 Comfort Inn, Hampton Inn, Home 2 Suites 🅾 AutoZone, CVS Drug, GNC, Goodyear/auto, Kroger/dsl, Petco
1	Craft Rd, **N** 🛏 Candlewood Suites 🅾 Camping World RV Ctr, Chevrolet, Hyundai, **S** ⛽ Shell
0mm	**Mississippi/Tennessee state line, I-22 begins/ends. US 78 continues wb.**

OLIVE BRANCH (vertical side text)

⬆N INTERSTATE 55

Exit #	Services
291.5mm	Mississippi/Tennessee state line
291	State Line Rd, Southaven, **E** ⛽ Exxon, RaceWay/dsl, Shell/dsl 🍴 Interstate BBQ, Little Caesar's, Subway, Tops BBQ, Waffle House 🛏 Days Inn, Quality Inn, Southern Inn, Super 8 🅾 Family$, Firestone/auto, Goodyear/auto, Kroger/dsl, Southaven RV Park, Walgreens, **W** ⛽ Exxon, Valero 🍴 Capt D's, Checkers, Dale's Rest., El Patron Mexican, Lucky China, Sonic, Taco Bell, Wendy's 🅾 BigLots, Fred's, Mainstreet Automotive, Rite Aid, tires, USPO, Walgreens
289	MS 302, to US 51, Horn Lake, **E** ⛽ BP/Circle K, Shell/Circle K 🍴 Abbays Rest., Backyard Burger, Baskin-Robbins, Buffalo Wild Wings, Burger King, Chick-fil-A, Chili's, Dunkin', Fazoli's, Firehouse Subs, Five Guys, Fox&Hound, Huey's Rest., IHOP, Jimmy John's, Krystal, Kublai Khan, Lenny's Subs, Logan's Roadhouse, Longhorn Steaks, McDonald's, Mi Pueblo, Nagoya Japanese, Naru Japanese, Newk's Eatery, O'Charley's, Olive Garden, On-the-Border, Outback Steaks, Red Lobster, Sonic, Starbucks

SOUTHAVEN (vertical side text)

INTERSTATE 55 Cont'd

289	Continued
	Steak'n Shake, Subway, Swanky's Tacos, Swanky's Tacos, TGIFriday's, Wendy's, Wing Stop, Wing Stop 🛏️ Candlewood Suites, Comfort Suites, Courtyard, Fairfield Inn, Hampton Inn, Hilton Garden, Holiday Inn, Holiday Inn Express, Home2Suites, Homewood Suites, Residence Inn ⓞ $Tree, Advance Parts, Aldi Foods, AT&T, Best Buy, Books-A-Million, Buick/GMC, Chevrolet, Chrysler/Dodge/Jeep, CVS Drug, Dillard's, Discount Tire, Ford, GNC, Gordman's, 🅷, JC Penney, Jo-Ann Fabrics, Lowe's, Marshall's, Nissan, Office Depot, Old Navy, PetCo, Sam's Club/gas, Tuesday Morning, URGENT CARE, Verizon, Walmart/Subway, W 🍴 BP/Circle K, Phillips 66/dsl, Shell/Circle K/dsl 🍴 Applebee's, Arby's, ChuckECheese's, Country Home Buffet, Cracker Barrel, Grand Buffet, Hardee's, Hooters, KFC, McDonald's, Memphis BBQ, Papa John's, Pizza Hut, Popeye's, Starbucks, Taco Bell, TX Roadhouse, Waffle House, Wendy's, Zaxby's 🛏️ Best Value Inn, Best Western, Comfort Inn, Drury Inn, EconoLodge, La Quinta, Motel 6, Sleep Inn ⓞ CVS Drug, Family$, Gateway Tires/repair, Home Depot, Kroger, Meineke, Save-a-Lot Foods, Target, Walgreens
287	Church Rd, E 🍴 Citgo/dsl 🍴 Area 50 Grill, Domino's ⓞ AutoZone, Tanger Outlets/famous brands, W 🍴 Citgo/dsl, Mapco/dsl/deli, Shell/Circle K/dsl 🍴 Boiling Point Seafood, Casa Mexicana, Dixie Queen, McDonald's, Sonic, Subway, Taco Bell, Three Guys Pizza, Waffle House 🛏️ Homegate Inn, Magnolia Inn ⓞ El Daze RV Camping (1mi), Family$, Fred's, Harley-Davidson, Jellystone Camping, Southaven RV Ctr, Walgreens
285mm	weigh sta both lanes
284	to US 51, Nesbit Rd, W 🍴 Shell 🍴 Happy Daze Dairybar ⓞ USPO
283	I-69, MS 304, Tunica
280	MS 304, US 51, Hernando, E 🍴 Exxon, Murphy USA/dsl 🍴 Arby's, Buon Cibo, Capt D's, Domino's, Fins Grill, Guadalajara Mexican, KFC, Royal Buffet, Sonic, Steak Escape, Taco Bell, Zaxby's 🛏️ Days Inn, Hampton Inn ⓞ $Tree, AT&T, GNC, Ultimate Tires/repair, URGENT CARE, Walgreens, Walmart/Subway, W 🍴 Mobil, Shell/Circle K/dsl 🍴 Brick Oven Rest., Coleman's BBQ, Lenny's Subs, Little Caesar's, McDonald's, Mi Pueblo, Mr Chen's, Papa John's, Pizza Hut, Subway, Taco Felix, Waffle House, Wendy's 🛏️ Super 8 ⓞ AutoZone, Bryant Repair, Desoto Museum, Fred's, Kroger/gas, NAPA, to Arkabutla Lake, USPO, vet
279mm	Welcome Ctr sb, full ♿ facilities, 🄲, 🄿, litter barrels, petwalk, RV dump, 24hr security
276mm	🆁🆂 nb, full ♿ facilities, 🄲, 🄿, litter barrels, petwalk, RV dump, 24hr security
273mm	Coldwater River
271	MS 306, Coldwater, W 🍴 Shell 🍴 Subway ⓞ Lake Arkabutla, Memphis S RV Park
265	MS 4, Senatobia, W 🍴 Marathon/dsl, 🄿🄸🄻🄾🅃/Huddle House/dsl/scales/24hr, Shell/dsl 🍴 Applebee's, Coleman's BBQ, Domino's, Hardee's, KFC, McDonald's, New China Buffet, Pizza Hut, Popeye's, Rio Lindo Mexican, Sonic, Subway, Taco Bell, Waffle House, Wendy's, Zaxby's 🛏️ Best Value Inn, Magnolia Inn ⓞ CarQuest, Fred's, 🅷, Kaye Mkt, USPO
263	rd 740, S Senatobia
257	MS 310, Como, E ⓞ N Sardis Lake, W 🍴 Citgo/dsl 🍴 Windy City Grille (1mi) ⓞ $General
252	MS 315, Sardis, E 🍴 Chevron/dsl, Local/dsl 🍴 McDonald's 🛏️ Lake Inn, Rodeway Inn ⓞ NAPA, repair, RV camping, Sardis Dam, to Kyle SP, W 🍴 BP/Subway/dsl, Shell/dsl 🍴 Sonic ⓞ $General, Fred's

B A T E S V I L L E

246	MS 35, N Batesville, E ⓞ to Sardis Lake, W 🍴 🄻🄾🅅🄴🅂 Loves/McDonald's/Subway/dsl/scales/24hr, Shell/dsl
243b a	MS 6, to Batesville, E 🍴 Marathon/dsl, Mobil/dsl, Murphy USA/dsl, RaceWay/dsl 🍴 Backyard Burger, Chili's, Mi Pueblo Mexican, Zaxby's 🛏️ Comfort Suites, Home 2 Suites ⓞ $Tree, 🅷, Lowe's, to Sardis Lake, to U of MS, Walmart/Subway, W 🍴 BP, Exxon/dsl, Phillips 66/dsl, Shell/dsl 🍴 Burger King, Burn's BBQ, Cafe Ole, Capt D's, Cracker Barrel, Domino's, Hardee's, Huddle House, KFC, Little Caesar's, McDonald's, New China, Pizza Hut, Popeye's, Sonic, Subway, Taco Bell, Waffle House, Wendy's, Yamato Hibachi 🛏️ Best Value Inn, Days Inn, EconoLodge, Hampton Inn, Holiday Inn ⓞ $General, AT&T, AutoZone, Factory Stores/famous brands, Family$, Fred's, Kroger/dsl, O'Reilly Parts, Piggly Wiggly, Save-a-Lot, URGENT CARE, USPO, Walgreens
240mm	🆁🆂 both lanes, full ♿ facilities, 🄲, 🄿, litter barrels, petwalk, RV dump, 24hr security
237	to US 51, Courtland, E 🍴 Pure/dsl, W ⓞ $General
233	to Enid Dam, E ⓞ RV camping, to Enid Lake
227	MS 32, Oakland, E ⓞ to Cossar SP, W 🍴 Sayle/Baskin Robbins/dsl, Shell/dsl 🍴 Country Catfish ⓞ $General
220	MS 330, Tillatoba, E 🍴 Conoco/rest./dsl/@
211	MS 7 N, to Coffeeville, E ⓞ Frog Hollow RV Park, W 🍴 Exxon/Aunt M's/dsl, Marathon/dsl
208	Papermill Rd, E 🍴 Monroe's/Chester's/dsl/scales ⓞ Grenada Airport
206	MS 8, MS 7 S, to Grenada, E 🍴 Exxon/dsl, Shell/dsl, Sprint 🍴 Applebee's, China Buffet, Church's, Great Wall Chinese, Jake&Rip's Catfish, La Cabana Mexican, Little Caesar's, McAlister's Deli, McDonald's, No Way Jose, Pizza Hut, Pizza Inn, Shoney's, Simply Southern Cafe, Subway, Taco Bell, Wendy's 🛏️ Baymont Inn, Best Value Inn, EconoLodge, Grenada Inn, Hampton Inn, Holiday Inn Express, Knights Inn, Relax Inn, Rodeway Inn ⓞ $General, $Tree, Advance Parts, AT&T, AutoZone, Chevrolet, CVS Drug, GNC, 🅷, O'Reilly Parts, SaveALot, to Grenada Lake/RV camping, Walmart/McDonald's, W 🍴 Exxon/Huddle House, Sayle/Baskin Robbins/dsl 🍴 Waffle House 🛏️ Comfort Inn, Hilltop Inn ⓞ Ford/Lincoln, Nissan, Toyota
199	Troutt Rd, S Grenada, E ⓞ to camp McCain
195	MS 404, Duck Hill, E ⓞ to Camp McCain, W 🍴 Conoco/dsl
185	US 82, Winona, E 🍴 Exxon, Shell/Kangaroo/Little Caesar's/dsl 🍴 Huddle House, KFC, McDonald's, Sonic, Subway, Waffle House 🛏️ Best Value Inn, Holiday Inn Express, Magnolia Lodge, Relax Inn ⓞ 🅷, W 🍴 🄿🄸🄻🄾🅃/Taco Bell/dsl/scales/24hr/@
174	MS 35, MS 430, Vaiden, E 🍴 35-55 Trkstp/Chester's/dsl/scales/24hr, Chevron/dsl, Shell ⓞ Vaiden Camping, W 🍴 Exxon/dsl
173mm	🆁🆂 sb, full ♿ facilities, 🄲, 🄿, litter barrels, petwalk, RV dump, 24hr security

G R E N A D A

🅖 = gas 🅕 = food 🅛 = lodging 🅞 = other 🆁🆂 = rest stop   Copyright 2022 - The Next EXIT ®

MS

INTERSTATE 55 Cont'd

Exit #	Services
164	to West, **W** 🅕 West Trkstp/dsl
163mm	🆁🆂 nb, full 🅱 facilities, 🄲, 🄰, litter barrels, petwalk, RV dump, 24hr security
156	MS 12, Durant, **E** 🅕 Shell/Chester's/dsl 🅕 Subway 🅛 Durant Motel/rest. (3mi), Oak Tree Inn, **W** 🅞 🅷 (7mi)
150	**E** 🅞 Holmes Co SP, RV camping
146	MS 14, Goodman, **W** 🅞 to Little Red Schoolhouse
144	MS 17, to Pickens, **W** 🅕 Marathon/Baskin-Robbins/dsl/24hr 🅞 to Little Red Schoolhouse
139	MS 432, to Pickens
133	Vaughan
128mm	**E** 🅞 to Jackson Zoo, **W** 🅕 RaceWay, Shell 🅕 McDonald's, Popeye's, Sonic 🅞 Family$
124	MS 16, to N Canton
119	MS 22, to MS 16 E, Canton, **E** 🅕 Exxon, Kangaroo/Subway/dsl, Marathon/dsl, Shell/Domino's, Valero/dsl 🅕 El Sombrero Mexican, McDonald's, Pizza Hut, Popeye's, Sonic, Waffle House, Wendy's 🅛 Best Value Inn, Best Western, Econolodge, Hampton Inn, Holiday Inn Express, La Quinta, Relax Inn, Super 8 🅞 $General Mkt, Family$, 🅷, Nissan, O'Reilly Parts, to Ross Barnett Reservoir, **W** 🅕 Chevron/KFC/dsl, Citgo, ♥Loves/Arby's/dsl/scales/24hr/@, Texaco/Penn's/dsl 🅕 Bumpers Drive-In, Two Rivers Steaks 🅞 Walmart
118a b	Nissan Parkway, **E** 🅞 to Nissan
114a b	Sowell Rd
112	US 51, Gluckstadt, **E** 🅕 Exxon/Krystal/dsl 🅕 Sonic 🅛 Super 8 🅞 Goodyear/auto, **W** 🅕 Shell/Pizza Hut/dsl 🅞 Camper Corral RV Ctr, vet
108	MS 463, Madison, **E** 🅕 Kangaroo/Mobil/dsl, Shell/dsl 🅕 Applebee's, Backyard Burger, Burger King, Chick-Fil-A, Chili's, Corner Bakery Café, Dickey's BBQ, El Potrillo, Jimmy John's, La Guadalupe Mexican, Little Caesar's, Longhorn Steaks, Subway 🅞 $Tree, AT&T, Best Buy, Dick's, GNC, Lowe's, Michael's, Office Depot, PetCo, SteinMart, Walmart, **W** 🅕 Exxon/KFC/dsl 🅕 BoneFish Grill, KFC, Nagoya Japanese, Papito's Grill, Pizza Inn, Schlotsky's, Subway, Tay's BBQ, Wendy's 🅛 Hilton Garden 🅞 CVS Drug, Home Depot, Kroger, Walgreens
107	Colony Park Blvd, Madison Ave, **E** 🅞 Sam's Club/dsl
105c b	Old Agency Rd, **E** 🅕 Chevron/dsl 🅛 Home2Suites 🅞 Honda, Hyundai, **W** 🅕 Biaggi's Ristorante, Five Guys, Panera Bread, PF Changs, Ruth's Chris Steaks, Smoothie King, Starbucks 🅛 Hyatt Place 🅞 Barnes&Noble, Fresh Mkt Foods, GNC
105a	Natchez Trace Pkwy
104	I-220, to W Jackson
103	County Line Rd, **E** 🅕 Chevron, Exxon/dsl, Murphy Express/dsl 🅕 Bop's Custard, Bulldog Grill, Burgers&Blues Cafe, Cane's, Chick-fil-A, ChuckECheese's, Drago's Rest., Fortune Chinese, Grand China, HoneyBaked Ham, Jason's Deli, KFC, King Buffet, Krispy Kreme, Papito's Grill, Pizza Hut, Popeye's, Taco Bell, Wendy's, Whataburger, Zaxby's 🅛 Cabot Lodge, Courtyard, Days Inn, EconoLodge, Extended Stay America, Hilton, Quality Inn, Red Roof Inn, Staybridge Suites 🅞 $Tree, Acura, Belk, BigLots, Cadillac, Dillard's, JC Penney, Lowe's, Marshall's, Old Navy, Ross, TJ Maxx, to Barnett Reservoir, Tuesday Morning, Verizon, Walmart, **W** 🅕 Logan's Roadhouse, Nagoya Japanese, Olive Garden, Red Lobster, Subway 🅛 Drury Inn, Holiday Inn Express, Motel 6 🅞 Home Depot, Jo-Ann Fabrics, Petsmart, Target, Upton Tire
102b	Beasley Rd, Adkins Blvd, **E** 🅕 Sunoco 🅕 Cracker Barrel, Outback Steaks, Twin Peaks Rest. 🅛 Super 8 🅞 Chevrolet, Ford, Nissan,

Exit #	Services
102b	Continued Toyota, **W** 🅕 Shell/dsl, Texaco/dsl 🅕 Baskin-Robbins, Burger King, Chili's, Fuddrucker's, IHOP, Luby's, McDonald's, Waffle House 🅛 Baymont Inn, Comfort Inn, Extended Stay America, Fairfield Inn, Howard Johnson, InTown Suites, La Quinta 🅞 CarMax, Chrysler/Dodge/Jeep, frontage rds access 102a, Mercedes, Save-A-Lot Foods
102a	Briarwood, **E** 🅛 Rodeway Inn 🅞 Buick/GMC, **W** 🅕 Capt D's, Popeye's 🅛 Clarion 🅞 Chrysler/Dodge/Jeep, Porsche
100	North Side Dr W, **E** 🅕 Chevron, Marathon/dsl, Sprint 🅕 Burger King, Char Rest., McAlister's Deli, Papa John's, Piccadilly's, Pizza Hut, Starbucks, Subway, Wendy's 🅛 Extended Stay America 🅞 $Tree, Audi, Books-A-Million, CVS Drug, Firestone/auto, Goodyear/auto, Jaguar/LandRover, Kroger/dsl, Office Depot, SteinMart, Verizon, vet, VW, Walgreens, Whole Foods Mkt, **W** 🅕 Exxon/dsl, FastLane, Shell 🅕 Domino's, Hooters, Waffle House 🅛 Select Motel, USA Inn
99	Meadowbrook Rd, Northside Dr E (from nb), **E** 🅕 Newk's Eatery
98c b	MS 25 N, Lakeland Dr, **E** 🅕 Shell/dsl 🅛 Parkside Inn 🅞 LaFleur's Bluff SP, museum, **W** 🅞 🄰, 🅷
98a	Woodrow Wilson Dr (exits left from nb) downtown
96c	Fortification St, **E** 🅛 Studio 6 Suites, **W** 🅞 Bellhaven College 🅷
96b	High St, Jackson, **E** 🅞 BMW, Chevrolet, Infiniti, Lexus, **W** 🅕 Exxon/Subway/dsl, Valero/Kangaroo/dsl 🅕 Arby's, Chimneyville Cafe, Domino's, Popeye's, Taco Bell, Waffle House, Wendy's, Whataburger 🅛 Best Value Inn, Best Western, Comfort Inn, Hampton Inn, Holiday Inn Express, Red Roof Inn, Regency Hotel 🅞 fairgrounds, Honda, 🅷, museum, st capitol, Subaru/Volvo
96a	Pearl St (from nb), Jackson, **W** downtown, access to same as 96b
94	(46 from nb), I-20 E, to Meridian, US 49 S
45b[I-20]	US 51, State St, **N** 🅕 Marathon, Petro/Iron Skillet/dsl/scales/24hr, Shell, **S** 🅕 Pilot/McDonald's/dsl/scales/24hr, downtown
45a	Gallatin St (from sb), **W** 🅞 Blue Beacon, **N** 🅕 Marathon, Petro/Iron Skillet/dsl/scales/24hr, Shell, **S** 🅕 Pilot/McDonald's/d 🅞 Nissan
92c	(44 from sb), I-20 W, to Vicksburg, US 49 N
92b	US 51 N, State St, Gallatin St
92a	McDowell Rd, 1 mi **E** Petro/Iron Skillet/dsl/scales/24hr Pilot/McDonald's/dsl, **W** 🅕 Citgo/dsl, Exxon, Family$, Marathon/dsl, Shell 🅕 McDonald's, Waffle House 🅞 Food Depot, Fred's, Rite Aid, Roses
90b	Daniel Lake Blvd (from sb), **W** 🅕 Shell 🅞 Harley-Davidson
90a	Savanna St, **E** 🅞 transmissions, **W** 🅕 Gas 🅞 Caney Creek F Ctr
88	Elton Rd, **W** 🅕 Exxon/dsl, Shell/Subway/dsl 🅞 Camping World RV Ctr
85	Byram, **E** 🅕 Blue Sky/dsl, Hungry Jack's/dsl 🅕 Daddio's BBQ, Krystal, Mexican Grill 🅛 Comfort Inn, Woodspring Suites, Swinging Bridge RV Park, **W** 🅕 Byram/dsl, Chevron/dsl, Exxon/dsl, Mobil/Kangaroo/dsl 🅕 Backyard Burger, Burger King, Capt D's, Domino's, KFC, Mazzio's, McAlister's Deli, McDonald's, New China, Newk's Eatery, Papa John's, Pizza Hut, Popeye's, Sonic, Subway, Taco Bell, Waffle House, Wendy's 🅛 Best Value Inn, Holiday Inn Express 🅞 $General, AutoZone, Family, Mkt Place Foods, NAPA, O'Reilly Parts, Tire Depot, Walgreens, Walmart/Subway
81	Wynndale Rd, **E** 🅞 repair, **W** 🅕 Chevron/dsl/24hr
78	Terry, **E** 🅕 Citgo/dsl, Texaco/Subway/dsl 🅞 Buick/Chevrolet/GMC (1mi), Fred's, USPO, **W** 🅕 Quick Trip 🅞 $General

CANTON

MADISON

JACKSON

INTERSTATE 55 Cont'd

Exit #	Services
72	MS 27, Crystal Springs, E 🅖 Exxon/Subway/dsl, Phillips 66/dsl 🅗 Louise's Pit BBQ, McDonald's, Popeye's 🅞 Ford
68	to US 51, S Crystal Springs, E 🅖 gas/dsl 🅞 Red Barn Produce, vet
65	to US 51, Gallman, E 🅖 Stuckey's/dsl
61	MS 28, Hazlehurst, E 🅖 Exxon/Circle K/Subway/dsl, Murphy Express/dsl, Phillips 66/dsl 🅗 Burger King, KFC/Taco Bell, Los Parrilleros, McDonald's, Pizza Hut, Sonic, Waffle House, Wendy's 🅗 Best Value Inn, Rodeway Inn, Western Inn 🅞 $General, $Tree, Advance Parts, AT&T, Family$, Fred's, 🅗, Piggly Wiggly, SaveALot, Verizon, Walgreens, Walmart
59	to S Hazlehurst
56	to Martinsville
54mm	🆁🆂 both lanes, full 🅗 facilities, 🅗, 🅗, litter barrels, petwalk, RV dump, vending, 24hr security
51	to Wesson, E 🅞 Lake Lincoln SP, W 🅖 Texaco/Country Jct Trkstp/dsl/rest.
48	Mt Zion Rd, to Wesson
42	to US 51, N Brookhaven, E 🅖 Exxon/Subway, Shell/Gridiron Grill/dsl/scales/24hr 🅞 🅗, W 🅗 Super 8
40	to MS 550, Brookhaven, E 🅖 Blue Sky, Exxon/Subway, Marathon/Domino's/dsl, Murphy USA/dsl, Shell/dsl 🅗 Bowie BBQ, Burger King, China Buffet, Cracker Barrel, DQ, El Dorado Mexican, Hudgey's Rest., KFC, Krystal, Little Caesar's, Little Tokyo, Los Parrilleros, McDonald's, Mitchell's Steaks, Pizza Hut, Popeye's, Sonic, Taco Bell, Waffle House, Wards Burgers, Wendy's 🅗 Best Value Inn, Comfort Inn, Hampton Inn, Holiday Inn Express, Lincoln Inn, Rodeway Inn, Spanish Inn 🅞 $General, $Tree, AT&T, AutoZone, Buick/Cadillac/Chevrolet/GMC, CarQuest, Family$, Ford/Lincoln, Fred's, Gene's Tires, GNC, Honda, 🅗, Nissan, O'Reilly Parts, Rite Aid, Save-A-Lot Foods, Toyota, Walgreens, Walmart/Subway, W 🅗 IHOP 🅞 Home Depot
38	US 84, S Brookhaven, W 🅖 Chevron/dsl/24hr
30	Bogue Chitto, Norfield, E 🅖 Phillips 66 🅗 Nick and Nino's, Reef Rest. 🅗 Ebassy Suites, Holiday Inn Express, Home2 Suites, Homewood Suites, W 🅗 Cracker Barrel, Waffle House, Wendy's 🅗 Drury Inn, Sleep In, Sonesta Inn 🅞 Toyota
24	Johnston Station, E 🅞 to Lake Dixie Springs
20b a	US 98 W, to Natchez, Summit, E 🅖 Marathon/dsl, Shell/dsl, Stop'n Shop/dsl, W 🅖 Exxon/Subway/dsl, ShawnMart/dsl
18	MS 570, Smithdale Rd, N McComb, E 🅖 Marathon, Murphy USA/dsl 🅗 Burger King, McDonald's, Piccadilly's, Ruby Tuesday 🅗 Holiday Inn Express 🅞 AT&T, Belk, Hobby Lobby, 🅗, JC Penney, Kia, Lowe's, Walgreens, Walmart/Subway, W 🅖 Chevron/Mr Whiskers/dsl 🅗 Applebee's, Arby's, El Dorado Mexican, Santa Fe Steaks 🅗 Comfort Inn, Deerfield Inn, Hampton Inn 🅞 Ford/Lincoln
17	Delaware Ave, McComb, E 🅖 Blue Sky, Chevron/dsl, Exxon/Penn's Rest., Marathon/Subway/dsl, Pump&Savor 🅗 Burger King, Domino's, Golden Corral, Kyoto Steaks, Little Caesar's, Pizza Hut, Popeye's, Smoothie King, Sonic, Taco Bell, Tortillo Soup, Waffle House, Wendy's 🅗 Best Western, Quality Inn 🅞 $General, AutoZone, Chrysler/Dodge/Jeep, CVS Drug, Family$, Fred's, 🅗, Kroger, McComb Mkt, O'Reilly Parts, Office Depot, Rite Aid, Verizon, W 🅗 Days Inn
15b a	US 98 E, MS 48 W, McComb, 1 mi E 🅖 Citgo/dsl, Exxon/Subway, Presley QuikStop/dsl, Pump&Savor, Shell 🅗 Church's, KFC 🅗 Camellian Motel 🅞 $General, $Tree, Advance Parts, Family$, tires, vet $Tree, W 🅗 Marathon/dsl
13	Fernwood Rd, E 🅞 truck repair, W 🅖 ❤Loves/Chester's/McDonald's/dsl/scales/24hr/@ 🅞 golf, to Percy Quin SP
10	MS 48, Magnolia, 1 mi E 🅖 Exxon/Subway/dsl, Marathon, Shell/dsl 🅞 RV camping Marathon
8	MS 568, Magnolia
4	Chatawa
3mm	Welcome Ctr nb, full 🅗 facilities, 🅗, 🅗, litter barrels, petwalk, RV dump, 24hr security
2mm	weigh sta nb
1	MS 584, Osyka, Gillsburg
0mm	Mississippi/Louisiana state line

INTERSTATE 59

Exit #	Services
172mm	Mississippi/Alabama state line
	I-59 S and I-20 W run together to Meridian. See I-20, exits 170mm-150.
142	to US 11, Dunns Falls, Savoy
137	to N Enterprise, to Stonewall
134	MS 513, S Enterprise, E 🅖 FastStop
126	MS 18, to Rose Hill, Pachuta, E 🅖 Alliance/dsl, Pachuta TP/dsl
118	to Vossburg, Paulding
113	MS 528, to Heidelberg, E 🅖 Chevron/dsl/24hr, Exxon/Subway/dsl, Valero/dsl 🅗 Ward's Burgers
109mm	parking area sb, litter barrels, no rest rooms
106mm	parking area nb, litter barrels, no restrooms
104	Sandersville
99	US 11, E 🅞 Sleepy Hollow RV Park (1mi)
97	US 84 E, E 🅖 Circle K/Subway/dsl, Exxon/Huddle House/dsl/scales 🅗 Hardee's, Ward's Burgers, W 🅖 Shell 🅗 KFC, Vic's Rest.
96b	MS 15 S, Cook Ave
96a	Masonite Rd, 4th Ave
95d	(from nb)
95c	Beacon St, Laurel, W 🅗 Burger King, Church's, McDonald's, Popeye's 🅗 TownHouse Motel 🅞 $General, Family$, Firestone/auto, Grocery Depot, 🅗, JC Penney, museum of art, NAPA, USPO
95b a	US 84 W, MS 15 N, 16th Ave, Laurel, 0-2 mi W 🅖 Alliance/dsl, Exxon/dsl, Fast Stop, Murphy Express/dsl, Shell 🅗 Applebee's, Arby's, Buffalo Wild Wings, Buffet Palace, Burger King, Cane's, Capt D's, Checkers, Chick-fil-A, China Town, Dickey's BBQ, Domino's, DQ, Hardee's, KFC, Laredo Grill, Little Caesar's, McDonald's, Mi Casita, Panda Express, Papa John's, Popeye's, Shipley's Donuts, Shoney's, Sonic, Subway, Taco Bell, Tokyo Grill, Waffle House, Ward's Burgers, Wendy's 🅗 Baymont Suites, Best Western, EconoLodge, Hampton Inn, Holiday Inn Express, Rodeway Inn, Super 8 🅞 $General, $Tree, Advance Parts, AT&T, auto tech, AutoZone, BigLots, Chevrolet, Chrysler/Dodge/Jeep/Toyota,

BROOKHAVEN

McCOMB

LAUREL

↑N INTERSTATE 59 Cont'd

LAUREL

Exit	Services
95b a	Continued CVS Drug, Ford/Lincoln, Grocery Depot, H, Kia, Kroger/dsl, Lowe's, Nissan, O'Reilly Parts, Office Depot, Piggly Wiggly, Roses, Tuesday Morning, Verizon, Walgreens, Walmart/Subway
93	US 11, S Laurel, **W** ⛽ Exxon/Subway/dsl, Shell/dsl 🍴 Hardee's ⊙ Southern Tires
90	US 11, Ellisville Blvd, **E** ⛽ Marathon/dsl 🍴 Huddle House, **W** ⛽ Valero/dsl
88	MS 588, MS 29, Ellisville, **E** ⛽ Chevron/dsl/24hr, Fast Mkt/dsl, Keith's/dsl 🍴 Domino's, KFC, Little Caesar's, McDonald's, Pizza Hut, Sonic, Subway, Ward's Burgers ⊙ $General, AutoZone, CashSaver, Ellisville Drug, Family$, NAPA, O'Reilly Parts, **W** ⛽ Shell/dsl 🛏 Millennium Inn
85	MS 590, to Ellisville, **W** ⛽ Texaco/dsl
80	to US 11, Moselle, **E** ⛽ Chevron/dsl/24hr
78	Sanford Rd
76	**W** ⊙ to Hattiesburg-Laurel Reg Airport
73	Monroe Rd, to Monroe
69	MS 42 E, Gandy Pkwy, to Petal, Eatonville
67b a	US 49, Hattiesburg, **E** ⛽ Clark's/dsl, Exxon, Exxon/dsl/scales, Shell, Texaco 🍴 Arby's, Burger King, Cracker Barrel, DQ, Krystal, McDonald's, Popeye's, Waffle House 🛏 Budget Inn, EconoLodge, Executive Inn, Holiday Inn, Howard Johnson, Magnuson, Quality Inn, Red Roof Inn, Sleep Inn, Sunset Inn, Super 8, University Inn ⊙ $General, Hattiesburg Cycles, **W** ⛽ Chevron, MapleLeaf/dsl, Pure/dsl, Shell/Subway, Stuckey's Express/dsl, Texaco, Valero 🍴 Sonic, Waffle House, Ward's Burgers, Wendy's 🛏 Candlewood Suites, DoubleTree Inn, Northgate Inn
65b a	US 98 W, Hardy St, Hattiesburg, **E** ⛽ Shell/dsl, Valero 🍴 Applebee's, Baskin Robbins, Buffalo Wild Wings, Cane's, Checkers, CiCi's Pizza, Cookout, Crab House, Crescent City Grill, Domino's, Ed's Burger Joint, Firehouse Subs, IHOP, Jimmy John's, Lenny's Subs, Little Caesar's, McDonald's, Papa John's, Pizza Hut, Qdoba, Smoothie King, Starbucks, Subway, Tabella Italian, Taco Bell, Topher's, Ward's Burgers 🛏 Courtyard, Days Inn, Fairfield Inn, Hotel Indigo, La Quinta, Residence Inn, Super 8, TownePlace Suites, Western Motel ⊙ Corner Mkt Foods, CVS Drug, Goodyear/auto, Home Depot, H, to USM, URGENT CARE, Verizon, vet, Walgreens, **W** ⛽ Chevron, Circle K, Exxon/Domino's, Shell/Jimmy John's/dsl 🍴 Arby's, Burger King, Chesterfield's Rest., Chick-fil-A, Chili's, China Buffet, ChuckECheese's, City Buffet, Dickey's BBQ, FireHouse Subs, Five Guys, Gatti Town Pizza, Georgia Blue Rest., Golden Corral, Hardee's, HoneyBaked Ham, Hooters, Krispy Kreme, Logan's Roadhouse, Longhorn Steaks, Marble Slab, McAlister's Deli, McDonald's, Newk's Eatery, O'Charley's, Olive Garden, Outback Steaks, Panda Express, Pepper's Deli, Pizza Hut, Plaid Rhino Burger, Popeye's, Red Lobster, Super King Asian, Taco Bell, TGIFriday's, Waffle House, Ward's Burgers, Wendy's, Which Wich?, Yamato Japan, Zaxby's 🛏 Baymont Inn, Best Western, Comfort Suites, Hampton Inn, Hilton Garden, Home 2 Suites, InTown Suites, Microtel, Red Lion Inn ⊙ $Tree, Aamco, Advance Parts, AT&T, AutoZone, Belk, Best Buy, BigLots, Books-A-Million, Dick's, Dillard's, Firestone/auto, Goodyear/auto, Hobby Lobby, H, JC Penney, Jo Ann, Kohl's, Lowe's, Michael's, Nissan, Office Depot, Old Navy, PetCo, Petsmart, Ross, Sam's Club/gas, SteinMart, Target, TJ Maxx, Tuesday Morning, Verizon, Walgreens, Walmart, Winn-Dixie
60	US 11, S Hattiesburg, **E** ⛽ Shell/TX BBQ/dsl, **W** ⛽ Circle K/Subway/dsl/24hr, Texaco, Valero/dsl ⊙ Freightliner, Peterbilt
59	US 98 E, to US 49, Lucedale, MS Gulf Coast
56mm	parking area both lanes, litter barrels, no restrooms

HATTIESBURG

Exit	Services
51	rd 589, to Purvis, **W** ⛽ Chevron/dsl/24hr, Pinebelt Oil/ds Shell/dsl (2mi) 🍴 Little Caesar's, McDonald's (2mi), Pizza Hu (2mi), to Little Black Cr Water Park
48mm	Little Black Creek
41	MS 13, to Lumberton, **W** ⛽ Marathon/dsl ⊙ $General, to Littl Black Cr Water Park
35	Hillsdale Rd, **E** 🛏 to Kings Arrow Ranch
32mm	Wolf River
29	rd 26, to Poplarville, **W** ⛽ 🅛 Loves/Arby's/dsl/scales/24h Pure/dsl ⊙ NAPA, tires/repair
27	MS 53, to Poplarville, Necaise, **W** ⛽ Chevron/dsl 🍴 McDonald's
19	to US 11, Millard
15	to McNeill, **W** ⛽ McNeill Trkstop/rest./dsl
10	to US 11, Carriere, **E** ⛽ Texaco/cafe/dsl ⊙ Clearwater RV Cam (5mi)
6	MS 43 N, N Picayune, **E** 🍴 Mi Sol Azteca, Paul's Pastries, **W** ⛽ Chevron/dsl 🍴 DQ, McDonald's, Sonic, Subway, Waffle Hous 🛏 Super 8 ⊙ Claiborne Hill Mkt, CVS Drug, Family$, H, Wa greens

PICAYUNE

Exit	Services
4	MS 43 S, to Picayune, **E** ⛽ Murphy USA/dsl, RaceTrac/d 🍴 McDonald's, Rio Grande Mexican, Ryan's ⊙ $Tree, AT& Buick/Cadillac/Chevrolet/GMC, Chrysler/Dodge/Jeep, GM Home Depot, Nissan, Verizon, Walgreens, Walmart, **W** ⛽ Exxon/dsl, Keith's/dsl, Shell/dsl 🍴 Applebee's, Burger Kin Domino's, Don's Seafood, Hardee's, IHOP, Little Caesar's, Ne Buffet City, Papa John's, Pizza Hut, Popeye's, Subway, Taco Bel Tokyo Grill, Waffle House, Wendy's 🛏 Days Inn, EconoLodg Heritage Inn, Holiday Inn Express ⊙ $General, Advance Part AutoZone, Family$, Ford/Lincoln, Gene's Tire/auto, H, O'Reill Parts, Paw Paw's RV Ctr, Shoppers Value, URGENT CARE
3mm	Welcome Ctr nb, full ♿ facilities, 🍴 vending, 🛏 litter barrel petwalk, RV dump
1.5mm	weigh sta both lanes
1	US 11, MS 607, **E** ⊙ NASA, **W** ⛽ Shell/dsl ⊙ $General
0mm	Mississippi/Louisiana state line, Pearl River

↑E INTERSTATE 220 (Jackson)

Exit #	Services
11mm	I-220 begins/ends on I-55, exit 104.
9	Hanging Moss Rd, County Line Rd, **E** ⛽ Marathon/dsl
8	Watkins Dr, **E** ⛽ Exxon/Subway, Shell/Chester's/dsl
5b a	US 49 N, Evers Blvd, to Yazoo City, **E** ⛽ Citgo 🍴 KFC, Sonic 🛏 Star Motel ⊙ $General, Family$, Food Depot/gas, **W** ⛽ $Ge eral, Exxon/Burger King, Forty Nine TS/Subway/dsl, Shell/Bask Robbin/dsl
3	Industrial Dr
2b a	Clinton Blvd, Capitol St Big Black River
1b a	US 80, **E** ⛽ Citgo/dsl, Shell 🍴 Capt D's, Country Fisherma DQ, KFC, McDonald's, Pizza Hut, Popeye's, Taco Bell, Wendy 🛏 Best Inn, Scottish Inn ⊙ AutoZone, Firestone/auto, N Transmission, UHaul, **W** ⛽ Citgo/dsl, Exxon/dsl 🍴 Arby Krystal ⊙ $General
0mm	I-220 begins/ends on I-20, exit 41.

NOTES

MISSOURI

➤N   INTERSTATE 29

Exit #	Services
124mm	Missouri/Iowa state line
123mm	Nishnabotna River
121.5mm	weigh sta both lanes
116	rd A, rd B, to Watson, **W** 🅾 fireworks
110	US 136, Rock Port, Phelps City, **E** 🏧 Sinclair/dsl 🏠 fireworks, Rockport Inn, to NW MO St U, **W** 🏧 Cenex/Godfather's/dsl/24hr, Phillips 66/Subway/dsl/24hr 🍴 McDonald's, Trails End Rest. 🏠 Super 8 🅾 fireworks, Rivers Edge RV Park, truck wash
109.5mm	Welcome Ctr sb, full ♿ facilities, info, 🍴, 🏠, litter barrels, petwalk
107	MO 111, to Rock Port
106.5mm	Rock Creek
102mm	Mill Creek
99	rd W, Corning
97mm	Tarkio River
92	US 59, to Fairfax, Craig, **W** 🏧 Sinclair/dsl
90.5mm	Little Tarkio Creek
86.5mm	Squaw Creek
84	MO 118, Mound City, **E** 🏧 Cenex/dsl, Schoonover Oil, Sinclair/Subway/dsl 🍴 Breadeaux Pizza, Casey's Rest., McDonald's, Quacker's Steaks, Senor Barrigas Mexican, Shakers Icecream 🏠 Audrey's Motel, Super 8 🅾 $General, Bumper Parts, USPO, **W** 🏧 BP/dsl 🅾 Big Lake SP (12mi)
82mm	truck parking both lanes, limited facilities
79	US 159, Rulo, **E** 🏧 Phillips 66 Trkstp/dsl/rest/RV dump/@, **W** 🅾 to Big Lake SP (12mi), to Squaw Creek NWR (3mi)
78mm	Kimsey Creek
75	US 59, to Oregon
67	US 59 N, to Oregon
66.5mm	Nodaway River
65	US 59, rd RA, to Fillmore, Savannah, **E** 🏧 Trex/dsl 🅾 antiques, fireworks
60	rd K, rd CC, Amazonia, **W** 🅾 Hunt's Fruit Barn
58.5mm	Hopkins Creek
56b a	I-229 S, US 71 N, US 59 N, to St Joseph, Maryville
55mm	Dillon Creek
53	US 59, US 71 bus, to St Joseph, Savannah, **E** 🅾 AOK Camping, **W** 🏧 Phillips 66/dsl 🅾 antiques, fireworks
50	US 169, St Joseph, King City, **1-3 mi W on Belt Hwy** 🏧 Cenex/dsl, Conoco, Shell, Sinclair/Subway/dsl 🍴 54th St Grill, Bob Evans, Buffalo Wild Wings, Cheddar's, Chick-fil-A, Chili's, Chipotle Mexican, Coldstone, Culver's, Famous Dave's, Hardee's, IHOP, KFC, McDonald's, Olive Garden, Panda Express, Ryan's, Sonic, Starbucks, Subway, Taco Bell 🏠 Candlewood Suites, Fairfield Inn, Holiday Inn Express 🅾 Advance Parts, Aldi Foods, AT&T, Autozone, Best Buy, Dick's, Home Depot, Kohl's, Lowe's, Michael's, Old Navy, Petco, Petsmart, Sam's Club/gas, Target, Tires+, TJ Maxx, URGENT CARE, Walgreens, Walmart/Subway
47	MO 6, Frederick Blvd, to Clarksdale, St Joseph, **E** 🏧 Conoco 🍴 Bandanas BBQ 🏠 Days Inn, Drury Inn 🅾 🏥, **W** 🏧 Sinclair/dsl 🍴 Applebee's, Arby's, Burger King, Cracker Barrel, Denny's, Dunkin', El Maguey Mexican, Fazoli's, Five Guys, Golden Corral, LJ Silver, McAlister's Deli, McDonald's, New China Super Buffet, Pancheros, Panera Bread, Papa John's, Papa Murphy's, Perkins, Pizza Hut, Red Lobster, Rib Crib BBQ, Sonic, Starbucks, Subway,

47	**Continued** Taco Bell, TX Roadhouse, Wendy's, Whiskey Creek Steaks 🏠 Best Value Inn, Hampton Inn, Motel 6, Quality Suites, Ramada, Stoney Creek Inn 🅾 $General, Apple Mkt Foods, BigLots, Buick/GMC, Chevrolet, CVS Drug, Dillard's, Firestone/auto, Ford/Lincoln, Hobby Lobby, Honda, HyVee Foods/dsl, JC Penney, Jo-Ann Fabrics, Nissan, Office Depot, Taco John's, Toyota, U-Haul, Verizon, vet, Walgreens
46b a	US 36, to Cameron, St Joseph, **E** 🅾 to MWSU, **1 mi W** on US 169 🏧 BP/dsl, FP/dsl, Murphy USA/dsl, Roadstar/dsl, Sinclair/dsl 🍴 Burger King, Jimmy John's, Pizza Hut, Taco John's, Wendy's 🅾 $General, Ace Hardware, AT&T, CVS, KIA, Klein RV Ctr, O'Reilly Parts, Walgreens, Walmart/Subway
44	US 169, to Gower, St Joseph, **E** 🏧 Loves/Arby's/dsl/scales/24hr, Phillips 66 🍴 Nelly's Mexican, Subway 🏠 Guesthouse Inn 🅾 dsl repair, **W** 🏧 Murphy USA/dsl, Shell/dsl/24hr 🍴 DQ, El Maguey, Goodcents Subs, McDonald's, San Jose Steaks, Sonic, Taco Bell, Waffle House 🅾 $Tree, Apple Mkt Foods, Chrysler/Dodge/Jeep, Harley-Davidson, Hyundai, Menards, Walmart/Subway
43	I-229 N, to St Joseph
39.5mm	Pigeon Creek
35	rd DD, Faucett, **W** 🏧 Farris Trkstp/dsl/motel/rest/24hr/@
33.5mm	Bee Creek
30	rd Z, rd H, Dearborn, New Market, **E** 🏧 Trex/Subway/dsl/24hr
29.5mm	Bee Creek
27mm	Rs both lanes, full ♿ facilities, 🍴, 🏠, litter barrels, vending, petwalk
25	rd E, rd U, to Camden Point, **E** 🏧 Trex/dsl
24mm	weigh sta nb/truck parking sb
20	MO 92, MO 273, to Atchison, Leavenworth, **W** 🏧 Trex/Dunkin'/dsl 🅾 antiques, to Weston Bend SP
19.5mm	Platte River

PLATTE CITY

INTERSTATE 29 Cont'd

Exit #	Services
19	rd HH, Platte City (sb returns at 18), **W** 🔲 Casey's, Platte-Clay Fuel/dsl 🍴 DQ, Maria's Mexican, Pizza Hut, Red Dragon Chinese, Roxanne's Cafe 🛏 Quality Inn, Travelodge ◻ $General, Airport RV Park, CarQuest, O'Reilly Parts, same as 18, USPO
18	MO 92, Platte City, **E** ◻ Basswood RV Park (5mi), **W** 🔲 Phillips 66/Jimmy John's, QT/dsl 🍴 Arby's, Burger King, China Wok, Culver's, DQ, El Maguey, GoodCents Subs, McDonald's, Pizza Hut/Taco Bell, Pizza Shoppe, Sonic, Starbucks, Subway, Waffle House, Wendy's 🛏 Ramada, Super 8 ◻ Buick/Chevrolet, Chrysler/Dodge/Jeep, CVS Drug, Ford, Goodyear/auto, PriceChopper Foods, same as 19, TrueValue, Verizon, Walgreens
17	I-435 S, to Topeka
15	Mexico City Ave, **W** 🛏 Marriott ◻ 🖘
14	I-435 E (from sb), to St Louis
13	to I-435 E, **E** 🛏 Extended Stay America, Fairfield Inn, Holiday Inn, Microtel, Quality Suites, Sheraton, Super 8, Surestay Plus, Towneplace Suites, **W** 🛏 Marriott ◻ KCI Airport
12	NW 112th St, **E** 🔲 BP, Phillips 66/dsl 🍴 Old Chicago Pizza 🛏 Best Western +, Candlewood Suites, Comfort Inn, Days Inn, Extended Stay America, Hampton Inn, Hilton, **W** 🛏 EconoLodge
10	Tiffany Springs Pkwy, **E** 🔲 Phillips 66/dsl 🍴 Beaches Cantina, SmokeBox BBQ 🛏 Embassy Suites, Holiday Inn Express, Homewood Suites, Residence Inn, **W** 🍴 Cracker Barrel, Ruby Tuesday, Waffle House, Wendy's 🛏 Chase Suites, Courtyard, Drury Inn, Extended Stay America, Hyatt Place, Sleep Inn ◻ Buick/GMC, Harley-Davidson, Honda, Lexus, Nissan, Toyota
9b a	MO 152, to Liberty, Topeka
8	MO 9, rd T, NW Barry Rd, **E** 🔲 Phillips 66/dsl 🍴 Applebee's, Big Biscuit, Burger King, Chick-fil-A, Chili's, China Wok, Chipotle Mexican, ChuckeCheese, Dickey's BBQ, Five Guys, Golden Corral, Honeybaked Cafe, Hong's Buffet, Hooters, Houlihan's, Jason's Deli, Kato Japanese, On the Border, Panchero's, Panda Express, Panera Bread, Papa Murphy's, Rally House, Sheridan's Custard, Starbucks, Subway, Taco Bell, Wendy's, Winstead's Rest. ◻ $Tree, AutoZone, Best Buy, Ford, Hobby Lobby, Home Depot, 🅷, HyVee/dsl, JC Penney, Lowe's, NTB, Petsmart, Ross, Target, Verizon, vet, Walmart, **W** 🔲 Phillips 66/dsl, QT/dsl 🍴 54th St Grill, A&W/LJSilver, Abuelo's, Arby's, Bar Louie, BoLings Chinese, Bravo Italian, Buffalo Wild Wings, Granite City, Hardee's, Hereford House, Jimmy John's, McDonald's, Minsky's Pizza, Noodles&Co, Outback Steaks, Rainbow Oriental, Smokehouse BBQ, Sonic, Stone Canyon Pizza, Taco Bueno 🛏 La Quinta, Motel 6, Super 8 ◻ AT&T, Barnes&Noble, CVS Drug, Dick's, Dillard's, Marshall's, Michael's, Old Navy, Staples, Tires+, Verizon
6	NW 72nd St, Platte Woods, **E** 🔲 Sinclair/dsl ◻ vet, **W** 🔲 Phillips 66 🍴 Iron Wok, Papa John's, Tasty Thai ◻ K-Mart
5	MO 45 N, NW 64th St, **W** 🔲 Shell/dsl 🍴 Bonefish Grill, Caribou Coffee, Chamas Brazilian Grill, Chipotle, Culver's, Goodcents Subs, IHOP, Luna Azteca, McDonald's, Papa Murphy's, Saki Asian, Starbucks, Subway, Taco Bell ◻ $General, CVS Drug, GNC, Hen House Mkt, HyVee, Sprouts Mkt, Tuesday Morning, vet
4	NW 56th St (from nb), **W** 🔲 Phillips 66
3c	rd A (from sb), Riverside, **W** 🔲 QT/dsl 🍴 Corner Café, Sonic ◻ Rverside Automotive, USPO
3b	I-635 S
3a	Waukomis Dr, rd AA (from nb)
2b	US 169 S (from sb), to KC
2a	US 169 N (from nb), to Smithville
1e	US 69, Vivion Rd, **E** 🔲 Phillips66/dsl 🍴 Steak'n Shake ◻ Cadillac/Chevrolet, Fiat, Home Depot, Lincoln, Subaru

KANSAS CITY

Exit #	Services
1d	MO 283 S, Oak Tfwy (from sb), **W** 🔲 BP/dsl 🍴 McDonald', Subway ◻ CVS, O'Reilly Parts
1c	Gladstone (from nb), **E** 🔲 Phillips 66 🍴 Arby's, Freddy's, Panda Express, Pizza Ranch, Taco Bueno, Wendy's ◻ BigLots, Discount Tire, 🅷, Lowe's, Petco, PriceChopper Foods, Sam's Club dsl
1b	I-35 N (from sb), to Des Moines
1a	Davidson Rd
8mm	I-35 N.
\multicolumn{2}{l}{I-29 and I-35 run together 6 mi. See Missouri Interstate 35, exits 3-8a.}

INTERSTATE 35

Exit #	Services
114mm	Missouri/Iowa state line
114	US 69, to Lamoni, **W** 🔲 Conoco/dsl/24hr
113.5mm	Zadie Creek
112mm	MO welcome ctr sb, full ♿ facilities, 🍴, 🏕, litter barrels, pe walk, wireless internet
110	weigh sta both lanes
106	rd N, Blythedale, **E** 🔲 Phillips 66/Dinner Bell Cafe/motel dsl/24hr/@, Phillips 66/fireworks 🛏 Eagles Landing Motel ◻ camping, dsl repair, **W** 🔲 Loves/Subway/dsl/scales/24h ◻ Eagle Ridge RV Park (2mi), fireworks
99	rd A, to Ridgeway, 5 mi **W** ◻ camping
94mm	E Fork Big Creek
93	US 69, Bethany
92	US 136, Bethany, **E** 🔲 Casey's/dsl/scales, Sinclair/Subway/d 🍴 KFC/Taco Bell, McDonald's 🛏 Budget Inn, **W** 🔲 BP/ds Casey's/dsl, Kum&Go/dsl, MFA 🍴 China King, DQ, Nopal Mexican, Pizza Hut, Sonic, TootToot Rest. 🛏 Comfort Inn, Super ◻ $General, 🅷, Peterbilt, Walmart
90mm	Pole Cat Creek
88	MO 13, to Bethany, Gallatin
84	rds AA, H, to Gilman City, **E** ◻ Crowder SP (24mi)
81mm	truck parking, limited facilities
80	rds B, N, to Coffey
78	rd C, Pattonsburg, **W** 🔲 gas/dsl
74.5mm	Grand River
72	rd DD
68	US 69, to Pattonsburg
64	MO 6, to Maysville, Gallatin
61	US 69, Winston, Gallatin, **E** 🔲 Shell/rest./dsl/24hr
54	US 36, Cameron, **E** 🔲 Shell/Baskin-Robbins/Wendy's/dsl/24h Sinclair/dsl/scales/24hr 🍴 McDonald's, Subway 🛏 Comfor Inn, Guesthouse Inn, Motel 6 ◻ 🅷, **W** 🔲 Valero/dsl 🍴 Burge King, Chinese Chef, DQ, El Maguey Mexican, KFC/Taco Bell, Pizza Hut, Sonic, Washington Street Rest. 🛏 Best Value Inn, Day Inn, EconoLodge, Super 8 ◻ Advance Parts, antiques, Buick Chevrolet/GMC, Cameron Mkt, O'Reilly Parts, Twin Creeks Tir USPO, Verizon, Walmart
52	rd BB, Lp 35, to Cameron, **E** ◻ 🅷, **W** 🔲 Casey's, same as 54 ◻ $General
49mm	Brushy Creek
48.5mm	Shoal Creek
48	US 69, Cameron, **E** ◻ to Wallace SP (2mi)
40	MO 116, Lathrop, **E** 🔲 Trex/Country Cafe/dsl ◻ antiques
34.5mm	Ⓡˢ both lanes, full ♿ facilities, 🍴, 🏕, litter barrels, vending petwalk
33	rd PP, Holt, **E** 🍴 auto repair, **W** 🔲 BP/dsl, Conoco/dsl 🛏 American Eagle Inn ◻ $General
30mm	Holt Creek

BETHANY

CAMERON

MO

INTERSTATE 35 Cont'd

K E A R N E Y

Exit #	Services
26	MO 92, Kearney, **E** 📶 Casey's/dsl, Phillips 66/dsl, QT/dsl 🍴 China Wok, Jimmy John's, McDonald's, Papa Murphy's, Pizza Hut, Sonic 🛏 Comfort Inn, Super 8 ⊡ CVS Drug, Price Chopper, to Watkins Mill SP, True Value, Verizon, **W** 📶🍴⛽/Taco Bell/dsl/scales/24hr 🍴 Arby's, Burger King, Hunan Garden Chinese, JJ's Homestead Rest., Pizza Shoppe, Stables Grill, Subway 🛏 EconoLodge, Quality Inn ⊡ Goodyear/auto, O'Reilly Parts, to Smithville Lake
22mm	parking area sb, weigh sta nb
20	US 69, MO 33, to Excelsior Springs, **E** ⊡ 🏥
17	MO 291, rd A, **1 mi E** 📶 BP, QT/dsl 🍴 A&W, CiCi's, Dickey's BBQ, Firehouse Subs, Hardee's, LJ Silver, McDonald's, Minsky's Pizza, Papa John's, Papa Murphy's, Perkins, Sonic, Subway, Taco Bell ⊡ $General, Chevrolet, Days Inn, Firestone/auto, KC Auto, Liberty RV Ctr, O'Reilly Parts, same as 16, Walgreens, **W** 📶 Phillips 66/dsl, QT 🍴 DQ, Masabi Japanese, McDonald's, Nicky's Pizza, Sonic, Subway, Zaxby's 🛏 Sleep Inn, Woodspring Suites ⊡ Price Chopper Foods, to KCI Airport, URGENT CARE, Walgreens
16	MO 152, Liberty, **E** 📶 EVC, Phillips 66 🍴 Baskin-Robbins, Chick-fil-A, CiCi's Pizza, Culver's, Domino's, Five Guys, IHOP, Jimmy John's, Margarita's, MOD Pizza, Olive Garden, Perkins, Pizza Hut, Pizza Ranch, Planet Sub, Red Robin, Starbucks, TX Roadhouse, Wendy's 🛏 Days Inn, Super 8 ⊡ Advance Parts, AutoZone, Chevrolet, CVS Drug, Dick's, Discount Tire, Firestone/auto, Gordman's, 🏥, Hy-Vee/gas, Lowe's, Ross, URGENT CARE, Walgreens, **W** 📶 Murphy USA/dsl, Phillips 66/dsl 🍴 54th St Grill, Applebee's, Arby's, Buffalo Wild Wings, Burger King, Cheddar's, Chili's, Chipotle Mexican, Corner Cafe, Cracker Barrel, Fanner's Grill, Freddy's Burgers, Jose Peppers, Joy Wok, KFC, LongHorn Steaks, McDonald's, Noodles&Co, Old Chicago Pizza, Panda Express, Panera Bread, PepperJax Grill, Qdoba, Steak'n Shake, Subway, Taco Bell, Ted's Cafe Escondido, Waffle House 🛏 Comfort Suites, Fairfield Inn, Hampton Inn, Holiday Inn Express ⊡ Aldi Foods, AT&T, Best Buy, Christian Bros Auto, Ford, Home Depot, JC Penney, Jiffy Lube, Kohl's, Michael's, NAPA, NTB, Office Depot, Petsmart, Sam's Club/dsl, Sprouts Mkt, Target, TJ Maxx, Tuesday Morning, URGENT CARE, Verizon, Walmart/Subway
14	US 69 (exits left from sb), Liberty Dr, to Glenaire, Pleasant Valley, **E** 📶 Phillips 66, Sinclair/dsl, **W** 📶 QT/dsl/scales/24hr
13	US 69 (from nb), to Pleasant Valley, **E** 📶 Phillips 66, Sinclair/dsl, **W** 📶 QT/dsl/scales/24hr
12 b a	I-435, to St Louis
11	US 69 N, Vivion Rd, **E** 📶 BP/dsl, Phillips 66/dsl 🍴 Church's, McDonald's, **W** 📶 QT/dsl 🍴 Sonic, Stroud's Rest., Subway ⊡ CVS Drug, O'Reilly Parts, USPO, vet
10	N Brighton Ave (from nb), **W** 📶 QT/dsl 🍴 Church's, Sonic ⊡ CVS Drug
9	MO 269 S, Chouteau Trfwy, **E** 📶 Phillips 66 🍴 IHOP, McDonald's, Ming Garden, Papa Murphy's, Subway, Wing Stop ⊡ Festival Foods, GNC, Harrah's Casino/rest., Target, **W** 🍴 Wendy's (1mi)
8c	MO 1, Antioch Rd, **E** 📶 Conoco/7-11 🍴 Domino's 🛏 Best Western ⊡ auto repair, **W** 📶 Phillips 66, QT 🍴 Dickey's BBQ, Waffle House ⊡ AT&T, Walgreens
8b	I-29 N, US 71 N, KCI ↗
	I-35 S and I-29 S run together 6 mi.
8a	Parvin Rd, **E** 📶 BP/dsl, Shell/dsl 🍴 Subway ⊡ O'Reilly Parts

K A N S A S   C I T Y

Exit #	Services
6b a	Armour Rd, **E** 📶 Phillips 66/dsl 🍴 Arby's, Burger King, Denny's, McDonald's, Quiznos, Subway 🛏 EconoLodge, La Quinta ⊡ 🏥, repair, to Riverboat Casino, **W** 📶 Flash/dsl, Phillips 66, QT 🍴 DQ, Jimmy John's, Lucky Dragon Chinese, Pizza Hut, Subway, Taco Bell, Wendy's 🛏 American Inn, Holiday Inn Express ⊡ URGENT CARE, USPO
5b	16th Ave industrial district
5a	Levee Rd, Bedford St industrial district
4.5mm	Missouri River
4b	Front St, **E** ⊡ Isle of Capri Riverboat Casino/rest.
4a	US 24 E, Independence Ave
3	I-70 E, US 71 S, to St Louis
2g	**I-35 N and I-29 N run together 6 mi.**
2e	Oak St, Grand-Walnut St, **E** 📶 Phillips 66 🛏 Marriott
2d	Main-Delaware, Wyandotte St downtown
2a	I-70 W, to Topeka
2y	US 169, Broadway to downtown
2w	12th St, Kemper Arena to downtown
2v	14th St to downtown
2u	I-70 E, to Broadway, **E** 🍴 Denny's
1e	US 69, Vivion Rd, **E** 📶 Sinclair/dsl
1d	20th St (from sb), **E** 📶 Phillips 66
1c	27th St, SW Blvd, W Pennway (from nb), **E** 📶 Phillips 66 ⊡ 🏥
1a	SW Trafficway (from sb)
0mm	Missouri/Kansas state line

INTERSTATE 44

S T   L O U I S

Exit #	Services
293mm	I-44 begins/ends on I-70, exit 249 in St Louis.
290a	I-55 S, to Memphis
290c	Gravois Ave (from wb), 12th St, **S** 🍴 Jack-in-the-Box
290b	18th St (from eb) downtown
289	Jefferson Ave, St Louis, **N** 📶 Phillips 66 🍴 Subway 🛏 Hotel Avyan, Residence Inn ⊡ Family$, SaveALot, **S** 📶 Conoco 🍴 Lee's Chicken, McDonald's ⊡ $General
288	Grand Blvd, St Louis, **N** 📶 BP 🛏 Water Tower Inn ⊡ 🏥, vet, **S** 🍴 Domino's, Jack-in-the-Box, Jimmy John's, Starbucks, Subway ⊡ Family$
287b a	Kingshighway, Vandeventer Ave, St Louis, **N** 📶 BP, QT/dsl ⊡ 🏥, Jiffy Lube, U-Haul, **S** ⊡ Chevrolet, to MO Botanical Garden
286	Hampton Ave, St Louis, **N** 📶 BP, Circle K, Mobil, Phillips 66 🍴 Courtesy Diner, Denny's, Jack-in-the-Box, McDonald's, Steak'n Shake, Subway, Taco Bell ⊡ zoo, **S** 📶 Circle K/dsl 🍴 Bartolino's Rest., Hardee's, Wendy's 🛏 Drury Inn, Holiday Inn, Red Roof Inn
285	SW Ave (from wb, no EZ return)
284b a	Arsenal St, Jamieson St
283	Shrewsbury (from wb) some services same as 282

MO

⬆️E INTERSTATE 44 Cont'd

Exit #	Services
282	Laclede Sta Rd, Murdock Ave (from eb), St Louis, N 🅟 BP 🍴 Frisco Cafe, Front Row Grill, Hwy 61 Roadhouse, Imo's Pizza, McDonald's, Racanelli's Pizza, Starbucks, Subway, Webster Wok Chinese 🅾 Subaru, vet
280	Elm Ave, St Louis, N 🅟 BP 🍴 Jamba Juice 🅾 Schnuck's Foods, 1 mi S 🅟 Shell/Circle K 🍴 Steak'n Shake 🅾 Walgreens
279	(from wb), Berry Rd
278	Big Bend Rd, St Louis, N 🍴 Culver's, Hardee's 🅾 🏥, Sam's Club/gas, URGENT CARE, S 🅟 Mobil/dsl, QT
277b	US 67, US 61, US 50, Lindbergh Blvd, N 🍴 Arby's, Blaze Pizza, Buffalo Wild Wings, Cane's, Chili's, Chipotle Mexican, Dunkin', Jason's Deli, Sonic, TX Roadhouse, White Castle 🛏 Best Western 🅾 $Tree, Aldi Foods, AT&T, AutoZone, Harley-Davidson, Hobby Lobby, 🏥, Lowe's Whse, Office Depot, Target, TJ Maxx, Walmart, S 🅟 Circle K/dsl, Phillips 66/dsl 🍴 Burger King, Chick-fil-A, Denny's, Five Guys, Fuddrucker's, Helen Fitzgerald's Grill, IHOP, Lion's Choice, Longhorn Steaks, Panda Express, St Louis Bread, Steak'n Shake, Subway, Walnut Grill 🛏 Days Inn/rest., Hilltop Hotel, Holiday Inn 🅾 Dobb's Auto/Tire, Home Depot, Marshall's, Old Navy, Petsmart, Ross, Stein Mart
277a	MO 366 E, Watson Rd access to same as 277b S
276b a	I-270, N to Chicago, S Memphis
275	N Highway Dr (from wb), Soccer Pk Rd, N 🅟 Road Ranger/Subway/dsl
274a b	Bowles Ave, N 🅟 Road Ranger/Subway/dsl, S 🅟 Phillips 66/dsl, QT/dsl 🍴 Bandana's BBQ, Cracker Barrel, Jack-in-the-Box, Krispy Kreme, McDonald's, White Castle 🛏 Drury Inn, Fairfield Inn, Holiday Inn Express, Motel 6, PearTree Inn, Stratford Inn, Super 8, TownePlace Suites
272	MO 141, Fenton, Valley Park, N 🅟 Motomart, S 🅟 Phillips 66/dsl, ZX 🍴 Bob Evans, Hardee's, Jimmy John's, Psghetti's, Ruby Tuesday, Starbucks, Steak'n Shake, Subway, Sugarfire BBQ, Taco Bell 🛏 Drury Inn, Hampton Inn 🅾 Save-A-Lot Foods
269	Antire Rd, Beaumont
266	Lewis Rd, N 🅾 golf, Rte 66 SP
266mm	Meramec River
265	Williams Rd (from eb)
264	MO 109, rd W, Eureka, N 🅟 Phillips 66/dsl 🍴 Arby's, Burger King, Culver's, Domino's, Jimmy John's, McDonald's, Pizza Hut, Poor Richard's, Smokers BBQ, St Louis Bread, Taco Bell, White Castle 🅾 AT&T, Byerly RV Ctr, O'Reilly Parts, Schnuck's Foods, to Babler SP, Valvoline, Verizon, S 🅟 QT/dsl 🅾 Walgreens
261	Lp 44, to Allenton, N 🅟 Motomart/McDonald's/dsl 🍴 China King, Denny's, Imo's Pizza, Lion's Choice, Steak'n Shake, Subway 🛏 Best Inn, Holiday Inn, Super 8 🅾 $Tree, AutoZone, Jellystone RV Camping, same as 264, to Six Flags, Walmart, S 🅟 Circle K/dsl, Circle K/dsl (2) 🅾 KOA
257	(256 from eb) Lp 44, Pacific, N 🅟 Phillips 66/dsl, 🚛/Subway/dsl/scales/24hr 🛏 Comfort Inn 🅾 fireworks, S 🅟 BP/dsl, Mobil/dsl, Motomart 🍴 Domino's, El Agave Mexican, Hardee's, KFC, McDonald's, New China, Pizza Hut, Taco Bell 🛏 Quality Inn 🅾 $General, B&H Foods, Chrysler/Dodge/Jeep, CVS Drug, O'Reilly Parts, SaveALot, st police
253	MO 100 E, to Gray Summit, S 🅟 Mobil/dsl 🅾 fireworks, Shaw Nature Preserve
251	MO 100 W, to Washington, N 🅟 BP/dsl, Mr Fuel/dsl/scales, Phillips 66/Burger King/dsl 🅾 $General, 🏥 (11mi)
247	US 50 W, rd AT, rd O, to Union, N 🅾 Pin Oak Creek RV Park, S 🅾 to Robertsville SP
247mm	Bourbeuse River

Exit #	Services
242	rd AH, to Hist Rte 66
240	MO 47, St Clair, N 🅟 Phillips 66/Taco Bell/dsl 🍴 Burger King 🅾 tire/auto, S 🅟 Mobil/dsl 🍴 Domino's, McDonald's, Subway 🛏 Budget Lodge, Super 8 🅾 $General, Country Mart Foods, NAPA, O'Reilly Parts, Save-A-Lot Foods, USPO
239	MO 30, rds AB, WW, St Clair, N 🅾 repair, S 🅟 Phillips 66/dsl
238mm	weigh sta both lanes
235mm	🆁🆂 both lanes (both lanes exit left), full ♿ facilities, 🍴🅟, litter barrels, vending, petwalk
230	rds W, Stanton, S 🅟 Amstar/fireworks 🅾 KOA, Meramec Caverns Camping (3mi), USPO
226	MO 185 S, Sullivan, N 🅟 FLYING J/Denny's/dsl/LP/scales/24hr 🅾 vet, S 🅟 Circle K/dsl 🍴 Applebee's, Arby's, China Buffet, DQ, Imo's Pizza, KFC, Little Caesar's, McDonald's, Starbucks, Subway, Taco Bell 🅾 $General, $Tree, Aldi Foods, AT&T, AutoZone, Lowe's, O'Reilly Parts, same as 225, to Meramec SP, Walmart
225	MO 185 N, rd D, Sullivan, N 🅟 Mobil, Phillips 66/dsl 🍴 Domino's, Du Kum Inn Rest., Jimmy John's 🛏 Baymont Inn, Best Value Inn, Motel 6, Super 8 🅾 Chevrolet/Buick/GMC, Chrysler/Dodge/Jeep, Ford, S 🅟 BP/Fas-Trip/dsl/café, ZX 🍴 Cracker Barrel, El Nopal Mexican, Jack-in-the-Box, Lion's Choice, Pizza Hut 🛏 Comfort Inn 🅾 city park, 🏥, same as 226
218	rds N, C, J, Bourbon, N 🅟 ZX/dsl 🛏 Budget Inn, S 🅟 Mobil/dsl 🍴 $General, Planet Sub, Subway 🅾 Blue Sprgs Camping (6mi), Bourbon RV Ctr, Riverview Ranch Camping (8mi), Sinks Drug, Town&Country Mkt
214	rd H, Leasburg, N 🅟 Mobil/dsl, S 🍴 Skippy's Rte 66 Rest. 🅾 to Onandaga Cave SP (7mi)
210	rd UU, N 🅾 Meremac Valley Resort, S 🍴 MO Hick BBQ (3mi) 🅾 winery
208	MO 19, Cuba, N 🅟 Midwest/Phillips 66/Dotty's Rest./dsl/scales/24hr/@ 🍴 Huddle House, Pizza Hut 🛏 Cuba Inn, Super 8 🅾 antiques, Blue Beacon, S 🅟 Casey's, Mobil/dsl 🍴 East Sun Chinese, Hardee's, Jack-in-the-Box, McDonald's, Sonic, Subway, Taco Bell 🛏 Days Inn 🅾 $General, $Tree, Mace Foods, O'Reilly Parts, to Ozark Nat Scenic Riverways (74mi), Walmart
203	rds F, ZZ, S 🅾 Rosatti Winery (2mi)
195	MO 8, MO 68, St James, Maramec Sprg Park, N 🅟 BP/Circle K/dsl, Mobil/dsl 🍴 China King, McDonald's, Pizza Hut, Sonic, Subway 🛏 Economy Inn, Greenstay Inn 🅾 $General, Ford, O'Reilly Parts, Ray's Tires, to Maremac Winery, tours ctr, S 🅟 Casey's/dsl, Phillips 66/dsl 🍴 Burger King 🛏 Finn's Motel 🅾 CountryMart Foods
189	rd V, Industrial Park Dr, Hypoint, N 🅟 💙Loves/McDonald's/Subway/dsl/scales/24hr, S 🅾 Mule Trading Post
186	US 63, MO 72, Rolla, N 🅟 Sinclair/dsl 🍴 Steak'n Shake 🛏 Drury Inn, Hampton Inn, Motel 6 🅾 Big O Tire, Kia, Kohl's, Lowe's, Nissan, Plaza Tire, S 🅟 BreakTime/dsl, Mobil/dsl, Phillips 66/dsl 🍴 Buffalo Wild Wings, Colton's Steaks, Donut King, IHOP, Koi Chinese, Lee's Chicken, Panera Bread, Starbucks 🛏 Budget Motel 🅾 🏥
185	rd E, to Rolla, N 🅾 hwy patrol, S 🅟 ZX 🍴 Arby's, DQ, Hardee's, Huddle House, Jimmy John's, Kyoto Japanese, LJ Silver, Papa John's, Subway, Taco Bell, Wendy's 🅾 CVS Drug, Ford, 🏥, Kroger, UMO at Rolla
184	US 63 S, to Rolla, N 🛏 Comfort Suites, Holiday Inn Express 🅾 Menards, Petsmart, Ross, TJ Maxx, S 🅟 MotoMart, ZX 🍴 Arby's, Bandana's BBQ, Denny's, Dickey's BBQ, Little Caesar's, LJ Silver, Lucky House Chinese, Maid-Rite, McDonald's, Penelope's Rest., Pizza Hut, Sirloin Stockade, Subway, Waffle House, Wendy's 🛏 Baymont Inn, Best Western, EconoLodge, Quality Inn

SULLIVAN

CUBA

ROLLA

INTERSTATE 44 Cont'd

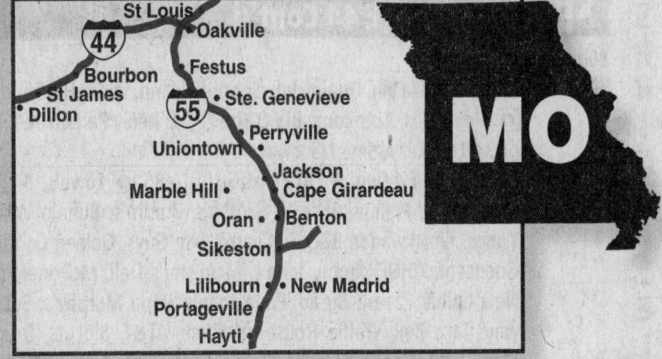

184 Continued
Sunset Inn, Super 8 ⊙ Buick/Cadillac/GMC, Chevrolet, city park, CVS Drug, 🏥, Kroger

179 rds T, C, to Doolittle, Newburg, S 📶 Phillips 66/dsl 🍴 Cookin' From Scratch Rest. ⊙ $General

178mm truck parking both lanes, restrooms

176 Sugar Tree Rd

172 rd D, Jerome

169 rd J

166 to Big Piney

164mm Big Piney River

163 MO 28, to Dixon, N 📶 Road Ranger/Chesters/Subway/dsl/scales/24hr, S 📶 Phillips 66/dsl 🛏 Best Western, Days Inn, Motel 6 ⊙ RV Park, Uranus Fudge Factory

161b a rd Y, to Ft Leonard Wood, N 📶 Mobil/dsl, Murphy USA/dsl, One Stop/dsl 🍴 Cracker Barrel, Domino's, Ocean Buffet, Papa Murphy's, Pizza Hut, Rte 66 Diner, Ruby Tuesday, Wendy's 🛏 Baymont Inn, Best Value Inn, Candlewood Suites, Comfort Inn, Fairfield Inn, Hampton Inn, Hawthorn Suites, Mainstay Suites, Red Roof Inn ⊙ Lowe's, Toyota, visitors ctr, Walmart/Subway, S 📶 Casey's/dsl, Kum&Go/dsl 🍴 Arby's, Buffalo Wild Wings, Cantina Bravo, Colton's Steaks, Culver's, Freddy's, Hardee's, Little Caesar's, McDonald's, Panera Bread, Papa John's, Starbucks, Subway, Taco Bell, Waffle House 🛏 Budget Inn, EconoLodge, Holiday Inn Express, Liberty Lodge, Quality Inn, ZLoft Hotel ⊙ $General, $Tree, AT&T, AutoZone, Chrysler/Dodge/Jeep, Family$, Ford/Lincoln, Mazda, NAPA, O'Reilly Parts, Verizon

159 Lp 44, to Waynesville, St Robert, N 🍴 DQ, Sonic 🛏 All Star Motel, Super 8 ⊙ auto repair, O'Reilly Parts, S 📶 Cenex/dsl 🍴 El Cabrito 🛏 Alliance Inn ⊙ Big O Tire, Cadillac/GMC

158mm Roubidoux Creek

156 rd H, Waynesville, N 📶 Express Stop/Burger King/dsl/e85, Gulf/dsl, Kum&Go/dsl 🍴 McDonald's, Subway ⊙ $General, Chevrolet, Price Cutter+

153 MO 17, to Buckhorn, N 🍴 Ft Wood Inn, S 📶 Gulf/dsl ⊙ Glen Oaks RV Park

150 MO 7, rd P to Richland

145 MO 133, rd AB, to Richland, N 📶 Sinclair/Oasis/cafe/dsl/24hr

143mm Gasconade River

140 rd N, to Stoutland, S 📶 Cenex/pizza/dsl

139mm Bear Creek

135 rd F, Sleeper

130 rd MM, N 📶 Cenex/dsl, Express Stop/Taco John's/dsl 🍴 Andy's Rest. 🛏 EconoLodge, Munger Moss Inn, S 📶 Kum&Go/dsl ⊙ 🏥

129 MO 5, MO 32, MO 64, to Hartville, Lebanon, N 🍴 Applebee's, Arby's, Bamboo Garden, Bandana's BBQ, Burger King, DQ, Elm St Eatery, Jimmy John's, KFC, Little Caesar's, LJ Silver, McDonald's, Papa Murphy's, Sonic, Steak'n Shake, Subway, Taco Bell, Wendy's ⊙ Aldi Foods, AT&T, AutoZone, Chevrolet, Ford, King Cashsaver, O'Reilly Parts, repair, Rte 66 Museum, to Bennett Sprgs SP, to Lake of the Ozarks, Verizon, Walgreens, Walnut Bowl Factory, S 📶 Cenex/dsl, Phillips 66/dsl 🍴 Capt D's, Denny's, Domino's, Hardee's, La Tolteca, Pizza Hut ⊙ $Tree, 🏥, Lowe's, O'Reilly Parts, Sawyer Tire/auto, Walmart/Subway

127 Lp 44, Lebanon, N 📶 Cenex/dsl, Gulf/B&D/J Diner/dsl/scales/24hr 🍴 Dowd's Catfish&BBQ, El Sombrero Mexican, Slim Chickens, Subway, Tequila Mexican, Waffle House 🛏 Best Value Inn, Days Inn, Hampton Inn, Holiday Inn Express, Midwest Inn, Rte 66 Motel, Super 8 ⊙ $General, Chrysler/Dodge/Jeep,

127 Continued
Cutlery/Walnut Bowl Outlet, Firestone/auto, S 📶 Conoco/McDonald's/dsl 🍴 Dickey's BBQ ⊙ Buick/Cadillac/GMC, Harley-Davidson, Russell Stover

123 County Rd, S ⊙ antiques, Happy Trails RV Ctr, Happy Trails RV Park

118 rds C, A, Phillipsburg, S 📶 Phillips 66 ⊙ Redmon's Gifts, tourist info

113 rds J, Y, Conway, N 📶 Conoco/dsl 🍴 Rockin Chair Café 🛏 Budget Inn ⊙ to Den of Metal Arts, S 📶 Sinclair/dsl ⊙ $General, SummerFresh Foods, USPO

111mm Rs both lanes, full 🚻 facilities, 🅲, vending, litter barrels, 🐾 petwalk, playground

108mm Bowen Creek

107 Sparkle Brooke Rd, Sampson Rd

106mm Niangua River

100 MO 38, rd W, Marshfield, N 📶 Murphy USA/dsl, Phillips 66 ⊙ $Tree, auto repair, Chevrolet, Chrysler/Dodge/Jeep, Ford, Walmart/Subway, S 📶 Casey's/dsl, Cenex/dsl, Shell/dsl 🍴 Burger King, DQ, El Charro, Golden China, Grillos Cafe, KFC/Rib Crib, McDonald's, Pizza Hut, Sonic, Subway, Taco Bell 🛏 Holiday Inn Express ⊙ $General, AutoZone, O'Reilly Parts, RV Express RV Park, Verizon, Walgreens

96 rd B, Northview, N ⊙ Rustic Meadows RV Park (2mi)

89mm weigh sta both lanes

88 MO 125, to Fair Grove, Strafford, N 📶 Loves/Hardee's/dsl/scales/rv dump/24hr, TA/Subway/Taco Bell/dsl/scales/24hr/@ 🍴 McDonald's ⊙ Camping World RV Ctr, truckwash, vet, S 📶 Breaktime/dsl, Kum&Go 🍴 Pizza Hut 🛏 Super 8 ⊙ $General, Strafford RV Park

84 MO 744, S ⊙ Peterbilt

82b a US 65, to Branson, Fedalia, S 📶 Kum&Go/dsl, Phillips 66/dsl 🍴 Waffle House ⊙ Bull Shoals Lake, Kenworth, st patrol, to Table Rock Lake

80b a rd H to Pleasant Hope, Springfield, N 📶 Conoco/rest./dsl/scales/24hr, Kum&Go/dsl, Shell/dsl, Sinclair, Tesla EVC 🍴 Tropical Cafe, Waffle House 🛏 Days Inn, Holiday Inn Express, Red Roof Inn, Super 8 ⊙ $General, S 📶 Casey's, Kum&Go/dsl, Phillips 66/dsl, Shell 🍴 Andy's Custard, Applebee's, Braum's, Burger King, Carriage House, Cracker Barrel, Culver's, El Maguey Mexican, Fazoli's, Freddy's, Hardee's, Hong Kong Inn, Houlihan's, Ichiban Buffet, Jose Locos, King's Asian Chef, Little Tokyo, LJ Silver, McDonald's, Panda Express, Pizza Hut, Rib Crib, Royal Buffet, Ruby Tuesday, Schlotzsky's, Shanghai Inn, Sonic, Steak'n Shake, Subway, Taco Bell, Whole Hog Cafe, Ziggies Cafe 🛏 Baymont Inn, Best Western, Campus Inn, Candlewood Suites, Comfort Inn, Dogwood Park Inn, Doubletree Hotel, Drury Inn, EconoLodge, Economy Inn, Fairfield Inn, Flagship Motel, Hampton Inn, Holiday Inn, Home 2 Suites, Lamplighter Hotel,

= gas = food = lodging = other = rest stop   Copyright 2022 - The Next EXIT ®

SPRINGFIELD

⬆E INTERSTATE 44 Cont'd

80b a	Continued Motel 6, Plaza Inn, Quality Inn, Springfield Inn, SpringHill Suites ⓞ Aldi Foods, AutoZone, Big O Tire, Ⓗ, O'Reilly Parts, Tire Express, U-Haul, Walmart/Subway
77	MO 13, KS Expswy, N 🅖 Kum&Go/dsl/e85 ⓞ Lowe's, S 🅖 Casey's/dsl, Phillips 66/dsl 🍴 Arby's, Braum's, Buffalo Wild Wings, Chuckwagon BBQ, El Charro, Five Guys, Golden Corral, Goodcents, IHOP, Jimmy John's, McAlister's Deli, McDonald's, New China, Panera Bread, Papa John's, Papa Murphy's, Subway, Taco Bell, Waffle House ⓞ $Tree, AT&T, BigLots, Drug Mart, GNC, Goodyear/auto, Hobby Lobby, PriceCutter Foods, Verizon, Walgreens, Walmart
75	US 160 W byp, to Willard, Stockton Lake, S 🅖 Kum&Go/dsl 🍴 Wendy's 🛏 Courtyard, La Quinta
72	MO 266, to Chesnut Expwy, S 🅖 Casey's, Cenex, ⭐FLYING J/ Wendy's/PJ Fresh/dsl/scales/24hr, Kum&Go/dsl/e85 🍴 Alli's Rest., Arby's, China Wok, Hardee's, KFC, LJ Silver, McDonald's, Pizza Hut, Plaza Mexico, Sonic, Subway, Taco Bell, Waffle House 🛏 Best Budget Inn, Best Western+, Redwood Motel ⓞ $General, AutoZone, city park, PriceCutter Foods
70	rds MM, B, N ⓞ fireworks, S ⓞ KOA (1mi), Wilson's Creek Nat Bfd (5mi)
69	to US 60, Springfield
67	rds N, T, Bois D' Arc, to Republic, S 🅖 Conoco/dsl 🛏 AmericInn (5mi) ⓞ art glass
66mm	Pond Creek
64.6mm	Dry Branch
64.5mm	Pickerel Creek
61	rds K, PP, N 🅖 Cenex/Hoods/dsl/scales/LP/24hr, Phillips 66 🛏 Hood I-44 Motel
58	MO 96, rds O, Z, to Carthage, Halltown, S 🅖 Shell/dsl ⓞ truck repair
57	to rd PP (from wb)
56.5mm	Turnback Creek
56mm	Goose Creek
52.5mm	truck parking both lanes
49	MO 174E, rd CCW, Chesapeake
46	MO 39, MO 265, Mt Vernon, Aurora, N 🅖 Casey's/dsl, Gulf/dsl, Kum&Go/dsl, TA/Conoco/Subway/dsl/scales/24hr/@ 🍴 Bamboo Garden Chinese, El Azteca Mexican, KFC/LJ Silver, Mazzio's, McDonald's, Pizza Hut, Sonic, Subway, Taco Bell 🛏 Best Western, USA Inn ⓞ $General, O'Reilly Parts, True Value, S 🅖 Cenex/dsl 🛏 Quality Inn ⓞ to Table Rock Lake
44	rd H, to Monett, Mt Vernon, N 🍴 Subway (1mi) ⓞ Mid-America Dental/Hearing, Walmart
43.5mm	Spring River
38	MO 97, to Stotts City, Pierce City, N 🅖 gas/dsl/repair/tires, S ⓞ U of MO SW Ctr (4mi)
33	MO 97 S, to Pierce City
29	rd U, to La Russell, Sarcoxie, N ⓞ antiques, Beagle Bay RV Camping, OzarkLand Gifts, S 🅖 Casey's (1mi), Kum&Go/Subway/dsl ⓞ antiques
29mm	Center Creek
26	MO 37, to Reeds, Sarcoxie, N ⓞ Bill's Truck/trailer repair
22	rd 100 N, N ⓞ Colaw RV Ctr, S ⓞ Consignment RV Sales
21mm	Jones Creek
18b a	I-49 N, US 71 N, MO 59 S, to Carthage, Neosho, N ⓞ Coachlight RV Ctr/Camping
15	MO 66 W, Lp 44 (from wb), Joplin, N 🛏 Tara Motel
15mm	Grove Creek
14mm	Turkey Creek

JOPLIN

13	Prigmore Ave, S 🅖 Skyline Travel Plaza/dsl/scales/24hr
11b a	I-49 S, US 71 S, MO 249 N, to Neosho, Ft Smith, S 🅖 ⭐FLYING J/ Denny's/dsl/LP/scales/24hr/@, Speedco ⓞ Blue Beacon, Goodyear Tires/repair, Kenworth
8b a	US 71, to Neosho, Joplin, N 🅖 Cenex/dsl, Conoco/dsl, Kum&Go/dsl, Phillips 66/dsl 🍴 Andy's Custard, Applebee's, Arby's, Billy Sims BBQ, Braum's, Buffalo Wild Wings, Burger King, Carino's Italian, Casa Montez Mexican, Cheddar's, Chick-fil-A, Chipotle, ChuckeCheese, CiCi's, Denny's, Domino's, El Vallarta Mexican, Firehouse Subs, First Watch, Five Guys, Freddy's, Golden Corral, Golden Dragon, Hardee's, HuHot, IHOP, Jimmy John's, Jimmy's Egg, Little Caesar's, Logan's Roadhouse, Longhorn Steaks, McAlister's, McDonald's, Old Chicago, Olive Garden, On the Border, Outback Steaks, Panda Express, Pizza Hut, Popeye's, Qdoba, Red Hot&Blue Grill, Red Lobster, Rib Crib, Schlotzsky's, Sonic, Starbucks, Steak'n Shake, Subway, Taco Bell, TX Roadhouse, Waffle House, Wasab Steaks, Wendy's 🛏 Best Western, Candlewood Suites, Comfort Inn, Days Inn, Drury Inn, EconoLodge, Fairfield Inn, Hampton Inn, Hilton Garden, Holiday Inn, Homewood Suites, La Quinta, Motel 6, Quality Inn, Residence Inn, Sunrise Inn, Super 8, Tru Hilton ⓞ $Tree, Aldi Foods, AT&T, AutoZone, Best Buy, Books-A-Million, Chrysler/Dodge/Jeep, Discount Tire, Firestone/auto, Food4Less, Ford/Lincoln, Freightliner, Goodyear/auto, Hobby Lobby, Home Depot, Honda, Hyundai, JC Penney, Jo-Ann Fabrics, Kia, Kohl's, Lowe's, Macy's, Mercedes, Michael's, Nissan, O'Reilly Parts, Office Depot, Petsmart, Ross, Sam's Club/gas, Subaru, Target, TJ Maxx, Toyota, Verizon, Walgreens, Walmart/Subway, S 🅖 Casey's 🍴 Cracker Barrel, Fazoli's 🛏 Microtel, TownePlace Suites ⓞ vet, Wheelen RV Ctr
6	MO 86, MO 43 N, to Racine, Joplin, N 🅖 Phillips 66 🍴 Jimmy John's, Moe's SW Grill, Schlotzsky's ⓞ CVS Drug, Walgreens, S 🅖 Kum&Go/dsl/e15 ⓞ Harley-Davidson, Ⓗ
5.5mm	Shoal Creek
4	MO 43 to Seneca, N 🅖 ❤Loves/Hardee's/dsl/scales/24hr, S 🅖 Conoco/Subway/dsl, Petro/Iron Skillet/Pizza Hut/Taco Bell/dsl/scales/24hr/@, 🅖/Wendy's/dsl/scales/24hr 🍴 McDonald's 🛏 Sleep Inn ⓞ $General, fireworks, IA 80 Truckomat, KOA
3mm	weigh sta both lanes
2mm	Welcome Ctr eb, full ♿ facilities, 🪑 litter barrels, 📞 vending, restrooms, truck parking wb
1	US 400, US 166W, to Baxter Springs, KS, N 🅖 Downstream/dsl ⓞ Downstream Casino/RV Park, Downstream RV Park, S ⓞ Sandstone Gardens
0mm	Missouri/Oklahoma state line

⬆N INTERSTATE 49

Exit #	Services
184	I-435, I-470
	I-49 begins/ends, continues N as US 71.
182	Red Bridge Rd, Longview Rd, E 🅖 Sinclair/dsl 🍴 McDonald's, Taco Bell ⓞ auto repair, W 🅖 Phillips 66/dsl 🛏 Woodspring Suites
181	Blue Ridge Blvd, E 🅖 Shell/dsl 🍴 Church's 🛏 Best Value Inn ⓞ NAPA, U-Haul, W 🅖 BP/dsl, Conoco/dsl 🍴 54th St Grill, Arby's, Chipotle, Hardee's, IHOP, KFC, McAlister's Deli, Papa John's, Petco, Pizza Hut, Starbucks, Wendy's ⓞ $Tree, Advance Parts, AT&T, AutoZone, Burlington Coats, CVS, GNC, Price Chopper, Tires+, TJ Maxx
180	(from sb), same as 181 w, W ⓞ Jerry's Auto Repair

INTERSTATE 49 Cont'd

Exit #	Services
179	Main St, E 🅿 Conoco 🍴 Burger King, Capestre Mexican, Capt D's, Popeye's, Providencia Pizzeria 🅾 $General, Firestone/auto, Holiday Inn Express, to Longview Lake CP, W 🅿 Phillips 66/dsl 🍴 Taco Bell, Waffle House 🅾 transmissions, USPO, Walgreens
178	140th St, W 🅿 Phillips 66/dsl 🍴 Pizza Hut 🅾 $General
177	MO 150, E 🅿 Phillips 66/dsl, QT/dsl 🍴 Sonic, Subway 🅾 Harley Davidson
176	155th St, to Belton, W 🅿 Cenex/dsl 🅾 $General
175	rd Y, 163rd St, Belton, E 🍴 Cracker Barrel 🏨 Hampton Inn 🅾 🄷, W 🅿 Phillips 66/dsl, QT/dsl 🍴 Fazoli's, Kneader's, Pizza Hut, Taco Bueno 🅾 AutoZone, CVS, Hobby Lobby, Marshall's, Menards, O'Reilly Parts, Petco, Price Chopper, Ross
174	MO 58, Belton, E 🅿 QT/dsl, Shell/dsl 🍴 Burger King, China Star, Church's, Firehouse Subs, Golden Corral, KFC, MOD Pizza, Panda Express, Papa John's, Pizza Hut, Qdoba, Steak'n Shake, Taco Bell, Waffle House, Wendy's 🏨 Quality Inn 🅾 Advance Parts, AT&T, Big O Tire, Chrysler/Dodge/Jeep, Firestone/auto, 🄷, Lowe's, Sam's Club/dsl, Transwest RV Ctr, Walmart/Subway, W 🍴 Applebee's, Arby's, Buffalo Wild Wings, Chipotle, Freddy's, Hawaiian Bros, HyVee/dsl, IHOP, Jimmy John's, Jose Pepper's, Longhorn Steaks, McDonald's, Panera Bread, Papa Murphy's, Pepper Jax Cafe, Starbucks, Subway, TX Roadhouse 🏨 EconoLodge, Fairfield Inn 🅾 $Tree, Aldi Foods, Discount Tire, Express Auto Service, GNC, Home Depot, Jo-Ann, Kohl's, Petsmart, Target, Verizon, Walgreens
172	N Cass Pkwy
168	Peculiar Way
167	MO C, J, Peculiar, E 🅿 Casey's, ⊘FLYING J/Denny's/dsl/Lp/scales/24hr 🍴 Subway 🏨 Highland Inn 🅾 Peculiar RV Park, W 🍴 Sonic 🅾 CountryMart/dsl, USPO
160	MO 291 N, Harrisonville, E 🅿 Casey's/dsl, Murphy USA, QT/dsl 🍴 Applebee's, Arby's, Branding Iron BBQ, Capt D's, El Maguey Mexican, Hardee's, Jimmy John's, KFC, McDonald's, Subway, Sunrise Chinese, Taco Bell, Wendy's 🏨 Best Value Inn, Budget Motel, Harrisonville Inn 🅾 $Tree, AT&T, GNC, 🄷, vet, Walmart, W 🅾 Ford
159	MO 2 W, 7 N, Mechanic St, Harrisonville, E 🅿 BP, Casey's/dsl, Phillips 66/dsl 🍴 Burger King, China Wok, DQ, Papa Murphy's, Pizza Hut, Starbucks 🅾 CVS, DLS Tire/auto, Price Chopper, Verizon, vet, Walgreens
158	MO 2 E, Commercial Blvd, Harrisonville, E 🅿 Conoco/dsl, Phillips 66 🍴 Best Burrito 🏨 Comfort Inn 🅾 Russell Stover, Sutherland's, W 🅿 Loves/McDonald's/Subway/dsl/scales/24hr
157mm	weigh sta both lanes
157	MO 7 S, to Clinton, E 🅾 🖪, W 🅿 BP/dsl, Sapp Bros/dsl/scales/24hr 🏨 Slumber Inn
153	307th St
148mm	S Grand River
147	MO A, B, Archie, Drexel, W 🅿 Phillips 66, Phillips 66/dsl 🍴 Mama's Kitchen, S 🅾 $General
144	MO E, AA, Crescent Hill
141	MO 18, Adrian, to Clinton, W 🅿 Casey's/dsl 🍴 Gray's Cafe 🅾 $General
136	rds D, F, Passaic, to Butler, W 🅾 McBee's Bratwurst/BBQ
131	MO 52 W, Butler, Amoret, E 🅿 Conoco 🍴 McDonald's, Pizza Hut, Sonic, Subway, Taco Bell 🏨 Days Inn, Super 8 🅾 $General, Chrysler/Dodge/Jeep/Ford, 🄷, O'Reilly Parts, Walmart, W 🍴 El Charro
130	US 71 Bus (from nb), to Butler
129	MO 52 E, Appleton City
120	rds B, A, Rich Hill, to Osceola, W 🅿 Phillips 66/dsl 🍴 Swope's Drive In 🅾 $General, Food Fair Mkt/drug
116	Rd TT, to Panama
112	Horton, W 🅾 Farm Mkt
110	Rd D, Stotesbury
107	Rd M, Compton Jct
103	Highland Ave, to Nevada, W 🅾 $General, Buick/Chevrolet/GMC, Osage Prairie RV Park
102a	US 54, Nevada, to El Dorado Springs, W 🅿 MFA/dsl/e85 🍴 54 Cafe 🅾 Centennial Park, Highly Tires
102b	49 Bus, W 🅾 same as 103
101	Rd K, Nevada, to Camp Clark, E 🅿 Conoco/dsl, W 🅿 Hot Spot/dsl, Murphy USA/dsl, ⬛/dsl/scales/24hr 🍴 Burger King, Buzz's BBQ, Pizza Hut, Sonic, Subway 🏨 Best Value Inn, Country Inn&Suites, Holiday Inn Express, Nevada Inn, Super 8 🅾 AutoZone, Chrysler/Dodge/Jeep/Ford, Verizon, Walmart/Subway, Wilson Tire
95	Rd E, Milo
91	Rds DD, BB, to Bellamy
88	Rds B, N, Sheldon, Bronaugh, E 🅾 to Stockton Lake (33 mi)
83	Rds C, V, Irwin
80	Rds EE, DD
77	US 160, Lamar, Mindenmines, E 🅿 Phillips 66, Sinclair/dsl/scales/24hr 🍴 Bamboo House, McDonald's, Pizza Hut, Sonic, Subway, Taco Bell, Taco Palace 🏨 Blue Top Inn, Super 8 🅾 $Tree, Blue Top Quiltshop, O'Reilly Parts, truckwash, W 🅿 Murphy USA/dsl, Phillips 66/Roady's/dsl 🍴 DQ 🅾 🄷, Lamar Truck tire, Walmart
74	30th Rd
70	MO 126, Golden City, Pittsburg
66	Rds K, H, Jasper, W 🅿 Judy's Trkstp/Cafe/dsl, Phillips 66/dsl 🅾 $General
63	Rds N, M
56	Garrison Ave (from sb), to Carthage, E 🏨 Best Inn (2mi)
55	Civil War Rd, to Carthage
53	MO 571 S, MO 96, MO 171 N, Central Ave, Carthage, E 🅿 Casey's/dsl, Phillips 66/dsl 🍴 Arby's, Boomer's BBQ, Burger King, LJ Silver, McDonald's, Sirloin Stockade, Sonic, Subway 🏨 Days Inn 🅾 $General, King Cashsaver
51	Fairview Ave, to Carthage
50	Rd HH, Fir Rd, E 🅿 Murphy USA, Phillips 66/McDonald's/dsl 🍴 Big Ben's BBQ, Hardee's, Iggy's Diner, KFC, Little Caesar's, Peck&Jen's Custard, Taco Bell, Wendy's 🏨 Quality Inn, Super 8 🅾 $General, $Tree, Aldi Foods, Chrysler/Dodge/Jeep, Ford, Lowe's, Verizon, Walgreens, Walmart/Subway, W 🅾 🄷
49	MO 571, Garrison Ave, to Carthage (from nb)
47	Cedar Rd, W 🅾 Coachlight RV Ctr/Park, Mid America RV Ctr

Side labels: BELTON, HARRISONVILLE, NEVADA, CARTHAGE

MO

ST LOUIS

▲N INTERSTATE 49 Cont'd

Exit #	Services
46mm	I-44, E to Springfield, W to Joplin. **I-49 and I-44 run together 7 mi. See I-44, exit 15.**
39b	I-44, E to Springfield, W to Joplin. **I-49 and I-44 run together 7 mi. See I-44, exit 15.**
39a	Rd FF, 32nd St, E 🅞 Kenworth, W 🅕 ⓕFLYING J/Denny's/dsl LP/scales/24hr 🅞 Blue Beacon, Goodyear Tires/repair, Speedco
35	Rd V, Diamond, E 🅞 G Washington Carver NM
33	MO 175, Gateway Dr, W 🅖 Phillips 66/dsl/deli 🅞 Shoal Creek RV Park
30	Iris Rd
27	MO 86, to Neosho, Racine, E 🅖 ❤Loves/McDonald's/Subway/dsl/scales/24hr, Phillips 66/dsl, W 🅞 Freightliner
24	US 60, to Neosho, Seneca, E 🅖 Kum&Go/dsl/e85, Murphy USA 🅕 Burger King, Burger King, Denny's, El Charro, KFC, LJ Silver, Taco Bell 🅛 Best Western, Super 8 🅞 $Tree, Aldi, Lowe's, Verizon, Walmart, W 🅞 Whispering Woods RV Park (12 mi)
20	Rd AA
17	Rds C, B, to Goodman, E 🅞 truck repair
16	MO 59 (from sb), Kelley Springs
10	MO 76, to Anderson, W 🅖 Cenex/Subway/dsl 🅕 Mazzio's 🅛 EconoLodge 🅞 Harps/dsl
7	Rd EE, to Pineville, Lanagan, E 🅞 Sugar Island Camping
5	Rd H, to Pineville
	I-49 begins/ends, US 71 continues S, W 🅞 Lazy Days Camping

▲N INTERSTATE 55

Exit #	Services
209mm	Missouri/Illinois state line at St. Louis, Mississippi River
209b	to I-70 W to Kansas City
209a	W 🅞 Busch Stadium, to Arch
208	Park Ave, 7th St, W 🅖 BP 🅕 Rally's, Taco Bell, White Castle 🅛 Hilton
207c b	I-44W, Truman Pkwy, to Tulsa
207a	Gravois St (from nb), E 🅖 Midwest Petroleum, W 🅕 A-1 Chinese Wok, Jack-in-the-Box
206c	Arsenal St, E 🅞 Anheuser-Busch Tour Ctr, W 🅖 Shell/dsl
206b	Broadway (from nb)
206a	Potomac St (from nb)
205	Gasconade, W 🅞 🅗
204	Broadway, E 🅖 Phillips 66, W 🅖 Conoco/dsl 🅕 Hardee's, McDonald's, Subway 🅞 Family$, O'Reilly Parts, Walgreens
203	Bates St, Virginia Ave, W 🅖 7-11, BP
202c	Loughborough Ave, W 🅕 Burger King, China King, Little Caesar's, Qdoba, St Louis Bread Co, Starbucks 🅞 AutoZone, Firestone/auto, Lowe's Whse, Schnuck's Foods
202b	Germania (from sb)
202a	Carondelet (from nb), Carondelet (from nb)
201b	Weber Rd
201a	Bayless Ave, E 🅖 BP 🅕 McDonald's, W 🅖 7-11/gas, Mobil/dsl 🅕 DQ, Jack-in-the-Box, Subway, Taco Bell 🅞 auto repair
200	Union Rd (from sb)
199	Reavis Barracks Rd, E 🅖 Shell/Circle K 🅕 STL BBQ
197	US 50, US 61, US 67, Lindbergh Blvd, E 🅖 Phillips 66 🅕 Applebee's, Arby's, Buffalo Wild Wings, ChuckeCheese, CiCi's, Dillard's, Hometown Buffet, HoneyBaked Ham, Hooters, IHOP, Imo's Pizza, KFC, Krispy Kreme, McAlister's, Noodles&Co, Penn Sta Subs, Qdoba, Starbucks, Steak'n Shake, Subway, Taco Bell, Tucker's Place, Wendy's 🅛 Holiday Inn 🅞 AT&T, Best Buy, Chrysler/Dodge/Jeep, CVS Drug, Dick's, Dobbs Tire, Ford/Lincoln,

197	Continued
	Home Depot, JC Penney, Jo-Ann Fabrics, Macy's, mall, Marshall's, NTB, Sears/auto, Verizon, vet, W 🅖 QT/dsl 🅕 Bob Evans, Culvers, Denny's, Golden Corral, O'Charley's, Panda Express, Pasta House 🅛 Best Value Inn 🅞 Aldi Foods, AT&T, CarMax, Chevrolet, Costco/gas, Honda, Hyundai, Kia, Mazda, Nissan, Target, VW
196b	I-270 W, to Kansas City
196a	I-255 E, to Chicago
195	Butler Hill Rd, E 🅖 Phillips 66 🅛 Hampton Inn 🅞 Advance Parts, Walgreens Popeye's, Holiday Inn Express, W 🅖 Phillips 66 🅕 Burger King, Hardee's, Subway, Taco Bell, Waffle House 🅞 Schnuck's Foods, tires/repair
193	Meramec Bottom Rd, E 🅖 QT/dsl 🅕 Cracker Barrel 🅛 Best Western 🅞 Midwest RV Ctr
191	MO 141, Arnold, E 🅖 QT 🅕 54th St Grill, Applebee's, Arby's, Bandana's BBQ, Capt D's, Chick-fil-A, China King, Denny's, Dunkin'/Baskin Robbins, Fazoli's, Five Guys, Jack-in-the-Box, Jimmy John's, Las Fuentes, Lee's Chicken, Lion's Choice, LJ Silver, McDonald's, Panda Express, Papa John's, Rally's, Starbucks, Steak'n Shake, Super China Buffet, Taco Bell, Terrazza Grill, Wendy's 🅛 Drury Inn, Pear Tree Inn 🅞 Aldi Foods, AT&T, CVS Drug, Dobbs Tire, Gordman's, Hobby Lobby, Kohl's, NAPA, O'Reilly Parts, PetCo, Shop'n Save Foods, vet, Walgreens, Walmart/Subway, W 🅖 Phillips 66/Circle K/dsl 🅕 Chili's, First Wok, Pasta House, Penn Sta Subs, Qdoba, St Louis Bread, Sunny St Cafe, TX Roadhouse 🅛 Woodspring Suites 🅞 $Tree, Dierberg's Foods, GNC, Lowe's, Office Depot, Petsmart, Ross, Verizon
190	Richardson Rd, E 🅖 BP/McDonald's, Hucks, Phillips 66/dsl, Shell/Circle K/dsl 🅕 Culver's, Domino's, DQ, Pizza Hut, Ponderosa, Taco Bell, White Castle 🅞 $Tree, Advance Parts, Auto Tire, Firestone, Save-A-Lot Foods, URGENT CARE, W 🅖 7-11, Phillips 66/dsl, Shell/Circle K/dsl 🅕 Burger King, Front Row Grill, Happy Wok, Imo's Pizza, McDonald's/playplace, Mr. Goodcents Subs, Ruby Tuesday, Waffle House 🅛 Quality Inn 🅞 Aamco, AutoZone, GNC, Home Depot, Plaza Tire, Schnuck's Foods, Target, Walgreens
186	Imperial, Kimmswick, E 🅖 Mobil, Shell/Circle K 🅕 Big Carl's BBQ, Blue Owl (1mi) 🅞 auto repair, W 🅖 Phillips 66/Jack-in-the-Box/dsl 🅕 China Wok, Domino's, Ginono's Grill, Papa John's, Scottie's Grill, Subway 🅞 to Mastodon SP, USPO
185	rd M, Barnhart, Antonia, W 🅖 Phillips 66, Phillips 66/dsl 🅞 Karsch's Mkt, USPO, Walgreens
180	rd Z, to Hillsboro, Pevely, E 🅖 Mobil/dsl 🅕 Burger King, Domino's, Main St BBQ, Pizza Hut, Subway, Taco Bell 🅞 $General, Queens Foods, W 🅖 Mr Fuel/dsl, Phillips 66/McDonald's/dsl/scales 🅛 Super 8 🅞 auto repair, rv camping
178	Herculaneum, E 🅖 QT/Wendy's/dsl/scales, Shell/Circle K 🅕 Cracker Barrel, DQ, Jack-in-the-Box, La Pachanga Mexican, Subway 🅞 Toyota Little Caesar's, W 🅞 Buick/GMC, Cadillac/Chevrolet, Ford, vet
175	rd A, Festus, E 🅖 Mobil, Murphy USA/dsl, Phillips 66/dsl 🅕 Arby's, Bob Evans, Burger King, Capt D's, China 1, Fazoli's, Hibachi Grill, Imo's Pizza, Jack-in-the-Box, McDonald's/playplace, Oriental Buffet, Panda Express, Papa John's, Sonic, St. Louis Bread Co, Steak'n Shake, Subway, Taco Bell, White Castle 🅛 La Quinta, Quality Inn 🅞 $Tree, Advance Parts, Aldi Foods, AT&T, AutoZone, CVS Drug, Dobbs Tire, GNC, Home Depot, Plaza Tire, Schnuck's Foods/gas, URGENT CARE, Walgreens, Walmart Verizon, W 🅖 Phillips 66/7-11/dsl, Phillips 66/Domino's/dsl 🅕 Hardee's, Jimmy John's, Ruby Tuesday, Waffle House, Whittaker's Pizza 🅛 Comfort Inn, Holiday Inn Express 🅞 Chrysler/Dodge/Jeep, Lowe's
174b a	US 67, Lp 55, Festus, Crystal City, E 🅖 Phillips 66/dsl 🅞 🅗
170	US 61, W 🅖 BP/dsl/LP 🅕 Gators Grill

⬆N   INTERSTATE 55 Cont'd

Exit #	Services
165	rd TT (from sb)
162	rds DD, OO
160mm	🆁🆂 nb/weigh sta sb, full 🅳 facilities, 🛒 litter barrels, 🅒, vending, petwalk
157	rd Y, Bloomsdale, E 🅖 Phillips 66/Subway, W 🅖 ❤Loves/ Chester's/McDonald's/dsl/scales/24hr
154	rd O, to St Genevieve
150	MO 32, rds B, A, to St Genevieve, E 🅖 BP 🍴 DQ 🅞 Hist Site (6mi), 🄷, W 🅖 Phillips 66/dsl 🅞 Hawn SP (11mi)
143	rds J, M, N, Ozora, W 🅖 Exxon/Subway/dsl/scales/24hr 🛏 Econolodge 🅞 truckwash
141	rd Z, St Mary
135	rd M, Brewer
129	MO 51, to Perryville, E 🅖 MotoMart/McDonald's/dsl 🍴 Burger King, KFC, Ponderosa, Taco Bell 🅞 Ford, 🄷, W 🅖 Rhodes/IMO's/dsl 🍴 China Buffet, Five Star Chinese, Subway 🛏 Comfort Inn, Days Inn, Holiday Inn, Super 8 🅞 AT&T, Buick/Chevrolet, Chrysler/Dodge/Jeep, Walmart
123	rd B, Biehle, W 🅖 Rhodes/dsl
119mm	Apple Creek
117	rd KK, to Appleton
111	rd E, Oak Ridge
110mm	🆁🆂 sb/full facilities, truck parking nb
105	US 61, Fruitland, E 🅖 Casey's, Phillips 66/dsl, Rhodes/dsl 🅞 $General, Purcell Tires/repair, Trail of Tears SP (11mi), W 🅖 D-Mart/dsl 🍴 Bavarian Halle, DQ, Pizza Inn 🛏 Drury Inn
102	LaSalle Ave, E Main St
99	US 61, MO 34, to Jackson, E 🅞 RV camping, W 🍴 Delmonico's Steaks 🛏 Comfort Suites 🅞 Hill Top RV, McDowell South RV Ctr
96	rd K, to Cape Girardeau, E 🅖 Phillips 66/dsl 🍴 Applebee's, Buffalo Wild Wings, Burger King, Chick-fil-A, China Town, CiCi's Pizza, Cracker Barrel, Daddy's Cheesecake, Denny's, Dexter BBQ, DQ, El Acapulco, Firehouse Subs, Golden Corral, Great Wall Chinese, Honey Baked Ham, IHOP, Logan's Roadhouse, O'Charley's, Olive Garden, Panera Bread, Papa Murphy's, Popeye's, Qdoba, Red Lobster, Ruby Tuesday, Starbucks, Steak'n Shake, Subway, Taco Bell, TX Roadhouse, Wendy's 🛏 Auburn Place, Drury Lodge/rest., Hampton Inn, Holiday Inn Express, PearTree Inn 🅞 AT&T, Barnes&Noble, Best Buy, BigLots, CVS Drug, Hobby Lobby, 🄷, JC Penney, Macy's, Old Navy, Schnuck's Foods, to SEMSU, Verizon, W 🅖 Shell 🍴 McDonald's/playplace, Outback Steaks, Penn Sta Subs, White Castle 🛏 Drury Suites, Quality Inn 🅞 $Tree, Chrysler/Dodge/Jeep, Honda, Hyundai, Kohl's, Lowe's, Mazda, Nissan, PetCo, Plaza Tire, Sam's Club, Sears Grand, Staples, Target, TJ Maxx, Toyota, Walmart/Subway
95	MO 74 E, E 🅖 Mercato/dsl 🛏 Candlewood Suites 🅞 URGENT CARE, W 🅞 Menard's
93a b	MO 74 W, Cape Girardeau
91	rd AB, to Cape Girardeau, E 🅖 Rhodes/IMO's/dsl 🍴 Staxx Diner 🅞 Harley-Davidson, tire repair, vet, W 🅞 🐾 Capetown RV Ctr
89	US 61, rds K, M, Scott City, E 🅖 Rhodes 🍴 Burger King, Ice Cream Corner, Las Brisas Mexican, Pizza Hut, Pizza Pro, Subway 🅞 $General, Bob's Foods, Medicap Drug, NAPA, Plaza Tire/auto
87	MO PP
80	MO 77, Benton, E 🅖 Express/dsl, W 🅖 Exxon/McDonald's/dsl 🍴 fireworks 🍴 Subway 🅞 antiques, winery (8mi)
69	rd HH, to Sikeston, Miner, E 🅞 Peterbilt, W 🅞 golf, 🄷
67	US 60, US 62, Miner, E 🅖 Breaktime/dsl 🛏 Best Value Inn, Best Western+, Motel 6 🅞 Hinton RV Park, 0-2 mi W 🅖 Conoco, Hucks, Jasper's Gas, Mobil, QuickCheck 🍴 Bo's BBQ, Buffalo Wild Wings, Burger King, Dexter BBQ, El Tapatio Mexican,

M I N E R	
67	Continued Lambert's Rest., Little Caesar's, McDonald's, Papa Murphy's, Pizza Hut, Pizza Inn, Ruby Tuesday, Sergio's Mexican, Sonic, Subway, Taco John's, Wendy's 🛏 Comfort Inn, Country Hearth Inn, Drury Inn, PearTree Inn, Super 8 🅞 $General, AutoZone, Buick/Chevrolet, Cadillac/GMC, CVS Drug, Family$, Food Giant, Food Giant, 🄷, Raben Tires, Sikeston Outlets/famous brands, Walgreens
66b	US 60 W, to Poplar Bluff, 3 mi W on US 61/62 🅖 ❤Loves/ Dunkin'/dsl/scales/24hr, Breaktime/E-85 🍴 A&W/LJ Silver, Applebee's, Arby's, China Buffet, Colton's Steaks, DQ, El Bracero Mexican, Hardee's, La Ruleta Mexican, McDonald's, Sonic, Taco Bell, Watami, Zaxby's 🛏 Days Inn, Hampton Inn, Holiday Inn Express 🅞 $Tree, Aldi Foods, AT&T, Chrysler/Dodge/Jeep, Ford/Lincoln, GNC, JC Penney, Lowe's, O'Reilly Parts, Walmart/Subway
66a	I-57 E, to Chicago, US 60 W
59mm	St Johns Bayou
58	MO 80, Matthews, E 🅖 TA/Taco Bell/dsl/scales/24hr/@ 🅞 to Big Oak Tree SP (24mi), truck repair, W 🅖 FLYING J/Denny's/dsl/LP/RV dump/scales/24hr, LNG, ❤Loves/Chester's/Subway/dsl/scales/24hr 🅞 repair
52	rd P, Kewanee, E 🅖 Mobil/BJ Trvl Ctr/BBQ/dsl
49	US 61, US 62, New Madrid, E 🅞 Hunter-Dawson HS (3mi)
44	US 61, US 62, Lp 55, New Madrid, E 🅞 Higgerson School Hust Site
42mm	🆁🆂 sb/full facilities, truck parking nb
40	rd EE, St Jude Rd, Marston, E 🅖 PILOT/Subway/dsl/scales/24hr 🛏 Hunter Lodge, W 🅖 MFA 🛏 Travelodge
32	US 61, MO 162, Portageville, W 🅖 Casey's, Phillips 66/dsl 🍴 China King, McDonald's, Sonic, Subway 🅞 $General
27	rds K, A, BB, to Wardell, E 🅞 RV camping (2mi), W 🅞 Delta Research Ctr
20mm	🆁🆂 nb, full 🅳 facilities, picnic table, litter barrels, 🅒, vending, petwalk
H A Y T I	19 MO 84, Hayti, E 🅖 Double Nickel/dsl, PILOT/Arby's/dsl/scales/24hr, Shell 🍴 KFC/Taco Bell, McDonald's, Pizza Hut 🛏 Quality Inn, Regency Motel 🅞 Lady Luck Casino/camping 🍴 Burger King, W 🅖 Exxon/Hayti Trvl Ctr/Subway/dsl, Phillips/dsl, R&P/dsl 🍴 Apple Barrel, Chubby's BBQ, Los Portales, Patty Ann's BBQ 🛏 Drury Inn 🅞 $General, CarQuest, Fred's Store, Hay's Foods, 🄷, repair, USPO
17b a	I-155 E, US 412, to TN
14	rds J, H, U, to Caruthersville, Braggadocio
10mm	weigh sta nb
8	US 61, MO 164, Steele, E 🅞 truck repair, W 🅖 Shell/Subway/dsl/scales 🛏 Deerfield Inn
4	rd E, to Holland, Cooter
3mm	truck parking both lanes
1	US 61, rd O, Holland, W 🅖 Shell/dsl/24hr
0mm	Missouri/Arkansas state line

☐ = gas ☐ = food ☐ = lodging ☐ = other ☐ = rest stop   Copyright 2022 - The Next EXIT ©

MO

INTERSTATE 57

Exit #	Services
22mm	Missouri/Illinois state line, Mississippi River
18.5mm	**weigh sta both lanes**
12	US 62, MO 77, Charleston, E ☐ *FLYING J*/Huddle House/dsl/scales/24hr ☐ Eagle Inn ☐ JSH Towing/repair, W ☐ Casey's/dsl ☐ Las Brisas Mexican, Waffle&Pancake House ☐ Super 8 ☐ vet
10	MO 105, Charleston, E ☐ Exxon/Boomland/dsl ☐ McDonald's, Wally's Eatery ☐ Boomland RV Park, W ☐ Casey's ☐ China Buffet, Pizza Hut, Subway ☐ Quality Inn ☐ city park, CountryMart Foods, Plaza Tire
4	rd B, Bertrand
1b a	I-55, N to St Louis, S to Memphis. I-57 begins/ends on I-55
	I-57 begins/ends on I-55, exit 66.

INTERSTATE 64

Exit #	Services
41mm	Missouri/Illinois state line, Mississippi River
40b a	Broadway St, to Stadium, to the Arch, N ☐ Hilton, Sheraton, stadium, S ☐ Dobb's Tire
40c	(from wb), I-44 W, I-55 S
39c	11th St (exits left) downtown
39b	14th St, N ☐ Sheraton, S ☐ BP downtown
39a	21st St, Market St (from wb), N ☐ Drury Inn, Hampton Inn
38d	Chestnut at 20th St, N ☐ Drury Inn, Hampton Inn
38c	Jefferson Ave, St Louis Union Sta, N ☐ Joplin House, S ☐ Residence Inn
38a	Forest Park Blvd (from wb), N ☐ Shell
37b a	Market St, Bernard St, Grand Blvd, N ☐ Shell ☐ Del Taco ☐ Adam's Mark Hotel, Courtyard, Drury Inn, Hampton Inn, Hyatt, Marriott
36d	Vandeventer Ave, Chouteau Ave
36b a	Kingshighway, N ☐ ☐, S ☐ BP
34d c	Hampton Ave, Forest Park, N ☐ museums, zoo, S ☐ BP, Mobil, Phillips 66 ☐ Courtesy Diner, Hardee's, Imo's Pizza, Jack-in-the-Box, Smokin' Al's BBQ, Steak'n Shake, Subway, Taco Bell ☐ Hampton Inn
34a	Oakland Ave, N ☐ BP ☐ Del Taco, Subway ☐ ☐
33d	McCausland Ave, N ☐ BP ☐ Del Taco
33c	Bellevue Ave, N ☐ ☐
33b	Big Bend Blvd
32b a	Eager Rd, Hanley Rd, S ☐ Shell ☐ Chick-fil-A, Chipotle, Lion's Choice, McDonald's, Panda Express, Subway, Trader Joe's ☐ Best Buy, Dierberg's Foods, Home Depot, Petco, Petsmart, REI, Target, Whole Foods Mkt
31b a	I-170 N, N ☐ Burger King, CA Pizza Kitchen, Cheesecake Factory, Dillard's, Five Guys, IHOP, Maggiano's, PF Chang's, St Louis Bread ☐ Homewood Suites ☐ CVS Drug, Macy's, mall, Nordstrom, Verizon, S ☐ Drury Inn ☐ Bonefish Grill, Chick-fil-A, Subway ☐ Dierberg's Foods, Michael's, Target
30	McKnight Rd
28b	Clayton Rd (from wb)
28a	US 67, US 61, Lindbergh Blvd, N ☐ Honda, S ☐ Bricktops, Brio Grill, Fleming's Rest., Schneithouse Rest., St Louis Bread, Starbucks, Tim Hortons ☐ Hilton ☐ Shnuck's Foods
27	Spoede Rd
26	rd JJ, Ballas Rd, N ☐ ☐, S ☐ ☐
25	I-270, N to Chicago, S to Memphis
24	Mason Rd, N ☐ Courtyard, Marriott ☐ hwy patrol, LDS Temple
23	Maryville Centre Dr (from wb), N ☐ Courtyard, Marriott

ST LOUIS

CHESTERFIELD

22	MO 141, N ☐ ☐, S ☐ Five Guys, Hot Wok
21	Timberlake Manor Pkwy
20	Chesterfield Pkwy (from wb) same as 19b a
19b a	MO 340, Chesterfield Pkwy, Olive Blvd, N ☐ BP, Shell ☐ Charlie Gitto's, Sheridan's Custard, Taco Bell ☐ DoubleTree Hotel, Hampton Inn, Homewood Suites, Residence Inn, SpringHill Suites ☐ Dobb's Tire, Schnucks Foods, USPO, Walgreens, S ☐ Mobil ☐ California Pizza Kitchen, Cheesecake Factory, Chili's, Edgewild Rest., PF Chang's, Twin Peaks ☐ Drury Plaza Hotel, Hyatt Place ☐ Dillard's, mall
17	Boones Crossing, Long Rd, Chesterfield Airport Rd, N ☐ Residence Inn ☐ Prestige Outlets/famous brands, S ☐ Mobil ☐ 54th St Grill, Bar Louie, Brickhouse Tavern, Buffalo Wild Wings, Cane's, Chick-fil-A, Culver's, East Coast Pizza, Five Guys, Fox&Hound, Hardee's, IHOP, Jason's Deli, Kaldi's Coffee, Lion's Choice, McDonald's, Mimi's Cafe, Old Spaghetti Factory, Olive Garden, Original Pancakes, Panda Express, Qdoba Mexican, Red Lobster, Red Robin, SmokeHouse Rest., Sonic, St Louis Bread, Steak'n Shake, Subway, Syberg's Cafe, Taco Bell, Wendy's ☐ Courtyard, Hampton Inn, Hilton Garden, Holiday Inn Express ☐ $Tree, Aldi Foods, AutoTire Care, AutoZone, Best Buy, Dick's, Dobb's Tire, Firestone/auto, Ford, GNC, Gordman's, Home Depot, Lowe's, Michael's, Old Navy, Petsmart, Ross, Sam's Club, Target, Verizon, Walgreens, Walmart, WorldMkt
16	Long Rd (from wb)
14	Chesterfield Airport Rd (from eb), S ☐ BP/dsl, Phillips 66/dsl ☐ Comfort Inn ☐ Premium Outlets/famous brands
13mm	Missouri River
11	Research Park Ctr Dr, S ☐ Wingate Inn
10	MO 94 (from wb), N ☐ Mercedes
9	rd k, O'Fallon, N ☐ Mobil, QT/dsl ☐ Arby's, Cracker Barrel, Culver's, Denny's, Las Margaritas, McDonald's, Starbucks, Subway, Walnut Grill, Wendy's ☐ Holiday Inn Express, Residence Inn, Sleep Inn, Staybridge Suites ☐ Chevrolet, Honda, ☐, Walgreens
6	rd DD, Wing Haven Blvd, N ☐ Phillips 66 ☐ Bristol Seafood, Hunan King, Massa's Italian, Outback Steaks, Subway ☐ Hilton Garden ☐ vet
4	rd N, N ☐ Phillips 66 ☐ Qdoba Mexican, Red Robin ☐ JC Penney, Petco, Shop'n Save, Target, S ☐ Murphy USA/dsl, Phillips 66 ☐ Arby's, El Maguay, Jack-in-the-Box, McDonald's, Sonic, St. Louis Bread Co., Starbucks, Steak'n Shake, Subway, Taco Bell, Wendy's, White Castle ☐ $Tree, Aldi Foods, AutoZone, Dobb's Tire, Firestone/auto, GNC, Lowe's, Walmart
2	Lake St. Louis Blvd, N ☐ Hucks/dsl ☐ BC's Rest., Max&Erma's ☐ Old Navy, Schnuck's Foods, Von Maur, Walgreens
1	Prospect Rd
0mm	I-70 E to St Louis, W to Kansas City

INTERSTATE 70

Exit #	Services
251.5mm	Missouri/Illinois state line, Mississippi River
251a	I-55 S, to Memphis, to I-44, to downtown/no return
249b	Tucker Blvd, downtown St Louis, S ☐ Mobil/dsl
249a	I-44 W, I-55 S
248b	St Louis Ave, Branch St
248a	Salisbury St, McKinley Br, S ☐ BP, Phillips 66
247	Grand Ave, N ☐ BP, Phillips 66/Subway/dsl ☐ Western Inn
246b	Adelaide Ave
246a	N Broadway, O'Fallon Park, N ☐ Loves/McDonald's/Subway/dsl/scales/24hr, Mobil/dsl ☐ Freightliner, truck tires
245b	W Florissant
245a	Shreve Ave, S ☐ BP

Copyright 2022 - The Next EXIT ® [gas] = gas [food] = food [lodging] = lodging [other] = other [Rs] = rest stop

INTERSTATE 70 Cont'd

Exit #	Services
244b	Kingshighway, 3/4 mi S [gas] BP [food] Burger King, McDonald's, Subway [other] Walgreens
244a	Bircher Blvd, Union Blvd, N [gas] BP/dsl, Mobil/dsl
243b	(243c from eb) Bircher Blvd
243a	Riverview Blvd
243	Goodfellow Blvd, N [gas] BP, Conoco/dsl
242b a	Jennings Sta Rd, S [lodging] Western Inn
241b	Lucas-Hunt Rd, N [gas] Shell/Circle K, 3/4 mi S [food] Church's, Lee's Chicken, McDonald's [other] Walgreens
241a	Bermuda Rd, S [other] [H]
240b a	Florissant Rd, N [gas] BP/McDonald's [other] Family$, Schnuck's Foods
239	N Hanley Rd, N [lodging] Hilton Garden, S [gas] BP
238c b	I-170 N, I-170 S, no return
238a	N [other] Lambert-St Louis Airport, S [lodging] Renaissance Hotel
237	Natural Bridge Rd (from eb), S [gas] Phillips 66, Shell [food] Church's, Jack-in-the-Box, Rally's, Steak'n Shake, Waffle House [lodging] Ramada Inn, Renaissance, Travelodge
236	Lambert-St Louis Airport, S [gas] BP/dsl [food] Bandana's BBQ, Golden Pancake, Lombardo's Café Rafferty's Rest., Subway [lodging] Best Value Inn, Drury Inn, Econolodge, Hampton Inn, Hilton, Holiday Inn, Holiday Inn Express, Marriott, Peartree Inn, Quality Inn
235c	Cypress Rd, rd B W, N [other] to [airport]
235b a	US 67, Lindbergh Blvd, N [lodging] Airport Plaza Hotel, S [food] Lion's Choice Rest., TGIFriday's [lodging] Crowne Plaza, Embassy Suites, Extended Stay America [other] Menard's
234	MO 180, St Charles Rock Rd, N [gas] BP, Phillips 66/dsl [food] A&W/LJ Silver, Applebee's, Arby's, Chimi's Mexican, Chipotle, Fazoli's, HomeTown Buffet, Imo's Pizza, Jack-in-the-Box, Jimmy John's, LoneStar Steaks, McDonald's, New China Buffet, Pizza Hut, Ponderosa, Red Lobster, St Louis Bread, Subway, Taco Bell, Wendy's, White Castle, Ya Hala Mediterranean [other] $Tree, Aldi Foods, AT&T, AutoZone, Best Buy, CVS Drug, Hobby Lobby, [H], Kohl's, Meineke, NTB, Office Depot, Petsmart, Save-A-Lot Foods, Target, Verizon, Walgreens, Walmart/Burger King, S [gas] QT [food] IHOP, Lion's Choice [other] Chrysler/Dodge/Jeep, Home Depot, Schnuck's, Shamel Tires/repair, Walgreens
232	I-270, N to Chicago, S to Memphis
231b a	Earth City Expwy, N [gas] Motomart, Phillips 66/Jack-in-the-Box/dsl [food] Malone's Grill, McDonald's [lodging] Candlewood Suites, Courtyard, Extended Stay America, Holiday Inn, Residence Inn, SpringHill Suites, S [gas] Mobil [food] Burger King, Dave&Buster's, Subway [lodging] Holiday Inn Express, Homewood Suites, La Quinta [other] Hollywood Casino/Hotel, Riverport Ampitheatre
230mm	Missouri River
229b a	5th St, St Charles, N [gas] BP, Mobil/dsl, Motomart/dsl [food] Bellacino's Italian, Buffalo Wild Wings, China House Buffet, Denny's, Dunkin', Firehouse Subs, Jack-in-the-Box, Lee's Chicken, Little Tokyo, McDonald's, Qdoba, Starbucks, TX Roadhouse, Waffle House [lodging] Best Value Inn, Best Western, Comfort Suites [other] Aldi Foods, Ameristar Casino, Bass Pro Shops, Gordman's, Walgreens, S [gas] QT/dsl [food] Bar Louie, Cracker Barrel, Five Guys, Tuscanos Brazilian [lodging] Drury Suites, Embassy Suites, Fairfield Inn
228	MO 94, to Weldon Springs, access to 227, St Charles, N [gas] Mobil/dsl, QT/dsl [food] Arby's, DQ, Imo's Pizza, Papa John's, Steak'n Shake [other] Advance Parts, AutoZone, CVS Drug, GNC, NAPA, Schnuck's, Valvoline, S [gas] Mobil/dsl, QT [food] Chinese Express, ChuckECheese, Fazoli's, Gingham's Rest., Grappa Grill, Jimmy John's, McAlister's Deli, Outback Steaks, Pizza Hut, Tilted Kilt [lodging] Intown Suites [other] $General, Dobb's Tire

227	Zumbehl Rd, access to 228, N [gas] Phillips 66/dsl, ZX [food] Culpepper's Grill [lodging] Super 8 [other] Ford, Lowe's, Sav-A-Lot Foods, S [gas] BP, Hucks/dsl [food] Applebee's, Big Woody's BBQ, Bob Evans, Capt D's, El Mariachi Mexican, Fratelli's Ristorante, Golden Corral, Hardee's, Hoho Chinese, Jack-in-the-Box, McDonald's, Papa Murphy's, Penn Sta Subs, Shogun, Smashburger, St Louis Bread, Subway, Taco Bell [lodging] Red Roof Inn, TownePlace Suites [other] $Tree, Dierberg's Foods, GNC, Jiffy Lube, Michael's, NTB, Petco, Petsmart, Sam's Club/gas, Schnuck's Foods, URGENT CARE, vet, Walgreens, Walmart
225	Truman Rd, to Cave Springs, N [gas] Phillips 66/dsl [lodging] Hampton Inn, Rodeway Inn [other] Buick/GMC, Cadillac, Harley Davidson, Indian Motorcycles, Mazda, Subaru, U-Haul, VW, S [gas] Conoco, QT [food] Advance Parts, Bandanas BBQ, Burger King, Chimi's Mexican, Culver's, Denny's, Hibachi Grill, Hooters, IHOP, Jack-in-the-Box, KFC, Lion's Choice Rest., LJ Silver, Longhorn Steaks, Los Chavez Mexican, McDonald's, O'Charley's, Pasta House, Red Lobster, Steak'n Shake, Subway, Taco Bell, Thai Kitchen, Wendy's, White Castle [lodging] Country Inn&Suites, Courtyard [other] AT&T, Batteries+Bulbs, Chrysler/Dodge/Jeep, Firestone, Hobby Lobby, Home Depot, [H], Kia, Office Depot, Shop'n Save, Target, TJ Maxx, URGENT CARE, Verizon
224	MO 370 E
222	Mid-Rivers Mall Dr, rd C, St Peters, N [gas] QT/dsl/24hr [food] Burger King [other] CarMax, Chevrolet, Honda, Lincoln, Toyota, S [gas] Mobil/dsl [food] Arby's, Bob Evans, Buffalo Wild Wings, Chili's, China Wok, Domino's, Fazoli's, HoneyBaked Ham, Joe's Crabshack, Max & Erma's, McDonald's/playplace, Olive Garden, Planet Sub, Qdoba, Red Robin, Ruby Tuesday, St Louis Bread, Steak'n Shake, Subway, Taco Bell, Wendy's [lodging] Drury Inn, Extended Stay America [other] Aldi Foods, Barnes&Noble, Best Buy, BigLots, Costco/gas, Dick's, Dillard's, Hyundai/Nissan/VW, JC Penney, JoAnn Fabrics, Kia, Macy's, Marshall's, NTB, Verizon
220	MO 79, to Elsberry, N [other] Cherokee Lakes Camping (7mi), S [gas] 7-11/gas, BP, Phillips 66/dsl [food] El Mezon, Gettemeier's Rest., Jack-in-the-Box, McDonald's/playplace, Pirrone's Pizzaria, Sonic, Subway [lodging] Days Inn [other] Dierberg's Foods, O'Reilly Parts, Walgreens
219	T R Hughes Blvd, S [gas] QT [lodging] Comfort Inn
217	rds K, M, O'Fallon, N [gas] Hucks/dsl [food] Baskin-Robbins, Burger King, Jack-in-the-Box, Piggy's BBQ, Pizza Hut/Taco Bell, Rally's, Sonic, Waffle House [other] Firestone, Jiffy Lube, O'Reilly Parts, S [gas] Mobil/dsl, Phillips 66/dsl, QT [food] Applebee's, Arby's, Bob Evans, Cappuccino's, Domino's, Fazoli's, Golden Corral, Jimmy John's, KFC, Lion's Choice Rest., McDonald's/playplace, Pantera's Pizza, Papa John's, Pizza Hut, Red Robin, St Louis Bread, Stefanina's Pizza, Subway, TX Roadhouse, Wendy's [other] Advance Parts, Aldi Foods, Auto Tire, AutoZone, CVS Drug, GNC, Home Depot, Lowe's, Meineke, Midas, Schnuck's Foods, Shop'n Save Foods, Verizon, Walgreens, Walmart

ST LOUIS (vertical side label)

ST CHARLES (vertical side label)

ST PETERS (vertical side label)

O'FALLON (vertical side label)

MO (map label)

🅖 = gas 🍴 = food 🛏 = lodging 🅞 = other 🆁🆂 = rest stop   Copyright 2022 - The Next EXIT

▲E INTERSTATE 70 Cont'd

Exit #	Services
216	Bryan Rd, N 🛏 Super 8 🅞 Ford, Peterbilt, St Louis RV Ctr, S 🍴 Conoco, Phillips 66/Jack-in-the-Box/dsl, QT 🍴 DQ, Little Caesar's, Mr. Goodcents, Wendy's
214	Lake St Louis, N 🍴 Phillips 66/McDonald's/dsl, S 🍴 Phillips 66/dsl, Shell/Circle K 🍴 Denny's, Hardee's 🛏 Best Value Inn 🅞 H
212	rd A, N 🛏 Economy Inn 🅞 Camping World, S 🍴 Mobil 🍴 Pizzamenti's Cafe 🛏 Regency Plaza Hotel 🅞 Chrysler/Dodge/Jeep
210 b a	I-64, US 40 E, US 61 N, S 🅞 H
209	rd Z, Church St, New Melle, N 🍴 DQ 🛏 Holiday Inn Express, S 🍴 Phillips 66/dsl 🍴 Stone Summit Steaks 🛏 Hampton Inn
208	Pearce Blvd, Wentzville Pkwy, Wentzville, N 🍴 Mobil/dsl, QT/dsl 🍴 54th St Grill, 88 China, Applebee's, Arby's, Bob Evans, Buffalo Wild Wings, Chick-fil-A, China Buffet, Culver's, Domino's, El Maguey, Fritz's Custard, Hardee's, Jack-in-the-Box, Jimmy John's, KFC, Lion's Choice, Little Caesar's, McDonald's, Olive Garden, Panda Express, Papa John's, Penn Sta., Pizza Hut, Pizza Pro, Ruby Tuesday, St Louis Bread, Starbucks, Steak'n Shake, Subway, Sunny St Cafe, Taco Bell, Waffle House, Wendy's, White Castle 🛏 Fairfield Inn 🅞 $General, AT&T, AutoZone, Chevrolet, Dick's, Dierberg's Foods, Dobb's Tire, GNC, Home Depot, H, Kohl's, Lowe's, Michael's, NAPA, O'Reilly Parts, Petsmart, Ross, Sam's Club/dsl, Save-A-Lot, Schnuck's Food, Target, URGENT CARE, Verizon, Walgreens, Walmart, S 🍴 BP/dsl 🍴 Bandana's BBQ, Chimi's FreshMex, IHOP, TX Roadhouse 🛏 Super 8 🅞 Hyundai, Thomas RV Ctr
206	new exit
204mm	weigh sta both lanes
203	rds W, T, Foristell, N 🍴 Mr Fuel/dsl/scales, TA/BP/Pizza Hut/Popeye's/Taco Bell/dsl/scales/24hr/@ 🛏 Quality Inn, S 🍴 Phillips 66/McDonald's/dsl 🅞 dsl repair
200	rds J, H, F (from wb), Wright City, N 🍴 Phillips 66/dsl 🍴 Ruiz Castillo's Mexican (1mi) 🅞 $General, S 🍴 BP 🍴 Subway 🛏 Super 7 Inn
199	rd J, H, F, Wright City, N 🍴 Shell/McDonald's/dsl 🅞 $General, S 🛏 Super 7 Inn 🅞 Volvo Trucks
198mm	🆁🆂 both lanes, full ♿ facilities, 🍴, 🖼, litter barrels, petwalk
193	MO 47, Warrenton, N 🍴 Fast Lane/DQ/dsl, Mobil/dsl 🍴 1st Wok, Applebee's, Burger King, China House, Dominos, DQ, El Jimador Mexican, Jack-in-the-Box, Little Caesar's, McDonald's, Pizza Hut, Subway, Waffle House, Wendy's 🛏 Best Value Inn, Holiday Inn Express, Super 8 🅞 Aldi Foods, AT&T, Mosers Foods, Walmart, S 🍴 BP/dsl, Conoco/dsl, Phillips 66/dsl 🍴 Denny's, Imo's Pizza, Papa John's, Taco Bell 🛏 Baymont Inn 🅞 AutoZone, CarQuest, Chevrolet, NAPA, O'Reilly Parts, Walgreens
188	rds A, B, to Truxton, S 🍴 ⊕FLYING J/Denny's/dsl/LP/RV Dump/scales/24hr 🛏 Budget Inn
183	rds E, NN, Y, Jonesburg, 1 mi N 🅞 Jonesburg Gardens Camping, S 🍴 Phillips 66/Chester's/dsl 🅞 USPO
179	rd F, High Hill, S 🛏 Colonial Inn, Motel 70
175	MO 19, New Florence, N 🍴 BP/dsl, Shell/dsl/24hr 🍴 Dad's Jct Cafe, McDonald's 🛏 Best Inn, Best Value Inn, Days Inn 🅞 auto repair, Stone Hill Winery/gifts (15mi), S 🍴 Loves/Arby's/Speedco/dsl/scales/24hr/@
170	MO 161, rd J, Danville, N 🍴 Red's/dsl 🅞 Kan-Do RV Park, to Graham Cave SP, S 🅞 Lazy Day RV Park
169.5mm	truck parking
168mm	Loutre River

Exit #	Services
167mm	truck parking eb
161	rds D, YY, Williamsburg, N 🍴 Cranes/mkt 🍴 Marlene's Res 🅞 USPO
155	rds A, Z, to Calwood, N 🅞 antiques
148	US 54, Kingdom City, N 🍴 BP/dsl, Phillips 66/Burger King dsl 🍴 Taco Bell 🅞 MO Tourism Ctr, to Mark Twain Lake, 🍴 Fast Lane/DQ/dsl, Gulf/Gasper's/Arby's/dsl/scales/@, Pet ro/Mobil/Iron Skillet/dsl/scales/24hr/@, Phillips 66/Subway dsl/scales/24hr 🍴 Denny's, McDonald's 🛏 Days Inn, Holiday Inn Express, Motel 6, Quality Inn, Super 8 🅞 Ozarkland Gifts, Wheeler's Truckwash
144	rds M, HH, to Hatton, S 🅞 fireworks
137	rds DD, J, to Millersburg, Stephens, S 🍴 Ranch House BBQ 🅞 antiques, Freightliner, to Little Dixie WA (4mi)
133	rd Z, to Centralia, N 🅞 Gander RV Ctr
131	Lake of the Woods Rd, N 🍴 BP, Phillips 66/Subway/dsl 🍴 Buckingham BBQ, George's Rest, Sonic 🛏 Super 8 🅞 Harley-Davidson, S 🍴 Conoco/dsl 🍴 Jimmy John's 🛏 Holiday In
128a	US 63, to Jefferson City, Columbia, N 🍴 CNG, Mobil/dsl, QT 🍴 Bandanas BBQ, Bob Evans, Burger King, China Garden, Cracker Barrel, Golden Corral, Hooters, KFC, McDonald's, Pizza Hut, Ruby Tuesday, Steak'n Shake, Taco Bell, Wendy's, White Castle 🛏 Best Western+, Fairfield Inn, Hampton Inn, Hilton Garden, Red Roof Inn, Residence Inn, SpringHill Suites, Super 8 🅞 Bass Pro Shop, Home Depot, Menard's, Pine Grove RV Park, S 🍴 BreakTime/dsl 🍴 Applebee's, Baskin-Robbins, Chili's, Chipotle Mexican, CiCi's, Culver's, El Maguey, Firehouse Subs, Five Guys, Freddy's, Good Cents Subs, Houlihan's, IHOP, Kobe Japanese, Little Caesar's, Longhorn Steaks, Panda Express, Panera Bread, Sonic, Starbucks, Subway, TGIFriday's 🛏 Country Inn& Suites, Drury Plaza, Motel 6, Quality Inn, Ramada, Staybridge Suites, Suburban Inn, Wingate Inn 🅞 $Tree, H, HyVee Foods, Lowe's/Subway, Patricia's Foods, Sam's Club, Staples, Verizon, Walmart/McDonald's
128	Lp 70 (from wb), same as 128a, Columbia, N 🍴 Shell 🍴 Hardee's 🅞 Honda, S 🛏 Eastwood Motel 🅞 Big O Tire, H, NAPA
127	MO 763, to Moberly, Columbia, N 🍴 Waffle House 🛏 Budget Host 🅞 Chrysler/Dodge/Jeep, Fiat, Hyundai, Mazda, Toyota, transmissions, VW, S 🍴 Phillips 66/dsl 🛏 Super 7 Motel
126	MO 163, Providence Rd, same as 127, Columbia, N 🍴 Phillips 66/dsl 🍴 Country Kitchen 🛏 Quality Inn, Red Roof Inn 🅞 CarQuest, McKnight Tire, S 🍴 BreakTime/dsl 🍴 Burger King, Carlito's Mexican, Church's, DQ, LJ Silver, McDonald's, Pizza Hut, Subway, Taco Bell 🅞 AutoZone, Buick/Cadillac/Chevrolet/GMC, H, Nissan, O'Reilly Parts
125	Lp 70, West Blvd, same as 124, Columbia, N 🛏 Comfort Suites, S 🍴 Phillips 66/dsl 🍴 Agave Mexican, Cheddar's, Domino's, Fazoli's, Imo's Pizza, JJ's Cafe, Olive Garden, Teppanyaki Grill 🛏 Days Inn 🅞 Aldi Foods, BMW, Firestone/auto, Kia, Mercedes, Mosers Foods, Subaru, U-Haul, vet
124	MO 740, rd E, Stadium Blvd, same as 125, Columbia, N 🛏 Extended Stay America, S 🍴 BreakTime, Phillips 66/dsl 🍴 Applebee's, ChuckECheese, Denny's, Five Guys, Hardee's, Jazz Kitchen, KFC, Lee's Chicken, McDonald's, Pancheros, Panera Bread, Pizza Hut, Red Lobster, Ruby Tuesday, Smokehouse BBQ, Sports Zone Grill, Steak'n Shake, Subway, Taco Bell, TX Roadhouse, Wendy's 🛏 Best Value Inn, Drury Inn, Holiday Inn, La Quinta, Royal Inn 🅞 $Tree, AT&T, Barnes&Noble, Best Buy, Dick's, Dillard's, Ford, Hobby Lobby, JC Penney, Marshalls, Michael's, Natural Grocers, O'Reilly Parts, Old Navy, PetCo, Petsmart, Target, to U of MO, URGENT CARE, Verizon
122mm	Perche Creek

Side markers: WENTZVILLE, WARRENTON, COLUMBIA, MO

INTERSTATE 70 Cont'd

Exit #	Services
121	US 40, rd UU, Midway, N ☐ Midway/dsl/rest., Phillips 66 ☐ Budget Inn ☐ tires/repair, S ☐ golf
117	rds J, O, to Huntsdale, Harrisburg
115	rd BB N, Rocheport, N ☐ to Katy Tr SP, winery
114.5mm	Missouri River
111	MO 98, MO 179, to Wooldridge, Overton, S ☐ Cenex/dsl/repair ☐ RV Park
106	MO 87, Bingham Rd, to Boonville, S ☐ Cenex/dsl
104mm	Ⓡˢ both lanes, full ☐ facilities, ☐, ☐, litter barrels, vending, petwalk
103	rd B, Main St, Boonville, N ☐ Breaktime, Casey's/dsl, Murphy USA/dsl ☐ China One Buffet, La Hacienda Mexican, McDonald's, Pizza Hut, Sonic, Subway, Taco Bell ☐ Days Inn, Super 8 ☐ ⒽⒾ NAPA, RV Express Camping, to Katy Tr SP, Walmart/Subway, S ☐ Cenex/dsl ☐ Rte B Cafe ☐ QT Inn ☐ Buick/Chevrolet/GMC
101	US 40, MO 5, to Boonville, N ☐ Pilot/Wendy's/dsl/24hr ☐ Arby's ☐ Comfort Inn, Holiday Inn Express, Isle of Capri Hotel (3mi) ☐ Buick/Cadillac/Chevrolet/GMC, Ford, Russell Stover Candies, S ☐ Loves/Hardee's/scales/dsl/24hr, to Lake of the Ozarks
98	MO 41, MO 135, Lamine, N ☐ tires, to Arrow Rock HS (13mi), S ☐ Conoco/Ma's Kettle/dsl, Settlers/dsl ☐ repair
93mm	Lamine River
89	rd K, to Arrow Rock, N ☐ to Arrow Rock HS
84	rd J, N ☐ truck repair, Valero/DQ/Stuckey's
78b a	US 65, to Marshall, N ☐ Conoco/dsl ☐ fireworks, RV Park
77mm	Blackwater River
74	rd YY, N ☐ Cenex/Betty's/cafe/dsl/repair/24hr ☐ Welcome Motel
71	rds EE, K, to Houstonia
66	MO 127, Sweet Springs, N ☐ Ⓗ, S ☐ BreakTime/dsl, Casey's/dsl ☐ Brownsville Sta Rest. ☐ Night Inn, Super 8 ☐ $General, Bumper Parts
65.5mm	Davis Creek
62	rds VV, Y, Emma
58	MO 23, Concordia, N ☐ TA/Country Pride/Subway/dsl/scales/24hr/@ ☐ El Patron, McDonald's ☐ $General, Bratchers Mkt, truck/RV wash, S ☐ Breaktime/dsl, Casey's/dsl, Cenex/dsl ☐ Dempsey's BBQ, Pizza Hut ☐ Best Value Inn, Budget Inn, Days Inn ☐ Bumper Parts
57.5mm	Ⓡˢ both lanes, full ☐ facilities, ☐, ☐, litter barrels, vending, petwalk
52	rd T, Aullville
49	MO 13, to Higginsville, N ☐ Casey's/dsl, Pilot/McDonald's/Subway/dsl/scales/24hr ☐ Sure Stay Inn ☐ to Confederate Mem, S ☐ Super 8 ☐ Great Escape RV Park
45	rd H, to Mayview
43mm	weigh sta both lanes
41	rds O, M, to Lexington, Mayview
38	MO 131 (from wb), same as 37, Odessa, S ☐ BP/dsl, Phillips 66/dsl, Shell ☐ McDonald's, Pizza Hut, Sonic, Subway, Taco John's, Thompson's Country Kitchen ☐ $General Mkt, $Tree, O'Reilly Parts
37	MO 131, same as 38, Odessa, N ☐ Country Gardens RV Park/dump, S ☐ BP/dsl, Phillips 66/dsl, Shell ☐ El Camino Real, McDonald's, Pizza Hut, Sonic, Subway, Taco John's, Thompson's Country Kitchen ☐ Parkside Inn ☐ $General Mkt, $Tree, fireworks, NAPA, O'Reilly Parts, Sunrise Mkt
35mm	truck parking both lanes

31	rds D, Z, to Bates City, Napoleon, N ☐ ♥Loves/Hardee's/dsl/scales/24hr ☐ Bates City RV Camping, S ☐ Valero/dsl ☐ Bates City BBQ ☐ fireworks
29.5mm	Horse Shoe Creek
28	rd H, rd F, Oak Grove, N ☐ TA/Country Pride/Popeye's/dsl/scales/24hr/@ ☐ Oak Grove Inn ☐ Blue Beacon, KOA, S ☐ Casey's, Petro/BP/Iron Skillet/DQ/Wendy's/scales/dsl/@, QT/dsl ☐ China Buffet, Hardee's, KFC/Taco Bell, McDonald's, Pizza Hut, PJ's Rest., Subway, Waffle House ☐ EconoLodge, Holiday Inn Express ☐ $Tree, Cash Saver Foods, Lake Paradise RV/Camping (9mi), O'Reilly Parts, SpeedCo Lube, Walgreens, Walmart
24	US 40, rds AA, BB, to Buckner, N ☐ Casey's/dsl, QT/dsl ☐ Papa Murphy's ☐ Best Value Inn, Comfort Inn ☐ LifeStyle RV Ctr, Price Chopper, vet S ☐ Conoco/Subway/dsl/scales/24hr, Temp Stop/Amoco/dsl ☐ McDonald's, Sonic ☐ Advance Parts, Trailside RV Park/Ctr
21	Adams Dairy Pkwy, N ☐ Camping World RV Ctr (1mi), S ☐ Murphy USA/dsl, Phillips 66/Burger King/dsl ☐ Arby's, Cane's, Chick-fil-A, Chipotle Mexican, Five Guys, Jersey Mike's, Olive Garden, Panda Express, Panera Bread, Pepper Jax Grill, Planet Sub, Sonic, Subway, Taco Bell, TX Roadhouse ☐ Courtyard ☐ AT&T, GNC, Gordman's, Home Depot, Kohl's, Michael's, NTB, PetCo, Ross, Target, TJ Maxx, Verizon, Walmart
20	MO 7, Blue Springs, N ☐ Phillips 66/dsl, QT/dsl ☐ Backyard Burger, China 1, Custard's, Dunkin', Goodcents Subs, Minsky's Pizza, Papa Murphy's, Rancho Grande, Sonic, Subway ☐ Best Value Inn, Days Inn, Econolodge, Rodeway Inn ☐ $General, Ace Hardware, CVS Drug, NAPA, O'Reilly Parts, PriceChopper Foods, Walgreens, Walmart Mkt, S ☐ BP/dsl, QT, Valero/dsl ☐ Applebee's, Big Biscuit, Denny's, Firehouse Subs, Jack-in-the-Box, Jimmy John's, KFC, LJ Silver, McDonald's, Original Pizza, Starbucks, Subway, Taco Bell, Taco Bueno, Wendy's, Winsteads Cafe, Zarda's BBQ ☐ Hampton Inn, Quality Inn ☐ Advance Parts, Aldi Foods, AutoZone, BigLots, Chevrolet, Firestone/auto, Goodyear/auto, Hobby Lobby, Ⓗ, Hy-Vee Foods/gas, Office Depot, Russell Stover, transmissions, URGENT CARE
18	Woods Chapel Rd, same as 20, N ☐ La Quinta, Motel 6, Super 8, Welcome Inn ☐ Harley-Davidson, S ☐ Conoco/dsl, Phillips 66/dsl, QT, QT (2) ☐ China Kitchen, KFC/Taco Bell, Las Playas Mexican, McDonald's, Pizza Hut, Sonic, Subway, Taco John's, Waffle House ☐ CVS Drug, Ford, Hyundai
17	Little Blue Pkwy, 39th St, N ☐ QT/dsl ☐ Black Bear Diner, Buffalo Wild Wings, Coldstone, DQ, Hereford House, Jimmy John's, Lion's Choice, On the Border, Saints Grill, Sonic, Twin Peaks, Wendy's ☐ Hilton Garden ☐ Ⓗ, Menard's, World Mkt, S ☐ QT ☐ Arby's, BD Mongolian, Carrabba's, Chipotle Mexican, Corner Cafe, Culver's, Golden Corral, Hooters, IHOP, Kobe Steaks, McDonald's, Outback Steaks, Panera Bread, Pie Five, Qdoba,

BOONEVILLE

CONCORDIA

ODESSA

BLUE SPGS

🅖 = gas 🍴 = food 🛏 = lodging 🅞 = other 🆁🆂 = rest stop   Copyright 2022 - The Next EXIT

INTERSTATE 70 Cont'd

17	Continued
	Red Robin, Subway, Whataburger 🛏 Candlewood Suites, Comfort Suites, Drury Inn, Holiday Inn Express, My Place 🅞 Carmax, Costco/gas, Lowe's
16mm	Little Blue River Little Blue River
15b	MO 291 N, Independence, **1 exit N on 39th St** 🅖 Phillips 66, QT 🍴 54th St Grill, Applebee's, Burger King, Chick-fil-A, Chili's, ChuckECheese, Famous Dave's, Fazoli's, Logan's Roadhouse, Longhorn Steaks, McDonald's, Noodles&Co, Perkins, Smokehouse BBQ, Starbucks, Taco Bell, Zio's Italian 🛏 Fairfield Inn, Residence Inn, Staybridge Suites 🅞 AT&T, AutoZone, Barnes&Noble, Best Buy, Dick's, Dillard's, 🅗, JC Penney, JoAnn, Kohl's, Macy's, Marshalls, NTB, Petsmart, Ross, Sam's Club/gas, Target, Walmart
15a	I-470 S, MO 291 S, to Lee's Summit, same as 14
14	Lee's Summit Rd, **1 mi N** 🍴 Longhorn Steaks, **S** 🅖 Tesla EVC 🍴 Cheddar's, Cracker Barrel, Los Cabos, Old Chicago, Pizza Ranch, Slim Chickens 🛏 Stoney Creek Hotel 🅞 Bass Pro Shops, Duluth Trading, Hobby Lobby, Home Depot
12	Noland Rd, Independence, **N** 🅖 Conoco/dsl, QT, Shell 🍴 China Town, Denny's, Domino's, Hardee's, Mr Goodcents, Pizza St, Sheridan's Custard, Sonic, Subway 🛏 Best Western, Super 8 🅞 $General, Advance Parts, Buick/GMC/Cadillac, Chevrolet, Chrysler/Jeep, CVS Drug, Firestone/auto, Ford, Office Depot, to Truman Library, TrueValue, Walgreens, Walmart Mkt, **S** 🅖 Phillips 66/Kicks 🍴 Arby's, Bandana's BBQ, Baskin Robbins, Burger King, HoneyBaked Ham, KFC/Taco Bell, Krispy Kreme, Ma Ma Garden, McDonald's, Olive Garden, Pizza Hut, Quiznos, Red Lobster, Ruby Tuesday, Steak'n Shake, Wendy's 🛏 American Inn, Best Value Inn, Days Inn, Quality Inn, Red Roof Inn 🅞 $Tree, BigLots, GNC, Gordman's, HyVee Foods/gas, Old Time Pottery, Petco, PriceChopper Mkt, Tires+, U-Haul
11	US 40, Blue Ridge Blvd, Independence, **N** 🅖 QT/dsl 🍴 A&W/LJ Silver, La Fuentes, Rosie's Cafe, Sonic, Subway, V's Italian, **S** 🅖 7-11, BP, Murphy USA/dsl, Sinclair 🍴 Applebee's, Big Boy Burgers, Chipotle Mexican, Church's, East Buffet, Firehouse Subs, IHOP, McDonald's, Papa John's, Samurai Chef, Starbucks 🅞 Family$, GNC, Lowe's, O'Reilly Parts, Verizon, vet, Walmart/Subway
10	Sterling Ave (from eb), same as 11
9	Blue Ridge Cutoff (from wb), **N** 🍴 Denny's 🛏 Hotel Lotus, Woodspring Suites, **S** 🅖 BP, Phillips 66/Subway 🍴 Taco Bell 🛏 Best Western 🅞 Sports Complex
8b a	I-435, N to Des Moines, S to Wichita
7b	Manchester Trafficway
7mm	Blue River
7a	US 40 E, 31st St
6	Van Brunt Blvd, **N** 🅖 Conoco/7-11, Phillips 66/dsl, **S** 🅖 BP 🍴 McDonald's 🅞 VA 🅗
5c	Jackson Ave (from wb)
5b	31st St (from eb)
5a	27th St (from eb)
4c	23rd Ave
4b	18th St
4a	Benton Blvd (from eb), Truman Rd, **N** 🅖 Super Stop/Wendy's/dsl 🍴 Subway 🅞 Advance Parts, Save-A-Lot Foods
3c	Prospect Ave, **N** 🅖 BP 🍴 Church's, **S** 🍴 McDonald's
3b	Brooklyn Ave (from eb), **N** 🅖 BP 🍴 Church's, **S** 🅖 Shell/dsl 🍴 McDonald's
3a	Paseo St, **S** 🅖 BP/dsl 🅞 tires
2m	US 71 S downtown
2l	I-670, to I-35 S

(left margin: MO INDEPENDENCE KANSAS CITY)

2j	11th St downtown
2g	I-29/35 N, US 71 N, to Des Moines
2h	US 24 E downtown
2e	MO 9 N, Oak St, **S** 🅖 Phillips 66 🛏 Marriott
2d	Main St downtown
2c	US 169 N, Broadway, **S** 🅖 Phillips 66 🛏 Marriott
2b	Beardsley Rd
2a	I-35 S, to Wichita
0mm	Missouri/Kansas state line, Kansas River

INTERSTATE 270 (St Louis)

Exit #	Services
15b a	I-55 N to Chicago, S to St Louis. **I-270 begins/ends in Illinois on I-55/I-70, exit 20.**
12	IL 159, to Collinsville, **1 mi N** 🅖 QT/dsl, ZX/dsl 🍴 Applebee's, Denny's, DQ, Hardee's, IHOP, Jack-in-the-box, Jimmy John's, KFC, Little Caesar's, Papa John's, Subway 🅞 Aldi Foods, AT&T, Chrysler/Dodge/Jeep, Home Depot, Lowe's, PetsMart, Sam's Club/dsl, Walgreens, Walmart, **S** 🅞 🅗
9	IL 157, to Collinsville, **N** 🍴 Comfort Inn, **S** 🅖 BP/dsl 🛏 Hampton Inn
7	I-255, to I-55 S to Memphis
6b a	IL 111, **N** 🅖 FLYING J/Denny's/dsl/scales/24hr 🍴 Hen House Rest. 🛏 Motel 6 🅞 Blue Beacon/scales, Speedco, truck/trailer repair, **S** 🅖 Mobil/dsl 🍴 Denny's, McDonald's/playplace, Taco Bell 🛏 Best Western+, Days Inn, Fairfield Inn, La Quinta, Super 8 🅞 to Pontoon Beach
4	IL 203, Old Alton Rd, to Granite City
3b a	IL 3, **N** 🅞 Riverboat Casino, **S** 🅖 Phillips 66 🍴 Hardee's, Waffle House 🛏 Budget Motel, EconoLodge, Economy Inn, Sun Motel 🅞 KOA, MGM Camping
2mm	Chain of Rocks Canal
0mm	Illinois/Missouri state line, Mississippi River
34	Riverview Dr, to St Louis, **N** **Welcome Ctr/🆁🆂 both lanes, full 🅥 facilities, info, litter barrels,** 🅥, 🛏 🅖 Moto Mart/Subway
33	Lilac Ave, **N** 🅞 USPO, **S** 🅖 Phillips 66/Jack-in-the-Box/dsl, QT/dsl/scales/24hr 🍴 Hardee's
32	Bellefontaine Rd, **N** 🅖 Shell/Circle K 🍴 China King, McDonald's, Pizza Hut, Steak'n Shake 🛏 Budget Inn 🅞 Advance Parts, Family$, Firestone/auto, Schnuck's Foods, **S** 🅖 BP 🍴 White Castle 🅞 Aldi Foods
31b a	MO 367, **N** 🅖 BP, QT/dsl 🍴 Jack-in-the-Box, Little Caesar's, McDonalds, Subway, Taco Bell 🅞 $General, CVS Drug, Family$, 🅗, Shop'n Save Foods, U-Haul, Walgreens
30b a	Hall's Ferry Rd, rd AC, **N** 🅖 Conoco/dsl, QT/dsl, Shell/dsl 🍴 Applebee's, Capt. D's, White Castle 🛏 Knights Inn 🅞 Ford/Lincoln, Kia, **S** 🅖 BP/dsl, Conoco, Phillips 66 🍴 China Wok, Church's, Cracker Barrel, IHOP, Steak'n Shake, Subway 🅞 AutoZone, Home Depot, Meineke, O'Reilly Parts, Shop'n Save Foods
29	W Florissant Rd, **N** 🍴 China Moon, Jack-in-the-Box, Lion's Choice, Pasta House 🅞 $General, Aldi Foods, Dobb's Tire/auto, Family$, Firestone, GNC, Ross, **S** 🅖 Phillips 66/dsl, QT/dsl 🍴 Arby's, Burger King, Domino's, Hibachi Grill, Krispy Kreme, Little Caesar's, McDonald's, Starbucks 🅞 $General, $Tree, AT&T, NTB, Sam's Club/gas, Walmart
28	Elizabeth Ave, Washington St, **N** 🅖 Phillips 66/dsl 🍴 Jack-in-the-Box, Subway, Taco Bell 🅞 Chevrolet, Schnuck's Foods, Walgreens
27	New Florissant Rd, rd N, **N** 🅞 CVS Drug, Shell/Circle K
26b	Graham Rd, N Hanley, **N** 🅖 Phillips 66/7-11/dsl 🍴 Arby's, LJ Silver, Starbucks 🛏 Quality Inn, Red Roof Inn 🅞 $Tree, 🅗, **S** 🍴 McDonald's 🛏 Days Inn 🅞 $General

(right margin: ST LOUIS)

INTERSTATE 270 (St Louis) Cont'd

Exit #	Services
26a	I-170 S
25b a	US 67, Lindbergh Blvd, **N** 🅖 BP, Phillips 66, QT/dsl 🅕 Bandana's BBQ, Burger King, Church's, Domino's, Five Guys, IHOP, Imo's Pizza, Jack-in-the-Box, Jimmy John's, McDonald's, Papa John's, Pizza Hut, Pueblo Nuevo Mexican, Starbucks, Subway, Taco Bell, Waffle House, Wendy's 🛏 Comfort Inn, Holiday Inn Express, InTown Suites, La Quinta 🅞 $General, AutoZone, Dierberg's Deli, Family$, Firestone/auto, Ford, GNC, Hyundai, NAPA, Nissan, O'Reilly Parts, Sav-a-Lot Foods, Schnuck's Foods, Toyota, Walgreens, **S** 🅕 Jimmy John's 🛏 Budget Inn, Crossland Suites 🅞 Honda, USPO, VW
23	McDonnell Blvd, **E** 🅕 Denny's, Quiznos 🛏 Motel 6, **W** 🅖 Mobil/dsl, QT/dsl 🅕 Arby's, Jack-in-the-Box, Lion's Choice, McDonald's, Steak'n Shake, Subway, Taco Bell 🅞 Buick/GMC
22b a	MO 370 W, to MO Bottom Rd
20c	MO 180, St Charles Rock Rd, **E** 🅖 BP, Phillips 66/dsl 🅕 A&W/LJ Silver, Applebees, Arby's, Chick-fil-A, Chimi's Mexican, Chipotle, Fazoli's, Hometown Buffet, Imo's Pizza, Jack-in-the-Box, Jimmy John's, Lonestar Steaks, McDonald's, New China Buffet, Pizza Hut, Qdoba, Red Lobster, St. Louis Bread, Subway, Taco Bell, Wendy's, White Castle, Ya Hala Mediterranean 🅞 $Tree, Aldi Foods, AT&T, AutoZone, Best Buy, CVS Drug, Hobby Lobby, 🅗, Kohl's, Meineke, NTB, Office Depot, Petsmart, Save-a-Lot, Target, Verizon, Walgreens, Walmart/Burger, **W** 🅕 QT 🅕 Bob Evans, Olive Garden, Waffle House 🛏 Best Value Inn, Motel 6, Super 8
20b a	I-70, E to St Louis, W to Kansas City
17	Dorsett Rd, **E** 🅕 Bandana's BBQ, Papa John's, Syberg's Grill, Waffle House 🛏 Drury Inn, Hampton Inn, Homewood Suites, **W** 🅖 Mobil, Phillips 66/dsl, Shell 🅕 Arby's, Denny's, Firehouse Subs, McDonald's, MOD Pizza, Steak'n Shake, Subway 🛏 Motel 6 🅞 GNC, Schnuck's Mkt, Walgreens
16b a	Page Ave, rd D, MO 364 W, **E** 🅖 BP, QT, Shell/Circle K/dsl 🅕 Hardee's, Hooters, McDonald's, Spazio Café, Starbucks 🛏 Comfort Inn, Courtyard, Days Inn, DoubleTree, Extended Stay America, Extended Stay America (2), Extended Stay America (3), Fairfield Inn, Hawthorn Suites, La Quinta, Red Roof Inn, Residence Inn, Sheraton, Sonesta Suites
14	MO 340, Olive Blvd, **E** 🅖 CVS Drug, Dierberg's Mkt, Phillips 66/dsl 🅕 Applebee's, AT&T, Bristol Cafe, Five Guys, Granite City, Lion's Choice Rest., McDonald's, Pasta House, Pei Wei, Pieology, Potbelly, Qdoba, Starbucks, Subway 🛏 Courtyard, Drury Inn 🅞 Aldi Foods, BMW/Audi/Infiniti, Chevrolet, Land Rover/Jaguar, Lexus, Mercedes, Verizon, **W** 🅖 Schnuck's Mkt 🅕 Coldstone, IMO's Pizza, Jet's Pizza, La Salsa, Subway, TGIFriday's 🅞 Dierberg's Foods, 🅗, Kohl's, vet, Walgreens
13	rd AB, Ladue Rd
12b a	I-64, US 40, US 61, E to St Louis, W to Wentzville, **E** 🅞 🅗
9	MO 100, Manchester Rd, **E** 🅕 Bravo, Cane's, Chick-fil-A, Elephant Bar, Five Guys, Imo's Pizza, J Gilbert's Rest., Jimmy John's, McAlister's Deli, McDonald's, Qdoba, Subway 🅞 Barnes&Noble, Dick's, Macy's, Nordstrom, Schnuck's, **W** 🅖 Shell 🅕 Red Robin
8	Dougherty Ferry Rd, **2 mi S** 🅖 Citgo/7-11, Mobil 🅕 McDonald's 🅞 🅗
7	Big Ben Rd, **N** 🅞 🅗
5b a	I-44, US 50, MO 366, E to St Louis, W to Tulsa
3	MO 30, Gravois Rd, **N** 🅖 BP, Phillips 66 🅕 Bandana BBQ, Olive Garden, Outback Steaks 🅞 Ford
2	MO 21, Tesson Ferry Rd, **N** 🅖 BP, Mobil 🅕 54th St Grill, Baskin Robbins, Burger King, Church's, Jack-in-the-Box, Jimmy John's, Joey B's, Olive Garden, Outback Steaks, Panda Chinese, Pizza Hut, Quizno's, Red Lobster, Shogun Japanese, Subway, Taco Bell, TGIFriday's, Waffle House, White Castle 🅞 Acura, AutoZone, Buick/GMC, Dobb's Auto, Honda, O'Reilly Parts, Schnuck's Foods, Shop'n Save, Toyota, Walgreens, **S** 🅖 Shell/Circle K/dsl 🅕 Chevy's Mexican, Dierberg's Foods, Little Caesar's
1b a	I-55 N to St Louis, S to Memphis

INTERSTATE 435 (Kansas City)

Exit #	Services
83	I-35, N to KS City, S to Wichita
82	Quivira Rd, Overland Park, **N** 🅕 Burger King, Cheddar's, Chick-fil-A, KFC, Mimi's Cafe, Outback Steaks, Sonic, Taco Bell 🅞 AT&T, Dillard's, 🅗, JC Penney, Macy's, Nordstrom's, Target, **S** 🅕 Boston Mkt, Domino's, McDonald's, Subway, Taco Bell, Wendy's 🛏 Extended Stay America 🅞 CVS Drug, Hen House Mkt
81	US 69 S, to Ft Scott
80	Antioch Rd
79	Metcalf Ave, **N** 🅖 Conoco/7-11, Phillips 66/dsl/repair 🅕 Buffalo Wild Wings, Carrabba's, Chartroose Caboose, ChuckECheese, D'Bronx Pizza, Denny's, Fox&Hound, Hardee's, Hooters, Jack-in-the-Box, Jose Pepper's, Krispy Kreme, Subway 🛏 Comfort Inn, Days Inn, Embassy Suites, Extended Stay America, Hampton Inn, Homewood Suites, La Quinta, Motel 6, Overland Park Place Hotel, Super 8 🅞 AAA, 🅗, Office Depot, vet, Walmart Mkt, **S** 🅕 Applebee's, McDonald's, Panera Bread 🛏 Drury Inn, Marriott, PearTree Inn
77b a	Nall Ave, Roe Ave, **N** 🅖 QT 🅕 Brobeck's BBQ, Freddy's, Sonic, Winstead's Grill 🛏 Best Value Inn 🅞 USPO, **S** 🅕 Corner Bakery Cafe, Wendy's 🛏 Chase Suite Hotel, Courtyard, Extended Stay America, Hilton Garden, Holiday Inn, Hyatt Place, Sheraton 🅞 Walgreens
75b	State Line Rd, **N** 🅖 Phillips 66 🅕 Applebee's, Gate's BBQ, Jimmy John's, McDonald's, Taco Bell 🅞 Buick/GMC/Cadillac, Goodyear/auto, Midas, O'Reilly Parts, PriceChopper Foods, **S** 🅖 QT/dsl 🅞 city park, 🅗
75a	Wornall Rd, **N** 🅖 QT 🅕 Applebee's, China King, Coach's Grill, Dunkin', Fuzzy's Taco Shop, McDonald's, Panera Bread, Pizza Hut, Subway 🅞 Acura, Audi, Chevrolet, Honda, Nissan, Price Chopper, Toyota, VW
74	Holmes Rd, **N** 🅖 Phillips 66/dsl 🅕 Subway, Thai House, **S** 🛏 Courtyard, Extended Stay America
73	103rd St (from wb)
71b a	I-470/US 50 E, I-49/US 71S

MO

KANSAS CITY

INTERSTATE 435 (Kansas City) Cont'd

Exit #	Services
70	Bannister Rd, **E** 🅿 Phillips 66 🍴 Walgreens, Wendy's, **W** 🍴 Taco Bell Ⓞ Firestone/auto, Home Depot
69	87th St., **E** 🅿 Conoco/dsl, QT 🍴 McDonald's 🛏 Advance Parts, Capital Inn, **W** 🛏 Days Inn
67	Gregory Blvd (same as 66a b), **W** Ⓞ Nature Ctr, zoo
66	MO 350 E, 63rd st
65	Eastwood Tfwy, **W** 🅿 Conoco 🍴 Church's, McDonald's, Peachtree Rest.
63c	Raytown Rd, Stadium Dr (nb only), **E** Ⓞ to Sports Complex
63b a	I-70, W to KC, E to St Louis
61	MO 78, **2 mi E** 🍴 Church's
60	MO 12 E, Truman Rd, 12th St, **E** 🅿 Phillips 66/dsl, **W** 🅿 QT
59	US 24, Independence Ave, **E** 🅿 QT Ⓞ to Truman Library, **W** 🍴 Hardee's Ⓞ CarQuest
57	Front St, **E** 🅿 ⓕFLYING J/Conoco/rest/dsl/scales/24hr Ⓞ Blue Beacon, Kenworth, **W** 🅿 Phillips 66/dsl, QT, Sinclair/dsl 🍴 Denny's, McDonald's, Smugglers Rest., Subway, Waffle House 🛏 Howard Johnson Plaza, Quality Inn Ⓞ URGENT CARE
56mm	Missouri River
55b a	MO 210, **E** 🅿 Phillips 66/dsl, 🏪PILOT/PJ Fresh/dsl/scales/24hr 🍴 Subway 🛏 Ameristar Hotel/Casino, Motel 6 Ⓞ Ford/Volvo/GMC/Mercedes Trucks, Riverboat Casino
54	48th St, Parvin Rd, **E** 🛏 Funpark, **W** 🅿 QT 🍴 All Star Grill, Taco Bell, Waffle House, Wendy's 🛏 Best Inn, Candlewood Suites, Comfort Inn, Days Inn, Hampton Inn, Holiday Inn, Hometowne Suites, SpringHill Suites, Super 8, SureStay Inn
52a	US 69, **E** 🅿 Phillips 66/dsl, **W** 🍴 McDonald's, Pizza Hut, Subway Ⓞ $General, Walgreens
52b	I-35, S to KC
51	Shoal Creek Dr, **W** Ⓞ LDS Temple
49b a	MO 152 E, to I-35 N, Liberty, **2 mi E** 🍴 54th St Grill, Applebee's, Bob Evans, Buffalo Wild Wings, Cracker Barrel, Longhorn Steaks, Steak'n Shake 🛏 Best Western, Comfort Inn, Fairfield Inn, Hampton Inn, Holiday Inn Express, Super 8
47	NE 96th St
46	NE 108th St
45	MO 291, NE Cookingham Ave, to I-35 N
42	N Woodland Ave
41b a	US 169, Smithville, **4 mi N** 🅿 Kum&Go 🍴 Burger King, McDonald's, Sonic 🛏 Super 8
40	NW Cookingham
37	NW Skyview Ave, rd C, **N** 🅿 Cenex (1mi), **S** Ⓞ golf (3mi)
36	to I-29 S, to KCI Airport, **N** 🅿 Cenex, **S** 🛏 Extended Stay America, Fairfield Inn, Holiday Inn, Marriott, Microtel, Plaza Hotel, Quality Suites, Sheraton, Super 8

Exit #	Services
31	I-29 N, to St Joseph, S to KC Prairie Creek
29	rd D, NW 120th St
24	MO 152, rd N, NW Berry Rd
22	MO 45, Weston, Parkville, **E** 🅿 The Station/DiBella's Pizza/dsl
20mm	Missouri/Kansas state line, Missouri River
18	KS 5 N, Wolcott Dr, **E** Ⓞ to Wyandotte Co Lake Park
16	Donohoo Rd
15b a	Leavenworth Rd, **E** 🅿 Conoco/Subway/dsl 🛏 Comfort Suites, Woodlands Racetrack
14b a	Parallel Pkwy, **E** Ⓞ Honda, Toyota, **W** 🅿 Phillips 66/7-11/Subway/dsl 🍴 Applebee's, Arby's, Bob Evans, Bryant's BBQ, Carino's Italian, Chick-fil-A, Chili's, Chipotle Mexican, Chuisano's Brick Oven, Culver's, Danny's Grill, Dave&Buster's, Five Guys, Fuddrucker's, Granite City Rest, Hooters, IHOP, Jack-in-the-Box, Jose Pepper's Grill, Longhorn Sreaks, McDonald's, Olive Garden, Panda Express, Panera Bread, Pizza Hut, Red Lobster, Sheridan's Custard, Sonic, Starbucks, Stix Asian, Taco Bell, Taco Bueno, Wendy's 🛏 Candlewood Suites, Country Inn&Suites, Holiday Inn Express, Residence Inn Ⓞ AT&T, JC Penney, Kohl's, NTB, Old Navy, Sam's Club/dsl, Target, TJ Maxx, Verizon, Walmart
13b a	US 24, US 40, State Ave, **E** 🍴 Frontier Steaks Ⓞ water park, **W** 🍴 Casa Agave, Famous Dave's BBQ, Lonestar Steaks 🛏 Best Western, Chateau Avalon, Great Wolf Lodge, Hampton Inn Ⓞ Cabela's, KS Race Track, Russell Stovers
12b a	I-70, KS Tpk, to Topeka, St Louis
11	Kansas Ave
9	KS 32, KS City, Bonner Springs, **W** 🅿 Phillips 66/dsl
8b	Woodend Rd, **E** Ⓞ Peterbilt, **W** 🅿 Shell/Subway/dsl/scales
8.8mm	Kansas River
8a	Holliday Dr, to Lake Quivira
6c	Johnson Dr
6b a	Shawnee Mission Pkwy, **E** 🍴 Chili's, Grand Wok, IHOP, McDonald's, Pizza Hut, Subway Ⓞ Aldi Foods, GNC, Home Depot, Kohl's, Lowe's, Michael's, NTB, Petsmart, Target, Walmart/Subway
5	Midland Dr, Shawnee Mission Park, **E** 🅿 Conoco, Phillips 66/7-11/Subway/dsl 🍴 Barley's Brewhaus, Chen's Kitchen, Eggtc, Jose Pepper's Grill, Minsky's Pizza, Paula&Bill's Ristorante, Wendy's 🛏 Hampton Inn, **W** 🍴 Hereford House 🛏 Courtyard, Holiday Inn Express
3	87th Ave, **E** 🅿 BP, Phillips 66/dsl 🍴 Freddy's, McDonald's, Panera Bread, Papa John's, Papa Murphy's, Sonic, Taco Bell Ⓞ Ace Hardware, Aldi Foods, Sprouts Mkt, Walgreens, **W** 🍴 Gambino's Pizza, Grand St Cafe, Hen House Mkt, Subway 🛏 Hyatt Place
2	95th St
1b	KS 10, to Lawrence
1a	Lackman Rd, **N** 🅿 Phillips 66/dsl 🛏 Suburban Lodge
0mm	I-435 begins/ends on I-35.

NOTES

MONTANA

⬆N   INTERSTATE 15

Exit #	Services
398mm	Montana/US/Canada Border, Sweetgrass
397	Sweetgrass, **W** Rs both lanes, full ♿ facilities, 🛆 litter barrels, petwalk, 🍴 Gastrak 🛏 Glocca Morra Motel/cafe ⊙ Duty Free
394	ranch access
389	MT 552, Sunburst, **W** 📇 CFN/dsl ⊙ Sunburst Mercantile, Sunburst RV Park, USPO
385	Swayze Rd
379	MT 215, MT 343, to Kevin, Oilmont, **W** 🍴 Four Corners Café
373	Potter Rd
369	Bronken Rd
366.5mm	weigh sta sb
364	Shelby, **E** ⊙ Lewis&Clark RV Park, **W** ⊙ ☇
363	US 2, Shelby, to Cut Bank, Shelby, **0-1 mi E** 📇 Cenex, Pilot/Exxon/Country Skillet/dsl/scales/24hr, Sinclair/dsl 🍴 Dash Drive-In, Dixie Inn Steaks, Kowloon Chinese, Pizza Hut, Subway, The Griddle 🛏 Comfort Inn, Crossroads Inn, Glacier Motel/RV Park, O'Haire Motel ⊙ Albertsons, CarQuest, city park, 🅗, Mark's Tire, Parts+, Shelby RV Park, TrueValue, USPO, visitor info, **W** 🛏 Best Western ⊙ to Glacier NP
361mm	parking area nb
358	Marias Valley Rd, to Golf Course Rd, **E** ⊙ camping
357mm	Marias River
352	Bullhead Rd
348	rd 44, to Valier, **W** ⊙ Lake Frances RA (15mi)
345	MT 366, Ledger Rd, **E** ⊙ to Tiber Dam (42mi)
339	Conrad, **E** Rs/weigh sta both lanes, full ♿ facilities, 🛆 litter barrels, petwalk, **W** 📇 Calumet/dsl, Cenex/dsl, Conoco/dsl, Exxon/Subway/dsl 🍴 A&W/Chester's, Home Cafe, Main Drive-In 🛏 Northgate Motel, Super 8 ⊙ Buick/Chevrolet/GMC, CarQuest, Conrad Tire/repair, Ford, 🅗, IGA Foods, museum, Olson's Drug, Pondera RV Park, TrueValue, USPO, vet, Village Drug, Westco RV Ctr
335	Midway Rd, Conrad, **4 mi W** 📇 gas 🍴 food 🛏 lodging ⊙ 🅗, RV camping
328	MT 365, Brady, **W** 📇 Mtn View Co-op/dsl ⊙ city park, USPO
321	Collins Rd
319mm	Teton River, Rs both lanes, full ♿ facilities, 🍴, 🛆 litter barrels, petwalk
313	MT 221, MT 379, Dutton, **W** 📇 Cenex/dsl 🍴 The Drive-In ⊙ city park, USPO
302	MT 431, Power
297	Gordon
290	US 89 N, rd 200 W, to Choteau, **W** 📇 Conoco/dsl, Sinclair/dsl/LP/RV dump ⊙ USPO
288mm	parking area both lanes
286	Manchester, **W** ⊙ livestock auction same as 290 (2mi)
282	US 87 N (from sb), NW bypass, **2-3 mi E** 📇 Conoco/dsl, Holiday/dsl 🍴 Arby's, Buffalo Wild Wings, Burger King, Little Caesar's, McDonald's, New Peking, Subway, Taco Bell, Taco John's 🛏 Days Inn ⊙ $Tree, Ace Hardware, Albertsons/Osco, O'Reilly Parts, Sam's Club/gas, Staples, Tire-Rama, TJ Maxx, Walgreens, Walmart
280	US 87 N, Central Ave W, Great Falls, **E** 📇 Loaf 'N Jug/dsl 🍴 A&W/KFC, Ford's Drive-In, Lippi's Kitchen, Papa John's 🛏 Alberta Inn, Central Motel, Days Inn (3mi), Staybridge Suites ⊙ city park, to Giant Sprgs SP, U-Haul/LP, vet, Whalen Tire
280mm	Sun River
278	US 89 S, rd 200 E, 10th Ave, Great Falls, **E** 📇 Calumet/dsl, Cenex/dsl, Conoco/dsl, Exxon/dsl, Holiday/Subway/dsl, Sinclair/dsl, Town Pump/dsl 🍴 4B's Rest., Applebee's, Arby's, Baskin-Robbins, Beef'O'Brady's, Best Wok, Boston's Pizza, Burger King, Café Rio, Chili's, Classic 50s Diner/casino, Coldstone, DQ, Fuddrucker's, Golden Corral, Hardee's, Jaker's Rest., JB's Rest., Jimmy John's, Little Caesar's, MacKenzie River Pizza, McDonald's, Ming's Chinese, Noodle Express, Papa John's, Papa Murphy's, Pita Pit, Pizza Hut, Sonic, Starbucks, Subway, Taco Bell, Taco Del Mar, Taco John's, Taco Treat, Wendy's, Wheat MT, ZPizza 🛏 Best Western, Comfort Inn, Comfort Inn (2), Extended Stay America, Fairfield Inn, Hampton Inn,

SHELBY

CONRAD

GREAT FALLS

⬆N INTERSTATE 15 Cont'd

278 Continued
Hilton Garden, Holiday Inn, Holiday Inn Express, La Quinta, Motel 6, Super 8, Western Motel 🅾 $Tree, Ace Hardware, Albertsons/Osco, AT&T, AT&T, AutoZone, Barnes&Noble, Big O Tire, BigLots, Cadillac/Chevrolet/Toyota, CarQuest, Chrysler/Dodge/Jeep, CVS Drug, Dick's RV Park, Firestone/auto, Ford, Gardner's RV Ctr, Harley-Davidson, Herberger's, Home Depot, Honda, 🅗, JC Penney, Jo-Ann Fabrics, KOA, Michael's, Midas, NAPA, Nissan, O'Reilly Parts, Old Navy, PetCo, Pierce RV Ctr, Ross, Scheels Sports, Smith's/dsl, Super 1 Foods, Target, Tire-Rama, to Malmstrom AFB, transmissions, USPO, Verizon, VW, Walgreens

277 Airport Rd, E 🅿 ⊕FLYING J/Denny's/dsl/scales/24hr, 🛢Conoco/Subway/casino/dsl/scales/24hr 🛏 Crystal Inn, W 🅾 ☕

275mm weigh sta nb

270 MT 330, Ulm, E 🅿 Cenex/dsl/LP 🅾 USPO, W 🍴 Beef'n Bone Steaks 🅾 to Ulm SP

256 rd 68, Cascade, 1/2 mi E 🅿 Sinclair/dsl 🍴 Angus Bear Cafe 🛏 Trout Flyshop 🅾 Tom's Foods, USPO

254 rd 68, Cascade, 1/2 mi E same as 256

250 local access

247 Hardy Creek, W 🅾 RV camping, to Tower Rock SP

246.5mm Missouri River

245mm scenic overlook sb

244 Canyon Access, 2 mi W 🍴 MO Inn Rest. 🅾 Prewett Creek Camping, rec area, RV camping

240 Dearborn, E 🅾 RV park

239mm Ⓡs both lanes, full ♿ facilities, 🛢, 🪑, litter barrels, petwalk

238mm Stickney Creek

236mm Missouri River

234 Craig, E 🍴 Izaak's Cafe, Trout Shop Café/lodge 🛏 Flyshop 🅾 boating, camping, rec area

228 US 287 N, to Augusta, Choteau

226 MT 434, Wolf Creek, E 🅿 Exxon/dsl 🍴 Oasis Café 🛏 Wolf Creek Angler 🅾 camping, to Holter Lake, W 🍴 Frenchman&Me Café 🅾 USPO

222mm parking area both lanes

219 Spring Creek, Recreation Rd (from nb), Spring Creek 🅾 boating, camping

218mm Little Prickly Pear Creek

216 Sieben

209 E 🅾 to Gates of the Mtns RA

202mm weigh sta sb

200 MT 279, MT 453, Lincoln Rd, W 🅿 Sinclair/Bob's Mkt/dsl 🍴 GrubStake Rest. 🅾 Lincoln Rd RV Park, to ski area

194 Custer Ave, E 🅿 Conoco/dsl 🍴 Chili's, Hardee's, IHOP, Nagoya Japanese, Qdoba 🛏 Comfort Suites, Residence Inn 🅾 Costco/gas, GNC, Hobby Lobby, Home Depot, Staples, Super 1 Foods, TJ Maxx, W 🅿 Cenex/dsl, Conoco/dsl, Exxon/dsl 🍴 Applebee's, Arby's, Buffalo Wild Wings, Burger King, DQ, Jade Garden, Mackenzie River Pizza, McDonald's, Panda Express, Papa Murphy's, Pizza Hut, Quiznos, Steve's Cafe, Subway, Taco Bell, Taco Del Mar 🛏 Holiday Inn Express 🅾 $Tree, Albertson's, AT&T, AutoZone, CVS Drug, Helena RV Park (5mi), Jo-Ann, Lowe's, Macy's, Murdoch's, Natural Grocers, PetCo, Petsmart, Ross, Target, Verizon

193 Cedar St, Helena, E 🅾 ☕, W 🅿 Conoco/dsl, Conoco/dsl, Exxon/dsl 🍴 Godfather's, Little Caesar's, Perkins, Steffano's Pizza, Subway, Taco John's 🛏 Quality Inn, Wingate Inn 🅾 Ace Hardware, Chevrolet/Buick/GMC, O'Reilly Parts, Tire Rama, USPO, vet

192b a US 12, US 287, Helena, Townsend, E 🅿 Cenex, Conoco/dsl 🍴 Burger King, Pizza Hut 🛏 Hampton Inn 🅾 Big Lots, Chrysler/Dodge/Jeep, D&D RV Ctr, Ford/Lincoln, Honda, Nissan, Schwab Tire, st patrol, Toyota, Walmart/Subway, W 🅿 Exxon/dsl, Holiday, Sinclair/dsl 🍴 DQ, Jimmy John's, L&D Chinese, McDonald's, Overland Express Rest., Papa John's, Papa Murphy's, Rte 12 Diner, Starbucks, Steve's Cafe, Taco John's, Taco Treat, Village Inn Pizza, Wendy's 🛏 Baymont Inn, Days Inn, Fairfield Inn, Howard Johnson, Jorgenson's Inn, La Quinta, Motel 6, Radisson, Shilo Inn, Super 8 🅾 Albertson's, CVS Drug, GNC, 🅗, J&s Tire/auto, Safeway/dsl, Verizon, Walgreens

190 S Helena, W 🅾 🅗

187 MT 518, Montana City, Clancy, E 🍴 Hugo's Pizza/casino, W 🅿 Cenex/dsl 🍴 Jackson Creek Cafe, MT City Grill 🛏 Elkhorn Inn

182 Clancy, E 🅾 Alhambra RV Park, W 🍴 Chubby's Grill, Legal Tender Rest. 🅾 to NF, USPO

178mm Ⓡs both lanes, full ♿ facilities, 🛢, 🪑, litter barrels, petwalk

176 Jefferson City NF access

174.5mm chain up area both lanes

168mm chainup area both lanes

164 rd 69, Boulder, E 🅿 Exxon/dsl/casino 🍴 Elkhorn Cafe, Joe's Pizza, Mtn Good Rest., The River Café 🅾 auto repair, RC RV camping, USPO

161mm parking area nb

160 High Ore Rd

156 Basin, E 🅾 camping, Merry Widow Health Mine/RV camping W 🅾 Basin Cr Pottery, USPO

154mm Boulder River

151 to Boulder River Rd, Bernice, W 🅾 camping, picnic area

148mm chainup area both lanes

143.5mm chainup area both lanes

138 Elk Park, W 🅾 Sheepshead Picnic Area, wildlife viewing

134 Woodville

133mm continental divide, elev 6368 continental divide

130.5mm scenic overlook sb

129 I-90 E, to Billings

I-15 S and I-90 W run together 8 mi.

127 Harrison Ave, Butte, E 🅿 Cenex/dsl, ConocoPhillips/dsl, Exxon/dsl, Exxon/dsl (2), Sinclair/dsl 🍴 A&W/KFC, Arby's, Asia Buffet, Buffalo Wild Wings, Burger King, MacKenzie River Pizza, McDonald's, MT Club Rest., Perkins, Pizza Hut, Pizza Ranch, Silver Bow Pizza, Starbucks, Subway, Taco Bell, Three Amigos, Wendy's 🛏 Best Western, Comfort Inn, Hampton Inn, Super 8 🅾 $Tree, American Car Care, Buick/Chevrolet/GMC, CarQuest, casinos, Chrysler/Dodge/Jeep, Ford, Hart's RV Ctr, Herberger's, Honda, Jo-Ann Fabrics, Kia, Murdoch's, NAPA, Petco, Rocky Mtn RV Ctr, Staples, Subaru, Toyota, Verizon, vet, Walmart/Subway, W 🅿 Cenex/dsl, Conoco/dsl 🍴 Derby Steaks, Domino's, DQ, El Taco Mexican, Hanging 5 Rest., Hardee's, John's Rest., Papa John's, Papa Murphy's, Quiznos, Royse's Burgers, Taco John's 🛏 Days Inn, Fairfield Inn, Holiday Inn Express, La Quinta, Quality Inn 🅾 Ace Hardware, AutoZone, Lisac's Tires, O'Reilly Parts, Safeway, Walgreens

126 Montana St, Butte, E 🅿 Conoco/dsl, Exxon/dsl, W 🍴 Chef's Garden Italian 🛏 Eddy's Motel 🅾 🅗, Safeway, Schwab Tire

124 I-115 (from eb), to Butte City Ctr

123mm weigh sta sb

122 Rocker, E 🅿 🛢/Conoco/McDonald's/Subway/dsl/scales/24hr 🛏 Econolodge 🅾 casino, weight sta nb, W 🅿 ⊕FLYING J/Exxon/rest./dsl/LP/24hr 🛏 Best Value Inn 🅾 2 Bar Lazy-H RV Camping

I-15 N and I-90 E run together 8 mi.

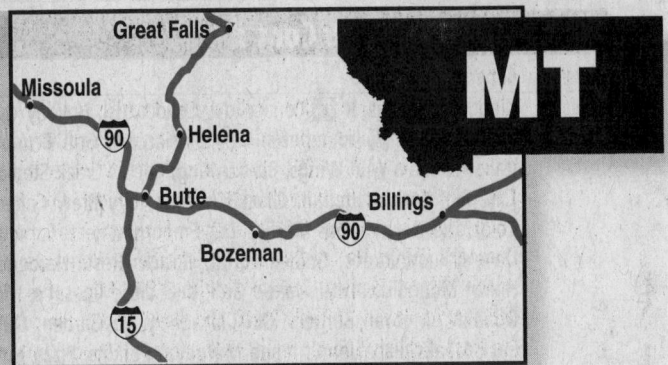

🔼N INTERSTATE 15 Cont'd

Exit #	Services
121	I-90 W, to Missoula
119	Silver Bow, W ⊙ Port of MT Transportation Hub
116	Buxton
112mm	Continental Divide, elevation 5879
111	Feely
109mm	🅁🅂/weigh sta both lanes, full ♿ facilities, 🍴, 🚻, litter barrels, petwalk
102	rd 43, to Wisdom, Divide, W ⊙ rv camping (2mi), to Big Hole Nat Bfd (62mi)
99	Moose Creek Rd
93	Melrose, W 🍴 Hitchin Post Rest., Melrose Café/grill/dsl 🛏 Great Waters Inn (5mi), Pioneer Mtn Cabins ⊙ Sportsman Motel/RV Park, Sunrise Flyshop, USPO
85.5mm	Big Hole River
85	Glen, E ⊙ Willis Sta RV camping (3mi)
74	Apex, Birch Creek
64mm	Beaverhead River
63	Lp 15, rd 41, Dillon, Twin Bridges, E 📌 Cenex/dsl/LP/RV Dump, Exxon/dsl, Phillips 66/dsl 🍴 4B's Rest., Lions Den, McDonald's, Pizza Hut, Subway 🛏 Best Western/rest., Fairbridge Inn, Motel 6, Quality Inn, Sundowner Motel, Super 8 ⊙ auto repair/tires, Buick/Chevrolet, CarQuest, city park, Family$, 🅗, KOA, Les Schwab Tire, Murdoch's, museum, NAPA, O'Reilly Parts, Safeway/dsl, W MT U
62	Lp 15, Dillon, E 🍴 DQ, Sparky's Rest., Taco John's 🛏 Flyshop Inn ⊙ 🅗, KOA, Southside RV Park, to W MT U, Van's/IGA Foods
60mm	Beaverhead River
59	MT 278, to Jackson, W ⊙ Bannack SP, Countryside RV Park/LP
56	Barretts, E ⊙ RV camping, W 📌 Sinclair/RV Park/dsl
55mm	parking area sb, litter barrels
52	Grasshopper Creek
51	Dalys (from sb, no return)
50mm	Beaverhead River
46mm	Beaverhead River
45mm	Beaverhead River
44	MT 324, E 🍴 Buffalo Lodge ⊙ Armstead RV Park, W ⊙ Clark Cyn Reservoir/RA, RV camping
38.5mm	Red Rock River
37	Red Rock
34mm	parking area both lanes, litter barrels, restrooms
29	Kidd
23	Dell, E 📌 Cenex/dsl 🍴 Yesterdays Calf-a ⊙ USPO
16.5mm	weigh sta both lanes
15	Lima, E 🅁🅂 both lanes, ♿ facilities, litter barrels, petwalk, 📌 Exxon/dsl, Tesla EVC 🍴 Jan's Café 🛏 Mtn View Motel/RV Park ⊙ ambulance, Big Sky Tire/auto, Ralph's Tire, USPO
9	Snowline
0	Monida, E ⊙ to Red Rock Lakes
0mm	Montana/Idaho state line, Monida Pass, elevation 6870

🔼E INTERSTATE 90

Exit #	Services
554.5mm	Montana/Wyoming state line
549	Aberdeen
544	Wyola
530	MT 463, Lodge Grass, 1 mi S 📌 food, gas/dsl, lodging
517.5mm	Little Bighorn River
514	Garryowen, N 📌 Conoco/Subway ⊙ Custer Bfd Museum, S ⊙ 7th Ranch RV camp (3mi)
511.5mm	Little Bighorn River

510	US 212 E, N 📌 Conoco/café/dsl/gifts ⊙ casino, 🅗, to Little Bighorn Bfd
509.5mm	weigh sta, both lanes exit left
509.3mm	Little Bighorn River
509	Crow Agency, N 📌 Conoco, S ⊙ to Bighorn Canyon NRA
503	Dunmore
498mm	Bighorn River
497	MT 384, 3rd St, Hardin, N ⊙ fireworks, S 🛏 Western Motel ⊙ Bighorn Cty Museum, 🅗
495	MT 47, City Ctr, Hardin, N 📌 Cenex/dsl, Loves/Hardee's/dsl/scales/24hr 🍴 Golden Bridge Chinese ⊙ KOA, S 📌 Cenex/dsl, Exxon/dsl, FLYING J/Conoco/Subway/dsl/LP/24hr 🍴 DQ, McDonald's, Pizza Hut, Taco John's 🛏 Rodeway Inn, Super 8, Western Motel ⊙ Chevrolet, Grand View Camping/RV Park, 🅗, Sunset Village RV Park
484	Toluca
478	Fly Creek Rd
477mm	🅁🅂 both lanes, full ♿ facilities, 🍴, 🚻, litter barrels, petwalk
469	Arrow Creek Rd
462	Pryor Creek Rd
456	I-94 E, to Bismarck, ND
455	Johnson Lane, N 📌 Pilot/Conoco/McDonald's/dsl/scales/24hr, S 📌 FLYING J/dsl/LP/scales/24hr, Exxon/A&W/dsl 🍴 Burger King, Domino's, DQ, Jin's Chinese, Subway 🛏 Holiday Inn Express ⊙ Bretz RV Ctr, Verizon, Whalen Tire
452	US 87 N, City Ctr, Billings, 2-4 mi N on US 87 📌 Cenex/dsl, Conoco/Arby's/dsl/LP, Holiday/dsl, 🍴 Applebee's, Arby's, Burger King, Domino's, DQ, Fuddrucker's, Godfather's, Golden Phoenix, Jimmy John's, MacKenzie River Pizza, McDonald's, Panda Express, Papa John's, Papa Murphy's, Pizza Hut, Sonic, Starbucks, Subway, Taco Bell, Taco John's, Wendy's 🛏 Boothill Inn, Country Inn&Suites, Heights Motel ⊙ Ace Hardware, Albertsons/Osco, American Spirit RV Ctr, AT&T, AutoZone, BigLots, CarQuest, CVS Drug, GNC, Metra Rv Ctr, O'Reilly Parts, Petsmart, Target, Tire Rama, U-Haul, Verizon, vet, Walgreens, Walmart, S 📌 Cenex/dsl ⊙ RV Camping
451.5mm	Yellowstone River
450	MT 3, 27th St, Billings, N 📌 Conoco/dsl 🍴 Blondy's Cafe, Pizza Hut 🛏 Doubletree, Vegas Motel ⊙ CarQuest, city park, 🅗, USPO, visitor ctr, S ⊙ KOA, Yellowstone River Camping
447	S Billings Blvd, N 📌 Conoco/Subway/dsl, Holiday/dsl 🍴 4B's Rest., Burger King, DQ, Fiddlers Green Grill, McDonald's, Popeye's, Taco Bell 🛏 Best Western/Kelly, Comfort Suites, Days Inn, Extended Stay America, Hampton Inn, Ledgestone Hotel, My Place, Sleep Inn, Super 8 🛏 Cabela's Sporting Goods, NAPA, Sam's Club/dsl, S ⊙ Freightliner, Kenworth, KOA (2mi), Yellowstone River Campground

DILLON

HARDIN

BILLINGS

🗒 = gas 🍴 = food 🛏 = lodging Ⓞ = other Ⓡ🅂 = rest stop Copyright 2022 - The Next EXIT

↑⬇Ⓔ	**INTERSTATE 90 Cont'd**

BILLINGS

Exit #	Services
446	King Ave, Billings, N 🗒 Conoco/dsl, Conoco/dsl, Holiday/dsl, Phillips 66/dsl 🍴 Applebee's, Arby's, Asian Sea Grill, Bruno's Italian, Buffalo Wild Wings, Burger King, Cactus Creek Steaks, Café Rio, Carino's Italian, ChuckECheese's, City Brew Coffee, Coldstone, Denny's, Dos Machos, DQ, Emporium Rest., Famous Dave's, Fuddrucker's, Golden Corral, Gusicks Rest., Hardee's, HuHot Mongolian, IHOP, Jake's Grill, KFC, Little Caesar's, McDonald's, MooYah Burgers, Old Chicago, Olive Garden, Outback Steaks, Papa John's, Papa Murphy's, Perkins, Pizza Hut, Pizza Ranch, Qdoba, Red Lobster, Rendezvous Grill, Starbucks, Subway, Taco Bell, Taco John's, TX Roadhouse, Wendy's 🛏 Baymont Inn, C'Mon Inn, Fairfield Inn, Hilton Garden, Lexington Inn, Quality Inn, Residence Inn, SpringHill Suites, TownePlace Suites, Western Executive Inn Ⓞ $Tree, Albertsons/Osco, AT&T, AutoZone, Barnes&Noble, Best Buy, Chevrolet, Chrysler/Dodge/Jeep, Costco/gas, Dillards, Ford, Hobby Lobby, Home Depot, JC Penney, JoAnn Fabrics, Kia, Lisac's Tire, Lowe's, Mercedes, Michael's, Natural Grocers, Nissan, O'Reilly Parts, Office Depot, Old Navy, Petsmart, Ross, Subaru, USPO, Verizon, vet, Walmart/Subway, World Mkt, S 🗒 Conoco/dsl 🍴 Cracker Barrel, Emporium Rest. 🛏 EconoLodge, Howard Johnson, Kelly Inn, La Quinta, Motel 6, Motel 6 (2), Radisson, Red Lion Inn Ⓞ Volvo/Mack Trucks
443	Zoo Dr, to Shiloh Rd, N 🗒 Holiday/dsl 🍴 Five Guys, MT Rib/Chophouse 🛏 Bighorn Resort/waterpark, Hampton Inn, Holiday Inn Express, Homewood Suites Ⓞ Honda, Hyundai/Volvo/Buick, Pierce RV Ctr, zoo, S Ⓞ Harley-Davidson, vet
439mm	weigh sta both lanes
437	E Laurel, S 🗒 TA/Sinclair/cafe/dsl/scales/casino/motel/RV Park/24hr
434	US 212, US 310, to Red Lodge, Laurel, N 🗒 Cenex/dsl, Conoco/dsl, Exxon/dsl 🍴 Beartooth Grill, City Brew Coffee, Gauica's Mexican, Hardee's, McDonald's, Pizza Hut, Subway, Taco Bell, Taco John's 🛏 Best Western, Locomotive Inn Ⓞ Ace Hardware, AutoZone, Chevrolet, CVS Drug, Ford, IGA Foods, O'Reilly Parts, Rapid Tire, Verizon, Walmart/Subway, S Ⓞ Riverside Park/RV Camping, to Yellowstone NP
433	Lp 90 (from eb) same as 434
426	Park City, S 🗒 Cenex/café/dsl/24hr, KwikStop 🍴 The Other Cafe Ⓞ USPO
419mm	Ⓡ🅂 both lanes, full 🚻 facilities, (🅲), 🗑, litter barrels, petwalk
408	rd 78, Columbus, N Ⓞ Mtn Range RV Park, S 🗒 Conoco, Pilot/Exxon/dsl/24hr 🍴 Bearstone Cafe, McDonald's, Subway 🛏 Big Sky Motel, Super 8 Ⓞ casino, city park, Family$, 🏥, IGA Foods, tires/repair, to Yellowstone
400	Springtime Rd
398mm	Yellowstone River
396	ranch access
392	Reed Point, N 🗒 Sure Stop/dsl Ⓞ Old West RV Park, USPO
384	Bridger Creek Rd
381mm	Ⓡ🅂 both lanes, full 🚻 facilities, (🅲), 🗑, litter barrels, petwalk
377	Greycliff, S Ⓞ KOA, Prairie Dog Town SP
370	US 191, Big Timber, 1 mi N 🗒 Sinclair/dsl 🛏 Grand Hotel, Lazy J Motel Ⓞ 🏥, Spring Creek RV Ranch (4mi), USPO, vet
369mm	Boulder River
367	US 191 N, Big Timber, N 🗒 Conoco/dsl, Exxon/dsl 🍴 Country Skillet 🛏 River Valley Inn, Super 8 Ⓞ CarQuest, Family$, historic site/visitor info, Spring Creek Camping (3mi)
362	De Hart
354	MT 563, Springdale

LIVINGSTON / BOZEMAN / BELGRADE

Exit #	Services
352	ranch access
350	East End access
343	Mission Creek Rd, N Ⓞ Ft Parker HS
340	US 89 N, to White Sulphur Sprgs, S Ⓞ ⊘
337	Lp 90, to Livingston, 2 mi N Ⓞ services in Livingston
333mm	Yellowstone River
333	US 89 S, Livingston, N 🍴 Clark's Rest., DQ, Mark's In&Out, Pizza Hut, Taco John's 🛏 Budget Host, Livingston Inn, Quality Inn, Rodeway Inn, Yellowstone Pioneer Lodge Ⓞ Ace Hardware, Chrysler/Dodge/Jeep, 🏥, Town&Country Foods, True Value Hardware, Verizon, Western Drug, S 🗒 Cenex/dsl, Conoco/dsl, Exxon/dsl 🍴 Arby's, McDonald's, Rosa's Pizza, Subway 🛏 Comfort Inn, Super 8 Ⓞ Albertsons/Osco, KOA (10mi), Osen RV Park/Lp, to Yellowstone, URGENT CARE, vet
330	Lp 90, Livingston, 1 mi N 🗒 Cenex/Yellowstone Trkstp/dsl/rest./24hr
326.5mm	chainup/chain removal area both lanes
324	ranch access
323mm	chainup/chain removal area wb
322mm	Bridger Mountain Range
321mm	turnouts/hist marker both lanes
319	Jackson Creek Rd
319mm	chainup area both lanes
316	Trail Creek Rd
313	Bear Canyon Rd, S Ⓞ Bear Canyon Camping
309	US 191 S, Main St, Bozeman, N Ⓞ Subaru, Sunrise RV Park, S 🗒 Cenex/dsl, Conoco/dsl, Exxon/dsl 🍴 MT AleWorks, Ranch House Motel, Western Heritage Inn Ⓞ East Main Food, 🏥, repair, Tire Rama, to Yellowstone
306	MT 205, N 7th, to US 191, Bozeman, N 🗒 Cenex 🍴 McDonald's, Panda Buffet 🛏 Fairfield Inn, La Quinta, Microtel, Motel 6, Ramada, Rodeway Inn, Super 8 Ⓞ Murdoch's, ski area, Whalen Tire, S 🗒 Conoco/Arby's/dsl, Exxon 🍴 Applebee's, Bar-3 BBQ, Dominos, DQ, Famous Dave's BBQ, Papa John's, Santa Fe Red's Cafe, Taco John's, Village Inn Pizza 🛏 Best Western, Bozeman Inn, Comfort Inn, Days Inn, Hampton Inn, Holiday Inn, Homewood Suites, Royal 7 Inn Ⓞ Big O Tire, Firestone/auto, Museum of the Rockies, U-Haul, Verizon, Walmart/McDonald's
305	MT412, N 19th Ave, N Ⓡ🅂, full 🚻 facilities, petwalk, 🗑/litter barrels 🗒 Exxon 🛏 Mountainview Inn, 0-2 mi S 🗒 Conoco/dsl 🍴 A&W/KFC, Buffalo Wild Wings, Carino's Italian, City Brew Coffee, Clarks Fork Rest., Corner Bakery Cafe, Five Guys, IHOP, Jimmy John's, Mongolian BBQ, Noodles&Co, Old Chicago Pizza, Olive Garden, Outback Steaks, Papa Murphy's, Starbucks, Subway, Wasabi Grill, Wendy's 🛏 C'mon Inn, Comfort Suites, Country Inn Suites, Hilton Garden, Holiday Inn Express, My Place Extended Stay, Residence Inn, SpringHill Suites Ⓞ AT&T, Costco/gas, Ford/Lincoln/RV Ctr, Home Depot, Lowe's, Michael's, Office Depot, Petsmart, REI, Ross, Smith's Foods/dsl, Staples, Target, TJMaxx, USPO, Verizon, vet, World MKT,
299	Airway Blvd, N Ⓞ ⊘
298	MT 291, rd 85, Belgrade, N 🗒 Cenex/dsl, Exxon/Subway/dsl 🍴 Burger King, DQ, McDonald's, Papa Murphy's, Pizza Hut, Rosa's Pizza, Starbucks, Taco Bell, Taco Time 🛏 Holiday Inn Express Ⓞ Albertson's/Osco, NAPA, Town&Country Foods, Verizon, Whalen Tire, S 🗒 FLYING J/Conoco/dsl/scales/LP, Pilot/Conoco/dsl/scales/24hr 🍴 Fiesta Mexicana 🛏 La Quinta, Quality Inn, Super 8 Ⓞ Freightliner, Harley-Davidson, repair, Tire Factory, to Yellowstone NP, TrueValue
292.5mm	Gallatin River

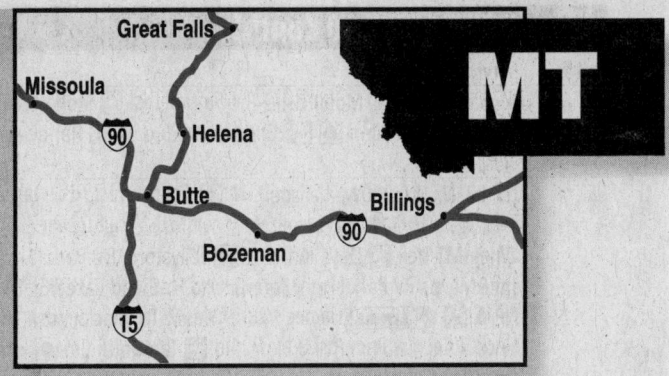

INTERSTATE 90 Cont'd

Exit #	Services
288	MT 288, MT 346, Manhattan, **N** 🅟 Conoco/Subway/dsl 🅞 RV camping
283	Logan, **S** 🅞 Madison Buffalo Jump SP (7mi)
279mm	Madison River
278	MT 205, rd 2, Three Forks, Trident, **N** 🅞 Missouri Headwaters SP, **S** 🅟 Conoco/dsl 🍴 Iron Horse Cafe 🏠 Broken Spur Motel, Lewis&Clark Motel, Sacajawea Hotel 🅞 CarQuest, golf
277.5mm	Jefferson River
274	US 287, to Helena, Ennis, **N** 🅟 Conoco/dsl 🍴 Wheat MT Bakery/deli 🏠 Ft 3 Forks Motel/RV Park 🅞 dsl repair, to Canyon Ferry SP, **S** 🅟 Pilot/Exxon/Subway/dsl/scales/24hr 🅞 Camp 3 Forks, Lewis&Clark Caverns SP, to Yellowstone NP
267	Milligan Canyon Rd
261.5mm	**chain-up area**
257mm	Boulder River
256	MT 359, Cardwell, **S** 🅟 Cenex/dsl/RV Park 🅞 Lewis&Clark Caverns SP, RV camping, to Yellowstone NP
249	rd 55, to rd 69, Whitehall, **S** 🅟 Exxon/dsl 🍴 A&W/KFC, Subway 🏠 Rodeway Inn 🅞 casino, Cliff's Tire/auto, to Virginia City NHS
241	Pipestone
240.5mm	**chainup/chain removal area both lanes**
238.5mm	**runaway ramp eb**
237.5mm	**pulloff eb**
235mm	**truck parking both lanes, litter barrels, restrooms**
233	Continental Divide, elev 6393, Homestake
230mm	**chain-up area both lanes**
228	MT 375, Continental Dr, **S** 🅟 Conoco/dsl 🅞 Harley-Davidson, Three Bears Foods
227	I-15 N, to Helena, Great Falls
	I-90 and I-15 run together 8 mi. See Montana I-15, exits 122-127.
123mm	**weight sta wb**
122	Rocker, **N** 🅟 🛢FLYING J/Exxon/rest./dsl/LP/24hr 🏠 Best Value Inn 🅞 2 Bar Lazy-H RV Camping, **S** 🅟 Pilot/Conoco/McDonald's/Subway/dsl/scales/24hr 🏠 EconoLodge 🅞 casino, weight sta eb
219	I-15 S, to Dillon, Idaho Falls
216	Ramsay
211	MT 441, Gregson, **3-5 mi S** food, lodging, Fairmont RV Park (Apr-Oct)
210.5mm	**parking area wb**, Pintlar Scenic route info
208	rd 1, Pintler Scenic Loop, Georgetown Lake RA, Opportunity, Anaconda, **S** 🆁🆂 both lanes, full ♿ facilities, petwalk, 🍽, litter barrels🅞 food, gas, 🅷, lodging, RV camp/dump, ski area
201	Warm Springs, **S** 🅞 MT ST 🅷
197	MT 273, Galen, **S** 🅞 to MT ST 🅷
195	Racetrack
187	Lp 90, Deer Lodge (no wb return), **2 mi S** 🏠 Travelodge 🅞 🅷, KOA (seasonal), Old MT Prison/auto museum, same as 184, Valley Foods
184	Deer Lodge, **S** 🅟 Conoco/dsl/casino, Exxon/dsl/casino, Sinclair/Subway/dsl 🍴 4B's Rest., A&W, McDonald's, Pizza Hut 🏠 Travelodge, Western Big Sky Inn 🅞 city park, Family$, Grant-Kohrs Ranch NHS, 🅷, Indian Creek Camping, KOA, Safeway/deli, Schwab Tire, USPO
179	Beck Hill Rd
175	US 12 E, Garrison, **N** 🅞 hist site, RiverFront RV Park
175mm	Little Blackfoot River
174	US 12 E (from eb), **S** 🍴 same as 175
170	Phosphate

Exit #	Services
166	Gold Creek, **S** 🅞 Camp Mak-A-Dream, USPO
162	Jens
154	to MT 1 (from wb), Drummond, **S** 🅟 Cenex/dsl, Conoco/dsl 🍴 Parker's Rest., Wagon Wheel Café 🏠 Drummond Motel, Sky Motel, Wagon Wheel Motel 🅞 city park, Front St Mkt, Georgetown Lake RA, Pintler Scenic Lp
153	MT 1 (from eb), **S** same as 154
150.5mm	**weigh sta both lanes**
143mm	🆁🆂 both lanes, full ♿ facilities, 🍽, 🍽, litter barrels, petwalk
138	Bearmouth Area, **N** 🅞 Chalet Bearmouth Camp/rest.
130	Beavertail Rd, **S** 🅞 to Beavertail Hill SP
128mm	**parking area both lanes, litter barrels/restrooms**
126	Rock Creek Rd, **S** 🅞 rec area
120	Clinton, **N** 🅟 Conoco/dsl 🍴 Poor Henry's Café (1mi W on frtg rd) 🅞 Clinton Market, **S** 🅞 USPO
113	Turah, **S** 🅟 Turah RV Park/gas
109.5mm	Clark Fork
109mm	Blackfoot River
109	MT 200 E, Bonner, **N** 🅟 Pilot/Exxon/Arby's/Subway/dsl/scales/casino/LP/24hr 🍴 River City Grill 🅞 hist site, USPO
108.5mm	Clark Fork
107	E Missoula, **N** 🅟 Ole's/Conoco/dsl, Sinclair 🍴 Reno Cafe 🏠 Aspen Motel 🅞 dsl repair
105	US 12 W, Missoula, **S** 🅟 Cenex/dsl, Conoco/dsl, Sinclair/dsl 🍴 Burger King, Five Guys, McDonald's, Pizza Hut, Qdoba, Subway, Taco Bell 🏠 Campus Inn, Comfort Inn, DoubleTree, Motel 6, Thunderbird Motel 🅞 Ace Hardware, Albertson's, Kingfisher Flyshop, O'Reilly Parts, U of MT, Verizon
104	Orange St, Missoula, **S** 🅟 Conoco/dsl 🍴 Pagoda Chinese, Taco John's 🏠 Mtn Valley Inn, Red Lion Inn 🅞 🅷, TireRama, to City Ctr
101	US 93 S, Reserve St, **N** 🅟 Conoco/dsl 🍴 Cracker Barrel, MacKenzie River Pizza, Starbucks 🏠 Best Western+, C'Mon Inn, Motel 6, My Place 🅞 ski area, **0-2 mi S** 🅟 Cenex/dsl/LP, Conoco/dsl, Domino's, Exxon/Subway/dsl 🍴 Arby's, Buffalo Wild Wings, Burger King, Cafe Rio, Chipotle, Coldstone, DQ, Famous Dave's BBQ, Freddy's, Fuddrucker's, HoagiVille, IHOP, Jimmy John's, Little Caesar's, McDonald's, MOD Pizza, MT Club Rest./casino, Old Chicago, Outback Steaks, Panda Express, Perkins, Pizza Hut, Popeye's, Quiznos, Rowdy's Cabin Rest., Stone Of Accord, Taco Bell, Taco Time/TCBY, Wendy's 🏠 Courtyard, EconoLodge, Hampton Inn, Hilton Garden, Holiday Inn Express, La Quinta, Quality Inn, Ruby's Inn/rest., Staybridge Suites, Super 8, TownePlace Suites, Travelers Inn 🅞 Albertson's, AT&T, Barnes&Noble, Best Buy, Bretz RV/Marine, Chevrolet/Cadillac, Costco/gas, dsl repair, Firestone/auto, GNC, Home Depot, Lowe's, Michael's, Old Navy, Petsmart, REI, Ross, Staples, Target, TJ Maxx, Verizon, VW, Walgreens, Walmart/Subway

BUTTE

DEER LODGE

MISSOULA

🔷 INTERSTATE 90 Cont'd

Exit #	Services
99	Airway Blvd, **S** 🅖 Mobil/dsl/24hr, Sinclair/dsl 🅛 Stone Creek Lodge, Wingate Inn 🅞 📶, Chrysler/Dodge/Jeep, Harley-Davidson, Kia
96	US 93 N, MT 200W, Kalispell, **N** 🅖 Conoco/rest.dsl/scales/24hr/@, *FLYING J*/Exxon/McDonald's/dsl/scales/24hr 🅕 WheatMT/deli 🅛 Days Inn/rest. 🅞 Jellystone RV Park (1mi), Jim&Mary's RV Park (1mi), Peterbilt, to Flathead Lake&Glacier NP, **S** 🅖 *Loves*/Hardee's/dsl/scales/24hr, Sinclair/dsl, TA/Sinclair/Country Pride/dsl/scales/24hr 🅛 Tamarack Inn 🅞 Harlow Truck Ctr, Kenworth
92.5mm	**inspection sta both lanes**
89	Frenchtown, **N** 🅞 to Frenchtown Pond SP, **S** 🅖 Conoco/dsl/café 🅕 Alcan Grill, Gammy's Cafe 🅞 Broncs Grocery/gas, USPO
85	Huson, **S** 🅖 gas 🅕 cafe 🅞 📶
82	Nine Mile Rd, **N** 🅞 food, Hist Ranger Sta/info, 📶
81.5mm	Clark Fork
80mm	Clark Fork
77	MT 507, Petty Creek Rd, Alberton, **S** 🅖 access to gas 🅕 food 🅛 lodging 🅞 📶
75	Alberton, **N** 🅖 Cenex/dsl 🅞 USPO, **S** 🅛 River Edge Rest. 🅞 casino, motel, RV camp
73mm	**parking area wb, litter barrels**
72mm	**parking area eb, litter barrels**
70	Cyr
70mm	Clark Fork
66	Fish Creek Rd
66mm	Clark Fork
61	Tarkio
59mm	Clark Fork
58mm	🆁🆂 **both lanes, full** 🅰 **facilities,** 📶, 🏕, **litter barrels, petwalk, NF camping (seasonal)**
55	Lozeau, Quartz
53.5mm	Clark Fork
49mm	Clark Fork
47	MT 257, Superior, **N** 🅖 Conoco/dsl, Durango's Rest./gas, Energy Partners/LP 🅛 Big Sky Motel, Hilltop Motel 🅞 Family Foods, 🏥, Mineral Drug, NAPA, USPO, **S** 🅖 *Pilot*/Exxon/dsl/casino/24hr
45mm	Clark Fork
43	Dry Creek Rd, **N** 🅞 NP camping (seasonal)
37	Sloway Area
34mm	Clark Fork
33	MT 135, St Regis, **N** 🅖 Conoco/rest/dsl/gifts, Exxon, Sinclair 🅕 Frosty Drive-In, Huck's Grill, Jasper's Rest., OK Café/casino 🅛 Little River Motel, St Regis Motel, Super 8 🅞 antiques, city park, Nugget Camground, St Regis Campground (seasonal), to Glacier NP, USPO
30	Two Mile Rd, **S** 🅞 fishing access
29mm	fishing access wb
26	Ward Creek Rd (from eb)
25	Drexel
22	Camels Hump Rd, Henderson, **N** 🅞 antiques (1mi), camping (seasonal)
18	DeBorgia, **N** 🅕 O'aces Rest. 🅞 Black Diamond Guest Ranch, USPO
16	Haugan, **N** 🅖 Exxon/dsl/24hr 🅛 50000 Silver $/motel/rest./casino/RV park
15mm	**weigh sta both lanes, exits left from both lanes**
10	Saltese, **N** 🅛 Mangold's Motel
10mm	St Regis River
5	Taft Area access to Hiawatha Trail
4.5mm	🆁🆂 **both lanes, chainup/removal, full** 🅰 **facilities,** 🏕, **litter barrels, petwalk**
0	Lookout Pass 🅞 access to Lookout Pass ski area/lodge, info
0mm	Montana/Idaho state line, Central/Pacific time zone, Lookout Pass elev 4680

🔷 INTERSTATE 94

Exit #	Services
250mm	Montana/North Dakota state line
248	Carlyle Rd
242	MT 7 (from wb), Wibaux, **S** 🆁🆂 **both lanes, full** 🅰 **facilities,** 📶, 🏕, **litter barrels,** 🅖 Amsler's/dsl, Cenex/dsl/service 🅕 Taste Hut 🅛 Beaver Creek Inn
241	MT 261 (from eb), to MT 7, Wibaux, **S** same as 242
240mm	**weigh sta both lanes**
236	ranch access
231	Hodges Rd
224	Griffith Creek, frontage road
222.5mm	Griffith Creek
215	MT 335, Glendive, City Ctr, **N** 🅖 Cenex/dsl 🅕 C's Family Cafe, Penny's Diner 🅛 Astoria Suites, Comfort Inn, Days Inn, Holiday Inn Express, Oak Tree Inn, Super 8 🅞 Glendive Camping (apr-oct), museum, Running's Hardware, **S** 🅖 Exxon/dsl, Holiday dsl 🅕 Subway 🅛 El Centro Motel, Glendive Inn, La Quinta 🅞 🏥, to Makoshika SP, Verizon
215mm	Yellowstone River
213	MT 16, to Sidney, Glendive, **N** 🅖 Town Pump/dsl/scales 🅞 state patrol, **S** 🅖 Cenex/dsl, Sinclair/dsl 🅕 Pizza Hut 🅛 Riverside Inn 🅞 Albertson's/Osco, Ford, K-Mart, NAPA, Reynolds Mkt
211	MT 200S (from wb, no EZ return), to Circle
210	Lp 94, to rd 200 S, W Glendive, **S** 🅖 Cenex/dsl, Exxon/dsl 🅞 Buick/Chevrolet, I-94 RV Park, Makoshika SP, Tire Rama
206	Pleasant View Rd
204	Whoopup Creek Rd
198	Cracker Box Rd
192	Bad Route Rd, **S** 🆁🆂/**weigh sta both lanes, full** 🅰 **facilities, weather info,** 📶, 🏕, **litter barrels, camping, petwalk**
187mm	Yellowstone River
185	MT 340, Fallon, **S** 🅕 café 🅞 📶
184mm	O'Fallon Creek
176	MT 253, Terry, **N** 🅖 Cenex/dsl, Four Corners/dsl 🅕 Dizzy Dine 🅛 Kempton Hotel 🅞 🏥, museum, Terry RV Oasis
170mm	Powder River
169	Powder River Rd
159	Diamond Ring
148	Valley Access
141	US 12 E, Miles City, **N** 🅞 RV Camping
138	rd 59, Miles City, **N** 🅖 Cenex/dsl, Conoco/dsl, *Pilot*/Exxon/dsl/24hr 🅕 4B's Rest., Arby's, Black Iron Grill, Boardwalk Rest., City Brew Coffee, DQ, Gallagher's Rest., Little Caesar's, McDonald's, Mexico Lindo, MT Rib&Chophouse, Pizza Hut, Subway, Taco John's, Wendy's 🅛 Best Western, EconoLodge, Motel 6, Sleep Inn 🅞 $Tree, Ace Hardware, Albertsons/Osco, Buick/Chevrolet, casinos, 🏥, Murdoch's, O'Reilly Parts, Verizon, Walmart, **S** 🅖 Cenex/dsl 🅕 New Hunan Chinese 🅛 Comfort Inn, Guesthouse Inn, MC Hotel, Super 8
137mm	Tongue River
135	Lp 94, Miles City, **N** 🅞 KOA (Apr-Oct)

MT

▲E   INTERSTATE 94 Cont'd

Exit #	Services
128	no services
126	Moon Creek Rd
117	Hathaway
114mm	Ⓡⓢ eb, full Ⓗ facilities, Ⓒ, ⌂, litter barrels, petwalk
113mm	Ⓡⓢ wb, full Ⓗ facilities, Ⓒ, ⌂, litter barrels, petwalk, overlook
106	Butte Creek Rd, to Rosebud, N ⓕ food Ⓞ Ⓒ
103	MT 446, MT 447, Rosebud Creek Rd, N ⓕ food Ⓞ Ⓒ
98.5mm	weigh sta both lanes
95	Forsyth, N ⓖ Exxon/dsl, Forsyth Watering Hole ⓕ DQ ⌂ Sundowner Inn Ⓞ Ford, Ⓗ, NAPA, to Rosebud RA, Van's/IGA, vet, S Ⓞ Wagon Wheel Camping
93	US 12 W, Forsyth, N ⓖ Exxon/dsl, Forsyth Watering Hole ⓕ Fitzgerald's Rest., Top That Eatery ⌂ Rails Inn, Restwel Inn, WestWind Motel Ⓞ Ⓗ
87	rd 39, to Colstrip
82	Reservation Creek Rd
72	MT 384, Sarpy Creek Rd
67	Hysham, 1-2 mi N ⓖ gas ⓕ food Ⓞ Ⓒ
65mm	Ⓡⓢ both lanes, full Ⓗ facilities, Ⓒ, ⌂, litter barrels, petwalk
63	ranch access
53	Bighorn access to Ⓒ
52mm	Bighorn River

Exit #	Services
49	MT 47, to Hardin, Custer, S ⓕ Ft Custer Café Ⓞ camping, to Little Bighorn Bfd
47	Custer, S ⓖ Cenex/Custer Sta/dsl ⓕ Jct City Saloon/café Ⓞ USPO
41.5mm	Ⓡⓢ wb, full Ⓗ facilities, Ⓒ, ⌂, litter barrels, petwalk
38mm	Ⓡⓢ eb, full Ⓗ facilities, Ⓒ, ⌂, litter barrels, petwalk
36	frontage rd, Waco
23	Pompeys Pillar, N Ⓞ Pompeys Pillar Nat Landmark
14	Ballentine, Worden, S ⓕ Long Branch Café/casino
6	MT 522, Huntley, N ⓕ Pryor Creek Café/casino, S ⓕ golf
0mm	I-90, E to Sheridan, W to Billings, **I-94 begins/ends on I-90, exit 456.**

FORSYTH

NOTES

NEBRASKA

NE

INTERSTATE 80

Exit #	Services
455mm	Nebraska/Iowa state line, Missouri River
454	13th St, N ⛽ BP/dsl, Midtown, Valero 🍴 Big Horn BBQ, Burger King, Jimmy John's, McDonald's/playplace 🛏 Comfort Inn 🅾 Family$, tires/repair, S 🍴 King Kong Burgers 🅾 Doorly Zoo
453	24th St (from eb)
452b	I-480 N, US 75 N, N 🅾 Eppley Airfield
452a	US 75 S
451	42nd St, N ⛽ BP/dsl 🅾 H, S ⛽ Phillips 66 🍴 Burger King, McDonald's, Taco Bell 🅾 Pitstop Lube
450	60th St, N ⛽ Phillips 66 🅾 NAPA, to U of NE Omaha, S ⛽ Casey'/dsl 🅾 transmissions
449	72nd St, to Ralston, N ⛽ BP, QT 🍴 Burger King, Spezia Italian 🛏 Baymont Inn, Best Value Inn, Comfort Inn, DoubleTree, Quality Inn, Ramada, Super 8 🅾 H, Walmart, S ⛽ Cenex/dsl 🍴 Anthony's Steaks
448	84th St, N ⛽ BP/dsl 🍴 Arby's, Crane Coffee, Denny's, Farmhouse Café, Great Wall Chinese, Husker Hounds, La Casa, Little Caesar's, McDonald's, Pizza Ranch, Subway, Taco Bell 🛏 Motel 6 🅾 Ace Hardware, Advance Parts, CVS Drug, Jensen's Tire/auto, Mangelson's Crafts, ShopKO, USPO, S ⛽ Kum&Go/dsl/e85, QT, Shell/dsl 🍴 Wendy's 🅾 Chevrolet, Kia
446	I-680 N, to Boystown
445	US 275, NE 92, I thru L St, N ⛽ Casey's/dsl 🍴 Buffalo Wings&Rings, Cheddar's, Famous Dave's BBQ, Hardee's, Jason's Deli, Noodles&Co, Pita Pit, Qdoba, SmashBurger, Starbucks, Wendy's 🛏 Carol Hotel 🅾 Book-A-Million, Buick/GMC, Home Depot, Michael's, Nelsen's RV Ctr, PetCo, Sam's Club/gas, Super Target, Verizon, Walmart, S ⛽ BP, QT/dsl 🍴 Arby's, Brew Burgers, Burger King, Dunkin', Godfather's Pizza, Hog Wild BBQ, Hunan Garden, Jimmy' Egg Cafe, Jimmy John's, LJ Silver, McDonald's, Runza, Subway, Taco Bell, Valentino's, Village Inn 🛏 Best Western, La Quinta, Motel 6, Super 8, Victorian Inn, Victorian Inn, Westmont Inn 🅾 Bag'n Save Foods, Family$, Jensen Automotive, O'Reilly Parts, URGENT CARE
444	Q St, N ⛽ Casey's/dsl
442	126th St, Harrison St, N 🅾 Chrysler/Dodge/Jeep, Toyota, VW, S ⛽ Phillips 66/dsl 🍴 Amigo's Mexican, Burger King, Coldstone, Dunkin', Houston's, Jimmy John's, Pizza West, Runza, Sonic, Summer Kitchen 🛏 Comfort Suites, Courtyard, Embassy Suites, Hampton Inn, My Place, Woodspring Suites 🅾 Cabela's, Costco/gas
440	NE 50, to Springfield, N ⛽ BP/dsl/e85, Phillips 66/dsl, Sapp Bros/Subway/dsl/24hr/@ 🍴 Azteca Mexican, Cracker Barrel, Hardee's, McDonald's 🛏 Countryside Suites, EconoLodge, Hometown Lodge, Motel 6, Quality Inn, Red Carpet Inn 🅾 Ford, tires, S ⛽ BP, to Platte River SP 🅾 H
439	439 NE 370, to Gretna, N ⛽ Kum&Go/dsl 🍴 Arby's, Taco John's 🛏 Holiday Inn Express 🅾 Walmart/Subway, S 🅾 H, museum, Volvo Trucks
432	US 6, NE 31, to Gretna, N ⛽ Pump&Pantry/dsl/24hr 🍴 McDonald's, Subway 🛏 Super 8 🅾 KOA, Nebraska X-ing/famous brands, S ⛽ FLYING J/Denny's/dsl/LP/24hr 🅾 to Schramm SP
431mm	📱 wb, full 🚻 facilities, info, litter barrels, petwalk, 🅲, 🚗
427mm	Platte River
426	NE 66, to Southbend, N 🅾 museum, rv camping, to Mahoney SP
425.5	📱 eb, full 🚻 facilities, litter barrels, petwalk, 🅲, 🚗, vending
420	NE 63, Greenwood, N ⛽ Cenex/cafe/dsl/scales/24hr 🅾 Pine Grove RV Park, S ⛽ Shell/dsl 🅾 antiques, to Platte River SP, WWII Museum

OMAHA

Exit #	Services
416mm	weigh sta both lanes
409	US 6, to E Lincoln, Waverly, N ⛽ Casey's (2mi) 🍴 McDonald (2mi), Subway (2mi), S 🅾 H
405	US 77 N, 56th St, Lincoln, S ⛽ Phillips 66 🅾 H, antique Freightliner, Peterbilt, truck service/wash/tires
403	27th St, Lincoln, 0-3 mi S ⛽ Mobil, Phillips 66/Subway/dsl Phillips 66/Wendy's/dsl, Shell 🍴 Amigos Mexican, Applebee Arby's, Asian Buffet, Burger King, Cane's, Carlos O'Kelly's, Chin Inn, CiCi's Pizza, Cracker Barrel, Culver's, daVinci's Italian, Dicl ey's BBQ, DQ, Fazoli's, Golden Corral, IHOP, Jimmy John's, Kir Kong Burger, Mazatlan Mexican, McDonald's, Papa John Papa Murphy's, Pizza Hut, Popeye's/Taco Inn, Ruby Tuesda Runza, Schlotzsky's, Sonic, Taco Bell, Taco John's, Village In 🛏 AmericInn, Best Western+, Country Inn&Suites, Countrysid Suites, Fairfield Inn, Hampton Inn, Holiday Inn Express, La Quir ta, Microtel, Motel 6, Quality Inn, Red Roof Inn, Sleep Inn, Sta bridge Suites, Super 8, TownePlace Suites, Woodspring Suite 🅾 $Tree, AutoZone, BMW, Buick/Chevrolet/GMC, Chrysler Dodge/Jeep, Ford/Lincoln, GNC, Gordman's, Haas Tire, Hom Depot, HyVee Foods, Lexus, Menards, Mercedes, Petsmar Sam's Club/dsl, ShopKO, Super Saver Foods, to U NE, Toyot URGENT CARE, Verizon, Walmart/McDonald's
401b	US 34 W, S 🅾 RV camping
401a	I-180, US 34 E, to 9th St, Lincoln
399	NW 12th St, Lincoln, N ⛽ Gulf/FatDogs/dsl, Phillips 66/dsl 🍴 Baskin-Robbins, Big Ten Subs, McDonald's 🛏 Best Value Inn Comfort Inn, Country Inn Suites, Fairfield Inn, Hampton In Holiday Inn Express, Horizon Inn, Luxury Inn, Quality Inn, Rode way Inn, Sunset Inn, Travelodge 🅾 to ⊙, S ⛽ Casey's/dsl 🍴 Subway 🛏 EconoLodge
397	US 77 S, to Beatrice
396	US 6, West O St (from eb), S 🛏 Rodeway Inn, Super 8
395	US 6, NW 48th St, S ⛽ Phillips 66/dsl, Shoemaker's/Shell/dsl scales/@ 🛏 Cobbler Inn 🅾 Harley-Davidson, truck repair
388	NE 103, to Crete, Pleasant Dale
382	US 6, Milford, S ⛽ Phillips 66/dsl
381mm	📱 eb, full 🚻 facilities, litter barrels, petwalk, 🅲, 🚗, vending
379	NE 15, to Seward, N 🅾 Buick/Chevrolet/GMC, Ford, H (3mi), ⛽ Shell/dsl
375mm	truck parking (wb)
373	80G, Goehner, N ⛽ gas
369	80E, Beaver Crossing, 3 mi S 🅾 H, food, RV camping
366	80F, to Utica
360	93B, to Waco, N ⛽ Phillips 66/Waco Rest/dsl/24hr, S 🅾 Double Nickel Camping
355mm	📱 wb, full 🚻 facilities, info, litter barrels, petwalk, 🅲, 🚗 vending
353	US 81, to York, N ⛽ Conoco/dsl, Pump-N-Pantry/e85, Sap pBros/Sinclair/Subway/scales/dsl, Shell/dsl 🍴 Arby's, Burge King, China Buffet, Dickey's BBQ, DQ, Golden Gate Chinese KFC/Taco Bell, La Carreta Mexican, McDonald's, Runza, Star bucks, Taco John's, The Kitchen, Wendy's 🛏 Best Value Inn Comfort Inn, Days Inn, Hampton Inn, Holiday Inn Express, Nev Victorian Inn, Super 8, Yorkshire Motel 🅾 H, Buick/GMC Chevrolet, Elms RV Park, Ford, RV Camp, Walmart/Subway, S ⛽ Petro/Phillips 66/Iron Skillet/Pizza Hut/dsl/24hr/@, Shell/Huddl House/dsl 🍴 Applebee's 🛏 Best Western+, Motel 6 🅾 Blu Beacon, Freightliner, tires/wash/lube
351mm	📱 eb, full 🚻 facilities, info, litter barrels, petwalk, 🅲, 🚗 vending

LINCOLN

YORK

NE

INTERSTATE 80 Cont'd

Exit #	Services
348	93E, to Bradshaw
342	93A, Henderson, N ⭕ Prairie Oasis Camping, S 🅿️ Henderson Trkstp/dsl 🍴 Subway 🏠 Sun Motel ⭕ 🄷
338	41D, to Hampton
332	NE 14, Aurora, **2-3 mi** N 🅿️ Casey's 🍴 McDonald's, Pizza Hut, Subway 🏠 Budget Host ⭕ 🄷, Ford, to Plainsman Museum, S 🅿️ ♥Loves/Arby's/dsl/scales/24hr
324	41B, to Giltner
318	NE 2, to Grand Island, S ⭕ KOA (seasonal)
317mm	🆁🆂 wb, **full** ♿ facilities, info, litter barrels, petwalk, 🄲, 🄰, vending
315mm	🆁🆂 eb, **full** ♿ facilities, info, litter barrels, petwalk, 🄲, 🄰, vending
314mm	Platte River
314	Locust Street, to Grand Island, **4-6** N ⭕ food, gas, lodging
312	US 34/281, to Grand Island, N 🅿️ Bosselman/Pilot/Little Caesar's/Subway/scales/dsl/24hr, Fat Dogs 🍴 Thunder Road Grill 🏠 Motel 6, USA Inn ⭕ 🄷, Mormon Island RA, to Stuhr Pioneer Museum, S 🅿️ Phillips 66/Arby's/dsl 🏠 Days Inn, Quality Inn/Riverfront Grille ⭕ Hastings Museum (15mi), Peterbilt
305	40C, to Alda, N 🅿️ Sinclair/dsl, TA/Country Pride/dsl/scales/24hr/@, S Crane Meadows Nature Ctr/🆁🆂
300	NE 11, Wood River, N ⭕ to Cheyenne SRA, S 🅿️ Pilot/Subway/dsl/scales/24hr 🏠 motel/RV park
291	10D, Shelton, N ⭕ War Axe SRA
285	10C, Gibbon, N 🅿️ Petro Oasis/dsl ⭕ RV camping, Windmill SP, S 🏠 Country Inn
279	NE 10, to Minden, N 🅿️ Conoco/dsl, S ⭕ Pioneer Village Camping (13mi)
275	NE 10, Kearney, N ⭕ Archway Mon
275mm	The Great Platte River Road Archway Monument
272	NE 44, Kearney, N 🅿️ Casey's, Casey's/dsl, Cenex/dsl, Phillips 66/Subway/dsl, Pump&Pantry/dsl 🍴 Amigo's, Angus Burger, Arby's, Burger King, Coppermill Steaks, DQ, Egg&I, El Limon, El Maguey, Firehouse Subs, Freddy's, Gourmet House Japanese, Hunan's Rest., King's Buffet, LJ Silver, McDonald's, Moe's SW, Old Chicago, Perkins, Pizza Hut, Red Lobster, Ruby Tuesday, Runza, Taco Bell, Taco John's, USA Steaks, Wendy's, Whiskey Creek 🏠 AmericInn, Candlewood Suites, Comfort Inn, Country Inn&Suites, Days Inn, EconoLodge, Fairfield Inn, Hampton Inn, Holiday Inn, Howard Johnson, La Quinta, Microtel, Midtown Western Inn, Motel 6, New Victorian Inn, Quality Inn, Ramada Inn, Rodeway Inn, Super 8, Western Inn South, Wingate Inn ⭕ 🄷, $General, Apache Camper Ctr, Boogaart's, Buick/Cadillac, Chevrolet, Chrysler/Dodge/Jeep,

Exit #	Services
272	Continued Kearney RV Park/camping, Museum of NE Art, to Archway Mon, U NE Kearney, Verizon, Walmart (3mi), S 🅿️ Conoco/dsl 🍴 Skeeter's BBQ 🏠 Best Western+, Holiday Inn Express
271mm	🆁🆂 wb, **full** ♿ facilities, info, litter barrels, petwalk, 🄲, 🄰
269mm	🆁🆂 eb, **full** ♿ facilities, info, litter barrels, petwalk, 🄲, 🄰
263	Rd 10 b, Odessa, N 🅿️ Sapp Bros./Apple Barrel Rest./dsl ⭕ UP Wayside
257	US 183, Elm Creek, N 🅿️ Pilot/Subway/dsl/scales/24hr 🏠 Rodeway Inn ⭕ Antique Car Museum, Sunny Meadows Camping, S ⭕ Nebraska Prairie Museum (9mi)
248	Overton, N 🅿️ Jay Bros/dsl
237	US 283, Lexington, N 🅿️ Casey's, Cenex/dsl, Gulf/dsl, Phillips 66/dsl 🍴 Arby's, Baskin-Robbins, Burger King, Delight Donuts, DQ, Hong Kong Buffet, Little Caesar's, McDonald's, Pizza Hut, San Pedro Mexican, Sonic, Wendy's 🏠 Comfort Inn, Days Inn, Econolodge, Holiday Inn Express, Minute Man Motel ⭕ 🄷, $General, $Tree, Advance Parts, Buick/Chevrolet, Military Vehicle Museum, O'Reilly Parts, Plum Creek Foods, Verizon, Walmart/Subway, S 🅿️ Sinclair/dsl/@ 🍴 Kirk's Café 🏠 Super 8 ⭕ to Johnson Lake RA (6mi)
231	Darr Rd
227mm	🆁🆂 both lanes, **full** ♿ facilities, info, litter barrels, petwalk, 🄲, 🄰, vending
222	NE 21, Cozad, N 🅿️ Casey's/dsl, Cenex/dsl 🍴 Burger King, DQ, Panda Buffet, Pizza Hut, Runza, Subway 🏠 Knights Inn, Rodeway Inn ⭕ 🄷, $General, Firestone/auto, museum
211	NE 47, Gothenburg, N 🅿️ Cenex/dsl, Cenex/dsl/24hr 🍴 Lasso Espresso, McDonald's, Mi Ranchito Mexican, NE Grill, Pizza Hut, Runza 🏠 Comfort Suites, Howard Johnson, Travel Inn ⭕ 🄷, Buick/Chevrolet, Carquest, Pony Express Sta Museum (1mi), S ⭕ Blue Heron Camping/Gas
199	Brady
194mm	🆁🆂 both lanes, **full** ♿ facilities, litter barrels, petwalk, 🄲, 🄰, vending
190	Maxwell, N 🅿️ Ranchland/dsl, S ⭕ RV camping, to Ft McPherson Nat Cemetary (2mi)
181mm	weigh sta both lanes
179	to US 30, N Platte, N 🅿️ Pump&Pantry/dsl 🏠 Comfort Inn, La Quinta, Motel 6, Tru Hilton ⭕ RV camping, S 🅿️ FLYING J/Denny's/dsl/scales/LP/RV dump/24hr, ♥Loves/McDonald's/Subway/dsl/scales/24hr ⭕ tire/lube/repair, truckwash
177	US 83, N Platte, N 🅿️ Cenex/dsl, Shell/dsl, Sinclair/dsl, U-Fillem 🍴 Amigo's Rest., Applebee's, Arby's, Burger King, Coldstone, DQ, Dunkin', Hunan Moon, Jimmy John's, KFC, King Buffet, Little Caesar's, LJ Silver/Taco Bell, McDonald's, Penny's Diner, Perkins, Pizza Hut, Qdoba, Quiznos, Ruby Tuesday, Runza, San Pedro Mexican,

AURORA

KEARNEY

LEXINGTON

N PLATTE

🅖 = gas 🍴 = food 🛏 = lodging 🅞 = other 🆁🆂 = rest stop   Copyright 2022 - The Next EXIT

INTERSTATE 80 Cont'd

N PLATTE

177	Continued
	Sonic, Starbucks, Subway, Wendy's, Whiskey Creek Steaks 🛏 Baymont Inn, Blue Spruce Motel, Fairfield Inn, Hampton Inn, Howard Johnson, Knights Inn, Motel 6, Quality Inn 🅞🅗, $General, $Tree, Advance Parts, Goodyear/auto, Harley-Davidson, Herberger's, Holiday RV Park, museum, Staples, SunMart Foods, Tire Pros, to Buffalo Bill's Ranch, Verizon, visitor ctr, Walgreens, Walmart/Subway, **S** 🅖 Cenex, Gulf/Taco Bell/dsl/24hr/@ 🅞 KJ's U-Fillem/Subway/dsl/RV dump 🍴 Taco John's 🛏 Best Western+, Comfort Inn, Days Inn, Holiday Inn Express, Super 8 🅞 Chevrolet/Cadillac, Chrysler/Dodge/Jeep, dsl repair, Ford/Lincoln, Hobby Lobby, Honda, Menards, Nissan, Seevers Tire/auto, to Lake Maloney RA, Toyota, vet, veterans memorial/info
164	56C, Hershey, **N** 🅖 Shell/Western Cafe/dsl/24hr/@ 🅞 KJ's Ranch Store
160mm	🆁🆂 both lanes, full 🦽 facilities, info, litter barrels, petwalk, 🚻, 🖼
158	NE 25, Sutherland, **N** 🛏 Park Motel (1mi) 🅞 RV camping, **S** 🅖 Sinclair/Godfather's Pizza/dsl 🅞 RV camping
149mm	Central/Mountain time zone
145	51C, Paxton, **N** 🅖 Shell/dsl/24hr 🛏 Days Inn 🅞 RV camping
133	51B, Roscoe
132mm	🆁🆂 wb, full 🦽 facilities, info, litter barrels, petwalk, 🚻, 🖼
126	US 26, NE 61, Ogallala, **N** 🅖 Casey's/dsl, Cenex/dsl, Kwik Stop, Sapp Bros/Shell/dsl/24hr, Watering Hole/dsl, Western/dsl 🍴 Arby's, Front Street Cafe, Golden Village Chinese, Margarita's, McDonald's, Peking Chinese, Pizza Hut, Runza, Spur Steaks, Valentino's 🛏 Days Inn, Lonesome Dove Lodge, Quality Inn, Travelodge 🅞🅗, $General, Bomgaars, Buick/Chevrolet/GMC, Chrysler/Dodge/Jeep, Firestone/auto, Ford/Lincoln, NAPA, O'Reilly Parts, SunMart Foods, to Lake McConaughy, U-Save Drug, Verizon, **S** 🅖 EVC, Gulf/Subway/dsl, TA/Country Pride/dsl/scales/24hr/@ 🍴 DQ, Mi Ranchito Mexican, Royal Buffet, Wendy's 🛏 Hampton Inn, Holiday Inn Express, Rodeway Inn, Super 8 🅞 Ace Hardware, Countryview Camping, Sleepy Sunflower RV Park, truck repair, Walmart/dsl
124mm	🆁🆂 eb, full 🦽 facilities, info, litter barrels, petwalk, 🚻, 🖼
117	51A, Brule, **N** 🍴 Happy Jack's/dsl 🅞 Riverside RV camping
107	25B, Big Springs, **N** 🅖 Big Springs/dsl, ⊕ *FLYING J*/Grandma Max's/Subway/dsl/scales/24hr/@ 🍴 Sam Bass' Steaks 🛏 Motel 6 🅞 truckwash, **S** 🅞 McGreer's Camping
102	I-76 S, to Denver
102mm	S Platte River
101	US 138, to Julesburg, **S** truck parking
99mm	scenic turnout eb
95	NE 27, to Julesburg
85	25A, Chappell, **N** 🅖 FVC/dsl/repair, Pump&Pantrydsl, Shell/dsl 🅞 Creekside RV Park/Camping, Super Foods, USPO, wayside park
76	17F, Lodgepole, **1 mi N** 🅞 gas/dsl, lodging
69	17E, to Sunol
61mm	🆁🆂 wb, full 🦽 facilities, litter barrels, petwalk, 🚻, 🖼, vending
59	US 385, 17J, Sidney, **N** 🅖 Gulf/dsl, Sapp Bros/Shell/dsl/24hr, Tesla EVC 🍴 Applebee's, Arby's, Buffalo Point Rest., China 1 Buffet, DQ, McDonald's, Mi Ranchito Mexican, Perkins, Pizza Hut, Runza, Sonic, Subway 🛏 Best Western+, Days Inn, Fairfield Inn, Hampton Inn, Motel 6, Quality Inn 🅞 auto/dsl repair, Bomgaars, Cabela's Outfitters/RV Park, Chrysler/Dodge/Jeep, Ford, RV camping (2mi), visitor ctr, Walmart, **S** 🅖 ♥ Love's /IHOP/dsl/scales/24hr, Shamrock/dsl 🛏 Comfort Inn, Country Inn Suites 🅞 auto tire/truck repair, truckwash
55	NE 19, to Sterling, Sidney
51.5mm	🆁🆂/hist marker eb, full 🦽 facilities, litter barrels, petwalk, 🚻, 🖼, vending

OGALLALA

SIDNEY

48	to Brownson
38	rd 17 b, Potter, **N** 🅖 FVC/dsl/LP 🅞 repair
29	53A, Dix, **1/2 mi N** 🅞 food, gas
22	53E, Kimball, **1-2 mi N** 🅖 Kwik Stop, Vince's/dsl 🍴 Pizza H Subway 🛏 Days Inn, Motel Kimball, Sleep4Less Motel 🅞 c park, Kimball RV Park (seasonal), Main St Mkt, NAPA
20	NE 71, Kimball, **0-2 mi N** 🅖 Conoco/dsl, FVC/dsl, Kwik Sto Vince's/dsl 🍴 O'Henry's Diner, Pizza Hut, Subway 🛏 1st In state Inn, Days Inn, Motel Kimball, Sleep4Less Motel, Super 8 🅞 city park, Kimball RV Park (seasonal), Main St Mkt, NAPA, Shopp
8	53C, to Bushnell
1	53B, Pine Bluffs, **1 mi N** 🅞 RV camping
0mm	Nebraska/Wyoming state line

KIMBALL

INTERSTATE 680 (Omaha)

Exit #	Services
	I-680 begins/ends on I-80, exit 27.
29b a	I-80, W to Omaha, E to Des Moines.
28	IA 191, to Neola, Persia
21	L34, Beebeetown
19mm	🆁🆂 wb, full 🦽 facilities, info, litter barrels, petwalk, 🚻, 🖼
16mm	🆁🆂 eb, full 🦽 facilities, info, litter barrels, petwalk, 🚻, 🖼
15mm	scenic overlook
71	I-29 N, to Sioux City
66	Honey Creek
3b a	(61 b a from wb) I-29, S to Council Bluffs, IA 988, to Crescent, 🅖 Casey's/dsl 🅞 to ski area
1	County Rd
14mm	Nebraska/Iowa state line, Missouri River, Mormon Bridge
13	US 75 S, 30th St, Florence, **E** 🅖 Shell/dsl 🍴 Enzo's, Zesto Din 🅞 HyVee Drug, LDS Temple, Mormon Trail Ctr, **W** 🅖 Florence/d
12	US 75 N, 48th St, **E** 🅖 Cenex/dsl 🍴 Burger King (2mi), Taco Be (2mi)
9	72nd St, **1-2 mi E** 🅖 Kwikshop 🍴 Burger King, Golden Corra Jimmy John's, KFC, Panda Express, Taco Bell, Village Inn 🅞🅗 Big Lots, Marshall's, Petsmart, Target, Walgreen, **W** 🅞 Cu ningham Lake RA
6	NE 133, Irvington, **E** 🅖 BP, MurphyUSA/dsl 🍴 Burger Kin Jimmy John's 🅞 $Tree, Verizon, Walmart/Subway/drugs/24h **W** 🍴 Legend's Grill, Villagio Pizzeria, Zesto Cafe 🛏 Fairfie Inn, Holiday Inn Express
5	Fort St, **W** 🅖 KwikShop, QT 🍴 Dunkin' 🅞 CVS Drug, HyVe Foods, Walgreens
4	NE 64, Maple St, **E** 🅖 BP, **W** 🅖 Kum&Go/dsl, Megasaver 🍴 Burger King, China 1, Godfather's Pizza, Jimmy John's, La Mes Mexican, McDonald's, Pizza Hut, Runza, Subway, Taco Bel Taco John's 🛏 Comfort Suites, La Quinta 🅞 $General, Famil Fare, O'Reilly Parts, vet
3	US 6, Dodge St, **E** 🍴 Cheesecake Factory, Granite City Rest JC Mandarin Chinese, Panera Bread, PF Chang's 🛏 AmericInn Marriott 🅞 AAA, Audi/VW, BMW, Dick's, Hyundai, Jaguar Land Rover, JC Penney, Mazda, Mini, Subaru, Von Maur, Whol Foods Mkt, **W** 🅖 Phillips 66 🍴 Burger King, Chick-fil-A, Chin Buffet, Cilantro's, DQ, Jimmy John's, McDonald's, Starbucks Subway, Which Wich? 🛏 Best Western, Hampton Inn, Sher aton, Super 8, TownPlace Suites 🅞 Cadillac, Chevrolet, Costco gas, Discount Tire, Menard's
2	Pacific St, **E** 🅖 Conoco 🍴 Subway, **W** 🅖 BP
1	NE 38, W Center Rd, **E** 🅖 Cenex/dsl 🍴 Don Carmelo's, Don& Millie's Rest., Subway, **W** 🅖 Phillips 66 🍴 Arby's, Burger King Dickey's BBQ, IHOP, Krispy Kreme, McAlister's Deli, Ozark BBQ Starbucks, Subway, Taco Bell, Wendy's 🅞 $Tree, Baker's Foods dsl, Office Depot, TJ Maxx, Tuesday Morning
0mm	I-680 begins/ends on I-80, exit 446.

OMAHA

NEVADA

▲N INTERSTATE 15

MESQUITE

Exit #	Services
123mm	Nevada/Arizona state line, Pacific/Mountain time zone
122	Lp 15, Mesquite, **E** NV Welcome Ctr both lanes, full ♿ facilities, petwalk, 🅶 Arco, Maverik/dsl, Shell/DQ/dsl 🍴 Alberto's Mexican, Cafe Rio, Canton Chinese, Cucina Italiano, Dominos, Golden West Rest./casino, Jack-in-the-Box, KFC, Los Lupes, Panda Garden, Peggy Sue's Cafe, Taco Bell 🏠 Best Western, Rising Star 🅾 $General, Ace Hardware, AutoZone, Big O Tire, CarQuest, city park, Smith's/Subway/dsl, Sun Resort RV Park, USPO, Walgreens **W** 🅶 76/dsl/LP/RV park 🍴 McDonald's, Starbucks 🏠 Eureka Motel/casino, Virgin River Hotel/casino
120	Lp 15, Mesquite, Bunkerville, **E** 🅶 Shell/dsl, Sinclair/dsl, Terrible's 🍴 McDonald's 🏠 Casablanca Resort/casino/RV Park, Oasis Resort RV Park 🅾 USPO, **W** 🅶 Chevron/dsl 🍴 Del Taco, Popeye's, Roberto's Tacos 🏠 Holiday Inn Express 🅾 🅷, $Tree, Ford/RV Ctr, Verizon, Walmart/Subway
118	Lower Flat Top Dr, **W** 🍴 *FLYING J*/dsl/scales24hr
112	NV 170, Riverside, Bunkerville
110mm	**truck parking both lanes, litter barrels**
100	to Carp, Elgin
96mm	**truck parking both lanes, litter barrels**
93	NV 169, to Logandale, Overton, **E** 🅶 Chevron (3mi) 🅾 Lake Mead NRA, Lost City Museum
91	NV 168, Glendale, **W** 🅶 Arco/dsl 🍴 Muddy River Rest. 🅾 USPO
90.5mm	Muddy River
90	NV 168 (from nb), Glendale, Moapa, **W** 🅶 gas 🅾 Moapa Indian Reservation, USPO
88	Hidden Valley
88mm	**parking area both lanes, litter barrels**
84	Byron
80	Ute
75	Valley of Fire SP, Lake Mead NRA, **E** 🅶 Chevron/dsl/24hr 🅾 casino, fireworks
64	US 93 N, Great Basin Hwy, to Ely, Great Basin NP, **W** 🅶 *Loves*/Subway/Godfather's/dsl/scales/24hr
60mm	**livestock check sta sb**
58	NV 604, Las Vegas Blvd, to Apex, Nellis AFB
54	Speedway Blvd, Hollywood Blvd, **E** 🅶 Petro/Sinclair/dsl/scales/24hr/@ 🍴 Race Day Cafe 🅾 Las Vegas Speedway, **W** 🅶 Speedee Mart/dsl
52	rd 215 W
50	Lamb Ave, **1-2 mi E** 🏠 Comfort Inn 🅾 Hitchin Post RV Park
48	Craig Rd, **E** 🅶 Arco, *PILOT*/KFC/Pizza Hut/dsl/scales/24hr, Shell, Sinclair/Subway/dsl 🍴 Burger King, Jack-in-the-Box, Taco Bell, Zapata's Cantina 🏠 Comfort Inn 🅾 7-11, Firestone/auto, Freightliner, to Nellis AFB, **W** 🅶 7-11 🍴 Cane's, Cannery Grill, Carl's Jr, Chipotle Mexican, Del Taco, Famous Dave's BBQ, Five Guys, In-N-Out, Jamba Juice, Marble Slab, Mulligan's, Panda Express, Sonic, Starbucks, Subway 🏠 Best Western, Hampton Inn, SpringHill Suites 🅾 Batteries&Bulbs, Lowe's, Sam's Club/gas
46	Cheyenne Ave, **E** 🍴 CiCi's Pizza, Marianna's Mkt, Panda Express, Subway, Taco Bell 🅾 $Tree, 7-11, NAPA, vet, **W** 🅶 7-11, Valero/Mortons/Subway/dsl/LP24hr 🍴 Denny's, McDonald's, Tacos El Gordo 🏠 Sunrise Inn 🅾 Aamco, Blue Beacon, dsl repair, Kenworth, SpeedCo, tires

LAS VEGAS

Exit #	Services
45	Lake Mead Blvd, **E** 🅶 Chevron, Rebel/dsl 🍴 Arby's, Burger King, Jack-in-the-Box, McDonald's 🅾 7-11, PepBoys, **W** 🅶 Arco/dsl
44	Washington Ave (from sb), **E** 🅾 casinos
43	D St (from nb), same as 44
42b a	I-515 to LV, US 95 N to Reno, US 93 S to Phoenix
41b a	NV 159, Charleston Blvd, **E** 🅶 7-11, Arco/dsl 🍴 Cheesecake Factory, Chipotle 🅾 Premium Outlets/famous brands, Walgreens, **W** 🅶 Chevron, Rebel/dsl 🍴 Carl's Jr, Del Taco, Jimmy John's, McDonald's, Starbucks, Wendy's 🅾 🅷, CVS Drug, Smith's Foods
40	Sahara Ave, **E** 🏠 Artisan Hotel 🅾 multiple casinos/hotels, The Strip, **W** 🅶 7-11, Arco/dsl, Chevron, Rebel/dsl, Shell 🍴 Carl's Jr, Chipotle Mexican, DQ, El Pollo Loco, In-N-Out, KFC, Landry's Seafood, Los Tacos, Macaroni Grill, McDonald's, Panda Express, PDQ Cafe, Pizza Hut, Shilla BBQ, Starbucks, Subway, TGIFriday's, Wendy's 🏠 Palace Sta. Hotel/Casino 🅾 $Tree, AT&T, casinos, CVS Drug, Mariana's Mkt, Office Depot, Ross, TJ Maxx
39	Spring Mtn Rd (from sb), **E** 🅾 multiple hotels/casinos, **W** 🍴 Multiple Asian Cuisine, Subway 🅾 Firestone/auto
38b a	Flamingo Rd, **E** 🅾 multiple casinos/hotels, The Strip, to UNLV, **W** 🅶 Chevron, Rebel/dsl 🍴 Burger King, McDonald's, Ricardo's Mexican, Sonic, Starbucks, Subway, TGIFriday's 🏠 Gold Coast Hotel, Palms Hotel, Rio Hotel 🅾 Smith's Foods

 = gas   = food = lodging = other = rest stop   Copyright 2022 - The Next EXIT

INTERSTATE 15 Cont'd

LAS VEGAS

Exit #	Services
37	Tropicana Ave, E Rebel Coco's Rest. Bellagio, Excaliber Hotel, Hooters Hotel/casino, Mandalay Bay, MGM Grand, Monte Carlo, Motel 6, Tropicana Hotel , multiple hotels/casinos, W Rebel/dsl, Shell/Subway, Standard, Texaco Burger King, Cane's, Dennys, In-N-Out, Jack-in-the-Box, McDonald's, Wendy's Budget Suites, Days Inn, Hampton Inn, La Quinta, Motel 6, Orleans Hotel, Siegel Suites
36	Russell Rd, E multiple hotels/casinos, to , W Chevron/Herbst/dsl Courtyard, Fairfield Inn, Holiday Inn Express, Residence Inn, Staybridge Suites
34	to I-215 E, Las Vegas Blvd, to The Strip, E McCarran Airport
33	NV 160, to Blue Diamond, Death Valley, E 7-11, Chevron/dsl, Rebel/dsl Bootlegger Bistro, Buffalo Wild Wings, Burger King, Cane's, Chili's, Chipotle Mexican, Denny's, Dickey's BBQ, Dunkin', Five Guys, Hawaiian BBQ, IHOP, Jersey Mikes, McDonald's, NY Pizza, Outback Steaks, Panda Express, Popeyes, Smashburger, Starbucks, Subway, Wienerschnitzel Baymont Inn, Budget Suites, Caribe Resort, Hilton Garden CVS Drug, factory outlet/famous brands, Oasis RV Resort, Smith's Foods, W Chevron/dsl, Shell, TA/Burger King/Subway/TacoTime/dsl/LP/scales/24hr/@ Cafe Rio, Carl's Jr, Chipotle, Del Taco, Domino's, Famous Dave's BBQ, In-N-Out, Jack-in-the-Box, McDonald's, Panda Express, Papa Murphy's, Subway Silverton Lodge/Casino AT&T, $Tree, 99c Store, Albertson's, Bass ProShops, BigLots, Discount Tire, GNC, Kohl's, Meineke, Office Depot, PetCo, Ross, Target, Verizon, Walgreens, WorldMkt
31	Silverado Ranch Blvd, E Steak'n Shake South Point Hotel/Casino
30	W Cactus Ave, W Chevron/dsl
27	NV 146, to Henderson, Lake Mead, Hoover Dam, 0-2 mi E Arco, Chevron/dsl, Shell Burger King, Jack-in-the-Box, Starbucks, Subway Best Western, Hampton Inn Camping World, casino, W vet
25	NV 161, Sloan, 1 mi E Camping World
24mm	bus/truck check sta nb
12	NV 161, to Goodsprings, Jean, E Shell/dsl Denny's Gold Strike Casino/hotel, NV Correctional, NV HP, skydiving, USPO, W Chevron/dsl/24hr
1	Primm, E Chevron/Subway/dsl, Texaco/dsl Carl's Jr, Dennys, KFC, Mad Greek Cafe, McDonald's, Panda Express, Starbucks, Taco Bell Buffalo Bill's Resort/casino, factory outlets, Primm Valley Resort/casino, W FLYING J/Subway/Qdoba/DQ/dsl/scales Whiskey Pete's Hotel/casino
0mm	Nevada/California state line

JEAN

INTERSTATE 80

WENDOVER

Exit #	Services
411mm	Nevada/Utah state line
410	US 93A, to Ely, W Wendover, S NV Welcome Ctr/info, full facilities Chevron/dsl, Pilot/Arby's/dsl/scales/24hr, Shell/Taco Time/dsl Burger King, McDonald's, Pizza Hut, Subway Knights Inn, Motel 6, Nugget Hotel/casino, Peppermill Hotel/casino/RV parking, Rainbow Hotel/casino, Red Garter Hotel/casino Best Hardware, city park, KOA, Smith's Foods/dsl
407	Ola, W Wendover
405mm	Pacific/Mountain time zone
398	to Pilot Peak
390mm	Silverzone Pass, elevation 5940
387	to Shafter

Exit #	Services
378	NV 233, to Montello, Oasis
376	to Pequop
373mm	both lanes, litter barrels, , rest rooms, Pequop Summ elev 6967
365	to Independence Valley, N prison camp
360	to Moor
354mm	parking area eb
352b a	US 93, Great Basin Hwy, E Wells, N Chevron/dsl/LP, Conoco/dsl, Petro/Dunkin'/dsl/café/casino Bella's Diner, Burg King/Subway Motel 6, Rest Inn Motel, Sharon Motel, Sup 8 Crossroads RV Park, repair, Tire Factory, S FLYING J dsl/scales/LP/casino/RV Dump/24hr, LNG, Loves/McDo alds/dsl/scales/24hr Hampton Inn Great Basin NP
351	W Wells, N Wells/dsl/LP Family$, Mtn Shadows Park, Roy's Foods, USPO, Well's Hardware, S Angel Lake R Park, to Angel Lake RA
348	to Beverly Hills, N RV camping
343	to Welcome, Starr Valley, N food , Welcome RV Pa
333	Deeth, Starr Valley
328	to River Ranch
321	NV 229, Halleck, Ruby Valley
318mm	N Fork Humboldt River
317	to Elburz
314	to Ryndon, Devils Gate, N Sinclair/cafe/dsl, S RV campir
312mm	check sta both lanes
310	to Osino, 4 mi S Valley View RV Park
303	E Elko, N Flyers/CFN/dsl, Sinclair/Arctic Circle/dsl/24 Wingers Holiday Inn Express, Home 2 Suites, Ledg stone Hotel, TownePlace Suites, S Chevron/dsl, Conoco dsl, Maverik/dsl, Sinclair/dsl Blue Moon Rest., Burg King, Chef Cheng's Chinese, Domino's, DQ, Garibaldi's Mex can, McDonald's/playplace, Monkey Sun Chinese, Pizza Bar Pizza Hut, Quiznos, Subway, Taco Time, Toki Ona Diner, We dy's Best Value Inn, Best Western, Budget Inn, Comfo Inn, Days Inn, High Desert Inn, Hilton Garden, Holiday M tel, Motel 6, Quality Inn, Red Lion Inn/casino, Sheraton Fo Points, Super 8, Travelodge , , Albertson's, AT&T, Big Tires, Buick/Cadillac/Chevrolet/GMC, Cal Ranch Store, ci park, Double Dice RV Park, Ford, Gold Country RV Park, Goo year/auto, Iron Horse RV Park, JC Penney, Kenworth, NE N Museum, Valley View RV Park
301	NV 225, Elko, N Maverik/dsl 9 Beans/Burrito, Arby' Burger King, Denny's, Greatwall Chinese, Jack-in-the-Bo Jimmy John's, Mattie's Grill, McDonald's/playplace, Pap Murphy's, Port of Subs, RoundTable Pizza Baymont In Shilo Inn Suites AT&T, GNC, Home Depot, JoAnn Fabric Marshall's, Petco, Raley's Foods, Ross, Verizon, Walmart/Su way, S Shell, Shell/dsl Costa Vida, Dos Amigos, KF Little Caesar's, Sergio's Mexican, Starbucks, Subway, Taco Be American Inn, Centre Motel, Economy Inn, Elko Inn, Esqui Inn, Hampton Inn, Manor Inn, Midtown Motel, Rodeway In Scottish Inn, Stampede Motel, Stockmen's Hotel/casino, Thu derbird Motel , , Advance Parts, , AutoZone, Cimarro West RV Park, CVS Drug, Family$, O'Reilly Parts, Smith's Foods dsl, transmission, Verizon
298	W Elko, S Sinclair/Port of Subs/dsl
292	to Hunter, N CA Trail Interpretive Ctr
285mm	Humboldt River, tunnel
282	NV 221, E Carlin, N prison area
280	NV 766, Carlin, N Pizza Factory Desert Gold RV Par dsl repair, S Chevron/dsl, Pilot/Subway/dsl/scales/24

WELLS

ELKO

CARLIN

🔼E INTERSTATE 80 Cont'd

280	Continued
	🍴 Chin's Cafe, Rigobertos Mexican, State Café/casino 🏠 Carlin Inn, Cavalier Motel 🅾 Ace Hardware, Family$, tires, USPO
279	NV 278 (from eb), to W Carlin, **1 mi S** 🍴 Flyers/dsl
271	to Palisade
270mm	**truck parking both lanes, litter barrels, Emigrant Summit, elevation 6114**
268	to Emigrant
261	NV 306, to Beowawe, Crescent Valley
259mm	🆁🆂 **both lanes, full ♿ facilities, litter barrels, petwalk,** 🄰
257mm	Humboldt River
254	to Dunphy
244	to Argenta
233	NV 304, to Battle Mountain, **N** 🍴 Conoco/dsl 🍴 Mama's Pizza/deli 🏠 Royal Inn 🅾 🅷 Ace Hardware, FoodTown
231	NV 305, Battle Mountain, **1 mi N** 🍴 ⊘FLYING J/76/Blimpie/dsl/casino/24hr, Chevron/dsl, Maverik/dsl 🍴 El Aguila Real, Hide-a-way Steaks, McDonald's, Ming Dynasty, Owl Rest., Pizza Factory, Port of Subs 🏠 Big Chief Motel, Nevada Hotel, Owl Motel, Super 8 🅾 🅷 city park, Family$, Mills Drug, NAPA, NAPA Care, Tire Factory, USPO
229	NV 304, W Battle Mountain, **N** 🍴 ⊘FLYING J/76/dsl/casino/scales/24hr, Shell/dsl 🍴 Colt Rest./casino 🏠 Big Chief Motel, Rodeway Inn 🅾 Colt RV camping, NAPA Care, Tire Factory
222	to Mote
216	Valmy, **N** 🍴 Chevron/USPO/dsl, **S** 🆁🆂 **both lanes, full ♿ facilities, litter barrels, petwalk,** 🄲, 🄰, **RV dump**
212	to Stonehouse
205	to Pumpernickel Valley
203	to Iron Point
200	**truck parking both lanes, litter barrels, Golconda Summit, elevation 5159**
194	Golconda, **N** 🅾 USPO
187	to Button Point, **N** 🆁🆂 **both lanes, full ♿ facilities, litter barrels, petwalk,** 🄲, 🄰, **RV dump**
180	NV 794, E Winnemucca Blvd
178	NV 289, Winnemucca Blvd, Winnemucca, **S** 🍴 Chevron/dsl, Maverik/dsl 🍴 Rte 66 Grill, Sonoma Grill 🏠 Budget Inn, Candlewood Suites, Cozy Motel, Frontier Motel, Valu Motel 🅾 🅷 Advance Parts, carwash
176	US 95 N, Winnemucca, **N** 🍴 Pacific Pride/dsl, **S** 🍴 ⊘FLYING J/dsl/LP/RV dump/24hr, Chevron/dsl/24hr, Conoco/dsl, G Gas, Kwik Serv/dsl 🍴 Burger King, China Garden, Dos Amigos Mexican, Dotty's, Griddle Rest., Jack-in-the-Box, KFC/LJ Silver, Little Caesar's, McDonald's/playplace, Pig BBQ, Pizza Hut, Port of Subs, RoundTable Pizza, Sid's Rest., Subway, Taco Bell, Taco Time 🏠 Best Western, Country Hearth Inn, Economy Inn, Holiday Inn Express, Holiday Motel, Model T Motel/casino/RVPark, Motel 6, Park Hotel, Pyrenees Motel, Quality Inn, Regency Inn, Santa Fe Inn, Scott Motel, Scottish Inn, Super 8, Winnemucca Inn/casino, Winner Hotel/casino 🅾 🅷 auto/truck repair, AutoZone, Ford, O'Reilly Parts, Ridley's Foods, RV camping, Schwab Tire, Verizon, Walmart/Subway
173	W Winnemucca, **N** 🍴 PILOT/Subway/dsl/scales/24hr, **S** 🅾 ⊙
168	to Rose Creek, **S** 🅾 prison area
158	to Cosgrave, **S** 🆁🆂 **both lanes, full ♿ facilities, litter barrels, petwalk,** 🄲, 🄰
151	Mill City, **N** 🍴 TA/Subway/Taco Bell/Fork/dsl/casino/24hr/@

149	NV 400, Mill City, **1 mi N** 🍴 TA/Subway/Taco Bell/Fork/dsl/24hr/@, **S** 🅾 Star Point Gen. Store/RV camping
145	Imlay, **S** 🅾 Star Peak RV Park
138	Humboldt
129	Rye Patch Dam, **N** 🅾 to Rye Patch SRA, **S** 🍴 Chevron/Rye Patch Trkstp/dsl
119	to Rochester, Oreana
112	to Coal Canyon, **S** 🅾 to correctional ctr
107	E Lovelock (from wb), same as 106
106	Main St, Lovelock, **N** 🍴 Chevron/dsl/LP, PJ's Gas/subs/dsl 🍴 Black Rock Grill, Cowpoke Cafe, McDonald's, Pizza Factory 🏠 Cadillac Inn, Covered Wagon Motel, Punch Inn/casino, Royal Inn, Super 10 Motel 🅾 🅷 auto care, city park/playground/restrooms, Family$, Lazy K Camping, Safeway Foods, USPO, **S** 🍴 Conoco/Port of Subs/dsl24hr
105	W Lovelock (from eb), **N** 🍴 Shop'n Go/dsl, Valero/dsl 🍴 La Casita Mexican 🏠 Lovelock Inn 🅾 🅷 Brookwood RV Park, museum, NAPA, same as 106
93	to Toulon, **S** 🅾 ⊙
83	US 95 S, to Fallon, **S** 🆁🆂 **both lanes, full ♿ facilities, litter barrels,** 🄲, 🄰
78	to Jessup
65	to Hot Springs, Nightingale
50	NV Pacific Pkwy, Fernley
48	US 50A, US 95A, to Fallon, E Fernley, **N** 🍴 ⊘FLYING J/Denny's/dsl/scales/Lp/24hr, **S** 🍴 Chevron/dsl, Shell/dsl 🍴 Burger King, Dotty's Grill, Jack-in-the-Box, KFC, Louie's China, McDonald's, Moto Japanese, Papa Murphy's, Pizza Factory, Pizza Hut, Port of Subs, Silverado Rest./casino, Starbucks, Taco Bell 🏠 Best Western, Super 8 🅾 $Tree, AutoZone, Chrysler/Dodge/Jeep, Lowe's, O'Reilly Parts, Raley's Mkt, tires, to Great Basin NP, URGENT CARE, USPO, Verizon, Walgreens, Walmart/Subway
46	US 95A, W Fernley, **N** 🍴 Loves/Arby's/dsl/scales/24hr, **S** 🍴 PILOT/DQ/Wendy's/dsl/scales/24hr 🏠 Comfort Suties 🅾 Blue Beacon, SpeedCo
45mm	Truckee River
43	to Pyramid Lake, Wadsworth, **N** 🍴 Pyramid Lake/dsl/RV camping
42mm	**check sta eb,** 🆁🆂 **wb, full ♿ facilities, litter barrels, petwalk,** 🄲, 🄰, **wireless internet**
40	Painted Rock
38	Orchard
36	Derby Dam
32	USA Pkwy, Tracy, Clark Station, **S** 🍴 Golden Gate/Port of Subs/dsl/scales 🍴 Philly's, Subway 🏠 Studio 6
28	NV 655, Waltham Way, Patrick
27mm	scenic view eb
25mm	**check sta wb**

= gas = food = lodging = other = rest stop Copyright 2022 - The Next EXIT

	INTERSTATE 80 Cont'd
Exit #	Services
23	Mustang, S Chevron/dsl/24hr
22	Lockwood
21	Vista Blvd, Greg St, Sparks, N Chevron/McDonald's, Qwik-Stop Del Taco Fairfield Inn, Woodspring Suites , S Petro/Iron Skillet/dsl/24hr/@ Super 8 Peterbilt, truckwash
20	Sparks Blvd, Sparks, N 7-11, Shell/dsl BJ's Rest., Buffalo Wild Wings, Burrito Bandito, Carl's Jr, Chick-fil-A, Chipotle, Fuddruckers, Jersey Mike's, Jimmy John's, Olive Garden, Outback Steaks, Panda Express, Papa John's, Popeye's, Starbucks, Subway, Taco Bell Hampton Inn, Residence Inn AT&T, Best Buy, Discount Tire, GNC, Lowe's, Old Navy, Petco, Scheel's Sports, Schwab Tire, Target, Tires+, TJ Maxx, Verizon, water funpark, S Petro/Iron Skillet/dsl/scales/24hr/@ Super 8 Freightliner
19	E McCarran Blvd, Sparks, N Arco, Chevron/dsl, Sinclair/dsl, TA/Fuddrucker's/dsl/scales/@ Applebee's, Baskin-Robbins, BJ's BBQ, Black Bear Diner, Burger King, Cane's, China King, Domino's, El Pollo Loco, Jack-in-the-Box, KFC, Little Caesar's, McDonald's, Pizza Hut, Pizza+, Port Of Subs, Sizzler, Taco Bell, Wendy's, Wienerschnitzel Aloha Inn, Sunrise Motel, Windsor Inn $Tree, 99c Store, AutoZone, BigLots, CVS Drug, Family$, Foodmaxx Foods, O'Reilly Parts, Ross, Victorian RV Park, S Denny's, Super Burrito Best Western+ NAPA
18	NV 445, Pyramid Way, Sparks, N 7-11 In-N-Out Bourbon Square Casino, Nugget Courtyard, S Nugget Hotel/casino
17	Rock Blvd, Nugget Ave, Sparks, N Arco, Chevron, V/dsl Safari Motel, Victorian Inn, Wagon Train Motel casinos, O'Reilly Parts, S Nugget Hotel/casino
16	B St, E 4th St, Victorian Ave, N Arco Jack's Cafe Motel 6 Rail City Casino, S Chevron/repair
15	I-580 S, US 395, to Carson City, Susanville, 0-1 mi S Best Western, Holiday Inn Express, Hyatt Place, La Quinta , Costco/gas, Grand Sierra Resort, USPO, Walmart/McDonald's

14	Wells Ave, Reno, N Motel 6, S Chevron/dsl Denny America's Best Inn, Days Inn, Ramada Inn auto repa Goodyear, Tire Pros
13	US 395, Virginia St, Reno, N Shell/dsl Taco Shop, , Circus Circus, to downtown hotels/casinos, to UNVR no, Walgreens
12	Keystone Ave, Reno, N Arco Pizza Hut, Starbuc Gateway Inn, Motel 6 7-11, CVS Drug, Raley's Food S Chevron/dsl Burger King, Jack-in-the-Box, KFC, Litt Caesar's, McDonald's, Port of Subs, Round Table Pizza, Ta Bell, Wendy's casinos, Keystone RV Park, Meineke, NAP O'Reilly Parts, SaveMart/drug
10	McCarran Blvd, Reno, N 7-11/dsl, Arco Applebee Asian Wok, Baskin-Robbins, Bully's Grill, Burger King, Carl's Chili's, Chipotle, Del Taco, El Pollo Loco, Hawaiian BBQ, IHC Jack-in-the-Box, KFC, Little Caesar's, McDonald's, Papa Mu phy's, Pizza+, Popeyes, Qdoba Mexican, RoundTable Pizz Silver Chop Chinese, Starbucks, Subway, Taco Bell, Tacos el R $Tree, AT&T, AutoZone, Big O Tires, Discount Tire, Kohl O'Reilly Parts, Petsmart, Ross, Safeway/dsl, SaveMart Food Staples, Tires+, Walgreens, Walmart/McDonald's, S 7-1 Home Depot, URGENT CARE, vet
9	Robb Dr, N Chevron/dsl, Maverik/dsl Bully's Grill, Burg Me, Casa Grande, China Kitchen, Dickey's BBQ, Domino's, Jimm John's, Moxie's Cafe, Port Of Subs, Starbucks, Subway Ham ton Inn CVS Drug, Raley's Foods/dsl, URGENT CARE
8	W 4th St (from eb), Robb Dr, Reno, S RV camping
7	Mogul
6.5mm	truck parking/hist marker/scenic view both lanes
5	to E Verdi (from wb no return), N Maria's Mexican
4.5mm	scenic view eb
4	Garson Rd, Boomtown, N Chevron/Boomtown Hotel/dsl/c sino Mel's Rest. Cabela's, KOA/RV dump
3.5mm	check sta eb
3	Verdi (from wb)
2.5mm	Truckee River
2	Lp 80, to Verdi, N Sinclair/dsl/24hr Jack-in-the-B Gold Ranch RV Resort/casino
0mm	Nevada/California state line

RENO

SPARKS

NV

NOTES

NEW HAMPSHIRE

🔼 INTERSTATE 89

LEBANON

Exit #	Services
61mm	New Hampshire/Vermont state line, Connecticut River
20(60)	NH 12A, W Lebanon, **E** 🅿 Sunoco 🍴 99 Rest., Chili's, Dunkin', KFC/Taco Bell, Lui Lui Pizza, Subway 🅾 GNC, Hannaford Foods, Jo-Ann Fabrics, LL Bean, Rite Aid, Shaw's Foods, TJ Maxx, Town Fair Tire, USPO, **W** 🅿 Tesla EVC 🍴 110 Grill, Applebee's, D'angelo's, Denny's, Five Guys, Koto Japanese, McDonald's, Moe's SW Grill, Panera Bread, Starbucks, Weathervane Seafood, Wendy's 🛏 Baymont Inn, Fireside Inn 🅾 $Tree, AT&T, Best Buy, BJ's Whse/dsl, CVS Drug, Home Depot, JC Penney, Kohl's, Michael's, Midas, Old Navy, Petsmart, PriceChopper Foods, Staples, Verizon, Walgreens, Walmart
19(58)	US 4, NH 10, W Lebanon, **E** 🅿 Gulf/dsl, Mobil 🍴 China Station 🅾 AutoZone, Family$, Ford, Harley-Davidson, Honda, Pricechopper Foods, **W** 🅿 Sunoco/Maplewoods/dsl 🅾 O'Reilly Parts
57mm	Welcome Ctr/🆁🆂/weigh sta sb, full ♿ facilities, litter barrels, petwalk, 🎮, 🍱, vending, weigh sta nb
18(56)	NH 120, Lebanon, **E** 🅿 Irving/dsl/scales 🛏 Courtyard (3mi), Hilton Garden, Quality Inn, Residence Inn (2mi) 🅾 🏥, Chrysler/Dodge/Jeep, Freightliner, Nissan, to Dartmouth Coll, Volvo/VW, Wilson Tire/repair, **W** 🅿 Mobil/Subway/dsl, Shell/dsl 🅾 U-Haul
17(54)	US 4, to NH 4A, Enfield, **E** 🅾 vet
16(52)	Eastman Hill Rd, **E** 🅿 Gulf/Subway/dsl, **W** 🅿 Mobil/Dunkin'/dsl 🅾 Whaleback Ski Area
15(50)	Montcalm
14(47)	NH 10 (from sb), N Grantham
13(43)	NH 10, Grantham, **E** 🅿 Irving/Gen Store/dsl, **W** 🅿 Irving/Circle K 🍴 Dunkin', Pizza Chef 🅾 vet
40mm	🆁🆂 nb, ull ♿ facilities, info, litter barrels, petwalk, 🎮, picnic table, vending
12A(37)	Georges Mills, **W** 🅾 food, lodging, 🎮, RV camping, to Sunapee SP
12(34)	NH 11 W, New London, **2 mi E** 🅿 Irving/dsl 🍴 McKenna Rest. 🛏 Maple Hill Country Inn, New London Inn 🅾 🏥
11(31)	NH 11 E, King Hill Rd, New London, **2-3 mi E** 🛏 Fairway Motel, New London Inn
10(27)	to NH 114, Sutton, **E** 🅾 to Winslow SP, **1 mi W** 🅾 to Wadleigh SP
26mm	🆁🆂 sb, full ♿ facilities, info, litter barrels, petwalk, 🎮, 🍱, vending
9(19)	NH 103, Warner, **E** 🅿 Irving/Circle K/Dunkin'/dsl, Shell/Subway/pizza 🍴 McDonald's 🅾 Aubuchon Hardware, MktBasket Foods, Rollins SP, **W** 🅾 to Sunapee SP
8(17)	NH 103 (from nb, no EZ return), Warner, **1 mi W** 🅿 gas 🍴 food 🅾 museum, to Rollins SP
15mm	Warner River
7(14)	NH 103, Davisville, **W** 🅾 Pleasant Lake Camping
12mm	Contoocook River
6(10)	NH 127, Contoocook, **E** 🅿 Sunoco 🍴 Everyday Cafe 🅾 vet, **W** 🅾 Elm Brook Park, Sandy Beach Camping (3mi)
5(8)	US 202 W, NH 9 (exits left from nb), Hopkinton, **W** 🍴 food 🅾 RV camping (seasonal)
4(7)	NH 103, Hopkinton (from nb, no EZ return), **E** 🅿 gas
3(4)	Stickney Hill Rd (from nb)**2(2)** NH 13, Clinton St, Concord, **E** 🅾 🏥, **W** 🅾 NH Audubon Ctr
1(1)	Logging Hill Rd, Bow, **E** 🅿 Mobil 🍴 Chen Yang Li Chinese 🛏 Hampton Inn
0mm	I-93 N to Concord, S to Manchester, **I-89 begins/ends on I-93, 36mm.**

WARNER

🔼 INTERSTATE 93

LITTLETON

Exit #	Services
2(11)	I-91, N to St Johnsbury, S to White River Jct. **I-93 begins/ends on I-91, exit 19.**
1(8)	VT 18, to US 2, to St Johnsbury, **2 mi E** 🅿 gas 🍴 food 🛏 camping, lodging
1mm	Welcome Ctr nb, full ♿ facilities, info, litter barrels, petwalk, 🎮, 🍱, vending, WiFi
131mm	Vermont/New Hampshire state line, Connecticut River, **exits 1-2 are in VT**
44(130)	NH 18, NH 135, **W** Welcome Ctr (8am-8pm)/scenic vista both lanes, full ♿ facilities, info, litter barrels, petwalk, 🎮, 🍱
43(125)	NH 135 (from sb), to NH 18, Littleton, **1-2 mi W** 🅾 🏥, same as 42
42(124)	US 302 E, NH 10 N, Littleton, **E** 🅿 Citgo/Quiznos, Cumberland Farms, Sunoco/dsl 🍴 Burger King, Deluxe Pizza, Dunkin', Littleton Diner, Pizza Hut, Subway 🛏 Littleton Motel 🅾 Family$, Rite Aid, USPO, Walgreens, **W** 🅿 Cumberland Farms/dsl, Mobil 🍴 99 Rest., Applebee's, Domino's, McDonald's 🛏 Hampton Inn 🅾 $Tree, Buick/Chevrolet, Chrysler/Dodge/Jeep/Fiat, Home Depot, KOA (5mi), Lowe's, O'Reilly Parts/VIP Service, Shaw's Foods/Osco Drug, Staples, Tire Whse, TJ Maxx, Town Fair Tire, Verizon, Walmart/Dunkin'
41(122)	US 302, NH 18, NH 116, Littleton, **E** 🅿 Irving/Circle K/dsl 🛏 Eastgate Motel/rest., Travel Inn 🅾 Littleton Food Co-op, **W** 🅾 NE Tire

🅿 = gas 🍴 = food 🛏 = lodging 🅞 = other Ⓡ🅢 = rest stop   Copyright 2022 - The Next EXIT

INTERSTATE 93 Cont'd

Exit #	Services
40(121)	US 302, NH 10 E, Bethlehem, **E** 🛏 Adair Country Inn/Rest. 🅞 to Mt Washington
39(119)	NH 116, NH 18 (from sb), N Franconia, Sugar Hill, **W** 🛏 lodging
38(117)	NH 116, NH 117, NH 142, NH 18, Sugar Hill, **E** 🛏 Best Western, **W** 🍴 DutchTreat Rest., Hungry Bear Café 🅞 Bode Hardware, Franconia Village Store, Frost Museum, Mac's Mkt, USPO
37(115)	NH 142, NH 18 (from nb), Franconia, Bethlehem, **W** 🛏 Hillwinds Lodge 🅞 Franstead Camping
36(114)	NH 141, to US 3, S Franconia, **W** 🍴 food 🛏 lodging 🅞 golf
35(113)	US 3 N (from nb), to Twin Mtn Lake
112mm	S Franconia, Franconia Notch SP begins sb
34c	NH 18, S Franconia, Echo Beach Ski Area, info, view area
34b	Cannon Mtn Tramway, **W** 🅞 Boise Rock, Lafayette Place Camping, Old Man Viewing
109mm	trailhead parking
108mm	Lafayette Place Camping, trailhead parking
107mm	The Basin, The Basin
34a	US 3, The Flume Gorge, camping (seasonal), info, The Flume Gorge
104mm	Franconia Notch SP begins nb
33(103)	US 3, N Woodstock, **E** 🅿 Irving/dsl 🍴 Fresolones Pizza, Longhorn Palace Rest. 🛏 Beacon Lodge, Days Inn, EconoLodge, Franconia Notch Motel, Green Village Cottages, Indian Head Resort, Mt Coolidge Motel, Pemi Motel, Profile Motel, Rodeway Inn, Woodward's Resort/Rest. 🅞 Indian Head viewing, to Franconia Notch SP, waterpark, **W** 🍴 Sunny Day Diner 🛏 Country Bumpkin Cottages/Camping, Cozy Cabins, Mt Liberty Cabins, White Mtn Motel/Cottages 🅞 Arnold's NAPACare, Clark's Trading Post, Tim's Repair, vet
32(101)	NH 112, Loon Mtn Rd, N Woodstock, **E** 🅿 BP/7-11/dsl, Citgo, Mobil/dsl 🍴 Black Mtn Burger, Cafe Nacho's, Cheng Garden Chinese, Common Man Rest., Dunkin', El Charro, Enzo's Pizza, Flapjack's Pancakes, GH Pizza, Gordi's Fish&Steaks, Gypsy Cafe, McDonald's, Subway, White Mtn Bagel Deli 🛏 Holiday Inn Express, Kancamagu's Lodge, Lincoln Sta. Lodge, Nordic Inn, South Mtn Resort 🅞 Aubuchon Hardware, Family$, NAPA, PriceChopper Foods, Rite Aid, USPO, **W** 🅿 Citgo 🍴 Imperial Chinese, Lafayette Dinner Train, Landmark II Rest., Peg's Café, Truant's Rest., Woodstock Inn Rest. 🛏 Alpine Lodge, Cascade Lodge 🅞 USPO
31(97)	to NH 175, Tripoli Rd, **W** 🅞 KOA (2mi)
30(95)	US 3, Woodstock, **E** 🍴 Lanterns End Grill 🛏 Jack-O-Lantern Inn/rest. 🅞 golf
29(89)	US 3, Thornton, **E** 🅞 Pemi River RV Park/LP, **W** 🛏 Gilcrest Motel
28(87)	NH 49, Campton, **E** 🅿 Gulf, Mobil 🍴 Dunkin', Exit 28 Pizza 🅞 Handy Man Hardware, USPO, **W** 🅿 Irving/dsl 🍴 Sunset Grill 🅞 Branch Brook Camping, Chelsey's Pizza, Mtn Vista RV Park, repair
27(84)	Blair Rd, Beebe River, **E** 🍴 Covered Bridge Farm Table 🛏 Days Inn, Red Sleigh Condos
26(83)	US 3, NH 25, NH 3A, Tenney Mtn Hwy, **W** 🛏 Common Man Inn, EconoLodge, Pilgrim Inn 🅞 🅷
25(81)	NH 175 (from nb), Plymouth, **W** 🅿 Citgo/dsl, Irving/Circle K/dsl 🍴 Downtown Pizza, Fracher's Diner, HongKong Garden, Lucky Dog Grill, Thai Smile 🅞 🅷, Chase St Mkt, Plymouth State U, USPO
24(76)	US 3, NH 25, Ashland, **E** 🅿 Irving/Circle K/dsl, Mobil, Racing Mart 🍴 Ashland Pizza, Burger King, Common Man Diner, Dunkin', La Catrina, Lucky Dragon Chinese, Village Grill 🛏 Comfort Inn 🅞 $General, Bob's Mkt, Jellystone RV Camp (4mi), repair, USPO

Exit #	Services
23(71)	NH 104, NH 132, to Mt Washington Valley, New Hampton, 🅿 Irving/Circle K/dsl, Mobil/dsl 🍴 Dunkin', Rossi Italia Subway 🅞 Jellystone, USPO
22(62)	NH 127, Sanbornton, **1-5 mi W** 🅞 🅷, food, gas/dsl, 🅒
61mm	Ⓡ🅢 sb, full ♿ facilities, info, litter barrels, petwalk, 🅒, 🅕 vending
20(57)	US 3, NH 11, NH 132, NH 140, Tilton, **E** 🅿 Irving/Circle K dsl/24hr, Shell/Subway/dsl 🍴 99 Rest., Applebee's, Burger King, Dunkin', Five Guys, Green Ginger Chinese, KFC, McDonald's, Starbucks, Taco Bell, Thai Cuisine, Tilt'n Diner, UNO, UperCrust Pizza, Wendy's 🛏 Hampton Inn, Holiday Inn Express, Super 8 🅞 BJ's Whse/gas, Hobby Lobby, Home Depot, Kohl's, Old Navy, O'Reilly Parts/VIP Service, Staples, Subaru, Tanger Outlet/famous brands, Verizon, Walgreens, **W** 🍴 Chili's, Pizza Hut 🅞 Chrysler/Dodge/Jeep, Ford, Kohl's, Lowe's, MktBasket Foods, Nissan, USPO, VW, Walmart/Subway
56mm	Winnipesaukee River
19(55)	NH 132 (from nb no ez return), Franklin, **W** 🅿 Gulf 🍴 Cia Italian 🅞 🅷, NH Vet Home
51mm	Ⓡ🅢 nb, full ♿ facilities, info, litter barrels, petwalk, 🅒, 🅕 vending
18(49)	to NH 132, Canterbury, **E** 🅞 to Shaker Village HS
17(46)	US 4 W, to US 3, NH 132, Boscawen, **W** 🅿 Mobil/Dunkin'
16(41)	NH 132, E Concord, **E** 🅿 Mobil/dsl 🅞 Quality Cash Mkt
15W(40)	US 202 W, to US 3, N Main St, Concord, **W** 🅿 Citgo, Cumberland/Dunkin', Speedway 🍴 Domino's, Friendly's 🛏 Courtyard/café
15E	I-393 E, US 4 E, to Portsmouth
14(39)	NH 9, Loudon Rd, Concord, **E** 🅿 Mobil, Shell/dsl 🍴 DQ, 99 Rest., Applebee's, Arnie's Place, B Good, Buffalo Wild Wings, Burger King, Chicago Grill, Chipotle, D'angelo's, Dunkin', Rodeo Mexican, Five Guys, Friendly's, LJ Silver/Taco Bell, Longhorn Steaks, McDonald's, Moritomo Japanese, Newick Lobster House, Olive Garden, Panera Bread, PapaGino's, Pizza Hut, Red Apple Buffet, Red Arrow Diner, Starbucks, Sunshine Oriental, TGIFriday's, Wendy's, Windmill Rest. 🅞 $Tree, 7-11, AAA, Ace Hardware, Advance Parts, Aldi Foods, AutoZone, Best Buy, BonTon, BooksAMillion, city park, CVS, Dick's, GNC, Hannaford Foods, Home Depot, Irving/Circle K/Subway/dsl, JC Penney, LLBean, Lowe's, Meineke, Michael's, Midas, Mkt Basket Foods, PetCo, Petsmart, Rite Aid, Sam's Club/gas, Shaws Food, Shaw's Foods (2), Shell/dsl, Staples, Target, TJ Maxx, TownFair Tire, URGENT CARE, USPO, Verizon, Walgreens, Walmart, **W** 🅿 Citgo, Cumberland, Speedway 🍴 Domino's, Tea Garden Rest. 🛏 Holiday Inn 🅞 hist sites, Jo-Ann, Marshall's, MktBasket, museum, to state offices
13(38)	to US 3, Manchester St, Concord, **E** 🅿 Cumberland, Sunoco dsl/deli 🍴 Beefside Rest., Brookside Pizza, Dunkin', Ichiban Japanese, Red Blazer Rest., Veano's Italian 🅞 Buick/GMC, Cadillac/Chevrolet, Chrysler/Dodge/Jeep, Harley-Davidson, Kia, Nissan, O'Reilly Parts/VIP Service, Outdoor RV Ctr Subaru, Stratham's Tire, Subaru, Tire Whse, Volvo, **W** 🅿 Mobil/dsl, Speedway/dsl 🍴 Burger King, Common Man Diner, D'angelo's, Dunkin', KFC, McDonald's 🛏 Best Western, Comfort Inn, Fairfield Inn, Residence Inn 🅞 🅷, Aubuchon Hardware, CVS Drug, Firestone, Goodyear/auto
12N(37)	NH 3A N, S Main, **E** 🅿 7-11, Irving/Subway/dsl/24hr 🍴 Dunkin' 🛏 Tru Hilton 🅞 Ford, Honda, Hyundai, Mazda, Toyota, **W** 🅞
12S	NH 3A S, Bow Junction, **E** 🅿 7-11, Irving/Circle K/Subway/dsl 🍴 Dunkin' 🛏 Tru Hilton 🅞 Ford/Mazda, Honda, Hyundai, Toyota
36mm	I-89 N to Lebanon, **toll road begins/ends**

NH

WOODSTOCK

CONCORD

Copyright 2022 - The Next EXIT ® 🅿 = gas 🍴 = food 🏠 = lodging 🅾 = other Ⓡs = rest stop

🔼N INTERSTATE 93 Cont'd

Exit #	Services
31mm	**Welcome Ctr both lanes, full facilities,** 🅿 Irving/dsl 🍴 Hi-Way Diner 🅾 General Store
11(28)	NH 3A, to Hooksett, 4 mi E 🅿 🍴 [img]/dsl/rest., **toll plaza**
28mm	I-293, Everett Tpk
10(27)	NH 3A, Hooksett, E 🅿 Irving/Circle K/dsl 🍴 Dunkin', Subway, Wendy's 🅾 Home Depot, Kohl's, Petco, Target, Verizon, W 🅿 Irving/Circle K/Dunkin'/dsl, Mr Gas 🅾 Bass Pro Shop, MktBasket Foods, Walmart/Subway
26mm	Merrimac River
9N S(24)	US 3, NH 28, Manchester, E 🅿 Irving/Dunkin'/Circle K/dsl 🏠 Fairfield Inn, W 🅿 Sunoco/dsl 🍴 Burger King, Cheng Du Chinese, Happy Garden Chinese, La Carreta Mexican, Lusia's Italian, Mr Mac's Cafe, PapaGino's, Puritan Rest., Shorty's Mexican, Subway, Villaggio Ristorante 🅾 Chrysler/Dodge/Jeep, city park, Hannaford Foods, Lincoln, O'Reilly Parts/VIP Service, U-Haul
8(23)	to NH 28a, Wellington Rd, W 🅾 🏠 Currier Gallery
7(22)	NH 101 E, to Portsmouth, Seacoast
6(21)	Hanover St, Candia Rd, Manchester, E 🍴 Dunkin', Wendy's 🅾 vet, W 🅿 Citgo, Mobil/dsl, Shell 🍴 Dunkin', McDonald's 🅾 🏠, GNC, Granite State Tire/auto, Hannaford Foods
19mm	I-293 W, to Manchester (from nb), 🅾 to 🔜
5(15)	NH 28, to N Londonderry, E 🅿 Irving/Dunkin'/dsl, Sunoco/dsl 🍴 Poor Boy's Diner, W 🅿 Shell/dsl 🍴 Subway 🏠 Sleep Inn
4(12)	NH 102, Derry, E 🅿 Mobil/dsl, Mutual, Rte 102, Shell/Dunkin'/dsl, Sunoco/dsl 🍴 Burger King, Cracker Barrel, Derry Rest., Juliano's Pizza, Subway 🅾 🏠, Advance Parts, R. Frost Farm, W 🅿 7-11, Global, Speedway 🍴 99 Rest., Dunkin', KFC/Taco Bell, La Carreta Mexican, McDonald's, PapaGino's, Starbucks, Wendy's 🅾 AT&T, Ford, GNC, Hannaford Foods, Home Depot, Mkt Basket Foods, O'Reilly Parts/VIP Service, Shaw's Foods, Staples, TJ Maxx, Town Fair Tire, USPO, Verizon
7mm	**weigh sta both lanes**
3(6)	NH 111, Windham, E 🅿 Mobil/McDonald's 🍴 House of Pizza, Windham Rest. 🅾 URGENT CARE, vet, W 🅿 B&H 🍴 33 Hilltop, Dunkin', Klemm's Bakery 🅾 Castleton Conference Ctr, CVS Drug, Osco Drug, Shaw's Foods, USPO
2(3)	to NH 38, NH 97, Salem, E 🍴 Tuscan Kitchen 🏠 Red Roof Inn, W 🍴 Blackwater Grill, Dunkin', Margarita's Cafe, Michael's Flatbread 🏠 Holiday Inn, La Quinta 🅾 URGENT CARE
1(2)	NH 28, Salem, E 🅿 Citgo/dsl, Gulf 🍴 99 Rest., Chili's, LJ Silver, Mary Ann's Diner, McDonald's, Panera Bread, PapaGino's, Taco Bell, T-Bones 🏠 Park View Inn 🅾 AT&T, Best Buy, Dick's, Home Depot, JC Penney, Kohl's, Lord&Taylor, Macy's, Marshall's, Meineke, Michael's, MktBasket Foods, NTB, PetCo, Petsmart, Staples, Target, TJ Maxx, TownFair Tire, Verizon, vet, Walgreens
1mm	**Welcome Ctr nb, full** ♿ **facilities, info, litter barrels, petwalk,** 🅿, 🚻, **vending**
0mm	New Hampshire/Massachusetts state line

🔼N INTERSTATE 95

Exit #	Services
17mm	New Hampshire/Maine state line, Piscataqua River
7 (16)	Market St, Portsmouth, Port Authority, E 🏠 Hampton Inn, Hilton Garden, Residence Inn, Sheraton, 0-2 mi W 🅿 BP, Mobil 🍴 Applebee's, D'Angelo, Dunkin', Panera Bread, Qdoba, Starbucks, Wendy's 🏠 Courtyard, Homewood Suites 🅾 $Tree, AutoZone, BJ's Whse/gas, Marshall's, MktBasket Foods, PepBoys, PetCo, Rite Aid, TJ Maxx, Verizon, vet, 🅾 waterfront hist sites
6(15)	Woodbury Ave (from nb), Portsmouth, E 🏠 Howard Johnson, W same as 7

5(14)	US 1, US 4, NH 16, The Circle, Portsmouth, E 🅿 Bypass Gas, Shell/dsl 🍴 Roudabout Diner 🏠 Anchorage Inn, Best Western+, Fairfield Inn, Holiday Inn, Howard Johnson, Port Inn 🅾 🏠, Buick/Cadillac/GMC, Chevrolet, U-Haul, W 🍴 Chipotle, Longhorn Steaks, McDonald's 🏠 Hampton Inn, Motel 6, Residence Inn 🅾 Barnes&Noble, Best Buy, Dick's, Ford/Lincoln, Home Depot, Kohl's, Mazda, Michael's, Nissan, Old Navy, Staples, Trader Joe's
4(13.5)	US 4 (exits left from nb), to White Mtns, Spaulding TPK, E 🅾 🏠, W 🅾 to Pease Int Trade Port
3a(13)	NH 33, Greenland
3b(12)	NH 33, to Portsmouth, E 🅾 🏠, 0-2 mi W 🅿 Sunoco/dsl, TA/Country Pride/dsl/scales/24hr/@ 🍴 Dunkin', McDonald's, Starbucks 🅾 Lowe's, Mercedes, Target, VW
6.5mm	**toll plaza**
2(6)	NH 101, to Hampton, W 🅾 🏠
4mm	Taylor River
1(1)	NH 107, to Seabrook, **toll rd begins/ends,** E 🅿 BP, Irving/Circle K/dsl, Mobil/dsl, Prime, Richdale, Shell, Sunoco/Subway/dsl 🍴 99 Rest., Applebee's, Burger King, Chili's, Dunkin', Five Guys, IHOP, KFC/Taco Bell, McDonald's, Outback Steaks, Panera Bread, Pizza Hut, Starbucks, Wendy's 🏠 Best Western Hampshire Inn, Holiday Inn Express 🅾 $Tree, Advance Parts, AutoZone, CVS Drug, Dick's, GNC, Hobby Lobby, Home Depot, Jo-Ann Fabrics, Kohl's, Lowe's, Meineke, MktBasket Foods, NTB, Petsmart, Staples, Sullivan Tire, TJ Maxx, TownFair Tire, Verizon, Walmart, W 🅿 Citgo 🍴 McGrath's Dining 🏠 Seabrook Inn 🅾 NAPA
.5mm	**Welcome Ctr nb, full** ♿ **facilities, litter barrels, petwalk,** 🅿, 🚻, **vending**
0mm	New Hampshire/Massachusetts state line

🔼N INTERSTATE 293 (Manchester)

Exit #	Services
8(9)	I-93, N to Concord, S to Derry. I-293 begins/ends on I-93, 28mm.
7(6.5)	NH 3A N, Dunbarton Rd (from nb)
6(6)	Amoskeag Rd, Singer Park, Manchester, E 🅿 Sunoco/dsl 🏠 La Quinta, W 🅿 Mobil, Shell/dsl 🍴 Dunkin', Hot Stone Pizza 🅾 🏠
5(5)	Granite St, Manchester (from nb, no EZ return), E 🍴 The Foundry 🏠 DoubleTree, W 🅿 7-11, Gulf 🍴 Dunkin', Subway 🅾 🏠, tires, Walgreens
4(4)	US 3, NH 3A, NH 114A, Queen City Br, E 🅿 7-11 🅾 Elliott 🏠, W 🅿 Mobil/dsl, Rapid Refill/dsl, Speedway/dsl 🍴 Applebee's, Burger King, Chen's Garden, D'angelo's, DQ, Dunkin', KC's Rib Shack, KFC, KFC, Little Caesar's, McDonald's, Panera Bread, Taco Bell, Wendy's 🏠 Comfort Inn, EconoLodge 🅾 $Tree, Family$, Subaru, Walmart

Vertical margin labels: MANCHESTER · DERRY · SALEM · PORTSMOUTH (left); PORTSMOUTH · SEABROOK · MANCHESTER (right)

■ = gas ⑪ = food ⌂ = lodging ⊙ = other Rs = rest stop   Copyright 2022 - The Next EXIT

⬆N INTERSTATE 293 (Manchester) Cont'd

Exit #	Services
3(3)	NH 101, **0-2 mi W on US 3** ⑪ Carrabba's, Chipotle, Dunkin', IHOP, Outback Steaks, Panera Bread, Starbucks, T-Bones, Whole Foods Mkt ⌂ Country Inn& Suites, Hampton Inn ⊙ CVS Drug, Hannaford's, Kohl's, Lexus, Lowe's, Marshall's, Mini, O'Reilly Parts/VIP Service, Rite Aid, Staples, Target, Trader Joe's, URGENT CARE, vet
2.5mm	Merrimac River
2(2)	NH 3A, Brown Ave, **S** ■ Mobil/dsl, Shell/Subway/dsl ⑪ Airport Diner, Dunkin', McDonald's ⌂ Holiday Inn, Homewood Suites, SpringHill Suites, Super 8 ⊙ Manchester Airport
1(1)	NH 28, S Willow Rd, **N** ■ Mobil/dsl, Sunoco/dsl ⑪ Boston Mkt, Burger King, Chipotle Mexican, CJ's Grill, Coldstone, Dunkin', Firehouse Subs, Five Guys, Friendly's, McDonald's, Panera Bread,

Exit #	Services
1(1)	Continued Papa John's, Pizza Hut, Sal's Pizza, Starbucks, Subway, Taco Be... Wendy's, Yee Dynasty Chinese ⌂ Fairfield Inn, Holiday Inn E... press, Quality Inn ⊙ H, $Tree, Aldi Foods, AT&T, AutoZon... Batteries+Bulbs, BJ's Whse, Buick/GMC, Chevrolet, CVS Dru... Hannaford Foods, Harley-Davidson, Home Depot, Kia, Mazd... Mercedes, Michael's, PepBoys, PetCo, Petsmart, Sullivan Tir... repair, TJ Maxx, TownFair Tire, U-Haul, URGENT CARE, Verizo... vet, VW, Walmart, **S** ■ Shell ⑪ '99 Rest., Bertucci's, Buffa... Wild Wings, ChuckeCheese, D'angelo's, FoodCourt, Great B... fet, La Carreta, Longhorn Steaks, Masa Japanese Steaks, Oli... Garden, Red Robin, TGIFriday's, TX Roadhouse ⌂ Courtya... TownePlace Suites ⊙ Barnes&Noble, Best Buy, BMW, CarMa... Ford, Hobby Lobby, Honda, Hyundai, JC Penney, Macy's, Nissa... NTB, Old Navy, Staples, Toyota
0mm	I-93, N to Concord, S to Derry. I-293 begins/ends on I-93.

NEW JERSEY

⬆E INTERSTATE 78

Exit #	Services
58b a	US 1N, US 9N, NJ Tpk
57	US 1S, US 9S, **N** ⌂ Doubletree, Howard Johnson, Ramada Inn, **S** ⌂ Courtyard, Fairfield Inn, SpringHill Suites ⊙ to Newark Airport
56	Clinton Ave (exits left from eb)
55	Irvington (from wb), **N** ■ Speedway/dsl ⑪ Burger King, Dunkin', Wendy's, White Castle ⊙ H, AutoZone
54	Hillside, Irvington (from eb), **N** ■ Speedway/dsl ⑪ Burger King, Dunkin', Wendy's, White Castle ⊙ H, AutoZone
52	Garden State Pkwy
50b a	Millburn (from wb), **N** ■ BP, Exxon, Lukoil ⑪ Manny's Wieners ⊙ Best Buy, Firestone/auto, Ford/Lincoln, Home Depot Superstore, Target, USPO, Whole Foods Mkt
49b a	NJ 124 (from eb), to Maplewood, same as 50b a
48	to NJ 24, to I-287 N, (exits left from eb), Springfield
48mm	I-78 eb divides into express & local
45	NJ 527 (from eb), Glenside Ave, Summit
44	(from eb), to Berkeley Heights, New Providence
43	to New Providence, Berkeley Heights
41	to Berkeley Heights, Scotch Plains
40	NJ 531, The Plainfields, **S** ⊙ H
36	NJ 651, to Warrenville, Basking Ridge, **N** ■ Exxon, Tesla EVC ⑪ Dunkin', **S** ■ Exxon
33	NJ 525, to Martinsville, Bernardsville, **N** ⑪ 3West Rest., LingLing Chinese, Starbucks ⌂ Courtyard ⊙ USGA Golf Museum, **S** ■ Exxon/7-11 ⑪ Chipotle, Panera Bread ⊙ Mavis Tire, Verizon
32mm	scenic overlook wb
29	I-287, to US 202, US 206, I-80, to Morristown, Somerville, **S** ⊙ H
26	NJ 523 spur, to North Branch, Lamington
24	NJ 523, to NJ 517, to Oldwick, Whitehouse, **2-3 mi S** ■ Exxon/dsl, Gulf/dsl ⑪ Readington Diner, Starbucks, Subway ⊙ Kings Mkt, Rite Aid, Walgreens
20b a	NJ 639 (from wb), to Cokesbury, Lebanon, **S** ■ Exxon, Sunoco ⑪ Dunkin', Janina Bistro, Kirsten's Italian ⌂ Courtyard ⊙ to Round Valley RA, vet
18	US 22 E, Annandale, Lebanon, **N** same as 17, **S** ⊙ H, Honda
17	NJ 31 S, Clinton, **N** ■ Exxon, Speedway, Valero/dsl ⑪ Baskin-Robbins/Dunkin', Finnigel's, McDonald's ⊙ Mavis Tire/auto, to Voorhees SP

Exit #	Services
16	NJ 31 N (from eb), Clinton, **N** same as 17
15	NJ 173 E, to Pittstown, Clinton, **N** ■ Express/repair, Shell/d... ⑪ Subway ⌂ Holiday Inn, **S** ⑪ Cracker Barrel, Frank's Ita... ian, Hunan Wok ⌂ Hampton Inn ⊙ H, GNC, ShopRite Food... TJ Maxx, Verizon, Walmart/Dunkin'
13	NJ 173 W (from wb), same as 12, **N** ⑪ Clinton Sta Diner
12	NJ 173, to Jutland, Norton, **N** ■ Clinton/dsl, Exxon/Dunkin... dsl, ▥▥/Subway/dsl/scales/24hr ⊙ to Spruce Run RA, ve... **S** ■ Shell ⑪ Bagelsmith Deli
11	NJ 173, West Portal, Pattenburg, **N** ■ Mobil, Shell/pizza/d... ⑪ American Spirits Rest., Chalet Rest. ⊙ Jugtown Campin... st police
8mm	Rs both lanes, litter barrels, no restrooms, ▦
7	NJ 173, to Bloomsbury, West Portal, **N** ⊙ RV camping, **S** ■ C... go/deli, ▥▥/Subway/dsl/scales/24hr, TA/Burger King/Count... Pride/dsl/scales/24hr/@
6mm	weigh sta both lanes
6	Warren Glen, Asbury (from eb)
4	Warren Glen, Stewartsville (from wb)
3	US 22, NJ 173, to Phillipsburg, **0-2 mi N** ■ BP/dsl, Penn Jerse... Trkstp/dsl/scales/24hr, Speedway/dsl, US/dsl, Wawa ⑪ A... plebee's, Chick-fil-A, Dunkin', Frank's Trattoria, IHOP, Key Ci... Diner, McDonald's, Panera Bread, Pizza Hut, Quaker Stea... Ruby Tuesday, Starbucks, Taco Bell, Teppanyaki, White Cast... ⌂ Best Value ⊙ H, $Tree, Advance Parts, Aldi, AutoZon... Best Buy, Hobby Lobby, Home Depot, Honda, Kohl's, Lowe'... Marshall's, Meineke, Michael's, Old Navy, PetCo, ShopRi... Foods, Stop&Shop, Target, Verizon, Walmart/Subway
0mm	New Jersey/Pennsylvania state line, Delaware River

⬆E INTERSTATE 80

Exit #	Services
	I-80 begins/ends on I-95, exit 69.
68	Leonia, Teaneck, **N** ⑪ Starbucks ⌂ Hampton Inn, Marrio... ⊙ H
68b a	I-95, N to New York, S to Philadelphia, to US 46
67	to Bogota (from eb)
66	Hudson St, to Hackensack
65	Green St, S Hackensack
64b a	NJ 17 S, to US 46 E, Newark, Paramus, **S** ■ BP/dsl ⑪ Crow... Nest Rest. ⌂ Hilton ⊙ Stop&Shop

NH NJ 3

NEWARK

CLINTON

CLINTON

▲E INTERSTATE 80 Cont'd

Exit #	Services
63	NJ 17 N, **N** 🚪 Amoco/7-11/dsl, BP, EVC, Exxon/dsl, Shell/dsl, Sunoco, Wawa/dsl 🍴 Boston Mkt, Chipotle, Longhorn Steaks, Outback Steaks, Starbucks ⬤ H, Acura, BMW, Harley-Davidson, Home Depot
62 b a	GS Pkwy, to Saddle Brook, **N** 🍴 Dunkin' 🛏 Garden Plaza, Marriott, **S** 🛏 Crowne Plaza
61	NJ 507, to Garfield, Elmwood Park, **N** ⬤ Marcal Paper Co
60	NJ 20, N to Hawthorne, **N** ⬤ H, Lowe's, Pepboys, Stern Tire/auto
59	Market St (from wb), to Paterson
58 b a	Madison Ave, to Paterson, Clifton, **S** ⬤ H
57c	Main St (from wb), to Paterson
57 b a	NJ 19 S, to Clifton, downtown Paterson
56 b a	Squirrelwood Rd, to Paterson, **S** 🚪 Lukoil/Dunkin'
55 b a	Union Blvd (from wb, no EZ return), Totowa, **N** 🚪 Shell/dsl, **S** 🛏 Holiday Inn ⬤ Cadillac
54	Minnisink Rd, to Paterson, **S** 🍴 Dunkin' ⬤ Home Depot
53	US 46 E, to NJ 3 (no eb return), to Wayne, Cliffton, **0-2 mi S** 🚪 Exxon 🍴 Applebee's, Bahama Breeze, Blaze Pizza, Brio Tuscan Grill, CA Pizza, Chipotle, IHOP, Olive Garden, Qdoba, Sonic, Starbucks, TGIFriday's ⬤ Bloomingdale's, Costco/gas, Hobby Lobby, JC Penney, Lord&Taylor, Macy's, Nissan, Office Depot, Old Navy
52	US 46, the Caldwells
48	to Montville (from wb), Pine Brook
47b	US 46 W, to Montclair, **N** 🚪 Sunoco 🍴 Five Guys, IHOP, Longhorn Steaks, Moe's SW, Wendy's 🛏 Holiday Inn, Travelodge ⬤ Home Depot, ShopRite Foods
47a	I-280 E, to The Oranges, Newark
45	to US 46, Lake Hiawatha, Whippany, **0-2 mi N on US 46** 🚪 BP/dsl, Gulf/dsl, Sunoco/dsl 🍴 Applebee's, Buffalo Wild Wings, Cuba Mia, Dunkin', Eccola Rest., Empire Diner, Five Guys, IHOP, Jasper Chinese, Longhorn Steaks, McDonald's, Moe's SW Grill, Outback Steaks, Panera Bread, Quin Dynasty, Sakura Japanese, Smashburger, Starbucks, Subway, Taco Bell, Wendy's 🛏 Budget Inn, Holiday Inn/rest., Ramada Ltd, Red Roof Inn, Travelodge ⬤ $Tree, Advance Parts, Firestone, Home Depot, Michael's, PepBoys, PetCo, ShopRite Foods, Staples, Verizon, Walgreens
43 b a	I-287, to US 46, Boonton, Morristown
42 b a	US 202, US 46, to Morris Plains, same as 39, Parsippany, **0-1 mi N on US 46** 🚪 76/Dunkin'/dsl, Exxon 🍴 Fuddrucker's, McDonald's, TGIFriday's, Wendy's 🛏 Courtyard, Days Inn, Fairfield Inn, Hampton Inn ⬤ Marshall's, Subaru
39	(38 from eb), US 46 E, to NJ 53, Denville, **0-2 mi N on US 46** 🚪 Citgo/dsl, Enrite Gas, Exxon, Speedway/Dunkin', Sunoco 🍴 Burger King, Casa Bella Italian, Charlie Brown's Steaks, Dunkin', Moe's SW Grill, Paul's Diner, Summit West Diner ⬤ H, Chevrolet, Verizon, Walgreens, **S** 🚪 Delta ⬤ Verizon
37	NJ 513, to Hibernia, Rockaway, **N** 🚪 Exxon/dsl, Shell 🍴 Dunkin', Hibernia Diner, River Barn Rest. 🛏 Hampton Inn, **S** 🚪 ⬤ H
35 b a	to Dover, Mount Hope, **S** 🚪 Exxon 🍴 Buffalo Wild Wings, Chipotle, Coldstone, Dunkin', Olive Garden, Red Robin, Riviera Mexican 🛏 Hilton Garden, Homewood Suites, TownePlace Suites ⬤ H, Best Buy, JC Penney, Lord&Taylor, Macy's, Michael's, Verizon
34 b a	NJ 15, to Sparta, Wharton, **N** 🚪 Exxon/dsl 🍴 Fortune Buffet ⬤ Rite Aid, USPO, **S** 🍴 Dunkin', Five Guys, Frank's Pizza, Panera Bread, Qdoba, Starbucks, Townsquare Diner ⬤ H, $Tree, Big Lots, Costco/gas, Dick's, Home Depot, Petsmart, ShopRite Foods, Target, Walmart/Subway

32mm	truck Rs wb
30	Howard Blvd, to Mt Arlington, **N** 🚪 Exxon/dsl, Quickchek Gas 🍴 Blossom Asian, Cracker Barrel, Davy's Hotdogs, Dunkin', Frank's Pizza 🛏 Courtyard, Holiday Inn Express ⬤ $Tree
28	US 46, to NJ 10, to Ledgewood, Lake Hopatcong, **1-2 mi S on US 46, NJ 10** 🚪 Speedway/dsl, Sunoco/dsl 🍴 Boston Mkt, Domino's, Dunkin', Fuddruckers, KFC, McDonald's, Muldoons Diner, Outback Steaks, Panera Bread, Red Lobster, Taco Bell, TGIFriday's, Wendy's, White Castle ⬤ AutoZone, Barnes&Noble, BJ's Whse, CVS Drug, Home Depot, Jo-Ann, Kohl's, Petco, ShopRite Foods, Toyota, Walgreens, Walmart
27	US 206 S, NJ 182, to Netcong, Somerville, **N** 🍴 Dunkin' ⬤ Ford, **S** 🚪 Shell/dsl 🍴 Applebee's, Chili's, Longhorn Steaks, McDonald's, Panera Bread, Subway, Wendy's 🛏 Extended Stay America ⬤ $Tree, Lowe's, Michael's, Old Navy, Petsmart, TJMaxx, Verizon, Walmart
26	US 46 W (from wb, no EZ return), to Budd Lake, same as 27, **S** 🚪 Conoco, Shell/dsl
25	US 206 N, to Newton, Stanhope, **1-2 mi N on US 206** 🚪 Exxon/dsl, Shell/dsl 🍴 Bellas Pizza, Blackforest Rest., Byram Diner, Dunkin', Empire Buffet, Frank's Pizza, McDonald's, Subway 🛏 Holiday Inn, Residence Inn ⬤ CVS Drug, Mavis Tire, Nissan, ShopRite Foods, to Waterloo Village, vet
23.5mm	Musconetcong River
21mm	⬤ picnic area both lanes, litter barrels, petwalk, 🚻, scenic overlook (eb)

🅟 = gas 🍴 = food 🛏 = lodging 🅞 = other 🆁🆂 = rest stop. Copyright 2022 - The Next EXIT

◆E INTERSTATE 80 Cont'd

Exit #	Services
19	NJ 517, to Hackettstown, Andover, N 🅟 Shell/dsl, **1-2 mi S** 🅟 Shell/dsl/repair 🍴 Terranova Pizza 🅞 🅷, 7-11, Stephen's SP, USPO
12	NJ 521, to Blairstown, Hope, N 🍴 Dunkin' 🅞 Harley-David-son, st police, S 🅟 US Gas 🍴 Hope Mkt Deli 🅞 Jenny Jump SF, Land of Make Believe, RV camping (5mi), USPO
7mm	🆁🆂 eb, full 🛏 facilities, info, litter barrels, petwalk, 🚻, 🅿, vending
6mm	scenic overlook wb, no trailers
4c	to NJ 94 N (from eb), to Blairstown
4b	to US 46 E, to Buttzville
4a	NJ 94, to US 46 E, to Portland, Columbia, N 🅟 TA/Pizza Hut/ Taco Bell/dsl/scales/24hr/@ 🍴 McDonald's 🅞 RV camping, S 🍴 Columbia Inn Rest. 🅞 USPO
3.5mm	Hainesburg Rd (from wb), accesses services at 4
2	**weigh sta eb**
1mm	N 🅞 Worthington SF
1	to Millbrook (from wb), N 🅞 Worthington SF
0mm	New Jersey/Pennsylvania state line, Delaware River

◆N INTERSTATE 95

Exit #	Services
124mm	New Jersey/New York state line, Hudson River, Geo Washing-ton Br
123mm	Palisades Pkwy (from sb)
73	NJ 67, Lemoine Ave, W 🅟 Sunoco 🍴 Five Guys, McDonald's 🅞 A&P Mkt, GNC, Verizon, Walgreens
72(122)	US 1, US 9, US 46, Ft Lee, E 🛏 Doubletree, W 🅟 Sunoco 🍴 McDonald's
71(121)	Broad Ave, Leonia, Englewood, E 🅟 Lukoil, W 🅟 Speedway 🛏 Holiday Inn
70(120)	to NJ 93, Leonia, Teaneck, W 🛏 Hampton Inn, Marriott
69(119)	I-80 W (from sb), to Paterson
68(118)	US 46, Challenger Blvd, Ridgefield Park, E 🅟 Exxon 🍴 Lan Garden Chinese 🛏 Day's Inn, Hampton Inn, Hilton Garden
117mm	**I-95 and NJ Turnpike run together sb.**

◆N NEW JERSEY TURNPIKE

Exit #	Services
	I-95 and NJ Turnpike run together sb.
18(117)	US 46 E, Ft Lee, Hackensack, **last exit before toll sb**
17(116)	Lincoln Tunnel
115mm	**Vince Lombardi Service Plaza nb, W** 🅟 Sunoco/dsl 🍴 Burger King, Nathan's, Popeye's
114mm	toll plaza, 🚻
16W(113)	NJ 3, Secaucus, Rutherford, E 🅟 Shell, Speedway 🛏 Hilton, W 🛏 Extended Stay America 🅞 Meadowlands
112mm	**Alexander Hamilton Service Area sb,** 🅟 Sunoco/dsl 🍴 Roy Rogers 🅞 gifts
16E(112)	NJ 3, Secaucus, E Lincoln Tunnel
15W(109)	I-280, Newark, The Oranges
15E(107)	US 1, US 9, Newark, Jersey City, E Lincoln Tunnel
14c	Holland Tunnel
14b	Jersey City
14a	Bayonne
14(105)	I-78 W, US 1, US 9, **2 mi** W 🛏 Courtyard, Fairfield Inn, Spring-Hill Suites 🅞 🖵
102mm	**Halsey Service Area,** 🅟 Sunoco/dsl 🍴 Roy Rogers, other ser-vices in Elizabeth

Exit #	Services
13a(102)	Elizabeth, E 🛏 Country Inn Suites, Courtyard, Embassy Suites, Extended Stay America, Residence Inn, W 🍴 McDonald' 🛏 Crowne Plaza, Days Inn, Hampton Inn, Hilton, Rennaisance services on US1/US9
13(100)	I-278, to Verrazano Narrows Bridge
12(96)	Carteret, Rahway, E 🍴 McDonald's 🛏 Holiday Inn 🅞 CV Drug, Walgreens, W 🛏 Executive Suites
93mm	**Cleveland Service Area nb, T Edison Service Area sb,** 🍴 Burg-er King, Dunkin', Popeye's, Roy Rogers, Sbarro's, Starbuck Starbucks
11(91)	US 9, Garden State Pkwy, to Woodbridge, E 🍴 McDon-ald's 🛏 Hampton Inn 🅞 $Tree, Home Depot, Walmart, W 🅟 Speedway/dsl 🛏 Residence Inn, The Forge Inn
10(88)	I-287, NJ 514, to Perth Amboy, E 🅟 Speedway/dsl 🛏 Court-yard, Edison Hotel
9(83)	US 1, NJ 18, to New Brunswick, E Brunswick, E 🅟 Gulf, Mo-bil/dsl, Speedway/dsl 🍴 Bone Fish Grill, Boston Mkt, Burg-er King, Carrabba's, Dunkin', Grand Buffet, Hooters, Jerse Mike's, KFC, McDonald's, Perkins, Popeye's, Starbucks 🛏 Days Hotel, Motel 6 🅞 $Tree, AT&T, Best Buy, Dick's, Kohl' Lowe's, Petsmart, ShopRite Foods, TJ Maxx, Walmart/Subwa W 🅟 Exxon 🍴 Famous Dave's, Houlihan's, On the Border 🛏 Hilton, Holiday Inn Express
79mm	**Kilmer Service Area nb, Kilmer Service Area,** 🍴 Burger King Cookies and Creamery, Sbarro, Starbucks 🅞 Sunoco/dsl
8a(74)	to Jamesburg, Cranbury, W 🛏 Courtyard, Crowne Plaza
72mm	**Pitcher Service Area,** 🅟 Sunoco/dsl 🍴 Cinnabon, Dick Clark AB Grill, Nathan's, Roy Rogers, Starbucks
8(67)	NJ 33, NJ 571, Highstown, E 🅟 Petro/dsl, Shell/Dunkin'/ds Speedway/dsl 🍴 Prestige Diner 🛏 Days Inn, Hampton Inn Holiday Inn 🅞 CVS Drug, vet, W 🛏 Quality Inn, Townhous Motel
7a(60)	I-195 W to Trenton, E to Neptune
59mm	**Richard Stockton Service Area sb** 🅟 Sunoco/dsl, 🍴 Burge King, Nathan's, Pizza Hut, Quiznos, Roy Rogers, Starbuck TCBY, **Woodrow Wilson Service Area nb** 🅟 Sunoco
7(54)	US 206, to Bordentown, to Ft Dix, McGuire AFB, to I-295, Trento W 🅟 AmeriGas, Delta/dsl, Exxon, Gulf, ♥Loves/Wendy' dsl/scales/24hr, Petro/Iron Skillet/dsl/scales/24hr/@, Sunoc Valero/dsl 🍴 Denny's, Dunkin', McDonald's 🛏 Best Wester Comfort Inn, Days Inn, Hampton Inn, Ramada Inn 🅞 WaWa
6(51)	I-276, to PA Tpk
5(44)	to Mount Holly, Willingboro, E 🅟 AJ's Gas/dsl 🍴 Applebee Charlie Brown's Steaks, Cracker Barrel, McDonald's, Recovery Gr 🛏 Best Western, Hampton Inn, Hilton Garden, Quality Inn 🅞 ve W 🅟 BP, Exxon/dsl, Valero/dsl 🍴 Burger King, China Hous Dunkin', IHOP, TGIFriday's 🛏 Courtyard, Holiday Inn Expre 🅞 $Tree, AT&T, Dick's, Home Depot, Kohl's, Motel 6, Target
39mm	**James Fenimore Cooper Service Area nb,** 🅟 Sunoco/d 🍴 Burger King, Cinnabon, Popeye's, Roy Rogers, TCBY 🅞 gif
4(34)	NJ 73, to Philadelphia, Camden, E 🅟 US Gas, WaWa/d 🍴 Applebee's, Chili's, Cracker Barrel, Dunkin', Kazumi, M Donald's, On-the-Border, Sage Rest., TGIFriday's, Wendy 🛏 Candlewood Suites, Comfort Inn, Extended Stay Americ Hampton Inn, Hilton Garden, Holiday Inn Express, Hyatt Hous Hyatt Place, Knights Inn, La Quinta, Rodeway Inn, Staybridg Suites, Wyndham Hotel 🅞 BMW, Cadillac, Lexus, Mini, Toyot Verizon, Whole Foods Mkt, W 🅟 Lukoil 🍴 Bob Evans, Mille Alehouse, Starbucks 🛏 aLoft, Courtyard, Fairfield Inn, Hot ML, Red Roof Inn, Super 8, Westin
30mm	**Walt Whitman Service Area sb, Walt Whitman Service Are** 🅟 Sunoco 🍴 Cinnabon, Nathan's, Roy Rogers, TCBY 🅞 gif

NJ

⬆N NEW JERSEY TURNPIKE Cont'd

Exit #	Services
3(26)	NJ 168, Atlantic City Expwy, Walt Whitman Br, Camden, Woodbury, E 🔲 Pioneer, WaWa/dsl 🔲 Antonietta's, Luigi's Pizza, Pat's Pizza, Phily Diner, Rita's Custard 🔲 Days Inn, La Quinta 🔲 Advance Parts, CVS Drug, Toyota, Walgreens, W 🔲 Riggins, Shell/dsl, Valero/dsl 🔲 Burger King, Club Diner, Dunkin', Vero Pizzaria, Wendy's 🔲 Bellmawr Motel, EconoLodge, Howard Johnson, Red Roof Inn, Super 8
2(13)	US 322, to Swedesboro, W 🔲 Shell/Dunkin'/dsl
5mm	Barton Service Area sb, Fenwick Service Area nb, 🔲 Sunoco/dsl 🔲 Burger King, Nathan's, Pizza Hut, Starbucks, TCBY
1(1.2)	Deepwater, W 🔲 Gulf, 🔲Pilot🔲/Subway/dsl/scales/24hr 🔲 Comfort Inn, Friendship Motor Inn, Holiday Inn Express, Red Carpet Inn
1mm	toll road begins/ends
2(I-295)	I-295 N divides from toll road, I-295 S converges with toll road.
1(I-295)	NJ 49, to Pennsville, E 🔲 WaWa/dsl 🔲 Applebee's, Burger King, Cracker Barrel, Dunkin', KFC/Taco Bell, McDonald's 🔲 Hampton Inn, Super 8 🔲 Peterbilt, W 🔲 Coastal 🔲 Seaview Motel
0mm	New Jersey/Delaware state line, Delaware River, Delaware Memorial Bridge

⬆N INTERSTATE 195

Exit #	Services
36	Garden State Parkway N. I-195 begins/ends on GS Pkwy, exit 98.
35b a	NJ 34, to Brielle, GS Pkwy S., Pt Pleasant, 0-2 mi S 🔲 Exxon/dsl, Getty/dsl, Lukoil/dsl 🔲 Legends Japanese
31b a	NJ 547, NJ 524, to Farmingdale, N 🔲 to Allaire SP
28b a	US 9, to Freehold, Lakewood, N 🔲 LukOil/7-11/dsl, WaWa/dsl 🔲 Ivy League Grill, Lino's Pizza, Stewart's Drive-In 🔲 At 9 Motel, S 🔲 Exxon, Gulf, LukOil, QuickChek/dsl, WaWa 🔲 Applebee's, Arby's, Baskin-Robbins/Dunkin', Boston Mkt, Chick-fil-A, China Moon, Chipotle, Dunkin', Five Guys, IHOP, Jersey Mike's Subs, Longhorn Steaks, Luigi's Pizza, McDonald's, Panera Bread, Pizza Hut, Ruby Tuesday, Sonic, Starbucks, Subway, Taco Bell 🔲 $Tree, Advance Parts, AT&T, Barnes&Noble, Best Buy, BJ's/dsl, CVS Drug, GNC, Hobby Lobby, Kohl's, Lowe's, Michael's, PepBoys, PetCo, Petsmart, repair, ShopRite Foods, Staples, Stop&Shop, Target, TJ Maxx, USPO, Verizon, vet, Walgreens, Walmart/McDonald's
22	to Jackson Mills, Georgia, N 🔲 to Turkey Swamp Park, 2 mi S 🔲 McDonald's 🔲 ShopRite Foods
21	NJ 526, NJ 527, to Jackson, Siloam
16	NJ 537, to Freehold, N 🔲 Citgo/dsl, Sunoco 🔲 FoodCourt, GianMarco's Pizza 🔲 H, Jackson Outlets/famous brands, S 🔲 WaWa/dsl 🔲 Burger King, Chicken Holiday, Dunkin', KFC/LJ Silver, McDonald's, McGinns Pizzaria, Rio Grande Mexican, Tommy's Rest. 🔲 Six Flags
11	NJ 524, Imlaystown, N 🔲 to Horse Park of NJ
8	NJ 539, Hightstown, Allentown, S 🔲 Shell (1mi), Valero/repair 🔲 Sam's Deli 🔲 vet
7	NJ 526, Robbinsville, Allentown, N 🔲 Hampton Inn, 1 mi S 🔲 La Piazza Ristorante
6	NJ Tpk, N to NY, S to DE Memorial Br
5b a	US 130, N 🔲 Delta/dsl/repair, Valero/dsl 🔲 Domino's, Dunkin', Rusert's Deli, ShrimpKing Rest., Taco Bell 🔲 Homewood Suites 🔲 AAA, vet, S 🔲 GS Fuel/dsl, WaWa/dsl 🔲 Chick-fil-A, Chili's, China Grill, Cracker Barrel, DQ, Jersey Mike's Subs, Longhorn Steaks, McDonald's, Outback Steaks, Panchero's, Panera Bread, Red Robin, Ruby Tuesday, Subway,

5b a	Continued
	TGIFriday's, Wendy's 🔲 Hilton Garden, Residence Inn 🔲 $Tree, AT&T, Barnes&Noble, BJ's Whse, GNC, Harry's Army Navy, Home Depot, Honda, Kohl's, Lowe's, Michael's, Old Navy, Petsmart, Ross, ShopRite Foods, Staples, to state aquarium, USPO, Verizon, Walmart
3b a	Hamilton Square, Yardville, N 🔲 H
2	US 206 S, S Broad St, Yardville, S 🔲 BP, Shell/dsl 🔲 Subway 🔲 $Tree, 7-11, CVS Drug, Rite Aid
1b a	US 206 (eb only), N 🔲 Circle Deli, Taco Bell 🔲 Advance Parts, Midas, S 🔲 Papa John's 🔲 ShopRite Foods
0mm	I-295, I-195 begins/ends.

⬆N INTERSTATE 287

Exit #	Services
68mm	New Jersey/New York state line
66	NJ 17 S, Mahwah, 1-3 mi E 🔲 Amoco/dsl, BP, Liberty/dsl, 🔲Pilot🔲/dsl, Sunoco/dsl, Valero/Subway/dsl 🔲 Boston Mkt, Burger King, Dunkin', McDonald's 🔲 Comfort Suites, Courtyard, Doubletree, Hampton Inn, Homewood Suites, Sheraton, Super 8 🔲 Buick/GMC, Cadillac, Chrysler/Dodge/Jeep, Home Depot, Honda, Hyundai
59	NJ 208 S, Franklin Lakes
58	US 202, Oakland, E 🔲 Lukoil/dsl 🔲 Jr's Pizza, Luca Pizza, Mike's Doghouse, Pizza Hut, Starbucks, Subway 🔲 $Tree, Staples, USPO, Walgreens, W 🔲 Exxon
57	Skyline Dr, Ringwood
55	NJ 511, Pompton Lakes, E 🔲 Frank's Pizza, Starbucks, Thatcher McGhee Eatery, Wendy's, W 🔲 Gulf/dsl 🔲 Baskin-Robbins, Burger King, Dunkin' 🔲 Holiday Inn Express 🔲 CVS Drug, Stop'n Shop
53	NJ 511A, rd 694, Bloomingdale, Pompton Lakes, E 🔲 Sunoco, Valero 🔲 Dunkin', Karen's Country Kitchen 🔲 USPO
52b a	NJ 23, Riverdale, Wayne, Butler, 0-3 mi E 🔲 Amoco/dsl, BP, BP/dsl, Delta, Sunoco 🔲 23 Buffet, Dunkin', Jersey Mike's, Moe's SW Grill, Pompton Queen Diner, Stefano's Pizza 🔲 H, 7-11, GNC, Honda, Kia, Pepboys, Stop&Shop, Subaru, TJ Maxx, Toyota, VW, W 🔲 Lukoil 🔲 Applebee's, Chili's, Dunkin, Flaming Grill, Santinas Pizza, Subway, Wendy's 🔲 Best Buy, BJ's Whse, Home Depot, Jo-Ann, Lowes Whse, Staples, Target, Walmart
47	US 202, Montville, Lincoln Park, E 🔲 Exxon 🔲 Harrigan's Rest., Montville Inn Rest.
45	Myrtle Ave, Boonton, W 🔲 Shell/dsl, Speedway 🔲 Dunkin', Jr's Pizza, McDonald's, Starbucks, Subway 🔲 Acme Mkt, Buick/Chevrolet, Verizon, Walgreens
43	Intervale Rd, to Mountain Lakes, E 🔲 Valero/dsl

NEW JERSEY TURNPIKE / MAHWAH (margin tabs)

◻ = gas   ◻ = food   ◻ = lodging   ◻ = other   ◻ = rest stop   Copyright 2022 - The Next EXIT

INTERSTATE 287 Cont'd

Exit #	Services
42	US 46, US 202 (from sb only), W◻ Conoco/Dunkin'/dsl, Exxon ◻ Fuddrucker's, McDonald's, TGIFriday's, Wendy's ◻ Courtyard, Day's Inn, Embassy Suites, Fairfield Inn, Hampton Inn ◻ CVS Drug, Marshall's, Subaru, USPO
41b a	I-80, E to New York, W to Delaware Water Gap
40	NJ 511, Parsippany Rd, to Whippany, W◻ Petro Hub, Shell/dsl, Woroco Gas ◻ Carrot Chinese, Frank&Son Pizza, Subway ◻ Embassy Suites (1mi) ◻ vet
39b a	NJ 10, Dover, Whippany, E ◻ Exxon, Quickchek/dsl ◻ Brookside Diner, Dunkin', Jersey Mike's, Palermo's Pizza, Pancake House, Whippany Diner ◻ CVS Drug, W◻ Liberty/dsl, Lukoil, Raceway ◻ Chick-fil-A, Chipotle, Dunkin', Smashburger, Subway, Wendy's, Zin Burger ◻ Best Value Inn, Hilton, Hyatt House, Marriott ◻ Barnes&Noble, Buick/GMC, GNC, Harley Davidson, Kohl's, Stop'n Shop, Verizon
37	NJ 24 E, Springfield
36b a	rd 510, Morris Ave, Lafayette
35	NJ 124, South St, Madison Ave, Morristown, E ◻ Friendly's ◻ Richie's Country Store, vet, W ◻ Best Western+ ◻ ◻, Rite Aid, Walgreens
33	Harter Rd
33mm	E truck ◻ nb, full ◻ facilities, litter barrels, petwalk, ◻, ◻, vending
30b a	to US 202, N Maple Ave, Basking Ridge, E ◻ The Ridge, W ◻ EVC, Gulf, Lukoil ◻ GrainHouse Rest., Vine Rest. ◻ Olde Mill Inn/rest.
26b a	rd 525 S, Mt Airy Rd, Liberty Corner, 3 mi E◻ Exxon ◻ Chipotle, Panera Bread ◻ Courtyard, Somerset Hotel
22b a	US 202, US 206, Pluckemin, Bedminster, E◻ Exxon, Exxon/dsl ◻ Coldstone, Dunkin', Golden Palace, Panchero's, Rocco's Pizza, Starbucks, Subway ◻ CVS Drug, Fresh Mkt, King's Foods, URGENT CARE, Verizon
21b a	I-78, E to NY, W to PA
17	US 206 (from sb), Bridgewater, W ◻ Exxon ◻ Buffalo Wild Wings, CA Pizza, Cheesecake Factory, Chipotle Mexican, Dunkin', KFC, Maggiano's Italian, McDonald's, Redstone, Seasons 52 Grill, Taco Bell, TGIFriday, Wendy's ◻ Marriott ◻ Best Buy, Bloomingdale's, Lord&Taylor, Macy's
14b a	US 22, to US 202/206, E ◻ Speedway/dsl ◻ Chevrolet/Lexus, W ◻ BP, Sunoco/dsl, Valero/dsl ◻ Houlihan's, Red Lobster ◻ Hampton Inn ◻ Acura, Chrysler/Dodge/Jeep, Fiat, Ford, Infiniti, Kia, Mercedes, Nissan, Volvo
13b a	NJ 28, Bound Brook, E◻ 76/dsl, BP/dsl ◻ 30 Burgers, Burger King, Dunkin', Frank's Pizza, Girasole Rest., Little Caesar's ◻ 7-11, AT&T, AutoZone, QuickChek Mkt, ShopRite Foods, Walgreens, W ◻ WaWa/dsl ◻ Applebee's, ChuckeCheese, McDonald's, Panchero's ◻ Hilton Garden ◻ ◻, 7-11, Costco, Home Depot, Marshall's, Michael's, Old Navy, PepBoys, PetsMart, Target
12	Weston Canal Rd, Manville, E◻ USPO, W ◻ Hooters ◻ Clarion
10	NJ 527, Easton Ave, New Brunswick, E ◻ Hotel Somerset, W ◻ Exxon ◻ Dunkin', Ichiban, Ruby Tuesday, Subway, Wild Ginger Asian ◻ Candlewood Suites, Comfort Inn, Courtyard, Doubletree, Extended Stay America, Fairbridge Inn, Fairfield Inn, Homewood Suites, Residence Inn, Sonesta Suites, SpringHill Suites ◻ ◻, Garden State Conv Ctr
9	NJ 514, River Rd, W◻ Delta ◻ Dunkin' ◻ Embassy Suites, Radisson
8.5mm	weigh sta nb
8	Possumtown Rd, Highland Park

Exit #	Services
7	S Randolphville Rd, Piscataway, E◻ Lukoil/dsl
6	Washington Ave, Piscataway, E◻ Shell/7-11/dsl ◻ Popeye ◻ AutoZone, W ◻ Applebee's, Chand Palace, Gourmet P za, Healthy Garden, Longhorn Steaks, Olive Garden, Pane Bread, Piscataway Pizza, Smashburger, Starbucks, Subw. TGIFriday's, Thai Basil ◻ 99c Depot, Aldi Foods, GNC, Low Whse, PetCo, same as 5, ShopRite Foods, Walmart/McDonal
5	NJ 529, Stelton Rd, Dunellen, E◻ BP/dsl, Gulf/dsl, Luko dsl ◻ Enzo's Pizza, KFC ◻ Red Carpet Inn ◻ Advan Parts, Goodyear/auto, Home Depot, Meineke, Stop'n Shop, ◻ Exxon, WaWa/dsl ◻ Brickhouse Rest., Burger King, Chip tle, Dunkin', El Toro Loco, Five Guys, Fontainbleu Diner, Gab eles Grill, Gianni Pizza, IHOP, Joe's Crabshack, Panda Expre Pizza Hut, Red Lobster, Red Robin, Taco Bell, Villa Pizza, We dy's, White Castle ◻ Garden Executive Hotel, Hampton Ir Holiday Inn, Motel 6, Woodspring Suites ◻ $Tree, Burlingt Coats, Dick's, Kohl's, Marshall's, Mavis Tire, NAPA, Pep Boy Staples, Target, Tuesday Morning, Verizon
4	Durham Ave (from nb, no EZ return), S Plainfield, E◻ Fu lOne/dsl ◻ McDonald's, Subway ◻ ◻, Firestone/auto
3	New Durham Rd (from sb), E◻ Shell, W ◻ Dunkin', R Onion Chinese ◻ Fairfield Inn, Home 2 Suites, Red Roof I ◻ Walgreens
2b a	NJ 27, Metuchen, New Brunswick, E ◻ Brownstone Grill, ◻ BP, Lukoil ◻ Dunkin' ◻ Costco/gas, Petsmart, USF Walmart/Subway
1b a	US 1, N◻ Exxon/dsl, Raceway/dsl, Shell, Tesla EVC ◻ Be hana, Cheesecake Factory, Dunkin', Famous Dave's BBQ, Ho lihan's, IHOP, Little Italy, Macaroni Grill, McDonald's, Men Park Diner, Panera Bread, Seasons 52 Grill, Sonic, White Cast ◻ Barnes&Noble, Firestone/auto, Goodyear/auto, Macy Midas, Nordstrom's, Target, S ◻ Shell/7-11/dsl ◻ Appl bee's, Boston Mkt, ChuckeCheese, Jersey Mike's, McDonald Starbucks, Zinburger ◻ Comfort Inn, Quality Inn ◻ $Tre AT&T, BJ's Whse, Home Depot, Infiniti, Land Rover/Jagua Porche, Mercedes, Office Depot, PepBoys, PetCo, Sam's Clu gas, Stop&Shop Foods, Volvo
0mm	I-287 begins/ends on NJ 440. I-95/NJ Tpk

INTERSTATE 295

Exit #	Services
77mm	New Jersey/Delaware state line, Delaware River, Delaware M morial Bridge
76	1 NJ 29, to Trenton, 2 mi W◻ st police museum
75	NJ 579, to Harbourton, E◻ LukOil (1mi) ◻ Dunkin', Red St Pizza ◻ 7-11, W◻ BP
73b a	Scotch Rd, E◻ Courtyard, W◻ ◻
72b a	NJ 31, to Ewing, Pennington, E◻ Citgo/repair, Exxon/repa LukOil/Dunkin'/dsl ◻ SpringHill Suites ◻ Robbins Drug, ◻ Exxon, LukOil/Blimpie/dsl ◻ Mizuki Asian, Starbuc ◻ ShopRite Foods, Stop&Shop Foods
71b a	Federal City Rd (sb only)
69b a	US 206, W◻ LukOil/dsl ◻ Fox's Pizza, Starbucks
68b a	NJ 583, NJ 546, to Princeton Pike
67b a	US 1, to Trenton, New Brunswick, E◻ Shell, WaWa/McDo ald's/dsl ◻ Michael's Diner ◻ Howard Johnson, Sleepy Ho low Motel ◻ Acura, 0-3 mi W ◻ LukOil/dsl ◻ Applebee' Bahama Breeze, Big Fish Bistro, Bonefish Grill, Brick House Ta ern, Brio Grille, Buffalo Wild Wings, Cheesecake Factory, Ch potle, ChuckECheese's, Corner Bakery Cafe, Dunkin', Firehous Subs, Hooters, Houlihan's, Jersey Mike's, Joe's Crabshac

Vertical labels: **PISCATAWAY**, **BRIDGEWATER**, **NJ**

⬆N INTERSTATE 295 Cont'd

67b a | Continued
Olive Garden, On-the-Border, Outback Steaks, Panera Bread, Pei Wei, PF Chang's, Red Lobster, Seasons 32, Smashburger, Starbucks, Subway, TGIFriday's, Wendy's 🛏 Clarion, Comfort Inn, Extended Stay America, Hyatt Place, Hyatt Regency, Red Roof Inn, Residence Inn Ⓞ $Tree, AT&T, Barnes&Noble, Best Buy, Buick/Cadillac/GMC, Chevrolet, Dick's, Firestone/auto, Hobby Lobby, Home Depot, JC Penney, Jo-Ann Fabrics, Kohl's, Lord&Taylor, Lowe's, Macy's, malls, Marshall's, Michael's, Mini, NTB, Old Navy, PepBoys, PetCo, Petsmart, REI, Ross, ShopRite Foods, Staples, Target, TJ Maxx, Trader Joe's, Verizon, Walmart, Wegman's Foods, Whole Foods Mkt

65b a | Sloan Ave, **E** ⛽ Exxon 🍴 Burger King, DeLorenzo's Pizza, Dunkin', Five Guys, New China Buffet, Subway, Taco Bell, Uno Grill Ⓞ Goodyear/auto, Risoldi's Mkt

64 | NJ 535 N (from sb), to NJ 33 E, same as 63

63b a | NJ 33 W, rd 535, Mercerville, Trenton, **E on rd 33** ⛽ Lukoil, Speedway/dsl, Valero 🍴 Applebee's, Lucky Star Buffet, McDonald's, Pizza Hut, Popeye's, Stewart's Rootbeer, Subway, Vincent's Pizza Ⓞ Ace Hardware, auto repair, CVS Drug, Ford/Subaru, Rite Aid, USPO, **W** ⛽ Exxon 🍴 Dunkin', White Horse Diner Ⓞ Advance Parts, Family$, transmissions, Walgreens, Walmart, WaWa

62 | Olden Ave N (from sb, no return), **W** ⛽ Delta, Exxon

61b a | Arena Dr, White Horse Ave, **W** Ⓞ 7-11

60b a | I-195, to I-95, W to Trenton, E to Neptune

58mm | scenic overlook both lanes

57b a | US 130, to US 206, **E** ⛽ Amera, Valero 🍴 Denny's, Dunkin', McDonald's, Rosario's Pizza 🛏 Best Western, Days Inn, Ramada Inn Ⓞ Aldi, **W** 🍴 Starbucks 🛏 Candlewood Suites Ⓞ Acme Foods, st police, Verizon

56 | to US 206 S (from nb, no return), to NJ Tpk, Ft Dix, McGuire AFB, **E** ⛽ ⬤Loves/Wendy's/dsl/scales/24hr, Petro/Iron Skillet/dsl/scales/24hr/@ 🛏 Days Inn, Hampton Inn Ⓞ Blue Beacon, same as 57, **W** 🛏 Candlewood Suites Ⓞ st police

52b a | rd 656, to Columbus, Florence, **3 mi E** ⛽ ⬤Loves/Wendy's/dsl/scales/24hr, Petro/Iron Skillet/dsl/scales/24hr/@

47b a | NJ 541, to Mount Holly, NJ Tpk, Burlington, **E** ⛽ BP, Exxon/dsl, Valero/dsl 🍴 Applebee's, Burger King, China House, Cracker Barrel, Dunkin', IHOP, Recovery Grill, TGIFriday's 🛏 Best Western, Courtyard, Hampton Inn, Hilton Garden, Holiday Inn Express, Motel 6, Quality Inn Ⓞ $Tree, AT&T, Dick's, Home Depot, Kohl's, Target, **W** ⛽ BP, Citgo/dsl, Gulf/dsl, WaWa/dsl 🍴 Checker's, Chick-fil-A, Dunkin', Kum Fong, Subway, Villa Pizza, Wendy's Ⓞ Ⓗ, AutoZone, Marshall's, ShopRite, Walmart/Subway

45b a | to Mt Holly, Willingboro, **W** ⛽ LukOil/dsl Ⓞ Ⓗ, auto repair

43b a | rd 636, to Rancocas Woods, Delran, **W** ⛽ Exxon 🍴 Carlucci's Rest.

40b a | NJ 38, to Mount Holly, Moorestown, **E** 🍴 Ruby Tuesday 🛏 Residence Inn, **W** ⛽ Amera/dsl, WaWa/dsl 🍴 Anthony's Pizza, Arby's, Chick-fil-A, Chipotle, Dunkin', Jimmy John's, Naf Naf Grill, Panera Bread, Qdoba, Starbucks, Subway, TGIFriday's, Wendy's 🛏 SpringHill Suites Ⓞ Ⓗ, Costco/gas, GNC, Jo-Ann Fabrics, Petsmart, Target, TJ Maxx, UHaul, Wegman's Foods

36b a | NJ 73, to NJ Tpk, Tacony Br, Berlin, **E** ⛽ LukOil/dsl 🍴 Bob Evans, Miller's Alehouse, Starbucks 🛏 aLoft, Courtyard, EconoLodge, Fairfield Inn, Hotel ML, Red Roof Inn, Super 8, TownePlace Suites, Westin, **W** ⛽ Citgo, Shell, WaWa/dsl 🍴 Bertucci's, Boscov's, Boston Mkt, Buffalo Wild Wings, Burger King, Chick-fil-A, Chipotle Mexican, Corner Cafe, Don Pablo, Dunkin', Five Guys, Friendly's, Jersey Mike's, Old Town Buffet,

---

36b a | Continued
Panera Bread, Pei Wei, Perkins, PJ Whelahin's, Popeye's, The Melting Pot, Uno Grill, Wendy's 🛏 Crossland Suites, Homewood Suites, Motel 6, Quality Inn Ⓞ $Tree, Acura, Advance Parts, AT&T, AutoZone, Barnes&Noble, Best Buy, Dick's, Fiat, Ford/Lincoln, Home Depot, Infiniti, Lord&Taylor, Lowe's, Marshall's, Michael's, Mr Tire, Old Navy, PepBoys, PepBoys, Petsmart, Ross, ShopRite Foods, Staples

34b a | NJ 70, to Camden, Cherry Hill, **E** ⛽ BP, Exxon, WaWa 🍴 Burger King, Dunkin', PJ Whelihans, Rock Hill Rest., Stacy's Korean BBQ 🛏 Extended Stay America, Residence Inn Ⓞ Mavis Tire, Tires+, **W** ⛽ Jersey Gas, LukOil, US Gas 🍴 Dunkin', Famous Dave's BBQ, Han Dynasty, McDonald's, Norma's Rest., Ponzio's Rest, Qdoba, Rita's, Salad Works, Seasons Pizza, Starbucks 🛏 Woodspring Suites Ⓞ Ⓗ, $Tree, AT&T, CVS Drug, Goodyear/auto, Mom's Mkt, Rite Aid, vet, WaWa, Whole Foods Mkt

32 | NJ 561, to Haddonfield, Voorhees, **E** ⛽ LukOil/dsl 🍴 Herman's Deli, Hunan Wok, Tucchi's Pizza, Vito's Pizza Ⓞ Ⓗ, $Tree, Trio Tire, USPO, **W** ⛽ Pioneer/dsl 🍴 Burger King, Dunkin', Subway, Tutti Toscani Ⓞ 7-11, Ford

31 | Woodcrest Station

30 | Warwick Rd (from sb)

29b a | US 30, to Berlin, Collingswood, **E** ⛽ Astro/dsl, Citgo/dsl, Valero/dsl, WaWa/dsl 🍴 Arby's, Church's, Dunkin', McDonald's, Popeye's, Wendy's, Wild Wing Cafe Ⓞ AutoZone, Home Depot, Lowe's, Petsmart, ShopRite

28 | NJ 168, to NJ Tpk, Belmawr, Mt Ephraim, **E** ⛽ Riggins, Shell/dsl, Valero/dsl 🍴 Burger King, Club Diner, Dunkin', Vero Pizzaria, Wendy's 🛏 Bellmawr Motel, EconoLodge, Howard Johnson, Red Roof Inn, Super 8, **W** ⛽ BP, Conoco, Speedway/dsl, WaWa/dsl 🍴 Applebee's, Arby's, Black Horse Diner, Chick-fil-A, Da Vinci'sRest., Domino's, Dunkin', Little Caesar's, McDonald's, Pizza Hut/Taco Bell, Sonic Ⓞ Acme Foods, AutoZone, Chrysler/Dodge, CVS Drug, Firestone/auto, Harley-Davidson, Meinke, Midas, Mr Tire, PepBoys, URGENT CARE, USPO, Walgreens, Walmart/Subway

26 | I-76, NJ 42, to I-676 (exits left from sb), Walt Whitman Bridge, Walt Whitman Bridge

25b a | NJ 47, to Westville, Deptford

24b a | NJ 45, NJ 551 (no EZ sb return), to Westville, **E** Ⓞ Ⓗ, AutoZone, **W** Ⓞ Chevrolet, Family$

23 | US 130 N, to National Park

22 | NJ 644, to Red Bank, Woodbury, **E** ⛽ Citgo 🍴 Dunkin', **1 mi W** ⛽ Crown Point Trkstp/dsl/@

21 | NJ 44 S, Paulsboro, Woodbury, **W** 🍴 WaWa, Wendy's 🛏 Westwood Motor Lodge

20 | NJ 44, rd 643, to National Park, Thorofare, **E** 🛏 Best Western, **W** 🛏 Red Bank Inn

19 | to NJ 44, rd 656, Mantua

🅖 = gas 🅕 = food 🛏 = lodging 🅞 = other 🆁🆂 = rest stop   Copyright 2022 - The Next EXIT

⬆🅝 INTERSTATE 295 Cont'd

Exit #	Services
18b a	rd 667, to rd 678, Clarksboro, Mt Royal, **E** 🅖 Exxon/dsl, TA/Shell/Country Pride/dsl/scales/@ 🅕 Dragon Nest Chinese, Dunkin', McDonald's 🅞 RV camping, **W** 🅖 Valero, WaWa/dsl
17	rd 680, to Mickleton, Gibbstown, **W** 🅕 Burger King, Domino's, Dunkin', Mr Bee's Deli 🅞 $General, Advance Parts, Family$, GNC, Rite Aid, ShopRite Foods
16b	rd 551, to Gibbstown, Mickleton
16a	rd 653, to Paulsboro, Swedesboro
15	rd 607, to Gibbstown
14	rd 684, to Repaupo
13	US 130 S, US 322 W, to Bridgeport (from sb, no return)
11	US 322 E, to Mullica Hill
10	Ctr Square Rd, to Swedesboro, **E** 🅖 Citgo/dsl, WaWa/dsl 🅕 Applebee's, Ciconte's Pizza, Dunkin', McDonald's, Wendy's 🛏 Hampton Inn, Holiday Inn, TownePlace Suites 🅞 Acme Foods/Sav-On, Firestone/auto, Rite Aid, URGENT CARE, Verizon, **W** 🅞 Camping World RV Supplies/service
7	to Auburn, Pedricktown
4	NJ 48, Woodstown, Penns Grove
3mm	weigh sta nb
2mm	🆁🆂 nb, full 🅰 facilities, info, litter barrels, 🅒 picnic table, ⬛ dump, vending
2c	to US 130 (from sb), Deepwater, **E** same as 2b, **W** 🅕 ✈FLYING Denny's/dsl/scales/LP/24hr, Sunoco/Dunkin'/dsl/scales/24hr
2b	US 40 E, to NJ Tpk, **E** 🅖 Gulf, PILOT/Subway/dsl/scales/24hr 🛏 Comfort Inn, Friendship Motor Inn, Holiday Inn Express, Red Carpet Inn, **W** same as 2c
2a	to Delaware Bridge, US 40 W (from nb)
1c	NJ 551 S, Hook Rd, to Salem, **E** 🛏 White Oaks Motel
1b	US 130 N (from nb), Penns Grove
1a	NJ 49 E, to Pennsville, Salem, **E** 🅖 WaWa/dsl 🅕 Applebee's, Burger King, Cracker Barrel, Dunkin', KFC/Taco Bell, McDonald's 🛏 Hampton Inn, Super 8 🅞 Peterbilt, **W** 🅕 Coastal/dsl 🛏 Seaview Motel
0mm	New Jersey/Pennsylvania state line, Delaware River

NOTES

NEW MEXICO

📍 INTERSTATE 10

Exit #	Services
164.5mm	New Mexico/Texas state line
164mm	**Welcome Ctr wb, full ♿ facilities, 🅒, 🛏, litter barrels, petwalk**
162	NM 404, Anthony, S 🅖 Alon/dsl 🅞 El Paso West RV Park, Family$
160mm	**weigh sta wb**
155	NM 227 W, to Vado, N 🅞 Western Sky's RV Park, S 🅖 Chevron/ El Viajero/dsl/scales/24hr, NTS/dsl/scales/24hr/@ 🅞 $General, El Camino Real HS
151	Mesquite
144	I-25 N, to Las Cruces
142	Rd 188, Rd 101, Valley Dr, Las Cruces, N 🅖 Chevron/dsl 🍴 Chilito's Mexican, Dick's Cafe, IHOP, Jimmy John's, Whataburger 🛏 Best Western, Courtyard, EconoLodge, Holiday Inn Express, Motel 6, Quality Inn, Ramada Inn, Super 8, Teakwood Inn 🅞 auto/RV repair/tires, Cadillac/Chevrolet, Dalmont's RV Camping, Ford/Lincoln, Honda, 🅷 Hyundai, Mazda, Nissan, NMSU, vet, S 🅖 Alon/dsl 🅞 USPO
140	NM 28, to Mesilla, Las Cruces, N 🅖 Alon/dsl 🍴 Applebee's, Blake's Lotaburger, BurgerTime, Cracker Barrel, Domino's, Golden Corral, K-Bob's, McDonald's, Murry Express, Starbucks, Subway 🛏 Best Value Inn, Days Inn, Drury Inn, Hampton Inn, La Quinta, SpringHill Suites 🅞 Buick/GMC, Kia, Toyota, VW, Walmart/McDonald's, S 🍴 LunaRossa Pizza 🛏 Comfort Inn 🅞 Harley-Davidson, Holiday World RV Ctr, Siesta RV Park, United RV Ctr
139	NM 292, Amador Ave, Motel Blvd, Las Cruces, N 🅖 Pilot 🍴 Subway/dsl/scales/24hr, TA/Burger King/Pizza Hut/Taco Bell/ dsl/24hr/scales/@, S 🍴 PitStop Café 🛏 Coachlight Inn/RV Park 🅞 NAPACare
138mm	Rio Grande River
135.5mm	**🆁🆂 eb, full ♿ facilities, 🛏, litter barrels, petwalk, scenic view**
135	US 70 E, to W Las Cruces, Alamogordo, 1 mi N 🅞 KOA
132	N 🅞 fairgrounds, to ✈, S 🅖 Loves/Subway/dsl/ scales/24hr
127	Corralitos Rd, N 🅖 Exxon 🅞 Bowlin's Trading Post, to fairgrounds
120.5mm	**insp sta wb**
116	NM 549
111mm	**parking area wb, litter barrels**
102	Akela, N 🅖 Exxon/dsl/gifts
85	East Motel Dr, Deming, S 🅖 Chevron/dsl, Conoco/dsl 🛏 Hampton Inn, Holiday Inn Express, La Quinta, Motel 6, Quality Inn 🅞 Buick/Cadillac/Chevrolet/GMC, Chrysler/Dodge/Jeep, Dreamcatcher RV Park
82b	Railroad Blvd, Deming, N 🅖 Chevron/dsl, S 🅖 Conoco/dsl 🍴 DQ, Golden Star Chinese, IHOP, KFC, Little Caesar's, Ranchers Grill, Wendy's 🛏 Days Inn, Grand Motel 🅞 $General, $Tree, AutoZone, Big O Tire, Deming Visitors Ctr, Little Vinyard RV Park, NAPA, O'Reilly Parts, Roadrunner RV Park, st police, Sunrise RV Park, to Rock Hound SP, Verizon, Wagon Wheel RV Park, Walmart/Subway
82a	US 180, NM 26, NM 11, Deming, N 🅖 Chevron/dsl 🍴 Blake's Lotaburger, S 🅖 Exxon, Phillips 66 🍴 Burger King, China Rest., Denny's, Domino's, KFC, Palma's Italian, Pizza Hut, Rancher's Grill, Si Senor 🛏 Butterfield Stage Motel 🅞 Budget Tire, CarQuest, 🅷 museum, Rockhound SP, to Pancho Villa SP, Walgreens

LAS CRUCES (left margin)

LORDSBURG (right margin)

NM

Exit #	Services
81	NM 11, W Motel Dr, Deming, S 🅖 Circle K/dsl, CNG 🍴 Benji's Rest, El Camino Real, McDonald's, Sonic, Subway, Taco Bell 🛏 Best Western, Comfort Inn, Deming Motel, Executive Motel, Super 8, Western Motel 🅞 81 Palms RV Park, city park, Hitchin Post RV Park, 🅷, Rock Hound SP, to Pancho Villa SP
68	NM 418, S 🅖 Petro/Iron Skillet/Starbucks/dsl/scales/24hr, tires/ repair
62	Gage, S 🅖 Butterfield Station/Exxon/DQ/dsl
61mm	**🆁🆂 wb, full ♿ facilities, 🛏, litter barrels, vending, petwalk**
55	Quincy
53mm	**🆁🆂 eb, full ♿ facilities, 🛏, litter barrels, vending, petwalk**
51.5mm	Continental Divide, elev 4585
49	NM 146 S, to Hachita, Antelope Wells
42	Separ, S 🅞 Bowlin's Continental Divide Trading Post/Gifts
34	NM 113 S, Muir, Playas
29	no service
24	US 70, E Motel Dr, Lordsburg, N 🅖 FLYING J/Denny's/dsl/LP/ scales/RV Dump/24hr, Pilot/Arby's/dsl/scales/24hr 🛏 American Motel 🅞 Horseman RV Park
23.5mm	**weigh sta both lanes**
22	NM 494, Main St, Lordsburg, N 🍴 McDonald's 🛏 Comfort Inn, Hampton Inn 🅞 $General, Family$, NAPA, Saucedo's Foods, USPO, S 🅖 Circle K/dsl 🍴 Kranberry's Rest. 🛏 EconoLodge, Motel 10, Motel 6, Plaza Inn 🅞 KOA
20b a	W Motel Dr, Lordsburg, N 🅖 Loves/Godfather's Pizza/Subway/scales/dsl 🛏 Days Inn, S Visitors Ctr/full ♿ facilities, info 🅖 Chevron/dsl/24hr
15	to Gary
11	NM 338 S, to Animas
5	NM 80 S, to Road Forks, S 🅞 dsl/tire repair, fireworks
3	Steins
0mm	New Mexico/Arizona state line

⊡ = gas ⊞ = food ⊟ = lodging ⊡ = other ⊠ = rest stop Copyright 2022 - The Next EXIT

INTERSTATE 25

Exit #	Services
460.5mm	New Mexico/Colorado state line
460	Raton Pass Summit, elev 7834, **weigh sta sb**, E ⊡ Cedar Rail Campground
454	2nd St, Lp 25, Raton, **2 mi** W ⊡ Crossroads ⊟ Budget Host ⊡ CarQuest, Ford, Ⓗ
452	NM 72 E, Raton, E ⊡ to Sugarite Canyon SP, W ⊡ Conoco
451	US 64 E, US 87 E, Raton, E ⊡ 87 Express/dsl, Chevron/dsl, CR/dsl/24hr ⊞ Subway ⊡ Summerlan RV Park, to Capulin Volcano NM, W ⊡ Conoco/dsl, CR/dsl, Loaf'n Jug/dsl, Shamrock ⊞ Arby's, Denny's, Domino's, JRs Burritos, K-Bob's Steaks, McDonald's, Sonic ⊟ Best Western+, Casa Lemus, Microtel, Oasis Motel/rest, Peak Inn, Quality Inn, Robin Hood Motel, Super 8, Travelodge ⊡ $General, Ace Hardware, AutoZone, Family$, Ⓗ, KOA, O'Reilly Parts, Super Save Foods, Visitor's Ctr/info
450	Lp 25, Raton, W ⊟ Holiday Inn Express, Oasis Motel/rest. ⊡ AutoZone, Ⓗ, KOA, vet
446	US 64 W, to Cimarron, Taos, **4 mi** W ⊡ camping, NRA Whittington Ctr
440mm	Canadian River
435	Tinaja
434.5mm	⊠ both lanes, full ♿ facilities, weather info, ⊞ litter barrels, petwalk
426	NM 505, Maxwell, W ⊡ Maxwell Station/dsl ⊡ to Maxwell Lakes, USPO
419	NM 58, to Cimarron, E ⊡ Chevron/Russell's/Subway/dsl/scales/24hr/@
414	US 56, Springer, **1 mi** E ⊡ Conoco/dsl, Crossroads/dsl ⊞ Minnie's Dairy Delite ⊟ Broken Arrow Motel, Oasis Motel ⊡ Old Santa Fe Trail RV Park
412	US 56 E, US 412 E, NM 21, NM 468, Springer, **1 mi** E ⊡ Alon ⊟ Brown Hotel/cafe ⊡ CarQuest, Family$, Springer Foods, USPO
404	NM 569, Colmor, Charette Lakes
393	Levy
387	NM 120, to Roy, Wagon Mound, E ⊡ Conoco/dsl, Phillips 66/dsl
376mm	⊠ sb, full ♿ facilities, ⊡, ⊞ litter barrels, petwalk, RV camp
374mm	⊠ nb, full ♿ facilities, ⊡, ⊞ litter barrels, petwalk, RV camp
366	NM 97, NM 161, Watrous, Valmora, W ⊡ Ft Union NM, Santa Fe Trail
364	NM 97, NM 161, Watrous, Valmora
361	no service
360mm	**parking area both lanes**
356	Onava, Onava
352	E ⊡ ⊟, RV camping
347	to NM 518, Las Vegas, **0-2 mi** W ⊡ Loves/Chester's/dsl/scales/24hr, Phillips 66/Burger King, Pino/dsl/rest. ⊞ Arby's, Hillcrest Rest., KFC, Little Moon Chinese, McDonald's, Sonic, Taco Bell, Wendy's ⊟ Best Western, Budget Inn, Comfort Inn, Days Inn, Palamino Inn, Regal Motel, Super 8 ⊡ Ⓗ, Storrie Lake SP
345	NM 65, NM 104, University Ave, Las Vegas, E ⊡ to Conchas Lake SP, W ⊡ Allsups, Crossroads/dsl ⊞ DQ, Hillcrest Rest., Johnny's Kitchen, KFC ⊟ El Fidel, Knights Inn ⊡ Hist. Old Town Plaza, Ⓗ
343	to NM 518 N, Las Vegas, E ⊡ Garcia Tires, **0-2 mi** W ⊡ Alon, Phillips 66/dsl ⊟ Holiday Inn Express, Thunderbird Motel ⊡ auto repair
339	US 84 S, to Santa Rosa, Romeroville, E ⊡ KOA, W ⊡ Phillips 66/Subway/dsl
335	Tecolote
330	Bernal

Exit #	Services
325mm	parking area both lanes, no rest rooms
323	NM 3 S, Villanueva, E ⊞ La Risa (1mi) ⊡ Madison Wine (6mi), to Villanueva SP/rv camping, USPO
319	San Juan, San Jose, W ⊡ Pecos River Sta.
307	NM 63, Rowe, Pecos, W ⊡ Hist Rte 66, Pecos NM same as 2...
299	NM 50, Glorieta, Pecos, W ⊡ Phillips 66 dsl (4mi), Shell (3r... ⊡ Glorieta Conf Ctr
297	Valencia
294	Apache Canyon, W ⊡ KOA, Rancheros Camping (Mar-N... (3mi)
290	US 285 S, to Lamy, S to Clines Corners, E ⊡ Phillips 66/... (1mi), W ⊞ Cafe Fina ⊡ KOA (3mi), Rancheros Camping (M... Nov)
284	NM 466, Old Pecos Trail, Santa Fe, W ⊡ Pecos Trail Inn/Cafe Harry's Roadhouse ⊡ Ⓗ, museums
282	US 84, US 285, St Francis Dr, W ⊡ Conoco/Wendy's/dsl, Mob... dsl ⊞ Church's
278	NM 14, Cerrillos Rd, Santa Fe, E ⊡ RV Ctr, **0-4 mi** W ⊡ Gia... dsl, Murphy Express/dsl, Phillips 66/dsl, Shell ⊞ Adelita's M... ican, Applebee's, Arby's, Blue Corn Cafe, Buffalo Wild Win... Bumble Bee's Baja Grill, Burger King, Denny's, Domino's, Fly... Tortilla, IHOP, KFC, Little Caesars, LJ Silver, Lotaburger, LuL... Chinese, McDonald's, Olive Garden, Outback Steaks, Panda... press, Panera Bread, Papa Murphy's, Pizza Hut, Ranch Ho... Steaks, Red Lobster, Schlotzsky's, Sonic, Starbucks, Taco B... Tortilla Flats ⊟ Best Western, Comfort Inn, Comfort Suit... Courtyard, Days Inn, Doubletree, EconoLodge, Fairfield I... Hampton Inn, Holiday Inn Express, Hyatt Place, La Quin... Motel 6, Quality Inn, Santa Fe Inn, Super 8, Tranquilla Inn... AAA, Albertson's, AT&T, Best Buy, BigLots, BMW, Buick/G... Cadillac/Chevrolet, Chrysler/Dodge/Jeep, CVS Drug, Dillar... Discount Tire, Firestone/auto, Ford/Lincoln, Harley-Davids... Home Depot, Honda, JC Penney, Jo-Ann Fabrics, Kohl's, La... Rover, Lexus, Los Campos RV Park, Lowe's, Mazda, Meced... Smart, Meineke, Michaels, Natural Grocers, Peerless Tire, P... ske, PepBoys, Petsmart, Ross, Sam's Club/gas, Santa Fe O... lets/famous brands, Sprouts Mkt, Staples, Subaru/VW, Targ... TJ Maxx, Tuesday Morning, Verizon, Volvo, Walgreens, Walm...
276b a	NM 599, to NM 14, to Madrid, E ⊡ Phillips 66/Allsup's ⊡ S... ta Fe Skies RV Park, **4 mi** W ⊡ Shell ⊡ Sunrise Springs
271	CR 50F, La Cienega
269mm	⊠ nb, full ♿ facilities, ⊡, ⊞ litter barrels, petwalk
267	Waldo Canyon Rd ⊡ insp sta., access to ⊠ nb
264	NM 16, Pueblo, W ⊡ to Cochiti Lake RA
263mm	Galisteo River
259	NM 22, to Santo Domingo Pueblo, W ⊡ Phillips 66/cafe/dsl... to Cochiti Lake RA (11mi)
257	Budaghers, W ⊡ Mormon Battalion Mon
252	San Felipe Pueblo, E ⊡ San Felipe TC/dsl ⊞ San Felipe Casi... rest.
248	Rte 66, Algodones
242	US 550, NM 44 W, NM 165 E, to Farmington, Aztec, **0-2 mi** W... Chevron/dsl, Conoco/dsl, M&M/Burger King/dsl, Phillips... dsl, Valero/dsl ⊞ Denny's, Guang Dong Chinese, IHOP, K... Lotaburger, McDonald's, Pizza Hut, Sonic, Starbucks, Subw... Taco Bell, Twisters, Wendy's ⊟ Days Inn, Holiday Inn Expr... Motel 6, Super 8 ⊡ $General, AutoZone, Casino, Home De... KOA, O'Reilly Parts, to Coronado SP, Walgreens, Walmart
240	NM 473, to Bernalillo, W ⊡ Conoco/dsl ⊞ Abuelita's Mexi... Range Café ⊡ KOA, to Coronado SP, USPO, vet
234	NM 556, Tramway Rd, E ⊡ Valero/Subway/dsl ⊡ casino, W... Phillips 66/dsl

Side labels: RATON, LAS VEGAS, SANTA FE, NM

INTERSTATE 25 Cont'd

Exit #	Services
233	Alameda Blvd, **E** 🅖 Chevron 🍴 Burger King 🏨 Comfort Suites, Motel 6, Staybridge Suites 🅞 Audi/Porsche, Lincoln, Meineke, Mercedes, Toyota, Volvo, **W** 🅖 Phillips 66/Circle K/dsl 🍴 Carl's Jr 🏨 Best Value, Holiday Inn Express 🅞 Balloon Fiesta Park, CarMax
232	Paseo del Norte, Paseo del Norte, **E** 🍴 Chick-fil-A, China Luck, Chipotle Mexican, Five Guys, Freddy's Steakburgers, Jason's Deli, Jimmy John's, McDonald's, Panda Express, Panera Bread, Starbucks, Subway, Tomato Cafe, Wendy's 🏨 Howard Johnson 🅞 Aloha RV Ctr, AutoZone, Discount Tire, Kohl's, Lowe's, Office Depot, Target, Verizon, Walgreens, **W** 🅖 Shell/Circle K 🍴 Arby's 🏨 Courtyard, Marriott
231	San Antonio Ave, **E** 🅖 Alon/7-11 🍴 Cracker Barrel, Denny's, Lotaburger 🏨 Comfort Suites, Hilton Garden, Homewood Suites, La Quinta, Quality Inn 🅞 🏨 USPO, **W** 🏨 Baymont Inn, Crossland Suites, LaQuinta 🅞 Mazda, VW
230	San Mateo Blvd, Osuna Rd, Albuquerque, **E** 🅖 Chevron, Circle K, Giant/dsl, Phillips 66/Circle K, Shell 🍴 Applebee's, Arby's, Azuma Grill, Bob's Burgers, Burger King, Chick-fil-A, Chili's, Cici's Pizza, Firehouse Subs, Furrs Buffet, Golden Corral, Hayashi, Hooters, Jack-in-the-Box, KFC, LJ Silver, McDonald's, Olive Garden, Papa John's, Pizza Hut/Taco Bell, Popeyes, Schlotzsky's, Sonic, Souper Salad, Starbucks, Subway, SweetTomatoes, Taco Bueno, Taco Cabana, Teriyaki Chicken, TX Roadhouse, Village Inn, Wendy's, Wienerschnitzel 🏨 Nativo Lodge 🅞 $Tree, Albertson's, AT&T, AutoZone, Brake Masters, Cadillac, CVS Drug, Fiat, Firestone, Firestone/auto, GNC, Just Brakes, Midas, NAPA, O'Reilly Parts, Peerless Tire, PepBoys, PetCo, Ross, Sprouts Mkt, Subaru, Tuesday Morning, U-Haul, Walgreens, **W** 🅖 Circle K/dsl, Valero/dsl 🍴 McDonald's, Quiznos, Weck's Breakfast/lunch, Whataburger 🏨 Studio 6 🅞 BMW/Mini
229	Jefferson St, **E** 🍴 ClaimJumper, Outback Steaks 🏨 Holiday Inn 🅞 same as 230, **W** 🍴 Boston's Pizza, Chama River Rest., Cheddar's, Chile Rio, Coldstone, Dickey's BBQ, Fox&Hound, Fuddrucker's, Genghis Grill, Mimi's Café, Nick&Jimmy's Grill, Pappadeaux, Pars Cuisine, PF Chang's, Plum Cafe Asian, Red Robin, Subway, Twin Peaks Rest., TX Land&Cattle Steaks 🏨 Drury Inn, Hampton Inn, Hampton Inn, Residence Inn, TownePlace Suites 🅞 Lexus
228	Montgomery Blvd, **E** 🅖 Alon/7-11/dsl, Chevron/dsl, Conoco/dsl 🍴 Fiestas Cantina, Lotaburger 🏨 Best Western 🅞 Discount Tire, 🏨, **W** 🅖 Shell/Circle K 🍴 Arby's, Carl's Jr, IHOP, McDonald's, Panda Express, Starbucks, Wendy's 🏨 InTowne Suite 🅞 Acura, Costco/gas, Ford, Home Depot, Infiniti, Office Depot, Petsmart, REI, Sam's Club/gas, Sportsman's Whse
227b	Comanche Rd, Griegos Rd, **E** 🅞 UPS Depot
227a	Candelaria Rd, Albuquerque, **E** 🅖 Circle K/dsl, Pump'n'Save/dsl, Shell, TA/Valero/Country Pride/dsl/scales/24hr/@ 🍴 Applebee's, Little Anita's, Mesa Grill, Range Cafe, Subway, Village Inn 🏨 Candlewood Suites, Crowne Plaza, Days Inn, Elegante Hotel, Fairfield Inn, Holiday Inn Express, La Quinta, Motel 1, Motel 76, Quality Inn, Rodeway Inn, Super 8, Travelodge 🅞 Kenworth, **W** 🅖 Chevron/dsl 🏨 Ambassador Inn, Rodeway Inn 🅞 Penske
226b a	I-40, E to Amarillo, W to Flagstaff
225	Lomas Blvd, **E** 🅖 Phillips 66 🏨 Plaza Inn/rest. 🅞 Chevrolet, **W** 🅖 FillUp, Shell/Circle K/McDonald's 🍴 Burger King, Carl's Jr, Starbucks 🏨 Embassy Suites 🅞 🏨
224	Lead Ave, Coal Ave, Grand Ave, Central Ave, **E** 🅖 Alon/7-11 🍴 66 Diner 🏨 Crossroads Motel 🅞 🏨, **W** 🍴 M&M 🏨 Best Value Inn, EconoLodge, Hotel Parq Central, Knights Inn
223	Chavez Ave, **E** 🏨 Motel 6 🅞 sports arena

(Map of New Mexico showing I-25 and I-40, with cities: Vallencitos, Arroyo Hondo, Springer, Miami, San Juan Pueblo, Ocate, Wagons Mound, Mora, Sapello, Santa Fe, Las Vegas, Pueblo, Trementia PO, Rio Rancho, Bernalillo, Villanueva, Cuervo, Stanley, Albuquerque, Santa Rosa, Belen, Vaughn, Mountainair)

NM

Exit #	Services
222b a	Gibson Blvd, **E** 🅖 Phillips 66/dsl 🍴 Applebee's, Buffalo Wild Wings, Burger King, Dion's Pizza, Fuddrucker's, IHOP, Subway, Village Inn, Waffle House 🏨 AmericInn, Best Western, Comfort Inn, Country Inn&Suites, Courtyard, Days Inn, Extended Stay America, Fairfield Inn, Hawthorn Suites, Hilton Garden, Holiday Inn Express, La Quinta, Quality Suites, Ramada Inn, Residence Inn, Sleep Inn, TownePlace Suites 🅞 🏨, Kirtland AFB, museum, vet, **W** 🅖 Alon/7-11/dsl 🍴 Church's, Lotaburger
221	Sunport, **E** 🏨 Holiday Inn, Homewood Suites, Hyatt Place, Staybridge Suites 🅞 ✈, USPO
220	Rio Bravo Blvd, Mountain View, **E** 🅞 golf, 1-2 mi **W** 🅖 Shell/dsl, Valero/dsl 🍴 Bob's Burgers, Burger King, Church's, KFC/Taco Bell, McDonald's, O'Reilly Parts, Pizza Hut, Subway 🅞 Albertsons/Sav-On, Family$, vet, Walgreens
215	NM 47, **E** 🅖 Isleta One Stop/dsl, Phillips 66/Subway/dsl 🅞 casino, golf, st police, to Isleta Lakes RA/RV Camping
214mm	Rio Grande
213	NM 314, Isleta Blvd, **W** 🅖 Chevron/Subway/dsl 🅞 $General, vet
209	NM 45, to Isleta Pueblo
203	NM 6, to Los Lunas, **E** 🅖 Chevron/dsl, Murphy USA/dsl, Shell/Circle K/Wendy's/dsl/24hr, Valero/dsl 🍴 Applebee's, Benny's Burger, Del Taco, Denny's, Sonic, Starbucks 🏨 Days Inn, Los Lunas Inn 🅞 AutoZone, Big O Tire, Chevrolet, Chrysler/Dodge/Jeep, Ford, Home Depot, Lowe's, URGENT CARE, Walgreens, **W** 🅖 Phillips 66/Subway/dsl 🍴 Carl's Jr, Chili's, Coldstone, KFC, Mariscos Altamar, Panda Express 🏨 Western Skies Inn 🅞 Buick/GMC, Discount Tire, Verizon, Walmart/McDonald's
195	Lp 25, Los Chavez, **1 mi E** 🅖 Roadrunner/grill/dsl 🍴 Pizza Hut/Taco Bell 🅞 Walmart/Subway
191	NM 548, Belen, **E** 🅖 Conoco/dsl, Loves/Arby's/dsl/scales/24hr 🍴 McDonald's, Pizza Hut 🏨 Super 8 🅞 $General, USPO, Walgreens, **W** 🍴 Rio Grande Diner 🏨 Holiday Inn Express, RV park
190	Lp 25, Belen, **1-2 mi E** 🅖 Conoco/dsl, Phillips 66 🍴 A&W/LJ Silver, McDonald's, Pizza Hut 🏨 Super 8 🅞 $General, Affordable Tire/repair, AutoZone, USPO, Walgreens
175	US 60, Bernardo, **E** 🅞 Salinas NM, **W** 🅞 Kiva RV Park
174mm	Rio Puerco
169	**E** 🍴 La Joya St Game Refuge 🅞 Sevilleta NWR
167mm	🆁🆂 both lanes, full 🚻 facilities, 📞, litter barrels, vending, petwalk
166mm	Rio Salado
165mm	weigh sta/parking area both lanes
163	San Acacia
156	Lemitar, **W** 🅖 Phillips 66/dsl/24hr
152	Escondida, **W** 🅞 to st police
150	US 60 W, Socorro, **W** 🅖 Chevron/dsl, Exxon/dsl, Phillips 66/dsl, Valero/dsl 🍴 Bodega Burger Co, Burger King, China Best, Denny's, Domino's, K-Bob's, Little Caesar's, Lotaburger, McDonald's,

ALBUQUERQUE (vertical side text, left margin)

ALBUQUERQUE (vertical side text, center)

BELEN (vertical side text)

SOCORRO (vertical side text)

NM

🅖 = gas   🍴 = food   🛏 = lodging   🅞 = other   🆁ˢ = rest stop   Copyright 2022 - The Next EXIT ®

INTERSTATE 25 Cont'd

150 Continued
Pizza Hut, Socorro Springs Rest., Sofia's Kitchen, Sonic, Subway 🛏 Best Value, Best Western, Comfort Inn, Days Inn, EconoLodge, Economy Inn, Holiday Inn Express, Sands Motel, Super 8 🅞 $General, Ace Hardware, AutoZone, Brooks Foods, CarQuest, Family$, Ford, NAPA, Smith's Foods, to NM Tech, Verizon, vet, Walmart

147 US 60 W, Socorro, W 🅖 Chevron/dsl, Conoco/dsl/LP, Pump-N-Save/dsl, Shell/Circle K/dsl 🍴 Arby's 🛏 Rodeway Inn 🅞 🅗 repair/transmissions, Socorro RV Park, to 🆁ˢ

139 US 380 E, to San Antonio, E 🅞 to Bosque Del Apache NWR

124 to San Marcial, E 🅞 Ft Craig, to Bosque del Apache NWR

115 NM 107, E 🍴 to Camino Real Heritage Ctr, Truck Plaza/dsl/rest./24hr

114mm 🆁ˢ both lanes, full 🦽 facilities, 🛢 litter barrels, petwalk, RV parking, vending

107mm 🅞 Nogal Canyon

100 Red Rock

92 Mitchell Point

90mm La Canada Alamosa, La Canada Alamosa

89 NM 181, to Cuchillo, to Monticello 🅞 RV Park (4mi)

83 NM 52, NM 181, to Cuchillo, **3 mi** E 🍴 Ivory Tusk Inn & Tavern 🛏 Elephant Butte Inn/rest. 🅞 Elephant Lake Butte SP, RV Park

82mm insp sta nb

79 Lp 25, to Truth or Consequences, E 🅖 Chevron/dsl, Circle K, Shell/dsl 🍴 Blakes's Lotaburger, Denny's, K-Bob's, La Cocina Mexican, Los Arcos Steaks, McDonald's, Pizza Hut, Sonic, Subway 🛏 Ace Lodge, Comfort Inn, Desert View Motel, Holiday Inn Express, Hot Springs Inn, Motel 6, Oasis Motel 🅞 $General, AutoZone, 🅗, O'Reilly Parts, to Elephant Butte SP, USPO, Verizon, Walmart

76 (75 from nb)Lp 25, to Williamsburg, E 🅖 Conoco/dsl, FillUp/dsl, Phillips 66/dsl, Shell/dsl 🍴 Maria's Mexican 🛏 Rio Grande Motel 🅞 Alco, auto/tire repair, Buick/Chevrolet/GMC, Cielo Vista RV Park, city park, Rio Grande RV Park, RJ RV Park, Shady Corner RV Park

71 Las Palomas

63 NM 152, to Hillsboro, Caballo, E 🅞 Lakeview RV Park/dsl/LP

59 rd 187, Arrey, Derry, E 🅞 to Caballo-Percha SPs

58mm Rio Grande

51 rd 546, to Arrey, Garfield, Derry

41 NM 26 W, Hatch, **1 mi** W 🅖 Alon/Subway/dsl 🍴 Burgers&More, Sparky's Cafe 🛏 Kings Pillow Inn 🅞 Chile Pepper Outlets, Franciscan RV Ctr, USPO

35 NM 140 W, Rincon

32 Upham

27mm scenic view nb, 🛢 litter barrels

26mm insp sta nb

23mm 🆁ˢ both lanes, full 🦽 facilities, 🛢 litter barrels, vending, petwalk

19 Radium Springs, W 🅞 Family$, Fort Selden St Mon, Leasburg SP, RV camping, USPO

9 Dona Ana, W 🅖 Chucky's/dsl, Circle K/dsl 🍴 Chachi's Mexican, Jake's Cafe 🅞 $General, Family$, RV camping, USPO

6 US 70, to Alamogordo, Las Cruces, E 🅖 Alon/dsl, Shell 🍴 Domino's, IHOP, Outback Steaks, Papa Johns, Peter Piper Pizza, Pizzaria Uno, Red Brick Pizza, Ruby Tuesday, Starbucks, Subway 🛏 Fairfield Inn, Holiday Inn Express, Motel 6, Staybridge Suites, Towneplace Suites 🅞 AT&T, 🅗, Sam's Club/gas, USPO, vet, W 🅖 Alon/dsl, Chevron, Shell/dsl, Valero/dsl 🍴 Burger King, BurgerTime, China Express, Domino's, DQ, Dunkin', KFC, Little Caesar's, Lotaburger, McDonald's, Sonic, Spanish Kitchen,

6 Continued
Subway, Taco Bell, Whataburger/24hr, Wienerschnitzel 🅞 $General, $Tree, Albertson's, AutoZone, CVS Drug, Family$, Kohl's, Lowe's, O'Reilly Parts, Verizon, vet, Walgreens

3 Lohman Ave, Las Cruces, E 🅖 Alon/dsl, Shell 🍴 Applebee's, Buffalo Wild Wings, Burger King, Cattle Baron Steaks, Chili's, Chucke Cheese, Dumkin Donuts, Empire Buffet, Farley's Grill, Fidencio's Mexican, Five Guys, Genghis Grill, Golden Corral, Hooters, Jack in-the-Box, Jason's Deli, KFC, McAlister's Deli, Olive Garden, Pecan Grill, Red Lobster, Sonic, Starbucks, Village Inn, Whataburger 🛏 Hotel Encanto 🅞 Albertsons, AutoZone, Barnes&Noble, Dick's, Dillard's, Discount Tire, Home Depot, JC Penney, mall, Marshalls, PetCo, Ross, Sears/auto, Target, W 🅖 Giant/dsl, Valero/dsl 🍴 Arby's, Carl's Jr, Corner Bakery Cafe, McDonald's, Papa Murphy's, Quiznos, Subway, Taco Bell, TX Roadhouse, Wendy's 🛏 Hampton Inn 🅞 AT&T, Best Buy, Big Lots, Brake Masters, Hobby Lobby, NAPA, Old Navy, PepBoys, Petsmart, Staples, URGENT CARE, Verizon, vet, Walgreens, Walmart

1 University Ave, Las Cruces, E 🍴 AlonSubway/dsl 🛏 Hilton Garden 🅞 golf, 🅗, museum, st police, W 🍴 Giant/dsl 🍴 Dublin Cafe, Lorenzo's Italian, McDonald's, Schlotsky's 🛏 Comfort Suites, Sleep Inn, Woodspring Suites 🅞 $Tree, Jo-Ann Fabrics, NMSU, Tuesday Morning

0mm I-25 begins/ends on I-10, exit 144 at Las Cruces.

INTERSTATE 40

Exit #	Services
373.5mm	New Mexico/Texas state line, Mountain/Central time zone
373mm	**Welcome Ctr wb, full 🦽 facilities, 🅒, 🛢 litter barrels, petwalk**
369	NM 93 S, NM 392 N, Endee, N 🍴 Chevron/Russell's Truck&Travel/Subway/dsl/scales/24hr
361	Bard
358mm	**weigh sta both lanes**
356	NM 469, San Jon, N 🍴 Phillips 66/Dhillon//cafe/dsl 🅞 repair, to Ute Lake SP, S 🍴 Valero/dsl 🛏 San Jon Motel 🅞 city park, USPO
343	no service
339	NM 278, N 🅞 🆁ˢ
335	Lp 40, E Tucumcari Blvd, Tucumcari, N 🍴 Conoco/dsl 🛏 Best Value, EconoLodge, Motel 6, Quality Inn, Rodeway Inn, Super 8 🅞 to Conchas Lake SP, S 🍴 KOA
333	US 54 E, Tucumcari, 0-1 mi N 🍴 ⊕FLYING J/Phillips 66/dsl/LP/scales/24hr, ♥Love's/Arbys/Chester's/Godfather's/dsl/scales 🛏 Fairfield Inn 🅞 city park, Mtn Rd RV Park, truck repair, truckwash
332	NM 209, NM 104, 1st St, Tucumcari, 0-2 mi N 🍴 Shell/Circle K, Subway/dsl, Valero/Allsups/dsl 🍴 Blake's Lotaburger, K-Bob's, McDonald's, Pizza Hut, Sonic, Taco Bell 🛏 Best Western, Days Inn, Desert Inn, Holiday Inn Express, La Quinta 🅞 $General, Ace Hardware, Dinosaur Museum, Family$, 🅗, Lowe's Foods, st police, to Conchas Lake SP
331	Camino del Coronado, Tucumcari
329	US 54, US 66 E, W Tucumcari Ave
321	Palomas
311	Montoya
302mm	**🆁ˢ both lanes, full 🦽 facilities, 🅒, 🛢 litter barrels, petwalk, RV dump**
300	NM 129, Newkirk, N 🍴 Rte 66/dsl 🅞 to Conchas Lake, USPO
291	to Rte 66, Cuervo, N 🍴 Cuervo Gas/repair
284	no service
277	US 84 S, to Ft Sumner, N 🍴 Phillips 66/dsl, 🅒🅒🅒/Subway/dsl/scales/24hr 🍴 Annie's Rest., DQ, Silver Moon Café

INTERSTATE 40 Cont'd

277	Continued
	Best Western, Budget Inn, Comfort Inn, Hampton Inn, Holiday Inn Express, Motel 6, Quality Inn Ⓞ NAPACare, S 🍴 ♥Loves/ Carl's Jr/dsl/24hr, TA/Shell/Subway/dsl/24hr/@ Ⓞ truck/tire repair
275	US 54 W, Santa Rosa, N 🍴 Chevron/dsl, Valero/Allsup's 🍴 Mc-Donald's, Rte 66 Rest., Santa Fe Grill 🛏️ Days Inn, Econolodge, La Quinta, Rodeway Inn Ⓞ Santa Rosa Camping, st police, S 🍴 Shell/Circle K/dsl 🍴 Joseph's Grill 🛏️ Laloma Motel/RV Park, Rodeway Inn, Sun'n Sand Motel/rest., Super 8, Tower Motel Ⓞ $General, CarQuest, city park, Family$, 🅷, NAPA, USPO
273.5mm	Pecos River
273	US 54 S, Santa Rosa, N 🍴 Santa Rosa Lake SP, S 🍴 Phillips 66/dsl 🛏️ Best Value Inn Ⓞ NAPACare, to Carlsbad Caverns NP
267	Colonias, N 🍴 Sinclair/dsl
263	San Ignacio
256	US 84 N, NM 219, to Las Vegas
252	no service
251.5mm	🆁🆂 both lanes, full ♿ facilities, 🍴, 🖼️, litter barrels, petwalk, RV dump
243	Milagro, N 🍴 Phillips 66/dsl
239	no service
234	N 🍴 Exxon/Flying C/DQ/dsl/gifts
230	NM 3, to Encino, N Ⓞ to Villanueva SP
226	no service
220mm	parking area both lanes, litter barrels
218b a	US 285, Clines Corners, N 🍴 Conoco/dsl/24hr, Phillips 66/dsl 🍴 Clines Corners Rest., Subway, S Ⓞ to Carlsbad Caverns NP
208	Wagon Wheel
207mm	🆁🆂 both lanes, full ♿ facilities, 🖼️, litter barrels, petwalk
203	no service
197	to Rte 66, Moriarty, 1-2 mi S 🍴 Lisa's TC/dsl/rest./@ Ⓞ auto/ RV repair, Glider Museum same as 194
196	NM 41, Howard Cavasos Blvd, N 🍴 Pilot/Subway/dsl/ scales/24hr, S 🍴 Lisa's TC/dsl, Phillips 66/Circle K/dsl 🍴 Blakes Lotaburger 🛏️ Quality Inn, Sunset Motel Ⓞ auto repair, city park, Family$, to Salinas NM (35mi), USPO
194	NM 41, Moriarty, S 🍴 Alon/7-11/dsl, Conoco/dsl, TA/Shell/ Burger King/Country Pride/Pizza Hut/dsl/24hr/scales/@ 🍴 Ar-by's, Chili Hills Mexican, El Comedor Mexican, KFC/Taco Bell, Subway 🛏️ Best Value Inn, Best Western, Motel 6, Ponderosa Motel, Super 8 Ⓞ $General, Chevrolet/GMC, Moriarty Foods, RV Ctr, URGENT CARE
187	NM 344, Edgewood, N 🍴 Conoco/DQ/dsl 🍴 Denny's Ⓞ Walmart/McDonald's, S 🍴 Phillips 66/dsl 🍴 Chili Hills Mexi-can, China Chef, Domino's, McDonald's, Pizza Barn, Sonic, Sub-way 🛏️ Comfort Inn Ⓞ $Tree, auto/rv repair, AutoZone, Ford, O'Reilly Parts, Rte 66 RV Park, RV Camping, Smith's Foods/dsl, USPO, Walgreens
181	NM 217, Sedillo, S 🍴 Route 66/dsl
178	Zuzax, S 🍴 Zuzax/dsl/repair Ⓞ Hidden Valley RV Park, Leisure Mtn RV Park
175	NM 337, NM 14, Tijeras, N Ⓞ to Cibola NF, Turquoise Trail RV Park, S 🍴 Subway Ⓞ USPO
170	Carnuel
167	Central Ave, to Tramway Blvd, S 🍴 Alon/7-11, Alon/7-11/dsl, Phillips 66/Circle K/dsl, Valvoline 🍴 Blakes Lotaburger, Happy Garden, KFC, McDonald's, Starbucks, Subway, Taco Bell, Waf-fle House 🛏️ Budget Host, Deluxe Inn, EconoLodge, Motel 6, Quality Inn, Rodeway Inn, Suburban Lodge, Woodspring Suites Ⓞ $Tree, Rocky Mtn RV/marine, Smith's/gas, Sprouts Mkt, to Kirtland AFB

166	Juan Tabo Blvd, N 🍴 Phillips 66/Circle K, Texaco/dsl 🍴 AA Buffet, Dominos, McDonald's, Olive Garden, Peter Piper Pizza, Pizza Hut, Starbucks, Subway, Taco Bell, Twisters Diner, Village Inn Rest., Weck's Rest., Wendy's 🛏️ Guest Gate Inn, Super 8 Ⓞ $General, Albertson's, Discount Tire, Family$, Hobby Lobby, Midas, Sav-On Drug, Tuesday Morning, vet, S 🍴 Sonic, Wie-nerschnitzel Ⓞ $General, Chisholm Trail RV Ctr, Holiday RV Ctr, KOA/LP, Myer's RV Ctr, repair
165	Eubank Blvd, N 🍴 Chevron, Phillips 66/Circle K 🍴 Applebee's, Owl Cafe, Panda Express, Sadie's Rest., Sonic 🛏️ Days Inn, Econolodge, Holiday Inn Express, Ramada Ⓞ $Tree, Best Buy, CarQuest, city park, PetCo, Target, S 🍴 Circle K/dsl, Conoco/dsl 🍴 Bob's Burgers, Boston Mkt, Burger King, Chick-fil-A, Chili's, Church's, Del Taco, Freddy's, IHOP, Jack-in-the-Box, Starbucks, Subway, Taco Bell, Taco Cabana, Twister's Burritos, Wendy's Ⓞ AutoZone, Costco/gas, Home Depot, O'Reilly Parts, Peerless Tires, Petsmart, repair, Ross, Sam's Club/gas, Toyota, Wal-greens, Walmart/McDonald's
164	Lomas Blvd, Wyoming Blvd, N 🍴 Circle K/dsl, Phillips 66/dsl 🍴 Black Angus, Chick-fil-A, Dickey's BBQ, Dominos, Furr's Buf-fet, Krispy Kreme, Subway, Wendy's Ⓞ $Tree, 🅷, NAPA, vet, Walgreens, Walmart, S Ⓞ Chrysler/Dodge/Jeep, Ford, Har-ley-Davidson, Honda, Hyundai, Kirtland AFB, Mazda, Subaru, transmissions, VW
162b a	Louisiana Blvd, N 🍴 BJ's Rest., Blaze Pizza, Bravo Italian, Buca Italian, CA Pizza Kitchen, Cheesecake Factory, Chili's, Chipot-le, Dave & Buster's, Elephant Bar Rest., Firehouse Subs, Five Guys, Fuddrucker's, Garduno's Mexican, Genghis Grill, Jasons Deli, La Madeleine, LePeep, Longhorn Steaks, Macaroni Grill, McAlister's Deli, Melting Pot, Ojos Locos, Panera Bread, Red Robin, Ruth's Chris, Seasons Grill 52, Starbucks, Subway 🛏️ Hil-ton Garden, Homewood Suites, Hyatt Place, Marriott, Sheraton Ⓞ AT&T, Barnes&Noble, Big O Tire, Dick's, Dillard's, Firestone/ auto, JC Penney, Kohl's, Macy's, Petsmart, Sears/auto, Target, TJ Maxx, Trader Joe's, Verizon, S 🍴 Shell 🍴 Burger King Ⓞ atomic museum
161b a	San Mateo Blvd, Albuquerque, N 🍴 Giant/dsl, Shell 🍴 Bob's Burgers, Denny's, Domino's, KFC, Pizza Hut, Starbucks, Subway, Taco Bell 🛏️ San Mateo Inn Ⓞ $Tree, Office Depot, Old Navy, Walmart Mkt, S 🍴 Chevron/dsl 🍴 Starbucks
160	Carlisle Blvd, Albuquerque, N 🍴 Circle K/gas, Murphy Express/ dsl, Shell, USA 🍴 Applebee's, Blakes Lotaburger, China Wok, Jack-in-the-Box, Little Anita's, McDonald's, Papa Murphy's, Range Cafe, Rudy's BBQ, Sonic, Subway, Twisters Grill, Vil-lage Inn Rest., Whataburger 🛏️ Best Value Inn, Candlewood Suites, Crowne Plaza, Days Inn, EconoLodge, Elegante Hotel, Fairfield Inn, Hampton Inn, Holiday Inn Express, La Quinta, Motel 6, Quality Inn, Residence Inn, Suburban Motel, Super 8, Wyndham Ⓞ AutoZone, Firestone/auto, Walgreens, Walmart,

NM

Ⓖ = gas Ⓕ = food Ⓛ = lodging Ⓞ = other Ⓡˢ = rest stop   Copyright 2022 - The Next EXIT ®

ALBUQUERQUE

	INTERSTATE 40 Cont'd
160	Continued
	S Ⓖ Chevron/dsl, Circle K Ⓕ Burger King Ⓛ Home 2 Suites Ⓞ Ⓗ, Whole Foods Mkt
159b c	I-25, S to Las Cruces, N to Santa Fe
158	6th St, 8th St, 12th St, Albuquerque, N Ⓖ Ⓕ Loves/Subway/ dsl Ⓞ $ General, U-Haul, S Ⓖ Chevron/dsl Ⓛ Comfort Inn
157b	12th St (from eb), N Ⓖ Four Winds/Burrito Co/dsl Ⓕ Laguna Burgers, McDonald's, Starbucks Ⓛ Holiday Inn Express Ⓞ Lowe's, Walgreens
157a	Rio Grande Blvd, Albuquerque, N Ⓖ Chevron Ⓕ Range Cafe, S Ⓖ Shell Ⓕ Ben Michaels, Blakes Lotaburger, Burger King, Little Anita's, Starbucks Ⓛ Best Western+/grill, Hotel Albuquerque Ⓞ repair
156mm	Rio Grande River
155	Coors Rd, Albuquerque, N Ⓖ Circle K, Mobil, Valero/dsl Ⓕ Applebee's, Arby's, Baskin-Robbins, Burger King, Chili's, Chipotle, Cracker Barrel, Golden Corral, IHOP, Krispy Kreme, McDonald's, Mimmo's Pizza, Panda Express, Panera Bread, Papa Murphy's, Sonic, Starbucks, Subway, Taco Cabana, Twisters Burritos, Wendy's, Wienerschnitzel, Wing Stop Ⓞ $Tree, AutoZone, Brake Masters, Family$, Firestone, GNC, Home Depot, Jiffy Lube, Verizon, Walgreens, Walmart/Subway, S Ⓖ Chevron/ dsl, Phillips 66/Circle K/dsl, Shell, Valero Ⓕ Altamar Mexican, Blakes Lotaburger, Buffalo Wild Wings, China Buffet, Del Taco, Denny's, Dion's, Freddy's, McDonald's, Papa John's, Pizza Hut/ Taco Bell, Subway, Twisters Burritos Ⓛ Days Inn, EconoLodge, Hampton Inn, La Quinta, Motel 6, Motel 76, Quality Inn, Rodeway Inn, Super 8 Ⓞ BigLots, Discount Tire, O'Reilly Parts
154	Unser Blvd, N Ⓖ Valero, Walmart/dsl Ⓕ McDonald's, Starbucks, Taco Bell Ⓞ GNC, to Petroglyph NM, Verizon, Walmart Mkt
153	98th St, S Ⓖ Ⓕ FLYING J/Denny's/dsl/LP/24hr, LNG, Valero-dsl Ⓕ Burger King, Church's, Godfather's, Jack-in-the-Box, Little Caesars, McDonald's, Starbucks, Subway, Wing Stop Ⓛ Microtel Ⓞ $Tree, AutoZone, truckwash/tire/lube
149	Central Ave, Paseo del Volcan, N Ⓞ Camping World, Enchanted Trails RV Camping, Freightliner, LaMesa RV Ctr, to Shooting Range SP, S Ⓖ Ⓕ Loves/Carl's Jr/dsl/scales/24hr Ⓞ American RV Park, High Desert RV Park
140.5mm	Rio Puerco River, N Ⓖ 66 Pit Stop
140	Rio Puerco, N Ⓖ 66 Pit Stop/dsl, S Ⓖ Rte 66 TC/DQ/Road Runner Cafe/hotel/casino/dsl/@
131	Canoncito
126	NM 6, to Los Lunas
120mm	Rio San Jose Rio San Jose
117	Mesita
114	NM 124, Laguna, 1/2 mi N Ⓖ 66 Pit Stop/dsl
113.5mm	scenic view both lanes, litter barrels
108	Casa Blanca, Paraje, S Ⓖ Rte 66 TC/DQ/dsl/24hr Ⓞ casino, Dancing Eagle Mkt, RV park
104	Cubero, Budville
102	Sky City Rd, Acomita, N Ⓖ Sky City/McDonald's/hotel/casino/dsl Ⓕ Huwak'a Rest. Ⓞ casino, RV Park/laundry, S Ⓡˢ both lanes, full ♿ facilities, Ⓒ, 🚮, litter barrels, petwalk, Ⓞ Ⓗ
100	San Fidel
96	McCartys
89	NM 117, to Quemado, N Ⓖ Sky City/Subway/dsl/gifts, S Ⓞ El Malpais NM
85	NM 122, NM 547, Grants, N Ⓖ Alon/dsl, Phillips 66/dsl, Shell/ dsl Ⓕ Asian Buffet, Blakes Lotaburger, Canton Cafe, Denny's, Pizza Hut, Subway, Taco Bell Ⓛ Best Western, Days Inn, Holiday Inn Express, Motel 6, Quality Inn, Sands Motel, Super 8,

GRANTS

GRANTS

85	Continued
	SureStay Ⓞ $Tree, AutoZone, Delta Tire, Ⓗ, O'Reilly Parts, repair/transmissions/towing, Walgreens, Walmart, S Ⓞ Lavaland RV Park
81b a	NM 53 S, Grants, N Ⓖ Phillips 66/dsl Ⓕ Domino's, KFC, McDonald's, Sonic Ⓞ Ford, Ⓗ, NAPA, USPO, S Ⓞ Blue Spruce RV Park, El Malpais NM, KOA/Cibola Sands RV Park
79	NM 122, NM 605, Milan, N Ⓖ Chevron/dsl, Ⓕ Loves/Chester's/Subway/dsl/scales/24hr Ⓕ DQ Ⓛ Crossroads Motel Ⓞ $ General, Bar-S RV Park, S Ⓖ Petro/Iron Skillet/dsl/scales/24hr/@ Ⓞ dsl repair, Speedco Lube
72	Bluewater Village, N Ⓖ Exxon/DQ/dsl
63	NM 412, Prewitt, S Ⓞ to Bluewater Lake SP (7mi)
53	NM 371, NM 612, Thoreau, N Ⓖ Giant/Blimpie/dsl Ⓞ Family$ NAPA, USPO
47	Continental Divide, elevation 7275, N Ⓖ Phillips 66 Ⓞ Continental Divide Trdg Post, towing/repair, S Ⓞ USPO
44	Coolidge
39	Refinery, N Ⓖ Ⓕ FLYING J/Subway/Dennys/dsl/scales/24hr/@
36	Iyanbito
33	NM 400, McGaffey, Ft Wingate, N Ⓞ museum, RV camping, to Red Rock SP
26	E 66th Ave, E Gallup, N Ⓖ Shell/Subway/dsl Ⓕ Denny's Ⓛ Comfort Suites, Holiday Inn Express, La Quinta, Sleep Inn, TownePlace Suites Ⓞ museum, Red Rock Camping, st police, to Red Rock SP, S on Rte 66 Ⓖ Conoco/dsl, Giant/dsl, Pronto Express, Shell/Ortega Gifts Ⓕ Blakes Lotaburger, Burger King, KFC, McDonald's, Sonic, Wendy's Ⓛ Days Inn, Fairfield Inn, Hacienda Motel, Roadrunner Motel Ⓞ $General, Family $, Ⓗ, Verizon
22	Montoya Blvd, Gallup, N Ⓡˢ both lanes, full facilities, info, S on Rte 66 Ⓖ Duke City/dsl, Gas Up, Giant/dsl, Phillips 66 Ⓕ Big Cheese Pizza, Church's, Domino's, DQ, Earl's Rest., Hong Kong Buffet, LJ Silver, Papa John's, Pizza Hut, Subway, Taco Bell Ⓛ Blue Spruce Motel, El Capitan Motel, El Rancho Motel/rest. Ⓞ Albertson's, O'Reilly Parts, Shop'n Save, Walgreens
20	US 491, to Shiprock, Gallup, N Ⓖ Alon/dsl, Giant/dsl Ⓕ Applebee's, Arby's, Big Cheese Pizza, Blakes Lotaburger, Burger King, CA Chinese, Carl's Jr., Church's, Cracker Barrel, Del Taco, Denny's, DQ, Freddy's, Golden Corral, KFC, King Dragon Chinese, Little Caesars, McDonald's, Panda Express, Pizza Hut, Sizzler, Sonic, Subway, Super Buffet, Taco Bell, Wendy's Ⓛ Comfort Inn, Hampton Inn, Hilton Garden, Quality Inn, SpringHill Suites Ⓞ $Tree, AT&T, AutoZone, Beall's, Big Lots, CarQuest, Chrysler/Dodge/Jeep, Family$, Hobby Lobby, Home Depot, JC Penney, Nissan, O'Reilly Parts, PepBoys, Safeway, Verizon, Walmart/McDonald's, S on Rte 66 Ⓖ Phillips 66/dsl Ⓕ Badlands Grill, Blakes Lotaburger, Don Diego's, El Charrito, El Sombrero Mexican, Garcia's Rest, McDonald's, Rte 66 Diner, Sonic Ⓛ Best Value Inn, Days Inn, Golden Desert Motel, Knights Inn, Rodeway Inn, Royal Holiday Motel, Super 8 Ⓞ Ford/Lincoln, Ⓗ, Tire Factory
16	NM 118, W Gallup, Mentmore, N Ⓖ Ⓕ Loves/Chester's/Subway/dsl/24hr, Navajo/dsl/24hr, TA/Country Pride/dsl/scales/24hr/@, USave Trkstp/dsl Ⓞ Ace Truck/dsl Service, Blue Beacon, NKS Truck Repair, S Ⓖ Conoco/dsl, Shell/dsl, Valero/Allsup's Ⓕ Taco Bell, Virgie's Mexican Ⓛ Budget Inn, EconoLodge, Hampton Inn, Knights Inn, Microtel, Motel 6, Red Roof Inn, Travelodge Ⓞ Family $, USA RV Park
12mm	inspection/weigh sta eb
8	to Manuelito
3mm	Welcome Ctr eb, full ♿ facilities, Ⓒ, 🚮, litter barrels, petwalk
0mm	New Mexico/Arizona state line

GALLUP

NEW YORK

⬆N   INTERSTATE 81

Exit #	Services
184mm	US/Canada border, New York state line. I-81 begins/ends.
183.5mm	US Customs (sb)
52(183)	Island Rd, to De Wolf Point, last US exit nb, last US exit nb
51(180)	Island Rd, to Fineview, Islands Parks, **E** 🏠 Torchlite Lodge 🅾 USPO, **W** 🅶 Sunoco Thousand Islands Park
179mm	St Lawrence River
178.5mm	Thousand Islands Toll Bridge Booth, **NY Welcome Ctr/**🆁🆂 sb, full ♿ facilities, litter barrels, petwalk, 🅲, 🏕
50NS(178)	NY 12, E to Alexandria Bay, W to Clayton, Thousand Island Region, **E** 🅶 Sunoco/dsl 🍴 Kountry Kottage Rest., Subway 🏠 PineHurst Motel 🅾 🏥, Chrysler/Dodge/Jeep, PriceChopper Mkt, st police, **W NY Welcome Ctr/**🆁🆂, 🅶 EVC, Mobil 🏠 Bridgeview Motel 🅾 vet
174mm	🆁🆂 nb, full ♿ facilities, litter barrels, petwalk, 🅲, 🏕, vending
49(171)	NY 411, to Theresa, Indian River Lake
168mm	parking area sb, picnic table
161mm	parking area nb
48a	I-781, CR 16, to Ft Drum
48(158)	US 11, NY 37, **E** 🅶 Circle K/dsl, Mobil/Dunkin'/dsl 🍴 Longway's Diner 🏠 Allen's Budget Motel, Royal Inn 🅾 Long-Park Tire
156.5mm	parking area both lanes
47(155)	NY 12, Bradley St, Watertown, **E** 🅶 Sunoco/Subway/dsl, Valero 🍴 Frosty Dairy Bar 🅾 🏥, Honda, **W** 🏠 Rainbow Motel
154.5mm	Black River
46(154)	NY 12F, Coffeen St, Watertown, **E** 🅶 Mobil/Dunkin/dsl 🍴 Cracker Barrel, Shorty's Diner 🅾 Home Depot, URGENT CARE, **W** 🅶 Sunoco/Tim Horton/dsl
45(152)	NY 3, to Arsenal St, Watertown, **E** 🅶 Mobil/Tim Horton/dsl, Sunoco, Tesla EVC 🍴 Apollo Rest., Applebee's, Arby's, Buffalo Wild Wings, Burger King, Camino Real, Chipotle Mexican, Daily Buffet, Denny's, Dunkin', Five Guys, Ichiban, Jreck Subs, KFC, Lotus Rest., McDonald's, Moe's SW Grill, Mustard Seed Cafe, Ruby Tuesday, Sonic, Starbucks, Taco Bell 🏠 Comfort Inn, EconoLodge, Fairfield Inn, Hampton Inn, Hilton Garden, Holiday Inn Express, Travelodge 🅾 $General, $Tree, Advance Parts, Aldi Foods, AT&T, AutoZone, BigLots, Jo-Ann Fabrics, Mavis Discount Tire, Midas, Monro, Mr Tire, PriceChopper Foods/24hr, Staples, TJ Maxx, USPO, Walgreens, **W** 🅶 Fastrac 🍴 Bob Evans, Olive Garden, Panera Bread, Pizza Hut, Red Lobster, Super Wok, TGIFriday's, TX Roadhouse 🏠 Ramada Inn 🅾 Best Buy, Burlington Coats, Dick's, GNC, Hannaford Foods, JC Penney, Kohl's, Lowe's, Michael's, Old Navy, PetCo, Sam's Club, Target, to Sackets Harbor, Verizon, Walmart/Dunkin'
149mm	parking area nb
44(148)	NY 232, to Watertown Ctr, 3 mi **E** 🅾 🏥
147mm	🆁🆂 sb, full ♿ facilities, litter barrels, petwalk, 🅲, 🏕, vending
43(146)	US 11, to Kellogg Hill
42(144)	NY 177, Adams Center, **E** 🅶 Sunoco/Mama Mia's Pizza/dsl 🅾 Harley Davidson, Tugger's Camping (12mi)
41(140)	NY 178, Adams, **E** 🅶 Sunoco/dsl 🍴 Dunkin', McDonald's 🅾 Willows on the Lake RV Park, **W** 🅾 KOA, st police
138mm	South Sandy Creek

40(135)	NY 193, to Ellisburg, Pierrepont Manor
134mm	parking area/🏕 both lanes
39(133)	Mannsville
38(131)	US 11
37(128)	Lacona, Sandy Creek, **E** 🍴 Two Bros Pizza 🏠 Harris Lodge 🅾 USPO, **W** 🅶 Mobil/dsl 🍴 New China One 🏠 Pink House Inn B&B 🅾 $General, CarQuest, Colonial Court Camping (3mi), Sandy Island Beach SP, Tops/dsl, USPO
36(121)	NY 13, Pulaski, **E** 🅶 Byrne Dairy/dsl, Valero 🍴 Ponderosa 🏠 Red Carpet Inn 🅾 Buick/Chevrolet, Ford, **W** 🅶 FasTrac/dsl, KwikFill/dsl 🍴 Arby's, Burger King, Dunkin', McDonald's, Paulanjo's Pizza, River House Rest., Stefano's Rest. 🏠 1880 House B&B, Super 8 🅾 Advance Parts, Aldi Foods, Family$, Kinney Drug, Mavis Tire, NAPA, Rite Aid, to Selkirk Shores SP, Top's Foods, URGENT CARE, Verizon
35(118)	to US 11, Tinker Tavern Rd, **E** 🅾 Streamside RV Park
34(115)	NY 104, to Mexico, **E** 🅶 Mobil/Maple View Rest./dsl/scales, **W** 🏠 Feeder Creek Lodge (5mi) 🅾 Jellystone Camping (9mi)
33(111)	NY 69, Parish, **E** 🅶 Sunoco/dsl/24hr 🍴 Grist Mill Rest. 🅾 $General, Up Country RV Park (8mi), **W** 🅶 Gulf, Mirabito/Dunkin'/dsl 🍴 Passarella Pizza 🅾 USPO
32(103)	NY 49, to Central Square, **E** 🅶 Mirabito/dsl 🍴 Good Golly's Rest. 🅾 Murphy's Automotive, **W** 🅶 Fastrac/gas 🍴 Burger King, Dunkin', McDonald's, Taco Bell 🅾 $Tree, Advance Parts, Ford, NAPA, Rite Aid, URGENT CARE, Verizon, Walmart/Subway
31(99)	to US 11, Brewerton, **E** 🅾 Oneida Shores Camping, **W** 🅶 Circle K/dsl, Mirabito/Tim Hortons/dsl 🍴 Dunkin', Lin Li's Chinese, Little Caesar's, McDonald's, Subway 🏠 Days Inn 🅾 $General, AT&T, Kinney Drugs, USPO, vet
30(96)	NY 31, to Cicero, **E** 🅶 Fastrac/dsl, Speedway/dsl 🍴 Arby's, Cracker Barrel, Dunkin', McDonald's, Sapori Pizza 🏠 Comfort Suites, Holiday Inn Express 🅾 $Tree, Aldi, **W** 🅶 Kwikfill 🍴 Cicero Diner, Cicero Pizza 🅾 Burdick's RV Ctr
29(93)	I-481 S, NY 481, to Oswego, Syracuse, 1 mi **W** on US 11 🅶 EVC, Speedway 🍴 Burger King, Chick-fil-A, Copper Top Tavern, Denny's, DQ, Dunkin', Jimmy John's, KFC, Little Caesar's, McDonald's, Moe's SW Grill, Panera Bread, Pizza Hut, Starbucks,

(left margin, vertical) WATERTOWN

(right margin, vertical) PULASKI

🅖 = gas 🅗 = food 🅐 = lodging 🅞 = other 🆁🆂 = rest stop   Copyright 2022 - The Next EXIT ®

⬆N INTERSTATE 81 Cont'd

29(93)	Continued
	Subway, Taco Bell, Tully's Rest., Wendy's 🅞 $General, $Tree, Advance Parts, AT&T, Audi/Porsche/VW, AutoZone, BMW, Buick/GMC, Chevrolet, Chrysler/Dodge/Jeep, Firestone/auto, GNC, Goodyear/auto, Home Depot, Hyundai, Kia, Lexus, Lincoln, Lowe's, Marshall's, Mavis Tire, Mazda, Midas, NAPA, Nissan, PepBoys, PriceChopper Foods, Rite Aid, Target, Toyota, Verizon, Walmart, Wegman's Foods
28(91)	N Syracuse, Taft Rd, **E** 🅖 Circle K/dsl, KwikFill, Sunoco/dsl 🅞 U-Haul, **W** 🅖 Sunoco/dsl 🅞 Auto Value Parts, USPO
27(90)	N Syracuse, **E** 🅞 ⛽
26(89)	US 11, Mattydale, **E** 🅖 Sunoco/Dunkin/dsl 🅗 Paladino's Pizza, Zebb's Deluxe Grill 🅐 Red Carpet Inn 🅞 $Tree, auto repair, BigLots, Dunn Tire/auto, GNC, Goodyear/auto, PetCo, Rite Aid, **W** 🅖 Delta Sonic/dsl 🅗 Applebee's, Arby's, Burger King, Camino Real, Denny's, Dunkin', Julie's Diner, McDonald's, Sonic, Subway, Taco Bell, Tim Hortons, Wendy's 🅐 Candlewood Suites, EconoLodge, Holiday Inn Express 🅞 Advance Parts, Aldi Foods, AT&T, Monro Auto, Mr Tire, Rite Aid, Sullivan's Car Care, Top's Foods
25a(88)	I-90, NY Thruway
25(87.5)	7th North St, **E** 🅖 ⛽/McDonald's/dsl/scales/24hr 🅞 NAPA Autocare, **W** 🅖 EVC, Sunoco/dsl 🅗 Burger King, Denny's, Dunkin', Little Caesar's, Subway, Tully's Rest. 🅐 Comfort Inn, Country Inn Suites, Hampton Inn, Maplewood Inn/cafe, Super 8, Tru Hilton
24(86)	NY 370 W, to Liverpool, same as 23
23(86)	NY 370 E, Hiawatha Blvd, **E** 🅗 Stella's Diner, Wendy's 🅞 Family$, **W** 🅖 EVC, Speedway/Dunkin' 🅗 Cheesecake Factory, Dave&Busters, Panera Bread, PF Chang's 🅞 Best Buy, Dick's, JC Penney, Lord&Taylor, Macy's, TJ Maxx
22(85)	NY 298, Court St
21(84.5)	Spencer St, Catawba St (from sb), industrial area
20(84)	I-690 W (from sb), Franklin St, West St
19(84)	I-690 E, Clinton St, Salina St, to E Syracuse
18(84)	Harrison St, Adams St, **E** 🅐 Crowne Plaza 🅞 🅷, to Syracuse U, **W** 🅞 Civic Ctr
17(82)	Brighton Ave, S Salina St, **W** 🅖 Conoco/Chicken Basket
16a(81)	I-481 N, to DeWitt
16(78)	US 11, to Nedrow, Onondaga Nation, **1-2 mi W** 🅖 Valero 🅗 McDonald's, Pizza Hut 🅞 $General, Aldi, Mr Tire
15(73)	US 20, La Fayette, **E** 🅖 Cirvle K/dsl 🅗 New LaFayette Inn, Old Tymes Rest. 🅞 $General, NAPA, st police, USPO, vet, **W** 🅗 McDonald's
71mm	truck insp sta both lanes
14(67)	NY 80, Tully, **E** 🅖 Circle K/deli/dsl 🅗 A Pizza More, Tasty China 🅐 Quality Inn 🅞 $General, Chevrolet, Kinney Drug, USPO, **W** 🅗 Burger King
13(63)	NY 281, Preble, **E** 🅖 Mirabito/Dunkin'/Subway/dsl 🅞 to Song Mtn Ski Resort
60mm	🆁🆂/truck insp nb, full 🅿 facilities, litter barrels, petwalk, 🅲, 🏕, vending
12(53)	US 11, NY 281, to Homer, **W** 🅖 KwikFill, Sunoco, Sunoco/Dunkin'/dsl 🅗 Little Italy 🅞 🅷, $General, st police, to Fillmore Glen SP
11(52)	NY 13, Cortland, **E** 🅗 Perkins 🅐 Clarion Inn, Holiday Inn Express, Quality Inn, **W** 🅖 Mobil/Dunkin'/dsl 🅗 Arby's, Denny's, Friendly's, McDonald's, Starbucks, Subway, Taco Bell, Wendy's 🅐 Hampton Inn, Ramada Inn, Red Roof Inn 🅞 Advance Parts, Family$, Jo-Ann Fabrics, Mr Tire, P&C Foods
10(50)	US 11, NY 41, to Cortland, McGraw, **W** 🅖 Pitstop/Dunkin'/dsl, Speedway/dsl/24hr, Sunoco 🅐 Cortland Motel, Motel 6

(left margin vertical labels: SYRACUSE, CORTLAND)

(center margin vertical label: BINGHAMTON)

9(38)	US 11, NY 221, **W** 🅖 Sunoco/XtraMart/dsl/24hr, Valero 🅗 NY Pizzaria, Reilly's Cafe 🅐 Greek Peak Lodge, Three Bear Inn/rest. 🅞 city park, Country Hills Camping, Maple Museum, Robinson's Repair, st police, USPO
33mm	🆁🆂 sb, full 🅿 facilities, litter barrels, petwalk, 🅲, 🏕, vending
8(30)	NY 79, to US 11, NY 26, NY 206 (no EZ return), Whitney Pt, **E** 🅖 Kwikfill, Speedway, Sunoco 🅗 Aiello's Ristorante, Arby's, Dunkin', McDonald's, Subway 🅐 Hotel Griffin 🅞 $General, Gregg's Mkt, NAPA, Parts+, to Dorchester Park, USPO
7(21)	US 11, Castle Creek, **W** 🅖 Mirabito/Subway/Tim Hortons/dsl
6(16)	US 11, to NY 12, I-88E, Chenango Bridge, **E on US 11** 🅖 Mirabito/dsl, Sunoco/dsl 🅗 Arby's, Burger King, Denny's, Dunkin', Grande Pizza, Moe's SW Grill, Subway, Wendy's 🅞 Advance Parts, AutoZone, Big E Tire/auto, Chrysler/Dodge/Jeep, CVS Drug, Lowe's, Mavis Tire, Monro, Mr Tire, Rite Aid, Valvoline, Verizon, Weis Foods, **W on US 11** 🅖 KwikFill, Tesla EVC, Wave/dsl 🅗 China Star, Nirchi's Pizza, Sonic, Spot Diner, Starbucks 🅐 Comfort Inn, Motel 6, Quality Inn 🅞 Aldi Foods, Harley Davidson
15mm	I-88 begins eb
5(14)	US 11, Front St, **1 mi W** 🅖 Mirabito/Subway/dsl, Sunoco, McDonald's/dsl, Tesla EVC 🅗 Applebee's, Cracker Barrel, Starbucks, Thai Front 🅐 EconoLodge, Fairfield Inn, Red Roof Inn 🅞 Cutler Botanical Garden
4(13)	NY 17, Binghamton
3(12)	Broad Ave, Binghamton, **W** 🅖 Mirabito 🅗 KFC 🅞 CVS Drug, Weis Mkt
3(10)	Industrial Park, same as 2
2(8)	US 11, NY 17, **1-2 mi W** 🅖 Loves/Wendy's/dsl/scales/24hr, Mirabito/Dunkin'/dsl, TA/Country Pride/dsl/scales/24hr/ 🅗 Burger King, McDonald's, Subway, Taco Bell 🅐 Del Motel
1(4)	US 11, NY 7, Kirkwood, **1-2 mi W** 🅖 Mirabito/dsl 🅐 Kirkwood Motel
2mm	Welcome ctr nb, full 🅿 facilities, litter barrels, petwalk, 🅲, 🏕, vending
1mm	truck insp sta nb
0mm	New York/Pennsylvania state line

➡E INTERSTATE 84

Exit #	Services
71.5mm	New York/Connecticut state line
69	US 6, US 202, NY 121 (from wb), N Salem, same as 20
68N	NY 22, Palling, **N** 🅖 Mobil, Shell/dsl, Valero 🅗 Dunkin', Portofinos 🅞 Ford, Honda, Subaru
68S	I-684, to NYC
65	NY 312, Carmel, **S** 🅗 Applebee's, Dunkin', Eveready Diner, Gaetano's Deli 🅞 🅷, DeCicco's Mkt, Home Depot, Kohl's, Marshall's, Michael's, Verizon
61	NY 311, Lake Carmel, **S** 🅗 La Famiglia
58	Ludingtonville Rd, **S** 🅖 Speedway/dsl, Sunoco/dsl 🅗 Cutillo Rest., Dunkin', Gappy's Pizza, Lou's Rest.
56mm	elevation 965 ft
55mm	🆁🆂 both lanes, full 🅿 facilities, litter barrels, petwalk, 🅲, 🏕, vending
52	Taconic Parkway, N to Albany, S to New York
50	CR 27, Lime Kiln NY, **3 mi N** 🅖 Shell 🅗 Dunkin' 🅐 Arbor Ridge Inn
46	US 9, to Poughkeepsie, **N** 🅖 Mobil/deli, Mobil/dsl, Phillips 66 🅗 Dunkin'/dsl 🅗 A&W/KFC, Boston Mkt, Charlie Brown's, Chipotle, Coldstone, Cracker Barrel, Fishkill Grill, Five Guys, Hudson Buffet, Panera Bread, Red Line Diner, Starbucks, Subway, Taco Bell, Wendy's 🅐 Courtyard, Extended Stay America, Extended

INTERSTATE 84 Cont'd

46 Continued
Stay America, Hampton Inn, Hawthorn Inn, Hilton Garden, Holiday Inn Express, Hyatt House, Magnuson Hotel, Ramada Inn, SpringHill Suites 🅞 AT&T, Sam's Club, Verizon, Walmart, **S** 🅖 Speedway/dsl 🅕 Maya Cafe, McDonald's 🅞 Home Depot

44 NY 52 E, Fishkill, **N** 🅖 Valero/dsl 🅕 Golden Buddha, Green Garden 🅞 CVS Drug, USPO, **S** 🅖 Mobil, Sunoco/dsl 🅕 84 Diner, Hometown Deli 🅛 Quality Inn

41 NY 9D, to Wappingers Falls, **1 mi N** 🅖 Gulf/dsl, Mobil/dsl

41mm toll booth

40mm Hudson River

39 US 9W, NY 32, to Newburgh, **N** 🅖 Citgo/dsl, Sunoco 🅕 Alexis Diner, Burger King, Domino's, Dunkin', Green Garden Chinese, KFC, McDonald's, New China, Papa John's, Pizza Hut, Planet Pizza, Subway 🅞 $Tree, Advance Parts, BigLots, Family$, Firestone/auto, Monro, PriceChopper Foods, Shop Rite Foods, Verizon, Walgreens, **S** 🅖 Citgo/dsl, Shell/dsl, Sunoco 🅕 Dunkin' 🅞 🅗

37 NY 52, to Walden, **N** 🅖 Conoco/dsl

36b NY 300, Newburgh, **N** 🅖 Mobil 🅕 DQ, Dunkin', Flaming Grill Buffet, Leo's Pizzaria, McDonald's, Newburgh Buffet, Perkins, Taco Bell, Wendy's 🅞 $Tree, AT&T, AutoZone, GNC, Marshall's, Mavis Tire, Midas, Office Depot, Stop&Shop Foods, Verizon, **S** 🅖 Mobil, Speedway/dsl, Sunoco/dsl 🅕 Applebee's, Burger King, Chili's, China City, Cosimos Ristorante, Denny's, Five Guys, IHOP, Ikaros Diner, Longhorn Steaks, Orange Hill Bistro, Panera Bread, Pizza Mia, Sonic, Starbucks, Subway, TGIFriday's, Union Sq Rest., Yobo Asian 🅛 Days Inn, Hampton Inn, Howard Johnson, Hudson Valley Hotel, Ramada Inn, Super 8 🅞 $General, Adam's Farm Mkt, Aldi Foods, Barnes&Noble, Buick/GMC, Cadillac/Chevrolet, Chrysler/Dodge/Jeep, Ford/Lincoln, Home Depot, Honda, Kohl's, Lowe's, Meineke, Michael's, Nissan, PetsMart, Target, Tesla EVC, Verizon, Walmart

36a I-87, NY Thruway, Albany, to NYC

34 NY 17K, to Newburgh, **N** 🅖 Mobil/dsl, Pilot/Arby's/dsl/scales/24hr 🅕 Airport Diner 🅛 Sheraton, **S** 🅖 Shell/Dunkin'/dsl 🅛 Courtyard, Hampton Inn, Howard Johnson 🅞 Toyota

32 NY 747, International Blvd, **S** 🅛 Homewood Suites 🅞 to Stewart Airport

28 NY 208, Maybrook, **N** 🅖 Mobil/dsl, Sunoco/dsl 🅕 Burger King, Dunkin', McDonald's 🅛 Holiday Inn Express 🅞 AutoPro Parts, Rite Aid, ShopRite Foods, Verizon, Walgreens, Winding Hills Camping, **S** 🅖 Speedway/dsl, TA/Shell/Country Pride/Pizza Hut/dsl/scales/24hr/@ 🅕 Renee's Deli, Subway 🅛 Super 8 🅞 Advance Parts, auto/truck repair, Blue Beacon, st police

24mm 🆁🆂 wb, full 🅗 facilities, litter barrels, petwalk, 🄲, 🄰, vending

19 NY 17, Middletown, **N** 🅖 Mobil/24hr, Tesla EVC 🅕 Americana Diner, Applebee's, Boston Mkt, Buffalo Wild Wings, Burger King, Chipotle, Cosimo's Italian, Denny's, Dunkin'/Baskin-Robbins, Five Guys, Fuji Japanese, Golden Corral, KFC, McDonald's, Olive Garden, Panera Bread, Pizza Hut, Popeye's, Red Lobster, Ruby Tuesday, Sonic, Starbucks, Subway, Taco Bell, TX Roadhouse, Wendy's, Youyou Asian 🅛 Home 2 Suites, Middletown Motel, Super 8 🅞 $Tree, Aldi Foods, AT&T, AutoZone, Best Buy, Big Lots, CVS Drug, Dick's, Firestone/auto, GNC, Hannaford Foods, Hobby Lobby, Home Depot, Honda, JC Penney, Jo-Ann Fabrics, Kohl's, Lowe's, Macy's, Marshall's, Mavis Tire/auto, Michael's, Midas, Old Navy, PetCo, PetsMart, PriceChopper Foods, Rite Aid, Sam's Club/dsl, ShopRite/gas, Staples, Target, Tire Discount, TJ Maxx, U-Haul, Verizon, Walmart/Subway, **S** 🅕 Chili's, D lux Diner, Dunkin', El Bandido Mexican, Outback Steaks, TGIFriday 🅛 Courtyard, Hampton Inn, Holiday Inn, Microtel 🅞 🅗, st police

17mm 🆁🆂 eb, full 🅗 facilities, litter barrels, petwalk, 🄲, 🄰, vending

15 US 6, to Middletown, **N** 🅖 Citgo/dsl, Mobil, QuickChek/dsl, Shell, Sunoco 🅕 DQ, Dunkin', IHOP, McDonald's, Peking Chinese, Rita's Custard, Subway, Taco Bell, Wendy's 🅛 Sleep Inn 🅞 $General, Acura, AutoZone, Buick/Chevrolet, Family$, Lexus, Mavis Discount Tire, Mazda, Meineke, Monro Automotive, NAPA, ShopRite Foods, Subaru, Verizon, VW, Walgreens, **S** 🅖 Geo/Dunkin'/dsl, Sunoco/dsl 🅛 Days Inn 🅞 Kia, Nissan, Toyota, USPO

4 Mountain Rd, **S** 🅕 Firehouse Deli

4mm elevation 1254 ft wb, 1272 ft eb

3mm parking area both lanes

1 US 6, NY 23, Port Jervis, **N** 🅕 Arlene'n Tom's Diner, Dunkin'/Baskin-Robbins 🅞 🅗, Ford, **S** 🅖 BP/dsl/LP, Citgo/dsl, Gulf/dsl, Pilot/Subway/dsl, Shell/dsl, Valero/dsl 🅕 DQ, McDonald's, Village Pizza 🅞 $Tree, GNC, ShopRite Foods, TJ Maxx

0mm New York/Pennsylvania state line, Delaware River

INTERSTATE 86

Exit #	Services
I-86 begins/ends on I-87, exit 16, toll booth	

131(379) NY 17, **N** 🅕 Chipotle, Food Court, Starbucks 🅞 Outlets/famous brands, **S** 🅞 EVC, Gulf/dsl 🅕 Chili's, Dunkin', El Castillo Mexican, IHOP, KFC/Taco Bell, Outback Steaks, Panera Bread, TGIFriday's, Uno Grill, Wendy's 🅛 Hampton Inn 🅞 $Tree, Best Buy, BJ's Whse, BMW, GNC, Home Depot, Kohl's, Mercedes, Michael's, Old Navy, Petsmart, Staples, Target, TJMaxx, Verizon, Walmart/Subway

130a(378) US 6, Bear Mtn, to West Point (from eb, no return)

130(377) NY 208, Monroe, Washingtonville, **N** 🅕 208 Grill, **S** 🅖 Exxon, Mobil/dsl, Sunoco/dsl 🅕 Burger King, Domino's, Dunkin', Empire Diner, Wayback Burger 🅞 $Tree, Rite Aid, ShopRite Foods, USPO, Verizon

129(375) Museum Village Rd

128(374) rd 51 (only from wb), Oxford Depot

127(373) Greycourt Rd (from wb only), Sugar Loaf, Warwick

126(372) NY 94 (no EZ wb return), Chester, Florida, **N** 🅖 Mobil, Shell, Sunoco/dsl 🅕 Bro Bruno Pizza, Burger King, Chester Diner, Dunkin', McDonald's, Subway, Taco Bell, Wendy's 🅛 Holiday Inn Express 🅞 CVS Drug, GNC, Goodyear/auto, Rite Aid, ShopRite Foods, USPO, Verizon, **S** 🅞 Lowe's

125(369) NY 17M E, South St

124(368) NY 17A, NY 207, **N** 🅖 Gulf/Dunkin'/dsl, Mobil/dsl, QuickChek/dsl 🅕 Burger King, Goshen Diner, Pizza Hut 🅞 AutoZone, CVS Drug, Verizon, **S** 🅛 Comfort Inn 🅞 Chrysler/Dodge/Jeep, Hyundai, URGENT CARE

123 US 6, NY 17M (wb only), Port Jervis

122a(367) Fletcher St, Goshen

MIDDLETOWN

NY

INTERSTATE 86 Cont'd

Exit #	Services
122(364)	rd 67, E Main St, Crystal Run Rd, N Chili's, D Lux Diner, Outback Steaks, TGIFriday's Courtyard, Hampton Inn, Holiday Inn, Microtel URGENT CARE, S El Bandido Rest.
121(363)	I-84, E to Newburgh, W to Port Jervis
120(363)	NY 211, N Mobil, Tesla EVC Buffalo Wild Wings, Cosimo's Ristorante, Fuji Japanese, Olive Garden Home 2 Suites, Middletown Motel, Super 8 Best Buy, Dick's, Hannaford's Foods, Honda, JC Penney, Lowe's, Macy's, Mavis Discount Tire, PetCo, Sam's Club/dsl, Target, S Americana Diner, Applebee's, Boston Mkt, Burger King, Chipotle, Denny's, Dunkin', Five Guys, Franco Di Roma Italian, Golden Corral, KFC, McDonald's, Panera Bread, Papa John's, Pizza Hut, Popeye's, Red Lobster, Ruby Tuesday, Sonic, Starbucks, Subway, Taco Bell, TX Roadhouse, Wendy's, Yu Yu Chinese $General, $Tree, Aldi Foods, AT&T, AutoZone, BigLots, CVS Drug, Firestone/auto, GNC, Hobby Lobby, Home Depot, Jo-Ann, Kohl's, Marshall's, Michael's, Midas, Old Navy, Petsmart, PriceChopper, ShopRite/gas, Staples, Tire Discount Ctr, TJMaxx, U-Haul, Verizon, Walmart/Subway
119(360)	NY 302, Circleville, to Pine Bush, Pine Bush, S Citgo/dsl, Exxon/Dunkin'/dsl Subway
118a(358)	NY 17M, Fair Oaks
118(358)	Fair Oaks, Circleville, N Economy Inn, S Citgo/dsl, Mobil/dsl
116(355)	NY 17K, Bloomingburg, N Mtn View Rest., S Citgo/dsl Quickway Diner
115	Burlingame Rd
114	Wurtsboro, Highview (from wb)
113(350)	US 209, Wurtsboro, Ellenville, N Mobil/dsl, Stewarts/gas Danny's Steaks Days Inn G-Mart Foods, S Giovanni's Café (2mi)
112(347)	Masten Lake, Yankee Lake, N Days Inn, S Yankee Lake
111(344)	(eb only), Wolf Lake, S Global/dsl
110(343)	Lake Louise Marie
109(342)	Rock Hill, Woodridge, N Citgo/dsl, EVC Bernie's Holiday Rest., Dunkin', Dutch's Cafe, Pizza Rock Sullivan Ramada Ace Hardware, auto repair, Hilltop Farms Camping (6mi), Super Mkt Trading Post, USPO, S Mobil/dsl Windsong B&B
108(341)	Bridgeville, same as 109
107(340)	Thompsonville, S Chevrolet, Chrysler/Dodge/Jeep, Toyota
106(339)	East Broadway, E. Broadway, N Ford/Lincoln, S Mobil/dsl Super 8 (2 mi) GMC Trucks, Hyundai, Toyota
105(337)	NY 42, Monticello, N Mobil/dsl Bro Bruno's Pizza, Burger King, China City, Dunkin', Giovanni's Rest., KFC, McDonald's, Subway, Taco Bell AutoZone, Home Depot, museum, ShopRite Foods, Walmart/McDonald's, S Citgo/dsl, Sunoco/dsl Monticello Diner, Pizza Hut, Stewart's, Wendy's EconoLodge, Heritage Inn, Super 8 Advance Parts, Family$, NAPA, Verizon, Walgreens
104(336)	NY 17B, Raceway, Monticello, S Citgo/dsl, Mobil/Subway/dsl Albella Rest., Colosseo Rest., Dunkin', Tilly's Diner Best Western, Raceway Motel AT&T, Swinging Bridge Camp
103	Rapp Rd (wb only)
102(332)	Harris, N
101(327)	Ferndale, Swan Lake, S Mobil/dsl
100(327)	NY 52 E, Liberty, N Citgo/dsl, Sam's, Sunoco Burger King, Dunkin', Joseph's Italian, Last Licks Cafe, Liberty Diner, McDonald's, Piccolo Italian, Pizza Hut, Subway, Taco Bell Days Inn, Knights Inn $Tree, Ace Hardware, Advance Parts, AutoZone, Rite Aid, ShopRite Foods, USPO, Verizon, S Lincoln Motel Buick/Cadillac, Chrysler/Dodge/Jeep, Ford/Lincoln, NAPA

WINDSOR

Exit #	Services
100a	NY 52 W (no wb return), Liberty, S st police
99(325)	NY 52 W, to NY 55, Liberty, S Sunoco Catskill Motel
98(321)	Cooley, Parksville, N Mobil/dsl
97(319)	Morsston
96(316)	Livingston Manor, S Citgo, EVC, Sunoco Robin Ho Diner Covered Bridge Camping, Mongaup Pond Campin Peck's Mkt, to Covered Bridge, USPO
313mm	eb, truck insp. sta, full facilities, litter barrels, petwal , , vending
94(311)	NY 206, Roscoe, Lew Beach, N Mobil/dsl, Sunoco/dsl, Te la EVC Raimondo's Diner, Roscoe Diner Creekside B& Reynolds House Motel, Rockland House Motel, Roscoe Mot Beaverkill St Camping (8mi), Roscoe Mkt, st police, USPO Mobil/dsl Tennanah Lake Motel
93(305)	to Cooks Falls (from wb)
92(303)	Horton, Cooks Falls, Colchester, S Sunoco/dsl Riversi Café/lodge Russell Brook Camping
90(297)	NY 30, East Branch, Downsville, N Sunoco Beaver-D Camping, Oxbow Camping, Peaceful Valley Camping, S Branch Motel
295mm	wb, full facilities, litter barrels, petwalk, , , vendin
89(293)	Fishs Eddy
87a(288)	NY 268 (from wb, no ez-return), same as 87
87(284)	NY 97, to NY 268, to NY 191, Hancock, Cadosia, S Mir bito/Subway/dsl, Sunoco, Valero McDonald's, New Chi Hancock House Hotel, Upper Delaware Inn Family NAPA, Rite Aid, Tops Foods
276mm	parking area wb
84(274)	Deposit, N Mirabito/dsl BC Pizza, Honey's Cafe, We dy's Deposit Motel, Laurel Bank Motel Family$, st poli
83(272)	Deposit, Oquaga Lake
82(270)	NY 41, McClure, Sanford, N Cornerstone Cafe au repair, Kellystone Park, Oquaga Creek SP, S Scott's Fam Resort Guestward Camping (3mi)
265mm	parking area eb, litter barrels,
81(263)	E Bosket Rd
80(261)	Damascus, N Mirabito/dsl auto repair, Forest Hill La Park Camping (3mi)
79(259)	NY 79, Windsor, N Sunoco/dsl China Star, Pizza Win Subway Big M Mkt, USPO, S Marian's Pizza/Su Windsor Diner $General, Lakeside Camping (8mi)
78(256)	Dunbar Rd, Occanum
77(254)	W Windsor, N Sunoco/dsl McDonald's $General
76(251)	Haskins Rd, to Foley Rd
75(250)	I-81 S, to PA (exits left from wb)
3	Colesville Rd (from eb), S /Wendy's/dsl/scale 24hr, Mirabito/Dunkin'/dsl, TA/Country Pride/dsl/scales/24 Subway
I-86/I-81 run together 4 miles.	
3	Broad Ave (from wb, no return)
4s	NY 7, I-86/I-81 run together 4 miles.
72(244)	I-81 N, US 11, Front St, Clinton St, (no wb re-entry)
71(242)	Airport Rd, Johnson City, S Mirabito Microtel Walm
70(241)	NY 201, Johnson City, N Mirabito, Speedway/dsl Arby Dunkin', Food&Fire BBQ, Friendly's, Great China, McDonal Papa John's, Pizza Hut, Ruby Tuesday, Taco Bell Baymont I Hampton Inn, La Quinta, Red Roof Inn $Tree, JC Penney, M vis Tire, Mr Tire, PetCo, Wegman's Foods, S Home Depot
69(239)	NY 17C
238mm	Susquehanna River
68(237)	NY 17C, Old Vestal Rd, (from eb, no re-entry)

▲🅴 INTERSTATE 86 Cont'd

Exit #	Services

67(236) NY 26, NY 434, Vestal, Endicott, **S on NY 434** 🅖 Mirabito/dsl, Mirabito/Dunkin', Speedway/dsl, Stop'N Gas 🍽 A&W/LJ Silver, Applebee's, Arby's, Blaze Pizza, Burger King, CA Grill, Chili's, ChuckECheese, Denny's, Dunkin', IHOP, Jimmy John's, KFC, McDonald's, Moe's SW Grill, Olive Garden, Outback Steaks, Panera Bread, Pudgie's Pizza, Red Lobster, Red Robin, Starbucks, Subway, Taco Bell, TGIFriday's, Wendy's 🏨 Candlewood Suites, Comfort Suites, Courtyard, Hampton Inn, Holiday Inn Express, Homewood Suites, Parkway Motel 🅞 $Tree, Aldi Foods, AT&T, Barnes&Noble, Best Buy, Big E Tire/auto, BigLots, Chrysler/Dodge/Jeep, CVS Drug, Dick's, Ford/Lincoln, Jo-Ann Fabrics, Kohl's, Lowe's, Mavis Tire, Michael's, Mr Tire, Nissan, Old Navy, Petsmart, Price Rite Foods, Rite Aid, Sam's Club, Staples, Target, TJ Maxx, U-Haul, USPO, Verizon, vet, Volvo, VW, Walmart/Dunkin', Wies Foods

66(231) NY 434, Apalachin, **S** 🅖 KwikFill 🍽 Big Dipper Drive-In, Blue Dolphin Diner, Dunkin', McDonald's, Perkins, Subway 🏨 Apalachin Inn, Comfort Inn

65(225) NY 17C, NY 434, Owego, **N** 🅖 Speedway 🍽 A&W/KFC, Arby's, McDonald's, Panda Wok, Subway, Wendy's 🏨 Hampton Inn, Holiday Inn Express, Treadaway Inn/rest. 🅞 $General, Buick/GMC, Hickories Park Camping, Mr Tire, Top's Foods, Verizon, **S** 🅞 st police

64(223) NY 96, Owego, **N** 🍽 Dunkin' 🅞 AutoZone, CVS Drug, Rite Aid, USPO, **S** 🅖 Mobil/dsl

222mm 🆁🆂 wb, full ♿ facilities, litter barrels, petwalk, 🅒, 🏕, vending

63(218) Lounsberry, **S** 🅖 Valero/rest./dsl/24hr

62(214) NY 282, Nichols, **S** 🅖 Citgo/pizza/dsl 🅞 Jim's RV Ctr, Tioga Downs Race Track (2mi)

212mm 🆁🆂 eb, full ♿ facilities, litter barrels, petwalk, 🅒, 🏕, vending

208mm Susquehanna River

61(206) NY 34, PA 199, Waverly, Sayre, **N** 🅞 $General, Goodyear/gas, **S** 🅖 Gulf 🏨 Best Western/rest. 🅞 Chrysler/Dodge/Jeep, Joe's RV Ctr, Nissan, Subaru

60(204) US 220, to Sayre, Waverly, **N** 🏨 O'brien's Inn, **S** 🅖 Citgo/dsl, Mirabito/Dunkin'/dsl, Tesla EVC 🍽 Wendy's (3mi) 🏨 Candlewood Suites, Comfort Inn, Hampton Inn 🅞 Advance Parts, Aldi Foods, Rite Aid, Top's Foods, Toyota

59a(202) Wilawana, **S** 🅖 Sunoco/Subway/dsl

59(200) NY 427, Chemung, **N** 🅖 Dandy/dsl

58a(197) to CR 60, Lowman

57(195) rd 2, Lowman, Wellsburg, **N** 🅞 Gardner Hill Campsites (4mi), USPO

56(190) Jerusalem Hill, **N** 🍽 Hilltop Rest., **S** 🅖 Citgo/dsl, Sunoco/Dandy Pizza/Subway/dsl 🍽 Dunkin', McDonald's 🏨 Holiday Inn, Mark Twain Motel (3mi) 🅞 🏥

54(186) NY 13, to Ithaca

53(185) Horseheads, **S** 🅖 Speedway/dsl 🍽 Burger King, Domino's, Dunkin', Guiseppe's Pizza, Lin Buffet, McDonald's, Rico's Pizza, Subway, Wendy's 🏨 Red Carpet Inn, Travelodge 🅞 Advance Parts, Family$, Rite Aid

52b(184) NY 14, to Watkins Glen, **N** 🍽 Friendly's 🏨 Knights Inn, Quality Inn, **S** 🍽 Denny's, Rita's Custard

52a(183) Commerce Ctr, **S** 🍽 Buffalo Wild Wings, Cracker Barrel, Red Robin, TX Roadhouse 🏨 Fairfield Inn 🅞 Aldi Foods, AT&T, Dick's, Jo-Ann Fabrics, Kohl's, Mavis Discount Tire, Petsmart, Walmart/McDonald's

51a(182) Chambers Rd, **N** 🅖 Sunoco/Subway/dsl 🍽 Chili's, Dunkin', McDonald's, Olive Garden, Outback Steaks, Red Lobster, Ruby Tuesday 🏨 Candlewood Suites, Country Inn&Suites, Courtyard,

51a(182) Continued
Hampton Inn, Hilton Garden 🅞 JC Penney, Nissan, **S** 🍽 Applebee's, Charley's Subs, Five Guys, Moe's SW, Mt Fuji Japanese, Old Country Buffet, Panera Bread, Popeye's, Taco Bell, TGIFriday's, Wendy's 🏨 EconoLodge 🅞 $Tree, Barnes&Noble, Best Buy, Buick/GMC/Cadillac, Field&Stream, Hobby Lobby, Honda, Hyundai, Lowe's, Michael's, Mr Tire, Old Navy, PetCo, Sam's Club, Staples, Subaru, Target, TJ Maxx, Top's Foods, Toyota, URGENT CARE, Verizon

50(180) Kahler Rd, **N** 🅞 to Airport

49(178) Olcott Rd, Canal St, Big Flats, **N** 🅞 🛩, antiques, **S** 🅖 Sunoco 🍽 Picnic Pizza 🏨 Comfort Suites 🅞 USPO

48(171) NY 352, E Corning, **N** 🅖 Citgo 🏨 Budget Inn, Gate House Motel 🅞 🏥

47(174) NY 352, Gibson, E Corning, **N** 🏨 Budget Inn, Gate House Motel

46(171) NY 414, to Watkins Glen, Corning, **N** 🅞 Ferenbaugh Camping (5mi), KOA (14mi), Watkins Glen Camping, **S** 🅖 Sunoco 🍽 Pizza Hut 🏨 Comfort Inn, Radisson, Staybridge Suites 🅞 Corning Glass Museum

45(170) NY 352, Corning, **S** 🅖 Fastrac 🍽 Bob Evans, Subway, Wendy's 🏨 Fairfield Inn 🅞 Advance Parts, AutoZone, Rite Aid, Tops/gas

44a I-99 S, US 15 S, NY 417 W, Gang Mills, **N** 🅖 Mobil 🍽 McDonald's, **S** 🅖 Gulf, Sunoco 🍽 Applebee's, Arby's, Taco Bell 🏨 Best Value Inn, Corning Inn, EconoLodge, Hampton Inn, Ramada Inn 🅞 $Tree, Aldi Foods, Buick/GMC, Chevrolet, Home Depot, Verizon, Walmart

43(167) NY 415, Painted Post, **N** 🅖 Citgo 🍽 Burger King 🅞 $General, AutoValue Parts, Big Lots, Firestone/auto, **S** 🅖 7-11 🍽 Denny's, Dunkin' 🏨 Hampton Inn, Holiday Inn Express

167mm parking area wb, litter barrels

42(165) Coopers Plains, **N** 🅞 st police

41(161) rd 333, Campbell, **N** 🅖 Sunoco/Subway/dsl 🅞 Camp Bell Camping (1mi), **S** 🅖 Sunoco 🅞 antiques, Cardinal Campsites (6mi)

160mm 🆁🆂 eb, full ♿ facilities, litter barrels, petwalk, 🅒, 🏕, vending

40(156) NY 226, Savona, **N** 🅖 Mobil/dsl 🅞 $General, King's Mkt

39(153) NY 415, Bath, **N** 🍽 Chat-a-Whyle Rest. (3mi) 🏨 National Hotel, **S** 🅞 Jellystone (2mi)

38(150) NY 54, to Hammondsport, Bath, **N** 🅖 Exxon/dsl, KwikFill 🍽 Arby's, Burger King, Dunkin', Ling Ling Chinese, McDonald's, Pizza Hut, Rico's Pizza, Subway, Taco Bell 🏨 Budget Inn, Days Inn, Microtel, Super 8 🅞 $General, Advance Parts, AT&T, Campers Haven Camping, Family$, Hickory Hill Camping (3mi), Meyer's RV Ctr, Monro, museum, Rite Aid, SaveALot, st police, to Keuka Lake, Top's Foods/gas, Verizon, Walgreens

147mm 🆁🆂 wb, full ♿ facilities, litter barrels, petwalk, 🅒, 🏕, vending

37(146) NY 53, to Prattsburg, Kanona, **S** 🅖 🛢🛢🛢/Subway/dsl/scales/24hr/@, Sunoco/Smokey's/dsl/scales 🅞 st police, USPO, Wilkin's RV Ctr (1mi)

NY

Side bar: V E S T A L · O W E G O · E L M I R A · C O R N I N G · B A T H

= gas   = food   = lodging   = other   = rest stop   Copyright 2022 - The Next EXIT

INTERSTATE 86 Cont'd

Exit #	Services
36(145)	I-390 N, NY 15, to Rochester
35(138)	Howard, S to Lake Demmon RA
34(130)	NY 36, Hornell, Arkport, 0-2 mi S KwikFill, Mobil/dsl Applebee's, Country Kitchen, Dunkin', McDonald's, Pizza Hut, Subway Days Inn, EconoLodge, Sunshine Motel $General, $Tree, Advance Parts, Aldi Foods, AutoZone, Chrysler/Dodge/Jeep, Ford/Nissan, GNC, Lowe's, NAPA, Verizon, Walmart/Subway, Wegman's Foods
125mm	scenic overlook eb
33(124)	NY 21, to Alfred, Almond, Andover, S 7-11/dsl Kanakadea Camping, Lake Lodge Camping (8mi), USPO
117mm	highest elevation on I-86, elev 2110 ft eb, 2080 ft wb
32(116)	W Almond
31(108)	Angelica, N Valero/dsl American House Inn
30(104)	NY 19, Belmont, Wellsville, N Letchworth SP (27mi), S , st police
101mm	eb, full facilities, litter barrels, petwalk, , , vending
29(99)	NY 275, to Bolivar, Friendship, S Miller&Brandes Gas, Mobil/Subway/dsl
28(92)	NY 305, Cuba, N Moonwink's Rest. EconoLodge $General, Maple Lane RV Park, S Sunoco/dsl, Valero/dsl Charlie's Chicken Pizza, McDonald's, Subway , Cuba Cheese Shop, Cuba Drug, Family$, Giant Foods
27(84)	NY 16, NY 446, Hinsdale, N food, S gas lodging
26(79)	NY 16, Olean, S 7-11 Burger King, Pizza Hut, Subway, Wendy's Holiday Inn Express
25(77)	Buffalo St, Olean, S Citgo/dsl , 2 mi S on NY 417 Tesla EVC Applebee's, Burger King, Coldstone/Tim Hortons, Domino's, Dunkin', Friendly's, Lakeview Chinese, Little Caesar's, McDonald's, Perkins, Subway Best Western+, Fairfield Inn, Microtel $Tree, Advance Parts, Aldi Foods, AT&T, BJ's Whse/gas, GNC, Home Depot, Jo-Ann Fabrics, KwikFill, Old Navy, St Bonaventure U, Staples, Tops Foods/gas, Verizon, Walmart/Subway
24(74)	NY 417, Allegany, S Mobil/7-11/dsl $General, to St Bonaventure U
73mm	wb, full facilities, litter barrels, petwalk,
23(68)	US 219 S, N M&M Jct./Subway/dsl, Sassy's Trkstp/dsl
66mm	Allegheny River
21(61)	US 219 N, Salamanca
20(58)	NY 417, NY 353, Salamanca, N Allegany Gas, Antone's Gas, Grand Ctr Sta, Nafco Quickstop/Burger King/24hr, Seneca OneStop/dsl/24hr Burger King, Little Caesar's, McDonald's Holiday Inn Express, Hotel Westgate AutoZone, Rail Museum, Seneca-Iroquis Museum, S casino
19(54)	N Red House Area, S Allegany SP
18(51)	NY 280, S Allegany SP, Quaker Run Area
17(48)	NY 394, Steamburg, S Steamburg, WW/dsl
16(41)	W Main St, Randolph, N Mobil/7-11/dsl R&M Rest. RV camping
40mm	parking area,
15(39)	School House Rd
39mm	parking area,
14(36)	US 62, Kennedy, 1 mi N Keystone Gas Office Pizza/Subs, S RV camping
32mm	Cassadaga Creek
13(31)	NY 394, Falconer, S Keystone, Mobil/dsl Burger King Budget Inn, Quality Inn CVS Drug, Harley-Davidson
12(28)	NY 60, Jamestown, N KwikFill/dsl st police, S Mobil/McDonald's/dsl Bob Evans, Tim Horton Comfort Inn, Hampton Inn, Holiday Inn Express
11(25)	to NY 430, Jamestown, S gas/dsl food lodging
22mm	Welcome ctr/ eb, full facilities, litter barrels, petwalk, , vending
10(21)	NY 430 W, Bemus Point
9(20)	NY 430 E (no EZ eb return), N Mobil/dsl Bemus Point Rest.
19mm	Chautauqua Lake
8(18)	NY 394, Mayville, N USPO, vet
7(15)	Panama
6(9)	NY 76, Sherman, N Keystone Gas $General, city park, NAPA, Sherman Drug, USPO
4(1)	NY 430, Findley Lake, N Holiday Inn Express, S Blue Heron Inn, Peek'n Peak Conference Ctr to Peek'n Peak Ski Area
0mm	New York/Pennsylvania state line. Exits 3-1 are in PA.
3	PA 89, North East, Wattsburg, N gas food
1b a	I-90, W to Erie, E to Buffalo.
	I-86 begins/ends on I-90, exit 37.

INTERSTATE 87

Exit #	Services
176mm	US/Canada Border, NY state line, I-87 begins/ends.
43(175)	US 9, Champlain, E Duty Free America, W Peterbilt Trk stp/deli/dsl/scales/24hr/@ repair
42(174)	US 11 S, to Rouse's Point, Champlain, E Irving/dsl, Sunoco Subway Empire Buffet, Pizza+ $General, $Tree, Ace Hardware, Chevrolet (3mi), Kinney Drug, PriceChopper, Rite Aid, USPO, W Mobil/dsl, Valero/dsl Dunkin', McDonald's, Nathan's
41(167)	NY 191, Chazy, E st police, W Miner Museum
162mm	both lanes full facilities, info, litter barrels, petwalk, ,
40(160)	NY 456, Beekmantown, E Mobil/dsl Conroy's Organic Pt Auroche Lodge, Stonehelm Motel/café, W Twin Elms Camping
39(158)	NY 314, Moffitt Rd, Plattsburgh Bay, E Mobil/dsl, Stewarts Dunkin', Gus' Rest Rip van Winkle Motel, Super 8 $General, Plattsburgh RV Park, to VT Ferry, W Shady Oaks Camping, to Adirondacks
38(154)	NY 22, NY 374, to Plattsburgh, E Mobil/dsl Subway Kinney Drug, W RV Store
37(153)	NY 3, Plattsburgh, E Stewarts #1 Chinese, Buffalo Wild Wings, Burger King, Chick-fil-A, China Buffet, Chipotle, Domino's, Dunkin', Five Guys, Golden Palace, Guiseppe's Pizza, Jade Buffet, KFC, Koto Japanese, McDonald's, Michigans+ Rest, Panera Bread, Perkins, Pizza Hut, Starbucks, Subway, Taco Bell, TX Roadhouse, Wendy's Comfort Inn, Holiday Inn , Aldi Foods, BigLots, Buick/GMC, Family$, Ford, GNC, Kinney Drug, Michael's, Petsmart, Sam's Club/dsl, Staples, TJ Maxx, TrueValue, Verizon, vet, Walgreens, Walmart, W Mobil/dsl, Shell, Sunoco/Lambo's Subs, Tesla EVC 99 Rest., Anthony's Rest., Applebee's, Butcher Block Rest., Dickey's BBQ, Dunkin', Friendly's, Ground Round, PriceChopper Mkt, Subway, Uno Best Value Inn, Best Western+, Days Inn, Hampton Inn, La Quinta, Microtel, Quality Inn $Tree, Advance Parts, AT&T, AutoZone, Best Buy, Dick's, Hannaford Foods, Harley-Davidson, Hobby Lobby, Honda, JC Penney, Kinney Drug, Lowe's, Midas, Prays Mkt, Target, vet
151mm	Saranac River
36(150)	NY 22, Plattsburgh AFB, E Mobil/dsl st police, U-Haul, W Shell/Dunkin'/dsl
146mm	nb, full facilities, litter barrels, petwalk, , truck insp sta both lanes

INTERSTATE 87 Cont'd

Exit #	Services
35(144)	NY 442, to Port Kent, Peru, **2-8 mi E** 🅾 Iroquois/Ausable Pines Camping, to VT Ferry, **W** 🅿 Mobil/Dunkin'/Subway/dsl, Mobil/repair 🍴 Dunkin', Livingood's Rest., McDonald's, Pasquale's Rest. 🅾 Aubuchon Hardware, Tops Foods, USPO
143mm	emergency 🅲 at 2 mi intervals begin sb/end nb
34(137)	NY 9 N, Ausable Forks, **E** 🅿 Sunoco/dsl 🍴 Big Daddy's BBQ, Pleasant Corner Rest., **W** 🅾 Ausable River RV Camping, auto repair, Prays Mkt
136mm	Ausable River
33(135)	US 9, NY 22, to Willsboro, **E** 🅿 gas/dsl 🍴 food 🏠 lodging 🅾 RV camping, to Essex Ferry
125mm	N Boquet River
32(124)	Lewis, **E** 🅾 RV Camping, **W** 🅿 Beavers 🍴 Trkstp Diner 🅾 RV Camping, st police
120mm	Boquet River
31(117)	NY 9 N, to Elizabethtown, Westport, **E** 🅿 Mobil/dsl 🏠 HillTop Motel 🅾 RV camp/dump, **W** 🅾 🏥, st police, vet
30(104)	US 9, NY 73, Keene Valley
99mm	℞s both lanes, full ♿ facilities, litter barrels, petwalk, 🅲, 🚻, trk insp sta
29(94)	N Hudson, **E** 🅾 Jellystone Camping, USPO, **W** 🅾 Blue Ridge Falls Camping
28(88)	NY 74 E, to Ticonderoga, Schroon Lake, **E** 🅿 Mt Severance Country Store, Sunoco/dsl 🏠 Maple Leaf Motel, Schroon Lake B&B 🅾 RV camp/dump, services on US 9, st police
83mm	parking area nb
27(81)	US 9 (from nb, no EZ return), Schroon Lake, **E** 🅿 to gas/dsl 🍴 food 🏠 lodging
26(78)	US 9 (from sb, no EZ return), Pottersville, Schroon Lake, **E** 🏠 Lee's Corner Motel 🅾 Wakonda Camping, **W** 🅿 Mobil/dsl 🍴 Black Bear Diner 🅾 USPO
25(73)	NY 8, Chestertown, **E** 🅿 Crossroads Country Store 🅾 Country Haven Camping, **W** 🅿 Stewart's/dsl
24(67)	Bolton Landing, **E** 🅾 RV camping
67mm	Schroon River
66mm	parking area sb, 🚻
64mm	parking area nb, 🚻
23(58)	to US 9, Diamond Point, Warrensburg, **W** 🅿 Citgo/dsl, Cumberland, Gulf, Stewarts, Sunoco/Dunkin'/dsl 🍴 Dragon Lee Chinese, George Henry's Rest., McDonald's, Subway 🏠 Super 8 🅾 Central Adirondack Tr, Family$, Ford, PriceChopper Foods, Riverview Camping, Schroon River Camping (3mi), ski area, Tops Foods
22(54)	US 9, NY 9 N, to Diamond Pt, Lake George, **E on US 9** 🍴 Gino&Tony's, Guiseppe's Pizza, Mario's Italian, Monte Cristo's, Moose Tooth Grill, Number 1 🏠 7 Dwarfs Motel, Admiral Motel, Balsam Motel, Barberry Ct, Best Value Inn, Blue Moon Motel, Brookside Motel, Courtyard, EconoLodge, Georgian Lakeside Resort, Heritage Motel, Lake Crest Inn, Lake George Inn, Lake Haven Motel, Lake Motel, Marine Village Resort, Motel Montreal, Nordick's Motel, Oasis Motel, O'Sullivan's Motel, Park Lane Motel, Sundowner Motel, Surfside Motel 🅾 multiple services, PriceChopper Foods, same as 21, **W** parking area both lanes
21(53)	NY 9 N, Lake Geo, Ft Wm Henry, **E on US 9** 🅿 Stewarts, Sunoco/dsl, Valero 🍴 A&W, Adirondack Brewery, Barnsider BBQ, Blacksmith Rest., Dining Room, DJ's Cafe, Gaslight Grill, Jasper's Steaks, Lobster Pot, Mama Riso's Italian, McDonald's, Mezzaluna's, Pizza Hut 🏠 Best Western, Ft William Henry Inn, Hampton Inn, Holiday Inn Resort, Lake View Inn, Lincoln Log Motel, Motel 6, Quality Inn, Rodeway Inn, Super 8, Tiki Hotel,

GLENS FALLS

LAKE GEORGE

21(53)	Continued Travelodge, Villager Motel, Windsor Hotel, Wingate Inn 🅾 city park, Harley-Davidson, King Phillip Camping, Lake George Camping, multiple services, Rite Aid, same as 22, USPO, waterpark, **W** 🅿 Mobil/dsl/LP 🏠 Kathy's Cottages
51mm	Adirondack Park
20(49)	NY 149, to Ft Ann, **E on US 9** 🅿 Mobil/Dunkin'/dsl, Sunoco/dsl 🍴 Blue Moose Rest., Frank's Pizza, Johnny Rocket's, Logjam Rest., Olde Post Grille, Subway 🏠 Clarion, Comfort Suites, French Mtn Inn, Great Escape Lodge, Mohican Motel 🅾 Factory Outlets/famous brands, Ledgeview RV Park (3mi), Six Flags Funpark, waterpark
19(47)	NY 254, Glens Falls, **E** 🅿 Mobil/dsl, Speedway, Sunoco, Tesla EVC 🍴 99 Rest., Ambrosia Diner, Burger King, Chicago Grill, Dickey's BBQ, Dunkin', Five Guys, Friendly's, Giavano's Pizza, Golden Corral, KFC, Liberty Pizza, McDonald's, Moe's SW Grill, Mr B's Rest., Old China Buffet, Olive Garden, Outback Steaks, Panera Bread, Papa John's, Pizza Hut, Red Lobster, Silo Rest., Starbucks, Subway, Taco Bell/LJ Silver, Wendy's 🏠 Alpen Haus Motel, Budget Inn, EconoLodge, Home 2 Suites, Quality Inn, Red Roof Inn, Sleep Inn 🅾 $Tree, Ace Hardware, Advance Parts, AT&T, AutoZone, Dick's, Goodyear, Hobby Lobby, Home Depot, JC Penney, Jo-Ann Fabrics, Meineke, Petco, Price Rite Foods, PriceChopper Foods, Rite Aid, Staples, Target, TJ Maxx, Tuesday Morning, USPO, Verizon, Walmart, **W** 🅿 Mobil/Dunkin'/Subway/dsl 🏠 Baymont Inn 🅾 st police
18(45)	Glens Falls, **E** 🅿 Cumberland Farms/Subway/e-85/dsl, Speedway/dsl, Sunoco/dsl 🍴 Dunkin', Pizza Hut, Steve's Place Rest., Subway 🏠 Days Inn, Fairfield Inn 🅾 🏥, $General, CVS Drug, Hannaford Foods, Toyota, U-Haul, Walgreens, **W** 🅿 Fastrac/dsl, Stewarts 🍴 McDonald's, Taco Bell 🏠 Holiday Inn Express 🅾 Super 8
43mm	℞s both lanes, full ♿ facilities, litter barrels, petwalk, 🅲, 🚻, vending
42mm	Hudson River
17(40)	US 9, S Glen Falls, **E** 🅿 Citgo/dsl, Exxon/Subway/dsl, Mobil, Speedway/dsl, Sunoco/dsl 🍴 Dunkin', Fitzgerald's Steaks 🏠 Budget Inn, Landmark Motel (1mi) 🅾 Adirondack RV Camp, **W** 🅾 Moreau Lake SP
16(36)	Ballard Rd, Wilton, **E** 🅾 Coldbrook Campsites, **W** 🅿 Mobil, Stewart's, Sunoco/Scotty's Rest./dsl/scales/24hr 🏠 Mt View Acres Motel 🅾 Alpin Haus RV Ctr, golf
15(30)	NY 50, NY 29, Saratoga Springs, **E** 🅿 Speedway/dsl, Sunoco 🍴 99 Rest., Applebee's, Burger King, Chipotle Mexican, Denny's, Dunkin', Five Guys, Friendly's, Golden Corral, Jersey Mike's, KFC/Taco Bell, McDonald's, Moe's SW Grill, Osaka, Panera Bread, Red Robin, Subway, Sunny Wok, TGIFriday's 🏠 Comfort Inn 🅾 AT&T, Barnes&Noble, Best Buy, BJ's Whse, Dick's, Ford, GNC, Hannaford Foods, Healthy Living Mkt,

🚉 = gas 🍴 = food 🛏 = lodging 🅾 = other 🆁🆂 = rest stop   Copyright 2022 - The Next EXIT ©

S A R A T O G A   S P R I N G S

N | INTERSTATE 87 Cont'd

15(30)	Continued Home Depot, JC Penney, Kohl's, Lowe's, Old Navy, Petsmart, PriceChopper Mkt, Rite Aid, Staples, Subaru, Target, TJ Maxx, Toyota, Walgreens, Walmart, **W** 🛏 Residence Inn 🅾 H
14(28)	NY 9P, Schuylerville, **2 mi W** 🛏 Hampton Inn, Holiday Inn 🅾 H, museum, racetrack
13(25)	US 9, Saratoga Springs, **E** 🍴 Andy's Grille, DeLucia's Deli 🛏 Budget Inn, Locust Grove Motel 🅾 Ballston Spa SP, Nissan, **W** 🚉 Mobil/dsl, Stewarts 🍴 13 North Rest., PJ's BBQ 🛏 Best Western+, Design Motel, Roosevelt Inn/rest., Top Hill Hotel 🅾 Saratoga SP
12(21)	NY 67, Malta, **E** 🚉 Citgo/dsl, Cumberland Farms/dsl, Sunoco/dsl 🍴 Bentley's Rest., Dunkin', KFC/Taco Bell, Malta Diner, McDonald's, Panera Bread, Starbucks, Subway 🛏 Fairfield Inn, Home 2 Suites 🅾 CVS Drug, GNC, PriceChopper Foods, Saratoga NHP, st police, Stewart's, Verizon, **W** 🛏 Hyatt Place 🅾 URGENT CARE
11(18)	Round Lake Rd, Round Lake, **W** 🚉 Gulf/dsl, Stewarts/dsl 🍴 Governor's Rest. 🅾 Hannaford Foods, Walgreens
10(16)	Ushers Rd, **E** 🚉 Speedway/Dunkin'/dsl, Xtra/dsl 🅾 auto repair, **W** 🅾 Stewarts
14mm	🆁🆂 nb, full ♿ facilities, info, litter barrels, petwalk, 🅲, 🏞, vending
9(13)	NY 146, Clifton Park, **E** 🚉 Speedway/Dunkin'/dsl, USA 🍴 Burger King, Caputo's Pizza, Chili's, Cracker Barrel, Delmonico's Steaks, Harborhouse Fish Fry, Mr Subb, Peddler's Grill, Pizza Hut, Red Robin, Snyder's Rest., Subway, Wheatfields Bistro 🛏 Holiday Inn Express, Park Manor Inn, Residence Inn 🅾 Advance Parts, Aldi Foods, AutoZone, BigLots, Goodyear/auto, Home Depot, Kohl's, Lowe's, Michael's, Midas, Petco, Red Roof Inn, Rite Aid, Target, **W** 🚉 Mobil, Sunoco/dsl 🍴 99 Rest., Bellini's Italian, Blaze Pizza, Brick House Pizza, Buffalo Wild Wings, Chipotle Mexican, Dunkin', East Wok, Five Guys, Friendly's, IHOP, La Fiesta, McDonald's, Moe's SW Grill, Olive Garden, Outback Steaks, Panera Bread, Pasta Pane, Salad Creations, Starbucks, Subway, Taco Bell, TGIFriday's, Wendy's 🛏 Best Western, Hampton Inn, Hilton Garden, Homewood Suites 🅾 $Tree, AT&T, Chevrolet, CVS Drug, Firestone/auto, GNC, Hannaford Foods, JC Penney, Jo-Ann Fabrics, Marshall's, Petsmart, PriceChopper Mkt, st police, Staples, Verizon, Walgreens
8a(12)	Grooms Rd, to Waterford
8(10)	Crescent, Vischer Ferry, **E** 🚉 Speedway/dsl 🍴 McDonald's 🅾 USPO, **W** 🚉 Stewart's/dsl, Sunoco 🍴 Dunkin', Mangia Pizza, Pancho's Mexican 🅾 CVS Drug
8mm	Mohawk River
7(7)	NY 7, Troy, **E on US 9 N** 🚉 Speedway/dsl 🍴 Century House, Mr Subb 🛏 Comfort Inn, Holiday Inn Express, Sycamore Motel 🅾 $General, Acura, Chrysler/Dodge/Jeep, Ford, Infiniti, Lexus, Nissan, Walgreens, **E on US 9 S** 🚉 Sunoco 🍴 BurgerFi, Dunkin', McDonald's, Red Robin, Subway 🅾 AT&T, AutoZone, Hobby Lobby, Marshall's
6(6)	NY 2, to US 9, same as 7, Schenectady, **E** 🚉 Mobil, Speedway 🍴 Applebee's, Boston Mkt, ChuckeCheese, Circle Diner, Jersey Mike's, Mr Subb, Panera Bread, Red Robin, Starbucks, Wendy's 🛏 Golden Circle Inn, La Quinta 🅾 $Tree, CVS Drug, Dick's, Field&Stream, GNC, Hannaford Foods, Home Depot, Lowe's, Mavis Discount Tire, Mkt Bistro, Petsmart, Sam's Club, Staples, Toyota, VW, Walmart/Subway, **W** 🚉 Mobil/dsl, Stewart's 🍴 Carrabba's, Chipotle Mexican, Denny's, DiBella's Subs, Dunkin', Ruby Tuesday, Sake Japanese, Sonic, Subway 🛏 Microtel, Quality Inn, Super 8, TownePlace Suites 🅾 Goodyear/auto, Michael's, Target, TJ Maxx, Verizon

A L B A N Y

5(5)	NY 155 E, Latham, **E** 🍴 DeeDee's Rest., Philly's Grill 🅾 USP(
4(4)	NY 155 W, Wolf Rd, **E on Wolf Rd** 🚉 Mobil/Subway, Speedway/dsl, Sunoco 🍴 99 Rest., Arby's, Capital Buffet, Chipotl(Mexican, CiCi's Pizza, Denny's, Dunkin', Honeybaked Ham Longhorn Steaks, Macaroni Grill, Maxie's Grill, McDonald's Moe's SW Grill, Olive Garden, Outback Steaks, Pizza Hut, Re(Lobster, Reel Seafood Co, Samurai, Smashburger, Starbucks Subway, Ted's Fishfry, TX Roadhouse, Whse Grill BBQ, Wolf 1-11 🛏 Courtyard, Fairfield Inn, Hampton Inn, Holiday Inn Home 2 Suites, Homewood Suites, Marriott, Red Lion Inn, Re(Roof Inn, Residence Inn, Staybridge Suites, SureStay+ 🅾 Chev rolet, CVS Drug, Firestone/auto, Hannaford Foods, Trader Joe's **W** 🍴 Blu Stone Bistro, Koto Japanese 🛏 Desmond Hotel, Ho tel Indigo 🅾 to Heritage Park
2(2)	NY 5, Central Ave, **E** 🚉 Mobil/dsl, Sunoco, Tesla EVC 🍴 BJ's Rest., Buca Italian, Cheesecake Factory, Chili's, Five Guys, Hon eybaked Ham, Hooters, IHOP, Panera Bread, PF Chang's, Star bucks, Taco Bell, Wendy's 🛏 Cocca's Inn, Holiday Inn Express Scottish Inn, SpringHill Suites, Staybridge Suites, Travelodge 🅾 Barnes&Noble, BJ's Whse/gas, Goodyear/auto, Jo-Ann Fabrics, LL Bean, Lowe's, Macy's, Marshall's, Mr Tire, PetCo Staples, Target, Whole Foods Mkt, **W** 🚉 Cumberland Farms dsl, Gulf/dsl, Mobil, USA/dsl 🍴 Brazilian Steaks, Delmonico's Steaks, DQ, Dunkin', La Fiesta Mexican, McDonald's, Moe's SW Grill, Mr Subb, Smokey Bones BBQ, Subway, Wendy's 🛏 Days Inn, EconoLodge, Howard Johnson, Motel 6, Quality Inn, Re(Carpet Inn 🅾 Advance Parts, AT&T, AutoZone, Buick/GMC, Ca dillac, Krause's Candy, Midas, PepBoys, ShopRite/gas, Subaru Verizon, Walgreens
1W(1)	NY State Thruway (from sb), I-87 S to NYC, I-90 W to Buffalo
1E(1)	I-90 E (from sb), to Albany, Boston
1S(1)	to US 20, Western Ave, **E on US 20** 🚉 Mobil 🍴 B Good, Blaze Pizza, Burger King, Chipotle Mexican, Coldstone, Dunkin', Five Guys, J&A Italian, Starbucks, TGIFriday's 🛏 Days Inn, Hampton Inn 🅾 AT&T, CVS Drug, USPO, Verizon, **W on US 20** 🚉 Mobil, USA 🍴 Capital City Diner, Dunkin', El Charro, Hana Grill, McDonald's 🛏 Homewood Suites, Tru Hilton 🅾 Adirondack Tires, PriceChopper Foods
1N(1)	I-87 N (from nb), to Plattsburgh
149	NY State Thruway goes west to Buffalo (I-90), S to NYC (I-87), I-87 N to Montreal
24(148)	I-90 and I-87 N
23(142)	I-787, to Albany, US 9, **E on US 9 W** 🚉 Cumberland Farms/ Dunkin'/dsl, Sunoco/dsl 🛏 Comfort Inn 🅾 transmissions, **W** 🚉 Stewarts 🍴 Johnny B's Diner 🛏 Quality Inn
139mm	parking area sb, litter barrel, 🏞
22(135)	NY 396, to Selkirk
21a(134)	I-90 E, to MA Tpk, Boston
127mm	**New Baltimore Travel Plaza both lanes,** 🚉 Mobil/dsl 🍴 Famous Famiglia, Quiznos, Roy Rogers, Starbucks, TCBY 🅾 atm, info, wi-fi
21b(124)	US 9 W, NY 81, to Coxsackie, **W** 🚉 21B Travel Plaza/rest./dsl/ scales/24hr, Sunoco/dsl 🍴 Dunkin', McDonald's 🛏 Best Western, Holiday Inn Express 🅾 Boat'n RV Whse, repair, vet
21(114)	NY 23, Catskill, **E** 🚉 Stewart's, Sunoco/dsl 🛏 Pelokes Motel (2mi) 🅾 Home Depot, to Rip van Winkle Br, visitors ctr, **W** 🍴 Anthony's Banquet Hall 🛏 Astoria Motel, Rip Van Winkle Motel 🅾 to Hunter Mtn/Windham Ski Areas
103mm	Malden Service Area nb, 🚉 Mobil/dsl 🍴 Carvel Ice Cream, Hotdogs, McDonald's 🅾 atm, **parking area sb,** 🅲
20(102)	NY 32, to Saugerties, **E** 🚉 Mobil/dsl, Stewart's, Sunoco 🍴 Dunkin', Frederico's Pizza, McDonald's, Pizza Star, Starway Café, Subway 🅾 Advance Parts, Big Lots, Chrysler/Dodge/Jeep,

NY

INTERSTATE 87 Cont'd

20(102)	Continued
	CVS Drug, Family$, PriceChopper Foods, Verizon, **W** 🅿 Speed-way/dsl, Sunoco/dsl 🍴 Michelle's Diner 🛏 Comfort Inn, Holiday Inn Express, Howard Johnson/rest. 🅾 Blue Mtn Campground (5mi), Brookside Campground (10mi), KOA (2mi), Rip Van Winkle Campground (3mi), to Catskills
99mm	parking area nb, litter barrels, 🚻, 🛏
96mm	**Ulster Travel Plaza sb,** 🅿 Sunoco/dsl 🍴 Burger King, Nathan's, Pizza Hut, Starbucks, TCBY 🅾 atm, 🚻, wi-fi
19(91)	NY 28, Rhinecliff Br, Kingston, **E** 🅿 QuickChek/dsl 🍴 Olympic Diner, Picnic Pizza, Stadium Diner 🛏 Best Western+, Super 8 🅾 access to I-587 E, Advance Parts, Advance Parts, CVS Drug, Hannaford Foods, Kia, Walgreens, **W** 🍴 Roudigan's Steaks 🛏 Motel 19, Quality Inn, Rodeway Inn 🅾 access to US 209, Camping World RV Ctr, Chrysler/Dodge/Jeep/Fiat, Ford, Nissan
18(76)	NY 299, to Poughkeepsie, New Paltz, **E** 🅿 Mobil, Shell/dsl 🛏 87 Motel, EconoLodge, Rodeway Inn 🅾 Lowe's, to Mid-Hudson Br, **W** 🅿 EVC, Sunoco 🍴 Burger King, Dunkin', Gadaletos Seafood, McDonald's, Pasquale's Pizza, Plaza Diner, Rino's Pizza, Rococo's Pizza, Subway 🛏 Best Value Inn, Hampton Inn 🅾 Advance Parts, AT&T, KOA (10mi), Midas, Rite Aid, ShopRite Foods, Tops Mkt, Verizon
66mm	**Modena service area sb,** 🅿 Sunoco/dsl 🍴 Carvel's Ice Cream, Chicago Grill, McDonald's, Moe's SW Grill 🅾 atm, UPS, wi-fi
65mm	**Plattekill Travel Plaza nb,** 🅿 Sunoco/dsl 🍴 Nathan's, Roy Rogers, Starbucks 🅾 atm, info, wi-fi
17(60)	I-84, NY 17K, to Newburgh, **E on NY 300 N** 🅿 Mobil 🍴 Buffalo Wild Wings, DQ, Dunkin', Flaming Grill, Joe's Deli, McDonald's, Newburgh Buffet, Perkins, Pizza Union, Taco Bell, Wendy's 🅾 $Tree, AT&T, AutoZone, BonTon, Marshall's, Mavis Tire, Midas, Office Depot, Stop&Shop, **E on NY 300 S** 🅿 Speedway/dsl, Sunoco/dsl, Tesla EVC 🍴 Applebee's, Burger King, Chili's, China City, Cosimos Ristorante, Denny's, Five Guys, IHOP, Ikaros Diner, Longhorn Steaks, Neptune Diner, Panera Bread, Pizza Mia, Sonic, Starbucks, Subway, TGIFriday's, Union Sq Rest., Yobo Asian 🛏 Days Inn, Hampton Inn, Howard Johnson, Hudson Valley Hotel, Ramada Inn, Super 8 🅾 $General, Adam's Food Mkt, Aldi Foods, Barnes&Noble, Buick/GMC, Cadillac/Chevrolet, Chrysler/Dodge/Jeep, Ford/Lincoln, Home Depot, Honda, Kohl's, Lowe's, Meineke, Michael's, Nissan, Petsmart, Target, Verizon, Walmart/McDonald's
16(45)	US 6, NY 17, to West Point, Harriman, **W** 🅿 Gulf/dsl 🍴 Applebee's, Chicago Grill, Chili's, Dunkin', KFC, Outback Steaks, Panera Bread, TGIFriday's, Wendy's 🛏 Days Inn, Hampton Inn 🅾 $Tree, Best Buy, BJ's Whse, BMW, GNC, Home Depot, Kohl's, Michaels, Old Navy, Petsmart, st police, Staples, Target, TJ Maxx, Verizon, Walmart/Subway, Woodbury Outlet/famous brands
34mm	**Ramapo Service Area sb,** 🅿 Sunoco/dsl 🍴 Carvel, McDonald's, Uno Pizza 🅾 atm, wi-fi
33mm	**Sloatsburg Travel Plaza nb,** 🅿 Sunoco/dsl 🍴 Burger King, Dunkin', Quiznos, Sbarro's 🅾 atm, gifts, info
15a(31)	NY 17 N, NY 59, Sloatsburg
15(30)	I-287 S, NY 17 S, to NJ. **I-87 S & I-287 E run together.**
14b(27)	Airmont Rd, Montebello, **E** 🛏 Crowne Plaza, **W on NY9** 🅿 Gulf/Dunkin'/dsl 🍴 Airmont Diner, AJ's, Bagel Boys Cafe, Le Brick, Starbucks, Sutter's Mill Rest. 🛏 Howard Johnson 🅾 🏥, ShopRite Foods, Tallman Tires, Walgreens, Walmart
14a(23)	Garden State Pkwy, to NJ, Chestnut Ridge
14(22)	NY 59, Spring Valley, Nanuet, **E** 🅿 76/dsl, Citgo/dsl, Shell/dsl 🍴 Burger King, Deliziosa Pizza, Domino's, IHOP, McDonald's, Planet Wings, Subway 🛏 Candlewood Suites, Quality Inn

14(22)	Continued
	🅾 BMW, Costco/gas, Lowe's, Maserati/Ferrari, Michael's, Target, **W** 🅿 76, Citgo, Gulf 🍴 Baskin-Robbins/Dunkin', ChuckeCheese, Dunkin', Franco's Pizza, KFC/Taco Bell, Nanuet Diner, Panera Bread, Red Lobster, Smashburger, Starbucks, White Castle, Zinburger 🛏 Days Inn, Hampton Inn, Hilton Garden 🅾 $Tree, AT&T, Barnes&Noble, Fairway Mkt, Home Depot, Macy's, Marshall's, Mavis Tires, Midas, PetCo, Staples, Stop&Shop Foods, Verizon
13(20)	Palisades Pkwy, N to Bear Mtn, S to NJ
12(19)	NY 303, Palisades Ctr Dr, W Nyack, **W** 🅿 Mobil 🍴 Buffalo Wild Wings, Cheesecake Factory, Outback Steaks, Panera Bread 🛏 Tappan Zee Hotel 🅾 Barnes&Noble, Best Buy, BJ's Whse, Dave&Buster's, Dick's, Home Depot, Lord&Taylor, Macy's, Mavis Tire/repair, Old Navy, Staples, Target, Verizon
11(18)	US 9W, to Nyack, **E** 🅿 Mobil, Shell/dsl 🛏 West Gate Inn 🅾 🏥, Walgreens, **W** 🅿 Shell/dsl 🍴 Dunkin', McDonald's 🛏 Super 8 🅾 J&L Repair/tire, Midas, Old World Food Mkt
10(17)	Nyack (from nb), same as 11
14mm	Hudson River, Tappan Zee Br
13mm	toll plaza
9(12)	to US 9, to Tarrytown, **E** 🅿 Shell, Speedway/dsl 🅾 CVS Drug, **W** 🅿 BP, EVC 🛏 DoubleTree Hotel 🅾 Honda, Mavis Tire
8(11)	I-287 E, to Saw Mill Pkwy, White Plains, **E** 🛏 Extended Stay America, Hampton Inn, Marriott, Sheraton
7a(10)	Saw Mill River Pkwy S, to Saw Mill River SP
7(8)	NY 9A (from nb), Taconic SP, Ardsley, **E** 🅾 🏥, **W** 🛏 Ardsley Acres Motel
6mm	**Ardsley Travel Plaza nb,** 🅿 Sunoco/dsl 🍴 Burger King, Popeye's 🅾 vending
5.5mm	toll plaza
6ba(5)	Stew Leonard Dr, to Ridge Hill, **W** 🅾 Costco, Home Depot, Stew Leonard's Farmfresh Foods
6(4.5)	Tuckahoe Dr, Yonkers, **E** 🅿 BP/repair 🍴 Marcellino's Pizza, McDonald's, Subway 🅾 ShopRite Foods/drug, **W** 🅿 Gulf, Mobil/dsl 🍴 Domino's, Dunkin', Kim Wei Chinese 🛏 Ramada Inn, Royal Regency Hotel
5(4.3)	NY 100 N (from nb), Central Park Ave, White Plains
4(4)	Cross Country Pkwy, Mile Sq Rd, **E** 🍴 Applebee's, Boston Mkt, Chipotle, Panda Express, Panera Bread, Red Lobster, Starbucks 🛏 Hyatt Place 🅾 Ford/Lincoln/Subaru, Macy's, Marshall's, TJ Maxx, **W** 🅿 BP, Shell/dsl, Shell/Dunkin'/dsl 🍴 Burger King 🅾 Chevrolet, Mavis Tire
3(3)	Mile Square Rd, **E** 🅾 Stop&Shop, **W** 🅿 Citgo
2(2)	Yonkers Ave (from nb), Westchester Fair, **E** 🅿 Mobil 🅾 Yonkers Speedway
1(1)	Hall Place, McLean Ave, **E** 🍴 Dunkin' 🅾 Acme Mkt/Subway
0mm	New York St Thruway and I-87 N run together to Albany.

=gas =food =lodging =other =rest stop   Copyright 2022 - The Next EXIT ®

INTERSTATE 87 Cont'd

Exit #	Services
14(11)	McLean Ave, E Acme/dsl Dunkin', Subway
13(10)	E 233rd, NE Tollway, service plaza both lanes, Gulf/Dunkin'
12(9.5)	Hudson Pkwy (from nb), Sawmill Pkwy
11(9)	Van Cortlandt Pk S
10(8.5)	W 230th St (from sb), W 240th (from nb), E Citgo, W Dunkin' , Marshall's, Target
9(8)	W Fordham Rd, E BP/dsl Dallas BBQ
8(7)	W 179th (from nb), W Roberto Clemente SP
7(6)	I-95, US 1, S to Trenton, NJ, N to New Haven, CT
6(5)	E 153rd t, River Ave, Stadium Rd, E Yankee Stadium
5(5)	E 161st, Macombs Dam Br, (exit 4 from nb), E AT&T, Best Buy, Michael's, Target, Yankee Stadium
3(3)	E 138th St, Madison Ave Br, E BP/dsl
2(2)	Willis Ave, 3rd Ave Br, E Mobil/dsl, W McDonald's
1(1)	Brook Ave, Hunts Point, E BP, W Speedway
0mm	I-87 begins/ends on I-278.

INTERSTATE 88

Exit #	Services
25a	I-90/NY Thruway. I-88 begins/ends on I-90, exit 25a.
117mm	toll booth (to enter or exit NY Thruway)
25(116)	NY 7, to Rotterdam, Schenectady, 3 mi S /Dunkin'/Subway/dsl/scales/24hr Peppino's Pizza Frosty Acres Camping
24(112)	US 20, NY 7, to Duanesburg, N Stewart's, Valero/dsl Duanesburg Diner, Dunkin' st police, S USPO
23(101)	NY 30, to Schoharie, Central Bridge, N Apple Food/dsl Hideaway Camping (2mi), Locust Park Camping, S Mobil/Subway/dsl Apple Barrel Cafe, Dunkin' Quality Inn, Wedgewood B&B (2mi)
22(95)	NY 7, NY 145, to Cobleskill, Middleburgh, 2-5 mi N Speedway/dsl, Stewart's/dsl, Sunoco Dunkin', Pizza Hut, Subway Colonial CT Motel, Super 8 , $General, $Tree, Advance Parts, AT&T, Buick/Chevrolet/GMC, Chrysler/Dodge/Jeep, Howe Caverns Camping, PriceChopper Foods, to Howe Caverns, Walmart/McDonald's, S Twin Oaks Camping (5mi)
21(90)	NY 7, NY 10, to Cobleskill, Warnerville, 2-3 mi N Mobil/dsl, Speedway/Dunkn'/dsl, Stewart's/dsl Arby's, Burger King, KFC/Taco Bell, McDonald's, Pizza Hut, Subway , $General, Ace Hardware, CVS Drug, Mavis Tire, NAPA, PriceChopper Foods, SavaLot, Walmart/McDonald's
20(87)	NY 7, NY 10, to Richmondville, S Mobil/dsl, Sunoco/dsl Reinhardt's Deli, Sub Express Countryside Inn USPO
79mm	wb, full facilities, litter barrels, petwalk, , , vending
19(76)	to NY 7, Worcester, N Stewart's, Sunoco/dsl
73mm	eb, full facilities, litter barrels
18(71)	to Schenevus, N Mirabito/dsl Schenevus Rest.
17(61)	NY 7, to NY 28 N, Colliersville, Cooperstown, N Sunoco Best Western (14mi), Redwood Inn to Baseball Hall of Fame
16(59)	NY 7, to Emmons, N Arby's, Brooks BBQ, Farmhouse Rest., Morey's Rest., Pizza Hut Amber Life Motel, Rainbow Inn PriceChopper Foods, Rite Aid
15	NY 28, NY 23, Oneonta, N Speedway Dunkin', KFC Townhouse Inn , Advance Parts, to Soccer Hall of Fame, USPO, S Mirabito/dsl, Speedway/dsl Applebee's, Buffalo Wild Wings, Burger King, Denny's, Five Guys, McDonald's, Moe's SW, Mt Fuji Japanese, Panera Bread, Subway, Taco Bell, Tim Horton, Wendy's Budget Inn, Courtyard, Holiday Inn Express, Quality Inn, Super 8 $Tree, Aldi Foods, AT&T,

Exit #	Services
15	Continued BJ's Whse/gas, Dick's, Ford, Hannaford Foods, Home Depot, JC Penney, Lowe's, Mr Tire, Petco, TJ Maxx, Verizon, Walmart
14(55)	Main St (from eb), Oneonta, N Stewart's, Sunoco Alfresco's Italian Advance Parts
13(53)	NY 205, 1-2 mi N Mirabito, Speedway, Valero/dsl DQ, Dunkin', McDonald's Celtic Motel, Hampton Inn, Motel 88 Buick/Cadillac/Chevrolet/GMC, Gilbert Lake SP (11mi), Honda, NAPA, Nissan, repair, Rite Aid, st police, Subaru, Verizon
12(47)	NY 7, to Otego, S Mirabito/Subway/Tim Hortons/dsl/24hr, Sunoco/dsl
42	wb, facilities, tables, litter barrels
11(40)	NY 357, to Unadilla, Delhi, S KOA
39mm	eb, full facilities, litter barrels, petwalk, , , vending
10(38)	NY 7, to Unadilla, 2 mi N KwikFill, Mirabito Country Motel (4mi) Family$, st police, USPO
9(33)	NY 8, to Sidney, N Citgo/dsl, Sunoco China Buffet, Little Caesar's, McDonald's, Pizza Hut, Subway Algonkin Motel, Country Motel, Super 8 , $General, Advance Parts, PriceChopper Foods, Tall Pines Camping, USPO
8(29)	NY 206, to Bainbridge, N Citgo/dsl, Sunoco Bob's Family Diner, China Star, Dunkin' Algonkin Motel, Susquehanna Motel Auto Parts+, Chevrolet/GMC, Family$, Riverside RV Park, USPO, S to Oquage Creek Park
7(22)	NY 41, to Afton, 1-2 mi N Mirabito, Sunoco/dsl Main St Grill, RiverClub Rest. Afton Golf/rest., Kellystone Park, Smith-Hale HS
6(16)	NY 79, to NY 7, Harpursville, Ninevah, S Mirabito/Subway/dsl Pantheon Rest. Family$, to Nathanial Cole Park
5(12)	Martin Hill Rd, to Belden, N Belden Hill Camping
4(8)	NY 7, to Sanitaria Springs, S Speedway/dsl
3(4)	NY 369, Port Crane, N to Chenango Valley SP, S Fastrac/dsl, KwikFill Subway
2(2)	NY 12a W, to Chenango Bridge, N Mirabito USPO
1(1)	NY 7 W (no wb return), to Binghamton
0mm	I-81, N to Syracuse, S to Binghamton. I-88 begins/ends on I-81.

INTERSTATE 90

Exit #	Services
0mm	New York/Massachusetts state line
0(B23)	NY 22, to Austerlitz, New Lebanon, W Stockbridge, N Citgo/dsl/scales/24hr, Loves /Dunkin'/Subway/dsl/scales/24hr, S Sunoco/dsl Berkshire Travel Lodge Woodland Hills Camp (3mi)
0(B17)	toll plaza,
0(B15)	NY 295, Taconic Pkwy, 1-2 mi S gas
0(B7)	US 9, NY Thruway W, to I-87, , toll booth
12(20)	US 9, to Hudson, N /Subway/dsl/scales/24hr, 0-3 mi S to Van Buren NHS
18.5mm	/weigh sta wb, full facilities, litter barrels, petwalk, , , vending
11(15)	US 9, US 20, E Greenbush, Nassau, N Speedway/dsl, Sunoco/dsl Dunkin' st police, S Stewart's Mercato's Pizza, My Place Host Field Inn, Knights Inn Rite Aid, USPO, vet
10(10)	Miller Rd, to E Greenbush, S Mobil/dsl Dunkin' Comfort Inn
9(9)	US 4, to Rensselaer, Troy, N Mobil/dsl Applebee's, Domino's, Dunkin', Five Guys, McDonald's, Moe's SW, OffShore Pier Rest., Panera Bread, Starbucks, Subway, Taco Bell, The Sports Grill Holiday Inn Express, Residence Inn $Tree, AT&T,

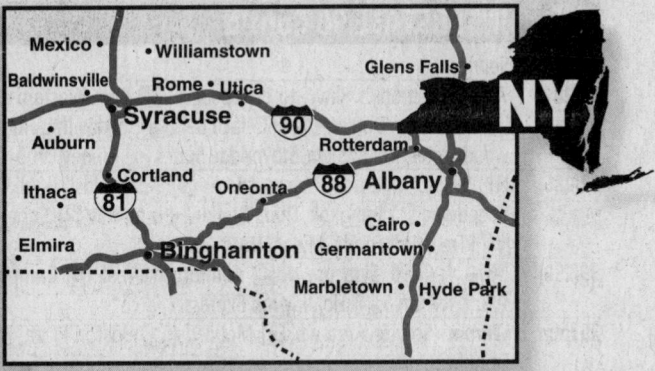

🚶🅴 INTERSTATE 90 Cont'd

9(9) Continued
CVS Drug, Home Depot, Mavis Tire/auto, PetsMart, Staples, Target, Walmart, **S** 🅿️ Mobil/dsl, Stewart's 🍴 Cracker Barrel, Denny's, Dunkin' 🏨 Hampton Inn 🅾️ Fairfield Inn

8(8) NY 43, Defreestville

7(7) Washington Ave (from eb), Rensselaer

6.5mm Hudson River

6a I-787, to Albany

6(4.5) US 9, Northern Blvd, to Loudonville, **N** 🅿️ Stewart's 🍴 Mr Subb, NY Pizza 🏨 Red Carpet Inn 🅾️ 🏥

5a(4.) Corporate Woods Blvd

5(3.5) Everett Rd, to NY 5, Central Ave, **S on NY 5** 🅿️ ShopRite, Speedway/dsl 🍴 Dunkin', Gateway Diner, Hokkaido Asian, Little Caesar's, McDonald's, Popeye's, Subway, Taco Bell 🏨 Motel 6, Ramada 🅾️ 🏥, $Tree, Aamco, Advance Parts, AutoZone, Chevrolet, Chrysler/Dodge/Jeep, CVS Drug, Fiat, Ford, Hannaford's Foods, Home Depot, Hyundai, Kia, Mavis Tire, Mazda, Monro, Nissan, PepBoys, PriceChopper Foods, Rite Aid, ShopRite Foods, Verizon

4(3) NY 85 S, to Slingerlands

3(2.5) **S** 🅾️ State Offices

2(2) Fuller Rd, Washington Ave, same as 1, **S on Washington** 🅿️ Sunoco/Subway 🍴 Dunkin' 🏨 Courtyard, CrestHill Suites, Extended Stay America, Fairfield Inn, Hilton Garden, Red Carpet Inn, TownePlace Suites 🅾️ same as 1S

1N(1) I-87 N, to Montreal, to Albany Airport

1S(1) US 20, Western Ave, **S** 🅿️ Mobil 🍴 Black&Blue Rest., Blaze Pizza, Burger King, Capital City Diner, Chipotle Mexican, Coldstone, Creo Rest., Dave&Buster's, Dunkin', Five Guys, Hana Grill, Ichiban Japanese, McDonald's, Moe's SW Grill, Panera Bread, Peaches Cafe, Provence Rest., Starbucks, TGIFriday's, Uno Grill 🏨 Hampton Inn, Residence Inn 🅾️ AT&T, Best Buy, CVS Drug, Dick's, Home Depot, JC Penney, Macy's, Michael's, Old Navy, PetsMart, PriceChopper Foods, USPO, Verizon, Walmart

24(149) I-87 N to Albany, Montreal, S to NYC

153mm **Guilderland Service Area eb,** 🅿️ Mobil/dsl 🍴 McDonald's

25(154) I-890, NY 7, NY 146, to Schenectady

25a(159) I-88 S, NY 7, to Binghamton, **S** 🅿️ Pilot/Dunkin'/Subway/dsl/scales/24hr

26(162) I-890, NY 5 S, Schenectady

168mm **Pattersonville Service Area wb,** 🅿️ Mobil/dsl 🍴 Hershey's, Roy Rogers, Starbucks 🅾️ atm, NY Mkt, wi-fi

172mm **Mohawk Service Area eb,** 🅿️ Mobil/dsl 🍴 McDonald's

27(174) NY 30, Amsterdam, **N** 🅿️ Mobil/dsl, Valero/Dunkin'/dsl 🏨 Knight Inn, Super 8 🅾️ Alpin Haus RV Ctr (3mi)

28(182) NY 30A, Fonda, **N** 🅿️ Citgo/rest/dsl/motel/24hr, Sunoco/dsl, TA/Country Pride/dsl/motel/scales/24hr/@ 🍴 Dunkin', McDonald's 🏨 Riverside Motel 🅾️ 🏥, st police, truck repair

184mm **parking area/truck insp area both lanes, litter barrels,** 🚻

187mm 🆁🆂 **wb, full facilities, living history site**

29(194) NY 10, Canajoharie, **N** 🅿️ Cumberland, Stewart's/dsl 🍴 McDonald's, Subway 🅾️ $General, BigLots, Rite Aid, Riverfront Park, USPO, **S** 🅿️ Beavers/dsl, Citgo/dsl, Sunoco 🍴 Mercato Pizza, Village Rest. 🅾️ USPO

210mm **Indian Castle Service area eb, Iroquois Service Area wb,** 🅿️ Mobil/dsl 🍴 Burger King, Hershey's Ice Cream, Roy Rogers, Starbucks 🅾️ atm, Dunkin', wi-fi

29a(211) NY 169, to Little Falls, **N** 🏨 Travelodge (3mi) 🅾️ 🏥, to Herkimer Home

30(220) NY 28, to Mohawk, Herkimer, **N** 🅿️ FasTrac/dsl, Stewart's, Sunoco/Subway/dsl 🍴 Applebee's, Burger King, Denny's, Dunkin', KFC/Taco Bell, McDonald's, Pizza Hut, Tony's Pizzaria, Vinny's Pizza 🏨 Budget Motel, Inn Towne Motel, Red Roof Inn 🅾️ $General, $Tree, Advance Parts, AutoZone, Mavis Tire/auto, Rite Aid, Verizon, vet, Walmart, **S** 🅿️ FasTrac 🍴 Little Caesar's, Red Apple Chinese 🅾️ Family$, to Cooperstown (Baseball Hall of Fame)

227mm **Schuyler Service Area wb,** 🅿️ Mobil/dsl 🍴 Breyer's, McDonald's 🅾️ atm, st police

31(233) I-790, NY 8, NY 12, to Utica, **N** 🅿️ Citgo/dsl, Fastrac, Sunoco 🍴 Applebee's, Burger King, Charlie's Pizza, Franco's Pizza, Good Friend Chinese 🅾️ $Tree, Aldi Foods, Bass Pro Shop, BigLots, BJ's Whse/gas, Lowe's, PriceChopper Foods, Rite Aid, Walmart/McDonald's, **S** 🅿️ Speedway/dsl 🍴 Babe's Grill, Delmonico's Steaks, Denny's, Dunkin', McDonald's, Moe's SW, Subway, Taco Bell, Wendy's 🏨 Best Western, Days Inn, EconoLodge, Fairfield Inn, Hampton Inn, Happy Journey Motel, Holiday Inn Epress, Red Roof Inn, Rest Inn 🅾️ AT&T

236mm I-790 (from eb), to Utica

237.5mm Erie Canal

238mm Mohawk River

32(243) NY 232, Westmoreland, **N** 🏨 Travel Inn, **S** 🅿️ Stewart's 🅾️ USPO

244mm **Oneida Service Area eb,** 🅿️ Sunoco/dsl 🍴 Burger King, Sbarro's, Starbucks 🅾️ atm, gifts

250mm **parking area eb, litter barrel,** 🚻, ♿

33(253) NY 365, to Vernon Downs, Verona, **N** 🅿️ SavOn Gas/Dunkin'/dsl 🏨 Inn at Turning Stone, **S** 🅿️ SavOn Gas/LP/repair 🍴 Dunkin', Recovery Grill 🏨 Fairfield Inn, La Quinta, Microtel 🅾️ 🏥, Turning Stone Casino

256mm **parking area wb, litter barrel,** 🚻, ♿

34(262) NY 13, to Canastota, **N** 🅾️ Verona Beach SP Camping, **S** 🅿️ SavOn/dsl 🍴 Dunkin', McDonald's 🏨 Days Inn, Graziano Motel/rest. 🅾️ Boxing Hall of Fame

266mm **Chittenango Service Area wb,** 🅿️ Sunoco/dsl 🍴 Sbarro's, Starbucks 🅾️ atm

34a(277) I-481, to Syracuse, Chittenango

35(279) NY 298, The Circle, Syracuse, **S** 🅿️ Xpress Mart 🍴 Burger King, Denny's, Dunkin', East Wok, Grimaldi's, Jimmy John's, Joey's Italian, Jreck Subs, McDonald's, Ruby Tuesday 🏨 Best Western+, Magnuson Inn, Best Value Inn, Candlewood Suites, Comfort Inn, Courtyard, Cresthill Suites, Days Inn, Doubletree Inn, Embassy Suites, Extended Stay America, Fairfield Inn, Hampton Inn, Hilton Garden, Homewood Suites, Motel 6, Quality Inn, Ramada, Red Roof Inn, Residence Inn, Rodeway Inn, SpringHill Suites 🅾️ Stevenson's Tire/auto, Verizon

280mm **Dewitt Service Area eb,** 🅿️ Sunoco/dsl 🍴 McDonald's

36(283) I-81, N to Watertown, S to Binghamton

NY

Exit #	Services

INTERSTATE 90 Cont'd

37(284) 7th St, Electronics Pkwy, to Liverpool, N 🛏 Best Western+, S 🅟 Speedway/Dunkin' 🍴 KFC/Taco Bell 🛏 Holiday Inn, Homewood Suites, Knights Inn, Staybridge Suites ◎ Kinney Drug

38(286) NY 57, to Liverpool, Syracuse, N 🅟 Fastrac/dsl, KwikFill, Speedway 🍴 Bangkok Thai, Dunkin', Pizza Hut 🛏 Super 8 ◎ $Tree, Aldi Foods, Midas, NAPA, Rite Aid

39(290) I-690, NY 690, Syracuse, N 🛏 Comfort Inn/rest. ◎ Camping World RV Ctr, S 🛏 Holiday Inn Express

292mm Warners Service Area wb, 🅟 Mobil/dsl 🍴 Boston Pizza, McDonald's

40(304) NY 34, to Owasco Lake, Weedsport, N ◎ Riverforest RV Park, S 🅟 Fastrac, KwikFill, Sunoco/dsl 🍴 Arby's, Arnold's Rest., Cj's Rest., DB's Drive-In, Dunkin', NY Pizzaria 🛏 Days Inn, Rodeway Inn ◎ $General, Ace Hardware, Bass Pro Shops (12mi), Kinney Drug, NAPA, USPO, Weedsport Foods

310mm Port Byron Service Area eb, 🅟 Mobil/dsl 🍴 Boston Pizza, Edy's Ice Cream

318mm parking area wb, litter barrels

41(320) NY 414, to Cayuga Lake, Waterloo, S 🅟 Byrne Dairy/dsl, Circle K/dsl, Petro/Iron Skillet/dsl/scales/24hr/@ 🍴 MaGee Country Diner 🛏 Hampton Inn (4mi), Microtel (4mi), Quality Inn (4mi) ◎ Cayuga Lake SP/camping, Waterloo Outlets/famous brands (3mi)

324mm Junius Ponds Service Area wb, 🅟 Sunoco/dsl 🍴 Dunkin', Roy Rogers ◎ atm, wi-fi

42(327) NY 14, to Geneva, Lyons, S 🅟 Mobil/7-11/dsl/scales 🛏 Belhurst (6mi), Best Value Inn (6mi), Days Inn (6mi), Hampton Inn (6mi), Ramada Inn (6mi) ◎ Junius Ponds RV Camping, Waterloo Outlets/famous brands (3mi)

337mm Clifton Springs Service Area eb, 🅟 Sunoco/dsl 🍴 Burger King, Sbarro's, Starbucks ◎ atm

43(340) NY 21, to Palmyra, Manchester, N ◎ Hill Cumorah LDS HS (2mi), S 🅟 Sunoco/dsl 🍴 Dunkin', McDonald's 🛏 Manchester Inn ◎ KOA (6mi)

44(347) NY 332, Victor, S 🅟 7-11/dsl, Mobil/Subway, Speedway, Sunoco/dsl 🍴 Burger King, Dunkin', KFC, McDonald's, Park Place Rest. 🛏 Budget Inn, Comfort Inn, Travelodge ◎ $General, $Tree, Aldi Foods, AutoZone, casino, CVS Drug, KOA (4mi), st police, Top's Foods

350mm Seneca Service Area wb, 🅟 Mobil/dsl 🍴 Checker's, Villa Pizza ◎ atm, wi-fi

45(351) I-490, NY 96, to Rochester, N 🅟 Mobil/dsl 🍴 BoneFish Grill, Champp's Grill, Chipotle, City Tavern, Distillery Rest., Five Guys, Longhorn Steaks, McDonald's, Moe's SW Grill, Olive Garden, Panera Bread, PF Chang's, Pi Craft Pizza, Starbucks, Subway 🛏 Hampton Inn, Springdale Farm B&B ◎ $Tree, AT&T, Best Buy, BJ's Whse/gas, Dick's, GNC, Home Depot, JC Penney, Kohl's, Lord&Taylor, Macy's, Michael's, Old Navy, Petsmart, Staples, Target, Verizon, Von Maur, Walmart, S 🅟 KwikFill/dsl 🍴 Burger King, Chili's, Denny's, Taco Bell, Wendy's 🛏 Best Western+, Holiday Inn Express, Homewood Suites, Microtel, Royal Inn ◎ Wilkins RV Ctr

353mm parking area eb, litter barrels

46(362) I-390, to Rochester, N on NY 253 W 🅟 Gulf/dsl, Mobil/dsl, Speedway/Dunkin'/dsl 🍴 McDonald's, Peppermint's Rest., Tim Hortons, Wendy's 🛏 Days Inn, Fairfield Inn, Microtel, Red Roof Inn, Super 8 ◎ Buick/GMC

366mm Scottsville Service Area eb, 🅟 Mobil/dsl 🍴 Arby's ◎ atm, info

376mm Ontario Service Area wb, 🅟 Sunoco/dsl 🍴 Boston Pizza, Edy's Ice Cream, McDonald's ◎ atm, wi-fi

47(379) I-490, NY 19, to Rochester, N 🅟 490 Truckstop/dsl 🛏 Edson House B&B ◎ Timberline Camping

48(390) NY 98, to Batavia, N 🛏 Fairbridge Inn, Hampton Inn, Holiday Inn Express, S 🅟 Citgo 🍴 Applebee's, Bob Evans, Five Guys, Subway, Taco Bell, Tim Horton's, Yume Asian Bistro 🛏 Best Western, Budget Inn, Days Inn, La Quinta, Quality Inn, Red Roof Inn, Relax Inn, Super 8 ◎ AT&T, AutoZone, BJ's Whse, Dick's, Home Depot, Kohl's, Marshall's, Michael's, PetCo, Rite Aid, Target, Tops Foods, Verizon, Walmart/Subway

397mm Pembroke Service Area eb, 🅟 Sunoco/dsl 🍴 Tim Hortons ◎ atm, gifts

48a(402) NY 77, Pembroke, S 🅟 FLYING J/Denny's/Subway/dsl/LP/scales/24hr, TA/Mobil/Country Pride/dsl/scales/24hr/@ 🍴 Subway 🛏 Darien Lake Lodge/camping, EconoLodge ◎ Sleepy Hollow Camping (8mi)

412mm Clarence Service Area wb, full ♿ facilities, 🅟 Sunoco/dsl 🍴 Arby's, Tim Hortons ◎ atm, info, wi-fi

49(417) NY 78, Depew, 0-3 mi N 🅟 Delta Sonic, Mobil/dsl, Sunoco Sunoco, Tesla EVC 🍴 Applebee's, Arby's, Burger King, Chili's, Chipotle, Cracker Barrel, Deep South Taco, Dibella's Subs, DQ, Duff's Wings, Dunkin', Firehouse Subs, Five Guys, Fuji Grill, Jimmy John's, KFC, La Divina Dos, La Tolteca, McDonald's, Mighty Taco, Moe's SW Grill, Old Country Buffet, Olive Garden, Panera Bread, Picasso's Pizza, Pizza Plant, Protocol Rest., Red Lobster, Russel's Steaks, Salsarita's, Santora's Pizza, Starbucks, Starbucks, Subway, Taco Bell, Ted's Hot-Dogs, Tim Horton, Tully's Rest., Wendy's 🛏 Clarion, Home 2 Suites, Motel 6, Salvatore's Hotel, SpringHill Suites, Staybridge Suites, Super 8, Tru Hilton ◎ $Tree, Acura, Advance Parts, Aldi Foods, AT&T, AutoZone, Barnes&Noble, Best Buy, BigLots, BJ's Whse/gas, Buick/GMC, Chevrolet, Chrysler/Dodge/Jeep, Dick's, Dunn Tire, Firestone/auto, Ford, Goodyear/auto, Hobby Lobby, Home Depot, Honda, Hyundai, JC Penney, Jo-Ann Fabrics, Kohl's, Lowe's, Marshall's, Mavis Tire, Michael's, Office Depot, PetCo, PetsMart, Rite Aid, SteinMart, Target, TJ Maxx, Top's Food/deli, Tuesday Morning, Verizon, vet, Walgreens, Walmart/Subway, Wegman's Foods, S 🅟 Kwikfill, Mobil/dsl 🍴 China 1, Italian Village, John&Mary's Cafe, McDonald's, Salvatore's Italian, Subway, Tim Horton 🛏 Garden Place Hotel, Hospitality Inn, La Quinta, Red Roof Inn ◎ $Tree, 7-11, Advance Parts, Mavis Tire, Top's Foods/gas

419mm toll booth

50(420) I-290 to Niagara Falls

50a(421) Cleveland Dr (from eb)

51(422) NY 33 E, Buffalo, S ◎ ⊙, st police

52(423) Walden Ave, to Buffalo, N 🍴 Applebee's, Burger King, Chipotle, Famous Dave's BBQ, IHOP, McDonald's, Ruby Tuesday, Starbucks, Subway, TGIFriday's, Tim Horton 🛏 Hampton Inn, Holiday Inn Express, Residence Inn ◎ $Tree, Aldi Foods, AT&T, AutoZone, Firestone/auto, Ford, Home Depot, Michael's, Office Depot, PetsMart, PriceRite Mkt, Target, Top's Foods, S 🅟 Delta Sonic, Jim's Trk Plaza/Sunoco/dsl/rest./scales/24hr, KwikFill 🍴 Alton's Rest., Bar Louie's, Bravo Italiano, Cheesecake Factory, Dick's, Dunkin', Five Guys, Gordon Biersch arrest., Longhorn Steaks, McDonald's, Melting Pot, Mighty Taco, Milton's Rest. Moe's SW, Olive Garden, Panera Bread, PF Chang's, Pizza Hut, Popeye's, Smokey Bones BBQ, Sonic, Taco Bell, Texas de Brazil Steaks, Tim Horton, Zahng's Buffet 🛏 Baymont Inn, Home 2 Suites, Millenium Hotel ◎ Best Buy, Burlington Coats, Cabela's, Dave&Buster's, Dunn Tire, JC Penney, Lord&Taylor, Macy's Marshall's, Mavis Tire, Sam's Club, Verizon

52a(424) William St

53(425) I-190, to Buffalo, Niagara Falls, N 🛏 Best Western+

54(428) NY 400, NY 16, to W Seneca, E Aurora

Sidebars: BATAVIA, DEPEW, BUFFALO, ROCHESTER, NY

🔼Ⓔ INTERSTATE 90 Cont'd

Exit #	Services
55(430)	US 219, Ridge Rd, Orchard Park, **S** 🅿 Delta Sonic, Sunoco 🍴 Denny's, Ferro's NY Pizza, Mighty Taco, Subway, Tim Horton, Wendy's 🛏 Country Inn&Suites, Hampton Inn, Staybridge Suites ⭕ $General, Aldi Foods, BigLots, Goodyear/auto, Home Depot, Mr Tire, Pepboys, Petco, Tops Foods/gas, Verizon, Wegman's Foods
431mm	toll booth
56(432)	NY 179, Mile Strip Rd, **N** 🅿 Gulf/dsl, Mobil, Sunoco 🍴 Blasdell Pizza, China King, DiPaolo's Rest., Odyssey Rest., Whse Rest. 🛏 EconoLodge ⭕ $General, Advance Parts, CVS Drug, repair, SaveALot Foods, USPO, **S** 🍴 Applebee's, Chipotle, ChuckeCheese, El Canelo Mexican, Firehouse Subs, Five Guys, McDonald's, Mongolian Buffet, Olive Garden, Outback Steaks, Panera Bread, Pizza Hut, Popeye's, Red Lobster, Starbucks, Subway, TGIFriday's, Wendy's ⭕ $Tree, Aldi Foods, Barnes&Noble, Best Buy, BJ's Whse, Firestone/auto, Hobby Lobby, Home Depot, JC Penney, Jo-Ann Etc, Old Navy, PepBoys, TJ Maxx, Wegman's Foods
57(436)	NY 75, to Hamburg, **N** 🅿 Mobil/Dunkin'/dsl 🍴 Arby's, Blasdell Pizza, Denny's, Hat Trix, McDonald's, Tim Horton, Uncle Joe's Diner, Waterstone Grill, Wendy's 🛏 Comfort Inn, Holiday Inn Express, Motel 6, Red Roof Inn ⭕ Chevrolet, Chrysler/Dodge/Jeep, Ford, Honda, Lowe's, Pepboys, transmissions, Walmart/Subway, **S** 🅿 Go Gas, Kwikfill/dsl, Mad J's 🍴 Burger King, Mexico City, Pizza Hut, Savory Cafe, Subway, Tim Horton 🛏 Hampton Inn, Quality Inn, Super 8 ⭕ $General, Advance Parts, AutoZone, Gander RV Ctr, Goodyear/auto, Monro Automotive, NAPA, USPO, vet
442mm	parking area both lanes, litter barrels
57a(445)	to Eden, Angola, **N** 🅿 Mobil/dsl
447mm	Angola Service Area both lanes, 🅿 Sunoco/dsl 🍴 McDonald's, Moe's SW Grill, Subway ⭕ atm, gifts, wi-fi
58(456)	US 20, NY 5, to Silver Creek, Irving, **N** 🅿 Kwikfill, Seneca Hawk Trkstp/dsl 🍴 Burger King, Colony Rest., McDonald's, Millie's Rest., Sunset Bay, Sunset Grill, Tim Hortons, Tom's Rest. 🛏 Lighthouse Inn ⭕ Ⓗ, auto repair, to Evangola SP, USPO
59(468)	NY 60, Fredonia, Dunkirk, **N** 🅿 Clarion (2mi), Dunkirk Motel (4mi) ⭕ Lake Erie SP/camping (7mi), **S** 🅿 Country Fair/dsl, Kwikfill/dsl 🍴 Applebee's, Arby's, Azteca Cantina, Bob Evans, Burger King, Denny's, Dunkin', KFC/Taco Bell, Little Caesar's, McDonald's, Pizza Hut, Subway, Tim Horton, Tim Hortons, Wendy's, Wing City Grille 🛏 Best Western, Econolodge/Suburban Lodge, Quality Inn ⭕ $General, $Tree, Advance Parts, Aldi Foods, AT&T, AutoZone, BigLots, Chrysler/Dodge/Jeep, Ford/Lincoln, GMC, GNC, Home Depot, Midas, Monro, Petsmart, Rite Aid, TJ Maxx, Tops Foods/gas, Verizon, Walmart/Subway
60(485)	NY 394, Westfield, **N** ⭕ Brookside Beach Camping, KOA, to Lake Erie SP/camping, **S** 🛏 Holiday Motel, Webb's Resort ⭕ Ⓗ
494mm	toll booth
61(495)	Shortman Rd, to Ripley, **N** ⭕ Lakeside RV Park
496mm	New York/Pennsylvania state line

🔼Ⓝ INTERSTATE 95

Exit #	Services
32mm	New York/Connecticut state line
22(30)	Midland Ave (from nb), Port Chester, Rye, **W** 🍴 Dunkin' 🛏 Courtyard ⭕ Ⓗ, Home Depot, Staples, Whole Foods Mkt
21(29)	I-287 W, US 1 N, to White Plains, Port Chester, Tappan Zee
20(28)	US 1 S (from nb), Port Chester, **E** 🅿 Shell ⭕ CVS Drug, Ford, Subaru, USPO

(map of New York State showing cities: Mexico, Williamstown, Baldwinsville, Rome, Utica, Glens Falls, Syracuse, 90, Auburn, Rotterdam, Cortland, 88, Albany, Ithaca, Oneonta, 81, Cairo, Germantown, Elmira, Binghamton, Marbletown, Hyde Park, **NY**)

19(27)	Playland Pkwy, Rye, Harrison
18b(25)	Mamaroneck Ave, to White Plains, **E** 🅿 Shell, Speedway 🍴 Domino's, Jimmy's Pizza ⭕ Mavis Tire
18a(24)	Fenimore Rd (from nb), Mamaroneck, **E** 🅿 Conoco, Gulf
17(20)	Chatsworth Ave (from nb, no return), Larchmont
19.5mm	toll plaza
16(19)	North Ave, Cedar St, New Rochelle, **E** 🍴 Applebee's, Buffalo Wild Wings, Subway, TX Roadhouse 🛏 Radisson, Residence Inn ⭕ ShopRite, Toyota, USPO, **W** ⭕ Ⓗ
15(16)	US 1, New Rochelle, The Pelhams, **E** 🅿 SuperGas, Wave/dsl 🍴 Dunkin', New China, New Rochelle Diner ⭕ AutoZone, Costco/gas, CVS Drug, Harley-Davidson, Home Depot, Walgreens, **W** ⭕ repair
14(15)	Hutchinson Pkwy (from sb), to Whitestone Br
13(16)	Conner St, to Mt Vernon, **E** 🅿 Gulf/dsl 🍴 Taco Bell 🛏 Ramada Inn, **W** 🅿 🍴 McDonald's 🛏 Holiday Motel ⭕ Ⓗ, Co-Op City Tire/auto, Pepboys
12(15.5)	Baychester Ave (exits left from nb)
11(15)	Bartow Ave, Co-op City Blvd, **E** 🍴 Bartow Pizza, Applebee's, Burger King, Dallas BBQ, McDonald's, Outback, Panera Bread, Popeye's, Red Lobster, Starbucks ⭕ $Tree, AT&T, JC Penney, Marshall's, Old Navy, Staples, Stop & Shop, Verizon, **W** 🅿 BP/Dunkin', Sunoco/dsl, Wave/dsl 🍴 ChuckeCheese, Dunkin', Joyful Dragon, Pizza Hut, TGIFriday's ⭕ Aldi Foods, Home Depot
10(14.5)	Gun Hill Rd (exits left from nb), **W** 🛏 Pelham Garden
9(14)	Hutchinson Pkwy
8c(13.5)	Pelham Pkwy W
8b(13)	Orchard Beach, City Island
8a(12.5)	Westchester Ave (from sb)
7c(12)	Pelham Bay Park (from nb), Country Club Rd
7b(11.5)	E Tremont (from sb), **W** ⭕ Super FoodTown
7a(11)	I-695 (from sb), to I-295 S, Throgs Neck Br
6b(10.5)	I-278 W (from sb), I-295 S (from nb)
6a(10)	I-678 S, Whitestone Bridge
5b(9)	Castle Hill Ave, **W** 🅿 Sunoco 🍴 McDonald's, Subway ⭕ $Tree
5a(8.5)	Westchester Ave, White Plains Rd
4b(8)	Bronx River Pkwy, Rosedale Ave, **E** 🅿 BP/Dunkin'
4a(7)	I-895 S, Sheridan Expsy
3(6)	3rd Ave, **W** ⭕ Ⓗ
2b(5)	Webster Ave, **W** ⭕ Ⓗ
2a(4)	Jerome Ave, to I-87
1c(3)	I-87, Deegan Expsy, to Upstate
1b(2)	Harlem River Dr
1a(1)	US 9, NY 9A, H Hudson Pkwy, 178th St, downtown
0mm	New York/New Jersey state line, Hudson River, Geo Washington Br

(side labels: HAMBURG, **FREDONIA**, **NYC AREA**)
(right margin tab: NY)

⬆E INTERSTATE 190 (Buffalo)

Exit #	Services
25.5mm	US/Canada Border, US Customs
25b a	R Moses Pkwy, NY 104, NY 265, Lewiston, **E** Ⓞ Ⓗ
24	NY 31, Witmer Rd, **E** Ⓞ Ⓗ, st police
23	NY 182, Porter Rd, Packard Rd, **E** 🅿 EVC, Sunoco/dsl 🍴 Applebee's, Burger King, Chili's, Chipotle, DQ, Five Guys, Longhorn Steaks, Mighty Taco, Olive Garden, Panera Bread, Subway, Tim Horton Ⓞ $Tree, Advance Parts, Big Lots, Chrysler/Dodge/Jeep, Fashion Outlets/famous brands, Firestone/auto, Goodyear/Auto, Hobby Lobby, Jo-Ann Fabrics, Marshall's, Mavis Tire, Mr Tire, NAPA, Petco, Sam's Club/gas, U-Haul, Verizon, Walmart/Subway, Wegman's, **W** 🍴 Wendy's Ⓞ Aldi Foods
22	US 62, Niagara Falls Blvd, **E** 🅿 Sunoco 🍴 Arby's, Bob Evans, Burger King, Denny's, Dunkin', KFC, Mandalay Rest., McDonald's, Pizza Hut, Popeye's, Starbucks, Subway, Taco Bell, Wendy's 🛏 Beat Value Inn, Budget Host, Caravan Motel, Hampton Inn, Pelican Motel, Quality Inn, Red Carpet Inn, Super 8, Swiss Cottage Inn Ⓞ $Tree, Advance Parts, AT&T, Dunn Tire, Ford, Rite Aid, Target, TJ Maxx, Top's Foods/gas, Walgreens, **W** 🛏 Comfort Inn, Econolodge, La Quinta Ⓞ Home Depot
21a	La Salle Expswy
21	NY 384, Buffalo Ave, R Moses Pkwy, **E** 🛏 Aashram Hotel, Sheraton, **W** 🅿 Gulf Ⓞ American Falls, casino, to NF SP
20.5mm	Niagara River East, **toll booth sb**
20b a	Long Rd, **E** 🛏 Budget Motel Ⓞ Kelly's Country Store
19	Whitehaven Rd, **E** 🅿 Noco Express/dsl 🍴 McDonald's 🛏 Chateau Motel (2mi) Ⓞ $Tree, funpark, KOA (1mi), Top's Foods/gas, **W** Ⓞ Chevrolet, Hyundai, Toyota, vet
18b a	NY 324 W, Grand Island Blvd, **E** 🅿 NOCO/dsl, Speedway/dsl 🍴 Burger King, McDonald's, Tim Horton, Wendy's 🛏 Chateau Motel, Grand Suites Ⓞ $Tree, Advance Parts, Tops/gas, **W** Ⓞ Beaver Island SP
17.5mm	Niagara River East, **toll booth**
17	NY 266, last free exit nb
16	I-290 E, to I-90, Albany
15	NY 324, Kenmore Ave, **E** 🅿 7-11 Ⓞ city park, **W** Ⓞ U-Haul
14	Ontario St, **E** 🅿 KwikFill 🍴 McDonald's, Tim Horton Ⓞ Advance Parts, Family$
13	(from nb), same as 14
12	Amherst St, (from nb), downtown
11	NY 198, Buffalo, **E** 🅿 First Line
9	Porter Ave, to Peace Bridge, Ft Erie
8	NY 266, Niagara St, **E** 🛏 Buffalo Grand Hotel, **W** 🛏 Courtyard, downtown
7	NY 5 W, Church St, Buffalo, downtown
6	Elm St, **E** Ⓞ Ⓗ, downtown, **W** Ⓞ Arena
5	Louisiana St, Buffalo, downtown
4	Smith St, Fillmore Ave, Buffalo, downtown
3	NY 16, Seneca St, from sb, **W** 🍴 Tim Horton
2	US 62, NY 354, Bailey Ave, Clinton St
1	Ogden St, **E** 🅿 Sunoco 🍴 Wendy's 🛏 Best Western+, Comfort Inn Ⓞ Big Lots, CVS Drug, Family$
.5mm	toll plaza nb
0mm	I-90. I-190 begins/ends on I-90, exit 53.

⬆E INTERSTATE 287 (New York City)

Exit #	Services
12	I-95, N to New Haven, S to NYC. I-287 begins/ends on I-95, exit 2
11	US 1, Port Chester, Rye, **N** 🅿 BP, Mobil, Sunoco 🍴 Burger King, Domino's, Dunkin', McDonald's, Popeye's, Port Chester Diner, Subway, Taco Bell 🛏 Courtyard Ⓞ Ⓗ, Goodyear/auto, Home Depot, Kohl's, Mavis Discount Tire, Nissan, Staples, Verzon, Whole Foods Mkt
10	Bowman Ave, Webb Ave
9N S	Hutchinson Pkwy, Merritt Pkwy, to Whitestone Br
9a	I-684, Brewster
8	Westchester Ave, to White Plains, **S** 🅿 BP, Mobil 🍴 Buffalo Wild Wings, Cheesecake Factory, Chipotle, Five Guys, Morton's Steaks, Panera Bread, PF Chang's, Westchester Burger C 🛏 Crowne Plaza Ⓞ Chrysler/Dodge/Jeep, Ⓗ, Neiman Marcus, Nordstrom, Stop&Shop Foods, Walmart, Westchester Ma Place, Whole Foods Mkt
7	Taconic Pkwy (from wb), to N White Plains
6	NY 22, White Plains
5	NY 100, Hillside Ave, **S** 🅿 Gulf, Lukoil 🍴 Applebee's, Chipotle, Dunkin', Planet Pizza, Smashburger, Subway Ⓞ Aamco, AutoZone, GNC, Lexus, Mazda, vet
4	NY 100A, Hartsdale, **N** 🅿 Shell Ⓞ Ⓗ, **S** 🅿 Mobil 🍴 Bamboo Garden Chinese, Burger King Ⓞ BMW/Mini, Jaguar, Mazda/Subaru, Staples
3	Sprain Pkwy, to Taconic Pkwy, NYC
2	NY 9A, Elmsford, **N** 🅿 BP, Citgo, Gulf, Mobil, Sunoco 🍴 Dunkin', Subway, Taco Bell Ⓞ Mavis Discount Tire, NAPA Sam's Club, **S** 🅿 Shell 🍴 Wendy's
1	NY 119, Tarrytown, **N** 🅿 Shell/dsl, Tesla EVC 🍴 Cooper's Mill, Qdoba, Ruth's Chris Steaks 🛏 Marriott, Sheraton, **S** 🅿 BP/ds 🍴 El Dorado Diner 🛏 Extended Stay America, Hampton Inn
0	I-287 runs with I-87 N.

⬆E INTERSTATE 290 (Buffalo)

Exit #	Services
8	I-90, NY Thruway, I-290 begins/ends on I-90, exit 50.
7b a	NY 5, Main St, **N** 🅿 Mobil/dsl, Sunoco 🍴 La Nova Pizza, Wings, McDonald's, Panera Bread, Starbucks, Tim Horton Wendy's 🛏 Hampton Inn, Wyndham Garden Ⓞ Tops Foods Walgreens, **S** 🅿 Valero 🛏 Hyatt Place
6	NY 324, NY 240, **N** 🅿 Marathon/dsl 🛏 Courtyard Ⓞ Cadillac, **S** 🍴 China Star, ChuckeCheese, McDonald's, Sheridan Rest., Subway Ⓞ 7-11, Aamco, CVS Drug, Hyundai, Kia/Mazda, Lexus, Nissan, Subaru, URGENT CARE, Walgreens
5b a	NY 263, to Millersport, **N** 🅿 Gulf 🍴 Santora's Pizza, Zetti's Pizza 🛏 Candlewood Suites, Comfort Inn, DoubleTree, Marriott, Red Roof+, Residence Inn, **S** 🅿 Mobil 🛏 Homewood Suites Ⓞ Mr Tire, Toyota, VW, Walgreens
4	I-990, to St U
3b a	US 62, to Niagara Falls Blvd, **N** 🅿 Mobil/7-11, Valero 🍴 Anderson's Rest., Bob Evans, Checkers, Dunkin', Just Pizza, Pancake House, Roadhouse Grill, Ted's Hot Dogs 🛏 Econolodge, Extended Stay America, Knight's Inn, La Quinta, Red Carpet Inn, Rodeway Inn, Sleep Inn Ⓞ CarMax, Chrysler/Dodge/Jeep, Home Depot, Honda, NAPA, Rite Aid, URGENT CARE, vet, **S** 🅿 Delta Sonic, Sunoco/dsl 🍴 Applebee's, Blaze Pizza, Bone-Fish Grill, Buffalo Wild Wings, Burger King, Carrabba's, Cheeburger, Chili's, Chipotle, Denny's, Dibella's Subs, Domino's,

◤E INTERSTATE 290 (Buffalo) Cont'd

3b a	**Continued**
	Five Guys, John's Pizza, McDonald's, Moe's SW Grill, Olive Garden, Outback Steaks, Panera Bread, Papa John's, PI Pizza, Starbucks, TGIFriday, Tim Horton, Tulley's 🏠 Days Inn, Royal Inn 🅾️ $Tree, AT&T, Barnes&Noble, Best Buy, BJ's/gas, Christmas Tree Shop, Dick's, Firestone/auto, GNC, Goodyear/auto, JC Penney, Jo-Ann Fabrics, Lowes Whse, Macy's, Michael's, Old Navy, Pepboys, PetCo, PetsMart, Target, TJ Maxx, Trader Joe's
2	NY 425, Colvin Blvd, **N** 🍴 Athena's Rest., KFC, McDonald's, Subway, Texas Roadhouse, Tim Horton, Wendy's 🅾️ 🏠, Big Lots, Family$, Top's Foods/gas, **S** 🅿️ KwikFill 🍴 Just Pizza 🅾️ Pepboys
1b a	Elmwood Ave, NY 384, NY 265, **N** 🅿️ KwikFill 🍴 Franco's Pizza, John's Pizza/Subs, Subway, Touch of Italy 🏠 Center Way Motel 🅾️ 🏠, $Tree, auto repair, Rite Aid, **S** 🅿️ Sunoco/dsl 🍴 Arby's
0mm	I-190. **I-290 begins/ends on I-190 in Buffalo.**

◤E INTERSTATE 390 (Rochester)

Exit #	Services
20b a	I-490. **I-390 begins/ends on I-490 in Rochester.**
19(75)	NY 33a, Chili Ave, **N** 🅾️ AutoZone, URGENT CARE, **S** 🅿️ Sunoco 🍴 Burger King, KFC, Little Caesar's, Pizza Hut, Subway 🏠 Motel 6, Quality Inn 🅾️ $General
18b a	NY 204, Brooks Ave, **N** 🏠 Ramada Inn, **S** 🏠 Fairfield Inn 🅾️ 🔄
17(73)	NY 383, Scottsville Rd, **S** 🅿️ 7-11/dsl, Fastrac/dsl
16(71)	NY 15a, to E Henryetta, **N** 🅾️ 🏠, Costco/gas, **S** 🍴 Delmonico's Rest., TGI Friday's 🏠 Country Inn&Suites, Courtyard, Hampton Inn, Holiday Inn Express 🅾️ Rite Aid
15(70)	I-590, Rochester
14(68)	NY 15a, NY 252, **E** 🍴 Dunkin', Gray's Cafe, Jeremiah's, Outback Steaks, Tully's Rest. 🏠 Extended Stay America, Residence Inn 🅾️ $Tree, Top's Foods/gas, **W** 🅿️ Mobil/dsl 🍴 Bar Louie, Boston Mkt, Buffalo Wild Wings, Burger King, Dunkin', Five Guys, Jimmy John's, Moe's SW, Sonic, Starbucks, Subway, Taco Bell 🏠 Best Western, DoubleTree Inn, Hampton Inn, Holiday Inn, Home 2 Suites 🅾️ Big Lots, Staples, Verizon
13(67)	Hylan Dr, **E** 🅿️ Fastrac/dsl 🍴 Cracker Barrel 🏠 Comfort Suites, Homewood Suites, **W** 🅿️ Mobil/dsl 🍴 Chili's, Chipotle, ChuckECheese, IHOP, Joe's Crabshack, Longhorn Steaks, McDonald's, Olive Garden, Panera Bread, Qdoba, Red Robin, Smashburger, Starbucks, Subway, Tim Hortons, TX Roadhouse, Uno Grill, Wendy's 🅾️ Aldi Foods, Best Buy, BJ's Whse, Dick's, JC Penney, Lowe's, Marshall's, Michael's, Old Navy, PepBoys, PetCo, Target, Walmart, Wegman's Foods
12(66)	I-90, NY Thruway, NY 253, **W** 🅿️ Gulf/dsl/scales, Mobil/dsl, Speedway 🍴 Lehigh Rest., McDonald's, Peppermint's Rest., Tim Hortons, Wendy's 🏠 Country Inn&Suites, Days Inn, Fairfield Inn, Microtel, Red Carpet Inn, Red Roof Inn, Super 8 🅾️ Buick/GMC
11(62)	NY 15, NY 251, Rush, Scottsville, **2 mi N** 🍴 McDonald's, Tim Hortons, Wendy's 🏠 Fairfield Inn, Red Roof Inn
10(55)	US 20, NY 5, Avon, Lima, **N** 🅿️ Exxon 🍴 Countryside Diner 🏠 CrestHill Inn, Stratford Inn, **S** 🅿️ Quicklee's/dsl 🍴 Avon Cafe (3mi), Dutch Hollow Cafe (3mi), McDonald's (3mi), Subway (3mi), Tom Wahls Cafe (3mi) 🏠 Avon Cedar Lodge (3mi) 🅾️ Chrysler/Dodge/Jeep, Ford, Sugar Creek Camping (3mi)

9mm	scenic area wb
9(52)	NY 15, **N** 🅿️ Mobil/Dunkin'/dsl 🍴 Fratelli's Rest., Lakeville Rest., McDonald's, Tee&Gee Cafe 🏠 Rodeway Inn 🅾️ Chevrolet
8(48)	US 20a, Geneseo, **N** 🅾️ Conesus Lake Camping, **2 mi S** 🅿️ Mobil/Dunkin' 🍴 Applebee's, Denny's, KFC/Taco Bell, McDonald's, Subway, Tim Hortons, Wendy's 🏠 Hampton Inn, Quality Inn 🅾️ $Tree, Aldi Foods, AT&T, AutoZone, GNC, Petsmart, Verizon, Walmart, Wegman's
7(39)	NY 63, NY 408, Geneseo, **N** 🅾️ st police, **S** 🅿️ Doughboys/dsl, KwikFill, Valero/dsl 🍴 Dunkin', McDonald's 🏠 Alligence B&B, Country Inn&Suites, Geneseo River Hotel/Rest., Greenway Motel 🅾️ Bonadonna Auto, Family$, Letchworth SP, Ridge Camping, Rite Aid, Save-A-Lot Foods
38mm	℞ₛ both lanes, full ♿ facilities, litter barrels, petwalk, 🍽️, vending
6(33)	NY 36, Mt Morris, Sonyea
5(26)	NY 36, Dansville, **N** 🅿️ KwikFill/dsl, Mobil/7-11/dsl 🍴 Arby's, Burger King, Dunkin', McDonald's, Pizza Hut, Subway, Taco Bell 🅾️ $Tree, Advance Parts, BigLots, Chevrolet, Chrysler/Dodge/Jeep, CVS Drug, Rite Aid, Save-A-Lot Foods, Top's Foods/gas, Verizon, **S** 🅿️ TA/Valero/Country Pride/dsl/scales/24hr/@
4(23)	NY 36, Dansville, **N** 🅿️ Sunoco/dsl 🏠 Logan's Inn 🅾️ 🏠, **S** 🅾️ Skybrook Camping, Stonybrook Park Camping, Sugar Creek Camping, Sunvalley Camping
3(17)	NY 15, NY 21, Wayland, **N** 🅾️ CarQuest (1mi), Holiday Hill Campground (7mi), st patrol
2(11)	NY 415, Cohocton, Naples, **N** 🅿️ Mobil (2mi) 🅾️ Tumble Hill Camping (3mi)
1(2)	NY 415, Avoca, **S** 🅿️ Arrowmart 🏠 Caboose Motel (3mi) 🅾️ $General, USPO (2mi)

I-390 begins/ends on I-86, exit 36.

◤E INTERSTATE 495 (Long Island)

Exit #	Services
	I-495 begins/ends on NY 25.
73	rd 58, Old Country Road, to Greenport, Orient, **0-2 mi E** 🅾️ Petsmart, **0-2 mi S** 🅿️ BP, Citgo, EVC, Mobil/dsl, Speedway/dsl 🍴 Applebee's, Buffalo Wild Wings, Chipotle, IHOP, Panera Bread, Starbucks, Taco Bell, TGIFriday's, Wendy's 🏠 Hilton Garden, Holiday Inn Express 🅾️ Aldi Foods, AT&T, Best Buy, Buick/GMC, Chevrolet, Costco/gas, CVS Drug, Dick's, Ford/Lincoln, Harley-Davidson, Home Depot, Honda, Kia/Mazda, Lowe's, Michael's, Nissan/Hyundai, PetCo, Stop&Shop, Subaru/VW, Tanger/famous brands, Target, Toyota, Volvo, Walgreens, Walmart/Subway
72	NY 25, (no ez eb return), Riverhead, Calverton (no EZ eb return), **N** 🅾️ funpark, **S** 🅿️ Speedway 🏠 Hotel Indigo 🅾️ Tanger/famous brands/foodcourt

(left margin, vertical) **ROCHESTER**

(right margin, vertical) **RIVERHEAD**

NY

☐ = gas ☐ = food ☐ = lodging ☐ = other ☐ = rest stop   Copyright 2022 - The Next EXIT

INTERSTATE 495 (Long Island) Cont'd

MEDFORD

Exit #	Services
71	NY 24, to Hampton Bays (no ez eb return), Calverton, **N** ☐ Exxon/dsl
70	NY 111, to Eastport, Manorville, **S** ☐ 7-11, Cumberland Farms /dsl, EVC ☐ McDonald's, Starbucks, Wendy's ☐ CVS Drug, King Kullen Food/drug
69	Wading River Rd, Center Moriches, **S** ☐ golf
68	NY 46, to Shirley, Wading River, **S** ☐ Mobil ☐ Carlo's Pizzeria ☐ 7-11
67	Yaphank Ave, **N** ☐ USPO
66	NY 101, Sills Rd, Yaphank, **N** ☐ Shell/dsl
65.5mm	parking area both lanes
65	Horse Block Rd, **N** ☐ Baskin-Robbins/Dunkin' ☐ $Tree
64	NY 112, to Coram, Medford, **N** ☐ Speedway ☐ DQ, Subway ☐ 7-11, Family$, Lowe's, Michael's, Sam's Club, Target, TJ Maxx, Verizon, Walgreens, **S** ☐ BP (2), BP/Dunkin', Sunoco/ dsl ☐ J&R Steaks, Starbucks ☐ Comfort Inn, Fairfield Inn ☐ 7-11, AutoZone
63	NY 83, N Ocean Ave, **N** ☐ Speedway/dsl, Stop'n Shop/gas ☐ Applebee's, Burger King, McDonald's, Starbucks, Taco Bell, TGIFriday's ☐ Hampton Inn ☐ 7-11, CVS Drug **S** ☐ BP/dsl, Gulf/dsl ☐ Sonoma Grill ☐ Ramada Plaza
62	Nicolls Rd, rd 97, to Blue Point, Stony Brook, **N** ☐ BP, **S** ☐ Chili's, On the Border, Subway, Wendy's ☐ Residence Inn
61	rd 19, to Patchogue, Holbrook, **N** ☐ Mobil, **S** ☐ BP/dsl, Speedway/dsl ☐ China 4, Greek Islands Rest., Joe's Pizza/Pasta, Outback Steaks, Subway ☐ 7-11, Advance Parts, CVS Drug
60	Ronkonkoma Ave, **N** ☐ USPO, **S** ☐ Mobil ☐ Red Lobster, Smokey Bones BBQ ☐ Courtyard, Homewood Suites
59	Ocean Ave, to Oakdale, Ronkonkoma, **S** ☐ BP/Dunkin', Sunoco ☐ Hilton Garden (2mi) ☐ 7-11
58	Old Nichols Rd, Nesconset, **N** ☐ Gulf/Dunkin' ☐ Starbucks ☐ Jake's 58 Hotel ☐ BJ's Whse
57	NY 454, Vets Hwy, to Hauppauge, **N** ☐ BP/dsl ☐ TGIFriday's, **S** ☐ BP, Mobil, Shell, Sunoco ☐ Dave&Buster's, Islandia Buffet ☐ Hampton Inn ☐ 7-11, AT&T, Mavis Tire, Stop&Shop Foods, TJ Maxx, Verizon, Walgreens, Walmart/McDonald's
56	NY 111, Smithtown, Islip, **N** ☐ BP/Dunkin' ☐ Tropical Smoothie, **S** ☐ Sunoco/dsl ☐ Steve's Italian ☐ Holiday Inn Express
55	rd 67, Motor Pkwy, Central Islip, **N** ☐ Mobil ☐ Chipotle, Dunkin', IHOP, Madison Steaks, Subway, **S** ☐ Shell/dsl
54	Wicks Rd
53	Sagkitos Pkwy, Bay Shore, Kings Park, Bayshore, **N** ☐ BP/7-11 ☐ Applebee's ☐ Radisson, **S** ☐ Mobil
52	rd 4, Commack Rd, N Babylon, Commack, **N** ☐ Citgo/dsl, Cumberland Farms, Shell/dsl ☐ Ara Greek Kitchen, Chick-fil-A, Premier Diner, Red Robin, Starbucks, Starbucks (2) ☐ Hampton Inn ☐ Costco, Home Depot, Jo-Ann, Kohl's, Lowe's, Marshall's, ShopRite Mkt, Verizon, Walmart

HICKSVILLE

Exit #	Services
51.5mm	LI Welcome Ctr eb, full facilities/parking area wb, litter barrels
51	NY 231, to Northport, Babylon
50	Bagatelle Rd, to Wyandanch
49N	NY 110 N, to Huntington, **N** ☐ Marriott, **S** ☐ Jewel Rest.
49S	NY 110 S, to Amityville
48	Round Swamp Rd, Old Bethpage, **S** ☐ Cumberland Farms/dsl ☐ Hilton Garden, Homewood Suites, Sheraton ☐ USPO
46	Sunnyside Blvd, Plainview, **N** ☐ Holiday Inn, **S** ☐ 7-11
45	Manetto Hill Rd, Plainview, Woodbury
44	NY 135, to Seaford, Syosset
43	S Oyster Bay Rd, to Syosset, Bethpage, **N** ☐ BP
42	Northern Pkwy, rd N, Hauppauge

Exit #	Services
41	NY 106, NY 107, Hicksville, Oyster Bay, **N** ☐ Starbucks, Whole Foods Mkt ☐ CVS Drug, Marshall's, USPO, **S** ☐ BP, Mobil, Sunoco ☐ Arby's, Boston Mkt, Broadway Diner, Chick-fil-A, Chipotle, Dunkin', Five Guys, McDonald's, On the Border, Red Lobster, Starbucks ☐ $Tree, AT&T, Goodyear/auto, Petco, Verizon
40	NY 25, Mineola, Syosset, **S** ☐ BP, Speedway/dsl ☐ Burger King, Dunkin', KFC, Kobe Hibachi, McDonald's, Wendy's ☐ Hampton Inn, Jericho Inn ☐ 7-11, Chrysler/Dodge/Jeep, Home Depot, Kohl's
39	Glen Cove Rd, **N** ☐ Mobil
38	(from eb)Northern Pkwy E, Meadowbrook Pkwy, to Jones Beach
37	Willis Ave, to Roslyn, Mineola, **N** ☐ BP, Shell ☐ Dunkin, Green Cactus Mexican, Skinny Pizza, **S** ☐ Mobil/dsl ☐ Lou Joe Rest.
36	Searingtown Rd, to Port Washington, **N** ☐ ☐
35	Shelter Rock Rd, Manhasset, **S** ☐ ☐
34	New Hyde Park Rd
33	Lakeville Rd, to Great Neck, **N** ☐ ☐
32	Little Neck Pkwy, **N** ☐ Shell/Burger King ☐ Centre Pizza, Chipotle, Five Guys, Panera Bread, Starbucks ☐ Petco, Verizon
31	Douglaston Pkwy, **S** ☐ BP/service ☐ Grimaldi's Pizza, Jade Asian ☐ Fairway Mkt, USPO, vet
30	E Hampton Blvd, Cross Island Pkwy
29	Springfield Blvd, **S** ☐ BP/Dunkin' ☐ Starbucks ☐ GNC
27	I-295, Clearview Expswy, Throgs Neck, **N** ☐ Barney's ☐ Blue Bay Diner ☐ 7-11, EVC
26	Francis Lewis Blvd
25	Utopia Pkwy, 188th St, **N** ☐ Citgo, Mobil ☐ Courtyard, Fairfield Inn, **S** ☐ Gas Sale/dsl, Gulf, Mobil ☐ Applebee's, Arby's, Dunkin', Five Guys, Hooters, Qdoba, Subway ☐ Wyndham Garden ☐ Michael's, USPO
24	Kissena Blvd, **N** ☐ BP/dsl ☐ Dunkin', Subway, **S** ☐ Mobil
23	Main St, **N** ☐ Lake Pavilion
22	Grand Central Pkwy, to I-678, College Pt Blvd, **N** ☐ Holiday Inn Express
21	108th St, **N** ☐ BP/7-11, Mobil ☐ Holiday Inn Express
19	NY 25, Queens Blvd, Woodhaven Blvd, to Rockaways, **N** ☐ Applebee's, Cheesecake Factory, Chick-fil-A, Longhorn Steaks, McDonald's, Olive Garden, Popeye's ☐ JC Penney, Macy's, **S** ☐ Mobil ☐ Burger King, Chipotle, Dallas BBQ, Starbucks, Subway ☐ Wyndham Garden ☐ Aldi Foods, Costco, CVS, Kohl's, Marshall's, Old Navy, TJ Maxx, USPO
18.5	69th Ave, Grand Ave (from wb)
18	Maurice St, **N** ☐ Exxon/Dunkin'/dsl ☐ Comfort Inn ☐ dsl repair, **S** ☐ ☐ Maspeth Deli, McDonald's ☐ Holiday Inn Express
17	48th St, to I-278, **N** ☐ Mobil ☐ City View Inn
16	I-495 begins/ends in NYC.

NOTES

NORTH CAROLINA

INTERSTATE 26

Exit #	Services
71mm	North Carolina/South Carolina state line
69mm	N Pacolet River
67.5mm	**Welcome Ctr wb, full ♿ facilities, litter barrels, 🏳 🏕**
67	US 74 E, to NC 108, Columbus, Tryon, **N** 📷 Shell/Fuji Express/dsl, Vgo/dsl 🍽 Cocula Mexican, Joy Wok, Larkin's Carolina Grill, McDonald's, Subway, Waffle House, Wendy's ⊙ Advance Parts, CVS Drug, Family$, Food Lion, **S** 📷 Exxon/dsl 🍽 KFC/Taco Bell, Mtn View Deli 🛏 Days Inn ⊙ 🏥, $General, Bi-Lo
59	Saluda, **N** 🛏 Saluda Mtn Lodge, **S** 📷 BP/dsl, Marathon/Subway/dsl 🍽 Crust&Kettle Cafe, Saluda Rest. 🛏 Orchard Inn B&B (2mi) ⊙ $General, AppleMill Outlet, Atkins Fruit, camping, repair, vet
56mm	⊙ Green River
54	US 25 (from eb), to Greenville, E Flat Rock, to Carl Sandburg Home
53.5mm	2130 ft, Eastern Continental Divide
53	Upward Rd, Hendersonville, **N** 📷 Marathon/Dunkin'/dsl 🍽 Waffle House, Zaxby's 🛏 Fairfield Inn, Mtn Inn&Suites ⊙ Bloomfields Giftshop, Lakewood RV Park, Wildflower RV Park, **S** 📷 Exxon/McDonald's, Shell/pizza 🍽 Cracker Barrel, Poplar Leaf Cafe, Subway 🛏 Holiday Inn Express, Quality Inn ⊙ repair, to Carl Sandburg Home
49b a	US 64, Hendersonville, **N** 📷 Marathon/dsl, Shell/dsl, Sunoco/dsl 🍽 Chick-fil-A, Golden Corral, Jack-in-the-Box, Moose Cafe, O'Charley's, Sonic, Starbucks, Waffle House, Zaxby's 🛏 Best Western, Hampton Inn, Quality Inn, Ramada Inn ⊙ $Tree, Advance Parts, Ingles/gas, PetCo, Sam's Club/gas, Staples, Walmart, World of Clothing, **S** 📷 Exxon/dsl/LP, Shell/dsl 🍽 Applebee's, Arby's, Binion's Roadhouse, Bojangles, Burger King, China Buffet, Denny's, Fatz Café, Hardee's, Harry's Rest., HoneyBaked Ham, KFC, Krispy Kreme, LJ Silver, Lon Sen Chinese, McDonald's, Outback Steaks, Pizza Hut, Subway, Taco Bell, Tequila's Grill, Wendy's 🛏 Days Inn, EconoLodge, Red Roof Inn ⊙ 🏥, Aldi Foods, Belk, BigLots, Bi-Lo Foods, Chrysler/Dodge/Jeep, Clark Tire/auto, CVS Drug, Family$, Home Depot, Jo-Ann, Lowe's, NAPA, TJ Maxx, Tuesday Morning, Verizon
46mm	**weigh sta both lanes, 🏳**
44	US 25, Fletcher, **N** 📷 Exxon/dsl 🍽 Hardee's, Subway ⊙ flea mkt/campground, vet, **S** 📷 Citgo/dsl, Shell/DQ/dsl/scales/24hr, Sonny's/dsl 🍽 Bojangles, Burger King, McDonald's, Valentina's Mexican 🛏 Mountain Inn&Suites ⊙ 🏥, Camping World RV Ctr, USPO
41mm	**🅁ₛ both lanes, full ♿ facilities, litter barrels, 🏳 🏕, vending**
40	NC 280, Arden, **N** 📷 Fastop/dsl, Shell/Arby's 🍽 Bojangles, Carrabba's, Casa Torres, Chili's, Cracker Barrel, Firehouse Subs, IHOP, Jersey Mike's, Little Caesar's, Lonestar Steaks, McDonald's, Moe's SW Grill, Olive Garden, Ruby Tuesday, Sonic, Tamarind Thai, Tokyo Express 🛏 Budget Motel, Clarion, Comfort Inn, Courtyard, EconoLodge, Hampton Inn, Knight's Inn ⊙ Acura/Honda, Aldi Foods, Best Buy, BigLots, Dick's, Lowe's, Marshalls, Michael's, Old Navy, Petsmart, Ross, Rutledge Lake RV Park, Target, World Mkt, **S** 📷 Citgo/dsl 🍽 Circle B Ranch BBQ, J&S Cafeteria 🛏 Fairfield Inn ⊙ Asheville Airport, BMW

Exit #	Services
37	NC 146, Skyland, **N** 📷 🍽 Arby's, Brixx Pizza, Broken Egg Cafe, Coldstone, Hickory Tavern, McDonald's, Neo Burrito, PF Chang's, Starbucks, Waffle House, Which Wich? 🛏 Hilton, Quality Inn ⊙ Barnes&Noble, CVS Drug, Ingles/gas, REI, **S** ⊙ Chevrolet
34mm	French Broad River
33	NC 191, Brevard Rd, 2 mi **N** ⊙ Asheville Farmers Mkt, Bear Creek RV Camp, Toyota, **S** 📷 Citgo, HotSpot/dsl 🍽 Apollo Flame, Harbor Inn Seafood, LJ Silver, McDonald's, Papa's Mexican, Ryan's, Shogun Buffet, Stoneridge Grill, Subway, Taco Bell, Waffle House 🛏 Comfort Suites, Country Inn&Suites, Fairfield Inn, Hampton Inn, Hilton Garden, Holiday Inn Express, Rodeway Inn ⊙ $Tree, Asheville Outlets, Belk, Dillards, Field&Stream, Ingles Foods/dsl, Kia, PetCo, to Blue Ridge Pkwy, Verizon
31b a	I-40, E to Statesville, W to Knoxville
27mm	I-240 E, Patton Ave
	I-26 and I-240 run together 3 mi. See NC I-240 exits 1-4
25	rd 251, **N** ⊙ to UNCA
24	Elk Mtn Rd, Woodfin
23	Merrimon Ave, N Asheville, **N** 📷 Gulf/dsl, HotSpot 🍽 Bellagio Bistro, Frank's Pizza, Moe's BBQ 🛏 Days Inn ⊙ camping, vet
21	New Stock Rd, **N** 📷 Citgo/dsl, Shell 🍽 Domino's, Granny's Kitchen, Pizza Hut ⊙ $General, Campfire Lodge RV Park, CVS, Ingles/gas
19b a	N US 25, W US 70, Marshall, **N** 📷 Shell/dsl 🍽 Arby's, Bojangles, Burger King, Chapala Mexican, IHOP, KFC, La Carreta Mexican, Little Caesars, McDonald's, Peking East, Subway, TCBY, Waffle House, Zaxby's ⊙ Ace Hardware, Advance Parts, Aldi Foods, AutoZone, BigLots, Ingles/dsl, Roses, URGENT CARE, Verizon, **S** 📷 Shell/DQ/dsl 🍽 Steak'n Shake ⊙ $Tree, CVS, Lowe's, Walmart/Subway
18	Weaverville (no EZ return from eb)
17	to Flat Creek
15	rd 197, to Jupiter, Barnardsville
13	Forks of Ivy, **N** 📷 Mkt Ctr/dsl, **S** 📷 Exxon/dsl
11	rd 213, to Mars Hill, Marshall, **N** ⊙ tires, **S** 📷 Exxon//Hardee's/dsl, TriCo 🍽 Bojangles, Osaka Japanese, Subway, Waffle House, Wagon Wheel Rest. 🛏 Comfort Inn ⊙ $General, CVS, Ingles/dsl, NAPA
9	Burnsville, Spruce Pine, **N** ⊙ to Mt Mitchell SP
7mm	runaway truck ramp eb, scenic overlook wb
6mm	**Welcome Ctr/🅁ₛ eb, full ♿ facilities**

(left margin, top to bottom) **HENDERSONVILLE**

(left margin, bottom) **ARDEN**

(center margin) **ASHEVILLE**

(right tab) **NC**

Ⓖ = gas Ⓕ = food 🏨 = lodging Ⓞ = other Ⓡ🅢 = rest stop   Copyright 2022 - The Next EXIT ®

INTERSTATE 26 Cont'd

Exit #	Services
5.5mm	runaway truck ramp eb
5mm	Buckner Gap, elev. 3370
3	to US 23 A, Wolf Laurel, **N** Ⓖ Exxon/dsl Ⓕ Little Creek Cafe Ⓞ to ski areas
2.5mm	eb runaway truck ramp
.5mm	eb brake insp sta
0mm	North Carolina/Tennessee state line

INTERSTATE 40

Exit #	Services
420mm	I-40 begins/ends at Wilmington, **Services N on US 17** Ⓕ Buffalo Wild Wings, Hiro Japanese Steaks 🏨 Hampton Inn, TX Roadhouse Ⓞ CarQuest, Home Depot, Hyundai, Kia, Kohl's, Land Rover, Mazda, Nissan, Subaru, Toyota, Volvo, **Services S on US 17** Ⓖ Exxon, Murphy USA/dsl Ⓕ Arby's, Bojangles, Bonefish Grill, Carrabba's, Chick-fil-A, ChopStix, Church's, Cracker Barrel, Dunkin', Elizabeth's Pizza, Hieronymus Seafood Co, Hooters, IHOP, Jason's Deli, McDonald's, Olive Garden, Sonic, Subway, Taco Bell, Waffle House 🏨 AmeriStay, Best Western+, Budgetel, Comfort Suites, Country Inn Suites, Days Inn, Extended Stay America, Holiday Inn, Jameson Inn, MainStay Suites, Quality Inn, Red Roof Inn, Rodeway Inn, Sleep Inn, Staybridge Suites, Travel Inn, Wingate Inn Ⓞ Advance Parts, AutoZone, Batteries+, Black's Tires/auto, Cadillac, Costco/gas, Petsmart, Target, URGENT CARE, VW, Walgreens, Walmart, **Services 2-4 mi S on US 117/NC 132** Ⓖ BP/dsl, Exxon/dsl Ⓕ Applebee's, Bojangles, Carolina Ale House, Chili's, CiCi's Pizza, College Diner, Cookout, Golden Corral, HoneyBaked Ham, Jersey Mike's, Jimmy John's, Kickback Jack's, Little Caesar's, McAlister's Deli, McDonald's, Mission BBQ, Okami Japanese, Outback Steaks, Starbucks, Wendy's 🏨 Baymont Inn, Comfort Inn, Courtyard, Holiday Inn Express Ⓞ $Tree, AT&T, Best Buy, Buick/GMC, Chevrolet, Chrysler/Dodge/Jeep, Dick's, Harris-Teeter, Honda, Jo-Ann, Lowe's Foods, Lowe's Whse, Mercedes, Old Navy, PetCo, Ross, Sam's Club/gas, Staples, TJ Maxx, to UNCW, Verizon
420b a	Gordon Rd, NC 132 N, **2 mi N** Ⓖ Shell/dsl Ⓞ KOA (4mi), **S** Ⓖ BP/dsl, Circle K/dsl, Go Gas/dsl Ⓕ China Wok, Dunkin', McDonald's, Subway, Taco Bell Ⓞ $General, Family$, Lowe's Foods, Rite Aid
416b a	I-140, US 17, to Topsail Island, New Bern, Myrtle Beach
414	Holly Shelter Rd, to Brunswick Co beaches, Castle Hayne, **S** Ⓖ BP, Circle K/dsl, GoGas/dsl Ⓕ Carolina Cafe, Domino's, Hardee's, Hwy 55 Cafe, Subway Ⓞ $General, CVS Drug, Fresh Foods IGA, USPO
413mm	NE Cape Fear River
408	NC 210, **N** Ⓞ Mack/Volvo/Isuzu, **S** Ⓖ Phoenix TC/Exxon/Subway/dsl/scales, Shell/Freshway Cafe/dsl, Speedway/Wendy's/dsl Ⓕ Hardee's, McDonald's Ⓞ Advance Parts, Family$, Food Lion, to Moore's Creek Nat Bfd/camping, USPO
398	NC 53, Burgaw, **2 mi S** Ⓖ Shell/dsl, Walmart/dsl Ⓕ Bojangles, Domino's, Hardee's, KFC, McDonald's, Subway, Taco Bell 🏨 Burgaw Motel Ⓞ Ⓗ, $Tree, Advance Parts, Food Lion, Walmart
390	to US 117, Wallace
385	NC 41, Wallace, **N** Ⓖ Exxon/Village Subs, Tesla EVC Ⓕ Bojangles, Mad Boar Rest. 🏨 Holiday Inn Express Ⓞ Lake Leamon Camping, **1.5 mi S** Ⓖ Murphy USA/dsl, Speedway/dsl Ⓕ Burger King, Domino's, McDonald's, Sensation Farmhouse Rest., Subway, Taco Bell, Zaxby's Ⓞ $General, $Tree, Food Lion, O'Reilly Parts, Verizon, Walgreens, Walmart/Subway
384	NC 11, Wallace
380	Rose Hill, **S** Ⓖ BP/Subway/dsl (1mi), Comco, Kwikstop (1mi) Ⓞ Duplin Winery, Family$
373	NC 24 E, NC 903, Magnolia, **N** Ⓖ BP/dsl, Exxon/dsl/e85 Ⓞ Ⓗ, Cowan Museum
369	US 117, Warsaw
364	NC 24, to NC 50, Clinton, **N** Ⓖ Pilot/Arby's/Dunkin'/dsl/24hr, **S** Ⓡ🅢 both lanes, full 🅶 facilities, litter barrels, petwalk, 🄲, 🅵, vending Ⓖ BP/dsl, Citgo Ⓕ Bojangles, Cookout, KFC, McDonald's, Smithfield's BBQ, Subway, Taco Bell, Waffle House, Wendy's 🏨 Best Value Inn, Quality Inn
355	NC 403, to US 117, Goldsboro, Faison, **3 mi N** Ⓖ Exxon
348	Suttontown Rd
343	US 701, Newton Grove, **1 mi N** Ⓖ Exxon/dsl, to Bentonville Bfd
341	NC 50, NC 55, to US 13, Newton Grove, **1.5 mi N** Ⓖ Exxon/dsl Ⓕ Hardee's Ⓞ Food Lion, **S** Ⓖ BP/McDonald's, Shell/Subway/dsl Ⓕ Smithfield BBQ Ⓞ Family Auto/tire
334	NC 96, Meadow, **S** Ⓖ Short Stop/dsl Ⓞ $General
328b a	I-95, N to Smithfield, S to Benson
325	NC 242, to US 301, to Benson, **S** Ⓖ Marathon/dsl
324mm	Ⓡ🅢 both lanes, full 🅶 facilities, litter barrels, no overnight parking, petwalk, 🄲, 🅵, vending
319	NC 210, McGee's Crossroads, **N** Ⓖ BP/BBQ/dsl, Shell/Dunkin'/dsl Ⓕ McDonald's Ⓞ Ⓗ, vet, **S** Ⓖ Mobil/dsl, Sheetz/dsl Ⓕ Bojangle's, China Star, Domino's, Italian Pizza/Pasta, KFC/Taco Bell, Subway, Wendy's Ⓞ $General, AutoZone, CVS Drug, Food Lion
312	NC 42, to Clayton, Fuquay-Varina, **N** Ⓖ Murphy Express/dsl, Speedway/Dunkin'/dsl/24hr, Speedway/Wendy's/dsl Ⓕ Applebee's, China King, Cookout, Cracker Barrel, Divano's Pizza, Fiesta Mexicana, Hibachi&Co, Hwy 55 Burger, Jersey Mike's Subs, King Chinese, Pizza Inn, Ruby Tuesday, Smithfield BBQ, Wendy's 🏨 Comfort Inn, Holiday Inn Express, Super 8, Woodspring Suites Ⓞ $Tree, JustTires, Lowe's, URGENT CARE, Verizon, Walmart/McDonald's, **S** Ⓖ BP/Subway/dsl, Exxon/Burger King, Marathon/dsl, Shell/dsl Ⓕ Bojangle's, Domino's, DQ, Jumbo China, KFC/Taco Bell, Little Caesar's, McDonald's, Snoopy's Hotdogs, Waffle House, Yummi Japan 🏨 Hampton Inn, Sleep Inn Ⓞ AutoZone, CVS Drug, Food Lion, vet, Walgreens
309	US 70 E, Goldsboro, Smithfield
306b a	US 70 E bus, to Smithfield, Garner, Goldsboro **1 mi N** Ⓖ Citgo/dsl, Kangaroo/Subway/dsl Ⓞ Chrysler/Dodge/Jeep, **S** Ⓖ Sheetz/dsl Ⓕ Blaze Pizza, Buffalo Bros Pizza, Buffalo Wild Wings, Carolina Alehouse, Char-Grill, Chick-fil-A, Chili's, Chipotle, City BBQ, Coldstone, Five Guys, Kaze Japanese, La Cocina Mexican, Logan's Roadhouse, Longhorn Steaks, McDonald's, Moe's SW Grill, New Japan Express, Panera Bread, Prima Vera Pizza, Red Robin, Starbucks, Subway, TGIFriday's, Wendy's, Zaxby's Ⓞ $Tree, AT&T, Best Buy, BJ's Whse/gas, Burlington, Cabela's, Dick's, GNC, Kohl's, Michael's, Petsmart, Ross, Staples, Target, TJ Maxx
303	Jones Sausage Rd, **N** Ⓖ Speedway/Dunkin'/dsl Ⓕ Bojangle's, Burger King, Smithfield BBQ, Subway, **S** Ⓖ Speedway/Dunkin'/dsl
301	I-440 E, US 64/70 E, to Wilson
300b a	Rock Quarry Rd, **N** Ⓞ SaveALot, **S** Ⓖ Exxon, Valero/dsl Ⓕ Burger King, Little Caesar's, Subway, Wang's Kitchen Ⓞ Family$, Food Lion, Rite Aid
299	Person St, Hammond Rd, Raleigh (no EZ return eb), **1 mi N** Ⓖ Shell/dsl Ⓞ to Shaw U

WILMINGTON

NC

INTERSTATE 40 Cont'd

Exit #	Services
298b a	US 401 S, US 70 E, NC 50, N 🅖 Shell/dsl 🛏 Red Roof Inn, S 🅖 BP/Circle K, Citgo, Exxon, Exxon/dsl, Mobil, Speedway/dsl 🍴 Baskin-Robbins/Dunkin', Bojangle's, Burger King, Cook-Out, Domino's, Golden Corral, Mi Rancho Mexican, Taco Bell, Waffle House 🛏 Claremont Inn, Comfort Inn, Super 8 🅞 AutoZone, Carquest, Family$, Meineke, O'Reilly Parts, Sam's Club/gas
297	Lake Wheeler Rd, N 🅖 Exxon 🍴 Subway 🅞 Farmer's Mkt, S 🅖 Marathon
295	Gorman St, 1 mi N 🅖 Exxon/dsl 🍴 Hardee's, Little Caesar's, Subway 🛏 Holiday Inn Express 🅞 Family$, to NCSU, Walgreens, S 🅖 Kangaroo
293	to I-440, US 1, US 64 W, Raleigh, S 🅖 Exxon, Shell 🍴 BJ's Rest., Bob Evans, Chick-fil-A, China King, Chipotle, Coldstone, Cook-Out, Dickey's BBQ, East Garden, Egg&I, HoneyBaked Ham, Jasmin, Jason's Deli, Jersey Mike's Subs, McDonald's, Moe's SW Grill, Noodles&Co, Olive Garden, Panera Bread, Red Lobster, Red Robin, Remington Grill, Ruby Tuesday, Starbucks, Subway, Sweet Tomatoes, Taco Bell, Waffle House, Wild Wing Cafe 🛏 Best Western, DoubleTree, Fairfield Inn, Hilton Garden, Holiday Inn, Red Roof Inn, SpringHill Suites 🅞 Best Buy, BJ's Whse, Dick's, Ford, GNC, Home Depot, Jo-Ann Fabrics, Kohl's, Lincoln, Lowe's, Marshalls, Mazda, Michael's, NTB, Office Depot, Old Navy, PetCo, Petsmart, REI, Ross, SteinMart, Target, Verizon, World Mkt
291	Cary Towne Blvd, Cary, 1 mi S 🅖 Circle K 🍴 Dave&Buster's, DQ, Five Guys, Jersey Mike's, La Madeleine, Macaroni Grill, McDonald's, On-the-Border, Pei Wei, Penn Sta Subs, Primo Pizza, Starbucks 🅞 AT&T, Barnes&Noble, Belk, Dillard's, Firestone, Harris Teeter, JC Penney, vet
290	NC 54, Cary, N 🅖 Sheetz/dsl 🍴 McDonald's 🅞 Hyatt Place, Wingate Inn, S 🅖 Shell/dsl 🛏 Hampton Inn
289	to I-440, Wade Ave, to Raleigh, N 🅞 🅷, Carter-Finley Stadium, museum, to fairgrounds
287	Harrison Ave, Cary, N 🅞 to Wm B Umstead SP, S 🅖 BP/Circle/dsl 🍴 An Cuisine, Bonefish Grill, Burger King, BurgerFi, Carolina Cafe, Chick-fil-A, Jersey Mike's, McDonald's, Moe's SW Grill, NY Pizza, Ruth's Chris Steaks, Starbucks, Subway, Thai Cuisine, Wendy's 🛏 Embassy Suites, Extended Stay America, Towne-Place Suites, Umstead Hotel 🅞 Bass Pro Shops, Mr Tire
285	Aviation Pkwy, to Morrisville, N 🅖 Sheetz/dsl 🛏 Hilton Garden 🅞 Raleigh/Durham Airport
284	Airport Blvd, N 🍴 Capital City Chophouse 🛏 Cambria Suites, Country Inn&Suites, Hyatt Place 🅞 to RDU Airport, S 🅖 BP/Circle/dsl, Mobil 🍴 Bojangles, Carmen's, Cracker Barrel, Hooters, KFC/Taco Bell, Los Tres Magueyes, Peng's Asian, TX Steaks, Waffle House, Wendy's 🛏 Courtyard, Days Inn, Extended Stay America, Fairfield Inn, Hampton Inn, Holiday Inn, Holiday Inn Express, La Quinta, Microtel, Residence Inn, Sheraton, Staybridge Suites 🅞 Morrisville Outlets/famous brands/food court
283	I-540 E, toll I-540 W, to US 70, Aviation Pkwy
282	Page Rd, S 🍴 Arby's, Bojangles, Jimmy John's, McDonald's, Mez Cafe, Page Road Grill, Starbucks 🛏 Comfort Suites, DoubleTree, Sheraton, Sleep Inn, Wingate Inn 🅞 Office Depot
281	Miami Blvd, N 🛏 Extended Stay America, Hilton Garden, Marriott, S 🅖 BP, Shell/dsl 🍴 Arby's, Bojangles, Burger King, McDonald's, Quiznos, Randy's Pizza, Serena, Subway, Tropical Smoothie, Wendy's, Wok'n Grill, Zaxby's 🛏 Extended Stay America, Holiday Inn Express, Homewood Suites, Hotel Indigo 🅞 Office Depot
280	Davis Dr, N 🅞 to Research Triangle
279b a	NC 147 N, Triangle Expwy, to Durham, N 🅞 🅷
278	NC 55, to NC 54, Apex, Foreign Trade Zone 93, N 🅖 Marathon 🍴 Jimmy's Hotdogs, Sansui Grill, Waffle House 🛏 Comfort Inn, DoubleTree, EconoLodge, La Quinta, Red Roof Inn, S 🅖 BP, Exxon/dsl, Mobil/dsl 🍴 Arby's, BBQ Pit, Bojangles, Brigs Rest., Capt D's, Chick-fil-A, Cinco de Mayo, CookOut, El Dorado Mexican, Golden Corral, Hardee's, Little Caesar's, McDonald's, Papa John's, Pizza Hut, Starbucks, Subway, Taco Bell, Thai 55, Wendy's, William's Kitchen 🛏 Candlewood Suites, Courtyard, Crossland Suites, Extended Stay America, Residence Inn 🅞 $Tree, Aamco, Advance Parts, AutoZone, BigLots, Colonial Tire, CVS Drug, Firestone/auto, Food Lion, Jiffy Lube, Just Tires, Meineke, NAPA, O'Reilly Parts, Precision Tune, Walgreens
276	Fayetteville Rd, N 🅖 Circle K/dsl, Exxon/Circle K/dsl 🍴 China Cafe, City BBQ, McDonald's, Melting Pot, Orient Garden, Ruby Tuesday, Waffle House, Wendy's 🅞 GNC, Kroger/dsl, Roses, to NC Central U, Walgreens, S 🍴 Bufflo Wild Wings, CA Pizza Kitchen, Champp's Rest, Cheesecake Factory, Chili's, Chipotle, Firebird's, Fork-in-the-Road Cafe, Jersey Mike's, Los Tres Mexican, Maggiano's, McAlister's Deli, Melting Pot, Moe's SW Grill, Panera Bread, PF Chang's, Ruth's Chris Steaks, Starbucks, Ted's MT Grill 🛏 Hilton Garden 🅞 AT&T, Barnes&Noble, Belk, Best Buy, Buick/Cadillac/GMC, Chevrolet, JC Penney, Macy's, Mercedes, Nordstrom, Old Navy, Porsche, REI, World Mkt
274	NC 751, to Jordan Lake, N 🅖 BP, Marathon 🍴 Asian Kitchen, Burger King, Char Grill, Denny's, Dunkin', Jimmy John's, KFC, Marco's Pizza, Taco Bell, Which Wich?, Wing Stop 🅞 Advance Parts, CVS Drug, Harris Teeter, Honda, Lexus, Rite Aid, Sheetz/dsl, URGENT CARE, Walgreens, S 🅖 BP 🍴 Bonefish Grill, Bruster's, Chick-fil-A, Penn Sta Subs, Subway, Town Hall Burger 🛏 Fairfield Inn, Hyatt 🅞 Aldi Foods, Michael's, PetCo, Target
273	NC 54, to Durham, UNC-Chapel Hill, N 🅖 BP/dsl, S 🅖 BP, Shell/dsl 🍴 Amante Pizza, Hardee's, Jersey Mike's, Nantucket Grill, New China 🛏 Courtyard (2mi), Hampton Inn, Holiday Inn Express
270	US 15, US 501, Chapel Hill, Durham, N 🍴 Applebee's, Bob Evans, Carrabba's, Chipotle, Dickey's BBQ, Firehouse Subs, Five Guys, Freddy's, Jason's Deli, Jimmy John's, McAlister's, Moe's SW Grill, NY Pizza, Outback Steaks, Panera Bread, Papa John's, PDQ, Philly Steaks, Red Robin, Starbucks, Xank's Japanese 🛏 Comfort Inn, Home 2 Suites, Homewood Suites, SpringHill Suites, Staybridge Suites 🅞 $Tree, AT&T, Barnes&Noble, Best Buy, Dick's, Home Depot, 🅷S, Kohl's, Kroger/dsl, Marshalls, Michael's, Old Navy, Petsmart, to Duke U, Verizon, Walmart/Subway, S 🅖 Petco 🍴 Hardee's, La Hacienda, McDonald's, Starbucks, Subway, Wendy's 🛏 Quality Inn, Red Roof Inn,

R A L E I G H

C A R Y

C H A P E L H I L L

C H A P E L H I L L

INTERSTATE 40 Cont'd

270	Continued
	Residence Inn, Sheraton, University Inn ⊡ Acura, Advance Parts, AutoZone, BMW, CVS Drug, Food Lion, Lowe's, Mr Tire, Subaru, Trader Joe's
266	NC 86, to Chapel Hill, **2 mi S** ⊞ BP, Exxon, Speedway/dsl ⊞ Jersey Mike's, Subway
263	New Hope Church Rd
261	Hillsborough, **1.5 mi N** ⊞ BP/Circle K, Citgo/dsl ⊞ McDonald's, Pizza Hut ⊠ Holiday Inn Express
259	I-85 N, to Durham
I-40 and I-85 run together 30 mi. See I-85, exits 131-161.	
226	McConnell Rd, **S** ⊞ Exxon
224	E Lee St, to US 29 N, to US 220 N, **N** ⊞ BP/dsl, Shell/dsl ⊠ Holiday Inn Express, Rodeway Inn
223	to N US 29, E US 70, N US 20, Reidsville
222	MLK Jr (from eb), Sanford, **S** ⊞ Arby's, Biscuitville, Burger King, McDonald's, Subway, Taco Bell ⊞ Domino's, Ocean Blue Seafood Rest., Wendy's ⊡ Advance Parts, CVS Drug, Food Lion, Hall Tire Co, Walmart Mkt
221	S Elm-Eugene St, **N** ⊞ Citgo/dsl, Valero ⊡ AutoZone, Family$, Food Lion, O'Reilly Parts, **S** ⊞ BP, Shell/dsl ⊠ EconoLodge, Super 8 ⊡ Home Depot
220	Randleman Rd, US 220 S, to Greensboro, Ashboro, **N** ⊞ Marathon/dsl, Valero ⊞ Biscuitville, Church's, KFC, McDonald's, Pizza Hut, Sub Sta 2, Subway ⊡ Greensboro Tire, Harley-Davidson, Rite Aid, Save-A-Lot, **S** ⊞ BP, Kangaroo ⊞ Cook-Out, Mayflower Seafood, Waffle House, Wendy's
219	US 29 S, W US 70, Highpoint (exits left from wb), Charlotte
218	US 220, Freeman Mill Rd, Ashboro
217	Highpoint Rd, Koury Blvd (from wb), **N** ⊞ Exxon, Shell/dsl ⊞ Biscuitville, Burger King, Chili's, Ham's Rest., Hooters, Ichiban Grill, J Butler's Grille, Little Caesar's, Olive Garden, Sakura Japanese, Santa Fe Mexican, Subway, Taco Bell ⊠ DoubleTree Hotel, Hampton Inn, Holiday Inn, Quality Inn, Red Roof Inn, Super 8 ⊡ $General, $Tree, Office Depot, **S** ⊞ Shell ⊞ Bonefish Grill, Carrabba's, Darryl's Grill, Jimmy John's, Krispy Kreme, McDonald's, Popeye's, Smokey Bones BBQ, Waffle House, Wendy's, Zaxby's ⊠ Baymont Inn, Best Western, Comfort Suites, Drury Inn, Howard Johnson, Ramada Inn, Sheraton, Studio 6 ⊡ Dillard's, Discount Tire, JC Penney, O'Reilly Parts, Walmart Mkt
216	(from eb), Greensboro, **N** ⊡ coliseum
214	Wendover Ave, **N** ⊞ Sheetz/dsl ⊞ Burger King, China Buffet, Coldstone, Jake's Diner, Mario's Pizza, Moe's SW Grill, New Orleans Rest., Noodles&Co, Panera Bread, Penn Sta Subs, Ruby Tuesday, Waffle House ⊠ Extended Stay, Fairfield Inn, Hilton Garden, Holiday Inn Express, Microtel ⊡ Audi, Costco/gas, CVS Drug, Ford, Nissan, PetCo, Staples, TJ Maxx, Verizon, VW, **S** ⊞ Applebee's, Arby's, Biscuitville, Bojangles, Chick-fil-A, Chipotle Mexican, CookOut, Cracker Barrel, Elizabeth's Pizza, Golden Corral, Golden Wok, IHOP, Jimmy John's, Kabuto Japanese, La Hacienda Mexican, Logan's Roadhouse, Longhorn Steaks, McDonald's, O'Charley's, Panda Express, Papa John's, Red Lobster, Steak'n Shake, Subway, Taco Bell, TGIFriday's, Tripp's Rest., Villarosa Italian ⊠ Comfort Inn, Comfort Inn, Courtyard, Extended Stay America, Hyatt Place, InTown Suites, La Quinta, SpringHill Suites, Suburban Inn, Wingate Inn ⊡ $Tree, AT&T, Best Buy, Buick/GMC, Chevrolet, Dick's, Field&Stream, GNC, Goodyear, Hobby Lobby, Home Depot, Kohl's, Land River/Jaguar, Lowe's, Mazda, Meineke, Michael's, Old Navy, Petsmart, Ross, Sam's Club/gas, Target, Walmart

G R E E N S B O R O

W I N S T O N • S A L E M

213	Guilford College Rd, **N** ⊞ BP/dsl ⊠ Wyndham Garden, **S** same as 214, ⊞ Sheetz ⊡ vet
212 b a	I-73, US 241 S, to I-85, to Bryan Blvd, Ashboro, **N** ⊡ to ⊞
211	Gallimore Dairy Rd, **N** ⊡ Freightliner
210	NC 68, to High Point, Piedmont Triad, **N** ⊞ Shell ⊞ Arby's, Carolina's Diner ⊠ Days Inn, Embassy Suites, Fairview Inn, Holiday Inn, Homewood Suites, Sleep Inn ⊡ Ford Trucks, Kenworth, to ⊞, **S** ⊞ Exxon/dsl ⊞ Bojangles, Dunkin', Fatz Cafe, McDonald's, Pizza Hut/Taco Bell, Pollo Pizza/Pasta, Ruby Tuesday, Shoney's, Subway, Wendy's ⊠ Best Western, Comfort Suites, Courtyard, Extended Stay America, Fairfield Inn, Hampton Inn, Hawthorn Suites, Hilton Garden, Holiday Inn Express, Home 2 Suites, Motel 6, Quality Inn, Red Roof Inn, Residence Inn, SpringHill Suites
208	Sandy Ridge Rd, **N** ⊞ Exxon/Subway/dsl, Sheetz/dsl, Speedway/dsl ⊡ Camping World RV Ctr, **S** ⊞ Shell/Circle K/dsl ⊡ Out Of Doors Mart
206	Lp 40 (from wb), to Kernersville, Winston-Salem, downtown
203	NC 66, to Kernersville, **N** ⊞ QM/Subway/dsl, Sheetz/dsl, Speedway/dsl ⊞ Capt Tom's Seafood, Clark's BBQ, Dairi-O, McDonald's, Wendy's ⊠ Hampton Inn, Sleep Inn ⊡ ⊞, Ford, NTB, **S** ⊞ Shell/dsl ⊠ Holiday Inn Express
201	Union Cross Rd, **N** ⊞ BP/dsl ⊞ Blue Naples Pizza, Burger King, China Café, Subway ⊡ CVS Drug, Food Lion, Walmart Mkt, **S** ⊞ Sheetz/dsl ⊞ Bojangle's
196	I-74, US 311 S, to High Point
195	US 311 N, NC 109, to Thomasville, **S** ⊞ Citgo, Speedway/dsl ⊡ Family$
193 b a	US 52, NC 8, to Lexington, **S** ⊞ Shell, Speedway/dsl ⊞ Hardee's
193 c	Silas Creek Pkwy (from eb), same as 192
192	NC 150, to Peters Creek Pkwy, **N** ⊞ Shell, Speedway ⊞ Bojangles, Burger King, Hero House Rest, Hong Kong Buffet, IHOP, KFC, Little Caesar's, Monterrey Mexican, Mr BBQ, Subway, Taco Bell, Tokyo Japanese ⊠ University Inn ⊡ $General, $Tree, Acura/Subaru, Audi, AutoZone, BigLots, Ford, Hamrick's, Hyundai, Infiniti, Mazda, Office Depot, Rite Aid, VW, **S** ⊞ BP, QM ⊞ Arby's, Baskin-Robbins/Dunkin', Cook-Out, Dairi-O, K&W Cafeteria, McDonald's, Papa John's, Pizza Hut, Waffle House, Wendy's, Zaxby's ⊠ Holiday Inn Express ⊡ Advance Parts, Aldi Foods, BMW/Mini, CVS Drug, Family$, Food Lion, Honda, Mock Tire, Toyota
190	Hanes Mall Blvd (from wb, no re-entry), **N** ⊞ Carolina Alehouse, Chipotle Mexican, Coldstone, Elizabeth's Pizza, Genghis Grill, Jimmy John's, McDonald's, Ruby Tuesday, TGI-Friday's, Tripp's Rest. ⊠ Best Western ⊡ ⊞, Belk, Dick's, Dillard's, Firestone/auto, JC Penney, Macy's, Marshalls, same as 189, **S** ⊞ Bad Daddy's Burger, Burger King, ChuckECheese, Outback Steaks, Pan Asian, Starbucks, Subway ⊠ Comfort Suites, Microtel
189	US 158, Stratford Rd, Hanes Mall Blvd, **N** ⊞ BJ's Rest., Bojangles, Chili's, Golden Corral, Honeybaked Ham, Olive Garden, Red Lobster, Red Robin, Taco Bell, TX Roadhouse ⊠ Courtyard, Fairfield Inn ⊡ ⊞, Belk, Buick/GMC, Cadillac, Chevrolet, Dillard's, JC Penney, Macy's, Walgreens, **S** ⊞ Shell ⊞ Applebee's, Bleu Rest., Brixx Pizza, Buffalo Wild Wings, Cheddar's, Chick-fil-A, Firebirds Grill, Five Guys, Hooters, Jason's Deli, Jersey Mike's, KFC/LJ Silver, Longhorn Steaks, Mario's Pizza, Moe's SW Grill, Panera Bread, Qdoba, Subway, Tin Tin Asian, Twin Peaks, Village Tavern, Which Wich?, Zaxby's ⊠ Extended Stay America, Hampton Inn, Hilton Garden, La Quinta, Residence Inn,

NC

◆E INTERSTATE 40 Cont'd

189 Continued
Sleep Inn, SpringHill Suites 🅾 $Tree, AT&T, Barnes&Noble, Best Buy, Costco/gas, CVS Drug, Discount Tire, Hobby Lobby, Home Depot, Kohl's, Lowe's, Michael's, NTB, Petsmart, Ross, Sam's Club/gas, Target, Verizon

188 US 421, to Yadkinville, to WFU (no EZ wb return), Winston-Salem, **1/2 mi N** off US 421 🅶 BP, Exxon, Kangaroo, Shell 🍴 Arby's, Burger King, Cook-Out, Dickey's BBQ, McDonald's, Starbucks, Waffle House, Wendy's 🅾 CarMax, Lexus, Mercedes, Verizon, vet, Walmart/Subway

184 to US 421, Clemmons, **N** 🍴 Mobil/7-11, Shell 🍴 Applebee's, Dairi-O, Dunkin', IHOP, K&W Cafe, KFC, Milner Bros Rest., Panera Bread, Steak Escape 🏨 Quality Inn, **S** 🍴 BP/dsl, Circle K, Speedway/dsl 🍴 Arby's, Biscuitville, Brick Oven Pizza, Burger King, Cracker Barrel, Domino's, Kimono Japanese, Krispy Kreme, Little Richard's BBQ, McDonald's, Mi Pueblo Mexican, Mtn Fried Chicken, Pizza Hut, Ruby Tuesday, Sonic, Starbucks, Subway, Taco Bell, Time to Eat Cafe, Waffle House, Wendy's 🏨 Super 8, Village Inn 🅾 $Tree, Advance Parts, AutoZone, BigLots, CVS Drug, GNC, Lowe's Foods, Meineke, NTB, O'Reilly Parts, Staples, USPO, Verizon, vet, Walgreens, Walmart Mkt

182 Bermuda Run, Tanglewood, **S** 🍴 Chang Thai, Jersey Mike's, Lee's Chinese, Monte De Rey Mexican, Papa John's, Subway 🅾 Harris-Teeter, Tanglewood Camping

182mm Yadkin River

180 NC 801, Tanglewood, **N** 🍴 Sheetz/dsl 🍴 Capt's Galley Seafood, Domino's, La Carreta Mexican, Subway 🏨 Hampton Inn 🅾 🅷, Lowe's Foods/dsl, Rite Aid, **S** 🍴 BP/McDonald's/dsl, Speedway/dsl 🍴 Asian View, Bojangles, Jade Garden, Miyabi Japanese, Venezia Italian, Wendy's, Zaxby's 🅾 $General, Ace Hardware, CVS Drug, Food Lion, Walgreens

177mm 🆁🆂 both lanes, full ♿ facilities, litter barrels, petwalk, 🄲, 🄰, vending

174 Farmington Rd, **N** 🍴 Shell/dsl, **S** 🅾 vineyards

170 US 601, Mocksville, **N** 🍴 Citgo/dsl, Murphy USA/dsl, TA/Shell/Country Pride/Popeye's/dsl/scales/24hr 🍴 JinJin Chinese, La Carreta Mexican 🅾 $Tree, Campers Inn RV Ctr, GNC, Verizon, Walmart/Subway, **S** 🍴 BP, Sheetz/dsl, Speedway/Taco Bell 🍴 Arby's, Bojangles, Burger King, China Grill, Domingo's Mexican, Dunkin', Dynasty Chinese, East Coast Grill, KFC, Marco's Pizza, McDonald's, Papa John's, Pizza Hut, Sagebrush Steaks, Shiki Japanese, Subway, Waffle House, Wendy's 🏨 Comfort Inn, Days Inn, HighWay Inn, Scottish Inn 🅾 🅷, $General, Advance Parts, Lowe's, O'Reilly Parts, USPO, vet, Walgreens

168 US 64, to Mocksville, **N** 🍴 Exxon/dsl 🅾 Lake Myers RV Resort (3mi), **S** 🍴 BP/dsl 🅾 🅷

162 US 64, Cool Springs, **N** 🅾 Lake Myers RV Resort (5mi), **S** 🍴 Shell/dsl 🅾 Midway Camping

161mm S Yadkin River

154 to US 64, Old Mocksville Rd, **N** 🅾 🅷, **S** 🍴 Citgo/dsl, Loves/McDonald's/dsl/scales/24hr 🍴 Jaybee's Hotdogs 🅾 repair/tires

153 US 64 (from eb), **1/2 mi S** 🍴 Citgo/dsl 🍴 Jaybee's Hotdogs 🅾 repair/tires

152b a I-77, S to Charlotte, N to Elkin

151 US 21, E Statesville, **N** 🍴 Marathon/DQ/dsl, Speedway/dsl 🍴 Applebee's, Baskin-Robbins/Dunkin', Bojangles, Chick-fil-A, Chili's, Cook-Out, Cracker Barrel, K&W Cafeteria, KFC, Logan's Roadhouse, McDonald's, Mi Pueblo Café, Red Lobster, Ruby Tuesday, Shiki Japanese, Sorrento's Italian, Taco Bell, Wendy's, Zaxby's 🏨 Days Inn, Sleep Inn 🅾 $Tree, Advance Parts, Aldi Foods, AutoZone, BigLots, Chevrolet, CVS Drug,

151 Continued
GNC, Hobby Lobby, Home Depot, Lowe's, Meineke, Michael's, NTB, Petsmart, Staples, TJ Maxx, URGENT CARE, Verizon, Verizon, Walmart/Subway, **S** 🍴 Exxon 🍴 BJ Hibachi, Greg's BBQ, Lonestar Steaks, Olde 1847 Pizza&Wing, Sonic, Waffle House 🏨 Holiday Inn Express, Masters Inn, Quality Inn 🅾 🅷, $General, URGENT CARE

150 NC 115, Statesville, **N** 🍴 BP/dsl, Citgo, Sheetz/dsl, Shell/Subway 🍴 Amalfi's Italian, Little Caesar's, Ol'Bob's BBQ, Waffle Shop 🅾 $General, CVS Drug, Food Lion, Fred's, museum

148 US 64, NC 90, W Statesville, **N** 🍴 Citgo/dsl, Shell 🍴 Arby's, BoxCar Grille, Burger King, McDonald's, Shiki Japanese, Subway, Village Inn Pizza 🏨 Economy Inn 🅾 $General, CVS Drug, Ingles Foods

146 Stamey Farm Rd, **N** 🅾 truck repair

144 Old Mountain Rd, **N** 🍴 Backyard's 🍴 Troy's Rest., **S** 🍴 BP/dsl, Shell/dsl

143mm weigh sta both lanes

141 Sharon School Rd, **N** 🍴 Citgo/dsl

140mm Catawba River

138 NC 10 W, Oxford School Rd, to Catawba, **N** 🍴 Valero/dsl

136mm 🆁🆂 both lanes, full ♿ facilities, litter barrels, petwalk, 🄲, 🄰, vending

135 Claremont, **S** 🍴 Shell/7-11 🍴 BoxCar Grille, Burger King, Hannah's BBQ, Hardee's, New Panda, Subway 🏨 Rodeway Inn 🅾 $General, Carolina Coach RV Ctr, Lowe's Foods

133 Rock Barn Rd, **N** 🍴 Shell/dsl, **S** 🍴 Liberty/Subway/dsl/scales/24hr

132 to NC 16, Taylorsville, **N** 🍴 Marathon/Kangaroo, Murphy USA/dsl, Shell/dsl 🍴 Burger King, Hwy 55 Cafe, Jin's Buffet, Subway, Zaxby's 🏨 Holiday Inn Express 🅾 $Tree, AT&T, AutoZone, Walmart

130 Old US 70, **N** 🍴 Jack-in-the-Box, Subway 🅾 repair, Verizon, vet, **S** 🍴 Citgo, Pure 🅾 USPO

128 US 321, Fairgrove Church Rd, Hickory, **N** 🍴 BP, Marathon/dsl, Shell 🍴 McDonald's, Waffle House 🅾 🅷, **S** 🍴 Citgo, Marathon/dsl 🍴 Dos Amigos, Nagano Japanese, Papa Pesto's Greek/Italian, Wendy's 🏨 Days Inn, La Quinta 🅾 Chrysler/Dodge/Jeep, to Catawba Valley Coll

126 to US 70, NC 155, **S** 🍴 Marathon/dsl 🍴 Applebee's, Bob Evans, Buffalo Wild Wings, Chili's, East Coast Wings, IHOP, Jason's Deli, Krispy Kreme, McDonald's, O'Charley's, Olive Garden, Panera Bread, Popeye's, Taco Bell 🏨 Holiday Inn Express 🅾 Barnes&Noble, Discount Tire, Hickory Furniture Mart, Lowe's, Michael's, PetCo, Ross, Sam's Club/gas, URGENT CARE, Walmart/McDonald's

125 Hickory, **N** 🍴 RaceWay/dsl 🍴 Bojangles, Dickey's BBQ, Golden Corral, Hardee's, Kickback Jack's Grill, Mellow Mushroom, Rancho Viejo, Starbucks, TX Roadhouse 🏨 Red Roof Inn

🅞 = gas 🅗 = food 🅛 = lodging 🅞 = other 🆁🆂 = rest stop   Copyright 2022 - The Next EXIT

▲E INTERSTATE 40 Cont'd

125	Continued
	🅞 $General, Aamco, Advance Parts, Firestone/auto, S 🅗 Shell/dsl, Speedway/dsl 🅗 Arby's, Atlanta Bread, Burger Fi, Carrabba's, Chick-fil-A, Chipotle, ChuckECheese, CiCi's Pizza, Coldstone, Cracker Barrel, Five Guys, Hooters, J&S Cafeteria, Jack-in-the-Box, KFC, Kobe Japanese, Longhorn Steaks, NY Hibachi Buffet, Outback Steaks, PDQ Rest., Red Lobster, Ruby Tuesday, Tony's Pizza, Waffle House, Wendy's, Which Wich?, Wild Wok, Zaxby's 🅛 Baymont Inn, Best Western, Courtyard, Crowne Plaza, Fairfield Inn, Hampton Inn, Hilton Garden, Quality Inn, Sleep Inn 🅞 $Tree, Aldi Foods, AT&T, Belk, Best Buy, Carmax, Dick's, Dillard's, Food Lion, Ford, Hamrick's, Harley-Davidson, Home Depot, Honda, JC Penney, Kohl's, Mazda, NAPA, Nissan, NTB, Office Depot, Old Navy, O'Reilly Parts, Petsmart, Sunrise Camping Ctr, Suzuki, Target, TJ Maxx, Toyota, Verizon
123	US 70/321, to NC 127, Hickory
121	Long View, N 🅞 Kenworth
119 b a	Hildebran, N 🅗 Shell/Subway 🅗 Bojangles, Hardee's 🅞 $General
118	Old NC 10, N 🅗 Pure, Shell/dsl
116	Icard, S 🅗 Marathon/McDonald's/dsl 🅗 Burger King, Granny's Kitchen 🅛 Icard Inn 🅞 USPO
113	Connelly Springs, N 🅗 Citgo/dsl 🅗 Patsy Ann's Rest, Subway 🅞 🅗, CVS Drug, Ford/Hyundai, Walgreens
112	Mineral Springs Mtn Rd, Valdese
111	Valdese
107	NC 114, to Drexel
106	Bethel Rd, S 🅗 Exxon/dsl 🅛 Economy Inn/rest.
105	NC 18, Morganton, N 🅗 BP/Dunkin'/dsl 🅗 Abele's Rest., Arby's, Capt D's, Cracker Barrel, Fatz Café, Harbor Inn Seafood, Las Salsas, McDonald's, Sonic, Wendy's, Zaxby's, Zeko's Italian 🅛 Hampton Inn 🅞 🅗, Chevrolet/Buick/GMC, S 🅗 Shell/dsl 🅗 El Paso Mexican, Sagebrush Steaks, Waffle House 🅛 Quality Inn, Sleep Inn 🅞 to South Mtns SP
104	Enola Rd, S 🅗 Chen's Garden 🅞 $Tree, BigLots, Food Lion
103	US 64, Morganton, N 🅗 Citgo/dsl, Exxon/dsl 🅗 Allison's Rest., Chick-fil-A, Cook-Out, Village Inn Pizza 🅛 Days Inn, S 🅗 Marathon, RaceWay/dsl 🅗 Bojangles, Butch's BBQ, Denny's, Hardee's, KFC, Subway, Taco Bell, Tokyo Diner 🅛 Comfort Inn 🅞 $General, Clark Tire/auto, Food Lion, Honda, Ingles Foods, Lowe's
100	Jamestown Rd, N 🅗 BP/dsl 🅗 Waffle Shop 🅞 Chrysler/Dodge/Jeep, Ford/Lincoln
98	Causby Rd, to Glen Alpine, S 🅞 B&B/food
96	Kathy Rd
94	Dysartsville Rd, Lake James, N 🅞 Lake James SP
90	Lake James, Nebo, N 🅗 Nebo/dsl 🅞 to Lake James SP, S 🅗 Marathon/dsl 🅞 Springs Creek RV Ctr
86	NC 226, to Spruce Pine, Marion, N 🅗 Exxon, ⬤Loves/Subway/Godfather's/dsl/scales/24hr 🅗 Hardee's, KFC, Waffle House 🅞 Jellystone RV Park (2mi)
85	US 221, Marion, N 🅛 Hampton Inn 🅞 to Mt Mitchell SP, S 🅗 Marathon/dsl 🅛 Best Value Inn, Super 8 🅞 $General
83	Ashworth Rd
82mm	🆁🆂 both lanes, full 🅗 facilities, litter barrels, petwalk, 🅲, 🅐, vending
81	Sugar Hill Rd, to Marion, N 🅗 BP/dsl, Murphy Express/dsl 🅗 Arby's, Bojangle's, Hwy 55 Cafe, Japanese Express, New China, Nopale's Mexican, Waffle House 🅞 🅗, $Tree, Chrysler/Dodge/Jeep, GNC, Walmart/Subway, S 🅗 🅛/Subway/dsl

76mm	Catawba River
75	Parker Padgett Rd, S 🅗 Exxon/Stuckey's/DQ/dsl
73	Old Fort, N 🅗 BP/dsl 🅗 Hardee's 🅞 Auto+, S 🅗 Sunoco/ds 🅗 McDonald's
72	US 70 (from eb), Old Fort, N 🅛 B&B
71mm	Pisgah NF, eastern boundary
67.5mm	truck 🆁🆂 eb
66	Ridgecrest, N 🅛 B&B
65	(from wb), to Black Mountain, Black Mtn Ctr
64	NC 9, Black Mountain, N 🅗 Shell/Subway 🅗 Pizza Hut, Starbucks 🅛 Hampton Inn, S 🅗 BP/dsl 🅗 Denny's, McDonald's Phil's BBQ, Starbucks, Taco Bell, Wendy's 🅛 Quality Inn 🅞 Ingles Foods/gas, Walgreens
63mm	Swannanoa River
59	Swannanoa, N 🅗 BP/Subway, Shell/dsl 🅗 Athens Pizza, Burger King, Don Chon Chinese, Papa John's 🅞 Ace Hardware, CVS Drug, Family$, Harley-Davidson, Ingles Foods/gas, KOA (2mi), Miles RV Ctr/Park, to Warren Wilson Coll, USPO, vet, S 🅞 Mama Gertie's Camping
55	US 70, E Asheville, N 🅗 BP, Citgo/Subway, Mobil 🅗 Arby's, Bojangles, Cocula Mexican, Domino's, Gondolier Italian, Waffle House, Zaxby's 🅛 Days Inn, Holiday Inn, Motel 6, Quality Inn 🅞 Family$, Folk Art Ctr, Go Groceries, Tap's RV park, to Mt Mitchell SP, VA 🅗, vet
53 b a	I-240 W, US 74 a, to Asheville, Bat Cave, S 🅗 Shell/dsl 🅗 Sonic, Subway 🅞 CVS Drug, Ingles, to Blue Ridge Pkwy, N on Fairview Rd 🅗 Ay Carumba Mexican, China Buffet, J&S Cafeteria, KFC, Little Caesars, McDonald's, Papa John's, Pizza Hut, Subway 🅛 Ramada Inn 🅞 $General, Advance Parts, Citgo/dsl, CVS Drug, Hamrick's, Home Depot, Meineke
51	US 25A, Sweeten Creek Rd, S 🅗 Subway 🅛 Brookstone Lodge
50	US 25, Asheville, N 🅗 Market Ctr, Shell, Shell/dsl 🅗 Arby's, Asaka Japanese, Chapala Mexican, Hardee's, Jimmy John's, L Silver, McDonald's, Moe's SW Grill, Ruth's Chris Steaks, Starbucks, Subway, TGIFriday's, TX Roadhouse, Wendy's, Zoe's Kitchen 🅛 Baymont Inn, Biltmore Village Lodge, Doubletree Inn, Grand Bohemian Hotel, Guesthouse Inn, Residence Inn 🅞 🅗, to Biltmore House, URGENT CARE, S 🅗 Speedway/dsl 🅗 Apollo Flame Rest., Atl Bread Co, Bojangles, Huddle House, Juicy Lucy's 🅞 Advance Parts, Ingles/deli
47mm	French Broad River
47	NC 191, W Asheville, N 🅞 Bear Creek RV Camping, S 🅗 BP/Subway 🅗 Moose Cafe 🅛 Comfort Suites, Country Inn&Suites, Fairfield Inn, Hampton Inn, Holiday Inn Express, Rodeway Inn 🅞 Audi/Porsche/VW, Farmer's Mkt, Ford, Nissan
46 b a	I-26 & I-240 E, 2 mi N multiple services from I-240
44	US 19, US 23, W Asheville, N 🅗 BP, Shell/DQ/dsl, Speedway/dsl 🅗 Applebee's, Arby's, Bojangle's, Burger King, Cracker Barrel, Dunkin', El Chapala Mexican, Fatz Cafe, Hardee's, IHOP, Subway, Waffle House, Wendy's, Yao Grill 🅛 Comfort Inn, Country Inn&Suites, Ramada Inn, Red Roof Inn, Rodeway Inn, Sleep Inn, Whispering Pines Motel 🅞 Chevrolet, Chrysler/Dodge/Jeep, Lowe's, Mazda/Mercedes, S 🅗 McDonald's, Zaxby's 🅛 Asheville Inn, Holiday Inn, Woodspring Suites 🅞 Bi-Lo Foods, CVS Drug, Home Depot
41mm	weigh sta both lanes
37	Candler, N 🅗 Sunoco, TA/Country Pride/dsl/scales/24hr/@ 🅞 Goodyear/truck tires, S 🅗 Exxon/dsl 🅛 Days Inn, Plantation Motel 🅞 $General, KOA
33	Newfound Rd, to US 74, S 🅗 Exxon
31	Rd 215, Canton, N 🅗 Sagebrush Steaks 🅛 Best Value Inn 🅞 URGENT CARE, S 🅗 BP/dsl, Marathon/DQ, Shell/d

* HICKORY, MORGANTON, NC; right margin: ASHEVILLE, ASHEVILLE*

INTERSTATE 40 Cont'd

31	Continued
	🍴 Arby's, Bojangles, Burger King, McDonald's, Starbucks, Subway, Taco Bell, Waffle House 🛏 Quality Inn 🅞 Ford, Ingles Foods/dsl, RV/truck repair
27	US 19/23, to Waynesville, Great Smokey Mtn Expswy, 3 mi S 🍴 Burger King, Coffee Cup Cafe, Subway 🛏 Super 8 🅞 🏥, $Tree, Food Lion, GNC, Lowe's, to WCU (25mi)
24	NC 209, to Lake Junaluska, N 🅖 Pilot/Subway/dsl/scales /24hr/@ 🛏 Midway Motel, S 🅖 Shell/cafe/dsl/24hr 🅞 🏥
20	US 276, to Maggie Valley, Lake Junaluska, S 🅖 BP/dsl, Exxon/dsl, Marathon (2mi) 🅞 Creekwood RV Park, Pride RV Resort, Winngray RV Park
16mm	Pigeon River
15	Fines Creek
13mm	Pisgah NF eastern boundary
10mm	🆁🆂 both lanes, full 🚻 facilities, litter barrels, petwalk, 🕴, 🐾, vending
7	Harmon Den
4mm	tunnel both lanes
0mm	North Carolina/Tennessee state line

INTERSTATE 74

Exit #	Services
23	US 220 S, I-70/73 begins/ends.
25	US 220 N, Ellerbe
28	to NC 73 W, Millstone Rd
30	Haywood Parker Rd
33	NC 73
35	Norman
39	Tabernacle Church Rd
41	US 220 S, US 220 A N, Candor
44	NC 211, Candor, Pinehurst, N 🅖 Exxon/dsl, Pilot/Dunkin'/Wendy's/dsl/scales/24hr, S 🅖 Citgo/dsl 🅞 $General
49	NC 24, 27, Troy, Carthage, S 🅖 Citgo 🍴 Bojangle's, Hardee's, Waffle House 🛏 Day Inn 🅞 $General
52	Star, Robbins
56	US 220 A, Ether, Steeds
58	Black Ankle Rd
60	🆁🆂/visitor ctr both lanes, full 🚻 facilities
61	NC 705, Seagrove, Robbins, N 🅖 Citgo/Hardee's/dsl
66	New Hope Church Rd
68	US 220, NC 134, Ulah, Troy
71	McDowell Rd, N 🅖 Tank$Tommy, S 🍴 K&W Cafeteria
72b a	US 64, NC 49, To Lexington, N 🅖 BP, Speedway/dsl 🍴 Arby's, Bamboo Garden, Biscuitville, Bojangle's, Burger King, Dunkin', Huddle House, McDonald's, Taco Bell, Wendy's 🛏 Comfort Inn 🅞 Lowe's Foods, S 🅖 Citgo/dsl 🍴 Subway 🛏 Randolph Inn 🅞 Food Lion
74	(exits left) Salisbury St, Sunset Ave
75	W Presnell St
76	Vision Dr
77	Spero Rd
79	Pineview St
86	(80 from wb) I-73 N (exits left from eb, runs with I-74)
84	US 311 S, Randleman, S 🅖 Citgo 🅞 USPO
79	Cedar Square Rd, Archdale
75	I-85, N to Greensboro, S to Charlotte
71b	I-85BR, US 29
71a	E Green St
70	MLK Dr, S 🅞 🏥

69	Greensboro Rd, Jamestown, N 🅖 Exxon 🍴 Bojangle's 🅞 Holiday Tire/auto, vet, S 🅖 Citgo 🍴 McDonald's 🅞 Family$, SaveALot
67	NC 68, Eastchester Dr, to I-40, S 🅖 Marathon/dsl 🍴 Barbarito's, Honeybaked Ham 🅞 URGENT CARE
66	Johnson St
65	US 311, N Main St, High Point, S 🅖 Sheetz/dsl 🍴 McDonald's 🅞 Aldi Foods
63	NC 66, Kernersville
60	High Point Rd
59	Union Cross Rd
56	Ridgewood Rd
I-74 begins/ends on I-40, exit 196.	
Future I-74 connects via US 52 to US 311 around Winston Salem	
122	Moore-RJR Dr, N 🅞 Hanging Rock SP
123	King, Tobaccoville, N 🅖 Exxon/7-11 🍴 Bojangle's, Burger King, KFC, Little Caesar's, Little Italy, McDonald's, Papa John's, Pizza Hut, Stratford BBQ, Subway, Taco Bell, Waffle House, Wendy's 🛏 Bestway Inn 🅞 $General, $Tree, Advance Parts, CVS Drug, Family$, Food Lion, Lowe's Foods, O'Reilly Parts, Rite Aid, USPO, vet, Walmart
127mm	scenic overlook wb
129	Pinnacle, N 🅖 BP/dsl, S 🅖 Marathon
131	Pilot Mtn SP
134	NC 268, Pilot Mtn, Elkin, N 🅖 Exxon/dsl 🍴 McDonald's, Mtn View Rest. 🛏 Econolodge 🅞 Advance Parts, S 🅖 Shell/Circle K/dsl, Speedway/Dunkin'/dsl 🍴 Wendy's
135	Pilot Mtn
136	Cook School Rd, N 🅖 Blue Mtn/dsl, Gas&Go 🅞 Ford
17	US 52 N, to Mt Airy
13	Park Dr
11	US 601, to Mt Airy, Dobson, N 🅖 Sheetz/dsl
8	Red Brush Rd, N 🅖 Shell/Circle K/dsl
6	NC 89, to Mt Airy, S 🅖 FLYING J/Brintle's Rest./dsl/scales/24hr/@, Marathon/Subway/dsl, Shell/Circle K/dsl 🍴 Copper Pot Rest. 🛏 Best Western
5	(101 from eb) I-77, N to Wytheville, S to Statesville
0mm	**I-74 begins/ends at NC state line, runs with I-77.**

INTERSTATE 77

Exit #	Services
105mm	North Carolina/Virginia state line
105mm	Welcome Ctr sb, full 🚻 facilities, info, litter barrels, petwalk, 🕴, 🐾, vending
103mm	weigh sta both lanes
101	I-74 E, to Mt Airy, Winston-Salem, Greensboro, E 🅞 🏥 (12mi)
100	NC 89, to Mt Airy, E 🅖 FLYING J/Brintle's Rest./dsl/scales/24hr/@, Marathon/Subway/dsl, Shell/Circle K/dsl 🍴 Copper Pot Rest. 🛏 Best Western 🅞 dsl repair, 🏥 (12mi)

K I N G
P I L O T   M T N

A S H E B O R O

NC

⬆N INTERSTATE 77 Cont'd

Exit #	Services
93	to Dobson, Surry, **E** 🅖 BP/DQ/dsl, Exxon/Circle K/dsl 🅕 Diner, Harvest Grill (2mi), Putters Grill 🄰 Hampton Inn, Surry Inn
85	NC 118, CC Camp Rd, to Elkin, **1-3 mi W** 🅖 Exxon/7-11/dsl, Murphy Express/dsl, Sheetz/dsl, Speedway/dsl 🅕 Burger King, KFC, Mazzini's Italian, McDonald's, Sonic, Taco Bell, Zaxby's 🄰 Fairfield Inn 🄾 🄷, $Tree, AT&T, BigLots, Food Lion, Lowe's, Rite Aid, Walmart/Subway
83	US 21 byp, to Sparta (from nb)
82.5mm	Yadkin River
82	NC 67, Elkin, **E** 🅖 BP/Subway/dsl, Citgo/Case Outlet/dsl, Exxon/dsl 🅕 Arby's, Cracker Barrel, Sixty Seven Pizza 🄰 Best Western 🄾 Holly Ridge Camping (8mi), **W** 🅖 Speedway/Dunkin'/dsl 🅕 Bojangles, Breakfastime, McDonald's, Valentino's Pizza, Waffle House, Wendy's 🄰 Days Inn, Hampton Inn, Quality Inn 🄾 $General, D-Rex Drug, Food Lion, URGENT CARE, vet
79	US 21 S, to Arlington, **E** 🅖 Citgo/Subway/dsl 🄰 Royal Inn, **W** 🅖 BP/dsl 🅕 Glenn's BBQ 🄰 Best Value Inn
73b a	US 421, to Winston-Salem, **1 mi E** 🅖 Exxon/Subway/7-11/dsl
72mm	🆁ₛ nb, full 🄯 facilities, litter barrels, petwalk, 🄲, 🄰, vending
65	NC 901, to Union Grove, Harmony, **E** 🄾 Van Hoy Farms Camping, **W** 🅖 BP/dsl, Exxon/Subway/7-11/dsl 🅕 Burger Barn 🄾 $General, Ace Hardware, Fiddler's Grove Camping (2mi)
63mm	🆁ₛ sb, full 🄯 facilities, litter barrels, petwalk, 🄲, 🄰, vending
59	Tomlin Mill Rd, **W** 🅖 Valero/dsl
58	🆁ₛ both lanes, full 🄯 facilities
56.5mm	S Yadkin River
54	US 21, to Turnersburg, **E** 🅖 Citgo, **W** 🅖 Exxon/7-11/dsl 🅕 Arby's, Baskin-Robbins/Dunkin', Chick-fil-A, CookOut, Golden Corral, Zaxby's
51b a	I-40, E to Winston-Salem, W to Hickory
50	E Broad St, Statesville, **E** 🅖 Citgo, Exxon/Kangaroo/dsl, Shell 🅕 Arby's, Bojangles, Burger King, Domino's, Dunkin'/Hungry Howie's, East Coast Grill, IHOP, Little Caesar's, Los Compadres Mexican, McDonald's, Papa John's, Papa Murphy's, Pizza Hut, Shanghai Buffet, Starbucks, Subway, Taco Bell, Wendy's 🄰 Brookwood Inn, Red Roof Inn 🄾 $General, $Tree, AT&T, Belk, Bi-Lo, Food Lion, Rite Aid, URGENT CARE
49b a	US 70, G Bagnal Blvd, to Statesville, **E** 🅖 BP, Citgo/dsl, Citgo/dsl, Marathon/dsl, Shell, Solo 🅕 KFC, Outback Steaks, Rice Fun Chinese, Subway, Village Inn Pizza, Waffle House 🄰 Best Value Inn, Best Western, Comfort Inn, Courtyard, Hampton Inn, Motel 6, Ramada Inn 🄾 auto repair, Camping World RV Ctr, Ford/Lincoln, Harley-Davidson, Honda, Nissan, Toyota, **W** 🅖 Citgo/dsl, Exxon/dsl 🄰 Hilton Garden, Microtel 🄾 Buick/GMC, Carquest, Chrysler/Dodge/Jeep
45	to Troutman, Barium Springs, **E** 🄾 KOA, RV Repair
42	US 21, NC 115, to Troutman, Oswalt, **E** 🅖 🅻ittle/Subway/Dunkin'/dsl/scales/24hr, Sheetz/dsl 🅕 Bojangles, McDonald's, Taco Bell, Wendy's 🄾 AutoZone, Lowe's, **W** 🅖 CNG, Exxon/dsl 🅕 Arby's 🄾 to Lake Norman SP
39mm	🆁ₛ both lanes, full 🄯 facilities, litter barrels, petwalk, 🄲, 🄰, vending
36	NC 150, Mooresville, **E** 🅖 Circle K/dsl, Exxon, QT/dsl, Shell/dsl 🅕 Applebee's, CookOut, Denny's, Domino's, Fat Boys Rest., Hong Mei Buffet, Pizza Hut, Pomodoro's, Popeyes, Sonny's BBQ, Taco Bell, Waffle House, Wendy's, Zaxby's 🄰 Days Inn, Fairfield Inn, Holiday Inn Express, Quality Inn 🄾 $Tree, Belk, Big Lots, Cadillac/Chevrolet, GNC, Jo-Ann Fabrics, Kia, Kohl's, Subaru, Tuesday Morning, URGENT CARE, Walmart/Subway,

Exit #	Services
36	Continued **W** 🅖 Circle K/dsl, Qt/dsl, Shell/dsl, Speedway/dsl 🅕 Baskin-Robbins/Dunkin', Bojangles, Buffalo Wild Wings, Charanda Mexican, Chick-fil-A, Chili's, Chipotle, Chopstix, Cracker Barrel, Duckworth's Grill, Firehouse Subs, Five Guys, Golden Corral, Hardee's, Hickory Tavern Grill, Hooters, IHOP, Iron Thunder Grill, LoneStar Steaks, McAlister's Deli, McDonald's, Moe's SW Cafe, Noodles&Co, O'Charley's, Panera Bread, Papa Murphy's, Red Robin, Rita's Custard, Sagebrush Steaks, Showmar's, Smoothie King, Sonic, Starbucks, Steak'n Shake, Subway 🄰 Carolina Inn, Hampton Inn, Sleep Inn, Wingate Inn 🄾 Advance Parts, AT&T, AutoZone, Best Buy, BJ's Whse/gas, CVS Drug, Dick's, Discount Tire, Food Lion, Hobby Lobby, Lowe's, Michael's, NTB, Old Navy, PetCo, Petsmart, Ross, Sam's Club/dsl, Staples, Target, TJ Maxx, Tuffy Auto, Verizon, vet, Walgreens, World Mkt
35	Brawley School Rd
33	US 21 N, **E** 🅖 Shell 🅕 Brusco's Pizza, China Express, DQ, Iron Grill Japanese, Jeffrey's Rest, Jets Pizza, McDonald's, Starbucks, Subway 🄰 Candlewood Suites, Hilton Garden, Spring Hill Suites, TownePlace Suites 🄾 🄷, **W** 🅖 Citgo/dsl, Marathon/dsl 🅕 Arby's, Baskin-Robbins/Dunkin', Sauza's Mexican 🄾 Food Lion, vet
31	Langtree Rd, **W** 🅖 Shell/dsl
30	Davidson, **E** 🅖 BP, Exxon/dsl 🅕 Char-Grill, Ming's Chinese, Subway 🄰 Homewood Suites 🄾 Harris-Teeter, to Davidson College, Woodie's Auto Service, **W** 🅕 North Harbor Rest
28	US 21 S, NC 73, Cornelius, Lake Norman, **E** 🅖 Cashion/dsl, Citgo 🅕 Acropolis Cafe 🄰 Days Inn, Hampton Inn 🄾 NAPA, vet, **W** 🅖 Marathon/Circle K 🅕 Asiana, Bojangles, Chicago Dog, Choplin's Rest., Domino's, Dragon Buffet, Fresh Chef Cafe, Honeybaked Ham, Jersey Mike's, Jimmy John's, KFC, Little Caesar's, Mac's BBQ, McAlister's Deli, McDonald's, Pizza Hut, Starbucks, Subway, Taco Bell, Waffle House, Wendy's 🄰 Clarion, Comfort Inn, EconoLodge, Microtel 🄾 $Tree, Chrysler/Dodge/Jeep, Fresh Mkt, Goodyear/auto, Hyundai, Infiniti, SteinMart, USPO, Walgreens
25	NC 73, Concord, Lake Norman, **E** 🅖 Exxon/7-11/dsl 🅕 Burger King, Chick-fil-A, Chili's, Duckworth's Grill, IHOP, Longhorn Steaks, McDonald's, Melting Pot, Moe's SW Grill, Panda Express, Panera Bread, Papa John's, Showmar's Rest., Starbucks, Subway, Zaxby's 🄰 Country Inn&Suites, Holiday Inn Express, Quality Inn 🄾 🄷, AAA, Advance Parts, AT&T, GNC, Harris-Teeter, Home Depot, Kohl's, Lowe's, Marshall's, PetCo, Staples, Target, Tuffy Auto, Verizon, vet, **W** 🅖 Shell/Circle K/dsl 🅕 Bob Evans, Bojangles, Bonefish Grill, Carrabba's, Chipotle, Hickory Tavern Grill, House of Taipei, Jason's Deli, Jimmy John's, Kabute Japanese, Outback Steaks, Qdoba, Red Rock's Cafe, Starbucks, Subway, Taco Mac, Viva Chicken, Which Wich?, Zoe's Kitchen 🄰 Candlewood Suites, Courtyard, Sleep Inn 🄾 Barnes&Noble, Dick's, Office Depot, to Energy Explorium, Walgreens, Whole Foods Mkt
23	Gilead Rd, to US 21, Huntersville, **E** 🅖 BP, Pittstop, Shell 🅕 Baskin-Robbins/Dunkin Dounuts, Bojangles, Chico's Mexican, CookOut, Hardee's, Huntersville Rest., Jersey Mike's, Little Caesar's, Rocky's Pizza, Romanello's Subs, Subway, Taco Bell, Waffle House, Wendy's 🄰 Best Western, Comfort Suites, Hampton Inn, Super 8 🄾 AutoZone, Buick/GMC, Food Lion, Ford, Goodyear/auto, Honda, Mazda, O'Reilly Parts, Rite Aid, Toyota, Tuesday Morning, USPO, vet, VW, **W** 🅖 Shell/7-11/dsl 🅕 Domino's, Firehouse Subs, Five Guys, Fusion Asian, Groucho's Deli, Hawthorne's Pizza, Killington's Rest., McDonald's, Papa Murphy's, Pizza Hut, Starbucks 🄾 🄷, Batteries+, CVS Drug, Earth Fare, GNC, Harris-Teeter, Publix, URGENT CARE, Walgreens

Vertical labels: ELKIN, STATESVILLE, MOORESVILLE, NC, MOORESVILLE, CONCORD

⬆N INTERSTATE 77 Cont'd

Exit #	Services
19b a	S I-485 Outer, Rd 115, to Spartanburg
18	Harris Blvd, Reames Rd, **E** 🅟 BP/Arby's, Shell/7-11/dsl 🍴 Azteca Mexican, Bob Evans, Hickory Tavern, Jack-in-the-Box, Jimmy John's, Subway, Waffle House 🛏 Comfort Suites, Courtyard, Fairfield Inn, Hilton Garden, Holiday Inn Express, Suburban Lodge 🅞 🏥, Advance Parts, Staples, to UNCC, Univ Research Park, URGENT CARE, **W** 🍴 Bravo Italian, Buffalo Wild Wings, Chick-fil-A, Chili's, East Coast Grill, Edomae Grill, Firebirds Grill, Firehouse Subs, Five Guys, Fox&Hound, Jersey Mike's, Mimi's Cafe, Moe's SW Grill, Olive Garden, On-the-Border, Panera bread, PF Chang's, Red Robin, Shane's Rib Shack, TGI Friday's, Wendy's 🛏 Drury Inn 🅞 $Tree, AT&T, Belk, Best Buy, Dick's, Dillard's, Discount Tire, Lowe's, Macy's, Old Navy, Petsmart, REI, Target, Verizon
16b a	US 21, Sunset Rd, **E** 🅟 Circle K, QT/dsl, Shell/7-11/dsl 🍴 Capt D's, Hardee's, KFC, McDonald's, Papa John's, Subway, Taco Bell, Wendy's 🛏 Days Inn, Super 8 🅞 $General, AutoZone, Just$ave Foods, NAPA, O'Reilly Parts, **W** 🅟 Circle K/dsl, Citgo/dsl, Shell/dsl/scales/24hr 🍴 Baskin-Robbins/Dunkin', Bojangles, Bubba's BBQ, CookOut, Denny's, Domino's, Jack-in-the-Box, Little Caesar's, Subway, Waffle House 🛏 Microtel, Sleep Inn 🅞 Advance Parts, Aldi Foods, CVS Drug, Family$, Food Lion, Meineke, Walgreens
13b a	I-85, S to Spartanburg, N to Greensboro
12	La Salle St, **W** 🅟 Marathon/dsl, Shell/dsl
11b a	I-277, Brookshire Fwy, NC 16
10b	Trade St, 5th St, **E** 🅞 to Discovery Place, **W** 🅟 Circle K 🍴 Bojangles, Church's 🅞 Family$
10a	US 21 (from sb), Moorhead St, downtown
9	I-277, US 74, to US 29, John Belk Fwy, downtown, **E** 🅞 🏥, stadium
8	Remount Rd (from nb, no re-entry)
7	Clanton Rd, **E** 🅟 QT/dsl, Shell/dsl 🛏 Quality Inn, Super 8 🅞 Family$, **W** 🅟 7-11/dsl, BP
6b a	US 521, Billy Graham Pkwy, **E** 🅟 Citgo, Exxon/dsl, Exxon/dsl (2), QT/dsl 🍴 Arby's, Azteca Mexican, Bojangles, Burger King, Capt D's, Carolina Prime Steaks, Domino's, Dragon House, Firehouse Subs, HoneyBaked Ham, IHOP, KFC, Papa John's, Tres Pesos Grill, Waffle House 🛏 Baymont Inn, Best Western, Clarion, Days Inn, Ramada, Sheraton 🅞 CVS Drug, Family$, Home Depot, TJ Maxx, to Queens Coll, Walgreens, **W** 🅟 Circle K 🛏 Courtyard, Embassy Suites, Extended Stay America, Hyatt House, InTowne Suites, La Quinta, Sleep Inn 🅞 ⊙
5	Tyvola Rd, **E** 🅟 Circle K, Exxon/7-11/dsl, Shell 🍴 Chili's, Kabuto, McDonald's, Sonny's BBQ, Subway 🛏 Cloverleaf Suites, Comfort Inn, Crowne Plaza, Extended Stay America, Hawthorn Suites, Hilton, Wyndham Garden 🅞 Aldi Foods, Costco/gas, Maserati, Meineke, Verizon, **W** 🛏 Extended Stay America, Home 2 Suites, Wingate Inn
4	Nations Ford Rd, **E** 🅟 Citgo, Shell/Circle K 🛏 Best Value Inn, Knights Inn, **W** 🅟 Mobil/Burger King
3	Arrowood Rd, **E** 🍴 Cafe South, Jack-in-the-Box, Sonic, Starbucks, Wendy's 🛏 Courtyard, Fairfield Inn, Holiday Inn Express, Hyatt Place, Mainstay Suites, Sonesta Suites, TownePlace Suites, **W** 🍴 Ruby Tuesday 🛏 Drury Inn, Hampton Inn
2	I-485
1.5mm	Welcome Ctr nb, full 🚻 facilities, info, litter barrels, petwalk, 🕿, 🚮, vending
1	Westinghouse Blvd, to I-485 (from nb), **E** 🅟 BP/dsl 🍴 Jack-in-the-Box, Subway, Waffle House 🛏 Super 8, **W** 🅟 Mobil/7-11/dsl
0mm	North Carolina/South Carolina state line

*(left margin: CHARLOTTE)*

⬆N INTERSTATE 85

Exit #	Services
234mm	North Carolina/Virginia state line
233	US 1, to Wise
231mm	**Welcome Ctr sb, full 🚻 facilities, litter barrels, petwalk, 🕿, 🚮**
229	Oine Rd, to Norlina, **E** 🅟 BP, **W** 🅞 SRA
226	Ridgeway Rd, **W** 🅞 to Kerr Lake, to SRA
223	Manson Rd, **E** 🅞 USPO, **W** 🅞 to Kerr Dam
220	US 1, US 158, Flemingtown Rd, to Middleburg, **E** 🅟 Mobil/dsl, **W** 🅟 Exxon/dsl/scales/truck wash 🛏 Chex Trkstp/motel/rest.
218	US 1 S (from sb exits left), to Raleigh
217	Nutbush Bridge, **E** 🅞 auto repair, **W** 🅞 Kerr Lake RA
215	US 158 BYP E, Henderson (no EZ return from nb), **E** 🅟 Citgo, Shell, Speedway/dsl 🍴 Burger King, Forsyth's BBQ, Golden China, Subway 🛏 Budget Host, EconoLodge, Scottish Inn 🅞 $General, Food Lion, repair/tires, Roses, services on US 158
214	NC 39, Henderson, **E** 🅟 BP, **W** 🅟 Mobil/dsl, Shell 🅞 to Kerr Lake RA
213	US 158, Dabney Dr, to Henderson, **E** 🅟 Marathon, Valero 🍴 Bamboo Garden, Big Cheese Pizza, Bojangles, Denny's, Domino's, Ichibar Chinese, KFC, McDonald's, Papa John's, Pino's Italian, Subway, Wendy's 🅞 Family$, Food Lion, Roses, vet, **W** 🅟 Shell 🍴 Chick-fil-A, Golden Corral, Mayflower Seafood, Pizza Hut, Ruby Tuesday, Smithfields BBQ, Taco Bell 🛏 Red Roof Inn 🅞 Advance Parts, Buick/Chevrolet/GMC, Chrysler/Dodge/Jeep, Ford/Lincoln, Lowe's, Rite Aid, Staples, Verizon
212	Ruin Creek Rd, **E** 🅟 Shell/dsl 🍴 Cracker Barrel, Mazatlan Mexican, Ribeye's, Waffle House 🅞 Toyota, **W** 🅟 Exxon/Burger King, Sheetz/dsl 🛏 Baymont Inn, Hampton Inn, Sleep Inn 🅞 🏥, $Tree, Belk, JC Penney, Walmart
209	Poplar Creek Rd, **W** 🅞 Vance-Granville Comm Coll
206	US 158, Oxford, **E** 🅟 Citgo, **W** 🅟 BP/dsl 🅞 ⊙
204	NC 96, Oxford, **E** 🅟 BP/dsl 🛏 Comfort Inn, King's Inn 🅞 Buick/Chevrolet/GMC, Ford, Honda, **W** 🅟 Shell, Speedway/dsl, Valero/Popeye's 🍴 Burger King, China Wok, CookOut, Domino's, KFC/Taco Bell, McDonald's, Pizza Hut, Subway, Wendy's 🛏 Clarion 🅞 🏥, GNC
202	US 15, Oxford, **W** 🅟 Murphy Express/dsl 🍴 Bojangles, Hwy 55 Cafe 🛏 Crown Motel (2mi) 🅞 $Tree, Verizon, Walmart
199mm	🆁🆂 both lanes, full 🚻 facilities, litter barrels, petwalk, 🕿, 🚮
198mm	Tar River
191	NC 56, Butner, **E** 🅟 BP/dsl, Speedway/dsl 🍴 Arby's, Bob's BBQ, Bojangles, Diner 56, Domino's, El Rio Mexican, KFC/Taco Bell, McDonald's, Pizza Hut, Pizza Mia, Sonic, Subway, Taste of China, Wendy's 🛏 Inn at Creedmoor 🅞 $General, $Tree, Advance Parts, AutoZone, Food Lion, M&H Tires, O'Reilly Parts, Rite Aid, to Falls Lake RA, Verizon, vet, **W** 🅟 Exxon, Shell/dsl 🍴 Hardee's, Old South Rest. 🛏 Best Western, EconoLodge, Quality Inn 🅞 auto repair

(right margin: HENDERSON, OXFORD, BUTNER)

*(right side: **NC**)*

🛒 = gas   🍴 = food   🏠 = lodging   🅾 = other   Rs = rest stop   Copyright 2022 - The Next EXIT

INTERSTATE 85 Cont'd

BUTNER / DURHAM

Exit #	Services
189	Butner, 1 mi **W** 🛒 BP/dsl, Exxon/dsl, Valero 🍴 BBQ Barn, Subway 🅾 repair, 1 mi **N** 🅾 $General
186b a	US 15, to Creedmoor, **E** 🛒 Variety Mart/dsl
185mm	Falls Lake
183	Redwood Rd
182	Red Mill Rd, **E** 🛒 Exxon/dsl 🅾 Kenworth/Isuzu Trucks
180	Glenn School Rd, **E** 🛒 Citgo/dsl 🍴 Hwy 55 Cafe 🅾 $Tree, AT&T, Verizon, Walmart/Subway
179	E Club Blvd, **E** 🛒 Exxon
178	US 70 E, to Raleigh, Falls Lake RA, Research Triangle, **E** 🅾 RDU Airport
177	Avondale Dr, NC 55, **W** 🛒 BP, Shell 🍴 American Hero, Arby's, Guanajuato, McDonald's, Subway, Waffle House 🅾 Advance Parts, AutoZone, Family$
176b a	Gregson St, US 501 N, **E** 🛒 Mobil 🍴 Burger King, Kickback Jack's, PanPan Diner, Randy's Pizza, Ruby Tuesday 🏠 Hampton Inn 🅾 **W** 🅾 H, Museum of Life&Science
175	Guess Rd, **E** 🛒 Citgo 🍴 Hog Heaven BBQ, Pad Thai 🏠 Holiday Inn Express, Super 8 🅾 Rite Aid, **W** 🛒 BP/dsl, Exxon/dsl, Pure/dsl 🍴 Bojangles, IHOP, Jimmy's Hotdogs, McDonald's, Popeye's, TX Roadhouse 🏠 Red Roof Inn 🅾 $Tree, Costco/gas, Family$, GNC, Home Depot, PetsMart, Ross, Verizon, vet
174a	Hillandale Rd, **W** 🛒 🍴 Bleu Olive, China King, El Corral, Pomodoro Italian 🏠 Comfort Inn, Courtyard 🅾 URGENT CARE, Walgreens
174b	US 15 S, US 501 S
173	US 15, US 501, US 70, Colemill Rd, W Durham, **E** 🛒 BP, Exxon/dsl, Mobil, Sheetz/dsl 🍴 Arby's, Biscuitville, Bojangles, Chick-fil-A, Cookout, Cracker Barrel, DogHouse Rest., Domino's, Japan Express, KFC/Taco Bell, Krispy Kreme, McDonald's, Shanghai Chinese, Subway, Waffle House, Wendy's, Zaxby's 🏠 Days Inn, Hilton, Motel 6, Quality Inn 🅾 H, $General, Advance Parts, AutoZone, CVS Drug, Mr Tire, O'Reilly Parts, Rite Aid
172	NC 147 S, to US 15 S, US 501 S (from nb), Durham
170	to NC 751, to Duke U (no EZ return from nb), **E** 🏠 Durham Skyland Inn, Scottish Inn, **W** 🅾 to Eno River SP
165	NC 86, to Chapel Hill, **E** 🛒 Eagles/Burger King/dsl, Sheetz/dsl 🍴 China Fuji, Hwy 55, Papa John's, Subway 🅾 $Tree, Advance Parts, Home Depot, vet, Walmart, **W** 🛒 BP/dsl 🅾 auto repair
164	Hillsborough, **E** 🛒 BP, Citgo/dsl 🍴 McDonald's 🏠 Holiday Inn Express, **W** 🛒 Shell 🍴 Bojangles, Colorado Burrito, Domino's, Hardee's, Jimmy's Hotdogs, KFC/Taco Bell, Pueblo Viejo Mexican, Subway, Waffle House, Wendy's 🏠 Microtel 🅾 $General, $Tree, AutoZone, Food Lion, Ford, Goodyear/auto
163	I-40 E, to Raleigh.
I-85 S and I-40 W run together 38 mi.	
161	to US 70 E, NC 86 N
160	to NC 86 N, Efland, **W** 🛒 Exxon/dsl 🍴 Missy's Grill 🅾 Andrew's Repair
158mm	**weigh sta both lanes**
157	Buckhorn Rd, **E** 🛒 BP/dsl, Petro/Marathon/Dunkin'/Iron Skillet/dsl/scales/24hr/@, **W** 🛒 Citgo
154	Mebane-Oaks Rd, **E** 🛒 Murphy USA/dsl, Sheetz/dsl 🍴 China Garden, Ciao Pizza, Hwy 55 Cafe, Starbucks, Subway, Taco Bell, Wendy's, Zaxby's 🅾 $Tree, AT&T, GNC, Walmart/Subway, **W** 🛒 BP, Shell/dsl, Speedway/dsl 🍴 Biscuitville, Blue Ribbon Diner, Bojangles, La Fiesta Mexican, McDonald's, Roma Pizza, Sake Japanese, Waffle House 🏠 Budget Inn 🅾 Advance Parts, AutoZone, CVS Drug, Lowe's Foods, Tanger Outlets/famous brands, URGENT CARE, Verizon, vet, Walgreens

MEBANE / BURLINGTON

Exit #	Services
153	NC 119, Mebane, **E** 🛒 BP/KFC/Pizza Hut/Taco Bell 🍴 Ann Maria's Pizza, Cracker Barrel, Hibachi, Hursey's BBQ, Jersey Mike's, La Cocina Mexican, Moe's SW Grill, Ruby Tuesday, Sakura Japanese, Smithfield's BBQ 🏠 Fairfield Inn, Hampton Inn, Holiday Inn Express 🅾 $General, Lowe's, O'Reilly Parts, vet, **W** 🛒 Exxon/Burger King 🍴 Asian Harbor, Catrina's, Domino's, Papa John's, Subway 🅾 Food Lion
152	Trollingwood Rd, **E** 🛒 ⛽/McDonald's/dsl/scales/24hr, 🛒 ♥Loves /Hardee's/dsl/scales/24hr
150	to Roxboro, Haw River, **W** 🛒 ⛽FLYING J/Denny's/dsl/LP/scales/24hr, ⛽/DQ/Wendy's/dsl/scales/24hr, SpeedC- 🏠 Days Inn 🅾 Blue Beacon
148	NC 54, Graham, **E** 🛒 BP/dsl, Exxon/Circle K, Shell/dsl 🍴 Waffle House 🏠 Quality Inn, **W** 🍴 AmMex 2 Cafe
147	NC 87, to Pittsboro, Graham, **E** 🛒 Sheetz/dsl 🍴 AnnaMaria's Pizzeria, Arby's, Bojangles, Great Wall Chinese, Guerrero Mexican, Pizza Hut, Popeye's, Subway, Wendy's 🅾 Advance Parts, AutoZone, Champion Tire/Repair, Family$, Food Lion, Ford, Jus Save, O'Reilly Parts, Rite Aid, **W** 🛒 Citgo/dsl, Exxon/dsl, Shell dsl 🍴 Biscuitville, Cook-Out, Golden China, La Fiesta Mexican, McDonald's, Taco Bell, Zaxby's 🅾 $General, CVS Drug, Verizon, Walgreens
145	NC 49, Burlington, **E** 🛒 BP/dsl, Sheetz/dsl, Shell/dsl 🍴 Cap D's 🏠 EconoLodge, Microtel, Motel 6 🅾 Harley-Davidson, **W** 🛒 BP/dsl 🍴 Biscuitville, Bojangles, Burger King, China Inn, Hardee's, KFC, Subway 🏠 Red Carpet Inn, Red Roof Inn, Royal Inn 🅾 $General, Chrysler/Dodge/Jeep, Family$, Food Lion, Rite Aid
143	NC 62, Burlington, **E** 🛒 Sav-Way 🍴 Hardee's, Waffle House, Wendy's 🅾 JR Outlet, to Alamance Bfd, **W** 🛒 Marathon, Sheetz/dsl 🍴 Biscuitville, Cutting Board Rest., K&W Cafeteria 🏠 Ramada Inn 🅾 $General, auto repair, Cadillac, Chevrolet, Food Lion, Ford, Home Depot, Mazda, vet
141	Huffman Mill Rd, Burlington, **E** 🛒 BP, Circle K 🍴 IHOP, Mayflower Seafood, Outback Steaks 🏠 Hampton Inn, Holiday Inn Express 🅾 H, Nissan, **W** 🍴 Applebee's, Arby's, Biscuitville, Bojangles, Cancun Mexican, Chick-fil-A, China Gate, Cook-Out, Cracker Barrel, East Coast Cafe, Fire Pit, Golden Corral, Grill 584, Hibachi Buffet, HoneyBaked Ham, Hooters, KFC, Krispy Kreme, La Cocina Mexican, Longhorn Steaks, McDonald's, Mellow Mushroom, O'Charley's, Panera Bread, Sal's Italian, Starbucks, Steak'n Shake, Subway, Taco Bell, Village Grill 🏠 Best Western+, Country Inn&Suites, Courtyard, Super 8 🅾 $Tree, Harris Teeter/dsl, Hyundai, Lowe's, Subaru/Volvo/VW, to Elon Coll, URGENT CARE, Verizon, Walgreens, Walmart/McDonald's
140	University Ave, **E** 🅾 H, Toyota, **W** 🍴 Brixx Pizza, Buffalo Wild Wings, Burger King, Chick-fil-A, Chili's, Coldstone, Freddy's, Jimmy John's, Little Italy, McDonald's, Moe's SW Grill, Olive Garden, Peking House, Red Bowl Asian, Red Lobster, Red Robin, San Marcos Mexican, Smithfield's BBQ, Starbucks, TX Roadhouse 🏠 Drury Inn 🅾 AT&T, Barnes&Noble, Belk, Best Buy, BJ's Whse/gas, Dick's, Dillard's, Discount Tire, GNC, Hobby Lobby, JC Penney, Kohl's, Michael's, Petsmart, Ross, Target, TJ Maxx, Verizon
139mm	Rs both lanes, full ♿ facilities, litter barrels, 🍴, 🐾, vending
138	NC 61, Gibsonville, **W** 🛒 TA/BP/Burger King/Popeye's/dsl/scales/24hr/@ 🅾 truckwash
135	Rock Creek Dairy Rd, **W** 🛒 Circle K, Citgo 🍴 Bojangles, China 1, Ciao Italian, Domino's, Guacamole Mexican, Jersey Mike's Subs, McDonald's, Osaka Japanese, Pizza Hut/Taco Bell, Subway, Zaxby's 🏠 Comfort Suites 🅾 $General, CVS Drug, Food Lion, Verizon

🅝 INTERSTATE 85 Cont'd

Exit #	Services
132	Mt Hope Church Rd, **E** 🛢 Shell/Subway/dsl 🍴 McDonald's, Pascali's Pizza, **W** 🛢 Liberty/dsl, 🛢/Wendy's/dsl/24hr ⌂ Hampton Inn
131	to I-85 S, to I-73 N, to US 421, Highpoint, Charlotte
129	Youngsmill Rd, **W** ◉ KOA (4mi)
128	Alamance Church Rd, **E** 🛢 Citgo/Subway/dsl
126b a	US 421, to Sanford, **E** ◉ Hagan Stone Park Camping, **W** 🛢 Circle K/dsl, Exxon/Circle K/dsl
124	S Elm, Eugene St, **E** 🛢 Murphy Express/dsl 🍴 Waffle House, **W** 🍴 Bamboo Grill, Bojangles, Cracker Barrel, Hwy 55 Cafe, McDonald's, Pizza Hut, Smithfield's BBQ, Starbucks, Subway, Taco Bell, Wendy's, Zaxby's ◉ AT&T, Lowe's, Verizon, Walmart/McDonald's
122c b a	US 220, to Greensboro, Asheboro (from sb)
121	I-40 W, I-73 N, to Winston-Salem
120	N US 29, E US 70, to I-40 W
119	Groometown Rd, from nb, **W** 🛢 Citgo/dsl
118	US 29 S, US 70 W, to High Point, Jamestown, **W** ⌂ Grandover Resort ◉ 🄷
115mm	Deep River
113c	I-74, US 311, Ashboro, to Winston-Salem
113a	NC 62, Archdale, **E** 🛢 Citgo/dsl, **W** 🛢 BP/dsl ⌂ Quality Inn
111	US 311, to High Point, Archdale, **E** 🛢 Sheetz/dsl 🍴 Bamboo Garden, Bojangles, Carolina's Diner, Hardee's, Pizza Hut, Subway, Taco Bell, Wendy's, Zaxby's ⌂ Days Inn ◉ $General, CVS Drug, Food Lion, Lowe's Foods, Walmart Mkt, **W** 🛢 Citgo, McDonald's, Mobil/dsl, Shell/Circle K/dsl, Valero/dsl 🍴 Biscuitville, Cabo Grill, Rancho Rest., Waffle House ⌂ Comfort Inn, Country Inn&Suites, Fairfield Inn, Hampton Inn, Holiday Inn Express ◉ 🄷, O'Reilly Parts, tires, USPO, vet
108	Hopewell Church Rd, Trinity
106	Finch Farm Rd, **E** 🛢 BP/dsl, **W** 🛢 Sheetz/dsl 🍴 BBQ Joe's, Subway (1mi)
103	NC 109, to Thomasville, **E** 🛢 Exxon/dsl, Mobil/7-11/dsl, Murphy USA/dsl, Sheetz/dsl 🍴 Arby's, Chen's Kitchen, Cookout Burgers, Elizabeth's Pizza, Subway, Taco Bell, Zaxby's ⌂ Staylodge ◉ $Tree, CVS Drug, Ingles Foods, Lidl Mkt, Walmart/McDonald's, **W** 🛢 Exxon/dsl, Fast Fuels/dsl, Shell, Speedway/dsl 🍴 BBQ Shack, Biscuitville, Bojangles, Burger King, China Garden, Denny's, E Coast Grill, Hardee's, Hunan Chinese, KFC, La Carreta Mexican, Little Caesar's, Mandarin Express, Mazatlan Mexican, McDonald's, Papa John's, Pizza Hut, Ruby Tuesday, Sonic, Sunrise Diner, Waffle House, Wendy's ⌂ Davidson Lodge, Quality Inn ◉ $General, Advance Parts, Aldi Foods, AutoZone, Family$, Food Lion, Mighty$, NAPA, NTB, O'Reilly Parts, Peebles, Rite Aid, UHaul, Verizon, Walgreens
102	Lake Rd, **W** 🛢 Marathon/dsl, Sunoco/dsl ⌂ Comfort Inn, Microtel ◉ 🄷
100mm	Ⓡ both lanes, full ♿ facilities, litter barrels, petwalk, 🍴, ⌂, vending
96	US 64, to Asheboro, Lexington, **E** 🛢 Citgo/dsl ◉ Modern Tire, NC Zoo, **W** 🛢 Exxon/dsl, Gulf/dsl 🍴 Randy's Rest. ◉ to Davidson Co Coll
94	Old US 64, **E** 🛢 Shell, **W** ◉ Timberlake Gallery
91	NC 8, to Southmont, **E** 🛢 BP/dsl, Citgo/dsl, Mobil/7-11 🍴 Biscuit King, Bojangle's, Christo Rest., Hunan Express, Kabuki Japanese, KFC, McDonald's, Ocean View Seafood, Subway, Waffle House, Wendy's ⌂ Days Inn, Red Roof Inn ◉ Food Lion, High Rock Lake Camping (7mi), Mock Tire, **W** 🛢 Exxon/dsl, Shell/dsl

91	Continued 🍴 Applebee's, Arby's, Burger King, Cagney's Kitchen, Chick-fil-A, Cracker Barrel, Golden Corral, La Carreta Mexican, Little Caesar's, Mi Pueblo, Pizza Hut (1mi), Subway, Taco Bell, Zaxby's ⌂ Country Hearth Inn, Quality Inn ◉ 🄷, $Tree, Belk, GNC, Lidl Mkt, Lowe's (1mi), Walgreens, Walmart
88	Linwood, **W** ⌂ Affordable Suites ◉ 🄷
87	US 29, US 70, US 52 (from nb), High Point, **W** ◉ 🄷, 🚬
86	Belmont Rd, **W** 🛢 Bill's Trkstp/dsl/scales/24hr/@
84	US 29 S, US 70 W, NC 150 (from nb), to Spencer
82	US 29, US 70 (from sb), to Spencer
81.5mm	Yadkin River
81	Long Ferry Rd, Spencer, **E** 🛢 BP/dsl
79	Spencer Shops SHS, Spencer, E Spencer, **1 mi W** 🛢 Citgo 🍴 Bojangles, Subway ◉ $General, Food Lion
76b a	US 52, to Albemarle, Salisbury, **E** 🛢 BP, Citgo 🍴 Applebee's, Buffalo Wild Wings, Capriano's, Chipotle, ColdStone, E Coast Grill, IHOP, Pancho Villa, Top China, Which Wich?, Zaxby's ⌂ Days Inn, Economy Inn, Happy Traveler Inn ◉ $Tree, Aldi Foods, AT&T, CVS Drug, Food Lion, GNC, Harley-Davidson, Lowe's, Marshall's, NTB, Old Navy, Petsmart, Rite Aid, Staples, Verizon, vet, Walgreens, **W** 🛢 Murphy Express/dsl, Shell/Circle K/dsl, Speedway/dsl 🍴 Blue Bay Seafood, Bojangles, Burger King, Capt D's, Chick-fil-A, China Buffet, Christo's Rest., Cookout, Cracker Barrel, Hardee's, HoneyBaked Ham, Jersey Mike's, KFC, Marco's Pizza, McDonald's, O'Charley's, Outback Steaks, Panera Bread, Papa John's, Pizza Hut, Starbucks, Taco Bell, Tokyo Express, Wendy's ⌂ Comfort Suites, Courtyard, Holiday Inn Express ◉ 🄷, Advance Parts, AutoZone, BigLots, Family$, Firestone/auto, Goodyear/auto, Office Depot, USPO, Walmart/Subway
75	US 601, Jake Alexander Blvd, **E** 🛢 Sheetz/dsl 🍴 Arby's, Breakfastime ⌂ Econolodge, Home 2 Suites ◉ Hall Automotive, to Dan Nicholas Park, **W** 🛢 BP, Citgo, Shell/dsl 🍴 Casa Grande Mexican, CiCi's Pizza, Ichiban Japanese, Nyoshi Japanese, Waffle House, Wendy's ⌂ Hampton Inn, Holiday Inn, Quality Inn ◉ Buick, Cadillac/Chevrolet, Chrysler/Dodge/Jeep, Ford, GMC, Honda, Kia, Nissan, Toyota
74	Julian Rd, **E** 🍴 Honeybaked Ham, Salsarita's ◉ Dick's, Hobby Lobby, **W** 🍴 Longhorn Steaks, Los Arcos, Olive Garden, Starbucks, Subway ◉ $Tree, Belk, Kohl's, Michael's
72	Peach Orchard Rd
71	Peeler Rd, **E** 🛢 Loves/Chester's/McDonald's/dsl/scales/24hr, **W** 🛢 Pilot/Dunkin'/Subway/dsl/scales/24hr 🍴 Bojangle's ◉ dsl repair
70	Webb Rd, **E** ◉ flea mkt, **W** 🛢 Shell/dsl ◉ st patrol
68	US 29, US 601, to Rockwell, China Grove, **W** 🛢 🍴 Bojangle's, Domino's, Gary's BBQ, Hardee's, Jimmie's Rest., Papa John's, Pizza Hut, Subway ◉ $General, AutoZone, Family$, Food Lion, Rite Aid

NC

⬆N INTERSTATE 85 Cont'd

Exit #	Services
63	Kannapolis, E 🛢 Pilot/Subway/dsl/scales 🍴 Waffle House 🛏 Motel 6, W 🛢 QT/dsl 🅾 URGENT CARE
60	Earnhardt Rd, Copperfield Blvd, E 🛢 Exxon/dsl, Shell/Circle K/dsl 🍴 Bojangles, Breakfast Time Rest., Copper Grill, Cracker Barrel, Waffle House 🛏 Country Inn&Suites, Hampton Inn, Sleep Inn 🅾 Ⓗ, Discount Tire, URGENT CARE, W 🛢 Shell/Kangaroo/dsl 🍴 Casa Grande Mexican, Dragon Wok, Dunkin', East Coast Wings, Firehouse Subs, Little Caesar's, Logan's Roadhouse, McDonald's, Ruby Tuesday, Steak'n Shake, Subway, Taco Bell, Wendy's 🛏 Holiday Inn Express 🅾 AT&T, Hobby Lobby, Kohl's, Lowe's, Petco, Sam's Club/gas, Walmart
59mm	🆁🆂 both lanes, full ♿ facilities, litter barrels, petwalk, Ⓒ, 🅿, vending
58	US 29, US 601, Concord, E 🛢 BP, Marathon/Circle K/dsl, Marathon/dsl, Shell/dsl 🍴 Applebee's, Capt D's, Chick-fil-A, Chili's, Chipotle, Freddy's, Golden Corral, Jimmy John's, McDonald's, Moe's SW Grill, Mr C's Rest., O'Charley's, Panera Bread, Popeye's, Starbucks, Subway, Wendy's 🛏 Best Value Inn, Quality Inn, Rodeway Inn 🅾 Ⓗ, Belk, Family$, Harris Teeter, JC Penney, Staples, Verizon, Walgreens, W 🛢 BP, QT/dsl, Speedway/dsl 🍴 CiCi's, IHOP 🛏 Comfort Inn, Econolodge, Microtel 🅾 $General, Ford, Home Depot, st patrol, vet
55	NC 73, to Davidson, Concord, E 🛢 Shell 🍴 McDonald's, W 🛢 Shell/Circle K/dsl 🛏 Days Inn
54	Kannapolis Pkwy, George W Lyles Pkwy, E 🛢 QT/dsl, SM/Subway/dsl 🍴 Bojangles, China Garden, Marco's Pizza, Off-the-Grill 🅾 Advance Parts, AutoZone, CVS Drug, Firestone/auto, Food Lion, Harris Teeter, URGENT CARE, vet, Walgreens, W 🛢 Circle K/dsl 🍴 Arby's, Asian Cafe, Buffalo Wild Wings, Chick-fil-A, Dunkin', Jersey Mike's, McDonald's, Mi Pueblo, Showmar's Rest., Starbucks, Zaxby's 🅾 $Tree, Best Buy, Dick's, Goodyear/auto, Marshall's, Petsmart, Steinmart, Super Target, Verizon
52	Poplar Tent Rd, E 🛢 Mobil/7-11/dsl 🍴 R&R BBQ 🅾 to Lowe's Speedway, W 🛢 Exxon/7-11/dsl
49	Bruton Smith Blvd, Concord Mills Blvd, E 🛢 BP/McDonalds, Mobil/7-11/dsl 🍴 Bojangles, Carrabba's, ChuckECheese, Cinco de Mayo Mexican, Cookout, Cracker Barrel, Firehouse Subs, Five Guys, Hooters, Hot Shots Grill, Jack-in-the-Box, KFC/Taco Bell, Ruby Tuesday, Sonic, Sonny's BBQ, Starbucks, Subway, Taco Bell, TX Land&Cattle Steaks, TX Roadhouse, Waffle House, Wendy's, Zaxby's 🛏 Comfort Suites, Courtyard, Embassy Suites, Great Wolf Lodge, Hampton Inn, Hilton Garden, Holiday Inn Express, Home Towne Suites, Homewood Suites, Residence Inn, Sleep Inn, SpringHill Suites, Wingate Inn 🅾 BJ's Whse/gas, Camping World, Camping World Resort (1.5mi), Chrysler/Dodge/Jeep, Harley-Davidson, Honda, Kia, to Lowe's Motor Speedway, Toyota, VW, W 🛢 Circle K/dsl 🍴 Bonefish Grill, Burger King, Carolina Alehouse, Charanda Mexican, Chick-fil-A, Chipotle, Dave&Buster's, Denny's, Dunkin', Foster's Grille, Freddy's, Jason's Deli, Jim'n Nick's BBQ, Jimmy John's, Mayflower Seafood, McAlisters Deli, Olive Garden, On-the-Border, Outback Steaks, Panera Bread, PDQ Cafe, Queen City Q, Razzoo's Cafe, Red Lobster, Steak'n Shake, Sticky Fingers, TGI Friday's, Tijuana Flats, Twin Peaks 🅾 $Tree, AT&T, BassPro Shops, Best Buy, BooksAMillion, Concord Mills Mall, Discount Tire, Firestone/auto, Goodyear/auto, Lowe's, Old Navy, PetCo, Ross, TJ Maxx, URGENT CARE, Verizon, Walmart/Subway

Exit #	Services
48	I-485, to US 29, to Rock Hill
46	Mallard Creek Church Rd, E 🛢 Exxon/7-11, Kangaroo, Speedway/dsl 🍴 China Cafe, Giacomos Pizza, Jack-in-the-Box, Wi Wing Cafe 🅾 Research Park, vet, W 🛢 Shell/Circle K 🍴 Faley's Pizzeria, Hickory Tavern, Rita's, Starbucks, Thai Tast Toyama Express, Zoe's Kitchen 🅾 PetCo, Trader Joe's
45b a	Harris Blvd, E 🍴 Applebee's, Bar Louie, Blaze Pizza, Boja gles, Buffalo Wild Wings, Burger King, Cheddar's, Chick-fil-A Chili's, China Buffet, China Palace, Chipotle, City BBQ, Dunkir Five Guys, IHOP, Jersey Mike's Subs, Jimmy John's, Los Arco McDonald's, Nakato Steaks, Noodles&Co, Panera Bread, Pap John's, Pei Wei, Picasso's Pizza, Qdoba, Shane's Rib Shac Shoney's, Showmar's Rest., Starbucks, Taco Bell, Taco Mac Gril TGIFriday's, Tijuana Flats, Tropical Cafe 🛏 Country Inn&Suite Courtyard, Drury Inn, Extended Stay America, Hampton Inn Hilton, Holiday Inn, Homewood Suites, Microtel, Residence Inn Sleep Inn 🅾 Ⓗ, Food Lion, Kohl's, Michael's, Office Depo Ross, Sam's Club, to Miz Scarlett's, to UNCC, U Research Par Verizon, Walgreens, Walmart/McDonald's, 0-2 mi W 🍴 Lon horn Steaks, Macaroni Grill, Red Robin, Tony's Pizza 🛏 Spring Hill Suites, TownePlace Suites 🅾 Harris Teeter, Rite Aid
43	University City Blvd, E 🛢 Circle K/dsl, Circle K/Subway/d 🍴 Chipotle, Culver's, Golden Corral, Honeybaked Ham, Outbac Steaks, Pablo's, Starbucks, Taco Bell, Zaxby's 🛏 Extended Sta America, Holiday Inn Express, InTowne Suites 🅾 AT&T, Chevro let, Discount Tire, Firestone/auto, GNC, Hobby Lobby, IKEA, Ma shall's, Old Navy, Petsmart, TJ Maxx, Walmart, World Mkt
42	US 29 (nb only)
41	Sugar Creek Rd, E 🛢 Shell/dsl, Exxon/7-11/gas 🍴 Bojangle McDonald's, Taco Bell, Wendy's 🛏 Best Value Inn, Brookwoo Inn, Continental Inn, Motel 6 🅾 Family$, W 🛢 Shell/Circle K dsl 🍴 Chicken Box Rest., Cookout, TX Ranch Steaks 🛏 Day Inn, Quality Inn, Red Roof Inn, Rodeway Inn, Super 8
40	Graham St, E 🛢 Exxon/7-11/dsl 🛏 Budget Inn 🅾 repai UPS, Volvo, Western Star, W 🛢 Marathon/dsl 🅾 Freightliner
39	Statesville Ave, E 🛢 Pilot/Subway/dsl/scales/24hr 🅾 Ad vance Parts, repair, W 🛢 Citgo/dsl, Shell/dsl 🍴 Bojangle 🅾 Family$
38	I-77, US 21, N to Statesville, S to Columbia
37	Beatties Ford Rd, E 🛢 7-11/dsl 🍴 Burger King, McDonald's Tops China 🅾 CVS Drug, Family$, Food Lion, USPO, W 🛢 Citg
36	NC 16, Brookshire Blvd, E 🛏 Rodeway Inn 🅾 repair, W 🛢 Exxon/7-11/dsl, Mobil/dsl, QT/dsl, RaceWay/dsl 🍴 Burg er King, Jack-in-the-Box, Subway 🅾 Family$, Griffin Tire
35	Glenwood Dr, E 🛢 Exxon 🛏 Knights Inn, W 🛢 Shell/dsl
34	NC 27, Freedom Dr, E 🛢 Citgo/dsl, Shell/Circle K 🍴 Beaure gard's Rest., Bojangles, Capt D's, Cookout, Domino's, KFC, Mc Donald's, Pizza Hut, Showmar's, Subway, Taco Bell, Wendy' 🅾 $Tree, Advance Parts, Aldi Foods, AutoZone, Family$, Good year/auto, URGENT CARE, Walgreens, W 🛏 Charlotte Express
33	US 521, Billy Graham Pkwy, E 🛢 Shell/dsl 🍴 Bojangles, KFC Taco Bell, McDonald's, Wendy's 🛏 Baymont Inn, Comfor Suites, Royal Inn, Sheraton, SpringHill Suites 🅾 🪧, W 🛢 Exx on/dsl 🍴 Cracker Barrel, Ichiban, Waffle House 🛏 EconoLodge Holiday Inn Express, La Quinta, Microtel, Motel 6, Quality Inn Suburban Lodge, Super 8
32	Little Rock Rd, E 🛢 Mobil/7-11/dsl 🛏 Airport Inn, Courtyard Hampton Inn, Holiday Inn, W 🛢 76/dsl, BP/dsl, Mobil/7-11 🍴 Arby's, Showmar's Rest., Subway 🛏 Country Inn&Suites Day's Inn, Wingate Inn 🅾 Family$, Food Lion, Griffin Tire Walgreens
30b a	I-485, to I-77, Pineville

CONCORD

CHARLOTTE

CHARLOTTE

CHARLOTTE

🔼N   INTERSTATE 85 Cont'd

Exit #	Services
29	Sam Wilson Rd, **W** 🛢 Loves/Chester's/dsl/scales/24hr, Shell/dsl, **S** 🅾 camping
28mm	weigh sta both lanes
27.5mm	Catawba River
27	NC 273, Mt Holly, **E** 🛢 BP/Dunkin'/dsl, Murphy USA/dsl 🍴 Arby's, Captain's Cap Seafood, Chick-fil-A, KFC, Pizza Hut, Sake Japanese, Starbucks, Subway, Taco Bell, Waffle House, Wendy's 🅾 Big Lots, CVS Drug, Family$, Firestone/auto, Lowe's, NAPA, Walgreens, Walmart/Subway, **W** 🛢 Citgo/dsl 🏠 Holiday Inn Express
26	NC 7, **E** 🛢 BP/dsl, Shell/Circle K/dsl 🍴 Bojangles, Estia's Rest., Hardee's, McDonald's, New China, Papa John's 🏠 Hampton Inn 🅾 $Tree, Advance Parts, Aldi Foods, AT&T, AutoZone, Ford, Verizon, **W** 🅾 Belmont Abbey Coll
24mm	South Fork River
23	NC 7, McAdenville, **W** 🛢 Exxon/dsl, Shell/Subway/dsl 🍴 Hardee's, Hillbilly's BBQ/Steaks
22	Cramerton, Lowell, **E** 🛢 Shell/Circle K/dsl, Speedway/dsl 🍴 Chick-fil-A, CiCi's, Denny's, Jack-in-the-Box, Jersey Mike's Subs, Moe's SW, Popeye's, Popeye's, Portofino's, Sakura Japanese, Schlotzsky's, Shane's Ribshack, Showmar's, Wild Wing Cafe, Zaxby's 🅾 Books-A-Million, Buick/Cadillac/Chevrolet/GMC, Honda, Kia, Kohl's, Lowe's, Old Navy, Petsmart, Sam's Club/gas, U-Haul
21	Cox Rd, **E** 🛢 Shell 🍴 Akropolis Cafe, Buffalo Wild Wings, Cheddar's, Chili's, Chipotle, ChuckeCheese, Cookout, Dynasty Buffet, Firehouse Subs, Five Guys, Golden Corral, Jimmy John's, Krispy Kreme, La Fuente, Logan's Roadhouse, Longhorn Steaks, McAlister's Deli, McDonald's, Noodles&Co, Olive Garden, On the Border, Panera Bread, Peking Garden, Qdoba, Ruby Tuesday, Starbucks, Steak'n Shake 🏠 Hilton Garden 🅾 $Tree, AT&T, Best Buy, Chrysler/Dodge/Jeep, Dick's, Discount Tire, Ford/Subaru, GNC, Hobby Lobby, Home Depot, Michael's, Nissan, NTB, Office Depot, O'Reilly Parts, PepBoys, Petco, Ross, Target, TJ Maxx, Verizon, vet, Walgreens, Walmart/Subway, **W** 🛢 Shell/dsl 🍴 Arby's, Brixx Pizza, IHOP 🏠 Super 8 🅾 🏩, $General, Medical Ctr Drug
20	NC 279, New Hope Rd, **E** 🛢 World 🍴 Capt D's, Dunkin', Jackson's Cafeteria, Los Arcos Mexican, McDonald's, O'Charley's, Red Lobster, Sake Japanese, Taco Bell, Tres Pesos, Wendy's 🅾 Advance Parts, AutoZone, Belk, Family$, Firestone/auto, Tuesday Morning, **W** 🍴 Bojangles, Cracker Barrel, Honeybaked Ham, KFC, Outback Steaks, TX Roadhouse, Waffle House 🏠 Best Western, Comfort Suites, Courtyard, Fairfield Inn, Hampton Inn 🅾 🏩, CarMax
19	NC 7, E Gastonia, **E** 🛢 Shell
17	US 321, Gastonia, **E** 🛢 Citgo/dsl/LP 🍴 Los Arcos Mexican 🏠 Days Inn, Woodspring Suites 🅾 Family$, **W** 🛢 QT/dsl, Shell/Circle K/dsl 🍴 Dunkin', Hardee's, Papa John's 🏠 Holiday Inn Express, Lakeside Lodge, Motel 6
14	NC 274, E Bessemer, **E** 🛢 Citgo/dsl, Murphy USA/dsl 🅾 Walmart, **W** 🛢 Citgo/dsl, Shell/Subway 🍴 Bojangles, Waffle House 🏠 Express Inn
13	Edgewood Rd, Bessemer City, **E** 🅾 to Crowders Mtn SP, **W** 🛢 Exxon/dsl
10b a	US 74 W, US 29, Kings Mtn
8	NC 161, to Kings Mtn, **E** 🏠 Holiday Inn Express 🅾 camping, **W** 🛢 BP/dsl 🍴 Los Tarascos, McDonald's, Subway, Taco Bell, Waffle House, Wendy's 🏠 Comfort Inn, Quality Inn 🅾 🏩, $General, Campers Inn RV Ctr
5	Dixon School Rd, **E** 🛢 Trkstp/dsl/24hr 🅾 truck/tire repair
4	US 29 S (from sb)
2.5mm	Welcome Ctr nb, full ♿ facilities, info, litter barrels, petwalk, 🚰, 🏧, vending
2	NC 216, Kings Mtn, **E** 🅾 to Kings Mtn Nat Military Park
0mm	North Carolina/South Carolina state line

🔼N   INTERSTATE 95

Exit #	Services
181mm	North Carolina/Virginia state line, **Welcome Ctr sb, full** ♿ facilities, litter barrels, petwalk, 🚰, 🏧, vending
180	NC 48, to Gaston, to Lake Gaston, Pleasant Hill, **W** 🛢 Pilot/Subway/dsl/scales/24hr
176	NC 46, to Garysburg, **W** 🛢 Shell/dsl 🍴 Burger King 🏠 Super 8
174mm	Roanoke River
173	US 158, Roanoke Rapids, Weldon, **E** 🛢 BP/dsl, Shell/dsl 🍴 Frazier's Rest., Ralph's BBQ, Waffle House 🏠 Days Inn, Econolodge, **W** 🛢 BP/dsl, Exxon/DQ/Stuckey's, Murphy USA/dsl, Sheetz/dsl, Shell/dsl 🍴 Applebee's, Arby's, Bojangles, Burger King, Carolina BBQ, Chick-fil-A, China Lin, Cookout, Cracker Barrel, Hardee's, Ichiban, KFC, Little Caesar's, Logan's Roadhouse, Mayflower Seafood, McDonald's, New China, Papa John's, Pizza Hut, Popeyes, Ruby Tuesday, San Jose Mexican, Starbucks, Subway, Subway, Taco Bell, TX Steaks, Waffle House, Wendy's, Zaxby's 🏠 Baymont Inn, Hampton Inn, Holiday Inn Express, Motel 6, Sleep Inn 🅾 🏩, $General, $Tree, Advance Parts, AutoZone, Belk, BigLots, Firestone/auto, Food Lion, GNC, Harley-Davidson, Honda, Lowe's, O'Reilly Parts, Rite Aid, Save a Lot Foods, Staples, Toyota, URGENT CARE, Verizon, Walgreens, Walmart
171	NC 125, Roanoke Rapids, **E** 🏠 Hilton Garden 🅾 Carolina Crossroads RV Resort, Roanoke Rapids Theater, **W** 🛢 Shell/dsl 🏠 Best Western 🅾 st patrol
168	NC 903, to Halifax, **E** 🛢 Exxon/Subway/dsl, Shell/Burger King/dsl, **W** 🛢 Oasis/Dunkin'/LP/dsl
160	NC 561, to Brinkleyville, **E** 🛢 Exxon, **W** 🛢 Shell/dsl
154	NC 481, to Enfield 1mi, **W** 🅾 KOA
151mm	weigh sta both lanes
150	NC 33, to Whitakers, **E** 🅾 golf, **W** 🛢 BP/Subway/DQ/Stuckey's/dsl
145	NC 4, to US 301, Battleboro, **E** 🛢 BP/dsl, Exxon/dsl, Marathon/dsl, Shell 🍴 Carolina BBQ, Denny's, Hardee's, Waffle House 🏠 Ashburn Inn, Best Western, Deluxe Inn, EconoLodge, Economy Inn, Quality Inn, Red Carpet Inn, Travelers Inn
142mm	Ⓡ🅂 both lanes, full ♿ facilities, litter barrels, petwalk, 🚰, 🏧, vending

ROANOKE RAPIDS

GASTONIA

NC

⛽ = gas 🍴 = food 🛏 = lodging Ⓞ = other 🆁🆂 = rest stop Copyright 2022 - The Next EXIT

INTERSTATE 95 Cont'd

Exit #	Services
141	NC 43, Red Oak, **E** ⛽ BP/dsl, Exxon/dsl/LP Ⓞ $General, Smith's Foods
138	US 64, **1 mi E** on Winstead ⛽ BP/dsl, Speedway/dsl 🍴 Bojangles, Cracker Barrel, Gardner's BBQ, Hardee's, Highway Diner, Outback Steaks, TX Steaks, Waffle House 🛏 Candlewood Suites, Comfort Inn, Country Inn&Suites, Courtyard, Doubletree, Hampton Inn, Holiday Inn, Residence Inn Ⓞ �H, Buick/GMC, Harley-Davidson, Honda, Rite Aid, to Cape Hatteras Nat Seashore, URGENT CARE
132	to NC 58, **E** ⛽ Pitstop/dsl, **1 mi W** ⛽ BP/dsl
128mm	Tar River
127	NC 97, to Stanhope, **E** Ⓞ ⊡
121	US 264a, Wilson, **0-4 mi E** ⛽ BP, Kangaroo/dsl/LP, Marathon, Murphy USA/dsl, Shell, Speedway/dsl 🍴 Applebee's, Arby's, Buffalo Wild Wings, Burger King, Chick-fil-A, Chili's, Chopstix, Cookout, Denny's, El Tapatio, Golden Corral, Hardee's, Hibachi Buffet, Jersey Mike's, KFC/LJ Silver, Kobe Express, Mama Mia's Pizzaria, McDonald's, Moe's SW Grill, Olive Garden, Quizno's, Red Chileez Grill, Ruby Tuesday, San Jose Mexican, Sonic, Starbucks, Subway, Teppanyaki, TX Steaks, Waffle House, Wendy's, Zaxby's's 🛏 Candlewood Suites, Hampton Inn, Quality Inn Ⓞ �H, $General, $Tree, Aldi Foods, AT&T, AutoZone, Belk, Best Buy, Big Lots, Chevrolet, Chrysler/Dodge/Jeep, Ford/Lincoln, GNC, Harris-Teeter, Hobby Lobby, Honda, Lowe's, Marshall's, Mr Tire, Nissan, O'Reilly Parts, Petsmart, Ross, Staples, Target, Toyota, URGENT CARE, Verizon, vet, Walmart, White's Tires, **W** ⛽ 🍴 Best-N-Burgers, Bojangles, Burger King, Cracker Barrel, McDonald's, Pino's Pizza 🛏 Comfort Suites, Country Inn&Suites, Fairfield Inn, Hampton Inn, Holiday Inn Express, Jameson Inn, Microtel, Sleep Inn Ⓞ to Country Dr Museum
119b a	I-795 S, US 264, US 117
116	NC 42, to Clayton, Wilson, **E** ⛽ Shell/dsl Ⓞ �H, **W** ⛽ Exxon/dsl Ⓞ Rock Ridge Camping (2mi)
107	US 301, Kenly, **E** ⛽ BP/dsl, Citgo, Exxon/McDonald's/dsl, Fuel Doc, PitStop 🍴 Andy's Cafe, Golden China, Nik's Pizza, Norman's BBQ, Subway 🛏 Budget Inn, Deluxe Inn, Quality Inn Ⓞ $General, CarQuest, Family$, Food Lion, Ford, O'Reilly Parts, Piggly Wiggly, Tobacco Museum
106	Truck Stop Rd, Kenly, **E** ⛽ ✈FLYING J/Denny's/dsl/LP/scales/24hr, **W** ⛽ Kenly 95/Petro/DQ/Subway/Wendy's/dsl/scales/24hr/@, 🅿🅸🅻🅾🆃/Arby's/dsl/scales/24hr 🍴 Waffle House 🛏 Days Inn, Motel 6 Ⓞ Blue Beacon, Speedco Lube, Truck-o-Mat
105.5mm	Little River
105	Bagley Rd, Kenly, **E** ⛽ Big Boys/Shell/105 Pizza/dsl/scales/24hr 🍴 Lowell Mill Rest.
102	Micro, **W** ⛽ Shop'N-Go 🍴 Backdoor Cafe Ⓞ $General, city park, USPO
101	Pittman Rd
99mm	🆁🆂 both lanes, full ♿ facilities, hist marker, litter barrels, petwalk, 🄲, vending
98	to Selma, **E** Ⓞ RVacation
97	US 70 A, to Pine Level, Selma, **E** ⛽ Mobil/dsl 🍴 Denny's, Robbins Nest Rest. 🛏 Days Inn Ⓞ J&R Outlet, **W** ⛽ BP/dsl, Exxon/dsl, Shell/dsl 🍴 Bojangles, Cookout, Don Beto's Tacos, KFC, McDonald's, Shoney's, Waffle House, Wendy's 🛏 EconoLodge, Hampton Inn, Masters Inn, Quality Inn Ⓞ �H

95	US 70, Smithfield, **E** 🛏 Best Value Inn, Village Motel, W ⛽ Sheetz/dsl, Speedway/dsl, Sunoco/dsl 🍴 Bob Evans, Burger King, Checker's, CiCi's Pizza, Coldstone, Cracker Barrel, Sombrero Mexican, Golden Corral, Outback Steaks, Ruby Tuesday, San Marcos Mexican, Subway, TX Steaks, Waffle House, Zaxby's 🛏 Baymont Inn, Best Western, Comfort Inn, Fairfield Inn, Sleep Inn, Super 8 Ⓞ �H, Ava Gardner Museum, Carolina Premium Outlets/famous brands, Harley-Davidson
93	Brogden Rd, Smithfield, **W** ⛽ BP/dsl, Citgo Ⓞ $General
91.5mm	Neuse River
90	US 301, US 701, to Newton Grove, **E** ⛽ BP/dsl, Valero/ds 🛏 Travelers Inn Ⓞ Happy Trails RV Park, Raleigh Oaks RV Resort, Ronnie's Tires, to Bentonville Bfd (14mi), **W** ⛽ Exxon/d 🍴 Holt Lake BBQ 🛏 Four Oaks Motel/RV Park
87	NC 96, Four Oaks, **W** ⛽ BP/dsl, Speedway/dsl, Walmart Express/dsl 🍴 McDonald's, Subway Ⓞ $General
81b a	I-40, E to Wilmington, W to Raleigh
79	NC 50, to NC 27, to NC 242, Benson, Newton Grove, **E** ⛽ Citgo/dsl, Short Stop/dsl 🍴 Char-Grill, Waffle House 🛏 Hampton Inn Ⓞ auto repair, **W** ⛽ Exxon/Burger King/dsl 🍴 China 8, Domino's, McDonald's, Pizza Hut, Subway, Taco Bell, White Swan BBQ 🛏 Days Inn Ⓞ Advance Parts, auto repair, Family$, Food Lion, Walgreens
78mm	Neuse River
77	Hodges Chapel Rd, **E** ⛽ 🅻🅾🆅🅴🆂/Subway/dsl/scales/R dump/24hr
75	Jonesboro Rd, **W** ⛽ Exxon/Milestone Diner, 🅿🅸🅻🅾🆃/Shell/DQ/Quiznos/dsl/scales/24hr/@
73	US 421, NC 55, to Dunn, Clinton, **E** 🍴 Cracker Barrel, Hwy 5 Cafe, McDonald's, Mi Casita Mexican, Panda House Chines Ⓞ Chevrolet, Chrysler/Dodge/Jeep, Family$, Food Lion, W ⛽ Exxon/dsl, Shell, Speedway/dsl 🍴 Bojangles, Burger King, El Charro Mexican, Fishing Chicken, Hot Dog&Hamburger Heavan, Sagebrush Steaks, Subway, Taco Bell, Triangle Waffl 🛏 Baymont Inn, Days Inn, Hampton Inn, Quality Inn, Super Ⓞ Charlie C's IGA, museum, to Campbell U.
72	Pope Rd, **E** 🛏 Comfort Inn, Royal Inn, **W** ⛽ BP, Pure/d 🍴 Brass Lantern Steaks 🛏 Fairfield Inn Ⓞ Cadillac/GMC
71	Longbranch Rd, **E** ⛽ 🅿🅸🅻🅾🆃/Circle K/Hardee's/dsl/scales/24hr **W** Ⓞ to Averasboro Bfd
70	SR 1811, **E** 🛏 Relax Inn
65	NC 82, Godwin, **E** Ⓞ Falcon Children's Home, **W** ⛽ Godwin Mart/dsl
61	to Wade, **E** ⛽ Lucky 7 Trkstp/dsl Ⓞ Fayetteville RV Resort Cottages, **W** ⛽ Exxon/dsl
58	US 13, to Newton Grove, I-295 to Fayetteville, **E** ⛽ Shell/dsl scales 🍴 Subway, Waffle House 🛏 Econolodge
56	Lp 95, to US 301 (from sb), Fayetteville, **W** ⛽ Circle K/ds Epco/dsl Ⓞ �H, Pope AFB, to Ft Bragg
55	NC 1832, Murphy Rd, **W** ⛽ Circle K/dsl, Epco/dsl
52	NC 24, Fayetteville, **W** Ⓞ botanical gardens, museum, Pop AFB, to Ft Bragg
49	NC 53, NC 210, Fayetteville, **E** ⛽ BP/dsl, BP/dsl, Exxon/dsl Marathon 🍴 Burger King, McDonald's, Pizza Hut, Taco Bell Waffle House 🛏 Days Inn, Deluxe Inn, Hampton Inn, Motel Tru Hilton Ⓞ $General, **W** ⛽ BP/Subway/dsl, Exxon/dsl, Sunoco/dsl 🍴 Bojangle's, Cracker Barrel, Ruby Tuesday 🛏 Baymont Inn, Comfort Inn, Doubletree, EconoLodge, Fairfield Inn Holiday Inn, Holiday Inn Express, Quality Inn, Red Roof Inn Sleep Inn, Super 8, Sure Stay Inn

Side labels: WILSON, KENLY (left column); SMITHFIELD, DUNN, FAYETTEVILLE (right column); NC

↑N INTERSTATE 95 Cont'd

Exit #	Services
48mm	Ⓡ both lanes, full ♿ facilities, litter barrels, petwalk, 🚻, 🏧, vending
47mm	Cape Fear River
46b a	NC 87, to Fayetteville, Elizabethtown, W ⊙ Ⓗ
44	Claude Lee Rd, W ⊙ Lazy Acres Camping, to 🚑
41	NC 59, to Hope Mills, Parkton, E 🏠 Circle K/Subway/dsl 🏠 Bojangles, W 🏠 BP/dsl 🏠 Grandsons Buffet ⊙ Camping World RV Ctr, Lake Waldo's Camping, Spring Valley RV Park
40	Lp 95, to US 301 (from nb), to Fayetteville, services on US 301 (5-7mi)
33	US 301, St Pauls, E 🏠 BP/dsl
31	NC 20, to St Pauls, Raeford, E 🏠 BP, Marathon/Huddle House/ dsl, Mobil/McDonald's, Valero 🏠 Burger King, Hardee's 🏨 Days Inn ⊙ Volvo Trucks, Walgreens, Walmart Mkt, W 🏠 BP/dsl, Sunoco 🏠 Taco Bell ⊙ Food Lion
25	US 301, E 🏠 Sun-Do/dsl
24mm	weigh sta both lanes
22	US 301, E 🏠 BP, Marathon, Shell/DQ 🏠 Burger King, Chick-fil-A, China Wok, Denny's, Firehouse Subs, Golden Corral, Hardee's, IHOP, Outback Steaks, Panera Bread, Papa John's, Pizza Hut, Ruby Tuesday, San Jose Mexican, Shogun, Smithfield BBQ, Starbucks, TX Steaks, Waffle House, Wendy's, Zaxby's 🏨 Best Western, Comfort Suites, Hampton Inn, Holiday Inn, Super 8 ⊙ $Tree, AT&T, Chrysler/Dodge/Jeep, Goodyear/auto, Honda, Lowe's, Lowe's Foods, McDonald's, Toyota, URGENT CARE, Verizon, Walmart/Subway, W 🏠 Gulf, Sun-Do/dsl, Sunoco/dsl 🏠 Bojangles 🏨 SpringHill Suites ⊙ Ford/Lincoln, Kia
20	NC 211, to NC 41, Lumberton, E 🏠 BP/dsl, Citgo/dsl, Liberty/ dsl 🏠 Arby's, Arnold's Rest., Bojangles, Burger King, Capt D's, Christopher's, CiCi's Pizza, Cook Out, Dunkin', Hardee's, Hong Kong Chinese, Hwy 55 Cafe, Kami Japanese, KFC, McDonald's, Shoney's, Sonic, Subway, Taco Bell, Tokyo Express, Village Sta. Rest., Waffle House 🏨 Deluxe Inn, Red Roof Inn ⊙ Ⓗ, Advance Parts, AutoZone, Belk, city park, CVS Drug, Food Lion/ deli, JC Penney, Nissan, O'Reilly Parts, Verizon, Walgreens, W 🏠 Marathon/dsl, Sun-do/dsl 🏠 Cracker Barrel, San Jose Mexican 🏨 Comfort Inn, Country Inn&Suites, Days Inn/rest., Fairfield Inn, Knights Inn
19	Carthage Rd, Lumberton, E 🏠 🏨 Rodeway Inn, W 🏠 Sunoco 🏨 Motel 6, Royal Inn
18mm	Lumber River
17	NC 72, Lumberton, Pembroke, E 🏠 Atkinson's/dsl, BP/dsl, Go-Gas/dsl, Mobil/dsl, Sunoco 🏠 Burger King, China Garden, Hardee's, Huddle House, McDonald's, Papa Bill's Ribs, Pizza Hut, Ruby Tuesday, Subway, Waffle House 🏨 Atkinson Inn, Budget Inn, Southern Inn ⊙ $General, $Tree, Advance Parts, AutoZone, CVS Drug, Food Lion, Walmart Mkt/dsl, W ⊙ KOA (3mi)
13	I-74, US 74, Rockingham, Wilmington, E ⊙ SE NC Beaches, U.S.S Wilmington
10	US 301, to Fairmont
7	to McDonald, Raynham
5mm	Welcome Ctr nb, full ♿ facilities, litter barrels, petwalk, 🚻, 🏧, vending
2	NC 130, to NC 904, Rowland
1b a	US 301, US 501, Dillon, E 🏠 Sunoco, Sunoco (2) 🏠 Hot Tamale Rest., Peddler Steaks, Pedro's Trkstp 🏨 Budget Motel, South-of-the-Border Motel ⊙ Pedro's Campground, W 🏠 Shell/dsl 🏠 Waffle House
0mm	North Carolina/South Carolina state line

←E→ INTERSTATE 240 (Asheville)

Exit #	Services
9mm	I-240 begins/ends on I-40, exit 53b a.
8	Fairview Rd, N 🏠 Shell/dsl 🏠 Ay Carumba, Cheddar's, China Buffet, Coldstone, J&S Cafeteria, KFC, Little Caesar's, McDonald's, Papa John's, Subway 🏨 Ramada Inn ⊙ $General, Advance Parts, Aldi Foods, Bi-Lo Foods, CVS Drug, Discount Tire, Hamrick's, Kohl's, Petsmart, U-Haul, Walmart/McDonald's, S 🏠 Citgo 🏠 Pizza Hut ⊙ Home Depot
7.5mm	Swannanoa River
7	US 70, N 🏠 Enmark 🏨 Best Western ⊙ Hyundai, Kia, Subaru, S 🏠 Shell/dsl 🏠 Applebee's, Bonefish Grill, Buffalo Wild Wings, Burger King, Carrabba's, Chick-fil-A, Chili's, Chucke-Cheese, Cici's Pizza, Cook Out, Cornerstone Rest., Cracker Barrel, DQ, Firehouse Subs, IHOP, Jersey Mike's Subs, Longhorn Steaks, McAlister's Deli, McDonald's, McDonald's, Mikado Japanese, O'Charley's, Olive Garden, Outback Steaks, Papa's Mexican, Red Lobster, Starbucks, Subway, Taco Bell, Waffle House, Wild Wok 🏨 Country Inn&Suites, Courtyard, Days Inn, EconoLodge, Extended Stay America, Hampton Inn, Holiday Inn, Homewood Suites, InTown Motor Inn, Mountaineer Inn, SpringHill Suites, Super 8 ⊙ $Tree, AT&T, Barnes&Noble, Belk, Best Buy, BigLots, Clark Tire/auto, Dick's, Dillards, Firestone/auto, Ingles Foods/ gas, JC Penney, Jo-Ann, Lowe's, Michael's, Midas, Office Depot, Old Navy, Ross, Target, TJ Maxx, Walgreens, Whole Foods Mkt
6	Tunnel Rd (from eb), same as 7
5b	US 70 E, US 74A, Charlotte St, N 🏠 Exxon, Shell 🏠 Charlotte St. Grill, Fuddruckers, Starbucks, Two Guys Hogi 🏨 B&B ⊙ vet, S 🏠 Chop House Rest. 🏨 Renaissance Hotel, Sheraton ⊙ Civic Ctr
5a	US 25, Merrimon Ave, N 🏠 Enmark, Exxon/dsl, Shell/dsl 🏠 Bojangles, Chick-fil-A ⊙ Green Life Foods, Harris Teeter, Staples, Trader Joe's
4c	Haywood St (no EZ return to eb), Montford, S 🏠 Carmel's Rest., Isa's Bistro, Roman's Deli 🏨 B&B, Hotel Indigo ⊙ downtown
4b	Patton Ave (from eb), downtown
4a	US 19 N, US 23 N, US 70 W, to Weaverville
3b	Westgate, N 🏠 Green Sage Cafe, Jason's Deli, Oriental Pavilion 🏨 Country Inn Suites, Crowne Plaza ⊙ CVS Drug, Earth-Fare Foods, Mr Transmission, Sam's Club/gas, Tuesday Morning
3a	US 19 S, US 23 S, W Asheville, N 🏠 Shell/dsl 🏠 A&W/LJ Silver, Bojangles, Burger King, CookOut, Denny's, Dragon China, El Que Pasa Mexican, Firehouse Subs, Green Tea Japanese, Jersey Mike's, KFC, Krispy Kreme, Little Caesar's, McDonald's, Neo Burrito, New 1 China, Papa John's, Pizza Hut, Sonic, Subway, Taco Bell, Wendy's, Yoshida Japanese, Zingers Cafe ⊙ $General, Advance Parts, Aldi Foods, AT&T, AutoZone, Clark Tire/auto, Ingles Foods, Sav-Mor Foods, URGENT CARE, vet, Walgreens

L U M B E R T O N

A S H E V I L L E

NC

[🅿] = gas [🍴] = food [🛏] = lodging [⊙] = other [Rs] = rest stop   Copyright 2022 - The Next EXIT ©

⬆️E INTERSTATE 240 (Asheville) Cont'd

Exit #	Services
2	US 19, US 23, W Asheville, N [🅿] Haywood Quickstop/dsl [🍴] Zia Mexican, S [⊙] B&B Drug
1c	Amboy Rd (from eb)
1b	NC 191, to I-40 E, Brevard Rd, S [⊙] camping, farmers mkt
1a	I-40 W, to Knoxville
0mm	I-240 begins/ends on I-40, exit 46b a.

⬆️E INTERSTATE 440 (Raleigh)

Exit #	Services
16	I-40. I-440 begins/ends on I-40.
15	Poole Rd, E [🅿] BP, Exxon, W [🅿] Circle K, Citgo/dsl, Valero/dsl [🍴] Burger King, Family$, Food Lion, KFC/Taco Bell, McDonald's, Subway, Wang's Kitchen
14	I-495, US 64/264, to Wilson, to Rocky Mount
13b a	US 64 bus, New Bern Ave, to Wilson, 0-2 mi E [🅿] BP/Circle K, Circle K, Exxon, Exxon/dsl, Murphy USA/dsl, Shell/dsl [🍴] Bojangles, Burger King, Domino's, McDonald's, Papa John's, Pizza Hut, Popeye's, Ruby Tuesday, Starbucks, Subway, Waffle House, Wendy's [🛏] Comfort Suites, Holiday Inn Express, Knights Inn, Microtel, Quality Inn [⊙] Advance Parts, AutoZone, CVS Drug, Firestone/auto, Food Lion, O'Reilly Parts, Plemmons RV Ctr, U-Haul, vet, Walgreens, Walmart, W [⊙] [H]
12	Yonkers Rd, Brentwood Rd
11b a	US 1, US 401, Capital Blvd N, N [🅿] BP, BP, Exxon, Mobil, Sunoco, Valero/dsl [🍴] Baskin-Robbins/Dunkin', Buffalo Bros Pizza, Burger King, ChuckeCheese, Cici's, Cookout, Golden Corral, IHOP, Mayflower Seafood, McDonald's, Outback Steaks, Popeye's, Starbucks, Taco Bell, Vallerta Mexican, Waffle House [🛏] Best Value Inn, Best Western, Extended Stay America, Holiday Inn, La Quinta, Motel 6, Quality Inn [⊙] $Tree, Advance Parts, AT&T, AutoZone, Food Lion, U-Haul
10	Wake Forest Rd, N [🍴] Bahama Breeze, Denny's [🛏] Days Inn, Extended Stay America, Hilton, Hyatt Place, Residence Inn [⊙] [H], CVS Drug, S [🅿] [🍴] Applebee's, Arby's, Biscuitville, BurgerFi, El Rodeo Mexican, Jersey Mike's, Jimmy John's, Jumbo China, McDonald's, Melting Pot Rest., Papa John's, Pizza Hut, Qdoba, Subway, Tropical Smoothie [🛏] Comfort Inn, Courtyard, Extended Stay America [⊙] Advance Parts, AutoZone, Buick/GMC, Costco/gas, Discount Tire, Hyundai, Mazda, Ross, Staples, Subaru, Trader Joe's
8b a	6 Forks Rd, North Hills, N [🅿] Exxon/repair, Tesla EVC [🍴] Bonefish Grill, Capital Grille, Chick-fil-A, Chuy's, Firebirds Grill, Five Guys, Fox&Hound Grille, Moe's SW Grill, Panera Bread, Pieola Pizza, Pieology, Ruths Chris Steaks, Starbucks, Zoe's Kitchen [🛏] AC Hotel Marriott, Hyatt House, Renaissance [⊙] AT&T, GNC, Harris Teeter, JC Penney, REI, Target
7b a	US 70, NC 50, Glenwood Ave, Crabtree Valley, N [🅿] BP (2), BP/dsl [🍴] Brio Grill, Cheesecake Factory, Fleming's, Kanki Japanese, McDonald's, Panera Bread, PF Chang's [🛏] Candlewood Suites, Courtyard, Embassy Suites, Fairfield Inn, Hampton Inn, Hilton Garden, Holiday Inn, La Quinta, Marriott, Residence Inn [⊙] Barnes&Noble, Belk, Best Buy, Macy's, McCormick&Shmicks, Old Navy
6	Ridge Rd (from nb), same as 7
5	Lake Boone Tr, W [🅿] Shell/Circle K [🍴] Chick-fil-A, McDonald's, Starbucks, Village Deli [⊙] [H], Food Lion, Rite Aid
4b a	to I-40 W, Wade Ave, to RDU

(side text, vertical) RALEIGH

(side text, vertical) CHARLOTTE

Exit #	Services
3	NC 54, Hillsboro St, E [🅿] BP, Exxon [🍴] Arby's, Bean Sprout Chinese, IHOP, Snoopy's Hotdogs, Waffle House [⊙] to Meredith Coll, to St Mary's, W [⊙] to Carter-Finley Stadium
2b a	Western Blvd, E [🅿] Domino's, Exxon, Shell/Circle K, Speedway/dsl [🍴] Amedeo's Italian, Bojangles, Cookout, Dunkin, McDonalds, Popeye's, Subway, Taco Bell, Wendy's [⊙] Advance Parts, Food Lion, Roses, Shaw U, to NCSU, vet
1d	Melbourne Rd (from sb)
1c	Jones-Franklin Rd
1b a	I-40. I-440 begins on I-40.

INTERSTATE 485 (Charlotte)

Exit #	Services
67	I-77, US 21, to Charlotte, Columbia, I-485 begins/ends.
65	South Blvd, N [🅿] Kangaroo [🍴] Chick-fil-A, Golden Corral, Hooters, McDonald's, Popeyes, Steak'n Shake, Wendy's [⊙] $Tree, Advance Parts, Big Lots, Chevrolet, Discount Tire, Honda, Jo Ann, Kohl's, Nissan, Old Navy, Petsmart, Ross, Subaru, Target, Toyota, Verizon, VW, World Mkt, S [🍴] Arby's [⊙] Cadillac, Car Max, Mercedes, NAPA, TreadQtrs Auto/tire, vet
64b a	rd 51, N [🅿] Exxon/dsl, Shell/Circle K/dsl [🍴] Bojangles, Chili's, CiCi's, CookOut, Firehouse Subs, Jimmy John's, K&W Cafeteria, KFC, McDonald's, Outback Steaks, Pizza Hut, Starbucks, Wendy's [🛏] Extended Stay America [⊙] [H], Aldi Foods, AutoZone, Bi-Lo, Family$, Firestone/auto, S [🍴] Kangaroo, Shell/7-11 [🍴] Applebee's, Buca Italian, Burger King, Capt D's, China Buffet, Harper's Rest., IHOP, Jason's Deli, Longhorn Steaks, McAlister's Deli, Olive Garden, Red Lobster, Sky Asian, Subway, Taco Bell [🛏] Comfort Suites, Hampton Inn, Hilton Garden, Holiday Inn Express, Quality Inn [⊙] $General, Barnes&Noble, Belk, Best Buy, Dick's, Dillard's, Food Lion, Home Depot, JC Penney, Macy's, Meineke, Midas, Office Depot, REI, Rite Aid, Sam's Club/gas, SteinMart, Tire Kingdom, TJ Maxx
61b a	US 521 S, Johnston Rd, N [🍴] Global Rest., Hickory Tavern, Red Robin, Ruby Tuesday, Sticky Fingers, Viva Chicken [🛏] Homewood Suites, SpringHill Suites [⊙] Earth Fare Foods, S [🍴] Kangaroo/dsl [🍴] 5 Guys Burgers, Duckworth's Grill, Mellow Mushroom Rest., Pei Wei, Starbucks, Stone Mtn Grill, Subway, Tony's Pizza, Vine American Kitchen [🛏] Ballantyne Hotel, Courtyard, Staybridge Suites [⊙] CVS Drug
59	Rea Rd, E [🅿] Exxon/7-11 [🍴] 1511 Cantina, Applebee's, Boneheads Grill, Chick-fil-A, City Tavern, Firebirds Grill, Marble Slab, Noodles Rest., Qdoba, Smashburger, Starbucks, True Pizza, Wendy's [🛏] Residence Inn [⊙] GNC, Goodyear/auto, Harris-Teeter, Michaels, Target, vet
57	Providence Rd, rd 16, E [🅿] Kangaroo/Wendy's [🍴] Hickory Tavern, Ilios Noche, Papa John's, Penn Sta, The Wok [⊙] Harris-Teeter, USPO, W [🅿] Exxon/7-11, Shell [🍴] BBQ Shack, BT Burger, Macaroni Grill, On the Border, Red Bowl Rest., Showmars Rest., Starbucks, Subway, Wolfman Pizza [⊙] CVS Drug, Harris-Teeter, Home Depot, Lowes Whse, Rite Aid, Staples, SteinMart, vet
52	E John St, to Matthews
51b a	US 74, to Charlotte, Monroe, E [🅿] Circle K/dsl [🛏] Country Inn&Suites, InTown Suites, Quality Inn [⊙] Toyota, W [🅿] Citgo/dsl, Exxon/7-11, Shell [🍴] Bojangles, Golden Corral, Pizza Hut, TX Roadhouse, Wendy's [🛏] Courtyard, EconoLodge, Microtel [⊙] [H], Aamco, AutoZone, Best Buy, Black's Auto/tire, Costco/gas, Firestone/auto, Lowe's Whse, Sam's Club/gas, Target, Tuesday Morning
49	Idlewild Rd, E [🅿] Exxon/7-11/dsl [🍴] Cactus Rose Mexican, China Cafe, Mama's Pizza [⊙] $Tree, GNC, Harris-Teeter, Meineke, Rite Aid

(side text, vertical) CHARLOTTE

(side text, vertical) NC

INTERSTATE 485 (Charlotte) Cont'd

Exit #	Services
47	Lawyers Rd, **E** 🅖 Gate/dsl 🍴 Bellacino's Pizza, Best China, Carnita's Mexican, Domino's, McDonald's, Subway 🅾 CVS Drug, Firestone/auto, Harris-Teeter, vet
44	rd 218, to Mint Hill, **W** 🅖 BP/dsl, Shell/7-11 🅾 $General, city park, CVS
43	rd 51, to Mint Hill
41	rd 24, rd 27, to Albemarle, **E** 🅖 Speedway/dsl 🍴 Bojangles
39	Harrisburg Rd, **W** 🅖 BP/EVC 🍴 China Garden, Papa John's, Wendy's 🅾 Food Lion
36	Rocky River Rd, **E** 🅖 BP/dsl, Gate/dsl 🍴 Best China, Bojangles, Capriccio Pizza, Subway 🅾 CVS Drug, Discount Tire, EMERGENCY, GNC, Harris-Teeter, Tuffy Auto
33	rd 49, to Harrisburg, **E** 🅖 Speedway/dsl 🍴 Cici's Pizza 🅾 Food Lion, USPO, **W** 🅖 BP, Circle K/dsl, Exxon/7-11, Shell/7-11/dsl 🍴 Arby's, Chopsticks, Domino's, Little Caesar's, Wendy's 🅾 Family$
32	US 29, **N** 🅖 QT/dsl 🅾 CVS Drug, Walmart Mkt, **S** 🅖 Exxon/7-11/dsl, Kangaroo, Speedway/dsl 🍴 Jack-in-the-Box 🅾 🏨, Tire Kingdom
30b a	I-85, N to High Point, S to Charlotte
28	Mallard Creek Rd
26	Benfield Rd, Prosperity Church Rd, Prosperity Ridge Rd, **N** 🅖 BP/dsl 🍴 Bojangle's, IHOP, Jersey Mike's, Papa Murphy's, Starbucks, Subway 🅾 Aldi Foods, Giffen Bros Automotive, Harris Teeter, Publix, Rite Aid, **S** 🅖 Shell/Circle K/dsl
23c	rd 115, to Huntersville, **N** 🅖 Shell/7-11/dsl 🅾 Audi, BMW, Lexus, Mercedes, Walmart
23b a	I-77, to Charlotte, Statesville
21	rd 24, Harris Blvd, **S** 🍴 Bravo Italian, Buffalo Wild Wings, Chick-fil-A, Chili's, East Coast Grill, Edomae Grill, Firebirds Grill, Firehouse Subs, Five Guys, Fox&Hound, Jersey Mike's, McDonald's, Mimi's Cafe, Moe's SW Grill, Olive Garden, On-the-Border, Panera bread, PF Chang's, Red Robin, Shane's Rib Shack, TGI Friday's, Wendy's 🛏 Drury Inn 🅾 $Tree, AT&T, Belk, Best Buy, Dick's, Dillard's, Discount Tire, Lowe's Whse, Macy's, Old Navy, Petsmart, REI, Target, Verizon

16	rd 16, to Newton, Brookshire Blvd, **E** 🅾 city park, **W** 🍴 Bojangles, Bull&Barrister Grille, Chick-fil-A, Domino's, Los Arcos, McDonald's, Papa John's, Pizza Hut, Red Bowl Asian, Subway, Wendy's 🅾 AT&T, AutoZone, Harris-Teeter, Rite Aid, URGENT CARE, vet, Walmart/Subway
14	rd 27, to Mt Holly Rd, **W** 🅖 BP (2mi) 🍴 Sonic (2mi) 🅾 Food Lion (2mi), Meineke (2mi)
12	Moores Chapel Rd, **E** 🍴 Jin Jin Chinese, Subway 🅾 Advance Parts, CVS Drug, Family$, Food Lion
10b a	I-85, to Spartanburg, Greensboro
9	US 29, US 74, Wilkinson Blvd, **S** 🍴 🅾 camping
6	West Blvd
4	rd 160, to Fort Mill, **N** 🅖 Exxon/7-11/dsl 🅾 CVS Drug, **S** 🅖 BP/dsl 🍴 Bojangles 🅾 Charlotte Premium Outlets/famous brands
3	Arrowood Rd, **S** 🍴 Quizno's, Siam Garden
1	S Tryon St, NC 49, **N** 🅖 Citgo, Exxon/7-11 🍴 Arby's, Bojangles, Chick-fil-A, Chili's, Dragon Buffet, IHOP, Lenny's Subs, Luigi's Pizza, McDonald's, O'Charley's, Panera Bread, Qdoba, Showmars Rest., Waffle House, Zaxby's 🅾 Family$, GNC, Lowe's Whse, Rite Aid, Walmart, **S** 🅖 Kangaroo/dsl, QT/dsl 🍴 Mac's BBQ, Applebee's, Baskin-Robbins/Dunkin', Burger King, Domino's, Don Pedro Mexican, Firehouse Subs, Fortune Cookie, Hungry Howie's, Joe Momma's Pizza, KFC, McAlister's Deli, Pan China, Portofino's, Starbucks, Subway, Taco Bell, Wild Wing Cafe 🛏 Hilton Garden, Homewood Suites 🅾 $Tree, AT&T, AutoZone, Discount Tire, Food Lion, NAPA, Office Depot, Tire Kingdom, Tuffy Auto, URGENT CARE

NOTES

📱 = gas 🍴 = food 🛏 = lodging 🄾 = other 🆁🆂 = rest stop Copyright 2022 - The Next EXIT

NORTH DAKOTA

🅝 INTERSTATE 29

Exit #	Services
218mm	US/Canada border, North Dakota state line
217mm	US Customs sb
216mm	historical site nb, tourist info sb
215	ND 59, rd 55, Pembina, **E** 📱 Gastrak/DutyFree Store/dsl, Gastrak/pizza/dsl/scales/24hr 🄾 Pembina State Museum/info
212	no service
208	rd 1, to Bathgate
203	US 81, ND 5, to Hamilton, Cavalier, **W** 🄾 to Icelandic SP (25 mi), **weigh sta both lanes**
200	no service
196	rd 3, Bowesmont
193	no service
191	rd 11, to St Thomas
187	ND 66, to Drayton, **E** 📱 Cenex/pizza/dsl/E-85, Tesoro/dsl 🛏 Motel 66 🄾 city park, USPO
184	to Drayton, **2 mi E** 📱 gas/dsl 🄾 USPO
180	rd 9
179mm	🆁🆂 both lanes (both lanes exit left), full ♿ facilities, litter barrels, petwalk, 🄲, 🛏, vending
176	ND 17, to Grafton, **10 mi W** 📱 gas 🍴 food 🛏 lodging 🄾 Ⓗ
172	65th St NE
168	rd 15, to Minto, Warsaw
164	57th St NE
161	ND 54, rd 19, to Ardoch, Oslo
157	32nd Ave
152	US 81, to Gilby, Manvel, **W** 📱 Manvel/dsl/food
145	US 81 bus, N Washington St, to Grand Forks
141	US 2, Gateway Dr, Grand Forks, **E** 📱 Cenex, Loaf'N Jug/dsl, University Sta/dsl 🍴 Burger King, Far East Buffet, Little Caesar's, McDonald's, Northside Cafe, Papa Murphy's, Subway, Taco John's 🛏 Best Value Inn, Budget Inn, EconoLodge, Grand Forks Inn, Ramada Inn, Select Inn, Super 8 🄾 Ⓗ, AT&T, Freightliner, Hugo's Foods, Kia, O'Reilly Parts, Subaru, to U of ND, transmissions, U-Haul, visitors ctr, **W** 📱 Simonson/café/dsl/24hr, StaMart/dsl/RV dump/scales/24hr/@ 🍴 Hardee's 🛏 Knights Inn 🄾 🛏, Budget RV Ctr, dsl repair, Mack/Volvo, NW Tire, to AFB, vet, Walmart/Subway
140	DeMers Ave, **E** 📱 Cenex/dsl, Loaf'N Jug/dsl, Valley Dairy 🍴 Red Pepper Cafe, Tim Hortons 🛏 Baymont Inn, Canada Inn, Expressway Suites, Hilton Garden, La Quinta, My Place Suites, Sleep Inn, Staybridge Suites 🄾 Ⓗ, Alerus Ctr, to U of ND
138	US 81, 32nd Ave S, **E** 📱 Cenex, Holiday/dsl 🍴 Applebee's, Arby's, Buffalo Wild Wings, Burger King, Cherry Berry Yogurt, Coldstone, Culver's, Denny's, DQ, Erbert&Gerbert's, Firehouse Subs, Five Guys, Ground Round, HuHot, IHOP, Jimmy John's, McDonald's, Noodles&Co, Olive Garden, Panera Bread, Papa Murphy's, Pizza Hut, Pizza Ranch, Qdoba Mexican, Red Lobster, Ruby Tuesday, Sakura Japanese, Starbucks, Subway, TX Roadhouse, Wendy's 🛏 Best Western, C'mon Inn, Country Inn&Suites, Days Inn, Fairfield Inn, Hampton Inn, Holiday Inn Express, Quality Inn, Rodeway Inn, SpringHill Suites 🄾 $Tree, AT&T, Best Buy, Chrysler/Dodge/Jeep, CVS Drug, Ford/Lincoln, Gordman's, Hobby Lobby, Hornbacher's Mkt, Hugo's Foods, JC Penney, Jo-Ann Fabrics, Kohl's, Lowe's, Menards, Michael's, Old Navy, PetCo, Sam's Club/gas, Scheel's, Target,

138	Continued
	Tire 1, Tires+, TJ Maxx, Toyota, Verizon, vet, Walmart/Subway, White Drug, car repair, Natural Grocers, **W** 📱 ⓕFLYING J/Subway/dsl/LP/scales/RV dump/24hr 🄾 Grand Forks Camping
130	ND 15, rd 81, Thompson, **1 mi W** 📱 gas 🍴 food
123	to Reynolds, **E** 🄾 to Central Valley School
120	truck insp sb
118	to Buxton
111	ND 200 W, to Cummings, Mayville, **W** 🄾 Big Top Fireworks, to Mayville St U
104	Hillsboro, **E** 📱 Casey's, Cenex/Burger King/dsl/LP/24hr 🍴 Subway 🛏 Hillsboro Inn 🄾 Ⓗ, Hillsboro Camping, USPO
100	ND 200 E, ND 200A, to Blanchard, Halstad
99mm	🆁🆂 both lanes, full ♿ facilities, litter barrels, petwalk, 🄲, 🛏 vending
92	rd 11, Grandin, **W** 📱 Stop&Shop/dsl
86	Gardner
78	Argusville
74.5mm	Sheyenne River
72	rd 17, rd 22, Harwood, **E** 📱 Cenex/pizza/dsl/LP/café/24hr
69	rd 20
67	US 81 bus, 19th Ave N, **1 mi E** 🍴 Applebee's, Buffalo Wild Wings, Burger King, McDonald's, Pizza Hut, Subway, Taco Bell 🛏 Candlewood Suites, Days Inn, Homewood Suites 🄾 CVS Drug, Hector Int Airport, VA Ⓗ
66	12th Ave N, **E** 📱 StaMart/dsl/scales/24hr 🍴 Marlin's Rest. 🛏 Woodspring Suites 🄾 Ⓗ, to ND St U, tuck repair, **W** 📱 Cenex/dsl 🍴 Arby's 🛏 Super 8
65	US 10, Main Ave, W Fargo, **E** 📱 Tesoro/dsl 🄾 CarQuest, NAPA, OK Tire, vet, **W** 📱 Cenex/Subway/dsl, Simonson/dsl 🍴 Hardee's, O'Kelly's Rest., Season Buffet Chinese 🛏 Biltmore on Main Inn 🄾 CarQuest, Honda, Kia, Lincoln, Mac Hardware, Mazda, Mercedes, O'Reilly Parts, Recreation RV Ctr, Toyota, VW
64	13th Ave, Fargo, **E** 📱 Don's, Exxon, Kum&Go/dsl, Petro Serve/dsl 🍴 Acapulco Mexican, Applebee's, Arby's, Buck Rest, Burger King, ChuckeCheese, DQ, Erbert&Gerbert's Sub, GreenMill Rest., Ground Round, Little Caesar's, Perkins, Sickie's Garage, Subway, Taco John's, Wendy's 🛏 AmericInn, Baymont Inn, Country Inn&Suites, Days Inn, EconoLodge, EconoLodge, Grand Inn, Motel 6, Quality Inn, Quality Suites, Super 8 🄾 AT&T, CashWise Foods/drug/gas, CVS Drug, Family's, Goodyear/auto, Meineke, O'Reilly Parts, Tires+/transmission, Tuesday Morning, Verizon, White Drug, **W** 📱 All-Stop/dsl, Casey's, Cenex 🍴 Applebee's, Arby's, Buffalo Wild Wings, Chili's, Culver's, Denny's, Domino's, DQ, Happy Joe's Pizza, KFC, Kobe Japanese, Kroll's Diner, LoneStar Steaks, Longhorn Steaks, McDonald's, Olive Garden, Osaka Japanese, Panchero's Mexican, Panera Bread, Paradiso Mexican, Pizza Hut, Red Lobster, Ruby Tuesday, Santa Lucia Cafe, Schlotzsky's, Spitfire Grill, Subway, Taco Bell, Taco John's, TX Roadhouse 🛏 Econolodge, Fairfield Inn, Fargo Inn, Holiday Inn, Holiday Inn Express, Kelly Inn, Ramada Inn, Red River Lodge 🄾 $Tree, Audi/VW, Barnes&Noble, Best Buy, BigLots, Cadillac/Chevrolet, Chrysler/Dodge/Jeep, Family Fare Mkt, GNC, Gordman's, Herberger's, Hobby Lobby, Hornbacher's Foods, Hyundai, JC Penney, Jo-Ann, Jo-Ann Fabrics, Kohl's, Lowe's, Macy's, Menards, Michael's, Natural Grocers, Nissan, Old Navy, PetCo, Petsmart, Sam's Club/gas, Target, TJ Maxx, USPO, Walgreens, Walmart/Subway

GRAND FORKS

FARGO

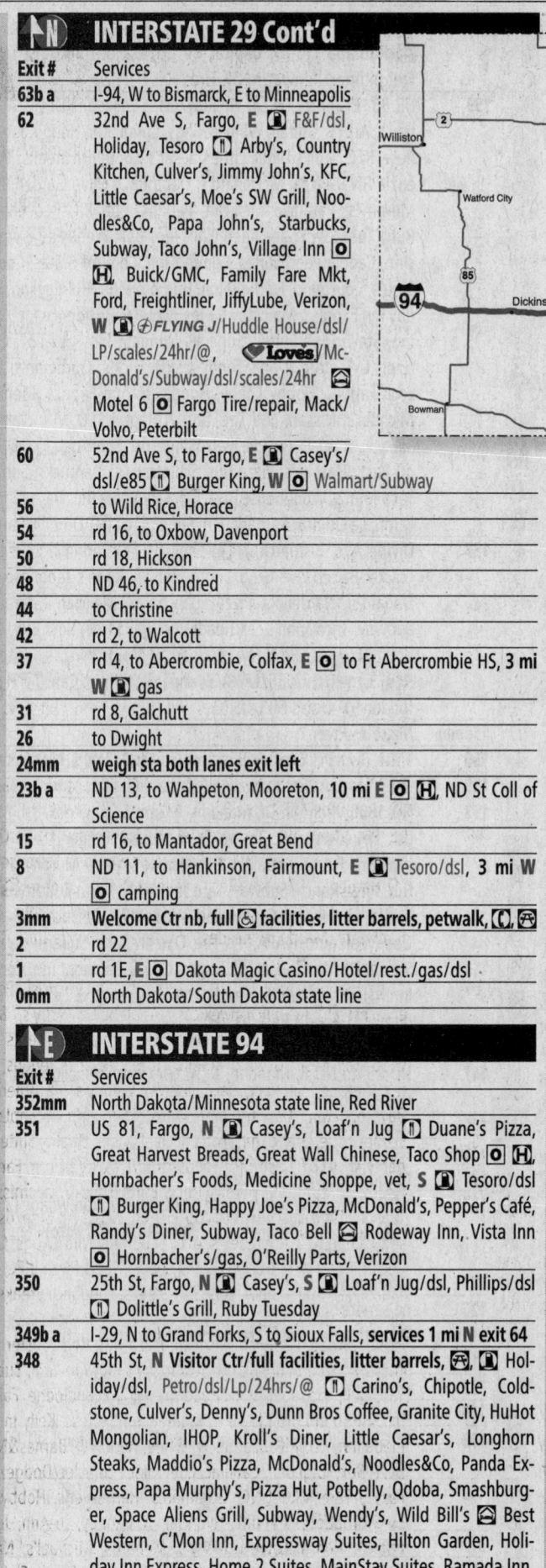

INTERSTATE 29 Cont'd

Exit #	Services
63b a	I-94, W to Bismarck, E to Minneapolis
62	32nd Ave S, Fargo, **E** 🅶 F&F/dsl, Holiday, Tesoro 🍴 Arby's, Country Kitchen, Culver's, Jimmy John's, KFC, Little Caesar's, Moe's SW Grill, Noodles&Co, Papa John's, Starbucks, Subway, Taco John's, Village Inn 🅞 🎗, Buick/GMC, Family Fare Mkt, Ford, Freightliner, JiffyLube, Verizon, **W** 🅶 *FLYING J*/Huddle House/dsl/ LP/scales/24hr/@, **Loves**/Mc-Donald's/Subway/dsl/scales/24hr 🛏 Motel 6 🅞 Fargo Tire/repair, Mack/ Volvo, Peterbilt
60	52nd Ave S, to Fargo, **E** 🅶 Casey's/ dsl/e85 🍴 Burger King, **W** 🅞 Walmart/Subway
56	to Wild Rice, Horace
54	rd 16, to Oxbow, Davenport
50	rd 18, Hickson
48	ND 46, to Kindred
44	to Christine
42	rd 2, to Walcott
37	rd 4, to Abercrombie, Colfax, **E** 🅞 to Ft Abercrombie HS, **3 mi** **W** 🅶 gas
31	rd 8, Galchutt
26	to Dwight
24mm	**weigh sta both lanes exit left**
23b a	ND 13, to Wahpeton, Mooreton, **10 mi E** 🅞 🎗, ND St Coll of Science
15	rd 16, to Mantador, Great Bend
8	ND 11, to Hankinson, Fairmount, **E** 🅶 Tesoro/dsl, **3 mi W** 🅞 camping
3mm	**Welcome Ctr nb, full ♿ facilities, litter barrels, petwalk, ⓒ, 🗑**
2	rd 22
1	rd 1E, **E** 🅞 Dakota Magic Casino/Hotel/rest./gas/dsl
0mm	North Dakota/South Dakota state line

INTERSTATE 94

Exit #	Services
352mm	North Dakota/Minnesota state line, Red River
351	US 81, Fargo, **N** 🅶 Casey's, Loaf'n Jug 🍴 Duane's Pizza, Great Harvest Breads, Great Wall Chinese, Taco Shop 🅞 🎗, Hornbacher's Foods, Medicine Shoppe, vet, **S** 🅶 Tesoro/dsl 🍴 Burger King, Happy Joe's Pizza, McDonald's, Pepper's Café, Randy's Diner, Subway, Taco Bell 🛏 Rodeway Inn, Vista Inn 🅞 Hornbacher's/gas, O'Reilly Parts, Verizon
350	25th St, Fargo, **N** 🅶 Casey's, **S** 🅶 Loaf'n Jug/dsl, Phillips/dsl 🍴 Dolittle's Grill, Ruby Tuesday
349b a	I-29, N to Grand Forks, S to Sioux Falls, **services 1 mi N exit 64**
348	45th St, **N Visitor Ctr/full facilities, litter barrels**, 🗑, 🍴 Holiday/dsl, Petro/dsl/Lp/24hrs/@ 🍴 Carino's, Chipotle, Coldstone, Culver's, Denny's, Dunn Bros Coffee, Granite City, HuHot Mongolian, IHOP, Kroll's Diner, Little Caesar's, Longhorn Steaks, Maddio's Pizza, McDonald's, Noodles&Co, Panda Express, Papa Murphy's, Pizza Hut, Potbelly, Qdoba, Smashburger, Space Aliens Grill, Subway, Wendy's, Wild Bill's 🛏 Best Western, C'Mon Inn, Expressway Suites, Hilton Garden, Holiday Inn Express, Home 2 Suites, MainStay Suites, Ramada Inn, Red Roof Inn, Staybridge Suites, Wingate Inn 🅞 Blue Beacon,

Exit #	Services
348	Continued Hobby Lobby, Home Depot, Kohl's, NAPA, Old Navy, Sam's Club, Scheel's Sports, Target, Tuffy Auto, Verizon, Walmart/ Subway, **S** 🍴 Casey's/DQ/dsl, Holiday 🍴 Applebee's, Famous Dave's BBQ, Five Guys, Hardee's, Korean BBQ, Mexican Village, Old Chicago Pizza, Pizza Ranch, Sonic, Taco John's, Taco Shop 🛏 AmericInn, Comfort Suites, Hampton Inn, La Quinta, Residence Inn, Sheraton, Sleep Inn 🅞 AT&T, Red River Zoo
347	9th St E, Veterans Blvd, **N** 🍴 Blarney Stone 🛏 Cambria Inn, Element Hotel, **S** 🅶 Casey's/dsl 🍴 Firehouse Subs, McDonald's, Papa John's, Subway, Taco Bell 🛏 Microtel, My Place Hotel 🅞 Cash Wise Foods/dsl, Costco/gas, 🎗
346b a	to Horace, W Fargo, **S** 🍴 repair, Tesoro/dsl 🅞 Harley Davidson
343	US 10, Lp 94, W Fargo, **N** 🅶 Cenex/dsl 🅞 Adventure RV Ctr, Pioneer Village, Red River Valley RV Park
342	38th St NE
342mm	**weigh sta wb**
340	to Kindred
338	Mapleton, **N** 🅶 Tesoro/dsl
337mm	**truck parking wb, litter barrels**
331	ND 18, to Leonard, Casselton, **N** 🅶 Tesoro/Subway/dsl 🍴 Country Kitchen 🛏 Days Inn/RV park
328	to Lynchburg
327mm	**truck parking eb, litter barrels**
324	Wheatland, to Chaffee
322	Absaraka
320	to Embden
317	to Ayr
314	ND 38 N, to Alice, Buffalo, **3 mi N** 🅶 gas 🍴 food
310	36th St SE
307	to Tower City, **N** 🅶 Cenex/café/dsl/RV Park/24hr, motel
304mm	🆁🆂 both lanes (both lanes exit left), full ♿ facilities, info, litter barrels, petwalk, ⓒ, 🗑, vending
302	ND 32, to Fingal, Oriska, **1 mi N** 🅞 city park
298	123rd Ave SE
296	121st Av SE
294	Lp 94, to Kathryn, Valley City, **N** 🅞 🎗, camping
292	Valley City, **N** 🍴 PetroServe/Tesoro/café/dsl 🍴 Sabir's Rest. 🛏 AmericInn, Grand Stay Hotel, Super 8, Wagon Wheel Inn/ rest. 🅞 🎗, Ford, to Bald Hill Dam, **S** 🅞 Ft Ransom SP (35mi)
291	Sheyenne River
290	Lp 94, Valley City, **N** 🅶 Casey's/dsl 🍴 Burger King, Kenny's Rest., Kirin House Chinese, Pizza Ranch, Subway 🅞 🎗,

ND

F A R G O

[⛽] = gas [🍴] = food [🛏] = lodging [O] = other [Rs] = rest stop   Copyright 2022 - The Next EXIT

↑E INTERSTATE 94 Cont'd

Exit	Services
290	Continued
	Buick/Chevrolet/GMC, Chrysler/Dodge/Jeep, Family$, Firestone/auto, NAPA, O'Reilly Parts, ShopKo
288	ND 1 S, to Oakes, S [O] Fort Ransom SP (36 mi)
283	ND 1 N, to Rogers
281	to Litchville, Sanborn, 1-2 mi N [⛽] gas [🍴] food [🛏] lodging
276	Eckelson, S [O] Prairie Haven Camping/gas/dsl
275mm	continental divide, elevation 1490
272	to Urbana
269	Spiritwood
262	Bloom, N [O] [🍴]
260	Jamestown, N [⛽] Casey's, Cenex/café/dsl/@ [🛏] Starlite Motel [O] to St [H]
259mm	James River
258	US 52 W, US 281, Jamestown, N [⛽] Exxon/TCBY/dsl, Tesoro/dsl [🍴] Arby's, DQ, Hardee's, McDonald's, Pizza Ranch, Subway, Taco Bell [🛏] Comfort Inn, Days Inn, Holiday Inn Express, Jamestown Motel [O] Buffalo Herd/museum, Buick/Chevrolet/GMC, Firestone/auto, NW Tire, O'Reilly Parts, Toyota, S [⛽] Shell/dsl [🍴] Applebee's, Burger King, Grizzly's Rest., Hong Kong Buffet, La Carreta Mexican, Paradiso Mexican, Perkins [🛏] EconoLodge, Fairfield Inn, Hampton Inn, My Place, Quality Inn, Super 8 [O] $Tree, AT&T, Chrysler/Dodge/Jeep, Ford/Lincoln, GNC, Harley-Davidson, Mac's Hardware, Menards, Verizon, Walmart
257	Lp 94 (from eb, exits left), to Jamestown, N [O] dsl repair
256	US 52 W, US 281 N, S [O] [H], Jamestown Campground/RV dump (1mi)
254mm	[Rs] both lanes, full [♿] facilities, litter barrels, petwalk, [🚻], [🖼], vending
251	Eldridge
248	74th Ave SE
245	70th Ave SE
242	Windsor
238	to Gackle, Cleveland
233	58th Ave SE
230	Medina, 1 mi N [⛽] Famer's Union/dsl/LP [🍴] DairyTreat [O] city park, Medina RV Park, USPO
228	ND 30 S, to Streeter
224mm	[Rs] wb, full [♿] facilities, litter barrels, petwalk, [🚻], [🖼], vending
221	Crystal Springs
221mm	[Rs] eb, full [♿] facilities, litter barrels, petwalk, [🚻], [🖼], vending
217	Pettibone
214	Tappen, S [⛽] gas/dsl/food
208	ND 3 S, Dawson, N [O] RV camping, 1/2 mi S [⛽] gas [🍴] food [O] RV camping, to Camp Grassick
205	Robinson
200	ND 3 N, to Tuttle, Steele, S [⛽] Shell/Subway/Pizza Hut/dsl [🛏] Cobblestone Inn [O] truckwash
195	20th Ave SE
190	Driscoll, S [🍴] food
182	US 83 S, ND 14, to Wing, Sterling, S [⛽] Cenex/dsl [🛏] Top's Motel (1mi)
176	McKenzie
170	Menoken, S [O] RV Park, to McDowell Dam
168mm	[Rs] both lanes, full [♿] facilities, litter barrels, petwalk, [🚻], [🖼], vending, wifi
161	Lp 94, Bismarck Expswy, Bismarck, N [⛽] Cenex/dsl/LP/24hr, Exxon/dsl [🛏] My Place [O] Peterbilt, Toyota, S [⛽] Holiday/dsl, Tesoro/Marlin's Rest./dsl/scales/24hr [🍴] McDonald's

Exit	Services
161	Continued
	[🛏] Ramada Ltd [O] Capital RV Ctr, Dakota Zoo, dsl repair Freightliner, Kenworth, OK Tires
159	US 83, Bismarck, N [⛽] Holiday/dsl, Simonson/dsl [🍴] Applebee's, Arby's, Buffalo Wings&Rings, China Star, Hong Kong Chinese, KFC, Kroll's Diner, Little Caesar's, Longhorn Steaks, MacKenzie River Pizza, McDonald's, Oahu BBQ, Olive Garden, Papa Murphy's, Paradiso Mexican, Perkins, Pita Pit, Red Lobster, Ruby Tuesday, Space Alien Grill, Taco Bell, Wendy's [🛏] AmericInn, Candlewood Suites, Comfort Inn, Comfort Suites, Country Suites, Courtyard, Fairfield Inn, Hampton Inn, Holiday Inn, Holiday Inn Express, Mainstay Suites, Motel 6, Residence Inn, Sleep Inn, Staybridge Suites, Super 8, Wingate Inn [O] AT&T, Chevrolet, CVS Drug, Dan's Foods/USPO, Dick's, Gordman's, Hancock Fabrics, Hobby Lobby, Honda, Jo-Ann Fabrics, Menards, Michael's, Nissan, NW Tire, Ross, UHaul, USPO, VW, Walmart, Subway, S [⛽] Exxon/dsl, PetroServe/dsl, Shell/dsl [🍴] DQ, East 40 Rest., Hardee's, Pizza Hut, Schlotzsky's, Starbucks, Subway, Taco John's, Woodhouse Rest. [🛏] Best Value Inn, Days Inn, Kelly Inn, La Quinta, Ramada Inn, Super 8 [O] [H], O'Reilly Parts
157	Divide Ave, Bismarck, N [⛽] Shell/dsl [🍴] Carino's, Coldstone, Cracker Barrel, Five Guys, Jimmy John's, Kobe's Japanese, McDonald's, Nardello's Pizza, Pancheros Mexican, Starbucks, Subway, Taco John's, TX Roadhouse [O] $Tree, Best Buy, GNC, Kohl's, Lowe's, Old Navy, Petsmart, TJ Maxx, Verizon, visitor ctr S [⛽] Cenex/dsl/E85/LP/RV Dump [🍴] Stadium Café [🛏] Hampton Inn [O] Dan's Mkt/USPO
156mm	Missouri River
156	I-194, Bismarck Expswy, Bismarck City Ctr, 1/2 mi S [O] Dakota Zoo
155	to Lp 94 (exits left from wb), Mandan, City Ctr, same as 153
153	ND 1806, Mandan Dr, Mandan, 1/2 mi S [⛽] Cenex/dsl, M&H dsl, PetroServe/dsl, Tesoro [🍴] Bonanza, Burger King, Dakota Farms Rest., Domino's, DQ, Hardee's, Papa Murphy's, Pizza Hut, Pizza Ranch, Subway, Taco John's [🛏] North Country Inn [O] Chevrolet, Dacotah Centennial Park, Family$, Ft Lincoln SP (5mi), Goodyear/auto, NAPA, NW Tire, O'Reilly Parts, Subaru, Verizon
152	Sunset Dr, Mandan, N [⛽] Tesoro/dsl [🛏] Baymont Inn, Comfort Inn [O] Thrifty White Drug, Walmart/Subway, S [⛽] Tesoro/RV dump [🍴] Fried's Rest. [O] [H]
152mm	scenic view eb
147	ND 25, to ND 6, Mandan, S [⛽] FLYING J/Shell/Subway/dsl/scales/24hr
140	to Crown Butte
135mm	scenic view wb, litter barrel
134	to Judson, Sweet Briar Lake
127	ND 31 N, to New Salem, N [O] Knife River Indian Village (35mi) S [⛽] Cenex/dsl, Tesoro/dsl [🍴] Sunset Cafe [🛏] Arrowhead Inn, café [O] DFC/dsl, vet, World's Largest Cow
123	to Almont
120	no service
119mm	[Rs] both lanes, full [♿] facilities, litter barrels, petwalk, [🚻], [🖼]
117	no service
113	no service
110	ND 49, to Glen Ullin
108	to Glen Ullin, Lake Tschida, 3 mi [⛽] gas [🍴] food [🛏] lodging [O] camping
102	Hebron, to Glen Ullin, to Lake Tschida, 3 mi S [⛽] gas [🍴] food [🛏] lodging [O] camping
97	Hebron, 2 mi N [⛽] gas [🍴] food [🛏] lodging
96.5mm	central/mountain time zone
90	no service

Side markers: JAMESTOWN, BISMARCK, MANDAN, HEBRON, ND

✈E INTERSTATE 94 Cont'd

Exit #	Services
84	ND 8, Richardton, N 🍴 Cenex/dsl Ⓞ 🅷 Schnell RA, Springfield Mkt, to Assumption Abbey
78	to Taylor
72	to Enchanted Hwy, Gladstone
64	Dickinson, S 🍴 Cenex/Tiger Truckstop/rest./dsl/24hr, Dakota Diner Ⓞ dsl repair, Ford/Lincoln, Honda, NW Tire, Toyota
61	ND 22, Dickinson, N 🍴 Cenex/dsl/LP, Mobil/Schlotsky's/dsl/scales/24hr, Simonson/dsl 🍴 Applebee's, Arby's, Burger King, City Brew Coffee, DQ, El Sombrero Mexican, Jimmy John's, Papa Murphy's, Pizza Ranch, Qdoba, Sakura Japanese, Sanford's Rest., Taco Bell, Taco John's, Wendy's 🏨 AmericInn, Astoria Suites, Best Western, Candlewood Suites, Comfort Inn, Hampton Inn, Holiday Inn Express, Microtel, My Place, Ramada, Red Roof Inn, TownePlace Suites Ⓞ AT&T, Cashwise Foods, Chevrolet/Cadillac, Family Fare Mkt, Goodyear/auto, Herberger's, Midas, O'Reilly Parts, Runnings Hardware, USPO, Verizon, Walmart/Subway, White Drug, S 🍴 Cenex/dsl, Conoco/repair, Holiday/dsl, Tesoro/Domino's/dsl 🍴 A&W/KFC, Country Kitchen, Don Pedro's Mexican, King Buffet, McDonald's, Perkins, Subway 🏨 La Quinta, Motel 6, Quality Inn, Relax Inn, Rodeway Inn, Travel Inn Ⓞ 🅷 Ace Hardware, museum, visitor info
59	Lp 94, to Dickinson, N 🍴 Buffalo Wild Wings 🏨 Hawthorn Suites, Woodspring Suites Ⓞ Family Fare/dsl, Menard's, Verizon, S Ⓞ camping, 🅷, to Patterson Lake RA, services in Dickinson
56	116th Ave
51	South Heart
42	US 85, to Grassy Butte, Belfield, Williston, N 🍴 MVP/dsl Ⓞ T Roosevelt NP (52mi), S 🍴 Cenex/dsl/24hr, Conoco/dsl 🍴 Trapper's Kettle Rest. 🏨 Trapper's Inn Ⓞ NAPA
36	Fryburg
32	T Roosevelt NP, N ℞ₛ both lanes, full facilities, scenic overlook
27	Lp 94, S Ⓞ Historic Medora (from wb), T Roosevelt NP
24.5mm	Little Missouri Scenic River
24	Medora, Historic Medora, S Ⓞ Chateau de Mores HS, T Roosevelt NP, visitors ctr
23	West River Rd (from wb)
22mm	scenic view eb
18	Buffalo Gap, N Ⓞ Buffalo Gap Camping (seasonal)
10	Sentinel Butte, Camel Hump Lake, S 🍴 gas
7	Home on the Range
1	ND 16, S Welcome/Visitor Ctr, full ♿ facilities, litter barrels, petwalk, 🍴 ⊕FLYING J/Subway/dsl/scales/LP/24hr, Cenex/dsl/LP/24hr 🏨 Buckboard Inn Ⓞ Beach RV Park
1mm	weigh sta eb, litter barrel
0mm	North Dakota/Montana state line

D I C K I N S O N

ND

NOTES

(blank lined note section)

🅟 = gas 🍴 = food 🛏 = lodging 🄾 = other 🆁🆂 = rest stop   Copyright 2022 - The Next EXIT

OHIO

🔼E INTERSTATE 70

B L A I N E

C A M B R I D G E

Exit #	Services
225.5mm	Ohio/West Virginia state line, Ohio River
225	US 250 W, OH 7, Bridgeport, N 🅟 Marathon, StarFire, Sunoco/dsl 🍴 DQ, Papa John's, Pizza Hut 🄾 Advance Parts, AutoZone, Family$, Meineke, NAPA, S 🅟 Clark, Exxon/dsl 🍴 Domino's
220	US 40, rd 214, N 🅟 Marathon, Sunoco/dsl 🛏 Comfort Inn, S 🅟 Exxon/dsl 🛏 Days Inn 🄾 vet
219	I-470 E, to Bel-Aire, Washington PA, (from eb)
218	Mall Rd, to US 40, to Blaine, N 🅟 BP, Exxon/Subway/dsl, Sheetz/dsl 🍴 Applebee's, Arby's, Burger King, DeFelice Pizza, Denny's, Eat'n Park, HoneyBaked Ham, King Buffet, Little Caesar's, Outback Steaks, Pizza Hut, Red Lobster, Starbucks, Steak'n Shake, Taco Bell, Tlaquepaque Mexican, Undo's Rest., W Texas Steaks, Wendy's 🛏 Best Value Inn, Hawthorn Suites, Holiday Inn Express, Knights Inn, Microtel, Red Roof Inn, Super 8, Wingate Inn 🄾 $General, $Tree, AAA, Advance Parts, Aldi Foods, AT&T, AutoZone, Buick/Cadillac/Chevrolet, CVS Drug, Kroger, Lowe's, Sam's Club, Staples, Stewarts RV Ctr, URGENT CARE, Verizon, Walmart/McDonald's, S 🍴 Bob Evans, Buffalo Wild Wings, Chipotle, Cracker Barrel, Garfield's Rest., KFC/LJ Silver, Longhorn Steaks, McDonald's, Osaka Steaks, Panera Bread, Starbucks, Zhuzi Chinese 🛏 Candlewood Suites, Fairfield Inn, Residence Inn 🄾 Boscov's, Chrysler/Dodge/Jeep, Jo-Ann Fabrics, Macy's, Marshall's, NTB
216	OH 9, St Clairsville, N 🅟 BP
215	National Rd, N 🍴 Burger King, Domino's, WenWu Chinese 🄾 Riesbeck's Foods, USPO
213	OH 331, Flushing, S 🅟 BP, Marathon/Subway/dsl, Sunoco/dsl
211mm	🆁🆂 both lanes, full ♿ facilities, litter barrels, petwalk, 🄲, 🄰, vending
208	OH 149, Morristown, N 🅟 Exxon/McDonald's/dsl 🍴 Schlepp's Rest. 🛏 Arrowhead Motel (1mi), Days Inn 🄾 $General, Cannonball Speedway, Ford/Lincoln, S 🅟 Marathon/Quiznos/dsl, Pilot/Subway/dsl/scales/24hr 🛏 Sleep Inn 🄾 Barkcamp SP, Harley-Davidson
204	US 40 E (from eb, no return), National Rd
202	OH 800, to Barnesville, S 🅟 Sunoco/dsl 🄾 🄷
198	rd 114, Fairview
193	OH 513, Middlebourne, N 🅟 BP, FuelMart/dsl 🄾 fireworks
189mm	🆁🆂 eb, full ♿ facilities, litter barrels, petwalk, 🄲, 🄰, vending
186	US 40, OH 285, to Old Washington, N 🅟 Marathon/dsl 🄾 $General, S 🅟 GoMart/dsl, Speedway/dsl/scales/24hr
180b a	I-77 N, to Cleveland, to Salt Fork SP, I-77 S, to Charleston
178	OH 209, Cambridge, 0-1 mi N 🅟 BP/dsl, Sheetz/dsl 🍴 Bob Evans, Coldstone/Tim Hortons, Cracker Barrel, Denny's, DQ, Forum Rest., KFC, McDonald's, Papa John's, Pizza Hut, Ruby Tuesday, Subway, Wendy's 🛏 Comfort Inn, Days Inn, Hampton Inn, Holiday Inn Express, Microtel, Quality Inn, Sleep Inn, Southgate Hotel 🄾 🄷, $General, Advance Parts, AutoZone, BigLots, Cash Saver Foods, Family$, Ford, O'Reilly Parts, Verizon, S 🅟 Murphy USA/dsl, Pilot/Subway/dsl/scales/24hr 🍴 Arby's, Buffalo Wild Wings, Burger King, Great Chinese, Little Caesar's, Taco Bell, Tlaquepaque Mexican 🛏 Baymont Inn 🄾 $Tree, Aldi Foods, AT&T, Chevrolet, Chrysler/Dodge/Jeep, Spring Valley RV Park (1mi), Verizon, Walmart/Subway
176	US 22, US 40, to Cambridge, N 🅟 Sunoco/dsl 🛏 Budget Inn 🄾 RV camping, st patrol, vet

Z A N E S V I L L E

173mm	weigh sta both lanes
169	OH 83, to Cumberland, New Concord, N 🅟 Marathon/dsl 🛏 Garland Hotel 🄾 John&Annie Glen Historic Site, RV camping, to Muskingum U
164	US 22, US 40, Norwich, N 🅟 🛏 Baker's Motel, Zane Gray Museum, S 🄾 antiques, pottery
163mm	🆁🆂 wb, full ♿ facilities, litter barrels, petwalk, 🄲, 🄰, vending
160	OH 797, Airport Rd, N 🅟 💚Loves/Arby's/dsl/scales/24hr, 🅟 BP, Marathon/Subway/dsl 🍴 Denny's, McDonald's, Wendy's 🛏 Best Western, Economy Inn, Kautilya Zanesville Hotel 🄾 🄷, st patrol
157	OH 93, Zanesville, N 🅟 BP, S 🅟 Marathon, Shell/dsl 🄾 st patrol
155	OH 60, OH 146, Underwood St, Zanesville, N 🍴 Bob Evans, Olive Garden, Oriental Buffet, Red Lobster, Steak'n Shake, Tumbleweed Grill 🛏 Hampton Inn, Holiday Inn Express, Quality Inn, Wingate Inn 🄾 🄷, Riesbeck's Mkt, USPO, S 🅟 Marathon/dsl 🍴 Cracker Barrel, Subway, Wendy's 🛏 Baymont Inn, Travel Inn 🄾 Rite Aid
154	5th St (from eb)
153b	Maple Ave (no EZ return from wb), N 🅟 🍴 DQ, Italian Eatery, Papa John's, Tee Jaye's Rest. 🄾 🄷, CVS Drug, Family$
153a	State St, N 🅟 Speedway/dsl 🄾 to Dillon SP (8mi), USPO
153mm	Licking River
152	US 40, National Rd, N 🅟 BP/A&W/Subway/dsl, Shell/dsl 🍴 McDonald's 🛏 Super 8
142	US 40 (from wb, no EZ return), Gratiot, N 🄾 RV camping
141	OH 668, US 40 (from eb, no return), to Gratiot, same as 142
132	OH 13, to Thornville, Newark, N 🄾 Dawes Arboretum (3mi), 🅟 BP, Shell 🍴 Subway (2mi)
131mm	🆁🆂 both lanes, full ♿ facilities, litter barrels, petwalk, 🄲, 🄰, vending
129b a	OH 79, to Buckeye Lake, Hebron, N 🍴 Subway 🛏 Best Western 🄾 Advance Parts, Kroger/gas, S 🅟 🍴 Donato's Pizza, McDonald's, Subway, Taco Bell, Wendy's 🛏 Motel 6 🄾 CarQuest, KOA (2mi)
126	OH 37, to Granville, Lancaster, N 🅟 Marathon/dsl, Pilot/Chester's/Subway/dsl/scales/24hr, S 🅟 IA 80 Truckomat/truck wash, TA/BP/Bob Evans/Popeye's/Sbarro's/dsl/scales/24hr 🛏 Deluxe Inn, Red Roof Inn 🄾 KOA
122	OH 158, to Baltimore, Kirkersville, N 🛏 Regal Inn, 🍴 FLYING J/Denny's/dsl/LP/scales/24hr 🄾 fireworks
118	OH 310, to Pataskala, N 🅟 BP/McDonald's, Shell/dsl, Speedway/dsl 🍴 DQ, S 🅟 BP/Duke's/Subway/dsl 🄾 RCD RV Ctr
112c	OH 204, to Blecklick Rd (from eb)
112	OH 256, to Pickerington, Reynoldsburg, N 🅟 BP, Shell/McDonald's 🍴 Buffalo Wild Wings, Chipotle Mexican, Culvers, Five Guys, IHOP, Logan's Roadhouse, Noodles&Co, O'Charley's, Olive Garden, Panera Bread, Penn Sta, Smokey Bones BBQ, Subway, TGIFriday's 🛏 Fairfield Inn, Holiday Inn Express 🄾 AT&T, Best Buy, Jo-Ann Fabrics, Marshall's, NTB, Old Navy, Petco, Petsmart, Sam's Club/gas, Staples, Target, Tire Discounters, Verizon, Walgreens, Walmart/Subway, S 🅟 Speedway/dsl 🍴 Arby's, Bob Evans, Cane's, Cold Stone, Cracker Barrel, Donato's Pizza, Firehouse Subs, Iron Chef, Jimmy John's, KFC, La Fogata Mexican, LJ Silver, Longhorn Steaks, Max&Erma's, Omezzo Italian, Red Robin, Skyline Chili, Starbucks, Steak'n Shake, Wendy's 🛏 Best Western, Comfort Inn, Hampton Inn 🄾 Advance Parts, Barnes&Noble, Kohl's, Kroger/E85, URGENT CARE, Verizon

OH

Copyright 2022 - The Next EXIT ®   🅿=gas 🍴=food 🏠=lodging 🅾=other Rs=rest stop

INTERSTATE 70 Cont'd

Exit #	Services
110	Brice Rd, to Reynoldsburg, **N** 🅿 Speedway/dsl, Sunoco 🍴 Burger King, Donato's, Genji Japanese, Golden China, Popeye's, Subway, TeeJaye's Rest., Tim Horton's, Waffle House 🏠 Days Inn, Extended Stay America, La Quinta, Red Roof Inn 🅾 BigLots, Family$, Goodyear/auto, Home Depot, O'Reilly Parts, **S** 🅿 BP, Speedway/dsl 🍴 Applebee's, Arby's, Asian Star, Boston Mkt, Chipotle Mexican, KFC, McDonald's, Starbucks, Subway, Taco Bell, Waffle House 🏠 Comfort Suites, Motel 6, Rodeway Inn 🅾 $Tree, Acura, Advance Parts, Aldi Foods, Family$, Fiat, Firestone/auto, Honda, Lowe's, Michael's, Toyota, Walgreens
108b a	I-270 N to Cleveland, access to 🅷, I-270 S to Cincinnati
107a	OH 317, Hamilton Rd, to Whitehall, **S** 🅿 Shell/dsl 🍴 Arby's, Burger King, Capt D's, ChuckeCheese, Ichiban Japanese, McDonald's, Papa John's, Pizza Hut, Popeye's, Red Lobster, Steak'n Shake, Taco Bell 🏠 Hampton Inn, InTown Suites 🅾 $General, AT&T, PepBoys
105a	US 33, to Lancaster, **2 mi N** 🍴 Tat Italian
105b	US 33, James Rd, Bexley, **N** 🍴 Tat Italian
103b a	Livingston Ave, to Capital University, **N** 🅿 Exxon, Speedway/dsl 🍴 Mr Hero Subs, Peking Dynasty, Popeye's, Subway, Taco Bell, Tim Horton's, Wendy's 🅾 auto repair, Katz Tires, **S** 🅿 Marathon, Shell 🍴 McDonald's, Rally's, White Castle 🅾 Family$
102	Kelton Ave, Miller Ave
101a	I-71 N, to Cleveland
100b	US 23, to 4th St, downtown
99c	Rich St, Town St (exits left from wb)
99b	OH 315 N, downtown
99a	I-71 S, to Cincinnati
98b	Mound St (from wb, no EZ return), **S** 🅿 Speedway 🍴 Little Caesar's, McDonald's, Rally's 🅾 Aldi Foods, Family$
98a	US 62, OH 3, Central Ave, to Sullivant, same as 98b
97	US 40, W Broad St, **N** 🍴 Arby's, Burger King, McDonald's, Subway, Taco Bell, Tim Horton's 🏠 Knights Inn, Motel 6 🅾 Aamco, CVS Drug, U-Haul, USPO
96	I-670 (exits left from eb), 🅾 to ✈
95	Hague Ave (from wb), **S** 🅿 Exxon
94	Wilson Rd, **N** 🅿 Marathon/Circle K/Subway/dsl, UDF, **S** 🅿 BP, Pilot/Wendy's/dsl/scales/24hr, Shell/dsl, Speedway 🍴 McDonald's, Waffle House 🏠 EconoLodge 🅾 vet
93b a	I-270, N to Cleveland, S to Cincinnati
91b a	to Hilliard, New Rome, **N** 🅿 GetGo, Shell, Speedway/dsl 🍴 Applebee's, Arby's, Buffalo Wild Wings, Burger King, Chick-fil-A, Chipotle, Cracker Barrel, Culver's, Daruma Japanese, Donato's Pizza, El Vaquero Mexican, Fazoli's, Firehouse Subs, Five Guys, Golden Chopsticks, Hot Head Burrito, IHOP, KFC, McDonald's, Olive Garden, Outback Steaks, Panda Express, Panera Bread, Perkins, Red Robin, Rooster's Rest., Skyline Chili, Subway, Supreme Buffet, Taco Bell, Tim Horton's/Coldstone, TX Roadhouse, Wendy's, White Castle, Wild Ginger Asian 🏠 Best Value Inn, Comfort Suites, Fairfield Inn, Hampton Inn, Hawthorn Inn, Holiday Inn, La Quinta, Motel 6, Red Roof Inn 🅾 $Tree, Advance Parts, AT&T, Dick's, Discount Tire, Firestone/auto, Ford, GNC, Kohl's, Marshall's, Meijer/dsl, Michael's, Midas,

91b a	Continued Old Navy, Petsmart, Sam's Club/gas, Target, URGENT CARE, Verizon, Walmart/Subway, **S** 🅿 BP/dsl, Marathon/dsl 🍴 Bob Evans, Handel's Ice Cream, Steak'n Shake 🏠 Best Western, Country Inn&Suites, Super 8
85	OH 142, to Plain City, W Jefferson, **N** 🅾 Prairie Oaks SP, **S** 🅾 Battelle Darby SP
80	OH 29, to Mechanicsburg, **S** 🅾 hwy patrol
79	US 42, to London, Plain City, **N** 🅿 Pilot/Arby's/dsl/scales/24hr 🍴 Waffle House 🅾 Camping World RV Ctr, truck/auto repair, **S** 🅿 Speedway/Subway/dsl, TA/BP/Pizza Hut/Popeye's/dsl/scales/24hr/@ 🍴 McDonald's, Taco Bell, Wendy's 🏠 Holiday Inn Express, Motel 6 🅾 🅷
72	OH 56, to London, Summerford, **N** 🅿 Marathon/Subway/dsl, **4 mi S** 🅾 🅷
71mm	Rs both lanes, full ♿ facilities, litter barrels, petwalk, 🐕, 🚮, vending
66	OH 54, to Catawba, South Vienna, **N** 🅿 Fuelmart/dsl/scales, **S** 🅿 Speedway/dsl
62	US 40, Springfield, **N** 🏠 Harmony Motel 🅾 🅷, antiques, auto repair, Harmony Farm Mkt, to Buck Creek SP, **S** 🅾 Beaver Valley Camping
59	OH 41, to S Charleston, **N** 🅾 🅷, Harley-Davidson, st patrol, **S** 🅿 BP/dsl, Loves/Subway/Wendy's/dsl/scales/24hr 🅾 antiques
54	OH 72, to Cedarville, Springfield, **N** 🅿 BP/dsl, Shell, Speedway/dsl, Sunoco/dsl 🍴 A&W/LJ Silver, Arby's, Bob Evans, Burger King, Cassano's Pizza/subs, Cracker Barrel, Domino's, Dunkin', El Toro Mexican, Hardee's, Lee's Chicken, Little Caesar's, McDonald's, Panda Chinese, Popeye's, Rally's, Rudy's Smokehouse, Subway, Taco Bell 🏠 Baymont Inn, Comfort Suites,

COLUMBUS AREA

SPRINGFIELD

OH

🅖 = gas 🅕 = food 🅛 = lodging 🅞 = other 🆁🆂 = rest stop   Copyright 2022 - The Next EXIT ®

⬆️E   INTERSTATE 70 Cont'd

SPRINGFIELD

Exit	Services
54	Continued
	Hampton Inn, Holiday Inn Express, Motel 6, Quality Inn, Red Roof Inn, USA Suites 🅞 🅗, Advance Parts, BigLots, Family$, Kroger/deli, Rite Aid, Walgreens, **S** 🅕 Marathon/dsl
52b a	US 68, to Urbana, Xenia, **S** 🅞 to John Bryan SP
48	OH 4 (from wb), to Enon, Donnelsville, **N** 🅞 camping, **S** 🅕 Speedway
47	OH 4 (from eb), to Springfield, **N** 🅞 Enon Beach Camping, **S** 🅕 Speedway
44	I-675 S, Spangler Rd, to Cincinnati
43mm	Mad River
41b a	OH 4, OH 235, to Dayton, New Carlisle, **N** 🅕 Shell/dsl 🅕 McDonald's, Taco Bell, Wendy's 🅞 Freightliner, Kenworth
38	OH 201, Brandt Pike, **N** 🅕 Marathon/dsl 🅞 Meijer/Subway/dsl/E85, **S** 🅕 Shell, UDF/dsl 🅕 Bob Evans, Hardee's, Sonic, Tim Horton's, Waffle House, Wendy's 🅛 Comfort Inn, Red Roof Inn 🅞 vet, Walmart
36	OH 202, Huber Heights, **N** 🅕 Speedway/dsl 🅕 Applebee's, Big Boy, Dragon City, El Toro Grill, Fazoli's, Firehouse Subs, Osaka Japanese, Steak'n Shake, Taco Bell, Waffle House 🅛 Baymont Inn 🅞 $Tree, AT&T, Big Lots, Dick's, GNC, Hobby Lobby, Kia, Kohl's, Lowe's, Marshall's, Petsmart, Staples, Target, Verizon, vet, **S** 🅕 BP/dsl, Marathon/dsl 🅕 Arby's, Buffalo Wild Wings, Burger King, Chipotle Mexican, CiCi's Pizza, IHOP, McDonald's, Panera Bread, Rooster's Rest., Skyline Chili, Subway, TGIFriday's, TX Roadhouse 🅛 Days Inn, Hampton Inn, Holiday Inn Express 🅞 Kroger/gas
33b a	I-75, N to Toledo, S to Dayton
32	to US 40, Vandalia, **N** 🅞 to Dayton Intn'l Airport
29	OH 48, to Dayton, Englewood, **N** 🅕 BP, Speedway/dsl, Sunoco/dsl, Valero 🅕 Arby's, Big Boy, Bob Evans, Buffalo Wild Wings, Company BBQ, Domino's, Firehouse Subs, Hot Head Burrito, Lee's Chicken, Perkins, Pizza Hut, Popeye's, Skyline Chili, Taco Bell, Tim Horton's, Tony's Italian, Wendy's, Yen Ching Chinese 🅛 Best Western+, Clarion, Hampton Inn 🅞 $Tree, Advance Parts, Aldi Foods, AutoZone, Family$, Grismer/auto, Midas, O'Reilly Parts, Petco, Verizon, vet, **S** 🅕 Chipotle, El Toro, McDonald's, MOD Pizza, Panera Bread, Starbucks, Steak'n Shake, Waffle House 🅛 Comfort Inn, Motel 6 🅞 🅗, AT&T, Meijer/dsl/E85
26	OH 49 S, **N** 🅕 Murphy USA/dsl 🅕 Bob Evans, La Rosa's Pizza, Sonic, Subway 🅞 URGENT CARE, Verizon, Walmart/Subway, **S** 🅕 Shell/dsl 🅕 Burger King, Wendy's
24	OH 49 N, to Greenville, Clayton, **N** 🅞 KOA (seasonal)
21	Arlington Rd, Brookville, **N** 🅕 Speedway/Subway/dsl, **S** 🅕 Speedway/dsl 🅕 Arby's, Brookville Grille, Great Wall Chinese, KFC/Taco Bell, K's Rest., Lee's Chicken, McDonald's, Pizza Hut, Rob's Rest., Subway, Waffle House, Wendy's 🅛 Brookville Inn, Holiday Inn Express 🅞 $General, Advance Parts, Brookville Parts, Chevrolet, Family$, IGA Foods, Rite Aid
14	OH 503, to West Alexandria, Lewisburg, **N** 🅕 Marathon/Subway/dsl 🅕 Dari Twist 🅛 Super Inn 🅞 $General, **S** 🅕 Sunoco/dsl
10	US 127, to Eaton, Greenville, **N** 🅕 TA/BP/Burger King/Subway/dsl/scales/24hr/@, **S** 🅕 🚆/Subway/dsl/scales/24hr 🅛 Budget Inn
3mm	Welcome Ctr eb/🆁🆂 both lanes, full 🚻 facilities, litter barrels, petwalk, 🅲, 🐾, vending
1	US 35 E (from eb), to Eaton, New Hope
0mm	Ohio/Indiana state line, Welcome Arch, **weigh sta eb**

DAYTON

OH

⬆️N   INTERSTATE 71

CLEVELAND

Exit #	Services
	I-71 begins/ends on I-90, exit 170 in Cleveland.
247b	I-90 W, I-490 E.
247a	W 14th, Clark Ave, **E** 🅕 Applebee's, Chipotle, Five Guys, IHOP, Panda Express, Taco Bell 🅞 Walmart
246	Denison Ave, Jennings Rd (from sb)
245	US 42, Pearl Rd, **E** 🅕 BP/7-11, Gas&Go 🅞 zoo, **W** 🅞 🅗
244	W 65th, Denison Ave (exits left from nb)
242b a	W 130th, to Bellaire Rd, **W** 🅕 Sunoco
240	W 150th, **E** 🅕 Marathon, Speedway/dsl, Sunoco 🅕 Burger King, Denny's, Happy's Pizza 🅛 Marriott 🅞 AutoZone, Goodyear/auto, Marc's Foods, **W** 🅕 BP/Subway/7-11/dsl 🅕 Hub Grill 🅛 La Quinta, Sheraton
239	OH 237 S (from sb), **W** 🅞 to ✈
238	I-480, Toledo, Youngstown, **W** 🅞 ✈
237	Snow Rd, Brook Park, **E** 🅕 GetGo, Marathon/Circle K, Shell 🅕 Arby's, Bob Evans, Burger King, Dunkin', Garden Rest. Goody's Rest., KFC, Little Caesar's, McDonald's, Rally's, Reddi Pizza, Subway, Taco Bell 🅛 Best Western, Holiday Inn Express, Howard Johnson 🅞 $General, $Tree, Advance Parts, Auto Zone, Conrad Tire/repair, CVS Drug, Giant Eagle, O'Reilly Parts, Rite Aid, **W** 🅞 to ✈
235	Bagley Rd, **E** 🅕 Bob Evans 🅞 Mr Tire, vet, **W** 🅕 BP/dsl, Gulf, Speedway/dsl 🅕 Aladdin's Eatery, Arby's, Baskin-Robbins, Dunkin', Burger King, Capri Pizza, Chipotle, Craft Brew Garden, Five Guys, Jimmy John's, Little Hong Kong, Max&Erma's, McDonald's, Olive Garden, Panera Bread, Penn Sta Subs, Perkins, Pizza Hut, Starbucks, Taco Bell, Zoup! 🅛 Comfort Inn, Courtyard, Crowne Plaza, Days Inn, Extended Stay America, Hampton Inn, Home 2 Suites, Motel 6, Red Roof Inn, Sonesta Inn, TownePlace Suites 🅞 🅗, Aldi Foods, Verizon
234	US 42, Pearl Rd, **E** 🅕 Shell/dsl, Sunoco/dsl 🅕 Hunan Chinese, Jet's Pizza, Katherine's Rest., Mr Hero, Santo's Italian, Three Bros Pizza 🅞 Audi/Porsche, Honda, **W** 🅕 Mobil/dsl, Sheetz/dsl, Tesla EVC 🅕 Buffalo Wild Wings, McDonald's 🅛 King Inn, La Siesta Motel 🅞 Home Depot, Lowe's, Walmart/Subway
233	I-80 and Ohio Tpk, to Toledo, Youngstown
231	OH 82, Strongsville, **E** 🅕 Shell 🅛 Holiday Inn, Super 🅞 Chevrolet, **W** 🅕 BP/7-11/dsl, Marathon/Subway/dsl 🅕 Applebee's, B Spot Burger, Buca Italian, Chick-fil-A, Chipotle, DiBella's Subs, Firehouse Subs, Houlihan's, Longhorn Steak, Macaroni Grill, Panera Bread, Red Lobster, Rosewood Grill, Samurai Japanese, Starbucks, TGIFriday, Zoup! 🅞 $Tree, AAA, AT&T, Best Buy, Costco/gas, Dick's, Dillard's, Heinen's Mkt, JC Penney, Kohl's, Macy's, Michael's, Midas, NTB, Old Navy, PetCo, Target, TJ Maxx, Verizon
226	OH 303, Brunswick, **E** 🅕 Shell/dsl 🅕 Antonio's Pizza 🅞 Chrysler/Dodge/Jeep, Hyundai, Subaru, Toyota, vet, VW, **W** 🅕 Speedway/dsl, Sunoco/dsl 🅕 Applebee's, Arby's, Bob Evans, Burger King, Chipotle, Georgio's Pizza, House of Pearl, KFC, McDonald's, Muchos Buenos Mexican, Panera Bread, Panini's Grill, Pizza Hut, Starbucks, Steak'n Shake, Subway, Taco Bell, Wendy's 🅛 Quality Inn 🅞 $General, Ford, Giant Eagle Mkt, GNC, Home Depot, Marc's Mkt, Verizon, Comfort Suites, Jersey Mike's
225mm	🆁🆂 nb, full 🚻 facilities, litter barrels, petwalk, 🅲, 🐾
224mm	🆁🆂 sb, full 🚻 facilities, litter barrels, petwalk, 🅲, 🐾
222	OH 3, Medina, Hinckley, **W** 🅞 st patrol
220	I-271 N, (from nb) to Erie, Pa
218	OH 18, to Akron, Medina, **E** 🅕 BP/dsl, Marathon/dsl, Sunoco/dsl 🅕 Baskin-Robbins/Dunkin', Burger King, DQ, Fresh Food Deli, Master Pizza, Pizza Hut 🅛 Holiday Inn Express, Quality Inn

STRONGSVILLE

INTERSTATE 71 Cont'd

AKRON

218	Continued
	Super 8 🅾 Kia, Nissan, Verizon, **W** 🚇 GetGo, Speedway/dsl 🍴 Arby's, Bob Evans, Brown Derby, Buffalo Wild Wings, Chipotle, Denny's, McDonald's, Rocknes Rest., Starbucks, Taco Bell, Waffle House, Wendy's 🏨 Fairfield Inn, Hampton Inn, Motel 6, Red Roof Inn 🅾 🅷 Aldi Foods, Buehler's Foods, Buick/Cadillac/GMC, Chrysler/Dodge/Jeep, Firestone/auto, Harley-Davidson, Honda, Verizon
209	I-76 E, to Akron, US 224, **W** 🍴 Pilot/Subway/dsl/scales/24hr, TA/Country Pride/Burger King/Popeye's/dsl/scales/24hr/@ 🍴 Arby's, McDonald's, Starbucks 🏨 Super 8 🅾 Blue Beacon, Chippewa Valley Camping (1mi), SpeedCo
204	OH 83, Burbank, **E** 🚇 BP/dsl, Duke/dsl, Loves/Hardee's/dsl/scales/24hr 🏨 Plaza Motel, **W** 🚇 Pilot/Wendy's/dsl/scales/24hr 🍴 Arby's, Bob Evans, Burger King, McDonald's 🅾 🅷, OH Sta Outlets/famous brands
198	OH 539, W Salem
196mm	Rs both lanes, full ♿ facilities, litter barrels, petwalk, 🅲, 🏕️, vending
196	OH 301 (from nb, no re-entry), W Salem
186	US 250, Ashland, **E** 🚇 Marathon 🍴 Grandpa's Village/cheese/gifts, Perkins 🅾 Hickory Lakes Camping (7mi), **W** 🚇 Goasis/BP/Pizza Hut/Popeye's/Starbucks/Taco Bell/dsl/24hr, Marathon/Subway/dsl 🍴 Buffalo Wild Wings, Chipotle, Denny's, Dunkin', Jake's Rest., McDonald's, Wendy's 🏨 Hampton Inn, Holiday Inn Express, Motel 6, Quality Inn, Super 8 🅾 🅷, $Tree, Aldi Foods, AT&T, Buehler's Foods, GNC, Home Depot, st patrol, to Ashland U, URGENT CARE, Verizon, Walmart/Subway

MANSFIELD

176	US 30, to Mansfield, **E** 🏨 Heritage Inn 🅾 fireworks
173	OH 39, to Mansfield
169	OH 13, Mansfield, **E** 🚇 Marathon/7-11/dsl, Murphy USA/dsl 🍴 Applebee's, Chipotle, Cracker Barrel, Steak'n Shake, Wendy's 🏨 Best Western, La Quinta 🅾 Mohican SP, Walmart/Subway, **W** 🚇 BP/7-11 🍴 Arby's, Bob Evans, Burger King, El Charrito Mexican, McDonald's, Subway, Taco Bell 🏨 Hampton Inn, Super 8, Travelodge 🅾 🅷, st patrol
165	OH 97, to Bellville, **E** 🚇 BP, Shell/Dunkin'/dsl, Speedway/dsl 🍴 Buckeye Express Diner, Burger King, Der Dutchman, KC's Rib House, McDonald's 🏨 Comfort Inn, Economy Inn, Mid Ohio Inn, Quality Inn 🅾 to Mohican SP, **W** 🚇 Loves/Subway/Taco John's/dsl/scales/24hr 🍴 Wendy's
151	OH 95, to Mt Gilead, **E** 🚇 Duke/BP/deli, Marathon, Tesla EVC 🍴 Eight Sisters Cafe, McDonald's, Wendy's 🏨 Best Western 🅾 st patrol, **W** 🚇 Shell/dsl, Sunoco/dsl/e85 🍴 Subway 🏨 Knights Inn 🅾 🅷, Mt Gilead SP (6mi)
149mm	truck parking both lanes
140	OH 61, Mt Gilead, **E** 🚇 Pilot/Arby's/dsl/scales/24hr, **W** 🚇 BP/Taco Bell, Marathon/Subway 🍴 Legacy Rest. 🅾 Cardinal Ctr Camping
131	US 36, OH 37, to Delaware, **E** 🚇 Flying J/Denny's/dsl/LP/scales/24hr/@, Pilot/Subway/dsl/scales/24hr 🍴 Burger King 🅾 Harley-Davidson, **W** 🚇 BP/dsl, Shell/Tim Hortons 🍴 Arby's, Bob Evans, Cracker Barrel, KFC/LJ Silver, McDonald's, Panera Bread, Starbucks, Taco Bell, Waffle House, Wendy's, White Castle 🏨 Hampton Inn, Holiday Inn Express, Travelodge 🅾 🅷, Alum Cr SP, Cross Creek Camping (6mi)
128mm	Rs both lanes, full ♿ facilities, litter barrels, petwalk, 🅲, 🏕️, vending
121	Polaris Pkwy, to Gemini Pl, **E** 🚇 BP, Shell/dsl, UDF 🍴 Bonefish Grill, Buffalo Wild Wings, Canes, Carfagna's Kitchen, El Alcapulco, Firehouse Subs, First Watch, Five Guys, McDonald's,

121	Continued
	Mellow Mushroom Pizza, Polaris Grill, Skyline Chili, Starbucks, Steak'n Shake, Subway, Tim Horton's 🏨 Fairfield Inn, Four Points Sheraton, Hampton Inn, Holiday Inn Express, Homewood Suites 🅾 Firestone/auto, Mr Tire, **W** 🚇 BP, Sunoco 🍴 Applebee's, Arby's, Bar Louie, Benihana, Bibibop Asian, BJ's Rest., Brio Grille, Burger King, CA Pizza, Cantina Laredo, Carrabba's, Charley Subs, CheeseCake Factory, Chick-fil-A, Chipotle Mexican, Coldstone, Corner Bakery Cafe, Dave&Buster's, Domino's, El Vaquero Mexican, Firebird's Grill, Honey Baked Ham, Jason's Deli, Jersey Mike's, Jimmy John's, Krispy Kreme, Marcella's Italian, Matt the Miller's Tavern, McDonald's, McKenzie River Pizza, Merlot's Rest., Mimi's Cafe, Mitchell Steaks, MOD Pizza, Molly Woo's, Noodles&Co, O'Charley's, Olive Garden, Panda Express, Panera Bread, Papa John's, Penn Sta Subs, Potbelly's, Qdoba, Quaker Steak, Red Lobster, Red Robin, Rooster's Grill, Sonic, Starbucks, Subway, Taco Bell, TX Roadhouse, Waffle House, Wendy's 🏨 Cambria Suites, Candlewood Suites, Comfort Inn, Extended Stay America, Hilton, Hilton Garden, Residence Inn, Staybridge Suites 🅾 AT&T, AutoZone, Barnes&Noble, Best Buy, BigLots, Cabela's, Costco/gas, Dick's, Field&Stream, funpark, GNC, Hobby Lobby, JC Penney, Jo-Ann Etc, Kroger/gas, Lowe's, Macy's, NTB, Old Navy, Petsmart, Target, TireDiscounters, TJ Maxx, Verizon, Von Maur, Walgreens, World Mkt
119b a	I-270, to Indianapolis, Wheeling
117	OH 161, to Worthington, **E** 🚇 BP/dsl, Shell, Speedway/dsl, Sunoco/dsl 🍴 Burger King, Carfagna's Italian, Casa Hacienda, China Dynasty, Chipotle, Dunkin'/Baskin Robbins, KFC, Massey's Pizza, McDonald's, Penn Sta Subs, Popeye's, Rally's, Red Lobster, Subway, Super Seafood Buffet, Taco Bell, Wendy's, White Castle 🏨 Best Value Inn, Haven Inn, Norwood Inn, Red Roof Inn 🅾 $General, auto repair, CVS Drug, Family$, Walgreens, **W** 🚇 Shell, Speedway/dsl 🍴 Asian Kitchen, China Jade, Domino's, McDonald's, Pizza Hut, Subway, Tim Hortons, Waffle House, Wendy's 🏨 Baymont Inn, Continent Inn, Crowne Plaza, Extended Stay America, Hawthorn Suites, Hometowne Studios, Super 8 🅾 Advance Parts, AutoZone, Chevrolet, Family$, Premier Tire
116	Morse Rd, Sinclair Rd, **E** 🚇 BP, Marathon/dsl, Shell/dsl, Speedway/dsl, Turkey Hill/dsl 🍴 Chipotle, Dunkin'/Robbins Robins, Jimmy John's, Little Caesar's, McDonald's, Papa John's, Subway, Taco Bell, Tim Horton's 🏨 Extend Suites 🅾 $General, $Tree, Buick/GMC, Chrysler/Dodge/Jeep, CVS Drug, Firestone/auto, Ford, Menard's, Mr Tire, PepBoys, Save-A-Lot Foods, URGENT CARE, **W** 🚇 Sunoco 🏨 Best Value Inn, Motel 6 🅾 NTB
115	Cooke Rd
114	N Broadway, **W** 🚇 Sunoco/dsl 🍴 Subway, Tim Horton
113	Weber Rd, **W** 🚇 Speedway/dsl 🅾 Advance Parts

OH

COLUMBUS AREA

OH

INTERSTATE 71 Cont'd

Exit #	Services
112	Hudson St, E Marathon, Shell/dsl Wendy's Holiday Inn Express Family$, W Aldi Foods, Lowe's, NTB
111	17th Ave, W McDonald's Comfort Suites, Days Inn
110b	11th Ave
110a	5th Ave, E Sunoco Royal Fish&Chicken, White Castle, W Exxon Burger King, Church's, KFC, Wendy's AutoZone
109a	I-670
109b	OH 3, Cleveland Ave
109c	Spring St (exits left from sb)
108b	US 40, Broad St, downtown
108a	Main St
101a[70]	I-70 E, US 23 N, to Wheeling
100b a[70]	US 23 S, Front St, High St, downtown
106a	I-70 W, to Indianapolis
106b	OH 315 N, Dublin St, Town St
105	Greenlawn, E Jimmy John's, White Castle Berliner Park, W Marathon
104	OH 104, Frank Rd, W Marathon/Subway/dsl/scales
101b a	I-270, Wheeling, Indianapolis
100	Stringtown Rd, E BP, Tesla EVC Bibibop Asian, Bob Evans, Buffalo Wings & Rings, Charley's Grilled Subs, Chick-fil-A, Chipotle, Coldstone, DQ, El Vaquero Mexican, Five Guys, Fusion Steaks, Honey Baked Ham, Jersey Mike's, Longhorn Steaks, O'Charley's, Olive Garden, Panda Express, Panera Bread, Red Robin, Roosters Grill, Smokey Bones BBQ, Sonic, Starbucks, Steak'n Shake, TX Roadhouse, White Castle Best Western, Candlewood Suites, Courtyard, Drury Inn, Fairfield Inn, Hampton Inn, Hilton Garden, Holiday Inn Express, La Quinta, Quality Inn, Red Roof Inn, SpringHill Suites AT&T, Best Buy, Dick's, Discount Tire, Firestone/auto, GNC, Hobby Lobby, Home Depot, Kohl's, Michael's, Petsmart, Staples, Target, TJ Maxx, Verizon, vet, Walmart/Subway, W BP, GetGo, Speedway/dsl, Sunoco/dsl, Turkey Hill/dsl Applebee's, Arby's, Cane's Chicken Fingers, China Bell, City BBQ, Cracker Barrel, Donato's Pizza, Fazoli's, Golden Corral, IHOP, KFC, Mariachi Mexican, Massey's Pizza, McDonald's, Papa John's, Pizza Hut, Rally's, Ruby Tuesday, Starbucks, Subway, Taco Bell, TeeJaye's Rest., Tim Horton, Waffle House, Wendy's Comfort Inn, Comfort Suites, Days Inn, Motel 6, Travelodge Advance Parts, Aldi Foods, AutoZone, BigLots, CVS Drug, Giant Eagle Foods, GNC, Goodyear/auto, Kroger/dsl, Tuffy Auto, USPO, Walgreens
97	OH 665, London-Groveport Rd, E Marathon/Circle K Arby's, Jimmy John's, KFC, McDonald's, Starbucks, Subway, Sunny St Cafe, Taco Bell, Tim Horton/Wendy's, Waffle House $Tree, Chevrolet, CVS Drug, Kroger/gas/e85, Meijer/e85, Tire Discounters, to Scioto Downs, URGENT CARE, Verizon, vet
94	US 62, OH 3, Orient, E $General, W Sunoco/Subway/dsl Eddie's Repair
84	OH 56, Mt Sterling, E BP/Subway/dsl to Deer Creek SP (9mi)
75	OH 38, Bloomingburg, E fireworks, W Sunoco/dsl
69	OH 41, OH 734, Jeffersonville, E FLYING J/Denny's/dsl/scales/LP/24hr , Walnut Lake Camping, W BP, Shell/Subway/dsl Arby's, Wendy's Quality Inn Family$, Buckeye RV Ctr, Buckeye RV Ctr
68mm	Rs both lanes, full facilities, litter barrels, petwalk, , vending

Exit #	Services
65	US 35, Washington CH, E Shell/dsl, Speedway/Speedy Caf dsl, TA/BP/Pizza Hut/Popeye's/dsl/scales/24hr/@ A&W/KF Bob Evans, Chipotle Mexican, LJ Silver/Taco Bell, McDonald Subway, Waffle House, Wendy's, Werner's BBQ Baymo Inn, Fairfield Inn, Hampton Inn , Tanger Outlets/famo brands, EVC, EVC, Starbucks, Starbucks, W Loves/Har ee's/dsl/scales/24hr EconoLodge
58	OH 72, to Sabina
50	US 68, to Wilmington, E , W BP/DQ/dsl, Hilton/Su way/dsl/scales/24hr, Shell/dsl Max&Erma's, McDonald Wendy's Holiday Inn, repair/tires Robert's Centre
49mm	weigh sta nb
45	OH 73, to Waynesville, E BP, Shell/dsl 73 Grill , Caesar Creek Camping (3mi), Caesar Creek SP (5mi), flea m
36	Wilmington Rd, E Olive Branch Camping, to Ft Ancient St Me
35mm	Little Miami River
34mm	Rs both lanes, full facilities, litter barrels, petwalk, , scenic view, vending
32	OH 123, to Lebanon, Morrow, E FLYING J/Wendy's/d scales/24hr, Marathon, Valero Country Kitchen M gan's Riverside Camping, 3 mi W Bob Evans, Skyline Chi
28	OH 48, S Lebanon, E Speedway/Speedy's Cafe/dsl Di ey's BBQ, Starbucks, White Castle $Tree, Kohl's, Lowe Petsmart, Target, Verizon, W hwy patrol
25	OH 741 N, Kings Mills Rd, E Shell/Popeye's/Dunkin', Spee way/dsl Buffalo Wings&Rings, Chipotle, DQ, El Rancho Nue Jimmy John's, McDonald's, Outback Steaks, Ruby Tuesday, Ta Bell, Wendy's Comfort Suites, Great Wolf Lodge, Kings Isla Resort, Residence Inn Harley-Davidson, USPO, Verizon, W Ameristop/Subway, BP Arby's, Big Boy, Burger King, Pane Bread, Perkins, Pizza Hut, Skyline Chili, Starbucks, Waffle Hou Woodhouse Kitchen Baymont Inn, Hampton Inn, Microtel, S per 8, Tru Hilton CarX, CVS Drug, GNC, Kroger/dsl, vet
24	Western Row, King's Island Dr (from nb), E Sunoco E Grill, Fantastic Wok King's Island Resort
19	US 22, Mason-Montgomery Rd, E Speedway/dsl A by's, Big Boy, Boston Mkt, Burger King, Cane's, Cracker Barr Dunkin', Flipdaddy's Burgers, Fricker's, Golden Corral, Hone Baked Ham, Hot Head Burrito, Iron Chef Grill, KFC, Longho Steaks, McDonald's, Olive Garden, Potbelly, Slim Chicke Taco Bell, Wendy's, White Castle Comfort Inn, Red R Inn, SpringHill Suites, TownePlace Suites Aldi Foods, AT& AutoZone, Barnes&Noble, Best Buy, Buick/GMC, Chevrol Chrysler/Dodge/Jeep, Costco/gas, Firestone/auto, Ford, GM Honda, Infiniti, JC Penney, Kia, Kohl's, Kroger, Lexus, Maze Meijer/dsl, Michael's, Nissan, Old Navy, Petco, Porsche, Su aru, Target, Tire Discounters, Tires+, Toyota, Tuffy Auto, USI Verizon, VW, Walgreens, W BP/dsl, Shell/Dunkin' Bla Pizza, Bravo Italian, Carrabba's, Chick-fil-A, Chipotle Mexica DiBella Subs, Dickey's BBQ, Firebirds Grill, Five Guys, F &Hound Grill, Graeter's Cafe, Hooters, IHOP, Jimmy John's, K wood's Kitchen, Maplewood Kitchen, McAlister's Deli, Missi BBQ, Noodles&Co, O'Charley's, Panda Express, Panera Brea Piada Italian, Popeye's, Qdoba, Red Robin, Rusty Bucket, S line Chili, Steak'n Shake, Taziki's Cafe, Waffle House, Wendy Zoup! Best Western, Drury Inn, Hilton Garden, Holiday Express, Homewood Suites, Hyatt Place, La Quinta, Marri Mason Inn Dick's, Hobby Lobby, Home Depot, Lowe's, M shall's, NAPA, Staples, vet, Walmart/Subway, Whole Foods M
17b a	I-275, to I-75, OH 32
15	Pfeiffer Rd, E , W BP, Shell/dsl, Sunoco/dsl B Evans, Buffalo Wild Wings, City BBQ, Firehouse Grill, Subw

INTERSTATE 71 Cont'd

15	Continued
	🏨 Comfort Inn, Courtyard, Embassy Suites, Holiday Inn Express, Quality Hotel, Red Roof Inn, SpringHill Suites, Wingate Inn
14	OH 126, Reagan Hwy, Blue Ash
12	US 22, OH 3, Montgomery Rd, E 🚪 BP/dsl, Shell/Dunkin'/Subway, Sunoco 🍴 Arby's, Bob Evans, Chipotle Mexican, Chuy's, Coopers Hawk, Currito, Delicious Coal Fired Pizza, Ember's, First Watch, Fusian, Jimmy John's, Outback Steaks, Panera Bread, Penn Sta Subs, Red Lobster 🏨 Hampton Inn 🅾 Tuesday Morning, W 🚪 BP, Marathon 🍴 Cheesecake Factory, Chick-fil-A, Chipotle, Honeybaked Ham, IHOP, Jersey Mike's, Maggiano's, McDonald's, Potbelly, Ruby Tuesday, Starbucks, Taziki's Grill, TX Roadhouse, Wendy's 🏨 Best Western+ 🅾 🅷, AT&T, Dick's, Dillard's, Firestone/auto, Fresh Mkt Foods, Macy's, Marshall's, Old Navy, PepBoys, Staples, Tire Discounters, TJ Maxx, Trader Joe's, Verizon
11	Kenwood Rd, (from nb), W 🅾 🅷, same as 12
10	Stewart Rd (from nb), to Silverton, E 🅾 BMW/Mini, W 🚪 Marathon/dsl
9	Redbank Rd, to Fairfax, (no ez sb return), E 🚪 UDF 🍴 Rally's
8	Kennedy Ave, Ridge Ave W, E 🚪 Meijer/dsl 🍴 IHOP 🏨 Motel 6 🅾 Kroger/dsl, Petsmart, Target, W 🚪 Marathon/dsl, Shell/Subway/Dunkin'/dsl 🍴 Gold Star Chili, Hooligan's, Jack-in-the-Box, LJ Silver, McDonald's, Wendy's, White Castle 🏨 Quality Inn 🅾 $Tree, Aldi Foods, Buick/GMC, Burlington Coats, Home Depot, Lowes Whse, Sumeral Tire
7	(from sb) OH 562, Ridge Ave E, Norwood
6	Edwards Rd, E 🚪 BP, Shell/Popeye's/Dunkin', Speedway/dsl 🍴 BJ's Rest., Boston Mkt, Bravo Italiana, Buca Italian, Buffalo Wild Wings, Capital Grille, Donato's, First Watch, Five Guys, J Alexander's Rest., Jason's Deli, Longhorn Steaks, Marco's Pizza, PF Chang's, Potbelly, Qdoba, Rusty Bucket, Seasons 52 Grill, Starbucks, The Pub 🏨 Courtyard 🅾 AT&T, GNC, Old Navy, REI, SteinMart, TJ Maxx, URGENT CARE, Whole Foods Mkt, W 🚪 Shell
5	Dana Ave, Montgomery Rd, W 🅾 Xavier Univ, Zoo
3	Taft Rd (from sb), W 🅾 U of Cincinnati
2	US 42, Reading Rd, Gilbert ave (from sb), E 🅾 art museum, W 🅾 🅷, ballpark stadium arena, downtown
1k j	I-471 S
1d	Main St, downtown
1c b	Pete Rose Way, Fine St, downtown, stadium
1a	I-75 N, US 50, to Dayton
1	**I-71 S and I-75 S run together.**
0mm	Ohio/Kentucky state line, Ohio River

INTERSTATE 74

Exit #	Services
20	I-75 (from eb), N to Dayton, S to Cincinnati, **I-74 begins/ends on I-75.**
19	Gilmore St, Spring Grove Ave
18	US 27 N, Colerain Ave
17	Montana Ave (from wb), N 🚪 BP
14	North Bend Rd, Cheviot, N 🚪 Shell, Speedway/dsl 🍴 Big Boy, Dunkin', Jersey Mike's, McDonald's, Papa John's, Skyline Chili, Subway, Taco Bell, Wendy's 🅾 Family$, Kroger, Petco, Sam's Club/gas, Tire Discounters, Verizon, Walgreens, S 🚪 Shell 🍴 Bob Evans 🅾 vet
11	Rybolt Rd, Harrison Pike, S 🚪 🍴 Chipotle, Longhorn Steaks, Marco's Pizza, McDonald's, Penn Sta Subs, Sakura Steaks, Skyline Chili, Starbucks, Wendy's, White Castle 🏨 Holiday Inn Express 🅾 AT&T, Kohl's, Meijer/gas, Verizon

9	I-275 N, to I-75, N to Dayton, (exits left from eb)
8mm	Great Miami River
7	OH 128, to Hamilton, Cleves, N 🚪 BP/dsl, Sunoco/dsl 🍴 Wendy's
5	I-275 S, to Kentucky
3	Dry Fork Rd, N 🚪 BP/dsl, S 🚪 Marathon/dsl, Shell/Dunkin'/dsl 🍴 Monk's Kitchen 🅾 vet
2mm	weigh sta eb
1	New Haven Rd, to Harrison, N 🚪 BP/dsl 🍴 Bob Evans, Buffalo Wild Wings, China Garden, Chipotle Mexican, Cracker Barrel, Dunkin', Little Caesar's, O'Charley's, Subway 🏨 Best Western+ 🅾 Ford, Home Depot, Kia, Remke Mkt, Staples, Tires+, URGENT CARE, Verizon, S 🚪 Circle K, Speedway/dsl, Sunoco-White Castle, UDF 🍴 A&W/KFC, Arby's, Big Boy, Burger King, Domino's, DQ, El Mariachi Cantina, Firehouse Subs, Freddy's, Happy Garden, Marco's Pizza, McDonald's, Penn Sta Subs, Pizza Hut, Skyline Chili, Taco Bell, Valle Escondidos, Waffle House, Wendy's 🏨 Holiday Inn Express, Super 8 🅾 $General, $Tree, Advance Parts, AT&T, AutoZone, BigLots, CVS Drug, Family$, Firestone/auto, GNC, Kroger/dsl, Meineke, NAPA, O'Reilly Parts, Sumerel Tire/auto, Tire Discounters, Walgreens
0mm	Ohio/Indiana state line

INTERSTATE 75

Exit #	Services
211mm	Ohio/Michigan state line
210	OH 184, Alexis Rd, to Raceway Park, W 🚪 BP/Circle K/dsl, Pilot/Subway/dsl/scales/24hr 🍴 Arby's, Bob Evans, Burger King, McDonald's, Taco Bell, Wendy's 🏨 Courtyard, Fairfield Inn, Hampton Inn, Holiday Inn Express 🅾 Aldi Foods, AutoZone, Meijer/dsl, Menards, URGENT CARE
210mm	Ottawa River
209	Ottawa River Rd (from nb), E 🚪 BP, Sunoco 🍴 China King, Little Caesar's, Marco's Pizza, River Diner 🅾 Kroger/e85, Rite Aid, Verizon, vet
208	I-280 S, to I-80/90, to Cleveland
207	Stickney Ave, Lagrange St, E 🚪 BP, Stop&Go 🍴 Arby's, KFC, Marco's Pizza, McDonald's, Wendy's 🅾 Family$, Rite Aid
206	to US 24, Phillips Ave, W 🅾 auto repair, transmissions
205b	Berdan Ave, E 🅾 🅷, W 🍴 Burger King, Subway 🅾 $General
205a	to Willys Pkwy, to Jeep Pkwy
204	I-475 W, to US 23 (exits left fom nb), to Maumee, Ann Arbor
203b	US 24, to Detroit Ave, W 🚪 Gas Express/dsl, Sunoco 🍴 KFC, McDonald's, Rally's, Wendy's 🅾 Family$, Rite Aid, U-Haul
203a	Bancroft St, downtown
202	Washington St, Collingwood Ave (from sb, no EZ return), E 🅾 🅷, $Tree, Art Museum, W 🍴 China Star, McDonald's 🅾 $General
201b a	OH 25, Collingwood Ave, W 🅾 Toledo Zoo
200	South Ave, Kuhlman Dr

OH

INTERSTATE 75 Cont'd

Exit #	Services
200mm	Maumee River
199	OH 65, Miami St, to Rossford, E 🛏 Days Inn
198	Wales Rd, Oregon Rd, to Northwood, E 🍴 Mobil/Subway/dsl, S&G/dsl 🍴 Arby's, Arturo's Kitchen, Coney Island, Fried Rice, Jimmy John's 🛏 Best Value Inn, BridgePointe Inn
197	Buck Rd, to Rossford, E 🍴 Shell/dsl 🍴 Tim Horton's, Wendy's, W 🍴 BP, Sunoco/dsl 🍴 Denny's, McDonald's, Subway 🛏 Knights Inn, Motel 6
195	to I-80/90, OH 795, OH Tpk (**toll**), Perrysburg, E 🍴 BP/Subway/dsl 🛏 Country Inn&Suites, Courtyard, Hampton Inn, Staybridge Suites 🅾 Bass Pro Shops, Camping World RV Ctr
193	US 20, US 23 S, Perrysburg, E 🍴 BP/dsl 🍴 Arby's, Big Boy, Bob Evans, Burger King, Chick-fil-A, Chili's, China City, Chipotle, Cocina de Carlos, Cracker Barrel, Dickey's BBQ, First Wok, Five Guys, Fricker's, IHOP, Jimmy John's, KFC, McDonald's, Panda Express, Panera Bread, Penn Sta Subs, Sonic, Starbucks, Subway, Taco Bell, Tim Horton's, Wendy's 🛏 Baymont Inn, Candlewood Suites, Comfort Suites, EconoLodge, Holiday Inn, Quality Inn 🅾 $Tree, Aldi Foods, Belle Tire, Best Buy, Discount Tire, GNC, Hobby Lobby, Home Depot, KOA (7mi), Kohl's, Kroger/gas/e85, Lowe's, Meijer/dsl, Michael's, Petsmart, Target, TJ Maxx, Tuffy, Walgreens, Walmart/Subway, W 🍴 Speedway/dsl 🛏 La Quinta 🅾 AutoZone, Harley-Davidson
192	I-475, US 23 N (exits left from nb), to Maumee, Ann Arbor
187	OH 582, to Luckey, Haskins
181	OH 64, OH 105, to Pemberville, Bowling Green, E 🛏 Holiday Inn Express 🅾 Meijer/dsl/e85, W 🍴 BP/dsl, Circle K/Subway/dsl, Speedway/dsl 🍴 Bob Evans, Buffalo Wild Wings, Burger King, Chipotle Mexican, Coldstone/Tim Horton's, El Zarape Mexican, Fricker's Rest., Jimmy John's, McDonald's, Panera Bread, Penn Sta Subs, Starbucks, Waffle House, Wendy's 🛏 Best Western, Days Inn, Fairfield Inn, Hampton Inn, Home 2 Suites 🅾 H, to Bowling Green State U, USPO, Verizon
179	US 6, to Fremont, Napoleon, E 🅾 museum
179mm	🆁🆂 both lanes, full ♿ facilities, litter barrels, petwalk, 📞, 🚮, vending
175mm	weigh sta nb
171	OH 25, Cygnet
168	Eagleville Rd, Quarry Rd, E 🍴 FuelMart/dsl
167	OH 18, to Fostoria, North Baltimore, E 🍴 Petro/BP/Iron Skillet/dsl/scales/24hr/@ 🍴 McDonald's, W 🍴 ♥Love's/Arby's/dsl/scales/24hr, Sunoco 🅾 $General, Great Scot Mkt
165mm	Rocky Ford River
164	OH 613, to McComb, Fostoria, E 🅾 RV camping, Van Buren SP, W 🍴 Pilot/Subway/Taco Bell/dsl/scales/24hr
162mm	weigh sta sb
161	rd 99, E 🍴 Shell/Subway/dsl, Speedway/Speedy's Cafe/dsl 🛏 Comfort Suites 🅾 Ford/Lincoln, hwy patrol, Kia, URGENT CARE, VW, W 🅾 antiques
159	US 224, OH 15, Findlay, E 🍴 Exxon/dsl, Marathon/dsl, Speedway/Speedy's Cafe/dsl 🍴 Burger King, Culver's, Dakota Grill, Fin's Seafood Grill, Jimmy John's, KFC/LJ Silver, McDonald's, Ming's Great Wall, Pizza Hut, Ralphie's, Steak'n Shake, Subway, Taco Bell, Wendy's 🛏 Drury Inn, Findlay Value Inn, Rodeway Inn, Super 8 🅾 H, Advance Parts, W 🍴 Murphy USA/dsl, Shell/dsl 🍴 Bob Evans, Coldstone/Tim Horton's, Cracker Barrel, Denny's, Hokkaido Steaks, Jac&Do's Pizza, Outback Steaks, Penn Sta Subs, Tony's Rest., TX Roadhouse, Waffle House 🛏 Country Inn&Suites, Hampton Inn, Hilton Garden, Holiday Inn Express, Quality Inn 🅾 AT&T, AutoZone, Best 1 Tires/repair, Chrysler/Dodge/Jeep, Peterbilt, Verizon, Walmart/Subway

Exit #	Services
158mm	Blanchard River
157	OH 12, Findlay, E 🍴 Marathon/dsl, W 🍴 Fricker's Re 🛏 EconoLodge 🅾 vet
156	US 68, OH 15, to Carey, E 🅾 🍴
153mm	🆁🆂 both lanes, full ♿ facilities, litter barrels, petwalk, 📞, 🚮 vending
145	OH 235, to Ada, Mount Cory, E 🅾 Twin Lakes Camping
142	OH 103, to Arlington, Bluffton, E 🍴 Fairway Inn, W 🍴 Marathon/Circle K/dsl, Shell 🍴 Arby's, McDonald's/rv parking Subway, Taco Bell, Wendy's 🛏 Comfort Inn 🅾 $General, au repair, to Bluffton U, vet
140	Bentley Rd, to Bluffton, W 🅾 🍴
135	OH 696, to US 30, to Delphos, Beaverdam, E 🍴 Speedway Speedy's Cafe/dsl/24hr, W 🍴 ✈FLYING J/Denny's/dsl/scale LP/24hr/@, Pilot/McDonald's/Subway/dsl/24hr/@ 🅾 $General, Blue Beacon, SpeedCo, tires, truck repair
134	Napolean Rd (no nb re-entry), to Beaverdam
130	Bluelick Rd, E 🍴 Clark
127b a	OH 81, to Ada, Lima, W 🍴 Fuelstop/dsl 🍴 Subway, Wa House 🛏 Comfort Inn, Red Carpet Inn
126mm	Ottawa River
125	OH 309, OH 117, Lima, E 🍴 Murphy USA/dsl, Speedway Speedy's Cafe/dsl 🍴 Applebee's, Bob Evans, Buffalo Wings Rings, Burger King, Capt D's, China Buffet, China Buffet, Cracker Barrel, El Cazadore, Hunan Garden, McDonald's, Olive Garden, Panera Bread, Red Lobster, Skyline Chili, Subway, Taco Bell, TX Roadhouse, Wendy's 🛏 Courtyard, Hampton Inn, Howard Johnson, Motel 6 🅾 $Tree, Aldi Foods, AT&T, BigLots, For Lincoln, Sam's Club/gas, Verizon, Walgreens, Walmart/Burger King, W 🍴 Arby's, Kewpee Hamburger's, Yamato Stea 🛏 Country Inn&Suites, Holiday Inn, Travelodge 🅾 H, $General, Advance Parts, Best 1 Tires/repair, O'Reilly Parts, Rite A Save-A-Lot Foods, Verizon
124	4th St, E 🅾 Ford/Lincoln, hwy patrol
122	OH 65, Lima, E 🍴 Speedway/Speedy Cafe/dsl, W 🍴 Marathon/Subway/dsl 🅾 Family$, Freightliner, truck repair, Volvo
120	Breese Rd, Ft Shawnee, W 🍴 Shawnee Fuelstop/dsl 🅾 H ley-Harley-Davidson
118	to Cridersville, W 🍴 Casey's/dsl, Fuelmart/Subway/dsl, Spee way/dsl 🅾 $General, Community Mkt, vet
114mm	🆁🆂 both lanes, ♿ facilities, litter barrels, pet walk, 📞, 🚮 vending
113	OH 67, to Uniopolis, Wapakeneta
111	Bellefontaine St, Wahpakeneta, E 🍴 TA/Hub Room Rest./dsl scales/@ 🛏 Red Roof Inn 🅾 KOA, truck tires, W 🍴 Clark/d Murphy USA/dsl, Shell 🍴 Arby's, Bob Evans, Burger King, Ca D's, DQ, El Azteca, Lucky Steer Rest., McDonald's, Pizza H Subway, Taco Bell, Waffle House, Wendy's 🛏 Best Weste Holiday Inn Express, Super 8 🅾 Advance Parts, Aldi Foods, C Drug, Lowe's, Neil Armstrong Museum, O'Reilly Parts, st pat URGENT CARE, Verizon, Walmart
110	US 33, to St Marys, Bellefontaine, E 🅾 hwy patrol, KOA
104	OH 219, W 🍴 Circle K/Subway/dsl, Gulf/dsl, Marath 🛏 Budget Host 🅾 $General
102	OH 274, to Jackson Ctr, New Breman, E 🅾 air stream tours, 🅾 bicycle museum
99	OH 119, to Minster, Anna, E 🍴 99/dsl, Marathon/dsl, 🍴 Shell, Speedway/Taco Bell/dsl 🍴 Subway, Wend 🅾 Family$, lube/wash/repair
94	rd 25A, Sidney, E 🍴 Marathon/deli
93	OH 29, to St Marys, Sidney, W 🅾 Camp Qtokee, Lake Loramie
92	OH 47, to Versailles, Sidney, E 🍴 Speedway/dsl 🍴 Arby China Garden, Coldstone, Fuji Steakhouse, Little Caesar's, S way, Time Horton's, Wendy's 🅾 H, Advance Parts, AutoZo

OH

P E R R Y S B U R G

F I N D L A Y

L I M A

S I D N E Y

⬆N INTERSTATE 75 Cont'd

92 Continued
CVS Drug, NAPA, URGENT CARE, Walgreens, **W** 📱 Murphy USA/dsl, Sunoco/dsl, VP 🍴 Applebee's, Big Boy, Bob Evans, Buffalo Wild Wings, Burger King, Cazadores Mexican, Chipotle, Culver's, Fricker's, Hong Kong Buffet, KFC, McDonald's, Perkins, Pizza Hut, Smokin Jo's BBQ, Taco Bell, Waffle House 🛏 Days Inn, Holiday Inn Express, Motel 6, Quality Inn, Super 8 ⊙ $Tree, Aldi Foods, AT&T, Buick/Cadillac/Chevrolet/GMC, Chrysler/Dodge/Jeep, Ford/Lincoln, Kroger/dsl, Lowe's, Menards, Verizon, Walmart/Subway

90 Fair Rd, to Sidney, **E** 📱 Sunoco/dsl, **W** 📱 Loves/Chester's/Godfather's/Hardee's/dsl/scales/24hr, Marathon/DQ/dsl 🛏 Hampton Inn

88mm Great Miami River

83 rd 25A, Piqua, **W** 📱 Sunoco/MaidRite Cafe/dsl ⊙ Chrysler/Dodge/Jeep, Sherry RV Ctr, to Piqua Hist Area

82 US 36, to Urbana, Piqua, **E** 📱 Marathon, Murphy USA/dsl 🍴 A&W/LJ Silver, Arby's, China East, China Garden, DQ, KFC, Subway, Taco Bell, Waffle House, Wendy's ⊙ $Tree, Aldi Foods, AT&T, BigLots, Harley-Davidson, Home Depot, JoAnn Fabrics, st patrol, Verizon, vet, Walmart/Subway, **W** 📱 Speedway 🍴 Bob Evans, Buffalo Wings&Rings, Cracker Barrel, McDonald's, Red Lobster 🛏 Budgetel, Comfort Inn, La Quinta ⊙ Elder Beerman, JC Penney, Sears/auto

81mm Rs both lanes, full 🚻 facilities, litter barrels, 🎁, 🛢, vending

78 rd 25A, **E** ⊙ H

74 OH 41, to Covington, Troy, **E** 📱 BP/dsl 🍴 Al's Pizza, Golden Bowl, Little Caesar's, McDonald's, Pizza Hut, Subway, Taco Bell ⊙ to Hobart Arena, URGENT CARE, vet, **W** 📱 Circle K/dsl, Shell, Speedway/dsl 🍴 Applebee's, Big Boy, Bob Evans, Buffalo Wild Wings, Burger King, Cassano's Pizza, Chick-fil-A, Chipotle Mexican, Culver's, Fazoli's, Fricker's, J's Cuisine, Jimmy John's, KFC, Logan's Roadhouse, Los Pitayos Mexican, Marion's Pizza, Outback Steaks, Panera Bread, Penn Sta Subs, Ruby Tuesday, Sakai Japanese, Skyline Chili, Starbucks, Steak'n Shake, Tim Horton 🛏 Comfort Suites, Fairfield Inn, Hampton Inn, Holiday Inn Express, Residence Inn, Super 9 ⊙ $General, $Tree, AT&T, AutoZone, GNC, Grismer Auto Service, Kohl's, Lowe's, Meijer/dsl, Petco, Staples, Tire Discounters, Verizon, Walmart/Subway

73 OH 55, to Ludlow Falls, Troy, **E** 📱 BP, Shell 🍴 Asian Cottage, Boston Stoker Coffee House, Honeybaked Ham, Hot Head Burrito, Lincoln Sq Rest., Papa John's, Starbucks, Subway, Waffle House, Wendy's 🛏 Budget Inn, Motel 6, Royal Inn ⊙ $General, Kroger/e85, Verizon

69 rd 25A, **E** 📱 Casey's/dsl, Circle K/dsl, Shell/dsl ⊙ Arbogast RV Ctr, Buick/GMC, Chrysler/Dodge/Jeep, Ford

68 OH 571, to West Milton, Tipp City, **E** 📱 BP/dsl, Shell, Speedway/dsl 🍴 Burger King, Cassano's Pizza, Domino's, Greenfire Bistro, Hickory River BBQ, Hong Kong Kitchen, Hot Head Burritos, McDonald's, Subway ⊙ AT&T, CVS Drug, Family$, FoodTown, Goodyear/auto, Honda, O'Reilly Parts, **W** 📱 Marathon, Speedway/dsl 🍴 Arby's, Big Boy, Bob Evans, Taco Bell, Wendy's 🛏 Holiday Inn Express, La Quinta ⊙ Lee's Garage, Menards, vet

64 Northwoods Blvd, **E** 🍴 El Toro Mexican, Fu Ying ⊙ $Tree, Kroger/dsl, **W** 📱 FLYING J/Subway/dsl/scales/RV dump/24hr

63 US 40, to Donnelsville, Vandalia, **E** 📱 Speedway/dsl 🍴 Bunker's Grill, Dragon China, Fricker's ⊙ AutoZone, O'Reilly Parts, repair, **W** 📱 BP/dsl, Shell, Speedway/dsl 🍴 Arby's, Burger King, Domino's, Hot Head Burrito, KFC/LJ Silver, McDonald's, Pizza Hut, Subway, Taco Bell, Waffle House, Wendy's 🛏 Super 8 ⊙ Goodyear/auto, Rite Aid

61b a I-70, E to Columbus, W to Indianapolis, to Dayton Int Airport

59 Wyse Rd, Benchwood Rd, **E** 🍴 Little York Pizza, Shen's 🛏 Hawthorn Suites, Knights Inn ⊙ BMW/Volvo/VW, Discount Tire, **W** 📱 Speedway/dsl, Valero/dsl 🍴 Arby's, Asian Buffet, Big Boy, Bob Evans, Burger King, Cassano's Pizza, Chick-fil-A, Chipotle Mexican, Coldstone, Cousin Vinny's Puzza, Cracker Barrel, El Toro Mexican, Fazoli's, Fricker's, Golden Corral, Hooters, Longhorn Steaks, McAlister's Deli, McDonald's, O'Charley's, Olive Garden, Outback Steaks, Panera Bread, Red Lobster, Red Robin, Ruby Tuesday, Sake Japanese, Skyline Chili, SmashBurger, SmokeyBones BBQ, Subway, Taco Bell, Tesla EVC, Tim Horton's 🛏 Comfort Inn, Courtyard, Days Inn, Drury Inn, Extended Stay America, Hampton Inn, Home 2 Suites, Motel 6, Quality Inn, Red Lion Inn, Red Roof Inn, Residence Inn, SpringHill Suites, TownePlace Suites ⊙ Office Depot, Sam's Club/gas, Verizon, Walmart/Subway

58 Needmore Rd, to Dayton, **E** 📱 BP/dsl, Shell/McDonald's 🍴 Hardee's ⊙ Goodyear/auto, to AF Museum, **W** 📱 Marathon/dsl, Speedway/Speedy's Cafe, Sunoco/dsl 🍴 A&W/LJ Silver, Church's, Domino's, Subway, Tim Horton's, Waffle House, Wendy's ⊙ $General, $Tree, Advance Parts, auto repair, AutoZone, Family$, Kroger/gas, Midas, O'Reilly Parts, USPO, vet

57b Wagner Ford Rd, Siebenthaler Rd, Dayton

57a Neva Rd

56 Stanley Ave, Dayton, **E** 📱 Shell, **W** 🍴 Dragon City Chinese, Great Steak, McDonald's, Pancake House, Taco Bell 🛏 Dayton Motel

55b a Keowee St, Dayton, downtown

54c OH 4 N, Webster St, to Springfield, downtown

54mm Great Miami River

54b OH 48, Main St, Dayton, **E** 📱 Chevrolet, Honda, **W** ⊙ H, Family$

54a Grand Ave, Dayton, downtown

53b OH 49, 1st St, Salem Ave, Dayton, downtown

53a OH 49, 3rd St, downtown

52b a US 35, E to Dayton, W to Eaton

51 Edwin C Moses Blvd, Nicholas Rd, **E** 🛏 Courtyard, Marriott ⊙ H, to U of Dayton, **W** 📱 BP/dsl, Loves/Hardee's/dsl/scales/24hr 🍴 McDonald's, Wendy's 🛏 Holiday Inn Express ⊙ SunWatch Indian Village

50b a OH 741, Kettering St, Dryden Rd, **E** ⊙ H, vet, **W** 📱 Marathon/dsl 🛏 Red Roof Inn

47 Dixie Dr, W Carrollton, Moraine, **E** 📱 Sunoco/dsl 🍴 Big Boy, Domino's, Waffle House ⊙ $General, auto repair, **W** 📱 Shell/dsl, Speedway/dsl 🍴 El Meson, KFC, McDonald's, Pizza Hut, Sonic, Taco Bell, Wendy's ⊙ $General, USPO

44 OH 725, to Centerville, Miamisburg, **E** 📱 BP/dsl, Shell, Speedway/dsl 🍴 Applebee's, Big Boy, Bonefish Grill, Bravo Italiana, Chick-fil-A, ChuckeCheese, Dunkin'/Baskin-Robbins, El Toro Mexican,

⬆️N INTERSTATE 75 Cont'd

44 Continued
Fazoli's, FirstWatch Cafe, Fricker's, Godfather's, Golden Corral, Hardee's, Jimmy John's, KFC, Logan's Roadhouse, Marion's Pizza, McDonald's, O'Charley's, Olive Garden, Outback Steaks, Panera Bread, Penn Sta Subs, PF Chang's, Red Lobster, Rusty Bucket Grill, Sake Japanese, Skyline Chili, SmashBurger, Starbucks, Steak'n Shake, Subway, Taco Bell, Waffle House, Wendy's 🅛 Comfort Suites, Courtyard, DoubleTree Suites, Extended Stay America, Hampton Inn, Hawthorn Suites, Homewood Suites, InTowne Suites, Motel 6, SpringHill Suites, Studio 6, Woodspring Suites 🅞 🅗, $Tree, Advance Parts, Aldi Foods, AT&T, Audi/VW/Porsche/Jaguar, Barnes&Noble, Best Buy, Burlington Coats, Dick's, Discount Tire, Grismer Auto Service, Hobby Lobby, Home Depot, Honda/Nissan/Mazda, JC Penney, Jo-Ann Fabrics, Kia, Lowe's, Macy's, Menard's, Michael's, Midas, Monro, Office Depot, PepBoys, Petsmart, Target, Tire Discounters, Toyota, Verizon, vet, Walmart, **W** 🅖 BP, Marathon, Shell/dsl 🅗 Bob Evans, LJ Silver, Perkins, Tim Horton's 🅛 Knights Inn, Quality Inn, Red Roof Inn, Super 8 🅞 🅗, $General, CarMax, Chevrolet, Ford, NAPA, transmissions

43 I-675 N, to Columbus

41 Austin Blvd, **E** 🅗 BJ's Rest., Broken Egg Cafe, Chipotle, Chuy's, Coldstone, Dewey's Pizza, Firebirds, Five Guys, Noodles&Co, Panera Bread, Spicy Olive 🅛 Hilton Garden 🅞 AT&T, Field&Stream, GNC, Kohl's, Kroger/dsl, TJ Maxx

38 OH 73, Springboro, Franklin, **E** 🅖 Shell, Speedway/dsl, Thornton's/dsl 🅗 Applebee's, Arby's, Bob Evans, Burger King, China Garden, Chipotle Mexican, KFC, LJ Silver, McDonald's, Papa John's, Pizza Hut, Popeye's, Skyline Chili, Starbucks, Subway, Taco Bell, Tim Horton's, Waffle House, Wendy's 🅛 Hampton Inn, Quality Inn 🅞 Kroger, O'Reilly Parts, Tire Discounters, USPO, vet, **W** 🅖 Murphy USA/dsl, Speedway/dsl, Sunoco 🅗 A&G Pizza, Big Boy, Domino's, El Vaquero Mexican, Gold-Star Chili, Lee's Chicken, McDonald's 🅛 EconoLodge, Holiday Inn Express 🅞 $General, $Tree, Auto Doc, AutoZone, NAPA, URGENT CARE, USPO, Walgreens, Walmart

36 OH 123, to Lebanon, Franklin, **E** 🅖 Marathon/Mom's Rest./dsl, 🅿🅸🅻🅾🆃/Subway/Pizza Hut/dsl/scales/24hr/@, Shell/Wendy's/dsl 🅗 McDonald's, Waffle House 🅛 Motel 6, **W** 🅖 Marathon/White Castle/dsl, Sunoco

32 OH 122, Middletown, **E** 🅗 McDonald's 🅛 Days Inn, Red Roof Inn, Super 8 🅞 🅗, CVS Drug, **W** 🅗 Applebee's, Arby's, Big Boy, Bob Evans, Cracker Barrel, El Rancho Grande, Fricker's, Golden Corral, GoldStar Chili, Hot Head Burritos, KFC, La Rosa's Pizza, O'Charley's, Olive Garden, Sonic, Wendy's, White Castle 🅛 Drury Inn, Fairfield Inn, Hampton Inn, Holiday Inn Express, Quality Inn 🅞 $General, Aldi Foods, AT&T, AutoZone, BigLots, Kohl's, Kroger/dsl, Lowe's, Meijer/dsl, Petco, Staples, Tire Discounters, URGENT CARE, Verizon, Walmart/Subway

29 OH 63, to Hamilton, Monroe, **E** 🅖 Shell/Popeye's/dsl 🅗 Burger King, Chipotle, Culver's, DQ, Dunkin', GoldStar Chili, Skyline Chili, Tim Horton/Wendy's, Waffle House 🅛 Comfort Inn 🅞 Premium Outlets/Famous Brands, Tire Discounters, Trader's World, **W** 🅖 Speedway/dsl 🅗 Froggy's, McDonald's, Richard's Pizza, Subway 🅛 Best Western, Motel 75 🅞 Honda

27.5mm 🆁🆂 both lanes, full ♿ facilities, info, litter barrels, petwalk, 🅒, 🅡, vending

24 OH 129 W, to Hamilton, **E** 🅛 Holiday Inn Express, Hyatt, **W** 🅖 Kroger/dsl, Tesla EVC, UDF 🅗 Buffalo Wings & Rings, Bibibop Asian, Big Boy, Brio Tuscan Grille, Burger King, Chick-fil-A, Coopers Hawk, Donato's Pizza, First Watch, Five Guys, Freddy's,

---

24 Continued
Grand Peking, Hot Head Burritos, Jets Pizza, Kona Grill, McDonald's, MOD Pizza, Popeye's, Qdoba, Rodizio Grill, Rusty Bucket Rest., Starbucks, Starbucks, Taco Bell 🅛 AC Marriott, Home 2 Suites 🅞 $Tree, Cabela's, CVS, Dick's, Dillard's, Kroger, Old Navy, Verizon

22 Tylersville Rd, to Mason, Hamilton, **E** 🅖 Marathon, Thornton's/dsl 🅗 Arby's, Bob Evans, BoneFish Grill, Burger King, Cane's, Chick-fil-A, Chipotle, City BBQ, Firehouse Subs, Fricker's, Graeter's Grill, IHOP, Jack-in-the-Box, Jimmy John's, KFC, LJ Silver, Longhorn Steaks, McAlister's Deli, McDonald's, Miyako Grill, Noodles&Co, Panda Express, Panera Bread, Perkins, Pizza Hut, Skyline Chili, SmashBurger, Soho Japanese, Starbucks, Taco Bell, Taziki Grill, TGIFriday's, Twin Dragon, Waffle House, Wayback Burger, Wendy's 🅞 🅗, AT&T, Big Lots, Discount Tire, Firestone/auto, Fresh Mkt, GNC, Home Depot, Kohl's, Kroger, Michael's, Office Depot, Petsmart, Target, TJ Maxx, URGENT CARE, Walgreens, **W** 🅗 Speedway/dsl 🅛 Sheraton 🅞 Aldi Foods, CarX, Lowe's, Meijer/dsl, Tire Discounters

21 Cin-Day Rd, **E** 🅗 Big Boy 🅛 Quality Inn, **W** 🅗 EVC, Shell/dsl, Speedway/dsl, UDF/Subway/dsl 🅗 Arby's, Domino's, Dunkin', El Rancho Nuevo, La Rosa's Pizza, Little Caesar's, Papa John's, Sonic, Tikka Grill, Waffle House, Wendy's, White Castle 🅞 AutoZone, Christian Bros Automotive, USPO, Walgreens, Walmart/Subway

19 Union Centre Blvd, to Fairfield, **E** 🅗 Bravo Italiana, Chuy's, Mitchell's Fish Mkt, Original Pancakes, Panera Bread, PF Chang's, Red Robin, Smokey Bones BBQ 🅞 AT&T, Barnes&Noble, Verizon, **W** 🅖 BP/dsl, Marathon/Circle K, Shell 🅗 Aladdin's Eatery, Applebee's, Bob Evans, Buffalo Wild Wings, Burger King, Chipotle Mexican, Dingle House, First Watch, Jag's Steaks, Jimmy John's, McDonald's, Mellow Mushroom, Palermo Italian, Rancho Nuevo, Skyline Chili, Starbucks, Subway, Tom+Chee, Uno, Wendy's, Yummy Bowl 🅛 Aloft, Comfort Inn, Courtyard, Hampton Inn, Hilton Garden, Holiday Inn, Homewood Suites, Marriott, Residence Inn, Staybridge Suites 🅞 IKEA, Mercedes, Monro, Volvo

16 I-275 to I-71, to I-74

15 Sharon Rd, to Sharonville, Glendale, **E** 🅖 Sunoco, Thornton's/dsl 🅗 Big Boy, Bob Evans, Cracker Barrel, Ruby Tuesday, Skyline Chili, Subway, Waffle House 🅛 Baymont Inn, Drury Inn, Hawthorn Suites, Hilton Garden, Holiday Inn Express, La Quinta, Quality Inn, Red Roof Inn, Travel Inn, **W** on Kemper 🅗 Sunoco 🅗 Burger King, Cane's, Chick-fil-A, Chili's, ChuckeCheese, Cindy Crab Seafood, Five Guys, Habaneros, LJ Silver, McDonald's, Panera Bread, Penn Sta Subs, Pizza Hut, Taco Bell, Tokyo Japanese, Vincenzo's Italian 🅛 Fairfield Inn, Home Towne Studios, LivInn Suites, Motel 6, Sharonville Hotel, Sonesta Suites 🅞 AT&T, Best Buy, Costco/gas, Hyatt Place Conv Ctr, Lowe's, Nissan, Sam's Club, Target

14 OH 126, to Woodlawn, Evendale, **E** 🅞 GE Plant, **W** 🅗 Sunoco/dsl

13 Shepherd Lane, to Lincoln Heights, **E** 🅞 GE Plant, **W** 🅗 Wendy's

12 Wyoming Ave, Cooper Ave, to Lockland, **W** 🅗 Marathon/dsl

10a OH 126, Ronald Reagan Hwy

10b Galbraith Rd (exits left from nb), Arlington Heights

9 OH 4, OH 561, Paddock Rd, Seymour Ave, **E** 🅞 to Cincinnati Gardens, **W** 🅞 fairgrounds

8 Towne St, Elmwood Pl (from nb)

7 OH 562, to I-71, Norwood, Cincinnati Gardens

6 Mitchell Ave, St Bernard, **E** 🅗 Mobil, Shell, Sunoco 🅗 Popeye's, White Castle 🅛 Quality Inn 🅞 to Cincinnati Zoo, Xavier U, Walgreens, **W** 🅖 BP/dsl 🅗 Gold Star Chili, McDonald's, Rally's 🅞 Advance Parts, Family$, Ford, Honda, Hyundai, Kia, Kroger, Tires+, **S** 🅞 AutoZone

⬆N INTERSTATE 75 Cont'd

Exit #	Services
4	I-74 W, US 52, US 27 N, to Indianapolis
3	to US 27 S, US 127 S, Hopple St, E 🍴 Big Boy, White Castle 🛏 Budget Host 🅾 �H, U of Cincinnati, W 🅿 Shell 🍴 Wendy's
2b	Harrison Ave, W 🅿 🅾 Family$, industrial district
2a	Western Ave, Liberty St (from sb)
1g	Ezzard Charles Dr ((from sb), W 🛏 Quality Inn
1f	US 50W, Freeman Ave (from sb), W 🅿 Marathon/dsl, Shell/Subway 🍴 Big Boy, Taco Bell, Wendy's, White Castle 🛏 Quality Inn 🅾 Ford, NAPA, USPO
1e	7th St (from sb), downtown
1c	5th St, E 🛏 Hilton, Hyatt, Millennium Hotel, Westin 🅾 to Duke Energy Center, downtown
1a	I-71 N, to Cincinnati, downtown, to stadium
0mm	Ohio/Kentucky state line, Ohio River

⬆E INTERSTATE 76

Exit #	Services
65	Ohio/Pennsylvania state line. **See OH TPK, exits 232-234.**
60mm	I-76 eb joins Ohio TPK **(toll)**
57	to OH 45, Bailey Rd, to Warren
54	OH 534, to Newton Falls, Lake Milton, N 🅾 RV camping, S 🅿 Sunoco/dsl 🅾 to Berlin Lake
52mm	Lake Milton
48	OH 225, to Alliance, N 🅾 to W Branch SP, S 🅾 to Berlin Lake, to Lake Milton SP
45mm	Rs both lanes, full ♿ facilities, litter barrels, petwalk, 🅲, 🖼
43	OH 14, to Alliance, Ravenna, N 🅾 to W Branch SP, S 🅿 Marathon/Subway/dsl 🍴 fireworks
38b a	OH 5, OH 44, to Ravenna, N 🅿 BP/dsl, Speedway/dsl 🍴 Arby's, McDonald's/rv parking, Wendy's, S 🅿 Marathon/Circle K 🍴 Cracker Barrel 🅾 �H, $General, auto parts, Giant Eagle Foods, RV camping
33	OH 43, to Hartville, Kent, N 🅿 BP/dsl 🍴 Los Girasoles Mexican 🛏 Comfort Inn, Days Inn, EconoLodge, Hampton Inn, Holiday Inn Express, Super 8 🅾 to Kent St U, S 🅿 Circle K, Speedway/dsl 🍴 Gionino's Pizza, McDonald's, Pizza Hut, Subway, Wendy's 🅾 $General, Goodyear Tire/brakes, vet
31	rd 18, Tallmadge, N 🅿 Murphy USA/dsl 🍴 #1 Chinese, Applebee's, Arby's, Beef'O'Brady's, Chipotle, DQ, La Terraza Mexican, Panera Bread 🅾 $Tree, AT&T, GNC, Kohl's, Lowe's, Marshall's, Petco, Verizon, Walmart/Subway
29	OH 532, Tallmadge, Mogadore
27	OH 91, Canton Rd, Gilchrist Rd, N 🍴 Bob Evans, S 🅿 Marathon/Subway/dsl 🍴 Hardee's 🛏 EconoLodge
26	OH 18, E Market St, Mogadore Rd, N 🅿 Marathon/dsl 🅾 Hamad Tire/repair, S 🍴 Arby's, Dunkin', McDonald's, Subway, Wendy's 🅾 $General
25b a	Martha Ave, General St, Brittain, N 🅿 Circle K/dsl 🛏 Hilton Garden 🅾 Mercedes, Toyota, S 🅾 Goodyear HQ
24	Arlington St, Kelly Ave, S 🅾 Goodyear HQ
23b	OH 8, Buchtell Ave, to Cuyahoga (exits left from eb), to U of Akron
23a	I-77 S, to Canton
22a	Main St, Broadway, N 🅾 Aldi Foods, downtown
21c	OH 59 E, Dart Ave, N 🅾 �H
21b	Lakeshore St, Bowery St (from eb)
21a	East Ave (from wb)
20	I-77 N (from eb), to Cleveland
19	Battles Ave, Kenmore Blvd
18	I-277, US 224 E, to Canton, Barberton

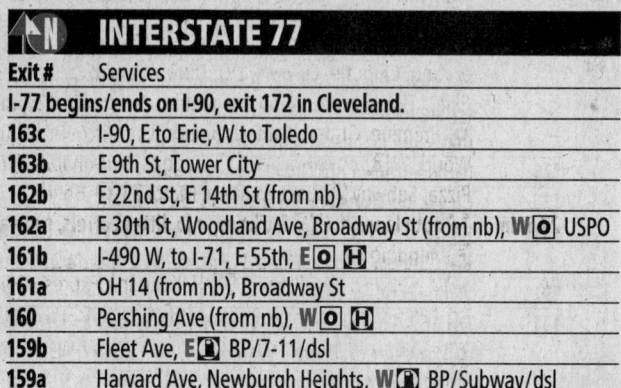

Exit #	Services
17b	OH 619, Wooster Rd, S 🅿 Sunoco/dsl 🅾 �H, tires/repair
17a	(from eb, no return) State St, to Barberton, S 🍴 Papa John's, Papa Roni's Pizza 🅾 �H, Walgreens
16	Barber Rd, S 🅿 Rocky's/dsl/e85 🍴 DQ, Tomaso's Italian 🅾 Chrysler/Dodge/Jeep
14	Cleve-Mass Rd, to Norton, S 🅿 BP/dsl, Circle K/dsl 🍴 Arby's, Casa Del Mar Mexican, Marco's Pizza, McDonald's, Ming Garden, Pizza Hut, Subway, Wendy's 🅾 $General, Ace Hardware, Acme Fresh Mkt, Advance Parts, CVS Drug, Ritzman Drug, USPO, Verizon
13b a	OH 21, N to Cleveland, S to Massillon
11	OH 261, Wadsworth, N 🅿 Speedway/dsl, S 🅿 GetGo/e85, Giant Eagle 🍴 Antonio's Pizza, Beef'O'Brady's, Wayback Burger 🅾 AAA, GNC, Kohl's, Lowe's, PetCo, Target, Verizon
9	OH 94, to N Royalton, Wadsworth, N 🅿 GetGo, Marathon/Circle K 🍴 Applebee's, Arby's, Bob Evans, Burger King, China Express, Chipotle Mexican, El Rincon Mexican, Galaxy Rest., Little Caesar's, Marie's Cafe, McDonald's, Panera Bread, Pizza Hut, Romeo's Pizza, Starbucks, Taco Bell, Wendy's 🛏 Comfort Inn, Holiday Inn Express 🅾 $Tree, Aldi Foods, BigLots, Buehler's Foods, DrugMart, Goodyear/auto, Home Depot, NTB, Verizon, Walmart/Subway, S 🅿 Marathon/DQ/dsl, Sunoco 🍴 Casa Del Rio, Dunkin', KFC, Papa John's 🛏 Legacy Inn 🅾 Advance Parts, auto repair, AutoZone, CVS Drug, Rite Aid, vet
7	OH 57, to Rittman, Medina, N 🅿 Marathon/dsl, S 🅾 �H, 🖼
6mm	weigh sta eb
2	OH 3, to Medina, Seville, N 🅿 Marathon/Circle K/dsl 🍴 Digsby Pizza, DQ, Hardee's, Huddle House, Subway 🛏 Hawthorn Suites, Quality Inn 🅾 Maple Lakes Camping (seasonal), S 🅿 Clark, Shell/dsl 🍴 #1 Chinese, E of Chicago Pizza, El Patron Mexican 🅾 $General
1	I-76 E, to Akron, US 224, W on US 224 🅿 Pilot/Subway/dsl/scales/24hr, TA/BP/Burger King/Popeye's/dsl/scales/24hr/@ 🍴 Arby's, McDonald's, Starbucks 🛏 Super 8 🅾 Blue Beacon, Chippewa Valley Camping (1mi), SpeedCo
0mm	**I-76 begins/ends on I-71, exit 209.**

⬆N INTERSTATE 77

Exit #	Services
I-77 begins/ends on I-90, exit 172 in Cleveland.	
163c	I-90, E to Erie, W to Toledo
163b	E 9th St, Tower City
162b	E 22nd St, E 14th St (from nb)
162a	E 30th St, Woodland Ave, Broadway St (from nb), W 🅾 USPO
161b	I-490 W, to I-71, E 55th, E 🅾 �H
161a	OH 14 (from nb), Broadway St
160	Pershing Ave (from nb), W 🅾 �H
159b	Fleet Ave, E 🅿 BP/7-11/dsl
159a	Harvard Ave, Newburgh Heights, W 🅿 BP/Subway/dsl

AKRON
OH

🅿 = gas 🍽 = food 🛏 = lodging 🅾 = other 🆁🆂 = rest stop   Copyright 2022 - The Next EXIT ⓡ

INTERSTATE 77 Cont'd

CLEVELAND

Exit #	Services
158	Grant Ave, Cuyahoga Heights
157	OH 21, OH 17 (from sb), Brecksville Rd
156	I-480, to Youngstown, Toledo
155	Rockside Rd, to Independence, **E** 🍽 Shell, Sunoco/dsl 🍽 Aladdin's, Bob Evans, Bonefish Grill, Chipotle, Delmonico's Steaks, Denny's, DiBella's Subs, Jimmy John's, McDonald's, Melt Grill, Outback Steaks, Panera Bread, Potbelly, Red Robin, Shula's Steaks, Starbucks, Wendy's, Winking Lizard Grill, Zoup! 🛏 Comfort Inn, DoubleTree, Embassy Suites, Holiday Inn, La Quinta, Red Roof Inn, SpringHill Suites 🅾 AT&T, Drugmart, to Cuyahoga Valley NP, Verizon, Walgreens, **W** 🍽 Applebee's, Longhorn Steaks, Wasabi Steaks 🛏 Courtyard, Crowne Plaza, Hampton Inn, Home 2 Suites, Hyatt Place, Residence Inn
153	Pleasant Valley Rd, to Independence, 7 Hills
151	Wallings Rd
149	OH 82, to Broadview Heights, Brecksville, **1 mi E** 🍽 Shell/dsl 🍽 Austin's Grille, Courtyard Cafe, Panera Bread, Sakura Japanese, Simon's Rest., Starbucks, Subway 🅾 CVS Drug, Marc's Foods, vet, Walgreens, **W** 🍽 BP, GetGo/dsl 🍽 Bob Evans, Chipotle, McDonald's, Starbucks, Wild Eagle Steaks 🅾 Giant Eagle Foods
147	to OH 21, Miller Rd (from sb)
146	I-80/Ohio Tpk, to Youngstown, Toledo
145	OH 21 (from nb), **E** 🍽 🍽/Wendy's/dsl/scales 🍽 Cozumel Mexican, Subway 🛏 Days Inn, Hampton Inn, Holiday Inn Express, Motel 6, Super 8
144	I-271 N, to Erie
143	OH 176, to I-271 S, **W** 🍽 Shell 🍽 McDonald's, Panda Chinese, Richfield Cafe, Subway, Teresa's Pizza
141mm	🆁🆂 both lanes, full ♿ facilities, litter barrels, petwalk, 🍽, 🅿, vending
138	Ghent Rd, **W** 🍽 Circle K/dsl 🍽 Gasoline Alley, Lanning's Rest.

FAIRLAWN

Exit #	Services
137b a	OH 18, to Fairlawn, Medina, **E** 🍽 Circle K, GetGo, Shell, Speedway 🍽 Applebee's, A-Wok, Bob Evans, Boston Mkt, Bravo Italiana, Burntwood Tavern, Chick-fil-A, Chili's, Chipotle Mexican, Coldstone, Cracker Barrel, Donato's Pizza, First Watch, Five Guys, Fleming's Steaks, Gionino's Pizza, HoneyBaked Ham, Hyde Park Grille, Jimmy John's, Macaroni Grill, McDonald's, Menchie's, Olive Garden, Pad Thai, Panera Bread, Penn Sta Subs, PF Chang's, Red Lobster, Robeck's FruitJuice, Starbucks, Steak'n Shake, Subway, Taco Bell, Wendy's, Winking Lizard Grill, Zoup! 🛏 Courtyard, DoubleTree, EconoLodge, Fairfield Inn, Hampton Inn, Hilton, Holiday Inn, Homewood Suites, Motel 6, Quality Inn 🅾 $Tree, Acme Fresh Mkt, Aldi Foods, AT&T, Barnes&Noble, Best Buy, Dick's, Dillard's, Earth Fare Foods, Ford, Giant Eagle Foods, Goodyear/auto, Hobby Lobby, Home Depot, JC Penney, Jo-Ann Fabrics, Lowe's, Macy's, Michael's, NTB, Old Navy, Petsmart, Sam's Club, Staples, TJ Maxx, Verizon, Walmart, World Mkt, **W** 🍽 Sunoco 🍽 DQ, Hooley House Rest., Kingfish Rest., Longhorn Steaks, Outback Steaks, Tres Potrillos, Wasabi Grill 🛏 Baymont Inn, Best Western+, Extended Stay America, Extended Stay America 2, Fairbridge Suites, Radisson, Residence Inn, Super 8 🅾 🏥
136	(exits left from nb) OH 21S, to Massillon
135	Cleveland-Massillon Rd (from nb, no return)
133	Ridgewood Rd, Miller Rd, **E** 🍽 Circle K/dsl, **W** 🍽 Old Carolina BBQ, Teresa's Pizza, Tiffany's Bakery 🅾 Conrad's Automotive
132	White Pond Dr, Mull Ave
131	OH 162, Copley Rd, **E** 🍽 Circle K 🍽 China Star, Little Caesar's 🅾 Save-A-Lot Foods, Walgreens, **W** 🍽 BP/dsl 🍽 McDonald's, Pizza Hut 🅾 vet

AKRON

Exit #	Services
130	OH 261, Wooster Ave, **E** 🍽 Circle K, Sunoco/dsl 🍽 Ann's Place, Burger King, Church's, McDonald's, New Ming Chinese, Rally's, Subway 🅾 Advance Parts, AutoZone, O'Reilly Parts, 🅾 Chevrolet, Toyota, U-Haul
129	I-76 W, to I-277, to Kenmore Blvd, Barberton

I-77 S and I-76 E run together. See I-76, exits 21a-22b.

Exit #	Services
125b	I-76 E, to Youngstown, I-77 and I-76 run together
125a	OH 8 N, to Cuyahoga Falls, 🅾 U of Akron
124b	Lover's Lane, Cole Ave
124a	Archwood Ave, Firestone Blvd (from sb)
123b	OH 764, Wilbeth Rd, **E** 🍽 DQ 🅾 to 🛏
123a	Waterloo Rd (from sb), **W** 🍽 BP, GetGo 🍽 Burger King, House of Hunan, Hungry Howies, Mi Casa, Papa John's, Rally's, Subway, Waterloo Rest. 🅾 $General, $Tree, Big Lots, Giant Eagle Foods, GNC, Marc's Mkt, Rite Aid, Walgreens
122b a	I-277, US 224 E, to Barberton, Mogadore
120	Arlington Rd, to Green, **E** 🍽 Speedway/dsl 🍽 Applebee's, Denny's, Golden Corral, IHOP, Jimmy John's, Mr Hero, Shogun, Starbucks, Waffle House 🛏 EconoLodge, Red Roof Inn 🅾 AT&T, AutoZone, Home Depot, Kohl's, O'Reilly Parts, Staples, Walmart/Subway, **W** 🍽 🍽 Bob Evans, Burger King, Chipotle Mexican, CiCi's Pizza, McDonald's, Panera Bread, Subway, Taco Bell, TGIFriday's, Wendy's 🛏 Fairfield Inn, Hampton Inn, Holiday Inn Express, Residence Inn, Woodspring Suites 🅾 $Tree, Acura, Buick/GMC, Camping World RV Ctr, Chevrolet, Circle K, GNC, Goodyear/auto, Honda, Hyundai, Infiniti, Lexus, Lowe's, Nissan, Subaru, Target, Verizon
118	OH 241, to OH 619, Massillon, **E** 🍽 Sheetz/dsl, Speedway/dsl 🍽 Gionino's Pizza, Handel's Ice Cream, Hunan Dragon, Subway, **W** 🍽 Circle K/dsl, GetGo, Tesla EVC 🍽 Arby's, DQ, Dunkin', Hungry Howie's, Jimmy John's, Kasai Japanese, Lucky Star Chinese, McDonald's, Menches Rest., Starbucks, Subway, Tom Chee Cafe 🛏 Cambria Suites, Super 8 🅾 🏥, $General, Acme Fresh Mkt, Advance Parts, Aldi Foods, Conrad Automotive, CVS Drug, Giant Eagle Foods
113	**W** 🛏 Hilton Garden 🅾 Akron-Canton Airport, General RV Ctr (2mi)
112	Shuffel St, **E** 🛏 Embassy Suites
111	Portage St, N Canton, **E** 🍽 Circle K, Sunoco/dsl, TA/Country Pride/dsl/scales/24hr/@ 🍽 Burger King, KFC, Palombo Italian, Quaker Steak, Subway, Sylvester's Italian 🅾 Mr Tire, TrueValue, **W** 🍽 BP/dsl, Speedway/dsl 🍽 Aladdin's Eatery, BJ's Rest., Bonefish Grill, Carrabba's, ChuckeCheese, Coldstone, Cracker Barrel, Dunkin'/Baskin-Robbins, Five Guys, IHOP, Longhorn Steaks, McDonald's, Menchie's, Outback Steaks, Panera Bread, Red Robin, Rockne's Cafe, Romeo's Pizza, Samantha's Rest., Starbucks, Taco Bell, Wasabi Japanese, Wendy's, Zoup 🛏 Best Western+, Microtel, Rodeway Inn 🅾 AAA, AT&T, Best Buy, BJ's Whse, Book A Million, Chevrolet, DrugMart, Giant Eagle Foods, Goodyear/auto, Harley-Davidson, Home Depot, Lowe's, Marshall's, Michael's, Old Navy, Sam's Club/gas, Walgreens, Walmart/Subway

CANTON

Exit #	Services
109b a	Everhard Rd, Whipple Ave, **E** 🍽 Marathon/Subway/dsl, Speedway/dsl 🍽 Denny's, Fat Head's Brewery, Fazoli's, Jersey Mike's, Moe's SW, Waffle House 🛏 Baymont Inn, Comfort Inn, Fairfield Inn, Hampton Inn, Home 2 Suites, Hyatt Place, Residence Inn, Staybridge Suites 🅾 Buick/GMC, Ford, **W** 🍽 Marathon 🍽 A-Japanese Steaks, Applebee's, Arby's, Bob Evans, Bravo Italian, Brown Derby, Buffalo Wild Wings, Buffet Dynasty, Burnt Wood Tavern, Cane's, Chick-fil-A, Chili's, Chipotle Mexican, CiCi's Pizza, DiBella Subs, Dunkin', Firehouse Subs, Golden Corral, HoneyBaked Ham, Jerzees Grille, Jimmy John's, Katana Buffet, KFC

OH

🔼🔽 INTERSTATE 77 Cont'd

109b a Continued

McDonald's, Mission BBQ, Mr Hero, Mulligan's, Olive Garden, Original Steaks & Hoagies, Panda Express, Panera Bread, Papa Bear's, Papa Gyros, Penn Sta Subs, Pizza Hut, Red Lobster, Robek's, Ruby Tuesday, Sahara Grill, Sakura Japanese, Starbucks, Steak'n Shake, Subway, Taco Bell, TGIFriday's, TX Roadhouse 🅛 Courtyard, Holiday Inn, Knights Inn, Quality Inn, Ramada, Red Roof Inn, SpringHill Suites 🅞 $Tree, Aldi Foods, AT&T, Burlington Coats, Dick's, Dillard's, Firestone/auto, Goodyear/auto, Jo-Ann Fabrics, Kohl's, Macy's, Magnuson, Marc's Foods, NTB, Petsmart, Target, TJ Maxx, Tuesday Morning, Verizon, World Mkt

107b a US 62, OH 687, Fulton Rd, to Alliance, **E** 🅖 Marathon/Circle K/Subway 🅕 Jerzee's Grille 🅞 city park, **W** 🅖 Circle K/Dunkin' 🅞 Pro Football Hall of Fame

106 13th St NW, **E** 🅞 🅷

105b OH 172, Tuscarawas, St, **E** 🅕 Lindsey's, McDonald's, **W** 🅕 KFC, Subway 🅞 AutoZone, CVS

105a 6th St SW (no EZ return from sb), **E** 🅖 Sunoco 🅕 McDonald's 🅞 Ford, **W** 🅕 Subway 🅞 🅷, AutoZone

104b a US 30, US 62, to E Liverpool, Massillon

103 OH 800 S, **E** 🅖 Marathon/Subway/dsl, Speedway 🅕 Arby's, DQ, Italo's Pizza, McDonald's, Peking Chinese, Taco Bell, Waffle House 🅞 $Tree, Advance Parts, auto repair, Family$, Goodyear/auto, O'Reilly Parts, Save-A-Lot Foods, **W** 🅞 Firestone

101 OH 627, to Faircrest St, **E** 🅖 Pilot/Subway/dsl/scales/24hr, Speedway/McDonald's 🅕 Wendy's 🅛 Fairfield Inn

99 Fohl Rd, to Navarre, **E** 🅞 KOA (4mi), **W** 🅖 Sunoco

93 OH 212, to Zoar, Bolivar, **E** 🅖 Speedway/dsl 🅕 McDonald's, Pizza Hut, Wendy's 🅛 Sleep Inn 🅞 $General, Giant Eagle Foods, NAPA, to Lake Atwood Region, vet, Zoar Tavern HS (3mi), **W** 🅖 Marathon/DQ/Subway/dsl

87 US 250W, to Strasburg, **W** 🅖 BP/Taco Bell/dsl, Marathon/dsl 🅕 Hardee's, Manor Rest., McDonald's, Subway 🅛 Ramada Ltd 🅞 Family$, Verizon

85 Schneiders Crossing Rd, to Dover, **E** 🅖 Marathon 🅕 Freddy's, Subway 🅞 Buehler's Mkt/gas

83 OH 39, OH 211, to Sugarcreek, Dover, **E** 🅖 BP/dsl, Speedway/Speedy's Cafe/dsl 🅕 Bob Evans, KFC, McDonald's, Shoney's, Wendy's 🅛 77 Inn/Grill 🅞 🅷, Chrysler/Dodge/Jeep, Flynn's Tires, Ford, Honda, Lincoln, Nissan, **W** 🅛 Comfort Inn, Country Inn&Suites 🅞 vet

81 US 250, to Uhrichsville, OH 39, New Philadelphia, **E** 🅖 Sheetz/dsl, Speedway 🅕 Buffalo Wild Wings, Burger King, Denny's, El San Jose Mexican, Hog Heaven BBQ, LJ Silver, Pizza Hut, Starbucks, Taco Bell, TX Roadhouse 🅛 Best Western, Hampton Inn, Holiday Inn Express, Schoenbrunn Inn, Travelodge 🅞 $General, $Tree, Advance Parts, Aldi Foods, BigLots, O'Reilly Parts, Walmart/Subway, **W** 🅖 Eagle TP/rest./dsl/scales/24hr 🅞 Harley-Davidson

73 OH 751, to rd 53, Stone Creek, **W** 🅖 Marathon/dsl

65 US 36, Port Washington, Newcomerstown, **W** 🅖 BP, Duke TP/rest./dsl, Speedway/Wendy's 🅕 McDonald's, Taco Bell 🅛 Hampton Inn, Super 8

64mm Tuscarawas River

54 OH 541, rd 831, to Plainfield, Kimbolton, **W** 🅖 BP

47 US 22, to Cadiz, Cambridge, **E** 🅞 to Salt Fork SP (6mi), **W** 🅖 BP/repair 🅞 🅷, to Glass Museum

46b a US 40, to Old Washington, Cambridge, **W** 🅖 Marathon/Wendy's/dsl, Speedway/dsl 🅕 Burger King, Hunan Chinese, Lee's Rest., LJ Silver, McDonald's 🅞 Family$, Riesbeck's Food

44b a I-70, E to Wheeling, W to Columbus

41 OH 209, OH 821, Byesville, **W** 🅖 BP, Circle K, Clark 🅕 McDonald's, Subway 🅞 $General, Family$, museum

39mm 🆁🆂 nb, full ♿ facilities, litter barrels, petwalk, 🅒, 🏕, vending

37 OH 313, Buffalo, **E** 🅖 🅕 Dough Boys Pizza, Subway 🅞 to Senecaville Lake, UPSO

36mm 🆁🆂 sb, full ♿ facilities, litter barrels, petwalk, 🅒, 🏕, vending

28 OH 821, Belle Valley, **E** 🅖 Sunoco/dsl 🅞 RV camping, to Wolf Run SP, USPO

25 OH 78, Caldwel, **E** 🅖 Pilot/Arby's/dsl/scales/24hr, Sunoco/Subway/dsl 🅕 DQ, Lori's Rest., McDonald's 🅛 Best Western, Days Inn, Microtel, **W** 🅛 Comfort Inn

16 OH 821, Macksburg

6 OH 821, to Devola, **E** 🅖 BP/Subway/dsl, **W** 🅖 Marathon/dsl/LP 🅞 🅷

3mm 🆁🆂 nb, full ♿ facilities, info, litter barrels, petwalk, 🅒, 🏕, vending

1 OH 7, to OH 26, Marietta, **E** 🅖 GoMart/dsl/24hr 🅕 DQ, IHOP, Subway 🅛 Baymont Inn, Comfort Suites, Fairfield Inn, Holiday Inn Express, Quality Inn, Red Roof Inn 🅞 $Tree, Aldi Foods, Buick/GMC, Cadillac/Chevrolet, Chrysler/Dodge/Jeep, Ford, Lincoln, GNC, Lowe's, Toyota, Walmart/McDonald's, **W** 🅖 BP/dsl, GetGo/dsl, Marathon/dsl, Speedway/dsl 🅕 Applebee's, Arby's, Biscuit World, Bob Evans, Burger King, Capt D's, China Fun, E Chicago Pizza, Empire Buffet, KFC, Las Trancas Mexican, Little Caesar's, LJ Silver, McDonald's, Napoli's Pizza, Papa John's, Pizza Hut, Qdoba, Shogun Hibachi, Shoney's, Subway, Taco Bell, Wendy's 🅛 Hampton Inn, Microtel, Super 8 🅞 Advance Parts, AT&T, AutoZone, Big Lots, Family$, JoAnn Fabrics, Kroger, Rite Aid, TrueValue, Verizon, Walgreens

0mm Ohio/West Virginia state line, Ohio River

🔼▶ INTERSTATE 80

Exit #	Services
237mm	Ohio/Pennsylvania state line
237mm	Welcome Ctr wb, full ♿ facilities, info, litter barrels, petwalk, 🅒, 🏕, vending
234b a	US 62, OH 7, Hubbard, to Sharon, PA, Hubbard, **N** 🅖 Flying J/Denny's/dsl/LP/scales/24hr, Shell/rest./dsl/scales/motel/24hr/@ 🅕 Arby's, Burger King, Dunkin', McDonald's, Waffle House 🅛 Best Western, Travelodge 🅞 Blue Beacon, Homestead RV Ctr., tire/dsl repair, **S** 🅖 Loves/Chester's/Subway/dsl/scales/ 24hr 🅞 Chevrolet
232mm	weigh sta wb
229	OH 193, Belmont Ave, to Youngstown, **N** 🅖 GetGo, Speedway/dsl 🅕 Chad Anthony's Italian, Fortune Garden, Handel's Ice Cream, Sta Square Italian, Subway 🅛 Comfort Suites, Hampton Inn, Motel 6, Rodeway Inn 🅞 Giant Eagle Foods,

MARIETTA

CAMBRIDGE

OH

▲E INTERSTATE 80 Cont'd

229	Continued
	S 🅖 BP/dsl, Shell 🍴 Arby's, Bob Evans, Denny's, El Tapatio, Golden Hunan Chinese, Happy Buffet, Jimmy's Italian, KFC, Little Caesar's, LJ Silver, McDonald's, Nonni's Ristorante, Pizza Hut, Señor Jalapeño Mexican, Subway, Taco Bell, Tim Horton, Uptown Pizza, Wendy's 🛏 Days Inn, Quality Inn Ⓞ $General, $Tree, Advance Parts, Aldi Foods, AutoZone, Firestone/auto, Goodyear/auto, O'Reilly Parts, Rite Aid, SaveALot Foods, USPO, vet, Walgreens, Walmart/Subway
228	OH 11, to Warren (exits left from eb), Ashtabula
227	US 422, Girard, Youngstown, N 🅖 Shell/dsl, Sunoco 🍴 Burger King, DQ, El Torero, JibJab Hotdogs, Subway
226	Salt Springs Rd, to I-680 (from wb), N 🅖 BP/Dunkin'/dsl, Sheetz/dsl 🍴 McDonald's, Waffle House Ⓞ vet, S 🅖 Mr Fuel/Road Rocket Diner/dsl/24hr, Petro/Shell/Iron Skillet/dsl/scales/24hr/@, 🅿️Pilot/Subway/dsl/scales/24hr Ⓞ Blue Beacon, Quality Truckwash, SpeedCo
224b	I-680 (from eb), to Youngstown
224a	OH 11 S, to Canfield
223	OH 46, to Niles, N 🅖 Country Fair/dsl, 🅿️Pilot/McDonald's/dsl/scales/24hr 🍴 Bob Evans, Dunkin', IceHouse Rest., Los Girasoles 🛏 California Palms, Candlewood Suites, Comfort Inn, Holiday Inn Express, S 🅖 BP/Subway/dsl, Sunoco, TA/Counry Pride/dsl/scales/24hr/@ 🍴 Arby's, Cracker Barrel, LJ Silver, Taco Bell, Perkins, Quaker Steak&Lube, Starbucks, Wendy's 🛏 Country Inn&Suites, Fairfield Inn, Hampton Inn, Quality Inn, Sleep Inn, Super 8 Ⓞ Freightliner, Harley-Davidson
221mm	Meander Reservoir
219mm	I-80 wb joins Ohio Tpk (toll)
	For I-80 exits 2-218, see Ohio Turnpike.

▲E INTERSTATE 90

Exit #	Services
244mm	Ohio/Pennsylvania state line
242mm	🆁🆂/weigh sta wb, full 🅰️ facilities, info, litter barrels, petwalk, Ⓒ, 🏧
241	OH 7, to Andover, Conneaut, N 🍴 Burger King, McDonald's (2mi) 🛏 Days Inn Ⓞ 🅷, AutoZone, Evergreen RV Park, S 🅖 ♥Loves♥/McDonald's/Subway/dsl/scales/24hr
235	OH 84, OH 193, to Youngstown, N Kingsville, N 🅖 Grab&Go/gas, Marathon/Circle K 🛏 Dav-Ed Motel Ⓞ Village Green Camping (2mi), S 🅖 Circle K/Subway/dsl, TA/BP/Burger King/dsl/scales/24hr/@ 🍴 Kay's Place Diner 🛏 Kingsville Motel Ⓞ towing/repair
228	OH 11, to Ashtabula, Youngstown, N Ⓞ 🅷 (4mi)
223	OH 45, to Ashtabula, N 🅖 *FLYING J*/Denny's/Shell/dsl/LP/scales/24hr 🛏 Austinburg Inn, Best Value Inn, Holiday Inn Express, Sleep Inn, S 🅖 🅿️Pilot/Subway/dsl/scales/24hr, SpeedCo 🍴 Burger King, Clay St Grill, McDonald's, Taco Bell, Waffle House 🛏 Hampton Inn Ⓞ auto repair
218	OH 534, Geneva, N 🅖 GetGo 🍴 Best Friend's Grill, Chop's Grille, McDonald's, Pizza Hut, Wendy's 🛏 Motel 6 Ⓞ 🅷, to Geneva SP, Willow Lake Camping (4mi), S 🅖 KwikFill, KwikFill/dsl/scales/24hr Ⓞ Kenisse's Camping
212	OH 528, to Thompson, Madison, N 🍴 McDonald's, Pizza Roto 🛏 Holiday Inn Express Ⓞ Mentor RV Ctr, S 🅖 Marathon/dsl Ⓞ KOA (4mi)
205	Vrooman Rd, 0-2 mi N Ⓞ Indian Point Park, Masons Landing Park, 0-2 mi S 🅖 BP/Subway/dsl, Marathon/dsl 🍴 Capps Pizza

200	OH 44, to Painesville, Chardon, S 🅖 BP/7-11/dsl, Shell/d 🍴 B2B Burgers, Chipotle, McDonald's, Paninis Grill, Piz Roto, Red Hawk Grille, Starbucks, Sunny St Cafe, Waffle Hous 🛏 Comfort Inn, Holiday Inn Express, Quail Hollow Reso Ⓞ 🅷, URGENT CARE, Verizon
198mm	🆁🆂 both lanes, full 🅰️ facilities, litter barrels, petwalk, Ⓒ, 🏧 vending
195	OH 615, Center St, Kirtland Hills, Mentor, 1-2 mi N 🛏 Be Western+
193	OH 306, to Mentor, Kirtland, 0-2 mi N 🅖 BP/7-11/dsl, She 🍴 McDonald's 🛏 Mentor Home Inn Ⓞ 🅷, S 🅖 Speedwa dsl 🍴 Burger King 🛏 Days Inn, Red Roof Inn Ⓞ Kirtlar Temple LDS Historic Site
190	Express Lane to I-271 (from wb)
189	OH 91, to Willoughby, Willoughby Hills, N 🅖 BP/7-11/d Shell/dsl 🍴 Applebee's, Big Cheese Pizza, Bob Evans, Ca Europa, Cracker Barrel, Peking Chef, Subway, TX Roadhous Wendy's 🛏 Courtyard, Motel 6, Travelodge Ⓞ 🅷, CVS Dru Walgreens, S Ⓞ BMW/Mini, Lexus
188	I-271 S, to Akron
187	OH 84, Bishop Rd, to Wickliffe, Willoughby, S 🅖 BP/7-11 dsl, Shell 🍴 Dunkin', Golden Mtn Chinese, McDonald's, Sul way, Tony's Pizza 🛏 Fairbridge Inn Ⓞ 🅷, $Tree, Chevrole CVS Drug, Giant Eagle Foods, Marc's Foods, Mazda/VW, NT O'Reilly Parts
186	US 20, Euclid Ave, N 🅖 Sunoco 🛏 EconoLodge, Quality Ir Ⓞ Ford, radiators/transmissions, Subaru, S 🅖 Shell 🍴 A by's, Asian Express, KFC, Popeye's, R-Ribs, Sidewalk Cafe, Tac Bell Ⓞ $General, Advance Parts, Family$, Firestone/aut Save-a-Lot Foods
185	OH 2 E (exits left from eb), to Painesville
184b	OH 175, E 260th St, N 🅖 Shell Ⓞ USPO, S Ⓞ auto/tire repa
184a	Babbitt Rd, N Ⓞ Buick/GMC
183	E 222nd St, N 🅖 repair, S 🅖 BP, Sunoco/dsl Ⓞ vet
182b a	185 St, 200 St, N 🅖 BP/7-11/dsl 🍴 Subway Ⓞ Home Dep Honda, Hyundai, S Ⓞ Marathon/dsl, Shell/dsl, Speedway/ds
181b a	E 156th St, S 🅖 BP/Mr Hero
180b a	E 140th St, E 152nd St
179	OH 283 E, to Lake Shore Blvd
178	Eddy Rd, to Bratenahl
177	University Circle, MLK Dr, N Ⓞ Cleveland Lake SP, S Ⓞ 🅷 Rockefeller Park
176	E 72nd St
175	E 55th St, Marginal Rds
174b	OH 2 W, to Lakewood, downtown, N Ⓞ Browns Stadium Rock&Roll Hall of Fame
174a	Lakeside Ave
173c	Superior Ave, St Clair Ave, N 🅖 BP, downtown
173b	Chester Ave, S 🅖 BP
173a	Prospect Ave (from wb), downtown
172d	Carnegie Ave, S 🅖 Shell/dsl 🍴 Burger King, KFC, McDonald Ⓞ Cadillac, downtown
172c b	E 9th St, S Ⓞ 🅷, to Cleveland St U
172a	I-77 S, to Akron
171b a	US 422, OH 14, Broadway St, Ontario St, N 🅖 🛏 Hilton Garde
171	Abbey Ave, downtown
170c b	I-71 S, to I-490
170a	US 42, W 25th St, S 🅖 Royal
169	W 44th St, W 41st St, N Ⓞ 🅷
167b a	OH 10, West Blvd, 98th St, to Lorain Ave, N Ⓞ 🅷, S 🅖 BP/d Ⓞ CVS Drug

YOUNGSTOWN

EUCLID

OH

INTERSTATE 90 Cont'd

Exit #	Services
166	W 117th St, **N** 🅿 BP/dsl, GetGo/dsl, Shell 🍴 Penn Sta Subs ⊡ Advance Parts, AutoZone, Giant Eagle Foods, Home Depot, Staples, Target, **S** 🅿 Gas USA ⊡ Monro
165	W 140th St, Bunts Rd, Warren Rd, **S** ⊡ Ⓗ
164	McKinley Ave, to Lakewood
162	Hilliard Blvd (from wb), to Westway Blvd, Rocky River, **S** 🅿 BP, Shell 🍴 Ferris Steaks, Joe's Rest. ⊡ USPO, vet
161	OH 2, OH 254 (from eb, no EZ return), Detroit Rd, Rocky River
160	Clague Rd (from wb), same as 159, **S** ⊡ Ⓗ
159	OH 252, Columbia Rd, **N** 🅿 EVC 🍴 Carrabba'a, Dave&Busters, Hooley House Grille, Outback Steaks, Si Senor 🛏 Courtyard, Super 8, TownePlace Suites ⊡ BMW, **S** 🅿 BP/7-11 🍴 Arby's, Domino's, Houlihan's, Jets Pizza, KFC, McDonald's, Panera Bread, Taco Bell, Urban Grill ⊡ Ⓗ, Chevrolet, NTB
156	Crocker Rd, Bassett Rd, Westlake, Bay Village, **N** 🅿 BP, Shell 🛏 DoubleTree, Extended Stay America, Holiday Inn Express, Red Roof Inn, Sonesta Suites, **S** 🅿 BP/7-11, Speedway 🍴 Aladdin's Eatery, Bar Louie, Bob Evans, Bonefish Grill, Brio, Cheesecake Factory, Don Ramon Mexican, First Watch, Five Guys, Jersey Mike's, Jimmy John's, McDonald's, Pizza by Robert, Robeks, Starbucks, Subway, TGIFriday's, Wendy's, Yard House, Zoup! 🛏 Hampton Inn, Hyatt Place ⊡ Ⓗ, Aldi Foods, Barnes & Noble, CVS Drug, Dick's, Fresh Thyme Mkt, Giant Eagle, GNC, Marc's Foods, Monro, Trader Joe's, Verizon
155	Nagel Rd, Avon Lake, **N** 🅿 GetGo/dsl 🛏 Residence Inn, **S** 🍴 Dunkin' ⊡ Drugmart, Meijer/dsl
153	OH 83, Avon Lake, **N** 🅿 Circle K/Dunkin'/dsl, GetGo/dsl 🍴 Arby's, Buffalo Wild Wings (2mi), Culver's, Fujiyama, King Yuan, Panda Express, Perkins, Rush Inn Grille, Wendy's ⊡ Ali Foods, AutoZone, Best Buy, Cabela's, Discount Tire, Duluth Trading, Firestone/auto, JC Penney, Lowe's, Menard's, PetCo, Walmart, **S** 🍴 Antonio's Pizza, Applebee's, Bob Evans, Burger King, Chipotle, Five Guys, IHOP, Jimmy John's, Mandarin House, Moe's SW Grill, Panera Bread, Penn Sta Subs, Red Robin, Starbucks, Subway, Taco Bell, Winking Lizard Tavern, Zoup! 🛏 Cambria Hotel ⊡ AT&T, Costco/gas, CVS Drug, GNC, Heinen's Mkt, Home Depot, Kohl's, Marc's Foods, Marshall's, Michael's, Old Navy, Target, USPO, Verizon, World Mkt
151	OH 611, Avon, **N** 🅿 BP/7-11/dsl, Pilot/Subway/dsl/24hr 🍴 McDonald's 🛏 Fairfield Inn, Woodspring Suites ⊡ Buick/GMC, Chevrolet, Harley-Davidson, NAPA, **S** 🅿 BJ's Whse/gas 🍴 Dunkin', Mulligan's Grille
148	OH 254, Sheffield, Avon, **N** 🅿 Quaker Steak&Lube 🛏 Homewood Suites ⊡ Ford, Kia, Mazda, Nissan, **S** 🅿 BP, GetGo, Sheetz/dsl, Speedway/dsl 🍴 Arby's, China Star, Cracker Barrel, KFC, Marco's Pizza, McDonald's, Panera Bread, Pizza Hut, Ruby Tuesday, Sorrento Pizzaria, Starbucks, Steak'n Shake, Subway, Sugarcreek Rest., Taco Bell, Wendy's ⊡ $General, $Tree, Aldi Foods, AutoZone, Drug Mart, Giant Eagle Mkt, Sam's Club/gas, Verizon
147mm	Black River
145	OH 57, to Lorain, I-80/Ohio Tpk E, Elyria, **N** 🍴 Burger King, George's Rest. ⊡ $General, Save-a-Lot, U-Haul, **S** 🅿 Speedway/dsl 🍴 Applebee's, Bob Evans, Buffalo Wild Wings, Burger King, Chipotle Mexican, Denny's, Golden Corral, Harry Buffalo, Honeybaked Ham, IHOP, McDonald's, Olive Garden, Red Lobster, Subway, TX Roadhouse, Wasabi Grill, Wendy's 🛏 Best Western, Country Inn&Suites, Days Inn, Hampton Inn, Quality Inn, Red Roof Inn ⊡ $General, $Tree, AT&T, Best Buy, Conrad's

145	Continued Automotive, Dick's, Firestone/auto, Giant Eagle Mkt, Home Depot, Honda, Hyundai, JC Penney, Jo-Ann Fabrics, Lowe's, Marc's Foods, Petsmart, Staples, Target, Tuffy Repair, Verizon
144	OH 2 W (from wb, no return), to Sandusky

I-90 wb joins Ohio Tpk. WB exits to Ohio/Indiana state line are on Ohio Turnpike, exits 142-0.

INTERSTATE 270 (Columbus)

Exit #	Services
55	I-71, to Columbus, Cincinnati
52b a	US 23, High St, Circleville, **N** 🅿 Marathon/Circle K, Speedway/dsl, Turkey Hill/dsl 🍴 Arby's, Bob Evans, Burger King, China City, KFC, Little Caesar's, LJ Silver, Los Mariachis, McDonald's, Pizza Hut, Ponderosa, Skyline Chili, Subway, Taco Bell, Tim Horton's, Waffle House, Wendy's, White Castle 🛏 Kozy Inn ⊡ $General, $Tree, Advance Parts, Aldi Foods, AutoZone, CVS Drug, Family$, Firestone/auto, Kroger/gas, Lowe's, NAPA, O'Reilly Parts, Walgreens, Walmart, **S** 🅿 BP/dsl ⊡ Kioto Downs
49	Alum Creek Dr, **N** 🅿 BP/dsl, Shell/dsl, Thornton's/dsl 🍴 Donato's Pizza, KFC/LJ Silver, Subway ⊡ $General, Family$, **S** 🅿 BP/dsl 🍴 Arby's, McDonald's, Taco Bell, Wendy's 🛏 Comfort Inn, Quality Inn
46b a	US 33, Bexley, Lancaster
43b a	I-70, E to Cambridge, W to Columbus
41b a	US 40, **E** 🅿 Shell, Speedway 🍴 Bob Evans, City BBQ, Honeybaked Ham, McDonald's, Outback Steaks, Rally's, Steak'n Shake, Taco Bell, Texas Roadhouse ⊡ auto repair, AutoZone, Family$, NAPA, TJ Maxx, Verizon, Walgreens, **W** 🅿 Shell/dsl, Speedway, UDF 🍴 Golden Corral, Hunan Chinese, McDonald's, Mi Mexico, Poblanos Mexican, Subway ⊡ $General, Family$
39	OH 16, Broad St, **E** 🅿 GetGo, Speedway/dsl 🍴 Arby's, Cane's, Chick-fil-A, Chipotle, Donato's Pizza, Dunkin', Five Guys, Hot Head Burrito, Jets Pizza, Jimmy John's, McDonald's, Noodles&Co, Panera Bread, Penn Sta Subs, Potbelly's, Sonic, Starbucks, Subway, Sunny St Cafe, Taco Bell, Tim Horton's, Waffle House, Wendy's, White Castle 🛏 Comfort Suites ⊡ Ⓗ, Giant Eagle Mkt, Goodyear/auto, Grismer Auto Service, Kroger, Menard's, URGENT CARE, Verizon, Walgreens, **W** 🅿 Shell, Speedway/dsl ⊡ Chevrolet
37	OH 317, Hamilton Rd, **E** 🅿 BP/dsl, Speedway/dsl 🍴 Arby's, Big Boy, Bob Evans, Burger King, Chinese Express, Chipotle, Dunkin', Firehouse Subs, Jersey Mike's, McDonald's, Panera Bread, Penn Sta Subs, Rusty Bucket, Starbucks, Taco Bell, Tim Horton's 🛏 Holiday Inn Express ⊡ Firestone/auto, GNC, Kroger/dsl, **W** 🛏 Fairfield Inn, Hampton Inn, Hilton Garden ⊡ Buick/GMC, Subaru/Jaguar/Porsche, Volvo, VW/Audi

OH

= gas ⊓ = food ⌂ = lodging ⊙ = other Ⓡ = rest stop Copyright 2022 - The Next EXIT

INTERSTATE 270 (Columbus) Cont'd

Exit #	Services
35b a	I-670W, US 62, E 🅖 Speedway/dsl ⊓ City BBQ, Little Caesar's, McDonald's, Tim Horton's ⊙ Advance Parts, AutoZone, CVS Drug, Family$, W I-670
33	Easton Way
32	Morse Rd, E 🅖 Marathon/DM, Speedway/dsl, UDF ⊙ CVS Drug, Mazda, Nissan, Toyota, W 🅖 BP, Shell/Subway, UDF/dsl ⊓ Abuelo's, Applebee's, BJ's Rest., Champp's Grill, Donato's Pizza, HomeTown Buffet, J Alexander's, Kobe Japanese, Logan's Roadhouse, McDonald's, On-the-Border, Papa John's, Pei Wei, Red Robin, Sakura Steaks, Smokey Bones, Steak'n Shake, Taco Bell, Wendy's ⌂ Courtyard, Extended Stay America, Hampton Inn, Holiday Inn Express, Residence Inn, Woodspring Suites ⊙ AT&T, Best Buy, Cadillac, Carmax, Costco/gas, Dick's, Discount Tire, Field&Stream, Infiniti, Jo-Ann Fabrics, Lexus, Lowe's Whse, Macy's, Mercedes, Michael's, Nordstrom's, NTB, Old Navy, Petsmart, REI, Sam's Club, Staples, Target, TJ Maxx, Trader Joe's, Verizon, Walmart/McDonald's, Whole Foods Mkt, World Mkt
30	OH 161 E to New Albany, W to Worthington
29	OH 3, Westerville, N 🅖 BP/dsl, Shell ⊓ Arby's, Bob Evans, Chipotle Mexican, City BBQ, Fazoli's, McDonald's, Pizza Hut, Tim Horton's, Wendy's ⌂ Red Roof Inn ⊙ Advance Parts, AT&T, Big Lots, CarQuest, Firestone/auto, Kohl's, Kroger, Marc's Mkt, vet, Walmart, S 🅖 Clark/dsl, Speedway/dsl ⊓ Carsoni's Italian, China House, Domino's, Subway ⊙ Aldi Foods, Family$, Grismer Tire/auto, Midas, Monro, USPO
27	OH 710, Cleveland Ave, N 🅖 Speedway/dsl ⊓ Subway, Wendy's ⌂ Ramada Inn ⊙ $General, CVS Drug, NAPA Autocare, Tuffy, S 🅖 Turkey Hill/dsl ⊓ El Rancho Allegre, McDonald's, O'Charley's ⌂ Embassy Suites ⊙ Home Depot
26	I-71, S to Columbus, N to Cleveland
23	US 23, Worthington, N ⊓ Bob Evans, Chipotle Mexican, Columbus Fish Mkt, Cucina Italiana, El Acapulco, Hyde Park Steaks, J Alexander's, J Gilbert's Steaks, Lotus Grill, Ruth's Chris Steaks, Starbucks, Subway, Sushiko Japanese, Winking Lizard ⌂ Courtyard, DoubleTree, Extended Stay America, Homewood Suites, Hyatt Place, Motel 6, Quality Inn, Red Roof Inn, Residence Inn, Sheraton, TownePlace Suites, Woodspring Suites, S 🅖 ⊓ Aladdin's Eatery, Buca Italian, Cosi Grill, Jimmy John's, McDonald's, Panera Bread, Piada Italian, Starbucks ⌂ Econolodge, Holiday Inn ⊙ Kroger
22	OH 315, N 🅖 BP/dsl, Marathon/dsl ⊓ Subway
20	Sawmill Rd, N 🅖 BP, Marathon/dsl ⊓ Burger King, IHOP, Logan's Roadhouse, Max&Erma's, McDonald's, Olive Garden, Papa John's, Subway, Taco Bell, Wendy's ⌂ Fairfield Inn ⊙ Buick/GMC, CVS Drug, Ford, Hyundai, Kroger/gas, Lincoln, Mazda, NTB, Subaru, vet, S 🅖 Shell, Speedway ⊓ Applebee's, Arby's, bd's Mongolian, Blue Ginger Asian, Bob Evans, Bonchon, Burger King, Cane's, Charlie's Subs, Chick-fil-A, Chili's, Chipotle Mexican, ChuckeCheese, El Vaquero Mexican, Firehouse Subs, Genji Japanese, Golden Corral, HoneyBaked Cafe, Jimmy John's, Joe's Crabshack, KFC, Krispy Kreme, McDonald's, Mellow Mushroom, Panera Bread, Pizza Hut, Red Lobster, Ruby Tuesday, Starbucks, Steak'n Shake, Subway, Ted's MT Grill, Vicenzos Italian ⌂ Cloverleaf Suites, Hampton Inn, Quality Inn ⊙ $Tree, Advance Parts, AT&T, AutoZone, Barnes&Noble, Big Lots, Cadillac/Honda, CarMax, Dick's, Discount Tire, Firestone/auto, GNC, Hobby Lobby, Home Depot, Infiniti, Jo-Ann Fabrics, Kohl's, Lexus, Lowe's Whse, Meijer, Meineke, Michael's, Mr Tire, Old Navy, PetCo, Petsmart, Sam's Club/gas, Staples, SteinMart, Target, Toyota, Trader Joe's, Verizon, vet, Whole Foods Mkt

Exit #	Services
17b a	US 33, Dublin-Granville Rd, E 🅖 Marathon, Sunoco ⊓ B Evans, Hyde Park Steaks, Jason's Deli, Max&Erma's, McDonald's, Pizza Hut, Subway ⌂ Courtyard, Crowne Plaza, Embas Suites, Extended Stay America, Hilton Garden, Red Roof In Residence Inn ⊙ CVS Drug, Fiat, Kroger, Mr Tire, USPO
15	Tuttle Crossing Blvd, E 🅖 BP, UDF ⊓ BJ's Rest., Bob Evan Boston Mkt, Chipotle Mexican, DiBella's Subs, House of Japa Longhorn Steaks, Macaroni Grill, McDonald's, Noodles&C Panera Bread, PF Chang's, River City Grill, Taco Bell, We dy's ⌂ Drury Inn, Homewood Suites, Hyatt Place, La Quint Marriott ⊙ JC Penney, W 🅖 Shell, Turkey Hill/Subway/c ⊓ Steak'n Shake, Uno Pizzaria ⌂ Staybridge Suites ⊙ Be Buy, NTB, vet, Walmart/Subway, World Mkt
13	Cemetery Rd, Fishinger Rd, E 🅖 Exxon/Subway, Shell, Spee way ⊓ Burger King, Carrabba's, Chipotle Mexican, Damon Dave&Buster's, Donato's Pizza, KFC, Lunada Mexican, Pane Bread, Skyline Chili, Spageddie's, Starbucks, Steak&Shake, Ti Horton's ⌂ Comfort Suites, Homewood Suites ⊙ $Tree, CV Drug, Discount Tire, GNC, Home Depot, Lowe's Whse, NT Staples, Tire Dicounters, Tuesday Morning, W 🅖 GetGo/d Speedway ⊓ Bob Evans, Marie's Scrambler, Max&Erma's, M Donald's, Rusty Bucket Rest., Tim Horton's, Wendy's ⌂ Ham ton Inn, Knights Inn ⊙ Giant Eagle Mkt, Nissan
10	Roberts Rd, E 🅖 Marathon, Thornton's/dsl ⊓ Subway, Ti Horton's, Wendy's ⌂ Woodspring Suites, W 🅖 Speedwa dsl ⊓ Tim Horton's, Waffle House ⌂ Courtyard, Quality In Royal Inn ⊙ CVS Drug, Family$, O'Reilly Parts
8	I-70, E to Columbus, W to Indianapolis
7	US 40, Broad St, E 🅖 BP, Speedway/dsl ⊓ Bob Evans, Bosto Mkt, Burger King, ChuckeCheese, McDonald's, Peacock Wes Popeye's, TeeJay's, White Castle ⊙ Advance Parts, Big Lot Buick/GMC, Chevrolet, GNC, Target, W 🅖 GetGo, Speedwa dsl, Thornton's ⊓ A&W/LJ Silver, Arby's, Canes, KFC, McDo ald's, Papa John's, Tim Horton's, Waffle House ⌂ Red Roof I ⊙ 🄷, CVS Drug, Family$, Giant Eagle Foods, Goodyear/au Home Depot, Jo-Ann Fabrics, O'Reilly Parts, Walgreens
5	Georgesville, E 🅖 Shell/dsl, Sunoco/dsl, UDF/dsl ⊓ Jimm John's, Starbucks ⊙ Verizon, Walmart, W ⊓ Applebee Arby's, Bob Evans, Buffalo Wild Wings, Chipotle Mexican, D Fiesta Mariachi, KFC/LJ Silver, McDonald's, O'Charley's, Re Lobster, Steak'n Shake, Subway, Taco Bell, Wendy's, Whi Castle ⊙ Advance Parts, AT&T, Chrysler/Dodge/Jeep, GN Honda, Hyundai/Subaru, Kia, Kroger/gas, Lowe's Whse, NT TireDiscounters, Toyota, VW
2	US 62, OH 3, Grove City, N 🅖 Turkey Hill/dsl ⌂ Woodsprir Suites, S 🅖 Marathon, Shell, Speedway/dsl ⊓ Big Boy, Bur er King, Domino's, Donato's Pizza, Little Caesar's, McDonald Subway, Tim Horton/Wendy's, Waffle House, Wedgewood Pi za ⊙ CVS Drug, Verizon
0mm	I-71

INTERSTATE 271 (Cleveland)

Exit #	Services
39mm	I-271 begins/ends on I-90, exit 188.
36	Wilson Mills Rd, Highland Hts, Mayfield, E 🅖 Shell ⊓ Ala din's Eatery, Austin's Steaks, Jersey Mike's, Yours Truly Res ⌂ Hilton Garden, Holiday Inn ⊙ Chrysler/Dodge/Jeep, CV Drug, Heinen's Mkt, vet, W 🅖 Marathon/dsl ⊓ Burgers Beer, Chipotle, Denny's, Hibachi Steaks, Panera Bread ⊙ B Lots, DrugMart, Home Depot, Kohl's, Tuesday Morning, Verizo
34	US 322, Mayfield Rd, E 🅖 BP/7-11, Circle K ⊓ Chipotle, DiBe la's Subs, FirstWatch, Five Guys, Fox&Hound Grille, Georgio's Pi za, Jimmy John's, Piccolo Italian, Scramblers, Starbucks, Subwa

OH

COLUMBUS

pyright 2022 - The Next EXIT ® ▢ = gas ▢ = food ⌂ = lodging ▢ = other Ⓡs = rest stop

⬆N INTERSTATE 271 (Cleveland) Cont'd

C L E V E L A N D

34	Continued
	Wendy's ▢ Ⓗ, Aldi Foods, CVS Drug, Marc's Foods, Michael's, Mr Tire, Old Navy, Rite Aid, Target, Tire Pros, Walmart, **W** ▢ Marathon, Shell, Speedway ▢ Arby's, Bob Evans, Burger King, Chick-fil-A, ChuckECheese, Dunkin', Firehouse Subs, Gaetano's Italian, McDonald's, Otani Japanese, Panera Bread, Penn Sta Subs, Pizza Hut, Sonic, Subway, Taco Bell, TGI Friday's ▢ $Tree, AT&T, AutoZone, Best Buy, Conrad's Tire/auto, Costco/gas, CVS Drug, Ford/Lincoln, Fresh Thyme Mkt, Giant Eagle Mkt, GNC, JoAnn Fabrics, Marshall's, Midas, Nissan, NTB, O'Reilly Parts, Petsmart, Staples, Verizon, World Mkt
32	Brainerd Rd, **E** ▢ Burntwood Tavern, J Alexander's ▢ Ⓗ, USPO
29	US 422 W, OH 87, Chagrin Blvd, Harvard Rd, **E** ▢ Shell, Speedway, Sunoco ▢ Bahama Breeze, Bob Evans, Bravo Italian, Chipotle, Corky&Lenny's Rest., McDonald's, Mitchell's Fish Mkt, Paladar Latin Kitchen, Pancake House, Red Lobster, Starbucks, Stone Oven, Tenas de Brazil, Wasabi Japanese, Wendy's ⌂ Courtyard, Extended Stay America, Extended Stay America, Fairfield Inn, Hampton Inn ▢ AT&T, Barnes&Noble, CVS Drug, Rite Aid, TJ Maxx, Trader Joe's, **W** ▢ BP/Subway, Shell/dsl ▢ Giovanni's Ristorante, Hyde Park Steaks, PF Chang's, Tres Potrillos, Winking Lizard Tavern ⌂ Clarion, DoubleTree, Embassy Suites, Home 2 Suites, Homewood Suites, Hotel Indigo, Residence Inn ▢ Ⓗ, Buick/GMC, Cadillac, Infiniti, NTB, Porsche, Verizon
28b	Harvard Rd, **E** ▢ Coopers Hawk, Firebirds, Syman's Tavern ⌂ Drury Inn ▢ REI, Verizon, Whole Foods Mkt, **W** ▢ Buffalo Wild Wings, Chick-fil-A, Chipotle, DiBella's Subs, Five Guys, Olive Garden, Panera Bread, Piada Italian, River City Grille, Robeks Cafe, Zoup! ⌂ Aloft, Marriott ▢ Ⓗ, Marshall's
28a	OH 175, Richmond Rd, Emery Rd, **E** ▢ BP, GetGo/dsl, Marathon/Circle K/Subway/dsl ▢ Baskin-Robbins/Dunkin', Don Ramon Mexican, Jimmy John's, McDonald's ▢ vet, **W** ▢ BJ's Whse
27b	I-480 W
27a	US 422 E, **E** ▢ CarMax, Chevrolet, Lowe's
26	Rockside Rd, **E** ▢ Speedway/dsl, Sunoco/dsl ▢ Burger King, Subway ▢ Family$
23	OH 14 W, Forbes Rd, Broadway Ave, **E** ▢ Sunoco ▢ B&M BBQ, McDonald's, Subway, Wendy's ⌂ Hampton Inn, Quality Inn ▢ Sam's Club/dsl, **W** ▢ Gasway, Marathon/Circle K/dsl
21	I-480 E, OH 14 E (from sb), to Youngstown
19	OH 82, Macedonia, **E** ▢ Speedway/dsl/e85 ▢ Dunkin', Penn Sta Subs, Pizza Hut, **W** ▢ Tesla EVC ▢ Antonio's Pizza, Applebee's, Arby's, Chick-fil-A, Chili's, Chipotle, Culver's, First Watch, Fuji Japanese, Golden Corral, Jersey Mike's, McDonald's, Outback Steaks, Panera Bread, Popeye's, Starbucks, Steak'n Shake, Taco Bell, Wendy's ▢ Aldi Foods, AT&T, Best Buy, Chevrolet, Discount Tire, Giant Eagle Foods, GNC, Hobby Lobby, Home Depot, Kohl's, Lowe's, NTB, O'Reilly Parts, PetCo, Petsmart, Target, Verizon, Verizon, Walgreens, Walmart/Subway
18b a	OH 8, Boston Hts, to Akron, (exits left from sb), **E** ▢ GetGo, Speedway/dsl ▢ Bob Evans, KFC ⌂ Country Inn&Suites, Key Inn, Knights Inn, La Quinta, **W** same as 19
12	OH 303, Richfield, Peninsula
10	I-77, to I-80, OH Tpk (from nb), to Akron, Cleveland
9	I-77 S, OH 176 (from nb), to Richfield
8mm	Ⓡs both lanes, full ⌂ facilities, litter barrels, petwalk, ▢, ▢
3	OH 94, to I-71 N, Wadsworth, N Royalton, **W** ▢ PetroUSA/dsl
0mm	I-271 begins/ends on I-71, exit 220.

M A C E D O N I A

INTERSTATE 275 (Cincinnati)

See Kentucky Interstate 275

⬆N INTERSTATE 280 (Toledo)

Exit #	Services
13	I-280 begins/ends on I-75, exit 208.
12	Manhattan Blvd, **E** ▢ Sunoco, **W** ▢ Sunoco/dsl
11	OH 25 S, Eerie St, **W** ▢ Huntington Ctr
10mm	Maumee River
9	OH 65, Front St, **E** ▢ Sunoco ▢ Subway, Tony Packo's Cafe, **W** ▢ Sunoco/dsl
8	Starr Ave, (from sb only)
7	OH 2, Oregon, **E** ▢ Circle K/dsl, Sunoco ▢ Arby's, Bob Evans, Briskets, Burger King, Coldstone/Tim Horton's, Empire, McDonald's, Sonic, Taco Bell, Wendy's ⌂ Comfort Inn, Hampton Inn, TownePlace Suites ▢ Ⓗ, Ford, to Maumee Bay SP, Walgreens
6	OH 51, Woodville Rd, Curtice Rd, **E** ▢ BP/dsl, Marathon ▢ Bob Evans, Burger King ▢ Menards, **W** ▢ Speedway/dsl ▢ Applebee's, Arby's, Big Boy, Gino's Pizza, KFC, LJ Silver, McDonald's, Subway, Taco Bell ⌂ Sleep Inn ▢ Ⓗ, $Tree, Advance Parts, Meijer/dsl, Midas, O'Reilly Parts
4	Walbridge
2	OH 795, Perrysburg, **W** ▢ Sunoco/dsl
1b	Bahnsen Rd, **E** ▢ ⚑FLYING J/Denny's/dsl/LP/scales/24hr ⌂ Best Value Inn, Regency Inn, **W** ▢ ❤Loves/Arby's/dsl/scales/24hr, Petro/BP/Iron Skillet/dsl/scales/24hr/@ ⌂ Budget Inn ▢ Blue Beacon, SpeedCo, Super 8
1a	I-280 begins/ends on I 80/90, OH Tpk, exit 71., **S** ▢ FuelMart/Subway/dsl/scales, Ⓟⓘⓛⓞⓣ/McDonald's/dsl/scales/24hr, TA/BP/Taco Bell/dsl/scales/24hr/@ ▢ KOA

⬆N INTERSTATE 475 (Toledo)

Exit #	Services
20	I-75. I-475 begins/ends on I-75, exit 204.
19	ProMedica Pky, Central Ave, **S** ▢ Burger King, Gino's Pizza, Subway ▢ Ⓗ
18b	Douglas Rd (from wb)
18a	OH 51 W, Monroe St
17	Secor Rd, **N** ▢ Marathon, Shell/dsl, Stop'n Shop, Sunoco ▢ Applebee's, Bambiño's Pizza, Bob Evans, Boston Mkt, Burger King, Famous Dave's BBQ, Hooters, KFC, Monroe St Diner, Netty's, Penn Sta Subs, Red Robin, Rudy's Hot Dogs, Tim Horton's ▢ Ⓗ, $Tree, Advance Parts, AT&T, Barnes&Noble, Best Buy, Jo-AnnFabrics, Kohl's, Kroger/dsl, O'Reilly Parts, Rite Aid, Walgreens, **S** ▢ ▢ Bubba's 33, Big Boy,

T O L E D O

INTERSTATE 475 (Toledo) Cont'd

17	Continued
	Chick-fil-A, Chipotle Mexican, El Vaquero, First Watch, Five Guys, Fusion, Jamba Juice, Jersey Mike's, McDonald's, Original Pancakes, Packo's, Piada Italian, Pizza Fire, Pizza Hut, Popeye's, Scrambler's, Sonic, Starbucks, Subway, Taco Bell, TX Roadhouse, Uncle John's Pancakes Courtyard, Hampton Inn, Holiday Inn Express, Quality Inn, Ramada Inn, Red Roof Inn Batteries+Bulbs, Costco/gas, Fresh Mkt, Home Depot, Rite Aid, Steinmart, U of Toledo
16	Talmadge Rd (from wb, no return), N BP/dsl, Speedway/dsl Arby's, Bar Louie, bd Mongolian BBQ, Bravo Italiana, Chick-fil-A, Chipotle, Coldstone, IHOP, J Alexander's, Jimmy John's, Longhorn Steaks, McDonald's, Panera Bread Dick's, JC Penney, Kohl's, Macy's, Old Navy
15	Corey Rd (from eb, no return)
14	US 23 N, to Ann Arbor
13	US 20, OH 120, Central Ave, E Speedway/dsl Bob Evans, Magic Wok, McDonald's, Rally's, Subway, Wendy's Buick/GMC, Cadillac, Chrysler/Dodge/Jeep, Fiat, Ford, Honda, Hyundai, Kia, Mazda, Nissan, Subaru, Toyota, Walmart, W BP, Speedway Buffalo Wild Wings, Chick-fil-A, Jimmy John's, KFC, Tim Horton's, Waffle House Lowe's, Verizon
8b a	OH 2, E BP/dsl Fire Station Grill, Penn Sta Subs, TGI-Friday's, TX Roadhouse Extended Stay America, Hawthorn Suites, Knights Inn, Red Roof Inn H, Home Depot, Kohl's, Old Navy, to OH Med Coll, W Speedway/dsl Arby's, Bob Evans, Boston Mkt, Burger King, Chick-fil-A, Chili's, Chipotle Mexican, Cinco de Mayo, Hot Head Burritos, IHOP, Jimmy John's, Little Caesar's, Magic Wok, Mancino's Pizza, Marco's Pizza, McDonald's, New Empire, Panda Express, Panera Bread, Starbucks, Subway, Taco Bell, Tim Horton's, Waffle House, Wendy's Courtyard, EconoLodge, Quality Inn $Tree, Aldi Foods, Best Buy, BigLots, Dick's, Firestone/auto, GNC, Kroger/dsl, Menard's, Michael's, Petsmart, Sam's Club/gas, Target, TJ Maxx, Verizon, Walmart/Subway
6	Dussel Dr, Salisbury Rd, to I-80-90/tpk, E Applebee's, Arby's, Bangkok Kitchen, Bluewater Grille, Buffalo Wild Wings, Coldstone, Cracker Barrel, Don Juan's, Gino's Pizza, Jimmy John's, Longhorn Steaks, Max&Erma's, McDonald's, Outback Steaks, Panera Bread, Rayoka Japanese, Rusty Taco, Sam's Diner, Scrambler's, Smokey Bones BBQ, Subway, Wendy's Country Inn&Suites, Courtyard, Extended Stay America, Fairfield Inn, Homewood Suites, Residence Inn, Super 8 Ford/Lincoln, W Bob Evans, Briarfield Café, Carrabba's, JoJo's Pizza Best Western Churchill's Mkt, vet
4	US 24, to Maumee, Napolean, N H, Toledo Zoo
3mm	Maumee River
2	OH 25, to Bowling Green, Perrysburg, N BP/dsl, Circle K/dsl, Shell American Table Rest., Arby's, Biggby Coffee, Dunkin', El Vaquero, Gino's Pizza, Jersey's Grill, Marco's Pizza, McDonald's, Subway, Wendy's Auto Value, Churchill's Mkt, Costco/dsl, GMC, Goodyear/auto, Hyundai, URGENT CARE, Volvo, VW, S Marathon, Speedway/dsl Bar Louie's, Biaggi's, Blue Pacific Grill, Bob Evans, Max&Erma's, Nagoya Japanese, Scrambler's, Starbucks, Taco Bell, Tea Tree Asian, Waffle House Economy Inn, Hilton Garden, Holiday Inn Express AT&T, Books-A-Million, GNC, Mytee Automotive, Tireman/auto, URGENT CARE, Verizon, vet
0mm	I-475 begins/ends on I-75, exit 192.

INTERSTATE 480 (Cleveland)

Exit #	Services
42	I-80, PA Tpk, I-480 begins/ends, 0-2 mi S BP, EVC, GetG Marathon/Circle K, Marathon/Circle K, Sheetz/24hr, Shell, Tes EVC Applebee's, Arby's, Baskin Robbins/Dunkin', Bob Evan Brown Derby Roadhouse, Buffalo Wild Wings, Burger King, Ch na Chef, Chipotle, Denny's, DQ, El Campesino, Fun Buffet, Hap Moose Grill, Honeybaked Ham, Jimmy John's, KFC, Little Ca sar's, McDonald's, Mr Hero, New Peking Chinese, Panda Expres Rockne's Grill, Ruby Tuesday, Sonic, Starbucks, Steak'n Shak Taco Bell, Wendy's Comfort Inn, Econolodge, Fairfield In Hampton Inn, Holiday Inn Express, Motel 6, Quality Inn, Town Place Suites, Wingate Inn H, $General, $Tree, Aldi Foods, A Seasons RV Ctr, AT&T, AutoZone, Giant Eagle Mkt, GNC, Hom Depot, Honda, Hyundai, Kia, Lowes Whse, Midas, Nissan, NT Save-a-Lot Foods, Staples, Target, Tire Source/auto, to Kent St U-Haul, USPO, Van's Tires, Verizon, vet, VW, Walgreens, Walma
41	Frost Rd, Hudson-Aurora
37	OH 91, Solon, Twinsburg, N Arby's, Brewster's, Chipotle, DC Mandarin Buffet, Panera Bread, Panini's Grill, Pizza Hut, Taco Be Comfort Suites, Giant Eagle Mkt, GNC, S BP/7-11
36	OH 82, Aurora, Twinsburg, N BP, McDonald's, Sheetz/d Burger King Super 8, S Cracker Barrel, Get'n G Wendy's Blue Canyon Rest. Hilton Garden
26	I-271, to Erie, PA
25a b c	OH 8, OH 43, Northfield Rd, Bedford, S Marathon, Shell, Su noco Giant Eagle Mkt
24	Lee Rd (from wb)
23	OH 14, Broadway Ave, N Marathon H, S Freightline
22	OH 17, Garanger, Maple Hts, Garfield Hts
21	Transportation Blvd, to E 98th St, N H, S GetGo Ap plebee's, Chipotle, Penn Sta Subs, Starbucks AT&T, Giar Eagle Foods, Verizon
20b a	I-77, Cleveland
17	OH 176, OH 17, Cleveland
16	OH 94, to OH 17 S, State Rd, N auto repair, Convenier Mart, transmissions, S BP/7-11, Sunoco/dsl Kia
15	US 42, Ridge Rd, N Applebee's, Baskin-Robbins/Dunkin Boston Mkt, CiCi's Pizza, Coldstone Creamery, Kintaro Hot Po McDonald's, Mr Hero, Penn Sta Subs, Pizza Hut, Plaza Nueve Rockne's Rest., Starbucks, TX Roadhouse $General, Gian Eagle Mkt, GNC, Lowe's, Marc's Foods, Michael's, TJMaxx, UR GENT CARE, USPO, Verizon, S GetGo, Speedway/Speedy Cafe/dsl Arby's, Denny's, DQ, Taco Bell, Wendy's $Tree Advance Parts, AT&T, Best Buy, Buick/GMC, Hyundai, Meineke Staples, Verizon, Walgreens
13	Teideman Rd, Brooklyn, S BP/dsl, Sheetz/dsl, Speedway dsl Buffalo Wild Wings, Burger King, Carrabba's, Chipotle Mexican, Cracker Barrel, Golden Corral, Hooley House Grill, Hun gry Howie's, Ice House Grill, IHOP, La Casa Mexican, LJ Silve McDonald's, Panera Bread, Subway, TGIFriday's Extende Stay America, Hampton Inn Aldi Foods, Home Depot, Jag uar, LandRover, Mazda, Sam's Club/gas, Volvo, Walmart
12b	W 150th, W130th, Brookpark, N Marathon Family$, S Marathon/dsl, Shell/dsl Big Boy, Bob Evans, Subway Best Value Inn Acura, Chevrolet, Chrysler/Dodge/Jeep Infiniti, Lexus, Mini, Toyota
11	I-71, Cleveland, Columbus
10	S Rd 237, Airport Blvd (wb only)
9	OH 17, Brookpark Rd, N Graytown Rd Tavern, Subway Hilton Garden, Woodspring Suites H, S 100th Bomb Group Rest. Sheraton
7	(wb only) Clague Rd, to WestLake

OH

⬛E INTERSTATE 480 (Cleveland) Cont'd

Exit #	Services
6	OH 252, Great Northern Blvd, to N Olmsted, **N** 🅿 BP, Shell, Speedway/dsl 🍴 Applebee's, Arby's, Bamboo Garden, BJ's Rest., Bob Evans, Boston Mkt, Brown Bag Burgers, Burger King, Chick-fil-A, Chili's, ChuckeCheese, Denny's, Famous Dave's, Five Guys, Frankie's Italian, Great Wall Buffet, Harry Buffalo, Jersey Mike's, Jimmy John's, Little Caesar's, Macaroni Grill, McAlister's Deli, Moe's SW Grill, Olive Garden, Panera Bread, Penn Sta Subs, Popeye's, Rail Burger Bar, Red Lobster, Red Robin, Ruby Tuesday, Scrambler's, Subway, Wendy's, Wild Mango Rest. 🛏 Candlewood Suites, Courtyard, Extended Stay America, Extended Stay America, Hampton Inn, La Quinta, Radisson 🅾 $Tree, Aldi Foods, AT&T, Best Buy, Big Lots, Buick/GMC/Cadillac, Chipotle Mexican, Conrad's Tire/auto, Dick's, Dillard's, Firestone/auto, Home Depot, Honda, Hyundai/VW, JC Penney, Jo-Ann Etc, Macy's, Marc's Foods, Monro, NTB, Petsmart, Subaru, Target, TJ Maxx, Toyota, Verizon, Walmart, World Mkt
3	Stearns Rd, **N** 🅾 🛏, **S** 🍴 Razzle's Cafe (2 mi) 🅾 CVS Drug (2 mi)
2	OH 10, Lorain Rd, to OH Tpk, **S** 🅿 BP, Sheetz/dsl, Speedway/dsl 🍴 Burger King, Chipotle, Dunkin', Gourme Rest., Lone Tree Tavern, McDonald's, Panera Bread, Taco Bell 🛏 Motel 6, Super 8
1	OH 10 W, to US 20 (from wb), Oberlin
0mm	OH 10, to Cleveland, **I-480 begins/ends on exit 151, OH Tpk**

⬛E INTERSTATE 680 (Youngstown)

Exit #	Services
14	OH 164, to Western Reserve Rd, **I-680 begins/ends on OH Tpk, exit 234, S** 🅿 Shell/Subway/dsl 🍴 Cafe 422, Carmella's Cafe, Dunkin', Ely's, McDonald's, Pizza Hut, Taco Bell, Wendy's 🅾 🛏
11b a	US 224, **S** 🅿 BP, GetGo, Shell/dsl 🍴 Aladdin's Eatery, Applebee's, Burger King, Chick-fil-A, Chipotle, Domino's, Dunkin', Honeybaked Ham, IHOP, Jersey Mike's, KFC, Longhorn Steaks, McDonald's, O'Charley's, Olive Garden, Outback Steaks, Panda Express, Panera Bread, Papa John's, Perkins, Primanti Bros, Red Lobster, Springfield Grill, Starbucks, Subway, Taco Bell, TX Roadhouse 🛏 Best Western+, Days Inn, Fairfield Inn, Hampton Inn, Holiday Inn, Red Roof Inn, Residence Inn 🅾 🛏, $Tree, Aldi Foods, AT&T, Best Buy, Big Lots, Giant Eagle, GNC, Hobby Lobby, Lowe's, Marc's Foods, Marshall's, NTB, Petsmart, Sam's Club/gas, Tuesday Morning, URGENT CARE, Walmart/Subway
9b a	OH 170, Midlothian Blvd, Struthers, **S** 🅿 Shell/dsl, Speedway/dsl 🍴 McDonald's, Subway 🅾 $General, Rite Aid, Walgreens
8	Shirley Rd, downtown
7	US 62, OH 7, South Ave, downtown
6b a	US 62, OH 7, Mkt St, downtown
5	Glenwood Ave, Mahoning Ave, downtown
4b a	OH 193, to US 422, Salt Springs Rd, **N** 🅾 🛏, museum
3c b	Belle Vista Ave, Connecticut Ave
3a	OH 711 E, to I-80 E
2	Meridian Rd, **S** 🅾 Ford/Peterbilt Trucks
1	OH 11

⬛E OHIO TURNPIKE

Exit #	Services
241mm	Ohio/Pennsylvania state line
239mm	toll plaza, 🍴
237mm	**Mahoning Valley Travel Plaza eb, Glacier Hills Travel Plaza wb,** 🅿 Sunoco/dsl/24hr 🍴 DQ (sb), Panera Bread (wb)
234	I-680 (from wb), to Youngstown

232	OH 7, to Boardman, Youngstown, **N** 🅿 Marathon/dsl, Sheetz 🍴 DQ, Los Gallos Mexican, Rita's Custard, Steamer's Stonewall Tavern 🛏 Budget Inn, Holiday Inn Express, Quality Inn, Skylight Inn 🅾 $General, antiques, **S** 🅿 🅿ilot/McDonald's/dsl/scales/24hr 🛏 Davis Motel, Liberty Inn
218	I-80 E, to Youngstown. OH Tpk runs with I-76 eb, I-80 wb. **Services S Mahoning Rd**
216	Lordstown (from wb), **N** 🅾 GM Plant
215	Lordstown (from eb), **N** 🅾 GM Plant
210mm	Mahoning River
209	OH 5, to Warren, **N** 🛏 Budget Lodge, **S** 🅿 Marathon/dsl 🛏 EconoLodge, Holiday Inn Express
197mm	**Portage Service Plaza wb, Bradys Leap Service Plaza eb,** 🅿 Sunoco/dsl/24hr 🍴 McDonald's, Starbucks
193	OH 44, to Ravenna
192mm	Cuyahoga River
187	OH 14 S, I-480, to Streetsboro, **0-2 mi S** 🅿 EVC, GetGo, Marathon/Circle K, Marathon/Circle K, Sheetz, Tesla EVC 🍴 Applebee's, Arby's, Baskin Robbins/Dunkin', Bob Evans, Brown Derby Roadhouse, Buffalo Wild Wings, Burger King, China Chef, Chipotle, Denny's, El Campesino, Fun Buffet, Happy Moose Grill, Honeybaked Ham, Jimmy John's, KFC, Little Caesar's, McDonald's, Mr Hero, New Peking Chinese, Panda Express, Rockne's Grill, Ruby Tuesday, Sonic, Starbucks, Steak'n Shake, Taco Bell, Wendy's 🛏 Comfort Inn, EconoLodge, Fairfield Inn, Hampton Inn, Holiday Inn Express, Motel 6, Quality Inn, TownePlace Suites, Wingate Inn 🅾 🛏, $General, $Tree, Aldi Foods, All Seasons RV Ctr, AT&T, AutoZone, Giant Eagle Mkt, GNC, Home Depot, Honda, Hyundai, Kia, Lowe's, Midas, NAPA, Nissan, NTB, Save-a-Lot Foods, Staples, Target, Tire Source/auto, to Kent St U, U-Haul, USPO, Van's Tires, Verizon, vet, VW, Walgreens, Walmart
180	OH 8, to I-90 E, **N** 🍴 Valley Jct Rest. 🛏 Baymont Inn 🅾 Costco/dsl, **S** 🅿 BP/dsl 🅾 to Cuyahoga Valley NRA
177mm	Cuyahoga River
173	OH 21, to I-77, **N** 🅿 🅿ilot/Wendy's/dsl/scales 🛏 Holiday Inn Express, Motel 6, **S** 🍴 Cozumel Mexican, Subway 🛏 Days Inn, Hampton Inn, Super 8
170mm	**Towpath Service Plaza eb, Great Lakes Service Plaza wb,** 🅿 Sunoco/dsl/24hr 🍴 Burger King, FoodCourt, Panera Bread, Pizza Hut, Starbucks
161	US 42, to I-71, Strongsville, **N on US 42** 🅿 Mobil/dsl, Sheetz/dsl 🍴 Buffalo Wild Wings, McDonald's, O'Charlie's 🛏 Kings Inn, La Siesta Motel 🅾 Home Depot, Lowe's, vet, Walmart/Subway, **S on US 42** 🛏 Elmhaven Motel 🅾 DQ, Fiat, J-Bella Rest., KFC, Marco's Pizza, Mr Hero, Olympia's Cafe, Staples, vet
152	OH 10, to Oberlin, I-480, Cleveland, **N** 🅿 BP, Sheetz/dsl, Speedway/dsl 🍴 Burger King, Chipotle, Dunkin', Gourme Rest., Lone Tree Tavern, McDonald's, Panera Bread, Taco Bell 🛏 Motel 6, Super 8

STREETSBORO

OH

⬆️🅔 OHIO TURNPIKE Cont'd

Exit #	Services
151	I-480 E (from eb), to Cleveland, N Ⓞ ✈
146mm	Black River
145	OH 57, to Lorain, to I-90, Elyria, N 🅖 Speedway/dsl 🍴 Applebee's, Bob Evans, Buffalo Wild Wings, Burger King, Chipotle Mexican, Denny's, Giant Eagle Mkt, Golden Corral, Harry Buffalo, Honeybaked Ham, IHOP, Jimmy John's, McDonald's, Olive Garden, Red Lobster, Subway, TX Roadhouse, Wasabi Grill, Wendy's 🛏 Courtyard, Best Western, Country Inn&Suites, Days Inn, Hampton Inn, Quality Inn, Red Roof Inn Ⓞ $General, $Tree, AT&T, Best Buy, Conrad's Automotive, Dick's, Firestone/auto, Home Depot, Honda, Hyundai, JC Penney, Jo-Ann Fabrics, Lowe's, Marc's Foods, Petsmart, Staples, Target, Tuffy, Verizon, S 🅖 Shell, Speedway/dsl 🛏 Super 8
142	I-90 (from eb, exits left), OH 2, to W Cleveland
140	OH 58, Amherst, N 🅖 Sunoco/Subway 🍴 DQ, Moosehead Grill Ⓞ $General, Chrysler/Dodge/Jeep, S Ⓞ Ford
139mm	Service Plaza both lanes, 🅖 Sunoco/dsl/24hr 🍴 Burger King, Panera Bread, Popeye's, Starbucks
135	rd 51, Baumhart Rd, to Vermilion
132mm	Vermilion River
118	US 250, to Norwalk, Sandusky, N 🅖 Circle K/dsl, Marathon/dsl 🍴 McDonald's, Subway 🛏 Country Inn Suites, Days Inn, Hampton Inn, Motel 6, Quality Inn, Red Roof Inn, Super 8 Ⓞ Milan RV Park, S 🛏 Colonial Inn Ⓞ to Edison's Birthplace
110	OH 4, to Bellevue
100mm	Service Plaza both lanes, 🅖 Sunoco/dsl/24hr 🍴 Burger King, Sbarro's, Starbucks
93mm	Sandusky River
91	OH 53, to Fremont, Port Clinton, N 🅖 Days Inn, 0-2 mi S 🅖 Murphy USA/dsl, Shell/Subway/dsl/24hr 🍴 Applebee's, Bob Evans, Buffalo Wild Wings, Burger King, Fricker's, Jimmy John's, McDonald's, Subway, Taco Bell 🛏 Comfort Inn, Delux Inn, Hampton Inn, Holiday Inn Express, Quality Inn Ⓞ 🏥, $Tree, Aldi Foods, AT&T, AutoZone, Ford/Lincoln, GNC, Lowe's, Rutherford B. Hayes Library, Staples, URGENT CARE, USPO, Verizon, vet, Walmart
81	OH 51, Elmore, Woodville, Gibsonburg
80.5mm	Portage River
77mm	Service Plaza both lanes, 🅖 Sunoco/dsl/24hr 🍴 Hardee's (eb), Red Burrito
71	I-280, OH 420, to Stony Ridge, Toledo, N 🅖 ⚡FLYING J/Denny's dsl/scales/LP/24hr, Loves/Arby's/dsl/scales/24hr, Petro BP/Iron Skillet/dsl/scales/24hr/@ 🛏 Best Value Inn, Budget Inn, Regency Inn, Super 8 Ⓞ Blue Beacon, SpeedCo, S 🅖 FuelMart/Subway/dsl/scales, 🚚/McDonald's/dsl/scales/24hr TA/BP/Taco Bell/dsl/scales/24hr/@ Ⓞ KOA
64	I-75 N, to Toledo, Perrysburg, S 🅖 BP/Subway/dsl 🛏 Country Inn&Suites, Courtyard, Hampton Inn, Staybridge Suites Ⓞ Bass Pro Shops, Camping World RV Ctr
63mm	Maumee River
59	US 20, to I-475, Maumee, Toledo, N 🅖 Shell/dsl, Speedway/dsl 🍴 Bob Evans, Golden Lily, Marco's Pizza, McDonald's, Nick's Cafe, Olive Garden, Steak'n Shake, Subway, Waffle House 🛏 Motel 6 Ⓞ $Tree, Goodyear/auto, Jo-Ann Fabrics, NAPA, O'Reilly Parts, Rite Aid, to Toledo Stadium, Walgreens S 🅖 Shell/dsl, Speedway/dsl 🍴 Big Boy, Chipotle Mexican, Deet's BBQ, Five Guys, Fricker's, La Fiesta Mexican, Packo's, Pizza Hut, Red Lobster, Schlotzsky's, Steak Escape, Taco Bell, Tim Horton's 🛏 Best Value Inn, Budget Inn, Comfort Inn, Comfort Inn, Days Inn, Hampton Inn, Holiday Inn, Home 2 Suites, Red Roof Inn Ⓞ antiques, AT&T, Ford, Honda, Kroger/dsl, Meijer/dsl, Toyota, Verizon, vet
52	OH 2, to Toledo, N 🍴 Loma Linda Mexican, S 🛏 Days Inn Ⓞ 🔧, RV/truck repair
39	OH 109, S 🅖 Country Corral/Winchester's Rest./dsl/scales/24hr
34	OH 108, to Wauseon, S 🅖 Sunoco/dsl/24hr 🍴 Blue Ribbon Diner 🛏 Days Inn, Holiday Inn Express, M Star Hotel, Rodeway Inn Ⓞ 🏥, 2 mi S on US 20A 🅖 Circle K, Murphy USA/dsl 🍴 Burger King, DQ, Kamwa Chinese, McDonald's, Pizza Hut, Subway, Taco Bell, Wendy's Ⓞ Ace Hardware, AutoZone, Rite Aid, Walmart
25	OH 66, Burlington, N Ⓞ Harrison Lake SP (3mi), S Ⓞ Sauder Village Museum/Inn
24.5mm	Tiffen River
20	Indian Meadow wb/Tiffen River eb Service Plaza, 🅖 Sunoco/dsl 🍴 Burger King (eb), Sbarro's, Starbucks
13	OH 15, to Bryan, Montpelier, S 🅖 Marathon/dsl, Sunoco 🍴 Four Seasons Rest., JJ Winn's Rest. 🛏 EconoLodge, Holiday Inn Express, Quality Inn, Rainbow Motel Ⓞ Hutch's Dsl Repair
11.5mm	St Joseph River
3mm	toll plaza, Ⓒ
2	OH 49, to US 20, N 🍴 Subway Ⓞ truck repair, truck wash
0mm	Ohio/Indiana state line

LORAIN

TOLEDO

WAUSEON

OH

NOTES

OKLAHOMA

🔼N INTERSTATE 35

Exit #	Services
236mm	Oklahoma/Kansas state line
235	**weigh sta sb**
231	US 177, Braman, E 🅿 Conoco/deli/dsl 🅾 casino
230	Braman Rd
229mm	Chikaskia River
225mm	**Welcome Ctr sb, full ♿ facilities, 🍴, 🛏, litter barrels, vending, petwalk**
222	OK 11, to Blackwell, Medford, Alva, Newkirk, E 🅿 Conoco/dsl, Shell/dsl 🍴 Braum's, Cobb's Rest., KFC/Taco Bell, Los Potros Mexican, McDonald's, Subway 🛏 Best Way Inn, Best Western, Econolodge, Holiday Inn Express, Sleep Inn 🅾 🄷
218	Hubbard Rd
217mm	**weigh sta both lanes**
214	US 60, to Tonkawa, Lamont, Ponka City, N OK Coll, E 🅾 RV Park, W 🅿 Casey's/dsl, 🍴/Taco Bell/dsl/scales/24hr, Shell/dsl 🛏 New Western Inn 🅾 casino
213mm	Salt Fork of Arkansas River
211	Fountain Rd, E 🅿 ♥Love's/Chester's/Subway/dsl/scales/24hr/RV Dump
209mm	**parking area, litter barrels**
203	OK 15, to Marland, Billings, E 🅿 Phillips 66/DQ/Subway/dsl/CNG/scales/24hr
199mm	Red Rock Creek
195mm	**parking area both lanes, litter barrels**
194b a	US 412, US 64 W, Cimarron Tpk, to Cimarron, Enid, W 🅾 Phillips U
193	Airport Rd (from nb, no return)
191mm	Black Bear Creek
186	US 64 E, to Fir St, Perry, E 🅿 Mobil/Subway/dsl 🍴 Braum's, McDonald's 🛏 Super 8 🅾 🄷, museum, W 🅿 Exxon/dsl 🛏 Comfort Suites, Holiday Inn Express, Microtel, Regency Inn 🅾 Chevrolet/Buick/GMC
185	US 77, to Covington, Perry, E 🛏 American Inn, W 🅿 Phillips 66/rest/motel/dsl/24hr
180	Orlando Rd
174	OK 51, to Stillwater, Hennessee, E 🅿 Phillips 66/dsl 🍴 Smokey Pokey Cafe 🛏 Fairfield Inn (12mi), Hampton Inn (12mi), La Quinta (12mi), Residence Inn (12mi) 🅾 Lake Carl Blackwell RV Park, to OSU
173mm	**parking area sb, litter barrels, parking only**
171mm	**parking area nb, litter barrels, parking only**
170	Mulhall Rd
166mm	Cimarron River
157	OK 33, to Cushing, Guthrie, E 🅿 ♥Love's/Carl's Jr/dsl/scales/24hr, Valero/Golden Chick/dsl 🅾 Langston U, W 🅿 ♥Love's/Subway/dsl, Road Star, Shell/dsl, Valero 🍴 Arby's, Braum's, El Rodeo Mexican, Pizza Hut, Sonic, The Ribshack 🛏 Best Value Inn, Hampton Inn, Holiday Inn Express, Interstate Motel, La Quinta, Sleep Inn 🅾 🄷, OK Terr Museum, RV camping
153	US 77 N (exits left from nb), Guthrie, W 🍴 McDonald's (3mi), Taco Bell (3mi) 🅾 Buick/Cadillac/GMC, Chevrolet, Chrysler/Dodge/Jeep, Ford
151	Seward Rd, E 🅿 Shell/cafe/dsl 🅾 Lazy E Arena (4mi), Pioneer RV park
146	Waterloo Rd, E 🅿 Phillips 66/dsl, Shell/Subway/dsl
143	Covell Rd, E 🅿 Phillips 66/dsl 🍴 Subway, W 🛏 Hilton Garden
142	Danforth Rd (from nb)
141	US 77 S, OK 66E, to 2nd St, Edmond, Tulsa, W 🅿 Conoco/dsl, Phillips 66/dsl 🛏 Best Western, Fairfield Inn, Hampton Inn, Holiday Inn Express, Home 2 Suites, La Quinta 🅾 🄷, vet
140	SE 15th St, Spring Creek, Arcadia Lake, Edmond Park, W 🅿 Phillips 66/Circle K/Subway/dsl 🍴 Braum's, Buffalo Wild Wings, Chick-fil-A, Whataburger 🅾 Sam's Club/dsl, Walmart
139	SE 33rd St
138d	Memorial Rd
138c	Sooner Rd (from sb)
138b	Kilpatrick Tpk
138a	I-44 Tpk E to Tulsa
I-35 S and I-44 W run together 8 mi.	
137	NE 122nd St, to OK City, E 🅿 PDQ/dsl, Shell/dsl 🍴 El Patio, IHOP 🛏 Budget Lodge, Hampton Inn, Sleep Inn, W 🅿 ⓕFLYING J/Huddle House/dsl/scales/LP/24hr, ♥Love's/Godfathers/Subway/dsl/24hr, Valero/dsl/scales 🍴 Cracker Barrel, McDonald's, Sonic, Waffle House 🛏 Baymont Inn, Best Value Inn, Days Inn, Economy Inn, Holiday Inn Express, Motel 6, Super 8 🅾 Abe's RV Park, Frontier City Funpark, Oklahoma Visitors Ctr/info/restrooms
136	Hefner Rd, W 🅿 Conoco/dsl, same as 137
135	Britton Rd
134	Wilshire Blvd, W 🛏 Executive Inn 🅾 Blue Beacon
I-35 N and I-44 E run together 8 mi.	
133	I-44 W, to Amarillo, W 🅾 Cowboy Hall of Fame, st capitol
132b	NE 63rd St (from nb), 1/2 mi E 🅿 Conoco/dsl 🍴 Braum's 🛏 Remington Inn
132a	NE 50th St, Remington Pk, W 🅾 funpark, museum, zoo
131	NE 36th St, W 🅿 Phillips 66/Circle K/dsl 🅾 45th Inf Division Museum
130	US 62 E, NE 23rd St, E 🅿 Shell/dsl, W 🅾 to st capitol
129	NE 10th St, E 🅿 Valero/McDonald's/dsl 🅾 Family$
128	I-40 E, to Ft Smith
127	Eastern Ave, OK City, W 🅿 Checkers/Subway/dsl/scales/24hr/@, Petro/Iron Skillet/dsl/24hr/@ 🍴 Waffle House 🛏 Comfort Inn, EconoLodge, Motel 6, Ramada 🅾 Lewis RV Ctr
126a	I-40, W to Amarillo, I-235 N, to st capitol
126b	I-35 S to Dallas
125d	SE 15th St, E 🅿 Conoco/dsl 🛏 Holiday Inn Express
125b	SE 22nd St (from nb)
125a	SE 25th same as 124b

OK

GUTHRIE

🅖 = gas 🅕 = food 🅛 = lodging 🅞 = other 🆁🆂 = rest stop   Copyright 2022 - The Next EXIT ®

INTERSTATE 35 Cont'd

Exit #	Services
124b	SE 29th St, **E** 🅕 China Queen, Denny's, El Sombrero, McDonald's, Sonic, Taco Bell 🅛 Best Value Inn, Days Inn, Plaza Inn, Royal Inn, **W** 🅖 Phillips 66/Circle K 🅕 Mama Lou's Rest. 🅛 Executive Inn, same as 125a
124a	Grand Blvd, **E** 🅛 Studio 6, Super 8, **W** 🅛 Drover's Inn
123b	SE 44th St, **E** 🅖 Shell 🅕 Domino's, Sonic 🅛 Best Value Inn, Courtesy Inn, Motel 6 🅞 $General, **W** 🅖 Phillips 66 🅕 Subway, Taco Mayo 🅞 $General, Family$, USPO
123a	SE 51st St, **E** 🅖 Conoco/dsl 🅛 Best Value Inn
122b	SE 59th St, **E** 🅖 Phillips 66/dsl, **W** 🅖 Shell/dsl, Valero/dsl 🅞 U-Haul
122a	SE 66th St, **E** 🅕 Burger King, Subway, TX Roadhouse 🅛 Fairfield Inn, Magnuson Hotel, Residence Inn, **W** 🅖 7-11 🅕 Arby's
121b	US 62 W, I-240 E
121a	SE 82nd St, (from sb), **W** 🅛 Days Inn, Rodeway Inn
120	SE 89th St, **E** 🅖 Valero/dsl/scales 🅛 Ford, **W** 🅖 Loves/Subway/dsl/24hr 🅞 Classic Parts
119b	N 27th St, **E** 🅖 Shell/Circle K/dsl 🅕 Starbucks, **W** 🅕 Pickles Rest.
119a	Shields Blvd (exits left from nb)
118	N 12th St, **E** 🅕 Mazzio's, Peking Buffet 🅛 Super 8, **W** 🅖 7-11, Shell, Valero/dsl 🅕 A&W/LJ Silver, Arby's, Braum's, Grandy's, KFC, Mamma Lou's, McDonald's, Papa John's, Subway, Taco Bell, Wendy's, Western Sizzlin 🅛 Best Western, Candlewood Suites, Econolodge, Hampton Inn, SpringHill Suites 🅞 $General, AutoZone, vet
117	OK 37, S 4th St, **W** 🅖 7-11, On Cue/dsl/CNG/e10 🅞 🅗 USPO
116	S 19th St, **E** 🅖 Sam's Club/dsl, Shell 🅕 Braum's, Garage Burgers, Genghis Grill, Jimmy John's, McDonald's, Ricky's Cafe, Slim Chickens, Taco Bell, Taco Bueno, Waffle House, Whataburger, Zaxby's 🅞 American Automotive, AT&T, Best Buy, Firestone/auto, GNC, Hobby Lobby, JC Penney, Office Depot, Petsmart, Ross, URGENT CARE, **W** 🅖 Murphy USA 🅕 Alfredo's Mexican, Applebee's, Arby's, Buffalo Wild Wings, Burger King, Cane's, Carl's Jr, Chick-fil-A, Chicken Express, Chili's, China House, Del Taco, DQ, Earl's Ribs, Firehouse Subs, Five Guys, Freddy's Custard, Furr's Buffet, Hollies Steaks, IHOP, Jack-in-the-Box, Jersey's Mike's Subs, Jimmy's Egg, Luigi's Bistro, Mazzio's, McAlister's Deli, Oliveto's Italian, Panda Express, Pei Wei, Qdoba Mexican, Schlotzsky's, Smashburger, Sonic, Starbucks, Subway, Taco Mayo, Tropical Cafe 🅛 La Quinta 🅞 $Tree, Aldi Foods, AT&T, AutoZone, Dick's, Discount Tire, Gordman's, Harley-Davidson, Home Depot, Kohl's, Lowe's, Target, Tires+, Verizon, Walmart
114	Indian Hill Rd, **E** 🅛 Woodspring Suites, **W** 🅕 Double Dave's Pizza 🅞 Cadillac, funpark
113	US 77 S (from sb, exits left), Norman
112	Tecumseh Rd, **W** 🅕 McDonald's, Sonic 🅞 CVS Drug, 🅗, Nissan, Toyota, URGENT CARE
110b a	Robinson St, **E** 🅕 Carl's Jr, Cheddar's, Chipotle, ChuckECheese, Five Guys, Logan's Roadhouse, Panda Express, Pei Wei, Qdoba Mexican, Sonic, Starbucks, Subway, Taco Bell, Wing Stop, Zio's Italian, Zoe's Kitchen 🅛 Embassy Suites, Holiday Inn Express, Motel 6 🅞 $Tree, AT&T, Buick/GMC, Crest Mkt, Discount Tire, Ford, GNC, Homeland Foods/gas, Honda, 🅗, Hyundai, Kohl's, Mazda, Michael's, Office Depot, PetCo, Target, Tires+, TJ Maxx, Verizon, VW, **W** 🅖 Conoco/Subway 🅕 Arby's, Braum's, Cafe Escondido, Chuy's Mexican, Cracker Barrel, Domino's, Jersey Mike's, Outback Steaks, Papa John's, Papa Murphy's, Rib Crib, Saltgrass Steaks, Waffle House, Yamato Steaks 🅛 Comfort Inn, Courtyard, Hilton Garden, Norman Hotel 🅞 Kia
109	Main St, **E** 🅖 Murphy USA/dsl, Phillips 66/dsl, Shell/Circle K, Sinclair 🅕 Arby's, Chick-fil-A, DQ, Golden Corral, Jimmy's Egg, Little Caesar's, Panera Bread, Subway, Waffle House, Wendy's, Whataburger, Zaxby's 🅛 Days Inn, EconoLodge, Super 8, Travelodge 🅞 Aldi Foods, AT&T, AutoZone, Best Buy, BigLots, Chrysler/Dodge/Jeep, Hobby Lobby, Kwik Kar, Lowe's, Tires+, Walmart/McDonald's, **W** 🅖 Conoco/Circle K/dsl 🅕 Applebee's, BJ's Brewhouse, Burger King, Cane's, Charleston's, Chili's, McDonald's, Olive Garden, Red Lobster 🅛 Fairfield Inn, Hampton Inn, La Quinta 🅞 Barnes&Noble, Dillard's, JC Penney, Jo-Ann, Old Navy, Sam's Club
108b a	OK 9 E, Norman, **E** 🅖 Conoco/Circle K 🅕 Braum's, Del Rancho Steaks, Schlotzsky's, Taco Bell 🅛 Sooner Legends Inn/rest. 🅞 $General, NAPA, O'Reilly Parts, to U of OK, **W** 🅕 Carino's Italian, IHOP, Jason's Deli, Red Robin 🅛 Country Inn&Suites, La Quinta 🅞 Chevrolet, Home Depot, Petsmart, Ross
107mm	Canadian River
106	OK 9 W, to Chickasha, **E** 🅞 Casino, **W** 🅖 Loves/Subway/dsl/24hr, Shell 🅕 McDonald's, Sonic 🅛 Sleep Inn 🅞 casino, URGENT CARE, vet
104	OK 74 S, Goldsby, **E** 🅞 Floyd's RV Ctr, **W** 🅖 CNG, Valero/dsl 🅕 Libby's Cafe
101	Ladd Rd
98	Johnson Rd, **E** 🅞 Funtown RV Ctr
95	US 77 (exits left from sb), Purcell, 1-3 mi **E** 🅖 Conoco/dsl 🅕 KFC, Mazzio's, Van's BBQ 🅞 $General, AutoZone, Ford, 🅗
91	OK 74, to OK 39, Maysville, **E** 🅖 Conoco/dsl, Murphy USA/dsl, Phillips 66/dsl 🅕 Braum's, McDonald's, New China, Subway, Taco Mayo 🅛 EconoLodge, Executive Inn, Ruby's Inn/rest. 🅞 AT&T, Walmart/Subway, **W** 🅖 Shell/dsl 🅕 A&W/LJ Silver, Taco Bell
86	OK 59, Wayne, Payne, **E** 🅞 American RV Park
79	OK 145 E, Paoli, **E** 🅖 Phillips 66/dsl
76mm	Washita River
74	Kimberlin Rd, to OK 19
72	OK 19, Paul's Valley, **E** 🅖 Conoco/dsl, Murphy USA/dsl, Sunoco/dsl/rest/24hr 🅕 Arby's, Braum's, Chicken Express, Green Tea Chinese, Happy Days Diner, KFC/Taco Bell, McDonald's, Riviera Maya, Snider's Buffet, Sonic, Subway, Tio's Mexican 🅛 American Inn, Best Value Inn, Comfort Inn, Days Inn, Hampton Inn, Holiday Inn Express, Relax Inn 🅞 AT&T, Buick/Cadillac/GMC, Chrysler/Dodge/Jeep, URGENT CARE, Walmart, **W** 🅖 Phillips 66/dsl/24hr, Shell/dsl 🅞 Ford/Lincoln, truckwash
70	Airport Rd, **E** 🅖 Loves/Burger King/dsl/LP/scales/24hr/@ 🅞 🅗, **W** 🅞 T&R RV Resort
66	OK 29, Wynnewood, **E** 🅛 Kent's Motel, **W** 🅖 Shell/dsl
64	OK 17A E, to Wynnewood, **E** 🅞 GW Exotic Animal Park
60	Ruppe Rd
59mm	🆁🆂 both lanes, full 🅿 facilities, 🄲, picnic table, litter barrels, petwalk, RV dump
55	OK 7, Davis, **E** 🅖 Conoco/dsl, Phillips 66/A&W/dsl/24hr 🅛 The Inn 🅞 to Chickasaw NRA, Treasure Valley Casino/Inn, **W** 🅖 Phillips 66/dsl 🅞 Chickasaw Nation Welcome Ctr, to Arbuckle Ski Area
54.5mm	Honey Creek Pass
53mm	weigh sta both lanes
51	US 77, Turner Falls, **E** 🅛 Arbuckle Mtn Motel, Mtnview Inn (3mi) 🅞 RV camping, to Arbuckle Wilderness, **W** 🅖 Sinclair/rv park
49mm	scenic turnout both lanes
47	US 77, Turner Falls Area
46mm	scenic turnout both lanes
42	OK 53 W, Springer, Comanche, **W** 🅖 Exxon/Subway/dsl

NORMAN

PAULS VALLEY

OKLAHOMA CITY

OK

INTERSTATE 35 Cont'd

Exit #	Services
40	OK 53 E, Gene Autry, **E** 🅖 Valero/dsl/café/24hr 🅞 Gene Autry Museum (8mi)
33	OK 142, Ardmore, **E** 🅖 Shell, Valero/dsl 🅕 IHOP, Jimmy's Egg Cafe 🅛 Best Value Inn, Courtyard, Holiday Inn, La Quinta, Nissan, Red Roof Inn, SpringHill Suites, Super 8 🅞 Honda, regional park, tires, **W** 🅖 FLYING J/Huddle House/dsl/LP/scales/24hr
32	12th St, Ardmore, **E** 🅖 Phillips 66/dsl, Shell 🅕 Arby's, Braum's, Chick-fil-A, Chili's, Cotton Patch Cafe, Freddy's, Quiznos, Rib Crib, Sakura Hibachi, Santa Fe Steaks, Starbucks, Whataburger 🅛 Baymont Inn, Candlewood Suites, La Quinta 🅞 $Tree, AT&T, Chevrolet, Hilton Garden, Hyundai, Lowe's, PetCo, Ross, Toyota, **W** 🅖 Loves/Godfather's/Subway/dsl/24hr/@ 🅕 McDonald's 🅛 Microtel
31 b a	US 70 W, OK 199 E, Ardmore, **E** 🅖 Shell/dsl, Valero/dsl 🅕 Applebee's, Burger King, Denny's, El Chico, El Tapatio, Interurban Grill, Jack-in-the-Box, KFC, McDonald's, Papa John's, Pizza Hut, Prairie Kitchen, Two Frogs Grill 🅛 Best Western+, Comfort Inn, Days Inn, Hampton Inn, Lexington Inn, Motel 6, Quality Inn 🅞 AutoZone, Econolodge, Kia, O'Reilly Parts, **W** 🅖 Conoco/dsl 🅞 Ardmore RV Park, Chrysler/Dodge/Jeep, Ford/Lincoln, vet
29	US 70 E, Ardmore, **E** 🅞 to Lake Murray SP/lodge (8mi), **W** 🅞 Hidden Lake RV Park
24	OK 77 S, **E** 🅞 By the Lake RV Park, Red River Livestock Mkt, to Lake Murray SP
22.5mm	Hickory Creek
21	Oswalt Rd, **W** 🅖 Valero/dsl 🅞 Ardmore Marietta RV Park
15	OK 32, Marietta, **E** 🅖 Valero/dsl/24hr 🅕 Carl's Jr, Homeland Foods, La Roca Mexican, McDonald's, Robertson's Sandwiches, Sonic, Subway 🅞 $General, 🏥, to Lake Texoma SP, **W** 🅖 Gulf/dsl, Shell/dsl
5	OK 153, Thackerville, **W** 🅞 Red River Ranch RV Park, Shorty's Foods/gas
3.5mm	Welcome Ctr nb, full ♿ facilities, 🅒, 🛢, litter barrels, vending, petwalk
3	Winstar Blvd, **E** 🅞 casino, same as 1
1	US 77 N, **E** 🅖 Phillips 66/dsl/CNG 🅕 Sonic 🅛 Best Western, Red River Suites, The Inn 🅞 RV park, Winstar Casino, **W** 🅞 Red River RV Resort (3mi)
0mm	Oklahoma/Texas state line, Red River

INTERSTATE 40

Exit #	Services
331mm	Oklahoma/Arkansas state line
330	OK 64D S (from eb), Ft Smith
329mm	weigh sta wb
325	US 64, Roland, Ft Smith, **N** 🅖 Cherokee Trkstp/Valero/Subway/dsl/scales/24hr 🅕 Four Star Diner 🅛 Best Value Inn, Cherokee Inn 🅞 casino, **S** 🅖 Phillips 66/dsl/scales, 🚍/Wendy's/dsl/scales/24hr, QS/dsl 🅕 Arby's, El Celaya Mexican, Mazzio's, McDonald's, Sonic, Subway, Taco Bell 🅛 Interstate Inn 🅞 $General, Marvin's Foods, O'Reilly Parts
321	OK 64b N, Muldrow, **S** 🅖 Arena/dsl 🅛 Executive Inn 🅞 truck parts/svc
316mm	🆁🆂 eb, full ♿ facilities, info, 🅒, 🛢, litter barrels, vending, petwalk
313mm	🆁🆂 wb, full ♿ facilities, info, 🅒, 🛢, litter barrels, vending, petwalk, RV dump
311	US 64, Sallisaw, **N** 🅖 Phillips 66/dsl, Sunoco/dsl 🅕 El Toro Mexican, Hardee's, KFC/Taco Bell, O'Reilly Parts, Pizza Hut,

Exit #	Services
311	Continued Simple Simon's Pizza 🅛 Motel 6, Sallisaw Inn 🅞 $General, AutoZone, Brushy Lake SP (10mi), 🏥, Sequoya's Home (12mi)
308	US 59, Sallisaw, **N** 🅖 Murphy USA/dsl, Sunoco/dsl 🅕 A&W/LJ Silver, Arby's, Asian Star, Braum's, Cazadore Mexican, China Harbor, Mazzio's, McDonald's, Roma's Italian, Sonic, Subway, Taco Bueno 🅛 Days Inn, Economy Inn, Golden Spur Motel, Super 8 🅞 $General, $Tree, AT&T, casino, 🏥, Verizon, Walmart/Subway, **S** 🅖 Valero/dsl 🅕 Chen's Garden 🅞 Buick/Chevrolet/GMC, Chrysler/Dodge/Jeep, Ford, KOA, to Kerr Lake, truck/tire repair
303	Dwight Mission Rd
297	OK 82 N, Vian, **N** 🅖 FL/dsl, Loves/Subway/dsl/24hr/@ 🅕 Simple Simon, Subway 🅞 Cherokee Landing SP (24 mi), IGA Foods, to Tenkiller Lake RA (12 mi), USPO, **S** 🅞 Sequoia NWR
291	OK 10 N, to Gore, **N** 🅞 Greenleaf SP (10mi), Tenkiller SP (21mi)
290mm	Arkansas River
287	OK 100 N, to Webbers Falls, **N** 🅖 Loves/Burger King/Subway/dsl/24hr 🅕 Cox's Buffet 🅞 Greenleaf SP, parts/tires/repair, Tenkiller SP
286	Muskogee Tpk, to Muskogee
284	Ross Rd
283mm	parking area both lanes, litter barrels
278	US 266, OK 2, Warner, **N** 🅖 Conoco, Sinclair/dsl (2), Sinclair/McDonald's/dsl 🅕 El Jaracho Mexican, Sonic, Subway 🅛 Ambassadors Inn & RV 🅞 $General
270	Texanna Rd, to Porum Landing, **S** 🅖 Campbell's/BBQ
265	US 69 bus, Checotah, **N** 🅖 Kwik'n Easy 🅕 Pizza Hut, Sonic, **S** 🅖 Phillips 66/dsl 🅛 Budget Inn 🅞 Chevrolet/Chrysler/Dodge/Jeep
264 b a	US 69, to Eufaula, 1 mi **N** 🅖 FLYING J/Denny's/dsl/LP/scales/24hr, Casey's/dsl, Phillips 66/dsl/24hr 🅕 Charlie's Chicken, McDonald's, Simple Simon's Pizza, Taco Bell 🅛 Best Value Inn 🅞 $General, AT&T, O'Reilly Parts, repair, TrueValue, Walmart/Subway
262	to US 266, Lotawatah Rd, **N** 🅖 Sunshine
261mm	Lake Eufaula
259	OK 150, to Fountainhead Rd, **S** 🅖 Fountain Head/dsl 🅛 Lake Eufaula Inn 🅞 to Lake Eufaula SP
255	Pierce Rd, **N** 🅞 KOA
251mm	🆁🆂 both lanes
247	Tiger Mtn Rd, **S** 🅞 Quilt Barn/antiques
240 b a	US 62 E, US 75 N, Henryetta, **N** 🅖 Conoco/dsl, Loves/dsl, Phillips 66, Shell 🅕 Arby's, Braum's, Classic Diner, El Charro Mexican, KFC, Mazzio's, McDonald's, Shoney's, Sonic, Subway, Taco Bell, Taco Bueno 🅛 Days Inn, Economy Inn, Relax Inn 🅞 Chevrolet, Chrysler/Dodge/Jeep, Ford, O'Reilly Parts, tires/repair, Walmart, **S** 🅞 Indian Nation Tpk
237	US 62, US 75, Henryetta, **N** 🅖 Kellogg/dsl 🅛 Green Country Inn 🅞 Henryetta RV Park (2mi), 🏥, **S** 🅛 Super 8
231	US 75 S, to Weleetka, **N** 🅖 Sinclair/dsl 🅕 Cowpoke's Cafe

INTERSTATE 40 Cont'd

Exit #	Services
227	Clearview Rd, S 🄾 casino
221	US 62, OK 27, Okemah, N 🅖 $General/dsl, Express/Subway/dsl/24hr, Phillips 66/McDonald's 🍴 Dairy Boy Drive-In, Mazzio's, Pepino's Mexican, Simple Simon's, Sonic 🛏 Days Inn 🄾 $General, Chevrolet, Homeland Foods, NAPA, TrueValue, S 🅖 ❤Loves/Chester Fried/dsl/24hr 🄾 casino, 🄷, truck repair
217	OK 48, to Bristow, Bearden, S 🅖 gas/dsl
216mm	N Canadian River
212	OK 56, to Cromwell, Wewoka, N 🄾 auto/tire repair, S 🅖 to Seminole Nation Museum (16mi), Valero/Chester's/dsl
208mm	Gar Creek
202mm	Turkey Creek
200	US 377, OK 99, to Little, Prague, N 🅖 Bar H Bar TC/Shell/dsl/RV park 🍴 RoadHouse Diner, S 🅖 Conoco/dsl, ❤Loves/Subway/dsl/24hr, Sinclair/dsl 🍴 Robertson's Ham Sandwiches, Roundup Rest/RV Park 🄾🄷
197mm	Ⓡ🅂 both lanes, full ♿ facilities, 🄲, 🚮, litter barrels, petwalk
192	OK 9A, Earlsboro, S 🅖 Valero/Baskin Robbins/dsl
189mm	N Canadian River
186	OK 18, to Shawnee, N 🅖 Phillips 66, Sinclair 🍴 Denny's 🛏 American Inn, Comfort Inn, Days Inn, Fairfield Inn, La Quinta, Quality Inn, Super 8, S 🅖 Shell/Domino's/dsl, Sinclair/dsl 🍴 Carl's Jr, Cazadorez, Sonic, Subway, Van's BBQ 🛏 Colonial Inn 🄾 Chrysler/Dodge/Jeep, Homeland Foods
185	OK 3E, Shawnee Mall Dr, to Shawnee, N 🅖 Murphy USA/dsl 🍴 Buffalo Wild Wings, Chili's, Garage Burgers, KFC, Panda Express, Red Lobster, Santa Fe Steaks, Taco Bueno, Wendy's 🛏 Holiday Inn Express 🄾 $Tree, AT&T, Chevrolet, Dillard's, Ford, JC Penney, Jo-Ann, Kohl's, Ross, Walgreens, Walmart/McDonald's, S 🅖 Circle K/dsl 🍴 Braum's, Burger King, Chick-fil-A, Cracker Barrel, Delta Cafe, Freddy's, IHOP, Mazzio's, McAlister's Deli, McDonald's, Popeye's, Qdoba, Rib Crib BBQ, Schlotzsky's, Sonic, Starbucks, Subway, Taco Bell, Whataburger 🛏 Hampton Inn 🄾 Aldi Foods, CVS Drug, Discount Tire, Hobby Lobby, Lowe's, O'Reilly Parts, Petsmart, Staples, TJ Maxx, Verizon
181	US 177, US 270, to Tecumseh, S 🅖 Shell/dsl 🍴 Rosa's Mexican 🄾 dsl repair, Prestige RV Ctr
180mm	N Canadian River
178	OK 102 S, Dale, N 🅖 Grand TC/Subway/hotel/casino/dsl
176	OK 102 N, McLoud Rd, S 🅖 ❤Loves/Subway/dsl/24hr, Sinclair/dsl 🍴 Curtis Watson Rest.
172	Newalla Rd, to Harrah
170	Kickapoo Turnpike to Tulsa
169	Peebly Rd
166	Choctaw Rd, to Woods, N 🅖 ❤Loves/McDonald's/Subway/dsl/scales/24hr 🄾 KOA, S 🅖 🄻🄸🄿🄿/Wendy's/dsl/scales/24hr 🍴 Sonic 🄾 to Lake Thunderbird SP (11mi)
165	I-240 W (from wb), to Dallas
162	Anderson Rd, N 🄾 Gander RV Ctr, LP
159b	Douglas Blvd, N 🅖 KFC, OnCue/dsl, Shell/Circle K/dsl 🍴 A&W/LJ Silver, Denny's, Freddy's, Jimmy John's, McDonald's, Pizza Hut, Sonic, Subway, Taco Bell, Whataburger 🄾 Eastland Hills RV Park, S 🄾 🄷, Tinker AFB
159a	Hruskocy Gate, N 🄾 Chrysler/Dodge/Jeep, same as 157, U-Haul, S 🄾 Tinker AFB, Gate 7
157c	Eaker Gate 🄾 Tinker AFB same as 159
157b	Air Depot Blvd, N 🅖 Shell/Circle K 🍴 Bricktown Brewery, Cane's, Cheddar's, Chick-fil-A, Chili's, Jack-in-the-Box, Logans Roadhouse, McAlister's Deli, Panda Express, Panera Bread, Pei Wei, Qdoba Grill, Santa Fe Steaks, Starbucks, Steak&Shake 🄾
157b	Continued AT&T, Best Buy, Dick's, Firestone/auto, GNC, JC Penney, Kohl's, Lowe's, Marshall's, O'Reilly Parts, Office Depot, Old Navy Petsmart, Target, Verizon, S 🄾 Tinker AFB, Gate 1
157a	SE 29th St, Midwest City, N 🅖 Shell/Circle K 🍴 On the Border 🛏 Best Western+, Traveler's Inn 🄾 O'Reilly Parts, S 🄾 Ford Sam's Club/gas
156b a	Sooner Rd, N 🅖 Conoco/Circle K, Gulf 🍴 Black Bear Diner, Waffle House 🛏 Hampton Inn, Hawthorn Suites, Holiday Inn Express, Home 2 Suites, La Quinta, Motel 6, Sheraton, Studio 6 🄾 Hobby Lobby, Home Depot, Walmart/Subway, S 🍴 Best China, Buffalo Wild Wings, Carl's Jr, Garage Grill, Hungry Howie's, Ted's Mexican 🛏 Candlewood Suites, SpringHill Suites, Super 8 🄾 AT&T, Chevrolet/GMC, Discount Tire, Tires+, Toyota, Verizon
155b	SE 15th St, Del City, N 🅖 Valero/dsl 🄾 Family$, 🄷, Nissan
155a	Sunny Lane Rd, Del City, N 🅖 Conoco/Subway/dsl 🄾 Hyundai, U-Haul, S 🍴 Braum's, Church's, Dunkin', Luigi's Pizza, Sonic 🄾 $General, $Tree
154	Reno Ave, Scott St, N 🛏 Woodspring Suites 🄾 vet, S 🍴 7-11
152	(153 from wb) I-35 N, to Wichita
127	Eastern Ave (from eb), Okla City, N 🅖 Checkers/Subway/dsl/scales/24hr, Petro/Iron Skillet/dsl/scales/@ 🍴 Waffle House 🛏 Comfort Inn, Econolodge, Motel 6 🄾 Lewis RV Ctr
151b c	I-35, S to Dallas, I-235 N, to downtown, N 🄾 to st capitol
151a	Lincoln Blvd, N 🅖 Casey's/Subway/Circle K/dsl 🍴 Earl's Rib Palace, Fuzzy's Taco Shop, McDonald's 🛏 Hampton Inn, Homewood Suites, Residence Inn 🄾 Bass Pro Shop, Bricktown Stadium
150c	Robinson Ave (from wb), OK City, N 🍴 Abuelo's Mexican, Bob's Steaks, Pearl's Crabtown, Spark, Starbuck's, Texadelphia, Yucatan Tacos 🛏 Courtyard, Hilton Garden, Residence Inn, Sheraton, SpringHill, Staybridge Suites 🄾 U-Haul
150b	Harvey Ave (from eb), N 🛏 Courtyard, Hilton Garden, Renaissance Hotel, Sheraton downtown
150a	Shields Blvd (from eb), N 🄾 to downtown
149b	Classen Blvd (from wb) same as 149a, to downtown
149a	Western Ave, Reno Ave, N 🅖 Conoco/dsl, Shell/dsl, VP/Subway/dsl 🍴 McDonald's, Sonic, Sweis Gyros, Taco Bell
148c	Virginia Ave (from wb) to downtown
148b	Penn Ave (from eb), N 🅖 Valero/dsl 🄾 Summit Truck Repair
148a	Agnew Ave, Villa Ave, N 🅖 VP/dsl
147c	May Ave
147b a	I-44, E to Tulsa, W to Lawton
146	Portland Ave (from eb, no return), N 🅖 Phillips 66/Subway/dsl 🍴 Taqueria Mexican 🄾 diesel repair
145	Meridian Ave, OK City, N 🅖 Casey's/Circle K/dsl, Shell/Circle K/dsl 🍴 Denny's, Earl's Ribs, Gopuram Indian, McDonald's, On the Border, Trapper's Rest. 🛏 Best Western, Biltmore Hotel, Days Inn, Extended Stay America, Howard Johnson, Red Roof Inn, Sonesta Suites, Studio 6, Super 8, S 🅖 Phillips 66/Circle K/dsl 🍴 Billy Sims BBQ, Burger King, Charleston Rest., Chili's, Cracker Barrel, Frosted Mug Grill, Golden Palace Chinese, IHOP, Mackie's Steaks, Red River Pizza, San Marcos Mexican, Sonic, Subway, Taco Bell, Waffle House, Whataburger, Zapata's, Zio's Italian 🛏 AmericInn, Baymont Inn, Comfort Suites, Comfort Suites (2), Country Inn&Suites, Courtyard, DoubleTree, Econo Lodge, Embassy Suites, Fairfield Inn, Governors Suites, Hampton Inn, Hilton Garden, Holiday Inn, Holiday Inn Express, Home 2 Suites, Hyatt Place, La Quinta, Meridian Inn, Motel 6, Oak Tree Inn, Ramada, Residence Inn, Sheraton, Sleep Inn, Staybridge Suites, TownePlace Suites, Tru, Wingate Inn, Woodspring Suites, Wyndham Garden 🄾 Boot Barn

SHAWNEE

OK

OKLAHOMA CITY

INTERSTATE 40 Cont'd

Exit #	Services
144	MacArthur Blvd, N 🅶 Casey's/dsl, Shell/Circle K/dsl 🍴 Applebee's, Arby's, Chick-fil-A, China One, Coldstone, Del Taco, Firehouse Subs, Five Guys, Freddy's, Golden Corral, Jack-in-the-Box, Jimmy John's, KFC, McDonald's, Olive Garden, Panda Express, Panera Bread, Qdoba, Schlotzsky's, Sonic, Starbucks, Taco Bueno, Twin Peaks, TX Roadhouse 🛏 SpringHill Suites 🅾 $Tree, AT&T, GNC, Hobby Lobby, Petsmart, Ross, Verizon, Walmart/McDonald's, S 🛏 Comfort Inn, Green Carpet Inn, Microtel, Travelers Inn 🅾 Sam's Club/gas
143	Rockwell Ave, N 🅶 7-11/dsl 🍴 Buffalo Wild Wings, Jersey Mike's, S&B's Burgers, Taco Bell 🛏 Best Western, Homewood Suites 🅾 Best Buy, Dick's, Discount Tire, Harley Davidson, Home Depot, McClain's RV Ctr, Tires+, S 🛏 Sands Motel/RV Park/LP 🅾 Rockwell RV Park
142	Council Rd, N 🅶 On Cue/dsl/CNG, Tesla EVC 🍴 BJ's Rest., Braum's, Garage Burgers, Jimmy's Egg, McDonald's, Subway, Taco Mayo, Ted's Mexican, Whataburger 🛏 Super 40 Inn 🅾 dsl repair, S 🅶 TA/Country Pride/dsl/scales/24hr/@ 🛏 Econo Inn 🅾 Council Rd RV Park, Ford/Peterbilt, truckwash
140	Morgan Rd, N 🅶 Pilot/McDonald's/dsl/24hr/@, TA/Popeye's/Fazoli's/dsl/24hr/@ 🅾 Blue Beacon, S 🅶 FLYING J/Huddle House/dsl /LP/scales/24hr, Loves/Subway/dsl/scales/24hr 🍴 Braum's Ice Cream, Sonic 🅾 Speedco
139	Kilpatrick Tpk
138	OK 4, to Yukon, Mustang, N 🍴 Catfish Cove 🛏 Best Value Inn, Comfort Suites, Motel 6 🅾 Chrysler/Dodge/Jeep, vet, S 🅶 Conoco/Circle K/dsl 🍴 Braum's, Burger King, Golden Chick, IHOP, Interurban Grill, Mama Mo's Pizza, McDonald's, Sonic, Subway, Taco Bell 🛏 Best Western+, Home 2 Suites, Hyatt Place, La Quinta 🅾 Aamco, CVS Drug, Homeland Food/drug, Mustang Run RV Park, URGENT CARE
137	Cornwell Dr, Czech Hall Rd, N 🅶 On Cue/dsl 🅾 Homeland Food/drug, URGENT CARE
136	OK 92, Garth Brooks Blvd, Yukon, N 🅶 Casey's, Murphy USA/dsl 🍴 A&W/LJ Silver, Braum's, Cane's, Chelino's Mexican, CiCi's Pizza, KFC, McDonald's, Popeye's, Primo's Italian, Subway, Waffle House, Wendy's 🛏 Hampton Inn 🅾 $Tree, AutoZone, Big O Tire, NAPA, repair, Sprouts Mkt, T-Mobile, Tuesday Morning, USPO, Walgreens, Walmart, S 🅶 Shell/dsl 🍴 Alfredo's Mexican, Arby's, Buffalo Wild Wings, Carino's Italian, Cheddar's, Chick-fil-A, Chicken Express, Chili's, Del Taco, DQ, Freddy's, Hideaway Pizza, Hooters, Jersey Mike's, Jimmy's Egg Café, Johnnie's Broiler, Logan's Roadhouse, Louie's Grill, McAlister's Deli, Panda Express, Pizza Hut, Rib Crib, Sonic, Starbucks, Taco Bueno, Tokyo Moon 🛏 Avid Hotel, Fairfield Inn, Holiday Inn Express, Sleep Inn 🅾 Aldi, AT&T, Big Lots, Discount Tire, Ford, GNC, Hobby Lobby, Ⓗ, Kohl's, Lowe's, lube & service, Marshall's, Petco, PetsMart, Ross, Staples, Target, Tires+
135	Frisco Rd
132	Cimarron Rd, S 🅾 🖵
130	Banner Rd, N 🅶 Shell/dsl
129mm	weigh st both lanes
127	S Radio Rd, S 🅶 Loves/Carl's Jr/dsl/scales/24hr
125	US 81, to El Reno, N 🅶 Loves/Subway/dsl, Phillips 66/dsl, Shell/dsl 🍴 Chelino's Mexican, China King, Swadley's BBQ, Taco Mayo 🛏 Best Value Inn, Economy Express, Ranger Motel 🅾 $General, Buick/GMC, Chevrolet, Chrysler/Dodge/Jeep, Ford/Lincoln
123	Country Club Rd, to El Reno, N 🅶 Casey's, Murphy USA/dsl, Shell/dsl, Valero/dsl 🍴 Arby's, Braum's, Burger King, Greatwall
123	Continued Chinese, KFC, Little Caesar's, McDonald's, Pizza Express, Pizza Hut, Subway, Taco Bell, Taco Bueno 🛏 Fairfield Inn, Hampton Inn, Home 2 Suites, Motel 6 🅾 AT&T, AutoZone, Ⓗ, Walgreens, Walmart, S 🍴 Denny's, MT Mikes Steaks 🛏 Baymont Inn, Best Western/RV Park, Days Inn, Holiday Inn Express, Regency Motel
119	Lp 40, to El Reno
115	US 270, to Calumet
111mm	picnic area eb, 🚻, litter barrels
108	US 281, to Geary, N 🅶 Shell/Subway/dsl/24hr 🅾 KOA/Indian Trading Post, to Roman Nose SP, S 🅶 Phillips 66/Pizza Inn/dsl
105mm	S Canadian River
104	Methodist Rd
101	US 281, OK 8, Hinton, N 🅾 Territory Rte 66 RV Park, to Roman Nose SP, S 🅶 Loves/Chester's/Godfather's/Sonic/dsl/scales 🍴 Subway 🛏 Hinton Country Inn, Sugar Creek Inn 🅾 casino, Chevrolet, to Red Rock Canyon SP
95	Bethel Rd
88	OK 58, to Hydro, Carnegie
84	Airport Rd, N 🅶 Phillips 66/dsl/CNG/scales/24hr 🍴 Lucille's Roadhouse 🛏 Holiday Inn Express, Travel Inn 🅾 Buick/Cadillac/Chevrolet/GMC, Ⓗ, Stafford Aerospace Museum, S 🛏 La Quinta 🅾 Chrysler/Dodge/Jeep, Ford/Lincoln
82	E Main St, Weatherford, N 🅶 Conoco/dsl, Phillips 66/dsl, Shell/dsl 🍴 Arby's, BBQ Shed, Braum's, Carl's Jr, Chicken Express, Hibachi Buffet, Jerry's Rest., KFC, Little Caesar's, McDonald's, Pizza Hut, Qdoba, Sonic, Subway, Taco Mayo 🛏 Best Western+, Comfort Inn, Fairfield Inn, Scottish Inn 🅾 $General, Ace Hardware, AT&T, GNC, Ⓗ, NAPA, O'Reilly Parts, Savealot Foods, to SW OSU, United Mkt, Walgreens, S 🛏 Tru Hotel 🅾 Walmart/Subway
80a	(from eb), N 🅶 Phillips/dsl 🍴 Casa Soto Mexican
81	E Main St (from eb) 🅾 same as 82
80	W Main St, Mountainview, Thomas, N 🛏 Best Value Inn 🅾 NAPAcare
71	Custer City Rd, N 🅶 Loves/Subway/dsl/24hr 🅾 Cherokee Trading Post/rest.
69	Lp 40 (from wb, no return), to Clinton
67.5mm	Washita River
66	US 183, Clinton, S 🅶 Shell/dsl 🅾 Ford
65a	10th St, Neptune Dr, Clinton, N 🍴 Branding Iron Rest., China King, Picante Grille 🛏 Days Inn, Relax Inn, Super 8 🅾 United Foods, S 🅶 Phillips 66/dsl 🛏 EconoLodge, Holiday Inn Express 🅾 Hargus RV Park
65	Gary Blvd, Clinton, N 🅶 Hutch/dsl 🍴 Braum's, Italian Villa, KFC/Taco Bell, LJ Silver, Mazzio's, McDonald's, MT Mike's, Palacios Mexican, Pizza Hut, Subway, Taco Mayo 🛏 Hampton Inn, Motel 6, Ramada Inn, Tradewinds Inn 🅾 $General, $Tree, Ⓗ, K-Mart, Rte 66 Museum, S 🛏 Holiday Inn Express, La Quinta

YUKON

EL RENO

WEATHERFORD

CLINTON

OK

←E INTERSTATE 40 Cont'd

Exit #	Services
62	Parkersburg Rd, S ⭕ Hargus RV Ctr
61	Haggard Rd
57	Stafford Rd
53	OK 44, Foss
50	Clinton Lake Rd, N ⭕ KOA/LP/dsl
47	Canute, S 🅿 Shell/dsl
41	OK 34 (exits left from eb), Elk City, N 🅿 Hutch's/dsl, Loves/Subway/dsl 🛏 Hiway Inn, La Quinta, Motel 6, Red Carpet Inn, Sleep Inn, Super 8 ⭕ Elk Run RV Park, 🅷
40	E 7th St, Elk City, N 🛏 Holiday Inn Express ⭕ Chrysler/Dodge/Jeep, S 🅿 Hutch's/dsl/CNG 🍴 Huddle House, Rib Crib 🛏 Hampton Inn ⭕ Hobby Lobby, same as 41, Walmart/McDonald's Wendy's
38	OK 6, Elk City, N 🅿 Conoco/dsl, Phillips 66/dsl 🍴 Arby's, Billy Sims BBQ, Boomtown Grill, China Super Buffet, LJ Silver, McDonald's, Western Sizzlin 🛏 Bedford Inn, Days Inn ⭕ Ace Hardware, Elk Creek RV Park, tires, S 🅿 Phillips 66/dsl 🛏 Best Western+, Clarion Inn, Comfort Inn ⭕ Elk City RV Ctr, to Quartz Mtn SP
34	Merritt Rd
32	OK 34 S (exits left from eb), Elk City
26	Cemetery Rd, N 🅿 Truck Stop 40/dsl ⭕ dsl repair, S 🅿 TA/Taco Bell/Subway/dsl/scales/24hr/@
25	Lp 40, Sayre, 1 mi N 🅿 Hutch's/dsl/CNG 🛏 Western Motel, Windgate Hotel ⭕ Bobcat Creek RV Park, Chevrolet/GMC, Ford, 🅷
23	OK 152, Sayre
22.5mm	N Fork Red River
20	US 283, Sayre, N 🅿 Flying J/Denny's/dsl/LP/RV dump/scales/24hr 🍴 McDonald's 🛏 AmericInn ⭕ to Washita Bfd Site (25mi), Truck lube, truckwash
14	Hext Rd
13.5mm	check sta both lanes, litter barrels
11	Lp 40, to Erick, Hext
10mm	Welcome Ctr eb/Rs, full 🅰 facilities, 🅲, 🅰, litter barrels, petwalk, RV dump
7	OK 30, Erick, N 🛏 Motel 6, S 🅿 Loves/Subway/dsl/scales 🍴 Simple Simon's Pizza 🛏 Days Inn
5	Lp 40, Honeyfarm Rd
1	weigh Sta eb
1	Texola, S ⭕ RV camping
0mm	Oklahoma/Texas state line

←E INTERSTATE 44

Exit #	Services
329mm	Oklahoma/Missouri state line
321mm	Spring River
314mm	Oklahoma Welcome Ctr wb, full facilities
313	OK 10, Miami, N 🅿 Loves/dsl, Phillips 66, Phillips 66/dsl 🍴 Donut Palace, Subway 🛏 Days Inn, Deluxe Inn, EconoLodge, Hampton Inn, Holiday Inn Express, Microtel, Motel 6 ⭕ auto repair, 🅷, Miami RV Park, to NE OK A&M Coll, S ⭕ Chrysler/Dodge/Jeep
312mm	Neosho River
302	US 59, US 69, Afton, S 🅿 Buffalo Ranch/Subway/dsl 🛏 Rte 66 Motel ⭕ $General
289	US 60, Vinita, N 🅿 Murphy USA/dsl 🍴 Braum's, Clanton's Cafe, McDonald's, Pizza Hut, Sonic, Subway, Woodshed Deli 🛏 Holiday Inn Express, Vinita Inn ⭕ $General, $Tree, Ace Hardware, Chevrolet, 🅷, O'Reilly Parts, st patrol, USPO, Walmart

---

Exit #	Services
288mm	service plaza both lanes 🅿 Kum&Go/dsl 🍴 McDonald's, Subway
286mm	toll plaza
283	US 69, Big Cabin, N 🅿 Big Cabin/Subway/dsl/scales/24hr/@ Loves/Carl's Jr/dsl/scales/24hr 🛏 Super 8 ⭕ Cabin R Park, trk repair
269	OK 28 (from eb, no re-entry), to Adair, Chelsea
255	OK 20, to Pryor, Claremore, 0-2 mi N 🅿 Kum&Go/dsl/e8 Murphy USA/dsl, QT/dsl 🍴 $General, Carl's Jr 🛏 Hampto Inn, Holiday Inn Express, Super 8, Travel Inn, Will Rogers In ⭕ 🅷, museum, to Rogers U, Walgreens, Walmart, Will Roger Memorial
248	to OK 266, Port of Catoosa, N 🅿 QT/dsl 🛏 Hampton Inn (4mi Microtel (2mi), Quality Inn (4mi), Will Rogers Inn (4mi) ⭕ Dave's RV Ctr
244mm	Kerr-McClellan Navigation System
241mm	Will Rogers Tpk begins eb, ends wb, 🅲
241	(35 from wb) OK 66 E, to Catoosa
241b	US 412 E (34 from wb), Choteau
240a	OK 167 N, 193rd E Ave, N 🍴 Freddy's, IHOP, McDonald's, O Joe's BBQ, Panda Express, Taco Bell, Taco Bueno, Waffle House Wendy's 🛏 Cherokee Inn/Casino, Fairfield Inn, Hampton Inn Hardrock Hotel/Casino, Homewood Suites, La Quinta ⭕ AT& GNC, Petco, Ross, Tate Boys Automotive, Walgreens, Walmar S 🅿 QT 🍴 Mazzio's, Port City Diner, Sonic, Subway 🛏 Comfor Suites, Holiday Inn Express, Motel 6 ⭕ $General, O'Reilly Parts tires/repair
238	161st E Ave, N 🅿 QT/dsl/scales/24hr ⭕ Cherokee Nation We come Ctr, truckwash, S 🍴 Arby's, Burger King 🛏 Microtel ⭕ truckwash
236b	I-244 W, to downtown Tulsa, N ⭕ ✈
236a	129th E Ave, N 🅿 Flying J/Denny's/dsl/LP/24hr ⭕ Souther Tire Mart, S 🍴 McDonald's
235	E 11th St, Tulsa, N 🅿 QT/dsl 🍴 Mazzio's, Sonic, Subway 🛏 Economy Inn, Executive Inn, Garnett Inn, Knights Inn, Travelodge ⭕ $General, O'Reilly Parts, Walgreens, S 🍴 Braum's ⭕ Whse Mkt
234b	same as 235
234a	US 169, N to Owasso, S to Broken Arrow, to ✈
233	E 21st St, N 🍴 Golden Corral ⭕ Camping World RV Ctr, Family$, S 🍴 El Chico
231	US 64, OK 51, to Muskogee, E 31st St, Memorial Dr, N 🅿 QT/dsl 🍴 Sonic, Speedy Gonzales Mexican, Subway 🛏 Delux Inn, Homestay Inn, Ramada Inn, Tulsa Inn ⭕ Walgreens, S 🅿 Shell Taco Silvia 🍴 Cracker Barrel, IHOP, McDonald's, Pizza Hut, Ruby Tuesday, Village Inn 🛏 Best Value Inn, Best Western+, Clarion, Comfort Suites, Courtyard, EconoLodge, Embassy Suites, Extended Stay America, Fairfield Inn, Hampton Inn, Quality Suites, Sleep Inn, Super 8 ⭕ Cavender's Boots, Chevrolet, Harley-Davidson, Nissan
230	E 41st St, Sheridan Rd, N 🅿 Shell 🍴 Carl's Jr, Chick-fil-A, Chipotle, Desi Wok, Jimmy John's, On-the-Border, Panera Bread, Schlotzsky's, Starbucks, Subway, Top That! Pizza ⭕ AT&T, Barnes&Noble, Cartec Automotive, JC Penney, Jo-Ann Fabrics, Michael's, Old Navy, Petco, Petsmart, Reasor's Foods, Ross, Verizon, S 🍴 Buffalo Wild Wings, Carino's Italian 🛏 La Quinta ⭕ Batteries+Bulbs, Best Buy, Home Depot
229	Yale Ave, Tulsa, N 🅿 Shell 🍴 El Chico, McDonald's, Subway ⭕ Firestone/auto, JC Penney, PetCo, S 🅿 Kum&Go/dsl/e85, QT 🍴 Andy's Custard, Applebee's, Arby's, Braum's, Cane's, Jack-in-the-Box, Outback Steaks, Qdoba, Red Lobster, Saltgrass Steaks, Sonic, Taco Bell, Village Inn 🛏 Comfort Inn, Hilton Garden, Holiday Inn Express, Motel 6, Red Roof Inn, Residence Inn ⭕ 🅷, Kia, vet

OK

🔷 INTERSTATE 44 Cont'd	

Exit #	Services
228	Harvard Ave, Tulsa, **N** ⛽ QT/dsl 🍴 Casa Tequila Mexican, McDonald's, NYC Pizza 🛏 Tradewinds Motel, **S** 🍴 A&W/LJ Silver, Chili's, Freckle's Frozen Custard, Jamil's Rest, Mario's Pizza, Papa John's, Starbucks, Subway 🛏 Wingate Inn ⊙ $Tree, Hobby Lobby, SteinMart
227	Lewis Ave, Tulsa, **S** 🍴 Goldie's Grill ⊙ Walgreens
226b	Peoria Ave, Tulsa, **N** ⛽ Kum&Go/dsl, QT/dsl 🍴 Arby's, Brookside Diner, Burger St., Charleston's Rest., China Wok, CiCi's, Egg Roll Express, Jimmy's Egg, KFC, Little Caesar's, Mazzio's, Pizza Hut, Sonic, Subway, Super Wok, Taco Bell, Taco Bueno 🛏 Peoria Inn ⊙ $Tree, Harley-Davidson, O'Reilly Parts, Reasor's Mkt, Robertson Tire, Verizon, Walmart Mkt, Whole Foods Mkt, **S** 🍴 Braum's, Golden Palace ⊙ $General, AutoZone, Family$, Walgreens
226a	Riverside Dr
225mm	Arkansas River
225	Elwood Ave, **N** ⊙ Chevrolet, Ford, **S** 🛏 Budget Inn
224b a	US 75, to Okmulgee, Bartlesville, **N** ⛽ QT/dsl 🍴 KFC, Mazzio's, Sonic ⊙ $General, vet, Whse Mkt, **S** 🛏 Royal Inn ⊙ Hurley RV Ctr
223c	33rd W Ave, Tulsa, **N** 🍴 Braum's, Domino's, **S** ⛽ Conoco 🍴 Rib Crib BBQ
223b	51st St (from wb)
223a	I-244 E, to Tulsa downtown
222c	(from wb), **S** 🛏 Value Inn
222b	55th Place, **N** 🛏 Capri Motel, Crystal Motel, **S** 🛏 Best Value Inn, Winston's Inn
222a	49th W Ave, Tulsa, **N** 🍴 Carl's Jr, Monterey Mexican, Subway 🛏 Gateway Motel, Interstate Inn, Motel 6 ⊙ $General, BigLots, Mack Trucks, **S** ⛽ QT/Kitchens/dsl/scales/24hr 🍴 Arby's, McDonald's, Taco Bueno, Waffle House 🛏 Comfort Inn, Super 8 ⊙ Buick/GMC, Freightliner, Kenworth
221a	57th W Ave, (from wb), **S** ⊙ Buick/GMC
221mm	**Turner Tkp begins wb, ends eb**
218	Creek Tpk E (from eb)
215	OK 97, to Sand Sprgs, Sapulpa, **S** ⛽ Kum&Go/dsl/e85 🍴 Freddie's Rest., Subway 🛏 Super 8 ⊙ 🅗, Hunter RV Ctr, Route 66 RV Park
211	OK 33, to Kellyville, Drumright, **S** ⊙ Heyburn Lake SP
207	no service
196	OK 48, Bristow, **S** ⛽ Kenny's/dsl, Phillips 66/dsl 🍴 Mazzio's, McDonald's, Pizza Hut, Sonic, Steak'nEgg Rest, Taco Mayo 🛏 Carolyn Inn ⊙ $General, $Tree, Ford, O'Reilly Parts, Walmart
182mm	**toll plaza**
179	OK 99, to Drumright, Stroud, **N** 🍴 Ranch House Rest. 🛏 Cattle Country Lodge, **S** ⛽ Kids/dsl, Phillips 66/Subway/dsl 🍴 5Star BBQ, Cozumel Mexican, Mazzio's, McDonald's, Pepe's Mexican, Sonic 🛏 Hampton Inn, Skyliner Motel, Sooner Motel ⊙ auto/tire repair, 🅗, USPO
178mm	**Hoback Plaza both lanes (exits left)** ⛽ Phillips 66/dsl 🍴 McDonald's
167mm	**service plaza (from eb)** ⛽ Phillips 66/dsl
166	OK 18, to Cushing, Chandler, **S** ⛽ Phillips 66/dsl 🍴 Sonic 🛏 Lincoln Motel ⊙ Chandler Tire, Chevrolet/GMC, Ford
158	OK 66, to Wellston, **N** ⛽ Phillips 66/Subway/dsl/24hr 🍴 Butcher BBQ ⊙ $General
147	N Luther Rd
146	Luther-Jones
138d	to Memorial Rd, to Enterprise Square
138a	I-35, I-44 E to Tulsa, Turner Tpk
	I-44 and I-35 run together 8 mi. Exits 137-134.

Exit #	Services
135mm	**Turner Tpk begins eb, ends wb**
135	Britton Rd
134	Wilshire Blvd, **N** 🛏 Executive Inn ⊙ Blue Beacon
130	I-35 S, to Dallas, access to services on I-35 S
129	MLK Ave, Remington Park, **N** 🛏 Park Hill Inn ⊙ Cowboy Museum, **S** 🍴 McDonald's, Sonic, Subway ⊙ Family$
128b	Kelley Ave, OK City, **N** ⛽ Conoco, VP/Subway/dsl 🍴 Gabriella's Italian
128a	Lincoln Blvd, **S** ⛽ Lincoln Mart/dsl 🛏 Lincoln Inn Express, Oxford Inn ⊙ st capitol
127	I-235 S, US 77, City Ctr, Broadway St, **N** ⛽ Conoco/Circle K, Shell/Circle K 🛏 Holiday Inn, Surestay ⊙ URGENT CARE
126	Western Ave, **S** 🛏 Sleep Inn
125c	NW Expressway (exits left from sb)
125	Classen Blvd, (exits left from wb), OK City, **N** 🍴 Cheesecake Factory, Chili's, Freebirds Burrito, Jamba Juice, Olive Garden, Pei Wei, Smashburger, Subway, Whiskey Cake Kitchen ⊙ AT&T, Dillard's, JC Penney, Macy's, Old Navy, Ross, Verizon, Walmart/McDonald's, **S** 🍴 IHOP, McDonald's, Milagro Mexican 🛏 Courtyard, Hyatt Place
125a	OK 3A, Penn Ave, to NW Expswy, **N** ⛽ VP Express, **S** ⛽ Shell/Circle K, Valero 🍴 Braum's ⊙ auto/tire repair, Family$
124	N May, **N** ⛽ Shell/Circle K/Subway 🍴 Azteca Mexican 🛏 Days Inn, Motel 6, Super 8 ⊙ O'Reilly Parts, Sam's Club/dsl, **S** ⛽ Valero 🍴 Dunkin', Jersey Mike's, Starbucks, Wendy's ⊙ Aamco, Advance Parts, Family$, Ford, Lowe's
123b	OK 66 W, NW 39th, to Warr Acres, **N** ⛽ 7-11, Shell, Valero/McDonald's/dsl 🍴 Braum's, Carl's Jr, Jimmy's Egg, Sonic 🛏 Hospitality Inn ⊙ Family$, U-Haul
123a	NW 36th St, **S** ⊙ Woodspring Suites
122	NW 23rd St, **N** ⛽ 7-11, Conoco/dsl 🍴 Church's, EggRoll King ⊙ Tires+, **S** ⛽ Conoco 🍴 Arby's, Sonic ⊙ Family$
121b a	NW 10th St, **N** ⛽ On Cue/dsl, **S** ⛽ 7-11, Shamrock ⊙ $General, fairgrounds, Family$, Whittaker's Foods
120b a	I-40, W to Amarillo, E to Ft Smith
119	SW 15th St
118	OK 152 W, SW 29th St, OK City, **E** ⛽ 7-11, Shamrock 🍴 A&W/LJ Silver, Burger King, CiCi's Pizza, Jimmy's Egg, KFC, McDonald's, Pizza Hut, Sonic, Subway, Taco Bueno ⊙ $General, $Tree, Advance Parts, AT&T, AutoZone, Buy-4-Less Foods, city park, O'Reilly Parts, Walgreens, **W** ⛽ Alon/dsl ⊙ city park, transmissions, U-Haul/LP
117	SW 44th St, **W** ⊙ auto repair
116b	Airport Rd (exits left from nb), **W** ⊙ ✈
116a	SW 59th St, **E** ⛽ Conoco/Circle K 🍴 Subway, Waffle House ⊙ Family$, **W** ⊙ Will Rogers Airport
115	I-240 E, US 62 E, to Ft Smith
114	SW 74th St, OK City, **E** ⛽ Valero/dsl 🍴 Braum's, Burger King, Perry's Rest. 🛏 Motel 6 ⊙ $General

INTERSTATE 44 Cont'd

Exit #	Services
113	SW 89th St, E 🛢 7-11, Loves/Subway/dsl, Valero/dsl 🍴 Sonic Ⓞ CVS Drug, 🏥
112	SW 104th St, E 🛢 Valero, Walmart/dsl 🍴 Arby's, McDonald's, Starbucks, Subway, Taco Bell Ⓞ $General, Crest Mkt, Firestone/auto, Verizon, Walmart
111	SW 119th St, E 🛢 7-11, On Cue/dsl 🍴 Little Caesar's, Sonic
110	OK 37 E, to Moore, E Ⓞ 🏥
109	SW 149th St, E 🍴 JR's Grill
108mm	S Canadian River
108	OK 37 W, to Tuttle, W 🛢 Conoco/dsl, Phillips 66/dsl 🍴 Arby's, Braum's, Carlito's Mexican, Jimmy's Egg, KFC/Taco Bell, Little Caesar's, McDonald's, New China, Sonic, The Pizza Shop, Tri City Diner Ⓞ $General, AT&T, AutoZone, O'Reilly Parts, Walgreens, Walmart/Subway
107	US 62 S (no wb return), to Newcastle, E 🛢 Loves/Subway/Dunkin'/dsl/scales/24hr 🏠 Comfort Inn, Newcastle Motel Ⓞ casino, Newcastle RV
99	H E Bailey Spur, rd 4, to Blanchard, Tuttle, Norman
97mm	toll booth
85.5mm	service plaza, both lanes exit left 🛢 Phillips 66/dsl 🍴 McDonald's
83	US 62, Chickasha, W 🛢 Jay's/dsl, Valero/dsl 🏠 Best Western+ Ⓞ Southern Plains Indian Museum (18mi)
80	US 81, Chickasha, E 🛢 Circle K/dsl, Shell/dsl 🍴 La Fiesta Mexican, Western Sizzlin 🏠 Best Value Inn, Fairfield Inn, Hampton Inn, Holiday Inn Express, Super 8 Ⓞ Buick/GMC, Cadillac/Chevrolet, Chrysler/Dodge/Jeep, vet, W 🛢 Griffith's Repair, Loves/dsl, Murphy USA/dsl, Valero 🍴 Arby's, Braum's, Chicken Express, China Dream, China Moon, Cotton Patch Cafe, Domino's, KFC, Little Caesar's, Mazzio's Pizza, McDonald's, New China, Pizza Hut, Sims BBQ, Sonic, Subway, Taco Bell, Taco Mayo, Tropical Cafe 🏠 Quality Inn, Ranch House Motel Ⓞ $General, $Tree, Ace Hardware, Aldi Foods, AT&T, AutoZone, Chickasha RV Park, CVS Drug, Ford, 🏥, O'Reilly Parts, Ralph&Son's Tires/repair, Save-A-Lot Foods, URGENT CARE, Verizon, Walgreens, Walmart/Subway
78	no service
66mm	toll plaza both lanes
62	to Cyril (from wb)
53	US 277, Elgin, Lake Ellsworth, E 🛢 Shamrock, Valero/McDonald's/dsl 🍴 Billy Sim's BBQ, China Garden, Sonic, Subway Ⓞ $General, Family$, tires
46	US 62 E, US 277, US 281, to Elgin, Apache, Comanche Tribe last free exit eb
45	OK 49, to Medicine Park, W 🛢 Loves/Subway/dsl/24hr 🍴 Burger King, Sonic Ⓞ $General, Wichita NWR
41	to Ft Sill, Key Gate, W Ⓞ Ft Sill Museum
40c	Gate 2, to Ft Sill
40a	to Cache
39	US 62 W, to Cache, E 🛢 Alon/dsl, W 🏠 Castle Inn
39b	US 281 (from sb) Ⓞ same as 39a
39a	US 281, Cache Rd (exits left from nb), Lawton, E 🛢 Alon/dsl, W 🛢 Stripes/dsl, Valero/dsl 🏠 Castle Inn Ⓞ $General
38	Cache Rd (exits left from nb)
37	Gore Blvd, Lawton, E 🛢 Apache/dsl 🍴 Braum's, Los Tres Amigos, Marco's Pizza, Sonic, Taco Mayo, URGENT CARE 🏠 Apache Casino/Hotel, Best Western+ Ⓞ casino, USPO, W 🍴 Cracker Barrel, Mike's Grille, Salas Cantina 🏠 Comfort Suites, Fairfield Inn, Hilton Garden, Holiday Inn Express, Homewood Suites, Sleep Inn, SpringHill Suites Ⓞ $Tree, AT&T, Chrysler/Dodge/Jeep, Dick's, Harley-Davidson, Jo-Ann, Kohl's, Nissan, Petco
36a	OK 7, Lee Blvd, Lawton, E 🛢 Phillips 66/dsl/repair, Barefoot/dsl, Shamrock/dsl 🍴 Braum's, Burger King, KFC, Taco Bell, Leo&Ken's Rest., McDonald's 🏠 Motel 6 Ⓞ $General, Advance Parts, ☑, CVS Drug, 🏥, vet
33	US 281, 11th St, Lawton, W Ⓞ ☑
30	OK 36 (last free exit sb), Geronimo
20.5mm	Elmer Graham Plaza (both lanes exit left) 🛢 Phillips 66/dsl 🍴 Back 40 BBQ Ⓞ info
20	OK 5, to Walters
19.5mm	toll plaza
5	US 277 N, US 281, Randlett, last free exit nb, E 🛢 Loves/Subway/dsl/scales/24hr
1	OK 36, to Grandfield, E 🛢 Comanche Nation TP/dsl, W Ⓞ Kiow Hotel/casino
0mm	Oklahoma/Texas state line, Red River

INTERSTATE 240 (Oklahoma City)

Exit #	Services
16mm	I-240 begins/ends on I-40.
14	Anderson Rd, S 🛢 Conoco/dsl
11b a	Douglas Blvd, N Ⓞ Tinker AFB
9	Air Depot Blvd
8	OK 77, Sooner Rd, N 🛢 Phillips 66/dsl/CNG/e85 🍴 Sonic Ⓞ URGENT CARE, S 🛢 Phillips 66/Popeye's/dsl, Valero/McDonald's/dsl Ⓞ 🏥
7	Sunnylane Ave, S 🛢 Valero/Subway/dsl 🏠 Woodspring Suite
6	Bryant Ave
5	S Eastern Ave
4c	Pole Rd, N 🍴 Burger King, Subway, TX Roadhouse 🏠 Fairfield Inn, Magnuson Hotel, Residence Inn
4b a	I-35, N to OK City, S to Dallas, US 77 S, US 62/77 N
3b	S Shields, N 🛢 Valero/dsl 🍴 Braum's Ⓞ Chrysler/Dodge/Jeep, Home Depot, S Ⓞ Discount Tire, Nissan, Subaru
3a	S Santa Fe, N Ⓞ Kia, S 🛢 Murphy USA/dsl 🍴 Chili's, IHOP, Jersey Mike's, Panda Express Ⓞ Lowe's, Staples, Walmart/McDonald's
2b	S Walker Ave, N 🛢 7-11, Shell/Circle K 🍴 Johnnie's Broiler, Rib Crib, S 🍴 Burger Joint, Carino's, ChuckeCheese, City Bites, Jimmy's Egg Grill, On-the-Border 🏠 Holiday Inn Express Ⓞ PepBoys
2a	S Western Ave, N 🛢 7-11, Conoco 🍴 Braum's, Burger King, CiCi's Pizza, House of Szechwan, Taste of China Ⓞ $General, Advance Parts, Hyundai, Tires+, vet, S 🛢 7-11, Valero/dsl 🍴 A&W/LJ Silver, Chick-fil-A, Garage Burgers, Grandy's, Hibachi Buffet, Jimmy John's, KFC, McDonald's, Popeye's, Red Lobster 🏠 Best Western, Comfort Inn, Hampton Inn, Home 2 Suites, Quality Inn Ⓞ Chevrolet, Honda, Office Depot
1c	S Penn Ave, N 🛢 Conoco/dsl 🍴 Cane's, Carl's Jr, Charleston's Rest., Denny's, Golden Corral, Hooters, Old Chicago Pizza, Olive Garden, Outback Steaks, Pioneer Pies, SaltGrass Steaks, Schlotsky's Ⓞ AT&T, Best Buy, BigLots, GNC, Green Acres Mkt, Hobby Lobby, Marshall's, Michaels, Old Navy, Petsmart, Ross, Verizon, S 🛢 Shell/Circle K 🍴 Hunan Buffet, Joe's Crabshack, Mazzio's, Papa John's, Starbucks, Subway, Taco Bueno, Western Sizzlin Ⓞ $Tree, URGENT CARE
1b	S May Ave, N 🛢 7-11/gas 🍴 Abel's Mexican, Jack-in-theBox, New Mandarin, Taco Bell, Waffle House Ⓞ O'Reilly Parts, S 🛢 Nova, Valero/dsl 🍴 Braum's, Burger King, Perry's Rest. 🏠 Cambridge Inn, Knights Inn Ⓞ $General
1a	I-44, US 62, I-240 begins ends on I-44.

OREGON

INTERSTATE 5

Exit #	Services
308.5mm	Oregon/Washington state line, Columbia River
308	Jansen Beach Dr, **E** 🅿 Chevron/dsl 🍴 Burger King, Hooters, Starbucks, Taco Bell 🛏 Oxford Suites, Red Lion 🅾 Safeway, **W** 🍴 BJ's Rest., Bradley's Grill, CJ's Deli, Denny's, Jersey Mike's, Jimmy John's, McDonald's, Panera Bread, Stanford's Rest., Starbucks, Subway 🅾 Best Buy, Burlington Coats, GNC, Home Depot, Jansen Beach RV Park, Michael's, Old Navy, PetCo, Ross, Staples, Target, TJ Maxx, Verizon
307	OR 99E S, MLK Blvd, Union Ave, Marine Dr (sb only), **E** 🅿 76/dsl, Jubitz Trvl Ctr/rest/dsl/@ 🍴 Pizza Mia, Portland Cascade Grill, Subway 🛏 Courtyard, Fairfield Inn, Portlander Inn, Residence Inn 🅾 Blue Beacon, truck repair, **W** 🅾 Expo Ctr
306b	Interstate Ave, Delta Park, **E** 🅿 Arco 🍴 Burger King, Burrito House, Elmer's, Mars Meadows Chinese, Shari's 🛏 Best Western, Days Inn, Motel 6 🅾 $Tree, Baxter Parts, Dick's, Lowe's, Portland Meadows, vet, Walmart
306a	Columbia (from nb), same as 306b
305b a	US 30, Lombard St (from nb, no return), **E** 🍴 Little Caesar's 🅾 Knecht's Parts, **W** 🅿 Astro/dsl, Shell/dsl 🍴 Panda Express, Subway, Wendy's 🅾 Fred Meyer
304	Rosa Parks Way, **W** 🅿 76/dsl, Arco 🍴 Nite Hawk Cafe 🛏 Viking Motel 🅾 U of Portland
303	Alberta St, Swan Island, **E** 🅾 🅷, **W** 🍴 Subway, Taco Bell 🛏 Monticello Motel, Westerner Motel 🅾 CarQuest
302b	I-405, US 30 W, **W** to ocean beaches
302a	Rose Qtr, City Ctr, **E** 🅿 76/Circle K/dsl, Shell/dsl 🍴 Bellagio's Pizza, Burger King, Chipotle Mexican, Jersey Mike's, McDonald's, Muchas Gracias, Qdoba Mexican, Starbucks, Wendy's 🛏 Courtyard, Crowne Plaza, Shiloh Inn 🅾 🅷, 7-11, Kia, Schwab Tire, Toyota, Verizon, Walgreens, **W** 🅾 coliseum
301	I-84 E, US 30 E, **services E off I-84 exits**
300	US 26 E (from sb), Milwaukie Ave, **W** 🛏 Hilton, Marriott
299b	I-405, US 26 W, to city ctr
299a	US 26 E, OR 43 (from nb), City Ctr, to Lake Oswego
298	Corbett Ave
297	Terwilliger Blvd, **W** 🍴 Baja Fresh, KFC, La Costita, Starbucks 🅾 🅷, Fred Meyer, to Lewis and Clark Coll.
296b	Multnomah Blvd (from sb), **W** 🅾 Safeway, same as 296a
296a	(from sb), Barbur, **W** 🅿 76/dsl, Chevron/dsl 🍴 Bellagio's Pizza, Frack Burger, Subway 🛏 Aladdin Inn, Budget Lodge, Capitol Hill Motel 🅾 7-11, AT&T, Schwab Tire
295	Capitol Hwy (from sb), Taylors Ferry Rd (from nb), **E** 🅿 Shell/dsl 🍴 McDonald's, Sho Japanese, Starbucks, Thai Orchid 🛏 Hospitality Inn, **W** 🍴 Taco Time, Wendy's 🅾 Walgreens
294	Barbur Blvd, OR 99W, to Tigard, **E** 🛏 Comfort Suites, **W** 🅿 76, Chevron, Shell 🍴 Arby's, Baja Fresh, Banning's Rest., Baskin-Robbins, Burger King, Buster's BBQ, Carl's Jr, Chang's Mongolian Grill, Gators Eatery, Jimmy John's, Mazatlan Mexican, McDonald's, Starbucks, Subway, Taco Bell 🛏 Quality Inn, Regency Inn 🅾 $Tree, Americas Tire, auto repair, Baxter Parts, Costco, Fred Meyer, JoAnn Fabrics, NAPA, PetCo, Petsmart, Schwab Tire, transmissions, U-Haul, vet, Walmart/Subway, Winco Foods

293	Haines St, **W** 🅾 Ford/Lincoln
292	OR 217, Kruse Way, Lake Oswego, **E** 🅿 Shell/dsl 🍴 Applebee's, Chevy's Mexican, Chipotle, Olive Garden, Oswego Grill, Potbelly, Stanford's Rest., Starbucks 🛏 Crowne Plaza, Fairfield Inn, Hilton Garden, Phoenix Inn, Residence Inn 🅾 LDS Temple, **W** 🛏 Extended Stay America 🅾 Lowe's
291	Carman Dr, **W** 🅿 76/dsl, Chevron 🍴 Burgerville, Domino's, El Sol De Mexico, Starbucks, Subway, Sweet Tomatoes 🛏 Courtyard, Holiday Inn Express 🅾 Home Depot, Office Depot
290	Lower Boonsferry Rd, Lake Oswego, **E** 🅿 Chevron/dsl, Space Age/dsl/LP 🍴 Arby's, Baja Fresh, Baskin-Robbins, Burger King, Cafe Yumm, Carl's Jr., Fuddruckers, Miller's Rest., Nicoli's Grill, Panda Express, Starbucks, Subway, Taco Bell 🛏 Motel 6 🅾 Dick's, Safeway Foods, See's Kitchen, Walgreens, **W** 🍴 CA Pizza Kitchen, Claim Jumper, Jamba Juice, Jimmy John's, McCormick&Schmick's, Pastini Pastaria, PF Chang's, Qdoba Mexican, Royal Panda, Starbucks, Twigs Bistro, Village Inn 🛏 Grand Hotel 🅾 Barnes&Noble, Verizon, Whole Foods Mkt
289	Tualatin, **E** 🅿 76, Shell/dsl 🍴 Chipotle Mexican, Famous Dave's BBQ, Jamba Juice, McDonald's, Panera Bread, Starbucks, Subway 🅾 🅷, 7-11, Best Buy, Old Navy, Petsmart, vet, **W** 🍴 Applebee's, Buffalo Wild Wings, Carl's Jr, Coldstone, Dickie Jo's Burgers, Hayden's Grill, Jack-in-the-Box, McDonald's, Outback Steaks, Pieology Pizzaria, Pizza Hut, Shari's, Starbucks, Subway, Taco Bell, Thai Rest., Wendy's 🛏 Century Hotel, Comfort Inn 🅾 Cabela's, Fred Meyer, Haggen's Foods, Michael's, New Seasons Mkt, O'Reilly Parts, PetCo, Staples, TJ Maxx
288	I-205, to Oregon City
286	Elligsen Rd, Boonsferry Rd, Stafford, **E** 🅿 76/dsl 🍴 Burger King, Cafe Yumm!, Moe's SW Grill, Panda Express, Pizza Schmizza, Starbucks, Subway, Zoup! 🛏 La Quinta, Motel 6 🅾 Chrysler/Dodge/Jeep, Costco/gas, Discount Tire, Ferrari/Maserati, Mercedes, Office Depot, Petsmart, Pheasant Ridge RV Resort, Target, **W** 🅿 Chevron/dsl 🍴 Boone Town Bistro, Carl's Jr 🛏 Holiday Inn/rest. 🅾 Audi, Camping World RV Ctr, Chevrolet, Nissan, Toyota

P O R T L A N D

OR

= gas   = food   = lodging   = other   = rest stop   Copyright 2022 - The Next EXIT®

INTERSTATE 5 Cont'd

Exit #	Services
283	Wilsonville, E Abella Italian, Arby's, Chipotle, Denny's, Jamba Juice, Jimmy John's, Juan Colorado, McDonald's, Noodles&Co, Papa Murphy's, Red Robin, Shari's, Starbucks, Subway, Taco Bell, Thai Rest., Wanker's Café, Wendy's, Wong's Chinese GuestHouse Inn, Quality Inn, SnoozInn $Tree, Ace Hardware, AT&T, Fry's Electronics, funpark, GNC, Honda, NAPA, Rite Aid, Safeway, Schwab Tire, URGENT CARE, USPO, vet, W Fred Meyer/dsl Baskin-Robbins, Biscuits Cafe, Boone's Jct Pizza, Burger King, Domino's, Hunan Kitchen, Little Caesar's, McMenamin's Rest., Oswego Grill, Perfect Pizza, Qdoba, RAM Rest., Sonic, Starbucks, Subway, Wow Burger Best Western Wilsonville 7-11, auto repair, Fred Meyer/dsl, O'Reilly Parts, Verizon, Walgreens
282.5mm	Willamette River
282	Charbonneau District, E Langdon Farms Rest. Langdon Farms Golf
281.5mm	both lanes, coffee, full facilities, info, litter barrels, petwalk, vending
278	Donald, E 76/dsl/LP Aurora Acres RV Park, W FLYING J/Subway/dsl/scales/24hr, TA/Country Pride/Popeye's/dsl/scales/24hr/@ NAPA Truck Parts, SpeedCo Lube, to Champoeg SP, truckwash
274mm	weigh sta both lanes
271	OR 214, Woodburn, E Arco/dsl, Chevron Burger King, Denny's, DQ, KFC, McDonald's, Subway, Taco Bell Best Western, Super 8 76/repair, Al's RV Ctr, vet, Walgreens, Walmart/McDonald's, W Shell/dsl Arby's, Elmer's, Jack-in-the-Box, Jamba Juice, Panera Bread, Starbucks La Quinta Ford, Woodburn Outlets/famous brands, Woodburn RV Park
263	Brooks, Gervais, E Brooks Mkt/deli, W Pilot/Subway/Taco Bell/dsl/LP/scales/24hr Carl's Jr., Chalet Rest. Antique Powerland Museum, Freightliner, Willamette Mission SP (4mi)
260b a	OR 99E, Chemawa Rd, Keizer, W Burger King, Firehouse Subs, Jamba Juice, McDonald's, Outback Steaks, Panda Express, Panera Bread, RoundTable Pizza, Starbucks, Subway, Taco Bell, Taco del Mar Holiday Inn Express AT&T, GNC, Lowe's, Marshall's, Michael's, Old Navy, PetCo, REI, Ross, Staples, Target, Verizon, World Mkt
259mm	45th parallel, halfway between the equator and N Pole
258	N Salem, E Figaro's Italian, Guesthouse Rest., McDonald's, Original Pancake House, Subway Best Western, Rodeway Inn 5 Star RV Park, Al's RV Ctr, Hwy RV Ctr, Roth's Foods, W 76, Arco, Pacific Pride/dsl, Shell/dsl Don Pedro Mexican, Jack-in-the-Box, LumYuen Chinese Motel 6, Travelers Inn Stuart's Parts, to st capitol
256	to OR 213, Market St, Salem, E Applebee's, Arby's, Baja Fresh, Blue Willow Rest., Burger King, Carl's Jr, China Buffet, Chipotle, Denny's, Elmer's, Five Guys, Izzy's Rest., Jack-in-the-Box, KFC, La Hacienda Mexican, McDonald's, Olive Garden, Sizzler, Starbucks, Subway, Taco Bell Capital Inn, Days Inn BigLots, Buick/GMC, Discount Tire, Firestone/auto, Fred Meyer/dsl, Kia, Midas, Schwab Tires, Verizon, Walgreens, W Arco, Pacific Pride/dsl, Shell/dsl Almost Home Rest., Baskin-Robbins, DQ, McDonald's, Newport Bay Seafood, Pietro's Pizza, Rockin-Rogers Diner, Subway Comfort Inn, DoubleTree, Holiday Lodge, Motel 6, Red Lion Hotel, Shilo Inn, Super 8 Mazda, vet
253	OR 22, Salem, Stayton, E Chevron, Shell/dsl, Space Age/dsl Burger King, Carls Jr, Las Polomas Mexican, McDonalds/playplace, Shari's, Subway $Tree, Home Depot,

---

Exit #	Services
253	Continued Salem Camping/RV Park, ShopKO, to Detroit RA, WinCo Foods, W Shell/dsl Carl's Jr, Denny's, DQ, Jack-in-the-Box, Panda Express, Popeyes, Taco Del Mar Best Western+, Comfort Suites, Hampton Inn, La Quinta, Residence Inn H, AAA, Chrysler/Jeep, Costco/gas, Lowe's, Nissan, Schwab Tire, st police, Walmart
252	Kuebler Blvd
249	to Salem, 2 mi W 76, Arco Arby's, Burger King, Carl's Jr Phoenix Inn Safeway/gas
248	Sunnyside, E Enchanted Forest Themepark, Willamette Valley Vineyards, W Pacific Pride/dsl
244	to N Jefferson, E Emerald Valley RV Park
243	Ankeny Hill
242	Talbot Rd
241mm	both lanes, full facilities, info, litter barrels, petwalk,
240.5mm	Santiam River
239	Dever-Conner
238	S Jefferson, Scio, W Loves/Arby's/dsl/scales/24hr
237	Viewcrest (from sb)
235	Millersburg
234	OR 99E, Albany, E Cascade Grill Comfort Suites, Holiday Inn Express, Knox Butte Camping/RV dump, W Chevron Burger King, Carl's Jr, DQ, Golden Town Buffet, McDonald's, Muchas Gracias, Subway, Taco Bell Budget Inn, Motel 6, Quality Inn, Super 8 H, Costco/gas, Kohl's, NAPA, to Albany Hist Dist
233	US 20, Albany, E 76/dsl, Chevron/dsl/LP Denny's, LumYuen Chinese Best Western+, Phoenix Inn, Rodeway Inn Blue Ox RV Park, Chevrolet, Home Depot, Honda, Lassen RV Ctr, st police, Toyota, Walmart, W Shell/dsl, Space Age/dsl Abby's Pizza, Arby's, Baskin-Robbins, Burgerville, Carl's Jr, El Trio Loco, Elmer's, Fox Den Pizza, Golden Wok, Jack-in-the-Box, Los Dos Amigos, Los Tequilos Mexican, Original Breakfast Cafe, Pizza Hut, Sizzler, Skipper's, Starbucks, Sweetwaters Rest., Taco Time, Wendy's Value Inn H, $Tree, Bi-Mart, CarQuest, Chrysler/Dodge/Hyundai/Jeep/Subaru, Fred Meyer/dsl, Hyundai, JoAnn Fabrics, Knechts's Parts, Old Navy, O'Reilly Parts, Rite Aid, Ross, Schwab Tires, Staples, Target, Walgreens
228	OR 34, to Lebanon, Corvallis, E 76/dsl, Leather's/dsl Pine Cone Cafe Mallard Creek Golf/RV Resort, W Arco/dsl, Chevron/CFN/A&W/dsl, Shell/dsl Subway KOA (5mi), to OSU
222mm	Butte Creek
216	OR 228, Halsey, Brownsville, E 76/Pioneer Villa TrkStp/deli/dsl/24hr/@ Travelodge, W Mobil/dsl parts/repair/towing
209	to Jct City, Harrisburg, W Diamond Hill RV Park
206mm	both lanes, full facilities, info, litter barrels, petwalk,
199	Coburg, E Fuel'n Go/dsl Premier RV Resort, W Shell/McDonald's/dsl, TA/Country Pride/Truck'n'Travel Motel/dsl/scales/24hr/@ Coburg Crossing Cafe Camping World, dsl repair, Eugene Kamping RV Park, Evert RV Ctr, Freightliner, hist dist, RV Corral, Volvo
197mm	McKenzie River
195b a	N Springfield, E Arco, Chevron/dsl Applebee's, Buffalo Wild Wings, Cafe Yummi, Carl's Jr, China Sun, Ciao Pizza, Denny's, Elmer's Rest., FarMan Chinese, Five Guys, Hacienda Amigo Mio, HomeTown Buffet, Hop Valley Rest., IHOP, Jack-in-the-Box, Jimmy John's, KFC, McDonald's, Outback Steaks, Panda Express, Roadhouse Grill, Shari's, Sizzler, Starbucks, Subway, Taco Bell,

Sidebar labels (vertical):
WILSONVILLE — OR — SALEM — ALBANY — SPRINGFIELD

⬆N INTERSTATE 5 Cont'd

Exit	Description
195b a	Continued Taco Grande 🛏 Best Western, Comfort Suites, Courtyard, Hilton Garden, Holiday Inn, Holiday Inn Express, Motel 6, Quality Inn, Super 8 ⊡ H, Best Buy, Cabela's, Kohl's, Michael's, Ross, st police, Staples, Target, USPO, Walmart Mkt, **W** 🍴 Taco Bell ⊡ Costco/gas, Office Depot, Petsmart, ShopKO, to 🏥
194b a	OR 126 E, I-105 W, Springfield, Eugene, **1 mi W** 🍴 76, Chevron, Mobil 🍴 Carl's Jr, MOD Pizza, PF Chang's, Starbucks 🛏 La Quinta, Residence Inn ⊡ Albertson's, Natural Grocers, Nissan, Old Navy, Subaru, U Of O
193mm	Willamette River
192	OR 99 (from nb), to Eugene, **E** 🛏 Candlewood Suites, Fairfield Inn, **W** 🍴 🍴 House Of Chen, Starbucks, Subway 🛏 Best Western, Days Inn, Holiday Inn Express, University Inn ⊡ Mkt Of Choice, to U of O
191	Glenwood, **W** 🍴 76/dsl, Shell/dsl/LP 🍴 Denny's 🛏 Comfort Suites, Motel 6
189	30th Ave S, Eugene, **E** 🍴 Shell/dsl/LP ⊡ Harley-Davidson, NW RV Supply, Shamrock RV Park, **W** 🍴 Chevron/dsl, SeQuntial/dsl
188b	OR 99 S (nb only), Goshen
188a	OR 58, OR 99 S to Oakridge, **E** ⊡ Deerwood RV Park, **W** 🍴 Pacific Pride/dsl ⊡ tires
186	Dillard Rd, to Goshen (from nb)
182	Creswell, **E** 🍴 DQ, Subway 🛏 Comfort Inn ⊡ $General, Bi-Mart, golf, OR RV Ctr, **W** 🍴 76/dsl, Arco/dsl 🍴 China Wok, Creswell Cafe, Figaro's Pizza, Joe's Diner, TJ's Rest. 🛏 Super 8 ⊡ $Tree, Creswell Automotive, Dari Mart, Meadowlark RV Park, NAPA
180mm	Coast Fork of Willamette River
178mm	🆁🆂 both lanes, coffee, full ♿ facilities, litter barrels, petwalk, 🚮, 🕿
176	Saginaw
175mm	Row River
174	Cottage Grove, **E** 🍴 Chevron/dsl/repair, Pacific Pride/dsl 🍴 Arby's, Chalerm Thai, Subway, Taco Bell 🛏 Village Resort/RV park ⊡ H, AutoZone, Chevrolet/GMC, Chrysler/Dodge/Jeep, Walmart, **W** 🍴 Chevron/dsl/LP, Mobil/dsl, Shell/dsl 🍴 Burger King, Carl's Jr, Jack-in-the-Box, KFC, McDonald's/RV parking, Papa Murphy's, Pinocchio's Pizza, Taco Time, Torero's Mexican, Vintage Rest. 🛏 Best Western, Quality Inn, Relax Inn ⊡ $Tree, Bi-Mart Foods, Grocery Outlet, O'Reilly Parts, Safeway/dsl, Walgreens
172	6th St (from sb), Cottage Grove Lake (from sb), **2 mi W** ⊡ Cottage Grove RV Village
170	to OR 99, London Rd (nb only), Cottage Grove Lake, **6 mi W** ⊡ Cottage Grove RV Village
163	Curtin, **E** 🛏 Stardust Motel ⊡ antiques, **W** ⊡ Pass Creek Park/camping
162	OR 38, OR 99, to Drain, Elkton
161	Anlauf (from nb)
160	Salt Springs Rd
159	Elk Creek, Cox Rd
154	Yoncalla, Elkhead
150	OR 99, to OR 38, Yoncalla, Red Hill, **W** ⊡ Eagle Valley RV Park
148	Rice Hill, **E** 🍴 Arco/LP, ⊛FLYING J/Denny's/Subway/dsl/scales/24hr, Pacific Pride/dsl 🍴 Ranch Rest. 🛏 Ranch Motel, Rodeway Inn ⊡ Rice Hill RV Park, towing/dsl repair, **W** 🍴 K-R Drive-In
146	Rice Valley
144mm	🆁🆂 sb, full ♿ facilities, litter barrels, petwalk, 🚮, 🕿
143mm	🆁🆂 nb, full ♿ facilities, litter barrels, petwalk, 🚮, 🕿

Exit	Description
142	Metz Hill
140	OR 99 (from sb), Oakland, **E** 🍴 Tolly's Rest. ⊡ Oakland Hist Dist
138	OR 99 (from nb), Oakland, **E** 🍴 Tolly's Rest. ⊡ Oakland Hist Dist
136	OR 138W, Sutherlin, **E** 🍴 Chevron/dsl, Mobil/dsl 🍴 Abby's Pizza, Apple Peddler Rest., Burger King, Domino's, McDonald's, Papa Murphy's, Pedotti's Italian, Sol de Sutherlin, Yummy House 🛏 Best Western+, Motel 6, Relax Inn ⊡ $Tree, Autocare, AutoZone, I-5 RV Ctr, NAPA, **W** 🍴 Shell/dsl 🍴 Dakota St Pizza, DQ, Si Casa Flores, Starbucks, Subway, Taco Bell ⊡ Hi-Way Haven RV Camp, Umpqua RV Park
135	Wilbur, Sutherlin, **E** 🍴 CFN/dsl, Shell/dsl/LP ⊡ vet
129	OR 99, Winchester, **E** 🍴 Del Ray Cafe ⊡ Kamper Korner RV Ctr (1mi), Rivers Edge RV Park, st police
129mm	N Umpqua River, N Umpqua River
127	Stewart Pkwy, Edenbower Rd, N Roseburg, **E** 🍴 Shell/dsl 🍴 Shari's Rest., Subway 🛏 Motel 6, Super 8 ⊡ Costco/gas, Home Depot, Honda, Lowe's, Mt Nebo RV Park, Verizon, **W** 🍴 Mobil, Valero/dsl 🍴 Applebee's, Del Taco, McDonald's/playplace, Red Robin, Subway, Yummy Chinese 🛏 Sleep Inn ⊡ H, Albertson's, Big O Tire, Macy's, Sherm's Foods, vet, Walmart
125	Garden Valley Blvd, Roseburg, **E** 🍴 Abby's Pizza, China Buffet, Elmer's, Gilberto's Mexican, Jack-in-the-Box, KFC, Los Dos Amigo's Mexican, McDonald's, Smokin' Friday BBQ, Sonic, Subway, Taco Bell 🛏 Comfort Inn, Hampton Inn, Quality Inn ⊡ AT&T, AutoZone, BigLots, Buick/Chevrolet/GMC, Ford/Lincoln, Honda, NAPA, Safeway/dsl, Toyota, U-Haul, Verizon, vet, Walgreens, **W** 🍴 Shell/LP/repair 🍴 Burger King, Carl's Jr, Fox Den Pizza, Panda Express, Pita Pit, Rodeo Steaks, RoundTable Pizza, Si Casa Flores Mexican, Sizzler, Starbucks, Wendy's 🛏 Best Western, Days Inn ⊡ H, $Tree, Bi-Mart Foods, Fred Meyer/dsl, JC Penney, JoAnn Fabrics, Marshall's, Michael's, O'Reilly Parts, PetCo, Rite Aid, Ross, Staples, Walgreens
124	OR 138, Roseburg, City Ctr, **E** 🍴 Chevron/dsl, Texaco/dsl 🍴 Denny's 🛏 Baymont Inn, Holiday Inn Express, Rodeway Inn, Travelodge ⊡ Rite Aid, **W** 🍴 76/dsl, Mobil/dsl 🍴 Charley's BBQ, Domino's, KFC/LJ Silver, Pete's Drive-In, Subway, Taco Time ⊡ Grocery Outlet, Harvard Ave Drug
123	Roseburg, **E** ⊡ camping, museum, to Umpqua Park
121	McLain Ave
120.5mm	S Umpqua River
120	OR 99 N (no EZ nb return), Green District, Roseburg, **E** 🛏 Rodeway Inn, Shady Oaks Motel, **W** ⊡ auto repair
119	OR 99 S, OR 42 W, Winston, **E** ⊡ Ingram Dist., **W** 🍴 Chevron/A&W/dsl, ⬥Loves/Arby's/dsl/scales/LP/24hr, Shell/dsl 🍴 McDonald's, Papa Murphy's, Subway, Taco Bell ⊡ $General, Ray's Foods, Rising River RV Park, Western Star RV Park
113	Clarks Branch Rd, Round Prairie, **W** 🛏 Quikstop Motel ⊡ On the River RV Park (2mi)
112.5mm	S Umpqua River

E
U
G
E
N
E

S
U
T
H
E
R
L
I
N

R
O
S
E
B
U
R
G

⛽ = gas 🍴 = food 🛏 = lodging ⊡ = other 🅁 = rest stop   Copyright 2022 - The Next EXIT ®

🔼 INTERSTATE 5 Cont'd

Exit #	Services
112	OR 99, OR 42, Dillard, E ⊡ Rivers West RV Park
111mm	weigh sta both directions
110	Boomer Hill Rd
108	Myrtle Creek, E ⛽ Chevron 🍴 Armando's Mexican, Golf Course Cafe, Subway, Tommy's Cafe ⊡ city park, Myrtle Creek RV Park, Ray's Foods
106	Weaver Rd
103	Tri City, Myrtle Creek, E ⊡ Tri-City RV Park, W ⛽ Chevron/A&W/dsl, Pacific Pride 🍴 McDonald's
102	Gazley Rd, E ⊡ Surprise Valley RV Park (1mi)
101.5mm	S Umpqua River
101	Riddle, Stanton Park, W ⊡ camping
99	Canyonville, E ⛽ Penny Pincher 🍴 Burger King, El Paraiso 🛏 7 Feathers Hotel/casino, Riverside Motel ⊡ Canyon Mkt, city park, W 🅁 7 Feathers Trkstp/café/dsl/scales/24hr/@ 🍴 Creekside Rest. 🛏 Holiday Inn Express ⊡ 7 Feathers RV Resort
98	OR 99, Canyonville, Days Creek, E ⛽ Arco/dsl, Mobil/dsl 🍴 Ken's Cafe, Papa Morgan's Rest., Subway 🛏 Leisure Inn ⊡ $General, auto repair, Canyonville Hardware, NAPA, Ray's Foods, USPO, vet, W ⊡ museum
95	Canyon Creek
90mm	Canyon Creek Pass, elevation 2020
88	Azalea
86	Barton Rd, Quine's Creek, E ⛽ Quines Creek/dsl ⊡ Heaven on Earth Rest./rest., Meadow Wood RV Park (3mi)
83	Barton Rd (from nb), E ⊡ Meadow Wood RV Park/camping
80	Glendale, W ⛽ Cow Creek/Lp/Rest.
79.5mm	Stage Road Pass, elevation 1830
78	Speaker Rd (from sb)
76	Wolf Creek, W ⛽ 76/deli/dsl, Pacific Pride/dsl, Shell/dsl 🍴 Wolf Creek Inn Rest. ⊡ Creekside RV park, USPO
74mm	Smith Hill Summit, elevation 1730
71	Sunny Valley, E ⛽ Covered Bridge Store/gas, W ⊡ Sunny Valley RV Park/motel
69mm	Sexton Mtn Pass, elevation 1960
66	Hugo, E ⊡ KOA, W ⊡ Pottsville Museum (3mi)
63mm	🅁 both lanes, full ♿ facilities, info, litter barrels, petwalk, 🚻, vending
61	Merlin, W ⛽ Valero/dsl ⊡ $General, Almeda RV Park, Beaver Creek RV Resort (2mi), OR RV Ctr, Ray's Foods, repair
58	OR 99, to US 199, Grants Pass, W ⛽ 76/Circle K/dsl, CFN/dsl, Chevron, Mobil/dsl, Shell/dsl/repair, TownePump Gas 🍴 Black Bear Diner, Burger King, Carl's Jr, China Hut, Denny's, DQ, In-N-Out, Jack-in-the-Box, McDonald's, Muchas Gracias Mexican, Nano's Mexican, Papa Murphy's, Sizzler, Subway, Taco Bell, Uptown Grill, Wendy's 🛏 Best Way Inn, Buona Sera Inn, Hampton Inn, Hawks Inn, La Quinta, Motel 6, Quality Inn, Red Lion Inn, Redwood Motel, Sunset Inn, Super 8, Sweet-Breeze Inn, Travelodge ⊡ 🏨, $Tree, AutoZone, Chevrolet/Honda, Chrysler/Dodge/Jeep, Jack's RV Resort, Nissan, repair, Rouge Valley RV Park, Schwab Tire, st police, towing
55	US 199, Redwood Hwy, E Grants Pass, W ⛽ Arco/dsl, Mobil/dsl 🍴 Abby's Pizza, Applebee's, Arby's, Carl's Jr, Elmer's, Jersey Mike's, KFC, Kobe Buffet, La Burrita, McDonald's, MOD Pizza, Panda Express, Pizza Hut, Shari's, Si Casa Flores Mexican, Starbucks, Subway, Taco Bell 🛏 Best Western, Holiday Inn Express ⊡ 🏨, $Tree, Albertson's, AT&T, BigLots, Fred Meyer/dsl, Grocery Outlet, Jo-Ann, Moon Mtn RV Park (2mi), O'Reilly Parts, Petco, Rite Aid, RiverPark RV Park (4mi), Ross, Siskiyou RV Ctr, Staples, Verizon, Walmart, Winco Foods

Exit #	Services
48	Rogue River, E ⛽ 76/dsl, Chevron/Circle K/dsl 🍴 Abby's Pizza, Cottage Cafe, Homestead Rest., Subway ⊡ $General, Ace Hardware, auto repair, Rogue River RA, vet, W 🍴 La Guayacama, Mkt Basket Deli 🛏 Bella Rosa Inn, Best Western ⊡ Bridgeview RV Park, Chinook Winds RV Park, visitors ctr/info, Whispering Pines RV Park
45b	W Valley of the Rogue SP/🅁 both lanes, camping, full ♿ facilities, litter barrels, petwalk, 🚻, 🚻
45mm	Rogue River
45a	OR 99, Savage Rapids Dam, E ⊡ Cypress Grove RV Park
43	OR 99, OR 234, to Crater Lake, Gold Hill, E 🛏 RoadRiver B&B, Rock Point RV Park
40	OR 99, OR 234, Gold Hill, E 🍴 Figaro's Pizza ⊡ $General, KOA, Lazy Acres Motel/RV Park, Running Salmon RV Park, W ⛽ Dardanelle's/gas ⊡ Dardanelle's Trailer Park
35	OR 99, Blackwell Rd, Central Point, 2-4 mi W ⛽ gas 🍴 food 🛏 lodging ⊡ Jacksonville Nat Hist Landmark, st police
33	Central Point, E ⛽ Chevron, LNG, 🅿Pilot/Subway/Taco Bell/dsl/scales/24hr 🍴 Burger King, KFC, Shari's Rest., Sonic 🛏 Candlewood Suites (2mi), Courtyard (2mi), Holiday Inn Express, La Quinta, Super 8 ⊡ Costco/dsl, funpark, W ⛽ 76/Circle K/dsl, Shell/dsl 🍴 Abby's Pizza, Little Caesar's, Mazatlan Mexican, McDonald's ⊡ Albertson's, AT&T, USPO
30	OR 62, to Crater Lake, Medford, E ⛽ Arco, Chevron/dsl, Witham Trkstp/rest./dsl/24hr/@ 🍴 Abby's Pizza, Applebee's, Asian Grill, Baskin Robbins, Buffalo Wild Wings, Burger King, Carl's Jr, Del Taco, Denny's, DQ, Elmer's, McDonald's, Olive Garden, Outback Steaks, Panda Express, Papa John's, Papa Murphy's, Pita Pit, Pizza Hut, Red Robin, RoundTable Pizza, Sizzler, Sonic, Starbucks, Subway, Taco Bell, Taco Delite, Thai Bistro, TX Roadhouse, Wayback Burger, Wendy's 🛏 Comfort Inn, Hampton Inn, Motel 6, Quality Inn, Ramada, Rogue Regency Hotel, Shilo Inn ⊡ 🏨, $Tree, AT&T, AutoZone, Barnes&Noble, Best Buy, BigLots, Bi-Mart, Chevrolet/Buick/GMC, Discount Tire, Food4Less, Ford/Lincoln, Fred Meyer/dsl, Hobby Lobby, JoAnn, Lowe's, Mazda, Mercedes, Michael's, NAPA, Office Depot, Old Navy, O'Reilly Parts, Petsmart, Ross, Safeway, Schwab Tire, st police, Subaru, TJ Maxx, USPO, Verizon, vet, Walmart/Subway, W ⛽ 76/dsl, Spirit/dsl 🍴 Chipotle, In-n-Out, Jack-in-the-Box, Kaleidoscope Pizza, KFC, MOD Pizza, Red Lobster, Subway, Wendy's ⊡ CarQuest, JC Penney, Kohl's, Macy's, Natural Grocers, Petco, REI, Target, Toyota, Trader Joe's, Verizon
27	Barnett Rd, Medford, E 🍴 Black Bear Diner, DQ 🛏 Best Western, Days Inn/rest., Hilton Garden, Homewood Suites, Motel 6, Travelers Inn ⊡ 🏨, W ⛽ 76/Circle K/dsl, Chevron/dsl 🍴 Abby's Pizza, Arby's, Burger King, Carl's Jr, Domino's, El Arriero Mexican, HomeTown Buffet, Jack-in-the-Box, KFC, McDonald's, McGrath's FishHouse, Panda Express, Pizza Hut, Rooster's Rest., Shari's, Starbucks, Subway, Taco Bell, Wendy's 🛏 Comfort Inn, Holiday Inn Express, Medford Inn, Royal Crest Motel, Sovana Inn, SpringHill Suites, TownePlace Suites ⊡ $Tree, AT&T, Fred Meyer/dsl, GNC, Grocery Outlet, Harry&David's, O'Reilly Parts, Staples, Verizon, Walgreens, Walmart/McDonald's, WinCo Foods
24	Phoenix, E ⛽ Petro/Iron Skillet/dsl/scales/RV dump/24hr/@, Shell/dsl 🛏 Best Value/PearTree RV park ⊡ Home Depot, Peterbilt, W ⛽ Chevron/Circle K/dsl 🍴 Amigos Mexican, Angelo's Pizza, Jack-in-the-Box, McDonald's ⊡ auto repair, Harley Davidson, Holiday RV Park, Ray's Foods, Rite Aid
22mm	🅁 sb, full ♿ facilities, litter barrels, petwalk, 🚻, 🚻, vending
21	Talent, W ⛽ 76/dsl, Chevron/dsl 🍴 Subway 🛏 GoodNight Inn ⊡ $General, Ashland Talent RV Resort, vet

OR

G R A N T S   P A S S

M E D F O R D

⬆N INTERSTATE 5 Cont'd

Exit #	Services
19	Valley View Rd, Ashland, **W** 🅖 76/dsl, Pacific Pride/dsl, Shell/dsl/LP 🅕 Burger King, El Tapatio Mexican 🏠 Comfort Inn, EconoLodge/RV Park 🅞 Acura, Chevrolet, Ford
18mm	**weigh sta both lanes**
14	OR 66, to Klamath Falls, Ashland, **E** 🅖 Chevron/dsl, Mobil/dsl/LP, Valero/dsl 🅕 El Paraiso Mexican, OakTree Rest. 🏠 Ashland Hills Inn & Suites, Best Western, Holiday Inn Express, Relax Inn 🅞 Emigrant Lake Camping (3mi), Glenyan RV Park (3mi), **W** 🅖 Arco, Shell 🅕 Señor Sam's Mexican, Subway, Taco Bell, Wendy's, Wild Goose Cafe 🏠 Rodeway Inn, Super 8 🅞 🅷 $Tree, Albertson's, AT&T, Bi-Mart, CarQuest, Rite Aid, Schwab Tire, Shop'n Kart, U-Haul, vet
12	🆁🆂 nb, full facilities
11	OR 99, Siskiyou Blvd (nb only, no return)
6	to Mt Ashland, **E** 🏠 Callahan's Siskiyou Lodge/rest. 🅞 ski area
4mm	Siskiyou Summit, elevation 4310, brake check both lanes
1	to Siskiyou Summit (from nb, no return)
0mm	Oregon/California state line

⬆E INTERSTATE 84

Exit #	Services
378mm	Oregon/Idaho state line, Snake River
377.5mm	Welcome Ctr wb, full ♿ facilities, info, litter barrels, petwalk, 🄲, 🄰, vending
376b a	US 30, to US 20/26, Ontario, Payette, **N** 🅖 Chevron/dsl 🅕 A&W/KFC, Burger King, Carl's Jr, China Buffet, Country Kitchen, Denny's, Domino's, DQ, Dutch Bros Coffee, Little Caesar's, McDonald's, Panda Express, Papa Murphy's, Starbucks, Subway, Taco Time, Wingers 🏠 Best Western, Clarion, Motel 6, Quality Inn, Red Lion Inn, Sleep Inn 🅞 $Tree, AT&T, GNC, Home Depot, st police, Staples, Toyota, Verizon, Walgreens, Walmart/Subway, Waremart, **S** 🅖 Arby's/dsl/scales/24hr, Sinclair/dsl 🅕 East Side Cafe, Gandolfo's Deli, Ogawa's Japanese, Sweet Caroline's, Taco Bell 🏠 Holiday Inn Express, OR Trail Motel, Stockman's Motel, Super 8 🅞 🅷 Commercial Tire, Les Schwab Tire, NAPA
374	US 30, OR 201, to Ontario, **N** 🅞 to Ontario SP, **S** 🅖 Loves/Chester's/Subway/dsl/scales/24hr/@, Pacific Pride 🏠 Budget Inn 🅞 🅷
373.5mm	Malheur River
371	Stanton Blvd, **2 mi S** 🅞 to correctional institution
362	Moores Hollow Rd
356	OR 201, to Weiser, ID, **3 mi N** 🅞 Catfish Junction RV Park, Oasis RV Park
354.5mm	weigh sta eb
353	US 30, to Huntington, **N** 🅞 info, RV camping, to Farewell Bend SP, **weigh sta wb**
351mm	Pacific/Mountain time zone
345	US 30, Lime, Huntington, **1 mi N** 🅖 gas 🅕 food 🏠 lodging 🅞 to Snake River Area, Van Ornum BFD
342	Lime (from eb)
340	Rye Valley
338	Lookout Mountain
337mm	Burnt River
335	to Weatherby, **N** 🆁🆂 both lanes, full ♿ facilities, litter barrels, **Oregon Trail Info, petwalk,** 🄰, **vending**
330	Plano Rd, to Cement Plant Rd, **S** 🅞 cement plant
329mm	pulloff eb
327	Durkee, **N** 🅖 Co-op/dsl/LP/café

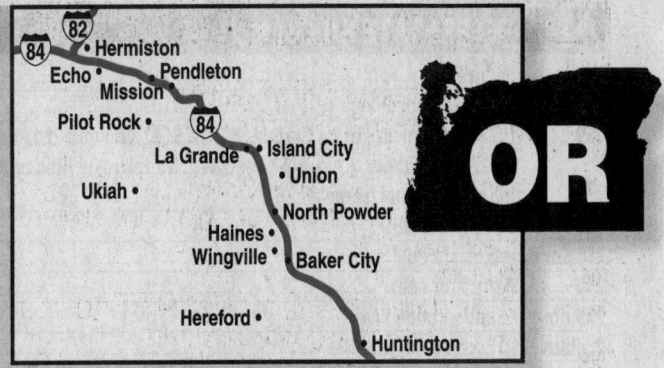

325mm	Pritchard Creek
321mm	Alder Creek
317	to Pleasant Valley (from wb)
315	to Pleasant Valley (from wb)
313	to Pleasant Valley (from eb)
306	US 30, Baker, **2-3 mi S** 🅖 Chevron/dsl 🏠 Baker City Motel, Bridge Street Hotel, OR Trail Motel/rest. 🅞 🅷, Les Schwab Tire, same as 304, to st police
304	OR 7, Baker, **N** 🅖 Chevron/dsl/24hr 🏠 Super 8, Welcome Inn 🅞 Grocery Outlet, **S** 🅖 Maverik/dsl, Shell/dsl, Sinclair/dsl/rest./scales/24hr, USA/dsl 🅕 Big Chief's BBQ, Golden Crown, McDonald's, Papa Murphy's, Pizza Hut, Rising Sun Chinese, Starbucks, Subway, Sumpter Jct Rest., Taco Time 🏠 Eldorado Inn, Geiser Grand Motel, Rodeway Inn, Sunridge Inn 🅞 🅷, $Tree, Albertson's, Bi-Mart, Carquest, CarQuest, city park, Mtn View RV Park/LP (3mi), museum, O'Reilly Parts, Paul's Transmissions/repair, Rite Aid, Safeway Foods, to hist dist, Verizon
302	OR 86 E to Richland, **S** 🅞 🅷, A Frame RV Park/LP, st police
298	OR 203, to Medical Springs
297mm	Baldock Slough
295mm	🆁🆂 both lanes, full ♿ facilities, info, litter barrels, petwalk, 🄲, 🄰, vending
289mm	Powder River
287.5mm	45th parallel, halfway between the equator and north pole
286mm	N Powder River
285	US 30, OR 237, North Powder, **N** 🏠 North Powder Motel/cafe, **S** 🅞 ski area, to Anthony Lakes
284mm	Wolf Creek
283	Wolf Creek Lane
278	Clover Creek
273	Frontage Rd
270	Ladd Creek Rd (from eb, no return)
269mm	🆁🆂 both lanes, full ♿ facilities, info, litter barrels, petwalk, 🄲, 🄰, vending
268	Foothill Rd
265	OR 203, LaGrande, **N** 🅞 ⬆, Eagles Hot Lake RV Park, **S** 🅖 FLYING J/rest./dsl/scales/24hr 🅕 SmokeHouse Rest. (2mi) 🅞 Freightliner
261	OR 82, LaGrande, **N** 🅖 Chevron/dsl, Shell/dsl 🅕 Denny's, Little Caesar's, Pizza Hut, Primo's Pizza, Starbucks, Taco Bell 🏠 LaGrande Inn 🅞 AT&T, Chrysler/Dodge/Jeep, Ford, Grocery Outlet, Thunder RV Ctr, Verizon, vet, Walmart/Subway, **S** 🅖 76/Baskin-Robbins/Subway/dsl, Chevron/dsl, Texaco/dsl 🅕 Chen's Chinese, Domino's, DQ, Dutch Bro's Coffee, KFC, La Fiesta Mexican, Local Harvest Eatery, McDonald's, Moy's Dynasty, Nell's Steakburger, Papa Murphy's, Taco Time, Wendy's 🏠 Best Western+, Royal Motel, Sandman Inn/Best Value, Super 8 🅞 🅷, $General, $Tree, Ace Hardware, E OR U, O'Reilly Parts, Rite Aid, Safeway/dsl, Schwab Tire, Wallowa Lake

⛽ = gas 🍴 = food 🛏 = lodging 🅾 = other 🆁🆂 = rest stop   Copyright 2022 - The Next EXIT

INTERSTATE 84 Cont'd

Exit #	Services
260mm	Grande Ronde River
259	US 30 E (from eb), to La Grande, **1-2 mi** S ⛽ Chevron/dsl, Mobil/dsl 🍴 Burger King 🛏 Greenwell Motel/rest., Rodeway Inn, Royal Motel, same as 261
257	Perry (from wb)
256.5mm	weigh sta eb
256	Perry (from eb)
255mm	Grande Ronde River
254mm	🅾 scenic wayside
252	OR 244, to Starkey, Lehman Sprgs, S 🅾 camping, chainup area, Hilgard SP
251mm	🅾 Wallowa-Whitman NF, eastern boundary
248	Spring Creek Rd, to Kamela, **3 mi** N 🅾 Oregon Trail Visitors Park
246mm	🅾 Wallowa-Whitman NF, western boundary
243	Summit Rd, Mt Emily Rd, to Kamela, **2 mi** N 🅾 Emily Summit SP, 🅾 Oregon Trail info
241mm	Summit of the Blue Mtns, elevation 4193
238	Meacham
234	Meacham, S 🅾 Emigrant Sprs SP
231.5mm	🅾 Umatilla Indian Reservation, eastern boundary
228mm	Deadman Pass, 🆁🆂 both lanes, full ♿ facilities, litter barrel, Oregon Trail info, petwalk, 🍴 (wb) picnic table, RV Dump (wb), vending
227mm	weigh sta wb, brake check area
224	Poverty Flats Rd, Old Emigrant Hill Rd, to Emigrant Springs SP
223mm	no restrooms, wb viewpoint
221.5mm	eb viewpoint, no restrooms
220mm	runaway truck ramp wb
216	Mission, McKay Creek, N ⛽ Arrowhead Trkstp/Pacific Pride/McDonald's/dsl/24hr 🍴 DQ, Subway 🅾 Wildhorse Casino/RV Park
213	US 30 (from wb), Pendleton, **3-5 mi** N ⛽ Chevron/dsl 🛏 Travelers Inn 🅾 Pendleton NHD
212mm	Umatilla Indian Reservation western boundary
210	OR 11, Pendleton, N 🅾 museum, st police, S ⛽ Chevron/Circle K/dsl, Sinclair/dsl/LP 🍴 Shari's/24hr 🛏 Best Western, Hampton Inn, Holiday Inn Express, Motel 6, Red Lion Inn/rest., Super 8 🅾 KOA
209	US 395, Pendleton, N ⛽ Space Age 🍴 Domino's, DQ, Jack-in-the-Box, KFC, Little Caesar's, Pizza Hut, Quiznos, Taco Bell 🛏 Oxford Suites, Travelodge 🅾 $Tree, AT&T, Dean's Mkt, Grocery Outlet, O'Reilly Parts, Rite Aid, Safeway/dsl, Verizon, Walgreens, Walmart/Subway, S ⛽ Astro/dsl, Sinclair/dsl 🍴 Abby's Pizza, Burger King, Denny's, Dickey's BBQ, McDonald's, Rooster's Rest, Starbucks, Subway, Wendy's 🛏 Motel 6 🅾 🏥, Les Schwab, Thompson RV Ctr
208mm	Umatilla River
207	US 30, W Pendleton, N ⛽ Sinclair/dsl/LP 🅾 Lookout RV Park, truck repair
202	Barnhart Rd, to Stage Gulch, N 🅾 Woodpecker Truck Repair
199	Stage Coach Rd, Yoakum Rd
198	Lorenzen Rd, McClintock Rd, N 🅾 trailer/reefer repair
193	Echo Rd, to Echo, 🅾 Oregon Trail Site
188	US 395 N, Hermiston, N ⛽ Chevron/dsl (5mi), 🟥/Subway/McDonald's/dsl/24hr/RV park 🍴 Denny's/24hr (5mi), Jack-in-the-Box (5mi), McDonald's (5mi), Shari's/24hr (5mi) 🛏 Best Western (5mi), Holiday Inn Express, Motel 6, Oxford Suites (5mi) 🅾 🏥(5mi), S 🅾 Echo HS, Henrietta RV Park (1mi)
187mm	🆁🆂 both lanes, full ♿ facilities, info, litter barrels, petwalk, 🍴 🛏

BOARDMAN

182	OR 207, to Hermiston, N ⛽ Space Age/A&W/dsl/LP/24🛏 Comfort Inn
180	Westland Rd, to Hermiston, McNary Dam, N 🅾 trailer repair, ⛽ Western Express/dsl 🅾 Freightliner
179	I-82 W, to Umatilla, Kennewick, WA
177	🅾 Umatilla Army Depot
171	Paterson Ferry Rd, to Paterson
168	US 730, to Irrigon, **8 mi** N 🅾 Green Acres RV Park, Oasis R Park, Oregon Trail info
165	Port of Morrow, S ⛽ Pacific Pride/dsl
164	Boardman, N ⛽ Chevron/Circle K/dsl, Sinclair/dsl 🍴 C& Drive-In, Smiley's Cafe, Sunrise Cafe, Village Rest. 🛏 Knight Inn, Riverview Motel 🅾 Boardman RV/Marina Park, city park USPO, S ⛽ Shell/dsl 🍴 Subway 🅾 Boardman Tire, NAPA, Oregon Trail Library, Rodeway Inn 🅾 Harvest Town Mkt
161mm	🆁🆂 both lanes, full ♿ facilities, litter barrels, petwalk, 🍴 🛏 vending
159	Tower Rd, S 🍴 ❤Loves/Carl's Jr/dsl/scales/24hr
151	Threemile Canyon
147	OR 74, to Ione, Blue Mtn Scenic Byway, Heppner, 🅾 Orego Trail Site
137	OR 19, Arlington, S ⛽ Shell/Circle K/dsl 🍴 Happy Canyon Cafe Pheasant Grill, Rivers Edge Deli 🛏 Rodeway Inn 🅾 Arlingto Hardware, Arlington RV Park/dump, city park, Thrifty Foods
136.5mm	viewpoint wb, 🛏 litter barrels
131	Woelpern Rd (from eb, no return)
129	Blalock Canyon, 🅾 Lewis&Clark Trail
123	Philippi Canyon, 🅾 Lewis&Clark Trail
114.5mm	John Day River
114	S 🅾 LePage Park
112	parking area both lanes, litter barrels, N 🅾 John Day Dam
109	Pendleton, N 🅾 John Day Visitor Ctr, S ⛽ Sinclair/ds 🍴 Bob's T-Bone, Bull Dog Diner 🛏 Hillview Motel, Tyee Mote 🅾 Ed's RV Park, Family Mkt/deli, Rufus RV Park
104	US 97, Biggs, N 🅾 Des Chutes Park Bridge, Maryhill Museum, ⛽ 76/Circle K/Noble Roman's/dsl/24hr, 🟥/McDonald's/dsl/scales/24hr, Shell/Subway/dsl 🍴 Linda's Rest. 🛏 Dinty' Motel, Three Rivers Inn 🅾 Dinty's Mkt, dsl/tire repair
100mm	Columbia River Gorge Scenic Area, Deschutes River
97	OR 206, Celilo, N 🅾 Celilo SP, restrooms, S 🅾 Deschutes SP Indian Village
92mm	pull off eb
88	N 🅾 to The Dalles Dam

THE DALLES

87	US 30, US 197, to Dufur, N ⛽ 76/dsl/24hr, Chevron/ds 🍴 McDonald's, Portage Grill 🛏 Comfort Inn, Shilo Inn 🅾 Columbia Hills RV Park, Lone Pine RV Park, st police, S 🍴 Big Jim's Drive-In 🛏 Celilo Inn
85	The Dalles, N Riverfront Park, litter barrels, 🍴 🛏 playground, restrooms, 🅾 marina, S ⛽ 76/dsl, Chevron, Sinclair 🍴 Burgerville, Canton Wok, Clock Tower Rest., Domino's, River Tap Rest. 🛏 Dalles Inn, Oregon Motel 🅾 🏥, AJ's Radiators, Dalles Parts, to Nat Hist Dist, TrueValue, USPO
83	(84 from wb) W The Dalles, N 🍴 Casa El Mirador 🛏 Legends Hotel/Casino 🅾 S-Point Automotive, S ⛽ Astro/dsl, Chevron/dsl, Fred Meyer/dsl 🍴 Burger King, Denny's, DQ, Dutch Bro's Coffee, Ixtapa Mexican, Jack-in-the-Box, KFC, McDonald's, Papa Murphy's, Pizza Hut, Shari's Rest., Starbucks, Subway, Taco Bell, Taco Time, The BBQ 🛏 Cousin's Inn/rest., Fairfield Inn, Motel 6, Super 8 🅾 🏥, $Tree, AT&T, AutoZone, Buick/Chevrolet/ GMC, Chrysler/Dodge/Jeep, Ford, Fred Meyer, Grocery Outlet, Honda, Jo-Ann Fabrics, Nissan, O'Reilly Parts, PetCo, Rite Aid Safeway/dsl, Staples, Subaru, Toyota, Verizon, Walgreens

OR

▲🇪 INTERSTATE 84 Cont'd

Exit #	Services
82	Chenowith Area, S 🅖 76/dsl 🅕 Spooky's Café 🅞 Bi-Mart Foods, Columbia Discovery Ctr, Home Depot, museum, same as 83
76	Rowena, N 🅞 Lewis & Clark info, Mayer SP, Memaloose SP, windsurfing
73mm	🆁 both lanes, full 🦽 facilities, litter barrels, petwalk, 🚻, 🛢, RV dump 🅞 camping, Memaloose SP
69	US 30, Mosier, S 🅞 USPO
66mm	N 🆁 wb full facilities, litter barrels, 🛢, 🅞 Koberg Beach SP
64	US 30, OR 35, to White Salmon, Hood River, N 🅖 Chevron/dsl, Shell 🅕 McDonald's, Riverside Grill, Starbucks 🆎 Best Western 🅞 marina, museum, st police, visitors info
63	Hood River, City Ctr, N 🅖 Valero/dsl 🆎 Hampton Inn, S 🅖 Astro 🅕 3 River's Grill, Andrew's Pizza, Big Horse Rest., Hood River Rest., Pietro's Pizza 🆎 Hood River Hotel, Oakstreet Hotel 🅞 🅗, USPO
62	US 30, Westcliff Dr, W Hood River, N 🅕 Charburger, White Buffalo Rest. 🆎 Columbia Gorge Hotel, Vagabond Lodge, S 🅖 76/dsl, Chevron/dsl/LP 🅕 Domino's, DQ, Egg River Cafe, HoHo Chinese, McDonald's, Pelinti Cafe, Red Carpet Cafe, Starbucks, Subway, Taco Bell 🆎 Holiday Inn Express, Prater's Motel, Riverview Lodge 🅞 🅗, AT&T, Les Schwab Tire, Rite Aid, Safeway, Verizon, Walmart
61mm	pulloff wb
60	service rd wb (no return)
58	Mitchell Point Overlook (from eb)
56	N 🅞 RV camping, Viento SP
55	Starvation Peak Tr Head (from eb), restrooms
54mm	weigh sta wb
51	Wyeth, S 🅞 camping
49mm	pulloff eb
47	Forest Lane, Hermon Creek (from wb), 🅞 camping
45mm	weigh sta eb
44	US 30, to Cascade Locks, N 🅖 Chevron/dsl, Shell/dsl 🅕 Bridgeside Rest., Cascade Inn Rest., Eastwind Drive-In, Waterfront Cafe 🆎 Best Western+, Bridge of the Gods Motel, Cascade Motel, Columbia Gorge Inn 🅞 Columbia Mkt, KOA, Stern Wheeler RV Park, to Bridge of the Gods, USPO
41	🅞 Eagle Creek RA (from eb), to fish hatchery
40	N 🅞 Bonneville Dam NHS, info, to fish hatchery
37	Warrendale (from wb)
35	Historic Hwy, Multnomah (exits left from both lanes), S 🅞 Ainsworth SP, Fishery RV Park, scenic loop highway, waterfall area
31	Multnomah Falls (exits left from both lanes), S 🅕 Multnomah Falls Lodge/Rest. (hist site) 🅞 camping
30	S 🅞 Benson SRA (from eb)
29	Dalton Point (from wb)
28	to Bridal Veil (7 mi return from eb), S 🅞 USPO
25	N 🅞 Rooster Rock SP
23mm	🅞 hist marker, viewpoint wb
22	Corbett, 2 mi S 🅖 Corbett Mkt 🅕 View Point Rest. 🅞 Crown Point RV Camping
19mm	🅞 Columbia River Gorge scenic area
18	Lewis&Clark SP, to Oxbow SP
17.5mm	Sandy River
17	Marine Dr, Troutdale, N 🅕 DQ 🆎 Comfort Inn, S 🅖 Chevron/dsl, 🅛Loves/Chester's/dsl/LP/scales/24hr, TA/Shell/Country Pride/Popeye's/Subway/dsl/scales/24hr/@ 🅕 Arby's, McDonald's, Shari's/24hr, Subway, Taco Bell 🆎 Holiday Inn Express, Motel 6 🅞 Premium Outlets/famous brands, Sandy Riverfront RV Resort

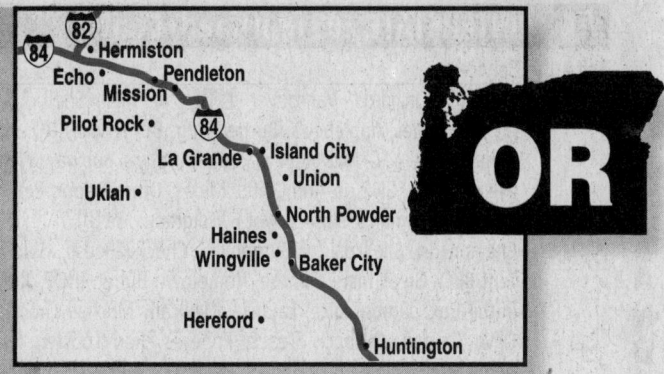

16	238th Dr, Fairview, N 🅖 Arco/dsl/24hr 🅕 Bronx Eatery, Burger King, Jack-in-the-Box 🆎 Travelodge 🅞 Camping World, Walmart/Subway, S 🅖 🅞 🅗
14	207th Ave, Fairview, N 🅖 Shell/dsl 🅕 Parkway Grill 🅞 auto repair, Portland RV Park, Rolling Hills RV Park
13	181st Ave, Gresham, N 🅖 Chevron/dsl 🆎 Hampton Inn, S 🅖 76, Arco, Shell 🅕 Burger King, Canton Pearl, Carl's Jr, Elmer's, McDonald's, Pizza Hut, Shari's, Subway, Wendy's 🆎 Bridgeway Inn, Days Inn, Extended Stay America, Portland Suites, Sheraton 🅞 $Tree, 7-11, U-Haul, vet
10	122nd Ave (from eb)
9	I-205, S to Salem, N to Seattle, to 🍃, (to 102nd Ave from eb)
8	I-205 N (from eb), N 🅞 to 🍃
7	Halsey St (from eb), Gateway Dist
6	I-205 S (from eb)
5	OR 213, to 82nd Ave (eb only), N 🆎 Days Inn, S 🅕 Eastern Cathay 🆎 Comfort Inn
4	68th Ave (from eb), to Halsey Ave
3	58th Ave (from eb), S 🅖 76, Shell/dsl 🅞 🅗, Fred Meyer
2	43rd Ave, 39th Ave, Halsey St, N 🅖 🅕 Burger King, Panera Bread, Starbucks 🆎 Banfield Motel 🅞 Rite Aid, Trader Joe's, S 🅞 🅗, same as 1
1	33rd Ave, Lloyd Blvd (eb only), downtown, N 🅖 Shell/dsl 🅕 Burger King, Starbucks 🅞 AT&T, S 🅕 Wendy's 🅞 Schwab Tire, same as 2
1	to downtown (wb only), N 🅕 Applebee's 🆎 Doubletree, Residence Inn 🅞 $Tree, Macy's, Marshall's, Nordstrom, Safeway, S 🅞 Cadillac
0mm	I-84 begins/ends on I-5, exit 301.

▲🇳 INTERSTATE 205 (Portland)

Exit #	Services
37mm	I-205 begins/ends on I-5. Exits 36-27 are in Washington.
36	NE 134th St (from nb), E 🅖 Chevron/dsl 🆎 Holiday Inn Express 🅞 🅗, W 🅖 7-11, Arco, Mobil, Shell 🅕 Applebee's, Baskin-Robbins, Billygan's Roadhouse, Burger King, Burgerville, El Tapatio, Jack-in-the-Box, McDonald's, Muchas Gracias, Panda Express, Papa Murphy's, PizzaSchmitzza, Round Table Pizza, Starbucks, Subway, Taco Bell 🆎 La Quinta, Shilo Inn, Vancouver Inn 🅞 99 RV Park, Albertson's, Fred Meyer, Safeway/dsl, Verizon, Walgreens
32	NE 83rd St, Anderson Rd, Battle Ground, W 🅖 Shell/dsl/24hr 🅕 Burger King, Emporor Chinese, Krispy Kreme, Panda Express, Starbucks, Subway, Taco Bell, Taste of China, Weinerschnitzel, Wendy's 🅞 Costco/gas, Home Depot, vet

🅿️ = gas 🍴 = food 🛏️ = lodging 🅾️ = other Ⓡ = rest stop Copyright 2022 - The Next EXIT

P O R T L A N D   A R E A

▲N INTERSTATE 205 (Portland) Cont'd

Exit #	Services
30c b a	WA 500, Orchards, Vancouver, **E** 🅿️ 76, Shell, Shell, USA 🍴 ABC Buffet, Applebee's, Burger King, Burgerville, DQ, Imperial Palace, KFC, McDonald's, Papa Murphy's, Subway, Wendy's 🅾️ 7-11, GNC, Jo-Ann Crafts, Midas, Office Depot, PetCo, repair, Sportsman's Whse, Toyota, Walgreens, **W** 🅿️ 7-11/dsl, Chevron/dsl, Shell/dsl 🍴 Burgerville, ChuckeCheese, Golden Tent BBQ, Great Taste Chinese, Hometown Buffet, IHOP, Jack-in-the-Box, Jamba Juice, LaCosta Mexican, Muchas Gracias, Olive Garden, Outback Steaks, Popeyes, Red Lobster, Red Robin, RoundTable Pizza, Shari's, Starbucks, Subway, Taco Bell 🛏️ Best Western, Comfort Suites, Day's Inn, Heathman Lodge, Holiday Inn Express, Howard Johnson's, Residence Inn, Staybridge Inn 🅾️ $Tree, Americas Tire, auto repair, Barnes&Noble, GNC, JC Penney, Macy's, Old Navy, Petsmart, Ross, Target, TJ Maxx, URGENT CARE, Verizon
28	Mill Plain Rd, **E** 🅿️ 76, Chevron 🍴 Applebee's, Baskin-Robbins, Breakfast At Valerie's, Burger King, Burgerville, DQ, Elmer's Rest., Irishtown Grill, Jimmy John's, Kings Buffet, McDonald's, McGrath's Fish House, Muchas Gracias Mexican, Pizza Hut, Shari's, Starbucks, Sweet Tomatoes, Taco Bell, Yummy Mongolian 🛏️ Best Western, DoubleTree Hotel, Extended Stay America, The Guesthouse Motel 🅾️ $Tree, 7-11, Fred Meyer/dsl, O'Reilly Parts, PetCo, Schwab Tire, Trader Joe's, **W** 🅿️ 7-11, 76 🍴 Arby's, Jack-in-the-Box, Little Caesar's, Subway 🅾️ Ⓗ, auto/tire repair, Walgreens, Walmart/McDonald's
27	WA 14, Vancouver, Camas, Columbia River Gorge
25mm	Oregon/Washington state line. Columbia River. **Exits 27-36 are in Washington.**
24	122nd Ave, Airport Way, **E** 🅿️ 7-11/dsl 🍴 Burger King, China Wok, Dutch Bros Coffee, Jack-in-the-Box, McDonald's, Panera Bread, Shari's, Subway 🛏️ Candlewood Suites, Clarion, Comfort Suites, Courtyard, Fairfield Inn, Hilton Garden, Holiday Inn Express, La Quinta, Shilo Inn/rest., SpringHill Suites, Staybridge Suites, Super 8 🅾️ Home Depot, Michael's, **W** 🍴 Buffalo Wild Wings, Famous Dave's, Red Robin 🛏️ Embassy Suites, Hampton Inn, Hyatt Place, Loft Hotel, Red Lion Hotel, Residence Inn, Sheraton/rest. 🅾️ ✈️, Best Buy, Marshall's, PetsMart, Ross, Staples
23b a	US 30 byp, Columbia Blvd, **E** 🍴 Leather's Fuel/dsl, Shell/dsl 🍴 Bill's Steaks, Elmer's Rest. 🛏️ Best Western, Comfort Inn, Econolodge, Quality Inn, Rodeway Inn, **W** 🛏️ Best Value Inn, Holiday Inn, Radisson, Ramada Inn
22	I-84 E, US 30 E, to The Dalles
21b	I-84 W, US 30 W, to Portland
21a	Glisan St, **E** on NE 102nd St 🅿️ 76, Arco 🍴 Applebee's, Carl's Jr, Izzy's Pizza, Jamba Juice, Starbucks, Subway 🅾️ Fred Meyer, Kohl's, Office Depot, Ross, WinCo Foods
20	Stark St, Washington St, **E** 🅿️ 76/7-11, Chevron/dsl 🍴 Arby's, Baja Fresh, Burger King, Denny's, Elmer's Rest., Hometown Buffet, Jack-in-the-Box, McMenamin's Rest., Old Chicago Pizza, Olive Garden, Panda Express, Portland Seafood Co, Red Robin, Saylor's, Starbucks, Subway, Village Inn 🛏️ Chestnut Tree Inn, Ramada 🅾️ $Tree, Big Lots, Home Depot, Target, Tuesday Morning, Verizon, **W** 🍴 Stark St Pizza, Taco Bell 🛏️ Motel 6 🅾️ 7-11
19	US 26, Division St, **E** 🅿️ Space Age/dsl 🅾️ Ⓗ, **W** 🅿️ Shell 🍴 Burgerville, ChuckeCheese, McDonald's
17	Foster Rd
16	Johnson Creek Blvd, **W** 🅿️ 76, Arco 🍴 Applebee's, Bajio, Burger King, Carl's Jr, Five Guys, Hog Wild BBQ, Jack-in-the-Box, Jimmy John's, Krispy Kreme, McDonald's, McDonald's, Outback

P O R T L A N D   A R E A

16	Continued
	Steaks, Panda Express, RoundTable Pizza, Starbucks, Taco Be 🅾️ 7-11, Best Buy, Dick's, Firestone/auto, Fred Meyer/ds Home Depot, Knecht's Parts, O'Reilly Parts, PetsMart, RV Ctr Trader Joe's, Walgreens, Walmart/Subway
14	Sunnyside Rd, **E** 🅿️ 76/dsl 🍴 A&W/KFC, Baja Fresh, Dom no's, Gustav's Grill, Jersey Mike's, McMenamin's, Papa John' Starbucks 🛏️ Clarion, Sunnyside Inn 🅾️ Ⓗ, Office Depot, 🅿️ Chevron/dsl 🍴 Burger King, CA Pizza Kitchen, Cheesecak Factory, Chick-fil-A, Chipotle, Claim Jumper, Dave&Buster' Denny's, DQ, Jimmy John's, McDonald's, Muchas Gracia Noodles&Co, Old Spaghetti Factory, Olive Garden, Paner Bread, Pieology Pizzaria, Pizza Hut, RAM Rest., Red Robi Stanford's Rest., Wendy's 🛏️ Courtyard, Monarch Hotel/res 🅾️ Barnes&Noble, Discount Tire, Hobby Lobby, JC Penney Kohl's, Macy's, Nordstroms, Old Navy, PetCo, REI, Target U-Haul, Verizon, World Mkt
13	OR 224, to Milwaukie, **W** 🅾️ CarMax, Lowe's
12	OR 213, to Milwaukie, **E** 🅿️ Chevron/dsl, Pacific Pride, She 🍴 Denny's, Elmer's, KFC, McDonald's, New Cathay Chinese Pronto Pizza, Subway, Taco Bell, Wendy's 🛏️ Clackamas Inr Hampton Inn 🅾️ $Tree, 7-11, Fred Meyer, USPO, **W** 🛏️ Comfo Suites
11	82nd Dr, Gladstone, **W** 🅿️ Arco, Chevron 🍴 High Rock Rest., McDonald's, Starbucks, Subway 🛏️ Holiday Inn Expres 🅾️ Harley-Davidson, Safeway
10	OR 213, Park Place, **E** 🅿️ Chevron/dsl 🅾️ Ⓗ, Home Depot, t Oregon Trail Ctr
9	OR 99E, Oregon City, **E** 🅿️ 76, Chevron/dsl 🍴 KFC 🅾️ Ⓗ, re pair, Subaru, **W** 🍴 La Hacienda Mexican, McDonald's, Shari's Starbucks, Subway, Thai Rest. 🛏️ Best Western+ 🅾️ $Tree AT&T, Firestone/auto, Michael's, Rite Aid, Ross, URGENT CARE
8.5mm	Willamette River
8	OR 43, W Linn, Lake Oswego, **E** 🅿️ 🅾️ museum, **W** 🅿️ Chev ron/dsl, Shell/dsl 🍴 Starbucks 🅾️ Mkt of Choice, USPO, Veri zon, vet
7mm	viewpoint nb, hist marker
6	10th St, W Linn St, **E** 🅿️ Chevron/LP 🍴 Five Guys, Ixtapa Mex ican, McDonald's, McMenamin's Rest., Papa Murphy's, Willa mette Coffee House 🅾️ Ace Hardware, Les Schwab, **W** 🍴 Bis cuit's Cafe, Subway
4mm	Tualatin River
3	Stafford Rd, Lake Oswego, **W** 🍴 Wanker's Country Store 🅾️ Ⓗ
0mm	I-205 begins/ends on I-5, exit 288.

NOTES

🅞🆁 (OR)

PENNSYLVANIA

⬆️Ｅ INTERSTATE 70

Exit #	Services
171mm	Pennsylvania/Maryland state line, **Welcome Ctr wb, full** 🖕 **facilities, info, litter barrels, petwalk,** 🔌 🚻 **vending**
168	US 522 N, Warfordsburg, **N** 🅿️ **Fuel/dsl, S** 🅾️ **fireworks**
163	PA 731 S, Amaranth
156	PA 643, Town Hill
153mm	🆁🆂 **eb, full** 🖕 **facilities, litter barrels, petwalk,** 🔌 🚻 **vending**
151	PA 915, Crystal Spring, **N** 🅾️ auto repair, **S** 🅾️ Country Store/ USPO
149	US 30 W, to Everett, S Breezewood (no immediate wb return), 3 mi **S** 🍴 McDonald's 🛏️ Wildwood Motel
147	US 30, Breezewood, **Services on US 30** 🅿️ Exxon/dsl, *FLYING J*/Perkins/dsl/scales/24hr, Sheetz/dsl, Shell, Shell/Dunkin'/Subway/dsl, Sunoco/dsl, TA/ Valero/Gateway Rest./Subway/dsl/scales/24hr/@ 🍴 Bob Evans, Classic American Diner, Hardee's, McDonald's, Pizza Hut, Starbucks, Subplicity, Taco Bell 🛏️ Best Western, EconoLodge, Holiday Inn Express, Quality Inn, Wiltshire Motel 🅾️ Blue Beacon
	I-70 and I-76/PA Tpk run together 71 mi. See I-76 PA/Tpk exits 148mm-75.
77	I-70 E runs with I-76/PA Turnpike eb
58	PA Tpk. I-70 E and I-76/PA Turnpike E run together.
57b a	I-70 W, US 119, PA 66 **(toll)**, New Stanton, **N** 🅿️ Exxon, Sheetz/ dsl 🍴 BBG Grill, Bob Evans, Eat'n Park, McDonald's, Pagano's Rest., Pizza Hut, Subway, Szechuan Wok, Wendy's 🛏️ Budget Inn, Comfort Inn, Days Inn, EconoLodge, Fairfield Inn, Garden Inn, Hampton Inn, Motel 6, Super 8, **S** 🅿️ Marathon/dsl, Sunoco/dsl 🍴 Cracker Barrel, La Tavola Ristorante 🅾️ $General, USPO
54	Madison, **N** 🅾️ KOA, **S** 🅾️ truck repair
53	Yukon
51b a	PA 31, West Newton, **S** 🅾️ Volvo/Mack
49	Smithton, **N** 🅿️ Citgo/rest./dsl/scales/@, *FLYING J*/Denny's/ dsl/LP/scales/24hr/@
46b a	PA 51, Pittsburgh, **N** 🅿️ Sunoco/dsl 🍴 Burger King 🛏️ Comfort Inn 🅾️ Buick/Cadillac/Chevrolet, Ford/Kia, Honda, **S** 🅿️ GetGo/dsl, PP/dsl 🍴 Clubhouse Grille 🛏️ Budget Inn, Clarion 🅾️ golf
44	Arnold City
43b a	(43 from eb) PA 201, to PA 837, Fayette City, **S** 🅿️ Exxon/dsl 🍴 A&W/LJ Silver, Burger King, Denny's, Domino's, Eat'n Park, Hibachi Buffet, Hoss' Rest., KFC, Little Bamboo, McDonald's, Old Mexico, Pizza Hut, Rita's Custard, Sonny's Grille, Starbucks, Subway, Taco Bell, Wendy's 🛏️ Candlewood Suites, Fairfield Inn, Hampton Inn, Holiday Inn Express 🅾️ $General, $Tree, Advance Parts, Aldi Foods, AT&T, BigLots, CVS Drug, Giant Eagle Foods, GNC, Jo-Ann Fabrics, Lowe's, NAPA, Staples, URGENT CARE, Verizon, Walmart
42a	Monessen
42	N Belle Vernon, **S** 🅿️ BP/McDonald's/7-11, Sunoco/dsl 🍴 DQ
41	PA 906, Belle Vernon

40mm	Monongahela River
40	PA 88, Charleroi, **N** 🅿️ Gulf, Sunoco 🍴 McDonald's, My Girl's Rest., Subway/TCBY 🅾️ 🇭 Rite Aid, Valley Tire
39	Speers, **S** 🅿️ Exxon/dsl
37b a	PA 43 **(toll)**, N to Pittsburgh, S to CA
36	Lover (from wb, no re-entry)
35	PA 481, Centerville
32b a	PA 917, Bentleyville, **S** 🅿️ BP/dsl, 🅿️ilot/DQ/Subway/dsl/ scales/24hr 🍴 Burger King, King's Rest., McDonald's, Pizza Hut 🛏️ Best Western, Holiday Inn Express 🅾️ $General, Advance Parts, AutoZone, Blue Beacon, Giant Eagle Foods, Rite Aid
31	to PA 136, Kammerer, **N** 🛏️ Carlton Motel
27	Dunningsville, **S** 🛏️ Avalon Motel
25	PA 519, to Eighty Four, **S** 🅿️ BP/7-11 Diner/dsl/24hr, Sunoco/dsl
21	I-79 S, to Waynesburg.
	I-70 W and I-79 N run together 3.5 mi.
20	PA 136, Beau St, **S** 🅾️ to Washington&Jefferson Coll
19b a	US 19, Murtland Ave, **N** 🅿️ BP/dsl, GetGo 🍴 Applebee's, Arby's, Asahi Buffet, Buffalo Wild Wings, Chick-fil-A, Cracker Barrel, Five Guys, Fusion Steaks, Ichiban Steaks, Jimmy John's, Krispy Kreme, Longhorn Steaks, Max&Erma's, McDonald's, Moe's SW Grill, Noodles&Co, Olive Garden, Outback Steaks, Panera Bread, Penn Sta Subs, Plaza Azteca, Red Lobster, Red Robin, Rita's Custard, Starbucks, Subway, Taco Bell, TGIFriday's, TX Roadhouse, Wong's Wok, Zoup! 🛏️ SpringHill Suites 🅾️ $Tree, Aldi Foods, AT&T, Dick's, Field&Stream, Ford, Giant Eagle Foods, GNC, Hobby Lobby, Honda, Hyundai, Kohl's, Lowe's, Mercedes, Michael's, Nissan, PetCo, Petsmart, Sam's Club/gas, Save-A-Lot Foods, Target, Toyota, URGENT CARE, Verizon, Walmart/McDonald's, **S** 🅿️ BP/dsl, Exxon/dsl, Sunoco, Sunoco/dsl 🍴 A&W/LJ Silver, Bob Evans, Donut Connection, Dunkin', Eat'n Park, Grand China, KFC, Old Mexico, Papa John's, Pizza Hut, Waffle House 🛏️ Hampton Inn, Motel 6 🅾️ 🇭 BigLots, Buick/GMC, Chevrolet, Firestone/auto, Home Depot, Jo-Ann Fabrics, Mazda, Pepboys, Staples, Subaru
18	I-79 N, to Pittsburgh.
	I-70 E and I-79 S run together 3.5 mi.

NEW STANTON

FAYETTE CITY

🅿 = gas 🍴 = food 🛏 = lodging Ⓞ = other Rs = rest stop   Copyright 2022 - The Next EXIT ®

⭐E INTERSTATE 70 Cont'd

Exit #	Services
17	PA 18, Jefferson Ave, Washington, N 🅿 GetGo/dsl 🍴 DQ, McDonald's Ⓞ Family$, Rite Aid, S 🅿 Sunoco/dsl 🍴 4Star Pizza, Burger King, China Express, Little Caesar's, Subway Ⓞ $General, Advance Parts, Advance Parts (2), AutoZone, CVS Drug, O'Reilly Parts, Shop'n Save Foods, USPO, Walgreens
16	Jessop Place, N 🅿 Dean's 🛏 Suburban Lodge, S Ⓞ auto/truck repair
15	US 40, Chesnut St, Washington, N Ⓞ Food Land, S 🅿 BP/7-11, Exxon/dsl, Marathon, Sunoco/dsl 🍴 Bob Evans, Denny's, Dunkin', Garfield's Rest., McDonald's, Taco Bell, Wendy's 🛏 Best Value Inn, Comfort Suites, Days Inn, Ramada Inn, Red Roof Inn Ⓞ Jo-Ann, Marshalls, Rite Aid, Ross
11	PA 221, Taylorstown, N 🅿 BP/dsl, S Ⓞ repair
6	PA 231, to US 40, Claysville, N 🅿 BP/dsl
5mm	Welcome Ctr eb, full 🚻 facilities, 🛏 litter barrels, petwalk, vending
1	W Alexander
0mm	Pennsylvania/Ohio state line

⭐E INTERSTATE 76

Exit #	Services
354mm	Pennsylvania/New Jersey state line, Delaware River, Walt Whitman Br
351	Front St, I-95 (from wb), N to Trenton, S to Chester
350	Packer Ave, 7th St, to I-95 (from eb), S 🛏 Holiday Inn Ⓞ to sports complex
349	to I-95, PA 611, Broad St, N 🅿 Citgo 🍴 Talk of the Town
348	PA 291, W to Chester (exits left from wb)
347a	to I-95 S (exits left from wb)
347b	Passyunk Ave, Oregon Ave, N 🍴 Burger King, KFC, Little Caesar's, McDonald's, Pizza Hut Ⓞ BJ's Whse, Home Depot, Ross, ShopRite, S Ⓞ FDR Park
346c	28th St, Vare Ave, Mifflin St (from wb)
346b	Grays Ferry Ave, University Ave, N 🍴 Fresh Grocer, Little Caesar's, McDonald's Ⓞ 🅷 USPO, S 🅿 76, Speedway/dsl 🍴 Dunkin'
346a	South St (exits left from wb)
345	30th St, Market St, downtown
344	I-676 E, US 30 E, to Philadelphia (no return from eb), N Ⓞ LDS Temple
343	Spring Garden St, Haverford
342	US 13, US 30 W, Girard Ave, N Ⓞ E Fairmount Park, S Ⓞ Philadelphia Zoo
341	Montgomery Dr, W River Dr, W Fairmount Park, S Ⓞ W Fairmount Park
340b	US 1 N, Roosevelt Blvd, to Philadelphia
339	US 1 S, S 🍴 CA Pizza Kitchen, Chili's, Chipotle Mexican, Houlihans, PeiWei Asian, Starbucks, TGIFriday's 🛏 Dave's Hotel Ⓞ Target, Verizon
340a	Lincoln Dr, Kelly Dr, to Germantown
338	Belmont Ave, Green Lane, S 🅿 76, Sunoco Ⓞ UHaul, WaWa
337	Hollow Rd (from wb), Gladwyne
332	PA 23 (from wb), Conshohocken, N 🛏 Marriott
331b a	I-476, PA 28 (from eb), to Chester, Conshohocken
330	PA 320, Gulph Mills, S Ⓞ to Villanova U
329	Weadley Rd (from wb), N 🅿 Exxon
328b a	US 202 N, to King of Prussia, N 🅿 Exxon/dsl, Lukoil, Shell, Sunoco, WaWa 🍴 Bahama Breeze, Baja Fresh, Burger King,

Exit #	Services
328b a	Continued
	CA Pizza Kitchen, Capital Grille, Champp's, Cheesecake Factory, Chili's, Fox&Hound, Hooters, Joe's Crabshack, Maggiano's, Morton's Steaks, Panera Bread, Red Lobster, Ruby's Diner, Ruth's Chris Steaks, Sullivan's Steaks 🛏 Best Western, Doubletree, Fairfield Inn, Hampton Inn, Holiday Inn Express, Hyatt, Inn of King of Prussia, Motel 6, Sheraton Ⓞ Best Buy, Bloomingdale's, Costco, Dick's, Home Depot, Lord&Taylor, Macy's, Neiman Marcus, Nordstrom, Old Navy, S 🛏 Crowne Plaza
327	US 202 S, to US 420 W, Goddard Blvd, Valley Forge Park, E Ⓞ Valley Forge Park
326	I-76 wb becomes I-76/PA Tpk to Ohio

For I-76 westbound to Ohio, see I-76/PA Turnpike.

⭐E INTERSTATE 76 (Turnpike)

Exit #	Services
	PA Tpk runs wb as I-276/I-95, eb ends on NJ Tpk.
6a(I-95)	US 130 exit is in NJ, to Bordentown, N Ⓞ $Tree, Rite Aid, S 🅿 Conoco/dsl, WaWa/dsl 🍴 Burger King, Dunkin'
355mm	PA Tpk/I-276 merges with I-95 N
352.5mm	toll plaza
352	PA 132, Street Rd, EZ tag only, from eb
351	US 1, to I-95, to Philadelphia, N 🍴 Bar Louie, Bertucci's, Chick-fil-A, Chipotle, Cracker Barrel, Jimmy John's, Longhorn Steaks, McDonald's, On The Border, Panda Express, Red Robin, Starbucks, Uno, Wendy's 🛏 Crowne Plaza Ⓞ Barnes&Noble, Buick/GMC, CVS Drug, Home Depot, Lowes Whse, Target, Walmart, S 🅿 7-11/dsl, Classic/wash, Sunoco/dsl 🍴 Dunkin' 🛏 Best Western, Comfort Inn, Courtyard, Hampton Inn, Knights Inn, Neshaminy Inn, Quality Inn, Radisson, Red Roof Inn Ⓞ Indian Motorcycles, Toyota
343	PA 611, Willow Grove, N 🅿 BP/dsl, Shell/dsl, Speedway/dsl, Sunoco 🍴 Carrabba's, Dunkin', Sonic 🛏 Courtyard, Fairfield Inn, SpringHill Suites Ⓞ 7-11, Home Depot, Lexus, NTB, S 🍴 Bonefish Grill, China Garden, Domino's, Dunkin', Ooka Japanese, Tony Roni's Pizza 🛏 Hampton Inn Ⓞ 7-11, Audi, Infiniti, Best Buy, PepBoys, repair, Staples, transmissions
340	to VA Dr, EZ tag only, from wb, no trucks, 🅿 WaWa/dsl, EZ tagholder only
339	PA 309, Ft Washington, N 🅿 LukOil/dsl 🍴 Friendly's, Subway 🛏 Best Western, Hilton Garden, Holiday Inn Express Ⓞ BMW, Mercedes, Volvo, WaWa
334	PA Tpk NE Extension, I-476, S to Philadelphia, N to Allentown
333	Germantown Pike, to Norristown, N 🅿 Lukoil, Sunoco 🍴 Azteca, Bertucci's, California Pizza Kitchen, Chipotle, Dave&Buster's, Dunkin', Elevation Burger, PF Chang's, Red Stone Grill, Starbucks, Zoup! 🛏 Courtyard, DoubleTree, Extended Stay America, SpringHill Suites Ⓞ 🅷 Boscov's, Verizon, Whole Foods, S 🅿 LukOil
328mm	King of Prussia Service Plaza wb, 🅿 Sunoco/dsl/24hr 🍴 Burger King, Starbucks
	PA Tpk runs eb as I-276, wb as I-76.
326	I-76 E, to US 202, I-476, Valley Forge, N 🅿 Shell 🛏 Radisson, S 🅿 Exxon, LukOil, Shell, Sunoco, WaWa 🍴 CA Pizza Kitchen, Cheesecake Factory, Chili's, Hooters, Maggiano's, Red Lobster, Ruth's Chris Steaks, Sullivan Steaks 🛏 Best Western, Hampton Inn, Holiday Inn Express, Hyatt, Inn of King of Prussia, Motel 6, Sheraton Ⓞ Best Buy, Costco, Dick's, Home Depot, Macy's, Neiman Marcus, Nordstrom, Walmart, Wegman's
325mm	Valley Forge Service Plaza eb, 🅿 Sunoco/dsl/24hr 🍴 Larson Grill, Starbucks

WASHINGTON

PHILADELPHIA

PA

INTERSTATE 76 (Turnpike) Cont'd

Exit #	Services
312	PA 100, to Downingtown, Pottstown, N 🅿 WaWa/dsl 🅾 Car-Sense, Harley-Davidson, S 🅿 Sunoco/dsl, WaWa 🍴 Applebee's, Chick-fil-A, Isaac's Deli, Red Robin, Starbucks, Uno Grill, Wendy's 🛏 Clarion, Comfort Suites, Extended Stay America, Fairfield Inn, Hampton Inn, Hilton Garden, Residence Inn 🅾 Giant Foods, Target, Walgreens
305mm	Camiel Service Paza wb, 🅿 Sunoco/dsl/24hr 🍴 Roy Rogers, Starbucks
298	I-176, PA 10, to Reading, Morgantown, N 🍴 Arby's, DQ, Dunkin', Sonic, Subway 🛏 USA Inn 🅾 $Tree, AutoZone, Lowe's, Mavis Tire, Verizon, Walmart, S 🅿 Exxon, Sheetz/dsl 🍴 McDonald's, Rita's Custard 🛏 Holiday Inn 🅾 Chevrolet, Rite Aid, USPO
290mm	Bowmansville Service Plaza eb, 🅿 Sunoco/dsl/24hr 🍴 Burger King, Hershey's, Starbucks
286	US 322, PA 272, to Reading, Ephrata, N 🅿 Citgo/dsl 🍴 Baskin-Robbins/Dunkin', Park Place Diner, Subway, Zia Maria's Eatery 🛏 Black Horse Inn/rest., S 🅿 Turkey Hill 🛏 Comfort Inn, Econolodge, Hampton Inn (11mi), Red Carpet Inn, Red Roof Inn
266	PA 72, to Lebanon, Lancaster, N 🅿 Speedway/dsl, Sunoco/Chester's 🍴 Comfort Inn 🛏 Holiday Inn Express (17 mi) 🅾 🏥, auto repair, Harley-Davidson, NAPA, S 🛏 Hampton Inn 🅾 Mt Hope Winery, Pinch Pond Camping
259mm	Lawn Service Plaza wb, 🅿 Sunoco/dsl/24hr 🍴 Burger King, Starbucks 🅾 RV dump
250mm	Highspire Service Plaza eb, 🅿 Sunoco/dsl/24hr 🍴 Starbucks, Steak'n Shake
247	I-283, PA 283, to Harrisburg, Harrisburg East, Hershey, N 🅿 Exxon/dsl, Sheetz/dsl, Sunoco 🍴 Bob Evans, Capitol Diner, Chick-fil-A, Chili's, Five Guys, Friendly's, Gilligan's Steaks, McDonald's, Moe's SW, Subway, Taco Bell, Wendy's 🛏 Best Western, Courtyard, Harrisburg Hotel, Holiday Inn, La Quinta, Red Lion, Red Roof Inn, Sheraton, Sleep Inn, Super 8 🅾 GNC, Harrisburg East Camping, JC Penney, Kia, Petco, Target, Verizon
246mm	Susquehannah River
242	I-83, Harrisburg West, N 🅿 Shell/dsl, Speedway, Sunoco 🍴 Bob Evans, John's Diner, McDonald's, Pizza Hut 🛏 Best Western, Budget Inn, Clarion Inn, Fairfield Inn, Holiday Inn Express, La Quinta, Motel 6, Quality Inn, Scottish Inn 🅾 vet, S 🅿 Rutter's/dsl 🛏 Days Inn, Red Carpet Inn
236	US 15, to Gettysburg, Gettysburg Pike, Harrisburg, N 🅿 Exxon, Gulf/dsl 🍴 Isaac's Rest, Marzoni's, McDonald's, Papa John's, Peppermill Rest, Subway, Subway (2) 🛏 Comfort Inn, Country Inn&Suites, Courtyard, EconoLodge, Hampton Inn, Homewood Suites, TownePlace Suites 🅾 🏥, U-Haul, vet, S 🅿 Sheetz 🍴 Arby's, Bros Pizza, Burger King, Cracker Barrel, Subway, Wendy's 🛏 Motel 6, Wingate Inn 🅾 $Tree, Giant Food/gas, GNC, Rite Aid
226	US 11, to I-81, to Harrisburg, Carlisle, N 🅿 🈁 FLYING J/Denny's/dsl/LP/scales/24hr/@, Gulf/dsl, ❤Loves/Wendy's/dsl/scales/24hr, Petro/Iron Skillet/dsl/scales/24hr/@, Pioneer/dsl, Sunoco/Subway/dsl 🍴 Arby's, Bob Evans, Carelli's Subs, Dunkin', Embers Steaks, McDonald's, Middlesex Diner, Rte 11 Diner, Waffle House 🛏 Best Value Inn, Days Inn, EconoLodge, Hampton Inn, Hotel Carlisle, Knights Inn, Quality Inn, Red Roof Inn, Residence Inn, Rodeway Inn, Super 8, Travelodge 🅾 Blue Beacon, S 🅿 Rutter's/dsl 🍴 Hoss' Rest. 🛏 Best Western, Holiday Inn Express, Motel 6 🅾 🏥, U-Haul, vet

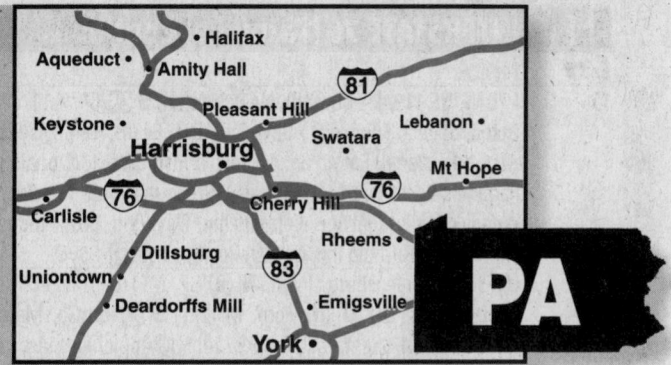

219mm	Plainfield Service Plaza eb, 🅿 Sunoco/dsl/24hr 🍴 Hershey's Ice Cream, Roy Rogers, Starbucks
203mm	Blue Mtn Service Plaza wb, 🅿 Sunoco/dsl/24hr 🍴 Hershy's Ice Cream, Pizza Hut, Roy Rogers, Starbucks
201	PA 997, to Shippensburg, Blue Mountain, S 🛏 Kenmar Motel 🅾 auto/truck repair
199mm	Blue Mountain Tunnel
197mm	Kittatinny Tunnel
189	PA 75, Willow Hill, S 🍴 Double Dip Drive-In, Pizza Star 🛏 Willow Hill Motel/rest.
187mm	Tuscarora Tunnel
180	US 522, Mt Union, Ft Littleton, N 🅿 Cutchall's/dsl, Noname/dsl 🍴 The Family Rest. 🛏 Downes Motel
172mm	Sideling Service Plaza both lanes, 🅿 Sunoco/dsl/24hr 🍴 Burger King, Famiglia Pizza, Hershey's, Popeye's, Starbucks
161	US 30, Breezewood, Services N on US 30 🅿 Exxon/dsl, 🈁FLYING J/Perkins/dsl/scales/24hr, Sheetz/dsl, Shell, Shell/Dunkin'/Subway/dsl, Sunoco/dsl, TA/Valero/Gateway Rest./Subway/dsl/scales/24hr/@ 🍴 Bob Evans, Classic American Diner, Hardee's, McDonald's, Pizza Hut, Starbucks, Subplicity, Taco Bell 🛏 Best Western, EconoLodge, Holiday Inn Express, Quality Inn, Wiltshire Motel 🅾 Blue Beacon
161mm	I-70 W and I-76/PA Turnpike W run together.
148mm	Midway Service Plaza both lanes, 🅿 Sunoco/dsl/24hr 🍴 Sbarro's, Starbucks, Steak'n Shake
146	I-99, US 220, Bedford, N 🅿 GetGo/McDonald's/dsl, PP/dsl, Sheetz/dsl/24hr, Shell/Subway/dsl 🍴 Bedford Diner, Clara's Place, Denny's, Ed's Steaks, Hoss' Rest., LJ Silver, Pizza Hut, Salsa's Mexican, Wendy's 🛏 Best Value Inn, Budget Host, Fairfield Inn, Quality Inn, Rodeway Inn, Travelodge 🅾 Blue Knob SP (15mi), to Shawnee SP (10mi), S 🛏 Hampton Inn
123mm	Allegheny Tunnel
112mm	Somerset Service Plaza both lanes, 🅿 Sunoco/dsl/24hr 🍴 Burger King, Pizza Hut, Popeye's, Starbucks
110	PA 601, to US 219, Somerset, N 🅿 KwikFill/dsl, Sheetz 🍴 Hoss' Rest., King's Rest., Pizza Hut 🛏 $Inn, Economy Inn 🅾 Advance Parts, Ford, tires, S 🅿 Somerset TravelCtr/dsl/@, Tesla EVC, Turkey Hill 🍴 Arby's, Bruster's Ice Cream, DQ, Eat'n Park, KFC, LJ Silver, McDonald's, Pine Grill, Ruby Tuesday, Starbucks, Subway, Summit Diner, Wendy's 🛏 Budget Host, Budget Inn, Comfort Inn, Days Inn, Econolodge, Hampton Inn, Holiday Inn Express, Quality Inn, Super 8 🅾 Harley-Davidson
91	PA 711, PA 31, to Ligonier, Donegal, N 🍴 Tall Cedars Rest., S 🅿 BP/McDonald's, Sunoco/dsl 🍴 DQ, Subway 🛏 Days Inn, Holiday Inn Express 🅾 camping, golf
78mm	New Stanton Service Plaza wb, 🅿 Sunoco/dsl/24hr 🍴 Burger King, Hershey's Ice Cream, Quiznos, Starbucks
	I-70 E runs with I-76/PA Turnpike eb.

HARRISBURG

BREEZEWOOD

PA

🅿 = gas 🍴 = food 🛏 = lodging 🄾 = other Ⓡs = rest stop Copyright 2022 - The Next EXIT

INTERSTATE 76 (Turnpike) Cont'd

Exit #	Services
75	I-70 W, US 119, PA 66 (toll), New Stanton, S 🅿 BP/7-11/dsl, Exxon, Sheetz, Sunoco 🍴 BBG Grill, Bob Evans, Campy's Pizza, Cracker Barrel, Eat'n Park, La Tavola Risorante, McDonald's, Pagano's Rest., Pizza Hut, Subway, Szechuan Wok, TJ's Rest., Wendy's 🛏 Budget Inn, Comfort Inn, Days Inn, EconoLodge, Express Inn, Fairfield Inn, Garden Inn, Super 8 🄾 USPO
67	US 30, to Greensburg, Irwin, N 🅿 BP/7-11/dsl, Sheetz/dsl 🍴 Domino's, DQ 🄾 Ⓗ, Ford, Mr Tire, S 🅿 GetGo, Marathon/7-11/dsl, Sheetz/dsl, Sunoco/24hr 🍴 Applebee's, Arby's, Atria's, Bob Evans, Burger King, Denny's, Double Wide Grill, Dunkin', Eat'n Park, Fire Pit Grill, Five Guys, KFC, Little Caesar's, McDonald's, Panera Bread, Pizza Hut, Starbucks, Subway, Taco Bell, Wendy's 🛏 Hampton Inn, Holiday Inn Express 🄾 $Tree, Advance Parts, Aldi Foods, AT&T, Giant Eagle Foods/24hr, GNC, Kohl's, Rite Aid, Target, Verizon, Walgreens, Walmart
61mm	parking area eb
57	I-376, US 22, to Pittsburgh, Monroeville, S 🅿 Marathon, Sheetz, Sunoco 🍴 Arby's, Blaze Pizza, Chick-fil-A, China Palace, Chipotle, Denny's, El Campesino, Five Guys, Golden Corral, Max&Erma's, McDonald's, Outback Steaks, Panda Express, Panera Bread, Penn Sta Subs, Primanti Bros, Red Lobster, Starbucks, Subway, Taco Bell, Wendy's 🛏 Comfort Suites, Courtyard, Day's Inn, Extended Stay America, Hampton Inn, Holiday Inn Express, Red Roof Inn 🄾 Ⓗ, AT&T, Big Lots, CVS Drug, GNC, Honda, Lowes Whse, Marshall's, NTB, Old Navy, Pet Land, PetCo, Rite Aid, to Heinz Field, URGENT CARE
49mm	Oakmont Service Plaza eb, 🅿 Sunoco/dsl/e85/24hr 🍴 Burger King, Starbucks 🄾 litter barrels, 🚮
48.5mm	Allegheny River
48	PA 28, to Pittsburgh, Allegheny Valley, New Kensington, N 🅿 Exxon, Sunoco 🄾 Rite Aid, S 🅿 GetGo, Marathon/dsl, Sheetz/dsl 🍴 Bob Evans, Burger King, Denny's, Dunkin', Gino Bro's Pizza, KFC, McDonald's, Pizza Hut, Primanti Bros, Subway, Wendy's 🛏 Day's Inn, Hampton Inn, Holiday Inn Express, Quality Inn, TownePlace Suites, Valley Motel 🄾 Advance Parts, AutoZone, Ford, Target
41mm	parking area/call box eb
39	PA 8, to Pittsburgh, Butler Valley, 0-1 mi N 🅿 Exxon, GetGo, Sheetz/dsl, Sunoco 🍴 Applebee's, Atria's Rest., Bruno's Pizza, Buffalo Wild Wings, Eat'n Park, King's Rest., McDonald's, Starbucks, Taco Bell, Wendy's 🛏 Quality Inn 🄾 $Tree, Advance Parts, Chrysler/Dodge/Jeep, Dunkin', Giant Eagle Foods, GNC, Kohl's, Lowes Whse, Petco, Shop'n Save Foods, Target, TJ Maxx, USPO, Walmart/Subway, S 🅿 BP, Sunoco/dsl 🍴 Arby's, Bruster's, Burger King, China Bistro, Domino's, KFC, Little Caesar's, McDonald's, Panera Bread, Pasquales Pizza, Pizza Hut, Primanti Bros, Starbucks, Subway, Vocelli Pizza 🄾 Ⓗ, AT&T, AutoZone, CVS Drug, Firestone/auto, Home Depot, Mr. Tire, NTB, O'Reilly Parts, Pepboys, Rite Aid, USPO
31mm	Toll Plaza wb
28	to I-79, to Cranberry, Pittsburgh, N 🅿 BP/7-11/dsl, GetGo, Marathon/dsl, Sheetz/dsl, Sunoco/dsl 🍴 Aladdin's Eatery, Arby's, Bob Evans, Boston Mkt, Bravo Italian, Buffalo Wild Wings, Burger King, Chipotle Mexican, Denny's, Domino's, Dunkin', Dynasty, Eat'n Park, Emiliano's, Firehouse Subs, Five Guys, HotDog Shoppe, Houlihan's, Ichiban Steakhouse, Jason's Deli, Jersey Mike's, Jimmy John's, Mad Mex, Max&Erma's, McDonald's, Monte Cello's Grill, Panda Express, Panera Bread, Perkins, Pizza Hut, Pizza Roma, Primanti Bros, Saga Steaks, Subway, Vocelli Pizza, Wendy's 🛏 Candlewood Suites, Clarion, Comfort Inn,

(left margin vertical text: PITTSBURGH CRANBERRY; PA)

28	Continued
	Doubletree, Hampton Inn, Hyatt Place, Motel 6, Quality Inn, Red Roof Inn, Residence Inn, Super 8, Woodspring Suites 🄾 $Tree, Aldi Foods, AT&T, AutoZone, Barnes&Noble, Best Buy, Costco gas, Field&Stream, Firestone/auto, Giant Eagle Foods, GNC, Home Depot, Jo-Ann Fabrics, Marshall's, Michael's, NAPA, Pep Boys, Petco, Rite Aid, Toyota, Tuesday Morning, USPO, Verizon, Walgreens, Walmart
23.5mm	pulloff eb
17mm	parking area eb
13.4mm	parking area eb
13mm	Beaver River
13	PA 8, to Ellwood City, Beaver Valley, N 🅿 Al's Corner 🍴 Subway 🛏 Beaver Falls Motel, Lark Motel, Park Inn 🄾 Ⓗ, 🛏 Super 8
10	PA 60 (toll), to New Castle, Pittsburgh, S 🄾 to ✈
6mm	pulloff eb
2mm	pulloff eb
1mm	toll plaza eb, toll plaza eb
0mm	Pennsylvania/Ohio state line

INTERSTATE 78

Exit #	Services
77mm	Pennsylvania/New Jersey state line, Delaware River
76mm	Welcome Ctr wb, toll booth wb, full 🛗 facilities, litter barrels, petwalk, 🄲, 🚮, vending
75	to PA 611, Easton, N 🅿 TurkeyHill/dsl 🍴 Dunkin', McDonald (1mi), Subway 🄾 Crayola Factory, CVS Drug, S 🅿 Exxon/dsl
71	PA 33, to Stroudsburg, 1 mi N on Freemansburg Ave 🍴 Chipotle, CJT Asian, Frank's Pizza, MOD Pizza, Panera Bread, Ruby Tuesday, Starbucks, TGIFriday's, TX Roadhouse, Wayback Burgers 🛏 Courtyard 🄾 Barnes&Noble, Best Buy, Dick's, Ⓗ, Lowe's, Michael's, Pet Supplies+, ShopRite Mkt, Staples, Verizon
67	PA 412, Hellertown, N 🅿 TurkeyHill/gas 🍴 Wendy's 🛏 Comfort Suites (3mi) 🄾 Ⓗ, Chevrolet, S 🅿 Citgo/dsl, Exxon/dsl, Sunoco 🍴 Bella's Ristorante, Dunkin', Papa John's, Rocco' Pizza, Roma Pizza, Vassi's Drive-In, Waffle House 🛏 Holiday Inn Express 🄾 7-11, CVS Drug, repair
60b a	PA 145 N, PA 309 S, South Fort St, Quakertown
59	to PA 145 (from eb), Summit Lawn
58	Emaus St (from wb), S 🅿 Gulf 🄾 $General
57	Lehigh St, N 🅿 Sunoco/dsl, WaWa/dsl 🍴 Arby's, China House, Dunkin', IHOP, Palumbo Pizza, Queen City Diner, Subway, Willy Joe's Rest. 🛏 Red Roof Inn 🄾 $Tree, AAA, BigLots, CVS Drug, Family$, Ford/Lincoln, Home Depot, Infiniti, Kia, Mavis Tires/repair, Redner's Whse, Toyota, VW, S 🅿 Sunoco, TurkeyHill, Valero 🍴 A1 Japanese, Bangkok, Brass Rail Rest., Domino's, Dunkin', McDonald's, Papa John's, Perkins, Pizza Hut/Taco Bell, Rodizio Grill, Rossi's Pizza, Starbucks, Subway, Tilted Kilt Eatery, Wendy's 🄾 Acura, AT&T, Audi/Mercedes/Porsche, BonTon, Bottom$ Mkt, Buick/GMC, Cadillac/Chevrolet, Chrysler/Dodge/Jeep, Honda, Hyundai, Kost Tire, Mazda, Midas, Ross, Staples, SteinMart, Verizon, Volvo, Williams Tire/auto
55	PA 29, Cedar Crest Blvd, N 🅿 Shell, S 🄾 Ⓗ
54b a	US 222, Hamilton Blvd, N 🅿 Speedway, WaWa/dsl 🍴 Bamboo Asian, Baskin-Robbins/Dunkin', Boston Mkt, Carrabba's, Gourmet Buffet, Ice Cream World, McDonald's, Menchie's, Perkins, Pizza Hut, Subway, TGIFriday's, Wendy's 🛏 Holiday Inn Express, Howard Johnson 🄾 Dorney Funpark, Office Depot, Rite Aid, USPO, Weis Foods, S 🅿 WaWa 🍴 Dunkin', Hunan Springs 🛏 Holiday Inn 🄾 Audi, Costco/gas, Subaru, Target
53	PA 309 (wb only)

(right margin vertical text: ALLENTOWN)

⭱E INTERSTATE 78 Cont'd

Exit #	Services
51	to I-476, US 22 E, PA 33 N (eb only), Whitehall
49b a	PA 100, Fogelsville, **N** 🅕 Arby's, Cracker Barrel, LJ Silver, Panda&Fish Chinese, Pizza Hut, Steak'n Shake, Windsor Deli 🏠 Comfort Inn, Hawthorn Inn 🅞 KOA (7mi), Mavis Tire/repair, Rite Aid, **S** 🅖 Shell/Dunkin', Sunoco, WaWa/dsl 🅕 Arooga's Grill, Burger King, Florence Italian, Starlite Diner, Taco Bell, Yocco's Hotdogs 🏠 Allentown Park Hotel, Hilton Garden, Holiday Inn, Sleep Inn, Staybridge Suites 🅞 Clover Hill Winery, st police, Toyota
45	PA 863, to Lynnport, **N** 🅖 Exxon/dsl, Sunoco/New Smithville Diner/dsl 🅞 truck service, **S** 🅕 Demarco's Italian 🏠 Super 8
40	PA 737, Krumsville, **N** 🅞 Pine Hill Campground, Robin Hill RV Park (4mi)
35	PA 143, Lenhartsville, **3 mi S** 🅞 Robin Hill Park
30	Hamburg, **S** 🅕 Hamburg Mkt
29b a	PA 61, to Reading, Pottsville, **N** 🅖 Shell/dsl, WaWa/dsl 🅕 Baskin-Robbins/Dunkin', Burger King, Cracker Barrel, Five Guys, JA Buffet, LJ Silver/Taco Bell, Logan's Roadhouse, McDonald's, Pizza Hut, Red Robin, Starbucks, Wendy's 🏠 Microtel 🅞 $Tree, Advance Parts, Aldi, AT&T, Boat'n RV Ctr RV, Cabela's Outdoor, GNC, Harley-Davidson (8mi), Hyundai, Lowe's, Pet Supplies+, Russell Stover, Toyota, Verizon, Walmart/Subway
23	Shartlesville, **N** 🅖 Chromeshop/dsl, ❤️Loves/McDonald's/Subway/dsl/scales/24hr 🅕 Dunkin' 🏠 Dutch Motel 🅞 Appalachian Campsites, **S** 🅕 Blue Mtn Family Rest. 🏠 Motel 6 🅞, antiques, camping, Dutch Haus/gifts, USPO
19	PA 183, Strausstown, **N** 🅖 🅞 Sheepskin Mkt, **S** 🅖 Power/dsl
17	PA 419, Rehrersburg, **N** 🅖 US Gas 🅞 truck/tire repair
16	Midway, **N** 🅖 Exxon/dsl, Sunoco/dsl 🅕 J&S Pizza, Midway Diner 🏠 Quality Inn
15	Grimes
13	PA 501, Bethel, **N** 🅖 Valero/dsl, **S** 🅖 Bethel/dsl, Sheetz/dsl 🅞 dsl repair, USPO
10	PA 645, Frystown, **S** 🅖 ⦿FLYING J/Huddle House/Subway/dsl/scales/24hr/@ 🏠 Travel Inn
6	(8 from wb, US 22)PA 343, Fredricksburg, **1 mi S** 🅖 PP/dsl, Redner's Whse/mkt 🅕 Esther's Rest. 🅞 KOA (5mi)

I-81. I-78 begins/ends on I-81, exit 89.

⭱N INTERSTATE 79

Exit #	Services
183b a	PA 5, 12th St, Erie, **E** 🅞 Ⓗ, Valley Tire, **W** 🅖 Country Fair/dsl, Gulf/dsl 🅕 Applebee's, Arby's, Bob Evans, Bruster's, Chipotle, Domino's, Dunkin', El Canelo Mexican, Five Guys, Hibachi Japanese, IHOP, Jimmy John's, KFC, McDonald's, Moe's SW Grill, Panera Bread, Pizza Hut, Popeye's, Serafini's, Starbucks, Taco Bell, Tim Hortons, Wendy's 🏠 Comfort Inn (2mi) 🅞 $General, $Tree, Advance Parts, Aldi Foods, BigLots, CVS Drug, Dunn Tire, Family$, Giant Eagle Foods, GNC, Save-a-Lot Foods, Tires-4-Less, to Presque Isle SP, Tuesday Morning, U-Haul, Verizon, vet
182	US 20, 26th St, **E** 🅖 Country Fair/dsl, KwikFill 🅕 Subway 🅞 Ⓗ, CVS Drug, Family$, Tops Foods/gas/24hr, **W** 🅖 Country Fair/dsl 🅕 Arby's, Burger King, DQ, Hong Kong Chinese, Hoss's Steaks, Hungry Howie's, Little Caesar's, LJ Silver, McDonald's, Pizza Pete's, Subway, Tim Hortons 🏠 Glass House Inn 🅞 $General, AT&T, AutoZone, Ford, Giant Eagle Foods, Monro, O'Reilly Parts, TrueValue, URGENT CARE, USPO, vet, Volvo

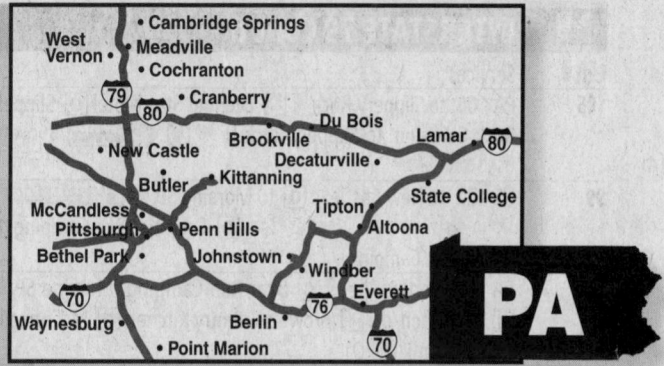

180	US 19, to Kearsarge, **E** 🅕 Aoyama Japanese, Arby's, Buffalo Wild Wings, Cheddar's, Coldstone, Firebirds Grill, Fox&Hound, KFC, Mad Mex, Max&Erma's, McDonald's, Moe's SW Grill, O'Charley's, Olive Garden, Outback Steaks, Primanti Bros, Red Lobster, Smokey Bones BBQ, Sonic, Starbucks, Wendy's 🏠 Candlewood Suites, Fairfield Inn, Homewood Suites, SpringHill Suites, TownePlace Suites 🅞 Ⓗ, Audi/Cadillac, Barnes&Noble, Chrysler/Dodge/Jeep, Dick's, Field & Stream, Firestone/auto, JC Penney, Macy's, Michael's, Petco, Rite Aid, Ross, TJ Maxx, Toyota, Verizon, **W** 🅕 Country Fair/dsl
178b a	I-90, E to Buffalo, W to Cleveland
174	to McKean, **E** 🅖 access to gas/dsl, **W** 🅞 KOA
166	US 6N, to Edinboro, **E** 🅖 Country Fair/dsl, Sheetz 🅕 McDonald's (3mi), TacoBell (2mi), Wendy's 🏠 Comfort Suites 🅞 Advance Parts, vet, Walmart/Subway
163mm	🆁🆂 both lanes, full ♿ facilities, litter barrels, petwalk, 🅒, 🄿, vending
154	PA 198, to Saegertown, Conneautville, **E** 🅞 Erie NWR (17mi)
147b a	US 6, US 19, US 322, to Meadville, **E** 🅖 Country Fair/dsl, GetGo, Sheetz/dsl 🅕 Applebee's, Arby's, Chovy's Italian, Cracker Barrel, DQ, Five Guys, Hoss's Rest., KFC, Perkins, Pizza Hut, Subway, Super China, Taco Bell 🏠 EconoLodge, Holiday Inn Express 🅞 Ⓗ, Advance Parts, AT&T, Family$, Giant Eagle Foods, Home Depot, Jo-Ann Fabrics, Save-a-Lot Foods, **W** 🅖 Sheetz/dsl 🅕 Burger King, Compadres Mexican, King's Rest., McDonald's, Red Lobster, Subway, Tim Hortons, Yuen's Garden 🏠 Hampton Inn, Quality Inn 🅞 $Tree, Aldi Foods, AutoZone, Buick/GMC, Chevrolet, GNC, to Pymatuning SP, Toyota, URGENT CARE, Verizon, Walmart/Subway
141	PA 285, to Geneva, **E** 🅞 to Erie NWR (20mi), **W** 🅖 Aunt Bee's Rest./dsl, Citgo/dsl
135mm	🆁🆂/weigh sta both lanes, full ♿ facilities, litter barrels, petwalk, 🅒, 🄿, vending
130	PA 358, to Sandy Lake, **W** 🅞 Ⓗ(13mi), to Goddard SP
121	US 62, to Mercer, **E** 🅞 Valley Tire, **W** 🅖 Sunoco/dsl 🅞 st police
116b a	I-80, E to Clarion, W to Sharon
113	PA 208, PA 258, to Grove City, **E** 🅖 Country Fair/dsl, Marathon/dsl 🅕 Compadres Mexican 🅞 Ⓗ, **W** 🅖 KwikFill/Subway, Sheetz/dsl, Tesla EVC 🅕 Eat'n Park, Hoss' Rest., McDonald's, My Bro's Place, Palato's Italian, Primanti Bros, Taco Bell, Timber Creek Rest., Wendy's 🏠 Best Western, Candlewood Suites, Comfort Inn, Hampton Inn, Holiday Inn Express, Microtel, Super 8, TownePlace Suites 🅞 KOA (3mi), Premium Outlets/famous brands
110mm	🆁🆂/weigh sta sb, full ♿ facilities, litter barrels, petwalk, 🅒, 🄿, vending
107mm	🆁🆂/weigh sta nb, full ♿ facilities, litter barrels, petwalk, 🅒, 🄿, vending

E R I E

M E A D V I L L E

PA

🛢 = gas 🍴 = food 🛏 = lodging ⭕ = other Rs = rest stop   Copyright 2022 - The Next EXIT ®

⬆N INTERSTATE 79 Cont'd

Exit #	Services
105	PA 108, to Slippery Rock, **E** 🛏 Evening Star Motel ⭕ Slippery Rock Camping, to Slippery Rock U, **W** 🛢 Loves/Subway/dsl/scales24hr
99	US 422, to New Castle, **E** ⭕ to Moraine SP, **W** 🛢 Pilot/McDonald's/Subway/dsl/scales/24hr ⭕ Coopers Lake Camping, to Rose Point Camping
96	PA 488, Portersville, **E** ⭕ Bear Run Camping, Moraine SP, **W** 🛢 Marathon/dsl 🍴 Brown's Country Kitchen ⭕ McConnell's Mill SP (3mi), USPO
88	(87 from nb) US 19, PA 68, Zelienople, **W** 🛢 Exxon/dsl 🍴 Burger King, Fox's Pizza, Log Cabin Inn Rest., Pizza Hut
85	(83 from nb), PA 528 (no quick return), to Evans City, **W** ⭕ Buick/GMC
83	PA 528, Evans City
80mm	weigh sta both lanes
78	(76 from nb, exits left from nb), US 19, PA 228, to Mars, access to I-76, PA TPK, **E** 🛢 GetGo/dsl, Gulf/7-11/dsl 🍴 Anthony's Pizza, Applebee's, Chick-fil-A, Cracker Barrel, DiBella's Subs, Firebirds, Jimmy Wan's Chinese, Juniper Grill, Longhorn Steaks, McDonald's, Moe's SW Grill, Noodles&Co, Olive Garden, Patron Mexican, Red Robin, River City Grille, Smokey Bones BBQ, Starbucks, Subway 🛏 Best Western+, Courtyard, Hilton Garden, Home 2 Suites, Marriott, TownePlace Suites ⭕ Dick's, GNC, Kohl's, Lowe's, Petsmart, Staples, Target, TJ Maxx, Verizon, on US 19, **W** 🍴 Aladdin's Eatery, Arby's, Bob Evans, Boston Mkt, Bravo Italian, Buffalo Wild Wings, Burger King, Chipotle Mexican, Denny's, Domino's, Dunkin', Dynasty, Eat'n Park, Emiliano's Mexican, Firehouse Subs, Five Guys, HotDog Shoppe, Houlihan's, Ichiban Steakhouse, Jason's Deli, Jersey Mike's, Jimmy John's, Mad Mex, Max&Erma's, McDonald's, Monte Cello's Grill, Panda Express, Panera Bread, Perkins, Pizza Hut, Pizza Roma, Primanti Bros, Saga Steaks, Subway, Vocelli Pizza, Wendy's 🛏 Candlewood Suites, Clarion, Comfort Inn, Doubletree, Hampton Inn, Hyatt Place, Motel 6, Quality Inn, Red Roof Inn, Residence Inn, Super 8, Woodspring Suites ⭕ H, $Tree, Aldi Foods, AT&T, AutoZone, Barnes&Noble, Best Buy, BP/7-11/dsl, Costco/gas, Field&Stream, Firestone/auto, GetGo, Giant Eagle Foods, GNC, Home Depot, Jo-Ann Fabrics, Marathon/dsl, Marshall's, Michael's, NAPA, PepBoys, PetCo, Rite Aid, Sheetz/dsl, Sunoco/dsl, Toyota, Tuesday Morning, USPO, Verizon, Walgreens, Walmart
77	I-76/Tpk, to Youngstown
75	US 19 S (from nb), to Warrendale, services on US 19
73	PA 910, to Wexford, **E** 🛢 🍴 Eat'n Park, Starbucks 🛏 EconoLodge ⭕ Rite Aid, **W** 🛢 Exxon/dsl, Sheetz/dsl, Tesla EVC 🛏 Hampton Inn
72	I-279 S (from sb, exits left), to Pittsburgh
68	Mt Nebo Rd, **E** 🛢 Sheetz/dsl
66	to PA 65, Emsworth
65	to PA 51, Coraopolis, Neville Island, **E** 🛢 Speedway/Speedway Cafe 🍴 Kings Grille 🛏 Fairfield Inn ⭕ Penske Trucks, **W** 🍴 Subway
64.5mm	Ohio River
64	PA 51 (from nb), to Coraopolis, McKee's Rocks
60	PA 60, Crafton, **E** 🛢 GetGo/dsl 🍴 Primanti Bros 🛏 Comfort Inn, EconoLodge, Hilltop Motel, Motel 6 ⭕ H, **W** 🍴 Juliano's Rest. ⭕ Meineke
59b	I-376 W, US 22 W, US 30 (from nb), **W** ⭕ ⊕
59a	I-376 E, to Pittsburgh
57	to Carnegie

(left margin vertical text: CRANBERRY)
(right side vertical text: PITTSBURGH, **WAYNESBURG**)

Exit #	Services
55	PA 50, to Heidelberg, **E on PA 50** 🛢 Advance Parts, Marathon/dsl, Sunoco 🍴 Arby's, Bob Evans, ChuckeCheese, Eat'n Park, Jersey Mike's, LJ Silver, McDonald's, Moe's SW, Panera Bread, Pizza Hut, Sonic, Starbucks, Subway, Taco Bell, TX Roadhouse, Walnut Grill, Wendy's ⭕ $Tree, BigLots, Firestone/auto, Ford, Giant Eagle Foods, GNC, Home Depot, Jo-Ann Fabrics, Lowe's, Mr Tire, Pepboys, Rite Aid, Shop'n Save, TJ Maxx, Tuesday Morning, Walgreens, Walmart
54	PA 50, to Bridgeville, **E** 🛢 BP/dsl, GetGo 🍴 Chipotle, Jimmy John's, McDonald's, Starbucks 🛏 Holiday Inn Express ⭕ H, Aldi Foods, Chevrolet, Midas, Monro, NAPA, Rite Aid, USPO, **W** 🛢 Sunoco/dsl 🍴 Five Guys 🛏 Hampton Inn
50mm	Rs/weigh sta both lanes, full ♿ facilities, litter barrels, petwalk, 🛢, 🐾, vending
48	South Pointe, **W** 🍴 Jackson's Rest., Subway 🛏 Holiday Inn Express, Hilton Garden, Homewood Suites
45	to PA 980, Canonsburg, **E** 🛢 Sheetz ⭕ Toyota, **W** 🛢 Citgo 🍴 Dunkin', Hogfathers BBQ, KFC/Taco Bell, Little Caesar's, McDonald's, Papa John's, Pizza Hut, Starbucks, Subway, WaiWa Grill, Wendy's 🛏 Super 8 ⭕ $General, Advance Parts, auto transmission repair, AutoZone, Walgreens
43	PA 519, Houston, **E** 🛢 BP/dsl, **W** 🛢 Sunoco ⭕ Freightliner
41	Race Track Rd, **E** 🛢 Marathon/dsl 🍴 Burger King, Dunkin' McDonald's, Waffle House, Wendy's 🛏 Cambria Suites, Candlewood Suites, Comfort Inn, Country Inn&Suites, Courtyard, Doubletree, Hampton Inn, Holiday Inn Express, Hyatt Place ⭕ Audi, Old Navy, racetrack, Tanger Outlets/famous brands, **W** 🛢 BP/dsl 🛏 Microtel ⭕ Trolley Museum
40	Meadow Lands, **W** ⭕ golf, racetrack, Trolley Museum (3mi)
38	I-70 W, to Wheeling
I-79 and I-70 run together 3.5 mi. See I-70, exits 19b-20.	
34	I-70 E, to Greensburg
33	US 40, to Laboratory, **W** ⭕ KOA
31mm	weigh sta sb
30	US 19, to Amity, **W** 🛢 Exxon/Subway/dsl
23	to Marianna, Prosperity
19	US 19, to PA 221, Ruff Creek, **W** 🛢 BP/dsl
14	PA 21, to Waynesburg, **E** 🛢 🍴 Bob Evans 🛏 Comfort Inn, Microtel ⭕ Walmart/Subway, **W** 🛢 BP/7-11/dsl, Exxon/dsl, GetGo, Marathon, Sheetz, Sunoco 🍴 Burger King, DQ, Golden Wok, Hardee's, KFC, Little Caesar's, McDonald's, Pizza Hut, Subway, Taco Bell, Wendy's 🛏 EconoLodge, Hampton Inn, Super 8 ⭕ H, $General, $Tree, Advance Parts, Aldi Foods, AT&T, AutoZone, BigLots, Cadillac/Chevrolet/Subaru, Chrysler/Dodge/Jeep, CVS Drug, Giant Eagle Foods, Rite Aid, st police, Subaru, Verizon
7	to Kirby
6mm	Welcome Ctr/weigh sta nb, full ♿ facilities, litter barrels, petwalk, 🛢, 🐾, vending
1	Mount Morris, **E** 🛢 Sunoco/Huddle House/dsl/scales/24hr ⭕ Honda/Mazda, **W** 🛢 Marathon/dsl
0mm	Pennsylvania/West Virginia state line

⬆E INTERSTATE 80

Exit #	Services
311mm	Pennsylvania/New Jersey state line, Delaware River
310.5	toll booth wb
310	PA 611, Delaware Water Gap, **Welcome Ctr**/Rs, **S** 🍴 Fuel Or Gulf 🍴 Apple Pie Bakery, Doughboys Pizza, Sango Kura
309	US 209 N, PA 447, to Marshalls Creek, **N** 🛢 Gulf 🍴 DC Dunkin', Huddle House, Landmark Cafe 🛏 Days Inn, Staybridge Suites ⭕ H

(left margin: **PA**)

S T R O U D S B U R G

INTERSTATE 80 Cont'd

Exit #	Services
308	East Stroudsburg, **N** ⛽ Exxon/Subs Now ⊙ Ⓗ, WaWa, **S** 🍴 Roasted Tomato Grill 🛏 Quality Inn, Super 8
307	PA 191, Broad St, **N** 🛏 Hampton Inn ⊙ Ⓗ, **S** ⛽ Sunoco 🍴 Compton's Rest. 🛏 Bridgeview Inn
306	Dreher Ave (from wb, no EZ return), **N** ⊙ WaWa
305	US 209, Main St, **N** ⛽ Gulf/dsl, Sunoco 🍴 Perkins 🛏 Pocono Plaza Inn, **S** ⛽ Exxon/dsl
304	US 209, to PA 33, 9th St (from wb)
303	9th St, (from eb), **N** 🍴 Burger King, Dunkin', Five Guys, McDonald's, Olive Garden, Panera Bread, Popeye's, Ruby Tuesday, TX Roadhouse, Wendy's ⊙ $Tree, Best Buy, BJ's/Subway/gas, Buick/GMC, Chevrolet, CVS Drug, Home Depot, Hyundai, JC Penney, Kia, Michael's, Midas, Old Navy, Petsmart, Staples, Target, Target, TJ Maxx, URGENT CARE, Walgreens, Weis Foods/gas
302	PA 611, to Bartonsville, **N** ⛽ Exxon/dsl 🍴 Chili's, Dunkin', East Gourmet Buffet, Frank's Pizza, Ichiban Steaks, Longhorn Steaks, Moe's SW Grill, Red Lobster, Red Robin, Sonic 🛏 Baymont Inn, Fairfield Inn, Hampton Inn, Howard Johnson, SpringHill Suites ⊙ $Tree, Advance Parts, AT&T, Dick's, Giant Foods/gas, Kohl's, Lowe's, Mavis Tire, URGENT CARE, Verizon
299	PA 715, Tannersville, **N** ⛽ Citgo/dsl, Mobil/Burger King/dsl, Tesla EVC, Turkey Hill 🍴 DQ, Dunkin', FoodCourt, Friendly's, Pocono Diner 🛏 Best Western+, Scotrun Motel ⊙ $General, CVS Drug, The Crossing Factory Outlet/famous brands, Weis Foods, **S** ⛽ Sunoco/dsl 🛏 Days Inn ⊙ to Big Pocono SP, to Camelback Ski Area
298	PA 611 (from wb), to Scotrun, **N** ⛽ Fill&Fly/dsl 🍴 Brick Oven Pizza 🛏 Great Wolf Lodge, Scotrun Diner/motel ⊙ to Mt Pocono
295mm	Ⓡⓢ eb, full ♿ facilities, litter barrels, petwalk, ⓒ, 🖼, vending
293	I-380 N, to Scranton, (exits left from eb)
284	PA 115, to Wilkes-Barre, Blakeslee, **N** ⛽ Citgo, WaWa/dsl 🍴 Dunkin' 🛏 Best Western ⊙ st police, **S** ⛽ Gulf/dsl ⊙ Fern Ridge Camping, to Pocono Raceway
277	PA 940, to PA Tpk (I-476), to Pocono, Lake Harmony, Allentown, **N** ⛽ WaWa 🍴 Arby's, Burger King, McDonald's 🛏 Comfort Inn, EconoLodge, Holiday Inn Express, Mtn Laurel Resort, Pocono Inn/Resort, Quality Inn, Split Rock Resort
274	PA 534, **N** ⛽ Hickory Run/Exxon/rest./dsl/scales/24hr, Sunoco/Subs Now/dsl/24hr ⊙ towing/repair, **S** ⊙ to Hickory Run SP (6mi)
273mm	Lehigh River
273	PA 940, PA 437, to Freeland, White Haven, **N** ⛽ Exxon, Fuel One, **S** 🍴 Powerhouse Eatery
270mm	Ⓡⓢ eb, full ♿ facilities, info, litter barrels, petwalk, ⓒ, 🖼, vending
262	PA 309, to Hazleton, Mountain Top, **N** ⛽ Citgo/Dunkin' 🍴 Mary's Rest., Wendy's 🛏 EconoLodge ⊙ auto/truck repair, Nescopeck SP (5mi), **S** ⛽ Valero/dsl 🛏 Holiday Inn Express
260 b a	I-81, N to Wilkes-Barre, S to Harrisburg
256	PA 93, to Nescopeck, Conyngham, **N** ⛽ Citgo/repair, Pilot/Subway/dsl/scales/24hr, **S** 🛏 Hampton Inn (4mi), Motel 6 ⊙ Ⓗ, towing/truck repair
251mm	Nescopeck River
246mm	Ⓡⓢ/weigh sta both lanes, full ♿ facilities, litter barrels, petwalk, ⓒ, 🖼, vending, weather info
242	PA 339, to Mainville, Mifflinville, **N** ⛽ Loves/Arby's/dsl/scales/24hr, Sunoco/Burger King/Subway/dsl 🍴 McDonald's 🛏 Super 8, **S** ⛽ Delta/dsl 🛏 Comfort Inn
241mm	Susquehanna River

H A Z L E T O N

Exit #	Services
241b a	US 11, to Berwick, Lime Ridge, Bloomsburg, **N** 🛏 Red Maple Inn (2mi) ⊙ Ⓗ, 2-5 mi **S** ⛽ Sheetz/dsl, Sunoco/Subs Now/dsl 🍴 Applebee's, Arby's, Burger King, China Queen, Domino's, Dunkin', Kemler's Rest., Little Caesar's, Marley's Grill, McDonald's, Morris Rest., Oliran Japanese, Pizza Hut, Rita's Custard, Subway, Taco Bell, Taste of Italy, Wendy's 🛏 Motel 6, Relax Inn ⊙ AAA, Ace Hardware, Advance Parts, BigLots, Buick/GMC, Cadillac/Chevrolet, CVS Drug, Ford/Honda, Giant Foods/gas, Kost Tire, Rite Aid, Staples, U-Haul, Verizon, Weis Foods/gas
236	PA 487, to Bloomsburg, Lightstreet, **N** ⛽ Tesla EVC 🛏 Fairfield Inn, **S** ⛽ Sunoco 🍴 Denny's 🛏 Hampton Inn, Turkey Hill Inn ⊙ Ⓗ, to Bloomsburg U
232	PA 42, Buckhorn, **N** ⛽ Exxon/Subs Now, TA/Country Pride/Subway/dsl/scales/24hr/@, Tesla EVC 🍴 Burger King, Cracker Barrel, KFC, Perkins, Quaker Steak&Lube, Ruby Tuesday, Starbucks, Wendy's 🛏 Holiday Inn Express, Quality Inn ⊙ AT&T, Home Depot, **S** 🍴 Gourmet Buffet, Olive Garden, Panera Bread 🛏 Comfort Suites ⊙ $Tree, Indian Head Camping (3mi), Lowe's, Marshall's, PetCo, Verizon, Walmart/McDonald's
224	PA 54, to Danville, **N** ⛽ Exxon/Subway/dsl 🛏 Quality Inn, **S** ⛽ Mobil/dsl 🍴 Friendly's, McDonald's 🛏 Best Western, Hampton Inn, Red Roof Inn, Super 8 ⊙ Ⓗ
219mm	Ⓡⓢ both lanes, full ♿ facilities, info, litter barrels, petwalk, ⓒ, 🖼, vending
215	PA 254, Limestonevill, **S** ⛽ FLYING J/Penn 80 Rest./Subway/dsl/scales/24hr/@ ⊙ Eagle Truckwash
212b a	I-180 W, PA 147 S, to Muncy, Williamsport, **S** ⛽ Sunoco (1mi)
210.5mm	Susquehanna River
210b a	US 15, to Williamsport, Lewisburg, **S** ⛽ Sunoco/dsl 🍴 Bonanza 🛏 Holiday Inn Express, Quality Inn ⊙ Ⓗ, KOA (5mi)
199	Mile Run
194mm	Ⓡⓢ/weigh sta both lanes, full ♿ facilities, litter barrels, petwalk, ⓒ, 🖼, vending
192	PA 880, to Jersey Shore, **N** ⛽ Sunoco/dsl ⊙ Ⓗ, **S** ⛽ Valero/dsl ⊙ towing/truck repair
185	PA 477, Logantown, **N** ⛽ Valero, **S** 🍴 Twilight Diner ⊙ RB Winter SP (12mi)
178	US 220, Lock Haven, 5 mi **N** ⛽ KwikFill/dsl, Sheetz/dsl 🍴 Little Caesar's, Original Italian Pizza, Ruby Tuesday ⊙ Ⓗ, $General, $Tree, Advance Parts, Lowe's, Walmart/Subway, Weis Foods
173	PA 64, Lamar, **N** ⛽ Pilot/Subway/dsl/scales/24hr 🍴 Cottage Rest., McDonald's 🛏 Hampton Inn, Quality Inn/rest. ⊙ repair, **S** ⛽ FLYING J/Denny's/Dunkin'/dsl/LP/scales/24hr, TA/Country Pride/dsl/scales/24hr/@, Valero
161	I-99, US 220 S, PA 26, to Bellafonte, **N** ⊙ Bellefonte Camping, KOA (2mi), **S** ⊙ to PSU
158	US 220 S, PA 150, to Altoona, Milesburg, **N** ⛽ Shell/Subway, TA/Country Pride/dsl/scales/24hr/@, Valero/dsl 🍴 McDonald's 🛏 Quality Inn

L A M A R

PA

🅖 = gas 🍴 = food 🛏 = lodging 🅞 = other 🆁🆂 = rest stop Copyright 2022 - The Next EXIT ®

INTERSTATE 80 Cont'd

Exit #	Services
147	PA 144, to Snow Shoe, N 🅖 Phillips 66/dsl/repair/24hr, Sunoco/dsl/24hr 🍴 Snow Shoe Rest., Snow Shoe Sandwich Shop, Subway 🅞 Hall's Foods, USPO
146mm	🆁🆂 both lanes, full 🅮 facilities, litter barrels, petwalk, 🅒, 🏕, vending
138mm	Moshannon River
133	PA 53, to Philipsburg, Kylertown, N 🅖 Exxon, KwikFill/motel/dsl/scales 🍴 Roadhouse Rest. 🅞 $General, Mtn View Mkt, USPO, S 🅞 🏥, Black Moshannon SP (9mi)
123	PA 970, to Shawville, Woodland, N 🅞 Woodland Camping, S 🅖 Gio's BBQ/dsl (2mi), PP/dsl 🅞 st police, USPO
120mm	Susquehanna River, W Branch
120	PA 879, Shawville, Clearfield, N 🅖 Sapp Bros/rest./dsl/scales/24hr/@ 🅞 Peterbilt, S 🅖 BP/dsl, Sheetz, Snappy's 🍴 Arby's, Burger King, Dunkin', Dutch Pantry, KFC, McDonald's 🛏 Best Western+, Comfort Inn, Hampton Inn, Holiday Inn Express, Red Roof Inn, Super 8 🅞 🏥, Lowe's, Walmart/Subway
111mm	highest point on I-80 east of Mississippi River, 2250 ft
111	PA 153, to Penfield, N 🅞 to Parker Dam, to SB Elliot SP, S 🅞 🏥
101	PA 255, Du Bois, N 🅖 Snappy's/Grille /dsl 🅞 camping, 1-2 mi S 🅖 Sheetz/dsl 🍴 A&W/LJ Silver, Burger King, Dunkin', Eat'n Park, Fusion Buffet, Italian Oven, Japan One, McDonald's, Napoli Pizzeria, Perkins, Pizza Hut, Red Lobster, Ruby Tuesday, Station 101 Grill, Subway, Taco Bell, Wendy's 🛏 Fairfield Inn, Hampton Inn, Homewood Suites 🅞 🏥, $General, $Tree, Aldi Foods, BigLots, CVS Drug, JC Penney, Jo-Ann Fabrics, Lowe's, Old Navy, PetCo, Rite Aid, Ross, st police, Staples, TJ Maxx, Verizon, Walmart/Subway
97	US 219, to Brockway, Du Bois, S 🅖 🛢/Arby's/dsl/scales/24hr, Sheetz/dsl/24hr 🍴 Dutch Pantry Rest., Hoss' Rest. (2mi) 🛏 Best Western (2mi), Clarion, Holiday Inn Express 🅞 🏥, Advance Parts (2mi), AutoZone (2mi), Freightliner
90	PA 830 E, N 🅞 Du Bois Regional Airport
87.5mm	🆁🆂 both lanes, full 🅮 facilities, litter barrels, petwalk, 🅒, 🏕, vending
86	PA 830, to Reynoldsville
81	PA 28, to Brookville, Hazen, S hist dist (2mi)
78	PA 36, to Sigel, Brookville, N 🅖 ⊘FLYING J/Denny's/dsl/LP/scales/24hr, TA/BP/Taco Bell/dsl/scales/24hr/@ 🍴 McDonald's, Pizza Hut 🛏 Super 8 🅞 NAPA, to Cook Forest SP, S 🅖 Get-Go/dsl, O Ring CNG, Sheetz/dsl 🍴 Arby's, Burger King, China Wok, Plyler's Buffet, Subway 🛏 Gold Eagle Inn, Rodeway Inn 🅞 $General, Chrysler/Dodge/Jeep, Family$, truckwash
73	PA 949, Corsica, N 🅞 to Clear Creek SP, S 🅞 USPO
70	US 322, to Strattanville
64	PA 66 S, to New Bethlehem, Clarion, N 🅞 to Clarion U
62	PA 68, to Clarion, N 🅖 BP, KwikFill/dsl 🍴 Applebee's, Arby's, Burger King, Cozumel, Eat'n Park, Hunan King, McDonald's, Perkins, Pizza Hut, RRR Roadhouse, Sakura Buffet, Subway, Taco Bell 🛏 Clarion, Hampton Inn, Holiday Inn Express, Motel 6, Quality Inn, Ramada 🅞 🏥, $Tree, Advance Parts, Aldi Foods, AT&T, AutoZone, JC Penney, Verizon, Walmart/Subway, S 🛏 Microtel
61mm	Clarion River
60	PA 66 N, to Shippenville, N 🅖 Jiffy/dsl 🅞 camping, to Cook Forest SP
56mm	weigh sta both lanes
53	to PA 338, to Knox, N 🅖 Satterlee Gas/dsl (cardlock) 🍴 Big Country Rest. 🅞 Countryside Crafts/Quilts, Wolf's Camping Resort, S 🅞 Good Tire Service

Exit #	Services
45	PA 478, to St Petersburg, Emlenton
44.5mm	Clarion River, Allegheny River
42	PA 38, to Emlenton, N 🅖 Exxon/Subway/dsl, 🛢/rest. dsl/scales/24hr 🛏 Emlenton Motel 🅞 Gaslight RV Park, truck RV repair
35	PA 308, to Clintonville, N 🅞 Family$
30.5mm	🆁🆂 both lanes, full 🅮 facilities, litter barrels, petwalk, 🅒, 🏕, vending
29	PA 8, to Franklin, Barkeyville, N 🅖 Speedway/Speedway Cafe dsl 🍴 Arby's, Burger King, King's Rest. 🛏 Motel 6, Quality Inn 🅞 Freightliner, S 🍴 Heath/dsl, KwikFill/dsl/scales/motel/24hr, TA/BP/Subway/dsl/scales/24hr/@ 🅞 to Slippery Rock U, truckwash
24	PA 173, to Grove City, Sandy Lake, S 🅞 🏥, Grove City Coll
19b a	I-79, N to Erie, S to Pittsburgh
15	US 19, to Mercer, N 🅖 PP/dsl, Shell 🍴 Burger King, Margarita King Mexican 🛏 Comfort Inn, 2 mi S 🍴 Iron Bridge Rest 🅞 KOA (4mi)
4b a	I-376, PA 60, to PA 18, to Sharon-Hermitage, New Castle, N 🅖 Sheetz/dsl, Sunoco/Subway/dsl 🛏 EconoLodge, Hampton Inn, Holiday Inn Express, Park Inn, Quality Inn, Red Roof Inn, Super 8, S 🍴 DQ, MiddleSex Diner 🅞 $General
2.5mm	Shenango River
1mm	Welcome Ctr eb, full 🅮 facilities, litter barrels, petwalk, 🅒, 🏕 vending
0mm	Pennsylvania/Ohio state line

INTERSTATE 81

Exit #	Services
233mm	Pennsylvania/New York state line
232mm	Welcome Ctr/weigh sta sb, full 🅮 facilities, litter barrels, petwalk, 🅒, 🏕
230	PA 171, Great Bend, E 🅖 Valero 🅞 Lakeside Camping (5mi) W 🅖 Exxon/Tim Hortons/dsl, Sunoco/dsl 🍴 Bluestone Pizz, Burger King, Dobb's Country Kitchen, Dunkin', McDonald's, Subway 🛏 Colonial Brick Motel 🅞 Family$, Reddon's Drug, Rob's Foods
223	PA 492, New Milford, E 🅞 East Lake Camping/RV Park (3mi) W 🅖 Citgo/dsl, Gulf/dsl 🍴 Green Gables Rest. 🛏 Blue Ridg Motel, Lynn Lee B&B (1.5mi)
219	PA 848, to Gibson, E 🅖 Sunoco/Burger King/dsl, W 🅖 ⊘FLYING J/Denny's/dsl/scales/24hr, Exxon/McDonald's dsl/24hr 🛏 Holiday Inn Express, st police
217	PA 547, Harford, E 🅖 Exxon/Subway/dsl/24hr, Mobil/dsl/24h
211	PA 92, Lenox, E 🅞 Elk Mtn Ski Area, Shady Rest Campin (3mi), W 🅖 Gulf/dsl, Pump-N-Pantry/dsl 🍴 Bingham's Res, Lenox Rest. 🅞 Lenox Drug
209mm	🆁🆂 sb, full 🅮 facilities, litter barrel, petwalk, 🅒, 🏕, vending
206	PA 374, to Glenwood, Lenoxville, E 🅖 Sunoco/dsl 🅞 to E Mountain Ski Resort
203mm	🆁🆂 nb, full 🅮 facilities, litter barrels, petwalk, 🅒, 🏕, vendin
202	PA 107, to Fleetville, Tompkinsville
201	PA 438, East Benton, W 🅖 Duchniks/dsl/repair 🍴 B&B Res
199	PA 524, Scott, E 🅖 Gulf/dsl, W 🅖 Exxon/Subway 🛏 Mot 81 🅞 to Lackawanna SP
197	PA 632, Waverly, E 🅞 Rite Aid, Weis Foods, W 🅖 Sunoc Doc's Deli 🛏 Camelot Inn/rest

D U B O I S B R O O K V I L L E C L A R I O N

PA

⬆N INTERSTATE 81 Cont'd

Exit #	Services
194	US 6, US 11, to I-476/PA Tpk, Clarks Summit, **W** 🅖 Exxon/dsl, Sheetz/dsl, Sunoco/dsl, Valero 🍴 Burger King, Dino&Francesco's, Domino's, DQ, Dunkin', Krispy Kreme, Kyoto Japanese, McDonald's, Moe's SW Grill, Starbucks, Starbucks, Subway, Sunny Chinese, Taco Bell, Waffle House, Wendy's 🏠 Comfort Inn, EconoLodge, Hampton Inn, Nichols Village Inn, Ramada Inn 🅞 Ace Hardware, Advance Parts, Kost Tire, Monro, Rite Aid, Verizon, Weis Mkt
191b a	US 6, US 11, to Carbondale, **E** 🅖 Sheetz/dsl, Sunoco 🍴 A&W/LJ Silver, Applebee's, Buffalo Wild Wings, Burger King, China Palace, Chipotle, ChuckECheese, Colarusso's Pizza, Denny's, DQ, Dunkin', Five Guys, HoneyBaked Ham, Jersey Mike's, La Tonalateca, McDonald's, Olive Garden, Panera Bread, Perkins, Perkins, Primanti Bros, Quaker Steak&Lube, Red Lobster, Red Robin, Rita's Custard, Roma Pizza, Royal Buffet, Ruby Tuesday, Starbucks, Subway, Taco Bell, TGIFriday's, TX Roadhouse, Uno Grill, Viewmont Diner 🏠 Days Inn, Holiday Inn Express, Home 2 Suites 🅞 $Tree, Aldi Foods, AT&T, Books-A-Million, Dick's, Field&Stream, Firestone/auto, Harley-Davidson, Hobby Lobby, Home Depot, Hyundai, JC Penney, Jo-Ann Crafts, Kohl's, Macy's, Marshall's, Michael's, Old Navy, PepBoys, Petsmart, Target, TJ Maxx, Verizon, Walmart, Wegman's Mkt, William's Tires, **W** 🅞 to Anthracite Museum
190	Main Ave, Dickson City, **E** 🍴 Wendy's 🏠 Fairfield Inn, Microtel, Residence Inn 🅞 auto repair, Best Buy, Ford, Lowe's, Sam's Club/gas, Staples, vet, **W** 🅞 Schiff's Mkt, Toyota
188	PA 347, Throop, **E** 🅖 Sheetz/dsl, Sunoco/dsl 🍴 McDonald's, Wendy's 🏠 Dunmore Inn, Quality Inn, Rodeway Inn, Sleep Inn 🅞 Advance Parts, BigLots, Kost Tire, Monro, Nissan, PriceChopper Foods, st police, URGENT CARE, **W** 🅖 Exxon/Subway/dsl 🍴 Burger King, Dunkin', Friendly's
187	to I-84, I-380, US 6 (no return from nb)
186	PA 435, Drinker St (from nb) **E** 🅖 Valero/dsl, **W** 🅖 Exxon/dsl
185	Central Scranton Expwy (exits left from nb), **W** 🅞 🍴 🅗
184	to PA 307, River St, **W** 🅖 Exxon/Subway/dsl, Valero, Vamco 🍴 Asian Taste, Dunkin' 🏠 Sheraton 🅞 🅗 $Tree, CVS Drug, Gerrity Foods
182	Davis St, Montage Mtn Rd, **E** 🅖 EVC, Exxon/Coldstone/Subway/dsl, Tesla EVC 🍴 Burger King, Food&Fire BBQ, Gourmet Slice Pizza, Harvest Seasonal Grill, Longhorn Steaks, Marzoni's Brick Oven, Nonno's Pizza, Panchero's Mexican, Panera Bread, Ruby Tuesday, Starbucks 🏠 Comfort Suites, Courtyard, Hampton Inn, SpringHill Suites, TownePlace Suites 🅞 AT&T, GNC, Verizon, **W** 🅖 Sunoco 🍴 Dunkin', Waffle House, Wendy's 🏠 EconoLodge 🅞 CVS Drug, USPO
180	to US 11, PA 502, to Moosic, (exits left from nb), **W** on US 11 🅖 Citgo/dsl, Sunoco 🍴 Subway
178b a	to US 11, Avoca, **E** 🏠 Best Western+, **W** 🅖 Petro/Shell/Iron Skillet/dsl/scales/24hr/@
175b a	PA 315 S, to I-476, Dupont, **E** 🅖 Exxon/Subway/dsl, Sunoco/dsl 🍴 Arby's, McDonald's, Perkins 🏠 Knights Inn 🅞 Volvo, **W** 🅖 🚛/Wendy's/dsl/scales/24hr 🍴 Burger King, Denny's, Star Asia Buffet, Taco Bell, Uncle Joe's Pizza 🏠 Holiday Inn Express 🅞 truck repair, Verizon, Walmart/Subway
170b a	PA 115, PA 309, Wilkes-Barre, **E** 🅖 Exxon/Subway/dsl, Sunoco/dsl, Tesla EVC 🏠 Holiday Inn, **W** 🅖 Citgo, Sunoco/dsl 🍴 Buffalo Wild Wings, Burger King, Denny's, Domino's, Dunkin', Friendly's, Grotto Pizza, Hardee's, Harvest Buffet, IHOP, Jersey Mike's, Longhorn Steaks, McDonald's, Moe's SW Grill, Red Lobster, Sonic, Taco Bell, TGIFriday's, Wendy's

S C R A N T O N

W I L K E S B A R R E

170b a	Continued 🏠 Days Inn, Extended Stay America, Fairfield Inn, Holiday Inn Express, Host Inn, Quality Inn, Red Roof Inn, Woodspring Suites 🅞 🅗 $General, AutoZone, Chevrolet, JC Penney, Macy's, to Pocono Downs, Williams Tire/auto
168	Highland Park Blvd, Wilkes-Barre, **W** 🅖 Sheetz/dsl, Sunoco/Subway/dsl, Tesla EVC 🍴 Applebee's, Bob Evans, Chili's, Chipotle, ChuckECheese, Cracker Barrel, Five Guys, King's Buffet, La Tolteca Mexican, Miller's Alehouse, Mizu Steaks, Nello's Pizza, Olive Garden, Outback Steaks, Popeye's, Red Robin, Smokey Bones BBQ, Starbucks, TX Roadhouse, Wendy's 🏠 Courtyard, Hampton Inn, Hilton Garden, Motel 6 🅞 AT&T, Barnes&Noble, Best Buy, Dick's, Firestone/auto, Home Depot, Kohl's, Kost Tire/auto, Lowe's, Marshall's, Michael's, Nissan, Old Navy, PepBoys, PetCo, Petsmart, PriceChopper, Ross, Sam's Club/gas, Staples, Target, TJ Maxx, Tuesday Morning, U-Haul, URGENT CARE, Verizon, Walgreens, Walmart/Subway, Wegman's Foods
165b a	PA 309 S, (exits left from nb), Wilkes-Barre, **W** 🅖 Citgo/dsl, Gulf 🍴 Dunkin', McDonald's, Perkins, Taco Bell 🏠 Comfort Inn, EconoLodge 🅞 $Tree, Advance Parts, Rite Aid
164	PA 29, to Nanticoke, Ashley
159	Nuangola, **W** 🅖 Valero/Subs Now/dsl 🅞 camping (10mi)
157mm	℞/weigh sta sb, full ♿ facilities, litter barrels, petwalk, ☏, 🛏, vending
156mm	℞/weigh sta nb, full ♿ facilities, litter barrels, petwalk, ☏, 🛏, vending
155	to Dorrance, **E** 🅖 Sunoco/dsl, **W** 🅞 Blue Ridge Plaza/dsl
151b a	I-80, E to Mountaintop, W to Bloomsburg
145	PA 93, W Hazleton, **E** 🅖 Sunoco/Dunkin'/dsl, TurkeyHill/dsl 🍴 Applebee's, Arby's, Bonanza, Damon's, Denny's, Five Stars Chinese, LJ Silver, McDonald's, Panera Bread, Perkins, Pizza Hut, Popeye's, Subway, Taco Bell, Wendy's 🏠 Comfort Inn, Fairfield Inn, Forest Hill Inn, Ramada Inn (2mi) 🅞 🅗 $Tree, Advance Parts, Aldi Foods, AT&T, Big Lots, Boscov's, Buick/Cadillac/GMC, Chrysler/Dodge/Jeep, Lowe's, Mazda, Michael's, Old Navy, Petsmart, st police, Verizon, Walmart/McDonald's, Weis Foods, **W** 🅖 JN Delimart 🍴 Damenti's, Top of the 80's 🏠 Candlewood Suites, Hampton Inn
143	PA 924, to Hazleton, **W** 🅖 Fuelon/Subs Now/dsl/scales, Sunoco/Subway, TurkeyHill/dsl 🍴 Burger King, Sonic 🏠 Residence Inn
141	PA 424, S Hazleton Beltway, **E** 🅞 Mt Laurel Motel
138	PA 309, to McAdoo, **2 mi E** 🏠 Pines Motel
134	to Delano
132mm	parking area/weigh sta both lanes
131b a	PA 54, Mahanoy City, **E** 🅞 to Tuscarora/Locust Lake SP, **W** 🍴 Gulf/dsl, Sunoco/dsl 🏠 Comfort Inn & Suites

H A Z L E T O N

PA

INTERSTATE 81 Cont'd

Exit #	Services
124b a	PA 61, to Frackville, **E** 🍴 Cracker Barrel, McDonald's 🛏 Holiday Inn Express 🅾 BigLots, **W** 🍴 Exxon, Gulf/dsl, Speedway 🍴 Anthony's Pizza, Dutch Kitchen, Subway 🛏 EconoLodge, Granny's Motel, Motel 6 🅾 🄷, Ken's Tire/auto, Rite Aid, st police
119	High Ridge Park Rd, to Gordon, **E** 🛏 Country Inn&Suites
116	PA 901, to Minersville, **E** 🍴 901 Rest.
112	PA 25, to Hegins, **W** 🅾 camping
107	US 209, to Tremont
104	PA 125, Ravine, **E** 🍴 Exxon/Burger King/dsl/scales/24hr 🅾 Echo Valley Campground
100	PA 443, to Pine Grove, **E** 🍴 Sunoco/dsl 🍴 Arby's, McDonald's 🛏 Comfort Inn, Seasons Inn 🅾 $General, **W** 🍴 ▦▦▦/DQ, Subway/dsl/scales/24hr, ▦▦▦/dsl 🍴 Diner 🛏 Hampton Inn 🅾 truckwash, vet
90	PA 72, to Lebanon, **E** 🍴 Exxon/Subway, ♥Loves/McDonald's/dsl/scales/24hr, Speedway/Dunkin'/dsl 🍴 Burger King, Wendy's 🛏 Days Inn, Fairfield Inn 🅾 KOA, st police, **W** 🛏 Comfort Inn
89	I-78 E, to Allentown
85b a	PA 934, to Annville, **2 mi W** 🍴 Funck's Rest. 🅾 to IndianTown Gap Nat Cem
80	PA 743, Grantville, **E** 🍴 Shell/dsl 🛏 Days Inn, Hampton Inn, **W** 🍴 Exxon/dsl 🍴 Italian Delight 🛏 Comfort Suites, Holiday Inn 🅾 racetrack
79mm	🆁🆂/weigh sta both lanes, full ♿ facilities, litter barrels, petwalk, 🄲, 🕭, vending
77	PA 39, to Hershey, **E** 🍴 ▦▦▦/Pizza Hut/dsl/scales/24hr, Sheetz/dsl 🍴 Hershey Rd Rest. 🛏 Country Inn&Suites, EconoLodge, La Quinta, Motel 6, Super 8 🅾 st police, to Hershey Attractions, **W** 🍴 ⊕FLYING J/Perkins/dsl/24hr/@, TA/Country Pride/dsl/scales/24hr/@ 🍴 McDonald's 🛏 Holiday Inn Express 🅾 Goodyear, SpeedCo, truck repair
72	to US 22, Linglestown, **E** 🍴 Sheetz/dsl, Speedway/Dunkin'/dsl, Sunoco/dsl 🍴 Burger King, Chipotle Mexican, Five Guys, McDonald's, Red Robin, Starbucks, Subway, Tonino's Pizza 🛏 Baymont Inn, Quality Inn 🅾 Advance Parts, Chrysler/Dodge/Jeep, Costco/gas, CVS Drug, Harley-Davidson, Hobby Lobby, Karn's Foods, Target, Toyota, U-Haul, **W** 🍴 Turkey Hill 🍴 Mikado Japanese 🛏 Candlewood Suites, Ramada Inn 🅾 $General
70	I-83 S, to York, 🅾 ⊖
69	Progress Ave, **E** 🍴 Cracker Barrel, Dunkin', Harvest Grill, Macaroni Grill, Starbucks, Tonino's Grill 🛏 Home 2 Suites 🅾 AT&T, CVS Drug, st police, Susquehanna Shoppes, **W** 🍴 Turkey Hill/dsl 🍴 Arby's, YP Rest. 🛏 Best Western, Hampton Inn, Red Roof Inn, SpringHill Suites
67b a	US 22, US 322 W, PA 230, Cameron St, to Lewistown
66	Front St, **E** 🅾 🄷, **W** 🍴 Exxon, Sunoco 🍴 Front St Diner, McDonald's, Pizza Hut, Simply Turkey, Two Guys Pizza, Wendy's 🛏 Best Value, Days Inn
65	US 11/15, to Enola, **1 mi E** 🍴 Sunoco/dsl, Tom's 🍴 Al's Pizza, China Taste, Domino's, DQ, Dunkin', McDonald's, Squeaky Rail Diner, Subway, Wendy's 🛏 Quality Inn 🅾 $Tree, Advance Parts, Fischer Parts, Rite Aid
61	PA 944, to Wertzville, **E** 🍴 Burger King, Taco Bell 🛏 Holiday Inn Express 🅾 🄷, AT&T, Giant/dsl, Weiss Mkt, **W** 🍴 Turkey Hill/dsl 🛏 Best Western+
59	PA 581, to US 11, to I-83, Harrisburg, **3 mi E on Carlisle Pk** 🍴 Sheetz/dsl, Sunoco 🍴 Applebee's, Burger King, Carrabba's, Denny's, Dunkin', McDonald's, Outback Steaks, TGIFriday's,

Left margin (vertical): **LEBANON**   **HARRISBURG**

Exit #	Services
59	Continued Wayback Burger, Wendy's 🛏 Park Inn 🅾 AutoZone, Buick/GMC, Home Depot, Hyundai, Lowe's, Nissan, NTB, Pepboys, Petsmart, TJ Maxx
57	PA 114, to Mechanicsburg, **2 mi E** 🍴 Sheetz/dsl 🍴 Alfredo'Pizza, Arby's, Dickey's BBQ, Great Wall Chinese, Isaac's Rest. KFC/LJ Silver, McDonald's, Olive Garden, Pizza Hut, Red Robin, Silver Spring Diner, Subway, Taco Bell 🛏 Home 2 Suites, La Quinta 🅾 CarMax, Giant Foods/gas, Sam's Club/gas, Walmar
52b a	US 11, to I-76/PA Tpk, Middlesex, **E** 🍴 ⊕FLYING J/Denny's dsl/scales/24hr/@, I-81/dsl, Sheetz/dsl, Tesla EVC 🍴 Dunkin Hickory Ridge, Middlesex Diner 🛏 Best Value Inn, Quality Inn Red Roof Inn, Super 8 🅾 🄷, **W** 🍴 Gulf, ♥Loves/Wendy's dsl/24hr, Petro/Iron Skillet/dsl/24hr/@, Rutters/dsl, Sunoco Subway/dsl 🍴 Arby's, Carelli's Subs, McDonald's, Miracle Mile Diner, Waffle House 🛏 Best Western, Comfort Inn, Day Inn, Diamond Carlisle Inn, EconoLodge, Hampton Inn, Holiday Inn Express, Motel 6, Residence Inn, Rodeway Inn, Travelodge 🅾 🄷, Blue Beacon
49	PA 74 (no EZ sb return), same as 48, **E** 🍴 Sheetz/dsl 🍴 Hardee's, **W** 🍴 Trindle Grill 🅾 AAA
48	PA 74, York Rd (no EZ nb return), **E** 🍴 Red Robin, Starbucks Subway 🛏 Microtel 🅾 $Tree, Aldi Foods, Kohl's, Michael's Petsmart, Rite Aid, Target, Verizon, **W** 🍴 Gulf/dsl, Speedwa 🍴 Burger King, Farmers Mkt Diner, Little Caesar's, McDonald's, Neato Burrito, Pizza Hut, Scalles Whse Rest., Taco Be 🅾 CVS Drug, Dunkin', Ford, Jo-Ann, Lowe's, Midas, Weis Mkt
47	PA 34, Hanover St, **E** 🍴 Chili's, Cracker Barrel 🛏 Sleep In 🅾 Home Depot, **W** 🍴 Applebee's, Bruster's/Nathan's, Chick fil-A, China Palace, Chipotle, DQ, Five Guys, Panera Bread Papa John's, Rita's Custard, Subway, Super Buffet, Vinny Rest., Wendy's 🅾 AT&T, CVS Drug, Rite Aid, Staples, TJ Maxx Walmart/McDonald's
45	College St, **E** 🍴 Gulf/dsl 🍴 Alfredo Pizza, Arby's, Hoss's Rest McDonald's, Subway, Walnut Bottom Diner 🛏 Hotel Ava, Super 8 🅾 🄷, Giant Food Mkt, Monro, Tire Pros, Verizon
44	PA 465, Allen Rd, to Plainfield, **E** 🛏 Country Inn&Suites, Fairfield Inn 🅾 🄷, st police, **W** 🍴 Sheetz/dsl 🍴 Burger King Subway
38.5mm	🆁🆂 both lanes, full ♿ facilities, litter barrels, petwalk, 🄲, 🕭
37	PA 233, to Newville, **E** 🅾 Pine Grove Furnace SP, **W** 🅾 C Denning SP
29	PA 174, King St, **E** 🍴 Sunoco/dsl 🛏 Rodeway Inn, **W** 🍴 Gul Rutter's/dsl 🍴 Bros Pizza, Burger King, China House, Domino's, KFC, Little Caesar's, Subway, Taco Bell, Wendy's 🛏 Be Western, Holiday Inn Express, Theo's Motel 🅾 $General, Advance Parts, Aldi Foods, AT&T, Cadillac/Chevrolet, CVS Drug Ford, Verizon, vet, Walmart
24	PA 696, Fayette St, **E** 🍴 Sheetz/dsl, **W** 🍴 Pacific Pride/dsl
20	PA 997, Scotland, **E** 🍴 Citgo/dsl 🍴 McDonald's 🛏 Comfort Inn, Super 8, **W** 🍴 Sunoco 🛏 Quality Inn
17	Walker Rd, **W** 🍴 Sheetz/dsl 🍴 Aki Japanese, Bruster's/Nathan's, Buffalo Wild Wings, Cafe del Sol, Chick-fil-A, Chipotle Mexican, Five Guys, Fuddrucker's, Jersey Mike's, Jimmy John's, Longhorn Steaks, MOD Pizza, Olive Garden, Panera Bread, Red Robin, Sonic, Starbucks, Subway, TGIFriday's, TX Roadhouse 🛏 Candlewood Suites, Country Inn&Suites, SpringHill Suites 🅾 Aldi Foods, AT&T, BJ's/dsl, Buick/Chevrolet/GMC, Ford, Giant Foods/gas, Kohl's, Michael's, Mr Tire, Petsmart, Staples, Target, URGENT CARE, Verizon

Right margin (vertical): CARLISLE

Left margin (bottom): PA

INTERSTATE 81 Cont'd

Exit #	Services
16	US 30, to Chambersburg, **E** 🅶 Sheetz/dsl 🍴 Arby's, Bonanza, Bro's Pizza, Burger King, Chris's Kitchen, Domino's, DQ, Dunkin', Hoss's Rest., KFC, Little Caesar's, Perkins, Popeye's, Supreme Buffet, Waffle House, Wendy's 🛏 Days Inn 🅾 $Tree, AAA, Dick's, Harley-Davidson, Hobby Lobby, Jo-Ann Fabrics, Lowe's, NAPA, Nissan/Toyota, Petco, TJ Maxx, U-Haul, vet, Walmart/Subway, **W** 🍴 Big Oak Cafe, Burger King, Chambersburg Diner, Copper Kettle, LJ Silver, McDonald's, Pizza Hut, Ruby Tuesday, Taco Bell 🛏 Best Western, Clarion, La Quinta 🅾 🏥, Advance Parts, AutoZone, Lincoln, Walgreens
14	PA 316, Wayne Ave, **E** 🅶 Sheetz/dsl 🍴 Bob Evans, Cracker Barrel 🛏 Baymont Inn, Hampton Inn, Red Carpet Inn, **W** 🅶 KwikFill 🍴 Applebee's, Arby's, China Wok, Denny's, Mario's Italian, Montezuma Mexican, Papa John's, Red Lobster, Stoner's Rest., Subway, Twin Dragon Chinese, Volcano Japanese, Wendy's 🛏 Holiday Inn Express, Motel 6, Red Roof Inn 🅾 $Tree, CVS Drug, Giant Foods/gas, GNC, Mr Tire, Save-a-Lot Foods, Verizon, Weis Mkt
12mm	weigh sta sb
10	PA 914, Marion
7mm	weigh sta nb
5	PA 16, Greencastle, **E** 🅶 Shell/dsl, Sunoco/grill/dsl, TA/Country Pride/dsl/scales/24hr/@ 🍴 Burger King, McDonald's, Taco Bell 🛏 Super 8 🅾 truckwash, Whitetail Ski Resort, **W** 🅶 Exxon/Dunkin'/dsl 🛏 Green Motel 🅾 AutoZone
3	US 11, **E** 🅶 Sunoco/dsl 🍴 Bro's Pizza 🛏 Comfort Inn 🅾 Bowers Tire/auto, **W** 🅶 Sheetz/dsl 🅾 Chevrolet
2mm	Welcome Ctr nb, full 🛗 facilities, litter barrels, petwalk, 🅲, 🛏, vending
1	PA 163, Mason-Dixon Rd, **W** 🍴 Hoffman's Grill 🛏 Stateline Inn 🅾 Keystone RV Ctr
0mm	Pennsylvania/Maryland state line, Mason-Dixon Line

INTERSTATE 83

Exit #	Services
51b a	I-83 begins/ends on I-81, exit 70.
50b a	US 22, Jonestown Rd, Harrisburg, **E** 🅶 Speedway/dsl, Sunoco/dsl, USA 🍴 Applebee's, Arby's, Buffalo Wild Wings, Chipotle Mexican, Cold Stone, Colonial Park Diner, Domino's, El Rodeo Mexican, Five Guys, Gilligan's Grill, Hibachi Grill, LJ Silver, Longhorn Steaks, McDonald's, Mission BBQ, Noodles&Co, Old Country Buffet, Olive Garden, Panera Bread, Pizza Hut, Red Lobster, Red Robin, Shogun Asian, Starbucks, Subway, Taco Bell, Wendy's 🅾 Advance Parts, Aldi Foods, AT&T, AutoZone, Best Buy, BooksAMillion, Boscov's, Costco/gas, Dick's, Ford, Goodyear/auto, Hobby Lobby, Home Depot, Jo-Ann, Kohl's, Marshall's, Meineke, Michael's, NTB, Old Navy, PepBoys, PetCo, Rite Aid, Ross, Shannon Tire/auto, Target, Tires+, U-Haul, Verizon, vet, Weis Foods, William's Tires/repair, **W** 🅶 Sunoco/dsl 🍴 Crave Diner, DQ, Dunkin', Gabriella's Italian, KFC, Roberto's Pizza 🅾 Rite Aid
48	Union Deposit Rd, **E** 🅶 Sunoco 🍴 Arby's, Burger King, Dunkin', Infinito's Buffet, Panera Bread 🛏 Best Western, Hampton Inn 🅾 🏥, $Tree, Giant Foods/gas, Rite Aid, Staples, URGENT CARE, **W** 🅶 Gulf/dsl, Sheetz/dsl, Tesla EVC 🍴 Chipotle, ChuckeCheese, Empire Asian Bistro, Great Wall Chinese, HFC Pizza, IHOP, Jimmy John's, McDonald's, Naples Pizza, New China, Outback Steaks, Rita's Ice Cream, Starbucks, Subway, TX Roadhouse, Waffle House, Wendy's 🛏 Country Inn&Suites,
48	**Continued** EconoLodge, Fairfield Inn, Holiday Inn Express 🅾 $General, $Tree, BigLots, Lowe's, PriceRite Foods, Weis Foods
47	(46b from nb), US 322 E, to Hershey, Derry St, **E** 🅶 Speedway/Dunkin' 🍴 Papa John's, Pizza Hut 🅾 Home Depot, Petsmart
46b a	I-283 S, to I-76/PA Tpk, **services E off I-283** 🅶 Sunoco/dsl 🍴 Bob Evans, Capitol Diner, Chick-fil-A, Chili's, Five Guys, Friendly's, Lancaster Brewing Rest., Leeds Rest., McDonald's, Moe's SW Grill, Subway 🛏 Courtyard, EconoLodge, Howard Johnson, La Quinta, Red Lion Inn, Red Roof Inn, Sheraton, Sleep Inn, Super 8 🅾 $General, GNC, JC Penney, Kia, Petco, Target, Verizon
45	Paxton St, **E** 🅶 Sheetz/dsl 🍴 Applebee's, Burger King, Cafe Fresco, Capt Don's Rest., Dunkin', Fiesta Mexico, Hibachi Buffet, McDonald's, Melting Pot, Papa Joe's Pizza, Pizza Hut, Qdoba, Ruby Tuesday, Starbucks, Tomato Pie Cafe 🛏 Hilton Garden, Homewood Suites, Towneplace Suites 🅾 $Tree, Advance Parts, AutoZone, Bass Pro Shops, Macy's, Meineke, Nissan, Subaru, Toyota
44b	17th St, 19th St, **E** 🅶 Sunoco, Turkey Hill 🍴 Dunkin', Hardee's, Kajimachi Japanese 🅾 Advance Parts, AutoZone, Buick/GMC, Firestone/auto, Honda, Hyundai, Midas
44a	PA 230, 13th St, Harrisburg, **E** 🅾 Family$, **W** 🅾 Chevrolet, VW, downtown
43	2nd St, Harrisburg, **W** 🛏 Crowne Plaza, Hilton 🅾 🏥, st capitol, downtown
42.5mm	Susquehanna River
42	Lemoyne
41b	Highland Park, **E** 🅶 Turkey Hill 🍴 Burger King, KFC, **W** 🅶 Sunoco 🍴 Vito's Italian 🅾 Ace Hardware, Weis Foods
41a	US 15, PA 581 W, to Gettysburg
40b	New Cumberland, **W** 🅶 Gulf/dsl 🍴 Cedar Cliff Pizza, McDonald's, New China, Starbucks, Subway 🅾 $General, CVS Drug
40a	Limekiln Rd, to Lewisberry, **E** 🅶 Shell/dsl, Sunoco 🍴 John's Diner, McDonald's, Pizza Hut 🛏 Budget Inn, Capital Inn, Clarion, Fairfield Inn, Holiday Inn Express, La Quinta, **W** 🅶 Speedway/Dunkin' 🛏 Best Western+, Motel 6, Scottish Inn 🅾 vet
39b	I-76/PA Tpk
39a	PA 114, Lewisberry Rd, **E** 🅶 EVC, Rutter's/dsl 🛏 Days Inn, Highland Inn, Red Carpet Inn
38	Reesers Summit
36	PA 262, Fishing Creek, **E** 🅶 Speedway/Dunkin' 🍴 Bruster's, Culhane's Steaks, Mamma's Pizza 🅾 CVS Drug
35	PA 177, Lewisberry, **E** 🍴 Patriot Pizza/subs, **W** 🅶 Exxon 🍴 Francesco's Pizza, Summit Rest.
34mm	parking area/weigh sta sb
34	Valley Green (from nb), same as 33

PA

gas = gas food = food lodging = lodging other = other Rs = rest stop Copyright 2022 - The Next EXIT

INTERSTATE 83 Cont'd

Exit #	Services
33	PA 392, Yocumtown, **E** Rutter's, Speedway/Dunkin'/dsl Brothers Pizzaria, Burger King, Hong Kong Buffet, KFC/Taco Bell, Maple Donuts, McDonald's, New China Buffet, Subway Value Inn $Tree, Advance Parts, AutoZone, GNC, Rite Aid, Verizon, Walmart/Subway
33mm	parking area/weigh sta nb
32	PA 382, Newberrytown, **E** Rutter's/deli/dsl/24hr, Sunoco/dsl, **W** Exxon/dsl
28	PA 295, Strinestown, **W** Rutter's/24hr 83 Diner, Wendy's
24	PA 238, Emigsville, **W** Sunoco/dsl Four Bros Rest.
22	PA 181, N George St, same as 21b, **E** Rutter's Comfort Inn, Homewood Suites
21b a	US 30, Arsenal Rd, to York, **E** Sheetz/dsl Cheddar's, Clock Diner, Qdoba, Starbucks Days Inn, EconoLodge, Motel 6, Sheraton, Tru Hilton AT&T, Buick/GMC, **W** Dickey's BBQ, Royal Farms/dsl, Rutter's/dsl, Sheetz/dsl Arby's, Bob Evans, Buffalo Wild Wings, Burger King, Chick-fil-A, Chili's, China Buffet, Chipotle, Denny's, Domino's, DQ, Dunkin', El Rodeo Mexican, Friendly's, Fujihana Japanese, Great Wall, Hardee's, Hoss's, Infinito's, Jersey Mike's, Jimmy John's, KFC, Little Caesar's, LJ Silver, Logan's Roadhouse, Lyndon Diner, Maple Donuts, McDonald's, Mission BBQ, MOD Pizza, Old Country Buffet, Olive Garden, Outback Steaks, Panera Bread, Pizza Hut, Quaker Steak, Rita's Custard, Smokey Bones BBQ, Subway, Taco Bell, Wendy's Best Western, La Quinta, Motel 6, Super 8, Wingate Inn $General, $Tree, Advance Parts, Aldi Foods, AutoZone, BJ's Whse/gas, BMW, Cadillac/Chevrolet, Chrysler/Dodge/Jeep, CVS Drug, Giant Foods/gas, Harley-Davidson, Honda, Kia, Kohl's, Lowe's, NTB, Old Navy, PepBoys, PetCo, Petsmart, Ross, Staples, Subaru, Target, TJ Maxx, URGENT CARE, Verizon, Walmart/McDonald's, Weis Foods/gas
19	PA 462, Market St, **E** Rutter's/dsl Applebee's, Arby's, Aroma Buffet, Buffalo Wild Wings, Chick-fil-A, ChuckECheese's, DQ, Dunkin', Fiesta Mexico, Firehouse Subs, Fuddruckers, Guadalajara Mexican, Jimmy John's, KFC, MOD Pizza, Moe's SW, Panera Bread, Papa John's, Red Lobster, Rita's Custard, Starbucks, Taco Bell, Tokyo Diner, Wendy's Quality Inn $General, $Tree, Advance Parts, Aldi Foods, Burlington Coats, Firestone/auto, Giant Foods/gas, Goodyear/auto, Home Depot, Lowe's, Meineke, Nissan, NTB, Petco, Sam's Club/gas, Verizon, Volvo, Walgreens, Walmart, Weis Mkt, **W** H
18	PA 124, Mt Rose Ave, Prospect St, **E** Rutters Arooga's Grille, Burger King, Five Guys, Nino's Pizza, Parma Pizza Grill, Pizza Hut $Tree, Grocery Outlet, Nello Tire
16b a	PA 74, Queen St, **E** Sunoco Baskin-Robbins/Dunkin', Cracker Barrel, IHOP, Imperial Gourmet, Isaac's Rest., JJ Panda, John's Pizza Shop, Maple Donuts, MOD Pizza, Primanti Bros, Starbucks, Stone Grille Country Inn&Suites, Hampton Inn, Home 2 Suites Giant Foods/gas, **W** Sheetz/dsl Chipotle, Infinito's Pizza, Jersey Mike's, Jimmy John's, Little Caesar's, McDonald's, Noodles&Co, Panera Bread, Pizza Hut/Taco Bell, Starbucks, Subway, Wendy's $General, $Tree, AT&T, CVS Drug, Jo-Ann Fabrics, Monro, Price Rite Foods, Tuesday Morning, vet, Walgreens, Weis Mkt
15	S George St, I-83 spur into York, **W** H
14	PA 182, Leader Heights, **E** Sheetz/dsl, Tesla EVC Arby's, Domino's, First Wok, Subway vet, **W** Rutter's McDonald's Holiday Inn Express Rite Aid
10	PA 214, Loganville, **W** Rutter's/dsl Mamma's Pizza Midway Motel st police, TrueValue
8	PA 216, Glen Rock, **W** Shrewsbury Mkt (2mi)

Exit #	Services
4	PA 851, Shrewsbury, **E** Tom's/dsl/24hr Bill Bateman Grill, Burger King, Cracker Barrel, Papa John's, Ruby Tuesda Hampton Inn Home Depot, TrueValue, **W** Exxon dsl Arby's, Chick-fil-A, Chipotle, Coachlight Rest., Emera Garden Chinese, Five Guys, KFC/Taco Bell, McDonald's, Pane Bread, Rita's Custard, Sons of Italy Pizzaria, Starbucks, Subwa Wendy's $Tree, AAA, Advance Parts, Giant Foods, GNC, N Tire, Saubel's Foods, Verizon, Walmart
2mm	Welcome Ctr nb, full facilities, litter barrels, petwalk, vending
0mm	Pennsylvania/Maryland state line

INTERSTATE 84

Exit #	Services
54mm	Pennsylvania/New York state line, Delaware River
53	US 6, PA 209, Matamoras, **Welcome Ctr/both lanes, full facilities, litter barrels, petwalk, , , vending, N** Go2 Shell, TurkeyHill/dsl The Grill, Two Rivers Grille App Inn AutoZone, fireworks, PriceChopper, **S** Sunoco/d Dunkin', Goodfella's Italian, McDonald's, Peking Garde Perkins, Roy Rogers, Subway, Taco Bell, Village Diner, Wayba Burger, Wendy's Best Western, Hampton Inn, Scottish Ir $Tree, Advance Parts, Home Depot, Lowe's, Mavis Tire auto, Staples, Tristate RV Park, Verizon, Walmart/Subway
46	US 6, to Milford, **N** Sunoco/dsl, 0-2 mi **S** Exxon/dsl, Gu TurkeyHill Apple Valley Rest., Chang Mao Chinese, Chir Buffet, Dimmick Inn Steaks Rodeway Inn Key Food Mk NAPA, Rite Aid, USPO
34	PA 739, to Lords Valley, Dingmans Ferry, **S** Mirabito/dsl, S noco/Dunkin'/dsl Bruno Pizza, McDonald's, Panda Chines Portobello's Family$, Rite Aid, Weis Foods
30	PA 402, to Blooming Grove, **N** st police, to Lake Walle paupack
26	PA 390, to Tafton, **N** Exxon/dsl Tanglewood Ski Are (4mi), to Lake Wallenpaupack, **S** to Promised Land SP
26mm	Rs/weigh sta both lanes, full facilities, litter barrels, pe walk, , , vending
20	PA 507, Greentown, **N** Exxon/dsl, Sunoco/Subwa John's Italian Animal Park (5mi)
17	PA 191, to Newfoundland, Hamlin, **N** Howe's/Exxon/ds scales/24hr Twin Rocks Diner Comfort Inn dsl repai
8	PA 247, PA 348, Mt Cobb, **N** Gulf/dsl, Sunoco/Burger King Tim Hortons/dsl $General
4	I-380 S, to Mount Pocono
2	PA 435 S, to Elmhurst
1	Tigue St, **N** Holiday Inn, **S** Valero/dsl
0mm	I-84 begins/ends on I-81, exit 54.

INTERSTATE 90

Exit #	Services
46mm	Pennsylvania/New York state line, **Welcome Ctr/weigh sta w full facilities, litter barrels, petwalk, , , vending**
45	US 20, to State Line, **N** KwikFill/dsl/scales McDonald's, Shell/Subway/dsl Red Carpet Inn fireworks, Niaga Falls Info
41	PA 89, North East, **N** Shell/repair New Harvest Res Holiday Inn Express, **S** Creekside Camping (4mi)
37	I-86 E, to Jamestown
35	PA 531, to Harborcreek, **N** TA/Country Pride/Pizza Hut/Su way/dsl/scales/24hr/@ Blue Beacon, dsl repair
32	PA 430, PA 290, to Wesleyville, **N** Country Fair, GetGo/dsl
29	PA 8, to Hammett, **N** Country Fair Wendy's H Best Value dsl repair

INTERSTATE 90 Cont'd

Exit #	Services
27	PA 97, State St, Waterford, N 🅖 Country Fair/dsl 🅕 Arby's, Barbato's Italian, Doc Holiday's Grill, McDonald's 🅛 Days Inn, La Quinta, Motel 6, Red Roof Inn 🅞 🅗, S 🅖 ⛽Pilot/Subway/ dsl/scales/24hr, Sheetz/dsl, Shell/Tim Hortons/dsl 🅕 Taco Bell 🅛 Baymont Inn, Quality Inn, Super 8 🅞 $General, casino
24	US 19, Peach St, to Waterford, N 🅖 Country Fair/dsl, Delta Sonic/Subway, GetGo/dsl, KwikFill, Tesla EVC 🅕 Applebee's, Burger King, Chick-fil-A, Chipotle Mexican, ChuckeCheese, Cracker Barrel, Dunkin', Eat'n Park, Five Guys, Golden Corral, KFC, Krispy Kreme, Longhorn Steaks, McDonald's, Olive Garden, Panera Bread, Quaker Steak&Lube, S&S Buffet, Starbucks, Steak'n Shake, Taco Bell, TGIFriday's, Tim Hortons, Torero's Mexican, TX Roadhouse 🅛 Courtyard, Hilton Garden 🅞 🅗, $Tree, Advance Parts, Aldi Foods, AT&T, Best Buy, Hobby Lobby, Home Depot, Jo-Ann Fabrics, Kohl's, Lowe's, Marshall's, Old Navy, Petsmart, Sam's Club/gas, Staples, Target, URGENT CARE, Verizon, Walmart/Subway, Wegman's Foods, S 🅖 Country Fair, Shell/Subway 🅕 Blotto's Grill, Bob Evans, IHOP 🅛 Best Western+, Comfort Inn, Country Inn&Suites, Hampton Inn, Holiday Inn Express, Home 2 Suites, Microtel, Residence Inn, Solstice Inn, Wingate Inn 🅞 waterpark
22b a	I-79, N to Erie, S to Pittsburgh, 3-5 mi N services in Erie
18	PA 832, Sterrettania, N 🅖 Marathon/dsl 🅞 Presque Passage RV Park, to Presque Isle SP, Waldameer Park (8mi), S 🅕 Beechwood Rest. 🅛 Quality Inn 🅞 golf, KOA, West Haven RV Park/camping
16	PA 98, to Franklin Center, Fairview, S 🅞 Follys Camping (2mi), Mar-Da-Jo-Dy Camping (5mi)
9	PA 18, to Girard, Platea, N 🅞 Fiesler's Service/repair/tires, st police, S 🅛 Green Roof Inn (2mi)
6	PA 215, to Albion, East Springfield, N 🅛 lodging
3	US 6N, to Cherry Hill, West Springfield, N 🅛 lodging on US 20
2.5mm	🆁🆂/weigh sta eb, full 🅗 facilities, info, litter barrels, petwalk, 🅒, 🛏, vending
0mm	Pennsylvania/Ohio state line

ERIE

INTERSTATE 95

Exit #	Services
	Pennsylvania/New Jersey state line, Delaware River. I-276 runs eb to NJ TPK.
42(I-95)	US 13, Delaware Valley, N 🅖 🅕 Dallas Diner, McDonald's 🅛 Motel 6 🅞 7-11, auto repair, U-Haul, S 🅖 G Fuel, LukOil/dsl, Sunoco/dsl, Valero/dsl, WaWa/dsl 🅕 Burger King, Dunkin', Golden Eagle Diner, Italian Family Pizza, Porfirio's Pizza 🅛 Rodeway Inn, Villager Lodge 🅞 $General, Meineke
40	(from nb) I-295 N, to NJ. I-95 N merges with PA Tpk/276 to NJ Tpk
39	PA 413, I-276, to Bristol Bridge, Burlington
37	PA 132, to Street Rd, W 🅖 BP/dsl, Liberty, Sunoco/dsl 🅕 Burger King, Chick-fil-A, China Sun Buffet, Dunkin', Golden Corral, Krispy Kreme, Little Caesar's, McDonald's, Popeye's, TX Roadhouse, Wendy's 🅞 $General, Advance Parts, Aldi Foods, GNC, Goodyear/auto, PepBoys, U-Haul, Walgreens, WaWa
35	PA 63, to US 13, Woodhaven Rd, Bristol Park, W 🅖 BP/Dunkin', Sunoco/dsl 🅕 Arby's, Bob Evans, Boston Mkt, Burger King, Dunkin', Grand China Buffet, KFC, McDonald's, Old Haven Pizza, Pizza Hut, Rita's Custard, Taco Bell, Wendy's 🅛 Holiday Inn Express 🅞 🅗, $Tree, Acme Foods, Dick's, Home Depot, Marshall's, NTB, TJ Maxx, Verizon, Walmart, WaWa
32	Academy Rd, W 🅖 Lukoil 🅕 Dunkin', KFC, McDonald's 🅞 🅗, AutoZone

PHILADELPHIA AREA

Exit #	Services
30	PA 73, Cottman Ave, W 🅖 Sunoco
27	Bridge St, W 🅖 7-11, Citgo/dsl, Exxon, Lukoil 🅕 Dunkin' 🅞 🅗, Rite Aid
26	to NJ 90, Betsy Ross Br, W 🅖 BP/Dunkin', Speedway, Sunoco/dsl, WaWa/dsl 🅕 Applebee's, Boston Mkt, Burger King, Chick-fil-A, KFC, McDonald's, Sonic, Taco Bell, Wendy's 🅞 $Tree, Advance Parts, Home Depot, Lowe's, Rite Aid, ShopRite Foods, Target, Walmart
25	Allegheny Ave, W 🅖 Sunoco/dsl 🅞 🅗, WaWa
23	Lehigh Ave, Girard Ave, E 🅞 casino, W 🅖 Exxon 🅕 Applebee's, Arby's, Coldstone, Dunkin', Rita's Custard 🅞 🅗, $Tree, AutoZone, CVS Drug, GNC, PepBoys, Rite Aid, WaWa/dsl
22	I-676, US 30, to Central Philadelphia, Independence Hall
20	Columbus Blvd, Penns Landing, 1-2 mi E on Columbus 🅖 BP, Liberty/WaWa/dsl 🅕 Burger King, Chick-fil-A, ChuckECheese, Dunkin', Famous Dave's BBQ, IHOP, Longhorn Steaks, McDonald's, Ruby Buffet, Wendy's 🅛 Holiday Inn Express 🅞 $Tree, Acme Mkt, AT&T, Best Buy, GNC, Home Depot, IKEA, Lowe's, Marshall's, Old Navy, PepBoys, Staples, Target, Verizon, Walmart, 1-2 mi W on Columbus 🅛 Marriott
19	I-76 E, to Walt Whitman Bridge, W 🅖 BP, Liberty, Sunoco/dsl 🅕 Dunkin', KFC, Little Caesar's, McDonald's, Popeye's 🅞 $General, Aldi Foods, to stadiums
17	PA 611, to Broad St, Pattison Ave, W 🅞 🅗, to Naval Shipyard, to stadium
15mm	Schuykill River
15	Enterprise Ave, Island Ave (from sb)
14	Bartram Ave, Essington Ave (from sb)
13	PA 291, to I-76 W (from nb), to Central Philadelphia, E 🅛 Aloft, Doubletree, Hawthorn Suites, Marriott, Renaissance Inn, Sheraton Four Points, Sheraton Suites, W 🅛 Residence Inn
12	Philadelphia Intl Airport, E services same as 10
10	PA 291, Bartrom Ave, (from nb), Cargo City, E 🅛 Marriott, Renaissance Hotel, W 🅖 WaWa/dsl 🅕 Ruby Tuesday 🅛 Courtyard, Embassy Suites, Extended Stay America, Extended Stay America, Fairfield Inn, Hampton Inn, Microtel 🅞 Heinz NWR
9b a	PA 420, to Essington, Prospect Park, E 🅖 Sunoco/dsl, Valero/dsl 🅕 Denny's, Lehmans Rest., Mel's Diner, Philly Diner 🅛 Clarion, La Quinta, Motel 6, Red Roof+, SpringHill Suites, Wyndham Garden 🅞 USPO, WaWa
8	to Chester Waterfront, Ridley Park, E 🅖 Royal Farms 🅕 Cracker Barrel, Wendy's 🅛 Microtel, SpringHill Suites, on US 13, W 🅕 Stargate Diner
7	I-476 N, to Plymouth, Meeting
6	PA 352, PA 320, to Edgmont Ave, E 🅕 McDonald's, Popeye's 🅞 $General, $Tree, AT&T, AutoZone, Shoprite, Walmart/Subway, W 🅛 Days Inn
5	Kerlin St (from nb), E 🅖 Sunoco

PA

🏔 INTERSTATE 95 Cont'd

Exit #	Services
4	US 322 E, to NJ, to Barry Bridge, **W** 🛏 Highland Motel
3	(from nb, no EZ return)US 322 W, Highland Ave, **E** 🅟 Sunoco/dsl 🅞 $General, Ford, Goodyear
2	PA 452, to US 322, Market St, **W** 🅟 Exxon/dsl, Royal Farms/dsl 🍴 Dunkin', McDonald's, Subway
1	Chichester Ave, **E** 🅟 Sunoco 🅞 fireworks, **W** 🍴 Dunkin' 🅞 transmissions, WaWa
0mm	Pennsylvania/Delaware state line, **Welcome Ctr/weigh sta nb, full ♿ facilities, litter barrels, petwalk,** 🅒, 🖼

🏔 INTERSTATE 99

Exit #	Services
85	**I-99 begins/ends on I-80, exit 161.**
83	PA 350, Bellefonte, **E** 🅟 Tesla EVC, Weis Foods/gas 🍴 Wendy's, **W** 🅟 Lyken's Mkt 🍴 Burger King, Pizza Hut, Sammi's Rest. 🅞 Rite Aid, TrueValue
81	PA 26 S, to PA 64, to Pleasant Gap
80	Harrison Rd (from nb, no re-entry)
78b a	PA 150, to Bellafonte, **W** 🅟 Sheetz/dsl 🍴 Dunkin' 🛏 EconoLodge 🅞 auto repair, Ford
76	Shiloh Rd, **E** 🅟 Sheetz/dsl 🍴 McDonald's, Perkins, Quaker Steak, Rey Azteca 🛏 Best Western+, Ramada 🅞 $Tree, AAA, Advance Parts, Barnes&Noble, BigLots, Chevrolet, Jo-Ann Fabrics, Ross, Sam's Club, Subaru, Walmart/Subway
74	Innovation Park, Beaver Stadium, Penn State U
73	US 322 E, Lewiston, State College
71	Woodycrest, Tofftrees, **E** 🅟 Sheetz/dsl 🍴 Applebee's, Chick-fil-A, Cracker Barrel, McDonald's, Olive Garden, Outback Steaks, Panda Express, Qdoba, Red Lobster, Starbucks, TX Roadhouse 🛏 Hampton Inn, Holiday Inn Express, SpringHill Suites 🅞 $Tree, Best Buy, Dick's, Kohl's, Michael's, PetCo, Target, Verizon, Walmart, Wegman's Foods, **W** 🍴 Down Under Cafe 🛏 Carnegie Inn, Toftrees Golf Resort
69	US 322 E, Valley Vista Dr, **E** 🅟 Sheetz/dsl 🅞 Home Depot, Lowe's
68	Skytop Mtn Rd, Grays Woods, Waddle
62	US 322 W, to Phillipsburg (from sb)
61	to US 322 W, Port Matilda, **E** 🅟 Lykens Mkt/Sub Express/dsl 🍴 Brother's Pizza 🛏 Port Matilda Hotel 🅞 USPO
52	PA 350, **W** 🅟 Snappy's/Subway/dsl
48	PA 453, Tyrone, **W** 🅟 Sheetz/dsl 🍴 Burger King, Nino's Pizza, Subway 🅞 🏥, Advance Parts, USPO
45	Tipton, Grazierville, **W** 🅟 Rossi's 🅞 🏥, DelGrosso's Funpark, Ford
41	PA 865 N, Bellwood, **E** 🅞 Ft Roberdeau HS (6mi), **W** 🅟 Martin Gen Store/dsl, Sheetz/dsl 🅞 DelGrosso's Funpark (3 mi)
39	PA 764 S, Pinecroft, **W** 🛏 Comfort Inn, Days Inn, Elizabeth Rest B&B 🅞 Martin's Foods, Oak Spring Winery
33	17th St, same as 32, Altoona, **W** 🅟 Sheetz/dsl 🅞 Aldi Foods, Lowe's, Railroader Museum, U-Haul
32	PA 36, Frankstown Rd, Altoona, **E** 🅟 GetGo, Sheetz/dsl 🍴 Chili's, Chipotle, DQ, Panera Bread, Subway, TX Roadhouse 🅞 Barnes&Noble, Best Buy, Boscov's, Canoe Cr SP, Dick's, Giant Eagle Foods, GNC, Home Depot, Kohl's, Michael's, PetCo, Ross, Staples, Verizon, **W** 🅟 Sheetz/dsl 🍴 ChuckeCheese, Dunkin', El Campesino Mexican, Five Guys, Honeybaked Ham, McDonald's, Olive Garden, Papa John's, Perkins, Pizza Hut, Popeye's, Red Lobster, Subway, Wendy's 🛏 EconoLodge,

Exit #	Services
32	Continued Quality Inn, Super 8 🅞 🏥, $Tree, AT&T, AutoZone, Chrysler Dodge/Jeep, CVS Drug, Jo-Ann Fabrics, Nissan, O'Reilly Parts, Rite Aid, Save-A-Lot, URGENT CARE, USPO, Walgreens
31	Plank Rd, Altoona, **E** 🍴 Chick-fil-A, Dunkin', Jethro's Rest, King's Rest., Outback Steaks 🛏 Altoona Grand Hotel, Courtyard, Holiday Inn Express 🅞 Field&Stream, Firestone/auto, Petco, Sam's Club/gas, st police, Target, TJ Maxx, Walmart/McDonald's, **W** 🍴 Applebee's, Arby's, Bob Evans, Burger King, Casa Valadez, Champs Grill, Chinese Gourmet, Cracker Barrel, Denny's, Eat'n Park, KFC, Little Caesar's, LJ Silver, Longhorn Steaks, Panda Express, Red Robin, Taco Bell 🛏 Hampton Inn, Motel 6 🅞 Advance Parts, BigLots, Buick/GMC, Hobby Lobby, JC Penney, Macy's, Martin's/gas, Monro, Verizon, Weis Foods
28	US 22, to Ebensburg, Holidaysburg
23	PA 36, PA 164, Roaring Spring, Portage, **E** 🅟 GetGo/dsl, Sheetz/24hr, Turkey Hill 🅞 🏥, truck repair, Walmart/Subway
15	Claysburg, King, Claysburg, King, **W** 🅟 Sheetz/dsl 🅞 $General
10	to Imler, **W** 🍴 Slick's Ivy Stone Rest. (2mi) 🅞 Blue Knob S (8mi)
7	PA 869, Osterburg, St Clairsville, **W** 🍴 Slick's Ivy Stone Res (2mi) 🅞 Blue Knob SP
3	PA 56, Johnstown, Cessna, **E** 🅞 st police, truck parts
1	I-70/76, **E** 🅟 GetGo/McDonald's/dsl, Pacific Pride/dsl, Sheetz/dsl, Shell/Subway/dsl 🍴 Arby's, Bedford Diner, Denny's, Ed Steaks, Hoss' Rest, Pizza Hut, Taco Bell, Wendy's 🛏 Budget Host, Fairfield Inn, Hampton Inn, Quality Inn, Rodeway Inn, Super 8

I-99 begins/ends on US 220.

🏔 INTERSTATE 295

Exit #	Services
10mm	Pennsylvania/New Jersey state line, Delaware River
10	PA 32, to New Hope, **W** 🅞 Washington Crossing Hist Park
9mm	**Welcome Ctr sb, full ♿ facilities, litter barrels, petwalk,** 🅒, 🖼 **vending**
8	PA 332, to Yardley, Newtown, **W** 🍴 Dunkin' 🛏 Hampton In 🅞 🏥, to Tyler SP
5b a	US 1, W to I-276/PA TPK, Langhorne, Oxford Valley, **W** 🅞 🏥
3	US 1 bus, to PA 413, Penndel, Levittown, **E** 🅟 Shell/7-11/dsl 🍴 Arrano Hibachi Steaks, ChuckECheese's, Dunkin', Friendly's, Hong Kong Pearl, Olive Garden, Panera Bread, Red Lobster, Ruby Tuesday, Subway, Uncle Bill's Homestyle, Wendy's 🅞 $Tree, Acura, Chevrolet, Chrysler/Dodge/Jeep, Firestone/auto, Ford, Goodyear/auto, Harley-Davidson, Honda, Hyundai, Kia, Lowe's, Marshall's, Redner's Whse Mkt, Sam's Club, Subaru, Subaru, Target, VW/Volvo, **W** 🍴 Denny's, McDonald's 🅞 🏥, Toyota, U-Haul

I-295 begins/ends on I-276/I-95/PA Tpk

🏔 INTERSTATE 476

Exit #	Services
131	US 11, US 6. **I-476 begins/ends on I-81. Services same as I-81 exit 194.**
122	Keyser Ave, Old Forge, Taylor
121mm	toll plaza
115	I-81, PA 315, Wyoming Valley, Pittston, **W** 🅟 Exxon/Subway/dsl, 🍴/Wendy's/dsl/scales/24hr, Sunoco/dsl 🍴 Arby's, Burger King, Denny's, McDonald's, Perkins 🛏 Holiday Inn Express, Knight's Inn 🅞 Volvo, Walmart/Subway

INTERSTATE 476 Cont'd

Exit #	Services
112mm	toll plaza
105	PA 115, Wilkes-Barre, Bear Creek, E 🅿 Exxon, Mobil 🍴 Dunkin'
95	I-80, PA 940, Pocono, Hazleton, W 🅿 WaWa 🍴 Arby's, Burger King, McDonald's 🛏 Comfort Inn, EconoLodge, Holiday Inn Express, Mtn Laurel Resort, Pocono Inn/Resort, Quality Inn, Split Rock Resort
87	PA 903, Jim Thorpe (tag holder only)
86mm	**Hickory Run Service Plaza both lanes,** 🅿 Sunoco/dsl 🍴 Burger King, Jamba Juice, Quizno's, Starbucks
74	US 209, Mahoning Valley, Lehighton, Stroudsburg, W 🍴 Citgo, Shell/Subway/dsl 🛏 Country Inn&Suites, Hampton Inn
71mm	Lehigh Tunnel
56	I-78, US 22, PA 309, Lehigh Valley, E 🅿 Tesla EVC 🍴 China House, Dunkin', Jamba Juice, Moe's SW, Red Robin, Subway, Trivet Diner, Wendy's, Zio's Pizza 🛏 Parkview Inn 🅾 BMW/ Mini, Lexus, Maserati, Staples, Tuesday Morning, on US 22, W 🅿 Exxon, Trexler Plaza 🍴 Chris Rest., Potsy Pizza 🛏 Holiday Inn Express, Motel 6 🅾 CVS Drug, Dan's Auto Repair, Jaguar, Land Rover, S 🍴 Dunkin'
56mm	**Allentown Service Plaza both lanes,** 🅿 Sunoco/dsl 🍴 Famiglia Pizza, Hershey's Ice Cream, Roy Rogers, Starbucks
44	PA 663, Quakertown, Pottstown, E 🅿 BP, Exxon/Subway/dsl, Wawa/dsl 🍴 Caitlyn&Cody's Diner, Dunkin', Faraco's Pizza 🛏 Hampton Inn, Holiday Inn Express, Quality Inn, SpringHill Suites 🅾 🎗

Exit #	Services
31	PA 63, Lansdale, E 🅿 Lukoil, Royal Farms 🍴 Margaritas Mexican, Osaka Japanese, The Mill Rest. 🛏 Courtyard, Holiday Inn 🅾 🎗, USPO, Walgreens, WaWa
20	Germantown Pike W, to I-276 W, PA Tpk W
19	Germantown Pike E
18b a	(18 from sb), Conshoshocken, Norristown, E 🅿 Lukoil, Sunoco 🍴 Andy's Diner, Burger King, Cracker Barrel, Domino's, Dunkin', Five Guys, Illiano's Pizza, McDonald's, Outback Steaks, Panera Bread, Qdoba, Rita's Ice Cream, Ruby Tuesday, Salad Works, Starbucks, Tony Roni Pizza 🛏 Hampton Inn 🅾 AT&T, Barnes&Noble, Best Buy, Dick's, Giant Foods, Lowe's, Marshall's, Old Navy, Petsmart, REI, Rite Aid, Ross, Target, Toyota, Verizon, Weis Mkt, W 🍴 Papa John's, Uno, Wendy's 🅾 Audi, BJ's Whse, Ford, Home Depot, Honda, Hyundai, IKEA, Kia, Mazda, Michael's, Nissan, Porsche
16b a	(16 from sb), I-76, PA 23, to Philadelpia, Valley Forge
13	US 30, E 🅿 Liberty 🍴 Campus Pizza, First Watch Cafe, Nova Grill, Snap Kitchen, Starbucks, Winger's 🅾 🎗, to Villanova U, USPO
9	PA 3, BrooUpper Darby, E 🍴 Barnaby's Rest. 🅾🎗 URGENT CARE
5	US 1, Lima, Springfield, E 🍴 Chipotle, Hibachi Japanese, Smashburger, Subway 🅾 AT&T, Giant Foods, Jo-Ann Fabrics, Marshall's, Old Navy, Staples, Verizon, Walmart
3	Baltimore Pike, Media, Swarthmore, E 🅿 Mobil/dsl 🍴 Carrabba's, Dunkin', Olive Garden, Outback Steaks, Panera Bread, Qdoba, Ruby Tuesday, Starbucks 🅾 🎗, Macy's, Swarthmore Coll, Target
1	McDade Blvd, E 🅿 Exxon 🍴 Dunkin', McDonald's, Panda Chinese 🅾 $Tree, CVS Drug
0mm	**I-476 begins/ends on I-95, exit 7.**

RHODE ISLAND

INTERSTATE 95

Exit #	Services
43mm	Rhode Island/Massachusetts state line
30(42)	East St, to Central Falls, E 🍴 Dunkin', Subway
29(41)	US 1, Cottage St, W 🍴 d'Angelo
28(40)	RI 114, School St, E 🅿 Sunoco 🅾 🎗, to hist dist, Yarn Outlet
27(39)	US 1, RI 15, Pawtucket, W 🅿 EVC, Shell/repair/dsl, Sunoco/dsl/24hr 🍴 Burger King, Dunkin', Murphy's Law 🛏 Hampton Inn
26(38)	RI 122, Lonsdale Ave (from nb), E 🅾 U-Haul
25(37)	US 1, RI 126, N Main St, Providence, E 🅿 Shell/dsl, Speedway/dsl 🍴 Chili's, Dunkin', Gregg's Rest. 🅾 🎗, $Tree, Firestone/auto, PepBoys, Walgreens, W 🅿 Speedway 🍴 Burger King, Chelo's Rest. 🅾 Aamco
24(36.5)	Branch Ave, Providence, W 🅿 Stop&Shop/gas 🍴 Wendy's 🅾 Home Depot, Stop&Shop, URGENT CARE, Walmart/Subway, downtown
23(36)	RI 146, RI 7, Providence, E 🅿 Mobil/dsl 🛏 Marriott, W 🅾 🎗, USPO
22(35.5)	US 6, RI 10, Providence, E 🍴 Cheesecake Factory, Dave&Buster's, Fleming's Steaks, Panera Bread, PF Chang's 🅾 CVS Drug, Macy's
21(35)	Broadway St, Providence, E 🍴 Starbucks 🛏 Hilton
20(34.5)	I-195, to E Providence, Cape Cod
19(34)	Eddy St, Allens Ave, to US 1, W 🍴 Dunkin', Wendy's 🅾🎗
18(33.5)	US 1A, Thurbers Ave, W 🅿 Shell/dsl 🍴 Burger King 🅾🎗
17(33)	US 1 (from sb), Elmwood Ave, W 🍴 Dunkin' 🅾 Tires Whse, USPO
16(32.5)	RI 10, Cranston, E 🅾 Williams Zoo/park

Exit #	Services
15(32)	Jefferson Blvd, E 🅿 Mobil 🍴 Dunkin', Shogun Steaks 🛏 Courtyard, La Quinta, Motel 6, W 🅾 Ryder Trucks
14(31)	RI 37, Post Rd, to US 1, W 🅿 Shell/dsl 🍴 Burger King 🅾 Aldi, CVS Drug, Ford/Lincoln, Mazda, Volvo
13(30)	TF Green Airport Connector Rd, E 🅿 Shell, Sunoco/Dunkin' 🍴 Bertucci's, Chelo's Grill, Chipotle, HoneyDew Donuts, IHOP, Subway, Tuscan Grille, Wendy's 🛏 Best Western, ExtendedStay

🅿 = gas   🍴 = food   🛏 = lodging   🅾 = other   Rs = rest stop   Copyright 2022 - The Next EXIT

⬆N INTERSTATE 95 Cont'd

13(30)	Continued
	America, Fairfield Inn, Hampton Inn, Hilton Garden, Holiday Inn Express, Homewood Suites, Radisson, Sheraton, Sonesta Suites 🅾 TF Green Airport
12b(29)	RI 2, I-295 N (from sb)
12a	RI 113 E, to Warwick, E 🅿 Shell/Dunkin'/dsl 🛏 Crowne Plaza Hotel 🅾 Lowe's, Stop&Shop, W 🅿 Sunoco 🍴 BJ's Rest., ChuckeCheese, On the Border, Wendy's 🅾 Kohl's, Walmart/Subway
11(29)	I-295 N (exits left from nb), to Woonsocket
10b a(28)	RI 117, to Warwick, W 🅾 H
9(25)	RI 4 S, E Greenwich
8b a(24)	RI 2, E Greenwich, E 🅿 Shell/dsl, Tesla EVC 🍴 Dunkin', McDonald's, Outback Steaks, Panera Bread, PieZone Pizza, TX Roadhouse 🛏 Extended Stay America 🅾 AT&T, CVS Drug, Dave's Mkt, 0-2 mi W 🅿 Sunoco/dsl 🍴 Applebee's, Carrabba's, Chick-fil-A, Chili's, Denny's, Dunkin', Five Guys, KFC, Moe's SW, Olive Garden, PapaGino's Pizza, Smokey Bones BBQ, Starbucks, TGIFriday's, Wendy's 🛏 SpringHill Suites 🅾 Acura, Aldi Foods, Arlington RV Ctr, Audi/Bentley/BMW/Inifinti/Lexus/Mini/Porsche, Barnes&Noble, Best Buy, Cadillac, Home Depot, Honda, Jaguar, Jo-Ann Fabrics, Land Rover, Lowe's, Mercedes, Michael's, Nissan, PepBoys, Petco, Petsmart, Staples, Stop&Shop/gas, Subaru, Target, vet, VW
7(21)	to Coventry, E 🅿 Mobil/dsl, W 🅿 Cumberland/dsl 🍴 Applebee's, Cracker Barrel, Denny's, Dunkin', McDonald's, Wendy's 🛏 Hampton Inn, Holiday Inn Express, Residence Inn 🅾 BJ's Whse/gas, CVS Drug, Firestone/auto, GNC, Home Depot, URGENT CARE, Verizon, Walmart/Subway
6a(20)	Hopkins Hill Rd, W 🍴 Dunkin' 🅾 park&ride
6(18)	RI 3, to Coventry, W 🅿 Petro, Shell/dsl/24hr, Sunoco/dsl 🍴 Dunkin', Gentleman Farmer Diner, Subway, Wicked Good Pizza 🛏 Best Western, Super 8 🅾 $General, TrueValue, vet
5b a(15)	RI 102, W 🅿 TA/Shell/Popeye's/dsl/scales/24hr 🍴 Dan's Rest. 🛏 Classic Motor Lodge
10mm	parking area both lanes
4(9)	RI 3, to RI 165 (from nb), Arcadia, W 🅾 Arcadia SP, camping
3b a(7)	RI 138 E, to Kingston, Wyoming, E 🍴 Dunkin', McDonald's, Village Pizza, Wendy's 🅾 Rite Aid, Stop&Shop/gas, vet, W 🅿 Cumberland/dsl, Mobil/Dunkin' 🍴 Bali Village Chinese, Dragon Palace, Subway, Wood River Inn Rest. 🛏 Stagecoach House B&B 🅾 $General, CVS Drug, Family$, NAPA, USPO
6mm	Welcome Ctr/weigh sta nb, full facilities
2(4)	Hope Valley
1(1)	RI 3, to Hopkinton, Westerly, E 🅾 H, beaches, RV camping, to Misquamicut SP
0mm	Rhode Island/Connecticut state line

⬆N INTERSTATE 295 (Providence)

Exit #	Services
4b a(4)	I-95, N to Boston, S to Providence. **I-295 begins/ends on I-95, exit 4 in MA. Exits 2-1 are in MA.**
2b a(2)	US 1, E 🅿 Mobil/Dunkin'/dsl 🍴 99 Rest., Chicago Grill, Chick-fil-A, Chipotle, ChuckeCheese, d'angelo, Five Guys, Friendly's, Longhorn Steaks, Moe's SW, Panera Bread, PapaGino's Italian, Ruby Tuesday, Smashburger, TGIFriday's 🅾 $Tree, AT&T, Best Buy, BJ's Whse, Buick/Chevrolet/GMC, CVS Drug, Dick's, Firestone/auto, JC Penney, Jo-Ann Fabrics, Lowe's, Macy's,

2b a(2)	Continued
	Marshall's, Michael's, Old Navy, Petco, Petsmart, Staple Stop&Shop/gas, Target, Verizon, Walmart/Dunkin', W 🍴 Gu Shell/dsl 🍴 Applebee's, Dunkin' 🛏 Holiday Inn Expres Knights Inn, Pineapple Inn 🅾 CarMax, CVS Drug, Nissan, Sub aru, Toyota
0mm	Rhode Island/Massachusetts state line. Exits 1-2 are in MA.
22(24)	RI 114, to Cumberland, E 🅿 Shell/dsl, Sunoco 🍴 Dunki HoneyDew Donuts 🅾 CVS Drug, Dave's Foods, USPO, W 🍴 Deli, Saki's Pizza/subs 🅾 Diamond Hill SP
20(21)	RI 122, E 🅿 Gulf 🍴 Bollywood Grill, Burger King, Dunki McDonald's 🅾 Verizon, W 🍴 Fortune House Chinese, Hone Dew Donuts, Paradise Pointe, Subway 🅾 AAA, Ace Hardwar CVS Drug, Rite Aid, Seabra Foods, URGENT CARE
20mm	Blackstone River
19.5mm	Rs nb, full facilities, weigh sta
18b a(19)	RI 146, Woonsocket, Lincoln, E 🅿 EVC, Sunoco/dsl 🍴 Asia Grill, Chili's, Dunkin', Five Guys, McDonald's, Panera Brea Starbucks 🛏 Courtyard 🅾 $Tree, AT&T, GNC, Marshall Stop&Shop/gas, Target
15b a(16)	RI 7, N Smithfield, E 🍴 Terrazza Ristorante 🛏 Home, Suites, W 🅿 7-11/dsl 🍴 Biagio's Pizza, Dunkin', Parent Rest. 🛏 Hampton Inn, Holiday Inn Express 🅾 Smith-Apple House
12b a(13)	US 44, Centerdale, E 🅿 Speedway 🍴 Cancun Mexica Dunkin', Parma Ristorante 🅾 H, NAPA, repair, W 🅿 Exxo dsl, Mobil, Shell/dsl 🍴 Applebee's, Burger King, Chelo's Gr Chicago Grill, Chili's, Chipotle, D'angelo, Domino's, Dunki KFC/Taco Bell, McDonald's, Panera Bread, PapaGino's, Soni Starbucks, Subway, TinTsin Chinese, Yamato Steaks 🅾 $Tre AT&T, Barnes&Noble, CVS Drug, Dave's Foods, Dick' Home Depot, Kohl's, Michael's, Old Navy, Rite Aid, Staple Stop&Shop, Target, TJ Maxx, to Powder Mill Ledges WR, U GENT CARE, Verizon
10	RI 5, Greenville Ave
9c(10)	US 6, to Providence, E 🅿 Shell/Dunkin' 🍴 Atwood Grill, Bur er King, Denny's, Dunkin', Five Guys, Hei Place, Jersey Mike KFC, Popeye's, Smashburger, Starbucks, Subway 🅾 AT&T, A toZone, BJ's Gas, Buick/GMC, Chevrolet, Chrysler/Dodge/Jee CVS Drug, Honda, Hyundai, Kia, Stop&Shop/gas, Town Fa Tire, USPO
9a(9)	US 6 E Expswy, E 🍴 Chipotle, McDonald's, Taco Bell 🅾 $Tre BJ's Whse, Home Depot, Petsmart
7(8)	🅾 RI Resource Recovery Industrial Park
6(7)	RI 14, Plainfield Pk, E 🅿 Speedway/dsl 🍴 McDonal 🅾 $Tree, Walmart/Subway, W 🅿 Gulf, Mobil/dsl/24 🍴 Dunkin', Palmieri Pizza, Subway 🅾 CVS Drug, repair
3b a(4)	rd 37, Phenix Ave, E 🅾 TF Green Airport
1b(2)	RI 2 S, to Warwick, E 🅿 EVC 🍴 Buffalo Wild Wings, Chica Grill, Longhorn Steaks, Red Robin 🛏 Extended Stay Ameri 🅾 $Tree, JC Penney, Macy's, Marshalls, Old Navy, Target, Ve izon, W 🅿 Mobil, Sunoco/Subway 🍴 BJ's Rest., Burger Kir Chili's, Chipotle Mexican, ChuckeCheese, Dunkin', McDonald Olive Garden, On-the-Border, Panera Bread, Smashburg Smokey Bones, Sonic, Starbucks, Subway, Taco Bell, We dy's 🅾 AT&T, AutoZone, Barnes&Noble, Best Buy, Chrysle Dodge/Keep/Kia, Dick's, Hobby Lobby, Home Depot, Jagu Kia, Kohl's, Petco, PetsMart, Price Rite Foods, Rite Aid, Staple Target, TJMaxx, TownFair Tire, Trader Joe's, Verizon, Walma Subway
1a(1)	RI 113 W, to W Warwick, same as 2
0mm	I-295 begins/ends on I-95, exit 11.

E GREENWICH

PROVIDENCE

RI

SOUTH CAROLINA

⬆E INTERSTATE 20

Exit #	Services
141b a	I-95, N to Fayetteville, S to Savannah. I-20 begins/ends on I-95, exit 160. See Interstate 95, exit 160a for services.
137	SC 340, to Timmonsville, Darlington, N 🅖 BP/dsl (1mi) 🅞 $General (1mi), S 🅖 Marathon
131	US 401, SC 403, to Hartsville, Lamar, N 🅖 Exxon/dsl 🅞 to Darlington Raceway, S 🅖 Shell/Markette/dsl
129mm	parking area both lanes, commercial vehicles only
123	SC 22, N 🅞 camping, Lee SP
121mm	Lynches River
120	SC 341, Bishopville, Elliot, N 🅖 BP/dsl 🅞 to Cotton Museum, S 🅖 Exxon/dsl 🅕 Taste of Country Rest. 🅛 Best Value Inn
116	US 15, to Sumter, Bishopville, N 🅖 Shell/KFC/dsl/24hr 🅕 McDonald's, Pizza Hut, Subway (1mi), Waffle House, Zaxby's 🅛 Red Roof Inn 🅞 to Cotton Museum, S 🅖 🅿🅸🅻🅾🆃/DQ/Wendy's/dsl/scales/24hr 🅕 Huddle House 🅞 Shaw AFB
108	SC 34, to SC 31, Manville, N 🅖 BP/dsl, S 🅖 Exxon/dsl
101	rd 329, Dr Humphries Rd
98	US 521, to Camden, N 🅖 BP/dsl, Exxon/McDonald's, Mobil/Circle K/dsl, Shell/dsl 🅕 Fatz Cafe, Waffle House 🅛 Comfort Suites, Hampton Inn, Holiday Inn Express 🅞 🅷, to Revolutionary War Park
96mm	Wateree River
93mm	🆁🆂 both lanes, full ♿ facilities, 🅲, vending, 🅟 litter barrels, petwalk
92	US 601, to Lugoff, N 🅖 Mobil, 🅿🅸🅻🅾🆃/DQ/Subway/dsl/scales/24hr, Shell/Bojangles/dsl 🅕 Hardee's, Waffle House 🅛 Days Inn, EconoLodge
87	SC 47, to Elgin, N 🅖 BP/dsl, Shell/dsl, S 🅖 ♥Love's/Hardee's/dsl/scales/24hr
82	SC 53, to Pontiac, N 🅖 Mobil, Shell 🅕 Blimpie, Burger King, Egg Roll Express 🅛 Woodspring Suites 🅞 $General, Harley-Davidson, vet, S 🅖 BP/dsl 🅞 Clothing World Outlet
80	Clemson Rd, N 🅖 Circle K, Exxon/dsl, Shell/Bojangles/dsl 🅕 China Garden, D's, Dunkin', Groucho's Deli, Henry's, J Peters Grill, Krispy Kreme, Maurice's BBQ, McDonald's, San Jose Mexican, Subway, Sumo Japanese, Travinia Italian, Waffle House, Zaxby's 🅛 Hampton Inn, Holiday Inn Express 🅞 CVS Drug, Firestone/auto, S 🅕 Wendy's 🅞 Chevrolet, Ft Jackson Nat Cem, Hyundai
76b	Alpine Rd, to Ft Jackson, N 🅞 Sesquicentennial SP
76a	(76 from eb), I-77, N to Charlotte, S to Charleston
74	US 1, Two Notch Rd, to Ft Jackson, N 🅖 Mobil/dsl 🅕 Chili's, Fazoli's, Hooters, IHOP, Lizard's Thicket, Outback Steaks, Waffle House 🅛 Best Western+, Comfort Suites, EconoLodge, Fairfield Inn, Hampton Inn, La Quinta, Microtel, Motel 6, Red Roof Inn 🅞 Home Depot, to Sesquicentennial SP, USPO, S 🅖 BP, Exxon, Shell 🅕 Applebee's, Bojangles, Brickhouse, China Garden, Church's, Harbor Inn Seafood, Hardee's, Honeybaked Ham, Jasmine Buffet, Maurice's BBQ, McDonald's, Monterrey Mexican, Substation II 🅛 Days Inn 🅞 Advance Parts, AT&T, AutoZone, Best Buy, Firestone/auto, Lowe's, Marshall's, Verizon
73b	SC 277 N, to I-77 N
73a	SC 277 S, to Columbia, S 🅞 🅷
72	SC 555, Farrow Rd

COLUMBIA

71	US 21, N Main, to Blythewood, Columbia, N 🅖 BP/dsl, Save-a-Ton/dsl, TA/Subway/Taco Bell/dsl/scales/24hr/@ 🅕 McDonald's 🅛 Days Inn 🅞 tires/repair, truckwash, S 🅖 Shell
70	US 321, Fairfield Rd, S 🅖 ⊘FLYING J/Denny's/dsl/LP/24hr, Exxon 🅕 Hardee's 🅛 Super 8 🅞 Blue Beacon, truck repair
68	SC 215, Monticello Rd, to Jenkinsville, N 🅖 Exxon/dsl, Shell/dsl, S 🅖 Shell/dsl
66mm	Broad River
65	US 176, Broad River Rd, to Columbia, N 🅖 BP, CK Mart, Exxon, Shell/Circle K 🅕 Bojangles, Rush's BBQ, Sonic, Subway, Waffle House 🅛 Economy Inn 🅞 $Tree, Aamco, CVS Drug, Family$, U-Haul, Walgreens, S 🅖 Speedway/dsl 🅕 Arby's, Baskin-Robbins/Dunkin', Chick-fil-A, Church's, KFC, Lizard's Thicket, McDonald's, Nick's, Ocean View Seafood, Ruby Tuesday, Sandy's HotDogs, Scholtzsky's, Taco Bell, Wendy's, Zaxby's 🅛 American Inn, InTown Suites, Ramada Ltd, Regency Inn, Royal Inn 🅞 $General, Advance Parts, Office Depot, PepBoys
64b a	I-26, US 76, E to Columbia, W to Greenville, Spartanburg
63	Bush River Rd, N 🅖 Shell/Circle K 🅕 Burger King, Cracker Barrel, Real Mexican, Subway 🅛 Quality Inn 🅞 CVS Drug, S 🅖 Marathon, Murphy USA/dsl, Sunoco/dsl 🅕 Fuddrucker's 🅛 Best Western, DoubleTree, Knights Inn, Sleep Inn 🅞 AutoZone, Hamrick's, Walmart
61	US 378, W Cola, N 🅖 Exxon, Murphy Express/dsl 🅕 Chick-Fil-A, Chili's, Jewell's BBQ, McDonald's, Starbucks, Substation II, Taco Bell 🅛 Wingate Inn 🅞 Honda, S 🅖 BP/dsl, Shell/Burger King/dsl 🅕 Waffle House 🅞 $General
58	US 1, W Columbia, N 🅖 Shell/Subway/dsl, Sunoco 🅕 Waffle House, S 🅖 Murphy Express/dsl 🅕 Bojangles, San Jose Mexican 🅛 Woodspring Suites 🅞 auto repair, County Tire
55	SC 6, to Lexington, N 🅖 BP/Circle K/dsl, QT/dsl 🅛 Best Western+, S 🅖 BP/dsl, Shell/Circle K/DQ/dsl 🅕 Bojangles, Dunkin', Great Wall Chinese, Maurice's BBQ, McDonald's, Waffle House, Wendy's 🅛 Days Inn 🅞 $General, CVS Drug

SC

📍E INTERSTATE 20 Cont'd

Exit #	Services
52.5mm	weigh sta wb
51	SC 204, to Gilbert, N 📗 Circle K/dsl, Shell/Subway/dsl/24hr 🍴 Burger King 🅾 John's RV Sales/Svc, S 📗 ♥Loves/Chester's/ McDonald's/dsl/scales/24hr, Shell/dsl 🍴 Arby's 🅾 $General
44	SC 34, to Gilbert, N 📗 44Trkstp/rest./dsl/24hr, BP/dsl
39	US 178, to Batesburg, N 📗 Exxon/dsl, S 📗 Marathon/dsl/ scales 🍴 Hillview Rest.
35.5mm	weigh sta eb
33	SC 39, to Wagener, N 📗 Cheapway/dsl, S 📗 Shell/Huddle House/dsl/scales
29	SC 49, Wire Rd
22	US 1, to Aiken, S 📗 BP/dsl, RaceWay/dsl, Shell/Circle K/dsl 🍴 Bojangle's, Burger King, Hardee's, McDonald's, Waffle House 🛏 Days Inn, Quality Inn 🅾 $General, Palmetto Lake RV Camping, to USC Aiken
20mm	parking area both lanes, commercial vehicles only
18	SC 19, to Aiken, S 📗 Shell/Subway/dsl 🍴 Waffle House 🛏 Deluxe Inn, Guest Inn 🅾 Ⓗ
11	Bettis Academy Rd, SC 144, Graniteville, N 📗 Shell/Huddle House/dsl/scales/24hr, S 📗 Pilot/Subway/dsl/scales/24hr 🍴 McDonald's
6	I-520 to N Augusta
5	US 25, SC 121, N 📗 BP/repair/dsl, Circle K/dsl, Shell/Circle K/ dsl/scales 🍴 Bojangles, Burger King, Checkers, Crazy Buffet, DQ, Jersey Mike's, Little Caesar's, McDonald's, Pablo's Mexican, Sonic, Subway, Wendy's, Zaxby's 🛏 Holiday Inn Express 🅾 $General, Advance Parts, Food Lion, GNC, Verizon, Walmart, S 📗 Marathon 🍴 Waffle House 🛏 Sleep Inn
1	SC 230, Martintown Rd, N Augusta, N 📗 Gas+/dsl, S 📗 Shell/ Circle K/Subway/dsl 🍴 Waffle House 🅾 to Garn's Place
.5mm	Welcome Ctr eb, full ♿ facilities, 🚻, 🛢, litter barrels, vending, petwalk
0mm	South Carolina/Georgia state line, Savannah River

📍E INTERSTATE 26

Exit #	Services
221	Meeting St, Charleston, E 🍴 Church's 🛏 Courtyard, Embassy Suites, Hampton Inn, Hyatt Place 🅾 Family$
	I-26 begins/ends on US 17 in Charleston, SC.
221b	US 17 N, to Georgetown
221a	US 17 S, to Kings St, to Savannah
220	Romney St (from wb)
219b	Morrison Dr, East Bay St (from eb), N 📗 Exxon
219a	Rutledge Ave (from eb, no EZ return), to The Citadel
218	Spruill Ave (from wb), N Charleston
217	N Meeting St (from eb)
216b a	SC 7, Cosgrove Ave, to US 17 S
215	SC 642, Dorchester Rd, N Charleston, N 📗 Cheapway/dsl 🛏 Charleston Grand, S 📗 BP/Circle K/dsl 🛏 Charleston Inn 🅾 Best Value Inn
213b a	Montague Ave, Mall Dr, N 🍴 Cowboys Brazilian, Hello Deli, Red Lobster 🛏 Courtyard, Marriott, Woodspring Suites 🅾 Charles Towne Square, S 📗 BP/Circle K/dsl, Mobil, Spinx/dsl 🍴 Arby's, Big Billy's Burgers, Bonefish Grill, Bufflo Wild Wings, Burger King, Chick-fil-A, Chipotle, CiCi's Pizza, Community Pizza, Domino's, Dunkin', Firehouse Subs, Five Guys, Golden Corral, Grand Buffet, IHOP, Jersey Mike's, Jim'N Nick's BBQ, Jimmy John's, La Hacienda, McAlister's Deli, McDonald's, Mellow Mushroom, Panda Express, Panera Bread, Sake Japanese, Starbucks,

Exit #	Services
213b a	Continued
	Steak'n Shake, Taste of Tokyo, Waffle House, Zaxby's 🛏 ALo, Comfort Inn, Crowne Plaza, EconoLodge, Embassy Suites, Extended Stay America, Extended Stay America (2), Fairfield In, Hampton Inn, Hilton Garden, Holiday Inn Express, Home 2 Suite, Homewood Suites, Hyatt Place, InTown Suites, Quality Inn, Residence Inn, Rodeway Inn, TownePlace Suites, Wingate Inn 🅾 $Tree, AT&T, Field&Stream, Old Navy, Sam's Club/gas, Staple, Tanger Outlet/Famous Brands, Verizon, vet, Walmart/Subway
212c b	I-526, E to Mt Pleasant, W to Savannah, S 🅾 🗨
212a	Remount Rd, Hanahan, N on US 52/78 📗 Sunoco/dsl 🍴 KF, Taco Bell 🅾 Advance Parts, AutoZone, Ford
211b a	Aviation Pkwy, N on US 52/78 📗 Citgo, Exxon 🍴 Arby's, Burger King, Capt D's, Church's, KFC, McDonald's, Nick's Gyro, Papa John's, Popeye's, Schlotzsky's, Smokey Bones, Sonic, Subway, Super Buffet, Taco Bell 🛏 Masters Inn 🅾 O'Reilly Par, PepBoys, U-Haul, USPO, S 📗 Circle K/dsl 🍴 Waffle House 🛏 Budget Inn
209	Ashley Phosphate Rd, to US 52, N 📗 Exxon, Kangaroo 🍴 Applebee's, Cane's, Carrabba's, Chick-fil-A, China Buffet, Chipotle Mexican, ChuckECheese, Coldstone, Denny's, Dickey's BBQ, Firehouse Subs, Five Guys, Hardee's, Hooters, Jersey Mike's Subs, Jimmy John's, King Street Grill, Longhorn Steaks, Los Reyes, Moe's SW Grill, Noisy Oyster, O'Charley's, Olive Garden, Outback Steak, Panda Express, Smokey Bones BBQ, Starbucks, Subway, Taco Bell, Waffle House, Wendy's, Wild Wing Cafe 🛏 Candlewoo Suites, Country Inn&Suites, DoubleTree, Extended Stay Ameri, Hawthorn Inn, Holiday Inn Express, InTown Suites, Red Roof I, Rodeway Inn, Suburban Inn, URGENT CARE 🅾 $General, $Tr, AT&T, Barnes&Noble, Belk, Best Buy, BigLots, Books-A-Milli, Dillard's, Firestone/auto, GNC, Hobby Lobby, Home Depot, Ⓗ, Penney, Lowe's, Michael's, Nissan, NTB, Office Depot, Old Na, Petco, Petsmart, Ross, Target, Toyota, Tuesday Morning, Ve, zon, Walgreens, Walmart/McDonald's, S 📗 BP, RaceWay/, Speedway/dsl, Sunoco/dsl 🍴 Bojangles, Cracker Barrel, IH, McDonald's, Osaka Asian, Ruby Tuesday, Waffle House 🛏 B, Western, Fairfield Inn, Hampton Inn, Hyatt Place, InTown Suit, La Quinta, Motel 6, Quality Inn, Relax Inn, Residence Inn, Sle, Inn, Staybridge Suites, Woodspring Suites
209a	to US 52 (from wb), to Goose Creek, Moncks Corner
205b a	US 78, to Summerville, N 📗 BP/Dunkin', Speedway/dsl, Sunoco/dsl 🍴 Arby's, Bruster's, Cook-Out, East Bay Deli, Firehouse Subs, Fortune Garden, Jersey Mike's, Sonic, Starbucks, Subway, Waffle House, Wendy's, Willie Jewell's BBQ, Zaxby's 🛏 Fairfield Inn, Hampton Inn, Holiday Inn Express, Wingate Inn 🅾 Charleston Southern U, CVS Drug, Family$, Ⓗ, S 📗 Citgo, Speedway/ dsl, Sunoco/dsl 🍴 Burger King, China Chef, KFC, Subway, Taco Bell 🅾 Advance Parts, CVS Drug, KOA, Piggly Wiggly
204mm	📸 eb, full ♿ facilities, vending, 🚻, 🛢, litter barrels, petw
203	College Park Rd, Ladson, N 📗 BP, Sunoco/dsl 🍴 McDonal, Waffle House 🛏 Best Western, Days Inn, S 📗 Spinx/dsl 🅾 K, (2mi)
202mm	📸 wb, full ♿ facilities, vending, 🚻, 🛢, litter barrels, petw
199b a	US 17 A, to Moncks Corner, Summerville, N 📗 BP, Kangaro, dsl, Marathon, Pilot/McDonald's/dsl/scales/24hr, Speedway/Dunkin'/dsl 🍴 Carolina Alehouse, China Chef, China W, KFC, Pizza Hut, Subway 🛏 Courtyard 🅾 $General, Advan, Parts, AutoZone, BiLo, Buick/GMC, CVS Drug, Family$, O'Re, Parts, vet, S 📗 Shell/Circle K 🍴 Applebee's, Atlanta Bread, jangles, Box Car Betty's, Burger King, Chick-fil-A, China Tok, Cracker Barrel, Domino's, Dunkin', Five Guys, Hardee's, IHOP, sey Mike's Subs, La Hacienda, Logan's Roadhouse, Marble S

opyright 2022 - The Next EXIT ® 🛢 = gas ⬜ = food 🛏 = lodging Ⓞ = other 📶 = rest stop

INTERSTATE 26 Cont'd

199b a Continued
McAlisters Deli, Mellow Mushroom, Moe's SW Grill, Newk's Eatery, O'Charleys, Panera Bread, Papa John's, Ruby Tuesday, Ryan's, Shoney's, Smashburger, Starbucks, Sticky Fingers, Waffle House, Which Wich?, Zaxby's 🛏 Comfort Inn, Comfort Suites, Country Inn&Suites, EconoLodge, Economy Inn, Hampton Inn, Holiday Inn Express, Quality Inn, Sleep Inn Ⓞ AT&T, Belk, Best Buy, Chrysler/Dodge/Jeep, Dick's, Earthfare Mkt, GNC, Home Depot, Jo-Ann, Kohl's, Lowe's, NTB, Petco, Petsmart, Ross, Staples, Target, TJ Maxx, Verizon, Walgreens, Walmart/McDonald's, World Mkt

194 SC 16, to Jedburg, **E** Ⓞ access to Foreign Trade Zone 21, **W** ⬜ *FLYING J*/PJ Fresh/Wendy's/dsl/scales/24hr

187 SC 27, to Ridgeville, St George, **N** ⬜ Shell, **S** ⬜ BP/dsl Ⓞ Francis Beidler Forest (10mi)

177 SC 453, to Holly Hill, Harleyville, **S** ⬜ Shell/dsl 🛏 Ashley Lodge/RV park

174mm weigh sta both lanes

172b a US 15, to Santee, St George, **S** ⬜ Horizon/Domino's/Subway/dsl/e-85/scales/24hr

169b a I-95, N to Florence, S to Savannah

165 SC 210, to Bowman, **N** ⬜ Exxon/dsl, **S** ⬜ BP/dsl

159 SC 36, to Bowman, **N** ⬜⬜/McDonald's/dsl/scales/24hr/@, **S** ⬜ Exxon

154b a US 301, to Santee, Orangeburg, **N** 🛏 Days Inn, **S** ⬜ Exxon, ♥ *Loves*/Chesters/Subway/dsl/scales/24hr, Shell/dsl ⬜ Waffle House

152mm 📶 wb, full 🚻 facilities, vending, 🅲, 🏞, litter barrels, petwalk

150mm 📶 eb, full 🚻 facilities, vending, 🅲, 🏞, litter barrels, petwalk

149 SC 33, to Cameron, to SC State Coll, Orangeburg Ⓞ Claflin Coll

145b a US 601, to Orangeburg, St Matthews, **S** ⬜ BP/dsl, Exxon, Shell, Sunoco/dsl, United/dsl ⬜ Burger King, Chick-fil-A, Cracker Barrel, Fatz Café, Hardee's, McDonald's, Ruby Tuesday, Seafood Academy, Subway, Waffle House, Wendy's, Zaxby's 🛏 Carolina Lodge, Comfort Inn, Country Inn&Suites, Days Inn, Fairfield Inn, Hampton Inn, Holiday Inn Express, Howard Johnson, Quality Inn, Sleep Inn, Southern Lodge Ⓞ $General, Cadillac/Chevrolet, Chrysler/Dodge/Jeep, Ford, Ⓗ, Nissan, Toyota

139 SC 22, to St Matthews, **S** ⬜ Horizon/e85, Mobil, ⬜⬜/Dunkin'/Arby's/dsl/scales/24hr Ⓞ Sweetwater Lake Camping (2.5mi)

136 SC 6, to North, Swansea, **N** ⬜ Exxon/dsl

129 US 21, **N** ⬜ Shell/dsl

125 SC 31, to Gaston, **N** Ⓞ Wolfe's Truck/trailer repair

123mm 📶 both lanes, full 🚻 facilities, vending, 🅲, 🏞, litter barrels, petwalk

119 US 176, US 21, to Dixiana, **S** ⬜ BP/Subway/dsl, Exxon/dsl

116 I-77 N, to Charlotte, US 76, US 378, to Ft Jackson

115 US 176, US 21, US 321, to Cayce, **N** ⬜ BP, Gulf, RaceWay, Shell/dsl ⬜ Pizza Hut, Waffle House Ⓞ $General, $Tree, Advance Parts, Bi-Lo, CVS Drug, Family$, Reid's Foods, **S** ⬜ ⬜⬜/DQ/Wendy's/dsl/scales/24hr, Shell/dsl ⬜ Bojangles, Carolina Wings, Great China, Hardee's, McDonald's, Sonic, Subway 🛏 Country Hearth Inn Ⓞ Firestone, Piggly Wiggly

113 SC 302, Cayce, **N** ⬜ Marathon, Mobil/Burger King, Sunoco/dsl ⬜ Waffle House 🛏 Airport Inn, Knights Inn, Masters Inn Ⓞ $General, AutoZone, O'Reilly Parts, Rite Aid, Save-A-Lot, Toyota, Walgreens, **S** ⬜ BP/dsl, RaceWay, Shell/Circle K ⬜ Lizard's Thicket, Shoney's, Subway, Waffle House 🛏 Carolina Lodge, Country Inn&Suites, Days Inn, Sleep Inn, Travelers Inn Ⓞ ⬀, NAPA

111b a US 1, to W Columbia, **N** ⬜ Murphy USA/dsl, RaceWay, Shell/Circle K/dsl ⬜ Chick-fil-A, Domino's, Dragon City Chinese, Hardee's, Little Caesar's, Maurice's BBQ, Moe's SW Grill, Ruby Tuesday, San Jose, Sonic, Subway, Tokyo Grill, Waffle House, Zaxby's 🛏 Clarion, Delta Motel, Quality Inn Ⓞ $General, $Tree, AT&T, Bi-Lo, GNC, Hobby Lobby, Pet Supplies+, to USC, Walgreens, Walmart, **S** ⬜ Speedway/dsl ⬜ Applebee's, China Chef, Fat Boy Greek, Popeye's, Wendy's Ⓞ Aldi Foods, BigLots, Family$, Lowe's, U-Haul

110 US 378, to W Columbia, Lexington, **N** ⬜ Grecian Gardens, Happy China, Lizard's Thicket, McDonald's, Rush's Rest., Subway, Waffle House 🛏 America's Inn, Hampton Inn, Holiday Inn Ⓞ CVS Drug, Family$, Food Lion, Toyota, **S** ⬜ Mobil/dsl, Shell/Circle K ⬜ Atlanta Bread, Bojangles, China Dragon, Firehouse Subs, La Fogata, Pizza Hut 🛏 Executive Inn Ⓞ Ⓗ, URGENT CARE

108b a I-126 to Columbia, Bush River Rd, **N** ⬜ BP, Exxon/dsl, Shell/dsl ⬜ Capt D's, Chick-fil-A, Hardee's, Ruby Tuesday, Schlotzsky's, Waffle House, Wendy's, Zaxby's 🛏 Comfort Inn, Embassy Suites, Extended Stay America, Homewood Suites Ⓞ $General, Advance Parts, Chrysler/Jeep/Dodge, Dodge/Ram, Firestone/auto, Ford/Lincoln, Hyundai, Kia, Mazda, Midas, Office Depot, Riverbanks Zoo, Verizon, **S** ⬜ City Gas, Murphy USA/dsl, Sunoco/dsl ⬜ Bamboo House, Fuddrucker's, Pizza Hut, Tokyo Grill 🛏 Baymont Inn, Best Western, DoubleTree, Hawthorn Suites, Knights Inn, Sleep Inn Ⓞ AutoZone, GNC, Hamrick's, Walmart

107b a I-20, E to Florence, W to Augusta

106b a St Andrews Rd, **N** ⬜ Exxon/dsl ⬜ ChuckECheese, IHOP, Karen's Kitchen, Papa John's, Seasoned with Soul, Sonic 🛏 Motel 6 Ⓞ $Tree, Camping World RV Ctr, CVS Drug, Infiniti, Nissan, Walgreens, **S** ⬜ BP/dsl, Shell, Speedway/dsl ⬜ Domino's, Maurice's BBQ, McDonald's, Ms. B's, Nick's Grill, Taqueria Jalisco, Tokyo Buffet, Waffle House, WG's Wings, Zaxby's 🛏 Red Roof Inn Ⓞ $General, KJ's IGA, Tire Kingdom

104 Piney Grove Rd, **N** ⬜ Sunoco/dsl ⬜ Hardee's, San Jose Mexican, Waffle House 🛏 Quality Inn Ⓞ Costco/gas, Sportsmans Whse, vet, **S** ⬜ Exxon, Shell/dsl 🛏 Country Inn&Suites, Microtel Ⓞ Carmax, Land Rover

103 Harbison Blvd, **N** ⬜ Applebee's, Hooters, Wendy's 🛏 Hampton Inn Ⓞ Chevrolet, funpark, Home Depot, Lowe's, **S** ⬜ Shell/Circle K, Speedway/Dunkin'/dsl ⬜ Bojangles, BoneFish Grill, Buffalo Wild Wings, Carolina Alehouse, Carrabba's, Casa Linda, Chick-fil-A, Chili's, Chipotle Mexican, Coldstone, Copper River Grill, Denny's, Fazoli's, Firehouse Subs, Five Guys, Flaming Grill, Honey Baked Ham, Huhot Mongolian, Jimmy John's, Longhorn Steaks, Macaroni Grill, Marble Slab, McAlister's Deli, McDonald's, Miyabi Japanese, Miyo's, Olive Garden, Outback Steaks, Panera Bread, Rioz Brazilian, Rita's Custard, Ruby Tuesday, Rush's BBQ, Ryan's, Sonic, Starbucks, Subway, Tokyo Grill,

(vertical text left margin) ORANGEBURG

(vertical text right margin) COLUMBIA

SC

⬆E INTERSTATE 26 Cont'd

103	Continued
	Tsunami Steaks, TX Roadhouse, Which Wich?, Wild Wing Cafe, Yamato Japanese 🛏 Comfort Suites, Fairfield Inn, Hilton Garden, Holiday Inn Express, Home Towne Suites, InTown Suites, Wingate Inn Ⓞ $Tree, AT&T, Belk, Best Buy, Buick/GMC, Dick's, Dillard's, Firestone/auto, Goodyear/auto, JC Penney, Kohl's, Marshalls, Michael's, Midas, NTB, Old Navy, Petsmart, Publix, Ross, Sam's Club/dsl, Staples, SteinMart, Target, TJ Maxx, Verizon, Walmart
102	SC 60, Ballentine, Irmo, N 🍴 Cracker Barrel 🛏 Extended Stay Deluxe, Hyatt Place Ⓞ 🅷, S 🅿 JP/dsl, Shell 🍴 Arby's, Bellacino's Pizza, Dunkin', Groucho's Deli, Marco's Pizza, Maurice's BBQ, Moe's SW Grill, Papa John's, Smashburger, Taco Bell, Zaxby's, Zoe's Kitchen 🛏 Residence Inn Ⓞ AAA, CVS Drug, Jiffy Lube, same as 103
101 b a	US 76, US 176, to N Columbia, 1/2 mi N 🅿 Shell/dsl 🍴 Bojangles, China House, Fatz Café, Jersey Mike's Subs, Silver Fox Grill Ⓞ $General, AutoZone, Food Lion, Harley-Davidson, Publix, Walgreens, S 🅿 7-11/dsl, BP, Circle K, Hickory Point/dsl 🍴 Burger King, Lucky's BurgerShack, Waffle House Ⓞ $General, Toyota
97	US 176, to Ballentine, Peak, N 🍴 China 1, Subway Ⓞ Food Lion, S 🅿 Sunoco/dsl 🍴 Burger King
94mm	weigh sta wb
91	SC 48, to Chapin, S 🅿 BP/dsl, Exxon/Taco Bell/dsl, Shell/dsl 🍴 Bojangles, Farm Boys BBQ, McDonald's, Waffle House Ⓞ to Dreher Island SP, URGENT CARE
85	SC 202, Little Mountain, Pomaria, S Ⓞ to Dreher Island SP
82	SC 773, to Prosperity, Pomaria, N 🅿 Exxon/Circle K/Subway/dsl/24hr, 🛢/Wendy's/dsl/scales/24hr 🍴 Waffle House
81mm	weigh sta eb
76	SC 219, to Pomaria, Newberry, N 🅿 ❤Loves/McDonald's/Chester's/dsl/scales/24hr, 0-2 mi S 🅿 BP, Murphy USA 🍴 Burger King, Wendy's 🛏 Hampton Inn (4mi), Holiday Inn Express, Home2 Suites Ⓞ to Newberry Opera House, Walmart
74	SC 34, to Newberry, N 🅿 BP/dsl, Shell/dsl 🍴 Bill&Fran's Café, S 🅿 Citgo/dsl 🍴 Arby's, Capt D's, Hardee's, McDonald's, Waffle House 🛏 Days Inn, Days Inn, Economy Inn Ⓞ 🅷, to Ninety-Six HS
72	SC 121, to Newberry, S 🅿 Citgo/dsl Ⓞ 🅷, to Newberry Coll
66	SC 32, to Jalapa
63.5mm	🆁🆂 both lanes, full 🚻 facilities, 🅲, vending, 🗑 litter barrels, petwalk
60	SC 66, to Joanna, S 🅿 BP/dsl Ⓞ Magnolia RV Park
54	SC 72, to Clinton, W 🅿 QT, N 🅿 BP/dsl, S 🅿 Citgo/dsl 🍴 Fatz Cafe, Zaxby's 🛏 Hampton Inn Ⓞ 🅷, to Presbyterian Coll
52	SC 56, to Clinton, N 🛢/Subway/dsl/scales/24hr 🍴 Blue Ocean Rest., McDonald's 🛏 Comfort Suites, Quality Inn, S 🅿 Citgo/dsl 🍴 Hardee's, Waffle House, Wendy's 🛏 Days Inn Ⓞ 🅷
51	I-385, to Greenville (from wb)
45.5mm	Enoree River
44	SC 49, to Cross Anchor, Union
41	SC 92, to Enoree, N 🅿 Valero
38	SC 146, to Woodruff, N 🅿 HotSpot/Shell/Hardee's/dsl/scales/24hr
35	SC 50, Walnut Grove Rd, to Woodruff, S 🅿 BP/dsl
33mm	S Tyger River
32mm	N Tyger River
28	US 221, to Spartanburg, N 🅿 Circle K/dsl/24hr, Shell/Subway/dsl 🍴 Bojangles, Burger King, Italian Pizza, Waffle House Ⓞ 🅷, Pine Ridge Camping (3mi), to Walnut Grove Plantation

IRMO (vertical label, left margin)
SPARTANBURG (vertical label, center margin)

22	SC 296, Reidville Rd, to Spartanburg, N 🅿 Exxon/dsl, Marathon/Kangaroo/dsl, Spinx/dsl 🍴 Arby's, Blue Bay Rest., Bruster's, Chief's Rest., Fatz Cafe, Fuddrucker's (1mi), Little Caesars, McDonald's, Outback Steaks, Substation II, Waffle House, Wasabi Japanese, Wayback Burger, Zaxby's Ⓞ $General, Advance Parts, to Croft SP, USPO, vet, S 🅿 7-11/dsl, QT/dsl, Sunoco/dsl 🍴 Clock Rest., Denny's, Domino's, Dunkin', El Limon Mexican, Hardee's, Hong Kong Express, Hunan K, Panda Garden, Papa John's, Subway 🛏 Sleep Inn, Southern Suites, Super 8 Ⓞ $General, Abbott Farms, Bi-Lo, CVS Drug, Hyundai, Mida, Rite Aid, Toyota, vet, VW, Walgreens
21 b a	US 29, to Spartanburg, N 🅿 Marathon/Circle K, Spinx/dsl 🍴 A&W/LJ Silver, Bojangles, Brasilia Steaks, Buffalo Wild Wing, Burger King, Chick-fil-A, Chipotle Mexican, ChuckECheese, Ci's, City Range Steaks, Corona Mexican, DQ, Firehouse Sub, FoodCourt, Golden Corral, Jack-in-the-Box, Jason's Deli, Jin J Buffet, Kanpai Tokyo, KFC, La Taverna Italian, Longhorn Steak, McAlister's Deli, Moe's SW Grill, O'Charley's, Olive Garden, Panera Bread, Pizza Hut, Red Bowl Asian, Red Lobster, Ru Tuesday, Ryan's, Starbucks, Subway, Wendy's 🛏 Comfo Suites, Hampton Inn, Hilton Garden, Holiday Inn Express, Residence Inn Ⓞ AT&T, Barnes&Noble, Belk, Best Buy, Costco/ga, Dick's, Dillard's, Discount Tire, Firestone/auto, Hamrick's, Hom Depot, JC Penney, Jo-Ann Fabrics, Lowe's, Meineke, Michael, Office Depot, Old Navy, Petsmart, Rite Aid, Ross, TJ Maxx, Tues day Morning, USPO, Verizon, Walmart/McDonald's, S 🅿 Marathon/dsl, Shell/dsl 🍴 Apollo's Pizza, Applebee's, Compadre TexMex, IHOP, McDonald's, Shogun Japanese, Starbucks, Ta Bell, Waffle House 🛏 Tru Hotel Ⓞ $Tree, Advance Parts, C Quest, Hobby Lobby, Ingles Foods/gas, Kohl's, Sam's Club/ga Target, TrueValue
19 b a	Lp I-85, Spartanburg, N 🅿 BP/dsl, Valero 🍴 Cracker Barr Subway 🛏 Residence Inn, S 🅿 Valero 🛏 Brookwood Inn
18 b a	I-85, N to Charlotte, S to Greenville
17	New Cut Rd, S 🅿 BP/dsl, Exxon/dsl 🍴 Burger King, Fatz Ca McDonald's, Waffle House 🛏 Days Inn, Howard Johnson, R Roof Inn, Rodeway Inn
16	John Dodd Rd, to Wellford, N 🅿 Exxon/Circle K/Aunt M's/ Ⓞ Camping World RV Ctr
15	US 176, to Inman, N 🅿 Breakers, Shell/Circle K/dsl/scales Waffle House Ⓞ 🅷, S 🅿 QT/dsl Ⓞ Simply RV Ctr
10	SC 292, to Inman, N 🅿 Shell/Hot Spot/Subway/dsl/scales/24
7.5mm	Lake William C. Bowman
5	SC 11, Foothills Scenic Dr, Chesnee, Campobello, N 🅿 Circle Subway/dsl/scales/24hr, S 🅿 Marathon/Li'l Cricket/dsl
3mm	Welcome Ctr eb, full 🚻 facilities, info, 🅲, 🗑, litter barre vending, petwalk, wi-fi
1	SC 14, to Landrum, S 🅿 Shell/Burger King/dsl 🍴 Bojangl China Cafe, Papa John's, Pizza Hut (1mi), Starbucks, Subway $General, Bi-Lo Foods, Ingles/café/gas, Verizon, vet
0mm	South Carolina/North Carolina state line

⬆N INTERSTATE 77

Exit #	Services
91mm	South Carolina/North Carolina state line
90	US 21, Carowinds Blvd, E 🅿 Mobil/Circle K/dsl, QT/dsl 🍴 jangles, Burger King, McDonald's, Zaxby's Ⓞ fireworks, 🅷, 🅿 Circle K/Subway, Exxon/7-11, QT/dsl, Shell/Circle K/We dy's/dsl 🍴 Cracker Barrel, Culver's, Famous Dave's, KFC, Mc SW, Panchito's Mexican 🛏 Best Western, Clarion, Comfort I Country Inn Suites, Motel 6, Quality Inn Ⓞ Cabela's, Carowi Camping, Carowinds Funpark

SC (logo, bottom left)

INTERSTATE 77 Cont'd

Exit #	Services
89.5mm	Welcome Ctr sb, full ♿ facilities, info, 🅒, vending, ⛱, litter barrels, petwalk/weigh sta nb
88	Gold Hill Rd, to Pineville, **E** 🅞 URGENT CARE, **W** 🅖 QT/dsl, Shell/dsl, Valero/dsl 🅕 Dunkin', Hardee's, Marco's Pizza 🅛 WingBonz Cantina 🅞 Chrysler/Dodge/Jeep, Fiat, Ford, Hyundai, KOA, Publix, vet
85	SC 160, Ft Mill, Tega Cay, **E** 🅖 Exxon 🅕 Brixx Pizza, Carolina Alehouse, Panera Bread, Smashburger, Starbucks 🅛 Courtyard 🅞 Ft Mill Drug, **W** 🅖 BP/dsl, QT/dsl, Shell/Circle K/dsl 🅕 Akahana Asian, Big Wok, Burger King, Charanda Mexican, Chick-fil-A, Empire Pizza, Fratelli's Italian, Jimmy John's, Killington's Rest., McAlister's Deli, Moe's SW Grill, Papa John's, Pizza Hut, Starbucks, Wendy's, Zaxby's 🅛 Hampton Inn, Holiday Inn Express 🅞 CVS Drug, Firestone/auto, Goodyear/auto, Harris-Teeter, Lowe's, Meineke, vet, Walgreens
84.5mm	weigh sta sb
83	SC 49, Sutton Rd, **W** 🅖 Loves/Chester/Subway/dsl/scales/24hr
82.5mm	Catawba River
82c	US 21, SC 161, Rock Hill, Ft Mill, **E** 🅖 Exxon 🅕 Freddy's, IHOP, Sonny's BBQ, Steak'n Shake, Zaxby's 🅛 Comfort Inn 🅞 Home Depot, Lidl, Petsmart, **W** 🅖 Mobil/dsl, QT/dsl, Shell/Circle K, Shell/dsl, Valero 🅕 Big Wok, Chinese Bistro Deli, Empire Pizza, Hooters, Krispy Kreme, McDonald's, Outback Steaks, Sonic, Starbucks 🅛 Courtyard 🅞 $General, Food Lion, 🏥, TreadQtrs Auto, Walgreens
82b a	**E** 🅖 Exxon 🅛 Comfort Inn, Ramada Inn, **W** 🅖 Shell/Circle K/dsl 🅕 Arby's, Bojangles, Burger King, Chick-fil-A, China Kitchen, CiCi's Pizza, Cookout, Fuji Japan, Golden Corral, HoneyBaked Ham, HongKong Chinese, Little Caesar's, Luigi& Sons Italian, Mario's Pizza, McDonald's, Nick's Gyros, Penn Sta. Subs, Pizza Hut, Popeye's, Rock Hill Diner, Sakura Japanese, Subway, Taco Bell, Waffle House, Wendy's 🅛 Baymont Inn, Best Way, Best Western, Country Inn&Suites, Days Inn, EconoLodge, Economy Express Inn, Howard Johnson, Microtel, Motel 6, Quality Inn, Red Roof Inn 🅞 $General, $Tree, Advance Parts, Aldi Foods, AutoZone, BigLots, Cadillac/Chevrolet, city park, Family$, Firestone/auto, Midas, NAPA, O'Reilly Parts, Office Depot, PepBoys, Publix, Verizon, York Co Museum
79	SC 122, Dave Lyle Blvd, to Rock Hill, **E** 🅖 BP/dsl, Murphy USA/dsl 🅕 Amber Buffet, Applebee's, Buffalo Wild Wings, Charanda Mexican, Chick-fil-A, Cracker Barrel, Five Guys, Hardee's, Jersey Mike's, Longhorn Steaks, Newk's Eatery, O'Charley's, Ruby Tuesday, TX Roadhouse 🅛 Comfort Suites, Fairfield Inn, Hampton Inn, Holiday Inn, Home 2 Suites, La Quinta, Staybridge Suites, TownePlace Suites, Tru, Wingate Inn 🅞 $Tree, AT&T, Belk, Buick/GMC, Discount Tire, Food Lion, Harley Davidson, Hobby Lobby, Honda, JC Penney, Kohl's, Lowe's, Meineke, Nissan, NTB, Sam's Club/dsl, Staples, Toyota, Verizon, Walmart, **W** 🅖 Circle K/dsl 🅕 Baskin Robins/Dunkin', Bob Evans, Chili's, DQ, Firehouse Subs, Jack-in-the-Box, McAlister's Deli, McDonald's, Mellow Mushroom Pizza, Moe's SW Grill, Olive Garden, Panera Bread, Subway, Taco Bell, Wendy's 🅛 Extended Stay America, Hilton Garden 🅞 Best Buy, Books-A-Million, Dick's, Ford, Michael's, Ross, Target, TJ Maxx, URGENT CARE
77	US 21, SC 5, to Rock Hill, **E** 🅖 BP/Subway/dsl, Pilot/dsl, QT/dsl 🅞 to Andrew Jackson SP (12mi), **W** 🅖 Valero/dsl 🅕 Waffle House 🅞 to Winthrop Coll
75	Porter Rd, **E** 🅖 Crown, fireworks
73	SC 901, to Rock Hill, York, **E** 🅖 Flying J/Denny's/dsl/scales/LP/24hr, Exxon/dsl, **W** 🅞 🏥
66mm	🆁🆂 both lanes, full ♿ facilities, 🅒, ⛱, litter barrels, vending, petwalk
65	SC 9, to Chester, Lancaster, **E** 🅖 BP/dsl, Citgo/dsl, QT/dsl, Shell/Subway/dsl 🅕 Bojangles, China Wok, Waffle House 🅛 Days Inn, EconoLodge 🅞 $General, IGA Foods/gas, **W** 🅖 Exxon/dsl 🅕 Burger King, Country Omelet, Front Porch Rest., KFC/Taco Bell, McDonald's, Zaxby's 🅛 Motel 6, Quality Inn, Super 8 🅞 🏥, vet
62	SC 56, to Fort Lawn, Richburg
55	SC 97, to Chester, Great Falls, **E** 🅖 Exxon/dsl, **W** 🅞 🏥, to Chester SP
48	SC 200, to Great Falls, **E** 🅖 Shell/Grand Central Rest./dsl/@, **W** 🅖 Pilot/Wendy's/DQ/dsl/scales/24hr
46	SC 20, to White Oak
41	SC 41, to Winnsboro, **E** 🅞 to Lake Wateree SP
34	SC 34, to Winnsboro, Ridgeway, **E** 🅖 Am Pm/dsl 🅛 Ridgeway Motel (1mi) 🅞 Bryan's Auto/tire, Ridgeway Camping (1mi), **W** 🅖 Exxon/dsl 🅕 Waffle House 🅛 Ramada Ltd
32	Peach Rd, Ridgeway 🅞 Little Cedar Creek Camping (2mi)
27	Blythewood Rd, **E** 🅖 BP/Dunkin', Exxon/Bojangles/dsl/24hr 🅕 Carolina Wings, China King, Hardee's, KFC/Pizza Hut, McDonald's, San Jose Mexican, Subway, Valentina's Greek, Waffle House, Wendy's 🅛 Comfort Inn, Days Inn, Holiday Inn Express 🅞 $General, IGA Foods, repair/tires, USPO, vet, **W** 🅕 Lizard's Thicket 🅞 Food Lion, Groucho's Deli
24	US 21, to Wilson Blvd., **E** 🅖 BP/dsl, Shell/Subway/dsl 🅞 auto repair, **W** 🅖 Exxon/dsl
22	Killian Rd, **E** 🅖 Mobil/Burger King/dsl, Murphy Express/dsl 🅕 Applebee's, Bojangles, Chick-fil-A, Firehouse Subs, Freddy's, Hardee's, McDonald's, Panda Express, Popeye's, Salsarita's, Steak'n Shake, Subway, Taco Bell, Tropical Cafe, Zaxby's 🅛 Hampton Inn 🅞 Acura, Aldi Foods, AutoZone, BMW, CVS Drug, Discount Tire, Firestone, Honda, Kia, Kroger/dsl, Lowe's, Mazda, Rite Aid, Subaru, Toyota, VW, Walgreens, **W** 🅕 China Dragon, Monterrey's Mexican 🅞 Lexus/Buick/GMC/Cadillac, Verizon, Walmart/McDonald's
19	SC 555, Farrow Rd, **E** 🅖 BP/dsl, Exxon, Shell/dsl 🅕 Bojangles, Cracker Barrel, Sonic, Subway, Wendy's 🅛 Courtyard, Hilton Garden, Residence Inn 🅞 🏥, Longs Drug, **W** 🅖 Shell/dsl 🅕 China Kitchen, Waffle House 🅞 SC Archives
18	to SC 277, to I-20 W (from sb), Columbia
17	US 1, Two Notch Rd, **E** 🅖 BP, Citgo, Exxon, Shell/Circle K 🅕 Arby's, Burger King, TX Roadhouse, Waffle House 🅛 Columbia NE Hotel, Holiday Inn Express, InTown Suites, Quality Inn 🅞 Family$, to Sesquicentennial SP, U-Haul, USPO, vet, Walgreens, **W** 🅖 Mobil 🅕 Chili's, Fazoli's, Hooters, IHOP, Lizard's Thicket,

SC

🅖 = gas 🍴 = food 🛏 = lodging 🄾 = other ℞ₛ = rest stop Copyright 2022 - The Next EXIT

🔼🅽 INTERSTATE 77 Cont'd

COLUMBIA

17	Continued Outback Steaks, Waffle House 🛏 Best Western+, Comfort Suites, EconoLodge, Fairfield Inn, Hampton Inn, La Quinta, Microtel, Red Roof Inn 🄾 Home Depot
16b a	I-20, W to Augusta, E to Florence, Alpine Rd
15b a	SC 12, to Percival Rd, W 🍴 Shell
13	Decker Blvd (from nb), W 🍴 El Cheapo, Spinx/dsl
12	Forest Blvd, Thurmond Blvd, E to Ft Jackson, W 🍴 Circle K/dsl, Shell/dsl/24hr 🍴 Chick-fil-A, Cookout, Domino's, Eastern Buffet, Golden Corral, Juicy Crab, McDonald's, Panera Bread, San Jose Rest., Sonic, Subway, Wendy's 🛏 Extended Stay America, Super 8 🄾 $Tree, AT&T, 🅷, museum, Sam's Club/gas, Tuesday Morning, Verizon, vet, Walmart
10	SC 760, Jackson Blvd, E to Ft Jackson, 2 mi W 🍴 Shell 🍴 Applebee's, Bojangles, Buffalo Wild Wings, Maurices BBQ, Moe's SW, Ruby Tuesday, Smashburger, Subway 🛏 EconoLodge 🄾 Bilo, Staples, Walgreens, Whole Foods Mkt
9b a	US 76, US 378, to Sumter, Columbia, 0-2 mi E 🍴 Citgo, Murphy USA/dsl, Shell, Shell/Burger King, Sunoco/dsl 🍴 Arby's, Bojangles, Capt D's, Chick-fil-A, Domino's, KFC, McDonald's, Popeye's, Ruby Tuesday, Rush's Rest., Sawasdee Kitchen, Shoney's, Subway, Taco Bell, Waffle House, Waffle House, Wendy's, Zaxby's 🛏 Baymont Inn, Candlewood Suites, Comfort Inn, Country Inn&Suites, Days Inn, Hampton Inn, Holiday Inn Express, Home 2 Suites, La Quinta, Microtel, Quality Inn, Sleep Inn, TownePlace Suites 🄾 $Tree, Advance Parts, Aldi Foods, AutoZone, CVS Drug, Family$, Firestone/auto, Ford, Lowe's, NTB, O'Reilly Parts, URGENT CARE, USPO, Verizon, Walmart, W 🍴 Circle K, Shell 🍴 Firehouse Subs, Hardee's, Jimmy John's, Krispy Kreme, MOD Pizza, Panera Bread, Sonic, Starbucks, Sub Station, Wendy's 🛏 Best Value Inn 🄾 $General, BigLots, GNC, Goodyear/auto, 🅷, Target, Walgreens
6b a	Shop Rd, W 🄾 fairgrounds, to USC Coliseum
5	SC 48, Bluff Rd, W 🍴 Loves/McDonald's/Subway/dsl/scales/24hr, Shell/Burger King/dsl 🍴 Bojangles (2mi) 🄾 $General, Petro/Starbucks/dsl/scales/24hr
3mm	Congaree River
2	SC 35, to Cayce, W Columbia, W 🛏 Courtyard
1	US 21, US 176, US 321 (from sb), Cayce, W accesses same as SC I-26, exit 115.
	I-77 begins/ends on I-26, exit 116.

🔼🅽 INTERSTATE 85

Exit #	Services
106.5mm	South Carolina/North Carolina state line
106	US 29, to Grover, W 🍴 Exxon/dsl, Hickory Point/gas, Mobil/dsl/fireworks, Pilot/Wendy's/DQ/dsl/scales/24hr
104	SC 99, Tribal Rd, E 🍴 Loves/McDonald's/Subway/dsl/scales/24hr, W 🄾 fireworks
103mm	Welcome Ctr sb, full 🛢 facilities, info, 🄲, 🚻, litter barrels, vending, petwalk
102	SC 198, to Earl, E 🍴 BP/dsl, Exxon 🍴 Hardee's, W 🍴 FLYING J/Denny's/dsl/scales/LP/24hr, Citgo/dsl 🍴 McDonald's, Waffle House
100mm	Buffalo Creek
100	SC 5, to Blacksburg, Shelby, W 🍴 Citgo, Exxon/dsl/scales/24hr
98	Frontage Rd (from nb)
97mm	Broad River
96	SC 18, E 🍴 Circle K/Krystal/dsl
95	SC 18, to Gaffney, E 🍴 Exxon/Circle K/dsl, PetroMax/dsl 🍴 Mr Waffle 🛏 Gaffney Inn, Shamrock Inn 🄾 🅷, to Limestone Coll

GAFFNEY
SPARTANBURG

92	SC 11, to Gaffney, E 🍴 Circle K/Subway/dsl, Fast Point/dsl, Murphy USA/dsl 🍴 Aegean Pizza, Applebee's, Bojangles, Burger King, Chick-fil-A, China Express, CookOut, Daddy Joe's BBQ, Domino's, Firehouse Subs, KFC, Little Caesar's, McDonald's, Olive Garden, Papa John's, Pete's, Pizza Hut, Popeye's, Sonic, Taco Bell, Waffle House, Wendy's, Wings Etc., Zaxby's 🛏 Baymont Inn, Super 8 🄾 $General, $Tree, Advance Parts, Aldi Foods, AT&T, Belk, BigLots, BiLo, Ingles Foods, Lowe's, O'Reilly Parts, to Limestone Coll, USPO, Verizon, Walgreens, Walmart, W 🍴 Fatz Cafe 🛏 EconoLodge, Quality Inn 🄾 Chevrolet, Foothills Scenic Hwy, to The Peach
90	SC 105, SC 42, to Gaffney, E 🍴 Pilot/Arby's/dsl/scales/24hr, QT/dsl 🍴 Bojangles, Clock Rest., Starbucks, Subway, Waffle House 🛏 Red Roof Inn, Sleep Inn, W 🍴 Citgo/dsl, Exxon/Burger King 🍴 Cracker Barrel, El Michoacan, Food Court, Outback Steaks 🛏 Hampton Inn 🄾 fruit stand, Gaffney Outlets/famous brands, Hamrick's
87	SC 39, E 🄾 KOA
83	SC 110, E 🄾 fruit stand, W 🍴 Westar/dsl/scales/24hr/@ 🄾 fruitstand, to Cowpens Bfd
82	Frontage Rd (from nb)
80.5mm	Pacolet River
80	SC 57, to Gossett, E 🍴 Hot Spot/Shell/dsl
78	US 221, Chesnee, E 🍴 Citgo/dsl 🍴 Hardee's 🛏 Red Roof Inn, W 🍴 Burger King, QT/dsl, RaceWay/dsl 🍴 Arby's, Bojangles, McDonald's, Southern BBQ, Subway, Waffle House, Wendy's 🛏 Hampton Inn, Holiday Inn Express 🄾 $General, Advance Parts, Harley-Davidson, Ingles Foods/cafe/dsl
77	Lp 85, Spartanburg services along Lp 85 exits E
75	SC 9, Spartanburg, E 🍴 Spinx/dsl 🍴 Denny's 🛏 Best Western 🄾 $General, W 🍴 QT/dsl, RaceWay/dsl 🍴 Bruster's, Capri Italian, CookOut, Copper River Grill, Fatz Café, Grapevine Rest, La Paz Mexican, McDonald's, Pizza Hut, Waffle House, Zaxby's 🛏 Comfort Inn, Days Inn 🄾 CVS Drug, Ingles/cafe/gas, Parr Automotive, USPO
72	US 176, to I-585, E 🄾 to USCS, Wofford/Converse Coll, W 🍴 Kangaroo/dsl, RaceWay/dsl 🍴 China Fun, El Limon Mexican, Subway, Waffle House 🄾 $General, Ingles Foods/cafe/gas
70b a	I-26, E to Columbia, W to Asheville
69	Lp 85, SC 41 (from nb), to Fairforest
68	SC 129, to Greer
67mm	N Tyger River
66	US 29, to Lyman, Wellford, E 🍴 Exxon/Subway/dsl 🍴 Waffle House
63	SC 290, to Duncan, E 🍴 Exxon/Circle K/dsl, QT/dsl, Spinx, Dunkin'/dsl 🍴 Bojangles, Chick-Fil-A, Clock Rest., Cracker Barrel, El Primo Mexican, Firehouse Subs, Fudd's Burger, KFC, Pasanos Italian, Pizza Inn, Sake Japanese, Starbucks, Taco Bell, Thai Garden, Waffle House, Zaxby's 🛏 Baymont Inn, Fairfield Inn, Hampton Inn, Home 2 Suites, Microtel, W 🍴 BP, Marathon/dsl, Pilot/Wendy's/dsl/scales/24hr, TA/BP/DQ/rest/dsl/scales/24hr/@ 🍴 Demetre's Grill, El Molcajete Mexican, Hardee's, McDonald's 🛏 Day's Inn, Holiday Inn Express, Quality Inn, Woodspring Suites 🄾 Blue Beacon, Sonny's RV Ctr, Speedco
62.5mm	S Tyger River
60	SC 101, to Greer, E 🍴 Marathon, QT/dsl 🍴 Landmark Diner, Subway, Theo's Rest, W 🍴 Spinx/Burger King/dsl 🍴 Bojangles, Waffle House 🛏 Super 8 🄾 BMW Visitor Ctr
58	Brockman-McClimon Rd
57	W 🄾 Greenville-Spartanburg Airport

SC

✈Ⓝ INTERSTATE 85 Cont'd

Exit #	Services

56 SC 14, to Greer, E🅿 Citgo/dsl 🅾🛏, W🅿 QT/dsl, Spinx/dsl 🅾 Goodyear Truck Tires, Ledford's Adventure RV Ctr

55mm Enoree River

54 Pelham Rd, E🅿 Exxon/Circle K, Stop-A-Minute/dsl 🍴 Burger King, Corona Mexican, Skin's Hotdogs, Waffle House 🛏 Best Western, Comfort Suites, W🅿 BP/dsl 🍴 Asian Kitchen, Bertolos Pizza, Bojangles, California Dreaming Rest., Chick-fil-A, Chophouse 47, Dunkin', Eggs Up Grill, Firehouse Subs, Five Guys, Frankie's Pizza, Hardee's, Jimmy John's, Joe's Crabshack, Joy of Tokyo, Logan's Roadhouse, Macaroni Grill, McDonald's, Moe's SW Grill, On the Border, Palmetto Alehouse, Panera Bread, PDQ Rest., Red Bowl Asian, Schlotzsky's, Starbucks, Taco Bell, Taziki's Cafe, Tropical Cafe, Wendy's 🛏 Courtyard, EconoLodge, Extended Stay America, Fairfield Inn, Hampton Inn, Holiday Inn Express, Home2 Suites, MainStay Suites, Marriott, Residence Inn, Wingate Inn, Wyndham Garden 🅾 Advance Parts, Bi-Lo, CVS Drug, EarthFare Foods, GNC, Goodyear/auto, Verizon, Walgreens, Walmart

51 I-385, SC 146, Woodruff Rd, E🍴 Brixx Pizza, Buffalo Wild Wings, Chipotle Mexican, Coldstone, Cracker Barrel, Fuddrucker's, Genghis Grill, IHOP, La Parrilla, Lieu's Bistro, Longhorn Steaks, Oriental House, Panera Bread, PF Chang's, Red Robin, Sticky Fingers 🛏 Drury Inn, Hampton Inn, Hilton Garden, Homewood Suites, Residence Inn, Staybridge Suites, Tru Hilton 🅾 Barnes&Noble, Best Buy, Dick's, Goodyear/auto, Hamrick's Outlet, Lowe's, Marshalls, PetCo, Petsmart, REI, Ross, Verizon, vet, Whole Foods Mkt, W🅿 QT/dsl, RaceWay/dsl 🍴 Bad Daddy's Burger, Carolina Alehouse, Carrabba's, Cheddars, Chuy's Mexican, Dave&Busters's, Firebirds, Grimaldi's, HuHot Mongolian, McDonald's, MidTown Deli, Panda Express, Ruby Tuesday, Ruth's Chris Steaks, Starbucks, Strossner's Cafe, Subway, TGIFriday's, Tin Lizzy's, Tropical Cafe, Tucanos Brazilian Grill, Twin Peaks Rest., Waffle House, Wild Wing Cafe, Yardhouse Rest., Zoe's Kitchen 🛏 Baymont Inn, Candlewood Suites, Comfort Inn, Crowne Plaza, Days Inn, Embassy Suites, Holiday Inn Express, La Quinta, Microtel, My Place 🅾 AT&T, Cabela's, Costco/gas, Firestone/auto, Home Depot, Old Navy, Target, Trader Joe's

48b a US 276, Greenville, E🅿 BP/dsl, QT/dsl 🍴 Waffle House 🛏 Red Roof Inn 🅾 BMW/Mini, CarMax, to ICAR, W🅿 Exxon/dsl 🍴 Arby's, Burger King, Happy China, Hooters, McDonald's, Olive Garden, Starbucks, Subway, Taco Bell 🛏 Country Inn&Suites, Embassy Suites 🅾 $Tree, Acura, Audi/Porsche/VW, Bi-Lo, Buick/GMC, Chevrolet/Cadillac, Chrysler/Dodge/Jeep, CVS Drug, Ford/Lincoln, GNC, Honda, Infiniti, Jaguar, Kia, Lexus, Mazda, Meineke, Mercedes, Michael's, Nissan, Office Depot, Old Time Pottery, PepBoys, Petsmart, SteinMart, Subaru, Toyota, Volvo

46c rd 291, Pleasantburg Rd, Mauldin Rd, W🅿 BP, Citgo/dsl, QT/dsl 🍴 Jack-in-the-Box, Papa John's, Subway 🛏 Greenville Inn, InTown Suites, Super Lodge, Woodspring Suites 🅾 Aamco, Advance Parts, Aldi, Home Depot, NTB, same as 46ba

46b a US 25 bus, Augusta Rd, E🅿 Mike&Jack/dsl, QT/dsl, Spinx/dsl, Vgo 🍴 Burger King, Waffle House 🛏 Country Hearth Inn, Southern Suites, W🛏 Economy Inn, Traveler's Inn 🅾 Home Depot, same as 46c

44 US 25, White Horse Rd, E🅿 Spinx/Subway/dsl, W🅿 Citgo/dsl, McDonald's, Fastfuels/dsl 🍴 Waffle House 🅾 Freightliner, 🛏

44a SC 20 (from sb), to Piedmont

42 I-185, to Greenville, I-185 S (toll), Columbia, W🅾🛏

40 SC 153, to Easley, E🅿 BP/dsl 🍴 Waffle House, W🅿 7-11/dsl, Citgo/dsl, QT/dsl, RaceWay/dsl, Spinx/dsl 🍴 Arby's, Big Clock, Bojangles, Burger King, Chick-Fil-A, Cracker Barrel, Dunkin', El Sureno Mexican, Firehouse Subs, Huddle House, KFC, Little Caesar's, Los Amigos, McDonald's, Papa John's, Pizza House, Pizza Hut, Subway, Taco Bell, Zaxby's 🛏 Best Western+, Comfort Suites, Executive Inn, Hampton Inn (4mi), Holiday Inn Express, Super 8 🅾 $General, Advance Parts, AutoZone, Bi-Lo, CVS Drug, O'Reilly Parts, Verizon, Walgreens, Walmart

39 SC 143, to Piedmont, E🅿 Vgo/dsl, W🅿 Shell/dsl

35 SC 86, to Easley, Piedmont, E🅿 BP/Subway (1.5mi), 🅿Pilot/ McDonald's/dsl/scales/24hr 🍴 Cancun Mexican, Hardee's (1.5mi), Sweet P's, Tony' Pizza 🅾 O'Reilly Parts, repair/tires, Walgreens, W🅿 QT/dsl, Spinx/dsl 🍴 Bojangles

34 US 29 (from sb), to Williamston

32 SC 8, to Pelzer, Easley, E🅿 7-11/dsl, Shell/dsl

27 SC 81, to Anderson, E🅿 BP/dsl, Exxon/dsl, Stop A Minit/dsl 🍴 Arby's, McDonald's, Papa's Mexican, Waffle House 🛏 Hampton Inn, Holiday Inn Express 🅾🛏

23mm 🆁🆂 sb, full 🛏 facilities, 🅲 vending, 🌲 litter barrels, petwalk

21 US 178, to Anderson, E🅿 BP/dsl, QT/dsl 🍴 Burger King, Waffle House

19b a US 76, SC 28, to Anderson, E🅿 Exxon/dsl, QT/dsl, Shell/dsl, Stop A Minit/dsl 🍴 Applebee's, Barbarito's, Bojangles, Carson Steaks, Chick-fil-A, Chili's, Chipotle, CookOut, Denny's, Five Guys, Fuddruckers, Golden Corral, Golden Corral, Grand China, Hardee's, Hardee's, Hibachi Grill, Jack-in-the-Box, Logan's Roadhouse, Longhorn Steaks, O'Charley's, Olive Garden, Panera Bread, Red Lobster, Starbucks, Tucker's Rest., TX Roadhouse, Zaxby's 🛏 Best Value Inn, Days Inn, Hilton Garden, Holiday Inn, Rodeway Inn, Super 8 🅾 $General, $Tree, Advance Parts, Aldi Foods, AT&T, Best Buy, Chrysler/Dodge/Jeep, Dick's, Ford/Mazda, GNC, Goodyear, Harley-Davidson, Hobby Lobby, Home Depot, Honda, Kohl's, Lowe's, Meineke, Michael's, Nissan, O'Reilly Parts, Office Depot, Old Navy, Petsmart, Publix/deli, Ross, Russell Stover, Sam's Club, Staples, Target, TJ Maxx, Toyota, Verizon, vet, Walmart/Subway, W🅿 RaceWay/dsl, Shell/McDonald's 🍴 Arby's, Cracker Barrel, Fatz Cafe, Hooters, J Peters Grill, Outback Steaks, Starbucks, Subway, Waffle House, Wendy's, Wild Wing Cafe 🛏 Baymont Inn, Comfort Suites, Country Inn&Suites, Fairfield Inn, Hampton Inn, Holiday Inn Express, Microtel, Residence Inn 🅾 to Clemson U (11mi)

18mm 🆁🆂 nb, full 🛏 facilities, 🅲 vending, 🌲 litter barrels, petwalk

15mm Lake Hartwell

14 SC 187, to Clemson, Anderson, E🅿 Marathon/dsl 🍴 Huddle House, W🍴 Mi Casa 🛏 Budget Inn 🅾 $General, to Clem Research Pk

12mm Seneca River, Lake Hartwell

SC

🔃 = gas 🍴 = food 🛏 = lodging ⊙ = other ℞s = rest stop Copyright 2022 - The Next EXIT

⬆N INTERSTATE 85 Cont'd

Exit #	Services
11	SC 24, SC 243, to Townville, **E** 🔃 Exxon/dsl, Sunoco/dsl 🍴 Subway ⊙ to Savannah River Scenic Hwy, **W** 🔃 Shell/dsl 🍴 Townville Cafe
9mm	weigh sta nb
4	SC 243, to SC 24, Fair Play, **E** 🔃 **Loves**/Arby's/dsl/scales/24hr, Mobil/dsl
2	SC 59, to Fair Play, **W** ⊙ fireworks
1	SC 11, to Walhalla, **W** 🍴 Gazebo Rest. ⊙ fireworks, to Lake Hartwell SP
.5mm	Welcome Ctr nb, full 🛁 facilities, info, 🍴, 🛒, litter barrels, vending, petwalk
0mm	South Carolina/Georgia state line, Lake Hartwell, Tugaloo River

⬆N INTERSTATE 95

Exit #	Services
198mm	South Carolina/North Carolina state line
196mm	Welcome Ctr sb, full 🛁 facilities, info, 🍴, vending, 🛒, litter barrels, petwalk
195mm	Little Pee Dee River
193	SC 9, SC 57, to N Myrtle Beach, Dillon, **E** 🔃 Exxon/dsl, Mobil/dsl, Murphy Express/dsl, Sunoco/dsl 🍴 B&C Steak/BBQ, Burger King, CookOut, Huddle House, Little Caesar's, Pizza Hut, Popeye's, Subway, Tokyo Cafe, Waffle House, Wendy's, Zaxby's 🛏 Best Value Inn, Days Inn, Quality Inn, Red Roof Inn, Taco Bell ⊙ $General, $Tree, Advance Parts, AutoZone, CVS Drug, fireworks, Food Lion, 🏥, O'Reilly Parts, SaveALot Foods, Walgreens, Walmart, **W** 🍴 Eastern Cafe Chines 🛏 Economy Inn ⊙ Bass Lake RV Camp/LP, **N** 🔃 Speedway/Speedy Cafe/dsl/24hr
190	SC 34, to Dillon, **W** 🔃 **Loves**/Arby's/dsl/scales/24hr
181	SC 38, Oak Grove, **E** 🔃 ⚘FLYING J/dsl/LP/scales/24hr, BP/Subway/dsl/24hr, Shell/McDonald's/dsl/24hr 🍴 Shuler's BBQ (5mi) ⊙ fireworks, **W** 🍴 ▦/DQ/Wendy's/dsl/scales/24hr 🛏 Best Western
175mm	Pee Dee River
170	SC 327, **E** 🔃 BP, ▦/Wendy's/dsl/scales/24hr 🍴 McDonald's, Subway, Waffle House, Zaxby's 🛏 Holiday Inn Express ⊙ Harley Davidson, Missile Museum, to Myrtle Beach, **W** 🔃 Buc-ee's
169	TV Rd, to Florence, **E** ⊙ dsl repair, Florence RV Park, **W** 🔃 BP, Petro/Shell/Iron Skillet/dsl/scales/24hr/@ 🛏 Best Value Inn ⊙ Blue Beacon, dsl repair, Peterbilt
164	US 52, to Darlington, Florence, **E** 🔃 Exxon/dsl, RaceWay, Shell/dsl 🍴 Cracker Barrel, McDonald's, Quincy's, Ruby Tuesday, Waffle House, Wendy's 🛏 Baymont Inn, Best Western, EconoLodge, Rodeway Inn, Suburban Lodge, Super 8 ⊙ Chrysler/Dodge/Jeep, 🏥, **W** 🔃 Mobil, ▦/Subway/Taco Bell/dsl, TA/BP/Popeye's/dsl/scales/@ 🍴 Arby's, Dickey's BBQ, Dunkin', Fatz Café, Hardee's, Krispy Kreme, Shoney's, Young's Pecans, Zaxby's 🛏 Comfort Suites, Country Inn&Suites, Days Inn, Hampton Inn, La Quinta, Microtel, Motel 6, Sleep Inn, Travel House Inn, Tru Hilton ⊙ to Darlington Raceway, transmissions
160b	I-20 W, to Columbia
160a	Lp 20, to Florence, **E** 🔃 Exxon/dsl, Murphy USA/dsl, Tesla EVC 🍴 Arby's, Bruster's Ice Cream, Buffalo Wild Wings, Burger King, Chick-fil-A, Chili's, Chipotle, ChuckeCheese, Firehouse Subs, Golden Corral, Hibachi Grill, Hwy 55 Cafe, IHOP, La Bamba Mexican, Longhorn Steaks, Mellow Mushroom, Olive Garden, Outback Steaks, Panera Bread, Percy&Willie's, Red Bowl Asian, Red Lobster, Ruby Tuesday, San Jose's, Subway, Taco Bell, Waffle House, Western Sizzlin, Which Wich? 🛏 Courtyard, Days Inn, Fairfield Inn, Hampton Inn, Hilton Garden,

Exit #	Services
160a	Continued Holiday Inn Express, Home 2 Hilton, Homewood Suites, Quality Inn, Red Roof Inn, Residence Inn, SpringHill Suites, Staybridge Suites, TownePlace Suites ⊙ $Tree, Aldi Foods, AT&T, Barnes&Noble, Belk, Best Buy, Big Lots, Dick's, Discount Tire, Hamrick's, Hobby Lobby, Home Depot, JC Penney, Kohl's, Lowes Whse, Petsmart, Sam's Club/dsl, Target, Verizon, Walmart
157	US 76, Timmonsville, Florence, **E** 🔃 Citgo/dsl, Kangaroo/dsl, Marathon/dsl, Shell/McDonald's 🍴 Peking Asian, Waffle House 🛏 Florence Inn, Travelodge ⊙ Abbott Farms Peaches, **W** 🔃 Mobil/dsl 🛏 Palmetto Inn, Swamp Fox Camping (1mi), Tree Top Inn ⊙ auto repair
153	Honda Way, **W** 🔃 Exxon/dsl ⊙ Honda Plant
150	SC 403, to Sardis, **E** 🔃 Mobil/dsl/scales 🍴 Hotplate Cafe 🛏 Budget Inn, **W** 🔃 Marathon/dsl
147mm	Lynches River
146	SC 341, to Lynchburg, Olanta, **E** 🛏 Relax Inn
141	SC 53, SC 58, to Shiloh, **E** ⊙ DonMar RV Ctr, to Woods Bay S **W** 🔃 Shell
139mm	℞s both lanes, full 🛁 facilities, 🍴, vending, 🛒, litter barrels, petwalk
135	US 378, to Sumter, Turbeville, **E** 🔃 BP/dsl, Citgo/dsl/24hr 🛏 Day's Inn, **W** 🔃 Exxon/Subway/dsl
132	SC 527, to Sardinia, Kingstree
130mm	Black River
122	US 521, to Alcolu, Manning, **W** 🔃 Exxon/dsl
119	SC 261, to Paxville, Manning, 0-1 mi **E** 🔃 Murphy USA/dsl, Shell/dsl, TA/BP/Pizza Hut/Popeye's/dsl/scales/24hr/@ 🍴 Bojangles, Burger King, CookOut, Huddle House, Mariachi's Mexican, McDonald's, Shoney's, Sonic, Subway, Taco Bell, Waffle House, Wendy's, Yucatan Mexican, Zaxby's 🛏 Baymont Inn, Days Inn, Hampton Inn, Quality Inn, SureStay ⊙ $General, AutoZone, Chrysler/Dodge/Jeep, CVS Drug, Ford, 🏥, O'Reilly Parts, truckwash, Verizon, Walmart, **W** 🔃 Enmarket/dsl/e85, Marathon 🛏 Super 8
115	US 301, to Summerton, Manning, **W** 🔃 Shell/dsl 🍴 Georgio's Rest 🛏 Ashburn Inn
108	rd 102, Summerton, **E** 🔃 BP/DQ, Citgo/dsl 🍴 TawCaw Campin (6mi), **W** 🔃 **Loves**/McDonald's/Subway/dsl/scales/24hr/ 🛏 Days Inn
102	US 15, US 301 N, to N Santee, **E** 🔃 Marathon/dsl 🛏 Santee Resort/Motel ⊙ KOA, Palmetto Shores Resort, **W** 🔃 Horizon/dsl/e85 ⊙ to Santee NWR
100mm	Lake Marion
99mm	℞s both lanes, full 🛁 facilities, 🍴, info, vending, 🛒, litter barrels, petwalk
98	SC 6, to Eutawville, Santee, **E** 🔃 BP/Bojangles, Citgo, Exxon, Mobil 🍴 Huddle House, Pizza Hut, Subway, Taco Bell 🛏 Best Western+, Clarion, Econolodge, Fairfield Inn, Hampton Inn, Red Roof Inn, Super 8, Travelodge ⊙ $General, IGA Foods, **W** 🔃 Horizon/dsl/e85, Marathon/dsl, Shell, Sunoco 🍴 Burger King, Cracker Barrel, McDonald's, Waffle House, Wendy's 🛏 Clarion Inn/rest., Comfort Inn, Holiday Inn, Knights Inn, Lake Marion Inn, Quality Inn ⊙ CarQuest, CVS Drug, Family$, Food Lion, Rivers Country Store, to Santee SP (3mi), USPO
97	US 301 S (from sb, no return), to Orangeburg
93	US 15, to Santee, Holly Hill
90	US 176, to Cameron, Holly Hill, **W** 🔃 Exxon/dsl
86b a	I-26, W to Columbia, E to Charleston
82	US 178, to Bowman, Harleyville, **E** 🔃 Enmarket/Subway ▦/Wendy's/DQ/Dunkin'/dsl/scales/24hr 🛏 Peachtree In **W** 🔃 Shell/dsl ⊙ tires/truck repair
77	US 78, to Bamberg, St George, **E** 🔃 Enmarket/Subway/dsl/e85, ⚘FLYING J/Denny's/dsl/scales/24hr, Monoco, Sunoco 🍴 Empire Chinese, Georgio's Rest., Hardee's, KFC, McDonald's

🔼Ⓝ INTERSTATE 95 Cont'd

77	Continued
	Pizza Hut, Skynyrd's Grill, Waffle House 🛏 Best Value Inn, Days Inn/RV Park, EconoLodge, Quality Inn Ⓞ $General, Ace Hardware, BiLo, Chevrolet/GMC, CVS Drug, Family$, USPO, W 🅿 BP, Shell/Taco Bell/dsl 🛏 Country Hearth Inn, Knights Inn
74mm	weigh sta nb, parking area sb, commercial vehicles only
68	SC 61, Canadys, E 🅿 BP, Crosco Express, Shell/Subway/dsl Ⓞ to Colleton SP (3mi)
62	McLeod Rd
57	SC 64, Lodge, Walterboro, E 🅿 Citgo/dsl, Horizon/e85, Shell/DQ, Sunoco/dsl 🍴 Arby's, Bojangles, Burger King, Capt D's, China Wok, Dimitrio's Rest., Domino's, Dunkin', EVC, Hardee's, Huddle House, McDonald's, Olde House Café, Starbucks, Subway, Taco Bell, Waffle House, Wendy's 🛏 Carolina Lodge, Sleep Inn, Southern Inn Ⓞ $General, Ace Hardware, Advance Parts, AutoZone, Belk, Family$, Ford, GNC, Ⓗ, O'Reilly Parts, W 🅿 Murphy USA/dsl 🍴 China Buffet, Fat Jack's, IHOP, KFC, Zaxby's 🛏 Super 8 Ⓞ $Tree, AT&T, PetCo, Verizon, Walmart
53	SC 63, to Varnville, Walterboro, Hampton, E 🅿 BP/McDonald's, Circle K/dsl, El Cheapo, Exxon, Shell/DQ 🍴 Ruby Tuesday, Shoney's, Waffle House 🛏 Baymont Inn, Best Western, Comfort Inn, EconoLodge, Palms Inn, Ramada Inn, Red Roof Inn, Rodeway Inn Ⓞ fireworks, W 🅿 Enmarket/dsl 🍴 Cracker Barrel 🛏 Days Inn, Hampton Inn, Holiday Inn Express, Microtel, Motel 6, Quality Inn Ⓞ New Green Acres Camping
47mm	🆁🆂 both lanes, full ♿ facilities, 🅲, vending, 🗑 litter barrels, petwalk
42	US 21, to Yemassee, Beaufort
40mm	Combahee River
38	SC 68, to Hampton, Yemassee, E 🅿 Enmarket/dsl/e85 Ⓞ Family$, W 🅿 BP/Subway/TCBY, Exxon/dsl, ❤Loves/dsl/scales/24hr 🍴Hardee's/dsl, Shell/dsl
33	US 17 N, to Beaufort, E 🅿 BP/dsl, Exxon/McDonald's, Marathon/Subway/TCBY, Shell 🍴 17 W Kitchen, Waffle House, Wendy's 🛏 Best Western, Hampton Inn, Motel 6, Red Roof Inn Ⓞ Confederate Railroad Museum, KOA, The Oaks RV Camping
30.5mm	Tullifinny River
29mm	Coosawhatchie River
28	SC 462, to Coosawhatchie, Hilton Head, Bluffton, W 🅿 Exxon/dsl, Gen Store
22	US 17, Ridgeland, W 🅿 Sunoco Ⓞ Ⓗ
21	SC 336, to Hilton Head, Ridgeland, E 🅿 Citgo/dsl, Marathon/dsl 🍴McDonald's, Wendy's Ⓞ Boat'n RV Whse, W 🅿 BP/DQ/dsl, Enmarket/dsl, Oyo Motel, Shell 🍴 Burger King, Chef Donald's, Hong Kong Chinese, KFC, Subway, Waffle House 🛏 Carolina Lodge, Days Inn, Quality Inn Ⓞ $General, Harvey's Foods, Ⓗ, Rite Aid
18	SC 13, to US 17, US 278, to Switzerland, Granville, Ridgeland
17mm	parking area both lanes, commercial vehicles only
8	US 278, to Bluffton, Hardeeville, E 🅿 BP/Burrito/dsl/scales, Circle K/McDonald's, Exxon 🍴 Dunkin', Waffle House Ⓞ Ⓗ, W 🅿 Horizon/Subway/dsl, Shell/dsl 🛏 Holiday Inn Express, Motel 6
5	US 17, US 321, to Savannah, Hardeeville, E 🅿 BP/dsl, Parker's/dsl, 🅿/Subway/dsl/scales/24hr 🍴 Chicken Lickin, Mi Tierrita Mexican, Waffle House 🛏 Days Inn, Economy Inn, Sleep Inn Ⓞ fireworks, to Savannah NWR, W 🅿 Butlers/dsl/repair, Octane/dsl, Speedway/dsl, Sunoco/dsl 🍴 Burger King, Wendy's 🛏 Best Western+, Deluxe Inn, Hardeeville Inn, Knights Inn, Magnolia Motel, Quality Suites, Red Roof Inn, Super 8, Travelodge Ⓞ $General, Advance Parts, Family$, fireworks, NAPA
4.5mm	Welcome Ctr nb, full ♿ facilities, info, 🅲, 🗑 litter barrels, vending, petwalk, wi-fi
4mm	weigh sta both lanes
0mm	South Carolina/Georgia state line, Savannah River

🔼Ⓝ INTERSTATE 385 (Greenville)

Exit #	Services
42	US 276, Stone Ave, to Travelers Rest, **I-385 begins/ends on US 276**, E Ⓞ CarQuest, vet, W 🅿 Spinx/dsl Ⓞ multiple services on US 276, to Greenville Zoo
40b a	SC 291, Pleasantburg Dr, E 🅿 Sunoco 🍴 Jack-in-the-Box, Little Caesar's, Olive Tree, S&S Cafeteria, Sonic, Starbucks, Subway, Taco Casa, Wendy's Ⓞ $Tree, CVS Drug, Family$, Furman U, to BJU, Walgreens, W 🅿 Citgo/dsl, QT/dsl 🍴 Domino's, Krispy Kreme 🛏 Phoenix Inn/Rest., Sleep Inn Ⓞ Cottman Transmissions, Midas
39	Haywood Rd, E 🅿 Spinx 🍴 Noodleville, Outback Steaks, Portofino's, Tony's Pizzeria 🛏 Clarion, Courtyard, Hawthorn Inn, Hilton, Hyatt Place, La Quinta Ⓞ Firestone/auto, USPO, W 🅿 Spinx/dsl 🍴 Applebee's, Backyard Burger, Burger King, Chick-fil-A, Chili's, Chipotle, ChuckeCheese, CiCi's Pizza, CityRange Steaks, Clock Rest., Copper River Grill, Don Pablo, Firehouse Subs, Five Guys, Fried Green Tomatoes, Grille 33, Habiba Mediterranean, Halton Country Buffet, Harbor Inn Seafood, Jason's Deli, Jimmy John's, Kanpai Tokyo, McAlister's Deli, Miyabi Japanese, Moe's SW Grill, Monterrey Mexican, Panera Bread, Papa's&Beer, Rafferdi's, Saskatoon Rest., Starbucks, Stax Grill, Steak'n Shake, Waffle House 🛏 Baymont Inn, Extended Stay America, Hampton Inn Ⓞ AT&T, Barnes&Noble, Belk, Dillard's, Discount Tire, JC Penney, Jo-Ann, Macy's, TJ Maxx, Verizon, vet
37	Roper Mtn Rd, W 🅿 Marathon/Kangaroo/dsl, QT/dsl, RaceWay/dsl 🍴 Carrabba's, Cheddar's, Chuy's Mexican, Dave&Busters, HuHot Mongolian, Krystal, McDonald's, MidTown Deli, Ruby Tuesday, Ruths Chris Steaks, Starbucks, Strossner's Cafe, Subway, TGI Friday's, Tucnos Brazilian Grill, Twin Peaks Rest., Waffle House, Yardhouse Rest. 🛏 Candlewood Suites, Comfort Inn, Crowne Plaza, Days Inn, Embassy Suites, Holiday Inn Express, La Quinta, Microtel Ⓞ AT&T, Cabela's, Costco/gas, Firestone/auto, Home Depot, Hyundai, Old Navy, Target, Trader Joe's
36b a	I-85, N to Charlotte, S to Atlanta
35	SC 146, Woodruff Rd, 0-2 mi E 🅿 Marathon, QT/dsl, Spinx 🍴 Applebee's, Bojangles, Bone Fish Grill, Boston Pizzeria, Bruster's, Chick-fil-A, Chili's, China Buffet, CookOut, Culver's, Dunkin', Epic Curean Rest., Firehouse Subs, Great Harvest Bread, Green Tomato Buffet, Hardee's, Hibachi Grill, Jersey Mike's, JP's 4 Corners SW Rest., KFC, Krispy Kreme, Little Caesar's, McAlister's Deli, McDonald's, Mimi's Japanese Steaks, Moe's SW Grill, Pizza Inn, Sonic, Starbucks, Stevi B's, Subway, Taco Bell, Topper's Rest., Travinia Italian, Waffle House, Wendy's, Your Pizza Pie, Zaxby's Ⓞ $Tree, AAA, Ace Hardware, Aldi Foods, Bi-Lo Foods, BigLots, Discount Tire, GNC, Hobby Lobby, Kohl's, O'Reilly Parts, Publix, Rite Aid, Sam's Club/gas, Save-a-Lot Foods, Staples, Tire Kingdom, URGENT CARE, USPO, Walmart, W 🅿 Red Robin 🍴 Brixx Pizza, Buffalo Wild Wings, Chipotle

SC

🅿 = gas   🍴 = food   🛏 = lodging   ⓞ = other   Rs = rest stop   Copyright 2022 - The Next EXIT

↑N INTERSTATE 385 (Greenville) Cont'd

35	Continued
	Mexican, Coldstone, Cracker Barrel, Fuddrucker's, Genghis Grill, IHOP, La Parrilla Mexican, Lieu's Bistro, Longhorn Steaks, Oriental House, Panera Bread, PF Chang's, Red Robin, Sticky Fingers, Which Wich? 🛏 Drury Inn, Hampton Inn, Hilton Garden, Homewood Suites, Residence Inn, Staybridge Suites, Tru Hilton ⓞ Barnes&Noble, Best Buy, Dick's, Goodyear/auto, Hamrick's Outlet, Lowe's, Marshall's, Petco, Petsmart, REI, Ross, Verizon, vet, Whole Foods Mkt, World Mkt
34	Butler Rd, Mauldin, E 🅿 Spinx/dsl 🍴 Arby's, W 🍴 Bojangles, Dino's Rest., Moretti's Pizzeria, Sub Sta. 2 ⓞ $General
33	Bridges Rd, Mauldin
31	I-185 toll, SC 417, to Laurens Rd, E 🅿 Marathon, Shell/dsl 🍴 Hardee's, McDonald's, Subway ⓞ BiLo, SaveALot Foods, W 🅿 Spinx/dsl
30	I-185 toll, US 276, Standing Springs Rd
29	Georgia Rd, to Simpsonville, W 🛏 Woodspring Suites
27	Fairview Rd, to Simpsonville, E 🅿 Shell 🍴 Carolina Rest., CoachHouse Rest., JB's BBQ, Little Caesar's, McDonald's, Milano Pizzeria, Subway 🛏 Palmetto Inn ⓞ $General, Advance Parts, AutoZone, Big Lots, CVS Drug, 🅗, O'Reilly Parts, W 🅿 Exxon, Murphy USA, Spinx/dsl 🍴 Anthony's Pizza, Applebee's, Arby's, AZ Steaks, Baskin-Robbins, Bellacino's, Bruster's, Burger King, Chick-fil-A, Cracker Barrel, Epic Buffet, Firehouse Subs, Five Guys, Hibachi House, Hungry Howie's, IHOP, Jack-in-the-Box, Jersey Mike's, KFC, La Fogata Mexican, Mad Cuban, McDonald's, Mei Mei House, Moe's SW Grill, O'Charley's, Panera Bread, Pizza Hut, Ruby Tuesday, Sonic, Starbucks, Subway, Taco Bell, Tequila's Mexican, Waffle House, Wendy's, Zaxby's 🛏 Comfort Suites, Days Inn, Hampton Inn, Holiday Inn Express, Motel 6, Quality Inn ⓞ $Tree, AT&T, Belk, Bi-Lo, CVS Drug, GNC, Goodyear/auto, Home Depot, Ingles Foods, Kohl's, Lowe's, Publix, Ross, Target, Tire Kingdom, TJ Maxx, URGENT CARE, USPO, Verizon, Walgreens, Walmart
26	Harrison Bridge Rd, W 🅿 7-11/dsl, QT/dsl same as 27
24	Fairview St, E 🅿 Marathon 🍴 Hardee's, Waffle House
23	SC 418, to Fountain Inn, Fork Shoals, E 🅿 Exxon/pizza/subs/dsl 🍴 Bojangles, Zaxby's ⓞ $General, O'Reilly Parts, USPO, W 🅿 Sunoco/dsl
22	SC 14 W, Old Laurens Rd, to Fountain Inn
19	SC 14 E, to Gray Court, Owings
16	SC 101, to Woodruff, Gray Court
10	rd 23, Barksdale, Ora
9	US 221, to Laurens, Enoree, E 🅿 S&H Trkstp/dsl 🍴 Waffle House 🛏 Budget Lodge, W ⓞ Walmart Dist Ctr
6mm	Rs both lanes (both lanes exit left), full 🛏 facilities, 🅟, vending, 🚮 litter barrels, petwalk
5	SC 49, to Laurens, Union
2	SC 308, to Clinton, Ora, W ⓞ 🅗, to Presbyterian Coll in Clinton
0mm	I-26 S to Columbia, I-385 begins/ends on I-26 at 52mm.

↑N INTERSTATE 526 (Charleston)

Exit #	Services
33mm	I-526 begins/ends.
32	US 17, N 🅿 Shell, Speedway/dsl 🍴 Atl Bread, Bojangles, Burger King, Burton's Grill, Cane's, Five Guys, Grimaldi's Brick Oven, IHOP, PF Chang's, Qdoba, Sonic, Taco Bell, TGIFriday, Zoe's Kitchen 🛏 Courtyard, Hampton Inn ⓞ Advance Parts, AT&T, Barnes&Noble, Belk, BiLo, Chevrolet, CVS Drug, GNC, Lowes Whse, Midas, Old Navy, Rite Aid, Tire Kingdom, TrueValue, Verizon, Walgreens, 0-1 mi S 🅿 Shell/Circle K, Sunoco/dsl

32	Continued
	🍴 Applebees, Arby's, Chick-fil-A, Cici's, Firehouse Subs, Hardee's, Huddle House, Jimmy John's, La Hacienda Mexican, Liberty Rest., McDonald's, Melvin's Ribs& Cue, Moe's SW Grill, Momma Goldberg's Deli, Outback Steaks, Sticky Fingers, Subway, Wendy's, Zeus Grill 🛏 Best Western, Clarion, Day's Inn, Extended Stay America, Hampton Inn, Hilton Garden, Holiday Inn, Holiday Inn Express, Mainstay Suites, Quality Inn, Red Roof Inn, Sleep Inn ⓞ $Tree, Bi-Lo, CVS Drug, Firestone/auto, Harris Teeter, Jiffy Lube, Marshall's, Michaels, NAPA, O'Reilly Parts, Office Depot, Petco, Publix, Staples, TJ Maxx, Trader Joe's, USPO, Verizon, vet, VW, Walmart, Whole Foods Mkt
28	Long Point Rd, N 🅿 Exxon, Shell 🍴 Another Broken Egg, Bamboo Garden, Chick-fil-A, McAlister's, Moe's SW Grill, Starbucks, Subway, Waffle House, Wendy's ⓞ Charles Pinckney NHS, CVS Drug, Harris Teeter Foods, PetsMart, Steinmart
26mm	Wando River
24	Daniel Island, S 🅿 Exxon 🍴 Domino's, Dragon Palace, Subway, Wasabi 🛏 Hampton Inn, Home 2 Suites ⓞ Publix
23b a	Clements Ferry Rd
21mm	Cooper River
20	Virginia Ave (from eb), S 🅿 Speedway Depot
19	N Rhett Ave, N 🅿 Exxon, Kangaroo/Subway/dsl, Pilot/Arby's/dsl/scales/24hr 🍴 Bojangles, Waffle House ⓞ Family$, Food Lion, S 🅿 Kwikstop
18b a	US 52, US 78, Rivers Ave, N 🅿 BP/dsl, Circle K/dsl ⓞ auto repair, Family$, H&L Foods, S 🅿 76/dsl 🛏 Woodspring Suites
17b a	I-26, E to Charleston, W to Columbia
16	Montague Ave, Airport Rd, S 🍴 Bonefish Grill, Chili's, Denny's, Jersey Mike's, La Hacienda, Panera Bread, Starbucks, Wendy's 🛏 Embassy Suites, Hilton Garden, Holiday Inn, Homewood Suites, Residence Inn ⓞ Sam's Club/gas, Staples, Tanger Outlet/famous brands, Walmart/Subway
15	SC 642, Dorchester Rd, Paramount Dr, N 🅿 Shell/Circle K [auto service, Family$, S 🅿 Citgo/dsl, Sunoco 🍴 Burger King, Checker's, Domino's, East Bay Deli, Huddle House, Little Caesar's, Pizza Hut, Subway 🛏 Airport Inn ⓞ Advance Parts, Bi-Lo Foods, CVS Drug, Family$, Food Lion, Harley-Davidson, U-Haul
14	Leeds Ave, S 🛏 Woodspring Suites ⓞ boat marina
13mm	Ashley River
11b a	SC 61, Ashley River Rd, N 🍴 Baron's Pizza, Chick-fil-A, McDonald's, O'Charley's ⓞ Food Lion, Home Depot, 🅗, Jo-Ann, Kohl's, Lowes Whse, Marshall's
10	US 17, SC 7, **services from US 17** E 🅿 BP 🍴 Bessinger's BBQ, Capt D's, Chick-fil-A, CookOut, Dunkin', Five Guys, Hopsing Asian, IHOP, King St Grille, Krispy Kreme, La Fontana Italia, McDonald's, Panera Bread, Red Lobster, Ruby Tuesday, Taco Bell 🛏 Best Western, Evergreen Motel, Holiday Inn Express, Motel 6, Sleep Inn, Town & Country Suites ⓞ AutoZone, Belk, BiLo, BMW/Mini, Buick/GMC/Cadillac, Chevrolet, Chrysler/Dodge/Jeep, Dick's, Dillard's, Ford/Lincoln, Honda, Hyundai, Infiniti, Jaguar/Range Rover/Porsche, JC Penney, Maserati, Mercedes, Nissan, Pepboys, Petsmart, Ross, Smart, Target, Tire Kingdom, vet, Volvo, **services from US 17** W 🅿 AMFlag, Shell, Circle K, Speedway/dsl 🍴 China Fun, Hardees, Inyabi Japanese, Subway, Waffle House 🛏 Comfort Suites, Econolodge, Hampton Inn, Hawthorn Suites, InTown Suites ⓞ Acura, Advance Parts, Audi, Carmax, Costco/gas, CVS Drug, DriveTime, Family$, Food Lion, Kia, Lexus, Toyota
9	I-526 begins/ends on US 17.

SC

SOUTH DAKOTA

S I S S E T O N

W A T E R T O W N

B R O O K I N G S

🧭 N INTERSTATE 29

Exit #	Services
253mm	South Dakota/North Dakota state line
251mm	**Welcome Ctr sb, full 🅰 facilities, info, [🄲], 🛋, litter barrels, pet-walk, RV dump**
246	SD 127, to Rosholt, New Effington, **3 mi** W [🅖] gas 🍴 food [🅞] RV camping, Sica Hollow SP (24mi)
242	110th St
235mm	weigh sta sb
232	SD 10, Sisseton, E [🅖] Dakota Connection/dsl/casino/24hr [🍴] Crossroads Cafe, **1-3 mi** W [🅖] Amstar/dsl, FuelMax/dsl, Sinclair/dsl/e85, Tesoro [🍴] Cottage Rest, DQ, Pizza Hut, Subway, Taco John's 🛏 Holiday Motel, I-29 Motel, Super 8 [🅞] Camp Dakotah, Family$, Ft Sisseton SP (35mi), [🄷], NAPA, Teals Mkt, to Roy Lake SP (25mi)
224	Peever, Sioux Tribal Hqtrs, E [🅖] I-29 Food'n Fill/dsl, W [🅞] Pickerel Lake (16mi)
213	SD 15, to Wilmot, E 🆁🆂 **both lanes, full 🅰 facilities, [🄲], 🛋, litter barrels, petwalk, RV dump, st patrol** [🅞] to Hartford Beach SP (17mi)
207	US 12, Summit, E [🅖] Cenex/Pizza Hut/Subway/dsl/24hr [🍴] County Line Camping (1mi), W [🅞] Blue Dog Fish Hatchery (15mi), Waubay NWR (19mi)
201	to Twin Brooks
193	SD 20, to South Shore, Stockholm
185	to Waverly, W [🅞] Dakota Sioux Casino/Cenex/rest. (4mi)
180	US 81 S, to Watertown, **5 mi** W [🅖] Sinclair [🅞][♿] Bramble Park Zoo
177	US 212, Watertown, E [🅖] Tesoro/Grainery Cafe/dsl/24hr 🛏 Holiday Inn Express [🅞] fireworks, truck repair, truck wash, WW Tires, **0-2 mi** W [🅖] Cenex/Subway/dsl, Cenex/Subway/dsl (2), Freedom/dsl, Sinclair/dsl, Tesoro/dsl [🍴] Applebee's, Arby's, Buffalo Wild Wings, Burger King, China Buffet, Culver's, Domino's, DQ, Firehouse Subs, Four Seasons Buffet, Godfather's, Guadalajara Mexican, Hardee's, IHOP, Jimmy John's, KFC, Little Caesar's, Marco's Pizza, McDonald's, Papa Murphy's, Perkins, Pizza Hut, Qdoba, Senor Max's Mexican, Starbucks, Subway, Taco Bell, Taco John's 🛏 Country Inn Suites, Days Inn, Econolodge, Hampton Inn, Quality Inn [🅞] $Tree, Advance Parts,

177	Continued AT&T, Chrysler/Dodge/Jeep, Ford/Lincoln, Goodyear/auto, Harley-Davidson, Herberger's, Hobby Lobby, [🄷], Hy-Vee Foods, Menards, NAPA, O'Reilly Parts, Target, Tires+, to Sandy Shore RA (10mi), Verizon, Walgreens, Walmart/Subway
164	SD 22, to Castlewood, Clear Lake, **9 mi** E [🅖] Cenex/dsl [🅞][🄷]
161mm	🆁🆂 **both lanes, full 🅰 facilities, [🄲], 🛋, litter barrels, vending, petwalk**
157	to Brandt
150	SD 28, SD 15 N, to Toronto, **7 mi** W [🅖] gas [🍴] food 🛏 lodging [🅞] Lake Poinsett RA (24 mi), SD Amateur Baseball Hall of Fame (24 mi)
140	SD 30, to White, Bruce, W [🅞] Oakwood Lakes SP (12mi)
133	US 14 byp, Brookings, E [🅞] WW Tires, W [🅞] Laura Ingalls Wilder Home (43 mi), museums, to SD St U
132	US 14, Lp 29, Brookings, E [🅖] Cenex/dsl [🍴] Applebee's, Whiskey Creek Grill 🛏 Fairfield Inn, Hampton Inn, Holiday Inn Express, My Place Hotel, Super 8, W [🅖] BP [🍴] Arby's, Backyard BBQ, Buffalo Wild Wings, Burger King, Culver's, DQ, Ground Round, Guadalajara Mexican, Hardee's, Jimmy John's, KFC, King's Wok, McDonald's, Papa John's, Papa Murphy's, Perkins, Pizza Ranch, Qdoba Mexican, Subway, Taco Bell 🛏 Comfort Suites, Days Inn, Econolodge, Quality Inn [🅞] Advance Parts, AT&T, Buick/Chevrolet/GMC, CarQuest, city park, [🄷], Lowe's, Verizon, Walmart/Subway
127	SD 324, to Elkton, Sinai
124mm	Big Sioux River
121	to Nunda, Ward, 🆁🆂 **both lanes, full 🅰 facilities, [🄲], 🛋, litter barrels, vending, petwalk, RV dump, st patrol**
114	SD 32, to Flandreau, **7 mi** E [🅖] Cenex [🍴] Subway 🛏 Sioux River Motel/RV park [🅞] Royal River Casino/hotel, Santee Tribal Hqtrs
109	SD 34, to Madison, Colman, **20 mi** W [🅖] Shell/Crossroads Rest./dsl, Sinclair/Prairie Jct/dsl [🅞] Dakota St U, museum, to Lake Herman SP
104	to Trent, Chester
103mm	**parking area both lanes**
98	SD 115 S, Dell Rapids, E [🅖] Cenex (3mi), Shell (3mi) [🍴] DQ (3mi), Pizza Ranch (3mi) 🛏 Bilmar Inn (3mi) [🅞] Chevrolet, dsl service, [🄷] (3mi), vet

🅿 = gas 🍽 = food 🛏 = lodging 🅾 = other ℞ = rest stop   Copyright 2022 - The Next EXIT

INTERSTATE 29 Cont'd

Exit #	Services
94	SD 114, to Baltic, **E** 🅿 Clark/dsl 🅾 to EROS Data Ctr (10mi), US Geological Survey (10mi)
86	to Renner, Crooks
84b a	I-90, W to Rapid City, E to Albert Lea
83	SD 38 W, 60th St, **E** 🅿 *FLYING J*/Denny's/dsl/LP/scales/24hr/@ 🍽 Burger King 🛏 Quality Suites 🅾 Freightliner, Harley-Davidson, Indian Motorcycles, Truckwash, **W** 🅾 fireworks, hwy patrol, Walmart/Subway
82	Benson Rd, **E** 🍽 BeefOBrady's 🛏 Fairfield Inn
81	SD 38 E, Russell St, Sioux Falls, **E** 🅿 BP, Food'n Fuel/Quiznos 🍽 Roll'n Pin Rest. 🛏 Arena Motel, Best Western+, Dakotah Lodge, Guesthouse Inn, Motel 6, Ramada Inn, Sheraton, Sioux Falls Inn, Sleep Inn, Super 8 🅾 golf, Schaap's RV Ctr, **W** 🍽 Subway
80	Madison St, **E** 🅿 Sinclair/dsl 🅾 to fairgrounds
79	SD 42, 12th St, **E** 🅿 BP, Freedom 🍽 Burger King, Burger Time, Fry'n Pan, Golden Harvest Chinese, KFC, McDonald's, Pizza Hut, Sneaky's Chicken, Subway, Taco Bell, Taco John's, Tomacelli's Pizza, Wendy's 🛏 Ramada, Woodspring Suites 🅾 $General, Ace Hardware, BMW/Cadillac/Mercedes, Chevrolet, city park, 🏥, Lewis Drug, NAPA, Nissan, to Great Plains Zoo/museum, Toyota, USPO, Walgreens, **W** 🅿 BP/dsl, Cenex/Chester's/dsl, Food'n Fuel 🍽 Hardee's 🅾 Meineke, Tower RV Park
78	26th St, Empire St, **E** 🅿 BP/dsl/e85 🍽 Buffalo Wild Wings, Carino's Italian, Carnaval Brazillian Grill, Chevy's Mexican, ChuckeCheese, Coldstone, Cracker Barrel, Culver's, Domino's, Granite City Rest., Outback Steaks, Puerto Vallarta, Ruby Tuesday, Sonic 🛏 ClubHouse Suites, Hampton Inn, Holiday Inn Express, StayBridge Suites 🅾 BigLots, Home Depot, Michael's, Petsmart, Sam's Club/gas, USPO, World Mkt, **W** 🍽 DQ, Papa John's, Starbucks 🛏 TownePlace Suites 🅾 Hy-Vee Foods/gas, Lowe's, Tuffy Auto, Verizon
77	41st St, Sioux Falls, **E** 🅿 BP, SA/dsl, Shell, Sinclair/dsl 🍽 Applebee's, Arby's, Burger King, Chili's, Firehouse Subs, Fry'n Pan Rest., Fuddrucker's, HuHot Mongolian, KFC, Lonestar Steaks, McDonald's, Old Chicago Pizza, Olive Garden, Pancake House, Panda Express, Papa Murphy's, Perkins, Pizza Hut, Pizza Ranch, Qdoba Mexican, Red Lobster, Starbucks, Subway, Szechwan Chinese, Taco Bell, Taco John's, TX Roadhouse, Valentino's, Wendy's 🛏 Best Western, Comfort Suites, Courtyard, Fairfield Inn, Microtel, MyPlace Hotel, Red Rock Inn, Residence Inn, SpringHill Suites, Super 8 🅾 Advance Parts, Barnes&Noble, Best Buy, Dick's, Ford/Lincoln, Goodyear/auto, Gordman's, Hy-Vee Foods/dsl, Hyundai, JC Penney, Kohl's, Macy's, Mazda, Menards, Old Navy, PetCo, Sears/auto, Target, Tires+, TJ Maxx, Verizon, Walgreens, Walmart/Subway, Younkers, **W** 🅿 Holiday/dsl 🍽 Burger King, Godfather's, IHOP, Little Caesar's, Perkins, Subway 🛏 AmericInn, Baymont Inn, Days Inn, La Quinta, Red Roof Inn 🅾 Lewis Drug, USPO
75	I-229 E, to I-90 E
73	Tea, **E** 🅿 Sinclair/dsl 🍽 Marlin's Rest. **W** 1.5mi 🅾 Red Barn Camping
71	to Harrisburg, Lennox, **E** 🅾 repair, **W** 🅾 RV camping
68	to Lennox, Parker
64	SD 44, Worthing, **W** 🅾 Buick/Chevrolet, New Prairie RV Ctr
62	US 18 E, to Canton, **E** 🅿 Cenex/pizza/dsl 🛏 Countryside RV park/motel
59	US 18 W, to Davis, Hurley
56	to Fairview, **E** 🅾 to Newton Hills SP (12mi)
53	to Viborg
50	to Centerville, Hudson
47	SD 46, to Irene, Beresford, **E** 🅿 BP/Burger King, Casey's/d Sinclair/dsl 🍽 Subway 🛏 Crossroads Motel, Super 8 🅾 $General, CarQuest, Chevrolet, Fiesta Foods, Jet Auto Repair, Lew Drug, **W** 🍽 Conoco/Dutch Rest./dsl/scales/24hr
42	to Alcester, Wakonda
41mm	truck check (from sb)
38	to Volin, **E** 🅾 to Union Co SP (3mi)
31	SD 48, to Akron, Spink
26	SD 50, to Vermillion, **E** Welcome Ctr/℞ both lanes, full ♿ facilities, info, 🍽, 🏥, litter barrels, petwalk, **W** 🅿 BP/Subway Pizza Hut/dsl 🍽 Burger King (6mi), Godfather's Pizza (6m Jimmy John's (6mi), Red Steakhouse (6mi), Subway (6mi), Ta John's (6mi) 🛏 Best Western (6mi), Comfort Inn (6mi), Holid Inn Express (6mi), Prairie Inn (6mi), Super 8 (6mi) 🅾 🏥 (6m Hy-Vee Foods (6mi), to Lewis & Clark RA (6mi), to U of SD (6m Walmart (6mi)
18	Lp 29, to Burbank, Elk Point, **E** 🅿 A-1/dsl, Casey's 🛏 Hom Towne Inn
15	to Elk Point, **E** 🅿 Kum&Go/Subway/dsl, **W** 🅾 fireworks
13mm	weigh sta nb, parking area sb
9	SD 105, Jefferson, **E** 🅿 Conoco/Choice Cut Rest.
4	North Shore Dr, McCook, **1 mi W** 🅾 Adams Homestead/natu preserve, KOA (seasonal)
2	SD 105, N Sioux City, **E** 🅿 Goode/casino/dsl/E10/20/30 🍽 M Donald's, Subway, Taco John's 🅾 fireworks, USPO, **W** 🅿 C sey's, Clark 🛏 Days Inn, Hampton Inn, Red Carpet Inn, Super 🅾 KOA
1	Dakota Dunes Blvd, **W** 🅿 Cenex/dsl 🍽 Graham's Grill Country Inn&Suites 🅾 Dakota Dunes Golf Resort
0mm	South Dakota/Iowa state line, Big Sioux River

INTERSTATE 90

Exit #	Services
412.5mm	South Dakota/Minnesota state line
412mm	Welcome Ctr wb/℞ eb, full ♿ facilities, info, 🍽, 🏥, litter ba rels, petwalk, RV dump (wb), weigh sta (wb)
410	Valley Springs, **N** 🅾 Palisades SP (7mi) **S** 🅿 gas 🍽 food Beaver Creek Nature Area
406	SD 11, Brandon, Corson, **N** 🅾 Palisades SP (10mi) **S** 🅿 BP/ Holiday/McDonald's/dsl, Local 🍽 Brandon Steaks, DQ, Gre Wall, Papa Murphy's, Pizza Hut, Pizza Ranch, Subway, Ta John's, Tailgator's Grill 🛏 Holiday Inn Express, Quality Inn Ace Hardware, Lewis Drug, Sturdevant's Parts, Sunshine Foo to Big Sioux RA (4mi), Verizon
402	EROS Data Ctr, **N** 🅾 Jellystone RV Park, tires
400	I-229 S
399	SD 115, Cliff Ave, Sioux Falls, **N** 🅾 Camping World, KOA **S** BP/Get'n Go/dsl, Conoco, Holiday/dsl/e85, *Loves*/Gran ma Max's/Subway/dsl/scales/24hr/@, Sinclair/dsl 🍽 Arby Burger King, McDonald's/truck parking, Perkins, Taco Bell, Ta John's 🛏 Cloud Nine Motel, Days Inn, EconoLodge, Super 8 Graham Tire, 🏥, Kenworth, Peterbilt, Volvo
398mm	Big Sioux River
396b a	I-29, N to Brookings, S to Sioux City
395	Marion Rd, Marion **S** 🅾 Walmart/Subway
390	SD 38, Hartford, **N** 🍽 Pizza Ranch (3mi) 🅾 Goos RV Ctr **S** Cowboy Town/dsl
387	rd 17, Hartford, **N** 🅿 BP/dsl 🍽 Midway Grill, Pizza Ran (1.6mi) 🛏 AmericInn
379	SD 19, Humboldt, **N** 🅿 Clark/dsl 🅾 USPO
375mm	E Vermillion River

SD

S I O U X   F A L L S

S I O U X   F A L L S

SD

INTERSTATE 90 Cont'd

Exit #	Services
374	to SD 38, Montrose, **5 mi S** ⊙ Battle Creek Res., Lake Vermillion RA, RV camping
368	Canistota, **5 mi S** 🏠 Best Western, Canistota Depot Inn, Ortman Hotel
364	US 81, to Yankton, Salem, **4 mi N** 🛢 Cenex 🏠 Home Motel ⊙ Camp America
363.5mm	W Vermillion River
363mm	🅿ˢ both lanes, full 🚹 facilities, 🎁, 🛒, litter barrels, vending, petwalk, RV dump, st patrol
357	to Bridgewater, Canova
353	Spencer, Emery **S** 🛢 FuelMart/Subway/dsl/casino/24hr
352mm	Wolf Creek
350	SD 25, Emery, Farmer, **N** ⊙ to DeSmet, Home of Laura Ingalls Wilder
344	SD 262, to Fulton, Alexandria **S** 🛢 Sinclair/dsl
337mm	parking area both lanes
335	Riverside Rd, **N** ⊙ KOA (1mi)
334.5mm	⊙ James River
332	SD 37 S, to Parkston, Mitchell, **N** 🛢 Cenex/Chester's/dsl, Clark, I-90/Holiday/Marlin's Rest./Subway/dsl/scales/24hr, Sinclair/Jimmy John's 🍴 Arby's, Cattleman's Club Steaks, Chef Louie Steaks, Corona Village Mexican, McDonald's, Perkins, Pizza Hut, Pizza Ranch, Starbucks, Twin Dragon Chinese 🏠 AmericInn, Corn Palace Inn, Days Inn, Quality Inn, Super 8/truck parking, Thunderbird Motel ⊙ Advance Parts, AutoZone, Chrysler/Dodge/Jeep, 🏥, Museum of Pioneer Life, O'Reilly Parts, Rondee's Campground, to Corn Palace, transmissions, URGENT CARE, Verizon, Walgreens **S** 🛢 Shell/Godfather's/Taco Bell/dsl/24hr 🍴 Culver's, Hardee's, Quiznos, Ruby Tuesday, Whiskey Creek Grill 🏠 Comfort Inn, Hampton Inn, Holiday Inn Express, Kelly Inn ⊙ $Tree, AT&T, Cabela's, Menards, Verizon, Walmart/Subway
330	SD 37 N, Mitchell, **N** 🛢 Cenex/Chester's/dsl, Shell/dsl, Sinclair/dsl 🍴 DQ 🏠 Budget Inn, Motel 6, Ramada Inn, Siesta Motel, Travelodge ⊙ County Fair Foods, 🏥, Jack's Campers/RV Ctr, Lewis Drug, Mr. Tire, museum, to Corn Palace, weigh sta **S** ⊙ Dakota RV Park
325	Betts Rd **S** ⊙ Famil-e-Fun Camping
319	Mt Vernon, **1 mi N** 🛢 Sinclair/dsl, Westey's One Stop/dsl
310	US 281, to Stickney **S** 🛢 Sinclair/Deli Depot/dsl/24hr ⊙ to Ft Randall Dam
308	Lp 90, to Plankinton, **N** 🛢 Sinclair/Al's Cafe/dsl 🏠 Cabin Fever Motel/RV Park, Smart Choice Inn ⊙ Gordy's Camping, Hills RV Park, repair, USPO
301.5mm	🅿ˢ both lanes, full 🚹 facilities, 🎁, 🛒, litter barrels, RV dump
296	White Lake, **1 mi N** 🛢 Hillman's/dsl 🏠 A-Z Motel ⊙ USPO **S** ⊙ Siding 36 Motel/RV Park
294mm	Platte Creek
289	SD 45 S, to Platte **S** ⊙ to Snake Cr/Platte Cr RA (25mi)
284	SD 45 N, Kimball, **N** 🛢 Clark, Conoco/Ditty's/Diner/dsl 🍴 Frosty King 🏠 Dakota Winds Motel, Westwood Inn ⊙ Parkway Campground, repair/tires **S** ⊙ tractor museum
272	SD 50, Pukwana, **2 mi N** 🛢 gas 🍴 food 🏠 lodging **S** ⊙ Snake/Platte Creek Rec Areas (25mi)
265	SD 50, Chamberlain, **N** 🛢 Cenex/DQ/dsl 🏠 AmericInn ⊙ 🏥, St Joseph Akta Lakota Museum (4mi), vet **S** 🛢 Speedway/dsl ⊙ Happy Camper Campground
264mm	🅿ˢ both lanes, full 🚹 facilities, scenic view, info, 🎁, 🛒, litter barrels
263	Chamberlain, **N** 🛢 Sinclair/dsl 🍴 McDonald's, Pizza Hut, Subway (1mi), Taco John's 🏠 Bel Aire Motel (1mi), Best Western (1mi), Super 8 ⊙ Crow Creek Sioux Tribal Hqtrs, SD Hall of Fame
262mm	Missouri River
260	SD 50, Oacoma, **N** 🛢 Phillips 66/Arby's/dsl, Shell/dsl, Sinclair/dsl 🏠 Al's Oasis/Motel/Camping/cafe/mkt, Baymont Inn, Cedar Shore Motel/Camping (3mi), Econolodge, Howard Johnson, Quality Inn ⊙ antiques, Buick/Chevrolet, Dakota Camping, Oasis Camping, Old West Trading Post
251	SD 47, to Winner, Gregory
248	SD 47, Reliance, **N** 🛢 Cenex (1mi), Farmer's Union/dsl (1mi) ⊙ Sioux Tribal Hqtrs, to Big Bend RA
241	to Lyman
235	SD 273, Kennebec, **N** 🛢 Clark/dsl 🍴 Hot Rods Steaks 🏠 Budget Host, Kings Inn ⊙ auto repair, KOA, USPO
226	US 183 S, Presho, **N** 🛢 Cenex/dsl, Sinclair/dsl 🏠 Hutch's Motel/café ⊙ New Frontier RV Park, pioneer museum, repair, vet
225	lp 90, Presho same as 226
221mm	🅿ˢ wb, full 🚹 facilities, info, 🎁, 🛒, litter barrels, RV dump, petwalk
220	no service
218mm	🅿ˢ eb, full 🚹 facilities, info, 🎁, 🛒, litter barrels, RV dump, petwalk
214	Vivian
212	US 83 N, SD 53, to Pierre, **N** 🛢 Sinclair/dsl ⊙ 🏥 (34mi)
208	no service
201	Draper
194mm	parking area both lanes
192	US 83 S, Murdo, **N** 🛢 🏪/Subway/dsl/Lp/scales/24hr, Pioneer/dsl 🍴 Buffalo Rest., Covered Wagon Cafe, Murdo Drive-In, Prairie Pizza, Rusty Spur Steaks, Star Rest. 🏠 American Inn, Best Western, Iversen Inn, Range Country Lodge, Sioux Motel, Super 8 ⊙ American RV Park/camping, auto museum, city park, Ford, Murdo Foods, USPO **S** 🏠 Country Inn ⊙ to Rosebud
191	Murdo, **N** same as 192
188mm	parking area both lanes
183	Okaton **S** ⊙ Ghost Town
177	no service
175mm	central/mountain timezone
172	to Cedar Butte
170	SD 63 N, to Midland, **N** 🛢 Conoco/dsl ⊙ 1880's Town, KOA
167mm	🅿ˢ wb, full 🚹 facilities, 🎁, 🛒, litter barrels, RV dump, petwalk
165mm	🅿ˢ eb, full 🚹 facilities, 🎁, 🛒, litter barrels, RV dump, petwalk
163	SD 63, Belvidere **S** 🛢 Belvidere Store/dsl 🍴 JR's Grill
152	Lp 90, Kadoka, **N** 🛢 Conoco/rest./dsl/24hr **S** ⊙ Badlands Petrified Gardens

MITCHELL

CHAMBERLAIN

MURDO

SD

INTERSTATE 90 Cont'd

Exit #	Services
150	SD 73 S, Kadoka, N 🛏 Dakota Inn/rest. S 🅿 Conoco/dsl, Sinclair/pizza/dsl 🍴 Subway, Sunset Grill 🛏 Best Value Inn, Budget Host, El Centro Motel/rest., Ponderosa Motel/RV Park, Wagon Wheel Motel, West Motel 🄾 Kadoka Kampground, repair, to Buffalo Nat Grasslands
143	SD 73 N, to Philip, 15 mi N 🄾 🄷
138mm	scenic overlook wb
131	SD 240, N 🄾 Minuteman Missle NHS S 🅿 Conoco 🛏 Badlands Inn (9mi), Cedar Pass Lodge/rest. (9mi) 🄾 Circle 10 Camping, KOA (11mi), Prairie Home NHS, to Badlands NP
129.5mm	scenic overlook eb
127	no service
121	Bigfoot Rd
116	239th St
112	US 14 E, to Philip
110	SD 240, Wall, N 🅿 Conoco/dsl, Exxon, Phillips 66/Subway 🍴 Cactus Cafe, DQ, Red Rock Rest., Roadtrip Cafe, Wall Drug Rest. 🛏 Ann's Motel, Best Value Inn, Best Western, Days Inn, EconoLodge, Fountain Hotel, Sunshine Inn, Super 8, The Wall Motel, Travelodge, Welsh Motel 🄾 Ace Hardware, Arrow Campground, Harley Davidson, National Grasslands Visitor Ctr, Pronto Parts, Sleepy Hollow RV Park/Camping, Wall Drug, Wall Foods, Wounded Knee Museum S 🛏 Frontier Cabins Motel 🄾 RV camping, to Badlands NP
109	W 4th Ave, Wall, 1-2 mi N access to same as 110
107	Cedar Butte Rd
101	Jensen Rd, to Schell Ranch
100mm	🆁🆂 both lanes, full 🚻 facilities, info, 🄲, 🏕, litter barrels, RV dump, vending, petwalk
99.5mm	Cheyenne River
98	Wasta, N 🅿 24 Express/dsl 🄾 USPO, Wasta RV Camping
90	173rd Ave, to Owanka
88	171st Ave (from eb, no re-entry)
84	167th Ave, N 🄾 Olde Glory Fireworks
78	161st Ave, New Underwood 1/2 mi S 🅿 Sinclair/dsl, Steve's General Store/dsl/motel/rest. 🍴 Harry's Hideaway Rest, 🛏 BJ's Motel 🄾 Boondocks Camping
69mm	parking area both lanes
67	to Box Elder, N 🅿 💚Loves/Hardee'sdsl/scales/24hr 🄾 Air&Space Museum, Ellsworth AFB, Speedco
63	(eb only) to Box Elder S 🅿 Phillips 66/dsl 🄾 Ellsworth AFB
61	Elk Vale Rd, N 🅿 Exxon/dsl, ⚡FLYING J/Conoco/CountryMkt/dsl/e-85/LP/RV dump/scales/24hr/@ 🍴 Sickies Burgers 🛏 Cambrian Suites, MainStay Suites, My Place 🄾 Black Hills Visitor Ctr, Cabela's, Dakota RV Ctr S 🅿 Conoco/dsl, Sinclair/dsl/e85 🍴 Arby's, Dakotah Steakhouse, Marco's Pizza, McDonald's, Perkins, Taco Bell 🛏 Baymont Inn, Best Western+, Comfort Suites, Courtyard Inn, Fairfield Inn, Home 2 Suites, La Quinta, Residence Inn, Sleep Inn 🄾 Freightliner, KOA (2mi seasonal)
60	Lp 90, to Mt Rushmore, Rapid City, N 🄾 Buick/GMC, Chevrolet, Ford/Lincoln, Great Western Tire, Honda, Kenworth/Volvo, Nissan, Toyota S 🅿 Holiday/dsl 🍴 Blaze Pizza, Culver's, Five Guys, Fuji Japanese Steaks, Gyro Hub, HuHot Mongolian, Jimmy John's, Longhorn Steaks, MacKenzie River, Noodles&Co, Old Chicago, On the Border, Panera Bread, Pizza Ranch, Popeyes, Qdoba Mexican, Starbucks, Storming Crab, Tropical Smoothies 🛏 Staybridge Suites 🄾 $Tree, Aamco, AT&T, dsl repair, Gordman's, 🄷, Menards, Michael's, Nat Coll of Mines/Geology, PetCo, Ross, Sam's Club/dsl, Scheel's Sports, Target, TJ Maxx, Verizon

Exit #	Services
59	La Crosse St, Rapid City, N 🅿 Mobil/dsl, Phillips 66 🍴 Burger King, Denny's, Fuddrucker's, Minerva's Rest., Outback Steak, Puerto Vallarta Mexican, Starbucks, TGIFriday's, TX Roadhouse 🛏 Best Western, Country Inn&Suites, EconoLodge, Hilton Garden, Holiday Inn Express, Serena Inn, Super 8 🄾 Herberger', Hobby Lobby, mall, st patrol S 🅿 Exxon/24hr, Sinclair 🍴 Arnold's Diner, China Wok, Golden Corral, Little Caesar's, Mill Stone Rest., Mongolian Grill, Pacific Rim Cafe, Perkins, Phil Ted's, Subway 🛏 AmericInn, Days Inn, Fair Value Inn, Foothill Inn, Grand Gateway Hotel, Hampton Inn, Microtel, Motel , Quality Inn, Ramada, Rodeway Inn, URGENT CARE 🄾 AT&, Walgreens, Walmart/McDonald's
58	Haines Ave, Rapid City, N 🅿 Yesway/dsl 🍴 Applebee's, Bob Cafe, Chili's, Hardee's, IHOP, Maple Street BBQ, Olive Garden, Red Lobster 🛏 Grand Stay Motel, Super 8 🄾 BAM!, Best Buy, JC Penney, Jo-Ann, Kohl's, Lowe's, Petsmart, Tires+, to Rushmore Mall S 🅿 Loaf'n Jug, Maverik/dsl 🍴 Papa John's, Pizza Hut, Taco John's, Wendy's 🄾 Family$, 🄷, URGENT CARE
57	I-190, US 16, to Rapid City, Mt Rushmore, 1 mi S on North St 🅿 Exxon 🍴 Panchero's Mexican 🛏 Holiday Inn, Howard Johnson, The Rushmore Hotel 🄾 Family Thrift Foods, Knecht Home Ct, Office Depot
55	Deadwood Ave, N 🄾 Dakota RV Ctr, Harley-Davidson/cafe 🅿 Pilot/Subway/dsl/scales/24hr/@ 🍴 Marlin's Rest. 🄾 dsl repair
52	Peaceful Pines Rd, Black Hawk, N 🄾 Lazy JD RV Park (4mi) Three Flags Camping (1mi) S 🍴 BJ's/dsl, Godfather's Pizza 🄾 Family$, USPO
48	Stagebarn Canyon Rd S 🅿 Conoco/Haggar's Mkt/food, Pit Stop/dsl 🍴 Pizza Hut 🛏 Summerset 🄾 $General, Camping World RV Ctr, O'Reilly Parts
46	Piedmont Rd, Elk Creek Rd, N 🍴 Elk Creek Steakhouse 🄾 Elk Creek RV Park, to Petrified Forest S 🅿 Sinclair/Papa John's, mart/dsl 🍴 Sacora Sta Rest. 🄾 Sacora Sta Camping
44	Bethlehem Rd S 🄾 Jack's RV Ctr (2mi)
42mm	parking area both lanes
40	Tilford S 🄾 RV Park
39mm	weigh sta eb
37	Pleasant Valley Rd, N 🄾 Kickstands Camp S 🄾 Bulldog Camping, Rush-No-More Camping
34	S 🄾 Black Hills Nat Cemetary, No Name City RV Park
32	SD 79, Jct Ave, Sturgis, N 🅿 Conoco/dsl, Exxon/dsl 🍴 Red' Grill, Taco John's 🛏 Sturgis Lodge 🄾 Ford, Grocery Mart, 🄷 NAPA, to Bear Butte SP, vet S 🅿 Mobil/Arby's/Papa John's/ds 🄾 Ford
30	US 14A W, SD 34E, to Deadwood, Sturgis, N 🅿 Cenex/dsl, Phillips 66/dsl 🍴 McDonald's, Pizza Hut, Shanghai Chinese, Sturgis Coffee Co 🄾 $General, CarQuest, Day's End Camping, Family$, Indian Motorcycles, O'Reilly Parts, tires, USPO S 🅿 Conoco/dsl, Ranch Mart 🍴 Burger King, DQ, Pizza Ranch, Subway 🛏 Baymont Inn Days Inn, Super 8 🄾 BMW Motorcycles, Chevrolet, Verizon
23	SD 34 W, to Belle Fourche, Whitewood, N 🄾 Northern Hills RV Ctr S 🅿 Howdy's/dsl, Mobil/Sonset Sta/dsl 🍴 Hideaway Dine 🛏 Tony's Motel 🄾 USPO
17	US 85 S, to Deadwood S 🅿 Cenex/dsl 🄾 Deadwood NL (17mi), Elkhorn Ridge RV Resort, KOA (9mi)
14	US 14A, Spearfish Canyon, N 🅿 FreshStart/dsl 🍴 Applebee's Culver's, Subway 🛏 Fairfield Inn, Hampton Inn, Holiday Inn, rest., Quality Inn 🄾 $Tree, AutoZone, Verizon, Walmart S 🅿 Phillips 66/dsl 🍴 KFC/LJ Silver, Perkins, Pizza Ranch, Roma' Rest. 🛏 Baymont Inn, Super 8, Travelodge 🄾 Ace Hardware, Bomgaars, Ford/Lincoln, transmissions

Vertical labels: KADOKA WALL RAPID CITY STURGIS

S P E A R F I S H

INTERSTATE 90 Cont'd

Exit #	Services
12	Jackson Blvd, Spearfish **S** 🅰 Conoco/dsl, Exxon, Loaf'n Jug, Phillips 66/dsl 🍴 Arby's, Barbacoa's, Domino's, Jade Palace Chinese, McDonald's, Millstone Rest., Papa Murphy's, Pizza Hut, Taco John's 🛏 Best Western O Black Hills St U, CarQuest, Chrysler/Dodge/Jeep, historic fish hatchery, 🅷, same as 10
10	US 85 N, to Belle Fourche **S** 🍴 Burger King, Cedar House Rest., City Brew, Golden Dragon Chinese, Little Caesar's, McDonald's, Philly Ted's, Qdoba, Subway, Taco Bell 🛏 Days Inn O Buick/ Chevrolet, Cadillac/GMC, 🅷, KOA, Safeway/dsl, same as 12, USPO, Walgreens
8	McGuigan Rd, W Spearfish **S** 🍴 Phillips 66/dsl O KOA (1mi)
2	1 mi **N** O McNenny St Fish Hatchery
1mm	Welcome Ctr eb, full 🅰 facilities, info, Ⓒ, 🚻, litter barrels, RV dump, petwalk
0mm	South Dakota/Wyoming state line

S I O U X   F A L L S

INTERSTATE 229 (Sioux Falls)

Exit #	Services
10b a	I-90 E and W. **I-229 begins/ends on I-90, exit 400.**
9	Benson Rd, **W** 🍴 Marlin's Rest., Sinclair/pizza/dsl 🍴 DQ, Jimmy John's O Ford Trucks, Western Star
7.5mm	Big Sioux River
7	Rice St, **E** winter sports, **W** to stockyards
6	SD 38, 10th St, **E** 🅰 Sinclair 🍴 A&W, Applebee's, Arby's, Denny's, Domino's, DQ, Fryn' Pan Rest., Jimmy John's, KFC, Pizza Hut, Pizza Ranch, Taco Bell, Tokyo Hibachi, Tomacelli's Italian 🛏 Super 8 O AT&T, AutoZone, Family$, Hy-Vee Foods, O'Reilly Parts, Sturdevant's Parts, USPO, Valvoline, vet, **W** 🍴 BP/dsl, Casey's/dsl, Shell 🍴 Burger King, BurgerTime, Hardee's, Little Caesar's, McDonald's, Pita Pit, Pizza Inn, Pizza Man, Puerto Vallarta, Qdoba Mexican, Subway, Taco John's 🛏 Rushmore Motel O Lewis Drug, vet
5.5mm	Big Sioux River
5	26th St, **E** 🅰 Holiday/dsl 🍴 Burger King, Cherry Creek Grill, Dario's Pizza, McDonald's, Saigon Panda O city park, **W** O 🅷

Exit #	Services
4	Cliff Ave, **E** 🍴 BP
3	SD 115, Lp 229, Minnesota Ave, **E** O city park, **W** 🅰 BP/dsl, Sinclair 🍴 Arby's, Burger King, Camilles Cafe, Culver's, DQ, Famous Dave's BBQ, Golden Bowl Chinese, Hardee's, Little Caesar's/TCBY, McDonald's, Subway O $Tree, Ace Hardware, Acura, Buick/GMC, Costco/gas, Hy-Vee Foods/dsl, Kia, Lewis Drug, Staples, tires, USPO, vet
2	Western Ave, **E** 🅰 Holiday/dsl 🍴 Bracco Cafe, DQ, Scooters Coffee, Starbucks, **W** 🅰 Cenex/dsl, Holiday 🍴 Buck's Roadhouse, Burger King, China Buffet, Huhot Mongolian, Lone Star Steaks, Papa Murphy's, PepperJax Grill, Perkins, Qdoba Mexican, Redrossa Pizza, Scheel's, Valentino's O Advance Parts, AutoZone, Best Buy, Goodyear/auto, Hancock Fabrics, 🅷, Tuesday Morning
1.5mm	Big Sioux River
1c	Louise Ave, **E** 🅰 Holiday/dsl 🛏 Comfort Suites, Hampton Inn, Holiday Inn Express, Homewood Suites O Chrysler/Dodge/ Jeep, Fiat, 🅷, Lewis Drug, **W** 🅰 BP 🍴 Burger King, Five Guys, Jimmy John's, Marco's Pizza, McDonald's, Noodles&Co, Panera Bread, Qdoba Mexican, Royal Palace, Spezia's Rest, Taco John's, Wendy's 🛏 Hilton Garden Inn O Barnes&Noble, Dick's, Honda, Hy-Vee Foods/dsl, JC Penney, Jo-Ann Fabrics, Kohl's, mall, Target, Verizon, Walgreens
1b a	I-29 N and S. **I-229 begins/ends on I-29, exit 75.**

NOTES

TN

TENNESSEE

C H A T T A N O O G A

⬆E	INTERSTATE 24
Exit #	Services
185b a	I-75, N to Knoxville, S to Atlanta. **I-24 begins/ends on I-75, exit 2 in Chattanooga.**
184	Moore Rd, S 🍴 Chef Lin's Buffet, Provino's Italian ⊙ $Tree, URGENT CARE
183	(183a from wb), Belvoir Ave, Germantown Rd
181a	US 41 S, to East Ridge (from eb), S 🍴 2503 Station Grill, Sugar's Ribs
181	Fourth Ave, to TN Temple U, Chattanooga, N 🅿 Citgo/dsl, Exxon/dsl, Hi-Tech Fuel, Stop'n Save 🍴 Bojangles, Burger King, Capt D's, Hunan Wok, Krystal, Subway, Waffle House 🛏 Chatt Inn ⊙ $General, Family$, Food City, Mack/Volvo Trucks, NAPA, O'Reilly Parts, repair, vet, S 🅿 Mystik
180b a	US 27 S, TN 8, Rossville Blvd, N ⊙ Best One Tires/service, to UT Chatt, S 🅿 Mapco/dsl, Mobil/dsl 🛏 Hamilton Inn ⊙ Family$, to Chickamauga Battlefield
178	US 27 N, Market St, to Lookout Mtn, Chattanooga, N 🅿 BP/dsl, Citgo 🛏 District 3 Hotel, Marriott, Staybridge Suites ⊙ Chevrolet, Ford/Lincoln, Midas, Nissan, to aquarium, to Chattanooga ChooChoo, U-Haul, S 🅿 RaceWay/dsl 🍴 KFC 🛏 Comfort Inn, Motel 6, Red Roof+
175	Browns Ferry Rd, to Lookout Mtn, N 🅿 BP, Spirit/dsl 🍴 China Gourmet 🛏 Best Value Inn, La Quinta ⊙ CVS Drug, vet, S 🅿 Mapco/dsl 🍴 Hardee's, McDonald's 🛏 Comfort Inn, EconoLodge, Travelodge ⊙ $General
174	US 11, US 41, US 64, Lookout Valley, N 🍴 Waffle House 🛏 Days Inn ⊙ Racoon Mtn Camping (1mi), st patrol, S 🅿 BP/dsl, Exxon/Circle K/dsl, Murphy USA/dsl 🍴 Cracker Barrel, Jack's Rest., Logan's Roadhouse, Los 3 Amigos, New China, Sonic, Taco Bell, Waffle House, Wendy's 🛏 Best Western, Budget Motel, Clarion, Country Inn&Suites, Fairfield Inn, Hampton Inn, Holiday Inn Express, Quality Inn, Red Roof Inn, Super 8 ⊙ $Tree, Ace Hardware, URGENT CARE, Verizon, Walmart/Subway
172mm	🆁🆂 eb, full 🚻 facilities, 🄲, 🄿, litter barrels, vending, petwalk
171mm	Tennessee/Georgia state line
169	GA 299, to US 11, N 🅿 Mapco/dsl, S 🅿 BP/Krispy Chicken/dsl/24hr, Citgo, 🄿🄸🄻🄾🅃/Subway/dsl/scales/24hr ⊙ $General
167	I-59 S, to Birmingham
167mm	Tennessee/Georgia state line, Central/Eastern time zone
161	TN 156, to Haletown, New Hope, N 🅿 Anchor Inn/dsl (1mi) ⊙ Hales Bar RV Park (2.5mi), S 🅿 Chevron/fireworks
160mm	Tennessee River/Nickajack Lake
159mm	Welcome Ctr wb/🆁🆂 eb, full 🚻 facilities, 🄲, vending, 🄿, litter barrels, petwalk
158	US 41, TN 27, Nickajack Dam, N 🅿 ❤Loves/McDonald's/Subway/dsl/scales/24hr, S ⊙ Shellmound Camping (2.5mi) 🅿 Speedway/Speedy's Cafe/24hr
155	TN 28, Jasper, N 🅿 Hi-Tech/dsl, Quality Inn 🍴 Hardee's, Western Sizzlin, S 🅿 BP/Mapco/dsl ⊙🄷
152	US 41, US 64, US 72, Kimball, S Pittsburg, N 🅿 Phillips 66/fireworks, RaceWay/dsl, Shell/dsl 🍴 A&W/LJ Silver, Arby's, China Buffet, Cracker Barrel, Domino's, El Toril, KFC, Krystal, Little Caesar's, McDonald's, Pizza Hut, Shoney's, Subway, Taco Bell, Waffle House, Wendy's 🛏 Best Value Inn, Comfort Inn, Hampton Inn, Holiday Inn Express, Super 8 ⊙ $Tree, Buick/Chevrolet/GMC, GNC, Lowe's, Walmart, S ⊙ Lodge Cast Iron, to Russell Cave NM
143	Martin Springs Rd, N 🅿 Citgo/dsl

M O N T E A G L E

M A N C H E S T E R

135	US 41 N, Monteagle, N 🅿 Marathon/dsl, 🄿🄸🄻🄾🅃/Wendy's/dsl/scales/24hr 🍴 High Point Rest., Rocky Top Rest., Shan Chinese ⊙ Family$, Monteagle Parts, USPO, S 🛏 Red Roof Inn
134	US 64, US 41A, to Sewanee, Monteagle, N 🅿 BP/Mapco/McDonald's/dsl 🍴 Sonic 🛏 American Eagle Inn ⊙ CVS Drug, to S Cumberland SP, S 🅿 Exxon/dsl, Marathon/Kangaroo 🍴 Hardee's, Pizza Hut, Smokehouse BBQ, Subway, Waffle House 🛏 Best Western, Mountain Inn, Super 8 ⊙ $General, Auto/tire repair, Fred's, Piggly Wiggly, to U of The South
133mm	🆁🆂 both lanes, full 🚻 facilities, 🄲, 🄿, litter barrels, vending, petwalk
128mm	Elk River
127	US 64, TN 50, to Winchester, Pelham, N 🅿 Citgo, Marathon/dsl, S 🅿 Gulf/dsl ⊙ to Tims Ford SP/RV camping
119mm	trucks only parking area both lanes
117	to Tullahoma ⊙ USAF Arnold Ctr, UT Space Institute
116mm	weigh sta both lanes
114	US 41, Manchester, N 🅿 Exxon/24 Truckers/scales/dsl, Marathon/dsl, Murphy USA/dsl, Shell/dsl 🍴 Great Wall Chinese, Logan's Roadhouse, O'Charley's, Potrillos Mexican, Starbucks 🛏 Comfort Suites, Holiday Inn Express, Motel 6, Quality Inn, Scottish Inn, Sleep Inn, Truckers Inn ⊙ $Tree, AT&T, Home Depot, KOA, Nissan, tire/truck repair, Toyota, Verizon, Walmart/Subway, S 🅿 Mobil/Circle K, RaceWay/dsl 🍴 Arby's, Baskin-Robbins, Bojangles, Burger King, Capt D's, Hong Kong Buffet, KFC, Krystal, McDonald's/playplace, Papa John's, Pizza Hut, Rafael Italian, Subway, Taco Bell, Waffle House, Wendy's 🛏 Days Inn, Microtel, Red Roof Inn, Regency Inn, Royal Inn ⊙ Advance Parts, AutoZone, Family$, Ford/Lincoln, O'Reilly Parts, Russell Stover, USPO, vet
111	TN 55, Manchester, N 🅿 BP/dsl, Co-op/dsl, Mobil/Circle K ⊙ 🄷, to Rock Island SP, vet, S 🍴 Hardee's, J&G Pizza/Steaks, Sonic ⊙ $General, Gateway Auto, Old Stone Fort SP, Rite Aid, to Jack Daniels Dist HS, Walgreens
110	TN 53, Manchester, N 🅿 Exxon, Mobil/Circle K/dsl, Petro/dsl 🍴 Cracker Barrel, Emma's Rest., Las Fajitas Mexican, Oak Rest. 🛏 Ambassador Inn, Econolodge, Economy Inn, Hampton Inn ⊙ 🄷, S 🅿 Shell/dsl 🍴 Los 3 Amigos, Prater's BBQ, Waffle House ⊙ repair
110mm	Duck River
105	US 41, N 🅿 Exxon/dsl, Marathon/dsl, S ⊙ Dickel HS, tire/repair, to Normandy Dam, Whispering Oaks Camping (1.5mi)
97	TN 64, to Shelbyville, Beechgrove, S 🅿 Marathon/dsl
89	Buchanan Rd, N 🅿 ❤Loves/McDonald's/dsl/scales/24hr 🍴 Subway, S 🅿 Shell/dsl ⊙ $General, A&L RV Ctr
84	Joe B. Jackson Pkwy, N 🍴 Subway
81	US 231, Murfreesboro, N 🅿 Exxon, Gulf/dsl, Mapco, Shell 🍴 Cathay Asian, Cracker Barrel, Krystal, Parthenon Grille, Shoney's, Sports Seasons Grill, Wendy's 🛏 Best Value Inn, Knights Inn, Quality Inn, Ramada Ltd, Regal Inn ⊙ Chrysler/Dodge/Jeep, Honda, 🄷, S 🅿 Kangaroo, Mapco/dsl, Mobil, 🄿🄸🄻🄾🅃/Arby's/scales/dsl/24hr 🍴 Bojangles, Burger King, La Siesta Mexican, McDonald's/playplace, Pizza Hut, Rick's BBQ, Sonic, Starbucks, Subway, Taco Bell, Waffle House, Whitt's BBQ, Zaxby's 🛏 Select Inn, Vista Suites ⊙ $General, Advance Parts, AutoZone, Discount Tire, Gateway Auto, Kroger/dsl, O'Reilly Parts, Rite Aid, Toyota, vet
80	New Salem Hwy, rd 99, S 🅿 Costco/gas, Speedway/Speedy's Cafe/dsl 🍴 Domino's, Marco's Pizza, Subway

TN

ⓔ INTERSTATE 24 Cont'd

MURFREESBORO

NASHVILLE

Exit #	Services
78	TN 96, to Franklin, Murfreesboro, **N** ⓖ Marathon, Murphy USA/dsl, Phillips 66/Church's/White Castle/dsl, Shell/Jack-in-the-Box ⓕ Arby's, Baskin-Robbins, Bonefish Grill, Buffalo Wild Wings, Carrabba's, Cheddar's, Chick-fil-A, Chipotle, Chophouse, ChuckECheese, Coconut Bay Cafe, Cracker Barrel, Egg&I Cafe, Fazoli's, Firehouse Subs, Five Guys, IHOP, Jason's Deli, Jim'n Nick's BBQ, Jimmy John's, KFC, McDonald's, Mi Patria, Moe's SW Grill, Old Chicago, Olive Garden, Outback Steaks, Panda Express, Panera Bread, Red Lobster, Red Robin, Sam's Grill, Samurai's Cuisine, Sandwich Factory, SmashBurger, Starbucks, Steak'n Shake, Subway, TGIFriday's, Waffle House, Wendy's, Zaxby's ⌂ Baymont Inn, Best Western, Candlewood Suites, Clarion, Comfort Suites, Country Inn&Suites, Days Inn, DoubleTree, EconoLodge, Fairfield Inn, Hampton Inn, Holiday Inn Express, Microtel, Motel 6, Red Roof Inn, Sleep Inn, Super 8 ⓞ $Tree, Aldi Foods, AT&T, Books-A-Million, Dillard's, Discount Tire, Firestone, Hobby Lobby, Home Depot, JC Penney, Jo-Ann Fabrics, Lowe's, Marshalls, NTB, Petsmart, Ross, Sears/auto, Staples, SteinMart, Target, TJ Maxx, to Stones River Bfd, Verizon, vet, Walgreens, Walmart, **S** ⓖ Kangaroo/dsl, Mapco, Marathon/dsl, Shell/dsl ⓕ auto repair, Camino Real Mexican, Capt D's, China Garden, Dos Rancheros, DQ, Hardee's, Jersey Mike's Subs, McDonald's, O'Charley's, Papa Murphy's, Pizza Garden, Pizza Hut, Sonic, Subway, Taco Bell, vet, Waffle House, Wasabi Japanese ⌂ Woodspring Suites ⓞ $General, AutoZone, Kohl's, Kroger/dsl, O'Reilly Parts, Old Time Pottery, Rite Aid, Sam's Club/gas, Walgreens
76	Fortress Blvd, Manson Pike, Medical Center Pkwy, **N** ⓖ Thornton's/dsl ⓕ Bar Louie, Chili's, Culver's, Genghis Grill, Longhorn Steaks, Macaroni Grill, Mimi's Cafe, Newk's Eatery, Peter D's, Starbucks, Subway, Which Wich? ⌂ Embassy Suites, Hilton Garden, Holiday Inn, Residence Inn ⓞ Barnes&Noble, Belk, Best Buy, Dick's, GNC, Ⓗ, Michael's, Old Navy, Petco, Tire Discounters, to Stones River Nat. Bfd, World Mkt, **S** ⓖ Exxon/dsl ⓕ Sonic ⓞ Chevrolet/Cadillac/GMC/Buick, Toyota
74b a	TN 840, to Lebanon, Franklin
70	TN 102, Lee Victory Pkwy, Almaville Rd, to Smyrna, **N** ⓖ Speedway/Speedy Cafe/dsl/scales ⓕ Asian Cafe, Bojangles, Mi Tierro Mexican, Naked Fish ⓞ Publix, **S** ⓖ Kangaroo/Little Caesar's/dsl, Mapco, Shell/dsl ⓕ Legends Steaks, McDonald's, Sonic, Subway ⌂ Deerfield Inn ⓞ $General
66	TN 266, Sam Ridley Pkwy, to Smyrna, **N** ⓖ Shell/dsl ⓕ A&W/LJ Silver, Arby's, Asuka Hibachi, Blue Coast Burrito, Buffalo Wild Wings, Cheddar's, Chick-fil-A, Chili's, Chipotle, CiCi's Pizza, DQ, Famous Dave's BBQ, Firehouse Subs, Five Guys, Hickory Falls Cafe,
66	Continued IHOP, Jersey Mike's Subs, Jim'n Nick's BBQ, Krispy Kreme, La Siesta Mexican, Logan's Roadhouse, Longhorn Steaks, Panda Express, Panera Bread, Papa Murphy's, Pollo Tropical, Razz Grill, Smoothie King, Sonic, Starbucks, Subway, Waffle House, Wendy's, Zaxby's ⓞ $General, $Tree, AT&T, CVS Drug, Discount Tire, Firestone/auto, GNC, Home Depot/gas, Ⓗ, Kohl's, Kroger/dsl, Lowe's, Nashville I-24 Camping (3mi), Petsmart, Publix, Ross, Staples, Target, Tire Discounters, URGENT CARE, Verizon, Walgreens, **S** ⓕ Cracker Barrel, O'Charley's, Ruby Tuesday ⌂ Candlewood Suites, Comfort Suites, Fairfield Inn, Hampton Inn, Hilton Garden, Holiday Inn Express, Home 2 Suites, La Quinta, Sleep Inn, TownePlace Suites
64	Waldron Rd, to La Vergne, **N** ⓖ Kangaroo, Kwik Sak, Pilot/Subway/dsl/scales/24hr ⓕ Arby's, Hardee's, Krystal, McDonald's, Waffle House ⌂ Comfort Inn, Quality Inn, Ramada Inn, **S** ⓖ Mapco/dsl ⓞ $General
62	TN 171, Old Hickory Blvd, **N** ⓖ Citgo/Subway/dsl, Shell/dsl, TA/BP/Burger King/Popeye's/dsl/scales/24hr/@ ⓕ Acapulco Burrito ⌂ Rodeway Inn
60	Hickory Hollow Pkwy, **N** ⓖ Exxon/dsl, Mapco, Thornton's/dsl ⓕ 360 Burger, Burger King, ChuckECheese, KFC/LJ Silver, Logan's Roadhouse, McDonald's/Playplace, New Century Buffet, O'Charley's, Red Lobster, Starbucks, Subway, Taco Bell, Wendy's, Zaxby's ⌂ Country Inn&Suites, Hampton Inn, Holiday Inn Express ⓞ Chevrolet, Chrysler/Dodge/Jeep, Family$, Firestone/auto, Kroger/gas, Mazda, Office Depot, **S** ⓖ BP/Quiznos/dsl, Shell/Dunkin' ⓕ Camino Real Mexican, Casa Fiesta Mexican, IHOP, Olive Garden, Shoney's, Steak'n Shake ⌂ Antioch Qtrs, Knights Inn, Super 8 ⓞ Home Depot, Kia, vet
59	TN 254, Bell Rd same as 60
56	TN 255, Harding Place, **N** ⓖ Delta/dsl, Exxon, Shell/dsl ⓕ Applebee's, Bar-B-Cutie, Chicago Gyros, Dunkin', KFC, McDonald's, Mikado Japanese, Pizza Hut/Taco Bell, Subway, Waffle House, Wendy's ⌂ Executive Inn, M Motel, Stay Lodge, Thrifty Inn ⓞ $Tree, Sam's Club/gas, **S** ⓖ Delta/dsl, Shell/dsl ⓕ Burger King, Hooters, Jack-in-the-Box, La Fiesta ⌂ Best Value Inn, Travelodge ⓞ Ⓗ
57	Haywood Lane, **N** ⓖ Kwik Sak/dsl ⓕ Hardee's, Whitt's BBQ ⓞ $General, Walgreens, **S** ⓖ Kangaroo, Shell
54b a	TN 155, Briley Pkwy ⓞ to Opryland
53	I-440 W, to Memphis
52	US 41, Murfreesboro Rd, **N** ⓖ Phillips 66/dsl, Shell ⓕ Waffle House ⌂ Best Western, Days Inn, Holiday Inn Express, Rodeway Inn, Super 8, **S** ⓖ Mapco/dsl, SpeedCo/dsl/e85 ⓕ BP/dsl ⓞ NAPA
52b a	I-40, E to Knoxville, W to Memphis

I-24 and I-40 run together 2 mi. See I-40, exits 212-213.

📷 = gas 🍴 = food 🏠 = lodging Ⓞ = other ℞ₛ = rest stop Copyright 2022 - The Next EXIT ©

TN

NASHVILLE

🔺Ⓔ INTERSTATE 24 Cont'd

Exit #	Services
50b	I-40 W
49	Shelby Ave, (from wb only), S 📷 Exxon Ⓞ to LP Field
48	James Robertson Pkwy, N 📷 Citgo, S 📷 Exxon, TA/Country Pride/dsl/24hr/@ 🍴 Gerst Haus Rest., Shoney's 🏠 La Quinta Inn & Suites, Quality Inn, Stadium Inn Ⓞ LP Stadium, st capitol
47a	US 31E
47	N 1st St, Jefferson St, N 📷 BP, Citgo, Zmart/dsl Ⓞ Family$, S 📷 Mystic Gas 🏠 Clarion, Knights Inn Ⓞ U-Haul
I-24 and I-65 run together. See I-65, exit 87 b a.	
44b a	I-65, N to Louisville, S to Nashville
43	TN 155, Briley Pkwy, Brick Church Pike
40	TN 45, Old Hickory Blvd, N 📷 Marathon/Subway/dsl, Phillips 66/dsl, Shell/dsl 🍴 El Rey Azteca 🏠 Super 8
35	US 431, to Joelton, Springfield, N Ⓞ🏥, S 📷 BP/Heritage TC/DQ/Subway/dsl, Shell/dsl, Tfuel/dsl 🍴 Family Rest., Mazatlan Mexican, McDonald's, Taco Bell 🏠 Days Inn Ⓞ $General, auto repair, OK Camping
31	TN 249, New Hope Rd, S 📷 Marathon/dsl, Shell/dsl 🍴 Jardin Mexican
24	TN 49, to Springfield, Ashland City, N 📷 Mapco/dsl, Marathon/Pizza Hut/dsl 🏠 Quality Inn Ⓞ🏥, S 📷 Shell/dsl, SS/Dunkin'/Wendy's/dsl 🍴 Burger King, Hardee's, KFC/Taco Bell, Sidelines Grill, Sonic, Subway 🏠 Hampton Inn Ⓞ $General Mkt, city park, Hill Foods, O'Reilly Parts, USPO, vet
19	TN 256, Maxey Rd, to Adams, N 📷 Phillips 66/dsl, S 📷 Shell/dsl Ⓞ $General
11	TN 76, to Adams, Clarksville, N 📷 Shell/dsl, S 📷 Citgo, Exxon/dsl 🍴 Domino's, El Rancho Grande, McDonald's, Pancho Villa Grille, Subway, Waffle House 🏠 Baymont Inn, Comfort Inn, Days Inn, Super 8 Ⓞ $General, 🏥, Publix, vet
9mm	Red River
8	TN 237, Rossview Rd, N 🍴 Burger King, Popeye's, S Ⓞ Dunbar Cave SP

CLARKSVILLE

4	US 79, to Clarksville, Ft Campbell, N 📷 Exxon/dsl, Shell/dsl 🍴 Cracker Barrel 🏠 Best Western+, Hilton Garden, Holiday Inn Express, Sleep Inn Ⓞ Sam's Club/gas, Spring Creek Camping (2mi), S 📷 BP/dsl, Murphy USA/dsl, Shell/Subway/dsl 🍴 Applebee's, Arby's, Baskin-Robbins, Buffalo Wild Wings, Burger King, Canela Mexican, Capt D's, Cheddar's, Chick-Fil-A, Chili's, China King, Chipotle, ChuckeCheese, Church's/White Castle, DQ, Fazoli's, Firehouse Subs, Golden Corral, Harbor Cafe, IHOP, Jersey Mike's, KFC, Krispy Kreme, Krystal, LJ Silver, Logan's Roadhouse, Longhorn Steaks, McDonald's, Moe's SW Grill, Noodles&Co, O'Charley's, Old Chicago Pizza, Olive Garden, Outback Steaks, Panera Bread, Rafferty's, Red Lobster, Shogun Japanese, Shoney's, Starbucks, Steak'n Shake, Subway, Taco Bell, Tilted Kilt, TX Roadhouse, Waffle House, Wendy's, Zaxby's 🏠 Baymont Inn, Best Inn, Best Value Inn, Candlewood Suites, Country Inn&Suites, Courtyard, Days Inn, EconoLodge, Fairfield Inn, Gateway Inn, Guesthouse Inn, Hampton Inn, Hometowne Suites, La Quinta, Mainstay Suites, Microtel, Quality Inn, Ramada Ltd, Red Roof Inn, Rodeway Inn, Super 8, Woodspring Suites Ⓞ $Tree, AT&T, Belk, Best Buy, Books-A-Million, Buick/GMC, Dick's, Firestone/auto, Goodyear/auto, Hobby Lobby, Home Depot, 🏥, Hyundai, JC Penney, Kohl's, Kroger/dsl, Lowe's, Mazda, Office Depot, Petco, Petsmart, Ross, Subaru, Target, TJ Maxx, to Austin Peay St U, to Land Between the Lakes, Toyota, U-Haul, Verizon, Walmart/McDonald's
1	TN 48, to Clarksville, Trenton, N 📷 Exxon/dsl, Shell/dsl Ⓞ Clarksville RV Camping, S 📷 Exxon/dsl, Shell/dsl 🍴 Bojangles,

---

1	Continued
	Burger King, Coldstone, Dunkin', El Bracero Mexican, Little Caesar's, Marco's Pizza, McDonald's, Sonic, Starbucks, Subway, Wendy's, Zaxby's Ⓞ $General, AT&T, AutoZone, Walgreens
.5mm	Welcome Ctr eb, full 🚻 facilities, 🍴 vending, 🗑 litter barrels, petwalk
0mm	Tennessee/Kentucky state line

🔺Ⓔ INTERSTATE 26

Exit #	Services
54.5mm	Tennessee/North Carolina state line
54mm	runaway truck ramp wb
52mm	runaway truck ramp wb, scenic overlook eb (no trucks)
50	Flag Pond Rd
47.5mm	scenic overlook wb (no trucks)
46mm	N Welcome Ctr/℞ₛ both lanes, full 🚻 facilities, 🗑 litter barrels, 🍴 petwalk
44mm	Higgins Creek
43	US 19 W, rd 352, Temple Hill Rd
42mm	S Indian Creek
40	Jackson-Love Hwy, Erwin, Jonesborough, N 📷 Valero/dsl 🏠 Mtn Inn Ⓞ🏥, Nolichucky Gorge Camping (2mi)
37	TN 81, rd 107, Erwin, Jonesborough, N 📷 Shell 🍴 Bojangles, Huddle House, McDonald's, Pal's Drive-Thru, Taco Bell Ⓞ🏥 USPO, Walgreens, S 🏠 Super 8 Ⓞ A. Johnson NHS (31mi), River Park Camping (5mi)
36	Main St, Erwin, N 📷 BP/dsl, Exxon/dsl/e-85 🍴 Azteca Mexican, Hardee's, KFC, Little Caesars, Pizza Hut, Subway, Wendy's Ⓞ $General, Advance Parts, AutoZone, Firestone, Rite Aid
34	Tinker Rd, N 📷 Murphy USA/dsl 🍴 Los Jalapenos, Primo's Pizza Ⓞ Walmart
32	rd 173, Unicoi Rd, to Cherokee NF, N 📷 Jerry's Mkt 🍴 Clarence's Drive-In, Whistle Stop Deli Ⓞ $General, Grandview Ranch Camping (7mi), USPO, S Ⓞ Woodsmoke Camping
27	rd 359 N, Okolona Rd, N 📷 BP 🏠 Budget Inn (3mi) Ⓞ truck repair
24	US 321, TN 67, Elizabethton, N 📷 Shell/Dunkin'/dsl Ⓞ Roan Mtn SP, S 📷 BP/dsl 🍴 Arby's, Burger King, Fox's Pizza, Little Caesar's, LJ Silver, Subway 🏠 Comfort Inn Ⓞ Advance Parts, CVS, Food City/gas, 🏥, Price Less Foods, to ETSU, Walgreens
23	rd 91, Market St, N 🍴 DQ, McDonald's, S Ⓞ museum
22	rd 400, Unaka Ave, Watauga Ave
20b a	US 11 E, US 19 N, to Roan St, N 📷 Shell/dsl, Sunoco/dsl 🍴 Arby's, Cootie Brown's Rest., Harbor House Seafood, Hardee's, Little Caesar's, LJ Silver, Mellow Mushroom Pizza, Moto Japanese, Peerless Rest., Perkins, Popeye's, Sonic 🏠 Best Western, Holiday Inn, Ramada Ltd, Super 8 Ⓞ Acura, Advance Parts, AT&T, AutoZone, BigLots, Ford, Fred's, Honda, Hyundai, Mazda, NAPA Repair, O'Reilly Parts, Subaru, Tuesday Morning, UHaul, VW, S 🍴 Applebees, Babylon Grill, Bojangles, Bonefish Grill, Brusco's Pizza, Fazoli's, Five Guys, Greg's Pizza, Hana Steaks, Hibachi Grill, Hooters, Jack's City Grill, KFC, Longhorn Steaks, McAlister's Deli, McDonald's, O'Charley's, Olive Garden, Papa Murphy's, Red Lobster, Shoney's, Smokey Bones BBQ, Starbucks, Subway, Taco Bell, TX Roadhouse, Zaxby's 🏠 Doubletree, Motel 6, Red Roof Inn Ⓞ $General, $Tree, Belk, Books-A-Million, CVS, Dick's, FreeService Tire/auto, JC Penney, Kroger, Office Depot, Sears/auto, Target, TJ Maxx, Verizon, Walgreens
19	TN 381, to St of Franklin Rd, to Bristol, N 📷 Murphy USA/dsl, Valero/McDonald's 🍴 Golden Corral, Honeybaked Ham, Logan's Roadhouse, Outback Steaks, Subway 🏠 Comfort Suites Ⓞ Walmart, 0-2 mi S 🍴 Amigo Mexican, Barberito's Grille,

ERWIN

JOHNSON CITY

TN

🔼🔽 INTERSTATE 26 Cont'd

19   **Continued**
Buffalo Wild Wings, Carrabba's, Cheddar's, Chick-fil-A, Chili's, ChuckECheese's, East Coast Wings, Fuddruckers, IHOP, Jason's Deli, Mad Greek, Ming's Asian, Panera Bread, Rita's Custard, Wendy's, Which Wich? 🛏 Courtyard, Hampton Inn, Sleep Inn 🅞 AT&T, Barnes&Noble, Best Buy, Home Depot, 🅗, Kohl's, Lowe's, Michael's, Natural Foods Mkt, Old Navy, PetsMart, Ross, Sam's Club/gas, Steinmart, USPO, Verizon, vet

17   Boone St, **N** 🅖 BP, QP/dsl 🍴 Beef'o Brady's, Bob Evans, Giovanni's Italian, Hardee's, McDonald's, Pal's Drive-in, Pizza+ 🅞 $General, Ingles Foods/dsl, **S** 🅖 Exxon/e-85, Shell/Subway/dsl 🍴 Cracker Barrel, Domino's, Poblano's Mexican, Waffle House, Wendy's 🛏 Holiday Inn Express, Quality Inn, Woodspring Suites

13   rd 75, Bobby Hicks Hwy, **N** 🅖 BP, Shell 🍴 Burger King, China Luck, DQ, La Carreta, McDonald's, Pal's Drive-Thru, Papa John's, Pizza Hut, Sicily Italian, Subway, Taco Bell, Yong Asian 🅞 $General, Advance Parts, Food City/gas, O'Reilly Parts, USPO, Walgreens, **S** 🅖 Exxon/dsl

10   Eastern Star Rd, **N** 🍴 Phil's Dream Pit BBQ

8 b a   I-81, to Bristol, Knoxville

6   rd 347, Rock Springs Rd, **S** 🅖 Rite Quik/dsl

5mm   Welcome Ctr/🆁🆂, full 🚻 facilities both lanes, 🚮, litter barrels, petwalk

4   TN 93, Wilcox Dr, **N** 🅖 BP/Subway, Mobil/McDonald's/dsl 🍴 Burger King, Hardee's, La Carreta Mexican, Pizza Hut, Wendy's 🛏 Comfort Suites, Hampton Inn, Holiday Inn Express, Quality Inn 🅞 $General, Cave's Drug, Price Less Foods, **S** 🅖 Exxon, Mobil/Arby's/dsl/e-85 🍴 Pizza+

3   Meadowview Pkwy, **N** 🛏 Marriott

1   US 11 W, West Stone Dr, **N** 🅖 Shell 🍴 Little Caesar's, Molcajete's Mexican 🛏 Super 8 🅞 🅗, Walgreens, **S** 🅖 Exxon, Murphy USA/dsl 🍴 Bojangles, China Star, Fatz Cafe, Sonic, Subway 🅞 $Tree, Lowe's, Walmart

I-26 begins/ends on US 23.

🔼🔽 INTERSTATE 40

Exit #	Services
451mm	Tennessee/North Carolina state line
451	Waterville Rd
447	Hartford Rd, **N** 🅖 Citgo/dsl, **S** 🅖 BP/dsl 🍴 Bean Tree Cafe, Pigeon River Smokehouse 🅞 Foxfire Camping, Shauan's Riverside RV Park, USPO, whitewater rafting
446mm	Welcome Ctr wb, full 🚻 facilities, 🅲, vending, 🚮, litter barrels, petwalk, NO TRUCKS
443	Foothills Pkwy, to Gatlinburg 🅞 Great Smoky Mtns NP
443mm	Pigeon River
440	US 321, to Wilton Spgs Rd, Gatlinburg, **N** 🅖 76/440 Trkstp/cafe/dsl, **S** 🅖 Marathon 🍴 Broasted Chicken 🅞 Arrow Creek Camping (14mi), CrazyHorse Camping (14mi)
439mm	Pigeon River
435	US 321, to Gatlinburg, Newport, **N** 🅖 Exxon/Biodsl/e-85, JSK Express, Marathon, Rite Quik/dsl, Weigel/dsl 🍴 Arby's, Burger King, Hardee's, KFC, Lois' Country Kitchen, McDonald's, Pizza Hut, SageBrush Steaks, Subway, Taco Bell 🛏 Motel 6 🅞 CVS Drug, 🅗, O'Reilly Parts, Town&Country Drug, USPO, Walgreens, **S** 🅖 Mobil/dsl, Murphy USA/dsl 🍴 Bojangle's, Brooklyn Pizza, Cracker Barrel, Monterrey Mexican, New China, Papa John's, Papa Murphy's, Portabella's, Ruby Tuesday, Waffle House, Wendy's 🛏 Best Western, Family Inn, Hampton Inn, Holiday Inn Express, Knights Inn, Quality Inn 🅞 $General, $Tree, AT&T, Lowe's, Save-A-Lot Foods, Verizon, Walmart/Subway

432 b a	US 70, US 411, US 25W, to Newport, **N** 🅖 Exxon/dsl, Marathon/dsl, TimeOut TC/BP/Huddle House/dsl/scales 🛏 Comfort Inn, Relax Inn 🅞 Buick/Chevrolet, Chrysler/Dodge/Jeep, KOA (2mi), Tana-See RV Park, truck service, Westgate Tire, **S** 🅖 Citgo/dsl, Marathon/dsl, Shell/dsl 🛏 Family Inn/rest. 🅞 $General
426mm	🆁🆂 wb, full 🚻 facilities, 🅲, vending, 🚮, litter barrels, petwalk
425mm	French Broad River
424	TN 113, Dandridge, **N** 🅖 Marathon/dsl
421	I-81 N, to Bristol
420mm	🆁🆂 eb, full 🚻 facilities, 🅲, vending, 🚮, litter barrels, petwalk
417	TN 92, Dandridge, **N** 🅖 Marathon/dsl, Pilot/Subway/dsl/scales/24hr/@ 🍴 Capt's Galley, Hardee's, McDonald's, Perkins, Ruby Tuesday, Taste of Dandridge 🛏 Rodeway Inn, **S** 🅖 Exxon/Wendy's/dsl, Marathon/dsl, Weigel's/dsl 🍴 Arby's, Bojangles, LJ Silver/Taco Bell, Shoney's, Waffle House 🛏 Hampton Inn, Holiday Inn Express, Jefferson Inn, Quality Inn, Super 8 🅞 Advance Parts
415	US 25W, US 70, to Dandridge, **S** 🅖 Marathon/dsl 🍴 Sonic (3mi)
412	Deep Sprgs Rd, to Douglas Dam, **N** 🅖 ♥Love's/Chester's/Subway/dsl/scales/24hr, Speedway/Speedy's Cafe/dsl
407	TN 66, to Sevierville, Pigeon Forge, Gatlinburg, **N** 🅖 Shell/Subway/dsl 🍴 Chophouse, Cracker Barrel, McDonald's, Uncle Buck's Grill 🛏 Best Value Inn, Fairfield Inn, Hampton Inn, Holiday Inn Express 🅞 Bass Pro Shops, Harley Davidson, RV Camping, Smoky Mtn Visitor's Ctr, **S** 🅖 BP/Subway/dsl, Exxon/dsl, Mobil/Dunkin'/dsl, Shell/Krystal/dsl 🍴 Burger King, FlapJack's, Wendy's 🛏 Best Western, Comfort Suites, Days Inn, Quality Inn 🅞 Chrysler/Dodge/Jeep, flea mkt, Russell Stover, RV Camping, TN Tourist Info, USPO multiple services/outlets
402	Midway Rd
398	Strawberry Plains Pk, **N** 🅖 BP/dsl, Citgo/dsl, Exxon/dsl, Shell/dsl 🍴 Aubrey's Rest., McDonald's, Outback Steaks, Waffle House, Wendy's 🛏 EconoLodge, Hampton Inn, Holiday Inn Express, Knight's Inn, Quality Inn, Red Roof Inn, Rodeway Inn, Super 8 🅞 TN RV Ctr, **S** 🅖 Pilot/Subway/dsl/scales/24hr, Weigel's 🍴 Arby's, Burger King, Cracker Barrel, Golden Wok Chinese, KFC, Krystal, Puleo's Grille, Taco Bell 🛏 Best Western, Comfort Suites, Fairfield Inn, La Quinta, Motel 6
395mm	🅞 Holston River
394	US 70, US 11E, US 25W, Asheville Hwy, **N** 🅖 BP, Pilot/dsl, Shell/dsl 🍴 Papa John's, Subway, Wendy's 🛏 Gateway Inn 🅞 Advance Parts, AutoZone, city park, **S** 🅖 Exxon, Mapco/dsl 🍴 Habaneros Mexican, Pizza Hut, Scott's Place, Waffle House 🛏 Days Inn 🅞 $General, CVS Drug, Family$, Kroger/gas, NAPA, vet, Walgreens
393	I-640 W, to I-75 N

K I N G S P O R T

N E W P O R T

D A N D R I D G E

🅖 = gas 🅗 = food 🅛 = lodging 🅞 = other 🆁🆂 = rest stop   Copyright 2022 - The Next EXIT

TN

INTERSTATE 40 Cont'd

Exit #	Services
392	US 11W, Rutledge Pike, **N** 🅖 Citgo/dsl 🅞 $General, truck repair, U-Haul, **S** 🅖 Shell 🅗 Buddy's BBQ, Hardee's, Shoney's 🅞 NAPA, Sav-A-Lot Foods, to Knoxville Zoo, transmissions
390	Cherry St, Knoxville, **N** 🅖 Marathon/dsl, Top Fuel Mart, Weigel's/Subway 🅗 Happy Garden Chinese 🅛 Knoxville Inn 🅞 tires, **S** 🅖 Exxon 🅗 Arby's, Little Caesar's, LJ Silver, McDonald's 🅛 Regency Inn 🅞 Advance Parts, Family$, O'Reilly Parts, vet, Walgreens
389	US 441 N, Broadway, 5th Ave, **N** 🅖 Pilot/dsl, Shell/dsl, Star 🅗 Burger King, KFC, Krystal, McDonald's, Sonic, Subway, Taco Bell, Wendy's 🅞 $General, Ace Hardware, Belew Drug, CVS Drug, Family$, Firestone/auto, Kroger/dsl, Save-A-Lot Foods, USPO, Walgreens/24hr
388	US 441 S (exits left from wb), **S** 🅛 Crowne Plaza, Hilton, Holiday Inn 🅞 downtown, to Smokey Mtns, to U of TN
387a	I-275 N, to Lexington
387	TN 62, 17th St, **N** 🅖 Gas'N Go, Pilot/dsl 🅛 Hamilton Inn, Royal Inn 🅞 $General, Food City, vet
386b a	US 129, University Ave, to UT
385	I-75 N, I-640 E
I-40 W and I-75 S run together 17 mi.	
383	Papermill Rd, **N** 🅛 Red Roof Inn, **S** 🅖 Exxon/dsl, Pilot/dsl 🅗 Barberitos, Buddy's BBQ, Burger King, Five Guys, Krispy Kreme, Sonic, Twin Peaks, Waffle House 🅛 Courtyard, Hampton Inn, Holiday Inn Express, Travelodge 🅞 Food City, same as 380, Walgreens
380	US 11, US 70, West Hills, **S** 🅖 Delta Express, Mapco/dsl 🅗 Arby's, Brazeiro's Brazilian Steaks, Brixx Pizza, Burro Flojo Mexican, Cheesecake Factory, Chick-fil-A, Chili's, Cookout, Doc's Grille, Dunkin', Firehouse Subs, Hardee's, Honeybaked Ham, Hooters, IHOP, Jets Pizza, Jimmy John's, Longhorn Steaks, McAlister's Deli, McDonald's, Mooyah Burger, Mr Gatti's, O'Charley's, Olive Garden, Papa John's, Penn Sta Subs, Petro's Chili, PF Chang's, Pizza Hut, PlumTree Chinese, Qdoba Mexican, Red Lobster, Salsarita's Cantina, Starbucks, Subway, Taco Bell, Tropical Smoothie Cafe, TX Roadhouse, Zaxby's 🅛 Extended Stay America, Ramada Inn 🅞 $Tree, AT&T, Barnes&Noble, Belk, Dillards, Food City, JC Penney, Kohl's, mall, O'Reilly Parts, Office Depot, Old Navy, Petsmart, REI, Ross, Sears/auto, Steinmart, Target, TJ Maxx, Trader Joe's, U-Haul, Walgreens, Whole Foods Mkt
379	Bridgewater Rd, **N** 🅖 Exxon/Subway/dsl, Pilot/McDonald's/dsl 🅗 Taco Bell 🅞 Sam's Club/gas, Walmart/Subway, **S** 🅖 Conoco/dsl, Marathon/dsl 🅗 Asia Kitchen, Buddy's BBQ, Burger King, Cheddar's, ChuckeCheese, CiCi's Pizza, Makino Japanese, Misaki Japanese, Shoney's, Sonic, Wendy's 🅛 In-Town Suites 🅞 Aamco, Advance Parts, AutoZone, Books-A-Million, Buick/GMC, Chrysler/Dodge/Jeep, Firestone/auto, Ford/Lincoln, Hyundai/Subaru, Mazda, Nissan, NTB, Tire Barn, Transmission World
378	Cedar Bluff Rd, **N** 🅖 Pilot/Taco Bell/dsl, Shell, Weigel's/dsl 🅗 Arby's, Burger King, Cracker Barrel, Dunkin', KFC, Little Caesar's, McDonald's, Old Mill Bread Co., Papa John's, Starbucks, Subway, Waffle House, Wendy's 🅛 Country Inn&Suites, Days Inn, Hampton Inn, Holiday Inn, Quality Inn 🅞 $General, 🅗, **S** 🅖 Exxon 🅗 Applebee's, Blaze Pizza, Cancun Mexican, Capt D's, Carrabba's, Chipotle, Chuy's Mexican, Famous Dave's BBQ, Firehouse Subs, Fuddrucker's, Hardee's, Jason's Deli, Koko Japanese, Krystal, La Rosa's, Lenny's Subs, Newk's Cafe, Outback Steaks, Panera Bread, Parkside Grill, Peerless Grill, Penn Sta. Subs, Pizza Hut, Puleo's Grill, Rafferty's, Salsarita's, Starbucks,

Exit #	Services
378	Continued
	Which Wich?, Zaxby's 🅛 Baymont Inn, Best Western, Comfort Inn, Courtyard, Embassy Suites, Extended Stay America, Hilton Garden, Home 2 Suites, Microtel, Motel 6, Red Roof Inn, Residence Inn, Towne Place Suites 🅞 $Tree, Aldi Foods, AT&T, Best Buy, Cadillac, Chevrolet, CVS Drug, Dick's, Fiat, Ford/Lincoln, GNC, Home Depot, Jo-Ann Fabrics, Kia, Kroger/dsl, Lowe's, Pepboys, Staples, Tuesday Morning, Volvo, Walgreens
376	I-140 E, TN 162 N, to Maryville, **N** to Oak Ridge Museum
374	TN 131, Lovell Rd, **N** 🅖 Shell/dsl, Speedway/Speedy Cafe/dsl, scales/24hr, TA/Country Pride/dsl/scales/24hr/@ 🅗 Bojangles, Subway, Waffle House 🅛 Econolodge 🅞 Harley-Davidson, **S** 🅖 Pilot/Wendy's/dsl/24hr 🅗 Abuelo's Mexican, Arby's, Baskin-Robbins, Bonefish Grill, Brixx Pizza, Buffalo Wild Wings, Calhoun's Rest., Chick-fil-A, Chipotle, Connor's Rest., Egg&I Cafe, Flemings, Hurricane Grill, IHOP, Jimmy John's, Kabuki Japanese, Krystal, Lenny's Subs, McAlister's Deli, McDonald's, Mimi's Cafe, Moe's SW Grill, Noodles&Co, O'Charley's, Olive Garden, Panera Bread, Pei Wei, Red Robin, Salsarita's Cantina, Smokey Mtn Brewery, Sonic, Starbucks, Steak'n Shake, Taco Bell, TX Roadhouse, Wasabi Japanese, Zoe's Kitchen 🅛 Budget Inn, Candlewood Suites, Homewood Suites, SpringHill Suites 🅞 $Tree, Advance Parts, AutoZone, Belk, Best Buy, BMW/Mini, CarMax, Costco/gas, EarthFare Foods, GNC, Hobby Lobby, Honda, 🅗, Land Rover, Lexus, Marshall's, Mercedes, Old Navy, Petsmart, Ross, Target, Toyota, Walgreens, Walmart/Subway, World Mkt
373	Campbell Sta Rd, **N** 🅖 Marathon/dsl, Shell/dsl 🅛 Comfort Suites, Country Inn&Suites, Fairfield Inn, Holiday Inn Express, Super 8 🅞 Buddy Gregg RV Ctr, **S** 🅖 Exxon/dsl, Pilot/dsl, Weigel's 🅗 Bad Daddy's Burger, Cracker Barrel, Dunkin', Hardee's, La Parrilla, Longhorn Steaks, Mellow Mushroom, Newk's Grill, Panda Express, Potbelly, Seasons Grille, Taco Boy, Wild Wing Cafe, Zaxby's 🅛 Clarion, Hampton Inn, Staybridge Suites 🅞 AT&T, JC Penney, Publix, Verizon, Walgreens
372mm	weigh sta both lanes
369	Watt Rd, **N** 🅖 FLYING J/Denny's/dsl/LP/scales/RV dump/ 24hr, Speedco 🅞 Blue Beacon, **S** 🅖 Petro/Iron Skillet/dsl/ scales/24hr/@, TA/Marathon/Burger King/Pizza Hut/Popeye's/ Subway/dsl/24hr/@ 🅞 Knoxville Coach & RV
I-40 E and I-75 N run together 17 mi.	
368	I-75 and I-40
364	US 321, TN 95, Lenoir City, Oak Ridge, **N** 🅞 Crosseyed Cricket Camping (2mi), 4-5 mi **S** 🅖 Loves/McDonald's/Subway/ dsl/24hr 🅗 Ruby Tuesday 🅛 Days Inn, EconoLodge, Hampton Inn, Holiday Inn Express
362	Industrial Park Rd
360	Buttermilk Rd, **N** 🅞 Soaring Eagle RV Park
356	TN 58 N, Gallaher Rd, to Oak Ridge, **N** 🅖 Marathon/dsl, Weigels/dsl 🅛 Motel 6 🅞 $General, 4 Seasons Camping
355	Lawnville Rd, **N** 🅖 Pilot/Subway/dsl
352	TN 58 S, Kingston, **N** 🅛 Lakeview Inn, **S** 🅖 Exxon/dsl, Mobil/dsl, RaceWay 🅗 Buddy's BBQ, Hardee's, Little Caesar's, McDonald's, Sonic, Subway, Taco Bell 🅛 Super 8 🅞 $General, Cash Saver Foods, Family$, Marina RV Park, to Watts Bar Lake, USPO
351mm	Clinch River
350	US 70, Midtown, **S** 🅖 Weigel's/dsl 🅗 Bojangles, Gondolier Italian, Subway, Zaxby's 🅞 AT&T, Caney Creek Camping (3mi), 🅗, Kroger, Lowe's, Walgreens
347	US 27, Harriman, **N** 🅖 Phillips 66/dsl 🅗 Hardee's, KFC, LJ Silver, Los Primos Mexican, McDonald's, Pizza Hut, Ruby Tuesday, Subway, Taco Bell, Wendy's 🅛 Days Inn 🅞 Big S Fork NRA, to Frozen Head SP, Verizon, **S** 🅖 Murphy USA/dsl, Shell/Krystal/dsl/24hr,

K N O X V I L L E

H A R R I M A N

🔼E INTERSTATE 40 Cont'd

347 **Continued**
Sunoco/dsl 🍴 Cancun Mexican, Capt D's, China King, Cracker Barrel, Domino's, McDonald's, Shoney's, Sonic 🛏 Comfort Inn, Holiday Inn Express, Quality Inn, Rodeway Inn ⊙ Ace Hardware, BigLots, 🅷, vet, Walmart

340 TN 299 N, Airport Rd

339.5mm eastern/central time zone line

338 TN 299 S, Westel Rd, **S** 🅿 Exxon/dsl, Sunoco/dsl ⊙ Boat-N-RV Ctr/Park

336mm parking area/weigh sta eb, litter barrel

329 US 70, Crab Orchard, **N** 🅿 Citgo/dsl, Marathon/dsl ⊙ KOA (4mi), **S** ⊙ Cumberland Trails SP, Wilson SP

327mm ℞s wb, full 🅰 facilities, 🍴, 🚻, litter barrels, petwalk, vending

324mm ℞s eb, full 🅰 facilities, 🍴, 🚻, litter barrels, petwalk, vending

322 TN 101, Peavine Rd, Crossville, **N** 🅿 Exxon/Subway/dsl, Volunteer/dsl 🍴 Hardee's, McDonald's 🛏 Holiday Inn Express ⊙ Deer Run RV Resort, KOA Camping, Roam-Roost RV Campground, to Fairfield Glade Resort, **S** 🅿 Shell/dsl 🍴 Cancun Mexican, Taco Bell 🛏 Comfort Suites, Hampton Inn, Super 8 ⊙ Chestnut Hill Winery, Cumberland Mtn SP, 🅷

320 TN 298, Crossville, **N** 🅿 🛢/Wendy's/dsl/scales/24hr 🍴 Butcher's Block Rest., Lefty's BBQ ⊙ antiques, winery, **S** 🅿 Shell/DQ/dsl, Speedway/dsl 🍴 Log Cabin Rest. ⊙ auto repair/ tires, Crossville Outlet/famous brands, 🅷, Save-A-Lot Foods

318mm Obed River

317 US 127, Crossville, **N** 🅿 Exxon/dsl, Shell/Circle K/dsl 🍴 Shoney's, Subway 🛏 Baymont Inn, Motel 6, Quality Inn ⊙ repair, to Big South Fork RA, to York SP, **0-2 mi S** 🅿 Jiffy, Marathon/dsl, Murphy USA/dsl, Shell 🍴 Arby's, Bojangles, Burger King, Cancun Mexican, Cracker Barrel, La Costa Mexican, McDonalds, Papa John's, Romo's Mexican, Ruby Tuesday, Ryan's, Sonic, Subway, Taco Bell, Tokyo Steaks, Vegas Steaks, Waffle House, Zaxby's 🛏 Economy Inn, Red Roof Inn ⊙ $General, $Tree, Buick/Cadillac/Chevrolet/GMC, Chrysler/Dodge/Jeep, Ford, GNC, 🅷, Lowe's, Rite Aid, Shadden Tires, Staples, to Cumberland Mtn SP, Verizon, Walgreens, Walmart

311 Plateau Rd, **S** 🅿 BP/dsl, Exxon/Hunt Bros Pizza

307mm parking area/weigh sta wb, litter barrels

301 US 70 N, TN 84, Monterey, **N** 🅿 Shell 🍴 Burger King, DQ, Rocky Pops BBQ/Catfish, Subway 🛏 Bethel Inn

300 US 70, Monterey, **N** 🅿 Citgo/dsl 🍴 DQ, Hardee's

291mm Falling Water River

290 US 70, Cookeville, **S** 🅿 Super/dsl 🍴 Fiesta Cancun 🛏 Alpine Suites

288 TN 111, to Livingston, Cookeville, Sparta, **N** Hull SP, **S** 🅿 Sunoco/dsl, Super Truck&TravelCtr/dsl/24hr 🍴 Subway 🛏 Fall Creek Inn

287 TN 136, Cookeville, **N** 🅿 Marathon/dsl, Murphy USA/dsl, Shell/dsl 🍴 Applebee's, Arby's, Baskin-Robbins, Blue Coast Burrito, Buffalo Wild Wings, Bully's Rest., Burger King, Capt D's, Cheddars, Chick-fil-A, Chili's, Cookout, Cracker Barrel, Dunkin', Fazoli's, Firehouse Subs, Fuji Japanese, Golden Corral, Hibachi Buffet, IHOP, Krystal, LJ Silver, Logan's Roadhouse, Longhorn Steaks, Marco's Pizza, McDonald's, Nick's Rest., O'Charley's, Olive Garden, Outback Steaks, Papa Murphy's, Pizza Hut, Red Lobster, Ruby Tuesday, Shoney's, Sonic, Starbucks, Steak'n Shake, Subway, Taco Bell, Wendy's 🛏 Best Value Inn, Best Western, Clarion, Comfort Inn, Comfort Suites, Days Inn, Hampton Inn, Red Roof Inn ⊙ Aldi Foods, BigLots, Firestone/auto, Harley-Davidson, JC Penney, Kroger/gas, Lowe's, Nissan, st patrol,

287 **Continued**
transmissions, Verizon, Walmart, **S** 🅿 Marathon/Godfather's/ dsl, 🛢/dsl 🍴 Gondola, KFC, Waffle House 🛏 Country Inn&Suites, Fairfield Inn, Holiday Inn Express, La Quinta, Motel 6, TownePlace Suites ⊙ Sam's Club/gas, URGENT CARE

286 TN 135, Burgess Falls Rd, **N** 🅿 Exxon, Gulf, RaceWay/dsl, Shell/dsl 🍴 Arby's, Hardee's, Waffle House ⊙ Chrysler/Dodge/Jeep, Ford/ Lincoln, Goodyear/auto, 🅷, Hyundai, Kia, to TTU, Toyota, USPO, **S** 🅿 Sunoco/dsl 🛏 Star Motor Inn ⊙ Burgess Falls SP (8mi)

280 TN 56 N, Baxter, **N** 🅿 ♥Loves/McDonalds/Subway/dsl/ scales/24hr, Speedway/dsl/24hr 🍴 Huddle House ⊙ Camp Discovery (2mi), Twin Lakes RV Park (2mi)

276 Old Baxter Rd

273 TN 56 S, to Smithville, **S** 🅿 Shell ⊙ Rose Garden Rest. ⊙ USPO

268 TN 96, Buffalo Valley Rd, **N** Grandville Marina Camping (11mi), **S** to Edgar Evins SP/RV camping

267mm Caney Fork River

267mm ℞s both lanes, full 🅰 facilities, info, 🍴, 🚻, litter barrels, petwalk, vending

266mm Caney Fork River

263mm Caney Fork River

258 TN 53, Gordonsville, **N** 🅿 Exxon/KFC/Taco Bell, Shell/dsl 🍴 McDonald's, Subway, Timberloft Café, Waffle House 🛏 Comfort Inn ⊙ to Cordell Hull Dam, **S** 🅿 Mobil/dsl, 🛢/Wendy's/dsl/scales/24hr 🍴 Arby's, Cornerstone Cafe, El Corral Mexican, KFC/Taco Bell ⊙ $General

254 TN 141, to Alexandria

252mm parking area/truck sta both lanes, 🚻, litter barrels

245 Linwood Rd

239 US 70, Lebanon, **N** 🅿 $General, RaceWay/dsl, Shell, **S** 🅿 Phillips 66/Uncle Pete's/dsl/scales 🍴 Jalisco Mexican

238 US 231, Lebanon, **N** 🅿 Exxon, Mapco/dsl, Murphy Express/dsl, Shell/dsl 🍴 Applebee's, Arby's, Chick-fil-A, Cici's Pizza, Cracker Barrel, Demo's Steaks, El Molino Mexican, Hardee's, Jack-in-the-Box, KFC, Logan's Roadhouse, Los Compadres, McDonald's, Panda Express, Pizza Hut, Ryan's, Shoney's, Starbucks, Subway, Sunset Rest., Taco Bell, Waffle House, Wendy's, White Castle, Whitt's BBQ, Zaxby's 🛏 Days Inn, EconoLodge, Executive Inn, Holiday Inn Express, Quality Inn, Ramada ⊙ $Tree, Aldi Foods, AT&T, Discount Tire, 🅷, Lowe's, to Bledsoe SP (23mi), Verizon, Walgreens, Walmart/Subway, **S.** 🅿 Citgo/Pizza Inn/Quiznos/ dsl, LNG, 🛢/Subway/DQ/dsl/scales/24hr, Shell/dsl, Speedway/dsl/e85 🍴 O'Charley's, Sonic 🛏 Comfort Suites, Knights Inn, La Quinta, Travel Inn ⊙ Family RV Ctr, Lebanon Outlets/famous brands, Shady Acres Camping, Timberline Campground, to Cedars of Lebanon SP

236 S Hartmann Dr, **N** 🅿 Mapco/dsl, Shell/dsl 🍴 Chili's, Outback Steaks, Subway 🛏 Fairfield Inn, Hampton Inn ⊙ Buick/Chevrolet/GMC, Home Depot, 🅷, Rose Tire

☐ = gas ☐ = food ☐ = lodging ☐ = other ☐ = rest stop Copyright 2022 - The Next EXIT

TN

▶E INTERSTATE 40 Cont'd

Exit #	Services
235	TN 840 W, to Murfreesboro
232	TN 109, to Gallatin, N ☐ Mapco/Quiznos/dsl Shell/McDonald's/dsl/24hr, Speedway/dsl, Thornton's/dsl ☐ Bellacino's Pizza, Coach's Grill, Sonic, Subway, Waffle House, Wendy's ☐ Sleep Inn, Woodspring Suites, S ☐ KOA (3mi)
228mm	truck sta, wb only
229b a	Beckwith Rd
226mm	truck sta
226	TN 171, Mt Juliet Rd, N ☐ BP/McDonald's/dsl, Exxon/dsl, Murphy Express/dsl, Shell/dsl ☐ Arby's, Capt D's, Cheddars, Don Pancho Mexican, Far East Buffet, Five Guys, Longhorn Steaks, Subway ☐ Comfort Suites ☐ $Tree, Aldi Foods, Firestone/auto, Lowe's, NTB, URGENT CARE, Walmart, S ☐ Mapco/Quiznos/dsl ☐ Blue Coast Burrito, Bonfire Japanese Steaks, Buffalo Wild Wings, Chick-fil-A, ChuckECheese, Cori's Dog House, Cracker Barrel, Firehouse Subs, Fulin's Asian, Jonathan's, Logan's Roadhouse, Marble Slab, Martin's BBQ, McDonald's, Mi Casa Mexican, NY Pizza, O'Charley's, Olive Garden, Panera Bread, Penn Sta Subs, Pizza Hut, Red Lobster, Red Robin, Salsarita's Cantina, Sonic, Steak'n Shake, Taco Bell, Taziki's Cafe, Waffle House, Wasabi Steaks, Wendy's, Which Wich?, Zaxby's ☐ Hampton Inn, Holiday Inn Express, Quality Inn ☐ AT&T, Belk, Best Buy, Books-A-Million, Dick's, Discount Tire, Ford, GNC, JC Penney, JoAnn Fabrics, Kroger/dsl, Old Navy, Petsmart, Publix, Ross, Staples, Target, Tire Discounters, TJ Maxx, to Long Hunter SP, Verizon, vet, Walgreens
221	TN 45 N, Old Hickory Blvd, to The Hermitage, **0-2 mi** N ☐ BP, Delta/dsl, Exxon, RaceWay/dsl ☐ Applebee's, Baskin-Robbins/Dunkin', Buffalo Wild Wings, Burger King, Chick-fil-A, Chili's, Cinco de Mayo, Domino's, DQ, Famous Dave's, Fazoli's, Firehouse Subs, Golden Corral, Hardee's, IHOP, Jack-in-the-Box, Jets Pizza, Las Palmas Mexican, O'Charley's, Outback Steaks, Panera Bread, Penn Sta Subs, Pizza Hut, Qdoba Mexican, Starbucks, Steak'n Shake, Subway, Taziki's Cafe, Waffle House ☐ Best Value Inn, Suburban Lodge, Super 8, Vista Inn ☐ Home Depot, ☐, Kroger, Lowe's, PetCo, Staples, Verizon, Walgreens, S ☐ Kwik Sak/dsl, Marathon/dsl, Phillips 66/White Castle, Shell/McDonald's
219	Stewart's Ferry Pike, N ☐ Mapco/dsl, S ☐ Mapco/Subway/dsl, Shell/dsl, Thornton's/dsl ☐ China King, Cracker Barrel, La Hacienda Mexican, Sal's Pizza, Subway, Waffle House ☐ Comfort Suites, Country Inn&Suites, Days Inn, EconoLodge, Family Inn, Motel 6, Sleep Inn ☐ $General, Food Lion, Fred's, vet
216	(216 c from eb) TN 255, Donaldson Pk, N ☐ BP/dsl, Mapco, RaceWay/dsl, Shell/dsl ☐ Arby's, Backyard Burger, Bar-B-Cutie, Darfon's, Jalisco Mexican, KFC, McDonald's, Panera Bread, Ruby Tuesday, Shoney's, Sonic, Subway, Taco Bell, Waffle House, Wendy's ☐ BNA Inn, Country Inn&Suites, Drury Inn, Hampton Inn, Holiday Inn Express, Hyatt Place, La Quinta, Radisson, Red Roof Inn, Sheraton, SpringHill Suites, Super 8 ☐ Advance Parts, USPO, Walgreens, S ☐ ☐ ☐
216b a	(from eb), S Nashville Intn'l Airport
215b a	TN 155, Briley Pkwy, to Opryland, **N on Elm Hill** ☐ Citgo, Mapco ☐ Jack-in-the-Box, Waffle House ☐ Alexis Inn, Baymont Inn, Club Hotel, Comfort Suites, Courtyard, Doubletree, Extended Stay, Hilton Garden, Holiday Inn, Homewood Suites, La Quinta, Marriott, Nashville Inn, Quality Inn, Residence Inn, TownePlace Suites ☐ URGENT CARE, S ☐ Phillips 66/dsl ☐ Dunkin', Mazatlan Mexican, Panda House, Subway ☐ Hamilton Inn, Hotel Preston

213	US 41 (from wb no return), to Spence Lane, N ☐ CNG ☐ Kenworth, S ☐ Phillips 66/dsl, Shell ☐ Waffle House ☐ Best Western, Days Inn, Holiday Inn Express, Rodeway Inn, same as 212, Super 8
213b	I-24 W
213a	I-24 E/I-440, E to Chattanooga
212	Fessler's Lane (from eb, no return), N ☐ Freightliner, Harley-Davidson, S ☐ BP/dsl, Mapco/dsl, Shell/Dunkin', SpeedCo dsl/e85 ☐ Burger King, McDonald's, Sonic, Wendy's ☐ Scottish Inn ☐ Chevrolet, NAPA, same as 213
211mm	Cumberland River
211b	I-24 W
211a	I-24E, I-40 W
210c	US 31 S, US 41A, 2nd Ave, 4th Ave, N ☐ Hilton, Renaissance Hotel, Sheraton, S museum
210b a	I-65 S, to Birmingham
209b a	US 70 S, Charlotte Ave, Nashville, N ☐ Exxon ☐ McDonald ☐ Sheraton ☐ Conv Ctr, Country Music Hall of Fame, Firestone Mazda, S ☐ Exxon ☐ Burger King, Jack Cawthon's BBQ, Krystal, Sonic, Subway, White Castle ☐ Comfort Inn, Hilton Garden ☐ Buick/GMC, Hyundai, Toyota, URGENT CARE, Walgreens
208b a	I-65, N to Louisville
207	28th Ave, Jefferson St, Nashville, N ☐ BP ☐ Subway, Wendy ☐ Family$, to TN St U, S ☐ ☐
206	I-440 E, to Knoxville
205	46th Ave, W Nashville, S ☐ Shell/dsl ☐ M L Rose Burgers, McDonald's ☐ USPO
204	TN 155, Briley Pkwy, S ☐ BP/dsl ☐ Burger King, China Buffet, Church's/White Castle, Cinco De Mayo, Domino's, Hattie B's Chicken, Jack-in-the-Box, KFC, Las Palmas, Papa John's, Shoney's, Subway, Waffle House, Wendell Smith's Rest., White Castle, Whitt's BBQ ☐ Best Western, Comfort Inn, Days Inn, Holiday Inn Express ☐ CVS Drug, Family$, Firestone/auto, Kroger/gas, O'Reilly Parts, PepBoys, Sav-a-lot Foods, Walgreens
201b a	US 70, Charlotte Pike, N ☐ Exxon, Shell/dsl, Thornton's/dsl ☐ Bojangles, Cracker Barrel, El Sombrero, Jim 'N Nick's BBQ, Krystal, Little Caesar's, Waffle House, Wayback Burger, Wendy's ☐ Super 8 ☐ GNC, Kwik Kar, Lowe's Whse, vet, Walmart/Subway S ☐ BP, Delta Express/dsl ☐ Arby's, Blue Coast Burrito, Buffalo Wild Wings, Chick-fil-A, Firehouse Subs, IHOP, Logan's Roadhouse, McDonald's, Pizza Hut, Red Robin, Taco Bell ☐ $Tree, AT&T, Best Buy, Big Lots, Books-A-Million, Costco/gas, Dick's, Firestone/auto, GNC, Marshall's, Old Navy, PetsMart, Publix, Ross, Target, Uhaul, URGENT CARE, Verizon, World Mkt
199	rd 251, Old Hickory Blvd, N ☐ Shell/dsl ☐ $General, S ☐ BP, Mapco/dsl ☐ Sonic, Subway
196	US 70, to Bellevue, Newsom Sta, N ☐ Mapco/dsl ☐ Shoney's, S ☐ BP, Mapco/dsl, Shell/dsl ☐ Arby's, Asihi Asian, Baskin Robbins, El Agavero, Jonathan's Grill, O'Charley's, Pizza Hut, Sir Pizza, Sonic, Subway, Taco Bell, Waffle House, Wendy's ☐ Hampton Inn, Microtel ☐ $Tree, AutoZone, Firestone/auto, Home Depot, Michael's, PetCo, Publix, Sears/auto, Staples, USPO, Verizon, Walgreens
195mm	Harpeth River
192	McCrory Lane, to Pegram, N ☐ Eddie's Mkt (1mi), **4 mi** S ☐ Loveless Cafe ☐ Natchez Trace Pkwy
190mm	Harpeth River
188mm	Harpeth River
188	rd 249, Kingston Springs, N ☐ BP, Mapco/Quiznos/dsl, Shell/Arby's/dsl ☐ El Jardin Mexican, McDonald's/playplace, Sonic, Subway ☐ Best Western, Mid-Town Inn, Relax Inn ☐ USPO, ☐ Petro/BP/Quick Skillet/dsl/scales/showers/24hr/@ ☐ vet

NASHVILLE

TN

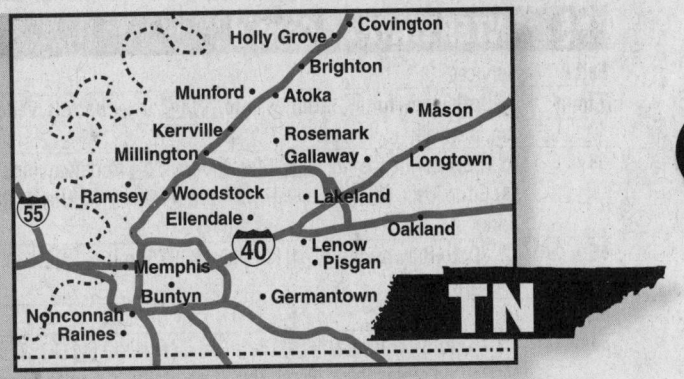

INTERSTATE 40 Cont'd

Exit #	Services
182	TN 96, to Dickson, Fairview, **N** 🅖 BP/dsl 🛏 Fairview Inn O M Bell SP (16mi), **S** 🅖 ✈ FLYING J/Denny's/dsl/LP/scales/24hr, Citgo/Backyard Burger/Dunkin'/dsl 🛏 Deerfield Inn
176	I-840
172	TN 46, to Dickson, **N** 🅖 Marathon/dsl, Pilot/Wendy's/dsl/ scales/24hr, Shell/Dunkin'/Taco Bell/dsl 🍴 Arby's, Bojangle's, Camino Real, Cracker Barrel, Hardee's, Logan's Roadhouse, McDonald's, Ruby Tuesday, Waffle House 🛏 Best Western, Comfort Inn, EconoLodge, Fairfield Inn, Hampton Inn, Motel 6, Rodeway Inn, South-Aire Inn, Super 8 O $General, auto repair, Chappell's Foods, Chevrolet/Buick/GMC, Dickson RV Park, Ford, H, Nissan, to M Bell SP, truck repair, **S** 🅖 Marathon/dsl, Shell/dsl 🍴 Colton's Steaks, O'Charley's, Sonic 🛏 Days Inn, Holiday Inn Express, Quality Inn
170	Rs both lanes, full ♿ facilities, 🅲, 🏞, litter barrels, vending, petwalk
166mm	Piney River
163	rd 48, to Dickson, **N** 🅖 ♥Loves/McDonald's/Subway/dsl/ scales/24hr, Phillips 66/dsl O tire repair, **S** 🅖 Shell O Pinewood Camping (7mi), Tanbark Camping
152	rd 230, Bucksnort, **N** 🅖 Sunoco/dsl 🛏 Rodeway Inn
149mm	Duck River
148	rd 50, Barren Hollow Rd, to Turney Center
143	TN 13, to Linden, Waverly, **N** 🅖 Pilot/Arby's/dsl/ scales/24hr, Shell 🍴 Jen's Rest, Log Cabin Rest., Loretta Lynn's Kitchen, McDonald's, Rochelle's BBQ 🛏 Days Inn, Holiday Inn Express, Knights Inn, Quality Inn O KOA/LP, **S** 🅖 Speedway/ dsl 🛏 Scottish Inn
141mm	Buffalo River
137	Cuba Landing, **N** O TN River RV Park, **S** 🍴 Cuba Landing Rest./ gas
133mm	Tennessee River
133	rd 191, Birdsong Rd, **9 mi N** 🛏 Good Sam RV Park, Songbird RV Resort/marina
131mm	Rs both lanes, full ♿ facilities, 🅲, vending, 🏞, litter barrels, petwalk
126	US 641, TN 69, to Camden, **N** 🅖 Marathon/Subway/dsl, Shell/ North 40/dsl 🍴 Burger Barn O $ General, Paris Landing SP, tire/truck repair, to NB Forrest SP, truck wash, **S** 🅖 ♥Loves/ Arby's/dsl/scales/24hr, Marathon/dsl, Shell/dsl 🛏 Days Inn O H, Mouse-tail Landing SP (24mi)
116	rd 114, **S** O RV camping, to Natchez Trace SP
110mm	Big Sandy River
108	TN 22, to Lexington, Parkers Crossroads, **N** 🅖 Marathon/ dsl/24hr, Phillips 66/dsl, Shell/McDonald's/dsl 🍴 DQ, Smarter's Rest, Subway 🛏 Knights Inn O city park, USPO, **S** 🅖 Exxon 🍴 Becky's Kitchen, Patty's Rest. 🛏 Best Value Inn O $ General, H, Parkers Crossroads Bfd Visitors Ctr, to Shiloh NMP (51mi)
103mm	parking area/truck sta eb, litter barrels
102mm	parking area/truck sta wb, litter barrels
101	rd 104, **N** 🅖 101 TP/Real Food/dsl/tires/24hr O golf (3mi)
93	rd 152, Law Rd, **N** 🅖 Phillips 66/deli/dsl/24hr, **S** 🅖 Shell/dsl
87	US 70, US 412, Jackson, **N** 🅖 Gulf/dsl, Mapco/Deli/dsl/e85, **S** 🅖 ♥Loves/Hardee's/dsl/scales/24hr, Skyline Express/dsl, Speedway/dsl/e85
85	Christmasville Rd, to Jackson, **N** 🅖 Exxon/dsl, Pilot/Denny's/dsl/scales/24hr, Speedway/dsl 🛏 Comfort Inn O $General, **S** 🅖 Shell/Pizza Pro/dsl 🍴 Burger King, Jack's, Jet's Pizza, Jiang Jun Chinese, Lenny's Subs, Los Portales, McDonald's, Reggi's BBQ, Sonic, Sparky's, Subway, Taco Bell, Waffle House 🛏 Holiday Inn Express O $Tree, Food Giant
83	Campbell st, **N** 🅖 Shell/Old Madina Mkt/dsl 🛏 Residence Inn, **S** 🛏 Courtyard, Hampton Inn
82 b a	US 45, Jackson, **N** 🅖 Dodge's/dsl, Marathon/dsl 🍴 Cracker Barrel 🛏 Best Value Inn, Knights Inn O Batteries+Bulbs, Smallwoods RV Ctr (4mi), **S** 🅖 Exxon, Hucks/dsl 🍴 Baskin-Robbins, Burger King, Catfish Galley, ChuckeCheese, DQ, KFC, Krystal, Little Caesar's, LJ Silver, Los Portales Mexican, McDonald's/ playplace, Papa John's, Pizza Hut, Popeye's, Sakura Japanese, Sonic, Starbucks, Subway, Taco Bell, Tulum Mexican, Waffle House, Wendy's 🛏 Executive Inn, La Quinta, Ramada Ltd, Scottish Inn, Travellers Motel O $General, $Tree, Advance Parts, AT&T, AutoZone, Belk, BigLots, Firestone/auto, Fred's, Goodyear/auto, JC Penney, Kroger/dsl, Macy's, O'Reilly Parts, Office Depot, Sears, vet
80 b a	US 45 Byp, Jackson, **0-2 mi N** 🅖 Exxon, Shell/dsl 🍴 Arby's, Asahi Japanese, Backyard Burger, Baskin-Robbins, Buffalo Wild Wings, Casa Adobe, Cheddar's, Chick-fil-A, Chili's, CookOut, Don Pancho, DQ, Dunkin', Fazoli's, Firehouse Subs, Five Guys, Flat Iron Grill, Fujiyama Japanese, Genghis Grill, HoneyBaked Ham, IHOP, Jason's Deli, Jersey Mike's, Jimmy John's, Lenny's Subs, Longhorn Steaks, Maggie Moo's, Marco's Pizza, McAlisters Deli, Moe's SW Grill, Olive Garden, Outback Steaks, Panda Express, Panera Bread, Perkins, Popeye's, Red Lobster, Red Robin, Snappy Tomato, Sonic, Starbucks, Steak'n Shake, Subway, TGIFriday's, Wendy's, Zaxby's 🛏 Baymont Inn, Fairfield Inn, Hilton Garden, Howard Johnson O $Tree, Aldi Foods, AT&T, AutoZone, Best Buy, Books-A-Million, Buick/Cadillac/ Chevrolet/GMC, CarMax, Dick's, Firestone/auto, Gateway Tires/repair, Hobby Lobby, Home Depot, JoAnn Fabrics, Kia, Kohl's, Lowe's, Marshall's, Nissan, Old Navy, Petsmart, Ross, Sam's Club/gas, SteinMart, Targwet, TJ Maxx, Toyota, Verizon, Walmart/gas, **S** 🅖 BP, G/dsl, Mobil/dsl, Shell/dsl 🍴 Arby's, Asia Garden, Baudo's Rest., Burger King, Checkers, Heavenly Ham, Logan's Roadhouse, McDonald's, O'Charley's, Old Hickory Steakhouse, Old Town Spaghetti, Pizza Hut, Red Bones Grill, Subway, Taco Bell, Waffle House 🛏 Best Western, Casey Jones Motel, Clarion, Comfort Suites, Days Inn, DoubleTree, EconoLodge, Jackson Hotel, Motel 6, Old Hickory Inn, Quality Inn, Super 8 O $General, Chickasaw SP, Chrysler/Dodge/Jeep, Ford/Lincoln, Harley-Davidson, Honda, H, Hyundai, to Pinson Mounds SP, Tuesday Morning
79	US 412, Jackson, **S** 🅖 Citgo/Subway/dsl, Exxon, Valero 🛏 Rodeway Inn O Jackson RV Park
78mm	Forked Deer River
76	rd 223, **S** 🍴 McKenzie BBQ (2.5mi) O McKellar-Sipes Airport, Whispering Pines RV Park
74	Lower Brownsville Rd

Ⓖ = gas Ⓕ = food Ⓛ = lodging Ⓞ = other Ⓡⓢ = rest stop Copyright 2022 - The Next EXIT

↑E INTERSTATE 40 Cont'd

Exit #	Services
73mm	Ⓡⓢ both lanes, full Ⓛ facilities, info, Ⓒ, Ⓐ, litter barrels, vending, petwalk
68	rd 138, Providence Rd, N Ⓕ Marathon/dsl Ⓛ Rodeway Inn, S Ⓕ Citgo/dsl, TA/Shell/Subway/dsl/scales/24hr/@ Ⓞ Joy-O RV Park
66	US 70, to Brownsville, N Ⓞ Ft Pillow SHP (51mi), S Ⓕ Exxon/dsl Ⓛ Motel 6
60	rd 19, Mercer Rd
56	TN 76, to Brownsville, N Ⓕ Delta/dsl, Marathon Ⓕ DQ, KFC, McDonald's/playplace, Pizza Hut, Taco Bell Ⓛ Comfort Inn, Days Inn, Econolodge, Rodeway Inn, S Ⓕ Exxon/Breakfast Cove/dsl, Valero
55mm	Hatchie River
52	TN 76, rd 179, Koko Rd, to Whiteville, S Ⓕ Koko Mkt
50mm	weigh sta both lanes
47	TN 179, to Stanton, Dancyville
42	TN 222, to Stanton, S Ⓕ Exxon/dsl, Ⓕⓘⓛⓔⓢ/Chester's/Subway/dsl/scales/24hr Ⓛ Deerfield Inn
35	TN 59, to Somerville, S Ⓕ Shelldsl/scales Ⓕ Longtown Rest.
29.5mm	Loosahatchie River
29	TN 196, Hickory Withe Rd
25	TN 205, Airline Rd, to Arlington, N Ⓕ Shell/dsl, S Ⓕ Exxon/Taco Bell/dsl Ⓞ vistor ctr
24	I-269, TN 385, rd 204, to Arlington, Millington, Collierville
20	Canada Rd, Lakeland, N Ⓕ Mobil/dsl, Shell/dsl Ⓕ Cracker Barrel, Waffle House Ⓛ Motel 6, Relax Inn, Super 8, S Ⓕ Exxon/Subway/dsl, fireworks Ⓞ Memphis East Camping
18	US 64, to Bartlett, N Ⓕ Shell/Burger King Ⓕ Abuelo's, Buffalo Wild Wings, El Porton Mexican, Firebird's Grill, Hooters, Longhorn Steaks, McAlister's Deli, O'Charley's, Olive Garden, Panera Bread, Steak'n Shake, TGI Friday's, TX Roadhouse Ⓛ Best Western, Fairfield Inn, Holiday Inn, Home 2 Suites, La Quinta, SpringHill Suites Ⓞ Buick/GMC, Firestone/auto, Lowe's, Pepboys, Sam's Club/gas, same as 16, Verizon, Walmart, S Ⓕ Circle K/dsl, Citgo, Marathon Ⓕ Backyard Burger, Dunkin', KFC, Lenny's Subs, Papa John's, Papa Murphy's, Pizza Hut, Subway, Zaxby's Ⓞ AT&T, Family$, Kroger/dsl, Sprouts Mkt, Walgreens
16b a	TN 177, to Germantown, N Ⓕ BP/Circle K, Shell/Circle K Ⓕ Abuelo's, Arby's, Bahama Breeze, Baskin Robbins, Buffalo Wild Wings, Burger King, Casa Mexicana, Cheesecake Factory, Chick-fil-A, Chili's, Colton's Steaks, Cook Out, Dave & Buster's, IHOP, J. Alexander's, Joe's Crabshack, Logan's Roadhouse, McDonald's/playplace, On-the-Border, Red Lobster, Red Sun Buffet, Redlands Grill, Starbucks, Subway, Taco Bell, TCBY, Tellini's Italian, Waffle House, Wendy's Ⓛ Extended Stay America, Hampton Inn, Hyatt Place Ⓞ $Tree, Barnes&Noble, Best Buy, BigLots, CarMax, Chevrolet, Chrysler/Dodge/Jeep, Dillard's, Ford, Hobby Lobby, Home Depot, Honda, Ⓗ, Hyundai, JC Penney, Macy's, Michael's, Nissan, Office Depot, Old Navy, Petsmart, Target, TJ Maxx, Walgreens, S Ⓕ BP/Circle K, Shell/Circle K Ⓕ Abbay's Rest., Arby's, Backyard Burger, Burger King, Cheddar's, ChuckeCheese, Corky's BBQ, Genghis Grill, Honeybaked Ham, Howard's Donuts, Jason's Deli, Jim'n Nick's BBQ, Jimmy John's, La Hacienda, Lenny's Subs, Little Caesar's, Margarita's Mexican, McDonald's, Newk's Cafe, Osaka, Pei Wei Chinese, Pyros Pizza, Shogun Japanese, Subway, Waffle House, Wendy's Ⓛ Comfort Suites, Country Inn & Suites, Hilton Garden, Microtel, Quality Suites Ⓞ Aldi Foods, AT&T, AutoZone, Costco/gas, Dick's, GNC, Gordman's, Kohl's, Kroger/gas, Marshall's, Rite Aid, Ross, Steinmart, Toyota, Tuesday Morning, URGENT CARE, Verizon, vet

M E M P H I S

15b a	Appling Rd, N Ⓕ BP/Circle K/dsl, Shell/dsl Ⓞ Ⓗ, S Ⓕ Marathon/dsl Ⓕ Subway Ⓞ Family $
14	Whitten Rd, N Ⓕ Mapco, Shell/Burger King, Valero/dsl, Walmart/dsl Ⓕ Hardee's, McDonald's, Sidecar Café, Taco Bell Ⓞ Firestone/auto, Harley-Davidson, Walmart, S Ⓕ BP/Circle K, Shell/Backyard Burger/dsl Ⓕ Dunkin', Subway, Supreme Hot Wings Ⓛ Candlewood Suites Ⓞ Family$, Walgreens
12	Sycamore View Rd, N Ⓕ Citgo/dsl, Murphy Express/dsl, Shell/dsl Ⓕ Capt D's, Church's, Cracker Barrel, IHOP, Krystal, McDonald's, Ruby Tuesday, Shoney's, Sonic, Starbucks, Taco Bell, Waffle House Ⓛ Baymont Inn, Best Value Inn, Comfort Inn, Extended Stay America, GardenTree Hotel, Motel 6, Red Roof Inn Ⓞ $General, AutoZone, Family$, Walgreens, S Ⓕ BP/Circle K/dsl, Exxon, Mapco Ⓕ Beijing Chinese, Burger King, Dos Amigos, Pizza Hut, Popeye's, Subway, Tops BBQ, Wendy's Ⓛ Budgetel, Days Inn, Econolodge, Fairfield Inn, Knights Inn, La Quinta, Memphis Inn, Quality Inn, Rodeway Inn Ⓞ Bass Pro Shops
10.5mm	Wolf River
10b a	(from wb) I-240 W around Memphis, I-40 E to Nashville
12c	(from eb) I-240 W, to Jackson, I-40 E to Nashville
12b	Sam Cooper Blvd (from eb)
12a	US 64/70/79, Summer Ave, N Ⓕ Mapco/dsl, Marathon/dsl Ⓕ Asian Palace, Waffle House Ⓛ Welcome Inn Ⓞ U-Haul, S Ⓕ Exxon Ⓕ McDonald's, Subway Ⓞ $Tree, Firestone/auto, Fred"
10	TN 204, Covington Pike, N Ⓕ BP/Circle K Ⓕ McDonald's, Wendy's Ⓞ Audi/VW, Buick/GMC, Chevrolet, Chrysler/Dodge/Jeep/Fiat, Honda, Hyundai, Kia, Mazda, Nissan, Sam's Club, Subaru, SuperLo Food
8b a	TN 14, Jackson Ave, N Ⓕ Citgo/dsl Ⓛ Motel 6, Sleep Inn Ⓞ Raleigh Tire, S Ⓕ Citgo/dsl, Valero Ⓞ AutoZone, Family$, O'Reilly Parts, repair
6	Warford Rd
5	Hollywood St, N Ⓕ Marathon, Valero/dsl Ⓕ Burger King, Popeye's Ⓞ Family$, S Ⓞ Memphis Zoo
3	Watkins St, N Ⓕ Highway/dsl, Jubilee/dsl, Marathon Ⓞ Family$, U-Haul
2a	rd 300, to US 51 N, Millington, N Ⓞ Meeman-Shelby SP
2	Smith Ave, Chelsea Ave, S Ⓕ Valero
1e	I-240 E
1d c b	US 51, Danny Thomas Blvd, N Ⓞ Ronald McDonald House, St Jude Research Ctr
1a	2nd St (from wb), downtown, S Ⓛ Crowne Plaza, Holiday Inn, Sheraton Ⓞ Conv Ctr
1	Riverside Dr, Front St (from eb), Memphis, S Ⓛ Comfort Inn, Courtyard, Sleep Inn Ⓞ Conv Ctr, Riverfront, Visitors Ctr
0mm	Tennessee/Arkansas state line, Mississippi River

↑N INTERSTATE 55

Exit #	Services
13mm	Tennessee/Arkansas state line, Mississippi River
12c	Delaware St, Memphis, W Ⓛ Super 8
12b	Riverside Dr, E TN Welcome Ctr, downtown Memphis
12a	E Crump Blvd (from nb), E Ⓕ Exxon Ⓕ Capt D's, KFC, LJ Silver, Taco Bell Ⓞ Family$
11	McLemore Ave, Presidents Island industrial area
10	S Parkway, 1/2 mi E Ⓕ Marathon/dsl
9	Mallory Ave industrial area
8	Horn Lake Rd (from sb)
7	US 61, 3rd St, E Ⓕ Exxon, Shell Ⓕ Church's, Interstate BBQ, McDonald's Ⓞ $Tree, AutoZone, Family$, Kroger, NAPA, Roses, Save-A-Lot Foods, Walgreens, W Ⓕ MapCo, Marathon/Chester's/dsl Ⓕ KFC, McDonald's, Subway Ⓛ Rest Inn Ⓞ Fuller SP, Indian Museum

MEMPHIS

INTERSTATE 55 Cont'd

Exit #	Services
6b a	I-240
5b	US 51 S, Elvis Presley Blvd, to Graceland, 0-2 mi W on US 51 🅕 Citgo/dsl, Dodge's/dsl, Exxon, Marathon, Shell/dsl 🅕 Baskin-Robbins, BJ's Wings, Burger King, Checker's, Exline Pizza, KFC, Krispy Kreme, Little Caesar's, McDonald's, Piccadilly's, Subway, Taco Bell 🅛 American Inn, Days Inn, Guesthouse at Graceland, Heartbreak Hotel/RV Park, Memory Lane Inn 🅞 $General, $Tree, Advance Parts, Aldi Foods, CVS, D&N RV Ctr, Family$, Ⓗ, Memphis Visitors Ctr, Presley RV Park, to Graceland, Walgreens
5a	Brooks Rd, E 🅖🅕 BP, Exxon, Mapco/dsl 🅕 Burger King, Papa John's, Popeye's 🅛 Airport Inn, Best Value Inn, Kings Hotel, Motel 6 🅞 Freightliner, Peterbilt
2b a	TN 175, Shelby Dr, Whitehaven, E 🅕 Citgo/Subway/dsl, Exxon, Phillips 66/dsl, Qmart/dsl 🅛 Colonial Inn, W 🅕 Exxon/dsl, Shell/dsl, Valero/dsl 🅕 Burger King, Dixie Queen Burgers, IHOP, McDonald's, Popeye's 🅞 $General, Family$, Kroger/gas, Save-a-Lot Foods, Toyota, U-Haul, Walgreens
0mm	Tennessee/Mississippi state line

INTERSTATE 65

Exit #	Services
121.5mm	Tennessee/Kentucky state line
121mm	Welcome Ctr sb, full 🅔 facilities, 🅕, 🅐, litter barrels, vending, petwalk
120	Highland Rd
119mm	weigh/insp sta both lanes
117	TN 52, Portland, E 🅖🅕 Exxon/Godfather's/Quiznos/dsl, Shell/dsl/fireworks 🅛 Comfort Suites 🅞 Bledsoe Cr SP (20mi), Ⓗ, W 🅕 Shell/dsl 🅛 Budget Host 🅞 fireworks
116mm	Red River
113mm	Red River
112	TN 25, Cross Plains, E 🅕 Shell/dsl/fireworks 🅞 $General, antiques, Bledsoe Cr SP (20mi), W 🅕 Mapco/Subway/dsl
108	TN 76, White House, E 🅕 Murphy USA/dsl, Nervous Charlie's/dsl, Shell, Speedway/dsl 🅕 A&W/KFC, Arby's, Bojangles, China Spring, Cracker Barrel, DQ, Dunkin', Hardee's, Little Caesar's, Los Agaves, McDonald's, Mr Wok, Papa Murphy's, Sonic, Subway, Taco Bell, Waffle House, Wendy's, Zaxby's 🅛 AT&T, Hampton Inn, Holiday Inn Express, Motel 6, Quality Inn 🅞 Ace Hardware, city park/playground, Kroger/gas, O'Reilly Parts, Rite Aid, USPO, Walgreens, Walmart/Subway, W 🅕 Loves/IHOP/dsl/scales/24hr, Shell/dsl 🅛 Days Inn
104	rd 257, Bethel Rd, W 🅕 Shell/dsl 🅞 Owl's Roost Camping
98	US 31 W, Millersville, E 🅕 Shell/dsl 🅕 Subway, Waffle House 🅞 $General, auto repair, Grand Ol' RV Resort, W 🅕 Marathon 🅛 Economy Inn 🅞 fireworks
97	rd 174, Long Hollow Pike, E 🅖🅕 BP/dsl, Exxon, Mapco 🅕 Arby's, Capt D's, Cracker Barrel, Domino's, Happy Asian, Kabuto Japanese, KFC, McDonald's, Papa Murphy's, Quiznos, Shoney's, Subway, Taco Bell, Waffle House, Wendy's 🅛 Baymont Inn, Courtyard, Days Inn, Hampton Inn, Quality Inn, Red Roof Inn, Somotel, TownePlace Suites 🅞 Kroger/dsl, USPO, Walgreens, W 🅕 Shell/dsl 🅕 Buck's BBQ, DQ, Hardee's, Krystal, Poncho Villa Grill, Sonic 🅛 La Quinta, Motel 6 🅞 Rite Aid, Walgreens
96	Rivergate Pky, E 🅕 Phillips 66/dsl, Shell/dsl 🅕 Checkers, Chicago Gyros, El Chico, Fuji Steaks, HoneyBaked Ham, Hooters, Las Palmas Mexican, McDonald's, O'Charley's, Pizza Hut, Subway, Wendy's 🅛 Best Value Inn, Comfort Suites, Country Inn Suites, Magnuson Hotel, Rodeway Inn 🅞 Dillard's, Ⓗ,

NASHVILLE

Exit #	Services
96	Continued JC Penney, Macy's, mall, W 🅕 Marathon, Volunteer E on Gallatin 🅕 Arby's, Bar-B-Cutie, Burger King, Chick-fil-A, Chili's, ChuckeCheese, CiCi's, Cookout, Domino's, Fazoli's, IHOP, Jersey Mike's, Jets Pizza, Jimmy John's, Krispy Kreme, Las Fiestas, Logan's Roadhouse, Longhorn Steaks, Olive Garden, Outback Steaks, Panda Express, Panera Bread, Pollo Tropical, Popeye's, Rafferty's, Red Lobster, Ryan's, Sonic, Starbucks, Steak'n Shake, Taco Bell, TGI Friday's, Zaxby's 🅞 $General, $Tree, $Tree, AT&T, Best Buy, Big Lots, Books-A-Million, Buick/GMC, CarMax, Chevrolet, Chrysler/Dodge/Jeep, CVS Drug, Dick's, Discount Tire, Firestone/auto, Goodyear/auto, Harley-Davidson, Hobby Lobby, Home Depot, Honda, Jo-Ann's Etc, Kia, Lowe's, Nissan, O'Reilly Parts, Office Depot, Old Navy, PepBoys, Petsmart, Target, TJ Maxx, Toyota, URGENT CARE, Verizon, VW, Walgreens, Walmart/Subway/gas
95	TN 386, Vietnam Veterans Blvd (from nb)
92	rd 45, Old Hickory Blvd, E 🅞 to Old Hickory Dam, W 🅞 Ⓗ
90b	TN 155 E, Briley Pkwy, E 🅞 to Opryland
90a	US 31W, US 41, Dickerson Pike, E 🅖🅕 Citgo/dsl, Delta/dsl, Exxon/dsl 🅕 Arby's, Capt D's, Chicago Gyros, China King, Church's, Domino's, Jay's Rest., KFC, Little Caesar's, McDonald's, Pizza Hut, Subway, Taco Bell, Waffle House, Wendy's 🅛 Days Inn, EconoLodge, Sleep Inn, Super 8 🅞 $General, Advance Parts, AutoZone, Family$, O'Reilly Parts, Walgreens, W 🅕 Murphy USA/dsl 🅞 $Tree, Lowe's, Walmart
88b a	I-24, W to Clarksville, E to Nashville
87b a	US 431, Trinity Lane, E 🅖🅕 BP, Loves/Subway/dsl/scales/24hr 🅕 Church's/White Castle, Krystal, Sonic 🅛 Cumberland Inn, Delux Inn 🅞 Piggly Wiggly, W 🅕 BP, Exxon, Shell/dsl, Victory/dsl 🅕 Fat Mo's, Jack-in-the-Box, Jack's BBQ, McDonald's, Subway, Taco Bell, Waffle House 🅛 Best Value Inn, Days Inn, EconoLodge, Halmark Inn, Howard Johnson, King's Inn, Magnuson Hotel, Ravin Hotel, Red Roof Inn, Regency Inn, Rodeway Inn 🅞 $General, Family$
86	I-24 E, to I-40 E, to Memphis
86mm	Cumberland River
85	US 41A, 8th Ave, E 🅖🅕 AutoZone 🅞 Kroger/gas, O'Reilly Parts, to st capitol, W 🅕 Exxon 🅕 Arby's, Jersey Mike's, McDonald's, Pizza Hut, Starbucks, Subway, Taco Bell, Wendy's, Wise Burger 🅛 Fairfield Inn, Millennium Hotel, SpringHill Suites 🅞 Cadillac, Honda, Lexus
84b a	I-40, E to Knoxville, W to Memphis
209[I-40]	US 70, Charlotte Ave, Church St, E 🅖🅕 Exxon 🅕 McDonald's 🅛 Sheraton 🅞 Firestone, W 🅕 Exxon, Shell/dsl 🅕 Burger King, Jack Cawthon's BBQ, Krystal, Sonic, Subway, White Castle 🅛 Comfort Inn, Hilton Garden 🅞 Hyundai, URGENT CARE, Walgreens
82b a	I-40, W to Memphis, E to Nashville

■ = gas ⑪ = food ⌂ = lodging ⊡ = other Ⓡs = rest stop   Copyright 2022 - The Next EXIT ®

TN

INTERSTATE 65 Cont'd

Exit #	Services
81	Wedgewood Ave, **W** ■ BP, Exxon, Shell/dsl ⑪ Burger King, Subway ⊡ $General, U-Haul
80	I-440, to Memphis, Knoxville
79	Armory Dr, **E on Powell** ■ Shell ⑪ Applebee's, Firehouse Subs, Jersey Mike's, Logan's Roadhouse, Panda Express, Panera Bread, Pizza Hut, Rafferty's, Subway, Taco Bell, Wendy's ⊡ BMW, CarMax, Home Depot, Michael's, Petsmart, Ross, Staples, TJ Maxx, Walmart
78b a	rd 255, Harding Place, **E** ■ Mapco, Pure, Shell ⑪ Beijing Chinese, Cracker Barrel, Sub House, Waffle House ⌂ La Quinta, Red Roof Inn ⊡ CVS Drug, URGENT CARE
74	TN 254, Old Hickory Blvd, to Brentwood, **E** ⑪ Coldstone, Fulin's Asian, Longhorn Steaks, Panera Bread, Qdoba Mexican, Waffle House ⌂ Best Western, Holiday Inn Express, Hyatt Place, Sheraton ⊡ GNC, Target, **W** ■ BP, Gulf, Shell/dsl, Twice Daily/dsl ⑪ Backyard Burger, Blaze Pizza, BurgerFi, Chick-fil-A, Chili's, Chipotle Mexican, Corky's BBQ, Dunkin' Donuts, FirstWatch, Five Guys, Jimmy John's, McAlister's Deli, McDonald's, Moe's SW Grill, Newk's Eatery, O'Charley's, Papa John's, Papa Murphy's, Pei Wei, Pizza Hut, Ruby Tuesday, Starbucks, Subway, Taco Bell, Taziki 's Cafe, Wendy's, Which Wich?, Zoe's ⌂ Baymont, Courtyard, Extended Stay (2), Extended Stay America, Hampton Inn, Hilton Garden, Hilton Suites, Mainstay Suites ⊡ Cadillac, CVS Drug, Firestone/auto, Fresh Mkt Foods, Kroger, Land Rover, Office Depot, PetCo, Publix, REI, TJ Maxx, Walgreens
71	TN 253, Concord Rd, to Brentwood
69	rd 441, Moores Lane, Galleria Blvd, **E** ■ MapCo/dsl, Shell, Tesla EVC ⑪ Amerigo's Grill, Baskin-Robbins, Cheddar's, Dicky's BBQ, Dunkin', Fuji Japanese, Hungry Howie's, Mexicali Grill, Outback Steaks, Papa Murphy's, Shogun Japanese, Sonic, Sportsman's Grille, Starbucks ⌂ Hilton Garden, Holiday Inn, Holiday Inn Express, Hyatt Place ⊡ Acura/Lexus, Advance Parts, Christian Bros. Auto, CVS Drug, Home Depot/dsl, Michael's, Petsmart, Publix, vet, Walgreens, **W** ■ BP, Shell/dsl ⑪ Backyard Burger, Buca Italian, Burger King, Capt D's, Cheesecake Factory, Chili's, Cracker Barrel, Famous Dave's, HoneyBaked Ham, Honeysuckle Grill, J Alexander's Rest., Krispy Kreme, Logan's Roadhouse, Macaroni Grill, McDonald's, Peking Palace, Pizza Hut/Taco Bell, Red Lobster, Schlotzsky's, Stoney River Steaks, Subway, Twin Peaks ⌂ Sleep Inn ⊡ $Tree, Barnes&Noble, Belk, Best Buy, Costco/gas, Dillard's, Discount Tire, Firestone/auto, JC Penney, Macy's, mall, NTB, Old Navy, Ross, Sears/auto, Target, UHaul
68b a	Cool Springs Blvd, **E** ⑪ Jersey Mike's, Noodles&Co, Swankys Tacos, Tupelo Honey Cafe ⌂ Courtyard, Embassy Suites, Marriott, Residence Inn, **W** ■ Exxon, Shell ⑪ BoneFish Grill, Burger Up, Canton Buffet, Carrabba's, Chick-fil-A, Chipotle, ChuckeCheese, Chuy's Mexican, Five Guys, Genghis Grill, Greek Cafe, J Christopher's, Jack-in-the-Box, Jason's Deli, Jersey Mike's, Jim 'N Nicks BBQ, Jimmy John's, Jonathan's Grille, Las Palmas, McAlister's Deli, McDonald's, Moe's SW Grill, Newk's Eatery, Old Chicago, Panda Express, Panera Bread, Papa John's, PF Chang's, Pie Five Pizza, Pizza Hut, Pollo Tropical, Saladworks, Sperry's, Starbucks, Subway, TGIFriday's, Wendy's, Which Wich, Wild Wing Cafe, Zoe's Kitchen ⌂ ALoft, Country Inn&Suites, Hampton Inn, TownePlace Suites ⊡ Acura, AT&T, Dick's, GNC, Harley-Davidson, Jo-Ann Fabrics, Kroger, Lowe's, Marshall's, Mazda, Office Depot, Sam's Club/gas, Staples, TJ Maxx, to Galleria Mall, Verizon, vet, Walgreens

BRENTWOOD

FRANKLIN

67	McEwen Dr, **E** ⌂ Homewood Suites, **W** ⑪ Blue Coast Burrito, Brick Top's, Buffalo Wild Wings, Culver's, Firehouse Subs, Granite City, Jamba Juice, Little Caesar's, Marco's Pizza, Pei Wei, Sonic, Subway, Tazikis Mediterranean Cafe ⌂ Drury Inn ⊡ CarMax, CVS, Kohl's, Petco, Toyota, Walmart, Whole Food Mkt
65	TN 96, to Murfreesboro, Franklin, **E** ■ Mapco, Shell/Krystal ⑪ Cracker Barrel, Sonic, Steak'n Shake ⌂ Best Value Inn, Comfort Inn, Days Inn, La Quinta, Ramada Inn ⊡ auto repair, Baymont Inn, Buick/GMC, Chevrolet, Honda, Kia, O'Reilly Parts, Subaru, URGENT CARE, Volvo, Walgreens, **W** ■ BP/dsl, Shell, Shell/dsl ⑪ Arby's, Backyard Burger, Bar-B-Cutie, Bleachers Sports Grill, El Agave Mexican, Franklin Chophouse, Franklin Chophouse, Guacamole Mexican, Hardee's, IHOP, Jersey Mike's, KFC, La Terraza Mexican, McDonald's, Nashville Pizza, O'Charley's, Pancho's Mexican, Papa John's, Shoney's, Starbucks, Subway, Taco Bell, Waffle House, Wendy's, Whitts BBQ, Zaxby's ⌂ Best Western, Best Western, Quality Inn ⊡ $General, $Tree, Aldi Foods, AT&T, BigLots, Chrysler/Dodge/Jeep, Discount Tire, Fiat, Ford/Lincoln, Hobby Lobby, Home Depot, Kroger/dsl, Publix/gas, Rite Aid, Sprouts Mkt, SteinMart, to Confederate Cem at Franklin, Tuesday Morning, Verizon, vet, Walgreens
64mm	Harpeth River
61	TN 248, Peytonsville Rd, to Spring Hill, **E** ■ TA/BP/Country Pride/dsl/scales/24hr/@, **W** ■ Mapco, Shell/dsl ⌂ Goose Creek Inn
59b a	I-840, Memphis, Knoxville
58mm	W Harpeth River
53	TN 396, Saturn Pkwy, Spring Hill, to TN Scenic Pkwy, Columbia
48mm	truck insp/weigh sta nb
46	US 412, TN 99, to Columbia, Chapel Hill, **E** ■ ♥Loves/Arbys/dsl/scales/24hr, Marathon/dsl ⌂ Sleep Inn ⊡ Harley-Davidson, Henry Horton SP, **W** ■ Citgo/Subway/dsl, Exxon, Shell, Stan's/Country Store ⑪ Burger King, Cracker Barrel, McDonald's, Waffle House ⌂ Best Value Inn, Comfort Inn, Comfort Suites, Fairfield Inn, Hampton Inn, Holiday Inn Express, Super 8 ⊡ Ⓗ
40.5mm	Duck River
37	TN 50, to Columbia, Lewisburg, **E** ⊡ Ⓗ, TN Walking Horse HQ, **W** ■ BP/dsl ⊡ to Polk Home
32	rd 373, to Lewisburg, Mooresville, **E** ■ BP/dsl
27	rd 129, to Lynnville, Cornersville, **E** ⊡ Texas T Camping
25mm	parking area sb
24mm	parking area nb
22	US 31A, to Pulaski, **E** ■ Tennesseean Trkstp/Exxon/Pop's BBQ/dsl/scales/24hr/@ ⑪ McDonald's, Subway ⌂ EconoLodge, **W** ■ ▦▦▦/dsl/scales/24hr, Shell/dsl
14	US 64, to Pulaski, **E** ■ Exxon/dsl, Shell/dsl ⑪ Sarge's Shack Rest. ⌂ Motel 6 ⊡ to Jack Daniels Distillery (30mi)
6	rd 273, Bryson, **E** ■ Shell/rest./dsl/repair ⌂ Best Value Inn ⊡ dsl repair, **W** ■ Marathon/dsl (2mi)
5mm	weigh sta nb
4mm	Elk River
3mm	Welcome Ctr nb, full ⌖ facilities, info, Ⓒ, ⏢, litter barrels, petwalk
1	US 31, rd 7, Ardmore, Ardmore, **E** ■ Chevron/dsl, Shell, Victory/Huddle House/dsl ⑪ Burger King, El Olmeca Mexican, Hardee's, KFC/Taco Bell, McDonald's, Sonic, Subway, Whitts BBQ ⊡ $General, $Tree, Daly Tire, O'Reilly Parts
0mm	Tennessee/Alabama state line

INTERSTATE 75

Exit #	Services
161.5mm	Tennessee/Kentucky state line
161mm	**Welcome Ctr sb, full ♿facilities, 🅒 vending, 🝙 litter barrels, petwalk**
160	**US 25W, Jellico, E🅟** Sunoco/dsl, VP/dsl, **W🅟** Exxon/Wendy's/dsl, Shell/Arby's/dsl 🅕 Hardee's, Heritage Pizza, McDonald's, Subway 🅛 Days Inn, Parkway Inn 🅞 fireworks, 🅗, to Indian Mtn SP
156	Rarity Mtn Rd
144	Stinking Creek Rd, **4 mi E🅟** Ride Royal Blue Camping
141	**TN 63, to Royal Blue, Huntsville, E🅟** Shell/dsl 🅕 El Rey Azteca, **W🅟** 🅿️Pilot/Subway/dsl/scales/24hr, TA/Shell/Popeye's/dsl 🅕 Hardee's 🅛 Comfort Inn 🅞 fireworks, repair/truckwash, to Big South Fork NRA
134	**US 25W, TN 63, Caryville, E🅟** Shell 🅕 Takumi Japanese, Waffle House 🅛 Hampton Inn, Holiday Inn Express, Red Roof Inn, Super 8 🅞 $General, Cumberland Gap NHP, 🅗, to Cove Lake SP, **W🅟** Exxon/dsl 🅕 Scotty's Hamburgers, Shoney's 🅛 Budget Host 🅞 USPO
129	**US 25W S, Lake City, W🅟** BP/dsl, Marathon/Sonic/dsl, 🅿️Pilot/dsl, Shell/dsl 🅕 Cracker Barrel, Domino's, Glenn's Pizza, KFC/Taco Bell, La Fiesta Mexican, McDonald's, Subway 🅛 Blue Haven Motel, Econolodge, Lamb's Inn/rest., Scottish Inn 🅞 $General, Family$, fireworks, same as 128
128	**US 441, to Lake City, E🅟** Sunoco 🅞 Mtn Lake Marina Camping (4mi), **W🅟** BP/dsl, Marathon, Weigel's/dsl 🅛 Blue Haven Motel 🅞 $General, Advance Parts, antique cars, Family$, same as 129, to Norris Dam SP
126mm	Clinch River
122	**TN 61, Bethel, Norris, E🅟** Mobil/dsl, Wiegel's/dsl 🅕 Shoney's 🅞 antiques, KOA, Museum of Appalachia, Toyota, **W🅟** BP/dsl, Exxon/Burger King/Subway/dsl, Git'n Go/dsl, Phillips 66/dsl, Shell/Baskin-Robbins 🅕 Arby's, Bojangles, Firehouse Subs, Golden Girls Rest., Gondolier Italian, Hardee's, Harrison's Grill, Krystal, LJ Silver, McDonald's, Petro's Chili, Waffle House, Wendy's, Zaxby's 🅛 Baymont Inn, Hampton Inn, Holiday Inn Express, Quality Inn, Red Roof Inn, Super 8 🅞 AT&T, Big Pine Ridge SP, Ford, Verizon, Walgreens, Walmart/McDonald's
117	**rd 170, Racoon Valley Rd, E🅟** BP/dsl/scales/24hr, **W🅛** Valley Inn 🅞 Racoon Valley RV Park, Volunteer RV Park
112	**rd 131, Emory Rd, to Powell, E🅟** 🅿️Pilot/DQ/Taco Bell/dsl, Shell/Buddy's BBQ/dsl 🅕 Arby's, Bruster's, Chick-fil-A, Cook-Out, Firehouse Subs, Five Guys, Jets Pizza, Krystal, McDonald's/playplace, Petro's Cafe, Ruby Tuesday, Starbucks, Steak'n Shake, Subway, Taco Bell, Wendy's, Zaxby's 🅛 Comfort Inn, Holiday Inn Express, La Quinta 🅞 CVS Drug, 🅗, Ingles/gas, O'Reilly Parts, Rigg's Drug, Verizon, **W🅟** Exxon/dsl, Shell/dsl, Weigel's/dsl 🅕 Aubrey's Rest., Hardee's, Shoney's, Waffle House 🅛 Super 8 🅞 Kroger/dsl
110	**Callahan Dr, E🅟** Weigel's/dsl 🅕 Archer's BBQ, Asian Cafe 🅛 Baymont Inn, Express Inn 🅞 Honda, **W🅛** Scottish Inn 🅞 Kia, Mack/Volvo
108	**Merchants Dr, E🅟** Delta/dsl, Marathon/dsl, Mobil/dsl, 🅿️Pilot/dsl 🅕 Applebee's, Cracker Barrel, El Chico, Hooters, Monterrey Mexican, O'Charley's, Pizza Hut, Puelo's Grill, Starbucks, Waffle House 🅛 Best Western, Clarion, Comfort Suites, Hampton Inn, Mainstay Suites, Quality Inn, Red Roof Inn, Sleep Inn 🅞 Ingles, Valvoline, **W🅟** Exxon/dsl, 🅿️Pilot/Domino's/dsl 🅕 Austin's Steaks, Burger King, Capt D's, Dunkin', IHOP, Mandarin House, McDonald's, Nixon's Deli, Outback Steaks, Red Lobster, Subway, Taco Bell 🅛 Best Value Inn, EconoLodge, Motel 6, Select Inn, Super 8 🅞 CVS Drug, Walgreens

K N O X V I L L E (vertical)

107	**I-640 & I-75**
3b[I-640]	**US 25W, (from nb), W🅞** Chevrolet, Ford, Nissan
1[I-640]	**rd 62, Western Ave, E🅕** Hardee's, Krystal 🅞 Advance Parts, Family$, O'Reilly Parts, **W🅟** Exxon/dsl, Marathon/dsl, RaceWay/dsl 🅕 Central Park, Firehouse Subs, KFC, Little Caesars, LJ Silver, McDonald's, Panda Chinese, Shoney's, Subway, Taco Bell, Wendy's 🅞 CVS Drug, Kroger/dsl, Walgreens
	I-75 and I-40 run together 17 mi. See I-40, exits 369 through 385.
84[368]	**I-40, W to Nashville, E to Knoxville**
81	**US 321, TN 95, to Lenoir City, E🅟** Exxon/Subway/dsl, Mobil, Murphy USA/dsl, Shell/Buddy's BBQ/TCBY/dsl, Shell/dsl, Weigel's/dsl 🅕 Arby's, Aubrey's Rest., Bella Hibachi, Bojangles, Burger King, Capt D's, Chick-fil-A, Chili's, China Buffet, Cinco Amigos Mexican, Cracker Barrel, Domino's, Dunkin', Firehouse Subs, Gondolier Italian, Hardee's, 🅗, KFC, McDonald's, Panda Express, Papa John's, Papa Murphy's, Pizza Hut, Shoney's, Starbucks, Subway, Taco Bell, Waffle House, Wendy's, Zaxby's 🅛 Fairfield Inn, Hampton Inn, Holiday Inn Express, King's Inn/rest. 🅞 $General Mkt, $Tree, Advance Parts, AT&T, AutoZone, Big Lots, CVS Drug, Food City/gas, Ford, Ft Loudon Dam, GNC, Great Smokies NP, Home Depot, Ingles, Lazy Acers RV Park (7mi), O'Reilly Parts, Verizon, Walgreens, Walmart/Subway, **W🅟** Citgo/dsl 🅕 Krystal, Ruby Tuesday 🅛 Comfort Inn, EconoLodge 🅞 Crosseyed Cricket Camping (6mi), Matlock Tires/Repair
76	**rd 324, Sugar Limb Rd, W🅞** to TN Valley Winery
74mm	Tennessee River
72	**TN 72, to Loudon, E🅟** Exxon/Wendy's/dsl, Shell/McDonald's, Weigel's/dsl 🅕 Bojangles, KFC, Romeo's Pizza, Taco Bell 🅛 Inn of Loudon, La Quinta 🅞 to Ft Loudon SP, **W🅟** Marathon 🅛 Best Value Inn 🅞 Express RV Park
68	**rd 323, to Philadelphia, E🅕** cheese factory/store (2mi)
62	**RD 322, Oakland Rd, to Sweetwater, E🅕** Dinner Bell Rest., **W🅞** KOA
60	**TN 68, Sweetwater, 0-2 mi E🅟** Citgo/dsl, Mobil, Sunoco, Weigel's 🅕 A&W/LJ Silver, Bradley's BBQ, Burger King, Domino's, Hardee's, Huddle House, KFC, Little Caesar's, McDonald's, Mexi Wings, Pizza Hut, Sonic, Subway, Taco Bell 🅛 Days Inn, Economy Inn, Guest Inn, Quality Inn 🅞 $General, $Tree, Ace Hardware, Advance Parts, Ford/Lincoln, 🅗, O'Reilly Parts, to Lost Sea Underground Lake, Verizon, Walgreens, **W🅟** Kangaroo/dsl, Marathon 🅛 Holiday Inn Express, Motel 6 🅞 flea mkt, to Watts Bar Dam, vet
56	**rd 309, Niota, E🅟** 🅿️Pilot/Wendy's/dsl/scales/24hr 🅞 TN Country Camping, **W🅞** repair
52	**rd 305, Mt Verd Rd, to Athens, E🅟** Marathon/dsl (2mi), Sunoco/dsl 🅕 Subway (2mi) 🅞 Overniter RV Park, **W🅟** BP 🅛 Athens Lodge

S W E E T W A T E R (vertical)

B E T H E L (vertical)

TN

⬆N INTERSTATE 75 Cont'd

Exit #	Services
49	TN 30, to Athens, E 🄿 Betty's BBQ, Exxon, Kangaroo, Mobil/dsl, Murphy USA/dsl 🍴 Applebee's, Arby's, Buddy's BBQ, Burger King, Capt D's, China Wok, Cookout, Dunkin', Firehouse Subs, Hardee's, KFC, Krystal, Little Caesar's, McDonald's, Mexi Wing, Ming Dynasty, Papa John's, Pizza Hut, Ruby Tuesday, Shoney's, Sonic, Subway, Subway, Taco Bell, Waffle House, Wendy's, Western Sizzlin, Zaxby's 🛏 Days Inn, EconoLodge, Hampton Inn, Holiday Inn Express, Motel 6, Scottish Inn, Super 8 🄾 $General, $Tree, Advance Parts, AT&T, Athens I-75 Camping, Belk, BigLots, GNC, 🄷, Russell Stover, Staples, to TN Wesleyan Coll, URGENT CARE, Verizon, Walgreens, Walmart/Subway, W 🄿 Mobil/dsl, Speedway/Speedy's Cafe/dsl 🍴 Cracker Barrel 🛏 Best Value Inn, Comfort Inn, Fairfield Inn
45mm	🆁🆂 both lanes, full 🚻 facilities, 🗑 litter barrels, 🅲 petwalk, vending
42	rd 39, Riceville Rd, E 🄿 Citgo/dsl 🛏 Relax Inn, Rice Inn (2mi) 🄾 $General (2mi)
36	rd 163, to Calhoun, E 🍴 Hardee's (3mi) 🄾 Hiwassee/Ocoee River SP
35mm	Hiwassee River
33	rd 308, to Charleston, E 🄿 Marathon/dsl 🍴 Hardee's, W 🄿 Loves/McDonald's/Subway/dsl/scales/24hr
27	Paul Huff Pkwy, 1 mi E 🄿 Murphy USA, Shell/dsl 🍴 Applebee's, Buffalo Wild Wings, Capt D's, Chili's, CiCi's, DQ, Fazoli's, Firehouse Subs, Five Guys, Golden Corral, IHOP, Little Caesar's, Longhorn Steaks, Marco's Pizza, McDonald's, O'Charley's, Olive Garden, Outback Steaks, Panera Bread, Papa Murphy's, Pita Pit, Pizza Hut, Royal Buffet, Six Happiness, Sonic, Starbucks, Steak'n Shake, Subway, Taco Bell 🛏 Baymont Inn, Holiday Inn Express 🄾 $Tree, Aldi Foods, auto repair/tires, AutoZone, Belk, Buick/Cadillac/GMC, CVS Drug, Discount Tire, Food Lion, Hobby Lobby, Home Depot, JC Penney, Lowe's, NTB, PetCo, Petsmart, Publix, Staples, TJ Maxx, Verizon, Walgreens, Walmart, W 🄿 EVC, Exxon/dsl, Orbit/dsl, Shell/Subway 🍴 Burger King, Denny's, Fulin's Asian, Hardee's, Honeybaked Ham, Shane's Ribshack, Waffle House, Wendy's 🛏 Clarion, Classic Suites, Hampton Inn, Quality Inn, Red Roof Inn, Royal Inn, Super 8 🄾 AT&T, Books-A-Million, Kohl's, Ross, Target
25	TN 60, Cleveland, E 🄿 Chevron/dsl, RaceWay/dsl, Shell/dsl, Sunoco/dsl 🍴 Bojangles, Burger King, Checkers, Cracker Barrel, Dunkin', Hardee's, Las Margaritas, McDonald's, Old Fort Rest., Sonic, Subway, Waffle House, Zaxby's 🛏 Days Inn, Douglas Inn, EconoLodge, Economy Inn, Fairfield Inn, Howard Johnson, Knights Inn, Motel 6 🄾 $General, Ace Hardware, BigLots, Cherokee Drug, 🄷, NAPA, to Lee Coll, Tuesday Morning, vet, W 🄿 BP 🛏 Cleveland Hotel, Comfort Inn, La Quinta, Mtn View Inn
23mm	truck/weigh sta nb
20	US 64 byp, to Cleveland, 1-4 mi E 🄿 FuelMart 🄾 Ford, Honda, Kia, W 🄿 Exxon/dsl, Loves/McDonald's/Subway/dsl/scales/24hr 🄾 fireworks, KOA (1mi), Toyota
16mm	scenic view sb
13mm	truck/weigh sta, litter barrels sb
11	US 11 N, US 64 E, Ooltewah, E 🄿 BP/Circle K, EVC, Mapco, Murphy USA/dsl, RaceWay/dsl 🍴 Arby's, Bojangles, Burger King, Chick-fil-A, China Rose, Cracker Barrel, El Cortes Mexican, Hardee's, Jersey Mike's, Little Caesar's, McDonald's, Panda Express, Pizza Hut, Puleo's Grille, Sonic, Starbucks, Subway, Taco Bell, Wendy's, Zaxby's 🛏 Hampton Inn, Holiday Inn Express, SpringHill Suites 🄾 $General, Ace Hardware, Aldi Foods, AutoZone,

11	Continued
	Food City, GNC, O'Reilly Parts, Verizon, vet, Walgreens, Walmart/Subway, W 🄿 BP/Circle K/Dunkin', Exxon/dsl 🍴 Beef'o Brady's, Krystal, Waffle House 🛏 Super 8 🄾 Publix, Tire Discounters, to Harrison Bay SP
9	TN 317, Apison Pk, Volkswagen Dr, E 🄿 Shell
7b a	US 11, US 64, Lee Hwy, E 🄿 Exxon/dsl, W 🄿 BP, EVC, EVC, Speedway/Speedy's Cafe/dsl 🍴 City Cafe, Waffle House 🛏 Airport Inn, Best Inn, Best Value Inn, Best Western, EconoLodge, Motel 6, Woodspring Suites 🄾 Denton's Repair, Harley-Davidson, Jaguar/Land Rover/Porsche/Infiniti
5	Shallowford Rd, same as 4a, E 🍴 Acropolis Grill, Arby's, Chuy's, CiCi's, Forbidden City Chinese, Imperial Garden, J. Alexanders, James Co Grill, Jersey Mike's, Krystal, McAlister's Deli, McDonald's, Mellow Mushroom Pizza, Miller's Alehouse, Newk's Eatery, Outback Steaks, Panda Express, Pier 88, Ruth's Chris Steaks, Smokey Bones BBQ, Starbucks, Steak'n Shake, Taco Bell, Zaxby's 🛏 Courtyard, Embassy Suites, Studio 6, Wingate Inn 🄾 Best Buy, Firestone/auto, Fresh Mkt, Hobby Lobby, Home Depot, Lowe's, Office Depot, Old Navy, Petco, Petsmart, Publix, REI, SteinMart, Target, Walgreens, Walmart/Subway, World Mkt, W 🄿 BP, Citgo/dsl, Exxon/dsl, Shell, Speedway/Speedy's Cafe/dsl 🍴 Cracker Barrel, Fazoli's, Firebox Grill, Fuji Steaks, O'Charley's, Papa John's, Shoney's, Sonic, Subway, TX Roadhouse, Waffle House, Wendy's 🛏 Athena Inn, Baymont Inn, Comfort Inn, Days Inn, Fairfield Inn, Hilton Garden, Holiday Inn, Home 2 Suites, Homewood Suites, La Quinta, La Quinta, MainStay Suites, Microtel, Quality Inn, Red Roof Inn, Residence Inn, Sleep Inn, Staybridge Suites, Super 8, SureStay+, TownePlace Suites, Travelodge, Tru Hilton 🄾 CarMax, CVS Drug, Family$, Food City, Goodyear/auto, 🄷, SaveALot, U of TN/Chatt
4a	(from nb) Hamilton Place Blvd, same as 5, E 🄿 Shell 🍴 Abuelo's, Acropolis, Big River Grille, BoneFish Grill, Capt D's, Carrabba's, Cheddar's, Cheesecake Factory, Chick-fil-A, Chili's, Chop House, DQ, El Meson Mexican, Firebirds, Firehouse Subs, Five Guys, Golden Corral, Hana Steak, Honeybaked Ham, Jason's Deli, Jim'n Nick's BBQ, McDonald's, Moe's SW Grill, Olive Garden, Outback Steaks, Panera Bread, PF Chang's, Red Lobster, Red Robin, Salsarita's Mexican, Shogun Japanese, Starbucks, Sticky Fingers BBQ, Taziki's Cafe 🛏 Hampton Inn, InTown Suites 🄾 $Tree, AT&T, Barnes&Noble, Belk, Big Lots, Dick's, Dillard's, Earthfare, Firestone/auto, JC Penney, Jo-Ann, Kohl's, Marshall's, Michael's, Pepboys, Ross, Staples, Target, TJ Maxx, Verizon, World Mkt
4	TN 153, Chickamauga Dam Rd, 🄾
3b a	TN 320, Brainerd Rd, E 🄿 BP/Circle K 🍴 Baskin-Robbins, Subway, W 🄾 BMW
2	I-24 W to I-59, to Chattanooga, Lookout Mtn
1.5mm	Welcome Ctr nb, full 🚻 facilities, 🅲 vending, 🗑 litter barrels, petwalk
1b a	US 41, Ringgold Rd, to Chattanooga, E 🄿 BP/Circle K, Shell/dsl 🍴 Buddy's BBQ, Chick-fil-A, Starbucks, Wendy's 🛏 Best Western+, EconoLodge, Hampton Inn, La Quinta, Motel 6, Quality Inn 🄾 Bass Pro Shops, Camping World RV Ctr/park, Family$, W 🄿 Citgo/dsl, Mapco/dsl, Valero/dsl 🍴 Arby's, Baskin-Robbins, Burger King, Cracker Barrel, Dunkin', Firehouse Subs, Hardee's, Krystal, Marco's Pizza, McDonald's, Pizza Hut, Popeye's, PortoFino Italian, Sonic, Subway, Taco Bell, Teriyaki House, Waffle House, Wally's Rest. 🛏 Budgetel, Fairfield Inn, Four A's Inn, Holiday Inn Express, Super 8, Waverly Motel 🄾 $General, Advance Parts, AutoZone, Family$, Food Lion, O'Reilly Parts, U-Haul, Walgreens
0mm	Tennessee/Georgia state line

ATHENS

CLEVELAND

CHATTANOOGA

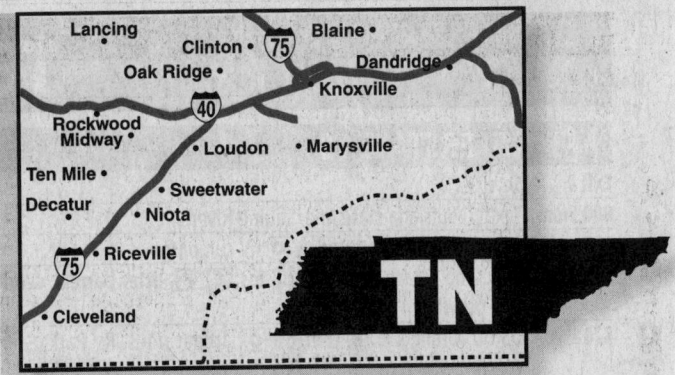

⬆N INTERSTATE 81

Exit #	Services
75mm	Tennessee/Virginia state line, **Welcome Ctr sb, full** ♿ **facilities, info,** 〔C〕, **vending,** 🧺 **litter barrels, petwalk**
74b a	US 11W, to Bristol, Kingsport, **E** 🏨 Fairfield Inn, Hampton Inn 〔O〕〔H〕, **W** 〔⛽〕 Tesla EVC, Valero/dsl 🍴 Aubrey's Rest., Bojangle's, Brusco's Pizza, Chick-fil-A, Drake's Rest., Jersey Mike's, La Carreta, McDonald's, Moe's SW, Outback Steaks, Pal's Drive-Thru, Panda Express, Starbucks, Steak'n Shake, Zaxby's 〔O〕 Bass Pro Shops, Belk, CarMax, Dick's, GNC, Marshall's, Michael's, Old Navy, Verizon
69	TN 394, to Blountville, **E** 〔⛽〕 BP/Subway/dsl 🍴 Arby's, Domino's 〔O〕 Advance Parts, Bristol Int Speedway, Lakeview RV Park (8mi), Shadrack Camping
66	rd 126, to Kingsport, Blountville, **W** 〔⛽〕 Shell/dsl 🍴 McDonald's
63	rd 357, **E** 〔⛽〕 BP/Krystal/dsl, Shell/Subway/dsl 🍴 Cracker Barrel, Wendy's 🏨 La Quinta, Sleep Inn 〔O〕 Hamricks, Tri-Cities Airport, **W** 〔⛽〕 Citgo/dsl 🏨 Econolodge 〔O〕 dsl repair, KOA, Rocky Top Camping
60mm	Holston River
59	rd 36, to Johnson City, Kingsport, **E** 〔⛽〕 Marathon/dsl 🏨 Super 8, **W** 〔⛽〕 Exxon/dsl, Marathon, Shell/dsl, Sunoco 🍴 Arby's, Fisherman's Dock Rest., Hardee's, HotDog Hut, Jersey Mike's Subs, La Carreta Mexican, Little Caesar's, Little Caesar's, McDonald's, Moto Japanese, Pal's Drive-Thru, Perkins, Pizza Hut, Plum Tree Rest., Raffaele's Pizza, Sonic, Subway, Taco Bell, The Shack BBQ, Zachary's Steaks 🏨 Comfort Inn, Motel 6 〔O〕 $General, Advance Parts, CVS Drug, Ingles/deli, Murphy's Automotive, O'Reilly Parts, to Warrior's Path SP, URGENT CARE, USPO, Verizon, Walgreens
57b a	I-26
56	Tri-Cities Crossing
50	TN 93, Fall Branch, **W** 〔O〕 auto auction, st patrol
44	Jearoldstown Rd, **E** 〔⛽〕 Marathon
41mm	〔Rs〕 sb, full ♿ facilities, 〔C〕, vending, 🧺 litter barrels, petwalk
38mm	〔Rs〕 nb, full ♿ facilities, 〔C〕, vending, 🧺 litter barrels, petwalk
36	rd 172, to Baileyton, **E** 〔⛽〕 Pilot/Subway/dsl/scales/24hr, **W** 〔⛽〕 Marathon/dsl, Shell/Subway/dsl/24hr, TA/Country Pride/dsl/scales/24hr/@ 🍴 Pizza+ 🏨 36 Motel 〔O〕 $General, Around Pond RV Park, Family$, KOA (2mi)
30	TN 70, to Greeneville, **E** 〔⛽〕 Marathon/DQ/Stuckey's/dsl
23	US 11E, to Greeneville, **E** 〔⛽〕 Marathon/Wendy's, Mobil/Subway/dsl 〔O〕 Crockett SP, to Andrew Johnson HS, Tri-Am RV Ctr, **W** 〔⛽〕 Exxon/DQ/dsl, Phillips 66/dsl/rest./scales 🍴 McDonald's, Pizza+, Taco Bell, Tony's Repair 🏨 Quality Inn, Super 8
21mm	weigh sta sb
15	rd 340, Fish Hatchery Rd
12	TN 160, to Morristown, **E** 〔⛽〕 Phillips 66/dsl, **W** 〔⛽〕 Gulf/dsl 🏨 Days Inn (6mi), Hampton Inn (12mi), Holiday Inn Express (5mi), Super 8 (5mi) 〔O〕 to Crockett Tavern HS
8	US 25E, to Morristown, **E** 🍴 Sonic (2mi), **W** 〔⛽〕 Weigel's/dsl 🍴 Bojangle's, Cracker Barrel, Fastop/Subway/dsl, Hardee's, McDonald's 🏨 Best Western+, Hampton Inn, Parkway Inn, Super 8 〔O〕 to Cumberland Gap NHP
4	rd 341, White Pine, **E** 〔⛽〕 Pilot/McDonald's/dsl/scales/24hr 🍴 Subway, **W** 〔⛽〕 Pilot/Dunkin'/Wendy's/dsl/scales/24hr 🍴 Taco Bell 🏨 Econolodge 〔O〕 to Panther Cr SP
2.5mm	〔Rs〕 sb, full ♿ facilities, 〔C〕, 🧺 litter barrels, vending, petwalk
1b a	I-40, E to Asheville, W to Knoxville. **I-81 begins/ends on I-40, exit 421.**

⬆N INTERSTATE 640 (Knoxville)

Exit #	Services
9mm	**I-640 begins/ends on I-40, exit 393.**
8	Millertown Pike, Mall Rd N, **N** 〔⛽〕 Exxon/DQ, Shell 🍴 Applebee's, Burger King, China Wok, Honeybaked Ham, KFC, Krystal, Mandarin Palace, McDonald's, Pizza Hut, Taco Bell, TX Roadhouse, Wendy's 〔O〕 $Tree, AT&T, Belk, Food City/dsl, Jo-Ann, Kohl's, Marshall's, Old Navy, Ross, Sam's Club/dsl, Target, Walmart, **S** 〔⛽〕 Shell/dsl 🍴 Amigo's, Cracker Barrel, Little Caesar's, O'Charley's, Sonic 〔O〕 Home Depot, Lowe's Whse, PepBoys
6	US 441, to Broadway, **N** 〔⛽〕 Citgo/dsl, Pilot/dsl 🍴 Arby's, Cancun Mexican, Chick-fil-A, Chop House, CiCi's, Firehouse Subs, Hardee's, Krispy Kreme, Lenny's Subs, LJ Silver, McDonald's, Panera Bread, Papa John's, Papa Murphy's, Penn Sta Subs, Ruby Tuesday, Sonic, Subway, Taco Bell 〔O〕 $General, Advance Parts, AutoZone, BigLots, CVS Drug, Firestone, Food City/gas, Kroger, O'Reilly Parts, repair/tires, Verizon, Walgreens, **S** 🍴 Bojangle's, Buddy's BBQ, Little Caesar's, Shoney's 〔O〕 $General, $Tree, Food City, Office Depot
3a	I-75 N to Lexington, I-275 S to Knoxville
3b	US 25W, Clinton Hwy, **N** 〔O〕 Chevrolet, Ford, Nissan, services on frontage rds
1	TN 62, Western Ave, **N** 〔⛽〕 Exxon/dsl, Marathon/dsl, Raceway/dsl 🍴 Central Park, Firehouse Subs, KFC, Little Caesars, LJ Silver, McDonald's, Panda Chinese, Shoney's, Subway, Taco Bell, Wendy's 〔O〕 CVS Drug, Kroger/dsl, Walgreens, **S** 🍴 Hardee's, Krystal 〔O〕 Advance Parts, Family$, O'Reilly Parts
	I-640 begins/ends on I-40, exit 385.

NOTES

= gas   = food   = lodging   = other   = rest stop   Copyright 2022 - The Next EXIT

TEXAS

INTERSTATE 10

Exit #	Services
880.5mm	Texas/Louisiana state line, Sabine River
880	Sabine River Turnaround, N ◻ RV camping
879mm	**Welcome Ctr wb, full ♿ facilities, ◻, ♻, litter barrels, vending, petwalk**
878	US 90, Orange, N ⛽ Gulf/dsl ◻ airboat rides, RV Park, S ◻ Western Store
877	TX 87, 16th St, Orange, N ⛽ Exxon/dsl, Shamrock/dsl 🍴 Little Caesar's, Pizza Hut, Subway 🛏 Hampton Inn ◻ Ace Hardware, Market Basket/deli, S ⛽ Get'n Go/dsl, Kwik Stop/dsl, Shell/dsl, Valero/dsl 🍴 2 Amigo's Mexican, Casa Ole, Church's, DQ, General Wok, Jack-in-the-Box, McDonald's, Popeye's, Sonic, Taco Bell ◻ $General, CVS Drug, Family$, Goodyear/auto, HEB Foods, Kroger/dsl, Modica Tires, O'Reilly Parts, Verizon, Walgreens
876	Adams Bayou, Frontage Rd, Adams Bayou, N 🍴 Gary's Café, Señor Toro's Mexican, Taste of Orange Rest., Waffle House 🛏 Best Price Motel, Best Texan Inn, Days Inn, EconoLodge, Executive Inn, Knights Inn, Motel 6 ◻ Toyota, S ⛽ Chevron/dsl 🛏 Holiday Inn Express, same as 877
875	FM 3247, MLK Dr, N ⛽ Exxon/dsl, S ◻ Chrysler/Dodge/Jeep, 🏥
874	US 90, Womack Rd, to Orange, S ◻ 🏥
873	TX 62, TX 73, to Bridge City, N ⛽ FLYING J/Denny's/dsl/LP/scales/24hr, Fuel Tec/dsl/24hr 🛏 Studio 6 ◻ Blue Beacon, Oak Leaf RV Park, S 🍴 Subway/Wendy's/dsl/scales/24hr, Shell/Church's/dsl, Valero/dsl 🍴 McDonald's, Sonic, Waffle House, Whataburger 🛏 Best Western, Comfort Inn, La Quinta
872	N Mimosa Ln, Jackson Dr, from wb
870	FM 1136
869	FM 1442, to Bridge City, S ⛽ Exxon/dsl
867	Frontage Rd (from eb)
865	Doty Rd (from wb), Frontage Rd
864	FM 1132, FM 1135, N 🛏 Budget Inn ◻ TX Star RV Park
862	Lakeside St, Timberlane Dr, N ⛽ Conoco
861	FM 105, Vidor, N ⛽ Chevron/dsl, Citgo/dsl, Conoco/dsl, Valero/dsl 🍴 Casa Ole, Domino's, DQ, Jack-in-the-Box, Little Caesars, McDonald's/playplace, Ming's Buffet, Novrosky's Burgers, Popeye's, Waffle House ◻ AutoZone, CVS, Mktbasket Foods, Modica Bros Tires, O'Reilly Parts, Verizon, Walgreens, Walmart, S ⛽ Citgo/dsl, Exxon/dsl 🍴 Burger King, Pizza Hut, Sonic, Subway, Taco Bell, Whataburger 🛏 Best Western+, Holiday Inn Express ◻ auto repair, Family$
860	Dewitt Rd, Frontage Rd, W Vidor, S ⛽ Citgo, Exxon, Mobil/dsl 🍴 Burger King, Pizza Hut, Sonic, Subway, Taco Bell, Whataburger 🛏 Best Western, Holiday Inn Express ◻ Family$, repair
859	Bonner Turnaround (from eb), Asher Turnaround (from wb), N ◻ Boomtown RV Park, S ⛽ Chevron/Gateway/dsl/24hr
858	Rose City
856	Old Hwy 90 (from eb), Rose City
855b	Magnolia St (from wb)
855a	US 90 bus, to downtown, Port of Beaumont
854	ML King Pkwy, Beaumont, N ⛽ Chevron/dsl, Valero/dsl 🍴 Jack-in-the-Box, S ⛽ Jet/dsl, Shamrock/dsl 🍴 McDonald's
853b	11th St, N ⛽ Valero/dsl 🍴 Cafe Del Rio, Red Lobster, Waffle House 🛏 Beaumont Lodge, Days Inn, EconoLodge, Holiday Inn, Merit Inn, Sleep Inn, Studio 6 ◻ MktBasket, S ⛽ Chevron/dsl, Shamrock 🍴 Checker's, Chula Vista Mexican, Dunkin', Jack-in-the-Box, Luby's 🛏 HomeBridge Suites, Rodeway Inn ◻ 🏥

853a	US 69 N, to Lufkin
852	Harrison Ave, Calder Ave, Beaumont, N ⛽ Shell/dsl, Valero/dsl 🍴 Casa Ole Mexican, Casa Tapatia Mexican, Chili's, Franie's Italian, Olive Garden, Saltgrass Steaks, Tony's BBQ, S 🍴 Church's, McDonald's 🛏 La Quinta, Scottish Inn ◻ 🏥
851	US 90, College St, N ⛽ Chevron/dsl, Exxon/dsl, Raceway/dsl 🍴 Carrabba's, Chicken Express, Floyd's Cajun Cafe, Golden Corral, Hooters, Lupe Tortilla, Outback Steaks, Sartin's Seafood, Tokyo Japanese, Waffle House 🛏 Howard Johnson, Quality Inn, Ramada, Red Roof Inn ◻ Advance Parts, AutoZone, Harley-Davidson, Indian Motorcycles, O'Reilly Parts, URGENT CARE, Verizon, Volvo Trucks, S ⛽ Exxon/dsl, Mobil, Shell/dsl 🍴 Cane's, Chick-fil-A, China Hut, DQ, IHOP, Pizza Hut, Sonic, Taco Bell, Wendy's, Whataburger 🛏 Best Value, Courtyard, Elegante Motel, Fairfield Inn, Regency Inn, Woodspring Suites ◻ $Tree, BMW, Chrysler/Dodge/Jeep, CVS Drug, Discount Tire, Firestone/auto, HEB Foods, Honda, 🏥, Mercedes, Nissan, NTB, Office Depot, Sam's Club/gas, U-Haul, VW, Walgreens
850	wb only, same as 851
849	US 69 S, Washington Blvd, to Port Arthur, N ◻ 🍴
848	Walden Rd, N ⛽ Shell/dsl 🍴 Pappadeaux Seafood, Sonic, Subway, Taco Bell 🛏 Comfort Suites, Holiday Inn/rest, La Quinta ◻ USPO, S ⛽ Chevron/dsl, Petro/Iron Skillet/dsl/scales/24hr/@, Shell/dsl 🍴 Cheddar's, Cracker Barrel, Jack-in-the-Box, Joe's Crabshack, Twin Peaks, Waffle House 🛏 Candlewood Suites, Executive Inn, Hampton Inn, Hilton Garden, Home 2 Suites, Homewood Suites, Residence Inn, Super 8
847	Brooks Rd (from wb), (845 from eb), S ◻ Gulf Coast RV Resort, Hidden Lake RV Park
845	TX 364
843	Smith Rd, N ⛽ Love's/Arby's/Chester's/Godfather's/dsl/scales/24hr
838	FM 365, Fannett, N 🍴 Alligator Park/Rest., Shell/Bar-H BBQ/gas ◻ T&T RV Park
837.5mm	no service
833	Hamshire Rd, N ⛽ Valero/Sonic/dsl
829	FM 1663, Winnie, N ⛽ Exxon/dsl, Mobil/Burger King/dsl, Shell/dsl/24hr 🍴 McDonald's, Taco Bell, Whataburger/24hr 🛏 Days Inn ◻ RV Park, S ⛽ Chevron/Chester's/dsl, Gulf/Subway/Pizza Hut/dsl/scales/24hr, Texaco/dsl 🍴 Al-T's Seafood, Exxon/dsl, Hart's Chicken, Jack-in-the-Box, Joe's Italian, Waffle House 🛏 Best Value Inn, Comfort Inn, Hampton Inn, Holiday Inn Express, La Quinta, Motel 6, Winnie Inn/RV Park ◻ Chrysler/Jeep/Dodge, 🏥
828	TX 73, TX 124 (from eb), to Winnie, S ◻ 🏥 same as 829
827	FM 1406
822	FM 1410
821	**insp sta wb**
819	Jenkins Rd, N ⛽ Chevron/Dunkin'/dsl, S ⛽ Exxon/Stuckey's/Chester's/dsl
817	FM 1724
814	Frontage Rd, from eb, 🅡🅢 **both lanes, full ♿ facilities, ♻, litter barrels**
813	TX 61 (from wb), Hankamer, N ⛽ Shell/dsl 🛏 Palace Inn, S ⛽ Exxon/DJ's Diner/dsl 🍴 McDonald's, same as 812
812	TX 61, Hankamer
811	Turtle Bayou Turnaround, S ⛽ Gator Jct/dsl ◻ Turtle Bayou RV Park
810	FM 563, to Anahuac, Liberty, S ⛽ Chevron/Blimpie/dsl, Texaco/Jack-in-the-Box/dsl

Sidebar labels: ORANGE · VIDOR · BEAUMONT · WINNIE · TX

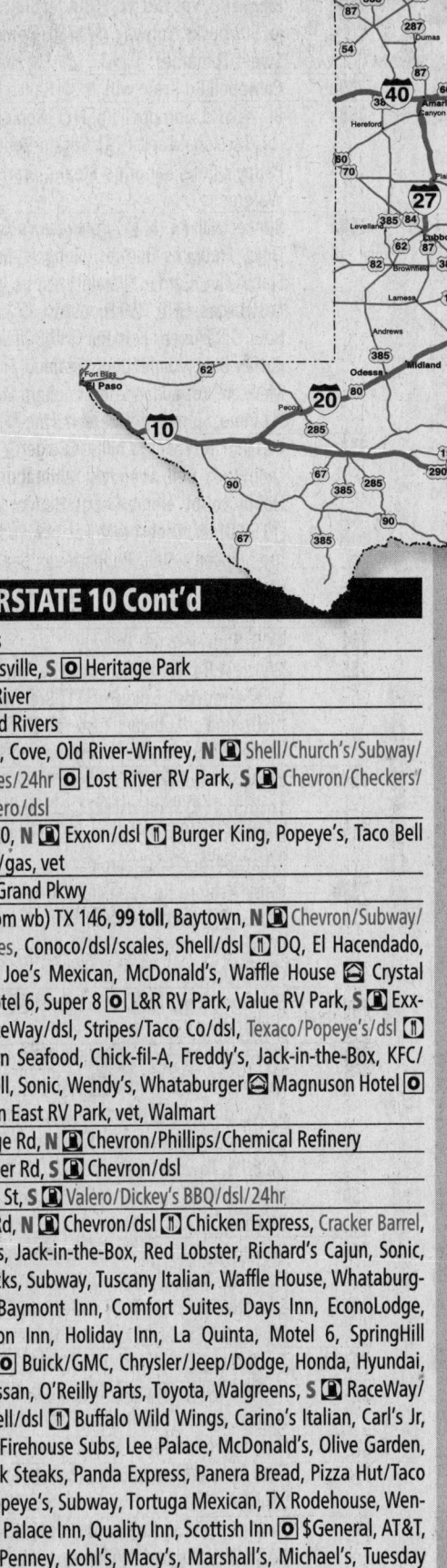

B A Y T O W N

🛣️ INTERSTATE 10 Cont'd

Exit #	Services
807	to Wallisville, **S** Ⓞ Heritage Park
805.5mm	Trinity River
804mm	Lost, Old Rivers
803	FM 565, Cove, Old River-Winfrey, **N** 🅿️ Shell/Church's/Subway/dsl/scales/24hr Ⓞ Lost River RV Park, **S** 🅿️ Chevron/Checkers/dsl, Valero/dsl
800	FM 3180, **N** 🅿️ Exxon/dsl 🍴 Burger King, Popeye's, Taco Bell Ⓞ HEB/gas, vet
799	TX 99, Grand Pkwy
797	(798 from wb) TX 146, **99 toll**, Baytown, **N** 🅿️ Chevron/Subway/dsl/scales, Conoco/dsl/scales, Shell/dsl 🍴 DQ, El Hacendado, Iguana Joe's Mexican, McDonald's, Waffle House 🏠 Crystal Inn, Motel 6, Super 8 Ⓞ L&R RV Park, Value RV Park, **S** 🅿️ Exxon, RaceWay/dsl, Stripes/Taco Co/dsl, Texaco/Popeye's/dsl 🍴 Baytown Seafood, Chick-fil-A, Freddy's, Jack-in-the-Box, KFC/Taco Bell, Sonic, Wendy's, Whataburger 🏠 Magnuson Hotel Ⓞ Houston East RV Park, vet, Walmart
796	Frontage Rd, **N** 🅿️ Chevron/Phillips/Chemical Refinery
795	Sjolander Rd, **S** 🅿️ Chevron/dsl
793	N Main St, **S** 🅿️ Valero/Dickey's BBQ/dsl/24hr
792	Garth Rd, **N** 🅿️ Chevron/dsl 🍴 Chicken Express, Cracker Barrel, Denny's, Jack-in-the-Box, Red Lobster, Richard's Cajun, Sonic, Starbucks, Subway, Tuscany Italian, Waffle House, Whataburger 🏠 Baymont Inn, Comfort Suites, Days Inn, EconoLodge, Hampton Inn, Holiday Inn, La Quinta, Motel 6, SpringHill Suites Ⓞ Buick/GMC, Chrysler/Jeep/Dodge, Honda, Hyundai, Kia, Nissan, O'Reilly Parts, Toyota, Walgreens, **S** 🅿️ RaceWay/dsl, Shell/dsl 🍴 Buffalo Wild Wings, Carino's Italian, Carl's Jr, Chili's, Firehouse Subs, Lee Palace, McDonald's, Olive Garden, Outback Steaks, Panda Express, Panera Bread, Pizza Hut/Taco Bell, Popeye's, Subway, Tortuga Mexican, TX Rodehouse, Wendy's 🏠 Palace Inn, Quality Inn, Scottish Inn Ⓞ $General, AT&T, Ⓗ, JC Penney, Kohl's, Macy's, Marshall's, Michael's, Tuesday Morning, Verizon
791	John Martin Rd, **S** 🅿️ Buc-ee's/dsl 🍴 Cheddar's, Saltgrass Steaks 🏠 Best Western+, Woodspring Suites Ⓞ Cadillac/Chevrolet, Ford
790	Ellis School Rd, **N** 🏠 Super 8
789	Thompson Rd, **N** 🅿️ ♥Loves/McDonald's/dsl/scales/24hr/@ 🏠 Super 8, **S** 🅿️ ⓕFLYING J/Denny's/dsl/scales/24hr/@, TA/Country Pride/dsl/scales/24hr/@ Ⓞ Blue Beacon, Truck Lube
788.5mm	Ⓡₛ eb, full 🚹 facilities, 🅿️, 🐾, litter barrels, petwalk
788	sp 330 (from eb), to Baytown
787	sp 330, Crosby-Lynchburg Rd, to Highlands, **N** 🅿️ Exxon/Domino's/dsl Ⓞ RV Camping (1mi), **S** 🅿️ Phillips 66/dsl 🍴 Four Corners BBQ Ⓞ to San Jacinto SP
786.5mm	San Jacinto River
786	Monmouth Dr
785	Magnolia Ave, to Channelview, **N** 🅿️ Shell/dsl/scales, **S** 🅿️ Exxon/dsl, truckwash
784	Cedar Lane, Bayou Dr, **N** 🅿️ Valero/dsl 🏠 Rodeway Inn, TX Inn
783	Sheldon Rd, **N** 🅿️ Chevron/dsl/24hr, Shell/dsl, Valero/dsl 🍴 Burger King, Church's, Jack-in-the-Box, Pizza Hut, Pizza Inn, Popeye's, Subway, Taco Bell, Whataburger 🏠 Days Inn, Grand Inn, Holiday Inn, Leisure Inn, Palace Inn, Parkway Inn, Travelers Inn Ⓞ AutoZone, Discount Tire, Family$, FoodFair, USPO, **S** 🅿️ Chevron/dsl, Texaco/dsl 🍴 McDonald's, Wendy's 🏠 Deluxe Inn, Fairfield Inn, Scottish Inn Ⓞ auto repair
782	Dell-Dale Ave, **N** 🅿️ Exxon/dsl 🏠 Dell-Dale Motel, Luxury Inn Ⓞ Ⓗ, **S** Ⓞ Channelview RV Ctr
781b	Market St, **N** 🏠 Clarion Ⓞ Ⓗ
781a	TX 8, Sam Houston Pkwy, **S** 🅿️ Gulf/dsl
780	(779a from wb) Uvalde Rd, Freeport St, **N** 🅿️ Chevron/dsl, Texaco/dsl 🍴 Capt Tom's Seafood, China Dragon, IHOP, Panda Express, Shipley Donuts, Sonic, Subway, Taco Cabana Ⓞ

⛽ = gas 🍴 = food 🛏 = lodging ⦿ = other Ⓡ = rest stop Copyright 2022 - The Next EXIT ®

TX

HOUSTON

↑E INTERSTATE 10 Cont'd

Exit	Description
780	Continued
	$Tree, Aamco, Ace Hardware, H, Office Depot, S 🍴 Baytown Seafood, Golden Corral, Whataburger ⦿ Firestone/auto, Home Depot, Sam's Club/gas, U-Haul, Verizon, Walmart/McDonald's
779b	N ⛽ Gulf, Valero/dsl 🍴 China Dragon, IHOP, Panda Express, Shipley's Donuts, Sonic, Subway, Taco Cabana 🛏 Interstate Motel ⦿ $Tree, Aamco, Ace Hardware, Office Depot
778b	Normandy St, N ⛽ Shell/Jack-in-the-Box, Texaco/dsl 🛏 La Quinta, S ⛽ Citgo/dsl 🍴 Cafe Ko, Church's 🛏 Normandy Inn
778a	FM 526, Federal Rd, Pasadena, N 🍴 Burger King, Casa Ole Mexican, KFC/Taco Bell, Pizza Hut, Popeye's, Subway, S ⛽ Shell/dsl 🍴 James Coney Island, Pappa's Seafood, Pappadeaux Seafood Kitchen, Pappas BBQ, Peking Bo Chinese, Saltgrass Steaks, Sonic, Swamp Shack Rest. 🛏 Lamplight Inn, Super 8 ⦿ AutoZone, Discount Tire, O'Reilly Parts, Scottish Inn
776b	John Ralston Rd, Holland Ave, N ⛽ Chevron/dsl, Exxon, Texaco 🍴 Chulas Mexican, Denny's, Fuddruckers, Luby's, Mambo Seafood, Pappasito's Cantina, Subway 🛏 Candlewood Suites, Comfort Inn, Day Inn, Palace Inn, Regency Inn ⦿ Family$, Fiesta Foods, NTB, URGENT CARE, S same as 778
776a	Mercury Dr, N 🍴 Arandas Mexican, Burger King, McDonald's, Tepatillan Mexican, TX Grill 🛏 Best Western, Hampton Inn, Motel 6, Premier Inn, Quality Inn ⦿ Volvo Trucks, S ⛽ Shell/dsl, Valero/dsl 🍴 Chili's, Cici's Pizza, Murphy's Deli 🛏 Holiday Inn Express ⦿ CVS Drug, URGENT CARE
775b a	I-610
774	Gellhorn (from eb) Blvd, S ⦿ Anheuser-Busch Brewery
773b	McCarty St, N ⛽ Chevron/dsl, Shell
773a	US 90A, N Wayside Dr, N ⛽ Speedy/dsl 🍴 Jack-in-the-Box, Whataburger, S ⛽ Chevron/dsl, Shell/dsl, Valero 🍴 Church's, Subway
772	Kress St, Lathrop St, N ⛽ Exxon, Pemex 🍴 Popeye's, S 🍴 7 Mares Seafood, Burger King
771b	Lockwood Dr, N ⛽ Chevron/Subway/dsl 🍴 McDonald's ⦿ Family$, Walgreens, S ⛽ Shell/dsl 🛏 Palace Inn
771a	Waco St
770c	US 59 N
770b	Jenson St, Meadow St, Gregg St
770a	US 59 S, to Victoria
769c	McKee St, Hardy St, Nance St downtown
769a	Smith St (from wb) to downtown
768b a	I-45, N to Dallas, S to Galveston
767b	Taylor St
767a	Studemont Dr, Yale St, Heights Blvd, S ⛽ Shell/dsl 🍴 Chick-fil-A, Chili's, Dickey's BBQ, KFC/Taco Bell, Panda Express, Subway ⦿ AT&T, Petsmart, Staples, Target
766	(from wb), Heights Blvd, Yale St
765b	N Durham Dr, N Shepherd Dr, N ⛽ Shell/dsl 🍴 Wendy's 🛏 Howard Johnson ⦿ vet, S ⛽ Valero/dsl 🍴 Saltgrass Steaks
765a	TC Jester Blvd, S ⛽ Exxon/dsl, Texaco/dsl 🍴 Golden Hunan, Starbucks ⦿ vet
764	Westcott St, Washington Ave, Katy Rd, N 🍴 Denny's 🛏 Hampton Inn, S ⛽ Chevron 🍴 IHOP, McDonald's 🛏 Scottish Inn
763	I-610
762	Silber Rd, Post Oak Rd, N 🍴 Chick-fil-A, Dave&Buster's, Jimmy John's, Panda Express, Red Robin, SteaKountry ⦿ Chrysler/Dodge/Jeep, Fiat, Firestone/auto, IKEA, Walmart, S 🍴 Jack-in-the-Box, Shipley Donuts 🛏 Crowne Plaza, Holiday Inn Express
761b	Antoine Rd, S ⛽ Exxon/dsl ⦿ CVS Drug
761a	Wirt Rd, Chimney Rock Rd, S ⛽ Exxon/dsl ⦿ CVS Drug
760	Bingle Rd, Voss Rd, N 🍴 Burger Shack, Hunan Chef, Pueblo Viejo, Starbucks, Subway ⦿ AT&T, Home Depot, S ⛽ Shell/dsl 🍴 Sweet Tomatoes
759	Campbell Rd (from wb), N ⦿ Ranch Mkt same as 758b
758b	Blalock Rd, Campbell Rd, N 🍴 Sonic ⦿ H, Lowe's, S ⛽ Chevron/McDonald's/dsl 🍴 Baskin-Robbins, Goode Co TX BBQ Pappy's Cafe, Saltgrass Steaks, Starbucks ⦿ cleaners, Kroger Walgreens
758a	Bunker Hill Rd, N 🍴 Boudreaux's Cajun, Dennys, Egg&I, Five Guys, Freebirds Burritos, Genghis Grill, Jimmy John's, Marble Slab, Olive Garden, Panda Express, Which Wich? ⦿ Best Buy Costco/gas, GNC, HEB Foods/dsl, Jo-Ann, Lowe's, Michael's, PepBoys, S 🍴 American Island Grill, Buffalo Wild Wings, Ciro's Italian Corner Bakery Cafe, Denis Seafood, Firehouse Subs, Guadalajara Mexican, Kobe Japanese, Longhorn Steaks, Lupe Tortilla, Russo's NY Pizza, Subway 🛏 Memorial Inn ⦿ Marshall's, Ross, Verizon
757	Gessner Rd, N 🍴 Chili's, Chulas Grill, McDonald's, Murphy's Deli, Taco Bell, Wendy's, Whataburger ⦿ AT&T, CVS Drug Hobby Lobby, Home Depot, Honda, Sam's Club/gas, U-Haul, S 🍴 59 Diner, Cheesecake Factory, Fuddrucker's, Goode Co. Seafood, Jason's Deli, Pappadeaux Seafood, Pappasito's, Perry's Steaks 🛏 Westin Hotel ⦿ Firestone/auto, Ford, H, Macy's Office Depot, Target
756	TX 8, Sam Houston Tollway
755	Willcrest Rd, N ⦿ Discount Tire, Lincoln, Mazda, NTB, U-Haul S ⛽ Citgo/dsl, Exxon/dsl 🍴 Brenner's Steaks, Denny's, IHOP McDonald's, Subway, Taste of TX 🛏 Candlewood Suites, Extended Stay America, Hampton Inn, Sheraton
754	Kirkwood Rd, N 🛏 Embassy Suites ⦿ Audi/Porsche, Lincoln, Toyota, S ⛽ Shell/dsl 🍴 Carrabba's, Prince's Burgers, Shipley Do-Nuts, Spicy Pickle, Starbucks, Taco Cabana, Twin Peaks, Whataburger ⦿ Chevrolet
753b	Dairy-Ashford Rd, N ⦿ Infiniti, Lexus, Nissan, Volvo, S ⛽ Exxon/dsl 🍴 Chili's, Hibachi Grill, Subway, TX Cattle Steaks 🛏 Courtyard, Hilton Garden, Holiday Inn Express ⦿ Cadillac, URGENT CARE
753a	Eldridge Pkwy, N ⛽ Conoco/dsl 🛏 Omni Hotel, S ⛽ Valero/dsl ⦿ Kwik Kar
751	TX 6, to Addicks, N ⛽ Shell 🍴 Bros Pizza, Cattlegard Rest. Quiznos, Waffle House 🛏 Drury Inn, Homewood Suites, Studio 6, Wyndham, S 🍴 North China, Salata, Subway 🛏 Beat Value, Extended Stay America, Fairfield Inn, Hyatt House, La Quinta Motel 6, TownePlace Suites ⦿ USPO
750	Park Ten Blvd, eb only, N 🛏 Red Roof Inn, S 🛏 Embassy Suites, Marriott ⦿ Acura, BMW, Buick/GMC, Hoover RV Ctr
748	Barker-Cypress Rd, N ⛽ Exxon/Subway 🍴 BurgerTex Grill, Coaches Grill, El Rancho Mexican, Firehouse Subs, Popeyes, Smoothie Factory, Tony's Mexican 🛏 Residence Inn ⦿ H, S 🍴 Cracker Barrel ⦿ Hyundai, Subaru, vet, VW
747b a	Fry Rd, N ⛽ Gulf/dsl, Shell/dsl 🍴 Applebee's, Arby's, Buffalo Wild Wings, Burger King, Chipotle, Denny's, DQ, Five Guys, Jimmy John's, McDonald's, Panda Express, Panera Bread, Pizza Hut, Smoothie King, Sonic, Souper Salad, Starbucks, Subway, Taco Bell, Waffle House, Whataburger 🛏 Candlewood Suites ⦿ AAA, Best Buy, HEB Food/gas, Hobby Lobby, Home Depot, Jo-Ann, Kohl's, Kroger/dsl, Ross, Sam's Club/gas, URGENT CARE, Verizon, vet, Walgreens, Walmart, S ⛽ Shell/dsl, Starbucks 🍴 Captain Tom's Seafood, Fazoli's, IHOP, McDonald's, Outback Steaks, Potbelly, Quiznos, Smashburger, Star Chinese, TX Mesquite Grill, Wendy's, Willie's 🛏 Woodspring Suites ⦿ AT&T, H, Katy Drug, Lowe's, NTB, Office Depot, Petsmart, Randall's Mkt, Target, TJ Maxx, U-Haul

🄴 INTERSTATE 10 Cont'd

Exit #	Services
746	W Green Blvd, N 🅖 RaceWay/dsl 🍴 BJ's Rest., Chang's Chinese, Cheddar's, Chuy's Mexican, Firehouse Subs, Kublai Khan Stirfry, Longhorn Steaks, Nagoya Japanese, Olive Garden, Orleans Seafood Kitchen, Springcreek BBQ, Stadia Grill, Steak'n Shake, TX Roadhouse, Wild Wings Cafe 🛏 Holiday Inn Express, Palace Inn, S 🍴 Carl's Jr, Jimmy Changas TexMex 🛏 Home2 🄾 Christian Bros Automotive, CVS Drug, Ford, Honda
745	Mason Rd, N 🄾 CarMax, S 🅖 Shell/dsl, Valero/dsl 🍴 Babin's Seafood, Blackeyed Pea, Burger King, Carino's Italian, Chick-fil-A, Chili's, CiCi's, Dickey's BBQ, DQ, El Patron Mexican, Freebirds Burrito, Hooters, Jack-in-the-Box, Jason's Deli, KFC, Landry's Seafood, Luby's, McDonald's, Panda Express, Papa John's, Pizza Hut, Popeye's, Rudy's BBQ/gas, SaltGrass Steaks, Schlotzsky's, Subway, Taco Bell, Taco Cabana, Whataburger, Which Wich? 🛏 Comfort Inn&Suites, Hampton Inn, La Quinta, Motel 6, Super 8 🄾 $Tree, 99c Store, AutoZone, Chevrolet, Chrysler/Dodge/Jeep, Discount Tire, Fiesta Foods, Firestone/auto, Goodyear/auto, HEB Food/gas, Kia, Toyota, transmissions, Walgreens
743	TX 99, Grand Pkwy, Peek Rd, N 🍴 La Madeleine, Red Robin 🄾 🄷, JC Penney, S 🍴 Freddy's Steakburgers, Subway 🄾 Costco/gas, URGENT CARE
741	(742 from wb) Katy-Fort Bend County Rd, Pin Oak Rd, S 🅖 Murphy USA/dsl, Shell/dsl, Texaco/dsl 🍴 Alegra Brazilian, Alicia's Mexican, Antonia's Rest, Chick-fil-A, ChuckECheese, CiCi's Pizza, Denny's, Fuddruckers, Jack-in-the-Box, Jimmy John's, JoJo's Mongolian Grill, KFC, LJ Silver/Taco Bell, Los Cucos, Pizza Hut, Popeyes, Rainforest Cafe, Red Lobster, Smashburger, Starbucks, Subway, Subway, TGIFriday's, Whataburger 🛏 Best Western, Comfort Suites, Country Inn & Suites, Courtyard, Hilton Garden, Holiday Inn, Homewood Suites, Residence Inn, SpringHill Suites 🄾 $Tree, AT&T, BassPro Shops, BooksAMillion, Discount Tire, HEB/dsl, 🄷, Katy Mills Outlet/famous brands, Marshall's, Nissan, Ross, URGENT CARE, Verizon, Walgreens, Walmart/McDonald's
740	FM 1463, N 🅖 Exxon/dsl, S 🅖 Shell/McDonald's/dsl 🍴 Starbucks
739	Cane Island Pkwy, N 🅖 Buc-ee's/dsl, S 🄾 Camping World
737	Pederson Rd, N 🅖 Buc-ee's/dsl, ♥Loves/Arby's/dsl/scales/24hr, S 🄾 Camping World RV Super Ctr, Holiday World RV Ctr
735	Igloo Rd
734	Woods Rd
732	FM 359, to Brookshire, N 🅖 FLYING J/Denny's/dsl/LP/scales/24hr/@, Exxon/Chester's/dsl, Shell 🍴 Church's, Orlando's Pizza, Subway 🛏 Executive Inn, S 🅖 Burger King, Chevron/dsl, Shell/McDonald's/dsl 🍴 Jack-in-the-Box, Popeye's, Taco Bell 🛏 Holiday Inn Express, Super 8 🄾 truck lube, truckwash
731	FM 1489, to Koomey Rd, N 🅖 Exxon/dsl 🍴 Ernesto's Mexican 🛏 Brooke Hotel 🄾 Houston W RV Park, S 🅖 Texaco/Dickey's BBQ/dsl 🛏 La Quinta
729	Peach Ridge Rd, Donigan Rd (730 from wb), S 🅖 Kathy's/dsl/rest./24hr
726	Chew Rd (from eb), S 🄾 golf
725	Mlcak Rd (from wb), S 🅖 Kathy 's Korner/dsl
723	FM 1458, to San Felipe, N 🅖 Exxon/Subway/dsl/scales/24hr 🄾 Peterbilt, to Stephen F Austin SP (3mi), S 🄾 Riverside Tire
721	(from wb) US 90, N 🅖 Shell/Chester's/dsl 🄾 Chrysler/Dodge/Jeep, Ford
720a	Outlet Ctr Dr, N 🅖 Shell/Chester's/dsl

S E A L Y

C O L U M B U S

Exit #	Services
720	TX 36, to Sealy, N 🅖 Shell/dsl 🍴 DQ, Hartz Chicken Buffet, McDonald's, Sonic, Tony's Rest. 🄾 $General, Jones RV Ctr, O'Reilly Parts, Walgreens, S 🅖 Chevron/Burger King/dsl, Murphy USA/dsl, Shell/dsl, Texaco/dsl 🍴 Cazadore's Mexican, Chicken Express, Domino's, Ernesto's Cantina, Hinze's BBQ, Jack-in-the-Box, Jin's Asian, Pizza Hut, Subway, Whataburger 🛏 Best Value Inn, Countryside Inn, Holiday Inn Express, Super 8 🄾 $Tree, Verizon, Walmart/Subway
718	US 90 (from eb), to Sealy, N 🅖 Valero/Huddle House/Subway/dsl, S 🅖 Exxon/Prasek's Smokehouse/dsl
716	Pyka Rd, N 🅖 Sunoco/dsl/rest./showers/24hr/@
713	Beckendorff Rd
709	FM 2761, Bernardo Rd, N 🅖 TA/Carl's Jr/Subway/Dunkin'/dsl/scales/24hr
704	FM 949, N 🄾 Happy Oaks RV Park (3mi)
699	FM 102, to Eagle Lake, N 🄾 Happy Oaks RV Park, S 🄾 Eagle Lake SP (14mi)
698	Alleyton Rd, N 🍴 Mikeska's BBQ, S 🅖 Shell/Taco Bell/BBQ/dsl, Valero/Subway/dsl 🄾 Chrysler/Dodge/Jeep, Ford
697mm	Little Colorado River
696	TX 71, Columbus, N 🅖 Exxon/Burger King/dsl, Shell/dsl 🍴 #1 Buffet, Blake St. Grill, Jack-in-the-Box, Pizza Hut, Schobel's Rest., Whataburger, Zapata Mexican 🛏 Columbus Inn, Holiday Inn Express 🄾 AT&T, AutoZone, HEB Foods, 🄷, Walmart, S 🅖 Chevron/dsl, Conoco/Church's/Subway/dsl, Phillips 66/dsl 🍴 Los Cabos Mexican, McDonald's, Nancy's Steaks, Sonic 🛏 Baymont Inn, Best Value, LaQuinta 🄾 Columbus RV Park
695	TX 71 (from wb), to La Grange
693	FM 2434, to Glidden
692mm	🆁🆂 both lanes, full 🛏 facilities, vending, 🍴, 🛏, litter barrels, RV dump, petwalk
689	US 90, to Hattermann Lane, N 🄾 Whispering Oaks RV Park
682	FM 155, to Wiemar, N 🅖 Shell/dsl, Valero/dsl 🍴 DQ, McDonald's, Subway/Texas Burger 🛏 Motel 6 🄾 $General, 🄷, Lowe's Mkt, Tire Pros, S 🅖 76/Church's/dsl/24hr, ♥Loves/Chester's/Wendy's/dsl/scales/24hr 🄾 Buick/Chevrolet/GMC
678mm	E Navidad River
677	US 90
674	US 77, Schulenburg, N 🅖 Pilot/Taco Bell/PJ Fresh/dsl/scales/24hr, Sunoco/Stripes/Taco Co 🍴 Oak Ridge Smokehouse 🛏 Best Value Inn, Executive Inn 🄾 Ford, Potter Country Store, S 🅖 Exxon/dsl, Holiday Inn Express, Valero/Subway 🍴 DQ, Los Agaves, Lucy's Grill, Taco Rodeo, Whataburger 🛏 Best Western+ 🄾 $General, Family$, O'Reilly Parts, Schulenberg RV Park
672mm	W Navidad River
668	FM 2238, to Engle
661	TX 95, FM 609, to Flatonia, N 🅖 Citgo/dsl, Valero/dsl 🍴 Jessito's Mexican, Joel's BBQ, Robert's Steaks 🄾 Flatonia RV Ranch (1mi),

INTERSTATE 10 Cont'd

Exit	Description
661	Continued
	S 🅖 Shell/McDonald's/Grumpy's Rest./motel/dsl, Valero 🍴 DQ, Subway 🛏 Best Western+, Carefree Inn, Sunset Inn 🅞 $General, NAPA
658mm	🆁🆂 both lanes, tables, litter barrels
653	US 90, Waelder, N 🅖 Shell/dsl
649	TX 97, to Waelder
642	TX 304, to Gonzales
637	FM 794, to Harwood
632	US 90/183, to Gonzales, N 🅖 ♥Love's/Subway/dsl/scales/24hr 🛏 Best Western+, Coachway Inn (2mi), La Quinta, S 🅖 Buc-ee's/dsl 🅞 camping, to Palmetto SP (5mi)
630mm	San Marcos River
628	TX 80, to Luling, N 🅖 Citgo (2mi), Valero/pizza/dsl/24hr 🅞 🅗, Riverbend RV Park
625	Darst Field Rd
624.5mm	Smith Creek
621mm	weigh sta both lanes
620	FM 1104
618mm	🆁🆂 both lanes, full 🖐 facilities, 🅒, 🅟, petwalk
617	FM 2438, to Kingsbury
614	toll 130 N, to Austin, Waco
612	US 90
611mm	Geronimo Creek
610	TX 123, to San Marcos, N 🅖 Exxon/Circle K/dsl, Shell/Subway/dsl 🍴 Chili's, Giuseppe Pizza, IHOP, Los Cucos Mexican, Starbucks 🛏 Comfort Inn, Days Inn, Hampton Inn, Holiday Inn Express, TownePlace Suites 🅞 Carters Tires, S 🅖 Valero/dsl 🍴 Taco Cabana 🅞 🅗
609	TX 123, Austin St, S 🅖 Phillips 66/dsl, Sunoco/dsl 🅞 Chevrolet, Home Depot
607	TX 46, FM 78, to New Braunfels, N 🅖 Valero/Jack-in-the-Box/dsl 🛏 Motel 6 🅞 Ford, S 🅖 Exxon/dsl, Shell/Circle K/dsl 🍴 Bill Miller BBQ, Dixie Grille, Garcia's Mexican, McDonald's, Subway, Whataburger 🛏 Best Value, La Quinta 🅞 Chrysler/Dodge/Jeep
605	FM 464, N 🅞 Twin Palms RV Park
605mm	Guadalupe River
604	FM 725, to Lake McQueeney, N 🅖 ♥Love's/Arby's/dsl/scales/24hr 🅞 Twin Palms RV Park
603	US 90 E, US 90A, to Seguin, N 🅞 D&A RV Park, Seguin RV Ctr, S 🅞 Explore USA RV Ctr
601	FM 775, to New Berlin, N 🅖 Chevron/Subway/dsl/scales/24hr
600	Schwab Rd
599	FM 465, to Marion
599mm	Santa Clara Creek
597	Santa Clara Rd, N 🅞 auto racetrack
595	Zuehl Rd
594mm	Cibolo Creek
593	FM 2538, Trainer Hale Rd, N 🅖 Texaco/dsl 🅞 tires, S 🅖 Exxon/Lucille's Rest./dsl/24hr
593mm	Woman Hollering Creek
591	FM 1518, to Schertz, N 🅖 Alamo Trvl Ctr/Shell/dsl 🅞 repair, S 🅖 Valero/Circle K/dsl/e85
589	Pfeil Rd, Graytown Rd
589mm	Salatrillo Creek
587	LP 1604, Randolph AFB, to Universal City, N 🅖 EVC/CNG, S 🅖 Shell/McDonald's/dsl 🍴 Whataburger
585.5mm	Escondido Creek
585	FM 1516, to Converse, N 🅖 Chevron/Church's/dsl/scales/24hr 🛏 Best Western+, S 🅞 Kenworth, Peterbilt/GMC/Freightliner

KIRBY
SAN ANTONIO

Exit	Description
585mm	Martinez Creek
583	Foster Rd, N 🅖 ⒡FLYING J/Denny's/dsl/LP/scales/24hr/@, Valero/Subway/dsl/24hr 🍴 Jack-in-the-Box 🛏 Comfort Inn, La Quinta 🅞 Blue Beacon, Speedco Lube, Tire Mart, S 🅖 TA/Chevron/Burger King/Pizza Hut/Popeye's/dsl/24hr/@
582.5mm	Rosillo Creek
582	Ackerman Rd, Kirby, N 🅖 PILOT/Subway/dsl/scales/24hr, S 🅖 Petro/Iron Skillet/dsl/scales/24hr/@ 🍴 El Rodeo Mexican 🛏 Knights Inn 🅞 Blue Beacon, Petrolube
581	I-410
580	LP 13, WW White Rd, N 🅖 Chevron/dsl, Valero/dsl 🍴 La Playa Seafood, Wendy's 🛏 Red Roof Inn, Rodeway Inn, Super 7 🅞 tires, S 🅖 Exxon/7-11, Valero 🍴 Bill Miller BBQ, El Rodeo Mexican, Lazaritas Mexican, McDonald's, Pizza Hut, Popeye's, Subway 🛏 Best Value, Motel 6, Super 8 🅞 Family$, Ford/Volvo Trucks, tires/repair
579	Houston St, N 🅖 Valero/dsl 🍴 Starbucks 🛏 Quality Inn 🅞 Penske, S 🅖 Chevron, Stripes/Valero/dsl 🛏 Days Inn, Knights Inn, Upland Inn
578	Pecan Valley Dr, ML King Dr, S 🅖 Shell/Subway/dsl
577	US 87 S, to Roland Ave, S 🍴 Whataburger 🛏 Best Western+, Super 8
576	New Braunfels Ave, Gevers St, S 🅖 Valero 🍴 McDonald's
575	Pine St, Hackberry St, S 🍴 Little Red Barn Steaks
574	I-37, US 281
573	Probandt St, N 🍴 Jack-in-the-Box, Miller's BBQ, S 🅖 Valero 🅞 tires/repair, to SA Missions HS
I-10 and I-35 run together 3 miles. See I-35, exits 156-154a.	
569c	Santa Rosa St 🅞 to Our Lady of the Lake U downtown
568	spur 421, Culebra Ave, Bandera Ave, S 🅞 to St Marys U
567	Lp 345, Fredericksburg Rd (from eb upper level accesses I-35 S, I-10 E, US 87 S, lower level accesses I-35 N)
566b	Fresno Dr, S 🅖 Exxon/dsl 🛏 Galaxy Inn
566a	West Ave, N 🅖 Exxon/7-11 🍴 DQ, Subway, Whataburger 🅞 CarCare
565c	(from wb), access to same as 565 a b, S 🅖 Shell 🍴 Jimador Mexican, Starbucks 🛏 La Quinta
565b	Vance Jackson Rd, N 🅖 Murphy USA/dsl 🍴 Bill Miller BBQ, IHOP 🛏 Comfort Inn, Days Inn, EconoLodge 🅞 Walmart, S 🅖 Shell/dsl 🛏 Holiday Inn Express
565a	Crossroads Blvd, Balcone's Heights, N 🅖 Shell/dsl 🛏 Howard Johnson 🅞 vet, S 🅖 Valero/dsl 🍴 Crossroads BBQ, Dave&Buster's, Denny's, El Pollo Loco, McDonald's, Whataburger 🛏 SpringHill Suites 🅞 Firestone/auto, Hobby Lobby, Mazda, Office Depot, Target
564b a	I-410, services off of I-410 W, Fredericksburg Rd
563	Callaghan Rd, N 🅖 Valero 🍴 Las Palapas Mexican, Subway 🛏 Embassy Suites, Marriott 🅞 $General, Ford, Sprouts Mkt, Toyota, S 🅖 Exxon/7-11 🍴 Mamacita's Rest. 🅞 Lowe's
561	Wurzbach Rd, N 🅖 Texaco/dsl 🍴 Bolo's Grille, Broadway 5050 Grill, County Line BBQ, Egg&I, Firehouse Subs, Fuddrucker's, Honeybaked Ham, Jason's Deli, Pappasito's Cantina, Popeye's, Sea Island Shrimphouse, Taste Of China, TX Land&Cattle, Wasabi Grill 🛏 Extended Stay America, Homewood Suites, Hyatt Place, Motel 6, Staybridge Suites 🅞 AutoZone, BigLots, HEB Food/gas, Office Depot, Porsche, Tuesday Morning, S 🅖 Shell/dsl 🍴 210 Ceviche Seafood, Alamo Café, Arby's, Chester's Burgers, China Sea, Church's, Denny's, El Taco Tote, Jack-in-the-Box, Mamma Margie's Mexican, McDonald's, Pizza Hut, Ruby Tuesday, Sumo Japanese, Taco Bell, Wendy's 🛏 Baymont Inn, Best Western, Candlewood Suites, Drury Inn, Hawthorn Suites, La Quinta, Motel 6, Sleep Inn 🅞 CarMax, 🅗

INTERSTATE 10 Cont'd

Exit #	Services
560b	Frontage Rd (from eb) same as 561
560a	Huebner Rd, **N** 🍴 CA Pizza Kitchen, Chipotle, Fare Wok, Genghis Grill, La Madeleine, Macaroni Grill, Panera Bread, Pericos Mexican, Salata, SaltGrass Steaks 🅾 Cadillac, Chrysler/Jeep/Dodge, Fiat, Nissan, Old Navy, Ross, **S** 🅿 Chevron, Exxon, Shell/Jack-in-the-Box/dsl 🍴 Cracker Barrel, Jim's Rest., Miller's BBQ 🛏 Days Inn, Quality Inn, TownePlace Suites
559	Lp 335, US 87, Fredericksburg Rd, **N** 🍴 Pearl Inn 🛏 Holiday Inn Express 🅾 Acura, **S** 🍴 Krispy Kreme, Shell/Jack-in-the-Box/dsl 🛏 Comfort Suites, Days Inn, HomeGate Studios, Rodeway Inn, SpringHill Suites 🅾 Infiniti
558	De Zavala Rd, **N** 🅿 Chevron, Shell/Subway 🍴 Bill Miller BBQ, Burger King, Carrabba's, Chick-fil-A, Chili's, Five Guys, Fox-&Hound, KFC/Taco Bell, Logan's Roadhouse, McDonald's, Outback Steaks, Sonic, Starbucks, Taco Cabana, The Earl of Sandwich, Wendy's 🅾 HEB Foods, Home Depot, Marshall's, PetCo, Petsmart, Steinmart, Target, **S** 🍴 IHOP, Popeye's, Schlotzsky's 🛏 Days Inn, SpringHill Suites, Studio 6 🅾 Discount Tire, Sam's Club/gas, Verizon, Walmart
557	Spur 53, **N** 🅿 Exxon/7-11/dsl 🍴 Cheddar's, Chuy's Mexican 🛏 Best Western, EconoLodge, Embassy Suites, Howard Johnson, Super 8 🅾 Audi, Chevrolet, Hyundai, Jaguar/Mazerati/Ferrari, **S** 🅿 Valero/Subway/dsl 🍴 A&W/LJ Silver, Cici's Pizza, Huhot Chinese, IHOP, Matamoro's Cantina, Quiznos, Twin Peaks, Whataburger, Zio's Italian 🛏 Holiday Inn 🅾 Costco/gas, Land Rover, Sams Club/gas, Univ of TX at San Antonio, Walmart
556b	Frontage Rd
556a	to Anderson Lp, **S** 🅾 to Seaworld, Six Flags
555	La Cantera Pkwy, **N** 🍴 54th St Rest., BJ's Rest., Bob's Chophouse, Chick-fil-A, Coldstone, Freddy's Steakburger, Islamorada Rest., Maggiano's Little Italy, McDonald's/playplace, Mimi's Cafe, Panera Bread, Popeye's, Potbelly, Red Robin, Sonic, Starbucks, Tiago's, Whataburger, Which Wich? 🛏 Courtyard, Hilton Garden, Residence Inn 🅾 $Tree, AT&T, Bass Pro Shops, Best Buy, Dick's, GNC, Hobby Lobby, JC Penney, Lowe's, Michaels, Old Navy, Petsmart, Ross, Staples, Target, TJ Maxx, World Mkt, **S** 🍴 Applebee's, Longhorn Steaks, Olive Garden, Red Lobster 🛏 Drury Inn, La Quinta, Motel 6 🅾 Honda, to La Cantera Pkwy
554	Camp Bullis Rd, **N** 🅿 Texaco/dsl 🅾 Russell CP, **S** 🅿 Shell/dsl 🛏 Rodeway Inn
552	Dominion Dr, Stonewall Pkwy, **S** 🍴 Aldo's Rest., Bourbon St. Kitchen, La Gloria 🅾 Audi, CVS Drug, Lexus, Subaru, VW
551	Boerne Stage Rd (from wb), to Leon Springs, **N** 🅿 Shamrock/dsl 🍴 Rudy's BBQ, Sonic, **S** 🍴 Las Palapas Mexican, Longhorns Rest., Papa Nacho's, Starbucks, Subway 🅾 CarX, GNC, HEB Foods/dsl, Tesla
550	FM 3351, Ralph Fair Rd, **N** 🅿 Exxon/McDonald's/dsl, Valero/dsl 🍴 Rudy's BBQ/gas, Willie's Cafe 🛏 La Quinta, **S** 🅿 Shell/Domino's/dsl 🍴 Bill Miller's BBQ, Laguna Madre, Schlotsky's, Taco Cabana, Whataburger 🅾 Walgreens, Walmart
546	Fair Oaks Pkwy, Tarpon Dr, **N** 🅿 Shell/dsl 🍴 Papa John's American Dream RV Ctr, CVS Drug, ExploreUSA RV Ctr, Harley-Davidson, vet, **S** 🅿 Chevron/dsl/café, Exxon/dsl/café 🅾 Belden's Automotive, Fair Oaks Automotive, Hoover RV Ctr
543	Boerne Stage Rd, to Scenic LP Rd, **N** 🅿 Valero/Circle K/Subway/dsl 🛏 Fairfield Inn 🅾 Ancira RV Ctr, Buick/GMC, Chevrolet, Chrysler/Dodge/Jeep, Ford, NAPA, tires/repair, to Cascade Caverns/camping (3mi), **S** 🅾 Explore USA RV Ctr, Infiniti, Mercedes, Nissan, Toyota
542	(from wb), **N** 🅿 Shamrock 🍴 Domino's, Pizza Hut, Subway, Wendy's 🅾 $Tree, Alamo Fiesta RV Park, O'Reilly Parts, same as 540, Verizon
540	TX 46, to New Braunfels, **N** 🅿 Exxon/Taco Bell/dsl, Murphy USA/dsl, Shell/dsl 🍴 Burger King, Centinela Mexican, Church's, Denny's, DQ, Guadalajara Mexican, Little Caesar's, Papa Murphy's, Pizza Hut, Shanghai Chinese, Sonic, Subway, Taco Cabana, Wendy's 🛏 Comfort Inn, Days Inn, Motel 6 🅾 AutoZone, Discount Tire, HEB Food/dsl, Verizon, vet, Walgreens, Walmart, **S** 🍴 Chili's, Starbucks, Whataburger 🛏 Hampton Inn 🅾 Home Depot, Ⓗ
539	Johns Rd, **N** 🛏 Best Western, **S** 🅿 Valero/dsl/LP
538mm	Cibolo Creek
538	Ranger Creek Rd
537	US 87, to Boerne
533	FM 289, Welfare, **N** 🍴 PoPo Family Rest. 🅾 Top of the Hill RV Park (1mi)
532mm	Little Joshua Creek
531mm	Ⓡ wb, tables, litter barrels
530mm	Big Joshua Creek
529.5mm	Ⓡ eb, tables, litter barrels
527	FM 1621 (from wb), to Waring
526.5mm	Holiday Creek
524	TX 27, FM 1621, to Waring, **N** 🅾 vet, **S** 🅿 Chevron, Shell/dsl
523.5mm	Guadalupe River
523	US 87 N, to Comfort, **N** 🅿 Chevron/Chicken Express/dsl, ♥Love's/McDonald's/Subway/dsl/scales/24hr, **S** 🅿 Exxon/dsl 🍴 DQ 🛏 Executive Inn 🅾 $General, RV Park/LP
521.5mm	Comfort Creek
520	FM 1341, to Cypress Creek Rd
515mm	Cypress Creek
514mm	Ⓡ both lanes, full ♿ facilities, vending, 🍴, 🚰, litter barrels, RV dump, petwalk, playground, wireless internet
508	TX 16, Kerrville, **N** 🅿 Exxon/dsl 🅾 Buick/Cadillac/Chevrolet, 0-2 mi **S** 🅿 Exxon, Shell/McDonald's/dsl/24hr, Stripes/Taco Co, Valero/dsl/e-85 🍴 Bella Sera Italian, Burger King, Chicken Express, Cracker Barrel, Good Taste Asian, IHOP, Jack-in-the-Box, Little Caesar's, Margarita's Mexican, McDonald's, Schlotzsky's, Sonic, Taco Bell, Taco Casa 🛏 Best Western, Days Inn, Hampton Inn, Holiday Inn Express, La Quinta, Motel 6, Quality Inn, Super 8, Yo Ranch Hotel 🅾 $Tree, Advance Parts, BigLots, Home Depot, Ⓗ, Kerrville RV Ctr, Lowe's, O'Reilly Parts, Walgreens
505	FM 783, to Kerrville, **S** 🅿 Exxon/dsl, 3 mi **S** on TX 27 🅿 Phillips 66/dsl, Stripes/Taco Co/dsl 🍴 Belle Vita, Billy Gene's Rest., Chick-fil-A, Chili's, CiCi's, Culver's, Del Norte Rest., Dickey's BBQ, DQ, Fuddruckers, Golden Chick, Mamacita's, McDonald's, Pizza Hut, Popeye's, Sonic, Starbucks, Subway, Taco Casa, Wendy's, Whataburger 🛏 Inn of the Hills 🅾 $General, AT&T, AutoZone, Chrysler/Dodge/Jeep, CVS Drug, Discount Tire, HEB Foods/gas, Take It Easy RV Resort, Tuesday Morning, Walmart/McDonald's

INTERSTATE 10 Cont'd

Exit #	Services
503.5mm	scenic views both lanes, litter barrels
501	FM 1338, N 🅞 Buckhorn RV Resort, S 🅞 KOA (2mi)
497mm	scenic views both lanes, 🛏, litter barrels
492	FM 479
490	TX 41
488	TX 27, to Ingram, Mountain Home
484	Midway Rd
477	US 290, to Fredericksburg
476.5mm	service rd eb
472	Old Segovia Rd
465	FM 2169, to Segovia, S 🅖 Phillips 66/rest./dsl 🛏 River Valley Inn/RV park
464.5mm	Johnson Fork Creek
462	US 83 S, to Uvalde
461mm	🛏 eb, tables, litter barrels
460	(from wb), to Junction
459mm	🛏 wb, tables, litter barrels
457	FM 2169, to Junction, N 🅖 Shell/dsl, S 🛏 Econolodge 🅞 RV camping, S. Llano River SP
456.5mm	Llano River
456	US 83/377, Junction, N 🅖 Alon/dsl, Chevron/dsl/24hr, Shell/McDonald's/dsl/24hr 🍽 Cooper's BBQ, Tia Nena's Mexican 🛏 Motel 6, S 🅖 Conoco/dsl, Exxon/dsl, Phillips 66/dsl, Pilot/Subway/PJ Fresh/dsl/scales/24hr 🍽 DQ, Isaack Rest., La Familia Mexican, Lum's BBQ, Sonic 🛏 Best Western, Holiday Inn Express, Lazy T Motel, Legends Inn, Rodeway Inn, Sun Valley Motel, The Hills Motel 🅞 $General, Best Hardware, Family$, 🅗, Lowe's Mkt, Plumley's Store, S Llano RV Park, to S Llano River SP
452.5mm	Bear Creek
451	RM 2291, to Cleo Rd
448mm	North Creek
445	RM 1674, S 🅞 camping
444.5mm	Stark Creek
442mm	Copperas Creek
442	RM 1674, to Ft McKavett, N 🅞 to Ft McKavett SHS
439mm	N Llano River
438	Lp 291 (from wb), to Roosevelt same as 437
437	Lp 291 (from eb, no EZ return), to Roosevelt, 1 mi N 🅖 Simon Bros Mercantile/dsl 🅞 USPO
429	RM 3130, to Harrell
423mm	parking area both lanes, litter barrels
420	RM 3130, to Baker Rd
412	Allison Rd, RM 3130
404	RM 3130, RM 864, N 🅞 to Ft McKavett St HS, 3 mi S 🅖 Loves/Chester's/dsl/scales/24hr, Stripes/Taco Co 🅞 🅗
400	US 277, Sonora, N 🅖 Road Ranger/Church's/desk 🍽 Sutton Co Steaks 🛏 Motel 6, S 🅖 Alon/7-11/dsl, Sunoco/dsl, Sunoco/Stripes/dsl 🍽 DQ, La Mexicana Rest., Pizza Hut, Sonic, Taco Grill 🛏 Quality Inn, Super 8, Surestay 🅞 Family$, USPO
399	(from eb) LP 467, Sonora, N 🛏 Motel 6, S 🅖 Sunoco/dsl, Sunoco/Stripes/Taco Co 🍽 DQ 🅞 🅗, RV camping
394mm	🆁🆂 both lanes, full ♿ facilities, 🕭, 🛏, litter barrel, petwalk, RV dump
392	RM 1989, Caverns of Sonora Rd, 8 mi S 🅞 Caverns of Sonora Camping
388	RM 1312 (from wb)
381	RM 1312 (from eb)
372	Taylor Box Rd, N 🅖 Exxon/rest./dsl/scales/24hr 🛏 Super 8 🅞 auto museum, Circle Bar RV Park
368	LP 466, N same as 365 & 363

365	TX 163, Ozona, N 🅖 Stripes/Godfather's/Taco Co/dsl, Sunoco dsl, Valero/dsl 🍽 Cafe Next Door, DQ, Sonic, Subway 🛏 Best Value Inn, Economy Inn/RV Park, Hampton Inn, Hillcrest Inn, Holiday Inn Express, Quality Inn 🅞 $General, dsl/auto repair 🅗, NAPA, to David Crockett Mon, S 🍽 Pilot/dsl, Sunoco Stripes 🍽 El Chato's 🅞 city park
363	Lp 466, to Ozona
361	RM 2083, Pandale Rd
357mm	Eureka Draw
351mm	Howard Draw
350	FM 2398, to Howard Draw
349mm	parking area wb, litter barrels
346mm	parking area eb, litter barrels
343	TX 290 W, S 🅞 Ft. Lancaster Historic Site
337	Live Oak Rd
336.5mm	Live Oak Creek
328	River Rd, Sheffield
327.5mm	Pecos River
325	TX 290, TX 349, to Iraan, Sheffield, N 🅞 🅗
320	Frontage Rd
314	Frontage Rd
309mm	🆁🆂 both lanes, full ♿ facilities, 🕭, 🛏, litter barrels, petwalk, wi-fi
307	US 190, FM 305, to Iraan, N 🅞 🅗
298	RM 2886
294	FM 11, Bakersfield, N 🅖 Exxon, S 🅖 Chevron/café/dsl 🅞 🕭
288	Ligon Rd, N many windmills
285	McKenzie Rd, S 🅞 Domaine Cordier Ste Genevieve Winery
279mm	🛏 eb, tables, litter barrels
277	FM 2023
273	US 67/385, to McCamey, 🛏 wb, tables, litter barrels
272	University Rd
264	Warnock Rd, N 🅞 Fort Stockton RV Park/Roadrunner Cafe
261	US 290 W, US 385 S, N 🅖 Exxon/dsl, S 🅖 Loves/Carl's Jr dsl/scales/24hr, Shell/dsl, Stripes/dsl 🍽 DQ, Pizza Hut, Sonic, Subway 🛏 All Inn, Budget Inn, Deluxe Inn, Executive Inn 🅞 🅗 RV camping, to Big Bend NP
259b a	(259 from eb) TX 18, FM 1053, Ft Stockton, N 🅖 Shell/Burger King/dsl 🅞 I-10 RV Park, S 🅖 Flying J/Subway/dsl/scales/24hr 🅞 🅗
257	US 285, to Pecos, Ft Stockton, N 🅖 Stripes/Sunoco/Taco Co/dsl/scales24hr 🅞 Camp Stockton RV Park, golf, S 🅖 Chevron/dsl/24hr, Exxon/dsl, Shell/dsl, Valero/dsl 🍽 Bush's Chicken, Dickey's BBQ, DQ, KFC/Taco Bell, Little Caesar's, McDonald's, Pecos Roadhouse, Pizza Hut, Pizza Pro, Sonic, Steak House, Subway 🛏 Atrium West Inn, Best Western+, Candlewood Suites, Days Inn, Fairfield Inn, Hampton Inn, La Quinta, Quality Inn, Texan Inn 🅞 $General, $Tree, Ace Hardware, Advance a Parts, AutoZone, Buick/Chevrolet, Comanche Land RV Park, Family$, Firestone/auto, Lowe's Foods, O'Reilly Parts, Williams Tires
256	to US 385 S, Ft Stockton, N 🅞 HillTop RV, S 🅖 Shell/dsl Walmart/dsl 🍽 Domino's, Howard's Drive-In, K-Bob's Steaks, Subway 🛏 Comfort Suites, Holiday Inn Express, Motel 6, Sleep Inn, Super 8 🅞 auto/RV repair, Big Bend NP, Chrysler/Jeep/Dodge, Ford, to Ft Stockton Hist Dist, vet, Walmart
253	FM 2037, to Belding
248	US 67, FM 1776, to Alpine, S 🅞 to Big Bend NP
246	Firestone
241	Kennedy Rd
235	Mendel Rd Welcome Ctr wb, full ♿ facilities, 🕭, 🛏, litter barrels, vending, petwalk
233mm	🆁🆂 both lanes, full ♿ facilities, 🕭, 🛏, litter barrels, petwalk

🚏E INTERSTATE 10 Cont'd

Exit #	Services
229	Hovey Rd
222	Hoefs Rd
214	(from wb), FM 2448
212	TX 17, FM 2448, to Pecos, **N** 🏕, litter barrels, **S** ⓕ Saddleback RV Camping, Valero/I-10 Fuel/café/dsl
209	TX 17, **S** ⓞ Ft Davis NHS, to Balmorhea SP, to Davis Mtn SP
206	FM 2903, to Balmorhea, Toyah, **2 mi S** ⓖ GasCard ⓕ Uncles Rest. ⓞ to Balmorhea SP, USPO
192	FM 3078, to Toyahvale, **S** ⓞ to Balmorhea SP
188	Giffin Rd
187	I-20, to Ft Worth, Dallas
186	I-10, E to San Antonio (from wb)
185mm	🏕 both lanes, tables, litter barrels
184	Springhills
181	Cherry Creek Rd, **S** ⓖ Chevron/dsl
176	TX 118, FM 2424, to Kent, **S** ⓞ Davis Mtn SP, Ft Davis, to McDonald Observatory
173	Hurd's Draw Rd
166	Boracho Sta
159	Plateau, **N** ⓖ Exxon/rest./dsl/24hr
153	Michigan Flat
146	Wild Horse Rd
146mm	weigh sta wb
145mm	Ⓡ both lanes, full & facilities, 🏕, litter barrels, petwalk, wi-fi
140b	Ross Dr, Van Horn, **N** ⓖ Loves/Subway/dsl/scales/24hr, Valero/dsl ⌂ Days Inn, Desert Inn, Sands Motel/rest. ⓞ Desert Willow RV Park, repair, **S** ⓞ Mountain View RV Park/dump
140a	US 90, TX 54, Van Horn Dr, **N** ⓖ Alon/dsl ⌂ Hotel El Capitan ⓞ Ⓗ, NAPA, **S** ⓖ 🏪/Wendy's/dsl/scales/24hr, Valero/dsl ⓕ Papa's Pantry ⓞ dsl/tire repair, RV Dump, Van Horn RV Park
138	Lp 10, to Van Horn, **N** ⓕ Chuy's Rest. ⌂ Budget Inn, EconoLodge, Economy Inn, Knights Inn, Motel 6, Red Roof Inn, Value Inn ⓞ $General, auto/dsl repair, city park, Oasis RV Park, Porter Foods, Southern Star RV Park, UPSO, visitor info, **S** ⓖ Chevron/dsl/24hr, Tesla EVC ⓕ McDonald's ⌂ Hampton Inn, Holiday Inn Express, Quality Inn, Super 8 ⓞ tires/repair
137mm	weigh sta eb
136mm	scenic overlook wb, 🏕, litter barrels
135mm	Mountain/Central time zone
133	(from wb) Frontage Rd
129	to Hot Wells, Allamore
108	to Sierra Blanca (from wb) same as 107
107	FM 1111, Sierra Blanca Ave, **N** ⓖ Exxon/Subway/dsl/24hr ⓕ Delfina's Mexican ⓞ to Hueco Tanks SP, truck/tire repair, USPO, **S** ⓖ Chevron/dsl ⌂ Americana Inn ⓞ Stagecoach Trading Post
105	(106 from wb) Lp 10, Sierra Blanca same as 107
102.5mm	insp sta eb
99	Lasca Rd, **N** 🏕 both lanes, tables, litter barrels, no restrooms
98mm	🏕 eb, litter barrels, no restrooms
95	Frontage Rd (from eb)
87	FM 34, **S** ⓖ TX 87/dsl
85	Esperanza Rd
81	FM 2217
78	TX 20 W, to McNary
77mm	truck parking area wb
72	spur 148, to Ft Hancock, **S** ⓖ Shell/dsl ⓕ Angie's Rest. ⌂ Ft Hancock Motel ⓞ Family$, USPO
68	Acala Rd
55	Tornillo
51mm	Ⓡ both lanes, full & facilities, 🏕, litter barrels, petwalk

VAN HORN (vertical left margin)

EL PASO (vertical left margin, lower)

Exit #	Services
49	FM 793, Fabens, **S** ⓖ Speedway/dsl ⓕ Church's, Little Caesar's, McDonald's, Subway ⌂ Fabens Inn/Cafe ⓞ Family$, San Eli Foods
42	FM 1110, to Clint, **S** ⓖ Express/Dickey's BBQ/dsl ⓕ Cotton Eyed Joe's, Mamacita's Rest. ⌂ Adobe Inn, Best Western, Cotton Valley Motel/RV Park/rest./dump
37	FM 1281, Horizon Blvd, **N** ⓖ FLYING J/Denny's/dsl/scales/24hr/@, Loves/Chester's/Subway/dsl/scales/24hr/@ ⌂ Americana Inn ⓞ Freightliner, RV Camping, Speedco Lube, **S** ⓖ Petro/Valero/Iron Skillet/Subway/dsl/scales/24hr/@ ⓕ McDonald's ⌂ Deluxe Inn ⓞ Blue Beacon
35	Eastlake Blvd.
34	TX 375, Americas Ave, **N** ⓖ Chevron/dsl, Valero/Subway/dsl ⌂ Motel 6, Woodspring Suites ⓞ Mission RV Camping, Peterbilt, U-Haul, **S** ⓞ El Paso Museum of Hist
32	FM 659, Zaragosa Rd, **N** ⓖ Alon/7-11 ⓕ Applebee's, Barrigos Mexican, BJ's Rest., Cheddar's, Chico's Tacos, Chipotle Mexican, Corner Bakery Cafe, Famous Dave's, Five Guys, Furr's Buffet, Genghis Grill, Great American Steaks, IHOP, Jaci-in-the-Box, Jason's Deli, Krispy Kreme, La Malinche Mexican, Logan's Roadhouse, Macaroni Grill, Mama Fu's Asian, McDonald's, Outback Steaks, Pei Wei, Peter Piper Pizza, Potbelly, Sonic, Starbucks, Taco Bell, Village Inn, Whataburger ⌂ Courtyard, Hampton Inn, Holiday Inn Express ⓞ AT&T, Chevrolet, Discount Tire, GNC, Kohl's, Lowe's, Michaels, Nissan, Office Depot, Ross, Walgreens, Which Wich?, World Mkt, **S** ⓖ Circle K/dsl ⓕ Gallego's Mexican ⓞ city park, vet, Volvo/Mack
30	Lee Trevino Dr, **N** ⓖ Exxon ⓕ Denny's, Los Canarios Mexican, Whataburger ⌂ La Quinta, Motel 6, Red Roof Inn, Studio 6 ⓞ Discount Tire, Firestone/auto, Ford, Home Depot, Kenworth/Ford Trucks, Lexus, Mazda, Toyota, **S** ⓞ Chrysler/Dodge/Jeep
29	Lomaland Dr, **S** ⓖ Alon/7-11 ⌂ Ramada ⓞ Harley-Davidson
28b	Yarbrough Dr, El Paso, **N** ⓖ Murphy USA, Shell/Coldstone/dsl, Texaco ⓕ Buffalo Wild Wings, Burger King, ChuckECheese, Corner Bakery, Dunkin', Grandy's, Hayashi Japanese, Hong Kong Buffet, LJ Silver, McDonald's, Peter Piper Pizza, Sonic, Subway, TX Roadhouse, Wendy's, Whataburger, Wienerschnitzel ⌂ Days Inn ⓞ AT&T, Big Lots, Ⓗ, Office Depot, Ranch Mkt, Ross, Walmart, **S** ⓕ Rudy's BBQ, Valero/dsl ⓕ Applebee's, Fuddrucker's, Julio's Cafe, La Malinche Mexican, Lin's Buffet, Pizza Hut, Rudy's BBQ/gas, Shangri-La, Villa Del Mar ⌂ Comfort Inn, InTown Suites, La Quinta ⓞ Ⓗ
28a	FM 2316, McRae Blvd, **N** ⓖ Texaco/dsl, Valero ⓕ Pizza Hut ⌂ La Quinta ⓞ Ⓗ, Jo-Ann Fabrics, Murphy USA/dsl, **S** ⓖ Circle K/dsl ⓕ Fuddruckers, Gabriel's Mexican, Pizza Hut ⌂ La Quinta, Quality Inn ⓞ NAPA, vet

(map inset: Lamesa, Big Spring, Stanton, Midland, Odessa, Monahans, Pyote, Thomtonville, Pecos, Barstow, Toyah, McCamey, Iraan, Ozona, Balmorhea, Fort Stockton, Sheffield, Fort Davis — with I-20, I-10 routes) **TX**

INTERSTATE 10 Cont'd

Exit #	Services
27	Hunter Dr, Viscount Blvd, N ⛽ Alon/7-11, Valero/dsl 🍽 Grand China Buffet, Taco Bell 🏨 La Quinta ⊙ $General, $Tree, Jo-Ann, S ⛽ Alon/7-11, Exxon/dsl 🍽 Whataburger ⊙ Family$, Food City
26	Hawkins Blvd, El Paso, N ⛽ Shamrock, Shell 🍽 Arby's, Chipotle Mexican, Firehouse Subs, Five Guys, Landry's Seafood, Luby's, Olive Garden, Starbucks, Twin Peaks ⊙ AT&T, Barnes&Noble, Best Buy, Dick's, Dillard's, JC Penney, Macy's, Old Navy, Petsmart, Sam's Club/gas, Steinmart, TJ Maxx, Verizon, Walgreens, Walmart, S ⛽ Circle K/dsl 🍽 McDonald's, Village Inn 🏨 Super 8 ⊙ Tony Lama Boots
25	Airway Blvd, N ⛽ Speedway/dsl 🍽 Carino's, Famous Dave's, Starbucks, Whataburger 🏨 Comfort Inn, Courtyard, Hampton Inn, Holiday Inn, Residence Inn ⊙ El Paso Airport, VW/Volvo/Mercedes, S ⛽ Chevron/Subway/dsl/24hr 🏨 Holiday Inn Express, Staybridge Suites
24b	Geronimo Dr, N 🍽 El Taco Tote, Taco Cabana 🏨 Wingate Inn ⊙ $Tree, Costco/gas, Kohl's, Marshall's, Office Depot, Ross, Target, Walgreens, S ⛽ Alon/7-11/dsl, Circle K 🍽 Denny's, IHOP 🏨 Embassy Suites, Hilton Garden, Homewood Suites, Hyatt Place, La Quinta ⊙ URGENT CARE
24a	Trowbridge Dr, N 🍽 Luby's, McDonald's, Whataburger ⊙ Ford, Nissan, Walgreens
23b	US 62/180, to Paisano Dr, N 🍽 Jack-in-the-Box, McDonald's, Whataburger 🏨 Budget Inn, Soluna Inn ⊙ Ford, to Carlsbad, U-Haul
23a	Raynolds St, S 🍽 Arby's 🏨 Best Value Inn, Motel 6 ⊙ 🏥
22b	US 54, Patriot Fwy
22a	Copia St, El Paso, N ⛽ Alon/7-11, Shamrock 🍽 KFC
21	Piedras St, El Paso, N 🍽 Burger King, McDonald's ⊙ Family$
20	Dallas St, Cotton St, N ⛽ Valero 🍽 Church's, Subway
19	TX 20, El Paso, downtown, N ⛽ Chevron, S 🏨 Camino Real Hotel, DoubleTree Inn, Holiday Inn Express
18b	Franklin Ave, Porfirio Diaz St
18a	Schuster Ave, N ⊙ Sun Bowl, S ⊙ to UTEP
16	Executive Ctr Blvd, N ⛽ Valero 🏨 Extend Suites
13b a	US 85, Paisano Dr, to Sunland Park Dr, N ⛽ Valero 🍽 $Tree, Barrigo's Café, Buffalo Wild Wings, Carino's Italian, ChuckE-Cheese, Corner Bakery Cafe, Five Guys, Grand China, IHOP, Olive Garden, PF Chang's, Red Lobster, Sonic, Whataburger ⊙ AT&T, Barnes&Noble, Best Buy, Dillard's, JC Penney, Marshall's, Michael's, Office Depot, Old Navy, Petsmart, Ross, Sprouts Mkt, Target, URGENT CARE, Verizon, vet, S ⛽ Shamrock/dsl, Shell 🍽 Bob-O's Funpark, La Malinche Mexican, Little Caesar's, McDonald's, Sonic, State Line BBQ, Subway 🏨 Best Western, Country Inn Suites, Extended Stay America, Quality Inn, Sleep Inn ⊙ Buick/GMC, Chrysler/Dodge/Jeep, Family$, Vista Mkt
12	Resler Dr (from wb)
11	TX 20, to Mesa St, Sunland Park, N ⛽ Chevron/dsl, Circle K, Circle K/dsl (2), Mobil/dsl 🍽 AJ's Diner, Chick-fil-A, Chili's, CiCi's, Coldstone, Cracker Barrel, El Taco Tote, Famous Dave's BBQ, Golden Corral, Krispy Kreme, Leo's Mexican, PacoWong's Chinese, Panda Express, Pei Wei, Popeye's, Schlotsky's, Souper Salad, Subway, Taco Bell, TX Roadhouse, Wendy's, Wienerschnitzel 🏨 Comfort Suites, EconoLodge, Fairfield Inn, La Quinta (2), LaQuinta, Red Roof Inn, SpringHill Suites ⊙ $General, Albertson's, BigLots, Family$, Firestone/auto, GNC, Home Depot, PepBoys, SteinMart, TirePros, USPO, Verizon, Walmart/McDonald's, S ⛽ Chevron/dsl, Valero/dsl 🍽 Ay Caramba Mexican, Burger King, Church's, Golden Buddha, Jack-in-the-Box, KFC, McDonald's, Pizza Hut,

11	Continued Starbucks, Subway, Taco Cabana, Village Inn 🏨 Days Inn, Motel 6, Travelodge ⊙ $General, $Tree, AutoZone, Big 8 Foods, Hobby Lobby, Martin Tires, Sam's Club/gas, Walgreens
9	Redd Rd, N ⛽ Circle K 🍽 Applebee's, Burger King, Double Dave's Pizza, Peter Piper Pizza, Starbucks, Subway ⊙ Albertson's, Ford, Kohl's, Lowe's, O'Reilly Parts, S ⛽ Circle K/dsl, Valero ⊙ Chevrolet, Honda, Mazda, URGENT CARE, VW, Walmart Mkt
8	Artcraft Rd, N ⛽ Walmart Gas/dsl 🍽 Cane's, Chipotle, McDonald's, Panda Express, Pieology, Starbucks, Taco Bell ⊙ AT&T, Cabela's, Petsmart, Ross, TJ Maxx, Tuesday Morning, Verizon, Walmart, S ⛽ Shell/dsl 🍽 Carl's Jr, Church's, Rudy's BBQ/dsl, Subway 🏨 Hampton Inn, Holiday Inn Express, Quality Inn ⊙ $Tree, Nissan
6	Lp 375, Transmountain Rd, to Canutillo, N ⛽ Speedway/DQ/dsl ⊙ Franklin Mtns SP, to Trans Mountain Rd, S ⛽ Martin Tire, Speedway/McDonald's 🍽 IHOP, Pizza Hut, Sonic, Starbucks, Whataburger ⊙ Discount Tire, El Paso Shops/Famous Brands, GNC
5mm	truck check sta eb
2	Westway, Vinton, N ⛽ Petro/Valero/Subway/dsl/scales/24hr ⊙ American RV Park, Camping World (1mi), PetroLube/tires, ⊙ truck repair/tires
1	S Welcome Ctr eb, full ♿ facilities, info, 🚻, 🏞, litter barrels, petwalk, weigh sta wb 🍽 Great American Steaks ⊙ Anthony RV Ctr, funpark
0	FM 1905, Anthony, N ⛽ ✈FLYING J/Denny's/dsl/LP/RV dump/24hr, ◆Loves/Chester's/McDonald's/dsl/scales/24hr 🍽 Carl's Jr 🏨 Best Value Inn, S ⛽ Alon/7-11/dsl, 🔶 Subway/Wendy's/dsl/24hr/@ 🍽 Burger King, KFC/Taco Bell 🏨 Best Western ⊙ $General, $Tree, Anthony RV Ctr, Big 8 Foods, funpark, tires, truckwash, Walgreens
0mm	Texas/New Mexico state line

INTERSTATE 20

Exit #	Services
636mm	Texas/Louisiana state line
635.5mm	Welcome Ctr/🅿️ wb, full ♿ facilities, 🚻, 🏞, litter barrels, petwalk
635	TX 9, TX 156, to Waskom, N ⛽ Chevron/Burger King/dsl, Exxon/McDonald's/dsl 🍽 DQ, Jim's BBQ ⊙ Family$, USPO
633	US 80, FM 9, FM 134, to Waskom, N ⛽ Shell 🍽 Catfish Village Rest., S ⊙ Miss Ellie's RV Park
628	to US 80, to Frontage Rd
624	FM 2199, to Scottsville
620	FM 31, to Elysian Fields, N ⊙ Timberline RV Park (3mi)
617	US 59, Marshall, 0-2 mi N ⛽ Exxon/dsl, Shell 🍽 Applebee's, Burger King, Cafe Italia, Catfish Express, Golden Chick, Golden Corral, IHOP, In Japan Steaks, Jalapeño Tree, KFC, Little Caesars, LJ Silver, McDonald's, Pizza Hut, Porky's Smokehouse, Sonic, Subway, Taco Bell, Waffle House, Wendy's, Whataburger 🏨 Baymont Inn, Best Western, Best Western, Comfort Suites, Days Inn, Fairfield Inn, Hampton Inn, Quality Inn ⊙ $General, Chevrolet, Chrysler/Dodge/Jeep, Ford/Lincoln, NAPA, Save-A-Lot Foods, Toyota, S ⛽ Chevron/dsl, Conoco/Pony Express/dsl/scales/@, Rudy's/dsl, Valero/dsl 🍽 JW's Diner 🏨 Best Value Inn, EconoLodge, Holiday Inn Express, La Quinta, Motel 6, Super 8 ⊙ Holiday Springs RV Park (2mi)
614	TX 43, to Marshall, S ⊙ to Martin Creek Lake SP
610	FM 3251
604	FM 450, Hallsville, N ⛽ Valero/dsl ⊙ 450 Hitchin' Post RV Park, to Lake O' the Pines

INTERSTATE 20 Cont'd

Exit #	Services
600mm	Mason Creek
599	FM 968, Longview, **N** 🅾 Kenworth, **S** ⛽ Exxon/Sonic/dsl, Valero Travel Plaza/@ 🅾 Cowboy RV Park (5mi), Goodyear Truck Tire, truck repair, truck/rv wash
596	US 259 N, TX 149, to Lake O' Pines, **N** 🍴 Exxon/Grandy's, dsl, Shell/Sonic/TX Smokehouse/dsl 🍴 Burger King, Denny's, Whataburger 🛏 Centerstone Suites, Microtel, Super 8 🅾 🏥, **S** ⛽ Valero/dsl 🍴 Cracker Barrel 🛏 Holiday Inn Express 🅾 to Martin Lake SP
595b a	TX 322, Estes Pkwy, **N** ⛽ Exxon/dsl, EZ Mart 🍴 Hajalmer's Rest., Jack-in-the-Box, McDonald's, Waffle House 🛏 Best Value Inn, Best Western, Express Inn, Guest Inn, Knight's Inn, La Quinta 🅾 Family$, **S** ⛽ Alon/dsl, Murphy USA/dsl 🍴 KFC/Taco Bell 🛏 Baymont Inn, Days Inn, Motel 6 🅾 auto repair, Walmart/Subway
593mm	Sabine River
591	FM 2087, FM 2011, **S** 🅾 Fernbrook RV Park (2mi)
589b a	US 259, TX 31, Kilgore (exits left from wb), **1-3 mi S** ⛽ Chevron/dsl, Exxon/dsl 🍴 Chili's, Kilgore Café, Mazzio's, McDonald's, Taco Bueno 🛏 Best Value Inn, Comfort Suites, Hampton Inn, Holiday Inn Express 🅾 AutoZone, Chevrolet, E Texas Oil Museum, Ford, O'Reilly Parts
587	TX 42, Kilgore, **N** ⛽ Exxon/dsl 🍴 Bodacious BBQ, **S** ⛽ Exxon/Wendy's/dsl 🍴 Denny's 🛏 Days Inn 🅾 Big Rig Lube, E TX Oil Museum, Walmart (3mi)
583	TX 135, to Kilgore, Overton, **N** ⛽ EZmart/dsl 🅾 Liberty City RV Park, Shallow Creek RV Resort
582	FM 3053, Liberty City
579	Joy-Wright Mtn Rd
575	Barber Rd
574mm	🆑 both lanes, ♿ accessible, tables, litter barrels
571b	FM 757, Omen Rd, to Starrville
571a	US 271, to Gladewater, Tyler, **S** ⛽ Cefco/Carl's Jr/Subway/dsl/scales/24hr, Shell/Sonic/Texas Smokehouse/dsl/scales/24hr
567	TX 155, Winona, **N** ⛽ Valero/dsl/24hr, **S** 🍴 DQ (2mi) 🛏 Best Value Inn 🅾 Freightliner, 🏥
565	FM 2015, to Driskill-Lake Rd
562	FM 14, **N** 🍴 Bodacious BBQ 🅾 to Tyler SP, **S** ⛽ 🅿/McDonald's/dsl/scales/24hr 🅾 Northgate RV Park (4mi)
560	Lavender Rd, **S** 🅾 5 Star RV Park (2 mi)
557	Jim Hogg Rd, **N** ⛽ 76/dsl 🅾 TX Rose RV Park
556	US 69, to Tyler, **N** ⛽ Gulf/dsl, Murphy USA/dsl, RaceWay/dsl 🍴 Burger King, Chicken Express, Chili's, Cole's Grill, Domino's, Eastern Buffet, IHOP, KFC\LJ Silver, McDonald's, Pizza Hut, Pizza Inn, Posado's Cafe, Sonic, Subway, Taco Bell 🛏 Best Western, Comfort Suites, Hampton Inn, La Quinta, Motel 6 🅾 $General, Family$, Fred's, Kwik Kar, Lowe's, Verizon, Walmart/Subway, **S** ⛽ Chevron/DQ, Exxon/dsl 🍴 Cracker Barrel, Wendy's 🛏 Best Value Inn
554	Harvey Rd
553	TX 49 S **(toll)**, CR 411
552	FM 849, **N** ⛽ Valero/dsl 🍴 Collin St Bakery, Subway 🅾 vet
548	TX 110, to Grand Saline, **N** ⛽ Exxon/dsl, **S** ⛽ Valero/dsl
546mm	cmv insp sta both lanes
544	Willow Branch Rd, **N** 🅾 Willow Branch RV Park
540	FM 314, to Van, **N** ⛽ Loves/Carl's Jr/dsl/scales/24hr, Loves/Arby's/dsl/scales/24hr 🍴 Bush's Chicken, DQ, Farmhouse Rest., Sonic, Soul Mans BBQ, Subway 🛏 Fairfield Inn, Van Inn
538mm	🆑 both lanes, full ♿ facilities, 🅲, vending, 🛒 litter barrels, petwalk
537	FM 773, FM 16
536	Tank Farm Rd
533	Oakland Rd, to Colfax, **N** ⛽ Shell/🅿/A&W/LJ Silver/dsl
530	FM 1255, Canton
528	FM 17, to Grand Saline, **N** 🅾 Chrysler/Dodge/Jeep
527	TX 19, **N** ⛽ Exxon/dsl 🍴 Bunker Rest., Chicken Express, Denny's, Jalapeño Tree, Whataburger 🛏 Motel 6, Quality Inn, Super 8, **S** ⛽ Circle K/dsl/24hr, Mobil/dsl, Shell/dsl 🍴 Dairy Palace, DJ's BBQ, DQ, King's Fish House, McDonald's, Subway, Taco Bell 🛏 Best Western, Days Inn 🅾 Ford, Mill Creek Ranch RV Resort, to First Monday SP
526	FM 859, to Edgewood, **N** 🅾 water park
523	TX 64, Wills Point, **N** ⛽ Shell/dsl/24hr 🍴 Duke's Rest., Taco Casa 🅾 Bluebird RV Park, repair
521	Myrtle Springs Rd, **S** 🅾 Explore USA RV Ctr, repair, RV camp/dump
519	Turner-Hayden Rd, **S** 🅾 Canton RV Park
516	FM 47, to Wills Point, **N** 🍴 Fourwinds Steaks to Lake Tawakoni, **S** ⛽ Texaco/dsl 🍴 Robertson's Café/gas 🛏 Interstate Motel
512	FM 2965, Hiram-Wills Point Rd
512mm	🅾 cmv inspection sta both lanes
509	Hiram Rd, **S** ⛽ Shell/dsl/cafe/24hr
506	FM 429, FM 2728, College Mound Rd, **N** 🅾 Blue Bonnet Ridge RV Park
503	Wilson Rd, **S** ⛽ TA/Shell/Country Pride/Pizza Hut/Subway/dsl/LP/24hr/@
501	TX 34, to Terrell, **N** ⛽ Exxon/dsl, QT/dsl/scales/24hr, Shell/Subway/dsl 🍴 Church's, Italrican Cafe, Schlotzsky's, Sonic, Starbucks, Steak&Grill, Waffle House 🛏 Baymont Inn, Days Inn, Gateway Inn, La Quinta, Motel 6, Quality Inn 🅾 Home Depot, 🏥, **S** ⛽ Circle K/dsl, Valero/dsl/24hr 🍴 Applebee's, Carmona's Cantina, IHOP, McDonald's, Wendy's 🛏 Holiday Inn Express, Super 8 🅾 Old Navy, Tanger Outlet/famous brands
499b	Rose Hill Rd, to Terrell
499a	to US 80, W to Dallas same as 498
498	FM 148, to Terrell, **N** ⛽ Buc-ee's/dsl, Exxon/Denny's/Subway/dsl, Shell/dsl 🍴 Cane's, Chick-fil-A, Chipotle, DQ, Freddy's, Panda Express, Soulman's BBQ, Starbucks, Taco Bueno, Taco Cabana, Whataburger 🛏 Fairfield Inn, Tru Hilton 🅾 Discount Tire, Marshall's, Petco, Verizon, **S** ⛽ Terrell RV Park
493	FM 1641, **S** ⛽ Exxon/Pizza Inn/Taco Mayo/dsl 🍴 Sonic
491	FM 2932, Helms Tr, to Forney, **N** ⛽ Shell/Subway/dsl
490	FM 741, to Forney
487	FM 740, to Forney, **S** 🅾 Forney RV park
483	Lawson Rd, Lasater Rd
482	Belt Line Rd, to Lasater, **N** ⛽ Exxon/dsl 🍴 Smokehouse BBQ, Sonic, **S** ⛽ Shell/KFC/Pizza Hut/Subway 🅾 RV park

TYLER (vertical, left margin)

CANTON (vertical, center margin)

TERRELL (vertical, center margin)

TX (tab, right margin)

[Legend icons]: = gas = food = lodging = other = rest stop   Copyright 2022 - The Next EXIT ®

DALLAS

INTERSTATE 20 Cont'd

Exit #	Services
481	Seagoville Rd, **N** Shell/Church's/Dickey's BBQ, Valero/dsl Motel 6, **S** Lindy's Rest.
480	I-635, N to Mesquite
479b a	US 175, **S** Marlow/dsl
477	St Augustine Rd, **N** Family$, **S** Shell/dsl Sonic
476	Dowdy Ferry Rd
474	TX 310 N, Central Expsy
473b a	JJ Lemmon Rd, I-45 N to Dallas, S to Houston
472	Bonnie View Rd, **N** FLYING J/Denny's/dsl/LP/24hr, Shell Jack-in-the-Box Express Inn Blue Beacon, Kenworth, Speedco Lube, **S** TA/Exxon/Burger King/Taco Bell/dsl/scales/24hr/@
470	TX 342, Lancaster Rd, **N** Chevron/dsl, Exxon/Popeye's/Subway/dsl/scales/24hr Soulman's BBQ, **S** /Wendy's/dsl/scales/24hr LJ Silver/Taco Bell, McDonald's, Sonic, Whataburger, William's Chicken Days Inn
468	Houston School Rd, **S** Exxon/dsl, QT/dsl Whataburger
467b a	I-35E, N to Dallas, S to Waco, **1 mi N** off of I-35E Chevron, Shell McDonald's
466	S Polk St, **N** Exxon/dsl, Texaco/dsl DQ, Sonic, Subway Family$, **S** Loves/Carl's Jr/dsl/scales/24hr
465	Wheatland/S Hampton Rds, **N** Shell/Subway Chick-fil-A, Chili's, Furr's Cafeteria $Tree, Aldi Foods, CVS Drug, GNC, Office Depot, Petsmart, Ross, Target, **S** Chevron/McDonald's, Murphy USA/dsl, QT/dsl, RaceWay/dsl Arby's, Burger King, Cheddar's, Jack-in-the-Box, Panda Express, Popeye's, Sonic, Spring Creek BBQ, Taco Bell, Wendy's Super 8 Home Depot, Honda, H, Hyundai, Kia, Lowe's, Nissan, Sam's Club/gas, Toyota, Walmart
464b a	US 67, Love Fwy
463	Camp Wisdom Rd, **N** Chevron/7-11, Exxon Catfish King Rest., Denny's, Taco Bell/LJ Silver, Taco Cabana Best Value Inn, Rodeway Inn, Royal Inn, Super 7 $Tree, Chrysler/Dodge/Jeep, **S** Shamrock Burger King, Chubby's Rest., Dave's BBQ, Olive Garden, Red Lobster, Subway, Tortilla Factory
462b a	Duncanville Rd (no EZ wb return), **S** QT, Shell/dsl Church's, Jack-in-the-Box, Los Lupes Mexican, Popeye's, Whataburger Hampton Inn, Hilton Garden, Motel 6 Firestone/auto, Kroger
461	Cedar Ridge Rd, **S** RaceWay/dsl
460	TX 408
458	Mt Creek Pkwy
457	FM 1382, to Grand Prairie, **N** Shell/7-11/dsl, Valero/dsl Waffle House, **S** RaceTrac/dsl Jack-in-the-Box to Joe Pool Lake
456	Carrier Pkwy, to Corn Valley Rd, **N** QT Chick-fil-A, Dickey's BBQ, Domino's, Don Pablo, Popeyes, Sonic, Starbucks, Taco Cabana, Whataburger AutoZone, Home Depot, Kohl's, Target, **S** Shell Baskin-Robbins, Boston Mkt, Chapp's Cafe, Cheddar's, Chili's, Chipotle, Denny's, IHOP, Little Caesar's, McDonald's, Spring Creek BBQ, Subway Holiday Inn Express Albertsons/gas, CVS Drug, GNC, Tom Thumb Foods/gas, Verizon, Walgreens
455	TX 151, **S** QT/dsl
454	Great Southwest Pkwy, **N** Exxon/dsl, Mobil/7-11/dsl Beto's, Carino's Italian, China Dragon, ChuckeCheese, DQ, Golden Corral, KFC, McDonald's, Taco Bell, Taco Bueno, TX Roadhouse, Waffle House, Wendy's, Wienerschnitzel Comfort Suites, Heritage Inn, Quality Inn Firestone/auto, Harley-Davidson, H, U-Haul, **S** 7-11, QT/dsl, Shell/Subway/dsl, Valero/dsl Applebee's, Arby's, Buffalo Wild Wings, Burger King,

FT WORTH

Exit #	Services
454	Continued Schlotzsky's, Sonic La Quinta, Super 8 $Tree, AT&T, Discount Tire, Kroger, Office Depot, Petsmart, RaceTrac/dsl, Sam's Club, to Joe Pool Lake, Walgreens, Walmart/McDonald's
453b a	TX 360
452	Frontage Rd
451	Collins St, New York Ave, **N** Exxon/dsl, RaceTrac/dsl, Rudy's Store/BBQ/dsl Cotton Patch Cafe, Golden Corral, Jack-in-the-Box, Whataburger Chrysler/Dodge/Jeep, Kia/Mazda, VW, URGENT CARE, **S** QT, Shell, Valero/dsl Chicken Express, KFC/Taco Bell, McDonald's, Sonic, Subway, Taco Bueno Hampton Inn Buick/GMC, Nissan
450	Matlock Rd, **N** Abuelo's Mexican, Bar Louie, BJ's Rest., Black eyed Pea, Bone Daddy's, Boomer Jack's Grill, Chuy's Mexican Coldstone, Dave&Buster's, Genghis Grill, Houlihan's, India Grill, Jason's Deli, Kincaide's Burgers, McAlister's Deli, Melting Pot, Mercado Juarez, Mimi's Cafe, PF Changs, Pluckers' Wings, Potbelly, Red Robin, Starbucks, Sweet Tomatoes, The Keg Steaks, Wendy's, Which Wich Courtyard, Quality Inn Residence Inn AT&T, Costco/gas, H, Jo-Ann Fabrics, Lowe's, Old Navy, Petsmart, Staples, World Mkt, **S** 7-11, RaceWay dsl, Shell/7-11 Joe's Pizza, Pizza Patron, Starbucks Fry's Electronics, O'Reilly Parts
449	FM 157, Cooper St, **N** Shell/dsl Cane's, Cheesecake Factory, Chili's, Corner Bakery, Grandy's, Honeybaked Ham, IHOP, In N-Out, McDonald's, Nagoya Japanese, On-the-Border, Outback Steaks, Pei Wei, Razzoo's Cajun Café, Red Lobster, Rockfish Seafood, Salt Grass Steaks, Souper Salad, Spaghetti Whse, Spring Creek BBQ, Whataburger Best Western, Days Inn, Holiday Inn Express, La Quinta, Studio 6, Super 8 Barnes&Noble, Best Buy, Dick's, Dillard's, Discount Tire, JC Penney, Macy's, mall, Michael's Office Depot, Sears/auto, Target, TJ Maxx, Verizon, **S** Shell Applebee's, Arby's, Boston Mkt, Burger St, Carl's Jr, Chick-fil-A, Chipotle, Denny's, El Arroyo, El Fenix Mexican, Lin's Buffet, LJ Silver, Macaroni Grill, McDonald's, Olive Garden, Panda Express, Peter Piper Pizza, Schlotsky's, Starbucks, Subway, Taco Bueno, Taco Cabana, TGIFriday InTown Suites, Microtel $Tree, AAA, Acura, Chevrolet, Ford, Hobby Lobby, Home Depot, Honda, Hyundai, NTB, Ross, Suzuki, Toyota, Walmart/McDonald's
448	Bowen Rd, **N** QT, RaceTrac/dsl Cracker Barrel, Sonic, **S** Shell
447	Kelly-Elliott Rd, Park Springs Blvd, **N** 7-11, Valero, **S** city park, Exxon/Subway
445	Green Oaks Blvd, **N** Conoco/dsl, Shell/7-11/dsl Arby's, Boston Mkt, Braum's, Burger St, Cafe Acapulco, Chapp's Cafe Chick-fil-A, Church's, CiCi's, Colter's BBQ, Fuzzy's Tacos, Hooters, Jack-in-the-Box, Jay Jay Rest., Joe's Pizza, Mijo's Cafe Quizno's, Schlotzsky's, Starbucks, Taco Bell, Taco Cabana, Taco Casa, Tai-Pan, Wendy's, Whataburger $Tree, Ace Hardware, Albertsons, AT&T, CVS Drug, Firestone, Kroger/dsl, Meineke, Office Depot, Verizon, Walgreens, **S** 7-11, Murphy Express dsl, QT/dsl, Valero/dsl Cheddar's, Corky's Pizza, Golden Buffet, IHOP, McDonald's, Pancho's Mexican, Panda Express, Sonic, Subway, Taco Bueno, Waffle House $General, Auto Zone, BigLots, Discount Tire, O'Reilly Parts, Tuesday Morning, vet, Walmart/Subway
444	US 287 S, to Waxahatchie same as 445, from eb
443	Bowman Springs Rd (from wb)
442b a	I-820 to Ft Worth, US 287 bus, **N** Valero Great Western Inn, Knights Inn, **S** QT/dsl
441	Anglin Dr, Hartman Lane, **N** Woodspring Suites, **S** Conoco/dsl

INTERSTATE 20 Cont'd

Exit #	Services
440b	Forest Hill Dr, **S** ⛽ Shell/7-11/dsl 🍴 Braum's, Capt D's, CiCi's Pizza, Jack-in-the-Box, Luby's, Sonic, Starbucks, Subway, Taco Bell 🏨 La Quinta ⊙ $General, $Tree, AutoZone, CVS Drug, Discount Tire, O'Reilly Parts, Super 1 Foods, Walgreens
440a	Wichita St, **N** ⛽ Chevron/dsl, QT/dsl 🍴 #1 Chinese, Starbucks, Taco Casa, Wendy's, **S** ⛽ Texaco/dsl, Valero 🍴 Chicken Express, Denny's, Domino's, McDonald's, Pizza Hut, Schlotzsky's, Taco Bueno, Whataburger 🏨 Best Western, Comfort Inn, Hampton Inn
439	Campus Dr, **N** ⊙ Chrysler/Dodge/Jeep, Ford, **S** ⊙ Sam's Club/gas
438	Oak Grove Rd, **S** ⛽ Valero
437	I-35W, N to Ft Worth, S to Waco
436b	Hemphill St, **N** ⛽ Shell/dsl, **S** ⊙ Chevrolet
436a	FM 731 (from eb), to Crowley Ave, **N** ⛽ Conoco/dsl, Valero/dsl 🍴 China Express ⊙ $General, Sav-a-Lot Foods, **S** 🍴 Burger-Box, Pizza Hut/Taco Bell, Subway ⊙ transmissions
435	McCart St, **N** ⛽ 76/dsl, Shamrock, **S** ⛽ Mobil/dsl
434b	Trail Lakes Dr, **S** ⛽ Shell 🍴 Sonic, Starbucks, Subway, Wendy's ⊙ CVS Drug, Family$
434a	Granbury Rd
433	Hulen St, **N** ⛽ Shell/dsl 🍴 Chef Chen, ChuckECheese, Honeybaked Ham, Hooters, Olive Garden, Papa Murphy's, Souper Salad, Subway, TX Roadhouse 🏨 TownePlace Suites ⊙ Albertsons, Home Depot, NTB, Petsmart, Sprouts Mkt, TJ Maxx, **S** 🍴 Abuelo's Mexican, BJ's Rest., Denny's, Five Guys, In-N-Out, Jack-in-the-Box, Kincaide's Burgers, McDonald's, Panera Bread, Pizza Inn, Potbelly, Red Lobster, Red Robin 🏨 Hampton Inn ⊙ Barnes&Noble, Dillard's, Hobby Lobby, Macy's, Michael's, Office Depot, Old Navy, Ross, Sears/auto
431	(432 from wb), TX 183, Bryant-Irvin Rd, **N** ⛽ Chevron 🍴 Chipotle Mexican, Genghis Grill, Keg Steaks, Mimi's Café, On-the-Border, Taste of Asia ⊙ Best Buy, Cavender's Boots, Kohl's, Lowe's, Petsmart, Sam's Club/gas, **S** ⛽ Chevron, Shell/dsl 🍴 Blackeyed Pea, Chick-fil-A, Chicken Express, Cousin's BBQ, Fox & Hound, Fuddruckers, IHOP, Jimmy John's, Lonestar Oysters, Outback Steaks, Pei Wei, Pizza Hut, Razzoo's Cajun, Rio Mambo, SaltGrass Steaks, Schlotzsky's, Sonic, Starbucks, Subway, Szechuan 🏨 Courtyard, Extended Stay America, Holiday Inn Express, Homewood Suites, Hyatt Place, La Quinta ⊙ AT&T, Costco/gas, Firestone/auto, Ford, Goodyear/auto, H, Infiniti, Kwik Kar, Lexus, Mazda, PetCo, Staples, Target, Verizon, Walgreens
430mm	Clear Fork Trinity River
429b	Winscott Rd, **N** ⛽ Circle K/dsl 🍴 Cracker Barrel 🏨 Best Western, Comfort Suites
429a	US 377, to Granbury, **S** ⛽ QT/dsl, RaceTrac/dsl, Shell/dsl, Valero 🍴 7-11/dsl, Arby's, Braum's, Burger King, Chick-fil-A, Chicken Express, Domino's, Golden Chick, Jack-in-the-Box, KFC/Taco Bell, McDonald's, NY Pizza, Panda Express, Pizza Hut, Ricky's BBQ, Sonic, Starbucks, Subway, Taco Casa, Taco Villa, Waffle House, Waffle House, Whataburger 🏨 Motel 6 ⊙ $General, AutoZone, CVS Drug, O'Reilly Parts, USPO, Walgreens, Walmart
428	I-820, N around Ft Worth
426	RM 2871, Chapin School Rd
425	Markum Ranch Rd, **S** ⛽ Shell/Taco Bell/Dunkin'/dsl/scales/24hr
421	I-30 E (from eb), to Ft Worth
420	FM 1187, Aledo, Farmer parking & ride
419mm	weigh sta eb
418	Ranch House Rd, Willow Park, **N** ⛽ Exxon/Taco Casa, Shell/dsl 🍴 Pizza Hut, Sonic, Subway, Whataburger, **S** ⛽ Chevron/dsl

418	Continued 🍴 Alex's Pizza, Chicken Express, Domino's, McDonald's, Railhead BBQ 🏨 Quality Inn ⊙ $General, Brookshire Foods/gas, Cowtown RV Park, Texas RV Outlet
417mm	**N** 🍴 Cafe 23:5, Sunny Street Cafe ⊙ H
415	FM 5, Mikus Rd, Annetta, **N** ⊙ vet, **S** ⛽ Shell/dsl ⊙ 415 RV Ctr
413	(414 from wb), US 180 W, Lake Shore Dr, **N** ⛽ Murphy USA/dsl, RaceTrac/dsl, Shell/dsl 🍴 Chick-fil-A, DQ, Golden Chick, McDonald's, Paleo's Pizza, Sonic, Subway, Taco Bell, Waffle House ⊙ Buick/Cadillac/Chevrolet/GMC, Ford, HEB Mkt, Hyundai, Lincoln, Nissan, Toyota, Verizon, Walgreens, Walmart/Subway, **S** ⛽ Valero/dsl
411	Service Rd (from wb), same as 413
410	Bankhead Hwy, **S** ⛽ Loves/Subway/dsl/24hr
409	FM 2552 N, Clear Lake Rd, **N** ⛽ Petro/Valero/Iron Skillet/dsl/24hr/@ 🍴 Antonio's Mexican, Granny's Kitchen, Jack-in-the-Box, Little Panda Chinese, Popeyes 🏨 Heritage Inn, Sleep-Go Motel ⊙ Blue Beacon, H, **S** ⛽ Shell/dsl
408	TX 171, FM 1884, FM 51, Tin Top Rd, Weatherford, **N** ⛽ Exxon, Mobil, Murphy USA/dsl 🍴 Applebee's, Baker's Ribs, Braum's, Buffalo Wild Wings, Cane's, Chicken Express, China Harbor, CiCi's Pizza, Cotton Patch Cafe, IHOP, Kincaide's Burgers, LJ Silver, Logan's Roadhouse, McAlister's Deli, McDonald's, MT Rest., Olive Garden, Panda Express, Rosa's Cafe, Schlotzsky's, Starbucks, Subway, Taco Bell, Taco Bueno, Taco Cabana, Whataburger, Wild Mushroom Steaks 🏨 La Quinta, Sleep Inn, Super 8 ⊙ $Tree, AT&T, AutoZone, Belk, Christian Bros Auto, Discount Tire, Firestone/auto, JC Penney, Just Brakes, Michael's, TJ Maxx, Verizon, Walgreens, Walmart/Subway, **S** ⛽ Exxon/Subway/dsl, Shell/Burger King/dsl 🍴 Chick-fil-A, Chili's, Chipotle, Cracker Barrel, Honey Bee Ham, On-the-Border, Tokyo Japanese Steaks, Waffle House, Whataburger 🏨 Best Western+, Candlewood Suites, Comfort Suites, Fairfield Inn, Hampton Inn, Holiday Inn Express, Motel 6, Quality Inn, Super Value Inn ⊙ Best Buy, GNC, Kohl's, Lowe's, NTB, Petsmart, Ross, Target, URGENT CARE
407	Tin Top Rd (from eb), **N** ⊙ Home Depot, **S** ⊙ KOA, same as 408
406	Old Dennis Rd, **N** ⛽ QT/dsl/scales/24hr, Truck'n Travel 🍴 Chuck Wagon Rest. 🏨 Quest Inn, **S** ⛽ Pilot/Wendy's/dsl/scales/24hr 🏨 EconoLodge, Quality 1 Motel ⊙ Boss Shop Repair, Honda
404	Williams Memorial Dr
402	(403 from wb), TX 312, to Weatherford
397	FM 1189, to Brock, **N** ⛽ Chevron/dsl ⊙ Oak Creek RV Park
394	FM 113, to Millsap
393mm	Brazos River
391	Gilbert Pit Rd
386	US 281, to Mineral Wells, Stephenville, **N** ⛽ Shell/Subway/dsl ⊙ Gilbert Pecans, **S** ⛽ Chevron/Maverick TC/Taco Casa/dsl, Sunoco/Stripes/Taco Co/dsl 🍴 DQ

WEATHERFORD

🡹E INTERSTATE 20 Cont'd

Exit #	Services
380	FM 4, Santo, S 🅞 RV Park
376	Blue Flat Rd, Panama Rd
373	TX 193, Gordon
370	TX 108 S, FM 919, Gordon, N 🅟 Texaco/Bar-B/dsl, S 🅟 Exxon/dsl 🅞 Cactus Rose RV Park, Longhorn Inn/Country Store
367	TX 108 N, Mingus, N 🅕 Smoke Stack Café 🅞 Thurber Sta, S 🅕 NY Hill Rest.
364mm	Palo Pinto Creek
363	Tudor Rd, 🏞, tables, litter barrels
362mm	Bear Creek, 🏞 both lanes, tables, litter barrels
361	TX 16, to Strawn
359mm	🆁🆂 wb, full 🅗 facilities, 🏞, litter barrels, petwalk
358	(from wb), Frontage Rd
356mm	Russell Creek
354	Lp 254, Ranger
353	🆁🆂 eb, full 🅗 facilities, 🏞, litter barrels, vending
351	(352 from wb), College Blvd
349	FM 2461, Ranger, N 🅟 Loves/Godfather's/Subway/dsl/scales/24hr 🅕 DQ 🅛 Rodeway Inn 🅞 RL RV Park, S 🅟 Phillips 66/dsl, repair
347	FM 3363 (from wb), Olden, S 🅕 Starr Stop Cafe
345	FM 3363 (from eb), Olden, S 🅕 Starr Stop Cafe
343	TX 112, FM 570, Eastland, Lake Leon, N 🅟 Alon/7-11/Subway, Murphy USA/dsl, Shell/Taco Casa/dsl 🅕 Chicken Express, Domino's, DQ, Heff's Burgers, McDonald's, Pizza Heaven, Pizza Hut, Sonic, Taco Bell 🅛 Holiday Inn Express, La Quinta, Super 8/RV park 🅞 $General, AT&T, AutoZone, Buick/Cadillac/Chevrolet/GMC, Chrysler/Dodge/Jeep, Ford, O'Reilly Parts, TrueValue, Walmart, S 🅟 Exxon/dsl 🅕 Pulido's Mexican 🅛 Budget Host, Days Inn
340	TX 6, Eastland, N 🅟 Valero/dsl 🅞 🅗
337	spur 490, N 🅞 The Wild Country RV Park
332	US 183, Cisco, N 🅟 Alon/Allsups/dsl 🅕 Chicken Express, DQ, Pizza Heaven, Sonic, Subway 🅛 Cisco Inn, Executive Inn/RV Park 🅞 $General, Family$, Hilton Mon (1mi), NAPA
330	TX 206, Cisco, N 🅟 Sunoco/Stripes/Tacos/dsl/scales/24hr 🅛 Lone Star Inn 🅞 🅗, S 🅟 FLYING J/Denny's/dsl/scales/24hr
329mm	🏞 wb, tables, litter barrels, 🅗 accessible
327mm	🏞 eb, tables, litter barrels, 🅗 accessible
324	Scranton Rd
322	Cooper Creek Rd
320	FM 880 N, FM 2945 N, to Moran
319	FM 880 S, Putnam, N 🅟 Fillin Sta/café 🅞 USPO
316	Brushy Creek Rd
313	FM 2228
310	Finley Rd
308	Lp 20, Baird
307	US 283, Clyde, N 🅟 Loves/Chester's/Subway/dsl/scales/24hr 🅕 DQ 🅛 Baird Motel/RV park/dump, S 🅟 Alon/Allsups/7-11, Conoco/dsl 🅕 Robertson's Café
306	FM 2047, Baird, N 🅞 Chevrolet/GMC, Hanner RV Ctr
303	Union Hill Rd
301	FM 604, Cherry Lane, N 🅟 Exxon/dsl 🅕 McDonald's, Sonic, Whataburger 🅞 NAPA, S 🅟 Alon/7-11, Alon/7-11/dsl 🅕 Chicken Express, Pizza House, Subway 🅞 Family$, United Mkt, USPO
300	FM 604 N, Clyde, N 🅞 Chrysler/Dodge/Jeep, S 🅟 Texaco/dsl 🅞 White's RV Park/dump
299	FM 1707, Hays Rd
297	FM 603, Eula Rd

296.5mm	🆁🆂 both lanes, full 🅗 facilities, 🅒, 🏞, litter barrels, petwalk wifi
294	Buck Creek Rd, N 🅞 Big Counry RV Ctr/park, Buck Creek RV Park/dump, S 🅞 Abilene RV Park
292b	Elmdale Rd
292a	Lp 20 (exits left from wb)
290	TX 36, Lp 322, S 🅞 🚲, zoo
288	TX 351, N 🅟 Alon/7-11/dsl, Murphy USA/dsl 🅕 Buffalo Wild Wings, Chick-fil-A, Chili's, Cracker Barrel, DQ, Golden Chick, Jason's Deli, Oscar's Mexican, Panda Express, Subway, Taco Casa, Wendy's 🅛 Comfort Suites, Courtyard, Days Inn, Executive Inn, Holiday Inn Express, Knights Inn, Quality Inn, Residence Inn, TownePlace Suites, Whitten Inn 🅞 $Tree, AT&T, Lowe's, Walmart/Subway, S 🅛 Super 8 🅞 🅗
286c	FM 600, Abilene, N 🅟 Alon/7-11/dsl, Alon/Allsups/dsl 🅕 Denny's 🅛 Best Western, Hampton Inn, Holiday Inn, La Quinta, 🅟 Alon/7-11/dsl 🅛 Sleep Inn
286	US 83, Pine St, Abilene, S 🅟 Alon/Allsups 🅛 Frontier Inn 🅞
285	Old Anson Rd, S 🅟 Alon/Allsups/dsl 🅛 Best Value Inn
283b	N US 277, U83, Anson
283a	US 277 S, US 83 (exits left from wb)
282	FM 3438, Shirley Rd, S 🅛 Motel 6 🅞 KOA
281	Fulwiler Rd, to Dyess AFB, S 🅞 to Dyess AFB
279	US 84 E, to Abilene, 1-3 mi S access to facilities
278	Lp 20, N 🅟 Conoco/dsl/24hr 🅞 dsl repair, S 🅟 Westgo TC/Phillips 66/Huddle House/dsl/scales/24hr/@ 🅞 Mack Trucks/Volvo
277	FM 707, Tye, N 🅟 FLYING J/Denny's/dsl/LP/24hr 🅞 Peterbilt, truck lube, Tye RV Park, S 🅟 Alon/7-11/dsl 🅞 Southern Tire Mart, USPO
274	Wells Lane
272	Wimberly Rd
270	FM 1235, Merkel, N 🅟 Alon/dsl/24hr, Conoco/dsl
269	FM 126, N 🅕 Sonic, Subway 🅛 Scottish Inn, S 🅟 Alon/7-11 dsl, Phillips 66/dsl 🅕 DQ, Skeet's BBQ 🅞 CarQuest, Family$
267	Lp 20, Merkel, S 1mi access to gas, food, lodging
266	Derstine Rd
264	Noodle Dome Rd
263	Lp 20, Trent, N 🅞 RV Park
262	FM 1085, S 🅟 Alon/7-11/dsl
261	Lp 20, Trent
259	Sylvester Rd
258	White Flat Rd oil wells
257mm	🆁🆂 both lanes, full 🅗 facilities, 🅒, vending, 🏞, litter barrel petwalk
256	Stink Creek Rd
255	Adrian Rd
251	Eskota Rd
249	FM 1856, N 🅞 Lonestar RV Park
247	TX 70 N, Sweetwater
246	Alabama Ave, Sweetwater
245	Arizona Ave (from wb) same as 244
244	TX 70 S, Sweetwater, N 🅟 Alon/7-11/dsl/24hr, Chevron, Subway/dsl, Murphy USA/dsl 🅕 Dickey's BBQ, Domino's, DQ, Golden Chick, McDonald's, Subway, Wendy's 🅛 Best Western+, Budget Inn, Motel 6, Quality Inn 🅞 AT&T, AutoZone, 🅗 Medicine Place Drug, Verizon, Walmart, S 🅟 Shell/dsl 🅕 Big Boy's BBQ, Buck's BBQ, Great Wall Buffet, Schlotzsky's, Skeet Grill, Taco Bell 🅛 Country Hearth Inn, Hampton Inn, Holiday Inn Express, La Quinta, Ranch House Motel/rest., Stay Express Inn 🅞 Chaparral RV Park, Ford, Rainbolt RV Park
243	Hillsdale Rd, Robert Lee St, N 🅞 Family RV Ctr

ABILENE

SWEETWATER

�¥E INTERSTATE 20 Cont'd

Exit #	Services
242	Hopkins Rd, **N** 🅖 **Loves**/Arby's/dsl/scales/24hr 🛏 Microtel, **S** 🍴 TA/Alon/Pizza Hut/Popeye's/dsl/scales/24hr/@ 🅾 Rolling Plains RV Park, truck wash, truck/tire repair
241	Lp 20, Sweetwater, **N** 🅖 gas 🍴 food 🛏 lodging, **S** 🅾 RV camping
240	Lp 170, **N** 🅾 ✈, camping
239	May Rd
238b a	US 84 W, Blackland Rd
237	Cemetery Rd
236	FM 608, Roscoe, **N** 🅖 Alon/dsl, Sunoco/Stripes/Taco Co/dsl 🅾 NAPA, **S** 🍴 Retta Mae's Rest
235	to US 84, Roscoe
230	FM 1230 many wind turbines
229mm	🆁🆂 wb, tables, litter barrels, ♿ accessible
228mm	🆁🆂 eb, tables, litter barrels, ♿ accessible
227	Narrell Rd
226b	Lp 20 (from wb), Loraine
226a	FM 644 N, Wimberly Rd
225	FM 644 S, **1 mi S** 🅖 access to gas 🍴 food
224	Lp 20, to Loraine, **1 mi S** 🅖 gas 🍴 food
223	Lucas Rd, **S** 🅾 223 RV Park
221	Lasky Rd
220	FM 1899
219	Lp 20, Country Club Rd, Colorado City
217	TX 208 S, **N** 🅖 Sunoco/Stripes/Taco Co/dsl/scales/24hr 🛏 La Quinta, **S** 🍴 Santiago's 🅾 Lone Wolf RV Park
216	TX 208 N, **N** 🅖 Chevron/Subway/dsl 🍴 DQ 🛏 Sleep Inn, **S** 🅖 Sunoco/Stripes/Taco Co/dsl 🍴 Golden Chick, Pizza Hut, Sonic 🛏 American Inn, Hotel Texas, Motel 6, Super 8 🅾 $General, City RV Park, 🅷, Parts+
215	FM 3525, Rogers Rd, **N** 🛏 Motel 6 Extended, **2 mi S** 🅖 access to gas 🍴 food 🅾 🅷
214.5mm	Colorado River
213	Lp 20, Enderly Rd, Colorado City
212	FM 1229
211mm	Morgan Creek
210	FM 2836, **S** 🅖 Country Store 🅾 camping, 🆁🆂, to Lake Colorado City SP
209	Dorn Rd
207	Lp 20, Westbrook
206	FM 670, to Westbrook
204mm	**N** full ♿ facilities, 🅲, 🆁🆂, litter barrels, petwalk
200	Conaway Rd
199	Iatan Rd
195	Frontage Rd (from eb)
194a	E Howard Field Rd
192	FM 821 many oil wells
191mm	🆁🆂 eb, full ♿ facilities, 🅲, 🆁🆂, litter barrels, petwalk
190	Snyder Field Rd
189	McGregor Rd
188	FM 820, Coahoma, **N** 🅖 Sunoco/Stripes/Taco Co/dsl 🍴 DQ 🛏 Coahoma Inn 🅾 Coahoma RV Park, USPO
186	Salem Rd, Sand Springs
184	Moss Lake Rd, Sand Springs, **N** 🅖 Alon/dsl 🅾 $General, **S** 🅾 RV camping
182	Midway Rd
181b	Refinery Rd, **N** 🅖 Alon Refinery
181a	FM 700, **N** 🅾 ✈, RV camping, **2 mi S** 🅾 🅷
179	US 80, Big Spring, **S** 🅖 Alon/7-11 🍴 Denny's 🛏 Camlot Inn, Quality Inn, Super 8 🅾 $General, Buick/Cadillac/Chevrolet

BIG SPRING

Exit #	Services
178	TX 350, Big Spring, **N** 🅖 Shell/dsl 🅾 tire/truck service, **S** 🅖 Pilot/McDonald's/dsl/scales/24hr
177	US 87, Big Spring, **N** 🅖 Exxon/dsl, TA/Subway/Popeye's/dsl/scales/24hr/@ 🍴 Texas Cajan Cafe 🛏 Advantage Inn, La Quinta, Plaza Inn, W Texas Inn, **S** 🅖 Alon/dsl, Sunoco/Stripes/dsl 🍴 Casa Blanca Mexican, DQ, McAlister's Deli, Starbucks 🛏 Baymont Inn, Best Western, Hampton Inn, Sleep Inn MainStay Suites, Spring City Inn, TownePlace Suites 🅾 Chrysler/Dodge/Jeep
176	TX 176, Andrews
174	Lp 20 E, Big Springs, **S** 🅖 Shell/dsl 🅾 ✈, Big Spring SP, 🅷
172	Cauble Rd
171	Moore Field Rd
169	FM 2599
168mm	🆁🆂 both lanes, tables, litter barrels
165	FM 818
158	Lp 20 W, to Stanton, **N** 🅾 RV camping
156	TX 137, Lamesa, **S** 🅖 Phillips 66/Stripes/Subway/dsl/24hr 🍴 Sonic 🛏 Comfort Inn, Stanton Inn, Super 8
154	US 80, Stanton, **2 mi S** 🅖 access to gas 🍴 food 🛏 lodging
151	FM 829 (from wb)
144	Loop 250, **2-3 mi N** 🅾 services in Midland
143mm	Frontage Rd (from eb)
142mm	🆁🆂 both lanes, tables, litter barrels, hits marker
140	FM 307 (from eb)
138	TX 158, FM 715, Greenwood, **N** 🅖 Pilot/dsl, Valero/dsl 🍴 KD's BBQ, Whataburger, **S** 🅖 Flying J/Moe's/dsl/scales/24hr, Sunoco/Stripes/Subway/dsl, Sunoco/Stripes/Taco Co/dsl 🛏 Baymont Inn
137	Old Lamesa Rd, **N** 🛏 Mainstay Suites
136	TX 349, Midland, **N** 🅖 Murphy USA/dsl, Sunoco/Stripes/Taco Co/dsl 🍴 Cici's Pizza, Domino's, IHOP, Jack-in-the-Box, Little Caesar's, McAlister's Deli, McDonald's, Sonic, Starbucks 🛏 Best Western+, Candlewood Suites, Comfort Inn, Country Inn&Suites, Holiday Inn Express, Microtel, Quality Inn, Super 8, West Texas Inn 🅾 $General, $Tree, Advance Parts, AutoZone, Chavez Tires, Discount Tire, Family$, Petroleum Museum, Verizon, Walmart/Subway, **S** 🅖 Daves Gas/NAPA/dsl, Exxon/Burger King/dsl, Pilot/dsl, Stripes/Taco Co/dsl
135	Cotton Flat Rd, **S** 🅾 🅷
134	Midkiff Rd, **0-1 mi N (Wall St)** 🅖 Alon/7-11, Exxon/dsl, Shell, Sunoco/Stripes/Subway/dsl 🍴 Denny's, DQ 🛏 Best Value Inn, Bradford Inn, Days Inn, Executive Inn, La Quinta, Studio 6, Super 8 🅾 Chevrolet, Chrysler/Dodge/Jeep, Ford/ Lincoln, Honda, 🅷, Midland RV Park, Subaru
131	TX 158, Midland, **N** 🅖 Super 7 Inn 🅾 Midland RV Park, **S** 🅖 **Loves**/Chester's/Subway/dsl/scales/24hr 🛏 Suburban Inn

MIDLAND

🛣 E INTERSTATE 20 Cont'd

Exit #	Services
126	FM 1788, N 🛢 🄿🄸🄻🄾🅃/McDonald's/dsl/scales/24hr, Sunoco/Stripes/Taco Co/dsl 🍴 Steak'n Shake, Subway 🅾 🍴, Carquest, Main Street Mkt/Subway/dsl, museum, Western Auto
121	Lp 338, Odessa, 0-3 mi N (TX 191) 🛢 Alon/7-11, Stripes/Taco Co/dsl 🍴 Carino's, Casa Ole, Cheddar's, Chili's, Dickey's BBQ, Domino's, Fazoli's, Five Guys, Fuddruckers, Genghis Grill, Golden Corral, Harigan's Grill, Hooters, IHOP, KFC, Logan's Roadhouse, McDonald's, Panda Express, Pizza Hut, Red Lobster, Rosa's Cafe, Schlotzsky's, Sonic, Subway, Twin Peaks Rest, Wendy's, Whataburger 🏠 Comfort Suites, Days Inn, Elegante Hotel, Fairfield Inn, Hampton Inn Express, Hilton Garden, Holiday Inn, Holiday Inn Express, La Quinta, Parkway Inn, Quality Inn, Sleep Inn, Studio 6, Super Inn 🅾 $General, $Tree, AT&T, Buick/GMC, Chevrolet, Dillard's, Hobby Lobby, Home Depot, Honda, Hyundai, JC Penney, Lowe's, Mazda, Mkt Street, Nissan, Sam's Club/gas, Staples, Target, Toyota, U of TX Permian Basin, USPO, Walmart/Subway, S 🛢 🄵🄻🅈🄸🄽🄶 J/McDonald's/dsl/scales/24hr
120	JBS Pkwy, N 🏠 Candlewood Suites, Comfort Inn, Staybridge Suites, Super 8 🅾 Mack/Volvo
118	FM 3503, Grandview Ave, N 🛢 Alon/dsl 🅾 Freightliner/Peterbilt
116	US 385, Odessa, N 🛢 Chevron/dsl, Stripes/Taco Co/dsl 🍴 DQ, La Margarita 🏠 Delux Inn, Ramada, Villa West Inn 🅾 $General, city park, Family$, 🄷, S 🛢 Alon/dsl, Valero/dsl 🏠 Holiday Inn Express, MainStay Suites, Motel 6
115	FM 1882, N 🛢 Sunoco/Stripes/Taco Co/dsl, S 🛢 🄻🄾🅅🄴🅂/McDonald's/Subway/dsl/scales/24hr 🅾 Blue Beacon
113	TX 302, Odessa
112	FM 1936, Odessa, N 🛢 Main Street Mkt/dsl
108	Moss Ave, Meteor Crater, N 🛢 Road Ranger/Church's/Subway/dsl/scales/24hr, S 🛢 🄿🄸🄻🄾🅃/PJ Fresh/Dunkin'/dsl/scales/24hr
104	FM 866, Meteor Crater Rd, Goldsmith, N 🅾 RV park
103.5mm	weigh sta both directions
101	FM 1601, to Fenwell, Penwell
93	FM 1053, to Ft Stockton
86	TX 41, N 🅾 Monahans Sandhills SP, S 🅾 🄿🄸🄻🄾🅃/Dunkin'/Subway/dsl/scales 24hr
83	US 80, Monahans, 2 mi N 🅾 🄷, RV camping
80	TX 18, Monahans, N 🛢 Chevron/dsl 🍴 Bar-H Steaks, DQ, Great Wall Buffet, McDonald's, Pappy's BBQ, Pizza Hut, Sonic 🏠 Candlewood Suites, Hampton Inn, Holiday Inn Express, Holiday Inn Express 🅾 $General, Family$, 🄷, Lowe's Foods, O'Reilly Parts, repair/tires, Verizon, S 🛢 Alon/dsl, Sunoco/Stripes/Subway/dsl, Texaco/Huddle House/dsl/24hr 🍴 Huddle House 🏠 Best Value Inn, Best Western+, Comfort Inn, Texan Inn 🅾 Buick/Chevrolet/GMC, Chrysler/Dodge/Jeep, RV Park, vet
79	Lp 464, Monahans, S 🏠 La Quinta
76	US 80, Monahans, 2 mi N 🅾 RV camping, to Million Barrel Museum
73	FM 1219, Wickett, N 🛢 Alon/Allsup's/dsl, S 🛢 Main St/Shell/Subway/dsl
70	TX 65
69.5mm	🆁🆂 both lanes, full ♿ facilities, 🚻, 🏭, litter barrels, petwalk, wi-fi
66	TX 115, FM 1927, to Pyote, N 🛢 Alon/dsl, S 🍴 🄿🄸🄻🄾🅃/dsl/scales/24hr
58	Frontage Rd, multiple oil wells
52	Lp 20 W, to Barstow
49	FM 516, to Barstow

48mm	Pecos River
44	Collie Rd
42	US 285, Pecos, N 🛢 ✈FLYING J/Denny's/dsl/scales/24hr, Alon, Sunoco/Stripes/dsl/e85 🍴 Alfredo's Mexican, Burger King, DQ, El Rodeo Mexican, Golden Palace Chinese, KFC, Pizza Hut, Sonic 🏠 Holiday Inn Express, Quality Inn, Staybridge Suites, Super 7, Travelodge, Woodspring Suites 🅾 AutoZone, museum, tire repair, Walmart, S 🛢 🄻🄾🅅🄴🅂/McDonald's/Subway/Chester's/dsl/scales/24hr/@ 🏠 Microtel
40	Country Club Dr, N 🛢 🍴 Dickey's BBQ, Domino's 🏠 Cobblestone Inn, Comfort Suites, Fairfield Inn 🅾 st patrol, S 🛢 Stripes. Subway 🍴 Alpine Lodge Rest. 🏠 Best Western+, La Quinta 🅾 municipal park, Pecos Park/Zoo, RV camping
39	TX 17, Pecos, N 🛢 🄿🄸🄻🄾🅃/Dunkin'/PJ Fresh/dsl/scales/24hr 🏠 Home 2 Suites 🅾 🄷, S 🛢 Sunoco/Stripes/Subway/dsl/24hr 🏠 Hampton Inn, La Bonita Inn 🅾 Buick/Chevrolet/GMC, Pecos Tire, Trapark RV Park
37	Lp 20 E
33	FM 869, N 🛢 Exxon/Subway/dsl, Shell/Whataburger/dsl 🍴 Bob's BBQ, DQ, Los Enchiladas, Pizza Boy, Sonic
29	Shaw Rd, S 🅾 to TX AM Ag Sta
25mm	🆁🆂 both lanes, tables, litter barrels, ♿ accessible
22	FM 2903, to Toyah, N 🛢 Valero/dsl
13	McAlpine Rd
7	Johnson Rd
3	Stocks Rd
	I-20 begins/ends on I-10, 187mm.

🛣 N INTERSTATE 27

Exit #	Services
	I-27 begins/ends on I-40, exit 70 in Amarillo.
123b	I-40, W to Albuquerque, E to OK City
123a	26th Ave, E 🛢 DJ Gas
122c	from sb only
122a	34th Ave, Tyler St, E 🅾 $General, Toot'n Totem 🍴 Sonic
122b	FM 1541, Washington St, Parker St, Moss Lane, W 🍴 Taco Bell, Thai Express
121a	Hawthorne Dr, Austin St, E 🏠 Amarillo Motel, W 🅾 Scottie' Transmissions
121b	Georgia St, E 🛢 Murphy USA/dsl 🅾 Buick/GMC, Honda, Mazda, Subaru, Walmart/McDonald's
120b	45th Ave, E 🍴 Waffle House 🅾 O'Reilly Parts, W 🛢 Toot'n Totum, Valero 🍴 Abuelo's Mexican, Donut Stop, Gatti's Pizza, Grandma's Cocina, McDonald's, Sonic, Whataburger 🅾 $General, Advance Parts, BMW, Chrysler/Dodge/Jeep, Drug Emporium, vet, Walgreens
120a	Republic Ave
119b a	(from sb) Western St, 58th Ave, E 🛢 Phillips 66/dsl 🍴 Sonic, Subway 🅾 $General, Fiesta Foods, W 🛢 Valero/dsl 🍴 Arby's, Braum's, Thai Palace, Wendy's 🅾 Aamco, U-Haul, USPO, Walgreens
119a	(from nb) W Hillside
117	Bell St, Arden Rd, W 🛢 Valero/dsl 🍴 Popeye's, Sonic 🅾 $General
116	Lp 335, Hollywood Rd, E 🛢 🄻🄾🅅🄴🅂/Subway/dsl/scales/24hr, Phillips 66/dsl 🍴 McDonald's, Waffle House, Whataburger 🏠 Comfort Suites, Motel 6, W 🏠 Holiday Inn Express 🅾 🄷 (8mi
115	Sundown Lane
113	McCormick Rd, E 🅾 $General, Ford, W 🅾 Family Camping Ctr
112	FM 2219, E 🅾 Stater's RV Ctr
111	Rockwell Rd, W 🅾 Buick/GMC
110	US 87 S, US 60 W, Canyon

Side tabs: TX, ODESSA, MONAHANS, PECOS, AMARILLO

▲N INTERSTATE 27 Cont'd

Exit #	Services
109	Buffalo Stadium Rd, W 🅾 stadium
108	FM 3331, Hunsley Rd
106	TX 217, to Palo Duro Cyn SP, Canyon, E 🅾 Palo Duro Canyon SP (10mi), Palo Duro RV Park, **3 mi** W 🍴 McDonald's 🛏 Best Western, Buffalo Inn, Holiday Inn Express 🅾 Plains Museum, to W TX A&M
103	FM 1541 N, Cemetery Rd
99	Hungate Rd
98mm	parking area both lanes, litter barrels
96	Dowlen Rd
94	FM 285, to Wayside
92	Haley Rd
90	FM 1075, Happy, W ⛽ gas/dsl
88b a	US 87 N, FM 1881, Happy same as 90
83	FM 2698
82	FM 214
77	US 87, Tulia
75	NW 6th St, Tulia, **1 mi** E ⛽ Phillips 66/dsl 🍴 Pizza Hut, Sonic 🛏 Lasso Motel, W same as 74
74	TX 86, Tulia, E 🛏 Lasso Motel 🅾 🇭, W ⛽ Pilot/Valero/Subway/dsl/scales/24hr 🛏 Executive Inn
70mm	parking area both lanes, litter barrels
68	FM 928
63	FM 145, Kress, **1 mi** E ⛽ gas/dsl 🍴 food 🅾 🇨
61	US 87, County Rd, N 🅾 $General
56	FM 788
54	FM 3183, to Plainview
53	Lp 27, Plainview, E 🅾 access to gas, camping, food, 🇭, lodging
51	Quincy St
50	TX 194, Plainview, E ⛽ Valero/dsl 🅾 🇭, to Wayland Bapt U
49	US 70, Plainview, E ⛽ AllStar/dsl, Allsup's, Cefco/dsl, Phillips 66/Stripes/dsl, Valero/dsl 🍴 910 Smokehouse BBQ, A&W/LJ Silver, Carlito's Mexican, China Dragon, Cotton Patch Café, Domino's, Leal's Mexican, Pizza Hut, Tokyo Japanese 🛏 Comfort Suites, Days Inn, Quality Inn 🅾 $Tree, AutoZone, Beall's, GNC, NAPA, O'Reilly Parts, United Foods, W ⛽ Allsup's/dsl, Murphy USA/dsl, Valero/dsl 🍴 Burger King, Chicken Express, Chili's, Dos Jefes, Empire Buffet, IHOP, McDonald's, Mia's Italian, Sonic, Subway, Taco Bell, Wendy's 🛏 Holiday Inn Express, Plainview Inn, Super 8 🅾 AT&T, GNC, Verizon, Walmart/McDonald's
48	FM 3466, Plainview (from nb), E 🅾 Chevrolet/Buick/GMC, Chrysler/Dodge/Jeep
45	Lp 27, to Plainview
43	FM 2337
41	County Rd
38	Main St
37	FM 1914, Cleveland St, W ⛽ Allsups/dsl 🅾 city park, Family$, Lowe's Foods
36	FM 1424, Hale Center
32	FM 37 W
31	FM 37 E
29mm	🆁🆂 both lanes, full ♿ facilities, 🇨, 🛒, litter barrels, petwalk, tornado shelter, vending
27	County Rd
24	FM 54, W 🅾 RV park/dump
22	Lp 369, Abernathy
21	FM 597, Main St, Abernathy, W ⛽ HH Farms/dsl 🍴 DQ 🅾 $General, USPO
20	FM 597, Abernathy (from nb)
17	CR 53

15	Lp 461, to New Deal same as 14
14	FM 1729, E ⛽ Alon/rest./dsl/scales/24hr
13	Lp 461, to New Deal
12	access rd (from nb)
11	FM 1294, Shallowater
10	Keuka St, E 🅾 Fed Ex
9	Airport Rd, E 🅾 ✈, W 🅾 Lubbock RV Park/LP/dump
8	FM 2641, Regis St, E 🅾 ✈, W ⛽ Loves/Subway/Chester's/dsl/scales/24hr
7	Yucca Lane, E 🅾 Pharr RV Ctr
6b a	Lp 289, Ave Q, Lubbock, E 🅾 Pharr RV
5	B. Holly Ave, Municipal Dr, E 🅾 Mackenzie SP, W 🅾 Civic Ctr
4	US 82, US 87, 4th St, to Crosbyton, E 🅾 funpark, W ⛽ Flying J/Subway/dsl/LP/scales/24hr 🅾 to TTU
3	US 62, TX 114, 19th St, Floydada, E ⛽ Phillips 66 🅾 NAPA
2	34th St, E ⛽ Phillips 66/dsl 🍴 Pete's Drive Inn, W ⛽ Valero 🍴 Josie's #5, Phillips 66, Subway 🅾 AutoZone, Raff&Hall Drug, U-Haul
1c	50th St, E ⛽ Buddy's 🍴 El Charro 🅾 Family$, W ⛽ Alon/7-11, Valero/dsl 🍴 A&W/LJ Silver, Bryan's Steaks, Burger King, China Star, Church's, Domino's, KFC, La Bella Pizza, McDonald's, Pizza Hut/Taco Bell, Subway, Wienerschnitzel 🛏 Howard Johnson, Microtel 🅾 $General, O'Reilly Parts, United Food/gas, USPO, Walgreens
1b	US 84, E 🛏 Best Value Inn, Days Inn, W 🛏 Best Western+, Country Inn Suites, EconoLodge, Holiday Inn Express, La Quinta, Motel 6, Quality Inn, Red Roof Inn, Super 8, Woodspring Suites 🅾 Chevrolet
1a	Lp 289
1	82nd St, W ⛽ Phillips 66/dsl, **I-27 begins/ends on US 87 at 82nd St in S Lubbock.**

▲E INTERSTATE 30

Exit #	Services
223mm	Texas/Arkansas state line
223b a	US 59, US 71, State Line Ave, Texarkana, N ⛽ Exxon/dsl, EZ Mart 🍴 Denny's, IHOP, Naaman's BBQ, Travelodge, Waffle House 🛏 Baymont Inn, Best Western+, Holiday Inn Express, Howard Johnson, Ramada, Ramada Inn, Red Roof Inn, Regency Inn, Super 8, Wyndham Garden 🅾 KOA, S ⛽ Chevron/dsl, Exxon, Murphy USA/dsl, RaceWay/dsl, Shell 🍴 Burger King, Cattleman's Steaks, China Inn, China King, El Chico, Fuzzy's Tacos, Hooters, KFC, Little Caesar's, LJ Silver, Marble Slab, McDonald's, Papa John's, Popeye's, Schlotzsky's, Slim Chickens, Sonic, Starbucks, Subway, Taco Bell, Wendy's, Whataburger 🛏 Ambassador Inn, Best Value Inn, Days Inn, EconoLodge, Executive Inn, Magnuson Hotel, Motel 6, Rodeway Inn 🅾 $General, $Tree, Albertson's/Sav-On, AutoZone, CVS Drug, O'Reilly Parts, VW, Walgreens, Walmart/Subway

PLAINVIEW (side tab)

LUBBOCK (side tab)

TX (side tab)

[gas] = gas　[food] = food　[lodging] = lodging　[O] = other　[Rs] = rest stop　Copyright 2022 - The Next EXIT ©

TX

TEXARKANA

INTERSTATE 30 Cont'd

Exit #	Services
223mm	Welcome Ctr wb, full [&] facilities, info, [C], [tel], litter barrels, vending, petwalk
222	TX 93, FM 1397, Summerhill Rd, N [gas] Shell, Valero/Subway/dsl [food] Applebee's, McDonald's, The One Buffet, Waffle House [lodging] Motel 6 [O] AT&T, Goodyear Truck Tire, Hyundai, URGENT CARE, S [gas] Exxon/dsl [food] Catfish King, Sonic [O] Ford, Gateway Tires, Nissan, Walmart Mkt/dsl
220b	FM 559, Richmond Rd, N [gas] Shell [food] Buffalo Wild Wings, Burger King, Cane's, Chick-fil-A, Chipotle, CiCi's Pizza, Coldstone Creamery, Cracker Barrel, Domino's, DQ, Fuji Grill, Genghis Grill, Gusano's Pizza, Jason's Deli, Jimmy John's, Larry's Pizza, Little Caesar's, Longhorn Steaks, McAlister's Deli, Mooyah Burgers, On-the-Border, Osaka Japanese, Papa Murphy's, Pizza Hut, Red Lobster, Reggie's Cafe, Ruby Tuesday, Schlotzsky's, Silver Star Smokehouse, Smashburger, Sonic, Starbucks, Steak'n Shake, Taco Bell, TaMolly's Mexican, TX Roadhouse, Wendy's, Wing Stop [lodging] Comfort Suites, Courtyard, Residence Inn, TownePlace Suites [O] $General, $Tree, AT&T, Best Buy, Chevrolet, Discount Tire, Home Depot, Honda, Kohl's, Kwik Kar, Office Depot, Old Navy, Petsmart, Sam's Club/gas, Super 1 Food/gas, Target, TJ Maxx, Verizon, Walmart Mkt/dsl, S [gas] Valero/dsl [food] Arby's, Chili's, ChuckeCheese, Firehouse Subs, Golden Chick, Golden Corral, Grandy's, Lee's China, McDonald's, Newk's, Olive Garden, Outback Steaks, Subway, Taco Bueno, Tacos 4Life [lodging] Candlewood Suites, Hampton Inn, Hilton Garden/Conv Ctr, Holiday Inn Express [O] Albertson's/Sav-On, AT&T, Books-A-Million, Cavender's Boots, CVS Drug, Dillard's, Hobby Lobby, JC Penney, Michael's, Ross, Tuesday Morning, Walgreens
220a	I-369 S, US 59 S, Texarkana
219	Pecan St, University Ave, S [gas] Exxon, Murphy USA [food] Subway, Wendy's [lodging] Country Inn&Suites, Fairfield Inn [O] Buick/GMC, Cadillac, Chrysler/Dodge/Jeep, Harley-Davidson, Kia, Lowe's, Mazda, Mercedes, vet, Walmart
218	FM 989, Nash, N [gas] Road Runner/dsl [food] Dixie Diner, S [gas] 76/ TX Best BBQ/Steak'n Shake/Golden Chick/Dunkin/dsl, Exxon/ Burger King/dsl [food] Sonic [O] GMC/Peterbilt, to Lake Patman, Toyota, USPO
213	FM 2253, Leary, S [gas] [Love's]/McDonald's/Subway/dsl/ scales/24hr
212	spur 74, S [O] Lone Star Army Ammo Plant
208	FM 560, Hooks, N [gas] Valero/dsl, S [gas] Truckstp/dsl/scales/24hr [food] DQ, Sonic [O] $General, Family$, Hooks Tire
207	rd 594, Red River Army Depot
206	TX 86, S [O] Red River Army Depot

NEW BOSTON

201	TX 8, New Boston, N [gas] Exxon/Burger King/dsl, Valero/dsl [food] Pitt Grill [lodging] Tex Inn [O] Chevrolet, Chrysler/Dodge/Jeep, S [gas] Murphy USA/dsl, Shell/dsl [food] $Tree, Catfish King, Church's, Domino's, DQ, KFC/Taco Bell, McDonald's, Pizza Hut, Randy's BBQ, Sonic [lodging] Best Value Inn, Bostonian Inn, Holiday Inn Express [O] Brookshire's Foods/gas, Ford, O'Reilly Parts, Verizon, Walmart/Subway
199	US 82, New Boston, 1/2 mi N [gas] VP/dsl, S [gas] Exxon/Denny's/dsl
198	TX 98, 1/2 mi N [gas] VP/dsl
193mm	Anderson Creek
192	FM 990
186	FM 561
181mm	Sulphur River
178	US 259, to DeKalb, Omaha
174mm	White Oak Creek
170	FM 1993

MT PLEASANT

165	FM 1001
162b a	US 271, FM 1402, FM 2152, Mt Pleasant, N [gas] Exxon/dsl [food] Applebee's, Blalock BBQ [lodging] Holiday Inn Express, Super 8 [O] $General, KOA, S [gas] Shell/dsl, Sunoco/Subway/dsl [food] Burger King, McDonald's, Popeye's, Sonic [lodging] Best Western [O] $General Cadillac/Chevrolet, Chrysler/Dodge/Jeep, Family$, Ford, [H], vet
160	US 271, FM 1734, Mt Pleasant, N [gas] Texaco/dsl [food] Senorita's Mexican [lodging] La Quinta [O] Buick/GMC (1mi), Lowe's, Rambling Fever RV Park (2mi), Toyota, S [gas] Exxon/dsl, Shell/dsl [food] IHOP Jalapeño Tree [lodging] Executive Inn, Hampton Inn, Motel 6, Quality Inn [O] Sandlin SP
158mm	weigh sta both lanes
156	Frontage Rd
153	spur 185, to Winfield, Miller's Cove, N [gas] Hana/Exxon/Winfield Café/dsl, Winfield/dsl
150	Ripley Rd, N [O] Lowe's Distribution
147	spur 423, N [gas] [Love's]/Chester's/Subway/dsl/scales/24hr [lodging] American Inn [O] tires/repair, S [gas] Duke's/Shell/Taco Casa, BBQ/dsl
146	TX 37, Mt Vernon, N [food] Sonic [O] $General, auto repair, Brookshire Foods/gas, O'Reilly Parts, S [gas] Cefco/Huddle House dsl/24hr, Exxon/dsl [food] Burger King, DQ, El Manna, McDonald's [lodging] Super 8 [O] auto/dsl repair, to Lake Bob Sandlin SP
142	County Line Rd (from eb)
141	FM 900, Saltillo Rd
136	FM 269, Weaver Rd
135	US 67 N
131	FM 69
127	US 67, Lp 301, N [lodging] Days Inn, Econolodge, Ferrari Inn, Motel 6 [O] [H], S [gas] Shell [lodging] Best Western
126	FM 1870, College St, S [gas] Shell [lodging] Best Western [O] Firestone auto, same as 127
125	Bill Bradford Rd same as 124

SULPHUR SPGS

124	TX 11, TX 154, Sulphur Springs, N [gas] Exxon/dsl [food] Bodacious BBQ, Broadway Buffet, Chicken Express, Don Ialo's Mexican, IHOP, Juan Pablo's Mexican, Metro Diner, Pizza Hut, Schlotzsky's, Soulman's BBQ, Subway, Wendy's [lodging] Hampton Inn, Holiday Inn Express, Royal Inn [O] $General, AutoZone, Brookshire's Foods/gas, CVS Drug, Family$, Ford/Lincoln, FSA Outlet/famous brands, [H], O'Reilly Parts, USPO, VF Outlet/famous brands, Walgreens, S [gas] Exxon/dsl, Murphy USA/dsl, Shell dsl [food] Braum's, Burger King, Chili's, Domino's, DQ, Furr's Rest, Jack-in-the-Box, McDonald's, Panda Express, Pizza Inn, Roma Italian, Sonic, Starbucks, Taco Bell/LJ Silver, Whataburger [O] AT&T, Cody Drug, Discount Wheel&Tire, Lowe's, Verizon, Walmart/Subway
123	FM 2297, League St, N [gas] Shamrock/dsl, Shell
122	TX 19, to Emory, N [gas] Shamrock/dsl [O] Chrysler/Dodge/Jeep, [H], to Cooper Lake SP, Travel Time RV Ctr, S [gas] CNG, [Love's] /Carl's Jr/dsl/scales/24hr, [Pilot]/Arby's/dsl/scales/24hr, Valero/dsl [O] dsl repair
120	US 67 bus
116	FM 2653, Brashear Rd, S [O] USPO
112	FM 499 (from wb)
111mm	[Rs] both lanes, full facilities
110	FM 275, Cumby, N [gas] Phillips 66/dsl, S [gas] Valero/dsl
104	FM 513, FM 2649, Campbell, S to Lake Tawakoni
101	TX 24, TX 50, FM 1737, to Commerce, N [gas] Exxon/dsl [O] to TX A&M-Commerce
97	Lamar St, N [gas] Exxon/dsl [lodging] Budget Inn, S [O] vet
96	Lp 302
95	Division St, S [O] [H]

INTERSTATE 30 Cont'd

Exit #	Services
94b	US 69, US 380, Greenville, N 🅿 Valero/dsl 🍴 Collin St Bakery, Golden Chick, Senorita's Mexican 🛏 Knights Inn, Royal Inn 🅾 🚑, S 🅿 Exxon, QT/dsl 🍴 Arby's, McDonald's, Racho Viejo 🛏 Economy Inn, Express Inn, Guest Inn, Motel 6, Super 8
94a	US 69, US 380, Greenville, S 🅿 QT/dsl, Valero/Subway/dsl 🅾 Chrysler/Dodge/Jeep
93b a	US 67, TX 34 N, N 🅿 Chevron/Taco Casa/dsl, Exxon/dsl, Race-Trac/dsl, Shell/dsl, Texaco 🍴 Applebee's, Braum's, Buffet Palace, Chick-fil-A, Chicken Express, Chipotle, CiCi's, Cotton Patch Cafe, DQ, El Fenix, Firehouse Subs, Grandy's, IHOP, Jack-in-the-Box, Jimmy John's, KFC, Little Caesar's, Panera Bread, Pizza Hut, Schlotzsky's, Sonic, Starbucks, Subway, Taco Bell, Taco Bueno, Tony's Italian, Wendy's, Whataburger 🛏 Hampton Inn 🅾 Aldi Foods, AT&T, Beall's, Belk, BigLots, Brookshire's Foods, Cavender's Outfitter, Discount Tire, Hobby Lobby, 🚑, Kwik Kar, Lowe's, Marshall's, O'Reilly Parts, Petco, Ross, Staples, URGENT CARE, USPO, Verizon, Walgreens, S 🅿 Exxon/dsl, Murphy USA/dsl, Shell/dsl 🍴 Burger King, Chili's, Cracker Barrel, Molina's Mexican, Panda Express, Papa John's, Popeye's, Red Lobster, Rib Crib BBQ, Shogun Hibachi, Soulman's BBQ, Subway, TaMolly's Mexican 🛏 Best Western+, Comfort Suites, Holiday Inn Express 🅾 $Tree, Buick/GMC, Ford/Lincoln, Home Depot, Hyundai, Nissan, NTB, Walmart
92	Stratton Pkwy, S 🅾 Chevrolet/Cadillac
90mm	Farber Creek
89	FM 1570, S 🛏 Luxury Inn
89mm	E Caddo Creek
87	FM 1903, N 🅿 Shell/dsl 🅾 fireworks, S 🅿 Pilot/McDonald's/dsl/scales/24hr, Texaco/Huddle House/dsl 🍴 Baker's Ribs 🅾 tire repair
87mm	Elm Creek
85	FM 36, Caddo Mills, N 🅾 Dallas NE RV Park
85mm	W Caddo Creek
83	FM 1565 N, N 🅿 Exxon/Pizza Inn/dsl
79	FM 2642, N 🅾 Budget RV Ctr, S 🅿 Buc-ee's 🅾 vet
77b	FM 35, Royse City, N 🅿 Texaco/Subway/dsl/scales/24hr 🍴 Soulman's BBQ 🅾 Family$
77a	TX 548, Royse City, N 🅿 Shell/dsl 🍴 Jack-in-the-Box, McDonald's 🛏 American Inn 🅾 AutoZone, tires, S 🅿 Exxon 🍴 Denny's, Pizza Hut, Rice Express, Sonic, Taco Bell 🛏 Holiday Inn Express
76	Campbell Blvd, N 🅿 Murphy Express/dsl 🍴 Arby's, Burger King, DQ, Palio's Pizza Cafe, Panda Express, Papa John's, Popeye's, Whataburger 🅾 AT&T, CVS Drug, Kwik Kar, O'Reilly Parts, URGENT CARE, Walmart/Subway
75	Campbell Rd (from wb, same as 76)
74	Frontage Rd (from eb)
73	FM 551, Fate
70	FM 549, N 🅾 Happy Trails RV Ctr, McLains RV Ctr, S 🅿 Loves/Carl's Jr./dsl/scales/24hr 🅾 Kia
69	(from wb), Frontage Rd, N 🛏 Super 8, S 🅾 Honda, Hyundai, Nissan, Nissan, Toyota
68	TX 205, to Rock Wall, N 🅿 7-11/dsl, Murphy USA/dsl, QT/dsl, Shell 🍴 Braum's, Chicken Express, Domino's, Joe Willy's Grill, Luigi's Italian, Starbucks, Subway, Taco Casa, Whataburger 🛏 Best Western+, Rockwall Inn, Woodspring Suites 🅾 Buick/GMC, Chevrolet, Chrysler/Dodge/Jeep, Ford, Hobby Lobby, vet, Walmart/Subway, S 🅿 RaceTrac/dsl, TA/Burger King/Starbucks/dsl/24hr/scales/@ 🍴 Cane's, Firehouse Subs, Freebird Burritos, In-N-Out, Luby's, Rosa's Cafe, Soulman's BBQ 🅾 Belk, Costco/gas, Jo-Ann Fabrics, Toyota
67b	FM 740, Ridge Rd, N 🅿 Chevron, Murphy USA/dsl 🍴 Buffet City, Culver's, Denny's, Edohana Hibachi, Grandy's, IHOP, LJ Silver, Logan's Roadhouse, McDonald's, Mellow Mushroom Pizza, Popeye's, Schlotzsky's, Steak'n Shake, Taco Bueno, Taco Cabana, Waffle House, Wendy's 🛏 Hampton Inn 🅾 Firestone/auto, Goodyear/auto, S 🅿 Exxon, Kroger/dsl, Shell 🍴 Applebee's, Bahama Buck's Ice Cream, Blackeyed Pea, Buffalo Wild Wings, Carino's Italian, Chick-fil-A, Chili's, Chipotle Mexican, ChuckeCheese, CiCi's, Cotton Patch Cafe, Dickey's BBQ, El Chico, Firehouse Subs, Five Guys, Freebirds Burrito, Jack-in-the-Box, Jimmy John's, La Madelein, Mi Cocina, Mooyah Burgers, Olive Garden, On-the-Border, Panda Express, Pizza Hut, Sonic, Soulman's BBQ, Starbucks, Subway, Taco Bell, Which Wich? 🛏 La Quinta 🅾 $Tree, AT&T, Beall's, Belk, Best Buy, CVS Drug, Dick's, Discount Tire, Home Depot, 🚑, JC Penney, Jo-Ann, Kohl's, Lowe's, Michael's, NTB, Old Navy, PetCo, Petsmart, Ross, Staples, SteinMart, Target, TJ Maxx, to Lake Tawakoni, URGENT CARE, Verizon, vet
67a	Horizon Rd, Village Dr, N 🍴 Genghis Grill, Kyoto Japanese, Saltgrass Steaks, Snuffer's Rest, Starbucks 🛏 Hampton Inn, S 🍴 Culpepper Steaks, Oar House 🛏 Hilton
66mm	Ray Hubbard Reservoir
64	Dalrock Rd, Rowlett, N 🅿 Shell/dsl, Valero/dsl 🍴 Alejandro's Grill, Church's, Dickey's BBQ 🛏 Comfort Suites 🅾 🚑
63mm	Ray Hubbard Reservoir
62	Bass Pro Dr, N 🛏 Quality Inn 🅾 to Hubbard RA, S 🅿 Shell/dsl, Texaco, Valero/dsl 🍴 CiCi's Pizza, Flying Saucer Grill, Islamadora Fish Co, Primo's Grille, TX Land&Cattle, Whataburger 🛏 Holiday Inn Express 🅾 Bass Pro Shops
61b	Bush Tpk
61a	Zion Rd (from wb), N 🅿 Exxon/dsl 🛏 Discovery Inn
60b	Bobtown Rd (eb only), N 🅿 7-11/dsl 🍴 Jack-in-the-Box 🛏 La Quinta, S 🅿 Shell 🍴 Subway
60a	Rose Hill Dr
59	Beltline Rd, Garland, N 🅿 7-11/dsl, QT 🍴 Chili's, China City, Denny's, IHOP, KFC, Little Caesar's, McDonald's, McDonald's, Moe's SW, Papa John's, Starbucks, Subway, Taco Bell, Taco Cabana, Taco Casa, Wendy's, Whataburger 🅾 Albertson's, Discount Tire, GNC, Tuesday Morning, Walgreens, Walmart, S 🅿 RaceTrac/dsl 🍴 Baker's Ribs, Carl's Jr, DQ, Sonic, Waffle House, Williams Chicken 🛏 Best Value Inn, Motel 6, Super 8 🅾 AT&T, Kroger
58	Northwest Dr, N 🅿 Shell, Valero/dsl 🅾 Hyundai, Nissan, S 🅿 Exxon/dsl, QT/dsl, Texaco 🍴 Jack-in-the-Box 🅾 Lowe's
56c b	I-635 S-N
56a	Galloway Ave, Gus Thomasson Dr (from eb), N 🅿 Star USA, Texaco, Valero/dsl 🍴 Golden Chick, KFC, McDonald's, Sonic, Taco Bell 🅾 AutoZone, USPO, Walgreens, S 🅿 7-11, Chevron

Left margin labels: GREENVILLE · ROCK WALL · ROCKWALL · GARLAND

INTERSTATE 30 Cont'd

56a	Continued
	🍴 Dicky's BBQ, Domino's, El Fenix, Grandy's, Hooters, Jack-in-the-Box, King Buffet, Luby's, Olive Garden, Outback Steaks, Posado's Cafe, Razzoo's Cajun, Red Lobster, Sports City Cafe, Subway, TGIFriday's, Wendy's 🛏 Courtyard, Crossland Suites, Delux Inn, Fairfield Inn 🅾 Aldi Foods, BigLots, Celebration Sta Funpark, Firestone/auto, Kroger/dsl, NTB, RV Max
55	Motley Dr, **N** 🅶 Shell/dsl 🛏 Astro Inn 🅾 to Eastfield Coll, **S** 🅶 Exxon/7-11 🛏 Microtel
54	Big Town Blvd, **N** 🅶 Valero/dsl 🛏 Mesquite Inn, **S** 🅾 Explore RV Ctr, Holiday World RV Ctr
53b	US 80 E (from eb), to Terrell
53a	Lp 12, Buckner, **N** 🛏 Holiday Inn Express, Super 8 🅾 Chevrolet, Toyota, **S** 🍴 Panda Express, Taco Cabana, Whataburger 🅾 $Tree, Sam's Club/gas, Staples, Walmart
51	(52 a from wb), Highland Rd, Jim Miller Blvd, **N** 🅶 Exxon/7-11 🍴 Country China, Denny's, McDonald's, Waffle House 🛏 Holiday Inn Express, Quality Inn, **S** 🅶 RaceWay/dsl, Shell/dsl 🍴 Burger King, Capt D's, CiCi's Pizza, Furr's Cafe, Grandy's, KFC, Popeye's, Subway, Taco Bell, Wendy's 🛏 Motel 6, Super 7 Inn 🅾 AutoZone, CVS Drug, O'Reilly Parts
50b a	Longview, Ferguson Rd, **N** 🅶 Texaco, **S** 🅾 Brake-O, U-Haul
49b	Dolphin Rd, Lawnview Ave, Samuell Ave, **N** 🅶 Shell 🛏 Best Value Inn
49a	Winslow St, **N** 🅶 Circle K, Shell/dsl 🍴 Jack-in-the-Box, McDonald's, **S** 🅶 Circle K, Shell/dsl 🅾 tires
48b	TX 78, E Grand, **N** 🅾 arboretum, **S** 🅾 fairpark
48a	Carroll Ave, Central Ave, Peak St, Haskell Ave, **N** 🅶 7-11, Shamrock, Valero 🅾 Hamm's Tires, 🏥, **S** 🍴 Joe's Rest
47	2nd Ave, **S** 🅶 Shell 🍴 McDonald's 🅾 Cotton Bowl, fairpark
46b	I-45, US 75, to Houston
46a	Central Expswy downtown
45	I-35E, N to Denton, to Commerce St, Lamar St, Griffin St, **S** 🅶 Gulf/dsl 🍴 McDonald's 🛏 Ambassador Inn
44b	I-35E S, Industrial Blvd
44a	I-35E N, Beckley Ave (from eb)
43b a	Sylvan Ave (from wb), **N** 🅶 Valero/dsl 🅾 Family$, 🏥, USPO
42	Hampton Rd
41	Westmoreland Ave
39	Cockrell Hill Rd, **N** 🅶 Shell/dsl 🍴 Grand China, IHOP, KFC/Taco Bell, Pollo Campero, Sonic, Wing Stop 🛏 Comfort Suites, Fairfield Inn, Hampton Inn 🅾 Staples, **S** 🅶 Murphy USA/dsl 🍴 Burger King, Chick-fil-A, Chili's, CiCi's, Dickey's BBQ, Golden Corral, Little Caesar's, Lucky Rice, McDonald's, New Buffet, Panda Express, Starbucks, Subway, Taco Cabana, Wendy's, Whataburger 🛏 Holiday Inn Express 🅾 $Tree, Best Buy, Lowe's, Ross, Walmart/McDonald's
38	Lp 12, **N** 🅶 Exxon/7-11, Texaco/dsl, VP/dsl 🍴 Burger King
36	MacArthur Blvd, **S** 🅾 U-Haul
34	Belt Line Rd, **N** 🅶 QT/dsl, RaceTrac/dsl 🛏 Studio 6, Super 8 🅾 Ford, Ripley's Museum, **S** 🅶 RaceTrac/dsl, Shell/Subway/dsl, Valero/dsl 🍴 Burger King, Popeye's, Schlotzsky's, Starbucks 🅾 city park, vet
32b a	George Bush Tpk, **toll**, **N** 🅶 Valero/dsl
30	TX 360, Six Flags Dr, Arlington Stadium, **N** 🅶 Shell, Valero/dsl 🍴 Boston's, Cracker Barrel, Grand Buffet, Saltgrass Steaks, Steak'n Shake, The Rock Grill, Wendy's 🛏 Best Inn, Budget Suites, Candlewood Suites, Crowne Plaza, Extended Stay America, Extended Stay America, Fairfield Inn, Hawthorn Suites, Hilton, Hilton Garden, Hyatt Place, Motel 6, Residence Inn, Studio 6, Wingate Inn, **S** 🅶 Shell/7-11/dsl, Valero 🍴 Denny's,

30	Continued
	Humperdink's Rest., Jack-in-the-Box, Mariano's Mexican, Mc Donald's, Red Neck Heaven Rest, Subway 🛏 Baymont Inn, Holiday Inn Express, Homewood Suites, Hyatt Place, Knight's Inn La Quinta, Quality Inn, Ranger Inn, Sleep Inn 🅾 Ford/Lincoln Six Flags Funpark
29	Ball Park Way, **N** 🅶 Chevron/7-11, QT, Valero/dsl 🍴 Dicky' BBQ, Rio Mambo, Sonic 🛏 Hampton Inn, SpringHill Suites Towneplace Suites 🅾 Auto Nation/Toyota, USPO, **S** 🍴 On-the-Border, Vila Brazil 🛏 Howard Johnson, Sheraton 🅾 Six Flag Funpark
28b a	FM 157, Collins St, **N** 🅶 Chevron/dsl 🍴 Chipotle, IHOP Mooyah Burgers, Pei Wei, Potbelly, Starbucks, Waffle House 🛏 EconoLodge, Holiday Inn 🅾 BMW, Cadillac, Chrysler/Dodge Jeep, Mini, Walmart, Whole Foods Mkt, **S** 🍴 Arby's, Asian Buffet, Blackeyed Pea, Blue Mesa Grill, Buffalo Wild Wings, Cane's Chili's, El Chico, Gino's East Pizzaria, Hooters, Jason's Deli, Joe' Crab Shack, Lupe's Grill, Olive Garden, Panda Express, Panera Bread, Pappadeaux, Pappasito's Cantina, Popeye's, Sherlock' Grill, Subway, Taco Bell, Taco Bueno, TGIFriday's, TX Land&Cattle, Wendy's, Which Wich? 🛏 Comfort Suites, Courtyard, Day Inn 🅾 $Tree, GNC, Home Depot, Michael's, Office Depot, Pep Boys, Petsmart, Ross, SteinMart, TX Stadium, Walgreens
27	Lamar Blvd, Cooper St, **N** 🅶 Gulf 🍴 Jack-in-the-Box, Subwa 🅾 BigLots, Family$, Kroger/dsl, vet, **S** 🅶 7-11, QT/dsl, Shell dsl 🍴 Burger King, Pappasito's Cantina, Tom's Burgers 🛏 Comfort Suites
26	Fielder Rd, **S** 🅾 to Six Flags (from eb)
25mm	Village Creek
24	Eastchase Pkwy, **N** 🍴 Jack-in-the-Box, Panda Express 🛏 L Quinta 🅾 CarMax, Lowe's, Sam's Club/gas, Verizon, Walmart McDonald's, **S** 🅶 Chevron/7-11/dsl, RaceTrac/dsl, Shell/7-11 dsl 🍴 Burger King, Chicken Express, CiCi's Pizza, IHOP, McDonald's, No Frills Grill, Pizza Hut, Schlotzsky's, Subway, Taco Bell Wendy's, Whataburger 🅾 $Tree, Aldi Foods, AT&T, GNC, Marshall's, Office Depot, Ross, Target
23	Cooks Lane, **S** 🅶 Shell/dsl
21c b	I-820
21a	Bridgewood Dr, **N** 🅶 Chevron/dsl 🍴 Braum's, Dickey's BBC Jack-in-the-Box, KFC, Luby's, Subway, Taco Casa, Wendy's 🅾 $General, Albertson's, Discount Tire, Firestone/auto, Home De pot, U-Haul, **S** 🅶 Conoco, Phillips 66/dsl, QT 🍴 Taco Bueno Whataburger/24hr
19	Brentwood Stair Rd (from eb), **N** 🅶 Shell, **S** 🅶 Shamrock, Texaco 🅾 Family$
18	Oakland Blvd, **N** 🅶 Circle K, Shell/dsl 🍴 Taco Bell, Waffl House 🛏 Motel 6
16c	Beach St, **S** 🅶 7-11 🛏 Motel 6, Stay Express Hotel
16b a	Riverside Dr (from wb), **S** 🛏 Great Western Inn
15b a	I-35W N to Denton, S to Waco
14b	Jones St, Commerce St, Ft Worth downtown
14a	TX 199, Henderson St, Ft Worth downtown
13b	TX 199, Henderson St, **N** 🛏 Holiday Inn Express, Omni, Sherato
13a	8th Ave, **N** 🛏 Holiday Inn Express
12b	Forest Park Blvd, **N** 🍴 Pappa's Burgers, Pappadeaux Café, Pa pasito's, **S** 🅾 🏥, URGENT CARE
12a	University Dr, City Parks, **S** 🛏 SpringHill Suites
11	Montgomery St, **S** 🅶 Shell/7-11/dsl 🍴 Railhead BBQ, Tac Bell, Whataburger
10	Hulen St, Ft Worth, **S** 🍴 Buttons Rest., Chick-fil-A, McDonald Mi Cocina, Potbelly, Smoothie King, Starbucks 🅾 Central Mk WorldMkt

Side labels: DALLAS, ARLINGTON, FT WORTH

TX

⬆️E INTERSTATE 30 Cont'd

Exit #	Services
9b	US 377, Camp Bowie Blvd, Horne St, N 🍴 Uncle Julio's Mexican, S 🅖 7-11, Exxon/7-11, Texaco/dsl 🍴 Campisi's Italian, Chipotle, Jack-in-the-Box, Jason's Deli, Jersey Mike's, Jimmy John's, McDonald's, Mexican Inn Cafe, Schlotzsky's, Smashburger, Sonic, Starbucks, Subway, Taco Bueno, Wendy's 🅞 AT&T, Batteries+Bulbs, URGENT CARE, Walgreens
9a	Bryant-Irvin Rd, S 🅖 same as 9b, Shell
8b	Ridgmar, Ridglea
8a	TX 183, Green Oaks Rd, N 🍴 Applebee's, Arby's, Asia Bowl, Cane's, Chick-fil-A, Chipotle, Cowtown BBQ, Del Taco, Don Pablo's, Firehouse Subs, Grand Buffet, Jack-in-the-Box, McDonald's, Olive Garden, Panda Express, Papa Murphy's, Sonic, Subway, Taco Bueno, Whataburger, Woody Creek BBQ 🏠 Courtyard 🅞 $Tree, Albertson's, Aldi Foods, AT&T, Best Buy, BigLots, Dillard's, Firestone/auto, JC Penney, Jo-Ann Fabrics, Lowe's, Neiman Marcus, NTB, Office Depot, Old Navy, PetCo, Petsmart, Ross, Sam's Club/gas, Sears/auto, Target, U-Haul, Verizon, Walmart/Subway, S 🏠 Fairfield Inn, Hampton Inn
7b a	Cherry Lane, TX 183, spur 341, to Green Oaks Rd, N 🍴 Shell/7-11, Texaco/dsl, Valero/dsl 🍴 ChuckECheese, IHOP, Popeye's, Subway, Wendy's 🏠 Comfort Inn, Motel 6, Scottish Inn 🅞 O'Reilly Parts, same as 8a, U-Haul, S 🍴 QT/dsl 🏠 Holiday Inn, Holiday Inn Express, La Quinta, Quality Inn, Super 8
6	Las Vegas Trail, N 🍴 Chevron/McDonald's/dsl, Conoco/dsl 🍴 Jack-in-the-Box, Waffle House 🏠 Days Inn 🅞 Hyundai, Lincoln, S 🍴 Shell/7-11/dsl, Texaco, Valero/dsl, vet 🏠 Best Value Inn, Knights Inn, Relax Inn 🅞 AutoZone, Kia
5b c	I-820 N and S
5a	Alemeda St (from eb, no EZ return)
3	RM 2871, Chapel Creek Blvd, S 🍴 Exxon/Church's/Subway/dsl 🍴 Sonic
2	spur 580 E
1b	Linkcrest Dr, S 🍴 Gulf/dsl
0mm	I-20 W. I-30 begins/ends on I-20, exit 421.

⬆️N INTERSTATE 35

Exit #	Services
504mm	Texas/Oklahoma state line, Red River
504	Frontage Rd, access to Texas Welcome Ctr
503mm	parking area both lanes
502mm	Welcome Ctr sb, TX Tourist Bureau/info, full ♿ facilities, 🅒, 🆁, litter barrels, wifi
501	FM 1202, Prime Outlets Blvd, E 🅞 Chrysler/Dodge/Jeep, Ford, W 🍴 Conoco/café/dsl 🍴 Applebee's, Cracker Barrel 🏠 Hampton Inn, La Quinta 🅞 Prime Outlets/famous brands, RV camping, Western Outfitter
500	FM 372, Gainesville, W 🍴 Hitchin' Post/Shell/dsl
498b a	US 82, to Wichita Falls, Gainesville, Sherman, E 🍴 Chevron/dsl/24hr, Shell/dsl, Valero/dsl 🍴 Luigi's Italian 🏠 Budget Host, Super 8 🅞 AT&T, ℍ, URGENT CARE, W 🍴 Exxon/dsl 🏠 Comfort Suites, Days Inn, Rodeway Inn
497	Frontage Rd, W 🍴 Valero/dsl
496b	TX 51, FM 51, California St, Gainesville, E 🍴 Chevron 🍴 Arby's, Braum's, Fera's Mexican, IHOP, McDonald's, Sonic, Starbucks, Starbucks, Taco Bell, Taco Casa, Wendy's 🏠 Holiday Inn Express, Quality Inn 🅞 Kwik Kar/auto, Lowe's Mkt, W 🍴 Valero 🍴 Chili's 🅞 N Central TX Coll
496a	to Weaver St
496mm	Elm Fork of the Trinity River

495	Frontage Rd
494	FM 1306
492mm	🆁 sb, tables, litter barrels
491	Spring Creek Rd
490mm	🆁 nb, tables, litter barrels
489	FM 1307 to Hockley Creek Rd
487	FM 922, Valley View, W 🍴 Shell/Subway/Taco Tico/dsl, Valero/dsl 🍴 DQ 🅞 USPO
486	Fm 1307, W 🍴 Texaco/dsl 🏠 Texas Inn 🅞 $General
485	Frontage Rd (from sb)
483	FM 3002, Lone Oak Rd, E 🍴 Shell/Church's/Subway/dsl 🅞 Roberts Lake SP, RV Guys
482	Chisam Rd
481	View Rd, W 🅞 McClain's RV Ctr
480	Lois Rd, E 🅞 Walmart Dist Ctr
479	Belz Rd, Sanger same as 478
478	FM 455, to Pilot Pt, Bolivar, E 🍴 QuickTrack, Shell/dsl 🍴 DQ, Fuzzy's Tacos, Miguelito's, Pizza Hut, Sonic, Subway, Taco Bell 🏠 Sanger Inn 🅞 RV park, USPO, W 🍴 Chevron/dsl, Conoco/Chicken Express/dsl 🍴 Domino's, Jack-in-the-Box, McDonald's 🅞 Chevrolet, Family$, Kwik Kar Lube, O'Reilly Parts, Ray Roberts Lake and SP, Super Save Foods, Verizon
477	Keaton Rd, E 🍴 Exxon/dsl
475b	Rector Rd
475a	FM 156, to Krum (from sb)
474	Cowling rd (from nb)
473	FM 3163, Milam Rd, E 🍴 Loves/Subway/dsl/scales/24hr
472	Ganzer Rd, W 🅞 Crandell RV Ctr
471	US 77, FM 1173, Lp 282, to Denton, Krum, E 🍴 TA/Pizza Hut/Taco Bell/dsl/scales/24hr/@ 🅞 ℍ, W 🍴 Loves/Godfather's/Subway/Wendy's/dsl/scales/24hr 🅞 Foster's Western Shop, to Camping World RV Supply
470	Lp 288 same services as 469 from sb
469	US 380, University Dr, to Decatur, McKinney, E 🍴 7-11/dsl, Chevron/Subway, RaceTrac/dsl 🍴 Braum's, Cane's, Chick-fil-A, Chili's, ChinaTown Café, Cowboy Chicken, Cracker Barrel, Dickey's BBQ, Freebird's Burrito, Luigi's Pizza, McDonald's, Mooyah, Panda Express, Panera Bread, Starbucks, Taco Cabana, Taco Casa, Villa Grande, Whataburger, WhichWich?, Wing Stop 🏠 Best Western, Fairfield Inn 🅞 Albertson's/Sav-On, AT&T, GNC, Jo-Ann Fabrics, Kohl's, Kwik Kar, PetCo, Ross, Sam's Club/gas, to TX Woman's U, URGENT CARE, Walmart/McDonald's, Winco Foods, W 🍴 Exxon/dsl, QT/dsl 🍴 Brisket Burger, Denny's, DQ, Shell/dsl, Waffle House 🏠 Comfort Inn, Days Inn, Holiday Inn Express, Howard Johnson, La Quinta, Motel 6, Woodspring Suites 🅞 Camping World RV Supply, ℍ, I-35 RV Ctr
468	FM 1515, Airport Rd, W Oak St, E 🅞 ℍ
467	I-35W, S to Ft Worth
	I-35 divides into E and W sb, converges into I-35 nb. See Texas I-35 W.

Vertical left margin: GAINESVILLE

Vertical right margin: DENTON

⛽ = gas 🍴 = food 🛏 = lodging ⊙ = other Ⓡⓢ = rest stop Copyright 2022 - The Next EXIT ©

INTERSTATE 35 Cont'd

Exit #	Services
466b	Ave D, **E** 🍴 Central Grill, Chicken Express, IHOP, Pancho's Mexican ⊙ $General, to NTSU
466a	McCormick St, **E** ⛽ EKon, Shell/7-11/dsl 🍴 Pancho's Mexican ⊙ $General
465b	US 377, Ft Worth Dr, **E** ⛽ RaceTrac/dsl, Valero 🍴 Layalina Mediterranean, Taco Bell, Whataburger 🛏 Motel 6, **W** ⛽ 7-11/dsl 🍴 Outback Steaks, Sonic 🛏 Knights Inn
465a	FM 2181, Teasley Ln, **E** ⛽ 7-11 🍴 Applebee's, Braum's, Carino's, ChuckeCheese, Domino's, Hooters, KFC, Little Caesar's, Pizza Hut, Subway 🛏 Hampton Inn, Quality Inn ⊙ Brookshires Foods, U-Haul, **W** ⛽ Exxon, Shell/dsl 🍴 La Milpa Mexican, Rudy's BBQ/gas 🛏 Best Value Inn, Super 8 ⊙ vet
464	US 77, Pennsylvania Dr, Denton same as 463
463	Lp 288, to McKinney, **E** ⛽ Murphy USA, RaceTrac/dsl 🍴 Arby's, Buffalo Wild Wings, Buffet King, Burger King, Carl's Jr, Chick-fil-A, Chipotle, CiCi's Pizza, Corner Bakery Cafe, Egg&I Cafe, El Fenix, Five Guys, Fuddrucker's, Golden Corral, Gulf Coast Kitchen, Jason's Deli, Jersey Mike's, Jimmy John's, LJ Silver, McAlister's Deli, McDonald's, Mooyah, Olive Garden, On-the-Border, Palio's Pizza, Panda Express, Pei Wei, Pollo Tropical, Red Lobster, Sonic, Starbucks, Taco Bell, TX Roadhouse, Wendy's, Whataburger 🛏 Best Western, Courtyard, Hilton Garden ⊙ $General, $Tree, AT&T, Barnes&Noble, Best Buy, BigLots, Burlington Coats, Dillard's, Discount Tire, Firestone/auto, Goodyear/auto, Hobby Lobby, Home Depot, JC Penney, Kroger/dsl, Kwik Kar, Lowe's, Macy's, Michael's, NTB, Office Depot, Old Navy, PetCo, Petsmart, Ross, Sears/auto, Staples, Target, TJ Maxx, Verizon, Walgreens, Walmart, **W** ⛽ Chevron/dsl 🍴 BJ's Rest., Bone Daddy's, Chili's, Chuy's Mexican, Fuzzy's Tacos, Jack-in-the-Box, Papa John's, Schlotzsky's, Wing Stop 🛏 Homewood Suites ⊙ EMERGENCY CARE, same as 464, vet
462	State School Rd, Mayhill Rd, **E** ⛽ QT 🍴 Dickey's BBQ, Subway 🛏 Residence Inn ⊙ 🅗, URGENT CARE, **W** ⛽ Exxon 🍴 Shogun Japanese, Sonic ⊙ Buick/GMC, Cadillac, Chevrolet, Chrysler/Dodge/Jeep, Honda, Toyota
461	Sandy Shores Rd, Post Oak Dr, **E** ⊙ Explore USA RV Ctr, Ford, Hyundai, vet, **W** ⊙ Christian Bros Auto, Chrysler/Dodge/Jeep, Kia, Mazda, Nissan, Subaru
460	Corinth Pkwy, **E** ⊙ McClains RV Ctr, **W** ⊙ Harley-Davidson
459	Frontage Rd, **W** ⊙ Destiny RV Resort
458	FM 2181, Swisher Rd, **E** ⛽ Circle K, QT/dsl 🛏 Best Western, Comfort Inn ⊙ O'Reilly Parts, **W** ⛽ Chevron/McDonald's, Exxon/7-11, Murphy USA/dsl 🍴 Chick-fil-A, Chicken Express, Denny's, IHOP, Jack-in-the-Box, KFC/Taco Bell, Los Cabos, Pizza Hut, Sonic, Starbucks, Subway, Wendy's, Whataburger ⊙ Albertson's, Aldi Foods, AT&T, AutoZone, Discount Tire, Firestone/auto, GNC, Kwik Kar, URGENT CARE, Verizon, Walgreens, Walmart
457b	Denton Rd, Hundley Dr, Lake Dallas
457a	Hundley Dr (from nb), Lake Dallas
456	Highland Village
456mm	Lewisville Lake
454b	Garden Ridge Blvd
454a	FM 407, Justin, **E** ⛽ Valero 🍴 Old House BBQ, **W** ⛽ QT/dsl 🍴 McDonald's, Subway
453	Valley Ridge Blvd, **E** ⊙ Ford, May's RV, **W** ⛽ Chevron/dsl 🍴 Burger King, Fat Cow BBQ, Subway ⊙ Home Depot, Kohl's, Lowe's, Staples
452	FM 1171, to Flower Mound, **E** 🍴 IHOP, Taco Bueno 🛏 Select Inn ⊙ 🅗, **W** ⛽ Shell 🍴 Buffet Palace, Burger King, Cane's,

Exit #	Services
452	Continued Chick-fil-A, Chipotle Mexican, CiCi's Pizza, Grandy's, Korne Cafe, McDonald's, Panda Express, Pizza Hut, Regal Buffet Smashburger, Sonic, Taco Bell, Taco Cabana, Whataburger ⊙ $Tree, Albertson's, CVS, DQ, Midas, PetCo, Sam's Club/gas same as 451, transmissions, U-Haul, URGENT CARE, Walmart
451	Fox Ave, **E** ⛽ Shell/dsl 🍴 Braum's, **W** ⛽ Chevron/dsl 🍴 Cracker Barrel, Starbucks 🛏 Baymont Inn, EconoLodge ⊙ VW
450	TX 121, Grapevine, **E** ⛽ 7-11, Exxon/dsl 🛏 Texan Inn ⊙ Chrysler/Dodge/Jeep, **W** ⛽ Chevron, Conoco/dsl 🍴 Burger King, Church's, Subway, Taco Bell, Waffle House ⊙ Firestone/auto, Kwik Kar, Nissan, Toyota
449	Corporate Drive, **E** ⛽ Valero/dsl 🍴 Hooters, Kyoto, On-the Border, Razzoo's Cajun 🛏 Extended Stay America, Motel Suburban Lodge ⊙ Cavender's Boots, Chevrolet, Honda, **W** ⛽ Valero 🍴 Cantina Loredo, Chili's, Denny's, El Fenix, Outback Steaks 🛏 Best Western ⊙ $Tree, Hobby Lobby, Jo-Ann Fabric Marshall's, NTB, Petsmart, Tuesday Morning
448b a	Round Grove Rd, TX 121, Rayburn Fwy, **E** ⛽ 7-11 🍴 A&W/KF Cane's, ChuckeCheese, Dickey's BBQ, Jack-in-the-Box, Joe Crabshack, LJ Silver/Taco Bell, Olive Garden, Pei Wei, Soup Salad, Starbucks, Subway, Taco Casa 🛏 Homewood Suites Honda, Ross, Target, **W** ⛽ Exxon/7-11, RaceTrac/dsl 🍴 Applebee's, Arby's, BJ's Grill, Buffalo Wild Wings, Chick-fil-A, Chipotle Mexican, Christina's Mexican, Cotton Patch Rest., Firehouse Subs, Five Guys, Freebirds Burrito, Honeybaked Ham, Jason Deli, Jimmy John's, La Madeline Bakery, Logan's Roadhouse Macaroni Grill, McDonald's, Panda Express, Panera Bread Penn Sta Subs, Popeye's, Red Lobster, Redneck Heaven BB Saltgrass Steaks, Schlotzsky's, Sonic, Spring Creek BBQ, Starbucks, Steak'n Shake, Subway, Taco Bueno, Taco Cabana, TG Friday's, Twin Peaks, Wendy's, Which Wich? 🛏 Comfort Suites Country Inn&Suites, Courtyard, Fairfield Inn, Hampton In Hilton Garden, Holiday Inn Express, Residence Inn, SpringHill Suites, TownePlace Suites ⊙ AT&T, Barnes&Noble, Best Bu Costco/gas, Dillard's, Discount Tire, JC Penney, Macy's, ma Michael's, Old Navy, Sears/auto, URGENT CARE, Verizon
447a	TX 121, Rayburn Fwy
446	Frankford Rd, **E** ⛽ RaceTrac 🍴 La Hacienda Ranch Grill
445b a	Pres Geo Bush Tpk
444	Whitlock Lane, Sandy Lake Rd, **E** ⛽ Shell 🍴 La Hacienda Rodeway Inn ⊙ Buick/GMC, Kia, **W** 🍴 McDonald's, Starbucks 🛏 Delux Inn ⊙ Harley-Davidson
443	Belt Line Rd, Crosby Rd, **E** ⛽ RaceTrac 🍴 Subway ⊙ Ford Hyundai, **W** ⛽ Shell ⊙ Chevrolet, U-Haul
442	Valwood Pkwy, **E** ⛽ Chevron/Subway/dsl, Conoco/dsl 🍴 D Grandy's, Jack-in-the-Box, Taco Bueno, Waffle House 🛏 Gue Inn, LoneStar Inn, Super 8, **W** ⛽ Gas/dsl ⊙ transmissions
441	Valley View Lane, **W** ⛽ Chevron, Shell/dsl 🛏 Best Value In Days Inn, Motel 6
440b	I-635 E
440c	I-635 W ⊙ to DFW Airport
439	Royal Lane, **E** ⛽ Shell/dsl, Valero/7-11/dsl, Wendy's 🍴 Mc Donald's, **W** ⛽ Chevron/7-11, Exxon/dsl 🍴 Jack-in-the-Box
438	Walnut Hill Lane, **E** ⛽ Chevron/dsl, Shell, Valero/dsl 🍴 Burg King, Denny's, Trail Dust Steaks, Wild Turkey Grill 🛏 Hampt Inn, La Quinta, Quality Inn, **W** ⛽ Gulf/dsl, Shell/dsl
437	Manana Rd (from nb) same as 438
436	TX 348, to DFW, Irving, **E** ⛽ Shell/dsl 🍴 Finish Line G IHOP, Starbucks, Waffle House 🛏 Baymont Inn, Best Weste Country Inn Suites, Days Inn, Elegante Hotel, Holiday Inn press, SpringHill Suites, Studio 6, **W** ⛽ Exxon/dsl, Valero/

L E W I S V I L L E

D A L L A S

TX

⬆N INTERSTATE 35 Cont'd

436	Continued
	🍴 Chili's, Gino's Pizzaria, Humperdinks, Jack-in-the-Box, Jason's Deli, Joe's Crabshack, Mambo Seafood, McDonald's, Ojos Locos Cantina, Olive Garden, Papadeaux Seafood, Pappa's BBQ, Pappas Bros Steaks, Pappasito's Mexican, Red Lobster, Taco Bell, TX L&C, Wendy's 🛏 Budget Suites, Century Inn
435	Harry Hines Blvd (from nb)
434b	Regal Row, E 🚹 Chevron/Grandy's/dsl 🍴 Sam's Grill, Whataburger 🛏 Motel 6, W 🛏 Ramada Inn
434a	Empire, Central, E 🚹 Shell/McDonald's 🍴 Kay's Rest, Sonic 🛏 Budget Suites, Candlewood Suites, InTown Suites, Wingate Inn 🄾 Office Depot, W 🚹 Exxon/dsl 🍴 Bombshells Rest., Burger King, Schlotzsky's, Taco Bell
433b	Mockingbird Lane, E 🚹 Shell/dsl 🍴 Jack-in-the-Box 🛏 Budget Suites, Comfort Inn, Crowne Plaza, Hawthorn Suites, Love Field Hotel, Residence Inn 🄾 Love Field Airport, W 🍴 Starbucks
433a	(432b from sb) TX 356, Commonwealth Dr
432a	Inwood Rd, E 🚹 Exxon/7-11 🄾 Chevrolet, 🄷, URGENT CARE, W 🚹 Shell, Texaco/Subway/dsl 🍴 Taco Cabana, Whataburger 🛏 Embassy Suites, Extended Stay America, Hampton Inn, Holiday Inn Express, Homewood Suites
431	Motor St, E 🚹 Chevron 🍴 Denny's 🄾 🄷, W 🚹 Shell/7-11 🍴 Alamo Rest 🛏 Marriott Suites
430c	Wycliff Ave, E 🛏 Holiday Inn, Renaissance Hotel, W 🛏 Hilton Anatole, Hilton Garden
430b	Mkt Ctr Blvd, E 🄾 World Trade Ctr, W 🚹 Shell 🍴 Denny's 🛏 Best Western, Courtyard, Days Inn, DoubleTree, Fairfield Inn, Sheraton Suites
430a	Oak Lawn Ave, E 🛏 Holiday Inn, W 🚹 Shell/dsl 🍴 Denny's, Medieval Times Rest. 🄾 to Merchandise Mart
429c	HiLine Ave (from nb)
429b	Continental Ave, Commerce St W, E 🍴 Hooters, W 🚹 Exxon, Shell 🍴 McDonald's, Popeye's downtown
429a	to I-45, US 75, to Houston
428e	Commerce St E, Reunion Blvd, Dallas downtown
428d	I-30 W, to Ft Worth
428a	I-30 E, to I-45 S
428b	Industrial Blvd, E 🚹 Exxon, W 🚹 Fuel City/dsl, Shamrock
427b	I-30 E
427a	Colorado Blvd, E 🄾 🄷
426c	Jefferson Ave, E 🚹 Shell/dsl
426b	TX 180 W, 8th St, E 🚹 Shell/dsl
426a	Ewing Ave, E 🍴 McDonald's, Popeye's
425c	Marsalis Ave, W 🚹 Chevron, GME Mart 🍴 Jack-in-the-Box
425b	Beckley Ave, 12th St, sb only, W 🚹 QT, Shell 🍴 Wendy's
425a	Zang Blvd same as 425b
424	Illinois Ave, E 🚹 Chevron 🍴 William's Chicken, W 🚹 Exxon/7-11 🍴 Burger King, Church's, Jack-in-the-Box, Little Caesar's, Pancake House, Popeye's, Sonic, Subway, Taco Bell 🛏 Oak Tree Inn 🄾 Kroger, Ross, Walgreens
423b	Saner Ave
423a	(422b from nb) US 67 S, Kiest Blvd, W 🚹 Shell/repair 🍴 Golden Chick, McDonald's, Subway
421b	Ann Arbor St, W 🚹 Exxon/dsl
421a	Lp 12E W, E 🚹 RaceWay/dsl 🛏 Motel 6, W 🚹 QT/dsl 🍴 IHOP, Subway 🄾 $Tree, Walmart
420	Laureland, E 🚹 7-11/dsl 🛏 Plaza Inn, W 🚹 Exxon/dsl, Texaco 🛏 Linfield Inn
419	Camp Wisdom Rd, E 🚹 Exxon 🍴 Jack-in-the-Box 🛏 Oak Cliff Inn, W 🚹 Chevron, Shell 🍴 McDonald's 🛏 Grand Inn 🄾 U-Haul

DALLAS (vertical text in left margin)

418c	Danieldale Rd (from sb)
418b	I-635/I-20 E, to Shreveport
418a	I-20 W, to Ft Worth
417	Wheatland Rd (from nb)
416	Wintergreen Rd, W 🚹 7-11 🍴 Cracker Barrel, Waffle House 🛏 Clarion, Days Inn, Hampton Inn, Holiday Inn Express
415	Pleasant Run Rd, E 🚹 Shell/dsl, Valero/Church's/dsl 🍴 Bienvenidos Mexican, Chicken Express, Chili's, CiCi's Pizza, Grandy's, IHOP, In-N-Out, Logan's Roadhouse, Sonic, Subway, Taco Cabana, Waffle House 🛏 Great Western Inn, Hwy Express Inn, Motel 6, Spanish Trails Motel 🄾 Family$, Home Depot, NAPA, W 🍴 Burger King, Dicky's BBQ, El Chico, KFC, LJ Silver, Luby's, McDonald's, On the Border, Outback Steaks, Pollo Tropical, Starbucks, Taco Bueno, Wendy's 🛏 Best Value Inn, La Quinta 🄾 AT&T, Chevrolet, Discount Tire, Firestone/auto, Ford, Kroger, Office Depot, Ross
414	FM 1382, Desoto Rd, Belt Line Rd, E 🚹 Murphy USA/dsl 🍴 Taco Bell, Whataburger 🄾 Verizon, Walmart/McDonald's, W 🚹 $Tree, QT/dsl
413	Parkerville Rd, W 🚹 Exxon/Subway/dsl 🄾 U-Haul
412	Bear Creek Rd, W 🚹 Shell/dsl 🍴 Jack-in-the-Box 🄾 transmissions
411	FM 664, Ovilla Rd, E 🚹 Exxon/dsl, Murphy USA/dsl, RaceTrac 🍴 Burger King, Denny's, Dickey's BBQ, DQ, LJ Silver/Taco Bell, McDonald's, Panda Express, Whataburger 🛏 Comfort Inn 🄾 Brookshire's Foods, CVS Drug, USPO, Walgreens, Walmart, W 🚹 Exxon/Subway, Valero
410	Red Oak Rd, E 🚹 Shell/Pizza Inn/Subway/dsl, Valero/dsl 🛏 Motel 6, W 🄾 Hilltop Travel Trailers
408	US 77, TX 342, to Red Oak, E 🄾 golf
406	Sterrett Rd, E 🄾 fireworks
405	FM 387, E 🚹 Phillips 66/dsl, QT/dsl
404	Lofland Rd, industrial area
403	US 287, to Ft Worth, E 🚹 Murphy USA/dsl, RaceTrac/dsl, Shell/dsl, Valero 🍴 A&W/LJ Silver, Carino's, Chick-fil-A, Chili's, Chipotle, Domino's, DQ, El Fenix, IHOP, Jack-in-the-Box, KFC, Logan's Roadhouse, McDonald's, Olive Garden, Panda Express, Pizza Hut, Starbuck's, Taco Bueno, Taco Cabana, Waffle House, Wendy's 🛏 Comfort Suites, Fairfield Inn, Hampton Inn, Holiday Inn Express, LaQuinta 🄾 Belk, Best Buy, Buick/GMC/Chevrolet, Discount Tire, Hobby Lobby, Home Depot, 🄷, JC Penney, Lowe's, Office Depot, Petsmart, Ross, Target, Walmart, W 🄾 Chrysler/Dodge/Jeep, Ford
401b	US 287 bus, Waxahatchie, E 🛏 Motel 6, Super 8
401a	Brookside Rd, E 🛏 Dallas Suites, Executive Inn
399b	FM 1446
399a	FM 66, FM 876, Maypearl, E 🛏 Texas Inn, W 🚹 Exxon/dsl, Shell/Sonic/dsl
397	to US 77, to Waxahachie

WAXAHATCHIE (vertical text in right margin)

⬆N INTERSTATE 35 Cont'd

Exit #	Services
391	FM 329, Forreston Rd
386	TX 34, Italy, **E** 🅖 ♥Loves/Carl's Jr/dsl/scales/24hr, Shell/Smokehouse BBQ/dsl 🅗 Sonic 🅞 $General, **W** 🅖 Exxon/Grandy's/McDonald's/dsl/scales 🅗 Pizza Inn, Subway, Taco Bell 🅐 Italy Inn 🅞 truckwash
384	Derrs Chapel Rd
381	FM 566, Milford Rd
377	FM 934
374	FM 2959, Carl's Corner, **W** 🅖 Petro/Exxon/Dunkin'/Iron Skillet/dsl/scales/24hr/@
373	I-35E
371	I-35 W. **I-35 divides into E and W nb, converges sb See Texas I-35 W.**
370	US 77 N, FM 579, Hillsboro, **E** 🅖 TA/Shell/Country Pride/Burger King/dsl/scales/24hr/@ 🅗 Rangers Cafe
368b	FM 286 (from sb), **E** 🅗 LoneStar Café, Taco Bell, Wendy's 🅐 Hampton Inn, **W** 🅖 Exxon, Valero/dsl 🅗 Braum's, El Conquistador Mexican, El Taco Jalisco, Pizza Hut, Up In Smoke BBQ 🅐 Best Value Inn, EconoLodge, La Quinta 🅞🅗
368a	TX 22, TX 171, to Whitney, **E** 🅖 7-11, ♥Loves/Chester's/Subway/dsl/scales/24hr 🅗 Dickey's BBQ, DQ, Golden Buffet, IHOP, McDonald's, Starbucks 🅐 Comfort Suites, Days Inn, Motel 6, Quality Inn, Super 8 🅞 Hillsboro Outlets/Famous Brands, **W** 🅖 7-11, Chevron/dsl, Mobil, Murphy USA/dsl 🅗 $Tree, Chicken Express, Jack-in-the-Box, Schlotzsky's, Sonic, Whataburger 🅐 Thunderbird Motel/rest. 🅞 AT&T, Chrysler/Dodge/Jeep, Ford, Walmart/Subway
367	Old Bynum Rd (from nb) same as 368
364b	TX 81 N, to Hillsboro (from nb, exits left)
364a	FM 310 (from sb)
363	CR 3111
362mm	🆁ₛ both directions, full facilities, 🖼, litter barrels, petwalk
359	FM 1304, **W** 🅖 Gulf/dsl/24hr 🅞 truckwash
358	FM 1242 E, Abbott, **E** 🅗 Still Smokin' BBQ
356	Co Rd 3102
355	County Line Rd, **E** 🅞 Waco North RV Park
354	Marable St, **E** 🅞 Waco North RV Park
353	FM 2114, West, **E** 🅖 Chevron/dsl, Shell/Czech Bakery 🅗 Bush's Chicken, Sonic, Subway 🅞 Ford, **W** 🅖 Exxon/Slovacek's/dsl 🅐 Best Western Czech Inn 🅞 Chevrolet, Vintage Automotive
351	FM 1858, **E** 🅞 tires/repair
349	Wiggins Rd
347	FM 3149, Tours Rd
346	Ross Rd, **W** 🅖 Exxon/Church's/dsl/24hr 🅞 antiques, I-35 RV Park/LP
345	Old Dallas Rd, **W** 🅞 I-35 RV Park/LP
345a	Frontage Rd, same as 345
343	FM 308, Elm Mott, **E** 🅖 Exxon/DQ, Shell/Jct Cafe/dsl/scales/24hr, **W** 🅞 $General
342b	US 77 bus, **W** 🅞 North Crest RV Park
342a	FM 2417, Crest Dr, **W** 🅖 Valero/dsl 🅗 Bush's Chicken, DQ 🅐 Motel 6 🅞 auto repair, Family$
341	Craven Ave, Lacy Lakeview, **E** 🅞 Freightliner, **W** 🅖 Chevron, Shell
340	Myers Lane (from nb)
339	to TX 6 S, FM 3051, Lake Waco, **E** 🅖 Murphy USA, Valero/dsl 🅗 Casa Ole, Cici's Pizza, Domino's, El Conquistador, Jack-in-the-Box, Luby's, Pizza Hut, Popeye's, Sonic, Subway, Wendy's, Whataburger, WingStop 🅐 Holiday Inn 🅞 $General, $Tree, Advance Parts, Discount Tire, Home Depot, NAPA, to 🅐, Walmart,
339	Continued **W** 🅖 7-11/dsl, Chevron, Shell, Valero/dsl 🅗 Burger King, Cracker Barrel, Heitmiller Steaks, KFC, McDonald's, Starbucks, Taco Bell 🅐 Fairfield Inn, Hampton Inn 🅞 AT&T, URGENT CARE
338b	Behrens Circle (from nb), same as 339, **E** 🅗 Jack-in-the-Box, Little Caesar's, Sonic 🅞 GNC, **W** 🅖 Shell/dsl/LP 🅗 Cracker Barrel 🅐 Best Western, Comfort Suites, Days Inn, Delta Inn, Hampton Inn, Knights Inn, Motel 6, Quality Inn
338a	US 84, to TX 31, Waco Dr, **E** 🅖 Chopstix 🅗 Collin St Bakery, Denny's, Subway 🅐 Woodspring Suites 🅞 AutoZone, Family$, HEB Food/gas, O'Reilly Parts, Sam's Club/gas, Tesla EVC, **W** 🅐 Comfort Suites 🅞🅗
337	US 77 business
335c	Lake Brazos Dr, MLK Blvd, **E** 🅞 Baylor Stadium, **W** 🅗 Buzzard Billy's 🅐 Red Roof Inn, Scottish Inn 🅞🅗
335mm	Brazos River
335b	FM 434, University Parks Dr, **E** 🅗 Starbucks 🅞 Baylor U, Texas Ranger Museum, **W** 🅖 7-11/dsl 🅗 In-N-Out, Jack-in-the-Box 🅐 Residence Inn
335a	4th St, 5th St, **E** 🅖 Exxon/Subway/dsl 🅗 IHOP 🅐 La Quinta 🅞 Baylor U, **W** 🅖 Valero/dsl 🅗 Cane's, Chick-fil-A, Fazoli's, Freddy's, LJ Silver, McAlister's Deli, McDonald's, Panera Bread, Papa John's, Sonic, Taco Bell, Taco Cabana, Wendy's, Whataburger 🅞 CVS Drug
334b	US 77 S, 17th St, 18th St, **E** 🅖 Shell/dsl, Valero/dsl 🅗 Burger King, Fuego Grill, Jimmy John's, Pizza Hut, Popeye's, Schlotzsky's, Vitek's BBQ 🅐 Budget Inn, Deluxe Inn, La Quinta, Super 8, **W** 🅖 Shell 🅗 Taquerias Mexican 🅞🅗
333a	Lp 396, Valley Mills Dr, **E** 🅖 7-11/dsl 🅗 El Chico, Elite Cafe, Rudy's BBQ/gas, Trujillo's Mexican, TX Roadhouse 🅐 Comfort Suites, Motel 6 🅞 Kia, Mazda, **W** 🅖 RaceWay/dsl, Valero/dsl 🅗 Bubba's Rest., Bush's Chicken, Catfish King, Chili's, Church's, George's Rest., Jack-in-the-Box, Little Caesar's, Pizza Patron, Potbelly, Sonic, Starbucks, Subway, Zoe's Kitchen 🅐 Home2 Suites 🅞 Aamco, Advance Parts, AutoZone, CVS Drug, Family$, HEB Foods/dsl, Lincoln, Walgreens
331	New Rd, **E** 🅖 Phillips 66/dsl 🅐 Candlewood Suites, New Road Inn, Relax Inn, Rodeway Inn, **W** 🅖 ⭐FLYING J/Denny's/dsl/scales/24hr 🅗 Burger King, Carl's Jr, Hooters, IHOP 🅐 Quality Inn 🅞 Harley Davidson
330	Lp 340, TX 6, **W** 🅖 Chevron/dsl 🅗 Buffalo Wild Wings, Bush's Chicken, Chuy's Mexican, Don Carlo's Mexican, Heitmiller Steaks, Logan's Roadhouse, Newk's Eatery, Panda Express, Panera Bread, Saltgrass Steaks, Sonic, Starbucks, Subway 🅐 Hampton Inn, Holiday Inn Express, Homewood Suites, TownePlace Suites 🅞 $Tree, AT&T, Belk, Best Buy, Cabela's, Cavender's Boots, Fiat/Alpha Romeo, Ford, Honda, 🅗, Hyundai, JoAnn, Kohl's, Marshall's, Nissan, Office Depot, Old Navy, PetCo, Ross, Toyota, URGENT CARE, World Mkt
328	FM 2063, FM 2113, Moody, **E** 🅖 🄿🄸🄻🄾🅃/Subway/Wendy's/dsl/scales/24hr/@ 🅗 McDonald's 🅐 Robinson Inn 🅞 Kenworth, 🅖 Shell/dsl, Valero/dsl 🅗 DQ 🅐 Ramada Inn, Sleep Inn
325	FM 3148, Moonlight Dr, **W** 🅖 Valero/dsl 🅞 FunTown RV Ctr
323	FM 2837 (from sb), Lorena, **W** 🅖 Brookshire Bros/Conoco/dsl 🅗 Pizza House, Sonic
322	Lorena, **E** 🅖 Phillips 66/dsl, **W** 🅗 Bush's Chicken, Pizza House 🅞 $General
321	Callan Ranch Rd
319	Woodlawn Rd
318b a	Bruceville
315	TX 7, FM 107, Eddy, **E** 🅖 Bruceville-Eddy RV Park, **W** 🅞 Family$, to Mother Neff SP
314	Old Blevins Rd

TEMPLE

INTERSTATE 35 Cont'd

Exit #	Services
311	Big Elm Rd, **E** 🅞 fireworks
308	FM 935, Troy, **E** 🅖 Love's/Subway/McDonald's/dsl/scales/24hr, Shell/dsl, Valero/dsl, **W** 🅞 $General, dsl repair
306	FM 1237, Pendleton, **W** 🅞 Goodyear Truck Tires
305	Berger Rd, **W** 🅞 Lucky's RV Park, repair
304	Lp 363, Dodgen Loop, **E** 🅖 Buc-ee's/dsl, **W** 🅖 Shell/Wendy's/dsl 🅞 Freightliner
303	spur 290, N 3rd St, Temple, **E** 🅖 S-2 Gas 🅐 Texas Inn
302	Nugent Ave, **E** 🅖 Exxon/dsl 🅐 Baymont Inn, Best Value Inn, EconoLodge, Motel 6, **W** 🅕 TX Roadhouse 🅐 Best Western, Days Inn, Knights Inn, Motel 6
301	TX 53, FM 2305, Adams Ave, **E** 🅖 Exxon/dsl, Valero 🅕 Arby's, Chick-fil-A, KFC, Little Caesar's, LJ Silver, McDonald's, Pizza Hut, Starbucks, Subway, Taco Bell, Whataburger 🅐 La Quinta 🅞 Advance Parts, HEB Foods/dsl, 🅗, O'Reilly Parts, URGENT CARE, **W** 🅕 TX Roadhouse 🅐 Best Western
300	Ave H, 49th –57th Sts, **E** 🅕 Clem Mikeskas BBQ
299	US 190 E, TX 36, **E** 🅖 Shell/dsl 🅕 Cracker Barrel, Jack-in-the-Box, Luby's, Olive Garden, Sol de Jalisco 🅐 Budget Inn, Residence Inn, Travelodge 🅞 AT&T, Chrysler/Dodge/Jeep, 🅗, Natural Grocers, Tires To You, URGENT CARE, Verizon, **W** 🅕 BJ's Rest., Chili's, Chipotle Mexican, Five Guys, IHOP, McDonald's, Subway, Taco Cabana 🅐 Hampton Inn 🅞 Best Buy, Firestone/auto, GNC, Home Depot, Michael's, Petsmart, Target
298	nb only, to Frontage Rd, **E** 🅕 Longhorn Steaks 🅐 Residence Inn
297	FM 817, Midway Dr, **E** 🅖 Phillips 66/dsl 🅕 Golden Corral 🅐 Holiday Inn, Super 8/rest. 🅞 Buick/GMC/Cadillac, Nissan, **W** 🅖 Valero/dsl 🅞 Goodyear/auto, VW
294b	FM 93, 6th Ave, **E** 🅖 Shell/dsl 🅕 McDonald's 🅞 Chevrolet, Ford/Lincoln, Toyota, **W** 🅕 Subway 🅐 River Forest Inn 🅞 Harley-Davidson, U of Mary Hardin Baylor
294a	Central Ave, **E** 🅕 Taco Bell, **W** 🅖 Shell/dsl 🅕 Burger King, El Mexicano Grill, Jimmy John's, Pizza Hut, Schlotzsky's, Schoepf's BBQ, Sonic, Starbucks, Whataburger 🅐 Knights Inn 🅞 AutoZone, city park, O'Reilly Parts, Parts+, USPO
293b	TX 317, FM 436, Main St
293a	US 190 W, to Killeen, Ft Hood
292	Lp 121 (same as 293a), **E** 🅖 Valero/dsl/24hr 🅐 Budget Host, **W** 🅖 7-11/dsl, Exxon/dsl 🅕 Oxbow Steaks 🅐 La Quinta 🅞 Belton RV Park, Sunbelt RV Ctr
290	Shanklin Rd
289	Tahuaya Rd
287	Amity Rd
286	FM 2484, **E** 🅖🅐 Days Inn, Holiday Inn Express, **W** 🅞 to Stillhouse Hollow Lake, Tranquil RV Park (2mi)
285	FM 2268, Salado, **E** 🅖 Conoco/dsl 🅕 Subway 🅐 Holiday Inn Express 🅞 Brookshire Foods/gas, **W** 🅖 Cefco/dsl, Gulf 🅕 Bush's Chicken, Robertson's Rest., Sonic
284	Stagecoach Rd, **E** 🅐 Stagecoach Inn, **W** 🅕 Johnny's Steaks
283	FM 2268, FM 2843, to Holland, Salado, **E** 🅐 Stagecoach Inn
282	FM 2115, **E** 🅖 Valero/dsl
281mm	🆁🆂 both lanes, full ♿ facilities, 🅲, 🄰, litter barrels, vending, petwalk, RV dump
280	Grainger Rd, Hackberry Rd, Prairie Dell
279	Hill Rd
277	Rd 305
275	FM 487, to Florence, Jarrell, **E** 🅖 Exxon/dsl 🅞 $General, **W** 🅖 Shell/dsl (2), Shell/Krispy Kreme/Pizza Inn/dsl 🅞 USPO
274	Rd 312, **E** 🅖 Exxon/Subway/dsl, FLYING J/Burger King/Denny's/dsl/scales 🅕 McDonald's

GEORGETOWN

Exit #	Services
271	Ronald Reagan Blvd, **W** 🅖 Shell/Subway/dsl/24hr
268	fm 972, Walburg, **E** 🅞 Crestview RV Ctr
266	TX 195, **E** 🅖 Phillips 66/dsl, Shell TC/dsl/scales/24hr, **W** 🅖 Shell/dsl
265	TX 130 Toll S, to Austin
264	Lp 35, Georgetown
262	RM 2338, Lake Georgetown, **E** 🅖 Valero 🅕 Chipotle Mexican, KFC, McDonald's, Papa John's, Pizza Hut, Sonic, Starbucks, Subway, Verts Grill 🅞 $Tree, CVS Drug, Parts+, URGENT CARE, **W** 🅕 DQ, Frankie's Pizza, Plaka Greek, Whataburger 🅐 Candlewood Suites, Georgetown Inn, Holiday Inn Express, La Quinta
261	TX 29, Georgetown, **E** 🅖 Shell/dsl 🅕 Applebee's, Burger King, Chili's, Domino's, Jack-in-the-Box, Jimmy John's, KFC, La Playa, McDonald's, Schlotzsky's, Taco Bell 🅐 Best Western, Comfort Suites, Hampton Inn 🅞 HEB Foods, Hobby Lobby, Midas, O'Reilly Parts, same as 262, Tuesday Morning, **W** 🅖 Murphy USA/dsl 🅕 Cane's, Carl's Jr, Casa Ole, Chick-fil-A, CiCi's, Cotton Patch Cafe, Five Guys, George's Rest., IHOP, Longhorn Steaks, Mama Fu's, McAlister's Deli, Panda Express, Panera Bread, Pie Five, Popeye's, Salsa's Mexican, Souper Salad, Starbucks, Taco Cabana, Wendy's 🅞 AT&T, Beall's, Best Buy, Discount Tire, Home Depot, Kohl's, Michael's, Natural Grocers, Office Depot, Old Navy, Petsmart, Ross, Target, TJ Maxx, Verizon, Walgreens, Walmart/McDonald's
260	RM 2243, Leander, **E** 🅞 🅗, USPO, **W** 🅖 Chevron/dsl, Exxon/dsl, Texaco 🅕 Jack-in-the-Box 🅐 Econolodge
259	Lp 35, **W** 🅞 RV Outlet Ctr, to Interspace Caverns
257	Westinghouse Rd, **E** 🅞 Buick/Chevrolet, Chrysler/Dodge/Jeep, Ford/Lincoln, Mazda, Mercedes, Subaru/Volvo, VW
256	RM 1431, Chandler Rd, **E** 🅕 BJ Rest., Chili's, Chipotle, Firehouse Subs, Freebirds Burrito, In-N-Out, Jamba Juice, Jimmy John's, La Madeleine, Mimi's Cafe, Mooyah Burger, Panda Express, Papa John's, Pei Wei, Razzoo's Cajun, Starbucks, Steak'n Shake, TGI Friday's, Which Wich?, Zoe's Kitchen 🅞 Bass Pro Shops, GNC, HEB/dsl, IKEA, JC Penney, Jo-Ann Fabrics, Mazda, Petsmart, REI, Ross, Round Rock Outlet/famous brands, Volvo, Walgreens
254	FM 3406, Round Rock, **E** 🅖 Chevron/dsl 🅕 Gatti's Pizza, Kerby Lane Cafe, La Tapatia, McDonald's, Saucy Rooster 🅐 Best Western 🅞 $General, Firestone/auto, Harley-Davidson, Honda, Hyundai, Kia, Toyota, **W** 🅖 EVC, Shell/dsl 🅕 Chuy's Mexican, Cover 3 Rest., Cracker Barrel, Denny's, Double Dave's Pizza, Jack Allen's Kitchen, Mellow Mushroom, Rudy's BBQ/gas, Salt Traders Rest., SaltGrass Steaks 🅐 Courtyard, Hilton Garden, Holiday Inn, Holiday Inn Express, La Quinta, Red Roof Inn, SpringHill Suites, Woodspring Suites 🅞 CVS Drug, GMC, Nissan
253b	US 79, to Taylor, **E** 🅖 Chevron/dsl/24hr, Texaco/dsl 🅕 Baskin-Robbins, Casa Garcia's, DQ, Fuddrucker's, KFC, La Tapatia, LJ Silver, Pizza Hut, Short Stop Dogs, Sirloin Stockade

ROUND ROCK

TX

TX

ROUND ROCK

⬆N INTERSTATE 35 Cont'd

253b Continued
🛏 Best Western, Wingate Inn 🅾 $General, Advance Parts, AutoZone, Beall's, Cottman Transmissions; Just Brakes, **W** 🍴 Shell/dsl 🍴 Gatti's Pizza, Hunan Lion, IHOP, La Margarita, Poke Joe's BBQ, Popeye's, Starbucks, Thundercloud Subs 🛏 Country Inn&Suites, La Quinta, Motel 6, Red Roof Inn, Woodspring Suites 🅾 $Tree, USPO

253a Frontage Rd, same as 253 b

252b a RM 620, **E** 🍴 Shell/dsl 🛏 Candlewood Suites, Extended Stay America 🅾 NAPA, **W** 🍴 Mobil/dsl 🍴 Corner Cafe Bakery, Freddy's Steakburgers, Jimmy John's, Little Caesar's, McDonald's, Starbucks, Wendy's 🛏 Comfort Suites, Staybridge Suites 🅾 Office Depot, Sprouts Mkt, Tuesday Morning

251 Lp 35, Round Rock, **E** 🍴 CiCi's Pizza, Outback Steaks, Papa John's, Pluckers Wings, Smokey Mo's BBQ, Whataburger 🛏 Residence Inn 🅾 Aamco, BigLots, Brake Check, **W** 🍴 Shell 🍴 Burger King, Jack-in-the-Box, Luby's, Taco Cabana 🛏 Days Inn, Marriott, Sleep Inn 🅾 Austin's Automotive, GNC, NTB, transmissions, Walgreens

250 TX 45, Lp 1, **E** 🍴 Chick-fil-A, Chili's, El Taquito, Firehouse Subs, Five Guys, Green Mesquite BBQ, Jason's Deli, Joe's Crabshack, Macaroni Grill, McDonald's, Panda Express, Subway, Twin Peaks Rest. 🛏 Hampton Inn, Homewood Suites, Residence Inn 🅾 $Tree, AT&T, Best Buy, Discount Tire, Home Depot, Michael's, Petsmart, Ross, Steinmart, Target, URGENT CARE, Walmart/Subway, **W** 🍴 Applebee's, Chipotle, Egg&I Cafe, Hooters, Jimmy John's, Logan's Roadhouse, Longhorn Steaks, Olive Garden, Red Lobster, Schlotzsky's, Tokyo Steaks 🛏 Extended Stay America, La Quinta 🅾 Barnes&Noble, Hobby Lobby, Kohl's, Lowe's, Marshall's, Old Navy, PetCo, Sam's Club, World Mkt

248 Grand Ave Pkwy, **E** 🍴 7-11/Subway/dsl, Citgo, Shell/dsl 🍴 Chucho's Mexican, Gatti's Pizza, Thundercloud Subs, TX Roadhouse 🛏 Comfort Suites 🅾 URGENT CARE, **W** 🍴 Exxon/McDonald's/dsl

247 FM 1825, Pflugerville, **E** 🍴 Exxon/7-11/dsl 🍴 Bombshells Rest., Burger King, Cheddar's, Domino's, FD's Grillhouse, Jack-in-the-Box, Subway, Taco Cabana, Wendy's 🛏 Comfort Suites 🅾 Firestone/auto, GNC, HEB Foods/gas, **W** 🍴 Exxon/7-11, Shell/Church's 🍴 KFC, Miller's BBQ, Sonic 🛏 Country Inn Suites 🅾 Goodyear, McSpadden Automotive, Tires4Less

246 Howard Lane, **E** 🍴 Citgo, Exxon/7-11/dsl 🍴 Arby's, Baby Acapulco, McDonald's, Subway, Wings'n More 🅾 Home Depot, Kohl's, NTB, **W** 🍴 Valero/dsl 🍴 IHOP, Whataburger 🛏 Sleep Inn 🅾 CarMax

245 FM 734, Parmer Lane, to Yager Lane (244 from nb), **E** 🍴 Carino's, Chick-fil-A, Chili's, Freebirds Burrito, In-N-Out, Jersey Mike's, Jimmy John's, Kublai Khan, Little Caesar's, Masala Wok, MOD Pizza, My Fit Grill, Panda Express, Pei Wei, Schlotzsky's, Souper Salad, Subway, Verts Grill, Zed's Rest 🛏 Homewood Suites 🅾 $Tree, HEB Food/E-85, Hobby Lobby, JC Penney, Kohl's, PetCo, Petsmart, Ross, Sears Grand, Verizon, **W** 🍴 Conoco/dsl, Exxon/7-11/dsl, Murphy USA/dsl 🍴 Buffalo Wild Wings, Golden Corral, Hoho Chinese, Red Robin 🛏 Courtyard, Fairfield Inn, Hilton Garden, Residence Inn, SpringHill Suites, Staybridge Suites 🅾 AT&T, CarMax, Discount Tire, Lowe's, Walmart/McDonald's

244 Tech Ridge Blvd, Yager Lane, (from nb), same as 245

243 Braker Lane, **E** 🍴 Valero/dsl 🍴 Whataburger 🅾 U-Haul, **W** 🍴 Citgo, Shell/dsl 🛏 Austin Motel, Woodspring Suites 🅾 $General

241 Rundberg Lane, **E** 🍴 Exxon/7-11 🍴 Grand China Buffet, Jack-in-the-Box 🛏 Extended Stay America, Orangewood Inn 🅾 $General, Chevrolet, U-Haul, **W** 🍴 Chevron, Shell 🛏 Austin Suites, Budget Inn, Budget Lodge, Economy Inn, Holiday Inn Express, Motel 6, Motel 6 (2), Red Roof Inn, Super 8

240a US 183, Lockhart, **E** 🍴 Exxon 🍴 Jack-in-the-Box 🛏 Days Inn, Orangewood Inn, **W** 🍴 Chevron/dsl 🛏 Motel 6, Red Roof Inn, Super 8

239 St John's Ave, **E** 🍴 Shell 🍴 Burger King, Chili's, Japon Japanese, Pappadeaux, Pappasito's Mexican 🛏 Crowne Plaza, Days Inn, DoubleTree, Drury Inn, Econolodge, Hampton Inn, Studio 6 🅾 USPO, **W** 🍴 Exxon/7-11, Mobil/dsl, Valero/dsl 🍴 Applebee's, Buffalo Wild Wings, Carrabba's, Denny's, IHOP, Ojos Locos, Panda Express, Wendy's 🛏 Best Value Inn, Comfort Inn, Country Inn&Suites, Courtyard, Holiday Inn, Hyatt Place, La Quinta, Motel 6, Ramada Inn 🅾 Ford, Office Depot

238b US 290 E, RM 222, same as 238a, Frontage Rds connect several exits

238a 51st St, **E** 🍴 Buffet King, Chipotle, Church's, CiCi's, Jamba Juice, La Madeleine, McDonald's, Papa John's, Pieology, SmashBurger, Subway, Tino's Greek, TX Steaks, Which Wich? 🛏 DoubleTree Hotel, Drury Inn, EconoLodge, Embassy Suites 🅾 $Tree, Advance Parts, AutoZone, Best Buy, Home Depot, Marshall's, Old Navy, Petsmart, Ross, Staples, Target, Walgreens, **W** 🍴 Shell 🍴 Baby Acapulco, Capt Benny's Seafood 🛏 Capital Inn, Courtyard, Fairfield Inn, Motel 6, Super 8

237b 51st St, same as 238a

237a Airport Blvd, **W** 🍴 In-N-Out, Jack-in-the-Box, Wendy's 🅾 GNC, Goodyear, HEB Foods, PetCo, Sears/auto

236.7 upper level is I-35 thru, lower level accesses downtown

236b 39th St, **E** 🍴 Chevron/dsl 🍴 Short Stop Burgers, Subway 🅾 Fiesta Foods, O'Reilly Parts, U-Haul, **W** 🍴 Shell/dsl 🅾 to U of TX

236a 26th-32nd Sts, **E** 🍴 Los Altos Mexican, Subway 🛏 Days Inn, 🛏 Rodeway Inn 🅾 Ⓗ

235b Manor Rd, **E** 🍴 Denny's 🛏 DoubleTree, **W** 🛏 Rodeway Inn 🅾 st capitol, U of TX same as 236a

235a MLK, 15th St, **W** 🅾 Ⓗ

234.9 upper level is I-35 thru, lower level accesses downtown

234c 11th St, 12th St, **E** 🍴 Chevron/dsl, Shell/dsl 🍴 Denny's, Wendy's 🛏 DoubleTree Hotel, Super 8 🅾 CVS Drug, **W** 🍴 Gulf/dsl, Shell 🛏 Hilton, Hilton Garden, La Quinta, Marriott, Omni Motel, Radisson, Sheraton 🅾 Ⓗ, museum, st capitol downtown

234b 8th-3rd St, **W** 🍴 IHOP

234a Cesar Chavez St, Holly St, **E** 🍴 Shell/dsl, **W** 🍴 Chevron/dsl 🛏 Holiday Inn downtown

233mm Little Colorado River

233 Riverside Dr, Town Lake, **E** 🍴 Gulf, Shell/dsl 🍴 Chipotle, Church's, MOD Pizza, Starbucks 🅾 AT&T, Walgreens

232b Woodland Ave

232a Oltorf St, **E** 🍴 Chevron/dsl, Gulf, Shell/dsl 🍴 Donn's BBQ, Luby's, Sonic 🛏 Best Value, Howard Johnson, La Quinta, Motel 6, Parkwest Inn, **W** 🍴 Conoco/dsl, Exxon/7-11 🍴 Denny's, Starbucks 🛏 Best Western, Simco Plaza

231 Woodward St, **E** 🛏 same as 232, Wyndham Garden, **W** 🅾 Home Depot, Walmart

230b a US 290 W, TX 71, Ben White Blvd, St Elmo Rd, **E** 🍴 Shell/Circle K/dsl 🛏 Baymont Inn, Courtyard, Fairfield Inn, Hampton Inn, Homewood Suites, Marriott, Omni Hotel, Quality Inn, Red Roof Inn, Residence Inn, SpringHill Suites 🅾 Acura, **W** 🍴 Burger King 🛏 Candlewood Suites, Days Inn, La Quinta 🅾 Audi, CarMax, Chrysler/Dodge/Jeep, Ford, Ⓗ, Hyundai, Kia, Mazda, Nissan, NTB, Toyota

AUSTIN

🔼 INTERSTATE 35 Cont'd

Exit #	Services
229	Stassney Lane, **W** 🍴 Buffalo Wild Wings, Chili's, Chipotle, Jimmy John's, Krispy Kreme, Logan's Roadhouse, Macaroni Grill, Pizza Hut, Trudy's Grill, Twin Peaks Rest., TX Cattle Co Steaks 🏠 Holiday Inn Express, Staybridge Suites 🅾 Fiesta Foods/gas, Lowe's
228	Wm Cannon Drive, **E** 🅿 Exxon, Valero 🍴 Applebee's, McDonald's, Subway, Taco Bell 🅾 Brake Check, Discount Tire, HEB Foods, Nissan, **W** 🅿 Shell/dsl 🍴 Burger King, China Harbor, Gatti's Pizza, Golden Corral, KFC, LJ Silver, Taco Cabana, Wendy's, Whataburger 🅾 Advance Parts, AT&T, BigLots, Chevrolet, Firestone
227	Slaughter Lane, Lp 275, S Congress, **E** 🅿 Shell/dsl 🍴 ChuckE-Cheese, Don Dario's, IHOP 🅾 Home Depot, Lone Star RV Resort, U-Haul, **W** 🅿 Murphy USA/dsl, Valero, Valero/dsl 🍴 Carino's, Chick-fil-A, Chili's, Chipotle Mexican, Fuddrucker's, Gatti Town, Jack-in-the-Box, Jason's Deli, Longhorn Steaks, Luby's, Mama Fu's, Miller BBQ, Panda Express, Serrano's Tex-Mex, Smashburger, Sonic, Starbucks, Steak'n Shake, Subway, Taco Bell, TGIFriday's, TX Roadhouse, Wendy's, Whataburger 🅾 $Tree, AT&T, Best Buy, Firestone/auto, GNC, Hobby Lobby, JC Penney, Jo-Ann, Marshall's, Petsmart, Ross, Sam's Club/dsl, Target, URGENT CARE, Verizon, VW, Walgreens, Walmart
226	Slaughter Creek Overpass
225	FM 1626, Onion Creek Pkwy, **E** 🅿 Texaco, Valero 🍴 Subway 🅾 Harley-Davidson
224	Frontage Rd (from nb)
223	FM 1327, rd 45 toll
221	Lp 4, Buda, **E** 🅿 Chevron/McDonald's 🍴 Starbucks 🏠 Best Value Inn, Candlewood Suites, Comfort Suites, Holiday Inn Express 🅾 Ford, Kenworth, **W** 🅿 Murphy USA/dsl, Shell/dsl 🍴 Arby's, Chili's, Cracker Barrel, Dan's Burgers, Domino's, Jack-in-the-Box, KFC/LJ Silver, Little Caesar's, Logan's Roadhouse, Miller BBQ, Papa John's, Pizza Hut, Sonic, Subway, Taco Bell, Whataburger, Zaxby's 🏠 Hampton Inn, Microtel 🅾 AT&T, AutoZone, Cabela's, HEB Food/dsl/E-85, O'Reilly Parts, USPO, Verizon, Walgreens, Walmart
220	FM 2001, Niederwald, **E** 🅿 Shell 🍴 Burger King 🅾 Camper Clinic RV Ctr, Marshall's RV Park, **W** 🅾 Crestview RV Ctr/Park, Peterbilt
217	Lp 4, Buda, **E** 🅿 Exxon/dsl 🏠 La Quinta 🅾 Mack/Volvo, **W** 🅿 Valero/dsl 🍴 Burger King 🏠 Quality Inn 🅾 Christian Bros Auto, Home Depot
215	Bunton Overpass, **E** 🅿 Exxon/KFC/LJ Silver, Walmart/dsl 🍴 Carl's Jr, Dickey's BBQ, Dunkin'/Baskin Robbins, Firehouse Subs, Pollo Tropical, Popeye's, Taco Bell, Taco Cabana, Wendy's 🏠 Hampton Inn 🅾 AT&T, Discount Tire, Firestone/auto, 🏥, Lowe's, Walgreens, Walmart, **W** 🅿 Conoco/dsl, Sunoco/Schlotzky's/dsl 🍴 Applebee's, Casa Garcia's, Chick-fil-A, Chicken Express, Five Guys, IHOP, Jack-in-the-Box, Jersey Mike's, Little Caesar's, Mama Fu's, McDonald's, MOD Pizza, Panda Express, Papa Murphy's, Starbucks, Subway, Whataburger 🏠 Comfort Suites 🅾 $Tree, Explore USA RV Ctr, GNC, HEB Foods/dsl/e85, Kohl's, PetCo, Ross, Target, URGENT CARE, Verizon
213	FM 150, Kyle, **E** 🅿 7-11/dsl, Valero/dsl 🍴 DQ 🅾 AutoZone, O'Reilly Parts, **W** 🅿 Conoco/dsl 🍴 Casa Maria Mexican 🅾 Advance Parts, CVS Drug, repair
210	Yarrington Rd, **E** 🅾 Hyundai, **W** 🅾 Buick/Chevrolet/GMC, Ford, Plum Creek RV Park
209	weight sta (sb only)
208mm	Blanco River

S A N   M A R C O S

Exit #	Services
208	Frontage Rd, Blanco River Rd, **W** 🏠 Hilton Garden 🅾 Buick/Chevrolet/GMC
206	Lp 82, Aquarena Springs Rd, **E** 🅿 Conoco, Valero/dsl 🅾 San Marcos RV Park, **W** 🅿 Exxon/dsl, Shell, Shell/dsl 🍴 Inn-N-Out, Pancake House, Pollo Tropical, Popeye's, Sonic 🏠 Best Value Inn, Howard Johnson, La Quinta, Motel 6, Quality Inn, Ramada Ltd, Rodeway Inn, Summit Inn, Super 8 🅾 to SW TX U
205	TX 80, TX 142, Bastrop, **E** 🅿 7-11/dsl, Exxon, Little Caesar's, RaceWay/dsl, Shell/dsl, Valero/dsl 🍴 Cane's, China Palace, Fazoli's, Freebirds Burrito, Jason's Deli, Pizza Hut, Subway, Wing Stop 🏠 Executive Inn, Fairfield Inn 🅾 $General, AutoZone, CVS Drug, Hobby Lobby, Verizon, Walmart, **W** 🅿 Valero 🍴 A&W/LJ Silver, Burger King, Church's, Chuy's, Five Guys, IHOP, Kobe Japanese, Logan's Roadhouse, McDonald's, Taco Cabana, Wendy's 🏠 Best Western, Budget Inn, Days Inn, Gateway Inn, Knights Inn, Red Roof Inn, Rodeway Inn 🅾 Brake Check, city park, HEB/gas, Office Depot, Walgreens
204mm	San Marcos River
204b	CM Allen Pkwy, **W** 🅿 Shell/dsl, Spirit/dsl 🍴 Casa Maria, DQ, Krispy Kreme, La Fonda Rest., Mazatlan, Plucker's Grill, Sonic 🏠 Best Western, EconoLodge 🅾 AutoZone, O'Reilly Parts, transmissions
204a	Lp 82, TX 123, to Seguin, **E** 🅿 Conoco, Exxon/dsl 🍴 54th St Grill, Burger King, Bush's Chicken, Carino's, Chicken Express, Chili's, Freddy's, Luby's, McDonald's, Newk's Eatery, Red Lobster, Starbucks, Whataburger 🏠 Comfort Suites, Hampton Inn, Wingate Inn 🅾 Aamco, 🏥
202	FM 3407, Wonder World Dr, **E** 🅿 Exxon/dsl, Shell/dsl 🍴 Carl's Jr, Chick-fil-A, Fuschaks BBQ, Jack-in-the-Box, Panera Bread, Taste of China, Wienerschnitzel 🏠 Comfort Inn 🅾 $Tree, Best Buy, Discount Tire, 🏥, Lowe's, Marshall's, Petsmart, Ross, Sams Club/gas, **W** 🅿 Valero/dsl 🍴 TX Roadhouse 🏠 Candlewood Suites, Country Inn&Suites, Holiday Inn Express 🅾 repair
201	McCarty Lane, **E** 🏠 Embassy Suites, **W** 🍴 Firehouse Subs, Panda Express, Sonic 🅾 AT&T, Beall's, Chrysler/Dodge/Jeep, Firestone/auto, JC Penney, Nissan, Target, URGENT CARE
200	Centerpoint Rd, **E** 🍴 Chipotle, Cracker Barrel, Outback Steaks, Subway, Taco Bell, Wendy's 🅾 GNC, Old Navy, San Marcos Outlets/famous brands, Tanger Outlet/famous brands, **W** 🅿 Sunoco/dsl 🍴 McDonald's, Starbucks, Subway, Whataburger, Zaxby's 🏠 Baymont Inn, Courtyard 🅾 Honda
199	Posey Rd, **E** 🅾 Tanger Outlets/famous brands, Toyota, same as 200
196	FM 1106, York Creek Rd, **W** 🅾 Canyon Trail RV Park
195	Watson Lane, Old Bastrop Rd
193	Conrads Rd, Kohlenberg Rd, **W** 🅿 TA/Shell/Country Fare/Popeye's/Subway/dsl/scales/24hr/@ 🅾 Camping World RV Ctr

= gas   = food   = lodging   = other   = rest stop   Copyright 2022 - The Next EXIT ®

TX

INTERSTATE 35 Cont'd

NEW BRAUNFELS

Exit #	Services
191	FM 306, FM 483, Canyon Lake, E Buc-ee's BJ's Rest, Las Palapas, Longhorn Steaks, Newk's Eatery, Panda Express, Panera Bread, Sea Island Shrimphouse, Shogun Japanese, Subway, Whataburger, Which Wich?, Willie's Grill AT&T, Belk, Best Buy, Dick's, GNC, Hobby Lobby, JC Penney, Petsmart, Ross, Target, TJ Maxx, URGENT CARE, Verizon, Walmart Dist Ctr, W Exxon/dsl Burger King, HEB/e85 Wingate Inn Nissan, transmissions
190c	Post Rd
190b	Frontage Rd, New Braunfels, E Evergreen RV Ctr
190a	Frontage Rd, same as 189
189	TX 46, Seguin, E Shell/dsl Chili's, Denny's, Golden Corral, Logan's Roadhouse, Olive Garden, Peter Piper Pizza, Sonic, Taco Palenque Best Value Inn, Courtyard, EconoLodge, Hampton Inn, La Quinta, Super 8, Travelodge Discount Tire, Home Depot, Kohl's, Office Depot, vet, W Texaco, Valero Applebee's, Bush's Chicken, Chipotle Mexican, IHOP, Mama Fu's, McDonald's, Miller's BBQ, Pizza Hut, Subway, Taco Bell, Taco Cabana, TJ's Burgers, Wendy's Baymont, Best Western, Candlewood Suites, Comfort Suites, Country Inn Suites, Days Inn, Edelweiss Inn, Fairfield Inn, Hilton Garden, Holiday Inn Express, Howard Johnson, Microtel, Motel 6, Quality Inn, Ramada Inn, Rodeway Inn, Sleep Inn H, Walgreens
188	Frontage Rd, W Garden Buffet, Mamacita's Rest. River Ranch Resort Hyundai, Tuesday Morning
188mm	Guadalupe River
187	FM 725, Lake McQueeny Rd, E A&W/LJ Silver, Arby's, Burger King, CiCi's, River Hofbrau, Whataburger $Tree, Aamco, BigLots, Chevrolet, Ford/Lincoln, Jeep, Meineke, vet, W Adobe Café, DQ, Jack-in-the-Box, Jason's Deli Budget Inn CVS Drug, H, River Ranch RV Resort
186	Walnut Ave, E Exxon/Subway, Murphy USA/dsl, Valero/dsl Carl's Jr, Chick-fil-A, Firehouse Subs, McDonald's, Popeye's, Schlotzsky's, Taco Bell Red Roof Inn Jo-Ann, Lowe's, Verizon, Walmart, W Shell/dsl Baskin-Robbins, Bonzai Japanese, Chicken Express, Panda Express, Papa John's, Papa Murphy's, Pollo Tropical, Starbucks $Tree, AutoZone, GNC, HEB Foods/gas, U-Haul, Walgreens
185	FM 1044
184	FM 482, Lp 337, Rueckle Rd, E Shell/dsl Hill Country RV Park, Kia, Mazda, W /McDonald's/Subway/dsl/scales Jack-in-the-Box
183	Solms Rd, W Exxon/Circle K/dsl
182	Engel Rd
180	Schwab Rd
178	FM 1103, Cibolo Rd, Hubertus Rd, E Exxon/7-11/dsl McDonald's Walgreens, W Valero/Subway/dsl
177	FM 482, FM 2252, W Stone Creek RV Park
176	Weiderstein Rd same as 175
175	FM 3009, Natural Bridge, E Valero/dsl Chili's, IHOP, Mama Margie's Mexican, McDonald's, Miller's BBQ, Schlotzsky's, Sonic, Taco Cabana Fairfield Inn, Hampton Inn HEB Food/dsl/E-85, Lowe's, Verizon, vet, W Murphy USA/dsl, Shell/dsl, Valero/Subway/dsl Abel's Diner, Arby's, Cane's, Chick-fil-A, Denny's, Domino's, Jack-in-the-Box, Jimmy John's, KFC/Pizza Hut/Taco Bell, Panda Express, Pollo Tropical, Starbucks, Wendy's, Whataburger, Wing Stop Best Western, La Quinta $Tree, URGENT CARE, Walmart/McDonald's
174b	Schertz Pkwy, E Shell Chevrolet, W Crestview RV Ctr

SAN ANTONIO

Exit #	Services
174a	FM 1518, Selma, E Phillips 66/dsl Rudy's BBQ Audi Buick/GMC, Honda, Subaru, W Comfort Inn Crestview RV Ctr
173	Old Austin Rd, Olympia Pkwy, E Baskin Robbins, Charley's Subs, Cheddar's, Chick-fil-A, Chili's, Chipotle Mexican, CiCi's Firehouse Subs, Five Guys, Freddy's, Genghis Grill, Hooters IHOP, Las Palapas, Macaroni Grill, Outback Steaks, Panda Express, Panera Bread, Papouli's Greek, Peter Piper Pizza, Red Robin, Sea Island Srimp, Starbucks, Subway, Wendy's Holiday Inn Express AT&T, Beall's, Best Buy, Costco/gas, Discount Tire, GNC, Hobby Lobby, Home Depot, Kohl's, Michael's NTB, Old Navy, Petsmart, Ross, Target, TJ Maxx, URGENT CARE Verizon, WorldMkt, W ChuckeCheese, Chuy's Mexican, Freebirds Burritos, Houlihan's Hampton Inn
172	TX 218, Anderson Lp, P Booker Rd, E Buffalo Wild Wings Coldstone, Gino's East Pizza, IHOP, Jimmy John's, TX Roadhouse, Zio's Hilton Garden, Woodspring Suites Nissan, to Randolph AFB, W Comfort Inn to SeaWorld
171	Topperwein Rd same as 170
170	Judson Rd, to Converse, E Carl's Jr, Denny's, Whataburger Great Value Inn, La Quinta Ford, H, Hyundai, Nissan, Toyota, W Exxon/7-11 Best Western Kia, Mazda, Sam's Club/gas
169	O'Conner Rd, Wurzbach Pkwy, E Exxon/7-11/dsl McDonald's, Quiznos, Subway, Taco Cabana Comfort Suites CarMax, Chrysler/Dodge/Jeep, Lowe's, Walgreens, W Shell/dsl Valero/dsl Jack-in-the-Box, Jim's Rest., Mi Casa Inn, Sonic Kia, Mazda
168	Weidner Rd, E Citgo/dsl Comfort Suites, Days Inn, W Chevron Econolodge, Super 8 Harley-Davidson, Volvo Trucks
167b	Thousand Oaks Dr, Starlight Terrace, E Valero/dsl
167a	Randolph Blvd, E Valero/dsl, W Days Inn, Delta Inn, Midtowne Suites, Motel 6
166	I-410 W, Lp 368 S, W to Sea World
165	FM 1976, Walzem Rd, E Shell, Valero/dsl Applebee's Baskin Robbins/Dunkin', Benny's, Buffalo Wild Wings, Burger King, Bush's Chicken, China Harbor, Church's, Domino's IHOP, In-n-Out, Jack-in-the-Box, KFC/Taco Bell, Las Palapas Mexican, Little Caesar's, LJ Silver, Luby's, McDonald's, Miller's BBQ, Olive Garden, Pizza Hut, Red Lobster, Ross, Shoney's Starbucks, Subway, Taco Cabana, Whataburger Drury Inn $Tree, 99c Store, AutoZone, Cavender's Boots, CVS Drug Discount Tire, Firestone/auto, HEB/dsl, Home Depot, Office Depot, PepBoys, Petsmart, Walgreens, Walmart/Subway/dsl W Sonic NTB
164b	Eisenhauer Rd, E Exxon/7-11 Hampton Inn, La Quinta Mainstay Suites, Super 8, Woodspring Suites $General
164a	Rittiman Rd, E Exxon/7-11, Shell/dsl, Valero/dsl Burger King, Church's, Cracker Barrel, Denny's, Hacienda Tapatia, Jack-in-the-Box, McDonald's, Taco Bell, Taco Cabana, Whataburger Best Western, Comfort Suites, Hallmark Inn, Hampton Inn La Quinta, Mainstay Suites, Motel 6, Motel 6 (2), Rittiman Inn Super 8, Travel Inn, Woodspring Suites, W Valero Big Miller BBQ, Popeye's, Sonic, Subway
163	I-410 S (162 from nb, exits left from sb)
161	Binz-Engleman Rd (from nb) same as 160
160	Splashtown Dr, E Valero/Subway/dsl/24hr Motel 6, W Grady's BBQ Best Value Inn, Budget Lodge, Days Inn, Howard Johnson, Microtel, Motel 6, Travelodge
159b	Walters St, E McDonald's, W EconoLodge to Ft Sam Houston

⬆️N	**INTERSTATE 35 Cont'd**

Exit #	Services
159a	New Braunfels Ave, **E** 🅿️ Shell/dsl, Texaco/Burger King 🅾️ auto/dsl repair, **W** 🅿️ Chevron/dsl, Valero/dsl 🍴 Miller BBQ, Sonic 🛏️ Antonian Suites 🅾️ to Ft Sam Houston
158c	N Alamo St, Broadway
158b	I-37 S, US 281 S, to Corpus Christi to Alamo
158a	US 281 N (from sb), to Johnson City
157b a	Brooklyn Ave, Lexington Ave, N Flores, **E** 🛏️ Super 8, **W** 🍴 Luby's 🅾️ 🅷 downtown
156	I-10 W, US 87, to El Paso
155b	Durango Blvd, **E** 🛏️ Best Western, Courtyard, Fairfield Inn, Holiday Inn, La Quinta, Residence Inn 🅾️ 🅷, **W** 🍴 McDonald's 🛏️ Candlewood Suites, Doubletree, Motel 6 downtown
155a	South Alamo St, **E** 🅿️ Exxon, Shell/dsl 🍴 Church's, Huevos Nuevos, McDonald's, Wendy's 🛏️ Best Western, Days Inn, Holiday Inn, La Quinta, Residence Inn, Travelodge 🅾️ Advance Parts, USPO, **W** 🛏️ Knights Inn
154b	S Laredo St, Ceballos St same as 155b
154a	Nogalitos St
153	I-10 E, US 90 W, US 87 🅾️ Lackland AFB, to Kelly AFB
152b	Malone Ave, Theo Ave, **E** 🍴 Taco Cabana, **W** 🅿️ Shell
152a	Division Ave, **E** 🅿️ Chevron 🍴 Bill Miller BBQ, Las Cazuelas Mexican, Whataburger/24hr 🛏️ Econolodge, **W** 🍴 Sonic 🅾️ transmissions
151	Southcross Blvd, **E** 🅿️ Exxon/7-11/dsl, Shell, **W** 🅿️ Shell/dsl 🍴 Mazatlan Mexican
150b	Lp 13, Military Dr, **E** 🅿️ Valero 🍴 Applebee's, Carl's Jr, Denny's, Don Pedro Mexican, Papa John's, Starbucks, Subway, Taco Cabana 🛏️ La Quinta 🅾️ AutoZone, Discount Tire, Meineke, U-Haul, **W** 🅿️ Exxon 🍴 Buffalo Wild Wings, Burger King, Chick-fil-A, Chili's, CiCi's, Freddy's Custard, Hungry Farmer Rest, IHOP, Jack-in-the-Box, KFC, Lin's Buffet, Little Caesar's, LJ Silver, Longhorn Steaks, Mama Margie's Mexican, McDonald's, Olive Garden, Panda Express, Popeye's, Red Lobster, Sea Island Shrimp House, Wendy's, Whataburger 🅾️ $Tree, AT&T, Dick's, Firestone/auto, HEB Foods, Home Depot, JC Penney, Lowe's, Macy's, mall, Office Depot, Old Navy, Ross, Sears/auto, Target, Verizon, Walgreens
150a	Zarzamora St (149 fom sb) same as 150b
149	Hutchins Blvd (from sb), **E** 🅿️ Valero/dsl 🛏️ Motel 6, Woodspring Suites, **W** 🅾️ Chevrolet, Ford, Honda, 🅷, Hyundai, Kia
148b	Palo Alto Rd
148a	TX 16 S, spur 422 (from nb), Poteet, **E** 🅿️ Chevron/dsl, Murphy USA/dsl 🍴 Golden Chick 🛏️ Days Inn 🅾️ CVS Drug, Walmart/Subway, **W** 🅾️ $General
147	Somerset Rd, **E** 🅿️ Shell/dsl 🅾️ Ford, **W** 🅾️ Chrysler/Dodge/Jeep
146	Cassin Rd (from nb)
145b	Lp 353 N
145a	I-410, TX 16
144	Fischer Rd, **E** 🅿️ Valero/7-11/Subway/dsl/scales/24hr 🛏️ D&D Motel, **W** 🅿️ 💙Loves/Carl's Jr/dsl/scales/24hr/@ 🅾️ Toyota
142	Medina River Turnaround (from nb)
141	Benton City Rd, Von Ormy, **E** 🅾️ USPO, **W** 🅿️ Shell/Parador Café/dsl
140	Anderson Lp, 1604, **E** 🅿️ Exxon/dsl/24hr 🍴 Burger King, **W** 🅿️ Pilot/Subway/dsl/scales/24hr 🅾️ Alamo River RV Resort, to Sea World
139	Kinney Rd
137	Shepherd Rd, **E** 🅾️ truck repair, **W** 🅿️ Exxon/Choke Canyon BBQ/dsl/24hr 🅾️ dsl repair

Exit #	Services
135	Luckey Rd
133	TX 132 S (from sb), Lytle same as 131
131	FM 3175, FM 2790, Benton City Rd, **E** 🛏️ Best Western, **W** 🅿️ HEB/dsl/24hr 🍴 Bill Miller BBQ, Little Caesar's, McDonald's, Sonic, Subway, Whataburger 🛏️ Days Inn/cafe 🅾️ $General, AutoZone, CVS Drug, Family$, HEB Food/dsl, USPO
129mm	Ⓡs both lanes, full ♿ facilities, 🚻, 🛏️, litter barrels, vending, petwalk
127	FM 471, Natalia, **W** 🅿️ 💙Loves/Subway/Wendy's/dsl/scales/24hr/@
125	FM 770
124	FM 463, Bigfoot Rd, **E** 🅾️ Ford
122	TX 173, Divine, **E** 🅿️ Exxon/dsl 🅾️ Chevrolet, Chrysler/Dodge/Jeep, **W** 🅿️ Chevron/McDonald's/Subway/dsl, Exxon, Shell/dsl 🍴 CCC Steaks, Church's, Pizza Hut, Sonic, Viva Zapatas Mexican 🛏️ Country Corner Inn 🅾️ O'Reilly Parts, Walmart/Subway
121	TX 132 N, Devine
118.5mm	weigh sta both lanes
114	FM 462, Yancey, Bigfoot, **E** 🅿️ Lucky/dsl, **W** 🅿️ Shell/dsl 🅾️ USPO
111	US 57, to Eagle Pass, **W** 🅿️ Road Ranger/Valero/Subway/Chester's/dsl/scales/24hr
104	Lp 35
101	FM 140, Pearsall, **E** 🅿️ Chevron/dsl 🍴 Cowpokes BBQ, Jalisco's Mexican 🛏️ Baymont Inn, Garden Inn, Hampton Inn, Pearsall Inn, Royal Inn 🅾️ HEB Foods/dsl, **W** 🅿️ Exxon/Subway/Church's/dsl/24hr, Petro/Valero/Iron Skillet/dsl/scales/24hr 🍴 Hungry Hunter Grill 🛏️ Days Inn, Holiday Inn Express, La Quinta, Rio Frio Motel, Southern Inn 🅾️ 🅷
99	FM 1581, to Divot, Pearsall
93mm	parking/🛏️ both lanes, ♿ accessible, litter barrels
91	FM 1583, Derby
90mm	Frio River
86	Lp 35, Dilley
85	FM 117, **E** 🍴 Garcia Café 🛏️ Best Western, Days Inn, Relax Inn, Super 8, **W** 🅿️ Exxon/dsl, Phillips 66/Church's/dsl/CNG/24hr 🍴 DQ 🛏️ Budget Inn, Sona Inn 🅾️ RV park
84	TX 85, Dilley, **E** 🅿️ Mobil/Burger King/dsl 🅾️ Chevrolet, 🅷, Lowe's Mkt/dsl, **W** 🅿️ Shell/Pollo Grande/dsl/24hr, Valero/Subway/dsl/24hr 🛏️ Best Value Inn, Executive Inn 🅾️ NAPA
82	County Line Rd, to Dilley, Dilley
77	FM 469, Millett
74	Gardendale
69	(68 from nb), Lp 35, Cotulla, **E** 🅿️ Phillips 66/dsl 🅾️ Family$, Lowe's Mkt, **W** 🅿️ ✈FLYING J/Subway/PJ Fresh/dsl/scales/24hr, Stripes/Taco Co/dsl/scales/24hr 🍴 McDonald's, Sonic 🛏️ Days Inn, Fairfield Inn, Mainstay Suites, Microtel
65	Lp 35, Cotulla

Vertical margin text (left): **SAN ANTONIO**
Vertical margin text (right): **PEARSALL**
Side tab: **TX**

🚗 = gas 🍴 = food 🏨 = lodging Ⓞ = other Ⓡs = rest stop   Copyright 2022 - The Next EXIT ®

⬆N INTERSTATE 35 Cont'd

Exit #	Services
67	FM 468, to Big Wells, **E** 🚗 Exxon/Wendy's/dsl/24hr, JJ's/dsl, Valero/deli/dsl/24hr 🍴 DQ, El Charro Mexican, Golden Chick, Pizza Hut, Subway, Taco Palenque 🏨 Baymont Inn, Candlewood Suites, Comfort Suites, Executive Inn, Hampton Inn, Holiday Inn Express, La Quinta, Quality Inn, Super 8, Village Inn Ⓞ truck repair, **W** 🚗 Chevron/dsl/scales/24hr 🍴 LaSalle Steakhouse 🏨 Best Western, Hotel Cotulla, Residency Suites Ⓞ Mack/Volvo
63	Elm Creek Interchange
59mm	Ⓡs both lanes, full ♿ facilities, 🍴, 🏞, litter barrels, vending, petwalk
56	FM 133, Artesia Wells
48	Caiman Creek Interchange
39	TX 44, Encinal, **E** 🚗 ♥Loves/Chester Fried/Subway/dsl/scales/24hr, Road Ranger/Church's/dsl/scales/24hr, **W** 🚗 Chevron/dsl
38	TX 44 (from nb), Encinal
32	San Roman Interchange
29mm	inspection sta nb
27	Callaghan Interchange
24	255 toll, Camino Colombia toll rd, to Monterrey
22	Webb Interchange
18	US 83 N, to Carrizo Springs, **E** TX Travel Info Ctr (8am-5pm)/Ⓡs, full facilities, 🏞, litter barrels, petwalk, wireless internet, **W** other RV Camping
14mm	parking area sb
12b	(13 from sb) Uniroyal Interchange, **E** 🚗 PILOT/McDonald's/Subway/dsl/scales/24hr Ⓞ Blue Beacon, Southern Tire Mart, **W** 🚗 FLYING J/Denny's/dsl/scales/24hr, TA/Burger King/Subway/Taco Bell/dsl/scales/24hr/@
12a	Port Loredo
10	Port Laredo Carriers Dr (from nb)
9	Industrial Blvd, to Bob Bullock Lp (from sb only)
8b	Lp 20 W, to Solidarity Bridge
8a	Lp 20 W, to to World Trade Bridge, Milo
5	San Isidro Pkwy
4b	Las Cruces Dr, **E** 🚗 Valero/dsl 🍴 El Pescador
4a	FM 1472
4	FM 1472, Del Mar Blvd, **E** 🚗 Exxon/Burger King/dsl 🍴 Applebee's, Carino's Italian, CiCi's, IHOP, Jack-in-the-Box, McDonald's, Quiznos, Whataburger 🏨 Extended Stay America, Hampton Inn Ⓞ Best Buy, BigLots, HEB Foods/gas, Marshall's, Old Navy, Target, **W** 🚗 La Noria/dsl 🏨 Days Inn Ⓞ Harley-Davidson
3b	Mann Rd, **E** 🍴 Buffalo Wild Wings, Krispy Kreme, Lin's Chinese 🏨 Residence Inn Ⓞ Ford/Lincoln, Honda, Kia, Lowe's, Mazda, URGENT CARE, **W** 🍴 Chili's, Golden Corral, Kettle Pancake House, Subway, Taco Palenque, TX Roadhouse, Whataburger 🏨 Best Value, Family Garden Inn, Gateway Inn, La Hacienda Motel, Monterey Inn, Motel 6, Red Roof Inn, SpringHill Suites Ⓞ $Tree, AT&T, Home Depot, Kohl's, Michael's, Office Depot, PetCo, Ross, Verizon, Walmart/McDonald's
3a	San Bernardo Ave, **E** 🍴 Chick-fil-A, ChuckECheese, El Taco Tote, Emperor Garden, Fuddrucker's, LJ Silver, Logan's Roadhouse, Luby's, Luby's, Olive Garden, Peter Piper Pizza, Red Lobster, Sirloin Stockade, Tony Roma's 🏨 Fairfield Inn Ⓞ $General, Advance Parts, HEB Foods/gas, K-Mart, Macy's, mall, NAPA, PepBoys, Sears/auto, SteinMart, **W** 🚗 Valero 🍴 Burger King, Danny's Rest., DQ, McDonald's, Pizza Hut, Popeye's, Taco Bell, Taco Palenque, Wendy's Ⓞ Family$, O'Reilly Parts, Sam's Club/gas

L A R E D O

2	US 59, Saunders Rd, **E** 🚗 Conoco, Shell 🍴 Jack-in-the-Box Ⓞ ♿, **W** 🍴 Exxon/Burger King/dsl, Shell/dsl 🍴 Church's, Denny's, Subway 🏨 Best Western, Courtyard, La Quinta, Ramada Plaza, Super8 Ⓞ Advance Parts, AutoZone, AutoZone, Mexico Insurance
1b	Park St, to Sanchez St, **W** 🚗 Conoco/dsl 🍴 La Mexicana Rest. Pizza Hut, Popeye's
1a	Victoria St, Scott St, Washington St (from sb), **E** 🚗 Valero, **W** 🚗 Chevron, Valero/dsl 🍴 Dos Marias, McDonald's, Wendy's Ⓞ Firestone/auto

I-35 begins/ends in Laredo at Victoria St, access to multiple services.

⬆N INTERSTATE 35 (West)

Exit #	Services
	I-35W begins/ends on I-35, exit 467.
85b	W Oak St, **E** Ⓞ ♿
85a	I-35E S
84	FM 1515, Bonnie Brae St, **E** Ⓞ ♿
82	FM 2449, to Ponder
79	Crawford Rd
76	FM 407, to Justin, Argyle, **W** 🚗 Exxon/dsl Ⓞ Paradise Mkt
76mm	🏞 both lanes, tables, litter barrels
74	FM 1171, to Lewisville
72	Dale Earnhardt Way, **W** 🏨 Marriott Ⓞ TX Motor Speedway
70	TX 114, to Dallas, Bridgeport, **E** 🚗 QT/dsl, Shell/BBQ/dsl, Valero/dsl/e85 🍴 BurgerIM, IHOP, Popeye's, Rosa's Cafe, Sonic 🏨 Holiday Inn Express, Home 2 Suites, La Quinta, Motel 6, Quality Inn Ⓞ Northlake RV Park, to DFW Airport, **W** 🚗 Buc-ee's/dsl EVC, EVC (2) 🍴 Buffalo Wild Wings, Cane's, Chick-fil-A, In-N-Out, Olive Garden, Panda Express, Smoothie King, Starbucks, Whataburger 🏨 Marriott Ⓞ Tanger Outlets/famous brands TX Motor Speedway, Verizon
68	Eagle Pkwy, **W** Ⓞ ♿
67	Alliance Blvd, **W** Ⓞ FedEx, to Alliance Airport
66	to Westport Pkwy, Keller-Haslet Rd, **E** 🏨 Hampton Inn, Hilton Garden, Residence Inn, **W** 🚗 7-11/Wendy's/dsl 🍴 Bryan' BBQ, Schlotzsky's, Snooty Pig, Subway, Taco Bueno Ⓞ USPO
65	TX 170 E, **E** 🚗 PILOT/McDonald's/dsl/scales/24hr 🍴 IHOP Ⓞ Cabela's/cafe
64	Golden Triangle Blvd, to Keller-Hicks Blvd, **E** 🚗 QT/dsl, RaceTrac/dsl/e85 Ⓞ Chrysler/Dodge/Jeep, Kia
63	Heritage Trace, Park Glen, **E** 🚗 7-11 🍴 BJ's Rest., Cheddar's, Chick-fil-A, Chipotle, Chuy's, Coldstone, Costa Vida, Cousin BBQ, Free Birds Burritos, Houlihan's, Jason's Deli, McAlister' Deli, McDonald's, Mi Cocina, Panera Bread, Pei Wei, Pie Five Razzoo's Cajun, Smoothie King, Starbucks, Subway, The Roc Kitchen, Which Wich?, Zoe's Kitchen 🏨 Courtyard Ⓞ Belk, Bes Buy, Dick's, GNC, JC Penney, Kroger/dsl, Petsmart, Verizon, **W** 🚗 7-11/dsl
62	North Tarrant Pkwy, **E** 🍴 54th St Grill, Chili's, Firehouse Sub Five Guys, Fuzzy's Tacos, HaNaBi Hibachi, Olive Garden, Piz za Inn, Pluckers, Thai Fusion Ⓞ ♿, **W** 🍴 Cane's, Chick-fil-A ChuckECheese, El Pollo Loco, In-N-Out, Jimmy John's, La Made leine, Old Chicago, Pollo Tropical, Potbelly, Starbucks, Taco Ca bana, Tom+Chee, Uncle Julio's, Wendy's Ⓞ $Tree, AT&T, Cost co/gas, Hobby Lobby, Old Navy, Petco, Ross, Target, TJ Max Tuesday Morning, URGENT CARE, Winco
60	US 287 N, US 81 N, to Decatur
59	Basswood (sb only), **E** 🚗 Chevron/Jack-in-the-Box/dsl 🍴 Chicken Express, DQ, Sonic, Subway, Taco Bell Ⓞ Home Depo NTB

INTERSTATE 35 (West) Cont'd

Exit #	Services
58	Western Ctr Blvd, **E** 🅖 7-11/dsl, Shell/Church's 🅕 Boomer-Jack's, Braum's, Brick House, Chili's, Denny's, Dublin Square Rest., Flips Grill, Genghis Grill, Jake's Burgers, Jimmy John's, On-the-Border, Posados Cafe, Rudy's BBQ, SaltGrass Steaks, Shady Oak Grill, Twin Peaks, Wendy's, Which Wich?, Wing Stop 🅛 Magnuson Hotel, Residence Inn 🅞 AT&T, **W** 🅕 Boston's, Firehouse Subs, Joe's Crabshack, McDonald's, Popeye's, Rosa's Cafe, Smoothie King, Starbucks, Subway, Waffle House, Whataburger 🅛 Comfort Inn, Holiday Inn Express, Staybridge Suites 🅞 repair, URGENT CARE
57b a	I-820 E&W
56b	Melody Hills Dr
56a	Meacham Blvd, **E** 🅖 Shell/7-11 🅛 Hilton Garden, Knights Inn, La Quinta, **W** 🅖 Texaco/dsl 🅕 Cracker Barrel, McDonald's, Subway 🅛 Holiday Inn, Quality Inn, Radisson, Super 8 🅞 USPO
55	Pleasantdale Ave (from nb)
54c	33rd St, Long Ave (from nb), **W** 🅖 Drivers TC/Subway/dsl/scales 🅛 Motel 6
54b a	TX 183, NE 28th St, **E** 🅖 Lisa's Chicken/dsl, **W** 🅖 QT/dsl 🅛 Stockyards Motel 6 Inn
53	North Side Dr, Yucca Dr, **E** 🅖 Shell/7-11/dsl, **W** 🅕 Mercado Juarez Café 🅛 Country Inn&Suites
53mm	Trinity River
52e	Carver St (from nb)
52d	Pharr St (exits left from nb)
52b	US 377N, Belknap
52a	US 377 N, TX 121, to DFW
51a	I-30 E, to Avalene (from nb) downtown Ft Worth
50c a	I-30 W, E to Dallas
50b	TX 180 E (from nb)
49b	Rosedale St, **E** 🅖 7-11/dsl 🅕 Jack-in-the-Box, **W** 🅞 🅗
49a	Allen Ave, **E** 🅖 Valero/dsl, **W** 🅞 🅗
48b	Morningside Ave (from sb) same as 48a
48a	Berry St, **E** 🅖 Chevron/McDonald's 🅞 AutoZone, El Rio Grande Foods, Family$, **W** 🅖 RaceTrac/dsl 🅞 U-Haul, zoo
47	Ripy St, **E** 🅞 transmissions
46b	Seminary Dr, **E** 🅖 RaceWay 🅕 Grandy's, Jack-in-the-Box, Taco Cabana, Whataburger 🅛 Days Inn, Delux Inn, Motel 6, Super 7 Inn 🅞 NAPA, **W** 🅖 Shell, Valero 🅕 Chalio Mexican, ChuckECheese, Denny's, Sonic, Wendy's 🅞 Firestone/auto, Pepboys, Ross
46a	Felix St, **E** 🅖 Valero 🅛 Dalworth Inn, **W** 🅕 Cesar's Tacos, McDonald's 🅞 Family$
45b a	I-20, E to Dallas, W to Abilene
44	Altamesa, **E** 🅛 Radisson, **W** 🅖 Conoco/dsl 🅕 Rig Steaks, Waffle House 🅛 Baymont Inn, Comfort Suites, Motel 6, South Lp Inn, Super 8
43	Sycamore School Rd, **W** 🅖 Exxon/7-11/dsl 🅕 Chicken Express, Jack-in-the-Box, Jimmy John's, Sonic, Subway, Whataburger 🅛 Scottish Inn 🅞 $General, Home Depot
42	Everman Pkwy, **E** 🅕 McDonald's, Starbucks, **W** 🅖 QT/dsl/scales, Shell/dsl
41	Risinger Rd, **E** 🅞 Chrysler/Dodge/Jeep, **W** 🅞 Camping World RV Service/Supplies, McClain's RV Ctr
40	Garden Acres Dr, **E** 🅖 Loves/Subway/dsl/scales/24hr 🅛 Motel 6 🅞 🅗, **W** 🅖 7-11/dsl 🅕 Chicken Express, Taco Bell
39	FM 1187, McAlister Rd, **E** 🅖 QT/dsl 🅞 🅗, **W** 🅖 Shell/dsl, Valero/dsl 🅕 Buffalo Wild Wings, Charley's Subs, Firehouse Subs,

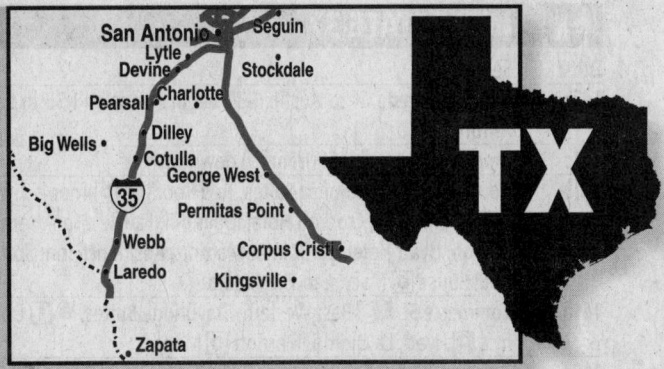

39	Continued Logan's Roadhouse, McAlister's Deli, Mooyah Burger, Olive Garden, Panda Express, Red Lobster, Subway, TGIFriday's, Waffle House 🅛 Magnuson 🅞 AT&T, Best Buy, Kohl's, Michael's, Old Navy, Petsmart, Ross, Staples, TJ Maxx, URGENT CARE, Verizon
38	Alsbury Blvd, **E** 🅖 Mobil/dsl 🅕 Chili's, Cracker Barrel, Hibachi Japanese, IHOP, McDonald's, Mexican Inn Cafe, On-the-Border, Our Place Grill, Outback Steaks, Spring Creek BBQ 🅛 Fairfield Inn, Hampton Inn, Holiday Inn Express, La Quinta, Super 8 🅞 Discount Tire, Ford, Lowe's Whse, **W** 🅖 7-11/dsl, RaceTrac/dsl 🅕 Applebee's, Arby's, Burger King, Chick-fil-A, Cotton Patch Cafe, Denny's, El Fenix, Sonic, Taco Cabana, Wendy's 🅞 Albertson's, Chevrolet, GNC, JC Penney, Michael's, PetsMart, Ross, URGENT CARE, vet
37	TX 174, Wilshire Blvd, to Cleburne, (from sb)
36	FM 3391, TX 174S, Burleson, **E** 🅖 7-11/dsl, Mobil 🅕 Miranda's Cantina, Sonic, Waffle House 🅛 Best Western, Days Inn, Quality Inn 🅞 Harley Davidson, Honda, Hyundai, Nissan, Sam's Club/dsl, **W** 🅞 $General, transmissions
35	Briaroaks Rd (from sb), **E** 🅞 same as 36, **W** 🅞 Mockingbird Hill RV Park (2mi)
32	Bethesda Rd, **E** 🅖 Valero 🅛 Five Star Inn 🅞 RV Ranch Park, **W** 🅞 Mockingbird Hill RV Park
30	FM 917, Mansfield, **E** 🅖 Shell/Sonic/dsl 🅞 $General, **W** 🅖 Shell/dsl
27	Rd 604, Rd 707
26b a	US 67, Cleburne, **E** 🅖 Chevron/dsl, Exxon/dsl, Texaco/dsl 🅕 Chicken Express, Domino's, DQ, Lin's Chinese, Little Caesar's, McDonald's, Pizza Hut, Sonic, Subway, Taco Bell, Waffle House, Whataburger 🅛 Comfort Inn, Holiday Inn Express, La Quinta, Motel 6, Super 8 🅞 $General, AutoZone, Brookshire Foods, Family$, Motor Home Specialists, Parts+, RV Tech Ctr, **W** 🅖 QT/dsl 🅕 Burger King 🅞 CVS Drug
24	FM 3136, FM 1706, Alvarado, **E** 🅖 Shell/LJ Silver/dsl/scales/24hr
21	Rd 107, to Greenfield
17	FM 2258
16	TX 81 S, Rd 201, Grandview
15	FM 916, Maypearl, **W** 🅖 Mobil/dsl, Shell/Burger King/dsl 🅕 Subway 🅞 USPO
12	FM 67
8	FM 66, Itasca, **W** 🅕 $General 🅞 Ford, 🅡🅢 litter barrels
7	FM 934, **E** 🅞 🅡🅢, litter barrels, **W** 🅖 Exxon/dsl 🅞 Golden Chick Cafe
3	FM 2959, **E** 🅞 to Hillsboro Airport
	I-35W begins/ends on I-35, 371mm.

TX

SAN ANTONIO

⊞Ⓝ INTERSTATE 37

Exit #	Services
142b a	I-35 S to Laredo, N to Austin. I-37 begins/ends on I-35 in San Antonio.
141c	Brooklyn Ave, Nolan St (from sb) downtown
141b	Houston St, E ⓐ Comfort Suites, Red Roof Inn ⊡ Theo's Tires, W ⓕ Denny's ⓐ Crockett Hotel, Days Inn, Fairfield Inn, Hampton Inn, Hyatt Hotel, La Quinta, Marriott, Residence Inn, SpringHill Suites ⊡ Macy's, to The Alamo
141a	Commerce St, E ⓐ Best Western, Staybridge Suites, W ⓕ Denny's ⓐ Hyatt, La Quinta, Marriott ⊡ Macy's
140b	Durango Blvd, E ⓕ Bill Miller BBQ ⊡ to Alamo Dome downtown
140a	Carolina St, Florida St, E ⓖ Shell/dsl
139	I-10 W, US 87, US 90, to Houston, W ⊡ to Sea World
138c	Fair Ave, Hackberry St, E ⓕ DQ, Jack-in-the-Box, La Tapatia Mexian, Popeye's ⊡ Brake Check, Family$, Home Depot, W ⓖ Exxon/7-11, Shell
138b	E New Braunfels Ave (from sb), E ⓕ Burger King, Chick-fil-A, IHOP, McDonald's, Taco Cabana, Wendy's ⊡ Beall's, HEB/dsl, Marshall's, W ⓖ Exxon ⓕ Sonic
138a	Southcross Blvd, W New Braunfels Ave, E ⓖ McDonald's, Taco Cabana, Wendy's ⓕ Golden Chick, Panda Express, W ⓖ Exxon ⓕ Burger King, Sonic
137	Hot Wells Blvd, E ⓖ Chevron/dsl, W ⓕ IHOP ⓐ Motel 6, Super 8
136	Pecan Valley Dr, E ⓖ Citgo/dsl ⓕ Church's, KFC/Taco Bell, Pizza Hut ⓐ Pecan Valley Inn ⊡ AutoZone, O'Reilly Parts, W ⊡ Ⓗ
135	Military Dr, Lp 13, E ⓖ Shell/dsl, Valero ⓕ Jack-in-the-Box, Rancho Grande ⓐ Quality Inn ⊡ CVS Drug, Mission Trail RV park, W ⓖ Valero/Subway/dsl ⓕ A&W/LJ Silver, Buffalo Wild Wings, Buffet Seafood, Burger King, Carino's Italian, Chaba Thai, Chick-fil-A, Chili's, Cracker Barrel, IHOP, Little Caesar's, Longhorn Cafe, Panda Express, Papa John's, Peter Piper Pizza, Sonic, Starbucks, Subway, Whataburger ⓐ Hampton Inn, Holiday Inn Express, La Quinta ⊡ $Tree, Advance Parts, AT&T, AutoZone, Best Buy, BigLots, Discount Tire, HEB Food/gas, Home Depot, Ⓗ, Lowe's, Office Depot, PetCo, Ross, Sam's Club/dsl, Target, to Brooks AFB, Walgreens, Walmart/McDonald's
133	I-410, US 281 S
132	US 181 S, to Floresville, E ⓖ Shell/7-11/dsl ⊡ $General
130	Donop Rd, Southton Rd, E ⓖ Valero/7-11/dsl ⓕ Tom's Burgers ⓐ Days Inn ⊡ Braunig Lake RV Resort, W ⓖ Shell/dsl ⊡ car/truckwash
127	San Antonio River Turnaround (from nb), Braunig Lake
127mm	San Antonio River
125	FM 1604, Anderson Lp, E ⓖ Mobil/dsl/24hr ⓕ Burger King ⊡ fireworks, W ⓖ Exxon/dsl, Ⓟⓘⓛⓞⓣ/Subway/dsl/scales/24hr, Shell/dsl ⓕ Miller's BBQ, Sonic, Whataburger ⊡ fireworks, tires
122	Priest Rd, Mathis Rd, E ⓖ Valero/dsl ⊡ $General
120	Hardy Rd
117	FM 536
113	FM 3006
112mm	ⓡ both lanes, tables, litter barrels
109	TX 97, to Floresville, E ⓖ Chevron/dsl, Exxon/dsl ⓕ Portrillo's Mexican ⊡ Chrysler/Dodge/Jeep
106	Coughran Rd
104	spur 199, Leal Rd, to Pleasanton (no immediate sb return) same as 103
103	US 281 N, Leal Rd, to Pleasanton, E ⓖ Valero/dsl ⓕ DQ, K&K Cafe ⓐ Kuntry Inn

Exit #	Services
98	TX 541, McCoy
92	US 281A, Campbellton
88	FM 1099, to FM 791, Campbellton
83	FM 99, Whitsett, Peggy, E ⓖ Shell/cafe/dsl, W ⓖ C Fuels/d Exxon/dsl ⓕ Choke Canyon BBQ
82mm	ⓡ sb, full ⓖ facilities, ⓒ, ⓡ, litter barrels
78mm	ⓡ nb, full ⓖ facilities, ⓒ, ⓡ, litter barrels
76	US 281A, FM 2049, Whitsett
75mm	truck weigh sta sb
74mm	truck weigh sta nb
72	US 281 S, Three Rivers, W ⓖ Loves/McDonald's/Subwa dsl/scales/24hr/@ ⓕ Sonic, Van's BBQ ⓐ Motel 6 ⊡ to R Grande Valley
69	TX 72, Three Rivers, W ⓖ Valero/Subway/dsl/24hr ⊡ Reba Rose RV Park, to Choke Cyn SP
65	FM 1358, Oakville, E ⓕ Van's BBQ
59	FM 799
56	US 59, George West, E ⓖ ⊞FLYING J/McDonald's/ds scales/24hr, Stripes/Taco Co/dsl/24hr, W g Shell/BBQ/dsl/24h Valero/Burger King/dsl/24hr
51	Hailey Ranch Rd
47	FM 3024, FM 534, Swinney Switch Rd, W ⓕ Swinney Switc Cafe ⊡ Mike's Mkt/gas, Mustang Hollow Camping (4mi)
44mm	parking area sb
42mm	parking area nb
40	FM 888
36	TX 359, to Skidmore, Mathis, W ⓖ Road Ranger/Subway/ds scales, Shell/McDonald's/dsl, Valero/dsl (1mi) ⓕ Pizza Hu Smolik's Smokehouse ⓐ La Quinta ⊡ Lake Corpus Christi SR
34	TX 359 W, E ⊡ Adventure TX RV Ctr/LP, W ⓖ Shell, Valero/d ⓕ Church's, Sonic ⓐ DQ, Pizza Hut ⊡ $General, O'Reilly Part to Lake Corpus Christi SP
31	TX 188, to Sinton, Rockport
22	TX 234, FM 796, to Odem, Edroy
20b	Cooper Rd
19.5mm	ⓡ both lanes, ⓖ accessible, tables, litter barrels
17	US 77 N, to Victoria
16	LaBonte Park, W info, ⓡ litter barrels
15	Sharpsburg Rd (from sb), Redbird Ln
14	I-69, US 77 S, Redbird Ln, to Kingsville, Robstown, 1 mi W o FM 624 ⓖ RaceWay/dsl, Shell/dsl, Valero/Burger King/dsl ⓕ Chili's, CiCi's, Denny's, El Tapatio Mexican, Good'n Crisp Chicke Miller's BBQ, Papa John's, Pizza Hut, Popeye's, Sonic, Subwa Whataburger, Wienerschnitzel ⓐ Comfort Inn, Holiday Inn E press ⊡ $General, $Tree, AT&T, AutoZone, Beall's, CVS Dru Discount Tire, Firestone/auto, GNC, Hobby Lobby, Home Depo Ⓗ, O'Reilly Parts, Petco, Ross, Verizon, Walmart/McDonald's
13b	Sharpsburg Rd (from nb)
13a	FM 1694, Callicoatte Rd, Leopard St
11b	FM 24, Violet Rd, Hart Rd, E ⓖ Shell/Subway/dsl ⓕ Chic en Shack, W ⓖ Exxon/dsl, Valero/dsl ⓕ Domino's, DQ, F Amancer Mexican, KFC/LJ Silver, Little Caesar's, McDonald' Pizza Hut, Schlotzsky's, Sonic, Subway, Taco Bell, Whataburg ⓐ Hampton Inn, Super 8 ⊡ Advance Parts, AutoZone, Family HEB Food/gas, O'Reilly Parts, Walgreens
11a	McKinzie Rd, E ⓖ Shell ⓕ Jack-in-the-Box ⓐ La Quinta, W Valero/dsl
10	Carbon Plant Rd
9	FM 2292, Up River Rd, Rand Morgan Rd, W ⓖ Valero/dsl ⓕ Whataburger
7	Suntide Rd, Tuloso Rd, Clarkwood Rd, W ⊡ CC RV Ctr, Freigh liner

INTERSTATE 37 Cont'd

Exit #	Services
6	Southern Minerals Rd, E 🅞 refinery
5	Corn Products Rd, Valero Way, E 🅞 Kenworth/Mack, W 🅖 Gascard/dsl 🍴 Jalisco II Rest. 🏠 Best Value, Howard Johnson, ValStay
4b	Lantana St, McBride Lane (from sb), W 🏠 Airport Inn, Motel 6
4a	TX 358, to Padre Island, W 🏠 Holiday Inn, Plaza Inn 🅞 Walmart (4mi)
3b	McBride Lane (from nb), W 🅞 Gulf Coast Racing
3a	Navigation Blvd, E 🅖 Valero/dsl 🏠 Rodeway Inn, W 🅖 Exxon/7-11/dsl 🍴 Denny's, La Milpas, Miller BBQ 🏠 Hampton Inn, Holiday Inn Express, Knights Inn, La Quinta, Super 8 🅞 CarQuest
2	Up River Rd, E 🅞 refinery, W 🍴 Mr G's BBQ
1e	Lawrence Dr, Nueces Bay Blvd, E 🅞 refinery, W 🅖 Valero 🍴 Church's 🏠 Red Roof Inn 🅞 Aamco, AutoZone, Firestone, HEB Foods, USPO
1d	Port Ave (from sb), W 🅖 Coastal, Shell 🍴 Vick's Burgers 🏠 EconoLodge 🅞 Port of Corpus Christi
1c	US 181, TX 286, Shoreline Blvd, Corpus Christi, W 🅞 🏥
1b	Brownlee St (from nb)
1a	Buffalo St (from sb) 🅖 Sunoco/dsl 🍴 Burger King, Joe's Crabshack, Landry's Seafood, Subway, Waterstreet Seafood, Whataburger 🏠 Bayfront Inn, Best Western, Holiday Inn, Omni Hotel, Super 8 🅞 U-Haul, USPO
	I-37 begins/ends on US 181 in Corpus Christi.

INTERSTATE 40

Exit #	Services
177mm	Texas/Oklahoma state line
176	spur 30 (from eb), to Texola
169	FM 1802, Carbon Black Rd
167	FM 2168, Daberry Rd
165mm	check sta wb
164	Lp 40 (from wb), to Shamrock, 1 mi S 🏠 EconoLodge 🅞 check sta eb, 🏥, museum
163	US 83, to Wheeler, Shamrock, N 🅖 Chevron/Taco Bell/dsl 🏠 Best Western+, Irish Inn 🅞 Ace Hardware, S 🅖 Conoco/dsl, Tesla EVC, Valero/Subway/dsl 🍴 McDonald's 🏠 EconoLodge, Holiday Inn Express, Sleep Inn, Western Motel 🅞 Family$
161	Lp 40, Rte 66 (from eb), to Shamrock
157	FM 1547, Lela, 1 mi S 🅞 TX RV Park
152	FM 453, Pakan Rd
148	FM 1443, Kellerville Rd
146	County Line Rd
143	Lp 40 (from wb), to McLean, N 🅖 to Rte 66
142	TX 273, FM 3143, to McLean, N 🅖 Conoco/dsl 🍴 Red River Steaks 🏠 Cactus Inn 🅞 RV Camping/dump, USPO
141	Rte 66 (from eb), McLean same as 142
135	FM 291, Rte 66, Alanreed, S 🅖 Conoco/motel/café/RV park/dump 🅞 USPO
132	Johnson Ranch Rd ranch access
131mm	🆁🆂 wb, full ♿ facilities, 🅫, 🏞, litter barrels, petwalk
129mm	🆁🆂 eb, full ♿ facilities, 🅫, 🏞, litter barrels, petwalk, playground
128	FM 2477, to Lake McClellan, N 🅞 Lake McClellan RA/RV Dump
124	TX 70 S, to Clarendon, S 🅞 RV camping/dump (11mi)
121	TX 70 N, to Pampa
114	Lp 40, Groom, N 🅞 dsl repair
113	FM 2300, Groom, N 🅖 Conoco, S 🅖 Phillips 66/dsl 🍴 DQ 🏠 Chalet Inn
112	FM 295, Groom, 1 mi S 🅖 gas 🅞 Biggest Cross
110	Lp 40, Rte 66
109	FM 294
105	FM 2880 grain silo
98	TX 207 S (from wb), to Claude
96	TX 207 N, to Panhandle, N 🅖 ❤Loves/Subway/dsl/24hr, S 🏠 Conway Inn/cafe, Executive Inn
89	FM 2161, to Rte 66
87	FM 2373
87mm	🆁🆂 both lanes, litter barrels
85	Amarillo Blvd, Durrett Rd access to camping
81	FM 1912, N 🅖 Valero/dsl
80	FM 228, N 🅞 AOK RV Park
78	US 287 S (from eb), FM 1258, Pullman Rd same as 77
77	FM 1258, Pullman Rd
76	spur 468, N 🅖 ⊕FLYING J/Denny's/dsl/LP/RV dump/scales/24hr, Phillips/dsl 🍴 Buffalo Wild Wings 🏠 Fairfield Inn, Holiday Inn Express, La Quinta 🅞 Mack/Volvo Trucks, S 🅖 Speedco 🅞 Custom RV Ctr, TX info
75	Lp 335, Lakeside Rd, N 🅖 PILOT/Subway/McDonald's/dsl/scales/24hr/@, Valero/dsl 🏠 Hampton Inn, Holiday Inn, Knights Inn, Super 8 🅞 KOA (2mi), Overnite RV Park, S 🅖 Petro/dsl/rest./scales/@ 🅞 Blue Beacon
74	Whitaker Rd, N 🍴 Big Texan Inn 🅞 RV camping, S 🅖 ❤Loves/Subway/dsl/scales/@, TA/Exxon/FoodCourt/dsl/scales/24hr/@ 🅞 Blue Beacon, Eagle Truckwash, Peterbilt
73	Eastern St, Bolton Ave, Amarillo, N 🅖 Toot'n Totum/dsl 🏠 Express Inn, Motel 6, Wood Spring Suites, S 🅖 CEFCO/dsl 🏠 Best Western
72b	Grand St, Amarillo, N 🅖 Valero/dsl 🍴 Henk's BBQ 🏠 Value Inn 🅞 O'Reilly Parts, S 🅖 Murphy USA/dsl, Phillips 66, Valero 🍴 Braum's, Chicken Express, McDonald's, Sonic, Starbucks, Subway, Taco Villa, Whataburger 🏠 Best Value Inn 🅞 $Tree, Advance Parts, Amigo's Foods, AutoZone, BigLots, Meineke, same as 73, URGENT CARE, Walmart
72a	Nelson St, N 🍴 Cracker Barrel 🏠 Ashmore Inn, Comfort Inn, La Kiva Hotel, Rest Inn, Sleep Inn, Super 8 🅞 Qtrhorse Museum, S 🅖 Valero/dsl 🍴 Domino's 🏠 Camelot Suites 🅞 transmissions
71	Ross St, Osage St, Amarillo, N 🅖 Chevron/dsl, Valero 🍴 Burger King, IHOP, KFC, McDonald's, Schlotsky's, Subway, Wienerschnitzel 🏠 Comfort Inn, Days Inn, Microtel, Quality Inn, Sheraton 🅞 Discount Tire, S 🍴 Arby's, Denny's, Fiesta Grande Mexican, Sonic, Taco Bell, Wendy's 🏠 Baymont Inn, La Quinta 🅞 Chevrolet, Ford, Hyundai, Sam's Club/gas, USPO
70	I-27 S, US 60 W, US 87, US 287, to Canyon, Lubbock to downtown Amarillo
69b	Washington St, Amarillo, S 🅖 TT/dsl 🍴 DQ 🅞 CVS Drug Subway
69a	Crockett St access to same as 68b

TX

AMARILLO

⬆E INTERSTATE 40 Cont'd

Exit #	Services
68b	Georgia St, **N** 🅖 TT/dsl ⯅ Dyer's BBQ, Schlotzky's, Sharky's Burrito Co, **S** 🅖 Valero ⯅ Burger King, Church's Chicken, Coldstone, Denny's, Firehouse Subs, Jersey Mike's, Pizza Hut, Sonic, Starbucks, TX Roadhouse, Whataburger 🅐 Holiday Inn Express 🅞 Home Depot, Office Depot, Walgreens
68a	Julian Blvd, Paramount Blvd, **N** ⯅ Chili's, Rosa's Cafe 🅐 same as 67, **S** 🅖 Valero ⯅ Burger King, Chick-Fil-A, Chipotle, Panda Express, Popeyes, Red Lobster, Ruby Tequila's Mexican, TX Roadhouse 🅐 Holiday Inn Express, Motel 6, Super 8, Travelodge 🅞 Home Depot, Office Depot Five Guys, Bubba's BBQ, El Patron
67	Western St, Amarillo, **N** 🅖 Phillips 66 ⯅ Braum's, Burger King, McAlister's Deli, McDonald's, Papa Murphy's, Sonic, Subway, Taco Bell, Wendy's Aspen Creek Grill, **S** 🅖 Murphy Express/dsl, Rudy's/BBQ/dsl, Valero ⯅ Blue Sky Rest., Cheddar's, IHOP, Jimmy John's, Olive Garden, Waffle House, Wienerschnitzel 🅐 Baymont Inn, Candlewood Suites, Comfort Suites, Staybridge Suites 🅞 Discount Tire, Firestone/auto, Michael's, O'Reilly Parts, Petco, same 68
66	Bell St, Amarillo, **N** 🅖 Cefco/dsl 🅐 Fairfield Inn, Red Roof Inn, Relax Inn, Residence Inn 🅞 Harley-Davidson, **S** ⯅ Donut Stop, Taco Bueno 🅞 CashSaver
65	Coulter Dr, Amarillo, **N** 🅖 Phillips 66/dsl ⯅ Arby's, Golden Corral, Subway, Taco Bell, Waffle House 🅐 Days Inn, Executive Inn, Holiday Inn, Holiday Inn Express, La Quinta 🅞 Cadillac/Chevrolet, Chrysler/Dodge/Jeep, Firestone/auto, 🅗, **S** 🅖 Chevron/Chicken Express/dsl ⯅ ChinaStar, CiCi's, Hoffbrau Steaks, Outback Steaks, Pizza Hut, Whataburger 🅐 5th Season Inn, Hampton Inn, Sleep Inn 🅞 AT&T, Goodyear/auto, Verizon
64	Soncy Rd, to Pal Duro Cyn, **N** ⯅ Fuddrucker's, Furr's Buffet, Jimmy John's, Lin's Chinese, Plaza Rest., Red Robin 🅐 Comfort Inn, Country Inn&Suites, Drury Inn, Hilton Garden, Holiday Inn, Homewood Suites 🅞 USPO Cavender's Boots, Discount Tire, Courtyard, Kabuki, SpringHill Suites, Longhorn Steaks, My Place, Saltgrass Steaks, Logan's Roadhouse, Extended Stay America, Tru, **S** 🅖 Valero/dsl/24hr ⯅ Applebee's, ChuckeCheese, DQ, Fazoli's, Hooters, Marble Slab Creamery, McAlisters Deli, McDonald's, On-the-Border, Pei Wei, Starbucks, Subway 🅞 $Tree, Barnes&Noble, Best Buy, Dillard's, Ford, Home Depot, JC Penney, Jo-Ann Fabrics, Kohl's, Lincoln, Old Navy, PetsMart, Ross, Sam's Club/dsl, Sears/auto, Target, Verizon, World Mkt
62b	Lp 40, Amarillo Blvd, **N** 🅞 Gander Outdoors, **S** 🅞 Sundown RV Resort
62a	Hope Rd, Helium Rd, **S** 🅞 Cadillac RV camping
60	Arnot Rd, **S** 🅖 ♥Love's/Subway/dsl 🅞 Oasis RV Resort/dump
57	RM 2381, Bushland, **N** 🅖 Falcon Stop/dsl 🅞 grain silos, **S** 🅖 Phillips 66/dsl ⯅ Bushland Burger, Joe's Pizza 🅞 USPO, vet
55mm	**parking area wb, litter barrels**
54	Adkisson Rd
53.5mm	**parking area eb, litter barrels**
49	FM 809, Wildorado, **S** 🅖 Crist Fuel/dsl/LP
42	Everett Rd
37	Lp 40 W, to Vega, **1 mi N** 🅐 Bonanza Motel 🅞 same as 36, Walnut RV Park
36	US 385, Vega, **N** 🅖 Alon/dsl, Shamrock, Valero/Allsup's/dsl/scales/24hr ⯅ DQ, Subway 🅐 Days Inn 🅞 RV Park $ General, **S** 🅖 ⯅/PJ Fresh/dsl/scales/24hr, Vega Trk Stop/cafe/dsl
35	to Rte 66, to Vega, **N** 🅐 Best Value Inn, Bonanza Motel (1mi) 🅞 same as 36, Walnut RV Park (1mi)

VEGA

WICHITA FALLS

32mm	🆁🆂 both lanes, litter barrels
28	to Rte 66, Landergin
23	to Adrian, Vega same as 22
22	TX 214, Adrian, **N** ⯅ Midpoint Cafe 🅞 auto repair, USPO, **S** 🅖 Valero/dsl
18	FM 2858, Gruhlkey Rd
15	Ivy Rd
13mm	🆁🆂 both lanes, tables, litter barrels
0	Lp 40, to Glenrio
0mm	Texas/New Mexico state line, Central/Mountain time zone

⬆E INTERSTATE 44

Exit #	Services
15mm	Texas/Oklahoma state line, Red River
14	Lp 267, E 3rd St, **W** 🅞 historical marker, KOA
13	Glendale St, **W** ⯅ Subway
12	Burkburnett, **E** 🅖 Valero/dsl 🅐 Best Western, **W** 🅖 Alon/7-11/dsl ⯅ Braum's, Chicken Express, Feedlot Rest., Lite Par Asian, McDonald's, Whataburger 🅞 Chevrolet, Ford, NAPA
11	FM 3429, Daniels Rd
9mm	🆁🆂 both lanes, tables, litter barrels, petwalk
7	East Rd
6	Bacon Switch Rd
5a	FM 3492, Missile Rd, **E** ⯅ El Mejicano Rest., Marco's Pizza 🅞 s patrol, **W** 🅖 Exxon/dsl
5	Access Rd
4	City Loop St
3c	FM 890, **W** 🅖 Murphy USA/dsl ⯅ Cracker Barrel, Golden Chick Jack-in-the-Box, KFC/Taco Bell, Parkway Grill, Subway 🅞 Walmart/Subway
3b	sp 325, Sheppard AFB
3a	US 287 N, to Amarillo, **W** 🅖 Shell/dsl ⯅ Carl's Jr 🅐 Howard Johnson
2	Maurine St, **E** 🅖 Alon/7-11/dsl 🅐 Best Value Inn, Executive Inn, Motel 6, Quality Inn 🅞 Chevrolet, Mazda/VW, **W** 🅖 Alon/7-11 ⯅ Denny's, LJ Silver, Whataburger 🅐 Candlewood Suites, Comfort Inn, La Quinta, Red Roof Inn, Super 8
1d	US 287 bus, Lp 370, **W** 🅖 Valero/dsl 🅐 Travelodge
1c	Texas Travel Info Ctr, **E** 🅖 $Saver
1b	Scotland Park (from nb)
1a	US 277 S, to Abilene, **W** ⯅ Arby's 🅐 EconoLodge
1	Holliday St, **W** 🅖 Valero/dsl ⯅ Arby's, Burger King, Carl's Jr IHOP, McDonald's, Subway 🅐 Delux Inn, EconoLodge 🅞 Family$, 🅗, Walgreens
0mm	Witchita Falls. **I-44 begins/ends on US 287.**

⬆N INTERSTATE 45

Exit #	Services
286	to I-35 E, to Denton. **I-45 begins/ends in Dallas.**
285	Bryan St E, US 75 N
284b a	I-30, W to Ft Worth, E to Texarkana, **E** 🅞 access to 🅗
283b	Pennsylvania Ave, to MLK Blvd, **E** ⯅ Kwikstop
283a	Lamar St
281	Overton St (from sb), **W** 🅖 Chevron
280	Illinois Ave, Linfield St, **E** 🅐 Star Motel, **W** 🅖 Exxon, Shell/dsl
279b a	Lp 12
277	Simpson Stuart Rd, **W** 🅞 to Paul Quinn Coll
276b a	I-20, W to Ft Worth, E to Shreveport
275	TX 310 N (from nb, no re-entry)
274	Dowdy Ferry Rd, Hutchins, **E** 🅖 Exxon/Subway/dsl, Shell/McDonald's/dsl 🅐 Gold Inn, La Quinta, Motel 6 🅞 auto repair, **W** 🅖 Top Fuel/dsl ⯅ DQ, Jack-in-the-Box, Whataburger

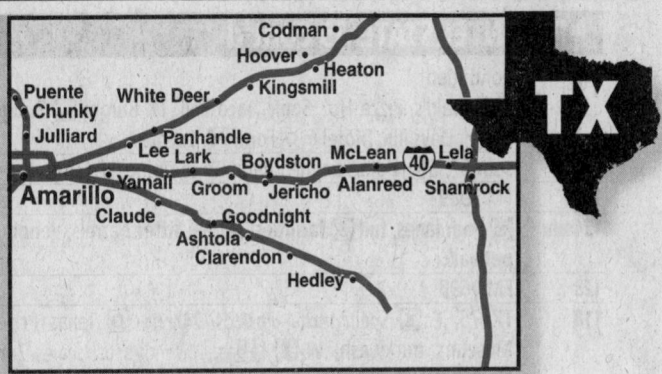

INTERSTATE 45 Cont'd

Exit #	Services
273	Wintergreen Rd, **W** 📱 QT/dsl/scales/24hr
272	Fulghum Rd, **E** 📱 Loves/Carl's Jr/dsl/scales/24hr, **W** 🅾 weigh sta both lanes
271	Pleasant Run Rd
270	Belt Line Rd, to Wilmer, **E** 📱 Chevron/Pizza Inn/dsl, **W** 📱 Exxon/Sonic/dsl, Shell/Church's/Subway/dsl 🍴 Denny's 🅾 $General, Family$, USPO
269	Mars Rd
268	Malloy Bridge Rd
267	Frontage Rd
266	FM 660, **E** 🍴 Jack-in-the-Box, **W** 📱 Valero/dsl 🍴 DQ, Pizza Hut
265	Lp 45, Ferris nb only
263a b	Lp 561
262	Frontage Rd
260	Lp 45, **E** 🍴 Traylor RV Park, **W** 📱 Shell/Sonic/dsl
259	FM 813, FM 878, Jefferson St
258	Lp 45, Palmer, **E** 📱 Chevron/Subway/dsl/scales/24hr 🅾 golf
255	FM 879, Garrett, **E** 📱 Exxon/dsl, **W** 📱 Chevron/dsl
253	Lp 45, **W** 📱 Shell/Subway/dsl
251b	TX 34, Ennis, **E** 📱 Alon/dsl, Cotton Patch Cafe, QT/dsl 🍴 Bubba's BBQ, McDonald's 🏠 Baymont Inn, Comfort Suites, Days Inn, Holiday Inn Express, La Quinta 🅾 Ford, URGENT CARE, **W** 📱 Chevron/dsl, Exxon/dsl/24hr, Murphy USA/dsl, Valero 🍴 Braum's, Burger King, Chili's, Chipotle, Denny's, Domino's, DQ, Golden Chick, Grand Buffet, Hilda's Kitchen, IHOP, Jack-in-the-Box, Little Caesar's, Papa John's, Sonic, Starbucks, Subway, Taco Bell, Taco Cabana, Tokyo Grill, Waffle House, Wall Chinese, Wendy's, Whataburger 🏠 Quality Inn 🅾 $Tree, AT&T, AutoZone, Beall's, Chevrolet, Chrysler/Dodge/Jeep, 🅷, RV camping, Walmart/McDonald's
251a	Creechville Rd, FM 1181, Ennis, **W** 🅾 🅷
249	FM 85, Ennis, **E** 🏠 Budget Inn, **W** 📱 Exxon/Subway/dsl 🅾 Blue Beacon, repair
247	US 287 N, to Waxahatchie
246	FM 1183, Alma, **E** 📱 Loves/Subway/dsl/scales/24hr, **W** 📱 Chevron/dsl
244	FM 1182
243	Frontage Rd
242	Calhoun St, Rice, **W** 📱 Shell/Sonic/dsl 🅾 Family$
239	FM 1126, **W** 📱 Conoco/dsl 🅾 Rendell RV Ctr
238	FM 1603, **E** 📱 Exxon/rest./dsl/24hr 🅾 Casita RV Trailers
237	Frontage Rd
235b	Lp I-45 (from sb), to Corsicana
235a	Frontage Rd
232	Roane Rd, E 5th Ave
231	TX 31, Corsicana, **E** 📱 Mobil/Taco Casa/dsl, Valero/dsl 🍴 Jack-in-the-Box 🏠 Best Western, La Quinta, Super 8 🅾 Buick/Cadillac/Chevrolet/GMC, **W** 📱 Exxon/dsl, Shell/Subway/dsl 🍴 Bill's Fried Chicken, McDonald's 🏠 Comfort Inn 🅾 Chrysler/Dodge/Jeep, Ford/Lincoln, 🅷, to Navarro Coll
229	US 287, Palestine, **E** 📱 Exxon/Wendy's/dsl, Shell/dsl 🍴 Applebee's, Chili's, Collin St Bakery, Denny's, DQ, Panda Express, Schlotsky's, Sonic, Subway, Taco Bell, Whataburger 🏠 Hampton Inn, Holiday Inn Express 🅾 Corsicana Outlets, Home Depot, Office Depot, Russell Stover Candies, **W** 🍴 Waffle House 🏠 Days Inn, Motel 6, Traveler's Inn
228b	Lp 45 (exits left from nb), Corsicana, **2 mi W** services in Corsicana
228a	15th St, Corsicana, **W** 🅾 Toyota
225	FM 739, Angus, **E** 📱 Conoco/dsl 🅾 RV park, to Chambers Reservoir
221	Frontage Rd
220	Frontage Rd
219b	Frontage Rd
219a	TX 14 (from sb), to Mexia, Richland, **W** 📱 Shell
218	FM 1394 (from nb), Richland, **W** 📱 Shell
217mm	Ⓡs both lanes, full 🅿 facilities, 📞, 🚻, litter barrels, vending, petwalk
213	TX 75 S, FM 246, to Wortham, **W** 📱 Exxon/dsl, Valero/dsl
211	FM 80, to Streetman, Kirvin
206	FM 833, **W** 🅾 I-45 RV Park (3mi)
198	FM 27, to Wortham, **E** 📱 Shell/Cole's BBQ 🍴 Gilberto's Mexican 🏠 La Quinta 🅾 🅷, **W** 📱 Cooper Farms/dsl, Loves/Burger King/dsl/scales/24hr 🏠 Budget Inn 🅾 I-45 RV Park (4mi)
197	US 84, Fairfield, **E** 📱 Chevron/dsl, Exxon/dsl, Shell/dsl 🍴 Bush's Chicken, DQ, Jack-in-the-Box, McDonald's, Sam's Rest., Something Different Rest, Sonic, Subway/TX Burger 🏠 Days Inn, Holiday Inn Express, Super 8 🅾 Brookshire Foods/gas, Chevrolet, Chrysler/Dodge/Jeep, Fred's Store, **W** 📱 Exxon/dsl, Shell/dsl 🍴 I-45 Rest., KFC/Taco Bell, Mesquite Grill, Pizza Hut, Ponte's Diner 🏠 Budgetel, Regency Inn 🅾 Ace Hardware, Ford
189	TX 179, to Teague, **E** 📱 Exxon/Dinner Bell Rest/dsl, **W** 📱 Valero/Chester's/Huddle House/dsl
180	TX 164, to Groesbeck
178	US 79, Buffalo, **E** 📱 Chevron/dsl, Conoco/dsl, Mobil/dsl, Shell/dsl 🍴 Pizza Hut, Subway/TX Burger 🅾 $General, Brookshire Foods/gas, Family$, **W** 📱 Exxon/Church's/Subway/Pizza Inn/dsl/scales, 🍴 /PJ Fresh/Taco Bell/dsl/scales/24hr, Texaco/dsl 🍴 Anthony's Rest., Dickey's BBQ, DQ, McDonald's, Rancho Viejo, Sonic 🏠 Best Value Inn, Hampton Inn, Quality Inn, Super 8
175mm	Bliss Creek
166mm	weigh sta sb
164	TX 7, Centerville, **E** 📱 Chevron, Shell/Woody's BBQ/dsl 🍴 Broken Star Cafe, Country Cousins BBQ, Subway/TX Burger 🏠 Days Inn, **W** 📱 CNG, Exxon, Shell/Woody's BBQ/dsl 🍴 DQ, Jack-in-the-Box, Roble's Mexican
160mm	🚻 sb, tables, litter barrels
159mm	Boggy Creek
156	FM 977, to Leona, **W** 📱 Exxon/dsl
155mm	🚻 nb, tables, litter barrels
152	TX OSR, to Normangee, **W** 📱 Shell/Arby's/dsl 🅾 Yellow Rose RV Park
146	TX 75
142	US 190, TX 21, Madisonville, **E** 📱 Buc-ees/dsl, Exxon/dsl 🍴 Dickey's BBQ, Shipley's Donuts, Subway 🏠 Best Western, Madisonville Inn 🅾 URGENT CARE, **W** 📱 Exxon, Mobil/Church's/dsl, Shell/Subway 🍴 Jack-in-the-Box, Lakeside Rest,

🅶 = gas 🍴 = food 🛏 = lodging 🅾 = other 🆁🆂 = rest stop   Copyright 2022 - The Next EXIT ®

INTERSTATE 45 Cont'd

HUNTSVILLE

142	Continued McDonald's, Pizza Hut, Sonic, Taco Bell, TX Burger 🛏 Budget Motel, Days Inn, Motel 6 🅾 Ford, 🅷 Toyota
136	spur 67, E 🅾 Home on the Range RV camping/LP (3mi)
132	FM 2989
124mm	🆁🆂 both lanes, full ♿ facilities, 🅲, 🛆 litter barrels, vending, petwalk
123	FM 1696
118	TX 75, E 🅶 Shell/Hitchin Post/dsl/24hr/@ 🅾 Texas Prison Museum, truckwash, W 🅶 ⬜/Wendy's/dsl/scales/24hr, Shell/Dickey's BBQ/Subway/dsl 🍴 Chicken Express
116	US 190, TX 30, E 🅶 Conoco/dsl, Phillips 66/dsl, Valero/dsl 🍴 Arby's, Bandera Grill, Church's, Golden Corral, Los Panchitos, Mama Juanita's, McDonald's, Popeye's, Schlotzsky's, Sonic, Whataburger 🛏 Days Inn, EconoLodge, Holiday Inn Express, La Quinta, Motel 6 🅾 AutoZone, Brookshire Foods/gas, Buick/Cadillac/Chevrolet/GMC, Cavander's Boots, Chrysler/Dodge/Jeep, CVS Drug, Family$, Firestone/auto, O'Reilly Parts, vet, Walgreens, W 🅶 Chevron/dsl, Exxon/dsl, Murphy USA/dsl, Shell 🍴 Bob Luby's Seafood, Buffalo Wild Wings, Burger King, Cane's, Chili's, Chipotle, Denny's, Five Guys, Grand Buffet, Hartz Chicken, IHOP, Jack-in-the-Box, Little Caesar's, Moe's SW, Olive Garden, Panda Express, Pizza Hut, Rodeo Mexican, Starbucks, Subway, Taco Bell, Wing Stop, Yummy Mongolian 🛏 Best Western, Hampton Inn 🅾 $Tree, AT&T, Discount Tire, GNC, Hobby Lobby, Home Depot, 🅷 JC Penney, Kroger/dsl, Marshall's, Office Depot, Petco, Ross, Target, USPO, Verizon, Walmart
114	FM 1374, E 🅶 Exxon/dsl, Shell 🍴 DQ, Margaritas Rest. 🛏 Red Roof Inn, Super 8, W 🅶 Texaco/dsl, Valero/dsl 🍴 Country Inn Steaks 🛏 Best Value Inn, Quality Suites 🅾 Ford, 🅷 Hyundai
113	TX 19 (from sb), Huntsville, W 🅾 Ford, Hyundai
112	TX 75, E 🍴 Big E's 🅾 Houston Statue, museum, to Sam Houston St U
109	Park 40, W 🅾 to Huntsville SP
103	FM 1374/1375 (from sb), to New Waverly, W 🅶 Chevron/Burger King/dsl
102	FM 1374/1375, TX 150 (from nb), to New Waverly, E 🅶 Valero/dsl (1mi) 🍴 Waverly Rest., W 🅶 Chevron/Burger King/dsl (1mi)
101mm	weigh sta nb
98	TX 75, Danville Rd, Shepard Hill Rd, E 🅾 Convenience RV Ctr/repair
97	Calvary Rd
95	Longstreet Rd, Calvary Rd, Willis, E 🅾 Holiday World, W 🅶 ❤Loves/Subway/Wendy's/dsl/scales/24hr
94	FM 1097, Longstreet Rd, to Willis, E 🅶 Kwik Stop/dsl 🍴 Jack-in-the-Box, Sonic, Taco Bell 🅾 $General, AutoZone, W 🅶 Chevron/Popeye's, Shell/dsl 🍴 Burger King, Chick-fil-A, Cilantros Mexican, Little Caesar's, McDonald's, Papa John's, Pizza Hut, Scholtzsky's, Shipley's Donuts, Subway, Whataburger, WingStop, Yummy Mongolian 🛏 Best Western 🅾 GNC, Kroger/dsl, Verizon, Walgreens
92	FM 830, Seven Coves Dr, W 🅾 Omega Farms RV Park (2mi), RV Park on the Lake (3mi), Thousand Trails Resort (2mi)
90	League Line Rd, E 🅶 Mobil/McDonald's, Shell/dsl 🍴 Mama Juanita's Mexican, Waffle House, Wendy's 🛏 Comfort Inn, Days Inn, La Quinta 🅾 Conroe Outlets/famous brands, W 🅶 Chevron/Jack-in-the-Box 🍴 Cracker Barrel
89	FM 3083, Teas Nursery Rd, Montgomery Co Park, E 🅶 Exxon/dsl 🍴 Applebee's, Buffalo Wild Wings, Popeye's, Red Lobster, Smokey Mo's BBQ 🛏 Fairfield Inn, Homewood Suites 🅾 AT&T, Kohl's, Old Navy, Petsmart, Ross, TJ Maxx, W 🍴 Firehouse Subs,

CONROE

89	Continued Olive Garden, Wengs Wok, Wild Ginger Japanese 🛏 Woodspring Suites 🅾 Cavender's Boots, JC Penney, Verizon
88	Lp 336, to Cleveland, Navasota, E 🅶 Valero/dsl 🍴 Arby's, Burger King, Carl's Jr, Chili's, China Delight, Denny's, Domino's, Dunkin'/Baskin Robbins, Los Cucos Mexican, Marble Slab Creamery, Margarita's Mexican, McDonald's, Papa John's, Pizza Hut, Potbelly, Sonic, Subway, Supreme Buffet, TX Roadhouse, Whataburger, Wing Stop 🛏 Hampton Inn, Holiday Inn Express 🅾 $Tree, Advance Parts, CVS Drug, Discount Tire, Discount Tire, GNC, HEB Foods/gas, Hobby Lobby, Kroger/gas, Michael's, vet, Walgreens, W 🅶 Chevron/24hr 🍴 Casa Ole Mexican, Culver's, Dickey's BBQ, Hunan Village, Jack-in-the-Box, KFC, Ryan's, Starbucks 🅾 99c Store, Big Lots, Lowe's, PetCo, Sam's Club/gas, Tuesday Morning, Walmart
87	TX 105, Conroe, E 🍴 Burger King, CiCi's, El Charrito, Freebirds Burrito, Golden Corral, La Mariposa, McDonald's, Outback Steaks, Popeye's, Saltgrass Steaks 🛏 Super 8 🅾 $General, CVS Drug, Firestone/auto, NTB, W 🅶 Exxon 🍴 Cane's, Chick-fil-A, Chipotle, El Bosque Mexican, Five Guys, Luby's, Panda Express, Panera Bread, Papa Murphy's, Schlotzsky's, Shogun Japanese, Smoothie King, Starbucks, Subway, Vero Italian, Whataburger 🅾 Best Buy, Buick/GMC, GNC, Home Depot, 🅷 Hyundai, Office Depot, Target, Verizon
85	FM 2854, Gladstell St, E 🅶 Shell/dsl 🅾 Ford, Honda, Kia, Nissan, UHaul, W 🅶 Valero 🛏 Best Value Inn, Motel 6 🅾 Chevrolet, Chrysler/Dodge/Jeep, DeMontrond RV Ctr, 🅷 Mazda, Toyota
84	TX 75 N, Frazier St, E 🅶 Chevron/dsl 🛏 Corporate Inn, Econolodge, W 🅶 Shell/dsl 🍴 China Buffet, IHOP, Incredible Pizza, Pizza Hut, Subway, Taco Cabana, Waffle House 🛏 Baymont Inn 🅾 Discount Tire, 🅷 Kroger/dsl, Verizon
83	Crighton Rd, Camp Strake Rd
82	River Plantation Dr
82mm	San Jacinto River
81	FM 1488, to Hempstead, Magnolia, E 🅶 Citgo/dsl, W 🅶 Valero/Subway/dsl 🅾 CamperLand RV Ctr
80	Needham Rd (from sb)
79	TX 242, Needham, E 🅶 Shell/McDonald's 🍴 Mama Juanita's Mexican, Mercedes 🛏 Best Western 🅾 Costco/dsl, Mini, VW, W 🅶 Exxon, Murphy USA/dsl 🍴 Arby's, Burger King, ChuckeCheese, Domino's, Dunkin', LJ Silver/Taco Bell, Outback Steaks, Panera Bread, Popeye's, Sonic, Starbucks, Subway, Taco Cabana, Twin Peaks, Wendy's, Whataburger, Willie's Grill, Wings'N More 🛏 Fairfield Inn, SpringHill Suites, TownPlace Suites 🅾 BMW/Mini, Firestone/auto, 🅷 Kohl's, Lowe's Whse, Walgreens, Walmart
78	Needham Rd (from sb), Tamina Rd access to same as 77
77	Woodlands Pkwy, Robinson, Chateau Woods, E 🅶 Chevron 🍴 Babin's Seafood, BJ's Rest., Buca Italian, Buffalo Wild Wings, Chuy's, El Bosque Mexican, Hooters, Lupe Tortilla, Mi Rancho Mexican, Pappadeaux, PeiWei, Red Robin, Saltgrass Steaks, Spring Creek BBQ, Subway 🛏 Best Value Inn, Courtyard, Holiday Inn 🅾 Discount Tire, GNC, Home Depot, Michael's, NTB, Old Navy, Petsmart, Sam's Club/gas, SteinMart, vet, Walgreens, W 🅶 Shell/dsl, Texaco, Valero/dsl, Valero/dsl 🍴 Blackeyed Pea, Brazilian Steaks, Cane's, Chick-fil-A, Chili's, Chipotle Mexican, Culver's, Denny's, Freebirds Burrito, Guadalajara Mexican, Jack-in-the-Box, Jason's Deli, Jimmy John's, Kirby's Steaks, Luby's, Olive Garden, Red Lobster, Sweet Tomatoes, TGIFriday's, Zoe's Kitchen 🛏 Clarion, Days Inn, Drury Inn, Hampton Inn, Homewood Suites, La Quinta, Marriott 🅾 Best Buy, Dillard's, HEB Foods, 🅷 Macy's, mall, Marshall's, Ross, Sears, Target, World Mkt

INTERSTATE 45 Cont'd

Exit #	Services
76	Research Forest Dr, Tamina Rd, **E** 🍴 Pappas BBQ 🅾 Firestone/auto, Office Depot, PepBoys, URGENT CARE, **W** 🅖 Shell/dsl 🍴 Bonefish Grill, Carrabba's, Firehouse Subs, Fukuda Japanese, IHOP, Landry's Seafood, Longhorn Steaks, Macaroni Grill, Noodles&Co, Olive Garden, Starbucks, Sweet Tomatoes, TGIFriday's 🏨 Courtyard, Residence Inn 🅾 JC Penney, Woodlands Mall
73	Rayford Rd, Sawdust Rd, **E** 🅖 Shell/dsl, Valero 🍴 Cane's, Hartz Chicken, Jack-in-the-Box, McDonald's, Popeye's, Sonic, Starbucks, Thomas BBQ 🏨 Holiday Inn Express, La Quinta 🅾 Aamco, AutoZone, O'Reilly Parts, Walgreens, **W** 🅖 Shell/dsl 🍴 Carrabba's, Gino's Pizza, IHOP, Pizza Hut 🏨 Extended Stay America, Super 8 🅾 Brake Check, Discount Tire, GNC, Harley-Davidson, HEB Foods, Jo-Ann
72a	Spring Crossing Dr, **W** 🅖 Texaco/dsl 🏨 Fairfield Inn
72b	to Hardy Toll Rd from sb
70b	Spring-Stuebner Rd, **E** 🏨 Hampton Inn 🅾 Vaughn RV Ctr
70a	FM 2920, to Tomball, **E** 🅖 Exxon/dsl, Rudy's BBQ/dsl, Shell/dsl 🍴 Arby's, Chick-fil-A, El Palenque Mexican, Golden Jade Chinese, Hartz Chicken, McDonald's, Subway, Taco Cabana, Wendy's, Whataburger, Zaxby's 🏨 Best Western, Comfort Suites 🅾 $Tree, Hyundai, Kohl's, Michael's, O'Reilly Parts, Ross, Toyota, Vaughn's RV Ctr, Verizon, Walmart, **W** 🅖 RaceWay 🏨 Palace Inn 🅾 U-Haul, vet
68	Holzwarth Rd, Cypress Wood Dr, **E** 🍴 Burger King, Freddy's, Golden Corral, Gringo's TexMex, McAlister's Deli, Pizza Hut/Taco Bell, Sonic, Starbucks 🅾 AT&T, Pepboys, **W** 🅖 Exxon/dsl, Murphy Express/dsl, Smashburger 🍴 Bombshells Rest., Cheddar's, Chipotle, Denny's, Dickey's BBQ, Firehouse Subs, Jack-in-the-Box, Lenny's Subs, Panera Bread, Pizza Hut, Popeye's, Razzoo's Cajun, Schlotsky's, Starbucks 🏨 EconoLodge, Motel 6, Scottish Inn 🅾 Advance Parts, Best Buy, Chrysler/Dodge/Jeep, Firestone/auto, Ford/Lincoln, Home Depot, Lowe's Whse, Office Depot, PetCo, Staples, Target, Walgreens
66	FM 1960, to Addicks, **E** 🅖 Chevron/dsl 🍴 Subway, TX Roadhouse 🅾 Acura, AT&T, BMW, Chevrolet, Honda, Mercedes, Petsmart, Subaru, **W** 🅖 Exxon, Valero 🍴 Chick-fil-A, Cilantros Mexican, Hooters, James Coney Island, McDonald's, Outback Steaks, Panda Express, Pollo Campero, Red Lobster 🏨 Baymont Inn, Fairfield Inn, Hampton Inn, Hilton Garden, Palace Inn, Quality Inn, Studio 6 🅾 $Tree, Audi, 🏥, Infiniti, Jaguar/LandRover, Kroger/dsl, Lexus, NTB, Porsche, U-Haul
64	Richey Rd, **E** 🍴 Buffalo Wild Wings, Olive Garden, Taco Bell 🏨 Best Value Inn, Downtowner Inn, Super 8 🅾 CarMax, Discount Tire, Sam's Club/dsl, **W** 🅖 ⛽FLYING J/Denny's/dsl/scales/24hr 🍴 Chula's Cantina, El Toro Loco, Joe's Crabshack, Lupe Tortilla, Mamacita's Mexican, Michoacan Rest, SaltGrass Steaks, Subway, Wings'n More 🏨 SpringHill Suites
63	Airtex Dr, **E** 🅖 Exxon/dsl, Sunoco/dsl, Valero/Church's 🍴 China Bear, Pappasito's Cantina 🏨 Comfort Suites, Woodspring Suites 🅾 Cadillac, LoneStar RV Ctr, Nissan, **W** 🅖 Exxon/dsl 🍴 Cracker Barrel, Jack-in-the-Box, Popeye's, Whataburger 🏨 Best Western, Holiday Inn Express, Sleep Inn
62	Rankin Rd, Kuykendahl, **E** 🏨 Best Classic Inn, Scottish Inn, **W** 🅖 Chevron/McDonald's, RaceWay/dsl, Shell 🍴 Shiply Donuts, Sonic 🏨 Extended Stay Amerca, Palace Inn, SunSuites 🅾 Buick/GMC, DeMontrond RV Ctr, Kia, Lamborghini, Volvo, VW, Walgreens

61	Greens Rd, **E** 🅖 Exxon 🍴 Brown Sugar's BBQ, IHOP, Luna's Mexican 🏨 Knights Inn 🅾 Dillard's, **W** 🍴 Luby's, Panda Chinese, Subway 🏨 Comfort Inn 🅾 99c Store, Burlington Coats
60c	Beltway E
60	(b a from nb) TX 525, **W** 🍴 Pappas Seafood 🅾 U-Haul
59	FM 525, West Rd, **E** 🅖 Shell/dsl, Shell/dsl/repair 🍴 A&W/LJ Silver, Burger King, China Border, CiCi's, Denny's, Domino's, Hanz Diner, Mambo Seafood, McDonald's, Michoacan Rest., Pizza Hut 🏨 Holiday Inn Express 🅾 AutoZone, Chrysler/Dodge/Jeep, Family$, Firestone/auto, **W** 🅖 Exxon/dsl, Shell/dsl 🍴 Chili's, Jalisco's Mexican, Panda Express, Papa John's Pizza, Starbucks, Subway, Taco Bell, Taco Cabana, Wendy's, Whataburger, Wing Stop 🏨 Best Value Inn 🅾 $Tree, AT&T, Best Buy, Discount Tire, Fry's Electronics, Home Depot, Office Depot, PepBoys, Ross, Verizon, Walmart
57	(b a from nb) TX 249, Gulf Bank Rd, Tomball, **E** 🅖 Chevron, Gulf/dsl, Texaco/Church's 🍴 Subway, **W** 🅖 Shell 🍴 Sonic, Tampico Seafood 🏨 Days Inn, Quality Inn 🅾 CVS Drug, Family$, Giant$
56	Canino Rd, **E** 🏨 Taj Inn Suites, **W** 🅖 Texaco 🍴 Denny's, Luby's 🏨 Deluxe Inn, Gulfwind Motel 🅾 Ford, Isuzu, Walgreens
55	(b a from nb) Little York Rd, Parker Rd, **E** 🅖 Chevron/dsl, Exxon/dsl, Texaco 🍴 Burger King, China One, McDonald's, Ranchero King Buffet, Subway, Whataburger 🅾 Advance Parts, Family$, FoodTown, **W** 🍴 KFC, La Chicken, Popeye's 🅾 Walgreens
54	Tidwell Rd, **E** 🅖 Exxon/dsl 🍴 Aunt Bea's Rest, Burger King, Chacho's Mexican, China Border, Pancho's Mexican, Thomas BBQ 🅾 99c Store, CVS Drug, **W** 🅖 Chevron, Shell 🍴 Hartz Chicken, McDonald's 🏨 Guest Motel, Southwind Motel, Symphony Inn, Town Inn 🅾 Family$, U-Haul
53	Airline Dr, **E** 🅾 Discount Tire, Fiesta Foods/drug, **W** 🅖 Citgo, Shell/dsl 🍴 Little Mexico, Whataburger 🏨 Best Value Inn, Luxury Inn, Palace Inn
52	(b a from nb) Crosstimbers Rd, **E** 🅖 Murphy Express/dsl 🍴 Baskin-Robbins, Burger King, Chick-fil-A, China Star, Chucke-Cheese, Cici's, IHOP, Jack-in-the-Box, James Coney Island, KFC, McDonald's, Ojos Locos Cantina, Panda Express, Pappas BBQ, Pizza Hut, Sonic, Subway, Taco Bell 🅾 $Tree, AT&T, CVS Drug, GNC, Marshall's, Ross, Verizon, Walmart, **W** 🏨 Texan Inn
51	I-610
50	(b a from nb) Patton St, Calvacade St, Link Rd, **E** 🅖 Citgo, Exxon, ⛽Loves/Wendy's/dsl/scales/24hr, Shell 🏨 Best Value Inn, Luxury Inn, **W** 🏨 Astro Inn 🅾 AutoZone, Family$, NAPA, USPO
49b	N Main St, Houston Ave, **E** 🅖 Citgo, ⛽Loves/Wendy's/dsl/scales/24hr 🏨 Best Value Inn, Luxury Inn, **W** 🅖 Exxon/dsl 🍴 Domino's, McDonald's, Subway, Whataburger/24hr 🏨 Sleep Inn 🅾 O'Reilly Parts

H O U S T O N

TX

TX

H O U S T O N

⬆N INTERSTATE 45 Cont'd

Exit #	Services
48b a	I-10, E to Beaumont, W to San Antonio
47d	Dallas St, Pierce St (from sb), E 🅾 🏥
47c	McKinney St (from sb, exits left)
47b	Houston Ave, Memorial Dr, W 🛏 DoubleTree downtown
47a	Allen Pkwy (exits left from sb)
46b a	US 59, N to Cleveland, S to Victoria, W 🛢 Chevron, Texaco 🍴 McDonald's 🅾 BMW
45b a	South St, Scott St, Houston, E 🛢 Phillips 66/Church's/dsl, Shell 🛏 Scott Inn, W 🛢 to TSU
44	Cullen Blvd, Houston, W 🛢 to U of Houston
43b	Telephone Rd, Houston, E 🛢 Valero/dsl
43a	Tellepsen St, E 🍴 Luby's, W 🅾 U of Houston
41b	US 90A, Broad St, S Wayside Dr, E 🛏 Houston Inn, Palace Inn 🅾 Walmart/McDonald's, W 🛢 Chevron/dsl, Exxon 🍴 Burger King, Chick-fil-A, Jack-in-the-Box, Little Caesar's, McDonald's, Taco Cabana 🅾 AT&T
41a	Woodridge Dr, E 🛢 Shell 🍴 Chinese Buffet, Church's, Denny's, James Coney Island, McDonald's, Pappa's Seafood House, Pizza Hut, Schlotsky's 🅾 King$, W 🍴 Bonebrake BBQ, Boudreaux Cajun, China Star, ChuckeCheese, CiCi's, Doneraki Mexican, IHOP, KFC/Taco Bell, Panda Express, Pappas BBQ, Sonic, Starbucks, Subway, Taco Palenque, Wendy's, Whataburger 🅾 Best Buy, HEB Food/gas, Home Depot, Lowe's, Marshall's, Office Depot, Old Navy, Ross, Verizon
40c	I-610 W
40b	I-610 E, to Pasadena
40a	Frontage Rd (from nb)
39	Park Place Blvd, Broadway Blvd, E 🛢 Shell/dsl, W 🛢 Pemex/dsl, Shell/dsl 🍴 Kelley's Rest., Papa John's, Subway 🅾 Chrysler/Dodge/Jeep, Family$
38b	Howard Dr, Bellfort Dr (from sb), E 🛢 Shell 🍴 Jack-in-the-Box, Wendy's, W 🛢 Shell/dsl, Texaco/dsl 🍴 Chilo's Seafood, VStar Seafood Buffet 🛏 Camelot Inn, Moonlight Inn, Mustang Inn, Palace Inn
38	TX 3, Monroe Rd, E 🛢 Shell/dsl, Sunoco/Stripes/dsl, Valero/dsl 🍴 DQ, Jack-in-the-Box, Ninfa's Mexican, Starbucks, Wendy's 🛏 Palace Inn 🅾 AutoZone, Family$, URGENT CARE, W 🛢 Chevron/dsl, Texaco/dsl 🍴 Mannie's Seafood, Pappa's BBQ, Subway 🛏 Holiday Inn Express, Sheraton 🅾 Firestone/auto, U-Haul
36	College Ave, Airport Blvd, E 🛢 Valero 🍴 Aranda's Bakery, Burger House, Church's, DQ, Jack-in-the-Box, Shipley Donuts, Subway, Waffle House 🛏 Holiday Inn Express 🅾 O'Reilly Parts, W 🛢 Gulf/dsl, Shell/dsl, Valero/dsl 🍴 Denny's, Denny's, Taco Cabana 🛏 Best Western, Comfort Suites, Courtyard, Days Inn, Drury Inn, Hampton Inn, Holiday Inn, La Quinta, Marriott, Motel 6, SpringHill Suites 🅾 Discount Tire
35	Edgebrook Dr, E 🛢 Chevron, RaceWay/dsl, Shell/dsl 🍴 Aranda's Mexican, Burger King, Chilo's Rest., Jack-in-the-Box, KFC, Popeye's, Subway, Taco Bell 🅾 Family$, Fiesta Foods, Firestone/auto, Office Depot, vet, W 🛢 Citgo/dsl 🍴 James Coney Island, Mambo Seafood, McDonald's, Pizza Hut, Whataburger 🅾 $General, Cavender's Boots, O'Reilly Parts, Verizon
34	S Shaver Rd, E 🛢 Conoco 🍴 McDonald's 🛏 Island Suites 🅾 Ford, Kia, Nissan, Toyota, W 🛢 MurphyUSA/dsl 🍴 Arby's, China Star Buffet, Chopstix, Ojos Locos, Pancho's Mexican, Pizza Patron, Starbucks, Subway, Wendy's 🅾 $Tree, 99c Store, AT&T, Discount Tire, Firestone/auto, GNC, Honda, Macy's, Marshall's, NTB, PetsMart, Ross, Staples, Walmart/McDonald's

L E A G U E   C I T Y

33	Fuqua St, E 🍴 Chili's, Denny's, Fuddrucker's, Las Haciendas, Luby's, Olive Garden, Schlotzky's, TGIFriday's 🛏 Studio 6, Sun Suites 🅾 Lincoln, Volvo, W 🍴 Bayou City Wings, Blackeyed Pea, Bombshells Grill, Boudreaux's, Casa Ole, Cici's Pizza, Fox &Hound, Golden Corral, Gringo's Mexican, IHOP, Joe's Crab shack, McDonald's, Outback Steaks, Subway, Taco Bell, Taco Cabana, TX Land&Cattle Steaks, Whataburger 🅾 Buick/GMC, CarMax, Chevrolet, Home Depot, Sam's Club/gas
32	Sam Houston Tollway
31	FM 2553, Scarsdale Blvd, W 🅾 Chevrolet
30	FM 1959, Dixie Farm Rd, Ellington Field, E 🛢 Shell/dsl 🍴 El Nopalito, Subway 🛏 Motel 6 🅾 Chrysler/Dodge/Jeep, Fiat, 🏥, Infiniti, Subaru, W 🛢 Exxon/dsl, RaceWay, Shell/dsl 🍴 Mc-Donald's, Popeye's 🛏 Palace Inn 🅾 Lonestar RV, VW
29	FM 2351, Clear Lake City Blvd, to Clear Lake RA, Friendswood W 🅾 Hyundai
27	El Dorado Blvd, E 🛢 Exxon/dsl 🍴 Carl's Jr, Chick-fil-A, Panera Bread, Starbucks, Taco Bell 🅾 Firestone/auto, Home Depot, W 🍴 Bar Louie, Kona Grill, Maggiano's, Perry's Steakhouse, Sonic, Subway, TX Roadhouse, Whataburger, Yardhouse Grill 🅾 Cadillac, Kohl's, Lexus, Sam's Club/gas, Walmart/McDonald's
26	Bay Area Blvd, E 🛢 Chevron 🍴 Bonefish Grill, Buffalo Wild Wings, Chick-fil-A, La Madeleine, Longhorn Steaks, Lupe Tortilla, Noodles&Co, Pei Wei, Potbelly, Red Lobster, Taco Cabana, TGIFriday's, Zio's Kitchen 🛏 Best Western, Hampton Inn, Hilton Garden, La Quinta 🅾 Barnes&Noble, Best Buy, 🏥, Lowe's, Michael's, Staples, to Houston Space Ctr, World Mkt, W 🛢 Valero/dsl 🍴 Burger King, Cheesecake Factory, Chick-fil-A, ChuckeCheese, Dave&Buster's, Denny's, Five Guys, Los Cucos, McDonald's, Olive Garden, Panda Express, PF Chang's, Starbucks, Subway, Zoe's Kitchen 🛏 Holiday Inn Express 🅾 AT&T, Dillard's, Fresh Mkt, JC Penney, Jo-Ann Fabrics, Macy's, mall, Marshall's, Office Depot, Old Navy, Petsmart, Ross, Sears/auto, Target, Verizon, vet
25	FM 528, NASA rd 1, E 🛢 Chevron/dsl, Valero/dsl 🍴 Bone Daddy's, Cheddar's, Chili's, Chuy's Mexican, Fuddrucker's, Las Hacienda Mexican, Luby's, Marble Slab, McAlister's Deli, Michiru Asian, Pappa's Seafood, Pappasito's Cantina, Rudy's BBQ/dsl, Saltgrass Steaks, Steak'n Shake, Twin Peaks Rest., Waffle House 🛏 Motel 6, SpringHill Suites 🅾 BigLots, Cavendar's Boots, Fry's Electronics, Hobby Lobby, Honda, 🏥, Mazda, W 🍴 Floyd's Cajun, Hooters, James Coney Island, Pappa's Cafe, Subway 🅾 Tuesday Morning
23	FM 518, League City, E 🛢 RaceWay/dsl, Shell/dsl 🍴 Center Buffet, La Brisa, Sonic, Subway 🅾 $Tree, Kroger, W 🛢 Chevron/dsl, Valero 🍴 Cracker Barrel, McDonald's, Taco Bell, Waffle House, Wendy's 🛏 Super 8 🅾 Discount Tire, Space Ctr RV Park, U-Haul
22	Calder Dr, Brittany Bay Blvd, E 🅾 BMW/Mini, Mercedes, Nissan, Toyota, W 🅾 Acura, Holiday World RV Ctr
20	FM 646, Santa Fe, Bacliff, E 🛢 MurphyUSA/dsl 🍴 Chick-fil-A, Cici's Pizza, Denny's, Five Guys, Freebirds Burrito, Jack-in-the-Box, Jimmy Changas, Logan's Roadhouse, Marble Slab, McDonald's, NY Pizzaria, Panda Express, Panera Bread, Pollo Tropical, Quaker Steak, Schlotzky's, Spring Creek BBQ, Subway, Whataburger, Which Wich? 🛏 Candlewood Suites, Hampton Inn 🅾 $Tree, AT&T, Best Buy, Firestone/auto, GNC, Hobby Lobby, Home Depot, JC Penney, Lowe's, Michael's, NTB, PetsMart, Ross, Staples, Target, TJ Maxx, URGENT CARE, Walmart/McDonald's, W 🛢 Chevron/dsl 🍴 888 Chinese Rest., Chili's, Subway, Taco Cabana 🅾 Cabela's, HEB Foods/gas, Kohl's, PetCo, Verizon, Walgreens

INTERSTATE 45 Cont'd

Exit #	Services
19	FM 517, Dickinson Rd, Hughes Rd, **E** 🍴 Jack-in-the-Box, Little Mexico 🅞 Buick/GMC, CVS Drug, Family$, Kia, **W** 🍴 Conoco/dsl, Shell/dsl 🍴 KFC, McDonald's, Pizza Hut, Sonic, Starbucks, Subway, Taco Bell, Wendy's, Whataburger/24hr 🏨 Days Inn 🅞 Chrysler/Dodge/Jeep, Ford, Kroger
17	Holland Rd, **W** 🍴 Buc-ee's/dsl 🅞 Tanger Outlets/Famous Brands, to Gulf Greyhound Park
16	FM 1764 E (from sb), Texas City same as 15
15	FM 2004, FM 1764, Hitchcock, **E** 🍴 Beyond Burger, Gringo's Cafe, Jack-in-the-Box, Olive Garden, Ryan's 🏨 Best Western, Fairfield Inn, Holiday Inn Express, Woodspring Suites 🅞 Chevrolet/Toyota, DeMontrond RV Ctr, 🅗, mall, **W** 🍴 Gulf/Subway, MurphyUSA/dsl, Shell 🍴 Best Wok, IHOP, Little Caesar's, Pizza Hut, Rose Garden Chinese, Sonic, Waffle House, Wendy's, Whataburger, WingStop 🅞 AT&T, Gulf Greyhound Park, Sam's Club/gas, URGENT CARE, Verizon, Walmart/McDonald's
13	Century Blvd, Delany Rd, **W** 🍴 Barcema's Mexican 🏨 Best Value Inn, Super 8 🅞 Lazy Days RV Park, VF Factory Outlet/famous brands
12	FM 1765, La Marque, **E** 🍴 Chevron/dsl 🍴 Domino's, Jack-in-the-Box, Kelley's Rest., Sonic 🅞 $General, CVS Drug, Family$, **W** 🍴 Texaco/dsl 🅞 Little Thicket RV Park, UHaul
11	Vauthier Rd
10	**E** 🍴 Exxon, Valero 🍴 KFC, McDonald's, PitStop BBQ, Subway, **W** 🍴 Shell/dsl 🅞 Hoover RV Ctr, Oasis RV Park
9	Frontage Rd (from sb, no return/turnaround)
8	Frontage Rd (from nb)
7c	Frontage Rd
7b	TX 146, TX 6 (exits left from nb), Texas City
7a	TX 146, TX 3
6	Frontage Rd (from sb)
5	Frontage Rd
4	Frontage Rd, Village of Tiki Island, **W Welcome Ctr** 🍴 Valero/dsl 🅞 public boat ramp
4mm	West Galveston Bay
1c	TX 275, FM 188 (from nb), Port Ind Blvd, Teichman Rd, Port of Galveston, **E** 🍴 Citgo, Exxon/dsl, Valero/dsl 🏨 Howard Johnson, Motel 6 🅞 Buick/Chevrolet/GMC, Ford, Toyota
1b	71st St (from sb), **E** 🍴 Best Value Inn, same as 1c
1a	TX 342, 61st St, to W Beach, **E** 🍴 RaceWay 🍴 Subway, WingStop 🏨 Candlewood Suites 🅞 Big Lots, Family$, GNC, Home Depot, NTB, PetsMart, Target, **0-2 mi W** 🍴 Chevron/dsl, Citgo, Exxon, Murphy USA/dsl, Shell/Burger King/dsl, Texaco/dsl, Valero 🍴 Cici's Pizza, Domino's, Golden Corral, Happy Buddah, Healthy Chinese, Jack-in-the-Box, Jimmy John's, KFC, Little Caesar's, Marble Slab, Mario's, McAlister's Deli, McDonald's, Papa John's, Popeye's, Schlotsky's, Sonic, Starbucks, Subway, Taco Bell, Taco Cabana, Waffle House, Whataburger, Yamato Japanese 🏨 Baymont Inn, Comfort Inn, Hilton, Quality Inn, Red Roof Inn, Rodeway Inn, SpringHill Suites, Super 8 🅞 $Tree, AT&T, AutoZone, CVS Drug, Family$, Firestone/auto, Kroger/dsl, KwikCar, Marshall's, O'Reilly Parts, Office Depot, Randall's Food/gas, Ross, Tuesday Morning, URGENT CARE, USPO, Verizon, Walgreens, Walmart

I-45 begins/ends on TX 87 in Galveston.

INTERSTATE 410 (San Antonio)

Exit #	Services
53	I-35, S to Laredo, N to San Antonio
51	FM 2790, Somerset Rd
49	TX 16 S, spur 422, **N** 🍴 Chevron, Texaco/dsl 🍴 Church's, Domino's, Sonic, Subway, Whataburger 🏨 Days Inn 🅞 🅗, to Palo Alto Coll, **S** 🍴 Valero/dsl 🍴 Jack-in-the-Box 🏨 Best Western
48	Zarzamora St, **S** 🍴 Valero/dsl
47	Turnaround (from eb)
46	Moursund Blvd
44	US 281 S, spur 536, Roosevelt Ave, **N** 🍴 Shell/McDonald's/dsl, Valero/dsl 🍴 Subway, **S** 🍴 Jack-in-the-Box 🏨 Holiday Inn Express
43	Espada Rd (from eb)
42	spur 122, S Presa Rd, **N** 🅞 to San Antonio Missions Hist Park, **S** 🍴 Valero/dsl
41	I-37, US 281 N
39	spur 117, WW White Rd
37	Southcross Blvd, Sinclair Rd, Sulphur Sprs Rd, **N** 🍴 Shell/dsl, Valero 🍴 Family$ 🅞 🅗
35	US 87, Rigsby Ave, **E** 🍴 Exxon/7-11, Murphy USA/dsl, Valero/dsl 🍴 Denny's, El Rodeo Mexican, Jack-in-the-Box, KFC/Taco Bell, McDonald's 🅞 $Tree, AT&T, Walmart/McDonald's, **W** 🍴 Chevron/dsl 🍴 Bill Miller BBQ, Burger King, Domino's, El Tapico Mexican, Habachi Buffet, Laguna Madre, Sonic, Taco Cabana, Whataburger 🏨 Days Inn, Holiday Inn Express 🅞 Aamco, Advance Parts, Gascard/dsl, U-Haul, vet, Walgreens
34	FM 1346, E Houston St, **W** 🍴 Valero/dsl 🅞 USPO
33	I-10 E, US 90 E, to Houston, I-10 W, US 90 W, to San Antonio
32	Dietrich Rd (from sb), FM 78 (from nb), to Kirby
31b	Lp 13, WW White Rd
31a	FM 78, Kirby
30	Binz-Engleman, Space Center Dr (from nb)

I-410 and I-35 run together 7 mi, See I-35, exits 161 thru 165.

27	I-35, N to Austin, S to San Antonio
26	Lp 368 S, Alamo Heights
25b	FM 2252, Perrin-Beitel Rd, **N** 🍴 Chevron/dsl, Valero/dsl 🍴 Carl's Jr, KFC/Taco Bell, Schlotsky's, Subway, Tastee-Freez/Wienerschnitzel 🏨 Budget Lodge 🅞 Brake Check, Family$, **S** 🍴 Jim's Rest.
25a	Starcrest Dr, **N** 🍴 Valero 🍴 Jack-in-the-Box 🏨 Travelodge 🅞 🅗
24	Harry Wurzbach Hwy, **N** 🍴 Taco Cabana, **S** 🍴 BBQ Sta. 🅞 VW
23	Nacogdoches Rd, **N** 🍴 Shell/dsl 🍴 Bill Miller BBQ, Church's, Formosa Chinese, IHOP, Jimmy John's, Luby's, Pizza Hut, Sonic 🏨 Crowne Plaza, **S** 🍴 Chevron/7-11 🅞 Volvo

INTERSTATE 410 (San Antonio) Cont'd

Exit #	Services
22	Broadway St, N 🅿 Shell/dsl 🍴 Chili's, Fuddrucker's, McDonald's 🛏 Cambria Suites, Courtyard, Home2 Suites, S 🅿 Citgo, Valero/dsl 🍴 Cane's, Chesters Hamburgers, Jim's Rest., Little Caesar's, Martha's Mexican, Taco Palenque, Whataburger 🛏 Residence Inn, SpringHill Suites, TownHouse Motel
21	US 281 S, Airport Rd, Jones Maltsberger Rd, N 🍴 Applebee's 🛏 Drury Suites, Hampton Inn, Holiday Inn, Holiday Inn Express, PearTree Inn, Sheraton, S 🅿 Murphy USA/dsl 🍴 Cracker Barrel, Logan's Roadhouse, Pappadeaux, Texas Land&Cattle, Whataburger 🛏 Best Western, Courtyard, Days Inn, Fairfield Inn, Home2 Suites, La Quinta, Staybridge Suites, TownePlace Suites 🅾 Nissan, TJ Maxx, Walmart/McDonald's/24hr
20	TX 537, N 🅿 Valero 🍴 Arby's, Chick-fil-A, Jack-in-the-Box, Jason's Deli, Rosario's Mexican, Subway, TGIFriday's, Wendy's 🛏 DoubleTree Hotel, Hilton 🅾 Barnes&Noble, Best Buy, Brake Check, Cavender's Boots, Chevrolet, Honda, Jo-Ann Fabrics, Lexus, Lincoln, Mazda, Mercedes, Office Depot, PetCo, Ross, Subaru, S 🍴 Cheesecake Factory, Chipotle, Dickey's BBQ, Earth Burger, Egg&I, El Pollo Loco, Freddy's, Jimmy John's, La Madeleine, Longhorn Steaks, Luby's, Panda Express, Starbucks, Taco Cabana, Twin Peaks 🛏 Aloft 🅾 AT&T, Chrysler/Dodge/Jeep, CVS Drug, Dillard's, JC Penney, Macy's, Saks 5th, Target, Verizon
19b	FM 1535, FM 2696, Military Hwy, N 🍴 Guajillos Mexican, Souper Salad, S 🍴 Denny's, Jim's Rest.
19a	Honeysuckle Lane, Castle Hills
17b	(18 from wb), S 🅿 Shell 🍴 Bill Miller BBQ, Burger King, Pollo Tropical, Subway 🅾 HEB Foods/gas, NAPA, vet
17	Vance Jackson Rd, N 🅿 Valero/dsl 🍴 Jack-in-the-Box, McDonald's, Sonic, Starbucks, Taco Cabana, Whataburger 🛏 Embassy Suites, Marriott 🅾 Aamco, AT&T, Discount Tire, S 🅿 Petronic, Shell 🍴 Church's, Subway 🅾 U-Haul
16b a	I-10 E, US 87 S, to San Antonio, I-10 W, to El Paso, US 87 N
15	Lp 345, Fredericksburg Rd, E 🅿 Citgo, EVC 🍴 Church's, Dave&Buster's, Denny's, El Pollo Loco, El Rodeo, Jack-in-the-Box, Jim's Rest., Luby's, McDonald's, Peter Piper Pizza, Taco Cabana, Wendy's, Whataburger 🛏 Best Value Inn, SpringHill Suites 🅾 Family$, Firestone/auto, Hobby Lobby, SteinMart, Target, W 🅿 Chevron/7-11/dsl 🅾 CVS Drug
14	(c b a from sb) Callaghan Rd, Babcock Ln, E 🅿 Chevron/dsl, Valero/dsl 🍴 Marie Callender's, Popeye's, Red Lobster, Whataburger 🛏 Best Western, Quality Inn 🅾 Hyundai, W 🅿 Exxon, Shell, Valero 🍴 Burger King, Chili's, ChopSticks Chinese, Ding-How Chinese, Golden Corral, Henry's Tacos, IHOP, Jack-in-the-Box, Jim's Rest, Joe's Crabshack, Las Palapas Mexican, Louie Italian, McDonald's, Nicha's Mexican, Pizza Hut, Quizno's, Subway, Taco Cabana, Wendy's 🅾 Cavander's Boots, Chevrolet, Home Depot, 🅷, NTB, Petsmart, Sam's Club/gas, Walmart/Subway/24hr
13	(b a from sb) TX 16 N, Bandera Rd, Evers Rd, Leon Valley, E 🍴 Outback Steaks, Panda Express 🅾 Audi, HEB Foods/dsl, Office Depot, Toyota, UHaul, W 🍴 Bill Miller BBQ, Henry's Tacos, Jim's Rest., Schlotzsky's, Sonic, Taco Cabana 🅾 Chevrolet
12	(from sb), W 🍴 Fortune Cookie Chinese, Jason's Deli, Ojos Locos, Olive Garden, Sea Island Shrimp House, Starbucks 🅾 $Tree, AT&T, Barnes&Noble, Best Buy, Marshall's, Michael's, Old Navy, Petco, Ross
11	Ingram Rd, E 🅿 Shell/dsl 🍴 KFC/Taco Bell, Los Roberto's, Saltgrass Steaks, TX Roadhouse, Vallarta Mexican 🛏 Comfort Suites, Courtyard, Days Inn, Holiday Inn Express, Red Roof Inn, Residence Inn 🅾 Aamco, Chrysler/Dodge/Jeep, Mazda, Nissan, W 🍴 Chick-fil-A, ChuckeCheese, Denny's, Fuddrucker's, Jack-in-the-Box, Whataburger 🛏 Best Western 🅾 Dillard's, Firestone/auto, JC Penney, Macy's, mall, Sears/auto
10	FM 3487, Culebra Rd, E 🍴 Denny's, J Anthony's Seafood, McDonald's, Wendy's 🛏 La Quinta, Ramada Ltd 🅾 Harley-Davidson, to St Mary's U, W 🅿 Phillips 66 🅾 Ford
9	(b a from sb) TX 151, E 🍴 Subway, W 🅿 Murphy USA/dsl 🍴 54th St Grill, Buffalo Wild Wings, Carino's Italian, Cheddar's, Chili's, Chipotle Mexican, Cracker Barrel, Dickey's BBQ, Firehouse Subs, IHOP, McAlister's Deli, Panda Express, Schlotsky's, Starbucks, TGIFriday's, Twin Peaks, Whataburger 🛏 Homewood Suites, Quality Inn, Sleep Inn, SpringHill Suites 🅾 $Tree, AT&T, GNC, Home Depot, Lowe's Whse, Office Depot, Petsmart, Ross, Target, to Sea World, URGENT CARE, Verizon, Walmart/McDonald's
7	(8 from sb) Marbach Dr, E 🅿 Exxon/7-11 🍴 Church's, Golden Wok, IHOP 🅾 PepBoys, W 🅿 Chevron/dsl, Shell/dsl 🍴 Burger King, Chick-fil-A, Jack-in-the-Box, Jim's Rest., Jimmy John's, KFC, LJ Silver, McDonald's, Peter Piper Pizza, Pizza Hut, Popeye's, Red Lobster, Sonic, Subway, Taco Bell, Taco Cabana, Whataburger/24hr 🛏 Knights Inn, Motel 6 🅾 $Tree, Advance Parts, BigLots, BrakeCheck, Discount Tire, Firestone/auto, HEB Foods/gas
6	US 90, E 🛏 Country Inn Motel 🅾 to Lackland AFB, W 🅿 Shell dsl, Valero/dsl 🛏 Best Western 🅾 Explore USA RV Ctr
4	Valley Hi Dr, to Del Rio, San Antonio, E 🅿 Valero/dsl 🍴 Burger King, Church's, Little Caesar's, McDonald's, Panda Express, Pizza Hut, Sonic, Subway 🅾 AutoZone, Family$, HEB Food/gas, O'Reilly Parts, W 🅿 Valero 🍴 Jack-in-the-Box 🅾 to Lackland AFB, Walgreens
3	(b a from sb) Ray Ellison Dr, Medina Base, E 🅿 Chevron/dsl, W 🅿 Exxon/dsl, Valero/Subway/dsl 🅾 Walmart/Subway
2	FM 2536, Old Pearsall Rd, E 🅿 Shell/dsl, Valero/dsl 🍴 Bill Miller BBQ, Church's, Domino's, Little Caesar's, McDonald's, Mexico Taqueria, Sonic, Subway 🅾 AutoZone, CVS Drug, O'Reilly Parts
1	Frontage Rd, W 🅾 Toyota

INTERSTATE 610 (Houston)

Exit #	Services
38c a	TX 288 N downtown, access to zoo
37	Scott St, N 🅿 Citgo, Exxon 🅾 Family$
36	FM 865, Cullen Blvd, N 🛏 Crystal Inn, S 🅿 Chevron/McDonald's, Shell 🛏 Cullen Inn
35	Calais Rd, Crestmont St, MLK Blvd, S 🅿 Shell 🍴 Subway
34	S Wayside Dr, Long Dr, N 🅿 Citgo, Shell/dsl, Sunoco/Stripes/dsl 🍴 Church's, S 🅿 Shell, Valero/dsl 🍴 Jack-in-the-Box 🅾 NAPA
33	Woodridge Dr, Telephone Rd, N 🅿 Shell/dsl 🍴 ChuckeCheese, Cici's Pizza, Doneraki Mexican, IHOP, KFC/Taco Bell, McDonald's, Panda Express, Pappas BBQ, Starbucks, Taco Palenque, Wendy's 🅾 Advance Parts, Best Buy, Brake Check, Harley Davidson, HEB Foods/gas, Lowe's, Marshall's, Old Navy, Ross, Verizon, S 🅿 Citgo/dsl 🍴 Spanky's Pizza
32b a	I-45, S to Galveston, N to Houston 🅾 to ♿
31	Broadway Blvd, S 🅿 Phillips 66/dsl, Valero/dsl
30c b	TX 225, to Pasadena San Jacinto Mon
29	Port of Houston Main Entrance

⬆E INTERSTATE 610 (Houston) Cont'd

Exit #	Services
28	Clinton Dr, W 🔳 Shell/Burger King/dsl to Galina Park
27	Turning Basin Dr industrial area
26b	Market St
26a	I-10 E, to Beaumont, I-10 W to downtown
24	(b a from sb) US 90 E, Wallisville Rd, E 🔳 Citgo/dsl, Gulf/dsl, ♥Loves/Arby's/dsl/scales/24hr, Pilot/McDonald's/dsl/scales, Valero/dsl, Valero/Hartz Chicken/dsl/scales/24hr 🍴 Chevron/dsl 🅾 Blue Beacon, W 🔳 Citgo/dsl
23b	N Wayside, N 🍴 Valero
23a	Kirkpatrick Blvd
22	Homestead Rd, Kelley St, N 🔳 Shell/dsl 🍴 Whataburger 🛏 Super 8, S 🔳 Chevron/Subway/dsl/scales
21	Lockwood Dr, W 🔳 Texaco/Subway/dsl, N 🔳 Chevron/McDonald's, Shell/dsl 🍴 Church's, Timmy Chan Chinese 🅾 Family$, Fiesta Foods, 🅷
20a b	US 59 to downtown
19b	Hardy Toll Rd
19a	Hardy St, Jensen Dr (from eb)
18	Irvington Blvd, Fulton St, N 🔳 Chevron, S 🔳 Shell/dsl
17b c	I-45, N to Dallas, S to Houston
17a	(eb only) Airline Dr, S 🔳 Shell/dsl 🍴 Jack-in-the-Box 🛏 Western Inn
16	(b a from eb) Yale St, N Main St, Shamrock, N 🔳 Exxon/dsl 🅾 Harley-Davidson, S 🔳 Texaco 🍴 Burger King, KFC/Taco Bell, Starbucks
15	TX 261, N Shepherd Dr, N 🍴 Five Guys, Gabby's BBQ, Sonic, Starbucks, Taco Cabana, S 🔳 Chevron/dsl, Shell 🍴 Chick-fil-A, Wendy's, Whataburger 🅾 Home Depot, PepBoys
14	Ella Blvd, N 🔳 Exxon 🍴 Cane's, Carl's Jr, El Pollo Loco, KFC, McDonald's, Popeye's, Taco Bell, S 🔳 Murphy USA/dsl, Shell 🍴 Chipotle, Thomas BBQ 🅾 BrakeCheck, CVS Drug, 🅷, Lowe's Whse, Office Depot
13c	TC Jester Blvd, N 🔳 Shell 🍴 Antone's Po' Boys, Denny's, Juanita's Mexican 🛏 Courtyard, SpringHill Suites, S 🔳 Phillips 66/dsl
13b a	US 290 (exits left from nb)
12	W 18th St, E 🍴 Applebee's, Whataburger, W 🔳 Shell 🍴 Burger King 🛏 Sheraton
11	I-10, W to San Antonio, E to downtown Houston
10	Woodway Dr, Memorial Dr, W 🔳 Chevron/Pizza Inn/dsl, Shell/dsl 🅾 Goodyear
9b	Post Oak Blvd, E 🛏 Drury Inn, Hampton Inn, La Quinta, W 🍴 McCormick&Schmick's Café, Starbucks
9a	San Felipe Rd, Westheimer Rd, FM 1093, E 🔳 Chevron/dsl, Shell 🍴 Grotto Rest., Jack-in-the-Box, Le Peep Cafe, Starbucks, Sullivan Steaks 🛏 Extended Stay America, Hampton Inn, La Quinta 🅾 CVS Drug, NTB, Target, W 🔳 Shell 🍴 CA Pizza Kitchen,

9a	Continued
	Five Guys, Jamba Juice, Panera Bread, Yia Yia Mary's 🛏 Courtyard, Extended Stay America, Marriott, Sheraton 🅾 AT&T, Best Buy, Dillard's, Nieman-Marcus, Whole Foods Mkt
8a	US 59, Richmond Ave, E 🛏 Extended Stay America 🅾 CVS Drug, W 🔳 Shell 🛏 Holiday Inn 🅾 Dillards
7	Bissonet St, West Park Dr, Fournace Place, E 🍴 Beudreax's Kitchen 🛏 Candlewood Suites 🅾 Home Depot, Petsmart, W 🔳 Shell/dsl/repair
6	Bellaire Blvd
5b	Evergreen St
5a	Beechnut St, E 🔳 Chevron 🍴 Boston Mkt, IHOP, Lowe's, McDonald's, Outback Steaks, Panda Express, Subway 🅾 Hobby Lobby, Verizon, W 🔳 AT&T, Phillips 66, Shell 🍴 Becks Prime, Chick-fil-A, Escalante Mexican Grill, Fadi's Grill, James Coney Island, La Madeleine, Los Tios Mexican, Saltgrass Steaks, Smoothie King, Starbucks 🅾 Best Buy, GNC, JC Penney, Marshall's, Old Navy, Ross, SteinMart, Target
4a	S Post Oak Rd, Brasswood, E 🍴 Outback Steaks, W 🅾 Target, Walmart
3	Stella Link Rd, N 🔳 Mobil 🍴 Domino's 🅾 99c Store, Discount Tire, O'Reilly Parts, S 🔳 Valero/dsl 🅾 Brake Check, vet
2	US 90A, N 🔳 Exxon/dsl, Mobil, Texaco, Valero 🍴 Burger King, Chacho's Cantina, Denny's/24hr, KFC, McDonald's, Popeye's, Starbucks, Subway, Wendy's 🛏 Holiday Inn Express 🅾 CVS Drug, Discount Tire, Family$, Ford, Honda, Mazda, Walgreens, S 🔳 Chevron/dsl 🍴 Golden Corral, Taco Bell, Whataburger/24hr 🛏 Candlewood Suites, CareFree Inn, Motel 6, Motel 6 (2), RainTree Inn 🅾 Nissan, to Buffalo Speedway
1c	Kirby Dr (from eb), N 🛏 Crowne Plaza, Quality Inn, Sterling Inn, S 🍴 Joe's Crabshack, Pappadeaux Seafood, Pappasito's Cantina 🅾 Cavender's Boots, Chevrolet, Hyundai, NTB, Toyota
1b a	FM 521, Almeda St, Fannin St, N 🔳 Chevron/dsl, Shell 🍴 Burger King 🅾 NRG Arena, S 🔳 Shell/dsl 🍴 McDonald's 🅾 Aamco, Chrysler/Dodge/Jeep, to Six Flags

H O U S T O N

NOTES

⊡ = gas ⊞ = food ⌂ = lodging ⊙ = other ⬚ = rest stop   Copyright 2022 - The Next EXIT

UTAH

UT

⬆N INTERSTATE 15

Exit #	Services
400.5mm	Utah/Idaho state line
398	Portage
392	UT 13 S, Plymouth, E ⊞ United/A&W/dsl
385	UT 30 E, to Riverside, Fielding, 1 mi E ⊞ Sinclair/Riverside Grill/dsl
381	Tremonton, Garland, 2 mi E ⊙ food, gas, ⒣ lodging
379	I-84 W, to Boise
376	UT 13, to Tremonton, 2-3 mi E ⊞ Texaco/Arby's/dsl/scales/24hr ⊞ JC'S Diner, Subway, Taco Time ⌂ Marble Motel, Sandman Motel (3mi)
372	UT 240, to UT 13, to rec area, Honeyville, E ⊙ Crystal Hot Springs Camping
370mm	⬚ sb, full ♿ facilities, info, ⓒ, ⬚ litter barrels, vending, petwalk
365	UT 13, Brigham City, W ⊙ to Golden Spike NHS
363	Forest St, Brigham City, E ⊞ ●Loves●/Carl's Jr/Subway/dsl/scales/24hr ⌂ Holiday Inn Express, W ⊙ Bear River Bird Refuge
362	US 91, to US 89, Brigham City, Logan, E ⊞ 7-11/dsl, Chevron/dsl, Exxon, Floriberto's Mexican, Phillips 66/dsl, USA ⊞ Burger King, Costa Vida, Domino's, Hunan Chinese, J&D's Rest., KFC/Taco Bell, McDonald's, Old Grist Mill Bread, Pizza Hut, Sonic, Subway, Taco Time, Wendy's, Wingers ⌂ Crystal Inn, Howard Johnson Express ⊙ $Tree, AT&T, AutoZone, Buick/Cadillac/Chevrolet, Golden Spike RV Park, ⒣, John Watson, Chiropractor (5mi), KOA (4mi), O'Reilly Parts, Schwab Tires, to Yellowstone NP via US 89, Verizon, Walmart/Subway, W ⊞ Maverick/DQ/dsl/scales/24hr ⌂ Days Inn
361mm	⬚ nb, full ♿ facilities, ⓒ, ⬚ litter barrels, vending, petwalk
359	Port of Entry both lanes
357	UT 315, to Willard, Perry, E ⊞ ⊘FLYING J/Subway/dsl/LP/scales/24hr ⊙ KOA (2mi), Willard Peak Camping
351	UT 126, to US 89, to Utah's Fruit Way, Willard Bay, W ⊙ Smith & Edwards Hardware
349	UT 134, N Ogden, Farr West, E ⊞ 7-11, EVC, Exxon/Wendy's/dsl, Maverik/dsl ⊞ Arby's, Bella's Mexican, Burger King, Del Taco, Domino's, Jumbo Burger, McDonald's, Subway, Taco Bell ⌂ Comfort Inn ⊙ Jiffylube, Wasatch View RV park, W ⊞ Chevron/dsl
346	to Harrisville, W ⊞ Cal Ranch, Chevron/Subway/dsl, dsl repair, Maverik/dsl ⊞ GriDeli's, Taco Time, Zhang's Chinese ⊙ vet
344	UT 39, 12th St, Ogden, E ⊞ 7-11/dsl, Chevron/dsl, Old Frontier ⌂ Best Western+ ⊙ to Ogden Canyon RA, W ⊞ One 9/Subway/Taco Bell/dsl/24hr ⌂ Sleep Inn ⊙ Sierra RV Ctr
343	UT 104, 21st St, Ogden, E ⊞ ⊘FLYING J/Denny's/dsl/LP/24hr, Phillips 66/dsl ⊞ Cactus Red's SW Grill, McDonalds ⌂ Comfort Suites, Holiday Inn Express, Motel 6, Woodspring Suites ⊙ RV Repair, W ⊞ Shell/Blimpie/dsl ⌂ Super 8 ⊙ Bideaux RV Ctr, Century RV Park
342	(from nb, no return) UT 53, 24th St, Ogden
341b a	UT 79 W, 31st St, Ogden, 1-2 mi E on Wall St ⊞ Longhorn Steaks ⊙ Big O Tires, Chevrolet, Costco/gas, Dillard's, Ford, ⒣, Hyundai, to Weber St U, W ⊙ ⊙ ⊘
340	I-84 E (from sb), to Cheyenne, Wyo
339	UT 26 (from nb), to I-84 E, Riverdale Rd, E ⊞ Exxon/dsl, Sinclair/dsl ⊞ Applebee's, Arby's, Buffalo Wild Wings, Carl's Jr, Chili's, Chipotle, Honeybaked Ham, IHOP, Jamba Juice, Jersey Mike's, Lucky Buffet, McDonald's, MOD Pizza, Starbucks, Subway, Sweet Burrito, Wendy's ⌂ Motel 6 ⊙ $Tree, Best Buy, Buick/GMC, Cadillac, Chrysler/Dodge/Jeep, Good Earth Natural Foods,

R O Y

339	Continued
	Gordman's, Harley-Davidson, Home Depot, Honda, Jo-A⸱, Fabrics, Kia, Maverik/dsl, Nissan, Petsmart, Sam's Club/ga⸱, Schwab Tire, Target, Toyota, Verizon, Walmart
338	UT 97, Roy, Sunset, E ⊙ Air Force Museum, W ⊞ 7-11, EVC, Ex⸱ on/dsl, Maverik/dsl, Sinclair/dsl ⊞ A&W/KFC, Arby's, Beez Caf⸱ Burger King, Five Star Thai, Greek Olive Rest., Japanese Wasab⸱ McDonald's, Papa Murphy's, Rancherito's Mexican, Taco Be⸱ Village Inn Rest., Wendy's ⊙ AutoZone, Citte RV Ctr, CVS Dru⸱ Harmon's Mkt, Midas, O'Reilly Parts, Sacco's Fresh Mkt, Schwa⸱ Tires, Smith's/dsl, transmissions, vet, vet, Walgreens
335	UT 103, Clearfield, E ⊞ Jimmy John's, Popeye's, Starbucks ⸱ Tru ⊙ Hill AFB, W ⊞ Phillips 66/dsl, Shell/dsl, Sinclair ⊞ Burg⸱ er King, Carl's Jr, KFC, McDonald's, Subway, Taco Bell, Winger⸱ ⌂ Ameri-Stay, Charin Inn, Days Inn ⊙ C&M Tires, U-haul
334	UT 193, Clearfield, E ⊞ Chevron/dsl, Maverik ⊙ to Hill AFB, W ⊞ 7-11, Maverik/dsl ⊙ AutoZone
332	UT 108, Syracuse, E ⊞ URGENT CARE ⊞ Applebee's, Boston ⸱ Rest., Cafe Rio, Carl's Jr, Chick-fil-A, Chili's, Chipotle, Cracke⸱ Barrel, Famous Dave's, Five Guys, Golden Corral, Hook&Re⸱ Seafood, Jimmy John's, Lucky Slice Pizza, MacCool's Grill, MO⸱ Pizza, Moe's SW, Noodles&Co, Outback Steaks, Panda Expres⸱ Papa Murphy's, Popeye's, Red Robin, Rumbi Island Grill, Soni⸱ Tepanyaki, Zupas Cafe ⌂ Courtyard, Fairfield Inn, Hampto⸱ Inn, Hilton Garden, Holiday Inn Express, Home 2 Suites, L⸱ Quinta, TownePlace Suites ⊙ Barnes&Noble, Lowe's Whse⸱ Michael's, Petco, Ross, Target, Tire Pros, Verizon, Walgreens, W⸱ ⊞ 7-11, Crown Burger, Exxon/Subway/dsl ⊞ Arby's, Burge⸱ King, McDonald's ⊙ Ford, ⒣, to Antelope Island
331	UT 232, UT 126, to I-84, Layton, E ⊞ Buffalo Wild Wings⸱ Costa Vida, Cupbop Korean, Denny's, Garcia's, Hook & Ree⸱ La Puente, McDonald's, Olive Garden, Red Lobster, Sizzle⸱ TX Roadhouse, Wendy's ⌂ Best Western+, Comfort Inn ⊙ $Tree, Dick's, JC Penney, to Hill AFB S Gate, W ⊞ Exxon/ds⸱ ⊞ Asian Buffet, Burger King, Cantina SW Grill, Coldstone, De⸱ Taco, HuHot Mongolian, IHOP, KFC, Krispy Kreme, Pace's Rest.⸱ Rancheritos Mexican, Taco Bell ⊙ AT&T, Big Lots, Buick/GMC⸱ Chevrolet, Chrysler/Dodge/Jeep, Discount Tire, FedEx, Hobby⸱ Lobby, Home Depot, Kia, Petsmart, Sam's Club/gas, Staples⸱ Walmart/McDonald's
330	Layton Pkwy, to UT 126, Layton, E ⊞ Black Bear Diner, Jerse⸱ Mike's, Little Orient Chinese, Mo' Bettah Hawaiian, Swig, Teri⸱ yaki Grill, Z Brothers Pizza ⊙ Tire Pros, WinCo Foods, W ⊞⸱ Cafe Sabor ⊙ Camping World RV Ctr
328	UT 273, Kaysville, E ⊞ 7-11/dsl, Chevron/McDonald's, EVC ⊞⸱ Big Daddy's Pizza, Domino's, Dylan's Drive-In, Granny Annie's⸱ Rest., Pizza Hut, Subway, Taco Time, Wendy's, Winger's ⊙⸱ AutoZone, Big O Tire, O'Reilly Parts, Schwab Tire, USPO, Wal⸱ greens, W ⊞ Maverick/dsl ⊙ Camping World
325mm	parking area both lanes
325	UT 225, Lagoon Dr, Farmington, E ⊞ Chevron ⊞ Subway ⌂⸱ Hampton Inn ⊙ camping, funpark, Mercedes, W ⊞ AT&T⸱ Blaze Pizza, Cafe Rio, Chick-fil-A, Costa Vida, Habit Burger, Mc⸱ Donald's, Panda Express, R&R BBQ, Starbucks, Subway, Zupas⸱ ⌂ Hyatt Place ⊙ Cabela's, Gordman's, Harmon's Mkt, Mar⸱ shall's, Old Navy, Petco, Ross
324	US 89 N, UT 225, Legacy Pkwy (from sb), E ⊞ Maverik/dsl⸱ Smith's Foods/dsl ⊞ Burger King, Chevron/dsl, Chopstix Chi⸱ nese, Javier's Mexican, Papa John's, Subway ⌂ Hampton Inn⸱ ⊙ Aunt Pam's, Burt Bros/Goodyear/auto, Mercedes, RV Park

B R I G H A M   C I T Y

O G D E N

L A Y T O N

K A Y S V I L L E

Copyright 2022 - The Next EXIT® 🅶 = gas 🍴 = food 🏠 = lodging 🅾 = other 🆁🆂 = rest stop

INTERSTATE 15 Cont'd

Exit #	Services
322	UT 227 (from nb), Lagoon Dr, to Farmington, E 🍴 Subway 🅾 Lagoon Funpark/RV Park
319	UT 105, Parrish Lane, Centerville, E 🅶 7-11/dsl, Chevron/Jimmy John's/dsl, Phillips 66/dsl 🍴 Arby's, Carl's Jr, Chick-fil-A, Chili's, Costa Vida, Domino's, DQ, IHOP, In-N-Out, Little Caesar's, McDonald's, Papa Murphy's, Rancheritos, Sonic, Starbucks, Subway, Taco Bell, Wendy's 🅾 $Tree, Dave's Auto Repair, Dick's Mkt, Home Depot, Jo-Ann, Kohl's, Land Rover, O'Reilly Parts, Petsmart, Schwab Tire, Target, Tire Factory, Walmart
317	US 89 S (exits left from sb), UT 131, 500W, S Bountiful, E 🅶 Chevron/dsl, Exxon/dsl, Sinclair/7-11/dsl 🍴 Chipotle, Culver's, Five Guys, Jimmy John's, Texas Roadhouse 🏠 Country Inn Suites 🅾 Chrysler/Dodge/Jeep, Costco/gas, Office Depot, PetCo, Verizon
316	UT 68, 500 S, W Bountiful, Woods Cross, E 🅶 Shell 🍴 Applebee's, Barbacoa Mexican, Cafe Rio, Carl's Jr, Chipotle, ChuckaRama, Coldstone, Del Taco, Five Guys, Jimmy John's, KFC, McDonald's, Mikado Japanese, Panda Express, Pizza Hut, Sizzler, Starbucks, Subway, Taco Bell, TX Roadhouse, Wendy's 🅾 $Tree, AT&T, AutoZone, Barnes&Noble, Costco/gas, GNC, 🅷, Lowe's, Michael's, O'Reilly Parts, Office Depot, Petco, Ross, Tire Pros, TJ Maxx, Walgreens, W 🅶 Phillips 66/A&W/dsl 🏠 InTown Suites 🅾 vet
315	26th S, N Salt Lake, E 🅶 Chevron/dsl, R&R BBQ, Sinclair 🍴 Apollo Burger, Arby's, Black Bear Diner, Cafe Zupas, Jersey Mike's, Kneaders Bakery Cafe, McDonald's, MOD Pizza, Nielsen's Frozen Custard, Pappa's Steaks, Starbucks, Subway, Taco Time, Village Inn, Wendy's 🏠 Best Western+, Comfort Inn 🅾 AT&T, Buick/GMC, Burt Bros Tires, Chevrolet, Discount Tire, Ford/Lincoln, Honda, Mazda, Nissan, Schwab Tire, Smith's Foods, Southfork Hardware, Toyota, Tunex, U-Haul, Verizon, Walgreens, W 🍴 IHOP, Lorena's Mexican 🏠 Hampton Inn, Motel 6
314	Center St, Cudahy Lane (from sb), N Salt Lake, E 🅶 Chevron
313	I-215 W (from sb), W 🅾 to ⊕
312	US 89 S, to Beck St, N Salt Lake
311	2300 N
310	900 W (from sb), W 🏠 Salt City Inn
309	600 N, E 🅾 downtown, 🅷, LDS Temple, W 🅾 to UT State Fair-Park
308	I-80 W, to Reno, W 🅾 ⊕
307	400 S downtown
306	600 S, SLC City Ctr, **1 mi** E 🅶 Chevron, Fastbreak/dsl, Maverik, Sinclair, Tesla EVC 🍴 Alberto's Mexican, Denny's, McDonald's, R&R BBQ, Starbucks, Street Tacos, Subway 🏠 Comfort Inn, Crystal Inn, DoubleTree, Grand America, Hampton Inn, Hilton Garden, Hotel RL, Little America, Motel 6, Quality Inn, Sheraton, SpringHill Suites 🅾 Hyundai, LDS Church Offices, to Temple Square, Toyota
305c-a	1300 S, 2100 S UT 201 W, SLC, downtown, E 🅶 Chevron/dsl/24hr 🍴 Carl's Jr, ChuckECheese, Dickey's BBQ, IHOP, Jimmy John's, McDonald's, Starbucks 🅾 $Tree, Best Buy, Costco/gas, Home Depot, Office Depot, PetsMart, Sams Club/dsl, U-Haul, Walmart, W 🅶 ⊕FLYING J/Denny's/dsl/LP/24hr 🅾 Blue Beacon
304	I-80 E, to Denver, Cheyenne
303	UT 171, 3300 S, S Salt Lake, E 🅶 7-11, Carl's Jr, Maverik/dsl 🍴 Apollo Burgers, Crown Burger, Jimmy John's, McDonald's, Starbucks, Taco Bell 🏠 InTowne Suites, Motel 6, W 🅶 Maverik 🅾 Buick/GMC
301	UT 266, 4500 S, Murray, Kearns, E 🅶 Maverik 🍴 McDonald's, Subway 🅾 Discount Tire, W 🅶 Chevron/Burger King/dsl, Shell/dsl, Speedway/dsl 🍴 Denny's, Wendy's 🏠 Fairfield Inn, Hampton Inn 🅾 Lowe's Whse
300	UT 173, 5300 S, Murray, Kearns, E 🏠 Holiday Inn Express 🅾 🅷, W 🅶 Chevron/dsl, Exxon/dsl, Holiday/dsl 🍴 Papa Murphy's, Subway 🏠 Comfort Inn, Quality Inn 🅾 Smith's Foods
298	I-215 E and W
297	UT 48, 7200 S, Midvale, E 🅶 Chevron, Phillips 66/dsl 🍴 Arctic Circle, Betos Mexican, Denny's, Korean BBQ, McDonald's, Mekong Café, Mi Rico Burrito, Midvale Mining Cafe, Sweet Ginger Chinese 🏠 Day's Inn, Discovery Inn, InTowne Suites, La Quinta, Motel 6, Park Inn 🅾 Family$, Schwab Tire, Solitude Ski Areas, to Brighton, vet, Walgreens, W 🅶 Chevron/dsl 🍴 Arby's, Culver's, Dunkin', Freddy's, Jimmy John's, Popeye's, Subway, WinCo Foods, Zaxby's 🏠 Staybridge Suites
295	UT 209, 9000 S, Sandy, E 🅶 Chevron/dsl, Sinclair/dsl 🍴 Arby's, Korean BBQ, Schlotzky's, Sconecutter's Rest., Sizzler, Starbucks, Subway 🏠 EconoLodge 🅾 Alta Ski Areas, Discount Tire, NAPA, Rio Rinto Stadium, to Snowbird, W 🅶 Maverik/dsl, Maverik/dsl (2), URGENT CARE 🍴 BMW Motorcycles 🅾 Aamco, Harley-Davidson, 🅷
293	106th S, Sandy, S Jordan, E 🅶 Exxon, Shell//dsl 🍴 Burger King, Carl's Jr, Carver's Steak & Seafood, Chick-fil-A, Chili's, Chipotle Mexican, Costa Vida, Dog Haus, El Pollo Loco, Firehouse Subs, Five Guys, HuHot, IHOP, Jamba Juice, Jim's Rest., Krispy Kreme, La Puente, Legends Grill, Los Cucos Mexican, Mimi's Cafe, Noodles&Co, Olive Garden, Pei Wei, Potbelly, Rumbi Island Grill, Slapfish, Sonic, Starbucks, Subway, Sunday Best, Sweet Tomatoes, Taco Bell, TX Roadhouse, Wendy's 🏠 Best Western+, Courtyard, Extended Stay America, Hampton Inn, Hilton Garden, Holiday Inn Express, Hyatt House, Residence Inn 🅾 Barnes&Noble, Chrysler/Dodge/Jeep, Goodyear/auto, Honda, JC Penney, Macy's, Mazda, Old Navy, Petsmart, REI, Subaru, Target, USPO, W 🅶 Tesla EVC 🍴 R&R BBQ 🏠 Embassy Suites, Holiday Inn, Sleep Inn, Super 8 🅾 Buick/GMC, Kia, VW

N SALT LAKE

SALT LAKE

SANDY

UT

☐ = gas ⊞ = food 🏨 = lodging ⊡ = other ℞ = rest stop   Copyright 2022 - The Next EXIT ®

INTERSTATE 15 Cont'd

Exit #	Services
292	UT 175, 11400 S, **E** ⊞ Buffalo Wild Wings, Freebirds Burrito, Habit Burger, Handel's Ice Cream, Jersey Mike's, McDonald's, Original Pancake House, Pizzeria Limone, Shake Shack, Taco Time, Toscano ⊡ AT&T, Best Buy, Costco/gas, Duluth Trading Post, Home Depot, Scheel's, **W** ☐ EVC, EVC (2) ⊡ CarMax, Chevrolet, Ford, Nissan, Sam's Club/dsl, Toyota, Walmart
291	UT 71, 12300 S, Draper, Riverton, **E** ☐ AT&T, Holiday/dsl ⊞ Arctic Circle, Astro Burger, Barbacoa, Black Bear Diner, Café Rio Mexican, Cafe Zupas, Chick-fil-A, Chuck-A-Rama, Coldstone, Corner Cafe, Costa Vida, Cubby's, Del Taco, Empire Wok, Goodwood BBQ, Guadalahonky's Mexican, In-N-Out, Jamba Juice, Jimmy John's, La Hacienda, McDonald's, Noodles&Co, Panda Express, Pizza Hut, Rancheritos, Rumbi Grill, Smashburger, Sonic, Teriyaki Grill, Waffle Love 🏨 Fairfield Inn, Quality Inn, Ramada, SpringHill Suites ⊡ $Tree, aquarium, AutoZone, Camping World RV Supplies (1mi), Discount Tire, GNC, Goodyear/auto, ℍ, JoAnn, Kohl's, Michael's, Mountain Shadows Camping, Office Depot, Petco, Ross, Smith's Foods, TJ Maxx, Verizon, **W** ☐ 7-11/dsl, Chevron ⊞ Port of Subs, Subway
289	Bangerter Hwy, **E** ⊞ Burger King, Kneaders, Little Caesar's, NY Pizza, Subway, Taco Time 🏨 TownePlace Suites ⊡ Harmon's Mkt, Walgreens, **W** ☐ Maverik/dsl ⊞ McDonald's 🏨 Hampton Inn, Homewood Suites ⊡ IKEA
288	UT 140, Bluffdale, **E** ☐ 7-11/dsl, Chevron/dsl, Maverik/dsl ⊡ General RV Ctr
284	UT 92, Timpanogas Hwy, to Alpine, Highland, **E** ☐ EVC ⊞ Blaze Pizza, Braza Grill, Cafe Rio, Chick-fil-A, Chipotle, Five Guys, Jamba Juice, Jersey Mike's, McDonald's, Panda Express, PDQ, Pieology, Rumbi, Slapfish, Taco Bell, Village Baker, Wendy's 🏨 Hilton Garden, Hyatt Place, Staybridge Suites ⊡ AT&T, Audi/Porsche, Cabela's, Harmon's Mkt, to Timpanogas Cave, Traverse Mtn Outlets/famous brands, **W** ☐ 7-11/Subway/dsl, Maverik/dsl ⊞ Arby's, Carl's Jr, Costa Vida, Cubby's Cafe, Del Taco, Dickey's BBQ, Firehouse Subs, JCW Burgers, JDawgs, Popeye's, Smashburger, Starbucks, Zaxby's, Zupas 🏨 Courtyard, Hampton Inn, Holiday Inn Express, Home 2 Suites, SpringHill Suites ⊡ Thanksgiving Point/café
283	Triumph Blvd, **E** ☐ EVC 🏨 Hilton Garden, **W** 🏨 Tru 🏨 Jaguar
282	2100 N, UT 194, Lehi, **E** ⊡ U-Haul, **W** ☐ Exxon/dsl
279	UT 73, to Lehi, **E** ☐ Texaco/dsl ⊞ Buffalo Wild Wings, Cafe Rio, Chili's, ChuckARama, Culver's, Del Taco, Denny's, El Pollo Loco, Hibachi House, Jimmy John's, Namasthe Cafe, One Man Band Diner, Panda Express, Popeye's, TX Roadhouse 🏨 Motel 6 ⊡ Costco/gas, Home Depot, Lowe's Whse, Petsmart, Schwab Tire, Verizon, Walgreens, Walmart/Burger King, **W** ☐ Chevron/dsl, CNG, Phillips 66/7-11/Wendy's ⊞ Arctic Circle, KFC/Pizza Hut, McDonald's, Moochie's, Noble Roman's Pizza, Papa Murphy's, Subway, Tepanyki Japanese 🏨 Best Western, Comfort Inn, Day's Inn ⊡ Big O Tire, Dave's Chiropractic, Macey's, O'Reilly Parts, USPO, vet
278	Main St, American Fork, **E** ☐ Chevron ⊞ Cafe Zupas, Chili's, Del Taco, In-N-Out, Olive Garden, Pier 49, Sonic, Zaxby's ⊡ $Tree, $Tree, Chrysler/Dodge/Jeep, Dick's Sports, Five Below, Home Depot, ℍ, Kia, Kohl's, Michaels, Office Depot, Old Navy, Subaru, T.J. Maxx, Target, Walmart, **W** ☐ Phillips 66/dsl 🏨 Woodspring Suites
276	5th E, Pleasant Grove, **E** ☐ Exxon, Phillips 66 ⊞ Arby's, Beto's, Carl's Jr, KFC, McDonald's, Starbucks, Subway, Taco Bell, Wendy's 🏨 Holiday Inn Express ⊡ CVS Drug, ℍ, Stewart's RV Ctr, **W** ⊡ Buick/GMC, Chevrolet, Ford, Land Rover
275	Pleasant Grove, **E** ☐ Holiday/dsl ⊞ Costa Vida, Jersey Mike's, Panda Express, R&R BBQ, Starbucks 🏨 Hyatt House ⊡ BMW, Macey's Foods
273	Orem, Lindon, **E** ☐ Chevron, Maverik/dsl ⊞ Costa Vida Mexican, Del Taco ⊡ Discount Tire, Home Depot, Hyundai, Lexus, Schwab Tire, **W** ⊡ Harley-Davidson
272	UT 52, to US 189, 8th N, Orem, **1 mi E** ☐ Maverik/dsl ⊞ Arby's, Culver's, McDonald's, Milagros, Sonic, Starbucks, Subway 🏨 Fairfield Inn, La Quinta, TownePlace Suites ⊡ Honda, ℍ, to Sundance RA, Winco Foods
271	Center St, Orem, **1-2 mi E** ☐ 7-11, Chevron ⊞ Burger King, ChuckECheese, McDonald's, Panda Express, Taco Bell, Wendy's, Zaxby's ⊡ ℍ, Target, USPO, **W** ☐ Maverik/dsl ⊞ DQ
269	UT 265, 12th St S, University Pkwy, **1-3 mi E** ☐ Chevron, EVC, Texaco/Wendy's/dsl ⊞ Applebee's, Arby's, Carrabba's, Chili's, Chipotle, El Pollo Loco, Golden Corral, HoneyBaked Ham, IHOP, In-n-Out, J Dawgs, Krispy Kreme, McDonald's, Noodles & Co., Outback Steaks, Pizza Hut, Sizzler, Starbucks, Thai Evergreen, Village Inn 🏨 Comfort Inn, Hampton Inn, La Quinta ⊡ $Tree, Barnes&Noble, Best Buy, Dick's, Hobby Lobby, Honda, Jo-Ann Fabrics, Lowe's Whse, Mazda, Michael's, Nissan, Office Depot, Old Navy, Petsmart, Ross, Staples, TJ Maxx, to BYU, Toyota, Tuesday Morning, Verizon, VW, Walmart, **W** ☐ Chevron/dsl, CNG ⊞ Domino's, Subway 🏨 Holiday Inn Express
265b a	UT 114, Center St, Provo, **1 mi E** ☐ Maverik/dsl, Salt ⊞ Joe Vera's Mexican 🏨 Marriott ⊡ auto repair, Fresh Mkt, ℍ, **W** ☐ Chevron, Phillips 66/7-11/Wendy's, Shell/dsl ⊞ Great Steak Rest., Subway 🏨 Best Value Inn ⊡ Lakeside RV Camping, to Utah Lake SP
263	US 189 N, University Ave, Provo, **E** ☐ Exxon/dsl, Maverik/dsl, Phillips 66/dsl, Shell/dsl ⊞ A&W/KFC, Arby's, Burger King, Cafe Rio, ChuckaRama, Kyoto, McDonald's, Papa Murphy's, Rancheritos, Ruby River Steaks, Sizzler, Subway, Taco Bell, Village Inn Rest., Wendy's 🏨 Fairfield Inn, Hampton Inn, Little Suites, Ramada, Residence Inn, Sleep Inn ⊡ $Tree, Dillard's, Discount Tire, Home Depot, JC Penney, Les Schwab, Ross, Sam's Club/gas, Staples, to BYU, transmissions
261	UT 75, Springville, **E** ☐ ⊕FLYING J/Denny's/dsl/scales/24hr, Maverik ⊞ McDonald's (1mi) 🏨 Best Western, Holiday Inn Express ⊡ KOA, RestStop
260	UT 77, Springville, Mapleton, **E** ☐ Phillips 66/7-11/dsl ⊞ Arby's, Del Taco, IHOP, Mongolian Grill, Papa John's, Pizza Hut, Taco Bell, Wendy's ⊡ Big O Tire, JiffyLube, Walmart/Subway, **W** ☐ Chevron/Subway/dsl, ◆Loves/Chester's/McDonald's/dsl/scales/24hr ⊞ Cracker Barrel 🏨 Days Inn, Microtel ⊡ Quality RV Ctr
257b a	US 6 E, UT 156, Spanish Fork, **E** ☐ Chevron/dsl, Fresh Mkt/gas, Sinclair, Tesoro/dsl, Texaco/dsl/LP ⊞ Amber Rest., Arby's, Burger King, Cafe Rio, Carl's Jr, China Wok, Costa Vida, Cubby's Cafe, Culver's, Five Guys, Italian Place, Jimmy John's, KFC, Kneaders, Little Caesar's, McDonald's, One Man Band Diner, Papa Murphy's, Pizza Factory, Rita's, Sonic, Starbucks, Subway, Taco Bell, Taco Time, Wendy's, Zupas Kitchen ⊡ $Tree, AT&T, AutoZone, Big O Tire, Cal Store, Costco/gas, GNC, Good Earth Mkt, Jo-Ann Fabrics, Macey's Foods, O'Reilly Parts, Verizon, Walmart/Subway, **W** ⊡ Chevrolet
253	UT 164, to Spanish Fork
250	UT 115, Payson, **E** ☐ Chevron/dsl ⊞ McDonald's, Subway 🏨 Quality Inn ⊡ ℍ, Mt Nebo Loop, O'Reilly Parts, Payson Foods, RiteAid
248	Payson, Salem, **E** ☐ Chevron/dsl, Exxon/Arby's/Subway/dsl ⊞ Costa Vida, Hunan City, Papa John's, Papa Murphy's, Pizza Hut, Taco Bell, Tsing Tao Asian ⊡ $Tree, AT&T, AutoZone, Big O Tire, Verizon, Walmart/Subway, **W** ☐ Phillips 66/Wendy's/7-11/dsl

Side tabs: UT · DRAPER · LEHI · OREM · PROVO · SPRINGVILLE

🛢 = gas 🍴 = food 🛏 = lodging 🔲 = other 🆁🆂 = rest stop

⬆ N INTERSTATE 15 Cont'd

Exit #	Services
244	US 6 W, Santaquin, E 🛢 Maverik/dsl 🍴 Cubby's Diner, DQ 🔲 Tire Trax Auto, TrueValue, W 🛢 Chevron/dsl, Sinclair/dsl 🍴 Brumby's Cafe, Family Tree Rest., Hot Rod Diner, Main St Pizza, Subway, Taco Time 🔲 auto/tire care, Family$, Ford, Main St Mkt, Nat Hist Area, USPO
242	to S Santaquin, W 🛢 Chevron/dsl
233	UT 54, Mona, W 🛢 Shell/Subway/dsl
228	UT 28, to Nephi, 2-4 mi W services
225	UT 132, Nephi, E 🛢 Exxon/dsl/LP 🍴 Main St Pizza, One Man Band Diner, Taco Time, W 🛢 Chevron/Arby's/dsl, Phillips 66/7-11/Wendy's/dsl 🛏 Economy Inn 🔲 Big O Tire, 🅗
222	UT 28, to I-70, Nephi, E 🛢 Chevron/dsl/24hr, Exxon/scales/dsl/24hr, Texaco/dsl 🍴 Burger King, Mickelson's Rest., Subway 🛏 Motel 6, National 9 Inn, Super 8 🔲 dsl repair, W 🛢 ✈FLYING J/Denny's/dsl/LP/scales/24hr 🍴 Lisa's Country Kitchen 🛏 Best Western, Safari Motel 🔲 dsl repair, High Country RV Park, 🅗
207	to US 89, Mills
202	Yuba Lake, 🔃 access to boating, camping, rec services
188	US 50 E, to I-70, Scipio, E 🛢 76/Subway/dsl, Texaco/dsl 🛏 Scipio Hotel, W 🛢 ✈FLYING J/DQ/dsl/rest stop/24hr
184	ranch exit
178	US 50, to Delta, W 🔲 to Great Basin NP
174	to US 50, Holden, W 🔲 to Great Basin NP
167	Lp 15, Fillmore, 0-3 mi E 🛢 Chevron/dsl, Sinclair/dsl 🍴 5 Buck Pizza 🛏 Best Western/rest. 🔲 CarQuest, city park, golf, Goodyear, 🅗, KOA (3mi), WagonsWest RV Park, W 🛢 Chevron/Subway/rest stop/dsl, Texaco/dsl 🍴 Carl's Jr 🔲 tires/repair
163	Lp 15, to UT 100, Fillmore, E 🛢 Conoco/Burger King/Costa Vida/dsl, Maverik/dsl 🍴 Hong Kong Chinese, Larry's Drive-In 🛏 Comfort Inn 🔲 🅗, KOA, W 🛢 Chevron/dsl/24hr 🛏 Travel & Rest Inn
158	UT 133, Meadow, E 🛢 Conoco/dsl, Shell/dsl
153mm	view area sb
151mm	view area nb
146	Kanosh, 2 mi E 🛢 gas 🔲 chainup area
138	ranch exit
135	Cove Fort Hist Site, E 🛢 Chevron/Subway/rest stop/dsl, repair/tires
132	I-70 E, to Denver, E 🔲 Capitol Reef NP, Fremont Indian SP
129	Sulphurdale 🔲 chainup area
125	ranch exit
120	Manderfield 🔲 chainup area nb
112	to UT 21, Beaver, Manderfield, E 🛢 Chevron/dsl, Conoco/dsl, Sinclair/dsl 🍴 Arshel's Café, Carl's Jr, Crazy Cow Cafe, Hunan Chinese, McDonald's, Subway 🛏 Beaver Lodge, Best Western, Country Inn, De Lano Motel/RV Park, Motel 6 🔲 auto/RV/dsl repair, Family$, Hometown Mkt, 🅗, KOA (1mi), W 🛢 ✈FLYING J/cafe/dsl/scales/24hr 🍴 Denny's, Wendy's 🛏 Days Inn, Super 8 🔲 to Great Basin NP
109	to UT 21, Beaver, E 🛢 Phillips 66/dsl, Shell/Burger King/dsl/RV dump, Spirit/dsl 🍴 United Camping 🛏 Best Western, Comfort Inn 🔲 auto repair, Cache Valley Cheese, 🅗, Mike's Foodtown, NAPA, W 🛢 Blu LNG, Chevron/DQ/dsl 🍴 KanKun Mexican, Timberline Rest. 🛏 Quality Inn 🔲 to Great Basin NP, truck wash
100	ranch exit
95	UT 20, to US 89, to Panguitch, E 🔲 Bryce Canyon NP
88mm	🆁🆂 both lanes, full ♿ facilities, 🔃, 🅿, litter barrel, petwalk, hist site
82	UT 271, Paragonah
78	UT 141, 1 mi E 🛢 Chevron/dsl, Maverik 🛏 Days Inn 🔲 NAPA, ski areas, W 🛢 TA/Subway/Taco Bell/LP/dsl/scales/24hr/@
75	UT 143, 2 mi E 🛢 Chevron, Maverik, Phillips 66/dsl 🛏 Days Inn 🔲 Parowan Mkt, to Brian Head/Cedar Breaks Ski Resorts
71	Summit
62	UT 130, Cedar City, E 🛢 🅛🅞🅥🅔🅢/Carl's Jr/Subway/dsl/scales/24hr, Phillips 66/dsl 🍴 Allberto's Mexican 🔲 Country Aire RV Park, 🅗, KOA (2mi), st patrol, W 🛢 Maverik/dsl, Shell/dsl/24hr/dsl repair/@ 🛏 Travelodge
59	UT 56, Cedar City, 0-2 mi E 🛢 Chevron/DQ/dsl, Conoco/dsl, Maverik, Phillips 66/dsl/LP, She'll/dsl 🍴 A&W/KFC, Arby's, Burger King, China Kitchen, Denny's, Depot Grill, Firehouse Subs, Great Harvest Bread Co., Hermie's Drive-In, Hong Kong Buffet, IHOP, Jimmy John's, Little Caesar's, McDonald's/playplace, Papa Murphy's, Pizza Factory, Sizzler, Sonny Boy's BBQ, Subway, Taco Bell, Valerie's Tacos, Wendy's, Zaxby's 🛏 Abbey Inn, Best Value Inn, Best Western, Quality Inn, Stratford Hotel 🔲 Buick/Chevrolet, Goodyear/auto, Lin's Mkt, Mr Tire, NAPA, Tire Pros, USPO, Verizon, W 🛢 Maverik/dsl, Sinclair/dsl 🍴 Subway 🛏 Motel 6, Ramada, Super 8
57	Lp 15, to UT 14, Cedar City, 0-2 mi E 🛢 Chevron/repair/24hr, Phillips 66/dsl, Shell, Sinclair/dsl 🍴 DQ, Golden Corral, Subway, Taco Time 🛏 Clarion, Comfort Inn, Courtyard, Holiday Inn Express, La Quinta, SpringHill Suites 🔲 $Tree, AutoZone, Big O Tire, Bryce Cyn, CAL Ranch, Duck Crk, 🅗, Jo-Ann Fabrics, NAPACare, Navajo Lake, O'Reilly Parts, Smith's Food/dsl, Staples, TJ Maxx, to Cedar Breaks, Verizon, W 🛢 Chevron/dsl, USA 🍴 Applebee's, Cafe Rio, Chili's, Costa Vida, Del Taco, Dickey's BBQ, Five Buck Pizza, Jack-in-the-Box, Lupita's Mexican, Ninja Japanese, Panda Express, Papa John's, Starbucks, Subway, Winger's 🛏 Hampton Inn 🔲 GNC, Home Depot, Tunex, Verizon, Walgreens, Walmart/McDonald's
51	Kanarraville, Hamilton Ft
44mm	🆁🆂 both lanes, full ♿ facilities, 🔃, 🅿, litter barrels, petwalk, hist site
42	New Harmony, Kanarraville, W 🛢 Shell/dsl
40	to Kolob Canyon, E 🔲 scenic drive, tourist info/🔃, Zion's NP
36	Black Ridge
33	Snowfield
31	Pintura
30	Browse
27	UT 17, Toquerville, E 🔲 Grand Canyon, Lake Powell, to Zion NP
23	Leeds, Silver Reef (from sb), 3 mi E 🔲 hist site, Leed's RV Park/gas, museum
22	Leeds, Silver Reef (from nb) same as 23
16	UT 9, to Hurricane, E 🛢 Texaco/dsl 🛏 Holiday Inn Express 🔲 Harley-Davidson, Walmart Dist Ctr
13	Washington Pkwy, E 🛢 Maverik/dsl 🍴 Black Bear Diner
10	Middleton Dr, Washington, E 🛢 Phillips 66/dsl, Sinclair/dsl, USA 🍴 Alvero's Mexican, Arby's, Arctic Circle, Benja's Thai, Bishop's Cafe, Buca Italian, Burger King, Costa Vida, Del Taco, Dickey's BBQ, Don Pedro's Mexican, El Pollo Loco, Freddy's,

= gas = food = lodging = other = rest stop   Copyright 2022 - The Next EXIT ©

INTERSTATE 15 Cont'd

10	**Continued**
	Hungry Howie's, IHOP, In-N-Out, Jack-in-the-Box, Jimmy John's, Little Caesar's, Mad Pita, McDonald's, Peppers Cantina, Pizza Factory, Pizza Hut, Qdoba, Red Robin, Royal Thai, Sonic, Subway, TX Roadhouse, Wendy's Country Inn&Suites, Quality Inn AAA, Albertsons/Sav-On, AutoZone, Barnes&Noble, Best Buy, Costco/gas, Dillard's, Discount Tire, Home Depot, JC Penney, Jo-Ann Fabrics, Kohl's, Natural Grocers, O'Reilly Parts, PetCo, Tunex, Verizon, vet, Walmart/Subway, **W** Chevron/dsl/LP, Texaco/dsl auto repair, St George RV Park/camping
8	St George Blvd, St George, **E** Chevron/Subway/dsl, Texaco/dsl Apollo Burger, Applebee's, Brick Oven, Buffalo Wild Wings, Carl's Jr, Chick-fil-A, Chick-fil-A, Chili's, Chipotle, ChuckaRama, Coldstone, Firehouse Subs, Five Guys, Golden Corral, Habit Burger, Iggy's Grill, Jimmy John's, Mongolian BBQ, Olive Garden, Outback Steaks, Panda Express, Paradise Bakery & cafe, Red Lobster, Smashburger, Starbucks, Subway, Village Inn Rest., Winger's Best Inn, Courtyard, Hampton Inn, Ramada Inn, TownePlace Suites $Tree, AT&T, Dick's, Harmon's Foods, , Lowe's, Old Navy, Petsmart, Ross, Staples, Sunrise Tire, Target, TJ Maxx, Tuesday Morning, Verizon, Zion Outlets/famous brands, **W** Conoco/dsl, Maverik, Shell/dsl, Sinclair/dsl, Texaco/dsl A&W/KFC, Burger King, Cafe Rio, Denny's, Iceberg Drive-In, Larsen's Drive-In, McDonald's, Ocean Buffet, Panda Garden, Papa John's, Port of Subs, Red Ginger Asian, Sakura Japanese, Taco Bell, Taco Time, Tropical Smoothie, vet, Wendy's Best Western, Chalet Motel, Coronada Inn, Days Inn, EconoLodge, Economy Inn, Knights Inn, Motel 6, Rodeway Inn, Sands Motel, SunTime Inn, Super 8 Auto Tech/tires, Big O Tire, Desert Coach RV Ctr, NAPA, O'Reilly Parts, Rite Aid, to LDS Temple
6	UT 18, Bluff St, St George, **E** Chevron/dsl/24hr, Sinclair/dsl, Texaco/dsl Cracker Barrel, Culver's, Jack-in-the-Box, Player's Grill, Rib Chop House, Subway Ambassador Inn, Comfort Inn, Fairfield Inn, Hilton Garden Buick/GMC, Hyundai, Kia, museum, Subaru, VW, **W** Shell, Texaco Arby's, Beijing Buffet, Black Bear Diner, Burger King, Denny's, Domino's, DQ, Jimmy John's, McDonald's, Pizza Hut, Ricardo's Rest., SF Pizza Best Value Inn, Best Western, Claridge Inn, Clarion Suites, Crystal Inn, Howard Johnson, Lexington Hotel, Quality Inn, St George Inn auto/truck repair, AutoZone, Big O Tire, Cadillac/Chevrolet, Camping World RV Ctr, Chrysler/Dodge/Jeep, Ford/Lincoln, funpark, Goodyear/auto, Honda, , K-Mart, Mazda, Nissan, TempleView RV Park, Toyota, U-Haul
5	Dixie Dr
4	Brigham Rd, Bloomington, 4 Bloomington, **E** /Burger King/dsl/scales/24hr La Quinta, **W** Chevron/Subway/Taco Time/dsl, USA/dsl Dickey's BBQ, Hungry Howie's, Peppers Cantina, Wendy's Wingate Inn Walmart/Subway
2	UT 7 E, Southern Pkwy, **E** , **W** Terrible Herbst/dsl Hampton Inn
1	Port of Entry/**weigh sta both lanes**
0mm	Utah/Arizona state line

INTERSTATE 70

Exit #	Services
232mm	Utah/Colorado state line
227	Westwater
221	ranch exit
214	to Cisco
204	UT 128, to Cisco
193	Yellowcat Ranch Exit
190mm	**Welcome Ctr wb, full facilities, vending, info, litter barrels**

187	Thompson, **N** Exxon/7-11/dsl Ballard RV Park
185mm	**parking area eb**
182	US 191 S, Crescent Jct, to Moab, **N** Papa Joe's, **S** te Arches/Canyonlands NP
181mm	**eb, full facilities, litter barrels, scenic view**
175	ranch exit
164	UT 19, Green River, 1-3 mi **N** Phillips 66/Burger King/dsl /Westwinds/rest/dsl/scales/24hr, Silver Eagle/Blimpie/dsl, Tesla EVC Tamarisk Rest. Best Value Inn, Comfort Inn, Holiday Inn Express, Knights Inn, Motel 6, River Terrace Inn, Super 8 KOA, Powell River Museum, same as 160, tires/repair
160	UT 19, Green River, 0-2 mi **N** Conoco/Arby's/dsl, /Subway/dsl Cathy's Pizza, Chowhound, La Veracruzana, Ray's Rest. Budget Inn, Robbers Roost, Sleepy Hollow Mote Ace Hardware, city park, Green River SP, NAPA/repair, same as 164, Shady Acres RV Park, USPO
157	US 6 W, US 191 N, to Price, Salt Lake
149	UT 24 W, to Hanksville, to Capitol Reef, Lake Powell Goblir Valley SP
146	view area, restrooms wb
144mm	runaway truck ramp eb
143mm	view area both lanes, restrooms
142mm	runaway truck ramp eb
138mm	brake test area, restrooms eb
131	Temple Mt Rd
122mm	**Ghost Rock View Area both lanes, restrooms**
116	to Moore, **N** view area both lanes
115	**N** view area eb
108	ranch exit
105mm	Salt Wash View Area both lanes
99	ranch exit
91	UT 10 N, UT 72, to Emery, Price, **12 mi N** gas, **S** to Capitol Reef NP
86mm	**S both lanes, full facilities, litter barrels, petwalk**
73	ranch exit
63	Gooseberry Rd
56	US 89 N, to Salina, US 50 W, to Delta, NEXT SERVICES 109 MI EB, 0-1 mi **N** Conoco/dsl, Maverik/dsl, Phillips 66/Carl's Jr/dsl, Sinclair/Burger King/dsl Denny's, El Mexicano Mexican, Losta Motsa Pizza, Mom's Cafe, Subway EconoLodge, Rodeway Inn, Super 8 Barretts Foods, Butch Cassidy RV Camp, Family$, NAPA, Peterbilt, truck/RV/auto repair, **S** /Arby's/dsl/scales/24hr, Xpress/Little Caesar's/dsl
48	UT 24, to US 50, Sigurd, Aurora, **1-2 mi S** gas food Capitol Reef NP, to Fishlake NF
40	Lp 70, Richfield, 0-2 mi **S** FLYING J/Pepperoni's/dsl/LP/rest./24hr, Chevron/dsl, Maverik/dsl, Texaco/dsl Arby's, Frontier Village Rest., Papa Murphy's, Subway, Taco Time Best Western, Budget Host, Days Inn/rest., Holiday Inn Express, Super 8 Big O Tire, Buick/Cadillac/Chevrolet/GMC, Chrysler/Dodge/Jeep, city park, Fresh Mkt, , IFA Store, NAPA, RV/truck repair, USPO
37	Lp 70, Richfield, 1-2 mi **S** Phillips 66/Wendy's/dsl, Silver Eagle/Burger King/dsl Dickey's BBQ, KFC/Taco Bell, Little Caesar's, Lotsa Motsa Pizza, McDonald's, Pizza Hut, Steve's Steaks, Wingers Comfort Inn, Fairfield Inn, Hampton Inn, Motel 6, New West Motel, Quality Inn, Royal Inn $Tree, Ace Hardware, AutoZone, Ford, golf, Home Depot, KOA, O'Reilly Parts, Pearson Tire, st patrol, to Fish Lake/Capitol Reef Parks, Verizon, Walmart/Subway
31	Elsinore, Monroe, **S** Silver Eagle/DQ/dsl
25	UT 118, Joseph, Monroe, **S** Flying U Country Store/dsl/RV park
23	US 89 S, to Panguitch, Bryce Canyon
17	**N** camping, chain-up area (WB), Fremont Indian SP, info, museum,

(side labels, top to bottom: **UT** · **ST GEORGE** · **GREEN RIVER** · **SALINA** · **RICHFIELD**)

◆E INTERSTATE 70 Cont'd

Exit #	Services
13mm	brake test area eb
7	Ranch Exit
3mm	Western Boundary Fishlake NF
1	N 🅖 Chevron/Subway/rest stop (2mi) 🅞 Historic Cove Fort
0mm	I-15, N to SLC, S to St George.
I-70 begins/ends on I-15, exit 132.	

◆E INTERSTATE 80

Exit #	Services
197mm	Utah/Wyoming state line Utah/Wyoming state line
191	Wahsatch
187	ranch exit
185	Castle Rock
182mm	Port of Entry/weigh sta wb
178	Emery (from wb)
170	Welcome Ctr wb/🆁🆂 eb, full ♿ facilities, 🅒, vending, 🏬, litter barrels, petwalk, RV dump
169	Echo
168	I-84 W, to Ogden, I-80 E, to Cheyenne
166	view area both lanes, litter barrels
162	Coalville, N 🅖 Phillips 66/dsl/mart 🏠 Best Western 🅞 CamperWorld RV Park, Holiday Hills RV Camp/LP, S 🅖 Chevron/dsl, Sinclair/dsl 🅕 Polar King, Subway 🅞 Griffith's Foods, NAPA, to Echo Res RA, USPO
155	UT 32 S, Wanship, S 🅖 Sinclair/dsl 🅞 to Rockport SP
150	🅞 toll gate promontory
146b a	US 40 E, to Heber, Provo, N 🅖 Sinclair/Blimpie/Pizza Hut/dsl, S 🅖 Phillips 66/7-11/dsl 🅞 Burt Bros Tires, Home Depot
146	view area/chain up wb
145	UT 224, Kimball Jct, to Park City, N 🅞 Chevrolet, Ford, Park City RV Park, vet, S 🅖 Chevron/dsl 🅕 Arby's, Cafe Rio, Coldstone, Del Taco, Five Guys, Ghidottis Italian, Great Harvest Bread Co, Hearth & Hill, I Love Moo, Loco Lizard Cantina, McDonald's, Panda Express, Protein Foundry, Red Rock Cafe, Sammy's Bistro, Starbucks, Subway, Szechwan Chinese, Taco Bell, Thai So Good, Vessel Kitchen, Wendy's, Whole Foods Mkt 🏠 AC Hotel, Best Western, Holiday Inn Express 🅞 Best Buy, Enterprise Car Rental, Michaels, Outlet Mall/famous brands, Petco, RV camping, Smith's Foods/dsl, Staples, TJ Maxx, to ski areas, USPO, visitors info, Walmart
144mm	view area eb
141	ranch exit, N 🅖 Phillips 66/Subway/dsl 🅞 Burt Bros Tires, to Jeremy Ranch, S 🅕 Billy Blanco Mexican 🅞 camping, Fresh Mkt, ski area
140	Parley's Summit, Parley's Summit, S 🅖 Sinclair/dsl 🅕 No Worries Café
137	Lamb's Canyon
134	UT 65, Emigration Canyon, East Canyon 🅞 Mountaindale RA
133	utility exit (from eb)
132	ranch exit
131	(from eb) Quarry
130	I-215 S (from wb)
129	UT 186 W, Foothill Dr, Parley's Way, N 🅞 🏥
128	I-215 S (from eb)
127	UT 195, 23rd E St, to Holladay
126	UT 181, 13th E St, to Sugar House, N 🅖 Chevron 🅕 A&W/KFC, Carl's Jr, Chick-fil-A, Olive Garden, Red Lobster, Sizzler, Taco Bell, Training Table, Wendy's 🏠 Extended Stay America 🅞 Verizon
125	UT 71, 7th E St, N 🅕 Dee's Rest., Jimmy John's, Little Caesar's, Olympian Rest., Starbucks 🅞 AT&T, Firestone, Pepboys

SALT LAKE CITY

KIMBALL JCT

124	US 89, S State St, N 🅖 7-11 🅕 Astro Burgers, Burger King, Strarbucks, Subway, Taco Bell 🅞 Access RV Ctr, Chrysler/Dodge/Jeep, Discount Tire, vet, S 🅕 A&W/KFC 🏠 Ramada Inn
123mm	I-15, N to Ogden, S to Provo
I-80 and I-15 run together approx 4 mi. See I-15, exits 305-307.	
121	600 S to City Ctr
120	I-15 N, to Ogden
118	UT 68, Redwood Rd, to N Temple, 0-1 mi N on N Temple 🅖 Chevron/Subway/dsl, Loves/Arby's/dsl/scales/24hr 🅕 A&W/KFC, Apollo Burger, Burger King, Carl's Jr, Denny's, Taco Bell, Wendy's 🏠 Airport Inn, Candlewood Suites, Comfort Suites, Holiday Inn Express, Motel 6, Radisson, Ramada 🅞 7-11, S 🅖 Maverik/dsl 🅞 🏥
117	I-215, N to Ogden, S to Provo
115b a	Bangerter Hwy, N to Salt Lake Airport
114	Wright Bros Dr (from wb), N same as 113
113	5600 W (from eb), N 🅖 EVC, Phillips 66/dsl 🅕 Perkins, Port of Subs, Subway 🏠 Best Western+, Comfort Suites, Courtyard, DoubleTree, Fairfield Inn, Hampton Inn, Hilton Garden, Holiday Inn, Homewood Suites, Hyatt Place, La Quinta, Microtel, Quality Inn, Ramada Inn, Residence Inn, Sheraton, SpringHill Suites, Super 8, Tru Hilton
111	7200 W
104	UT 202, Saltair Dr, to Magna, N 🅞 beaches, Great Salt Lake SP
102	UT 201 (from eb), to Magna
101mm	view area wb
99	UT 36, to Tooele, S 🅖 FLYING J/Denny's/dsl/scales/LP/24hr, Chevron/Subway/dsl, TA/Burger King/Taco Bell/dsl/scales/24hr/@, Texaco/dsl 🅕 Del Taco, McDonald's 🏠 Comfort Inn/Suites, Oquirrh Motel/RV Park 🅞 🏥, SpeedCo
94mm	New Exit
88	to Grantsville
84	UT 138, to Grantsville, Tooele
77	UT 196, to Rowley, Dugway
70	to Delle, S 🅖 Delle/Tesoro/café/dsl
62	to Lakeside, Eagle Range 🅞 military area
56	to Aragonite
55mm	🆁🆂 both lanes, full ♿ facilities, 🅒, 🏬, litter barrels, petwalk, vending
49	to Clive
41	Knolls
26mm	architectural point of interest
10mm	🆁🆂 both lanes, full ♿ facilities, 🅒, 🏬, litter barrels, vending, petwalk, observation area
4	Bonneville Speedway, N 🅖 Sinclair/dsl/café/24hr
3mm	weigh sta both lanes, Port of Entry
2	UT 58 (no EZ wb return), Wendover, S 🅖 Shell/dsl, Sinclair/dsl 🅕 Subway 🏠 Best Western+, Bonneville Inn, Knights Inn, Motel 6, Nugget Hotel/casino, Quality Inn, Super 8, Western Ridge Motel 🅞 auto repair, Carquest, Family$, KOA, Montego Bay Hotel/Casino, USPO
0mm	Utah/Nevada state line, Mountain/Pacific time zone

⛽ = gas   🍴 = food   🛏 = lodging   🅾 = other   Rs = rest stop   Copyright 2022 - The Next EXIT ®

🔼E INTERSTATE 84

Exit #	Services
120	**I-84 begins/ends on I-80, exit 168 near Echo, Utah.**
115	Ut 65 S, to Henefer, Echo, to Henefer, Echo, **1/2 mi** S 🅾 Grump's Gen Store/gas, to E Canyon SP, USPO
112	UT 86 E, Henefer, S ⛽ gas 🍴 food 🛏 lodging
111	Croydon
111mm	🅾 Devil's Slide Scenic View
108	Taggart
106	ranch exit
103	UT 66, Morgan, N 🅾 Ford, S ⛽ Phillips 66/7-11/dsl, Texaco/dsl 🍴 J's Drive-in, Spring Chicken Café, Subway 🅾 Ace Hardware, city park, E Canyon SP, Family$, Ridley's Mkt, URGENT CARE, USPO
96	Peterson, N ⛽ Sinclair/dsl (3mi) 🅾 Nordic Valley Ski Areas, Powder Mtn, to Snow Basin, S ⛽ Phillips 66/dsl
94mm	Rs wb, full ♿ facilities, 🍽 litter barrels, petwalk
92	UT 167 (from eb), to Huntsville, N ⛽ Sinclair/dsl (2mi) 🅾 city park (2mi), to ski areas
91mm	S Rs eb, full ♿ facilities, 🍽 litter barrels, petwalk
87b a	US 89, to Ogden, Layton, Ogden, N 🍴 Best Western, McDonald's (2mi), Wendy's (2mi) 🅾 Cheese Outlet, Goodyear/auto, S 🅾 to Hill AFB
85	S Weber, Uintah
81	to I-15 S, UT 26, Riverdale Rd, N ⛽ Exxon/dsl, Maverik/dsl, Sinclair/dsl 🍴 Applebee's, Arby's, Buffalo Wild Wings, Carl's Jr, Chili's, Chipotle, El Pollo Loco, Habit Burger, Honeybaked Ham, IHOP, Jamba Juice, Jersey Mike's, Lucky Buffet, McDonald's, MOD Pizza, Starbucks, Subway, Sweet Burrito, Wendy's 🅾 $Tree, AT&T, Best Buy, Buick/GMC, Good Earth Foods, Gordman's, Harley-Davidson, Hobby Lobby, Home Depot, Honda, Jo-Ann, Kia, Lowe's Whse, Nissan, PepBoys, Petsmart, Sam's Club/gas, Schwab Tire, Target, Toyota, Verizon, Walmart/McDonald's, S 🛏 Motel 6 🅾 Chrysler/Dodge/Jeep
	I-84 and I-15 run together. See I-15, exits 344 through 379.
41	I-15 N to Pocatello
40	UT 102, Tremonton, Bothwell, N ⛽ Chevron/Poblano's/dsl/wash/24hr, Maverik/dsl, Sinclair/Burger King/dsl/scales/@, Tesla EVC 🍴 Denny's, McDonald's, Wendy's 🛏 Hampton Inn, Western Inn 🅾 C&R Rv Ctr, �H (4mi), O'Reilly Parts, RV/truck/tire repair, S 🅾 to Golden Spike NHS
39	to Garland, Bothwell, N 🅾 �H
32	ranch exit
26	UT 83 S, to Howell, S 🅾 to Golden Spike NHS
24	to Valley
20	to Blue Creek
17	ranch exit
16	to Hansel Valley (from wb)
12	ranch exit
7	Snowville, N ⛽ (Flying J)/Pepperoni's/dsl/LP/24hr, Sinclair/A&W/dsl 🍴 Mollie's Café, Ranch House Diner 🛏 Outsiders Inn 🅾 city park, Lotti-Dell RV camping, USPO
5	UT 30, to Park Valley
0mm	Utah/Idaho state line

🔼N INTERSTATE 215

Exit #	Services
29	**I-215 begins/ends on I-15.**
28	UT 68, Redwood Rd, E 🅾 Pony Express RV Park, W ⛽ (Flying J)/Pepperoni's/dsl/LP/@, Maverik/dsl 🍴 Lotus Chinese
26	Legacy Pkwy
25	22nd N
23	7th N, E ⛽ Exxon/dsl, ♥Love's/Arbys/dsl/scales/24hr (1.5 mi), Maverik 🍴 Denny's, KFC, Little Caesar's, McDonald's, Papa Murphy's, Subway, Taco Bell, Wendy's 🛏 Motel 6 🅾 $Tree, Family$, Super Saver Mkt, W 🛏 Airport Inn, Candlewood Suites, Comfort Suites, Holiday Inn Express, Radisson
22b a	I-80, W to Wendover, E to Cheyenne
21	California Ave, E ⛽ Sapp Bros/Sinclair/Burger King/dsl/@, Tesoro/7-11/dsl 🍴 RV/Truckwash, W ⛽ Chevron/dsl 🍴 Port of Subs
20b a	UT 201, W to Magna, 21st S, W ⛽ Maverik/dsl 🍴 Del Taco 🅾 Goodyear, Kenworth
18	UT 171, 3500 S, W Valley, E ⛽ 7-11 🍴 Applebee's, Chili's, Costa Vida Mexican, Cracker Barrel, Greek Souvlaki, IHOP, Kowloon Cafe 🛏 Baymont Inn, Country Inn Suites, Crystal Inn, Extended Stay America, Holiday Inn Express, La Quinta, Sleep Inn, Staybridge Suites 🅾 �H, PepBoys, W 🍴 AT&T, Cafe Rio, In-N-Out, Jimmy John's, Olive Garden, Pizza Hut, Red Robin, Smashburger, TGIFriday's, Wendy's, Winger's, Zupas 🛏 Embassy Suites 🅾 Big O Tire, Costco/gas, CVS Drug, JC Penney, Office Depot, Petco, Ross, Staples, Verizon
15	UT 266, 47th S, E ⛽ 7-11, Conoco/dsl 🍴 Dee's Rest., KFC, Mad Greek, Pizza Hut, Taco Time, Village Inn, Wendy's 🅾 Fresh Mkt, Goodyear/auto, Rite Aid, Walgreens, W ⛽ Chevron/dsl 🍴 Arby's, Arctic Circle, Tammie's Diner 🅾 vet ⛽ Sinclair/dsl
13	UT 68, Redwood Rd, E ⛽ Chevron, Shell/dsl 🍴 Apollo Burger, Applebee's, Arby's, Burger King, Carl's Jr, City Buffet, Dickey's BBQ, Domino's, Francesco's Rest., Freebirds Burrito, Honey Baked Ham, McDonald's/playplace, Panda Express, Starbucks, Subway, TX Roadhouse 🛏 Extended Stay America 🅾 $Tree, AT&T, Harmon's Mkt, Jo-Ann Fabrics, PetsMart, Ross, Verizon, Walmart/McDonald's
12	I-15, N to SLC, S to Provo
11	same as 10 (from eb)
10	UT 280 E, E ⛽ Tesoro 🍴 Papa John's 🅾 AutoZone, Sam's Club/gas, W 🍴 A&W/KFC, Applebee's, Arby's, Braza Grill, Brio Grill, CA Pizza, Cheesecake Factory, ChuckARama, Corner Bakery Cafe, Jason's Deli, Macaroni Grill, McDonald's, Olive Garden, Panda Express, Red Lobster, Red Robin, RedRock Cafe, Starbucks, Subway, Taco Bell, Verizon, Village Inn 🅾 Dillard's, Firestone/auto, Honda, �H, Marshalls, Midas, Nordstrom, Pepboys, Sprouts Mkt
9	Union Park Ave, E 🍴 Applebee's, Bucca Italian, Buffalo Wild Wings, Cafe Rio, Carl's Jr, Chick-fil-A, Chili's, Chipotle, Denny's, Dickey's BBQ, Famous Dave's BBQ, Firehouse Subs, Five Guys, Longhorn Steaks, Noodles&Co, Panda Express, Pei Wei, Smashburger, Subway, Wendy's 🛏 Hawthorn Suites, Super 8 🅾 $Tree, Barnes&Noble, Dick's, GNC, Gordman's, Home Depot, Michaels, Old Navy, Petco, Ross, Smith's Foods, Target, TJ Maxx, Verizon, Walmart/Subway, W ⛽ Shell 🛏 Crystal Inn, Motel 6 Extended 🅾 Firestone/auto 🅾 Office Depot
8	UT 152, 2000 E, E ⛽ Chevron 🍴 KFC, McDonald's, Sonic, Taco Bell 🅾 Whole Foods Mkt, W ⛽ Phillips 66/dsl 🍴 Subway, Wendy's 🅾 Discount Tire
6	6200 S, E 🍴 Jimmy John's, Luna Blanca, Pie Five, Starbucks, Trio Cafe, Zupas 🛏 Hyatt Place, Residence Inn 🅾 Alta, Brighton, Snowbird, Solitude/ski areas
5	UT 266, 45th S (from sb), Holladay, W ⛽ Sinclair
4	39th S, E ⛽ Chevron/dsl, Sinclair/dsl 🍴 Barbacoa Grill, Rocky Mtn Pizza, Subway 🅾 Ace Hardware, Dan's Mkt, W 🅾 �H
3	33rd S, Wasatch, W ⛽ Cafe Rio, Smith's/dsl 🍴 Five Guys, KFC, Taco Bell, McDonald's, Shivers Burgers, Wendy's 🅾 Petsmart, REI, Smith's Mkt
2	I-80 W
0	**I-215 begins/ends on I-80, exit 130.**

Side tabs: **UT** · **RIVERDALE** · **SALT LAKE CITY**

VERMONT

◤N   INTERSTATE 89

Exit #	Services
130mm	US/Canada Border, Vermont state line, **I-89 begins/ends.**
22(129)	US 7 S, Highgate Springs, **E** 🅖 Irving/dsl 🅞 DutyFree
129mm	Latitude 45 N, midway between N Pole and Equator
128mm	Rock River
21(123)	US 7, VT 78, Swanton, **E** 🅖 Shell/dsl, **W** 🅖 Mobil/Subway/dsl, Shell, Sunoco/dsl 🍴 Dunkin', McDonald's, Pam's Pizza, Shaggy's Snack Bar 🅞 $General, Auchubon Hardware, Hannaford Foods, NAPA
20(118)	US 7, VT 207, St Albans, **E** 🅞 Chevrolet, Toyota, **W** 🅖 Mobil/Subway/dsl, Sunoco 🍴 Burger King, Dunkin', KFC/Taco Bell, McDonald's, Oriental Kitchen, Pizza Hut 🅞 🄷 Advance Parts, AT&T, Aubuchon Hardware, Buick/GMC/Cadillac, Ford, Hannaford Foods, Jo-Ann Fabrics, Kinney Drug, PriceChopper Foods, TJ Maxx, URGENT CARE, Verizon, Walmart/Subway
19(114)	US 7, VT 36, VT 104, St Albans, **W** 🅖 Mobil/dsl, Shell/dsl 🍴 Dunkin', Subway 🛏 La Quinta 🅞 🄷 st police, vet
111mm	🆁🆂 both lanes, full ♿ facilities, info, litter barrels, petwalk, 🅒, 🚮, vending, wifi
18(107)	US 7, VT 104A, Georgia Ctr, **E** 🅖 Mobil/dsl, Shell/dsl 🍴 GA Farmhouse Rest. 🅞 $General, GA Auto Parts, repair, USPO
17(98)	US 2, US 7, **E** 🅖 Mobil, Shell/dsl 🅞 camping (4mi), **W** 🅞 camping (6mi)
96mm	weigh sta both lanes
16(92)	US 7, US 2, Winooski, **E** 🅖 Mobil 🍴 Lighthouse Rest. 🛏 Hampton Inn 🅞 Costco/gas, CVS Drug, Osco Drug, Shaw's Foods, **W** 🅖 Citgo, Shell/dsl 🍴 Athens Diner, Burger King, McDonald's, Subway 🛏 Motel 6, Quality Inn
15(91)	VT 15 (from nb no return), Winooski, **E** 🛏 Days Inn, Handys Extended Stay Suites 🅞 to St Michael's Coll, **W** 🅖 Mobil/dsl, Shell
90mm	Winooski River
14(89)	US 2, Burlington, **E** 🅖 Gulf, Mobil, Shell/dsl, Sunoco/dsl, Sunoco/repair, Valero 🍴 Al's Cafe, Applebee's, Chicken Charlie's, Dukes Public House, Dunkin', Hana Japanese, IHOP, Leonardo's Pizza, McDonald's, Moe's SW Grill, Outback Steaks, Pulcinella's, Rotisserie, Starbucks, Subway, Wind Jammer Rest., Zachary's Pizza 🛏 Anchorage Inn, Best Western+, Comfort Inn, Delta Hotel, Holiday Inn, Homewood Suites, La Quinta 🅞 Aubuchon Hardware, Barnes&Noble, CVS, Hannaford Foods, Healthy Living Mkt, JC Penney, Jo-Ann Fabrics, Kohl's, Midas, PriceChopper, Rite Aid, Target, Trader Joe's, USPO, **W** 🅖 Mobil/dsl, Shell 🛏 DoubleTree 🅞 🄷 Advance Parts, Michael's, PetCo, Staples, to UVT, Verizon
13(87)	I-189, to US 7, Burlington, **2 mi W on US 7 N** 🅖 Citgo/dsl, Sunoco/dsl 🍴 Buffalo Wild Wings, China Express, Chipotle, Five Guys, Starbucks, Subway 🅞 $Tree, GNC, Hyundai/Subaru, Kinney Drug, PriceChopper Mkt, Shaw's Foods, TJ Maxx, USPO, Walgreens, **2 mi W on US 7 S** 🅖 Gulf, Irving, Mobil/dsl, Shell/dsl, Sunoco 🍴 Burger King, Chicago Grill, Denny's, Koto Japanese, Lakeview House Rest., McDonald's, Olive Garden, Panera Bread, Pauline's Cafe, Zen Garden 🛏 Comfort Suites, Holiday Inn Express, North Star Motel, Travelodge 🅞 Acura/Audi, Advance Parts, Buick/Cadillac/GMC, Chevrolet, Chrysler/Dodge, Ford, Hannaford Foods, Jeep, Lowe's, Nissan, O'Reilly Parts, Tire Whse, Toyota, URGENT CARE, Verizon, VW
12(84)	VT 2A, to US 2, to Essex Jct, Williston, **E** 🅞 EVC, Mobil, Sunoco/Dunkin'/dsl 🍴 99 Rest., Chili's, Friendly's, Longhorn Steaks, Moe's SW Grill, Panera Bread, Starbucks, TX Roadhouse,
12(84)	Continued VT Taphouse 🛏 Fairfield, TownePlace Suites 🅞 Best Buy, CVS Drug, Dick's, Hannaford Foods, Home Depot, Marshall's, Natural Provisions Mkt, Old Navy, Petsmart, Shaws Foods/Osco, st police, Staples, Town Fair Tire, Verizon, Walmart, **W** 🛏 Courtyard, Sonesta Suites
82mm	🆁🆂 both lanes (7am-11pm), full ♿ facilities, litter barrels, petwalk, 🅒, 🚮, vending, WiFi
11(79)	US 2, to VT 117, Richmond, **W** 🅖 Mobil/dsl
67mm	parking area/weigh sta sb
66mm	weigh sta nb
10(64)	VT 100, to US 2, Waterbury, **E** 🅖 Mobil/dsl, Shell/dsl 🍴 Hong Kong Chinese, Thai Smile 🛏 Best Western+, Fairfield Inn 🅞 Shaws Foods/Osco Drug, TrueValue, **W** 🅖 Citgo/dsl 🍴 Maxi's Rest., Zachary's Pizza 🅞 USPO
9(59)	US 2, to VT 100B, Middlesex, **W** 🅖 EVC 🍴 Red Hen Baking Co 🅞 museum, st police
8(53)	US 2, Montpelier, **1 mi E** 🅖 Citgo, Cumberland Farms /dsl, Mobil/dsl, Shell/dsl 🍴 China Star, Domino's, Dunkin', Julio's, Sarducci's Rest. 🛏 Capitol Plaza Hotel 🅞 Aubuchon Hardware, camping (6mi), O'Reilly Parts, Rite Aid, Shaw's Foods, Sunoco/repair, to VT Coll
7(50)	VT 62, to US 302, Barre, **E** 🅖 Tesla EVC, Irving/dsl 🍴 Applebee's 🛏 Comfort Suites, Hilltop Inn 🅞 🄷 camping (7mi), Honda, JC Penney, Shaw's Foods, Subaru, Toyota, Walmart
6(47)	VT 63, to VT 14, S Barre, **4 mi E** camping, food, gas, info, lodging
5(43)	VT 64, to VT 12, VT 14, Williamstown, **6 mi E** camping, food, gas/dsl, lodging, **W** to Norwich U
41mm	highest elevation on I-89, 1752 ft
34.5mm	weigh sta both lanes
4(31)	VT 66, Randolph, **E** 🅞 RV camping (seasonal 1mi), **W** 🅖 Mobil/Subway/dsl 🍴 lodging (3mi), McDonald's 🅞 🄷 RV camping (5mi)

◻ = gas ◻ = food ◻ = lodging ◻ = other ◻ = rest stop   Copyright 2022 - The Next EXIT ®

VT

⬆N INTERSTATE 89 Cont'd

Exit #	Services
30mm	parking area sb
3(22)	VT 107, Bethel, E ◻ Irving/dsl ◻ Village Pizza ◻ to Jos Smith Mon (8mi), **1 mi W** ◻ Irving/dsl/LP ◻ st police, vet
14mm	White River
2(13)	VT 14, VT 132, Sharon, W ◻ Gulf/dsl ◻ Jos Smith Mon (6mi), Sharon Country Store, USPO
9mm	◻/weigh sta both lanes (7am-11pm), full ◻ facilities, info, litter barrels, ◻, ◻, vending, wi-fi
7mm	White River
1(4)	US 4, to Woodstock, Quechee, **3 mi E** ◻ Fairfield Inn, Hampton Inn, Holiday Inn Express, Super 8
1mm	I-91, N to St Johnsbury, S to Brattleboro
0mm	Vermont/New Hampshire state line, Connecticut River

⬆N INTERSTATE 91

Exit #	Services
178mm	US/Canada Border, Vermont state line, I-91 begins/ends.
29(177)	US 5, Derby Line, E ◻ Dutyfree, **1 mi W** ◻ Irving/Circle K/dsl ◻ city park
176.5mm	Welcome Ctr sb, full ◻ facilities, info, litter barrels, Midpoint between the Equator and N Pole, petwalk, ◻, ◻, wi-fi
28(172)	US 5, VT 105, Derby Ctr, E ◻ Gulf, repair, Sunoco/dsl/dsl ◻ Cow Palace Rest. ◻ auto/tire service, USPO, W ◻ Irving/Hoagie's Pizza, Mobil/dsl ◻ China Moon, Dunkin', McDonald's, Roasters Cafe, VT Pie&Pasta ◻ 4 Seasons ◻ ◻, $General, $Tree, Advance Parts, Chrysler/Dodge/Jeep, Kinney Drug, O'Reilly Parts, PriceChopper Foods, Rite Aid, Shaw's Foods, st police, Verizon
27(170)	VT 191, to US 5, VT 105, Newport, **3 mi W** ◻ ◻, Border Patrol, camping, info
167mm	parking area/weigh sta both directions
26(161)	US 5, VT 58, Orleans, E ◻ Pit Stop, Sunoco/dsl ◻ Subway ◻ Family$, Thibaults Mkt, TrueValue, USPO
156.5mm	Barton River
25(156)	VT 16, Barton, **1 mi E** ◻ Irving/Circle K/dsl ◻ Parson's Corner Rest. ◻ C&C Foods, Kinney Drug, O'Reilly Parts, USPO
154mm	parking area nb
150.5mm	highest elevation on I-91, 1856 ft
143mm	scenic overlook nb
141mm	◻ sb, full ◻ facilities, info, litter barrels, ◻, ◻
24(140)	VT 122, Wheelock, **2 mi E** food, gas, lodging
23(137)	US 5, to VT 114, Lyndonville, E ◻ Irving/dsl, Mobil/Dunkin' ◻ Hoagie's Pizza, Lyndon Buffet, McDonald's, Miss Lyndonville Diner, Pizza Man ◻ Colonnade Inn ◻ $General, CarQuest, Kinney Drug, Rite Aid, TrueValue, White Mkt Foods, W ◻ Lyndon Motel
22(132)	to US 5, St Johnsbury, **1-2 mi E** ◻ Sunoco/dsl ◻ KFC/Taco Bell, Kham's Cuisine, Pizza Hut ◻ ◻, Buick/GMC, Chrysler/Dodge/Jeep, Kinney Drug, O'Reilly Parts, PriceChopper Foods, repair, Subaru
21(131)	US 2, to VT 15, St Johnsbury, **1-2 mi E** services
20(129)	US 5, to US 2, St Johnsbury, E ◻ Mobil, Sunoco/dsl, Valero/dsl ◻ Anthony's Diner, Domino's, Dunkin', East Garden Chinese, Subway, Winegate Rest. ◻ welcome ctr, Family$, Kevin's Repair, NAPA, Rite Aid, W ◻ Comfort Inn ◻ st police
19(128)	I-93 S to Littleton NH
122mm	scenic view nb
18(121)	to US 5, Barnet, E ◻ camping (5mi), W ◻ camping (5mi)
115mm	parking area sb

D E R B Y   C T R

S T   J O H N S B U R Y

113mm	parking area nb
17(110)	US 302, to US 5, Wells River, NH, E ◻ ◻ (5mi), W ◻ Mobil/P&H Trkstp/rest./dsl/scales/24hr ◻ camping (9mi)
100mm	◻ nb, parking area sb, full ◻ facilities, info, litter barrels, petwalk, ◻, ◻
16(98)	VT 25, to US 5, Bradford, E ◻ Mobil/dsl/LP/café ◻ Hungry Bear Grill ◻ Bradford Motel ◻ Family$, Hannaford Foods, Kinney Drug, NAPA, O'Reilly Parts, Pierson Farm Mkt, W st police
15(92)	Fairlee, E ◻ Irving/dsl, Mobil/7-11, Sunoco/dsl ◻ Fairlee Diner, Lunchbox Deli ◻ $General, USPO, Wings Mkt/deli, W ◻ golf
14(84)	VT 113, to US 5, Thetford, **1 mi E** ◻ food, Rest-n-Nest Camping, W ◻ camping
13(75)	US 5, VT 10a, Hanover, NH, E ◻ ◻, to Dartmouth, W ◻ Citgo ◻ Norwich Inn Rest. ◻ auto service, USPO
12(72)	US 5, White River Jct, Wilder, E ◻ Cumberland Farms/dsl, Mobil
11(71)	US 5, White River Jct, E ◻ Mobil/dsl, Shell/Subway/dsl ◻ China Moon, Crossroads Country Café, McDonald's ◻ Comfort Inn ◻ Chevrolet, Hyundai, Subaru, Toyota, USPO, W ◻ Sunoco/dsl ◻ Dunkin' ◻ Fairfield Inn, Hampton Inn, Holiday Inn Express, Super 8, White River Inn ◻ ◻
10N(70)	I-89 N, to Montpelier
10S	I-89 S, to NH, ◻
68mm	Welcome Ctr sb, full facilities, weigh sta nb
9(60)	US 5, VT 12, Hartland, E ◻ ◻, W ◻ Mobil (1mi) ◻ Hartland Diner
8(51)	US 5, VT 12, VT 131, Ascutney, E ◻ Irving/Subway, Sunoco/dsl ◻ Ascutney House Rest. ◻ ◻, Getaway Camping (2mi), USPO
7(42)	US 5, VT 106, VT 11, Springfield, W ◻ Irving/Circle K/Subway/dsl/scales/24hr ◻ Holiday Inn Express ◻ ◻ (5mi)
39mm	weigh sta both lanes, weigh sta sb
6(34)	US 5, VT 103, to Bellows Falls, Rockingham, E ◻ Shell/dsl ◻ Leslie's Rest. ◻ Rodeway Inn, W ◻ Sunoco/dsl
5(29)	VT 121, to US 5, to Bellows Falls, Westminster, **3 mi E** food, gas, lodging, ◻
24mm	parking area both lanes
22mm	weigh sta sb
20mm	weigh sta nb
4(18)	US 5, Putney, E ◻ Putney Inn/rest., W ◻ Rod's/repair, Sunoco/dsl/24hr ◻ Putney Diner, Putney Food Coop/deli ◻ Putney Gen Store/deli, USPO
3(11)	US 5, VT 9 E, Brattleboro, E ◻ Agway/dsl, Citgo/dsl, Mobil/dsl, Sunoco ◻ 99 Rest., China Buffet, Dunkin', Fast Eddy Cafe, KFC, McDonald's, Panda North, Ramunto's Brick Oven, Taco Bell, Village Pizza, Wendy's ◻ Black Mtn Inn, Colonial Motel, Comfort Inn, Covered Bridge Inn, Hampton Inn, Holiday Inn Express, Motel 6, Quality Inn ◻ Advance Parts, Aldi Foods, AT&T, Buick/Chevrolet/GMC, Chrysler/Dodge/Jeep, Family$, Ford, GNC, Hannaford Foods, O'Reilly Parts, Staples, Subaru, TrueValue, URGENT CARE, USPO, Verizon
2(9)	VT 9 W, to rd 30, Brattleboro, W ◻ VT Country Deli ◻ to Marlboro Coll
1(7)	US 5, Brattleboro, E ◻ Gulf/dsl, Irving/Circle K/dsl, Mobil/Dunkin', Shell/Subway/dsl ◻ Domino's, FC Chinese, VT Inn Pizza ◻ EconoLodge ◻ ◻, $Tree, PriceChopper Mkt, Rite Aid, to Ft Dummer SP, vet, Walgreens
6mm	Welcome Ctr nb, full ◻ facilities, info, litter barrels, petwalk, ◻, ◻, playground, vending, wi-fi
0mm	Vermont/Massachusetts state line

B R A T T L E B O R O

⬆N INTERSTATE 93

See New Hampshire Interstate 93

VIRGINIA

VA

↑E INTERSTATE 64

Exit #	Services
299b a	I-264 E, to Portsmouth. I-64 begins/ends on I-264.
297	US 13, US 460, Military Hwy, N 🅿 7-11, Exxon 🍴 McDonald's, Papa John's
296b a	US 17, to Portsmouth, N 🅿 7-11 🍴 Hardee's, McDonald's, Papa John's, Pizza Hut, Subway, Zino's Cafe 🏠 Comfort Inn 🅾 $General, Food Lion, USPO, vet
294mm	S Br Elizabeth River
292	VA 190, to VA 104 (from eb, no EZ return), Dominion Blvd, S 🅿 7-11 🍴 #1 China, Burger King, Royal China, Subway 🅾 Family$, Food Lion
291b a	I-464 N, VA 104 S, to Elizabeth City, Outer Banks, same services as 292
290b a	VA 168, Battlefield Blvd, to Nag's Head, Manteo, N 🍴 Burger King 🏠 Woodspring Suites 🅾 $General, BigLots, Kroger, Merchant's Auto Ctr, NAPA, S 🅿 7-11, BP/DQ, Shell 🍴 Applebee's, Baskin-Robbins, Burger King, Carrabba's, Chick-fil-A, ChuckECheese's, CookOut, Denny's, Dunkin', Five Guys, Golden Corral, Grand China Buffet, Hardee's, Hunan Wok, Jade Garden, Little Caesar's, Panda Express, Sonic, Starbucks, Taco Bell, TGI-Friday's, Tropical Smoothie Café, TX Roadhouse, Waffle House, Wendy's, Wildwing Café 🏠 Hampton Inn, InTown Suites, Quality Inn, Studios For Less 🅾 🏥, $Tree, AT&T, Goodyear/auto, Home Depot, Kohl's, Lowe's, Nissan, Rite Aid, Sam's Club/gas, USPO, vet, Walgreens, Walmart
289b a	Greenbrier Pkwy, N 🅿 7-11, Citgo/dsl, WaWa/dsl 🍴 Burger King, McDonald's, Subway, Taco Bell, Wendy's 🏠 Extended Stay America, Hampton Inn, Holiday Inn Express, Marriott, Red Roof Inn, Staybridge Suites, Wingate Inn 🅾 Acura, auto repair, Chevrolet, Chrysler/Jeep, Dodge, Ford, GMC, Hyundai, JoAnn Fabrics, Kia, Lincoln, Mazda, Toyota, U-Haul, vet, VW, S 🅿 7-11 🍴 Abuelo's Mexican, Baker's Crust, Boston Mkt, Buffalo Wild Wings, Chipotle, Coldstone, Cracker Barrel, Fazoli's, Firehouse Subs, Hooters, Jason's Deli, Jersey Mike's Subs, Jimmy John's, Joe's Crabshack, Kyoto Japanese, Los Burritos, McDonald's, Moe's SW, Olive Garden, Panera Bread, Pizza Hut, Pop's Diner, Qdoba, Red Robin, Ruby Tuesday, Smokey Bones BBQ, Starbucks, Subway, Tropical Smoothie, Zero's Subs, Zoe's Kitchen 🏠 Aloft Hotel, Comfort Suites, Courtyard, Extended Stay, Fairfield Inn, Hilton Garden, Homewood Suites, Residence Inn, SpringHill Suites, Sun Suites 🅾 AT&T, Barnes&Noble,

289b a	Continued
	Best Buy, Dillard's, Food Lion, Harris Teeter, Macy's, Marshall's, Michael's, Office Depot, Old Navy, Petsmart, Ross, Steinmart, Target, TJ Maxx, Verizon, Walgreens
286b a	Indian River Rd, N 🅿 BP/dsl, Gulf, SkyMart/dsl, Speedway/dsl 🍴 Dunkin', Golden China, Hardee's 🅾 CVS, S 🅿 Exxon/dsl 🍴 CookOut, Ellen's BBQ, Oriental Cuisine, Oriental Cuisine, Waffle House 🅾 7-11
285mm	E Branch Elizabeth River
284a	I-264, to Norfolk, to VA Beach (exits left from eb)
284b	Newtown Rd
282	US 13, Northampton Blvd, N 🅿 Citgo/dsl 🍴 Krispy Kreme, McDonald's, Starbucks, Taco Bell, Wendy's 🏠 Quality Inn, Sleep Inn 🅾 to Chesapeake Bay Br Tunnel
281	VA 165, Military Hwy (no EZ eb return), N 🅿 Shell/dsl 🏠 EconoLodge 🅾 Aamco, Chysler/Dodge/Jeep, Fiat, S 🅿 7-11, Citgo 🍴 Burger King, Chick-fil-A, CookOut, Firehouse Subs, Hooters, IHOP, Jersey Mike's Subs, Jimmy John's, KFC, Little Caesar's, Logan's Roadhouse, Max&Erma's, Panera Bread, Qdoba, Ruby Tuesday, Sonic, Starbucks, Taco Bell, Wendy's 🏠 Candlewood Suites, Days Inn, Doubletree, Hampton Inn, Holiday Inn, Holiday Inn Express, InTown Suites, La Quinta, Residence Inn 🅾 BJ's Whse/dsl, FarmFresh Foods, Food Lion, GNC, Home Depot, Lowe's, Nissan, Pep Boys, Petco, Petsmart, Target, TJ Maxx, Verizon, Walgreens, Walmart/Subway
279	Norview Ave, N 🅿 WaWa/dsl 🍴 China House, Franco's Italian, Golden Corral, Pizza Hut, Wendy's 🅾 $General, $Tree, 7-11/dsl, Food Lion, Tire City, to 🛫 & botanical garden
278	VA 194 S (no EZ return)
277b a	VA 168, to Tidewater Dr, N 🅿 7-11, Shell 🍴 Bojangles, Domino's, Fuddrucker's, Hardee's, Ruby Tuesday 🅾 Advance Parts, Food Lion, Walmart/Subway, S 🅾 Honda
276c	to US 460 W, VA 165, Little Creek Rd, (from wb only), N 🅿 Race Coast/dsl, S 🅿 BP, Shell 🍴 Firehouse Subs, KFC, McDonald's, Moe's SW, Papa John's, Starbucks, Taco Bell, Wendy's 🅾 AutoZone, FarmFresh Foods, GNC, Harris Teeter, Kroger, Rite Aid, USPO, Walgreens
276b a	I-564 to Naval Base (exits left from wb)
274	Bay Ave (from wb), S 🅾 to Naval Air Sta
273	US 60, 4th View St, Oceanview, N 🅿 7-11/dsl 🏠 Economy Inn, Motel 6 🅾 Oceanview Pier
272	W Ocean View Ave, N 🍴 Willoughby Seafood, S 🍴 Sunset Grill
270mm	Chesapeake Bay Tunnel

NORFOLK

🅿 = gas   🍴 = food   🛏 = lodging   🄾 = other   🆁🆂 = rest stop   Copyright 2022 - The Next EXIT

INTERSTATE 64 Cont'd

Exit #	Services
269mm	weigh sta eb
268	VA 169 E, to Buckroe Beach, Ft Monroe, N 🅿 Citgo 🍴 Hardee's, McDonald's, S 🄾 to VA Air&Space Ctr
267	US 60, to VA 143, Settlers Ldg Rd, S 🍴 Golden City Chinese, Subway, Tropical Smoothie 🄾 🛏, to Hampton U
265c	(from eb), to Armistead Ave, N 🄾 to Langley AFB
265b a	VA 134, VA 167, to La Salle Ave, N 🅿 Citgo, RaceWay/dsl 🛏 Super 8 🄾 Home Depot, S 🅿 Citgo 🍴 KFC/Taco Bell, McDonald's 🄾 Advance Parts, Family$
264	I-664, to Newport News, Suffolk
263b a	US 258, VA 134, Mercury Blvd, to James River Br, N 🅿 7-11, BP, Exxon/dsl, Miller's/dsl, Shell 🍴 Abuelo's Mexican, Applebee's, Bojangles, Boston Mkt, Burger King, Chick-fil-A, Chili's, China Wok, Chipotle Mexican, Denny's, Dog House, El Azteca, Firehouse Subs, Five Guys, Golden Corral, Hooters, IHOP, Jason's Deli, McDonald's, Olive Garden, Outback Steaks, Panera Bread, Parklane Rest., Pizza Hut, Rally's, Red Lobster, Starbucks, Subway, Taco Bell, Tokyo Japanese, Waffle House, Wendy's 🛏 Best Western, Courtyard, Days Inn, Embassy Suites, Holiday Inn Express, Quality Inn, Red Roof Inn 🄾 $Tree, AT&T, Barnes&Noble, Chevrolet/Mazda, FarmFresh Foods, Food Lion, Ford, GNC, Goodyear/auto, JC Penney, Jo-Ann Fabrics, Marshall's, Michael's, NAPA, Nissan, Office Depot, PetCo, Ross, Target, U-Haul, USPO, Verizon, Volvo, Walgreens, Walmart, S 🅿 Citgo/dsl, Miller's/dsl, WaWa/dsl 🍴 Burritos Mexican, Chick-fil-A, CiCi's Pizza, Coldstone, Cracker Barrel, Domino's, Dunkin', Joe's Crabshack, La Parrilla, Little Caesar's, Longhorn Steaks, Pizza Hut, Rita's, Sonic, Steak'n Shake, Waffle House, Zaxby's 🛏 Ambassador Inn Suites, Hilton Garden, InTown Suites, Relax Inn, SpringHill Suites 🄾 $General, 7-11, Aamco, Advance Parts, BassPro Shop, BigLots, BJ's Whse/Subway/gas, CVS Drug, Firestone/auto, Lowe's, Office Depot, PepBoys, Toyota, Walmart Mkt
262	VA 134, Magruder Blvd (from wb, no EZ return), N 🅿 7-11, Exxon 🛏 Country Inn&Suites, Suburban Lodge 🄾 Audi, Hyundai, Mercedes
261b a	Center Pkwy, to Hampton Roads, N 🛏 Candlewood Suites, Hampton Inn (2mi), S 🅿 7-11, Shell 🍴 Anna's Italian, ChuckE-Cheese's, Fortune Garden Chinese, Gus's NY Pizza, McDonald's, Peking Chinese, Pizza Hut/Taco Bell, Plaza Azteca, Ruby Tuesday, Subway 🄾 $Tree, FarmFresh Foods, Food Lion, GNC, Rite Aid, TJMaxx
258b a	US 17, J Clyde Morris Blvd, N 🅿 BP, Shell/dsl 🍴 Domino's, New China, Waffle House 🛏 BudgetLodge, Country Inn&Suites, Holiday Inn Express, Host Inn, PointPlaza Hotel, Quality Inn 🄾 7-11, Advance Parts, Family$, Food Lion, S 🅿 Kangaroo, WaWa/dsl 🍴 Angelo's Steaks, Burger King, DQ, KFC/Taco Bell, McDonald's, Papa John's, Starbucks, Subway, Vinny's Pizza, Wendy's 🛏 Motel 6 🄾 🛏, museum, Rite Aid, Subaru, VW
256b a	Victory Blvd, Oyster Point Rd, N 🅿 Kangaroo/dsl, Murphy USA/dsl 🍴 Arby's, Burger King, Chick-fil-A, China Ocean, Hardee's, McDonald's, Panda Express, Pizza Hut, Ruby Tuesday, Saisaki Asian, Sonic, Starbucks, Subway, Three Amigos Mexican, TX Roadhouse, Uno Grill 🛏 CandleWood Suites, Courtyard, Hampton Inn, Hilton Garden, Staybridge Suites, TownePlace Suites 🄾 $Tree, FarmFresh Foods, GNC, Goodyear/auto, Kroger, Walgreens, Walmart, S 🛏 Crestwood Suites, Jameson Inn
255b a	VA 143, to Jefferson Ave, N 🅿 Exxon/dsl, Shell/dsl 🍴 Chili's, CookOut, Donato's Pizza, Firehouse Subs, Five Guys, Golden Corral, HoneyBaked Ham, Hooters, Jason's Deli, Longhorn Steaks, McDonald's, Moe's SW Grill, Olive Garden, Panera Bread, Papa John's, Red City Buffet, Red Lobster, Smokey Bones BBQ, Sonic, Starbucks 🛏 Comfort Suites 🄾 🛏, Acura, Buick/Cadillac/GMC, Chrysler/Dodge/Jeep, FarmFresh Foods deli, Fiat, GNC, Home Depot, Kohl's, Lowe's, Michael's, PetCo, Ross, Sam's Club/gas, TJ Maxx, Trader Joe's, Tuesday Morning, Walgreens, Walmart, S 🍴 Applebee's, Buffalo Wild Wings, Carrabba's, Cheddar's, Chick-fil-A, Chipotle Mexican, Coldstone, Cracker Barrel, KFC, McDonald's, Outback Steaks, Red Robin, Starbucks, Subway, Taco Bell, TGIFriday's, Waffle House, Wendy's 🛏 Best Western, Comfort Inn, Courtyard, Extended Stay America, Hampton Inn, Microtel, Residence Inn 🄾 7-11, Barnes&Noble, Best Buy, Costco/dsl, Dick's, Dillard's, Fresh Mkt, JC Penney, Macy's, Petsmart, Target, Verizon, World Mkt
250b a	to US Army Trans Museum, N 🅿 7-11/gas, Dodge's Store, Exxon/dsl, Sunoco 🍴 Hardee's, Subway 🄾 B&L Auto Repair, Newport News Campground/Park (1mi), to Yorktown Victory Ctr, 🛏 Ft Eustis Inn, Holiday Inn Express, Mulberry Inn 🄾 7-11
247	VA 143, to VA 238 (no EZ return wb), N 🅿 7-11/gas 🄾 to Yorktown, S 🄾 to Jamestown Settlement
243	VA 143, to Williamsburg, exits left from wb, S same as 242a
242b a	VA 199, to US 60, to Williamsburg, N 🛏 Wyndham Garden 🄾 Best Buy, Dick's, Kohl's, Target, to Yorktown NHS, water funpark, 1 mi S 🅿 7-11/gas, Sunoco, WaWa/dsl 🍴 China Cuisine, Doraldo's Italian, KFC, McDonald's, Sportsmans Grille, Starbucks, Subway, Taco Bell, Wendy's, Whaling Co Rest 🛏 Country Inn&Suites, Courtyard, Quality Inn 🄾 Busch Gardens, to Jamestown NHS, to William&Mary Coll
238	VA 143, to Colonial Williamsburg, Camp Peary, 2-3 mi S on US 60 🅿 Exxon/7-11, Shell 🍴 Aberdeen Barn Rest., Applebee's, Arby's, Chili's, Chipotle Mexican, Cracker Barrel, DQ, Firehouse Subs, Five Guys, Golden Corral, Hooters, IHOP, Jefferson Steaks, KFC, Kyoto, McDonald's, Outback Steaks, Pancake House, Pizza Hut, Plaza Azteca, Red Hot&Blue, Sal's Rest., Seafare Rest. Smokehouse Grill, Subway, Taco Bell, Uno Grille, Wendy's 🛏 Best Inn, Best Western, Comfort Inn, Country Inn&Suites, Days Inn, EconoLodge, Embassy Suites, Fairfield Inn, Hampton Inn, Hampton Inn, Hilton Garden, Holiday Inn Express, Holiday Inn/rest., Homewood Suites, La Quinta, Quality Inn, Residence Inn, Sleep Inn, SpringHill Suites, Travelodge 🄾 🛏, Anvil Camping (4mi), CVS Drug, Goodyear/auto
234	VA 646, to Lightfoot, 1-2 mi N 🄾 KOA, 2-3 mi S 🅿 Exxon/dsl, Shell/dsl 🍴 Burger King, Chick-fil-A, China Wok, Hardee's, IHOP, McDonald's, Sonic, Starbucks, Subway 🛏 Great Wolf Lodge, Holiday Inn Express, Super 8 🄾 🛏, $Tree, Ford, Home Depot, Lowe's, PetCo, Ross, Toyota, USPO, Walmart, Williamsburg Campark
231b a	VA 607, to Norge, Croaker, N 🅿 7-11/gas 🄾 to York River SP, 1-3 mi S on US 60 🅿 Shell/dsl 🍴 Candle Light Kitchen, China Star, Daddy-O's Pizza, Jimmy's Grill, Pizza Hut 🛏 EconoLodge 🄾 American Heritage RV Park, CVS Drug, FarmFresh Deli/gas, Food Lion, Honda, Hyundai, USPO
227	VA 30, to US 60, to West Point, Toano, S 🅿 Shell/dsl, Star Subway/dsl 🍴 McDonald's
220	VA 33 E, to West Point, N 🅿 Mobil/dsl
214	VA 155, to New Kent, Providence Forge, S 🅿 Exxon/DQ/dsl 🍴 Antonio's Pizza, Tops China
213mm	🆁🆂 both lanes, full 🛏 facilities, litter barrels, petwalk, 🅿, 🍴 vending

VA

HAMPTON

WILLIAMSBURG

INTERSTATE 64 Cont'd

Exit #	Services
211	VA 106, to Talleysville, to James River Plantations, **S** 🍴 ❤️Love's/Arby's/dsl/scales/24hr, 🄿🄸🄻🄾🅃/Subway/dsl/scales/24hr 🍴 Burger King
205	VA 33, VA 249, to US 60, Bottoms Bridge, Quinton, **N** 🍴 Exxon/dsl, Star Express, Valero 🍴 Julio's Mexican, Maria's Italian, Panda Garden, Pizza Hut, Subway, Wendy's ⬛ Food Lion, Verizon, **S** 🍴 FasMart, Shell/dsl 🍴 Bojangle's, McDonald's ⬛ Food Lion, Rite Aid
204mm	Chickahominy River
203mm	weigh sta both lanes
200	I-295, N to Washington, S to Rocky Mount, to US 60
197 b a	VA 156, Airport Dr, to Highland Springs, **N** 🍴 Shell/dsl, Valero 🍴 Antonio's Pizza, Domino's, Hardee's, Subway, Tops China ⬛ $General, 7-11, Advance Parts, CVS Drug, Farmers Foods, **S** 🍴 BP, Chubby's/dsl, Shell/7-11, WaWa 🍴 Arby's, Burger King, Mexico Rest., Pizza Hut, Roberto's Italian, The Patron, Waffle House 🛏 All Day Inn, Best Value Inn, Courtyard, EconoLodge, Hampton Inn, Hilton Garden, Holiday Inn, Holiday Inn Express, Homewood Suites, Microtel, Motel 6, Quality Inn, Red Roof Inn, Super 8 ⬛ to ✈
195	Laburnum Ave, **N** ⬛ auto repair, **S** 🍴 7-11, Exxon, WaWa/dsl 🍴 Applebee's, Capt D's, Chick-fil-A, China King, CiCi's Pizza, CookOut, Cracker Barrel, Firehouse Subs, Five Guys, Hardee's, IHOP, KFC, Little Caesar's, Longhorn Steaks, McDonald's, Olive Garden, Panera Bread, Papa John's, Popeye's, Qdoba Mexican, Red Lobster, Steak'n Shake, Subway, Taco Bell, TGIFriday's, Wendy's 🛏 Hyatt Place, Sheraton ⬛ $General, $Tree, AT&T, CarQuest, CVS Drug, GNC, JC Penney, Kroger, Lowe's, Michael's, Petsmart, Publix, Target, Walgreens
193 b a	VA 33, Nine Mile Rd, **N** 🍴 Exxon/Subway/dsl, Sunoco/dsl ⬛ PepBoys, **S** ⬛ 🄷
192	US 360, to Mechanicsville, **N** 🍴 Exxon/dsl, Shell 🍴 McDonald's ⬛ Tuffy Repair, **S** 🍴 Shell, Valero
190	I-95 S, to Petersburg, 5th St. **S** 🛏 Hilton, Marriott ⬛ coliseum, st capitol
	I-64 and I-95 run together, see VA I-95 exits 76-78.
187	I-95 N (exits left from eb), to Washington.
186	I-195, to Powhite Pkwy, from wb, Richmond
185 b a	US 33, Staples Mill Rd, Dickens Rd
183 c	from wb, US 250 W, Broad St, Glenside Dr N, same as exit 183
183 b a	US 250, Broad St E, Glenside Dr S., **N** 🍴 Sheetz/dsl 🍴 McDonald's, Mission BBQ, Nanking, Olive Garden, Subway, Taco Bell, TGIFriday's, Waffle House 🛏 Best Western, Econolodge/Rodeway, Embassy Suites, Hampton Inn, Knights Inn, Residence Inn, Super 8, Woodspring Suites ⬛ AutoZone, Honda, vet, Volvo, **S** 🍴 Chipotle, Denny's, Jersey Mike's, O'Charley's, Plaza Azteca, Starbucks 🛏 Candlewood Suites, Courtyard, Westin ⬛ 🄷, Aldi Foods, Home Depot, Target, to U of Richmond, vet, Walmart
181 b a	Parham Rd, **N** 🍴 Citgo, Exxon ⬛ Chrysler/Dodge/Jeep
180	Gaskins Rd, **N** 🍴 BP, Shell/dsl 🍴 Applebee's, Coldstone, Cracker Barrel, Dickey's BBQ, Golden Corral, IHOP, Kickback Jack's Rest., McDonald's, O'Charley's, Pizza Hut, Starbucks, Subway, Taco Bell 🛏 7-11, Exxon, Fairfield Inn, Holiday Inn Express, Mapco, SpringHill Suites ⬛ $Tree, Advance Parts, AutoZone, Costco/gas, Goodyear/auto, Kroger/gas, Lowe's, Martin's Foods, Mazda, Michael's, Sam's Club/gas, Tesla
178 b a	US 250, Broad St, Short Pump, **N** 🍴 7-11, Exxon, Wawa/dsl 🍴 Blaze Pizza, BurgerWorks, Capital Alehouse, Chipotle Mexican, Corner Bakery Cafe, DQ, Dunkin', Firehouse Subs, Five Guys, Hondo's Rest., Joey's Hotdogs, Leonardo's Pizza,

Exit #	Services
178 b a	Continued Moe's SW Grill, Noodles, Panera Bread, Potbelly, Silver Diner, Starbucks, Taziki's 🛏 Comfort Suites, Courtyard, Extended Stay America, Hampton Inn, Hilton Garden, Homestead Suites, Hyatt Place, Residence Inn ⬛ CarMax, CVS Drug, Firestone/auto, Ford, Marshall's, Ross, Verizon, **S** 🍴 7-11, Shell 🍴 Arby's, Bertucci's, BJ's Rest., Bonefish Grill, Buffalo Wild Wings, Burger King, Capt D's, Carolina Alehouse, Carrabba's, Cheesecake Factory, Chick-fil-A, Chili's, Chipotle Mexican, Chuy's Mexican, Dave&Buster's, Domino's, Genghis Grill, HoneyBaked Ham, Jason's Deli, Jersey Mike's Subs, Jimmy John's, Kanpai, KFC, Kona Grill, LJSilver, Longhorn Steaks, Maggiano's Italian, McDonald's, Olive Garden, Panda Express, Panera Bread, Plaza Azteca, Qdoba, Shula's Steaks, Sonic, Starbucks, Taco Bell, TGIFriday's, Wendy's 🛏 Candlewood Suites, Hilton, Hyatt House, Wingate Inn ⬛ $Tree, AT&T, Barnes&Noble, Best Buy, Buick/Chevrolet/GMC, CarQuest, Dick's, Dillard's, GNC, Hobby Lobby, Home Depot, Kohl's, Kroger, Lowe's, Macy's, Martin's Foods, Nissan, Nordstrom, NTB, Petco, Petsmart, REI, Staples, Steinmart, Target, Tom Leonard's Mkt, Trader Joe's, Verizon, Walmart, Whole Foods Mkt, World Mkt
177	I-295, to I-95 N to Washington, to Norfolk, VA Beach, Williamsburg
175	VA 288, Chesterfield
173	VA 623, to Rockville, Manakin, 0-2 mi **S** 🍴 Exxon/dsl, Shell/dsl, Valero/Subway/dsl 🍴 McDonald's, Sunset Grill, Taco Bell ⬛ $General, Food Lion, vet
169mm	Ⓡ🅂 both lanes, full 🦽 facilities, litter barrels, petwalk, 🍴, 🅿, vending
167	VA 617, to Goochland, Oilville, **N** 🍴 Exxon/dsl, **S** 🍴 BP/dsl
159	US 522, to Goochland, Gum Spring, **N** 🍴 Exxon/dsl, **S** 🍴 BP/DQ/dsl, Citgo
152	VA 629, Hadensville, 1 mi **S** 🍴 BP, Liberty
148	VA 605, Shannon Hill
143	VA 208, to Louisa, Ferncliff, **N** ⬛ Small Country Camping (7mi), **S** 🍴 Citgo/dsl, Exxon/dsl
136	US 15, to Gordonsville, Zion Crossroads, **N** 🍴 Sheetz/dsl 🍴 Arby's, Dunkin', IHOP, Lelo's Pizza, Popeye's, Subway, Taco Bell, Wendy's 🛏 Best Western+ ⬛ Advance Parts, Lowe's, Verizon, Walmart, **S** 🍴 BP/McDonald's/dsl/24hr, Exxon/Burger King/dsl, Shell/dsl/scales 🍴 Crescent Rest.
129	VA 616, Keswick, Boyd Tavern
124	US 250, to Shadwell, 2 mi **N** 🍴 BP, Exxon, Mobil/dsl, Shell, Speedway 🍴 Applebee's, Bojangle's, Burger King, Chick-fil-A, Chipotle, Dunkin', Guadalajara Mexican, Hardee's, Jersey Mike's, Jimmy John's, McDonald's, Shadwell's Rest., Starbucks, Taco Bell, TipTop Rest., Wendy's 🛏 Hilton Garden ⬛ 🄷, Audi/VW, BMW, CarMax, Ford, Giant Foods, Kia, Mercedes, Porsche, Rite Aid, Toyota, **S** 🛏 Comfort Inn
123mm	Rivanna River

RICHMOND

CHARLOTTESVILLE

[gas] = gas [food] = food [lodging] = lodging [other] = other [Rs] = rest stop   Copyright 2022 - The Next EXIT

INTERSTATE 64 Cont'd

Exit #	Services
121	VA 20, to Charlottesville, Scottsville, N [food] BP/dsl, S [other] KOA (10mi), to Monticello
120	VA 631, 5th St, to Charlottesville, N [gas] Exxon/dsl, Sunoco/dsl [food] Burger King, Domino's, Hardee's, Subway, Taco Bell, Waffle House [lodging] Holiday Inn, Sleep Inn [other] CVS Drug, Family$, Food Lion
118b a	US 29, to Lynchburg, Charlottesville, N [gas] [other] [H], services N on US 220, to UVA
114	VA 637, to Ivy
113mm	[Rs] wb, full [&] facilities, litter barrels, petwalk, [C], [A], vending
111mm	Mechum River
108mm	Stockton Creek
107	US 250, Crozet, 1 mi N [gas] BP/dsl, Citgo, Exxon/dsl, 1 mi S [other] Misty Mtn Camping
105mm	[Rs] eb, full [&] facilities, litter barrels, petwalk, [C], [A], vending
104mm	scenic area eb, litter barrels, no truck or buses
100mm	scenic area eb, hist marker, litter barrels, no truck or buses
99	US 250, to Waynesboro, Afton, N [lodging] Colony Motel [other] Skyline Drive, to Blue Ridge Pkwy, to Shenandoah NP, S [lodging] Afton Inn
96	VA 622, to Lyndhurst, Waynesboro, 3 mi N [gas] Shell, Speedway [lodging] Quality Inn [other] Waynesboro Camping
95mm	South River
94	US 340, to Stuarts Draft, Waynesboro, N [gas] 7-11/dsl, Exxon/dsl [food] Applebee's, Buffalo Wild Wings, Cracker Barrel, Five Guys, Golden Corral, KFC, Outback Steaks, Panera Bread, Pizza Hut, Plaza Azteca, Ruby Tuesday, Silk Road Rest., Sonic, Starbucks, Waffle House, Wendy's [lodging] Best Western+, Comfort Inn, Days Inn, Holiday Inn Express, Residence Inn, Super 8 [other] [H], Home Depot, Lowe's, Martin's Food/gas, Verizon, vet, Walmart, Waynesboro N 340 Camping (9mi), S [gas] Mobil/dsl [food] Chick-fil-A, McAlister's Deli, McDonald's [other] Aldi Foods, AT&T, Books-A-Million, GNC, Kohl's, Michael's, Petsmart, Ross, Target
91	Va 608, to Stuarts Draft, Fishersville, N [gas] Citgo/Subway (1mi), Shell/dsl [lodging] Hampton Inn [other] [H], Eaver's Tires, S [gas] Sheetz/dsl [food] McDonald's, Wendy's [other] Shenadoah Acres Camping (8mi), Walnut Hills Camping (9mi)
89mm	Christians Creek
87	I-81, N to Harrisonburg, S to Roanoke
I-64 and I-81 run together 20 miles. See I-81, exits 195-220.	
55	US 11, to VA 39, N [gas] Exxon [food] Burger King, Crystal Chinese, Naples Pizza, Ruby Tuesday, Waffle House [lodging] Best Western+, Sleep Inn, Super 8, Wingate Inn [other] $Tree, Ford, Lowe's, Stonewall Jackson Museum, Verizon, Walmart, S [gas] Marathon/7-11/Subway, Mobil/DQ/dsl [food] Applebee's, Country Cookin [lodging] Best Western, Comfort Inn, Country Inn&Suites, Holiday Inn Express, Motel 6
50	US 60, rd 623, to Kerrs Creek, Lexington
43	rd 780, to Goshen
35	VA 269, rd 850, Longdale Furnace
33mm	truck [Rs] eb
29	VA 269, VA 42 E, S [gas] Sunoco/dsl
27	US 60 W, US 220 S, VA 629, Clifton Forge, N [other] to Douthat SP, S [gas] BP/dsl, Exxon [food] Bella Pizza, Pizza Hut (2mi) [other] CVS Drug, Family$, Kroger
24	US 60, US 220, Clifton Forge, 1 mi S [gas] Shell/dsl [food] DQ, Hardee's [other] auto repair
21	to rd 696, Low Moor, N [gas] Loves/McDonald's/Subway/dsl/scales/24hr, S [gas] Exxon [food] Penny's Diner [lodging] Travelodge [other] [H]

COVINGTON (vertical side label)

Exit #	Services
16	US 60 W, US 220 N, to Hot Springs, Covington, N [gas] BP/Subway/dsl, Exxon/dsl, Shell [food] Burger King, Cucci's, San Jua Mexican, Western Sizzlin [lodging] Best Value Inn, Hampton Inn Magnuson Hotel, Pinehurst Hotel [other] to ski area, S [food] McDonald's [lodging] Compare Inn, [food] Taco Bell
14	VA 154, to Hot Springs, Covington, N [gas] Citgo, Exxon/Arby' [food] KFC, LJ Silver, Subway, Wendy's [other] $General, Advanc Parts, AutoZone, CVS Drug, Family$, Food Lion, URGENT CARE Verizon, S [food] Applebee's, China House, Trani's Grille [other] $Tree Chevrolet, Walmart
10	US 60 E, VA 159 S, Callaghan, S [gas] Marathon/dsl/LP
7	rd 661
2.5mm	Welcome Ctr eb, full [&] facilities, litter barrels, no trucks, pet walk, [C], [A]
1	Jerry's Run Trail, N to Allegheny Trail
0mm	Virginia/West Virginia state line

INTERSTATE 66

Exit #	Services
77mm	Constitution Ave, to Lincoln Mem. I-66 begins/ends in Washington, DC.
76mm	Potomac River, T Roosevelt Memorial Bridge
75	US 50 W (from eb), to Arlington Blvd, G Wash Pkwy, I-395, US 1 S Iwo Jima Mon
73	US 29, Lee Hwy, Key Bridge, to Rosslyn, N [lodging] Marriott, [lodging] Holiday Inn
72	to US 29, Lee Hwy, Spout Run Pkwy (from eb, no EZ return), N [gas] Shell [lodging] Virginia Inn, S [food] Starbucks, Tarbouch Gri [other] CVS Drug, Giant Foods, Walgreens
71	VA 120, Glebe Rd (no EZ return from wb), N [other] [H], S [gas] Sunoco [food] Booeymonger Grill, IHOP, Melting Pot, PF Chang [lodging] Comfort Inn, Holiday Inn
69	US 29, Sycamore St, Falls Church, N [gas] Exxon/7-11, S [lodging] EconoLodge [other] vet
68	Westmoreland St (from eb), same as 69
67	to I-495 N (from wb), to Baltimore, Dulles Airport
66b a	VA 7, Leesburg Pike, to Tysons Corner, Falls Church, N [gas] Exxon, Sunoco [food] China King, Jason's Deli, Ledo Pizza, Noodles& Co, Starbucks, Subway, Tara Thai [other] 7-11, Trader Joe's, Verizon, Whole Foods Mkt, S [gas] Citgo [food] Baja Fresh, Domino's, Jimmy John's, McDonald's, Starbucks, Subway [other] CVS Drug Giant Foods, GNC, Kia, Staples, vet, Volvo
64b a	I-495 S, to Richmond
62	VA 243, Nutley St, to Vienna, S [gas] Citgo [food] Baja Fresh, Domino's, McDonald's, Starbucks, Subway [other] CVS Drug, Michael's, Safeway Foods/gas, Walgreens
60	VA 123, to Fairfax, S [gas] Exxon, Shell, Sunoco [food] 29 Diner, Denny's, Freddy's Steakburgers, Fuddruckers, Hooters, McDonald's, Outback Steaks, Panera Bread, Papa John's, Red Lobster Smashburger, Subway [lodging] Best Western, Hampton Inn, Holiday Inn Express, Residence Inn [other] Chevrolet, CVS Drug, Kia, Mazda, Rite Aid, Subaru, to George Mason U, Toyota
57b a	US 50, to Dulles Airport, N [food] Brio Tuscan, Cheesecake Factory [lodging] Extended Stay America, Marriott [other] access to same as 55 JC Penney, Lord&Taylor, Macy's, S [gas] BP, Shell/dsl [food] Chipotle Chuy's, Jimmy John's, McDonald's, Wendy's [lodging] Comfort Inn rest., Courtyard, SpringHill Suites [other] AT&T, Ford, Giant Foods Honda, Nissan, NRA Museum, VW/Volvo, Walmart
55	Fairfax Co Pkwy, to US 29, N [gas] Exxon, Sunoco [food] Applebee's Blue Iguana Café, Burger King, Cantina Italiana, Chick-fil-A Chipotle, Dunkin', Guapo's, Jason's Deli, Jersey Mike's, Joe' Crabshack, Logan's Roadhouse, McDonald's, Noodles&Co

DC AREA (vertical side label)

VA (side tab)

WAYNESBORO (vertical side label)

LEXINGTON (vertical side label)

⬆🅴 INTERSTATE 66 Cont'd

M A N A S S A S *(vertical side label)*

55	Continued
	Olive Garden, Pizza Hut, Red Robin, Starbucks, Subway, Taco Bell, Wendy's 🛏 Hyatt Regency, Residence Inn ⊙ 🅗, Best Buy, BJ's Whse/gas, Dick's, Fair Oaks Mall, GNC, Kohl's, Michael's, Petsmart, Target, Verizon, Walmart, Whole Foods Mkt, World Mkt
53b a	VA 28, to Centreville, **S** same as 52, Dulles Airport, Manassas Museum
52	US 29, to Bull Run Park, Centreville, **N** 🅿 Sunoco/dsl ⊙ Bull Run Park/RV Dump, Goodyear/auto, **S** 🅿 Exxon, Sunoco/dsl 🍽 Charlie Chang's, Dickey's BBQ, Five Guys, IHOP, My Thai, Pancho Villa, Panda Express, Pizza Hut, Starbucks, Subway ⊙ $Tree, Advance Parts, AT&T, Giant Foods, SpringHill Suites, Trader Joe's, USPO, vet, Walgreens
49mm	℞ both lanes, full (facilities) facilities, litter barrels, petwalk, 🅲, 🅿
47b a	VA 234, to Manassas, **N** 🅿 Shell/dsl 🍽 Cracker Barrel, Golden Corral, Jerry's Subs, Uno, Wendy's 🛏 Courtyard, Holiday Inn Express, La Quinta, Wyndham Garden ⊙ Duluth Trading Co, Kohl's, Manassas Nat Bfd, Old Navy, **S** 🅿 7-11, BP, Exxon, RaceWay/dsl, Shell/repair, Sunoco 🍽 Arby's, Baja Fresh, Bob Evans, Burger King, Cafe Rio, Checker's, Chick-fil-A, Chili's, China Palace, Chipotle Mexican, ChuckECheese's, CiCi's, City Grille, Coldstone, Denny's, Domino's, DQ, Dunkin', Firehouse Subs, Food Lion, Great American Buffet, Hibachi Buffet, Hooters, IHOP, Jersey Mike's, Jimmy John's, KFC, Logan's Roadhouse, McDonald's, Olive Garden, Panda Express, Panera Bread, Papa John's, Pizza Hut, Pollo Campero, Popeye's, Potbelly's, Red Hot&Blue BBQ, Red Lobster, Starbucks, Subway, Subway, Taco Bell, TGIFriday's, Wendy's 🛏 Best Western, Comfort Suites, Days Inn, Hampton Inn, Holiday Inn, Quality Inn, Red Roof Inn, Residence Inn, Woodspring Suites ⊙ $Tree, Advance Parts, Aldi Foods, AT&T, AutoZone, Barnes&Noble, Best Buy, Buick/GMC, Burlington Coats, Chevrolet, Costco/gas, CVS Drug, Dick's, Family$, Giant Foods, GNC, Home Depot, Honda, Lowe's, Macy's, Marshall's, Merchant Auto Ctr, Michael's, Mr Tire, NTB, Office Depot, PepBoys, Petsmart, Reines RV Ctr, Ross, Shopper's Foods, Staples, Toyota, Tuesday Morning, URGENT CARE, Verizon, vet, Walgreens, Walmart
44	VA 234 S, Manassas, **S** ⊙ to Bristoe Sta Bfd SP
43b a	US 29, to Warrenton, Gainesville, **S** 🅿 7-11, BJ's/gas, Sunoco/dsl, WaWa 🍽 BJ's Rest, Burger King, Chick-fil-A, Chili's, Chipotle, Coldstone, Domino's, Famous Dave's, Firebirds Grill, Five Guys, Grafton St Rest., IHOP, Joe's Pizza/Subs, KFC, McDonald's, MOD Pizza, Out of the Blue Seafood, Panera Bread, Pei-Wei, Potbelly, Qdoba, Smashburger, Starbucks, Subway, Taco Bell, Uncle Julio's 🛏 Hampton Inn, SpringHill Suites, Woodspring Suites ⊙ Advance Parts, Best Buy, Cabela's, CVS Drug, Giant Food/drug, GNC, Lowe's, Petsmart, Piedmont Tire/auto, Target, Verizon, Walgreens
40	US 15, Haymarket, **N** ⊙ Greenville Farms Camping (5mi), 🅗, **S** 🅿 Sheetz/dsl 🍽 Burapa Cafe, Chick-fil-A, Foster's Grill, Giuseppe's Italian, Little Caesar's, McDonald's, Papa John's, Penn Sta Subs, Starbucks, Subway, Young Chow Cafe ⊙ CVS Drug, Food Lion, Kohl's, Verizon, Walmart
31	VA 245, to Old Tavern, **1 mi N** 🅿 Sunoco/dsl ⊙ USPO
28	US 17 S, Marshall, **N** 🅿 BP/McDonald's/dsl 🍽 Anthony's Pizza, Foster's Grille, Great Wall Chinese, Old Salem Cafe, Subway ⊙ Food Lion, vet
27	VA 55 E, Rd 647, Marshall, **1 mi N** 🅿 Citgo/dsl, Exxon/dsl/LP 🍽 Marshall Diner
23	US 17 N, VA 55, Delaplane (no re-entry from eb)

(map graphic of Virginia showing Richmond area with labels: Manquin, Buckeye, Mechanicsville, Tuckahoe, Richmond, Quinton, Oakland, Lee Park, Brookbury, Glendale, Beulah, Fair Hill, Chester, Walthall, Hopewell, Colonial Heights, Petersburg, Prince George, Fort Davis, Burgess — routes 95, 64, 295, VA)

20mm	Goose Creek
18	VA 688, Markham
13	VA 79, to VA 55, Linden, Front Royal, **S** 🅿 7-11/dsl, Exxon/dsl 🍽 Applehouse Rest./BBQ/gifts ⊙ Skyline Drive, to Shenandoah NP
11mm	Manassas Run
7mm	Shenandoah River
6	US 340, US 522, to Winchester, Front Royal, **N** 🅿 7-11, Mobil/7-11/dsl 🍽 Applebee's, Checkers, China City Buffet, Cracker Barrel, IHOP, Ledo Pizza, Los Potrillos, McAlister's Deli, Mikado, Panda Express, Roy Rogers, Starbucks, TGIFriday's, Tropical Cafe 🛏 TownePlace Suites ⊙ $Tree, Aldi Foods, AT&T, Buick/GMC, Ford, GNC, Lowe's, PetCo, Staples, Target, URGENT CARE, Walmart, **S** 🅿 7-11, Exxon/Dunkin'/Subway, Shell 🍽 McDonald's 🛏 Hampton Inn ⊙ Poe's Southfork Camping (2mi)
1b a	I-81, N to Winchester, S to Roanoke
0mm	I-66 begins/ends on I-81, exit 300.

⬆🅽 INTERSTATE 77

Exit #	Services
67mm	Virginia/West Virginia state line, East River Mtn
66	VA 598, to East River Mtn
64	US 52, VA 61, to Rocky Gap
62	VA 606, to South Gap
62mm	**Welcome Ctr sb, full 🅿 facilities, info, litter barrels, petwalk, 🅲, 🅿, vending**
59mm	℞ nb, full 🅿 facilities, litter barrels, petwalk, 🅲, 🅿, vending
58	US 52, to Bastian, **E** 🅿 BP/Front Porch Cafe/dsl, **W** 🅿 Exxon/Circle K, ❤Love's/Arby's/dsl/scales/24hr
56mm	runaway ramp nb
52	US 52, VA 42, Bland, **E** 🅿 Sunoco 🍽 Subway ⊙ $General, **W** 🅿 Circle K/DQ/dsl 🛏 Big Walker Motel
51.5mm	weigh sta both lanes
48mm	Big Walker Mtn
47	VA 717, 6 mi **W** ⊙ to Deer Trail Park/NF Camping
41	VA 610, Peppers Ferry, Wytheville, **E** 🍽 Sagebrush Steaks 🛏 Best Western, Sleep Inn, Super 8, **W** 🅿 Exxon/dsl/scales/24hr, TA/BP/Country Pride/Popeye's/Subway/Taco Bell/dsl/scales/24hr/@ 🍽 Southern Diner 🛏 Comfort Suites, Country Inn&Suites, Fairfield Inn, Hampton Inn, Ramada Inn, Tru Hilton
40	I-81 S, to Bristol, US 52 N
	I-77 and I-81 run together 9 mi. See I-81, exits 73-80.
32	I-81 N, to Roanoke
26mm	New River
24	VA 69, to Poplar Camp, **E** ⊙ New River Trail Info Ctr, to Shot Tower HP, **W** 🅿 Circle K/Subway/dsl
19	VA 620, **W** ⊙ 🛏

W Y T H E V I L L E *(vertical side label)*

VA *(side tab)*

= gas ⑪ = food 🏨 = lodging 🄾 = other ℞ = rest stop   Copyright 2022 - The Next EXIT

INTERSTATE 77 Cont'd

Exit #	Services
14	US 58, US 221, to Hillsville, Galax, E ⛽ Mobil/Subway ⑪ Peking Palace 🏨 Red Carpet Inn 🄾 H, LakeRidge RV Resort (14mi), W ⛽ BP, Exxon/dsl, Gulf/dsl/24hr ⑪ McDonald's, Pizza Inn, Shoney's, TCBY, Wendy's 🏨 Comfort Inn, Hampton Inn, Holiday Inn Express, Motel 6, Quality Inn, Super 8 🄾 Carrollwood Camping, Chevrolet
8	VA 148, VA 775, to Fancy Gap, E ⛽ Gulf ⑪ Fancy Gap Cafe (2mi) 🏨 Lakeview Motel/rest., Mountain Top Motel 🄾 $General, Chance's Creek RV Ctr, KOA (2mi), to Blue Ridge Pkwy, USPO, W ⛽ BP/dsl, Exxon/Circle K/dsl 🏨 Countryview Inn, Scottish Inn
6.5mm	runaway truck ramp sb
4.5mm	runaway truck ramp sb
3mm	runaway truck ramp sb
1	VA 620, E ⛽ ♥Love's/McDonald's/Subway/dsl/scales/24hr
.5mm	Welcome Ctr nb, full 🚻 facilities, info, litter barrels, petwalk, 🚮, 🏕
0mm	Virginia/North Carolina state line

INTERSTATE 81

Exit #	Services
324mm	Virginia/West Virginia state line
323	rd 669, to US 11, Whitehall, E ⛽ Exxon, W ⛽ ◆FLYING J/Denny's/Subway/dsl/LP/scales/24hr
321	rd 672, Clearbrook, E ⛽ Citgo/Old Stone Cafe/dsl ⑪ Woolen Mills Grill
320mm	Welcome Ctr sb, full 🚻 facilities, litter barrels, petwalk, 🚮, 🏕, vending
317	US 11, Stephenson, E ⑪ Chick-fil-A, Guan's Garden, Las Trancas, McDonald's, Subway, Tropical Smoothie Café, TX Roadhouse 🄾 AT&T, Lowe's, Petsmart, Target, Verizon, W ⛽ Exxon/Dunkin'/dsl, Sheetz, Shell/7-11/Burger King, Sunoco/dsl ⑪ Denny's, Pizza Hut/Taco Bell 🏨 Comfort Inn, EconoLodge, Holiday Inn Express (3mi) 🄾 H, Candy Hill Camping
315	VA 7, Winchester, E ⛽ Exxon, Sheetz/dsl ⑪ Bamboo Garden, Ledo's Pizza, Little Caesars, Sonic, Starbucks, Waffle House 🏨 TownePlace Suites 🄾 $Tree, Chrysler/Dodge/Jeep, GNC, Goodyear/auto, Martin's Foods/gas, PetCo, URGENT CARE, Walgreens, W ⛽ Exxon/Dunkin'/Subway, Liberty/dsl, Shell/dsl ⑪ 5 Guys Burgers, Apple Blossom Diner, Arby's, Camino Real Mexican, KFC, McDonald's, NIK Italian, Pizza Hut, Wendy's 🏨 Hampton Inn, Winchester Inn 🄾 AutoZone, CVS Drug, Family$, Food Lion, Food Maxx, Sharp Shopper Mkt, TrueValue
314mm	Abrams Creek
313	US 17/50/522, Winchester, E ⛽ Exxon/Baskin-Robbins/Dunkin'/Subway, Liberty/dsl, Mobil/7-11/dsl, Shell/dsl ⑪ Apple Valley Diner, Chinatown, Cracker Barrel, Golden Corral, Hibachi Grill, IHOP, Los Tolteco's Mexican, TX Steaks, Umberto's Pizza 🏨 Aloft Hotel, Candlewood Suites, Fairfield Inn, Holiday Inn, Red Roof Inn, Sleep Inn, Super 8, Travelodge 🄾 BigLots, Costco/gas, Food Lion, Jo-Ann Fabrics, Nissan, vet, W ⑪ Sheetz/dsl ⑪ Bob Evans, Buca Italian, Chili's, China Jade, China Wok, Chipotle Mexican, ChuckECheese's, CiCi's, Coldstone, Dickey's BBQ, Five Guys, Glory Days Grill, Ichiban Japanese, Jimmy John's, KFC, Longhorn Steaks, McDonald's, Okinawa Steaks, Olive Garden, Panera Bread, Perkins, Rancho Mexican, Red Lobster, Roy Rogers, Ruby Tuesday, Subway, Taco Bell, TGIFriday's, Waffle House, Wendy's 🏨 Best Western, Hampton Inn, Hilton Garden, Wingate Inn 🄾 $Tree, AT&T, Belk, Best Buy,
313	Continued Books-A-Million, Dick's, Hobby Lobby, Home Depot, JC Penney, Kohl's, Lowe's, Martin's Foods, Merchants Tire, Michael's, Old Navy, PepBoys, Petsmart, Ross, Staples, Target, TJ Maxx, to Shenandoah U, URGENT CARE, Verizon, Walgreens, Walmart
310	VA 37, to US 50W, W ⛽ Citgo/dsl, Shell/7-11/dsl ⑪ Carrraba's, McDonald's, Outback Steaks, Subway 🏨 Country Inn& Suites 🄾 H, Aldi Foods, Camping World, Candy Hill Camping (6mi), CarQuest, Honda, Volvo, VW
307	VA 277, Stephens City, E ⛽ Liberty/dsl, Shell/Burger King/dsl, Shell/Subway/dsl ⑪ Arby's, China House, Del Rio Mexican, Domino's, Ginger Asian, KFC/Taco Bell, McDonald's, Pizza Hut, Roma Italian, Waffle House, Wendy's 🏨 Comfort Inn, Holiday Inn Express 🄾 $General, 7-11, Advance Parts, AutoZone, Food Lion, Martin's Foods/gas, Rite Aid, Verizon, W ⛽ Exxon, Dunkin', Sheetz/dsl
304mm	weigh sta both lanes
302	rd 627, Middletown, E ⛽ Exxon/dsl, W ⛽ 7-11, Liberty/dsl ⑪ McDonald's 🏨 Econolodge 🄾 $General, to Wayside Theatre
300	I-66 E, to Washington, Shenandoah NP, Skyline Dr
298	US 11, Strasburg, E ⛽ Exxon/McDonald's/dsl/LP, Shell/7-11/dsl ⑪ Anthony's Pizza, Arby's, Burger King, Castiglia Italian, Ciro's Pizza, Denny's, Golden China, Great Wall Buffet 🏨 Fairfield Inn, Ramada Inn 🄾 Advance Parts, Family$, Food Lion, Verizon, W 🄾 Battle of Cedar Grove Camping, to Belle Grove Plantation
296	US 48, VA 55, Strasburg, E 🄾 museums
291	rd 651, Toms Brook, E 🏨 Budget Inn (3mi), W ⑪ ♥Love's /Arby's/dsl/scales/24hr, 🅿️TA/DQ/Subway/dsl/scales/24hr 🄾 truckwash/repair
283	VA 42, Woodstock, E ⛽ Liberty/7-11, Sheetz, Shell/Dunkin ⑪ Arby's, Burger King, China Wok, KFC, Las Trancas, McDonald's, Pizza Hut, Taco Bell, Tony's Pizza, Wendy's 🏨 Comfort Inn, Hampton Inn, Holiday Inn Express 🄾 H, CVS Drug, Family$, Food Lion, Rite Aid, to Massanutten Military Academy, W ⛽ Exxon/dsl, Sunoco ⑪ China Wok, Cracker Barrel, Domino's, Paisano's Pizza, Subway 🄾 $Tree, Ford, Lowe's, NAPA CarQuest, Walmart
279	VA 185, rd 675, Edinburg, E ⛽ Exxon/dsl, Shell/dsl ⑪ Sal's Italian Bistro 🄾 auto repair, Creekside Camping (2mi), USPO
277	rd 614, Bowmans Crossing
273	VA 292, RD 703, Mt Jackson, E ⛽ 7-11, Exxon/dsl, Liberty/dsl/scales/24hr, Sheetz/dsl/scales/24hr ⑪ Burger King, China King, Denny's, Italian Touch, Subway 🏨 Motel 6 🄾 $General, Food Lion, to Mt Jackson Hist Dist, USPO
269	rd 730, to US 11, Shenandoah Caverns, E ⛽ Shell/dsl, W 🄾 Shenandoah Valley Camping
269mm	N Fork Shenandoah River
264	US 211, New Market, E ⛽ Exxon/Subway/dsl, Liberty/dsl, Mobil/dsl, Shell/dsl ⑪ Appleseed's Rest., Burger King, Italian Job, McDonald's 🏨 Quality Inn 🄾 Endless Caverns Camping, Skyline Dr, to Shenandoah NP, W ⛽ 7-11 🏨 Days Inn 🄾 to New Market Bfd SHP
262mm	℞ both lanes, full 🚻 facilities, litter barrels, petwalk, 🚮, 🏕 vending
257	US 11, VA 259, to Broadway, 3-5 mi E ⛽ Liberty/7-11/Burger King/dsl 🄾 Endless Caverns Camping, KOA
251	US 11, Harrisonburg, W ⛽ Exxon/dsl, 🅿️TA/Subway/dsl/scales/24hr 🏨 Economy Inn
247b a	US 33, Harrisonburg, E ⛽ Citgo/dsl, Exxon/dsl, Royal/dsl, Sheetz/dsl, Shell/dsl, Walmart ⑪ Applebee's, Aroma Buffet, Bob Evans, Bravo Italian, Bruster's, Buffalo Wild Wings,

WOODSTOCK

WINCHESTER

Copyright 2022 - The Next EXIT ®   🅖 = gas   🅕 = food   🅗 = lodging   🅞 = other   🆁🆂 = rest stop

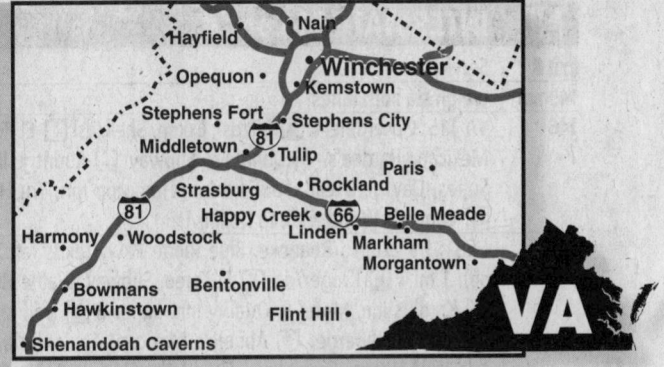

⬆N   INTERSTATE 81 Cont'd

H A R R I S O N B U R G

247b a   Continued
Burger King, Chick-fil-A, Chili's, Chipotle, CiCi's Pizza, Cook Out, Domino's, Dunkin', El Charro Mexican, Firehouse Subs, Five Guys, Franco's Pizza, Golden Corral, Great Wok, IHOP, Jess' Lunch, Jimmy John's, McAlister's Deli, McDonald's, O'Charley's, O'Neill's Grill, Outback Steaks, Panera Bread, Qdoba, Quaker Steak&Lube, Red Lobster, Ruby Tuesday, South Fork BBQ, Subway, Taco Bell, Tilted Kilt, TX Roadhouse, Waffle House, Wendy's, Which Wich?, Wood Grill Buffet 🅗 Best Western, Candlewood Suites, Comfort Inn, Courtyard, Doubletree, EconoLodge, Fairfield Inn, Hampton Inn, Motel 6, Quality Inn, Residence Inn, Sleep Inn 🅞 $Tree, AT&T, Barnes&Noble, Belk, Best Buy, Books-A-Million, Cadillac/Chevrolet, Costco/gas, Dick's, Firestone/auto, Home Depot, JC Penney, Kohl's, Kroger, Lowe's, Martin's Foods/gas, Michael's, Nissan, Old Navy, PetCo, Petsmart, Ross, Staples, Target, TJ Maxx, to Shenandoah NP, to Skyline Dr, Tuesday Morning, URGENT CARE, Verizon, Walmart/ McDonald's, **W** 🅖 Exxon/dsl, Liberty/dsl, Royal/dsl, Sheetz/ dsl 🅕 Arby's, Ciro's Pizza, DQ, Dragon Palace, Golden China, Hardee's, KFC, Kyoto, L'Italia, Little Caesars, McDonald's, Papa John's, Sam's Hotdogs, Subway 🅞 Advance Parts, BigLots, CVS Drug, Family$, Food Lion, URGENT CARE

245   VA 659, Port Republic Rd, **E** 🅕 Campus Corner, Exxon/dsl, Liberty/dsl, Royal/dsl 🅕 China Express, Corgan's Publick House, El Charro, McDonald's, Subway, Tropical Smoothie, Vito's Italian 🅗 Days Inn 🅞 🅗, CVS Drug, Food Lion, **W** 🅕 Asian City, Jimmy John's, Starbucks 🅞 to James Madison U

243   US 11, to Harrisonburg, 0-2 mi **W** 🅖 Exxon/dsl, Harrisonburg Travel Ctr/diner/dsl/scales, Liberty, Sheetz/dsl, Shell/7-11/dsl 🅕 Burger King, Cracker Barrel, Griddle&Grill, McDonald's, Pano's Rest., Pizza Hut, Subway, Taco Bell 🅗 Country Inn Suites, Hampton Inn, Holiday Inn Express, Microtel, Motel 6, Ramada Inn, Super 8 🅞 $General, Advance Parts, AutoZone, CarMax, Family$, Ford, Honda, Hyundai, Kia, Lincoln, Subaru, Toyota, USPO

240   VA 257, rd 682, Mount Crawford, **E** 🅖 Shell/7-11/dsl 🅕 McDonald's, **W** 🅖 Exxon/Burger King/dsl (1mi)

235   VA 256, Weyers Cave, **E** 🅖 Shell/dsl, **W** 🅖 BP/Subway/dsl, Exxon/dsl 🅞 Freightliner, to Grand Caverns

232mm   🆁🆂 both lanes, full 🅗 facilities, litter barrels, petwalk, 🅲, 🏃, vending

227   rd 612, Verona, **E** 🅖 BP/Subway/dsl 🅕 Waffle Inn, **W** 🅖 7-11/Wendy's, Exxon, Shell/dsl 🅕 Burger King, Ciro's Pizza, Hardee's, McDonald's 🅗 Knights Inn 🅞 $General, antiques, Food Lion, Good Sam RV Park (3mi), Rite Aid

225   VA 262, Woodrow Wilson Pkwy, **E** 🅗 Motel 6, **W** 🅗 Days Inn, Holiday Inn/rest.

222   US 250, Staunton, **E** 🅖 BP, Royal/dsl 🅕 Cracker Barrel, Hometown Grill, McDonald's, Mrs Rowe's Rest., TX Steaks 🅗 Best Western, Red Roof Inn, Sleep Inn, **W** 🅖 Sheetz, Speedway/ dsl 🅕 Baskin-Robbins/Dunkin', Burger King, Chili's, Country Cookin, Firehouse Subs, KFC, Massaki Japanese, Pizza Hut, Starbucks, Waffle House 🅗 Comfort Inn, EconoLodge 🅞 American Frontier Culture Museum, AT&T, auto repair, AutoZone, Lowe's, Martin's Foods/gas, Toyota, URGENT CARE, Walmart/Subway

221   I-64 E, to Charlottesville, Skyline Dr, Shenandoah NP

220   VA 262, to US 11, Staunton, **1 mi W** 🅖 Citgo, Exxon, Shell 🅕 A&W/LJ Silver, Applebee's, Arby's, Burger King, CiCi's Pizza, El Puerto, Jimmy John's, Kathy's Rest., Kline's Dairy Bar, Maria's Italian, McDonald's, Papa John's, Red Lobster, Sam's HotDogs, Sauced Grill, Subway, Taco Bell, Wendy's 🅗 Budget Inn, Hampton Inn 🅞 $General, $Tree, Advance Parts, Belk,

S T A U N T O N

---

220   Continued
Buick/GMC, Cadillac/Chevrolet, Chrysler/Dodge/Jeep, CVS Drug, Food Lion, Ford/Lincoln, Harley-Davidson, Honda, Hyundai, JC Penney, Kia/Mazda, Kroger/dsl, Nissan, NTB, Obaugh RV Ctr, Petco, Staples, Subaru, TJ Maxx, Verizon, vet, VW

217   Rd 654, to Mint Spring, Stuarts Draft, **E** 🅕 GB/dsl 🅗 Days Inn, **W** 🅖 Exxon/Circle K/dsl/24hr, Liberty/LP 🅗 Relax Inn 🅞 KOA

213b a   US 11, US 340, Greenville, **E** 🅕 BP/Subway, ⬤Loves/McDonalds/dsl/scales/24hr, 🅿🅸🅻🅾🆃/Arby's/scales/ds/24hr, Shell 🅕 Edelweiss Rest. 🅗 Hometowne Inn 🅞 KOA (3mi)

205   Rd 606, Raphine, **E** 🅕 BP/dsl, Exxon/Burger King/dsl, Fuel City/ Smiley's BBQ/dsl/24hr, Petro/Iron Skillet/Papa John's/Popeye's/ Subway/dsl/scales/24hr/@ 🅞 Blue Beacon, **W** 🅕 🅿🅸🅻🅾🆃 Wendy's/dsl/scales/24hr 🅗 Comfort Inn/rest. 🅞 Peterbilt

200   RD 710, Fairfield, **E** 🅕 BP/McDonald's/dsl, Pure 🅕 Frank's Pizza, **W** 🅖 Exxon/Subway/dsl, Shell/dsl

199mm   🆁🆂 sb, full 🅗 facilities, litter barrels, petwalk, 🅲, 🏃, vending

195   US 11, Lee Hwy, **E** 🅗 Maple Hall Country Inn, **W** 🅖 Exxon/dsl, TA/Shell/IHOP/dsl/scales/24hr/@ 🅗 Days Inn, Howard Johnson, Quality Inn 🅞 Lee-Hi Camping, repair

191   I-64 W (exits left from nb), US 60, to Charleston

188b a   US 60, to Lexington, Buena Vista, **3-5 mi E** 🅖 BP, Exxon 🅕 Burger King, Hardee's 🅗 Buena Vista Inn 🅞 $General, Family$, Food Lion, to Blue Ridge Pkwy, to Glen Maury Park, to Stonewall Jackson Home, **W** 🅖 Exxon/dsl, Exxon/McDonald's/ dsl 🅕 Hardee's, Pizza Hut, Taco Bell 🅗 Hampton Inn 🅞 🅗, Food Lion, Marshall Museum, to Washington&Lee U, VMI

180   US 11, Natural Bridge, (180a exits left from sb), **E** 🅗 Relax Inn 🅞 Cave Mtn NF, Jellystone Camping, **W** 🅖 Shell/dsl 🅕 Pink Cadillac Diner 🅗 Budget Inn 🅞 KOA

175   US 11 N, to Glasgow, Natural Bridge, **E** 🅖 Exxon 🅗 Natural Bridge Hotel/rest. (2mi) 🅞 Jellystone Camping (6.5mi), to James River RA

168   VA 614, US 11, Blue Ridge Pkwy, Arcadia, **E** 🅖 Shell/dsl 🅕 Mtn View Rest. 🅗 Wattstull Inn 🅞 Middle Creek Camping (6mi), **2 mi W** 🅖 Exxon 🅕 Burger King

167   US 11 (from sb), Buchanan

162   US 11, Buchanan, **E** 🅖 Exxon/dsl 🅞 to BR Pkwy, **W** 🅖 Citgo/ Subway

158mm   🆁🆂 sb, full 🅗 facilities, litter barrels, petwalk, 🅲, 🏃, vending

156   RD 640, to US 11, **E** 🅖 Exxon/Brugh's Mill/dsl

150   US 11/220, to Fincastle, **E** 🅖 Circle K/dsl/24hr, Dodge's/dsl, 🅿🅸🅻🅾🆃/Subway/dsl/24hr 🅕 Angelle's Diner, Bella Pizza, Country Cookin, Cracker Barrel, Hardee's, McDonald's, Shoney's, Taco Bell 🅗 Comfort Inn, Holiday Inn Express, Motel 6, Quality Inn, Red Roof Inn 🅞 $General Mkt, Berglund RV Ctr, truckwash, **W** 🅖 BP/dsl, Exxon/dsl, GB 🅕 Bojangle's, Little Caesar's, Pancho's Mexican, Pizza Hut, Three Lil' Pigs BBQ, Wendy's 🅗 Howard Johnson, Super 8 🅞 Kroger/dsl, Verizon, vet

L E X I N G T O N

🅶 = gas 🍴 = food 🛏 = lodging 🅾 = other 🆁🆂 = rest stop   Copyright 2022 - The Next EXIT ©

INTERSTATE 81 Cont'd

Exit #	Services
149mm	weigh sta both lanes
146	VA 115, Cloverdale, **E** 🅶 BP/dsl, Exxon, Shell/dsl 🍴 El Rodeo Mexican, Hardee's, McDonald's, Subway 🛏 Country Inn&-Suites, Days Inn/rest., Fairfield Inn, Hampton Inn, Tru Hilton 🅾 Camping World, CVS, to Hollins U
143	I-581, US 220, to Roanoke, Blue Ridge Pkwy (exits left from sb), **1 mi E** 🅶 Kroger/dsl 🍴 El Toreo, Subway, Waffle House 🛏 Knights Inn, Motel 6, Quality Inn, Super 8 🅾 Honda, **2-3 mi E on Hershberger** 🍴 Abuelo's Mexican, Applebee's, Buffalo Wild Wings, Carrabba's, Cheddar's, Chick-fil-A, Hardee's, IHOP, Logan's Roadhouse, Longhorn Steaks, O'Charley's, Olive Garden, Panera Bread, Red Palace Chinese, Red Robin, Rodio Grande, Shaker's, Smokey Bones BBQ, Starbucks, TGIFriday's, Zaxby's 🛏 Best Western+, Comfort Inn, Courtyard, Extended Stay America, Hampton Inn, Holiday Inn, Home 2 Suites, Hyatt Place, MainStay Suites, Residence Inn, Sheraton 🅾 $Tree, AT&T, Barnes&Noble, Belk, Best Buy, BigLots, Dick's, Exxon, Home Depot, Macy's, Michael's, Murphy USA/dsl, NTB, Old Navy, Petsmart, Shell, Staples, Target, U-Haul, Verizon, Walmart
141	VA 419, Salem, **E** 🅶 Liberty/7-11/dsl, Marathon/Burger King 🍴 Hardee's, IHOP, McDonald's, Starbucks 🛏 Baymont Inn, Days Inn, Fairfield Inn, Holiday Inn Express, La Quinta 🅾 🇭, Chevrolet, GNC, Kroger/gas, **1 mi W** 🅶 BP/Subway/dsl, Citgo 🍴 Billy's Barn Rest.
140	VA 311, Salem, **1 mi E** 🍴 Mac&Bob's Cafe, **1 mi W** 🅶 BP/Subway/dsl, Citgo 🍴 Billy's Barn Rest., Hanging Rock Grill/golf
137	VA 112, VA 619, Salem, **E** 🅶 BP, Exxon/dsl, Go-Mart, Marathon, Sheetz/dsl 🍴 Angelle's Diner, Anthony's Cafe, Applebee's, Arby's, Bojangle's, Burger King, Chick-fil-A, Denny's, DQ, Dunkin', Dynasty Buffet, El Rodeo Mexican, Firehouse Subs, Hardee's, Jimmy John's, K&W Cafeteria, KFC, Mamma Maria Italian, McDonald's, Omelette Shoppe, Pizza Hut, Starbucks, Subway, Taco Bell, Tokyo Express, Waffle House, Wendy's, Zaxby's 🛏 Comfort Suites, Motel 6, Quality Inn, Super 8 🅾 $General, $Tree, Aamco, Advance Parts, AutoZone, BigLots, Food Lion, Goodyear, Kroger/dsl, Lowe's, NTB, O'Reilly Parts, Verizon, Walgreens, Walmart/Subway, **W** 🛏 Hampton Inn, Howard Johnson
132	VA 647, to Dixie Caverns, **E** 🅶 Citgo/dsl 🛏 Blue Jay Motel 🅾 Dixie Caverns Camping
129mm	🆁🆂 nb, full ♿ facilities, litter barrels, petwalk, 🅲, 🛒, vending
128	US 11, VA 603, Ironto, **E** 🅶 Shell, **W** 🅶 Exxon/Dixie's/Subway/dsl/24hr
118c b a	US 11/460, Christiansburg, **E** 🅶 Shell/dsl 🍴 Cracker Barrel, Denny's 🛏 Days Inn, Fairfield Inn, Holiday Inn Express, Homewood Suites, Quality Inn, Super 8, Wyndham, **W** 🅶 Exxon/Subway/dsl, Liberty/7-11/dsl, Shell 🍴 Country Cookin, Hardee's, LJ Silver, McDonald's, Pizza Hut, Ruby Tuesday, Wendy's 🛏 EconoLodge, Shayona Inn 🅾 🇭, $General, Advance Parts, Chevrolet, Chrysler/Dodge/Jeep, Food Lion, Ford, Honda, Hyundai, Kia, Subaru, to VA Tech, Toyota
114	VA 8, Christiansburg, **E** to Blue Ridge Pkwy, **0-1 mi W** 🅶 Citgo/dsl 🍴 Burger King, Pizza Inn, Subway 🛏 Budget Inn 🅾 $General Mkt, USPO
109	VA 177, VA 600, **E** 🅾 🇭, **0-2 mi W** 🅶 Exxon/dsl, Marathon 🛏 Best Western, Comfort Inn, La Quinta, Super 8 (2mi) 🅾 Buick/Cadillac/Chevrolet
107mm	🆁🆂 both lanes, full ♿ facilities, litter barrels, petwalk, 🅲, 🛒, vending
105	VA 232, RD 605, to Radford, **2-4 mi W** 🅶 Citgo, Exxon/dsl 🍴 Sal's Italian 🛏 Executive Motel 🅾 museum

Exit #	Services
101	RD 660, to Claytor Lake SP, **E** 🛏 Claytor Lake Inn, Sleep Inn 🅾 repair, **W** 🅶 Exxon/DQ/dsl, Shell/Omelette Shoppe/Taco Bell/dsl/scales/@
98	VA 100 N, to Dublin, **E** 🅶 Exxon/Subway/dsl, Marathon 🍴 Bojangles, Shoney's 🛏 Hampton Inn, Holiday Inn Express, Quality Inn 🅾 to Wilderness Rd Museum, **W** 🅶 Liberty/dsl, Marathon/dsl, Shell/Papa John's/dsl 🍴 Arby's, Burger King, Domino's, El Ranchero Mexican, Fatz Cafe, McDonald's, Waffle House, Wendy's 🛏 Super 8 🅾 $General, NAPA, O'Reilly Parts, Verizon, Walmart/Subway
94b a	VA 99 N, to Pulaski, **0-3 mi W** 🅶 BP, Exxon/dsl, Speedway/dsl 🍴 China Wall, Compadre's Mexican, Domino's, Hardee's, KFC, Kimono Japanese, Little Caesar's, McDonald's, Sonic, Subway, Taco Bell, Wendy's 🅾 🇭, $General, Advance Parts, CVS, Family$, Food Lion, O'Reilly Parts
92	Rd 658, to Draper, **E** 🅶 🅾 to New River Trail SP
89b a	US 11 N, VA 100, to Pulaski, **E** 🅾 auto/truck repair
86	Rd 618, Service Rd, **W** 🅶 Sunoco/Appletree Rest./dsl 🅾 repair
84	Rd 619, to Grahams Forge, **W** 🅶 Exxon/Circle K/DQ/dsl/24hr, Love's/Chester's/Subway/dsl/scales/24hr 🛏 Fox Mtn Inn, Trail Motel
	I-81 S and I-77 N run together 9 mi.
81	I-77 S, to Charlotte, Galax, to Blue Ridge Pkwy
80	US 52 S, VA 121 N, to Ft Chiswell, **E** 🅶 FLYING J/Denny's/dsl/scales/24hr/@, Exxon/Burger King/dsl 🍴 Wendy's 🛏 Hampton Inn, Super 8 🅾 Blue Beacon, Ft Chiswell RV Park, NAPA, **W** 🅶 Circle K/dsl, Citgo 🍴 McDonald's 🛏 Comfort Inn 🅾 Speedco
77	Service Rd, **E** 🅶 FLYING J/Denny's/dsl/scales/LP/RV Dump/24hr, Circle K/Subway/dsl/24hr, Speedway/Dunkin'/dsl 🍴 Burger King 🅾 KOA, **W** 🅶 Exxon/dsl, 🚚/Arby's/DQ/dsl/scales/24hr 🅾 st police
73	US 11 S, Wytheville, **E** 🅶 Exxon/dsl, Go-Mart 🍴 Applebee's, Bob Evans, Cracker Barrel, Dawghouse, El Puerto Mexican, Hardee's, Papa John's, Peking Chinese, Shoney's, Sonic, Waffle House, Wendy's 🛏 Budget Host, Days Inn, EconoLodge, Holiday Inn Express, La Quinta, Motel 6, Quality Inn, Red Roof Inn, Rodeway Inn, Travelodge 🅾 🇭, $General, AutoZone, Buick, Chevrolet/GMC, CVS Drug, Food Lion, Ford, Goodyear/auto, Harley-Davidson, Nissan, Rite Aid, Rural King
	I-81 N and I-77 S run together 9 mi.
72	I-77 N, to Bluefield, **1 mi N on I-77 exit 41 E** 🍴 Sagebrush Steaks, 🛏 Best Western, Sleep Inn, Super 8, **1 mi N on I-77 exit 41 W** 🅶 Exxon/Circle K/dsl/24hr, TA/Country Pride/Popeye's/Subway/Taco Bell/dsl/scales/24hr/@ 🍴 Southern Diner 🛏 Comfort Suites, Country Inn&Suites, Fairfield Inn, Hampton Inn, Ramada/rest., Tru Hilton
70	US 21/52, Wytheville, **E** 🅶 BP/dsl, Sheetz/dsl 🍴 Bojangle's, China Wok, El Patio Mexican, KFC/Taco Bell, Little Caesar's, McDonald's, Ruby Tuesday, Starbucks, Subway, Tokyo Japanese, Wendy's 🅾 🇭, $Tree, Food Lion, GNC, Lowe's, O'Reilly Parts, PetCo, Verizon, Walmart/Subway, **W** 🅶 Kangaroo 🛏 Comfort Inn
67	US 11 (from nb, no re-entry), to Wytheville
61mm	🆁🆂 nb, full ♿ facilities, litter barrels, NO TRUCKS, petwalk, 🅲, 🛒, vending
60	VA 90, Rural Retreat, **E** 🅶 Shell/dsl 🍴 Dutch Pantry, McDonald's 🅾 $General, camping, to Rural Retreat Lake
54	rd 683, to Groseclose, **E** 🅶 Exxon, Sunoco/dsl 🍴 The Barn Rest. 🛏 Relax Inn 🅾 Settler's Museum
53.5mm	🆁🆂 sb, full ♿ facilities, litter barrels, petwalk, 🅲, 🛒, vending
50	US 11, Atkins, **W** 🅶 Circle K/Subway/dsl/24hr, Exxon 🛏 Comfort Inn 🅾 NAPA Care

(vertical side labels: ROANOKE, SALEM, CHRISTIANSBURG, WYTHEVILLE, VA)

🔼Ⓝ INTERSTATE 81 Cont'd

Exit #	Services
47	US 11, to Marion, **W** 🛢 Citgo/Subway, Gas'N Go, Shell/dsl 🍴 Arby's, Bojangle's, Burger King, Charley's Philly Steaks, China House, KFC/Taco Bell, Little Caesar's, McDonald's, Mi Puerto Mexican, Pizza Hut, Sonic, Wendy's 🏠 Best Value Inn, EconoLodge, Travel Inn 🅾 🏨 $General, $Tree, Advance Parts, AutoZone, Buick/Chevrolet/GMC, CVS Drug, Food City, Food Lion, Ford, Ingles, Marion Drug, O'Reilly Parts, to Hungry Mother SP (4mi), Verizon, Walgreens, Walmart
45	VA 16, Marion, **E** 🛢 Valero/dsl 🅾 Mt Rogers NRA, to Grayson Highlands SP, **W** 🛢 Sunoco 🍴 Hardee's 🅾 NAPA, USPO
44	US 11, Marion, **W** 🅾 $General, Vet
39	US 11, rd 645, Seven Mile Ford, **W** 🅾 Interstate Camping
35	VA 107, Chilhowie, **E** 🍴 Chilhowie Pizza, Hardee's 🏠 Knights Inn, **W** 🛢 Exxon/dsl, Gas'N Go, Mobil/Main St Mkt, Shell/dsl 🍴 McDonald's, Riverfront Rest., Subway, Taco Bell 🅾 $General, Food City, Greever's Drugs, USPO
32	US 11, to Chilhowie
29	VA 91, to Damascus, Glade Spring, **E** 🛢 Marathon/Subway/dsl, Petro/Iron Skillet/dsl/24hr/@, Valero/Wendy's 🍴 Giardino's Italian, Pizza+ 🏠 EconoLodge, Knights Inn 🅾 $General, Peterbilt, **W** 🛢 Exxon, Shell/dsl, Spirit 🍴 El Burrito Loco 🅾 vet
26	rd 737, Emory, **W** 🍴 Macado's (1mi) 🅾 to Emory&Henry Coll, USPO (1mi)
24	VA 80, Meadowview Rd, **E** 🛢 ❤Loves/McDonald's/Subway/dsl/scales/24hr, **W** 🍴 Harvest Table
22	rd 704, Enterprise Rd, **E** 🛢 Marathon/dsl 🅾 🏨
19	US 11/58, to Abingdon, **E** 🛢 Shell/Subway/Dunkin'/dsl, Walmart/dsl 🍴 Bojangle's, DQ, McDonald's, Pizza+ 🅾 $Tree, Lowe's, to Mt Rogers NRA, URGENT CARE, vet, Walmart, **W** 🛢 BP/dsl, Exxon/dsl, Marathon/Huddle House 🍴 Bella's Pizza, Burger King, Cracker Barrel, Harbor House Seafood, Papa Tom's Cantina, Pita's 🏠 Country Inn Suites, Fairfield Inn, Quality Inn, Red Roof Inn 🅾 $General
17	US 58A, VA 75, Abingdon, **E** 🛢 Mobil/dsl 🍴 Domino's, LJ Silver 🏠 Hampton Inn, **W** 🛢 Exxon, Gas'n Go 🍴 Arby's, Capt D's, Charley's Philly Steaks, China Wok, Fuji Express, Hardee's, Little Caesar's, Los Arcos, McDonald's, Papa John's, Shoney's, Subway, Taco Bell, Wendy's 🏠 Super 8 🅾 Advance Parts, Food City, GNC, Kroger/dsl
14	US 19, VA 140, Abingdon, **W** 🛢 BP/dsl, Exxon, Shell/dsl 🍴 McDonald's, Milano's Italian, Moon Dog Cafe, Subway 🏠 Comfort Inn, Comfort Suites 🅾 Chevrolet, Ford/Lincoln, Riverside Camping (10mi)
13.5mm	🅡ˢ nb, TRUCKERS ONLY, full 🦽 facilities, litter barrels, 🇨, 🚮, vending
13	VA 611, to Lee Hwy, **W** 🛢 Shell/dsl 🅾 Kenworth, Mack, Volvo
10	US 11/19, Lee Hwy, **W** 🛢 Exxon, Marathon/dsl, Shell/dsl 🏠 Deluxe Inn, Economy Inn, Evergreen Inn, Red Carpet Inn
7	Old Airport Rd, **E** 🛢 Shell/dsl 🍴 Bojangles, Cheddar's, Cracker Barrel, Sonic 🏠 Days Inn, Hilton Garden, **W** 🛢 Marathon, Sunoco/Wendy's, Valero/dsl 🍴 Chick-fil-A, Chili's, Cook-Out, Domino's, El Patio Mexican, Five Guys, Golden Corral, IHOP, Jersey Mike's Subs, Kobe Japanese, Logan's Roadhouse, Los Arcos, Mellow Mushroom, O'Charley's, Olive Garden, Pal's Drive-In, Perkins, Red Lobster, Starbucks, Subway, Taco Bell 🏠 Courtyard, Holiday Inn, Motel 6, Quality Inn 🅾 $General, $Tree, Advance Parts, AT&T, AutoZone, Best Buy, Books-A-Million, Food City/gas, Home Depot, Office Depot, Petsmart, Ross, Sam's Club/gas, Sugar Hollow Camping, Target, TJ Maxx, Verizon, Walmart

Exit #	Services
5	US 11/19, Lee Hwy, **E** 🛢 Shell 🍴 Arby's, Burger King, Hardee's, KFC, LJ Silver, McDonald's, Shoney's 🏠 Budget Inn, Red Roof Inn 🅾 Harley-Davidson, O'Reilly Parts, Price Less Foods, USPO, **W** 🛢 Exxon/dsl, Sheetz/dsl 🍴 Buffalo Wild Wings, Zaxby's 🏠 Comfort Inn 🅾 Aldi Foods, Buick/GMC, Cabela's, Hobby Lobby, Kings Tire, Lowe's
3	I-381 S, to Bristol, **1 mi E** 🛢 Gas'n Go/dsl, Mobil/dsl, Shell/dsl 🍴 Krystal, Subway 🏠 EconoLodge 🅾 Food City, vet
1b a	US 58/421, Bristol, **1 mi E** 🛢 5 Mart/dsl, Exxon/dsl, Shell 🍴 Burger King, Capt D's, KFC, McDonald's, Sonic, Subway, Taco Bell, Wendy's 🏠 Rodeway Inn 🅾 🏨 $Tree, Chrysler/Dodge/Jeep, CVS Drug, Kroger/dsl, Toyota, UHaul, Verizon, vet, Walgreens
0mm	Virginia/Tennessee state line, **Welcome Ctr nb, NO TRUCKS, full** 🦽 **facilities, info, litter barrels, petwalk,** 🇨, 🚮, **vending**

🔼Ⓝ INTERSTATE 85

Exit #	Services
I-85 begins/ends on I-95.	
69	US 301, I-95 N, Wythe St, Washington St, Petersburg
68	I-95 S, US 460 E, to Norfolk, Crater Rd
65	Squirrel Level Rd, **E** 🅾 to Richard Bland Coll, **W** 🛢 BP
63b a	US 1, to Petersburg, **E** 🛢 Chubby's/dsl, Exxon/KFC/dsl, Shell/Burger King/dsl 🍴 Hardee's, Taco Bell, Waffle House 🏠 Holiday Inn Express 🅾 $General, **W** 🛢 🍴 McDonald's
61	US 460, to Blackstone, **E** 🛢 Mapco/Subway/dsl 🍴 Joe's Rest., **W** 🅾 📶, auto repair
55mm	🅡ˢ both lanes, full 🦽 facilities, litter barrels, petwalk, 🇨, 🚮, vending
53	VA 703, Dinwiddie, **W** 🛢 Exxon/dsl 🅾 to 5 Forks Nat Bfd
52mm	Stony Creek
48	VA 650, DeWitt
42	VA 40, McKenney, **W** 🛢 BP, Citgo, Exxon
40mm	Nottoway River
39	VA 712, to Rawlings, **W** 🛢 Davis TC/Exxon/Dunkin'/Subway/dsl/scales/24hr, Race-In/Nottoway Rest.
34	VA 630, Warfield, **W** 🛢 Exxon/dsl
32mm	🅡ˢ both lanes, full 🦽 facilities, litter barrels, petwalk, 🇨, 🚮, vending
28	US 1, Alberta, **W** 🛢 Exxon 🅾 Family Dollar
27	VA 46, to Lawrenceville, **E** 🅾 to St Paul's Coll
24	VA 644, to Meredithville
22mm	weigh sta both lanes
20mm	Meherrin River
15	US 1, to South Hill, **E** 🛢 Hines, **W** 🛢 Hot Food/dsl, ❤Loves/Subway/McDonald's/dsl/scales/24hr 🍴 El Saucito, Kahill's Rest. 🏠 Holiday Inn Express

⮕N INTERSTATE 85 Cont'd

SOUTH HILL

Exit #	Services
12	US 58, VA 47, to South Hill, **E** 🅖 Exxon/dsl, ▢/Shell/dsl, RaceWay, Sunoco/dsl 🍴 Applebee's, Arby's, Bojangles, Domino's, Five Guys, Glass House Grill, Luca's Italian, Papa John's, Sonic 🛏 Best Western+, Comfort Inn, Fairfield Inn, Hampton Inn 🅞 $Tree, Verizon, Walmart/Subway, **W** 🅖 Exxon, Kangaroo/dsl 🍴 Brian's Steaks, Burger King, Cracker Barrel, Hardee's, KFC/Taco Bell, McDonald's, New China, Pizza Hut, Subway, Wendy's 🛏 Best Value Inn, Days Inn, Quality Inn 🅞 🅗, $General, AutoZone, CVS Drug, Family$, Food Lion, Home Depot, O'Reilly Parts, Roses
4	VA 903, to Bracey, Lake Gaston, **E** 🅖 Exxon/Simmon's/dsl/scales/24hr/@, Sunoco/Subway/Papa John's/dsl 🍴 Huddle House, Top This Pizza 🅞 $General, Americamps Camping (5mi), **W** 🅖 Shell/Pizza Hut/Quizno's 🛏 Lake Gaston Inn
3mm	Lake Gaston
1mm	**Welcome Ctr nb, full ♿ facilities, litter barrels, petwalk, 🍴, 🏧, vending**
0mm	Virginia/North Carolina state line

⮕N INTERSTATE 95

DC AREA

Exit #	Services
178mm	Virginia/Maryland state line, Potomac River, W Wilson Br
177c b a	US 1, to Alexandria, Ft Belvoir, **E** 🍴 Great American Steaks 🛏 Budget Host, Hampton Inn, Red Roof Inn, Relax Inn 🅞 Chevrolet, Chrysler/Dodge/Jeep, **W** 🅖 Liberty/repair, Speedway
176b a	VA 241, Telegraph Rd, **E** 🅖 BP, Speedway/dsl, **W** 🍴 Ted's MT Grill 🛏 Courtyard, Extended Stay America, Holiday Inn, SpringHill Suites
174	Eisenhower Ave Connector, to Alexandria
173	rd 613, Van Dorn St, to Franconia, **E** 🛏 Comfort Inn, **1 mi W** 🅖 Exxon, Shell 🍴 Dunkin', Jerry's Subs, McDonald's, Red Lobster 🅞 Aamco, Giant Foods, NTB
170a	I-495 N, **I-495 & I-95 N run together to MD**, to Rockville.
170b	I-395 N, to Washington
169b a	rd 644, Springfield, Franconia, **E** 🍴 Bertucci's, Dunkin', Houlihan's, Silver Diner, Starbucks, Subway, TGIFriday's 🛏 Best Western, Comfort Inn, Courtyard, Extended Stay America, Hampton Inn, Hilton 🅞 🅗, AT&T, Barnes&Noble, Best Buy, Dick's, Firestone/auto, Ford, Home Depot, JC Penney, Macy's, Michael's, Nissan, Old Navy, Petsmart, Staples, Subaru, Target, **W** 🅖 BP, Shell, Sunoco 🍴 Blue Pearl Buffet, Chick-fil-A, Chipotle Mexican, Deliah's Grill, Domino's, Dunkin', Five Guys, Hard Times Cafe, KFC, McDonald's, Noodles&Co, Outback Steaks, Panda Express, Popeye's, Starbucks, Subway 🛏 Holiday Inn Express, Homewood Suites, Motel 6, Residence Inn, TownePlace Suites 🅞 7-11, Advance Parts, CarQuest, Chrysler/Dodge/Jeep, CVS Drug, Giant Foods, GNC, Goodyear/auto, Mr Tire, Toyota, Trader Joe's, USPO, Verizon, vet, VW
167	VA 617, Backlick Rd (from sb), **W** 🅖 InterFuel/dsl
166b a	VA 7100, Newington, to Ft Belvoir, **E** 🅖 Pkwy Express 🍴 Wendy's 🛏 Embassy Suites 🅞 NTB, Toyota, U-Haul, **W** 🅖 Exxon/7-11/dsl 🍴 McDonald's 🅞 Costco
163	VA 642, Lorton, **E** 🅖 Shell/repair, Sunoco/dsl 🅞 auto repair, **W** 🅖 Shell/dsl 🍴 Antoneli's Pizza, Burger King, Gunston Wok, Kabob Factory Rest.
161	US 1 S (exits left from sb, no reentry nb), to Ft Belvoir, Mt Vernon, Woodlawn Plantation, Gunston Hall
160.5mm	Occoquan River

DUMFRIES

Exit #	Services
160b a	VA 123 N, Woodbridge, Occoquan, **E** 🅖 Sunoco 🍴 Taco Be... 🛏 Hampton Inn, Quality Inn 🅞 Aldi Foods, Food Lion, M... Transmissions, **W** 🅖 Exxon/repair/dsl, Fast Fuels, Shell/d... 🍴 KFC, Madigan's Waterfront Rest., McDonald's, VA Gri... Wendy's 🅞 7-11, same as 161
158b a	VA 294, Prince William Pkwy, Woodbridge, **W** 🅖 7-11, Exxon... Shell, Sunoco/dsl 🍴 Bonefish Grill, Boston Mkt, Bungalow Al... house, Chick-fil-A, Chipotle Mexican, ChuckeCheese, Coldston... Famous Dave's BBQ, Firehouse Subs, Hooters, IHOP, Macaron... Grill, McDonald's, Noodles&Co, Old Country Buffet, On-the... Border, Panda Express, Panera Bread, Qdoba, Red Lobster, Re... Robin, Smokey Bones BBQ, Starbucks, Taco Bell, TGIFriday'... Wendy's 🛏 Country Inn&Suites, Courtyard, Fairfield Inn, Ho... iday Inn Express, Residence Inn, SpringHill Suites 🅞 $Tree, A... vance Parts, Best Buy, CarMax, Dick's, GNC, JC Penney, Lowe... Michael's, Office Depot, Petsmart, Sam's Club/gas, Shopper... Foods, Target, Verizon, Walmart/Subway
156	VA 784, Potomac Mills, **E** 🍴 Brixx Woodfired Grill, Firebirds Gri... PF Chang's, Potbelly, Starbucks, Travinia Italian, Uncle Julio's Gri... Zoe's Kitchen 🛏 Hilton Garden, Homewood Suites 🅞 🅗, AT&... Old Navy, REI, to Leesylvania SP, Wegman's Mkt, **W** 🅖 Mobi... dsl, Shell/dsl, Sunoco/dsl 🍴 Bahama Breeze, Bob Evans, Bobby... Burger, Buffalo Wild Wings, Burger King, Char Broil Grill, Chees... cake Factory, Chili's, China King Buffet, Denny's, Domino's, D... Guapo's, Hard Times Cafe, Los Amigos, McDonald's, Olive Ga... den, Outback Steaks, Paisano's, Popeye's, Sakura Japanese, Si... ver Diner, Subway, Wendy's 🛏 Best Western, Wytestone Suite... 🅞 Costco/gas, Family$, Firestone/auto, IKEA, Jo-Ann Fabric... Marshalls, Nordstrom Rack, NTB, Potomac Mills Outlets/Famou... Brands, Staples, Tuesday Morning, U-Haul, vet
154mm	🆁🆂/weigh sta both lanes
152	VA 234, Dumfries, to Manassas, **E** 🅖 BP/dsl, Express, Ex... on/dsl, Shell/dsl, Valero/Subway 🍴 Applebee's, China On... KFC, McDonald's, Ruby Tuesday, Taco Bell 🛏 Sleep Inn, S... per 8 🅞 7-11, Food Lion, Meineke, NAPA Autocare, Walmar... Weems-Botts Museum, **W** 🅖 7-11, Exxon 🍴 Asian Pa... Chick-fil-A, Cracker Barrel, Five Guys, IHOP, Jerry's Subs, Mon... Clair Rest., Panera Bread, Starbucks, Subway, Tiziano Italia... Waffle House 🛏 Comfort Inn, Days Inn, EconoLodge, Hamptc... Inn, Holiday Inn 🅞 AT&T, Prince William Camping, Rite Ai... Shoppers Foods, Target, URGENT CARE
150	VA 619, Quantico, to Triangle, **E** 🍴 Dunkin', McDonald... 🛏 Ramada Inn 🅞 7-11, to Marine Corps Base, **W** Prince W... liam Forest Park
148	to Quantico (2mi), **E** 🅖 Gulf/dsl 🍴 Subway 🛏 Courtya... 🅞 to Marine Corps Base
143b a	to US 1, VA 610, Aquia, **E** 🅖 7-11, Exxon/Circle K/dsl, Vale... 🍴 Carlos O'Kelly's, El Gran Charro, KFC, McDonald's, Mick... Rest., Papa John's, Pizza Hut, Ruby Tuesday, Subway 🛏 Be... Western, Fairfield Inn, Hampton Inn, Staybridge Suites, Su... urban Extended Stay, Towne Place Suites 🅞 Aquia Pin... Camping, Nissan, Rite Aid, Tires+, **W** 🅖 7-11, Exxon/d... Kangaroo, WaWa 🍴 5 Guys Burgers, Applebee's, Baskin-Ro... bins/Dunkin', Bob Evans, Buffalo Wild Wings, Burger Kin... Chick-fil-A, Chili's, China Wok, CiCi's, Firehouse Subs, Hardee... Hibachi Buffet, IHOP, Jersey Mike's, Jimmy the Greek, Kob... Japanese, Little Caesar's, McDonald's, Moe's SW Grill, Outba... Steaks, Pancho Villa, Panera Bread, Popeye's, Starbucks, Tac... Bell, Umi Japanese, Wendy's 🛏 Comfort Inn, Country Inn... Suites, Quality Inn, Super 8, Wingate Inn 🅞 $General, $Tre... Aldi Foods, AutoZone, Best Buy, CVS Drug, Giant Foods, GNC... Home Depot, Kohl's, Lowe's, Merchant's Tire, Michael's, PetC...

INTERSTATE 95 Cont'd

143b a Continued
Petsmart, Ross, Shopper's Foods, Staples, Target, TJ Maxx, Toyota, URGENT CARE, Verizon, Walmart/McDonald's

140 VA 630, Stafford, E 📱 7-11, Sunoco/dsl, Valero 🍴 McDonald's Ⓞ 🏠, W 🍴 Exxon/dsl, Shell/dsl

137mm Potomac Creek

136 rd 8900, Centreport, **2 mi** E 📱 Valero/dsl, W 🔧

133b a US 17 N, to Warrenton, E 📱 Exxon/dsl 🍴 Arby's 🏠 Knights Inn, Motel 6 Ⓞ 7-11, auto/truck repair, CarQuest, W 📱 East-Coast/Subway/dsl, Shell/dsl, WaWa/dsl 🍴 Aladin Grill, Burger King, Dunkin', Hardee's, McDonald's, Pancho Villa Mexican, Panera Bread, Perkins, Ponderosa, Popeye's, Sam's Pizza&Subs, Subway, Taco Bell, Waffle House, Wendy's 🏠 Best Value Inn, Clarion, Comfort Suites, Country Inn&Suites, Days Inn, Holiday Inn Express, Quality Inn, Sleep Inn, Super 8, Super Value Inn, Wingate Inn Ⓞ Advance Parts, AutoZone, Blue Beacon, Food Lion, Honda, Petsmart, Target, Verizon

132.5mm Rappahannock River

132mm ℞ sb, full 🚻 facilities, litter barrels, petwalk, 🎁, 🏠, vending

130b a VA 3, to Fredericksburg, E 📱 BP/dsl, Gulf/dsl, Shell/dsl, Wawa 🍴 Aladin Cafe, Arby's, Bob Evans, Dixie Bones BBQ, Dunkin', Friendly's, Honeybaked Ham, KFC, Lonestar Steaks, McDonald's, Pizza King, Popeye's, Shoney's, Starbucks, Subway, Teppanyaki Buffet, Wendy's 🏠 Best Western, Quality Inn Ⓞ 🏠, AutoZone, Batteries+Bulbs, BigLots, Home Depot, PepBoys, Staples, Tuesday Morning, U-Haul, Verizon, W 📱 Exxon/dsl, Murphy USA, Sheetz/dsl, Valero, WaWa 🍴 5 Guys Burgers, A&W/LJ Silver, Applebee's, BoneFish Grill, Bravo!, Buffalo Wild Wings, Burger King, Cancun Mexican, Carrabba's, Checker's, Cheeburger Cheeburger, Chick-fil-A, Chili's, Chipotle Mexican, ChuckeCheese, CiCi's Pizza, Cracker Barrel, Dunkin', Firebirds Grill, Firehouse Subs, Hibachi Buffet, IHOP, Jimmy John's, Joe's Crabshack, Krispy Kreme, Logan's Roadhouse, McDonald's, Melting Pot, Noodles&Co, O'Charley's, Olive Garden, Outback Steaks, Pancho Villa, Panda Express, Panera Bread, Park Lane Grill, Peter Chang, Potbelly, Qdoba, Quaker Steak, Red Lobster, Ruby Tuesday, Ryan's, Sam's Pizza, Santa Fe Grill, Shane's Ribshack, Smokey Bones BBQ, Starbucks, Subway, Taco Bell, TGIFriday's, Tito's Diner, TX Roadhouse 🏠 Best Western, Hampton Inn, Hilton Garden, Homewood Suites, Hospitality House, Residence Inn, Super 8, WoodSpring Inn Ⓞ $General, $Tree, AAA, Aldi Foods, AT&T, AutoZone, Barnes&Noble, Belk, Best Buy, BJ's Whse, Books A Million, Costco/gas, CVS Drug, Dick's, Food Lion, GNC, Hobby Lobby, JC Penney, Kohl's, Lowe's, Macy's, Meineke, Mercedes, Merchants Tire, Michael's, NTB, Office Depot, Old Navy, Petsmart, Target, Verizon, vet, Volvo, Walmart, Wegman's Foods, Yankee Candle

126 US 1, US 17 S, to Fredericksburg, E 📱 7-11/dsl, BP/dsl, Exxon/Circle K, Gulf/dsl, Shell/dsl, Wawa 🍴 Arby's, Denny's, DQ, Friendly's, Golden Corral, Hardee's, Hooters, McDonald's, Pizza Hut, Poncho Villa Mexican, Ruby Tuesday, Subway, Taco Bell, Vita Felice Italian, Waffle House 🏠 Best Value Inn, Country Inn&Suites, Days Inn/rest., EconoLodge, Fairfield Inn, Hampton Inn, Howard Johnson, Knights Inn, Motel 6, Royal Inn, TownePlace Suites Ⓞ 🏠, $General, $Tree, Advance Parts, Aldi Foods, AutoZone, BMW Cycles, Buick/GMC, Chrysler/Dodge/Jeep, CVS Drug, Family$, Fiat, Food Lion, Hyundai, Kia, Little Tires, Mazda, Midas, Nissan, Rite Aid, Subaru, Tires+, VW, W 📱 7-11, 95 Fuel Stop/dsl, Exxon/Circle K, WaWa/dsl 🍴 5 Guys Burgers,

FREDERICKSBURG

126 Continued
Applebee's, Arby's, Asian Diner, Bob Evans, Buffalo Wild Wings, Burger King, Chick-fil-A, Chili's, China King, Chipotle Mexican, Coldstone Creamery, Cracker Barrel, Dickey's BBQ, El Charro Mexican, Famous Dave's BBQ, Firehouse Subs, Golden China, KFC, Kobe Japanese, Legends Grill, Longhorn Steaks, Mad Crab Grill, McDonald's, Mexico Rest., Mimi's Cafe, Panera Bread, Papa John's, Red Robin, Salsarita's Cantina, Sonic, Starbucks, Steak'n Shake, Subway, Taco Bell, Wendy's 🏠 Candlewood Suites, Holiday Inn Express, Sleep Inn, WyteStone Suites Ⓞ AT&T, Carmax, CVS Drug, Dick's, Firestone/auto, GNC, Jo-Ann Fabrics, Kohl's, Lowe's, Marshalls, Merchant Tire/auto, Petsmart, Rite Aid, Ross, Staples, Target, URGENT CARE, USPO, Verizon, vet, Walmart/Subway, World Mkt

118 VA 606, to Thornburg, E 📱 Shell/dsl Ⓞ Camping World, to Stonewall Jackson Shrine, W 📱 7-11, Citgo/dsl, Exxon, Shell/DQ/dsl, Valero 🍴 Angela's Italian, Domino's, McDonald's, Subway, Taco Bell 🏠 Best Western+, Holiday Inn Express, Quality Inn Ⓞ $General, Family$, Food Lion, KOA (7mi), to Lake Anna SP, USPO

110 VA 639, to Ladysmith, E 📱 Shell/dsl, W 📱 Citgo/dsl, Exxon/dsl 🍴 Domino's, Guiseppe's Rest., Lin's Gourmet, McDonald's, Subway, Timbers Rest. Ⓞ $General, Family$, Food Lion, Lady Smith Drug, Lady Smith Tire/repair, Verizon

108mm ℞ both lanes, full 🚻 facilities, litter barrels, pet walk, 🎁, 🏠, vending

104 VA 207, to US 301, Bowling Green, E 📱 Exxon/dsl, ⭐FLYING J/Golden Corral/dsl/Lp/scales/24hr/@, Gulf/7-11/dsl, ❤Love's/DQ/Subway/dsl/scales/24hr, Mr Fuel/dsl, Valero/dsl 🍴 Arby's, McDonald's, Wendy's 🏠 Knights Inn, Super 8 Ⓞ Blue Beacon, SpeedCo, to Ft AP Hill, W 📱 ⭐FLYING J/Denny's/dsl/scales/RV dump/24hr, Exxon/dsl 🍴 Waffle House 🏠 City Studio, Comfort Inn, Days Inn/rest., EconoLodge Ⓞ CarQuest, USPO

98 VA 30, Doswell, E 📱 7-11, Doswell TP/motel/dsl/scales/24hr/@, Exxon 🍴 Burger King, Denny's 🏠 Best Western, Country Inn&Suites, Days Inn, La Quinta Ⓞ Camp Wilderness, King's Dominion Camping, to King's Dominion Funpark, truckwash/service

92 VA 54, Ashland, E 📱 Sunoco, W 📱 7-11/dsl, EC/Krispy Kreme/dsl, Exxon/Subway, Kangeroo/dsl, Shell/dsl, Sunoco/Circle K/dsl, TA/Valero/Country Pride/dsl/scales/24hr/@ 🍴 Anthony's Pizza, Applebee's, Arby's, Brickoven Rest., Burger King, Capt D's, Chick-fil-A, China Wok, Cracker Barrel, DQ, El Azteca, GNC, Hardee's, Jersey Mike's Subs, KFC/LJ Silver, McDonald's, New China Buffet, Pizza Hut, Ponderosa, Ruby Tuesday, Starbucks, Taco Bell, Tops China, Waffle House, Wendy's 🏠 Apple Garden Inn, Ashland Inn, Days Inn, EconoLodge, Hampton Inn, Holiday Inn Express, Howard Johnson, Motel 6, Sleep Inn, Super 8 Ⓞ $General, $Tree, Ace Hardware, Advance Parts, AutoZone, Buick/GMC, CarQuest, CVS Drug, Family$, Food Lion, Martin's Foods/dsl, O'Reilly Parts, Rite Aid, Tuesday Morning, Verizon, Walmart/Subway

INTERSTATE 95 Cont'd

Exit #	Services
89	VA 802, to Lewistown Rd, **E** 🅖 Shell, TA/Pizza Hut/Popeye's/dsl/scales/24hr/@ 🅞 Americamps RV Camp, **W** 🅕 Bojangles, Dunkin', Subway, Wendy's 🅛 Country Inn Suites 🅞 Bass Pro Shops, Harley Davidson, Kosmo Village Camping, McGeorge's RV Ctr
86b a	VA 656, Elmont, to Atlee **E** 🅖 Sheetz/dsl, Valero/dsl 🅕 Burger King, Mario's Italian, McDonald's, Pizza Hut, Subway 🅞 CVS Drug, Food Lion, tire/auto repair, vet, **W** 🅕 Wawa/dsl 🅕 Applebee's, Arby's, BBQ, Buffalo Wild Wings, Chick-fil-A, Chili's, Chipotle Mexican, CiCi's Pizza, Coldstone Creamery, Famous Dave's BBQ, Firehouse Subs, Halligan BBQ, Jade Chinese, Jersey Mike's Subs, McDonald's, O'Charley's, O'Dragon Buffet, Panera Bread, Papa John's, Pizzaro, Plaza Azteca Mexican, Red Robin, Roda Japanese, Shoney's, Sonic, Starbucks, Subway, TX Roadhouse, Wendy's 🅛 Candlewood Suites, Comfort Suites, Courtyard, Hampton Inn, SpringHill Suites 🅞 $Tree, 7-11, AT&T, Barnes&Noble, Best Buy, Burlington, Dick's, Firestone/auto, GNC, Goodyear/auto, Home Depot, JC Penney, Martin's Foods, Merchant's Tire, Michael's, Petsmart, Ross, Shell/dsl, Target, Tire America, Walgreens
84b a	I-295 W, to I-64, to Norfolk
83b a	VA 73, Parham Rd, **W** 🅖 7-11, Exxon/DQ, Shell/dsl, Wawa 🅕 Aunt Sarah's, Burger King, Firehouse Subs, Frida's Cafe, Hardee's, Hawks BBQ, KFC/Taco Bell, McDonald's, Popeyes, River City Diner, Starbucks, Subway, Waffle House, Wendy's 🅛 Best Value Inn, Best Western, Cavalier Motel, Days Inn, EconoLodge, Knights Inn, Quality Inn, Sleep Inn 🅞 $Tree, BigLots, Food Lion, Lowe's, Verizon, Walmart
82	US 301, Chamberlayne Ave, **E** 🅖 BP/dsl, Sunoco/dsl, Valero/dsl, Wawa 🅕 KFC, McDonald's, Pizza Hut/Taco Bell, Subway 🅛 Super 8 🅞 $Tree, Family$, Food Lion, USPO, **W** 🅖 Exxon/Circle K
81	US 1, Chamberlayne Ave (from nb), same as 82
80	Hermitage Rd, Lakeside Ave (from nb, no return), **W** 🅖 Citgo/Subway 🅞 Ginter Botanical Gardens, Goodyear/auto
79	I-64 W, to Charlottesville, I-195 S, to U of Richmond
78	Boulevard (no EZ nb return), **E** 🅖 🅛 Clarion, **W** 🅞 🅗, stadium, to VA HS
76	Chamberlayne Ave, Belvidere, **E** 🅞 🅗, VA Union U
75	I-64 E, VA Beach, to Norfolk, 🆁🆂
74c	US 33, US 250 W, to Broad St, **W** 🅞 🅗, Museum of the Confederacy, st capitol
74b	Franklin St, **E** 🅞 Richmond Nat Bfd Park
74a	I-195 N, to Powhite Expswy, downtown
73.5mm	James River
73	Maury St, to US 60, US 360, industrial area
69	VA 161, Bells Rd, **E** Port of Richmond, **W** 🅖 Exxon/dsl, Shell/dsl 🅕 McDonald's, Subway 🅛 Candlewood Suites, Hampton Inn, Holiday Inn, Red Roof Inn
67b a	VA 895 (**toll** E), VA 150, to Chippenham Pkwy, Falling Creek, **W** 🅖 BP/dsl, RaceWay/dsl, Shell/dsl 🅕 Burger King, Hardee's 🅞 Food Lion, U-Haul
64	VA 613, to Willis Rd, **E** 🅖 BP, Exxon/Circle K/dsl 🅕 Waffle House 🅛 Best Value Inn, Knights Inn, **W** 🅖 7-11, Citgo/dsl, Shell/dsl, Sunoco 🅕 Burger King, Maury's BBQ, McDonald's, Subway 🅛 Country Inn&Suites, La Quinta, Sleep Inn, VIP Inn 🅞 Drewry's Bluff Bfd, flea mkt
62	VA 288 N, to Chesterfield, Powhite Pkwy, **W** 🅞 to 🆁🆂

Exit #	Services
61b a	VA 10, Chester, **E** 🅖 RaceWay/dsl 🅕 Don Pepe Mexican Hardee's 🅛 Comfort Inn, Courtyard, Hampton Inn, Holiday Inn Express, Homewood Suites, Quality Inn 🅞 🅗, City Point NHS, Petersburg NBF, to James River Plantations, **W** 🅖 Exxon Circle K/dsl, Gulf/dsl, Mobil/Circle K/dsl, Shell/dsl, Sunoco/dsl 🅕 Applebee's, Bojangles, Brass Monkey Grill, Buffalo Wild Wings, Burger King, Capt D's, Chili's, Chipotle, CiCi's Pizza Cracker Barrel, Denny's, Don Papa Mexican, Friendly's, Hardee's Hooters, IHOP, KFC, Logan's Roadhouse, McDonald's, O'Charley's, Panera Bread, Peking Chinese, Pizza Hut, Shoney's, Sonic, Starbucks, Subway, Taco Bell, The Patron Cantina, Wendy's 🅛 Country Inn&Suites, Days Inn, Fairfield Inn, InTowne Suites Suburban Lodge, Super 8 🅞 $General, $Tree, Aamco, AT&T Big Lots, Chevrolet, CVS Drug, Food Lion, GNC, Home Depot Kohl's, Kroger/gas, Lowe's, Martin's Foods, NAPA, PetCo, Rite Aid, Target, to Pocahontas SP, Verizon
58	VA 746, to Ruffinmill Rd, **E** 🅖 Loves/Wendy's/dsl/scales/24hr 🅞 Honda, Hyundai, Kia, Nissan, Subaru, Toyota, VW, **W** 🅖 7-11, Exxon/Subway/dsl, Wawa/dsl 🅕 McDonald's 🅛 Candlewood Suites, Comfort Inn, EconoLodge 🅞 Family$
54	VA 144, Temple Ave, Hopewell, to Ft Lee, **E** 🅖 Exxon/Burger King, Sheetz/dsl, Shell, Sunoco/Circle K/dsl, Wawa/dsl 🅕 Applebee's, Arby's, Buffalo Wild Wings, Chick-fil-A, China Buffet Chipotle, CiCi's Pizza, Denny's, Firehouse Subs, Five Guys, Golden Corral, Great China, IHOP, Jimmy John's, Longhorn Steaks McDonald's, Olive Garden, Outback Steaks, Panera Bread, Pizza Hut, Red Lobster, Ruby Tuesday, Sonic, Starbucks, Subway Taco Bell, TX Roadhouse, Wendy's 🅛 Comfort Suites, Hampton Inn, Hilton Garden, Holiday Inn, Woodspring Suites 🅞 $Tree AAA, AT&T, Best Buy, BooksAMillion, Dick's, Discount Tire Home Depot, JC Penney, Jo-Ann Fabrics, Macy's, Marshall's Michael's, NTB, Old Navy, Petsmart, Sam's Club/gas, Staples Target, Verizon, Walmart/Subway, **W** 🅖 Circle K/dsl 🅕 DQ Hardee's, Waffle House 🅞 to VSU, U-Haul
53	S Park Blvd, **E** same as 54
52.5mm	Appomattox River
52	Washington St, Wythe St, **E** 🅖 Marathon/dsl, Valero/dsl 🅕 Jade Garden 🅛 Knights Inn, Royal Inn 🅞 Petersburg Nat'l Bfd, **W** 🅖 Liberty 🅞 🅗
51	I-85 S, to South Hill, US 460 W
50d	Wythe St, (from nb), same as 52
50b c	**E** 🅖 7-11 🅛 Flagship Inn
50a	US 301, US 460 E, to Crater Rd, County Dr, **E** 🅖 BP, RaceWay/dsl, Star Express 🅕 Hardee's 🅛 American Inn, Budget Inn California Inn, EconoLodge 🅞 🅗
48b a	Wagner Rdon Crater Rd, **W** 🅖 Gulf/dsl, Wawa 🅕 Arby's, Bojangles, Burger King, Capt D's, KFC, King's BBQ, Little Caesar's Pizza Hut, Plaza Mexico, Subway, Taco Bell, Taste of China 🅛 Country Inn&Suites, Super 8 🅞 $General, $Tree, Advance Parts, 🅗, Martin's Foods, O'Reilly Parts, PepBoys, USPO, Verizon, Walgreens, Walmart
47	VA 629, to Rives Rd, **W** 🅖 Citgo, Shell/dsl 🅕 Bojangles, KFC Outlaw's Rest. 🅛 Heritage Motel 🅞 Ace Hardware, same as 48 on US 301, Softball Hall of Fame Museum, Walmart
46	I-295 N (exits left from sb), to Washington
45	US 301, **E** 🅖 Shell/dsl, **W** 🅖 Exxon/Circle K 🅕 Lighthouse Rest., Nanny's Rest., Steven Kent Rest. 🅛 Comfort Inn, Days Inn, Hampton Inn, Holiday Inn Express, Howard Johnson, Quality Inn
41	US 301, VA 35, VA 156, **E** 🅖 Exxon/dsl/scales/24hr 🅕 Nino's N Italian Rest. 🅛 EconoLodge 🅞 South 40 camp resort, **W** 🅛 Travelers Inn

INTERSTATE 95 Cont'd

Exit #	Services
40mm	weigh sta both lanes
37	US 301, Carson, **W** 🔲 BP/dsl, Shell/dsl
36mm	Ⓡs nb, full 🚻 facilities, litter barrel, petwalk, 🏧, 🏞, vending
33	VA 602, **W** 🔲 Davis/Exxon/Subway/Starbucks/dsl/scales/24hr, Moble/Wendys/dsl 🍴 Denny's, Little Italy, Popeye's 🛏 Hampton Inn, Sleep Inn
31	VA 40, Stony Creek, to Waverly, **W** 🔲 Citgo/dsl, Shell/dsl 🍴 Tastee Hut 🅾 Family$
24	VA 645
20	VA 631, Jarratt, **W** 🔲 Exxon/Blimpie/Pizza Hut/dsl/24hr, Sunoco/dsl 🅾 $General, Ford
17	US 301, **1 mi E** 🛏 Knights Inn, Reste Motel 🅾 Jellystone Park Camping
13	VA 614, to Emporia, **E** 🔲 Exxon/Chester's/dsl, Shell/dsl
12	US 301 (from nb)
11b a	US 58, Emporia, to South Hill, **E** 🔲 Citgo/Burger King, Exxon/Blimpie/LJ Silver, Shell/dsl 🍴 Applebee's, Arby's, Carolina BBQ, Cracker Barrel, Domino's, Hardee's, KFC, McDonald's, Pizza Hut, Taco Bell, Wendy's, Wong's Garden 🛏 Country Inn&Suites, Fairfield Inn, Rodeway Inn 🅾 �H, Advance Parts, Buick/Chevrolet/GMC, CVS Drug, Family$, Food Lion, NAPA, O'Reilly Parts, Rite Aid, Verizon, Walmart, **W** 🔲 Exxon, 🅿Pilot/Sadler/5 Guys Burgers/dsl/scales/24hr/@, Race-In/Quiznos/dsl 🍴 Bojangles, Pino's Pizza, Shoney's 🛏 Best Western, Days Inn, Hampton Inn, Holiday Inn Express, Quality Inn, Sleep Inn
8	US 301, **E** 🔲 Citgo, Simmons/Exxon/Huddle House/dsl/scales/24hr 🛏 Motel 6, Red Carpet Inn 🅾 truck repair
4	VA 629, to Skippers, **E** 🔲 ❤Loves/McDonald's/dsl/scales/24hr, 🅿Pilot/Dunkin'/Subway/dsl/scales/24hr, Shell/IHOP, **W** 🛏 AmericanInn
3.5mm	Fountain's Creek
.5mm	**Welcome Ctr nb, full 🚻 facilities, litter barrels, petwalk, 🏧, 🏞, vending**
0mm	Virginia/North Carolina state line

INTERSTATE 264 (Norfolk)

Exit #	Services
23mm	I-264 begins/ends. 🔲 BP, Shell 🅾 convention ctr
22	Birdneck Rd, **N** 🍴 Pizza Hut 🅾 museum, vet, **S** 🔲 Shell/dsl 🍴 Dunkin', Max&Erma's, McDonald's/playplace, Subway 🛏 DoubleTree 🅾 Family$, Food Lion, O'Reilly Parts
21	VA Beach Blvd, First Colonial Rd, **N** 🔲 BP, Shell 🍴 Applebee's, Arby's, Burger King, Chick-fil-A, China Wok, Chipotle, DQ, Five Guys, IHOP, KFC, McDonald's, Moe's SW Grill, Otani Japanese, Outback Steaks, Panera Bread, Pizza Hut, Plaza Azteca, Schlotzsky's, Shogun Japanese, Sonic, Starbucks, Subway, Taco Bell, Virginian Steaks, Wendy's, Zero's Subs 🅾 Advance Parts, CVS, GNC, JoAnn Fabrics, Kroger/dsl, Michael's, Office Depot, Petsmart, Rite Aid, SteinMart, Target, Toyota, Trader Joe's, USPO, Verizon, vet, Walgreens, Whole Foods Mkt, **S** 🔲 Shell, Wawa/dsl 🅾 7-11, CarQuest, Firestone/auto, NAPA
20	US 58 E, to VA Beach Blvd (eb only), **N** 🔲 Kangaroo, Wawa/dsl 🍴 Bojangle's, Capt. George's Seafood, China Moon, Hardee's, Ruby Tuesday, Starbucks, Subway 🅾 7-11, Family$, Food Lion, Kia/Lincoln, Lowe's, PepBoys, TJ Maxx, Tuesday Morning, vet

19	Lynnhaven Pkwy, **N** 🔲 7-11, Wawa 🍴 Ensenada Mexican, Iggle's, Lucky Express, Subway 🅾 Audi, Chevrolet, Ford, Hobby Lobby, Hyundai, Jaguar, Porsche, Subaru, VW, **S** 🍴 Five Guys, McDonald's, Olive Garden, Starbucks, Taco Bell 🅾 Walmart
18	Rosemont, **N** 🔲 Exxon 🍴 Bonefish Grill, Burger King, Denny's, Hardee's, Jade Garden, KFC, LJ Silver, McDonald's, Mi Casita Mexican, Papa John's, Pizza Hut, Starbucks, Taco Bell, Wendy's, Zero's Subs 🛏 EconoLodge 🅾 $Tree, Acura, AutoZone, BJ's Whse/gas, CarMax, Chrysler/Dodge/Jeep, Food Lion, Home Depot, Honda, Kroger, Merchant's Tire/Auto, Nissan, Petsmart, Rite Aid, Sam's Club/gas, Walgreens, **S** 🔲 Speedway/dsl, Wawa/dsl 🍴 Four Seasons Chinese 🅾 $General, CVS
17.5mm	inspection sta wb only
17a b	Independance Blvd, **N** 🔲 Exxon 🍴 Bahama Breeze, Cheesecake Factory, Chipotle, IHOP, Jason's Deli, Macaroni Grill, Max&Erma's, McDonald's, Mission BBQ, Panera Bread, PF Chang's, Ruby Tuesday, Smokey Bones BBQ, Starbucks, Taco Bell, Village Inn, Wendy's 🛏 Candlewood Suites, Crowne Plaza, Days Inn, Extended Stay, Hilton Garden, Motel 6, Westin 🅾 Barnes&Noble, Best Buy, Dick's, Kohl's, Michael's, Old Navy, Steinmart, Target, Walgreens, **S** 🔲 7-11, Exxon/dsl, Wawa/dsl 🍴 Arby's, Azteca Mexican, Domino's, Firehouse Subs, Golden Corral, Hardee's, KFC, Panda China, Quiznos, Starbucks, Subway, Taco Bell, TX Roadhouse, Zero Subs 🛏 InTown Suites 🅾 $General, auto repair, Food Lion, Mazda, Rite Aid, vet
16	Witchduck Rd
15a b	Newtown Rd, **N** 🍴 Capt D's, Domino's, McDonald's, Taco Bell, Wendy's 🛏 Homewood Suites, TownePlace Suites 🅾 7-11, AutoZone, **S** 🔲 BP, Shell 🍴 Denny's 🛏 Courtyard, Hampton Inn, Holiday Inn, La Quinta, Red Roof Inn, SpringHill Suites 🅾 7-11, Rite Aid
14b a	I-64, US 13, to Military Hwy
13	US 13, Military Hwy, **N** 🔲 Shell 🍴 Arby's, Boston Mkt, Lonestar Steaks, Mongolian BBQ, Norfolk Garden Korean, Piccadilly, Schlotzsky's 🛏 Days Inn, EconoLodge, Motel 6, Ramada Ltd 🅾 Costco/gas, CVS, Firestone/auto, Ross
12	Ballentine Blvd, **N** 🅾 �H, Norfolk SU
11b a	US 460, VA 166/168, Brambleton Ave, Campostello Rd, **N** 🔲 7-11 🍴 Chick-fil-A
10	Tidewater Dr, City Hall Ave, exits left from eb, **N** 🔲 Shell 🍴 McDonald's, Popeye's
9	St Paul's Blvd, Waterside Dr, **S** 🅾 to Harbor Park Stadium
8	I-464 S, to Chesapeake
7.5mm	tunnel
7b a	VA 141, Effingham St, Crawford St, **N** 🔲 Shell 🅾 Naval �H, **S** 🔲 Citgo 🅾 Shipyard
6	Des Moines Ave (from eb)

[P] = gas [food] = food [lodging] = lodging [O] = other [Rs] = rest stop   Copyright 2022 - The Next EXIT ®

INTERSTATE 264 (Norfolk) Cont'd

Exit #	Services
5	US 17, Frederick Blvd, **N** [P] WaWa/dsl [food] Chick-fil-A, Dunkin', IHOP, Little Caesar's, Rally's, Taco Bell, Wendy's [O] [H], Advance Parts, CVS Drug, Kroger, to Midtown Tunnel, Walgreens, Walmart, **S** [P] [O] Harley-Davidson
4	VA 337, Portsmouth Blvd
3	Victory Blvd, **N** [P] 7-11, Exxon, Shell, WaWa/dsl [food] Bojangles, Capt D's, CookOut, Domino's, DQ, Firehouse Subs, KFC, Krispy Kreme, McDonald's, Pizza Hut, Ruby Tuesday, Taco Bell, Tops China, Wendy's [O] $Tree, Advance Parts, AutoZone, BigLots, Lowe's, PepBoys, **S** [P] Royal Farms/dsl, Valero/dsl
2b a	Greenwood Dr
0mm	I-264 begins/ends on I-64, exit 299.

INTERSTATE 295 (Richmond)

Exit #	Services
53b a	I-64, W to Charlottesville, E to Richmond, to US 250, I-295 begins/ends.
51b a	Nuckols Rd, **1 mi N** [P] Miller's/dsl, Valero [food] Cheeburger, Chen's Chinese, Home Team Grill, McDonald's, Nonna's Pizzaria, Pizza Hut, Rico's Mexican, Samurai Japanese, Starbucks, Subway, Tropical Smoothie Cafe [O] CVS Drug, Food Lion, Walgreens, **S** [P] Exxon/Mkt Cafe [O] USPO
49b a	US 33, Richmond, **S** [food] JJ's Grille, Little Angela's, Little Caesar's, Little Szechuan, Nuevo Mexico [O] $ General, 7-11, CVS
45b a	Woodman Rd, **1-2 mi S** [P] 7-11 [food] Little Caesar's [O] $General, CVS Drug, Meadow Farm Museum
43	I-95, US 1, N to Washington, S to Richmond (exits left from nb), **N on US 1** [P] Shell/dsl [food] Applebee's, Arby's, BBQ, Buffalo Wild Wings, Chick-fil-A, Chili's, Chipotle Mexican, Coldstone, Famous Dave's BBQ, Firehouse Subs, McDonald's, O'Charley's, O'Dragon buffet, Panera Bread, Papa John's, Pizzaro, Plaza Azteca Mexican, Red Robin, Roda Japanese, Shoney's, Starbucks, Subway, TX Roadhouse, Wendy's [lodging] Candlewood Suites, Comfort Suites, Courtyard, Hampton Inn, SpringHill Suites [O] $Tree, AT&T, Barnes&Noble, Best Buy, Burlington, Dick's, Firestone/auto, GNC, Goodyear/auto, Home Depot, JC Penney, Macy's, Martin's Foods, Merchant's Tire, Michael's, Petsmart, Ross, Target, Tire America, Walgreens, **1-2 mi S** [P] 7-11, Shell, WaWa [food] Aunt Sarah's, Burger King, Frida's Mexican, Hardee's, KFC/Taco Bell, McDonald's, Ming's Dynasty, Starbucks, Subway, Waffle House, Wendy's [lodging] Best Value Inn, Cavalier Motel, Days Inn, EconoLodge, Knights Inn, Sleep Inn [O] $Tree, Food Lion, Lowe's, Walmart
41b a	US 301, VA 2, **E** [P] BP/dsl, Valero/dsl, WaWa/dsl [food] Bojangles, Burger King, China Kitchen, Dunkin', Marty's Grill, McDonald's, Popeye's, Stevi B's, Subway, Tropical Smoothie Cafe, Wendy's, Zheng Chinese [O] $General, AT&T, AutoZone, Kroger/gas, URGENT CARE, Verizon, vet, Walgreens, **0-4 mi W** [P] Exxon/dsl [food] Friendly's [lodging] Holiday Inn, Super 8, Travelodge
38b a	VA 627, Pole Green Rd, **0-1 mi E** [P] 7-11, Exxon/dsl, Sunoco/dsl [food] Antonio's Pizza, Bell Cafe, Bruster's, Chen's Rest., Mimmo's Rest., Patron Mexican, Subway [O] Food Lion, vet, **W** [P] 7-11, Valero [food] Pasta House [O] CVS, [H]
37b a	US 360, **E** [P] BP, Shell/dsl, Valero [food] Applebee's, Arby's, Buffalo Wild Wings, Burger King, Chick-fil-A, Cookout, Cracker Barrel, DQ, Franco's, Gus' Italian, IHOP, Jersey Mike's, KFC, McDonald's, Mexico Rest., Moe's SW Grill, Noodles&Co, Outback Steaks, Panera Bread, Papa John's, Peking Chinese, Pizza Hut, Roma Italian, Ruby Tuesday, Shoney's, Starbucks, Subway, Taco Bell, Waffle House, Wendy's [lodging] Hampton Inn,

Exit #	Services
37b a	**Continued** Holiday Inn Express [O] $Tree, Advance Parts, Aldi Foods, AT&T, Best Buy, BJ's Whse/gas, CVS, Food Lion, GNC, Home Depot, Kohl's, Marshall's, Old Navy, Petsmart, Target, Verizon, Walgreens, Walmart/Burger King, **W** [P] 7-11, Sunoco/dsl, Valero/dsl [O] $General, to Mechanicsville
34b a	VA 615, Creighton Rd, **E** [P] 7-11, Valero
31b a	VA 156, **E** [P] Exxon/dsl [O] to Cold Harbor Bfd, **W** [P] Shel (4mi), Valero [food] Hardee's (4mi) [lodging] Courtyard (4mi) EconoLodge (4mi), Holiday Inn Express (4mi), Motel 6 (4mi)
28	I-64, to US 60, **W** [O] museum
25	Rd 895 W (**toll**), to Richmond
22b a	VA 5, Charles City, **E** [P] Exxon/dsl [food] DQ [O] Shirley Plantation, **W** [P] Valero/Subway/dsl [food] China Taste, Portabella's Cafe [O] Food Lion, Richmond Nat Bfd, Rite Aid
18mm	James River
16	Rivers Bend Blvd
15b a	VA 10, Hopewell, **E** [P] BP/dsl [food] Burger King [O] [H], James River Plantations, **W** [P] EC/Subway/dsl, Exxon/McDonald's dsl, Sheetz, WaWa/dsl [food] Cesare's Ristorante, Chen's Rest. Jalapeno's, Rivers Bend Grill, Taco Bell, Wendy's, Wing's Pizza [lodging] Hyatt Place, Residence Inn [O] CVS Drug, Food Lion
13mm	Appomattox River
9b a	VA 36, Hopewell, **E** [P] Citgo, Gulf, WaWa/dsl [food] Bojangles, El Nopal, Hardee's, KFC, Little Caesar's, McDonald's, Rosa's Italian [lodging] Best Western, EconoLodge, Fairfield Inn, StayOver Suites [O] $General, Advance Parts, AutoZone, Family$, O'Reilly Parts Verizon, vet, Walgreens, **W** [P] BP/dsl, Exxon, Shell/dsl, Sunoco/dsl [food] Burger King, Denny's, DQ, Dragon Express, Dunkin' Kanpai Japanese, McDonald's, Papa John's, Pizza Hut, Ruby Tuesday, Shoney's, Starbucks, Subway, Taco Bell, Top's China Waffle House, Wendy's [lodging] Baymont Inn, Candlewood Suites Hampton Inn, Quality Inn [O] $Tree, Chevrolet, Family$, Food Lion, Rite Aid, to Petersburg Nat Bfd, U-Haul, US Army Museum
5.5mm	Blackwater Swamp
3b a	US 460, Petersburg, to Norfolk, **E** [P] EC/Subway/dsl, Pilot Wendy's/dsl/scales/24hr [food] Prince George BBQ, **1-2 mi** [P] BP/dsl [food] McDonald's
1	I-95, N to Petersburg, S to Emporium, I-295 begins/ends.

INTERSTATE 495 (DC)

Exit #	Services
57	I-95 S, I-395 N, I-95 N. **I-495 & I-95 N run together. See MD I-95 exits 25b a-2b a.**
54b a	VA 620, Braddock Rd, **S** [P] Shell/dsl [food] Hong Kong Expres [O] 7-11, Ctr for the Arts, Geo Mason U, NTB, Rite Aid, Safeway Foods, USPO
52b a	VA 236, Little River Tpk, Fairfax, **E** [P] Liberty/dsl, Sunoco repair [food] Chicken Loco, KFC/Taco Bell, Little Caesar's, McDonald's, Wendy's [O] $Tree, 7-11, Advance Parts, GNC, Petco Safeway Foods
51	VA 657, Gallows Rd, **W** [P] Exxon [O] [H], 7-11
50b a	US 50, Arlington Blvd, Fairfax, Arlington, **E** [lodging] Marriott, **W** [P] Shell, Sunoco/dsl [food] Chevy's Mexican, Five Guys, Grevey' Rest., Jasmine Garden, McDonald's, Panda Express, Panera Bread, Papa John's, Starbucks, Sweetwater Tavern, UNO Grill Wendy's [lodging] Residence Inn [O] [H], CVS Drug, Midas, Staples Target, URGENT CARE, vet
49c b a	I-66 (exits left from both lanes), to Manassas, Front Royal
47b a	VA 7, Leesburg Pike, Tysons Corner, Falls Church, **E** [lodging] Westin **W** [P] BP/dsl, Exxon, Shell/dsl [food] BJ's Rest., Chili's, Jimm John's, McDonald's, Olive Garden, On-the-Border, Panera Bread

(side margin labels: VA / MECHANICSVILLE / HOPEWELL / WASHINGTON AREA)

WASHINGTON AREA

🔼N INTERSTATE 495 (DC) Cont'd

47b a	Continued Silver Diner, Starbucks, Subway, Wendy's 🛏 Embassy Suites, Hilton Garden 🅾 AT&T, Best Buy, Bloomingdale's, Buick/Chevrolet/GMC, Chrysler/Dodge/Jeep, CVS Drug, Marshall's, Mr Tire, PetCo, Petsmart, Staples, Subaru/VW, TJ Maxx
46b a	VA 123, Chain Bridge Rd, W 🚗 Gulf/dsl, Sunoco/dsl 🍴 Cheesecake Factory, Maggiano's, PF Chang's 🛏 Courtyard, Crowne Plaza 🅾 Macy's
45b a	VA 267 W (toll), to I-66 E, to Dulles Airport
44	VA 193, Langley
43	G Washington Mem Pkwy, no trucks
42mm	Virginia/Maryland state line, Potomac River. **Exits 41-27 are in Maryland.**
41	Clara Barton Pkwy, Carderock, Great Falls, no trucks
40	Cabin John Pkwy, Glen Echo (from sb), no trucks
39	MD 190, River Rd, Washington, Potomac
38	I-270, to Frederick
36	MD 187, Old Georgetown Rd, S 🅾 H
35	(from wb), I-270
34	MD 355, Wisconsin Ave, Bethesda
33	MD 185, Connecticut Ave, N 🅾 LDS Temple, S 🚗 Citgo/repair, Giant/dsl, Liberty 🍴 Chevy Chase Mkt, Starbucks
31b a	MD 97, Georgia Ave, Silver Spring, N 🅾 H, S 🚗 BP/dsl, Exxon/dsl, Shell, W Express/dsl 🍴 Armand's Pizza, Domino's, Mayflower Chinese 🅾 CVS Drug, Snider's Foods, Staples, vet
30b a	US 29, Colesville, N 🚗 BP/dsl, Citgo, Shell 🍴 Chipotle, McDonald's, Papa John's, Red Maple Asian, Starbucks, Subway 🅾 7-11/Jerry's Subs, CVS Drug, Safeway Foods
29b a	MD 193, University Blvd
28b a	MD 650, New Hampshire Ave, N 🚗 BP, Exxon/dsl, Shell/repair 🍴 Domino's, Quizno's, Starbucks, Urban BBQ 🅾 7-11, CVS Drug, Safeway Foods
27	I-95, N to Baltimore, S to Richmond.
	I-495 & I-95 S run together. See MD I-95, exits 25b a-2b a.

🔼N INTERSTATE 664 (Norfolk)

PORTSMOUTH

Exit #	Services
15b a	I-64 to Chesapeake, I-264 E to Portsmouth & Norfolk. **I-664 begins/ends on I-64, exit 299.**
13b a	US 13, US 58, US 460, Military Hwy, E 🚗 Shell/Frank's/dsl 🛏 Bowers Hill Inn
12	VA 663, Dock Landing Rd
11b a	VA 337, Portsmouth Blvd, E 🚗 7-11, Citgo, Shell/dsl, Speedway 🍴 Applebee's, Arby's, Buffet City, Burger King, Chick-fil-A, Chili's, ChuckECheese, DQ, Dunkin', Five Guys, Golden Corral, IHOP, McDonald's, Olive Garden, Outback Steaks, Piccadilly, Pizza Hut, Pizza Hut, Red Lobster, Red Robin, Starbucks, Subway, Taco Bell, Wendy's 🛏 Extended Stay 4 Less, Hampton Inn, Holiday Inn Express 🅾 $Tree, AutoZone, Best Buy, Big Lots, BJ's Whse/gas, Buick, Firestone/auto, Food Lion, Ford, Home Depot, Merchant's Auto Ctr, Michael's, Old Navy, Petsmart, Ross, Sam's Club/gas, Target, Tuesday Morning, Walmart, W 🚗 7-11 🍴 Burger King, Cracker Barrel, Old Bay Seafood, Subway, Waffle House 🛏 Candlewood Suites, Fairfield Inn 🅾 Lowe's
10	VA 659, Pughsville Rd, E 🚗 7-11, Citgo, Shell 🍴 La Tolteca 🅾 Food Lion, Rite Aid, vet
9b a	US 17, US 164, E 🚗 7-11, Speedway/dsl, Wawa 🍴 Burger King, Capt D's, Domino's, DQ, Dunkin', Great Wall Chinese, KFC, McDonald's, Papa John's, Pizza Hut, Sonic, Taco Bell, Waffle House, Wendy's 🛏 Budget Lodge, Extended Stay America,

9b a	Continued Sleep Inn, Studios & Suites for Less, Super 8 🅾 $Tree, Advance Parts, Chevrolet, Honda, Hyundai, Kia, NAPA, Nissan, O'Reilly Parts, tires, Toyota, W 🍴 Buffalo Wild Wings, Subway 🛏 Comfort Suites, Hilton Garden 🅾 H, Harris Teeter, to James River Br
8b a	VA 135, College Dr, E 🚗 7-11, Murphy USA/dsl 🍴 Applebee's, Arby's, Chick-fil-A, Chipotle, Firehouse Subs, IHOP, McDonald's, Panda Express, Panera Bread, Ruby Tuesday, Subway, Taco Bell, TX Roadhouse, Wendy's, Zaxby's 🅾 Dick's, Discount Tire, Food Lion, GNC, Kohl's, Petsmart, Rite Aid, TJ Maxx, Walmart, W 🍴 Riverstone Chophouse 🛏 Courtyard, TownePlace Suites
11.5mm	insp sta nb
9mm	James River
8mm	tunnel
7	Terminal Ave
6	25th St, 26th St, E 🚗 7-11 🍴 McDonald's, W 🍴 Subway
5	US 60 W, 35th St, Jefferson Ave, E 🚗 Fast&Easy 🍴 #1 Chinese, Church's, King's Pizza 🅾 Hornsby Tire
4	Chesnut Ave, Roanoke Ave
3	Aberdeen Rd, W 🚗 7-11 🍴 Hardee's, McDonald's, Wendy's
2	Powhatan Pkwy, E 🚗 7-11, 1-2 mi W 🍴 Coldstone, Joe's Crabshack, Longhorn Steaks 🛏 Hilton Garden, SpringHill Suites 🅾 Bass Pro Shop, BJ's Whse/gas, Lowe's
1b a	I-64, W to Richmond, E to Norfolk. **I-664 begins/ends on I-64.**

NOTES

WASHINGTON

INTERSTATE 5

Exit #	Services
277mm	USA/Canada Border, Washington state line, customs
276	WA 548 S, Blaine, E 📱 Chevron/dsl, Exxon/dsl, Mobil/dsl, Shell/dsl 🍴 Big Al's Diner 🏠 Northwoods Motel ⭕ Duty Free, NAPA, to Peace Arch SP, W **Welcome Ctr**, 📱 Chevron/dsl/repair 🍴 Back Forest Steaks, Chada Thai, Edaleen Dairy, Ocean Bay Chinese, Pasa Del Norte, Pizza Factory, Railway Cafe, Starbucks, Tony's Cafe 🏠 Anchor Inn, Bay Side Motel, Cottage by the Bay B&B, International Motel, Sunset Inn ⭕ Blaine Marine Park, USPO
275	WA 543 N (from nb, no return), E 📱 Chevron/dsl, Mkt/dsl, Shell/dsl 🍴 Burger King, Subway ⭕ $Tree, Border Tire, Cost-Cutter Foods, Rite Aid, truck customs
274	Peace Portal Drive (from nb, no return), Blaine, W 📱 Shell/dsl 🍴 Lizzie's Cafe ⭕ Semi-ah-moo Resort
270	Birch Bay, Lynden, W 📱 Shell/Domino's/Subway/dsl 🍴 Bob's Burgers, Jack-in-the-Box, Subway 🏠 Semi-ah-moo Resort ⭕ Birch Bay Mkt, Thousand Trails Camping, vet
269mm	Welcome Ctr sb, full ♿ facilities, info, litter barrels, petwalk, 🚻, 🐾, vending
267mm	Rs nb, full ♿ facilities, info, litter barrels, petwalk, 🚻, 🐾, vending
266	WA 548 N, Grandview Rd, Custer, W 📱 Arco ⭕ Birch Bay SP
263	Portal Way, E 📱 Pacific Pride/dsl, Shell/dsl 🍴 El Nopal Mexican ⭕ AA RV Park, Cedars RV Park
263mm	Nooksack River
262	Main St, Ferndale, E 📱 Chevron/dsl, ▱▱▱/Subway/dsl/scales/24hr 🍴 McDonald's 🏠 Super 8 ⭕ GCR Tires, vet, W 📱 Gull/dsl, Shell/dsl 🍴 Bob's Burgers, Domino's, DQ, Jack-in-the-Box, Papa Murphy's, Sonic, Starbucks, Taco Time 🏠 Motel 6 ⭕ $Tree, Grocery Outlet, Haggen's Foods, NAPA, O'Reilly Parts, Schwab Tire, Verizon, vet, Walgreens
260	Slater Rd, Lummi Island, E 📱 Arco/dsl ⭕ antiques, El Monte RV Ctr, **4 mi** W 🏠 Silver Reef Hotel/Casino ⭕ Lummi Ind Res
258	Bakerview Rd, E 🍴 Asian Fusion, Five Guys, IHOP, Jack-in-the-Box, Papa Murphy's, Port of Subs, Starbucks, Subway, Taco Time 🏠 La Quinta ⭕ Costco/dsl, Fred Meyer/dsl, Verizon, W 📱 76/7-11, Arco, Mkt/dsl 🍴 Mykono's Greek Rest. 🏠 Holiday Inn Express, Hotel Bellingham, Shamrock Motel ⭕ 🏥, Bellingham RV Park, st patrol
257	Northwest Ave, E 🍴 Jack-in-the-Box, Starbucks 🏠 Home 2 Hilton, La Quinta, SpringHill Suites, TownePlace Suites ⭕ Cadillac/Chevrolet
256b	Bellis Fair Mall Pkwy (from nb), E ⭕ JC Penney, Target
256a	WA 539 N, Meridian St, E 📱 Shell/dsl, Super Gas/dsl 🍴 Arby's, Asian 1, Boston's Rest., Buffalo Wild Wings, Burger King, China Palace, Chipotle, Denny's, Domino's, DQ, Jimmy John's, Lilia's Mexican, McDonald's, Mi Mexico, Olive Garden, Red Robin, Shari's, Starbucks, Subway, Taco Bell, Taco Time, Thai House Rest., Wendy's, Wonderful Buffet 🏠 Baymont Inn, Best Western, Comfort Inn, Holiday Inn Express, Oxford Suites, Quality Inn ⭕ $Tree, AT&T, Barnes&Noble, Best Buy, Dick's, Hobby Lobby, Home Depot, JC Penney, Kohl's, Macy's, Marshall's, Michael's, Midas, O'Reilly Parts, Office Depot, O'Reilly Parts, PetCo, Petsmart, Rite Aid, Ross, Schwab Tire, Sierra Trading Post, Target, TJ Maxx, U-Haul, Verizon, Walgreens, Walmart/McDonald's, WinCo Foods, W 🍴 Slo Pitch Grill 🏠 EconoLodge, Rodeway Inn

Exit #	Services
255	WA 542 E, Sunset Dr, Bellingham, E 📱 76, Chevron/dsl, Shell/dsl 🍴 A&W/KFC, Applebee's, El Gitano Mexican, Hawaii BBQ, Jack-in-the-Box, Panda Express, Panda Palace, RoundTable Pizza, Starbucks, Taco Bell ⭕ Jo-Ann Fabrics, Lowe's, Rite Aid, Safeway/dsl, to Mt Baker, Tuesday Morning, USPO, Verizon, Walgreens, W ⭕ 🏥
254	Iowa St, State St, Bellingham, E 📱 76, Mobil/dsl ⭕ Audi/VW, Chrysler/Dodge/Jeep, Honda, Hyundai, Kia, Mercedes, Nissan, Subaru, Toyota, Volvo, W 📱 Chevron/dsl, Shell 🍴 DQ, McDonald's, Starbucks, Subway ⭕ AutoZone, Ford, Midas, NAPA, O'Reilly Parts
253	Lakeway Dr, Bellingham, E 🍴 Little Caesar's, Papa John's, Papa Murphy's, Port of Subs, Rhodes Cafe, Sol de Mexico, Subway, Woods Coffee 🏠 Guesthouse Inn, Sheraton Four Point ⭕ 7-11, Discount Tire, Fred Meyer/dsl, URGENT CARE, Whole Foods Mkt, W same as 252
252	Samish Way, Bellingham, E same as 253, W 📱 76, Chevron/dsl, SuperGas/dsl 🍴 Boomers Drive-In, Busara Thai Cuisine, Domino's, El Agave, El Albanil Mexican, Five Columns Greek, Kyoto Steaks, McDonald's, Pizza Hut, Sehome Diner, Starbucks, Subway, Taco Time, Wendy's 🏠 Bay City Motel, Bellingham Lodge, Cascade Inn, Coachman Inn, Days Inn, Motel 6, Villa Inn ⭕ $Tree, Ace Hardware, AT&T, Haggen Foods, REI, Rite Aid, URGENT CARE, vet, Walgreens
250	WA 11 S, Chuckanut Dr, Bellingham, Fairhaven Hist Dist, W 📱 Arco, Shell/repair 🍴 Starbucks, Subway ⭕ to Alaska Ferry, to Larrabee SP
246	N Lake Samish, E ⭕ Lake Padden RA, W 📱 Shell/dsl
242	Nulle Rd, S Lake Samish
240	Alger, E 📱 Shell/dsl/LP/RV dump 🍴 Alger Grille 🏠 Whispering Firs Motel/RV Parking
238mm	Rs both lanes, full ♿ facilities, litter barrels, petwalk, 🚻, 🐾, vending
236	Bow Hill Rd, E ⭕ Skagit Hotel Casino/rest./dsl/LP
235mm	weigh sta sb
234mm	Samish River
232	Cook Rd, Sedro-Woolley, E 📱 Chevron/dsl, Shell/dsl, Tesla EV 🍴 Bob's Burgers, Jack-in-the-Box, Starbucks, Subway 🏠 Fairfield Inn ⭕ 🏥, KOA (3mi)
231	WA 11 N, Chuckanut Dr, E ⭕ Camping World RV Ctr, Halterman's RV Ctr, Kia, vet, W ⭕ st patrol, to Larrabee SP (14mi)
230	WA 20, Burlington, E 📱 Chevron, Shell/dsl 🍴 Applebee's, Carino's Italian, Jack-in-the-Box, Mi Mexico, MOD Pizza, Outback Steaks, Papa Murphy's, Pizza Factory, Pizza Hut/Taco Bell, Popeye's, Red Robin, Starbucks 🏠 Cocusa Motel, Sterling Motel ⭕ 🏥, $Tree, 7-11, AutoZone, Fred Meyer/dsl, Haggen Foods, JC Penney, Macy's, Schwab Tire, Skagit Transmissions, Target, to N Cascades NP, Walgreens, W 📱 Pacific Pride/dsl 🍴 McDonald's 🏠 Holiday Inn Express ⭕ Harley-Davidson, Hyundai, to San Juan Ferry
229	George Hopper Rd, E 📱 Arco, Mobil/dsl 🍴 Carl's Jr, Chipotle, Mexican, Five Guys, Jamba Juice, Jimmy John's, McDonald's, Olive Garden, Panera Bread, Sakura Japanese, Shari's, Starbucks, Subway, Taco Del Mar, Wendy's 🏠 Candlewood Suites, Hampton Inn ⭕ AT&T, Best Buy, Costco/gas, Dick's, Discount Tire, Home Depot, Kohl's, Michael's, Old Navy, Outlet Shops/famous brands, Petsmart, Ross, See's Candies, Verizon, vet, W ⭕ Chrysler/Jeep/Dodge, Ford/Lincoln, Honda, Mazda, Nissan, Subaru, Toyota, VW

WA

🔼 INTERSTATE 5 Cont'd

Exit #	Services
228mm	Skagit River
227	WA 538 E, College Way, Mt Vernon, **E** 🍴 A&W, Big Scoop Rest., Denny's, Dragon Inn, El Gitano, Firehouse Subs, Hong Kong Rest., Jack-in-the Box, Jersey Mike's, KFC, Max Dale's Steak Chops, Moreno's Mexican, Papa Murphy's, Pizza Hut, Riverside Cafe, RoundTable Pizza, Starbucks, Subway, Taco Bell, Taco Time 🏠 Days Inn, West Winds Motel 🅞 $Tree, Ace Hardware, AutoZone, Grocery Outlet, Hobby Lobby, Jo-Ann Fabrics, Motorworks, Office Depot, O'Reilly Parts, PepBoys, PetCo, Rite Aid, Safeway/dsl, Tire Factory, Verizon, **W** 🍴 APP/dsl, Shell/dsl 🍴 Arby's, Burger King, Burgermaster, DQ, Fortune Chinese, IHOP, Los Compadres, Panda Express, Royal Star Buffet 🏠 Best Western, Quality Inn, Tulip Inn 🅞 Blade RV Ctr, Chevrolet, Lowe's, Riverbend RV Park, URGENT CARE, Walmart/Subway
226	WA 536 W, Kincaid St, **E** 🅞 🏠, **W** 🍴 Old Towne Grainery Rest., Skagit River Brewing Co 🅞 City Ctr, NAPA, Red Apple Mkt, visitor info
225	Anderson Rd, **E** 🍴 76/dsl 🅞 CarQuest, Country Motorhomes, **W** 🍴 Chevron 🅞 Evert's RV Ctr, Freightliner, Poulsbo RV Ctr
224	WA 99 S (from nb, no return), S Mt Vernon, **E** food, gas/dsl
221	WA 534 E, Conway, Lake McMurray, **E** 🍴 76/dsl 🅞 farmers mkt, **W** 🍴 76/dsl, Chevron/dsl/LP 🍴 Conway Deli 🏠 Channel Lodge/Rest. (11mi) 🅞 Blake's RV Park/marina (6mi), USPO
218	Starbird Rd
215	300th NW, **W** 🍴 Interstate/dsl
214mm	weigh sta nb
212	WA 532 W, Stanwood, Bryant, **W** 🍴 76/dsl, Shell/Burger Stop/dsl 🅞 Camano Island SP (19mi)
210	236th NE, **E** 🅞 Angel Winds Casino, River Rock/dsl
209mm	Stillaguamish River
208	WA 530, Silvana, Arlington, **E** 🍴 76, A1/dsl, Arco/dsl, Chevron/dsl, 🚚/PJ Fresh/dsl/scales/24hr 🍴 Denny's, Subway 🏠 Arlington Motel 🅞 Chevrolet, to N Cascades Hwy, **W** 🍴 Mobil/dsl
207mm	🆁🆂 both lanes, coffee, full 🏠 facilities, litter barrels, petwalk, 🍴, 🏠, RV dump, vending

206	WA 531, Lakewood, **E** 🍴 7-11, 76/dsl, Arco, Shell 🍴 Alfy's Pizza, Buzz Inn Steaks, Domino's, Jack-in-the-Box, Jersey Mike's, Jimmy John's, KFC, Little Caesar's, McDonald's, Moose Creek BBQ, Olympia Pizza, Panda Express, Papa Murphy's, Peking Palace, Starbucks, Subway, Taco Time, Wendy's 🏠 Best Western+, Quality Inn, Wyndham Garden 🅞 $Tree, AT&T, Chrysler/Dodge/Jeep, Ford, Harley-Davidson, Honda, Jo-Ann Fabrics, Lowe's, O'Reilly Parts, Rite Aid, Safeway/dsl, Schwab Tire, vet, Walmart/Subway, **W** 🍴 Bonefish Grill, Boston's, Buffalo Wild Wings, Burger King, Chipotle, Coldstone, Firehouse Subs, Five Guys, Hop Jack's, IHOP, Jamba Juice, MOD Pizza, Outback Steaks, Pizza Hut, Popeye's, Qdoba, Red Robin, Starbucks, Taco Bell, Taco Bell 🅞 AT&T, Best Buy, Costco/gas, Dick's, Discount Tire, Firestone/auto, Hobby Lobby, Marshall's, Michael's, Office Depot, PetCo, Target, to Wenburg SP, Tuesday Morning, Verizon
202	116th NE, **E** 🍴 Shell/dsl 🍴 Arby's, Blazing Onion Burger, Carl's Jr, DQ, Papa John's, Popeye's, Sonic, Starbucks, Subway, Taco Bell 🏠 Home 2 Suites 🅞 $Tree, Kohl's, Petsmart, Rite Aid, Ross, URGENT CARE, Verizon, WinCo Foods, **W** 🍴 Chevron/dsl, Donna's Trkstp/Gull/dsl/scales/24hr/@ 🍴 McDonald's, Olive Garden, RAM Rest. 🅞 Seattle Outlets/famous brands, st patrol, Tulalip Resort/Casino
200	88th St NE, Quil Ceda Way, **E** 🍴 7-11, Shell/dsl/LP 🍴 Applebee's, Jersey Mike's, Mkt St Cafe, Starbucks 🏠 Holiday Inn Express 🅞 Haggen's Foods, **W** 🍴 USA 🍴 Bob's Burgers, Panera Bread, Port of Subs 🅞 Cabela's, casino, Home Depot, Walmart/McDonald's
199	WA 528 E, Marysville, Tulalip, **E** 🍴 76, Arco, Chevron/dsl, Shell/dsl 🍴 Burger King, Don's Rest./24hr, DQ, Jack-in-the-Box, Jimmy John's, Las Margaritas Mexican, MOD Pizza, Subway 🏠 Village Motel/Rest. 🅞 Albertson's, AT&T, Big Lots, JC Penney, Petco, Rite Aid, Staples, Verizon, Walgreens, **W** 🍴 76, Chevron/dsl 🍴 McDonald's, Taco Time, Wendy's 🏠 Quality Inn 🅞 casino, Chevrolet, Robinson RV Ctr, Subaru, to Tulalip Indian Res
198	Port of Everett (from sb), Steamboat Slough, st patrol
195mm	Snohomish River
195	Port of Everett (from nb), Marine View Dr
194	US 2 E, Everett Ave, **W** 🍴 Shell/dsl 🅞 City Ctr, Schwab Tire
193	WA 529, Pacific Ave (from nb), **W** 🍴 🍴 Denny's, Hunan Palace 🏠 Best Western, Delta Hotel, Travelodge 🅞 🏠, Lowe's

▲▼ INTERSTATE 5 Cont'd

Exit #	Services
192	Broadway, to 41st St, **W** 🅿 76/dsl, Chevron, Shell 🍴 Buzz Inn Steaks, IHOP, Little Caesar's, Quiznos, Starbucks, Subway 🛏 Travelodge 🅾 City Ctr, Verizon
189	WA 526 W, WA 527, Everett Mall Way, Everett, **E** 🅿 Arco, Chevron, Shell/dsl 🍴 Alfy's Pizza, Burger King, Buzz Inn Steaks, Subway, Wendy's 🛏 EconoLodge, Extended Stay America 🅾 Costco/gas, vet, WinCo Foods, **W** 🅿 Shell/dsl 🍴 Bob's Burgers, Buffalo Wild Wings, Famous Dave's, Jack-in-the-Box, Jimmy John's, Olive Garden 🛏 Days Inn, Extended Stay America, Woodspring Suites 🅾 Best Buy, Michael's, Petsmart, TJ Maxx, Verizon, Walmart
188mm	🆁🆂/weigh sta sb, coffee, full ♿ facilities, info, litter barrels, 🚻, 🛒, RV dump
186	WA 96, 128th SW, **E** 🅿 76/dsl, Shell/dsl, Texaco 🍴 O'Donnells Rest. 🛏 Quality Inn 🅾 Lakeside RV Park, **W** 🅿 Arco, Chevron, Shell 🍴 A&W/KFC, Acropolis Pizza, Denny's, Dickey's BBQ, DQ, McDonald's, Ming Dynasty, Papa John's, Pizza Hut, Starbucks, Subway, Taco Bell, Taco Time 🛏 Holiday Inn Express, La Quinta, Motel 6 🅾 $Tree, Albertson's/Sav-on, Maple RV Park, PepBoys, vet
183	164th SW, **E** 🅿 Arco, Shell/dsl 🍴 Jack-in-the-Box, Panda Express, Quiznos, Starbucks, Subway, Taco Del Mar, Taco Time 🅾 Walgreens, Walmart, **W** 🅿 Chevron/dsl 🍴 Five Guys, MOD Pizza, Subway 🅾 Fred Meyer/dsl, vet
182	WA 525, Alderwood Mall Blvd, to Alderwood Mall, **E** I-405 S, to Bellevue, **W** 🅿 Arco 🍴 Anthony's SeafoodGrill, Azteca Mexican, Buffalo Wild Wings, Cafe Rio, Claim Jumper, Fatburger, Jersey Mike's, Keg Steaks, Macaroni Grill, Panera Bread, PF Chang's, Qdoba Mexican, Red Robin, TCBY 🛏 Homewood Suites, Residence Inn 🅾 JC Penney, Kohl's, Macy's, Nordstrom, REI, Rite Aid, Ross, See's Candies, Target, vet, World Mkt
181	44th Ave W, to WA 524, Lynnwood, **E** 🅿 76/dsl, Arco, Shell 🍴 Chick-fil-A, Jimmy John's, Little Caesar's, McDonald's/playplace, Old Spaghetti Factory, Starbucks 🛏 Embassy Suites, Extended Stay America, Hampton Inn, Holiday Inn Express 🅾 Albertson's, Barnes&Noble, Best Buy, Jaguar, Land Rover, Lowe's, Old Navy, O'Reilly Parts, PetCo, Staples, Verizon, vet, Whole Foods Mkt, **W** 🅿 76/dsl, Arco, Shell/repair 🍴 Applebee's, Arby's, Buca Italian, Chipotle Mexican, ChuckeCheese, Denny's, Ezell's Chicken, Harbour Buffet, IHOP, Jack-in-the-Box, KFC, McDonald's, Olive Garden, Panda Express, Red Lobster, Rock Woodfire Pizza, Starbucks, Subway, Taco Bell, Taco del Mar, Taco Time, Todo Mexico, Wendy's, Zeeks Pizza 🛏 Best Value Inn, Best Western, Courtyard, La Quinta 🅾 7-11, Fred Meyer/dsl, Goodyear/auto, Grocery Outlet, Schwab Tire, URGENT CARE, USPO, vet
179	220th SW, Mountlake Terrace, Mountlake Terrace, **W** 🅿 Shell/dsl 🍴 Azteca Mexican, Port of Subs, Subway 🅾 🏥, vet
178	236th St SW (from nb), Mountlake Terrace
177	WA 104, Edmonds, **E** 🅿 Chevron/dsl, Shell/dsl 🍴 Domino's, Gabriel's Fire BBQ, Mazatlan Mexican, McDonald's/playplace, Pagliacchi Pizza, Starbucks, Subway, Time Out Burger, Todo Mexico 🛏 Motel 6 🅾 O'Reilly Parts, RiteAid, Thriftway Foods, URGENT CARE
176	NE 175th St, Aurora Ave N, to Shoreline, **E** 🅾 Safeway/dsl
175	WA 523, NE 145th, 5th Ave NE
174	NE 130th, Roosevelt Way
173	1st Ave NE, Northgate Way, **E** 🅿 EVgo EVC 🍴 Azteca Mexican, BlueFin Grill, CA Pizza Kitchen, Chipotle Mexican, Domino's, Five Guys, Gate Buffet, Jimmy John's, Mama Stortini's, Ram Rest.,
173	Continued Red Robin, Stanford's Rest. 🅾 Barnes&Noble, Best Buy, Dick's Discount Tire, JC Penney, Macy's, Nordstrom, Old Navy, Petco, Ross, Target, Verizon, **W** 🅿 76, Chevron, Shell/dsl 🍴 McDonald's, Saffron Grill, Starbucks 🛏 Hotel Nexus 🅾 7-11
172	N 85th, Aurora Ave
171	WA 522, Lake City Way, Bothell
170	Ravenna Blvd, **E** 🅿 Shell/dsl
169	NE 45th, NE 50th, **E** 🅿 Chevron, Shell 🍴 Qdoba, Subway 🅾 🏥, PetCo, U of WA, vet, **W** 🅾 to Seattle Pacific U, zoo
168b	WA 520, to Bellevue
168a	Lakeview Blvd, downtown
167	Mercer St (exits left from nb), Fairview Ave, Seattle Ctr
166	Olive Way, Stewart St, **E** 🅾 🏥, **W** 🛏 SpringHill Suites 🅾 Honda
165a	Seneca St (exits left from nb), James St, **E** 🅾 🏥
165b	Union St, **E** 🛏 Homewood Suites, **W** 🍴 Ruth's Chris Steak 🛏 Crowne Plaza, Hilton, Renaissance Inn, Sheraton
164b	4th Ave S, to Kingdome, downtown
164a	I-90 E, to Spokane, downtown
163	6th Ave, S Spokane St, W Seattle Br, Columbian Way, **1 mi W** 🅾 4th Ave S 🅿 Arco/dsl, Gull/dsl, Shell 🍴 Arby's, Burger King, Denny's, Jack-in-the-Box, KFC, McDonald's, Starbucks, Subway, Taco Bell 🅾 Costco/gas, Pepboys, USPO
162	Corson Ave, Michigan St (exits left from nb), same as 161
161	Swift Ave, Albro Place, **W** 🅿 76/dsl, Shell/dsl 🍴 Starbucks 🛏 Georgetown Inn 🅾 Verizon
158	Pacific Hwy S, E Marginal Way, **W** 🅿 Chevron/dsl 🅾 NAPA
157	ML King Way
156	WA 539 N, Interurban Ave (no EZ return to sb), Tukwila, 🅿 Pacific Pride/dsl 🍴 Billy Baroos Rest., **W** 🅿 76/dsl, Shell/dsl 🍴 Jack-in-the-Box, Quiznos, Starbucks, Sunny Teriyaki 🛏 Days Inn
154b	WA 518, Burien, **W** 🛏 Extended Stay America
154a	I-405, N to Bellevue
153	S Center Pkwy, (from nb), **E** 🅿 Chevron/dsl 🍴 Applebee's, Azteca Mexican, Bahama Breeze, BJ's Rest., Buffalo Wild Wings, Burger King, CA Pizza Kitchen, Cheesecake Factory, Chipotle Mexican, ClaimJumper, Coldstone, Duke's ChowderHouse, Famous Dave's, Five Guys, Grazie Ristorante, IHOP, Jamba Juice, Mayflower of China, McDonald's, Mizuki Buffet, Mizuki Japanese Steaks, Mongolian Grill, Old Spaghetti Factory, Olive Garden, Outback Steaks, Panda Express, Panera Bread, Qdoba Mexican, Red Robin, Simply Thai, Sizzler, Stanford's Rest., Starbucks, Subway, Thai Cuisine, Zoopa 🛏 DoubleTree Inn, Holiday Inn Express, Hotel Interurban 🅾 $Tree, Acura, AT&T, Barnes&Noble, Best Buy, Big Lots, Firestone/auto, JC Penney, Jo-Ann Fabrics, Kohl's, Lowe's, Macy's, Michael's, Nordstrom, Nordstrom Rack, Office Depot, Old Navy, PetCo, Petsmart, REI, Ross, See's Candies, Target, Tuesday Morning, Verizon, World Mkt
152	S 188th, Orillia Rd, **W** 🅿 76/dsl 🍴 Dave's Diner, Denny's, Jack-in-the-Box, Taco Bell 🛏 DoubleTree Hotel, Hampton Inn, La Quinta, Motel 6 🅾 city park, to 🌊
151	S 200th, Military Rd, **E** 🅿 76/Subway/dsl 🛏 Motel 6, 🅿 7-11, 76, Chevron 🍴 IHOP 🛏 Best Value Inn, Best Western, Comfort Inn, Country Inn Suites, Days Inn, Fairfield Inn, Hampton Inn, Holiday Inn Express, Residence Inn, Sleep Inn 🅾 AutoZone, city park, O'Reilly Parts, U-Haul
149	WA 516, to Kent, Des Moines, **E** 🛏 Century Motel 🅾 Poulsbo RV Ctr, **W** 🅿 Arco, Chevron/dsl, Shell/dsl 🍴 Church's, Los Cabos Mexican, McDonald's, Pizza Hut, Starbucks, Subway 🛏 Garden Suites, Kings Arms Motel 🅾 $Tree, Lowe's, Meineke, to Saltwater SP, Walgreens

INTERSTATE 5 Cont'd

Exit #	Services
147	S 272nd, **E** 🅖 Chevron/dsl, **W** on Pacific Hwy 🅖 Arco, Shell/dsl 🅕 Jack-in-the-Box, Little Caesar's, McDonald's, Papa Murphy's, Starbucks, Subway, Taco Bell 🅞 AutoZone, Bartell Drug, Safeway
143	S 320th, Federal Way, **W** 🅖 76/dsl, Arco 🅕 Applebee's, Azteca Mexican, Black Angus, Black Bear Diner, Buffalo Wild Wings, Cafe Rio, Chick-fil-A, Chipotle Mexican, Church's, Coldstone, Denny's, Domino's, Grand Peking, Ivar's Seafood, Jasmine Mongolian, Jimmy John's, McDonald's, Mika Japanese Buffet, Old Country Buffet, Panda Express, Panera Bread, Papa Murphy's, Qdoba Mexican, Ram Rest., Red Lobster, Red Robin, Starbucks, Subway, Taco Time, Tokyo Japanese Steaks, Village Inn, Wendy's 🅛 Best Western+, Clarion, Comfort Inn, Courtyard, Extended Stay America, Hampton Inn 🅞 AT&T, Barnes&Noble, Best Buy, Campeon Mkt, Dick's, Jo-Ann Fabrics, Kohl's, Macy's, Marlene's Natural Mkt, Michael's, O'Reilly Parts, PetCo, Petsmart, Rite Aid, Ross, Safeway/dsl, Target, TJ Maxx, to Dash Point SP, Trader Joe's, Tuesday Morning, Verizon, Walmart/McDonald's
142b a	WA 18 E, S 348th, Enchanted Pkwy, **E** 🅞 funpark, **W** 🅖 Chevron, Shell/dsl 🅕 Arby's, Biscuits Cafe, Burger King, Del Taco, Denny's, Jack-in-the-Box, Jamba Juice, Jimmy Mac's Roadhouse, KFC, McDonald's, Olive Garden, Panda Express, Popeye's, Puerta Vallarta, Quiznos, RoundTable Pizza, Shari's, Starbucks, Subway, Taco Bell, Taco Del Mar, Taco Time, Thai Bistro, The Rock Pizza, Time Out Grill 🅛 Day's Inn, Quality Inn, Red Lion Inn 🅞 🅷, AT&T, Chevrolet, Costco/gas, Discount Tire, Hobby Lobby, Home Depot, Lowe's, Office Depot, O'Reilly Parts, Pepboys, Schwab Tire, UHaul, Verizon, Walmart/Subway
140mm	🆁🆂 both lanes, full facilities, litter barrels, petwalk, RV dump, weigh sta nb
137	WA 99, Fife, Milton, **E** 🅖 76/dsl, Chevron/dsl, Shell 🅕 DQ, Johnny's Rest., Warthog BBQ 🅛 Motel 6 🅞 Acura, Cadillac, RV Country, visitor info, **W** 🅖 76/dsl, 76/dsl 🅕 Arby's, Denny's, Fife Thai Rest., Jersey Mike's, KFC, McDonald's, Pick Quick Burgers, Pizza Hut, Poodle Dog, Sapporo Japanese, Starbucks, Subway, Taco Bell, Taco Time, Wendy's 🅛 Days Inn, EQC Motel/casino, Quality Inn 🅞 7-11, Audi/Porsche, Mercedes, O'Reilly Parts, Schwab Tire, Tacoma RV Ctr, Verizon
136b a	Port of Tacoma, **E** 🅖 CFN/dsl 🅞 Baydos RV Ctr, BMW, Costco, Honda, I-5 Motors, Mini, Peterbilt, **W** 🅖 76/dsl, Gull/dsl, ♥Love's/Chester's/Subway/dsl/scales/LP/RV dump/24hr, Shell/dsl 🅕 Jack-in-the-Box 🅛 Extended Stay America, Guesthouse Inn, Port of Tacoma Inn, Rodeway Inn, Sunshine Motel, Travelodge 🅞 Fife RV Ctr, Goodyear/biodsl, Harley-Davidson, Johnson RV Ctr, Land Rover/Jaguar/Lexus, Meineke, NAPA, Poulsbo RV Ctr, truck repair, Volvo
135	Bay St, Puyallup, **E** 🅖 76/Tahoma Express 🅞 Majestic RV Park (4mi), **W** 🅕 Subway 🅛 La Quinta 🅞 to Tacoma Dome
134	Portland Ave (from nb), same as 135
133	WA 7, I-705, **W** 🅛 Best Western, Courtyard, Holiday Inn Express 🅞 City Ctr, museum, Tacoma Dome
132	WA 16 W, S 38th, Gig Harbor, to Bremerton, **W** 🅕 Adriatic Grill, BJ's Rest., Buffalo Wild Wings, Chipotle, Five Guys, Jamba Juice, Jimmy John's, Krispy Kreme, Panera Bread, Red Robin, Wendy's 🅞 $Tree, Best Buy, Costco/gas, Firestone/auto, Ford/Toyota, Goodyear/auto, JC Penney, JoAnn Fabrics, Macy's, Nordstrom, Old Navy, PetCo, REI, to Pt Defiance Pk/Zoo, Verizon, World Mkt
130	S 56th, Tacoma Mall Blvd, **W** 🅖 Shell/dsl 🅕 Axteca Mexican, ChuckeCheese, Jack-in-the-Box 🅛 Extended Stay America
129	S 72nd, S 84th, **E** 🅖 Chevron, Valero 🅕 Applebee's, Burger King, DQ, Elmer's, Famous Dave's, IHOP, Jack-in-the-Box, Jimmy John's, Mongolian Grill, Olive Garden, Popeye's, Red Lobster, RoundTable Pizza, Shari's, Starbucks, Subway 🅛 Hampton Inn, Motel 6, Shilo Inn 🅞 Bass Pro Shops, WinCo Foods, **W** 🅕 Hooters 🅛 Clarion 🅞 Home Depot, to Steilacoom Lake
128	S 84th St (from nb), same as 129, **E** 🅖 76, Shell/dsl 🅕 Denny's, Ginger Palace, Greatwall Chinese, Subway 🅛 American Lodge, Comfort Inn, Crossland Suites, Econolodge, Hampton Inn, Holiday Inn Express, Howard Johnson, Red Lion Hotel, Rothem Inn, Travelodge, **W** 🅖 Shell/dsl 🅞 $Tree, Discount Tire
127	WA 512, S Tacoma Way, Puyallup, Mt Ranier, **W** 🅖 7-11, 76/7-11, Arco/dsl 🅕 AAA Buffet, DQ, Ivar's Seafood, Mazatlan Mexican, McDonald's, Sizzler, Starbucks, Taco Time, Wendy's 🅛 Candlewood Suites, Western Inn 🅞 Advance Parts, Grocery Outlet, O'Reilly Parts
125	to McChord AFB, Lakewood, **W** 🅖 76/Circle K/dsl, Chevron, Mobil, Shell/dsl 🅕 A&W/KFC, Carr's Rest., Church's, Denny's, Greek Cafe, Jack-in-the-Box, Pizza Hut, Subway, Wendy's 🅛 Holiday Inn Express, Home Motel, TownePlace Suites 🅞 🅷, 7-11, Aamco, Ford, NAPA, O'Reilly Parts, tires/repair, U-Haul
124	Gravelly Lake Dr, **W** 🅖 76/Circle K, Arco/repair 🅕 El Toro Mexican, Pizza Casa, same as 125
123	Thorne Lane, Tillicum Lane
122	Berkeley St, Camp Murray, **W** 🅖 Chevron/repair 🅕 Gertie's Grill, Jack-in-the-Box, KFC, McDonald's, Papa John's, Popeye's, Starbucks, Subway, Taco Bell 🅞 7-11, AutoZone
120	Ft Lewis, **E** 🅞 Ft Lewis Military Museum
119	Du Pont Rd, Steilacoom, **E** to Ft Lewis, **W** 🅖 🅕 Happy Teriyaki, Starbucks, Subway 🅛 Hampton Inn, Home 2 Suites
118	Center Dr, **W** 🅖 Chevron/dsl 🅕 Farrelli's Pizza, Fortune Cookie Chinese, Jack-in-the-Box, Koko's Wok, McDonald's, McNamara's Eatery, Pizza Hut, Quiznos, Starbucks, Subway, Super Buffet, Viva Mexico 🅛 Best Western, Fairbridge Inn, Fairfield Inn
117mm	weigh sta nb
116	Mounts Rd, Old Nisqually, **E** 🅞 golf, **W** 🅕 Eagles Pride Grill
115mm	Nisqually River
114	Nisqually, **E** 🅖 Arco/dsl, Chevron/repair/Lp 🅕 Medicine Creek Cafe, Nisqually Grill 🅞 Nisqually Auto Repair, Nisqually RV Park, River Bend RV Park (3mi), WLYH RV Park (2mi)
111	WA 510 E, Marvin Rd, to Yelm, **E** 🅖 76/Circle K, Chevron/dsl, Shell/dsl 🅕 Burger King, Chipotle, Coldstone, Domino's, Firehouse Subs, Hawk's Prairie Rest./casino, Jack-in-the-Box, Jamba Juice, Jersey Mike's, KFC/LJ Silver, Lemon Grass Rest., McDonald's, Panda Express, Panera Bread, Papa Murphy's, Popeye's, Puerto Vallarta, RAM Rest., Red Robin, Starbucks,

T A C O M A (vertical left margin)

OLYMPIA

🔼 INTERSTATE 5 Cont'd

111 Continued
Subway, Super Buffet, Taco Del Mar, Taco Time, Vinny's NY Pizza 🛏 Best Western+, Day's Inn ⬛ $Tree, AT&T, Best Buy, BigLots, Costco/gas, Grocery Outlet, Harley Davidson, Home Depot, O'Reilly Parts, Petco, Rite Aid, Safeway/gas, Schwab Tire, Verizon, Walgreens, Walmart/Subway, WLYH RV Park (2mi), **W** 🔋 7-11/dsl 🍴 Mayan Mexican, Meconi's Subs ⬛ Cabela's, Tolmie SP (5mi)

109 Martin Way, Sleator-Kenny Rd, **E** 🍴 Main Chinese Buffet, Taco Bell, The Rock Pizza ⬛ Discount Tire, **W** 🔋 76/dsl, Shell/dsl 🍴 Brewery City Pizza, Burger King, Casa Mia, Denny's, Domino's, El Serape Mexican, Jimmy John's, Red Lobster, Shari's, Subway 🛏 Comfort Inn, La Quinta, Quality Inn, Ramada Inn, Super 8 ⬛ 🇭, Point S Tire

108 Sleater-Kinney Rd, **E** 🔋 Shell/dsl 🍴 Applebee's, Arby's, Carl's Jr, McDonald's/playplace, Pizza Hut/Taco Bell, Starbucks, Wendy's 🛏 Candlewood Suites, Holiday Inn Express ⬛ $Tree, Firestone/auto, Fred Meyer/dsl, GNC, Kohl's, Marshall's, Michael's, Office Depot, Petsmart, Rite Aid, Target, Tuesday Morning, Verizon, **W** 🔋 Arco/dsl, Shell 🍴 Casa Mia, Dirty Dave's, El Serape Mexican, Jack-in-the-Box, Panda Express, Starbucks, Subway 🛏 Hampton Inn, Ramada Inn ⬛ 🇭, AT&T, Lowe's, Point S Tires, Safeway/gas, same as 109

107 Pacific Ave, **E** 🔋 Shell/dsl/E-85 🍴 DQ, Fajita Grill, Izzy's Pizza, Shari's, Subway, Taco Time ⬛ Albertson's, Home Depot, Ross, vet, **W** ⬛ 🇭, Coumbs RV Ctr

105 St Capitol, **W** 🔋 76/Subway/dsl, Chevron/dsl 🛏 Quality Inn ⬛ to St Capitol

104 US 101 N, W Olympia, to Aberdeen, **W** 🔋 7-11, Arco, Chevron/dsl, Shell/Oly Burger/dsl 🍴 Jack-in-the-Box 🛏 Extended Stay America, Red Lion Hotel ⬛ Buick/GMC, Chevrolet/Cadillac, Ford, Honda, Hyundai, Kia, Lincoln/Mazda, Nissan, Subaru, VW

103 2nd Ave, Deschutes Ave, to hist dist

102 Trosper Rd, Black Lake, **E** 🔋 Shell 🍴 Brewery City Pizza, Burger King, DQ, El Sarape Mexican, Jack-in-the-Box, KFC, McDonald's, Starbucks, Subway, Taco Bell, Taco Time 🛏 Best Western, Motel 6, Tumwater Inn ⬛ O'Reilly Parts, Schwab Tire, Tumwater Auto Repair, Verizon, **W** 🔋 Chevron, Mobil 🍴 Best Buffet, Little Caesar's, Panda Express, Papa Murphy's, Pizza Hut, Starbucks, Subway, Taco Del Mar, The Brick Rest. ⬛ Albertson's, Alderbrook RV Park, AutoZone, Costco/gas, Fred Meyer/dsl, GNC, Home Depot, URGENT CARE, Walgreens, Walmart

101 Tumwater Blvd, **E** 🔋 Chevron, Shell/dsl 🍴 DQ (1mi), Inferno's Pizza, Meconi's Pizza, Red Wagon Burgers 🛏 Comfort Inn, GuestHouse Inn, Olympia Camping ⬛ 7-11, USPO

99 WA 121 S, 93rd Ave, Scott Lake, **E** 🔋 🍴 Blimpie/McDonald's/Subway/dsl/scales/24hr ⬛ Ace Hardware, American Heritage Camping, Olympia Camping

95 WA 121, Littlerock, **3 mi E** 🍴 Millersylvania SP, RV camping, **W** 🔋 Chevron/dsl (3mi) 🍴 Farmboy Drive-In ⬛ Freightliner

93.5mm 🆁🆂 sb, coffee, full ♿ facilities, info, litter barrels, petwalk, 🕿, 🚮, vending

91mm 🆁🆂 nb, coffee, full ♿ facilities, info, litter barrels, petwalk, 🕿, 🚮, vending

88 US 12, Rochester, **E** ⬛ Blair's I-5 RV Ctr, I-5 Truckwash, **W** 🔋 Arco, CFN/dsl, Chehalis/Burger King/dsl, Chevron/dsl, Shell 🍴 DQ, Figaro's Pizza, Jack-in-the-Box, Jack-in-the-Box, Mariachi Mexican, McDonald's, Quiznos, Starbucks 🛏 Fairfield Inn, Great Wolf Lodge ⬛ auto repair, Outback RV Park (2mi)

CENTRALIA

82 Harrison Ave, Factory Outlet Way, Centralia, **E** 🔋 Arco 🍴 Burger King, Burgerville, Casa Ramos Mexican, DQ, Jimmy John's, Panda Chinese, Papa Pete's Pizza, Peking House Chinese, Pizza Hut, Quiznos, Thai Dish, Wendy's 🛏 Centralia Inn, King Oscar Motel, Motel 6, Quality Inn ⬛ AutoZone, VF/famous brands, **W** 🔋 Chevron/dsl, Mobil/dsl, Texaco 🍴 Arby's, Bill&Bea's Country Cousin Rest., Denny's, Domino's, Jack-in-the-Box, McDonald's, Papa Murphy's, Starbucks, Subway, Taco Bell 🛏 Motel 6 ⬛ AT&T, Centralia Outlets/famous brands, city park, Midway RV Park, O'Reilly Parts, Rite Aid, Safeway/dsl, Schwab Tire, Verizon

82mm Skookumchuck River

81 WA 507, Mellen St, **E** 🔋 Chevron/dsl, Shell/dsl 🍴 Subway 🛏 Empress Inn, Lakeview Inn, Pepper Tree Motel/RV Park, dump, **W** ⬛ 🇭

79 Chamber Way, **E** 🔋 Mobil/dsl 🍴 Jalisco Mexican ⬛ Chrysler/Dodge/Jeep/Fiat, museum, Tires, Inc., vet, visitor info, 🔋 Chevron/dsl/LP/e85 🍴 Applebee's, Burger King, McDonald's, Sonic, Starbucks, Subway, Taco Bell, Taco Del Mar, Wendy's ⬛ $Tree, GNC, Grocery Outlet, Home Depot, Michael's, O'Reilly Parts, st patrol, Toyota, Verizon, Walgreens, Walmart, McDonald's

77 WA 6 W, Chehalis, **E** 🔋 76/dsl, Cenex/dsl/LP 🍴 Dairy Bar, Jeremy's Cafe 🛏 Holiday Inn Express ⬛ NAPA, Schwab Tire, USPO, **W** ⬛ Rainbow Falls SP (16mi), truck parts, veterans museum

76 13th St, **E** 🔋 Arco, Chevron/dsl 🍴 Denny's, Jack-in-the-Box, Kit Carson Rest., Subway 🛏 Best Western+, Econolodge, Relax Inn ⬛ Awesome I-5 RV Ctr/RV dump, Baydo's RV Ctr, Ford, ⬛ RV park/dump

74 Labree Rd

72 Rush Rd, Napavine, **E** 🔋 Shell/dsl/scales 🍴 Burger King, McDonald's, RibEye Rest., Subway ⬛ Country Canopy RV Ctr/repair, **W** 🔋 Loves/Carl's Jr/dsl/scales/24hr, Shell/dsl 🍴 Arby's, Starbucks, Taco Bell

72mm Newaukum River

71 WA 508 E, Onalaska, Napavine, **E** 🔋 76/dsl ⬛ KC Truck Parts

68 US 12 E, Morton, **E** 🔋 Arco/dsl, Texaco/dsl 🍴 Spiffy's Rest. ⬛ Mt Ranier NP, to Lewis&Clark SP, **W** 🔋 76/rest./dsl

63 WA 505, Winlock, **W** 🔋 Shell/Chesters/dsl/LP

60 Toledo Vader Rd, Toledo

59 WA 506 W, Vader, **E** 🔋 Shell/dsl 🍴 Beesley's Cafe ⬛ RV Park, **W** 🔋 Chevron/Subway/dsl 🍴 Country House Rest.

59mm Cowlitz River

57 Jackson Hwy, Barnes Dr, **E** ⬛ R&R Tires, **W** 🔋 Texaco/Gee Cee's/café/dsl/scales/24hr/@ ⬛ repair, RV camping

55mm 🆁🆂 both lanes, full ♿ facilities, litter barrels, petwalk, 🕿, 🚮, vending

52 Barnes Dr, Toutle Park Rd, **E** ⬛ Paradise Cove RV Park/general store, **W** ⬛ Toutle River RV Resort

50mm Toutle River

49 WA 504 E, Castle Rock, **E** 🔋 Chevron/dsl/LP, Shell/dsl 🍴 49er Diner, Burger King, C&L Burgers, El Compadre Mexican, Papa Pete's Pizza, Subway 🛏 7 West Motel, Mt St Helens Motel, Timberland Inn ⬛ Seaquest SP (5mi), **W** 🍴 McDonald's ⬛ visitor info

48 Castle Rock, **E** ⬛ Cedars RV Park/dump, **W** ⬛ city park

46 Pleasant Hill Rd, Headquarters Rd, **E** ⬛ Cedars RV Park/dump

44mm weigh sta sb, weigh sta sb

42 Bridge Dr, Lexington, **W** 🔋 Chevron/dsl 🍴 Subway ⬛ auto repair

40 to WA 4, Kelso-Longview, **W** 🔋 Texaco 🛏 Econolodge

= gas = food = lodging = other Rs = rest stop

INTERSTATE 5 Cont'd

K E L S O

Exit #	Services
39	WA 4, Kelso, to Longview, E ⛽ Arco, Shell 🍴 Denny's, Jack-in-the-Box, McDonald's, Shari's, Starbucks, Subway, Taco Time 🛏 Motel 6, Red Lion Hotel, Super 8 ⬛ $Tree, Brook Hollow RV Park, city park, Rite Aid, Verizon, W 🍴 Burger King, DQ, Fiesta Bonita Mexican, Izzy's Pizza, Panera Bread, Red Lobster, Taco Bell 🛏 Comfort Inn, GuestHouse Inn ⬛ JC Penney, museum, Safeway/dsl, Target
36	WA 432 W, to WA 4, to US 30, Kelso, E ⬛ U-Neek RV Ctr, W ⬛ RV Camping, Toyota
32	Kalama River Rd, E 🍴 Fireside Café ⬛ Camp Kalama RV Park/camping/gifts
31mm	Kalama River

K A L A M A

Exit #	Services
30	Kalama, E ⛽ Chevron/dsl 🍴 Burger Bar, Columbia Rest., Lucky Dragon Chinese, Playa Azul Mexican, Poker Pete's Pizza, Subway 🛏 Motel 6 ⬛ antiques, Godfrey's Drug, USPO, W ⛽ Spirit/dsl 🛏 McMenamin's Kalamazoo Inn ⬛ RV camping
27	Todd Rd, Port of Kalama, E ⛽ Rebel/Shell/café/dsl/24hr
22	Dike Access Rd, W 🍴 Taco Bell ⬛ Columbia Riverfront RV Park, O'Reilly Parts, Schwab Tire, Verizon, Walmart/Subway
21	WA 503 E, Woodland, E ⛽ Arco/dsl, Chevron, Pacific Pride/dsl, Shell/LP/dsl 🍴 America's Diner, Burgerville, Casa Tapatia, DQ, Fat Moose Grill, Grocery Outlet, Guilliano's Pizza, Mali Thai, Oak-Tree Rest., Rosie's Rest. 🛏 Best Western, Lewis River Inn, Rodeway Inn ⬛ Ace Hardware, Hi-School Drug, Woodland Shores RV Park, W ⛽ Astro 🍴 Antony's Pizzaria, Carl's Jr, Guadalajara Mexican, Los Pepes Mexican, McDonald's, Papa Murphy's, Starbucks, Subway ⬛ $Tree, NAPA, repair/tires, Safeway/dsl
20mm	N Fork Lewis River
18mm	E Fork Lewis River
16	NW La Center Rd, La Center, E ⛽ Shell/dsl 🍴 Twin Dragons Rest. (2mi) ⬛ Paradise Point SP, Tri-Mountain Golf/rest., W 🛏 Ilani Casino/Hotel
15mm	weigh sta nb
14	WA 501 S, Pioneer St, Ridgefield, E ⛽ Arco 🍴 Country Café, Papa Pete's Pizza, Subway, Teriyaki Thai ⬛ Big Fir RV Park (4mi), Ridgefield WR, to Battleground Lake SP (14mi), Tri-Mountain RV Park, vet, W ⛽ Chevron/dsl
13mm	Rs sb, full ♿ facilities, info, litter barrels, petwalk, 🍴, 🏞, RV dump, vending
11	WA 502, Battleground, Rs nb, full ♿ facilities, info, litter barrels, petwalk, 🏞, RV dump, vending
9	NE 179th St, W ⛽ Chevron/dsl ⬛ RV Park
7	I-205 S (from sb), to I-84, WA 14, NE 134th St, E ⛽ 7-11, Arco, Mobil 🍴 Applebee's, Billygan's Roadhouse, Burger King, Burgerville, Jack-in-the-Box, McDonald's, Muchas Gracias, Panda Express, Round Table Pizza, Starbucks, Subway, Taco Bell 🛏 Holiday Inn Express, Quality Inn, Shilo Inn ⬛ 🏥, 99 RV Park, Albertson's, Safeway/dsl, Verizon, Walgreens, W ⛽ Shell 🍴 Baskin-Robbins, Bruchi's, El Tapatio, Garlic Jim's Pizza, Papa Murphy's, PizzaSchmitzza, Planet Thai, Starbucks, Subway 🛏 La Quinta ⬛ AT&T, Fred Meyer, URGENT CARE
5	NE 99th St, E 🍴 Burgerville, Carl's Jr, Del Taco, Domino's, Fat Dave's Rest., Popeyes, Quiznos ⬛ 7-11, AutoZone, Harley-Davidson, Walgreens, Walmart/Subway, Winco Foods/gas, W ⛽ Arco/dsl, Chevron/dsl 🍴 Applebee's, Bortolami's Pizza, McDonald's, Subway, Taco Del Mar ⬛ $Tree, Grocery Outlet, Kohl's, Office Depot, PetCo, Target, Verizon
4	NE 78th St, Hazel Dell, E ⛽ 7-11, 76 🍴 Baja Fresh, Baskin-Robbins, Burger King, Canton Chinese, Don Pedro Mexican, Dragon Buffet, Izzy's Grill, KFC, McDonald's, Muchas Gracias

V A N C O U V E R

Exit #	Services
4	Continued Mexican, PeachTree Rest., Pizza Hut, Skipper's, Starbucks, Subway, Taco Bell 🛏 Quality Inn ⬛ Aamco, AT&T, CarQuest, CostLess Parts, Firestone, Fred Meyer, Jo-Ann, O'Reilly Parts, Tire Factory, U-Haul, W ⛽ Shell/dsl/LP 🍴 Buffalo Wild Wings, Chipotle Mexican, Five Guys, Jack-in-the-Box, Jazzy John's BBQ, Jimmy John's, Little Caesar's, Panda Express, Pita Pit, RoundTable Pizza, Starbucks, Wendy's ⬛ GNC, Hancock Fabrics, Natural Grocers, Petsmart, Ross, Safeway, Tuesday Morning
3	NE Hwy 99, Main St, Hazel Dell, E ⛽ 7-11 🍴 Muchas Gracias Mexican, Pizza Hut, Skippers, W ⛽ Arco/dsl, Chevron/dsl 🍴 Papa Murphy's ⬛ Safeway, transmissions
2	WA 500 E, 39th St, to Orchards
1d	E 4th, Plain Blvd W, to WA 501, Port of Vancouver
1c	Mill Plain Blvd, City Ctr, E ⬛ Clark Coll, W ⛽ Chevron 🍴 Black Angus 🛏 Comfort Inn ⬛ st patrol
1b	6th St, E 🍴 Joe's Crabshack, Who Song & Larry's Mexican, W 🛏 EconoLodge, Hilton, Red Lion Hotel
1a	WA 14 E, to Camus, E ⬛ 🏥, W 🛏 EconoLodge, Hilton
0mm	Washington/Oregon state line, Columbia River

INTERSTATE 82

Exit #	Services
11mm	I-82 Oregon begins/ends on I-84, exit 179.
10	Westland Rd, E ⬛ to Umatilla Army Depot
5	Power Line Rd
1.5mm	Umatilla River
1	US 395/730, Umatilla, E 🍴 Jack-in-the-Box (5mi) 🛏 Best Western (8mi), Motel 6 (8mi), Oxford Inn (5mi), Quality Inn/rest. (2mi) ⬛ Hatrock Camping (8mi), to McNary Dam, W Welcome Ctr, , weigh sta ⛽ Chevron/dsl, Mobil/Subway/dsl, Shell/Crossroads Trkstp/dsl/rest./24hr 🛏 Tillicum Motel, Umatilla Inn ⬛ Harvest Foods, st police, Umatilla Marina/RV Park, USPO
132mm	Washington/Oregon state line, Columbia River
131	WA 14 W, to McNary Dam, Plymouth, N ⬛ RV camping
130mm	weigh sta wb
122	Coffin Rd
114	Locust Grove Rd

K E N N E W I C K

Exit #	Services
113	US 395 N, to I-182, Kennewick, Pasco, st patrol, 2-4 mi N ⛽ Exxon/Circle K/dsl, Metro/dsl, USA/dsl 🍴 A&W/KFC, Azteca Mexican, Bob's Burgers, Burger King, Carl's Jr, Costa Vida, Denny's, Dickey's BBQ, DQ, Jack-in-the-Box, Little Caesar's, McDonald's, Original Pancake House, Osaka Asian, Panda Express, Papa John's, Starbucks, Subway, Taco Bell, Taco Bell 🛏 Baymont Inn, Best Western+, Comfort Suites, Hampton Inn, La Quinta, Motel 6 ⬛ 🏥, AT&T, Blue Dog RV Ctr, Fred Meyer/dsl, GNC, Harley-Davidson, Home Depot, PetCo, Rite Aid, Safeway/dsl, st patrol, Traveland RV Ctr, Verizon, vet, Walgreens, Walmart/Subway

🅴 INTERSTATE 82 Cont'd

Exit #	Services
109	Badger Rd, W Kennewick, **N** 🛢️ Exxon/Subway/dsl, Sunmart/dsl 🍴 Silo Grill 🛏️ Quality Inn (3mi), Red Lion Hotel (3mi), Super 8 (3mi), **S** Ⓞ Columbia Sun RV Park
104	Dallas Rd, **3 mi N** 🛢️ Conoco/dsl
102	I-182, US 12 E, to US 395, Richland, Pasco, Spokane, services in Richland
96	WA 224 E, Benton City, **N** 🛢️ Conoco/cafe/dsl Ⓞ Beach RV Park
93	Yakitat Rd
88	Gibbon Rd
82	WA 22, WA 221, Mabton, **S** 🛢️ Conoco/dsl Ⓞ 🄷 (2mi), museum (2mi), to WAS U Research (2mi), to Wine Tasting
82mm	Yakima River
80	Gap Rd, **S** 🆁🆂 both lanes, full ♿ facilities, litter barrels, 🅲, 🅰, **rv dump**, 🛢️ Chevron/dsl, ♥Loves/Carl's Jr/dsl/scales/24hr, Pacific Pride/dsl, Shell/dsl/scales 🍴 Barn Rest., Burger King, Domino's, Dutch Bros Coffee, El Rancho Alegre, Golden Horse Chinese, KFC/Taco Bell, McDonald's, Starbucks, Subway 🛏️ Best Western+, Holiday Inn Express, Vintners Inn Ⓞ 🄷, Ford, Schwab Tire, ShopKO, URGENT CARE, Verizon, Wine Country RV Park
76mm	weigh sta eb
75	County Line Rd, Grandview, **S** 🛢️ Cenex/Deli/dsl, Safeway/dsl 🍴 Papa Murphy's Ⓞ O'Reilly Parts, same as 73
73	Stover Rd, Wine Country Rd, Grandview, **S** 🛢️ Chevron/Subway/dsl, Conoco/dsl 🍴 10-4 Café, DQ, Eli&Kathy's Rest., Garcia's Mexican, New Hong Kong 🛏️ Apple Valley Motel, Grandview Motel Ⓞ Chrysler/Dodge/Jeep, IGA Mercado, RV park/dump, Safeway/dsl, Schwab Tire
69	WA 241, to Sunnyside, **N** 🛢️ Arco/dsl, Shell/dsl/scales/24hr 🍴 A&W, Burger King, Carl's Jr, China Buffet, El Charrito Mexican, Green Olive Cafe, KFC, Little Caesar's, McDonald's, Mongolian BBQ, Panda Garden, Papa Murphy's, Pizza Hut, Popeye's, Subway, Taco Bell 🛏️ Best Western+, Quality Inn Ⓞ $Tree, AT&T, auto repair, AutoZone, Buick/Chevrolet, Fiesta Foods, GNC, Grocery Outlet, JC Penney, Nissan, O'Reilly Parts, Rite Aid, Ross, Walmart/Subway
67	Sunnyside, Port of Sunnyside, **N** 🛢️ Chevron/CFN/dsl, Conoco/dsl/e85 🍴 Jack-in-the-Box Ⓞ 🄷, BiMart Foods, **S** Ⓞ Dari-Gold Cheese
63	Outlook, Sunnyside, **3 mi N** 🍴 Snipe's Rest. 🛏️ Rodeway Inn, Sunnyside Inn Ⓞ Sunnyside RV Park
58	WA 223 S, to Granger, **S** 🛢️ Arco/dsl/tacos, Conoco/dsl
54	Division Rd, Yakima Valley Hwy, to Zillah, **S** Ⓞ Teapot Dome NHS
52	Zillah, Toppenish, **N** 🛢️ 76/dsl, Chevron/Circle K/dsl, Shell/Circle K/dsl 🍴 El Porton Mexican, McDonald's, Pizza Hut, Subway 🛏️ Best Western+
50	WA 22 E, to US 97 S, Toppenish, **3-4 mi S** 🍴 Legends Buffet/casino, McDonald's 🛏️ Quality Inn Ⓞ 🄷, Murals Museum, RV Park, to Yakima Nation Cultural Ctr
44	Wapato, **N** 🛢️ Donald Store/dsl
40	Thorp Rd, Parker Rd, Yakima Valley Hwy
39mm	Yakima River
38	Union Gap (from wb), **1 mi S** Ⓞ gas, lodging, museum
37	US 97 (from eb), **S** 🛢️ Conoco/dsl
36	Valley Mall Blvd, Yakima, **S** 🛢️ Arco/dsl, Cenex/dsl, Chevron/Gearjammer/Subway/dsl/scales/24hr/@ 🍴 A&W/KFC, Applebee's, Buffalo Wild Wings, Burger King, Carl's Jr, Denny's, El Porton Mexican, Famous Dave's, Jack-in-the-Box, Krispy Kreme,

Exit #	Services
36	Continued
	McDonald's, Miner's Drive-In, Old Country Buffet, Old Town St Rest., Outback Steaks, Panda Express, Panera Bread, SeaGalley Rest., Shari's, Starbucks, Subway, Taco Bell 🛏️ Best Western+ Quality Inn, Super 8 Ⓞ AT&T, Best Buy, Cabela's, Canopy R Ctr, Costco/gas, Dick's, Frank's Tire, Gap Autoparts, Hobby Lob by, Home Depot, JC Penney, Kohl's, Lowe's, Macy's, Marshall's Michael's, Office Depot, Old Navy, PetCo, Petsmart, Rite Ai Ross, st patrol, TJ Maxx, Toyota, URGENT CARE, Verizon, WinC Foods
34	WA 24 E, Nob Hill Blvd, Yakima, **N** Ⓞ dsl/repair, Sportsman S **S** 🛢️ 76/dsl, Arco/dsl, CFN/dsl, Nob Hill/dsl Ⓞ 🄷, 19th Ho RV Park, Circle K, Fiesta Foods, Freightliner, Kenworth, O'Reill Parts, Peterbilt, Volvo
33	Yakima Ave, Yakima, **N** 🛢️ Chevron/dsl, Shell/dsl 🍴 Burge King, El Mirador Mexican 🛏️ Baymont Inn, My Place, Oxfor Inn&Suites Ⓞ Chevrolet, Honda, Walmart/McDonald's, 🛢️ 7-11, Arco 🍴 Bob's Burgers, Domino's, DQ, Pizza Hut, Tac Bell 🛏️ Fairfield Inn, Hilton Garden, Holiday Inn, Howard Johnson, Ledgestone Hotel, Motel 6, Red Lion Hotel, Red Roof In Ⓞ $Tree, BigLots, Schwab Tire, Target
31b a	US 12 W, N 1st St, to Naches, **S** 🛢️ Arco/dsl, Conoco/dsl, She 🍴 Golden Moon Chinese, Jack-in-the-Box, Mel's Diner, N Teryaki, Red Lobster, Subway, Tammy's Mexican, Waffle's Ca 🛏️ Best Western+, Budget Inn, Days Inn, Econolodge, Econom Inn, Fairbridge Inn, Red Apple Motel, Sun Country Inn, Sunshin Motel, Yakima Inn Ⓞ Harley-Davidson, Trailer Inns RV Park
30	WA 823 N, Rest Haven Rd, to Selah
29	E Selah Rd, **N** Ⓞ fruits/antiques
26	WA 821 N, to WA 823, Canyon Rd, **N** 🛢️ Chevron/Noble R mans/Subway/dsl
24mm	🆁🆂 eb, full ♿ facilities, litter barrels, 🅰, RV dump
23mm	Selah Creek
22mm	🆁🆂 wb, full ♿ facilities, litter barrels, 🅰, RV dump
21mm	S Umptanum Ridge, elevation 2265
19mm	Burbank Creek
17mm	N Umptanum Ridge, elevation 2315
15mm	Lmuma Creek
11	Military Area, Military Area
8mm	Manastash Ridge, elevation 2672, view point both lanes
3	WA 821 S, Thrall Rd
0mm	I-90, E to Spokane, W to Seattle. **I-82 begins/ends on I-90, exit 11**

🅴 INTERSTATE 90

Exit #	Services
300mm	Washington/Idaho state line, Spokane River
299	State Line, Port of Entry, **N** 🍴 Panda Express Ⓞ Cabela Walmart/Subway
297	weigh sta wb
296	Otis Orchards, Liberty Lakes, **N** 🛢️ 76/dsl 🍴 Legend's Gr 🛏️ Best Western+ Ⓞ Buick/GMC, Kia, Mercedes, Porsche, 🛢️ Cenex/dsl, Chevron/LP 🍴 Barlow's Rest., Carl's Jr, Din How Asian, Domino's, Field House Pizza, Jimmy John's, McDo ald's, Papa Murphy's, Pizza Hut, Starbucks, Subway, Taco Be Taco Time 🛏️ Quality Inn Ⓞ Safeway, Home Depot, O'Rei Parts, Peterbilt, RnR RV Ctr, TireRama, URGENT CARE, vet, Wa greens, Yoke's Mkt
294	Country Vista Dr, Appleway Ave
293	Barker Rd, Greenacres, **N** 🛢️ Chevron/Trkstp/dsl/scales, Con co/dsl 🍴 Wendy's Ⓞ Camping World RV Ctr, Freedom RV C Harley-Davidson, **S** 🛢️ Exxon/Subway/dsl, Mobil/dsl Ⓞ N RV Ctr, repair, USPO

Side tabs: WA, SUNNYSIDE, YAKIMA

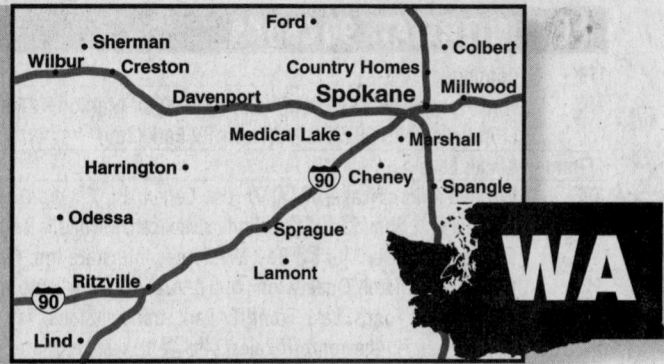

INTERSTATE 90 Cont'd

Exit #	Services
291b	Sullivan Rd, Veradale, N 🅕 Arby's, Hong Kong Buffet, Krispy Kreme, Outback Steaks, Panera Bread 🅛 Hampton Inn, My Place, Oxford Suites, Residence Inn 🅞 AT&T, Barnes&Noble, Best Buy, Jo-Ann Fabrics, Verizon, S 🅖 Chevron/dsl, Conoco/dsl 🅕 DQ, Five Guys, Jack-in-the-Box, Jimmy John's, KFC, Little Caesar's, Max Rest., McDonald's, Mongolian BBQ, Noodle Express, Panda Express, Pizza Hut, Pizza Pipeline, RoundTable Pizza, Schlotzsky's, Shari's, Starbucks, Subway, Taco Bell, Wendy's, Zelia's Cafe 🅛 Mirabeau Park Hotel, Ramada Inn 🅞 $Tree, Ace Hardware, Fred Meyer/dsl, GNC, Hancock Fabrics, Kohl's, Lowe's, Michael's, NAPA, PetCo, Petsmart, Ross, Schwab Tire, USPO, Walgreens, Walmart/McDonald's
291a	Evergreen Rd, N 🅕 Azteca Mexican, Black Angus, Boston's Rest, Buffalo Wild Wings, Cafe Rio, Honeybaked Ham, IHOP, Red Robin, Twigs Bistro 🅞 Dick's, Hobby Lobby, JC Penney, Macy's, Old Navy, Staples, TJ Maxx, S 🅖 Exxon/dsl, Maverik/dsl
289	WA 27 S, Pines Rd, Opportunity, N 🅖 Sam's/dsl 🅕 Black Pearl Rest., Subway 🅞 7-11, S 🅖 Cenex, Conoco/dsl, Holiday/dsl 🅕 Applebee's, DQ, Jack-in-the-Box, Jimmy John's, Qdoba Mexican 🅛 Comfort Inn 🅞 🅗 NW Auto, repair, Walgreens
287	Argonne Rd, Millwood, N 🅖 Holiday/dsl 🅕 Burger King, Caruso's Sandwiches, Denny's, Domino's, DQ, Jack-in-the-Box, Longhorn BBQ, McDonald's, Panda Express, Papa Murphy's, Pizza Hut, Starbucks, Subway, Taco Time, Timber Creek Grill, Wendy's 🅛 Baymont Inn, Motel 6, Super 8 🅞 $Tree, Albertson's, O'Reilly Parts, Savon, URGENT CARE, Verizon, vet, Walgreens, Yoke's Foods, S 🅖 Cenex/dsl, Conoco 🅕 Casa de Oro Mexican, Jimmy John's, Little Caesar's, Starbucks 🅛 Fairfield Inn, Holiday Inn Express 🅞 Ace Hardware, Rite Aid, Safeway
286	Broadway Ave, N 🅖 ⊕FLYING J/Conoco/rest./dsl/LP/scales/24hr/@, Chevron/dsl 🅕 Goodyear, Smacky's Cafe, Zip's Burgers 🅛 Rodeway Inn 🅞 International Trucks, Kenworth, Schwab Tire, S 🅞 7-11
285	Sprague Ave, N 🅕 Dragon Garden Chinese, IHOP, Jack-in-the-Box, McDonald's, Panda Express, Starbucks, Subway, Wendy's 🅛 ParkLane Motel/RV Park 🅞 $Tree, Advance Parts, AutoZone, Costco/gas, Home Depot, Lowe's, O'Reilly Parts, Verizon, Volvo Trucks, Walmart, S 🅖 Conoco 🅕 Burger Express, Cottage Cafe, Puerta Vallarta Mexican, Starbucks, Taco Time 🅞 Acura, CarMax, Chevrolet, Chrysler/Dodge, Ford, Honda, Hyundai, Mazda, Nissan, Toyota, transmissions, vet
284	Havana St (from eb, no EZ return), N 🅖 Mobil/dsl, S 🅖 Conoco/dsl 🅞 Fred Meyer/dsl
283b	Freya St, Thor St, N 🅖 Chevron/dsl, Mobil/dsl, S 🅖 Conoco/dsl 🅞 Fred Meyer/dsl
283a	Altamont St
282b	2nd Ave, N 🅖 Conoco/dsl 🅛 Ramada Inn 🅞 Office Depot
282a	WA 290 E, Trent Ave, Hamilton St, N 🅖 Conoco/dsl 🅛 Comfort Inn 🅞 Office Depot
281	US 2, US 395, to Colville, N 🅖 7-11, Conoco, Exxon, Mobil/dsl 🅕 Arby's, Dick's Hamburgers, Frankie Doodles Rest., Starbucks, Taco Time 🅛 Days Inn, FairBridge Inn 🅞 Firestone/auto, Schwab Tire, U-Haul, S 🅛 Quality Inn 🅞 🅗 URGENT CARE
280b	Lincoln St, N 🅖 76/dsl, Chevron 🅕 Atilano's Mexican, Carl's Jr, Domino's, Jack-in-the-Box, McDonald's, Molly's Rest., Taco Bell, Thai Cuisine, Zip's Burgers 🅞 Honda, Lexus, Subaru, Toyota, Troy's Tire, S 🅞 🅗
280a	Spokane, downtown, N 🅖 76/dsl, Chevron/McDonald's/dsl, Conoco 🅕 Frank's Diner, Jenny's Diner, Pizza Hut, Subway 🅞 Grocery Outlet
279	US 195 S, Pullman, to Colfax
277b a	US 2 W (no ez wb return), to Grand Coulee Dam, N 🅛 Blvd Motel, EconoLodge, Hampton Inn, Motel 6, Quality Inn 🅞 Fairchild AFB
276	Geiger Blvd, N 🅖 ⊕FLYING J/dsl/LP/24hr 🅕 Denny's, Subway 🅛 Airway Express Inn, Best Western+ 🅞 st patrol, USPO, S 🅖 Conoco/dsl
272	WA 902, Medical Lake, N 🅖 Mobil/dsl 🅞 Overland Sta/RV Park, S 🅖 Exxon/Subway/dsl, Petro/Iron Skillet/Subway/dsl/scales/24hr/@ 🅕 McDonald's 🅛 Super 8 🅞 Freightliner, Ponderosa Falls RV Resort, Speedco, truck repair
270	WA 904, Cheney, Four Lakes, S 🅖 🅛 Holiday Inn Express (4mi), Willow Springs Motel (6mi) 🅞 E WA U, Peaceful Pines RV Park (7mi)
264	WA 902, Salnave Rd, to Cheney, Medical Lake, 2 mi N camping
257	WA 904, Tyler, to Cheney, S 🅞 Peaceful Pines RV Park (10mi), to Columbia Plateau Trail SP, Tyler RV Park
254	Fishtrap, S 🅞 Fishtrap RV camping/tents
245	WA 23, Sprague, S 🅖 Chevron/dsl 🅕 Viking Drive-In 🅛 Sprague Motel/RV park 🅞 4 Seasons RV Park (6mi), Sprague Lake Resort/RV Park
242mm	℞ₛ both lanes, full ♿ facilities, litter barrels, petwalk, 🄲, 🄿, RV dump (eb), tourist/weather info
231	Tokio, N 🅞 weigh sta both lanes, S 🅖 Templin's Café/CFN/dsl 🅞 RV Park
226	Schoessler Rd
221	WA 261 S, Ritzville, City Ctr, N 🅖 Chevron/McDonald's, Conoco/dsl, Exxon/Circle K/Subway/dsl 🅕 Cow Creek Cafe/gifts, Ritz Roadhouse, Starbucks, Taco Del Mar, Zip's Rest. 🅛 Best Western, Days Inn/RV park, Empire Motel, Top Hat Motel 🅞 🅗, hist dist, S 🅖 ♥Love's/Carl's Jr/dsl/scales/24hr
220	to US 395 S, Ritzville, N 🅖 Bronco/dsl, Texaco/dsl 🅕 Jake's Cafe 🅛 Top Hat Motel 🅞 Days Inn/RV Park, Harvest Foods, NAPA, Schwab Tire, st patrol
215	Paha, Packard
206	WA 21, Odessa, to Lind
199mm	℞ₛ both lanes, full ♿ facilities, litter barrels, petwalk, 🄲, 🄿, RV dump, vending
196	Deal Rd, to Schrag
188	U Rd, to Warden, Ruff
184	Q Rd
182	O Rd, to Wheeler
179	WA 17, Moses Lake, N 🅖 Chevron/dsl, Conoco/Subway/dsl, Ernie's Trkstp/76/café/dsl/24hr, Sunval/dsl, Texaco/dsl 🅕 Arby's, Bob's Cafe, Burger King, Carl's Jr., Denny's, DQ, Dragon Express, McDonald's, Shari's, Starbucks, Subway, Taco Bell, Wendy's 🅛 Comfort Suites, El Rancho Motel, Fairfield Inn, Holiday Inn Express, Moses Lake Inn, Ramada Inn, Sure Stay Inn+, Wingate Inn 🅞 🅗, $Tree, Chevrolet, Chrysler/Dodge/Jeep,

🅿 = gas 🍴 = food 🛏 = lodging 🅾 = other ℞ = rest stop   Copyright 2022 - The Next EXIT

⬆E INTERSTATE 90 Cont'd

179	Continued Ford, Honda, Lowe's, Toyota, vet, **S**🅾 I-90 RV, Mardon RV Park (15mi), Potholes SP (22mi), Willows RV Park (2mi)
177mm	Moses Lake
176	WA 171, Moses Lake, **N**🅿 76/dsl, Cenex/dsl, Chevron/dsl, Shell, SP/dsl, Sunval/dsl 🍴 El Rodeo Mexican, Michael's Rest., Subway, Taco Del Mar 🛏 Best Western+, Interstate Inn, Motel 6, Oasis Motel, Quality Inn 🅾 🏥, AAA RV Park, auto repair, Harvest Foods, Lake Front RV Park, transmissions, vet, **S** 🅿 Half-Sun TP/Chevron/dsl/scales/24hr 🛏 Lakeshore Motel
175	Westshore Dr (from wb), to Mae Valley, **N**🅾 Blue Heron SP, **S** 🅾 st patrol
174	Mae Valley, **N** 🅾 Suncrest Resort/RV, **S** 🅿 Chevron/dsl 🅾 Pier 4 RV Park, st patrol
169	Hiawatha Rd
164	Dodson Rd, **N**🅾 Sunbasin RV park/camp (1mi)
162mm	℞ wb, full 🚻 facilities, litter barrels, petwalk, 🎣, 🛢, RV dump
161mm	℞ eb, full 🚻 facilities, litter barrels, petwalk, 🎣, 🛢, RV dump
154	Adams Rd
151	WA 281 N, to Quincy, **N**🅿 Shell/pizza/subs/dsl 🅾 🏥 (12mi), Shady Grove RV park, to Grand Coulee Dam
149	WA 281 S, George, **N**🅾 🏥 (12mi), **S**🅿 BW&M/Chester's/dsl, Shree's Trkstp/Subway/dsl/scales/24hr
143	Silica Rd, **N**🅾 to The Gorge Ampitheatre
139mm	**N**🅾 Wild Horses Mon, scenic view both lanes
137	WA 26 E, to WA 243, Othello, Richland
137mm	Columbia River
136	Huntzinger Rd, Vantage, **N**🅿 Chevron/dsl/24hr 🍴 Blustery's Burger Drive-in, Golden Harvest Rest. 🅾 Riverstone Vantage Resort/RV Park, to Ginkgo SP, Vantage Gen. Store, **S**🅾 to Wanapum SP (3mi)
126mm	Ryegrass, elevation 2535, ℞ both lanes, full 🚻 facilities, litter barrels, petwalk, 🎣, 🛢
115	Kittitas, **N**🅿 Shell/dsl/LP 🍴 Main Stop Rest. 🅾 Olmstead Place SP, UHaul
110	I-82 E, US 97 S, to Yakima
109	Canyon Rd, Ellensburg, **N**🅿 76, Astro/dsl, Chevron, Exxon/Circle K 🍴 Arby's, Burger King, Carl's Jr, Fiesta Mexican, Jimmy John's, Los Cabos Mexican, McDonald's, Oyama Japanese, Papa Murphy's, RanchHouse Rest., Roadhouse Grill, Rodeo City BBQ, Starbucks, Subway, Taco Bell, Taco Del Mar, Teriyaki Wok, Wendy's, Westside Pizza 🛏 Best Western+, Comfort Inn, Holiday Inn Express, Red Lion Inn, Super 8 🅾 🏥, Advance Parts, AutoZone, Chevrolet, NAPA, O'Reilly Parts, Rite Aid, Schwab Tire, Super 1 Foods, TrueValue, **S** 🅿 Conoco/Sak's/dsl/scales/LP/24hr 🍴 Buzz Inn Steaks 🛏 Days Inn/RV park
106	US 97 N, to Wenatchie, **N** 🅿 76/dsl, Chevron/dsl, Conoco/dsl, ♥Loves/Subway/dsl/scales/24hr 🍴 DQ, IHOP, Perkins 🛏 Econolodge, Hampton Inn 🅾 Buick/Cadillac/GMC, Canopy Country RV Ctr, Chrysler/Dodge/Jeep, truck repair, Truck/RV Wash, **S** 🅾 KOA, st patrol
101	Thorp Hwy, **N**🅿 Arco/dsl 🅾 antiques/fruits/vegetables
93	Elk Heights Rd, Taneum Creek
92.5mm	Elk Heights, elev 2359
89mm	Indian John Hill, elevation 2141, ℞ both lanes, full 🚻 facilities, litter barrels, petwalk, 🎣, 🛢, RV dump, vending
85	WA 970, WA 903, to Wenatchie, **N**🅿 76/dsl, Gas Save/dsl, Shell/dsl 🍴 Cottage Café, Giant Burger, Homestead BBQ 🛏 Aster Inn, Chalet Motel, Cle Elum Traveler's Inn, EconoLodge 🅾 Trailer Corral RV Park, vet

84	Cle Elum (from eb, return at 85), **N**🅿 Chevron/dsl, Short Stop, Subway/dsl, Warrior's/dsl 🍴 Best Thai, Burger King, Caboose Grill, DQ, El Caporal Mexican, Los Cabos Mexican, MaMa Vallones, McDonald's, Sunset Café, Taco Bell 🛏 Best Western Snowcap, Stewart Lodge, Timber Lodge Inn 🅾 $Tree, Cle Elum Hardware, museum, Safeway/dsl, URGENT CARE, USPO
81mm	Cle Elum River
80	Roslyn, Salmon la Sac, **N**🛏 Suncadia Resort/rest. (4mi)
80mm	**weigh sta both lanes**
78	Golf Course Rd, **S**🅾 Sun Country Golf/RV Park
74	W Nelson Siding Rd
71	Easton, **S** 🅿 Easton Store/dsl/LP 🛏 Easton Motel 🅾 Iron Horse SP, John Wayne Tr, USPO
71mm	Yakima River
70	Sparks Rd, Easton, Lake Easton SP, **N**🍴 Shell/RV Town/dsl, café 🍴 Backwoods Cafe, Mtn High Burger 🅾 repair, Silver Ridge Ranch RV Park, **S** 🅾 Lake Easton RV Camping, Lake Easton SP
63	Cabin Creek Rd
62	Stampede Pass, elev 3750, to Lake Kachess, **N** Lake Kachess Lodge
54	Hyak, Gold Creek, **S** Ski Area
53	Snoqualmie Pass, elev 3022, **S** 🅿 Chevron 🍴 Summit Pancake House 🛏 Summit Lodge 🅾 info, Lee's Summit Mkt, to rec areas
52	W Summit (from eb), same as 53
47	Tinkham Rd, Denny Creek, Asahel Curtis, **N**🅾 chain area, 🅾 RV camping/dump
45	USFS Rd 9030, **N**🅾 to Lookout Point Rd
42	Tinkham Rd
38	**N**🅾 fire training ctr
35mm	S Fork Snoqualmie River
34	468th Ave SE, Edgewick Rd, **N**🅿 Gull/dsl/deli, Shell/dsl, TA Country Pride/Popeyes/dsl only/24hr/@, Warriors/dsl 🛏 Edgewick Inn 🅾 Norwest RV Park
32	436th Ave SE, **1 mi N**🅾 Snoqualmie Ranger Sta, gas, lodging, **S** 🍴 Riverbend Cafe 🅾 Iron Horse SP (3mi)
31	WA 202 W, North Bend, Snoqualmie, **N**🅿 Chevron/dsl, Shell/dsl 🍴 Arby's, Blimpie, Burger King, Los Cabos, McDonald's, Mongolian Grill, Papa Murphy's, Starbucks, Subway, Taco Time 🛏 North Bend Motel, Sallish Lodge, Sunset Motel 🅾 🏥, NorthBend Outlets/famous brands, O'Reilly Parts, Safeway/dsl
27	North Bend, Snoqualmie (from eb), **N** 🍴 Woodman's Steak 🅾 🏥
25	WA 18 W, Snoqualmie Pkwy, Tacoma, to Auburn, **N**🅿 Shell/dsl/e85 (1.5mi) 🅾 weigh sta
22	Preston, **N**🅿 Shell/dsl 🍴 Rhodes BBQ, Subway 🅾 LP, USPO, **S**🅾 Blue Sky RV Park
20	High Point Way
18	E Sunset Way, Issaquah, **S**🅿 Shell (1mi) 🍴 Flying Pie Pizza, Las Margaritas, Mandarin Garden, Stan's BBQ, Sunset Alehouse 🅾 $Tree
17	E Sammamish Rd, Front St, Issaquah, **N** 🅿 🍴 Coho Cafe, Coldstone, Fatburger, Ivan's Rest., Jamba Juice, Krispy Kreme, McDonald's, Panda Express, Papa John's, Qdoba Mexican, Starbucks, Subway 🅾 AT&T, Bartell Drug, Best Buy, Fred Meyer, Home Depot, URGENT CARE, Walgreens, **S**🅿 Arco/dsl, Cenex/dsl, Chevron/dsl, Shell/dsl 🍴 Boehms Chocolates, Domino's, Stan's BBQ, Subway, XXX Rootbeer 🅾 Big O Tire
15	WA 900, Issaquah, Renton, **N**🅿 Arco/dsl, Chevron 🍴 IHOP, O'Char Thai, Red Robin, Taco Time, Tully's Coffee 🛏 Holiday Inn, Motel 6 🅾 Barnes&Noble, Big Lots, Costco/gas, Lowe's

Side tab labels: MOSES LAKE, ELLENSBURG, WA, CLE ELUM, ISSAQUAH

I
S
S
A
Q
U
A
H

▲E INTERSTATE 90 Cont'd

15 Continued
Michael's, Office Depot, PCC Natural Mkt, Petsmart, to Lk Sammamish SP, **S** 🅿️ Shell/dsl 🍴 12th Ave Cafe, Baskin-Robbins, Burger King, Cafe Rio, Chipotle Mexican, Corner Cafe Bakery, Dickey's BBQ, Five Guys, Frankie's Pizza, Issaquah Cafe, Jack-in-the-Box, Jamba Juice, Jersey Mike's, KFC/Taco Bell, La Venadita, McDonald's, Panera Bread, Papa Murphy's, Potbelly, Starbucks, Starbucks (2), Subway, Taco Time, The Egg&Us Rest., Tuttabella Pizza, WildFin Grill 🛏️ Hilton Garden, Homewood Suites Ⓞ Chevrolet, Firestone/auto, Ford, GNC, Hobby Lobby, O'Reilly Parts, PetCo, QFC Foods, REI, Rite Aid, Ross, Safeway, See's Candies, Target, Trader Joe's, USPO, Verizon

13 SE Newport Way, W Lake Sammamish, **S** 🅿️ 76/dsl 🍴 Starbucks, Subway Ⓞ Matthew's Thriftway Mkt, vet

11 SE 150th, 156th, 161st, Bellevue, **N** 🅿️ Shell 🍴 Cypress Coffee, DQ, Jack-in-the-Box, Lil' Jon Rest., McDonald's, Shibuya Grill, Starbucks, Subway 🛏️ Embassy Suites, Hyatt House, Quality Inn, Silver Cloud Inn Ⓞ 7-11, LDS Temple, Nissan, Subaru/ VW, Toyota, vet, **S** 🅿️ 76, Chevron, Shell/dsl, Standard/dsl 🍴 Domino's, Outback Steaks, Pizza Hut, Starbucks 🛏️ Larkspur Landing Suites Ⓞ Honda, O'Reilly Parts, Rite Aid, Safeway, Trailer Inn RV Park

10 I-405, N to Bellevue, S to Renton, services located off I-405 S, exit 10

S
E
A
T
T
L
E

9 Bellevue Way

8 E Mercer Way, Mercer Island

7c 80th Ave SE (exits left from wb)

7b a SE 76th Ave, 77th Ave, Island Crest Way, Mercer Island, **S** 🅿️ Chevron/dsl, Shell/dsl 🍴 McDonald's, Qdoba, Starbucks, Subway, Thai Rest. Ⓞ New Seasons Mkt, QFC Mkt, Walgreens

6 W Mercer Way (from eb), same as 7

5mm Lake Washington

3b a Ranier Ave, Seattle, downtown, **N** 🅿️ Shell/dsl

2c b I-5, N to Vancouver, S to Tacoma

2a 4th Ave S, to stadiums

0 I-90 begins/ends on I-5, exit 164.

▲E INTERSTATE 182 (Richland)

Exit #	Services
	I-182 begins/ends on US 395 N.

14b a US 395 N, WA 397 S, OR Ave, **N** 🅿️ *Flying J*/dsl/scales/24hr, King City/Shell/rest/dsl/@ 🍴 Burger King, Subway Ⓞ Arrowhead RV Park, Freightliner, Peterbilt, **S** 🛏️ Knights Inn

13 N 4th Ave, Cty Ctr, **N** 🅿️ CFN/dsl 🛏️ Airport Motel, Starlite Motel, **S** 🅿️ 76/dsl, Chevron/dsl Ⓞ 🅷, Green Tree RV park, Tire Pros, vet

12b N 20th Ave, **N** 🛏️ Best Western+, Red Lion Hotel

12a US 395 S, Court St, **S on Court St** 🅿️ Chevron, Circle K/dsl, Conoco, Exxon/Jack-in-the-Box, Petro, Shell/dsl, USA 🍴 A&W/ KFC, Andy's Rest., Baskin-Robbins, Burger King, Domino's, El Mirador Mexican, Little Caesar's, McDonald's, Oriental Express, Papa Murphy's, Pizza Hut, RoundTable Pizza, Subway, Taco Bell, Wendy's Ⓞ $Tree, Albertson's, AutoZone, Blue Dog RV Ctr, Cadillac/Chevrolet, Dean RV Ctr, Ford, Hyundai, Mazda, Nissan, Rite Aid, U-Haul, USPO, Walgreens

9 rd 68, Trac, **N** 🅿️ Exxon/Circle K/dsl, Maverik/dsl, Porter's/dsl 🍴 Antonio's Pizza, Applebee's, Arby's, Bruchi's, Cousin's Rest., Dickey's BBQ, Domino's, DQ, Fiesta Mexican, Hacienda del Sol,

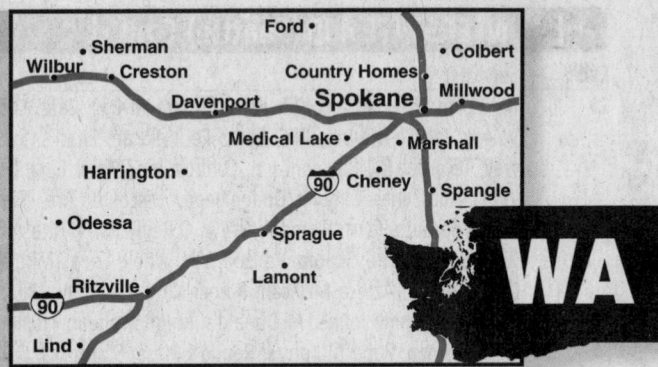

R
I
C
H
L
A
N
D

WA

9 Continued
IHOP, Jack-in-the-Box, Little Caesar's, McDonald's, Panda Express, Pier 39 Seafood, Pita Pit, Pizza Hut, Shakey's Pizza, Sonic, Starbucks, Subway, Taco Bell 🛏️ Hampton Inn, Holiday Inn Express, MyPlace Ⓞ $Tree, AT&T, Discount Tire, Firestone/auto, Franklin County RV Park, Grocery Outlet, Lowe's, O'Reilly Parts, Schwab Tire, URGENT CARE, Verizon, Walgreens, Walmart/Subway, Yokes Foods, **S** 🅿️ Maverik/dsl

7 Broadmoor Blvd, **N** 🛏️ Sleep Inn Ⓞ Camping World, GNC, Subaru, vet, **S** 🅿️ Exxon/Circle K/dsl Ⓞ Broadmoor RV Ctr, KOA

6.5mm Columbia River

5b a WA 240 E, Geo Washington Way, to Kennewick, **N** 🅿️ Conoco/ dsl 🍴 Anthony's Rest., Applebee's, Jack-in-the-Box, Starbucks 🛏️ Courtyard, Economy Inn, Hampton Inn, Red Lion Hotel, Shilo Inn, TownePlace Suites Ⓞ $Tree, AT&T, Winco Foods

4 WA 240 W, **N** 🅿️ Shell/dsl 🍴 El Porton Mexican, McDonald's, Starbucks Ⓞ BMW, Fred Meyer/dsl

3.5mm Yakima River

3 Keene Rd, Queensgate, **N** 🅿️ Exxon/Circle K, Maverik/dsl, USA/dsl 🍴 A&W/KFC, Bob's Burgers, Burger King, Costa Vida, Dickey's BBQ, Fiesta Mexican, Five Guys, Krispy Kreme, LJ Silver, McDonald's, Panda Express, Panera Bread, Qdoba, Starbucks, Sterling's Rest., Stick+Stone Pizza, Subway, Taco Bell Ⓞ AT&T, GNC, Home Depot, Marshall's, PetCo, Ross, Schwab Tire, Target, Tire Factory, Verizon, Walmart/Subway, **S** 🅿️ Chevron/dsl 🍴 MOD Pizza Ⓞ tires/repair

0mm I-182 begins/ends on I-82, exit 102.

▲N INTERSTATE 405 (Seattle)

Exit #	Services
30	I-5, N to Canada, S to Seattle, **I-405 begins/ends on I-5, exit 182.**

26 WA 527, Bothell, Mill Creek, **E** 🍴 McDonald's, Rama House Thai, Starbucks 🛏️ Extended Stay America, **W** 🅿️ Shell/ dsl 🍴 Applebee's, Arby's, Bamboo House, Bangkok Cafe, Baskin-Robbins, Bonefish Grill, Chick-fil-A, Crystal Creek Cafe, Five Guys, Grazie Ristorante, Imperial Wok, Jack-in-the-Box, Jimmy John's, Little Caesar's, MOD Pizza, Outback Steaks, Papa Murphy's, Qdoba Mexican, Starbucks, Subway, Taco Bell, Taco Time, Wendy's, Zeek's Pizza 🛏️ Comfort Inn, Extended Stay America, Hilton Garden, Holiday Inn Express Ⓞ 7-11, Bartell Drug, Goodyear/auto, Lake Pleasant RV Park, QFC Foods, Rite Aid, URGENT CARE, vet

24 NE 195th St, Beardslee Blvd, **E** 🅿️ Chevron/dsl 🍴 Subway, Teryaki Etc. 🛏️ Country Inn&Suites, Red Lion Inn, Residence Inn Ⓞ Exotic vet

23b WA 522 W, Bothell

23a WA 522 E, to WA 202, Woodinville, Monroe

22 NE 160th St, **E** 🅿️ Chevron, Shell/dsl 🍴 Top Mkt/deli

SEATTLE

WA

INTERSTATE 405 (Seattle) Cont'd

Exit #	Services
20	NE 124th St, **E** 🛢 Arco, Shell/dsl 🍴 Brown Bag Cafe, Cafe Veloce, Jack-in-the-Box, KFC, Santa Fe Mexican, Shari's, Subway, Taco Bell 🛏 Baymont Inn, Comfort Inn, Motel 6 Ⓞ Ⓗ, 7-11, AutoZone, Chrysler/Dodge/Jeep, Discount Tire, Fiat, Firestone/auto, Ford, Hyundai, NAPA, O'Reilly Parts, Rite Aid, Ross, Schwab Tire, Toyota, Verizon, VW, Whole Foods Mkt, **W** 🛢 76/dsl 🍴 Azteca Mexican, Burger King, Five Guys, Izumi Japanese, Jimmy John's, McDonald's, Mediterranean Kitchen, Olive Garden, Papa Murphy's, Romio's Pizza, Starbucks, Subway, Taco Del Mar, Taco Time, Wendy's 🛏 Courtyard Ⓞ AT&T, Buick/GMC, Fred Meyer/dsl, GNC, QFC Foods
18	WA 908, Kirkland, Redmond, **E** 🛢 76/Circle K/dsl, Chevron, Texaco/dsl 🍴 Baskin-Robbins, Little Caesar's, McDonald's, Starbucks, Subway, Taco Time, Tres Hermanos Ⓞ Chevrolet, Costco, Honda, Kia, Mazda, PepBoys, PetCo, Safeway, Tuesday Morning, U-Haul, URGENT CARE, vet, Walgreens, **W** 🛢 Shell/dsl 🍴 Acropolis Pizza, Papa John's, Starbucks, Subway, Wendy's Ⓞ QFC Foods, Tire Pros
17	NE 70th Pl
14b a	WA 520, Seattle, Redmond
13b	NE 8th St, **E** 🛢 Arco, Chevron/dsl, Shell/dsl 🍴 Burger King, Chick-fil-A, Taco del Mar 🛏 Hotel 116 Ⓞ Ⓗ, Bartell Drugs, Best Buy, Cadillac, Chevrolet, Ford, Home Depot, Infiniti, Mercedes, Porsche, Volvo, Whole Foods Mkt, **W** 🍴 Starbucks, Subway 🛏 Courtyard, Hyatt
13a	NE 4th St, **E** 🛏 Extended Stay America, Hampton Inn Ⓞ Chrysler/Dodge/Jeep, Lexus, **W** 🍴 Azteca Mexican, Subway 🛏 Hilton, Hotel Bellevue, Marriott, Red Lion/Bellevue Inn, Residence Inn, Sheraton
12	SE 8th St, **W** 🛏 Residence Inn
11	I-90, E to Spokane, W to Seattle
10	Cold Creek Pkwy, Factoria, **E on Factoria Blvd** 🛢 76, Chevron 🍴 Applebee's, Burger King, Chipotle, Coldstone, Domino's, El Tapatio Mexican, Goldberg's Rest., Great Harvest Bread, Jamba Juice, Jimmy John's, KFC, McDonald's, MOD Pizza,
10	Continued Novilhos Brazilian Steaks, Panda Express, Panera Bread, Ricardo's Mexican, Romio's Pizza, Shanghai Cafe, Starbucks, Subway, Taco Bell, Taco Time, Thai Ginger, Tokyo Japanese Ⓞ 7-11, AT&T, Bartell Drug, Midas, Old Navy, O'Reilly Parts, PetCo, QFC Foods, Rite Aid, Safeway, Target, TJ Maxx, Verizon, Walmart
9	112th Ave SE, Newcastle, Ⓒ
7	NE 44th St, **E** 🍴 Denny's, McDonald's, Starbucks, Subway, Taco Del Mar, Teriyaki Wok 🛏 EconoLodge
6	NE 30th St, **E** 🛢 Arco, **W** 🛢 Chevron/dsl, Shell/dsl Ⓞ 7-11
5	WA 900 E, Park Ave N, Sunset Blvd NE, **W** 🍴 Five Guys, Jimmy John's, Panda Express, Panera Bread, Potbelly, Red Robin, Torero's Mexican 🛏 Hampton Inn, Hyatt House, Residence Inn Ⓞ AT&T, Dick's, Fry's Electronics, GNC, Lowe's, Marshall's, Petsmart, Ross, Staples, Target, Verizon, World Mkt
4	WA 169 S, Wa 900 W, Renton, **E** 🍴 Shari's 🛏 Quality Inn Ⓞ Aqua Barn Ranch Camping, **W** 🍴 Burger King, Pizza Dudes, Subway 🛏 Renton Inn Ⓞ $Tree, 7-11
2	WA 167, Rainier Ave, to Auburn, **E** 🛏 Hilton Garden, Larkspur Landing, SpringHill Suites, TownePlace Suites Ⓞ Ⓗ, **W** 🛢 Arco/dsl, Chevron, Chevron, Mobil/dsl 🍴 A&W/KFC, Applebee's, Baskin-Robbins, Chipotle, Domino's, IHOP, Jack-in-the-Box, Jimmy John's, Jimmy Mac's Roadhouse, King Buffet, Little Caesar's, Mazatlan Mexican, McDonald's, Papa Murphy's, Pizza Hut, Popeye's, Sonic, Starbucks, Subway, Taco Bell, Taco Time, Wendy's, Yankee Grill 🛏 Red Lion Hotel Ⓞ AutoZone, Buick/Cadillac/GMC, Chevrolet, Chrysler/Dodge/Jeep, Discount Tire, Firestone/auto, Ford, Fred Meyer/dsl, Hyundai, Kia, Mazda, Midas, O'Reilly Parts, Safeway/gas, Schwab Tire, Subaru, Toyota, vet, Walgreens, Walmart
1	WA 181 S, Tukwila, **E** 🛢 Chevron/dsl 🍴 Jack-in-the-Box, Taco Bell, Wendy's 🛏 Courtyard, Embassy Suites, Extended Stay America, Hampton Inn, Ramada, Residence Inn, Woodspring Suites Ⓞ 7-11, **W** 🛢 🍴 Subway, Taco Del Mar 🛏 Comfort Suites, Homewood Suites Ⓞ fun center
0mm	I-5, N to Seattle, S to Tacoma, WA 518 W. **I-405 begins/ends on I-5, exit 154.**

NOTES

WEST VIRGINIA

🅴 INTERSTATE 64

Exit #	Services
184mm	West Virginia/Virginia state line
183	VA 311, (from eb, no reentry), Crows (from eb)
181	US 60, WV 92 (no ez wb return), White Sulphur Springs, **0-2 mi** **N** 📷 GoMart/dsl, Marathon/Godfather's, Shell 🍴 April's Pizzaria, Hardee's 🏠 Budget Inn, Greenbrier Resort, Old White Motel Ⓞ autocare, Family$, Food Lion, Rite Aid, ski area, to Midland Trail, USPO
179mm	Welcome Ctr wb, full 🚻 facilities, info, litter barrels, petwalk, Ⓒ 🖼
175	US 60, WV 92, Caldwell, **N** 📷 Exxon, Shell/Subway/dsl, Sunoco/Mountaineer Mart/dsl 🍴 Cook's Country Kitchen, McDonald's, Wendy's Ⓞ $General, **S** Ⓞ Greenbrier SF
173mm	Greenbrier River
169	US 219, Lewisburg, Hist Dist, **N** 📷 Shell 🍴 Biscuit World 🏠 Relax Inn Ⓞ Federated Parts, **S** 📷 Exxon/dsl, Gomart, Shell, Walmart/dsl 🍴 Applebee's, Arby's, Bellacino's, Bob Evans, China Palace, Dickey's BBQ, Hardee's, Papa John's, Ruby Tuesday, Shoney's, Subway, Taco Bell 🏠 Fairfield Inn, Hampton Inn, Holiday Inn Express, Quality Inn, Super 8 Ⓞ 🅷 $Tree, AT&T, AutoZone, Buick/Chevrolet, Ford, Lowe's, URGENT CARE, Verizon, Walmart
161	WV 12, Alta, **S** 📷 Citgo/dsl 🍴 Alta Sta/cafe Ⓞ Greenbrier River Camping (14mi)
156	US 60, Midland Trail, Sam Black Church, **N** 📷 Exxon/Arby's/dsl, Shell/dsl
150	rd 29, rd 4, Dawson, **S** 📷 Exxon 🍴 Cheddar's Cafe 🏠 Dawson Inn Ⓞ RV camping
147mm	runaway truck ramp wb
143	WV 20, Green Sulphur Springs, **N** 📷 Liberty/dsl
139	WV 20, Sandstone, Hinton, **S** 📷 Citgo/dsl Ⓞ Blue Stone SP (16mi), Richmonds Store/USPO, to Pipestem Resort Park (25 mi)
138mm	New River
136mm	runaway truck ramp eb
133.1mm	Sandstone Mtn, elev 2765
133	WV 27, Pluto Rd, Bragg, **S** RV camping, mandatory truck stop eb
129	WV 9, Shady Spring, **N** Ⓞ to Grandview SP, **S** 📷 Exxon/dsl, Shell/dsl 🍴 Subway Ⓞ Little Beaver SP
125b a	WV 307, Airport Rd, Beaver, **N** 📷 Shell/dsl 🍴 Biscuit World 🏠 Sleep Inn, **1 mi S** 📷 GoMart/gas, Marathon/dsl, Sheetz/dsl 🍴 Arby's, Dickey's BBQ, DQ, El Mariachi, Hardee's, KFC, Little Caesar's, LJ Silver, McDonald's, Subway, Wendy's Ⓞ Advance Parts, CVS Drug, Family$, Kroger, USPO, Walgreens
124	US 19, Eisenhower Dr, E Beckley, **1-2 mi N** 📷 GoMart/gas 🍴 Capt D's, Raleigh Diner 🏠 Green Bank Motel, Microtel Ⓞ 🅷, $General, last exit before **toll** rd wb
121	I-77 S, to Bluefield
	I-64 and I-77 run together 61 mi. See I-77, exits 42 through 100.
59	I-77 N (from eb), to I-79
58c	US 60, Washington St, **N** 📷 BP, Exxon, GoMart/dsl Ⓞ Family$, **S** 🍴 5th Quarter Steaks, Capt D's, Panera Bread, Shoney's, Wendy's 🏠 Courtyard, Embassy Suites, Hampton Inn, Holiday Inn Express, Marriott Ⓞ 🅷, civic ctr, Goodyear/auto, Macy's, mall

58b	US 119 N (from eb), Charleston, downtown, same as 58c
58a	US 119 S, WV 61, MacCorkle Ave
56	Montrose Dr, **N** 📷 Exxon/dsl, Marathon/dsl, Speedway/dsl 🍴 Hardee's, Los Agaves Mexican 🏠 Holiday Inn, Microtel, Wingate Inn Ⓞ $General, Acura, Advance Parts, Chevrolet, Dodge, Hyundai, Kia, NAPA, Rite Aid, VW
55	Kanawha Tpk (from wb)
54	US 60, MacCorkle Ave, **N** 🍴 Burger King, Casa Garcia, Graziano's Pizza, Krispy Kreme, Subway Ⓞ $Tree, AT&T, Kroger/dsl, TJ Maxx, **S** 🍴 Bob Evans, Husson's Pizza, KFC, LJ Silver, McDonald's, Pizza Hut, Schlotzsky's, Taco Bell, Wendy's Ⓞ 🅷, Aamco, Family$, Harley-Davidson, Honda, Mazda, URGENT CARE
53	Roxalana Rd, to Dunbar, **S** 📷 GoMart/dsl 🍴 BiscuitWorld, Capt D's, Gino's Pizza, Graziano's Pizza, Los Agaves, McDonald's, Subway, Wendy's 🏠 Dunbar Plaza Motel, Super 8 Ⓞ $General, Advance Parts, Aldi Foods, CVS Drug, Family$, Jo-Ann Fabrics, Kroger/dsl, NTB, Rite Aid
50	VW 25, Institute, **S** 📷 GoMart/dsl
47b a	WV 622, Goff Mtn Rd, **N** 📷 Exxon/dsl, GoMart, Speedway/dsl 🍴 BiscuitWorld, Bob Evans, Capt D's, Domino's, Gino's Pizza, Little Caesar's, McDonald's, Papa John's, Pizza Hut, Subway, Taco Bell, Wendy's 🏠 Motel 6 Ⓞ Advance Parts, AT&T, Autozone, Family$, Kroger/gas, Rite Aid, Save-a-Lot, URGENT CARE, Walgreens, **S** 🍴 Arby's, Asian Buffet, Barnyard BBQ, Buffalo Wild Wings, Burger King, Cracker Barrel, Golden Corral, HoneyBaked Ham, La Roca Mexican, Sakura Japanese, TGIFriday's 🏠 Comfort Inn, Holiday Inn Express, Sleep Inn Ⓞ $Tree, Lowe's, Staples, Walmart
45	WV 25, Nitro, **N** 📷 🛢/Arby's/dsl/scales/24hr Ⓞ Chevrolet, **S** 📷 Exxon/dsl, GoMart, Speedway/dsl 🍴 BiscuitWorld, Checker's, DQ, Gino's Pizza, McDonald's, Subway, Wendy's Ⓞ $General

L E W I S B U R G

C H A R L E S T O N

WV

🚗 = gas 🍴 = food 🛏 = lodging 🅾 = other 🅁ₛ = rest stop   Copyright 2022 - The Next EXIT ®

INTERSTATE 64 Cont'd

Exit #	Services
44.3mm	Kanawha River
44	US 35, St Albans, S🚗 Shell/7-11/dsl
40	US 35 N, Winfield, Pt Pleasant, S🚗 Sheetz/dsl, Speedway/dsl 🍴 DQ
39	WV 34, Winfield, N🚗 BP/Arby's, GoMart/dsl 🍴 Applebee's, Bob Evans, Rio Grande Mexican, Taste of Asia 🛏 Holiday Inn Express, Red Roof Inn 🅾 $General, $Tree, Advance Parts, Aldi Foods, BigLots, Elder-Beerman, GNC, Home Depot, USPO, S🚗 GoMart, TA/Country Pride/dsl/scales/24hr/@ 🍴 Biscuit World, Burger King, Capt D's, China Chef, El Rancho Grande, Fat Patty's, Fireside Grille, Gino's Pizza, Graziano's Pizza, KFC, McDonald's, Penn Sta., Subway, Taco Bell, TCBY, Wendy's 🛏 Hampton Inn 🅾 AT&T, AutoZone, Kroger/dsl, Rite Aid, URGENT CARE, Verizon
38mm	weigh sta both lanes
35mm	🅁ₛ both lanes, full 🛢 facilities, litter barrels, petwalk, 🐾, 🏕, vending
34	WV 19, Hurricane, N🍴 Arby's, KFC, Taco Bell 🅾 $Tree, Chevrolet, Chrysler/Dodge/Jeep, Ford, Martin RV Ctr, Walmart/Subway, S🚗 Exxon/Dunkin', Go-Mart, Sheetz/dsl 🍴 BiscuitWorld/Gino's Pizza, China Wok, Little Caesar's, McDonald's, Mi Pueblito, Pizza Hut, Subway 🛏 American Inn, Budget Inn 🅾 Rite Aid, USPO, vet, Walgreens
28	US 60, Milton, 0-2 mi S🚗 Exxon, Go-Mart, Marathon/dsl, Sheetz/dsl 🍴 Biscuit World, McDonald's, Pizza Hut, Subway, Taco Bell, Wendy's 🅾 $General, Advance Parts, AutoZone, CVS Drug, Family$, Jim's Camping (2mi), KOA (3mi), NAPA, Piggly Wiggly, Rite Aid, Save-A-Lot foods, USPO
20	US 60, Mall Rd, Barboursville, N🍴 Applebee's, Bob Evans, Buffalo Wild Wings, Burger King, Chick-fil-A, Chili's, Chipotle, IHOP, Logan's Roadhouse, McDonald's, Olive Garden, Panera Bread, Qdoba Mexican, Ruby Tuesday, Super China, Wendy's 🛏 Comfort Inn 🅾 BAM!, Best Buy, Dick's, Drug Emporium, Elder-Beerman, Firestone/auto, Hobby Lobby, JC Penney, JoAnn Fabrics, Kohl's, Lowe's, Macy's, Michael's, NTB, Old Navy, Walmart/Subway, S🚗 BP/dsl, Sheetz/dsl 🍴 Cracker Barrel, Fat Patty's, Outback Steaks, Shogun Japanese, Sonic, Steak&Shake, Subway, Taco Bell 🛏 Best Western, Hampton Inn, Holiday Inn 🅾 Toyota
18	US 60, to WV 2, Barboursville, N🍴 Bellacino's, O'Charley's, Starbucks 🅾 $Tree, Home Depot, Marshall's, Office Depot, Petco, Target, S🚗 Shell/7-11 🍴 Biscuit World, Gino's, Giovanni's Pizza, Hardee's, Papa John's 🅾 Food Fair, Kia, Kroger/gas, NAPA, Rite Aid, Walgreens
15	US 60, 29th St E, N🚗 GoMart/dsl, Shell/dsl, Speedway/dsl 🍴 #1 Kitchen, Arby's, Biscuit World, Burger King, Honeybaked Ham, Subway, Waffle House, Wendy's 🛏 Huntington Motel, Quality Inn 🅾 $General, AT&T, BigLots, NAPA, Save-a-Lot Foods, st police, Verizon, Walmart/McDonald's, S🚗 Exxon 🍴 Fazoli's, Golden Corral, KFC, Little Caesar's, Marco's Pizza, McDonald's, Penn Sta., Taco Bell 🛏 Days Inn, Red Roof Inn 🅾 Buick/Cadillac/GMC, CVS Drug, Honda, Nissan, Subaru, VW
11	WV 10, Hal Greer Blvd, 0-2 mi N🚗 Marathon/Subway 🍴 Arby's, Baskin-Robbins, Biscuit World, Bob Evans, El Ranchito Mexican, Frostop Drive-In, McDonald's, Papa John's, Ritzy's Cafe, Wendy's 🛏 Fairfield Inn, Hampton Inn, Ramada Ltd, Super 8, TownePlace Suites 🅾 🏥, AutoZone, Chrysler/Dodge/Jeep, Rite Aid, S🅾 Beech Fork SP (8mi)
10mm	Welcome Ctr eb, full 🛢 facilities, litter barrels, petwalk, 🐾, 🏕, vending

Exit #	Services
8	WV 152 S, WV 527 N, N🅾 URGENT CARE, vet, S🚗 GoMart/dsl, Speedway/dsl
6	US 52 N, W Huntington, Chesapeake, N🚗 Sheetz/dsl, Speedway/dsl 🍴 Pizza Hut, Shoney's, Wendys 🅾 $General, AutoZone, BigLots, Family$, Save-A-Lot Foods
1	US 52 S, Kenova, 0-1 mi N🚗 Exxon, Shell/dsl 🍴 Burger King, Evaroni's Pizza, Gino's Pizza, Hermanos Nunez Mexican, McDonald's, Stewart's Hotdogs, Taco Bell 🛏 Hollywood Mote 🅾 $General, Advance Parts, CVS Drug, NAPA, Save-A-Lot, USPO
0mm	West Virginia/Kentucky state line, Big Sandy River

INTERSTATE 68

Exit #	Services
32mm	West Virginia/Maryland state line
31mm	Welcome Ctr wb, full 🛢 facilities, litter barrels, petwalk, 🐾, 🏕, vending
29	rd 5, Hazelton Rd, N🚗 Sunoco/dsl 🛏 Microtel (1mi), 🅾 Big Bear Camping (3mi), Pine Hill RV Camp (4mi)
23	WV 26, Bruceton Mills, N🚗 BFS/Subway/dsl/24hr, Sunoco Little Sandy's Rest./dsl/24hr 🍴 Mill Stone Rest. 🛏 Maple Leaf Motel 🅾 antiques, Auto+ Parts, Family$, USPO
18mm	Laurel Run
17mm	runaway truck ramp eb
16mm	weigh sta wb
15	WV 73, WV 12, Coopers Rock, N🅾 Chestnut Ridge SF, Sand Springs Camping (2mi)
12mm	runaway truck ramp wb
10	WV 43 N, to rd 857, Fairchance Rd, Cheat Lake, N🚗 BFS/DQ/ Little Caesar's/dsl, Exxon/dsl 🍴 Angelo's Pizza, Dragon Cafe 🅾 USPO, vet, S🍴 Burger King 🛏 Lakeview Resort
9mm	Cheat Lake
7	rd 705, Pierpont Rd, N🚗 BFS/Little Caesar's/Subway/TCBY, Exxon/Taco Bell/dsl 🍴 Fox's Pizza Den, Fujiyama Steaks, Honeybaked Ham, IHOP, McDonald's, Outback Steaks, Ruby Tuesday, Wendy's 🛏 Holiday Inn Express, Super 8 🅾 🏥, Books-A-Million, Family$, GNC, Lowe's, Michael's, Shop'n Save Foods, to WVU Stadium, S🚗 Sunoco/dsl 🍴 Apple Annie's, Don Patron Mexican, Rita's Custard 🅾 Chrysler/Dodge
4	rd 7, to Sabraton, N🚗 BFS/Subway/dsl, Sheetz/dsl 🍴 Arby's, Burger King, Dunkin', Hardee's, KFC, LJ Silver, McDonald's, Popeye's, Shoney's, Wendy's 🛏 SpringHill Suites, Suburban Lodge 🅾 $General, $Tree, Advance Parts, AutoZone, CVS Drug, Family$, Kroger/dsl, NAPA, Save-A-Lot Foods, USPO, S🚗 Marathon/Circle K, Sunoco/dsl 🍴 China City
3mm	Decker's Creek
1	US 119, Morgantown, N🚗 Go-Mart/dsl 🛏 Morgantown Inn/ rest., Quality Inn 🅾 tires, S🚗 Sheetz/dsl, Tesla EVC 🍴 Denny's, Mariachi Loco 🅾 $Tree, to Tygart L SP, Walmart/Subway
0mm	I-79, N to Pittsburgh, S to Clarksburg. I-68 begins/ends on I-79, exit 148.

INTERSTATE 70

Exit #	Services
14mm	West Virginia/Pennsylvania state line
13.5mm	Welcome Ctr wb, full 🛢 facilities, litter barrels, petwalk, 🐾, 🏕, vending
11	WV 41, Dallas Pike, N🚗 TA/Country Pride/dsl/scales/24hr/@ 🛏 Comfort Inn, S🚗 Exxon, Marathon/DQ/dsl 🛏 EconoLodge 🅾 RV camping
10	rd 65, to Cabela Dr, N🚗 Sheetz/dsl 🍴 Applebee's, Bob Evans, Cheddar's, Coldstone, Eat'n Park, El Paso Mexican, Five Guys,

⬆️E INTERSTATE 70 Cont'd

10   Continued
Fusion Steaks, Jimmy John's, Logan's Roadhouse, McDonald's, Olive Garden, Panera Bread, Primanti Bros, Quaker Steak, TX Roadhouse, Wendy's 🛏 Fairfield Inn, Hampton Inn, Hawthorn Suites, Microtel 🅞 AT&T, Best Buy, Books-A-Million, Cabela's, GNC, JC Penney, Kohl's, Old Navy, PetCo, Russell Stover Candies, Target, TJ Maxx, Verizon, Walmart/Subway, **S** 🅖 Sheetz/dsl 🛏 Holiday Inn Express, Suburban Lodge 🅞 Buick/GMC, Chevrolet, Ford/Lincoln, Honda, Hyundai, Nissan, Toyota

5   US 40, WV 88 S, Tridelphia, **N** 🅖 Marathon/dsl 🅕 Pizza Hut, Subway, Wendy's 🛏 Super 8 🅞 Chrysler/Dodge/Jeep, Family$, Riesbeck's Foods, Subaru/VW, URGENT CARE, vet, **S** 🅖 Marathon/dsl 🅕 Arby's, DQ, McDonald's, Undo's Rest. 🅞 Advance Parts, AT&T, AutoZone, museum, Rite Aid

5a   I-470 W, to Columbus

4   WV 88 N (from eb), Elm Grove, same as 5

3.5mm   weigh sta eb

2b   Washington Ave, **N** 🅞 $General, **S** 🅕 Figaretti's Italian 🅞 🇭

2a   rd 88 N, to Oglebay Park, **N** 🅖 Marathon/dsl, Sheetz 🅕 AC Buffet, Bob Evans, DeFelice Bros Pizza, Hardee's, Little Caesar's, Papa John's, Perkins, Subway, Tim Hortons 🛏 Hampton Inn, SpringHill Suites 🅞 Advance Parts, CVS Drug, Kroger/gas, NTB, URGENT CARE, Verizon

1b   US 250 S, WV 2 S, S Wheeling

1mm   tunnel

1a   US 40 E, WV 2 N, Main St, downtown, **S** 🛏 Knights Inn

0   (from wb)US 40 W, Zane St, Wheeling Island, **N** 🅖 Exxon/dsl 🅕 Burger King, KFC

0mm   West Virginia/Ohio state line, Ohio River

⬆️N INTERSTATE 77

Exit #	Services
186mm	West Virginia/Ohio state line, Ohio River
185	WV 14, WV 31, Williamstown, **W** WV Welcome Ctr/🆁🆂, full facilities, info, litter barrels, 🏞, 🅖 Clark, GoMart/dsl, Shell (1mi) 🅕 Dutch Pantry 🛏 Econolodge/Rodeway Inn 🅞 Glass Factory Tours
179	WV 2 N, WV 68 S, to Waverly, **E** 🅖 Exxon/dsl 🅞 🍽️, **W** 🅖 BP/dsl 🅕 Burger King, Hardee's (3mi) 🛏 Red Carpet Inn, Sleep Inn 🅞 🇭
176	US 50, 7th St, Parkersburg, **E** to North Bend SP, **W** 🅖 BP/7-11, GoMart 🅕 Domino's, DQ, Hardee's, Little Caesar's, McDonald's, Mountaineer Rest./24hr, Omelette Shoppe, Wendy's 🛏 Economy Inn, Travelodge 🅞 Advance Parts, AutoZone, Chrysler/Dodge/Jeep, CVS Drug, Family$, Ford/Lincoln, Honda, Hyundai, Kroger/dsl, Mercedes, NAPA, Rite Aid, to Blennerhassett Hist Park, Toyota
174	WV 47, Staunton Ave, **1 mi E** 🅖 GoMart/Sub Express/dsl 🅞 $General
174mm	Little Kanawha River
173	WV 95, Camden Ave, **E** 🅖 Marathon/dsl, **1-4 mi W** 🅖 🅕 Hardee's 🛏 Blennerhassett Hotel 🅞 🇭
170	WV 14, Mineral Wells, **E** 🅖 BP/dsl/repair, GoMart/Taco Bell/dsl, Liberty Trkstp/dsl/24hr 🅕 McDonald's, Wendy's 🛏 Comfort Suites, Hampton Inn, **W** 🅕 Cracker Barrel, Napoli's Pizza 🛏 Holiday Inn Express, Microtel, Mineral Wells Inn
169mm	weigh sta both lanes, 🅒
166mm	🆁🆂 both lanes, full 🅖 facilities, litter barrels, petwalk, 🅒, 🏞, RV dump, vending

161	WV 21, Rockport, **W** 🅖 Marathon/dsl
154	WV 1, Medina Rd
146	WV 2 S, Silverton, Ravenswood, **E** 🅞 Ruby Lake Camping (4mi), **W** 🅖 Exxon/DQ, Marathon/dsl 🅕 McDonald's (3mi), Subway (4mi), Wendy's (3mi) 🛏 Scottish Inn
138	US 33, Ripley, **E** 🅖 BP/dsl, Marathon/dsl, Murphy USA/dsl, Sheetz/dsl 🅕 Arby's, KFC, Las Trancas Mexican, LJ Silver, McDonald's, Pizza Hut, Taco Bell, Wendy's 🛏 Holiday Inn Express, Super 8 🅞 $Tree, AutoZone, Family$, Kroger/dsl, NAPA, Rite Aid, Sav-A-Lot Foods, Verizon, Walmart/Subway, **W** 🅖 Exxon/dsl 🅕 Bob Evans, Ponderosa, Shoney's, Subway 🛏 Quality Inn 🅞 🇭
132	WV 21, Fairplain, **E** 🅖 BP/7-11/dsl, GoMart/dsl, Speedway/dsl/24hr 🅕 Burger King, Fratello's Italian 🅞 $General, Ford, Statts Mills RV Park (6mi), **W** 🅖 ❤️Loves/Chester's/McDonald's/dsl/scales/24hr
124	WV 34, Kenna, **E** 🅖 Exxon 🅕 Your Family Rest.
119	WV 21, Goldtown, same as 116
116	WV 21, Haines Branch Rd, Sissonville, **4 mi E** 🅞 Rippling Waters Camping
114	WV 622, Pocatalico Rd, **E** 🅖 BP/dsl 🅞 $General
111	WV 29, Tuppers Creek Rd, **W** 🅖 BP/Subway/dsl 🅕 Gino's (2mi), McDonald's (2mi), Tudor's Biscuit World, Wendy's (2mi)
106	WV 27, Edens Fork Rd, **W** 🅖 Marathon/dsl/country store 🛏 Sunset Motel (3mi)
104	I-79 N, to Clarksburg
102	US 119 N, Westmoreland Rd, **E** 🅖 BP/7-11, GoMart 🅕 Hardee's 🅞 Foodland/gas
101	I-64, **E** to Beckley, **W** to Huntington
100	Broad St, Capitol St, **W** 🅕 Subway 🛏 Best Western, Charleston Capitol Hotel, Marriott 🅞 🇭, Cadillac/GMC, Firestone, Rite Aid, USPO
99	WV 114, Capitol St, **E** 🅞 🍽️, **W** 🅖 BP/7-11, Exxon/Noble Roman's 🅕 Domino's, McDonald's, Wendy's 🅞 st capitol, to museum
98	35th St Bridge (from sb), **W** 🅖 Shell/7-11/dsl 🅕 Husson's Pizza, KFC, McDonald's, Steak Escape, Subway, Taco Bell, Wendy's 🅞 🇭, Rite Aid, to U of Charleston
97	US 60 W (from nb), Kanawha Blvd
96	US 60 E, Midland Trail, Belle, **W** 🅕 Anchor Pizza, Biscuit World, Gino's 🛏 Budget Host
96mm	**W Va Turnpike begins/ends.**
95.5mm	Kanawha River
95	WV 61, to MacCorkle Ave, **E** 🅖 GoMart/dsl/24hr, Marathon/Subway/dsl 🅕 Bob Evans, IHOP, McDonald's, TX Steaks 🛏 Country Inn&Suites, Days Inn, Holiday Inn Express, Knights Inn, Motel 6, Red Roof Inn 🅞 Advance Parts, AutoZone, **W** 🅖 Exxon/dsl, GoMart, Shell/7-11/dsl 🅕 Applebee's, Arby's,

Left margin: **WHEELING**   **PARKERSBURG**   Right margin: **CHARLESTON**   **WV**

⬆🅽 INTERSTATE 77 Cont'd

95	Continued
	Bojangle's, Burger King, Capt D's, China Buffet, Cracker Barrel, Firehouse Subs, Fujiyama Japanese, Hooters, La Carreta, Little Caesar's, Pizza Hut, Taco Bell 🅾 $Tree, AT&T, Drug Emporium, GNC, Kings Tire, Kroger/dsl, Lowe's, Piggly Wiggly, URGENT CARE, Verizon, vet
89	WV 61, WV 94, to Marmet, **E** 🅶 Exxon/Subway/dsl/24hr, GoMart/dsl, Sunoco/dsl 🍽 BiscuitWorld, Gino's Pizza, Hardee's, LJ Silver, Wendy's 🅾 $General, Family$, Ford, Kroger/dsl, NAPA, USPO
85	US 60, WV 61, East Bank, **E** 🅶 Marathon/dsl, Shell/Arby's/dsl 🍽 Gino's Pizza, McDonald's, Shoney's 🅾 $General, Chevrolet, Rite Aid
82.5mm	toll booth
79	Cabin Creek Rd, Sharon
74	WV 83, Paint Creek Rd
72mm	**Morton Service Area nb,** 🅶 Exxon/dsl 🍽 Burger King, Hershey's Ice Cream, KFC, Pizza Hut, Starbucks 🅾 atm
69mm	🆁🆂 sb, full 🛗 facilities, litter barrels, 🚻, 🛄
66	WV 15, to Mahan
60	WV 612, Oak Hill, to Mossy, **1/2 mi E** 🅶 Exxon/dsl 🅾 RV camping
56.5mm	toll plaza
54	rd 2, rd 23, Pax, **E** 🅶 Corner/dsl
48	US 19, N Beckley, **1-4 mi E on US 19/WV 16** 🅶 Exxon/Subway, Sheetz/dsl 🍽 Bob Evans, Buffalo Wild Wings, Burger King, Cheddar's, Chick-fil-A, Chili's, Dickey's BBQ, Five Guys, Honeybaked Ham, LJ Silver, Logan's Roadhouse, McDonald's, Olive Garden, Panera Bread, Peking Buffet, Qdoba, Rally's, Ryan's, Starbucks, Subway, Taco Bell, Wendy's 🛏 Days Inn 🅾 $General, $Tree, Advance Parts, AT&T, AutoZone, Belk, BigLots, Buick/GMC, Chevrolet, Chrysler/Dodge/Jeep, CVS Drug, Dick's, Food Lion, Goodyear/auto, Hobby Lobby, Honda, Hyundai, JC Penney, Jo-Ann Fabrics, Kia/Subaru, Kohl's, Kroger/gas, Lowe's, NAPA, Nissan, Petsmart, Rite Aid, RV Ctr, Sam's Club/gas, Staples, TJ Maxx, Toyota, U-Haul, Walgreens, Walmart
45mm	**Tamarack Service Area both lanes, W** 🅶 Exxon/dsl 🍽 Burger King, Hershey's Ice Cream, Quiznos, Sbarro's, Starbucks 🅾 gifts
44	WV 3, Beckley, **E** 🅶 Exxon/dsl, Marathon/dsl, Shell/Dickey's BBQ 🍽 Applebee's, Bojangle's, Burger King, Campestre Mexican, DQ, Fujiyama Japanese, Hooters, IHOP, McDonald's, Omelet Shoppe, Outback Steaks, Pizza Hut 🛏 Courtyard, EconoLodge, Fairfield Inn, Howard Johnson, Quality Inn/rest., Super 8, Travelodge 🅾 🏥, Advance Parts, CVS Drug, Kroger/gas, Rite Aid, Tires, URGENT CARE, **W** 🅶 BP/Subway/dsl, Go-Mart/dsl 🍽 Bob Evans, Cracker Barrel, Pasquale Italian, Ruby Tuesday, Sam's Hotdogs, TX Steaks, Wendy's 🛏 Baymont Inn, Comfort Inn, Country Inn&Suites, Hampton Inn, Holiday Inn, Microtel
42	WV 16, WV 97, to Mabscott, **2 mi E** 🅾 🏥, **W** 🅶 BP/dsl, Go-Mart 🍽 Arby's, Gino's Pizza/Biscuit World, Subway 🅾 AutoValue Repair, O'Reilly Parts, USPO, Walmart/Subway
40	I-64 E, to Lewisburg
30mm	toll booth
28	WV 48, to Ghent, **E** 🅶 Exxon/dsl, Marathon/dsl 🍽 Subway 🛏 Appalachian Resort Inn (12mi), Glade Springs Resort (1mi) 🅾 to ski area, **W** 🛏 Knight's Inn
26.5mm	elevation 3252, Flat Top Mtn
20	US 19, to Camp Creek, **E** 🅶 Exxon/dsl, **W** 🅾 Camp Creek SP/RV camping

18.5mm	Bluestone River, scenic overlook/**parking area/weigh sta sb**
17mm	**Bluestone Service Area/weigh sta nb, full** 🛗 **facilities,** 🆁🆂 **scenic view,** 🅶 Exxon/dsl 🍽 Blimpie, Hershey's Ice Cream, Starbucks, Uno Pizza 🅾 atm/fax
14	WV 20, Athens Rd, **E** 🅾 Pipestem Resort SP, to Concord U
9mm	**WV Turnpike begins/ends.**
9	US 460, Princeton, **E Welcome Ctr/Rest Area both lanes, full** 🛗 **facilities,** 🆁🆂 **litter barrels, petwalk,** 🍽 Walmart/dsl 🍽 Campestre Mexican, Kimono Japanese, Outback Steaks, Ryan's 🛏 Country Inn&Suites, Fairfield Inn 🅾 $Tree, AT&T, URGENT CARE, Verizon, Walmart/Subway, **W** 🍽 BP/dsl, Exxon, Sheetz/dsl, Shell/Subway 🍽 Applebee's, Arby's, Bob Evans, Bojangles, Capt D's, Chick-fil-A, Chili's, Cracker Barrel, Dolly's Diner, DQ, Hardee's, McDonald's, Shoney's, Starbucks, Taco Bell, TX Steaks, Wendy's 🛏 Days Inn, Eden Rock Motel, Hampton Inn, Holiday Inn Express, Microtel, Quality Inn, Sleep Inn, Turnpike Motel 🅾 🏥, Hyundai, Lowe's
7	WV 27, Twelve Mile Rd
5	WV 112 (from sb, no re-entry), to Ingleside
3mm	East River
1	US 52 N, to Bluefield, **4 mi W** 🍽 KFC/LJ Silver, Wendy's 🛏 EconoLodge, Quality Inn 🅾 🏥, to Bluefield St Coll
0mm	West Virginia/Virginia state line, East River Mtn

⬆🅽 INTERSTATE 79

Exit #	Services
160mm	West Virginia/Pennsylvania state line
159	Welcome Ctr sb, full 🛗 facilities, info, litter barrels, petwalk 🚻, 🛄, vending
155	US 19, WV 7, **0-3 mi E** 🅶 GetGo, Sheetz/dsl 🍽 Cheddar's, Chili's, Chipotle, CiCi's Pizza, Cracker Barrel, Evergreen Buffet, Golden Corral, Longhorn Steaks, McDonald's, Olive Garden, Red Lobster, Starbucks, TX Roadhouse 🛏 Best Western, EconoLodge, Fairfield Inn 🅾 🏥, $Tree, Barnes&Noble, Best Buy, Buick/Chevrolet/GMC, CVS Drug, Dick's, Giant Eagle Foods, GNC, Old Navy, PetCo, Sam's Club/dsl, Target, TJ Maxx, to WVU, Walmart/Subway, **W** 🅶 BFS/dsl 🍽 Burger King, DQ, Firehouse Subs, Little Caesar's, Tim Hortons 🛏 Candlewood Suites, La Quinta 🅾 Harley-Davidson, Hobby Lobby
153	University Towne Ctr, **E** 🍽 Buffalo Wild Wings, Fusion Japanese, Wendy's 🛏 Courtyard, Hampton Inn 🅾 Kia
152	US 19, to Morgantown, **E** 🅶 BFS/dsl, Exxon 🍽 Arby's, China Wok, McDonald's, Pizza Hut, Subway, Taco Bell 🛏 EconoLodge 🅾 Advance Parts, BigLots, URGENT CARE, **W** 🍽 Bob Evans, Burger King, Garfield's Rest. 🛏 Microtel 🅾 Belk, Elder-Beerman, JC Penney, Lowe's, Sears/auto
150mm	Monongahela River
148	I-68 E, to Cumberland, MD, **1 mi E** 🅶 Go-Mart/dsl, Sheetz/dsl, Tesla EVC 🍽 Denny's, Mariachi Loco, Subway 🛏 Morgantown Motel, Quality Inn, Ramada Inn 🅾 $Tree, tires, to Tygart Lake SP, Walmart
146	WV 77, to Goshen Rd, **W** 🅶 🅻🅾🆅🅴🆂/deli/dsl/scales/24hr (RV accessible dsl only)
141mm	weigh sta both lanes
139	WV 33, E Fairmont, **E** 🅶 Sunoco, **W** 🅶 Exxon, K&T/dsl/scales 🅾 repair, RV camping, to Prickett's Ft SP
137	WV 310, to Fairmont, **E** 🅶 Exxon/dsl, Sunoco 🛏 Clarion 🅾 to Valley Falls SP, vet, **W** 🅶 Shell/dsl 🍽 Domino's, KFC, McDonald's, Subway, Wendy's 🅾 🏥, $General, Advance Parts, Family$, Shop'n Save Foods
136	rd 273, Fairmont
135	WV 64, Pleasant Valley Rd

⬆N INTERSTATE 79 Cont'd

Exit #	Services
133	Kingmont Rd, **E** 🅖 Exxon/Fazoli's/dsl, Marathon/Subway/dsl 🅕 Cracker Barrel 🅛 Hampton Inn, Holiday Inn Express, Super 8, **W** 🅖 Shell/Quiznos/dsl 🅞 DJ's Diner 🅛 Quality Inn
132	US 250, S Fairmont, **E** 🅖 BFS/DQ/dsl, Walmart/dsl 🅕 Applebee's, Arby's, Bob Evans, Colasessano's Italian, Dutchman's Daughter, El Rey Mexican, Firehouse Subs, Grand China, Hardee's, Little Caesar's, McDonald's, Mi Pueblo, Subway, Taco Bell 🅛 Days Inn, Fairfield Inn, Microtel, Red Roof Inn 🅞 $General, Ace Hardware, Advance Parts, Chrysler/Dodge/Jeep, GNC, NAPA, Sav-A-Lot Foods, Shop'n Save, to Tygart Lake SP, Walmart/Subway, **W** 🅖 Exxon/dsl, GoMart/dsl, Sunoco/dsl 🅕 Burger King, Steak Escape 🅞 🅷, AT&T, Buick/GMC, Ford/Lincoln, Toyota, Trailer City RV Ctr
125	WV 131, Saltwell Rd, to Shinnston, **E** 🅕 Oliverio's Rest. (4mi) 🅞 Kia, **W** 🅖 BFS/Burger King/dsl, Exxon/dsl
124	rd 279, Jerry Dove Dr, **E** 🅖 BFS, Exxon/Dunkin'/dsl 🅕 Buffalo Wild Wings, DQ, Firehouse Subs, Little Caesar's, Mi Margherita 🅛 Microtel, Wingate Inn, **W** 🅖 Sheetz/dsl 🅕 IHOP, Subway, TGIFriday 🅛 Comfort Suites, Courtyard, Hawthorn Suites, Holiday Inn Express 🅞 🅷
123mm	🆁🆂 both lanes, full ♿ facilities, info, litter barrels, petwalk, 🅲, 🏕, RV dump, vending
121	WV 24, Meadowbrook Rd, **E** 🅖 GoMart, Sheetz/dsl 🅕 Biscuit World, Bob Evans, Gino's Pizza 🅛 Hampton Inn 🅞 Hyundai/Subaru, **W** 🅖 Exxon/dsl 🅕 Burger King, Garfield's Rest., Outback Steaks 🅛 Super 8 🅞 Dick's, Honda, JC Penney, Jo-Ann Fabrics, Marshall's, NTB, Old Navy, Target
119	US 50, to Clarksburg, **E** 🅕 A&W/LJ Silver, Brickside Grille, Chick-fil-A, Denny's, Eat'n Park, Grand China, KFC, Las Trancas, Little Caesar's, McDonald's, McDonald's (2), Panera Bread, Pizza Hut, Primanti Bros, Starbucks, Taco Bell, TX Roadhouse, Wendy's 🅛 Best Western+, Days Inn, Sleep Inn, SpringHill Suites, Sutton Inn, Townplace Suites 🅞 $Tree, Advance Parts, Autozone, BigLots, Family$, GNC, Home Depot, Kohl's, Kroger/dsl, Lowe's, Monro, Sam's Club/gas, URGENT CARE, USPO, Verizon, Walgreens
117	WV 58, to Anmoore, **E** 🅖 BFS/dsl 🅕 Applebee's, Arby's, Burger King, Honeybaked Ham, Ruby Tuesday, Ryan's, Subway 🅛 Hilton Garden 🅞 Aldi Foods, AT&T, El Rey Mexican, Staples, Walmart/Subway
115	WV 20, Nutter Fort, to Stonewood, **E** 🅖 BP/7-11/dsl, Exxon/dsl 🅞 $General, Stonewood Bulk Foods, **W** 🅛 Greenbrier Motel (5mi)
110	Lost Creek, **E** 🅖 General Store/dsl 🅞 USPO
105	WV 7, to Jane Lew, **E** 🅖 Jane Lew Trkstp/dsl/rest., Valero/dsl/rest. 🅛 Days Inn, **W** 🅖 GoMart 🅞 $General, Kenworth/Mack/Volvo
99	US 33, US 119, to Weston, **E** 🅖 GoMart/dsl, Marathon/DQ/Little Caesars/dsl, Sheetz/dsl 🅕 Burger King, Gino's Pizza, McDonald's, Patron Mexican, Peking Buffet, Steer Steakhouse, Subway 🅛 Hampton Inn (9mi), Holiday Inn Express, Quality Inn/rest., Super 8 🅞 $Tree, Advance Parts, Blackwater Falls, GNC, to Canaan Valley Resort, Walmart/dsl, **0-2 mi W** 🅖 Exxon/Arby's, Go-Mart 🅕 Domino's, Giovanni's, Hardee's, KFC, LJ Silver, Pizza Hut, Subway, Wendy's 🅞 🅷, $General, Chrysler/Dodge/Fiat, CVS Drug, Ford, NAPA, NAPACare, Rite Aid, Save-a-Lot
96	WV 30, to S Weston, **E** 🅞 Broken Wheel Camping, to S Jackson Lake SP
91	US 19, to Roanoke, **E** 🅖 Marathon/dsl 🅕 Stillwaters Rest. 🅞 camping, to S Jackson Lake SP

85mm	🆁🆂 both lanes, full ♿ facilities, info, litter barrels, petwalk, 🅲, 🏕, RV dump, vending
79.5mm	Little Kanawha River
79	WV 5, Burnsville, **E** 🅖 Exxon 🅛 79er Motel/rest. 🅞 Burnville Dam RA, **W** 🅖 GoMart 🅞 Cedar Cr SP
76mm	Saltlick Creek
67	WV 4, to Flatwoods, **E** 🅖 BP/Arby's/dsl, Go-Mart/dsl, Shell/dsl 🅕 Custard Stand, KFC/Taco Bell, McDonald's, Subway 🅛 Day's Hotel 🅞 antiques, Buick/Chevrolet, KOA, to Sutton Lake RA, **W** 🅖 Exxon/dsl, 🛢Moe's SW Grill/dsl/scales/24hr 🅕 China Buffet, Shoney's, Starbucks, Wendy's 🅞 Bulk Foods, Flatwood Factory Stores, Walmart
62	WV 4, Gassaway, to Sutton, **E** 🅖 Elk Motel 🅞 Sutton Lake Camping, **W** 🅖 GoMart 🅕 LJ Silver, Pizza Hut 🅛 Microtel 🅞 🅷, AutoZone, CVS Drug, Ford, Kroger/deli
57	US 19 S, to Beckley
52mm	Elk River
51	WV 4, to Frametown, **E** antiques, food
49mm	🆁🆂 both lanes, full ♿ facilities, litter barrels, petwalk, 🅲, 🏕, RV dump, vending
46	WV 11, Servia Rd
40	WV 16, to Big Otter, **E** 🅖 GoMart/dsl, **W** 🅖 Exxon/dsl
34	WV 36, to Wallback, 10 mi **E** 🅕 BiscuitWorld, Gino's Diner, Subway
25	WV 29, to Amma, **E** 🅖 Exxon/dsl
19	US 119, VW 53, to Clendenin, **E** 🅖 BP/7-11/dsl 🅞 Rite Aid (3mi), Speedway/dsl (3mi)
9	WV 43, to Elkview, **E** 🅖 GoMart/dsl 🅕 Burger King, Penn Sta Subs 🅞 AutoZone, **W** 🅖 Exxon/Arby's/dsl, Speedway/dsl 🅕 La Carreta, Little Caesar's, McDonald's, Picanha Steaks, Subway 🅛 La Quinta 🅞 $Tree, Advance Parts, AT&T, CVS Drug, Kroger/dsl
5	WV 114, to Big Chimney, 1 mi **E** 🅖 Exxon 🅕 Hardee's 🅞 Rite Aid, Smith's Foods
1	US 119, Mink Shoals, **E** 🅕 Harding's Family Rest. 🅛 Sleep Inn
0	I-77, S to Charleston, N to Parkersburg. **I-79 begins/ends on I-77, exit 104.**

⬆N INTERSTATE 81

Exit #	Services
26mm	West Virginia/Maryland state line, Potomac River
25mm	Welcome Ctr sb, full ♿ facilities, info, litter barrels, petwalk, 🅲, 🏕
23	US 11, Marlowe, Falling Waters, **E** 🅖 Exxon/AC&T/Subway/dsl 🅕 Kings Rest., Red Lantern Chinese 🅞 $General, Falling Waters Camping (1mi), Food Lion, **W** 🅖 BP/dsl 🅞 7-11, Outdoor Express RV Ctr

CLARKSBURG

CHARLESTON

🛢️ = gas 🍽️ = food 🏠 = lodging 🅾️ = other Ⓡ🅢 = rest stop   Copyright 2022 - The Next EXIT ©

INTERSTATE 81 Cont'd
Exit #   Services

20 WV 901, Spring Mills Rd, **E** 🛢️ Sheetz/dsl 🍽️ China Spring, Cinco de Mayo, Little Caesar's, McDonald's, Pizza Montese, Popeye's, Tokyo Cafe 🏠 Motel 6 🅾️ $Tree, Advance Parts, Walmart/Subway, **W** 🛢️ Shell/dsl 🍽️ Burger King, Domino's 🏠 Quality Inn

16 WV 9, N Queen St, Berkeley Springs, **E** 🛢️ Crown/dsl, Exxon/Subway/dsl, Sheetz 🍽️ Arby's, China King, Domino's, Dunkin', Hoss's, KFC, La Trattoria, LJ Silver, McDonald's, Meridian Cafe, Mrs McCracken's Diner, Pizza Hut, Popeye's, Rita's Custard, Subway, Taco Bell, Waffle House 🏠 Care Free Inn, Comfort Inn, Knights Inn, Super 8 🅾️ Advance Parts, Aldi Foods, AutoZone, BigLots, Carquest, CVS Drug, Family$, Food Lion, URGENT CARE, USPO, Walgreens, **W** 🛢️ Shell/Subway/dsl

14 rd 13, Dry Run Rd, **E** 🅾️ 🏥, **W** 🅾️ Butler's Farm Mkt (1mi)

13 rd 15, Kings St, Martinsburg, **E** 🛢️ BP/Subway/dsl, Sheetz/dsl 🍽️ Applebee's, Buffalo Wild Wings, Burger King, Cracker Barrel, Daily Grind, Fiesta Tapatia, Golden Corral, Jerry's Subs, Kobe Japanese, Las Trancas, Outback Steaks, Pizza Hut, Wendy's

13 Continued 🏠 Days Inn, Fairfield Inn, Holiday Inn/rest. 🅾️ 🏥, Chevrolet, Toyota, Office Depot, Walmart

12 WV 45, Winchester Ave, **E** 🛢️ Sheetz/dsl, Shell/dsl, Sunoco/ds 🍽️ Arby's, Asian Garden, Bob Evans, Chick-fil-A, China City Buffet Chipotle, Five Guys, McDonald's, Olive Garden, Panda Express Panera Bread, Papa John's, Ruby Tuesday, Ryan's, Taco Bell, Waffle House 🏠 Hampton Inn 🅾️ Advance Parts, AutoZone, BonTon Food Lion, Lowe's, Martin's Foods/gas, Nahkeeta Camping, W 🍽️ Ledo Pizza, Logan's Roadhouse, Subway, Tropical Smoothie 🏠 Hilton Garden 🅾️ $Tree, AT&T, Best Buy, Books-A-Million Dick's, GNC, Michael's, Petsmart, Target, TJ Maxx, URGENT CAR

8 rd 32, Tablers Sta Rd, **E** 🛢️ Sheetz/dsl

5 WV 51, Inwood, to Charles Town, **E** 🛢️ 7-11, BP, Liberty, Sheetz dsl, Shell/dsl 🍽️ Arby's, Burger King, Domino's, DQ, McDonald's, Pizza Hut, Pizza Oven, Subway, Waffle House 🏠 Hampton Inn 🅾️ Advance Parts, CVS Drug, Family$, Food Lion, NAPA Rite Aid, URGENT CARE, USPO, **W** 🅾️ Lazy-A Camping (9mi)

2mm Welcome Ctr/weigh sta nb, full ♿ facilities, info, litter barrels petwalk, 📞, 🚻, vending

0mm West Virginia/Virginia state line

NOTES

WISCONSIN

🅝 INTERSTATE 39

Exit #	Services
211	US 51, rd K, Merrill, **2 mi W** 🅖 Cenex 🍴 Chip's Burgers, Hardee's, Pine Ridge Rest., Pizza Hut 🅞 ✈
208	WI 64, WI 17, Merrill, **E** 🍴 KFC, Taco Bell, **W** 🅖 KwikTrip/dsl, Mobil/Arby's/dsl 🍴 China Inn, Culver's, Los Mezcales, Mama De Luca's Pizza, McDonald's, Subway 🛏 Americinn, Cobblestone Inn, EconoLodge 🅞 $Tree, Chrysler/Dodge/Jeep, 🅷 O'Reilly Parts, to Council Grounds SP, Verizon, Walmart
206mm	Wisconsin River
205	US 51, rd Q, Merrill, **E** 🅖 BP/Hwy 51/rest./dsl/24hr 🅞 fireworks
197	rd WW, to Brokaw, **W** 🅖 Mobil/dsl
194	US 51, rd U, rd K, Wausau, **E** 🅖 F&F/dsl, KwikTrip/dsl 🍴 McDonald's, Subway, Taco Bell, **W** 🍴 BP/Arby's/dsl 🅞 Ford, Kia, Nissan, Subaru, Toyota
193	Bridge St, **E** 🅞 CVS Drug, **W** 🅞 🅷
192	WI 29 W, WI 52 E, Wausau, to Chippewa Falls same as 191 b
191b	Sherman St, **E** 🅖 BP, Holiday/dsl, Shell 🍴 Applebee's, Buffalo Wild Wings, Great Dane Rest., Jimmy John's, King Buffet, Little Caesar's, McDonald's, Milwaukee Burger Co, Noodles&Co, Panera Bread, Papa Murphy's, Pizza Hut, Qdoba, Starbucks, Subway, Toppers Pizza 🛏 Courtyard, Hampton Inn, La Quinta, Motel 6, Plaza Hotel, Super 8 🅞 County Mkt/USPO, Trig's Foods, Walgreens, **W** 🅖 KwikTrip/dsl 🍴 2510 Deli, Hardee's 🅞 Cadillac, Home Depot, Honda, 🅷, Menards
191a	WI 29, Chippewa Falls
190mm	Rib River
190	rd NN, **E** 🅖 BP/Burger King 🍴 El Tequila Salsa, IHOP 🛏 Hilton Garden, **W** 🍴 The Store/Subway/dsl 🛏 Quality Inn 🅞 Granite Mtn Ski Area, Rib Mtn Ski Area, st patrol
188	rd N, **E** 🅖 KwikTrip/dsl 🍴 Dunkin', Fazoli's, HuHot, McDonald's, Olive Garden, Panda Express, Red Robin, Rococo Pizza, Ropa Pizza, Starbucks, TX Roadhouse 🛏 Days Inn 🅞 $Tree, Aldi Foods, AT&T, Audi/VW, Barnes&Noble, Best Buy, Chevrolet, Dick's, GNC, Gordman's, Hobby Lobby, Hyundai, JoAnn Fabrics, King's RV Ctr, Kohl's, Michael's, Old Navy, PetCo, Petsmart, Sam's Club/gas/dsl, Tires+, TJ Maxx, Walmart/Subway, **W** 🅞 Rib Mtn SP
187mm	I-39 begins/ends. Freeway continues N as US 51.
187	WI 29 E, to Green Bay
186mm	Wisconsin River
185	US 51, Rothschild, Kronenwetter, **E** 🅖 BP/dsl 🍴 Arby's, Culver's, Denny's, Green Mill Rest., Subway, Wausau Grill 🛏 Best Western+, EconoLodge, Grand Lodge, Holiday Inn, Motel 6, Stoney Creek Inn 🅞 Harley-Davidson, Pick'n Save Foods
181	Maple Ridge Rd, Kronenwetter, Mosinee, **E** 🅞 Peterbilt, vet, Volvo, **W** 🅞 Kenworth
179	WI 153, Mosinee, **W** 🅖 BP/Subway/dsl, KwikTrip/dsl, Shell/dsl 🍴 McDonald's, StageStop Rest. 🛏 Quality Inn 🅞 vet
175	WI 34, Knowlton, to WI Rapids, **1 mi W** 🅞 Mullins Cheese Factory
171	rd DB, Knowlton, **W** 🅖 gas 🍴 food 🛏 lodging 🅞 Rivers Edge Camping
165	US 10 W, to Marshfield (no nb re-entry)
163	Casimir Rd
161	US 51, Stevens Point, **W** 🅖 BP, Kwik Trip/dsl, The Store 🍴 Burger King, China Wok, Coldstone, Cousins Subs, Culver's, Hardee's, Jimmy John's, KFC, McDonald's, Michele's Rest., Noodles&Co, Perkins, Pizza Hut, Rococo's Pizza, Starbucks, Subway, Taco Bell, Topper's Pizza 🛏 Baymont Inn, Country Inn&Suites, Days Inn 🅞 $Tree, Trig's Foods, Verizon
159	WI 66, Stevens Point, **W** 🅖 KwikTrip/dsl 🅞 Ford, Honda, 🅷, Hyundai, Nissan, VW
158	US 10, Stevens Point, **E** 🅖 F&F/dsl, KwikTrip/dsl/e85, Mobil/dsl, The Store/Subway/dsl 🍴 Amber Grill, Arby's, Asian Buffet, Buffalo Wild Wings, Burger King, Culver's, DQ, El Mezcal Mexican, Fazoli's, Grazie's Grill, McDonald's, Qdoba, Taco Bell 🛏 Fairfield Inn, Holiday Inn, Holiday Inn Express 🅞 Aldi Foods, Chrysler/Dodge/Jeep, Target, Verizon, **W** 🅖 BP/dsl 🍴 Hilltop Grill 🛏 EconoLodge, La Quinta
156	rd HH, Whiting, **E** 🅖 The Store/Subway/dsl 🍴 Charcoal Grill, Chili's, McDonald's, Monk's Grill, Panda Express, Panera Bread, Pizza Ranch, Starbucks 🅞 $Tree, AT&T, Best Buy, GNC, JoAnn Fabrics, Kohl's, Lowe's, Michael's, PetCo, Staples, TJ Maxx, Walmart/Subway
153	rd B, Plover, **W** 🅖 BP, Kwik Trip/dsl, Mobil/Dunkin'/dsl 🍴 Arby's, Bamboo House, Burger King, Culver's, Happy Wok, IHOP, Jimmy John's, KFC, McDonald's, Papa Murphy's, Subway, Taco Bell, Tempura House Asian 🛏 AmericInn, Comfort Inn, Hampton Inn 🅞 city park, Copp's Foods, dsl repair, Menards, NAPA, Toyota, Verizon, vet
151	WI 54, to Waupaca, **E** 🅖 KwikTrip/rest./dsl/scales/24hr 🍴 Four Star Family Rest., Shooter's Rest. 🛏 Best Western, Super 8 🅞 tires/repair

WASSAU (vertical left margin)

STEVENS PT (vertical center margin)

WI

P O R T A G E

INTERSTATE 39 Cont'd

Exit #	Services
143	rd W, Bancroft, to WI Rapids, **E** 🅿 Citgo/dsl 🍴 Pop A Top Grill 🅾 USPO
139	rd D, Almond
136	WI 73, Plainfield, to WI Rapids, **E** 🅿 BP/dsl 🍴 Budda's Grill 🅾 service/repair, **W** 🅿 Citgo/Subway/dsl
131	rd V, Hancock, **E** 🅿 Citgo 🍴 Smiley's Diner 🅾 Oasis Camping
127mm	weigh sta both lanes (exits left)
124	WI 21, Coloma, **E** 🅿 Mobil/A&W/dsl 🍴 Red Hill Cafe, Subway 🛏 Mecan Inn (4mi) 🅾 Coloma Camping, **W** 🅿 BP/Chester's/dsl 🅾 Buick/Chevrolet
120mm	🆁🆂 sb, full ♿ facilities, 🅲, 🚻, vending, litter barrels, petwalk
118mm	🆁🆂 nb, full ♿ facilities, 🅲, 🚻, vending, litter barrels, petwalk
113	rd E, rd J, Westfield, **W** 🅿 BP/Burger King, Cenex, Mobil/dsl 🍴 McDonald's, Subway 🛏 Pioneer Motel/rest. 🅾 city park, Family$
106	WI 82 W, WI 23 E, Oxford, **E** 🛏 Crossroads Motel, **W** 🅿 Citgo/dsl
104	(from nb, no EZ return) rd D, Packwaukee
100	WI 23 W, rd P, Endeavor, **E** 🅿 BP/dsl
92	US 51 S, Portage, **E** 🅿 KwikTrip/dsl 🍴 Asian Express, Culver's, Dino's Rest., Jimmy John's, KFC, La Tolteca Mexican, McDonald's, Papa Murphy's, Pizza Ranch, Subway, Suzy's Steaks, Taco Bell 🛏 Best Western, Ridge Motel, Sunset Motel, Super 8 🅾 $Tree, Aldi Foods, AutoZone, Chrysler/Dodge/Jeep, Festival Foods, Ford/Lincoln, GNC, 🅷, Walgreens, Walmart
89b a	WI 16, to WI 127, Portage, **E** 🅿 BP/dsl 🍴 Hitching Post Eatery
88.5mm	Wisconsin River
87	WI 33, Portage, **W** ski area
86mm	Baraboo River
85	Cascade Mt Rd
84	I-39, I-90 & I-94 run together sb/eb.

INTERSTATE 41

Exit #	Services
171	I-43 S, to Milwaukee, US 41/141 N, to Marinette
170	US 141 S, Velp Ave, **E** 🅿 Mobil 🍴 Burger King, Taco Bell, **W** 🅿 BP/A&W/dsl, Shell/dsl 🍴 Gilligan's Rest., Julie's Rest., McDonald's, River St Grill, Sunny Chinese, Watering Hole Rest. 🛏 AmericInn 🅾 Bumper Parts, CVS Drug, Family$, Harley Davidson
168c b	WI 29, WI 32, Shawano Ave, Dousman St, **E** 🅿 KwikTrip, Tesla EVC 🛏 Comfort Suites 🅾 Buick/Cadillac/GMC, Meijer
168	WI 32, WI 54, Mason St, **E** 🍴 Pizza Hut 🅾 Home Depot, **W** 🅿 Mobil, Shell/Papa John's/dsl 🍴 Bon Orient Buffet, Chili's, Fazoli's, Hardee's, Little Caesar's, Los Banditos, McDonald's, Schlotsky's 🅾 Festival Foods, GNC, O'Reilly Parts, Petco, Sam's Club, Walmart/Subway
167	CR VK, Lombardi Ave, Hazelwood Ln, **E** 🅿 Shell 🍴 Chucke-Cheese, Margaritas, Red Lobster 🅾 Cabela's, Lambeau Field, Pick'n Save
165	WI 172, to I-43
164	CR AAA, Oneida St, Waube Ln, **E** 🅿 KwikTrip/dsl, Shell/dsl 🍴 Applebee's, Cousins Subs, Culver's, Denny's, Domino's, Five Guys, Grazie's Italian, Olive Garden, Perkins, Starbucks, Subway, Wendy's 🛏 Baymont Inn, Comfort Inn, Delta Hotel, EconoLodge, Fairfield Inn, Hampton Inn, Holiday Inn, Motel 6, Super 8 🅾 $Tree, Honda, Jo-Ann, **W** 🅿 BP/dsl, KwikTrip 🍴 Erbert & Gerbert's 🛏 Country Inn Suites, Microtel
163b	WI 32 N, Green Bay
163a	CR G, Main Ave, **E** 🅿 Shell/dsl, Tobacco Outlet/dsl 🍴 Burger King, Dunkin', Jimmy John's, McDonald's, Papa John's, Papa Murphy's,

G R E E N B A Y

A P P L E T O N

Exit #	Services
163a	**Continued** Starbucks, Subway 🅾 Aldi Foods, AutoZone, CVS Drug, Festiva Foods, Peterbilt, USPO, Walgreens, **W** 🅿 BP/A&W/Taco Bell/dsl, scales 🅾 UHaul
161	CR F, Scheuring Rd, De Pete, **E** 🅿 KwikTrip/Arby's/dsl, Shell dsl 🍴 Culver's, DQ 🛏 Sleep Inn 🅾 $Tree, Menard's, Verizon Walmart/Subway, **W** 🍴 Plank Road Rest.
157	CR S, Freedom, **W** 🅿 KwikTrip/dsl
154	CR U, Wrightstown
153	weigh sta nb
150	CR J, Kaukauna, **E** 🅾 Chrysler/Dodge/Jeep, **W** 🅿 BP/dsl 🅾 Freightliner
148	WI 55, Seymour, Kaukauna, **E** 🅿 KwikTrip/dsl, Shell/Arby's/ds 🛏 Days Inn, **W** 🅾 Chevrolet/Buick/GMC
146	CR N, Little Chute, Kimberly, **E** 🅿 BP/McDonald's/Subway/dsl, Shell/dsl 🍴 Burger King, Culver's, Taco Bell, Tom's Drive In 🛏 Country Inn Suites, **W** 🅾 Simon's Cheese Store
145	WI 441 S
144	CR E, Ballard Rd, **E** 🅿 Shell/dsl 🍴 Baskin Robbins, Hardee's McDonald's 🅾 🅷, **W** 🛏 AmericInn, Cambria Suites
142	WI 47, Richmond St, Black Creek, **E** 🅿 Mobil 🍴 Arby's, Fazoli's, Jimmy John's, Little Caesar's, McDonald's, Starbucks, Taco Bel 🛏 Snug In Motel 🅾 Kohl's, Walgreens, **W** 🅿 KwikTrip/dsl 🅾 Meijer/dsl
139	WI 15, CR OO, Northland Ave, Greenville, Hortonville, **W** 🅿 EVC KwikTrip/dsl 🅾 Acura, BMW, Hyundai, Infiniti, Land Rover/ Jaguar/Porsche, Lexus, Mazda, Mercedes, Mini, Nissan, Volvo, VW/Audi
138	WI 96, Wisconsin Ave, Fremont, **E** 🅿 KwikTrip/dsl 🍴 Arby's, Culver's, Famous Dave's, Golden Corral, Wendy's 🛏 Comfort Suites 🅾 CarX, Home Depot, Petsmart, Sam's Club, Woodman's, **W** 🅿 Mobil 🍴 Cheddar's, Chili's, IHOP, Jimmy John's, Noodles&Co, Olive Garden, Osaka Japanese, Papa Murphy's, Qdoba, Red Lobster, Schlotsky's, Solea Mexican Grill, Starbucks, TGI Friday, Walmart/Subway 🛏 Holiday Inn, Wingate Inn 🅾 $Tree, AT&T, Best Buy, Costco/dsl, Dick's, Discount Tire, JC Penney, Jo-Ann, Macy's, Menard's, Michael's, Petco, Scheel's, Target, Tires+, TJ Maxx, Verizon, Walgreens
137	WI 125, College Ave, **E** 🅿 BP/dsl, KwikTrip, Mobil 🍴 Applebee's, Burger King, Chick-fil-A, Denny's, HuHot, McDonald's, Panda Express, Panera Bread, Perkins, Popeye's, Starbucks, Subway, Taco Bell, TX Roadhouse 🛏 Baymont Inn, Clarion, La Quinta, Motel 6, Quality Inn, Rodeway Inn, Super 8 🅾 Big Lots, Chrysler/Dodge/Jeep, Firestone/auto, Ford, Goodyear/ auto, Honda, Kia, Office Depot, Subaru, Woodman's Gas, **W** 🅿 KwikTrip/dsl 🍴 Asian Garden, Buffalo Wild Wings, Chipotle, ChuckECheese, Fairfield Inn, Fazoli's, Five Guys, Machine Shed Rest., Outback Steaks, TGIFriday's 🛏 AmericInn, Candlewood Suites, Country Inn Suites, DoubleTree, GrandStay Suites, Hampton Inn, Home 2 Suites, Microtel, Residence Inn 🅾 Barnes&Noble, Hobby Lobby, Old Navy, USPO, vet
136	CR BB, Prospect Ave, **W** 🅿 BP, Mobil/Subway 🅾 Van Zealand Autocare
134	US 10 E, WI 441 N
133	CR II, Winchester Rd
132	Main St, Oak Ridge Rd (no return nb or sb), **E** 🅿 BP/dsl, Citgo/ dsl 🍴 Bradke's Rest. 🅾 Chevrolet/Buick/Cadillac
131	WI 114, CR JJ, Winneconne Ave, Hilbert, Sherwood, **E** 🅿 Citgo/ dsl, Fox Point, KwikTrip/dsl 🍴 Cousins Subs, Ground Round, Hardee's, KFC, Little Caesar's, McDonald's, Papa Murphy's, Pizza Hut, Starbucks, Subway 🛏 Best Western, Days Inn 🅾 $Tree, Advance Parts, Aldi Foods, CVS Drug, Festival Foods, Firestone/auto,

Copyright 2022 - The Next EXIT ® 🅖 = gas 🍴 = food 🏠 = lodging 🄾 = other 🆁🆂 = rest stop

⊕N INTERSTATE 41 Cont'd

131	**Continued** Ford/Lincoln, GNC, Pick'n Save, **W** 🍴 A&W, Applebee's, Arby's, Culver's, Jimmy John's, Perkins, Qdoba, Taco Bell 🄾 AT&T, Kohl's, Verizon, Walgreens, Walmart/Subway
129	Bell St, Breezewood Ln, **W** 🍴 Mobil 🍴 Solea Mexican
124	WI 76, Jackson St, **E** 🍴 Mobil, **W** 🍴 KwikTrip/dsl/CNG, Ole & Lena's 🄾 truck repair
120	US 45, US 10 W, New London
119	WI 21, Omro Rd, Oshkosh, **E** 🍴 DQ 🏠 La Quinta, **W** 🍴 KwikTrip/dsl, Shell/McDonald's 🍴 Cousins Subs, Culver's, Panera Bread, Papa Murphy's, Rocky Rococo Pizza, Subway, Wendy's 🏠 Holiday Inn Express 🄾 Chevrolet/Buick/GMC/Cadillac, Dick's, Festival Foods, 🅗, Lowe's, Menard's, Verizon, Walgreens
117	9th Ave, **E** 🍴 KwikTrip/dsl 🍴 Benvenuto's Italian, Buffalo Wild Wings, China King, Cousins Subs, Golden Corral, IHOP, Jimmy John's, Little Caesar's, McDonald's, Olive Garden, Pizza Hut, Potbelly, Qdoba, Red Robin, Starbucks, Taco Bell 🏠 Comfort Suites 🄾 AT&T, Best Buy, CVS Drug, Duluth Trading, Hobby Lobby, Jo-Ann, Ross, TJ Maxx, Verizon, Walgreens, **W** 🍴 Burger King, Domino's, Huhot, Perkins, Pizza Ranch 🄾 Goodyear/auto, NAPA, Walmart/Subway
116	WI 44, WI 91, S Park Ave, Ripon Rd, **E** 🍴 BP/dsl, Mobil/dsl 🍴 Applebee's, Arby's, Culver's, Durango's, Fazoli's, Firehouse Subs, Friar Tuck's Rest., Hangar Grill, Hardee's, Noodles&Co, Subway 🏠 Cobblestone Inn, Fairfield Inn, Hilton Garden, Super 8 🄾 $Tree, Advance Parts, air museum, 🛒, Aldi Foods, CarX, GNC, Petco, Pick'n Save, Target, Tires+, **W** 🍴 KwikTrip/dsl, Shell/dsl 🍴 Johnny Rockets 🏠 Hawthorn Suites 🄾 Honda, Kia, Nissan, Oshkosh Outlets/famous brands, Subaru, Toyota, vet, VW
113	WI 26, CR N, Rosendale, Waupun, Pickett, **E** 🄾 Sleepy Hollow Camping (2mi), **W** 🍴 Planeview/Subway/dsl/scales/24hr 🏠 Cobblestone Inn
106	CR N, Van Dyne
101	CR OO, Winnebago St, **E** 🍴 BP/Rest./dsl/scales 🄾 Mack/Volvo, truck wash
99	WI 23, Johnson St, Rosendale, Ripon, **E** 🍴 11:11 Burger, Ala Roma Pizza, Applebee's, Buffalo Wild Wings, Burger King, DQ, Faro's Rest., Fazoli's, Hardee's, KFC, McDonald's, Panda Express, Panera Bread, Popeye's, Qdoba, Rocky Rococo Pizza, Schriener's Rest., Starbucks 🏠 Days Inn, Hampton Inn, Super 8 🄾 AT&T, AutoZone, Best Buy, Jo-Ann, Kohl's, Pick'n Save, Staples, TJ Maxx, **W** 🍴 KwikTrip/dsl, Shell/Subway/dsl 🍴 Arby's, Culver's, Pizza Hut, Pizza Ranch 🄾 $Tree, Aldi Foods, CarX, Chevrolet/Buick/GMC/Cadillac, Ford, Harley Davidson, Mazda, Menard's, Petsmart, Target, Verizon, Walmart/Subway
98	CR D, Military Rd, **E** 🍴 McDonald's 🏠 Microtel 🄾 F&F/dsl, Schiek's Campers, **W** 🍴 BP/dsl 🍴 Rolling Meadows Rest. 🏠 Comfort Inn, Holiday Inn Express, Radisson 🄾 Chrysler/Dodge/Jeep, st patrol
97	CR VVV, Hickory St, **E** 🍴 KwikTrip/dsl, Pump&Pantry/dsl, **W** 🍴 ⬥Loves/Subway/dsl/scales/24hr 🏠 Country Inn Suites
95	US 152, Madison, Manitowoc, **E** 🄾 🅗
92	CR B, Oakfield, Eden, **E** 🄾 Breezy Hill Camping (2 mi)
87	WI 49, CR KK, Brownsville, Waupun
85	WI 67, Lomira, Campbellsport, **E** 🍴 Exxon/dsl, **W** 🍴 BP/Taco Bell/dsl, Shell/Subway/dsl 🍴 Bublitz's Rest., McDonald's 🏠 AmeriVu Inn 🄾 $General, Ford, Piggly Wiggly
82.5mm	🆁🆂 both lanes, full 🛗 facilities, 🗑 litter barrels, petwalk
81	WI 28, Mayville, Kewaskum
76	CR D, **W** 🄾 fireworks

72	WI 33, CR W, West Bend, Allenton, **W** 🍴 BP/dsl, Mobil 🍴 Alma's Cafe, Subway
68	CR K, **W** 🍴 Mobil/dsl 🍴 MJ Stevens Rest.
66	WI 144, West Bend, Slinger, **W** 🄾 Freedom RV Ctr, Held's Cheese/sausage, Slinger Speedway
64	WI 60, to Jackson, Slinger, Hartford, **E** 🄾 Scenic RV Ctr, **W** 🍴 BP/dsl, KwikTrip/dsl 🍴 Burger King, China Town, Cousins Subs, Polanco's Mexican 🄾 Chevrolet, Chrysler/Dodge/Jeep, 🅗, O'Reilly Parts, Piggly Wiggly, Schaefer's Service Ctr
60	CR FD, to WI 145, Richfield, **E** 🍴 Mobil/dsl/e85 🄾 Cabela's, **W** 🍴 BP/McDonald's/dsl/scales/24hr
59	(from nb) US 45 W
57	WI 167, Holy Hill Rd, **E** 🍴 Mobil/Subway/dsl, **W** 🍴 BP 🍴 Sawmill Rest.
54	WI 167, CR Y, Lannon Rd, Germantown, **E** 🍴 KwikTrip/dsl 🏠 Best Western, Country Inn Suites
52	CR Q, County Line Rd, **E** 🍴 Briscoe Co Wood Grill, **W** 🍴 Mobil/dsl, Speedway/dsl 🍴 Applebee's, Arby's, Buffalo Wild Wings, Burger King, Cracker Barrel, Jimmy John's, KFC, McDonald's, Panda Express, Pizza Hut/Taco Bell, Qdoba, Starbucks, Wendy's 🏠 Holiday Inn Express, Super 8 🄾 AT&T, Best Buy, Costco/dsl, Hobby Lobby, Kohl's, Metro Mkt, Target
51b a	Pilgrim Rd, **W** 🍴 KwikTrip 🍴 Kraverz Custard, Toppers 🄾 AutoZone
50b a	WI 74 W, WI 100 E, Menomonee Falls, **E** 🄾 Buick/GMC, Ford, **W** 🍴 BP 🏠 De Martinis Pizza 🄾 Monro
48	WI 145, **E** 🄾 Aldi Foods, Sam's Club/gas, Woodman's Mkt/gas
47b	CR PP, Good Hope Rd, **E** 🍴 Broken Egg, Cousins Subs, Point Burger Bar 🏠 Comfort Suites, Hilton Garden 🄾 CarMax, Chevrolet, Mazda, Nissan, Toyota
47	WI 175, Appleton Ave
46	CR E, Silver Spring Dr, **E** 🍴 Marathon/dsl, Mobil/dsl 🍴 Athens Rest., Cousins Subs, KFC, McDonald's, Subway, Taco Bell, Wendy's 🏠 Hampton Inn, Quality Inn 🄾 Goodyear/auto, Harley Davidson, Petro Mart, **W** 🍴 Speedway/dsl 🍴 Domino's 🏠 Hyatt Place
45	CR EE, Hampton Ave, **E** 🍴 Citgo, **W** 🍴 BP/dsl
44	WI 190, Capitol Dr, **E** 🍴 Subway 🄾 Walgreens, **W** 🍴 Arby's, Burger King, Chick-fil-A, Chipotle, Culver's, Jimmy John's, McDonald's, Noodles&Co, Potbelly's, Qdoba, Starbucks, Taco Bell 🄾 Advance Parts, GNC, Home Depot, Metro Mkt, O'Reilly Parts, Petco, Ross, Target
43	Burleigh St, **E** 🍴 Corner Bakery Cafe, Osgood's Rest., Pizza Man 🏠 Homewood Suites 🄾 Dick's, 🅗, Meijer, Old Navy, TJ Maxx, **W** 🍴 Wendy's 🏠 Cousins Subs 🄾 Aldi Foods, Firestone/auto, Lowe's
42b	North Ave W, **E** 🍴 BP 🍴 Buffalo Wild Wings, Cheesecake Factory, Dave&Buster's, Denny's, Five Guys, Maggiano's, Panera Bread, PF Chang's, Potbelly, Texas de Brazil 🏠 Extended Stay America, Holiday Inn Express, Radisson 🄾 Barnes&Noble, Best Buy, Macy's, Nordstrom's, Walgreens, **W** 🍴 Papa John's 🄾 vet

🅿 = gas 🍴 = food 🏨 = lodging 🅾 = other ℞ = rest stop   Copyright 2022 - The Next EXIT

🏕N INTERSTATE 41 Cont'd

Exit #	Services
42a	WI 100, Mayfair Rd, North Ave E (from nb), E 🍴 Dave&Buster's 🅾 Walgreens, W 🍴 Firehouse Subs 🏨 Crowne Plaza 🅾 Kia, Pick'n Save, USPO
40	Watertown Plank Rd, Swan Blvd, E 🅾 🔣, W 🏨 Crowne Plaza
39	US 18, Wisconsin Ave, Bluemound Rd, E 🅾 🔣
1b a	I-94
1d	WI 53, Greenfield Ave, E 🍴 Jets Pizza, Subway 🅾 CVS Drug, Family$, W 🅿 Speedway/dsl 🍴 DQ, Fazoli's, Las Fajitas, McDonald's, Starbucks, Wendy's 🅾 O'Reilly Parts
1e	(from sb) Lincoln Ave, E 🅾 same as 2 E
2a	(from sb) National Rd (wb)
2b	(from sb) Oklahoma Ave, E 🅿 Citgo 🅾 auto repair, 🔣
3	Beloit Rd
4	I-41 S runs with I-43 N/I-894 E, then I-94 E. See I-43 exits 5-9 and I-94 exits 316-347.
0mm	Wisconsin/Illinois state line

🏕N INTERSTATE 43

Exit #	Services
192mm	I-43 begins/ends at Green Bay on US 41.
192b	US 41 S, US 141 S, to Appleton, 1 mi S services on Velp Ave 🅿 BP/A&W/dsl, Express/dsl, Mobil, Shell/dsl 🍴 Burger King, Gilligan's Rest., Julie's Cafe, McDonald's, Riverstreet Grill, Sunny Chinese, Taco Bell, Watering Hole Rest 🏨 AmericInn 🅾 Bay Parts, Bumper Parts, CVS Drug, Family$, Harley-Davidson, Trans Motive Auto
192a	US 41 N, US 141 N
189	Atkinson Dr, to Velp Ave, Port of Green Bay, W 🅿 Shell/dsl
188mm	Fox River
187	East Shore Dr, Webster Ave, W 🅿 Shell/dsl/24hr, Tesla EVC 🍴 McDonald's, Subway, Wendy's 🏨 Hampton Inn, Hyatt 🅾 🔣
185	WI 54, WI 57, University Ave, to Algoma, E 🅾 U of WI GB, W 🅿 EVC, Festival Foods, KwikTrip, Shell/A&W 🍴 Domino's, Subway, Taco Bell 🅾 Family$, University Mkt, Walgreens
183	Mason St, rd V, E 🍴 Culver's, Mackinaw's Grill 🏨 Country Inn&Suites, Super 8 🅾 🔣, URGENT CARE, 1 mi W 🅿 BP, Mobil/dsl, Shell 🍴 Applebee's, Arby's, Burger King, China Buffet, Dunkin', Fazoli's, Green Tea Chinese, KFC, Little Caesar's, McDonald's, Noodles&Co, Papa John's, Papa Murphy's, Perkins, Pizza Ranch, Qdoba, Starbucks, Taco Bell 🅾 $General, $Tree, Advance Parts, Aldi Foods, AutoZone, Batteries+Bulbs, Chevrolet, Chrysler/Dodge/Jeep, Family$, Hobby Lobby, Kohl's, Mazda, Nissan, O'Reilly Parts, PetCo, Pick'n Save, Ross, Subaru, Tires+, Walgreens, Walmart/Subway
181	Eaton Rd, rd JJ, E 🅿 BP/McDonald's/dsl 🍴 Bellevue Cafe, Hardee's, Jimmy John's, Luigi's, Taco John's 🅾 Ford/Kia, Home Depot, W 🅿 Shell, Subway 🍴 A&W, Ravine Grill 🏨 AmericInn 🅾 Farm&Fleet/gas, Festival Foods, Menards
180	WI 172 W, to US 41, 5 mi W 🅿 BP/Taco Bell/24hr, Citgo/Country Express/dsl/scales/24hr, KwikTrip/dsl, Shell/Subway/dsl 🍴 Buffalo Wild Wings, Burger King, McDonald's, Tucson's Rest. 🏨 Holiday Inn Express 🅾 AT&T, Costco/gas, Discount Tire, GNC, 🔣, Pick'n Save, Target, to stadium, Verizon, Walgreens multiple services
178	US 141, to WI 29, rd MM, Bellevue, E 🅿 Shell/Arby's/dsl 🍴 Little Caesar's
171	WI 96, rd KB, Denmark, E 🅿 BP/dsl 🍴 Blossom's Cheese, DeGrande Rest, McDonald's, Subway 🅾 Shady Acres Camping

168mm	℞ both lanes, full 🔣 facilities, 🔣 vending, 🔣 litter barrels, petwalk
166mm	Devils River
164	WI 147, rd Z, Maribel, W 🅿 BP/dsl
160	rd K, Kellnersville
157	rd V, Hillcrest Rd, Francis Creek, E 🅿 Citgo/Subway/dsl, Marathon/diner/dsl
154	US 10 W, WI 310, Two Rivers, to Appleton, E 🅾 🔣
153mm	Manitowoc River
152	US 10 E, WI 42 N, rd JJ, Manitowoc, E 🍴 TimeOut Grill 🅾 antiques, 🔣, maritime museum
149	US 151, WI 42 S, Manitowoc, E 🅿 BP, Citgo/dsl, KwikTrip/dsl, Mobil, Shell/dsl 🍴 A&W, Applebee's, Arby's, Buffalo Wild Wings, Burger King, Culver's, DQ, El Tequila, Fork&Knife Rest., Four Seasons Rest., Frier Tuck's Sandwiches, Hardee's, Hong Kong Buffet, Jimmy John's, KFC, Little Caesar's, McDonald's, Noodles&Co, Panda Express, Papa Murphy's, Perkins, Pizza Ranch, Qdoba, Starbucks, Taco Bell, Wendy's 🏨 Harbor Town Inn, Holiday Inn, Quality Inn 🅾 $Tree, Advance Parts, Aldi Foods, AutoZone, Buick/Cadillac/Chevrolet/GMC, Chrysler/Dodge/Jeep, Family$, Festival Foods, GNC, Goodyear/auto, Hobby Lobby, 🔣, Kohl's, Lowe's, O'Reilly Parts, PetCo, Pick'n Save, USPO, Verizon, vet, Walgreens, Walmart/Subway, W 🅿 Shell/McDonald's 🍴 Subway 🏨 AmericInn 🅾 Harley-Davidson, Menards
144	rd C, Newton, E 🅿 Mobil/dsl
142mm	weigh sta sb
137	rd XX, Cleveland, E 🅿 Citgo/Subway/dsl 🅾 Kunes Co RV Ctr
128	WI 42, Howards Grove, E 🅿 BP/dsl/24hr, KwikTrip/dsl 🍴 Culver's, Hardee's, Harry's Diner, Shuff's Rest., TX Roadhouse 🏨 Quality Inn 🅾 Pomp's Tire, W 🅿 Mobil/dsl/scales 🅾 Menards, Walmart/Subway
126	WI 23, Sheboygan, E 🅿 BP, KwikTrip/dsl, Tesla EVC 🍴 Applebee's, Cousins Subs, Culver's, McDonald's, New China, Noodles&Co, Panera Bread, Pizza Hut, Pizza Ranch 🏨 La Quinta, Super 8 🅾 Aldi Foods, Batteries+Bulbs, BigLots, Festival Foods, Ford/Kia, Goodyear/auto, Honda, 🔣, Hyundai/Mazda, Kohl's, NAPA, Subaru, Toyota
123	WI 28, rd A, Sheboygan, E 🅿 Citgo/dsl/24hr, Mobil/McDonald's/dsl 🍴 Coldstone, Jimmy John's, Perkins, Qdoba, Rocky Rococo's Pizza, Starbucks, Subway, Wendy's 🏨 AmericInn, Holiday Inn Express 🅾 Harley-Davidson/Cruisers Burgers, Walmart/Subway, W 🍴 Arby's, Buffalo Wild Wings, Chili's, Starbucks 🅾 $Tree, AT&T, Best Buy, GNC, Home Depot, Jo-Ann Fabrics, Petsmart, Target, TJ Maxx
120	rds OK, V, Sheboygan, E 🅿 KwikTrip/dsl, ♥Love's/Hardee's/Subway/dsl/scales/24hr 🍴 Parkside Rest. 🏨 Sleep Inn 🅾 camping, Nissan, to Kohler-Andrae SP, VW, 1 mi W 🅾 Horn's RV Ctr
116	rd AA, Foster Rd, Oostburg, W 🅿 Sunoco 🍴 Judi's Place Rest., Pizza Ranch, Subway 🅾 Piggly Wiggly/gas
113	WI 32 N, rd LL, Cedar Grove, W 🅿 Citgo/dsl/repair, Mobil/dsl, Sunoco/Fueling Depot 🍴 Country Grove Rest. (1mi), Sunrise Rest. 🏨 Lakeview Motel
107	rd D, Belgium, E 🏨 Lake Church Inn/grill 🅾 Harrington Beach SP, W 🅿 BP/McDonald's/dsl/24hr, How-Dea Trkstp/Hobo's Korner Kitchen/dsl/scales, Mobil/dsl/24hr 🍴 Kyote's Grill, Subway 🏨 Belgium Inn 🅾 repair, USPO
100	WI 32 S, WI 84 W, Port Washington, E 🅿 BP/dsl, Mobil 🍴 Arby's, McDonald's, Pizza Hut, Subway 🏨 Country Inn&Suites, Holiday Inn (2mi) 🅾 Allen-Edmonds Shoes, Goodyear/auto, Piggly Wiggly, True Value, vet, W 🏨 Hundred Mile House Rest.

Side labels: MANITOWOC, WI, GREEN BAY

⬆N INTERSTATE 43 Cont'd

Exit #	Services
97	(from nb, exits left), WI 57, Fredonia
96	WI 33, to Saukville, **E** 🍴 Culver's (1mi) 🅾 Advance Parts, Best Hardware, Buick/Cadillac/Chevrolet, Camping World RV Ctr, Chrysler/Dodge/Jeep, Ford, O'Reilly Parts, Piggly Wiggly, Walgreens, Walmart, **W** 🅶 Exxon/McDonald's, KwikTrip/dsl 🍴 Domino's, DQ, Lam's Chinese, Papa Murphy's, Subway, Taco Bell 🛏 Motel 6 🅾 repair/tires
93	WI 32 N, WI 57 S, Grafton, **2 mi E** 🅶 BP 🅾 vet
92	WI 60, rd Q, Grafton, **E** 🍴 BP/dsl 🍴 GhostTown Rest., Water St Rest. 🛏 Hampton Inn, TownePlace Suites, **W** 🅶 Citgo/DQ/dsl 🍴 Charcoal Grill, Firehouse Subs, Noodles&Co, Qdoba, Starbucks, Subway 🛏 Comfort Inn 🅾 Aldi Foods, AT&T, Costco/gas, Dick's, Home Depot, 🚻, Kohl's, Meijer, Michael's, Petsmart, Target, Verizon
89	rd C, Cedarburg, **W** 🍴 Mobil/dsl 🅾 🚻
85	WI 57 S, WI 167 W, Mequon Rd, **W** 🍴 BP, Mobil, Shell 🍴 Caribou Coffee, Chancery Rest., Cousins Subs, Culver's, First Watch Cafe, Jimmy John's, Leonardo's Pizza, McDonald's, Noodles&Co, Panera Bread, Papa Murphy's, Pizza Hut, Starbucks, Taco Bell 🛏 Chalet Motel 🅾 Ace Hardware, AT&T, 🚻, Marshall's, Metro Mkt, Sendik's Foods, Verizon, vet, Walgreens
83	rd W, Port Washington Rd (from nb only)
82b a	WI 32 S, WI 100, Brown Deer Rd, **E** 🍴 BP, Mobil/dsl 🍴 Baskin-Robbins, Benji's Deli, Jose's Blue Sombrero, Maxfield's Pancakes, McDonald's, Noodles&Co, Peking Chef, Qdoba, Starbucks, Subway, Toppers Pizza 🅾 Best Buy, CVS Drug, GNC, Land's Inlet, Walgreens
80	Good Hope Rd, **E** 🍴 Mobil 🍴 Dr Dawg, Jimmy John's, King's Wok, Samurai Japanese 🛏 Fairfield Inn, Residence Inn 🅾 Pick'n Save, to Cardinal Stritch U
78	Silver Spring Dr, **E** 🍴 BP, Mobil 🍴 Arby's, Bar Louie, Boston Mkt, Buffalo Wild Wings, CA Pizza Kitchen, Cheesecake Factory, Cousins Subs, Devon Steaks, Fiddleheads Coffee, Five Guys, Kopp's Custard, McDonald's, Panera Bread, Papa Murphy's, Perkins, Potbelly, Qdoba, Taco Bell 🛏 La Quinta, Motel 6 🅾 AT&T, Barnes&Noble, Batteries+Bulbs, Goodyear/auto, Kohl's, Nissan, Trader Joe's, USPO, Verizon, Walgreens, **W** 🅾🚻
77b a	(from nb), **E** 🍴 Anchorage Rest., Solly's Grille 🛏 Holiday Inn
76b a	WI 57, WI 190, Green Bay Ave, **E** 🅾 Home Depot, **W** 🍴 BP/dsl 🍴 Burger King
75	Atkinson Ave, Keefe Ave, **E** 🍴 Mobil, **W** 🍴 BP
74	Locust St
73c	North Ave (rom sb), **E** 🍴 Wendy's, **W** 🍴 McDonald's
73b	North Ave (from nb) downtown
73a	WI 145 E, 4th St (exits left from sb), Broadway downtown
72c	Wells St, **E** 🛏 Doubletree, Hilton 🅾 Civic Ctr, 🚻, museum
72b	(from sb), I-94 W, to madison
72a	(310c from nb, exits left from sb), I-794 E, I-94 W to Madison, to Lakefront downtown
311	WI 59, National Ave, 6th St downtown
312a	Lapham Blvd, Mitchell St, **W** 🍴 BP, Citgo
312b	(from nb), Becher St, Lincoln Ave
314a	Holt Ave, **E** 🍴 SP Mart/dsl 🍴 Applebee's, Arby's, China King, Jimmy John's, Little Caesar's, Rosati's Pizza, Starbucks, Subway, Taco Bell, Wendy's 🅾 AutoZone, Family$, Home Depot, Pick'n Save Foods, Piggly Wiggly, Target, vet, **W** 🅾🚻, to Alverno Coll
314b	Howard Ave
10b	I-94 S to Chicago, **E** 🅾 ♿
9b a	WI 241, 27th St, **E** 🍴 Flying Eagle, Saifron/dsl 🍴 Arby's, Benny's Cafe, Dunkin', Famous Dave's, Sonic, Subway 🛏 Suburban
9b a	Continued Motel 🅾 AutoZone, Subaru, USPO, Walgreens, **W** 🍴 Buffalo Wild Wings, Chipotle Mexican, Denny's, Jimmy John's, McDonald's, New China, Omega Rest., Panda Express, Papa John's, Rich's Cakes, Starbucks, Taco Bell, Wong's Wok, Zebb's Rest 🛏 Quality Inn, Rodeway Inn 🅾 $Tree, AAA, Advance Parts/Meineke, AutoZone, Chevrolet, CVS Drug, Firestone/auto, Ford, Goodyear/auto, 🚻, Kohl's, Marshall's, Michael's, Pick'n Save Foods, Ross, Walgreens, Walmart
8a	WI 36, Loomis Rd, **E** 🍴 BP/dsl, Citgo 🍴 Los Mariachi's 🅾 Aldi Foods, Walgreens, **W** 🍴 Griddler's Cafe 🅾 to Alverno Coll
7	60th St, **E** 🍴 Speedway/dsl 🍴 Culver's, Subway 🅾 Harley-Davidson, Meijer/dsl, **W** 🍴 Speedway/dsl
5b	76th St (from sb, no EZ return), **E** 🍴 Speedway/dsl 🍴 Applebee's, Bakers Square, Burger King, Carrabba's Italian, Chick-fil-A, Cousins Subs, El Beso, Habaneros, Jersey Mike's, Jimmy John's, Kopp's Burgers, Kyoto Japanese, Longhorn Steaks, McDonald's, Noodles&Co, Old Country Buffet, Olive Garden, Panda Express, Panera Bread, Qdoba, Red Lobster, Red Robin, Ruby Tuesday, Starbucks, TGIFriday's, Topper's Pizza, Traditional Pancake House, Wendy's 🅾 $Tree, AT&T, Barnes&Noble, Best Buy, Firestone/auto, Goodyear/auto, JC Penney, Jo-Ann Fabrics, Macy's, Midas, PetCo, Petsmart, Sendik's Food Mkt, TJ Maxx, Tuesday Morning, Verizon, Walmart, **W** 🍴 Arby's, Pizza Hut, Subway 🅾 Advance Parts, Family$, Pick'n Save Foods, USPO, Walgreens
5a	WI 24 W, Forest Home Ave, **E** 🍴 Citgo/dsl 🍴 Outback Steaks, Portillo's 🅾 Boerner Botanical Gardens, Fresh Thyme Mkt, Kohl's, Marshall's, Ross, Welk's Auto
61	(4 from sb), I-894/US 45 N, I-43/US 45 S
60	US 45 S, WI 100, 108th St (exits left from sb), **E** 🍴 BP, Citgo, Marathon, Mobil 🍴 A&W, Amore Italian, Ann's Italian, Burger King, Chipotle Mexican, Confucious Chinese, Cousins Subs, Culver's, Dunkin', George Webb Rest., McDonald's, Noodles&Co, Open Flame Grill, Papa Murphy's, Starbucks, Subway, Taco Bell 🅾 $Tree, AutoZone, Chevrolet, O'Reilly Parts, Pick'n Save, USPO, vet, Walgreens, **W** 🍴 Andy's/dsl 🍴 Denny's, Forum Rest., McDonald's, Organ Piper Pizza, Subway 🅾 Aldi Foods, Goodyear/auto, NAPA, Nissan, vet, Walgreens, Walmart/Subway
59	WI 100, Layton Ave (from nb, exits left), same as 60, Hales Corner, **W** 🍴 BP/Cousins Subs
57	Moorland Rd, **E** 🍴 KwikTrip/dsl 🍴 Applebee's, Stonefire Pizza Co, TX Roadhouse, Zaffiro's Pizza 🛏 La Quinta 🅾 Costco/dsl, **W** 🍴 Speedway/dsl 🍴 Arby's, Buffalo Wild Wings, Cocina Real, Panera Bread, Papa John's, Point Burger 🛏 Holiday Inn Express 🅾 Firestone/auto, GNC, Michael's, Target
54	rd Y, Racine Ave, **1-2 mi E** 🍴 BP/dsl, KwikTrip 🅾 Cousins Subs, Culver's, McDonald's, Piggly Wiggly, Walgreens

⬆N INTERSTATE 43 Cont'd

Exit #	Services
50	WI 164, Big Bend, W 🅿 KwikTrip/dsl/e85 🍴 McDonald's, Subway
44mm	Fox River
43	WI 83, Mukwonago, E 🅿 BP/dsl 🅾 Aldi Foods, Chevrolet, Chrysler/Dodge/Jeep, Home Depot, 🏥, Walmart, W 🅿 Citgo 🍴 Boneyard Grille, Chen's Kitchen, Domino's, DQ, Starbucks, Taco Bell 🛏 Baymont Inn
38	WI 20, East Troy, W 🅿 ▥▥▥/Road Ranger/Subway/dsl/24hr, Shell/McDonald's 🍴 Ale Sta Rest., Cousins Subs, Dos Amigos, Genoa Pizza, LD's BBQ, Roma's Ristorante 🅾 $General, Carquest
36	WI 120, East Troy, E 🛏 Alpine Valley Resort, W 🛏 Quality Inn Suites
33	Bowers Rd, E 🅾 to Alpine Valley Music Theatre
32mm	🆁🆂 both lanes, full ♿ facilities, 🅲, 🕭, litter barrels, vending, petwalk
29	WI 11, Elkhorn, W 🅾 fairgrounds
27b a	US 12, to Lake Geneva, E 🅾 🏥
25	WI 67, Elkhorn, E 🅿 ❤Loves/Hardee's/dsl/scales/24hr, Mobil/dsl 🛏 AmericInn 🅾 Buick/Chevrolet/GMC, Chrysler/Dodge/Jeep, vet, W 🅿 Speedway/dsl/24hr 🍴 Burger King, Subway 🛏 Hampton Inn (2mi) 🅾 Kunes Country RV Ctr
21	WI 50, Delavan, E 🍴 Brodie's Beef, Chili's, China 1, Culver's, Domino's, Jimmy John's, Panera Bread, Papa Murphy's, Starbucks, Subway, Yoshi Japanese 🅾 Aldi Foods, AT&T, F&F Tires, Kohl's, Lowe's, Petsmart, Verizon, Walmart, W 🍴 Mobil/Dunkin'/dsl 🍴 KFC, Little Caesar's, McDonald's, Perkins, Wendy's 🛏 Comfort Suites, Super 8 🅾 $Tree, AutoZone, Cadillac/Chevrolet, Ford/Lincoln, GNC, NAPA, O'Reilly Parts, Piggly Wiggly, Walgreens
17	rd X, Delavan, Darien, W 🅿 BP/dsl
15	US 14, Darien, E 🅿 Mobil/dsl 🍴 West Wind Diner
6	WI 140, Clinton, E 🅿 Citgo/Subway/TCBY/dsl 🅾 $General, Ford
2	rd X, Hart Rd, E 🍴 Butterfly Fine Dining
1b a	I-90, E to Chicago, W to Madison, S 🅿 Mobil/McDonald's, ▥▥▥/Taco Bell/dsl/scales/24hr, Shell, Speedway/dsl 🍴 Applebee's, Arby's, Buffalo Wild Wings, Culver's, Doc's Rest., Dunkin', Jimmy John's, Little Caesar's, Little Mexico, Noodles&Co, Qdoba, Road Dawg Rest., Starbucks, Subway, Wendy's 🛏 Baymont Inn, Fairfield Inn, Hampton Inn, Holiday Inn Express, Home 2 Suites, Quality Inn, Rodeway Inn, Super 8 🅾 $Tree, Aldi Foods, AT&T, Buick/GMC, Cadillac/Chevrolet, GNC, Menards, NTB, O'Reilly Parts, Walmart

I-43 begins/ends on I-90, exit 185 in Beloit.

⬆E INTERSTATE 90

Exit #	Services
187mm	Wisconsin/Illinois state line, I-90 & I-39 run together nb.
187mm	Welcome Ctr wb, full ♿ facilities, info, 🅲, 🕭, litter barrels, vending, petwalk
185b	I-43 N, to Milwaukee
185a	WI 81, Beloit, S 🅿 Mobil/McDonald's/dsl, ▥▥▥/Taco Bell/dsl/scales/24hr, Shell, Speedway/dsl 🍴 Applebee's, Arby's, Buffalo Wild Wings, Culver's, Doc's Rest., Dunkin', Jimmy John's, Little Caesar's, Little Mexico, Noodles&Co, Papa Murphy's, Qdoba, Road Dawg Rest., Starbucks, Subway, Wendy's 🛏 Baymont Inn, Fairfield Inn, Hampton Inn, Holiday Inn Express, Home 2 Suites, Quality Inn, Rodeway Inn, Super 8 🅾 $Tree, Aldi Foods, AT&T, Buick/GMC, Cadillac/Chevrolet, GNC, Menards, NTB, O'Reilly Parts, Walmart

Exit #	Services
183	Shopiere Rd, rd S, to Shopiere, S 🅾 🏥, repair
181mm	weigh sta, wb
177	WI 11 W, Janesville, 2 mi S 🅿 KwikTrip/dsl 🅾 S WI Airport, to Blackhawk Tec Coll
175b a	WI 11 E, Janesville, to Delavan, N 🅿 BP/Subway/dsl 🛏 Baymont Inn 🅾 🏥, vet, S 🛏 Lannon Stone Motel 🅾 city park
171c b	US 14, WI 26, Janesville, N 🅿 TA/Mobil/Wendy's/dsl/scales/24hr/@ 🍴 Coldstone, Cozumel Mexican, Golden Corral, IHOP, Starbucks, Subway, TX Roadhouse 🛏 Holiday Inn Express, Microtel 🅾 Aldi Foods, Best Buy, GNC, Home Depot, Michael's, NTB, Old Navy, PetCo, Staples, TJ Maxx, S 🅿 Citgo, Exxon/dsl, KwikTrip/dsl 🍴 Applebee's, Arby's, Buffalo Wild Wings, Burger King, Chipotle, ChuckeCheese, Culver's, Dunkin', Famous Dave's, Fazoli's, Fuji Steaks, Hacienda Real, Hardee's, Jersey Mike's, Jimmy John's, KFC, Mac's Pizza, McDonald's, Milio's Sandwiches, Milwaukee Grill, Mo's Taasbag, Noodles&Co, Olive Garden, Panda Express, Panera Bread, Papa Murphy's, Peking Chinese, Pizza Hut, Prime Quarter Steaks, Qdoba Mexican, Red Robin, Road Dawg Eatery, Subway, Taco Bell, Taco John's, Tacos Neno, Toppers Pizza 🛏 Quality Inn, Super 8, TownePlace Suites 🅾 $Tree, Aldi Foods, AT&T, AutoZone, Big Lots, CarQuest, CVS Drug, Dick's Sports, F&F, Festival Foods, Ford/Lincoln, Harley-Davidson, Hobby Lobby, 🏥, Hyundai, Jo-Anne Fabric, Kohl's, mall, Mazda, Menards, Nissan/Kia/Subaru, O'Reilly Parts, Target, Toyota, USPO, Verizon, Walgreens
171a	WI 26, N 🅿 BP/dsl 🍴 Cracker Barrel 🛏 Hampton Inn, Motel 6, Ramada/rest. 🅾 Chrysler/Dodge/Jeep, Sam's Club, URGENT CARE, VW, Walgreens, Walmart, S same as 171c b
168mm	🆁🆂 eb, full ♿ facilities, 🅲, 🕭, litter barrels, vending, petwalk
163.5mm	Rock River
163	WI 59, Edgerton, to Milton, N 🅿 Mobil/Subway/dsl, Shell/Dunkin'/Taco John's/dsl 🍴 Blue Gilly's Rest., Culver's, McDonald's, WI Cheese Store 🛏 Quality Inn 🅾 KOA, marina
160	US 51S, WI 73, WI 106, Oaklawn Academy, to Deerfield, S 🅿 BP/dsl/scales/rest./24hr/@ 🅾 Creek View Camping (2mi), 🏥
156	US 51N, to Stoughton, S 🛏 Coachman's Inn/rest., 🏥
147	rd N, Cottage Grove, to Stoughton, S 🅿 BP/Arby's/dsl, Road Ranger/Subway/dsl/scales, Roady's 🅾 Badgerland Camping (2mi), Lake Kegonsa SP
146mm	weigh sta eb
142b a	(142a exits left from wb) US 12, US 18, Madison, to Cambridge, N 🅿 BP/dsl 🍴 Roadhouse Rest. 🛏 Best Value Inn, Magnuson Grand Hotel 🅾 casino, Harley-Davidson, S 🅿 Citgo/dsl, Phillips 66/Arby's/dsl, Shell/dsl 🍴 Denny's 🛏 Days Inn, Sleep Inn 🅾 🏥, Menards, UWI
138a	I-94, E to Milwaukee, W to La Crosse (exits left from eb)

I-90 W and I-94 W run together for 93 miles.

Exit #	Services
138b	WI 30, Madison, S 💬
135c b	US 151, Madison, N 🅿 BP/dsl 🍴 Erin's Pub, Happy Wok, Milio's Sandwiches, Uno Pizzaria 🛏 Cambria Suites, Courtyard, Fairfield Inn, GrandStay Suites, Holiday Inn, Staybridge Suites 🅾 Buick/GMC, Chrysler/Dodge/Jeep, Ford, Honda, Hyundai, Kia, Mazda, Nissan, Subaru, Toyota
135a	US 151, Madison, N 🍴 Chick-fil-A, S 🅿 BP, Citgo, Mobil, Shell 🍴 Applebee's, Arby's, Arod's TexMex, Buffalo Wild Wings, Chili's, Chipotle Mexican, Cracker Barrel, Culver's, Denny's, Dickey's BBQ, DoLittle's Woodfire Grill, Dumpling House, Hardee's, Hooters, IHOP, Jimmy John's, McDonald's, Moka, Noodles&Co, Olive Garden, Outback Steaks, Panera Bread, Perkins, Pizza Hut, Popeye's, Potbelly, Qdoba, Red Lobster, Red Robin, Starbucks, Sumo Steaks, Taco Bell, Takumi Japanese, TGIFriday's, Toppers's Pizza, TX Roadhouse, Wendy's 🛏 Best Western

INTERSTATE 90 Cont'd

135a **Continued**
Comfort Inn, Crowne Plaza Hotel/rest., EconoLodge, Hampton Inn, Howard Johnson, Microtel, Motel 6, Premier, Quality Inn, Red Roof Inn, Residence Inn, Rodeway Inn, Super 8 🅾 $Tree, Aldi Foods, AT&T, Barnes&Noble, Best Buy, Burlington Coats, city park, Dick's, Firestone/auto, Goodyear/auto, Gordman's, Hobby Lobby, Home Depot, Hy-Vee Foods, JC Penney, JoAnn Fabrics, Kohl's, Marshalls, Michaels, Office Depot, Old Navy, Petsmart, st patrol, Target, Tesla EVC, Verizon

132 US 51, Madison, De Forest, **N** 🅶 Shell/Pinecone Rest/dsl/24hr 🅾 Gander RV Ctr, **S** 🅶 TA/Subway/Popeye's/dsl/scales/24hr/@ 🅾 Freightliner/GMC/Volvo/White, Goodyear, Peterbilt, WI RV World

131 WI 19, Waunakee, **N** 🅶 Kwik Trip/dsl, Mobil/dsl, Speedway/ dsl 🍴 A&W, McDonald's, Rodeside Grill 🛏 Days Inn, Super 8 🅾 fireworks, Kenworth, Mousehouse Cheesehaus, truckwash, **S** 🅶 F&F/dsl

126 rd V, De Forest, to Dane, **N** 🅶 BP/A&W/Rococo's/dsl, Phillips 66/Arby's/dsl 🍴 Casey's, Culver's, McDonald's, Subway, Taco Bell 🛏 Holiday Inn Express 🅾 Cheese Chalet, KOA, **S** 🅶 Exxon, Shell 🛏 Comfort Inn 🅾 dsl/tire repair

119 WI 60, Arlington, to Lodi, **S** 🅶 Mobil/A&W/Cousins Subs/dsl 🍴 A&W, Rococo's Pizza 🛏 Quality Inn 🅾 dsl/tire repair

115 rd CS, Poynette, to Lake Wisconsin, **N** 🅶 BP/dsl 🍴 McDonald's, Subway 🅾 auto repair, dsl truck/trailer repair, Smokey Hollow Camping, **S** 🅶 Loves/Hardee's/dsl/scales/24hr

113mm 🆁🆂 both lanes, full 🦽 facilities, 🎁, 🛥, litter barrels, vending, petwalk

111mm Wisconsin River

108b a I-39 N, WI 78, to US 51 N, to Wis Dells, Portage, **N** 🅾 🏨, **S** 🅶 BP, Mobil, Petro/Iron Skillet/DQ/Subway/dsl/24hr/@ 🛏 Comfort Suites, Days Inn 🅾 Blue Beacon

106mm Baraboo River

106 WI 33, Portage, **N** 🅾 🏨, **S** 🅶 BP 🅾 Circus World Museum, Devil's Lake SP, SkyHigh Camping, to Cascade Mtn Ski Area, Wayside Park

92 US 12, to Baraboo, **N** 🅶 BP/dsl, Citgo/Subway/dsl, Exxon, Mobil/Dunkin'/dsl/24hr 🍴 Buffalo Phil's Grille, Burger King, Cheese Factory Rest, Cracker Barrel, Culver's, Denny's, Domino's, Famous Dave's BBQ, Field's Steaks, Green Owl Pizza, Marley's Rest., McDonald's, Milio's, Monk's Grill, Noodles&Co, Pizza Ranch, Ponderosa, R Place Italian, Sarento's Italian, Starbucks, Taco Bell, Uno Grill, Wintergreen Grill 🛏 Alakai Hotel, Country Squire Motel, Dell Creek Motel, Glacier Canyon Lodge, Grand Marquis Inn, Great Wolf Lodge, Holiday Inn Express, Kalahari Resort, Ramada, Wilderness Hotel, Wintergreen Hotel 🅾 Dells Outlets, Mkt Square Cheese, URGENT CARE, Verizon, **S** 🛏 Motel 6 🅾 🏨, Jellystone Camping, Mirror Lake SP, Red Oak Camping, Scenic Traveler RV Ctr

89 WI 23, Lake Delton, **N** 🅶 KwikTrip/dsl, Spirit 🍴 Brathouse Grill, Denny's Diner, Howie's Rest., KFC, Moosejaw Pizza 🛏 Best Value Inn, Hilton Garden, Malibu Inn, Olympia Motel, Twi-Lite Inn 🅾 Crystal Grand Music Theatre, Jellystone Camping, USPO, **S** 🍴 Dunkin', McDonald's 🅾 $Tree, Country Roads RV Park, Home Depot, Jo-Ann, Kohl's, Springbrook Camping, Walmart/Subway

87 WI 13, Wisconsin Dells, **N** 🅶 Citgo/dsl, Mobil/Arby's/dsl, Shell/Dunkin' 🍴 Applebee's, Bunyan's Rest., Burger King, Coldstone, Culver's, Denny's, IHOP, Jimmy John's, McDonald's, Mexicali Rose Rest., Perkins, Starbucks, Taco Bell, Wei's Chinese 🛏 Ambers Resort, AmericInn, Baymont Inn, Best Western,

---

87 **Continued**
Econolodge, Polynesian Hotel, Quality Inn, Super 8 🅾 golf, info, KOA, Sherwood Forest Camping, Walgreens, waterpark

85 US 12, WI 16, Wisconsin Dells, **0-3 mi N** 🛏 Fairview Motel 🅾 KOA, Sherwood Forest Camping, Standing Rock Camping, to Rocky Arbor SP, **S** 🅶 BP/dsl 🛏 Arrowhead Camping, Days End Motel, Edge-O-the-Dell RV Camping, Summer Breeze Resort

79 rd HH, Lyndon Sta, **S** 🅶 BP/Subway/dsl/24hr

76mm 🆁🆂 wb, full 🦽 facilities, 🎁, 🛥, litter barrels, vending, petwalk

74mm 🆁🆂 eb, full 🦽 facilities, 🎁, 🛥, litter barrels, vending, petwalk

69 WI 82, Mauston, **N** 🅶 Mauston TP/BP/Taco Bell/24hr, Pilot, Wendy's/dsl/scales/24hr, Shell/24hr 🍴 China Buffet, Family Rest. 🛏 Best Western Oasis, Quality Inn, Super 8 🅾 Carr Valley Cheese, to Buckhorn SP, **S** 🅶 KwikTrip/Denny's/dsl/scales/24hr, Mobil, Speedway 🍴 Culver's, Hardee's, Log Cabin Deli, McDonald's, Pizza Hut, Roman Castle Rest., Subway 🛏 Alaskan Inn 🅾 $General, Buick/Chevrolet, Family$, Festival Foods, 🏨, K-Mart, O'Reilly Parts, Verizon, vet, Walgreens

61 WI 80, New Lisbon, to Necedah, **N** 🅶 BP/dsl, Shell/McDonald's/ dsl 🛏 AmericInn, Edge O' the Woods Motel 🅾 Buckhorn SP, Chrysler/Dodge/Jeep, fireworks, Ford, **S** 🅶 KwikTrip/24hr 🅾 city park, Elroy-Sparta ST Tr, USPO

55 rd C, Camp Douglas, **N** 🅾 to Camp Williams, Volk Field, wayside, **S** 🅶 Arco/Quiznos/dsl, BP/dsl 🅾 to Mill Bluff SP

48 rd PP, Oakdale, **N** 🅶 Road Ranger/Subway/dsl/scales/24hr 🅾 antiques, KOA, truck/car wash, **S** 🅶 Loves/Hardee's/dsl/ scales/24hr 🅾 Mill Bluff SP, repair

45 I-94 W, to St Paul

I-90 E and I-94 E run together for 93 miles.

43 US 12, WI 16, Tomah, **N** 🅶 BP/dsl, KwikTrip/dsl/24hr 🍴 Burnstadt's Café, DQ 🛏 Daybreak Inn, Rest Well Motel 🅾 Burnstadt's Mkt, 🏨, vet

41 WI 131, Tomah, to Wilton, **N** 🅶 KwikTrip/dsl/24hr, Mobil/dsl 🍴 Burnstadts Cafe 🛏 Daybreak Inn 🅾 vet

28 WI 16, Sparta, Ft McCoy, **N** 🅶 BP/diner/dsl/scales 🛏 Best Western 🅾 🏨

25 WI 27, Sparta, to Melvina, **N** 🅶 Cenex/Arby's/dsl, KwikTrip/dsl, Mobil/Taco Bell, Shell/dsl 🍴 Burger King, Culver's, DQ, KFC, McDonald's, Pizza Hut, Sparta Rest., Subway 🛏 Country Inn, Super 8 🅾 $General, $Tree, Buick/Chevrolet, Family$, Ford, Hansens IGA, 🏨, O'Reilly Parts, Walgreens, Walmart/Subway

22mm 🆁🆂 wb, full 🦽 facilities, 🎁, 🛥, litter barrels, vending, petwalk

20mm 🆁🆂 eb, full 🦽 facilities, 🎁, 🛥, litter barrels, vending, petwalk

15 WI 162, Bangor, to Coon Valley, **N** 🅶 gas

12 rd C, W Salem, **N** 🅶 Cenex/cafe/dsl/24hr 🅾 Coulee Region RV Ctr, NAPA, Neshonoc Camping, **S** 🅶 BP/Subway/dsl 🛏 AmericInn 🅾 Peterbilt

10mm weigh sta eb

[Icon] = gas [Icon] = food [Icon] = lodging [Icon] = other [Icon] = rest stop   Copyright 2022 - The Next EXIT ©

INTERSTATE 90 Cont'd

Exit #	Services
5	WI 16, La Crosse, **N** [food] Arby's, BA Burrito, Buffalo Wild Wings, Ciatti's Italian, Coldstone, Manny's Mexican, Outback Steaks [lodging] Baymont Inn, Hampton Inn, Microtel [other] $Tree, Aldi Foods, Freightliner, Home Depot, Walmart/Subway, Woodman's Foods/gas/lube, **S** [gas] Kwik Trip/dsl/24hr [food] Bamboo House, Burracho's Mexican Grill, Carlos O'Kelly's, ChuckeCheese, Culver's, Fazoli's, HuHot Grill, Jimmy John's, McDonald's, Olive Garden, Perkins, Starbucks, TGIFriday's, TX Roadhouse [lodging] Holiday Inn Express [other] Barnes&Noble, Best Buy, Chevrolet, Dick's, F&F, Ford/Lincoln, Hobby Lobby, [H], JC Penney, Kohl's, Michael's, Target, Walgreens
4	US 53 N, WI 16, to WI 157, La Crosse, **N** [other] Harley-Davidson, **S** [gas] Kwik Trip, TO [food] Applebee's, Burger King, Caribou Coffee, China Inn, Cousins Subs, Famous Dave's BBQ, Grizzly's Rest., Panera Bread, Papa Murphy's, Red Lobster, Rococo's Pizza, Shogun Hibachi, Subway, Taco Bell, Wendy's [lodging] Comfort Inn [other] Festival Food/24hr, GNC, Goodyear/auto, [H], La Crosse River St Trail, Office Depot, Old Navy, PetCo, Petsmart, Sam's Club, Tires+, TJ Maxx, Verizon
3	US 53 S, WI 35, to La Crosse, **S** [gas] Clark/dsl, Kwik Trip [food] Econolodge, Hardee's, KFC, La Crosse Rest., McDonald's, North Country Steaks, Perkins, Pizza Hut, Subway [lodging] Best Value Inn, Best Western, Motel 6, Quality Inn, Settle Inn, Super 8 [other] to Great River St Trail, U-Haul, Viterbo Coll, Walgreens
2.5mm	Black River
2	rd B, French Island, **N** [other][food], **S** [gas] BP/dsl [lodging] Days Inn/rest. [other] Quillin's Mkt
1mm	Welcome Ctr eb, full [&] facilities, info, [C], [food], litter barrels, vending, petwalk
0mm	Wisconsin/Minnesota state line, Mississippi River

INTERSTATE 94

Exit #	Services
349mm	Wisconsin/Illinois state line, weigh sta nb
348.5mm	weigh sta wb
347	WI 165, rd Q, Lakeview Pkwy, **E** Welcome Ctr nb, full [&] facilities, [food], litter barrels, petwalk, [gas] BP/dsl [food] Chancery Rest., Culver's, McDonald's [lodging] Radisson [other] Old Navy, Premium Outlets/famous brands
345	rd C, **E** [lodging] Holiday Inn Express (1mi)
345mm	Des Plaines River
344	WI 50, Lake Geneva, to Kenosha, **1 mi E** [food] Buffalo Wild Wings, Cheddar's, Cousins Subs, Dickey's BBQ, Famous Dave's, Mobil/dsl, Noodles&Co, Olive Garden, Panda Express, Perkins, Pizza Hut, Shell/Dunkin'/dsl, Sparti's Gyros, Starbucks, Subway, Tuscany Bistro, TX Roadhouse, White Castle, Woodman's/gas [lodging] Candlewood Suites, Holiday Inn Express, La Quinta, Super 8 [other] AT&T, Best Buy, Chevrolet, Dick's, GNC, [H], JC Penney, Petsmart, Target, Verizon, Walgreens, **W** [gas] BP/dsl, Speedway/dsl [food] Arby's, Birchwood Grill, Cracker Barrel, KFC, McDonald's, Phoenix Rest., Wendy's [lodging] Best Western, Comfort Inn, Country Inn&Suites, Hampton Inn, Value Inn [other] BratStop Cheese Store, CarMax, Honda, Nissan, Subaru, Toyota
342	WI 158, to Kenosha, **E** Harley-Davidson, **W** antiques
340	WI 142, rd S, to Kenosha, **E** [gas] Kenosha TP/BP/Subway/dsl/E85/LP/scales/24hr [other][H], **W** [food] Mars Cheese Castle Rest. [lodging] Oasis Inn [other] Fun Time RV Ctr, to Bong RA
339	rd E
337	rd KR, to Mt Pleasant, **W** [food] Apple Holler Rest./orchard

Exit #	Services
335	WI 11, to Mt Pleasant, Burlington, to Racine
333	WI 20, Waterford, to Racine, **E** [gas] KwikTrip/dsl [food] Burger King, McDonald's [lodging] Days Inn Excel Inn, Holiday Inn Express [other][H], Toyota, **W** [gas] Citgo/Wendy's/dsl/24hr, Petro/Mobil/Iron Skillet/dsl/scales/24hr/@ [food] Chicken'n Waffles, Culver's, Route 20 Outhouse Grill, Subway [lodging] Quality Inn [other] Burlington RV Ctr, visitor info
329	rd K, Thompsonville, to Racine, **E** [gas][food]/Arby's/Subway/dsl/scales/24hr [food] A&W [other] dsl repair
328mm	weigh sta eb
327	rd G, **W** fireworks
326	7 Mile Rd, **E** [gas] BP, Mobil/dsl [other] Jellystone Park, **W** [other] Seven Mile Fair
325	WI 241 N (from wb), to 27th St
322	WI 100, to Ryan Rd, **E** [gas] KwikTrip/dsl [food] McDonald's, Wendy's [other] dsl repair, **W** [gas] Loves/Denny's/dsl/LP/scales/RV dump/24hr, Mobil, [food]/Subway/dsl/LP/scales/24hr, Shell [food] A&W/KFC/dsl [food] Arby's, Cousins Subs, Dish Bakery, Dunkin', Perkins, Starbucks, Yen Hwa Chinese [lodging] Staybridge Suites Value Inn [other] AutoZone, Blue Beacon, Freightliner/repair, [H] Pick'n Save, vet, Walgreens
321	Drexel Ave
320	rd BB, Rawson Ave, **E** [gas] BP/7-11/dsl, Mobil [food] Applebee's Burger King [lodging] La Quinta
319	rd ZZ, College Ave, **E** [gas] Shell/Subway, Speedway/dsl [food] Branded Steer Rest., McDonald's [lodging] Candlewood Suites Comfort Suites, Country Inn&Suites, Crowne Plaza, Days Inn EconoLodge, Fairfield Inn, Hampton Inn, Holiday Inn Express MainStay Suites, Motel 6, Red Roof Inn [other] Burlington Coats, **W** [gas] Royal
318	WI 119, **E** [other][food]
317	I-43, I-894 (from wb)
316	I-43 S, I-894 W (I-94 exits left from eb), to Beloit, **E** [gas] Clark/dsl [food] Martino's Hotdogs
314b	Howard Ave, to Milwaukee, **W** to Alverno Coll
314a	Holt Ave, **E** [gas] SP Mart/dsl [food] Applebee's, Arby's, China King Little Caesar's, Starbucks, Subway, Wendy's [other] $General, Family$, Home Depot, Pick'n Save Foods, Sentry Foods, Target, vet **W** [other][H] to Alverno Coll
312b a	Becher St, Mitchell St, Lapham Blvd, **W** [gas] BP, Citgo
311	WI 59, National Ave, 6th St downtown
310a	13th St (from eb), **E** [other][H]
310b	I-43 N, to Green Bay
310c	I-794 E, **E** [lodging] Hilton [other] Lake Michigan Port of Entry, to downtown
309b	26th St, 22nd St, Clybourn St, St Paul Ave, **N** [other][H], to Marquette U
309a	35th St, **N** [other] URGENT CARE
308c b	US 41
308a	VA Ctr, **S** [other] Miller Park
307b	68th-70th St, Hawley Rd
307a	68th-70th St
306	WI 181, to 84th St, **N** [other][H], **S** [other] Olympic Training Facility
305b	I-41 N, US 45 N, to Fond du Lac, **N** [other][H]
305a	I-894 S, I-41 S, US 45 S, to Chicago, **S** [other] to [food]
304b a	WI 100, **N** [gas] 7-11, Amstar/dsl, BP, Shell/dsl [food] Cousins Subs Domino's, Ghengis Khan BBQ, Habanero's Mexican, Honey Baked Cafe, Jimmy John's, Mo's Irish Grill, Peony Chinese, Qdoba, Rococo's, Starbucks, Subway, Taco Bell [lodging] Crowne Plaza Forty Winks Inn [other][H], zoo, **S** [gas] Amstar, BP/dsl, Speedway/dsl [food] Culver's, DQ, Fazoli's, McDonald's, Pallas Rest., Starbucks Toppers Pizza, Wendy's [lodging] Days Inn [other] Aldi Foods, Midas O'Reilly Parts, Sam's Club, U-Haul, Walgreens

INTERSTATE 94 Cont'd

Exit #	Services
301b a	Moorland Rd, N ⛽ BP/dsl, Mobil 🍴 Bakers Square, Bravo Italiano, Buffalo Wild Wings, Chipotle, CiCi's, Cooper's Hawk, Culver's, Five Guys, Fleming's Rest., Food Court, Fuddrucker's, Hooters, Jamba Juice, Jersey Mike's, Marty's Pizza/subs, McDonald's, Mitchell's Fish Mkt, Noodles&Co, Original Pancake House, Qdoba, Red Robin, Starbucks, Stir Crazy, Subway, TGIFriday's 🛏 Courtyard, Sheraton, TownePlace Suites ⬜ AT&T, Barnes&Noble, CVS Drug, F&F Tire, Firestone/auto, Fresh Mkt Foods, Goodyear/auto, JC Penney, Jo-Ann Fabrics, mall, Metro Mkt, Michael's, Office Depot, PetCo, Petsmart, SteinMart, TJ Maxx, Verizon, vet, Walgreens, World Mkt, S 🍴 Champp's Grill, Outback Steaks, Panera Bread, Starbucks 🛏 Best Western Midway, Brookfield Suites, Country Inn&Suites, Residence Inn ⬜ golf, Pick'n Save Foods, Walgreens, Walmart
297	WI 164 S, US 18, rd JJ, Blue Mound Rd, Barker Rd, 0-2 mi N ⛽ BP, Clark 🍴 Applebee's, BoneFish Grill, Boston Mkt, Brookfield Rest., Bullwinkle's Rest., Carrabba's, Chili's, ChuckECheese's, Cousins Subs, Emperors Kitchen, George Webb Rest., Hom Woodfired Grill, Jimmy John's, Jose's Mexican, KFC, Kopp's Custard, Laredo's Mexican, Mama Mia's, McDonald's, Melting Pot, Olive Garden, Perkins, Potbelly, Starbucks, Subway 🛏 DoubleTree, Extended Stay America, Hampton Inn, La Quinta, Motel 6, Quality Inn ⬜ $Tree, Acura, Advance Parts, Aldi Foods, Best Buy, GNC, Hobby Lobby, 🅷, Lexus/Mazda/VW, Meineke, Metro Mkt, S ⛽ Clark, PDQ 🍴 Arby's, Burger King, Chancery Rest., Cousin's Subs, Culver's, Famous Dave's BBQ, La Fuente Mexican, McDonald's, Meiji Chinese, New China, Oscar's Burgers, Papa Murphy's, Sonic, Starbucks, Subway, Taco Bell, Topper's Pizza, TX Roadhouse, Wendy's 🛏 Baymont Inn, Extended Stay America, Super 8 ⬜ AT&T, Buick/GMC, Cadillac, CarMax, Chevrolet, Farm&Fleet, Firestone/auto, Ford, Home Depot, Honda, Hyundai, Infiniti/Maserati/Mercedes/Porsche, Jaguar/Land Rover/Volvo, Kia, Kohl's, Menards, Midas, Nissan, Sam's Club, st patrol, Subaru, Target, Tires+, Walgreens, Woodman's/gas
295	rd F, to WI 74, Waukesha, N ⛽ KwikTrip/dsl 🍴 Jimmy John's 🛏 Marriott, S ⬜ 🅷, to Carroll U
294	WI 164, rd J S, to Waukesha, N ⛽ Mobil/Subway/dsl 🍴 Machine Shed Rest., Thunder Bay Grille 🛏 Holiday Inn, Wildwood Lodge, S ⬜ Expo Ctr, Peterbilt
293c	WI 16 W, Pewaukee (from wb), N ⬜ GE Plant
293b a	rd T, Wausheka, Pewaukee, S ⛽ KwikTrip/dsl, Mobil 🍴 Arby's, Asian Fusion, Canyon City Wood Grill, Cousins Subs, Culver's, Denny's, Dunkin', Feng's Kitchen, Jimmy John's, McDonald's, Mr. Wok, Papa Murphy's, Qdoba, Rococo's Pizza, Spring City Rest., Subway, Taco Amigo, Topper's Pizza, Weissgerber's Gasthaus Rest., Wendy's 🛏 Best Western ⬜ $Tree, AutoZone, CVS Drug, Firestone/auto, GNC, Goodharvest Mkt, Jo-Ann Fabrics, Office Depot, Pick'n Save Foods, Verizon, Walgreens
291	rd G, rd TT, N 🛏 Country Springs Inn
290	rd SS, Pewaukee
287	WI 83, Hartland, to Wales, N 🍴 Applebee's, Five Guys, Hardee's, McDonald's, Noodles&Co, Panera Bread, Perkins, Qdoba, Starbucks, Water St Brewery/rest. 🛏 Country Pride Inn, Holiday Inn Express ⬜ Albrecht's Mkt, Best Buy, GNC, Kohl's, Marshalls, Verizon, Walgreens, S ⛽ BP, PDQ/dsl/24hr 🍴 Burger King, Coldstone, DQ, Jimmy John's, Marty's Pizza, Pacific Asian Bistro, Pizza Hut, Rocky Rococo Pizza, StoneCreek Coffee, Subway 🛏 La Quinta ⬜ $Tree, Ace Hardware, Home Depot, PetCo, Target, Tires+, vet, Walmart/Subway

Exit #	Services
285	rd C, Delafield, N ⛽ BP/dsl, Mobil/deli 🛏 Delafield Hotel ⬜ to St John's Military Academy, S ⬜ to Kettle Moraine SF
283	rd P, to Sawyer Rd
282	WI 67, Dousman, to Oconomowoc, 0-2 mi N ⛽ KwikTrip/dsl, Mobil 🍴 Chili's, Cousins Subs, Culver's, Eat Smart Cafe, Feng's Kitchen, Jimmy John's, Pizza Hut, Qdoba, Quiznos, Rococo's Pizza, Rosati's Pizza, Starbucks, Stone Creek Coffee, Subway 🛏 Hilton Garden, Olympia Resort ⬜ Ace Hardware, Aldi Foods, AT&T, Brennan's Mkt, Ford, GNC, K-Mart, Pick'n Save, vet, Walgreens, S 🛏 Staybridge Suites ⬜ Harley-Davidson, 🅷, Old World WI HS (13mi), to Kettle Moraine SF (8mi)
277	Willow Glen Rd (from eb, no return)
275	rd F, Ixonia, to Sullivan, N ⛽ Mobil/dsl ⬜ Concord Gen Store, S ⬜ camping
267	WI 26, Johnson Creek, to Watertown, N ⛽ BP/McDonald's/dsl, Shell/dsl/rest./scales/24hr 🍴 Arby's, Hi-Way Harry's Cafe 🛏 Comfort Suites, Days Inn ⬜ Goodyear/auto, Johnson Creek Outlet Ctr/famous brands, Old Navy, S ⛽ KwikTrip/dsl 🍴 Culver's, Qdoba, Starbucks, Subway, Taco Bell ⬜ 🅷, Kohl's, Menards, to Aztalan SP
266mm	Rock River
264mm	Ⓡ🅂 wb, full ♿ facilities, 🅲, 🛋, litter barrels, vending, petwalk
263mm	Crawfish River
261mm	Ⓡ🅂 eb, full ♿ facilities, 🅲, 🛋, litter barrels, vending, petwalk
259	WI 89, Lake Mills, to Waterloo, N ⛽ Mobil/rest/dsl/24hr 🛏 Best Value Inn ⬜ truck repair, S ⛽ BP/dsl/E85, KwikTrip/dsl 🍴 Jimmy John's, McDonald's, Pizza Pit, Subway 🛏 Pyramid Motel/RV park ⬜ Ace Hardware, Buick/Chevrolet, Country Campers, to Aztalan SP, URGENT CARE, vet, Walgreens
250	WI 73, Deerfield, to Marshall
244	rd n, Sun Prairie, Cottage Grove, N ⛽ BP/dsl 🍴 Subway, S ⛽ BP/dsl, KwikTrip 🍴 Arby's
240	I-90 E.
I-94 and I-90 run together 93 miles. See I-90, exits 48-138.	
147	I-90 W, to La Crosse, I-94 and I-90 run together 93 miles
143	US 12, WI 21, Tomah, N ⛽ Shell/dsl 🍴 A&W/LJ Silver, Perkins 🛏 AmericInn, Best Western, Microtel, Super 8 ⬜ Humbird Cheese/gifts, U-Haul, S ⛽ BP, KwikTrip/Denny's/dsl/scales/24hr 🍴 Arby's, China Buffet, Culver's, Dunkin', KFC, McDonald's, Papa Murphy's, Pizza Hut, Starbucks, Subway, Taco Bell 🛏 Cranberry Lodge, EconoLodge, Hampton Inn, Quality Inn ⬜ $Tree, Ace Hardware, Advance Parts, Aldi Foods, Burger King, Chrysler/Dodge/Jeep, ECV, Ford, GMC, 🅷, NAPA, O'Reilly Parts, to Ft McCoy (9mi), Verizon, Walmart/Subway
135	rd EW, Warrens, N ⛽ BP/Chesters/dsl 🛏 3 Bears Resort ⬜ Jellystone Camping, S 🍴 Bog Rest.
128	rd O, Millston, N ⬜ Black River SF, camping, S ⛽ Cenex/dsl ⬜ USPO

Map labels: Hixton, Stevens Point, Amherst, De Pere, Green Bay, Denmark, Millston, Plainfield, Appleton, Oshkosh, Sparta, Tomah, Richford, New Lisbon, 90, Fond du Lac, Plymouth, La Valle, Dekorra, West Bend, Baraboo, 39, Watertown, Menomonee Falls, Madison, 94, Milwaukee, New Berlin, Edgerton, Caledonia, Janesville, 43, Dubuque, Beloit

WI

WAUKESHA

TOMAH

WI

🅿 = gas ⑪ = food 🛏 = lodging Ⓞ = other 🆁🆂 = rest stop Copyright 2022 - The Next EXIT

INTERSTATE 94 Cont'd

Exit #	Services
123mm	🆁🆂/scenic view both lanes, full 🚻 facilities, ⓒ, 🖼, litter barrels, vending, petwalk
116	WI 54, N 🅿 Cenex/Subway/Taco Johns/dsl/LP ⑪ Perkins 🛏 AmericInn, Comfort Inn, SureStay Plus/rest. Ⓞ Black River RA, Parkland Camp, S 🅿 ✈FLYING J/Denny's/dsl/24hr/@, Kwik-Trip/dsl ⑪ Arby's, Burger King, Culver's, McDonald's, Oriental Kitchen, Pizza Hut 🛏 Days Inn Ⓞ $General, Buick/Chevrolet/GMC, Walmart/Subway
115mm	Black River
115	US 12, WI 27, Black River Falls, to Merrillan, S 🅿 Holiday/dsl ⑪ Hardee's, KFC, Subway, Sunrise Rest. Ⓞ Ace Hardware, Gordy's Mkt, Harley-Davidson, Ⓗ
105	to WI 95, Hixton, to Alma Center, N 🛏 Motel 95/camping Ⓞ KOA (3mi), S 🅿 Cenex/dsl, Clark/dsl/24hr ⑪ Timber Valley Rest. Ⓞ city park, USPO
98	WI 121, Northfield, Pigeon Falls, to Alma Center, S 🅿 Cenex/dsl Ⓞ auto/truck repair
88	US 10, Osseo, to Fairchild, N 🅿 BP/DQ, TA/Osseo Rest./dsl/scales/24hr ⑪ Hardee's, Moe's Diner 🛏 10-7 Inn, Super 8 Ⓞ Chevrolet, Ford, Stoney Cr RV Park, S 🅿 Speedway/dsl ⑪ McDonald's, Subway, Taco John's 🛏 Osseo Inn Ⓞ Family$, Ⓗ
81	rd HH, rd KK, Foster, S 🅿 Cenex/dsl/LP ⑪ Foster Cheesehaus
70	US 53, Eau Claire, S Ⓞ Gander Outdoors, st police N off Golf Rd 🅿 Holiday/dsl ⑪ Applebee's, Asia Palace, Buffalo Wild Wings, Caribou Coffee, Chipotle, Coldstone, Culver's, Fazoli's, Fired Up Pizza, Firehouse Subs, Fuji Steaks, Grizzly's Grill, HuHot Chinese, Jade Garden, Jimmy John's, Johnny's Italian Steaks, Mancino's, Manny's Grill, McDonald's, Noodles&Co, Olive Garden, Panera Bread, Papa Murphy's, TGIFriday's, TX Roadhouse 🛏 Baymont Inn, Country Inn&Suites, Grandstay, Holiday Inn Ⓞ $Tree, Aldi Foods, AT&T, Bam!, Best Buy, JC Penney, Jo-Ann Fabrics, Kohl's, Menards, Michael's, PetCo, Petsmart, Ross, Sam's Club, Scheel's Sports, Target, TJ Maxx, Tuesday Morning, Verizon, Walmart/Subway, Younkers
68	WI 93, to Eleva, N 🅿 Holiday, KwikTrip/dsl ⑪ Burger King, Cousins Subs, DQ, Famous Dave's BBQ, Great Harvest Bread Co, Hardee's, Red Robin 🛏 EconoLodge Ⓞ BigLots, Chrysler/Dodge/Jeep, Festival Foods, Firestone/auto, Goodyear/auto, Gordy's Mkt, Kia, NAPA, Nissan, Subaru, transmissions, vet, S 🅿 Holiday/dsl 🛏 Metropolis Resort Ⓞ Audi/VW, Ford/Lincoln, Honda, Hyundai
65	WI 37, WI 85, Eau Claire, to Mondovi, N 🅿 Holiday/dsl, Kwik-Trip/dsl ⑪ Arby's, China Buffet, Godfather's Pizza, Green Mill Rest., Hardee's, Jimmy John's, Mancino's, McDonald's, Pizza Hut, Randy's Rest., Red Lobster, Starbucks, Subway, Taco Bell, Wendy's 🛏 Best Value Inn, Best Western, Clarion, Hampton Inn, Motel 6, Plaza Hotel, Quality Inn, Scottish Inn, Super 8 Ⓞ Adams Automotive, Gordy's Mkt, Ⓗ, Verizon, Walgreens, S Ⓞ tires
64mm	Chippewa River
59	to US 12, rd EE, to Eau Claire, N 🅿 Holiday/Burger King/dsl/24hr, Holiday/Subway/dsl/24hr ⑪ Dana's Grill, McDonald's, North Crossing Rest. 🛏 AmericInn, Days Inn, Knights Inn Ⓞ Freightliner, Ⓗ, Mack/Volvo Trucks, Peterbilt, S Ⓞ dsl repair
52	US 12, WI 29, WI 40, Elk Mound, to Chippewa Falls, S 🅿 U-Fuel/e85
49mm	weigh sta wb
45	rd B, Menomonie, N 🅿 Cenex/Subway/dsl/scales/24hr, 🔴Loves/Hardee's/dsl/scales/24hr ⑪ Exit 45 Rest., S 🅿 KwikTrip/dsl/scales/24hr ⑪ Cantinas Grill 🛏 Quality Inn Ⓞ Ⓗ, Kenworth/dsl repair, truckwash, Walmart Dist Ctr

Exit #	Services
44mm	Red Cedar River
43mm	🆁🆂 both lanes, full 🚻 facilities, ⓒ, 🖼, litter barrels, vending, petwalk, weather info
41	WI 25, Menomonie, N 🅿 Cenex/Dunkin'/E85 ⑪ Applebee', Caribou Coffee, China Buffet, Los Cabos Mexican, Menomine Rest., Papa Murphy's, Pizza Hut, Subway Ⓞ Aldi Foods, AT& Twin Springs Camping, Walmart/Subway, S 🅿 F&F/dsl, Holida Speedway/dsl ⑪ Arby's, Denny's, Dickey's BBQ, Jimmy John' Little Caesar's, McDonald's, Perkins, Starbucks, Taco Bell, Tac John's, Wendy's 🛏 AmericInn, Best Western+, Hampton Inn Motel 6, Super 8 Ⓞ $Tree, Advance Parts, Buick/GMC, Che rolet, Chrysler/Dodge/Jeep, Ford, Ⓗ, Mkt Place Foods, O'Reil Parts, Tesla EVC, to Red Cedar St Tr, Verizon, Walgreens
32	rd Q, to Knapp
28	WI 128, Wilson, Elmwood, to Glenwood City, N 🅿 KwikTrip Denny's/dsl/24hr, S Ⓞ camping, dsl repair, Eau Galle RA
24	rd B, to Baldwin, N 🅿 BP 🛏 Woodville Motel Ⓞ $General, S 🅿 camping, Eau Galle RA
19	US 63, Baldwin, to Ellsworth, N 🅿 Freedom/dsl, KwikTrip/Sub way/dsl ⑪ A&W, Culver's, DQ, Hardee's, McDonald's 🛏 Col blestone Ⓞ Ⓗ, S 🛏 Baymont Ⓞ fireworks
16	rd T, Hammond
10	WI 65, Roberts, to New Richmond, N 🅿 BP/dsl (2mi), ✈FLYING McDonald's/dsl/scales/24hr ⑪ Barnboard Rest. (2mi), S 🅿 Freightliner
8mm	weigh sta eb
4	US 12, rd U, Somerset, N 🅿 Holiday/dsl, TA/Country Pride/ds scales/24hr/@ 🛏 Regency Inn Ⓞ to Willow River SP, vet
3	WI 35 S, to River Falls, S Ⓞ U of WI River Falls
2	rd F, Carmichael Rd, Hudson, N 🅿 BP/repair, Freedom/dsl, Ho iday ⑪ Applebee's, Caribou Coffee, Culver's, Domino's, Fiest Loca, Jimmy John's, KFC, Papa Murphy's, Taco John's 🛏 Roy Inn Ⓞ $Tree, Family Fresh Foods, GNC, repair, Target, Verizo Walgreens, S 🅿 F&F/dsl, Holiday/dsl, KwikTrip/dsl, Shell ⑪ Arby's, Buffalo Wild Wings, Burger King, Caribou Coffee, Ch potle Mexican, Coldstone, Denny's, Five Guys, Green Mill Res Jersey Mike's, Kingdom Buffet, Kirin Ichiban, Leeann`Chin, Li tle Caesar's, McDonald's, Noodles&Co, Panda Express, Pane Bread, Perkins, Pita Pit, Pizza Hut, Popeye's, Sapporo Japanes Smashburger, Starbucks, Subway, Taco Bell, Wendy's 🛏 Am ericInn, Best Western/Tesla EVC, Comfort Suites, Hampton In Hudson House Hotel, Quality Inn, Super 8 Ⓞ Aldi Foods, AT& AutoZone, Chevrolet/GMC, Chrysler/Dodge/Jeep, County M Foods, Ford, Home Depot, Ⓗ, Menards, NAPA, O'Reilly Part TirePros, Tires+, to Kinnickinnic SP, USPO, Verizon, Walmart
1	WI 35 N, Hudson, 1 mi N 🅿 Freedom/dsl, Holiday ⑪ Carbone Pizzeria, DQ
0mm	Wisconsin/Minnesota state line, St Croix River

MENOMONIE

HUDSON

WI

EAU CLAIRE

NOTES

WYOMING

⬛N INTERSTATE 25

Exit #	Services
300	I-90, E to Gillette, W to Billings. **I-25 begins/ends on I-90, exit 56.**
299	US 16, Buffalo, **E** 🅖 Exxon/dsl, Maverik/dsl 🅕 Winchester Steaks 🅐 Buffalo Inn, Hampton Inn, Holiday Inn Express, SureStay 🅞 Bighorn Tire, Deer Park Camping, KOA, vet, **W** 🅖 Cenex/dsl/24hr 🅕 Bozeman Tr Steaks, Dash Inn Rest., Domino's, Hardee's, McDonald's, Pizza Hut, Sub Shop, Subway, Taco John's 🅐 Alamo Inn, Days Inn, Quality Inn, Rodeway WYO Motel, Super 8 🅞 Ace Hardware, Family$, 🅗, Indian RV Camp, O'Reilly Parts, to Yellowstone
298	US 87, Buffalo, **W** Nat Hist Dist Info
291	Trabing Rd
280	Middle Fork Rd
274mm	parking area both lanes, litter barrels
265	Reno Rd
254	Kaycee, **E** 🅖 Exxon/dsl 🅕 Country Inn Diner, Invasion Rest. 🅐 Cassidy Inn Motel, Siesta Motel 🅞 Kaycee Gen. Store, museum, NAPA Repair, Powder River RV Park, USPO, **W** 🅡ˢ both lanes, full 🅰 facilities, 🄲, 🛆, litter barrels, petwalk 🅖 Sinclair/pizza/subs/dsl/LP/motel 🅞 KC RV Park
249	TTT Rd
246	Powder River Rd
235	Tisdale Mtn Rd
227	WY 387 N, Midwest, Edgerton Oil Field Museum
223	no service
219mm	parking area both lanes
216	Ranch Rd
210	Horse Ranch Creek Rd, Midwest, Edgerton
197	Ormsby Rd
191	Wardwell Rd, to Bar Nunn, **W** 🅖 Loaf'N Jug/dsl 🅞 KOA
189	US 20, US 26 W, to Shoshone, **W** 🅞 🚢 Port of Entry
188b	WY 220, Poplar St, **E** 🅕 McDonald's, The Fort Eatery 🅐 Hampton Inn, Hilton Garden, La Quinta, Motel 6, Quality Inn, Ramkota Hotel, **W** 🅖 Exxon 🅕 Burger King, Casper's Rest., DQ 🅞 Harley-Davidson, to Ft Casper HS
188a	Center St, Casper, **E** 🅖 Conoco/dsl, Shell/dsl 🅕 Taco John's 🅐 National 9 Inn, Ramada, **W** 🅕 La Cocina, Starbucks, Subway 🅐 Days Inn, Parkway Plaza Motel/cafe 🅞 USPO
187	McKinley St, Casper, **E** 🅐 Ranch House Motel
186	US 20, US 26, US 87, Yellowstone St, **E** 🅞 city park, dsl repair, transmissions/repair, **W** 🅖 Exxon 🅞 auto repair, Chevrolet/Subaru, 🅗, Kia, O'Reilly Parts
185	WY 258, Wyoming Blvd, E Casper, **E** 🅖 Kum&Go/dsl, Loaf'n Jug/dsl 🅕 Applebee's, IHOP, Outback Steaks, Southern BBQ HQ, TX Roadhouse 🅐 Baymont Inn, C'mon Inn, Comfort Inn, Super 8 🅞 Murdoch's Ranch Store, Smith RV Ctr, vet, **W** 🅖 ⭐FLYING J/Conoco/Subway/dsl/LP/scales/24hr, Exxon/dsl 🅕 Arby's, Buffalo Wild Wings, Burger King, Denny's, DQ, Five Guys, Hamburger Stand, Hardee's, KFC/LJ Silver, Koto Japanese,

185	Continued McDonald's, Mongolian Grill, Old Chicago Grill, Olive Garden, On The Border, Perkins, Pizza Hut, Pizza Ranch, Qdoba, Red Lobster, Sanford's Cafe, Starbucks, Taco Bell, Taco John's, Village Inn, Wendy's 🅐 Candlewood Suites, Courtyard, Holiday Inn Express, Rodeway Inn 🅞 AutoZone, Best Buy, Dick's, Home Depot, JC Penney, Macy's, Natural Grocers, Nissan, PetCo, Plains Tire, Ridley's Foods/dsl, Ross, Sam's Club/gas, Staples, Target, to Oregon Tr, Verizon, Walgreens, Walmart
182	WY 253, Brooks Rd, Hat Six Rd, **E** 🅖 Sinclair/Lou's Rest/dsl 🅕 Sonic 🅐 Sleep Inn 🅞 Rivers Edge Camping, to Wilkins SP, **W** 🅕 FireRock Rest., Keg&Cork Rest., Subway, Wyo Aleworks 🅐 Best Western+, Holiday Inn, Mainstay Suites 🅞 Buick/Cadillac/GMC, Chrysler/Dodge/Jeep, 🅗, Kohl's, Marshall's, Menards, Petsmart, Toyota, Verizon, VW
171mm	parking area both lanes
165	Glenrock, **E** same as 160, dinosaur museum
160	US 87, US 20, US 26, E Glenrock, **E** 🅞 Deer Creek Village Camping, to Johnston Power Plant
156	Bixby Rd
154	Barber Rd
153mm	parking area both lanes
151	Natural Bridge
150	Inez Rd
146	La Prele Rd
140	WY 59, Douglas, **E** 🅖 Conoco/Subway/dsl, Maverik/dsl, Shell/dsl 🅕 Arby's, La Costa Mexican, McDonald's, Taco John's 🅐 Douglas Inn, Hampton Inn, Holiday Inn Express, Sleep Inn, Super 8 🅞 city park, 🅗, KOA, Lone Tree Village RV Park, Pioneer Museum, WY St Fair
135	US 20, US 26, US 87, Douglas, **E** 🅖 Juanita's/dsl, Loaf'n Jug/dsl, Sinclair/rest./dsl/24hr 🅕 4 Seasons Chinese, Pizza Hut, Plains Trading Post Rest., Starbucks, Village Inn 🅐 1st Interstate Inn, 4 Winds Motel, Budget Inn Express, Plains Motel

Side labels: BUFFALO · CASPER · DOUGLAS

INTERSTATE 25 Cont'd

135	Continued
	Ⓞ Douglas Hardware, Family$, Ⓗ, O'Reilly Parts, repair, Safeway Foods/dsl, Verizon
129mm	**parking area both lanes**
126	US 18, US 20 E, Orin, **E** Orin Jct Rest Area both lanes, full Ⓐ facilities, Ⓒ, Ⓐ, litter barrels, petwalk, RV dump Ⓕ Sinclair/Orin Jct Trkstp/dsl/café
125mm	N Platte River
111	Glendo, **E** Ⓕ Sinclair/dsl Ⓕ Glendo Marina Café Ⓞ Glendo Lakeside RV camping, to Glendo SP, USPO
104	to Middle Bear
100	Cassa Rd, **W** Ⓞ RV Park
94	El Rancho Rd
92	US 26 E, Dwyer, **E** Ⓡˢ both lanes, full Ⓐ facilities, Ⓐ litter barrel, petwalk, RV dump, Ft Laramie NHS, to Guernsey SP
87	Johnson Rd
84	Laramie River Rd
84mm	Laramie River
80	US 87, Laramie Power Sta, Wheatland, Laramie Power Sta, **E** Ⓕ Sinclair/A&W/Chester's/dsl, Tesla EVC Ⓕ Pizza Hut Ⓛ Best Western, Heartland Inn, Super 8 Ⓞ Arrowhead RV Park, Buick/Cadillac/Chevrolet, CarQuest, Chrysler/Dodge/Jeep, Family$, Ford, museum, O'Reilly Parts, Safeway Foods, same as 78
78	US 87, Wheatland, **E** Ⓕ Conoco/dsl, FVC/dsl, Maverik/dsl Ⓕ Arby's, Burger King, Subway, Taco John's, Western Sky's Diner Ⓛ Motel 6, West Winds Motel, WY Motel Ⓞ Ⓗ, visitors ctr, Wheatland Country Store, **W** Ⓕ Exxon/dsl, Sinclair/dsl Ⓞ Mtn View RV Park
73	WY 34 W, to Laramie
70	Bordeaux Rd
68	Antelope Rd
66	Hunton Rd
65.5mm	**parking area both lanes**
65	Slater Rd
64mm	Richeau Creek
57	TY Basin Rd, Chugwater
54	Lp 25, Chugwater, **E** Ⓡˢ both lanes, full Ⓐ facilities, litter barrels, petwalk, Ⓒ, Ⓐ, RV camping, RV dump, Ⓕ Chugwater Gas&Go/dsl Ⓛ Buffalo Lodge/Grill
47	Bear Creek Rd
39	Little Bear Community
36mm	Little Bear Creek
34	Nimmo Rd
33mm	Horse Creek
29	Whitaker Rd
25	ranch exit
21	Ridley Rd
17	US 85 N, to Torrington, **W** Ⓕ Little Bear Rest. (2mi)
16	WY 211, Horse Creek Rd
13	Vandehei Ave, **E** Ⓕ Loaf'n Jug/Subway, Maverik/dsl Ⓕ Mr Jim's Pizza, Silvermine Subs, **W** Ⓕ Sinclair/dsl
12	Central Ave, Cheyenne, **E** Ⓕ Exxon/dsl, Loaf'n Jug Ⓕ Arby's, Godfather's, McDonald's, Pizza Hut, Starbucks, Subway, Taco John's Ⓛ Hampton Inn, Rodeway Inn Ⓞ Albertsons, Big O Tire, Frontier Days Park, Ⓗ
11b	Warren AFB, Gate 1, Randall Ave, **E** Ⓞ museum, to WY St Capitol
10b d	Warren AFB, Gate 2, Missile Dr, WY 210, HappyJack Rd, **W** Ⓞ to Curt Gowdy SP
9	US 30, W Lincolnway, Cheyenne, **E** Ⓕ Exxon/Downhome Diner/dsl Ⓕ Outback Steaks Ⓛ Best Value Inn, Candlewood Suites,

9	Continued
	Days Inn, Fairfield Inn, Holiday Inn Express, La Quinta, Luxury Inn, Motel 6, My Place, Super 8, SureStay+, Towne Place Suit Ⓞ Buick/Cadillac/GMC, Chevrolet, Ford/Lincoln, Home Dep Honda, Hyundai, Nissan, Subaru, Toyota, **W** Ⓕ Little Americ Sinclair/dsl/rest./motel/@
8d b	I-80, E to Omaha, W to Laramie
7	WY 212, College Dr, **E** Ⓕ ♥Loves/Wendy's/d scales/24hr/@, Sinclair/Subway/dsl/24hr Ⓕ Arby's Ⓞ A-B Park (2mi), **W** Ⓕ ⊕FLYING J/Denny's/dsl/LP/scales/24hr/@ Ⓕ McDonald's Ⓛ Quality Inn Ⓞ Blue Beacon, truck repair
6.5mm	Port of Entry nb
4	High Plains Rd, **WY Welcome Ctr, rest/info ctr, both lanes,** Ⓐ facilities, Ⓒ, Ⓐ, litter barrels, petwalk
2	WY 223, Terry Ranch Rd, 2 mi **E** Ⓞ Terry Bison Ranch camping
0mm	Wyoming/Colorado state line

INTERSTATE 80

Exit #	Services
402mm	Wyoming/Nebraska State line
401	WY 215, Pine Bluffs, **N** Ⓕ Exxon/Subway/dsl, Sinclair/A&W dsl/24hr/@ Ⓕ Cafe 307, Rock Ranch Grill Ⓛ Gator's Motel NAPA, Pine Bluff RV Park, USPO, **S** Welcome Ctr/Ⓡˢ both lan full Ⓐ facilities, info, Ⓒ, playground, nature trail, Ⓐ, lit barrels, petwalk
391	Egbert
386	WY 213, WY 214, Burns, **N** Ⓕ Antelope Trkstp/dsl/cafe
377	WY 217, Hillsdale, **N** Ⓕ TA/Burger King/Taco Bell/d scales/24hr/@ Ⓞ Wyo RV Camping
372mm	Port of Entry wb, **truck insp**
370	US 30 W, Archer, **N** Ⓕ Sapp Bros/T-Joe's Rest./dsl/scales/24hr Ⓛ Rodeway Inn Ⓞ fireworks, repair, RV park
367	Campstool Rd, **N** Ⓕ ♦Pilot♦/Subway/dsl/scales/24hr Ⓛ B Western+ Ⓞ KOA (seasonal), Volvo Trucks, **S** Ⓞ to Wyomi Hereford Ranch
364	WY 212, to E Lincolnway, Cheyenne, **N** Ⓞ Walmart/dsl, **S** Ⓞ Camping (4mi), Peterbilt, **1-2 mi N on Lincolnway** Ⓕ Exxon/c Kum&Go/dsl, Loaf'n Jug/Subway Ⓕ Burger King, KFC, McDc ald's, Shari's Rest., Subway, Taco Bell, Wendy's Ⓞ $Tree, A toZone, Big O Tire, BigLots, Family$, Harley-Davidson, Hob Lobby, Ⓗ, Murdoch's Ranch Store, O'Reilly Parts, Sierra Tradi Post, Walgreens
362	US 85, I-180, to Central Ave, Cheyenne, Greeley, **1 mi N** Ⓕ Kum&Go/dsl Ⓕ Arby's, Carls' Jr, Hacienda Mexican, Jim John's, Papa John's, Village Inn Ⓞ CarQuest, Family$, Ⓗ, n seum, st capitol, Verizon, **S** Ⓕ Exxon/dsl, Loaf'n Jug/dsl, S clair/dsl Ⓕ Burger King, Little Caesar's, Pizza Hut, Sonic, Su way, Taco John's Ⓛ Comfort Inn, Holiday Inn, Roundup Mot SpringHill Suites Ⓞ AutoZone, Family$, Hideaway RV Villag Safeway Foods/gas, transmissions
359c a	I-25, US 87, N to Casper, S to Denver
358	US 30, W Lincolnway, Cheyenne, **N** Ⓕ Exxon/dsl/24hr, Lit America/Sinclair/dsl/motel/@ Ⓕ Outback Steaks Ⓛ Best Val Inn, Candlewood Suites, Days Inn, Fairfield Inn, Hampton I Holiday Inn Express, La Quinta, Luxury Inn, Motel 6, My Pla Inn, Super 8, TownPlace Suites Ⓞ Buick/GMC/Cadillac, Che rolet, Ford/Lincoln, Home Depot, Honda, Ⓗ, Hyundai, Maz Nissan, Subaru, Toyota
357	Wy 222, Roundtop Rd

↑E	**INTERSTATE 80 Cont'd**
Exit #	**Services**
348	Otto Rd
345	Warren Rd, **N truck parking**
342	Harriman Rd
339	Remount Rd
335	Buford, **S**🅖 Phin Deli/dsl
333mm	**parking area both lanes**, point of interest
329	Vedeauwoo Rd, **N** camping, **S** to Ames Monument, Nat Forest RA
323	WY 210, Happy Jack Rd, **N**🆁🆂 **both lanes, full** ♿ **facilities**, 🅒, 🏠, **litter barrels, petwalk**, 🅞 Lincoln Monument, elev. 8640, to Curt Gowdy SP
322mm	**chain up area both lanes**
316	US 30 W, Grand Ave, Laramie, **0-2 mi N**🅖 Exxon/dsl, Loaf'N Jug, USA Gas 🅕 Almanza's Mexican, Applebee's, Arby's, Burger King, Chili's, Dickey's BBQ, Hong Kong Buffet, Jimmy John's, Luciano's Italian, McAlister's Deli, McDonald's, Mr Jim's Pizza, Papa Murphy's, Perkins, Sonic, Starbucks, Subway, Taco Bell, Taco John's, Village Inn, Wendy's 🏠 AmericInn, Hampton Inn, Hilton Garden, Holiday Inn, Quality Inn 🅞 $Tree, AT&T, Buick/Chevrolet/GMC, Ford/Lincoln, GNC, 🅗, Ridley's Mkt, to UW, Toyota, URGENT CARE, Verizon, Walgreens, Walmart/Subway
313	US 287, to 3rd St, Laramie, Port of Entry, **N**🅖 Exxon, GasaMat, Loaf'N Jug, Phillips 66/dsl, Shell/dsl 🅕 Chuck Wagon Rest., Corona Village Mexican, Qdoba 🏠 Laramie Valley Inn, Motel 8, Sunset Inn 🅞 Honda, 🅗, Laramie Plains Museum, NAPA, Nissan, **S**🅖 Motel 6, Ramada Inn 🅞 USPO
312mm	Laramie River
311	WY 130, WY 230, Snowy Range Rd, Laramie, **N**🏠 WY Terr Park, **S**🅖 Conoco/dsl, Exxon/Chester's/Papa John's/dsl, Phillips 66/dsl 🅕 McDonald's, Subway 🏠 Best Value Inn, repair/tires, to Snowy Range Ski Area
310	Curtis St, Laramie, **N** 🅖 🅛Loves🅛/Carl's Jr/Subway/dsl/scales/24hr/@, 🅟Pilot🅟/Wendy's/dsl/scales/24hr/@ 🏠 Best Western, Days Inn, EconoLodge, Super 8 🅞 🅗, KOA, repair, **S**🅖 Blue Beacon, Petro/Iron Skillet/dsl/scales/24hr/@ 🏠 Comfort Inn, Fairfield Inn 🅞 Chrysler/Dodge/Jeep
307mm	**parking area both lanes**
297	WY 12, Herrick Lane
290	Quealy Dome Rd, **S**🅖 A&C Truckstop/dsl
279	Cooper Cove Rd
272mm	Rock Creek
272	WY 13, to Arlington, **N** gas, RV camping
267	🆁🆂 **both lanes, full facilities**
262mm	**parking area both lanes**
260	CR 402
259mm	E Fork Medicine Bow River
257mm	Medicine Bow River
255	WY 72, Elk Mtn, to Hanna, **N**🅖 Conoco/dsl, **S**🏠 Elk Mtn Hotel/rest
238	Peterson Rd
235	WY 130, S US 30/87, **N**🅖 Shell/dsl
229mm	N Platte River
228	🆁🆂 **both lanes**, 🏠, **litter barrels, petwalk**
221	E Sinclair, **N**🅖 Sinclair/rest/dsl/24hr 🅞 camping, to Seminoe SP
219	W Sinclair, **N**🅞 camping, to Seminoe SP
215	Cedar St, Rawlins, **N** 🅖 Conoco/dsl, KFC/Taco Bell, Sinclair/dsl 🅕 Asian Bistro, Burger King, McDonald's, Penny's Diner, Pizza Hut, Subway, Taco John's 🏠 1st Choice Inn, Comfort Inn,

215	Continued
	Econolodge, Fairfield Inn, Hampton Inn, Holiday Inn Express, Magnuson Inn, OakTree Inn, Rawlings Western Lodge 🅞 Bomgaars, Buick/Chevrolet/GMC, CarQuest, Chrysler/Dodge/Jeep, City Mkt/dsl, Do-It Hardware, Frontier Prison NHS, museum, O'Reilly Parts, to Yellowstone/Teton NP, Walmart/dsl
214	Higley Blvd, Rawlins, **N**🅖 Microtel 🅞 KOA, **S**🅖 TA/Conoco/Subway/dsl/scales/24hr/@ 🏠 Best Value Inn
211	WY 789, to US 287 N, Spruce St, Rawlins, **N**🅖 Conoco/dsl, Exxon/dsl, Loaf'n Jug, Sinclair/dsl 🅕 Cappy's Rest., Four Season Rest. 🏠 Best Western, Express Inn, La Bella, Motel 7, Rodeway Inn, Super 8, Travelodge 🅞 Family$, 🅗, Red Desert Rose Camping, V1/LP, Verizon
209	Johnson Rd, **N**🅖 ⚡FLYING J/Denny's/dsl/LP/scales/24hr
206	Hadsell Rd (no return)
205.5mm	continental divide, elev 7000
204	Knobs Rd
201	Daley Rd
196	Riner Rd
190mm	**parking area wb, litter barrels**
189mm	**parking area eb,** 🏠, **litter barrels**
187	WY 789, Creston, Baggs Rd
184	Continental Divide Rd
173	Wamsutter, **N** 🅖 🅛Loves🅛/Chester's/Subway/dsl/24hr/@, **S** 🅖 Conoco/dsl/repair/café/24hr 🅕 Broadway Café, Southern Comfort Cafe 🏠 Wamsutter Motel
165	Red Desert
158	Tipton Rd continental divide, elev 6930
156	GL Rd
154	BLM Rd
152	Bar X Rd
150	Table Rock Rd
146	Patrick Draw Rd
144mm	🆁🆂 **both lanes, full** ♿ **facilities**, 🅒, 🏠, **litter barrels, petwalk**
143mm	**parking area both lanes, litter barrels**
142	Bitter Creek Rd
139	Red Hill Rd
136	Black Butte Rd
133mm	**parking area both lanes**
130	Point of Rocks, **N**🅖 Conoco/dsl 🅞 RV Park
122	WY 371, to Superior
111	Airport Rd, Baxter Rd, **S**🏠
107	Pilot Butte Ave, Rock Springs, **S**🅖 Kum&Go/dsl/e85, Sinclair/dsl 🅕 Pizza Hut 🏠 Sands Inn/cafe, Springs Motel
104	US 191 N, Elk St, Rock Springs, **N**🅖 ⚡FLYING J/Denny's/dsl/LP/24hr, Chevron/dsl/24hr, Conoco/dsl, Exxon, Kum&Go/dsl/e85, Mobil/dsl 🅕 McDonald's, Pasta Veloce, Renegade Rest.,

Left margin vertical: **LARAMIE**

Right margin vertical: **RAWLINS** ... **ROCK SPGS**

📻 = gas ⑪ = food 🛏 = lodging ⊙ = other 🆁 = rest stop   Copyright 2022 - The Next EXIT

INTERSTATE 80 Cont'd

ROCK SPGS

Exit	Services
104	Continued
	Santa Fe SW Grill, Subway, Taco Time 🛏 Best Western, EconoLodge/rest. ⊙ Buick/GMC, to Teton/Yellowstone Nat Parks via US 191, truck repair, **S** 📻 Exxon/dsl 🛏 Days Inn
103	College Dr, Rock Springs, **S** 📻 Loaf'n Jug/dsl ⑪ Domino's ⊙ 🄷, W WY Coll
102	WY 430, Dewar Dr, Rock Springs, **N** 📻 Exxon, Loaf'N Jug/dsl, Sinclair/dsl, Tesla EVC ⑪ Applebee's, KFC/LJ Silver, Sapporo Japanese, Taco Time 🛏 Baymont Inn, Clarion, Comfort Inn, Motel 6 ⊙ $Tree, Cadillac/Chevrolet, Chrysler/Dodge, Herberger's, Home Depot, JC Penney, Jo-Ann, Murdoch's, Petco, Ross, Smith's Foods, TJ Maxx, **S** 📻 Dickey's BBQ, Kum&Go/dsl, Loaf'N Jug/dsl, Sinclair/dsl ⑪ Arby's, Bonsai Chinese, Burger King, Cafe Rio, Chopstix Chinese, Dickey's BBQ, Golden Corral, IHOP, Jimmy John's, Little Caesar's, McDonald's, Papa Murphy's, Pizza Hut, Quizno's, Sonic, Starbucks, Subway, Taco Bell, Village Inn, Wendy's, Winger's, Wonderful House Chinese 🛏 Hampton Inn, Holiday Inn, Holiday Inn Express, Homewood Suites, Motel 8, My Place, Quality Inn, Super 8, Western Inn ⊙ Albertsons/Sav-on, AutoZone, Big O Tire, Family$, Ford/ Lincoln, 🄷, NAPA, Nissan, O'Reilly Parts, Staples, Verizon, Walgreens, Walmart/Subway
100	new exit
99	US 191 S, E Flaming Gorge Rd, **N** ⊙ KOA (1mi), **S** 📻 Shell/ A&W/dsl/24hr/@ ⑪ Log Inn Rest., Ted's Rest. ⊙ fireworks, truck repair
94mm	Kissing Rock

GREEN RIVER

Exit	Services
91	US 30, to WY 530, Green River, **2 mi S** 📻 Loaf'N Jug/dsl, Maverik/dsl ⑪ Arctic Circle, McDonald's, Pizza Hut, Subway, Taco Time 🛏 Coachman Inn, Mustang Inn, Super 8 ⊙ Expedition NHS, Family$, same as 89, to Flaming Gorge NRA
89	US 30, Green River, **S** 📻 Exxon/dsl ⑪ Penny's Diner, Pizza Hut, Staci Ann's Cafe 🛏 Hampton Inn, OakTree Inn, Super 8, Western Inn ⊙ Adam's RV Service, The Travel Camp, to Flaming Gorge NRA
87.5mm	Green River
85	Covered Wagon Rd, **S** 📻 ♥Loves/Carl's Jr/Speedco/dsl/ scales/24hr ⊙ Adams RV parts/service, The Travel Camp
83	WY 372, La Barge Rd, **N** to Fontenelle Dam
78	(from wb)
77mm	Blacks Fork River
72	Westvaco Rd
71mm	**parking area both lanes**
68	Little America, **N** 📻 Sinclair/Little America Hotel/rest./dsl/24hr/@ ⊙ RV camping
66	US 30 W, to Teton, Yellowstone, Fossil Butte NM, Kemmerer
61	Cedar Mt Rd, to Granger
60mm	**parking area both lanes**
53	Church Butte Rd
49mm	**parking area wb**
48	Lp 80, Lyman, Ft Bridger, Hist Ft Bridger
45mm	Blacks Fork River
41	WY 413, Lyman, **N** 📻 Gas'n Go/cafe/dsl, **S** 🆁 both lanes, full 🚻 facilities, [C], 🅿, litter barrels, petwalk, ⑪ Taco Time ⊙ Gateway Inn (2mi), KOA (1mi)
39	WY 412, WY 414, to Carter, Mountain View
34	Lp 80, to Ft Bridger, **S** 🛏 Wagon Wheel Motel ⊙ Ft Bridger NHS, Ft Bridger RV Camp, to Flaming Gorge NRA
33.5mm	**parking area eb**

EVANSTON

Exit	Services
33	Union Rd
30	Bigelow Rd, **N** 📻 TA/Shell/Burger King/Taco Bell/Fork In the Road/dsl/scales/24hr/@, **S** fireworks
28	French Rd
28mm	French Rd, **parking area both lanes**
24	Leroy Rd
23	Bar Hat Rd
21	Coal Rd
18	US 189 N, to Kemmerer, to Nat Parks Fossil Butte NM
15	Guild Rd (from eb)
14mm	**parking area both lanes**
13	Divide Rd
10	Painter Rd, to Eagle Rock Ski Area
6	US 189, Bear River Dr, Evanston, **N** 📻 [Maverik]/Subway/dsl/ scales/24hr, Shell/dsl ⑪ Don Pedro's Mexican, Jody's Dine, Thai Won 🛏 Grizzly Inn, Motel 6, Prairie Inn, Travelodge ⊙ Phillips RV Park, repair/tires, truck wash, Wyo Downs Race track (10mi), **S** Welcome Ctr both lanes, full 🚻 facilities, [C], 🅿, litter barrels, petwalk, RV dump (seasonal), playground, Bear River SP
5	WY 89, Evanston, **N** 📻 Chevron/Taco Time/dsl, Maverik/dsl ⑪ Arby's, Costa Vida, DragonWall Chinese, Jimmy John's, McDonald's, Papa Murphy's, Subway, Wendy's 🛏 EconoLodge ⊙ $Tree, AutoZone, Chevrolet, GNC, 🄷, Jiffy Lube, Murdoch', NAPA, O'Reilly Parts, Verizon, Walmart/Subway, **S** ⊙ WY St 🄷
3	US 189, Harrison Dr, Evanston, **N** 📻 ⊘FLYING J/Subway/dsl/ scales/24hr, Chevron/dsl, Shell, Sinclair, Tesla EVC ⑪ JB's, Lotty's Rest., TC's Rest., Wally's Burgers 🛏 Best Western/rest, Comfort Inn, Days Inn, Hampton Inn, HillCrest Motel, Holiday Inn Express, Howard Johnson, Quality Inn, Super 8 ⊙ Chrysler/ Dodge/Jeep, USPO, **S** ⑪ KFC/Taco Bell ⊙ fireworks, 🄷
.5mm	Port of Entry eb, **weigh sta wb**
0mm	Wyoming/Utah state line

INTERSTATE 90

SUNDANCE

Exit #	Services
207mm	Wyoming/South Dakota state line
205	Beulah, **N** 📻 Sinclair/dsl/LP ⑪ Buffalo Jump Rest. 🛏 Sand Creek Trading Post/gas/cafe ⊙ Beulah Campground, USPO, Ranch A NHP (5mi)
204.5mm	Sand Creek
199	WY 111, to Aladdin, **N** Welcome ctr/🆁 (both directions), full 🚻 facilities, 🅿, litter barrels, [C], petwalk, to Devil's Tower NM, to Vore Buffalo Jump NHP (2mi),
191	Moskee Rd
189	US 14 W, Sundance, **N** 📻 Conoco/dsl/24hr 🛏 Best Western ⊙ 🄷, Mt View Camping, museum, to Devil's Tower NM, **S** 🆁 both lanes, full 🚻 facilities, info, [C], 🅿, litter barrels, playground, petwalk, RV dump, port of entry/**weigh sta**
187	WY 585, Sundance, **N** 📻 Fresh Start/dsl, Sinclair/dsl, Yeswa 🛏 Bear Lodge, Best Western, Budget Host Arrowhead, Dec Lodge ⊙ auto repair, Decker's Foods, 🄷, museum, NAPA, Devil's Tower
185	to WY 116, to Sundance, **S** 📻 Conoco/dsl, same as 187
178	Coal Divide Rd
177mm	**parking area both lanes**
172	Inyan Kara Rd
171mm	**parking area both lanes, litter barrels**
165	Pine Ridge Rd, to Pine Haven, **N** to Keyhole SP, Cedar Ridge R Park (10mi)

� INTERSTATE 90 Cont'd

Exit #	Services
163mm	parking area both lanes
160	Wind Creek Rd
154	US 14, US 16, **S** 🅶 Sinclair/dsl 🍴 Donna's Diner, Subway 🛏 Cozy Motel, Moorcourt Motel, Rangeland Motel/RV Park, Wyo Motel 🅾 city park, Diehl's Foods/gas, museum, USPO
153	US 16 E, US 14, W Moorcroft, **N** 🆁🆂 both lanes, full ♿ facilities, ☎, 📷, litter barrels, petwalk, **S** same as 154
152mm	Belle Fourche River
141	Rozet, **S** 🅾 All Seasons RV Park (3.5mi)
138mm	parking area both lanes
132	Wyodak Rd
129	Garner Lake Rd, **S** 🛏 Arbuckle Lodge 🅾 auto repair, Crazy Woman Camping (3mi), Harley-Davidson, High Plains Camping
128	US 14, US 16, Gillette, **N** 🅶 Kum&Go, Maverik/dsl, MG Oil/dsl, Sinclair/Papa John's/dsl 🍴 Mona's American/Mexican, Taco John's, Village Inn 🛏 Howard Johnson, Mustang Motel, National 9 Inn, Quality Inn 🅾 Crazy Woman Camping (2mi), East Side RV Ctr., Port of Entry, **S** 🛏 Arbuckle Lodge 🅾 High Plains Camping
126	WY 59, Gillette, **N** 🅶 Cenex/dsl, Loaf'N Jug, Sinclair/Papa John's/dsl 🍴 China King Buffet, Hardee's, Little Caesar's, McDonald's, Pizza Carrello, Pokey's BBQ, Prime Rib Rest., Starbucks, Subway 🛏 Best Value Inn 🅾 city park, Family$, Smith's Foods, Tire Factory, Verizon, **S** 🅶 🔶FLYING J/dsl/24hr, Exxon, Loaf'N Jug/dsl 🍴 A&W/LJ Silver, Adriano's Italian, Applebee's, Arby's, Armando's Taco, Buffalo Wild Wings, Burger King, DQ, Goodtimes Grill/Taco John's, Great Wall Chinese, Jimmy John's, KFC, Las Margarita's Mexican, Old Chicago Grill, Papa Murphy's, Perkins, Pizza Hut, Qdoba Mexican, Ruby Tuesday, Smiling Moose Deli, Subway, Taco Bell, Wendy's, Wyo Rib Chophouse 🛏 Candlewood Suites, Country Inn&Suites, Days Inn, Fairfield Inn, Holiday Inn Express, Home 2 Suites, La Quinta, Oak Tree Inn, Ramada Plaza, Wingate Inn 🅾 $Tree, Albertson's, AT&T, AutoZone, Big O Tire, city park, GNC, Goodyear Truck Tire, Home Depot, Jo-Ann, Menards, Midas, O'Reilly Parts, Office Depot, Osco Drug, Petco, Plains Tire, Tire-O-Rama, Verizon, vet, Walgreens, Walmart/Subway
124	WY 50, Gillette, **N** 🅶 Kum&Go/dsl, Shell/Burger King/dsl, Sinclair/Papa John's/dsl 🍴 Hong Kong Rest., Los Compadres Mexican, Pizza Hut, Sherpa Indian, Subway 🛏 Best Western/rest., Budget Inn, Comfort Inn, Hampton Inn, Motel 6, Super 8, TownePlace Suites 🅾 Crazy Woman Camping, Don's Foods, Ford, 🏥, **S** 🅶 Kum&Go/dsl 🍴 McDonald's 🅾 Bighorn Tire, Buick/Chevrolet/GMC, Chrysler/Dodge/Jeep
116	Force Rd
113	Wild Horse Creek Rd
106	Kingsbury Rd
102	Barber Creek Rd
91	Dead Horse Creek Rd
89mm	Powder River
88	Powder River Rd, **N** 🆁🆂 both lanes, full ♿ facilities, litter barrels, petwalk, ☎, 📷, RV Park
82	Indian Creek Rd
77	Schoonover Rd
73.5mm	Crazy Woman Creek
73	Crazy Woman Creek Rd
69	Dry Creek Rd
68.5mm	parking area wb
65	Red Hills Rd, Tipperary Rd
60mm	parking area both lanes, litter barrels

58	US 16, to Ucross, Buffalo, 0-3 mi **S** 🅶 Cenex/dsl/24hr, Exxon/dsl, Maverik/dsl 🍴 Bozeman Tr Steaks, Dash Inn Rest., Hardee's, McDonald's, Pizza Hut, Sub Shop, Subway, Taco John's, Winchester Steaks 🛏 Buffalo Inn, Comfort Inn, Days Inn, Hampton Inn, Holiday Inn Express, Quality Inn, Rodeway WYO Motel, Super 8 🅾 Ace Hardware, Bighorn Tire, Deer Park Camping, Family$, 🏥, Indian RV Camp, KOA, Nat Hist Dist, O'Reilly Parts, Verizon, vet
56b	I-25 S, US 87 S, to Buffalo
56a	25 Bus, 90 Bus, to Buffalo (from eb), **services 2 mi S**
53	Rock Creek Rd
51	Lake DeSmet, **1 mi N** 🅶 Lake Stop gas/motel/cafe 🅾 Lake DeSmet RV park
47	Shell Creek Rd
44	US 87 N, Piney Creek Rd, to Story, Banner, **N** 🅾 Ft Phil Kearney, museum, **5 mi S** Wagon Box Cabins/Rest.
39mm	scenic turnout wb
37	Prairie Dog Creek Rd, to Story
33	Meade Creek Rd, to Big Horn
31mm	parking area eb
25	US 14 E, Sheridan, **N** 🛏 Quality Inn 🅾 Dalton's RV Ctr, **S** 🅶 Cenex/dsl, Exxon/dsl, Holiday/dsl, Maverik/dsl 🍴 Arby's, Burger King, Goodtimes/Taco John's, Jimmy John's, Little Caesar's, Los Agaves, McDonald's, Ole's Pizza, Papa John's, Papa Murphy's, Perkins, Qdoba, Starbucks, Subway, Taco Bell, Wendy's 🛏 Candlewood Suites, Days Inn, Fairfield Inn, Holiday Inn, Holiday Lodge, Mill Inn 🅾 $Tree, Ace Hardware, 🔧, Albertson's/Osco Drug, AT&T, AutoZone, Buick/GMC, Chrysler/Dodge/Jeep, Firestone/auto, Ford/Lincoln, GNC, Goodyear/auto, Home Depot, Midas, NAPA, O'Reilly Parts, Petco, Sheridan Coll, Tire-Rama, to Hist Dist, Toyota, Verizon, vet, Walgreens, Walmart/Subway
23	WY 336, 5th St, Sheridan, **N** 🆁🆂 both lanes, full ♿ facilities, 📷, litter barrels, petwalk, RV dump 🅶 Rock Stop/Subway/dsl 🛏 Comfort Inn,, **S** 🅶 Cenex, Holiday/dsl, Tesla EVC 🍴 DQ, La Herradura Mexican, Pad Thai, Powder River Pizza, Silver Spur Cafe, Wyoming's Chop House 🛏 Alamo Motel, Baymont, Best Value Inn, Best Western, Hampton Inn, Sheridan Inn 🅾 city park, Honda, 🏥, Peter D's RV Park, radiators, Sheridan Cty Museum
20	to Main St, Sheridan, **N** 🅾 KOA, **S** 🅶 Common Cents/dsl, Pizza Hut 🍴 Krispy Krunchy Chicken, McDonald's 🛏 Bramble Motel, Budget Inn, Super 8
16	to Decker, Montana port of entry
15mm	Tongue River
14	WY 345, Acme Rd
9	US 14 W, Ranchester, **1 mi S** 🅶 Conoco/dsl 🅾 Conner Bfd NHS, Foothills Campground, Lazy R Campground, to Yellowstone/Teton NPs, Western Motel
1	Parkman
0mm	Wyoming/Montana state line

Copyright 2022 - The Next EXIT

NOTES

Copyright 2022 - The Next EXIT ®

Assist A Fellow Traveler with...

Published annually, the Next EXIT® provides the best USA Interstate Highway Information available. Order your next copy of the Next EXIT® for yourself or for someone special.

Visit **www.theNextExit.com** to order the **newest edition of the Next EXIT®**

Printed and digital options both available.

We are the Next EXIT,® the most complete guide for services on the interstate.

www.thenextexit.com | 1-800-nex-EXIT